WHITAKER'S CONCISE ALMANA

CW01476677

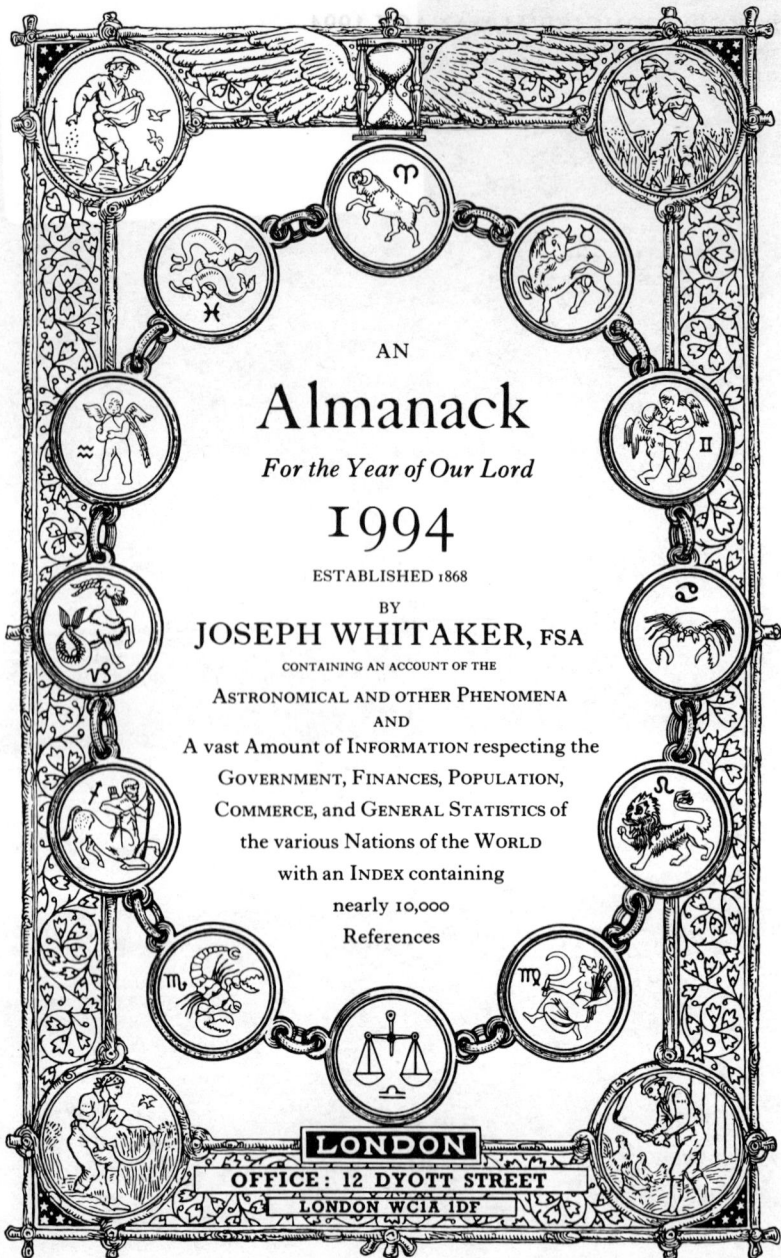

AN

Almanack

For the Year of Our Lord

1994

ESTABLISHED 1868

BY

JOSEPH WHITAKER, FSA

CONTAINING AN ACCOUNT OF THE

ASTRONOMICAL AND OTHER PHENOMENA

AND

A vast Amount of INFORMATION respecting the
GOVERNMENT, FINANCES, POPULATION,
COMMERCE, and GENERAL STATISTICS of
the various Nations of the WORLD
with an INDEX containing
nearly 10,000
References

LONDON

OFFICE: 12 DYOTT STREET
LONDON WC1A 1DF

The traditional design of the title page for Whitaker's Almanack which has appeared in each edition since 1868

Whitaker's Concise Almanack

1994

J. WHITAKER & SONS LTD

12 DYOTT STREET · LONDON WCIA IDF

J. WHITAKER AND SONS LTD
12 Dyott Street, London WC1A 1DF

Whitaker's Almanack published annually since 1868
© 126th edition J. Whitaker and Sons Ltd 1993

Concise Almanack (672 pages)
0 85021 240 5

Designed by Douglas Martin
Jacket design by Carroll Associates
Typeset by Clowes Computer Composition
Printed and bound in Great Britain by
Clays Ltd, St Ives PLC

Contents

Preface

TO THE 126TH ANNUAL VOLUME 1994

The last edition of Whitaker's Almanack broke with tradition, introducing the first change of size and layout in 125 years. The many letters we received from readers in response to the changes were almost universally positive, welcoming the improved legibility and clarity of the pages. It was a very gratifying response for all involved in introducing the new format, and we were grateful also for the comments and suggestions that helped us in refining aspects of the design for this edition.

Resisting the temptation to rest on our laurels after last year, a number of new items and revisions are included in the 126th edition of Whitaker. A new article about intellectual property describes the operation of copyright, patents, trade marks and design registration in the United Kingdom. The funding of the royal family, heatedly debated in the past year, is the subject of a revised and expanded article on royal finances. Also the subject of debate was the General Synod's vote in favour of ordaining women as priests; events leading to the vote and subsequent developments are summarized at the beginning of the Church of England section. Summaries of the Calcutt report on press self-regulation and the various discussion documents about the future of the BBC are included in the Media section, and the recommendations of the Royal Commission on Criminal Justice are included with White Papers, etc.

The replacement of the community charge by the council tax has occasioned a rewrite and expansion of the information about local government. The Countries of the World section has expanded with the inclusion of new entries for all the former Soviet and former Yugoslav republics, the separated Czech and Slovak republics and the newly independent Eritrea.

As ever, we wish to thank the many organizations and individuals who have provided us with information for this edition and whose assistance has been invaluable.

12 DYOTT STREET   HILARY MARSDEN
LONDON WC1A 1DF   *Editor*
TEL 071-836 8911

OCTOBER 1993

The Year 1994

CHRONOLOGICAL CYCLES AND ERAS

Dominical Letter	B
Epact	17
Golden Number (Lunar Cycle)	XIX
Julian Day, 1 January (from noon)	2,449,354
Julian Period	6707
Roman Indiction	2
Solar Cycle	15

	Beginning
Japanese year Heisei 6	1 January
Regnal year 43	6 February
Chinese year of the Dog	10 February
Indian (Saka) year 1916	22 March
Hindu new year	11 April
Sikh new year	13 April
Muslim year AH 1415	10 June
Jewish year AM 5755	6 September
Roman year 2747 AUC	

RELIGIOUS CALENDARS

Epiphany	6 January
Makara Sankranti	14 January
Birthday of Guru Gobind Singh Ji	19 January
Ramadan, first day	12 February
Sarasvati-puja	15 February
Ash Wednesday	16 February
Shivaratri	10 March
Holi	26 March
Passover, first day	27 March
Good Friday	1 April
Easter Day (Western churches)	3 April
Easter Day (Greek Orthodox)	3 April
Baisakhi Mela	13 April
Ramanavami	20 April
Rogation Sunday	8 May
Ascension Day	12 May
Feast of Weeks, first day	16 May
Pentecost (Whit Sunday)	22 May
Idu-l-kabir	*c.* 22 May
Trinity Sunday	29 May
Corpus Christi	2 June
Martyrdom of Guru Arjan Dev Ji	13 June
Raksha-bandhan	21 August
Janmashtami	29 August
Ganesh Chaturthi, first day	9 September
Yom Kippur (Day of Atonement)	15 September
Feast of Tabernacles, first day	20 September
Navaratri festival, first day	5 October
Durga-puja	11 October
Dasara	13 October
Diwali (Hindu) begins	1 November
Diwali (Sikh)	3 November
Diwali Day (Hindu), last day	4 November
Birthday of Guru Nanak Dev Ji	18 November
First Sunday in Advent	27 November
Chanucah, first day	28 November
Martyrdom of Guru Teg Bahadur Ji	7 December
Christmas Day	25 December

CIVIL CALENDAR

Accession of Queen Elizabeth II	6 February
Duke of York's birthday	19 February
St David's Day	1 March
Prince Edward's birthday	10 March
Commonwealth Day	14 March
St Patrick's Day	17 March
Birthday of Queen Elizabeth II	21 April
St George's Day	23 April
Coronation of Queen Elizabeth II	2 June
Duke of Edinburgh's birthday	10 June
The Queen's Official Birthday	11 June
Princess of Wales' birthday	1 July
Queen Elizabeth the Queen Mother's birthday	4 August
Princess Royal's birthday	15 August
Princess Margaret's birthday	21 August
Lord Mayor's Day	12 November
Remembrance Sunday	13 November
Prince of Wales' birthday	14 November
Wedding Day of Queen Elizabeth II	20 November
St Andrew's Day	30 November

LEGAL CALENDAR

LAW TERMS

Hilary Term	11 January to 30 March
Easter Term	12 April to 27 May
Trinity Term	7 June to 30 July
Michaelmas Term	1 October to 21 December

QUARTER DAYS

England, Wales and Northern Ireland

Lady	25 March
Midsummer	24 June
Michaelmas	29 September
Christmas	25 December

TERM DAYS

Scotland

Candlemas	28 February
Whitsunday	28 May
Lammas	28 August
Martinmas	28 November
Removal Terms	28 May, 28 November

1994

JANUARY

Sunday	2	9	16	23	30
Monday	3	10	17	24	31
Tuesday	4	11	18	25	
Wednesday	5	12	19	26	
Thursday	6	13	20	27	
Friday	7	14	21	28	
Saturday	1	8	15	22	29

FEBRUARY

Sunday		6	13	20	27
Monday		7	14	21	28
Tuesday	1	8	15	22	
Wednesday	2	9	16	23	
Thursday	3	10	17	24	
Friday	4	11	18	25	
Saturday	5	12	19	26	

MARCH

Sunday		6	13	20	27
Monday		7	14	21	28
Tuesday	1	8	15	22	29
Wednesday	2	9	16	23	30
Thursday	3	10	17	24	31
Friday	4	11	18	25	
Saturday	5	12	19	26	

APRIL

Sunday		3	10	17	24
Monday		4	11	18	25
Tuesday		5	12	19	26
Wednesday		6	13	20	27
Thursday		7	14	21	28
Friday	1	8	15	22	29
Saturday	2	9	16	23	30

MAY

Sunday	1	8	15	22	29
Monday	2	9	16	23	30
Tuesday	3	10	17	24	31
Wednesday	4	11	18	25	
Thursday	5	12	19	26	
Friday	6	13	20	27	
Saturday	7	14	21	28	

JUNE

Sunday		5	12	19	26
Monday		6	13	20	27
Tuesday		7	14	21	28
Wednesday	1	8	15	22	29
Thursday	2	9	16	23	30
Friday	3	10	17	24	
Saturday	4	11	18	25	

JULY

Sunday		3	10	17	24	31
Monday		4	11	18	25	
Tuesday		5	12	19	26	
Wednesday		6	13	20	27	
Thursday		7	14	21	28	
Friday	1	8	15	22	29	
Saturday	2	9	16	23	30	

AUGUST

Sunday		7	14	21	28
Monday	1	8	15	22	29
Tuesday	2	9	16	23	30
Wednesday	3	10	17	24	31
Thursday	4	11	18	25	
Friday	5	12	19	26	
Saturday	6	13	20	27	

SEPTEMBER

Sunday		4	11	18	25
Monday		5	12	19	26
Tuesday		6	13	20	27
Wednesday		7	14	21	28
Thursday	1	8	15	22	29
Friday	2	9	16	23	30
Saturday	3	10	17	24	

OCTOBER

Sunday	2	9	16	23	30
Monday	3	10	17	24	31
Tuesday	4	11	18	25	
Wednesday	5	12	19	26	
Thursday	6	13	20	27	
Friday	7	14	21	28	
Saturday	1	8	15	22	29

NOVEMBER

Sunday		6	13	20	27
Monday		7	14	21	28
Tuesday	1	8	15	22	29
Wednesday	2	9	16	23	30
Thursday	3	10	17	24	
Friday	4	11	18	25	
Saturday	5	12	19	26	

DECEMBER

Sunday		4	11	18	25
Monday		5	12	19	26
Tuesday		6	13	20	27
Wednesday		7	14	21	28
Thursday	1	8	15	22	29
Friday	2	9	16	23	30
Saturday	3	10	17	24	31

PUBLIC HOLIDAYS

	England and Wales	Scotland	Northern Ireland
New Year	3 January	3, 4 January	3 January
St Patrick's Day	—	—	17 March
*Good Friday	1 April	1 April	1 April
Easter Monday	4 April	—	4 April
May Day	2 May	30 May	2 May
Spring	30 May	2 May	30 May
Battle of Boyne	—	—	12 July
Summer	29 August	1 August	29 August
*Christmas	26, 27 December	26, 27 December	26, 27 December

* In England, Wales, and Northern Ireland, Christmas Day and Good Friday are common law holidays.
 In the Channel Islands, Liberation Day (9 May) is a bank and public holiday.

1995

JANUARY

Sunday	1	8	15	22	29
Monday	2	9	16	23	30
Tuesday	3	10	17	24	31
Wednesday	4	11	18	25	
Thursday	5	12	19	26	
Friday	6	13	20	27	
Saturday	7	14	21	28	

FEBRUARY

Sunday		5	12	19	26
Monday		6	13	20	27
Tuesday		7	14	21	28
Wednesday	1	8	15	22	
Thursday	2	9	16	23	
Friday	3	10	17	24	
Saturday	4	11	18	25	

MARCH

Sunday		5	12	19	26
Monday		6	13	20	27
Tuesday		7	14	21	28
Wednesday	1	8	15	22	29
Thursday	2	9	16	23	30
Friday	3	10	17	24	31
Saturday	4	11	18	25	

APRIL

Sunday		2	9	16	23	30
Monday		3	10	17	24	
Tuesday		4	11	18	25	
Wednesday		5	12	19	26	
Thursday		6	13	20	27	
Friday		7	14	21	28	
Saturday	1	8	15	22	29	

MAY

Sunday		7	14	21	28
Monday	1	8	15	22	29
Tuesday	2	9	16	23	30
Wednesday	3	10	17	24	31
Thursday	4	11	18	25	
Friday	5	12	19	26	
Saturday	6	13	20	27	

JUNE

Sunday		4	11	18	25
Monday		5	12	19	26
Tuesday		6	13	20	27
Wednesday		7	14	21	28
Thursday	1	8	15	22	29
Friday	2	9	16	23	30
Saturday	3	10	17	24	

JULY

Sunday		2	9	16	23	30
Monday		3	10	17	24	31
Tuesday		4	11	18	25	
Wednesday		5	12	19	26	
Thursday		6	13	20	27	
Friday		7	14	21	28	
Saturday	1	8	15	22	29	

AUGUST

Sunday		6	13	20	27
Monday		7	14	21	28
Tuesday	1	8	15	22	29
Wednesday	2	9	16	23	30
Thursday	3	10	17	24	31
Friday	4	11	18	25	
Saturday	5	12	19	26	

SEPTEMBER

Sunday		3	10	17	24
Monday		4	11	18	25
Tuesday		5	12	19	26
Wednesday		6	13	20	27
Thursday		7	14	21	28
Friday	1	8	15	22	29
Saturday	2	9	16	23	30

OCTOBER

Sunday	1	8	15	22	29
Monday	2	9	16	23	30
Tuesday	3	10	17	24	31
Wednesday	4	11	18	25	
Thursday	5	12	19	26	
Friday	6	13	20	27	
Saturday	7	14	21	28	

NOVEMBER

Sunday		5	12	19	26
Monday		6	13	20	27
Tuesday		7	14	21	28
Wednesday	1	8	15	22	29
Thursday	2	9	16	23	30
Friday	3	10	17	24	
Saturday	4	11	18	25	

DECEMBER

Sunday		3	10	17	24	31
Monday		4	11	18	25	
Tuesday		5	12	19	26	
Wednesday		6	13	20	27	
Thursday		7	14	21	28	
Friday	1	8	15	22	29	
Saturday	2	9	16	23	30	

PUBLIC HOLIDAYS

	England and Wales	Scotland	Northern Ireland
New Year	2 January	2, 3 January	2 January
St Patrick's Day	—	—	17 March
*Good Friday	14 April	14 April	14 April
Easter Monday	17 April	—	17 April
May Day	†	29 May	†
Spring	29 May	1 May	29 May
Battle of Boyne	—	—	12 July
Summer	28 August	7 August	28 August
*Christmas	25, 26 December	25, 26 December	25, 26 December

† In 1993 it was proposed that the May Day bank holiday in England, Wales and Northern Ireland should be abolished and replaced by an autumn bank holiday from 1995. No further details were available at the time of going to press.

FORTHCOMING EVENTS 1994

This is the UN International Year for the Family, the EC Year of Food and Nutrition, and the Arts Council Year for Drama, based in the city of Manchester.
The European City of Culture 1994 is Copenhagen.
* Provisional dates

6–16 January	London International Boat Show Earls Court, London
10–13 March	Cruft's Dog Show National Exhibition Centre, Birmingham
17 March–10 April	Ideal Home Exhibition Earls Court, London
20–22 March	London International Book Fair Olympia, London
7–13 April	International Antiques Fair National Exhibition Centre, Birmingham
29 April–21 May	Mayfest 1994 Glasgow
29 April–8 October	Pitlochry Festival Theatre season Pitlochry, Tayside
May–September	Chichester Festival Theatre season, West Sussex
11–15 May	Royal Windsor Horse Show Home Park, Windsor
26–27 May	Chelsea Flower Show Royal Hospital, Chelsea
27 May–12 June	Bath International Festival Bath
28 May–25 August	Glyndebourne Festival Opera season Glyndebourne, Lewes, East Sussex
June–August	Royal Academy Summer Exhibition Piccadilly, London
10–26 June	Aldeburgh Festival of Music and Arts, Suffolk
11 June	Trooping the Colour Horse Guards Parade, London
*13–31 July	Buxton Festival Derbyshire
4–7 July	The Royal Show Stoneleigh Park, Kenilworth, Warks
*15–23 July	Welsh Proms 1994 St David's Hall, Cardiff
15 July– 10 September	Promenade Concerts season Royal Albert Hall, London
19–30 July	Royal Tournament Earls Court, London
30 July–6 August	Royal National Eisteddfod of Wales Neath, West Glamorgan
*5–27 August	Edinburgh Military Tattoo Edinburgh Castle
12 August	Battle of Flowers Jersey
14 August– 3 September	Edinburgh International Festival
21–26 August	Three Choirs Festival Hereford
2 September– *6 November	Blackpool Illuminations
3 September	Braemar Royal Highland Gathering Braemar, Aberdeenshire
*16–24 September	Southampton International Boat Show Western Esplanade, Southampton

22–30 October	British International Motor Show National Exhibition Centre, Birmingham
6 November	London to Brighton Veteran Car Run
*7–22 November	London International Film Festival
12 November	Lord Mayor's Procession and Show City of London
17–27 November	Huddersfield Contemporary Music Festival
27–31 November	Royal Smithfield Show and Agricultural Machinery Exhibition, Earls Court, London

SPORTS EVENTS

15 January	Rugby Union: France v. Ireland Parc des Princes, Paris Wales v. Scotland Cardiff Arms Park
5 February	Rugby Union: Ireland v. Wales Lansdowne Road, Dublin Scotland v. England Murrayfield, Edinburgh
19 February	Rugby Union: Wales v. France Cardiff Arms Park England v. Ireland Twickenham, London
5 March	Rugby Union: Ireland v. Scotland Lansdowne Road, Dublin France v. England Parc des Princes, Paris
19 March	Rugby Union: Scotland v. France Murrayfield, Edinburgh England v. Wales Twickenham, London
26 March	University Boat Race Putney to Mortlake, London
16 April–2 May	Snooker: World Professional Championships Crucible Theatre, Sheffield
17 April	Athletics: London Marathon
30 April	Rugby League: Challenge Cup final Wembley Stadium, London
5–8 May	Badminton Horse Trials Badminton, Avon
7 May	Rugby Union: Pilkington Cup final Twickenham, London
14 May	Football: FA Cup final Wembley Stadium, London
15 May	Welsh FA Cup final Cardiff Arms Park
*19 May	Cricket: One-day International England v. New Zealand Edgbaston, Birmingham
*21 May	Cricket: One-day International England v. New Zealand Lord's, London
21 May	Football: Scottish FA Cup final Hampden Park, Glasgow
29 May–11 June	Cycling: Open Tour of Britain (formerly Milk Race)
30 May–4 June	Golf: British Amateur Championship Nairn

30 May–10 June	International TT Motorcycle Races Isle of Man
*2–6 June	Cricket: 1st Test Match England v. New Zealand Trent Bridge, Nottingham
*16–20 June	Cricket: 2nd Test Match England v. New Zealand Lord's, London
20 June–3 July	Lawn Tennis Championships Wimbledon, London
29 June–3 July	Henley Royal Regatta Henley-on-Thames
*30 June–5 July	Cricket: 3rd Test Match England v. New Zealand Old Trafford, Manchester
*9 July	Cricket: Benson & Hedges Cup final Lord's, London
*9–23 July	Shooting: NRA Imperial Meetings Bisley Camp, Woking, Surrey
*10 July	British Formula 1 Grand Prix Silverstone, Northants
14–17 July	Golf: Open Championship Turnberry, Ayrshire
*21–25 July	Cricket: 1st Test Match England v. South Africa Lord's, London
30 July–6 August	Yachting: Cowes Week Isle of Wight
*4–8 August	Cricket: 2nd Test Match England v. South Africa Headingley, Leeds
*18–22 August	Cricket: 3rd Test Match England v. South Africa The Oval, London
*25 August	Cricket: One-day International England v. South Africa Edgbaston, Birmingham
*27 August	Cricket: One-day International England v. South Africa Old Trafford, Manchester
1–4 September	Eventing: Burghley Horse Trials Burghley, Lincs
*3 September	Cricket: NatWest Trophy final Lord's, London
*4–10 October	Horse of the Year Show Wembley Arena, London

HORSE-RACING

17 March	Cheltenham Gold Cup Cheltenham
26 March	Lincoln Handicap Doncaster
9 April	Grand National Aintree
28 April	One Thousand Guineas Newmarket
30 April	Two Thousand Guineas Newmarket
1 June	The Derby Epsom
2 June	Coronation Cup Epsom
4 June	The Oaks Epsom
14–17 June	Royal Ascot
23 July	King George VI and Queen Elizabeth Diamond Stakes Ascot

10 September	St Leger Doncaster
1 October	Cambridgeshire Handicap Newmarket
15 October	Cesarewitch Newmarket

The horse-racing fixtures are the copyright of The Jockey Club.

CENTENARIES OF 1994

1494

20 April	Johannes Agricola, German Protestant reformer, born
4 May	Christopher Columbus landed in Jamaica

1594

2 February	Giovanni Palestrina, Italian composer, born
31 May	Jacopo Tintoretto, Venetian artist, died
22 November	Sir Martin Frobisher, navigator and explorer, died
5 December	Gerardus Mercator, Flemish mathematician and geographer, died

1694

27 July	Bank of England established by charter
21 November	François-Marie Voltaire, French philosopher, born
22 November	John Tillotson, Archbishop of Canterbury, died
28 December	Queen Mary II died

1794

16 January	Edward Gibbon, writer and historian, died
5 April	Georges Jacques Danton, French Revolutionary leader, executed
8 May	Antoine Lavoisier, French chemist, executed
1 June	Battle of the Glorious First of June
28 July	Maximilien Robespierre, French Revolutionary leader, executed

1894

1 January	Manchester Ship Canal opened to traffic
10 February	Harold Macmillan, 1st Earl of Stockton, Prime Minister 1957–63, born
21 February	Andres Segovia, Spanish classical guitarist, born
10 April	Ben Nicholson, artist, born
17 April NS	Nikita Krushchev, Soviet leader, born
23 June	King Edward VIII, later Duke of Windsor, born
30 June	Tower Bridge, London, opened
26 July	Aldous Huxley, author, born
1 August	Start of Sino-Japanese War
13 September	J. B. Priestley, author, born
14 October	e. e. cummings, American poet, born
20 November	Anton Rubinstein, Russian pianist and composer, died
24 November	Herbert Sutcliffe, cricketer, born
3 December	Robert Louis Stevenson, poet and author, died
7 December	Ferdinand de Lesseps, French diplomatist and maker of the Suez Canal, died
8 December	James Thurber, American humorist, born
20 December	Sir Robert Menzies, Australian Prime Minister 1939–41 and 1949–66, born
29 December	Christina Rossetti, poet and hymn writer, died
30 December	Amelia Bloomer, women's rights campaigner, died

CENTENARIES OF 1995

1695

21 November	Henry Purcell, composer, died

1795

3 January	Josiah Wedgwood, potter, died
19 May	James Boswell, biographer of Dr Johnson, died
13 June	Thomas Arnold, headmaster of Rugby, born
31 October	John Keats, poet, born
4 December	Thomas Carlyle, essayist and historian, born

1895

1 January	J. Edgar Hoover, American head of the FBI for nearly fifty years, born
24 January	Lord Randolph Churchill, politician, died
1 February	John Ford, American film director, born
10 March	Charles Frederick Worth, costumier, died
25 April	Sir Stanley Rous, founder member of the Football Association, born
29 April	Sir Malcolm Sargent, conductor, born
6 May	Rudolf Valentino, film actor, born
15 May	Joseph Whitaker, publisher, founder and first editor of *Whitaker's Almanack*, died
24 June	Jack Dempsey, American boxer, born

10 July	Carl Orff, German composer, born
12 July	Oscar Hammerstein, American librettist, born
	Kirsten Flagstad, Norwegian opera singer, born
26 July	Robert Graves, poet and novelist, born
5 August	Friedrich Engels, German socialist, died
29 August	Founding of Northern Rugby Football Union (known since 1922 as the Rugby Football League) at the George Hotel, Huddersfield
28 September	Louis Pasteur, French chemist, died
4 October	Buster Keaton, American film comedian, born
8 October	Juan Peron, Argentine soldier and politician, born
15 October	First British Motor Show, at Tunbridge Wells
25 October	Sir Charles Halle, pianist and conductor, died
16 November	Paul Hindemith, German composer, born
27 November	Alexandre Dumas (younger), French novelist, playwright and essayist, died
14 December	King George VI born
	Paul Éluard, French poet, born
29 December	Jameson Raid in Transvaal, South Africa
30 December	L. P. Hartley, novelist, born

Astronomy

The following pages give astronomical data for each month of the year 1994. There are four pages of data for each month. All data are given for oh Greenwich Mean Time (GMT), i.e. at the midnight at the beginning of the day named. This applies also to data for the months when British Summer Time is in operation (for dates, *see* below).

The astronomical data are given in a form suitable for observation with the naked eye or with a small telescope. These data do not attempt to replace the *Astronomical Almanac* for professional astronomers.

A fuller explanation of how to use the astronomical data is given on pages 71–3.

CALENDAR FOR EACH MONTH

The calendar for each month shows dates of religious, civil and legal significance for the year 1994.

The days in bold type are the principal holy days and the festivals and greater holy days of the Church of England as set out in the calendar of the *Alternative Service Book 1980*. Observance of certain festivals and greater holy days is transferred if the day falls on a principal holy day. The calendar shows the date on which holy days and festivals are to be observed in 1994.

The days in small capitals are dates of significance in the calendars of non-Anglican denominations and non-Christian religions.

The days in italic type are dates of civil and legal significance. The royal anniversaries shown in italic type are the days on which the Union flag is to be flown.

The rest of the calendar comprises days of general interest and the dates of birth or death of well-known people.

Fuller explanations of the various calendars can be found under Time Measurement and Calendars (pages 81–9).

The Zodiacal signs through which the Sun is passing during each month are illustrated. The date of transition from one sign to the next, to the nearest hour, is also given.

The longest day of the year, measured from sunrise to sunset, is at the summer solstice. For the remainder of this century the longest day in the United Kingdom will fall each year on 21 June. *See also* page 81.

The shortest day of the year is at the winter solstice. For the remainder of this century the shortest day in the United Kingdom will fall on 21 December in 1996, 1997, 2000, and on 22 December in 1994, 1995, 1998, 1999. *See also* page 81.

The equinox is the point at which day and night are of equal length all over the world. *See also* page 81.

In popular parlance, the seasons in the northern hemisphere comprise the following months:

Spring	March April May
Summer	June July August
Autumn	September October November
Winter	December January February

BRITISH SUMMER TIME

British Summer Time is the legal time for general purposes during the period in which it is in operation. During this period, clocks are kept one hour ahead of Greenwich Mean Time. The hour of changeover is 01h Greenwich Mean Time. The duration of Summer Time in 1994 is:

March 27 01h GMT to October 23 01h GMT

SEASONS

The seasons are defined astronomically as follows:

Spring	from the vernal equinox to the summer solstice
Summer	from the summer solstice to the autumnal equinox
Autumn	from the autumnal equinox to the winter solstice
Winter	from the winter solstice to the vernal equinox

The seasons in 1994 are:

Northern hemisphere

Vernal equinox	March 20d 20h GMT
Summer solstice	June 21d 15h GMT
Autumnal equinox	September 23d 06h GMT
Winter solstice	December 22d 02h GMT

Southern hemisphere

Autumnal equinox	March 20d 20h GMT
Winter solstice	June 21d 15h GMT
Vernal equinox	September 23d 06h GMT
Summer solstice	December 22d 02h GMT

January 1994

FIRST MONTH, 31 DAYS. *Janus*, god of the portal, facing two ways, past and future

Sun's Longitude 300° ≈ 20ᵈ07ʰ

1	*Saturday*	**The Naming of Jesus.** E. M. Forster *b*. 1879	*week 52 day 1*
2	*Sunday*	**2nd S. after Christmas.** Isaac Asimov *b*. 1920	*week 1 day 2*
3	*Monday*	*Bank Holiday in the UK.* Lord Haw Haw *exec*. 1946	3
4	*Tuesday*	*Bank Holiday in Scotland.* Jacob Grimm *b*. 1785	4
5	*Wednesday*	Edward the Confessor *d*. 1066	5
6	*Thursday*	**The Epiphany.** Gustave Doré *b*. 1833	6
7	*Friday*	Francis Poulenc *b*. 1899. Trevor Howard *d*. 1988	7
8	*Saturday*	Giotto (Ambrogio di Bondone) *d*. 1337	8
9	*Sunday*	**1st S. after Epiphany.** Sir Robert Mayer *d*. 1985	*week 2 day 9*
10	*Monday*	Penny post introduced 1840. Sinclair Lewis *d*. 1951	10
11	*Tuesday*	*Hilary Law Sittings begin.* William James *b*. 1842	11
12	*Wednesday*	Herman Goering *b*. 1893. Dame Agatha Christie *d*. 1976	12
13	*Thursday*	Stephen Foster *d*. 1864	13
14	*Friday*	Albert Schweitzer *b*. 1875. Lewis Carroll *d*. 1898	14
15	*Saturday*	Martin Luther King *b*. 1929	15
16	*Sunday*	**2nd S. after Epiphany.** Start of Prohibition (USA) 1920	*week 3 day 16*
17	*Monday*	Rutherford B. Hayes *d*. 1893. Clyde Walcott *b*. 1926	17
18	*Tuesday*	William of Prussia proclaimed first German Emperor 1871	18
19	*Wednesday*	Sir Henry Bessemer *b*. 1813	19
20	*Thursday*	Sir Roy Welensky *b*. 1907. Edmund Blunden *d*. 1974	20
21	*Friday*	Lenin *d*. 1924. Jack Nicklaus *b*. 1940	21
22	*Saturday*	Francis Bacon *b*. 1561. Queen Victoria *d*. 1901	22
23	*Sunday*	**3rd S. after Epiphany.** Vietnam War Treaty 1973	*week 4 day 23*
24	*Monday*	William Congreve *b*. 1670. Edward Jenner *d*. 1823	24
25	*Tuesday*	**Conversion of St Paul.** Robert Burns *b*. 1759	25
26	*Wednesday*	Proclamation of Republic of India 1950	26
27	*Thursday*	Mozart *b*. 1756. Verdi *d*. 1901	27
28	*Friday*	Henry VII *b*. 1457. Henry VIII *d*. 1547	28
29	*Saturday*	Frederick Delius *b*. 1862. H. E. Bates *d*. 1974	29
30	*Sunday*	**9th S. before Easter.** Stanley Holloway *d*. 1982	*week 5 day 30*
31	*Monday*	Guy Fawkes *exec*. 1606. Anna Pavlova *b*. 1885	31

ASTRONOMICAL PHENOMENA

d	h	
1	12	Mars in conjunction with Mercury. Mars 0°.8 N.
2	06	Earth at perihelion (147 million km)
3	20	Mercury in superior conjunction
6	05	Mars in conjunction with Venus. Mars 0°.3 S.
6	21	Jupiter in conjunction with Moon. Jupiter 3° N.
11	08	Neptune in conjunction with Sun
11	16	Mars in conjunction with Moon. Mars 5° S.
11	21	Venus in conjunction with Moon. Venus 5° S.
12	10	Mercury in conjunction with Moon. Mercury 6° S.
12	17	Uranus in conjunction with Sun
14	19	Saturn in conjunction with Moon. Saturn 6° S.
17	02	Venus in superior conjunction

CONSTELLATIONS

The following constellations are near the meridian at

	d	h		d	h
December	1	24	January	16	21
December	16	23	February	1	20
January	1	22	February	15	19

Draco (below the Pole), Ursa Minor (below the Pole), Camelopardus, Perseus, Auriga, Taurus, Orion, Eridanus and Lepus

MINIMA OF ALGOL

d	h	d	h	d	h
2	04.6	13	15.9	25	03.2
5	01.4	16	12.7	28	00.0
7	22.2	19	09.5	30	20.8
10	19.1	22	06.3		

THE MOON

Phases, Apsides and Node	d	h	m
☾ Last Quarter	5	00	01
● New Moon	11	23	10
☽ First Quarter	19	20	27
○ Full Moon	27	13	23
Perigee (370,142 km)	6	01	16
Apogee (404,362 km)	19	05	15
Perigee (367,408 km)	31	03	43

Mean longitude of ascending node on January 1, 241°

THE SUN   s.d. 16′.3

Day	Right Ascension	Dec. —	Equation of time	Rise 52°	Rise 56°	Transit	Set 52°	Set 56°	Sidereal time	Transit of First Point of Aries
	h m s	° ′	m s	h m	h m	h m	h m	h m	h m s	h m s
1	18 44 59	23 02	− 3 18	8 08	8 31	12 04	15 59	15 36	6 41 40	17 15 30
2	18 49 23	22 57	− 3 46	8 08	8 31	12 04	16 00	15 37	6 45 37	17 11 34
3	18 53 48	22 52	− 4 14	8 08	8 31	12 04	16 01	15 38	6 49 34	17 07 38
4	18 58 12	22 46	− 4 42	8 08	8 30	12 05	16 02	15 40	6 53 30	17 03 42
5	19 02 36	22 40	− 5 09	8 07	8 30	12 05	16 04	15 41	6 57 27	16 59 46
6	19 06 59	22 33	− 5 36	8 07	8 29	12 06	16 05	15 43	7 01 23	16 55 50
7	19 11 22	22 26	− 6 02	8 07	8 29	12 06	16 06	15 44	7 05 20	16 51 54
8	19 15 44	22 18	− 6 28	8 06	8 28	12 07	16 08	15 46	7 09 16	16 47 58
9	19 20 06	22 10	− 6 53	8 06	8 27	12 07	16 09	15 47	7 13 13	16 44 02
10	19 24 28	22 01	− 7 18	8 05	8 26	12 08	16 10	15 49	7 17 09	16 40 06
11	19 28 49	21 52	− 7 43	8 04	8 26	12 08	16 12	15 51	7 21 06	16 36 10
12	19 33 09	21 43	− 8 06	8 04	8 25	12 08	16 13	15 52	7 25 03	16 32 14
13	19 37 29	21 33	− 8 30	8 03	8 24	12 09	16 15	15 54	7 28 59	16 28 19
14	19 41 48	21 23	− 8 52	8 02	8 23	12 09	16 16	15 56	7 32 56	16 24 23
15	19 46 06	21 12	− 9 14	8 01	8 22	12 09	16 18	15 58	7 36 52	16 20 27
16	19 50 24	21 01	− 9 35	8 01	8 20	12 10	16 19	16 00	7 40 49	16 16 31
17	19 54 41	20 50	− 9 56	8 00	8 19	12 10	16 21	16 02	7 44 45	16 12 35
18	19 58 57	20 38	−10 15	7 59	8 18	12 10	16 23	16 03	7 48 42	16 08 39
19	20 03 13	20 25	−10 35	7 58	8 17	12 11	16 24	16 05	7 52 38	16 04 43
20	20 07 28	20 13	−10 53	7 56	8 15	12 11	16 26	16 07	7 56 35	16 00 47
21	20 11 42	20 00	−11 10	7 55	8 14	12 11	16 28	16 09	8 00 32	15 56 51
22	20 15 55	19 46	−11 27	7 54	8 12	12 12	16 29	16 11	8 04 28	15 52 55
23	20 20 08	19 33	−11 43	7 53	8 11	12 12	16 31	16 13	8 08 25	15 48 59
24	20 24 20	19 19	−11 58	7 52	8 09	12 12	16 33	16 16	8 12 21	15 45 04
25	20 28 31	19 04	−12 13	7 50	8 08	12 12	16 35	16 18	8 16 18	15 41 08
26	20 32 41	18 49	−12 26	7 49	8 06	12 13	16 37	16 20	8 20 14	15 37 12
27	20 36 50	18 34	−12 39	7 48	8 04	12 13	16 38	16 22	8 24 11	15 33 16
28	20 40 59	18 19	−12 51	7 46	8 03	12 13	16 40	16 24	8 28 07	15 29 20
29	20 45 06	18 03	−13 02	7 45	8 01	12 13	16 42	16 26	8 32 04	15 25 24
30	20 49 13	17 47	−13 13	7 43	7 59	12 13	16 44	16 28	8 36 01	15 21 28
31	20 53 19	17 30	−13 22	7 42	7 57	12 13	16 46	16 30	8 39 57	15 17 32

DURATION OF TWILIGHT (in minutes)

Latitude	52°	56°	52°	56°	52°	56°	52°	56°
	1 January		11 January		21 January		31 January	
Civil	41	47	40	45	38	43	37	41
Nautical	84	96	82	93	80	90	78	87
Astronomical	125	141	123	138	120	134	117	130

THE NIGHT SKY

Mercury passes through superior conjunction on the 3rd and remains too close to the Sun for observation for most of January. However, for the last three or four days of the month it should be possible to detect Mercury low above the SW horizon at the end of evening civil twilight: its magnitude is − 0.9.

Venus is at superior conjunction on the 17th and is unsuitably placed for observation throughout the month.

Mars passed through conjunction towards the end of last month and remains too close to the Sun for observation throughout January.

Jupiter, magnitude − 1.9, is a bright object, visible for several hours in the SE sky before sunrise. Jupiter is in Libra.

The Moon, just after Last Quarter, will be seen in the vicinity of the planet on the mornings of the 6th and 7th.

Saturn is an evening object in the SW sky, magnitude + 0.9. It is only seen at a low altitude and by the end of January it is a difficult object to detect, being very low on the horizon by the time that the twilight has faded sufficiently for it to be seen. Saturn is in the constellation of Aquarius. The thin crescent Moon passes 6° north of Saturn on the evening of the 14th.

THE MOON

Day	RA	Dec.	Hor. par.	Semi- diam.	Sun's co- long.	PA of Bright Limb	Phase	Age	Rise 52°	Rise 56°	Transit	Set 52°	Set 56°
	h m	°	′	′	°	°	%	d	h m	h m	h m	h m	h m
1	9 17	+10.6	58.3	15.9	132	114	89	18.6	20 44	20 39	2 40	9 39	9 46
2	10 09	+ 5.9	58.6	16.0	144	115	82	19.6	22 03	22 02	3 31	10 02	10 05
3	11 01	+ 0.8	58.9	16.0	156	115	72	20.6	23 21	23 25	4 21	10 25	10 23
4	11 54	− 4.3	59.1	16.1	168	115	61	21.6	—	—	5 11	10 47	10 42
5	12 47	− 9.2	59.2	16.1	180	113	50	22.6	0 41	0 49	6 02	11 13	11 03
6	13 42	−13.6	59.2	16.1	193	110	39	23.6	2 00	2 13	6 56	11 42	11 27
7	14 39	−17.3	59.2	16.1	205	107	28	24.6	3 18	3 36	7 51	12 17	11 58
8	15 37	−19.9	59.1	16.1	217	103	18	25.6	4 33	4 54	8 48	13 01	12 39
9	16 37	−21.3	58.8	16.0	229	99	11	26.6	5 39	6 02	9 47	13 54	13 31
10	17 37	−21.4	58.5	15.9	241	97	5	27.6	6 35	6 57	10 45	14 57	14 35
11	18 36	−20.1	58.0	15.8	253	100	1	28.6	7 20	7 40	11 41	16 07	15 48
12	19 32	−17.8	57.5	15.7	266	177	0	0.0	7 56	8 12	12 34	17 19	17 05
13	20 26	−14.5	56.9	15.5	278	237	1	1.0	8 24	8 36	13 23	18 32	18 21
14	21 17	−10.6	56.2	15.3	290	242	5	2.0	8 48	8 56	14 10	19 43	19 37
15	22 05	− 6.3	55.6	15.2	302	243	10	3.0	9 09	9 13	14 55	20 52	20 49
16	22 51	− 1.9	55.1	15.0	314	243	17	4.0	9 28	9 28	15 38	21 59	22 01
17	23 37	+ 2.5	54.6	14.9	327	244	24	5.0	9 47	9 44	16 20	23 05	23 11
18	0 21	+ 6.8	54.4	14.8	339	245	33	6.0	10 06	9 59	17 02	—	—
19	1 07	+10.8	54.2	14.8	351	247	42	7.0	10 28	10 17	17 45	0 10	0 20
20	1 53	+14.3	54.3	14.8	3	250	52	8.0	10 52	10 38	18 30	1 15	1 29
21	2 41	+17.3	54.5	14.9	15	253	61	9.0	11 21	11 04	19 17	2 19	2 36
22	3 31	+19.6	54.9	15.0	27	256	70	10.0	11 57	11 36	20 06	3 22	3 42
23	4 23	+21.0	55.4	15.1	39	260	78	11.0	12 41	12 19	20 58	4 21	4 43
24	5 17	+21.4	56.1	15.3	52	264	86	12.0	13 35	13 13	21 51	5 15	5 37
25	6 12	+20.7	56.8	15.5	64	267	92	13.0	14 39	14 19	22 45	6 01	6 22
26	7 08	+18.9	57.6	15.7	76	267	97	14.0	15 50	15 33	23 38	6 41	6 58
27	8 03	+16.0	58.2	15.9	88	251	99	15.0	17 06	16 54	—	7 14	7 27
28	8 59	+12.1	58.8	16.0	100	146	100	16.0	18 26	18 18	0 32	7 42	7 51
29	9 53	+ 7.5	59.3	16.2	112	124	97	17.0	19 46	19 43	1 24	8 07	8 12
30	10 47	+ 2.4	59.6	16.2	124	120	92	18.0	21 07	21 09	2 16	8 30	8 31
31	11 41	− 2.8	59.7	16.3	137	118	85	19.0	22 28	22 35	3 07	8 54	8 50

MERCURY

Day	RA	Dec.	Diam.	Phase	Transit	5° high 52°	5° high 56°
	h m	°	″	%	h m	h m	h m
1	18 38	−24.8	5	100	11 58	9 11	9 53
3	18 52	−24.7	5	100	12 04	14 53	14 12
5	19 06	−24.5	5	100	12 11	15 02	14 21
7	19 21	−24.1	5	100	12 17	15 12	14 32
9	19 35	−23.7	5	100	12 23	15 22	14 45
11	19 49	−23.2	5	99	12 30	15 33	14 58
13	20 03	−22.6	5	98	12 36	15 45	15 12
15	20 18	−21.8	5	98	12 42	15 58	15 27
17	20 32	−21.0	5	96	12 49	16 11	15 42
19	20 46	−20.1	5	95	12 55	16 25	15 58
21	20 59	−19.0	5	93	13 00	16 39	16 14
23	21 13	−17.9	5	91	13 06	16 52	16 30
25	21 26	−16.7	6	87	13 11	17 06	16 45
27	21 39	−15.4	6	83	13 16	17 19	17 00
29	21 50	−14.1	6	78	13 19	17 31	17 14
31	22 02	−12.7	6	72	13 22	17 42	17 27

VENUS

Day	RA	Dec.	Diam.	Phase	Transit	5° high 52°	5° high 56°
	h m	°	″	%	h m	h m	h m
1	18 28	−23.6	10	100	11 47	14 45	14 08
6	18 56	−23.4	10	100	11 55	14 56	14 19
11	19 23	−22.8	10	100	12 03	15 09	14 34
16	19 50	−21.9	10	100	12 10	15 23	14 52
21	20 17	−20.8	10	100	12 17	15 40	15 11
26	20 43	−19.4	10	100	12 23	15 57	15 31
31	21 08	−17.8	10	100	12 29	16 15	15 52

MARS

Day	RA	Dec.	Diam.	Phase	Transit	5° high 52°	5° high 56°
1	18 40	−24.0	4	100	11 58	9 03	9 42
6	18 56	−23.7	4	100	11 55	8 57	9 35
11	19 13	−23.3	4	100	11 52	8 51	9 27
16	19 30	−22.8	4	100	11 48	8 43	9 17
21	19 46	−22.2	4	100	11 45	8 35	9 07
26	20 03	−21.5	4	100	11 42	8 25	8 56
31	20 19	−20.7	4	100	11 39	8 15	8 44

SUNRISE AND SUNSET

	London 0°05′ 51°30′		Bristol 2°35′ 51°28′		Birmingham 1°55′ 52°28′		Manchester 2°15′ 53°28′		Newcastle 1°37′ 54°59′		Glasgow 4°14′ 55°52′		Belfast 5°56′ 54°35′	
	h m	h m	h m	h m	h m	h m	h m	h m	h m	h m	h m	h m	h m	h m
1	8 06	16 02	8 16	16 12	8 18	16 04	8 25	16 00	8 31	15 49	8 47	15 54	8 46	16 09
2	8 06	16 03	8 16	16 13	8 18	16 05	8 25	16 01	8 31	15 50	8 47	15 55	8 46	16 10
3	8 06	16 04	8 16	16 14	8 18	16 07	8 25	16 03	8 31	15 51	8 47	15 56	8 46	16 11
4	8 06	16 05	8 15	16 15	8 18	16 08	8 24	16 04	8 30	15 53	8 46	15 58	8 45	16 12
5	8 05	16 06	8 15	16 17	8 17	16 09	8 24	16 05	8 30	15 54	8 46	15 59	8 45	16 14
6	8 05	16 08	8 15	16 18	8 17	16 10	8 24	16 06	8 30	15 55	8 45	16 00	8 44	16 15
7	8 05	16 09	8 14	16 19	8 17	16 12	8 23	16 08	8 29	15 57	8 45	16 02	8 44	16 16
8	8 04	16 10	8 14	16 20	8 16	16 13	8 23	16 09	8 28	15 58	8 44	16 03	8 43	16 18
9	8 04	16 12	8 13	16 22	8 16	16 14	8 22	16 11	8 28	16 00	8 43	16 05	8 43	16 19
10	8 03	16 13	8 13	16 23	8 15	16 16	8 21	16 12	8 27	16 01	8 43	16 07	8 42	16 21
11	8 02	16 14	8 12	16 25	8 14	16 17	8 21	16 14	8 26	16 03	8 42	16 08	8 41	16 22
12	8 02	16 16	8 12	16 26	8 14	16 19	8 20	16 15	8 25	16 05	8 41	16 10	8 40	16 24
13	8 01	16 17	8 11	16 28	8 13	16 20	8 19	16 17	8 24	16 06	8 40	16 12	8 39	16 26
14	8 00	16 19	8 10	16 29	8 12	16 22	8 18	16 18	8 23	16 08	8 39	16 14	8 39	16 27
15	8 00	16 20	8 09	16 31	8 11	16 23	8 17	16 20	8 22	16 10	8 38	16 15	8 38	16 29
16	7 59	16 22	8 09	16 32	8 10	16 25	8 16	16 22	8 21	16 12	8 37	16 17	8 36	16 31
17	7 58	16 24	8 08	16 34	8 09	16 27	8 15	16 23	8 20	16 13	8 35	16 19	8 35	16 33
18	7 57	16 25	8 07	16 35	8 08	16 28	8 14	16 25	8 19	16 15	8 34	16 21	8 34	16 35
19	7 56	16 27	8 06	16 37	8 07	16 30	8 13	16 27	8 18	16 17	8 33	16 23	8 33	16 36
20	7 55	16 28	8 05	16 39	8 06	16 32	8 12	16 29	8 16	16 19	8 31	16 25	8 32	16 38
21	7 54	16 30	8 04	16 40	8 05	16 34	8 11	16 31	8 15	16 21	8 30	16 27	8 30	16 40
22	7 53	16 32	8 02	16 42	8 04	16 35	8 09	16 32	8 14	16 23	8 29	16 29	8 29	16 42
23	7 51	16 34	8 01	16 44	8 03	16 37	8 08	16 34	8 12	16 25	8 27	16 31	8 28	16 44
24	7 50	16 35	8 00	16 45	8 01	16 39	8 07	16 36	8 11	16 27	8 26	16 33	8 26	16 46
25	7 49	16 37	7 59	16 47	8 00	16 41	8 05	16 38	8 09	16 29	8 24	16 35	8 25	16 48
26	7 48	16 39	7 57	16 49	7 59	16 42	8 04	16 40	8 08	16 31	8 22	16 37	8 23	16 50
27	7 46	16 40	7 56	16 51	7 57	16 44	8 02	16 42	8 06	16 33	8 21	16 39	8 22	16 52
28	7 45	16 42	7 55	16 52	7 56	16 46	8 01	16 44	8 05	16 35	8 19	16 41	8 20	16 54
29	7 43	16 44	7 53	16 54	7 54	16 48	7 59	16 46	8 03	16 37	8 17	16 44	8 19	16 56
30	7 42	16 46	7 52	16 56	7 53	16 50	7 58	16 47	8 01	16 39	8 15	16 46	8 17	16 58
31	7 41	16 48	7 50	16 58	7 51	16 52	7 56	16 49	7 59	16 41	8 14	16 48	8 15	17 00

JUPITER

Day	RA	Dec.	Transit	5° high 52°	5° high 56°
	h m	° ′	h m	h m	h m
1	14 30.9	−13 40	7 48	3 37	3 54
11	14 36.6	−14 05	7 14	3 06	3 24
21	14 41.4	−14 26	6 40	2 34	2 52
31	14 45.3	−14 42	6 04	2 00	2 19

Diameters – equatorial 35″ polar 33″

SATURN

Day	RA	Dec.	Transit	5° high 52°	5° high 56°
	h m	° ′	h m	h m	h m
1	21 58.9	−13 51	15 15	19 25	19 08
11	22 02.7	−13 30	14 39	18 51	18 35
21	22 06.9	−13 07	14 04	18 19	18 03
31	22 11.3	−12 43	13 29	17 46	17 31

Diameters – equatorial 16″ polar 14″
Rings – major axis 36″ minor axis 7″

URANUS

Day	RA	Dec.	Transit	10° high 52°	10° high 56°
	h m	° ′	h m	h m	h m
1	19 33.6	−22 09	12 50	10 33	11 30
11	19 36.1	−22 04	12 13	9 55	10 51
21	19 38.6	−21 58	11 36	9 17	10 12
31	19 41.1	−21 52	10 59	8 39	9 33

Diameter 4″

NEPTUNE

Day	RA	Dec.	Transit	10° high 52°	10° high 56°
	h m	° ′	h m	h m	h m
1	19 28.1	−21 16	12 44	10 18	11 07
11	19 29.7	−21 13	12 07	9 39	10 28
21	19 31.3	−21 10	11 29	9 01	9 50
31	19 32.9	−21 06	10 51	8 23	9 11

Diameter 2″

February 1994

SECOND MONTH, 28 DAYS. *Februa*, Roman festival of Purification

Sun's Longitude 330° ♓ 18ᵈ21ʰ

1	Tuesday	Sir Stanley Matthews b. 1915	*week 5 day 32*
2	Wednesday	**Presentation of Christ.** Fritz Kreisler b. 1875	33
3	Thursday	Beau Nash d. 1762. Walter Bagehot b. 1826	34
4	Friday	End of sweet rationing 1953	35
5	Saturday	Sir John Pritchard b. 1921	36
6	Sunday	**8th S. before Easter.** *Queen's Accession 1952*	*week 6 day 37*
7	Monday	Sir Thomas More b. 1478. Mrs Ann Radcliffe d. 1823	38
8	Tuesday	Mary, Queen of Scots *exec.* 1587	39
9	Wednesday	Alban Berg b. 1885. Jim Laker b. 1922	40
10	Thursday	*Chinese Year of the Dog.* Samuel Plimsoll b. 1824	41
11	Friday	Lateran Treaty signed 1929. Mary Quant b. 1934	42
12	Saturday	RAMADAN begins. Abraham Lincoln b. 1809	43
13	Sunday	**7th S. before Easter.** Massacre of Glencoe 1692	*week 7 day 44*
14	Monday	St Valentine's Day. Francesco Cavalli b. 1602	45
15	Tuesday	Shrove Tuesday. Sir Ernest Shackleton b. 1874	46
16	Wednesday	**Ash Wednesday.** Angela Carter d. 1992	47
17	Thursday	Molière d. 1673. Heinrich Heine d. 1856	48
18	Friday	Queen Mary b. 1516. Michelangelo Buonarroti d. 1564	49
19	Saturday	*Duke of York b. 1960.* Cdr. Robert Peary d. 1920	50
20	Sunday	**1st S. in Lent.** Dame Marie Rambert b. 1888	*week 8 day 51*
21	Monday	Andres Segovia b. 1894. W. H. Auden b. 1907	52
22	Tuesday	1st Baron Baden-Powell b. 1857	53
23	Wednesday	George Watts b. 1817. Sir Adrian Boult d. 1983	54
24	Thursday	Wilhelm Grimm b. 1786. Joseph Rowntree d. 1925	55
25	Friday	Pierre Renoir b. 1841. Tennessee Williams d. 1983	56
26	Saturday	Victor Hugo b. 1802. Sir Harry Lauder d. 1950	57
27	Sunday	**2nd S. in Lent.** Lawrence Durrell b. 1912	*week 9 day 58*
28	Monday	Relief of Ladysmith 1900	59

ASTRONOMICAL PHENOMENA

d	h	
1	18	Saturn in conjunction with Mercury. Saturn 1° S.
3	07	Jupiter in conjunction with Moon. Jupiter 3° N.
4	21	Mercury at greatest elongation E.18°
9	16	Mars in conjunction with Moon. Mars 6° S.
11	03	Venus in conjunction with Moon. Venus 6° S.
11	09	Saturn in conjunction with Moon. Saturn 6° S.
11	21	Mercury in conjunction with Moon. Mercury 2° S.
14	03	Saturn in conjunction with Venus. Saturn 0°.05 N.
16	17	Venus in conjunction with Mercury. Venus 5° S.
19	08	Saturn in conjunction with Mercury. Saturn 5° S.
20	08	Mercury in inferior conjunction
21	17	Saturn in conjunction with Sun
28	01	Mars in conjunction with Mercury. Mars 4° S.

CONSTELLATIONS

The following constellations are near the meridian at

	d	h		d	h
January	1	24	February	15	21
January	16	23	March	1	20
February	1	22	March	16	19

Draco (below the Pole), Camelopardus, Auriga, Taurus, Gemini, Orion, Canis Minor, Monoceros, Lepus, Canis Major and Puppis

MINIMA OF ALGOL

d	h	d	h	d	h
2	17.6	14	04.9	22	19.4
5	14.4	17	01.7	25	16.2
8	11.3	19	22.6	28	13.0
11	08.1				

THE MOON

Phases, Apsides and Node	d	h	m
☾ Last Quarter	3	08	06
● New Moon	10	14	30
☽ First Quarter	18	17	47
○ Full Moon	26	01	15
Apogee (404,980 km)	16	01	35
Perigee (361,845 km)	27	22	08

Mean longitude of ascending node on February 1, 239°

THE SUN

s.d. 16′.2

Day	Right Ascension	Dec.	Equation of time	Rise 52°	Rise 56°	Transit	Set 52°	Set 56°	Sidereal time	Transit of First Point of Aries
	h m s	° ′	m s	h m	h m	h m	h m	h m	h m s	h m s
1	20 57 25	17 13	− 13 31	7 40	7 55	12 14	16 47	16 33	8 43 54	15 13 36
2	21 01 29	16 56	− 13 39	7 39	7 53	12 14	16 49	16 35	8 47 50	15 09 40
3	21 05 33	16 39	− 13 46	7 37	7 52	12 14	16 51	16 37	8 51 47	15 05 44
4	21 09 36	16 21	− 13 53	7 36	7 50	12 14	16 53	16 39	8 55 43	15 01 49
5	21 13 38	16 03	− 13 58	7 34	7 48	12 14	16 55	16 41	8 59 40	14 57 53
6	21 17 39	15 45	− 14 03	7 32	7 45	12 14	16 57	16 43	9 03 36	14 53 57
7	21 21 40	15 27	− 14 07	7 30	7 43	12 14	16 59	16 46	9 07 33	14 50 01
8	21 25 40	15 08	− 14 10	7 29	7 41	12 14	17 00	16 48	9 11 30	14 46 05
9	21 29 39	14 49	− 14 13	7 27	7 39	12 14	17 02	16 50	9 15 26	14 42 09
10	21 33 37	14 29	− 14 14	7 25	7 37	12 14	17 04	16 52	9 19 23	14 38 13
11	21 37 34	14 10	− 14 15	7 23	7 35	12 14	17 06	16 54	9 23 19	14 34 17
12	21 41 31	13 50	− 14 15	7 21	7 33	12 14	17 08	16 57	9 27 16	14 30 21
13	21 45 27	13 30	− 14 15	7 19	7 30	12 14	17 10	16 59	9 31 12	14 26 25
14	21 49 22	13 10	− 14 13	7 18	7 28	12 14	17 12	17 01	9 35 09	14 22 29
15	21 53 16	12 50	− 14 11	7 16	7 26	12 14	17 14	17 03	9 39 05	14 18 34
16	21 57 10	12 29	− 14 08	7 14	7 24	12 14	17 15	17 05	9 43 02	14 14 38
17	22 01 03	12 08	− 14 05	7 12	7 21	12 14	17 17	17 08	9 46 59	14 10 42
18	22 04 55	11 47	− 14 00	7 10	7 19	12 14	17 19	17 10	9 50 55	14 06 46
19	22 08 47	11 26	− 13 55	7 08	7 17	12 14	17 21	17 12	9 54 52	14 02 50
20	22 12 38	11 05	− 13 49	7 06	7 14	12 14	17 23	17 14	9 58 48	13 58 54
21	22 16 28	10 43	− 13 43	7 04	7 12	12 14	17 25	17 16	10 02 45	13 54 58
22	22 20 17	10 21	− 13 36	7 01	7 09	12 14	17 26	17 19	10 06 41	13 51 02
23	22 24 06	9 59	− 13 28	6 59	7 07	12 13	17 28	17 21	10 10 38	13 47 06
24	22 27 54	9 37	− 13 20	6 57	7 05	12 13	17 30	17 23	10 14 34	13 43 10
25	22 31 42	9 15	− 13 11	6 55	7 02	12 13	17 32	17 25	10 18 31	13 39 14
26	22 35 29	8 53	− 13 01	6 53	7 00	12 13	17 34	17 27	10 22 28	13 35 19
27	22 39 15	8 31	− 12 51	6 51	6 57	12 13	17 36	17 29	10 26 24	13 31 23
28	22 43 01	8 08	− 12 40	6 49	6 55	12 13	17 37	17 31	10 30 21	13 27 27

DURATION OF TWILIGHT (in minutes)

Latitude	52°	56°	52°	56°	52°	56°	52°	56°
	1 February		11 February		21 February		28 February	
Civil	37	41	35	39	34	38	34	38
Nautical	77	86	75	83	74	81	73	81
Astronomical	117	130	114	126	113	125	112	124

THE NIGHT SKY

Mercury, being at greatest eastern elongation (18°) on the 4th, is visible as an evening object, magnitude −0.8 to + 2.0, for the first half of the month. It may be seen low above the WSW horizon around the time of end of evening civil twilight. If conditions are very good on the evening of the 11th it may be possible to see the thin sliver of the New Moon, just over one day old, about 3° to the right of Mercury, just before setting in the west. On the evening of the 1st Mercury passes only 1° north of Saturn, though this event is unlikely to be detected without optical aid.

Venus is too close to the Sun for observation at first. However, during the last ten days of the month it is visible in the evenings for a short while after sunset, though only about 5° above the WSW horizon. The magnitude of Venus is −3.9.

Mars remains too close to the Sun for observation.

Jupiter, magnitude −2.1, is a brilliant object in the SE sky in the mornings. On the morning of the 3rd, the Moon, at Last Quarter, will be seen passing 3° south of the planet. On the last day of the month Jupiter reaches its first stationary point and will then commence its retrograde motion.

Saturn has come to the end of its evening apparition and will not be seen again until April.

Zodiacal Light. The evening cone may be observed in the western sky after the end of twilight from the beginning of the month until the 11th and again after the 26th. This faint phenomenon is only visible in good conditions, in the absence of both moonlight and artificial lighting.

THE MOON

Day	RA	Dec.	Hor. par.	Semi-diam.	Sun's co-long.	PA of Bright Limb	Phase	Age	Rise 52°	Rise 56°	Transit	Set 52°	Set 56°
	h m	°	'	'	°	°	%	d	h m	h m	h m	h m	h m
1	12 35	− 7.9	59.6	16.2	149	115	76	20.0	23 48	—	3 59	9 19	9 10
2	13 30	−12.5	59.4	16.2	161	113	65	21.0	—	0 00	4 52	9 47	9 34
3	14 26	−16.3	59.2	16.1	173	109	54	22.0	1 07	1 23	5 47	10 20	10 03
4	15 24	−19.2	58.8	16.0	185	104	43	23.0	2 22	2 42	6 43	11 00	10 40
5	16 22	−20.9	58.4	15.9	197	100	32	24.0	3 30	3 52	7 40	11 49	11 27
6	17 21	−21.3	58.0	15.8	210	95	22	25.0	4 28	4 51	8 37	12 48	12 25
7	18 19	−20.5	57.6	15.7	222	91	14	26.0	5 16	5 37	9 32	13 53	13 33
8	19 15	−18.6	57.1	15.6	234	89	7	27.0	5 55	6 12	10 25	15 03	14 47
9	20 09	−15.7	56.6	15.4	246	90	3	28.0	6 26	6 39	11 16	16 14	16 02
10	21 00	−12.0	56.1	15.3	258	108	1	29.0	6 51	7 01	12 03	17 25	17 17
11	21 49	− 7.9	55.6	15.2	270	203	0	0.4	7 13	7 19	12 49	18 35	18 31
12	22 36	− 3.6	55.2	15.0	283	232	2	1.4	7 33	7 35	13 32	19 43	19 43
13	23 21	+ 0.9	54.8	14.9	295	238	6	2.4	7 53	7 51	14 15	20 49	20 53
14	0 07	+ 5.2	54.4	14.8	307	241	11	3.4	8 12	8 07	14 57	21 55	22 03
15	0 52	+ 9.3	54.2	14.8	319	244	18	4.4	8 33	8 24	15 40	23 00	23 12
16	1 38	+13.0	54.1	14.8	331	247	25	5.4	8 56	8 43	16 24	—	—
17	2 25	+16.1	54.2	14.8	344	251	34	6.4	9 23	9 07	17 10	0 04	0 20
18	3 14	+18.6	54.5	14.8	356	255	43	7.4	9 55	9 36	17 57	1 07	1 25
19	4 04	+20.3	54.9	14.9	8	259	53	8.4	10 35	10 13	18 47	2 07	2 28
20	4 56	+21.1	55.4	15.1	20	263	62	9.4	11 23	11 01	19 38	3 02	3 24
21	5 50	+20.9	56.2	15.3	32	268	72	10.4	12 20	12 00	20 31	3 51	4 12
22	6 45	+19.6	57.0	15.5	44	272	80	11.4	13 27	13 09	21 24	4 33	4 52
23	7 40	+17.2	57.9	15.8	57	275	88	12.4	14 40	14 26	22 17	5 09	5 24
24	8 35	+13.8	58.7	16.0	69	276	94	13.4	15 58	15 48	23 10	5 40	5 51
25	9 30	+ 9.5	59.5	16.2	81	270	98	14.4	17 19	17 14	—	6 07	6 14
26	10 25	+ 4.5	60.1	16.4	93	210	100	15.4	18 42	18 41	0 03	6 32	6 34
27	11 21	− 0.7	60.5	16.5	105	132	99	16.4	20 05	20 10	0 56	6 56	6 54
28	12 16	− 6.0	60.6	16.5	117	121	94	17.4	21 29	21 38	1 50	7 22	7 15

MERCURY

Day	RA	Dec.	Diam.	Phase	Transit	5° high 52°	5° high 56°
	h m	°	"	%	h m	h m	h m
1	22 07	−12.1	6	69	13 23	17 48	17 33
3	22 16	−10.7	7	61	13 24	17 56	17 43
5	22 24	− 9.5	7	53	13 24	18 02	17 51
7	22 29	− 8.4	8	43	13 21	18 05	17 55
9	22 33	− 7.4	8	34	13 16	18 04	17 55
11	22 34	− 6.7	9	24	13 08	18 00	17 51
13	22 32	− 6.3	9	16	12 58	17 51	17 42
15	22 28	− 6.3	10	9	12 45	17 38	17 29
17	22 22	− 6.5	10	4	12 31	17 21	17 12
19	22 14	− 7.0	10	1	12 15	17 02	16 53
21	22 06	− 7.7	11	1	11 59	7 15	7 25
23	21 58	− 8.6	11	3	11 43	7 04	7 15
25	21 50	− 9.5	11	6	11 28	6 54	7 06
27	21 44	−10.3	10	10	11 15	6 46	6 58
29	21 40	−11.1	10	15	11 03	6 38	6 52
31	21 38	−11.8	10	20	10 54	6 32	6 47

VENUS

Day	RA	Dec.	Diam.	Phase	Transit	5° high 52°	5° high 56°
	h m	°	"	%	h m	h m	h m
1	21 13	−17.4	10	100	12 30	16 18	15 56
6	21 38	−15.6	10	100	12 35	16 36	16 17
11	22 03	−13.5	10	100	12 40	16 54	16 38
16	22 27	−11.3	10	99	12 44	17 12	16 58
21	22 50	− 9.0	10	99	12 48	17 29	17 18
26	23 14	− 6.5	10	99	12 51	17 46	17 38
31	23 37	− 4.0	10	98	12 55	18 03	17 57

MARS

Day	RA	Dec.	Diam.	Phase	Transit	5° high 52°	5° high 56°
1	20 22	−20.5	4	100	11 38	8 13	8 42
6	20 38	−19.6	4	100	11 34	8 03	8 29
11	20 54	−18.5	4	100	11 31	7 52	8 16
16	21 10	−17.4	4	99	11 27	7 40	8 02
21	21 26	−16.3	4	99	11 23	7 28	7 48
26	21 41	−15.0	4	99	11 18	7 15	7 34
31	21 56	−13.7	4	99	11 14	7 03	7 19

SUNRISE AND SUNSET

	London		Bristol		Birmingham		Manchester		Newcastle		Glasgow		Belfast	
	0°05′	51°30′	2°35′	51°28′	1°55′	52°28′	2°15′	53°28′	1°37′	54°59′	4°14′	55°52′	5°56′	54°35′
	h m	h m	h m	h m	h m	h m	h m	h m	h m	h m	h m	h m	h m	h m
1	7 39	16 49	7 49	17 00	7 50	16 54	7 54	16 51	7 58	16 43	8 12	16 50	8 13	17 02
2	7 38	16 51	7 47	17 01	7 48	16 55	7 53	16 53	7 56	16 45	8 10	16 52	8 12	17 04
3	7 36	16 53	7 46	17 03	7 46	16 57	7 51	16 55	7 54	16 47	8 08	16 54	8 10	17 06
4	7 34	16 55	7 44	17 05	7 45	16 59	7 49	16 57	7 52	16 49	8 06	16 57	8 08	17 08
5	7 33	16 57	7 43	17 07	7 43	17 01	7 48	16 59	7 50	16 51	8 04	16 59	8 06	17 10
6	7 31	16 59	7 41	17 09	7 41	17 03	7 46	17 01	7 48	16 54	8 02	17 01	8 04	17 12
7	7 29	17 00	7 39	17 10	7 39	17 05	7 44	17 03	7 46	16 56	8 00	17 03	8 02	17 14
8	7 28	17 02	7 37	17 12	7 38	17 07	7 42	17 05	7 44	16 58	7 58	17 05	8 00	17 16
9	7 26	17 04	7 36	17 14	7 36	17 09	7 40	17 07	7 42	17 00	7 56	17 07	7 58	17 18
10	7 24	17 06	7 34	17 16	7 34	17 11	7 38	17 09	7 40	17 02	7 54	17 10	7 56	17 21
11	7 22	17 08	7 32	17 18	7 32	17 13	7 36	17 11	7 38	17 04	7 51	17 12	7 54	17 23
12	7 20	17 10	7 30	17 20	7 30	17 14	7 34	17 13	7 36	17 06	7 49	17 14	7 52	17 25
13	7 19	17 11	7 28	17 21	7 28	17 16	7 32	17 15	7 34	17 08	7 47	17 16	7 50	17 27
14	7 17	17 13	7 27	17 23	7 26	17 18	7 30	17 17	7 32	17 10	7 45	17 18	7 48	17 29
15	7 15	17 15	7 25	17 25	7 24	17 20	7 28	17 19	7 30	17 13	7 42	17 21	7 46	17 31
16	7 13	17 17	7 23	17 27	7 22	17 22	7 26	17 21	7 27	17 15	7 40	17 23	7 44	17 33
17	7 11	17 19	7 21	17 29	7 20	17 24	7 24	17 23	7 25	17 17	7 38	17 25	7 41	17 35
18	7 09	17 20	7 19	17 31	7 18	17 26	7 22	17 25	7 23	17 19	7 36	17 27	7 39	17 37
19	7 07	17 22	7 17	17 32	7 16	17 28	7 20	17 27	7 21	17 21	7 33	17 29	7 37	17 39
20	7 05	17 24	7 15	17 34	7 14	17 30	7 18	17 29	7 18	17 23	7 31	17 31	7 35	17 41
21	7 03	17 26	7 13	17 36	7 12	17 31	7 15	17 31	7 16	17 25	7 28	17 34	7 32	17 43
22	7 01	17 28	7 11	17 38	7 10	17 33	7 13	17 33	7 14	17 27	7 26	17 36	7 30	17 45
23	6 59	17 29	7 09	17 40	7 08	17 35	7 11	17 35	7 11	17 29	7 24	17 38	7 28	17 47
24	6 57	17 31	7 07	17 41	7 06	17 37	7 09	17 37	7 09	17 31	7 21	17 40	7 26	17 49
25	6 55	17 33	7 05	17 43	7 04	17 39	7 07	17 39	7 07	17 33	7 19	17 42	7 23	17 51
26	6 53	17 35	7 02	17 45	7 01	17 41	7 04	17 40	7 04	17 35	7 16	17 44	7 21	17 53
27	6 50	17 37	7 00	17 47	6 59	17 43	7 02	17 42	7 02	17 37	7 14	17 46	7 19	17 55
28	6 48	17 38	6 58	17 48	6 57	17 44	7 00	17 44	7 00	17 40	7 11	17 49	7 16	17 57

JUPITER

Day	RA	Dec.	Transit	5° high	
				52°	56°
	h m	° ′	h m	h m	h m
1	14 45.7	−14 44	6 01	1 57	2 15
11	14 48.4	−14 54	5 24	1 21	1 40
21	14 50.0	−14 59	4 46	0 44	1 03
31	14 50.3	−14 59	4 08	0 05	0 24

Diameters – equatorial 38″ polar 36″

SATURN

Day	RA	Dec.	Transit	5° high	
				52°	56°
	h m	° ′	h m	h m	h m
1	22 11.7	−12 40	13 26	17 43	17 27
11	22 16.3	−12 15	12 51	17 11	16 56
21	22 21.0	−11 49	12 16	16 39	16 24
31	22 25.6	−11 24	11 42	16 06	15 52

Diameters – equatorial 15″ polar 14″
Rings – major axis 35″ minor axis 6″

URANUS

Day	RA	Dec.	Transit	10° high	
				52°	56°
	h m	° ′	h m	h m	h m
1	19 41.3	−21 52	10 56	8 35	9 29
11	19 43.7	−21 46	10 19	7 57	8 51
21	19 45.9	−21 41	9 42	7 19	8 12
31	19 47.9	−21 36	9 04	6 41	7 33

Diameter 4″

NEPTUNE

Day	RA	Dec.	Transit	10° high	
				52°	56°
	h m	° ′	h m	h m	h m
1	19 33.1	−21 06	10 47	8 19	9 07
11	19 34.5	−21 03	10 10	7 41	8 28
21	19 35.9	−21 00	9 32	7 02	7 49
31	19 37.1	−20 57	8 54	6 23	7 10

Diameter 2″

March 1994

THIRD MONTH, 31 DAYS. *Mars*, Roman god of battle

Sun's Longitude 0° ♈ 20ᵈ 20ʰ

1	*Tuesday*	St David's Day. David Niven *b*. 1910	*week* 9 *day* 60
2	*Wednesday*	Cardinal Archbishop of Westminster *b*. 1923	61
3	*Thursday*	William Macready *b*. 1793. Sir Henry Wood *b*. 1869	62
4	*Friday*	Patrick Moore *b*. 1923. Jim Clark *b*. 1936	63
5	*Saturday*	Henry II *b*. 1133. Josef Stalin *d*. 1953	64
6	*Sunday*	**3rd S. in Lent.** Cyrano de Bergerac *b*. 1619	*week* 10 *day* 65
7	*Monday*	First patent of Bell telephone 1876	66
8	*Tuesday*	Kenneth Grahame *b*. 1859. Hector Berlioz *d*. 1869	67
9	*Wednesday*	Amerigo Vespucci *b*. 1451. Yuri Gagarin *b*. 1934	68
10	*Thursday*	*Prince Edward b. 1964.* Owen Brannigan *b*. 1908	69
11	*Friday*	Sir Malcolm Campbell *b*. 1885	70
12	*Saturday*	Cesare Borgia *d*. 1507. Thomas Arne *b*. 1710	71
13	*Sunday*	**4th S. in Lent.** Mothering Sunday	*week* 11 *day* 72
14	*Monday*	Commonwealth Day. Maxim Gorky *b*. 1868	73
15	*Tuesday*	Julius Caesar *assass.* 44 BC	74
16	*Wednesday*	Aubrey Beardsley *d*. 1898	75
17	*Thursday*	St Patrick's Day. *Bank Holiday in Northern Ireland*	76
18	*Friday*	Nikolai Rimsky-Korsakov *b*. 1844	77
19	*Saturday*	**St Joseph of Nazareth.** Dr David Livingstone *b*. 1813	78
20	*Sunday*	**5th S. in Lent.** Dame Vera Lynn *b*. 1917	*week* 12 *day* 79
21	*Monday*	Sharpeville Massacre, South Africa 1960	80
22	*Tuesday*	Sir Anthony van Dyck *b*. 1599	81
23	*Wednesday*	Princess Eugenie of York *b*. 1990	82
24	*Thursday*	Union of English and Scottish crowns 1603	83
25	*Friday*	**The Annunciation.** Treaty of Rome 1957	84
26	*Saturday*	A. E. Housman *b*. 1859. Sir Noël Coward *d*. 1973	85
27	*Sunday*	**Palm Sunday.** PASSOVER begins	*week* 13 *day* 86
28	*Monday*	Dame Flora Robson *b*. 1902	87
29	*Tuesday*	John Major *b*. 1943. Joyce Cary *d*. 1957	88
30	*Wednesday*	*Hilary Law Sittings end.* Paul Verlaine *b*. 1844	89
31	*Thursday*	**Maundy Thursday.** René Descartes *b*. 1596	90

ASTRONOMICAL PHENOMENA

d	h	
2	15	Jupiter in conjunction with Moon. Jupiter 2° N.
10	01	Mercury in conjunction with Moon. Mercury 4° S.
10	18	Mars in conjunction with Moon. Mars 6° S.
10	23	Saturn in conjunction with Moon. Saturn 6° S.
13	12	Venus in conjunction with Moon. Venus 5° S.
14	05	Saturn in conjunction with Mars. Saturn 0°.3 S.
19	02	Mercury at greatest elongation W.28°
20	20	Equinox
24	10	Saturn in conjunction with Mercury. Saturn 0°.2 N.
29	22	Jupiter in conjunction with Moon. Jupiter 2° N.

CONSTELLATIONS

The following are near the meridian at

	d	h		d	h
February	1	24	March	16	21
February	15	23	April	1	20
March	1	22	April	15	19

Cepheus (below the Pole), Camelopardus, Lynx, Gemini, Cancer, Leo, Canis Minor, Hydra, Monoceros, Canis Major and Puppis

MINIMA OF ALGOL

d	h	d	h	d	h
3	09.8	14	21.1	23	11.6
6	06.7	17	18.0	26	08.4
9	03.5	20	14.8	29	05.2
12	00.3				

THE MOON

Phases, Apsides and Node	d	h	m
☾ Last Quarter	4	16	53
● New Moon	12	07	05
☽ First Quarter	20	12	14
○ Full Moon	27	11	10
Apogee (405,892 km)	15	17	12
Perigee (357,959 km)	28	06	13

Mean longitude of ascending node on March 1, 238°

THE SUN   s.d. 16′.1

Day	Right Ascension	Dec.	Equation of time	Rise 52°	Rise 56°	Transit	Set 52°	Set 56°	Sidereal time	Transit of First Point of Aries
	h m s	° ′	m s	h m	h m	h m	h m	h m	h m s	h m s
1	22 46 46	−7 45	−12 29	6 46	6 52	12 12	17 39	17 34	10 34 17	13 23 31
2	22 50 31	−7 23	−12 17	6 44	6 50	12 12	17 41	17 36	10 38 14	13 19 35
3	22 54 15	−7 00	−12 05	6 42	6 47	12 12	17 43	17 38	10 42 10	13 15 39
4	22 57 59	−6 37	−11 52	6 40	6 45	12 12	17 45	17 40	10 46 07	13 11 43
5	23 01 43	−6 14	−11 39	6 38	6 42	12 12	17 46	17 42	10 50 03	13 07 47
6	23 05 26	−5 50	−11 26	6 35	6 40	12 11	17 48	17 44	10 54 00	13 03 51
7	23 09 08	−5 27	−11 12	6 33	6 37	12 11	17 50	17 46	10 57 56	12 59 55
8	23 12 50	−5 04	−10 57	6 31	6 34	12 11	17 52	17 48	11 01 53	12 55 59
9	23 16 32	−4 40	−10 43	6 29	6 32	12 11	17 53	17 50	11 05 50	12 52 04
10	23 20 14	−4 17	−10 28	6 26	6 29	12 10	17 55	17 53	11 09 46	12 48 08
11	23 23 55	−3 53	−10 12	6 24	6 27	12 10	17 57	17 55	11 13 43	12 44 12
12	23 27 36	−3 30	− 9 57	6 22	6 24	12 10	17 59	17 57	11 17 39	12 40 16
13	23 31 16	−3 06	− 9 41	6 20	6 21	12 10	18 01	17 59	11 21 36	12 36 20
14	23 34 57	−2 42	− 9 24	6 17	6 19	12 09	18 02	18 01	11 25 32	12 32 24
15	23 38 37	−2 19	− 9 08	6 15	6 16	12 09	18 04	18 03	11 29 29	12 28 28
16	23 42 16	−1 55	− 8 51	6 13	6 14	12 09	18 06	18 05	11 33 25	12 24 32
17	23 45 56	−1 31	− 8 34	6 10	6 11	12 08	18 07	18 07	11 37 22	12 20 36
18	23 49 35	−1 08	− 8 17	6 08	6 08	12 08	18 09	18 09	11 41 19	12 16 40
19	23 53 14	−0 44	− 7 59	6 06	6 06	12 08	18 11	18 11	11 45 15	12 12 45
20	23 56 53	−0 20	− 7 42	6 03	6 03	12 08	18 13	18 13	11 49 12	12 08 49
21	0 00 32	+0 03	− 7 24	6 01	6 00	12 07	18 14	18 15	11 53 08	12 04 53
22	0 04 11	+0 27	− 7 06	5 59	5 58	12 07	18 16	18 17	11 57 05	12 00 57
23	0 07 49	+0 51	− 6 48	5 56	5 55	12 07	18 18	18 19	12 01 01	11 57 01
24	0 11 28	+1 14	− 6 30	5 54	5 53	12 06	18 20	18 21	12 04 58	11 53 05
25	0 15 06	+1 38	− 6 12	5 52	5 50	12 06	18 21	18 23	12 08 54	11 49 09
26	0 18 44	+2 02	− 5 53	5 50	5 47	12 06	18 23	18 25	12 12 51	11 45 13
27	0 22 23	+2 25	− 5 35	5 47	5 45	12 05	18 25	18 27	12 16 48	11 41 17
28	0 26 01	+2 49	− 5 17	5 45	5 42	12 05	18 26	18 30	12 20 44	11 37 21
29	0 29 39	+3 12	− 4 58	5 43	5 39	12 05	18 28	18 32	12 24 41	11 33 25
30	0 33 17	+3 35	− 4 40	5 40	5 37	12 05	18 30	18 34	12 28 37	11 29 30
31	0 36 56	+3 59	− 4 22	5 38	5 34	12 04	18 32	18 36	12 32 34	11 25 34

DURATION OF TWILIGHT (in minutes)

Latitude	52°	56°	52°	56°	52°	56°	52°	56°
	1 March		11 March		21 March		31 March	
Civil	34	38	34	37	34	37	34	38
Nautical	73	81	73	80	74	82	76	84
Astronomical	112	124	113	125	116	129	120	136

THE NIGHT SKY

Mercury is unsuitably placed for observation throughout the month.

Venus, magnitude −3.9, is visible as an evening object, low in the western sky after sunset. On the evening of the 13th, the thin crescent Moon is near the planet.

Mars is still too close to the Sun for observation.

Jupiter, magnitude −2.3, is a brilliant morning object in the constellation of Libra. Jupiter is now visible from the early evening onwards as it moves towards opposition in April. On the night of the 2nd to 3rd and again on the 29th to 30th the gibbous Moon will be seen passing about 3° south of the planet. The four Galilean satellites are readily observable with a small telescope, or a good pair of binoculars provided that they are held rigidly. Times of eclipses and shadow transits of these satellites are given on page 70.

Saturn remains too close to the Sun for observation throughout the month.

Zodiacal Light. The evening cone may be observed stretching up from the western horizon, along the ecliptic, after the end of twilight, from the beginning of the month until the 13th and again after the 27th.

THE MOON

Day	RA	Dec.	Hor. par.	Semi- diam.	Sun's co- long.	PA of Bright Limb	Phase	Age	Rise 52°	Rise 56°	Transit	Set 52°	Set 56°
	h m	°	′	′	°	°	%	d	h m	h m	h m	h m	h m
1	13 13	−10.9	60.5	16.5	129	116	88	18.4	22 51	23 05	2 45	7 50	7 39
2	14 11	−15.1	60.1	16.4	142	111	79	19.4	—	—	3 41	8 22	8 07
3	15 10	−18.3	59.6	16.2	154	106	69	20.4	0 10	0 28	4 38	9 01	8 42
4	16 09	−20.3	59.0	16.1	166	101	58	21.4	1 21	1 43	5 36	9 48	9 27
5	17 08	−21.1	58.3	15.9	178	95	47	22.4	2 23	2 45	6 33	10 44	10 22
6	18 06	−20.6	57.6	15.7	190	90	36	23.4	3 14	3 35	7 29	11 47	11 26
7	19 02	−18.9	57.0	15.5	202	86	26	24.4	3 55	4 13	8 22	12 54	12 37
8	19 56	−16.3	56.5	15.4	215	83	18	25.4	4 28	4 42	9 12	14 04	13 50
9	20 47	−12.9	55.9	15.2	227	81	11	26.4	4 55	5 06	10 00	15 14	15 04
10	21 35	− 9.0	55.5	15.1	239	81	5	27.4	5 18	5 25	10 45	16 22	16 17
11	22 22	− 4.8	55.1	15.0	251	87	2	28.4	5 39	5 42	11 29	17 30	17 29
12	23 08	− 0.5	54.7	14.9	263	122	0	29.4	5 58	5 58	12 12	18 37	18 39
13	23 53	+ 3.8	54.4	14.8	276	219	1	0.7	6 18	6 14	12 54	19 43	19 49
14	0 39	+ 8.0	54.2	14.8	288	237	3	1.7	6 38	6 30	13 37	20 48	20 58
15	1 24	+11.7	54.1	14.7	300	244	7	2.7	7 00	6 49	14 20	21 52	22 06
16	2 11	+15.0	54.0	14.7	312	248	12	3.7	7 26	7 11	15 05	22 55	23 12
17	2 59	+17.7	54.1	14.7	324	253	19	4.7	7 56	7 39	15 52	23 55	—
18	3 49	+19.7	54.4	14.8	337	258	27	5.7	8 33	8 12	16 40	—	0 15
19	4 39	+20.7	54.8	14.9	349	263	36	6.7	9 16	8 55	17 29	0 51	1 13
20	5 32	+20.9	55.3	15.1	1	267	45	7.7	10 09	9 48	18 20	1 42	2 03
21	6 25	+20.0	56.0	15.3	13	272	55	8.7	11 09	10 50	19 11	2 26	2 45
22	7 18	+18.1	56.9	15.5	25	276	65	9.7	12 17	12 01	20 03	3 03	3 20
23	8 12	+15.2	57.8	15.7	38	280	75	10.7	13 31	13 19	20 55	3 36	3 49
24	9 06	+11.3	58.8	16.0	50	282	84	11.7	14 49	14 41	21 47	4 04	4 13
25	10 01	+ 6.7	59.7	16.3	62	283	91	12.7	16 10	16 07	22 40	4 30	4 35
26	10 56	+ 1.6	60.5	16.5	74	280	97	13.7	17 33	17 35	23 34	4 55	4 55
27	11 51	− 3.7	61.0	16.6	86	261	100	14.7	18 58	19 05	—	5 20	5 16
28	12 49	− 8.8	61.2	16.7	98	136	99	15.7	20 24	20 36	0 29	5 48	5 39
29	13 48	−13.4	61.2	16.7	110	116	96	16.7	21 47	22 04	1 27	6 19	6 06
30	14 48	−17.1	60.8	16.6	123	108	91	17.7	23 05	23 25	2 26	6 57	6 40
31	15 50	−19.6	60.2	16.4	135	102	83	18.7	—	—	3 26	7 43	7 22

MERCURY

Day	RA	Dec.	Diam.	Phase	Transit	5° high 52°	5° high 56°
	h m	°	″	%	h m	h m	h m
1	21 40	−11.1	10	15	11 03	6 38	6 52
3	21 38	−11.8	10	20	10 54	6 32	6 47
5	21 38	−12.3	9	25	10 46	6 27	6 42
7	21 39	−12.7	9	30	10 40	6 23	6 39
9	21 41	−12.9	9	35	10 35	6 19	6 35
11	21 46	−13.0	8	39	10 31	6 16	6 32
13	21 51	−13.0	8	43	10 29	6 14	6 29
15	21 57	−12.9	8	47	10 27	6 11	6 27
17	22 04	−12.6	8	50	10 27	6 09	6 24
19	22 12	−12.2	7	54	10 27	6 06	6 21
21	22 20	−11.8	7	57	10 27	6 04	6 18
23	22 29	−11.2	7	60	10 28	6 01	6 15
25	22 38	−10.5	7	62	10 30	5 59	6 12
27	22 48	− 9.8	7	65	10 32	5 56	6 08
29	22 58	− 8.9	6	67	10 34	5 54	6 05
31	23 09	− 7.9	6	69	10 37	5 51	6 01

VENUS

Day	RA	Dec.	Diam.	Phase	Transit	5° high 52°	5° high 56°
	h m	°	″	%	h m	h m	h m
1	23 27	− 5.0	10	98	12 53	17 57	17 49
6	23 50	− 2.5	10	98	12 57	18 13	18 08
11	0 13	+ 0.1	10	98	13 00	18 29	18 27
16	0 36	+ 2.6	10	97	13 02	18 46	18 45
21	0 58	+ 5.2	10	97	13 05	19 02	19 03
26	1 21	+ 7.7	10	96	13 09	19 18	19 21
31	1 44	+10.1	10	95	13 12	19 33	19 39

MARS

Day	RA	Dec.	Diam.	Phase	Transit	5° high 52°	5° high 56°
1	21 50	−14.3	4	99	11 16	7 08	7 25
6	22 06	−12.9	4	99	11 11	6 55	7 11
11	22 21	−11.5	4	99	11 06	6 42	6 56
16	22 35	−10.1	4	99	11 02	6 29	6 41
21	22 50	− 8.6	4	99	10 57	6 15	6 26
26	23 05	− 7.1	4	98	10 52	6 02	6 11
31	23 19	− 5.6	4	98	10 46	5 48	5 56

SUNRISE AND SUNSET

	London		Bristol		Birmingham		Manchester		Newcastle		Glasgow		Belfast	
	0°05′	51°30′	2°35′	51°28′	1°55′	52°28′	2°15′	53°28′	1°37′	54°59′	4°14′	55°52′	5°56′	54°35′
	h m	h m	h m	h m	h m	h m	h m	h m	h m	h m	h m	h m	h m	h m
1	6 46	17 40	6 56	17 50	6 55	17 46	6 57	17 46	6 57	17 42	7 09	17 51	7 14	17 59
2	6 44	17 42	6 54	17 52	6 53	17 48	6 55	17 48	6 55	17 44	7 06	17 53	7 11	18 01
3	6 42	17 44	6 52	17 54	6 50	17 50	6 53	17 50	6 52	17 46	7 04	17 55	7 09	18 03
4	6 40	17 45	6 50	17 55	6 48	17 52	6 51	17 52	6 50	17 48	7 01	17 57	7 07	18 05
5	6 37	17 47	6 47	17 57	6 46	17 54	6 48	17 54	6 47	17 50	6 59	17 59	7 04	18 07
6	6 35	17 49	6 45	17 59	6 44	17 55	6 46	17 56	6 45	17 52	6 56	18 01	7 02	18 09
7	6 33	17 51	6 43	18 01	6 41	17 57	6 43	17 58	6 42	17 54	6 54	18 03	6 59	18 11
8	6 31	17 52	6 41	18 02	6 39	17 59	6 41	18 00	6 40	17 56	6 51	18 05	6 57	18 13
9	6 29	17 54	6 39	18 04	6 37	18 01	6 39	18 01	6 37	17 58	6 49	18 08	6 54	18 15
10	6 26	17 56	6 36	18 06	6 34	18 03	6 36	18 03	6 35	18 00	6 46	18 10	6 52	18 17
11	6 24	17 58	6 34	18 08	6 32	18 04	6 34	18 05	6 32	18 02	6 43	18 12	6 49	18 19
12	6 22	17 59	6 32	18 09	6 30	18 06	6 32	18 07	6 30	18 04	6 41	18 14	6 47	18 21
13	6 20	18 01	6 30	18 11	6 27	18 08	6 29	18 09	6 27	18 06	6 38	18 16	6 44	18 23
14	6 17	18 03	6 27	18 13	6 25	18 10	6 27	18 11	6 25	18 08	6 36	18 18	6 42	18 25
15	6 15	18 04	6 25	18 14	6 23	18 12	6 24	18 13	6 22	18 10	6 33	18 20	6 39	18 27
16	6 13	18 06	6 23	18 16	6 20	18 13	6 22	18 14	6 20	18 12	6 30	18 22	6 37	18 29
17	6 11	18 08	6 21	18 18	6 18	18 15	6 20	18 16	6 17	18 14	6 28	18 24	6 34	18 31
18	6 08	18 10	6 18	18 20	6 16	18 17	6 17	18 18	6 15	18 16	6 25	18 26	6 32	18 33
19	6 06	18 11	6 16	18 21	6 13	18 19	6 15	18 20	6 12	18 18	6 23	18 28	6 29	18 35
20	6 04	18 13	6 14	18 23	6 11	18 20	6 12	18 22	6 10	18 20	6 20	18 30	6 27	18 37
21	6 02	18 15	6 12	18 25	6 09	18 22	6 10	18 24	6 07	18 21	6 17	18 32	6 24	18 39
22	5 59	18 16	6 09	18 26	6 06	18 24	6 07	18 26	6 05	18 23	6 15	18 34	6 22	18 41
23	5 57	18 18	6 07	18 28	6 04	18 26	6 05	18 27	6 02	18 25	6 12	18 36	6 19	18 43
24	5 55	18 20	6 05	18 30	6 02	18 27	6 03	18 29	5 59	18 27	6 09	18 38	6 17	18 44
25	5 52	18 21	6 02	18 31	5 59	18 29	6 00	18 31	5 57	18 29	6 07	18 40	6 14	18 46
26	5 50	18 23	6 00	18 33	5 57	18 31	5 58	18 33	5 54	18 31	6 04	18 42	6 12	18 48
27	5 48	18 25	5 58	18 35	5 55	18 33	5 55	18 35	5 52	18 33	6 02	18 44	6 09	18 50
28	5 46	18 26	5 56	18 36	5 52	18 34	5 53	18 37	5 49	18 35	5 59	18 46	6 07	18 52
29	5 43	18 28	5 53	18 38	5 50	18 36	5 50	18 38	5 47	18 37	5 56	18 48	6 04	18 54
30	5 41	18 30	5 51	18 40	5 48	18 38	5 48	18 40	5 44	18 39	5 54	18 50	6 02	18 56
31	5 39	18 31	5 49	18 41	5 45	18 40	5 46	18 42	5 42	18 41	5 51	18 52	5 59	18 58

JUPITER

Day	RA	Dec.	Transit	5° high	
				52°	56°
	h m	° ′	h m	h m	h m
1	14 50.4	−14 59	4 15	0 13	0 32
11	14 49.7	−14 55	3 35	23 29	23 47
21	14 47.9	−14 45	2 54	22 46	23 04
31	14 44.9	−14 30	2 12	22 02	22 20

Diameters – equatorial 42″ polar 39″

SATURN

Day	RA	Dec.	Transit	5° high	
				52°	56°
	h m	° ′	h m	h m	h m
1	22 24.7	−11 29	11 49	7 25	7 39
11	22 29.2	−11 03	11 14	6 47	7 01
21	22 33.7	−10 38	10 39	6 10	6 23
31	22 37.9	−10 14	10 04	5 33	5 45

Diameters – equatorial 15″ polar 14″
Rings – major axis 35″ minor axis 5″

URANUS

Day	RA	Dec.	Transit	10° high	
				52°	56°
	h m	° ′	h m	h m	h m
1	19 47.5	−21 37	9 12	6 49	7 41
11	19 49.4	−21 33	8 34	6 10	7 02
21	19 50.9	−21 29	7 57	5 32	6 23
31	19 52.1	−21 26	7 18	4 53	5 44

Diameter 4″

NEPTUNE

Day	RA	Dec.	Transit	10° high	
				52°	56°
	h m	° ′	h m	h m	h m
1	19 36.9	−20 57	9 01	6 31	7 18
11	19 38.0	−20 55	8 23	5 52	6 39
21	19 38.9	−20 52	7 45	5 14	6 00
31	19 39.6	−20 51	7 06	4 35	5 21

Diameter 2″

April 1994

FOURTH MONTH, 30 DAYS. *Aperire*, to open; Earth opens to receive seed

Sun's Longitude 30° ♉ 20ᵈ 08ʰ

1	*Friday*	**Good Friday.** *Public Holiday in the UK*	*week* 13 *day* 91
2	*Saturday*	**Easter Eve.** Sergei Rachmaninoff *b.* 1873	92
3	*Sunday*	**Easter Day.** Brahms *d.* 1897	*week* 14 *day* 93
4	*Monday*	*Bank Holiday in England, Wales and Northern Ireland*	94
5	*Tuesday*	Sir Joseph Lister *b.* 1827. Chiang Kai-shek *d.* 1975	95
6	*Wednesday*	Cdr. Peary reaches North Pole 1909	96
7	*Thursday*	William Godwin *d.* 1836	97
8	*Friday*	El Greco *d.* 1614. Mary Pickford *b.* 1893	98
9	*Saturday*	National Gallery opened 1838	99
10	*Sunday*	**1st S. after Easter.** Evelyn Waugh *d.* 1966	*week* 15 *day* 100
11	*Monday*	Abdication of Napoleon 1814	101
12	*Tuesday*	*Easter Law Sittings begin*	102
13	*Wednesday*	Lord North *b.* 1732. Thomas Jefferson *b.* 1743	103
14	*Thursday*	Simone de Beauvoir *d.* 1986	104
15	*Friday*	Joe Davis *b.* 1901. Sinking of the Titanic 1912	105
16	*Saturday*	Culloden 1746. Sir Charles Chaplin *b.* 1889	106
17	*Sunday*	**2nd S. after Easter.** Benjamin Franklin *d.* 1790	*week* 16 *day* 107
18	*Monday*	Irish Free State becomes Republic of Ireland 1949	108
19	*Tuesday*	David Ricardo *b.* 1772. Lord Byron *d.* 1824	109
20	*Wednesday*	Napoleon III *b.* 1808. Bram Stoker *d.* 1912	110
21	*Thursday*	*Queen Elizabeth II b. 1926*	111
22	*Friday*	Henry Fielding *b.* 1707. Sir Henry Royce *d.* 1933	112
23	*Saturday*	St George's Day. Dame Ngaio Marsh *b.* 1899	113
24	*Sunday*	**3rd S. after Easter.** Sir Stafford Cripps *b.* 1889	*week* 17 *day* 114
25	*Monday*	**St Mark.** ANZAC landings at Gallipoli 1915	115
26	*Tuesday*	David Hume *b.* 1711. Eugene Delacroix *b.* 1798	116
27	*Wednesday*	Samuel Morse *b.* 1791. William Macready *d.* 1873	117
28	*Thursday*	Mutiny on the Bounty 1789	118
29	*Friday*	Duke Ellington *b.* 1899. Glen Byam Shaw *d.* 1986	119
30	*Saturday*	George Headley *b.* 1909. George Balanchine *d.* 1983	120

Astronomical Phenomena

d	h	
4	21	Mars in conjunction with Mercury. Mars 1° N.
7	10	Saturn in conjunction with Moon. Saturn 6° S.
8	21	Mars in conjunction with Moon. Mars 5° S.
9	04	Mercury in conjunction with Moon. Mercury 6° S.
12	23	Venus in conjunction with Moon. Venus 1° S.
26	04	Jupiter in conjunction with Moon. Jupiter 3° N.
30	09	Jupiter at opposition
30	10	Mercury in superior conjunction

Constellations

The following constellations are near the meridian at

	d	h
March	1	24
March	16	23
April	1	22
April	15	21
May	1	20
May	16	19

Cepheus (below the Pole), Cassiopeia (below the Pole), Ursa Major, Leo Minor, Leo, Sextans, Hydra and Crater

Minima of Algol

d	h	d	h	d	h
1	02.1	12	13.3	24	00.6
3	22.9	15	10.2	26	21.4
6	19.7	18	07.0	29	18.2
9	16.5	21	03.8		

The Moon

Phases, Apsides and Node	d	h	m
☾ Last Quarter	3	02	55
● New Moon	11	00	17
☽ First Quarter	19	02	34
○ Full Moon	25	19	45
Apogee (406,468 km)	11	23	49
Perigee (356,929 km)	25	17	17

Mean longitude of ascending node on April 1, 236°

THE SUN
s.d. 16'.0

Day	Right Ascension	Dec. +	Equation of time	Rise 52°	Rise 56°	Transit	Set 52°	Set 56°	Sidereal time	Transit of First Point of Aries
	h m s	° ′	m s	h m	h m	h m	h m	h m	h m s	h m s
1	0 40 34	4 22	−4 04	5 36	5 31	12 04	18 33	18 38	12 36 30	11 21 38
2	0 44 13	4 45	−3 46	5 33	5 29	12 04	18 35	18 40	12 40 27	11 17 42
3	0 47 52	5 08	−3 28	5 31	5 26	12 03	18 37	18 42	12 44 23	11 13 46
4	0 51 31	5 31	−3 11	5 29	5 24	12 03	18 38	18 44	12 48 20	11 09 50
5	0 55 10	5 54	−2 53	5 26	5 21	12 03	18 40	18 46	12 52 16	11 05 54
6	0 58 49	6 17	−2 36	5 24	5 18	12 02	18 42	18 48	12 56 13	11 01 58
7	1 02 29	6 39	−2 19	5 22	5 16	12 02	18 44	18 50	13 00 10	10 58 02
8	1 06 08	7 02	−2 02	5 20	5 13	12 02	18 45	18 52	13 04 06	10 54 06
9	1 09 48	7 24	−1 46	5 17	5 11	12 02	18 47	18 54	13 08 03	10 50 10
10	1 13 28	7 47	−1 29	5 15	5 08	12 01	18 49	18 56	13 11 59	10 46 15
11	1 17 09	8 09	−1 13	5 13	5 05	12 01	18 50	18 58	13 15 56	10 42 19
12	1 20 50	8 31	−0 57	5 11	5 03	12 01	18 52	19 00	13 19 52	10 38 23
13	1 24 31	8 53	−0 42	5 08	5 00	12 01	18 54	19 02	13 23 49	10 34 27
14	1 28 12	9 15	−0 27	5 06	4 58	12 00	18 56	19 04	13 27 45	10 30 31
15	1 31 54	9 36	−0 12	5 04	4 55	12 00	18 57	19 06	13 31 42	10 26 35
16	1 35 36	9 58	+0 03	5 02	4 53	12 00	18 59	19 08	13 35 39	10 22 39
17	1 39 18	10 19	+0 17	5 00	4 50	12 00	19 01	19 10	13 39 35	10 18 43
18	1 43 01	10 40	+0 31	4 58	4 48	11 59	19 02	19 12	13 43 32	10 14 47
19	1 46 44	11 01	+0 44	4 55	4 45	11 59	19 04	19 14	13 47 28	10 10 51
20	1 50 28	11 22	+0 57	4 53	4 43	11 59	19 06	19 16	13 51 25	10 06 56
21	1 54 11	11 42	+1 10	4 51	4 40	11 59	19 07	19 18	13 55 21	10 03 00
22	1 57 56	12 03	+1 22	4 49	4 38	11 59	19 09	19 21	13 59 18	9 59 04
23	2 01 40	12 23	+1 34	4 47	4 36	11 58	19 11	19 23	14 03 14	9 55 08
24	2 05 26	12 43	+1 45	4 45	4 33	11 58	19 13	19 25	14 07 11	9 51 12
25	2 09 11	13 03	+1 56	4 43	4 31	11 58	19 14	19 27	14 11 08	9 47 16
26	2 12 57	13 22	+2 07	4 41	4 28	11 58	19 16	19 29	14 15 04	9 43 20
27	2 16 44	13 41	+2 17	4 39	4 26	11 58	19 18	19 31	14 19 01	9 39 24
28	2 20 31	14 00	+2 26	4 37	4 24	11 57	19 19	19 33	14 22 57	9 35 28
29	2 24 19	14 19	+2 35	4 35	4 21	11 57	19 21	19 35	14 26 54	9 31 32
30	2 28 07	14 38	+2 44	4 33	4 19	11 57	19 23	19 37	14 30 50	9 27 36

DURATION OF TWILIGHT (in minutes)

Latitude	52°	56°	52°	56°	52°	56°	52°	56°
	1 April		11 April		21 April		30 April	
Civil	34	38	35	40	37	42	39	44
Nautical	76	85	79	90	84	96	89	105
Astronomical	121	137	128	148	138	167	152	200

THE NIGHT SKY

Mercury is not suitably placed for observation in April, passing through superior conjunction on the 30th.

Venus, magnitude −3.9, continues to be visible for a short time in the evenings, low in the western sky after sunset. On the evening of the 12th the thin crescent Moon, less than two days old, will be seen approaching Venus.

Mars continues to remain too close to the Sun for observation.

Jupiter reaches opposition on the last day of the month and therefore is visible throughout the hours of darkness. Jupiter is in Libra and a magnificent object in the night sky, magnitude −2.5. The Full Moon passes 3° south of the planet in the early hours of the 26th.

Saturn is still too close to the Sun for observation during the first half of the month. Later, it gradually becomes visible as a difficult morning object, low in the SE sky before the morning twilight inhibits observation. Its magnitude is +1.0. Saturn is in the constellation of Aquarius.

THE MOON

Day	RA h m	Dec. °	Hor. par. '	Semi- diam. '	Sun's co- long. °	PA of Bright Limb °	Phase %	Age d	Rise 52° h m	Rise 56° h m	Transit h m	Set 52° h m	Set 56° h m
1	16 51	−20.8	59.4	16.2	147	96	73	19.7	0 13	0 34	4 25	8 37	8 15
2	17 51	−20.6	58.5	15.9	159	90	62	20.7	1 09	1 30	5 23	9 39	9 19
3	18 49	−19.2	57.7	15.7	171	85	51	21.7	1 54	2 13	6 18	10 47	10 29
4	19 43	−16.8	56.9	15.5	184	81	41	22.7	2 30	2 45	7 09	11 56	11 42
5	20 35	−13.6	56.2	15.3	196	78	31	23.7	2 59	3 10	7 58	13 06	12 55
6	21 24	− 9.8	55.5	15.1	208	75	22	24.7	3 23	3 31	8 44	14 14	14 08
7	22 11	− 5.7	55.0	15.0	220	74	14	25.7	3 44	3 49	9 27	15 22	15 19
8	22 57	− 1.5	54.6	14.9	232	75	8	26.7	4 04	4 05	10 10	16 28	16 29
9	23 42	+ 2.8	54.3	14.8	245	77	4	27.7	4 24	4 21	10 52	17 33	17 38
10	0 27	+ 6.9	54.1	14.7	257	85	1	28.7	4 44	4 37	11 35	18 38	18 47
11	1 12	+10.7	54.0	14.7	269	155	0	29.7	5 05	4 55	12 18	19 43	19 55
12	1 59	+14.2	53.9	14.7	281	240	1	1.0	5 30	5 17	13 03	20 46	21 02
13	2 46	+17.0	54.0	14.7	293	250	4	2.0	5 59	5 42	13 48	21 47	22 06
14	3 36	+19.1	54.1	14.8	306	257	8	3.0	6 33	6 14	14 36	22 44	23 05
15	4 26	+20.4	54.4	14.8	318	262	14	4.0	7 14	6 53	15 25	23 36	23 58
16	5 17	+20.8	54.8	14.9	330	267	21	5.0	8 03	7 42	16 14	—	—
17	6 09	+20.2	55.3	15.1	342	272	29	6.0	9 00	8 40	17 04	0 22	0 42
18	7 02	+18.6	55.9	15.2	355	277	39	7.0	10 03	9 46	17 54	1 01	1 19
19	7 54	+16.1	56.7	15.4	7	281	49	8.0	11 12	10 59	18 44	1 34	1 49
20	8 46	+12.7	57.6	15.7	19	284	60	9.0	12 26	12 16	19 35	2 03	2 14
21	9 39	+ 8.5	58.5	15.9	31	287	70	10.0	13 43	13 38	20 25	2 29	2 36
22	10 32	+ 3.7	59.4	16.2	43	288	80	11.0	15 02	15 02	21 17	2 54	2 56
23	11 26	− 1.4	60.3	16.4	55	288	88	12.0	16 25	16 29	22 11	3 18	3 16
24	12 22	− 6.5	60.9	16.6	68	286	95	13.0	17 49	17 59	23 07	3 44	3 38
25	13 20	−11.4	61.3	16.7	80	279	99	14.0	19 15	19 29	—	4 14	4 03
26	14 21	−15.6	61.4	16.7	92	139	100	15.0	20 37	20 56	0 06	4 48	4 33
27	15 23	−18.6	61.2	16.7	104	105	98	16.0	21 53	22 14	1 07	5 31	5 12
28	16 27	−20.4	60.6	16.5	116	97	93	17.0	22 57	23 18	2 09	6 23	6 02
29	17 29	−20.7	59.8	16.3	129	90	86	18.0	23 48	—	3 10	7 25	7 03
30	18 30	−19.6	58.9	16.0	141	85	77	19.0	—	0 08	4 08	8 33	8 13

MERCURY

Day	RA h m	Dec. °	Diam. "	Phase %	Transit h m	5° high 52° h m	5° high 56° h m
1	23 14	− 7.4	6	71	10 38	5 50	5 59
3	23 25	− 6.4	6	73	10 41	5 47	5 55
5	23 26	− 5.2	6	75	10 45	5 44	5 52
7	23 48	− 4.0	6	77	10 49	5 41	5 47
9	0 00	− 2.7	6	80	10 53	5 38	5 43
11	0 12	− 1.3	6	82	10 57	5 35	5 39
13	0 24	+ 0.1	5	84	11 02	5 32	5 35
15	0 37	+ 1.6	5	87	11 07	5 29	5 31
17	0 50	+ 3.2	5	89	11 12	5 27	5 27
19	1 04	+ 4.8	5	91	11 18	5 24	5 23
21	1 18	+ 6.4	5	94	11 24	5 22	5 20
23	1 32	+ 8.1	5	95	11 31	5 20	5 16
25	1 47	+ 9.9	5	97	11 38	5 18	5 13
27	2 03	+11.6	5	99	11 46	5 16	5 10
29	2 18	+13.3	5	100	11 54	5 15	5 07
31	2 35	+15.0	5	100	12 02	18 52	19 02

VENUS

Day	RA h m	Dec. °	Diam. "	Phase %	Transit h m	5° high 52° h m	5° high 56° h m
1	1 49	+10.6	10	95	13 13	19 37	19 42
6	2 12	+12.9	11	94	13 16	19 52	20 00
11	2 36	+15.1	11	94	13 20	20 08	20 18
16	3 00	+17.1	11	93	13 25	20 24	20 35
21	3 24	+18.9	11	92	13 30	20 39	20 52
26	3 49	+20.6	11	91	13 35	20 54	21 09
31	4 15	+22.0	11	90	13 41	21 08	21 25

MARS

Day	RA h m	Dec. °	Diam. "	Phase %	Transit h m	5° high 52° h m	5° high 56° h m
1	23 22	− 5.3	4	98	10 45	5 45	5 53
6	23 37	− 3.7	4	98	10 40	5 32	5 38
11	23 51	− 2.1	4	98	10 35	5 18	5 23
16	0 05	− 0.6	4	98	10 29	5 05	5 08
21	0 19	+ 1.0	4	97	10 24	4 51	4 53
26	0 34	+ 2.5	4	97	10 18	4 38	4 39
31	0 48	+ 4.1	4	97	10 13	4 24	4 24

SUNRISE AND SUNSET

	London		Bristol		Birmingham		Manchester		Newcastle		Glasgow		Belfast	
	0°05′	51°30′	2°35′	51°28′	1°55′	52°28′	2°15′	53°28′	1°37′	54°59′	4°14′	55°52′	5°56′	54°35′
	h m	h m	h m	h m	h m	h m	h m	h m	h m	h m	h m	h m	h m	h m
1	5 36	18 33	5 46	18 43	5 43	18 41	5 43	18 44	5 39	18 43	5 48	18 54	5 57	19 00
2	5 34	18 35	5 44	18 45	5 41	18 43	5 41	18 46	5 37	18 45	5 46	18 56	5 54	19 02
3	5 32	18 36	5 42	18 46	5 38	18 45	5 38	18 47	5 34	18 47	5 43	18 59	5 52	19 04
4	5 30	18 38	5 40	18 48	5 36	18 47	5 36	18 49	5 31	18 49	5 41	19 01	5 49	19 06
5	5 27	18 40	5 37	18 50	5 34	18 48	5 34	18 51	5 29	18 51	5 38	19 03	5 47	19 07
6	5 25	18 41	5 35	18 51	5 31	18 50	5 31	18 53	5 26	18 53	5 35	19 05	5 44	19 09
7	5 23	18 43	5 33	18 53	5 29	18 52	5 29	18 55	5 24	18 55	5 33	19 07	5 42	19 11
8	5 21	18 45	5 31	18 55	5 27	18 54	5 26	18 57	5 21	18 57	5 30	19 09	5 39	19 13
9	5 18	18 47	5 29	18 56	5 24	18 55	5 24	18 58	5 19	18 59	5 28	19 11	5 37	19 15
10	5 16	18 48	5 26	18 58	5 22	18 57	5 22	19 00	5 16	19 00	5 25	19 13	5 34	19 17
11	5 14	18 50	5 24	19 00	5 20	18 59	5 19	19 02	5 14	19 02	5 23	19 15	5 32	19 19
12	5 12	18 52	5 22	19 01	5 18	19 01	5 17	19 04	5 11	19 04	5 20	19 17	5 30	19 21
13	5 10	18 53	5 20	19 03	5 15	19 02	5 15	19 06	5 09	19 06	5 18	19 19	5 27	19 23
14	5 08	18 55	5 18	19 05	5 13	19 04	5 12	19 07	5 07	19 08	5 15	19 21	5 25	19 25
15	5 05	18 57	5 15	19 06	5 11	19 06	5 10	19 09	5 04	19 10	5 13	19 23	5 22	19 27
16	5 03	18 58	5 13	19 08	5 09	19 08	5 08	19 11	5 02	19 12	5 10	19 25	5 20	19 28
17	5 01	19 00	5 11	19 10	5 06	19 09	5 05	19 13	4 59	19 14	5 08	19 27	5 18	19 30
18	4 59	19 02	5 09	19 11	5 04	19 11	5 03	19 15	4 57	19 16	5 05	19 29	5 15	19 32
19	4 57	19 03	5 07	19 13	5 02	19 13	5 01	19 17	4 55	19 18	5 03	19 31	5 13	19 34
20	4 55	19 05	5 05	19 15	5 00	19 15	4 59	19 18	4 52	19 20	5 00	19 33	5 10	19 36
21	4 53	19 07	5 03	19 16	4 58	19 16	4 56	19 20	4 50	19 22	4 58	19 35	5 08	19 38
22	4 51	19 08	5 01	19 18	4 56	19 18	4 54	19 22	4 47	19 24	4 55	19 37	5 06	19 40
23	4 49	19 10	4 59	19 20	4 53	19 20	4 52	19 24	4 45	19 26	4 53	19 39	5 04	19 42
24	4 47	19 12	4 57	19 21	4 51	19 22	4 50	19 26	4 43	19 28	4 50	19 41	5 01	19 44
25	4 45	19 13	4 55	19 23	4 49	19 23	4 48	19 27	4 41	19 30	4 48	19 43	4 59	19 46
26	4 43	19 15	4 53	19 25	4 47	19 25	4 46	19 29	4 38	19 32	4 46	19 45	4 57	19 48
27	4 41	19 17	4 51	19 26	4 45	19 27	4 43	19 31	4 36	19 34	4 43	19 47	4 55	19 49
28	4 39	19 18	4 49	19 28	4 43	19 28	4 41	19 33	4 34	19 35	4 41	19 49	4 52	19 51
29	4 37	19 20	4 47	19 30	4 41	19 30	4 39	19 35	4 32	19 37	4 39	19 51	4 50	19 53
30	4 35	19 21	4 45	19 31	4 39	19 32	4 37	19 36	4 29	19 39	4 36	19 53	4 48	19 55

JUPITER

Day	RA	Dec.	Transit	5° high	
				52°	56°
	h m	° ′	h m	h m	h m
1	14 44.6	−14 28	2 08	21 58	22 16
11	14 40.6	−14 09	1 24	21 12	21 30
21	14 36.0	−13 47	0 41	20 26	20 43
31	14 31.0	−13 24	23 52	19 40	19 56

Diameters – equatorial 44″ polar 41″

SATURN

Day	RA	Dec.	Transit	5° high	
				52°	56°
	h m	° ′	h m	h m	h m
1	22 38.4	−10 12	10 00	5 29	5 42
11	22 42.3	− 9 50	9 25	4 51	5 04
21	22 46.0	− 9 30	8 49	4 14	4 26
31	22 49.2	− 9 12	8 13	3 36	3 48

Diameters – equatorial 16″ polar 14″
Rings – major axis 36″ minor axis 4″

URANUS

Day	RA	Dec.	Transit	10° high	
				52°	56°
	h m	° ′	h m	h m	h m
1	19 52.2	−21 26	7 15	4 50	5 40
11	19 53.1	−21 24	6 36	4 11	5 01
21	19 53.7	−21 22	5 57	3 32	4 22
31	19 53.8	−21 22	5 18	2 53	3 43

Diameter 4″

NEPTUNE

Day	RA	Dec.	Transit	10° high	
				52°	56°
	h m	° ′	h m	h m	h m
1	19 39.7	−20 51	7 02	4 31	5 17
11	19 40.1	−20 49	6 23	3 52	4 38
21	19 40.3	−20 49	5 44	3 13	3 59
31	19 40.3	−20 49	5 05	2 33	3 19

Diameter 2″

May 1994

II

FIFTH MONTH, 31 DAYS. *Maia*, goddess of growth and increase

Sun's Longitude 60° II 21^{d}07^h

1	*Sunday*	**4th S. after Easter.** Great Exhibition opened 1851	*week* 18 *day* 121
2	*Monday*	**SS Philip and James.** *Bank Holiday in the UK*	122
3	*Tuesday*	Festival of Britain opened 1951	123
4	*Wednesday*	Start of the General Strike 1926	124
5	*Thursday*	Field Marshal Earl Wavell *b.* 1883	125
6	*Friday*	First four-minute mile run 1954	126
7	*Saturday*	Robert Browning *b.* 1812. Kitty Godfree *b.* 1896	127
8	*Sunday*	**5th S. After Easter.** Friedrick von Hayek *b.* 1899	*week* 19 *day* 128
9	*Monday*	Joseph Gay-Lussac *d.* 1850. Glenda Jackson *b.* 1936	129
10	*Tuesday*	Fred Astaire *b.* 1899. Sir Henry Stanley *d.* 1904	130
11	*Wednesday*	Spencer Perceval *assass.* 1812	131
12	*Thursday*	**Ascension Day.** Collapse of General Strike 1926	132
13	*Friday*	John Nash *d.* 1835. Sir Frank Brangwyn *b.* 1867	133
14	*Saturday*	**St Matthias.** Eric Morecombe *b.* 1926	134
15	*Sunday*	**S. after Ascension Day.** James Mason *b.* 1909	*week* 20 *day* 135
16	*Monday*	FEAST OF WEEKS begins. John Sell Cotman *b.* 1782	136
17	*Tuesday*	Summer Time Act came into force 1916	137
18	*Wednesday*	Pope John Paul II *b.* 1920	138
19	*Thursday*	Anne Boleyn *exec.* 1536. John Betjeman *d.* 1984	139
20	*Friday*	First Chelsea Flower Show 1913	140
21	*Saturday*	Albrecht Dürer *b.* 1471. Henry VI *killed* 1471	141
22	*Sunday*	**Pentecost (Whit Sunday).** Laurence Olivier *b.* 1907	*week* 21 *day* 142
23	*Monday*	Coalition Ministry dissolved 1945	143
24	*Tuesday*	British Legion founded 1921	144
25	*Wednesday*	Pedro Caldéron de la Barca *d.* 1681	145
26	*Thursday*	Last public hanging in England 1868	146
27	*Friday*	*Easter Law Sittings end.* Isadora Duncan *b.* 1878	147
28	*Saturday*	George I *b.* 1660. Earl Russell *d.* 1878	148
29	*Sunday*	**Trinity Sunday.** Mt Everest conquered 1953	*week* 22 *day* 149
30	*Monday*	*Bank Holiday in the UK.* Alfred Austin *b.* 1835	150
31	*Tuesday*	Jutland 1916. Sir Angus Wilson *d.* 1991	151

ASTRONOMICAL PHENOMENA

d	h	
4	21	Saturn in conjunction with Moon. Saturn 6° S.
8	00	Mars in conjunction with Moon. Mars 4° S.
10		Annular eclipse of Sun (*see* page 66)
11	22	Mercury in conjunction with Moon. Mercury 3° N.
13	07	Venus in conjunction with Moon. Venus 4° N.
17	20	Pluto at opposition
23	09	Jupiter in conjunction with Moon. Jupiter 3° N.
25		Partial eclipse of Moon (*see* page 66)
30	07	Mercury at greatest elongation E. 23°

CONSTELLATIONS

The following constellations are near the meridian at

	d	h		d	h
April	1	24	May	16	21
April	15	23	June	1	20
May	1	22	June	15	19

Cepheus (below the Pole), Cassiopeia (below the Pole), Ursa Minor, Ursa Major, Canes Venatici, Coma Berenices, Bootes, Leo, Virgo, Crater, Corvus and Hydra

MINIMA OF ALGOL

Algol is inconveniently situated for observation during May.

THE MOON

Phases, Apsides and Node	d	h	m
☾ Last Quarter	2	14	32
● New Moon	10	17	07
☽ First Quarter	18	12	50
○ Full Moon	25	03	39
Apogee (406,423 km)	9	02	18
Perigee (358,816 km)	24	02	55

Mean longitude of ascending node on May 1, 235°

THE SUN   s.d. 15′.8

Day	Right Ascension	Dec. +	Equation of time	Rise 52°	Rise 56°	Transit	Set 52°	Set 56°	Sidereal time	Transit of First Point of Aries
	h m s	° ′	m s	h m	h m	h m	h m	h m	h m s	h m s
1	2 31 56	14 56	+2 51	4 31	4 17	11 57	19 24	19 39	14 34 47	9 23 41
2	2 35 45	15 14	+2 59	4 29	4 15	11 57	19 26	19 41	14 38 43	9 19 45
3	2 39 35	15 32	+3 05	4 27	4 12	11 57	19 28	19 43	14 42 40	9 15 49
4	2 43 25	15 50	+3 12	4 25	4 10	11 57	19 29	19 45	14 46 37	9 11 53
5	2 47 16	16 07	+3 17	4 23	4 08	11 57	19 31	19 47	14 50 33	9 07 57
6	2 51 07	16 24	+3 22	4 22	4 06	11 57	19 33	19 49	14 54 30	9 04 01
7	2 54 59	16 41	+3 27	4 20	4 04	11 57	19 34	19 51	14 58 26	9 00 05
8	2 58 52	16 58	+3 31	4 18	4 02	11 56	19 36	19 53	15 02 23	8 56 09
9	3 02 45	17 14	+3 34	4 16	3 59	11 56	19 38	19 55	15 06 19	8 52 13
10	3 06 39	17 30	+3 37	4 15	3 57	11 56	19 39	19 57	15 10 16	8 48 17
11	3 10 34	17 46	+3 39	4 13	3 55	11 56	19 41	19 59	15 14 12	8 44 21
12	3 14 29	18 01	+3 40	4 11	3 53	11 56	19 42	20 00	15 18 09	8 40 26
13	3 18 24	18 16	+3 41	4 10	3 52	11 56	19 44	20 02	15 22 06	8 36 30
14	3 22 20	18 31	+3 42	4 08	3 50	11 56	19 45	20 04	15 26 02	8 32 34
15	3 26 17	18 45	+3 42	4 07	3 48	11 56	19 47	20 06	15 29 59	8 28 38
16	3 30 14	19 00	+3 41	4 05	3 46	11 56	19 49	20 08	15 33 55	8 24 42
17	3 34 12	19 13	+3 40	4 04	3 44	11 56	19 50	20 10	15 37 52	8 20 46
18	3 38 10	19 27	+3 38	4 02	3 42	11 56	19 52	20 12	15 41 48	8 16 50
19	3 42 09	19 40	+3 36	4 01	3 41	11 56	19 53	20 13	15 45 45	8 12 54
20	3 46 08	19 53	+3 33	3 59	3 39	11 56	19 54	20 15	15 49 41	8 08 58
21	3 50 08	20 05	+3 30	3 58	3 37	11 57	19 56	20 17	15 53 38	8 05 02
22	3 54 09	20 18	+3 26	3 57	3 36	11 57	19 57	20 19	15 57 35	8 01 06
23	3 58 10	20 29	+3 22	3 56	3 34	11 57	19 59	20 20	16 01 31	7 57 11
24	4 02 11	20 41	+3 17	3 54	3 33	11 57	20 00	20 22	16 05 28	7 53 15
25	4 06 13	20 52	+3 11	3 53	3 31	11 57	20 01	20 24	16 09 24	7 49 19
26	4 10 15	21 03	+3 05	3 52	3 30	11 57	20 03	20 25	16 13 21	7 45 23
27	4 14 18	21 13	+2 59	3 51	3 28	11 57	20 04	20 27	16 17 17	7 41 27
28	4 18 22	21 23	+2 52	3 50	3 27	11 57	20 05	20 28	16 21 14	7 37 31
29	4 22 26	21 33	+2 45	3 49	3 26	11 57	20 06	20 30	16 25 10	7 33 35
30	4 26 30	21 42	+2 37	3 48	3 25	11 57	20 08	20 31	16 29 07	7 29 39
31	4 30 35	21 51	+2 29	3 47	3 23	11 58	20 09	20 33	16 33 04	7 25 43

DURATION OF TWILIGHT (in minutes)

Latitude	52°	56°	52°	56°	52°	56°	52°	56°
	1 May		11 May		21 May		31 May	
Civil	39	45	41	49	44	53	46	57
Nautical	90	106	97	121	106	143	116	TAN
Astronomical	154	209	179	TAN	TAN	TAN	TAN	TAN

THE NIGHT SKY

Mercury is at greatest eastern elongation (23°) on the 30th and thus is visible in the evenings, magnitude −1.1 to +0.6, after the first ten days of the month. It may be detected low above the WNW horizon around the time of end of evening civil twilight. This evening apparition is the most favourable one of the year for observers in the northern hemisphere. Mercury will be passing about 8° north of Aldebaran on the 14th to 16th.

Venus is a brilliant object, magnitude −3.9, visible in the western sky for nearly two hours after sunset. The New Moon will be seen near the planet on the 12th to 13th. Venus passes 6° north of Aldebaran on the 5th.

Mars is unsuitably placed for observation.

Jupiter, magnitude −2.4, is only just past opposition and therefore continues to be visible throughout the hours of darkness. The Moon, near Full, is close to Jupiter on the 23rd.

Saturn, magnitude +1.0, is a morning object, visible in the SE sky for a while before dawn, though never at any great altitude. The thin crescent Moon will be seen near Saturn on the mornings of the 4th and 5th.

Eclipse. A partial eclipse of the Moon occurs on the 25th, visible from the British Isles (see page 66 for details).

THE MOON

Day	RA	Dec.	Hor. par.	Semi-diam.	Sun's co-long.	PA of Bright Limb	Phase	Age	Rise 52°	Rise 56°	Transit	Set 52°	Set 56°
	h m	°	′	′	°	°	%	d	h m	h m	h m	h m	h m
1	19 27	−17.5	57.9	15.8	153	80	67	20.0	0 29	0 45	5 03	9 44	9 28
2	20 21	−14.4	57.0	15.5	165	76	56	21.0	1 01	1 14	5 54	10 55	10 43
3	21 11	−10.7	56.2	15.3	177	73	46	22.0	1 27	1 36	6 41	12 05	11 57
4	21 59	− 6.7	55.5	15.1	189	71	36	23.0	1 50	1 55	7 26	13 13	13 09
5	22 46	− 2.4	54.9	15.0	202	70	27	24.0	2 10	2 12	8 09	14 20	14 20
6	23 31	+ 1.8	54.5	14.8	214	70	19	25.0	2 29	2 28	8 51	15 25	15 29
7	0 16	+ 6.0	54.2	14.8	226	71	12	26.0	2 49	2 44	9 34	16 30	16 37
8	1 01	+ 9.9	54.0	14.7	238	73	7	27.0	3 10	3 02	10 16	17 34	17 46
9	1 47	+13.4	54.0	14.7	251	76	3	28.0	3 34	3 22	11 00	18 38	18 53
10	2 34	+16.3	54.0	14.7	263	80	0	29.0	4 01	3 46	11 46	19 40	19 58
11	3 23	+18.6	54.1	14.7	275	254	0	0.3	4 34	4 15	12 33	20 39	20 59
12	4 13	+20.1	54.3	14.8	287	264	2	1.3	5 13	4 53	13 22	21 33	21 54
13	5 05	+20.7	54.6	14.9	300	269	5	2.3	6 00	5 38	14 11	22 21	22 41
14	5 57	+20.4	55.0	15.0	312	274	10	3.3	6 54	6 34	15 01	23 01	23 20
15	6 49	+19.0	55.5	15.1	324	278	16	4.3	7 55	7 37	15 51	23 36	23 52
16	7 41	+16.7	56.0	15.3	336	283	25	5.3	9 02	8 47	16 40	—	—
17	8 32	+13.6	56.7	15.4	349	286	34	6.3	10 12	10 01	17 29	0 06	0 18
18	9 24	+ 9.7	57.4	15.6	1	289	44	7.3	11 25	11 19	18 18	0 32	0 40
19	10 15	+ 5.3	58.2	15.9	13	290	55	8.3	12 41	12 39	19 07	0 56	1 00
20	11 07	+ 0.4	59.0	16.1	25	291	66	9.3	13 59	14 02	19 58	1 20	1 20
21	12 00	− 4.6	59.8	16.3	37	291	77	10.3	15 20	15 27	20 51	1 44	1 40
22	12 56	− 9.4	60.5	16.5	50	289	86	11.3	16 43	16 55	21 47	2 10	2 02
23	13 54	−13.8	60.9	16.6	62	287	93	12.3	18 06	18 23	22 46	2 41	2 28
24	14 55	−17.4	61.1	16.6	74	284	98	13.3	19 26	19 46	23 48	3 19	3 02
25	15 58	−19.8	61.0	16.6	86	300	100	14.3	20 37	20 58	—	4 06	3 46
26	17 02	−20.7	60.6	16.5	98	86	99	15.3	21 36	21 57	0 50	5 04	4 42
27	18 04	−20.2	59.9	16.3	110	83	95	16.3	22 23	22 41	1 52	6 10	5 50
28	19 05	−18.4	59.1	16.1	123	79	89	17.3	23 00	23 14	2 50	7 23	7 05
29	20 01	−15.6	58.1	15.8	135	75	81	18.3	23 29	23 40	3 44	8 37	8 23
30	20 55	−12.0	57.2	15.6	147	72	72	19.3	23 54	—	4 35	9 50	9 40
31	21 45	− 8.0	56.3	15.3	159	69	62	20.3	—	0 00	5 22	11 00	10 55

MERCURY

Day	RA	Dec.	Diam.	Phase	Transit	5° high 52°	5° high 56°
	h m	°	″	%	h m	h m	h m
1	2 35	+15.0	5	100	12 02	18 52	19 02
3	2 51	+16.6	5	99	12 11	19 10	19 22
5	3 08	+18.2	5	98	12 20	19 28	19 41
7	3 25	+19.6	5	95	12 29	19 45	20 00
9	3 43	+20.9	5	91	12 39	20 02	20 18
11	3 59	+22.1	6	87	12 48	20 18	20 35
13	4 16	+23.1	6	81	12 56	20 32	20 51
15	4 32	+23.9	6	76	13 04	20 45	21 04
17	4 48	+24.6	6	70	13 12	20 56	21 16
19	5 02	+25.0	6	65	13 18	21 05	21 26
21	5 16	+25.4	7	59	13 24	21 13	21 34
23	5 29	+25.6	7	54	13 29	21 18	21 40
25	5 41	+25.6	7	49	13 33	21 22	21 43
27	5 52	+25.6	8	44	13 35	21 24	21 45
29	6 02	+25.4	8	40	13 37	21 24	21 45
31	6 10	+25.2	8	35	13 37	21 22	21 43

VENUS

Day	RA	Dec.	Diam.	Phase	Transit	5° high 52°	5° high 56°
	h m	°	″	%	h m	h m	h m
1	4 15	+22.0	11	90	13 41	21 08	21 25
6	4 41	+23.1	11	89	13 47	21 21	21 39
11	5 07	+24.0	12	88	13 53	21 33	21 52
16	5 33	+24.6	12	87	14 00	21 43	22 03
21	6 00	+24.9	12	85	14 07	21 52	22 12
26	6 26	+25.0	12	84	14 14	21 58	22 19
31	6 52	+24.7	13	82	14 20	22 02	22 22

MARS

Day	RA	Dec.	Diam.	Phase	Transit	5° high 52°	5° high 56°
1	0 48	+ 4.1	4	97	10 13	4 24	4 24
6	1 02	+ 5.6	4	97	10 07	4 11	4 10
11	1 16	+ 7.1	4	97	10 01	3 58	3 55
16	1 30	+ 8.5	4	96	9 56	3 45	3 41
21	1 44	+ 9.9	4	96	9 50	3 32	3 27
26	1 59	+11.3	4	96	9 45	3 20	3 14
31	2 13	+12.6	4	96	9 40	3 07	3 00

SUNRISE AND SUNSET

	London		Bristol		Birmingham		Manchester		Newcastle		Glasgow		Belfast	
	0°05′	51°30′	2°35′	51°28′	1°55′	52°28′	2°15′	53°28′	1°37′	54°59′	4°14′	55°52′	5°56′	54°35′
	h m	h m	h m	h m	h m	h m	h m	h m	h m	h m	h m	h m	h m	h m
1	4 33	19 23	4 43	19 33	4 37	19 34	4 35	19 38	4 27	19 41	4 34	19 55	4 46	19 57
2	4 31	19 25	4 41	19 35	4 35	19 35	4 33	19 40	4 25	19 43	4 32	19 57	4 44	19 59
3	4 29	19 26	4 39	19 36	4 33	19 37	4 31	19 42	4 23	19 45	4 30	19 59	4 42	20 01
4	4 27	19 28	4 37	19 38	4 31	19 39	4 29	19 44	4 21	19 47	4 28	20 01	4 40	20 03
5	4 25	19 30	4 36	19 40	4 29	19 40	4 27	19 45	4 19	19 49	4 25	20 03	4 38	20 05
6	4 24	19 31	4 34	19 41	4 28	19 42	4 25	19 47	4 17	19 51	4 23	20 05	4 36	20 06
7	4 22	19 33	4 32	19 43	4 26	19 44	4 23	19 49	4 15	19 53	4 21	20 07	4 33	20 08
8	4 20	19 34	4 30	19 44	4 24	19 45	4 21	19 51	4 13	19 55	4 19	20 09	4 32	20 10
9	4 19	19 36	4 29	19 46	4 22	19 47	4 20	19 52	4 11	19 56	4 17	20 11	4 30	20 12
10	4 17	19 38	4 27	19 47	4 20	19 49	4 18	19 54	4 09	19 58	4 15	20 13	4 28	20 14
11	4 15	19 39	4 25	19 49	4 19	19 50	4 16	19 56	4 07	20 00	4 13	20 15	4 26	20 16
12	4 14	19 41	4 24	19 51	4 17	19 52	4 14	19 58	4 05	20 02	4 11	20 17	4 24	20 17
13	4 12	19 42	4 22	19 52	4 15	19 54	4 13	19 59	4 03	20 04	4 09	20 19	4 22	20 19
14	4 11	19 44	4 21	19 54	4 14	19 55	4 11	20 01	4 01	20 06	4 07	20 21	4 20	20 21
15	4 09	19 45	4 19	19 55	4 12	19 57	4 09	20 03	3 59	20 07	4 05	20 22	4 19	20 23
16	4 08	19 47	4 18	19 57	4 11	19 58	4 08	20 04	3 58	20 09	4 04	20 24	4 17	20 24
17	4 06	19 48	4 16	19 58	4 09	20 00	4 06	20 06	3 56	20 11	4 02	20 26	4 15	20 26
18	4 05	19 50	4 15	20 00	4 08	20 01	4 04	20 07	3 54	20 13	4 00	20 28	4 14	20 28
19	4 03	19 51	4 13	20 01	4 06	20 03	4 03	20 09	3 53	20 14	3 58	20 30	4 12	20 29
20	4 02	19 53	4 12	20 02	4 05	20 04	4 01	20 11	3 51	20 16	3 57	20 31	4 10	20 31
21	4 01	19 54	4 11	20 04	4 04	20 06	4 00	20 12	3 50	20 18	3 55	20 33	4 09	20 33
22	3 59	19 55	4 10	20 05	4 02	20 07	3 59	20 14	3 48	20 19	3 53	20 35	4 07	20 34
23	3 58	19 57	4 08	20 07	4 01	20 09	3 57	20 15	3 47	20 21	3 52	20 37	4 06	20 36
24	3 57	19 58	4 07	20 08	4 00	20 10	3 56	20 17	3 45	20 22	3 50	20 38	4 05	20 37
25	3 56	19 59	4 06	20 09	3 58	20 11	3 55	20 18	3 44	20 24	3 49	20 40	4 03	20 39
26	3 55	20 01	4 05	20 10	3 57	20 13	3 53	20 19	3 42	20 25	3 47	20 41	4 02	20 40
27	3 54	20 02	4 04	20 12	3 56	20 14	3 52	20 21	3 41	20 27	3 46	20 43	4 01	20 42
28	3 53	20 03	4 03	20 13	3 55	20 15	3 51	20 22	3 40	20 28	3 45	20 44	4 00	20 43
29	3 52	20 04	4 02	20 14	3 54	20 17	3 50	20 23	3 39	20 30	3 44	20 46	3 58	20 45
30	3 51	20 05	4 01	20 15	3 53	20 18	3 49	20 25	3 38	20 31	3 42	20 47	3 57	20 46
31	3 50	20 07	4 00	20 16	3 52	20 19	3 48	20 26	3 36	20 32	3 41	20 49	3 56	20 47

JUPITER

Day	RA	Dec.	Transit	5° high	
				52°	56°
	h m	° ′	h m	h m	h m
1	14 31.0	−13 24	23 52	4 08	3 52
11	14 26.1	−13 01	23 08	3 27	3 11
21	14 21.5	−12 39	22 24	2 45	2 29
31	14 17.6	−12 22	21 41	2 04	1 48

Diameters – equatorial 44″ polar 42″

SATURN

Day	RA	Dec.	Transit	5° high	
				52°	56°
	h m	° ′	h m	h m	h m
1	22 49.2	− 9 12	8 13	3 36	3 48
11	22 52.0	− 8 58	7 37	2 58	3 10
21	22 54.3	− 8 46	7 00	2 20	2 31
31	22 56.0	− 8 38	6 22	1 42	1 53

Diameters – equatorial 17″ polar 15″
Rings – major axis 38″ minor axis 3″

URANUS

Day	RA	Dec.	Transit	10° high	
				52°	56°
	h m	° ′	h m	h m	h m
1	19 53.8	−21 22	5 18	2 53	3 43
11	19 53.7	−21 23	4 39	2 13	3 03
21	19 53.1	−21 25	3 59	1 34	2 24
31	19 52.3	−21 27	3 19	0 54	1 45

Diameter 4″

NEPTUNE

Day	RA	Dec.	Transit	10° high	
				52°	56°
	h m	° ′	h m	h m	h m
1	19 40.3	−20 49	5 05	2 33	3 19
11	19 40.1	−20 49	4 25	1 54	2 40
21	19 39.6	−20 50	3 45	1 14	2 00
31	19 39.0	−20 52	3 05	0 34	1 21

Diameter 2″

♊ June 1994 ♋

SIXTH MONTH, 30 DAYS. *Junius*, Roman *gens* (family)

Sun's Longitude 90° ♋ 21ᵈ15ʰ

1	*Wednesday*	John Masefield *b.* 1878. Sir Hugh Walpole *d.* 1941	*week* 22 *day* 152
2	*Thursday*	**Corpus Christi.** *Coronation Day 1953*	153
3	*Friday*	Jefferson Davis *b.* 1808. Samuel Plimsoll *d.* 1898	154
4	*Saturday*	Giovanni Casanova de Seingalt *d.* 1798	155
5	*Sunday*	**2nd S. after Pentecost.** Adam Smith *b.* 1723	*week* 23 *day* 156
6	*Monday*	Pierre Corneille *b.* 1606. Carl Jung *d.* 1961	157
7	*Tuesday*	*Trinity Law Sittings begin.* Paul Gauguin *b.* 1848	158
8	*Wednesday*	John Smeaton *b.* 1724. Thomas Paine *d.* 1809	159
9	*Thursday*	George Stephenson *b.* 1781. Angus McBean *d.* 1990	160
10	*Friday*	MUSLIM NEW YEAR (1415). *Duke of Edinburgh b. 1921*	161
11	*Saturday*	**St Barnabas.** Queen's Official Birthday	162
12	*Sunday*	**3rd S. after Pentecost.** Leon Goossens *b.* 1897	*week* 24 *day* 163
13	*Monday*	W. B. Yeats *b.* 1865. Sir Henry Segrave *b.* 1930	164
14	*Tuesday*	Harriet Beecher Stowe *b.* 1811	165
15	*Wednesday*	Magna Carta sealed 1215. Watt Tyler *exec.* 1381	166
16	*Thursday*	Field Marshal Earl Alexander of Tunis *d.* 1969	167
17	*Friday*	Edward I *b.* 1239. Joseph Addison *d.* 1719	168
18	*Saturday*	Waterloo 1815. Samuel Butler *d.* 1902	169
19	*Sunday*	**4th S. after Pentecost.** Blaise Pascal *b.* 1623	*week* 25 *day* 170
20	*Monday*	Errol Flynn *b.* 1909. Sir Charles Groves *d.* 1992	171
21	*Tuesday*	Prince William of Wales *b.* 1982	172
22	*Wednesday*	Rider Haggard *b.* 1856. Judy Garland *d.* 1969	173
23	*Thursday*	Edward VIII *b.* 1894. Sir Leonard Hutton *b.* 1916	174
24	*Friday*	**St John the Baptist.** John Hampden *d.* 1643	175
25	*Saturday*	Earl Mountbatten of Burma *b.* 1900	176
26	*Sunday*	**5th S. after Pentecost.** Gilbert White *d.* 1793	*week* 26 *day* 177
27	*Monday*	Harriet Martineau *d.* 1876. Helen Keller *b.* 1880	178
28	*Tuesday*	Treaty of Versailles signed 1919	179
29	*Wednesday*	**St Peter.** Trades unions legalized 1871	180
30	*Thursday*	William Barents *d.* 1597. Tower Bridge opened 1894	181

ASTRONOMICAL PHENOMENA

d	h	
1	07	Saturn in conjunction with Moon. Saturn 6° S.
6	03	Mars in conjunction with Moon. Mars 2° S.
10	23	Mercury in conjunction with Moon. Mercury 3° N.
12	10	Venus in conjunction with Moon. Venus 7° N.
19	15	Jupiter in conjunction with Moon. Jupiter 3° N.
21	15	Solstice
25	10	Mercury in inferior conjunction
28	16	Saturn in conjunction with Moon. Saturn 6° S.

CONSTELLATIONS

The following constellations are near the meridian at

	d	h
May	1	24
May	16	23
June	1	22
June	15	21
July	1	20
July	16	19

Cassiopeia (below the Pole), Ursa Minor, Draco, Ursa Major, Canes Venatici, Bootes, Corona, Serpens, Virgo and Libra

MINIMA OF ALGOL

Algol is inconveniently situated for observation during June.

THE MOON

Phases, Apsides and Node	d	h	m
☾ Last Quarter	1	04	02
● New Moon	9	08	26
☽ First Quarter	16	19	57
○ Full Moon	23	11	33
☾ Last Quarter	30	19	31
Apogee (405,693 km)	5	12	38
Perigee (362,954 km)	21	06	43

Mean longitude of ascending node on June 1, 233°

THE SUN   s.d. 15′.8

Day	Right Ascension	Dec. +	Equation of time	Rise 52°	Rise 56°	Transit	Set 52°	Set 56°	Sidereal time	Transit of First Point of Aries
	h m s	° ′	m s	h m	h m	h m	h m	h m	h m s	h m s
1	4 34 40	21 59	+2 20	3 46	3 22	11 58	20 10	20 34	16 37 00	7 21 47
2	4 38 46	22 08	+2 11	3 45	3 21	11 58	20 11	20 35	16 40 57	7 17 51
3	4 42 52	22 15	+2 01	3 45	3 20	11 58	20 12	20 37	16 44 53	7 13 56
4	4 46 58	22 23	+1 51	3 44	3 19	11 58	20 13	20 38	16 48 50	7 10 00
5	4 51 05	22 30	+1 41	3 43	3 18	11 58	20 14	20 39	16 52 46	7 06 04
6	4 55 12	22 36	+1 31	3 43	3 18	11 59	20 15	20 40	16 56 43	7 02 08
7	4 59 20	22 42	+1 20	3 42	3 17	11 59	20 16	20 41	17 00 39	6 58 12
8	5 03 28	22 48	+1 08	3 42	3 16	11 59	20 17	20 42	17 04 36	6 54 16
9	5 07 36	22 54	+0 57	3 41	3 16	11 59	20 18	20 43	17 08 33	6 50 20
10	5 11 44	22 58	+0 45	3 41	3 15	11 59	20 18	20 44	17 12 29	6 46 24
11	5 15 53	23 03	+0 33	3 40	3 14	12 00	20 19	20 45	17 16 26	6 42 28
12	5 20 02	23 07	+0 21	3 40	3 14	12 00	20 20	20 46	17 20 22	6 38 32
13	5 24 11	23 11	+0 08	3 40	3 14	12 00	20 20	20 47	17 24 19	6 34 36
14	5 28 20	23 14	−0 04	3 40	3 13	12 00	20 21	20 47	17 28 15	6 30 40
15	5 32 29	23 17	−0 17	3 39	3 13	12 00	20 22	20 48	17 32 12	6 26 45
16	5 36 38	23 20	−0 30	3 39	3 13	12 01	20 22	20 49	17 36 08	6 22 49
17	5 40 48	23 22	−0 43	3 39	3 13	12 01	20 23	20 49	17 40 05	6 18 53
18	5 44 57	23 24	−0 56	3 39	3 13	12 01	20 23	20 49	17 44 02	6 14 57
19	5 49 07	23 25	−1 09	3 39	3 13	12 01	20 23	20 50	17 47 58	6 11 01
20	5 53 16	23 26	−1 22	3 39	3 13	12 01	20 24	20 50	17 51 55	6 07 05
21	5 57 26	23 26	−1 35	3 40	3 13	12 02	20 24	20 50	17 55 51	6 03 09
22	6 01 36	23 26	−1 48	3 40	3 13	12 02	20 24	20 51	17 59 48	5 59 13
23	6 05 45	23 26	−2 01	3 40	3 14	12 02	20 24	20 51	18 03 44	5 55 17
24	6 09 54	23 25	−2 14	3 40	3 14	12 02	20 24	20 51	18 07 41	5 51 21
25	6 14 04	23 24	−2 26	3 41	3 14	12 03	20 24	20 51	18 11 37	5 47 25
26	6 18 13	23 22	−2 39	3 41	3 15	12 03	20 24	20 51	18 15 34	5 43 30
27	6 22 22	23 20	−2 52	3 42	3 15	12 03	20 24	20 50	18 19 31	5 39 34
28	6 26 31	23 18	−3 04	3 42	3 16	12 03	20 24	20 50	18 23 27	5 35 38
29	6 30 40	23 15	−3 16	3 43	3 17	12 03	20 24	20 50	18 27 24	5 31 42
30	6 34 48	23 12	−3 28	3 43	3 17	12 04	20 23	20 49	18 31 20	5 27 46

DURATION OF TWILIGHT (in minutes)

Latitude	52°	56°	52°	56°	52°	56°	52°	56°
	1 June		11 June		21 June		30 June	
Civil	47	58	48	61	49	63	49	62
Nautical	117	TAN	125	TAN	128	TAN	125	TAN
Astronomical	TAN	TAN	TAN	TAN	TAN	TAN	TAN	TAN

THE NIGHT SKY

Mercury may possibly be detected, magnitude +1, low above the WNW horizon, around the time of end of evening civil twilight, for the first week of the month. For the remainder of June it is unsuitably placed for observation, inferior conjunction occurring on the 25th.

Venus, magnitude −4.0, is visible in the western sky in the evenings. Although it is continuing to increase its eastern elongation from the Sun, the period available for observation actually decreases slightly during the month because it is moving southwards in declination and also because the Sun is setting about a quarter of an hour later at the end of the month than it is at the beginning. The three-day-old Moon will be seen near Venus on the 11th to 12th.

Mars, magnitude +1.2, is very gradually emerging from the long morning twilight. It will not be an' easy object to detect, low above the eastern horizon before the sky gets too bright.

Jupiter is a brilliant evening object in Virgo, magnitude −2.3. By the end of the month it will be too low in the south-west for observation after midnight. It is slowing down in its retrograde path and is virtually stationary by the end of the month. The gibbous Moon is near the planet on the 19th.

Saturn is a morning object, in Aquarius, reaching its first stationary point on the 23rd. It is gradually becoming visible for longer each night and by the end of June should be visible low above the ESE horizon shortly before midnight. Its magnitude is +0.9. On the morning of the 1st the Moon, near Last Quarter, passes 6° north of the planet. The Moon is again in the vicinity of Saturn on the mornings of the 28th and 29th.

THE MOON

Day	RA h m	Dec. °	Hor. par. '	Semi-diam. '	Sun's co-long. °	PA of Bright Limb °	Phase %	Age d	Rise 52° h m	Rise 56° h m	Transit h m	Set 52° h m	Set 56° h m
1	22 32	− 3.7	55.6	15.1	171	68	52	21.3	0 15	0 18	6 06	12 08	12 07
2	23 18	+ 0.6	55.0	15.0	184	68	42	22.3	0 35	0 35	6 49	13 15	13 17
3	0 03	+ 4.9	54.5	14.8	196	68	33	23.3	0 55	0 51	7 32	14 20	14 26
4	0 49	+ 8.8	54.2	14.8	208	69	24	24.3	1 16	1 08	8 14	15 25	15 35
5	1 35	+12.5	54.1	14.7	220	71	16	25.3	1 38	1 27	8 58	16 29	16 42
6	2 22	+15.6	54.1	14.7	233	73	10	26.3	2 04	1 50	9 43	17 32	17 49
7	3 10	+18.1	54.2	14.8	245	75	5	27.3	2 35	2 17	10 29	18 32	18 52
8	4 00	+19.8	54.4	14.8	257	76	2	28.3	3 12	2 52	11 18	19 28	19 49
9	4 52	+20.7	54.7	14.9	269	59	0	29.3	3 56	3 35	12 07	20 18	20 40
10	5 44	+20.6	55.1	15.0	282	289	0	0.6	4 48	4 27	12 58	21 02	21 22
11	6 36	+19.5	55.5	15.1	294	284	3	1.6	5 48	5 29	13 48	21 39	21 56
12	7 29	+17.4	55.9	15.2	306	286	7	2.6	6 53	6 37	14 38	22 10	22 24
13	8 21	+14.5	56.4	15.4	318	289	13	3.6	8 03	7 51	15 27	22 38	22 47
14	9 12	+10.8	57.0	15.5	331	291	21	4.6	9 15	9 07	16 15	23 02	23 07
15	10 03	+ 6.5	57.6	15.7	343	293	30	5.6	10 29	10 25	17 04	23 25	23 26
16	10 53	+ 1.8	58.2	15.9	355	293	41	6.6	11 44	11 45	17 53	23 48	23 45
17	11 45	− 3.1	58.8	16.0	7	293	52	7.6	13 02	13 07	18 43	—	—
18	12 38	− 7.9	59.4	16.2	19	292	63	8.6	14 21	14 31	19 36	0 13	0 06
19	13 34	−12.3	59.9	16.3	32	290	74	9.6	15 42	15 56	20 32	0 40	0 29
20	14 32	−16.1	60.2	16.4	44	287	84	10.6	17 01	17 19	21 30	1 14	0 58
21	15 32	−18.9	60.4	16.5	56	284	91	11.6	18 15	18 36	22 31	1 55	1 36
22	16 35	−20.5	60.3	16.4	68	282	97	12.6	19 20	19 41	23 33	2 46	2 24
23	17 38	−20.6	60.1	16.4	80	295	100	13.6	20 13	20 33	—	3 47	3 26
24	18 39	−19.4	59.5	16.2	93	58	100	14.6	20 55	21 12	0 33	4 58	4 38
25	19 38	−17.0	58.8	16.0	105	68	97	15.6	21 28	21 41	1 30	6 12	5 56
26	20 34	−13.6	58.0	15.8	117	68	92	16.6	21 56	22 04	2 23	7 27	7 16
27	21 26	− 9.6	57.2	15.6	129	67	85	17.6	22 19	22 24	3 13	8 41	8 33
28	22 16	− 5.3	56.4	15.4	141	66	77	18.6	22 40	22 41	4 00	9 52	9 48
29	23 03	− 0.9	55.6	15.2	154	65	68	19.6	23 00	22 58	4 44	11 00	11 01
30	23 49	+ 3.4	55.0	15.0	166	66	58	20.6	23 21	23 15	5 28	12 07	12 12

MERCURY

Day	RA h m	Dec. °	Diam. "	Phase %	Transit h m	5° high 52° h m	5° high 56° h m
1	6 14	+25.0	8	33	13 37	21 21	21 41
3	6 21	+24.6	9	29	13 36	21 17	21 36
5	6 27	+24.2	9	25	13 33	21 11	21 30
7	6 31	+23.7	10	22	13 29	21 04	21 22
9	6 34	+23.2	10	18	13 24	20 55	21 13
11	6 36	+22.7	11	14	13 18	20 45	21 02
13	6 36	+22.2	11	11	13 10	20 33	20 50
15	6 35	+21.6	11	8	13 01	20 21	20 37
17	6 33	+21.1	12	6	12 50	20 07	20 22
19	6 30	+20.6	12	4	12 39	19 53	20 08
21	6 26	+20.1	12	2	12 27	19 38	19 52
23	6 21	+19.7	12	1	12 14	19 23	19 37
25	6 16	+19.3	12	1	12 02	19 08	19 22
27	6 11	+19.0	12	1	11 49	4 43	4 30
29	6 07	+18.8	12	2	11 37	4 32	4 19
31	6 03	+18.7	11	4	11 25	4 21	4 08

VENUS

Day	RA h m	Dec. °	Diam. "	Phase %	Transit h m	5° high 52° h m	5° high 56° h m
1	6 58	+24.6	13	82	14 21	22 03	22 23
6	7 24	+24.0	13	81	14 28	22 05	22 24
11	7 49	+23.1	13	79	14 33	22 04	22 22
16	8 14	+21.9	14	78	14 38	22 02	22 18
21	8 38	+20.5	14	76	14 43	21 58	22 13
26	9 02	+18.9	15	74	14 47	21 52	22 05
31	9 25	+17.1	15	73	14 50	21 45	21 56

MARS

Day	RA h m	Dec. °	Diam. "	Phase %	Transit h m	5° high 52° h m	5° high 56° h m
1	2 16	+12.8	4	96	9 38	3 05	2 58
6	2 30	+14.1	4	95	9 33	2 53	2 45
11	2 45	+15.2	4	95	9 28	2 41	2 32
16	2 59	+16.4	5	95	9 23	2 30	2 19
21	3 14	+17.4	5	95	9 17	2 19	2 08
26	3 28	+18.4	5	94	9 12	2 09	1 56
31	3 43	+19.3	5	94	9 07	1 58	1 45

SUNRISE AND SUNSET

	London 0°05′ 51°30′		Bristol 2°35′ 51°28′		Birmingham 1°55′ 52°28′		Manchester 2°15′ 53°28′		Newcastle 1°37′ 54°59′		Glasgow 4°14′ 55°52′		Belfast 5°56′ 54°35′	
	h m	h m	h m	h m	h m	h m	h m	h m	h m	h m	h m	h m	h m	h m
1	3 49	20 08	3 59	20 18	3 51	20 20	3 47	20 27	3 35	20 34	3 40	20 50	3 55	20 49
2	3 48	20 09	3 58	20 19	3 51	20 21	3 46	20 28	3 34	20 35	3 39	20 51	3 54	20 50
3	3 48	20 10	3 58	20 20	3 50	20 22	3 45	20 29	3 34	20 36	3 38	20 53	3 53	20 51
4	3 47	20 11	3 57	20 21	3 49	20 23	3 45	20 30	3 33	20 37	3 37	20 54	3 52	20 52
5	3 46	20 12	3 56	20 22	3 48	20 24	3 44	20 32	3 32	20 39	3 36	20 55	3 52	20 53
6	3 46	20 13	3 56	20 23	3 48	20 25	3 43	20 33	3 31	20 40	3 35	20 56	3 51	20 54
7	3 45	20 14	3 55	20 23	3 47	20 26	3 43	20 33	3 30	20 41	3 35	20 57	3 50	20 55
8	3 45	20 14	3 55	20 24	3 47	20 27	3 42	20 34	3 30	20 42	3 34	20 58	3 50	20 56
9	3 44	20 15	3 54	20 25	3 46	20 28	3 42	20 35	3 29	20 43	3 33	20 59	3 49	20 57
10	3 44	20 16	3 54	20 26	3 46	20 29	3 41	20 36	3 29	20 43	3 33	21 00	3 49	20 58
11	3 43	20 17	3 54	20 27	3 45	20 29	3 41	20 37	3 28	20 44	3 32	21 01	3 48	20 59
12	3 43	20 17	3 53	20 27	3 45	20 30	3 40	20 38	3 28	20 45	3 32	21 02	3 48	21 00
13	3 43	20 18	3 53	20 28	3 45	20 31	3 40	20 38	3 27	20 46	3 32	21 03	3 48	21 00
14	3 43	20 19	3 53	20 28	3 45	20 31	3 40	20 39	3 27	20 46	3 31	21 03	3 47	21 01
15	3 43	20 19	3 53	20 29	3 44	20 32	3 40	20 39	3 27	20 47	3 31	21 04	3 47	21 01
16	3 42	20 20	3 53	20 29	3 44	20 32	3 40	20 40	3 27	20 48	3 31	21 04	3 47	21 02
17	3 42	20 20	3 53	20 30	3 44	20 33	3 39	20 40	3 27	20 48	3 31	21 05	3 47	21 02
18	3 42	20 20	3 53	20 30	3 44	20 33	3 39	20 41	3 27	20 48	3 31	21 05	3 47	21 03
19	3 43	20 21	3 53	20 31	3 44	20 34	3 39	20 41	3 27	20 49	3 31	21 06	3 47	21 03
20	3 43	20 21	3 53	20 31	3 44	20 34	3 40	20 41	3 27	20 49	3 31	21 06	3 47	21 04
21	3 43	20 21	3 53	20 31	3 45	20 34	3 40	20 42	3 27	20 49	3 31	21 06	3 47	21 04
22	3 43	20 21	3 53	20 31	3 45	20 34	3 40	20 42	3 27	20 49	3 31	21 06	3 47	21 04
23	3 43	20 22	3 53	20 31	3 45	20 34	3 40	20 42	3 27	20 50	3 31	21 07	3 48	21 04
24	3 44	20 22	3 54	20 31	3 45	20 35	3 41	20 42	3 28	20 50	3 32	21 07	3 48	21 04
25	3 44	20 22	3 54	20 31	3 46	20 35	3 41	20 42	3 28	20 50	3 32	21 07	3 48	21 04
26	3 44	20 22	3 55	20 31	3 46	20 34	3 41	20 42	3 29	20 50	3 33	21 06	3 49	21 04
27	3 45	20 22	3 55	20 31	3 47	20 34	3 42	20 42	3 29	20 49	3 33	21 06	3 49	21 04
28	3 45	20 21	3 56	20 31	3 47	20 34	3 42	20 42	3 30	20 49	3 34	21 06	3 50	21 04
29	3 46	20 21	3 56	20 31	3 48	20 34	3 43	20 41	3 30	20 49	3 34	21 06	3 50	21 03
30	3 47	20 21	3 57	20 31	3 48	20 34	3 44	20 41	3 31	20 49	3 35	21 05	3 51	21 03

JUPITER

Day	RA	Dec.	Transit	5° high 52°	56°
	h m	° ′	h m	h m	h m
1	14 17.2	−12 20	21 36	1 59	1 44
11	14 14.3	−12 07	20 54	1 18	1 04
21	14 12.4	−12 00	20 13	0 38	0 23
31	14 11.6	−11 59	19 33	23 54	23 39

Diameters – equatorial 42″ polar 39″

SATURN

Day	RA	Dec.	Transit	5° high 52°	56°
	h m	° ′	h m	h m	h m
1	22 56.2	− 8 37	6 18	1 38	1 49
11	22 57.3	− 8 33	5 40	0 59	1 10
21	22 57.8	− 8 32	5 01	0 20	0 31
31	22 57.7	− 8 35	4 22	23 37	23 48

Diameters – equatorial 17″ polar 16″
Rings – major axis 40″ minor axis 3″

URANUS

Day	RA	Dec.	Transit	10° high 52°	56°
	h m	° ′	h m	h m	h m
1	19 52.2	−21 28	3 15	0 50	1 41
11	19 51.1	−21 31	2 34	0 10	1 01
21	19 49.7	−21 35	1 54	23 26	0 22
31	19 48.2	−21 39	1 13	22 46	23 38

Diameter 4″

NEPTUNE

Day	RA	Dec.	Transit	10° high 52°	56°
	h m	° ′	h m	h m	h m
1	19 38.9	−20 52	3 01	0 30	1 17
11	19 38.1	−20 54	2 21	23 47	0 37
21	19 37.1	−20 56	1 41	23 07	23 54
31	19 36.0	−20 59	1 01	22 27	23 14

Diameter 2″

July 1994

SEVENTH MONTH, 31 DAYS. *Julius* Caesar, formerly *Quintilis*, fifth month of Roman pre-Julian calendar

Sun's Longitude 120° ♌ 23ᵈ02ʰ

1	Friday	*Princess of Wales b. 1961.* Boyne 1690	week 26 day 182
2	Saturday	Sir Tyrone Guthrie *b.* 1900. Ernest Hemingway *d.* 1961	183
3	Sunday	**St Thomas. 6th S. after Pentecost**	week 27 day 184
4	Monday	Independence Day, USA. Louis Armstrong *b.* 1900	185
5	Tuesday	National Health Service started 1948	186
6	Wednesday	Beatrix Potter *b.* 1866. Otto Klemperer *d.* 1973	187
7	Thursday	Gustave Mahler *b.* 1860. Sir Arthur Conan Doyle *d.* 1930	188
8	Friday	Edward, the Black Prince *d.* 1376	189
9	Saturday	Ottorino Respighi *b.* 1879. Edward Heath *b.* 1916	190
10	Sunday	**7th S. after Pentecost.** John Calvin *b.* 1509	week 28 day 191
11	Monday	Robert the Bruce *b.* 1274. Oudenarde 1708	192
12	Tuesday	*Bank Holiday in Northern Ireland*	193
13	Wednesday	Jean-Paul Marat *assass.* 1793	194
14	Thursday	Fête Nationale, France. Emmeline Pankhurst *b.* 1858	195
15	Friday	St Swithin's Day. Inigo Jones *b.* 1573	196
16	Saturday	Mary Baker Eddy *b.* 1821. Miles Copeland *b.* 1913	197
17	Sunday	**8th S. after Pentecost.** Hardy Amies *b.* 1909	week 29 day 198
18	Monday	Dr W. G. Grace *b.* 1848. Sir Stanley Rous *d.* 1986	199
19	Tuesday	*Mary Rose* sank 1545. Edgar Degas *b.* 1834	200
20	Wednesday	Sir Edmund Hillary *b.* 1919	201
21	Thursday	Tate Gallery opened 1897. First men on the moon 1969	202
22	Friday	**St Mary Magdalen.** Revd William Spooner *b.* 1844	203
23	Saturday	Gen. Ulysses Grant *d.* 1885	204
24	Sunday	**9th S. after Pentecost.** Peter Sellers *d.* 1980	week 30 day 205
25	Monday	**St James.** S. T. Coleridge *d.* 1834	206
26	Tuesday	George Borrow *d.* 1881. Aldous Huxley *b.* 1894	207
27	Wednesday	Bank of England established 1694	208
28	Thursday	J. S. Bach *d.* 1750. Gerard Manley Hopkins *b.* 1844	209
29	Friday	Defeat of Spanish Armada 1588. Robert Schumann *d.* 1856	210
30	Saturday	*Trinity Law Sittings end.* William Penn *d.* 1718	211
31	Sunday	**10th S. after Pentecost.** St Ignatius Loyola *d.* 1556	week 31 day 212

ASTRONOMICAL PHENOMENA

d	h	
5	05	Mars in conjunction with Moon. Mars 0°.3 N.
5	19	Earth at aphelion (152 million km)
7	13	Mercury in conjunction with Moon. Mercury 1° S.
12	07	Venus in conjunction with Moon. Venus 6° N.
14	16	Neptune at opposition
16	21	Jupiter in conjunction with Moon. Jupiter 2° N.
17	04	Uranus at opposition
17	14	Mercury at greatest elongation W. 21°
25	23	Saturn in conjunction with Moon. Saturn 6° S.

CONSTELLATIONS

The following constellations are near the meridian at

	d	h
June	1	24
June	15	23
July	1	22
July	16	21
August	1	20
August	16	19

Ursa Minor, Draco, Corona, Hercules, Lyra, Serpens, Ophiuchus, Libra, Scorpius and Sagittarius

MINIMA OF ALGOL

d	h	d	h	d	h
1	20.2	13	07.4	24	18.6
4	17.0	16	04.2	27	15.5
7	13.8	19	01.0	30	12.3
10	10.6	21	21.8		

THE MOON

Phases, Apsides and Node	d	h	m
● New Moon	8	21	37
☽ First Quarter	16	01	12
○ Full Moon	22	20	16
☾ Last Quarter	30	12	40
Apogee (404,677 km)	3	04	40
Perigee (367,865 km)	18	17	31
Apogee (404,086 km)	30	22	56

Mean longitude of ascending node on July 1, 232°

THE SUN

s.d. 15′.8

Day	Right Ascension	Dec. +	Equation of time	Rise 52°	Rise 56°	Transit	Set 52°	Set 56°	Sidereal time	Transit of First Point of Aries
	h m s	° ′	m s	h m	h m	h m	h m	h m	h m s	h m s
1	6 38 57	23 08	− 3 40	3 44	3 18	12 04	20 23	20 49	18 35 17	5 23 50
2	6 43 05	23 04	− 3 52	3 45	3 19	12 04	20 23	20 49	18 39 13	5 19 54
3	6 47 13	23 00	− 4 03	3 46	3 20	12 04	20 22	20 48	18 43 10	5 15 58
4	6 51 21	22 55	− 4 14	3 46	3 21	12 04	20 22	20 47	18 47 06	5 12 02
5	6 55 28	22 50	− 4 25	3 47	3 22	12 05	20 21	20 47	18 51 03	5 08 06
6	6 59 35	22 44	− 4 35	3 48	3 23	12 05	20 21	20 46	18 55 00	5 04 10
7	7 03 42	22 38	− 4 45	3 49	3 24	12 05	20 20	20 45	18 58 56	5 00 15
8	7 07 48	22 31	− 4 55	3 50	3 25	12 05	20 20	20 44	19 02 53	4 56 19
9	7 11 54	22 25	− 5 05	3 51	3 26	12 05	20 19	20 43	19 06 49	4 52 23
10	7 15 59	22 17	− 5 14	3 52	3 27	12 05	20 18	20 42	19 10 46	4 48 27
11	7 20 05	22 10	− 5 22	3 53	3 29	12 05	20 17	20 41	19 14 42	4 44 31
12	7 24 09	22 02	− 5 30	3 54	3 30	12 06	20 16	20 40	19 18 39	4 40 35
13	7 28 13	21 53	− 5 38	3 55	3 31	12 06	20 16	20 39	19 22 35	4 36 39
14	7 32 17	21 45	− 5 45	3 56	3 33	12 06	20 15	20 38	19 26 32	4 32 43
15	7 36 20	21 36	− 5 52	3 58	3 34	12 06	20 14	20 36	19 30 29	4 28 47
16	7 40 23	21 26	− 5 58	3 59	3 36	12 06	20 13	20 35	19 34 25	4 24 51
17	7 44 25	21 16	− 6 03	4 00	3 37	12 06	20 11	20 34	19 38 22	4 20 55
18	7 48 27	21 06	− 6 09	4 01	3 39	12 06	20 10	20 32	19 42 18	4 17 00
19	7 52 28	20 56	− 6 13	4 03	3 40	12 06	20 09	20 31	19 46 15	4 13 04
20	7 56 28	20 45	− 6 17	4 04	3 42	12 06	20 08	20 29	19 50 11	4 09 08
21	8 00 28	20 33	− 6 20	4 05	3 44	12 06	20 07	20 28	19 54 08	4 05 12
22	8 04 28	20 22	− 6 23	4 07	3 45	12 06	20 05	20 26	19 58 05	4 01 16
23	8 08 27	20 10	− 6 26	4 08	3 47	12 06	20 04	20 25	20 02 01	3 57 20
24	8 12 25	19 58	− 6 27	4 09	3 49	12 06	20 03	20 23	20 05 58	3 53 24
25	8 16 22	19 45	− 6 28	4 11	3 51	12 06	20 01	20 21	20 09 54	3 49 28
26	8 20 19	19 32	− 6 29	4 12	3 52	12 06	20 00	20 19	20 13 51	3 45 32
27	8 24 16	19 19	− 6 29	4 14	3 54	12 06	19 58	20 18	20 17 47	3 41 36
28	8 28 12	19 05	− 6 28	4 15	3 56	12 06	19 57	20 16	20 21 44	3 37 40
29	8 32 07	18 51	− 6 27	4 17	3 58	12 06	19 55	20 14	20 25 40	3 33 44
30	8 36 02	18 37	− 6 25	4 18	4 00	12 06	19 54	20 12	20 29 37	3 29 49
31	8 39 56	18 23	− 6 22	4 20	4 01	12 06	19 52	20 10	20 33 34	3 25 53

DURATION OF TWILIGHT (in minutes)

Latitude	52°	56°	52°	56°	52°	56°	52°	56°
	1 July		11 July		21 July		31 July	
Civil	48	61	46	58	44	53	41	49
Nautical	124	TAN	116	TAN	107	144	98	122
Astronomical	TAN	TAN	TAN	TAN	TAN	TAN	180	TAN

THE NIGHT SKY

Mercury, although reaching greatest western elongation (21°) on the 17th, will be a very difficult object to observe from the British Isles because of the long duration of twilight. It may be possible to detect it low above the ENE horizon at the time of beginning of morning civil twilight, within a day or so of the 21st.

Venus, magnitude −4.1, continues to be visible as a brilliant object low in the western sky after sunset. The crescent Moon is near the planet on the evenings of the 11th and 12th. On the evening of the 10th, Venus will be seen passing 1° north of Regulus, though closest approach occurs before sunset.

Mars is visible as a morning object, magnitude +1.2. Mars is in Taurus, passing between the Hyades and the Pleiades early in the month. On the morning of the 5th the old crescent Moon will be seen approaching Mars.

Jupiter, magnitude −2.1, continues to be visible as a brilliant evening object. It reaches its second stationary point on the 2nd, resuming its direct motion. On the evening of the 16th the Moon, at First Quarter, passes 3° south of the planet.

Saturn, magnitude +0.8, continues to be visible as a morning object in Aquarius. The gibbous Moon is near Saturn on the morning of the 26th.

Uranus is at opposition on the 17th, in Sagittarius. Uranus is barely visible to the naked eye since its magnitude is +5.6, but it is readily located with small optical aid.

Neptune is at opposition on the 14th, also in Sagittarius. It is not visible to the naked eye since its magnitude is +7.9.

THE MOON

Day	RA	Dec.	Hor. par.	Semi-diam.	Sun's co-long.	PA of Bright Limb	Phase	Age	Rise 52°	Rise 56°	Transit	Set 52°	Set 56°
	h m	°	′	′	°	°	%	d	h m	h m	h m	h m	h m
1	0 35	+ 7.5	54.6	14.9	178	67	48	21.6	23 43	23 33	6 10	13 12	13 21
2	1 21	+11.3	54.3	14.8	190	69	39	22.6	—	23 54	6 54	14 17	14 29
3	2 08	+14.6	54.2	14.8	203	71	30	23.6	0 07	—	7 38	15 20	15 36
4	2 56	+17.3	54.2	14.8	215	74	22	24.6	0 36	0 19	8 24	16 22	16 40
5	3 45	+19.3	54.4	14.8	227	77	14	25.6	1 10	0 51	9 12	17 20	17 40
6	4 36	+20.5	54.7	14.9	239	79	8	26.6	1 51	1 30	10 01	18 13	18 34
7	5 28	+20.7	55.1	15.0	252	81	4	27.6	2 41	2 19	10 52	19 00	19 20
8	6 21	+19.9	55.6	15.2	264	74	1	28.6	3 38	3 18	11 43	19 40	19 57
9	7 15	+18.1	56.1	15.3	276	352	0	0.1	4 42	4 25	12 33	20 13	20 28
10	8 07	+15.4	56.6	15.4	288	302	1	1.1	5 51	5 38	13 24	20 42	20 53
11	8 59	+11.8	57.1	15.6	301	297	5	2.1	7 04	6 54	14 13	21 08	21 15
12	9 51	+ 7.6	57.6	15.7	313	296	11	3.1	8 18	8 13	15 02	21 32	21 35
13	10 42	+ 3.0	58.1	15.8	325	296	18	4.1	9 34	9 33	15 51	21 55	21 54
14	11 34	− 1.8	58.5	15.9	337	295	28	5.1	10 50	10 54	16 41	22 19	22 13
15	12 26	− 6.6	58.9	16.0	349	294	38	6.1	12 08	12 16	17 32	22 45	22 35
16	13 20	−11.1	59.2	16.1	2	292	50	7.1	13 26	13 39	18 25	23 15	23 01
17	14 16	−15.0	59.4	16.2	14	289	61	8.1	14 44	15 01	19 21	23 52	23 34
18	15 14	−18.1	59.6	16.2	26	285	72	9.1	15 58	16 18	20 19	—	—
19	16 14	−20.0	59.6	16.2	38	281	82	10.1	17 05	17 27	21 19	0 37	0 17
20	17 15	−20.7	59.5	16.2	51	277	90	11.1	18 02	18 23	22 18	1 32	1 11
21	18 16	−20.0	59.2	16.1	63	276	96	12.1	18 49	19 07	23 16	2 37	2 17
22	19 16	−18.1	58.8	16.0	75	283	99	13.1	19 26	19 41	—	3 49	3 32
23	20 12	−15.1	58.2	15.9	87	10	100	14.1	19 56	20 07	0 11	5 04	4 50
24	21 06	−11.4	57.6	15.7	99	55	98	15.1	20 22	20 28	1 02	6 18	6 09
25	21 57	− 7.2	56.9	15.5	112	60	94	16.1	20 44	20 47	1 51	7 31	7 26
26	22 46	− 2.7	56.2	15.3	124	62	89	17.1	21 05	21 04	2 37	8 42	8 41
27	23 33	+ 1.7	55.5	15.1	136	63	82	18.1	21 26	21 21	3 22	9 50	9 53
28	0 20	+ 6.0	55.0	15.0	148	65	73	19.1	21 47	21 39	4 05	10 57	11 04
29	1 06	+ 9.9	54.6	14.9	160	67	64	20.1	22 11	21 59	4 49	12 02	12 13
30	1 53	+13.4	54.3	14.8	173	69	55	21.1	22 38	22 23	5 33	13 07	13 21
31	2 40	+16.3	54.3	14.8	185	72	46	22.1	23 09	22 51	6 18	14 09	14 26

MERCURY

Day	RA	Dec.	Diam.	Phase	Transit	5° high 52°	5° high 56°
	h m	°	″	%	h m	h m	h m
1	6 03	+18.7	11	4	11 25	4 21	4 08
3	6 00	+18.7	11	6	11 14	4 10	3 57
5	5 58	+18.8	11	9	11 05	4 00	3 47
7	5 58	+19.0	10	12	10 57	3 50	3 37
9	5 58	+19.2	10	16	10 50	3 42	3 29
11	6 01	+19.5	9	20	10 45	3 35	3 21
13	6 04	+19.9	9	25	10 41	3 29	3 15
15	6 10	+20.3	8	30	10 39	3 24	3 09
17	6 17	+20.7	8	36	10 38	3 21	3 06
19	6 25	+21.1	8	41	10 39	3 19	3 03
21	6 35	+21.4	7	48	10 41	3 19	3 03
23	6 46	+21.7	7	54	10 45	3 20	3 04
25	6 58	+21.9	6	61	10 50	3 24	3 07
27	7 12	+22.0	6	68	10 56	3 29	3 12
29	7 27	+22.0	6	75	11 03	3 36	3 20
31	7 43	+21.8	6	81	11 11	3 46	3 29

VENUS

Day	RA	Dec.	Diam.	Phase	Transit	5° high 52°	5° high 56°
	h m	°	″	%	h m	h m	h m
1	9 25	+17.1	15	73	14 50	21 45	21 56
6	9 48	+15.1	16	71	14 53	21 37	21 46
11	10 09	+13.0	16	69	14 55	21 27	21 34
16	10 30	+10.7	17	67	14 56	21 17	21 22
21	10 51	+ 8.4	17	65	14 57	21 05	21 09
26	11 11	+ 6.0	18	63	14 57	20 53	20 55
31	11 31	+ 3.5	19	61	14 57	20 41	20 40

MARS

Day	RA	Dec.	Diam.	Phase	Transit	5° high 52°	5° high 56°
1	3 43	+19.3	5	94	9 07	1 58	1 45
6	3 58	+20.1	5	94	9 02	1 49	1 34
11	4 12	+20.8	5	94	8 57	1 39	1 24
16	4 27	+21.5	5	94	8 52	1 30	1 14
21	4 42	+22.0	5	93	8 47	1 22	1 05
26	4 57	+22.5	5	93	8 42	1 14	0 57
31	5 11	+22.9	5	93	8 37	1 07	0 49

SUNRISE AND SUNSET

	London 0°05′ 51°30′		Bristol 2°35′ 51°28′		Birmingham 1°55′ 52°28′		Manchester 2°15′ 53°28′		Newcastle 1°37′ 54°59′		Glasgow 4°14′ 55°52′		Belfast 5°56′ 54°35′	
	h m	h m	h m	h m	h m	h m	h m	h m	h m	h m	h m	h m	h m	h m
1	3 47	20 21	3 57	20 30	3 49	20 33	3 44	20 41	3 32	20 48	3 36	21 05	3 52	21 03
2	3 48	20 20	3 58	20 30	3 50	20 33	3 45	20 40	3 33	20 48	3 37	21 04	3 53	21 02
3	3 49	20 20	3 59	20 30	3 51	20 33	3 46	20 40	3 34	20 47	3 38	21 04	3 53	21 02
4	3 49	20 20	4 00	20 29	3 51	20 32	3 47	20 39	3 34	20 47	3 39	21 03	3 54	21 01
5	3 50	20 19	4 00	20 29	3 52	20 32	3 48	20 39	3 35	20 46	3 40	21 03	3 55	21 01
6	3 51	20 18	4 01	20 28	3 53	20 31	3 49	20 38	3 36	20 45	3 41	21 02	3 56	21 00
7	3 52	20 18	4 02	20 28	3 54	20 30	3 50	20 38	3 37	20 45	3 42	21 01	3 57	20 59
8	3 53	20 17	4 03	20 27	3 55	20 30	3 51	20 37	3 39	20 44	3 43	21 00	3 58	20 58
9	3 54	20 17	4 04	20 26	3 56	20 29	3 52	20 36	3 40	20 43	3 44	20 59	4 00	20 58
10	3 55	20 16	4 05	20 26	3 57	20 28	3 53	20 35	3 41	20 42	3 45	20 58	4 01	20 57
11	3 56	20 15	4 06	20 25	3 58	20 27	3 54	20 34	3 42	20 41	3 47	20 57	4 02	20 56
12	3 57	20 14	4 07	20 24	3 59	20 27	3 55	20 33	3 43	20 40	3 48	20 56	4 03	20 55
13	3 58	20 13	4 08	20 23	4 00	20 26	3 56	20 32	3 45	20 39	3 49	20 55	4 04	20 54
14	3 59	20 12	4 09	20 22	4 02	20 25	3 57	20 31	3 46	20 38	3 51	20 54	4 06	20 53
15	4 00	20 11	4 11	20 21	4 03	20 24	3 59	20 30	3 47	20 37	3 52	20 53	4 07	20 51
16	4 02	20 10	4 12	20 20	4 04	20 23	4 00	20 29	3 49	20 35	3 54	20 51	4 08	20 50
17	4 03	20 09	4 13	20 19	4 05	20 21	4 01	20 28	3 50	20 34	3 55	20 50	4 10	20 49
18	4 04	20 08	4 14	20 18	4 07	20 20	4 03	20 27	3 52	20 33	3 57	20 48	4 11	20 48
19	4 05	20 07	4 15	20 17	4 08	20 19	4 04	20 25	3 53	20 31	3 58	20 47	4 13	20 46
20	4 07	20 06	4 17	20 16	4 09	20 18	4 06	20 24	3 55	20 30	4 00	20 46	4 14	20 45
21	4 08	20 05	4 18	20 15	4 11	20 17	4 07	20 23	3 56	20 28	4 02	20 44	4 16	20 43
22	4 09	20 03	4 19	20 13	4 12	20 15	4 08	20 21	3 58	20 27	4 03	20 42	4 17	20 42
23	4 11	20 02	4 21	20 12	4 13	20 14	4 10	20 20	3 59	20 25	4 05	20 41	4 19	20 40
24	4 12	20 01	4 22	20 11	4 15	20 12	4 11	20 18	4 01	20 24	4 07	20 39	4 20	20 39
25	4 13	19 59	4 23	20 09	4 16	20 11	4 13	20 17	4 03	20 22	4 08	20 37	4 22	20 37
26	4 15	19 58	4 25	20 08	4 18	20 10	4 14	20 15	4 04	20 20	4 10	20 36	4 24	20 36
27	4 16	19 57	4 26	20 06	4 19	20 08	4 16	20 14	4 06	20 19	4 12	20 34	4 25	20 34
28	4 18	19 55	4 28	20 05	4 21	20 06	4 18	20 12	4 08	20 17	4 14	20 32	4 27	20 32
29	4 19	19 54	4 29	20 03	4 22	20 05	4 19	20 11	4 09	20 15	4 15	20 30	4 29	20 30
30	4 21	19 52	4 31	20 02	4 24	20 03	4 21	20 09	4 11	20 13	4 17	20 28	4 30	20 29
31	4 22	19 50	4 32	20 00	4 25	20 02	4 22	20 07	4 13	20 11	4 19	20 26	4 32	20 27

JUPITER

Day	RA	Dec.	Transit	5° high 52°	56°
	h m	° ′	h m	h m	h m
1	14 11.6	−11 59	19 33	23 54	23 39
11	14 12.0	−12 04	18 54	23 15	23 00
21	14 13.5	−12 15	18 17	22 36	22 21
31	14 16.1	−12 31	17 40	21 57	21 42

Diameters – equatorial 38″ polar 36″

SATURN

Day	RA	Dec.	Transit	5° high 52°	56°
	h m	° ′	h m	h m	h m
1	22 57.7	− 8 35	4 22	23 37	23 48
11	22 57.0	− 8 42	3 42	22 58	23 09
21	22 55.7	− 8 53	3 01	22 18	22 29
31	22 53.8	− 9 06	2 20	21 38	21 50

Diameters – equatorial 18″ polar 17″
Rings – major axis 42″ minor axis 4″

URANUS

Day	RA	Dec.	Transit	10° high 52°	56°
	h m	° ′	h m	h m	h m
1	19 48.2	−21 39	1 13	3 35	2 43
11	19 46.5	−21 43	0 32	2 54	2 01
21	19 44.8	−21 47	23 47	2 12	1 19
31	19 43.2	−21 52	23 06	1 30	0 36

Diameter 4″

NEPTUNE

Day	RA	Dec.	Transit	10° high 52°	56°
	h m	° ′	h m	h m	h m
1	19 36.0	−20 59	1 01	3 30	2 43
11	19 34.9	−21 01	0 20	2 50	2 02
21	19 33.8	−21 04	23 36	2 09	1 21
31	19 32.6	−21 06	22 55	1 28	0 40

Diameter 2″

August 1994

EIGHTH MONTH, 31 DAYS. Julius Caesar *Augustus*, formerly *Sextilis*, sixth month of Roman pre-Julian calendar

Sun's Longitude 150° ♍ 23ᵈ09ʰ

1	*Monday*	*Bank Holiday in Scotland.* Herman Melville *b.* 1819	*week* 31 *day* 213
2	*Tuesday*	Sir Arthur Bliss *b.* 1891, Enrico Caruso *d.* 1921	214
3	*Wednesday*	Sir Roger Casement *exec.* 1916. Colette *d.* 1954	215
4	*Thursday*	*Queen Elizabeth the Queen Mother b. 1900*	216
5	*Friday*	Guy de Maupassant *b.* 1850. Richard Burton *d.* 1984	217
6	*Saturday*	**The Transfiguration.** Sir Alexander Fleming *b.* 1881	218
7	*Sunday*	**11th S. after Pentecost.** Sidney Buller *d.* 1970	*week* 32 *day* 219
8	*Monday*	Princess Beatrice of York *b.* 1988	220
9	*Tuesday*	Singapore became independent 1965	221
10	*Wednesday*	Charles Keene *b.* 1823. James Whistler *b.* 1834	222
11	*Thursday*	Sir Angus Wilson *b.* 1913. Andrew Carnegie *d.* 1919	223
12	*Friday*	Thomas Bewick *b.* 1753. Ian Fleming *d.* 1964	224
13	*Saturday*	John Logie Baird *b.* 1888. Jules Massenet *d.* 1912	225
14	*Sunday*	**12th S. after Pentecost.** Leonard Woolf *d.* 1969	*week* 33 *day* 226
15	*Monday*	*Princess Royal b. 1950.* James Keir Hardie *b.* 1856	227
16	*Tuesday*	Robert van Bunsen *d.* 1899. Georgette Heyer *b.* 1902	228
17	*Wednesday*	Wilfrid Scawen Blunt *b.* 1840	229
18	*Thursday*	Godfrey Evans *b.* 1920. Sir Frederick Ashton *d.* 1988	230
19	*Friday*	Sir Henry Wood *d.* 1944. Bill Clinton *b.* 1946	231
20	*Saturday*	Raymond Poincaré *b.* 1860. Rajiv Gandhi *b.* 1944	232
21	*Sunday*	**13th S. after Pentecost.** *Princess Margaret b. 1930*	*week* 34 *day* 233
22	*Monday*	Richard III *d.* 1485. Henri Cartier-Bresson *b.* 1908	234
23	*Tuesday*	1st Duke of Buckingham *assass.* 1628	235
24	*Wednesday*	**St Bartholomew.** Eruption of Mt Vesuvius AD 79	236
25	*Thursday*	Leonard Bernstein *b.* 1918. Liberation of Paris 1944	237
26	*Friday*	Prince Albert *b.* 1819. Sir Francis Chichester *d.* 1972	238
27	*Saturday*	Earl Mountbatten of Burma *assass.* 1979	239
28	*Sunday*	**14th S. after Pentecost.** Goethe *b.* 1749	*week* 35 *day* 240
29	*Monday*	*Bank Holiday in England, Wales and Northern Ireland*	241
30	*Tuesday*	Mary Wollstonecraft Shelley *b.* 1797	242
31	*Wednesday*	Théophile Gautier *b.* 1811. John Ford *d.* 1973	243

ASTRONOMICAL PHENOMENA

d	h	
3	05	Mars in conjunction with Moon. Mars 3° N.
6	20	Mercury in conjunction with Moon. Mercury 6° N.
10	21	Venus in conjunction with Moon. Venus 3° N.
13	01	Mercury in superior conjunction
13	06	Jupiter in conjunction with Moon. Jupiter 2° N.
22	05	Saturn in conjunction with Moon. Saturn 6° S.
24	23	Venus at greatest elongation E. 46°

CONSTELLATIONS

The following constellations are near the meridian at

	d	h
July	1	24
July	16	23
August	1	22
August	16	21
September	1	20
September	15	19

Draco, Hercules, Lyra, Cygnus, Sagitta, Ophiuchus, Serpens, Aquila and Sagittarius

MINIMA OF ALGOL

d	h	d	h	d	h
2	09.1	13	20.3	25	07.5
5	05.9	16	17.1	28	04.4
8	02.7	19	13.9	31	01.2
10	23.5	22	10.7		

THE MOON

Phases, Apsides and Node	d	h	m
● New Moon	7	08	45
☽ First Quarter	14	05	57
○ Full Moon	21	06	47
☾ Last Quarter	29	06	41
Perigee (369,464 km)	12	23	10
Apogee (404,343 km)	27	17	52

Mean longitude of ascending node on August 1, 230°

THE SUN   s.d. 15′.8

Day	Right Ascension	Dec. +	Equation of time	Rise 52°	Rise 56°	Transit	Set 52°	Set 56°	Sidereal time	Transit of First Point of Aries
	h m s	° ′	m s	h m	h m	h m	h m	h m	h m s	h m s
1	8 43 50	18 08	−6 19	4 21	4 03	12 06	19 50	20 08	20 37 30	3 21 57
2	8 47 42	17 53	−6 16	4 23	4 05	12 06	19 49	20 06	20 41 27	3 18 01
3	8 51 35	17 37	−6 12	4 24	4 07	12 06	19 47	20 04	20 45 23	3 14 05
4	8 55 27	17 22	−6 07	4 26	4 09	12 06	19 45	20 02	20 49 20	3 10 09
5	8 59 18	17 06	−6 02	4 27	4 11	12 06	19 43	20 00	20 53 16	3 06 13
6	9 03 08	16 49	−5 56	4 29	4 13	12 06	19 42	19 58	20 57 13	3 02 17
7	9 06 58	16 33	−5 49	4 31	4 15	12 06	19 40	19 56	21 01 09	2 58 21
8	9 10 48	16 16	−5 42	4 32	4 17	12 06	19 38	19 53	21 05 06	2 54 25
9	9 14 37	15 59	−5 34	4 34	4 19	12 05	19 36	19 51	21 09 03	2 50 29
10	9 18 25	15 42	−5 26	4 35	4 20	12 05	19 34	19 49	21 12 59	2 46 34
11	9 22 12	15 24	−5 17	4 37	4 22	12 05	19 32	19 47	21 16 56	2 42 38
12	9 25 59	15 06	−5 07	4 39	4 24	12 05	19 30	19 44	21 20 52	2 38 42
13	9 29 46	14 48	−4 57	4 40	4 26	12 05	19 28	19 42	21 24 49	2 34 46
14	9 33 32	14 30	−4 47	4 42	4 28	12 05	19 26	19 40	21 28 45	2 30 50
15	9 37 17	14 11	−4 35	4 43	4 30	12 04	19 24	19 37	21 32 42	2 26 54
16	9 41 02	13 53	−4 24	4 45	4 32	12 04	19 22	19 35	21 36 38	2 22 58
17	9 44 46	13 34	−4 11	4 47	4 34	12 04	19 20	19 33	21 40 35	2 19 02
18	9 48 30	13 15	−3 58	4 48	4 36	12 04	19 18	19 30	21 44 31	2 15 06
19	9 52 13	12 55	−3 45	4 50	4 38	12 04	19 16	19 28	21 48 28	2 11 10
20	9 55 56	12 36	−3 31	4 52	4 40	12 03	19 14	19 25	21 52 25	2 07 15
21	9 59 38	12 16	−3 17	4 53	4 42	12 03	19 12	19 23	21 56 21	2 03 19
22	10 03 20	11 56	−3 02	4 55	4 44	12 03	19 10	19 21	22 00 18	1 59 23
23	10 07 01	11 36	−2 47	4 56	4 46	12 03	19 08	19 18	22 04 14	1 55 27
24	10 10 42	11 15	−2 31	4 58	4 48	12 02	19 06	19 16	22 08 11	1 51 31
25	10 14 22	10 55	−2 15	5 00	4 50	12 02	19 03	19 13	22 12 07	1 47 35
26	10 18 02	10 34	−1 58	5 01	4 52	12 02	19 01	19 11	22 16 04	1 43 39
27	10 21 42	10 13	−1 41	5 03	4 54	12 02	18 59	19 08	22 20 00	1 39 43
28	10 25 21	9 52	−1 24	5 05	4 56	12 01	18 57	19 05	22 23 57	1 35 47
29	10 29 00	9 31	−1 06	5 06	4 58	12 01	18 55	19 03	22 27 54	1 31 51
30	10 32 38	9 10	−0 48	5 08	5 00	12 01	18 52	19 00	22 31 50	1 27 55
31	10 36 17	8 48	−0 30	5 10	5 02	12 00	18 50	18 58	22 35 47	1 24 00

DURATION OF TWILIGHT (in minutes)

Latitude	52°	56°	52°	56°	52°	56°	52°	56°
	1 August		11 August		21 August		31 August	
Civil	41	48	39	45	37	42	35	40
Nautical	97	120	89	106	83	96	79	89
Astronomical	177	TAN	153	205	138	166	127	147

THE NIGHT SKY

Mercury is unsuitably placed for observation, superior conjunction occurring on the 13th.

Venus is visible low in the western sky after sunset, magnitude −4.6. Although greatest eastern elongation (46°) occurs on the 24th, Venus is only visible for a short time after sunset. The thin crescent Moon will be seen passing 3°south of Venus on the evening of the 10th. On the evening of the last day of the month Venus passes 0°.7 south of Spica, though this event is only likely to be seen with optical aid, as the two objects are less than 10° above the WSW horizon at sunset.

Mars, magnitude +1.2, is visible in the SE sky in the mornings. During the month Mars moves from·Taurus into Gemini. On the morning of the 3rd the old crescent Moon will be seen approaching the planet.

Jupiter is a brilliant object in the SW sky in the evenings, magnitude −1.9. Early in the month Jupiter passes from Virgo into Libra. The crescent Moon will be seen near the planet on the evenings of the 12th and 13th.

Saturn, magnitude +0.6, is approaching opposition and is therefore visible throughout the hours of darkness. On the morning of the 22nd the gibbous Moon passes 6° north of the planet.

Meteors. The maximum of the famous Perseid meteor shower occurs on the night of the 12th to 13th. As the crescent Moon sets in the early evening, there will be no interference by moonlight. The parent comet of this shower (Comet Swift-Tuttle) returned to perihelion in the autumn of 1992 and its next return is expected in 2126.

THE MOON

Day	RA h m	Dec. °	Hor. par. ′	Semi-diam. ′	Sun's co-long. °	PA of Bright Limb °	Phase %	Age d	Rise 52° h m	Rise 56° h m	Transit h m	Set 52° h m	Set 56° h m
1	3 29	+18.6	54.4	14.8	197	76	36	23.1	23 47	23 27	7 05	15 08	15 28
2	4 19	+20.0	54.6	14.9	209	80	27	24.1	—	—	7 53	16 03	16 24
3	5 11	+20.6	55.0	15.0	221	83	19	25.1	0 33	0 12	8 43	16 53	17 13
4	6 04	+20.2	55.5	15.1	234	87	12	26.1	1 26	1 06	9 34	17 36	17 54
5	6 57	+18.7	56.1	15.3	246	88	6	27.1	2 28	2 10	10 25	18 12	18 28
6	7 50	+16.4	56.8	15.5	258	86	2	28.1	3 36	3 21	11 16	18 44	18 56
7	8 43	+13.1	57.4	15.6	270	58	0	29.1	4 48	4 37	12 07	19 12	19 20
8	9 36	+ 9.0	58.0	15.8	283	321	1	0.6	6 03	5 56	12 57	19 37	19 41
9	10 28	+ 4.5	58.5	15.9	295	304	3	1.6	7 19	7 17	13 47	20 01	20 01
10	11 21	− 0.4	58.9	16.0	307	299	9	2.6	8 37	8 39	14 37	20 25	20 21
11	12 14	− 5.3	59.1	16.1	319	297	16	3.6	9 56	10 02	15 29	20 51	20 43
12	13 08	− 9.9	59.3	16.2	332	294	25	4.6	11 15	11 26	16 22	21 20	21 08
13	14 03	−14.0	59.3	16.2	344	290	36	5.6	12 32	12 48	17 17	21 54	21 38
14	15 01	−17.2	59.3	16.2	356	286	47	6.6	13 47	14 06	18 14	22 36	22 17
15	16 00	−19.4	59.2	16.1	8	282	59	7.6	14 55	15 16	19 12	23 27	23 06
16	17 00	−20.4	59.0	16.1	21	277	70	8.6	15 55	16 16	20 10	—	—
17	17 59	−20.1	58.7	16.0	33	272	79	9.6	16 44	17 03	21 07	0 27	0 06
18	18 58	−18.7	58.3	15.9	45	269	88	10.6	17 24	17 40	22 01	1 34	1 15
19	19 54	−16.1	57.9	15.8	57	268	94	11.6	17 56	18 09	22 53	2 46	2 31
20	20 48	−12.7	57.4	15.6	69	272	98	12.6	18 24	18 32	23 43	3 59	3 48
21	21 40	− 8.7	56.9	15.5	81	306	100	13.6	18 47	18 52	—	5 12	5 05
22	22 29	− 4.4	56.3	15.3	94	40	99	14.6	19 09	19 10	0 30	6 23	6 20
23	23 17	− 0.0	55.8	15.2	106	56	97	15.6	19 30	19 27	1 15	7 33	7 34
24	0 04	+ 4.3	55.2	15.1	118	61	92	16.6	19 52	19 45	1 59	8 41	8 46
25	0 50	+ 8.4	54.8	14.9	130	64	86	17.6	20 15	20 05	2 43	9 47	9 56
26	1 37	+12.0	54.5	14.8	142	67	79	18.6	20 40	20 27	3 27	10 52	11 04
27	2 25	+15.2	54.3	14.8	155	71	71	19.6	21 10	20 53	4 12	11 55	12 10
28	3 13	+17.6	54.2	14.8	167	75	62	20.6	21 45	21 26	4 58	12 55	13 14
29	4 02	+19.4	54.4	14.8	179	79	53	21.6	22 26	22 06	5 46	13 52	14 12
30	4 53	+20.2	54.7	14.9	191	83	43	22.6	23 16	22 55	6 34	14 43	15 04
31	5 45	+20.2	55.1	15.0	203	87	34	23.6	—	23 54	7 24	15 28	15 48

MERCURY

Day	RA h m	Dec. °	Diam. ″	Phase %	Transit h m	5° high 52° h m	5° high 56° h m
1	7 51	+21.6	6	84	11 15	3 51	3 35
3	8 07	+21.2	5	89	11 24	4 03	3 47
5	8 25	+20.5	5	93	11 34	4 16	4 01
7	8 42	+19.7	5	96	11 43	4 30	4 16
9	8 59	+18.8	5	98	11 52	4 45	4 32
11	9 16	+17.7	5	99	12 01	19 00	19 11
13	9 32	+16.5	5	100	12 09	19 01	19 11
15	9 48	+15.2	5	100	12 17	19 01	19 10
17	10 03	+13.8	5	99	12 24	19 01	19 09
19	10 18	+12.4	5	98	12 31	19 00	19 06
21	10 32	+10.9	5	96	12 37	18 58	19 04
23	10 46	+ 9.4	5	95	12 43	18 56	19 00
25	10 59	+ 7.8	5	94	12 48	18 54	18 56
27	11 12	+ 6.3	5	92	12 53	18 50	18 52
29	11 24	+ 4.8	5	90	12 58	18 47	18 47
31	11 36	+ 3.3	5	89	13 01	18 43	18 42

VENUS

Day	RA h m	Dec. °	Diam. ″	Phase %	Transit h m	5° high 52° h m	5° high 56° h m
1	11 35	+ 3.0	19	60	14 57	20 38	20 37
6	11 54	+ 0.6	20	58	14 56	20 24	20 21
11	12 12	− 1.9	21	56	14 55	20 10	20 05
16	12 30	− 4.4	22	53	14 53	19 56	19 48
21	12 48	− 6.8	23	51	14 51	19 40	19 31
26	13 05	− 9.2	25	48	14 49	19 25	19 13
31	13 22	−11.4	26	45	14 46	19 08	18 54

MARS

Day	RA h m	Dec. °	Diam. ″	Phase %	Transit h m	5° high 52° h m	5° high 56° h m
1	5 14	+23.0	5	93	8 36	1 05	0 47
6	5 29	+23.3	5	92	8 31	0 58	0 40
11	5 43	+23.5	5	92	8 26	0 52	0 33
16	5 58	+23.6	5	92	8 21	0 45	0 27
21	6 12	+23.7	5	92	8 15	0 40	0 21
26	6 26	+23.6	5	91	8 10	0 34	0 16
31	6 40	+23.5	5	91	8 04	0 29	0 11

SUNRISE AND SUNSET

	London		Bristol		Birmingham		Manchester		Newcastle		Glasgow		Belfast	
	0°05′	51°30′	2°35′	51°28′	1°55′	52°28′	2°15′	53°28′	1°37′	54°59′	4°14′	55°52′	5°56′	54°35′
	h m	h m	h m	h m	h m	h m	h m	h m	h m	h m	h m	h m	h m	h m
1	4 24	19 49	4 34	19 59	4 27	20 00	4 24	20 05	4 15	20 10	4 21	20 24	4 34	20 25
2	4 25	19 47	4 35	19 57	4 29	19 58	4 26	20 04	4 16	20 08	4 23	20 22	4 36	20 23
3	4 27	19 45	4 37	19 55	4 30	19 56	4 27	20 02	4 18	20 06	4 25	20 20	4 37	20 21
4	4 28	19 44	4 38	19 54	4 32	19 55	4 29	20 00	4 20	20 04	4 26	20 18	4 39	20 19
5	4 30	19 42	4 40	19 52	4 33	19 53	4 31	19 58	4 22	20 02	4 28	20 16	4 41	20 17
6	4 31	19 40	4 41	19 50	4 35	19 51	4 32	19 56	4 24	20 00	4 30	20 14	4 43	20 15
7	4 33	19 38	4 43	19 48	4 37	19 49	4 34	19 54	4 26	19 58	4 32	20 12	4 44	20 13
8	4 34	19 37	4 44	19 47	4 38	19 47	4 36	19 52	4 27	19 56	4 34	20 10	4 46	20 11
9	4 36	19 35	4 46	19 45	4 40	19 45	4 38	19 50	4 29	19 53	4 36	20 07	4 48	20 09
10	4 37	19 33	4 47	19 43	4 41	19 43	4 39	19 48	4 31	19 51	4 38	20 05	4 50	20 07
11	4 39	19 31	4 49	19 41	4 43	19 41	4 41	19 46	4 33	19 49	4 40	20 03	4 52	20 05
12	4 40	19 29	4 51	19 39	4 45	19 40	4 43	19 44	4 35	19 47	4 42	20 01	4 54	20 03
13	4 42	19 27	4 52	19 37	4 46	19 38	4 44	19 42	4 37	19 45	4 44	19 58	4 55	20 01
14	4 44	19 25	4 54	19 35	4 48	19 35	4 46	19 40	4 38	19 43	4 46	19 56	4 57	19 58
15	4 45	19 23	4 55	19 33	4 50	19 33	4 48	19 38	4 40	19 40	4 48	19 54	4 59	19 56
16	4 47	19 21	4 57	19 31	4 51	19 31	4 50	19 36	4 42	19 38	4 50	19 51	5 01	19 54
17	4 48	19 19	4 59	19 29	4 53	19 29	4 51	19 34	4 44	19 36	4 52	19 49	5 03	19 52
18	4 50	19 17	5 00	19 27	4 55	19 27	4 53	19 31	4 46	19 33	4 54	19 47	5 05	19 49
19	4 52	19 15	5 02	19 25	4 56	19 25	4 55	19 29	4 48	19 31	4 55	19 44	5 06	19 47
20	4 53	19 13	5 03	19 23	4 58	19 23	4 57	19 27	4 50	19 29	4 57	19 42	5 08	19 45
21	4 55	19 11	5 05	19 21	5 00	19 21	4 58	19 25	4 52	19 26	4 59	19 39	5 10	19 43
22	4 56	19 09	5 06	19 19	5 01	19 19	5 00	19 22	4 53	19 24	5 01	19 37	5 12	19 40
23	4 58	19 07	5 08	19 17	5 03	19 16	5 02	19 20	4 55	19 22	5 03	19 35	5 14	19 38
24	5 00	19 05	5 10	19 15	5 05	19 14	5 04	19 18	4 57	19 19	5 05	19 32	5 15	19 35
25	5 01	19 03	5 11	19 13	5 06	19 12	5 05	19 16	4 59	19 17	5 07	19 30	5 17	19 33
26	5 03	19 00	5 13	19 10	5 08	19 10	5 07	19 13	5 01	19 14	5 09	19 27	5 19	19 31
27	5 04	18 58	5 14	19 08	5 10	19 08	5 09	19 11	5 03	19 12	5 11	19 25	5 21	19 28
28	5 06	18 56	5 16	19 06	5 11	19 05	5 11	19 09	5 05	19 10	5 13	19 22	5 23	19 26
29	5 08	18 54	5 18	19 04	5 13	19 03	5 12	19 06	5 07	19 07	5 15	19 20	5 25	19 23
30	5 09	18 52	5 19	19 02	5 15	19 01	5 14	19 04	5 08	19 05	5 17	19 17	5 27	19 21
31	5 11	18 50	5 21	18 59	5 16	18 59	5 16	19 02	5 10	19 02	5 19	19 14	5 28	19 19

JUPITER

Day	RA	Dec.	Transit	5° high	
				52°	56°
	h m	° ′	h m	h m	h m
1	14 16.5	− 12 33	17 36	21 54	21 38
11	14 20.2	− 12 54	17 01	21 16	21 00
21	14 24.8	− 13 19	16 26	20 39	20 22
31	14 30.2	− 13 48	15 52	20 02	19 45

Diameters – equatorial 35″ polar 33″

SATURN

Day	RA	Dec.	Transit	5° high	
				52°	56°
	h m	° ′	h m	h m	h m
1	22 53.6	− 9 07	2 16	21 34	21 46
11	22 51.3	− 9 23	1 34	20 54	21 06
21	22 48.7	− 9 40	0 52	20 14	20 26
31	22 45.9	− 9 58	0 10	19 33	19 46

Diameters – equatorial 19″ polar 17″
Rings – major axis 43″ minor axis 5″

URANUS

Day	RA	Dec.	Transit	10° high	
				52°	56°
	h m	° ′	h m	h m	h m
1	19 43.0	− 21 52	23 02	1 26	0 32
11	19 41.4	− 21 56	22 21	0 44	23 46
21	19 40.0	− 21 59	21 40	0 03	23 04
31	19 38.8	− 22 02	21 00	23 18	22 22

Diameter 4″

NEPTUNE

Day	RA	Dec.	Transit	10° high	
				52°	56°
	h m	° ′	h m	h m	h m
1	19 32.5	− 21 07	22 51	1 24	0 36
11	19 31.5	− 21 09	22 11	0 43	23 50
21	19 30.6	− 21 11	21 31	0 02	23 09
31	19 29.8	− 21 13	20 51	23 18	22 29

Diameter 2″

September 1994

NINTH MONTH, 30 DAYS. *Septem* (seven), seventh month of Roman pre-Julian calendar

Sun's Longitude 180° ♎ 23ᵈ06ʰ

1	*Thursday*	Edward Alleyn *b.* 1566. James Corbett *b.* 1866	*week 35 day 244*
2	*Friday*	Baron de Coubertin *d.* 1937. Laura Riding *d.* 1991	245
3	*Saturday*	Start of Second World War 1939	246
4	*Sunday*	**15th S. after Pentecost.** Albert Schweitzer *d.* 1965	*week 36 day 247*
5	*Monday*	Jesse James *b.* 1847. Sir Douglas Bader *d.* 1982	248
6	*Tuesday*	JEWISH NEW YEAR (5755). Marquis de La Fayette *b.* 1757	249
7	*Wednesday*	Elizabeth I *b.* 1533. Catherine Parr *d.* 1548	250
8	*Thursday*	**Blessed Virgin Mary.** Richard I *b.* 1157	251
9	*Friday*	Henri de Toulouse-Lautrec *d.* 1901	252
10	*Saturday*	Treaty of St Germain signed 1919	253
11	*Sunday*	**16th S. after Pentecost.** David Ricardo *d.* 1823	*week 37 day 254*
12	*Monday*	Cleopatra's Needle erected, London, 1878	255
13	*Tuesday*	J. B. Priestly *b.* 1894. John Smith *b.* 1938	256
14	*Wednesday*	Duke of Wellington *d.* 1852. Sir Peter Scott *b.* 1909	257
15	*Thursday*	YOM KIPPUR. Prince Henry of Wales *b.* 1984	258
16	*Friday*	Henry V *b.* 1387. Fire of Moscow 1812	259
17	*Saturday*	Sir Frederick Ashton *b.* 1904. Stirling Moss *b.* 1929	260
18	*Sunday*	**17th S. after Pentecost.** Dr Samuel Johnson *b.* 1709	*week 38 day 261*
19	*Monday*	Poitiers 1356. Sir James Dewar *b.* 1842	262
20	*Tuesday*	FEAST OF TABERNACLES begins	263
21	*Wednesday*	**St Matthew.** Gustav Holst *b.* 1874	264
22	*Thursday*	Zutphen 1586. Michael Faraday *b.* 1791	265
23	*Friday*	Baroness Orczy *b.* 1865. Sigmund Freud *d.* 1939	266
24	*Saturday*	Horace Walpole *b.* 1717. Scott Fitzgerald *b.* 1896	267
25	*Sunday*	**18th S. after Pentecost.** Samuel Butler *d.* 1680	*week 39 day 268*
26	*Monday*	Sir Barnes Wallis *b.* 1887. Béla Bartok *d.* 1945	269
27	*Tuesday*	George Cruikshank *b.* 1792. Dame Gracia Fields *d.* 1979	270
28	*Wednesday*	Georges Clemenceau *b.* 1841. Miles Davis *d.* 1991	271
29	*Thursday*	**St Michael and all Angels.** Mrs Gaskell *b.* 1810	272
30	*Friday*	Lord Raglan *b* 1788. Rudolf Diesel *d.* 1913	273

ASTRONOMICAL PHENOMENA

d	h	
1	02	Mars in conjunction with Moon. Mars 4° N.
1	17	Saturn at opposition
7	07	Mercury in conjunction with Moon. Mercury 3° N.
9	02	Venus in conjunction with Moon. Venus 2° S.
9	19	Jupiter in conjunction with Moon. Jupiter 1° N.
18	08	Saturn in conjunction with Moon. Saturn 6° S.
23	06	Equinox
26	16	Mercury at greatest elongation E. 26°
28	22	Venus at greatest brilliancy
29	20	Mars in conjunction with Moon. Mars 6° N.
29	22	Jupiter in conjunction with Venus. Jupiter 7° N.

CONSTELLATIONS

The following constellations are near the meridian at

	d	h		d	h
August	1	24	September	15	21
August	16	23	October	1	20
September	1	22	October	16	19

Draco, Cepheus, Lyra, Cygnus, Vulpecula, Sagitta, Delphinus, Equuleus, Aquila, Aquarius and Capricornus

MINIMA OF ALGOL

d	h	d	h	d	h
2	22.0	14	09.2	22	23.6
5	18.8	17	06.0	25	20.5
8	15.6	20	02.8	28	17.3
11	12.4				

THE MOON

Phases, Apsides and Node	d	h	m
● New Moon	5	18	33
☽ First Quarter	12	11	34
○ Full Moon	19	20	01
☾ Last Quarter	28	00	23
Perigee (365,148 km)	8	14	23
Apogee (405,245 km)	24	12	03

Mean longitude of ascending node on September 1, 228°

THE SUN   s.d. 15′.9

Day	Right Ascension	Dec.	Equation of time	Rise 52°	Rise 56°	Transit	Set 52°	Set 56°	Sidereal time	Transit of First Point of Aries
	h m s	° ′	m s	h m	h m	h m	h m	h m	h m s	h m s
1	10 39 55	+8 27	−0 11	5 11	5 04	12 00	18 48	18 55	22 39 43	1 20 04
2	10 43 32	+8 05	+0 08	5 13	5 06	12 00	18 46	18 53	22 43 40	1 16 08
3	10 47 10	+7 43	+0 27	5 14	5 07	11 59	18 43	18 50	22 47 36	1 12 12
4	10 50 47	+7 21	+0 46	5 16	5 09	11 59	18 41	18 47	22 51 33	1 08 16
5	10 54 24	+6 59	+1 06	5 18	5 11	11 59	18 39	18 45	22 55 29	1 04 20
6	10 58 00	+6 36	+1 26	5 19	5 13	11 58	18 36	18 42	22 59 26	1 00 24
7	11 01 37	+6 14	+1 46	5 21	5 15	11 58	18 34	18 40	23 03 23	0 56 28
8	11 05 13	+5 52	+2 06	5 23	5 17	11 58	18 32	18 37	23 07 19	0 52 32
9	11 08 49	+5 29	+2 27	5 24	5 19	11 57	18 29	18 34	23 11 16	0 48 36
10	11 12 25	+5 06	+2 48	5 26	5 21	11 57	18 27	18 32	23 15 12	0 44 40
11	11 16 00	+4 44	+3 08	5 27	5 23	11 57	18 25	18 29	23 19 09	0 40 45
12	11 19 36	+4 21	+3 29	5 29	5 25	11 56	18 23	18 26	23 23 05	0 36 49
13	11 23 11	+3 58	+3 51	5 31	5 27	11 56	18 20	18 24	23 27 02	0 32 53
14	11 26 47	+3 35	+4 12	5 32	5 29	11 56	18 18	18 21	23 30 58	0 28 57
15	11 30 22	+3 12	+4 33	5 34	5 31	11 55	18 16	18 18	23 34 55	0 25 01
16	11 33 57	+2 49	+4 55	5 36	5 33	11 55	18 13	18 16	23 38 52	0 21 05
17	11 37 32	+2 26	+5 16	5 37	5 35	11 55	18 11	18 13	23 42 48	0 17 09
18	11 41 07	+2 03	+5 38	5 39	5 37	11 54	18 08	18 10	23 46 45	0 13 13
19	11 44 42	+1 39	+5 59	5 40	5 39	11 54	18 06	18 08	23 50 41	0 09 17
20	11 48 17	+1 16	+6 20	5 42	5 41	11 53	18 04	18 05	23 54 38	0 05 21
21	11 51 53	+0 53	+6 42	5 44	5 43	11 53	18 01	18 02	23 58 34	{ 0 01 25 / 23 57 30 }
22	11 55 28	+0 30	+7 03	5 45	5 45	11 53	17 59	18 00	0 02 31	23 53 34
23	11 59 03	+0 06	+7 24	5 47	5 46	11 52	17 57	17 57	0 06 27	23 49 38
24	12 02 39	−0 17	+7 45	5 49	5 48	11 52	17 54	17 55	0 10 24	23 45 42
25	12 06 14	−0 41	+8 06	5 50	5 50	11 52	17 52	17 52	0 14 20	23 41 46
26	12 09 50	−1 04	+8 27	5 52	5 52	11 51	17 50	17 49	0 18 17	23 37 50
27	12 13 26	−1 27	+8 48	5 54	5 54	11 51	17 47	17 47	0 22 14	23 33 54
28	12 17 02	−1 51	+9 08	5 55	5 56	11 51	17 45	17 44	0 26 10	23 29 58
29	12 20 39	−2 14	+9 28	5 57	5 58	11 50	17 43	17 41	0 30 07	23 26 02
30	12 24 15	−2 37	+9 48	5 59	6 00	11 50	17 40	17 39	0 34 03	23 22 06

DURATION OF TWILIGHT (in minutes)

Latitude	52°	56°	52°	56°	52°	56°	52°	56°
	1 September		11 September		21 September		30 September	
Civil	35	39	34	38	34	37	34	37
Nautical	79	89	76	84	74	82	73	80
Astronomical	127	146	120	135	115	129	113	126

THE NIGHT SKY

Mercury, despite reaching greatest eastern elongation (26°) on the 26th, is unsuitably placed for observation.

Venus is a magnificent object in the SW sky in the early evenings for a very short time after sunset, its magnitude being −4.6. The crescent Moon will be seen in the vicinity of Venus on the evenings of the 8th and 9th. Venus is gradually drawing closer to the Sun and is unlikely to be seen after the first fortnight in September.

Mars continues to be visible as a morning object in Gemini, magnitude +1.1. During the second part of September it will be seen passing south of the Heavenly Twins, Castor and Pollux. By the end of the month it should be visible low above the ENE horizon by midnight. The reddish tint of Mars should assist in its identification. On the morning of the 1st and again on the mornings of the 29th and 30th the old Moon will be seen near the planet.

Jupiter, magnitude −1.8, is a bright evening object in the SW sky but is now coming to the end of its evening apparition and before the end of September it will be lost to view in the evening twilight. The crescent Moon passes 2° south of the planet on the evening of the 9th.

Saturn reaches opposition on the first day of the month and is therefore visible throughout the hours of darkness. Its magnitude is +0.5. On the morning of the 18th the Moon, near Full, will be seen passing 6° north of the planet.

Zodiacal Light. The morning cone may be seen stretching up from the eastern horizon along the ecliptic before the beginning of morning twilight, from the 4th until the 17th.

THE MOON

Day	RA	Dec.	Hor. par.	Semi-diam.	Sun's co-long.	PA of Bright Limb	Phase	Age	Rise 52°	Rise 56°	Transit	Set 52°	Set 56°
	h m	°	′	′	°	°	%	d	h m	h m	h m	h m	h m
1	6 37	+19.2	55.7	15.2	216	91	25	24.6	0 13	—	8 14	16 08	16 25
2	7 30	+17.2	56.4	15.4	228	95	17	25.6	1 17	1 01	9 05	16 41	16 55
3	8 23	+14.3	57.2	15.6	240	97	10	26.6	2 27	2 14	9 56	17 11	17 21
4	9 16	+10.6	58.0	15.8	252	96	4	27.6	3 41	3 32	10 46	17 38	17 44
5	10 09	+ 6.2	58.7	16.0	265	85	1	28.6	4 58	4 53	11 37	18 03	18 05
6	11 02	+ 1.4	59.4	16.2	277	348	0	0.2	6 17	6 17	12 29	18 28	18 26
7	11 56	− 3.6	59.8	16.3	289	306	2	1.2	7 37	7 41	13 22	18 54	18 48
8	12 52	− 8.4	60.0	16.4	301	297	7	2.2	8 58	9 07	14 16	19 23	19 12
9	13 48	−12.8	60.0	16.4	314	292	14	3.2	10 18	10 32	15 11	19 56	19 42
10	14 47	−16.3	59.9	16.3	326	287	23	4.2	11 36	11 53	16 09	20 37	20 18
11	15 46	−18.8	59.6	16.2	338	282	33	5.2	12 47	13 07	17 07	21 25	21 05
12	16 46	−20.1	59.1	16.1	350	277	45	6.2	13 49	14 10	18 05	22 22	22 01
13	17 46	−20.1	58.7	16.0	2	272	56	7.2	14 41	15 01	19 02	23 27	23 07
14	18 44	−18.9	58.2	15.8	15	267	67	8.2	15 23	15 40	19 57	—	—
15	19 40	−16.6	57.6	15.7	27	263	77	9.2	15 58	16 11	20 48	0 36	0 20
16	20 34	−13.5	57.1	15.6	39	261	85	10.2	16 26	16 36	21 38	1 47	1 35
17	21 25	− 9.8	56.6	15.4	51	260	92	11.2	16 51	16 57	22 25	2 59	2 50
18	22 14	− 5.7	56.1	15.3	63	261	96	12.2	17 13	17 16	23 10	4 09	4 05
19	23 02	− 1.4	55.7	15.2	76	272	99	13.2	17 35	17 33	23 55	5 18	5 18
20	23 49	+ 2.9	55.2	15.0	88	3	100	14.2	17 56	17 51	—	6 26	6 30
21	0 36	+ 7.0	54.8	14.9	100	55	99	15.2	18 19	18 10	0 38	7 33	7 40
22	1 23	+10.8	54.5	14.8	112	64	96	16.2	18 43	18 31	1 23	8 38	8 49
23	2 10	+14.1	54.3	14.8	124	69	91	17.2	19 11	18 56	2 07	9 42	9 56
24	2 58	+16.8	54.1	14.7	136	74	85	18.2	19 44	19 26	2 53	10 43	11 01
25	3 47	+18.7	54.1	14.7	149	78	77	19.2	20 23	20 03	3 39	11 41	12 00
26	4 37	+19.8	54.3	14.8	161	83	69	20.2	21 09	20 48	4 27	12 34	12 54
27	5 28	+20.1	54.6	14.9	173	87	60	21.2	22 02	21 42	5 16	13 21	13 41
28	6 19	+19.4	55.1	15.0	185	92	50	22.2	23 01	22 44	6 05	14 02	14 20
29	7 10	+17.9	55.7	15.2	197	96	40	23.2	—	23 53	6 54	14 38	14 53
30	8 02	+15.4	56.5	15.4	210	100	31	24.2	0 07	—	7 44	15 08	15 20

MERCURY

Day	RA	Dec.	Diam.	Phase	Transit	5° high 52°	5° high 56°
	h m	°	″	%	h m	h m	h m
1	11 42	+ 2.5	5	88	13 03	18 41	18 39
3	11 53	+ 1.0	5	86	13 07	18 37	18 34
5	12 05	− 0.5	5	84	13 10	18 32	18 28
7	12 15	− 1.9	5	82	13 13	18 28	18 22
9	12 26	− 3.3	6	81	13 15	18 23	18 16
11	12 36	− 4.7	6	79	13 18	18 18	18 10
13	12 46	− 6.1	6	77	13 20	18 12	18 03
15	12 56	− 7.4	6	75	13 21	18 07	17 56
17	13 05	− 8.6	6	73	13 23	18 01	17 50
19	13 14	− 9.8	6	70	13 24	17 55	17 43
21	13 23	−11.0	6	68	13 24	17 49	17 35
23	13 31	−12.1	6	65	13 25	17 43	17 28
25	13 39	−13.1	7	62	13 24	17 37	17 21
27	13 46	−14.0	7	59	13 24	17 31	17 13
29	13 53	−14.8	7	55	13 22	17 24	17 06
31	13 59	−15.5	7	51	13 20	17 18	16 58

VENUS

Day	RA	Dec.	Diam.	Phase	Transit	5° high 52°	5° high 56°
	h m	°	″	%	h m	h m	h m
1	13 25	−11.9	27	45	14 45	19 05	18 50
6	13 41	−14.0	28	42	14 41	18 48	18 30
11	13 56	−16.0	30	39	14 37	18 30	18 10
16	14 11	−17.9	33	35	14 31	18 12	17 49
21	14 23	−19.6	35	32	14 24	17 53	17 26
26	14 35	−21.0	38	28	14 15	17 33	17 03
31	14 44	−22.3	41	24	14 04	17 12	16 39

MARS

Day	RA	Dec.	Diam.	Phase	Transit	52°	56°
1	6 43	+23.5	5	91	8 03	0 28	0 10
6	6 56	+23.3	5	91	7 57	0 23	0 05
11	7 10	+23.1	5	91	7 50	0 19	0 01
16	7 23	+22.7	6	90	7 44	0 14	23 56
21	7 36	+22.4	6	90	7 37	0 10	23 52
26	7 48	+22.0	6	90	7 30	0 05	23 48
31	8 01	+21.5	6	90	7 22	0 00	23 44

SUNRISE AND SUNSET

	London		Bristol		Birmingham		Manchester		Newcastle		Glasgow		Belfast	
	0°05′	51°30′	2°35′	51°28′	1°55′	52°28′	2°15′	53°28′	1°37′	54°59′	4°14′	55°52′	5°56′	54°35′
	h m	h m	h m	h m	h m	h m	h m	h m	h m	h m	h m	h m	h m	h m
1	5 12	18 47	5 22	18 57	5 18	18 56	5 18	18 59	5 12	19 00	5 21	19 12	5 30	19 16
2	5 14	18 45	5 24	18 55	5 20	18 54	5 19	18 57	5 14	18 57	5 23	19 09	5 32	19 14
3	5 16	18 43	5 26	18 53	5 21	18 52	5 21	18 55	5 16	18 55	5 25	19 07	5 34	19 11
4	5 17	18 41	5 27	18 51	5 23	18 49	5 23	18 52	5 18	18 52	5 27	19 04	5 36	19 09
5	5 19	18 38	5 29	18 48	5 25	18 47	5 25	18 50	5 20	18 50	5 29	19 01	5 38	19 06
6	5 20	18 36	5 30	18 46	5 26	18 45	5 26	18 47	5 21	18 47	5 30	18 59	5 39	19 04
7	5 22	18 34	5 32	18 44	5 28	18 42	5 28	18 45	5 23	18 45	5 32	18 56	5 41	19 01
8	5 23	18 32	5 34	18 42	5 30	18 40	5 30	18 43	5 25	18 42	5 34	18 54	5 43	18 59
9	5 25	18 29	5 35	18 39	5 31	18 38	5 31	18 40	5 27	18 39	5 36	18 51	5 45	18 56
10	5 27	18 27	5 37	18 37	5 33	18 35	5 33	18 38	5 29	18 37	5 38	18 48	5 47	18 54
11	5 28	18 25	5 38	18 35	5 35	18 33	5 35	18 35	5 31	18 34	5 40	18 46	5 48	18 51
12	5 30	18 22	5 40	18 32	5 36	18 31	5 37	18 33	5 33	18 32	5 42	18 43	5 50	18 49
13	5 31	18 20	5 42	18 30	5 38	18 28	5 38	18 30	5 35	18 29	5 44	18 41	5 52	18 46
14	5 33	18 18	5 43	18 28	5 40	18 26	5 40	18 28	5 36	18 27	5 46	18 38	5 54	18 44
15	5 35	18 16	5 45	18 25	5 41	18 23	5 42	18 25	5 38	18 24	5 48	18 35	5 56	18 41
16	5 36	18 13	5 46	18 23	5 43	18 21	5 44	18 23	5 40	18 22	5 50	18 33	5 58	18 38
17	5 38	18 11	5 48	18 21	5 45	18 19	5 45	18 21	5 42	18 19	5 52	18 30	5 59	18 36
18	5 39	18 09	5 49	18 19	5 46	18 16	5 47	18 18	5 44	18 16	5 54	18 27	6 01	18 33
19	5 41	18 06	5 51	18 16	5 48	18 14	5 49	18 16	5 46	18 14	5 56	18 25	6 03	18 31
20	5 43	18 04	5 53	18 14	5 50	18 12	5 51	18 13	5 48	18 11	5 58	18 22	6 05	18 28
21	5 44	18 02	5 54	18 12	5 51	18 09	5 52	18 11	5 49	18 09	6 00	18 19	6 07	18 26
22	5 46	17 59	5 56	18 09	5 53	18 07	5 54	18 08	5 51	18 06	6 02	18 17	6 09	18 23
23	5 47	17 57	5 57	18 07	5 55	18 04	5 56	18 06	5 53	18 04	6 03	18 14	6 10	18 21
24	5 49	17 55	5 59	18 05	5 56	18 02	5 58	18 03	5 55	18 01	6 05	18 11	6 12	18 18
25	5 51	17 52	6 01	18 02	5 58	18 00	5 59	18 01	5 57	17 58	6 07	18 09	6 14	18 16
26	5 52	17 50	6 02	18 00	6 00	17 57	6 01	17 59	5 59	17 56	6 09	18 06	6 16	18 13
27	5 54	17 48	6 04	17 58	6 01	17 55	6 03	17 56	6 01	17 53	6 11	18 04	6 18	18 11
28	5 55	17 46	6 06	17 56	6 03	17 53	6 05	17 54	6 03	17 51	6 13	18 01	6 20	18 08
29	5 57	17 43	6 07	17 53	6 05	17 50	6 06	17 51	6 04	17 48	6 15	17 58	6 22	18 06
30	5 59	17 41	6 09	17 51	6 06	17 48	6 08	17 49	6 06	17 46	6 17	17 56	6 23	18 03

JUPITER

Day	RA	Dec.	Transit	5° high	
				52°	56°
	h m	° ′	h m	h m	h m
1	14 30.8	−13 51	15 49	19 58	19 41
11	14 37.1	−14 23	15 16	19 22	19 04
21	14 44.0	−14 57	14 43	18 46	18 27
31	14 51.5	−15 32	14 12	18 10	17 51

Diameters – equatorial 33″ polar 31″

SATURN

Day	RA	Dec.	Transit	5° high	
				52°	56°
	h m	° ′	h m	h m	h m
1	22 45.6	−10 00	0 06	4 38	4 26
11	22 42.8	−10 18	23 20	3 55	3 42
21	22 40.1	−10 34	22 38	3 11	2 58
31	22 37.6	−10 48	21 56	2 28	2 14

Diameters – equatorial 19″ polar 17″
Rings – major axis 43″ minor axis 5″

URANUS

Day	RA	Dec.	Transit	10° high	
				52°	56°
	h m	° ′	h m	h m	h m
1	19 38.7	−22 02	20 56	23 14	22 18
11	19 37.9	−22 04	20 15	22 33	21 38
21	19 37.3	−22 05	19 36	21 53	20 57
31	19 37.1	−22 05	18 56	21 14	20 18

Diameter 4″

NEPTUNE

Day	RA	Dec.	Transit	10° high	
				52°	56°
	h m	° ′	h m	h m	h m
1	19 29.7	−21 14	20 47	23 14	22 25
11	19 29.1	−21 15	20 07	22 34	21 44
21	19 28.8	−21 16	19 27	21 54	21 05
31	19 28.6	−21 17	18 48	21 14	20 25

Diameter 2″

October 1994

TENTH MONTH, 31 DAYS. *Octo* (eight), eighth month of Roman pre-Julian calendar

Sun's Longitude 210° ♏ 23ᵈ 16ʰ

1	*Saturday*	*Michaelmas Law Sittings begin.* Henry III *b.* 1207	*week* 39 *day* 274
2	*Sunday*	**19th S. after Pentecost.** Richard III *b.* 1452	*week* 40 *day* 275
3	*Monday*	Reunification of Germany 1990	276
4	*Tuesday*	Max Planck *d.* 1947. *Sputnik I* launched 1957	277
5	*Wednesday*	Jacques Offenbach *d.* 1880. *R101* disaster 1930	278
6	*Thursday*	Jenny Lind *b.* 1820. Thor Heyerdahl *b.* 1914	279
7	*Friday*	Archbishop Laud *b.* 1573. Edgar Allen Poe *d.* 1849	280
8	*Saturday*	Kathleen Ferrier *d.* 1953. Clement Attlee *d.* 1967	281
9	*Sunday*	**20th S. after Pentecost.** John Lennon *b.* 1940	*week* 41 *day* 282
10	*Monday*	Jean Watteau *b.* 1684. Harold Pinter *b.* 1930	283
11	*Tuesday*	Camperdown 1797. James Joule *d.* 1889	284
12	*Wednesday*	Edward VI *b.* 1537. Vaughan Williams *b.* 1872	285
13	*Thursday*	Anatole France *d.* 1924. Lady Thatcher *b.* 1925	286
14	*Friday*	Dame Edith Evans *d.* 1976. Bing Crosby *d.* 1977	287
15	*Saturday*	First British Motor Show 1895	288
16	*Sunday*	**21st S. after Pentecost.** Oscar Wilde *b.* 1854	*week* 42 *day* 289
17	*Monday*	Saratoga 1777. Frederic Chopin *d.* 1849	290
18	*Tuesday*	**St Luke.** Canaletto *b.* 1697. Charles Gounod *d.* 1893	291
19	*Wednesday*	Charles I *b.* 1600. Jacqueline du Pré *d.* 1987	292
20	*Thursday*	Viscount Palmerston *b.* 1784. Bud Flanagan *d.* 1968	293
21	*Friday*	Alfred Nobel *b.* 1833. Aberfan disaster 1966	294
22	*Saturday*	Thomas Sheraton *d.* 1806. Paul Cézanne *d.* 1906	295
23	*Sunday*	**9th S. before Christmas.** Robert Bridges *b.* 1844	*week* 43 *day* 296
24	*Monday*	George Cadbury *d.* 1922. UN formally established 1945	297
25	*Tuesday*	Agincourt 1415. Georges Bizet *b.* 1838	298
26	*Wednesday*	Domenico Scarlatti *b.* 1685. William Hogarth *d.* 1764	299
27	*Thursday*	Theodore Roosevelt *b.* 1858	300
28	*Friday*	**SS Simon and Jude.** Statue of Liberty unveiled 1886	301
29	*Saturday*	Republic of Turkey proclaimed 1923	302
30	*Sunday*	**8th S. before Christmas.** George II *b.* 1683	*week* 44 *day* 303
31	*Monday*	Hallowmass Eve. Chiang Kai-shek *b.* 1887	304

ASTRONOMICAL PHENOMENA

d	h	
6	19	Mercury in conjunction with Moon. Mercury 3° S.
7	12	Jupiter in conjunction with Moon. Jupiter 0°.7 N.
7	13	Venus in conjunction with Moon. Venus 7° S.
15	04	Jupiter in conjunction with Venus. Jupiter 8° N.
15	11	Saturn in conjunction with Moon. Saturn 6° S.
21	05	Mercury in inferior conjunction
28	09	Mars in conjunction with Moon. Mars 7° N.

CONSTELLATIONS

The following constellations are near the meridian at

	d	h
September	1	24
September	15	23
October	1	22
October	16	21
November	1	20
November	15	19

Ursa Major (below the Pole), Cepheus, Cassiopeia, Cygnus, Lacerta, Andromeda, Pegasus, Capricornus, Aquarius and Piscis Austrinus

MINIMA OF ALGOL

d	h	d	h	d	h
1	14.1	13	01.3	24	12.6
4	10.9	18	18.9	27	09.4
7	07.7	21	15.8	30	06.2
10	04.5				

THE MOON

Phases, Apsides and Node	d	h	m
● New Moon	5	03	55
☽ First Quarter	11	19	17
○ Full Moon	19	12	18
☾ Last Quarter	27	16	44
Perigee (360,244 km)	6	14	06
Apogee (406,098 km)	22	01	52

Mean longitude of ascending node on October 1, 227°

THE SUN

s.d. 16′.1

Day	Right Ascension	Dec. −	Equation of time	Rise 52°	Rise 56°	Transit	Set 52°	Set 56°	Sidereal time	Transit of First Point of Aries
	h m s	° ′	m s	h m	h m	h m	h m	h m	h m s	h m s
1	12 27 52	3 01	+10 07	6 00	6 02	11 50	17 38	17 36	0 38 00	23 18 11
2	12 31 30	3 24	+10 27	6 02	6 04	11 49	17 36	17 33	0 41 56	23 14 15
3	12 35 07	3 47	+10 46	6 04	6 06	11 49	17 34	17 31	0 45 53	23 10 19
4	12 38 45	4 10	+11 04	6 05	6 08	11 49	17 31	17 28	0 49 49	23 06 23
5	12 42 23	4 34	+11 23	6 07	6 10	11 48	17 29	17 26	0 53 46	23 02 27
6	12 46 02	4 57	+11 41	6 09	6 12	11 48	17 27	17 23	0 57 43	22 58 31
7	12 49 41	5 20	+11 58	6 10	6 14	11 48	17 24	17 20	1 01 39	22 54 35
8	12 53 20	5 43	+12 15	6 12	6 16	11 48	17 22	17 18	1 05 36	22 50 39
9	12 57 00	6 05	+12 32	6 14	6 18	11 47	17 20	17 15	1 09 32	22 46 43
10	13 00 40	6 28	+12 48	6 16	6 20	11 47	17 18	17 13	1 13 29	22 42 47
11	13 04 21	6 51	+13 04	6 17	6 22	11 47	17 15	17 10	1 17 25	22 38 51
12	13 08 02	7 14	+13 20	6 19	6 24	11 47	17 13	17 08	1 21 22	22 34 56
13	13 11 44	7 36	+13 35	6 21	6 27	11 46	17 11	17 05	1 25 18	22 31 00
14	13 15 26	7 59	+13 49	6 22	6 29	11 46	17 09	17 03	1 29 15	22 27 04
15	13 19 08	8 21	+14 03	6 24	6 31	11 46	17 07	17 00	1 33 12	22 23 08
16	13 22 52	8 43	+14 17	6 26	6 33	11 46	17 04	16 58	1 37 08	22 19 12
17	13 26 35	9 05	+14 29	6 28	6 35	11 45	17 02	16 55	1 41 05	22 15 16
18	13 30 20	9 27	+14 42	6 29	6 37	11 45	17 00	16 53	1 45 01	22 11 20
19	13 34 04	9 49	+14 53	6 31	6 39	11 45	16 58	16 50	1 48 58	22 07 24
20	13 37 50	10 11	+15 04	6 33	6 41	11 45	16 56	16 48	1 52 54	22 03 28
21	13 41 36	10 32	+15 15	6 35	6 43	11 45	16 54	16 45	1 56 51	21 59 32
22	13 45 23	10 53	+15 25	6 36	6 45	11 45	16 52	16 43	2 00 47	21 55 36
23	13 49 10	11 15	+15 34	6 38	6 47	11 44	16 50	16 41	2 04 44	21 51 41
24	13 52 58	11 36	+15 42	6 40	6 49	11 44	16 48	16 38	2 08 41	21 47 45
25	13 56 47	11 56	+15 50	6 42	6 51	11 44	16 46	16 36	2 12 37	21 43 49
26	14 00 37	12 17	+15 57	6 44	6 54	11 44	16 44	16 34	2 16 34	21 39 53
27	14 04 27	12 38	+16 03	6 45	6 56	11 44	16 42	16 31	2 20 30	21 35 57
28	14 08 18	12 58	+16 09	6 47	6 58	11 44	16 40	16 29	2 24 27	21 32 01
29	14 12 10	13 18	+16 13	6 49	7 00	11 44	16 38	16 27	2 28 23	21 28 05
30	14 16 03	13 38	+16 17	6 51	7 02	11 44	16 36	16 24	2 32 20	21 24 09
31	14 19 56	13 58	+16 20	6 53	7 04	11 44	16 34	16 22	2 36 16	21 20 13

DURATION OF TWILIGHT (in minutes)

Latitude	52°	56°	52°	56°	52°	56°	52°	56°
	1 October		11 October		21 October		31 October	
Civil	34	37	34	37	34	38	36	40
Nautical	73	80	73	80	74	81	75	83
Astronomical	113	125	112	124	113	124	114	126

THE NIGHT SKY

Mercury is unsuitably placed for observation at first, passing through inferior conjunction on the 21st. However, for the last few days of the month it becomes visible as a morning object low in the eastern sky, around the time of beginning of morning civil twilight. By the last day of the month its magnitude has brightened to +0.3.

Venus is unsuitably placed for observation. Although it is still almost 40° from the Sun at the beginning of the month, its declination of −23° completely nullifies this apparently favourable elongation, as seen from the latitudes of the British Isles.

Mars, magnitude +0.9, is a morning object in Cancer.

Mars is visible in the SE sky during the early hours, crossing the meridian around daybreak. The Moon, at Last Quarter, will be seen approaching the planet on the morning of the 28th.

Jupiter is unsuitably placed for observation.

Saturn, magnitude +0.6, is an evening object in Aquarius. On the morning of the 15th the gibbous Moon will be seen in the vicinity of the planet. The rings of Saturn present a beautiful spectacle to the observer, even with only a small telescope, though they are now noticeably thinner than they were a few years ago, as the Earth passes through the ring plane next year.

THE MOON

Day	RA h m	Dec. °	Hor. par.	Semi-diam. ′	Sun's co-long. °	PA of Bright Limb °	Phase %	Age d	Rise 52° h m	Rise 56° h m	Transit h m	Set 52° h m	Set 56° h m
1	8 54	+12.0	57.4	15.6	222	102	22	25.2	1 18	1 07	8 34	15 36	15 44
2	9 47	+ 8.0	58.3	15.9	234	104	13	26.2	2 32	2 25	9 24	16 02	16 06
3	10 40	+ 3.4	59.2	16.1	246	104	7	27.2	3 49	3 47	10 15	16 27	16 27
4	11 34	− 1.5	59.9	16.3	258	100	2	28.2	5 09	5 11	11 07	16 53	16 49
5	12 29	− 6.5	60.5	16.5	271	60	0	29.2	6 31	6 38	12 02	17 21	17 13
6	13 27	−11.1	60.8	16.6	283	301	1	0.8	7 54	8 06	12 59	17 54	17 41
7	14 26	−15.0	60.8	16.6	295	290	5	1.8	9 16	9 32	13 58	18 33	18 16
8	15 27	−18.0	60.6	16.5	307	283	11	2.8	10 32	10 51	14 58	19 20	19 00
9	16 29	−19.7	60.1	16.4	319	227	20	3.8	11 40	12 01	15 58	20 16	19 55
10	17 31	−20.0	59.5	16.2	332	272	30	4.8	12 37	12 57	16 57	21 19	21 00
11	18 30	−19.1	58.8	16.0	344	266	41	5.8	13 23	13 40	17 53	22 28	22 11
12	19 27	−17.1	58.0	15.8	356	262	52	6.8	14 00	14 14	18 46	23 39	23 26
13	20 22	−14.2	57.3	15.6	8	258	63	7.8	14 30	14 40	19 35	—	—
14	21 13	−10.6	56.7	15.4	20	255	73	8.8	14 55	15 02	20 23	0 50	0 41
15	22 03	− 6.6	56.1	15.3	33	254	81	9.8	15 18	15 22	21 08	2 00	1 55
16	22 50	− 2.4	55.5	15.1	45	253	89	10.8	15 40	15 39	21 52	3 09	3 07
17	23 37	+ 1.8	55.1	15.0	57	254	94	11.8	16 01	15 57	22 36	4 16	4 18
18	0 23	+ 6.0	54.7	14.9	69	257	98	12.8	16 23	16 16	23 19	5 22	5 28
19	1 09	+ 9.8	54.4	14.8	81	269	100	13.8	16 47	16 36	—	6 28	6 37
20	1 56	+13.2	54.2	14.8	93	57	100	14.8	17 14	17 00	0 04	7 32	7 45
21	2 44	+16.0	54.1	14.7	106	72	98	15.8	17 45	17 28	0 49	8 34	8 50
22	3 33	+18.2	54.0	14.7	118	78	95	16.8	18 21	18 03	1 35	9 33	9 52
23	4 23	+19.5	54.0	14.7	130	83	90	17.8	19 05	18 44	2 23	10 27	10 47
24	5 13	+20.0	54.2	14.8	142	88	83	18.8	19 54	19 35	3 10	11 16	11 36
25	6 04	+19.6	54.5	14.9	154	93	75	19.8	20 51	20 32	3 59	11 59	12 17
26	6 54	+18.3	55.0	15.0	166	97	67	20.8	21 53	21 37	4 47	12 36	12 52
27	7 45	+16.2	55.6	15.1	179	101	57	21.8	22 59	22 47	5 35	13 07	13 21
28	8 36	+13.2	56.3	15.3	191	104	47	22.8	—	—	6 24	13 36	13 45
29	9 26	+ 9.5	57.2	15.6	203	107	37	23.8	0 10	0 01	7 12	14 01	14 07
30	10 17	+ 5.3	58.1	15.8	215	108	27	24.8	1 23	1 19	8 01	14 26	14 28
31	11 10	+ 0.6	59.1	16.1	227	109	17	25.8	2 40	2 40	8 52	14 51	14 49

MERCURY

Day	RA h m	Dec. °	Diam. ″	Phase %	Transit h m	5° high 52° h m	5° high 56° h m
1	13 59	−15.5	7	51	13 20	17 18	16 58
3	14 04	−16.1	8	47	13 17	17 11	16 50
5	14 08	−16.6	8	42	13 13	17 04	16 43
7	14 11	−16.9	8	36	13 07	16 57	16 35
9	14 12	−17.0	9	30	13 00	16 49	16 28
11	14 11	−16.8	9	24	12 51	16 42	16 21
13	14 09	−16.4	9	18	12 40	16 34	16 14
15	14 04	−15.7	10	11	12 28	16 27	16 08
17	13 58	−14.7	10	6	12 13	16 19	16 02
19	13 50	−13.4	10	2	11 57	7 44	8 00
21	13 42	−11.9	10	0	11 41	7 19	7 33
23	13 33	−10.4	10	1	11 25	6 54	7 07
25	13 26	− 9.0	10	5	11 11	6 32	6 43
27	13 22	− 7.8	9	12	10 59	6 13	6 24
29	13 19	− 7.0	9	20	10 49	6 00	6 09
31	13 20	− 6.6	8	30	10 42	5 50	5 59

VENUS

Day	RA h m	Dec. °	Diam. ″	Phase %	Transit h m	5° high 52° h m	5° high 56° h m
1	14 44	−22.3	41	24	14 04	17 12	16 39
6	14 50	−23.2	45	19	13 51	16 51	16 15
11	14 53	−23.8	49	15	13 34	16 30	15 52
16	14 53	−23.9	52	10	13 13	16 08	15 30
21	14 49	−23.5	56	6	12 49	15 48	15 11
26	14 41	−22.6	59	3	12 21	15 29	14 55
31	14 31	−21.1	61	1	11 52	15 12	14 42

MARS

Day	RA h m	Dec. °	Diam. ″	Phase %	Transit h m	5° high 52° h m	5° high 56° h m
1	8 01	+21.5	6	90	7 22	0 00	23 44
6	8 13	+21.0	6	90	7 15	23 55	23 40
11	8 24	+20.5	6	89	7 07	23 50	23 35
16	8 36	+19.9	6	89	6 58	23 45	23 31
21	8 47	+19.3	7	89	6 49	23 39	23 26
26	8 57	+18.7	7	89	6 40	23 33	23 21
31	9 07	+18.1	7	89	6 31	23 27	23 15

SUNRISE AND SUNSET

	London		Bristol		Birmingham		Manchester		Newcastle		Glasgow		Belfast	
	0°05′	51°30′	2°35′	51°28′	1°55′	52°28′	2°15′	53°28′	1°37′	54°59′	4°14′	55°52′	5°56′	54°35′
	h m	h m	h m	h m	h m	h m	h m	h m	h m	h m	h m	h m	h m	h m
1	6 00	17 39	6 10	17 49	6 08	17 46	6 10	17 46	6 08	17 43	6 19	17 53	6 25	18 01
2	6 02	17 36	6 12	17 46	6 10	17 43	6 12	17 44	6 10	17 41	6 21	17 50	6 27	17 58
3	6 04	17 34	6 14	17 44	6 12	17 41	6 14	17 42	6 12	17 38	6 23	17 48	6 29	17 56
4	6 05	17 32	6 15	17 42	6 13	17 39	6 15	17 39	6 14	17 35	6 25	17 45	6 31	17 53
5	6 07	17 30	6 17	17 40	6 15	17 36	6 17	17 37	6 16	17 33	6 27	17 43	6 33	17 51
6	6 09	17 27	6 19	17 37	6 17	17 34	6 19	17 34	6 18	17 30	6 29	17 40	6 35	17 48
7	6 10	17 25	6 20	17 35	6 18	17 32	6 21	17 32	6 20	17 28	6 31	17 37	6 37	17 46
8	6 12	17 23	6 22	17 33	6 20	17 29	6 23	17 30	6 22	17 25	6 33	17 35	6 39	17 43
9	6 14	17 21	6 24	17 31	6 22	17 27	6 24	17 27	6 24	17 23	6 35	17 32	6 40	17 41
10	6 15	17 19	6 25	17 29	6 24	17 25	6 26	17 25	6 26	17 21	6 37	17 30	6 42	17 38
11	6 17	17 16	6 27	17 26	6 25	17 23	6 28	17 23	6 27	17 18	6 39	17 27	6 44	17 36
12	6 19	17 14	6 29	17 24	6 27	17 20	6 30	17 20	6 29	17 16	6 41	17 25	6 46	17 33
13	6 20	17 12	6 30	17 22	6 29	17 18	6 32	17 18	6 31	17 13	6 43	17 22	6 48	17 31
14	6 22	17 10	6 32	17 20	6 31	17 16	6 34	17 16	6 33	17 11	6 45	17 20	6 50	17 29
15	6 24	17 08	6 34	17 18	6 33	17 14	6 35	17 13	6 35	17 08	6 47	17 17	6 52	17 26
16	6 25	17 06	6 35	17 16	6 34	17 11	6 37	17 11	6 37	17 06	6 49	17 15	6 54	17 24
17	6 27	17 03	6 37	17 14	6 36	17 09	6 39	17 09	6 39	17 04	6 51	17 12	6 56	17 22
18	6 29	17 01	6 39	17 11	6 38	17 07	6 41	17 07	6 41	17 01	6 53	17 10	6 58	17 19
19	6 31	16 59	6 41	17 09	6 40	17 05	6 43	17 04	6 43	16 59	6 56	17 07	7 00	17 17
20	6 32	16 57	6 42	17 07	6 41	17 03	6 45	17 02	6 45	16 56	6 58	17 05	7 02	17 15
21	6 34	16 55	6 44	17 05	6 43	17 01	6 47	17 00	6 47	16 54	7 00	17 03	7 04	17 12
22	6 36	16 53	6 46	17 03	6 45	16 59	6 48	16 58	6 49	16 52	7 02	17 00	7 06	17 10
23	6 38	16 51	6 47	17 01	6 47	16 56	6 50	16 56	6 51	16 50	7 04	16 58	7 08	17 08
24	6 39	16 49	6 49	16 59	6 49	16 54	6 52	16 53	6 53	16 47	7 06	16 55	7 10	17 05
25	6 41	16 47	6 51	16 57	6 50	16 52	6 54	16 51	6 55	16 45	7 08	16 53	7 12	17 03
26	6 43	16 45	6 53	16 55	6 52	16 50	6 56	16 49	6 57	16 43	7 10	16 51	7 14	17 01
27	6 45	16 43	6 54	16 53	6 54	16 48	6 58	16 47	6 59	16 41	7 12	16 49	7 16	16 59
28	6 46	16 41	6 56	16 51	6 56	16 46	7 00	16 45	7 01	16 38	7 14	16 46	7 18	16 57
29	6 48	16 39	6 58	16 49	6 58	16 44	7 02	16 43	7 03	16 36	7 16	16 44	7 20	16 55
30	6 50	16 38	7 00	16 48	7 00	16 42	7 04	16 41	7 05	16 34	7 19	16 42	7 22	16 52
31	6 52	16 36	7 01	16 46	7 01	16 40	7 06	16 39	7 07	16 32	7 21	16 40	7 24	16 50

JUPITER

Day	RA	Dec.	Transit	5° high	
				52°	56°
	h m	° ′	h m	h m	h m
1	14 51.5	−15 32	14 12	18 10	17 51
11	14 59.4	−16 08	13 40	17 35	17 15
21	15 07.8	−16 43	13 09	17 00	16 39
31	15 16.4	−17 19	12 39	16 25	16 03

Diameters – equatorial 31″ polar 29″

SATURN

Day	RA	Dec.	Transit	5° high	
				52°	56°
	h m	° ′	h m	h m	h m
1	22 37.6	−10 48	21 56	2 28	2 14
11	22 35.6	−10 59	21 15	1 45	1 32
21	22 34.1	−11 07	20 34	1 04	0 50
31	22 33.1	−11 12	19 54	0 23	0 09

Diameters – equatorial 18″ polar 17″
Rings – major axis 42″ minor axis 6″

URANUS

Day	RA	Dec.	Transit	10° high	
				52°	56°
	h m	° ′	h m	h m	h m
1	19 37.1	−22 05	18 56	21 14	20 18
11	19 37.2	−22 05	18 17	20 35	19 39
21	19 37.7	−22 03	17 38	19 56	19 01
31	19 38.6	−22 01	17 00	19 18	18 23

Diameter 4″

NEPTUNE

Day	RA	Dec.	Transit	10° high	
				52°	56°
	h m	° ′	h m	h m	h m
1	19 28.6	−21 17	18 48	21 14	20 25
11	19 28.7	−21 17	18 08	20 35	19 46
21	19 29.0	−21 17	17 29	19 56	19 07
31	19 29.6	−21 16	16 51	19 17	18 28

Diameter 2″

November 1994

ELEVENTH MONTH, 30 DAYS. *Novem* (nine), ninth month of Roman pre-Julian calendar

Sun's Longitude 240° ♐ 22ᵈ 13ʰ

1	*Tuesday*	**All Saints.** First premium bonds sold 1956	*week* 44 *day* 305
2	*Wednesday*	All Souls. Marie Antoinette *b.* 1755	306
3	*Thursday*	First dog in space 1957	307
4	*Friday*	Felix Mendelssohn *d.* 1847. Gabriel Fauré *d.* 1924	308
5	*Saturday*	Gunpowder Plot 1605. Robert Maxwell *d.* 1991	309
6	*Sunday*	**7th S. before Christmas.** Kate Greenaway *d.* 1901	*week* 45 *day* 310
7	*Monday*	October Revolution in Russia 1917 NS	311
8	*Tuesday*	César Franck *d.* 1890. Munich Putsch 1923	312
9	*Wednesday*	Edward VII *b.* 1841. Neville Chamberlain *d.* 1940	313
10	*Thursday*	Sir Jacob Epstein *b.* 1880. Sir Gordon Richards *d.* 1986	314
11	*Friday*	Armistice Day. Sören Kierkegaard *d.* 1855	315
12	*Saturday*	Mrs Gaskell *d.* 1865. Baroness Orczy *d.* 1947	316
13	*Sunday*	**6th S. before Christmas.** Archbishop Carey *b.* 1935	*week* 46 *day* 317
14	*Monday*	*Prince of Wales b. 1948.* Harold Larwood *b.* 1904	318
15	*Tuesday*	Brazil declared a Republic 1889	319
16	*Wednesday*	Paul Hindemith *b.* 1895. Clark Gable *d.* 1960	320
17	*Thursday*	Relief of Lucknow 1857. Eric Gill *d.* 1940	321
18	*Friday*	Sir David Wilkie *b.* 1785. Francis Thompson *d.* 1907	322
19	*Saturday*	Franz Schubert *d.* 1828. Sir Basil Spence *d.* 1976	323
20	*Sunday*	**5th S. before Christmas.** *Queen's Wedding Day 1947*	*week* 47 *day* 324
21	*Monday*	Natalia Makarova *b.* 1940. Edward Bawden *d.* 1989	325
22	*Tuesday*	George Eliot *b.* 1819. President Kennedy *assass.* 1963	326
23	*Wednesday*	Diane Quick *b.* 1946. Roald Dahl *d.* 1990	327
24	*Thursday*	Laurence Sterne *b.* 1713. Erskine Childers *exec.* 1922	328
25	*Friday*	Harley Granville-Barker *b.* 1877. Sir Anton Dolin *d.* 1983	329
26	*Saturday*	William Cowper *b.* 1731. John McAdam *d.* 1836	330
27	*Sunday*	**1st S. in Advent.** Anders Celsius *b.* 1701	*week* 48 *day* 331
28	*Monday*	CHANUCAH begins. Founding of Royal Society 1660	332
29	*Tuesday*	Claudio Monteverdi *d.* 1643. Louisa M. Alcott *b.* 1832	333
30	*Wednesday*	**St Andrew.** Cardinal Wolsey *d.* 1530. Mark Twain *b.* 1835	334

ASTRONOMICAL PHENOMENA

d	h	
2	07	Mercury in conjunction with Moon. Mercury 4° N.
2	23	Venus in inferior conjunction
3	12	Venus in conjunction with Moon. Venus 5° S.
3		Total eclipse of Sun (*see* page 66)
4	08	Jupiter in conjunction with Moon. Jupiter 0°.1 N.
6	01	Mercury at greatest elongation W. 19°
11	16	Saturn in conjunction with Moon. Saturn 6° S.
13	18	Venus in conjunction with Mercury. Venus 5° S.
17	20	Jupiter in conjunction with Sun
20	13	Pluto in conjunction with Sun
25	15	Mars in conjunction with Moon. Mars 7° N.
28	17	Jupiter in conjunction with Mercury. Jupiter 0°.4 N.
30	13	Venus in conjunction with Moon. Venus 2° N.

CONSTELLATIONS

The following constellations are near the meridian at

	d	h		d	h
October	1	24	November	15	21
October	16	23	December	1	20
November	1	22	December	16	19

Ursa Major (below the Pole), Cepheus, Cassiopeia, Andromeda, Pegasus, Pisces, Aquarius and Cetus

MINIMA OF ALGOL

d	h	d	h	d	h
2	03.0	13	14.3	25	01.5
4	23.8	19	07.9	27	22.3
7	20.6	22	04.7	30	19.2
10	17.5				

THE MOON

Phases, Apsides and Node	d	h	m
● New Moon	3	13	36
☽ First Quarter	10	06	14
○ Full Moon	18	06	57
☾ Last Quarter	26	07	04
Perigee (357,240 km)	3	23	39
Apogee (406,347 km)	18	05	08

Mean longitude of ascending node on November 1, 225°

THE SUN
s.d. 16'.2

Day	Right Ascension	Dec. −	Equation of time	Rise 52°	Rise 56°	Transit	Set 52°	Set 56°	Sidereal time	Transit of First Point of Aries
	h m s	° ′	m s	h m	h m	h m	h m	h m	h m s	h m s
1	14 23 50	14 17	+16 23	6 54	7 06	11 44	16 32	16 20	2 40 13	21 16 17
2	14 27 45	14 36	+16 24	6 56	7 08	11 44	16 30	16 18	2 44 09	21 12 21
3	14 31 41	14 55	+16 25	6 58	7 11	11 44	16 29	16 16	2 48 06	21 08 26
4	14 35 38	15 14	+16 25	7 00	7 13	11 44	16 27	16 14	2 52 03	21 04 30
5	14 39 35	15 32	+16 24	7 02	7 15	11 44	16 25	16 12	2 55 59	21 00 34
6	14 43 34	15 51	+16 22	7 03	7 17	11 44	16 23	16 10	2 59 56	20 56 38
7	14 47 33	16 09	+16 20	7 05	7 19	11 44	16 22	16 07	3 03 52	20 52 42
8	14 51 33	16 26	+16 16	7 07	7 21	11 44	16 20	16 06	3 07 49	20 48 46
9	14 55 33	16 44	+16 12	7 09	7 23	11 44	16 18	16 04	3 11 45	20 44 50
10	14 59 35	17 01	+16 07	7 11	7 26	11 44	16 17	16 02	3 15 42	20 40 54
11	15 03 37	17 18	+16 01	7 12	7 28	11 44	16 15	16 00	3 19 38	20 36 58
12	15 07 41	17 34	+15 54	7 14	7 30	11 44	16 14	15 58	3 23 35	20 33 02
13	15 11 45	17 50	+15 47	7 16	7 32	11 44	16 12	15 56	3 27 32	20 29 06
14	15 15 50	18 06	+15 39	7 18	7 34	11 44	16 11	15 54	3 31 28	20 25 11
15	15 19 55	18 22	+15 29	7 19	7 36	11 45	16 09	15 53	3 35 25	20 21 15
16	15 24 02	18 37	+15 19	7 21	7 38	11 45	16 08	15 51	3 39 21	20 17 19
17	15 28 09	18 52	+15 09	7 23	7 40	11 45	16 07	15 49	3 43 18	20 13 23
18	15 32 18	19 07	+14 57	7 25	7 42	11 45	16 05	15 48	3 47 14	20 09 27
19	15 36 27	19 21	+14 44	7 26	7 44	11 45	16 04	15 46	3 51 11	20 05 31
20	15 40 36	19 35	+14 31	7 28	7 46	11 46	16 03	15 45	3 55 07	20 01 35
21	15 44 47	19 49	+14 17	7 30	7 48	11 46	16 02	15 43	3 59 04	19 57 39
22	15 48 59	20 02	+14 02	7 31	7 50	11 46	16 00	15 42	4 03 01	19 53 43
23	15 53 11	20 15	+13 46	7 33	7 52	11 46	15 59	15 40	4 06 57	19 49 47
24	15 57 24	20 27	+13 29	7 35	7 54	11 47	15 58	15 39	4 10 54	19 45 51
25	16 01 38	20 39	+13 12	7 36	7 56	11 47	15 57	15 38	4 14 50	19 41 56
26	16 05 53	20 51	+12 54	7 38	7 58	11 47	15 56	15 36	4 18 47	19 38 00
27	16 10 08	21 02	+12 35	7 39	7 59	11 48	15 55	15 35	4 22 43	19 34 04
28	16 14 25	21 13	+12 15	7 41	8 01	11 48	15 55	15 34	4 26 40	19 30 08
29	16 18 42	21 24	+11 55	7 42	8 03	11 48	15 54	15 33	4 30 36	19 26 12
30	16 22 59	21 34	+11 34	7 44	8 05	11 49	15 53	15 32	4 34 33	19 22 16

DURATION OF TWILIGHT (in minutes)

Latitude	52°	56°	52°	56°	52°	56°	52°	56°
	1 November		11 November		21 November		30 November	
Civil	36	40	37	41	38	43	39	45
Nautical	75	84	78	87	80	90	82	93
Astronomical	115	127	117	130	120	134	123	137

THE NIGHT SKY

Mercury is at greatest western elongation (19°) on the 6th. Thus it is a morning object at first, visible low above the eastern horizon around the time of beginning of morning civil twilight. During its period of visibility its magnitude brightens from +0.1 to −0.8. On the morning of the 2nd it may be possible to glimpse the old crescent Moon, only 1.2 days before New, below and to the right of the planet. Do not confuse Mercury with Venus when the two planets are near each other on the 13th to 14th, Mercury passing north of Venus. Mercury passes 4° north of Spica on the 3rd.

Venus is unsuitably placed for observation at first, inferior conjunction occurring on the 2nd. However, after the first ten days of the month Venus becomes visible low above the SE horizon before dawn, magnitude −4.6. The old crescent Moon will be seen approaching Venus on the morning of the 30th.

Mars brightens during the month, its magnitude changing from +0.7 to +0.3. Early in the month it moves from Cancer into Leo. The Moon, near Last Quarter, will be seen in the vicinity of the planet on the mornings of the 25th and 26th.

Jupiter is in conjunction with the Sun on the 17th and therefore unsuitably placed for observation.

Saturn, magnitude +0.8, is still an evening object in Aquarius, though no longer visible after midnight. It resumes its direct motion after reaching its second stationary point on the 9th. The Moon, near First Quarter, will be seen passing 6° north of the planet on the early evening of the 11th.

THE MOON

Day	RA	Dec.	Hor. par.	Semi-diam.	Sun's co-long.	PA of Bright Limb	Phase	Age	Rise 52°	Rise 56°	Transit	Set 52°	Set 56°
	h m	°	′	′	°	°	%	d	h m	h m	h m	h m	h m
1	12 04	− 4.3	60.0	16.3	239	109	10	26.8	3 59	4 04	9 44	15 17	15 11
2	13 00	− 9.1	60.7	16.5	252	107	4	27.8	5 22	5 31	10 40	15 48	15 37
3	13 59	−13.4	61.2	16.7	264	102	1	28.8	6 45	6 59	11 38	16 24	16 09
4	15 00	−16.8	61.4	16.7	276	284	0	0.4	8 06	8 24	12 40	17 07	16 49
5	16 04	−19.1	61.2	16.7	288	277	3	1.4	9 21	9 41	13 42	18 01	17 41
6	17 08	−20.0	60.7	16.5	300	271	9	2.4	10 25	10 46	14 44	19 04	18 44
7	18 10	−19.5	60.0	16.4	313	265	17	3.4	11 18	11 36	15 43	20 14	19 56
8	19 10	−17.7	59.2	16.1	325	261	26	4.4	11 59	12 15	16 39	21 27	21 12
9	20 07	−15.0	58.2	15.9	337	256	37	5.4	12 32	12 44	17 32	22 40	22 29
10	21 00	−11.5	57.4	15.6	349	253	47	6.4	13 00	13 08	18 20	23 51	23 44
11	21 51	− 7.5	56.5	15.4	1	251	58	7.4	13 24	13 28	19 06	—	—
12	22 39	− 3.4	55.8	15.2	14	250	68	8.4	13 45	13 46	19 51	1 00	0 57
13	23 26	+ 0.9	55.2	15.1	26	249	77	9.4	14 07	14 04	20 34	2 08	2 09
14	0 12	+ 5.0	54.8	14.9	38	250	84	10.4	14 28	14 22	21 18	3 14	3 19
15	0 58	+ 8.9	54.4	14.8	50	251	91	11.4	14 51	14 41	22 01	4 19	4 27
16	1 44	+12.4	54.2	14.8	62	252	95	12.4	15 17	15 04	22 46	5 23	5 35
17	2 32	+15.3	54.0	14.7	74	253	99	13.4	15 46	15 30	23 32	6 26	6 41
18	3 20	+17.7	54.0	14.7	86	243	100	14.4	16 21	16 03	—	7 26	7 44
19	4 10	+19.2	54.0	14.7	99	92	100	15.4	17 02	16 42	0 19	8 22	8 42
20	5 00	+20.0	54.1	14.7	111	92	97	16.4	17 50	17 30	1 07	9 13	9 34
21	5 51	+19.8	54.3	14.8	123	95	94	17.4	18 44	18 25	1 55	9 58	10 17
22	6 41	+18.8	54.6	14.9	135	99	88	18.4	19 44	19 27	2 44	10 37	10 54
23	7 32	+16.8	55.0	15.0	147	103	81	19.4	20 48	20 35	3 32	11 10	11 24
24	8 22	+14.1	55.5	15.1	159	106	73	20.4	21 55	21 46	4 19	11 38	11 49
25	9 11	+10.7	56.2	15.3	171	109	63	21.4	23 06	23 00	5 06	12 04	12 11
26	10 01	+ 6.7	56.9	15.5	184	111	53	22.4	—	—	5 53	12 28	12 32
27	10 51	+ 2.3	57.8	15.7	196	112	43	23.4	0 18	0 16	6 41	12 52	12 51
28	11 42	− 2.3	58.7	16.0	208	112	32	24.4	1 33	1 36	7 31	13 16	13 12
29	12 36	− 7.0	59.6	16.2	220	111	22	25.4	2 51	2 58	8 23	13 43	13 35
30	13 32	−11.5	60.4	16.5	232	110	13	26.4	4 12	4 23	9 18	14 15	14 03

MERCURY

Day	RA	Dec.	Diam.	Phase	Transit	5° high 52°	5° high 56°
	h m	°	″	%	h m	h m	h m
1	13 21	− 6.6	8	35	10 40	5 48	5 57
3	13 25	− 6.7	7	45	10 36	5 45	5 54
5	13 31	− 7.2	7	54	10 35	5 46	5 56
7	13 38	− 7.8	7	62	10 35	5 50	6 00
9	13 47	− 8.7	6	69	10 36	5 56	6 07
11	13 57	− 9.7	6	75	10 38	6 03	6 16
13	14 08	−10.8	6	80	10 41	6 12	6 26
15	14 19	−11.9	6	84	10 44	6 22	6 37
17	14 30	−13.0	5	87	10 48	6 33	6 49
19	14 42	−14.2	5	90	10 52	6 44	7 02
21	14 54	−15.3	5	92	10 56	6 56	7 15
23	15 06	−16.4	5	94	11 00	7 07	7 28
25	15 19	−17.4	5	95	11 05	7 19	7 42
27	15 31	−18.4	5	96	11 10	7 31	7 55
29	15 44	−19.4	5	97	11 14	7 43	8 09
31	15 57	−20.3	5	98	11 19	7 55	8 23

VENUS

Day	RA	Dec.	Diam.	Phase	Transit	5° high 52°	5° high 56°
	h m	°	″	%	h m	h m	h m
1	14 29	−20.8	61	1	11 45	8 23	8 52
6	14 18	−18.8	62	1	11 15	7 39	8 03
11	14 09	−16.7	60	3	10 47	6 56	7 17
16	14 03	−14.9	57	6	10 21	6 18	6 36
21	14 00	−13.3	54	10	10 00	5 47	6 03
26	14 02	−12.3	50	14	9 42	5 22	5 37
31	14 07	−11.7	46	19	9 27	5 04	5 19

MARS

Day	RA	Dec.	Diam.	Phase	Transit	5° high 52°	5° high 56°
1	9 09	+18.0	7	89	6 29	23 26	23 14
6	9 19	+17.4	7	89	6 19	23 19	23 08
11	9 28	+16.8	7	89	6 08	23 12	23 01
16	9 37	+16.3	8	89	5 57	23 04	22 53
21	9 45	+15.8	8	89	5 45	22 55	22 45
26	9 52	+15.3	8	90	5 33	22 45	22 36
31	9 59	+14.8	9	90	5 20	22 34	22 25

SUNRISE AND SUNSET

	London		Bristol		Birmingham		Manchester		Newcastle		Glasgow		Belfast	
	0°05′	51°30′	2°35′	51°28′	1°55′	52°28′	2°15′	53°28′	1°37′	54°59′	4°14′	55°52′	5°56′	54°35′
	h m	h m	h m	h m	h m	h m	h m	h m	h m	h m	h m	h m	h m	h m
1	6 53	16 34	7 03	16 44	7 03	16 39	7 07	16 37	7 10	16 30	7 23	16 37	7 26	16 48
2	6 55	16 32	7 05	16 42	7 05	16 37	7 09	16 35	7 12	16 28	7 25	16 35	7 28	16 46
3	6 57	16 30	7 07	16 40	7 07	16 35	7 11	16 33	7 14	16 26	7 27	16 33	7 30	16 44
4	6 59	16 29	7 09	16 39	7 09	16 33	7 13	16 31	7 16	16 24	7 29	16 31	7 32	16 42
5	7 00	16 27	7 10	16 37	7 11	16 31	7 15	16 29	7 18	16 22	7 31	16 29	7 34	16 40
6	7 02	16 25	7 12	16 35	7 12	16 29	7 17	16 28	7 20	16 20	7 33	16 27	7 36	16 38
7	7 04	16 23	7 14	16 34	7 14	16 28	7 19	16 26	7 22	16 18	7 36	16 25	7 38	16 37
8	7 06	16 22	7 16	16 32	7 16	16 26	7 21	16 24	7 24	16 16	7 38	16 23	7 40	16 35
9	7 07	16 20	7 17	16 30	7 18	16 24	7 23	16 22	7 26	16 14	7 40	16 21	7 42	16 33
10	7 09	16 19	7 19	16 29	7 20	16 23	7 25	16 21	7 28	16 12	7 42	16 19	7 44	16 31
11	7 11	16 17	7 21	16 27	7 22	16 21	7 27	16 19	7 30	16 10	7 44	16 17	7 46	16 29
12	7 13	16 16	7 23	16 26	7 23	16 20	7 28	16 17	7 32	16 09	7 46	16 15	7 48	16 28
13	7 14	16 14	7 24	16 24	7 25	16 18	7 30	16 16	7 34	16 07	7 48	16 14	7 49	16 26
14	7 16	16 13	7 26	16 23	7 27	16 17	7 32	16 14	7 36	16 05	7 50	16 12	7 51	16 24
15	7 18	16 11	7 28	16 22	7 29	16 15	7 34	16 13	7 38	16 04	7 52	16 10	7 53	16 23
16	7 20	16 10	7 29	16 20	7 31	16 14	7 36	16 11	7 40	16 02	7 54	16 08	7 55	16 21
17	7 21	16 09	7 31	16 19	7 32	16 12	7 38	16 10	7 42	16 00	7 56	16 07	7 57	16 20
18	7 23	16 07	7 33	16 18	7 34	16 11	7 40	16 08	7 44	15 59	7 58	16 05	7 59	16 18
19	7 25	16 06	7 35	16 16	7 36	16 10	7 41	16 07	7 46	15 57	8 00	16 04	8 01	16 17
20	7 26	16 05	7 36	16 15	7 38	16 08	7 43	16 06	7 48	15 56	8 02	16 02	8 03	16 15
21	7 28	16 04	7 38	16 14	7 39	16 07	7 45	16 04	7 49	15 55	8 04	16 01	8 05	16 14
22	7 30	16 03	7 39	16 13	7 41	16 06	7 47	16 03	7 51	15 53	8 06	15 59	8 07	16 13
23	7 31	16 02	7 41	16 12	7 43	16 05	7 48	16 02	7 53	15 52	8 08	15 58	8 08	16 11
24	7 33	16 01	7 43	16 11	7 44	16 04	7 50	16 01	7 55	15 51	8 10	15 57	8 10	16 10
25	7 34	16 00	7 44	16 10	7 46	16 03	7 52	16 00	7 57	15 50	8 12	15 55	8 12	16 09
26	7 36	15 59	7 46	16 09	7 47	16 02	7 53	15 59	7 59	15 48	8 14	15 54	8 14	16 08
27	7 37	15 58	7 47	16 08	7 49	16 01	7 55	15 58	8 00	15 47	8 16	15 53	8 15	16 07
28	7 39	15 57	7 49	16 07	7 51	16 00	7 57	15 57	8 02	15 46	8 17	15 52	8 17	16 06
29	7 40	15 56	7 50	16 07	7 52	15 59	7 58	15 56	8 04	15 45	8 19	15 51	8 19	16 05
30	7 42	15 56	7 52	16 06	7 54	15 59	8 00	15 55	8 05	15 44	8 21	15 50	8 20	16 04

JUPITER

Day	RA	Dec.	Transit	5° high	
				52°	56°
	h m	° ′	h m	h m	h m
1	15 17.3	−17 22	12 36	8 49	9 11
11	15 26.2	−17 56	12 05	8 23	8 46
21	15 35.2	−18 29	11 35	7 56	8 20
31	15 44.3	−19 00	11 04	7 30	7 55

Diameters – equatorial 31″ polar 29″

SATURN

Day	RA	Dec.	Transit	5° high	
				52°	56°
	h m	° ′	h m	h m	h m
1	22 33.0	−11 12	19 50	0 19	0 05
11	22 32.8	−11 12	19 10	23 36	23 22
21	22 33.2	−11 08	18 31	22 57	22 43
31	22 34.2	−11 00	17 53	22 20	22 06

Diameters – equatorial 18″ polar 16″
Rings – major axis 40″ minor axis 6″

URANUS

Day	RA	Dec.	Transit	10° high	
				52°	56°
	h m	° ′	h m	h m	h m
1	19 38.7	−22 01	16 56	19 14	18 19
11	19 39.9	−21 58	16 18	18 37	17 42
21	19 41.5	−21 54	15 40	18 00	17 06
31	19 43.3	−21 49	15 02	17 23	16 30

Diameter 4″

NEPTUNE

Day	RA	Dec.	Transit	10° high	
				52°	56°
	h m	° ′	h m	h m	h m
1	19 29.6	−21 16	16 47	19 14	18 24
11	19 30.4	−21 14	16 08	18 35	17 46
21	19 31.4	−21 12	15 30	17 57	17 09
31	19 32.6	−21 10	14 52	17 20	16 31

Diameter 2″

December 1994

TWELFTH MONTH, 31 DAYS. *Decem* (ten), tenth month of Roman pre-Julian calendar

Sun's Longitude 270° ♑ 22ᵈ02ʰ

1	Thursday	Edmund Campion *exec.*1581. Queen Alexandra *b.* 1844	week 48 day 335
2	Friday	Napoleon Bonaparte crowned Emperor 1804	336
3	Saturday	Lord Leighton *b.* 1830. Mary Baker Eddy *d.* 1910	337
4	Sunday	**2nd S. in Advent.** Thomas Carlyle *b.* 1795	week 49 day 338
5	Monday	Walt Disney *b.* 1901. Claude Monet *d.* 1926	339
6	Tuesday	Warren Hastings *b.* 1732. Anthony Trollope *d.* 1882	340
7	Wednesday	Pearl Harbor 1941. Gordon Pirie *d.* 1991	341
8	Thursday	Jean Sibelius *b.* 1865. John Lennon *d.* 1980	342
9	Friday	John Milton *b.* 1608. R. A. Butler *b.* 1902	343
10	Saturday	Alfred Nobel *d.* 1896. Nobel Prizes first awarded 1901	344
11	Sunday	**3rd S. in Advent.** Colley Cibber *d.* 1757	week 50 day 345
12	Monday	Edvard Munch *b.* 1863. Douglas Fairbanks *d.* 1939	346
13	Tuesday	Abel Tasman discovered New Zealand 1642	347
14	Wednesday	C. P. E. Bach *d.* 1788. Andrei Sakharov *d.* 1989	348
15	Thursday	Harold Abrahams *b.* 1899. Grigori Rasputin *assass.* 1916	349
16	Friday	Jane Austen *b.* 1775. Somerset Maugham *d.* 1965	350
17	Saturday	Sir Herbert Beerbohm Tree *b.* 1853	351
18	Sunday	**4th S. in Advent.** Charles Wesley *b.* 1707	week 51 day 352
19	Monday	Leonid Brezhnev *b.* 1906. Stella Gibbons *d.* 1989	353
20	Tuesday	Sir Robert Menzies *b.* 1894. Bill Brandt *d.* 1983	354
21	Wednesday	*Michaelmas Law Sittings end.* Scott Fitzgerald *d.* 1940	355
22	Thursday	J. Arthur Rank *b.* 1888. Samuel Beckett *d.* 1989	356
23	Friday	Thomas Malthus *d.* 1834. Théophile Gautier *d.* 1872	357
24	Saturday	Christmas Eve. James Joule *b.* 1886	358
25	Sunday	**Christmas Day.** Sir Charles Chaplin *d.* 1977	week 52 day 359
26	Monday	**St Stephen.** Boxing Day. *Bank Holiday in the UK*	360
27	Tuesday	**St John the Evangelist.** *Bank Holiday in the UK*	361
28	Wednesday	**Holy Innocents.** Sir Arthur Eddington *b.* 1882	362
29	Thursday	Jameson Raid 1895. Harold Macmillan *d.* 1986	363
30	Friday	Rudyard Kipling *b.* 1865. Richard Rodgers *d.* 1979	364
31	Saturday	Peter May *b.* 1929. Sir Malcolm Campbell *d.* 1948	365

ASTRONOMICAL PHENOMENA

d	h	
2	05	Jupiter in conjunction with Moon. Jupiter 0°.5 S.
2	13	Mercury in conjunction with Moon. Mercury 2° S.
9	00	Saturn in conjunction with Moon. Saturn 6° S.
9	11	Venus at greatest brilliancy
14	03	Mercury in superior conjunction
22	02	Solstice
23	10	Mars in conjunction with Moon. Mars 8° N.
29	04	Venus in conjunction with Moon. Venus 3° N.
30	01	Jupiter in conjunction with Moon. Jupiter 1° S.

CONSTELLATIONS

The following constellations are near the meridian at

	d	h		d	h
November	1	24	December	16	21
November	15	23	January	1	20
December	1	22	January	16	19

Ursa Major (below the Pole), Ursa Minor (below the Pole), Cassiopeia, Andromeda, Perseus, Triangulum, Aries, Taurus, Cetus and Eridanus

MINIMA OF ALGOL

d	h	d	h	d	h
3	16.0	12	06.4	23	17.7
6	12.8	15	03.3	26	14.5
9	09.6	20	20.9	29	11.3

THE MOON

Phases, Apsides and Node	d	h	m
● New Moon	2	23	54
☽ First Quarter	9	21	06
○ Full Moon	18	02	17
☾ Last Quarter	25	19	06
● New Moon	32	10	56
Perigee (357,264 km)	2	12	19
Apogee (406,019 km)	15	07	47
Perigee (360,488 km)	30	23	04

Mean longitude of ascending node on December 1, 223°

THE SUN   s.d. 16′.3

Day	Right Ascension	Dec. —	Equation of time	Rise 52°	Rise 56°	Transit	Set 52°	Set 56°	Sidereal time	Transit of First Point of Aries
	h m s	° ′	m s	h m	h m	h m	h m	h m	h m s	h m s
1	16 27 18	21 44	+ 11 12	7 45	8 06	11 49	15 52	15 31	4 38 30	19 18 20
2	16 31 37	21 53	+ 10 49	7 47	8 08	11 49	15 52	15 30	4 42 26	19 14 24
3	16 35 56	22 02	+ 10 26	7 48	8 10	11 50	15 51	15 30	4 46 23	19 10 28
4	16 40 17	22 10	+ 10 03	7 49	8 11	11 50	15 51	15 29	4 50 19	19 06 32
5	16 44 38	22 18	+ 9 38	7 51	8 13	11 51	15 50	15 28	4 54 16	19 02 36
6	16 48 59	22 26	+ 9 13	7 52	8 14	11 51	15 50	15 27	4 58 12	18 58 41
7	16 53 21	22 33	+ 8 48	7 53	8 16	11 51	15 49	15 27	5 02 09	18 54 45
8	16 57 43	22 40	+ 8 22	7 54	8 17	11 52	15 49	15 26	5 06 06	18 50 49
9	17 02 06	22 46	+ 7 56	7 56	8 18	11 52	15 49	15 26	5 10 02	18 46 53
10	17 06 30	22 52	+ 7 29	7 57	8 20	11 53	15 49	15 26	5 13 59	18 42 57
11	17 10 53	22 57	+ 7 02	7 58	8 21	11 53	15 48	15 25	5 17 55	18 39 01
12	17 15 18	23 02	+ 6 34	7 59	8 22	11 54	15 48	15 25	5 21 52	18 35 05
13	17 19 42	23 07	+ 6 06	8 00	8 23	11 54	15 48	15 25	5 25 48	18 31 09
14	17 24 07	23 11	+ 5 38	8 01	8 24	11 55	15 48	15 25	5 29 45	18 27 13
15	17 28 32	23 14	+ 5 09	8 02	8 25	11 55	15 49	15 25	5 33 41	18 23 17
16	17 32 57	23 18	+ 4 41	8 02	8 26	11 56	15 49	15 25	5 37 38	18 19 21
17	17 37 23	23 20	+ 4 12	8 03	8 27	11 56	15 49	15 25	5 41 35	18 15 26
18	17 41 49	23 22	+ 3 42	8 04	8 28	11 57	15 49	15 25	5 45 31	18 11 30
19	17 46 15	23 24	+ 3 13	8 05	8 28	11 57	15 49	15 26	5 49 28	18 07 34
20	17 50 41	23 25	+ 2 43	8 05	8 29	11 58	15 50	15 26	5 53 24	18 03 38
21	17 55 07	23 26	+ 2 14	8 06	8 30	11 58	15 50	15 26	5 57 21	17 59 42
22	17 59 33	23 26	+ 1 44	8 06	8 30	11 59	15 51	15 27	6 01 17	17 55 46
23	18 04 00	23 26	+ 1 14	8 07	8 31	11 59	15 51	15 28	6 05 14	17 51 50
24	18 08 26	23 25	+ 0 44	8 07	8 31	12 00	15 52	15 28	6 09 10	17 47 54
25	18 12 53	23 24	+ 0 14	8 07	8 31	12 00	15 53	15 29	6 13 07	17 43 58
26	18 17 19	23 23	− 0 15	8 08	8 31	12 01	15 53	15 30	6 17 04	17 40 02
27	18 21 45	23 21	− 0 45	8 08	8 32	12 01	15 54	15 31	6 21 00	17 36 06
28	18 26 11	23 18	− 1 15	8 08	8 32	12 01	15 55	15 31	6 24 57	17 32 11
29	18 30 37	23 15	− 1 44	8 08	8 32	12 02	15 56	15 32	6 28 53	17 28 15
30	18 35 03	23 12	− 2 13	8 08	8 32	12 02	15 57	15 33	6 32 50	17 24 19
31	18 39 29	23 08	− 2 42	8 08	8 32	12 03	15 58	15 35	6 36 46	17 20 23

DURATION OF TWILIGHT (in minutes)

Latitude	52°	56°	52°	56°	52°	56°	52°	56°
	1 December		11 December		21 December		31 December	
Civil	40	45	41	47	41	47	41	47
Nautical	82	93	84	96	85	97	84	96
Astronomical	123	138	125	141	126	142	125	141

THE NIGHT SKY

Mercury is unsuitably placed for observation, superior conjunction occurring on the 14th.

Venus is a brilliant object, attaining its greatest brilliancy (magnitude −4.6) on the 9th. It completely dominates the SE sky for several hours before sunrise. On the morning of the 29th, the waning crescent Moon will be seen 4°–5° below the planet and observers who enjoy detecting Venus in daylight can use the Moon as a guide on that morning, just after sunrise. Observers with telescopes will notice that the phase of Venus increases noticeably during the month.

Mars is now visible from the late evening onwards, its magnitude brightening from +0.3 to −0.3 during the month. Mars is now in Leo and around the 8th will be seen passing 2° north of Regulus. It should be noted that Mars is a whole magnitude brighter than Regulus. On the morning of the 23rd the gibbous Moon will be seen approaching Mars, closest approach occurring after sunrise.

Jupiter is too close to the Sun for observation for the first ten days of the month but then emerges from the morning twilight to become visible low in the SE sky for a while before dawn. Its magnitude is −1.8.

Saturn, magnitude +1.0, continues to be visible as an evening object in the SW sky, in Aquarius. The Moon, near First Quarter, will be seen near the planet on the evening of the 8th.

Meteors. The maximum of the well-known Geminid meteor shower occurs during the early hours of the 14th. Bright moonlight will be a considerable hindrance to observation until shortly after 04h.

THE MOON

Day	RA	Dec.	Hor. par.	Semi-diam.	Sun's co-long.	PA of Bright Limb	Phase	Age	Rise 52°	Rise 56°	Transit	Set 52°	Set 56°
	h m	°	'	'	°	°	%	d	h m	h m	h m	h m	h m
1	14 31	−15.3	61.0	16.6	245	108	6	27.4	5 34	5 49	10 17	14 54	14 37
2	15 33	−18.2	61.3	16.7	257	108	2	28.4	6 53	7 12	11 19	15 42	15 22
3	16 38	−19.8	61.3	16.7	269	189	0	0.0	8 04	8 25	12 23	16 41	16 20
4	17 42	−19.9	61.0	16.6	281	258	2	1.0	9 04	9 24	13 25	17 49	17 30
5	18 45	−18.7	60.4	16.5	293	257	6	2.0	9 53	10 10	14 25	19 04	18 47
6	19 45	−16.2	59.5	16.2	306	254	13	3.0	10 31	10 45	15 21	20 20	20 07
7	20 42	−12.9	58.6	16.0	318	251	21	4.0	11 02	11 12	16 13	21 35	21 26
8	21 35	− 8.9	57.6	15.7	330	249	31	5.0	11 28	11 34	17 02	22 47	22 42
9	22 25	− 4.7	56.7	15.5	342	248	41	6.0	11 51	11 53	17 48	23 56	23 56
10	23 13	− 0.4	55.9	15.2	354	247	51	7.0	12 12	12 11	18 32	—	—
11	0 00	+ 3.9	55.2	15.0	6	247	61	8.0	12 34	12 29	19 16	1 04	1 07
12	0 46	+ 7.8	54.7	14.9	19	248	70	9.0	12 56	12 48	19 59	2 10	2 17
13	1 32	+11.5	54.3	14.8	31	250	79	10.0	13 21	13 09	20 44	3 14	3 25
14	2 19	+14.6	54.1	14.7	43	252	86	11.0	13 49	13 34	21 29	4 18	4 32
15	3 07	+17.1	54.0	14.7	55	254	92	12.0	14 21	14 04	22 16	5 19	5 36
16	3 57	+18.9	54.0	14.7	67	255	96	13.0	15 00	14 41	23 03	6 17	6 36
17	4 47	+19.9	54.1	14.8	79	251	99	14.0	15 45	15 25	23 52	7 10	7 30
18	5 38	+20.0	54.3	14.8	91	195	100	15.0	16 38	16 18	—	7 57	8 17
19	6 29	+19.2	54.6	14.9	103	115	99	16.0	17 36	17 19	0 41	8 38	8 56
20	7 20	+17.5	54.9	15.0	116	110	96	17.0	18 40	18 25	1 29	9 13	9 29
21	8 10	+14.9	55.3	15.1	128	112	92	18.0	19 46	19 35	2 17	9 43	9 56
22	9 00	+11.7	55.8	15.2	140	112	86	19.0	20 55	20 48	3 04	10 10	10 19
23	9 49	+ 7.9	56.4	15.4	152	113	78	20.0	22 06	22 02	3 51	10 34	10 39
24	10 38	+ 3.6	57.0	15.5	164	114	69	21.0	23 18	23 19	4 38	10 57	10 58
25	11 28	− 0.9	57.6	15.7	176	114	59	22.0	—	—	5 25	11 20	11 18
26	12 19	− 5.4	58.4	15.9	188	113	48	23.0	0 33	0 37	6 15	11 45	11 39
27	13 12	− 9.8	59.1	16.1	201	112	37	24.0	1 49	1 58	7 06	12 14	12 03
28	14 08	−13.8	59.8	16.3	213	109	26	25.0	3 07	3 21	8 01	12 47	12 33
29	15 07	−17.0	60.3	16.4	225	106	17	26.0	4 25	4 42	9 00	13 29	13 10
30	16 09	−19.2	60.7	16.5	237	103	9	27.0	5 39	5 59	10 01	14 20	14 00
31	17 12	−20.0	60.8	16.6	249	103	3	28.0	6 45	7 05	11 03	15 23	15 02

MERCURY

Day	RA	Dec.	Diam.	Phase	Transit	5° high 52°	5° high 56°
	h m	°	"	%	h m	h m	h m
1	15 57	−20.3	5	98	11 19	7 55	8 23
3	16 10	−21.1	5	99	11 25	8 06	8 37
5	16 23	−21.9	5	99	11 30	8 18	8 50
7	16 36	−22.6	5	99	11 35	8 29	9 03
9	16 49	−23.2	5	100	11 41	8 40	9 16
11	17 03	−23.8	5	100	11 46	8 50	9 29
13	17 17	−24.2	5	100	11 52	9 00	9 41
15	17 30	−24.6	5	100	11 58	9 10	9 52
17	17 44	−24.9	5	100	12 04	14 50	14 06
19	17 58	−25.1	5	100	12 10	14 54	14 10
21	18 12	−25.2	5	99	12 16	14 59	14 15
23	18 26	−25.2	5	99	12 23	15 06	14 21
25	18 40	−25.1	5	98	12 29	15 13	14 29
27	18 55	−24.9	5	98	12 35	15 22	14 39
29	19 09	−24.6	5	97	12 41	15 31	14 50
31	19 23	−24.3	5	96	12 48	15 41	15 02

VENUS

Day	RA	Dec.	Diam.	Phase	Transit	5° high 52°	5° high 56°
	h m	°	"	%	h m	h m	h m
1	14 07	−11.7	46	19	9 27	5 04	5 19
6	14 15	−11.6	42	24	9 16	4 52	5 06
11	14 25	−11.8	39	28	9 07	4 44	4 59
16	14 38	−12.4	36	32	9 00	4 41	4 56
21	14 52	−13.1	34	36	8 55	4 40	4 57
26	15 08	−14.0	31	39	8 51	4 43	5 00
31	15 26	−15.0	29	42	8 49	4 47	5 06

MARS

Day	RA	Dec.	Diam.	Phase	Transit	5° high 52°	5° high 56°
1	9 59	+14.8	9	90	5 20	22 34	22 25
6	10 05	+14.4	9	90	5 07	22 23	22 14
11	10 11	+14.1	9	91	4 52	22 10	22 02
16	10 15	+13.9	10	92	4 37	21 56	21 48
21	10 19	+13.7	10	92	4 21	21 40	21 32
26	10 22	+13.7	11	93	4 04	21 23	21 15
31	10 23	+13.7	11	94	3 46	21 05	20 57

SUNRISE AND SUNSET

	London		Bristol		Birmingham		Manchester		Newcastle		Glasgow		Belfast	
	0°05′	51°30′	2°35′	51°28′	1°55′	52°28′	2°15′	53°28′	1°37′	54°59′	4°14′	55°52′	5°56′	54°35′
	h m	h m	h m	h m	h m	h m	h m	h m	h m	h m	h m	h m	h m	h m
1	7 43	15 55	7 53	16 05	7 55	15 58	8 01	15 54	8 07	15 44	8 23	15 49	8 22	16 03
2	7 45	15 54	7 54	16 05	7 57	15 57	8 03	15 53	8 09	15 43	8 24	15 48	8 24	16 02
3	7 46	15 54	7 56	16 04	7 58	15 57	8 04	15 53	8 10	15 42	8 26	15 47	8 25	16 02
4	7 47	15 53	7 57	16 04	7 59	15 56	8 06	15 52	8 12	15 41	8 27	15 47	8 27	16 01
5	7 49	15 53	7 58	16 03	8 01	15 56	8 07	15 52	8 13	15 41	8 29	15 46	8 28	16 00
6	7 50	15 53	8 00	16 03	8 02	15 55	8 08	15 51	8 14	15 40	8 30	15 45	8 29	16 00
7	7 51	15 52	8 01	16 02	8 03	15 55	8 10	15 51	8 16	15 40	8 32	15 45	8 31	15 59
8	7 52	15 52	8 02	16 02	8 04	15 54	8 11	15 50	8 17	15 39	8 33	15 44	8 32	15 59
9	7 53	15 52	8 03	16 02	8 06	15 54	8 12	15 50	8 18	15 39	8 34	15 44	8 33	15 59
10	7 55	15 51	8 04	16 02	8 07	15 54	8 13	15 50	8 20	15 39	8 36	15 43	8 35	15 58
11	7 56	15 51	8 05	16 01	8 08	15 54	8 14	15 50	8 21	15 38	8 37	15 43	8 36	15 58
12	7 57	15 51	8 06	16 01	8 09	15 54	8 16	15 50	8 22	15 38	8 38	15 43	8 37	15 58
13	7 57	15 51	8 07	16 01	8 10	15 54	8 17	15 50	8 23	15 38	8 39	15 43	8 38	15 58
14	7 58	15 51	8 08	16 01	8 11	15 54	8 18	15 50	8 24	15 38	8 40	15 43	8 39	15 58
15	7 59	15 51	8 09	16 02	8 12	15 54	8 18	15 50	8 25	15 38	8 41	15 43	8 40	15 58
16	8 00	15 52	8 10	16 02	8 12	15 54	8 19	15 50	8 26	15 38	8 42	15 43	8 41	15 58
17	8 01	15 52	8 11	16 02	8 13	15 54	8 20	15 50	8 27	15 38	8 43	15 43	8 41	15 58
18	8 02	15 52	8 11	16 02	8 14	15 54	8 21	15 50	8 27	15 39	8 44	15 43	8 42	15 58
19	8 02	15 52	8 12	16 03	8 15	15 55	8 22	15 50	8 28	15 39	8 44	15 44	8 43	15 59
20	8 03	15 53	8 13	16 03	8 15	15 55	8 22	15 51	8 29	15 39	8 45	15 44	8 44	15 59
21	8 03	15 53	8 13	16 03	8 16	15 56	8 23	15 51	8 29	15 40	8 46	15 44	8 44	15 59
22	8 04	15 54	8 14	16 04	8 16	15 56	8 23	15 52	8 30	15 40	8 46	15 45	8 45	16 00
23	8 04	15 54	8 14	16 04	8 17	15 57	8 24	15 52	8 30	15 41	8 47	15 45	8 45	16 00
24	8 05	15 55	8 15	16 05	8 17	15 57	8 24	15 53	8 31	15 41	8 47	15 46	8 45	16 01
25	8 05	15 56	8 15	16 06	8 18	15 58	8 24	15 54	8 31	15 42	8 47	15 47	8 46	16 02
26	8 05	15 56	8 15	16 06	8 18	15 59	8 25	15 54	8 31	15 43	8 47	15 47	8 46	16 03
27	8 06	15 57	8 16	16 07	8 18	15 59	8 25	15 55	8 31	15 44	8 48	15 48	8 46	16 03
28	8 06	15 58	8 16	16 08	8 18	16 00	8 25	15 56	8 32	15 44	8 48	15 49	8 46	16 04
29	8 06	15 59	8 16	16 09	8 18	16 01	8 25	15 57	8 32	15 45	8 48	15 50	8 46	16 05
30	8 06	16 00	8 16	16 10	8 18	16 02	8 25	15 58	8 32	15 46	8 48	15 51	8 46	16 06
31	8 06	16 01	8 16	16 11	8 18	16 03	8 25	15 59	8 31	15 48	8 48	15 52	8 46	16 07

JUPITER

Day	RA	Dec.	Transit	5° high	
				52°	56°
	h m	° ′	h m	h m	h m
1	15 44.3	−19 00	11 04	7 30	ʻ7 55
11	15 53.4	−19 28	10 34	7 03	7 29
21	16 02.2	−19 54	10 04	6 36	7 03
31	16 10.8	−20 18	9 33	6 08	6 36

Diameters – equatorial 31″ polar 29″

SATURN

Day	RA	Dec.	Transit	5° high	
				52°	56°
	h m	° ′	h m	h m	h m
1	22 34.2	−11 00	17 53	22 20	22 06
11	22 35.9	−10 49	17 15	21 43	21 30
21	22 38.2	−10 34	16 38	21 08	20 55
31	22 41.0	−10 16	16 02	20 33	20 20

Diameters – equatorial 17″ polar 15″
Rings – major axis 38″ minor axis 5″

URANUS

Day	RA	Dec.	Transit	10° high	
				52°	56°
	h m	° ′	h m	h m	h m
1	19 43.3	−21 49	15 02	17 23	16 30
11	19 45.3	−21 44	14 25	16 47	15 54
21	19 47.5	−21 39	13 48	16 11	15 19
31	19 49.9	−21 33	13 11	15 35	14 44

Diameter 4″

NEPTUNE

Day	RA	Dec.	Transit	10° high	
				52°	56°
	h m	° ′	h m	h m	h m
1	19 32.6	−21 10	14 52	17 20	16 31
11	19 33.9	−21 07	14 14	16 42	15 54
21	19 35.4	−21 04	13 36	16 05	15 17
31	19 36.9	−21 01	12 58	15 28	14 40

Diameter 2″

RISING AND SETTING TIMES

Table 1. Semi-diurnal arcs (hour angles at rising/setting)

Dec.	Latitude 0° h m	10° h m	20° h m	30° h m	40° h m	45° h m	50° h m	52° h m	54° h m	56° h m	58° h m	60° h m	Dec.
0°	6 00	6 00	6 00	6 00	6 00	6 00	6 00	6 00	6 00	6 00	6 00	6 00	0°
1°	6 00	6 01	6 01	6 02	6 03	6 04	6 05	6 05	6 06	6 06	6 06	6 07	1°
2°	6 00	6 01	6 03	6 05	6 07	6 08	6 10	6 10	6 11	6 12	6 13	6 14	2°
3°	6 00	6 02	6 04	6 07	6 10	6 12	6 14	6 15	6 17	6 18	6 19	6 21	3°
4°	6 00	6 03	6 06	6 09	6 13	6 16	6 19	6 21	6 22	6 24	6 26	6 28	4°
5°	6 00	6 04	6 07	6 12	6 17	6 20	6 24	6 26	6 28	6 30	6 32	6 35	5°
6°	6 00	6 04	6 09	6 14	6 20	6 24	6 29	6 31	6 33	6 36	6 39	6 42	6°
7°	6 00	6 05	6 10	6 16	6 24	6 28	6 34	6 36	6 39	6 42	6 45	6 49	7°
8°	6 00	6 06	6 12	6 19	6 27	6 32	6 39	6 41	6 45	6 48	6 52	6 56	8°
9°	6 00	6 06	6 13	6 21	6 31	6 36	6 44	6 47	6 50	6 54	6 59	7 04	9°
10°	6 00	6 07	6 15	6 23	6 34	6 41	6 49	6 52	6 56	7 01	7 06	7 11	10°
11°	6 00	6 08	6 16	6 26	6 38	6 45	6 54	6 58	7 02	7 07	7 12	7 19	11°
12°	6 00	6 09	6 18	6 28	6 41	6 49	6 59	7 03	7 08	7 13	7 20	7 26	12°
13°	6 00	6 09	6 19	6 31	6 45	6 53	7 04	7 09	7 14	7 20	7 27	7 34	13°
14°	6 00	6 10	6 21	6 33	6 48	6 58	7 09	7 14	7 20	7 27	7 34	7 42	14°
15°	6 00	6 11	6 22	6 36	6 52	7 02	7 14	7 20	7 27	7 34	7 42	7 51	15°
16°	6 00	6 12	6 24	6 38	6 56	7 07	7 20	7 26	7 33	7 41	7 49	7 59	16°
17°	6 00	6 12	6 26	6 41	6 59	7 11	7 25	7 32	7 40	7 48	7 57	8 08	17°
18°	6 00	6 13	6 27	6 43	7 03	7 16	7 31	7 38	7 46	7 55	8 05	8 17	18°
19°	6 00	6 14	6 29	6 46	7 07	7 21	7 37	7 45	7 53	8 03	8 14	8 26	19°
20°	6 00	6 15	6 30	6 49	7 11	7 25	7 43	7 51	8 00	8 11	8 22	8 36	20°
21°	6 00	6 16	6 32	6 51	7 15	7 30	7 49	7 58	8 08	8 19	8 32	8 47	21°
22°	6 00	6 16	6 34	6 54	7 19	7 35	7 55	8 05	8 15	8 27	8 41	8 58	22°
23°	6 00	6 17	6 36	6 57	7 23	7 40	8 02	8 12	8 23	8 36	8 51	9 09	23°
24°	6 00	6 18	6 37	7 00	7 28	7 46	8 08	8 19	8 31	8 45	9 02	9 22	24°
25°	6 00	6 19	6 39	7 02	7 32	7 51	8 15	8 27	8 40	8 55	9 13	9 35	25°
26°	6 00	6 20	6 41	7 05	7 37	7 57	8 22	8 35	8 49	9 05	9 25	9 51	26°
27°	6 00	6 21	6 43	7 08	7 41	8 03	8 30	8 43	8 58	9 16	9 39	10 08	27°
28°	6 00	6 22	6 45	7 12	7 46	8 08	8 37	8 52	9 08	9 28	9 53	10 28	28°
29°	6 00	6 22	6 47	7 15	7 51	8 15	8 45	9 01	9 19	9 41	10 10	10 55	29°
30°	6 00	6 23	6 49	7 18	7 56	8 21	8 54	9 11	9 30	9 55	10 30	12 00	30°
35°	6 00	6 28	6 59	7 35	8 24	8 58	9 46	10 15	10 58	12 00	12 00	12 00	35°
40°	6 00	6 34	7 11	7 56	8 59	9 48	12 00	12 00	12 00	12 00	12 00	12 00	40°
45°	6 00	6 41	7 25	8 21	9 48	12 00	12 00	12 00	12 00	12 00	12 00	12 00	45°
50°	6 00	6 49	7 43	8 54	12 00	12 00	12 00	12 00	12 00	12 00	12 00	12 00	50°
55°	6 00	6 58	8 05	9 42	12 00	12 00	12 00	12 00	12 00	12 00	12 00	12 00	55°
60°	6 00	7 11	8 36	12 00	12 00	12 00	12 00	12 00	12 00	12 00	12 00	12 00	60°
65°	6 00	7 29	9 25	12 00	12 00	12 00	12 00	12 00	12 00	12 00	12 00	12 00	65°
70°	6 00	7 56	12 00	12 00	12 00	12 00	12 00	12 00	12 00	12 00	12 00	12 00	70°
75°	6 00	8 45	12 00	12 00	12 00	12 00	12 00	12 00	12 00	12 00	12 00	12 00	75°
80°	6 00	12 00	12 00	12 00	12 00	12 00	12 00	12 00	12 00	12 00	12 00	12 00	80°

Table 2. Correction for Refraction and Semi-diameter

	m	m	m	m	m	m	m	m	m	m	m	m	
0°	3	3	4	4	4	5	5	5	6	6	6	7	0°
10°	3	3	4	4	4	5	5	6	6	6	7	7	10°
20°	4	4	4	4	5	5	6	7	7	8	8	9	20°
25°	4	4	4	4	5	6	7	8	8	9	11	13	25°
30°	4	4	4	5	6	7	8	9	11	14	21	—	30°

NB: Regarding Table 1. If latitude and declination are of the same sign, take out the respondent directly. If they are of opposite signs, subtract the respondent from 12h.
Examples:

Lat.	Dec.	Semi-diurnal arc
+52°	+20°	7h 51m
+52°	−20°	4h 09m

SUNRISE AND SUNSET

The local mean time of sunrise or sunset may be found by obtaining the hour angle from Table 1 and applying it to the time of transit. The hour angle is negative for sunrise and positive for sunset. A small correction to the hour angle, which always has the effect of increasing it numerically, is necessary to allow for the Sun's semi-diameter (16′) and for refraction (34′); it is obtained from Table 2. The resulting local mean time may be converted into the standard time of the country by taking the difference between the longitude of the standard meridian of the country and that of the place, adding it to the local mean time if the place is west of the standard meridian, and subtracting it if the place is east.

Example – Required the New Zealand Mean Time (12h fast on GMT) of sunset on May 23 at Auckland, latitude 36° 50′ S. (or minus), longitude 11h 39m E. Taking the declination as $+20°.6$ (page 33), we find

	h	m
Tabular entry for 30° Lat. and Dec. 20°, opposite signs	+ 5	11
Proportional part for 6° 50′ of Lat.	−	15
Proportional part for 0°.6 of Dec.	−	2
Correction (Table 2)	+	4
Hour angle	4	58
Sun transits (page 33)	11	57
Longitudinal correction	+	21
New Zealand Mean Time	17	16

MOONRISE AND MOONSET

It is possible to calculate the times of moonrise and moonset using Table 1, though the method is more complicated because the apparent motion of the Moon is much more rapid and also more variable than that of the Sun.

The parallax of the Moon, about 57′, is near to the sum of the semi-diameter and refraction but has the opposite effect on these times. It is thus convenient to neglect all three quantities in the method outlined below.

TABLE 3. LONGITUDE CORRECTION

X \ A	40m	45m	50m	55m	60m	65m	70m
h	m	m	m	m	m	m	m
1	2	2	2	2	3	3	3
2	3	4	4	5	5	5	6
3	5	6	6	7	8	8	9
4	7	8	8	9	10	11	12
5	8	9	10	11	13	14	15
6	10	11	13	14	15	16	18
7	12	13	15	16	18	19	20
8	13	15	17	18	20	22	23
9	15	17	19	21	23	24	26
10	17	19	21	23	25	27	29
11	18	21	23	25	28	30	32
12	20	23	25	28	30	33	35
13	22	24	27	30	33	35	38
14	23	26	29	32	35	38	41
15	25	28	31	34	38	41	44
16	27	30	33	37	40	43	47
17	28	32	35	39	43	46	50
18	30	34	38	41	45	49	53
19	32	36	40	44	48	51	55
20	33	38	42	46	50	54	58
21	35	39	44	48	53	57	61
22	37	41	46	50	55	60	64
23	38	43	48	53	58	62	67
24	40	45	50	55	60	65	70

Notation

φ = latitude of observer

λ = longitude of observer (measured positively towards the west)

T_{-1} = time of transit of Moon on previous day

T_0 = time of transit of Moon on day in question

T_1 = time of transit of Moon on following day

δ_0 = approximate declination of Moon

δ_R = declination of Moon at moonrise

δ_S = declination of Moon at moonset

h_0 = approximate hour angle of Moon

h_R = hour angle of Moon at moonrise

h_S = hour angle of Moon at moonset

t_R = time of moonrise

t_S = time of moonset

Method

1. With arguments φ, δ_0 enter Table 1 on page 64 to determine h_0 where h_0 is negative for moonrise and positive for moonset.

2. Form approximate times from
$$t_R = T_0 + \lambda + h_0$$
$$t_S = T_0 + \lambda + h_0$$

3. Determine δ_R, δ_S for times t_R, t_S respectively.

4. Re-enter Table 1 on page 64 with –
   (a) arguments φ, δ_R to determine h_R
   (b) arguments φ, δ_S to determine h_S

5. Form $t_R = T_0 + \lambda + h_R + AX$
$$t_S = T_0 + \lambda + h_S + AX$$

where $A = (\lambda + h)$

and $X = (T_0 - T_{-1})$ if $(\lambda + h)$ is negative
$X = (T_1 - T_0)$ if $(\lambda + h)$ is positive

AX is the respondent in Table 3.

Example – To find the times of moonrise and moonset at Vancouver ($\varphi = +49°$, $\lambda = +8h\ 12m$) on 1994 January 10. The starting data (page 18) are

$T_{-1} = 9h\ 47m$
$T_0 = 10h\ 45m$
$T_1 = 11h\ 41m$
$\delta = -21°$

1. $h_0 = 4h\ 15m$
2. Approximate values
   $t_R = 10d\ 10h\ 45m + 8h\ 12m + (-4h\ 15m)$
   $= 10d\ 14h\ 42m$
   $t_S = 10d\ 10h\ 45m + 8h\ 12m + (+4h\ 15m)$
   $= 10d\ 23h\ 12m$
3. $\delta_R = -20°.6$
   $\delta_S = -20°.2$
4. $h_R = -4h\ 17m$
   $h_S = +4h\ 20m$
5. $t_R = 10d\ 10h\ 45m + 8h\ 12m + (-4h\ 17m) + 9m$
   $= 10d\ 14h\ 49m$
   $t_S = 10d\ 10h\ 45m + 8h\ 12m + (+4h\ 20m) + 29m$
   $= 10d\ 23h\ 46m$

To get the LMT of the phenomenon the longitude is subtracted from the GMT thus:
Moonrise = 10d 14h 49m − 8h 12m = 10d 06h 37m
Moonset = 10d 23h 46m − 8h 12m = 10d 15h 34m

ECLIPSES AND OCCULTATIONS 1994

ECLIPSES

There will be three eclipses during 1994, two of the Sun and one of the Moon. (Penumbral eclipses are not mentioned in this section as they are difficult to observe).

1. An annular eclipse of the Sun on May 10 is visible as a partial eclipse from the eastern Pacific including Hawaii, northern Siberia, North and Central America and the extreme northern edge of Colombia and Venezuela, the West Indies, the Atlantic Ocean, the Arctic Ocean, Greenland, Iceland, western Europe (including the British Isles), and north-west and west Africa. The eclipse begins at 14h 12m and ends at 20h 11m. The track of the annular phase crosses North America from lower California to Nova Scotia and then crosses the North Atlantic to Morocco. The annular phase begins at 15h 21m and ends at 19h 02m. The maximum duration of the annular phase is 6m 14s.

At Greenwich the partial eclipse begins at 17h 36m and ends (at sunset) at 19h 31m. At Edinburgh the partial eclipse begins at 17h 31m and ends at 19h 25m. As seen from the British Isles, approximately half of the Sun is obscured at maximum.

2. A partial eclipse of the Moon on May 25 is visible from Europe (including the British Isles), the Atlantic Ocean, Africa, Madagascar, Iceland, southern Greenland, Antarctica, the Americas (except the extreme north-west) and the Pacific Ocean. The eclipse begins at 02h 37m and ends at 04h 23m. For most of the British Isles, except the extreme south-west of England and Wales, and also for Ireland, the Moon will have set before the eclipse ends.

3. A total eclipse of the Sun on November 3 is visible as a partial eclipse from the eastern South Pacific Ocean, Central and South America, the Atlantic Ocean, part of Antarctica, southern Africa, and Madagascar. The path of totality crosses southern Peru, southern Bolivia, Paraguay, and southern Brazil. The eclipse begins at 11h 05m and ends at 16h 13m. The total phase begins at 12h 02m and ends at 15h 16m. The maximum duration is 4m 23s.

LUNAR OCCULTATIONS

Observations of the times of occultations are made by both amateur and professional astronomers. Such observations are later analysed to yield accurate positions of the Moon; this is one method of determining the difference between ephemeris time and universal time.

Many of the observations made by amateurs are obtained with the use of a stop-watch which is compared with a time-signal immediately after the observation. Thus an accuracy of about one-fifth of a second is obtainable, though the observer's personal equation may amount to one-third or one-half of a second.

The list on page 67 includes most of the occultations visible under favourable conditions in the British Isles. No occultation is included unless the star is at least 10° above the horizon and the Sun sufficiently far below the horizon to permit the star to be seen with the naked eye or with a small telescope. The altitude limit is reduced from 10° to 2° for stars and planets brighter than magnitude 2.0 and such occultations are also predicted in daylight.

The column Phase shows (i) whether a disappearance (D) or reappearance (R) is to be observed; and (ii) whether it is at the dark limb (D) or bright limb (B). The column headed 'El. of Moon' gives the elongation of the Moon from the Sun, in degrees. The elongation increases from 0° at New Moon to 180° at Full Moon and on to 360° (or 0°) at New Moon again. Times and position angles (P), reckoned from the

north point in the direction north, east, south, west, are given for Greenwich (lat. 51° 30′, long. 0°) and Edinburgh (lat. 56° 00′, long. 3° 12′ west).

The coefficients a and b are the variations in the GMT for each degree of longitude (positive to the west) and latitude (positive to the north) respectively; they enable approximate times (to within about 1m generally) to be found for any point in the British Isles. If the point of observation is $\Delta\lambda$ degrees west and $\Delta\phi$ degrees north, the approximate time is found by adding $a.\Delta\lambda + b.\Delta\phi$ to the given GMT.

Example: the reappearance of ZC668 on October 23 at Liverpool, found from both Greenwich and Edinburgh.

	Greenwich	Edinburgh
	°	°
Longitude	0.0	+3.2
Long. of Liverpool	+3.0	+3.0
$\Delta\lambda$	+3.0	−0.2
Latitude	+51.5	+56.0
Lat. of Liverpool	+53.4	+53.4
$\Delta\phi$	+1.9	−2.6
	h m	h m
GMT	3 32.8	3 23.8
$a.\Delta\lambda$	− 4.8	+ 0.3
$b.\Delta\phi$	− 1.5	+ 2.9
	3 26.5	3 27.0

If the occultation is given for one station but not the other, the reason for the suppression is given by the following code:

N = star not occulted

A = star's altitude less than 10° (2° for bright stars and planets)

S = Sun not sufficiently below the horizon

G = occultation is of very short duration

In some cases the coefficients a and b are not given; this is because the occultation is so short that prediction for other places by means of these coefficients would not be reliable.

LUNAR OCCULTATIONS 1994

Date		ZC No.	Mag.	Phase	El. of Moon	GREENWICH UT	a	b	P	EDINBURGH UT	a	b	P
					°	h m	m	m	°	h m	m	m	°
January	2	1495	5.9	R.D.	232					1 12.9			220
	15	3326	6.4	D.D.	46	18 47.5	−0.8	−1.5	87	18 39.6	−0.7	−1.0	71
	16	3455	6.4	D.D.	57	19 21.6	−0.7	−0.7	65	19 17.2	−0.6	−0.3	49
	16	3453	4.9	D.D.	57	19 27.0	−0.5	0.8	27	19 32.4			3
	17	29	7.2	D.D.	69	21 27.7	−0.4	−0.6	57	21 24.6	−0.4	−0.2	42
	21	497	6.5	D.D.	113	22 39.0	−0.7	−3.6	135	22 22.9	−0.9	−2.4	118
	22	628	4.8	D.D.	123	21 22.6	−1.6	1.1	51	21 25.2	−1.4	2.4	32
	24	915	4.7	D.D.	146	N				19 42.0			153
February	17	455	6.1	D.D.	81	21 23.4	−0.8	−1.1	75	21 16.8	−0.8	−0.8	63
	20	873	7.9	D.D.	115	23 7.8	0.0	−3.8	156	22 51.9	−0.4	−2.9	143
	21	892	6.6	D.D.	116	2 3.1	−0.2	−0.9	60	1 58.1	−0.3	−0.9	54
	21	894	4.6	D.D.	117	2 31.8	−0.1	−0.8	55	2 27.7	−0.2	−0.8	49
	21	1006	6.9	D.D.	125	18 30.0	−1.4	0.4	106	18 29.2	−1.1	1.0	92
	22	1038	6.8	D.D.	128	1 9.4	−0.4	−1.8	106	1 0.2	−0.5	−1.7	101
	22	1141	5.6	D.D.	137	19 23.1	−1.3	0.0	117	19 20.7	−1.1	0.6	103
	23	1281	6.4	D.D.	152	22 57.4	−1.3	−0.9	110	22 49.9	−1.3	−0.5	102
March	18	691	6.6	D.D.	73	22 52.2	0.4	−2.4	131	22 42.6	0.1	−2.3	123
	22	1212	7.1	D.D.	117	19 22.9			170	S			
	22	1234	6.1	D.D.	120	23 46.9	−1.1	−0.9	68	23 39.5	−1.2	−0.8	62
April	16	913	5.2	D.D.	64	21 45.2	−0.3	−1.3	75	21 38.3	−0.5	−1.2	69
	21	1543	6.6	D.D.	127	24 5.6	−0.7	−1.7	110	23 56.0	−0.7	−1.6	107
	22	1639	7.0	D.D.	138	20 22.3	−0.8	−1.2	151	S			
	22	1655	6.7	D.D.	140	23 27.3	−1.0	−1.4	117	23 18.3	−1.0	−1.2	114
	23	1670	5.1	D.D.	141	2 33.0	−0.2	−2.3	161	2 22.2	−0.3	−2.1	155
	28	2376	4.6	R.D.	212	2 31.7	−1.5	−0.1	266	2 26.9	−1.3	0.0	270
May	18	1495	5.9	D.D.	96	23 32.4	−0.3	−1.5	88	23 24.3	−0.4	−1.6	85
	19	1605	6.2	D.D.	108	22 55.6	−1.1	−0.9	60	22 48.1	−1.2	−0.8	55
	20	1723	7.1	D.D.	121	21 54.8	−1.1	−1.4	124	21 45.7	−1.0	−1.2	121
	21	1845	6.5	D.D.	135	22 34.5			186	22 21.9			179
	28	2791	5.4	R.D.	220	1 25.7	−1.4	0.9	251	1 25.6	−1.2	0.9	255
June	1	3320	5.3	R.D.	269	1 59.2	−0.6	2.1	225	2 6.7	−0.5	2.0	230
	18	1930	5.6	D.D.	117	20 49.5	−1.5	−0.6	93	S			
	21	2217	5.5	D.D.	146	0 24.5	−0.7	−0.1	38	0 23.0			25
	21	2376	4.6	D.D.	159	22 24.1	−1.4	−0.1	105	22 19.9	−1.2	0.1	102
July	18	2307	4.1	D.D.	127	20 34.2	−1.6	0.2	69	S			
	18	2310	4.6	D.D.	127	20 52.7	−1.4	−0.5	108	S			
	20	2633	4.0	D.D.	155	22 25.9	−1.5	−0.2	102	22 20.9	−1.3	0.0	97
	20	2638	5.4	D.D.	155	23 26.1	−1.0	0.4	39	23 25.0	−0.8	0.5	29
August	13	2119	6.7	D.D.	85	20 20.1	−1.0	−1.5	111	A			
	14	2267	5.1	D.D.	99	21 34.9	−0.9	−1.3	94	21 26.4	−0.9	−1.2	88
	24	105	4.6	R.D.	223	22 20.0	−0.9	1.1	296	22 21.9	−0.9	1.0	308
	31	895	5.9	R.D.	291	4 0.2	−1.4	−0.7	319	N			
October	10	2642	7.1	D.D.	77	18 21.1	−1.9	−1.8	136	18 9.8	−1.5	−1.0	125
	13	3093	4.5	D.D.	116	22 39.3	−0.4	0.4	32	22 41.6	−0.1	1.1	12
	17	3494	4.6	D.D.	153	3 13.3	−0.3	−1.2	78	3 7.5	−0.3	−0.9	64
	23	668	3.6	R.D.	219	3 32.8	−1.6	−0.8	273	3 23.8	−1.4	−1.1	287
	28	1318	5.7	R.D.	276	5 1.8	−1.0	−2.1	336	4 46.3			357
November	11	3320	5.3	D.D.	111	23 56.1	−0.7	−3.6	124	23 41.8	−0.6	−2.2	103
	12	3444	6.5	D.D.	122	23 23.3	−0.6	0.5	32	23 26.4	−0.3	1.6	11
	13	6	6.9	D.D.	131	19 44.9	−1.9	0.2	98	19 42.0	−1.4	0.8	85
	14	103	6.1	D.D.	141	17 26.0	−0.7	1.9	71	17 32.7	−0.5	2.0	64
	14	105	4.6	D.D.	142	18 8.4	−0.2	3.0	14	18 23.3			357
December	8	3259	7.4	D.D.	76	17 32.8	−1.3	0.5	55	17 32.2	−1.0	0.7	44
	12	209	7.2	D.D.	123	20 6.4	−1.6	0.5	74	20 5.2	−1.2	1.0	60
	21	1332	5.7	R.D.	223	21 5.1	−0.3	−0.4	329	A			

MEAN PLACES OF STARS 1994.5

Name	Mag.	RA (h m)	Dec. (° ')	Spectrum	Name	Mag.	RA (h m)	Dec. (°)	Spectrum
α And *Alpheratz*	2.1	0 08.1	+29 04	A0p	γ Corvi	2.6	12 15.5	−17 31	B8
β Cassiopeiae *Caph*	2.3	0 08.9	+59 07	F5	α Crucis	1.0	12 26.3	−63 04	B1
γ Pegasi *Algenib*	2.8	0 13.0	+15 09	B2	γ Crucis	1.6	12 30.9	−57 05	M3
β Mensae	2.9	0 25.5	−77 17	G0	γ Centauri	2.2	12 41.2	−48 56	A0
α Phoenicis	2.4	0 26.0	−42 20	K0	γ Virginis	2.7	12 41.4	− 1 25	F0
α Cassiopeiae *Schedar*	2.2	0 40.2	+56 30	K0	β Crucis	1.3	12 47.4	−59 40	B1
β Ceti *Diphda*	2.0	0 43.3	−18 01	K0	ε Ursae Majoris *Alioth*	1.8	12 53.8	+55 59	A0p
γ Cassiopeiae*	Var.	0 56.4	+60 41	B0p	α Canum Venaticorum	2.9	12 55.8	+38 21	A0p
β Andromedae *Mirach*	2.1	1 09.4	+35 35	M0	ζ Ursae Majoris *Mizar*	2.1	13 23.7	+54 57	A2p
δ Cassiopeiae	2.7	1 25.5	+60 12	A5	α Virginis *Spica*	1.0	13 24.9	−11 08	B2
α Eridani *Achernar*	0.5	1 37.5	−57 16	B5	ε Centauri	2.6	13 39.5	−53 26	B1
β Arietis *Sheratan*	2.6	1 54.3	+20 47	A5	η Ursae Majoris *Alkaid*	1.9	13 47.3	+49 20	B3
γ Andromedae *Almak*	2.3	2 03.6	+42 18	K0	β Centauri *Hadar*	0.6	14 03.4	−60 21	B1
α Arietis *Hamal*	2.0	2 06.9	+23 26	K2	θ Centauri	2.1	14 06.4	−36 21	K0
α Ursae Minoris *Polaris*	2.0	2 25.9	+89 14	F8	α Bootis *Arcturus*	0.0	14 15.4	+19 12	K0
β Persei *Algol**	Var.	3 07.8	+40 56	B8	α Centauri *Rigil Kent*	0.1	14 39.2	−60 49	G0
α *Persei Mirfak*	1.8	3 23.9	+49 51	F5	ε Bootis	2.4	14 44.7	+27 06	K0
η Tauri *Alcyone*	2.9	3 47.2	+24 05	B5p	β UMi *Kochab*	2.1	14 50.7	+74 11	K5
α Tauri *Aldebaran*	0.9	4 35.6	+16 30	K5	α CrB *Alphecca*	2.2	15 34.5	+26 44	A0
β Orionis *Rigel*	0.1	5 14.3	− 8 12	B8p	β Trianguli Australis	3.0	15 54.7	−63 25	F0
α Aurigae *Capella*	0.1	5 16.3	+46 00	G0	δ Scorpii	2.3	16 00.0	−22 36	B0
γ Orionis *Bellatrix*	1.6	5 24.8	+ 6 21	B2	β Scorpii	2.6	16 05.1	−19 47	B1
β Tauri *Elnath*	1.7	5 25.9	+28 36	B8	γ Ursae Minoris	3.1	15 20.7	+71 51	A2
δ Orionis	2.2	5 31.7	− 0 18	B0	α Scorpii *Antares*	1.0	16 29.1	−26 25	M0
α Leporis	2.6	5 32.5	−17 50	F0	α Trianguli Australis	1.9	16 48.1	−69 01	K2
ε Orionis	1.7	5 35.9	− 1 12	B0	ε Scorpii	2.3	16 49.8	−34 17	K0
ζ Orionis	1.8	5 40.5	− 1 57	B0	α Herculis†	Var.	17 14.4	+14 24	M3
κ Orionis	2.1	5 47.5	− 9 40	B0	λ Scorpii	1.6	17 33.2	−37 06	B2
α Orionis *Betelgeuse**	Var.	5 54.9	+ 7 24	M0	α Ophiuchi *Rasalhague*	2.1	17 34.7	+12 34	A5
β Aurigae *Menkalinan*	1.9	5 59.1	+44 57	A0p	θ Scorpii	1.9	17 36.9	−43 00	F0
β CMa *Mirzam*	2.0	6 22.5	−17 57	B1	κ Scorpii	2.4	17 42.1	−39 02	B2
α Carinae *Canopus*	−0.7	6 23.8	−52 42	F0	γ Draconis	2.2	17 56.5	+51 29	K5
γ Geminorum *Alhena*	1.9	6 37.4	+16 24	A0	ε Sgr *Kaus Australis*	1.9	18 23.8	−34 23	A0
α Canis Majoris *Sirius*	−1.5	6 44.9	−16 43	A0	α Lyrae *Vega*	0.0	18 36.8	+38 47	A0
ε Canis Majoris	1.5	6 58.4	−28 58	B1	σ Sagittarii	2.0	18 54.9	−26 18	B3
δ Canis Majoris	1.9	7 08.2	−26 23	F8p	β Cygni *Albireo*	3.1	19 30.5	+27 57	K0
α Geminorum *Castor*	1.6	7 34.2	+31 54	A0	α Aquilae *Altair*	0.8	19 50.5	+ 8 51	A5
α CMi *Procyon*	0.4	7 39.0	+ 5 14	F5	α Capricorni	3.8	20 17.7	−12 34	G5
β Geminorum *Pollux*	1.1	7 45.0	+28 02	K0	γ Cygni	2.2	20 22.0	+40 14	F8p
ζ Puppis	2.3	8 03.4	−39 59	Od	α Pavonis	1.9	20 25.2	−56 45	B3
γ Velorum	1.8	8 09.4	−47 19	Oap	α Cygni *Deneb*	1.3	20 41.2	+45 16	A2p
ε Carinae	1.9	8 22.4	−59 30	K0	α Cephei *Alderamin*	2.4	21 18.4	+62 34	A5
δ Velorum	2.0	8 44.6	−54 41	A0	ε Pegasi	2.4	21 43.9	+ 9 51	K0
λ Velorum *Suhail*	2.2	9 07.8	−43 25	K5	δ Capricorni	2.9	21 46.7	−16 09	A5
β Carinae	1.7	9 13.1	−69 42	A0	α Gruis	1.7	22 07.9	−46 59	B5
ι Carinae	2.2	9 16.9	−59 15	F0	δ Cephei†	3.7	22 29.0	+58 23	†
κ Velorum	2.6	9 21.9	−54 59	B3	β Gruis	2.1	22 42.3	−46 55	M3
α Hydrae *Alphard*	2.0	9 27.3	− 8 38	K2	α PsA *Fomalhaut*	1.2	22 57.3	−29 39	A3
α Leonis *Regulus*	1.3	10 08.1	+12 00	B8	β Pegasi *Scheat*	2.4	23 03.5	+28 03	M0
γ Leonis *Algeiba*	1.9	10 19.7	+19 52	K0	α Pegasi *Markab*	2.5	23 04.5	+15 11	A0
β Ursae Majoris *Merak*	2.4	11 01.5	+56 25	A0					
α Ursae Majoris *Dubhe*	1.8	11 03.4	+61 47	K0					
δ Leonis	2.6	11 13.8	+20 33	A3					
β Leonis *Denebola*	2.1	11 48.8	+14 36	A2					
γ Ursae Majoris *Phecda*	2.4	11 53.5	+53 44	A0					

*γ Cassiopeiae, 1993 mag. 2.5. β Persei, mag. 2.1 to 3.4.
α Orionis, mag. 0.1 to 1.2.
†α Herculis, mag. 3.1 to 3.9. δ Cephei, mag. 3.7 to 4.4,
Spectrum F5 to G0.

The positions of heavenly bodies on the celestial sphere are defined by two co-ordinates, right ascension and declination, which are analogous to longitude and latitude on the surface of the Earth. If we imagine the plane of the terrestrial equator extended indefinitely, it will cut the celestial sphere in a great circle known as the celestial equator. Similarly the plane of the Earth's orbit, when extended, cuts in the great circle called the ecliptic. The two intersections of these circles are known as the First Point of Aries and the First Point of Libra. If from any star a perpendicular be drawn to the celestial equator, the length of this perpendicular is the star's declination. The arc, measured eastwards along the equator from the First Point of Aries to the foot of this perpendicular, is the right ascension. An alternative definition of right ascension is that it is the angle at the celestial pole (where the Earth's axis, if prolonged, would meet the sphere) between the great circles to the First Point of Aries and to the star.

The plane of the Earth's equator has a slow movement, so that our reference system for right ascension and declination is not fixed. The consequent alteration in these quantities from year to year is called precession. In right ascension it is an increase of about 3s a year for equatorial stars, and larger or smaller changes in either direction for stars near the poles, depending on the right ascension of the star. In declination it varies between $+20''$ and $-20''$ according to the right ascension of the star.

A star or other body crosses the meridian when the sidereal time is equal to its right ascension. The altitude is then a maximum, and may be deduced by remembering that the altitude of the elevated pole is numerically equal to the latitude, while that of the equator at its intersection with the meridian is equal to the co-latitude, or complement of the latitude.

Thus in London (lat. 51° 30′) the meridian altitude of Sirius is found as follows:

	°	′
Altitude of equator	38	30
Declination south	16	43
Difference	21	47

The altitude of Capella (Dec. $+45°\ 59'$) at lower transit is:

	°	′
Altitude of pole	51	30
Polar distance of star	44	00
Difference	7	30

The brightness of a heavenly body is denoted by its magnitude. Omitting the exceptionally bright stars Sirius and Canopus, the twenty brightest stars are of the first magnitude, while the faintest stars visible to the naked eye are of the sixth magnitude. The magnitude scale is a precise one, as a difference of five magnitudes represents a ratio of 100 to 1 in brightness. Typical second magnitude stars are Polaris and the stars in the belt of Orion. The scale is most easily fixed in memory by comparing the stars with Norton's *Star Atlas* (*see* page 71). The stars Sirius and Canopus and the planets Venus and Jupiter are so bright that their magnitudes are expressed by negative numbers. A small telescope will show stars down to the ninth or tenth magnitude, while stars fainter than the twentieth magnitude may be photographed by long exposures with the largest telescopes.

MEAN AND SIDEREAL TIME

Acceleration					Retardation				
h	m s	m s	s		h	m s	m s	s	
1	0 10	0 00	0		1	0 10	0 00	0	
2	0 20	3 02	1		2	0 20	3 03	1	
3	0 30	9 07	2		3	0 29	9 09	2	
4	0 39	15 13	3		4	0 39	15 15	3	
5	0 49	21 18	4		5	0 49	21 21	4	
6	0 59	27 23	5		6	0 59	27 28	5	
7	1 09	33 28	6		7	1 09	33 34	6	
8	1 19	39 34	7		8	1 19	39 40	7	
9	1 29	45 39	8		9	1 28	45 46	8	
10	1 39	51 44	9		10	1 38	51 53	9	
11	1 48	57 49	10		11	1 48	57 59	10	
12	1 58	60 00			12	1 58	60 00		
13	2 08				13	2 08			
14	2 18				14	2 18			
15	2 28				15	2 27			
16	2 38				16	2 37			
17	2 48				17	2 47			
18	2 57				18	2 57			
19	3 07				19	3 07			
20	3 17				20	3 17			
21	3 27				21	3 26			
22	3 37				22	3 36			
23	3 47				23	3 46			
24	3 57				24	3 56			

The length of a sidereal day in mean time is 23h 56m 04s.09. Hence 1h MT = 1h + 9s.86 ST and 1h ST = 1h − 9s.83 MT.

To convert an interval of mean time to the corresponding interval of sidereal time, enter the acceleration table with the given mean time (taking the hours and the minutes and seconds separately) and add the acceleration obtained to the given mean time. To convert an interval of sidereal time to the corresponding interval of mean time, take out the retardation for the given sidereal time and subtract.

The columns for the minutes and seconds of the argument are in the form known as critical tables. To use these tables, find in the appropriate left-hand column the two entries between which the given number of minutes and seconds lies; the quantity in the right-hand column between these two entries is the required acceleration or retardation. Thus the acceleration for 11m 26s (which lies between the entries 9m 07s and 15m 13s) is 2s. If the given number of minutes and seconds is a tabular entry, the required acceleration or retardation is the entry in the right-hand column above the given tabular entry, e.g. the retardation for 45m 46s is 7s.

Example – Convert 14h 27m 35s from ST to MT

	h	m	s
Given ST	14	27	35
Retardation for 14h		2	18
Retardation for 27m 35s			5
Corresponding MT	14	25	12

For further explanation, *see* pages 73–4.

ECLIPSES AND SHADOW TRANSITS OF JUPITER'S SATELLITES 1994

GMT	Sat.	Phen.
d h m		
JANUARY		
3 05 50	I	Ec.D.
3 06 19	II	Sh.E.
4 05 13	I	Sh.E.
10 04 17	III	Ec.D.
10 06 32	I	Sh.I.
10 06 33	III	Ec.R.
10 07 43	I	Ec.D.
11 04 57	I	Sh.I.
11 07 06	I	Sh.E.
18 06 50	I	Sh.I.
19 03 39	II	Ec.D.
19 04 04	I	Ec.D.
19 06 02	II	Ec.R.
20 03 28	I	Sh.E.
26 05 57	I	Ec.D.
26 06 15	II	Ec.D.
27 03 12	I	Sh.I.
27 05 22	I	Sh.E.
28 03 13	II	Sh.E.
28 04 17	III	Sh.E.
FEBRUARY		
3 05 06	I	Sh.I.
3 07 15	I	Sh.E.
4 03 26	II	Sh.I.
4 05 46	II	Sh.E.
4 06 03	III	Sh.I.
10 06 59	I	Sh.I.
11 04 11	I	Ec.D.
11 05 59	I	Sh.I.
12 03 37	I	Sh.E.
13 03 07	II	Ec.R.
15 02 17	III	Ec.R.
18 06 03	I	Ec.D.
19 03 21	I	Sh.I.
19 05 30	I	Sh.E.
20 03 20	II	Ec.D.
20 05 43	II	Ec.R.
22 04 01	III	Ec.D.
22 06 13	III	Ec.R.
26 05 14	I	Sh.I.
27 02 24	I	Ec.D.
27 05 56	II	Ec.D.
28 01 52	I	Sh.E.
MARCH		
1 02 40	II	Sh.E.
6 04 17	I	Ec.D.
7 01 36	I	Sh.I.
7 03 45	I	Sh.E.
8 02 53	II	Sh.I.
8 05 13	II	Sh.E.
12 01 51	III	Sh.I.
12 04 00	III	Sh.E.
13 06 10	I	Ec.D.
14 03 29	I	Sh.I.
14 05 39	I	Sh.E.
15 00 39	I	Ec.D.
15 05 26	I	Sh.I.
16 00 07	I	Sh.E.
17 00 24	II	Ec.D.
19 05 49	III	Sh.I.
21 05 23	I	Sh.I.
22 02 32	I	Ec.D.
22 23 51	I	Sh.I.
23 02 01	I	Sh.E.
24 03 00	II	Ec.D.
25 23 36	II	Sh.E.
29 04 25	I	Ec.D.
29 23 49	III	Ec.D.
30 01 45	I	Sh.I.
30 01 58	III	Ec.R.
30 03 55	I	Sh.E.
30 22 53	I	Ec.D.
31 05 35	II	Ec.D.
APRIL		
1 23 49	II	Sh.I.
2 02 10	II	Sh.E.
6 03 38	I	Sh.I.
6 03 46	III	Ec.D.
7 00 47	I	Ec.D.
7 22 07	I	Sh.I.
8 00 17	I	Sh.E.
9 02 23	II	Sh.I.
9 04 44	II	Sh.E.
14 02 40	I	Ec.D.
15 00 00	I	Sh.I.
15 02 11	I	Sh.E.
16 04 57	II	Sh.I.
16 21 41	III	Sh.I.
16 23 48	III	Sh.E.
18 00 04	II	Ec.D.
21 04 34	I	Ec.D.
22 01 54	I	Sh.I.
22 04 04	I	Sh.E.
22 23 02	I	Ec.D.
23 22 33	I	Sh.E.
24 01 40	III	Sh.I.
24 03 46	III	Sh.E.
25 02 40	II	Ec.D.
26 20 49	II	Sh.I.
26 23 10	II	Sh.E.
29 03 48	I	Sh.I.
30 00 56	I	Ec.D.
30 03 06	I	Ec.R.
30 22 17	I	Sh.I.
MAY		
1 00 27	I	Sh.E.
1 21 35	I	Ec.R.
3 23 23	II	Sh.I.
4 01 45	II	Sh.E.
4 21 46	III	Ec.R.
5 20 54	II	Ec.R.
8 00 11	I	Sh.I.
8 02 21	I	Sh.E.
8 23 29	I	Ec.R.
9 20 50	I	Sh.E.
11 01 58	II	Sh.I.
12 01 44	III	Ec.R.
12 23 30	II	Ec.R.
15 02 05	I	Sh.I.
16 01 23	I	Ec.R.

GMT	Sat.	Phen.
16 20 34	I	Sh.I.
16 22 44	I	Sh.E.
20 02 05	II	Ec.R.
23 22 28	I	Sh.I.
24 00 38	I	Sh.E.
24 21 46	I	Ec.R.
28 22 49	II	Sh.E.
29 21 33	III	Sh.I.
29 23 36	III	Sh.I.
31 00 23	I	Sh.I.
31 23 41	I	Ec.R.
JUNE		
1 21 01	I	Sh.E.
4 23 04	II	Sh.I.
5 01 25	II	Sh.E.
6 01 31	III	Sh.I.
8 22 55	I	Sh.E.
13 23 08	II	Ec.R.
15 22 40	I	Sh.I.
16 00 49	I	Sh.E.
16 21 36	III	Ec.R.
16 21 59	I	Ec.R.
23 23 31	III	Ec.D.
23 23 54	I	Ec.R.
24 21 13	I	Sh.E.
29 22 33	II	Sh.E.
JULY		
1 23 07	I	Sh.E.
6 22 48	II	Sh.I.
8 22 53	I	Sh.I.
9 22 13	I	Ec.R.
11 21 26	III	Sh.I.
15 22 46	II	Ec.R.
17 21 25	I	Sh.E.
24 21 11	I	Sh.I.
29 21 30	III	Ec.R.
AUGUST		
16 20 00	II	Ec.D.
17 20 47	I	Ec.R.

Jupiter's satellites transit across the disk from east to west, and pass behind the disk from west to east. The shadows that they cast also transit across the disk. With the exception at times of Satellite IV, the satellites also pass through the shadow of the planet, i.e. they are eclipsed. Just before opposition the satellite disappears in the shadow to the west of the planet and reappears from occultation on the east limb. Immediately after opposition the satellite is occulted at the west limb and reappears from eclipse to the east of the planet. At times approximately two to four months before and after opposition, both phases of eclipses of Satellite III may be seen. When Satellite IV is eclipsed, both phases may be seen.

The times given refer to the centre of the satellite. As the satellite is of considerable size, the immersion and emersion phases are not instantaneous. Even when the satellite enters or leaves the shadow along a radius of the shadow, the phase can last for several minutes. With satellite IV, grazing phenomena can occur so that the light from the satellite may fade and brighten again without a complete eclipse taking place.

The list of phenomena gives most of the eclipses and shadow transits visible in the British Isles under favourable conditions.

Ec. = Eclipse	R. = Reappearance	
Sh. = Shadow transit	I. = Ingress	
D. = Disappearance	E. = Egress	

EXPLANATION OF ASTRONOMICAL DATA

Positions of the heavenly bodies are given only to the degree of accuracy required by amateur astronomers for setting telescopes, or for plotting on celestial globes or star atlases. Where intermediate positions are required, linear interpolation may be employed.

Definitions of the terms used cannot be given here. They must be sought in astronomical literature and textbooks. Probably the best source for the amateur is Norton's *Star Atlas and Reference Handbook* (Longman, 18th edition, 1989; £18.99), which contains an introduction to observational astronomy, and a series of star maps for showing stars visible to the naked eye. Certain more extended ephemerides are available in the British Astronomical Association Handbook, an annual popular among amateur astronomers. (Secretary: Burlington House, Piccadilly, London, wiv 9AG)

A special feature has been made of the times when the various heavenly bodies are visible in the British Isles. Since two columns, calculated for latitudes 52° and 56°, are devoted to risings and settings, the range 50° to 58° can be covered by interpolation and extrapolation. The times given in these columns are Greenwich Mean Times for the meridian of Greenwich. An observer west of this meridian must add his/her longitude (in time) and vice versa.

In accordance with the usual convention in astronomy, + and − indicate respectively north and south latitudes or declinations.

All data are, unless otherwise stated, for oh Greenwich Mean Time (GMT), i.e. at the midnight at the beginning of the day named.

PAGE ONE OF EACH MONTH

The calendar for each month is explained on page 15.

Under the heading Astronomical Phenomena will be found particulars of the more important conjunctions of the Sun, Moon and planets with each other, and also the dates of other astronomical phenomena of special interest.

The Constellations listed each month are those that are near the meridian at the beginning of the month at 22h local mean time. Allowance must be made for British Summer Time if necessary. The fact that any star crosses the meridian 4m earlier each night or 2h earlier each month may be used, in conjunction with the lists given each month, to find what constellations are favourably placed at any moment. The table preceding the list of constellations may be extended indefinitely at the rate just quoted.

Times of Minima of Algol are approximate times of the middle of the period of diminished light.

The principal phases of the Moon are the GMTs when the difference between the longitude of the Moon and that of the Sun is 0°, 90°, 180° or 270°. The times of perigee and apogee are those when the Moon is nearest to, and farthest from, the Earth, respectively. The nodes or points of intersection of the Moon's orbit and the ecliptic make a complete retrograde circuit of the ecliptic in about 19 years. From a knowledge of the longitude of the ascending node and the inclination, whose value does not vary much from 5°, the path of the Moon among the stars may be plotted on a celestial globe or star atlas.

PAGE TWO OF EACH MONTH

The Sun's semi-diameter, in arc, is given once a month.

The right ascension and declination (Dec.) is that of the true Sun. The right ascension of the mean Sun is obtained by applying the equation of time, with the sign given, to the right ascension of the true Sun, or, more easily, by applying

12h to the column Sidereal Time. The direction in which the equation of time has to be applied in different problems is a frequent source of confusion and error. Apparent Solar Time is equal to the Mean Solar Time plus the Equation of Time. For example at noon on August 8 the Equation of Time is −5m 38s and thus at 12h Mean Time on that day the Apparent Time is 12h − 5m 38s = 11h 54m 22s.

The Greenwich Sidereal Time at oh and the Transit of the First Point of Aries (which is really the mean time when the sidereal time is oh) are used for converting mean time to sidereal time and vice versa.

The GMT of transit of the Sun at Greenwich may also be taken as the local mean time (LMT) of transit in any longitude. It is independent of latitude. The GMT of transit in any longitude is obtained by adding the longitude to the time given if west, and vice versa.

LIGHTING-UP TIME

The legal importance of Sunrise and Sunset is that the Road Vehicles Lighting Regulations 1989 (SI 1989 No. 1796) make the use of front and rear position lamps on vehicles compulsory during the period between sunset and sunrise. Headlamps on vehicles are required to be used during the hours of darkness on unlit roads or whenever visibility is seriously reduced. The hours of darkness are defined in these regulations as the period between half an hour after sunset and half an hour before sunrise.

In all laws and regulations 'sunset' refers to the local sunset, i.e. the time at which the Sun sets at the place in question. This common-sense interpretation has been upheld by legal tribunals. Thus the necessity for providing for different latitudes and longitudes, as already described, is evident.

SUNRISE AND SUNSET

The times of Sunrise and Sunset are those when the Sun's upper limb, as affected by refraction, is on the true horizon of an observer at sea-level. Assuming the mean refraction to be 34′, and the Sun's semi-diameter to be 16′, the time given is that when the true zenith distance of the Sun's centre is 90° + 34′ + 16′ or 90° 50′, or, in other words, when the depression of the Sun's centre below the true horizon is 50′. The upper limb is then 34′ below the true horizon, but is brought there by refraction. It is true, of course, that an observer on a ship might see the Sun for a minute or so longer, because of the dip of the horizon, while another viewing the sunset over hills or mountains would record an earlier time. Nevertheless, the moment when the true zenith distance of the Sun's centre is 90° 50′ is a precise time dependent only on the latitude and longitude of the place, and independent of its altitude above sea-level, the contour of its horizon, the vagaries of refraction or the small seasonal change in the Sun's semi-diameter; this moment is suitable in every way as a definition of sunset (or sunrise) for all statutory purposes. (For further information, *see* footnote.)

SUNRISE, SUNSET AND MOONRISE, MOONSET

The tables have been constructed for the meridian of Greenwich, and for latitudes 52° and 56°. They give Greenwich Mean Time (GMT) throughout the year. To obtain the GMT of the phenomenon as seen from any other latitude and longitude in the British Isles, first interpolate or extrapolate for latitude by the usual rules of proportion. To the time thus found, the longitude (expressed in time) is to be added if west (as it usually is in Great Britain) or subtracted if east. If the longitude is expressed in degrees and minutes of arc, it must be converted to time at the rate of 1° = 4m and 15′ = 1m.

A method of calculating rise and set times for other places in the world is given on pages 64 and 65.

TWILIGHT

Light reaches us before sunrise and continues to reach us for some time after sunset. The interval between darkness and sunrise or sunset and darkness is called twilight. Astronomically speaking, twilight is considered to begin or end when the Sun's centre is 18° below the horizon, as no light from the Sun can then reach the observer. As thus defined, twilight may last several hours; in high latitudes at the summer solstice the depression of 18° is not reached, and twilight lasts from sunset to sunrise.

The need for some sub-division of twilight is met by dividing the gathering darkness into four steps.

(1) *Sunrise or Sunset*, defined as above.
(2) *Civil twilight*, which begins or ends when the Sun's centre is 6° below the horizon. This marks the time when operations requiring daylight may commence or must cease. In England it varies from about 30 to 60 minutes after sunset and the same interval before sunrise.
(3) *Nautical twilight*, which begins or ends when the Sun's centre is 12° below the horizon. This marks the time when it is, to all intents and purposes, completely dark.
(4) *Astronomical twilight*, which begins or ends when the Sun's centre is 18° below the horizon. This marks theoretical perfect darkness. It is of little practical importance, especially if nautical twilight is tabulated.

To assist observers the durations of civil, nautical and astronomical twilights are given at intervals of ten days. The beginning of a particular twilight is found by subtracting the duration from the time of sunrise, while the end is found by adding the duration to the time of sunset. Thus the beginning of astronomical twilight in latitude 52°, on the Greenwich meridian, on March 11 is found as 06h 24m − 113m = 04h 31m and similarly the end of civil twilight as 17h 57m + 34m = 18h 31m.

The letters TAN (twilight all night) are printed when twilight lasts all night.

Under the heading The Night Sky will be found notes describing the position and visibility of all the planets and also of other phenomena.

PAGE THREE OF EACH MONTH

The Moon moves so rapidly among the stars that its position is given only to the degree of accuracy that permits linear interpolation. The right ascension (RA) and declination (Dec.) are geocentric, i.e. for an imaginary observer at the centre of the Earth. To an observer on the surface of the Earth the position is always different, as the altitude is always less on account of parallax, which may reach 1°.

The lunar terminator is the line separating the bright from the dark part of the Moon's disk. Apart from irregularities of the lunar surface, the terminator is elliptical, because it is a circle seen in projection. It becomes the full circle forming the limb, or edge, of the Moon at New and Full Moon. The selenographic longitude of the terminator is measured from the mean centre of the visible disk, which may differ from the visible centre by as much as 8°, because of libration.

Instead of the longitude of the terminator the Sun's selenographic co-longitude (Sun's co-long.) is tabulated. It is numerically equal to the selenographic longitude of the morning terminator, measured eastwards from the mean centre of the disk. Thus its value is approximately 270° at New Moon, 360° at First Quarter, 90° at Full Moon and 180° at Last Quarter.

The Position Angle (PA) of the Bright Limb is the position angle of the midpoint of the illuminated limb, measured eastwards from the north point on the disk. The column Phase shows the percentage of the area of the Moon's disk

illuminated; this is also the illuminated percentage of the diameter at right angles to the line of cusps. The terminator is a semi-ellipse whose major axis is the line of cusps, and whose semi-minor axis is determined by the tabulated percentage; from New Moon to Full Moon the east limb is dark, and vice versa.

The times given as moonrise and moonset are those when the upper limb of the Moon is on the horizon of an observer at sea-level. The Sun's horizontal parallax (Hor. par.) is about 9″, and is negligible when considering sunrise and sunset, but that of the Moon averages about 57′. Hence the computed time represents the moment when the true zenith distance of the Moon is 90° 50′ (as for the Sun) minus the horizontal parallax. The time required for the Sun or Moon to rise or set is about four minutes (except in high latitudes). *See also* page 65 and footnote on page 71.)

The GMT of transit of the Moon over the meridian of Greenwich is given; these times are independent of latitude, but must be corrected for longitude. For places in the British Isles it suffices to add the longitude if west, and vice versa. For more remote places a further correction is necessary because of the rapid movement of the Moon relative to the stars. The entire correction is conveniently determined by first finding the west longitude λ of the place. If the place is in west longitude, λ is the ordinary west longitude; if the place is in east longitude λ is the complement to 24h (or 360°) of the longitude and will be greater than 12h (or 180°). The correction then consists of two positive portions, namely λ and the fraction $\lambda/24$ (or $\lambda°/360$) multiplied by the difference between consecutive transits. Thus for Sydney, New South Wales, the longitude is 10h 05m east, so $\lambda = 13$h 55m and the fraction $\lambda/24$ is 0.58. The transit on the local date 1994 January 4 is found as follows:

		d	h	m
GMT of transit at Greenwich	Jan.	3	04	21
λ			13	55
0.58 × (5h 11m − 4h 21m)				29
GMT of transit at Sydney		3	18	25
Corr. to NSW Standard Time			10	00
Local standard time of transit		4	04	25

As is evident, for any given place the quantities λ and the correction to local standard time may be combined permanently, being here 23h 55m.

Positions of Mercury are given for every second day, and those of Venus and Mars for every fifth day; they may be interpolated linearly. The diameter (Diam.) is given in seconds of arc. The phase is the illuminated percentage of the disk. In the case of the inner planets this approaches 100 at superior conjunction and 0 at inferior conjunction. When the phase is less than 50 the planet is crescent-shaped or horned; for greater phases it is gibbous. In the case of the exterior planet Mars, the phase approaches 100 at conjunction and opposition, and is a minimum at the quadratures.

Since the planets cannot be seen when on the horizon, the actual times of rising and setting are not given; instead, the time when the planet has an apparent altitude of 5° has been tabulated. If the time of transit is between 00h and 12h the time refers to an altitude of 5° above the eastern horizon; if between 12h and 24h, to the western horizon. The phenomenon tabulated is the one that occurs between sunset and sunrise. The times given may be interpolated for latitude and corrected for longitude as in the case of the Sun and Moon.

The GMT at which the planet transits the Greenwich meridian is also given. The times of transit are to be corrected to local meridians in the usual way, as already described.

PAGE FOUR OF EACH MONTH

The GMTs of sunrise and sunset for seven towns, whose adopted positions in longitude (W.) and latitude (N.) are given immediately below the name, may be used not only for these phenomena, but also for lighting-up times, which, under the Road Vehicles Lighting Regulations 1989, are from sunset to sunrise throughout the year. (*See* page 71 for a fuller explanation.)

The particulars for the four outer planets resemble those for the planets on Page Three of each month, except that, under Uranus and Neptune, times when the planet is 10° high instead of 5° high are given; this is because of the inferior brightness of these planets. The diameters given for the rings of Saturn are those of the major axis (in the plane of the planet's equator) and the minor axis respectively. The former has a small seasonal change due to the slightly varying distance of the Earth from Saturn, but the latter varies from zero when the Earth passes through the ring plane every 15 years to its maximum opening half-way between these periods. The rings were open at their widest extent in 1988.

TIME

From the earliest ages, the natural division of time into recurring periods of day and night has provided the practical time-scale for the everyday activities of the human race. Indeed, if any alternative means of time measurement is adopted, it must be capable of adjustment so as to remain in general agreement with the natural time-scale defined by the diurnal rotation of the Earth on its axis. Ideally the rotation should be measured against a fixed frame of reference; in practice it must be measured against the background provided by the celestial bodies. If the Sun is chosen as the reference point, we obtain Apparent Solar Time, which is the time indicated by a sundial. It is not a uniform time but is subject to variations which amount to as much as a quarter of an hour in each direction. Such wide variations cannot be tolerated in a practical time-scale, and this has led to the concept of Mean Solar Time in which all the days are exactly the same length and equal to the average length of the Apparent Solar Day.

The positions of the stars in the sky are specified in relation to a fictitious reference point in the sky known as the First Point of Aries (or the Vernal Equinox). It is therefore convenient to adopt this same reference point when considering the rotation of the Earth against the background of the stars. The time-scale so obtained is known as Apparent Sidereal Time.

GREENWICH MEAN TIME

The daily rotation of the Earth on its axis causes the Sun and the other heavenly bodies to appear to cross the sky from east to west. It is convenient to represent this relative motion as if the Sun really performed a daily circuit around a fixed Earth. Noon in Apparent Solar Time may then be defined as the time at which the Sun transits across the observer's meridian. In Mean Solar Time, noon is similarly defined by the meridian transit of a fictitious Mean Sun moving uniformly in the sky with the same average speed as the true Sun. Mean Solar Time observed on the meridian of the transit circle telescope of the Old Royal Observatory at Greenwich is called Greenwich Mean Time (GMT). The mean solar day is divided into 24 hours and, for astronomical and other scientific purposes, these are numbered 0 to 23, commencing at midnight. Civil time is usually reckoned in two periods of 12 hours, designated a.m. (*ante meridiem*, i.e. before noon) and p.m. (*post meridiem*, i.e. after noon).

UNIVERSAL TIME

Before 1925 January 1, GMT was reckoned in 24 hours commencing at noon; since that date it has been reckoned from midnight. In view of the risk of confusion in the use of the designation GMT before and after 1925, the International Astronomical Union recommended in 1928 that astronomers should employ the term Universal Time (UT) or Weltzeit (WZ) to denote GMT measured from Greenwich Mean Midnight.

In precision work it is necessary to take account of small variations in Universal Time. These arise from small irregularities in the rotation of the Earth. Observed astronomical time is designated UT0. Observed time corrected for the effects of the motion of the poles (giving rise to a 'wandering' in longitude) is designated UT1. There is also a seasonal fluctuation in the rate of rotation of the Earth arising from meteorological causes, often called the annual fluctuation. UT1 corrected for this effect is designated UT2 and provides a time-scale free from short-period fluctuations. It is still subject to small secular and irregular changes.

APPARENT SOLAR TIME

As has been mentioned above, the time shown by a sundial is called Apparent Solar Time. It differs from Mean Solar Time by an amount known as the Equation of Time, which is the total effect of two causes which make the length of the apparent solar day non-uniform. One cause of variation is that the orbit of the Earth is not a circle, but an ellipse, having the Sun at one focus. As a consequence, the angular speed of the Earth in its orbit is not constant; it is greatest at the beginning of January when the Earth is nearest the Sun.

The other cause is due to the obliquity of the ecliptic; the plane of the equator (which is at right angles to the axis of rotation of the Earth) does not coincide with the ecliptic (the plane defined by the apparent annual motion of the Sun around the celestial sphere) but is inclined to it at an angle of 23° 26'. As a result, the apparent solar day is shorter than average at the equinoxes and longer at the solstices. From the combined effects of the components due to obliquity and eccentricity, the equation of time reaches its maximum values in February (-14 minutes) and early November ($+16$ minutes). It has a zero value on four dates during the year, and it is only on these dates (approximately April 15, June 14, September 1, and December 25) that a sundial shows Mean Solar Time.

SIDEREAL TIME

A sidereal day is the duration of a complete rotation of the Earth with reference to the First Point of Aries. The term sidereal (or 'star') time is perhaps a little misleading since the time-scale so defined is not exactly the same as that which would be defined by successive transits of a selected star, as there is a small progressive motion between the stars and the First Point of Aries due to the precession of the Earth's axis. This makes the length of the sidereal day shorter than the true period of rotation by 0.008 seconds. Superimposed on this steady precessional motion are small oscillations called nutation, giving rise to fluctuations in apparent sidereal time amounting to as much as 1.2 seconds. It is therefore customary to employ Mean Sidereal Time, from which these fluctuations have been removed. The conversion of GMT to Greenwich sidereal time (GST) may be performed by adding the value of the GST at 0h on the day in question (Page Two of each month) to the GMT converted to sidereal time using the table on page 69.

Example – To find the GST at August 8d 02h 41m 11s GMT

	h	m	s
GST at 0h	21	05	06
GMT	2	41	11
Acceleration for 2h			20
Acceleration for 41m 11s			7
Sum = GST =	23	46	44

If the observer is not on the Greenwich meridian then his/her longitude, measured positively westwards from Greenwich, must be subtracted from the GST to obtain Local Sidereal Time (LST). Thus, in the above example, an observer 5h east of Greenwich, or 19h west, would find the LST as 4h 46m 44s.

EPHEMERIS TIME

In the study of the motions of the Sun, Moon and planets, observations taken over an extended period are used in the preparation of tables giving the apparent position of the body each day. A table of this sort is known as an ephemeris, and may be used in the comparison of current observations with tabulated positions. A detailed examination of the observations made over the past 300 years shows that the Sun, Moon and planets appear to depart from their predicted positions by amounts proportional to their mean motions. The only satisfactory explanation is that the time-scale to which the observations were referred was not as uniform as had been supposed. Since the time-scale was based on the rotation of the Earth, it follows that this rotation is subject to irregularities. The fact that the discrepancies between the observed and ephemeris positions were proportional to the mean motions of the bodies made it possible to secure agreement by substituting a revised time-scale and recomputing the ephemeris positions. The time-scale which brings the ephemeris into agreement with the observations is known as Ephemeris Time (ET).

The second of ET is defined in terms of the annual motion of the Earth in its orbit around the Sun (1/31556925.9747 of the tropical year for 1900 January 0d 12h ET). The precise determination of ET from astronomical observations is a lengthy process, as the accuracy with which a single observation of the Sun can be made is far less than that obtainable in, for instance, a comparison between clocks. It is therefore necessary to average the observations over an extended period. Largely on account of its faster motion, the position of the Moon may be observed with greater accuracy, and a close approximation to Ephemeris Time may be obtained by comparing observations of the Moon with its ephemeris position. Even in this case, however, the requisite standard of accuracy can only be achieved by averaging over a number of years.

In 1976 the International Astronomical Union adopted a new dynamical time-scale for general use whose scale unit is the SI second (see under Atomic Time). ET is now of little more than historical interest.

ATOMIC TIME

The fundamental standards of time and frequency must be defined in terms of a periodic motion adequately uniform, enduring and measurable. Progress has made it possible to use natural standards, such as atomic or molecular oscillations. Continuous oscillations are generated in an electrical circuit, the frequency of which is then compared or brought into coincidence with the frequency characteristic of the absorption or emission by the atoms or molecules when they change between two selected energy levels. The National Physical Laboratory routinely uses clocks of high stability produced by locking a quartz oscillator to the frequency defined by a caesium atomic beam.

International Atomic Time (TAI), established through international collaboration, is formed by combining the readings of many caesium clocks and was set close to the astronomically-based Universal Time (UT) near the beginning of 1958. It was formally recognized in 1971 and since 1988 January 1 has been maintained by the International Bureau of Weights and Measures (BIPM). The second markers are generated according to the SI definition of the second adopted in 1967 at the 13th General Conference of Weights and Measures: 'The second is the duration of 9 192 631 770 periods of the radiation corresponding to the transition between the two hyperfine levels of the ground state of the caesium-133 atom.'

Civil time in almost all countries is now based on Co-ordinated Universal Time (UTC), which differs from TAI by an integer number of seconds (determined from studies of the rate of rotation of the Earth) so that UTC does not depart from UT by more than 0.9s. UTC was designed to make both atomic time and UT accessible with accuracies appropriate for most users.

RADIO TIME-SIGNALS

UTC is made generally available through time-signals and standard frequency broadcasts such as MSF in the UK, CHU in Canada and WWV and WWVH in the USA. These are based on national time-scales that are maintained in close agreement with UTC and provide traceability to the national time-scale and to UTC. The markers of seconds in the UTC scale coincide with those of TAI.

As the rate of rotation of the Earth is variable, the time-signals are adjusted by the introduction of a leap second when necessary in order that UTC shall not depart from UT by more than 0.9s. For convenience, leap seconds are introduced when necessary on the last second of the third, sixth, ninth or twelfth month, but preferably on December 31 and/or June 30. In the case of a positive leap second, 23h 59m 60s is followed one second later by 0h 0m 00s of the first day of the month. In the case of a negative leap second, 23h 59m 58s is followed one second later by 0h 0m 00s of the first day of the month. Notices concerning the insertion of leap seconds in UTC are issued by the International Earth Rotation Service at the Observatoire de Paris.

To disseminate the national time-scale in the UK, special signals are broadcast on behalf of the National Physical Laboratory from the BT (British Telecom) radio station at Rugby. The signals are controlled from a caesium beam atomic frequency standard and consist of a standard frequency carrier of 60 kHz (MSF) which switches off for half a second to denote the passing of one minute, and for a tenth of a second to denote the passing of one second. Also transmitted are two binary coded decimal (BCD) time codes giving time of day and calendar information. Summer and winter time changes are encoded on instruction from the British Government. Other broadcast signals in the UK include the BBC six pips signal, the BT Speaking Clock and a coded time-signal on the BBC 198 kHz Droitwich transmitter, which is used for timing in the electricity supply industry. From 1972 January 1 the six pips on the BBC have consisted of five short pips from second 55 to second 59 followed by one lengthened pip, the start of which indicates the exact minute. From 1990 February 5 these signals have been controlled by the BBC with respect to the broadcast MSF signal and are thus traceable to the National Physical Laboratory. Formerly they were generated by the Royal Greenwich Observatory. The BT Speaking Clock is connected to the National Physical Laboratory caesium beam atomic frequency standard at the Rugby radio station.

Accurate timing may also be obtained from the signals of

international navigation systems, such as the ground-based Loran-C or Omega, or satellite-based Global Positioning System (GPS) of the USA or the Russian GLONASS system.

STANDARD TIME

In the year 1880 it was enacted by statute that the word 'time', when it occurred in any legal document relating to Great Britain, was to be interpreted, unless otherwise specifically stated, as the mean time of the Greenwich meridian. Summer time is the legal time during the period in which its use is ordained.

Since the year 1883 the system of standard time by zones has been gradually accepted, and now throughout the world a standard time which differs from that of Greenwich by an integral number of hours, either fast or slow, is used. (For time zones of countries of the world, *see* Index.)

Variations from the standard time of some countries occur during part of the year; they are decided annually and are usually referred to as Summer Time or Daylight Saving Time.

The large territories of the United States and Canada are divided into zones approximately 7.5° on either side of central meridians.

At the 180th meridian the time can be either 12 hours fast on Greenwich Mean Time or 12 hours slow, and a change of date occurs. The internationally-recognized date or calendar line is a modification of the 180th meridian, drawn so as to include islands of any one group on the same side of the line, or for political reasons. The line is indicated by joining up the following co-ordinates:

Lat.	Long.	Lat.	Long.
60° S.	180°	48° N.	180°
51° S.	180°	53° N.	170° E.
45° S.	172.5° W.	65.5° N.	169° W.
15° S.	172.5° W.	75° N.	180°
5° S.	180°		

BRITISH SUMMER TIME

In 1916 an Act ordained that during a defined period of that year the legal time for general purposes in Great Britain should be one hour in advance of Greenwich Mean Time. The Summer Time Acts 1922 to 1925 defined the period during which Summer Time was to be in force, stabilizing practice until the Second World War.

During the war the duration of Summer Time was extended and in the years 1941–5 and in 1947 Double Summer Time (two hours in advance of Greenwich Mean Time) was in force. After the war, Summer Time was extended in each year from 1948–52 and 1961–4 by Order in Council.

Between 1968 October 27 and 1971 October 31 clocks were kept one hour ahead of Greenwich Mean Time throughout the year. This was known as British Standard Time, although Greenwich Mean Time remained the standard time of Great Britain.

The most recent legislation is the Summer Time Act 1972, which enacted that 'the period of summer time for the purposes of this Act is the period beginning at two o'clock, Greenwich mean time, in the morning of the day after the third Saturday in March or, if that day is Easter Day, the day after the second Saturday in March, and ending at two o'clock, Greenwich mean time, in the morning of the day after the fourth Saturday in October.'

The duration of Summer Time can be varied by Order in Council and in recent years alterations have been made to bring the operation of Summer Time in Britain closer to similar provisions in other countries of the European Community. The latest Order in Council is the Summer Time Order 1992, stipulating that the duration of Summer

Time in 1994 will be from March 27 to October 23. As in recent years, the hour of changeover will be 01h Greenwich Mean Time.

The duration of Summer Time in the following years was:

1990 March 25–October 28
1991 March 31–October 27
1992 March 29–October 25
1993 March 28–October 24
1994 March 27–October 23

MEAN REFRACTION

Alt.	Ref.		Alt.	Ref.		Alt.	Ref.	
° ′	′		° ′	′		° ′	′	
1 20		21	3 12		13	7 54		6
1 30		20	3 34		12	9 27		5
1 41		19	4 00		11	11 39		4
1 52		18	4 30		10	15 00		3
2 05		17	5 06		9	20 42		2
2 19		16	5 50		8	32 20		1
2 35		15	6 44		7	62 17		0
2 52		14	7 54			90 00		
3 12								

The refraction table is in the form of a critical table (*see* page 69)

ASTRONOMICAL CONSTANTS

Solar Parallax	8″.794
Astronomical unit	149597870 km
Precession for the year 1994	50″.289
Precession in Right Ascension	3s.075
Precession in Declination	20″.044
Constant of Nutation	9″.202
Constant of Aberration	20″.496
Mean Obliquity of Ecliptic (1994)	23° 26′ 24″
Moon's Equatorial Hor. Parallax	57′ 02″.70
Velocity of light in vacuo per second	299792.5 km
Solar motion per second	20.0 km
Equatorial radius of the Earth	6378.140 km
Polar radius of the Earth	6356.755 km
North Galactic Pole (IAU standard)	
RA 12h 49m (1950.0). Dec. 27°.4 N.	
Solar Apex	RA 18h 06m Dec. +30°

Length of Year (in mean solar days)

Tropical	365.24220
Sidereal	365.25636
Anomalistic	365.25964
(perihelion to perihelion)	
Eclipse	346.6200

Length of Month (mean values)	d	h	m	s
New Moon to New	29	12	44	02.9
Sidereal	27	07	43	11.5
Anomalistic	27	13	18	33.2
(perigee to perigee)				

ELEMENTS OF THE SOLAR SYSTEM

Orb	Mean distance from Sun (Earth=1)	km 10⁶	Sidereal period y	Sidereal period d	Synodic period days	Incl. of orbit to ecliptic ° ′	Diameter km	Mass (Earth=1)	Period of rotation on axis d h m
Sun	—	—	—	—	—	—	1,392,000	332,948	25 09
Mercury	0.39	58		88	116	7 00	4,880	0.055	59
Venus	0.72	108		225	584	3 24	12,100	0.815	243
Earth	1.00	150	1	0	—	—	12,756eq	1.00	23 56
Mars	1.52	228	1	322	780	1 51	6,790	0.107	24 37
Jupiter	5.20	778	11	315	399	1 18	{ 142,800eq 134,200p	318 {	9 50 9 56
Saturn	9.54	1427	29	167	378	2 29	{ 120,000eq 108,000p	95 {	10 14 10 38
Uranus	19.19	2870	84	6	370	0 46	52,000	14.6	16–28
Neptune	30.07	4497	164	288	367	1 46	48,400	17.2	18–20
Pluto	39.46	5950	247	255	367	17 09	2,445	0.01	6 09

eq equatorial, *p* polar

THE SATELLITES

Name	Star mag.	Mean distance from primary km	Sidereal period of revolution d
EARTH			
Moon	—	384,400	27.322
MARS			
Phobos	12	9,400	0.319
Deimos	13	23,500	1.262
JUPITER			
XVI Metis	17	128,000	0.295
XV Adrastea	19	129,000	0.298
V Amalthea	14	181,000	0.498
XIV Thebe	15	222,000	0.675
I Io	5	422,000	1.769
II Europa	5	671,000	3.551
III Ganymede	5	1,070,000	7.155
IV Callisto	6	1,880,000	16.689
XIII Leda	20	11,090,000	239
VI Himalia	15	11,480,000	251
X Lysithea	18	11,720,000	259
VII Elara	17	11,740,000	260
XII Ananke	19	21,200,000	631
XI Carme	18	22,600,000	692
VIII Pasiphae	18	23,500,000	735
IX Sinope	18	23,700,000	758
SATURN			
Pan	—	134,000	0.575
Atlas	18	138,000	0.602
Prometheus	16	139,000	0.613
Pandora	16	142,000	0.629
Epimetheus	15	151,000	0.694
Janus	14	151,000	0.695
Mimas	13	186,000	0.942
Enceladus	12	238,000	1.370
Tethys	10	295,000	1.888
Telesto	19	295,000	1.888
Calypso	18	295,000	1.888
Dione	10	377,000	2.737
Helene	18	377,000	2.737
Rhea	10	527,000	4.518
Titan	8	1,222,000	15.945

Name	Star mag.	Mean distance from primary km	Sidereal period of revolution d
SATURN			
Hyperion	14	1,481,000	21.278
Iapetus	11	3,561,000	79.331
Phoebe	16	12,952,000	550.3
URANUS			
Cordelia	—	49,800	0.330
Ophelia	—	53,800	0.372
Bianca	—	59,200	0.433
Juliet	—	61,800	0.464
Desdemona	—	62,700	0.474
Rosalind	—	64,400	0.493
Portia	—	66,100	0.513
Cressida	—	69,900	0.558
Belinda	—	75,300	0.622
Puck	—	86,000	0.762
Miranda	17	129,000	1.414
Ariel	14	191,000	2.520
Umbriel	15	266,000	4.144
Titania	14	436,000	8.706
Oberon	14	583,000	13.463
NEPTUNE			
Naiad	—	48,000	0.30
Thalassa	—	50,000	0.31
Despina	—	52,000	0.33
Galatea	—	62,000	0.43
Larissa	—	74,000	0.55
Proteus	—	118,000	1.12
Triton	14	355,000	5.877
Nereid	19	5,510,000	360.21
PLUTO			
Charon	17	19,600	6.387

THE EARTH

The shape of the Earth is that of an oblate spheroid or solid of revolution whose meridian sections are ellipses not differing much from circles, whilst the sections at right angles are circles. The length of the equatorial axis is about 12,756 kilometres, and that of the polar axis is 12,714 kilometres. The mean density of the Earth is 5.5 times that of water, although that of the surface layer is less. The Earth and Moon revolve about their common centre of gravity in a lunar month; this centre in turn revolves round the Sun in a plane known as the ecliptic, that passes through the Sun's centre. The Earth's equator is inclined to this plane at an angle of 23.4°. This tilt is the cause of the seasons. In mid-latitudes, and when the Sun is high above the Equator, not only does the high noon altitude make the days longer, but the Sun's rays fall more directly on the Earth's surface; these effects combine to produce summer. In equatorial regions the noon altitude is large throughout the year, and there is little variation in the length of the day. In higher latitudes the noon altitude is lower, and the days in summer are appreciably longer than those in winter.

The average velocity of the Earth in its orbit is 30 kilometres a second. It makes a complete rotation on its axis in about 23h 56m of mean time, which is the sidereal day. Because of its annual revolution round the Sun, the rotation with respect to the Sun, or the solar day, is more than this by about four minutes (*see* page 73). The extremity of the axis of rotation, or the North Pole of the Earth, is not rigidly fixed, but wanders over an area roughly 20 metres in diameter.

TERRESTRIAL MAGNETISM

A magnetic compass points along the horizontal component of a magnetic line of force. These directions converge on the 'magnetic dip-poles', the places where a freely suspended magnetized needle would become vertical. Not only do the positions of these poles change with time, but their exact locations are ill-defined, particularly so in the case of the north dip-pole where the lines of force on the north side of it, instead of converging radially, tend to bunch into a channel. Although it is therefore unrealistic to attempt to specify the locations of the dip-poles exactly, the present adopted positions are 78°.2 N., 103°.7 W. and 64°.8 S., 138°.8 E. The two magnetic dip-poles are thus not antipodal, the line joining them passing the centre of the Earth at a distance of about 1,200 kilometres. The distances of the magnetic dip-poles from the north and south geographical poles are about 1,400 and 2,700 kilometres respectively.

There is also a 'magnetic equator', at all points of which the vertical component of the Earth's magnetic field is zero and a magnetized needle remains horizontal. This line runs between 2° and 10° north of the geographical equator in the eastern hemisphere, turns sharply south off the West African coast, and crosses South America through Brazil, Bolivia and Peru; it recrosses the geographical equator in mid-Pacific.

Reference has already been made to secular changes in the Earth's field. The following table indicates the changes in magnetic declination (or variation of the compass). Similar, though much smaller, changes have occurred in 'dip' or magnetic inclination. Secular changes differ throughout the world. Although the London observations strongly suggest a cycle with a period of several hundred years, an exact repetition is unlikely.

London		Greenwich	
1580	11° 15′ E.	1850	22° 24′ W.
1622	5° 56′ E.	1900	16° 29′ W.
1665	1° 22′ W.	1925	13° 10′ W.
1730	13° 00′ W.	1950	9° 07′ W.
1773	21° 09′ W.	1975	6° 39′ W.

In order that up-to-date information on the variation of the compass may be available, many governments publish magnetic charts on which there are lines (isogonic lines) passing through all places at which specified values of declination will be found at the date of the chart.

In the British Isles, isogonic lines now run approximately north-east to south-west. Though there are considerable local deviations due to geological causes, a rough value of magnetic declination may be obtained by assuming that at 50° N. on the meridian of Greenwich, the value in 1994 is 3° 33′ west and allowing an increase of 12′ for each degree of latitude northwards and one of 22′ for each degree of longitude westwards. For example, at 53° N., 5° W., declination will be about 3° 33′ + 36′ + 110′, i.e. 5° 59′ west. The average annual change at the present time is about 8′ decrease.

The number of magnetic observatories is about 200, widely scattered over the globe. There are three in Great Britain run by the British Geological Survey: at Hartland, North Devon; at Eskdalemuir, Dumfriesshire; and at Lerwick, Shetland Islands. The following are some recent annual mean values of the magnetic elements for Hartland.

Year	Declination West	Dip or inclination	Horizontal force	Vertical force
	° ′	° ′	oersted	oersted
1955	10 30	66 49	0.1859	0.4340
1960	9 59	66 44	0.1871	0.4350
1965	9 30	66 34	0.1887	0.4354
1970	9 06	66 26	0.1903	0.4364
1975	8 32	66 17	0.1921	0.4373
1980	7 44	66 10	0.1933	0.4377
1985	6 56	66 08	0.1938	0.4380
1990	6 15	66 10	0.1939	0.4388
1992	6 00	66 09	0.1941	0.4392

The normal world-wide terrestrial magnetic field corresponds approximately to that of a very strong small bar magnet near the centre of the Earth but with appreciable smooth spatial departures. The origin and slow secular change of the normal field are not fully understood but are generally ascribed to electric currents associated with fluid motions in the Earth's core. Superimposed on the normal field are local and regional anomalies whose magnitudes may in places exceed that of the normal field; these are due to the influence of mineral deposits in the Earth's crust. A small proportion of the field is of external origin, mostly associated with electric currents in the ionosphere. The configuration of the external field and the ionization of the atmosphere depend on the incident particle and radiation flux from the Sun. There are, therefore, short-term and non-periodic as well as diurnal, 27-day, seasonal and 11-year periodic changes in the magnetic field, dependent upon the position of the Sun and the degree of solar activity.

MAGNETIC STORMS

Occasionally, sometimes with great suddenness, the Earth's magnetic field is subject for several hours to marked disturbance. During a very large storm in March 1989 the declination at Lerwick changed by almost 8° in less than an hour. In many instances, such disturbances are accompanied by widespread displays of aurorae, marked changes in the incidence of cosmic rays, an increase in the reception of 'noise' from the Sun at radio frequencies together with rapid changes in the ionosphere and induced electric currents within the Earth which adversely affect radio and telegraphic communications. The disturbances are caused by changes in the stream of neutral and ionized particles which emanates from the Sun and through which the Earth is continuously passing. Some of these changes are associated with visible eruptions on the Sun, usually in the region of sun-spots. There is a marked tendency for disturbances to recur after intervals of about 27 days, the apparent period of rotation of the Sun on its axis, which is consistent with the sources being located on particular areas of the Sun.

ARTIFICIAL SATELLITES

To consider the orbit of an artificial satellite, it is best to imagine that one is looking at the Earth from a distant point in space. The Earth would then be seen to be rotating about its axis inside the orbit described by the rapidly revolving satellite. The inclination of a satellite orbit to the Earth's equator (which generally remains almost constant throughout the satellite's lifetime) gives at once the maximum range of latitudes over which the satellite passes. Thus a satellite whose orbit has an inclination of 53° will pass overhead all latitudes between 53° S. and 53° N., but would never be seen in the zenith of any place nearer than these latitudes. If we consider a particular place on the earth, whose latitude is less than the inclination of the satellite's orbit, then the Earth's rotation carries this place first under the northbound part of the orbit and then under the southbound portion of the orbit, these two occurrences being always less than 12 hours apart for satellites moving in direct orbits (i.e. to the east). (For satellites in retrograde orbits, the words 'northbound' and 'southbound' should be interchanged in the preceding statement.) As the value of the latitude of the observer increases and approaches the value of the inclination of the orbit, so this interval gets shorter until (when the latitude is equal to the inclination) only one overhead passage occurs each day.

OBSERVATION OF SATELLITES

The regression of the orbit around the Earth causes alternate periods of visibility and invisibility, though this is of little concern to the radio or radar observer. To the visual observer the following cycle of events normally occurs (though the cycle may start in any position): invisibility, morning observations before dawn, invisibility, evening observations after dusk, invisibility, morning observations before dawn, and so on. With reasonably high satellites and for observers in high latitudes around the summer solstice, the evening observations follow the morning observations without inter-

ruption as sunlight passing over the polar regions can still illuminate satellites which are passing over temperate latitudes at local midnight. At the moment all satellites rely on sunlight to make them visible, though a satellite with a flashing light has been suggested for a future launching. The observer must be in darkness or twilight in order to make any useful observations and the durations of twilight and the sunrise, sunset times given on Page Two of each month will be a useful guide.

Some of the satellites are visible to the naked eye and much interest has been aroused by the spectacle of a bright satellite disappearing into the Earth's shadow. The event is even more fascinating telescopically as the disappearance occurs gradually as the satellite traverses the Earth's penumbral shadow, and during the last few seconds before the eclipse is complete the satellite may change colour (in suitable atmospheric conditions) from yellow to red. This is because the last rays of sunlight are refracted through the denser layers of our atmosphere before striking the satellite.

Some satellites rotate about one or more axes so that a periodic variation in brightness is observed. This was particularly noticeable in several of the Soviet satellites.

Satellite research has provided some interesting results. Among them may be mentioned a revised value of the Earth's oblateness, 1/298.2, and the discovery of the Van Allen radiation belts.

LAUNCHINGS

Apart from their names, e.g. Cosmos 6 Rocket, the satellites are also classified according to their date of launch. Thus 1961 α refers to the first satellite launching of 1961. A number following the Greek letter indicated the relative brightness of the satellites put in orbit. From the beginning of 1963 the Greek letters were replaced by numbers and the numbers by roman letters e.g. 1963–01A. For all satellites successfully injected into orbit the table gives the designation and names of the main objects (in the order A, B, C . . . etc.), the launch date and some initial orbital data. These are the inclination to the equator (i), the nodal period of revolution (P), the eccentricity (e), and the perigee height.

Although most of the satellites launched are injected into orbits less than 1,000 km high there are an increasing number of satellites in geostationary orbits, i.e. where the orbital inclination is zero, the eccentricity close to zero, and the period of revolution is 1436.1 minutes. Thus the satellite is permanently situated over the equator at one selected longitude at a mean height of 35,786 km. Already this geostationary band is crowded; for example, the television satellite Astra 1A (1988–109B) has been placed only 0°.2 away from the communication satellite Arabsat 1A (1985–15A).

ARTIFICIAL SATELLITE LAUNCHES 1992

Desig-nation	Satellite	Launch date	i	P	e	Perigee height
			°	m		km
1992–						
21	Telecom 2B, Inmarsat 2F-4	April 15	0.1	1436.0	0.000	35777
22	Progress-M 12, rocket	April 19	51.6	90.5	0.003	279
23	USA 81, rocket	April 25				
24	Resurs-F14, rocket	April 29	82.1	89.2	0.000	231
25	Cosmos 2185, rocket	April 29	70.0	89.4	0.005	211
26	STS 49, Intelsat 6F-3	May 7	28.3	91.4	0.001	344
27	Palapa 7, rocket	May 14	0.2	1436.1	0.000	35777

Desig- nation	Satellite	Launch date	i	P	e	Perigee height
1992–			°	m		km
28	SROSS-C, rocket	May 20	46.0	91.2	0.013	250
29	Cosmos 2186, rocket	May 28	62.8	89.8	0.013	182
30	Cosmos 2187–2194, rocket	June 3	74.0	114.7	0.005	1402
31	EUVE	June 7	30.2	92.4	0.018	282
32	Intelsat K	June 10	2.7	1100.5	0.195	22065
33	Resurs F-15. rocket, engine	June 23	82.3	89.1	0.000	226
34	STS 50	June 25	28.5	90.4	0.000	300
35	Progress M-13, rocket	June 30	51.6	90.9	0.002	309
36	Cosmos 2195, rocket	July 1	82.9	104.8	0.004	958
37	DSCS 3B-02, IABS-02	July 2				
38	SAMPEX	July 3	81.7	96.8	0.013	515
39	Navstar 2A-05, rocket	July 7	55.0	717.9	0.008	19960
40	Cosmos 2196, launcher rocket, launcher, rocket	July 8	62.9	717.1	0.737	590
41	Insat 2A, Eutelsat 2 F-4	July 9	0.2	1438.4	0.007	35537
42	Cosmos 2197–2202, rocket	July 13	82.6	114.0	0.001	1397
43	Gorizont 26, launcher	July 14	1.5	1435.7	0.000	35762
44	Geotail, rocket	July 24	28.6	12346.6	0.963	185
45	Cosmos 2203, rocket	July 24	62.8	89.5	0.009	190
46	Soyuz TM15, rocket	July 27	51.6	88.3	0.001	190
47	Cosmos 2204–2206	July 30	64.8	675.8	0.000	19121
48	Cosmos 2207, rocket, engine	July 30	82.3	90.5	0.009	237
49	STS 46, Eureca 1	July 31	28.5	88.9	0.001	228
50	Molniya 1–84, launcher rocket, launcher, rocket	August 6	62.8	717.7	0.736	632
51	China 35, rocket	August 9	63.1	89.7	0.013	172
52	Topex/Poseidon, Uribyol 1, S80/T	August 10	66.1	112.1	0.001	1317
53	Cosmos 2208, rocket	August 12	74.0	100.9	0.001	788
54	Optus B1, rocket	August 13	0.3	1436.0	0.003	35675
55	Progress M-14, rocket	August 15	51.6	90.9	0.005	288
56	Resurs-F 16, rocket, Pion 5, Pion 6, engine	August 19	82.6	89.1	0.001	221
57	Satcom C4, rocket	August 31	0.1	1430.2	0.005	35470
58	Navstar 2A-06, rocket	September 9	54.8	722.9	0.012	19980
59	Cosmos 2209, launcher	September 10	1.3	1435.9	0.001	35764
60	Hispasat 1A, Satcom 3C	September 10	0.0	1436.2	0.000	35783
61	STS 47	September 12	57.0	90.6	0.001	299
62	Cosmos 2210, rocket	September 22	67.2	89.8	0.013	175
63	Mars Observer	September 25	(interplanetary space probe)			
64	Freja, China 38, rocket	October 6	63.0	109.0	0.077	596
65	Foton 5, rocket, engine	October 8	62.8	90.3	0.010	220
66	DFS 3, rocket	October 12	0.0	1436.0	0.000	35778
67	Molniya 3–42, launcher rocket, launcher, rocket	October 14	62.8	717.7	0.742	477
68	Cosmos 2211–2216, rocket	October 20	82.6	114.0	0.001	1400
69	Cosmos 2217, launcher rocket, launcher, rocket	October 21	62.9	717.8	0.737	599
70	STS 52, Lageos 2, CTA, IRIS, LAS	October 22	28.5	88.5	0.001	206
71	Progress M-15, rocket	October 27	51.6	90.4	0.004	269
72	Galaxy 7	October 28	0.1	1436.0	0.002	35715
73	Cosmos 2218, rocket	October 29	82.9	105.0	0.003	968
74	Ekran 20, launcher	October 30	1.6	1428.2	0.001	35575
75	Resurs-500, rocket, engine	November 15	82.6	89.5	0.009	187
76	Cosmos 2219, rocket	November 17	71.0	102.0	0.000	849
77	Cosmos 2220, rocket	November 20	67.1	89.6	0.013	167
78	MST 1	November 21	96.7	92.4	0.008	331
79	Navstar 2A-07, rocket	November 23	54.8	714.7	0.007	19926
80	Cosmos 2221, rocket	November 24	82.5	97.8	0.002	636

Desig-nation	Satellite	Launch date	i	P	e	Perigee height
1992-			°	m		km
81	Cosmos 2222, launcher rocket, launcher, rocket	November 25	62.9	708.1	0.735	591
82	Gorizont 27, launcher	November 27	1.5	1468.9	0.002	36358
83	USA 86	November 28				
84	Superbird A1	December 1	0.1	1436.0	0.001	35759
85	Molniya 3–43, launcher rocket, launcher, rocket	December 2	62.8	717.4	0.744	413
86	STS 53, DoD-1	December 2	57.0	92.0	0.001	369
87	Cosmos 2223, rocket	December 9	64.7	89.0	0.007	178
88	Cosmos 2224, launcher	December 17	2.3	1443.3	0.001	35882
89	Navstar 2A-08	December 18	54.7	717.9	0.001	20039
90	Optus B2	December 21	28.1	96.9	0.059	208
91	Cosmos 2225, rocket	December 22	64.9	89.7	0.007	214
92	Cosmos 2226, rocket	December 22	73.6	116.1	0.003	1478
93	Cosmos 2227, rocket	December 25	71.0	102.0	0.000	849
94	Cosmos 2228, rocket	December 25	82.5	97.8	0.003	633
95	Cosmos 2229, rocket	December 29	62.8	90.4	0.012	218
1993-						
01	Cosmos 2230	January 1	82.9	98.5	0.002	971
02	Molniya 1-85	January 13	62.8	735.5	0.741	608
03	STS 54, TDRS 6	January 13	28.5	90.4	0.001	296
04	Cosmos 2231	January 19	67.2	89.6	0.014	166
05	Soyuz TM-16	January 24	51.6	88.5	0.002	189
06	Cosmos 2232	January 26	62.8	709.6	0.736	591
07	USA 88	February 3	34.8	356.4	0.607	174
08	Cosmos 2233	February 9	82.9	104.8	0.004	956
09	OXP-1, SCD 1	February 9	25.0	99.8	0.005	721
10	Cosmos 2234–2236	February 17	64.9	670.0	0.001	18972
11	Astro D	February 20	31.1	96.3	0.008	532
12	Progress M-16	February 21	51.6	88.6	0.004	186
13	Raduga 29	March 25	1.4	1454.0	0.004	35980
14	START 1	March 25	75.8	101.5	0.020	684
15	UHF-F1	March 25	27.3	192.9	0.404	219
16	Cosmos 2237	March 26	71.0	102.0	0.000	850
17	USA 90	March 30	34.8	356.7	0.606	188
18	Cosmos 2238	March 30	65.0	92.8	0.001	404
19	Progress M-17	March 31	51.6	90.1	0.005	249
20	Cosmos 2239	April 1	82.9	104.8	0.002	970
21	Cosmos 2240	April 2	62.8	89.5	0.009	187
22	Cosmos 2241	April 6	62.9	706.0	0.733	631
23	STS 56	April 8	57.0	90.3	0.001	288
24	Cosmos 2242	April 19	82.5	97.8	0.002	635
25	Molniya 3-44	April 21	62.9	735.3	0.741	606

Time Measurement and Calendars

MEASUREMENTS OF TIME

Measurements of time are based on the time taken by the earth to rotate on its axis (day); by the moon to revolve round the earth (month); and by the earth to revolve round the sun (year). From these, which are not commensurable, certain average or mean intervals have been adopted for ordinary use.

THE DAY

The day begins at midnight and is divided into 24 hours of 60 minutes, each of 60 seconds. The hours are counted from midnight up to 12 noon (when the sun crosses the meridian), and these hours are designated a.m. (*ante meridiem*); and again from noon up to 12 midnight, which hours are designated p.m. (*post meridiem*), except when the 24-hour reckoning is employed. The 24-hour reckoning ignores a.m. and p.m., and the hours are numbered 0 to 23 from midnight.

Colloquially the 24 hours are divided into day and night, day being the time while the sun is above the horizon (including the four stages of twilight defined on page 72). Day is subdivided further into morning, the early part of daytime, ending at noon; afternoon, from noon to about 6 p.m.; and evening, which may be said to extend from 6 p.m. until midnight. Night, the dark period between day and day, begins at the close of astronomical twilight (*see* page 72) and extends beyond midnight to sunrise the next day.

The names of the days are derived from Old English translations or adaptations of the Roman titles.

Sunday	Sun	Sol
Monday	Moon	Luna
Tuesday	Tiw/Tyr (god of war)	Mars
Wednesday	Woden/Odin	Mercury
Thursday	Thor	Jupiter
Friday	Frigga/Freyja (goddess of love)	
		Venus
Saturday	Saeternes	Saturn

THE WEEK

The week is a period of seven days.

THE MONTH

The month in the ordinary calendar is approximately the twelfth part of a year, but the lengths of the different months vary from 28 (or 29) days to 31.

THE YEAR

The equinoctial or tropical year is the time that the earth takes to revolve round the sun from equinox to equinox, i.e. 365.24219 mean solar days, or 365 days 5 hours 48 minutes and 45 seconds.

The calendar year usually consists of 365 days, but a year containing 366 days is called bissextile (*see* Roman Calendar) or leap year, one day being added to the month of February, so that a date 'leaps over' a day of the week.

A year is a leap year if the date of the year is divisible by four without remainder, unless it is the last year of the century. The last year of a century is a leap year only if its number is divisible by 400 without remainder, e.g. the years 1800 and 1900 had only 365 days but the year 2000 will have 366 days.

THE SOLSTICE

A solstice is the point in the tropical year at which the sun attains its greatest distance, north or south, from the Equator. In the northern hemisphere the furthest point north of the Equator marks the summer solstice and the furthest point south the winter solstice.

The date of the solstice varies according to locality. For example, if the summer solstice falls on 21 June late in the day by Greenwich time, that day will be the longest of the year at Greenwich though it may be by only a second, but it will fall on 22 June, local date, in Japan, and so 22 June will be the longest day there. The date of the solstice is also affected by the length of the tropical year, which is 365 days 6 hours less about 11 minutes 15 seconds. If a solstice happens late on 21 June in one year, it will be nearly six hours later in the next (unless the next year is a leap year), i.e. early on 22 June, and that will be the longest day.

This delay of the solstice does not continue because the extra day in leap year brings it back a day in the calendar. However, because of the 11 minutes 15 seconds mentioned above, the additional day in leap year brings the solstice back too far by 45 minutes, and the time of the solstice in the calendar is earlier, in a four-year pattern, as the century progresses. The last year of a century is in most cases not a leap year, and the omission of the extra day puts the date of the solstice later by about six hours too much. Compensation for this is made by the fourth centennial year being a leap year. The solstice has become earlier in date throughout this century and, because the year 2000 is a leap year, the solstice will get earlier still throughout the 21st century.

Similar considerations apply to the day of the winter solstice, the shortest day of the year. The difference due to locality also prevails in the same sense as for the longest day.

At Greenwich the sun sets at its earliest by the clock about ten days before the shortest day. The daily change in the time of sunset is due in the first place to the sun's movement southwards at this time of the year, which diminishes the interval between the sun's transit and its setting. However, the daily decrease of the Equation of Time causes the time of apparent noon to be continuously later day by day. This in a measure counteracts the first effect. The rates of the change of these two quantities are not equal, nor are they uniform, but are such that their combination causes the date of earliest sunset to be 12 or 13 December at Greenwich. In more southerly latitudes the effect of the movement of the sun is less, and the change in the time of sunset depends on that of the Equation of Time to a greater degree, and the date of earliest sunset is earlier than it is at Greenwich. For example, on the Equator it is about 1 November.

THE EQUINOX

The equinox is the point at which the sun crosses the Equator and day and night are of equal length all over the world. This occurs in March and September.

DOG DAYS

The days about the heliacal rising of the Dog Star, noted from ancient times as the hottest period of the year in the northern hemisphere, are called the Dog Days. Their incidence has been variously calculated as depending on the Greater or Lesser Dog Star (Sirius or Procyon) and their duration has been reckoned as from 30 to 54 days. A generally accepted period is from 3 July to 15 August.

CHRISTIAN CALENDAR

In the Christian chronological system the years are distinguished by cardinal numbers before or after the birth of Christ, the period being denoted by the letters BC (Before Christ) or, more rarely, AC (*Ante Christum*), and AD (*Anno Domini* – In the Year of Our Lord). The correlative dates of the epoch are the fourth year of the 194th Olympiad, the 753rd year from the foundation of Rome, AM 3761 (Jewish chronology), and the 4714th year of the Julian period.

The system was introduced into Italy in the sixth century. Though first used in France in the seventh century, it was not universally established there until about the eighth century. It has been said that the system was introduced into England by St Augustine (AD 596), but it was probably not generally used until some centuries later. It was ordered to be used by the Bishops at the Council of Chelsea (AD 816). The actual date of the birth of Christ is somewhat uncertain.

THE JULIAN CALENDAR

In the Julian calendar all the centennial years were leap years, and for this reason towards the close of the sixteenth century there was a difference of ten days between the tropical and calendar years; the equinox fell on 11 March of the calendar, whereas at the time of the Council of Nicaea (AD 325), it had fallen on 21 March. In 1582 Pope Gregory ordained that 5 October should be called 15 October and that of the end-century years only the fourth should be a leap year (*see* page 81).

THE GREGORIAN CALENDAR

The Gregorian calendar was adopted by Italy, France, Spain and Portugal in 1582, by Prussia, the Roman Catholic German states, Switzerland, Holland and Flanders on 1 January 1583, by Poland in 1586, Hungary in 1587, the Protestant German and Netherland states and Denmark in 1700, and by Great Britain and Dominions (including the North American colonies) in 1752, by the omission of eleven days (3 September being reckoned as 14 September). Sweden omitted the leap day in 1700 but observed leap days in 1704 and 1708, and reverted to the Julian calendar by having two leap days in 1712; the Gregorian calendar was adopted in 1753 by the omission of eleven days (18 February being reckoned as 1 March). Japan adopted the calendar in 1872, China in 1912, Bulgaria in 1915, Turkey and Soviet Russia in 1918, Yugoslavia and Romania in 1919, and Greece in February 1923.

In the same year that the change was made in England from the Julian to the Gregorian calendar, the beginning of the new year was also changed from 25 March to 1 January (*see* page 86).

THE ORTHODOX CHURCHES

Some Orthodox Churches still use the Julian reckoning, but the majority of Greek Orthodox Churches and the Romanian Orthodox Church have adopted a modified 'New Calendar', observing the Gregorian calendar for fixed feasts and the Julian for movable feasts.

The Orthodox Church year begins on 1 September. There are four fast periods, and in addition to Pascha (Easter), twelve great feasts, as well as numerous commemorations of the saints of the Old and New Testaments throughout the year.

THE DOMINICAL LETTER

The Dominical Letter is one of the letters A–G which are used to denote the Sundays in successive years. If the first day of the year is a Sunday the letter is A; if the second, B; the third, C; and so on. Leap year requires two letters, the first for 1 January to 29 February, the second for 1 March to 31 December (*see* page 84).

EPIPHANY

The feast of the Epiphany, commemorating the manifestation of Christ, later became associated with the offering of gifts by the Magi. The day was of exceptional importance from the time of the Council of Nicaea (AD 325), as the primate of Alexandria was charged at every Epiphany feast with the announcement in a letter to the churches of the date of the forthcoming Easter. The day was of considerable importance in Britain as it influenced dates, ecclesiastical and lay, e.g. Plough Monday, when work was resumed in the fields, falls upon the Monday in the first full week after Epiphany.

LENT

The Teutonic word *Lent*, which denotes the fast preceding Easter, originally meant no more than the spring season; but from Anglo-Saxon times at least it has been used as the equivalent of the more significant Latin term Quadragesima, meaning the 'forty days' or, more literally, the fortieth day. Ash Wednesday is the first day of Lent, which ends at midnight before Easter Day.

PALM SUNDAY

Palm Sunday, the Sunday before Easter and the beginning of Holy Week, commemorates the triumphal entry of Christ into Jerusalem and is celebrated in Britain (when palm is not available) by branches of willow gathered for use in the decoration of churches on that day.

MAUNDY THURSDAY

Maundy Thursday is the day before Good Friday, the name itself being a corruption of *dies mandati* (day of the mandate) when Christ washed the feet of the disciples and gave them the mandate to love one another.

EASTER DAY

Easter Day is the first Sunday after the full moon which happens upon, or next after, the 21st day of March; if the full moon happens upon a Sunday, Easter Day is the Sunday after.

This definition is contained in an Act of Parliament (24 Geo. II c. 23) and explanation is given in the preamble to the Act that the day of full moon depends on certain tables that have been prepared. These are the tables whose essential points are given in the early pages of the Book of Common Prayer. The moon referred to is not the real moon of the heavens, but a hypothetical moon on whose 'full' the date of Easter depends, and the lunations of this 'calendar' moon consist of twenty-nine and thirty days alternately, with certain necessary modifications to make the date of its full agree as nearly as possible with that of the real moon, which is known as the Paschal Full Moon. As at present ordained, Easter falls on one of 35 days (22 March to 25 April).

A FIXED EASTER

On 15 June 1928 the House of Commons agreed to a motion for the third reading of a bill proposing that Easter Day shall, in the calendar year next but one after the commencement of the Act and in all subsequent years, be the first Sunday after the second Saturday in April. Easter would thus fall between 9 and 15 April (inclusive), that is, on the second or third Sunday in April. A clause in the Bill provided that before it shall come into operation, regard shall be had to any opinion expressed officially by the various Christian churches. Efforts by the World Council of Churches to secure a unanimous choice of date for Easter by its member churches have so far been unsuccessful.

ROGATION DAYS

Rogation Days are the Monday, Tuesday and Wednesday preceding Ascension Day and in the fifth century were ordered by the Church to be observed as public fasts with solemn processions and supplications. The processions were discontinued as religious observances at the Reformation, but survive in the ceremony known as 'Beating the Parish Bounds'. Rogation Sunday is the Sunday before Ascension Day.

EMBER DAYS

The Ember Days at the four seasons are the Wednesday,

Friday and Saturday (a) before the third Sunday in Advent, (b) before the second Sunday in Lent, and (c) before the Sundays nearest to the festivals of St Peter and of St Michael and All Angels.

TRINITY SUNDAY

Trinity Sunday is eight weeks after Easter Day, on the Sunday following Pentecost (Whit Sunday). Subsequent Sundays are reckoned in the Book of Common Prayer calendar of the Church of England as 'after Trinity'.

Thomas Becket (1118–70) was consecrated Archbishop of Canterbury on the Sunday after Whit Sunday and his first act was to ordain that the day of his consecration should be held as a new festival in honour of the Holy Trinity. The observance thus originated spread from Canterbury throughout the whole of Christendom.

MOVABLE FEASTS TO THE YEAR 2026

Year	Ash Wednesday	Easter	Ascension	Pentecost (Whit Sunday)	Sundays after Pentecost	Advent Sunday
1994	16 February	3 April	12 May	22 May	21	27 November
1995	1 March	16 April	25 May	4 June	20	3 December
1996	21 February	7 April	16 May	26 May	21	1 December
1997	12 February	30 March	8 May	18 May	22	30 November
1998	25 February	12 April	21 May	31 May	20	29 November
1999	17 February	4 April	13 May	23 May	21	28 November
2000	8 March	23 April	1 June	11 June	19	3 December
2001	28 February	15 April	24 May	3 June	20	2 December
2002	13 February	31 March	9 May	19 May	22	1 December
2003	5 March	20 April	29 May	8 June	19	30 November
2004	25 February	11 April	20 May	30 May	20	28 November
2005	9 February	27 March	5 May	15 May	22	27 November
2006	1 March	16 April	25 May	4 June	20	3 December
2007	21 February	8 April	17 May	27 May	21	2 December
2008	6 February	23 March	1 May	11 May	23	30 November
2009	25 February	12 April	21 May	31 May	20	29 November
2010	17 February	4 April	13 May	23 May	21	28 November
2011	9 March	24 April	2 June	12 June	18	27 November
2012	22 February	8 April	17 May	27 May	21	2 December
2013	13 February	31 March	9 May	19 May	22	1 December
2014	5 March	20 April	29 May	8 June	19	30 November
2015	18 February	5 April	14 May	24 May	21	29 November
2016	10 February	27 March	5 May	15 May	22	27 November
2017	1 March	16 April	25 May	4 June	20	3 December
2018	14 February	1 April	10 May	20 May	22	2 December
2019	6 March	21 April	30 May	9 June	19	1 December
2020	26 February	12 April	21 May	31 May	20	29 November
2021	17 February	4 April	13 May	23 May	21	28 November
2022	2 March	17 April	26 May	5 June	19	27 November
2023	22 February	9 April	18 May	28 May	21	3 December
2024	14 February	31 March	9 May	19 May	22	1 December
2025	5 March	20 April	29 May	8 June	19	30 November
2026	18 February	5 April	14 May	24 May	21	29 November

NOTES

Ash Wednesday (first day in Lent) can fall at earliest on 4 February and at latest on 10 March
Mothering Sunday (fourth Sunday in Lent) can fall at earliest on 29 February and at latest on 4 April
Easter Day can fall at earliest on 22 March and at latest on 25 April
Ascension Day is forty days after Easter Day and can fall at earliest on 30 April and at latest on 3 June

Pentecost (Whit Sunday) is seven weeks after Easter and can fall at earliest on 10 May and at latest on 13 June
Trinity Sunday is the Sunday after Whit Sunday
Corpus Christi falls on the Thursday after Trinity Sunday
Sundays after Pentecost – there are not less than 18 and not more than 23
Advent Sunday is the Sunday nearest to 30 November

EASTER DAYS AND DOMINICAL LETTERS 1500 TO 2030

	1500–1599	1600–1699	1700–1799	1800–1899	1900–1999	2000–2030
March						
d 22	1573	1668	1761	1818		
e 23	1505/16	1600	1788	1845/56	1913	2008
f 24		1611/95	1706/99		1940	
g 25	1543/54	1627/38/49	1722/33/44	1883/94	1951	
A 26	1559/70/81/92	1654/65/76	1749/58/69/80	1815/26/37	1967/78/89	
b 27	1502/13/24/97	1608/87/92	1785/96	1842/53/64	1910/21/32	2005/16
c 28	1529/35/40	1619/24/30	1703/14/25	1869/75/80	1937/48	2027
d 29	1551/62	1635/46/57	1719/30/41/52	1807/12/91	1959/64/70	
e 30	1567/78/89	1651/62/73/84	1746/55/66/77	1823/34	1902/75/86/97	
f 31	1510/21/32/83/94	1605/16/78/89	1700/71/82/93	1839/50/61/72	1907/18/29/91	2002/13/24
April						
g 1	1526/37/48	1621/32	1711/16	1804/66/77/88	1923/34/45/56	2018/29
A 2	1553/64	1643/48	1727/38/52(NS)	1809/20/93/99	1961/72	
b 3	1575/80/86	1659/70/81	1743/63/68/74	1825/31/36	1904/83/88/94	
c 4	1507/18/91	1602/13/75/86/97	1708/79/90	1847/58	1915/20/26/99	2010/21
d 5	1523/34/45/56	1607/18/29/40	1702/13/24/95	1801/63/74/85/96	1931/42/53	2015/26
e 6	1539/50/61/72	1634/45/56	1729/35/40/60	1806/17/28/90	1947/58/69/80	
f 7	1504/77/88	1667/72	1751/65/76	1822/33/44	1901/12/85/96	
g 8	1509/15/20/99	1604/10/83/94	1705/87/92/98	1849/55/60	1917/28	2007/12
A 9	1531/42	1615/26/37/99	1710/21/32	1871/82	1939/44/50	2023
b 10	1547/58/69	1631/42/53/64	1726/37/48/57	1803/14/87/98	1955/66/77	
c 11	1501/12/63/74/85/96	1658/69/80	1762/73/84	1819/30/41/52	1909/71/82/93	2004
d 12	1506/17/28	1601/12/91/96	1789	1846/57/68	1903/14/25/36/98	2009/20
e 13	1533/44	1623/28	1707/18	1800/73/79/84	1941/52	
f 14	1555/60/66	1639/50/61	1723/34/45/54	1805/11/16/95	1963/68/74	
g 15	1571/82/93	1655/66/77/88	1750/59/70/81	1827/38	1900/06/79/90	2001
A 16	1503/14/25/36/87/98	1609/20/82/93	1704/75/86/97	1843/54/65/76	1911/22/33/95	2006/17/28
b 17	1530/41/52	1625/36	1715/20	1808/70/81/92	1927/38/49/60	2022
c 18	1557/68	1647/52	1731/42/56	1802/13/24/97	1954/65/76	
d 19	1500/79/84/90	1663/74/85	1747/67/72/78	1829/35/40	1908/81/87/92	
e 20	1511/22/95	1606/17/79/90	1701/12/83/94	1851/62	1919/24/30	2003/14/25
f 21	1527/38/49	1622/33/44	1717/28	1867/78/89	1935/46/57	2019/30
g 22	1565/76	1660	1739/53/64	1810/21/32	1962/73/84	
A 23	1508	1671		1848	1905/16	2000
b 24	1519	1603/14/98	1709/91	1859		2011
c 25	1546	1641	1736	1886	1943	

HINDU CALENDAR

The Hindu calendar is a lunar calendar of twelve months, each containing 29 days, 12 hours. Each month is divided into a light fortnight (Shukla or Shuddha) and a dark fortnight (Krishna or Vadya) based on the waxing and waning of the moon. In most parts of India the month starts with the light fortnight, i.e. the day after the new moon, although in some regions it begins with the dark fortnight, i.e. the day after the full moon.

The new year begins in the month of Chaitra (March/April) and ends in the month of Phalgun (March). The twelve months, Chaitra, Vaishakh, Jyeshtra, Ashadh, Shravan, Bhadrapad, Ashvin, Kartik, Margashirsh, Paush, Magh and Phalgun, have Sanskrit names derived from twelve asterisms (constellations). There are regional variations to the names of the months but the Sanskrit names are understood throughout India.

Whenever the difference between the Hindu year of 360 lunar days (354 days 8 hours solar time) and the 365 days 6 hours of the solar year reaches the length of one Hindu lunar month (29 days 12 hours), a 'leap' month is added to the Hindu calendar.

The leap month may be added at any point in the Hindu year. The name given to the month varies according to when it occurs but is taken from the month immediately following it. Leap months occur in 1993–4 (Bhadrapad), 1996–7 (Ashadh) and 1999–2000 (Jyeshtra).

The days of the week are called Raviwar (Sunday), Somawar (Monday), Mangalwar (Tuesday), Budhawar (Wednesday), Guruwar (Thursday), Shukrawar (Friday) and Shaniwar (Saturday). The names are derived from the Sanskrit names of the Sun, the Moon and five planets, Mars, Mercury, Jupiter, Venus and Saturn.

Most fasts and festivals are based on the lunar calendar but a few are determined by the apparent movement of the Sun, e.g. Sankranti, which is celebrated on 14/15 January to mark the start of the Sun's apparent journey northwards and a change of season.

Festivals celebrated throughout India are Chaitra (the New Year), Raksha-bandhan (the renewal of the kinship bond between brothers and sisters), Navaratri (a nine-night festival dedicated to the goddess Parvati), Dasara (the victory of Rama over the demon army), Diwali (a festival of lights), Makara Sankranti, Shivaratri (dedicated to Shiva), and Holi (a spring festival).

Regional festivals are Durga-puja (dedicated to the goddess Durga (Parvati)), Sarasvati-puja (dedicated to the goddess

Sarasvati), Ganesh Chaturthi (worship of Ganesh on the fourth day (Chaturthi) of the light half of Bhadrapad), Ramanavami (the birth festival of the god Rama) and Janmashtami (the birth festival of the god Krishna).

The main festivals celebrated in Britain are Navaratri, Dasara, Durga-puja, Diwali, Holi, Sarasvati-puja, Ganesh Chaturthi, Raksha-bandhan, Ramanavami and Janmashtami.

The dates of the main festivals in 1994 are given on page 9.

JEWISH CALENDAR

The story of the Flood in the Book of Genesis relates that the Flood began on the 17th day of the second month, that after the end of 150 days the waters were abated, and that on the 17th day of the seventh month the Ark rested on Mount Ararat. This indicates the use of a calendar of some kind and that the writers recognized thirty days as the length of a lunation. However, after the diaspora, Jewish communities were left in considerable doubt as to the times of fasts and festivals. This led to the formation of the Jewish calendar as used today. It is said that this was done in AD 358 by Rabbi Hillel II, a descendant of Gamaliel, though some assert that it did not happen until much later.

The calendar is luni-solar, and is based on the lengths of the lunation and of the tropical year as found by Hipparchus (c.120 BC), which differ little from those adopted at the present day. The year AM 5754 (1993–4) is the 16th year of the 303rd Metonic (Minor or Lunar) cycle of 19 years and the 14th year of the 206th Solar (or Major) cycle of 28 years since the Era of the Creation. Jews hold that the Creation occurred at the time of the autumnal equinox in the year known in the Christian calendar as 3760 BC (954 of the Julian period). The epoch or starting point of Jewish chronology corresponds to 7 October 3761 BC. At the beginning of each solar cycle, the Tekufah of Nisan (the vernal equinox) returns to the same day and to the same hour.

The hour is divided into 1080 minims, and the month between one new moon and the next is reckoned as 29 days, 12 hours, 793 minims. The normal calendar year, called a Common Regular year, consists of 12 months of 30 days and 29 days alternately. Since twelve months such as these comprise only 354 days, in order that each of them shall not diverge greatly from an average place in the solar year, a thirteenth month is occasionally added after the fifth month of the civil year (which commences on the first day of the month Tishri, or as the penultimate month of the ecclesiastical year (which commences on the first day of month Nisan). The years when this happens are called Embolismic or leap years.

Of the 19 years that form a Metonic cycle, seven are leap years; they occur at places in the cycle indicated by the numbers 3, 6, 8, 11, 14, 17 and 19, these places being chosen so that the accumulated excesses of the solar years should be as small as possible.

A Jewish year is of one of the following six types:

Minimal Common	353 days
Regular Common	354 days
Full Common	355 days
Minimal Leap	383 days
Regular Leap	384 days
Full Leap	385 days.

The Regular year has alternate months of 30 and 29 days. In a Full year, whether common or leap, Marcheshvan, the second month of the civil year, has 30 days instead of 29; in

Minimal years Kislev, the third month, has 29 instead of 30. The additional month in leap years is called Adar I and precedes the month called Adar in Common years. Adar II is called Ve-Adar, in leap years, and the usual Adar festivals are kept in Ve-Adar. Adar I and Adar II always have 30 days, but neither this, nor the other variations mentioned, is allowed to change the number of days in the other months which still follow the alternation of the normal twelve.

These are the main features of the Jewish calendar, which must be considered permanent because as a Jewish law it cannot be altered except by a great Sanhedrin.

The Jewish day begins between sunset and nightfall. The time used is that of the meridian of Jerusalem, which is 2h 21m in advance of Greenwich Mean Time. Rules for the beginning of sabbaths and festivals were laid down for the latitude of London in the eighteenth century and hours for nightfall are now fixed annually by the Chief Rabbi.

JEWISH CALENDAR 5754–5

AM 5754 (754) is a Full Common year of 12 months, 51 sabbaths and 354 days. AM 5755 (755) is a Regular Leap year of 13 months, 55 sabbaths and 384 days.

Jewish Month	AM 5754	AM 5755
Tishri 1	16 September 1993	6 September 1994
Marcheshvan 1	16 October	6 October
Kislev 1	15 November	4 November
Tebet 1	15 December	4 December
Shebat 1	13 January 1994	2 January 1995
*Adar 1	12 February	1 February
Ve-Adar 1		3 March
Nisan 1	13 March	1 April
Iyar 1	12 April	1 May
Sivan 1	11 May	30 May
Tammuz 1	10 June	29 June
Ab 1	9 July	28 July
Elul 1	8 August	27 August

*Known as Adar Rishon in leap years.

JEWISH FASTS AND FESTIVALS

For dates of principal festivals in 1994, see page 9

Tishri 1–2	Rosh Hashanah (New Year)
Tishri 3	*Fast of Gedaliah
Tishri 10	Yom Kippur (Day of Atonement)
Tishri 15–21	Succoth (Feast of Tabernacles)
Tishri 21	Hoshana Rabba
Tishri 22	Shemini Atseret (Solemn Assembly)
Tishri 23	Simchat Torah (Rejoicing of the Law)
Kislev 25	Chanukah (Dedication of the Temple) begins
Tebet 10	Fast of Tebet
†Adar 13	§Fast of Esther
†Adar 14	Purim
†Adar 15	Shushan Purim
Nisan 15–22	Pesach (Passover)
Sivan 6–7	Shavuot (Feast of Weeks)
Tammuz 17	*Fast of Tammuz
Ab 9	*Fast of Ab

*If these dates fall on the sabbath the fast is kept on the following day
†Ve-Adar in leap years
§This fast is observed on Adar 11 (or Ve-Adar 11 in leap years) if Adar 13 falls on a sabbath

THE MUSLIM CALENDAR

The Muslim era is dated from the *Hijrah*, or flight of the Prophet Muhammad from Mecca to Medina, the corresponding date of which in the Julian calendar is 16 July AD 622. Hijrah years (AH) are used principally in Iran, Turkey, Egypt, Malaysia, various Arab states and certain parts of India. The dating system was adopted about AD 639, commencing with the first day of the month Muharram. Muharram precedes the month in which the Hijrah took place and was recognized as the beginning of the year because it followed the month of pilgrimage.

The calendar is a lunar calendar and consists of twelve months containing an alternate sequence of 30 and 29 days, with the intercalation of one day at the end of the twelfth month at stated intervals in each cycle of 30 years. The object of the intercalation is to reconcile the date of the first day of the month with the date of the actual new moon.

Some adherents still take the date of the evening of the first physical sighting of the crescent of the New Moon as that of the first of the month. For this reason, the beginning of a new month and the date of religious festivals can vary by a few days from the published calendars.

In each cycle of 30 years, 19 years are common and contain 354 days, and 11 years are intercalary (leap years) of 355 days, the latter being called *kabishah*. The mean length of the Hijrah years is 354 days 8 hours 48 minutes and the period of mean lunation is 29 days 12 hours 44 minutes.

To ascertain if a year is common or kabishah, divide it by 30: the quotient gives the number of completed cycles and the remainder shows the place of the year in the current cycle. If the remainder is 2, 5, 7, 10, 13, 16, 18, 21, 24, 26 or 29, the year is kabishah and consists of 355 days.

MUSLIM CALENDAR 1414–15

Hijrah year 1414 AH (remainder 4) is a common year; 1415 AH (remainder 5) is a kabishah year.

Month (length)	1414 AH	1415 AH
Muharram (30)	21 June 1993	10 June 1994
Safar (29)	21 July	10 July
Rabi' I (30)	19 August	8 August
Rabi' II (29)	18 September	7 September
Jumada I (30)	17 October	7 October
Jumada II (29)	16 November	5 November
Rajab (30)	15 December	4 December
Shaabân (29)	14 January 1994	3 January 1995
Ramadân (30)	12 February	1 February
Shawwâl (29)	14 March	3 March
Dhû'l-Qa'da (30)	12 April	1 April
Dhû'l-Hijjah (29 or 30)	12 May	1 May

MUSLIM FESTIVALS

Ramadan is a month of fasting for all Muslims because it is the month in which the revelation of the *Qur'an* (Koran) began. During Ramadan Muslims abstain from food, drink and sexual pleasure from dawn until after sunset throughout the month.

The two major festivals are *Idu-l-fitr* and *Idu-l-adha*. Idu-l-fitr marks the end of the Ramadan fast and is celebrated on the day after the sighting of the new moon of the following month. Idu-l-adha, the festival of sacrifice (also known as the great festival), celebrates the submission of the Prophet Ibrahim (Abraham) to Allah. Idu-l-adha falls on the tenth day of Dhul-Hijjah, coinciding with the day when those on *hajj* (pilgrimage to Mecca) sacrifice animals.

Other days accorded special recognition are:

Muharram 1	New Year's Day
Muharram 10	Ashura (the day Prophet Nuh left the Ark and Prophet Musa was saved from Pharaoh (Sunni), the death of the Prophet's grandson Husain (Shi'ite))
Rabi'u-l-Awwal (Rabi I) 12	Mawlidu-n-Nabiyy (birthday of the Prophet Muhammad)
Rajab 27	Laylatu-l-Isra wa l-Miraj (Night of the Journey and Ascension)
Ramadan Odd-numbered nights in the last 10 of the month	Laylatu-l-Qadr (Night of Power)
Dhu'l-Hijjah 10	Idu-l-adha (Festival of Sacrifice)

THE SIKH CALENDAR

The Sikh calendar is a lunar calendar of 365 days divided into 12 months. The length of the months varies between 29 and 32 days.

There are no prescribed feast days and no fasting periods. The main celebrations are Baisakhi Mela (the new year and the anniversary of the founding of the Khalsa), Diwali Mela (festival of light), Hola Mohalla Mela (a spring festival held in the Punjab), and the Gurpurbs (anniversaries associated with the ten Gurus).

The dates of the major celebrations in 1994 are given on page 9.

CIVIL AND LEGAL CALENDAR

THE HISTORICAL YEAR

Before the year 1752, two calendar systems were in use in England. The civil or legal year began on 25 March, while the historical year began on 1 January. Thus the civil or legal date 24 March 1658, was the same day as the historical date 24 March 1659; and a date in that portion of the year is written as 24 March 165⅞, the lower figure showing the historical year.

THE NEW YEAR

In England in the seventh century, and as late as the thirteenth, the year was reckoned from Christmas Day, but in the twelfth century the Anglican Church began the year with the feast of the Annunciation of the Blessed Virgin (Lady Day) on 25 March and this practice was adopted generally in the fourteenth century. The civil or legal year in the British Dominions (exclusive of Scotland) began with 'Lady Day' until 1751. But in and since 1752 the civil year has begun with 1 January. Certain dividends are still paid by the Bank of England on dates based on Old Style. New Year's Day in Scotland was changed from 25 March to 1 January in 1600.

On the continent of Europe, 1 January was adopted as the first day of the year by Venice in 1522, Germany in 1544, Spain, Portugal, and the Roman Catholic Netherlands in 1556, Prussia, Denmark and Sweden in 1559, France in 1564, Lorraine in 1579, the Protestant Netherlands in 1583, Russia in 1725, and Tuscany in 1751.

REGNAL YEARS

The regnal years are the years of a sovereign's reign, and each begins on the anniversary of his or her accession, e.g. regnal year 43 of the present Queen begins on 6 February 1994.

The system was used for dating Acts of Parliament until 1962. The Summer Time Act 1925, for example, is quoted as 15 and 16 Geo. V c. 64, because it became law in the parliamentary session which extended over part of both of these regnal years. Acts of a parliamentary session during which a sovereign died were usually given two year numbers, the regnal year of the deceased sovereign and the regnal year of his or her successor. Acts passed in 1952 were dated 16 Geo. VI and 1 Elizabeth II. Since 1962, Acts of Parliament have been dated by the calendar year.

QUARTER AND TERM DAYS

Holy days and saints days were the normal factors in early times for setting the dates of future and recurrent appointments. The quarter days in England and Wales are the feast of the Annunciation (25 March), the feast of St John the Baptist (24 June) and the feast of St Michael and All Angels (29 September).

The term days in Scotland are Candlemas (the feast of the Purification), Whitsunday, Lammas (Loaf Mass), and Martinmas (St Martin's Day). These fell on 2 February, 15 May, 1 August and 11 November respectively. However, by the Term and Quarter Days (Scotland) Act 1990, the dates of the term days were changed to 28 February (Candlemas), 28 May (Whitsunday), 28 August (Lammas) and 28 November (Martinmas).

RED-LETTER DAYS

Red-letter days were originally the holy days and saints days indicated in early ecclesiastical calendars by letters printed in red ink. The days to be distinguished in this way were approved at the Council of Nicaea in AD 325.

These days still have a legal significance, as judges of the Queen's Bench Division wear scarlet robes on red-letter days falling during the law sittings. The days designated as red-letter days for this purpose are:

Holy and saints days
Conversion of St Paul, the Purification, Ash Wednesday, the Annunciation, the Ascension, the feasts of St Mark, SS Philip and James, St Matthias, St Barnabas, St Peter, St Thomas, St James, St Luke, SS Simon and Jude, All Saints, St Andrew.

Civil calendar
The anniversary of The Queen's accession, The Queen's birthday, The Queen's official birthday, The Queen's coronation, the birthday of the Duke of Edinburgh, the birthday of Queen Elizabeth the Queen Mother, the birthday of the Prince of Wales, St David's Day and Lord Mayor's Day.

PUBLIC HOLIDAYS

Public holidays are divided into two categories, common law, and statutory. Common law holidays are holidays 'by habit and custom'; in England, Wales and Northern Ireland these are Good Friday and Christmas Day.

Statutory public holidays, known as bank holidays, were first established by the Bank Holidays Act 1871. They were, literally, days on which the banks (and other public institutions) were closed and financial obligations due on that day were payable the following day. The legislation currently governing public holidays in the United Kingdom is the Banking and Financial Dealings Act 1971. It stipulates which days are to be public holidays in England, Wales, Scotland and Northern Ireland.

Certain holidays (indicated by * below) are granted annually by royal proclamation, either throughout the United Kingdom or in any place in the United Kingdom. The public holidays are:

England and Wales
*New Year's Day
Easter Monday
*The first Monday in May
The last Monday in May
The last Monday in August
26 December, if it is not a Sunday
27 December when 25 or 26 December is a Sunday

Scotland
New Year's Day, or if it is a Sunday, 2 January
2 January, or if it is a Sunday, 3 January
Good Friday
The first Monday in May
*The last Monday in May
The first Monday in August
Christmas Day, or if it is a Sunday, 26 December
*Boxing Day – if Christmas Day falls on a Sunday, 26 December is given in lieu and an alternative day is given for Boxing Day

Northern Ireland
*New Year's Day
17 March, or if it is a Sunday, 18 March
Easter Monday
*The first Monday in May
The last Monday in May
*12 July, or if it is a Sunday, 13 July
The last Monday in August
26 December, if it is not a Sunday
27 December if 25 or 26 December is a Sunday
For dates of public holidays in 1994 and 1995, see pages 10–11.

CHRONOLOGICAL CYCLES AND ERAS

SOLAR (OR MAJOR) CYCLE

The solar cycle is a period of twenty-eight years, in any corresponding year of which the days of the week recur on the same day of the month.

METONIC (LUNAR, OR MINOR) CYCLE

In the year 432 BC, Meton, an Athenian astronomer, found that 235 lunations are very nearly, though not exactly, equal in duration to 19 solar years, and, hence, after 19 years the phases of the Moon recur on the same days of the month (nearly). The dates of full moon in a cycle of 19 years were inscribed in figures of gold on public monuments in Athens, and the number showing the position of a year in the cycle is called the golden number of that year.

JULIAN PERIOD

The Julian period was proposed by Joseph Scaliger in 1582. The period is 7980 Julian years, and its first year coincides with the year 4713 BC. The figure of 7980 is the product of the number of years in the solar cycle, the Metonic cycle and the cycle of the Roman indiction ($28 \times 19 \times 15$).

ROMAN INDICTION

The Roman indiction is a period of fifteen years, instituted for fiscal purposes about AD 300.

EPACT

The epact is the age of the calendar Moon, diminished by one day, on 1 January, in the ecclesiastical lunar calendar.

CHINESE CALENDAR

A lunar calendar was the sole calendar in use in China until 1911, when the government adopted the new (Gregorian) calendar for official and most business activities. The Chinese tend to follow both calendars, the lunar calendar playing an important part in personal life, e.g. birth celebrations, festivals, marriages; and in rural villages the lunar calendar dictates the cycle of activities, denoting the change of weather and farming activities.

The lunar calendar is used in Hong Kong, Singapore, Malaysia, Tibet and elsewhere in south-east Asia. The calendar has a cycle of 60 years. The new year begins at the first new moon after the sun enters the sign of Aquarius, i.e. the new year falls between 21 January and 19 February in the Gregorian calendar.

Each year in the Chinese calendar is associated with one of 12 animals: the rat, the ox, the tiger, the rabbit, the dragon, the snake, the horse, the goat or sheep, the monkey, the chicken or rooster, the dog, and the pig.

The date of the Chinese new year and the astrological sign for the years 1994–2000 are:

1994	10 February	Dog
1995	31 January	Pig
1996	19 February	Rat
1997	7 February	Ox
1998	28 January	Tiger
1999	16 February	Rabbit
2000	5 February	Dragon

COPTIC CALENDAR

In the Coptic calendar, which is used by part of the population of Egypt and Ethiopia, the year is made up of 12 months of 30 days each, followed, in general, by five complementary days. Every fourth year is an intercalary or leap year and in these years there are six complementary days. The intercalary year of the Coptic calendar immediately precedes the leap year of the Julian calendar. The era is that of Diocletian or the Martyrs, the origin of which is fixed at 29 August AD 284 (Julian date).

INDIAN ERAS

In addition to the Muslim reckoning there are six eras used in India. The principal astronomical system was the Kaliyuga era, which appears to have been adopted in the fourth century AD. It began on 18 February 3102 BC. The chronological system of northern India, known as the Vikrama Samvat era, prevalent in western India, began on 23 February 57 BC. The year AD 1994 is, therefore, the year 2051 of the Vikrama era.

The Saka era of southern India dating from 3 March AD 78, was declared the uniform national calendar of the Republic of India with effect from 22 March 1957, to be used concurrently with the Gregorian calendar. As revised, the year of the new Saka era begins at the spring equinox, with five successive months of 31 days and seven of 30 days in ordinary years, and six months of each length in leap years. The year AD 1994 is 1916 of the revised Saka era.

The Saptarshi era dates from the moment when the Saptarshi, or saints, were translated and became the stars of the Great Bear in 3076 BC.

The Buddhists reckoned from the death of Buddha in 543 BC (the actual date being 487 BC); and the epoch of the Jains was the death of Vardhamana, the founder of their faith, in 527 BC.

JAPANESE CALENDAR

The Japanese calendar is essentially the same as the Gregorian calendar, the years, months and weeks being of the same length and beginning on the same days as those of the Gregorian calendar. The numeration of the years is different, for Japanese chronology is based on a system of epochs or periods, each of which begins at the accession of an Emperor or other important occurrence. The method is not unlike the former British system of regnal years, but differs from it in that each year of a period closes on 31 December. The Japanese chronology begins about AD 650 and the three latest epochs are defined by the reigns of Emperors, whose actual names are not necessarily used:

Epoch
Taishō 1 August 1912 to 25 December 1926
Shōwa 26 December 1926 to 7 January 1989
Heisei 8 January 1989

Hence the year Heisei 5 begins on 1 January 1994.

The months are not named. They are known as First Month, Second Month, etc., First Month being the equivalent to January. The days of the week are Nichiyōbi (Sun-day), Getsuyōbi (Moon-day), Kayōbi (Fire-day), Suiyōbi (Water-day), Mokuyōbi (Wood-day), Kinyōbi (Metal-day), Doyōbi (Earth-day).

THE MASONIC YEAR

Two dates are quoted in warrants, dispensations, etc., issued by the United Grand Lodge of England, those for the current year being expressed as *Anno Domini* 1994 – *Anno Lucis* 5994. This *Anno Lucis* (year of light) is based on the Book of Genesis 1:3, the 4000 year difference being derived, in modified form, from *Ussher's Notation*, published in 1654, which places the Creation of the World in 4004 BC.

OLYMPIADS

Ancient Greek chronology was reckoned in Olympiads, cycles of four years corresponding with the periodic Olympic Games held on the plain of Olympia in Elis once every four years, the intervening years being the first, second, etc., of the Olympiad which received the name of the victor at the Games. The first recorded Olympiad is that of Choroebus, 776 BC.

ZOROASTRIAN CALENDAR

Zoroastrians, followers of the Iranian prophet Zarathushtra (known to the Greeks as Zoroaster) are mostly to be found in Iran and in India, where they are known as Parsis.

The Zoroastrian era dates from the coronation of the last Zoroastrian Sasanian king in AD 631. The Zoroastrian calendar is divided into twelve months, each comprising 30 days, followed by five holy days of the Gathas at the end of each year to make the year consist of 365 days.

In order to synchronize the calendar with the solar year of 365 days, an extra month was intercalated once every 120 years. However, this intercalation ceased in the twelfth century and the New Year, which had fallen in the spring, slipped back until it now falls in August. Because intercalation ceased at different times in Iran and India, there was one month's difference between the calendar followed in Iran (Kadmi calendar) and by the Parsis (Shenshai calendar).

In 1906 a group of Zoroastrians decided to bring the calendar back in line with the seasons again and restore the New Year to 21 March each year (Fasli calendar).

The Shenshai calendar (New Year in August) is mainly used by Parsis. The Fasli calendar (New Year, 21 March) is mainly used by Zoroastrians living in Iran, in the Indian subcontinent, or away from Iran.

THE ROMAN CALENDAR

Roman historians adopted as an epoch the foundation of Rome, which is believed to have happened in the year 753 BC. The ordinal number of the years in Roman reckoning is followed by the letters AUC (*ab urbe condita*), so that the year 1994 is 2747 AUC (MMDCCXLVII). The calendar that we know has developed from one established by Romulus, who is said to have used a year of 304 days divided into ten months, beginning with March. To this Numa added January and February, making the year consist of 12 months of 30 and 29 days alternately, with an additional day so that the total was 355. It is also said that Numa ordered an intercalary month of 22 or 23 days in alternate years, making 90 days in eight years, to be inserted after 23 February.

However, there is some doubt as to the origination and the details of the intercalation in the Roman calendar. It is certain that some scheme of this kind was inaugurated and not fully carried out, for in the year 46 BC Julius Caesar, who was then Pontifex Maximus, found that the calendar had been allowed to fall into some confusion. He therefore sought the help of the Egyptian astronomer Sosigenes, which led to the construction and adoption (45 BC) of the Julian calendar, and, by a slight alteration, to the Gregorian calendar now in use. The year 46 BC was made to consist of 445 days and is called the Year of Confusion.

In the Roman (Julian) calendar the days of the month were counted backwards from three fixed points, or days, and an intervening day was said to be so many days before the next coming point, the first and last being counted. These three points were the Kalends, the Nones, and the Ides. Their positions in the months and the method of counting from them will be seen in the table below. The year containing 366 days was called *bissextilis annus*, as it had a doubled sixth day (*bissextus dies*) before the March Kalends on 24 February – *ante diem sextum Kalendas Martias*, or a.d. VI Kal. Mart.

Present days of the month	*March, May, July, October have thirty-one days*	*January, August, December have thirty-one days*	*April, June, September, November have thirty days*	*February has twenty-eight days, and in leap year twenty-nine*
1	Kalendis	Kalendis	Kalendis	Kalendis
2	VI ⎱	IV ⎱ ante	IV ⎱ ante	IV ⎱ ante
3	V ⎰ ante	III ⎰ Nonas	III ⎰ Nonas	III ⎰ Nonas
4	IV ⎱ Nonas	pridie Nonas	pridie Nonas	pridie Nonas
5	III ⎰	Nonis	Nonis	Nonis
6	pridie Nonas	VIII ⎱	VIII ⎱	VIII ⎱
7	Nonis	VII	VII	VII
8	VIII ⎱	VI ⎱ ante	VI ⎱ ante	VI ⎱ ante
9	VII	V ⎰ Idus	V ⎰ Idus	V ⎰ Idus
10	VI ⎱ ante	IV	IV	IV
11	V ⎰ Idus	III ⎰	III ⎰	III ⎰
12	IV	pridie Idus	pridie Idus	pridie Idus
13	III ⎰	Idibus	Idibus	Idibus
14	pridie Idus	XIX ⎱	XVIII ⎱	XVI ⎱
15	Idibus	XVIII	XVII	XV
16	XVII ⎱	XVII	XVI	XIV
17	XVI	XVI	XV	XIII
18	XV	XV	XIV	XII
19	XIV	XIV	XIII	XI
20	XIII	XIII	XII	X ⎰ ante Kalendas
21	XII	XII ⎱ ante Kalendas	XI ⎰ ante Kalendas	IX ⎰ Martias
22	XI ⎱ ante Kalendas	XI ⎰ (of the month	X ⎰ (of the month	VIII
23	X ⎰ (of the month	X ⎰ following)	IX ⎰ following)	VII
24	IX ⎰ following)	IX	VIII	*VI
25	VIII	VIII	VII	V
26	VII	VII	VI	IV
27	VI	VI	V	III ⎰
28	V	V	IV ⎱	pridie Kalendas
29	IV	IV ⎰	III ⎰	Martias
30	III ⎰	III ⎰	pridie Kalendas	
31	pridie Kalendas (Aprilis, Iunias, Sextilis, Novembris)	pridie Kalendas (Februarias, Septembris, Ianuarias)	(Maias, Quinctilis, Octobris, Decembris)	* (repeated in leap year)

Calendar for Any Year 1770–2030

To select the correct calendar for any year between 1770 and 2030,
consult the index below
* leap year

Year		Year		Year		Year		Year		Year		Year		Year	
1770	C	1803	M	1836	L*	1869	K	1902	G	1935	E	1968	D*	2001	C
1771	E	1804	B*	1837	A	1870	M	1903	I	1936	H*	1969	G	2002	E
1772	H*	1805	E	1838	C	1871	A	1904	L*	1937	K	1970	I	2003	G
1773	K	1806	G	1839	E	1872	D*	1905	A	1938	M	1971	K	2004	J*
1774	M	1807	I	1840	H*	1873	G	1906	C	1939	A	1972	N*	2005	M
1775	A	1808	L*	1841	L*	1874	I	1907	E	1940	D*	1973	C	2006	A
1776	D*	1809	A	1842	M	1875	K	1908	H*	1941	G	1974	E	2007	C
1777	G	1810	C	1843	A	1876	N*	1909	K	1942	I	1975	G	2008	F*
1778	I	1811	E	1844	D*	1877	C	1910	M	1943	K	1976	J*	2009	I
1779	K	1812	H*	1845	G	1878	E	1911	A	1944	N*	1977	M	2010	K
1780	N*	1813	K	1846	I	1879	G	1912	D*	1945	C	1978	A	2011	M
1781	C	1814	M	1847	K	1880	J*	1913	G	1946	E	1979	C	2012	B*
1782	E	1815	A	1848	N*	1881	M	1914	I	1947	G	1980	F*	2013	E
1783	G	1816	D*	1849	C	1882	A	1915	K	1948	J*	1981	I	2014	G
1784	J*	1817	G	1850	E	1883	C	1916	N*	1949	M	1982	K	2015	I
1785	M	1818	I	1851	G	1884	F*	1917	C	1950	A	1983	M	2016	L*
1786	A	1819	K	1852	J*	1885	I	1918	E	1951	C	1984	B*	2017	A
1787	C	1820	N*	1853	M	1886	K	1919	G	1952	F*	1985	E	2018	C
1788	F*	1821	C	1854	A	1887	M	1920	J*	1953	I	1986	G	2019	G
1789	I	1822	E	1855	C	1888	B*	1921	M	1954	K	1987	I	2020	H*
1790	K	1823	G	1856	F*	1889	E	1922	A	1955	M	1988	L*	2021	K
1791	M	1824	J*	1857	I	1890	G	1923	C	1956	B*	1989	A	2022	M
1792	B*	1825	M	1858	K	1891	I	1924	F*	1957	E	1990	C	2023	A
1793	E	1826	A	1859	M	1892	L*	1925	I	1958	G	1991	E	2024	D*
1794	G	1827	C	1860	B*	1893	A	1926	K	1959	I	1992	H*	2025	G
1795	I	1828	F*	1861	E	1894	C	1927	M	1960	L*	1993	K	2026	I
1796	L*	1829	I	1862	G	1895	E	1928	B*	1961	A	1994	M	2027	K
1797	A	1830	K	1863	I	1896	H*	1929	E	1962	C	1995	A	2028	N*
1798	C	1831	M	1864	L*	1897	K	1930	G	1963	E	1996	D*	2029	C
1799	B*	1832	B*	1865	A	1898	M	1931	I	1964	H*	1997	G	2030	E
1800	G	1833	E	1866	C	1899	A	1932	L*	1965	K	1998	I		
1801	I	1834	G	1867	E	1900	C	1933	A	1966	M	1999	K		
1802	K	1835	I	1868	H*	1901	E	1934	C	1967	A	2000	N*		

A

```
        January              February            March
Sun.   1  8 15 22 29        5 12 19 26         5 12 19 26
Mon.   2  9 16 23 30        6 13 20 27         6 13 20 27
Tue.   3 10 17 24 31        7 14 21 28         7 14 21 28
Wed.   4 11 18 25       1  8 15 22         1  8 15 22 29
Thur.  5 12 19 26       2  9 16 23         2  9 16 23 30
Fri.   6 13 20 27       3 10 17 24         3 10 17 24 31
Sat.   7 14 21 28       4 11 18 25         4 11 18 25

        April                May                 June
Sun.   2  9 16 23 30        7 14 21 28         4 11 18 25
Mon.   3 10 17 24       1  8 15 22 29        5 12 19 26
Tue.   4 11 18 25       2  9 16 23 30        6 13 20 27
Wed.   5 12 19 26       3 10 17 24 31        7 14 21 28
Thur.  6 13 20 27       4 11 18 25       1  8 15 22 29
Fri.   7 14 21 28       5 12 19 26       2  9 16 23 30
Sat.   1  8 15 22 29        6 13 20 27         3 10 17 24

        July                 August              September
Sun.   2  9 16 23 30        6 13 20 27         3 10 17 24
Mon.   3 10 17 24 31        7 14 21 28         4 11 18 25
Tue.   4 11 18 25       1  8 15 22 29        5 12 19 26
Wed.   5 12 19 26       2  9 16 23 30        6 13 20 27
Thur.  6 13 20 27       3 10 17 24 31        7 14 21 28
Fri.   7 14 21 28       4 11 18 25       1  8 15 22 29
Sat.   1  8 15 22 29        5 12 19 26         2  9 16 23 30

        October              November            December
Sun.   1  8 15 22 29        5 12 19 26         3 10 17 24 31
Mon.   2  9 16 23 30        6 13 20 27         4 11 18 25
Tue.   3 10 17 24 31        7 14 21 28         5 12 19 26
Wed.   4 11 18 25       1  8 15 22 29        6 13 20 27
Thur.  5 12 19 26       2  9 16 23 30        7 14 21 28
Fri.   6 13 20 27       3 10 17 24       1  8 15 22 29
Sat.   7 14 21 28       4 11 18 25       2  9 16 23 30
```

B (LEAP YEAR)

```
        January              February            March
Sun.   1  8 15 22 29        5 12 19 26         4 11 18 25
Mon.   2  9 16 23 30        6 13 20 27         5 12 19 26
Tue.   3 10 17 24 31        7 14 21 28         6 13 20 27
Wed.   4 11 18 25       1  8 15 22 29        7 14 21 28
Thur.  5 12 19 26       2  9 16 23         1  8 15 22 29
Fri.   6 13 20 27       3 10 17 24         2  9 16 23 30
Sat.   7 14 21 28       4 11 18 25         3 10 17 24 31

        April                May                 June
Sun.   1  8 15 22 29        6 13 20 27         3 10 17 24
Mon.   2  9 16 23 30        7 14 21 28         4 11 18 25
Tue.   3 10 17 24       1  8 15 22 29        5 12 19 26
Wed.   4 11 18 25       2  9 16 23 30        6 13 20 27
Thur.  5 12 19 26       3 10 17 24 31        7 14 21 28
Fri.   6 13 20 27       4 11 18 25       1  8 15 22 29
Sat.   7 14 21 28       5 12 19 26       2  9 16 23 30

        July                 August              September
Sun.   1  8 15 22 29        5 12 19 26         2  9 16 23 30
Mon.   2  9 16 23 30        6 13 20 27         3 10 17 24
Tue.   3 10 17 24 31        7 14 21 28         4 11 18 25
Wed.   4 11 18 25       1  8 15 22 29        5 12 19 26
Thur.  5 12 19 26       2  9 16 23 30        6 13 20 27
Fri.   6 13 20 27       3 10 17 24 31        7 14 21 28
Sat.   7 14 21 28       4 11 18 25       1  8 15 22 29

        October              November            December
Sun.   7 14 21 28       4 11 18 25         2  9 16 23 30
Mon.   1  8 15 22 29        5 12 19 26         3 10 17 24 31
Tue.   2  9 16 23 30        6 13 20 27         4 11 18 25
Wed.   3 10 17 24 31        7 14 21 28         5 12 19 26
Thur.  4 11 18 25       1  8 15 22 29        6 13 20 27
Fri.   5 12 19 26       2  9 16 23 30        7 14 21 28
Sat.   6 13 20 27       3 10 17 24       1  8 15 22 29
```

EASTER DAYS

March 26	1815, 1826, 1837, 1967, 1978, 1989
April 2	1809, 1893, 1899, 1961
April 9	1871, 1882, 1939, 1950, 2023
April 16	1775, 1786, 1797, 1843, 1854, 1865, 1911, 1922, 1933, 1995, 2006, 2017
April 23	1905

EASTER DAYS

April 1	1804, 1888, 1956
April 8	1792, 1860, 1928, 2012
April 22	1832, 1984

C

	January	February	March
Sun.	7 14 21 28	4 11 18 25	4 11 18 25
Mon.	1 8 15 22 29	5 12 19 26	5 12 19 26
Tue.	2 9 16 23 30	6 13 20 27	6 13 20 27
Wed.	3 10 17 24 31	7 14 21 28	7 14 21 28
Thur.	4 11 18 25	1 8 15 22	1 8 15 22 29
Fri.	5 12 19 26	2 9 16 23	2 9 16 23 30
Sat.	6 13 20 27	3 10 17 24	3 10 17 24 31

	April	May	June
Sun.	1 8 15 22 29	6 13 20 27	3 10 17 24
Mon.	2 9 16 23 30	7 14 21 28	4 11 18 25
Tue.	3 10 17 24	1 8 15 22 29	5 12 19 26
Wed.	4 11 18 25	2 9 16 23 30	6 13 20 27
Thur.	5 12 19 26	3 10 17 24 31	7 14 21 28
Fri.	6 13 20 27	4 11 18 25	1 8 15 22 29
Sat.	7 14 21 28	5 12 19 26	2 9 16 23 30

	July	August	September
Sun.	1 8 15 22 29	5 12 19 26	2 9 16 23 30
Mon.	2 9 16 23 30	6 13 20 27	3 10 17 24
Tue.	3 10 17 24 31	7 14 21 28	4 11 18 25
Wed.	4 11 18 25	1 8 15 22 29	5 12 19 26
Thur.	5 12 19 26	2 9 16 23 30	6 13 20 27
Fri.	6 13 20 27	3 10 17 24 31	7 14 21 28
Sat.	7 14 21 28	4 11 18 25	1 8 15 22 29

	October	November	December
Sun.	7 14 21 28	4 11 18 25	2 9 16 23 30
Mon.	1 8 15 22 29	5 12 19 26	3 10 17 24 31
Tue.	2 9 16 23 30	6 13 20 27	4 11 18 25
Wed.	3 10 17 24 31	7 14 21 28	5 12 19 26
Thur.	4 11 18 25	1 8 15 22 29	6 13 20 27
Fri.	5 12 19 26	2 9 16 23 30	7 14 21 28
Sat.	6 13 20 27	3 10 17 24	1 8 15 22 29

EASTER DAYS

March 25	1883, 1894, 1951
April 1	1866, 1877, 1923, 1934, 1945, 2018, 2029
April 8	1787, 1798, 1849, 1855, 1917, 2007
April 15	1770, 1781, 1827, 1838, 1900, 1906, 1979, 1990, 2001
April 22	1810, 1821, 1962, 1973

E

	January	February	March
Sun.	6 13 20 27	3 10 17 24	3 10 17 24 31
Mon.	7 14 21 28	4 11 18 25	4 11 18 25
Tue.	1 8 15 22 29	5 12 19 26	5 12 19 26
Wed.	2 9 16 23 30	6 13 20 27	6 13 20 27
Thur.	3 10 17 24 31	7 14 21 28	7 14 21 28
Fri.	4 11 18 25	1 8 15 22	1 8 15 22 29
Sat.	5 12 19 26	2 9 16 23	2 9 16 23 30

	April	May	June
Sun.	7 14 21 28	5 12 19 26	2 9 16 23 30
Mon.	1 8 15 22 29	6 13 20 27	3 10 17 24
Tue.	2 9 16 23 30	7 14 21 28	4 11 18 25
Wed.	3 10 17 24	1 8 15 22 29	5 12 19 26
Thur.	4 11 18 25	2 9 16 23 30	6 13 20 27
Fri.	5 12 19 26	3 10 17 24 31	7 14 21 28
Sat.	6 13 20 27	4 11 18 25	1 8 15 22 29

	July	August	September
Sun.	7 14 21 28	4 11 18 25	1 8 15 22 29
Mon.	1 8 15 22 29	5 12 19 26	2 9 16 23 30
Tue.	2 9 16 23 30	6 13 20 27	3 10 17 24
Wed.	3 10 17 24 31	7 14 21 28	4 11 18 25
Thur.	4 11 18 25	1 8 15 22 29	5 12 19 26
Fri.	5 12 19 26	2 9 16 23 30	6 13 20 27
Sat.	6 13 20 27	3 10 17 24 31	7 14 21 28

	October	November	December
Sun.	6 13 20 27	3 10 17 24	1 8 15 22 29
Mon.	7 14 21 28	4 11 18 25	2 9 16 23 30
Tue.	1 8 15 22 29	5 12 19 26	3 10 17 24 31
Wed.	2 9 16 23 30	6 13 20 27	4 11 18 25
Thur.	3 10 17 24 31	7 14 21 28	5 12 19 26
Fri.	4 11 18 25	1 8 15 22 29	6 13 20 27
Sat.	5 12 19 26	2 9 16 23 30	7 14 21 28

EASTER DAYS

March 24	1799
March 31	1771, 1782, 1793, 1839, 1850, 1861, 1907
	1918, 1929, 1991, 2002, 2013
April 7	1822, 1833, 1901, 1985
April 14	1805, 1811, 1895, 1963, 1974
April 21	1867, 1878, 1889, 1935, 1946, 1957, 2019, 2030

D (LEAP YEAR)

	January	February	March
Sun.	7 14 21 28	4 11 18 25	3 10 17 24 31
Mon.	1 8 15 22 29	5 12 19 26	4 11 18 25
Tue.	2 9 16 23 30	6 13 20 27	5 12 19 26
Wed.	3 10 17 24 31	7 14 21 28	6 13 20 27
Thur.	4 11 18 25	1 8 15 22 29	7 14 21 28
Fri.	5 12 19 26	2 9 16 23	1 8 15 22 29
Sat.	6 13 20 27	3 10 17 24	2 9 16 23 30

	April	May	June
Sun.	7 14 21 28	5 12 19 26	2 9 16 23 30
Mon.	1 8 15 22 29	6 13 20 27	3 10 17 24
Tue.	2 9 16 23 30	7 14 21 28	4 11 18 25
Wed.	3 10 17 24	1 8 15 22 29	5 12 19 26
Thur.	4 11 18 25	2 9 16 23 30	6 13 20 27
Fri.	5 12 19 26	3 10 17 24 31	7 14 21 28
Sat.	6 13 20 27	4 11 18 25	1 8 15 22 29

	July	August	September
Sun.	7 14 21 28	4 11 18 25	1 8 15 22 29
Mon.	1 8 15 22 29	5 12 19 26	2 9 16 23 30
Tue.	2 9 16 23 30	6 13 20 27	3 10 17 24
Wed.	3 10 17 24 31	7 14 21 28	4 11 18 25
Thur.	4 11 18 25	1 8 15 22 29	5 12 19 26
Fri.	5 12 19 26	2 9 16 23 30	6 13 20 27
Sat.	6 13 20 27	3 10 17 24 31	7 14 21 28

	October	November	December
Sun.	6 13 20 27	3 10 17 24	1 8 15 22 29
Mon.	7 14 21 28	4 11 18 25	2 9 16 23 30
Tue.	1 8 15 22 29	5 12 19 26	3 10 17 24 31
Wed.	2 9 16 23 30	6 13 20 27	4 11 18 25
Thur.	3 10 17 24 31	7 14 21 28	5 12 19 26
Fri.	4 11 18 25	1 8 15 22 29	6 13 20 27
Sat.	5 12 19 26	2 9 16 23 30	7 14 21 28

EASTER DAYS

March 24	1940
March 31	1872, 2024
April 7	1776, 1844, 1912, 1996
April 14	1816, 1968

F (LEAP YEAR)

	January	February	March
Sun.	6 13 20 27	3 10 17 24	2 9 16 23 30
Mon.	7 14 21 28	4 11 18 25	3 10 17 24 31
Tue.	1 8 15 22 29	5 12 19 26	4 11 18 25
Wed.	2 9 16 23 30	6 13 20 27	5 12 19 26
Thur.	3 10 17 24 31	7 14 21 28	6 13 20 27
Fri.	4 11 18 25	1 8 15 22 29	7 14 21 28
Sat.	5 12 19 26	2 9 16 23	1 8 15 22 29

	April	May	June
Sun.	6 13 20 27	4 11 18 25	1 8 15 22 29
Mon.	7 14 21 28	5 12 19 26	2 9 16 23 30
Tue.	1 8 15 22 29	6 13 20 27	3 10 17 24
Wed.	2 9 16 23 30	7 14 21 28	4 11 18 25
Thur.	3 10 17 24	1 8 15 22 29	5 12 19 26
Fri.	4 11 18 25	2 9 16 23 30	6 13 20 27
Sat.	5 12 19 26	3 10 17 24 31	7 14 21 28

	July	August	September
Sun.	6 13 20 27	3 10 17 24 31	7 14 21 28
Mon.	7 14 21 28	4 11 18 25	1 8 15 22 29
Tue.	1 8 15 22 29	5 12 19 26	2 9 16 23 30
Wed.	2 9 16 23 30	6 13 20 27	3 10 17 24
Thur.	3 10 17 24 31	7 14 21 28	4 11 18 25
Fri.	4 11 18 25	1 8 15 22 29	5 12 19 26
Sat.	5 12 19 26	2 9 16 23 30	6 13 20 27

	October	November	December
Sun.	5 12 19 26	2 9 16 23 30	7 14 21 28
Mon.	6 13 20 27	3 10 17 24	1 8 15 22 29
Tue.	7 14 21 28	4 11 18 25	2 9 16 23 30
Wed.	1 8 15 22 29	5 12 19 26	3 10 17 24 31
Thur.	2 9 16 23 30	6 13 20 27	4 11 18 25
Fri.	3 10 17 24 31	7 14 21 28	5 12 19 26
Sat.	4 11 18 25	1 8 15 22 29	6 13 20 27

EASTER DAYS

March 23	1788, 1856, 2008
April 6	1828, 1980
April 13	1884, 1952
April 20	1924

G

January / February / March

	January	February	March
Sun.	5 12 19 26	2 9 16 23	2 9 16 23 30
Mon.	6 13 20 27	3 10 17 24	3 10 17 24 31
Tue.	7 14 21 28	4 11 18 25	4 11 18 25
Wed.	1 8 15 22 29	5 12 19 26	5 12 19 26
Thur.	2 9 16 23 30	6 13 20 27	6 13 20 27
Fri.	3 10 17 24 31	7 14 21 28	7 14 21 28
Sat.	4 11 18 25	1 8 15 22	1 8 15 22 29

April / May / June

	April	May	June
Sun.	6 13 20 27	4 11 18 25	1 8 15 22 29
Mon.	7 14 21 28	5 12 19 26	2 9 16 23 30
Tue.	1 8 15 22 29	6 13 20 27	3 10 17 24
Wed.	2 9 16 23 30	7 14 21 28	4 11 18 25
Thur.	3 10 17 24	1 8 15 22 29	5 12 19 26
Fri.	4 11 18 25	2 9 16 23 30	6 13 20 27
Sat.	5 12 19 26	3 10 17 24 31	7 14 21 28

July / August / September

	July	August	September
Sun.	6 13 20 27	3 10 17 24 31	7 14 21 28
Mon.	7 14 21 28	4 11 18 25	1 8 15 22 29
Tue.	1 8 15 22 29	5 12 19 26	2 9 16 23 30
Wed.	2 9 16 23 30	6 13 20 27	3 10 17 24
Thur.	3 10 17 24 31	7 14 21 28	4 11 18 25
Fri.	4 11 18 25	1 8 15 22 29	5 12 19 26
Sat.	5 12 19 26	2 9 16 23 30	6 13 20 27

October / November / December

	October	November	December
Sun.	5 12 19 26	2 9 16 23 30	7 14 21 28
Mon.	6 13 20 27	3 10 17 24	1 8 15 22 29
Tue.	7 14 21 28	4 11 18 25	2 9 16 23 30
Wed.	1 8 15 22 29	5 12 19 26	3 10 17 24 31
Thur.	2 9 16 23 30	6 13 20 27	4 11 18 25
Fri.	3 10 17 24 31	7 14 21 28	5 12 19 26
Sat.	4 11 18 25	1 8 15 22 29	6 13 20 27

EASTER DAYS

March 23	1845, 1913
March 30	1777, 1823, 1834, 1902, 1975, 1986, 1997
April 6	1806, 1817, 1890, 1947, 1958, 1969
April 13	1800, 1873, 1879, 1941
April 20	1783, 1794, 1851, 1862, 1919, 1930, 2003, 2014, 2025

I

January / February / March

	January	February	March
Sun.	4 11 18 25	1 8 15 22	1 8 15 22 29
Mon.	5 12 19 26	2 9 16 23	2 9 16 23 30
Tue.	6 13 20 27	3 10 17 24	3 10 17 24 31
Wed.	7 14 21 28	4 11 18 25	4 11 18 25
Thur.	1 8 15 22 29	5 12 19 26	5 12 19 26
Fri.	2 9 16 23 30	6 13 20 27	6 13 20 27
Sat.	3 10 17 24 31	7 14 21 28	7 14 21 28

April / May / June

	April	May	June
Sun.	5 12 19 26	3 10 17 24 31	7 14 21 28
Mon.	6 13 20 27	4 11 18 25	1 8 15 22 29
Tue.	7 14 21 28	5 12 19 26	2 9 16 23 30
Wed.	1 8 15 22 29	6 13 20 27	3 10 17 24
Thur.	2 9 16 23 30	7 14 21 28	4 11 18 25
Fri.	3 10 17 24	1 8 15 22 29	5 12 19 26
Sat.	4 11 18 25	2 9 16 23 30	6 13 20 27

July / August / September

	July	August	September
Sun.	5 12 19 26	2 9 16 23 30	6 13 20 27
Mon.	6 13 20 27	3 10 17 24 31	7 14 21 28
Tue.	7 14 21 28	4 11 18 25	1 8 15 22 29
Wed.	1 8 15 22 29	5 12 19 26	2 9 16 23 30
Thur.	2 9 16 23 30	6 13 20 27	3 10 17 24
Fri.	3 10 17 24 31	7 14 21 28	4 11 18 25
Sat.	4 11 18 25	1 8 15 22 29	5 12 19 26

October / November / December

	October	November	December
Sun.	4 11 18 25	1 8 15 22 29	6 13 20 27
Mon.	5 12 19 26	2 9 16 23 30	7 14 21 28
Tue.	6 13 20 27	3 10 17 24	1 8 15 22 29
Wed.	7 14 21 28	4 11 18 25	2 9 16 23 30
Thur.	1 8 15 22 29	5 12 19 26	3 10 17 24 31
Fri.	2 9 16 23 30	6 13 20 27	4 11 18 25
Sat.	3 10 17 24 31	7 14 21 28	5 12 19 26

EASTER DAYS

March 22	1818
March 29	1807, 1891, 1959, 1970
April 5	1795, 1801, 1863, 1874, 1885, 1931, 1942, 1953, 2015, 2026
April 12	1789, 1846, 1857, 1903, 1914, 1925, 1998, 2009
April 19	1778, 1829, 1835, 1981, 1987

H (LEAP YEAR)

January / February / March

	January	February	March
Sun.	5 12 19 26	2 9 16 23	1 8 15 22 29
Mon.	6 13 20 27	3 10 17 24	2 9 16 23 30
Tue.	7 14 21 28	4 11 18 25	3 10 17 24 31
Wed.	1 8 15 22 29	5 12 19 26	4 11 18 25
Thur.	2 9 16 23 30	6 13 20 27	5 12 19 26
Fri.	3 10 17 24 31	7 14 21 28	6 13 20 27
Sat.	4 11 18 25	1 8 15 22 29	7 14 21 28

April / May / June

	April	May	June
Sun.	5 12 19 26	3 10 17 24 31	7 14 21 28
Mon.	6 13 20 27	4 11 18 25	1 8 15 22 29
Tue.	7 14 21 28	5 12 19 26	2 9 16 23 30
Wed.	1 8 15 22 29	6 13 20 27	3 10 17 24
Thur.	2 9 16 23 30	7 14 21 28	4 11 18 25
Fri.	3 10 17 24	1 8 15 22 29	5 12 19 26
Sat.	4 11 18 25	2 9 16 23 30	6 13 20 27

July / August / September

	July	August	September
Sun.	5 12 19 26	2 9 16 23 30	6 13 20 27
Mon.	6 13 20 27	3 10 17 24 31	7 14 21 28
Tue.	7 14 21 28	4 11 18 25	1 8 15 22 29
Wed.	1 8 15 22 29	5 12 19 26	2 9 16 23 30
Thur.	2 9 16 23 30	6 13 20 27	3 10 17 24
Fri.	3 10 17 24 31	7 14 21 28	4 11 18 25
Sat.	4 11 18 25	1 8 15 22 29	5 12 19 26

October / November / December

	October	November	December
Sun.	4 11 18 25	1 8 15 22 29	6 13 20 27
Mon.	5 12 19 26	2 9 16 23 30	7 14 21 28
Tue.	6 13 20 27	3 10 17 24	1 8 15 22 29
Wed.	7 14 21 28	4 11 18 25	2 9 16 23 30
Thur.	1 8 15 22 29	5 12 19 26	3 10 17 24 31
Fri.	2 9 16 23 30	6 13 20 27	4 11 18 25
Sat.	3 10 17 24 31	7 14 21 28	5 12 19 26

EASTER DAYS

March 29	1812, 1964
April 5	1896
April 12	1868, 1936, 2020
April 19	1772, 1840, 1908, 1992

J (LEAP YEAR)

January / February / March

	January	February	March
Sun.	4 11 18 25	1 8 15 22 29	7 14 21 28
Mon.	5 12 19 26	2 9 16 23	1 8 15 22 29
Tue.	6 13 20 27	3 10 17 24	2 9 16 23 30
Wed.	7 14 21 28	4 11 18 25	3 10 17 24 31
Thur.	1 8 15 22 29	5 12 19 26	4 11 18 25
Fri.	2 9 16 23 30	6 13 20 27	5 12 19 26
Sat.	3 10 17 24 31	7 14 21 28	6 13 20 27

April / May / June

	April	May	June
Sun.	4 11 18 25	2 9 16 23 30	6 13 20 27
Mon.	5 12 19 26	3 10 17 24 31	7 14 21 28
Tue.	6 13 20 27	4 11 18 25	1 8 15 22 29
Wed.	7 14 21 28	5 12 19 26	2 9 16 23 30
Thur.	1 8 15 22 29	6 13 20 27	3 10 17 24
Fri.	2 9 16 23 30	7 14 21 28	4 11 18 25
Sat.	3 10 17 24	1 8 15 22 29	5 12 19 26

July / August / September

	July	August	September
Sun.	4 11 18 25	1 8 15 22 29	5 12 19 26
Mon.	5 12 19 26	2 9 16 23 30	6 13 20 27
Tue.	6 13 20 27	3 10 17 24 31	7 14 21 28
Wed.	7 14 21 28	4 11 18 25	1 8 15 22 29
Thur.	1 8 15 22 29	5 12 19 26	2 9 16 23 30
Fri.	2 9 16 23 30	6 13 20 27	3 10 17 24
Sat.	3 10 17 24 31	7 14 21 28	4 11 18 25

October / November / December

	October	November	December
Sun.	3 10 17 24 31	7 14 21 28	5 12 19 26
Mon.	4 11 18 25	1 8 15 22 29	6 13 20 27
Tue.	5 12 19 26	2 9 16 23 30	7 14 21 28
Wed.	6 13 20 27	3 10 17 24	1 8 15 22 29
Thur.	7 14 21 28	4 11 18 25	2 9 16 23 30
Fri.	1 8 15 22 29	5 12 19 26	3 10 17 24 31
Sat.	2 9 16 23 30	6 13 20 27	4 11 18 25

EASTER DAYS

March 28	1880, 1948
April 4	1920
April 11	1784, 1852, 2004
April 18	1824, 1976

K

	January	February	March
Sun.	3 10 17 24 31	7 14 21 28	7 14 21 28
Mon.	4 11 18 25	1 8 15 22	1 8 15 22 29
Tue.	5 12 19 26	2 9 16 23	2 9 16 23 30
Wed.	6 13 20 27	3 10 17 24	3 10 17 24 31
Thur.	7 14 21 28	4 11 18 25	4 11 18 25
Fri.	1 8 15 22 29	5 12 19 26	5 12 19 26
Sat.	2 9 16 23 30	6 13 20 27	6 13 20 27

	April	May	June
Sun.	4 11 18 25	2 9 16 23 30	6 13 20 27
Mon.	5 12 19 26	3 10 17 24 31	7 14 21 28
Tue.	6 13 20 27	4 11 18 25	1 8 15 22 29
Wed.	7 14 21 28	5 12 19 26	2 9 16 23 30
Thur.	1 8 15 22 29	6 13 20 27	3 10 17 24
Fri.	2 9 16 23 30	7 14 21 28	4 11 18 25
Sat.	3 10 17 24	1 8 15 22 29	5 12 19 26

	July	August	September
Sun.	4 11 18 25	1 8 15 22 29	5 12 19 26
Mon.	5 12 19 26	2 9 16 23 30	6 13 20 27
Tue.	6 13 20 27	3 10 17 24 31	7 14 21 28
Wed.	7 14 21 28	4 11 18 25	1 8 15 22 29
Thur.	1 8 15 22 29	5 12 19 26	2 9 16 23 30
Fri.	2 9 16 23 30	6 13 20 27	3 10 17 24
Sat.	3 10 17 24 31	7 14 21 28	4 11 18 25

	October	November	December
Sun.	3 10 17 24 31	7 14 21 28	5 12 19 26
Mon.	4 11 18 25	1 8 15 22 29	6 13 20 27
Tue.	5 12 19 26	2 9 16 23 30	7 14 21 28
Wed.	6 13 20 27	3 10 17 24	1 8 15 22 29
Thur.	7 14 21 28	4 11 18 25	2 9 16 23 30
Fri.	1 8 15 22 29	5 12 19 26	3 10 17 24 31
Sat.	2 9 16 23 30	6 13 20 27	4 11 18 25

EASTER DAYS

March 28	1869, 1875, 1937, 2027
April 4	1779, 1790, 1847, 1858, 1915, 1926, 1999 2010, 2021
April 11	1773, 1819, 1830, 1841, 1909, 1971, 1982, 1993
April 18	1802, 1813, 1897, 1954, 1965
April 25	1886, 1943

M

	January	February	March
Sun.	2 9 16 23 30	6 13 20 27	6 13 20 27
Mon.	3 10 17 24 31	7 14 21 28	7 14 21 28
Tue.	4 11 18 25	1 8 15 22	1 8 15 22 29
Wed.	5 12 19 26	2 9 16 23	2 9 16 23 30
Thur.	6 13 20 27	3 10 17 24	3 10 17 24 31
Fri.	7 14 21 28	4 11 18 25	4 11 18 25
Sat.	1 8 15 22 29	5 12 19 26	5 12 19 26

	April	May	June
Sun.	3 10 17 24	1 8 15 22 29	5 12 19 26
Mon.	4 11 18 25	2 9 16 23 30	6 13 20 27
Tue.	5 12 19 26	3 10 17 24 31	7 14 21 28
Wed.	6 13 20 27	4 11 18 25	1 8 15 22 29
Thur.	7 14 21 28	5 12 19 26	2 9 16 23 30
Fri.	1 8 15 22 29	6 13 20 27	3 10 17 24
Sat.	2 9 16 23 30	7 14 21 28	4 11 18 25

	July	August	September
Sun.	3 10 17 24 31	7 14 21 28	4 11 18 25
Mon.	4 11 18 25	1 8 15 22 29	5 12 19 26
Tue.	5 12 19 26	2 9 16 23 30	6 13 20 27
Wed.	6 13 20 27	3 10 17 24 31	7 14 21 28
Thur.	7 14 21 28	4 11 18 25	1 8 15 22 29
Fri.	1 8 15 22 29	5 12 19 26	2 9 16 23 30
Sat.	2 9 16 23 30	6 13 20 27	3 10 17 24

	October	November	December
Sun.	2 9 16 23 30	6 13 20 27	4 11 18 25
Mon.	3 10 17 24 31	7 14 21 28	5 12 19 26
Tue.	4 11 18 25	1 8 15 22 29	6 13 20 27
Wed.	5 12 19 26	2 9 16 23 30	7 14 21 28
Thur.	6 13 20 27	3 10 17 24	1 8 15 22 29
Fri.	7 14 21 28	4 11 18 25	2 9 16 23 30
Sat.	1 8 15 22 29	5 12 19 26	3 10 17 24 31

EASTER DAYS

March 27	1785, 1842, 1853, 1910, 1921, 2005
April 3	1774, 1825, 1831, 1983, 1994
April 10	1803, 1814, 1887, 1898, 1955, 1966, 1977
April 17	1870, 1881, 1927, 1938, 1949, 2022
April 24	1791, 1859, 2011

L (LEAP YEAR)

	January	February	March
Sun.	3 10 17 24 31	7 14 21 28	6 13 20 27
Mon.	4 11 18 25	1 8 15 22 29	7 14 21 28
Tue.	5 12 19 26	2 9 16 23	1 8 15 22 29
Wed.	6 13 20 27	3 10 17 24	2 9 16 23 30
Thur.	7 14 21 28	4 11 18 25	3 10 17 24 31
Fri.	1 8 15 22 29	5 12 19 26	4 11 18 25
Sat.	2 9 16 23 30	6 13 20 27	5 12 19 26

	April	May	June
Sun.	3 10 17 24	1 8 15 22 29	5 12 19 26
Mon.	4 11 18 25	2 9 16 23 30	6 13 20 27
Tue.	5 12 19 26	3 10 17 24 31	7 14 21 28
Wed.	6 13 20 27	4 11 18 25	1 8 15 22 29
Thur.	7 14 21 28	5 12 19 26	2 9 16 23 30
Fri.	1 8 15 22 29	6 13 20 27	3 10 17 24
Sat.	2 9 16 23 30	7 14 21 28	4 11 18 25

	July	August	September
Sun.	3 10 17 24 31	7 14 21 28	4 11 18 25
Mon.	4 11 18 25	1 8 15 22 29	5 12 19 26
Tue.	5 12 19 26	2 9 16 23 30	6 13 20 27
Wed.	6 13 20 27	3 10 17 24 31	7 14 21 28
Thur.	7 14 21 28	4 11 18 25	1 8 15 22 29
Fri.	1 8 15 22 29	5 12 19 26	2 9 16 23 30
Sat.	2 9 16 23 30	6 13 20 27	3 10 17 24

	October	November	December
Sun.	2 9 16 23 30	6 13 20 27	4 11 18 25
Mon.	3 10 17 24 31	7 14 21 28	5 12 19 26
Tue.	4 11 18 25	1 8 15 22	6 13 20 27
Wed.	5 12 19 26	2 9 16 23 30	7 14 21 28
Thur.	6 13 20 27	3 10 17 24	1 8 15 22 29
Fri.	7 14 21 28	4 11 18 25	2 9 16 23 30
Sat.	1 8 15 22 29	5 12 19 26	3 10 17 24 31

EASTER DAYS

March 27	1796, 1864, 1932, 2016
April 3	1836, 1904, 1988
April 17	1808, 1892, 1960

N (LEAP YEAR)

	January	February	March
Sun.	2 9 16 23 30	6 13 20 27	5 12 19 26
Mon.	3 10 17 24 31	7 14 21 28	6 13 20 27
Tue.	4 11 18 25	1 8 15 22 29	7 14 21 28
Wed.	5 12 19 26	2 9 16 23	1 8 15 22 29
Thur.	6 13 20 27	3 10 17 24	2 9 16 23 30
Fri.	7 14 21 28	4 11 18 25	3 10 17 24 31
Sat.	1 8 15 22 29	5 12 19 26	4 11 18 25

	April	May	June
Sun.	2 9 16 23 30	7 14 21 28	4 11 18 25
Mon.	3 10 17 24	1 8 15 22 29	5 12 19 26
Tue.	4 11 18 25	2 9 16 23 30	6 13 20 27
Wed.	5 12 19 26	3 10 17 24 31	7 14 21 28
Thur.	6 13 20 27	4 11 18 25	1 8 15 22 29
Fri.	7 14 21 28	5 12 19 26	2 9 16 23 30
Sat.	1 8 15 22 29	6 13 20 27	3 10 17 24

	July	August	September
Sun.	2 9 16 23 30	6 13 20 27	3 10 17 24
Mon.	3 10 17 24 31	7 14 21 28	4 11 18 25
Tue.	4 11 18 25	1 8 15 22 29	5 12 19 26
Wed.	5 12 19 26	2 9 16 23 30	6 13 20 27
Thur.	6 13 20 27	3 10 17 24 31	7 14 21 28
Fri.	7 14 21 28	4 11 18 25	1 8 15 22 29
Sat.	1 8 15 22 29	5 12 19 26	2 9 16 23 30

	October	November	December
Sun.	1 8 15 22 29	5 12 19 26	3 10 17 24 31
Mon.	2 9 16 23 30	6 13 20 27	4 11 18 25
Tue.	3 10 17 24 31	7 14 21 28	5 12 19 26
Wed.	4 11 18 25	1 8 15 22 29	6 13 20 27
Thur.	5 12 19 26	2 9 16 23 30	7 14 21 28
Fri.	6 13 20 27	3 10 17 24	1 8 15 22 29
Sat.	7 14 21 28	4 11 18 25	2 9 16 23 30

EASTER DAYS

March 26	1780
April 2	1820, 1972
April 9	1944
April 16	1876, 2028
April 23	1848, 1916, 2000

GEOLOGICAL TIME

The earth is thought to have come into existence approximately 4,600 million years ago, but for nearly half this time, the Archean era, it was uninhabited. Life is generally believed to have emerged in the succeeding Proterozoic era. The Archean and the Proterozoic eras are often together referred to as the Precambrian.

Although primitive forms of life, e.g. algae and bacteria, existed during the Proterozoic era, it is not until the strata of Palaeozoic rocks is reached that abundant fossilized remains appear, initially of small shellfish, followed by plants, primitive fishes and, in the Devonian period (c.400 million BC), land-living plants and amphibia.

Since the Precambrian, there have been three great geological eras:

PALAEOZOIC ('ancient life')
c.570–c.250 million BC

Cambrian - Mainly sandstones, slate and shales; limestones in Scotland. Shelled fossils and invertebrates, e.g. trilobites and brachiopods appear
Ordovician - Mainly shales and mudstones, e.g. in north Wales; limestones in Scotland
Silurian - Shales, mudstones and some limestones, found mostly in Wales and southern Scotland
Devonian - Old red sandstone, shale, limestone and slate, e.g. in south Wales and the West Country. 'The age of fishes' – proliferation of fish fossils. First traces of land-living life
Carboniferous - Coal-bearing rocks, millstone grit, limestone and shale
Permian - Marls, sandstones and clays, named after the area of Russia where these strata are widespread. First large-scale appearance of reptile fossils

There were two great phases of mountain building in the Palaeozoic era: the Caledonian, characterized in Britain by NE–SW lines of hills and valleys; and the later Hercyian, widespread in west Germany and adjacent areas, and in Britain exemplified in E.–W. lines of hills and valleys.

The end of the Palaeozoic era was marked by the extensive glaciations of the Permian period in the southern continents and the decline of amphibians. It was succeeded by an era of warm conditions.

MESOZOIC ('middle forms of life')
c.250–c.65 million BC

Triassic - Mostly sandstone, e.g. in the West Midlands
Jurassic - Mainly limestones and clays, typically displayed in the Jura mountains, and in England in a NE–SW belt from Lincolnshire and the Wash to the Severn and the Dorset coast
Cretaceous - Mainly chalk, clay and sands, e.g. in Kent and Sussex

Giant reptiles were dominant during the Mesozoic era, but it was at this time that marsupial mammals first appeared, as well as Archaeopteryx lithographica, the earliest known species of bird. Coniferous trees and flowering plants also developed during the era and, with the birds and the mammals, were the main species to survive into the Caenozoic (or Cenozoic) era. The giant reptiles became extinct.

CAENOZOIC ('recent life')
from c.65 million BC

Eocene - The emergence of new forms of life, i.e. existing species

Oligocene - Fossils of a few still existing species
Miocene - Fossil remains show a balance of existing and extinct species
Pliocene - Fossil remains show a majority of still existing species
Pleistocene - The majority of remains are those of still existing species
Holocene - The present, post-glacial period. Existing species only, except for a few exterminated by man

In the last 25 million years, from the Miocene through the Pliocene periods, the Alpine-Himalayan and the circum-Pacific phases of mountain building reached their climax. During the Pleistocene period ice sheets repeatedly locked up masses of water as land ice; its weight depressed the land, but the locking-up of the water lowered the sea-level by 100–200 metres. The glaciations and interglacials of the Ice Age are extremely difficult to date and classify, but recent scientific opinion considers the Pleistocene period to have begun approximately 1.7 million years ago. The last glacial retreat, merging into the Holocene period, was 10,000 years ago.

HUMAN DEVELOPMENT

Any consideration of the history of mankind must start with the fact that all members of the human race belong to one species of animal, i.e. Homo sapiens, the definition of a species being in biological terms that all its members can interbreed. As a species of mammal it is possible to group man with other similar types, known as the primates. Amongst these is found a sub-group, the apes, which includes, in addition to man, the chimpanzees, gorillas, orang-utans and gibbons. All lack a tail, have shoulder blades at the back, and a Y-shaped chewing pattern on the surface of their molars, as well as showing the more general primate characteristics of four incisors, a thumb which is able to touch the fingers of the same hand, and finger and toe nails instead of claws. All the factors available to scientific study suggest that human beings have chimpanzees and gorillas as their nearest relatives in the animal world. However, there remains the possibility that there once lived creatures, now extinct, which were closer to modern man than the chimpanzees and gorillas, and which shared with modern man the characteristics of having flat faces (i.e. the absence of a pronounced muzzle), being bipedal, and possessing large brains.

There are two broad groups of extinct apes recognized by specialists. First the ramapithecines, the remains of which, mainly jaw fragments, have been found in east Africa, Asia, and Turkey. They lived about 14 to 8 million years ago, and from the evidence of their teeth it seems they chewed more in the manner of modern man than the other presently living apes. The second group, the australopithecines, have left much more numerous remains amongst which sub-groups may be detected, although the geographic spread is limited to south and east Africa. Living between 5 and 1.5 million years ago, they were closer relatives of modern man to the extent that they walked upright, did not have an extensive muzzle, and had similar types of pre-molars. The first australopithecine remains were recognized at Taung in South Africa in 1924, and subsequent discoveries include those at the famous site of Olduvai Gorge in Tanzania. Perhaps the most impressive discovery was made at Hadar in Ethiopia in 1974 when about half a skeleton, known as 'Lucy', was found.

Also in east Africa, between 2 million and 1.5 million years ago, lived a hominid group which not only walked upright, had a flat face, and a large brain case, but also made simple pebble and flake stone tools. On present evidence these habilines seem to have been the first people to make tools, however crude. This facility is related to the larger brain size and human beings are the only animals to make implements to be used in other processes. These early pebble tool users, because of their distinctive characteristics, have been grouped as a separate sub-species, now extinct, of the genus *Homo*, and are known as *Homo habilis*.

The use of fire, again a human characteristic, is associated with another group of extinct hominids whose remains, about a million years old, are found in south and east Africa, China, Indonesia, north Africa and Europe. No doubt the mastery of the techniques of making fire helped the colonization of the colder northern areas and in this respect the site of Vertesszollos in Hungary is of particular importance. *Homo erectus* is the name given to this group of fossils and it now includes a number of famous individual discoveries from earlier decades, for example, Solo Man, Heidelberg Man, and especially Peking Man who lived at the cave site at Choukoutien which has yielded evidence of fire and burnt bone.

The well-known group, Neanderthal Man, or *Homo sapiens neandertalensis*, is an extinct form of modern man who lived between about 100,000 and 40,000 years ago, thus spanning the last Ice Age. Indeed, its ability to adapt to the cold climate on the edge of the ice sheets is one of its characteristic features, the remains being found only in Europe, Asia and the Middle East. Complete neandertal skeletons were found during excavations at Tabun in Israel, together with evidence of tool-making and the use of fire. Distinguished by very large brains, it seems that neanderthal man was the first to develop recognizable social customs, especially deliberate burial rites. Why the neanderthalers became extinct is not clear, but it may be connected with the climatic changes at the end of the Ice Ages, which would have seriously affected their food supplies; possibly they became too specialized for their own good.

The Swanscombe skull is the only known human fossil remains found in England. Some specialists see Swanscombe Man (or, more probably, woman) as a neanderthaler. Others group these remains together with the Steinheim skull from Germany, seeing both as a separate sub-species. Unfortunately there is too little evidence as yet on which to form a final judgement.

Modern Man, *Homo sapiens sapiens*, the surviving sub-species of *Homo sapiens*, had evolved to our present physical condition and had colonized much of the world by about 30,000 years ago. There are many previously distinguished individual specimens, for example Cromagnon Man, which may now be grouped together as *Homo sapiens sapiens*. It was modern man who spread to the American continent by crossing the landbridge between Siberia and Alaska and thence moved south through North America and into South America. Equally it is modern man who over the last 30,000 years has been responsible for the major developments in technology, art and civilization generally.

One of the problems for those studying fossil man is the lack in many cases of sufficient quantities of fossil bone for analysis. It is important that theories should be tested against evidence, and not the evidence made to fit the theory. The celebrated Piltdown hoax is perhaps the best-known example of 'fossils' being forged to fit what was seen in some quarters as the correct theory of man's evolution.

CULTURAL DEVELOPMENT

The Eurocentric bias of early archaeologists meant that the search for a starting point for the development and transmission of cultural ideas, especially by migration, trade and warfare, concentrated unduly on Europe and the Near East. The Three Age system, whereby pre-history was divided into a Stone Age, a Bronze Age, and an Iron Age, was devised by Christian Thomsen, curator of the National Museum of Denmark in the early nineteenth century, to facilitate the classification of the museum's collections. The descriptive adjectives referred to the materials from which the implements and weapons were made, and came to be regarded as the dominant features of the societies to which they related. The refinement of the Three Age system once dominated archaeological thought and still remains a generally accepted concept in the popular mind. However, it is now seen by archaeologists as an inadequate model for human development.

Common sense alone suggests that there were no complete breaks between one so-called Age and another, any more than contemporaries would have regarded 1485 as a complete break between medieval and modern English history. Nor can the Three Age system be applied universally. In some areas it is necessary to insert a Copper Age, while in Africa south of the Sahara there would seem to be no Bronze Age at all; in Australia, Old Stone Age societies survived, while in South America, New Stone Age communities existed into modern times. The civilizations in other parts of the world clearly invalidate a Eurocentric theory of human development.

The concept of the 'Neolithic revolution', associated with the domestication of plants and animals, was a development of particular importance in the human cultural pattern. It reflected change from the primitive hunter/gatherer economies to a more settled agricultural way of life and therefore, so the argument goes, made possible the development of urban civilization. However, it can no longer be argued that this 'revolution' took place only in one area from which all development stemmed. Though it appears that the cultivation of wheat and barley was first undertaken, together with the domestication of cattle and goats/sheep in the Fertile Crescent, there is evidence that rice was first deliberately planted and pigs domesticated in south-east Asia, maize first cultivated in Central America, and llamas first domesticated in South America. It has been recognized increasingly in recent years that cultural changes can take place independently of each other in different parts of the world at different rates and different times. There is no need for a general diffusionist theory.

Although scholars will continue to study the particular societies which interest them, it may be possible to obtain a reliable chronological framework, in absolute terms of years, against which the cultural development of any particular area may be set. The development and refinement of radio-carbon dating and other scientific methods of producing absolute chronologies is enabling the cross-referencing of societies to be undertaken. As the techniques of dating become more rigorous in application and the number of scientifically obtained dates increases, the attainment of an absolute chronology for prehistoric societies throughout the world comes closer to being achieved.

Tidal Tables

CONSTANTS

The constant tidal difference may be used in conjunction with the time of high water at a standard port shown in the predictions data (pages 98–109) to find the time of high water at any of the ports or places listed below.

EXAMPLE

Required times of high water at Stranraer at 1 *January* 1994
Appropriate time of high water at *Greenock*

	Morning tide 1 *January*	0232 hrs
Tidal difference		− 0020 hrs
High water at *Stranraer*		0212 hrs

The columns headed 'Springs' and 'Neaps' show the height, in metres, of the tide above datum for mean high water springs and mean high water neaps respectively.

* data very approximate
† data for first high water springs only
H. Harbour

Port		Diff.	Springs	Neaps
		h m	m	m
Aberdeen	Leith	−1 19	4.3	3.4
Aberdovey	Liverpool	−3 01	5.0	3.5
Aberystwyth	Liverpool	−3 31	5.0	3.5
Aldeburgh	London	−3 05	2.8	2.7
Alloa	Leith	+0 49	5.6	4.2
Amlwch	Liverpool	−0 35	7.2	5.7
Anstruther Easter	Leith	−0 22	5.5	4.4
Antwerp (Prosperpolder)	London	+0 50	5.8	4.8
Appledore	Avonmouth	−1 16	7.5	5.2
Arbroath	Leith	−0 33	5.0	4.1
Ardrossan	Greenock	−0 15	3.2	2.7
*Arundel	London	−2 04	3.2	2.1
Avonmouth	Avonmouth	0 00	13.2	9.8
Ayr	Greenock	−0 25	3.0	2.6
Baie de Lampaul	London	+2 30	7.4	5.8
Ballycotton	Avonmouth	−1 47	4.2	3.2
Banff	Leith	−2 44	3.5	2.8
Bantry	Liverpool	+5 55	3.3	2.4
Bardsey Island	Liverpool	−3 20	4.4	3.2
Barmouth	Liverpool	−2 58	5.0	3.5
Barnstaple	Avonmouth	−1 01	4.1	1.4
Barrow (Docks)	Liverpool	0 00	9.3	7.1
Barry	Avonmouth	−0 22	11.4	8.5
Belfast	London	−2 47	3.5	3.0
Berwick	Leith	−0 03	4.7	3.8
Bideford	Avonmouth	−1 16	5.9	3.6
Blackpool	Liverpool	−0 10	8.9	7.0
Blacktoft	Hull	+0 31	5.7	3.9
Blakeney	Hull	+0 46	3.4	2.0
Blyth	Leith	+0 51	5.0	3.9
Boscastle	Avonmouth	−1 21	7.3	5.6
Boulogne	London	−2 44	8.9	7.2
Bovisand Pier	London	+3 55	5.3	4.3
Bowling	Greenock	+0 15	4.0	3.4
Braye (Alderney)	London	+5 33	6.3	4.7
Brest	London	+2 28	7.5	5.9
Bridgwater	Avonmouth	−0 22	4.6	1.7
Bridlington	Leith	+2 04	6.1	4.7
Bridport (W. Bay)	London	+4 37	4.1	3.0
Brighton	London	−2 51	6.6	5.0
Buckie	Leith	−2 56	4.1	3.2
Bude Haven	Avonmouth	−1 34	7.7	5.8
Bull Sand Fort	Hull	−0 44	6.9	5.5
Burntisland	Leith	0 00	5.6	4.5
Calais	London	−2 04	7.1	5.9
Campbeltown	Greenock	+0 07	2.9	2.6
Cape Cornwall	Avonmouth	−2 31	6.0	4.3
Cardiff (Penarth)	Avonmouth	−0 15	12.2	9.2
Cardigan Port	Liverpool	−3 38	4.7	3.4
Carmarthen	Avonmouth	−0 49	2.6	0.4
Cayeux	London	−2 55	10.2	7.9
Chatham	London	−1 08	6.0	4.9
Chepstow	Avonmouth	+0 20	No data	
Cherbourg	London	−6 00	6.4	5.0
Chester	Liverpool	+1 05	4.0	2.0
Chichester H.	London	−2 40	4.9	4.0
†Christchurch H.	London	−5 08	1.8	1.4
Cobh	Liverpool	−5 55	4.2	3.2
Coulport	Greenock	−0 05	3.4	2.9
Coverack	Avonmouth	−2 02	5.3	4.2
Cowes	London	−2 38	4.2	3.5
Cromarty	Leith	−2 56	4.3	3.4
Cromer	Hull	+0 15	5.2	4.1
Dartmouth	London	+4 25	4.9	3.8
Deal	London	−2 37	6.1	5.0
Dieppe	London	−3 03	9.3	7.2
Dingle H.	Liverpool	+5 34	3.9	2.8
Donegal H.	Liverpool	−5 24	3.9	3.0
Douglas (IOM)	Liverpool	−0 04	6.9	5.4
Dover	London	−2 52	6.7	5.3
Duclair	London	−1 48	7.5	6.3
Duddon Bar	Liverpool	+0 03	8.5	6.6
Dunbar	Leith	−0 07	5.2	4.2
Dundalk (Sldr's Pt)	Liverpool	+0 21	5.1	4.2
Dundee	Leith	+0 11	5.4	4.3
Dungeness	London	−3 04	7.7	5.9
Dunkirk	London	−1 54	5.8	4.8
Eastbourne	London	−2 51	7.4	5.5
East Loch Tarbert	Greenock	+0 05	3.4	2.9
Exmouth Dock	London	+4 55	4.0	2.8
Eyemouth	Leith	−0 20	4.7	3.7
Falmouth	London	+3 35	5.3	4.2
Ferryside	Avonmouth	−0 59	6.7	4.5
Filey Bay	Leith	+1 51	5.8	4.9
Fishguard	Liverpool	−4 01	4.8	3.4
Folkestone	London	−3 04	7.1	5.7
Formby	Liverpool	−0 12	9.0	7.3
Fowey	London	+3 53	5.4	4.3
Fraserburgh	Leith	−2 29	3.7	2.9
†Freshwater Bay	London	−4 48	2.6	2.3
Galway	Liverpool	−6 08	5.1	3.9
Glasgow	Greenock	+0 26	4.7	4.1
Goole	Hull	+1 00	5.7	3.7
Gorleston	London	−5 00	2.4	2.0
Granton	Leith	0 00	5.6	4.5
Granville	London	+4 32	13.0	9.8
Grimsby	Hull	−0 27	7.0	5.6
Hartlepool	Leith	+0 57	5.4	4.2
Harwich	London	−2 06	4.0	3.4
Hastings	London	−2 57	7.5	5.8
Haverfordwest	Liverpool	−4 51	2.2	0.3

Port	Diff. h m	Springs m	Neaps m
Hestan Islet	Liverpool +0 25	8.3	6.3
Holyhead	Liverpool −0 50	5.6	4.4
Hook of Holland	London −0 01	2.1	1.7
†Hurst Point	London −3 53	2.7	2.3
Ijmuiden	London +1 03	2.0	1.6
Ilfracombe	Avonmouth −1 12	9.2	6.9
Inveraray	Greenock +0 11	3.3	3.0
Invergordon	Leith −2 48	4.4	3.5
Ipswich	London −1 46	4.2	3.4
Itchenor	London −2 38	4.8	3.8
Kinsale	Liverpool −6 07	4.0	3.2
Kirkcudbright	Liverpool +0 15	7.5	5.9
Kirkwall	Leith −4 15	2.9	2.2
Knights Town	Liverpool +5 32	3.6	2.8
Lamlash	Greenock −0 26	3.2	2.7
Le Havre	London −3 55	7.9	6.6
Lerwick	Leith −3 48	2.2	1.6
Limerick Dock	Liverpool −4 27	6.1	4.6
Littlehampton	London −2 39	5.9	4.5
Lizard Point	Avonmouth −2 17	5.3	4.2
Llanddwyn Island	Liverpool −1 55	4.9	3.9
Llanelli	Avonmouth −0 57	7.8	5.8
Loch Moidart	Greenock +5 58	4.8	3.5
Londonderry	London −5 37	2.7	2.1
Looe	London +3 55	5.4	4.2
Lossiemouth	Leith −3 01	4.1	3.2
Lowestoft	London −4 25	2.4	2.1
Lulworth Cove	London +4 59	2.3	1.5
Lundy Island	Avonmouth −1 24	8.0	5.9
Lyme Regis	London +4 55	4.3	3.1
†Lymington	London −3 48	3.0	2.6
Margate	London −1 53	4.8	3.9
Maryport	Liverpool +0 24	8.6	6.6
Menai Bridge	Liverpool −0 30	7.3	5.8
Mevagissey	London +3 53	5.4	4.3
Middlesbrough	Leith +1 08	5.6	4.5
Milford Haven	Liverpool −5 08	7.0	5.2
Minehead	Avonmouth −0 40	10.6	7.9
Montrose	Leith −0 19	4.8	3.9
Morecambe	Liverpool +0 07	9.5	7.4
Mostyn Quay	Liverpool −0 17	8.5	6.7
Newburgh	Leith +0 48	4.1	3.0
Newcastle upon Tyne	Leith +0 53	5.3	4.1
Newhaven	London −2 46	6.7	5.1
Newlyn	Avonmouth −2 25	5.6	4.4
Newport (Gwent)	Avonmouth −0 15	12.1	8.8
Newquay	Avonmouth −1 59	7.0	5.3
New Quay, Cardigan Bay	Liverpool −3 31	4.9	3.4
North Shields	Leith +0 50	5.0	3.9
North Sunderland	Leith +0 04	4.8	3.7
N. Woolwich	London −0 20	7.0	5.9
Oban	Greenock +5 43	4.0	2.9
Old Lynn Road	Hull +0 07	7.3	5.8
Orfordness	London −2 50	2.8	2.7
Ostend	London −1 32	5.1	4.2
Padstow	Avonmouth −1 46	7.3	5.6
Peel (IOM)	Liverpool −0 02	5.3	4.2
Peterhead	Leith −1 59	3.8	3.1
Plymouth	London +4 05	5.5	4.4
†Poole (Entrance)	London −5 18	2.0	1.6
Porlock Bay	Avonmouth −0 50	10.2	7.6
Porthcawl	Avonmouth −0 54	9.9	7.5
Portmadoc	Liverpool −2 46	5.1	3.4
Portland	London +5 09	2.1	1.4
Portpatrick	Liverpool +0 22	3.8	3.0
Portsmouth	London −2 38	4.7	3.8
Port Talbot	Avonmouth −0 54	9.6	7.3
Preston	Liverpool +0 10	5.3	3.3
Pwllheli	Liverpool −3 08	5.0	3.4
Ramsey (IOM)	Liverpool +0 10	7.6	5.9
Ramsgate	London −2 32	4.9	3.8
*Rosslare H.	Liverpool −5 24	1.9	1.4
Rosyth	Leith +0 09	5.8	4.7
Ryde	London −2 38	4.5	3.7
St Helier	London +4 48	11.1	8.1
St Ives	Avonmouth −1 56	6.6	4.9
St Malo	London +4 27	12.2	9.2
St Peter Port	London +4 54	9.3	7.0
Salcombe	London +4 10	5.3	4.1
Saltash	London +4 10	5.6	4.5
Scarborough	Leith +1 33	5.7	4.6
Scheveningen	London +1 02	2.1	1.6
Scrabster	Leith −6 06	5.0	4.0
Seaham	Leith +0 54	5.2	4.1
Selsey Bill	London −2 43	5.3	4.4
Sennen Cove	Avonmouth −2 31	6.1	4.8
Sharpness Dock	Avonmouth +0 42	9.3	5.6
Sheerness	London −1 19	5.7	4.8
Shoreham	London −2 44	6.3	4.9
Silloth	Liverpool +0 35	9.2	7.1
Southampton (1st high water)	London −2 54	4.5	3.7
Southend	London −1 23	5.7	4.8
Southwold	London −3 50	2.5	2.2
Stirling	Leith +1 15	2.9	1.6
Stonehaven	Leith −1 09	4.5	3.6
Stornoway	Liverpool −4 16	4.8	3.7
Stranraer	Greenock −0 20	3.0	2.5
Stromness	Leith −5 26	3.6	2.7
Sunderland	Leith +0 49	5.2	4.2
†Swanage	London −5 28	2.0	1.6
Swansea	Avonmouth −0 51	9.5	7.2
Tarn Point	Liverpool +0 05	8.3	6.4
Tay River (Bar)	Leith −0 19	5.2	4.2
Tees River (Entrance)	Leith +1 09	5.5	4.3
Teignmouth	London +4 37	4.8	3.6
Tenby	Avonmouth −1 06	8.4	6.3
Tilbury	London −0 49	6.4	5.4
Tobermory	Liverpool −5 11	4.4	3.3
Torquay	London +4 40	4.9	3.7
†Totland Bay	London −4 08	2.7	2.3
Troon	Greenock −0 25	3.2	2.7
Truro	London +3 43	3.5	2.4
Walton-on-Naze	London −2 10	4.2	3.4
Waterford	Liverpool −4 58	4.6	3.5
Weston-s.-Mare	Avonmouth −0 25	12.0	8.8
*Wexford H.	Liverpool −5 04	1.7	1.4
Whitby	Leith +1 23	5.6	4.3
Whitehaven	Liverpool +0 10	8.0	6.3
Wick	Leith −3 26	3.5	2.8
Wisbech Cut	Hull +0 03	7.0	5.1
Workington	Liverpool +0 21	8.2	6.4
Worthing	London −2 39	6.2	4.7
†Yarmouth (IOW)	London −3 43	3.1	2.5
Youghal	Liverpool −5 50	4.0	3.1

The tidal predictions for London Bridge, Avonmouth, Liverpool, Hull, Leith and Dun Laoghaire have been computed by the Proudman Oceanographic Laboratory, copyright reserved. The tidal predictions for Greenock have been computed by the Hydrographer of the Navy, Crown copyright reserved.

JANUARY 1994   *High water*   GMT

		London Bridge *Datum of predictions 3.20 m below				Avonmouth *Datum of predictions 6.50 m below				Liverpool *Datum of predictions 4.93 m below				Hull (*Albert Dock*) *Datum of predictions 3.90 m below			
		hr	ht m	hr	ht m	hr	ht m	hr	ht m	hr	ht m	hr	ht m	hr	ht m	hr	ht m
1	Saturday	03 45	7.2	16 10	7.3	09 12	13.4	21 37	13.0	00 59	9.2	13 17	9.4	08 20	7.3	20 28	7.5
2	Sunday	04 23	7.1	16 51	7.2	09 53	13.2	22 18	12.7	01 41	9.1	13 58	9.3	09 01	7.3	21 09	7.4
3	Monday	05 02	6.9	17 33	6.9	10 36	12.8	23 02	12.2	02 25	8.9	14 43	9.1	09 44	7.1	21 53	7.3
4	Tuesday	05 43	6.7	18 21	6.6	11 21	12.2	23 48	11.6	03 14	8.7	15 34	8.8	10 31	6.8	22 42	7.0
5	Wednesday	06 32	6.5	19 17	6.4	——	—	12 13	11.6	04 07	8.4	16 31	8.5	11 26	6.6	23 41	6.8
6	Thursday	07 33	6.3	20 26	6.3	00 46	11.0	13 17	11.1	05 12	8.1	17 40	8.2	——	—	12 34	6.4
7	Friday	08 49	6.3	21 41	6.4	01 56	10.7	14 33	11.0	06 27	8.0	18 59	8.1	00 54	6.6	13 52	6.4
8	Saturday	10 09	6.4	22 54	6.5	03 15	10.9	15 49	11.2	07 41	8.1	20 13	8.3	02 16	6.6	15 08	6.5
9	Sunday	11 25	6.5	——	—	04 28	11.4	17 02	11.7	08 47	8.5	21 18	8.6	03 37	6.7	16 14	6.8
10	Monday	00 01	6.6	12 31	6.7	05 34	12.1	18 05	12.3	09 45	8.9	22 14	8.9	04 45	6.9	17 09	7.1
11	Tuesday	00 57	6.7	13 24	6.8	06 32	12.7	18 58	12.7	10 35	9.3	23 04	9.1	05 40	7.1	17 54	7.3
12	Wednesday	01 47	6.8	14 12	7.0	07 19	13.2	19 43	13.0	11 22	9.5	23 47	9.2	06 27	7.2	18 36	7.5
13	Thursday	02 29	7.0	14 54	7.2	08 02	13.4	20 24	13.1	——	—	12 03	9.6	07 10	7.2	19 14	7.6
14	Friday	03 08	7.1	15 34	7.3	08 41	13.4	21 01	13.1	00 27	9.2	12 42	9.6	07 48	7.1	19 50	7.7
15	Saturday	03 46	7.2	16 12	7.3	09 18	13.2	21 34	12.8	01 03	9.1	13 19	9.4	08 24	7.1	20 27	7.6
16	Sunday	04 21	7.1	16 48	7.1	09 51	12.8	22 05	12.3	01 38	8.9	13 54	9.1	08 58	6.9	21 01	7.5
17	Monday	04 55	6.9	17 23	6.8	10 22	12.2	22 34	11.7	02 12	8.6	14 29	8.8	09 32	6.7	21 36	7.2
18	Tuesday	05 29	6.6	18 01	6.5	10 53	11.5	23 03	11.1	02 47	8.2	15 07	8.4	10 05	6.5	22 14	6.9
19	Wednesday	06 07	6.4	18 42	6.2	11 26	10.8	23 37	10.4	03 27	7.8	15 49	7.9	10 43	6.2	22 57	6.5
20	Thursday	06 53	6.0	19 31	5.9	——	—	12 05	10.1	04 13	7.4	16 41	7.5	11 30	5.9	23 52	6.0
21	Friday	07 48	5.7	20 30	5.7	00 23	9.8	13 04	9.5	05 13	7.1	17 49	7.2	——	—	12 36	5.7
22	Saturday	08 54	5.5	21 32	5.6	01 36	9.4	14 28	9.5	06 31	7.0	19 06	7.2	01 11	5.8	13 56	5.7
23	Sunday	10 00	5.5	22 37	5.8	03 05	9.7	15 49	10.0	07 48	7.3	20 18	7.5	02 30	5.8	15 09	5.9
24	Monday	11 08	5.7	23 42	6.1	04 18	10.6	16 53	10.9	08 49	7.8	21 12	8.0	03 40	6.0	16 10	6.3
25	Tuesday	——	—	12 11	6.1	05 16	11.6	17 47	11.8	09 36	8.3	21 59	8.5	04 36	6.4	16 57	6.6
26	Wednesday	00 38	6.5	13 03	6.6	06 06	12.4	18 36	12.5	10 20	8.8	22 41	8.9	05 23	6.7	17 40	7.0
27	Thursday	01 26	6.8	13 48	7.0	06 53	13.0	19 21	13.0	11 01	9.2	23 22	9.3	06 05	7.0	18 18	7.3
28	Friday	02 09	7.2	14 32	7.4	07 36	13.5	20 03	13.4	11 42	9.6	——	—	06 44	7.3	18 56	7.6
29	Saturday	02 50	7.4	15 14	7.6	08 19	13.8	20 44	13.7	00 03	9.5	12 21	9.8	07 24	7.6	19 32	7.9
30	Sunday	03 29	7.5	15 53	7.6	08 59	14.0	21 23	13.7	00 43	9.6	13 02	9.9	08 03	7.7	20 11	8.0
31	Monday	04 07	7.4	16 34	7.4	09 40	13.9	22 03	13.4	01 26	9.6	13 42	9.8	08 42	7.6	20 51	7.9

FEBRUARY 1994   *High water*   GMT

		London Bridge				Avonmouth				Liverpool				Hull (*Albert Dock*)			
1	Tuesday	04 45	7.2	17 16	7.1	10 19	13.4	22 42	12.8	02 08	9.4	14 26	9.5	09 23	7.4	21 34	7.7
2	Wednesday	05 27	7.0	18 01	6.7	11 02	12.7	23 24	12.0	02 51	9.0	15 12	9.1	10 08	7.1	22 22	7.3
3	Thursday	06 12	6.7	18 52	6.4	11 48	11.8	——	—	03 42	8.6	16 06	8.5	10 59	6.7	23 19	6.9
4	Friday	07 10	6.4	19 55	6.3	00 15	11.1	12 46	11.0	04 42	8.1	17 15	8.0	——	—	12 02	6.4
5	Saturday	08 23	6.2	21 08	6.2	01 24	10.5	14 02	10.4	05 58	7.8	18 41	7.7	00 32	6.4	13 22	6.2
6	Sunday	09 45	6.2	22 27	6.3	02 48	10.4	15 29	10.5	07 23	7.8	20 05	7.8	02 04	6.3	14 48	6.3
7	Monday	11 09	6.3	23 43	6.5	04 12	10.9	16 50	11.2	08 37	8.2	21 14	8.2	03 34	6.4	16 00	6.6
8	Tuesday	——	—	12 18	6.6	05 23	11.8	17 55	12.0	09 36	8.7	22 07	8.6	04 42	6.6	16 56	6.9
9	Wednesday	00 43	6.9	13 13	6.9	06 19	12.6	18 46	12.6	10 26	9.1	22 52	9.0	05 33	6.8	17 40	7.2
10	Thursday	01 33	6.9	13 59	7.1	07 05	13.1	19 28	13.0	11 08	9.4	23 32	9.1	06 15	7.0	18 19	7.4
11	Friday	02 13	7.0	14 39	7.2	07 45	13.3	20 04	13.1	11 46	9.5	——	—	06 51	7.1	18 54	7.6
12	Saturday	02 50	7.1	15 15	7.3	08 20	13.4	20 37	13.2	00 07	9.2	12 21	9.5	07 25	7.2	19 28	7.7
13	Sunday	03 24	7.2	15 48	7.2	08 52	13.3	21 06	13.1	00 39	9.1	12 53	9.4	07 57	7.2	20 02	7.7
14	Monday	03 55	7.1	16 19	7.1	09 23	13.1	21 34	12.8	01 10	9.0	13 24	9.2	08 27	7.1	20 34	7.6
15	Tuesday	04 26	7.0	16 49	6.9	09 50	12.6	22 00	12.2	01 40	8.8	13 57	8.9	08 56	7.0	21 06	7.3
16	Wednesday	04 57	6.8	17 22	6.7	10 17	11.9	22 26	11.6	02 09	8.5	14 29	8.6	09 27	6.8	21 40	7.0
17	Thursday	05 32	6.6	17 58	6.4	10 45	11.1	22 53	10.8	02 42	8.2	15 04	8.1	10 00	6.5	22 18	6.5
18	Friday	06 11	6.2	18 38	6.1	11 14	10.3	23 27	10.1	03 19	7.7	15 46	7.6	10 38	6.1	23 02	6.1
19	Saturday	06 56	5.9	19 26	5.8	11 55	9.7	——	—	04 09	7.3	16 47	7.1	11 27	5.8		
20	Sunday	07 52	5.5	20 27	5.5	00 22	9.6	13 11	9.2	05 23	7.0	18 11	6.9	00 06	5.7	12 51	5.5
21	Monday	09 05	5.4	21 43	5.5	01 59	9.4	15 01	9.5	06 55	7.0	19 38	7.2	01 45	5.6	14 24	5.7
22	Tuesday	10 26	5.6	23 04	5.8	03 37	10.2	16 19	10.6	08 12	7.5	20 44	7.8	03 05	5.9	15 33	6.2
23	Wednesday	11 42	6.0	——	—	04 46	11.4	17 20	11.7	09 08	8.2	21 35	8.4	04 10	6.3	16 29	6.5
24	Thursday	00 10	6.3	12 39	6.6	05 42	12.4	18 12	12.7	09 55	8.8	22 20	9.0	05 00	6.7	17 13	7.0
25	Friday	01 02	6.8	13 27	7.1	06 32	13.2	19 00	13.4	10 38	9.3	23 01	9.4	05 42	7.1	17 54	7.4
26	Saturday	01 45	7.3	14 11	7.5	07 17	13.8	19 43	13.8	11 20	9.8	23 43	9.8	06 23	7.5	18 32	7.8
27	Sunday	02 27	7.5	14 53	7.7	08 00	14.2	20 24	14.1	——	—	12 01	10.1	07 01	7.8	19 11	8.1
28	Monday	03 07	7.7	15 34	7.7	08 41	14.4	21 04	14.1	00 24	9.9	12 43	10.1	07 41	7.9	19 50	8.2

JANUARY 1994   *continued*

	GREENOCK *Datum of predictions 1.62 m below*				LEITH *Datum of predictions 2.90 m below*				DUN LAOGHAIRE †Datum of predictions 0.20 m above			
	hr	ht m	hr	ht m	hr	ht m	hr	ht m	hr	ht m	hr	ht m
1 Saturday	02 32	3.2	14 33	3.8	04 35	5.5	16 49	5.5	01 13	3.9	13 33	4.2
2 Sunday	03 13	3.2	15 14	3.8	05 17	5.4	17 31	5.4	01 59	3.9	14 19	4.1
3 Monday	03 55	3.2	15 55	3.7	06 04	5.3	18 18	5.3	02 51	3.8	15 11	4.1
4 Tuesday	04 39	3.2	16 40	3.6	06 53	5.1	19 10	5.2	03 47	3.7	16 08	4.0
5 Wednesday	05 29	3.1	17 30	3.4	07 49	5.0	20 10	5.0	04 50	3.7	17 15	3.9
6 Thursday	06 26	3.0	18 29	3.3	08 54	4.9	21 20	4.9	06 00	3.6	18 28	3.9
7 Friday	07 40	2.9	19 46	3.1	10 03	4.8	22 36	4.9	07 10	3.7	19 40	3.9
8 Saturday	09 12	3.0	21 25	3.1	11 13	4.9	23 49	5.0	08 14	3.8	20 43	4.0
9 Sunday	10 20	3.2	22 37	3.2	—	—	12 18	5.1	09 13	4.0	21 42	4.0
10 Monday	11 13	3.4	23 34	3.3	00 53	5.2	13 14	5.3	10 05	4.2	22 34	4.1
11 Tuesday	12 01	3.6	—	—	01 48	5.4	14 03	5.5	10 52	4.3	23 21	4.1
12 Wednesday	00 26	3.3	12 46	3.7	02 34	5.5	14 48	5.6	11 35	4.3	—	—
13 Thursday	01 14	3.4	13 28	3.8	03 18	5.5	15 32	5.6	00 05	4.1	12 13	4.4
14 Friday	01 55	3.4	14 06	3.8	04 00	5.5	16 12	5.6	00 43	4.0	12 51	4.3
15 Saturday	02 32	3.4	14 42	3.8	04 39	5.4	16 52	5.5	01 19	3.9	13 29	4.2
16 Sunday	03 07	3.4	15 17	3.8	05 17	5.2	17 31	5.3	01 57	3.8	14 08	4.1
17 Monday	03 43	3.4	15 53	3.7	05 55	5.0	18 09	5.1	02 38	3.7	14 52	3.9
18 Tuesday	04 20	3.4	16 31	3.5	06 36	4.8	18 51	4.9	03 22	3.5	15 41	3.7
19 Wednesday	04 59	3.3	17 12	3.3	07 19	4.6	19 36	4.7	04 15	3.4	16 37	3.5
20 Thursday	05 43	3.2	17 58	3.1	08 07	4.5	20 28	4.5	05 17	3.3	17 41	3.4
21 Friday	06 32	3.1	18 51	2.9	09 02	4.4	21 26	4.4	06 28	3.3	18 52	3.3
22 Saturday	07 30	3.0	19 58	2.8	10 03	4.3	22 35	4.3	07 35	3.3	19 58	3.4
23 Sunday	08 42	3.0	21 28	2.8	11 13	4.4	23 48	4.5	08 35	3.4	20 52	3.4
24 Monday	09 59	3.1	22 43	2.9	—	—	12 22	4.7	09 23	3.6	21 40	3.6
25 Tuesday	10 53	3.3	23 33	3.0	00 50	4.7	13 15	5.0	10 04	3.7	22 19	3.7
26 Wednesday	11 36	3.4	—	—	01 36	5.0	13 59	5.2	10 40	3.9	22 56	3.8
27 Thursday	00 17	3.1	12 17	3.5	02 19	5.3	14 38	5.4	11 14	4.0	23 32	3.9
28 Friday	00 59	3.2	12 57	3.6	02 58	5.5	15 15	5.6	11 50	4.2	—	—
29 Saturday	01 40	3.2	13 38	3.8	03 36	5.6	15 51	5.7	00 10	4.0	12 28	4.3
30 Sunday	02 19	3.3	14 19	3.8	04 15	5.7	16 31	5.8	00 51	4.1	13 11	4.3
31 Monday	02 56	3.3	14 59	3.9	04 57	5.6	17 13	5.7	01 36	4.1	13 57	4.3

NOTES:
*Difference of height in metres from Ordnance datum (Newlyn)
†Difference of height in metres from Ordnance datum (Dublin)
hr hour
m metres

FEBRUARY 1994   *continued*

	GREENOCK				LEITH				DUN LAOGHAIRE			
1 Tuesday	03 34	3.3	15 39	3.8	05 42	5.5	17 58	5.6	02 22	4.0	14 47	4.2
2 Wednesday	04 14	3.3	16 21	3.7	06 30	5.3	18 50	5.3	03 15	3.9	15 44	4.1
3 Thursday	04 57	3.2	17 08	3.5	07 22	5.0	19 49	5.0	04 16	3.7	16 53	3.9
4 Friday	05 47	3.1	18 00	3.2	08 24	4.8	21 01	4.8	05 28	3.7	18 10	3.8
5 Saturday	06 50	2.9	19 06	3.0	09 36	4.7	22 24	4.7	06 45	3.6	19 25	3.7
6 Sunday	08 49	2.9	21 22	2.9	10 55	4.7	23 44	4.8	07 56	3.7	20 35	3.8
7 Monday	10 08	3.1	22 36	3.0	—	—	12 08	4.9	09 01	3.9	21 37	3.9
8 Tuesday	11 02	3.4	23 31	3.1	00 50	5.0	13 08	5.1	09 56	4.1	22 30	4.0
9 Wednesday	11 50	3.5	—	—	01 42	5.2	13 56	5.3	10 43	4.2	23 13	4.0
10 Thursday	00 18	3.2	12 34	3.6	02 26	5.4	14 38	5.5	11 22	4.3	23 49	4.0
11 Friday	01 02	3.3	13 14	3.7	03 04	5.4	15 18	5.6	11 56	4.3	—	—
12 Saturday	01 39	3.3	13 50	3.7	03 39	5.4	15 53	5.5	00 20	3.9	12 28	4.2
13 Sunday	02 11	3.3	14 22	3.7	04 12	5.4	16 26	5.5	00 50	3.9	13 01	4.2
14 Monday	02 42	3.4	14 54	3.7	04 46	5.3	17 00	5.4	01 20	3.8	13 37	4.1
15 Tuesday	03 13	3.4	15 26	3.6	05 20	5.1	17 35	5.2	01 57	3.7	14 15	3.9
16 Wednesday	03 45	3.4	16 00	3.5	05 56	4.9	18 12	5.0	02 36	3.6	15 00	3.7
17 Thursday	04 21	3.3	16 37	3.3	06 36	4.7	18 54	4.7	03 22	3.5	15 51	3.5
18 Friday	05 01	3.2	17 20	3.1	07 19	4.5	19 41	4.5	04 16	3.3	16 51	3.4
19 Saturday	05 47	3.0	18 12	2.8	08 10	4.3	20 37	4.3	05 25	3.2	18 04	3.3
20 Sunday	06 43	2.9	19 15	2.7	09 11	4.2	21 46	4.2	06 46	3.2	19 20	3.3
21 Monday	07 51	2.8	20 40	2.7	10 21	4.3	23 04	4.3	07 58	3.3	20 24	3.4
22 Tuesday	09 11	2.9	22 17	2.8	11 41	4.5	—	—	08 51	3.4	21 15	3.5
23 Wednesday	10 20	3.1	23 11	3.0	00 18	4.6	12 44	4.8	09 36	3.6	21 56	3.7
24 Thursday	11 09	3.3	23 56	3.1	01 10	5.0	13 32	5.2	10 13	3.9	22 33	3.9
25 Friday	11 53	3.5	—	—	01 53	5.3	14 13	5.5	10 51	4.1	23 10	4.0
26 Saturday	00 38	3.2	12 37	3.6	02 33	5.6	14 51	5.8	11 28	4.3	23 48	4.1
27 Sunday	01 19	3.3	13 20	3.7	03 12	5.8	15 29	5.9	—	—	12 07	4.4
28 Monday	01 58	3.3	14 02	3.8	03 53	5.8	16 10	6.0	00 27	4.2	12 50	4.5

MARCH 1994   *High water*   GMT

		London Bridge			Avonmouth			Liverpool			Hull (*Albert Dock*)		
		Datum of predictions 3.20 m below			*Datum of predictions* 6.50 m below			*Datum of predictions* 4.93 m below			*Datum of predictions* 3.90 m below		
		hr m	ht	hr m	ht	hr m	ht	hr m	ht	hr m	ht	hr m	ht
1	Tuesday	03 46	7.7	16 14	7.5	09 20	14.2	21 43	13.8	01 06	9.9	13 24	10.0	08 20	7.9	20 33	8.1
2	Wednesday	04 27	7.5	16 57	7.2	10 01	13.7	22 21	13.1	01 47	9.6	14 08	9.7	09 02	7.6	21 18	7.8
3	Thursday	05 11	7.2	17 40	6.8	10 42	12.8	23 03	12.1	02 30	9.2	14 53	9.1	09 46	7.2	22 07	7.3
4	Friday	05 58	6.8	18 29	6.5	11 26	11.7	23 51	11.1	03 19	8.7	15 48	8.4	10 35	6.8	23 04	6.7
5	Saturday	06 55	6.5	19 27	6.2	—	—	12 22	10.7	04 19	8.1	16 57	7.8	11 37	6.3	—	—
6	Sunday	08 04	6.2	20 37	6.1	00 58	10.4	13 39	10.1	05 36	7.6	18 27	7.4	00 19	6.2	12 54	6.1
7	Monday	09 24	6.1	21 57	6.1	02 26	10.1	15 11	10.2	07 04	7.6	19 55	7.6	02 00	6.0	14 27	6.1
8	Tuesday	10 49	6.3	23 20	6.3	03 54	10.7	16 35	11.0	08 22	8.0	21 03	8.1	03 29	6.1	15 43	6.4
9	Wednesday	—	—	12 00	6.7	05 06	11.7	17 37	11.9	09 21	8.5	21 52	8.5	04 31	6.4	16 36	6.8
10	Thursday	00 22	6.7	12 55	7.0	05 59	12.5	18 25	12.6	10 07	8.9	22 34	8.8	05 17	6.7	17 20	7.1
11	Friday	01 12	6.9	13 40	7.2	06 43	13.0	19 04	12.9	10 47	9.2	23 09	9.0	05 55	6.9	17 56	7.3
12	Saturday	01 52	7.1	14 18	7.2	07 21	13.2	19 39	13.0	11 22	9.4	23 42	9.1	06 29	7.0	18 30	7.5
13	Sunday	02 27	7.1	14 50	7.2	07 55	13.2	20 09	13.1	11 56	9.4	—	—	07 00	7.2	19 04	7.6
14	Monday	03 00	7.1	15 21	7.1	08 24	13.2	20 37	13.1	00 11	9.1	12 27	9.3	07 28	7.3	19 36	7.6
15	Tuesday	03 28	7.1	15 48	7.1	08 52	13.1	21 04	12.9	00 41	9.1	12 56	9.2	07 57	7.2	20 07	7.5
16	Wednesday	03 56	7.0	16 16	7.0	09 20	12.7	21 29	12.5	01 09	8.9	13 26	9.0	08 26	7.1	20 40	7.2
17	Thursday	04 27	6.9	16 47	6.8	09 47	12.1	21 56	11.9	01 37	8.7	13 57	8.6	08 55	6.9	21 12	6.9
18	Friday	05 02	6.7	17 20	6.6	10 14	11.3	22 24	11.2	02 08	8.4	14 30	8.2	09 25	6.6	21 47	6.5
19	Saturday	05 39	6.5	17 57	6.4	10 42	10.6	22 55	10.5	02 43	8.0	15 10	7.8	09 58	6.2	22 28	6.1
20	Sunday	06 21	6.1	18 41	6.0	11 19	10.0	23 42	10.0	03 28	7.6	16 04	7.3	10 42	5.9	23 24	5.8
21	Monday	07 12	5.8	19 34	5.7	—	—	12 23	9.5	04 33	7.2	17 25	7.0	11 48	5.6	—	—
22	Tuesday	08 19	5.6	20 51	5.5	01 04	9.6	14 09	9.5	06 04	7.1	18 56	7.2	00 58	5.6	13 36	5.6
23	Wednesday	09 46	5.7	22 23	5.7	02 52	10.1	15 41	10.5	07 28	7.5	20 08	7.8	02 28	5.8	14 54	6.0
24	Thursday	11 08	6.1	23 37	6.3	04 11	11.3	16 48	11.7	08 33	8.1	21 04	8.4	03 36	6.3	15 53	6.5
25	Friday	—	—	12 11	6.7	05 11	12.4	17 44	12.7	09 25	8.8	21 52	9.1	04 31	6.7	16 42	7.0
26	Saturday	00 32	6.8	13 02	7.2	06 05	13.3	18 33	13.5	10 12	9.4	22 35	9.6	05 16	7.2	17 26	7.4
27	Sunday	01 19	7.2	13 47	7.5	06 53	13.9	19 18	14.0	10 55	9.9	23 19	9.9	05 58	7.6	18 06	7.9
28	Monday	02 02	7.5	14 29	7.7	07 38	14.3	20 02	14.2	11 39	10.1	—	—	06 37	7.8	18 49	8.1
29	Tuesday	02 43	7.7	15 11	7.7	08 20	14.4	20 42	14.2	00 01	10.1	12 22	10.2	07 17	8.0	19 32	8.2
30	Wednesday	03 25	7.7	15 53	7.5	09 01	14.2	21 22	13.9	00 45	10.0	13 06	10.0	07 59	7.9	20 17	8.0
31	Thursday	04 10	7.6	16 37	7.3	09 43	13.6	22 03	13.2	01 27	9.7	13 51	9.6	08 41	7.7	21 04	7.7

APRIL 1994   *High water*   GMT

		London Bridge			Avonmouth			Liverpool			Hull (*Albert Dock*)		
1	Friday	04 57	7.3	17 22	6.9	10 25	12.7	22 46	12.2	02 12	9.3	14 39	9.0	09 26	7.3	21 56	7.1
2	Saturday	05 47	6.9	18 11	6.5	11 11	11.6	23 35	11.2	03 01	8.8	15 34	8.3	10 17	6.8	22 55	6.5
3	Sunday	06 43	6.6	19 04	6.2	—	—	12 06	10.6	04 02	8.2	16 42	7.7	11 16	6.4	—	—
4	Monday	07 45	6.3	20 08	6.0	00 40	10.4	13 18	10.0	05 15	7.7	18 08	7.4	00 11	6.0	12 27	6.1
5	Tuesday	08 58	6.1	21 24	6.0	02 02	10.2	14 45	10.1	06 39	7.6	19 31	7.5	01 48	5.8	13 56	6.1
6	Wednesday	10 23	6.2	22 51	6.2	03 26	10.6	16 07	10.8	07 55	7.9	20 37	7.9	03 09	6.0	15 15	6.3
7	Thursday	11 34	6.6	23 56	6.6	04 36	11.5	17 07	11.7	08 54	8.3	21 27	8.3	04 08	6.3	16 10	6.6
8	Friday	—	—	12 29	7.0	05 31	12.2	17 55	12.3	09 41	8.7	22 06	8.6	04 53	6.5	16 53	6.9
9	Saturday	00 46	6.9	13 13	7.2	06 15	12.6	18 34	12.6	10 20	8.9	22 41	8.9	05 30	6.7	17 31	7.1
10	Sunday	01 27	7.0	13 51	7.2	06 51	12.8	19 08	12.7	10 55	9.1	23 13	9.0	06 02	7.0	18 05	7.3
11	Monday	02 02	7.0	14 23	7.1	07 25	12.8	19 39	12.9	11 27	9.2	23 43	9.1	06 32	7.1	18 39	7.4
12	Tuesday	02 32	7.0	14 51	7.0	07 55	12.8	20 06	12.9	11 58	9.1	—	—	07 00	7.2	19 11	7.4
13	Wednesday	03 00	7.0	15 17	7.0	08 24	12.8	20 34	12.9	00 12	9.1	12 29	9.1	07 28	7.2	19 43	7.3
14	Thursday	03 29	6.9	15 46	7.0	08 52	12.6	21 02	12.6	00 41	9.0	13 00	8.9	07 57	7.1	20 17	7.0
15	Friday	04 02	6.9	16 17	6.9	09 22	12.1	21 32	12.0	01 12	8.8	13 31	8.6	08 27	6.9	20 51	6.7
16	Saturday	04 37	6.8	16 52	6.8	09 51	11.5	22 03	11.5	01 42	8.6	14 06	8.3	08 59	6.6	21 26	6.4
17	Sunday	05 15	6.6	17 29	6.5	10 25	10.9	22 38	10.9	02 19	8.3	14 47	8.0	09 33	6.3	22 08	6.2
18	Monday	05 57	6.4	18 10	6.2	11 04	10.3	23 26	10.4	03 04	7.9	15 41	7.6	10 17	6.1	23 03	5.9
19	Tuesday	06 46	6.1	19 02	5.9	—	—	12 04	9.9	04 04	7.6	16 52	7.3	11 17	5.8	—	—
20	Wednesday	07 49	5.9	20 12	5.7	00 37	10.1	13 31	9.9	05 23	7.4	18 15	7.4	00 19	5.8	12 44	5.8
21	Thursday	09 11	5.9	21 42	5.8	02 10	10.4	15 01	10.6	06 45	7.7	19 28	7.9	01 49	5.9	14 09	6.0
22	Friday	10 33	6.3	22 59	6.3	03 32	11.3	16 11	11.6	07 54	8.2	20 29	8.5	02 58	6.3	15 13	6.5
23	Saturday	11 39	6.8	—	—	04 38	12.3	17 11	12.6	08 51	8.8	21 21	9.1	03 57	6.8	16 08	7.0
24	Sunday	00 00	6.7	12 34	7.3	05 34	13.1	18 05	13.3	09 42	9.4	22 09	9.5	04 46	7.2	16 57	7.4
25	Monday	00 52	7.1	13 21	7.4	06 26	13.7	18 53	13.8	10 30	9.8	22 55	9.9	05 31	7.5	17 44	7.7
26	Tuesday	01 37	7.3	14 06	7.4	07 14	14.0	19 39	14.0	11 18	10.0	23 40	10.0	06 15	7.7	18 30	8.0
27	Wednesday	02 22	7.5	14 50	7.5	08 00	14.1	20 23	14.1	—	—	12 04	10.0	06 57	7.8	19 17	8.0
28	Thursday	03 08	7.6	15 35	7.4	08 44	13.9	21 05	13.8	00 25	9.9	12 50	9.8	07 41	7.8	20 06	7.8
29	Friday	03 56	7.6	16 20	7.3	09 27	13.4	21 49	13.1	01 10	9.7	13 37	9.4	08 24	7.6	20 55	7.4
30	Saturday	04 45	7.4	17 06	7.0	10 12	12.6	22 34	12.3	01 58	9.3	14 26	8.9	09 11	7.3	21 47	6.9

MARCH 1994 *continued*

		GREENOCK				LEITH				DUN LAOGHAIRE			
		*Datum of predictions 1.62 m below				*Datum of predictions 2.90 m below				†Datum of predictions 0.20 m above			
		hr	ht m	hr	ht m	hr	ht m	hr	ht m	hr	ht m	hr	ht m
1	Tuesday	02 35	3.4	14 43	3.8	04 35	5.8	16 53	5.9	01 09	4.2	13 36	4.4
2	Wednesday	03 11	3.4	15 23	3.8	05 20	5.6	17 41	5.7	01 57	4.1	14 26	4.3
3	Thursday	03 49	3.4	16 05	3.6	06 08	5.3	18 33	5.4	02 48	4.0	15 25	4.1
4	Friday	04 30	3.3	16 50	3.4	07 00	5.0	19 35	5.0	03 48	3.8	16 37	3.8
5	Saturday	05 19	3.1	17 42	3.1	08 02	4.7	20 48	4.7	05 02	3.7	17 55	3.7
6	Sunday	06 19	2.9	18 50	2.8	09 15	4.6	22 12	4.6	06 22	3.6	19 14	3.6
7	Monday	08 26	2.8	21 21	2.8	10 36	4.6	23 34	4.7	07 38	3.7	20 29	3.7
8	Tuesday	09 52	3.0	22 27	2.9	11 55	4.8	———	—	08 48	3.8	21 32	3.8
9	Wednesday	10 45	3.3	23 16	3.1	00 40	4.9	12 56	5.0	09 45	4.0	22 20	3.8
10	Thursday	11 31	3.4	———	—	01 29	5.1	13 42	5.2	10 30	4.1	22 58	3.9
11	Friday	00 00	3.2	12 14	3.5	02 09	5.3	14 21	5.4	11 05	4.1	23 29	3.9
12	Saturday	00 40	3.2	12 53	3.5	02 42	5.3	14 56	5.4	11 36	4.1	23 55	3.9
13	Sunday	01 14	3.2	13 28	3.5	03 15	5.3	15 29	5.5	———	—	12 05	4.1
14	Monday	01 44	3.3	13 59	3.5	03 44	5.3	16 01	5.4	00 20	3.9	12 35	4.1
15	Tuesday	02 13	3.3	14 29	3.4	04 17	5.3	16 34	5.3	00 50	3.9	13 08	4.0
16	Wednesday	02 41	3.4	14 59	3.4	04 49	5.1	17 07	5.2	01 23	3.8	13 45	3.9
17	Thursday	03 12	3.4	15 32	3.3	05 24	5.0	17 42	5.0	02 01	3.7	14 28	3.7
18	Friday	03 46	3.3	16 09	3.1	06 01	4.8	18 22	4.8	02 45	3.6	15 16	3.5
19	Saturday	04 23	3.2	16 50	2.9	06 40	4.6	19 05	4.5	03 37	3.4	16 14	3.4
20	Sunday	05 07	3.0	17 41	2.7	07 28	4.4	20 00	4.3	04 40	3.2	17 22	3.2
21	Monday	06 01	2.8	18 45	2.6	08 27	4.3	21 06	4.2	05 55	3.2	18 40	3.2
22	Tuesday	07 08	2.8	20 06	2.6	09 37	4.2	22 24	4.3	07 14	3.2	19 49	3.3
23	Wednesday	08 28	2.8	21 40	2.7	10 56	4.4	23 40	4.6	08 14	3.4	20 43	3.5
24	Thursday	09 42	3.0	22 40	2.9	———	—	12 05	4.4	09 03	3.6	21 28	3.7
25	Friday	10 38	3.2	23 27	3.1	00 37	5.0	12 58	5.2	09 46	3.9	22 07	3.9
26	Saturday	11 26	3.4	———	—	01 24	5.4	13 42	5.5	10 26	4.1	22 47	4.1
27	Sunday	00 10	3.2	12 13	3.5	02 06	5.6	14 23	5.8	11 05	4.3	23 25	4.2
28	Monday	00 53	3.3	12 59	3.6	02 47	5.8	15 05	6.0	11 48	4.5	———	—
29	Tuesday	01 33	3.4	13 44	3.7	03 29	5.9	15 50	6.0	00 06	4.3	12 33	4.5
30	Wednesday	02 12	3.4	14 27	3.7	04 14	5.8	16 36	5.9	00 48	4.3	13 19	4.4
31	Thursday	02 49	3.5	15 09	3.6	04 59	5.6	17 27	5.7	01 36	4.2	14 14	4.3

NOTES:
*Difference of height in metres from Ordnance datum (Newlyn)
†Difference of height in metres from Ordnance datum (Dublin)
hr hour
m metres

APRIL 1994 *continued*

		GREENOCK				LEITH				DUN LAOGHAIRE			
1	Friday	03 28	3.5	15 52	3.5	05 48	5.3	18 22	5.3	02 26	4.1	15 14	4.0
2	Saturday	04 10	3.3	16 39	3.2	06 41	5.0	19 24	4.9	03 27	3.9	16 24	3.8
3	Sunday	04 58	3.1	17 34	2.9	07 43	4.7	20 34	4.6	04 40	3.7	17 41	3.6
4	Monday	05 59	2.9	18 50	2.7	08 55	4.5	21 53	4.5	06 00	3.6	19 00	3.5
5	Tuesday	07 47	2.8	20 57	2.7	10 12	4.5	23 10	4.6	07 16	3.7	20 14	3.6
6	Wednesday	09 23	3.0	22 02	2.9	11 28	4.7	———	—	08 28	3.8	21 15	3.7
7	Thursday	10 19	3.2	22 50	3.0	00 15	4.8	12 29	4.9	09 24	3.9	22 00	3.8
8	Friday	11 05	3.3	23 31	3.1	01 04	5.0	13 17	5.0	10 07	3.9	22 36	3.8
9	Saturday	11 47	3.3	———	—	01 43	5.1	13 56	5.2	10 44	4.0	23 03	3.8
10	Sunday	00 09	3.1	12 27	3.3	02 17	5.2	14 31	5.3	11 13	4.0	23 28	3.8
11	Monday	00 43	3.1	13 02	3.2	02 48	5.2	15 04	5.3	11 41	3.9	23 55	3.9
12	Tuesday	01 14	3.2	13 33	3.2	03 18	5.3	15 36	5.3	———	—	12 12	3.9
13	Wednesday	01 43	3.2	14 03	3.1	03 50	5.3	16 08	5.2	00 24	3.9	12 44	3.9
14	Thursday	02 11	3.3	14 34	3.1	04 22	5.1	16 43	5.1	00 58	3.8	13 20	3.8
15	Friday	02 42	3.3	15 08	3.1	04 57	5.0	17 19	5.0	01 36	3.8	14 04	3.7
16	Saturday	03 16	3.3	15 45	3.0	05 33	4.8	17 58	4.8	02 19	3.6	14 51	3.5
17	Sunday	03 52	3.2	16 28	2.8	06 12	4.7	18 41	4.6	03 09	3.5	15 47	3.4
18	Monday	04 33	3.0	17 19	2.7	06 57	4.5	19 34	4.4	04 05	3.3	16 50	3.3
19	Tuesday	05 24	2.9	18 22	2.6	07 53	4.4	20 35	4.4	05 12	3.2	18 00	3.3
20	Wednesday	06 30	2.8	19 37	2.6	09 01	4.3	21 47	4.4	06 26	3.3	19 09	3.4
21	Thursday	07 48	2.8	20 58	2.7	10 14	4.5	23 00	4.7	07 33	3.4	20 07	3.5
22	Friday	09 04	3.0	22 04	2.8	11 24	4.8	———	—	08 26	3.6	20 56	3.7
23	Saturday	10 06	3.2	22 55	3.0	00 02	5.0	12 22	5.1	09 16	3.9	21 42	3.9
24	Sunday	10 58	3.3	23 41	3.1	00 54	5.3	13 11	5.5	10 01	4.1	22 23	4.1
25	Monday	11 47	3.4	———	—	01 39	5.6	13 57	5.8	10 47	4.3	23 05	4.2
26	Tuesday	00 26	3.3	12 37	3.5	02 23	5.8	14 44	5.9	11 32	4.4	23 48	4.3
27	Wednesday	01 10	3.4	13 25	3.6	03 08	5.8	15 33	6.0	———	—	12 19	4.4
28	Thursday	01 51	3.5	14 12	3.6	03 54	5.8	16 22	5.8	00 33	4.3	13 09	4.4
29	Friday	02 32	3.5	14 57	3.3	04 42	5.6	17 14	5.6	01 19	4.3	14 02	4.2
30	Saturday	03 12	3.5	15 42	3.3	05 31	5.3	18 11	5.3	02 11	4.2	15 02	4.0

MAY 1994   *High water*   GMT

Day	LONDON BRIDGE				AVONMOUTH				LIVERPOOL				HULL (*Albert Dock*)			
	Datum of predictions 3.20 m below				*Datum of predictions 6.50 m below*				*Datum of predictions 4.93 m below*				*Datum of predictions 3.90 m below*			
	hr	m (ht)	hr	m (ht)	hr	m (ht)	hr	m (ht)	hr	m (ht)	hr	m (ht)	hr	m (ht)	hr	m (ht)
1 Sunday	05 36	7.1	17 54	6.7	10 59	11.6	23 23	11.4	02 47	8.9	15 19	8.3	10 00	6.9	22 45	6.4
2 Monday	06 28	6.7	18 43	6.4	11 51	10.8	——	—	03 43	8.4	16 23	7.8	10 53	6.6	23 52	6.0
3 Tuesday	07 24	6.4	19 40	6.1	00 20	10.7	12 53	10.2	04 48	7.9	17 36	7.5	11 56	6.3	—	—
4 Wednesday	08 27	6.2	20 46	5.9	01 29	10.3	14 06	10.1	06 01	7.7	18 52	7.5	01 15	5.8	13 11	6.1
5 Thursday	09 42	6.2	22 07	6.0	02 45	10.5	15 23	10.5	07 14	7.8	19 58	7.7	02 33	5.8	14 31	6.2
6 Friday	10 59	6.4	23 20	6.3	03 56	11.0	16 26	11.1	08 15	8.0	20 50	8.1	03 33	6.0	15 34	6.4
7 Saturday	11 56	6.7	——	—	04 52	11.6	17 17	11.7	09 05	8.3	21 32	8.4	04 19	6.3	16 22	6.6
8 Sunday	00 14	6.6	12 42	6.9	05 38	12.0	17 59	12.1	09 46	8.6	22 09	8.6	04 59	6.6	17 03	6.8
9 Monday	00 56	6.7	13 20	6.9	06 19	12.2	18 34	12.3	10 24	8.7	22 42	8.8	05 33	6.8	17 40	7.0
10 Tuesday	01 33	6.8	13 52	6.9	06 54	12.3	19 08	12.5	10 59	8.9	23 15	8.9	06 04	6.9	18 15	7.1
11 Wednesday	02 04	6.8	14 22	6.9	07 26	12.4	19 39	12.6	11 32	8.9	23 47	9.0	06 33	7.0	18 49	7.1
12 Thursday	02 34	6.8	14 51	6.9	07 59	12.5	20 10	12.7	—	—	12 05	8.9	07 03	7.1	19 24	7.0
13 Friday	03 07	6.9	15 22	6.9	08 30	12.4	20 42	12.6	00 18	9.0	12 39	8.8	07 35	7.0	19 59	6.9
14 Saturday	03 42	6.9	15 57	6.9	09 04	12.2	21 16	12.3	00 52	8.9	13 13	8.7	08 07	6.9	20 34	6.7
15 Sunday	04 20	6.9	16 33	6.8	09 39	11.8	21 51	11.9	01 26	8.7	13 51	8.5	08 42	6.7	21 13	6.5
16 Monday	04 59	6.8	17 09	6.7	10 17	11.4	22 31	11.5	02 05	8.5	14 33	8.2	09 19	6.5	21 57	6.4
17 Tuesday	05 40	6.7	17 50	6.4	10 59	10.9	23 19	11.0	02 50	8.3	15 24	7.9	10 04	6.3	22 48	6.2
18 Wednesday	06 28	6.4	18 39	6.2	11 54	10.6	——	—	03 45	8.0	16 27	7.8	10 57	6.1	23 51	6.1
19 Thursday	07 27	6.2	19 42	6.0	00 20	10.8	13 03	10.5	04 52	7.9	17 39	7.8	—	—	12 06	6.1
20 Friday	08 40	6.2	21 04	6.1	01 36	10.9	14 21	10.8	06 05	8.0	18 50	8.0	01 07	6.2	13 25	6.2
21 Saturday	09 59	6.4	22 21	6.3	02 54	11.3	15 34	11.4	07 16	8.3	19 55	8.5	02 20	6.4	14 34	6.5
22 Sunday	11 08	6.7	23 29	6.7	04 03	12.0	16 39	12.2	08 18	8.7	20 53	8.9	03 22	6.7	15 36	6.9
23 Monday	——	—	12 07	7.0	05 04	12.7	17 37	12.9	09 15	9.2	21 45	9.3	04 18	7.0	16 34	7.3
24 Tuesday	00 27	6.9	13 00	7.1	06 02	13.1	18 30	13.3	10 09	9.5	22 34	9.6	05 09	7.3	17 27	7.5
25 Wednesday	01 19	7.0	13 48	7.1	06 54	13.4	19 19	13.6	10 59	9.7	23 23	9.8	05 56	7.5	18 19	7.7
26 Thursday	02 08	7.2	14 33	7.2	07 43	13.6	20 07	13.7	11 49	9.7	——	—	06 41	7.6	19 08	7.6
27 Friday	02 56	7.4	15 19	7.2	08 31	13.5	20 52	13.6	00 10	9.8	12 38	9.6	07 25	7.6	19 57	7.5
28 Saturday	03 45	7.5	16 04	7.2	09 16	13.2	21 37	13.1	00 57	9.7	13 24	9.3	08 10	7.5	20 47	7.2
29 Sunday	04 33	7.4	16 49	7.1	10 01	12.6	22 21	12.5	01 44	9.4	14 12	8.9	08 55	7.4	21 34	6.9
30 Monday	05 20	7.2	17 34	6.8	10 45	11.9	23 06	11.7	02 30	9.0	15 01	8.4	09 40	7.1	22 25	6.5
31 Tuesday	06 08	6.9	18 19	6.5	11 30	11.1	23 55	11.1	03 19	8.6	15 53	8.0	10 28	6.8	23 19	6.1

JUNE 1994   *High water*   GMT

Day	LONDON BRIDGE				AVONMOUTH				LIVERPOOL				HULL (*Albert Dock*)			
1 Wednesday	06 57	6.6	19 07	6.2	——	—	12 18	10.6	04 14	8.2	16 51	7.6	11 20	6.5	——	—
2 Thursday	07 51	6.3	20 05	6.0	00 49	10.6	13 15	10.2	05 13	7.8	17 57	7.4	00 20	5.9	12 22	6.2
3 Friday	08 54	6.1	21 12	5.9	01 52	10.3	14 23	10.1	06 21	7.7	19 06	7.5	01 34	5.8	13 32	6.1
4 Saturday	10 06	6.1	22 30	6.0	03 01	10.4	15 32	10.4	07 26	7.7	20 05	7.7	02 42	5.8	14 45	6.1
5 Sunday	11 13	6.3	23 34	6.2	04 04	10.8	16 29	10.9	08 23	7.9	20 54	8.0	03 37	6.0	15 44	6.3
6 Monday	——	—	12 04	6.5	04 57	11.2	17 19	11.5	09 11	8.2	21 36	8.3	04 22	6.3	16 34	6.4
7 Tuesday	00 22	6.4	12 46	6.6	05 42	11.6	18 01	11.9	09 55	8.4	22 14	8.6	05 02	6.6	17 16	6.6
8 Wednesday	01 02	6.5	13 21	6.7	06 25	11.9	18 40	12.2	10 33	8.6	22 51	8.8	05 37	6.7	17 54	6.8
9 Thursday	01 37	6.6	13 55	6.8	07 03	12.1	19 15	12.4	11 09	8.7	23 26	8.9	06 11	6.9	18 30	6.8
10 Friday	02 13	6.7	14 30	6.9	07 39	12.3	19 52	12.6	11 46	8.8	——	—	06 43	7.0	19 07	6.9
11 Saturday	02 50	6.8	15 07	6.9	08 14	12.4	20 28	12.7	00 01	9.0	12 22	8.9	07 17	7.0	19 43	6.9
12 Sunday	03 29	6.9	15 43	6.9	08 52	12.4	21 05	12.7	00 36	9.0	12 59	8.8	07 52	7.0	20 21	6.9
13 Monday	04 07	7.0	16 20	6.9	09 30	12.3	21 44	12.5	01 14	9.0	13 38	8.7	08 30	6.9	21 02	6.8
14 Tuesday	04 47	7.0	16 57	6.8	10 10	12.0	22 25	12.1	01 54	8.8	14 20	8.6	09 09	6.8	21 44	6.7
15 Wednesday	05 27	6.8	17 36	6.6	10 52	11.6	23 10	11.8	02 37	8.7	15 08	8.4	09 51	6.7	22 31	6.5
16 Thursday	06 12	6.6	18 21	6.4	11 40	11.2	——	—	03 27	8.5	16 02	8.2	10 39	6.6	23 24	6.4
17 Friday	07 04	6.4	19 17	6.3	00 02	11.4	12 36	10.9	04 24	8.3	17 05	8.1	11 37	6.5	——	—
18 Saturday	08 11	6.3	20 29	6.2	01 05	11.2	13 46	10.9	05 30	8.2	18 15	8.1	00 29	6.3	12 47	6.4
19 Sunday	09 25	6.4	21 49	6.4	02 19	11.2	15 01	11.2	06 42	8.3	19 24	8.3	01 42	6.4	14 00	6.6
20 Monday	10 38	6.6	23 02	6.5	03 32	11.6	16 10	11.7	07 51	8.5	20 29	8.7	02 51	6.6	15 12	6.8
21 Tuesday	11 44	6.7	—	—	04 39	12.0	17 14	12.3	08 56	8.8	21 27	9.0	03 56	6.8	16 19	7.0
22 Wednesday	00 08	6.7	12 42	6.8	05 44	12.5	18 13	12.8	09 55	9.1	22 20	9.4	04 52	7.1	17 20	7.2
23 Thursday	01 06	6.8	13 34	6.8	06 41	12.9	19 07	13.2	10 48	9.3	23 11	9.6	05 42	7.3	18 12	7.4
24 Friday	01 58	6.9	14 22	6.9	07 34	13.1	19 55	13.5	11 39	9.4	23 58	9.7	06 29	7.5	19 01	7.4
25 Saturday	02 46	7.2	15 07	7.1	08 20	13.2	20 40	13.5	—	—	12 25	9.4	07 12	7.6	19 48	7.3
26 Sunday	03 32	7.4	15 49	7.2	09 04	13.1	21 23	13.2	00 43	9.7	13 10	9.2	07 55	7.6	20 33	7.2
27 Monday	04 17	7.4	16 31	7.2	09 44	12.8	22 04	12.8	01 27	9.5	13 52	8.9	08 37	7.5	21 15	6.9
28 Tuesday	04 59	7.3	17 11	7.0	10 24	12.2	22 43	12.2	02 09	9.2	14 34	8.6	09 18	7.3	21 57	6.6
29 Wednesday	05 42	7.0	17 51	6.7	11 00	11.6	23 21	11.5	02 51	8.8	15 17	8.2	10 00	7.1	22 39	6.3
30 Thursday	06 24	6.6	18 34	6.4	11 38	10.9	——	—	03 35	8.4	16 03	7.8	10 43	6.7	23 24	6.1

MAY 1994   *continued*

		GREENOCK				LEITH				DUN LAOGHAIRE			
		hr	m (ht)	hr	m (ht)	hr	m (ht)	hr	m (ht)	hr	m (ht)	hr	m (ht)
1	Sunday	03 55	3.4	16 32	3.1	06 26	5.1	19 10	4.9	03 09	4.0	16 08	3.7
2	Monday	04 43	3.2	17 28	2.9	07 26	4.8	20 13	4.7	04 15	3.8	17 19	3.5
3	Tuesday	05 42	3.0	18 35	2.8	08 31	4.6	21 20	4.5	05 29	3.7	18 32	3.4
4	Wednesday	07 00	2.9	20 00	2.7	09 39	4.5	22 31	4.5	06 43	3.6	19 42	3.5
5	Thursday	08 38	2.9	21 17	2.8	10 48	4.6	23 34	4.7	07 52	3.6	20 40	3.5
6	Friday	09 43	3.0	22 10	2.9	11 51	4.7	——	—	08 49	3.7	21 27	3.6
7	Saturday	10 32	3.1	22 54	3.0	00 27	4.8	12 43	4.8	09 36	3.7	22 04	3.7
8	Sunday	11 16	3.1	23 34	3.0	01 11	4.9	13 26	5.0	10 14	3.8	22 34	3.7
9	Monday	11 56	3.1	——	—	01 48	5.0	14 03	5.1	10 48	3.8	23 03	3.8
10	Tuesday	00 11	3.1	12 33	3.0	02 20	5.1	14 38	5.1	11 20	3.8	23 34	3.9
11	Wednesday	00 44	3.1	13 06	3.0	02 54	5.2	15 12	5.2	11 52	3.8	——	—
12	Thursday	01 15	3.2	13 38	2.9	03 26	5.2	15 47	5.1	00 05	3.9	12 26	3.8
13	Friday	01 45	3.3	14 11	3.0	04 01	5.1	16 22	5.1	00 38	3.9	13 02	3.7
14	Saturday	02 17	3.3	14 48	2.9	04 36	5.0	16 59	5.0	01 16	3.8	13 44	3.7
15	Sunday	02 53	3.3	15 27	2.9	05 11	4.9	17 38	4.9	01 59	3.7	14 29	3.6
16	Monday	03 30	3.3	16 11	2.8	05 51	4.8	18 22	4.8	02 45	3.6	15 21	3.5
17	Tuesday	04 10	3.1	17 02	2.7	06 36	4.7	19 11	4.7	03 37	3.5	16 18	3.4
18	Wednesday	04 57	3.0	18 01	2.7	07 28	4.6	20 10	4.6	04 36	3.4	17 21	3.4
19	Thursday	05 57	2.9	19 07	2.6	08 30	4.6	21 15	4.6	05 40	3.4	18 26	3.4
20	Friday	07 09	2.9	20 17	2.7	09 37	4.6	22 24	4.8	06 48	3.5	19 30	3.5
21	Saturday	08 27	3.0	21 27	2.8	10 45	4.8	23 28	5.0	07 51	3.7	20 25	3.7
22	Sunday	09 35	3.1	22 25	2.9	11 49	5.1	——	—	08 48	3.9	21 16	3.9
23	Monday	10 33	3.2	23 16	3.1	00 25	5.3	12 46	5.4	09 40	4.1	22 04	4.1
24	Tuesday	11 26	3.3	——	—	01 14	5.5	13 38	5.6	10 30	4.2	22 51	4.2
25	Wednesday	00 04	3.2	12 18	3.4	02 02	5.6	14 28	5.8	11 20	4.3	23 35	4.3
26	Thursday	00 51	3.4	13 10	3.4	02 49	5.7	15 19	5.8	——	—	12 09	4.3
27	Friday	01 36	3.5	14 00	3.4	03 37	5.7	16 10	5.7	00 21	4.4	12 59	4.3
28	Saturday	02 18	3.6	14 47	3.4	04 26	5.6	17 02	5.5	01 08	4.3	13 51	4.1
29	Sunday	02 59	3.6	15 34	3.3	05 17	5.4	17 54	5.3	01 57	4.2	14 45	3.9
30	Monday	03 42	3.5	16 21	3.2	06 09	5.2	18 47	5.0	02 50	4.1	15 44	3.7
31	Tuesday	04 28	3.4	17 11	3.0	07 04	5.0	19 43	4.8	03 47	3.9	16 44	3.5

NOTES:

GREENOCK — *Datum of predictions 1.62 m below
LEITH — *Datum of predictions 2.90 m below
DUN LAOGHAIRE — †Datum of predictions 0.20 m above

*Difference of height in metres from Ordnance datum (Newlyn)
†Difference of height in metres from Ordnance datum (Dublin)
hr hour
m metres

JUNE 1994   *continued*

		GREENOCK				LEITH				DUN LAOGHAIRE			
1	Wednesday	05 19	3.2	18 05	2.9	08 00	4.8	20 40	4.6	04 50	3.7	17 48	3.4
2	Thursday	06 18	3.0	19 01	2.8	08 58	4.6	21 40	4.5	05 57	3.6	18 52	3.4
3	Friday	07 27	2.9	20 04	2.8	09 58	4.5	22 41	4.5	07 04	3.5	19 52	3.4
4	Saturday	08 48	2.9	21 13	2.8	11 02	4.5	23 41	4.6	08 05	3.5	20 43	3.5
5	Sunday	09 53	2.9	22 11	2.9	——	—	12 01	4.6	08 58	3.5	21 27	3.6
6	Monday	10 42	2.9	22 58	3.0	00 32	4.7	12 51	4.7	09 43	3.6	22 05	3.7
7	Tuesday	11 26	2.9	23 39	3.0	01 15	4.9	13 35	4.9	10 23	3.6	22 41	3.8
8	Wednesday	12 05	2.9	——	—	01 55	5.0	14 14	5.0	10 58	3.6	23 14	3.8
9	Thursday	00 16	3.1	12 42	2.9	02 31	5.1	14 51	5.1	11 35	3.7	23 48	3.9
10	Friday	00 49	3.2	13 17	2.9	03 06	5.2	15 27	5.1	——	—	12 09	3.7
11	Saturday	01 22	3.3	13 54	2.9	03 43	5.2	16 03	5.1	00 21	3.9	12 45	3.7
12	Sunday	01 57	3.3	14 32	2.9	04 18	5.2	16 41	5.1	00 58	3.9	13 24	3.7
13	Monday	02 34	3.4	15 13	2.9	04 55	5.1	17 19	5.1	01 38	3.9	14 08	3.7
14	Tuesday	03 12	3.4	15 56	2.9	05 33	5.0	18 02	5.0	02 22	3.8	14 55	3.6
15	Wednesday	03 52	3.3	16 43	2.9	06 16	5.0	18 50	4.9	03 09	3.8	15 47	3.6
16	Thursday	04 37	3.2	17 35	2.8	07 05	4.9	19 43	4.8	04 02	3.7	16 44	3.5
17	Friday	05 29	3.1	18 33	2.8	08 02	4.8	20 45	4.8	05 01	3.7	17 48	3.5
18	Saturday	06 31	3.0	19 37	2.7	09 05	4.8	21 51	4.8	06 10	3.7	18 53	3.6
19	Sunday	07 47	3.0	20 51	2.8	10 15	4.9	22 57	4.9	07 20	3.7	19 58	3.7
20	Monday	09 07	3.0	22 00	2.9	11 26	5.0	23 59	5.1	08 25	3.9	20 55	3.9
21	Tuesday	10 14	3.1	22 58	3.1	——	—	12 29	5.2	09 24	4.0	21 49	4.0
22	Wednesday	11 12	3.2	23 49	3.3	00 56	5.3	13 26	5.4	10 19	4.1	22 38	4.2
23	Thursday	12 07	3.3	——	—	01 48	5.5	14 19	5.6	11 11	4.2	23 25	4.3
24	Friday	00 37	3.4	13 01	3.3	02 35	5.6	15 08	5.7	——	—	12 00	4.2
25	Saturday	01 23	3.5	13 51	3.3	03 25	5.7	15 57	5.6	00 10	4.4	12 48	4.1
26	Sunday	02 06	3.6	14 37	3.3	04 12	5.6	16 45	5.5	00 54	4.4	13 36	4.0
27	Monday	02 46	3.6	15 20	3.3	05 00	5.5	17 31	5.3	01 38	4.3	14 21	3.9
28	Tuesday	03 26	3.6	16 01	3.3	05 48	5.3	18 19	5.1	02 23	4.1	15 08	3.7
29	Wednesday	04 07	3.5	16 44	3.2	06 34	5.1	19 05	4.8	03 11	4.0	15 58	3.6
30	Thursday	04 50	3.3	17 28	3.1	07 22	4.9	19 53	4.6	04 04	3.8	16 53	3.4

JULY 1994   *High water*   GMT

Day	London Bridge *Datum of predictions 3.20 m below* hr m	hr m	Avonmouth *Datum of predictions 6.50 m below* hr m	hr m	Liverpool *Datum of predictions 4.93 m below* hr m	hr m	Hull (*Albert Dock*) *Datum of predictions 3.90 m below* hr m	hr m
1 Friday	07 10 6.3	19 23 6.1	00 02 10.8	12 19 10.4	04 24 8.0	16 57 7.5	11 34 6.4	— —
2 Saturday	08 05 6.0	20 22 5.9	00 51 10.3	13 14 10.0	05 22 7.6	18 01 7.3	00 19 5.8	12 36 6.1
3 Sunday	09 05 5.9	21 28 5.8	01 55 9.9	14 24 9.9	06 28 7.4	19 12 7.4	01 25 5.7	13 48 5.9
4 Monday	10 10 5.9	22 37 5.8	03 06 10.0	15 36 10.2	07 37 7.5	20 13 7.6	02 37 5.8	14 59 6.0
5 Tuesday	11 13 6.0	23 40 6.0	04 12 10.5	16 38 10.9	08 37 7.8	21 05 8.0	03 40 6.1	16 03 6.1
6 Wednesday	— —	12 07 6.2	05 09 11.1	17 30 11.5	09 27 8.1	21 49 8.4	04 31 6.3	16 53 6.4
7 Thursday	00 29 6.2	12 50 6.4	05 56 11.6	18 15 12.1	10 10 8.4	22 30 8.7	05 11 6.6	17 35 6.6
8 Friday	01 12 6.4	13 33 6.7	06 41 12.0	18 57 12.5	10 49 8.7	23 08 9.0	05 49 6.8	18 13 6.8
9 Saturday	01 54 6.7	14 12 6.9	07 22 12.4	19 36 12.8	11 27 8.9	23 44 9.2	06 25 7.0	18 50 6.9
10 Sunday	02 34 6.9	14 53 7.0	08 02 12.6	20 16 13.0	— —	12 05 9.0	07 00 7.2	19 28 7.1
11 Monday	03 14 7.1	15 31 7.1	08 41 12.8	20 55 13.2	00 22 9.3	12 45 9.1	07 36 7.3	20 06 7.2
12 Tuesday	03 53 7.2	16 06 7.1	09 19 12.9	21 34 13.1	01 00 9.3	13 24 9.1	08 14 7.3	20 45 7.2
13 Wednesday	04 31 7.2	16 42 7.0	09 58 12.7	22 14 12.8	01 40 9.3	14 05 9.0	08 52 7.3	21 26 7.1
14 Thursday	05 11 7.0	17 20 6.8	10 38 12.3	22 56 12.4	02 20 9.1	14 49 8.8	09 33 7.1	22 08 6.9
15 Friday	05 53 6.7	18 01 6.6	11 20 11.8	23 41 11.8	03 05 8.9	15 38 8.5	10 18 7.0	22 57 6.7
16 Saturday	06 41 6.5	18 53 6.4	— —	12 09 11.2	03 57 8.6	16 34 8.2	11 11 6.7	23 56 6.4
17 Sunday	07 41 6.3	20 01 6.3	00 36 11.3	13 12 10.8	05 01 8.3	17 44 8.0	— —	12 18 6.5
18 Monday	08 54 6.3	21 22 6.3	01 48 10.9	14 31 10.8	06 15 8.1	19 00 8.1	01 10 6.3	13 36 6.4
19 Tuesday	10 10 6.4	22 42 6.4	03 06 11.0	15 47 11.2	07 34 8.1	20 12 8.4	02 27 6.4	15 01 6.5
20 Wednesday	11 23 6.5	23 57 6.6	04 22 11.4	17 00 11.8	08 46 8.4	21 15 8.8	03 40 6.6	16 17 6.8
21 Thursday	— —	12 28 6.7	05 33 12.0	18 04 12.5	09 48 8.8	22 12 9.2	04 41 6.9	17 17 7.0
22 Friday	00 57 6.7	13 23 6.8	06 33 12.5	18 57 13.1	10 41 9.1	23 01 9.5	05 31 7.2	18 08 7.2
23 Saturday	01 49 6.9	14 09 6.9	07 24 12.9	19 43 13.4	11 27 9.3	23 44 9.7	06 15 7.4	18 51 7.3
24 Sunday	02 36 7.1	14 51 7.1	08 07 13.2	20 26 13.5	— —	12 10 9.3	06 56 7.6	19 32 7.3
25 Monday	03 18 7.3	15 31 7.2	08 47 13.2	21 04 13.4	00 27 9.7	12 49 9.2	07 35 7.7	20 10 7.2
26 Tuesday	03 57 7.3	16 09 7.2	09 23 13.0	21 40 13.1	01 04 9.6	13 27 9.0	08 13 7.7	20 48 7.1
27 Wednesday	04 35 7.2	16 44 7.0	09 56 12.6	22 14 12.5	01 42 9.3	14 02 8.8	08 51 7.5	21 23 6.9
28 Thursday	05 11 7.0	17 19 6.8	10 26 12.0	22 45 11.8	02 18 9.0	14 37 8.4	09 29 7.2	21 58 6.6
29 Friday	05 47 6.7	17 56 6.5	10 56 11.3	23 17 11.0	02 56 8.6	15 15 8.0	10 07 6.9	22 36 6.3
30 Saturday	06 27 6.4	18 39 6.2	11 28 10.6	23 54 10.3	03 36 8.1	16 00 7.6	10 49 6.4	23 20 6.0
31 Sunday	07 13 6.1	19 33 5.9	— —	12 09 10.0	04 27 7.6	16 57 7.3	11 42 6.0	— —

AUGUST 1994   *High water*   GMT

Day	London Bridge hr m	hr m	Avonmouth hr m	hr m	Liverpool hr m	hr m	Hull (*Albert Dock*) hr m	hr m
1 Monday	08 09 5.8	20 36 5.6	00 46 9.6	13 12 9.5	05 30 7.2	18 11 7.1	00 20 5.7	12 56 5.7
2 Tuesday	09 11 5.7	21 42 5.5	02 03 9.4	14 41 9.6	06 49 7.1	19 31 7.3	01 36 5.7	14 14 5.7
3 Wednesday	10 16 5.7	22 52 5.7	03 29 9.8	16 00 10.3	08 04 7.4	20 34 7.7	02 52 5.8	15 30 5.9
4 Thursday	11 25 5.9	23 57 5.9	04 36 10.6	17 00 11.3	09 01 7.8	21 25 8.2	03 56 6.2	16 28 6.2
5 Friday	— —	12 22 6.2	05 31 11.5	17 51 12.1	09 48 8.3	22 07 8.7	04 45 6.5	17 14 6.5
6 Saturday	00 48 6.3	13 09 6.6	06 19 12.2	18 36 12.7	10 28 8.7	22 47 9.1	05 26 6.8	17 54 6.8
7 Sunday	01 33 6.7	13 52 7.0	07 03 12.7	19 18 13.1	11 08 9.1	23 25 9.4	06 04 7.1	18 32 7.1
8 Monday	02 13 7.1	14 32 7.2	07 43 13.1	19 59 13.5	11 46 9.3	— —	06 40 7.4	19 08 7.4
9 Tuesday	02 54 7.4	15 10 7.4	08 24 13.4	20 38 13.7	00 03 9.6	12 25 9.5	07 15 7.6	19 45 7.5
10 Wednesday	03 34 7.5	15 46 7.4	09 02 13.5	21 18 13.7	00 42 9.7	13 04 9.5	07 53 7.7	20 23 7.5
11 Thursday	04 12 7.4	16 24 7.3	09 40 13.3	21 57 13.4	01 21 9.7	13 44 9.3	08 31 7.7	21 04 7.4
12 Friday	04 51 7.1	17 02 7.0	10 19 12.8	22 36 12.7	02 01 9.5	14 26 9.1	09 13 7.5	21 44 7.2
13 Saturday	05 33 6.8	17 44 6.8	10 59 12.1	23 20 12.0	02 44 9.1	15 12 8.7	09 58 7.2	22 32 6.8
14 Sunday	06 18 6.5	18 35 6.5	11 45 11.3	— —	03 35 8.7	16 09 8.3	10 50 6.8	23 28 6.5
15 Monday	07 16 6.2	19 42 6.3	00 12 11.1	12 46 10.7	04 38 8.2	17 20 7.9	11 58 6.4	— —
16 Tuesday	08 26 6.1	21 03 6.2	01 22 10.5	14 07 10.4	05 58 7.8	18 43 7.9	00 43 6.2	13 26 6.2
17 Wednesday	09 45 6.2	22 27 6.3	02 48 10.4	15 33 10.8	07 26 7.8	20 02 8.2	02 10 6.3	15 02 6.3
18 Thursday	11 05 6.4	23 44 6.6	04 14 11.0	16 50 11.7	08 42 8.2	21 07 8.7	03 27 6.5	16 15 6.6
19 Friday	— —	12 14 6.7	05 26 11.8	17 54 12.6	09 41 8.6	22 00 9.1	04 29 6.9	17 11 6.9
20 Saturday	00 46 6.9	13 09 6.9	06 23 12.6	18 44 13.2	10 30 9.0	22 47 9.5	05 17 7.2	17 56 7.1
21 Sunday	01 37 7.1	13 54 7.0	07 08 13.0	19 26 13.4	11 12 9.2	23 27 9.7	05 58 7.5	18 36 7.2
22 Monday	02 20 7.2	14 33 7.1	07 48 13.2	20 04 13.5	11 50 9.3	— —	06 36 7.6	19 11 7.3
23 Tuesday	02 58 7.3	15 10 7.2	08 23 13.3	20 40 13.5	00 04 9.7	12 25 9.3	07 12 7.7	19 45 7.3
24 Wednesday	03 34 7.3	15 43 7.2	08 55 13.2	21 12 13.2	00 39 9.6	12 57 9.1	07 48 7.7	20 17 7.2
25 Thursday	04 06 7.1	16 14 7.1	09 25 12.9	21 41 12.7	01 12 9.4	13 28 8.9	08 23 7.6	20 49 7.0
26 Friday	04 37 6.9	16 45 6.9	09 53 12.3	22 10 12.0	01 44 9.0	13 59 8.6	08 58 7.3	21 20 6.8
27 Saturday	05 09 6.7	17 20 6.7	10 18 11.6	22 36 11.2	02 18 8.7	14 33 8.3	09 32 6.9	21 53 6.5
28 Sunday	05 44 6.5	18 00 6.4	10 45 10.9	23 06 10.4	02 54 8.2	15 11 7.8	10 10 6.4	22 29 6.1
29 Monday	06 24 6.2	18 45 6.0	11 17 10.1	23 44 9.6	03 36 7.7	16 00 7.4	10 53 5.9	23 17 5.8
30 Tuesday	07 12 5.8	19 41 5.6	— —	12 06 9.5	04 35 7.2	17 11 7.0	11 58 5.6	— —
31 Wednesday	08 12 5.5	20 50 5.4	00 51 9.1	13 36 9.2	05 57 6.9	18 41 7.1	00 37 5.5	13 34 5.4

JULY 1994 *continued*

	GREENOCK *Datum of predictions 1.62 m below*				LEITH *Datum of predictions 2.90 m below*				DUN LAOGHAIRE †Datum of predictions 0.20 m above			
	hr	ht m	hr	ht m	hr	ht m	hr	ht m	hr	ht m	hr	ht m
1 Friday	05 37	3.1	18 14	3.0	08 13	4.7	20 45	4.5	05 02	3.6	17 51	3.4
2 Saturday	06 29	3.0	19 03	2.9	09 06	4.5	21 41	4.4	06 08	3.4	18 53	3.3
3 Sunday	07 29	2.8	20 01	2.8	10 05	4.4	22 42	4.4	07 16	3.4	19 54	3.4
4 Monday	08 49	2.7	21 14	2.8	11 10	4.4	23 45	4.5	08 18	3.4	20 48	3.5
5 Tuesday	10 07	2.8	22 20	2.9	——	—	12 13	4.5	09 13	3.4	21 36	3.6
6 Wednesday	11 00	2.8	23 09	3.1	00 41	4.7	13 05	4.7	10 00	3.5	22 17	3.7
7 Thursday	11 44	2.9	23 50	3.1	01 28	4.9	13 49	4.9	10 41	3.5	22 54	3.8
8 Friday	12 24	2.9	——	—	02 09	5.1	14 28	5.1	11 17	3.6	23 28	3.9
9 Saturday	00 26	3.2	13 03	2.9	02 47	5.2	15 06	5.2	11 50	3.7	——	—
10 Sunday	01 02	3.3	13 40	3.0	03 23	5.3	15 43	5.3	00 02	3.9	12 26	3.8
11 Monday	01 39	3.4	14 18	3.0	04 00	5.4	16 19	5.3	00 37	4.0	13 02	3.8
12 Tuesday	02 17	3.5	14 57	3.0	04 35	5.4	16 56	5.3	01 13	4.1	13 43	3.8
13 Wednesday	02 56	3.5	15 38	3.1	05 14	5.4	17 41	5.3	01 55	4.1	14 28	3.8
14 Thursday	03 35	3.5	16 20	3.0	05 56	5.3	18 27	5.2	02 41	4.0	15 16	3.8
15 Friday	04 17	3.4	17 06	3.0	06 43	5.2	19 18	5.0	03 33	4.0	16 11	3.7
16 Saturday	05 04	3.3	17 57	2.9	07 36	5.0	20 16	4.9	04 30	3.9	17 12	3.6
17 Sunday	05 59	3.1	18 56	2.8	08 41	4.9	21 22	4.8	05 40	3.8	18 24	3.6
18 Monday	07 07	3.0	20 16	2.8	09 54	4.8	22 34	4.8	06 56	3.7	19 34	3.7
19 Tuesday	08 45	2.9	21 44	2.9	11 11	4.9	23 42	5.0	08 08	3.8	20 38	3.9
20 Wednesday	10 07	3.0	22 46	3.1	——	—	12 22	5.1	09 13	3.9	21 36	4.0
21 Thursday	11 09	3.1	23 39	3.3	00 44	5.2	13 21	5.3	10 12	4.0	22 29	4.2
22 Friday	12 03	3.2	——	—	01 38	5.4	14 11	5.5	11 04	4.1	23 15	4.3
23 Saturday	00 27	3.5	12 54	3.3	02 26	5.6	14 56	5.6	11 52	4.1	23 59	4.4
24 Sunday	01 12	3.6	13 41	3.3	03 12	5.7	15 40	5.6	——	—	12 34	4.0
25 Monday	01 53	3.7	14 21	3.3	03 56	5.7	16 22	5.5	00 37	4.4	13 12	4.0
26 Tuesday	02 30	3.7	14 58	3.3	04 38	5.6	17 04	5.3	01 15	4.3	13 50	3.9
27 Wednesday	03 06	3.7	15 33	3.3	05 20	5.4	17 44	5.1	01 52	4.2	14 26	3.8
28 Thurday	03 41	3.6	16 10	3.3	06 01	5.2	18 25	4.9	02 34	4.0	15 09	3.6
29 Friday	04 18	3.4	16 48	3.3	06 41	5.0	19 07	4.7	03 18	3.8	15 55	3.5
30 Saturday	04 58	3.2	17 30	3.2	07 26	4.7	19 53	4.5	04 09	3.6	16 51	3.4
31 Sunday	05 43	3.0	18 16	3.0	08 16	4.5	20 45	4.4	05 11	3.4	17 55	3.3

NOTES:
*Difference of height in metres from Ordnance datum (Newlyn)
†Difference of height in metres from Ordnance datum (Dublin)
hr hour
m metres

AUGUST 1994 *continued*

	GREENOCK				LEITH				DUN LAOGHAIRE			
1 Monday	06 36	2.8	19 08	2.9	09 12	4.3	21 44	4.3	06 25	3.3	19 06	3.3
2 Tuesday	07 41	2.7	20 11	2.9	10 17	4.3	22 50	4.4	07 40	3.3	20 11	3.4
3 Wednesday	09 20	2.7	21 33	2.9	11 31	4.4	——	—	08 43	3.3	21 06	3.5
4 Thursday	10 38	2.8	22 37	3.1	00 02	4.6	12 34	4.6	09 35	3.4	21 53	3.6
5 Friday	11 25	3.0	23 22	3.2	00 58	4.8	13 22	4.9	10 19	3.5	22 31	3.8
6 Saturday	12 06	3.0	——	—	01 43	5.1	14 03	5.2	10 54	3.6	23 03	3.9
7 Sunday	00 01	3.3	12 45	3.1	02 23	5.3	14 42	5.4	11 28	3.8	23 36	4.0
8 Monday	00 41	3.4	13 23	3.1	03 01	5.5	15 19	5.5	——	—	12 00	3.9
9 Tuesday	01 20	3.5	14 00	3.2	03 36	5.6	15 57	5.6	00 10	4.2	12 37	4.0
10 Wednesday	01 59	3.6	14 37	3.2	04 12	5.7	16 36	5.6	00 48	4.2	13 16	4.0
11 Thursday	02 38	3.7	15 15	3.3	04 52	5.7	17 19	5.5	01 30	4.3	13 59	4.0
12 Friday	03 17	3.7	15 54	3.2	05 35	5.6	18 05	5.4	02 16	4.2	14 48	4.0
13 Saturday	03 58	3.6	16 35	3.2	06 23	5.4	18 54	5.2	03 08	4.1	15 43	3.9
14 Sunday	04 42	3.4	17 23	3.1	07 18	5.1	19 52	4.9	04 07	3.9	16 46	3.8
15 Monday	05 33	3.1	18 20	2.9	08 24	4.9	20 59	4.8	05 19	3.8	18 00	3.7
16 Tuesday	06 38	2.9	19 47	2.9	09 43	4.7	22 15	4.8	06 43	3.7	19 14	3.7
17 Wednesday	08 44	2.8	21 34	3.0	11 06	4.8	23 31	4.9	07 59	3.7	20 24	3.9
18 Thursday	10 11	3.0	22 36	3.2	——	—	12 18	5.0	09 09	3.8	21 26	4.0
19 Friday	11 07	3.1	23 26	3.4	00 36	5.2	13 15	5.3	10 09	3.9	22 19	4.2
20 Saturday	11 56	3.2	——	—	01 29	5.4	14 02	5.4	10 58	4.0	23 03	4.3
21 Sunday	00 12	3.6	12 42	3.3	02 14	5.6	14 42	5.5	11 39	4.0	23 42	4.3
22 Monday	00 56	3.6	13 22	3.3	02 55	5.7	15 20	5.5	——	—	12 13	4.0
23 Tuesday	01 35	3.7	13 58	3.4	03 34	5.7	15 57	5.5	00 14	4.3	12 44	3.9
24 Wednesday	02 09	3.7	14 29	3.4	04 11	5.6	16 32	5.4	00 47	4.2	13 13	3.9
25 Thursday	02 41	3.6	15 01	3.4	04 48	5.4	17 09	5.2	01 20	4.1	13 47	3.9
26 Friday	03 13	3.6	15 34	3.4	05 24	5.3	17 45	5.0	01 58	4.0	14 25	3.8
27 Saturday	03 46	3.4	16 05	3.4	06 02	5.0	18 25	4.8	02 40	3.8	15 09	3.7
28 Sunday	04 22	3.3	16 48	3.3	06 44	4.8	19 08	4.6	03 29	3.6	16 01	3.5
29 Monday	05 04	3.1	17 33	3.1	07 31	4.5	19 57	4.5	04 26	3.4	17 02	3.4
30 Tuesday	05 55	2.8	18 25	3.0	08 26	4.3	20 55	4.3	05 37	3.3	18 18	3.3
31 Wednesday	07 00	2.7	19 27	2.9	09 30	4.2	22 01	4.3	07 02	3.2	19 33	3.3

SEPTEMBER 1994   *High water*   GMT

		London Bridge			Avonmouth			Liverpool			Hull (*Albert Dock*)	
		*Datum of predictions 3.20 m below			*Datum of predictions 6.50 m below			*Datum of predictions 4.93 m below			*Datum of predictions 3.90 m below	
		hr m	hr m		hr m	hr m		hr m	hr m		hr m	hr m
1	Thursday	09 25 5.5	22 07 5.5		02 41 9.3	15 19 9.9		07 26 7.1	19 59 7.5		02 06 5.6	14 54 5.7
2	Friday	10 44 5.7	23 22 5.9		04 03 10.2	16 29 11.0		08 32 7.7	20 54 8.1		03 18 6.0	15 58 6.1
3	Saturday	11 51 6.1	— —		05 03 11.4	17 23 12.1		09 19 8.3	21 39 8.7		04 14 6.4	16 48 6.5
4	Sunday	00 19 6.4	12 42 6.6		05 52 12.4	18 11 13.0		10 02 8.8	22 20 9.2		04 57 6.9	17 28 6.9
5	Monday	01 06 6.9	13 26 7.1		06 39 13.0	18 56 13.5		10 42 9.3	22 59 9.6		05 37 7.3	18 06 7.3
6	Tuesday	01 49 7.3	14 06 7.4		07 21 13.5	19 38 13.9		11 22 9.6	23 39 9.9		06 15 7.6	18 43 7.6
7	Wednesday	02 30 7.5	14 46 7.6		08 02 13.8	20 19 14.1		— —	12 01 9.8		06 51 7.8	19 21 7.8
8	Thursday	03 10 7.6	15 24 7.6		08 41 13.9	20 58 14.1		00 18 10.0	12 41 9.8		07 31 8.0	19 59 7.8
9	Friday	03 49 7.5	16 03 7.5		09 20 13.7	21 37 13.7		00 59 10.0	13 23 9.7		08 10 7.9	20 40 7.6
10	Saturday	04 30 7.2	16 45 7.2		09 58 13.1	22 18 12.9		01 41 9.7	14 05 9.3		08 54 7.7	21 22 7.3
11	Sunday	05 13 6.8	17 30 6.9		10 41 12.3	23 02 11.9		02 26 9.2	14 53 8.9		09 41 7.3	22 10 6.9
12	Monday	06 00 6.5	18 24 6.5		11 27 11.4	23 55 11.0		03 18 8.6	15 49 8.3		10 36 6.7	23 06 6.5
13	Tuesday	06 56 6.2	19 30 6.3		— —	12 29 10.6		04 23 8.0	17 02 7.9		11 45 6.2	
14	Wednesday	08 04 6.0	20 47 6.2		01 07 10.3	13 52 10.3		05 49 7.6	18 28 7.8		00 20 6.2	13 26 6.0
15	Thursday	09 21 6.1	22 10 6.3		02 34 10.2	15 20 10.7		07 19 7.7	19 49 8.1		01 52 6.2	14 59 6.2
16	Friday	10 44 6.3	23 27 6.7		04 03 10.9	16 38 11.7		08 32 8.1	20 53 8.7		03 13 6.5	16 07 6.5
17	Saturday	11 54 6.7	— —		05 11 11.9	17 37 12.6		09 28 8.6	21 43 9.1		04 12 6.8	16 57 6.8
18	Sunday	00 28 7.0	12 49 7.0		06 04 12.6	18 25 13.2		10 12 9.0	22 26 9.4		04 59 7.2	17 38 7.0
19	Monday	01 17 7.3	13 33 7.2		06 47 13.0	19 04 13.4		10 51 9.2	23 04 9.6		05 38 7.4	18 13 7.1
20	Tuesday	01 58 7.3	14 12 7.2		07 24 13.2	19 39 13.4		11 25 9.3	23 39 9.6		06 13 7.6	18 44 7.2
21	Wednesday	02 34 7.3	14 46 7.2		07 56 13.2	20 11 13.3		11 57 9.3	— —		06 49 7.7	19 17 7.3
22	Thursday	03 07 7.2	15 15 7.2		08 26 13.1	20 42 13.2		00 11 9.5	12 27 9.2		07 22 7.6	19 46 7.3
23	Friday	03 36 7.0	15 45 7.1		08 54 12.9	21 11 12.8		00 42 9.3	12 56 9.0		07 56 7.5	20 16 7.1
24	Saturday	04 03 6.9	16 14 6.9		09 19 12.5	21 37 12.1		01 13 9.0	13 26 8.8		08 28 7.2	20 45 6.9
25	Sunday	04 33 6.8	16 48 6.7		09 46 11.9	22 04 11.4		01 44 8.7	13 57 8.5		09 02 6.8	21 15 6.6
26	Monday	05 06 6.6	17 26 6.5		10 12 11.1	22 31 10.5		02 18 8.3	14 32 8.1		09 36 6.4	21 47 6.3
27	Tuesday	05 43 6.3	18 08 6.2		10 42 10.4	23 04 9.8		02 57 7.8	15 15 7.6		10 15 6.0	22 28 5.9
28	Wednesday	06 25 6.0	18 57 5.8		11 24 9.8	23 59 9.3		03 50 7.3	16 17 7.2		11 09 5.6	23 30 5.6
29	Thursday	07 17 5.6	19 59 5.6		— —	12 37 9.4		05 06 7.0	17 46 7.1		— —	12 43 5.4
30	Friday	08 27 5.4	21 22 5.6		01 42 9.2	14 28 9.7		06 38 7.1	19 12 7.5		01 17 5.6	14 11 5.6

OCTOBER 1994   *High water*   GMT

		London Bridge			Avonmouth			Liverpool			Hull (*Albert Dock*)	
		hr m	hr m		hr m	hr m		hr m	hr m		hr m	hr m
1	Saturday	09 59 5.6	22 42 5.9		03 20 10.0	15 50 10.9		07 51 7.6	20 15 8.1		02 34 5.9	15 19 6.1
2	Sunday	11 13 6.1	23 46 6.5		04 26 11.3	16 49 12.1		08 46 8.3	21 04 8.7		03 34 6.4	16 12 6.6
3	Monday	— —	12 08 6.9		05 21 12.4	17 41 13.0		09 31 8.9	21 49 9.3		04 24 6.9	16 57 7.0
4	Tuesday	00 38 7.0	12 56 7.1		06 09 13.2	18 29 13.7		10 13 9.4	22 31 9.8		05 06 7.3	17 38 7.4
5	Wednesday	01 23 7.4	13 38 7.5		06 56 13.7	19 14 14.1		10 55 9.8	23 13 10.1		05 47 7.7	18 18 7.7
6	Thursday	02 05 7.6	14 19 7.7		07 38 14.0	19 56 14.3		11 37 10.0	23 56 10.2		06 27 7.9	18 56 7.9
7	Friday	02 46 7.6	15 01 7.8		08 20 14.1	20 38 14.2		— —	12 18 10.0		07 10 8.1	19 36 7.9
8	Saturday	03 28 7.5	15 45 7.7		09 01 13.9	21 20 13.7		00 39 10.1	13 02 9.9		07 53 8.0	20 17 7.7
9	Sunday	04 10 7.3	16 31 7.4		09 41 13.3	22 03 13.0		01 24 9.7	13 47 9.5		08 40 7.7	21 02 7.4
10	Monday	04 57 6.9	17 20 7.0		10 25 12.5	22 50 12.0		02 12 9.2	14 36 9.0		09 29 7.2	21 50 7.0
11	Tuesday	05 46 6.6	18 17 6.7		11 14 11.5	23 44 11.0		03 05 8.6	15 34 8.5		10 26 6.7	22 46 6.6
12	Wednesday	06 39 6.2	19 19 6.4		— —	12 09 10.6		04 12 7.9	16 44 8.0		11 37 6.2	23 55 6.3
13	Thursday	07 42 6.1	20 27 6.2		00 51 10.3	13 34 10.4		05 33 7.6	18 07 7.9		— —	13 17 6.0
14	Friday	08 53 6.0	21 46 6.3		02 14 10.2	14 58 10.8		06 59 7.7	19 24 8.1		01 25 6.2	14 41 6.1
15	Saturday	10 16 6.2	23 04 6.6		03 36 11.0	16 12 11.6		08 09 8.0	20 27 8.5		02 47 6.4	15 46 6.4
16	Sunday	11 29 6.6	— —		04 45 11.7	17 10 12.4		09 04 8.5	21 18 8.9		03 47 6.7	16 35 6.7
17	Monday	00 04 7.0	12 24 7.0		05 37 12.4	17 58 12.9		09 46 8.8	22 00 9.2		04 35 7.0	17 14 7.0
18	Tuesday	00 52 7.2	13 09 7.1		06 19 12.8	18 37 13.0		10 24 9.0	22 37 9.3		05 14 7.2	17 48 7.0
19	Wednesday	01 34 7.3	13 47 7.2		06 56 12.9	19 12 13.0		10 58 9.2	23 11 9.3		05 51 7.4	18 19 7.2
20	Thursday	02 08 7.2	14 19 7.1		07 26 12.9	19 45 13.0		11 29 9.2	23 43 9.3		06 25 7.4	18 49 7.3
21	Friday	02 39 7.1	14 49 7.1		07 56 13.0	20 14 12.9		11 58 9.2	— —		06 58 7.4	19 17 7.2
22	Saturday	03 05 7.0	15 17 7.0		08 24 12.9	20 42 12.6		00 15 9.2	12 28 9.1		07 32 7.3	19 46 7.1
23	Sunday	03 32 6.9	15 48 6.9		08 52 12.6	21 11 12.2		00 46 9.0	12 59 8.9		08 04 7.0	20 14 7.0
24	Monday	04 03 6.8	16 23 6.8		09 20 12.1	21 40 11.6		01 17 8.7	13 30 8.7		08 37 6.8	20 45 6.7
25	Tuesday	04 37 6.7	17 01 6.6		09 50 11.5	22 11 10.9		01 52 8.4	14 04 8.3		09 12 6.4	21 18 6.4
26	Wednesday	05 13 6.5	17 42 6.4		10 22 10.9	22 46 10.3		02 30 8.0	14 46 8.0		09 51 6.1	21 57 6.1
27	Thursday	05 53 6.2	18 27 6.1		11 04 10.3	23 37 9.8		03 19 7.6	15 41 7.6		10 41 5.8	22 50 5.8
28	Friday	06 41 5.9	19 24 5.9		— —	12 06 9.9		04 26 7.3	16 55 7.4		11 51 5.7	
29	Saturday	07 42 5.7	20 39 5.8		00 56 9.6	13 36 10.0		05 47 7.3	18 18 7.6		00 12 5.7	13 22 5.8
30	Sunday	09 08 5.7	22 02 6.1		02 30 10.1	15 04 10.8		07 03 7.7	19 28 8.1		01 43 5.9	14 34 6.1
31	Monday	10 30 6.1	23 11 6.5		03 44 11.3	16 11 11.9		08 05 8.3	20 25 8.7		02 49 6.3	15 33 6.6

SEPTEMBER 1994   *continued*

	GREENOCK *Datum of predictions 1.62 m below*				LEITH *Datum of predictions 2.90 m below*				DUN LAOGHAIRE †Datum of predictions 0.20 m above			
	hr	m	hr	m	hr	m	hr	m	hr	m	hr	m
1 Thursday	08 26	2.7	20 42	2.9	10 45	4.3	23 17	4.5	08 12	3.3	20 33	3.4
2 Friday	10 12	2.8	21 58	3.1	11 58	4.6	—	—	09 08	3.4	21 22	3.6
3 Saturday	11 00	3.0	22 50	3.3	00 23	4.8	12 51	4.9	09 52	3.5	22 00	3.8
4 Sunday	11 41	3.1	23 33	3.4	01 12	5.2	13 35	5.3	10 27	3.7	22 34	3.9
5 Monday	12 19	3.2	—	—	01 53	5.5	14 14	5.5	11 00	3.9	23 07	4.1
6 Tuesday	00 15	3.5	12 58	3.3	02 31	5.7	14 54	5.7	11 34	4.0	23 45	4.3
7 Wednesday	00 58	3.6	13 36	3.3	03 09	5.9	15 32	5.8	—	—	12 10	4.1
8 Thursday	01 39	3.7	14 13	3.4	03 47	6.0	16 12	5.8	00 24	4.4	12 51	4.2
9 Friday	02 20	3.8	14 50	3.4	04 31	5.9	16 56	5.7	01 06	4.4	13 34	4.2
10 Saturday	03 00	3.7	15 28	3.4	05 16	5.8	17 42	5.5	01 55	4.3	14 22	4.1
11 Sunday	03 40	3.6	16 09	3.4	06 06	5.5	18 33	5.2	02 50	4.2	15 18	4.0
12 Monday	04 24	3.4	16 55	3.2	07 04	5.1	19 32	5.0	03 53	3.9	16 24	3.9
13 Tuesday	05 15	3.1	17 53	3.0	08 14	4.8	20 42	4.8	05 11	3.7	17 41	3.8
14 Wednesday	06 23	2.8	19 27	2.9	09 36	4.7	22 01	4.7	06 35	3.6	18 57	3.8
15 Thursday	08 51	2.8	21 19	3.1	10 57	4.8	23 19	4.9	07 55	3.6	20 09	3.9
16 Friday	10 04	3.0	22 19	3.3	—	—	12 08	5.0	09 06	3.7	21 13	4.0
17 Saturday	10 55	3.2	23 08	3.5	00 23	5.1	13 03	5.2	10 03	3.9	22 05	4.1
18 Sunday	11 39	3.3	23 52	3.6	01 14	5.4	13 46	5.4	10 47	3.9	22 47	4.2
19 Monday	12 19	3.4	—	—	01 57	5.5	14 23	5.5	11 21	3.9	23 20	4.2
20 Tuesday	00 34	3.6	12 56	3.4	02 34	5.6	14 56	5.5	11 49	3.9	23 49	4.2
21 Wednesday	01 11	3.6	13 28	3.4	03 09	5.6	15 29	5.5	—	—	12 13	3.9
22 Thursday	01 44	3.5	13 58	3.4	03 44	5.5	16 03	5.4	00 19	4.1	12 41	4.0
23 Friday	02 14	3.5	14 28	3.5	04 18	5.4	16 35	5.3	00 51	4.1	13 12	3.9
24 Saturday	02 45	3.5	14 59	3.5	04 53	5.3	17 10	5.1	01 27	4.0	13 51	3.9
25 Sunday	03 17	3.4	15 33	3.5	05 30	5.1	17 48	4.9	02 08	3.8	14 34	3.8
26 Monday	03 52	3.2	16 10	3.4	06 09	4.8	18 29	4.7	02 57	3.6	15 23	3.6
27 Tuesday	04 32	3.1	16 53	3.2	06 54	4.6	19 17	4.5	03 51	3.4	16 21	3.4
28 Wednesday	05 22	2.9	17 45	3.1	07 48	4.4	20 11	4.4	04 58	3.3	17 31	3.3
29 Thursday	06 28	2.7	18 48	3.0	08 49	4.3	21 18	4.4	06 21	3.2	18 48	3.3
30 Friday	07 48	2.7	20 00	3.0	10 01	4.4	22 31	4.5	07 34	3.3	19 51	3.4

NOTES:
*Difference of height in metres from Ordnance datum (Newlyn)
†Difference of height in metres from Ordnance datum (Dublin)
hr hour
m metres

OCTOBER 1994   *continued*

	GREENOCK				LEITH				DUN LAOGHAIRE			
1 Saturday	09 28	2.8	21 16	3.1	11 16	4.6	23 41	4.8	08 31	3.4	20 42	3.6
2 Sunday	10 26	3.0	22 15	3.3	—	—	12 16	5.0	09 16	3.6	21 23	3.8
3 Monday	11 09	3.2	23 03	3.5	00 34	5.2	13 04	5.4	09 54	3.8	22 01	4.0
4 Tuesday	11 49	3.3	23 48	3.6	01 19	5.5	13 46	5.7	10 30	4.0	22 40	4.2
5 Wednesday	12 29	3.4	—	—	02 00	5.8	14 26	5.9	11 07	4.2	23 20	4.4
6 Thursday	00 33	3.7	13 09	3.5	02 42	6.0	15 08	6.0	11 46	4.3	—	—
7 Friday	01 19	3.7	13 49	3.6	03 25	6.1	15 50	5.9	00 03	4.5	12 28	4.4
8 Saturday	02 02	3.8	14 27	3.6	04 11	6.0	16 35	5.8	00 50	4.5	13 13	4.4
9 Sunday	02 44	3.7	15 07	3.6	05 00	5.8	17 23	5.6	01 41	4.4	14 04	4.3
10 Monday	03 26	3.6	15 48	3.5	05 54	5.5	18 15	5.3	02 38	4.1	15 01	4.1
11 Tuesday	04 12	3.4	16 36	3.4	06 54	5.1	19 17	5.0	03 46	3.9	16 07	4.0
12 Wednesday	05 05	3.1	17 35	3.2	08 03	4.9	20 27	4.8	05 02	3.7	17 21	3.8
13 Thursday	06 21	2.9	19 04	3.1	09 20	4.7	21 41	4.8	06 24	3.6	18 38	3.8
14 Friday	08 30	2.9	20 50	3.1	10 38	4.8	22 56	4.9	07 45	3.6	19 49	3.9
15 Saturday	09 41	3.0	21 53	3.3	11 45	5.0	23 59	5.1	08 52	3.7	20 52	4.0
16 Sunday	10 30	3.2	22 42	3.5	—	—	12 39	5.2	09 45	3.8	21 43	4.0
17 Monday	11 12	3.3	23 27	3.5	00 51	5.3	13 22	5.3	10 24	3.9	22 23	4.1
18 Tuesday	11 50	3.4	—	—	01 34	5.4	13 59	5.4	10 56	3.9	22 54	4.1
19 Wednesday	00 07	3.5	12 25	3.4	02 11	5.4	14 31	5.4	11 21	3.9	23 22	4.0
20 Thursday	00 45	3.4	12 57	3.4	02 45	5.5	15 02	5.4	11 45	4.0	23 53	4.0
21 Friday	01 18	3.4	13 27	3.5	03 19	5.4	15 34	5.4	—	—	12 14	4.0
22 Saturday	01 48	3.4	13 57	3.5	03 51	5.4	16 07	5.3	00 26	4.0	12 47	4.0
23 Sunday	02 19	3.3	14 29	3.6	04 26	5.3	16 42	5.2	01 01	3.9	13 24	3.9
24 Monday	02 51	3.3	15 02	3.6	05 03	5.1	17 19	5.0	01 43	3.8	14 06	3.8
25 Tuesday	03 28	3.2	15 39	3.5	05 42	4.9	17 56	4.9	02 29	3.6	14 54	3.7
26 Wednesday	04 08	3.1	16 20	3.4	06 26	4.7	18 41	4.7	03 22	3.5	15 48	3.5
27 Thursday	04 56	2.9	17 08	3.2	07 15	4.6	19 36	4.5	04 24	3.3	16 48	3.4
28 Friday	05 59	2.8	18 08	3.1	08 14	4.5	20 38	4.5	05 34	3.3	17 57	3.4
29 Saturday	07 13	2.8	19 18	3.0	09 22	4.5	21 47	4.6	06 46	3.3	19 02	3.4
30 Sunday	08 35	2.8	20 33	3.1	10 34	4.7	22 56	4.9	07 47	3.4	19 58	3.6
31 Monday	09 44	3.0	21 39	3.3	11 37	5.0	23 56	5.2	08 36	3.6	20 47	3.8

NOVEMBER 1994   *High water*   GMT

		LONDON BRIDGE *Datum of predictions 3.20 m below				AVONMOUTH *Datum of predictions 6.50 m below				LIVERPOOL *Datum of predictions 4.93 m below				HULL (*Albert Dock*) *Datum of predictions 3.90 m below			
		hr	m ht	hr	m ht	hr	m ht	hr	m ht	hr	m ht	hr	m ht	hr	m ht	hr	m ht
1	Tuesday	11 33	6.6	—	—	04 45	12.2	17 09	12.9	08 57	8.9	21 17	9.3	03 44	6.8	16 24	7.0
2	Wednesday	00 07	7.0	12 25	7.1	05 38	13.1	18 01	13.6	09 45	9.4	22 03	9.7	04 35	7.3	17 10	7.4
3	Thursday	00 56	7.3	13 13	7.4	06 29	13.7	18 50	14.0	10 30	9.8	22 49	10.0	05 21	7.6	17 52	7.7
4	Friday	01 41	7.4	13 58	7.6	07 15	14.0	19 36	14.2	11 15	10.1	23 36	10.1	06 08	7.9	18 34	7.9
5	Saturday	02 25	7.5	14 43	7.7	08 00	14.1	20 21	14.1	—	—	12 00	10.1	06 54	8.0	19 17	7.9
6	Sunday	03 08	7.5	15 31	7.7	08 44	14.0	21 06	13.7	00 24	10.0	12 45	9.9	07 41	7.9	20 02	7.8
7	Monday	03 55	7.3	16 20	7.5	09 29	13.5	21 53	13.0	01 10	9.7	13 33	9.6	08 30	7.6	20 47	7.5
8	Tuesday	04 42	7.1	17 11	7.3	10 15	12.7	22 39	12.1	02 01	9.2	14 23	9.2	09 20	7.2	21 34	7.2
9	Wednesday	05 32	6.8	18 04	6.9	11 04	11.9	23 31	11.3	02 54	8.6	15 18	8.7	10 15	6.7	22 26	6.8
10	Thursday	06 22	6.5	19 00	6.6	—	—	12 01	11.1	03 55	8.1	16 21	8.3	11 20	6.2	23 27	6.5
11	Friday	07 17	6.2	20 01	6.3	00 30	10.6	13 05	10.7	05 05	7.7	17 32	8.0	—	—	12 43	6.0
12	Saturday	08 20	6.1	21 11	6.2	01 39	10.3	14 20	10.7	06 22	7.6	18 46	8.0	00 40	6.3	14 06	6.0
13	Sunday	09 36	6.1	22 28	6.4	02 56	10.6	15 33	11.1	07 33	7.8	19 52	8.2	02 04	6.3	15 11	6.2
14	Monday	10 55	6.3	23 33	6.7	04 05	11.1	16 35	11.7	08 30	8.2	20 46	8.5	03 12	6.5	16 03	6.4
15	Tuesday	11 54	6.7	—	—	05 02	11.7	17 24	12.2	09 17	8.5	21 31	8.7	04 05	6.7	16 45	6.6
16	Wednesday	00 24	7.0	12 41	6.9	05 47	12.2	18 06	12.4	09 56	8.7	22 10	8.9	04 49	6.9	17 20	6.8
17	Thursday	01 04	7.1	13 20	7.0	06 25	12.4	18 44	12.5	10 31	8.9	22 45	9.0	05 27	7.0	17 52	7.0
18	Friday	01 41	7.0	13 54	7.0	06 58	12.6	19 18	12.6	11 04	9.1	23 19	9.1	06 04	7.1	18 23	7.1
19	Saturday	02 11	7.0	14 25	7.0	07 31	12.7	19 50	12.6	11 34	9.1	23 51	9.0	06 39	7.1	18 53	7.2
20	Sunday	02 40	7.0	14 56	7.0	08 00	12.7	20 20	12.5	—	—	12 07	9.1	07 11	7.1	19 21	7.1
21	Monday	03 10	6.9	15 29	6.9	08 30	12.6	20 51	12.3	00 25	8.9	12 38	9.0	07 45	7.0	19 52	7.0
22	Tuesday	03 43	6.9	16 06	6.9	09 02	12.4	21 25	11.9	00 57	8.8	13 12	8.8	08 19	6.8	20 26	6.9
23	Wednesday	04 17	6.8	16 42	6.8	09 36	12.0	21 58	11.5	01 34	8.5	13 47	8.6	08 55	6.6	21 01	6.7
24	Thursday	04 54	6.6	17 22	6.6	10 12	11.5	22 38	11.0	02 12	8.3	14 27	8.3	09 36	6.4	21 40	6.5
25	Friday	05 32	6.4	18 05	6.4	10 55	11.0	23 24	10.5	02 57	8.0	15 17	8.1	10 22	6.2	22 28	6.2
26	Saturday	06 14	6.2	18 56	6.2	11 47	10.7	—	—	03 53	7.7	16 17	7.9	11 17	6.0	23 30	6.1
27	Sunday	07 09	6.0	20 02	6.1	00 23	10.2	12 56	10.5	05 01	7.6	17 27	7.9	—	—	12 27	6.0
28	Monday	08 23	5.9	21 21	6.2	01 41	10.3	14 17	10.9	06 15	7.8	18 41	8.2	00 46	6.1	13 45	6.2
29	Tuesday	09 46	6.1	22 34	6.5	03 01	10.9	15 30	11.6	07 24	8.2	19 48	8.6	02 02	6.4	14 51	6.5
30	Wednesday	10 58	6.5	23 37	6.9	04 08	11.8	16 35	12.4	08 23	8.8	20 47	9.0	03 08	6.7	15 51	6.9

DECEMBER 1994   *High water*   GMT

		LONDON BRIDGE				AVONMOUTH				LIVERPOOL				HULL (*Albert Dock*)			
1	Thursday	11 58	6.9	—	—	05 09	12.7	17 34	13.1	09 18	9.2	21 41	9.5	04 07	7.1	16 45	7.3
2	Friday	00 32	7.1	12 52	7.1	06 05	13.3	18 29	13.6	10 09	9.6	22 33	9.7	05 03	7.5	17 33	7.5
3	Saturday	01 23	7.2	13 42	7.3	06 56	13.8	19 21	13.8	10 58	9.9	23 22	9.9	05 55	7.7	18 19	7.7
4	Sunday	02 09	7.2	14 32	7.5	07 45	14.0	20 09	13.9	11 46	10.0	—	—	06 44	7.8	19 03	7.8
5	Monday	02 56	7.3	15 19	7.6	08 31	14.0	20 56	13.7	00 11	9.8	12 34	10.0	07 34	7.7	19 48	7.8
6	Tuesday	03 42	7.3	16 09	7.6	09 18	13.7	21 41	13.2	01 00	9.6	13 20	9.8	08 21	7.5	20 31	7.7
7	Wednesday	04 28	7.3	16 58	7.4	10 03	13.1	22 26	12.5	01 48	9.2	14 08	9.4	09 09	7.2	21 16	7.5
8	Thursday	05 15	7.0	17 47	7.1	10 49	12.4	23 11	11.8	02 37	8.8	14 57	9.0	09 58	6.8	22 04	7.2
9	Friday	06 00	6.7	18 36	6.8	11 37	11.6	23 59	11.0	03 28	8.3	15 49	8.5	10 50	6.4	22 55	6.8
10	Saturday	06 49	6.4	19 28	6.4	—	—	12 29	11.0	04 24	7.9	16 48	8.1	11 49	6.1	23 52	6.5
11	Sunday	07 42	6.1	20 29	6.2	00 53	10.5	13 29	10.6	05 29	7.6	17 54	7.8	—	—	13 03	5.9
12	Monday	08 47	6.0	21 39	6.1	01 59	10.2	14 38	10.5	06 41	7.5	19 03	7.8	01 03	6.2	14 17	5.9
13	Tuesday	10 04	6.0	22 52	6.3	03 12	10.4	15 47	10.8	07 47	7.7	20 06	7.9	02 20	6.2	15 19	6.1
14	Wednesday	11 18	6.2	23 49	6.5	04 17	10.8	16 45	11.2	08 42	8.0	20 58	8.2	03 27	6.3	16 10	6.3
15	Thursday	—	—	12 10	6.5	05 09	11.4	17 34	11.7	09 27	8.3	21 43	8.4	04 19	6.5	16 52	6.6
16	Friday	00 35	6.7	12 53	6.6	05 54	11.9	18 18	12.0	10 06	8.6	22 23	8.7	05 04	6.6	17 28	6.8
17	Saturday	01 13	6.8	13 30	6.7	06 33	12.2	18 56	12.2	10 41	8.9	22 59	8.8	05 45	6.8	18 02	7.0
18	Sunday	01 47	6.9	14 04	6.8	07 08	12.5	19 31	12.4	11 16	9.0	23 33	8.9	06 20	6.9	18 33	7.1
19	Monday	02 19	6.9	14 39	6.9	07 42	12.6	20 04	12.5	11 49	9.1	—	—	06 54	7.0	19 04	7.2
20	Tuesday	02 54	7.0	15 15	7.0	08 16	12.7	20 38	12.5	00 08	8.9	12 22	9.1	07 28	7.0	19 36	7.2
21	Wednesday	03 29	7.0	15 52	7.0	08 49	12.8	21 13	12.4	00 43	8.9	12 57	9.1	08 03	7.0	20 11	7.2
22	Thursday	04 04	6.9	16 30	7.0	09 26	12.6	21 50	12.2	01 19	8.8	13 33	8.9	08 41	7.0	20 48	7.1
23	Friday	04 40	6.8	17 06	6.9	10 04	12.3	22 28	11.8	01 57	8.6	14 12	8.8	09 20	6.8	21 26	6.9
24	Saturday	05 15	6.7	17 47	6.7	10 43	11.9	23 09	11.3	02 39	8.4	14 54	8.6	10 01	6.6	22 10	6.8
25	Sunday	05 54	6.5	18 32	6.4	11 28	11.4	23 56	10.9	03 27	8.2	15 46	8.4	10 49	6.5	23 00	6.6
26	Monday	06 41	6.3	19 30	6.2	—	—	12 23	11.1	04 23	8.0	16 47	8.2	11 45	6.3	—	—
27	Tuesday	07 45	6.1	20 43	6.2	01 00	10.6	13 34	10.9	05 32	8.0	17 58	8.2	00 02	6.4	12 57	6.3
28	Wednesday	09 07	6.1	21 59	6.4	02 19	10.7	14 54	11.2	06 46	8.1	19 14	8.3	01 18	6.4	14 13	6.4
29	Thursday	10 26	6.4	23 11	6.7	03 34	11.3	16 07	11.8	07 55	8.4	20 23	8.6	02 34	6.6	15 23	6.7
30	Friday	11 37	6.7	—	—	04 43	12.1	17 14	12.4	08 58	8.9	21 25	9.0	03 47	6.9	16 25	7.0
31	Saturday	00 14	6.9	12 39	6.9	05 47	12.8	18 15	13.0	09 55	9.3	22 21	9.4	04 52	7.2	17 19	7.3

NOVEMBER 1994 *continued*

		GREENOCK *Datum of predictions 1.62 m below				LEITH *Datum of predictions 2.90 m below				DUN LAOGHAIRE †Datum of predictions 0.20 m above			
		hr	ht m	hr	ht m	hr	ht m	hr	ht m	hr	ht m	hr	ht m
1	Tuesday	10 34	3.2	22 33	3.5	———	—	12 30	5.4	09 22	3.8	21 32	4.1
2	Wednesday	11 19	3.4	23 22	3.6	00 47	5.5	13 17	5.7	10 03	4.1	22 16	4.3
3	Thursday	12 02	3.5	———	—	01 34	5.8	14 00	5.9	10 44	4.3	23 01	4.4
4	Friday	00 11	3.7	12 45	3.6	02 20	6.0	14 44	6.0	11 27	4.4	23 48	4.5
5	Saturday	00 59	3.7	13 28	3.7	03 06	6.1	15 29	6.0	———	—	12 12	4.5
6	Sunday	01 46	3.7	14 09	3.8	03 56	6.0	16 17	5.8	00 37	4.5	12 58	4.5
7	Monday	02 31	3.7	14 51	3.8	04 46	5.8	17 06	5.6	01 31	4.3	13 50	4.4
8	Tuesday	03 17	3.6	15 34	3.7	05 41	5.5	17 59	5.4	02 28	4.1	14 45	4.2
9	Wednesday	04 04	3.4	16 21	3.6	06 41	5.2	19 00	5.1	03 34	3.9	15 48	4.1
10	Thursday	04 59	3.2	17 18	3.4	07 46	4.9	20 06	4.9	04 47	3.6	16 57	3.9
11	Friday	06 07	3.0	18 29	3.2	08 54	4.8	21 13	4.8	06 03	3.5	18 08	3.8
12	Saturday	07 32	3.0	20 01	3.2	10 03	4.7	22 21	4.8	07 17	3.5	19 18	3.8
13	Sunday	08 57	3.0	21 16	3.3	11 09	4.8	23 26	4.9	08 22	3.6	20 21	3.8
14	Monday	09 53	3.2	22 11	3.3	———	—	12 05	5.0	09 13	3.7	21 12	3.9
15	Tuesday	10 37	3.3	22 57	3.4	00 20	5.0	12 51	5.1	19 54	3.8	21 54	3.9
16	Wednesday	11 17	3.4	23 40	3.4	01 07	5.2	13 32	5.2	10 27	3.9	22 29	3.9
17	Thursday	11 54	3.4	———	—	01 46	5.2	14 07	5.3	10 54	3.9	23 00	3.9
18	Friday	00 18	3.3	12 29	3.5	02 23	5.3	14 40	5.3	11 24	4.0	23 34	3.9
19	Saturday	00 54	3.3	13 00	3.5	02 56	5.3	15 12	5.4	11 55	4.0	———	—
20	Sunday	01 25	3.2	13 31	3.6	03 30	5.3	15 46	5.3	00 06	3.9	12 27	4.0
21	Monday	01 57	3.2	14 03	3.6	04 05	5.2	16 19	5.2	00 43	3.8	13 02	4.0
22	Tuesday	02 31	3.2	14 38	3.6	04 42	5.1	16 56	5.1	01 23	3.7	13 44	3.9
23	Wednesday	03 08	3.2	15 15	3.6	05 20	5.0	17 33	5.0	02 06	3.6	14 28	3.8
24	Thursday	03 49	3.1	15 55	3.5	06 02	4.9	18 15	4.9	02 55	3.5	15 16	3.6
25	Friday	04 35	3.0	16 38	3.4	06 49	4.8	19 04	4.8	03 50	3.4	16 09	3.5
26	Saturday	05 30	2.9	17 30	3.2	07 43	4.7	20 02	4.7	04 50	3.4	17 09	3.5
27	Sunday	06 35	2.9	18 33	3.2	08 45	4.7	21 06	4.7	05 55	3.4	18 14	3.6
28	Monday	07 46	2.9	19 46	3.2	09 53	4.8	22 14	4.9	07 00	3.5	19 17	3.7
29	Tuesday	08 59	3.0	21 01	3.3	10 59	5.0	23 20	5.1	07 59	3.7	20 15	3.9
30	Wednesday	10 00	3.2	22 04	3.4	11 58	5.3	———	—	08 51	3.9	21 09	4.1

NOTES:
*Difference of height in metres from Ordnance datum (Newlyn)
†Difference of height in metres from Ordnance datum (Dublin)
hr hour
m metres

DECEMBER 1994 *continued*

		GREENOCK				LEITH				DUN LAOGHAIRE			
1	Thursday	10 52	3.3	22 59	3.5	00 19	5.4	12 50	5.5	09 39	4.1	22 00	4.3
2	Friday	11 40	3.5	23 52	3.6	01 12	5.7	13 39	5.7	10 26	4.3	22 50	4.4
3	Saturday	12 26	3.6	———	—	02 03	5.9	14 26	5.9	11 11	4.4	23 38	4.4
4	Sunday	00 44	3.6	13 12	3.8	02 52	6.0	15 12	5.9	11 58	4.5		
5	Monday	01 35	3.6	13 56	3.9	03 43	6.0	16 01	5.9	00 28	4.4	12 45	4.5
6	Tuesday	02 23	3.6	14 39	3.9	04 34	5.8	16 52	5.7	01 20	4.3	13 34	4.5
7	Wednesday	03 09	3.6	15 22	3.9	05 27	5.6	17 44	5.5	02 15	4.1	14 26	4.3
8	Thursday	03 55	3.5	16 07	3.8	06 22	5.3	18 39	5.3	03 12	3.8	15 22	4.1
9	Friday	04 44	3.3	16 56	3.6	07 18	5.0	19 36	5.0	04 15	3.6	16 22	3.9
10	Saturday	05 36	3.2	17 51	3.4	08 16	4.8	20 35	4.9	05 22	3.5	17 28	3.8
11	Sunday	06 33	3.1	18 54	3.2	09 16	4.7	21 37	4.7	06 31	3.5	18 36	3.7
12	Monday	07 38	3.0	20 14	3.1	10 19	4.6	22 41	4.7	07 35	3.5	19 40	3.7
13	Tuesday	08 53	3.1	21 30	3.1	11 21	4.7	———	—	08 31	3.6	20 36	3.7
14	Wednesday	09 56	3.2	22 27	3.2	———	—	12 16	4.9	09 17	3.7	21 23	3.7
15	Thursday	10 44	3.3	23 14	3.2	00 37	4.9	13 04	5.0	09 56	3.8	22 04	3.7
16	Friday	11 26	3.4	23 56	3.2	01 22	5.0	13 43	5.1	10 31	3.9	22 41	3.8
17	Saturday	12 04	3.5	———	—	02 02	5.1	14 20	5.2	11 05	4.0	23 17	3.8
18	Sunday	00 35	3.2	12 38	3.5	02 38	5.2	14 54	5.3	11 38	4.0	23 50	3.8
19	Monday	01 10	3.2	13 10	3.6	03 12	5.3	15 29	5.3	———	—	12 12	4.0
20	Tuesday	01 42	3.2	13 43	3.6	03 47	5.3	16 03	5.3	00 24	3.8	12 44	4.0
21	Wednesday	02 16	3.2	14 18	3.7	04 22	5.2	16 38	5.3	01 01	3.8	13 20	4.0
22	Thursday	02 53	3.2	14 56	3.7	05 00	5.2	17 13	5.2	01 41	3.7	14 01	3.9
23	Friday	03 32	3.2	15 34	3.6	05 40	5.1	17 52	5.1	02 25	3.7	14 45	3.8
24	Saturday	04 14	3.1	16 15	3.5	06 23	5.0	18 36	5.0	03 15	3.6	15 36	3.7
25	Sunday	05 00	3.0	17 00	3.4	07 14	4.9	19 28	4.9	04 09	3.5	16 32	3.7
26	Monday	05 54	3.0	17 53	3.3	08 10	4.8	20 27	4.9	05 11	3.5	17 34	3.7
27	Tuesday	06 56	2.9	18 55	3.2	09 13	4.8	21 36	4.9	06 18	3.5	18 43	3.8
28	Wednesday	08 11	2.9	20 18	3.2	10 22	4.9	22 49	5.0	07 25	3.7	19 51	3.9
29	Thursday	09 29	3.1	21 39	3.2	11 30	5.1	23 59	5.2	08 26	3.9	20 51	4.0
30	Friday	10 31	3.3	22 44	3.3	———	—	12 29	5.3	09 22	4.1	21 47	4.2
31	Sat·day	11 24	3.5	23 41	3.4	01 00	5.5	13 22	5.5	10 12	4.3	22 41	4.3

World Geographical Statistics

THE EARTH

The shape of the Earth is that of an oblate spheroid or solid of revolution whose meridian sections are ellipses, whilst the sections at right angles are circles.

DIMENSIONS

Equatorial diameter = 12,756.28 km (7,926.38 miles)
Polar diameter = 12,713.50 km (7,899.80 miles)
Equatorial circumference = 40,075.01 km (24,901.45 miles)
Polar circumference = 40,008.00 km (24,859.82 miles)

The equatorial circumference is divided into 360 degrees of longitude, which is measured in degrees, minutes and seconds east or west of the Greenwich meridian (0°) to 180° (the meridian 180° E. coinciding with 180° W.). This was internationally ratified in 1884.

Distance north and south of the Equator is measured in degrees, minutes and seconds of latitude. The Equator is 0°, the North Pole is 90° N. and the South Pole is 90° S. The Tropics lie at 23° 26′ N. (Tropic of Cancer) and 23° 26′ S. (Tropic of Capricorn). The Arctic Circle lies at 66° 34′ N. and the Antarctic Circle at 66° 34′ S. (NB The Tropics and the Arctic and Antarctic circles are of variable latitude due to the mean obliquity of the Ecliptic; the values given are for 1994.5.)

AREA, ETC.

The surface area of the Earth is 510,069,120 km² (196,938,800 miles²), of which the water area is 70.92 per cent and the land area is 29.08 per cent.

The velocity of a given point of the Earth's surface at the Equator exceeds 1,000 miles an hour (24,901.45 miles in 24 hours, viz 1,037.56 mph); the Earth's velocity in its orbit round the Sun averages 66,629 mph (584,081,400 miles in 365.256363 days). The Earth is distant from the Sun 92,955,900 miles, on average.

Source: Royal Greenwich Observatory

OCEAN AREAS

	Area km²	miles²
Pacific	166,240,000	64,186,300
Atlantic	86,550,000	33,420,000
Indian	73,427,000	28,350,500
Arctic	13,223,700	5,105,700

GREATEST OCEAN DEPTHS

Greatest depth location	Depth metres	feet
Mariana Trench (Pacific)	10,916	35,839
Puerto Rico Trench (Atlantic)	8,605	28,232
Java Trench (Indian)	7,125	23,376
Eurasian Basin (Arctic)	5,450	17,880

SEA AREAS

	Area km²	miles²
South China	2,974,600	1,148,500
Caribbean	2,515,900	971,400
Mediterranean	2,509,900	969,100
Bering	2,226,100	873,000
Gulf of Mexico	1,507,600	582,100
Okhotsk	1,392,000	537,500
Japan	1,015,000	391,100
Hudson Bay	730,100	281,900
East China	664,600	256,600
Andaman	564,880	218,100
Black Sea	507,900	196,100
Red Sea	453,000	174,900
North Sea	427,100	164,900
Baltic Sea	382,000	147,500
Yellow Sea	294,000	113,500
Persian Gulf	230,000	88,800

THE CONTINENTS

There are six geographic continents, though America is often divided politically into North and Central America, and South America.

AFRICA is surrounded by sea except for the narrow isthmus of Suez in the north-east, through which is cut the Suez Canal. The Equator passes through the middle of the continent. Its extreme longitudes are 17° 20′ W. at Cape Verde, Senegal, and 51° 24′ E. at Ras Hafun, Somalia. The extreme latitudes are 37° 20′ N. at Cape Blanc, Tunisia, and 34° 50′ S. at Cape Agulhas, South Africa, about 4,400 miles apart.

NORTH AMERICA, including Mexico, is surrounded by ocean except in the south, where the isthmian states of CENTRAL AMERICA link North America with South America. Its extreme longitudes are 168° 5′ W. at Cape Prince of Wales, Alaska, and 55° 40′ W. at Cape Charles, Newfoundland. The extreme continental latitudes are Point Barrow, Alaska (71°22′ N.) and 14°22′ N. at Ocós in the south of Mexico. The West Indies, about 65,000 square miles in area, extend from about 27° N. to 10° N. latitude.

SOUTH AMERICA lies mostly in the southern hemisphere; the Equator passes through the north of the continent. It is surrounded by ocean except where it is joined to Central America in the north by the narrow isthmus through which is cut the Panama Canal. Its extreme longitudes are 34° 47′ W. at Cape Branco in Brazil and 81° 20′ W. at Punta Pariña, Peru. The extreme latitudes are 12° 25′ N. at Punta Gallinas, Colombia, and 55° 59′ S. at Cape Horn, Chile.

ANTARCTICA lies almost entirely within the Antarctic Circle (66° 34′ S.) and is the largest of the world's glaciated areas. The continent has an area of about 5.5 million square miles, 99 per cent of which is permanently ice-covered. The ice amounts to some 7.2 million cubic miles and represents more than 90 per cent of the world's fresh water. The environment is too hostile for unsupported human habitation. *See also* Countries of the World.

ASIA is the largest continent and occupies almost a third of the world's land surface. The extreme longitudes are about 26° E. on the west coast of Asia Minor and 169° 40′ W. at Mys Dežneva (East Cape), Russia, a distance of about 6,000 miles. Its extreme northern latitude is 77° 45′ N. at Cape Čeljuskin, Russia, and it extends over 5,000 miles south to about 1° 15′ N. of the Equator. The islands of Japan, the Philippines and Indonesia ring the continent to the east and south-east.

AUSTRALIA is the smallest of the continents and lies in the southern hemisphere. It is entirely surrounded by ocean. Its extreme longitudes are 113° 9′ E. at Steep Point and 153° 38′ E. at Cape Byron. The extreme latitudes are 10° 40′ S. at Cape York and 39° S. at South East Point.

EUROPE, including European Russia, is the smallest continent in the northern hemisphere. Its extreme latitudes are 71° 11′ N. at North Cape in Norway, and 36° 23′ N. at Cape Matapan in southern Greece, a distance of about 2,400 miles. Its breadth from Cape da Roca in Portugal (9° 30′ W.) in the west to the Urals in the east is about 3,300 miles. The division between Europe and Asia is generally regarded as being the Ural Mountains and, in the south, the valley of the Manych, which stretches from the Caspian Sea to the mouth of the Don.

	Area km²	miles²
Asia	43,998,000	16,988,000
*America	41,918,000	16,185,000
Africa	29,800,000	11,506,000
Antarctica	c.13,600,000	c.5,500,000
†Europe	9,699,000	3,745,000
Australia	7,618,493	2,941,526

*North and Central America has an area of 24,255,000 km² (9,365,000 miles²)
†Includes 5,571,000 km² (2,151,000 miles²) of CIS territory west of the Ural Mountains

GLACIATED AREAS

It is estimated that 15,600,000 km² (6,020,000 miles²) or 10.51 per cent of the world's land surface is permanently covered with ice.

	Area km²	miles²
South Polar regions	13,597,000	5,250,000
North Polar regions (incl. Greenland or Kalaallit Nunaat)	1,965,000	758,500
Alaska-Canada	58,800	22,700
Asia	37,800	14,600
South America	11,900	4,600
Europe	10,700	4,128
New Zealand	984	380
Africa	238	92

PENINSULAS

	Area km²	miles²
Arabian	3,250,000	1,250,000
Southern Indian	2,072,000	800,000
Alaskan	1,500,000	580,000
Labradorian	1,300,000	500,000
Scandinavian	800,300	309,000
Iberian	584,000	225,500

LARGEST ISLANDS

Island (and Ocean)	Area km²	miles²
Greenland (Arctic)	2,175,500	840,000
New Guinea (Pacific)	792,500	306,000
Borneo (Pacific)	725,450	280,100
Madagascar (Indian)	587,040	226,658
Baffin Island (Arctic)	507,528	195,928
Sumatra (Indian)	427,350	165,000
Honshu (Pacific)	227,413	87,805
*Great Britain (Atlantic)	218,040	84,186
Victoria Island (Arctic)	217,290	83,895
Ellesmere Island (Arctic)	196,235	75,767
Sulawesi (Celebes) (Indian)	178,700	69,000
South Island, NZ (Pacific)	151,010	58,305
Java (Indian)	126,650	48,900
Cuba (Atlantic)	114,525	44,218
North Island, NZ (Pacific)	114,050	44,035
Newfoundland (Atlantic)	108,855	42,030
Luzon (Pacific)	105,880	40,880
Iceland (Atlantic)	103,000	39,770
Mindanao (Pacific)	95,247	36,775
Ireland (Atlantic)	82,462	31,839

*Mainland only

LARGEST DESERTS

	Area (approx.) km²	miles²
The Sahara (N. Africa)	8,400,000	3,250,000
Australian Desert	1,550,000	600,000
Arabian Desert	1,300,000	500,000
*The Gobi (Mongolia/China)	1,170,000	450,000
Kalahari Desert (Botswana/ Namibia/S. Africa)	520,000	200,000
Sonoran Desert (USA/Mexico)	310,000	120,000
Namib Desert (Namibia)	310,000	120,000
†Kara Kum (Turkmenistan)	270,000	105,000
Thar Desert (India/Pakistan)	260,000	100,000
Somali Desert (Somalia)	260,000	100,000
Atacama Desert (Chile)	180,000	70,000
†Kyzyl Kum (Kazakhstan/ Uzbekistan)	180,000	70,000
Dasht-e Lut (Iran)	52,000	20,000
Mojave Desert (USA)	35,000	13,500
Desierto de Sechura (Peru)	26,000	10,000

*Including the Takla Makan – 320,000 km² (125,000 miles²)
†Together known as the Turkestan Desert

DEEPEST DEPRESSIONS

	Maximum depth below sea level	
	metres	feet
Dead Sea (Jordan/Israel)	395	1,296
Turfan Depression (Sinkiang, China)	153	505
Qattara Depression (Egypt)	132	436
Mangyshlak peninsula (Kazakhstan)	131	433
Danakil Depression (Ethiopia)	116	383
Death Valley (California, USA)	86	282
Salton Sink (California, USA)	71	235
W. of Ustyurt plateau (Kazakhstan)	70	230
Prikaspiyskaya Nizmennost' (Russia/ Kazakhstan)	67	220
Lake Sarykamysh (Uzbekistan/ Turkmenistan)	45	148
El Faiyûm (Egypt)	44	147
Valdies peninsula, Lago Enriquillo (Dominican Republic)	40	131

The world's largest exposed depression is the Prikaspiyskaya Nizmennost' covering the hinterland of the northern third of the Caspian Sea, which is itself 28 m (92 ft) below sea level
Western Antarctica and Central Greenland largely comprise crypto-depressions under ice burdens. The Antarctic Wilkes subglacial basin has a bedrock 2,341 m (7,680 ft) below sea-level. In Greenland (lat. 73° N., long. 39° W.) the bedrock is 365 m (1,197 ft) below sea-level

LONGEST MOUNTAIN RANGES

Range (location)	Length	
	km	miles
Cordillera de Los Andes (W. South America)	7,200	4,500
Rocky Mountains (W. North America)	4,800	3,000
Himalaya-Karakoram-Hindu Kush (S. Central Asia)	3,800	2,400
Great Dividing Range (E. Australia)	3,600	2,250
Trans-Antarctic Mts (Antarctica)	3,500	2,200
Atlantic Coast Range (E. Brazil)	3,000	1,900
West Sumatran-Javan Range (Indonesia)	2,900	1,800
Aleutian Range (Alaska and NW Pacific)	2,650	1,650
Tien Shan (S. Central Asia)	2,250	1,400
Central New Guinea Range (Irian Jaya/ Papua New Guinea)	2,000	1,250

HIGHEST MOUNTAINS

The world's 8,000-metre mountains (with six subsidiary peaks) are all in the 3,800 km (2,400 mile) long Himalaya-Karakoram-Hindu Kush range of south central Asia.

Mountain	Height	
	metres	feet
Mt Everest*	8,848	29,028
K2	8,607	28,238

Mountain	Height	
	metres	feet
Kangchenjunga	8,597	28,208
Lhotse	8,511	27,923
Makalu I	8,481	27,824
Lhotse Shar	8,383	27,504
Dhaulagiri I	8,167	26,795
Manaslu I (Kutang I)	8,156	26,760
Cho Oyu	8,153	26,750
Nanga Parbat (Diamir)	8,125	26,660
Annapurna I	8,091	26,546
Gasherbrum I (Hidden Peak)	8,068	26,470
Broad Peak I	8,046	26,400
Shisha Pangma (Gosainthan)	8,046	26,398
Gasherbrum II	8,034	26,360
Annapurna East	8,010	26,280
Makalu South-East	8,010	26,280
Broad Peak Central	8,000	26,246

*Named after Sir George Everest (1790–1866), Surveyor-General of India 1830–43, in 1863. He pronounced his name Eve-rest

The culminating summits in the other major mountain ranges are:

Mountain (range or country)	Height	
	metres	feet
Pik Pobeda (Tien Shan)	7,439	24,406
Cerro Aconcagua (Cordillera de Los Andes)	6,960	22,834
Mt McKinley, S. Peak (Alaska Range)	6,194	20,320
Kilimanjaro (Tanzania)	5,894	19,340
Hkakabo Razi (Myanmar)	5,881	19,296
Citlaltépetl (Orizaba) (Sierra Madre Oriental, Mexico)	5,699	18,700
El'brus, W. Peak (Caucasus)	5,663	18,481
Vinson Massif (E. Antarctica)	4,897	16,067
Puncak Jaya (Central New Guinea Range)	4,884	16,023
Mt Blanc (Alps)	4,807	15,771
Klyuchevskaya Sopka (Kamchatka peninsula, Russia)	4,750	15,584
Ras Dashan (Ethiopian Highlands)	4,620	15,158
Zard Kûh (Zagros Mts, Iran)	4,547	14,921
Mt Kirkpatrick (Trans Antarctic)	4,529	14,860
Mt Belukha (Altai Mts, Russia/ Kazakhstan)	4,505	14,783
Mt Elbert (Rocky Mountains)	4,400	14,433
Mt Rainier (Cascade Range, N. America)	4,392	14,410
Nevado de Colima (Sierra Madre Occidental, Mexico)	4,268	14,003
Jebel Toubkal (Atlas Mts, N. Africa)	4,165	13,665
Kinabalu (Crocker Range, Borneo)	4,101	13,455
Kerinci (West Sumatran-Javan Range, Indonesia)	3,800	12,467
Jabal an Nabī Shu'ayb (N. Tihāmat, Yemen)	3,760	12,336
Teotepec (Sierra Madre del Sur, Mexico)	3,703	12,149
Thaban Ntlenyana (Drakensberg, South Africa)	3,482	11,425
Pico de Bandeira (Atlantic Coast Range)	2,890	9,482
Shishaldin (Aleutian Range)	2,861	9,387
Kosciusko (Great Dividing Range)	2,228	7,310

HIGHEST VOLCANOES

Volcano (last major eruption) and location	Height metres	feet
Guallatiri (1993), Andes, Chile	6,060	19,882
Lascar (1991), Andes, Chile	5,990	19,652
Cotopaxi (1975), Andes, Ecuador	5,897	19,347
Tupungatito (1986), Andes, Chile	5,640	18,504
Nevado del Ruiz, Colombia (1985, 1992)	5,400	17,716
Sangay (1988), Andes, Ecuador	5,230	17,159
Guagua Pichincha (1988), Andes, Ecuador	4,784	15,696
Purace (1977), Colombia	4,756	15,601
Klyuchevskaya Sopka (1991), Kamchatka peninsula, Russia	4,750	15,584
Nevado de Colima (1991), Mexico	4,268	14,003
Galeras (1991), Colombia	4,266	13,996
Mauna Loa (1987), Hawaii Is.	4,170	13,680
Cameroon (1982), Cameroon	4,070	13,354
Acatenango (1972), Guatemala	3,960	12,992
Fuego (1991), Guatemala	3,835	12,582
Kerinci (1987), Sumatra, Indonesia	3,800	12,467
Erebus (1991), Ross Island, Antarctica	3,794	12,450
Tacana (1988), Guatemala	3,780	12,400
Santiaguito (1902, 1991), Guatemala	3,768	12,362
Rindjani (1966), Lombok, Indonesia	3,726	12,224
Semeru (1991), Java, Indonesia	3,675	12,060
Nyirgongo (1977), Zaïre	3,475	11,400
Koryakskaya (1957), Kamchatka, Russia	3,456	11,339
Irazú (1992), Costa Rica	3,432	11,260
Slamet (1988), Java, Indonesia	3,428	11,247
Spurr (1953), Alaska, USA	3,374	11,069
Mt Etna (1169, 1669, 1992), Sicily, Italy	3,369	11,053
Raung (1991), Java, Indonesia	3,322	10,932
Shiveluch (1964), Kamchatka, Russia	3,283	10,771
Agung (1964), Bali, Indonesia	3,142	10,308
Llaima (1990), Chile	3,128	10,239
Redoubt (1991), Alaska, USA	3,108	10,197
Tjareme (1938), Java, Indonesia	3,078	10,098
Iliamna (1978), Alaska, USA	3,076	10,092
On-Taka (1991), Japan	3,063	10,049
Nyamuragira (1991), Zaire	3,056	10,028

OTHER NOTABLE VOLCANOES

	Height metres	feet
Tambora (1815), Sumbawa, Indonesia	2,850	9,353
Mt St Helens (1980, 1986), Washington State, USA	2,530	8,300
Pinatubo (1991), Philippines	1,758	5,770
Hekla (1981), Iceland	1,491	4,892
Mt Pelée (1902), Martinique	1,397	4,583
Mt Unzen (1991), Kyushu, Japan	1,360	4,462
Vesuvius (AD 79, 1944), Italy	1,280	4,198
Kilauea (1988), Hawaii, USA	1,242	4,077
Stromboli (1992), Lipari Is., Italy	926	3,038
Krakatau (1883), Sunda Strait, Indonesia	804	2,640
Santoriní (Thíra) (1628 BC), Aegean Sea, Greece	566	1,857
Vulcano (Monte Aria), Lipari Is., Italy	499	1,637
Tristan da Cunha (1961), South Atlantic	243	800
Surtsey (1963–7), off Iceland	173	568

LARGEST LAKES

The areas of some of these lakes are subject to seasonal variation.

	Area km²	miles²	Length km	miles
Caspian Sea – Iran/Azerbaijan/Russia/Turkmenistan/Kazakhstan	371,000	143,000	1,171	728
Superior – Canada/USA	82,100	31,700	563	350
Victoria – Uganda/Tanzania/Kenya	69,500	26,828	362	225
Huron – Canada/USA	59,570	23,000	331	206
Michigan – USA	57,750	22,300	494	307
Aral Sea – Kazakhstan/Uzbekistan	40,400	15,600	331	235
Tanganyika – Zaïre/Tanzania/Zambia/Burundi	32,900	12,700	675	420
*Baykal (Baikal) – Russia	31,500	12,162	635	395
Great Bear – Canada	31,328	12,096	309	192
Malawi – Tanzania/Malawi/Mozambique	28,880	11,150	580	360
Great Slave – Canada	28,570	11,031	480	298
Erie – Canada/USA	25,670	9,910	388	241
Winnipeg – Canada	24,390	9,417	428	266
Ontario – Canada/USA	19,550	7,550	310	193
Balkhash – Kazakhstan	18,427	7,115	605	376
Ladozhskoye (Ladoga) – Russia	17,700	6,835	200	124

UNITED KINGDOM (BY COUNTRY)

	Area km²	miles²	Length km	miles
Lough Neagh – Northern Ireland	381.73	147.39	28.90	18.00
Loch Lomond – Scotland	71.12	27.46	36.44	22.64
Windermere – England	14.74	5.69	16.90	10.50
Lake Vyrnwy – Wales (artificial)	4.53	1.75	7.56	4.70
Llyn Tegid (Bala) – Wales (natural)	4.38	1.69	5.80	3.65

*World's deepest lake (1,940 m/6,365 ft)

LONGEST RIVERS

River (source and outflow)	Length km	miles
Nile (Bahr-el-Nil) (R. Luvironza, Burundi – E. Mediterranean Sea)	6,670	4,145
Amazon (Amazonas) (Lago Villafro, Peru – S. Atlantic Ocean)	6,648	4,007
Mississippi-Missouri (R. Red Rock, Montana – Gulf of Mexico)	5,970	3,710

River (source and outflow)	Length km	miles
Yenisey-Angara (W. Mongolia – Kara Sea)	5,540	3,442
Yangtze-Kiang (*Chang Jiang*) (Kunlun Mts, W. China – Yellow Sea)	5,530	3,436
Ob'-Irtysh (W. Mongolia – Kara Sea)	5,410	3,362
Huang He (*Yellow River*) (Bayan Har Shan range, central China – Yellow Sea)	4,830	3,000
Zaire (*Congo*) (R. Lualaba, Zaire-Zambia – S. Atlantic Ocean)	4,700	2,920
Amur-Argun (R. Argun, Khingan Mts, N. China – Sea of Okhotsk)	4,670	2,903
Lena-Kirenga (R. Kirenga, W. of Lake Baykal – Arctic Ocean)	4,345	2,700
Mackenzie-Peace (Tatlatui Lake, British Columbia – Beaufort Sea)	4,240	2,635
Mekong (Lants'ang, Tibet – South China Sea)	4,184	2,600
Niger (Loma Mts, Guinea – Gulf of Guinea, E. Atlantic Ocean)	4,184	2,600
Rió de la Plata-Paraná (R. Paranáiba, central Brazil – S. Atlantic Ocean)	4,000	2,485
Murray-Darling (SE Queensland – Lake Alexandrina, S. Australia)	3,750	2,330
Volga (Valdai plateau – Caspian Sea)	3,690	2,293
Zambezi (NW Zambia – S. Indian Ocean)	3,540	2,200

OTHER NOTABLE RIVERS

	Length km	miles
St Lawrence (Minnesota, USA – Gulf of St Lawrence)	3,130	1,945
Ganges-Brahmaputra (R. Matsang, SW Tibet – Bay of Bengal)	2,900	1,800
Indus (R. Sengge, SW Tibet – N. Arabian Sea)	2,880	1,790
Danube (*Donau*) (Black Forest, SW Germany – Black Sea)	2,850	1,770
Tigris-Euphrates (R. Murat, E. Turkey – Persian Gulf)	2,740	1,700
Irrawaddy (R. Mali Hka, N. Burma – Andaman Sea)	2,090	1,300
Don (SE of Novomoskovsk – Sea of Azov)	1,969	1,224

BRITISH ISLES

	Length km	miles
Shannon (Co. Cavan, Rep. of Ireland – Atlantic Ocean)	386	240
Severn (Powys, Wales – Bristol Channel)	354	220
Thames (Gloucestershire, England – North Sea)	346	215
Tay (Perthshire, Scotland – North Sea)	188	117
Clyde (Lanarkshire, Scotland – Firth of Clyde)	158	98½
Tweed (Peeblesshire, Scotland – North Sea)	155	96½
Bann (Upper and Lower) (Co. Down, N. Ireland – Atlantic Ocean)	122	76

GREATEST WATERFALLS – BY HEIGHT

Waterfall (river and location)	Total drop metres	feet	Greatest single leap metres	feet
Angel (Carrao, Venezuela)	979	3,212	807	2,648
Tugela (Tugela, S. Africa)	947	3,110	410	1,350
Utigård (Jostedal Glacier, Norway)	800	2,625	600	1,970
Mongefossen (Monge, Norway)	774	2,540	—	—
Yosemite (Yosemite Creek, USA)	739	2,425	435	1,430
Østre Mardøla Foss (Mardals, Norway)	656	2,154	296	974
Tyssestrengane (Tysso, Norway)	646	2,120	289	948
Cuquenán (Arabopó, Venezuela)	610	2,000	—	—
Sutherland (Arthur, NZ)	580	1,904	248	815
*Kjellfossen (Naeröfjord, Norway)	561	1,841	149	490

BRITISH ISLES (BY COUNTRY)

Waterfall (river and location)	Total drop metres	feet	Greatest single leap metres	feet
Eas a' Chuàl Aluinn (Glas Bheinn, Sutherland, Scotland)	200	658		
Powerscourt Falls (Dargle, Co. Wicklow, Rep. of Ireland)	106	350		
Pistyll-y-Llyn (Powys/ Dyfed border, Wales)	c.73	230–240	(cascades)	
Pistyll Rhyadr (Clwyd/ Powys border, Wales)	71.5	235	(single leap)	
Caldron Snout (R. Tees, Cumbria/Durham, England)	60	200	(cascades)	

*Volume often so low the fall atomizes into a 'bridal veil'

GREATEST WATERFALLS – BY VOLUME

Waterfall (river and location)	Mean annual flow m³/sec	galls/sec
Boyoma (R. Lualaba, Zaïre)	c.17,000	c.3,750,000
*Guairá (Alto Paraná, Brazil/ Paraguay)	13,300	2,930,000
Khône (Mekong, Laos)	11,500	2,530,000
Niagara (Horseshoe) (R. Niagara/Lake Erie–Lake Ontario)	3,000	670,000
Paulo Afonso (R. São Francisco, Brazil)	2,750	605,000
Urubupunga (Alto Paraná, Brazil)	2,800	625,000
Cataratas del Iguazú (R. Iguaçu, Brazil/ Argentina)	1,725	380,000
Patos-Maribando (Rio Grande, Brazil)	1,500	330,000
Victoria (*Mosi-oa-tunya*) (R. Zambezi, Zambia/ Zimbabwe)	1,000	220,000
Churchill (R. Churchill, Canada)	975	215,000
Kaieteur (R. Potaro, Guyana)	660	145,000

*Peak flow 50,000 m³/sec, 11,000,000 galls/sec

TALLEST INHABITED BUILDINGS

Building and city	Height metres	feet
Sears Tower, Chicago[1]	443	1,454
World Trade Center, New York[2]	417	1,368
Empire State Building, New York[3]	381	1,250
Bank of China, Hong Kong	368	1,209
Amoco Building, Chicago	346	1,136
John Hancock Center, Chicago	343	1,127
C. & S. Plaza, Atlanta	320	1,050
Chrysler Building, New York	319	1,046
Central Plaza, Hong Kong	313	1,028
First Interstate World Center, Los Angeles	310	1,017
Texas Commerce Tower, Houston	305	1,002
State University, Moscow[4]	302	994

[1] With TV antennae 475.18 m/1,559 ft
[2] With TV antennae, 521.2 m/1,710 ft; second tower, 415 m/1,362 ft
[3] With TV tower (added 1950–1), 430.9 m/1,414 ft
[4] Including spire

TALLEST STRUCTURES

Structure and location	Height metres	feet
*Warszawa Radio Mast, Konstantynow, Poland	646	2,120
KTHI-TV Mast, Fargo, North Dakota	629	2,063
CN Tower, Metro Centre, Toronto, Canada	555	1,822

*Collapsed during renovation, August 1991

LONGEST BRIDGES – BY SPAN

Bridge and location	Length metres	feet
SUSPENSION SPANS		
Humber Estuary, Humberside, England	1,410	4,626
Verrazano Narrows, Brooklyn–Staten I, USA	1,298	4,260
Golden Gate, San Francisco Bay, USA	1,280	4,200
Mackinac Straits, Michigan, USA	1,158	3,800
Bosporus, Istanbul, Turkey	1,074	3,524
George Washington, Hudson River, New York City, USA	1,067	3,500
Ponte 25 Abril (Tagus), Lisbon, Portugal	1,013	3,323
Firth of Forth (road), nr Edinburgh, Scotland	1,006	3,300
Severn River, Severn Estuary, England	988	3,240

The Akashi-Kaikyo road bridge (1988–98) will have a main span of 1,990 m/6,528 ft

Bridge and location	Length metres	feet
CANTILEVER SPANS		
Pont de Québec (rail-road), St Lawrence, Canada	548.6	1,800

Bridge and location	Length metres	feet
Ravenswood, W. Virginia, USA	525.1	1,723
Firth of Forth (rail), nr. Edinburgh, Scotland	521.2	1,710
Minato, Osaka, Japan	510.0	1,673
Commodore Barry, Chester, Pennsylvania, USA	494.3	1,622
Greater New Orleans, Louisiana, USA	480.0	1,575
Howrah (rail-road), Calcutta, India	457.2	1,500
STEEL ARCH SPANS		
New River Gorge, Fayetteville, W. Virginia, USA	518.2	1,700
Bayonne (Kill van Kull), Bayonne, NJ– Staten I, USA	503.5	1,652
Sydney Harbour, Sydney, Australia	502.9	1,650

The 'floating' bridging at Evergreen, Seattle, Washington State, USA, is 3,839 m/12,596 ft long
The longest stretch of bridgings of any kind are those between Mandeville and Jefferson, Louisiana, USA; the Lake Pontchartrain Causeway II 38.422 km/23.87 miles and Causeway I 38.352 km/23.83 miles

LONGEST VEHICULAR TUNNELS

Tunnel and location	Length km	miles
*Seikan (rail), Tsugaru Channel, Japan	53.90	33.49
Moscow metro, Belyaevo–Medved Kovo, Moscow, Russia	30.70	19.07
Northern line tube, East Finchley– Morden, London	27.84	17.30
Oshimizu, Honshū, Japan	22.17	13.78
Simplon II (rail), Brigue, Switzerland– Iselle, Italy	19.82	12.31
Simplon I (rail), Brigue, Switzerland– Iselle, Italy	19.80	12.30
Shin-Kanmon (rail), Kanmon Strait, Japan	18.68	11.61
Great Appennine (rail), Vernio, Italy	18.49	11.49
St Gotthard (road), Göschenen– Airolo, Switzerland	16.32	10.14
Rokko (rail), Ōsaka–Kōbe, Japan	16.09	10.00

*Sub-aqueous

The twin rail Eurotunnel under the English Channel between Cheriton, Kent and Sargette, near Calais, is due to open for freight in December 1993 and for passengers in mid 1994. The tunnels are 49.94 km/31.03 miles in length. Holing through was achieved on 30 October 1990
The longest non-vehicular tunnelling in the world is the Delaware Aqueduct in New York State, USA, constructed in 1937–44 to a length of 168.9 km/105 miles

BRITISH RAIL TUNNELS

	miles	yards
Severn, Bristol – Newport	4	484
Totley, Manchester – Sheffield	3	950
Standedge, Manchester – Huddersfield	3	66
Sodbury, Swindon – Bristol	2	924
Disley, Stockport – Sheffield	2	346
Ffestiniog, Llandudno – Blaenau Ffestiniog	2	338
Bramhope, Leeds – Harrogate	2	241
Cowburn, Manchester – Sheffield	2	182

LONGEST SHIP CANALS

Canal (opening date)	Length km	miles	Min. depth metres	feet
White Sea-Baltic (formerly Stalin) (1933) Canalized river; canal 51.5 km/32 miles	227	141.00	5.0	16.5
*Suez (1869) Links Red and Mediterranean Seas	162	100.60	12.9	42.3
V. I. Lenin Volga-Don (1952) Links Black and Caspian Seas	100	62.20	n/a	n/a
Kiel (or North Sea) (1895) Links North and Baltic Seas	98	60.90	13.7	45.0
*Houston (1940) Links inland city with sea	91	56.70	10.4	34.0
Alphonse XIII (1926) Gives Seville access to sea	85	53.00	7.6	25.0
Panama (1914) Links Pacific Ocean and Caribbean Sea; lake chain, 78.9 km/49 miles dug	82	50.71	12.5	41.0
Manchester Ship (1894) Links city with Irish Channel	64	39.70	8.5	28.0
Welland (1931) Circumvents Niagara Falls and Rapids	45	28.00	8.8	29.0
Brussels (Rupel Sea) (1922) Renders Brussels an inland port	32	19.80	6.4	21.0

*Has no locks

The first section of China's Grand Canal, running 1,780 km/1,107 miles from Beijing to Hangchou, was opened AD 610 but in undredged parts is today only 1.8 m/6 ft deep

The longest boat canal in the world is the Volga-Baltic canal from Astrakhan to St Petersburg with 2,300 route km/1,850 miles

The Seven Wonders of the World

I. THE PYRAMIDS OF EGYPT

The pyramids are found from Gizeh, near Cairo, to a southern limit 60 miles distant. The oldest is that of Zoser, at Saqqara, built c.2650 BC. The Great Pyramid of Cheops (built c.2580 BC) covers more than 13.12 acres and was originally 481 ft in height and 756 × 756 ft at the base.

II. THE HANGING GARDENS OF BABYLON

These adjoined Nebuchadnezzar's palace, 60 miles south of Baghdad. The terraced gardens, ranging from 75 ft to 300 ft above ground level, were watered from storage tanks on the highest terrace.

III. THE TOMB OF MAUSOLUS

Built at Halicarnassus, in Asia Minor, by the widowed Queen Artemisia about 350 BC. The memorial originated the term mausoleum.

IV. THE TEMPLE OF ARTEMIS AT EPHESUS

Ionic temple erected about 350 BC in honour of the goddess and burned by the Goths in AD 262.

V. THE COLOSSUS OF RHODES

A bronze statue of Apollo, set up about 280 BC. According to legend it stood at the harbour entrance of the seaport of Rhodes.

VI. THE STATUE OF ZEUS

Located at Olympia in the plain of Elis, and constructed of marble inlaid with ivory and gold by the sculptor Phidias, about 430 BC.

VII. THE PHAROS OF ALEXANDRIA

A marble watch tower and lighthouse on the island of Pharos in the harbour of Alexandria, built c.270 BC.

Distances from London by Air

The list of the distances in statute miles from London, Heathrow, to various cities (airport) abroad has been supplied by the publishers of *IATA/ IAL Air Distances Manual*, Southall, Middx.

To	Miles
Abidjan	3,197
Abu Dhabi	3,425
Addis Ababa	3,675
Adelaide	1,011
Aden	3,670
Algiers	1,035
Amman	2,287
Amsterdam	230
Ankara	1,770
Athens	1,500
Atlanta	4,198
Auckland	11,404
Baghdad	2,551
Bahrain	3,163
Baku	2,485
Bangkok	5,928
Barbados	4,193
Barcelona	712
Basle	447
Beijing/Peking	5,063
Beirut	2,161
Belfast	325
Belgrade	1,056
Berlin (Tegel)	588
Bermuda	3,428
Berne	476
Bogota	5,262
Bombay	4,478
Boston	3,255
Brasilia	5,452
Bratislava	817
Brisbane	10,273
Brussels	217
Bucharest	1,307
Budapest	923
Buenos Aires	6,915
Cairo	2,194
Calcutta	4,958
Calgary	4,357
Canberra	10,563
Cape Town	6,011
Caracas	4,639
Casablanca	1,300
Chicago (O'Hare)	3,941
Cologne	331
Colombo	5,411
Copenhagen	608
Dakar	2,706
Dallas (Fort Worth)	4,736
Dallas (Lovefield)	4,732
Damascus	2,223
Dar-es-Salaam	4,662
Darwin	8,613
Delhi	4,180

To	Miles
Denver	4,668
Detroit	3,754
Dhahran	3,143
Dhaka	4,976
Doha	3,253
Dubai	3,414
Dublin	279
Durban	5,937
Düsseldorf	310
Entebbe	4,033
Frankfurt	406
Freetown	3,046
Geneva	468
Gibraltar	1,084
Gothenburg (Landvetter)	664
Hamburg	463
Harare	5,156
Havana	4,647
Helsinki (Vantaa)	1,147
Hobart	10,826
Ho Chi Minh City	6,345
Hong Kong	5,990
Honolulu	7,220
Houston (Intercontinental)	4,821
Houston (William P. Hobby)	4,837
Islamabad	3,767
Istanbul	1,560
Jakarta	7,295
Jeddah	2,947
Johannesburg	5,634
Kabul	3,558
Karachi	3,935
Kathmandu	4,570
Khartoum	3,071
Kiev (Borispol)	1,357
Kiev (Julyany)	1,337
Kingston, Jamaica	4,668
Kuala Lumpur	6,557
Kuwait	2,903
Lagos	3,107
Larnaca	2,036
Lima	6,303
Lisbon	972
Lomé	3,129
Los Angeles	5,439
Madras	5,113
Madrid	773
Malta	1,305
Manila	6,685
Marseilles	614
Mauritius	6,075
Melbourne (Essendon)	10,504
Melbourne (Tullamarine)	10,499
Mexico City	5,529
Miami	4,414
Milan	609
Minsk	1,176
Montego Bay	4,687
Montevideo	6,841
Montreal (Mirabel)	3,241

To	Miles
Moscow (Sheremetievo)	1,557
Munich (Franz Josef Strauss)	584
Muscat	3,621
Nairobi	4,248
Naples	1,011
Nassau	4,333
New York (J. F. Kennedy)	3,440
Nice	645
Oporto	806
Oslo (Fornebu)	722
Ottawa	3,321
Palma, Majorca	836
Paris (Charles de Gaulle)	215
Paris (Le Bourget)	215
Paris (Orly)	227
Perth, Australia	9,008
Port of Spain	4,404
Prague	649
Pretoria	5,602
Reykjavik	1,167
Rhodes	1,743
Rio de Janeiro	5,745
Riyadh	3,067
Rome (Fiumicino)	895
St John's, Newfoundland	2,308
St Petersburg	1,314
Salzburg	651
San Francisco	5,351
Sao Paulo	5,892
Sarajevo	1,017
Seoul	5,507
Shanghai	5,725
Shannon	369
Singapore	6,756
Sofia	1,266
Stockholm (Arlanda)	908
Suva	10,119
Sydney	10,568
Tangier	1,120
Tehran	2,741
Tel Aviv	2,227
Tokyo (Narita)	5,956
Toronto	3,544
Tripoli	1,468
Tunis	1,137
Turin (Caselle)	570
Ulan Bator	4,340
Valencia	826
Vancouver	4,707
Venice (Tessera)	715
Vienna (Schwechat)	790
Vladivostok	5,298
Warsaw	912
Washington	3,665
Wellington	11,692
Yangon/Rangoon	5,582
Yokohama (Aomori)	5,637
Yokohama (Kanagawa)	5,938
Zagreb	848
Zürich	490

The United Kingdom

The United Kingdom comprises Great Britain (England, Wales and Scotland) and Northern Ireland. The Isle of Man and the Channel Islands are Crown dependencies with their own legislative systems, and not a part of the United Kingdom.

AREA AS AT 31 MARCH 1981

	Land miles²	km²	*Inland water miles²	km²	Total miles²	km²
United Kingdom	93,027	240,939	1,242	3,218	94,269	244,157
England	50,085	129,720	293	758	50,377	130,478
Wales	7,968	20,636	50	130	8,018	20,766
Scotland	29,767	77,097	653	1,692	30,420	78,789
†Northern Ireland	5,215	13,506	246	638	5,461	14,144
Isle of Man	—	—	—	—	221	572
Channel Islands	—	—	—	—	75	194

*Excluding tidal water
†Excluding certain tidal waters that are parts of statutory areas in Northern Ireland

POPULATION

The first official census of population in England, Wales and Scotland was taken in 1801 and a census has been taken every ten years since, except in 1941 when there was no census because of war. The last official census in the United Kingdom was taken on 21 April 1991 and the next is due in April 2001.

The first official census of population in Ireland was taken in 1841. However, all figures given below refer only to the area which is now Northern Ireland. Figures for Northern Ireland in 1921 and 1931 are estimates based on the censuses taken in 1926 and 1937 respectively.

Estimates of the population of England before 1801, calculated from the number of baptisms, burials and marriages, are:

1570	4,160,221	1670	5,773,646
1600	4,811,718	1700	6,045,008
1630	5,600,517	1750	6,517,035

Thousands	United Kingdom Total	Male	Female	England and Wales Total	Male	Female	Scotland Total	Male	Female	Northern Ireland Total	Male	Female
CENSUS RESULTS 1801–1991												
1801	—	—	—	8,893	4,255	4,638	1,608	739	869	—	—	—
1811	13,368	6,368	7,000	10,165	4,874	5,291	1,806	826	980	—	—	—
1821	15,472	7,498	7,974	12,000	5,850	6,150	2,092	983	1,109	—	—	—
1831	17,835	8,647	9,188	13,897	6,771	7,126	2,364	1,114	1,250	—	—	—
1841	20,183	9,819	10,364	15,914	7,778	8,137	2,620	1,242	1,378	1,649	800	849
1851	22,259	10,855	11,404	17,928	8,781	9,146	2,889	1,376	1,513	1,443	698	745
1861	24,525	11,894	12,631	20,066	9,776	10,290	3,062	1,450	1,612	1,396	668	728
1871	27,431	13,309	14,122	22,712	11,059	11,653	3,360	1,603	1,757	1,359	647	712
1881	31,015	15,060	15,955	25,974	12,640	13,335	3,736	1,799	1,936	1,305	621	684
1891	34,264	16,593	17,671	29,003	14,060	14,942	4,026	1,943	2,083	1,236	590	646
1901	38,237	18,492	19,745	32,528	15,729	16,799	4,472	2,174	2,298	1,237	590	647
1911	42,082	20,357	21,725	36,070	17,446	18,625	4,761	2,309	2,452	1,251	603	648
1921	44,027	21,033	22,994	37,887	18,075	19,811	4,882	2,348	2,535	1,258	610	648
1931	46,038	22,060	23,978	39,952	19,133	20,819	4,843	2,326	2,517	1,243	601	642
1951	50,225	24,118	26,107	43,758	21,016	22,742	5,096	2,434	2,662	1,371	668	703
1961	52,709	25,481	27,228	46,105	22,304	23,801	5,179	2,483	2,697	1,425	694	731
1971	55,515	26,952	28,562	48,750	23,683	25,067	5,229	2,515	2,714	1,536	755	781
1981	55,848	27,104	28,742	49,155	23,873	25,281	5,131	2,466	2,664	*1,533	750	783
1991	56,467	27,344	29,123	49,890	24,182	25,707	4,999	2,392	2,606	1,578	769	809
†RESIDENT POPULATION: PROJECTIONS (MID-YEAR)												
1991	57,561	28,099	29,463	50,903	24,865	26,038	5,068	2,452	2,615	1,590	781	809
2001	59,174	29,069	30,105	52,526	25,819	26,708	5,026	2,449	2,577	1,622	802	820
2011	60,033	29,630	30,403	53,510	26,423	27,087	4,900	2,400	2,500	1,623	806	816
2021	60,743	30,049	30,694	54,411	26,927	27,484	4,727	2,322	2,405	1,605	800	805
2031	61,068	30,213	30,855	54,977	27,208	27,769	4,524	2,224	2,300	1,567	782	785

* figures include 44,500 non-enumerated persons   † projections are 1989 based
Source: HMSO – *Annual Abstract 1993*; OPCS – Census reports

ISLANDS: Census Results 1901-91

	Isle of Man			Jersey			*Guernsey		
	Total	Male	Female	Total	Male	Female	Total	Male	Female
1901	54,752	25,496	29,256	52,576	23,940	28,636	40,446	19,652	20,794
1911	52,016	23,937	28,079	51,898	24,014	27,884	41,858	20,661	21,197
1921	60,284	27,329	32,955	49,701	22,438	27,263	38,315	18,246	20,069
1931	49,308	22,443	26,865	50,462	23,424	27,038	40,643	19,659	20,984
1951	55,123	25,749	29,464	57,296	27,282	30,014	43,652	21,221	22,431
1961	48,151	22,060	26,091	57,200	27,200	30,000	45,068	21,671	23,397
1971	56,289	26,461	29,828	72,532	35,423	37,109	51,458	24,792	26,666
1981	64,679	30,901	33,778	77,000	37,000	40,000	53,313	25,701	27,612
1991	69,788	33,693	36,095	84,082	40,862	43,220	58,867	28,297	30,570

* Population of Guernsey, Herm, Jethou and Lithou. Figures for 1901-71 record all persons present on census night; census figures for 1981 and 1991 record all persons resident in the islands on census night.

Source: 1991 Census

RESIDENT POPULATION

MID-YEAR ESTIMATE

	1981	1991p
United Kingdom	56,352,000	57,649,000
England	46,820,000	48,069,000
Wales	2,814,000	2,886,000
Scotland	5,180,000	5,100,000
Northern Ireland	1,538,000	1,594,000

p provisional
Source: HMSO - *Annual Abstract of Statistics 1993*

BY AGE AND SEX 1991p

Males	Under 16	Over 65
United Kingdom	6,023,000	3,650,000
England	4,983,000	3,072,000
Wales	304,000	199,000
Scotland	525,000	299,000
Northern Ireland	211,000	80,000

Females	Under 16	Over 60
United Kingdom	5,708,000	6,934,000
England	4,720,000	5,789,000
Wales	287,000	375,000
Scotland	499,000	611,000
Northern Ireland	201,000	159,000

p provisional
Source: HMSO - *Population Trends 72*

BY ETHNIC GROUP (1991 Census (Great Britain))

Ethnic group	Estimated population	Percentage
Caribbean	500,000	16.6
African	212,000	7
Other black	178,000	5.9
Indian	840,000	27.9
Pakistani	477,000	15.8
Bangladeshi	163,000	5.4
Chinese	157,000	5.2
Other Asian	198,000	6.6
Other	290,000	9.6
Total ethnic minority groups	3,015,000	100
White	51,874,000	—
All ethnic groups	54,889,000	—

Source: HMSO - *Population Trends 72*

AVERAGE DENSITY

	Persons per hectare	
	1981	1991
England	3.55	3.61
Wales	1.34	1.36
Scotland	0.66	0.65
Northern Ireland	1.12	1.11

Sources: OPCS - Census reports

IMMIGRATION 1991

Acceptances for settlement in the UK by nationality

Region	Number of persons
Europe: total	5,530
European Community	1,420
Other Western Europe	3,000
Eastern Europe	1,110
Americas: total	7,220
USA	3,910
Canada	680
Africa: total	9,580
Asia: total	24,900
Indian sub-continent	14,290
Middle East	2,900
Australasia: total	2,440
Other	2,780
Stateless	1,430
Total	53,900
Foreign	22,850
Commonwealth	31,060
Old Commonwealth	3,120
New Commonwealth	27,930

Source: HMSO - *Annual Abstract of Statistics 1993*

LIVE BIRTHS AND BIRTH RATES 1991

	Live births	Birth rate*
United Kingdom	793,000	13.8
England and Wales	699,000	13.7
Scotland	67,000	13.1
Northern Ireland	26,000	16.5

*Live births per 1,000 population
Source: HMSO - *Annual Abstract of Statistics 1993*

LEGAL ABORTIONS 1991 (ENGLAND AND WALES)

Age group	Number†
Under 16	3,080
16–19	30,750
20–34	113,600
35–44	17,730
45 and over	400
Age not stated	20
Total	165,500

† provisional
Source: HMSO – *Population Trends 72*

BIRTHS OUTSIDE MARRIAGE (UK)

Age group	1981	1991
Under 20	30,000	50,000
20–24	33,000	87,000
25–29	16,000	58,000
Over 30	13,000	41,000
Total	91,000	236,000

Source: HMSO – *Annual Abstract of Statistics 1993*

MARRIAGE AND DIVORCE 1990

	Marriages	Divorces*
United Kingdom	375,410	—
England and Wales	331,150	153,386
Scotland	34,672	12,272
Northern Ireland	9,588	2,591

*Decrees absolute granted (in Northern Ireland, divorce petitions filed)
Source: HMSO – *Annual Abstract of Statistics 1993*

DEATHS AND DEATH RATES 1991

Males	Deaths	Death rate*
United Kingdom	314,427p	11.2p
England and Wales	277,582	—
Scotland	29,312	—
Northern Ireland	7,533p	—
Females		
United Kingdom	331,754p	10.6p
England and Wales	292,462	—
Scotland	31,729	—
Northern Ireland	7,563p	—

* Deaths per 1,000 population
p provisional
Source: HMSO – *Annual Abstract of Statistics 1993*

INFANT MORTALITY 1991

Deaths of infants under 1 year of age per 1,000 live births

	Number
United Kingdom	7.4p
England and Wales	7.4
Scotland	7.1
Northern Ireland	7.4p

p provisional
Source: HMSO – *Annual Abstract of Statistics 1993*

EXPECTATION OF LIFE   LIFE TABLES 1988–90 (INTERIM FIGURES)

	England and Wales		Scotland		Northern Ireland	
Age	Male	Female	Male	Female	Male	Female
0	73.0	78.5	70.8	76.6	71.3	77.2
5	68.8	74.2	66.6	72.2	67.1	72.9
10	63.9	69.2	61.6	67.2	62.2	67.9
15	58.9	64.3	56.7	62.3	57.2	63.0
20	54.1	59.4	51.9	57.4	52.5	58.1
25	49.3	54.4	47.2	52.5	47.8	53.2
30	44.5	49.5	42.4	47.6	43.0	48.3
35	39.7	44.6	37.7	42.7	38.3	43.4
40	35.0	39.8	33.0	38.0	33.6	38.6
45	30.3	35.1	28.4	33.2	29.0	33.8
50	25.8	30.5	24.0	28.7	24.5	29.2
55	21.5	26.0	19.9	24.3	20.2	24.9
60	17.5	21.7	16.2	20.2	16.4	20.7
65	14.0	17.8	12.9	16.5	13.0	16.9
70	11.0	14.2	10.2	13.2	10.2	13.4
75	8.4	11.0	7.8	10.2	7.8	10.2
80	6.4	8.2	5.9	7.6	5.7	7.4
85	4.9	5.9	4.4	5.4	4.1	5.1

Source: HMSO – *Annual Abstract of Statistics 1993*

DEATHS ANALYSED BY CAUSE 1991

	England & Wales	Scotland	N. Ireland†
TOTAL DEATHS	570,044	61,041	15,096
DEATHS FROM NATURAL CAUSES	549,706	58,509	14,377
Infections and parasitic diseases	2,406	310	44
Intestinal infectious diseases	169	14	1
Tuberculosis of respiratory system	334	46	6
Other tuberculosis, including late effects	240	38	2
Whooping cough	—	—	—
Meningococcal infection	170	10	6
Measles	1	1	—
Malaria	11	1	—
Syphilis	15	2	—
Neoplasms	145,355	15,031	3,551
Malignant neoplasm of stomach	8,427	833	233
Malignant neoplasm of trachea, bronchus and lung	34,190	4,209	787
Malignant neoplasm of breast	13,869	1,282	342
Malignant neoplasm of uterus	3,163	294	66
Leukaemia	3,687	268	83
Benign and unspecified neoplasms	1,337	112	38
Endocrine, nutritional and metabolic diseases and immunity disorders	10,538	776	68
Diabetes mellitus	8,087	530	41
Nutritional deficiencies	109	6	1
Other metabolic and immunity disorders	1,664	197	23
Diseases of blood and blood-forming organs	2,446	170	31
Anaemias	1,110	68	18
Mental disorders	13,500	1,110	68
Diseases of nervous system and sense organs	11,889	947	168
Meningitis	233	26	10
Diseases of the circulatory system	261,834	29,166	6,983
Rheumatic heart disease	2,193	180	56
Hypertensive disease	3,340	316	67
Ischaemic heart disease	150,090	16,866	4,223
Diseases of pulmonary circulation and other forms of heart disease	18,820	2,234	627
Cerebrovascular disease	68,669	7,968	1,711
Diseases of the respiratory system	63,273	7,068	2,494
Influenza	248	28	5
Pneumonia	28,504	3,785	1,684
Bronchitis, emphysema	6,773	378	150
Asthma	1,884	161	47
Diseases of the digestive system	18,508	2,059	395
Ulcer of stomach and duodenum	4,304	368	98
Appendicitis	108	10	2
Hernia of abdominal cavity and other intestinal obstruction	1,967	176	45
Chronic liver disease and cirrhosis	3,102	476	60
Diseases of the genito-urinary system	6,964	805	272
Nephritis, nephrotic syndrome and nephrosis	3,234	541	183
Hyperplasia of prostate	413	12	8
Complications of pregnancy, childbirth, etc.	45	9	1
Abortion	6	—	—
Diseases of the skin and subcutaneous tissue	930	82	36
Diseases of the musculo-skeletal system	5,417	270	54
Congenital anomalies	1,643	193	90
Certain conditions originating in the perinatal period	250	213	82
Birth trauma, hypoxia, birth asphyxia and other respiratory conditions	78	105	31
Signs, symptoms and ill-defined conditions	5,208	300	40
Sudden infant death syndrome	912	90	15
DEATHS FROM INJURY AND POISONING	17,286	2,532	719
All accidents	11,049	1,734	492
Motor vehicle accidents	4,470	513	195
Suicide and self-inflicted injury	3,893	525	129
All other external causes	2,344	273	98

† provisional

Source: HMSO – *Annual Abstract of Statistics 1993*

The National Flag

The national flag of the United Kingdom is the Union Flag, generally known as the Union Jack. (The name 'Union Jack' derives from the use of the Union Flag on the jack-staff of naval vessels.)

The Union Flag is a combination of the cross of St George, patron saint of England, the cross of St Andrew, patron saint of Scotland, and a cross similar to that of St Patrick, patron saint of Ireland.

Cross of St George: cross Gules in a field Argent (red cross on a white ground).

Cross of St Andrew: saltire Argent in a field Azure (white diagonal cross on a blue ground).

Cross of St Patrick: saltire Gules in a field Argent (red diagonal cross on a white ground).

The Union Flag was first introduced in 1606 after the union of the kingdoms of England and Scotland under one sovereign. The cross of St Patrick was added in 1801 after the union of Great Britain and Ireland.

DAYS FOR FLYING FLAGS

The correct orientation of the Union Flag when flying is with the broader diagonal band of white uppermost in the hoist (i.e. near the pole) and the narrower diagonal band of white uppermost in the fly (i.e. farthest from the pole).

It is the practice to fly the Union Flag daily on some Customs Houses. In all other cases, flags are flown on government buildings by command of The Queen.

Days for hoisting the Union Flag are notified to the Department of the Environment by The Queen's command and communicated by the department to the other government departments. On the days appointed, the Union Flag is flown on all government buildings in London and elsewhere in the United Kingdom from 8 a.m. to sunset.

The Queen's Accession	6 February
Birthday of The Duke of York	19 February
St David's Day (in Wales only)	1 March
Birthday of The Prince Edward	10 March
Commonwealth Day (1994)	14 March
Birthday of The Queen	21 April
St George's Day (in England only)	23 April
Where a building has two or more flagstaffs, the Cross of St George may be flown in addition to the Union Flag, but not in a superior position	
Coronation Day	2 June
Birthday of The Duke of Edinburgh	10 June
The Queen's Official Birthday (1994)	11 June
Birthday of The Princess of Wales	1 July
Birthday of Queen Elizabeth the Queen Mother	4 August
Birthday of The Princess Royal	15 August
Birthday of The Princess Margaret	21 August
Remembrance Sunday (1994)	13 November
Birthday of The Prince of Wales	14 November

The Queen's Wedding Day	20 November
St Andrew's Day (in Scotland only)	30 November
The occasion of the opening and closing of Parliament by The Queen, whether or not Her Majesty performs the ceremony in person (on government buildings in the Greater London area only)	

FLAGS AT HALF-MAST

Flags are flown at half-mast on the following occasions:

(a) From the announcement of the death up to the funeral of the Sovereign, except on Proclamation Day, when flags are hoisted right up from 11 a.m. to sunset

(b) The funerals of members of the Royal Family, subject to special commands from The Queen in each case

(c) The funerals of foreign rulers, subject to special commands from The Queen in each case

(d) The funerals of Prime Ministers and ex-Prime Ministers of the United Kingdom

(e) Other occasions by special command of The Queen

On occasions when days for flying flags coincide with days for flying flags at half-mast, the following rules are observed. Flags are flown:

(a) although a member of the Royal Family, or a near relative of the Royal Family, may be lying dead, unless special commands be received from The Queen to the contrary

(b) although it may be the day of the funeral of a foreign ruler

If the body of a very distinguished subject is lying at a government office, the flag may fly at half-mast on that office until the body has left (provided it is a day on which the flag would fly) and then the flag is to be hoisted right up. On all other government buildings the flag will fly as usual.

THE ROYAL STANDARD

The Royal Standard is hoisted only when The Queen is actually present in the building, and never when Her Majesty is passing in procession.

The Royal Family

(see page 135)

THE SOVEREIGN

ELIZABETH II, by the Grace of God, of the United Kingdom of Great Britain and Northern Ireland and of her other Realms and Territories Queen, Head of the Commonwealth, Defender of the Faith

Her Majesty Elizabeth Alexandra Mary of Windsor, elder daughter of King George VI and of HM Queen Elizabeth the Queen Mother
Born 21 April 1926, at 17 Bruton Street, London W1
Ascended the throne 6 February 1952
Crowned 2 June 1953, at Westminster Abbey
Married 20 November 1947, in Westminster Abbey, HRH The Duke of Edinburgh
Official residences: Buckingham Palace, London SW1; Windsor Castle, Berks; Palace of Holyroodhouse, Edinburgh
Private residences: Sandringham, Norfolk; Balmoral Castle, Aberdeenshire
Office: Buckingham Palace, London SW1A 1AA. Tel: 071-930 4832

HUSBAND OF HM THE QUEEN

HRH THE PRINCE PHILIP, DUKE OF EDINBURGH, KG, KT, OM, GBE, AC, QSO, PC, Ranger of Windsor Park
Born 10 June 1921, son of Prince and Princess Andrew of Greece and Denmark (*see* page 135), naturalized a British subject 1947, created Duke of Edinburgh, Earl of Merioneth and Baron Greenwich 1947

CHILDREN OF HM THE QUEEN

HRH THE PRINCE OF WALES (Prince Charles Philip Arthur George), KG, KT, GCB and Great Master of the Order of the Bath, AK, QSO, PC, ADC(P)
Born 14 November 1948, created Prince of Wales and Earl of Chester 1958, succeeded as Duke of Cornwall, Duke of Rothesay, Earl of Carrick and Baron Renfrew, Lord of the Isles and Prince and Great Steward of Scotland 1952
Married 29 July 1981 Lady Diana Frances Spencer, now HRH The Princess of Wales (*born* 1 July 1961, youngest daughter of the 8th Earl Spencer and the Hon. Mrs Shand Kydd), *separated* 1992
Issue:
(1) HRH Prince William of Wales (Prince William Arthur Philip Louis), *born* 21 June 1982
(2) HRH Prince Henry of Wales (Prince Henry Charles Albert David), *born* 15 September 1984
Residences of the Prince of Wales: St James's Palace, London SW1; Highgrove, Doughton, Tetbury, Glos.
Residence of the Princess of Wales: Kensington Palace, London W8 4PU
Office: St James's Palace, London SW1A 1BS. Tel: 071-930 4832

HRH THE PRINCESS ROYAL (Princess Anne Elizabeth Alice Louise), GCVO
Born 15 August 1950, declared The Princess Royal 1987

Married (1) 14 November 1973 Captain Mark Anthony Peter Phillips, CVO (*born* 22 September 1948); marriage dissolved 1992; (2) 12 December 1992 Commander Timothy James Hamilton Laurence, MVO (*born* 1 March 1955)
Issue:
(1) Peter Mark Andrew Phillips, *born* 15 November 1977
(2) Zara Anne Elizabeth Phillips, *born* 15 May 1981
Residence: Gatcombe Park, Minchinhampton, Glos.
Office: Buckingham Palace, London SW1A 1AA. Tel: 071-930 4832

HRH THE DUKE OF YORK (Prince Andrew Albert Christian Edward), CVO, ADC(P)
Born 19 February 1960, created Duke of York, Earl of Inverness and Baron Killyleagh 1986
Married 23 July 1986 Sarah Margaret Ferguson, now HRH The Duchess of York (*born* 15 October 1959, younger daughter of Major Ronald Ferguson and Mrs Hector Barrantes), *separated* 1992
Issue:
(1) HRH Princess Beatrice of York (Princess Beatrice Elizabeth Mary), *born* 8 August 1988
(2) HRH Princess Eugenie of York (Princess Eugenie Victoria Helena), *born* 23 March 1990
Residences: Buckingham Palace, London SW1; Sunninghill Park, Ascot, Berks.
Office: Buckingham Palace, London SW1A 1AA. Tel: 071-930 4832

HRH THE PRINCE EDWARD (Prince Edward Antony Richard Louis), CVO
Born 10 March 1964
Residence and Office: Buckingham Palace, London SW1A 1AA. Tel: 071-930 4832

SISTER OF HM THE QUEEN

HRH THE PRINCESS MARGARET, COUNTESS OF SNOWDON (Princess Margaret Rose), CI, GCVO, Royal Victorian Chain, Dame Grand Cross of the Order of St John of Jerusalem
Born 21 August 1930, younger daughter of King George VI and HM Queen Elizabeth the Queen Mother
Married 6 May 1960 Antony Charles Robert Armstrong-Jones, GCVO (*born* 7 March 1930, created Earl of Snowdon 1961, Constable of Caernarvon Castle); marriage dissolved 1978
Issue:
(1) David Albert Charles, Viscount Linley, *born* 3 November 1961
(2) Lady Sarah Armstrong-Jones (Sarah Frances Elizabeth), *born* 1 May 1964
Residence and Office: Kensington Palace, London W8 4PU. Tel: 071-930 3141

MOTHER OF HM THE QUEEN

HM QUEEN ELIZABETH THE QUEEN MOTHER (Elizabeth Angela Marguerite), Lady of the Garter, Lady of the Thistle, CI, GMVO, GBE, Dame Grand Cross of the Order of St John, Royal Victorian Chain, Lord Warden and

Admiral of the Cinque Ports and Constable of Dover Castle
Born 4 August 1900, youngest daughter of the 14th Earl of
Strathmore and Kinghorne
Married 26 April 1923 (as Lady Elizabeth Bowes-Lyon)
Prince Albert, Duke of York, afterwards King George VI
(*see* page 134)
Residences: Clarence House, St James's Palace, London SW1;
Royal Lodge, Windsor Great Park, Berks; Castle of Mey,
Caithness
Office: Clarence House, St James's Palace, London SW1A
1BA. Tel: 071-930 3141

AUNT OF HM THE QUEEN

HRH PRINCESS ALICE, DUCHESS OF GLOUCESTER
(Alice Christabel), GCB, CI, GCVO, GBE, Grand Cordon of
Al Kamal
Born 25 December 1901, third daughter of the 7th Duke of
Buccleuch and Queensberry
Married 6 November 1935 (as Lady Alice Montagu-
Douglas-Scott) Prince Henry, Duke of Gloucester, third son
of King George V (*see* page 134)

COUSINS OF HM THE QUEEN

HRH THE DUKE OF GLOUCESTER (Prince Richard
Alexander Walter George), GCVO, Grand Prior of the Order
of St John of Jerusalem
Born 26 August 1944
Married 8 July 1972 Birgitte Eva van Deurs, now HRH The
Duchess of Gloucester, GCVO (*born* 20 June 1946, daughter
of Asger Henriksen and Vivian van Deurs)
Issue:
(1)   Earl of Ulster (Alexander Patrick Gregers Richard),
      born 24 October 1974
(2)   Lady Davina Windsor (Davina Elizabeth Alice
      Benedikte), *born* 19 November 1977
(3)   Lady Rose Windsor (Rose Victoria Birgitte Louise),
      born 1 March 1980
Residences: Kensington Palace, London W8 4PU; Barnwell
Manor, Peterborough, Northants. PE8 5PJ
Office: Kensington Palace, London W8 4PU. Tel: 071-937
6374

HRH THE DUKE OF KENT (Prince Edward George
Nicholas Paul Patrick), KG, GCMG, GCVO, ADC(P)
Born 9 October 1935
Married 8 June 1961 Katharine Lucy Mary Worsley, now
HRH The Duchess of Kent, GCVO (*born* 22 February 1933,
daughter of Sir William Worsley, Bt.)
Issue:
(1)   Earl of St Andrews (George Philip Nicholas), *born* 26
      June 1962, *married* 9 January 1988 Sylvana Tomaselli,
      and has issue, Edward Edmund Maximilian George,
      Baron Downpatrick, *born* 2 December 1988; Lady
      Marina Charlotte Alexandra Katharine Windsor, *born*
      30 September 1992
(2)   Lady Helen Taylor (Helen Marina Lucy), *born* 28
      April 1964, *married* 18 July 1992 Timothy Verner
      Taylor
(3)   Lord Nicholas Windsor (Nicholas Charles Edward
      Jonathan), *born* 25 July 1970
Residences: York House, St James's Palace, London SW1 1BQ;
Crocker End House, Nettlebed, Oxon.
Office: York House, St James's Palace, London SW1A 1BQ.
Tel: 071-930 4872

HRH PRINCESS ALEXANDRA, THE HON. LADY OGILVY
(Princess Alexandra Helen Elizabeth Olga Christabel), GCVO
Born 25 December 1936
Married 24 April 1963 The Hon. Sir Angus Ogilvy, KCVO
(*born* 14 September 1928, second son of 12th Earl of Airlie)
Issue:
(1)   James Robert Bruce Ogilvy, *born* 29 February 1964,
      married 30 July 1988 Julia Rawlinson
(2)   Marina Victoria Alexandra, Mrs Mowatt, *born* 31 July
      1966, *married* 2 February 1990 Paul Mowatt, and has
      issue, Zenouska Mowatt, *born* 26 May 1990; a son,
      born 4 June 1993
Residence: Thatched House Lodge, Richmond Park, Surrey
Office: 22 Friary Court, St James's Palace, London SW1A 1BJ.
Tel: 071-930 1860

HRH PRINCE MICHAEL OF KENT (Prince Michael
George Charles Franklin), KCVO
Born 4 July 1942
Married 30 June 1978 Baroness Marie-Christine Agnes
Hedwig Ida von Reibnitz, now HRH Princess Michael of
Kent (*born* 15 January 1945, daughter of Baron Gunther von
Reibnitz)
Issue:
(1)   Lord Frederick Windsor (Frederick Michael George
      David Louis), *born* 6 April 1979
(2)   Lady Gabriella Windsor (Gabriella Marina Alexandra
      Ophelia), *born* 23 April 1981
Residences: Kensington Palace, London W8 4PU; Nether
Lypiatt Manor, Stroud, Glos.
Office: Kensington Palace, London W8 4PU. Tel: 071-938
3519

ORDER OF SUCCESSION

---

1   HRH The Prince of Wales
2   HRH Prince William of Wales
3   HRH Prince Henry of Wales
4   HRH The Duke of York
5   HRH Princess Beatrice of York
6   HRH Princess Eugenie of York
7   HRH The Prince Edward
8   HRH The Princess Royal
9   Peter Phillips
10   Zara Phillips
11   HRH The Princess Margaret, Countess of Snowdon
12   Viscount Linley
13   Lady Sarah Armstrong-Jones
14   HRH The Duke of Gloucester
15   Earl of Ulster
16   Lady Davina Windsor
17   Lady Rose Windsor
18   HRH The Duke of Kent
19   Baron Downpatrick
20   Lady Marina Charlotte Windsor
21   Lord Nicholas Windsor
22   Lady Helen Taylor
23   Lord Frederick Windsor
24   Lady Gabriella Windsor
25   HRH Princess Alexandra, the Hon. Lady Ogilvy
26   James Ogilvy
27   Marina, Mrs Paul Mowatt

The Earl of St Andrews and HRH Prince Michael of Kent
lost the right of succession to the throne under the Act of
Settlement 1701, through marriage to a Roman Catholic.
However, their children and descendants remain in
succession, provided that they are in communion with the
Church of England

Royal Households

THE QUEEN'S HOUSEHOLD

Lord Chamberlain, The Earl of Airlie, KT, GCVO, PC
Lord Steward, The Viscount Ridley, KG, TD
Master of the Horse, The Lord Somerleyton
Treasurer of the Household, G. Knight, MP
Comptroller of the Household, D. Lightbown, MP
Vice-Chamberlain, S. Chapman, MP

Gold Stick, Maj.-Gen. Lord Michael Fitzalan-Howard,
    GCVO, CB, CBE, MC; Gen. Sir Desmond Fitzpatrick, GCB,
    DSO, MBE, MC
Vice-Adm. of the United Kingdom, Adm. Sir Anthony
    Morton, GBE, KCB
Rear-Adm. of the United Kingdom, Adm. Sir James Eberle,
    GCB
First and Principal Naval Aide-De-Camp, Adm. Sir
    Benjamin Bathurst, GCB
Flag Aide de Camp, Adm. Sir John Kerr, KCB
Aides-de-Camp-General, Gen. Sir Peter Inge, GCB; Gen. Sir
    Michael Wilkes, KCB, CBE; Gen. Sir Charles Guthrie, KCB,
    LVO, OBE
Air Aides-de-Camp, Air Chief Marshal Sir Michael Graydon,
    GCB, CBE; Air Chief Marshal Sir Andrew Wilson, KCB, AFC

Mistress of the Robes, The Duchess of Grafton, GCVO
Ladies of the Bedchamber, The Countess of Airlie, CVO; The
    Lady Farnham
Extra Ladies of the Bedchamber, The Marchioness of
    Abergavenny, DCVO; The Dowager Countess of Cromer,
    CVO
Women of the Bedchamber, Hon. Mary Morrison, DCVO;
    Lady Susan Hussey, DCVO; Mrs John Dugdale, DCVO; The
    Lady Elton
Extra Women of the Bedchamber, Mrs John Woodroffe, CVO;
    Lady Rose Baring, DCVO; Mrs Michael Wall, DCVO; Lady
    Abel Smith, DCVO; Mrs Robert de Pass
Equerries, Lt.-Col. B. A. Stewart-Wilson, CVO; Capt.
    J. Patrick; Capt. P. Hopkins (temp.)
Extra Equerries, Vice-Adm. Sir Peter Ashmore, KCB, KCVO,
    DSC; Lt.-Col. The Lord Charteris of Amisfield, GCB, GCVO,
    OBE, QSO, PC; Maj.-Gen. Sir Simon Cooper, KCVO; Air
    Cdre the Hon. T. Elworthy, CBE; The Rt Hon. Sir Robert
    Fellowes, KCB, KCVO; Sir Edward Ford, KCB, KCVO, ERD;
    Rear-Adm. Sir John Garnier, KCVO, CVO; Rear-Adm. Sir
    Paul Greening, GCVO; Brig. Sir Geoffrey Hardy-Roberts,
    KCVO, CB, CBE; The Rt. Hon. Sir William Heseltine, GCB,
    GCVO, AC, QSO; Rear-Adm. Sir Hugh Janion, KCVO;
    Lt.-Col. Sir John Johnston, GCVO, MC; Lt.-Col. A. Mather,
    OBE; Sir Peter Miles, KCVO; Lt.-Col. Sir John Miller,
    GCVO, DSO, MC; Air Cdre Sir Dennis Mitchell, KBE, CVO,
    DFC, AFC; The Lord Moore of Wolvercote, GCB, GCVO,
    CMG, QSO; Lt.-Gen. Sir John Richards, KCB; Lt.-Col.
    W. H. M. Ross, OBE; Air Vice-Marshal Sir John Severne,
    KCVO, OBE, AFC; Gp Capt P. Townsend, CVO, DSO, DFC;
    Rear-Adm. Sir Richard Trowbridge, KCVO; Lt.-Col.
    G. West, CVO; Air Cdre Sir Archie Winskill, KCVO, CBE,
    DFC, AE; Rear-Adm. R. Woodard

THE PRIVATE SECRETARY'S OFFICE
Buckingham Palace, London SW1A 1AA

Private Secretary to The Queen, The Rt Hon. Sir Robert
    Fellowes, KCB, KCVO

Deputy Private Secretary, Sir Kenneth Scott, KCVO, CMG
Assistant Private Secretary, R. B. Janvrin, LVO
Press Secretary, C. V. Anson, LVO
Deputy Press Secretary, G. Crawford
Assistant Press Secretary, Miss P. Russell-Smith
Chief Clerk, Mrs G. S. Coulson, MVO
Secretary to the Private Secretary, Mrs J. Bean, LVO
Clerks, Miss A. Freeman; Mrs A. Galletly; Miss H. Spiller;
    Miss H. Staveley; Mrs E. Walsh Waring; Miss P. Brown;
    Miss M. Edwards; Mrs N. Miller; Mrs P. Penfold; Miss
    N. Thompson
Press Office, Miss K. McGrigor, MVO; Mrs G. Middleburgh;
    Mrs R. Murdo-Smith, LVO; Miss C. Sillars
Lady-in-Waiting's Office, Mrs D. Phillips; Mrs J. Vince

THE QUEEN'S ARCHIVES
Round Tower, Windsor Castle, Berks

Keeper of The Queen's Archives, The Rt Hon. Sir Robert
    Fellowes, KCB, KCVO
Assistant Keeper, O. Everett, CVO
Registrar, Lady de Bellaigue, MVO
Assistant Registrar, Miss P. Clark
Curator of the Photographic Collection, Miss F. Dimond, LVO

THE PRIVY PURSE AND TREASURER'S OFFICE
Buckingham Palace, London SW1A 1AA

Keeper of the Privy Purse and Treasurer to The Queen, Maj.
    Sir Shane Blewitt, KCVO
Deputy Keeper of the Privy Purse and Deputy Treasurer,
    J. Parsons, LVO
Chief Accountant and Paymaster, D. Walker, LVO
Personnel Officer, Miss P. Lloyd
Assistant Chief Accountant and Paymaster, Miss R. Ward
Assistant Personnel Officer, Mrs C. Jones
Clerks, Mrs C. Auton, MVO; I. Biss; Mrs N. Broad; J. Curr;
    Miss N. Mooney; Miss C. Robinson; Miss G. Wickham,
    MVO; Miss P. Green
Land Agent, Sandringham, J. Major
Resident Factor, Balmoral, M. Leslie, LVO

FINANCE AND PROPERTY SERVICES

Director of Finance and Property Services, M. Peat
Deputy Director, Property Services, J. H. Tiltman
Superintending Architect, S. Dhargalkar
Senior Architect, Miss H. Bell
Property Administrator, Miss M. Green
Deputy Property Administrator, M. Bourke
Fire Precautions and Health and Safety Manager,
    G. Griffiths, MVO
Maintenance Manager, Buckingham Palace, R. Brown
Maintenance Manager, St James's and Kensington Palaces,
    R. Mole.
Assistant Maintenance Managers, M. Harmer; A. Ryan
Assistant Property Administrator, Mrs H. Dunlop
Management Auditor, I. McGregor
Assistant Management Auditor, Mrs D. Mowbray
Information Systems Manager, I. Hardy
Clerks, Mrs. J. Hillyer; Mrs C. Sharma; Mrs J. Thomas; Miss
    R. Wickenden

WINDSOR CASTLE
Maintenance Manager, E. Norton
Deputy Maintenance Manager, P. Godwin
Administrative Assistant, Mrs C. Crook

ROYAL ALMONRY

High Almoner, The Rt. Revd the Lord Bishop of St Albans
Hereditary Grand Almoner, The Marquess of Exeter
Sub-Almoner, Revd W. Booth
Secretary, P. Wright, CVO
Assistant Secretary, C. Williams, RVM

THE LORD CHAMBERLAIN'S OFFICE

Buckingham Palace, London SWIA IAA

Comptroller, Lt.-Col. M. Ross, OBE
Assistant Comptroller, Lt.-Col. A. Mather, OBE
Secretary, P. D. Hartley, MVO
Assistant Secretary, J. Spencer, MVO
State Invitations Assistant, vacant
Clerks, Miss L. Connor; Miss L. Dove; Mrs S. Scott; Miss
   A. Utting
Permanent Lords-in-Waiting, Lt.-Col. The Lord Charteris of
   Amisfield, GCB, GCVO, OBE, QSO, PC; The Lord Moore of
   Wolvercote, GCB, GCVO, CMG, QSO
Lords-in-Waiting, The Viscount Boyne; The Lord Camoys;
   The Viscount Long, CBE; The Viscount Astor; The
   Viscount St Davids; The Viscount Goschen
Baroness-in-Waiting, The Baroness Trumpington
Gentlemen Ushers, C. Greig, CVO, CBE; Gp Capt J. Slessor;
   Maj. N. Chamberlayne-Macdonald, LVO, OBE; Air
   Marshal Sir Roy Austen-Smith, KBE, CB, DFC; Vice-Adm.
   Sir David Loram, KCB, LVO; Capt. M. Barrow, DSO, RN;
   Capt. M. Fulford-Dobson, RN; Lt.-Gen. Sir Richard
   Vickers, KCB, LVO, OBE; Air Vice-Marshal B. Newton, CB,
   OBE; Col. M. Havergal, OBE
Extra Gentlemen Ushers, Maj. T. Harvey, CVO, DSO;
   Maj.-Gen. Sir Cyril Colquhoun, KCVO, CB, OBE; Lt.-Col.
   Sir John Hugo, KCVO, OBE; Vice-Adm. Sir Ronald
   Brockman, KCB, CSI, CIE, CVO, CBE; Air Marshal Sir
   Maurice Heath, KBE, CB, CVO; Sir James Scholtens, KCVO;
   Sir Patrick O'Dea, KCVO; Brig.-Gen. S. Cooper, CVO, OBE,
   CD; Adm. Sir David Williams, GCB; H. Davis, CVO, CM;
   Maj.-Gen. R. Reid, CVO, MC, CD; Lt.-Cdr. J. Holdsworth,
   CVO, OBE, RN; Col. G. Leigh, CVO, CBE; Lt.-Cdr. Sir
   Russell Wood, KCVO, VRD; Air Chief Marshal Sir Neville
   Stack, KCB, CVO, CBE, AFC; Maj.-Gen. Sir Desmond Rice,
   KCVO, CBE; Lt.-Col. Sir Julian Paget, Bt., CVO; S. W. F.
   Martin, CVO
Gentleman Usher to the Sword of State, Gen. Sir Edward
   Burgess, KCB, OBE
Gentleman Usher of the Black Rod, Adm. Sir Richard
   Thomas, KCB, OBE
Serjeants-at-Arms, D. Walker, LVO; Maj. B. Eastwood, MVO,
   MBE; P. Hartley, MVO

Marshal of the Diplomatic Corps, Vice-Adm. Sir James
   Weatherall, KBE
Vice-Marshal, A. St J. H. Figgis, CMG

Constable and Governor of Windsor Castle, Gen. Sir Patrick
   Palmer, KBE
Keeper of the Jewel House, Tower of London, Maj.-Gen.
   C. Tyler, CB
Master of The Queen's Music, Malcolm Williamson, CBE, AO
Poet Laureate, Ted Hughes, OBE
Bargemaster, R. Crouch
Warden of the Swans, Prof. C. Perrins, CVO
Marker of the Swans, D. Barber
Superintendent of the State Apartments, St James's Palace,
   vacant

ECCLESIASTICAL HOUSEHOLD

THE COLLEGE OF CHAPLAINS

Clerk of the Closet, Rt. Revd Bishop of Chelmsford

Deputy Clerk of the Closet, Revd W. Booth
Chaplains to The Queen, Revd A. H. H. Harbottle, LVO;
   Ven. D. N. Griffiths, RD; Revd Canon A. Glendining,
   LVO; Revd Canon J. V. Bean; Revd K. Huxley; Ven.
   P. Ashford; Revd Canon D. C. Gray, TD; Ven. D. Scott;
   Revd Canon E. James; Revd Canon J. Hester; Revd
   S. Pedley; Revd D. Tonge; Revd Canon N. M. Ramm;
   Revd Canon M. A. Moxon; Revd Canon
   R. T. W. McDermid; Revd Canon G. Murphy, LVO;
   Revd Canon R. H. C. Lewis; Revd D. J. Burgess; Revd
   E. R. Ayerst; Revd R. S. Clarke; Revd Canon C. J. Hill;
   Revd Canon K. Pound; Revd J. Haslam; Revd Canon
   G. Hall; Revd Canon A. C. Hill; Revd J. C. Priestley;
   Revd Canon J. O. Colling; Revd Canon G. Jones; Revd
   Canon D. G. Palmer; Revd Canon D. H. Wheaton; Revd
   Canon P. Boulton; Revd Canon R. A. Bowden; Revd
   Canon E. Buchanan; Revd Canon S. Goodridge; Revd
   J. Robson; Revd Canon J. Stanley
Extra Chaplains, Revd Canon J. S. D. Mansel, KCVO, FSA;
   Preb. S. A. Williams, CVO; Ven. E. J. G. Ward, LVO; Revd
   J. R. W. Stott; Revd Canon A. D. Caesar, CVO

CHAPELS ROYAL

Dean of the Chapels Royal, The Bishop of London
Sub-Dean of Chapels Royal, Revd W. Booth
Priests in Ordinary, Revd G. Watkins; Revd H. Mead; Revd
   S. E. Young
Organist, Choirmaster and Composer, R. J. Popplewell, MVO,
   FRCO, FRCM
Domestic Chaplain, Buckingham Palace, Revd W. Booth
Domestic Chaplain, Windsor Castle, The Dean of Windsor
Domestic Chaplain, Sandringham, Revd Canon G. R. Hall
Chaplain, Royal Chapel, Windsor Great Park, Revd Canon
   M. Moxon
Chaplain, Hampton Court Palace, Revd Canon M. Moore
Chaplain, Tower of London, Revd Canon
   J. G. M. W. Murphy, LVO
Organist and Choirmaster, Hampton Court Palace, Gordon
   Reynolds, LVO

MEDICAL HOUSEHOLD

Head of the Medical Household and Physician to The Queen,
   R. Thompson, DM, FRCP
Physician, R. W. Davey, MB, BS
Serjeant Surgeon, B. T. Jackson, MS, FRCS
Surgeon Oculist, P. Holmes Sellors, LVO, BM, B.ch., FRCS
Surgeon Gynaecologist, M. E. Setchell, FRCS, FRCOG
Surgeon Dentist, N. A. Sturridge, CVO, LDS, BDS, DDS
Orthopaedic Surgeon, R. H. Vickers, MA, BM, B.ch., FRCS
Physician to the Household, J. Cunningham, DM, FRCP
Surgeon to the Household, A. A. M. Lewis, MB, FRCS
Surgeon Oculist to the Household, T. J. ffytche, FRCS
Apothecary to The Queen and to the Household,
   N. R. Southward, LVO, MB, B.chir.
Apothecary to the Household at Windsor, J. H. D. Briscoe,
   MB, B.chir., D.obst.
Apothecary to the Household at Sandringham,
   I. K. Campbell, MB, BS, FRCGP
Coroner of The Queen's Household, J. Burton, CBE, MB, BS

CENTRAL CHANCERY OF THE ORDERS OF
KNIGHTHOOD

St James's Palace, London SWI

Secretary, Lt.-Col. A. Mather, OBE
Assistant Secretary, Miss R. Wells, MVO
Clerks, J. Bagwell Purefoy; Miss F. Bean; Mrs T. Isaac; Miss
   S. Koller, MVO; J. McGurk, MVO; D. Pogson; Miss
   A Weatherall

THE HONOURABLE CORPS OF GENTLEMEN-AT-ARMS
St James's Palace, London SW1

Captain, The Lord Hesketh
Lieutenant, Lt.-Col. Sir James Scott, Bt.
Standard Bearer, Maj. Sir Fergus Matheson of Matheson,
Bt.
Clerk of the Cheque and Adjutant, Col. T. Hall
Harbinger, Brig. A. N. Breitmeyer

Gentlemen of the Corps

Colonels, Sir Piers Bengough, KCVO, OBE; Hon. N. Crossley,
TD; T. Wilson; D. Fanshawe, OBE; J. Baker; R. ffrench
Blake; Sir William Mahon, Bt.
Lieutenant-Colonels, R. Mayfield, DSO; B. Lockhart; Hon.
P. H. Lewis; R. Macfarlane; Hon. G. B. Norrie;
J. H. Fisher, OBE; R. Ker, MC; P. Chamberlin
Majors, J. A. J. Nunn; Sir Philip Duncombe, Bt.; I. B.
Ramsden, MBE; M. J. Drummond-Brady; A. Arkwright;
G. M. B. Colenso-Jones; T. Gooch, MBE; J. B. B.
Cockcroft; C. J. H. Gurney; J. R. E. Nelson; P. D.
Johnson
Captain, The Lord Monteagle of Brandon

THE QUEEN'S BODY GUARD OF THE YEOMEN OF THE
GUARD
St James's Palace, London SW1

Captain, The Earl of Strathmore and Kinghorne
Lieutenant, Col. A. B. Pemberton, CVO, MBE
Clerk of the Cheque and Adjutant, Col. G. W. Tufnell
Ensign, Lt.-Col. S. Longsdon
Exons, Maj. C. Marriott; Maj. C. Enderby

MASTER OF THE HOUSEHOLD'S
DEPARTMENT

BOARD OF GREEN CLOTH
Buckingham Palace, London SW1A 1AA

Master of the Household, Maj.-Gen. Sir Simon Cooper, KCVO
Deputy Master of the Household, Lt.-Col. B. A. Stewart-
Wilson, CVO
Assistants to the Master of the Household, M. T. Parker, MVO;
P. Jackson
Chief Clerk, M. C. W. N. Jephson, MVO
Chief Housekeeper, Miss H. Colebrook
Deputy to Assistant F, M. Bovaird
Senior Clerk G, S. Stacey
Clerks, Miss S. Bell; Miss S. Derry, LVO; Miss S. Fergus,
MVO; Miss S. Hargreaves; Miss E. Henderson
Flower Arranger, Mrs P. Pentney
Palace Steward, A. Jarred, RVM
Royal Chef, L. Mann, RVM
Superintendent, Windsor Castle, Maj. B. Eastwood, MVO, MBE
Superintendent, The Palace of Holyroodhouse, Lt.-Col.
D. Anderson

ROYAL MEWS DEPARTMENT
Buckingham Palace, London SW1W 0QH

Crown Equerry, Lt.-Col. S. Gilbart-Denham
Veterinary Surgeon, P. Scott Dunn, LVO, MRCVS
Superintendent Royal Mews, Buckingham Palace, Maj.
A. Smith, MBE
Comptroller of Stores, Maj. L. Marsham, MVO
Chief Clerk, P. Almond, MVO
Deputy Chief Clerk, A. Marshall
Assistant Chief Clerk, Mrs J. Clark

THE ROYAL COLLECTION TRUST
St James's Palace, London SW1

*Director of Royal Collection and Surveyor of The Queen's
Works of Art,* Sir Geoffrey de Bellaigue, KCVO, FBA, FSA
Deputy Director (Finance), J. Parsons, LVO
Surveyor of The Queen's Pictures, C. Lloyd
Surveyor Emeritus of The Queen's Pictures, Sir Oliver Millar,
GCVO, FBA, FSA
Librarian, The Royal Library, Windsor Castle, O. Everett,
CVO
Deputy Surveyor of The Queen's Works of Art, H. Roberts,
FSA
Librarian Emeritus, Sir Robin Mackworth-Young, GCVO, FSA
Director of Media Affairs, R. Arbiter
Curator of the Print Room, The Hon. Mrs Roberts, MVO
Administrator and Assistant to The Surveyors (Military),
D. Rankin-Hunt, MVO, TD
Assistant to The Surveyor of The Queen's Pictures, C. Noble,
MVO
Secretary to the Director, Miss C. Paybody
Exhibitions Assistant (Pictures), Hon. C. Neville
Senior Picture Restorer, Miss V. Pemberton-Pigott, MVO
Chief Restorer, Old Master Drawings, M. Warnes, MVO
Senior Furniture Restorer, E. Fancourt, RVM
Armourer, J. Jackson, RVM
Chief Binder, R. Day, MVO, RVM
Deputy Curator of the Print Room, Mrs H. Ryan, MVO
Assistant Curator (Exhibitions), Miss T.-M. Morton
Bibliographer, Miss B. Wright, MVO
Superintendent Royal Collection Hampton Court Palace,
J. Cowell, MVO
Computer Systems Manager, S. Patterson
Financial Controller, Mrs G. Johnson
Accountant, Miss M. O'Connell

ROYAL COLLECTION ENTERPRISES LTD

Managing Director, M. E. K. Hewlett
Secretary to the Managing Director, Mrs C. Murphy, MVO
Finance Director, Mrs G. Johnson
Retail Manager, S. R. Spencer
Administrator Public Enterprises, Buckingham Palace, Miss
J. Grist
Administrator Public Enterprises, Windsor Castle, Mrs
A. Laing
Assistant Administrator Public Enterprises, Windsor Castle,
Mrs H. Tarrant
Head of Photographic Services, Miss G. Campling
Merchandise Consultant, Mrs K. Munro

ASCOT OFFICE
St James's Palace, London SW1
Tel 071-930 9882

Her Majesty's Representative at Ascot, Col. Sir Piers
Bengough, KCVO, OBE
Secretary, Miss L. Thompson-Royds

THE QUEEN'S HOUSEHOLD IN
SCOTLAND

Hereditary Lord High Constable, The Earl of Erroll
Hereditary Master of the Household, The Duke of Argyll
Lord Lyon King of Arms, Sir Malcolm Innes of Edingight,
KCVO, WS

Hereditary Bearer of the Royal Banner of Scotland, The Earl of Dundee
Hereditary Bearer of the Scottish National Flag, The Earl of Lauderdale
Hereditary Keepers:
Palace of Holyroodhouse, The Duke of Hamilton and Brandon
Falkland Palace, M. Crichton-Stuart
Stirling Castle, The Earl of Mar and Kellie
Dunstaffnage Castle, The Duke of Argyll
Dunconnel Castle, Sir Fitzroy Maclean, Bt., CBE
Hereditary Carver, Sir Ralph Anstruther, GCVO, MC
Keeper of Dumbarton Castle, Brig. A. S. Pearson, CB, DSO, OBE, MC, TD
Governor of Edinburgh Castle, Maj.-Gen. M. Scott, CBE, DSO
Historiographer, vacant
Botanist, Prof. D. Henderson, CBE, FRSE
Painter and Limner, D. A. Donaldson, RSA, RP
Sculptor in Ordinary, Prof. Sir Eduardo Paolozzi, CBE, RA
Astronomer, vacant
Heralds and Pursuivants, see page 287.

ECCLESIASTICAL HOUSEHOLD
Dean of the Chapel Royal, Very Revd W. J. Morris, DD, LL.D
Dean of the Order of the Thistle, The Very Revd G. I. Macmillan
Chaplains in Ordinary, Very Revd W. J. Morris, DD, LL.D.; Revd J. McLeod; Very Revd G. I. Macmillan; Revd M. D. Craig; Revd W. B. R. Macmillan, LL.D, DD.; Revd J. L. Weatherhead; Revd A. S. Todd, DD; Revd C. Robertson; Revd J. A. Simpson; Revd N. W. Drummond
Extra Chaplains, Very Revd R. W. V. Selby Wright, CVO, TD, DD, FRSE, FSAScot.; Very Revd W. R. Sanderson, DD; Very Revd R. L. Small, CBE, DD; Revd T. J. T. Nicol, MVO, MBE, MC, TD; Very Revd Prof. J. McIntyre, CVO, DD, FRSE; Revd C. Forrester-Paton; Revd H. W. M. Cant; Very Revd R. A. S. Barbour, KCVO, MC, DD; Revd K. MacVicar, MBE, DFC, TD; Very Revd W. B. Johnston, DD; Revd A. J. C. Macfarlane; Revd M. I. Levison
Domestic Chaplain, Balmoral, Revd J. A. K. Angus, LVO, TD

MEDICAL HOUSEHOLD
Physicians in Scotland, P. Brunt, MD, FRCP; A. L. Muir, MD, FRCP
Surgeons in Scotland, I. B. Macleod, MB, ch.B., FRCS; J. Engeset, ch.M., FRCS
Apothecary to the Household at Balmoral, D. J. A. Glass, MB, ch.B.
Apothecary to the Household at the Palace of Holyroodhouse, Dr J. Cormack, MD, FRCGP.

THE QUEEN'S BODY GUARD FOR SCOTLAND
ROYAL COMPANY OF ARCHERS
Archers' Hall, Edinburgh
Captain-General and Gold Stick for Scotland, Col. the Lord Clydesmuir, KT, CB, MBE, TD
Captains, Maj. the Lord Home of the Hirsel, KT; The Duke of Buccleuch and Queensberry, KT, VRD; Maj. Sir Hew Hamilton-Dalrymple, Bt., KCVO; Maj. the Earl of Wemyss and March, KT
Lieutenants, The Earl of Airlie, KT, GCVO; Capt. Sir Iain Tennant, KT; Capt. N. E. F. Dalrymple-Hamilton, CVO, MBE, DSC, RN; The Marquess of Lothian, KCVO
Ensigns, Cdre Sir John Clerk of Penicuik, Bt., CBE, VRD; The Earl of Elgin and Kincardine, KT; Col. G. R. Simpson, DSO, LVO, TD; Maj. Sir David Butter, KCVO, MC

Brigadiers, The Earl of Minto, OBE; Maj.-Gen. Sir John Swinton, KCVO, OBE; Gen. Sir Michael Gow, GCB; The Hon. Lord Elliott, MC; Maj. the Hon. Sir Lachlan Maclean, Bt.; The Rt. Hon. Lord Younger of Prestwick, KCVO, TD; Capt. G. Burnet, LVO; The Duke of Montrose; Lt.-Gen. Sir Norman Arthur, KCB; The Hon. Sir William Macpherson of Cluny, TD; Sir David Nickson, KBE; Maj. the Lord Glenarthur; Earl of Dalkeith
Adjutant, Maj. the Hon. Sir Lachlan Maclean, Bt.
Surgeon, Dr P. A. P. Mackenzie, TD
Chaplain, Very Revd R. Selby Wright, CVO, TD, DD, FRSE
President of the Council and Silver Stick for Scotland, Maj. Sir Hew Hamilton-Dalrymple, Bt., KCVO
Vice-President, Capt. Sir Iain Tennant, KT
Secretary, Col. H. F. O. Bewsher, LVO, OBE
Treasurer, J. Martin Haldane

HOUSEHOLD OF THE PRINCE PHILIP, DUKE OF EDINBURGH

Treasurer, Sir Brian McGrath, KCVO
Private Secretary, Brig. M. G. Hunt-Davis, CBE
Equerry, Wg Cdr. C. H. Moran
Extra Equerries, J. B. V. Orr, CVO; Sir Richard Davies, KCVO, CBE; Lord Buxton of Alsa; Brig. C. Robertson, CVO
Temporary Equerries, Maj. I. Grant, RM; Capt. G. Inglis-Jones; Capt. E. Bearcroft
Chief Clerk and Accountant, V. G. Jewell, MVO

HOUSEHOLD OF QUEEN ELIZABETH THE QUEEN MOTHER

Lord Chamberlain, The Earl of Crawford and Balcarres, PC
Private Secretary, Comptroller and Equerry, Capt. Sir Alastair Aird, KCVO
Assistant Private Secretary and Equerry, Maj. R. Seymour, CVO
Treasurer and Equerry, Maj. Sir Ralph Anstruther, Bt., GCVO, MC
Equerry, Capt. the Hon. E. Dawson-Damer (*temp.*)
Extra Equerries, Maj. Sir John Griffin, KCVO; The Lord Sinclair, CVO; Maj. W. Richardson, LVO; Maj. D. McMicking, LVO; Capt. A. Windham, LVO
Apothecary to the Household, Dr N. Southward, LVO, MB, B.chir.
Surgeon-Apothecary to the Household (Royal Lodge, Windsor), Dr J. Briscoe, D.obst.
Mistress of the Robes, vacant
Ladies of the Bedchamber, The Dowager Viscountess Hambleden, GCVO; The Lady Grimthorpe, CVO
Women of the Bedchamber, Dame Frances Campbell-Preston, DCVO; Lady Angela Oswald, LVO; The Hon. Mrs Rhodes; Mrs Michael Gordon-Lennox
Extra Women of the Bedchamber, Lady Victoria Wemyss, CVO; Lady Jean Rankin, DCVO; Miss Jane Walker-Okeover; Lady Margaret Colville; Lady Elizabeth Basset, DCVO
Clerk Comptroller, M. Blanch, CVO
Clerk Accountant, J. P. Kyle, LVO
Information Officer, Mrs R. Murphy, LVO
Clerks, Miss F. Fletcher, MVO; Mrs W. Stevens

HOUSEHOLD OF THE PRINCE AND PRINCESS OF WALES

Private Secretary and Treasurer to The Prince of Wales, Cdr. R. J. Aylard, RN
Private Secretary to the Princess of Wales, P. Jephson
Deputy Private Secretary to The Prince of Wales, S. Lamport.
Assistant Private Secretaries to The Prince of Wales,
  H. Merrill; Miss B. Harley
Press Secretary to the Prince of Wales, A. Percival
Assistant Press Secretary to the Prince of Wales, Miss
  A. Henney
Press Secretary to the Princess of Wales, G. Crawford
Equerry to The Prince of Wales, Cdr. R. Fraser
Equerry to The Princess of Wales, Capt. E. Musto, RM
Extra Equerries to The Prince of Wales, The Hon. Edward
  Adeane, CVO; Maj.-Gen. Sir Christopher Airy, KCVO, CBE;
  Sqn. Ldr. Sir David Checketts, KCVO; Sir David Landale,
  KCVO; Sir John Riddle, Bt., CVO; G. J. Ward, CBE; Col.
  J. Q. Winter, LVO
Ladies-in-Waiting, Miss Anne Beckwith-Smith, LVO;
  Viscountess Campden; Mrs Max Pike; Miss Alexandra
  Loyd; Mrs James Lonsdale
Extra Lady-in-Waiting, Lady Sarah McCorquodale
Secretary to the Duchy of Cornwall and Keeper of the Records,
  J. N. C. James, CBE

HOUSEHOLD OF THE DUKE AND DUCHESS OF YORK

*Private Secretary, Treasurer and Extra Equerry to the Duke
  and Duchess of York*, Capt. N. Blair, RN
*Comptroller and Assistant Private Secretary to the Duke and
  Duchess of York*, Mrs Jonathan Mathias
Equerry to The Duke of York, Capt. R. Maitland-Titterton
Extra Equerry, Maj. G. W. McLean

HOUSEHOLD OF THE PRINCE EDWARD

Private Secretary, Lt.-Col. S. G. O'Dwyer
Assistant Private Secretary, Mrs R. Warburton, MVO

HOUSEHOLD OF THE PRINCESS ROYAL

Private Secretary, Lt.-Col. P. Gibbs, LVO
Assistant Private Secretary, The Hon. Mrs Louloudis
Ladies-in-Waiting, Mrs Richard Carew Pole, LVO; Mrs
  Andrew Feilden, LVO; The Hon. Mrs Legge-Bourke, LVO;
  Mrs William Nunneley; Mrs Timothy Holderness-
  Roddam; Mrs Charles Ritchie; Mrs David Bowes Lyon
Extra Ladies-in-Waiting, Miss Victoria Legge-Bourke, LVO;
  Mrs Malcolm Innes, LVO; The Countess of Lichfield

HOUSEHOLD OF THE PRINCESS MARGARET, COUNTESS OF SNOWDON

Private Secretary and Comptroller, The Lord Napier and
  Ettrick, KCVO
Lady-in-Waiting, The Hon. Mrs Whitehead, LVO

Extra Ladies-in-Waiting, Lady Elizabeth Cavendish, LVO;
  Lady Aird, LVO; Mrs Robin Benson, LVO, OBE; Lady Juliet
  Townsend, LVO; Mrs Jane Stevens, LVO; The Hon. Mrs
  Wills, LVO; The Lady Glenconner, LVO; The Countess
  Alexander of Tunis, LVO; Mrs Charles Vyvyan

HOUSEHOLD OF THE DUKE AND DUCHESS OF GLOUCESTER

Private Secretary, Comptroller and Equerry, Maj.
  N. M. L. Barne
Assistant Private Secretary to The Duchess of Gloucester, Miss
  Suzanne Marland
Extra Equerry, Lt.-Col. Sir Simon Bland, KCVO
Ladies-in-Waiting, Mrs Michael Wigley, CVO; Mrs Euan
  McCorquodale, LVO; Mrs Howard Page
Extra Lady-in-Waiting, Miss Jennifer Thomson
Temporary Lady-in-Waiting, The Lady Camoys

HOUSEHOLD OF PRINCESS ALICE, DUCHESS OF GLOUCESTER

Private Secretary, Comptroller and Equerry, Maj.
  N. M. L. Barne
Extra Equerry, Lt.-Col. Sir Simon Bland, KCVO
Ladies-in-Waiting, Dame Jean Maxwell-Scott, DCVO; Mrs
  Michael Harvey
Extra Ladies-in-Waiting, Miss Diana Harrison; The Hon.
  Jane Walsh, LVO; Miss Jane Egerton-Warburton, LVO

HOUSEHOLD OF THE DUKE AND DUCHESS OF KENT

Private Secretary, Cdr. R. M. Walker
Extra Equerries, Lt.-Cdr. Sir Richard Buckley, KCVO; Cdr.
  R. M. Walker
Temporary Equerry, Capt. A. Tetley
Ladies-in-Waiting, Mrs Fiona Henderson, CVO; Mrs David
  Napier, LVO; Mrs Colin Marsh, LVO; Mrs Peter Wilmot-
  Sitwell, LVO; Mrs Julian Tomkins; Mrs Peter Troughton

HOUSEHOLD OF PRINCE AND PRINCESS MICHAEL OF KENT

Personal Secretary, Miss E. Moore-Searson
Equerry, Lt.-Col. Sir Christopher Thompson, Bt.
Ladies-in-Waiting, The Hon. Mrs Sanders; Miss Anne
  Frost; Lady Thompson
Extra Lady-in-Waiting, Mrs J. Fellowes

HOUSEHOLD OF PRINCESS ALEXANDRA, THE HON. LADY OGILVY

Comptroller and Private Secretary, Rear-Adm. Sir John
  Garnier, KCVO, CBE
Extra Equerry, Maj. Sir Peter Clarke, KCVO
Lady-in-Waiting, Lady Mary Mumford, LVO
Extra Ladies-in-Waiting, Mrs Peter Afia; Lady Mary
  Colman; Lady Nicholas Gordon Lennox; The Hon. Lady
  Rowley; Dame Mona Mitchell, DCVO

Royal Finances

FUNDING

THE CIVIL LIST

The Civil List dates back to the late 17th century, when it was used by the Sovereign to pay the salaries of judges, ambassadors and other government offices as well as the expenses of the royal household. In 1760 on the accession of George III it was decided that the Civil List would be provided by Parliament in return for the King surrendering the hereditary revenues of the Crown. Each sovereign since then has agreed to continue the arrangement.

The Civil List paid to The Queen is charged on the Consolidated Fund. Until 1972, the amount of money allocated annually under the Civil List was set for the duration of a reign. The system was then altered to a fixed annual payment for ten years but from 1975 high inflation made an annual review necessary. The system of payments reverted to the practice of a fixed annual payment for ten years from 1 January 1991.

The Civil List Acts provide for other members of the royal family to receive parliamentary annuities from government funds to meet the expenses of carrying out their official duties. Since 1975 The Queen has reimbursed the Treasury for the annuities paid to the Duke of Gloucester, the Duke of Kent and Princess Alexandra. In November 1992 it was announced that from 1 April 1993 The Queen will reimburse all the annuities except those paid to Queen Elizabeth Queen Mother and the Duke of Edinburgh.

The Prince of Wales does not receive a parliamentary annuity. He derives his income from the revenues of the Duchy of Cornwall and these monies meet the official and private expenses of the Prince of Wales and his family.

The annual payments for the years 1991–2000 are:

The Queen	£7,900,000
Queen Elizabeth the Queen Mother	643,000
The Duke of Edinburgh	359,000
*The Duke of York	249,000
*The Prince Edward	96,000
*The Princess Royal	228,000
*The Princess Margaret, Countess of Snowdon	219,000
*Princess Alice, Duchess of Gloucester	87,000
*The Duke of Gloucester	175,000
*The Duke of Kent	236,000
*Princess Alexandra	225,000
	10,237,000
*Refunded to the Treasury	1,515,000
Total	8,722,000

GRANT-IN-AID

Grant-in-aid is voted annually by Parliament to pay for the upkeep of the royal palaces which are used as royal residences or for official or ceremonial purposes.

THE PRIVY PURSE

The funds received by the Privy Purse pay for official expenses incurred by The Queen as head of state and for some of The Queen's private expenditure. The revenues of the Duchy of Lancaster are the principal source of income for the Privy Purse. The revenues of the Duchy were retained by George III in 1760 when the hereditary revenues were surrendered in exchange for the Civil List.

PERSONAL INCOME

The Queen's personal income derives mostly from investments, and is used to meet private expenditure.

DEPARTMENTAL VOTES

Other items of expenditure connected with the official duties of the royal family which fall on votes of government departments include:

The Royal Yacht; The Queen's Flight (Ministry of Defence)
Marshal of the Diplomatic Corps; overseas visits at the request of government departments (Foreign and Commonwealth Office)
Royal palaces (Department of National Heritage)
The Royal Train (Department of Transport)
Central Chancery of the Orders of Knighthood (HM Treasury)

TAXATION

The Sovereign is not legally liable to pay income tax, capital gains tax or inheritance tax. After income tax was reintroduced in 1842 some income tax was paid voluntarily by the Sovereign but over a long period these payments were phased out. In November 1992 the Prime Minister announced that The Queen had offered to pay tax on a voluntary basis from 6 April 1993, and that the Prince of Wales also wished to pay tax on a voluntary basis on his income from the Duchy of Cornwall. (He is already taxed in all other respects.)

The provisions for The Queen and the Prince of Wales to pay tax were set out in a Memorandum of Understanding on Royal Taxation presented to Parliament on 11 February 1993. The main provisions are that The Queen will pay income tax and capital gains tax in respect of her private income and assets, and on the proportion of the income and capital gains of the Privy Purse used for private purposes. Inheritance tax will be paid on The Queen's assets, except for those which pass to the next Sovereign, whether automatically or by gift or bequest. The Prince of Wales will pay income tax on income from the Duchy of Cornwall used for private purposes.

The Prince of Wales has confirmed that he intends to pay tax on the same basis following his accession to the throne.

Other members of the royal family are subject to tax as for any taxpayer.

Military Ranks and Titles

THE QUEEN

Lord High Admiral of the United Kingdom

Colonel-in-Chief
The Life Guards; The Blues and Royals (Royal Horse Guards and 1st Dragoons); The Royal Scots Dragoon Guards (Carabiniers and Greys); The Queen's Royal Lancers; Royal Tank Regiment; Corps of Royal Engineers; Grenadier Guards; Coldstream Guards; Scots Guards; Irish Guards; Welsh Guards; The Royal Welch Fusiliers; The Queen's Lancashire Regiment; The Argyll and Sutherland Highlanders (Princess Louise's); The Royal Green Jackets; Adjutant-General's Corps; The Governor-General's Horse Guards (of Canada); The King's Own Calgary Regiment; Canadian Forces Military Engineers Branch; Royal 22e Regiment (of Canada); Governor-General's Foot Guards (of Canada); The Canadian Grenadier Guards; Le Regiment de la Chaudiere (of Canada); 2nd Bn Royal New Brunswick Regiment (North Shore); The 48th Highlanders of Canada; The Argyll and Sutherland Highlanders of Canada (Princess Louise's); The Calgary Highlanders; Royal Australian Engineers; Royal Australian Infantry Corps; Royal Australian Army Ordnance Corps; Royal Australian Army Nursing Corps; The Corps of Royal New Zealand Engineers; Royal New Zealand Infantry Regiment; Royal New Zealand Army Ordnance Corps; Royal Malta Artillery; The Malawi Rifles

Captain-General
Royal Regiment of Artillery; The Honourable Artillery Company; Combined Cadet Force; Royal Regiment of Canadian Artillery; Royal Regiment of Australian Artillery; Royal Regiment of New Zealand Artillery; Royal New Zealand Armoured Corps

Patron
Royal Army Chaplains' Department

Air Commodore-in-Chief
Royal Auxiliary Air Force; Royal Air Force Regiment; Royal Observer Corps; Air Reserve (of Canada); Royal Australian Air Force Reserve

Commandant-in-Chief
Royal Air Force College, Cranwell

Hon. Air Commodore
RAF Marham

HM QUEEN ELIZABETH THE QUEEN MOTHER

Colonel-in-Chief
1st The Queen's Dragoon Guards; The Queen's Royal Hussars (The Queen's Own and Royal Irish); 9th/12th Royal Lancers (Prince of Wales's); The King's Regiment; The Royal Anglian Regiment; The Light Infantry; The Black Watch (Royal Highland Regiment); Royal Army Medical Corps; The Black Watch (Royal Highland Regiment) of Canada; The Toronto Scottish Regiment; Canadian Forces Medical Services; Royal Australian Army Medical Corps; Royal New Zealand Army Medical Corps

Hon. Colonel
The Royal Yeomanry; The London Scottish; Inns of Court and City Yeomanry

Commandant-in-Chief
Women's Royal Naval Service; Women's Royal Air Force; RAF Central Flying School

HRH THE PRINCE PHILIP, DUKE OF EDINBURGH

Admiral of the Fleet
Field Marshal
Marshal of the Royal Air Force

Admiral of the Fleet, Royal Australian Navy
Field Marshal, Australian Military Forces
Marshal of the Royal Australian Air Force

Admiral of the Fleet, Royal New Zealand Navy
Field Marshal, New Zealand Army
Marshal of the Royal New Zealand Air Force

Captain-General, Royal Marines

Admiral
Royal Canadian Sea Cadets

Colonel-in-Chief
The Duke of Edinburgh's Royal Regiment (Berkshire and Wiltshire); Queen's Own Highlanders (Seaforth and Camerons); Corps of Royal Electrical and Mechanical Engineers; Intelligence Corps; Army Cadet Force; The Royal Canadian Regiment; The Royal Hamilton Light Infantry (Wentworth Regiment) (of Canada); The Cameron Highlanders of Ottawa; The Queen's Own Cameron Highlanders of Canada; The Seaforth Highlanders of Canada; The Royal Canadian Army Cadets; The Royal Australian Corps of Electrical and Mechanical Engineers; The Australian Cadet Corps; The Royal New Zealand Corps of Electrical and Mechanical Engineers

Deputy Colonel-in-Chief
The Queen's Royal Hussars (The Queen's Own and Royal Irish)

Colonel
Grenadier Guards

Hon. Colonel
Edinburgh and Heriot-Watt Universities Officers' Training Corps; The Trinidad and Tobago Regiment

Air Commodore-in-Chief
Air Training Corps; Royal Canadian Air Cadets

Hon. Air Commodore
RAF Kinloss

HRH THE PRINCE OF WALES

Captain, Royal Navy
Group Captain, Royal Air Force

Colonel-in-Chief
The Royal Dragoon Guards; The Cheshire Regiment; The Royal Regiment of Wales (24th/41st Foot); The

Gordon Highlanders; The Parachute Regiment; 2nd King Edward VII's Own Gurkha Rifles (The Sirmoor Rifles); Army Air Corps; The Royal Canadian Dragoons; Lord Strathcona's Horse (Royal Canadians); Royal Regiment of Canada; Royal Winnipeg Rifles; Royal Australian Armoured Corps; 2nd Bn The Royal Pacific Islands Regiment

Colonel
Welsh Guards

Air Commodore-in-Chief
Royal New Zealand Air Force

Hon. Air Commodore
RAF Brawdy; RAF Valley

HRH THE PRINCESS OF WALES

Colonel-in-Chief
The Light Dragoons; The Princess of Wales's Royal Regiment (Queen's and Royal Hampshires); The Princess of Wales's Own Regiment (of Canada); The West Nova Scotia Regiment (of Canada); The Royal Australian Survey Corps

Hon. Air Commodore
RAF Wittering

HRH THE DUKE OF YORK

Lieutenant-Commander, Royal Navy

Admiral
Sea Cadet Corps

Colonel-in-Chief
The Staffordshire Regiment (The Prince of Wales's); The Royal Irish Regiment (27th (Inniskilling), 83rd, 87th and The Ulster Defence Regiment); Canadian Airborne Regiment

HRH THE PRINCESS ROYAL

Chief Commandant
Women's Royal Naval Service

Colonel-in-Chief
The King's Royal Hussars; Royal Corps of Signals; The Royal Scots (The Royal Regiment); The Worcestershire and Sherwood Foresters Regiment (29th/45th Foot); The Royal Logistic Corps; 8th Canadian Hussars (Princess Louise's); Canadian Forces Communications and Electronics Branch; The Grey and Simcoe Foresters; The Royal Regina Rifle Regiment; Royal Newfoundland Regiment; Royal Australian Corps of Signals; Royal New Zealand Corps of Signals; Royal New Zealand Nursing Corps

Hon. Colonel
London University Officers' Training Corps

Hon. Air Commodore
RAF Lyneham

Commandant-in-Chief
Women's Transport Service (FANY)

HRH THE PRINCESS MARGARET, COUNTESS OF SNOWDON

Colonel-in-Chief
The Royal Highland Fusiliers (Princess Margaret's Own Glasgow and Ayrshire Regiment); Queen Alexandra's Royal Army Nursing Corps; The Highland Fusiliers of Canada; The Princess Louise Fusiliers; The Bermuda Regiment

Deputy Colonel-in-Chief
The Royal Anglian Regiment

Hon. Air Commodore
RAF Coningsby

HRH PRINCESS ALICE, DUCHESS OF GLOUCESTER

Air Chief Marshal

Colonel-in-Chief
The King's Own Scottish Borderers; Royal Australian Corps of Transport; Royal New Zealand Corps of Transport

Deputy Colonel-in-Chief
The King's Royal Hussars; The Royal Anglian Regiment

Air Chief Commandant
Women's Royal Air Force

HRH THE DUKE OF GLOUCESTER

Colonel-in-Chief
The Gloucestershire Regiment

Deputy Colonel-in-Chief
The Royal Logistic Corps

Hon. Colonel
Royal Monmouthshire Royal Engineers (Militia)

Hon. Air Commodore
RAF Odiham

HRH THE DUCHESS OF GLOUCESTER

Colonel-in-Chief
Royal Australian Army Educational Corps; Royal New Zealand Educational Corps

Deputy Colonel-in-Chief
Adjutant-General's Corps

HRH THE DUKE OF KENT

Field Marshal
Hon. Air Vice-Marshal

Colonel-in-Chief
The Royal Regiment of Fusiliers; The Devonshire and Dorset Regiment; The Lorne Scots Regiment (Peel, Dufferin and Hamilton Regiment)

Colonel
Scots Guards

Hon. Air Commodore
RAF Leuchars

HRH THE DUCHESS OF KENT

Hon. Major-General

Colonel-in-Chief
The Prince of Wales's Own Regiment of Yorkshire

Deputy Colonel-in-Chief
The Royal Dragoon Guards; Adjutant-General's Corps;
The Royal Logistic Corps

HRH PRINCE MICHAEL OF KENT

Major (retd), The Royal Hussars (Prince of Wales's Own)

Hon. Auxiliary Commodore
Royal Naval Auxiliary Service

HRH PRINCESS ALEXANDRA, THE HON.
LADY OGILVY

Patron
Queen Alexandra's Royal Naval Nursing Service

Colonel-in-Chief
The King's Own Royal Border Regiment; The Queen's
Own Rifles of Canada; The Canadian Scottish Regiment
(Princess Mary's)

Deputy Colonel-in-Chief
The Queen's Royal Lancers; The Light Infantry

Deputy Hon. Colonel
The Royal Yeomanry

Patron and Air Chief Commandant
Princess Mary's Royal Air Force Nursing Service

The Royal Arms

ENGLAND

1st and 4th quarters (representing England) – Gules, three
lions passant guardant in pale Or
2nd quarter (representing Scotland) – Or, a lion rampant
within a double tressure flory counterflory Gules
3rd quarter (representing Ireland) – Azure, a harp Or,
stringed Argent
The whole shield is encircled with the Garter

SCOTLAND

The Royal Arms shown with the Lion of Scotland in the 1st
and 4th quarters, and the Lions of England in the 2nd
quarter
The whole shield is encircled with the Thistle

SUPPORTERS (ENGLAND)

Dexter (right) – a lion rampant guardant Or, imperially
crowned (shown in Scotland on the sinister)
Sinister (left) – a unicorn Argent, armed, crined, and
unguled Or, gorged with a coronet composed of crosses
patées and fleurs-de-lis, a chain affixed, passing between
the forelegs, and reflexed over the back (shown in
Scotland on the dexter and imperially crowned)

CRESTS

England – the Royal Crown Proper thereon a lion statant
guardant Or imperially crowned also Proper
Scotland – upon an imperial crown Proper a lion sejant
affrontée Gules imperially crowned Or, holding in the
dexter paw a sword and in the sinister a sceptre erect, also
Proper
Ireland – a tower triple-towered of the First, from the portal
a hart springing Argent, attired and hooved Or

BADGES

England – the red and white rose united, slipped and leaved
proper
Scotland – a thistle, slipped and leaved proper
Ireland – a shamrock leaf slipped vert; also a harp or,
stringed argent
United Kingdom – the rose of England, the thistle of
Scotland, and the shamrock of Ireland engrafted on the
same stem proper, and an escutcheon charged as the
Union Flag (all ensigned with the Royal Crown)
Wales – upon a mount vert a dragon passant, wings elevated
gules

The House of Windsor

King George V assumed by royal proclamation (17 June 1917) for his House and family, as well as for all descendants in the male line of Queen Victoria who are subjects of these realms, the name of Windsor.

KING GEORGE V (George Frederick Ernest Albert), second son of King Edward VII, born 3 June 1865; married 6 July 1893 HSH Princess Victoria Mary Augusta Louise Olga Pauline Claudine Agnes of Teck (Queen Mary, born 26 May 1867; died 24 March 1953); succeeded to the throne 6 May 1910; died 20 January 1936. Issue:

1. HRH PRINCE EDWARD Albert Christian George Andrew Patrick David, born 23 June 1894, succeeded to the throne as King Edward VIII, 20 January 1936; abdicated 11 December 1936; created Duke of Windsor, 1936; married 3 June 1937, Mrs Wallis Warfield (Her Grace The Duchess of Windsor, born 19 June 1896; died 24 April 1986), died 28 May 1972

2. HRH PRINCE ALBERT Frederick Arthur George, born 14 December 1895, created Duke of York 1920; married 26 April 1923, Lady Elizabeth Bowes-Lyon, youngest daughter of the 14th Earl of Strathmore and Kinghorne (HM Queen Elizabeth the Queen Mother, see page 123–4), succeeded to the throne as King George VI, 11 December 1936; died 6 Feburary 1952, having had issue (see page 123)

3. HRH PRINCESS (Victoria Alexandra Alice) MARY (Princess Royal), born 25 April 1897, married 28 February 1922, Viscount Lascelles, later the 6th Earl of Harewood (1882–1947), died 28 March 1965. Issue:

   (1) George Henry Hubert Lascelles, 7th Earl of Harewood, KBE, born 7 February 1923; married (1) 29 September 1949, Maria (Marion) Stein (marriage dissolved 1967); issue, (a) David Henry George, Viscount Lascelles, born 21 October 1950; (b) James

Edward, born 5 October 1953; (c) (Robert) Jeremy Hugh, born 14 February 1955; (2) 31 July 1967, Mrs Patricia Tuckwell; issue, (d) Mark Hubert, born 5 July 1964

   (2) Gerald David Lascelles, born 21 August 1924, married (1) 15 July 1952, Miss Angela Dowding (marriage dissolved 1978); issue, (a) Henry Ulick, born 19 May 1953; (2) 17 November 1978, Mrs Elizabeth Colvin; issue, (b) Martin David, born 9 February 1962

4. HRH PRINCE HENRY William Frederick Albert, born 31 March 1900, created Duke of Gloucester, Earl of Ulster and Baron Culloden 1928, married 6 November 1935, Lady Alice Christabel Montagu-Douglas-Scott, daughter of the 7th Duke of Buccleuch (HRH Princess Alice, Duchess of Gloucester, see page 124); died 10 June 1974. Issue:

   (1) HRH Prince William Henry Andrew Frederick, born 18 December 1941; accidentally killed 28 August 1972

   (2) HRH Prince Richard Alexander Walter George (HRH The Duke of Gloucester), see page 124

5. HRH PRINCE GEORGE Edward Alexander Edmund, born 20 December 1902, created Duke of Kent, Earl of St Andrews and Baron Downpatrick 1934, married 29 November 1934, HRH Princess Marina of Greece and Denmark (born 30 November OS, 1906; died 27 August 1968); killed on active service, 25 August 1942. Issue:

   (1) HRH Prince Edward George Nicholas Paul Patrick (HRH The Duke of Kent), see page 124

   (2) HRH Princess Alexandra Helen Elizabeth Olga Christabel (HRH Princess Alexandra, the Hon. Lady Ogilvy), see page 124

   (3) HRH Prince Michael George Charles Franklin (HRH Prince Michael of Kent), see page 124

6. HRH PRINCE JOHN Charles Francis, born 12 July 1905; died 18 January 1919

Descendants of Queen Victoria

QUEEN VICTORIA (Alexandrina Victoria), born 24 May 1819; succeeded to the throne 20 June 1837; married 10 February 1840 (Francis) Albert Augustus Charles Emmanuel, Duke of Saxony, Prince of Saxe-Coburg and Gotha (HRH Albert, Prince Consort, born 26 August 1819, died 14 December 1861); died 22 January 1901. Issue:

1. HRH PRINCESS VICTORIA Adelaide Mary Louisa (Princess Royal) (1840–1901), m. 1858, Frederic (1831–88), Emperor of Germany March–June 1888. Issue:

   (1) HIM Wilhelm II (1859–1941), Emperor of Germany 1888–1918, m. (1) 1881 Princess Augusta Victoria of Schleswig-Holstein-Sonderburg-Augustenburg (1858–1921); (2) 1922 Princess Hermine of Reuss (1887–1947). Issue:

   (a) Prince Wilhelm (1882–1951), Crown Prince 1888–1918, m. 1905 Duchess Cecilie of Mecklenburg-Schwerin; issue: Prince Wilhelm (1906–40); Prince Ludwig Ferdinand (b. 1907), m. 1938 Grand Duchess Kira (see page 135); Prince Hubertus (1909–50); Prince Friedrich Georg (1911–66); Princess Alexandrine Irene (1915–); Princess Cecilie (1917–75)

   (b) Prince Eitel-Friedrich (1883–1942), m. 1906 Duchess Sophie of Oldenburg (marriage dissolved 1926)

   (c) Prince Adalbert (1884–1948), m. 1914 Duchess Adelheid of Saxe-Meiningen; issue: Princess Victoria Marina (1917–81); Prince Wilhelm Victor (1919–89)

   (d) Prince August Wilhelm (1887–1949), m. 1908 Princess Alexandra of Schleswig-Holstein-Sonderburg-Glücksburg (marriage dissolved 1920); issue: Prince Alexander (1912–85)

   (e) Prince Oskar (1888–1958), m. 1914 Countess von Ruppin; issue: Prince Oskar (1915–39); Prince Burchard (1917–); Princess Herzeleide (1918–89); Prince Wilhelm (b. 1922)

   (f) Prince Joachim (1890–1920), m. 1916 Princess Marie of Anhalt; issue: Prince Karl (1916–75)

   (g) Princess Viktoria Luise (1892–1980), m. 1913 Ernst, Duke of Brunswick 1913–18 (1887–1953); issue: Prince Ernst (1914–87); Prince Georg (b. 1915), m. 1946 Princess Sophie of Greece (see page 135) and has issue (two sons, one daughter); Princess Frederika (1917–81), m. 1938 Paul I, King of the Hellenes (see page 135); Prince Christian (1919–81); Prince Welf Heinrich (b. 1923)

   (2) Princess Charlotte (1860–1919), m. 1878 Bernhard, Duke of Saxe-Meiningen 1914 (1851–1914). Issue: Princess Feodora (1879–1945), m. 1898 Prince Heinrich XXX of Reuss

   (3) Prince Heinrich (1862–1929), m. 1888 Princess Irene of Hesse (see page 135). Issue:

   (a) Prince Waldemar (1889–1945), m. Princess Calixsta of Lippe

   (b) Prince Sigismund (1896–1978), m. Princess Charlotte of Saxe-Altenburg; issue: Princess Barbe (b. 1920); Prince Alfred (b. 1924)

   (c) Prince Heinrich (1900–4)

   (4) Prince Sigismund (1864–6)

   (5) Princess Victoria (1866–1929), m. (1) 1890, Prince Adolf of Schaumburg-Lippe (1859–1916); (2) 1927 Alexander Zubkov

   (6) Prince Joachim Waldemar (1868–79)

   (7) Princess Sophie (1870–1932), m. 1889 Constantine I (1868–1923), King of the Hellenes 1913–17, 1920–3. Issue:

   (a) George II (1890–1947), King of the Hellenes 1923–4 and 1935–47, m. 1921 Princess Elisabeth of Roumania (marriage dissolved 1935), (see page 135)

   (b) Alexander I (1893–1920), King of the Hellenes 1917–20, m.

1919 Aspasia Manos; *issue:* Princess Alexandra (1921–93), *m.*
1944 King Petar II of Yugoslavia (*see* below)
(c) Princess Helena (1896–1982), *m.* 1921 King Carol of
Roumania (*see* below), (marriage dissolved 1928)
(d) Paul I (1901–64), King of the Hellenes 1947–64, *m.* 1938
Princess Frederika of Brunswick (*see* page 134); *issue:* King
Constantine II (*b.* 1940), *m.* 1964 Princess Anne-Marie of
Denmark (*see* page 136), and has issue (three sons, two
daughters); Princess Sophie (*b.* 1938), *m.* 1962 Juan Carlos I of
Spain (*see* page 136); Princess Irene (*b.* 1942)
(e) Princess Irene (1904–74), *m.* 1939 4th Duke of Aosta; *issue:*
Prince Amedeo (*b.* 1943)
(f) Princess Katherine (Lady Katherine Brandram) (*b.* 1913),
m. 1947 Major R. C. A. Brandram, MC, TD; *issue:* R. Paul G. A.
Brandram (*b.* 1948)
(8) Princess Margarethe (1872–1954), *m.* 1893 Prince Friedrich
Karl of Hesse (1868–1940). *Issue:*
(a) Prince Friedrich Wilhelm (1893–1916)
(b) Prince Maximilian (1894–1914)
(c) Prince Philipp (1896–1980), *m.* 1925 Princess Mafalda of
Italy; *issue:* Prince Moritz (*b.* 1926); Prince Heinrich (*b.* 1927);
Prince Otto (*b.* 1937); Princess Elisabeth (*b.* 1940)
(d) Prince Wolfgang (*b.* 1896), *m.* (1) 1924 Princess Marie
Alexandra of Baden; (2) 1948 Ottilie Möller
(e) Prince Richard (1901–)
(f) Prince Christoph (1901–43), *m.* 1930 Princess Sophie of
Greece (*see* below) and has issue (two sons, three daughters)

2. HRH PRINCE ALBERT EDWARD (HM KING EDWARD VII), *b.* 9
November 1841, *m.* 1863 HRH Princess Alexandra of Denmark
(1844–1925), *succeeded* to the throne 22 January 1901, *d.* 6 May 1910.
Issue:
(1) Albert Victor, Duke of Clarence and Avondale (1864–92)
(2) George (HM KING GEORGE V) (*see* page 134)
(3) Louise (1867–1931) Princess Royal 1905–31, *m.* 1889 1st
Duke of Fife (1849–1912). *Issue:*
(a) Princess Alexandra, Duchess of Fife (1891–1959), *m.* 1913
Prince Arthur of Connaught (*see* page 136)
(b) Princess Maud (1893–1945), *m.* 1923 11th Earl of Southesk
(1893–1992); *issue:* The Duke of Fife (*b.* 1929)
(4) Victoria (1868–1935)
(5) Maud (1869–1938), *m.* 1896 Prince Charles of Denmark
(1872–1957), later King Haakon VII of Norway 1905–57. *Issue:*
(a) Olav V, King of Norway 1957–91 (1903–91), *m.* 1929
Princess Märtha of Sweden (1901–54); *issue:* Princess Ragnhild
(*b.* 1930); Princess Astrid (*b.* 1932); Harald V, King of Norway
(*b.* 1937)
(6) Alexander (6–7 April 1871)

3. HRH PRINCESS ALICE Maud Mary (1843–78), *m.* 1862 Prince
Louis (1837–92), Grand Duke of Hesse 1877–92. *Issue:*
(1) Victoria (1863–1950), *m.* 1884 *Admiral of the Fleet* Prince
Louis of Battenberg (1854–1921), *cr.* 1st Marquess of Milford
Haven 1917. *Issue:*
(a) Alice (1885–1969), *m.* 1903 Prince Andrew of Greece
(1882–1944); *issue:* Princess Margarita (1905–81) *m.* 1931
Prince Gottfried of Hohenlohe-Langenburg (*see* below); Princess
Theodora (1906–69), *m.* Prince Berthold of Baden (1906–63)
and has issue (2 sons, one daughter); Princess Cecilie (1911–37),
m. George, Grand Duke of Hesse (*see* below); Princess Sophie (*b.*
1914), *m.* (1) 1930 Prince Christoph of Hesse (*see* above); (2)
1946 Prince Georg of Hanover (*see* page 134); Prince Philip,
Duke of Edinburgh (*b.* 1921) (*see* page 123)
(b) Louise (1889–1965), *m.* 1923 Gustaf VI Adolf (1882–1973),
King of Sweden 1950–73
(c) George, 2nd Marquess of Milford Haven (1892–1938), *m.*
1916 Countess Nadejda, daughter of Grand Duke Michael of
Russia; *issue:* Lady Tatiana (1917–88); David Michael, 3rd
Marquess (1919–70)
(d) Louis, 1st Earl Mountbatten of Burma (1900–79), *m.* 1922
Edwina Ashley, daughter of Lord Mount Temple; *issue:* Patricia,
Countess Mountbatten of Burma (*b.* 1924), Pamela (*b.* 1929)
(2) Elizabeth (1864–1918), *m.* 1884 Grand Duke Sergius of Russia
(1857–1905)
(3) Irene (1866–1953), *m.* 1888 Prince Heinrich of Prussia (*see*
page 134)
(4) Ernst Ludwig (1868–1937), Grand Duke of Hesse 1892–1918,
m. (1) 1894 Princess Victoria Melita of Saxe-Coburg (*see* below),
(marriage dissolved 1901); (2) 1905 Princess Eleonore of Solms-
Hohensolmslich. *Issue:*
(a) Princess Elizabeth (1895–1903)

(b) George, Grand Duke of Hesse (1906–37), *m.* Princess
Cecilie of Greece (*see* above), and had issue, 2 sons, accidentally
killed with parents 1937
(c) Ludwig, Grand Duke of Hesse (1908–68), *m.* 1937
Margaret, daughter of 1st Lord Geddes
(5) Frederick William (1870–3)
(6) Alix (Tsaritsa of Russia) (1872–1918), *m.* 1894 Nicholas II
(1868–1918) Tsar of All the Russias 1894–1917, assassinated 16
July 1918. *Issue:*
(a) Grand Duchess Olga (1895–1918)
(b) Grand Duchess Tatiana (1897–1918)
(c) Grand Duchess Marie (1899–1918)
(d) Grand Duchess Anastasia (1901–18)
(e) Alexis, Tsarevich of Russia (1904–18)
(7) Marie (1874–8)

4. HRH PRINCE ALFRED Ernest Albert, Duke of Edinburgh, *Admiral
of the Fleet* (1844–1900), *m.* 1874 Grand Duchess Marie
Alexandrovna of Russia (1853–1920); succeeded as Duke of Saxe-
Coburg and Gotha 22 August 1893. *Issue:*
(1) Alfred (Prince of Saxe-Coburg) (1874–99)
(2) Marie (1875–1938), *m.* 1893 Ferdinand (1865–1927), King of
Roumania (*see* below). *Issue:*
(a) Carol II (1893–1953), King of Roumania 1930–40, *m.* (2)
1921 Princess Helena of Greece (*see* above), (marriage dissolved
1928); *issue:* Michael (*b.* 1921), King of Roumania 1927–30,
1940–7, *m.* 1948 Princess Anne of Bourbon-Parma, and has
issue (five daughters)
(b) Elisabeth (1894–1956), *m.* 1921 George II, King of the
Hellenes (*see* page 134)
(c) Marie (1900–61), *m.* 1922 Alexander (1888–1934), King of
Yugoslavia 1921–34; *issue:* Petar II (1923–70), King of
Yugoslavia 1934–45, *m.* 1944 Princess Alexandra of Greece (*see*
above) and has issue (one son); Prince Tomislav (*b.* 1928), *m.* (1)
1957 Princess Margarita of Baden (daughter of Princess
Theodora of Greece and Prince Berthold of Baden, *see* above);
(2) 1982 Linda Bonney; and has issue (three sons, one daughter);
Prince Andrej (1929–90), *m.* (1) Princess Christina of Hesse
(daughter of Prince Christoph of Hesse and Princess Sophie of
Greece, *see* above); (2) 1963 Princess Kira-Melita of Leiningen
(*see* below); and has issue (three sons, one daughter)
(d) Prince Nicolas (1903–)
(e) Princess Ileana (1909–91), *m.* (1) 1931 Archduke Anton of
Austria; (2) 1954 Dr Stefan Issarescu; *issue:* Archduke Stefan (*b.*
1932); Archduchess Maria Ileana (1933–59); Archduchess
Alexandra (*b.* 1935); Archduke Dominic (*b.* 1937); Archduchess
Maria Magdalena (*b.* 1939); Archduchess Elisabeth (*b.* 1942)
(f) Prince Mircea (1913–16)
(3) Victoria Melita (1876–1936), *m.* (1) 1894 Grand Duke Ernst of
Hesse (*see* above) (marriage dissolved 1901); (2) 1905 the Grand
Duke Kirill of Russia (1876–1938). *Issue:*
(a) Marie Kirillovna (1907–51), *m.* 1925 Prince Friedrich Karl
of Leiningen; *issue:* Prince Emich (*b.* 1926); Prince Karl (*b.*
1928); Princess Kira-Melita (*b.* 1930), *m.* Prince Andrej of
Yugoslavia (*see* above); Princess Margarita (*b.* 1932); Princess
Mechtilde (*b.* 1936); Prince Friedrich (*b.* 1938)
(b) Kira Kirillovna (1909–67), *m.* 1938 Prince Ludwig of
Prussia (*see* page 134); *issue:* Prince Friedrich Wilhelm (*b.* 1939);
Prince Michael (*b.* 1940); Princess Marie (*b.* 1942); Princess Kira
(*b.* 1943); Prince Louis Ferdinand (1944–77); Prince Christian
(*b.* 1946); Princess Xenia (*b.* 1949)
(c) Vladimir Kirillovich (1917–92), *m.* 1948 Princess Leonida
Bagration-Mukhransky; *issue:* Grand Duchess Maria (*b.* 1953),
m. and has issue
(4) Alexandra (1878–1942), *m.* 1896 Ernst, Prince of Hohenlohe
Langenburg. *Issue:*
(a) Gottfried (1897–1960), *m.* 1931 Princess Margarita of
Greece (*see* above); *issue:* Prince Kraft (*b.* 1935), Princess Beatrix
(*b.* 1936), Prince George (*b.* 1938), Prince Ruprecht and Prince
Albrecht (*b.* 1944)
(b) Marie (1899–1967), *m.* 1916 Prince Frederick of Schleswig-
Holstein-Sonderburg-Glücksburg; *issue:* Prince Peter (1922–80);
Princess Marie (*b.* 1927)
(c) Princess Alexandra (1901–63)
(d) Princess Irma (1902–)
(5) Princess Beatrice (1884–1966), *m.* 1909 Alfonso of Orleans,
Infante of Spain. *Issue:*
(a) Prince Alvaro (*b.* 1910), *m.* 1937 Carla Parodi-Delfino; *issue:*
Princess Gerarda (*b.* 1939); Prince Alonso (1941–75); Princess
Beatriz (*b.* 1943); Prince Alvaro (*b.* 1947)

(b) Prince Alonso (1912–36)
(c) Prince Ataulfo (1913–)

5. HRH PRINCESS HELENA Augusta Victoria (1846–1923), m. 1866 Prince Christian of Schleswig-Holstein-Sonderburg-Augustenburg (1831–1917). Issue:
(1) Prince Christian Victor (1867–1900)
(2) Prince Albert (1869–1931), Duke of Schleswig-Holstein 1921–31
(3) Princess Helena (1870–1948)
(4) Princess Marie Louise (1872–1956), m. 1891 Prince Aribert of Anhalt (marriage dissolved 1900)
(5) Prince Harold (12–20 May 1876)

6. HRH PRINCESS LOUISE Caroline Alberta (1848–1939), m. 1871 the Marquess of Lorne, afterwards 9th Duke of Argyll (1845–1914); without issue

7. HRH PRINCE ARTHUR William Patrick Albert, Duke of Connaught, Field Marshal (1850–1942), m. 1879 Princess Louisa of Prussia (1860–1917). Issue:
(1) Margaret (1882–1920), m. 1905 Crown Prince Gustaf Adolf (1882–1973), afterwards King of Sweden 1950–73. Issue:
    (a) Gustaf Adolf, Duke of Västerbotten (1906–47), m. 1932 Princess Sibylla of Saxe-Coburg-Gotha (see below); issue: Princess Margaretha (b. 1934); Princess Birgitta (b. 1937); Princess Désirée (b. 1938); Princess Christina (b. 1943); Carl XVI Gustaf, King of Sweden (b. 1946)
    (b) Count Sigvard Bernadotte (b. 1907); m., issue: Count Michael (b. 1944)
    (c) Princess Ingrid (Queen Mother of Denmark) (b. 1910), m. 1935 Frederick IX (1899–72), King of Denmark 1947–72; issue: Margrethe II, Queen of Denmark (b. 1940); Princess Benedikte (b. 1944); Princess Anne-Marie (b. 1946), m. 1964 Constantine II of Greece (see page 135)
    (d) Prince Bertil, Duke of Halland (b. 1912), m. 1976 Mrs Lilian Craig
    (e) Count Carl Bernadotte (b. 1916), m. (1) 1946 Mrs Kerstin Johnson; (2) 1988 Countess Gunnila Busler
(2) Arthur (1883–1938), m. 1913 HH the Duchess of Fife (see page 135). Issue:
    Alastair Arthur, Duke of Connaught (1914–43)

(3) (Victoria) Patricia (1886–1974), m. 1919 Adm. Hon. Sir Alexander Ramsay. Issue:
    Alexander Ramsay of Mar (b. 1919), m. 1956 Hon. Flora Fraser (Lady Saltoun)

8. HRH PRINCE LEOPOLD George Duncan Albert, Duke of Albany (1853–84), m. 1882 Princess Helena of Waldeck (1861–1922). Issue:
(1) Alice (1883–1981), m. 1904 Prince Alexander of Teck (1874–1957), cr. 1st Earl of Athlone 1917. Issue:
    (a) Lady May (b. 1906), m. 1931 Sir Henry Abel-Smith, KCMG, KCVO, DSO; issue: Anne (b. 1932); Richard (b. 1933); Elizabeth (b. 1936)
    (b) Rupert, Viscount Trematon (1907–28)
    (c) Prince Maurice (March–September 1910)
(2) Charles Edward (1884–1954), Duke of Albany 1884 until title suspended 1917, Duke of Saxe-Coburg-Gotha 1900–18, m. 1905 Princess Victoria Adelheid of Schleswig-Holstein-Sonderburg-Glücksburg. Issue:
    (a) Prince Johann (1906–72), and has issue
    (b) Princess Sibylla (1908–72) m. 1932 Prince Gustav Adolf of Sweden (see above)
    (c) Prince Dietmar (1909–)
    (d) Princess Caroline (1912–83)
    (e) Prince Friedrich (b. 1918)

9. HRH PRINCESS BEATRICE Mary Victoria Feodore (1857–1944), m. 1885 Prince Henry of Battenberg (1858–96). Issue:
(1) Alexander, 1st Marquess of Carisbrooke (1886–1960), m. 1917 Lady Irene Denison. Issue:
    Lady Iris Mountbatten (1920–82)
(2) Victoria Eugénie (1887–1969), m. 1906 Alfonso XIII (1886–1941) King of Spain 1886–1931. Issue:
    (a) Prince Alfonso (1907–38)
    (b) Prince Jaime (1908–75)
    (c) Princess Beatrice (b. 1909)
    (d) Princess Maria (b. 1911)
    (e) Prince Juan (1913–93) Count of Barcelona, and has issue: Princess Maria (b. 1936); Juan Carlos I, King of Spain (b. 1938), m. 1962 Princess Sophie of Greece (see page 135) and has issue (1 son, 2 daughters); Princess Margarita (b. 1939)
    (f) Prince Gonzale (1914–34)
(3) Major Lord Leopold Mountbatten (1889–1922)
(4) Maurice (1891–1914), died of wounds received in action

English Kings and Queens 927 TO 1603

HOUSES OF CERDIC AND DENMARK

Reign
927–939   ÆTHELSTAN
            Second son of Edward the Elder, by Ecgwynn, and grandson of Alfred
            Acceded to Wessex and Mercia c.924, established direct rule over Northumbria 927, effectively creating the Kingdom of England
            Reigned 15 years
939–946   EDMUND I
            Born 921, fourth son of Edward the Elder, by Eadgifu
            Married (1) Ælfgifu (2) Æthelflæd
            Killed aged 25, reigned 6 years
946–955   EADRED
            Fifth son of Edward the Elder, by Eadgifu
            Reigned 9 years
955–959   EADWIG
            Born before 943, son of Edmund and Ælfgifu
            Married Ælfgifu
            Reigned 3 years
959–975   EDGAR I
            Born 943, son of Edmund and Ælfgifu
            Married (1) Aethelflæd (2) Wulfthryth (3) Ælfthryth
            Died aged 32, reigned 15 years

975–978   EDWARD I (the Martyr)
            Born c.962, son of Edgar and Æthelflæd
            Assassinated aged c.16, reigned 2 years
978–1016   ÆTHELRED (the Unready)
            Born c.968/969, son of Edgar and Ælfthryth
            Married (1) Ælfgifu (2) Emma, daughter of Richard I, count of Normandy
            1013–14 dispossessed of kingdom by Swegn Forkbeard (king of Denmark 987–1014)
            Died aged c.47, reigned 38 years
1016   EDMUND II (Ironside)
            Born before 993, son of Æthelred and Ælfgifu
            Married Ealdgyth
            Died aged over 23, reigned 7 months (April–November)
1016–1035 CNUT (Canute)
            Born c.995, son of Swegn Forkbeard, king of Denmark, and Gunhild
            Married (1) Ælfgifu (2) Emma, widow of Æthelred the Unready
            Gained submission of West Saxons 1015, Northumbrians 1016, Mercia 1016, king of all England after Edmund's death
            King of Denmark 1019–35, king of Norway 1028–35
            Died aged c.40, reigned 19 years

1035–1040   HAROLD I (Harefoot)
Born c.1016/17, son of Cnut and Ælfgifu
Married Ælfgifu
1035 recognized as regent for himself and his brother
Harthacnut; 1037 recognized as king
Died aged c.23, reigned 4 years

1040–1042   HARTHACNUT
Born c.1018, son of Cnut and Emma
Titular king of Denmark from 1028
Acknowledged king of England 1035–7 with Harold I
as regent; effective king after Harold's death
Died aged c.24, reigned 2 years

1042–1066   EDWARD II (the Confessor)
Born between 1002 and 1005, son of Æthelred the
Unready and Emma
Married Eadgyth, daughter of Godwine, earl of Wessex
Died aged over 60, reigned 23 years

1066   HAROLD II (Godwinesson)
Born c.1020, son of Godwine, earl of Wessex, and
Gytha
Married (1) Eadgyth (2) Ealdgyth
Killed in battle aged c.46, reigned 10 months (January–
October)

THE HOUSE OF NORMANDY

1066–1087   WILLIAM I (the Conqueror)
Born 1027/8, son of Robert I, duke of Normandy;
obtained the Crown by conquest
Married Matilda, daughter of Baldwin, count of
Flanders
Died aged c.60, reigned 20 years

1087–1100   WILLIAM II (Rufus)
Born between 1056 and 1060, third son of William I;
succeeded his father in England only
Killed aged c.40, reigned 12 years

1100–1135   HENRY I (Beauclerk)
Born 1068, fourth son of William I
Married (1) Edith or Matilda, daughter of Malcolm III
of Scotland (2) Adela, daughter of Godfrey, count of
Louvain
Died aged 67, reigned 35 years

1135–1154   STEPHEN
Born not later than 1100, third son of Adela, daughter
of William I, and Stephen, count of Blois
Married Matilda, daughter of Eustace, count of
Boulogne
1141 (February–November) held captive by adherents
of Matilda, daughter of Henry I, who contested the
crown until 1153
Died aged over 53, reigned 18 years

THE HOUSE OF ANJOU (PLANTAGENETS)

1154–1189   HENRY II (Curtmantle)
Born 1133, son of Matilda, daughter of Henry I, and
Geoffrey, count of Anjou
Married Eleanor, daughter of William, duke of
Aquitaine, and divorced queen of Louis VII of France
Died aged 56, reigned 34 years

1189–1199   RICHARD I (Coeur de Lion)
Born 1157, third son of Henry II
Married Berengaria, daughter of Sancho VI, king of
Navarre
Died aged 42, reigned 9 years

1199–1216   JOHN (Lackland)
Born 1167, fifth son of Henry II
Married (1) Isabella or Avisa, daughter of William, earl
of Gloucester (divorced) (2) Isabella, daughter of
Aymer, count of Angoulême
Died aged 48, reigned 17 years

1216–1272   HENRY III
Born 1207, son of John and Isabella of Angoulême

Married Eleanor, daughter of Raymond, count of
Provence
Died aged 65, reigned 56 years

1272–1307   EDWARD I (Longshanks)
Born 1239, eldest son of Henry III
Married (1) Eleanor, daughter of Ferdinand III, king
of Castile (2) Margaret, daughter of Philip III of
France
Died aged 68, reigned 34 years

1307–1327   EDWARD II
Born 1284, eldest surviving son of Edward I and
Eleanor
Married Isabella, daughter of Philip IV of France
Deposed January 1327, killed September 1327 aged 43,
reigned 19 years

1327–1377   EDWARD III
Born 1312, eldest son of Edward II
Married Philippa, daughter of William, count of
Hainault
Died aged 64, reigned 50 years

1377–1399   RICHARD II
Born 1367, son of Edward (the Black Prince), eldest
son of Edward III
Married (1) Anne, daughter of Emperor Charles IV
(2) Isabelle, daughter of Charles VI of France
Deposed September 1399, killed February 1400 aged
33, reigned 22 years

THE HOUSE OF LANCASTER

1399–1413   HENRY IV
Born 1366, son of John of Gaunt, fourth son of Edward
III, and Blanche, daughter of Henry, duke of
Lancaster
Married (1) Mary, daughter of Humphrey, earl of
Hereford (2) Joan, daughter of Charles, king of
Navarre, and widow of John, duke of Brittany
Died aged c.47, reigned 13 years

1413–1422   HENRY V
Born 1387, eldest surviving son of Henry IV and Mary
Married Catherine, daughter of Charles VI of France
Died aged 34, reigned 9 years

1422–1471   HENRY VI
Born 1421, son of Henry V
Married Margaret, daughter of René, duke of Anjou
and count of Provence
Deposed March 1461, restored October 1470
Deposed April 1471, killed May 1471 aged 49, reigned
39 years

THE HOUSE OF YORK

1461–1483   EDWARD IV
Born 1442, eldest son of Richard of York, who was the
grandson of Edmund, fifth son of Edward III, and the
son of Anne, great-granddaughter of Lionel, third son
of Edward III
Married Elizabeth Woodville, daughter of Richard,
Lord Rivers, and widow of Sir John Grey
Acceded March 1461, deposed October 1470, restored
April 1471
Died aged 40, reigned 21 years

1483   EDWARD V
Born 1470, eldest son of Edward IV
Deposed June 1483, died probably July–September
1483, aged 12, reigned 2 months (April–June)

1483–1485   RICHARD III
Born 1452, fourth son of Richard of York and brother
of Edward IV
Married Anne Neville, daughter of Richard, earl of
Warwick, and widow of Edward, Prince of Wales, son
of Henry VI
Killed in battle aged 32, reigned 2 years

THE HOUSE OF TUDOR

1485–1509	HENRY VII *Born* 1457, son of Margaret Beaufort, great-granddaughter of John of Gaunt, fourth son of Edward III, and Edmund Tudor, earl of Richmond *Married* Elizabeth, daughter of Edward IV *Died* aged 52, *reigned* 23 years
1509–1547	HENRY VIII *Born* 1491, second son of Henry VII *Married* (1) Catherine, daughter of Ferdinand II, king of Aragon, and widow of his elder brother Arthur (divorced) (2) Anne, daughter of Sir Thomas Boleyn (executed) (3) Jane, daughter of Sir John Seymour (died in childbirth) (4) Anne, daughter of John, duke of Cleves (divorced) (5) Catherine Howard, niece of the Duke of Norfolk (executed) (6) Catherine, daughter of Sir Thomas Parr and widow of Lord Latimer *Died* aged 55, *reigned* 37 years
1547–1553	EDWARD VI *Born* 1537, son of Henry VIII and Jane Seymour *Died* aged 15, *reigned* 6 years
1553	JANE *Born* 1537, daughter of Frances, daughter of Mary Tudor, the younger sister of Henry VIII, and Henry Grey, duke of Suffolk *Married* Lord Guildford Dudley, son of the Duke of Northumberland *Deposed* July 1553, *executed* February 1554 aged 16, *reigned* 14 days
1553–1558	MARY I *Born* 1516, daughter of Henry VIII and Catherine of Aragon *Married* Philip II of Spain *Died* aged 42, *reigned* 5 years
1558–1603	ELIZABETH I *Born* 1533, daughter of Henry VIII and Anne Boleyn *Died* aged 69, *reigned* 44 years

British Kings and Queens SINCE 1603

THE HOUSE OF STUART

1603–1625	JAMES I (VI OF SCOTLAND) *Born* 1566, son of Mary, queen of Scots and granddaughter of Margaret Tudor, elder daughter of Henry VII, and Henry Stewart, Lord Darnley *Married* Anne, daughter of Frederick II of Denmark *Died* aged 58, *reigned* 22 years (*see also* page 140)
1625–1649	CHARLES I *Born* 1600, second son of James I *Married* Henrietta Maria, daughter of Henry VI of France *Executed* 1649 aged 48, *reigned* 23 years COMMONWEALTH DECLARED 19 May 1649 1649–53 Government by a council of state 1653–8 Oliver Cromwell, *Lord Protector* 1658–9 Richard Cromwell, *Lord Protector*
1660–1685	CHARLES II *Born* 1630, eldest son of Charles I *Married* Catherine, daughter of John IV of Portugal *Died* aged 54, *reigned* 24 years
1685–1688	JAMES II (VII of Scotland) *Born* 1633, second son of Charles I *Married* (1) Lady Anne Hyde, daughter of Edward, earl of Clarendon (2) Mary, daughter of Alphonso, duke of Modena Reign ended with flight from kingdom December 1688 *Died* 1701 aged 67, *reigned* 3 years INTERREGNUM 11 December 1688 to 12 February 1689
1689–1702	WILLIAM III *Born* 1650, son of William II, prince of Orange, and Mary Stuart, daughter of Charles I *Married* Mary, elder daughter of James II *Died* aged 51, *reigned* 13 years
and 1689–1694	MARY II *Born* 1662, elder daughter of James II and Anne *Died* aged 32, *reigned* 5 years
1702–1714	ANNE *Born* 1665, younger daughter of James II and Anne *Married* Prince George of Denmark, son of Frederick III of Denmark *Died* aged 49, *reigned* 12 years

THE HOUSE OF HANOVER

1714–1727	GEORGE I (Elector of Hanover) *Born* 1660, son of Sophia (daughter of Frederick, elector palatine, and Elizabeth Stuart, daughter of James I) and Ernest Augustus, elector of Hanover *Married* Sophia Dorothea, daughter of George William, duke of Lüneburg-Celle *Died* aged 67, *reigned* 12 years
1727–1760	GEORGE II *Born* 1683, son of George I *Married* Caroline, daughter of John Frederick, margrave of Brandenburg-Anspach *Died* aged 76, *reigned* 33 years
1760–1820	GEORGE III *Born* 1738, son of Frederick, eldest son of George II *Married* Charlotte, daughter of Charles Louis, duke of Mecklenburg-Strelitz *Died* aged 81, *reigned* 59 years REGENCY 1811–20 Prince of Wales regent owing to the insanity of George III
1820–1830	GEORGE IV *Born* 1762, eldest son of George III *Married* Caroline, daughter of Charles, duke of Brunswick-Wolfenbüttel *Died* aged 67, *reigned* 10 years
1830–1837	WILLIAM IV *Born* 1765, third son of George III *Married* Adelaide, daughter of George, duke of Saxe-Meiningen *Died* aged 71, *reigned* 7 years
1837–1901	VICTORIA *Born* 1819, daughter of Edward, fourth son of George III *Married* Prince Albert of Saxe-Coburg and Gotha *Died* aged 81, *reigned* 63 years

THE HOUSE OF SAXE-COBURG AND GOTHA

1901–1910 EDWARD VII
Born 1841, eldest son of Victoria and Albert
Married Alexandra, daughter of Christian IX of
Denmark
Died aged 68, reigned 9 years

THE HOUSE OF WINDSOR

1910–1936 GEORGE V
Born 1865, second son of Edward VII
Married Victoria Mary, daughter of Francis, duke of
Teck
Died aged 70, reigned 25 years

1936 EDWARD VIII
Born 1894, eldest son of George V
Married (1937) Mrs Wallis Warfield
Abdicated 1936, died 1972 aged 77, reigned 10 months
(20 January to 11 December)

1936–1952 GEORGE VI
Born 1895, second son of George V
Married Lady Elizabeth Bowes-Lyon, daughter of 14th
Earl of Strathmore and Kinghorne (see also pages
123–4)
Died aged 56, reigned 15 years

1952– ELIZABETH II
Born 1926, elder daughter of George VI
Married Philip, son of Prince Andrew of Greece (see
also page 123)
WHOM GOD PRESERVE

Kings and Queens of Scots 1016 TO 1603

Reign
1016–1034 MALCOLM II
Born c.954, son of Kenneth II
Acceded to Alba 1005, secured Lothian c.1016,
obtained Strathclyde for his grandson Duncan c.1016,
thus forming the Kingdom of Scotland
Died aged c.80, reigned 18 years

1034–1040 DUNCAN I
Son of Bethoc, daughter of Malcolm II, and Crinan
Married a cousin of Siward, earl of Northumbria
Reigned 5 years

1040–1057 MACBETH
Born c.1005, son of a daughter of Malcolm II and
Finlaec, mormaer of Moray
Married Gruoch, granddaughter of Kenneth III
Died aged c.52, reigned 17 years

1057–1058 LULACH
Born c.1032, son of Gillacomgan, mormaer of Moray,
and Gruoch (and stepson of Macbeth)
Died aged c.26, reigned 7 months (August–March)

1058–1093 MALCOLM III (Canmore)
Born c.1031, elder son of Duncan I
Married (1) Ingibiorg (2) Margaret (St Margaret),
granddaughter of Edmund II of England
Killed in battle aged c.62, reigned 35 years

1093–1097 DONALD III BÁN
Born c.1033, second son of Duncan I
Deposed May 1094, restored November 1094, deposed
October 1097, reigned 3 years

1094 DUNCAN II
Born c.1060, elder son of Malcolm III and Ingibiorg
Married Octreda of Dunbar
Killed aged c.34, reigned 6 months (May–November)

1097–1107 EDGAR
Born c.1074, second son of Malcolm III and Margaret
Died aged c.32, reigned 9 years

1107–1124 ALEXANDER I (The Fierce)
Born c.1077, fifth son of Malcolm III and Margaret
Married Sybilla, illegitimate daughter of Henry I of
England
Died aged c.47, reigned 17 years

1124–1153 DAVID I (The Saint)
Born c.1085, sixth son of Malcolm III and Margaret
Married Matilda, daughter of Waltheof, earl of
Huntingdon
Died aged c.68, reigned 29 years

1153–1165 MALCOLM IV (The Maiden)
Born c.1141, son of Henry, earl of Huntingdon, second
son of David I
Died aged c.24, reigned 12 years

1165–1214 WILLIAM I (The Lion)
Born c.1142, brother of Malcolm IV
Married Ermengarde, daughter of Richard, viscount of
Beaumont
Died aged c.72, reigned 49 years

1214–1249 ALEXANDER II
Born 1198, son of William I
Married (1) Joan, daughter of John, king of England
(2) Marie, daughter of Ingelram de Coucy
Died aged 50, reigned 34 years

1249–1286 ALEXANDER III
Born 1241, son of Alexander II and Marie
Married (1) Margaret, daughter of Henry III of
England (2) Yolande, daughter of the Count of Dreux
Killed accidentally aged 44, reigned 36 years

1286–1290 MARGARET (The Maid of Norway)
Born 1283, daughter of Margaret (daughter of
Alexander III) and Eric II of Norway
Died aged 7, reigned 4 years

FIRST INTERREGNUM 1290–2
Throne disputed by 13 competitors. Crown awarded to
John Balliol by adjudication of Edward I of England

THE HOUSE OF BALLIOL

1292–1296 JOHN (Balliol)
Born c.1250, son of Dervorguilla, great-great-
granddaughter of David I, and John de Balliol
Married Isabella, daughter of John, earl of Surrey
Abdicated 1296, died 1313 aged c.63, reigned 3 years

SECOND INTERREGNUM 1296–1306
Edward I of England declared John Balliol to have
forfeited the throne for contumacy in 1296 and took
the government of Scotland into his own hands

THE HOUSE OF BRUCE

1306–1329 ROBERT I (Bruce)
Born 1274, son of Robert Bruce and Marjorie, countess
of Carrick, and great-grandson of the second daughter

of David, earl of Huntingdon, brother of William I
Married (1) Isabella, daughter of Donald, earl of Mar
(2) Elizabeth, daughter of Richard, earl of Ulster
Died aged 54, reigned 23 years

1329–1371   DAVID II
Born 1324, son of Robert I and Elizabeth
Married (1) Joanna, daughter of Edward II of England
(2) Margaret Drummond, widow of Sir John Logie
(divorced)
Died aged 46, reigned 41 years

1332 Edward Balliol, son of John Balliol, crowned
King of Scots September, expelled December
1333–6 Edward Balliol restored as King of Scots

THE HOUSE OF STEWART

1371–1390   ROBERT II (Stewart)
Born 1316, son of Marjorie, daughter of Robert I, and
Walter, High Steward of Scotland
Married (1) Elizabeth, daughter of Sir Robert Mure of
Rowallan (2) Euphemia, daughter of Hugh, earl of
Ross
Died aged 74, reigned 19 years

1390–1406   ROBERT III
Born c.1337, son of Robert II and Elizabeth
Married Annabella, daughter of Sir John Drummond of
Stobhall
Died aged c.69, reigned 16 years

1406–1437   JAMES I
Born 1394, son of Robert III
Married Joan Beaufort, daughter of John, earl of
Somerset
Assassinated aged 42, reigned 30 years

1437–1460   JAMES II
Born 1430, son of James I
Married Mary, daughter of Arnold, duke of Gueldres
Killed accidentally aged 29, reigned 23 years

1460–1488   JAMES III
Born 1452, son of James II
Married Margaret, daughter of Christian I of Denmark
Assassinated aged 36, reigned 27 years

1488–1513   JAMES IV
Born 1473, son of James III
Married Margaret Tudor, daughter of Henry VII of
England
Killed in battle aged 40, reigned 25 years

1513–1542   JAMES V
Born 1512, son of James IV
Married (1) Madeleine, daughter of Francis I of France
(2) Mary of Lorraine, daughter of the Duc de Guise
Died aged 30, reigned 29 years

1542–1567   MARY
Born 1542, daughter of James V and Mary
Married (1) the Dauphin, afterwards Francis II of
France (2) Henry Stewart, Lord Darnley (3) James
Hepburn, earl of Bothwell
Abdicated 1567, prisoner in England from 1568,
executed 1587, reigned 24 years

1567–1625   JAMES VI (and I of England)
Born 1566, son of Mary, queen of Scots, and Henry,
Lord Darnley
Acceded 1567 to the Scottish throne, reigned 58 years
Succeeded 1603 to the English throne, so joining the
English and Scottish crowns in one person. The two
kingdoms remained distinct until 1707 when the
parliaments of the kingdoms became conjoined
For British Kings and Queens since 1603, see pages
138–9

Welsh Sovereigns and Princes

Wales was ruled by sovereign princes from the earliest times until the
death of Llywelyn in 1282. The first English Prince of Wales was the
son of Edward I, who was born in Caernarvon town on 25 April 1284.
According to a discredited legend, he was presented to the Welsh
chieftains as their prince, in fulfilment of a promise that they should
have a prince who 'could not speak a word of English' and should be
native born. This son, who afterwards became Edward II, was created
'Prince of Wales and Earl of Chester' at the Lincoln Parliament on 7
February 1301.

The title Prince of Wales is borne after individual conferment and is
not inherited at birth, though some Princes have been declared and
styled Prince of Wales but never formally so created (s.). The title was
conferred on Prince Charles by The Queen on 26 July 1958. He was
invested at Caernarvon on 1 July 1969.

INDEPENDENT PRINCES AD 844 TO 1282

844–878	Rhodri the Great
878–916	Anarawd, son of Rhodri
916–950	Hywel Dda, the Good
950–979	Iago ab Idwal (or Ieuaf)
979–985	Hywel ab Ieuaf, the Bad
985–986	Cadwallon, his brother
986–999	Maredudd ab Owain ap Hywel Dda
999–1008	Cynan ap Hywel ab Ieuaf
1018–1023	Llywelyn ap Seisyll
1023–1039	Iago ab Idwal ap Meurig
1039–1063	Gruffydd ap Llywelyn ap Seisyll
1063–1075	Bleddyn ap Cynfyn
1075–1081	Trahaern ap Caradog
1081–1137	Gruffydd ap Cynan ab Iago
1137–1170	Owain Gwynedd

1170–1194	Dafydd ab Owain Gwynedd
1194–1240	Llywelyn Fawr, the Great
1240–1246	Dafydd ap Llywelyn
1246–1282	Llywelyn ap Gruffydd ap Llywelyn

ENGLISH PRINCES SINCE 1301

1301	Edward (Edward II)
1343	Edward the Black Prince, s. of Edward III
1376	Richard (Richard II), s. of the Black Prince
1399	Henry of Monmouth (Henry V)
1454	Edward of Westminster, son of Henry VI
1471	Edward of Westminster (Edward V)
1483	Edward, son of Richard III (d. 1484)
1489	Arthur Tudor, son of Henry VII
1504	Henry Tudor (Henry VIII)
1610	Henry Stuart, son of James I (d. 1612)
1616	Charles Stuart (Charles I)
c.1638 (s.)	Charles (Charles II)
1688 (s.)	James Francis Edward (The Old Pretender) (d. 1766)
1714	George Augustus (George II)
1729	Frederick Lewis, s. of George II (d. 1751)
1751	George William Frederick (George III)
1762	George Augustus Frederick (George IV)
1841	Albert Edward (Edward VII)
1901	George (George V)
1910	Edward (Edward VIII)
1958	Charles Philip Arthur George

The Peerage

and Members of the House of Lords

The rules which govern the creation and succession of peerages are extremely complicated. There are, technically, five separate peerages, the Peerage of England, of Scotland, of Ireland, of Great Britain, and of the United Kingdom. The Peerage of Great Britain dates from 1707 when an Act of Union combined the two Kingdoms of England and Scotland and separate peerages were discontinued. The Peerage of the United Kingdom dates from 1801 when Great Britain and Ireland were combined under an Act of Union. Some Scottish peers have received additional peerages of Great Britain or of the United Kingdom since 1707, and some Irish peers additional peerages of the United Kingdom since 1801.

The Peerage of Ireland was not entirely discontinued from 1801 but holders of Irish peerages, whether pre-dating or created subsequent to the Union of 1801, are not entitled to sit in the House of Lords if they have no additional English, Scottish, Great Britain or United Kingdom peerage. However, they are eligible for election to the House of Commons and to vote in Parliamentary elections, which other peers are not. An Irish peer holding a peerage of a lower grade which enables him to sit in the House of Lords is introduced there by the title which enables him to sit, though for all other purposes he is known by his higher title.

In the Peerage of Scotland there is no rank of Baron; the equivalent rank is Lord of Parliament, abbreviated to 'Lord' (the female equivalent is 'Lady'). All peers of England, Scotland, Great Britain or the United Kingdom who are 21 years or over, and of British, Irish or Commonwealth nationality are entitled to sit in the House of Lords.

No fees for dignities have been payable since 1937. The House of Lords surrendered the ancient right of peers to be tried for treason or felony by their peers in 1948.

HEREDITARY WOMEN PEERS

Most hereditary peerages pass on death to the nearest male heir, but there are exceptions, and several are held by women (*see* pages 149 and 161).

A woman peer in her own right retains her title after marriage, and if her husband's rank is the superior she is designated by the two titles jointly, the inferior one last. Her hereditary claim still holds good in spite of any marriage whether higher or lower. No rank held by a woman can confer any title or even precedence upon her husband but the rank of a hereditary woman peer in her own right is inherited by her eldest son (or perhaps daughter).

Since the Peerage Act 1963, hereditary women peers in their own right have been entitled to sit in the House of Lords, subject to the same qualifications as men.

LIFE PEERS

Since 1876 non-hereditary or life peerages have been conferred on certain eminent judges to enable the judicial functions of the House of Lords to be carried out. These Lords are known as Lords of Appeal or law lords and, to date, such appointments have all been male.

Since 1958 life peerages have been conferred upon distinguished men and women from all walks of life, giving them seats in the House of Lords in the degree of Baron or Baroness. They are addressed in the same way as hereditary Lords and Barons, and their children have similar courtesy titles.

PEERAGES EXTINCT SINCE THE LAST EDITION

EARLDOMS: Amherst (*cr.* 1826)
LIFE PEERAGES: Ewart-Biggs (*cr.* 1981); Hatch of Lusby (*cr.* 1978); Franks (*cr.* 1962); Ashby (*cr.* 1973); Airey of Abingdon (*cr.* 1979); Leatherland (*cr.* 1964); Willis (*cr.* 1963); Edmund-Davies (*cr.* 1974); Lloyd of Hampstead (*cr.* 1965); Bernstein (*cr.* 1969), Pennock (*cr.* 1982); Ridley of Liddesdale (*cr.* 1992); Underhill (*cr.* 1979); Bacon (*cr.* 1970); Zuckerman (*cr.* 1971); Elworthy (*cr.* 1972); Ross of Newport (*cr.* 1987), Gormley (*cr.* 1982); Strauss (*cr.* 1979); Winstanley (*cr.* 1975); Craigton (*cr.* 1959); Kadoorie (*cr.* 1981)

DISCLAIMER OF PEERAGES

The Peerage Act 1963 enables peers to disclaim their peerages for life. Peers alive in 1963 could disclaim within twelve months after the passing of the Act (31 July 1963); a person subsequently succeeding to a peerage may disclaim within twelve months (one month if an MP) after the date of succession, or of reaching 21, if later. The disclaimer is irrevocable but does not affect the descent of the peerage after the disclaimant's death, and children of a disclaimed peer may, if they wish, retain their precedence and any courtesy titles and styles borne as children of a peer. The disclaimer permits the disclaimant to sit in the House of Commons if elected as an MP.

EARLS: Durham (1970); Home (1963); Sandwich (1964)
VISCOUNTS: Hailsham (1963); Stansgate (1963)
BARONS: Altrincham (1963); Archibald (1975); Merthyr (1977); Reith (1972); Sanderson of Ayot (1971); Silkin (1972)

PEERS WHO ARE MINORS (i.e. under 21 years of age)

EARLS: Craven (*b.* 1989)
BARONS: Gretton (*b.* 1975)

CONTRACTIONS AND SYMBOLS

s.   Scottish title
I.   Irish title
*   The peer holds also an Imperial title, specified after the name by Engl., Brit. or UK
°   there is no 'of' in the title
b.   born
s.   succeeded
m.   married
w.   widower or widow
M.   minor
†   *heir* not ascertained at time of going to press

Hereditary Peers

ROYAL DUKES

Style, His Royal Highness The Duke of __
Style of address (formal) May it please your Royal Highness; *(informal)* Sir

Created	Title, order of succession, name, etc.	Heir
1947	*Edinburgh* (1st), The Prince Philip, Duke of Edinburgh, *(see* page 123)	The Prince of Wales
1337	*Cornwall,* Charles, Prince of Wales, *s.* 1952 *(see* page 123)	†
1398	*Rothesay,* Charles, Prince of Wales, *s.* 1952 *(see* page 123)	†
1986	*York* (1st), The Prince Andrew, Duke of York *(see* p. 123)	None
1928	*Gloucester* (2nd), Prince Richard, Duke of Gloucester, *s.* 1974 *(see* page 124)	Earl of Ulster *(see* page 124)
1934	*Kent* (2nd), Prince Edward, Duke of Kent, *s.* 1942 *(see* page 124)	Earl of St Andrews *(see* page 124)

† The title is not hereditary but is held by the Sovereign's eldest son from the moment of his birth or the Sovereign's accession

DUKES

Coronet, Eight strawberry leaves
Style, His Grace the Duke of __
Wife's style, Her Grace the Duchess of __
Eldest son's style, Takes his father's second title as a courtesy title
Younger sons' style, 'Lord' before forename and family name
Daughters' style, 'Lady' before forename and family name
For forms of address, *see* page 220

Created	Title, order of succession, name, etc.	Eldest son or heir
1868 I.*	*Abercorn* (5th), James Hamilton (6th *Brit. Marq.,* 1790, and 14th *Scott. Earl,* 1606, both *Abercorn), b.* 1934, *s.* 1979, *m.*	Marquess of Hamilton, *b.* 1969.
1701 S.*	*Argyll,* Ian Campbell (12th *Scottish* and 5th *UK Duke,* 1892, both *Argyll), b.* 1937, *s.* 1973, *m.*	Marquess of Lorne, *b.* 1968.
1703 S.	*Atholl* (10th), George Iain Murray, *b.* 1931, *s.* 1957.	John *M., b.* 1929.
1682	*Beaufort* (11th), David Robert Somerset, *b.* 1928, *s.* 1984, *m.*	Marquess of Worcester, *b.* 1952.
1694	*Bedford* (13th), John Robert Russell, *b.* 1917, *s.* 1953, *m.*	Marquess of Tavistock, *b.* 1940.
1663 S.*	*Buccleuch* (9th) & *Queensberry* (11th) (1684), Walter Francis John Montagu Douglas Scott, KT, VRD (8th *Engl. Earl, Doncaster,* 1662), *b.* 1923, *s.* 1973, *m.*	Earl of Dalkeith, *b.* 1954.
1694	*Devonshire* (11th), Andrew Robert Buxton Cavendish, MC, PC, *b.* 1920, *s.* 1950, *m.*	Marquess of Hartington, *b.* 1944.
1900	*Fife* (3rd), James George Alexander Bannerman Carnegie (12th *Scott. Earl, Southesk,* 1633, *s.* 1992), *b.* 1929, *s.* 1959. *(see* page 135).	Earl of Southesk, *b.* 1961.
1675	*Grafton* (11th), Hugh Denis Charles FitzRoy, KG, *b.* 1919, *s.* 1970, *m.*	Earl of Euston, *b.* 1947.
1643 S.*	*Hamilton* (15th) & *Brandon* (12th) (*Brit.* 1711), Angus Alan Douglas Douglas-Hamilton (*Premier Peer of Scotland), b.* 1938, *s.* 1973, *m.*	Marquess of Douglas and Clydesdale, *b.* 1978.
1766 I.*	*Leinster* (8th), Gerald FitzGerald (*Premier Duke and Marquess of Ireland;* 8th *Brit. Visct., Leinster,* 1747), *b.* 1914, *s.* 1976, *m.*	Marquess of Kildare, *b.* 1948.
1719	*Manchester* (12th), Angus Charles Drogo Montagu, *b.* 1938, *s.* 1985, *m.*	Viscount Mandeville, *b.* 1962.
1702	*Marlborough* (11th), John George Vanderbilt Henry Spencer-Churchill, *b.* 1926, *s.* 1972, *m.*	Marquess of Blandford, *b.* 1955.
1707 S.*	*Montrose* (8th), James Graham (6th *Brit. Earl, Graham,* 1722), *b.* 1935, *s.* 1992, *m.*	Marquess of Graham, *b.* 1973.
1483	*Norfolk* (17th), Miles Francis Stapleton Fitzalan-Howard, KG, GCVO, CB, CBE, MC (*Premier Duke;* 12th *Eng. Baron Beaumont,* 1309, *s.* 1971; 4th *UK Baron Howard of Glossop,* 1869, *s.* 1972), *b.* 1915, *s.* 1975, *m. Earl Marshal*.	Earl of Arundel and Surrey, *b.* 1956.
1766	*Northumberland* (11th), Henry Alan Walter Richard Percy, *b.* 1953, *s.* 1988.	Lord Ralph G.A.P., *b.* 1956.
1675	*Richmond* (10th) & *Gordon* (5th) (*UK* 1876), Charles Henry Gordon Lennox (10th *Scott. Duke, Lennox,* 1675), *b.* 1929, *s.* 1989, *m.*	Earl of March and Kinrara, *b.* 1955.

Created	Title, order of succession, name, etc.	Eldest son or heir
1707 S.*	Roxburghe (10th), Guy David Innes-Ker (5th UK Earl, Innes, 1837), b. 1954, s. 1974, m. (Premier Baronet of Scotland).	Marquess of Bowmont and Cessford, b. 1981.
1703	Rutland (10th), Charles John Robert Manners, CBE, b. 1919, s. 1940, m.	Marquess of Granby, b. 1959.
1684	St Albans (14th), Murray de Vere Beauclerk, b. 1939, s. 1988, m.	Earl of Burford, b. 1965.
1547	Somerset (19th), John Michael Edward Seymour, b. 1952, s. 1984, m.	Lord Seymour, b. 1982.
1833	Sutherland (6th), John Sutherland Egerton, TD (5th UK Earl, Ellesmere, 1846, s. 1944), b. 1915, s. 1963, m.	Francis R. E., b. 1940.
1814	Wellington (8th), Arthur Valerian Wellesley, KG, LVO, OBE, MC (9th Irish Earl, Mornington, 1760), b. 1915, s. 1972, m.	Marquess of Douro, b. 1945.
1874	Westminster (6th), Gerald Cavendish Grosvenor, b. 1951, s. 1979, m.	Earl Grosvenor, b. 1991.

MARQUESSES

Coronet, Four strawberry leaves alternating with four silver balls
Style, The Most Hon. the Marquess (of) __ . In Scotland the spelling 'Marquis' is preferred for pre-Union creations
Wife's style, The Most Hon. the Marchioness (of) __
Eldest son's style, Takes his father's second title as a courtesy title
Younger sons' style, 'Lord' before forename and family name
Daughters' style, 'Lady' before forename and family name
For forms of address, see page 220

Created	Title, order of succession, name, etc.	Eldest son or heir
1916	Aberdeen and Temair (6th), Alastair Ninian John Gordon (12th Scott. Earl, Aberdeen, 1682), b. 1920, s. 1984, m.	Earl of Haddo, b. 1955.
1876	Abergavenny (5th), John Henry Guy Nevill, KG, OBE, b. 1914, s. 1954, m.	Christopher G. C. N., b. 1955.
1821	Ailesbury (8th), Michael Sidney Cedric Brudenell-Bruce, b. 1926, s. 1974	Earl of Cardigan, b. 1952.
1831	Ailsa (7th), Archibald David Kennedy, OBE, (19th Scott. Earl, Cassillis, 1509), b. 1925, s. 1957, m.	Earl of Cassillis, b. 1956.
1815	Anglesey (7th), George Charles Henry Victor Paget, b. 1922, s. 1947, m.	Earl of Uxbridge, b. 1950.
1789	Bath (7th), Alexander George Thynn, b. 1932, s. 1992, m.	Viscount Weymouth, b. 1974.
1826	Bristol (7th), (Frederick William) John Augustus Hervey, b. 1954, s. 1985.	Lord F. W. C. Nicholas W. H., b. 1961.
1796	Bute (7th), John Colum Crichton-Stuart (12th Scott. Earl, Dumfries, 1633), b. 1958, s. 1993, m.	Earl of Dumfries, b. 1989.
1812	°Camden (6th), David George Edward Henry Pratt, b. 1930, s. 1983.	Earl of Brecknock, b. 1965.
1815	Cholmondeley (7th), David George Philip Cholmondeley (11th Irish Viscount, Cholmondeley, 1661), b. 1960, s. 1990. Lord Great Chamberlain.	Charles G. C., b. 1959.
1816 I.*	°Conyngham (7th), Frederick William Henry Francis Conyngham (7th UK Baron, Minster, UK 1821), b. 1924, s. 1974, m.	Earl of Mount Charles, b. 1951.
1791 I.*	Donegall (7th), Dermot Richard Claud Chichester, LVO (7th Brit. Baron, Fisherwick, 1790, 6th Brit. Baron, Templemore, 1831), b. 1916, s. to Marquessate, 1975: to Templemore Barony, 1953, m.	Earl of Belfast, b. 1952.
1789 I.*	Downshire (8th), (Arthur) Robin Ian Hill (8th Brit. Earl, Hillsborough, 1772), b. 1929, s. 1989, m.	Earl of Hillsborough, b. 1959.
1801 I.*	Ely (8th) Charles John Tottenham (8th UK Baron, Loftus, 1801), b. 1913, s. 1969, m.	Viscount Loftus, b. 1943.
1801	Exeter (8th), (William) Michael Anthony Cecil, b. 1935, s. 1988, m.	Lord Burghley, b. 1970.
1800 I.*	Headfort (6th), Thomas Geoffrey Charles Michael Taylour (4th UK Baron, Kenlis, 1831), b. 1932, s. 1960, m.	Earl of Bective, b. 1959.
1793	Hertford (8th), Hugh Edward Conway Seymour (9th Irish Baron, Conway, 1712), b. 1930, s. 1940, m.	Earl of Yarmouth, b. 1958.
1599 S.*	Huntly (13th), Granville Charles Gomer Gordon (Premier Marquess of Scotland) (5th UK Baron, Meldrum, 1815), b. 1944, s. 1987, m.	Earl of Aboyne, b. 1973.
1784	Lansdowne (8th), George John Charles Mercer Nairne Petty-Fitzmaurice, PC (8th Irish Earl, Kerry, 1723), b. 1912, s. 1944, w.	Earl of Shelburne, b. 1941.
1902	Linlithgow (4th), Adrian John Charles Hope (10th Scott. Earl, Hopetoun 1703), b. 1946, s. 1987, m.	Earl of Hopetoun, b. 1969.
1816 I.*	Londonderry (9th), Alexander Charles Robert Vane-Tempest-Stewart (6th UK Earl, Vane, 1823), b. 1937, s. 1955, m.	Viscount Castlereagh, b. 1972.
1701 S.*	Lothian (12th), Peter Francis Walter Kerr, KCVO (6th UK Baron, Kerr, 1821), b. 1922, s. 1940, m.	Earl of Ancram, MP, b. 1945.

Created	Title, order of succession, name, etc.	Eldest son or heir
1917	Milford Haven (4th), George Ivar Louis Mountbatten, b. 1961, s. 1970, m.	Earl of Medina, b. 1991.
1838	Normanby (4th), Oswald Constantine John Phipps, KG, CBE (8th Irish Baron, Mulgrave, 1767), b. 1912, s. 1932, m.	Earl of Mulgrave, b. 1954.
1812	Northampton (7th), Spencer Douglas David Compton, b. 1946, s. 1978, m.	Earl Compton, b. 1973.
1825 I.*	Ormonde (7th), James Hubert Theobald Charles Butler, MBE (7th UK Baron, Ormonde, 1821), b. 1899, s. 1971, w.	None to Marquessate. To Earldoms of Ormonde and Ossory, Viscount Mountgarret, b. 1936 (see p. 151).
1682 S.	Queensberry (12th), David Harrington Angus Douglas, b. 1929, s. 1954.	Viscount Drumlanrig, b. 1967.
1926	Reading (4th), Simon Charles Henry Rufus Isaacs, b. 1942, s. 1980, m.	Viscount Erleigh, b. 1986.
1789	Salisbury (6th), Robert Edward Peter Cecil, b. 1916, s. 1972, m.	Viscount Cranborne, b. 1946 (see also Baron Cecil, page 154).
1800 I.*	Sligo (11th), Jeremy Ulick Browne (11th UK Baron, Monteagle, 1806), b. 1939, s. 1991, m.	Sebastian U. B., b. 1964.
1787	°Townshend (7th), George John Patrick Dominic Townshend, b. 1916, s. 1921, w.	Viscount Raynham, b. 1945.
1694 S.*	Tweeddale (13th), Edward Douglas John Hay (4th UK Baron, Tweeddale, 1881), b. 1947, s. 1979.	Lord Charles D. M. H., b. 1947.
1789 I.*	Waterford (8th), John Hubert de la Poer Beresford (8th Brit. Baron, Tyrone, 1786), b. 1933, s. 1934, m.	Earl of Tyrone, b. 1958.
1551	Winchester (18th), Nigel George Paulet (Premier Marquess of England), b. 1941, s. 1968, m.	Earl of Wiltshire, b. 1969.
1892	Zetland (4th), Lawrence Mark Dundas (6th UK Earl of Zetland, 1838, 7th Brit. Baron Dundas, 1794), b. 1937, s. 1989, m.	Earl of Ronaldshay, b. 1965.

EARLS

Coronet, Eight silver balls on stalks alternating with eight gold strawberry leaves
Style, The Right Hon. the Earl (of) __
Wife's style, The Right Hon. the Countess (of) __
Eldest son's style, Takes his father's second title as a courtesy title
Younger sons' style, 'The Hon.' before forename and family name
Daughters' style, 'Lady' before forename and family name
For forms of address, see page 220

Created	Title, order of succession, name, etc.	Eldest son or heir
1639 S.	Airlie (13th), David George Coke Patrick Ogilvy, KT, GCVO, PC, b. 1926, s. 1968, m. Lord Chamberlain.	Lord Ogilvy, b. 1958.
1696	Albemarle (10th), Rufus Arnold Alexis Keppel, b. 1965, s. 1979.	Crispian W. J. K., b. 1948.
1952	°Alexander of Tunis (2nd), Shane William Desmond Alexander, b. 1935, s. 1969, m.	Hon. Brian J. A., b. 1939.
1662 S.	Annandale and Hartfell (11th), Patrick Andrew Wentworth Hope Johnstone, b. 1941, claim established 1985, m.	Lord Johnstone, b. 1971.
1789 I.	°Annesley (10th), Patrick Annesley, b. 1924, s. 1979, m.	Hon. Philip H.A., b. 1927.
1785 I.	Antrim (9th), Alexander Randal Mark McDonnell, b. 1935, s. 1977, m. (Viscount Dunluce.)	Hon. Randal A. St J. M., b. 1967.
1762 I.*	Arran (9th), Arthur Desmond Colquhoun Gore (5th UK Baron Sudley, 1884), b. 1938, s. 1983, m.	Paul A. G., CMG, CVO, b. 1921.
1955	°Attlee (3rd), John Richard Attlee, b. 1956, s. 1991, m.	None.
1714	Aylesford (11th), Charles Ian Finch-Knightley, b. 1918, s. 1958, m.	Lord Guernsey, b. 1947.
1937	°Baldwin of Bewdley (4th), Edward Alfred Alexander Baldwin, b. 1938, s. 1976, m.	Viscount Corvedale, b. 1973.
1922	Balfour (4th), Gerald Arthur James Balfour, b. 1925, s. 1968, m.	Eustace A. G. B., b. 1921.
1772	°Bathurst (8th), Henry Allen John Bathurst, b. 1927, s. 1943, m.	Lord Apsley, b. 1961.
1919	°Beatty (3rd), David Beatty, b. 1946, s. 1972, m.	Viscount Borodale, b. 1973.
1797 I.	Belmore (8th), John Armar Lowry-Corry, b. 1951, s. 1960, m.	Viscount Corry, b. 1985.
1739 I.*	Bessborough, Frederick Edward Neuflize Ponsonby (10th Irish and 2nd UK Earl, 1937, both Bessborough), b. 1913, s. 1956, m.	To Irish Earldom and UK Barony only, Arthur M. L. P., b. 1912.
1815	Bradford (7th), Richard Thomas Orlando Bridgeman, b. 1947, s. 1981, m.	Viscount Newport, b. 1980.
1677 S.	Breadalbane and Holland (10th), John Romer Boreland Campbell, b. 1919, s. 1959.	None.
1469 S.*	Buchan (17th), Malcolm Harry Erskine, (8th UK Baron Erskine 1806), b. 1930, s. 1984, m.	Lord Cardross, b. 1960.

Created	Title, order of succession, name, etc.	Eldest son or heir
1746	Buckinghamshire (10th), (George) Miles Hobart-Hampden, b. 1944, s. 1983, m.	Sir John Hobart, Bt., b. 1945.
1800	°Cadogan (7th), William Gerald Charles Cadogan, MC, b. 1914, s. 1933, m.	Viscount Chelsea, b. 1937.
1878	°Cairns (6th), Simon Dallas Cairns, CBE, b. 1939, s. 1989, m.	Viscount Garmoyle, b. 1965.
1455 S.	Caithness (20th), Malcolm Ian Sinclair, PC, b. 1948, s. 1965, m.	Lord Berriedale, b. 1981.
1800 I.	Caledon (7th), Nicholas James Alexander, b. 1955, s. 1980, m.	Viscount Alexander, b. 1990.
1661	Carlisle (12th), Charles James Ruthven Howard, MC (12th Scott. Baron, Ruthven of Freeland, 1651), b. 1923, s. 1963, m.	Viscount Morpeth, b. 1949.
1793	Carnarvon (7th), Henry George Reginald Molyneux Herbert, KCVO, KBE, b. 1924, s. 1987, m.	Lord Porchester, b. 1956.
1748 I.*	Carrick (10th), David James Theobald Somerset Butler (4th UK Baron, Butler, 1912), b. 1953, s. 1992, m.	Viscount Ikerrin, b. 1975.
1800 I.	°Castle Stewart (8th), Arthur Patrick Avondale Stuart, b. 1928, s. 1961, m.	Viscount Stuart, b. 1953.
1814	°Cathcart (6th), Alan Cathcart, CB, DSO, MC (15th Scott. Baron, Cathcart, 1447), b. 1919, s. 1927, m.	Lord Greenock, b. 1952.
1647 I.	Cavan (13th), Roger Cavan Lambart, b. 1944, s. 1988.	Arthur O. R. L., b. 1909.
1827	°Cawdor (7th), Colin Robert Vaughan Campbell, b. 1962, s. 1993.	Hon. Frederick W. C., b. 1965.
1801	Chichester (9th), John Nicholas Pelham, b. 1944, s. 1944, m.	Richard A. H. P., b. 1952.
1803 I.*	Clancarty (8th), William Francis Brinsley Le Poer Trench (7th UK Visct. Clancarty, 1823), b. 1911, s. 1975, m.	Nicholas P. R. Le P. T., b. 1952.
1776 I.*	Clanwilliam (7th), John Herbert Meade (5th UK Baron Clanwilliam, 1828), b. 1919, s. 1989, m.	Lord Gillford, b. 1960.
1776	Clarendon (7th), George Frederick Laurence Hyde Villiers, b. 1933, s. 1955, m.	Lord Hyde, b. 1976.
1620 I.*	Cork (13th) & Orrery (13th)(I. 1660), Patrick Reginald Boyle (9th Brit. Baron, Boyle of Marston, 1711), b. 1910, s. 1967, m.	Hon. John W. B., DSC, b. 1916.
1850	Cottenham (8th), Kenelm Charles Everard Digby Pepys, b. 1948, s. 1968, m.	Viscount Crowhurst, b. 1983.
1762 I.*	Courtown (9th), James Patrick Montagu Burgoyne Winthrop Stopford (8th Brit. Baron, Saltersford, 1796), b. 1954, s. 1975, m.	Viscount Stopford, b. 1988.
1697	Coventry (11th), George William Coventry, b. 1934, s. 1940, m.	Viscount Deerhurst, b. 1957.
1857	°Cowley (7th), Garret Graham Wellesley, b. 1934, s. 1975, m.	Viscount Dangan, b. 1965.
1892	Cranbrook (5th), Gathorne Gathorne-Hardy, b. 1933, s. 1978, m.	Lord Medway, b. 1968.
1801	Craven (9th), Benjamin Robert Joseph Craven, b. 1989, s. 1990, M.	Rupert J. E. C., b. 1926.
1398 S.*	Crawford (29th) & Balcarres (12th) (S. 1651), Robert Alexander Lindsay, PC (Premier Earl on Union Roll, 5th UK Baron, Wigan, 1826, and Baron Balniel (Life Peer)), b. 1927, s. 1975, m.	Lord Balniel, b. 1958.
1861	Cromartie (5th), John Ruaridh Blunt Grant Mackenzie, b. 1948, s. 1989, m.	Viscount Tarbat, b. 1987.
1901	Cromer (4th), Evelyn Rowland Esmond Baring, b. 1946, s. 1991, m.	Hon. Vivian J. R. B., b. 1950.
1633 S.*	Dalhousie (16th), Simon Ramsay, KT, GCVO, GBE, MC (4th UK Baron, Ramsay, 1875), b. 1914, s. 1950, m.	Lord Ramsay, b. 1948.
1725 I.*	Darnley (11th), Adam Ivo Stuart Bligh (20th Engl. Baron, Clifton of Leighton Bromswold, 1608), b. 1941, s. 1980, m.	Lord Clifton of Rathmore, b. 1968.
1711	Dartmouth (9th), Gerald Humphry Legge, b. 1924, s. 1962, m.	Viscount Lewisham, b. 1949.
1761	°De La Warr (11th), William Herbrand Sackville, b. 1948, s. 1988, m.	Lord Buckhurst, b. 1979.
1622	Denbigh (11th) & Desmond (10th) (I. 1622), William Rudolph Michael Feilding, b. 1943, s. 1966, m.	Viscount Feilding, b. 1970.
1485	Derby (18th), Edward John Stanley, MC, b. 1918, s. 1948, w.	Edward R. W. S., b. 1962.
1553	Devon (17th), Charles Christopher Courtenay, b. 1916, s. 1935, m.	Lord Courtenay, b. 1942.
1800 I.*	Donoughmore (8th), Richard Michael John Hely-Hutchinson (8th UK Visct., Hutchinson, 1821), b. 1927, s. 1981, m.	Viscount Suirdale, b. 1952.
1661 I.*	Drogheda (12th), Henry Dermot Ponsonby Moore (3rd UK Baron, Moore, 1954), b. 1937, s. 1989, m.	Viscount Moore, b. 1983.
1837	Ducie (7th), David Leslie Moreton, b. 1951, s. 1991, m.	Lord Moreton, b. 1981.
1860	Dudley (4th), William Humble David Ward, b. 1920, s. 1969, m.	Viscount Ednam, b. 1947.
1660 S.*	Dundee (12th), Alexander Henry Scrymgeour (2nd UK Baron, Glassary, 1954), b. 1949, s. 1983, m.	Lord Scrymgeour, b. 1982.
1669 S.	Dundonald (15th), Iain Alexander Douglas Blair Cochrane, b. 1961, s. 1986, m.	Lord Cochrane, b. 1991.
1686 S.	Dunmore (11th), Kenneth Randolph Murray, b. 1913, s. 1981, w.	Viscount Fincastle, b. 1946.
1822 I.	Dunraven and Mount-Earl (7th), Thady Windham Thomas Wyndham-Quin, b. 1939, s. 1965, m.	None.
1833	Durham. Disclaimed for life 1970. (Antony Claud Frederick Lambton, b. 1922, s. 1970, m.)	Hon. Edward R. L., b. 1961.
1837	Effingham (6th), Mowbray Henry Gordon Howard (16th Engl. Baron, Howard of Effingham, 1554), b. 1905, s. 1946, m.	Lt.-Cdr. David P. M. A. H., b. 1939.

Created	Title, order of succession, name, etc.	Eldest son or heir
1507 S.*	*Eglinton* (18th) & *Winton* (9th) (1600), Archibald George Montgomerie (6th *UK Earl, Winton*, 1859), b. 1939, s. 1966, m.	Lord Montgomerie, b. 1966.
1733 I.*	*Egmont* (11th), Frederick George Moore Perceval (9th *Brit. Baron, Lovel & Holland*, 1762), b. 1914, s. 1932, m.	Viscount Perceval, b. 1934.
1821	*Eldon* (5th), John Joseph Nicholas Scott, b. 1937, s. 1976, m.	Viscount Encombe, b. 1962.
1633 S.*	*Elgin* (11th), & *Kincardine* (15th) (s. 1647), Andrew Douglas Alexander Thomas Bruce (4th *UK Baron, Elgin*, 1849), KT, b. 1924, s. 1968, m.	Lord Bruce, b. 1961.
1789 I.*	*Enniskillen* (7th), Andrew John Galbraith Cole (5th *UK Baron, Grinstead*, 1815) b. 1942, s. 1989, m.	Arthur G. C., b. 1920.
1789 I.*	*Erne* (6th), Henry George Victor John Crichton (3rd *UK Baron, Fermanagh*, 1876), b. 1937, s. 1940, m.	Viscount Crichton, b. 1971.
1452 S.	*Erroll* (24th), Merlin Sereld Victor Gilbert Hay, b. 1948, s. 1978, m. Hereditary Lord High Constable and Knight Marischal of Scotland.	Lord Hay, b. 1984.
1661	*Essex* (10th), Robert Edward de Vere Capell, b. 1920, s. 1981, m.	Viscount Malden, b. 1944.
1711	°*Ferrers* (13th), Robert Washington Shirley, PC, b. 1929, s. 1954, m.	Viscount Tamworth, b. 1952.
1789	°*Fortescue* (8th), Charles Hugh Richard Fortescue, b. 1951, s. 1993, m.	Hon. Martin D. F., b. 1924.
1841	*Gainsborough* (5th), Anthony Gerard Edward Noel, b. 1923, s. 1927, m.	Viscount Campden, b. 1950.
1623 S.*	*Galloway* (13th), Randolph Keith Reginald Stewart (6th *Brit. Baron, Stewart of Garlies*, 1796), b. 1928, s. 1978, m.	Andrew C. S., b. 1949.
1703 S.*	*Glasgow* (10th), Patrick Robin Archibald Boyle (4th *UK Baron, Fairlie*, 1897), b. 1939, s. 1984, m.	Viscount of Kelburn, b. 1978.
1806 I.*	*Gosford* (7th), Charles David Nicholas Alexander John Sparrow Acheson (5th *UK Baron, Worlingham*, 1835), b. 1942, s. 1966, m.	Hon. Patrick B. V. M. A., b. 1915.
1945	*Gowrie* (2nd), Alexander Patric Greysteil Hore-Ruthven, PC (3rd *UK Baron, Ruthven of Gowrie*, 1919), b. 1939, s. 1955, m.	Viscount Ruthven of Canberra, b. 1964.
1684 I.*	*Granard* (10th), Peter Arthur Edward Hastings Forbes, (5th *UK Baron, Granard*, 1806), b. 1957, s. 1992, m.	Viscount Forbes.
1833	°*Granville* (5th), Granville James Leveson-Gower, MC, b. 1918, s. 1953, m.	Lord Leveson, b. 1959.
1806	°*Grey* (6th), Richard Fleming George Charles Grey, b. 1939, s. 1963, m.	Philip K. G., b. 1940.
1752	*Guilford* (9th), Edward Francis North, b. 1933, s. 1949, w.	Lord North, b. 1971.
1619 S.	*Haddington* (13th), John George Baillie-Hamilton, b. 1941, s. 1986, m.	Lord Binning, b. 1985.
1919	°*Haig* (2nd), George Alexander Eugene Douglas Haig, OBE, b. 1918, s. 1928, m.	Viscount Dawick, b. 1961.
1944	*Halifax* (3rd), Charles Edward Peter Neil Wood (5th *UK Viscount, Halifax*, 1866), b. 1944, s. 1980, m.	Lord Irwin, b. 1977.
1898	*Halsbury* (3rd), John Anthony Hardinge Giffard, FRS, FEng., b. 1908, s. 1943, w.	Adam E. G., b. 1934.
1754	*Hardwicke* (10th), Joseph Philip Sebastian Yorke, b. 1971, s. 1974.	Richard C. J. Y., b. 1916.
1812	*Harewood* (7th), George Henry Hubert Lascelles, KBE, b. 1923, s. 1947, m. (See also page 134).	Viscount Lascelles, b. 1950.
1742	*Harrington* (11th), William Henry Leicester Stanhope (8th *Brit. Viscount, Stanhope of Mahon*, 1717), b. 1922, s. 1929, m.	Viscount Petersham, b. 1945.
1809	*Harrowby* (7th), Dudley Danvers Granville Coutts Ryder, TD, b. 1922, s. 1987, m.	Viscount Sandon, b. 1951.
1605 S.	*Home*. Disclaimed for life 1963. (see Lord Home of the Hirsel, page 164.)	Hon. David A. C. D.-H., b. 1943.
1821	°*Howe* (7th), Frederick Richard Penn Curzon, b. 1951, s. 1984, m.	Charles M. P. C., b. 1967.
1529	*Huntingdon* (16th), William Edward Robin Hood Hastings Bass, b. 1948, s. 1990, m.	Hon. Simon A. R. H. H. B., b. 1950.
1885	*Iddesleigh* (4th), Stafford Henry Northcote, b. 1932, s. 1970, m.	Viscount St Cyres, b. 1957.
1756	*Ilchester* (9th), Maurice Vivian de Touffreville Fox-Strangways, b. 1920, s. 1970, m.	Hon. Raymond G. F.-S., b. 1921.
1929	*Inchcape* (3rd), Kenneth James William Mackay, b. 1917, s. 1939, m.	Viscount Glenapp, b. 1943.
1919	*Iveagh* (4th), Arthur Edward Rory Guinness, b. 1969, s. 1992.	Hon. Rory M. B. G., b. 1974.
1925	°*Jellicoe* (2nd), George Patrick John Rushworth Jellicoe, KBE, DSO, MC, PC, b. 1918, s. 1935, m.	Viscount Brocas, b. 1950.
1697	*Jersey* (9th), George Francis Child-Villiers (12th *Irish Visct., Grandison*, 1620), b. 1910, s. 1923, m.	Viscount Villiers, b. 1948.
1822 I.	*Kilmorey* (6th), Richard Francis Needham, MP, b. 1942, s. 1977, m.	Viscount Newry and Morne, b. 1966.
1866	*Kimberley* (4th), John Wodehouse, b. 1924, s. 1941, m.	Lord Wodehouse, b. 1951.
1768 I.	*Kingston* (11th), Barclay Robert Edwin King-Tenison, b. 1943, s. 1948, m.	Viscount Kingsborough, b. 1969.
1633 S.*	*Kinnoull* (15th), Arthur William George Patrick Hay (9th *Brit. Baron, Hay of Pedwardine*, 1711), b. 1935, s. 1938, m.	Viscount Dupplin, b. 1962.
1677 S.*	*Kintore* (13th), Michael Canning William John Keith (3rd *UK Viscount Stonehaven*, 1938), b. 1939, s. 1989, m.	Lord Inverurie, b. 1976.
1914	°*Kitchener of Khartoum* (3rd), Henry Herbert Kitchener, TD, b. 1919, s. 1937.	None.
1756 I.	*Lanesborough* (9th), Denis Anthony Brian Butler, TD, b. 1918, s. 1950.	Maj. Henry A. B. C. B., b. 1909.

Created	Title, order of succession, name, etc.	Eldest son or heir
1624 S.	*Lauderdale* (17th), Patrick Francis Maitland, *b.* 1911, *s.* 1968, *m.*	Viscount Maitland, *b.* 1937.
1837	*Leicester* (6th), Anthony Louis Lovel Coke, *b.* 1909, *s.* 1976, *m.*	Viscount Coke, *b.* 1936.
1641 S.	*Leven* (14th) & *Melville* (13th) (s. 1690), Alexander Robert Leslie Melville, *b.* 1924, *s.* 1947, *m.*	Lord Balgonie, *b.* 1954.
1831	*Lichfield* (5th), Thomas Patrick John Anson, *b.* 1939, *s.* 1960.	Viscount Anson, *b.* 1978.
1803 I.*	*Limerick* (6th), Patrick Edmund Pery, KBE (6th *UK Baron, Foxford,* 1815), *b.* 1930, *s.* 1967, *m.*	Viscount Glentworth, *b.* 1963.
1572	*Lincoln* (18th), Edward Horace Fiennes-Clinton, *b.* 1913, *s.* 1988, *m.*	Hon. Edward G. *F.-C.*, *b.* 1943.
1633 S.	*Lindsay* (16th), James Randolph Lindesay-Bethune, *b.* 1955, *s.* 1989, *m.*	Viscount Garnock, *b.* 1990.
1626	*Lindsey* (14th) *and Abingdon* (9th) (1682), Richard Henry Rupert Bertie, *b.* 1931, *s.* 1963, *m.*	Lord Norreys, *b.* 1958.
1776 I.	*Lisburne* (8th), John David Malet Vaughan, *b.* 1918, *s.* 1965, *m.*	Viscount Vaughan, *b.* 1945.
1822 I.*	*Listowel* (5th), William Francis Hare, GCMG, PC, (3rd *UK Baron, Hare,* 1869), *b.* 1906, *s.* 1931, *m.*	Viscount Ennismore, *b.* 1964.
1905	*Liverpool* (5th), Edward Peter Bertram Savile Foljambe, *b.* 1944, *s.* 1969, *m.*	Viscount Hawkesbury, *b.* 1972.
1945	°*Lloyd George of Dwyfor* (3rd), Owen Lloyd George, *b.* 1924, *s.* 1968, *m.*	Viscount Gwynedd, *b.* 1951.
1785 I.*	*Longford* (7th), Francis Aungier Pakenham, KG, PC (6th *UK Baron, Silchester,* 1821; 1st *UK Baron, Pakenham,* 1945), *b.* 1905, *s.* 1961, *m.*	Thomas F. D. *P.*, *b.* 1933.
1807	*Lonsdale* (7th), James Hugh William Lowther, *b.* 1922, *s.* 1953, *m.*	Viscount Lowther, *b.* 1949.
1838	*Lovelace* (5th), Peter Axel William Locke King (12th *Brit. Baron, King,* 1725), *b.* 1951, *s.* 1964, *m.*	None.
1795 I.*	*Lucan* (7th), Richard John Bingham (3rd *UK Baron, Bingham,* 1934), *b.* 1934, *s.* 1964, *m.*	Lord Bingham, *b.* 1967.
1880	*Lytton* (5th), John Peter Michael Scawen Lytton (18th *Engl. Baron, Wentworth,* 1529), *b.* 1950, *s.* 1985, *m.*	Viscount Knebworth, *b.* 1989.
1721	*Macclesfield* (9th), Richard Timothy George Mansfield Parker, *b.* 1943, *s.* 1992, *m.*	Hon. David J. G. *P.*, *b.* 1945.
1800	*Malmesbury* (6th), William James Harris, TD, *b.* 1907, *s.* 1950, *m.*	Viscount FitzHarris, *b.* 1946.
1776 & 1792	*Mansfield and Mansfield* (8th), William David Mungo James Murray (14th *Scott. Visct., Stormont,* 1621), *b.* 1930, *s.* 1971, *m.*	Viscount Stormont, *b.* 1956.
1565 S.	*Mar* (13th) & *Kellie* (15th) (s. 1616), John Francis Hervey Erskine, *b.* 1921, *s.* 1955, *m.*	Lord Erskine, *b.* 1949.
1785 I.	*Mayo* (10th), Terence Patrick Bourke, *b.* 1929, *s.* 1962, *m.*	Lord Naas, *b.* 1953.
1627 I.*	*Meath* (14th), Anthony Windham Normand Brabazon (5th *UK Baron, Chaworth,* 1831), *b.* 1910, *s.* 1949, *m.*	Lord Ardee, *b.* 1941.
1766 I.	*Mexborough* (8th), John Christopher George Savile, *b.* 1931, *s.* 1980, *m.*	Viscount Pollington, *b.* 1959.
1813	*Minto* (6th), Gilbert Edward George Lariston Elliot-Murray-Kynynmound, OBE, *b.* 1928, *s.* 1975, *m.*	Viscount Melgund, *b.* 1953.
1562 S.*	*Moray* (20th) Douglas John Moray Stuart (12th *Brit. Baron, Stuart of Castle Stuart,* 1796), *b.* 1928, *s.* 1974, *m.*	Lord Doune, *b.* 1966.
1815	*Morley* (6th), John St Aubyn Parker, *b.* 1923, *s.* 1962, *m.*	Viscount Boringdon, *b.* 1956.
1458 S.	*Morton* (22nd), John Charles Sholto Douglas, *b.* 1927, *s.* 1976, *m.*	Lord Aberdour, *b.* 1952.
1789	*Mount Edgcumbe* (8th), Robert Charles Edgcumbe, *b.* 1939, *s.* 1982, *m.*	Piers V. *E.*, *b.* 1946.
1831	*Munster* (7th), Anthony Charles FitzClarence, *b.* 1926, *s.* 1983, *m.*	None.
1805	°*Nelson* (9th), Peter John Horatio Nelson, *b.* 1941, *s.* 1981, *m.*	Viscount Merton, *b.* 1971.
1660 S.	*Newburgh* (12th), Prince Filippo Giambattista Camillo Francesco Aldo Maria Rospigliosi, *b.* 1942, *s.* 1986, *m.*	Princess Benedetta F. M. *R.*, *b.* 1974.
1827 I.	*Norbury* (6th), Noel Terence Graham-Toler, *b.* 1939, *s.* 1955, *m.*	Viscount Glandine, *b.* 1967.
1806 I.*	*Normanton* (6th), Shaun James Christian Welbore Ellis Agar (9th *Brit. Baron, Mendip,* 1791, 4th *UK Baron, Somerton,* 1873), *b.* 1945, *s.* 1967, *m.*	Viscount Somerton, *b.* 1982.
1647 S.	*Northesk* (13th), Robert Andrew Carnegie, *b.* 1926, *s.* 1975, *m.*	Lord Rosehill, *b.* 1954.
1801	*Onslow* (7th), Michael William Coplestone Dillon Onslow, *b.* 1938, *s.* 1971, *m.*	Viscount Cranley, *b.* 1967.
1696 S.	*Orkney* (8th), Cecil O'Bryen Fitz-Maurice, *b.* 1919, *s.* 1951, *m.*	O. Peter *St John, b.* 1938.
1925	*Oxford and Asquith* (2nd), Julian Edward George Asquith, KCMG, *b.* 1916, *s.* 1928, *m.*	Viscount Asquith, OBE, *b.* 1952.
1929	°*Peel* (3rd), William James Robert Peel (4th *UK Viscount Peel,* 1895), *b.* 1947, *s.* 1969, *m.*	Viscount Clanfield, *b.* 1976.
1551	*Pembroke* (17th) & *Montgomery* (14th) (1605), Henry George Charles Alexander Herbert, *b.* 1939, *s.* 1969.	Lord Herbert, *b.* 1978.
1605 S.	*Perth* (17th), John David Drummond, PC, *b.* 1907, *s.* 1951, *m.*	Viscount Strathallan, *b.* 1935.
1905	*Plymouth* (3rd), Other Robert Ivor Windsor-Clive (15th *Engl. Baron, Windsor,* 1529), *b.* 1923, *s.* 1943, *m.*	Viscount Windsor, *b.* 1951.
1785 I.	*Portarlington* (7th), George Lionel Yuill Seymour Dawson-Damer, *b.* 1938, *s.* 1959, *m.*	Viscount Carlow, *b.* 1965.

Created	Title, order of succession, name, etc.	Eldest son or heir
1689	*Portland* (11th), Count Henry Noel Bentinck, *b.* 1919, *s.* 1990, *m.*	Viscount Woodstock, *b.* 1953.
1743	*Portsmouth* (10th), Quentin Gerard Carew Wallop, *b.* 1954, *s.* 1984, *m.*	Viscount Lymington, *b.* 1981.
1804	*Powis* (8th), John George Herbert (9th *Irish Baron, Clive,* 1762), *b.* 1952, *s.* 1993, *m.*	Viscount Clive, *b.* 1979.
1765	*Radnor* (8th), Jacob Pleydell-Bouverie, *b.* 1927, *s.* 1968, *m.*	Viscount Folkestone, *b.* 1955.
1831 I.*	*Ranfurly* (7th), Gerald Françoys Needham Knox (8th *UK Baron, Ranfurly,* 1826), *b.* 1929, *s.* 1988, *m.*	Viscount Northland, *b.* 1957.
1771 I.	*Roden* (9th), Robert William Jocelyn, *b.* 1909, *s.* 1956, *w.*	Viscount Jocelyn, *b.* 1938.
1801	*Romney* (7th), Michael Henry Marsham, *b.* 1910, *s.* 1975, *m.*	Julian C. *M., b.* 1948.
1703 S.*	*Rosebery* (7th), Neil Archibald Primrose (3rd *UK Earl, Midlothian,* 1911), *b.* 1929, *s.* 1974, *m.*	Lord Dalmeny, *b.* 1967.
1806 I.	*Rosse* (7th), William Brendan Parsons, *b.* 1936, *s.* 1979, *m.*	Lord Oxmantown, *b.* 1969.
1801	*Rosslyn* (7th), Peter St Clair-Erskine, *b.* 1958, *s.* 1977, *m.*	Lord Loughborough, *b.* 1986.
1457 S.	*Rothes* (21st), Ian Lionel Malcolm Leslie, *b.* 1932, *s.* 1975, *m.*	Lord Leslie, *b.* 1958.
1861	°*Russell* (5th), Conrad Sebastian Robert Russell, *b.* 1937, *s.* 1987, *m.*	Viscount Amberley, *b.* 1968.
1915	°*St Aldwyn* (3rd), Michael Henry Hicks Beach, b. 1950, *s.* 1992, *m.*	Hon. David S. *H. B., b.* 1955.
1815	*St Germans* (10th), Peregrine Nicholas Eliot, *b.* 1941, *s.* 1988.	Lord Eliot, *b.* 1966.
1660	*Sandwich.* Disclaimed for life 1964. ((*Alexander*) *Victor* (*Edward Paulet*) *Montagu, b.* 1906, *s.* 1962.)	John E. H. *M., b.* 1943.
1690	*Scarbrough* (12th), Richard Aldred Lumley (13th *Irish Visct., Lumley,* 1628), *b.* 1932, *s.* 1969, *m.*	Viscount Lumley, *b.* 1973.
1701 S.	*Seafield* (13th), Ian Derek Francis Ogilvie-Grant, *b.* 1939, *s.* 1969, *m.*	Viscount Reidhaven, *b.* 1963.
1882	*Selborne* (4th), John Roundell Palmer, KBE, FRS, *b.* 1940, *s.* 1971, *m.*	Viscount Wolmer, *b.* 1971.
1646 S.	*Selkirk* (10th), (George) Nigel Douglas-Hamilton, KT, GCMG, GBE, AFC, AE, PC, QC, *b.* 1906, *s.* 1940, *m.*	The Master of Selkirk, *b.* 1939.
1672	*Shaftesbury* (10th), Anthony Ashley-Cooper, *b.* 1938, *s.* 1961, *m.*	Lord Ashley, *b.* 1977.
1756 I.*	*Shannon* (9th), Richard Bentinck Boyle (8th *Brit. Baron Carleton,* 1786), *b.* 1924, *s.* 1963.	Viscount Boyle, *b.* 1960.
1442	*Shrewsbury & Waterford* (22nd) (I. 1446), Charles Henry John Benedict Crofton Chetwynd Chetwynd-Talbot (*Premier Earl of England and Ireland; Earl Talbot,* 1784), *b.* 1952, *s.* 1980, *m.*	Viscount Ingestre, *b.* 1978.
1961	*Snowdon* (1st), Antony Charles Robert Armstrong-Jones, GCVO, *b.* 1930, *m.* (*see also* page 123).	Viscount Linley, *b.* 1961 (*see also* page 123).
1880	°*Sondes* (5th), Henry George Herbert Milles-Lade, *b.* 1940, *s.* 1970.	None.
1765	°*Spencer* (9th), Charles Edward Maurice Spencer, *b.* 1964, *s.* 1992, *m.*	G. C. Robert M. *S., b.* 1932.
1703 S.*	*Stair* (13th), John Aymer Dalrymple, KCVO, MBE (6th *UK Baron, Oxenfoord,* 1841), *b.* 1906, *s.* 1961, *m.*	Viscount Dalrymple, *b.* 1961.
1984	*Stockton* (2nd), Alexander Daniel Alan Macmillan, *b.* 1943, *s.* 1986.	Viscount Macmillan of Ovenden, *b.* 1974.
1821	*Stradbroke* (6th), Robert Keith Rous, *b.* 1937, *s.* 1983, *m.*	Viscount Dunwich, *b.* 1961.
1847	*Strafford* (8th), Thomas Edmund Byng, *b.* 1936, *s.* 1984, *m.*	Viscount Enfield, *b.* 1964.
1606 S.*	*Strathmore & Kinghorne* (18th), Michael Fergus Bowes Lyon (16th *Scottish Earl, Strathmore,* 1677, & 18th *Kinghorne,* 1606; 5th *UK Earl, Strathmore & Kinghorne,* 1937), *b.* 1957, *s.* 1987, *m.*	Lord Glamis, *b.* 1986.
1603	*Suffolk* (21st) & *Berkshire* (14th) (1626), Michael John James George Robert Howard, *b.* 1935, *s.* 1941, *m.*	Viscount Andover, *b.* 1974.
1955	*Swinton* (2nd), David Yarburgh Cunliffe-Lister, *b.* 1937, *s.* 1972, *m.*	Hon. Nicholas J. *C.-L., b.* 1939.
1714	*Tankerville* (10th), Peter Grey Bennet, *b.* 1956, *s.* 1980.	Revd the Hon. George A. G. *B., b.* 1925.
1822	°*Temple of Stowe* (8th), (Walter) Grenville Algernon Temple-Gore-Langton, *b.* 1924, *s.* 1988, *m.*	Lord Langton, *b.* 1955.
1815	*Verulam* (7th), John Duncan Grimston (11th *Irish Visct., Grimston,* 1719; 16th *Scott. Baron, Forrester of Corstorphine,* 1633), *b.* 1951, *s.* 1973, *m.*	Viscount Grimston, *b.* 1978.
1729	°*Waldegrave* (12th), Geoffrey Noel Waldegrave, KG, GCVO, TD, *b.* 1905, *s.* 1936, *m.*	Viscount Chewton, *b.* 1940.
1759	*Warwick* & °*Brooke* (8th) (*Brit.* 1746), David Robin Francis Guy Greville (8th *Earl Brooke* and 8th *Earl of Warwick*), *b.* 1934, *s.* 1984.	Lord Brooke, *b.* 1957.
1633 S.*	*Wemyss* (12th) & *March* (8th) (S. 1697), Francis David Charteris, KT (5th *UK Baron, Wemyss,* 1821), *b.* 1912, *s.* 1937, *w.*	Lord Neidpath, *b.* 1948.
1621 I.	*Westmeath* (13th), William Anthony Nugent, *b.* 1928, *s.* 1971, *m.*	Hon. Sean C. W. *N., b.* 1965.
1624	*Westmorland* (15th), David Anthony Thomas Fane, GCVO, *b.* 1924, *s.* 1948, *m.*	Lord Burghersh, *b.* 1951.
1876	*Wharncliffe* (5th), Richard Alan Montagu Stuart Wortley, *b.* 1953, *s.* 1987, *m.*	Viscount Carlton, *b.* 1980.
1801	*Wilton* (7th), Seymour William Arthur John Egerton, *b.* 1921, *s.* 1927, *m.*	Baron Ebury, *b.* 1934 (*see* page 155).
1628	*Winchilsea* (16th) & *Nottingham* (11th) (1675), Christopher Denys Stormont Finch Hatton, *b.* 1936, *s.* 1950, *m.*	Viscount Maidstone, *b.* 1967.

Created	Title, order of succession, name, etc.	Eldest son or heir
1766 I.	°*Winterton* (8th), (Donald) David Turnour, *b.* 1943, *s.* 1991, *m.*	Robert C. *T., b.* 1950.
1956	*Woolton* (3rd), Simon Frederick Marquis, *b.* 1958, *s.* 1969, *m.*	None.
1837	*Yarborough* (8th), Charles John Pelham, *b.* 1963, *s.* 1991, *m.*	Lord Worsley, *b.* 1990.

COUNTESSES IN THEIR OWN RIGHT

Style, The Right Hon. the Countess (of) ___
Husband, Untitled
Children's style, As for children of an Earl
For forms of address, *see* page 220

Created	Title, order of succession, name, etc.	Eldest son or heir
1643 S.	*Dysart* (11th in line), Rosamund Agnes Greaves, *b.* 1914, *s.* 1975.	Lady Katherine *Grant of Rothiemurchus, b.* 1918.
1633 S.	*Loudoun* (13th in line), Barbara Huddleston Abney-Hastings, *b.* 1919, *s.* 1960, *m.*	Lord Mauchline, *b.* 1942.
c.1115 S.	*Mar* (31st in line), Margaret of Mar (*Premier Earldom of Scotland*), *b.* 1940, *s.* 1975, *m.*	Mistress of Mar, *b.* 1963.
1947	°*Mountbatten of Burma* (2nd in line), Patricia Edwina Victoria Knatchbull, CBE, *b.* 1924, *s.* 1979, *m.*	Lord Romsey, *b.* 1947 (*see also* page 153).
c.1235 S.	*Sutherland* (24th in line), Elizabeth Millicent Sutherland, *b.* 1921, *s.* 1963, *m.*	Lord Strathnaver, *b.* 1947.

VISCOUNTS

Coronet, Sixteen silver balls
Style, The Right Hon. the Viscount ___
Wife's style, The Right Hon. the Viscountess ___
Children's style, 'The Hon.' before forename and family name
In Scotland, the heir apparent to a Viscount may be styled 'The Master of ___ (title of peer)'
For forms of address, *see* page 220

Created	Title, order of succession, name, etc.	Eldest son or heir
1945	*Addison* (4th), William Matthew Wand Addison, *b.* 1945, *s.* 1992, *m.*	Hon. Paul W. *A., b.* 1973.
1946	*Alanbrooke* (3rd), Alan Victor Harold Brooke, *b.* 1932, *s.* 1972.	None.
1919	*Allenby* (3rd), Lt.-Col. Michael Jaffray Hynman Allenby, *b.* 1931, *s.* 1984, *m.*	Hon. Henry J. H. *A., b.* 1968.
1911	*Allendale* (3rd), Wentworth Hubert Charles Beaumont, *b.* 1922, *s.* 1956, *m.*	Hon. Wentworth P. I. *B., b.* 1948.
1642 S.	*of Arbuthnott* (16th), John Campbell Arbuthnott, CBE, DSC, *b.* 1924, *s.* 1966, *m.*	Master of Arbuthnott, *b.* 1950.
1751 I.	*Ashbrook* (10th), Desmond Llowarch Edward Flower, KCVO, MBE, *b.* 1905. *s.* 1936, *m.*	Hon. Michael L. W. *F., b.* 1935.
1917	*Astor* (4th), William Waldorf Astor, *b.* 1951, *s.* 1966, *m.*	Hon. William W. *A., b.* 1979.
1781 I.	*Bangor* (8th), William Maxwell David Ward, *b.* 1948, *s.* 1993, *m.*	Hon. Edward N. *W., b.* 1953.
1925	*Bearsted* (4th), Peter Montefiore Samuel, MC, TD, *b.* 1911, *s.* 1986, *m.*	Hon. Nicholas A. *S., b.* 1950.
1963	*Blakenham* (2nd), Michael John Hare, *b.* 1938, *s.* 1982, *m.*	Hon. Caspar J. *H., b.* 1972.
1935	*Bledisloe* (3rd), Christopher Hiley Ludlow Bathurst, QC, *b.* 1934, *s.* 1979.	Hon. Rupert E. L. *B., b.* 1964.
1712	*Bolingbroke* (7th) & *St John* (8th) (1716), Kenneth Oliver Musgrave St John, *b.* 1927, *s.* 1974.	Hon. Henry F. *St J., b.* 1957.
1960	*Boyd of Merton* (2nd), Simon Donald Rupert Neville Lennox-Boyd, *b.* 1939, *s.* 1983, *m.*	Hon. Benjamin A. *L.-B., b.* 1964.
1717 I.*	*Boyne* (10th), Gustavus Michael George Hamilton-Russell (4th *UK Baron, Brancepeth,* 1866), *b.* 1931, *s.* 1942, *m.*	Hon. Gustavus M. S. *H.-R., b.* 1965.
1929	*Brentford* (4th), Crispin William Joynson-Hicks, *b.* 1933, *s.* 1983, *m.*	Hon. Paul W. *J.-H., b.* 1971.
1929	*Bridgeman* (3rd), Robin John Orlando Bridgeman, *b.* 1930, *s.* 1982, *m.*	Hon. William O. C. *B., b.* 1968.

Created	Title, order of succession, name, etc.	Eldest son or heir
1868	*Bridport* (4th), Alexander Nelson Hood (7th *Duke of Brontë in Sicily*, 1799, *and* 6th *Irish Baron Bridport*, 1794), *b.* 1948, *s.* 1969, *m.*	Hon. Peregrine A. N. *H.*, *b.* 1974.
1952	*Brookeborough* (3rd), Alan Henry Brooke, *b.* 1952, *s.* 1987, *m.*	Hon. Christopher A. *B.*, *b.* 1954.
1933	*Buckmaster* (3rd), Martin Stanley Buckmaster, OBE, *b.* 1921, *s.* 1974.	Hon. Colin J. *B.*, *b.* 1923.
1939	*Caldecote* (2nd), Robert Andrew Inskip, KBE, DSC, FEng., *b.* 1917, *s.* 1947, *m.*	Hon. Piers J. H. *I.*, *b.* 1947.
1941	*Camrose* (2nd), (John) Seymour Berry, TD, *b.* 1909, *s.* 1954, *m.*	Baron Hartwell, MBE, TD, *b.* 1911 (*see* page 164).
1954	*Chandos* (3rd), Thomas Orlando Lyttelton, *b.* 1953, *s.* 1980, *m.*	Hon. Oliver A. *L.*, *b.* 1986.
1665 I.	*Charlemont* (14th), John Day Caulfeild (18th *Irish Baron, Caulfeild of Charlemont*, 1620), *b.* 1934, *s.* 1985, *m.*	Hon. John D. *C.*, *b.* 1966.
1921	*Chelmsford* (3rd), Frederic Jan Thesiger, *b.* 1931, *s.* 1970, *m.*	Hon. Frederic C. P. *T.*, *b.* 1962.
1717 I.	*Chetwynd* (10th), Adam Richard John Casson Chetwynd, *b.* 1935, *s.* 1965, *m.*	Hon. Adam D. *C.*, *b.* 1969.
1911	*Chilston* (4th), Alastair George Akers-Douglas, *b.* 1946, *s.* 1982, *m.*	Hon. Oliver I. *A.-D.*, *b.* 1973.
1902	*Churchill* (3rd), Victor George Spencer (5th *UK Baron Churchill*, 1815), *b.* 1934, *s.* 1973.	None to Viscountcy. To Barony, Richard H. R. *S.*, *b.* 1926.
1718	*Cobham* (11th), John William Leonard Lyttelton (8th *Irish Baron, Westcote*, 1776), *b.* 1943, *s.* 1977, *m.*	Hon. Christopher C. *L.*, *b.* 1947.
1902	*Colville of Culross* (4th), John Mark Alexander Colville, QC (13th *Scott. Baron, Colville of Culross*, 1604), *b.* 1933, *s.* 1945, *m.*	Master of Colville, *b.* 1959.
1826	*Combermere* (5th), Michael Wellington Stapleton-Cotton, *b.* 1929, *s.* 1969, *m.*	Hon. Thomas R. W. *S.-C.*, *b.* 1969.
1917	*Cowdray* (3rd), Weetman John Churchill Pearson, TD (3rd *UK Baron, Cowdray*, 1910), *b.* 1910, *s.* 1933, *m.*	Hon. Michael O. W. *P.*, *b.* 1944.
1927	*Craigavon* (3rd), Janric Fraser Craig, *b.* 1944, *s.* 1974.	None.
1886	*Cross* (3rd), Assheton Henry Cross, *b.* 1920, *s.* 1932.	None.
1943	*Daventry* (3rd), Francis Humphrey Maurice FitzRoy Newdegate, *b.* 1921, *s.* 1986, *m.*	Hon. James E. *F.N.*, *b.* 1960.
1937	*Davidson* (2nd), John Andrew Davidson, *b.* 1928, *s.* 1970, *m.*	Hon. Malcolm W. M. *D.*, *b.* 1934.
1956	*De L'Isle* (2nd), Philip John Algernon Sidney, MBE, (7th *Baron De L'Isle and Dudley*, 1835), *b.* 1945, *s.* 1991, *m.*	Hon. Philip W. E. *S.*, *b.* 1985.
1776 I.	*De Vesci* (7th), Thomas Eustace Vesey (8th *Irish Baron, Knapton*, 1750), *b.* 1955, *s.* 1983, *m.*	Hon. Oliver I. *V.*, *b.* 1991.
1917	*Devonport* (3rd), Terence Kearley, *b.* 1944, *s.* 1973.	Chester D. H. *K.*, *b.* 1932.
1964	*Dilhorne* (2nd), John Mervyn Manningham-Buller, *b.* 1932, *s.* 1980, *m.*	Hon. James E.*M.-B.*, *b.* 1956.
1622 I.	*Dillon* (22nd), Henry Benedict Charles Dillon, *b.* 1973, *s.* 1982.	Hon. Richard A. L. *D.*, *b.* 1948.
1785 I.	*Doneraile* (10th), Richard Allen St Leger, *b.* 1946, *s.* 1983, *m.*	Hon. Nathaniel W. R. St J. *St L.*, *b.* 1971.
1680 I.*	*Downe* (11th), John Christian George Dawnay (4th *UK Baron, Dawnay*, 1897), *b.* 1935, *s.* 1965, *m.*	Hon. Richard H. *D.*, *b.* 1967.
1959	*Dunrossil* (2nd), John William Morrison, CMG, *b.* 1926, *s.* 1961, *m.*	Hon. Andrew W. R. *M.*, *b.* 1953.
1964	*Eccles* (1st), David McAdam Eccles, CH, KCVO, PC, *b.* 1904, *m.*	Hon. John D. *E.*, CBE, *b.* 1931.
1897	*Esher* (4th), Lionel Gordon Baliol Brett, CBE, *b.* 1913. *s.* 1963, *m.*	Hon. Christopher L. B. *B.*, *b.* 1936.
1816	*Exmouth* (10th), Paul Edward Pellew, *b.* 1940, *s.* 1970, *m.*	Hon. Edward F. *P.*, *b.* 1978.
1620 S.	*Falkland* (15th), Lucius Edward William Plantagenet Cary (*Premier Scottish Viscount on the Roll*), *b.* 1935, *s.* 1984, *m.*	Master of Falkland, *b.* 1963.
1720	*Falmouth* (9th), George Hugh Boscawen (26th *Eng. Baron, Le Despencer*, 1264), *b.* 1919, *s.* 1962, *m.*	Hon. Evelyn A. H. *B.*, *b.* 1955.
1918	*Furness* (2nd), William Anthony Furness, *b.* 1929, *s.* 1940.	None.
1720 I.*	*Gage* (7th), George John St Clere Gage, (6th *Brit. Baron, Gage*, 1790), *b.* 1932, *s.* 1982.	Hon. H. Nicolas *G.*, *b.* 1934.
1727 I.	*Galway* (12th), George Rupert Monckton-Arundell, *b.* 1922, *s.* 1980, *m.*	Hon. J. Philip *M.*, *b.* 1952.
1478 I.*	*Gormanston* (17th), Jenico Nicholas Dudley Preston (*Premier Viscount of Ireland*; 5th *UK Baron, Gormanston*, 1868), *b.* 1939, *s.* 1940, *w.*	Hon. Jenico F. T. *P.*, *b.* 1974.
1816 I.	*Gort* (8th), Colin Leopold Prendergast Vereker, *b.* 1916, *s.* 1975, *m.*	Hon. Foley R.S.P.*V.*, *b.* 1951.
1900	*Goschen* (4th), Giles John Harry Goschen, *b.* 1965, *s.* 1977, *m.*	None.
1849	*Gough* (5th), Shane Hugh Maryon Gough, *b.* 1941, *s.* 1951.	None.
1937	*Greenwood* (2nd), David Henry Hamar Greenwood, *b.* 1914, *s.* 1948.	Hon. Michael G. H. *G.*, *b.* 1923.
1929	*Hailsham.* Disclaimed for life 1963. (*see* Lord Hailsham of St Marylebone, page 164.)	Hon. Douglas M. *Hogg*, QC, MP, *b.* 1945.
1891	*Hambleden* (4th), William Herbert Smith, *b.* 1930, *s.* 1948, *m.*	Hon. William H. B. *S.*, *b.* 1955.
1884	*Hampden* (6th), Anthony David Brand, *b.* 1937, *s.* 1975.	Hon. Francis A. *B.*, *b.* 1970.
1936	*Hanworth* (2nd), David Bertram Pollock, *b.* 1916, *s.* 1936, *m.*	Hon. David S. G. *P.*, *b.* 1946.
1791 I.	*Harberton* (10th), Thomas de Vautort Pomeroy, *b.* 1910, *s.* 1980, *m.*	Hon. Robert W. *P.*, *b.* 1916.
1846	*Hardinge* (6th), Charles Henry Nicholas Hardinge, *b.* 1956, *s.* 1984, *m.*	Hon. Andrew H. *H.*, *b.* 1960.

Created	Title, order of succession, name, etc.	Eldest son or heir
1791 I.	*Hawarden* (9th), (Robert) Connan Wyndham Leslie Maude, *b.* 1961, *s.* 1991.	Hon. Thomas P. C. *M.*, *b.* 1964.
1960	*Head* (2nd), Richard Antony Head, *b.* 1937, *s.* 1983, *m.*	Hon. Henry J. *H.*, *b.* 1980.
1550	*Hereford* (18th), Robert Milo Leicester Devereux (*Premier Viscount of England*), *b.* 1932, *s.* 1952.	Hon. Charles R. de B. *D.*, *b.* 1975.
1842	*Hill* (8th), Antony Rowland Clegg-Hill, *b.* 1931, *s.* 1974.	Peter D. R. C. *C.-H.*, *b.* 1945.
1796	*Hood* (7th), Alexander Lambert Hood (7th *Irish Baron, Hood,* 1782), *b.* 1914, *s.* 1981, *m.*	Hon. Henry L. A. *H.*, *b.* 1958.
1956	*Ingleby* (2nd), Martin Raymond Peake, *b.* 1926, *s.* 1966, *m.*	None.
1945	*Kemsley* (2nd), (Geoffrey) Lionel Berry, *b.* 1909, *s.* 1968, *m.*	Richard G. *B.*, *b.* 1951.
1911	*Knollys* (3rd), David Francis Dudley Knollys, *b.* 1931, *s.* 1966, *m.*	Hon. Patrick N. M. *K.*, *b.* 1962.
1895	*Knutsford* (6th), Michael Holland-Hibbert, *b.* 1926, *s.* 1986, *m.*	Hon. Henry T. *H.-H.*, *b.* 1959.
1945	*Lambert* (3rd), Michael John Lambert, *b.* 1912, *s.* 1989, *m.*	None.
1954	*Leathers* (2nd), Frederick Alan Leathers, *b.* 1908, *s.* 1965, *m.*	Hon. Christopher G. *L.*, *b.* 1941.
1922	*Leverhulme* (3rd), Philip William Bryce Lever, KG, TD, *b.* 1915, *s.* 1949, *w.*	None.
1781 I.	*Lifford* (9th), (Edward) James Wingfield Hewitt, *b.* 1949, *s.* 1987, *m.*	Hon. James T. W. *H.*, *b.* 1979.
1921	*Long* (4th), Richard Gerard Long, CBE, *b.* 1929, *s.* 1967, *m.*	Hon. James R. *L.*, *b.* 1960.
1957	*Mackintosh of Halifax* (3rd), (John) Clive Mackintosh, *b.* 1958, *s.* 1980, *m.*	Hon. Thomas H. G. *M.*, *b.* 1985.
1955	*Malvern* (3rd), Ashley Kevin Godfrey Huggins, *b.* 1949, *s.* 1978.	Hon. M. James *H.*, *b.* 1928.
1945	*Marchwood* (3rd), David George Staveley Penny, *b.* 1936, *s.* 1979, *m.*	Hon. Peter G. *M.*, *b.* 1965.
1942	*Margesson* (2nd), Francis Vere Hampden Margesson, *b.* 1922, *s.* 1965, *m.*	Capt. Hon. Richard F. D. *M.*, *b.* 1960.
1660 I.*	*Massereene* (14th) & *Ferrard* (7th) (1797), John David Clotworthy Whyte-Melville Foster Skeffington (7th *UK Baron, Oriel,* 1821), *b.* 1940, *s.* 1993, *m.*	Hon. Charles *S.*, *b.* 1973.
1802	*Melville* (9th), Robert David Ross Dundas, *b.* 1937, *s.* 1971, *m.*	Hon. Robert H. K. *D.*, *b.* 1984.
1916	*Mersey* (4th), Richard Maurice Clive Bigham, *b.* 1934, *s.* 1979, *m.*	Hon. Edward J. H. *B.*, *b.* 1966.
1717 I.*	*Midleton* (12th), Alan Henry Brodrick (9th *Brit. Baron, Brodrick of Peper Harow,* 1796), *b.* 1949, *s.* 1988, *m.*	Hon. Ashley R. *B.*, *b.* 1980.
1962	*Mills* (3rd), Christopher Philip Roger Mills, *b.* 1956, *s.* 1988, *m.*	None.
1716 I.	*Molesworth* (11th), Richard Gosset Molesworth, *b.* 1907, *s.* 1961, *w.*	Hon. Robert B. K. *M.*, *b.* 1959.
1801 I.*	*Monck* (7th), Charles Stanley Monck (4th *UK Baron, Monck,* 1866), *b.* 1953, *s.* 1982.	Hon. George S. *M.*, *b.* 1957.
1957	*Monckton of Brenchley* (2nd), Gilbert Walter Riversdale Monckton, CB, OBE, MC, *b.* 1915, *s.* 1965, *m.*	Hon Christopher W. *M.*, *b.* 1952.
1935	*Monsell* (2nd), Henry Bolton Graham Eyres Monsell, *b.* 1905, *s.* 1969.	None.
1946	*Montgomery of Alamein* (2nd), David Bernard Montgomery, CBE, *b.* 1928, *s.* 1976, *m.*	Hon. Henry D. *M.*, *b.* 1954.
1550 I.*	*Mountgarret* (17th), Richard Henry Piers Butler (4th *UK Baron, Mountgarret,* 1911), *b.* 1936, *s.* 1966, *m.*	Hon. Piers J. R. *B.*, *b.* 1961.
1952	*Norwich* (2nd), John Julius Cooper, CVO, *b.* 1929, *s.* 1954, *m.*	Hon. Jason C. D. B. *C.*, *b.* 1959.
1651 S.	*of Oxfuird* (13th), George Hubbard Makgill, *b.* 1934, *s.* 1986, *m.*	Master of Oxfuird, *b.* 1969.
1873	*Portman,* (9th), Edward Henry Berkeley Portman, *b.* 1934, *s.* 1967, *m.*	Hon. Christopher E. B. *P.*, *b.* 1958.
1743 I.*	*Powerscourt* (10th), Mervyn Niall Wingfield (4th *UK Baron, Powerscourt,* 1885), *b.* 1935, *s.* 1973, *m.*	Hon. Mervyn A. *W.*, *b.* 1963.
1900	*Ridley* (4th), Matthew White Ridley, KG, TD, *b.* 1925, *s.* 1964, *m.* Lord Steward.	Hon. Matthew W. *R.*, *b.* 1958.
1960	*Rochdale* (2nd), St John Durival Kemp, *b.* 1938, *s.* 1993, *m.*	Hon. Jonathan H. D. *K.*, *b.* 1961.
1919	*Rothermere* (3rd), Vere Harold Esmond Harmsworth, *b.* 1925, *s.* 1978, *w.*	Hon. H. Jonathan E. V. *H.*, *b.* 1967.
1937	*Runciman of Doxford* (3rd), Walter Garrison Runciman, CBE, FBA (4th *UK Baron, Runciman,* 1933), *b.* 1934, *s.* 1989, *m.*	Hon. David W. *R.*, *b.* 1967.
1918	*St Davids* (3rd), Colwyn Jestyn John Philipps (20th *Engl. Baron Strange of Knokin,* 1299, 8th *Engl. Baron Hungerford,* 1426, *and De Moleyns,* 1445), *b.* 1939, *s.* 1991, *m.*	Hon. Rhodri C. *P.*, *b.* 1966.
1801	*St Vincent* (7th), Ronald George James Jervis, *b.* 1905, *s.* 1940, *m.*	Hon. Edward R. J. *J.*, *b.* 1951.
1937	*Samuel* (3rd), David Herbert Samuel, PH.D., *b.* 1922, *s.* 1978, *m.*	Hon. Dan J. *S.*, *b.* 1925.
1911	*Scarsdale* (3rd), Francis John Nathaniel Curzon (7th *Brit. Baron, Scarsdale,* 1761), *b.* 1924, *s.* 1977, *m.*	Hon. Peter G. N. *C.*, *b.* 1949.
1905	*Selby* (4th), Michael Guy John Gully, *b.* 1942, *s.* 1959, *m.*	Hon. Edward T. W. *G.*, *b.* 1967.
1805	*Sidmouth* (7th), John Tonge Anthony Pellew Addington, *b.* 1914, *s.* 1976, *w.*	Hon. Jeremy F. *A.*, *b.* 1947.
1940	*Simon* (2nd), John Gilbert Simon, CMG, *b.* 1902, *s.* 1954, *m.*	Hon. Jan D. *S.*, *b.* 1940.
1960	*Slim* (2nd), John Douglas Slim, OBE, *b.* 1927, *s.* 1970, *m.*	Hon. Mark W. R. *S.*, *b.* 1960.
1954	*Soulbury* (2nd), James Herwald Ramsbotham, *b.* 1915, *s.* 1971, *w.*	Hon. Sir Peter E. *R.*, GCMG, GCVO, *b.* 1919.
1776 I.	*Southwell* (7th), Pyers Anthony Joseph Southwell, *b.* 1930, *s.* 1960, *m.*	Hon. Richard A. P. *S.*, *b.* 1956.
1942	*Stansgate.* Disclaimed for life 1963. (*Rt. Hon. Anthony Neil Wedgwood Benn,* MP, *b.* 1925, *s.* 1960, *m.*)	Stephen M. W. *B.*, *b.* 1951.

Created	Title, order of succession, name, etc.	Eldest son or heir
1959	Stuart of Findhorn (2nd), David Randolph Moray Stuart, b. 1924, s. 1971, m.	Hon. J. Dominic S., b. 1948.
1957	Tenby (3rd), William Lloyd George, b. 1927, s. 1983, m.	Hon. Timothy H. G. L. G., b. 1962.
1952	Thurso (2nd), Robin Macdonald Sinclair, b. 1922, s. 1970, m.	Hon. John A. S., b. 1953.
1983	Tonypandy (1st), (Thomas) George Thomas, PC, b. 1909.	None.
1721	Torrington (11th), Timothy Howard St George Byng, b. 1943, s. 1961, m.	John L. B., MC, b. 1919.
1936	Trenchard (3rd), Hugh Trenchard, b. 1951, s. 1987, m.	Hon. Alexander T. T., b. 1978.
1921	Ullswater (2nd), Nicholas James Christopher Lowther, b. 1942, s. 1949, m.	Hon. Benjamin J. L., b. 1975.
1621 I.	Valentia (15th), Richard John Dighton Annesley, b. 1929, s. 1983, m.	Hon. Francis W. D. A., b. 1959.
1964	Watkinson (1st), Harold Arthur Watkinson, CH, PC, b. 1910, m.	None.
1952	Waverley (3rd), John Desmond Forbes Anderson, b. 1949, s. 1990.	None.
1938	Weir (3rd), William Kenneth James Weir, b. 1933, s. 1975, m.	Hon. James W. H. W., b. 1965.
1983	Whitelaw (1st), William Stephen Ian Whitelaw, KT, CH, MC, PC, b. 1918, m.	None.
1918	Wimborne (3rd), Ivor Fox-Strangways Guest (4th UK Baron, Wimborne, 1880), b. 1939, s. 1967, m.	Hon. Ivor M.V.G., b. 1968.
1923	Younger of Leckie (3rd), Edward George Younger, OBE, TD, b. 1906, s. 1946, w.	Baron Younger of Prestwick, KCVO, TD, PC, b. 1931 (see page 166).

BARONS/LORDS

Coronet, Six silver balls
Style, The Right Hon. the Lord ___. In the Peerage of Scotland there is no rank of Baron; the equivalent rank is Lord of Parliament (see page 141) and Scottish peers should always be styled 'Lord', never 'Baron'
Wife's style, The Right Hon. the Lady ___
Children's style, 'The Hon.' before forename and family name
In Scotland, the heir apparent to a Lord may be styled 'The Master of ___ (title of peer)'
For forms of address, see page 220

Created	Title, order of succession, name, etc.	Eldest son or heir
1911	Aberconway (3rd), Charles Melville McLaren, b. 1913, s. 1953, m.	Hon. H. Charles M., b. 1948.
1873	Aberdare (4th), Morys George Lyndhurst Bruce, KBE, PC, b. 1919, s. 1957, m.	Hon. Alastair J. L. B., b. 1947.
1835	Abinger (8th), James Richard Scarlett, b. 1914, s. 1943, m.	Hon. James H. S., b. 1959.
1869	Acton (4th), Richard Gerald Lyon-Dalberg-Acton, b. 1941, s. 1989, m.	Hon. John C. F. H. L.-D.-A., b. 1966.
1887	Addington (6th), Dominic Bryce Hubbard, b. 1963, s. 1982.	Hon. Michael W. L. H., b. 1965.
1955	Adrian (2nd), Richard Hume Adrian, FRS, b. 1927, s. 1977, m.	None.
1907	Airedale (4th), Oliver James Vandeleur Kitson, b. 1915, s. 1958.	None.
1896	Aldenham (6th), and Hunsdon of Hunsdon (4th) (1923), Vicary Tyser Gibbs, b. 1948, s. 1986, m.	Hon. Humphrey W. F. G., b. 1989.
1962	Aldington (1st), Toby Austin Richard William Low, KCMG, CBE, DSO, TD, PC, b. 1914, m.	Hon Charles H. S. L., b. 1948.
1945	Altrincham. Disclaimed for life 1963. (John Edward Poynder Grigg, b. 1924, s. 1955, m.)	†
1929	Alvingham (2nd), Maj.-Gen. Robert Guy Eardley Yerburgh, CBE, b. 1926, s. 1955, m.	Capt. Hon. Robert R. G. Y., b. 1956.
1892	Amherst of Hackney (4th), William Hugh Amherst Cecil, b. 1940, s. 1980, m.	Hon. H. William A. C., b. 1968.
1881	Ampthill (4th), Geoffrey Denis Erskine Russell, CBE, b. 1921, s. 1973.	Hon. David W. E. R., b. 1947.
1947	Amwell (3rd), Keith Norman Montague, b. 1943, s. 1990, m.	Hon. Ian K. M., b. 1973.
1863	Annaly (6th), Luke Richard White, b. 1954, s. 1990, m.	Hon. Luke H. W., b. 1990.
1949	Archibald. Disclaimed for life 1975. (George Christopher Archibald, b. 1926, s. 1975, m.)	None.
1885	Ashbourne (4th), Edward Barry Greynville Gibson, b. 1933, s. 1983, m.	Hon. Edward C. d'O. G., b. 1967.
1835	Ashburton (7th), John Francis Harcourt Baring, KCVO, b. 1928, s. 1991, m.	Hon. Mark F. R. B., b. 1958.
1892	Ashcombe (4th), Henry Edward Cubitt, b. 1924, s. 1962, m.	Mark E. C., b. 1964.
1911	Ashton of Hyde (3rd), Thomas John Ashton, TD, b. 1926, s. 1983, m.	Hon. Thomas H. A., b. 1958.
1800 I.	Ashtown (7th), Nigel Clive Crosby Trench, KCMG, b. 1916, s. 1990, m.	Hon. Roderick N. G. T., b. 1944.
1956	Astor of Hever (3rd), John Jacob Astor, b. 1946, s. 1984, m.	Hon. Charles G. J. A., b. 1990.
1789 I.*	Auckland (9th), Ian George Eden (9th Brit. Baron, Auckland, 1793), b. 1926, s. 1957, m.	Hon. Robert I. B. E., b. 1962.

Created	Title, order of succession, name, etc.	Eldest son or heir
1313	*Audley* (25th), Richard Michael Thomas Souter, *b.* 1914, *s.* 1973, *m.*	Three co-heiresses.
1900	*Avebury* (4th), Eric Reginald Lubbock, *b.* 1928, *s.* 1971, *m.*	Hon. Lyulph A. J. L., *b.* 1954.
1718 I.	*Aylmer* (13th), Michael Anthony Aylmer, *b.* 1923, *s.* 1982, *m.*	Hon. A. Julian A., *b.* 1951.
1929	*Baden-Powell* (3rd), Robert Crause Baden-Powell, *b.* 1936, *s.* 1962, *m.*	Hon. David M. B.-P., *b.* 1940.
1780	*Bagot* (9th), Heneage Charles Bagot, *b.* 1914, *s.* 1979, *m.*	Hon. C. H. Shaun B., *b.* 1944.
1953	*Baillieu* (3rd), James William Latham Baillieu, *b.* 1950, *s.* 1973, *m.*	Hon. Robert L. B., *b.* 1979.
1607 S.	*Balfour of Burleigh* (8th), Robert Bruce, *b.* 1927, *s.* 1967, *m.*	Hon. Victoria B., *b.* 1973.
1945	*Balfour of Inchrye* (2nd), Ian Balfour, *b.* 1924, *s.* 1988, *m.*	None.
1924	*Banbury of Southam* (3rd), Charles William Banbury, *b.* 1953, *s.* 1981.	None.
1698	*Barnard* (11th), Harry John Neville Vane, TD, *b.* 1923, *s.* 1964, *m.*	Hon. Henry F. C. V., *b.* 1959.
1887	*Basing* (5th), Neil Lutley Sclater-Booth, *b.* 1939, *s.* 1983, *m.*	Hon. Stuart W. S.-B., *b.* 1969.
1917	*Beaverbrook* (3rd), Maxwell William Humphrey Aitken, *b.* 1951, *s.* 1985, *m.*	Hon. Maxwell F. A, *b.* 1977.
1647 S.	*Belhaven and Stenton* (13th), Robert Anthony Carmichael Hamilton, *b.* 1927, *s.* 1961, *m.*	Master of Belhaven, *b.* 1953.
1848 I.	*Bellew* (7th), James Bryan Bellew, *b.* 1920, *s.* 1981, *m.*	Hon. Bryan E. B., *b.* 1943.
1856	*Belper* (4th), (Alexander) Ronald George Strutt, *b.* 1912, *s.* 1956.	Hon. Richard H. S., *b.* 1941.
1938	*Belstead* (2nd), John Julian Ganzoni, PC, *b.* 1932, *s.* 1958.	None.
1421	*Berkeley* (18th), Anthony Fitzhardinge Gueterbock, OBE, *b.* 1939, *s.* 1992, *m.*	Hon. Thomas F. G., *b.* 1969.
1922	*Bethell* (4th), Nicholas William Bethell, MEP, *b.* 1938, *s.* 1967, *m.*	Hon. James N. B., *b.* 1967.
1938	*Bicester* (3rd), Angus Edward Vivian Smith, *b.* 1932, *s.* 1968.	Hugh C. V. S., *b.* 1934.
1903	*Biddulph* (5th), (Anthony) Nicholas Colin Maitland Biddulph, *b.* 1959, *s.* 1988, *m.*	Hon. William I. R. M.B., *b.* 1963.
1938	*Birdwood* (3rd), Mark William Ogilvie Birdwood, *b.* 1938, *s.* 1962, *m.*	None.
1958	*Birkett* (2nd), Michael Birkett, *b.* 1929, *s.* 1962, *m.*	Hon. Thomas B., *b.* 1982.
1907	*Blyth* (4th), Anthony Audley Rupert Blyth, *b.* 1931, *s.* 1977, *m.*	Hon. Riley A. J. B., *b.* 1955.
1797	*Bolton* (7th), Richard William Algar Orde-Powlett, *b.* 1929, *s.* 1963, *m.*	Hon. Harry A. N. O.-P., *b.* 1954.
1452 S.	*Borthwick* (23rd), John Henry Stuart Borthwick, TD, *b.* 1905, *claim* succeeded 1986, *w.*	Master of Borthwick, *b.* 1940.
1922	*Borwick* (4th), James Hugh Myles Borwick, MC, *b.* 1917, *s.* 1961, *m.*	Hon. George S. B., *b.* 1922.
1761	*Boston* (10th), Timothy George Frank Boteler Irby, *b.* 1939, *s.* 1978, *m.*	Hon. George W. E. B. I., *b.* 1971.
1942	*Brabazon of Tara* (3rd), Ivon Anthony Moore-Brabazon, *b.* 1946, *s.* 1974, *m.*	Hon. Benjamin R. M.-B., *b.* 1983.
1880	*Brabourne* (7th), John Ulick Knatchbull, CBE, *b.* 1924, *s.* 1943, *m.*	Lord Romsey, *b.* 1947 (*see* page 149).
1925	*Bradbury* (2nd), John Bradbury, *b.* 1914, *s.* 1950, *m.*	Hon. John B., *b.* 1940.
1962	*Brain* (2nd), Christopher Langdon Brain, *b.* 1926, *s.* 1966, *m.*	Hon. Michael C. B., DM, *b.* 1928.
1938	*Brassey of Apethorpe* (3rd), David Henry Brassey, *b.* 1932, *s.* 1967, *m.*	Hon. Edward B., *b.* 1964.
1788	*Braybrooke* (10th), Robin Henry Charles Neville, *b.* 1932, *s.* 1990, *m.*	George N., *b.* 1943.
1957	*Bridges* (2nd), Thomas Edward Bridges, GCMG, *b.* 1927, *s.* 1969, *m.*	Hon. Mark T. B., *b.* 1954.
1945	*Broadbridge* (3rd), Peter Hewett Broadbridge, *b.* 1938, *s.* 1972, *m.*	Martin H. B., *b.* 1929.
1933	*Brocket* (3rd), Charles Ronald George Nall-Cain, *b.* 1952, *s.* 1967, *m.*	Hon. Alexander C. C. N.-C., *b.* 1984.
1860	*Brougham and Vaux* (5th), Michael John Brougham, *b.* 1938, *s.* 1967.	Hon. Charles W. B., *b.* 1971.
1945	*Broughshane* (2nd), Patrick Owen Alexander Davison, *b.* 1903, *s.* 1953, *m.*	Hon. W. Kensington D., DSO, DFC, *b.* 1914.
1776	*Brownlow* (7th), Edward John Peregrine Cust, *b.* 1936, *s.* 1978, *m.*	Hon. Peregrine E. Q. C., *b.* 1974.
1942	*Bruntisfield* (2nd), John Robert Warrender, OBE, MC, TD, *b.* 1921, *s.* 1993, *m.*	Hon. Michael J. V. W., *b.* 1949.
1950	*Burden* (2nd), Philip William Burden, *b.* 1916, *s.* 1970, *m.*	Hon. Andrew P. B., *b.* 1959.
1529	*Burgh* (7th), Alexander Peter Willoughby Leith, *b.* 1935, *s.* 1959, *m.*	Hon. A. Gregory D. L., *b.* 1958.
1903	*Burnham* (6th), Hugh John Frederick Lawson, *b.* 1931, *s.* 1993, *m.*	Hon. Harry F. A. L., *b.* 1968.
1897	*Burton* (3rd), Michael Evan Victor Baillie, *b.* 1924, *s.* 1962, *m.*	Hon. Evan M. R. B., *b.* 1949.
1643	*Byron* (13th), Robert James Byron, *b.* 1950, *s.* 1989, *m.*	Hon. Charles R. G. B., *b.* 1990.
1937	*Cadman* (3rd), John Anthony Cadman, *b.* 1938, *s.* 1966, *m.*	Hon. Nicholas A. J. C., *b.* 1977.
1796	*Calthorpe* (10th), Peter Waldo Somerset Gough-Calthorpe, *b.* 1927, *s.* 1945, *m.*	None.
1945	*Calverley* (3rd), Charles Rodney Muff, *b.* 1946, *s.* 1971, *m.*	Hon. Jonathan E. M., *b.* 1975.
1383	*Camoys* (7th), (Ralph) Thomas Campion George Sherman Stonor, *b.* 1940, *s.* 1976, *m.*	Hon. R. William R. T. S., *b.* 1974.
1715 I.	*Carbery* (11th), Peter Ralfe Harrington Evans-Freke, *b.* 1920, *s.* 1970, *m.*	Hon. Michael P. E.-F., *b.* 1942.
1834 I.*	*Carew* (6th), William Francis Conolly-Carew, CBE (6th *UK. Baron, Carew*, 1838), *b.* 1905, *s.* 1927, *w.*	Hon. Patrick T. C.-C., *b.* 1938.
1916	*Carnock* (4th), David Henry Arthur Nicolson, *b.* 1920, *s.* 1982.	Nigel N., MBE, *b.* 1917.
1796 I.*	*Carrington* (6th), Peter Alexander Rupert Carington, KG, GCMG, CH, MC, PC (6th *Brit. Baron, Carrington*, 1797), *b.* 1919, *s.* 1938, *m.*	Hon. Rupert F. J. C., *b.* 1948.
1812 I.	*Castlemaine* (8th), Roland Thomas John Handcock, MBE, *b.* 1943, *s.* 1973, *m.*	Hon. Ronan M. E. H., *b.* 1989.

Created	Title, order of succession, name, etc.	Eldest son or heir
1936	Catto (2nd), Stephen Gordon Catto, b. 1923, s. 1959, m.	Hon. Innes G. C., b. 1950.
1918	Cawley (3rd), Frederick Lee Cawley, b. 1913, s. 1954, m.	Hon. John F. C., b. 1946.
1603	Cecil, a subsidiary title of the Marquess of Salisbury. His heir Viscount Cranborne was given a Writ in Acceleration in this title to enable him to sit in the House of Lords whilst his father is still alive (see also page 144)	
1937	Chatfield (2nd), Ernle David Lewis Chatfield, b. 1917, s. 1967, m.	None.
1858	Chesham (6th), Nicholas Charles Cavendish, b. 1941, s. 1989, m.	Hon. Charles G. C. C., b. 1974.
1945	Chetwode (2nd), Philip Chetwode, b. 1937, s. 1950, m.	Hon. Roger C., b. 1968.
1945	Chorley (2nd), Roger Richard Edward Chorley, b. 1930, s. 1978, m.	Hon. Nicholas R. D. C., b. 1966.
1858	Churston (5th), John Francis Yarde-Buller, b. 1934, s. 1991, m.	Hon. Benjamin F. A. Y.-B., b. 1974.
1946	Citrine (2nd), Norman Arthur Citrine, b. 1914, s. 1983, m.	Hon. Ronald E. C., b. 1919.
1800 I.	Clanmorris (8th), Simon John Ward Bingham, b. 1937, s. 1988, m.	Robert D. de B. B., b. 1942.
1672	Clifford of Chudleigh (14th), Thomas Hugh Clifford, b. 1948, s. 1988, m.	Hon. Alexander T. H. C., b. 1985.
1299	Clinton (22nd), Gerard Nevile Mark Fane Trefusis, b. 1934, title called out of abeyance 1965, m.	Hon. Charles P. R. F. T., b. 1962.
1955	Clitheroe (2nd), Ralph John Assheton, b. 1929, s. 1984, m.	Hon. Ralph C. A., b. 1962.
1919	Clwyd (3rd), (John) Anthony Roberts, b. 1935, s. 1987, m.	Hon. J. Murray R., b. 1971.
1948	Clydesmuir (2nd), Ronald John Bilsland Colville, KT, CB, MBE, TD, b. 1917, s. 1954, m.	Hon. David R. C., b. 1949.
1960	Cobbold (2nd), David Antony Fromanteel Lytton Cobbold, b. 1937, s. 1987, m.	Hon. Henry F. L. C., b. 1962.
1919	Cochrane of Cults (4th), (Ralph Henry) Vere Cochrane, b. 1926, s. 1990, m.	Hon. Thomas H. V. C., b. 1957.
1954	Coleraine (2nd), (James) Martin (Bonar) Law, b. 1931, s. 1980, m.	Hon. James P. B. L., b. 1975.
1873	Coleridge (5th), William Duke Coleridge, b. 1937, s. 1984, m.	Hon. James D. C., b. 1967.
1946	Colgrain (3rd), David Colin Campbell, b. 1920, s. 1973, m.	Hon. Alastair C. L. C., b. 1951.
1917	Colwyn (3rd), (Ian) Anthony Hamilton-Smith, CBE, b. 1942, s. 1966, m.	Hon. Craig P. H.-S., b. 1968.
1956	Colyton (1st), Henry Lennox d'Aubigné Hopkinson, CMG, PC, b. 1902, m.	Alisdair J. M. H., b. 1958.
1841	Congleton (8th), Christopher Patrick Parnell, b. 1930, s. 1967, m.	Hon. John P. C. P., b. 1959.
1927	Cornwallis (3rd), Fiennes Neil Wykeham Cornwallis, OBE, b. 1921, s. 1982, m.	Hon. F. W. Jeremy C., b. 1946.
1874	Cottesloe (4th), John Walgrave Halford Fremantle, GBE, TD, b. 1900, s. 1956, m.	Cdr. Hon. John T. F., b. 1927.
1929	Craigmyle (3rd), Thomas Donald Mackay Shaw, b. 1923, s. 1944, m.	Hon. Thomas C. S., b. 1960.
1899	Cranworth (3rd), Philip Bertram Gurdon, b. 1940, s. 1964, m.	Hon. Sacha W. R. G., b. 1970.
1959	Crathorne (2nd), Charles James Dugdale, b. 1939, s. 1977, m.	Hon. Thomas A. J. D., b. 1977.
1892	Crawshaw (4th), William Michael Clifton Brooks, b. 1933, s. 1946.	Hon. David G. B., b. 1934.
1940	Croft (2nd), Michael Henry Glendower Page Croft, b. 1916, s. 1947, w.	Hon. Bernard W. H. P. C., b. 1949.
1797 I.	Crofton (7th), Guy Patrick Gilbert Crofton, b. 1951, s. 1989, m.	Hon. E. Harry P. C., b. 1988.
1375	Cromwell (7th), Godfrey John Bewicke-Copley, b. 1960, s. 1982, m.	Hon. Thomas D. B.-C., b. 1964.
1947	Crook (2nd), Douglas Edwin Crook, b. 1926, s 1989, m.	Hon. Robert D. E. C., b. 1955.
1920	Cullen of Ashbourne (2nd), Charles Borlase Marsham Cokayne, MBE, b. 1912, s. 1932, m.	Hon. Edmund W. M. C., b. 1916.
1914	Cunliffe (3rd), Roger Cunliffe, b. 1932, s. 1963, m.	Hon. Henry C., b. 1962.
1927	Daresbury (3rd), Edward Gilbert Greenall, b. 1928, s. 1990, m.	Hon. Peter G. G., b. 1953.
1924	Darling (2nd), Robert Charles Henry Darling, b. 1919, s. 1936, m.	Hon. R. Julian H. D., b. 1944.
1946	Darwen (3rd), Roger Michael Davies, b. 1938, s. 1988, m.	Hon. Paul D., b. 1962.
1923	Daryngton (2nd), Jocelyn Arthur Pike Pease, b. 1908, s. 1949.	None.
1932	Davies (3rd), David Davies, b. 1940, s. 1944, m.	Hon. David D. D., b. 1975.
1812 I.	Decies (7th), Marcus Hugh Tristram de la Poer Beresford, b. 1948, s. 1992, m.	Hon. Robert M. D. de la P. B., b. 1988.
1299	de Clifford (27th), John Edward Southwell Russell, b. 1928, s. 1982, m.	Hon. William S. R., b. 1930.
1851	De Freyne (7th), Francis Arthur John French, b. 1927, s. 1935, m.	Hon. Fulke C. A. J. F., b. 1957.
1821	Delamere (5th), Hugh George Cholmondeley, b. 1934, s. 1979, m.	Hon. Thomas P. G. C., b. 1968.
1838	de Mauley (6th), Gerald John Ponsonby, b. 1921, s. 1962, m.	Col. Hon. Thomas M. P., TD, b. 1930.
1937	Denham (2nd), Bertram Stanley Mitford Bowyer, KBE, PC, b. 1927, s. 1948, m.	Hon. Richard G. G. B., b. 1959.
1834	Denman (5th), Charles Spencer Denman, CBE, MC, TD, b. 1916, s. 1971, w.	Hon. Richard T. S. D., b. 1946.
1885	Deramore (6th), Richard Arthur de Yarburgh-Bateson, b. 1911, s. 1964, m.	None.
1887	De Ramsey (4th), John Ailwyn Fellowes, b. 1942, s. 1993, m.	Hon. Freddie J. F., b. 1978.
1264	de Ros (28th), Peter Trevor Maxwell, b. 1958, s. 1983, m. (Premier Baron of England).	Hon. Finbar J. M., b. 1988.
1881	Derwent (5th), Robin Evelyn Leo Vanden-Bempde-Johnstone, LVO, b. 1930, s. 1986, m.	Hon. Francis P. H. V.-B.-J., b. 1965.
1831	de Saumarez (7th), Eric Douglas Saumarez, b. 1956, s. 1991, m.	Hon. Victor T. S., b. 1956.
1910	de Villiers (3rd), Arthur Percy de Villiers, b. 1911, s. 1934.	Hon. Alexander C. de V., b. 1940.

Created	Title, order of succession, name, etc.	Eldest son or heir
1930	*Dickinson* (2nd), Richard Clavering Hyett Dickinson, *b.* 1926, *s.* 1943, *m.*	Hon. Martin H. *D.*, *b.* 1961.
1620 I. ⎫	*Digby* (12th), Edward Henry Kenelm Digby (6th *Brit. Baron, Digby*), *b.*	Hon. Henry N. K. *D.*, *b.* 1954.
1765* ⎭	1924, *s.* 1964, *m.*	
1615	*Dormer* (16th), Joseph Spencer Philip Dormer, *b.* 1914, *s.* 1975.	Geoffrey H. *D.*, *b.* 1920.
1943	*Dowding* (3rd), Piers Hugh Tremenheere Dowding, *b.* 1948, *s.* 1992.	Hon. Mark D. J. *D.*, *b.* 1949.
1800 I.	*Dufferin and Clandeboye.* Heir had not established claim at time of going to press.	Sir John Blackwood, Bt., *b.* 1944.
1929	*Dulverton* (3rd), (Gilbert) Michael Hamilton Wills, *b.* 1944, *s.* 1992, *m.*	Hon. Robert A. H. *W.*, *b.* 1983.
1800 I.	*Dunalley* (7th), Henry Francis Cornelius Prittie, *b.* 1948, *s.* 1992, *m.*	Hon. Joel H. *P.*, *b.* 1981.
1324 I.	*Dunboyne* (28th), Patrick Theobald Tower Butler, VRD, *b.* 1917, *s.* 1945, *m.*	Hon. John F. *B.*, *b.* 1951.
1802	*Dunleath* (5th), Michael Henry Mulholland, *b.* 1915, *s.* 1993, *w.*	Hon. Brian H. *M.*, *b.* 1950.
1439 I.	*Dunsany* (19th), Randal Arthur Henry Plunkett (20th *Irish Baron Killeen,* 1449), *b.* 1906, *s.* 1957, *m.*	Hon. Edward J. C. *P.*, *b.* 1939.
1780	*Dynevor* (9th), Richard Charles Uryan Rhys, *b.* 1935, *s.* 1962.	Hon. Hugo G. U. *R.*, *b.* 1966.
1857	*Ebury* (6th), Francis Egerton Grosvenor, *b.* 1934, *s.* 1957, *m.*	Hon. Julian F. M. *G.*, *b.* 1959.
1963	*Egremont* (2nd), & *Leconfield* (7th) (1859), John Max Henry Scawen Wyndham, *b.* 1948, *s.* 1972, *m.*	Hon. George R. V. *W.*, *b.* 1983.
1643	*Elibank* (14th), Alan D'Ardis Erskine-Murray, *b.* 1923, *s.* 1973, *m.*	Master of Elibank, *b.* 1964.
1802	*Ellenborough* (8th), Richard Edward Cecil Law, *b.* 1926, *s.* 1945, *w.*	Maj. Hon. Rupert E. H. *L.*, *b.* 1955.
1509 S.*	*Elphinstone* (18th), James Alexander Elphinstone (4th *UK Baron Elphinstone,* 1885), *b.* 1953, *s.* 1975, *m.*	Master of Elphinstone, *b.* 1980.
1934	*Elton* (2nd), Rodney Elton, TD, *b.* 1930, *s.* 1973, *m.*	Hon. Edward P. *E.*, *b.* 1966.
1964	*Erroll of Hale* (1st), Frederick James Erroll, TD, PC, *b.* 1914, *m.*	None.
1964	*Erskine of Rerrick* (2nd), Iain Maxwell Erskine, *b.* 1926, *s.* 1980.	None.
1627 S.	*Fairfax of Cameron* (14th), Nicholas John Albert Fairfax, *b.* 1956, *s.* 1964, *m.*	Hon. Edward N. T. *F.*, *b.* 1984.
1961	*Fairhaven* (3rd), Ailwyn Henry George Broughton, *b.* 1936, *s.* 1973, *m.*	Hon. James H. A. *B.*, *b.* 1963.
1916	*Faringdon* (3rd), Charles Michael Henderson, *b.* 1937, *s.* 1977, *m.*	Hon. James H. *H.*, *b.* 1961.
1756 I.	*Farnham* (12th), Barry Owen Somerset Maxwell, *b.* 1931, *s.* 1957, *m.*	Hon. Simon K. *M.*, *b.* 1933.
1856 I.	*Fermoy* (6th), Patrick Maurice Burke Roche, *b.* 1967, *s.* 1984.	Hon. E. Hugh B. *R.*, *b.* 1972.
1826	*Feversham* (6th), Charles Antony Peter Duncombe, *b.* 1945, *s.* 1963, *m.*	Hon. Jasper O. S. *D.*, *b.* 1968.
1798 I.	*ffrench* (8th), Robuck John Peter Charles Mario ffrench, *b.* 1956, *s.* 1986, *m.*	Hon. John C. M. J. F. *ff.*, *b.* 1928.
1909	*Fisher* (3rd), John Vavasseur Fisher, DSC, *b.* 1921, *s.* 1955, *m.*	Hon. Patrick V. *F.*, *b.* 1953.
1295	*Fitzwalter* (21st), (Fitzwalter) Brook Plumptre, *b.* 1914, *title called out of abeyance,* 1953, *m.*	Hon. Julian B. *P.*, *b.* 1952.
1776	*Foley* (8th), Adrian Gerald Foley, *b.* 1923, *s.* 1927, *m.*	Hon. Thomas H. *F.*, *b.* 1961.
1445 S.	*Forbes* (22nd), Nigel Ivan Forbes, KBE (*Premier Baron of Scotland*), *b.* 1918, *s.* 1953, *m.*	Master of Forbes, *b.* 1946.
1821	*Forester* (8th), (George Cecil) Brooke Weld-Forester, *b.* 1938, *s.* 1977, *m.*	Hon. C. R. George *W.-F.*, *b.* 1975.
1922	*Forres* (4th), Alastair Stephen Grant Williamson, *b.* 1946, *s.* 1978, *m.*	Hon. George A. M. *W.*, *b.* 1972.
1917	*Forteviot* (4th), John James Evelyn Dewar, *b.* 1938, *s.* 1993, *m.*	Hon. Alexander J. E. *D.*, *b.* 1971.
1951	*Freyberg* (3rd), Valerian Bernard Freyberg, *b.* 1970, *s.* 1993.	None.
1917	*Gainford* (3rd), Joseph Edward Pease, *b.* 1921, *s.* 1971, *m.*	Hon. George *P.*, *b.* 1926.
1818 I.	*Garvagh* (5th), (Alexander Leopold Ivor) George Canning, *b.* 1920, *s.* 1956, *m.*	Hon. Spencer G. S. de R. *C.*, *b.* 1953.
1942	*Geddes* (3rd), Euan Michael Ross Geddes, *b.* 1937, *s.* 1975, *m.*	Hon. James G. N. *G.*, *b.* 1969.
1876	*Gerard* (5th), Anthony Robert Hugo Gerard, *b.* 1949, *s.* 1992, *m.*	Hon. Rupert B. C. *G.*, *b.* 1981.
1824	*Gifford* (6th), Anthony Maurice Gifford, QC, *b.* 1940, *s.* 1961, *m.*	Hon. Thomas A. *G.*, *b.* 1967.
1917	*Gisborough* (3rd), Thomas Richard John Long Chaloner, *b.* 1927, *s.* 1951, *m.*	Hon. T. Peregrine L. *C.*, *b.* 1961.
1960	*Gladwyn* (1st), (Hubert Miles) Gladwyn Jebb, GCMG, GCVO, CB, *b.* 1900, *w.*	Hon. Miles A. G. *J.*, *b.* 1930.
1899	*Glanusk* (4th), David Russell Bailey, *b.* 1917, *s.* 1948, *m.*	Hon. Christopher R. *B.*, *b.* 1942.
1918	*Glenarthur* (4th), Simon Mark Arthur, *b.* 1944, *s.* 1976, *m.*	Hon. Edward A. *A.*, *b.* 1973.
1911	*Glenconner* (3rd), Colin Christopher Paget Tennant, *b.* 1926, *s.* 1983, *m.*	Hon. Charles E. P. *T.*, *b.* 1957.
1964	*Glendevon* (1st), John Adrian Hope, PC, *b.* 1912, *m.*	Hon. Julian J. S. *H.*, *b.* 1950.
1922	*Glendyne* (3rd), Robert Nivison, *b.* 1926, *s.* 1967, *m.*	Hon. John *N.*, *b.* 1960.
1939	*Glentoran* (2nd), Daniel Stewart Thomas Bingham Dixon, KBE, PC (NI), *b.* 1912, *s.* 1950, *w.*	Hon. Thomas R. V. *D.*, CBE, *b.* 1935.
1909	*Gorell* (4th), Timothy John Radcliffe Barnes, *b.* 1927, *s.* 1963, *m.*	Hon. Ronald A. H. *B.*, *b.* 1931.
1953	*Grantchester* (2nd), Kenneth Bent Suenson-Taylor, CBE, QC, *b.* 1921, *s.* 1976, *m.*	Hon. Christopher J. S-.*T.*, *b.* 1951.
1782	*Grantley* (7th), John Richard Brinsley Norton, MC, *b.* 1923, *s.* 1954, *m.*	Hon. Richard W. B. *N.*, *b.* 1956.
1794 I.	*Graves* (8th), Peter George Wellesley Graves, *b.* 1911, *s.* 1963, *w.*	Evelyn P. *G.*, *b.* 1926.
1445 S.	*Gray* (22nd), Angus Diarmid Ian Campbell-Gray, *b.* 1931, *s.* 1946, *w.*	Master of Gray, *b.* 1964.

Created	Title, order of succession, name, etc.	Eldest son or heir
1950	*Greenhill* (3rd), Malcolm Greenhill, *b.* 1924, *s.* 1989.	None.
1927	*Greenway* (4th), Ambrose Charles Drexel Greenway, *b.* 1941, *s.* 1975, *m.*	Hon. Mervyn S. K. *G.*, *b.* 1942.
1902	*Grenfell* (3rd), Julian Pascoe Francis St Leger Grenfell, *b.* 1935, *s.* 1976, *m.*	Francis P. J. *G.*, *b.* 1938.
1944	*Gretton* (4th), John Lysander Gretton, *b.* 1975, *s.* 1989, *M.*	None.
1397	*Grey of Codnor* (5th), Charles Legh Shuldham Cornwall-Legh, CBE, AE, *b.* 1903, *title called out of abeyance* 1989, *m.*	Hon. Richard H. *C.-L.*, *b.* 1936.
1955	*Gridley* (2nd), Arnold Hudson Gridley, *b.* 1906, *s.* 1965, *m.*	Hon. Richard D. A. *G.*, *b.* 1956.
1964	*Grimston of Westbury* (2nd), Robert Walter Sigismund Grimston, *b.* 1925, *s.* 1979, *m.*	Hon. Robert J. S. *G.*, *b.* 1951.
1886	*Grimthorpe* (4th), Christopher John Beckett, OBE, *b.* 1915, *s.* 1963, *m.*	Hon. Edward J. *B.*, *b.* 1954.
1945	*Hacking* (3rd), Douglas David Hacking, *b.* 1938, *s.* 1971, *m.*	Hon. Douglas F. *H.*, *b.* 1968.
1950	*Haden-Guest* (4th), Peter Haden Haden-Guest, *b.* 1913, *s.* 1987, *m.*	Hon. Christopher *H.-G.*, *b.* 1948.
1886	*Hamilton of Dalzell* (4th), James Leslie Hamilton, *b.* 1938, *s.* 1990, *m.*	Hon. Gavin G. *H.*, *b.* 1968.
1874	*Hampton* (6th), Richard Humphrey Russell Pakington, *b.* 1925, *s.* 1974, *m.*	Hon. John H. A. *P.*, *b.* 1964.
1939	*Hankey* (2nd), Robert Maurice Alers Hankey, KCMG, KCVO, *b.* 1905, *s.* 1963, *m.*	Hon. Donald R. A. *H.*, *b.* 1938.
1958	*Harding of Petherton* (2nd), John Charles Harding, *b.* 1928, *s.* 1989, *m.*	Hon. William A. J. *H.*, *b.* 1969.
1910	*Hardinge of Penshurst* (3rd), George Edward Charles Hardinge, *b.* 1921, *s.* 1960, *m.*	Hon. Julian A. *H.*, *b.* 1945.
1876	*Harlech* (6th), Francis David Ormsby-Gore, *b.* 1954, *s.* 1985, *m.*	Hon. Jasset D. C. *O.-G.*, *b.* 1986.
1939	*Harmsworth* (3rd), Thomas Harold Raymond Harmsworth, *b.* 1939, *s.* 1990, *m.*	Hon. Dominic M. E. *H.*, *b.* 1973.
1815	*Harris* (6th), George Robert John Harris, *b.* 1920, *s.* 1984.	Derek M. *H.*, *b.* 1916.
1954	*Harvey of Tasburgh* (2nd), Peter Charles Oliver Harvey, *b.* 1921, *s.* 1968, *m.*	Charles J. G. *H.*, *b.* 1951.
1295	*Hastings* (22nd), Edward Delaval Henry Astley, *b.* 1912, *s.* 1956, *m.*	Hon. Delaval T. H. *A.*, *b.* 1960.
1835	*Hatherton* (8th), Edward Charles Littleton, *b.* 1950, *s.* 1985, *m.*	Hon. Thomas E. *L.*, *b.* 1977.
1776	*Hawke* (11th), Edward George Hawke, *b.* 1950, *s.* 1992.	None.
1927	*Hayter* (3rd), George Charles Hayter Chubb, KCVO, CBE, *b.* 1911, *s.* 1967, *m.*	Hon. G. William M. *C.*, *b.* 1943.
1945	*Hazlerigg* (2nd), Arthur Grey Hazlerigg, MC, TD, *b.* 1910, *s.* 1949, *w.*	Hon. Arthur G. *H.*, *b.* 1951.
1797 I.	*Headley* (7th), Charles Rowland Allanson-Winn, *b.* 1902, *s.* 1969, *w.*	Hon. Owain G. *A.-W.*, *b.* 1906.
1943	*Hemingford* (3rd), (Dennis) Nicholas Herbert, *b.* 1934, *s.* 1982, *m.*	Hon. Christopher D. C. *H.*, *b.* 1973.
1906	*Hemphill* (5th), Peter Patrick Fitzroy Martyn Martyn-Hemphill, *b.* 1928, *s.* 1957, *m.*	Hon. Charles A. M. *M.-H.*, *b.* 1954.
1799 I.*	*Henley* (8th), Oliver Michael Robert Eden (6th *UK Baron, Northington*, 1885), *b.* 1953, *s.* 1977, *m.*	Hon. John W. O. *E.*, *b.* 1988.
1800 I.*	*Henniker* (8th), John Patrick Edward Chandos Henniker-Major, KCMG, CVO, MC (4th *UK Baron, Hartismere*, 1866), *b.* 1916, *s.* 1980, *m.*	Hon. Mark I. P. C. *H.-M.*, *b.* 1947.
1886	*Herschell* (3rd), Rognvald Richard Farrer Herschell, *b.* 1923, *s.* 1929, *m.*	None.
1935	*Hesketh* (3rd), Thomas Alexander Fermor-Hesketh, PC, *b.* 1950, *s.* 1955, *m.*	Hon. Frederick H. *F.-H.*, *b.*1988.
1828	*Heytesbury* (6th), Francis William Holmes à Court, *b.* 1931, *s.* 1971, *m.*	Hon. James W. *H. à C.*, *b.* 1967.
1886	*Hindlip* (5th), Henry Richard Allsopp, *b.* 1912, *s.* 1966, *m.*	Hon. Charles H. *A.*, *b.* 1940.
1950	*Hives* (2nd), John Warwick Hives, CBE, *b.* 1913, *s.* 1965, *m.*	Matthew P. *H.*, *b.* 1971.
1912	*Hollenden* (3rd), Gordon Hope Hope-Morley, *b.* 1914, *s.* 1977, *m.*	Hon. Ian H. *H.-M.*, *b.* 1946.
1897	*HolmPatrick* (4th), Hans James David Hamilton, *b.* 1955, *s.* 1991, *m.*	Hon. Ion H. J. *H.*, *b.* 1956.
1933	*Horder* (2nd), Thomas Mervyn Horder, *b.* 1910, *s.* 1955.	None.
1797 I.	*Hotham* (8th), Henry Durand Hotham, *b.* 1940, *s.* 1967, *m.*	Hon. William B. *H.*, *b.* 1972.
1881	*Hothfield* (6th), Anthony Charles Sackville Tufton, *b.* 1939, *s.* 1991, *m.*	Hon. William S. *T.*, *b.* 1977.
1597	*Howard de Walden* (9th), John Osmael Scott-Ellis, TD (5th *UK Baron, Seaford*, 1826), *b.* 1912, *s.* 1946, *m.*	To Barony of Howard de Walden, four co-heiresses. To Barony of Seaford, Colin H. F. *Ellis*, *b.* 1946.
1930	*Howard of Penrith* (2nd), Francis Philip Howard, *b.* 1905, *s.* 1939, *m.*	Hon. Philip E. *H.*, *b.* 1945.
1960	*Howick of Glendale* (2nd), Charles Evelyn Baring, *b.* 1937, *s.* 1973, *m.*	Hon. David E. C. *B.*, *b.* 1975.
1796 I.	*Huntingfield* (6th), Gerard Charles Arcedeckne Vanneck, *b.* 1915, *s.* 1969, *m.*	Hon. Joshua C. *V.*, *b.* 1954.
1866	*Hylton* (5th), Raymond Hervey Jolliffe, *b.* 1932, *s.* 1967, *m.*	Hon. William H. M. *J.*, *b.* 1967.
1933	*Iliffe* (2nd), Edward Langton Iliffe, *b.* 1908, *s.* 1960, *m.*	Robert P. R. *I.*, *b.* 1944.
1543 I.	*Inchiquin* (18th), Conor Myles John O'Brien, *b.* 1943, *s.* 1982.	Murrough R. *O'B.*, *b.* 1910.
1962	*Inchyra* (2nd), Robert Charles Reneke Hoyer Millar, *b.* 1935, *s.* 1989, *m.*	Hon. C. James C. H. *M.*, *b.* 1962.
1964	*Inglewood* (2nd), (William) Richard Fletcher-Vane, MEP, *b.* 1951, *s.* 1989, *m.*	Hon. Henry W. F. *F.-V.*, *b.* 1990.
1919	*Inverforth* (4th), Andrew Peter Weir, *b.* 1966, *s.* 1982.	Hon. John V. *W.*, *b.* 1935.
1941	*Ironside* (2nd), Edmund Oslac Ironside, *b.* 1924, *s.* 1959, *m.*	Hon. Charles E. G. *I.*, *b.* 1956.

Created	Title, order of succession, name, etc.	Eldest son or heir
1952	*Jeffreys* (3rd), Christopher Henry Mark Jeffreys, *b.* 1957, *s.* 1986, *m.*	Hon. Arthur M. H. *J.*, *b.* 1989.
1906	*Joicey* (5th), James Michael Joicey, *b.* 1953, *s.* 1993, *m.*	Hon. William J. *J.*, *b.* 1990.
1937	*Kenilworth* (4th), (John) Randle Siddeley, *b.* 1954, *s.* 1981, *m.*	Hon. William R. J. *S.*, *b.* 1992.
1935	*Kennet* (2nd), Wayland Hilton Young, *b.* 1923, *s.* 1960, *m.*	Hon. W. A. Thoby *Y.*, *b.* 1957.
1776 I.*	*Kensington* (8th), Hugh Ivor Edwardes (5th *UK Baron, Kensington*, 1886), *b.* 1933, *s.* 1981, *m.*	Hon. W. Owen A. *E.*, *b.* 1964.
1951	*Kenswood* (2nd), John Michael Howard Whitfield, *b.* 1930, *s.* 1963, *m.*	Hon. Michael C. *W.*, *b.* 1955.
1788	*Kenyon* (6th), Lloyd Tyrell-Kenyon, *b.* 1947, *s.* 1993, *m.*	Hon. Lloyd N. *T.-K.*, *b.* 1972.
1947	*Kershaw* (4th), Edward John Kershaw, *b.* 1936, *s.* 1962, *m.*	Hon. John C. E. *K.*, *b.* 1971.
1943	*Keyes* (2nd), Roger George Bowlby Keyes, *b.* 1919, *s.* 1945, *m.*	Hon. Charles W. P. *K.*, *b.* 1951.
1909	*Kilbracken* (3rd), John Raymond Godley, DSC, *b.* 1920, *s.* 1950.	Hon. Christopher J. *G.*, *b.* 1945.
1900	*Killanin* (3rd), Michael Morris, MBE, TD, *b.* 1914, *s.* 1927, *m.*	Hon. G. Redmond F. *M.*, *b.* 1947.
1943	*Killearn* (2nd), Graham Curtis Lampson, *b.* 1919, *s.* 1964, *m.*	Hon. Victor M. G. *A.*, *b.* 1941.
1789 I.	*Kilmaine* (7th), John David Henry Browne, *b.* 1948, *s.* 1978, *m.*	Hon. John F. S. *B.*, *b.* 1983.
1831	*Kilmarnock* (7th), Alastair Ivor Gilbert Boyd, *b.* 1927, *s.* 1975, *m.*	Hon. Robin J. *B.*, *b.* 1941.
1941	*Kindersley* (3rd), Robert Hugh Molesworth Kindersley, *b.* 1929, *s.* 1976, *m.*	Hon. Rupert J. M. *K.*, *b.* 1955.
1223 I.	*Kingsale* (35th), John de Courcy (*Premier Baron of Ireland*), *b.* 1941, *s.* 1969.	Nevinson R. *de C.*, *b.* 1920.
1682 S.*	*Kinnaird* (13th), Graham Charles Kinnaird (5th *UK Baron, Kinnaird*, 1860), *b.* 1912, *s.* 1972, *m.*	None.
1902	*Kinross* (5th), Christopher Patrick Balfour, *b.* 1949, *s.* 1985, *m.*	Hon. Alan I. *B.*, *b.* 1978.
1951	*Kirkwood* (3rd), David Harvie Kirkwood, PH.D., *b.* 1931, *s.* 1970, *m.*	Hon. James S. *K.*, *b.* 1937.
1800 I.	*Langford* (9th), Geoffrey Alexander Rowley-Conwy, OBE, *b.* 1912, *s.* 1953, *m.*	Hon. Owain G. *R.-C.*, *b.* 1958.
1942	*Latham* (2nd), Dominic Charles Latham, *b.* 1954, *s.* 1970.	Anthony M. *L.*, *b.* 1954.
1431	*Latymer* (8th), Hugo Nevill Money-Coutts, *b.* 1926, *s.* 1987, *m.*	Hon. Crispin J. A. N. *M.-C.*, *b.* 1955.
1869	*Lawrence* (5th), David John Downer Lawrence, *b.* 1937, *s.* 1968.	None.
1947	*Layton* (3rd), Geoffrey Michael Layton, *b.* 1947, *s.* 1989, *m.*	Hon. David *L.*, MBE, *b.* 1914.
1839	*Leigh* (5th), John Piers Leigh, *b.* 1935, *s.* 1979, *m.*	Hon. Christopher D. P. *L.*, *b.* 1960.
1962	*Leighton of St Mellons* (2nd), (John) Leighton Seager, *b.* 1922, *s.* 1963, *m.*	Hon. Robert W. H. L. *S.*, *b.* 1955.
1797	*Lilford* (7th), George Vernon Powys, *b.* 1931, *s.* 1949, *m.*	Hon. Mark V. *P.*, *b.* 1975.
1945	*Lindsay of Birker* (2nd), Michael Francis Morris Lindsay, *b.* 1909, *s.* 1952, *m.*	Hon. James F. *L.*, *b.* 1945.
1758 I.	*Lisle* (7th), John Nicholas Horace Lysaght, *b.* 1903, *s.* 1919, *m.*	Patrick J. *L.*, *b.* 1931.
1850	*Londesborough* (9th), Richard John Denison, *b.* 1959, *s.* 1968, *m.*	Hon. James F. *D.*, *b.* 1990.
1541 I.	*Louth* (16th), Otway Michael James Oliver Plunkett, *b.* 1929, *s.* 1950, *m.*	Hon. Jonathan O. *P.*, *b.* 1952.
1458 S.*	*Lovat* (15th), Simon Christopher Joseph Fraser, DSO, MC, TD (4th *UK Baron, Lovat*, 1837), *b.* 1911, *s.* 1933, *m.*	Master of Lovat *b.* 1939.
1946	*Lucas of Chilworth* (2nd), Michael William George Lucas, *b.* 1926, *s.* 1967, *m.*	Hon. Simon W. *L.*, *b.* 1957.
1663	*Lucas* (11th) & *Dingwall* (8th) (*Scottish Lordship* 1609), Ralph Matthew Palmer, *b.* 1951, *s.* 1991, *m.*	Hon. Lewis E. *P.*, *b.* 1987
1929	*Luke* (2nd), Ian St John Lawson-Johnston, KCVO, TD, *b.* 1905, *s.* 1943, *m.*	Hon. Arthur C. St J. *L.-J.*, *b.* 1933.
1914	*Lyell* (3rd), Charles Lyell, *b.* 1939, *s.* 1943.	None.
1859	*Lyveden* (6th), Ronald Cecil Vernon, *b.* 1915, *s.* 1973, *m.*	Hon. Jack L. *V.*, *b.* 1938.
1959	*MacAndrew* (3rd), Christopher Anthony Colin MacAndrew, *b.* 1945, *s.* 1989, *m.*	Hon. Oliver C. J. *M.*, *b.* 1983.
1776 I.	*Macdonald* (8th), Godfrey James Macdonald of Macdonald, *b.* 1947, *s.* 1970, *m.*	Hon. Godfrey E. H. T. *M.*, *b.* 1982.
1949	*Macdonald of Gwaenysgor* (2nd), Gordon Ramsay Macdonald, *b.* 1915, *s.* 1966, *m.*	None.
1937	*McGowan* (3rd), Harry Duncan Cory McGowan, *b.* 1938, *s.* 1966, *m.*	Hon. Harry J. C. *M.*, *b.* 1971.
1922	*Maclay* (3rd), Joseph Paton Maclay, *b.* 1942, *s.* 1969, *m.*	Hon. Joseph P. *M.*, *b.* 1977.
1955	*McNair* (3rd), Duncan James McNair, *b.* 1947, *s.* 1989, *m.*	Hon. Thomas J. *M.*, *b.* 1990.
1951	*Macpherson of Drumochter* (2nd), (James) Gordon Macpherson, *b.* 1924, *s.* 1965, *m.*	Hon. James A. *M.*, *b.* 1979.
1937	*Mancroft* (3rd), Benjamin Lloyd Stormont Mancroft, *b.* 1957, *s.* 1987, *m.*	None.
1807	*Manners* (5th), John Robert Cecil Manners, *b.* 1923, *s.* 1972, *m.*	Hon. John H. R. *M.*, *b.* 1956.
1922	*Manton* (3rd), Joseph Rupert Eric Robert Watson, *b.* 1924, *s.* 1968, *m.*	Capt. Hon. Miles R. M. *W.*, *b.* 1958.
1908	*Marchamley* (3rd), John William Tattersall Whiteley, *b.* 1922, *s.* 1949, *m.*	Hon. William F. *W.*, *b.* 1968.
1964	*Margadale* (1st), John Granville Morrison, TD, *b.* 1906, *w.*	Hon. James I. *M.*, TD, *b.* 1930.
1961	*Marks of Broughton* (2nd), Michael Marks, *b.* 1920, *s.* 1964.	Hon. Simon R. *M.*, *b.* 1950.
1964	*Martonmere* (2nd), John Stephen Robinson, *b.* 1963, *s.* 1989.	David A. *R.*, *b.* 1965.
1776 I.	*Massy* (9th), Hugh Hamon John Somerset Massy, *b.* 1921, *s.* 1958, *m.*	Hon. David H. S. *M.*, *b.* 1947.
1935	*May* (3rd), Michael St John May, *b.* 1931, *s.* 1950, *m.*	Hon. Jasper B. St J. *M.*, *b.* 1965.
1928	*Melchett* (4th), Peter Robert Henry Mond, *b.* 1948, *s.* 1973.	None.

Created	Title, order of succession, name, etc.	Eldest son or heir
1925	*Merrivale* (3rd), Jack Henry Edmond Duke, *b.* 1917, *s.* 1951, *m.*	Hon. Derek J. P. *D.*, *b.* 1948.
1911	*Merthyr.* Disclaimed for life 1977. (*Trevor Oswin Lewis, Bt.*, CBE, *b.* 1935, *s.* 1977, *m.*)	David T. *L.*, *b.* 1977.
1919	*Meston* (3rd), James Meston, *b.* 1950, *s.* 1984, *m.*	Hon. Thomas J. D. *M.*, *b.* 1977.
1838	*Methuen* (6th), Anthony John Methuen, *b.* 1925, *s.* 1975.	Hon. Robert A. H. *M.*, *b.* 1931.
1711	*Middleton* (12th), (Digby) Michael Godfrey John Willoughby, MC, *b.* 1921, *s.* 1970, *m.*	Hon. Michael C. J. *W.*, *b.* 1948.
1939	*Milford* (2nd), Wogan Philipps, *b.* 1902, *s.* 1962, *m.*	Hon. Hugo J. L. *P.*, *b.* 1929.
1933	*Milne* (2nd), George Douglass Milne, TD, *b.* 1909, *s.* 1948, *m.*	Hon. George A. *M.*, *b.* 1941.
1951	*Milner of Leeds* (2nd), Arthur James Michael Milner, AE, *b.* 1923, *s.* 1967, *m.*	Hon. Richard J. *M.*, *b.* 1959.
1947	*Milverton* (2nd), Revd Fraser Arthur Richard Richards, *b.* 1930, *s.* 1978, *m.*	Hon. Michael H. *R.*, *b.* 1936.
1873	*Moncreiff* (5th), Harry Robert Wellwood Moncreiff, *b.* 1915, *s.* 1942, *w.*	Hon. Rhoderick H. W. *M.*, *b.* 1954.
1884	*Monk Bretton* (3rd), John Charles Dodson, *b.* 1924, *s.* 1933, *m.*	Hon. Christopher M. *D.*, *b.* 1958.
1885	*Monkswell* (5th), Gerard Collier, *b.* 1947, *s.* 1984, *m.*	Hon. James A. *C.*, *b.* 1977.
1728	*Monson* (11th), John Monson, *b.* 1932, *s.* 1958, *m.*	Hon. Nicholas J. *M.*, *b.* 1955.
1885	*Montagu of Beaulieu* (3rd), Edward John Barrington Douglas-Scott-Montagu, *b.* 1926, *s.* 1929, *m.*	Hon. Ralph *D.-S.-M.*, *b.* 1961.
1839	*Monteagle of Brandon* (6th), Gerald Spring Rice, *b.* 1926, *s.* 1946, *m.*	Hon. Charles J. S. *R.*, *b.* 1953.
1943	*Moran* (2nd), (Richard) John (McMoran) Wilson, KCMG, *b.* 1924, *s.* 1977, *m.*	Hon. James M. *W.*, *b.* 1952.
1918	*Morris* (3rd), Michael David Morris, *b.* 1937, *s.* 1975, *m.*	Hon. Thomas A. S. *M.*, *b.* 1982.
1950	*Morris of Kenwood* (2nd), Philip Geoffrey Morris, *b.* 1928, *s.* 1954, *m.*	Hon. Jonathan D. *M.*, *b.* 1968.
1945	*Morrison* (2nd), Dennis Morrison, *b.* 1914, *s.* 1953.	None.
1831	*Mostyn* (5th), Roger Edward Lloyd Lloyd-Mostyn, MC, *b.* 1920, *s.* 1965, *m.*	Hon. Llewellyn R. L. *L.-M.*, *b.* 1948.
1933	*Mottistone* (4th), David Peter Seely, CBE, *b.* 1920, *s.* 1966, *m.*	Hon. Peter J. P. *S.*, *b.* 1949.
1945	*Mountevans* (3rd), Edward Patrick Broke Evans, *b.* 1943, *s.* 1974, *m.*	Hon. Jeffrey de C. R. *E.*, *b.* 1948.
1283	*Mowbray* (26th), *Segrave* (27th) (1283), & *Stourton* (23rd) (1448), Charles Edward Stourton, CBE, *b.* 1923, *s.* 1965, *m.*	Hon. Edward W. S. *S.*, *b.* 1953.
1932	*Moyne* (3rd), Jonathan Bryan Guinness, *b.* 1930, *s.* 1992, *m.*	Hon. Jasper J. R. *G.*, *b.* 1954.
1929	*Moynihan*, the 3rd Baron died November 1991. His trustees recognized Daniel Antony Patrick Berkeley Moynihan, (*b.* January 1991) as the financial heir of the 3rd Baron but the succession to the title is not settled.	
1781 I.	*Muskerry* (9th), Robert Fitzmaurice Deane, *b.* 1948, *s.* 1988, *m.*	Hon. Jonathan F. *D.*, *b.* 1986.
1627 S.	*Napier* (14th) & *Ettrick* (5th) (*UK* 1872), Francis Nigel Napier, KCVO, *b.* 1930, *s.* 1954, *m.*	Master of Napier, *b.* 1962.
1868	*Napier of Magdala* (6th), Robert Alan Napier, *b.* 1940, *s.* 1987, *m.*	Hon. James R. *N.*, *b.* 1966.
1940	*Nathan* (2nd), Roger Carol Michael Nathan, *b.* 1922, *s.* 1963, *m.*	Hon. Rupert H. B. *N.*, *b.* 1957.
1960	*Nelson of Stafford* (2nd), Henry George Nelson, FEng., *b.* 1917, *s.* 1962, *m.*	Hon. Henry R. G. *N.*, *b.* 1943.
1959	*Netherthorpe* (3rd), James Frederick Turner, *b.* 1964, *s.* 1982, *m.*	Hon. Patrick A. *T.*, *b.* 1971.
1946	*Newall* (2nd), Francis Storer Eaton Newall, *b.* 1930, *s.* 1963, *m.*	Hon. Richard H. E. *N.*, *b.* 1961.
1776 I.	*Newborough* (7th), Robert Charles Michael Vaughan Wynn, DSC, *b.* 1917, *s.* 1965, *m.*	Hon. Robert V. *W.*, *b.* 1949.
1892	*Newton* (5th), Richard Thomas Legh, *b.* 1950, *s.* 1992, *m.*	Hon. Piers R. *L.*, *b.* 1979.
1930	*Noel-Buxton* (3rd), Martin Connal Noel-Buxton, *b.* 1940, *s.* 1980, *m.*	Hon. Charles C. *N.-B.*, *b.* 1975.
1957	*Norrie* (2nd), (George) Willoughby Moke Norrie, *b.* 1936, *s.* 1977, *m.*	Hon. Mark W. J. *N.*, *b.* 1972.
1884	*Northbourne* (5th), Christopher George Walter James, *b.* 1926, *s.* 1982, *m.*	Hon. Charles W. H. *J.*, *b.* 1960.
1866	*Northbrook* (6th), Francis Thomas Baring, *b.* 1954, *s.* 1990, *m.*	None.
1878	*Norton* (7th), John Arden Adderley, OBE, *b.* 1915, *s.* 1961, *m.*	Hon. James N. A. *A.*, *b.* 1947.
1906	*Nunburnholme* (4th), Ben Charles Wilson, *b.* 1928, *s.* 1974.	Hon. Charles T. *W.*, *b.* 1935.
1950	*Ogmore* (2nd), Gwilym Rees Rees-Williams, *b.* 1931, *s.* 1976, *m.*	Hon. Morgan R.-*W.*, *b.* 1937.
1870	*O'Hagan* (4th), Charles Towneley Strachey, MEP, *b.* 1945, *s.* 1961, *m.*	Hon. Richard T. *S.*, *b.* 1950.
1868	*O'Neill* (4th), Raymond Arthur Clanaboy O'Neill, TD, *b.* 1933, *s.* 1944, *m.*	Hon. Shane S. C. *O'N.*, *b.* 1965.
1836 I.*	*Oranmore and Browne* (4th), Dominick Geoffrey Edward Browne (2nd *UK Baron Mereworth*, 1926), *b.* 1901, *s.* 1927, *m.*	Hon. Dominick G. T. *B.*, *b.* 1929.
1933	*Palmer* (4th), Adrian Bailie Nottage Palmer, *b.* 1951, *s.* 1990, *m.*	Hon. Hugo B. R. *P.*, *b.* 1980.
1914	*Parmoor* (4th), (Frederick Alfred) Milo Cripps, *b.* 1929, *s.* 1977.	M. Anthony L. *C.*, CBE, DSO, TD, QC, *b.* 1913.
1937	*Pender* (3rd), John Willoughby Denison-Pender, *b.* 1933, *s.* 1965, *m.*	Hon. Henry J. R. *D.-P.*, *b.* 1968.
1866	*Penrhyn* (6th), Malcolm Frank Douglas-Pennant, DSO, MBE, *b.* 1908, *s.* 1967, *m.*	Hon. Nigel *D.-P.*, *b.* 1909.
1603	*Petre* (18th), John Patrick Lionel Petre, *b.* 1942, *s.* 1989, *m.*	Hon. Dominic W. *P.*, *b.* 1966.
1918	*Phillimore* (4th), Claud Stephen Phillimore, *b.* 1911, *s.* 1990, *m.*	Hon. Francis S. *P.*, *b.* 1944.
1945	*Piercy* (3rd), James William Piercy, *b.* 1946, *s.* 1981.	Hon. Mark E. P. *P.*, *b.* 1953.

Created	Title, order of succession, name, etc.	Eldest son or heir
1827	Plunket (8th), Robin Rathmore Plunket, b. 1925, s. 1975, m.	Hon. Shaun A. F. S. P., b. 1931.
1831	Poltimore (7th), Mark Coplestone Bampfylde, b. 1957, s. 1978, m.	Hon. Henry A. W. B., b. 1985.
1690 S.	Polwarth (10th), Henry Alexander Hepburne-Scott, TD, b. 1916, s. 1944, m.	Master of Polwarth, b. 1947.
1930	Ponsonby of Shulbrede (4th), Frederick Matthew Thomas Ponsonby, b. 1958, s. 1990.	None.
1958	Poole (2nd), David Charles Poole, b. 1945, s. 1993, m.	Hon. Oliver J. P., b. 1972.
1852	Raglan (5th), FitzRoy John Somerset, b. 1927, s. 1964.	Hon. Geoffrey S., b. 1932.
1932	Rankeillour (4th), Peter St Thomas More Henry Hope, b. 1935, s. 1967.	Michael R. H., b. 1940.
1953	Rathcavan (2nd), Phelim Robert Hugh O'Neill, PC (NI), b. 1909, s. 1982, m.	Hon. Hugh D. T. O'N., b. 1939.
1916	Rathcreedan (3rd), Christopher John Norton, b. 1949, s. 1990, m.	Hon. Adam G. N., b. 1952.
1868 I.	Rathdonnell (5th), Thomas Benjamin McClintock–Bunbury, b. 1938, s. 1959, m.	Hon. William L. M.-B., b. 1966.
1911	Ravensdale (3rd), Nicholas Mosley, MC, b. 1923, s. 1966, m.	Hon. Shaun N. M., b. 1949.
1821	Ravensworth (8th), Arthur Waller Liddell, b. 1924, s. 1950, m.	Hon. Thomas A. H. L., b. 1954.
1821	Rayleigh (6th), John Gerald Strutt, b. 1960, s. 1988, m.	Hon. John F. S., b. 1993.
1937	Rea (3rd), John Nicolas Rea, MD, b. 1928, s. 1981, m.	Hon. Matthew J. R., b. 1956.
1628 S.	Reay (14th), Hugh William Mackay, b. 1937, s. 1963, m.	Master of Reay, b. 1965.
1902	Redesdale (6th), Rupert Bertram Mitford, b. 1967, s. 1991.	None.
1940	Reith. Disclaimed for life 1972. (Christopher John Reith, b. 1928, s. 1971, m.)	Hon. James H. J. R., b. 1971.
1928	Remnant (3rd), James Wogan Remnant, CVO, b. 1930, s. 1967, m.	Hon. Philip J. R., b. 1954.
1806 I.	Rendlesham (8th), Charles Anthony Hugh Thellusson, b. 1915, s. 1943, w.	Hon. Charles W. B. T., b. 1954.
1933	Rennell (3rd), (John Adrian) Tremayne Rodd, b. 1935, s. 1978, m.	Hon. James R. D. T. R., b. 1978.
1964	Renwick (2nd), Harry Andrew Renwick, b. 1935, s. 1973, m.	Hon. Robert J. R., b. 1966.
1885	Revelstoke (4th), Rupert Baring, b. 1911, s. 1934.	Hon. John B., b. 1934.
1905	Ritchie of Dundee (5th), (Harold) Malcolm Ritchie, b. 1919, s. 1978, m.	Hon. C. Rupert R. R., b. 1958.
1935	Riverdale (2nd), Robert Arthur Balfour, b. 1901, s. 1957, m.	Hon. Mark R. B., b. 1927.
1961	Robertson of Oakridge (2nd), William Ronald Robertson, b. 1930, s. 1974, m.	Hon. William B. E. R., b. 1975.
1938	Roborough (3rd), Henry Massey Lopes, b. 1940, s. 1992, m.	Hon. Massey J. H. L., b. 1969.
1931	Rochester (2nd), Foster Charles Lowry Lamb, b. 1916, s. 1955, m.	Hon. David C. L., b. 1944.
1934	Rockley (3rd), James Hugh Cecil, b. 1934, s. 1976, m.	Hon. Anthony R. C., b. 1961.
1782	Rodney (10th), George Brydges Rodney, b. 1953, s. 1992.	Hon. Michael C. R., b. 1926.
1651 S.*	Rollo (13th), Eric John Stapylton Rollo (4th UK Baron, Dunning, 1869), b. 1915, s. 1947, m.	Master of Rollo, b. 1943.
1959	Rootes (3rd), Nicholas Geoffrey Rootes, b. 1951, s. 1992, m.	William B. R., b. 1944.
1796 I.*	Rossmore (7th), William Warner Westenra (6th UK Baron, Rossmore, 1838), b. 1931, s. 1958, m.	Hon. Benedict W. W., b. 1983.
1939	Rotherwick (2nd), (Herbert) Robin Cayzer, b. 1912, s. 1958, w.	Hon. H. Robin C., b. 1954.
1885	Rothschild (4th), (Nathaniel Charles) Jacob Rothschild, b. 1936, s. 1990, m.	Hon. Nathaniel P. V. J. R., b. 1971.
1911	Rowallan (4th), John Polson Cameron Corbett, b. 1947, s. 1993, m.	Hon. Jason W. P. C. C., b. 1972.
1947	Rugby (3rd), Robert Charles Maffey, b. 1951, s. 1990, m.	Hon. Timothy J. H. M., b. 1975.
1919	Russell of Liverpool (3rd), Simon Gordon Jared Russell, b. 1952, s. 1981, m.	Hon. Edward C. S. R., b. 1985.
1876	Sackville (6th), Lionel Bertrand Sackville-West, b. 1913, s. 1965, m.	Hugh R. I. S.-W., MC, b. 1919.
1964	St Helens (2nd), Richard Francis Hughes-Young, b. 1945, s. 1980, m.	Hon. Henry H.-Y., b. 1986.
1559	St John of Bletso (21st), Anthony Tudor St John, b. 1957, s. 1978.	Edmund O. St J., b. 1927.
1887	St Levan (4th), John Francis Arthur St Aubyn, DSC, b. 1919, s. 1978, m.	Hon. O. Piers St A., MC, b. 1920.
1885	St Oswald (5th), Derek Edward Anthony Winn, b. 1919, s. 1984, m.	Hon. Charles R. A. W., b. 1959.
1960	Sanderson of Ayot. Disclaimed for life 1971. (Alan Lindsay Sanderson, b. 1931, s. 1971, m.)	Hon. Michael S., b. 1959.
1945	Sandford (2nd), Revd John Cyril Edmondson, DSC, b. 1920, s. 1959, m.	Hon. James J. M. E., b. 1949.
1871	Sandhurst (5th), (John Edward) Terence Mansfield, DFC, b. 1920, s. 1964, m.	Hon. Guy R. J. M., b. 1949.
1802	Sandys (7th), Richard Michael Oliver Hill, b. 1931, s. 1961, m.	Marcus T. H., b. 1931.
1888	Savile (3rd), George Halifax Lumley-Savile, b. 1919, s. 1931.	Hon. Henry L. T. L.-S., b. 1923.
1447	Saye and Sele (21st), Nathaniel Thomas Allen Fiennes, b. 1920, s. 1968, m.	Hon. Richard I. F., b. 1959.
1932	Selsdon (3rd), Malcolm McEacharn Mitchell-Thomson, b. 1937, s. 1963, m.	Hon. Callum M. M. M.-T., b. 1969.
1916	Shaughnessy (3rd), William Graham Shaughnessy, b. 1922, s. 1938, m.	Hon. Michael J. S., b. 1946.
1946	Shepherd (2nd), Malcolm Newton Shepherd, PC, b. 1918, s. 1954, m.	Hon. Graeme G. S., b. 1949.
1964	Sherfield (1st), Roger Mellor Makins, GCB, GCMG, FRS, b. 1904, w.	Hon. Christopher J. M., b. 1942.

Created	Title, order of succession, name, etc.	Eldest son or heir
1902	*Shuttleworth* (5th), Charles Geoffrey Nicholas Kay-Shuttleworth, *b.* 1948, *s.* 1975, *m.*	Hon. Thomas E. *K.-S.*, *b.* 1976.
1950	*Silkin*. Disclaimed for life 1972. (*Arthur Silkin, b.* 1916, *s.* 1972, *m.*)	Hon. Christopher L. *S.*, *b.* 1947.
1963	*Silsoe* (2nd), David Malcolm Trustram Eve, QC, *b.* 1930, *s.* 1976, *m.*	Hon. Simon R. T. *E.*, *b.* 1966.
1947	*Simon of Wythenshawe* (2nd), Roger Simon, *b.* 1913, *s.* 1960, *m.*	Hon. Matthew *S.*, *b.* 1955.
1449 s.	*Sinclair* (17th), Charles Murray Kennedy St Clair, CVO, *b.* 1914, *s.* 1957, *m.*	Master of Sinclair, *b.* 1968.
1957	*Sinclair of Cleeve* (3rd), John Lawrence Robert Sinclair, *b.* 1953, *s.* 1985.	None.
1919	*Sinha* (4th), Susanta Prasanna Sinha, *b.* 1953, *s.* 1989, *m.*	Hon. A. K. *S.*, *b.* 1930.
1828	*Skelmersdale* (7th), Roger Bootle-Wilbraham, *b.* 1945, *s.* 1973, *m.*	Hon. Andrew *B.-W.*, *b.* 1977.
1916	*Somerleyton* (3rd), Savile William Francis Crossley, *b.* 1928, *s.* 1959, *m.* Master of the Horse.	Hon. Hugh F. S. *C.*, *b.* 1971.
1784	*Somers* (8th), John Patrick Somers Cocks, *b.* 1907, *s.* 1953, *m.*	Philip S. *S. C.*, *b.* 1948.
1780	*Southampton* (6th), Charles James FitzRoy, *b.* 1928, *s.* 1989, *m.*	Hon. Edward C. *F.*, *b.* 1955.
1959	*Spens* (3rd), Patrick Michael Rex Spens, *b.* 1942, *s.* 1984, *m.*	Hon. Patrick N. G. *S.*, *b.* 1968.
1640	*Stafford* (15th), Francis Melfort William Fitzherbert, *b.* 1954, *s.* 1986, *m.*	Hon. Benjamin J. B. *F.*, *b.* 1983.
1938	*Stamp* (4th), Trevor Charles Bosworth Stamp, MD, FRCP, *b.* 1935, *s.* 1987, *m.*	Hon. Nicholas C. T. *S.*, *b.* 1978.
1839	*Stanley of Alderley* (8th) & *Sheffield* (8th) (1738 I.), Thomas Henry Oliver Stanley (7th *UK Baron Eddisbury*, 1848), *b.* 1927, *s.* 1971, *m.*	Hon. Richard O. *S.*, *b.* 1956.
1318	*Strabolgi* (11th), David Montague de Burgh Kenworthy, *b.* 1914, *s.* 1953, *m.*	Andrew D. W. *K.*, *b.* 1967.
1954	*Strang* (2nd), Colin Strang, *b.* 1922, *s.* 1978, *m.*	None.
1955	*Strathalmond* (3rd), William Roberton Fraser, *b.* 1947, *s.* 1976, *m.*	Hon. William G. *F.*, *b.* 1976.
1936	*Strathcarron* (2nd), David William Anthony Blyth Macpherson, *b.* 1924, *s.* 1937, *m.*	Hon. Ian D. P. *M.*, *b.* 1949.
1955	*Strathclyde* (2nd), Thomas Galloway Dunlop du Roy de Blicquy Galbraith, *b.* 1960, *s.* 1985, *m.*	Hon. Charles W. du R. de B. *G.*, *b.* 1962.
1900	*Strathcona and Mount Royal* (4th), Donald Euan Palmer Howard, *b.* 1923, *s.* 1959, *m.*	Hon. D. Alexander S. *H.*, *b.* 1961.
1836	*Stratheden* & *Campbell* (1841) (6th), Donald Campbell, *b.* 1934, *s.* 1987, *m.*	Hon. David A. *C.*, *b.* 1963.
1884	*Strathspey* (6th), James Patrick Trevor Grant of Grant, *b.* 1943, *s.* 1991, *m.*	Hon. Michael P. F. *G.*, *b.* 1953.
1838	*Sudeley* (7th), Merlin Charles Sainthill Hanbury-Tracy, *b.* 1939, *s.* 1941.	D. Andrew J. *H-T.*, *b.* 1928.
1786	*Suffield* (11th), Anthony Philip Harbord-Hamond, MC, *b.* 1922, *s.* 1951, *m.*	Hon. Charles A. A. *H.-H.*, *b.* 1953.
1893	*Swansea* (4th), John Hussey Hamilton Vivian, *b.* 1925, *s.* 1934, *m.*	Hon. Richard A. H. *V.*, *b.* 1957.
1907	*Swaythling* (4th), David Charles Samuel Montagu, *b.* 1928, *s.* 1990, *m.*	Hon. Charles E. S. *M.*, *b.* 1954.
1919	*Swinfen* (3rd), Roger Mynors Swinfen Eady, *b.* 1938, *s.* 1977, *m.*	Hon. Charles R. P. S. *E.*, *b.* 1971.
1935	*Sysonby* (3rd), John Frederick Ponsonby, *b.* 1945, *s.* 1956.	None.
1831 I.	*Talbot of Malahide* (10th), Reginald John Richard Arundell, *b.* 1931, *s.* 1987, *w.*	Hon. Richard J. T. *A.*, *b.* 1957.
1946	*Tedder* (2nd), John Michael Tedder, SC.D., PH.D., D.SC., *b.* 1926, *s.* 1967, *m.*	Hon. Robin J. *T.*, *b.* 1955.
1884	*Tennyson* (5th), Mark Aubrey Tennyson, DSC, *b.* 1920, *s.* 1991, *m.*	Lt.-Cdr. James A. *T.*, DSC, *b.* 1913.
1918	*Terrington* (4th), (James Allen) David Woodhouse, *b.* 1915, *s.* 1961, *m.*	Hon. C. Montague *W.*, DSO, OBE, b. 1917.
1940	*Teviot* (2nd), Charles John Kerr, *b.* 1934, *s.* 1968, *m.*	Hon. Charles R. *K.*, *b.* 1971.
1616	*Teynham* (20th), John Christopher Ingham Roper-Curzon, *b.* 1928, *s.* 1972, *m.*	Hon. David J. H. I. *R.-C.*, *b.* 1965.
1964	*Thomson of Fleet* (2nd), Kenneth Roy Thomson, *b.* 1923, *s.* 1976, *m.*	Hon. David K. R. *T.*, *b.* 1957.
1792	*Thurlow* (8th), Francis Edward Hovell-Thurlow-Cumming-Bruce, KCMG, *b.* 1912, *s.* 1971, *w.*	Hon. Roualeyn R. *H.-T.-C.-B.*, *b.* 1952.
1876	*Tollemache* (5th), Timothy John Edward Tollemache, *b.* 1939, *s.* 1975, *m.*	Hon. Edward J. H. *T.*, *b.* 1976.
1564 s.	*Torphichen* (15th), James Andrew Douglas Sandilands, *b.* 1946, *s.* 1975, *m.*	Douglas R. A. *S.*, *b.* 1926.
1947	*Trefgarne* (2nd), David Garro Trefgarne, PC, *b.* 1941, *s.* 1960, *m.*	Hon. George G. *T.*, *b.* 1970.
1921	*Trevethin* (4th), *and Oaksey* (2nd), John Geoffrey Tristram Lawrence, OBE (2nd *UK Baron, Oaksey*, 1947), *b.* 1929, *s.* 1971, *m.*	Hon. Patrick J. T. *L.*, *b.* 1960.
1880	*Trevor* (4th), Charles Edwin Hill-Trevor, *b.* 1928, *s.* 1950, *m.*	Hon. Marke C. *H.-T.*, *b.* 1970.
1461 I.	*Trimlestown* (20th), Anthony Edward Barnewall, *b.* 1928, *s.* 1990, *m.*	Hon. Raymond C. *B.*, *b.* 1930.
1940	*Tryon* (3rd), Anthony George Merrik Tryon, *b.* 1940, *s.* 1976, *m.*	Hon. Charles G. B. *T.*, *b.* 1976.
1935	*Tweedsmuir* (2nd), John Norman Stuart Buchan, CBE, CD, *b.* 1911, *s.* 1940, *m.*	Hon. William *B.*, *b.* 1916.
1523	*Vaux of Harrowden* (10th), John Hugh Philip Gilbey, *b.* 1915, *s.* 1977, *m.*	Hon. Anthony W. *G.*, *b.* 1940.
1800 I.	*Ventry* (8th), Andrew Wesley Daubeny de Moleyns, *b.* 1943, *s.* 1987, *m.*	Hon. Francis W. *D. de M.*, *b.* 1965.
1762	*Vernon* (10th), John Lawrance Vernon, *b.* 1923, *s.* 1963, *m.*	Col. William R. D. *Vernon-Harcourt*, OBE, *b.* 1909.
1922	*Vestey* (3rd), Samuel George Armstrong Vestey, *b.* 1941, *s.* 1954, *m.*	Hon. William G. *V.*, *b.* 1983.
1841	*Vivian* (6th), Nicholas Crespigny Laurence Vivian, *b.* 1935, *s.* 1991, *m.*	Hon. Charles H. C. *V.*, *b.* 1966.

Created	Title, order of succession, name, etc.	Eldest son or heir
1934	Wakehurst (3rd), (John) Christopher Loder, b. 1925, s. 1970, m.	Hon. Timothy W. L., b. 1958.
1723	Walpole (10th), Robert Horatio Walpole (8th Brit. Baron Walpole of Wolterton, 1756), b. 1938, s. 1989, m.	Hon. Jonathan R. H. W., b. 1967.
1780	Walsingham (9th), John de Grey, MC, b. 1925, s. 1965, m.	Hon. Robert de G., b. 1969.
1936	Wardington (2nd), Christopher Henry Beaumont Pease, b. 1924, s. 1950, m.	Hon. William S. P., b. 1925.
1792 I.	Waterpark (7th), Frederick Caryll Philip Cavendish, b. 1926, s. 1948, m.	Hon. Roderick A. C., b. 1959.
1942	Wedgwood (4th), Piers Anthony Weymouth Wedgwood, b. 1954, s. 1970, m.	John W., CBE, MD, b. 1919.
1861	Westbury (5th), David Alan Bethell, MC, b. 1922, s. 1961, m.	Hon. Richard N. B., MBE, b. 1950.
1944	Westwood (3rd), (William) Gavin Westwood, b. 1944, s. 1991, m.	Hon. William F. W., b. 1972.
1935	Wigram (2nd), (George) Neville (Clive) Wigram, MC, b. 1915, s. 1960, w.	Maj. Hon. Andrew F. C. W., MVO, b. 1949.
1491	Willoughby de Broke (21st), Leopold David Verney, b. 1938, s. 1986, m.	Hon. Rupert G. V., b. 1966.
1946	Wilson (2nd), Patrick Maitland Wilson, b. 1915, s. 1964, w.	None.
1937	Windlesham (3rd), David James George Hennessy, CVO, PC, b. 1932, s. 1962, w.	Hon. James R. H., b. 1968.
1951	Wise (2nd), John Clayton Wise, b. 1923, s. 1968, m.	Hon. Christopher J. C. W., PH.D., b. 1949.
1869	Wolverton (7th), Christopher Richard Glyn, b. 1938, s. 1988, m.	Hon. Andrew J. G., b. 1943.
1928	Wraxall (2nd), George Richard Lawley Gibbs, b. 1928, s. 1931.	Hon. Sir Eustace H. B. G., KCVO, CMG, b. 1929.
1915	Wrenbury (3rd), John Burton Buckley, b. 1927, s. 1940, m.	Hon. William E. B., b. 1966.
1838	Wrottesley (6th), Clifton Hugh Lancelot de Verdon Wrottesley, b. 1968, s. 1977.	Hon. Stephen J. W., b. 1955.
1919	Wyfold (3rd), Hermon Robert Fleming Hermon-Hodge, b. 1915, s. 1942.	None.
1829	Wynford (8th), Robert Samuel Best, MBE, b. 1917, s. 1943, m.	Hon. John P. B., b. 1950.
1308	Zouche (18th), James Assheton Frankland, b. 1943, s. 1965, m.	Hon. William T. A. F., b. 1984.

BARONESSES/LADIES IN THEIR OWN RIGHT

Style, The Right Hon. the Lady __, *or* The Right Hon. the Baroness __, according to her preference. Either style may be used, except in the case of Scottish titles (indicated by s.), which are not baronies (*see* page 141) and whose holders are always addressed as Lady
Husband, Untitled
Children's style, As for children of a Baron
For forms of address, *see* page 220.

Created	Title, order of succession, name, etc.	Eldest son or heir
1455	Berners, in abeyance between two co-heiresses, daughters of the late Baroness Berners, died 1992.	
1529	Braye (8th in line), Mary Penelope Aubrey–Fletcher, b. 1941, s. 1985, m.	Two co-heiresses.
1321	Dacre (27th in line), Rachel Leila Douglas-Home, b. 1929, title called out of abeyance, 1970, w.	Hon. James T. A. D.-H., b. 1952.
1332	Darcy de Knayth (18th in line), Davina Marcia Ingrams, b. 1938, s. 1943, w.	Hon. Caspar D. I., b. 1962.
1439	Dudley (14th in line), Barbara Amy Felicity Hamilton, b. 1907, s. 1972, m.	Hon. Jim A. H. Wallace, b. 1930.
1490 S.	Herries of Terregles (14th in line), Anne Elizabeth Fitzalan-Howard, b. 1938, s. 1975, m.	Lady Mary Mumford, CVO, b. 1940.
1602 S.	Kinloss (12th in line), Beatrice Mary Grenville Freeman-Grenville, b. 1922, s. 1944, m.	Master of Kinloss, b. 1953.
1681 S.	Nairne (12th in line), Katherine Evelyn Constance Bigham (Katherine, Viscountess Mersey), b. 1912, s. 1944, w.	The Viscount Mersey, b. 1934 (see page 151).
1445 S.	Saltoun (20th in line), Flora Marjory Fraser, b. 1930, s. 1979, m.	Hon. Katharine I. M. I. F., b. 1957.
1489 S.	Sempill (20th in line), Ann Moira Sempill, b. 1920, s. 1965, w.	Master of Sempill, b. 1949.
1628	Strange (16th in line), (Jean) Cherry Drummond of Megginch, b. 1928, title called out of abeyance, 1986, m.	Hon. Adam H. D. of M., b. 1953.
1544–5	Wharton (11th in line), Myrtle Olive Felix Robertson, b. 1934, title called out of abeyance, 1990, m.	Hon. Myles C. D. R., b. 1964.
1313	Willoughby de Eresby (27th in line), (Nancy) Jane Marie Heathcote-Drummond-Willoughby, b. 1934, s. 1983.	Two co-heiresses.

Life Peers

Between 1 September 1992 and 31 August 1993, the conferment of 16 life peerages was announced, three under the Appellate Jurisdiction Act 1876 and 13 under the Life Peerages Act 1958:

NEW LORDS OF APPEAL IN ORDINARY: (announced 10 September 1992) the Rt. Hon. Sir Harry Woolf; (22 July 1993) *the Rt. Hon. Sir Anthony Lloyd; *the Rt. Hon. Sir Michael Nolan

NEW YEAR HONOURS (31 December 1992): the Rt. Hon. Shirley Williams

THE QUEEN'S BIRTHDAY HONOURS (12 June 1993): Sir Richard Attenborough, CBE; Sir Ralf Dahrendorf, KBE; the Rt. Hon. Robert (Robin) Leigh-Pemberton; Sir Yehudi Menuhin, OM, KBE

'WORKING' PEERS (13 August 1993): *Miss Brenda Dean; *Mrs Joyce Gould; *Mrs Doreen Miller, MBE; *the Rt. Hon. Sir Paul Dean; *Simon Haskel; *Anthony Lester, QC; *Robert Dixon Smith; *Sir Christopher Tugendhat

*No title gazetted at time of going to press

CREATED UNDER THE APPELLATE JURISDICTION ACT 1876 (AS AMENDED)

BARONS

Created
1986   *Ackner,* Desmond James Conrad Ackner, PC, *b.* 1920, *m.*
1981   *Brandon of Oakbrook,* Henry Vivian Brandon, MC, PC, *b.* 1920, *m.*
1980   *Bridge of Harwich,* Nigel Cyprian Bridge, PC, *b.* 1917, *m.*
1982   *Brightman,* John Anson Brightman, PC, *b.* 1911, *m.*
1991   *Browne-Wilkinson,* Nicolas Christopher Henry Browne-Wilkinson, PC, *b.* 1930, *m.* Lord of Appeal in Ordinary.
1957   *Denning,* Alfred Thompson Denning, PC, *b.* 1899, *w.*
1986   *Goff of Chieveley,* Robert Lionel Archibald Goff, PC, *b.* 1926, *m.* Lord of Appeal in Ordinary.
1985   *Griffiths,* (William) Hugh Griffiths, MC, PC, *b.* 1923, *m.*
1987   *Jauncey of Tullichettle,* Charles Eliot Jauncey, PC, *b.* 1925, *m.* Lord of Appeal in Ordinary.
1977   *Keith of Kinkel,* Henry Shanks Keith, PC, *b.* 1922, *m.* Lord of Appeal in Ordinary.
1979   *Lane,* Geoffrey Dawson Lane, AFC, PC, *b.* 1918, *m.*
1992   *Mustill,* Michael John Mustill, PC, *b.* 1931, *m.* Lord of Appeal in Ordinary.
1986   *Oliver of Aylmerton,* Peter Raymond Oliver, PC, *b.* 1921, *m.*
1980   *Roskill,* Eustace Wentworth Roskill, PC, *b.* 1911, *m.*
1977   *Scarman,* Leslie George Scarman, OBE, PC, *b.* 1911, *m.*
1992   *Slynn of Hadley,* Gordon Slynn, PC, *b.* 1930, *m.* Lord of Appeal in Ordinary.
1982   *Templeman,* Sydney William Templeman, MBE, PC, *b.* 1920, *w.* Lord of Appeal in Ordinary.
1964   *Wilberforce,* Richard Orme Wilberforce, CMG, OBE, PC, *b.* 1907, *m.*
1992   *Woolf,* Harry Kenneth Woolf, PC, *b.* 1933, *m.* Lord of Appeal in Ordinary.

CREATED UNDER THE LIFE PEERAGES ACT 1958

BARONS

Created
1974   *Alexander of Potterhill,* William Picken Alexander, PH.D., *b.* 1905, *m.*
1988   *Alexander of Weedon,* Robert Scott Alexander, QC, *b.* 1936, *m.*
1976   *Allen of Abbeydale,* Philip Allen, GCB, *b.* 1912, *m.*
1961   *Alport,* Cuthbert James McCall Alport, TD, PC, *b.* 1912, *w.*
1992   *Amery of Lustleigh,* Julian Amery, PC, *b.* 1919, *w.*
1965   *Annan,* Noel Gilroy Annan, OBE, *b.* 1916, *m.*
1992   *Archer of Sandwell,* Peter Kingsley Archer, PC, QC, *b.* 1926, *m.*
1992   *Archer of Weston-super-Mare,* Jeffrey Howard Archer, *b.* 1940, *m.*
1970   *Ardwick,* John Cowburn Beavan, *b.* 1910, *m.*
1988   *Armstrong of Ilminster,* Robert Temple Armstrong, GCB, CVO, *b.* 1927, *m.*
1992   *Ashley of Stoke,* Jack Ashley, CH, PC, *b.* 1922, *m.*
1993   *Attenborough,* Richard Samuel Attenborough, CBE, *b.* 1923, *m.*
1967   *Aylestone,* Herbert William Bowden, CH, CBE, PC, *b.* 1905, *m.*
1982   *Bancroft,* Ian Powell Bancroft, GCB, *b.* 1922, *m.*
1974   *Banks,* Desmond Anderson Harvie Banks, CBE, *b.* 1918, *m.*
1974   *Barber,* Anthony Perrinott Lysberg Barber, TD, PC, *b.* 1920, *m.*
1992   *Barber of Tewkesbury,* Derek Coates Barber, *b.* 1918, *m.*
1983   *Barnett,* Joel Barnett, PC, *b.* 1923, *m.*
1982   *Bauer,* Prof. Peter Thomas Bauer, D.SC., *b.* 1915.
1967   *Beaumont of Whitley,* Revd Timothy Wentworth Beaumont, *b.* 1928, *m.*
1979   *Bellwin,* Irwin Norman Bellow, *b.* 1923, *m.*
1981   *Beloff,* Max Beloff, *b.* 1913, *m.*
1981   *Benson,* Henry Alexander Benson, GBE, *b.* 1909, *m.*
1971   *Blake,* Robert Norman William Blake, FBA, *b.* 1916, *m.*
1983   *Blanch,* Rt. Revd Stuart Yarworth Blanch, PC, *b.* 1918, *m.*
1978   *Blease,* William John Blease, *b.* 1914, *m.*
1980   *Boardman,* Thomas Gray Boardman, MC, TD, *b.* 1919, *m.*
1986   *Bonham-Carter,* Mark Raymond Bonham Carter, *b.* 1922, *m.*
1976   *Boston of Faversham,* Terence George Boston, QC, *b.* 1930, *m.*
1984   *Bottomley,* Arthur George Bottomley, OBE, PC, *b.* 1907, *m.*
1972   *Boyd-Carpenter,* John Archibald Boyd-Carpenter, PC, *b.* 1908, *m.*
1992   *Braine of Wheatley,* Bernard Richard Braine, PC, *b.* 1914, *w.*
1987   *Bramall,* Edwin Noel Westby Bramall, KG, GCB, OBE, MC, *Field Marshal, b.* 1923, *m.*
1976   *Briggs,* Asa Briggs, *b.* 1921, *m.*

Created

1976   *Brimelow*, Thomas Brimelow, GCMG, OBE, *b.* 1915, *m.*

1975   *Brookes*, Raymond Percival Brookes, *b.* 1909, *m.*

1979   *Brooks of Tremorfa*, John Edward Brooks, *b.* 1927, *m.*

1974   *Bruce of Donington*, Donald William Trevor Bruce, *b.* 1912, *m.*

1976   *Bullock*, Alan Louis Charles Bullock, FBA, *b.* 1914, *m.*

1988   *Butterfield*, (William) John (Hughes) Butterfield, OBE, DM, *b.* 1920, *m.*

1985   *Butterworth*, John Blackstock Butterworth, CBE, *b.* 1918, *m.*

1978   *Buxton of Alsa*, Aubrey Leland Oakes Buxton, MC, *b.* 1918, *m.*

1987   *Callaghan of Cardiff*, (Leonard) James Callaghan, KG, PC, *b.* 1912, *m.*

1984   *Cameron of Lochbroom*, Kenneth John Cameron, PC, *b.* 1931, *m.*

1981   *Campbell of Alloway*, Alan Robertson Campbell, QC, *b.* 1917, *m.*

1974   *Campbell of Croy*, Gordon Thomas Calthrop Campbell, MC, PC, *b.* 1921, *m.*

1966   *Campbell of Eskan*, John (Jock) Middleton Campbell, *b.* 1912, *w.*

1987   *Carlisle of Bucklow*, Mark Carlisle, QC, PC, *b.* 1929, *m.*

1983   *Carmichael of Kelvingrove*, Neil George Carmichael, *b.* 1921.

1975   *Carr of Hadley*, (Leonard) Robert Carr, PC, *b.* 1916, *m.*

1987   *Carter*, Denis Victor Carter, *b.* 1932, *m.*

1977   *Carver*, (Richard) Michael (Power) Carver, GCB, CBE, DSO, MC, *Field Marshal*, *b.* 1915, *m.*

1990   *Cavendish of Furness*, (Richard) Hugh Cavendish, *b.* 1941, *m.*

1982   *Cayzer*, (William) Nicholas Cayzer, *b.* 1910, *m.*

1964   *Chalfont*, (Alun) Arthur Gwynne Jones, OBE, MC, PC, *b.* 1919, *m.*

1985   *Chapple*, Frank Joseph Chapple, *b.* 1921, *m.*

1978   *Charteris of Amisfield*, Martin Michael Charles Charteris, GCB, GCVO, OBE, PC, Royal Victorian Chain, *b.* 1913, *m.*

1963   *Chelmer*, Eric Cyril Boyd Edwards, MC, TD, *b.* 1914, *m.*

1987   *Chilver*, (Amos) Henry Chilver, FRS, FEng., *b.* 1926, *m.*

1977   *Chitnis*, Pratap Chidamber Chitnis, *b.* 1936, *m.*

1992   *Clark of Kempston*, William Gibson Haig Clark, PC, *b.* 1917, *m.*

1979   *Cledwyn of Penrhos*, Cledwyn Hughes, CH, PC, *b.* 1916, *m.*

1990   *Clinton-Davis*, Stanley Clinton Davis, *b.* 1928, *m.*

1978   *Cockfield*, (Francis) Arthur Cockfield, PC, *b.* 1916, *m.*

1987   *Cocks of Hartcliffe*, Michael Francis Lovell Cocks, PC, *b.* 1929, *m.*

1980   *Coggan*, Rt. Revd (Frederick) Donald Coggan, PC, Royal Victorian Chain, *b.* 1909, *m.*

1964   *Collison*, Harold Francis Collison, CBE, *b.* 1909, *m.*

1987   *Colnbrook*, Humphrey Edward Gregory Atkins, KCMG, PC, *b.* 1922, *m.*

1981   *Constantine of Stanmore*, Theodore Constantine, CBE, AE, *b.* 1910, *w.*

1992   *Cooke of Islandreagh*, Victor Alexander Cooke, OBE, *b.* 1920, *m.*

1991   *Craig of Radley*, David Brownrigg Craig, GCB, OBE, *Marshal of the Royal Air Force*, *b.* 1929, *m.*

Created

1987   *Crickhowell*, (Roger) Nicholas Edwards, PC, *b.* 1934, *m.*

1978   *Croham*, Douglas Albert Vivian Allen, GCB, *b.* 1917, *m.*

1974   *Cudlipp*, Hugh Cudlipp, OBE, *b.* 1913, *m.*

1979   *Dacre of Glanton*, Hugh Redwald Trevor-Roper, *b.* 1914, *m.*

1993   *Dahrendorf*, Ralf Dahrendorf, KBE, Ph.D., D. Phil., FBA, *b.* 1929, *m.*

1986   *Dainton*, Frederick Sydney Dainton, PH.D., SC.D., FRS, *b.* 1914, *m.*

1983   *Dean of Beswick*, Joseph Jabez Dean, *b.* 1922.

1986   *Deedes*, William Francis Deedes, MC, PC, *b.* 1913, *m.*

1976   *Delfont*, Bernard Delfont, *b.* 1909, *m.*

1991   *Desai*, Prof. Meghnad Jagdishchandra Desai, PH.D., *b.* 1940, *m.*

1970   *Diamond*, John Diamond, PC, *b.* 1907, *m.*

1967   *Donaldson of Kingsbridge*, John George Stuart Donaldson, OBE, *b.* 1907, *m.*

1988   *Donaldson of Lymington*, John Francis Donaldson, PC, *b.* 1920, *m.*

1985   *Donoughue*, Bernard Donoughue, D.Phil., *b.* 1934.

1987   *Dormand of Easington*, John Donkin Dormand, *b.* 1919, *m.*

1992   *Eatwell*, John Leonard Eatwell, *b.* 1945.

1983   *Eden of Winton*, John Benedict Eden, PC, *b.* 1925, *m.*

1992   *Elis-Thomas*, Dafydd Elis Elis-Thomas, *b.* 1946, *m.*

1985   *Elliott of Morpeth*, Robert William Elliott, *b.* 1920, *m.*

1981   *Elystan-Morgan*, Dafydd Elystan Elystan-Morgan, *b.* 1932, *m.*

1980   *Emslie*, George Carlyle Emslie, MBE, PC, *b.* 1919, *m.*

1983   *Ennals*, David Hedley Ennals, PC, *b.* 1922, *m.*

1992   *Ewing of Kirkford*, Harry Ewing, *b.* 1931, *m.*

1983   *Ezra*, Derek Ezra, MBE, *b.* 1919, *m.*

1983   *Fanshawe of Richmond*, Anthony Henry Fanshawe Royle, KCMG, *b.* 1927, *m.*

1992   *Finsberg*, Geoffrey Finsberg, MBE, *b.* 1926, *m.*

1983   *Fitt*, Gerard Fitt, PC, *b.* 1926, *m.*

1979   *Flowers*, Brian Hilton Flowers, FRS, *b.* 1924, *m.*

1967   *Foot*, John Mackintosh Foot, *b.* 1909, *m.*

1982   *Forte*, Charles Forte, *b.* 1908, *m.*

1989   *Fraser of Carmyllie*, Peter Lovat Fraser, QC, PC, *b.* 1945, *m.*

1974   *Fraser of Kilmorack*, (Richard) Michael Fraser, CBE, *b.* 1915, *m.*

1982   *Gallacher*, John Gallacher, *b.* 1920, *m.*

1979   *Galpern*, Myer Galpern, *b.* 1903.

1992   *Geraint*, Geraint Wyn Howells, *b.* 1925, *m.*

1975   *Gibson*, (Richard) Patrick (Tallentyre) Gibson, *b.* 1916, *m.*

1979   *Gibson-Watt*, (James) David Gibson-Watt, MC, PC, *b.* 1918, *m.*

1992   *Gilmour of Craigmillar*, Ian Hedworth John Little Gilmour, PC, *b.* 1926, *m.*

1977   *Glenamara*, Edward Watson Short, CH, PC, *b.* 1912, *m.*

1965   *Goodman*, Arnold Abraham Goodman, CH, *b.* 1913.

1987   *Goold*, James Duncan Goold, *b.* 1934, *m.*

1976   *Grade*, Lew Grade, *b.* 1906, *m.*

1983   *Graham of Edmonton*, (Thomas) Edward Graham, *b.* 1925, *m.*

1967   *Granville of Eye*, Edgar Louis Granville, *b.* 1899, *m.*

1983   *Gray of Contin*, James (Hamish) Hector Northey Gray, PC, *b.* 1927, *m.*

1974   *Greene of Harrow Weald*, Sidney Francis Greene, CBE, *b.* 1910, *m.*

Created

1974   Greenhill of Harrow, Denis Arthur Greenhill, GCMG, OBE, *b.* 1913, *m.*

1975   Gregson, John Gregson, *b.* 1924.

1968   Grey of Naunton, Ralph Francis Alnwick Grey, GCMG, GCVO, OBE, *b.* 1910, *m.*

1991   Griffiths of Fforestfach, Brian Griffiths, *b.* 1941, *m.*

1983   Grimond, Joseph Grimond, TD, PC, *b.* 1913, *m.*

1970   Hailsham of St Marylebone, Quintin McGarel Hogg, KG, CH, PC, *b.* 1907, *m.*

1983   Hanson, James Edward Hanson, *b.* 1922, *m.*

1974   Harmar-Nicholls, Harmar Harmar-Nicholls, *b.* 1912, *m.*

1974   Harris of Greenwich, John Henry Harris, *b.* 1930, *m.*

1979   Harris of High Cross, Ralph Harris, *b.* 1924, *m.*

1968   Hartwell, (William) Michael Berry, MBE, TD, *b.* 1911, *w.*

1971   Harvey of Prestbury, Arthur Vere Harvey, CBE, *b.* 1906, *m.*

1974   Harvington, Robert Grant Grant-Ferris, AE, PC, *b.* 1907, *m.*

1990   Haslam, Robert Haslam, *b.* 1923, *m.*

1992   Hayhoe, Bernard John (Barney) Hayhoe, PC, *b.* 1925, *m.*

1992   Healey, Denis Winston Healey, CH, MBE, PC, *b.* 1917, *m.*

1984   Henderson of Brompton, Peter Gordon Henderson, KCB, *b.* 1922, *m.*

1979   Hill-Norton, Peter John Hill-Norton, GCB, *Admiral of the Fleet, b.* 1915, *m.*

1967   Hirshfield, Desmond Barel Hirshfield, *b.* 1913, *m.*

1979   Holderness, Richard Frederick Wood, PC, *b.* 1920, *m.*

1991   Hollick, Clive Richard Hollick, *b.* 1945, *m.*

1990   Holme of Cheltenham, Richard Gordon Holme, CBE, *b.* 1936, *m.*

1974   Home of the Hirsel, Alexander Frederick Douglas-Home, KT, PC, *b.* 1903, *w.*

1979   Hooson, (Hugh) Emlyn Hooson, QC, *b.* 1925, *m.*

1974   Houghton of Sowerby, (Arthur Leslie Noel) Douglas Houghton, CH, PC, *b.* 1898, *m.*

1992   Howe of Aberavon, (Richard Edward) Geoffrey Howe, PC, QC, *b.* 1926, *m.*

1992   Howell, Denis Herbert Howell, PC, *b.* 1923, *m.*

1978   Howie of Troon, William Howie, *b.* 1924, *m.*

1961   Hughes, William Hughes, CBE, PC, *b.* 1911, *m.*

1966   Hunt, (Henry Cecil) John Hunt, KG, CBE, DSO, *b.* 1910, *m.*

1980   Hunt of Tanworth, John Joseph Benedict Hunt, GCB, *b.* 1919, *m.*

1978   Hunter of Newington, Robert Brockie Hunter, MBE, FRCP, *b.* 1915, *m.*

1978   Hutchinson of Lullington, Jeremy Nicolas Hutchinson, QC, *b.* 1915, *m.*

1982   Ingrow, John Aked Taylor, OBE, TD, *b.* 1917, *m.*

1987   Irvine of Lairg, Alexander Andrew Mackay Irvine, QC, *b.* 1940, *m.*

1968   Jacques, John Henry Jacques, *b.* 1905, *m.*

1988   Jakobovits, Immanuel Jakobovits, *b.* 1921, *m.*

1987   Jay, Douglas Patrick Thomas Jay, PC, *b.* 1907, *m.*

1987   Jenkin of Roding, (Charles) Patrick (Fleeming) Jenkin, PC, *b.* 1926, *m.*

1987   Jenkins of Hillhead, Roy Harris Jenkins, PC, *b.* 1920, *m.*

1981   Jenkins of Putney, Hugh Gater Jenkins, *b.* 1908, *w.*

1981   John-Mackie, John John-Mackie, *b.* 1909, *m.*

1987   Johnston of Rockport, Charles Collier Johnston, TD, *b.* 1915, *m.*

Created

1987   Joseph, Keith Sinjohn Joseph, CH, PC, *b.* 1918, *m.*

1991   Judd, Frank Ashcroft Judd, *b.* 1935, *m.*

1976   Kagan, Joseph Kagan, *b.* 1915, *m.*

1980   Keith of Castleacre, Kenneth Alexander Keith, *b.* 1916, *m.*

1985   Kimball, Marcus Richard Kimball, *b.* 1928, *m.*

1983   King of Wartnaby, John Leonard King, *b.* 1918, *m.*

1993   Kingsdown, Robert (Robin) Leigh-Pemberton, PC, *b.* 1927, *m.*

1965   Kings Norton, Harold Roxbee Cox, PH.D., FEng., *b.* 1902, *m.*

1975   Kirkhill, John Farquharson Smith, *b.* 1930, *m.*

1974   Kissin, Harry Kissin, *b.* 1912, *m.*

1987   Knights, Philip Douglas Knights, CBE, QPM, *b.* 1920, *m.*

1991   Laing of Dunphail, Hector Laing, *b.* 1923, *m.*

1990   Lane of Horsell, Peter Stewart Lane, *b.* 1925, *w.*

1992   Lawson of Blaby, Nigel Lawson, PC, *b.* 1932, *m.*

1979   Lever of Manchester, Harold Lever, PC, *b.* 1914, *m.*

1982   Lewin, Terence Thornton Lewin, KG, GCB, LVO, DSC, *Admiral of the Fleet, b.* 1920, *m.*

1989   Lewis of Newnham, Jack Lewis, FRS, *b.* 1928, *m.*

1974   Lovell-Davis, Peter Lovell Lovell-Davis, *b.* 1924, *m.*

1979   Lowry, Robert Lynd Erskine Lowry, PC, PC(NI), *b.* 1919, *w. Lord of Appeal in Ordinary.*

1984   McAlpine of West Green, (Robert) Alistair McAlpine, *b.* 1942, *m.*

1988   Macaulay of Bragar, Donald Macaulay, QC, *b.* 1933.

1975   McCarthy, William Edward John McCarthy, *b.* 1925, *m.*

1976   McCluskey, John Herbert McCluskey, *b.* 1929, *m.*

1989   McColl of Dulwich, Ian McColl, FRCS, FRCSE, *b.* 1933, *m.*

1966   McFadzean, William Hunter McFadzean, KT, *b.* 1903, *m.*

1991   Macfarlane of Bearsden, Norman Somerville Macfarlane, *b.* 1926, *m.*

1978   McGregor of Durris, Oliver Ross McGregor, *b.* 1921, *m.*

1982   McIntosh of Haringey, Andrew Robert McIntosh, *b.* 1933, *m.*

1991   Mackay of Ardbrecknish, John Jackson Mackay, *b.* 1938, *m.*

1979   Mackay of Clashfern, James Peter Hymers Mackay, PC, *b.* 1927, *m. Lord High Chancellor.*

1988   Mackenzie-Stuart, Alexander John Mackenzie Stuart, , *b.* 1924, *m.*

1974   Mackie of Benshie, George Yull Mackie, CBE, DSO, DFC, *b.* 1919, *m.*

1982   MacLehose of Beoch, (Crawford) Murray MacLehose, KT, GBE, KCMG, KCVO, *b.* 1917, *m.*

1967   Mais, Alan Raymond Mais, GBE, TD, ERD, FEng., *b.* 1911, *m.*

1991   Marlesford, Mark Shuldham Schreiber, *b.* 1931, *m.*

1981   Marsh, Richard William Marsh, PC, *b.* 1928, *m.*

1985   Marshall of Goring, Walter Charles Marshall, CBE, FRS, *b.* 1932, *m.*

1987   Mason of Barnsley, Roy Mason, PC, *b.* 1924, *m.*

1980   Matthews, Victor Collin Matthews, *b.* 1919, *m.*

1983   Maude of Stratford-upon-Avon, Angus Edmund Upton Maude, TD, PC, *b.* 1912, *m.*

1981   Mayhew, Christopher Paget Mayhew, *b.* 1915, *m.*

1985   Mellish, Robert Joseph Mellish, PC, *b.* 1913, *m.*

1993   Menuhin, Yehudi Menuhin, OM, KBE, *b.* 1916, *m.*

1992   Merlyn-Rees, Merlyn Merlyn-Rees, PC, *b.* 1920, *m.*

1978   Mishcon, Victor Mishcon, *b.* 1915, *m.*

1981   Molloy, William John Molloy, *b.* 1918.

Created

1992   *Moore of Lower Marsh*, John Edward Michael Moore, PC, *b*. 1937, *m*.

1986   *Moore of Wolvercote*, Philip Brian Cecil Moore, GCB, GCVO, CMG, PC, *b*. 1921, *m*.

1990   *Morris of Castle Morris*, Brian Robert Morris, D.Phil., *b*. 1930, *m*.

1985   *Morton of Shuna*, Hugh Drennan Baird Morton, *b*. 1930, *m*.

1971   *Moyola*, James Dawson Chichester-Clark, PC (NI), *b*. 1923, *m*.

1984   *Mulley*, Frederick William Mulley, PC, *b*. 1918, *m*.

1985   *Murray of Epping Forest*, Lionel Murray, OBE, PC, *b*. 1922, *m*.

1964   *Murray of Newhaven*, Keith Anderson Hope Murray, KCB, Ph.D., *b*. 1903.

1979   *Murton of Lindisfarne*, (Henry) Oscar Murton, OBE, TD, PC, *b*. 1914, *m*.

1975   *Northfield*, (William) Donald Chapman, *b*. 1923.

1966   *Nugent of Guildford*, (George) Richard (Hodges) Nugent, PC, *b*. 1907, *m*.

1973   *O'Brien of Lothbury*, Leslie Kenneth O'Brien, GBE, PC, *b*. 1908, *m*.

1976   *Oram*, Albert Edward Oram, *b*. 1913, *m*.

1971   *Orr-Ewing*, (Charles) Ian Orr-Ewing, OBE, *b*. 1912, *m*.

1992   *Owen*, David Anthony Llewellyn Owen, PC, *b*. 1938, *m*.

1991   *Palumbo*, Peter Garth Palumbo, *b*. 1935, *m*.

1992   *Parkinson*, Cecil Edward Parkinson, PC, *b*. 1931, *m*.

1975   *Parry*, Gordon Samuel David Parry, *b*. 1925, *m*.

1990   *Pearson of Rannoch*, Malcolm Everard MacLaren Pearson, *b*. 1942, *m*.

1979   *Perry of Walton*, Walter Laing Macdonald Perry, OBE, FRS, FRSE, *b*. 1921, *m*.

1987   *Peston*, Maurice Harry Peston, *b*. 1931, *m*.

1983   *Peyton of Yeovil*, John Wynne William Peyton, PC, *b*. 1919, *m*.

1975   *Pitt of Hampstead*, David Thomas Pitt, *b*. 1913, *m*.

1992   *Plant of Highfield*, Prof. Raymond Plant, Ph.D., *b*. 1945, *m*.

1959   *Plowden*, Edwin Noel Plowden, GBE, KCB, *b*. 1907, *m*.

1987   *Plumb*, (Charles) Henry Plumb, MEP, *b*. 1925, *m*.

1981   *Plummer of St Marylebone*, (Arthur) Desmond (Herne) Plummer, TD, *b*. 1914, *m*.

1973   *Porritt*, Arthur Espie Porritt, GCMG, GCVO, CBE, *b*. 1900, *m*.

1990   *Porter of Luddenham*, George Porter, OM, FRS, *b*. 1920, *m*.

1992   *Prentice*, Reginald Ernest Prentice, PC, *b*. 1923, *m*.

1987   *Prior*, James Michael Leathes Prior, PC, *b*. 1927, *m*.

1975   *Pritchard*, Derek Wilbraham Pritchard, *b*. 1910, *m*.

1982   *Prys-Davies*, Gwilym Prys Prys-Davies, *b*. 1923, *m*.

1987   *Pym*, Francis Leslie Pym, MC, PC, *b*. 1922, *m*.

1982   *Quinton*, Anthony Meredith Quinton, *b*. 1925, *m*.

1978   *Rawlinson of Ewell*, Peter Anthony Grayson Rawlinson, PC, QC, *b*. 1919, *m*.

1976   *Rayne*, Max Rayne, *b*. 1918, *m*.

1983   *Rayner*, Derek George Rayner, *b*. 1926.

1987   *Rees*, Peter Wynford Innes Rees, PC, QC, *b*. 1926, *m*.

1988   *Rees-Mogg*, William Rees-Mogg, *b*. 1928, *m*.

1970   *Reigate*, John Kenyon Vaughan-Morgan, PC, *b*. 1905, *m*.

1991   *Renfrew of Kaimsthorn*, (Andrew) Colin Renfrew, FBA, *b*. 1937, *m*.

1979   *Renton*, David Lockhart-Mure Renton, KBE, TD, PC, QC, *b*. 1908, *w*.

Created

1990   *Richard*, Ivor Seward Richard, PC, QC, *b*. 1932, *m*.

1979   *Richardson*, John Samuel Richardson, LVO, MD, FRCP, *b*. 1910, *w*.

1983   *Richardson of Duntisbourne*, Gordon William Humphreys Richardson, KG, MBE, TD, PC, *b*. 1915, *m*.

1987   *Rippon of Hexham*, (Aubrey) Geoffrey (Frederick) Rippon, PC, QC, *b*. 1924, *m*.

1992   *Rix*, Brian Norman Roger Rix, CBE, *b*. 1924, *m*.

1961   *Robens of Woldingham*, Alfred Robens, PC, *b*. 1910, *m*.

1992   *Rodger of Earlsferry*, Alan Ferguson Rodger, PC, QC, FBA, *b*. 1944, *Lord Advocate*.

1992   *Rodgers of Quarry Bank*, William Thomas Rodgers, PC, *b*. 1928, *m*.

1977   *Roll of Ipsden*, Eric Roll, KCMG, CB, *b*. 1907, *m*.

1991   *Runcie*, Rt Revd Robert Alexander Kennedy Runcie, MC, PC, Royal Victoria Chain, *b*. 1921, *m*.

1975   *Ryder of Eaton Hastings*, Sydney Thomas Franklin (Don) Ryder, *b*. 1916, *m*.

1962   *Sainsbury*, Alan John Sainsbury, *b*. 1902, *w*.

1989   *Sainsbury of Preston Candover*, John Davan Sainsbury, KG, *b*. 1927, *m*.

1987   *St John of Fawsley*, Norman Antony Francis St John-Stevas, PC, *b*. 1929.

1985   *Sanderson of Bowden*, Charles Russell Sanderson, *b*. 1933, *m*.

1979   *Scanlon*, Hugh Parr Scanlon, *b*. 1913, *m*.

1976   *Schon*, Frank Schon, *b*. 1912, *m*.

1978   *Sefton of Garston*, William Henry Sefton, *b*. 1915, *m*.

1958   *Shackleton*, Edward Arthur Alexander Shackleton, KG, OBE, PC, *b*. 1911, *m*.

1989   *Sharp of Grimsdyke*, Eric Sharp, CBE, *b*. 1916, *m*.

1959   *Shawcross*, Hartley William Shawcross, GBE, PC, QC, *b*. 1902, *w*.

1980   *Sieff of Brimpton*, Marcus Joseph Sieff, OBE, *b*. 1913, *m*.

1971   *Simon of Glaisdale*, Jocelyn Edward Salis Simon, PC, *b*. 1911, *m*.

1991   *Skidelsky*, Robert Jacob Alexander Skidelsky, D.Phil., *b*. 1939, *m*.

1978   *Smith*, Rodney Smith, KBE, FRCS, *b*. 1914, *m*.

1965   *Soper*, Revd Donald Oliver Soper, Ph.D., *b*. 1903, *m*.

1990   *Soulsby of Swaffham Prior*, Ernest Jackson Lawson Soulsby, Ph.D., *b*. 1926, *m*.

1983   *Stallard*, Albert William Stallard, *b*. 1921, *m*.

1991   *Sterling of Plaistow*, Jeffrey Maurice Sterling, CBE, *b*. 1934, *m*.

1987   *Stevens of Ludgate*, David Robert Stevens, *b*. 1936, *m*.

1992   *Stewartby*, (Bernard Harold) Ian (Halley) Stewart, RD, PC, FBA, FRSE, *b*. 1935, *m*.

1981   *Stodart of Leaston*, James Anthony Stodart, PC, *b*. 1916, *m*.

1983   *Stoddart of Swindon*, David Leonard Stoddart, *b*. 1926, *m*.

1969   *Stokes*, Donald Gresham Stokes, TD, FEng., *b*. 1914, *m*.

1971   *Tanlaw*, Simon Brooke Mackay, *b*. 1934, *m*.

1978   *Taylor of Blackburn*, Thomas Taylor, CBE, *b*. 1929, *m*.

1992   *Taylor of Gosforth*, Peter Murray Taylor, PC, *b*. 1930, *m*., *Lord Chief Justice of England*.

1968   *Taylor of Gryfe*, Thomas Johnston Taylor, *b*. 1912, *m*.

1982   *Taylor of Hadfield*, Francis Taylor, *b*. 1905, *m*.

1992   *Tebbit*, Norman Beresford Tebbit, CH, PC, *b*. 1931, *m*.

Created
1971   *Seear,* (Beatrice) Nancy Seear, PC, *b.* 1913.
1967   *Serota,* Beatrice Serota, DBE, *b.* 1919, *m.*
1973   *Sharples,* Pamela Sharples, *b.* 1923, *m.*
1974   *Stedman,* Phyllis Stedman, OBE, *b.* 1916, *w.*
1992   *Thatcher,* Margaret Hilda Thatcher, OM, PC, *b.* 1925, *m.*
1980   *Trumpington,* Jean Alys Barker, *b.* 1922, *w.*
1985   *Turner of Camden,* Muriel Winifred Turner, *b.* 1927, *m.*

Created
1974   *Vickers,* Joan Helen Vickers, DBE, *b.* 1907.
1985   *Warnock,* Helen Mary Warnock, DBE, *b.* 1924, *m.*
1970   *White,* Eirene Lloyd White, *b.* 1909, *w.*
1993   *Williams of Crosby,* Shirley Vivien Teresa Brittain Williams, PC, *b.* 1930, *m.*
1971   *Young,* Janet Mary Young, PC, *b.* 1926, *m.*

Lords Spiritual

The Lords Spiritual are the Archbishops of Canterbury and York and 24 diocesan bishops of the Church of England. The Bishops of London, Durham and Winchester always have seats in the House of Lords; the other 21 seats are filled by the remaining diocesan bishops in order of seniority. The Bishop of Sodor and Man and the Bishop of Gibraltar are not eligible to sit in the House of Lords.

ARCHBISHOPS

Style, The Most Revd and Right Hon. the Lord Archbishop of __
Addressed as Archbishop *or,* Your Grace

Introduced to House of Lords
1991   *Canterbury* (103rd), George Leonard Carey, PC, PH.D., *b.* 1935, *m. Consecrated Bishop of Bath and Wells* 1987, *trans.* 1991.
1973   *York* (95th), John Stapylton Habgood, PC, ph.D., *b.* 1927, *m. Consecrated Bishop of Durham* 1973, *trans.* 1983.

BISHOPS

Style, The Right Revd the Lord Bishop of __
Addressed as My Lord
elected = date of election as diocesan bishop

Introduced to House of Lords
1990   *London* (131st), David Michael Hope, PC, *b.* 1940, *cons.* 1985, *elected* 1985, *trans.* 1991.
1984   *Durham* (92nd), David Edward Jenkins, *b.* 1925, *m., cons.* 1984, *elected* 1984.
1982   *Winchester* (95th), Colin Clement Walter James, *b.* 1926, *m., cons.* 1973, *elected* 1977, *trans.* 1985.
1979   *Chichester* (102nd), Eric Waldram Kemp, DD, *b.* 1915, *m., cons.* 1974, *elected* 1974.
1980   *Liverpool* (6th), David Stuart Sheppard, *b.* 1929, *m., cons.* 1969, *elected* 1975.
1984   *Ripon* (11th), David Nigel de Lorentz Young, *b.* 1931, *m., cons.* 1977, *elected* 1977.
1985   *Chelmsford* (7th), John Waine, *b.* 1930, *m., cons.* 1975, *elected* 1978, *trans.* 1986.
1985   *Sheffield* (5th), David Ramsay Lunn, *b.* 1930, *cons.* 1980, *elected* 1980.
1985   *St Albans* (8th), John Bernard Taylor, *b.* 1929, *m., cons.* 1980, *elected* 1980.

1985   *Newcastle* (10th), Andrew Alexander Kenny Graham, *b.* 1929, *cons.* 1977, *elected* 1981.
1986   *Salisbury* (76th), John Austin Baker, *b.* 1928, *m., cons.* 1982, *elected* 1982.
1987   *Worcester* (111th), Philip Harold Ernest Goodrich, *b.* 1929, *m., cons.* 1973, *elected* 1982.
1987   *Chester* (39th), Michael Alfred Baughen, *b.* 1930, *m., cons.* 1982, *elected* 1982.
1988   *Guildford* (7th), Michael Edgar Adie, *b.* 1929, *m., cons.* 1983, *elected* 1983.
1988   *Southwark* (7th), Robert Kerr Williamson, *b.* 1932, *m., cons.* 1984, *elected* 1984, *trans.* 1991.
1989   *Lichfield* (97th), Keith Norman Sutton, *b.* 1934, *m., cons.* 1978, *elected* 1984.
1989   *Peterborough* (36th), William John Westwood, *b.* 1925, *m., cons.* 1975, *elected* 1984.
1989   *Portsmouth* (7th), Timothy John Bavin, *b.* 1935, *cons.* 1974, *elected* 1985.
1989   *Exeter* (69th), (Geoffrey) Hewlett Thompson, *b.* 1929, *m., cons.* 1974, *elected* 1985.
1990   *Bristol* (54th), Barry Rogerson, *b.* 1936, *m., cons.* 1979, *elected* 1985.
1991   *Coventry* (7th), Simon Barrington-Ward, *b.* 1930, *m., cons.* 1985, *elected* 1985.
1991   *Norwich* (70th), Peter John Nott, *b.* 1933, *m., cons.* 1977, *elected* 1985.
1991   *St Edmundsbury and Ipswich* (8th), John Dennis, *b.* 1931, *m., cons.* 1979, *elected* 1986.
1993   *Lincoln* (70th), Robert Maynard Hardy, *b.* 1936, *m., cons.* 1980, *elected* 1986.

Bishops awaiting seats, in order of seniority
Oxford (41st), Richard Douglas Harries, *b.* 1936, *m., cons.* 1987, *elected* 1987.
Birmingham (7th), Mark Santer, *b.* 1936, *m., cons.* 1981, *elected* 1987.
Derby (5th), Peter Spencer Dawes, *b.* 1928, *m., cons.* 1988, *elected* 1988.
Southwell (9th), Patrick Burnet Harris, *b.* 1934, *m., cons.* 1973, *elected* 1988.
Rochester (105th), (Anthony) Michael (Arnold) Turnbull, *b.* 1935, *m., cons.* 1988, *elected* 1988.
Blackburn (7th), Alan David Chesters, *b.* 1937, *m., cons.* 1989, *elected* 1989.
Carlisle (65th), Ian Harland, *b.* 1932, *m., cons.* 1985, *elected* 1989.
Truro (13th), Michael Thomas Ball, *b.* 1932, *cons.* 1980, *elected* 1990.
Ely (67th), Stephen Whitefield Sykes, *b.* 1939, *m., cons.* 1990, *elected* 1990.

Hereford (103rd), John Keith Oliver, *b.* 1935, *m.*, cons. 1990, *elected* 1990.
Leicester (5th), Thomas Frederick Butler, *b.* 1940, *m.*, cons. 1985, *elected* 1991.
Bath and Wells (77th), James Lawton Thompson, *b.* 1936, *m.*, cons. 1978, *elected* 1991.
Wakefield (11th), Nigel Simeon McCulloch, *b.* 1942, *m.*, cons. 1986, *elected* 1992.

Bradford (8th), David James Smith, *b.* 1935, *m.*, cons. 1987, *elected* 1992.
Manchester (10th), Christopher John Mayfield, *b.* 1935, *m.*, cons. 1985, *elected* 1993.
Gloucester (39th), David Edward Bentley, *b.* 1935, *m.*, cons. 1986, *elected* 1993.

Prime Ministers since 1782

Over the centuries there has been some variation in the determination of the dates of appointment of Prime Ministers. Where possible, the date given is that on which a new Prime Minister kissed the Sovereign's hands and accepted the commission to form a ministry. However, until the middle of the 19th century the dating of a commission or transfer of seals could be the date of taking office. Where the composition of the Government changed, e.g. became a coalition, but the Prime Minister remained the same, the date of the change of government is given.

The Marquess of Rockingham, *Whig*, 27 March 1782
The Earl of Shelburne, *Whig*, 4 July 1782
The Duke of Portland, *Coalition*, 2 April 1783
William Pitt, *Tory*, 19 December 1783
Henry Addington, *Tory*, 17 March 1801
William Pitt, *Tory*, 10 May 1804
The Lord Grenville, *Whig*, 11 February 1806
The Duke of Portland, *Tory*, 31 March 1807
Spencer Perceval, *Tory*, 4 October 1809
The Earl of Liverpool, *Tory*, 8 June 1812
George Canning, *Tory*, 10 April 1827
Viscount Goderich, *Tory*, 31 August 1827
The Duke of Wellington, *Tory*, 22 January 1828
The Earl Grey, *Whig*, 22 November 1830
The Viscount Melbourne, *Whig*, 16 July 1834
The Duke of Wellington, *Tory*, 17 November 1834
Sir Robert Peel, *Tory*, 10 December 1834
The Viscount Melbourne, *Whig*, 18 April 1835
Sir Robert Peel, *Tory*, 30 August 1841
Lord John Russell (subsequently the Earl Russell), *Whig*, 30 June 1846
The Earl of Derby, *Tory*, 23 February 1852
The Earl of Aberdeen, *Peelite*, 19 December 1852
The Viscount Palmerston, *Liberal*, 6 February 1855
The Earl of Derby, *Conservative*, 20 February 1858
The Viscount Palmerston, *Liberal*, 12 June 1859
The Earl Russell, *Liberal*, 29 October 1865

The Earl of Derby, *Conservative*, 28 June 1866
Benjamin Disraeli, *Conservative*, 27 February 1868
William Gladstone, *Liberal*, 3 December 1868
Benjamin Disraeli, *Conservative*, 20 February 1874
William Gladstone, *Liberal*, 23 April 1880
The Marquess of Salisbury, *Conservative*, 23 June 1885
William Gladstone, *Liberal*, 1 February 1886
The Marquess of Salisbury, *Conservative*, 25 July 1886
William Gladstone, *Liberal*, 15 August 1892
The Earl of Rosebery, *Liberal*, 5 March 1894
The Marquess of Salisbury, *Conservative*, 25 June 1895
Arthur Balfour, *Conservative*, 12 July 1902
Sir Henry Campbell-Bannerman, *Liberal*, 5 December 1905
Herbert Asquith, *Liberal*, 7 April 1908
Herbert Asquith, *Coalition*, 25 May 1915
David Lloyd-George, *Coalition*, 7 December 1916
Andrew Bonar Law, *Conservative*, 23 October 1922
Stanley Baldwin, *Conservative*, 22 May 1923
Ramsay MacDonald, *Labour*, 22 January 1924
Stanley Baldwin, *Conservative*, 4 November 1924
Ramsay MacDonald, *Labour*, 5 June 1929
Ramsay MacDonald, *Coalition*, 24 August 1931
Stanley Baldwin, *Coalition*, 7 June 1935
Neville Chamberlain, *Coalition*, 28 May 1937
Winston Churchill, *Coalition*, 10 May 1940
Winston Churchill, *Conservative*, 23 May 1945
Clement Attlee, *Labour*, 26 July 1945
Sir Winston Churchill, *Conservative*, 26 October 1951
Sir Anthony Eden, *Conservative*, 6 April 1955
Harold Macmillan, *Conservative*, 10 January 1957
Sir Alec Douglas-Home, *Conservative*, 19 October 1963
Harold Wilson, *Labour*, 16 October 1964
Edward Heath, *Conservative*, 19 June 1970
Harold Wilson, *Labour*, 4 March 1974
James Callaghan, *Labour*, 5 April 1976
Margaret Thatcher, *Conservative*, 4 May 1979
John Major, *Conservative*, 28 November 1990

COURTESY TITLES

From this list it will be seen that, for example, the Marquess of Blandford is heir to the Dukedom of Marlborough, and Viscount Amberley to the Earldom of Russell. Titles of second heirs are also given, and the courtesy title of the father of a second heir is indicated by *; e.g., Earl of Burlington, eldest son of *Marquess of Hartington For forms of address, *see* page 220.

MARQUESSES

Blandford – *Marlborough, D.*
Bowmont and Cessford – *Roxburghe, D.*
Douglas and Clydesdale – *Hamilton, D.*
*Douro – *Wellington, D.*
*Graham – *Montrose, D.*
Granby – *Rutland, D.*
Hamilton – *Abercorn, D.*
*Hartington – *Devonshire, D.*
*Kildare – *Leinster, D.*
Lorne – *Argyll, D.*
*Tavistock – *Bedford, D.*
*Worcester – *Beaufort, D.*

EARLS

*Aboyne – *Huntly, M.*
Altamont – *Sligo, M.*
Ancram – *Lothian, M.*
Arundel and Surrey – *Norfolk, D.*
*Bective – *Headfort, M.*
*Belfast – *Donegall, M.*
*Brecknock – *Camden, M.*
Burford – *St Albans, D.*
Burlington – *Hartington, M.*
*Cardigan – *Ailesbury, M.*
Cassillis – *Ailsa, M.*
Compton – *Northampton, M.*
*Dalkeith – *Buccleuch, D.*
*Dumfries – *Bute, M.*
*Euston – *Grafton, D.*
Glamorgan – *Worcester, M.*
Grosvenor – *Westminster, D.*
*Haddo – *Aberdeen and Temair, M.*
Hillsborough – *Downshire, M.*
Hopetoun – *Linlithgow, M.*
March and Kinrara – *Richmond, D.*
*Mount Charles – *Conyngham, M.*
Mornington – *Douro, M.*
Mulgrave – *Normanby, M.*
Offaly – *Kildare, M.*
Ronaldshay – *Zetland, M.*
*St Andrews – *Kent, D.*
*Shelburne – *Lansdowne, M.*
*Southesk – *Fife, D.*

Sunderland – *Blandford, M.*
*Tyrone – *Waterford, M.*
Ulster – *Gloucester, D.*
*Uxbridge – *Anglesey, M.*
Wiltshire – *Winchester, M.*
Yarmouth – *Hertford, M.*

VISCOUNTS

Amberley – *Russell, E.*
Andover – *Suffolk and Berkshire, E.*
Anson – *Lichfield, E.*
Asquith – *Oxford & Asquith, E.*
Boringdon – *Morley, E.*
Borodale – *Beatty, E.*
Boyle – *Shannon, E.*
Brocas – *Jellicoe, E.*
Calne and Calstone – *Shelburne, E.*
Campden – *Gainsborough, E.*
Carlow – *Portarlington, E.*
Carlton – *Wharncliffe, E.*
Castlereagh – *Londonderry, M.*
Chelsea – *Cadogan, E.*
Chewton – *Waldegrave, E.*
Chichester – *Belfast, E.*
Clanfield – *Peel, E.*
Clive – *Powis, E.*
Coke – *Leicester, E.*
Corry – *Belmore, E.*
Corvedale – *Baldwin of Bewdley, E.*
Cranborne – *Salisbury, M.*
Cranley – *Onslow, E.*
Crichton – *Erne, E.*
Crowhurst – *Cottenham, E.*
Dalrymple – *Stair, E.*
Dangan – *Cowley, E.*
Dawick – *Haig, E.*
Deerhurst – *Coventry, E.*
Drumlanrig – *Queensberry, M.*
Dunwich – *Stradbroke, E.*
Dupplin – *Kinnoull, E.*
Ebrington – *Fortescue, E.*
Ednam – *Dudley, E.*
Emlyn – *Cawdor, E.*
Encombe – *Eldon, E.*
Ennismore – *Listowel, E.*
Enfield – *Strafford, E.*
Erleigh – *Reading, M.*
Feilding – *Denbigh, E.*
Fincastle – *Dunmore, E.*

FitzHarris – *Malmesbury, E.*
Folkestone – *Radnor, E.*
Forbes – *Granard, E.*
Garmoyle – *Cairns, E.*
Garnock – *Lindsay, E.*
Glandine – *Norbury, E.*
Glenapp – *Inchcape, E.*
Glentworth – *Limerick, E.*
Grimstone – *Verulam, E.*
Gwynedd – *Lloyd George of Dwyfor, E.*
Hawkesbury – *Liverpool, E.*
Ikerrin – *Carrick, E.*
Ingestre – *Shrewsbury, E.*
Ipswich – *Euston, E.*
Jocelyn – *Roden, E.*
Kelburn – *Glasgow, E.*
Kingsborough – *Kingston, E.*
Knebworth – *Lytton, E.*
Lascelles – *Harewood, E.*
Lewisham – *Dartmouth, E.*
Linley – *Snowdon, E.*
Loftus – *Ely, M.*
Lowther – *Lonsdale, E.*
Lumley – *Scarbrough, E.*
Lymington – *Portsmouth, E.*
Macmillan of Ovenden – *Stockton, E.*
Maidstone – *Winchilsea and Nottingham, E.*
Maitland – *Lauderdale, E.*
Malden – *Essex, E.*
Mandeville – *Manchester, D.*
Medina – *Milford Haven, M.*
Melgund – *Minto, E.*
Merton – *Nelson, E.*
Moore – *Drogheda, E.*
Morpeth – *Carlisle, E.*
Mount Stuart – *Dumfries, E.*
Newport – *Bradford, E.*
Newry and Mourne – *Kilmorey, E.*
Northland – *Ranfurly, E.*
Parker – *Macclesfield, E.*
Perceval – *Egmont, E.*
Petersham – *Harrington, E.*
Pollington – *Mexborough, E.*
Raynham – *Townshend, M.*
Reidhaven – *Seafield, E.*
Ruthven of Canberra – *Gowrie, E.*
St Cyres – *Iddesleigh, E.*
Sandon – *Harrowby, E.*
Savernake – *Cardigan, E.*

Slane – *Mount Charles, E.*
Somerton – *Normanton, E.*
Stopford – *Courtown, E.*
Stormont – *Mansfield, E.*
Strathallan – *Perth, E.*
Stuart – *Castle Stewart, E.*
Suirdale – *Donoughmore, E.*
Tamworth – *Ferrers, E.*
Tarbat – *Cromartie, E.*
Vaughan – *Lisburne, E.*
Villiers – *Jersey, E.*
Weymouth – *Bath, M.*
Windsor – *Plymouth, E.*
Wolmer – *Selborne, E.*
Woodstock – *Portland, E.*

BARONS (LORD –)

Aberdour – *Morton, E.*
Apsley – *Bathurst, E.*
Ardee – *Meath, E.*
Ashley – *Shaftesbury, E.*
Balgonie – *Leven & Melville, E.*
Balniel – *Crawford and Balcarres, E.*
Berriedale – *Caithness, E.*
Bingham – *Lucan, E.*
Binning – *Haddington, E.*
Brooke – *Warwick, E.*
Bruce – *Elgin, E.*
Buckhurst – *De La Warr, E.*
Burghersh – *Westmorland, E.*
Burghley – *Exeter, M.*
Cardross – *Buchan, E.*
Carnegie – *Southesk, E.*
Clifton of Rathmore – *Darnley, E.*
Cochrane – *Dundonald, E.*
Courtenay – *Devon, E.*
Dalmeny – *Rosebery, E.*
Doune – *Moray, E.*
Downpatrick – *St Andrews, E.*
Eliot – *St Germans, E.*
Erskine – *Mar & Kellie, E.*
Eskdail – *Dalkeith, E.*
Fintrie – *Graham, M.*
Formartine – *Haddo, E.*
Gillford – *Clanwilliam, E.*
Glamis – *Strathmore, E.*
Greenock – *Cathcart, E.*
Guernsey – *Aylesford, E.*
Hay – *Erroll, E.*
Herbert – *Pembroke, E.*
Howland – *Tavistock, M.*
Hyde – *Clarendon, E.*

Inverurie – *Kintore, E.*
Irwin – *Halifax, E.*
Johnstone – *Annandale and Hartfell, E.*
Kenlis – **Bective, E.*
Langton – *Temple of Stowe, E.*
La Poer – **Tyrone, E.*
Leslie – *Rothes, E.*
Leveson – *Granville, E.*
Loughborough – *Rosslyn, E.*

Maltravers – **Arundel and Surrey, E.*
Mauchline – *Loudoun, C.*
Medway – *Cranbrook, E.*
Montgomerie – *Eglinton and Winton, E.*
Moreton – *Ducie, E.*
Naas – *Mayo, E.*
Neidpath – *Wemyss & March, E.*
Norreys – *Lindsey & Abingdon, E.*

North – *Guilford, E.*
Ogilvy – *Airlie, E.*
Oxmantown – *Rosse, E.*
Paget de Beaudesert – **Uxbridge, E.*
Porchester – *Carnarvon, E.*
Ramsay – *Dalhousie, E.*
Romsey – *Mountbatten of Burma, C.*
Rosehill – *Northesk, E.*
Scrymgeour – *Dundee, E.*

Seymour – *Somerset, D.*
Strathnaver – *Sutherland, C.*
Wodehouse – *Kimberley, E.*
Worsley – *Yarborough, E.*

PEERS' SURNAMES WHICH DIFFER FROM THEIR TITLES

The following symbols indicate the rank of the peer holding each title:
C. Countess
D. Duke
E. Earl
M. Marquess
V. Viscount
* Life Peer
Where no designation is given, the title is that of an hereditary Baron or Baroness

Abney-Hastings – *Loudoun, C.*
Acheson – *Gosford, E.*
Adderley – *Norton*
Addington – *Sidmouth, V.*
Agar – *Normanton, E.*
Aitken – *Beaverbrook*
Akers-Douglas – *Chilston, V.*
Alexander – *A. of Potterhill**
Alexander – *A. of Tunis, E.*
Alexander – *A. of Weedon**
Alexander – *Caledon, E.*
Allen – *A. of Abbeydale**
Allen – *Croham**
Allanson-Winn – *Headley*
Allsopp – *Hindlip*
Amery – *A. of Lustleigh**
Anderson – *Waverley, V.*
Annesley – *Valentia, V.*
Anson – *Lichfield, E.*
Archer – *A. of Sandwell**
Archer – *A. of Weston-super-Mare**
Armstrong – *A. of Ilminster**
Armstrong-Jones – *Snowdon, E.*
Arthur – *Glenarthur*
Arundell – *Talbot of Malahide*
Ashley – *A. of Stoke**
Ashley-Cooper – *Shaftesbury, E.*
Ashton – *A. of Hyde*
Asquith – *Oxford & Asquith, E.*

Assheton – *Clitheroe*
Astley – *Hastings*
Astor – *A. of Hever*
Atkins – *Colnbrook**
Aubrey-Fletcher – *Braye*
Bailey – *Glanusk*
Baillie – *Burton*
Baillie Hamilton – *Haddington, E.*
Baldwin – *B. of Bewdley, E.*
Balfour – *B. of Inchrye*
Balfour – *Kinross*
Balfour – *Riverdale*
Bampfylde – *Poltimore*
Banbury – *B. of Southam*
Barber – *B. of Tewkesbury**
Baring – *Ashburton*
Baring – *Cromer, E.*
Baring – *Howick of Glendale*
Baring – *Northbrook*
Baring – *Revelstoke*
Barker – *Trumpington**
Barnes – *Gorell*
Barnewall – *Trimlestown*
Bathurst – *Bledisloe, V.*
Beauclerk – *St Albans, D.*
Beaumont – *Allendale, V.*
Beaumont – *B. of Whitley**
Beavan – *Ardwick**
Beckett – *Grimthorpe*
Bellow – *Bellwin**
Benn – *Stansgate, V.*
Bennet – *Tankerville, E.*
Bentinck – *Portland, E.*
Beresford – *Decies*
Beresford – *Waterford, M.*
Berry – *Camrose, V.*
Berry – *Hartwell**
Berry – *Kemsley, V.*
Bertie – *Lindsey, E.*
Best – *Wynford*
Bethell – *Westbury*
Bewicke-Copley – *Cromwell*
Bigham – *Mersey, V.*
Bigham – *Nairne*
Bingham – *Clanmorris*
Bingham – *Lucan, E.*
Blackwood – *Dufferin & Clandeboye*
Bligh – *Darnley, E.*

Bootle-Wilbraham – *Skelmersdale*
Boscawen – *Falmouth, V.*
Boston – *Boston of Faversham**
Bourke – *Mayo, E.*
Bowden – *Aylestone**
Bowes Lyon – *Strathmore, E.*
Bowyer – *Denham*
Boyd – *Kilmarnock*
Boyle – *Cork & Orrery, E.*
Boyle – *Glasgow, E.*
Boyle – *Shannon, E.*
Brabazon – *Meath, E.*
Braine – *B. of Wheatley**
Brand – *Hampden, V.*
Brandon – *B. of Oakbrook**
Brassey – *B. of Apethorpe*
Brett – *Esher, V.*
Bridge – *B. of Harwich**
Bridgeman – *Bradford, E.*
Brodrick – *Midleton, V.*
Brooke – *Alanbrooke, V.*
Brooke – *Brookeborough, V.*
Brooke – *B. of Ystradfellte**
Brooks – *B. of Tremorfa**
Brooks – *Crawshaw*
Brougham – *Brougham and Vaux*
Broughton – *Fairhaven*
Browne – *Kilmaine*
Browne – *Oranmore and Browne*
Browne – *Sligo, M.*
Bruce – *Aberdare*
Bruce – *Balfour of Burleigh*
Bruce – *B. of Donington**
Bruce – *Elgin and Kincardine, E.*
Brudenell-Bruce – *Ailesbury, M.*
Buchan – *Tweedsmuir*
Buckley – *Wrenbury*
Butler – *Carrick, E.*
Butler – *Dunboyne*
Butler – *Lanesborough, E.*
Butler – *Mountgarret, V.*
Butler – *Ormonde, M.*
Buxton – *B. of Alsa**
Byng – *Strafford, E.*
Byng – *Torrington, V.*

Callaghan – *C. of Cardiff**
Cameron – *C. of Lochbroom**
Campbell – *Argyll, D.*
Campbell – *Breadalbane and Holland, E.*
Campbell – *C. of Alloway**
Campbell – *C. of Croy**
Campbell – *C. of Eskan**
Campbell – *Cawdor, E.*
Campbell – *Colgrain*
Campbell – *Stratheden and Campbell*
Campbell-Gray – *Gray*
Canning – *Garvagh*
Capell – *Essex, E.*
Carington – *Carrington*
Carlisle – *C. of Bucklow**
Carmichael – *C. of Kelvingrove**
Carnegie – *Fife, D.*
Carnegie – *Northesk, E.*
Carr – *C. of Hadley**
Cary – *Falkland, V.*
Castle – *C. of Blackburn**
Caulfeild – *Charlemont, V.*
Cavendish – *C. of Furness**
Cavendish – *Chesham*
Cavendish – *Devonshire, D.*
Cavendish – *Waterpark*
Cayzer – *Rotherwick*
Cecil – *Amherst of Hackney*
Cecil – *Exeter, M.*
Cecil – *Rockley*
Cecil – *Salisbury, M.*
Chalker – *C. of Wallasey**
Chaloner – *Gisborough*
Chapman – *Northfield**
Charteris – *C. of Amisfield**
Charteris – *Wemyss and March, E.*
Cheshire – *Ryder of Warsaw**
Chetwynd-Talbot – *Shrewsbury, E.*
Chichester – *Donegall, M.*
Chichester-Clark – *Moyola**
Child-Villiers – *Jersey, E.*
Cholmondeley – *Delamere*
Chubb – *Hayter*
Clark – *C. of Kempston**
Clegg-Hill – *Hill, V.*

Parker – *Macclesfield, E.*
Parker – *Morley, E.*
Parnell – *Congleton*
Parsons – *Rosse, E.*
Paulet – *Winchester, M.*
Peake – *Ingleby, V.*
Pearson – *Cowdray, V.*
Pearson – *P. of Rannoch**
Pease – *Daryngton*
Pease – *Gainford*
Pease – *Wardington*
Pelham – *Chichester, E.*
Pelham – *Yarborough, E.*
Pellew – *Exmouth, V.*
Penny – *Marchwood, V.*
Pepys – *Cottenham, E.*
Perceval – *Egmont, E.*
Percy – *Northumberland, D.*
Perry – *P. of Southwark**
Perry – *P. of Walton**
Pery – *Limerick, E.*
Peyton – *P. of Yeovil**
Philipps – *Milford*
Philipps – *St Davids, V.*
Phipps – *Normanby, M.*
Pitt – *P. of Hampstead**
Plant – *P. of Highfield**
Platt – *P. of Writtle**
Pleydell-Bouverie –
  Radnor, E.
Plummer – *P. of St
  Marylebone**
Plumptre – *Fitzwalter*
Plunkett – *Dunsany*
Plunkett – *Louth*
Pollock – *Hanworth, V.*
Pomeroy – *Harberton, V.*
Ponsonby – *Bessborough, E.*
Ponsonby – *de Mauley*
Ponsonby – *P. of Shulbrede*
Ponsonby – *Sysonby*
Porter – *P. of Luddenham**
Powys – *Lilford*
Pratt – *Camden, M.*
Preston – *Gormanston, V.*
Primrose – *Rosebery, E.*
Prittie – *Dunalley*
Ramsay – *Dalhousie, E.*
Ramsbotham – *Soulbury,
  V.*
Rawlinson – *R. of Ewell**
Rees-Williams – *Ogmore*
Renfrew – *R. of
  Kaimsthorn**
Rhys – *Dynevor*
Richards – *Milverton*
Richardson – *R. of
  Duntisbourne**
Rippon – *R. of Hexham**
Ritchie – *R. of Dundee*
Robens – *R. of
  Woldingham**
Roberts – *Clwyd*
Robertson – *R. of Oakridge*
Robertson – *Wharton*
Robinson – *Martonmere*
Robson – *R. of Kiddington**
Roche – *Fermoy*
Rodd – *Rennell*
Rodger – *R. of Earlsferry**

Rodgers – *R. of Quarry
  Bank**
Roll – *R. of Ipsden**
Roper-Curzon – *Teynham*
Rospigliosi – *Newburgh, E.*
Rous – *Stradbroke, E.*
Rowley-Conwy – *Langford*
Royle – *Fanshawe of
  Richmond**
Runciman – *R. of Doxford,
  V.*
Russell – *Ampthill*
Russell – *Bedford, D.*
Russell – *de Clifford*
Russell – *R. of Liverpool*
Ryder – *Harrowby, E.*
Ryder – *R. of Eaton
  Hastings**
Ryder – *R. of Warsaw**
Sackville – *De La Warr, E.*
Sackville-West – *Sackville*
Sainsbury – *S. of Preston
  Candover**
St Aubyn – *St Levan*
St Clair – *Sinclair*
St Clair-Erskine – *Rosslyn,
  E.*
St John – *Bolingbroke and St
  John, V.*
St John – *St John of Blesto*
St John-Stevas – *St John of
  Fawsley**
St Leger – *Doneraile, V.*
Samuel – *Bearsted, V.*
Sanderson – *S. of Ayot*
Sanderson – *S. of Bowden**
Sandilands – *Torphichen*
Saumarez – *De Saumarez*
Savile – *Mexborough, E.*
Scarlett – *Abinger*
Schreiber – *Marlesford**
Sclater-Booth – *Basing*
Scott – *Eldon, E.*
Scott-Ellis – *Howard de
  Walden*
Scrymgeour – *Dundee, E.*
Seager – *Leighton of St
  Mellons*
Seely – *Mottistone*
Sefton – *S. of Garston**
Seymour – *Hertford, M.*
Seymour – *Somerset, D.*
Sharp – *S. of Grimsdyke**
Shaw – *Craigmyle*
Shirley – *Ferrers, E.*
Short – *Glenamara**
Siddeley – *Kenilworth*
Sidney – *De L'Isle, V.*
Sieff – *S. of Brimpton**
Simon – *S. of Glaisdale**
Simon – *S. of Wythenshawe*
Sinclair – *Caithness, E.*
Sinclair – *S. of Cleeve*
Sinclair – *Thurso, V.*
Skeffington – *Massereene,
  V.*
Slynn – *S. of Hadley**
Smith – *Bicester*
Smith – *Hambleden, V.*

Smith – *Kirkhill**
Somerset – *Beaufort, D.*
Somerset – *Raglan*
Souter – *Audley*
Spencer – *Churchill, V.*
Spencer-Churchill –
  Marlborough, D.
Spring Rice – *Monteagle of
  Brandon*
Stanhope – *Harrington, E.*
Stanley – *Derby, E.*
Stanley – *Stanley of Alderley
  & Sheffield*
Stapleton-Cotton –
  Combermere, V.
Sterling – *S. of Plaistow**
Stevens – *S. of Ludgate**
Stewart – *Galloway, E.*
Stewart – *Stewartby**
Stodart – *S. of Leaston**
Stoddart – *S. of Swindon**
Stonor – *Camoys*
Stopford – *Courtown, E.*
Stourton – *Mowbray*
Strachey – *O'Hagan*
Strutt – *Belper*
Strutt – *Rayleigh*
Stuart – *Castle Stewart, E.*
Stuart – *Moray, E.*
Stuart – *S. of Findhorn, V.*
Suenson-Taylor –
  Grantchester
Taylor – *Ingrow**
Taylor – *T. of Blackburn**
Taylor – *T. of Gosforth**
Taylor – *T. of Gryfe**
Taylor – *T. of Hadfield**
Taylour – *Headfort, M.*
Temple-Gore-Langton –
  Temple of Stowe, E.
Tennant – *Glenconner*
Thellusson – *Rendlesham*
Thesiger – *Chelmsford, V.*
Thomas – *T. of Gwydir**
Thomas – *T. of
  Swynnerton**
Thomas – *Tonypandy, V.*
Thomson – *T. of Fleet*
Thomson – *T. of Monifieth**
Thynn – *Bath, M.*
Thynne – *Bath, M.*
Tottenham – *Ely, M.*
Trefusis – *Clinton*
Trench – *Ashtown*
Trevor-Roper – *Dacre of
  Glanton**
Tufton – *Hothfield*
Turner – *Netherthorpe*
Turner – *T. of Camden**
Turnour – *Winterton, E.*
Turton – *Tranmire**
Tyrell-Kenyon – *Kenyon*
Vanden-Bempde-Johnstone
  – *Derwent*
Vane – *Barnard*
Vane – *Inglewood*
Vane-Tempest-Stewart –
  Londonderry, M.
Vanneck – *Huntingfield*

Vaughan – *Lisburne, E.*
Vaughan-Morgan –
  Reigate*
Vereker – *Gort, V.*
Verney – *Willoughby de
  Broke*
Vernon – *Lyveden*
Vesey – *De Vesci, V.*
Villiers – *Clarendon, E.*
Vivian – *Swansea*
Wade – *W. of Chorlton**
Walker – *W. of Worcester**
Wallace – *W. of Campsie**
Wallace – *W. of Coslany**
Wallop – *Portsmouth, E.*
Walton – *W. of Detchant**
Ward – *Bangor, V.*
Ward – *Dudley, E.*
Warrender – *Bruntisfield*
Watson – *Manton*
Wedderburn – *W. of
  Charlton**
Weir – *Inverforth*
Weld-Forester – *Forester*
Wellesley – *Cowley, E.*
Wellesley – *Wellington, D.*
Westenra – *Rossmore*
White – *Annaly*
White – *W. of Hull**
Whiteley – *Marchamley*
Whitfield – *Kenswood*
Williams – *Berners*
Williams – *W. of Crosby**
Williams – *W. of Elvel**
Williams – *W. of Mostyn**
Williamson – *Forres*
Willoughby – *Middleton*
Wills – *Dulverton*
Wilson – *Moran*
Wilson – *Nunburnholme*
Wilson – *W. of Langside**
Wilson – *W. of Rievaulx**
Wilson – *W. of Tillyorn**
Windsor – *Gloucester, D.*
Windsor – *Kent, D.*
Windsor-Clive – *Plymouth,
  E.*
Wingfield – *Powerscourt, V.*
Winn – *St Oswald*
Wodehouse – *Kimberley, E.*
Wolfson – *W. of
  Sunningdale**
Wood – *Halifax, E.*
Wood – *Holderness**
Woodhouse – *Terrington*
Wyatt – *W. of Weeford**
Wyndham – *Egremont &
  Leconfield*
Wyndham-Quin –
  Dunraven, E.
Wynn – *Newborough*
Yarde-Buller – *Churston*
Yerburgh – *Alvingham*
Yorke – *Hardwicke, E.*
Young – *Kennet*
Young – *Y. of Dartington**
Young – *Y. of Graffham**
Younger – *Y. of Leckie, V.*
Younger – *Y. of Prestwick**

Orders of Chivalry

THE MOST NOBLE ORDER OF THE GARTER (1348)

KG

Ribbon, Blue
Motto, Honi soit qui mal y pense
(*Shame on him who thinks evil of it*)
The number of Knights Companions
is limited to 24

SOVEREIGN OF THE ORDER
The Queen

LADY OF THE GARTER
HM Queen Elizabeth the Queen
Mother, 1936

ROYAL KNIGHTS
HRH The Duke of Edinburgh, 1947
HRH The Prince of Wales, 1958
HRH The Duke of Kent, 1985

EXTRA KNIGHTS COMPANIONS
AND LADIES
HRH Princess Juliana of the
Netherlands, 1958
HRH The Grand Duke of
Luxembourg, 1972
HM The Queen of Denmark, 1979
HM The King of Sweden, 1983
HM The King of Spain, 1988
HM The Queen of the Netherlands,
1989

KNIGHTS AND LADY COMPANIONS
Sir Cennydd Traherne, 1970
The Earl Waldegrave, 1971
The Earl of Longford, 1971
The Lord Shackleton, 1974
The Marquess of Abergavenny, 1974
The Lord Wilson of Rievaulx, 1976
The Duke of Grafton, 1976
The Lord Hunt, 1979
The Duke of Norfolk, 1983
The Lord Lewin, 1983
The Lord Richardson of
Duntisbourne, 1983
The Marquess of Normanby, 1985
The Lord Carrington, 1985
The Lord Callaghan of Cardiff, 1987
The Viscount Leverhulme, 1988
The Lord Hailsham of St Marylebone,
1988
Lavinia, Duchess of Norfolk, 1990
The Duke of Wellington, 1990
Field Marshal Lord Bramall, 1990
Sir Edward Heath, 1992
The Viscount Ridley, 1992

The Lord Sainsbury of Preston
Candover, 1992

Prelate, The Bishop of Winchester
Chancellor, The Marquess of
Abergavenny, KG, OBE
Register, The Dean of Windsor
Garter King of Arms, C. M. J. F. Swan,
CVO, Ph.D., FSA
Gentleman Usher of the Black Rod,
Adm. Sir Richard Thomas, KCB,
OBE
Secretary, D. H. B. Chesshyre, LVO

THE MOST ANCIENT AND MOST NOBLE ORDER OF THE THISTLE (REVIVED 1687)

KT

Ribbon, Green
Motto, Nemo me impune lacessit (*No
one provokes me with impunity*)
The number of Knights is limited to
16

SOVEREIGN OF THE ORDER
The Queen

LADY OF THE THISTLE
HM Queen Elizabeth the Queen
Mother, 1937

ROYAL KNIGHTS
HRH The Duke of Edinburgh, 1952
HRH The Prince of Wales, Duke of
Rothesay, 1977

KNIGHTS
The Lord Home of the Hirsel, 1962
The Earl of Wemyss and March, 1966
The Earl of Dalhousie, 1971
The Lord Clydesmuir, 1972
Sir Donald Cameron of Lochiel, 1973
The Earl of Selkirk, 1976
The Lord McFadzean, 1976
The Hon. Lord Cameron, 1978
The Duke of Buccleuch and
Queensberry, 1978
The Earl of Elgin and Kincardine,
1981
The Lord Thomson of Monifieth, 1981
The Lord MacLehose of Beoch, 1983
The Earl of Airlie, 1985
Capt. Sir Iain Tennant, 1986
The Viscount Whitelaw, 1990

Chancellor, The Duke of Buccleuch
and Queensberry

Dean, The Very Revd G. I. Macmillan
Secretary and Lord Lyon King of Arms,
Sir Malcolm Innes of Edingight,
KCVO, WS
Usher of the Green Rod, Rear- Admiral
D.A. Dunbar-Nasmith, CB, DSC

THE MOST HONOURABLE ORDER OF THE BATH (1725)

GCB *Military*   GCB *Civil*

GCB, Knight (or Dame) Grand Cross
KCB, Knight Commander
DCB, Dame Commander
CB, Companion

Ribbon, Crimson
Motto, Tria juncta in uno (*Three joined
in one*)
Remodelled 1815, and enlarged many
times since. The Order is divided into
civil and military divisions. Women
became eligible for the Order from 1
January 1971

THE SOVEREIGN

GREAT MASTER AND FIRST OR
PRINCIPAL KNIGHT GRAND CROSS
HRH The Prince of Wales, KG, KT,
GCB

Dean of the Order, The Dean of
Westminster
Bath King of Arms, Air Chief Marshal
Sir David Evans, GCB, CBE
Registrar and Secretary, Rear-Adm. D.
E. Macey, CB
Genealogist, C. M. J. F. Swan, CVO,
Ph.D., FSA
Gentleman Usher of the Scarlet Rod, Air
Vice-Marshal Sir Richard Peirse,
KCVO, CB
Deputy Secretary, The Secretary of the
Central Chancery of the Orders of
Knighthood
Chancery, Central Chancery of the
Orders of Knighthood, St James's
Palace, London SW1A 1BH

THE ORDER OF MERIT
(1902)

OM *Military*   OM *Civil*

OM

Ribbon, Blue and crimson

This Order is designed as a special distinction for eminent men and women without conferring a knighthood upon them. The Order is limited in numbers to 24, with the addition of foreign honorary members. Membership is of two kinds, military and civil, the badge of the former having crossed swords, and the latter oak leaves

THE SOVEREIGN
HRH THE DUKE OF EDINBURGH, 1968
Dorothy Hodgkin, 1965
Dame Veronica Wedgwood, 1969
Sir Isaiah Berlin, 1971
Sir George Edwards, 1971
Sir Alan Hodgkin, 1973
The Lord Todd, 1977
Revd Prof. Owen Chadwick, KBE, 1983
Sir Andrew Huxley, 1983
Sir Michael Tippett, 1983
Frederick Sanger, 1986
Air Commodore Sir Frank Whittle, 1986
The Lord Menuhin, 1987
Prof. Sir Ernst Gombrich, 1988
Dr Max Perutz, 1988
Dame Cicely Saunders, 1989
The Lord Porter of Luddenham, 1989
Rt. Hon. Baroness Thatcher, 1990
Dame Joan Sutherland, 1991
Prof. Francis Crick, 1991
Dame Ninette de Valois, 1992
Sir Michael Atiyah, 1992
Honorary Member, Mother Teresa, 1983

Secretary and Registrar, Sir Edward Ford, KCB, KCVO, ERD
Chancery, Central Chancery of the Orders of Knighthood, St James's Palace, London SW1A 1BH

THE MOST EXALTED ORDER OF THE STAR OF INDIA (1861)

GCSI, Knight Grand Commander
KCSI, Knight Commander
CSI, Companion

Ribbon, Light blue, with white edges
Motto, Heaven's Light our Guide

THE SOVEREIGN
Registrar, The Secretary of the Central Chancery of the Orders of Knighthood
No conferments have been made since 1947

THE MOST DISTINGUISHED ORDER OF ST MICHAEL AND ST GEORGE (1818)

GCMG   KCMG

GCMG, Knight (or Dame) Grand Cross
KCMG, Knight Commander
DCMG, Dame Commander
CMG, Companion

Ribbon, Saxon blue, with scarlet centre
Motto, Auspicium melioris aevi (*Token of a better age*)

THE SOVEREIGN
GRAND MASTER
HRH The Duke of Kent, KG, GCMG, GCVO, ADC
Prelate, The Rt. Revd the Bishop of Coventry
Chancellor, The Lord Carrington, KG, GCMG, CH, MC, PC
Secretary, Sir David Gillmore, KCMG
Registrar, Sir John Graham, Bt., GCMG
King of Arms, Sir Oliver Wright, GCMG, GCVO, DSC
Gentleman Usher of the Blue Rod, Sir John Margetson, KCMG
Dean, The Dean of St Paul's
Deputy Secretary, The Secretary of the Central Chancery of the Orders of Knighthood
Chancery, Central Chancery of the Orders of Knighthood, St James's Palace, London SW1A 1BH

THE MOST EMINENT ORDER OF THE INDIAN EMPIRE
(1868)

GCIE, Knight Grand Commander
KCIE, Knight Commander
CIE, Companion

Ribbon, Imperial purple
Motto, Imperatricis auspiciis (*Under the auspices of the Empress*)

THE SOVEREIGN
Registrar, The Secretary of the Central Chancery of the Orders of Knighthood
No conferments have been made since 1947

THE IMPERIAL ORDER OF THE CROWN OF INDIA (1877)
FOR LADIES

CI

Badge, the royal cipher in jewels within an oval, surmounted by an heraldic crown and attached to a bow of light blue watered ribbon, edged white
The honour does not confer any rank or title upon the recipient
No conferments have been made since 1947

HM The Queen, 1947
HM Queen Elizabeth the Queen Mother, 1931
HRH The Princess Margaret, Countess of Snowdon, 1947
HRH The Princess Alice, Duchess of Gloucester, 1937
HH Maharani of Travancore, 1929

THE ROYAL VICTORIAN ORDER (1896)

GCVO   KCVO

GCVO, Knight or Dame Grand Cross
KCVO, Knight Commander
DCVO, Dame Commander
CVO, Commander
LVO, Lieutenant
MVO, Member

Ribbon, Blue, with red and white edges
Motto, Victoria

THE SOVEREIGN
GRAND MASTER
HM Queen Elizabeth the Queen Mother
Chancellor, The Lord Chamberlain
Secretary, The Keeper of the Privy Purse
Registrar, The Secretary of the Central Chancery of the Orders of Knighthood
Chaplain, The Revd J. Robson
Hon. Genealogist, D. H. B. Chesshyre, LVO

THE MOST EXCELLENT ORDER OF THE BRITISH EMPIRE (1917)

GBE　　　　KBE

The Order was divided into military and civil divisions in December 1918

GBE, Knight or Dame Grand Cross
KBE, Knight Commander
DBE, Dame Commander
CBE, Commander
OBE, Officer
MBE, Member

Ribbon, Rose pink edged with pearl grey with vertical pearl stripe in centre (military division); without vertical pearl stripe (civil division)
Motto, For God and the Empire

THE SOVEREIGN

GRAND MASTER
HRH The Prince Philip, Duke of Edinburgh, KG, KT, OM, GBE, PC, FRS
Prelate, The Bishop of London
King of Arms, Admiral Sir Anthony Morton, GBE, KCB
Registrar, The Secretary of the Central Chancery of the Orders of Knighthood
Secretary, Sir Robin Butler, GCB, CVO
Dean, The Dean of St Paul's
Gentleman Usher of the Purple Rod, Sir Robin Gillett, Bt., GBE, RD
Chancery, Central Chancery of the Orders of Knighthood, St James's Palace, London SW1A 1BH

ORDER OF THE COMPANIONS OF HONOUR (1917)

CH

Ribbon, Carmine, with gold edges
This Order consists of one class only and carries with it no title. The number of awards is limited to 65 (excluding honorary members)

Anthony, Rt. Hon. John, 1981
Ashley of Stoke, The Lord, 1975
Aylestone, The Lord, 1975
Baker, Rt. Hon. Kenneth, 1992
Brenner, Sydney, 1986
Brooke, Rt. Hon. Peter, 1992
Carrington, The Lord, 1983

Casson, Sir Hugh, 1984
Cledwyn of Penrhos, The Lord, 1976
de Valois, Dame Ninette, 1981
Eccles, The Viscount, 1984
Fraser, Rt. Hon. Malcolm, 1977
Freud, Lucian, 1983
Gielgud, Sir John, 1977
Glenamara, The Lord, 1976
Goodman, The Lord, 1972
Gorton, Rt. Hon. Sir John, 1971
Hailsham of St Marylebone, The Lord, 1974
Hawking, Prof. Stephen, 1989
Healey, The Lord, 1979
Houghton of Sowerby, The Lord, 1967
Jones, James, 1977
Joseph, The Lord, 1986
King, Rt. Hon. Tom, 1992
Lange, Rt. Hon. David, 1989
Needham, Joseph, 1992
Pasmore, Victor, 1980
Perutz, Prof. Max, 1975
Popper, Prof. Sir Karl, 1982
Powell, Anthony, 1987
Powell, Sir Philip, 1984
Pritchett, Sir Victor, 1992
Runciman, Hon. Sir Steven, 1984
Rylands, George, 1987
Sanger, Frederick, 1981
Sisson, Charles, 1993
Smith, Arnold Cantwell, 1975
Somare, Rt. Hon. Sir Michael, 1978
Talboys, Rt. Hon. Sir Brian, 1981
Tebbit, The Lord, 1987
Thorneycroft, The Lord, 1979
Tippett, Sir Michael, 1979
Trudeau, Rt. Hon. Pierre, 1984
Watkinson, The Viscount, 1962
Whitelaw, The Viscount, 1974
Widdowson, Dr Elsie, 1993
Honorary Members, Lee Kuan Yew, 1970; Dr Joseph Luns, 1971

Secretary and Registrar, The Secretary of the Central Chancery of the Orders of Knighthood

THE DISTINGUISHED SERVICE ORDER (1886)

DSO

Ribbon, Red, with blue edges
Bestowed in recognition of especial services in action of commissioned officers in the Navy, Army and Royal Air Force and (since 1942) Mercantile Marine. The members are Companions only. A Bar may be awarded for any additional act of service

THE IMPERIAL SERVICE ORDER (1902)

ISO

Ribbon, Crimson, with blue centre
Appointment as Companion of this Order is open to members of the Civil Services whose eligibility is determined by the grade they hold. The Order consists of The Sovereign and Companions to a number not exceeding 1,900, of whom 1,300 may belong to the Home Civil Services and 600 to Overseas Civil Services. The Prime Minister announced in March 1991 that no further recommendations for appointments to the Order will be made.

Secretary, Sir Robin Butler, GCB, CVO
Registrar, The Secretary of the Central Chancery of the Orders of Knighthood, St James's Palace, London SW1A 1BH

THE ROYAL VICTORIAN CHAIN (1902)

It confers no precedence on its holders

HM THE QUEEN
HM Queen Elizabeth the Queen Mother, 1937
HRH Princess Juliana of the Netherlands, 1950
HM The King of Thailand, 1960
HIH The Crown Prince of Ethiopia, 1965
HM The King of Jordan, 1966
HM King Zahir Shah of Afghanistan, 1971
HM The Queen of Denmark, 1974
HM The King of Nepal, 1975
HM The King of Sweden, 1975
The Lord Coggan, 1980
HM The Queen of the Netherlands, 1982
General Antonio Eanes, 1985
HM The King of Spain, 1986
HM The King of Saudi Arabia, 1987
HRH The Princess Margaret, Countess of Snowdon, 1990
The Lord Runcie, 1991
The Lord Charteris of Amisfield, 1992
HE François Mitterrand, 1992
HE Richard von Weizsäcker, 1992

Baronetage and Knightage

BARONETS

Style, 'Sir' before forename and surname, followed by 'Bt.'
Wife's style, 'Lady' followed by surname
For forms of address, *see* page 220

There are five different creations of Baronetcies: Baronets of England (creations dating from 1611); Baronets of Ireland (creations dating from 1619); Baronets of Scotland or Nova Scotia (creations dating from 1625); Baronets of Great Britain (creations after the Act of Union 1707 which combined the kingdoms of England and Scotland); and Baronets of the United Kingdom (creations after the union of Great Britain and Ireland in 1801).

Badge of Ulster   *Badge of Baronets of Nova Scotia*

Badge of Baronets of the United Kingdom

The patent of creation limits the destination of a baronetcy, usually to male descendants of the first baronet, although special remainders allow the baronetcy to pass, if the male issue of sons fail, to the male issue of daughters of the first baronet. In the case of baronetcies of Scotland or Nova Scotia, a special remainder of 'heirs male and of tailzie' allows the baronetcy to descend to heirs general, including women. There are four existing Scottish baronets with such a remainder, one of whom, the holder of the Dunbar of Hempriggs creation, is a Baronetess.

The Official Roll of Baronets is kept at the Home Office by the Registrar of the Baronetage. Anyone who considers that he is entitled to be entered on the Roll may petition the Crown through the Home Secretary. Every person succeeding to a Baronetcy must exhibit proofs of succession to the Home Secretary. A person whose name is not entered on the Official Roll will not be addressed or mentioned by the title of Baronet in any official document, nor will he be accorded precedence as a Baronet.

BARONETCIES EXTINCT SINCE THE LAST EDITION
Bowman (*cr.* 1961); Moore (*cr.* 1923)

Registrar of the Baronetage, R. M. Morris
Assistant Registrar, Mrs F. G. Bright
Office, Home Office, Queen Anne's Gate, London SW1H 9AT. Tel: 071-273 3498

KNIGHTS

Style, 'Sir' before forename and surname, followed by appropriate post-nominal initials if a Knight Grand Cross, Knight Grand Commander or Knight Commander
Wife's style, 'Lady' followed by surname
For forms of address, *see* page 220

The prefix 'Sir' is not used by knights who are clerics of the Church of England, who do not receive the accolade. Their wives are entitled to precedence as the wife of a knight but not to the style of 'Lady'.

ORDERS OF KNIGHTHOOD

Knight Grand Cross, Knight Grand Commander, and Knight Commander are the higher classes of the Orders of Chivalry (*see* pages 174–6). Honorary knighthoods of these Orders may be conferred on men who are citizens of countries of which The Queen is not head of state. As a rule, the prefix 'Sir' is not used by honorary knights.

KNIGHTS BACHELOR

The Knights Bachelor do not constitute a Royal Order, but comprise the surviving representation of the ancient State Orders of Knighthood. The Register of Knights Bachelor, instituted by James I in the 17th century, lapsed, and in 1908 a voluntary association under the title of The Society of Knights (now The Imperial Society of Knights Bachelor by royal command) was formed with the primary objects of continuing the various registers dating from 1257 and obtaining the uniform registration of every created Knight Bachelor. In 1926 a design for a badge to be worn by Knights Bachelor was approved and adopted; in 1974 a neck badge and miniature were added.

Knight Principal, Col. Sir Colin Cole, KCB, KCVO, TD
Chairman of Council, Sir David Napley
Prelate, Rt. Revd and Rt. Hon. The Bishop of London
Hon. Registrar, Sir Kenneth Newman, GBE, QPM
Hon. Treasurer, The Lord Lane of Horsell
Clerk to the Council, R. M. Esden
Office, 21 Old Buildings, Lincoln's Inn, London WC2A 3UJ

LIST OF BARONETS AND KNIGHTS
Revised to 31 August 1993

Peers are not included in this list

Abal, Sir Tei, Kt., CBE
Abbott, Sir Albert Francis, Kt., CBE
Abdy, Sir Valentine Robert Duff, Bt. (1850)
Abel, Sir Seselo (Cecil) Charles Geoffrey, Kt., OBE
Abeles, Sir (Emil Herbert) Peter, Kt.
Abell, Sir Anthony Foster, KCMG
Abercromby, Sir Ian George, Bt. (s. 1636)
Abraham, Sir Edward Penley, Kt., CBE, FRS
Acheson, *Prof.* Sir (Ernest) Donald, KBE
Ackers, Sir James George, Kt.
Ackroyd, Sir John Robert Whyte, Bt. (1956)
Acland, Sir Antony Arthur, GCMG, GCVO
Acland, *Maj.* Sir (Christopher) Guy (Dyke), Bt., MVO (1890)
Acland, Sir John Dyke, Bt. (1644)
Acland, *Maj.-Gen.* Sir John Hugh Bevil, KCB, CBE
Acton, Sir Harold Mario Mitchell, Kt., CBE
Adam, Sir Christopher Eric Forbes, Bt. (1917)
Adams, Sir Philip George Doyne, KCMG
Adams, Sir William James, KCMG
Adamson, Sir (William Owen) Campbell, Kt.
Adrien, *Hon.* Sir Maurice Latour-, Kt.
Adye, Sir John Anthony, KCMG
Agnew, Sir Crispin Hamlyn, Bt. (s. 1629)
†Agnew, *Maj.* Sir George Keith, Bt., TD (1895)
Agnew, Sir (William) Godfrey, KCVO, CB
Ah-Chuen, Sir Moi Lin Jean Etienne, Kt.
Aiken, *Air Chief Marshal* Sir John Alexander Carlisle, KCB
Ainsworth, Sir (Thomas) David, Bt. (1916)
Aird, *Capt.* Sir Alastair Sturgis, KCVO
Aird, Sir (George) John, Bt. (1901)
Airey, Sir Lawrence, KCB
Airy, *Maj.-Gen.* Sir Christopher John, KCVO, CBE
Aisher, Sir Owen Arthur, Kt.
Aitchison, Sir Charles Walter de Lancey, Bt. (1938)
Aitken, Sir Robert Stevenson, Kt., MD, D.phil.
Akehurst, *Gen.* Sir John Bryan, KCB, CBE
Albert, Sir Alexis François, Kt., CMG, VRD
Albu, Sir George, Bt. (1912)
Alcock, *Air Chief Marshal* Sir (Robert James) Michael, KBE, CB
Aldous, *Hon.* Sir William, Kt.
Alexander, Sir Alexander Sandor, Kt.
Alexander, Sir Charles Gundry, Bt. (1945)

Alexander, Sir Claud Hagart-, Bt. (1886)
Alexander, Sir Douglas, Bt. (1921)
Alexander, Sir (John) Lindsay, Kt.
Alexander, *Prof.* Sir Kenneth John Wilson, Kt.
Alexander, Sir Michael O'Donal Bjarne, GCMG
Alexander, Sir Norman Stanley, Kt., CBE
†Alexander, Sir Patrick Desmond William Cable-, Bt. (1809)
Allan, Sir Anthony James Allan Havelock-, Bt. (1858)
Allard, Sir Gordon Laidlaw, Kt.
Allen, *Rear-Adm.* Sir David, KCVO, CBE
Allen, *Prof.* Sir Geoffrey, Kt., ph.D., FRS
Allen, *Hon.* Sir Peter Austin Philip Jermyn, Kt.
Allen, Sir Richard Hugh Sedley, KCMG
Allen, Sir William Guilford, Kt.
Allen, Sir (William) Kenneth (Gwynne), Kt.
Alleyne, Sir George Allanmoore Ogarren, Kt.
Alleyne, *Revd* Sir John Olpherts Campbell, Bt. (1769)
Alliance, Sir David, Kt., CBE
Allinson, Sir (Walter) Leonard, KCVO, CMG
Alliott, *Hon.* Sir John Downes, Kt.
Alment, Sir (Edward) Anthony John, Kt.
Althaus, Sir Nigel Frederick, Kt.
Ambo, *Rt. Revd* George, KBE
Amies, Sir (Edwin) Hardy, KCVO
Amis, Sir Kingsley William, Kt., CBE
Amory, Sir Ian Heathcoat, Bt. (1874)
Anderson, *Prof.* Sir (James) Norman (Dalrymple), Kt., OBE, QC, FBA
Anderson, *Maj.-Gen.* Sir John Evelyn, KBE
Anderson, Sir John Muir, Kt., CMG
Anderson, *Hon.* Sir Kevin Victor, Kt.
Anderson, *Vice-Adm.* Sir Neil Dudley, KBE, CB
Anderson, *Prof.* Sir (William) Ferguson, Kt., OBE
Anderton, Sir (Cyril) James, Kt., CBE, QPM
Andrew, Sir Robert John, KCB
Andrews, Sir Derek Henry, KCB, CBE
Andrews, *Hon.* Sir Dormer George, Kt.
Angus, Sir Michael Richardson, Kt.
Annesley, Sir Hugh Norman, Kt., QPM
Ansell, *Col.* Sir Michael Picton, Kt., CBE, DSO
Anson, *Vice-Adm.* Sir Edward Rosebery, KCB
Anson, Sir John, KCB
Anson, *Rear-Adm.* Sir Peter, Bt., CB (1831)
Anstey, *Brig.* Sir John, Kt., CBE, TD
Anstruther, *Maj.* Sir Ralph Hugo, Bt. GCVO, MC (s. 1694)
Antico, Sir Tristan Venus, Kt.

Antrobus, Sir Philip Coutts, Bt. (1815)
Appleyard, Sir Raymond Kenelm, KBE
Arbuthnot, Sir Keith Robert Charles, Bt. (1823)
Arbuthnot, Sir William Reierson, Bt. (1964)
Archdale, *Capt.* Sir Edward Folmer, Bt., DSC, RN (1928)
Archer, *Gen.* Sir (Arthur) John, KCB, OBE
Arculus, Sir Ronald, KCMG, KCVO
Armitage, *Air Chief Marshal* Sir Michael John, KCB, CBE
Armstrong, Sir Andrew Clarence Francis, Bt., CMG (1841)
Armstrong, Sir Thomas Henry Wait, Kt., D.Mus.
Armytage, Sir John Martin, Bt. (1738)
Arnold, *Rt. Hon.* Sir John Lewis, Kt.
Arnold, Sir Malcolm Henry, Kt., CBE
Arnold, Sir Thomas Richard, Kt., MP
Arnott, Sir Alexander John Maxwell, Bt. (1896)
Arnott, *Prof.* Sir (William) Melville, Kt., TD, MD
Arrindell, Sir Clement Athelston, GCMG, GCVO, QC
Arthur, *Lt.-Gen.* Sir (John) Norman Stewart, KCB
Arthur, Sir Stephen John, Bt. (1841)
Ash, *Prof.* Sir Eric Albert, Kt., CBE, FRS, FEng.
Ashburnham, Sir Denny Reginald, Bt. (1661)
Ashe, Sir Derick Rosslyn, KCMG
Ashley, Sir Bernard Albert, Kt.
Ashmore, *Admiral of the Fleet* Sir Edward Beckwith, GCB, DSC
Ashmore, *Vice-Adm.* Sir Peter William Beckwith, KCB, KCVO, DSC
Ashworth, Sir Herbert, Kt.
Aske, *Revd* Sir Conan, Bt. (1922)
Askew, Sir Bryan, Kt.
Asscher, *Prof.* (Adolf) William, Kt., MD, FRCP
Astley, Sir Francis Jacob Dugdale, Bt. (1821)
Aston, Sir Harold George, Kt., CBE
Aston, *Hon.* Sir William John, KCMG
Astor, *Hon.* Sir John Jacob, Kt., MBE
Astwood, *Hon.* Sir James Rufus, Kt.
Astwood, *Lt.-Col.* Sir Jeffrey Carlton, Kt., CBE, ED
Atcherley, Sir Harold Winter, Kt.
Atiyah, Sir Michael Francis, Kt., OM, ph.D., FRS
Atkinson, *Air Marshal* Sir David William, KBE
Atkinson, Sir Frederick John, KCB
Atkinson, Sir John Alexander, KCB, DFC
Atkinson, Sir Robert, Kt., DSC, FEng.
Attenborough, Sir David Frederick, Kt., CVO, CBE, FRS
Atwell, Sir John William, Kt., CBE, FRSE, FEng.
Atwill, Sir (Milton) John (Napier), Kt.
Audland, Sir Christopher John, KCMG

Beavis, *Air Chief Marshal* Sir Michael Gordon, KCB, CBE, AFC

Becher, Sir William Fane Wrixon, Bt., MC (1831)

Beck, Sir Edgar Charles, Kt., CBE, FEng.

Beck, Sir Edgar Philip, Kt.

Beckett, *Capt.* Sir (Martyn) Gervase, Bt., MC (1921)

Beckett, Sir Terence Norman, KBE, FEng.

Bedingfeld, *Capt.* Sir Edmund George Felix Paston-, Bt. (1661)

Beecham, Sir John Stratford Roland, Bt. (1914)

Beeley, Sir Harold, KCMG, CBE

Beetham, *Marshal of the Royal Air Force* Sir Michael James, GCB, CBE, DFC, AFC

Beevor, Sir Thomas Agnew, Bt. (1784)

Begg, Sir Neil Colquhoun, KBE

Begg, *Admiral of the Fleet* Sir Varyl Cargill, GCB, DSO, DSC

Beit, Sir Alfred Lane, Bt. (1924)

Beith, Sir John Greville Stanley, KCMG

Belch, Sir Alexander Ross, Kt., CBE, FRSE

Beldam, *Rt. Hon.* Sir (Alexander) Roy (Asplan), Kt.

Belich, Sir James, Kt.

Bell, Sir Gawain Westray, KCMG, CBE

Bell, Sir (George) Raymond, KCMG, CB

Bell, Sir John Lowthian, Bt. (1885)

Bell, *Hon.* Sir Rodger, Kt.

Bell, Sir Timothy John Leigh, Kt.

Bell, Sir (William) Ewart, KCB

Bell, Sir William Hollin Dayrell Morrison-, Bt. (1905)

Bellew, Sir Henry Charles Gratton-, Bt. (1838)

Bellinger, Sir Robert Ian, GBE

Bellingham, Sir Noel Peter Roger, Bt. (1796)

Bengough, *Col.* Sir Piers, KCVO, OBE

Benn, Sir (James) Jonathan, Bt. (1914)

Bennett, Sir Charles Moihi Te Arawaka, Kt., DSO

Bennett, *Air Vice-Marshal* Sir Erik Peter, KBE, CB

Bennett, *Rt. Hon.* Sir Frederic Mackarness, Kt.

Bennett, Sir Hubert, Kt.

Bennett, Sir John Mokonuiarangi, Kt.

Bennett, *Gen.* Sir Phillip Harvey, KBE, DSO

Bennett, Sir Reginald Frederick Brittain, Kt., VRD

Bennett, Sir Ronald Wilfrid Murdoch, Bt. (1929)

Benson, Sir Christopher John, Kt.

Benson, Sir (William) Jeffrey, Kt.

Bentley, Sir William, KCMG

Beresford, Sir (Alexander) Paul, Kt., MP

Berger, *Vice-Adm.* Sir Peter Egerton Capel, KCB, MVO, DSC

Berghuser, *Hon.* Sir Eric, Kt., MBE

Berlin, Sir Isaiah, Kt., OM, CBE

Bernard, Sir Dallas Edmund, Bt. (1954)

Berney, Sir Julian Reedham Stuart, Bt. (1620)

Berrill, Sir Kenneth Ernest, GBE, KCB

Berriman, Sir David, Kt.

Berry, *Prof.* Sir Colin Leonard, Kt., FRCPath.

Berthon, *Vice-Adm.* Sir Stephen Ferrier, KCB

Berthoud, Sir Martin Seymour, KCVO, CMG

Best, Sir Richard Radford, KCVO, CBE

Bethune, Sir Alexander Maitland Sharp, Bt. (s. 1683)

Bethune, *Hon.* Sir (Walter) Angus, Kt.

Bevan, Sir Martyn Evan Evans, Bt. (1958)

Bevan, Sir Timothy Hugh, Kt.

Beverley, *Lt.-Gen.* Sir Henry York La Roche, KCB, OBE, RM

Beynon, *Prof.* Sir (William John) Granville, Kt., CBE, PH.D., D.SC., FRS

Bibby, Sir Derek James, Bt., MC (1959)

Bickersteth, *Rt. Revd* John Monier, KCVO

Biddulph, Sir Ian D'Olier, Bt. (1664)

Bide, Sir Austin Ernest, Kt.

Bidwell, Sir Hugh Charles Philip, GBE

Biggam, Sir Robin Adair, Kt.

Biggs, *Vice-Adm.* Sir Geoffrey William Roger, KCB

Biggs, Sir Norman Paris, Kt.

Billière, *Gen.* Sir Peter Edgar de la Cour de la, KCB, KBE, DSO, MC

Bing, Sir Rudolf Franz Josef, KBE

Bingham, *Hon.* Sir Eardley Max, Kt., QC

Bingham, *Rt. Hon.* Sir Thomas Henry, Kt.

Birch, Sir John Allan, KCVO, CMG

Birch, Sir Roger, Kt., CBE, QPM

Bird, Sir Richard Geoffrey Chapman, Bt. (1922)

Birkin, Sir John Christian William, Bt. (1905)

Birkin, Sir (John) Derek, Kt., TD

Birkmyre, Sir Archibald, Bt. (1921)

Birley, Sir Derek Sydney, Kt.

Birrell, Sir James Drake, Kt.

Birtwistle, Sir Harrison, Kt.

Bishop, Sir Frederick Arthur, Kt., CB, CVO

Bishop, Sir George Sidney, Kt., CB, OBE

Bishop, Sir Michael David, Kt., CBE

Bisson, *Rt Hon.* Sir Gordon Ellis, Kt.

Black, *Prof.* Sir Douglas Andrew Kilgour, Kt., MD, FRCP

Black, Sir James Whyte, Kt., FRCP, FRS

Black, *Adm.* Sir (John) Jeremy, GCB, DSO, MBE

Black, Sir Robert Brown, GCMG, OBE

Black, Sir Robert David, Bt. (1922)

Blacker, *Lt.-Gen.* Sir (Anthony Stephen) Jeremy, KCB, CBE

Blacker, *Gen.* Sir Cecil Hugh, GCB, OBE, MC

Blackett, Sir George William, Bt. (1673)

Blacklock, *Surgeon Capt. Prof.* Sir Norman James, KCVO, OBE

Blackman, Sir Frank Milton, KCVO, OBE

Blackwell, Sir Basil Davenport, Kt., FEng.

Blackwood, Sir John Francis, Bt. (1814)

Blair, Sir Alastair Campbell, KCVO, TD, WS

Blair, *Lt.-Gen.* Sir Chandos, KCVO, OBE, MC

Blair, Sir Edward Thomas Hunter, Bt. (1786)

Blake, Sir Alfred Lapthorn, KCVO, MC

Blake, Sir Francis Michael, Bt. (1907)

Blake, Sir (Thomas) Richard (Valentine), Bt. (I. 1622)

Blaker, Sir John, Bt. (1919)

Blaker, *Rt. Hon.* Sir Peter Allan Renshaw, KCMG

Blakiston, Sir Ferguson Arthur James, Bt. (1763)

Bland, Sir (Francis) Christopher (Buchan), Kt.

Bland, Sir Henry Armand, Kt., CBE

Bland, *Lt.-Col.* Sir Simon Claud Michael, KCVO

Blelloch, Sir John Nial Henderson, KCB

Blennerhassett, Sir (Marmaduke) Adrian Francis William, Bt. (1809)

Blewitt, *Maj.* Sir Shane Gabriel Basil, KCVO

Blofield, *Hon.* Sir John Christopher Calthorpe, Kt.

Blois, Sir Charles Nicholas Gervase, Bt. (1686)

Blomefield, Sir Thomas Charles Peregrine, Bt. (1807)

Bloomfield, Sir Kenneth Percy, KCB

Blosse, *Capt.* Sir Richard Hely Lynch-, Bt. (1622)

Blount, Sir Walter Edward Alpin, Bt., DSC (1642)

Blunden, Sir George, Kt.

†Blunden, Sir Philip Overington, Bt. (I. 1766)

Blunt, Sir David Richard Reginald Harvey, Bt. (1720)

Blyth, Sir James, Kt.

Boardman, *Prof.* Sir John, Kt., FSA, FBA

Boardman, Sir Kenneth Ormrod, Kt.

Bodilly, *Hon.* Sir Jocelyn, Kt., VRD

Bodmer, Sir Walter Fred, Kt., PH.D., FRS

Body, Sir Richard Bernard Frank Stewart, Kt., MP

Boevey, Sir Thomas Michael Blake Crawley-, Bt. (1784)

Bogarde, Sir Dirk (Derek Niven van den Bogaerde), Kt.

Boileau, Sir Guy (Francis), Bt. (1838)

Boles, Sir Jeremy John Fortescue, Bt. (1922)

Boles, Sir John Dennis, Kt., MBE

Bolland, Sir Edwin, KCMG
Bollers, *Hon.* Sir Harold Brodie Smith, Kt.
Bolton, Sir Frederic Bernard, Kt., MC
Bona, Sir Kina, KBE
Bonallack, Sir Richard Frank, Kt., CBE
Bond, Sir Kenneth Raymond Boyden, Kt.
Bondi, *Prof.* Sir Hermann, KCB, FRS
Bonham, *Maj.* Sir Antony Lionel Thomas, Bt. (1852)
Bonsall, Sir Arthur Wilfred, KCMG, CBE
Bonsor, Sir Nicholas Cosmo, Bt., MP (1925)
Boolell, Sir Satcam, Kt.
Boon, Sir Peter Coleman, Kt.
Boord, Sir Nicolas John Charles, Bt. (1896)
Boorman, *Lt.-Gen.* Sir Derek, KCB
Booth, Sir Angus Josslyn Gore-, Bt. (I. 1760)
Booth, Sir Christopher Charles, Kt., MD, FRCP
Booth, Sir Douglas Allen, Bt. (1916)
Booth, Sir Gordon, KCMG, CVO
Booth, Sir Robert Camm, Kt., CBE, TD
Boothby, Sir Brooke Charles, Bt. (1660)
Boreel, Sir Francis David, Bt. (1645)
Boreham, Sir (Arthur) John, KCB
Boreham, *Hon.* Sir Leslie Kenneth Edward, Kt.
Bornu, The Waziri of, KCMG, CBE
Borrie, Sir Gordon Johnson, Kt., QC
Borthwick, Sir John Thomas, Bt. MBE (1908)
Bossom, *Hon.* Sir Clive, Bt. (1953)
Boswall, Sir (Thomas) Alford Houstoun-, Bt. (1836)
Boswell, *Lt.-Gen.* Sir Alexander Crawford Simpson, KCB, CBE
Bosworth, Sir Neville Bruce Alfred, Kt., CBE
Bottomley, Sir James Reginald Alfred, KCMG
Boughey, Sir John George Fletcher, Bt. (1798)
Boulton, Sir Clifford John, KCB
Boulton, Sir (Harold Hugh) Christian, Bt. (1905)
Boulton, Sir William Whytehead, Bt., CBE, TD (1944)
Bourn, Sir John Bryant, KCB
Bourne, Sir (John) Wilfrid, KCB
Bovell, *Hon.* Sir (William) Stewart, Kt.
Bowater, Sir Euan David Vansittart, Bt. (1939)
Bowater, Sir (John) Vansittart, Bt. (1914)
Bowden, Sir Frank, Bt. (1915)
Bowen, Sir Geoffrey Fraser, Kt.
Bowen, Sir Mark Edward Mortimer, Bt. (1921)
Bowen, *Hon.* Sir Nigel Hubert, KBE
†Bowlby, Sir Richard Peregrine Longstaff, Bt. (1923)
Bowman, Sir Jeffery Haverstock, Kt.
Bowman, Sir John Paget, Bt. (1884)

Bowmar, Sir Charles Erskine, Kt.
Bowness, Sir Alan, Kt., CBE
Bowness, Sir Peter Spencer, Kt., CBE
Boxer, *Air Vice-Marshal* Sir Alan Hunter Cachemaille, KCVO, CB, DSO, DFC
Boyce, Sir Robert Charles Leslie, Bt. (1952)
Boyd, Sir Alexander Walter, Bt. (1916)
Boyd, Sir John Dixon Iklé, KCMG
Boyd, Sir (John) Francis, Kt.
Boyd, *Prof.* Sir Robert Lewis Fullarton, Kt., CBE, D.SC., FRS
Boyes, Sir Brian Gerald Barratt-, KBE
Boyle, Sir Stephen Gurney, Bt. (1904)
Boyne, Sir Henry Brian, Kt., CBE
Boynton, Sir John Keyworth, Kt., MC
Boyson, *Rt. Hon.* Sir Rhodes, Kt., MP
Brabham, Sir John Arthur, Kt., OBE
Bradbeer, Sir John Derek Richardson, Kt., OBE
Bradbury, *Surgeon Vice-Adm.* Sir Eric Blackburn, KBE, CB
Bradford, Sir Edward Alexander Slade, Bt. (1902)
Bradley, Sir Burton Gyrth Burton-, Kt., OBE
Bradman, Sir Donald George, Kt.
Bradshaw, Sir Kenneth Anthony, KCB
Bradshaw, *Lt.-Gen.* Sir Richard Phillip, KBE
Brain, Sir (Henry) Norman, KBE, CMG
Braithwaite, Sir (Joseph) Franklin Madders, Kt.
Braithwaite, Sir Rodric Quentin, KCMG
Bramall, Sir (Ernest) Ashley, Kt.
Bramley, *Prof.* Sir Paul Anthony, Kt.
Branch, Sir William Allan Patrick, Kt.
Brancker, Sir (John Eustace) Theodore, Kt., QC
Branigan, Sir Patrick Francis, Kt., QC
Bray, Sir Theodor Charles, Kt., CBE
Braynen, Sir Alvin Rudolph, Kt.
Bremridge, Sir John Henry, KBE
Brennan, *Hon.* Sir (Francis) Gerard, KBE
Brett, Sir Charles Edward Bainbridge, Kt., CBE
Brickwood, Sir Basil Greame, Bt. (1927)
Bridges, *Hon.* Sir Phillip Rodney, Kt., CMG
Brierley, Sir Ronald Alfred, Kt.
Bright, Sir Keith, Kt.
Brinckman, Sir Theodore George Roderick, Bt. (1831)
Brisco, Sir Donald Gilfrid, Bt. (1782)
†Briscoe, Sir John James, Bt. (1910)
Brise, Sir John Archibald Ruggles-, Bt., CB, OBE, TD (1935)
Bristow, *Hon.* Sir Peter Henry Rowley, Kt.
Brittan, *Rt. Hon.* Sir Leon, Kt., QC
Brittan, Sir Samuel, Kt.
Britton, Sir Edward Louis, Kt., CBE
Broackes, Sir Nigel, Kt.
†Broadbent, Sir Andrew George, Bt. (1893)

Broadhurst, *Air Chief Marshal* Sir Harry, GCB, KBE, DSO, DFC, AFC
Brocklebank, Sir Aubrey Thomas, Bt. (1885)
Brockman, *Vice-Adm.* Sir Ronald Vernon, KCB, CSI, CIE, CVO, CBE
Brockman, *Hon.* Sir Thomas Charles Drake-, Kt., DFC
Brodie, Sir Benjamin David Ross, Bt. (1834)
Brogan, *Lt.-Gen.* Sir Mervyn Francis, KBE, CB
Bromhead, Sir John Desmond Gonville, Bt. (1806)
Bromley, Sir Rupert Charles, Bt. (1757)
Bromley, Sir Thomas Eardley, KCMG
Brook, Sir Robin, Kt., CMG, OBE
†Brooke, Sir Alistair Weston, Bt. (1919)
Brooke, Sir Francis George Windham, Bt. (1903)
Brooke, *Hon.* Sir Henry, Kt.
Brooke, Sir Richard Neville, Bt. (1662)
Brookes, Sir Wilfred Deakin, Kt., CBE, DSO
Brooksbank, Sir (Edward) Nicholas, Bt. (1919)
Broom, *Air Marshal* Sir Ivor Gordon, KCB, CBE, DSO, DFC, AFC
Broomfield, Sir Nigel Hugh Robert Allen, KCMG
Broughton, *Air Marshal* Sir Charles, KBE, CB
†Broughton, Sir David Delves, Bt. (1661)
Broun, Sir Lionel John Law, Bt. (s. 1686)
Brown, Sir Allen Stanley, Kt., CBE
Brown, Sir (Arthur James) Stephen, KBE
Brown, *Adm.* Sir Brian Thomas, KCB, CBE
Brown, *Lt.-Col.* Sir Charles Frederick Richmond, Bt. (1863)
Brown, Sir (Cyril) Maxwell Palmer, KCB, CMG
Brown, Sir David, Kt.
Brown, *Vice-Adm.* Sir David Worthington, KCB
Brown, Sir Derrick Holden-, Kt.
Brown, Sir Douglas Denison, Kt.
Brown, *Hon.* Sir Douglas Dunlop, Kt.
Brown, *Prof.* Sir (Ernest) Henry Phelps, Kt., MBE, FBA
Brown, Sir (Frederick Herbert) Stanley, Kt., CBE, FENG.
Brown, *Prof.* Sir (George) Malcolm, Kt., FRS
Brown, Sir George Noel, Kt.
Brown, Sir John Douglas Keith, Kt.
Brown, Sir John Gilbert Newton, Kt., CBE
Brown, Sir Mervyn, KCMG, OBE
Brown, *Hon.* Sir Ralph Kilner, Kt., OBE, TD
Brown, Sir Robert Crichton-, KCMG, CBE, TD
Brown, *Rt. Hon.* Sir Simon Denis, Kt.
Brown, *Rt. Hon.* Sir Stephen, Kt.

Brown, Sir Thomas, Kt.

Brown, Sir William Brian Piggott-, Bt. (1903)

Browne, *Rt. Hon.* Sir Patrick Reginald Evelyn, Kt., OBE, TD

Brownrigg, Sir Nicholas (Gawen), Bt. (1816)

Bruce, Sir (Francis) Michael Ian, Bt. (s. 1628)

Bruce, Sir Hervey James Hugh, Bt. (1804)

Bruce, *Rt. Hon.* Sir (James) Roualeyn Hovell-Thurlow-Cumming-, Kt.

Brunner, Sir John Henry Kilian, Bt. (1895)

Brunton, Sir (Edward Francis) Lauder, Bt. (1908)

Brunton, Sir Gordon Charles, Kt.

Bryan, Sir Arthur, Kt.

Bryan, Sir Paul Elmore Oliver, Kt., DSO, MC

Bryce, *Hon.* Sir (William) Gordon, Kt., CBE

Bryson, *Adm.* Sir Lindsay Sutherland, KCB, FEng.

Buchan, Sir John, Kt., CMG

Buchanan, Sir Andrew George, Bt. (1878)

Buchanan, Sir Charles Alexander James Leith-, Bt. (1775)

Buchanan, *Prof.* Sir Colin Douglas, Kt., CBE

Buchanan, *Vice-Adm.* Sir Peter William, KBE

Buchanan, Sir Robert Wilson (Robin), Kt.

Buchanan, Sir (Ranald) Dennis, Kt., MBE

Buck, Sir (Philip) Antony (Fyson), Kt., QC

Buckley, *Rt. Hon.* Sir Denys Burton, Kt., MBE

Buckley, Sir John William, Kt.

Buckley, *Lt.-Cdr.* Sir (Peter) Richard, KCVO

Buckley, *Hon.* Sir Roger John, Kt.

Bulkeley, Sir Richard Thomas Williams-, Bt. (1661)

Bull, Sir Simeon George, Bt. (1922)

Bull, Sir Walter Edward Avenon, KCVO

Bullard, Sir Julian Leonard, GCMG

Bullus, Sir Eric Edward, Kt.

Bulmer, Sir William Peter, Kt.

Bultin, Sir Bato, Kt., MBE

Bunbury, Sir Michael William, Bt. (1681)

Bunbury, Sir (Richard David) Michael Richardson-, Bt. (i. 1787)

Bunch, Sir Austin Wyeth, Kt., CBE

Bunting, Sir (Edward) John, KBE

Bunyard, Sir Robert Sidney, Kt., CBE, QPM

Burbidge, Sir Herbert Dudley, Bt. (1916)

Burbury, *Hon.* Sir Stanley Charles, KCMG, KCVO, KBE

Burdett, Sir Savile Aylmer, Bt. (1665)

Burgen, Sir Arnold Stanley Vincent, Kt., FRS

Burgess, *Gen.* Sir Edward Arthur, KCB, OBE

Burgh, Sir John Charles, KCMG, CB

Burke, Sir James Stanley Gilbert, Bt. (i. 1797)

Burke, Sir (Thomas) Kerry, Kt.

Burley, Sir Victor George, Kt., CBE

Burman, Sir (John) Charles, Kt.

Burnet, Sir James William Alexander (Sir Alastair Burnet), Kt.

Burnett, *Air Chief Marshal* Sir Brian Kenyon, GCB, DFC, AFC

Burnett, Sir David Humphery, Bt., MBE, TD (1913)

Burnett, Sir John Harrison, Kt.

Burnett, Sir Walter John, Kt.

Burney, Sir Cecil Denniston, Bt. (1921)

Burns, Sir Terence, Kt.

Burns, *Maj.-Gen.* Sir (Walter Arthur) George, GCVO, CB, DSO, OBE, MC

Burrell, Sir John Raymond, Bt. (1774)

Burrenchobay, Sir Dayendranath, KBE, CMG, CVO

Burrows, Sir Bernard Alexander Brocas, GCMG

Burston, Sir Samuel Gerald Wood, Kt., OBE

Burt, *Hon.* Sir Francis Theodore Page, KCMG

Burton, Sir Carlisle Archibald, Kt., OBE

Burton, Sir George Vernon Kennedy, Kt., CBE

Burton, *Air Marshal* Sir Harry, KCB, CBE, DSO

Burton, Sir Michael St Edmund, KCVO, CMG

Busby, Sir Matthew, Kt., CBE

Bush, *Adm.* Sir John Fitzroy Duyland, GCB, DSC

Butler, *Rt. Hon.* Sir Adam Courtauld, Kt.

Butler, Sir Clifford Charles, Kt., Ph.D., FRS

Butler, Sir (Frederick) (Edward) Robin, GCB, CVO

Butler, Sir Michael Dacres, GCMG

Butler, Sir (Reginald) Michael (Thomas), Bt. (1922)

Butler, *Hon.* Sir Richard Clive, Kt.

Butler, *Col.* Sir Thomas Pierce, Bt., CVO, DSO, OBE (1628)

Butt, Sir (Alfred) Kenneth Dudley, Bt. (1929)

Butter, *Maj.* Sir David Henry, KCVO, MC

Butterworth, Sir (George) Neville, Kt.

Buxton, *Hon.* Sir Richard Joseph, Kt.

Buxton, Sir Thomas Fowell Victor, Bt. (1840)

Buzzard, Sir Anthony Farquhar, Bt. (1929)

Byatt, Sir Hugh Campbell, KCVO, CMG

Byers, Sir Maurice Hearne, Kt., CBE, QC

Byford, Sir Lawrence, Kt., CBE, QPM

Byrne, Sir Clarence Askew, Kt., OBE, DSC

Cable, Sir James Eric, KCVO, CMG

Cadbury, Sir (George) Adrian (Hayhurst), Kt.

Cadell, *Vice-Adm.* Sir John Frederick, KBE

Cadogan, *Prof.* Sir John Ivan George, Kt., CBE, FRS, FRSE

Cadwallader, Sir John, Kt.

Cahn, Sir Albert Jonas, Bt. (1934)

Cain, Sir Edward Thomas, Kt., CBE

Cain, Sir Henry Edney Conrad, Kt.

Caine, Sir Michael Harris, Kt.

Caines, Sir John, KCB

Cairncross, Sir Alexander Kirkland, KCMG

Calcutt, Sir David Charles, Kt., QC

Calderwood, Sir Robert, Kt.

Caldwell, *Surgeon Vice-Adm.* Sir (Eric) Dick, KBE, CB

Callaghan, Sir Allan Robert, Kt., CMG

Callaghan, Sir Bede Bertrand, Kt., CBE

Callard, Sir Eric John, Kt., FEng.

Callaway, *Prof.* Sir Frank Adams, Kt., CMG, OBE

Calley, Sir Henry Algernon, Kt., DSO, DFC

Callinan, Sir Bernard James, Kt., CBE, DSO, MC

Calne, *Prof.* Sir Roy Yorke, Kt., FRS

Calthorpe, Sir Euan Hamilton Anstruther-Gough-, Bt. (1929)

Cameron of Lochiel, Sir Donald Hamish, KT, CVO, TD

Cameron, Sir (Eustace) John, Kt., CBE

Cameron, *Hon.* Sir John, KT, DSC, QC (Lord Cameron)

Cameron, Sir John Watson, Kt., OBE

Campbell, Sir Alan Hugh, GCMG

Campbell, Sir Colin Moffat, Bt., MC (s. 1668)

†Campbell, Sir Lachlan Philip Kemeys, Bt. (1815)

Campbell, Sir Ian Tofts, Kt., CBE, VRD

Campbell, Sir Ilay Mark, Bt. (1808)

Campbell, Sir Matthew, KBE, CB, FRSE

Campbell, Sir Niall Alexander Hamilton, Bt. (1831)

Campbell, Sir Robin Auchinbreck, Bt. (s. 1628)

Campbell, Sir Thomas Cockburn-, Bt. (1821)

Campbell, *Hon.* Sir Walter Benjamin, Kt.

Campbell, *Hon.* Sir William Anthony, Kt.

Campion, Sir Harry, Kt., CB, CBE

†Carden, Sir Christopher Robert, Bt. (1887)

Carden, Sir John Craven, Bt. (i. 1787)

Carew, Sir Rivers Verain, Bt. (1661)

Carey, Sir Peter Willoughby, GCB

Carlill, *Vice-Adm.* Sir Stephen Hope, KBE, CB, DSO

Carlisle, Sir John Michael, Kt.

Carmichael, Sir David Peter William Gibson-Craig-, Bt. (s. 1702 and 1831)

Carmichael, Sir John, KBE

Carnac, *Revd Canon* Sir (Thomas) Nicholas Rivett-, Bt. (1836)

Carnegie, *Lt.-Gen.* Sir Robin Macdonald, KCB, OBE

Carnegie, Sir Roderick Howard, Kt.

Carnwath, Sir Andrew Hunter, KCVO

Caro, Sir Anthony Alfred, Kt., CBE

Carpenter, *Very Revd* Edward Frederick, KCVO

Carpenter, *Lt.-Gen.* the Hon. Sir Thomas Patrick John Boyd-, KBE

Carr, Sir (Albert) Raymond (Maillard), Kt.

Carr, *Air Marshal* Sir John Darcy Baker-, KBE, CB, AFC

Carrick, *Hon.* Sir John Leslie, KCMG

Carsberg, *Prof.* Sir Bryan Victor, Kt.

Carswell, *Hon.* Sir Robert Douglas, Kt.

Carter, Sir Charles Frederick, Kt., FBA

Carter, Sir Derrick Hunton, Kt., TD

Carter, Sir John, Kt., QC

Carter, Sir John Alexander, Kt.

Carter, Sir Philip David, Kt., CBE

Carter, Sir Richard Henry Alwyn, Kt.

Carter, Sir William Oscar, Kt.

Cartland, Sir George Barrington, Kt., CMG

Cartledge, Sir Bryan George, KCMG

Cary, Sir Roger Hugh, Bt. (1955)

Casey, *Rt. Hon.* Sir Maurice Eugene, Kt.

Cash, Sir Gerald Christopher, GCMG, GCVO, OBE

Cass, Sir Geoffrey Arthur, Kt.

Cass, Sir John Patrick, Kt., OBE

Cassel, Sir Harold Felix, Bt., TD, QC (1920)

Cassels, *Field Marshal* Sir (Archibald) James Halkett, GCB, KBE, DSO

Cassels, Sir John Seton, Kt., CB

Cassels, *Adm.* Sir Simon Alastair Cassillis, KCB, CBE

Cassidi, *Adm.* Sir (Arthur) Desmond, GCB

Casson, Sir Hugh Maxwell, CH, KCVO, PPRA, FRIBA

Cater, Sir Jack, KBE

Cater, Sir John Robert, Kt.

Catford, Sir (John) Robin, KCVO, CBE

Catherwood, Sir (Henry) Frederick (Ross), Kt., MEP

Catling, Sir Richard Charles, Kt., CMG, OBE

Cato, *Hon.* Sir Arnott Samuel, KCMG

Caughey, Sir Thomas Harcourt Clarke, KBE

Caulfield, *Hon.* Sir Bernard, Kt.

Cave, Sir Charles Edward Coleridge, Bt. (1896)

Cave, Sir (Charles) Philip Haddon-, KBE, CMG

Cave, Sir Robert Cave-Browne-, Bt. (1641)

Cawley, Sir Charles Mills, Kt., CBE, Ph.D.

Cayley, Sir Digby William David, Bt. (1661)

Cayzer, Sir James Arthur, Bt. (1904)

Cazalet, *Hon.* Sir Edward Stephen, Kt.

Cazalet, Sir Peter Grenville, Kt.

Cecil, *Rear-Adm.* Sir (Oswald) Nigel Amherst, KBE, CB

Chacksfield, *Air Vice-Marshal* Sir Bernard Albert, KBE, CB

Chadwick, *Revd Prof.* Henry, KBE

Chadwick, *Hon.* Sir John Murray, Kt., ED

Chadwick, Sir Joshua Kenneth Burton, Bt. (1935)

Chadwick, *Revd Prof.* (William) Owen, OM, KBE, FBA

Chan, *Rt. Hon.* Sir Julius, KBE

Chance, Sir (George) Jeremy ffolliott, Bt. (1900)

Chandler, Sir Colin Michael, Kt.

Chandler, Sir Geoffrey, Kt., CBE

Chaney, *Hon.* Sir Frederick Charles, KBE, AFC

Chaplin, Sir Malcolm Hilbery, Kt., CBE

Chapman, Sir David Robert Macgowan, Bt. (1958)

Chapman, Sir George Alan, Kt.

Chapple, *Field Marshal* Sir John Lyon, GCB, CBE

Charles, Sir Joseph Quentin, Kt.

Charnley, Sir (William) John, Kt., CB, FEng.

Chatfield, Sir John Freeman, Kt., CBE

Chaytor, Sir George Reginald, Bt. (1831)

Checketts, *Sqn. Ldr.* Sir David John, KCVO

Checkland, Sir Michael, Kt.

Cheetham, Sir Nicolas John Alexander, KCMG

Chessells, Sir Arthur David (Tim), Kt.

Chesterman, Sir (Dudley) Ross, Kt., Ph.D.

Chesterton, Sir Oliver Sidney, Kt., MC

Chetwood, Sir Clifford Jack, Kt.

Chetwynd, Sir Arthur Ralph Talbot, Bt. (1795)

Cheung, Sir Oswald Victor, Kt., CBE

Cheyne, Sir Joseph Lister Watson, Bt., OBE (1908)

Chichester, Sir (Edward) John, Bt. (1641)

Child, Sir (Coles John) Jeremy, Bt. (1919)

Chilton, *Brig.* Sir Frederick Oliver, Kt., CBE, DSO

Chilwell, *Hon.* Sir Muir Fitzherbert, Kt.

Chinn, Sir Trevor Edwin, Kt., CVO

Chipperfield, Sir Geoffrey Howes, KCB

Chitty, Sir Thomas Willes, Bt. (1924)

Cholmeley, Sir Montague John, Bt. (1806)

Christie, Sir George William Langham, Kt.

Christie, *Hon.* Sir Vernon Howard Colville, Kt.

Christie, Sir William, Kt., MBE

Christison, *Gen.* Sir (Alexander Frank) Philip, Bt., GBE, CB, DSO, MC (1871)

Christopherson, Sir Derman Guy, Kt., OBE, D.Phil., FRS, FEng.

Chung, Sir Sze-yuen, GBE, FEng.

Clapham, Sir Michael John Sinclair, KBE

Clark, Sir Colin Douglas, Bt. (1917)

Clark, Sir Francis Drake, Bt. (1886)

Clark, Sir John Allen, Kt.

Clark, *Prof.* Sir John Grahame Douglas, Kt., CBE

Clark, Sir John Stewart-, Bt., MEP (1918)

Clark, Sir Robert Anthony, Kt., DSC

Clark, Sir Robin Chichester-, Kt.

Clark, Sir Terence Joseph, KBE, CMG, CVO

Clark, Sir Thomas Edwin, Kt.

Clarke, *Hon.* Sir Anthony Peter, Kt.

Clarke, Sir (Charles Mansfield) Tobias, Bt. (1831)

Clarke, *Prof.* Sir Cyril Astley, KBE, MD, SC.D., FRS, FRCP

Clarke, Sir Ellis Emmanuel Innocent, GCMG

Clarke, Sir (Henry) Ashley, GCMG, GCVO

Clarke, Sir Jonathan Dennis, Kt.

Clarke, *Maj.* Sir Peter Cecil, KCVO

Clarke, Sir Robert Cyril, Kt.

Clarke, Sir Rupert William John, Bt., MBE (1882)

Clay, Sir Richard Henry, Bt. (1841)

Clayton, Sir David Robert, Bt., (1732)

Clayton, Sir Robert James, Kt., CBE, FEng.

Cleaver, Sir Anthony Brian, Kt.

Clegg, Sir Walter, Kt.

Cleminson, Sir James Arnold Stacey, KBE, MC

Clerk, Sir John Dutton, Bt., CBE, VRD (s. 1679)

Clerke, Sir John Edward Longueville, Bt. (1660)

Clifford, Sir Roger Joseph, Bt. (1887)

Clothier, Sir Cecil Montacute, KCB, QC

Clucas, Sir Kenneth Henry, KCB

Clutterbuck, *Vice-Adm.* Sir David Granville, KBE, CB

Coates, Sir Ernest William, Kt., CMG

Coates, Sir Frederick Gregory Lindsay, Bt. (1921)

Coats, Sir Alastair Francis Stuart, Bt. (1905)

Coats, Sir William David, Kt.

Cobban, Sir James Macdonald, Kt., CBE, TD

Cochrane, Sir (Henry) Marc (Sursock), Bt. (1903)

Cockburn, Sir John Elliot, Bt. (s. 1671)

Cockburn, Sir Robert, KBE, CB, Ph.D., FEng.

Cockcroft, Sir Wilfred Halliday, Kt., D.Phil.

Cockerell, Sir Christopher Sydney, Kt., CBE, FRS

Cockram, Sir John, Kt.

Cockshaw, Sir Alan, Kt., FEng.

Codrington, Sir Simon Francis Bethell, Bt. (1876)

Codrington, Sir William Alexander, Bt. (1721)

Coghill, Sir Egerton James Nevill Tobias, Bt. (1778)

Cohen, Sir Edward, Kt.

Cohen, Sir Ivor Harold, Kt., CBE, TD

Cohen, Sir Stephen Harry Waley-, Bt. (1961)

Coldstream, Sir George Phillips, KCB, KCVO, QC

Cole, Sir (Alexander) Colin, KCB, KCVO, TD

Cole, Sir David Lee, KCMG, MC

Cole, Sir (Robert) William, Kt.

Coles, Sir (Arthur) John, KCMG

Colfox, Sir (William) John, Bt. (1939)

Collett, Sir Christopher, GBE

Collett, Sir Ian Seymour, Bt. (1934)

Collins, Sir Arthur James Robert, KCVO

Collins, Sir John Alexander, Kt.

Collyear, Sir John Gowen, Kt., FEng.

Colman, Hon. Sir Anthony David, Kt.

Colman, Sir Michael Jeremiah, Bt. (1907)

Colquhoun, Maj.-Gen. Sir Cyril Harry, KCVO, CB, OBE

Colquhoun of Luss, Sir Ivar Iain, Bt. (1786)

Colt, Sir Edward William Dutton Bt. (1694)

Colthurst, Sir Richard La Touche, Bt. (1744)

Combs, Sir Willis Ide, KCVO, CMG

Compston, Vice-Adm. Sir Peter Maxwell, KCB

Compton, Sir Edmund Gerald, GCB, KBE

Comyn, Hon. Sir James, Kt.

Conant, Sir John Ernest Michael, Bt. (1954)

Connell, Hon. Sir Michael Bryan, Kt.

Conran, Sir Terence Orby, Kt.

Cons, Hon. Sir Derek, Kt.

Constable, Sir Robert Frederick Strickland-, Bt. (1641)

Cook, Prof. Sir Alan Hugh, Kt.

Cook, Sir Christopher Wymondham Rayner Herbert, Bt. (1886)

Cooke, Sir Charles Fletcher-, Kt., QC

Cooke, Lt.-Col. Sir David William Perceval, Bt. (1661)

Cooke, Sir Howard Felix Hanlan, GCMG, ON, CD

Cooke, Rt. Hon. Sir Robin Brunskill, KBE

Cooksey, Sir David James Scott, Kt.

Cooley, Sir Alan Sydenham, Kt., CBE

Coop, Sir Maurice Fletcher, Kt.

Cooper, Rt. Hon. Sir Frank, GCB, CMG

Cooper, Sir (Frederick Howard) Michael Craig-, Kt., CBE, TD

Cooper, Gen. Sir George Leslie Conroy, GCB, MC

Cooper, Sir Louis Jacques Blom-, Kt., QC

Cooper, Sir Patrick Graham Astley, Bt. (1821)

Cooper, Sir Richard Powell, Bt. (1905)

Cooper, Maj.-Gen. Sir Simon Christie, KCVO

Cooper, Sir William Daniel Charles, Bt. (1863)

Coote, Sir Christopher John, Bt., Premier Baronet of Ireland (1. 1621)

Copas, Most Revd Virgil, KBE, DD

Cope, Rt. Hon. Sir John Ambrose, Kt., MP

Copisarow, Sir Alcon Charles, Kt.

Corbet, Sir John Vincent, Bt., MBE (1808)

Corby, Sir (Frederick) Brian, Kt.

Corfield, Rt. Hon. Sir Frederick Vernon, Kt., QC

Corfield, Sir Kenneth George, Kt.

Corley, Sir Kenneth Sholl Ferrand, Kt.

Cormack, Sir Magnus Cameron, KBE

Corness, Sir Colin Ross, Kt.

Cornford, Sir (Edward) Clifford, KCB, FEng.

Cornforth, Sir John Warcup, Kt., CBE, D.Phil., FRS

Corry, Sir William James, Bt. (1885)

Cortazzi, Sir (Henry Arthur) Hugh, GCMG

Cory, Sir (Clinton Charles) Donald, Bt. (1919)

Costar, Sir Norman Edgar, KCMG

Cotter, Lt.-Col. Sir Delaval James Alfred, Bt., DSO (1. 1763)

Cotterell, Sir John Henry Geers, Bt. (1805)

Cotton, Sir John Richard, KCMG, OBE

Cotton, Hon. Sir Robert Carrington, KCMG

Cottrell, Sir Alan Howard, Kt., Ph.D., FRS, FEng.

Cotts, Sir (Robert) Crichton Mitchell, Bt. (1921)

Coulson, Sir John Eltringham, KCMG

Couper, Sir (Robert) Nicholas (Oliver), Bt. (1841)

Court, Rt. Hon. Sir Charles Walter Michael, KCMG, OBE

Coutts, Sir David Burdett Money-, KCVO

Couzens, Sir Kenneth Edward, KCB

Covacevich, Sir (Anthony) Thomas, Kt., DFC

Coward, Vice-Adm. Sir John Francis, KCB, DSO

Cowdrey, Sir (Michael) Colin, Kt., CBE

Cowen, Rt. Hon. Prof. Sir Zelman, GCMG, GCVO, QC

Cowie, Sir Thomas (Tom), Kt., OBE

Cowperthwaite, Sir John James, KBE, CMG

Cox, Prof. Sir David Roxbee, Kt., FRS

Cox, Sir (Ernest) Gordon, KBE, TD, D.Sc., FRS

Cox, Sir Geoffrey Sandford, Kt., CBE

Cox, Sir (George) Trenchard, Kt., CBE, FSA

Cox, Vice-Adm. Sir John Michael Holland, Kt.

Cox, Sir Mencea Ethereal, Kt.

Cradock, Rt. Hon. Sir Percy, GCMG

Craig, Sir (Albert) James (Macqueen), GCMG

Cramer, Hon. Sir John Oscar, Kt.

Crane, Sir James William Donald, Kt., CBE

Craufurd, Sir Robert James, Bt. (1781)

Craven, Air Marshal Sir Robert Edward, KBE, CB, DFC

Crawford, Prof. Sir Frederick William, Kt., FEng.

Crawford, Hon. Sir George Hunter, Kt.

Crawford, Sir (Robert) Stewart, GCMG, CVO

Crawford, Vice-Adm. Sir William Godfrey, KBE, CB, DSC

Crawshay, Col. Sir William Robert, Kt., DSO, ERD, TD

Creagh, Maj.-Gen. Sir (Kilner) Rupert Brazier-, KBE, CB, DSO

Cresswell, Hon. Sir Peter John, Kt.

Crichton, Sir Andrew James Maitland-Makgill-, Kt.

Crill, Sir Peter Leslie, Kt., CBE

Cripps, Sir Cyril Humphrey, Kt.

Crisp, Sir (John) Peter, Bt. (1913)

Critchett, Sir Ian (George Lorraine), Bt. (1908)

Croft, Sir Owen Glendower, Bt. (1671)

Croft, Sir Thomas Stephen Hutton, Bt. (1818)

†Crofton, Sir Hugh Denis, Bt. (1801)

Crofton, Prof. Sir John Wenman, Kt.

Crofton, Sir Malby Sturges, Bt. (1838)

Croker, Sir Walter Russell, KBE

Crookenden, Lt.-Gen. Sir Napier, KCB, DSO, OBE

Cross, Sir Barry Albert, Kt., CBE, FRS

Cross, *Air Chief Marshal* Sir Kenneth Brian Boyd, KCB, CBE, DSO, DFC

Crossland, *Prof.* Sir Bernard, Kt., CBE, FEng.

Crossland, Sir Leonard, Kt.

Crossley, Sir Nicholas John, Bt. (1909)

Crouch, Sir David Lance, Kt.

Cruthers, Sir James Winter, Kt.

Cubbon, Sir Brian Crossland, GCB

Cubitt, Sir Hugh Guy, Kt., CBE

Cuckney, Sir John Graham, Kt.

Cullen, Sir (Edward) John, Kt., F.Eng.

Cumming, Sir William Gordon Gordon-, Bt. (1804)

Cuninghame, Sir John Christopher Foggo Montgomery-, Bt. (NS 1672)

†Cuninghame, Sir William Henry Fairlie-, Bt. (S. 1630)

Cunliffe, Sir David Ellis, Bt. (1759)

Cunningham, Sir Charles Craik, GCB, KBE, CVO

Cunningham, *Lt.-Gen.* Sir Hugh Patrick, KBE

Cunynghame, Sir Andrew David Francis, Bt. (S. 1702)

Curle, Sir John Noel Ormiston, KCVO, CMG

Curran, Sir Samuel Crowe, Kt., D.SC., Ph.D., FRS, FRSE, FEng.

Currie, *Prof.* Sir Alastair Robert, Kt., FRCP, FRCPE, FRSE

†Currie, Sir Donald Scott, Bt. (1847)

Currie, Sir Neil Smith, Kt., CBE

Curtis, Sir Barry John, Kt.

Curtis, Sir (Edward) Leo, Kt.

Curtis, *Hon.* Sir Richard Herbert, Kt.

Curtis, Sir William Peter, Bt. (1802)

Curtiss, *Air Marshal* Sir John Bagot, KCB, KBE

Curwen, Sir Christopher Keith, KCMG

Cuthbertson, Sir Harold Alexander, Kt.

Cutler, Sir (Arthur) Roden, VC, KCMG, KCVO, CBE

Cutler, Sir Charles Benjamin, KBE, ED

Cutler, Sir Horace Walter, Kt., OBE

Dacie, *Prof.* Sir John Vivian, Kt., MD, FRS

Dalais, Sir Adrien Pierre, Kt.

Dale, Sir William Leonard, KCMG

Dalrymple, *Maj.* Sir Hew Fleetwood Hamilton-, Bt., KCVO (S. 1697)

Dalton, Sir Alan Nugent Goring, Kt., CBE

Dalton, *Vice-Adm.* Sir Geoffrey Thomas James Oliver, KCB

Daly, *Lt.-Gen.* Sir Thomas Joseph, KBE, CB, DSO

Dalyell, Sir Tam, Bt., MP (NS 1685)

Daniel, Sir Goronwy Hopkin, KCVO, CB, D.Phil.

Daniell, Sir Peter Averell, Kt., TD

Danks, Sir Alan John, KBE

Darby, Sir Peter Howard, Kt., CBE, QFSM

Darell, Sir Jeffrey Lionel, Bt., MC (1795)

Dargie, Sir William Alexander, Kt., CBE

Dark, Sir Anthony Michael Beaumont-, Kt.

Darling, Sir Clifford, Kt.

Darling, Sir James Ralph, Kt., CMG, OBE

Darling, *Gen.* Sir Kenneth Thomas, GBE, KCB, DSO

Darlington, *Rear-Adm.* Sir Charles Roy, KBE

Darvall, Sir (Charles) Roger, Kt., CBE

Dashwood, Sir Francis John Vernon Hereward, Bt., *Premier Baronet of Great Britain* (1707)

Dashwood, Sir Richard James, Bt. (1684)

Daunt, Sir Timothy Lewis Achilles, KCMG

David, Sir Jean Marc, Kt., CBE, QC

Davidson, Sir Robert James, Kt., FEng.

Davie, Sir Antony Francis Ferguson-, Bt. (1847)

Davies, *Air Marshal* Sir Alan Cyril, KCB, CBE

Davies, *Hon.* Sir (Alfred William) Michael, Kt.

Davies, Sir Alun Talfan, Kt., QC

Davies, Sir David Henry, Kt.

Davies, *Hon.* Sir (David Herbert) Mervyn, Kt., MC, TD

Davies, *Vice-Adm.* Sir Lancelot Richard Bell, KBE

Davies, Sir Oswald, Kt., CBE

Davies, Sir Peter Maxwell, Kt., CBE

Davies, Sir Richard Harries, KCVO, CBE

Davies, Sir Victor Caddy, Kt., OBE

Davis, Sir Charles Sigmund, Kt., CB

Davis, Sir Colin Rex, Kt., CBE

Davis, *Hon.* Sir (Dermot) Renn, Kt., OBE

Davis, Sir (Ernest) Howard, Kt., CMG, OBE

Davis, Sir John Gilbert, Bt. (1946)

Davis, Sir Maurice Herbert, Kt., OBE

Davis, Sir Rupert Charles Hart-, Kt.

Davis, *Hon.* Sir Thomas Robert Alexander Harries, KBE

Davis, Sir (William) Allan, GBE

Davison, *Rt. Hon.* Sir Ronald Keith, GBE, CMG

Dawbarn, Sir Simon Yelverton, KCVO, CMG

Dawson, Sir Anthony Michael, KCVO, MD, FRCP

Dawson, *Hon.* Sir Daryl Michael, KBE, CB

Dawson, Sir Hugh Michael Trevor, Bt. (1920)

Dawson, *Air Chief Marshal* Sir Walter Lloyd, KCB, CBE, DSO

Dawtry, Sir Alan (Graham), Kt., CBE, TD

Day, Sir Derek Malcolm, KCMG

Day, Sir (Judson) Graham, Kt.

Day, Sir Michael John, Kt., OBE

Day, Sir Robin, Kt.

Deakin, Sir (Frederick) William (Dampier), Kt., DSO

Dean, *Rt. Hon.* Sir (Arthur) Paul, Kt.

Dean, Sir Patrick Henry, GCMG

Deane, *Hon.* Sir William Patrick, KBE

Dearing, Sir Ronald Ernest, Kt., CB

de Bellaigue, Sir Geoffrey, KCVO

Debenham, Sir Gilbert Ridley, Bt. (1931)

de Deney, Sir Geoffrey Ivor, KCVO

Deer, Sir (Arthur) Frederick, Kt., CMG

de Hoghton, Sir (Richard) Bernard (Cuthbert), Bt. (1611)

De la Bère, Sir Cameron, Bt. (1953)

de la Mare, Sir Arthur James, KCMG, KCVO

Delamere, Sir Monita Eru, KBE

de la Rue, Sir Andrew George Ilay, Bt. (1898)

Dellow, Sir John Albert, Kt., CBE

de Lotbinière, *Lt.-Col.* Sir Edmond Joly, Kt.

Delve, Sir Frederick William, Kt., CBE

de Montmorency, Sir Arnold Geoffroy, Bt. (I. 1631)

Denholm, Sir John Ferguson (Ian), Kt., CBE

Denman, Sir (George) Roy, KCB, CMG

Denny, Sir Alistair Maurice Archibald, Bt. (1913)

Denny, Sir Anthony Coningham de Waltham, Bt. (I. 1782)

Dent, Sir John, Kt., CBE, FEng.

Dent, Sir Robin John, KCVO

Denton, *Prof.* Sir Eric James, Kt., CBE, FRS

Derbyshire, Sir Andrew George, Kt.

Derham, Sir Peter John, Kt.

de Trafford, Sir Dermot Humphrey, Bt. (1841)

Deverell, Sir Colville Montgomery, GBE, KCMG, CVO

Devesi, Sir Baddeley, GCMG, GCVO

De Ville, Sir Harold Godfrey Oscar, Kt., CBE

Devitt, Sir Thomas Gordon, Bt. (1916)

de Waal, Sir (Constant Henrik) Henry, KCB, QC

Dewey, Sir Anthony Hugh, Bt. (1917)

Dewhurst, *Prof.* Sir (Christopher) John, Kt.

d'Eyncourt, Sir Mark Gervais Tennyson-, Bt. (1930)

Dhenin, *Air Marshal* Sir Geoffrey Howard, KBE, AFC, GM, MD

Dhrangadhra, HH the Maharaja Raj Saheb of, KCIE

Dibela, *Hon.* Sir Kingsford, GCMG

Dick, Sir John Alexander, Kt., MC, QC

Dickenson, Sir Aubrey Fiennes Trotman-, Kt.

Dickinson, Sir Harold Herbert, Kt.

Dickinson, Sir Samuel Benson, Kt.

Dilbertson, Sir Geoffrey, Kt., CBE

Dilke, Sir John Fisher Wentworth, Bt. (1862)

Dill, Sir Nicholas Bayard, Kt., CBE

Dillon, *Rt. Hon.* Sir (George) Brian (Hugh), Kt.

Dillon, Sir John Vincent, Kt., CMG

Dillon, Sir Max, Kt.

Diver, *Hon.* Sir Leslie Charles, Kt.

Dixon, Sir Jonathan Mark, Bt. (1919)

Djanogly, Sir Harry Ari Simon, Kt., CBE

Dobbs, *Capt.* Sir Richard Arthur Frederick, KCVO

Dobson, *Vice-Adm.* Sir David Stuart, KBE

Dobson, Sir Denis William, KCB, OBE, QC

Dobson, *Gen.* Sir Patrick John Howard-, GCB

Dobson, Sir Richard Portway, Kt.

Dodds, Sir Ralph Jordan, Bt. (1964)

Dodson, Sir Derek Sherborne Lindsell, KCMG, MC

Dodsworth, Sir John Christopher Smith-, Bt. (1784)

Doll, *Prof.* Sir (William) Richard (Shaboe), Kt., OBE, FRS, DM, MD, D.SC.

Dollery, Sir Colin Terence, Kt.

Donald, Sir Alan Ewen, KCMG

Donald, *Air Marshal* Sir John George, KBE

Donne, *Hon.* Sir Gaven John, KBE

Donne, Sir John Christopher, Kt.

Dookun, Sir Dewoonarain, Kt.

Dorey, Sir Graham Martyn, Kt.

Dorman, *Lt.-Col.* Sir Charles Geoffrey, Bt., MC (1923)

Dorman, Sir Maurice Henry, GCMG, GCVO

Dougherty, *Maj.-Gen.* Sir Ivan Noel, Kt., CBE, DSO, ED

Doughty, Sir William Roland, Kt.

Douglas, Sir (Edward) Sholto, Kt.

Douglas, Sir Robert McCallum, Kt., OBE

Douglas, *Hon.* Sir Roger Owen, Kt.

Douglas, *Rt. Hon.* Sir William Randolph, KCMG

Dover, *Prof.* Sir Kenneth James, Kt., D.Litt., FBA, FRSE

Down, Sir Alastair Frederick, Kt., OBE, MC, TD

Downes, Sir Edward Thomas, Kt., CBE

Downey, Sir Gordon Stanley, KCB

Downs, Sir Diarmuid, Kt., CBE, FEng.

Downward, Sir William Atkinson, Kt.

Dowson, Sir Philip Manning, Kt., CBE, ARA

Doyle, Sir Reginald Derek Henry, Kt., CBE

D'Oyly, Sir Nigel Hadley Miller, Bt. (1663)

Drake, Sir (Arthur) Eric (Courtney), Kt., CBE

Drake, *Hon.* Sir (Frederick) Maurice, Kt., DFC

Drew, Sir Arthur Charles Walter, KCB

Dreyer, *Adm.* Sir Desmond Parry, GCB, CBE, DSC

Drinkwater, Sir John Muir, Kt., QC

Driver, Sir Antony Victor, Kt.

Driver, Sir Eric William, Kt.

Drury, Sir (Victor William) Michael, Kt., OBE

Dryden, Sir John Stephen Gyles, Bt. (1733 and 1795)

du Cann, *Rt. Hon.* Sir Edward Dillon Lott, KBE

Duckmanton, Sir Talbot Sydney, Kt., CBE

Duckworth, *Maj.* Sir Richard Dyce, Bt. (1909)

du Cros, Sir Claude Philip Arthur Mallet, Bt. (1916)

Duff, *Rt. Hon.* Sir (Arthur) Antony, GCMG, CVO, DSO, DSC

Duffell, *Lt.-Gen.* Sir Peter Royson, KCB, CBE, MC

Duffus, *Hon.* Sir William Algernon Holwell, Kt.

Duffy, Sir (Albert) (Edward) Patrick, Kt., Ph.D.

Dugdale, Sir William Stratford, Bt., MC (1936)

Dunbar, Sir Archibald Ranulph, Bt. (S. 1700)

Dunbar, Sir David Hope-, Bt. (S. 1664)

Dunbar, Sir Drummond Cospatrick Ninian, Bt., MC (S. 1698)

Dunbar, Sir Jean Ivor, Bt. (S. 1694)

Dunbar of Hempriggs, Dame Maureen Daisy Helen (Lady Dunbar of Hempriggs), Btss. (S. 1706)

Duncan, Sir James Blair, Kt.

Duncombe, Sir Philip Digby Pauncefort-, Bt. (1859)

Dundas, Sir Hugh Spencer Lisle, Kt., CBE, DSO, DFC

Dunham, Sir Kingsley Charles, Kt., Ph.D., FRS, FRSE, FEng.

Dunlop, Sir Thomas, Bt. (1916)

Dunlop, Sir William Norman Gough, Kt.

Dunn, *Air Marshal* Sir Eric Clive, KBE, CB, BEM

Dunn, *Lt.-Col.* Sir (Francis) Vivian, KCVO, OBE

Dunn, *Air Marshal* Sir Patrick Hunter, KBE, CB, DFC

Dunn, *Rt. Hon.* Sir Robin Horace Walford, Kt., MC

Dunnett, Sir (Ludovic) James, GCB, CMG

Dunning, Sir Simon William Patrick, Bt. (1930)

Dunphie, *Maj.-Gen.* Sir Charles Anderson Lane, Kt., CB, CBE, DSO

Dunstan, *Lt.-Gen.* Sir Donald Beaumont, KBE, CB

†Duntze, Sir Daniel Evans, Bt. (1774)

Dupre, Sir Tumun, Kt., MBE

Dupree, Sir Peter, Bt. (1921)

Durand, Sir Edward Alan Christopher David Percy, Bt. (1892)

Durant, Sir (Robert) Anthony (Bevis), Kt.,

Durham, Sir Kenneth, Kt.

Durie, Sir Alexander Charles, Kt., CBE

Durkin, *Air Marshal* Sir Herbert, KBE, CB

Durrant, Sir William Henry Estridge, Bt. (1784)

Duthie, *Prof.* Sir Herbert Livingston, Kt.

Duthie, Sir Robert Grieve (Robin), Kt., CBE

Duval, Sir (Charles) Gaetan, Kt.

Duxbury, *Air Marshal* Sir (John) Barry, KCB, CBE

Dyer, *Prof.* Sir (Henry) Peter (Francis) Swinnerton-, Bt., KBE, FRS (1678)

Dyke, Sir David William Hart, Bt. (1677)

Dyson, *Hon.* Sir John Anthony, Kt.

Earle, Sir (Hardman) George (Algernon), Bt. (1869)

East, Sir (Lewis) Ronald, Kt., CBE

Easton, Sir Robert William Simpson, Kt., CBE

Eastwood, Sir John Bealby, Kt.

Eaton, *Adm.* Sir Kenneth John, KCB

Eberle, *Adm.* Sir James Henry Fuller, GCB

Ebrahim, Sir (Mahomed) Currimbhoy, Bt. (1910)

Eburne, Sir Sidney Alfred William, Kt., MC

Eccles, Sir John Carew, Kt., D.Phil., FRS

Echlin, Sir Norman David Fenton, Bt. (I. 1721)

Eckersley, Sir Donald Payze, Kt., OBE

†Edge, Sir William, Bt. (1937)

Edmenson, Sir Walter Alexander, Kt., CBE

Edmonstone, Sir Archibald Bruce Charles, Bt. (1774)

Edwardes, Sir Michael Owen, Kt.

Edwards, Sir Christopher John Churchill, Bt. (1866)

Edwards, Sir George Robert, Kt., OM, CBE, FRS, FEng.

Edwards, Sir (John) Clive (Leighton), Bt. (1921)

Edwards, Sir Llewellyn Roy, Kt.

Edwards, *Prof.* Sir Samuel Frederick, Kt., FRS

Egan, Sir John Leopold, Kt.

Egerton, Sir John Alfred Roy, Kt.

Egerton, Sir (Philip) John (Caledon) Grey-, Bt. (1617)

Egerton, Sir Seymour John Louis, GCVO

Egerton, Sir Stephen Loftus, KCMG

Eggleston, *Hon.* Sir Richard Moulton, Kt.

Eichelbaum, *Rt. Hon.* Sir Thomas, GBE

Eliott of Stobs, Sir Charles Joseph Alexander, Bt. (S. 1666)

Ellerton, Sir Geoffrey James, Kt., CMG, MBE

Elliot, Sir Gerald Henry, Kt.

Elliott, Sir Clive Christopher Hugh, Bt. (1917)

Elliott, Sir Randal Forbes, KBE

Elliott, *Prof.* Sir Roger James, Kt., FRS

Elliott, Sir Ronald Stuart, Kt.

Ellis, Sir John Rogers, Kt., MBE, MD, FRCP

Ellis, Sir Ronald, Kt., FEng.

Ellison, *Col.* Sir Ralph Harry Carr-, Kt., TD

Elphinstone, Sir John, Bt. (S. 1701)

Elphinstone, Sir (Maurice) Douglas (Warburton), Bt., TD (1816)

Elton, Sir Arnold, Kt., CBE

Elton, Sir Charles Abraham Grierson, Bt. (1717)

Elton, *Prof.* Sir Geoffrey Rudolph, Kt., FBA

Elwood, Sir Brian George Conway, Kt., CBE

Elworthy, Sir Peter Herbert, Kt.

Elyan, Sir (Isadore) Victor, Kt.

Emery, *Rt. Hon.* Sir Peter Frank Hannibal, Kt., MP

Empson, *Adm.* Sir (Leslie) Derek, GBE, KCB

Emson, *Air Marshal* Sir Reginald Herbert, KBE, CB, AFC

Engineer, Sir Noshirwan Phirozshah, Kt.

Engle, Sir George Lawrence Jose, KCB, QC

English, Sir Cyril Rupert, Kt.

English, Sir David, Kt.

English, Sir Terence Alexander Hawthorne, KBE, FRCS

Entwistle, Sir (John Nuttall) Maxwell, Kt.

Epstein, *Prof.* Sir (Michael) Anthony, Kt., CBE, FRS

Ereaut, Sir (Herbert) Frank Cobbold, Kt.

Errington, *Col.* Sir Geoffrey Frederick, Bt. (1963)

Errington, Sir Lancelot, KCB

Erskine, Sir (Thomas) David, Bt. (1821)

Esmonde, Sir Thomas Francis Grattan, Bt. (I. 1629)

Espie, Sir Frank Fletcher, Kt., OBE

Esplen, Sir John Graham, Bt. (1921)

Eustace, Sir Joseph Lambert, GCMG, GCVO

Evans, Sir Anthony Adney, Bt. (1920)

Evans, *Rt. Hon.* Sir Anthony Howell Meurig, Kt., RD

Evans, *Air Chief Marshal* Sir David George, GCB, CBE

Evans, *Air Chief Marshal* Sir David Parry-, GCB, CBE

Evans, Sir Francis Loring Gwynne-, Bt. (1913)

Evans, *Hon.* Sir Haydn Tudor, Kt.

Evans, Sir Richard Mark, KCMG, KCVO

Evans, Sir (Robert) Charles, Kt.

Evans, Sir (William) Vincent (John), GCMG, MBE, QC

Eveleigh, *Rt. Hon.* Sir Edward Walter, Kt., ERD

Everard, *Maj.-Gen.* Sir Christopher Earle Welby-, KBE, CB

Everard, Sir Robin Charles, Bt. (1911)

Everson, Sir Frederick Charles, KCMG

Every, Sir Henry John Michael, Bt. (1641)

Ewans, Sir Martin Kenneth, KCMG

Ewart, Sir (William) Ivan (Cecil), Bt., DSC (1887)

Ewbank, *Hon.* Sir Anthony Bruce, Kt.

Ewin, Sir (David) Ernest Thomas Floyd, Kt., OBE, MVO

Ewing, *Vice-Adm.* Sir (Robert) Alastair, KBE, CB, DSC

Ewing, Sir Ronald Archibald Orr-, Bt. (1886)

Eyre, Sir Graham Newman, Kt., QC

Eyre, *Maj.-Gen.* Sir James Ainsworth Campden Gabriel, KCVO, CBE

Eyre, Sir Reginald Edwin, Kt.

Faber, Sir Richard Stanley, KCVO, CMG

Fadahunsi, Sir Joseph Odeleye, KCMG

Fagge, Sir John William Frederick, Bt. (1660)

Fairbairn, *Hon.* Sir David Eric, KBE, DFC

Fairbairn, Sir (James) Brooke, Bt. (1869)

Fairbairn, Sir Nicholas Hardwick, Kt., QC, MP

Fairclough, Sir John Whitaker, Kt., FEng.

Fairgrieve, Sir (Thomas) Russell, Kt., CBE, TD

Fairhall, *Hon.* Sir Allen, KBE

Fairweather, Sir Patrick Stanislaus, KCMG

Falconer, *Hon.* Sir Douglas William, Kt., MBE

Falk, Sir Roger Salis, Kt., OBE

Falkiner, Sir Edmond Charles, Bt. (I. 1778)

Falkner, Sir (Donald) Keith, Kt.

Fall, Sir Brian James Proetel, KCMG

Falle, Sir Samuel, KCMG, KCVO, DSC

Fareed, Sir Djamil Sheik, Kt.

Farmer, Sir (Lovedin) George Thomas, Kt.

Farndale, *Gen.* Sir Martin Baker, KCB

Farquhar, Sir Michael Fitzroy Henry, Bt. (1796)

Farquharson, *Rt. Hon.* Sir Donald Henry, Kt.

Farquharson, Sir James Robbie, KBE

Farr, Sir John Arnold, Kt.

Farrer, Sir Charles Matthew, KCVO

Farrington, Sir Henry Francis Colden, Bt. (1818)

Fat, Sir (Maxime) Edouard (Lim Man) Lim, Kt.

Faulkner, Sir Eric Odin, Kt., MBE

Faulkner, Sir (James) Dennis (Compton), Kt., CBE, VRD

Fawcus, Sir (Robert) Peter, KBE, CMG

Fawkes, Sir Randol Francis, Kt.

Fay, Sir (Humphrey) Michael Gerard, Kt.

Fayrer, Sir John Lang Macpherson, Bt. (1896)

Fearn, Sir (Patrick) Robin, KCMG

Feilden, Sir Bernard Melchior, Kt., CBE

Feilden, Sir Henry Wemyss, Bt., (1846)

Feldman, Sir Basil Samuel, Kt.

Fell, Sir Anthony, Kt.

Fellowes, *Rt. Hon.* Sir Robert, KCB, KCVO

Fenn, Sir Nicholas Maxted, KCMG

Fennell, *Hon.* Sir (John) Desmond Augustine, Kt., OBE

Fennessy, Sir Edward, Kt., CBE

†Ferguson, Sir Ian Edward Johnson-, Bt. (1906)

Fergusson of Kilkerran, Sir Charles, Bt. (S. 1703)

Fergusson, Sir Ewan Alastair John, GCMG, GCVO

Fergusson, Sir James Herbert Hamilton Colyer-, Bt. (1866)

Feroze, Sir Rustam Moolan, Kt., FRCS

Ferris, *Hon.* Sir Francis Mursell, Kt., TD

ffolkes, Sir Robert Francis Alexander, Bt., OBE (1774)

Field, Sir Malcolm David, Kt.

Fielding, Sir Colin Cunningham, Kt., CB

Fielding, Sir Leslie, KCMG

Fiennes, Sir John Saye Wingfield Twisleton-Wykeham-, KCB, QC

Fiennes, Sir Maurice Alberic Twisleton-Wykeham-, Kt.

Fiennes, Sir Ranulph Twisleton-Wykeham-, Bt., OBE (1916)

Figg, Sir Leonard Clifford William, KCMG

Figgess, Sir John George, KBE, CMG

Figures, Sir Colin Frederick, KCMG, OBE

Fingland, Sir Stanley James Gunn, KCMG

Finlay, Sir David Ronald James Bell, Bt. (1964)

Finley, Sir Peter Hamilton, Kt., OBE, DFC

Firth, *Prof.* Sir Raymond William, Kt., Ph.D., FBA

Fish, Sir Hugh, Kt., CBE

Fisher, Sir George Read, Kt., CMG

Fisher, *Hon.* Sir Henry Arthur Pears, Kt.

Fisher, Sir Nigel Thomas Loveridge, Kt., MC

Fison, Sir (Richard) Guy, Bt., DSC (1905)

Fitch, *Adm.* Sir Richard George Alison, KCB

†Fitzgerald, *Revd* (Sir) Daniel Patrick, Bt. (1903)

FitzGerald, Sir George Peter Maurice, Bt., MC (*The Knight of Kerry*) (1880)

FitzHerbert, Sir Richard Ranulph, Bt. (1784)

Fitzpatrick, *Gen.* Sir (Geoffrey Richard) Desmond, GCB, DSO, MBE, MC

Fitzpatrick, *Air Marshal* Sir John Bernard, KBE, CB

Flanagan, Sir James Bernard, Kt., CBE

Flavelle, Sir (Joseph) David Ellsworth, Bt. (1917)

Fleming, *Instructor Rear-Adm.* Sir John, KBE, DSC

Fletcher, Sir Henry Egerton Aubrey-, Bt. (1782)

Fletcher, Sir James Muir Cameron, Kt.

Fletcher, Sir Leslie, Kt., DSC

Fletcher, *Air Chief Marshal* Sir Peter Carteret, KCB, OBE, DFC, AFC

Floissac, *Hon.* Sir Vincent Frederick, Kt., CMG, OBE, QC

Floyd, Sir Giles Henry Charles, Bt. (1816)

Foley, Sir (Thomas John) Noel, Kt., CBE

Follett, *Prof.* Sir Brian Keith, Kt., FRS

Foot, Sir Geoffrey James, Kt.

Foots, Sir James William, Kt.

Forbes, *Hon.* Sir Alastair Granville, Kt.

Forbes, *Maj.* Sir Hamish Stewart, Bt., MBE, MC (1823)

†Forbes of Craigievar, Sir John Alexander Cumnock Forbes-Sempill, Bt. (S. 1630)

Forbes, *Vice-Adm.* Sir John Morrison, KCB

Forbes, *Hon.* Sir Thayne John, Kt.

†Forbes of Pitsligo, Sir William Daniel Stuart-, Bt. (S. 1626)

Ford, Sir Andrew Russell, Bt. (1929)

Ford, Sir David Robert, KBE, LVO, OBE

Ford, *Maj.* Sir Edward William Spencer, KCB, KCVO

Ford, *Air Marshal* Sir Geoffrey Harold, KBE, CB, FEng.

Ford, *Prof.* Sir Hugh, Kt., FRS, FEng.

†Ford, Sir James Anson St Clair-, Bt. (1793)

Ford, Sir John Archibald, KCMG, MC

Ford, Sir Richard Brinsley, Kt., CBE

Ford, *Gen.* Sir Robert Cyril, GCB, CBE

Foreman, Sir Philip Frank, Kt., CBE, FEng.

Forman, Sir John Denis, Kt., OBE

Forrest, *Prof.* Sir (Andrew) Patrick (McEwen), Kt.

Forrest, *Rear-Adm.* Sir Ronald Stephen, KCVO

Forster, Sir Archibald William, Kt., FEng.

Forster, Sir Oliver Grantham, KCMG, MVO

Forwood, Sir Dudley Richard, Bt. (1895)

Foster, *Prof.* Sir Christopher David, Kt.

Foster, Sir John Gregory, Bt. (1930)

Foster, Sir Norman Robert, Kt.

Foster, Sir Robert Sidney, GCMG, KCVO

Foulis, Sir Ian Primrose Liston-, Bt. (S. 1634)

Foulkes, Sir Nigel Gordon, Kt.

Fowden, Sir Leslie, Kt., FRS

Fowke, Sir David Frederick Gustavus, Bt. (1814)

Fowler, Sir (Edward) Michael Coulson, Kt.

Fowler, *Rt. Hon.* Sir (Peter) Norman, Kt., MP

Fox, Sir (Henry) Murray, GBE

Fox, Sir (John) Marcus, Kt., MBE, MP

Fox, *Rt. Hon.* Sir Michael John, Kt.

Fox, Sir Paul Leonard, Kt., CBE

Frame, Sir Alistair Gilchrist, Kt., FEng.

France, Sir Arnold William, GCB

France, Sir Christopher Walter, KCB

Francis, Sir Horace William Alexander, Kt., CBE, FEng.

Frank, Sir Douglas George Horace, Kt., QC

Frank, Sir (Frederick) Charles, Kt., OBE, FRS

Frank, Sir Robert Andrew, Bt. (1920)

Frankel, Sir Otto Herzberg, Kt., D.SC., FRS

Franklin, Sir Eric Alexander, Kt., CBE

Franklin, Sir Michael David Milroy, KCB, CMG

Franks, Sir Arthur Temple, KCMG

Fraser, Sir Angus McKay, KCB, TD

Fraser, Sir Charles Annand, KCVO

Fraser, *Gen.* Sir David William, GCB, OBE

Fraser, *Air Marshal Revd* Sir (Henry) Paterson, KBE, CB, AFC

Fraser, Sir Ian, Kt., DSO, OBE

Fraser, Sir Ian James, Kt., CBE, MC

Fraser, Sir (James) Campbell, Kt.

Fraser, *Prof.* Sir James David, Bt. (1943)

Fraser, Sir William Kerr, GCB

Frederick, Sir Charles Boscawen, Bt. (1723)

Freeland, Sir John Redvers, KCMG

Freeman, Sir James Robin, Bt. (1945)

Freeman, Sir Ralph, Kt., CVO, CBE, FEng.

Freer, *Air Chief Marshal* Sir Robert William George, GBE, KCB

Freeth, *Hon.* Sir Gordon, KBE

French, *Hon.* Sir Christopher James Saunders, Kt.

Fretwell, Sir (Major) John (Emsley), GCMG

Freud, Sir Clement Raphael, Kt.

Froggatt, Sir Leslie Trevor, Kt.

Froggatt, Sir Peter, Kt.

Frossard, Sir Charles Keith, KBE

Frost, Sir David Paradine, Kt., OBE

Frost, *Hon.* Sir (Thomas) Sydney, Kt.

Fry, *Hon.* Sir William Gordon, Kt.

Fryberg, Sir Abraham, Kt., MBE

Fuchs, Sir Vivian Ernest, Kt., PH.D.

Fuller, *Hon.* Sir John Bryan Munro, Kt.

Fuller, Sir John William Fleetwood, Bt. (1910)

Fung, *Hon.* Sir Kenneth Ping-Fan, Kt., CBE

Furness, Sir Stephen Roberts, Bt. (1913)

Gadsden, Sir Peter Drury Haggerston, GBE, FEng.

Gage, Sir Berkeley Everard Foley, KCMG

Gairy, *Rt. Hon.* Sir Eric Matthew, Kt.

Gaius, *Rt. Revd* Saimon, KBE

Gallwey, Sir Philip Frankland Payne-, Bt. (1812)

Gamble, Sir David Hugh Norman, Bt. (1897)

Ganilau, *Ratu* Sir Penaia Kanatabatu, GCMG, KCVO, KBE, DSO

Gardiner, Sir George Arthur, Kt., MP

Gardner, Sir Douglas Bruce Bruce-, Bt. (1945)

Gardner, Sir Edward Lucas, Kt., QC

Garland, *Hon.* Sir Patrick Neville, Kt.

Garland, *Hon.* Sir Ransley Victor, KBE

Garlick, Sir John, KCB

Garner, Sir Anthony Stuart, Kt.

Garnier, *Rear-Adm.* Sir John, KCVO, CBE, LVO

Garrett, *Hon.* Sir Raymond William, Kt., AFC

Garrioch, Sir (William) Henry, Kt.

Garrod, *Lt.-Gen.* Sir (John) Martin Carruthers, KCB, OBE

Garthwaite, Sir William Francis Cuthbert, Bt., DSC (1919)

Gaskell, Sir Richard Kennedy Harvey, Kt.

Gatehouse, *Hon.* Sir Robert Alexander, Kt.

Geddes, Sir (Anthony) Reay (Mackay), KBE

George, Sir Arthur Thomas, Kt.

Gerken, *Vice-Adm.* Sir Robert William Frank, KCB, CBE

Gery, Sir Robert Lucian Wade-, KCMG, KCVO

Gethin, Sir Richard Joseph St Lawrence, Bt. (I. 1665)

Ghurburrun, Sir Rabindrah, Kt.

Gibb, Sir Francis Ross (Frank), Kt., CBE, FEng.

Gibbings, Sir Peter Walter, Kt.

Gibbon, *Gen.* Sir John Houghton, GCB, OBE

Gibbons, Sir (John) David, KBE

Gibbons, Sir William Edward Doran, Bt. (1752)

Gibbs, *Hon.* Sir Eustace Hubert Beilby, KCVO, CMG

Gibbs, *Rt. Hon.* Sir Harry Talbot, GCMG, KBE

Gibbs, *Field Marshal* Sir Roland Christopher, GCB, CBE, DSO, MC

Gibson, Sir Alexander Drummond, Kt., CBE

Gibson, Sir Christopher Herbert, Bt. (1931)
Gibson, *Revd* Sir David, Bt. (1926)
Gibson, *Vice-Adm.* Sir Donald Cameron Ernest Forbes, KCB, DSC
Gibson, *Rt. Hon.* Sir Peter Leslie, Kt.
Gibson, *Rt. Hon.* Sir Ralph Brian, Kt.
Giddings, *Air Marshal* Sir (Kenneth Charles) Michael, KCB, OBE, DFC, AFC
Gielgud, Sir (Arthur) John, Kt., CH
Giffard, Sir (Charles) Sydney (Rycroft), KCMG
Gilbert, *Air Chief Marshal* Sir Joseph Alfred, KCB, CBE
†Gilbey, Sir Walter Gavin, Bt. (1893)
Giles, *Rear-Adm.* Sir Morgan Charles Morgan-, Kt., DSO, OBE, GM
Gill, Sir Anthony Keith, Kt., F.Eng.
Gillett, Sir Robin Danvers Penrose, Bt., GBE, RD (1959)
Gillmore, Sir David Howe, KCMG
Gilmour, *Col.* Sir Allan Macdonald, KCVO, OBE, MC
Gilmour, Sir John Edward, Bt., DSO, TD (1897)
Gina, Sir Lloyd Maepeza, KBE
Gingell, *Air Chief Marshal* Sir John, GBE, KCB, KCVO
Girolami, Sir Paul, Kt.
Gladstone, Sir (Erskine) William, Bt. (1846)
Glasspole, Sir Florizel Augustus, GCMG, GCVO
Glen, Sir Alexander Richard, KBE, DSC
Glenn, Sir (Joseph Robert) Archibald, Kt., OBE
Glidewell, *Rt. Hon.* Sir Iain Derek Laing, Kt.
Glock, Sir William Frederick, Kt., CBE
Glover, *Gen.* Sir James Malcolm, KCB, MBE
Glover, Sir Victor Joseph Patrick, Kt.
Glyn, Sir Alan, Kt., ERD
Glyn, Sir Anthony Geoffrey Leo Simon, Bt. (1927)
Glyn, Sir Richard Lindsay, Bt. (1759 and 1800)
Goad, Sir (Edward) Colin (Viner), KCMG
Godber, Sir George Edward, GCB, DM
Goff, Sir Robert (William) Davis-, Bt. (1905)
Gohel, Sir Jayvantsinhji Kayaji, Kt., CBE
Gold, Sir Arthur Abraham, Kt., CBE
Gold, Sir Joseph, Kt.
Goldberg, *Prof.* Sir Abraham, Kt., MD, DSC, FRCP
Golding, Sir John Simon Rawson, Kt., OBE
Goldman, Sir Samuel, KCB
Goldsmith, Sir James Michael, Kt.
Gombrich, *Prof.* Sir Ernst Hans Josef, Kt., OM, CBE, Ph.D., FBA, FSA
Gooch, Sir (Richard) John Sherlock, Bt. (1746)
Gooch, Sir Trevor Sherlock (Sir Peter), Bt. (1866)

Goodall, Sir (Arthur) David Saunders, GCMG
Goodenough, Sir Richard Edmund, Bt. (1943)
Goodhart, Sir Philip Carter, Kt.
Goodhart, Sir Robert Anthony Gordon, Bt. (1911)
Goodhart, Sir William Howard, Kt., QC
Goodhew, Sir Victor Henry, Kt.
Goodison, Sir Alan Clowes, KCMG
Goodison, Sir Nicholas Proctor, Kt.
Goodson, Sir Mark Weston Lassam, Bt. (1922)
Goodwin, Sir Matthew Dean, Kt., CBE
Goody, *Most Revd* Launcelot John, KBE
Goold, Sir George Leonard, Bt. (1801)
Gordon, Sir Alexander John, Kt., CBE
Gordon, Sir Andrew Cosmo Lewis Duff-, Bt. (1813)
Gordon, Sir Charles Addison Somerville Snowden, KCB
Gordon, Sir Keith Lyndell, Kt., CMG
Gordon, Sir (Lionel) Eldred (Peter) Smith-, Bt. (1838)
Gordon, Sir Robert James, Bt. (s. 1706)
Gordon, Sir Sidney Samuel, Kt., CBE
Gordon Lennox, Lord Nicholas Charles, KCMG, KCVO
Gore, Sir Richard Ralph St George, Bt. (I. 1622)
Goring, Sir William Burton Nigel, Bt. (1627)
Gorton, *Rt. Hon.* Sir John Grey, GCMG, CH
Goschen, Sir Edward Christian, Bt., DSO (1916)
Gosling, Sir (Frederick) Donald, Kt.
Goswell, Sir Brian Lawrence, Kt.
Goulding, Sir (Ernest) Irvine, Kt.
Goulding, Sir (William) Lingard Walter, Bt. (1904)
Gourlay, *Gen.* Sir (Basil) Ian (Spencer), KCB, OBE, MC, RM
Gourlay, Sir Simon Alexander, Kt.
Govan, Sir Lawrence Herbert, Kt.
Gow, *Gen.* Sir (James) Michael, GCB
Gow, Sir Leonard Maxwell Harper, Kt., MBE
Gowans, Sir James Learmonth, Kt., CBE, FRCP, FRS
Gowans, *Hon.* Sir (Urban) Gregory, Kt.
Graaff, Sir de Villiers, Bt., MBE (1911)
Grabham, Sir Anthony Henry, Kt.
Graham, Sir Alexander Michael, GBE
Graham, Sir Charles Spencer Richard, Bt. (1783)
Graham, Sir James Bellingham, Bt. (1662)
Graham, Sir James Thompson, Kt., CMG
Graham, Sir John Alexander Noble, Bt., GCMG (1906)
Graham, Sir John Moodie, Bt. (1964)
Graham, Sir (John) Patrick, Kt.
Graham, Sir Norman William, Kt., CB

Graham, Sir Peter, KCB, QC
Graham, Sir Peter Alfred, Kt., OBE
Graham, *Lt.-Gen.* Sir Peter Walter, KCB, CBE
†Graham, Sir Ralph Stuart, Bt. (1629)
Graham, *Hon.* Sir Samuel Horatio, Kt., CMG, OBE
Grandy, *Marshal of the Royal Air Force* Sir John, GCB, GCVO, KBE, DSO
Grant, Sir Archibald, Bt. (s. 1705)
Grant, Sir Clifford, Kt.
Grant, Sir (John) Anthony, Kt., MP
Grant, Sir (Matthew) Alistair, Kt.
Grant, Sir Patrick Alexander Benedict, Bt. (s. 1688)
Gray, Sir John Archibald Browne, Kt., SC.D., FRS
Gray, *Vice-Adm.* Sir John Michael Dudgeon, KBE, CB
Gray, *Lt.-Gen.* Sir Michael Stuart, KCB, OBE
Gray, Sir William Hume, Bt. (1917)
Gray, Sir William Stevenson, Kt.
Graydon, *Air Chief Marshal* Sir Michael James, GCB, CBE
Grayson, Sir Jeremy Brian Vincent Harrington, Bt. (1922)
Green, Sir Allan David, KCB, QC
Green, Sir (Edward) Stephen (Lycett), Bt., CBE (1886)
Green, *Hon.* Sir Guy Stephen Montague, KBE
Green, Sir Kenneth, Kt.
Green, Sir Owen Whitley, Kt.
Green, Sir Peter James Frederick, Kt.
Greenaway, Sir Derek Burdick, Bt., CBE (1933)
Greenborough, Sir John, KBE
Greenbury, Sir Richard, Kt.
Greene, Sir (John) Brian Massy-, Kt.
Greengross, Sir Alan David, Kt.
Greening, *Rear-Adm.* Sir Paul Woollven, GCVO
Greenwell, Sir Edward Bernard, Bt. (1906)
Gregson, Sir Peter Lewis, KCB
Grenside, Sir John Peter, Kt., CBE
Grey, Sir Anthony Dysart, Bt. (1814)
Grey, Sir Roger de, KCVO, PRA
Grierson, Sir Michael John Bewes, Bt. (s. 1685)
Grierson, Sir Ronald Hugh, Kt.
Grieve, *Prof.* Sir Robert, Kt.
Griffin, *Adm.* Sir Anthony Templer Frederick Griffith, GCB
Griffin, *Maj.* Sir (Arthur) John (Stewart), KCVO
Griffin, Sir (Charles) David, Kt., CBE
Griffiths, Sir Eldon Wylie, Kt.
Griffiths, Sir (Ernest) Roy, Kt.
Griffiths, Sir John Norton-, Bt. (1922)
Grimwade, Sir Andrew Sheppard, Kt., CBE
Grindrod, *Most Revd* John Basil Rowland, KBE
Grinstead, Sir Stanley Gordon, Kt.
Grose, *Vice-Adm.* Sir Alan, KBE
Grotrian, Sir Philip Christian Brent, Bt. (1934)

Grove, Sir Charles Gerald, Bt. (1874)
Grove, Sir Edmund Frank, KCVO
Grugeon, Sir John Drury, Kt.
Grylls, Sir (William) Michael (John), Kt., MP
Guinness, Sir Alec, Kt., CBE
Guinness, Sir Howard Christian Sheldon, Kt., VRD
Guinness, Sir Kenelm Ernest Lee, Bt. (1867)
Guise, Sir John Grant, Bt. (1783)
Gujadhur, Sir Radhamohun, Kt., CMG
Gull, Sir Rupert William Cameron, Bt. (1872)
Gunn, Prof. Sir John Currie, Kt., CBE
Gunn, Sir William Archer, KBE, CMG
†Gunning, Sir Charles Theodore, Bt. (1778)
Gunston, Sir John Wellesley, Bt. (1938)
Guthrie, Gen. Sir Charles Ronald Llewelyn, KCB, LVO, OBE
Guthrie, Sir Malcolm Connop, Bt., (1936)
Guy, Gen. Sir Roland Kelvin, GCB, CBE, DSO
Habakkuk, Sir John Hrothgar, Kt., FBA
Hackett, Gen. Sir John Winthrop, GCB, CBE, DSO, MC
Hadlee, Sir Richard John, Kt., MBE
Hadley, Sir Leonard Albert, Kt.
Hadow, Sir Gordon, Kt., CMG, OBE
Hadow, Sir (Reginald) Michael, KCMG
Hague, Prof. Sir Douglas Chalmers, Kt., CBE
Halberg, Sir Murray Gordon, Kt., MBE
Hale, Prof. Sir John Rigby, Kt.
Hall, Sir Arnold Alexander, Kt., FRS, FEng.
Hall, Sir Basil Brodribb, KCB, MC, TD
Hall, Air Marshal Sir Donald Percy, KCB, CBE, AFC
Hall, Sir Douglas Basil, Bt., KCMG (s. 1687)
Hall, Sir Ernest, Kt., OBE
Hall, Sir (Frederick) John (Frank), Bt. (1923)
Hall, Sir John, Kt.
Hall, Sir John Bernard, Bt. (1919)
Hall, Sir Peter Edward, KBE, CMG
Hall, Sir Peter Reginald Frederick, Kt., CBE
Hall, Sir Robert de Zouche, KCMG
Hall, Brig. Sir William Henry, KBE, DSO, ED
Halliday, Vice-Adm. Sir Roy William, KBE, DSC
Hallinan, Sir (Adrian) Lincoln, Kt.
Halpern, Sir Ralph Mark, Kt.
Halsey, Revd Sir John Walter Brooke, Bt. (1920)
Halstead, Sir Ronald, Kt., CBE
Ham, Sir David Kenneth Rowe-, GBE
Hambling, Sir (Herbert) Hugh, Bt. (1924)
Hamburger, Sir Sidney Cyril, Kt., CBE
Hamer, Hon. Sir Rupert James, KCMG, ED

Hamill, Sir Patrick, Kt., QPM
Hamilton, Sir Edward Sydney, Bt. (1776 and 1819)
Hamilton, Sir James Arnot, KCB, MBE, FEng.
Hamilton, Adm. Sir John Graham, GBE, CB
Hamilton, Sir Malcolm William Bruce Stirling-, Bt. (s. 1673)
Hamilton, Sir Michael Aubrey, Kt.
Hamilton, Sir (Robert Charles) Richard Caradoc, Bt. (s. 1646)
Hammett, Hon. Sir Clifford James, Kt.
Hammick, Sir Stephen George, Bt. (1834)
Hampshire, Sir Stuart Newton, Kt., FBA
Hanbury, Sir John Capel, Kt., CBE
Hancock, Sir David John Stowell, KCB
Hancock, Air Marshal Sir Valston Eldridge, KBE, CB, DFC
Hand, Most Revd Geoffrey David, KBE
Handley, Sir David John Davenport-, Kt., OBE
Hanham, Sir Michael William, Bt., DFC (1667)
Hanley, Sir Michael Bowen, KCB
Hanmer, Sir John Wyndham Edward, Bt. (1774)
Hannam, Sir John Gordon, Kt., MP
Hannay, Sir David Hugh Alexander, KCMG
Hanson, Sir Anthony Leslie Oswald, Bt. (1887)
Hanson, Sir (Charles) John, Bt. (1918)
Hardcastle, Sir Alan John, Kt.
Harders, Sir Clarence Waldemar, Kt., OBE
Hardie, Sir Charles Edgar Mathewes, Kt., CBE
Hardie, Sir Douglas Fleming, Kt., CBE
Harding, Sir Christopher George Francis, Kt.
Harding, Sir George William, KCMG, CVO
Harding, Marshal of the Royal Air Force Sir Peter Robin, GCB
Harding, Sir Roy Pollard, Kt., CBE
Hardinge, Sir Robert Arnold, Bt. (1801)
Hardman, Sir Henry, KCB
Hardy, Sir David William, Kt.
Hardy, Sir James Gilbert, Kt., OBE
Hardy, Sir Rupert John, Bt. (1876)
†Hare, Sir Philip Leigh, Bt. (1818)
Harford, Sir James Dundas, KBE, CMG
Harford, Sir (John) Timothy, Bt. (1934)
Hargroves, Brig. Sir Robert Louis, Kt., CBE
Harington, Gen. Sir Charles Henry Pepys, GCB, CBE, DSO, MC
Harington, Sir Nicholas John, Bt. (1611)
Harland, Air Marshal Sir Reginald Edward Wynyard, KBE, CB
Harman, Gen. Sir Jack Wentworth, GCB, OBE, MC

Harman, Hon. Sir Jeremiah LeRoy, Kt.
Harmer, Sir Frederic Evelyn, Kt., CMG
Harmsworth, Sir Hildebrand Harold, Bt. (1922)
Harpham, Sir William, KBE, CMG
Harris, Prof. Sir Alan James, Kt., CBE, FEng.
Harris, Sir Anthony Kyrle Travers, Bt. (1953)
Harris, Prof. Sir Charles Herbert Stuart-, Kt., CBE, MD
Harris, Prof. Sir Henry, Kt., FRCP, FRCPath., FRS
Harris, Lt.-Gen. Sir Ian Cecil, KBE, CB, DSO
Harris, Sir Jack Wolfred Ashford, Bt. (1932)
Harris, Air Marshal Sir John Hulme, KCB, CBE
Harris, Sir Philip Charles, Kt.
Harris, Sir Ronald Montague Joseph, KCVO, CB
Harris, Sir William Gordon, KBE, CB, FEng.
Harrison, Prof. Sir Donald Frederick Norris, Kt., FRCS
Harrison, Sir Ernest Thomas, Kt., OBE
Harrison, Sir Francis Alexander Lyle, Kt., MBE, QC
Harrison, Surgeon Vice-Adm. Sir John Albert Bews, KBE
Harrison, Hon. Sir (John) Richard, Kt., ED
Harrison, Hon. Sir Michael Guy Vicat, Kt.
Harrison, Sir Michael James Harwood, Bt. (1961)
Harrison, Prof. Sir Richard John, Kt., FRS
Harrison, Sir (Robert) Colin, Bt. (1922)
Harrop, Sir Peter John, KCB
Hartley, Air Marshal Sir Christopher Harold, KCB, CBE, DFC, AFC
Hartley, Sir Frank, Kt., CBE, Ph.D.
Hartopp, Sir John Edmund Cradock-, Bt. (1796)
Hartwell, Sir Brodrick William Charles Elwin, Bt. (1805)
Harvey, Sir Charles Richard Musgrave, Bt. (1933)
Haskard, Sir Cosmo Dugal Patrick Thomas, KCMG, MBE
Haslam, Hon. Sir Alec Leslie, Kt.
Haslam, Rear-Adm. Sir David William, KBE, CB
Hassan, Sir Joshua Abraham, GBE, KCMG, LVO, QC
Hassett, Gen. Sir Francis George, KBE, CB, DSO, MVO
Hastings, Sir Stephen Lewis Edmonstone, Kt., MC
Hatty, Hon. Sir Cyril James, Kt.
Haughton, Sir James L., Kt., CBE, QPM
Havelock, Sir Wilfred Bowen, Kt.
Hawkins, Sir Arthur Ernest, Kt.

†Hawkins, Sir Howard Caesar, Bt. (1778)
Hawkins, Sir Paul Lancelot, Kt., TD
Hawley, Sir Donald Frederick, KCMG, MBE
†Hawley, Sir Henry Nicholas, Bt. (1795)
Haworth, Sir Philip, Bt. (1911)
Hawthorne, *Prof.* Sir William Rede, Kt., CBE, SC.D., FRS, FEng.
Hay, Sir David Osborne, Kt., CBE, DSO
Hay, Sir David Russell, Kt., CBE, FRCP, MD
Hay, Sir Hamish Grenfell, Kt.
Hay, Sir James Brian Dalrymple-, Bt. (1798)
†Hay, Sir John Erroll Audley, Bt. (s. 1663)
†Hay, Sir Ronald Frederick Hamilton, Bt. (s. 1703)
Haydon, Sir Walter Robert, KCMG
Hayes, Sir Brian David, GCB
Hayes, Sir Claude James, KCMG
Hayes, *Vice-Adm.* Sir John Osier Chattock, KCB, OBE
Hayr, *Air Marshal* Sir Kenneth William, KCB, KBE, AFC
Hayter, Sir William Goodenough, KCMG
Hayward, Sir Anthony William Byrd, Kt.
Hayward, Sir Jack Arnold, Kt., OBE
Hayward, Sir Richard Arthur, Kt., CBE
Haywood, Sir Harold, KCVO, OBE
Head, Sir Francis David Somerville, Bt. (1838)
Healey, Sir Charles Edward Chadwyck-, Bt. (1919)
Heap, Sir Desmond, Kt.
Heath, *Rt. Hon.* Sir Edward Richard George, KG, MBE, MP
Heath, Sir Mark Evelyn, KCVO, CMG
Heath, *Air Marshal* Sir Maurice Lionel, KBE, CB, CVO
Heathcote, *Brig.* Sir Gilbert Simon, Bt., CBE (1733)
Heathcote, Sir Michael Perryman, Bt. (1733)
Heatley, Sir Peter, Kt., CBE
Heaton, Sir Yvo Robert Henniker-, Bt. (1912)
Heiser, Sir Terence Michael, GCB
Hele, Sir Ivor Thomas Henry, Kt., CBE
Hellaby, Sir (Frederick Reed) Alan, Kt.
Henderson, Sir Denys Hartley, Kt.
Henderson, Sir (John) Nicholas, GCMG, KCVO
Henderson, Sir William MacGregor, Kt., D.SC., FRS
Henley, Sir Douglas Owen, KCB
Henley, *Rear-Adm.* Sir Joseph Charles Cameron, KCVO, CB
Hennessy, Sir James Patrick Ivan, KBE, CMG
Hennessy, Sir John Wyndham Pope-, Kt., CBE, FBA, FSA

†Henniker, Sir Adrian Chandos, Bt. (1813)
Henry, Sir Denis Aynsley, Kt., OBE, QC
Henry, *Rt. Hon.* Denis Robert Maurice, Kt.
Henry, *Hon.* Sir Geoffrey Arama, KBE
Henry, Sir James Holmes, Bt., CMG, MC, TD, QC (1923)
Henry, *Hon.* Sir Trevor Ernest, Kt.
Hepburn, Sir John Alastair Trant Kidd Buchan-, Bt. (1815)
Herbecq, Sir John Edward, KCB
Herbert, *Adm.* Sir Peter Geoffrey Marshall, KCB, OBE
Hermon, Sir John Charles, Kt., OBE, QPM
Heron, Sir Conrad Frederick, KCB, OBE
Herries, Sir Michael Alexander Robert Young-, Kt., OBE, MC
Hervey, Sir Roger Blaise Ramsay, KCVO, CMG
Heseltine, *Rt. Hon.* Sir William Frederick Payne, GCB, GCVO
Hetherington, Sir Arthur Ford, Kt., DSC, FEng.
Hetherington, Sir Thomas Chalmers, KCB, CBE, TD, QC
Heward, *Air Chief Marshal* Sir Anthony Wilkinson, KCB, OBE, DFC, AFC
Hewetson, Sir Christopher Raynor, Kt., TD
Hewett, Sir Peter John Smithson, Bt., MM (1813)
Hewitt, Sir (Cyrus) Lenox (Simson), Kt., OBE
Hewitt, Sir Nicholas Charles Joseph, Bt. (1921)
†Heygate, Sir Richard John Gage, Bt. (1831)
Heyman, Sir Horace William, Kt.
Heywood, Sir Peter, Bt. (1838)
Hezlet, *Vice-Adm.* Sir Arthur Richard, KBE, CB, DSO, DSC
Hibbert, Sir Jack, KCB
Hibbert, Sir Reginald Alfred, GCMG
Hickey, Sir Justin, Kt.
Hickman, Sir (Richard) Glenn, Bt. (1903)
Hidden, *Hon.* Sir Anthony Brian, Kt.
Hielscher, Sir Leo Arthur, Kt.
Higgins, Sir Christopher Thomas, Kt.
Higgins, *Rt. Hon.* John Patrick Basil (Eoin), Kt.
Higgins, *Rt. Hon.* Sir Terence Langley, KBE, MP
Higginson, Sir Gordon Robert, Kt., PH.D., FEng.
Higgs, Sir (John) Michael (Clifford), Kt.
Hildyard, Sir David Henry Thoroton, KCMG, DFC
Hill, Sir Alexander Rodger Erskine-, Bt. (1945)
Hill, Sir Arthur Alfred, Kt., CBE
Hill, Sir Brian John, Kt.
Hill, Sir James Frederick, Bt. (1917)

Hill, Sir John McGregor, Kt., PH.D., FEng.
Hill, Sir John Maxwell, Kt., CBE, DFC
†Hill, Sir John Rowley, Bt. (I. 1779)
Hill, *Vice-Adm.* Sir Robert Charles Finch, KBE
Hillary, Sir Edmund, KBE
Hillhouse, Sir (Robert) Russell, KCB
Hills, Sir Graham John, Kt.
Hilton, *Col.* Sir Peter, KCVO, MC
Himsworth, Sir Harold Percival, KCB, MD, FRS
Hine, *Air Chief Marshal* Sir Patrick Bardon, GCB, GBE
Hines, Sir Colin Joseph, Kt., OBE
Hinsley, *Prof.* Sir Francis Harry, Kt., OBE, FBA
Hirsch, *Prof.* Sir Peter Bernhard, Kt., PH.D., FRS
Hirst, *Rt. Hon.* Sir David Cozens-Hardy, Kt.
Hirst, Sir Michael William, Kt.
Hoare, Sir Peter Richard David, Bt. (1786)
Hoare, Sir Timothy Edward Charles, Bt. (I. 1784)
Hobart, Sir John Vere, Bt. (1914)
Hobday, Sir Gordon Ivan, Kt.
Hobhouse, Sir Charles John Spinney, Bt. (1812)
Hobhouse, *Rt. Hon.* Sir John Stewart, Kt.
Hockaday, Sir Arthur Patrick, KCB, CMG
Hockley, *Gen.* Sir Anthony Heritage Farrar-, GBE, KCB, DSO, MC
Hodge, Sir John Rowland, Bt., MBE (1921)
Hodge, Sir Julian Stephen Alfred, Kt.
Hodges, *Air Chief Marshal* Sir Lewis MacDonald, KCB, CBE, DSO, DFC
Hodgkin, *Prof.* Sir Alan Lloyd, OM, KBE, FRS, SC.D.
Hodgkin, Sir Gordon Howard Eliot, Kt., CBE
Hodgkinson, *Air Chief Marshal* Sir (William) Derek, KCB, CBE, DFC, AFC
Hodgson, Sir Maurice Arthur Eric, Kt., FEng.
Hodgson, *Hon.* Sir (Walter) Derek (Thornley), Kt.
Hodson, Sir Michael Robin Adderley, Bt. (I. 1789)
Hoffenberg, *Prof.* Sir Raymond, KBE
Hoffman, *Rt. Hon.* Sir Leonard Hubert, Kt.
Hogg, *Maj.* Sir Arthur Ramsay, Bt., MBE (1846)
Hogg, Sir Christopher Anthony, Kt.
Hogg, Sir Edward William Lindsay-, Bt. (1905)
Hogg, *Vice-Adm.* Sir Ian Leslie Trower, KCB, DSC
Hogg, Sir John Nicholson, Kt., TD
Holcroft, Sir Peter George Culcheth, Bt. (1921)
Holden, Sir David Charles Beresford, KBE, CB, ERD
Holden, Sir Edward, Bt. (1893)

Holden, Sir John David, Bt. (1919)
Holder, Sir John Henry, Bt. (1898)
Holder, *Air Marshal* Sir Paul Davie, KBE, CB, DSO, DFC, Ph.D.
Holderness, Sir Richard William, Bt. (1920)
Holdsworth, Sir (George) Trevor, Kt.
Holland, *Hon.* Sir Christopher John, Kt.
Holland, Sir Clifton Vaughan, Kt.
Holland, Sir Geoffrey, KCB
Holland, Sir Guy (Hope), Bt. (1917)
Holland, Sir Kenneth Lawrence, Kt., CBE, QFSM
Holland, Sir Philip Welsby, Kt.
Holliday, *Prof.* Sir Frederick George Thomas, Kt., CBE, FRSE
Hollings, *Hon.* Sir (Alfred) Kenneth, Kt., MC
Hollis, *Hon.* Sir Anthony Barnard, Kt.
Hollom, Sir Jasper Quintus, KBE
Holloway, *Hon.* Sir Barry Blyth, KBE
Holm, Sir Carl Henry, Kt., OBE
Holmes, *Prof.* Sir Frank Wakefield, Kt.
Holmes, Sir Maurice Andrew, Kt.
Holmes, Sir Peter Fenwick, Kt., MC
Holroyd, *Air Marshal* Sir Frank Martyn, KBE, CB
Holt, *Prof.* Sir James Clarke, Kt.
Home, Sir William Dundas, Bt. (s. 1671)
Honeycombe, *Prof.* Sir Robert William Kerr, Kt., FRS, FEng.
Honywood, Sir Filmer Courtenay William, Bt. (1660)
Hood, Sir Alexander William Fuller-Acland-, Bt. (1806)
Hood, Sir Harold Joseph, Bt., TD (1922)
Hookway, Sir Harry Thurston, Kt.
Hoole, Sir Arthur Hugh, Kt.
Hooper, Sir Leonard James, KCMG, CBE
Hope, Sir (Charles) Peter, KCMG, TD
Hope, Sir John Carl Alexander, Bt. (s. 1628)
Hope, Sir Robert Holms-Kerr, Bt. (1932)
Hopkin, Sir David Armand, Kt.
Hopkin, Sir (William Aylsham) Bryan, Kt., CBE
Hopkins, Sir Anthony Philip, Kt., CBE
Hopkins, Sir James Sidney Rawdon Scott-, Kt., MEP
Hordern, Sir Michael Murray, Kt., CBE
Hordern, *Rt. Hon.* Sir Peter Maudslay, Kt., MP
Horlick, *Vice-Adm.* Sir Edwin John, KBE, FEng.
Horlick, Sir John James Macdonald, Bt. (1914)
Hornby, Sir Derek Peter, Kt.
Hornby, Sir Simon Michael, Kt.
Horne, Sir Alan Gray Antony, Bt. (1929)
Horsfall, Sir John Musgrave, Bt., MC, TD (1909)

Horsley, *Air Marshal* Sir (Beresford) Peter (Torrington), KCB, CBE, MVO, AFC
Hort, Sir James Fenton, Bt. (1767)
Hoskyns, Sir Benedict Leigh, Bt. (1676)
Hoskyns, Sir John Austin Hungerford Leigh, Kt.
Hotung, Sir Joseph Edward, Kt.
Houghton, Sir John Theodore, Kt., CBE, FRS
†Houldsworth, Sir Richard Thomas Reginald, Bt. (1887)
Hounsfield, Sir Godfrey Newbold, Kt., CBE
House, *Lt.-Gen.* Sir David George, GCB, KCVO, CBE, MC
Houssemayne du Boulay, Sir Roger William, KCVO, CMG
Howard, Sir (Hamilton) Edward de Coucey, Bt., GBE (1955)
Howard, *Prof.* Sir Michael Eliot, Kt., CBE, MC
Howard, *Maj.-Gen.* Lord Michael Fitzalan-, GCVO, CB, CBE, MC
Howell, Sir Ralph Frederic, Kt., MP
Howells, Sir Eric Waldo Benjamin, Kt., CBE
Howard, Sir Walter Stewart, Kt., MBE
Howie, Sir James William, Kt., MD
Howlett, *Gen.* Sir Geoffrey Hugh Whitby, KBE, MC
Hoyle, *Prof.* Sir Fred, Kt., FRS
Hoyos, *Hon.* Sir Fabriciano Alexander, Kt.
Huckle, Sir (Henry) George, Kt., OBE
Huddie, Sir David Patrick, Kt., FEng.
Hudleston, *Air Chief Marshal* Sir Edmund Cuthbert, GCB, CBE
Hudson, Sir Havelock Henry Trevor, Kt.
Hudson, *Lt.-Gen.* Sir Peter, KCB, CBE
Huggins, *Hon.* Sir Alan Armstrong, Kt.
Hugh-Jones, Sir Wynn Normington, Kt., MVO
Hughes, Sir David Collingwood, Bt. (1773)
Hughes, *Prof.* Sir Edward Stuart Reginald, Kt., CBE
Hughes, Sir Jack William, Kt.
Hughes, *Air Marshal* Sir (Sidney Weetman) Rochford, KCB, CBE, AFC
Hughes, Sir Trevor Denby Lloyd-, Kt.
Hughes, Sir Trevor Poulton, KCB
Hugo, *Lt.-Col.* Sir John Mandeville, KCVO, OBE
Hull, *Prof.* Sir David, Kt.
Hulse, Sir (Hamilton) Westrow, Bt. (1739)
Hulton, Sir Geoffrey Alan, Bt. (1905)
Hume, Sir Alan Blyth, Kt., CB
Humphreys, Sir Olliver William, Kt., CBE
Humphreys, Sir (Raymond Evelyn) Myles, Kt.
Hunn, Sir Jack Kent, Kt., CMG
Hunt, Sir David Wathen Stather, KCMG, OBE

Hunt, Sir John Leonard, Kt., MP
Hunt, *Adm.* Sir Nicholas John Streynsham, GCB, LVO
Hunt, Sir Rex Masterman, Kt., CMG
Hunt, Sir Robert Frederick, Kt., CBE, FEng.
Hunter, *Hon.* Sir Alexander Albert, KBE
Hunter, Sir Ian Bruce Hope, Kt., MBE
Hurrell, Sir Anthony Gerald, KCVO, CMG
Hutchinson, *Hon.* Sir Ross, Kt., DFC
Hutchison, *Lt.-Cdr.* Sir (George) Ian Clark, Kt., RN
Hutchison, *Hon.* Sir Michael, Kt.
Hutchison, Sir Peter, Bt., CBE (1939)
Hutchison, Sir Peter Craft, Bt. (1956)
Hutton, *Rt. Hon.* Sir (James) Brian Edward, Kt.
Huxley, *Prof.* Sir Andrew Fielding, Kt., OM, FRS
Huxtable, *Gen.* Sir Charles Richard, KCB, CBE
Hyatali, *Hon.* Sir Isaac Emanuel, Kt.
Hyslop, Sir Robert John (Robin) Maxwell-, Kt.
Ibbs, Sir (John) Robin, KBE
Ihaka, *Ven.* Sir Kingi Matutaera, Kt., MBE
Imbert, Sir Peter Michael, Kt., QPM
Imray, Sir Colin Henry, KBE, CMG
Inch, Sir John Ritchie, Kt., CVO, CBE
Inge, *Gen.* Sir Peter Anthony, GCB
Ingham, Sir Bernard, Kt.
Ingilby, Sir Thomas Colvin William, Bt. (1866)
Inglis, Sir Brian Scott, Kt.
Inglis of Glencorse, Sir Roderick John, Bt. (s. 1703)
Ingram, Sir James Herbert Charles, Bt. (1893)
Inkin, Sir Geoffrey David, Kt., OBE
†Innes, Sir David Charles Kenneth Gordon, Bt. (NS 1686)
Innes of Edingight, Sir Malcolm Rognvald, KCVO
Innes, Sir Peter Alexander Berowald, Bt. (s. 1628)
Inniss, *Hon.* Sir Clifford de Lisle, Kt.
Irish, Sir Ronald Arthur, Kt., OBE
Irvine, *Dr* Sir Robin Orlando Hamilton, Kt.
Irving, Sir Charles Graham, Kt.
Isaacs, Sir Kendal George Lamon, KCMG, CBE, QC
Isham, Sir Ian Vere Gyles, Bt. (1627)
Jack, *Hon.* Sir Alieu Sulayman, Kt.
Jack, Sir David, Kt., CBE, FRS, FRSE
Jack, Sir David Emmanuel, GCMG, MBE
Jackson, *Air Chief Marshal* Sir Brendan James, GCB
Jackson, Sir (John) Edward, KCMG
Jackson, *Hon.* Sir Lawrence Walter, KCMG
Jackson, Sir Michael Roland, Bt. (1902)
Jackson, Sir Nicholas Fane St George, Bt. (1913)
Jackson, Sir Robert, Bt. (1815)

Jackson, *Gen.* Sir William Godfrey Fothergill, GBE, KCB, MC

Jackson, Sir William Thomas, Bt. (1869)

Jacob, Sir Isaac Hai, Kt., QC

Jacob, *Hon.* Sir Robert Raphael Hayim (Robin), Kt.

Jacobi, *Dr* Sir James Edward, Kt., OBE

Jacobs, Sir David Anthony, Kt.

Jacobs, *Hon.* Sir Kenneth Sydney, KBE

Jacobs, Sir Piers, KBE

Jacobs, Sir Wilfred Ebenezer, GCMG, GCVO, OBE, QC

Jacomb, Sir Martin Wakefield, Kt.

Jaffray, Sir William Otho, Bt. (1892)

Jakeway, Sir (Francis) Derek, KCMG, OBE

James, Sir Cynlais Morgan, KCMG

James, Sir Gerard Bowes Kingston, Bt. (1823)

James, Sir Robert Vidal Rhodes, Kt.

James, Sir Stanislaus Anthony, GCMG, OBE

Jamieson, *Air Marshal* Sir David Ewan, KBE, CB

Janion, *Rear-Adm.* Sir Hugh Penderel, KCVO

Jansen, Sir Ross Malcolm, KBE

Jardine, Sir Andrew Colin Douglas, Bt. (1916)

Jardine, *Maj.* Sir (Andrew) Rupert (John) Buchanan-, Bt., MC (1885)

Jardine of Applegirth, Sir Alexander Maule, Bt. (s. 1672)

Jarratt, Sir Alexander Anthony, Kt., CB

Jarrett, Sir Clifford George, KBE, CB

Jawara, *Hon.* Sir Dawda Kairaba, Kt.

Jay, Sir Antony Rupert, Kt., CVO

Jeewoolall, Sir Ramesh, Kt.

Jefferson, Sir George Rowland, Kt., CBE, FEng.

Jefferson, Sir Mervyn Stewart Dunnington-, Bt. (1958)

Jeffries, *Hon.* Sir John Francis, Kt.

Jehangir, Sir Hirji, Bt. (1908)

Jejeebhoy, Sir Rustom, Bt. (1857)

Jellicoe, Sir Geoffrey Alan, Kt., CBE, FRIBA

Jenkins, Sir Brian Garton, GBE

Jenkins, Sir Michael Romilly Heald, KCMG

Jenkins, Sir Owain Trevor, Kt.

Jenkinson, Sir John Banks, Bt. (1661)

Jenks, Sir Richard Atherley, Bt. (1932)

Jennings, Sir Albert Victor, Kt.

Jennings, Sir Raymond Winter, Kt., QC

Jennings, *Prof.* Sir Robert Yewdall, Kt., QC

Jephcott, Sir (John) Anthony, Bt. (1962)

Jessel, Sir Charles John, Bt. (1883)

Jewkes, Sir Gordon Wesley, KCMG

Joel, *Hon.* Sir Asher Alexander, KBE

John, Sir Rupert Godfrey, Kt.

†Johnson, Sir Allen Antony Wynn, Bt. (1818)

Johnson, *Rt. Hon.* Sir David Powell Croom-, Kt., DSC, VRD

Johnson, *Gen.* Sir Garry Dene, KCB, OBE, MC

Johnson, Sir John Rodney, KCMG

Johnson, Sir Peter Colpoys Paley, Bt. (1755)

Johnson, *Hon.* Sir Robert Lionel, Kt.

Johnson, Sir Ronald Ernest Charles, Kt., CB

Johnston, Sir Alexander, GCB, KBE

Johnston, Sir (David) Russell, Kt., MP

Johnston, Sir John Baines, GCMG, KCVO

Johnston, *Lt.-Col.* Sir John Frederick Dame, GCVO, MC

Johnston, *Lt.-Gen.* Sir Maurice Robert, KCB, OBE

Johnston, Sir Thomas Alexander, Bt. (s. 1626)

Johnstone, Sir Frederic Allan George, Bt. (s. 1700)

Johnstone, Sir (John) Raymond, Kt., CBE

Jolliffe, Sir Anthony Stuart, GBE

Jones, *Gen.* Sir (Charles) Edward Webb, KCB, CBE

Jones, Sir Christopher Lawrence-, Bt. (1831)

Jones, Sir David Akers-, KBE, CMG

Jones, *Air Marshal* Sir Edward Gordon, KCB, CBE, DSO, DFC

Jones, Sir (Edward) Martin Furnival, Kt., CBE

Jones, Sir Ewart Ray Herbert, Kt., D.SC., Ph.D., FRS

Jones, Sir Francis Avery, Kt., CBE, FRCP

Jones, Sir Gordon Pearce, Kt.

Jones, Sir Harry Ernest, Kt., CBE

Jones, Sir James Duncan, KCB

Jones, Sir (John) Derek Alun-, Kt.

Jones, Sir John Henry Harvey-, Kt., MBE

Jones, Sir (John) Kenneth (Trevor), Kt., CBE, QC

Jones, Sir John Lewis, KCB, CMG

Jones, Sir John Prichard-, Bt. (1910)

Jones, Sir Keith Stephen, Kt.

Jones, *Hon.* Sir Kenneth George Illtyd, Kt.

Jones, *Air Marshal* Sir Laurence Alfred, KCB, CB, AFC

Jones, Sir (Owen) Trevor, Kt.

Jones, Sir (Peter) Hugh (Jefferd) Lloyd-, Kt.

Jones, Sir Richard Anthony Lloyd, KCB

Jones, Sir Robert Edward, Kt.

Jones, Sir Simon Warley Frederick Benton, Bt. (1919)

Jones, Sir (Thomas) Philip, Kt., CB

Jones, Sir (William) Emrys, Kt.

Jones, *Hon.* Sir William Lloyd Mars-, Kt., MBE

Jordan, *Air Marshal* Sir Richard Bowen, KCB, DFC

Joughin, Sir Michael, Kt., CBE

Jowitt, *Hon.* Sir Edwin Frank, Kt.

Judge, *Hon.* Sir Igor, Kt.

Jugnauth, *Rt. Hon.* Sir Anerood, KCMG, QC

Jungius, *Vice-Adm.* Sir James George, KBE

Junor, Sir John Donald Brown, Kt.

Jupp, *Hon.* Sir Kenneth Graham, Kt., MC

Kaberry, *Hon.* Sir Christopher Donald, Bt. (1960)

Kadoorie, Sir Horace, CBE

Kalo, Sir Kwamala, Kt., MBE

Kan Yuet-Keung, Sir, GBE

Kapi, *Hon.* Sir Mari, Kt., CBE

Katsina, The Emir of, KBE, CMG

Katz, Sir Bernard, Kt., FRS

Kavali, Sir Thomas, Kt., OBE

Kawharu, *Prof.* Sir Ian Hugh, Kt.

Kay, *Prof.* Sir Andrew Watt, Kt.

Kay, *Hon.* Sir John William, Kt.

Kaye, Sir David Alexander Gordon, Bt. (1923)

Kaye, Sir Emmanuel, Kt., CBE

Kaye, Sir John Phillip Lister Lister-, Bt. (1812)

Keane, Sir Richard Michael, Bt. (1801)

Keating, Sir Edgar Mayne, Kt., CBE

Keeble, Sir (Herbert Ben) Curtis, GCMG

Keith, *Prof.* Sir James, KBE

Kellett, Sir Brian Smith, Kt.

Kellett, Sir Stanley Charles, Bt. (1801)

Kelly, *Rt. Hon.* Sir (John William) Basil, Kt.

Kelly, Sir William Theodore, Kt., OBE

Kemball, *Air Marshal* Sir (Richard) John, KCB, CBE

Kemp, Sir (Edward) Peter, KCB

Kendrew, Sir John Cowdery, Kt., CBE, SC.D., FRS

Kenilorea, *Rt. Hon.* Sir Peter, KBE

Kennard, *Lt.-Col.* Sir George Arnold Ford, Bt. (1891)

Kennaway, Sir John Lawrence, Bt. (1791)

Kennedy, Sir Clyde David Allen, Kt.

Kennedy, Sir Francis, KCMG, CBE

Kennedy, *Hon.* Sir Ian Alexander, Kt.

†Kennedy, Sir Michael Edward, Bt., (1836)

Kennedy, *Rt. Hon.* Sir Paul Joseph Morrow, Kt.

Kennedy, *Air Chief Marshal* Sir Thomas Lawrie, GCB, AFC

Kennedy-Good, Sir John, KBE

Kenny, Sir Anthony John Patrick, Kt., D.Phil., D.Litt., FBA

Kenny, *Gen.* Sir Brian Leslie Graham, GCB, CBE

Kent, Sir Harold Simcox, GCB, QC

Kenyon, Sir George Henry, Kt.

Kermode, Sir (John) Frank, Kt., FBA

Kermode, Sir Ronald Graham Quale, KBE

Kerr, *Hon.* Sir Brian Francis, Kt.

Kerr, *Adm.* Sir John Beverley, GCB

Kerr, Sir John Olav, KCMG

Kerr, *Rt. Hon.* Sir Michael Robert Emanuel, Kt.

Kerruish, Sir (Henry) Charles, Kt., OBE

Kerry, Sir Michael James, KCB, QC

Kershaw, Sir (John) Anthony, Kt., MC

Keswick, Sir John Chippendale Lindley, Kt.

Kidd, Sir Robert Hill, KBE, CB

Kidu, Hon. Sir Buri (William), Kt.

Kikau, Ratu Sir Jone Latianara, KBE

Kiki, Hon. Sir (Albert) Maori, KBE

Kilfedder, Sir James Alexander, Kt., MP

Killen, Hon. Denis James, KCMG

Killick, Sir John Edward, GCMG

Kilpatrick, Prof. Sir Robert, Kt., CBE

Kimber, Sir Charles Dixon, Bt. (1904)

Kinahan, Sir Robert George Caldwell, Kt., ERD

King, Sir Albert, Kt., OBE

King, Gen. Sir Frank Douglas, GCB, MBE

King, Sir John Christopher, Bt. (1888)

King, Vice-Adm. Sir Norman Ross Dutton, KBE

King, Sir Richard Brian Meredith, KCB, MC

King, Sir Wayne Alexander, Bt. (1815)

Kingman, Prof. Sir John Frank Charles, Kt., FRS

Kingsland, Sir Richard, Kt., CBE, DFC

Kingsley, Sir Patrick Graham Toler, KCVO

Kinloch, Sir David, Bt. (s. 1686)

†Kinloch, Sir David Oliphant, Bt. (1873)

Kipalan, Sir Albert, Kt.

Kirby, Hon. Sir Richard Clarence, Kt.

Kirkpatrick, Sir Ivone Elliott, Bt. (s. 1685)

Kirkwood, Hon. Sir Andrew Tristram Hammett, Kt.

Kirwan, Sir (Archibald) Laurence Patrick, KCMG, TD

Kitcatt, Sir Peter Julian, Kt., CB

Kitson, Gen. Sir Frank Edward, GBE, KCB, MC

Kitson, Sir Timothy Peter Geoffrey, Kt.

Kitto, Rt. Hon. Sir Frank Walters, KBE

Kleinwort, Sir Kenneth Drake, Bt. (1909)

Klug, Sir Aaron, Kt.

Knight, Sir Allan Walton, Kt., CMG

Knight, Sir Arthur William, Kt.

Knight, Sir Harold Murray, KBE, DSC

Knight, Air Chief Marshal Sir Michael William Patrick, KCB, AFC

Knill, Sir John Kenelm Stuart, Bt. (1893)

Knott, Sir John Laurence, Kt., CBE

Knowles, Sir Charles Francis, Bt. (1765)

Knowles, Sir Leonard Joseph, Kt., CBE

Knowles, Sir Richard Marchant, Kt.

Knox, Sir Bryce Muir, KCVO, MC, TD

Knox, Sir David Laidlaw, Kt., MP

Knox, Hon. Sir John Leonard, Kt.

Knox, Hon. Sir William Edward, Kt.

Koraea, Sir Thomas, Kt.

Kornberg, Prof. Sir Hans Leo, Kt., D.SC., SC.D., Ph.D., FRS

Korowi, Sir Wiwa, GCMG

Krusin, Sir Stanley Marks, Kt., CB

Kulukundis, Sir Elias George (Eddie), Kt., OBE

Kurongku, Most. Revd Peter, KBE

Labouchere, Sir George Peter, GBE, KCMG

Lacon, Sir Edmund Vere, Bt. (1818)

Lacy, Sir Hugh Maurice Pierce, Bt. (1921)

Lacy, Sir John Trend, Kt., CBE

Lagesen, Air Marshal Sir Philip Jacobus, KCB, DFC, AFC

Laidlaw, Sir Christophor Charles Fraser, Kt.

Laing, Sir (John) Maurice, Kt.

Laing, Sir (William) Kirby, Kt., FEng.

Lake, Sir (Atwell) Graham, Bt. (1711)

Laker, Sir Frederick Alfred, Kt.

Lakin, Sir Michael, Bt. (1909)

Laking, Sir George Robert, KCMG

Lamb, Sir Albert (Larry), Kt.

Lamb, Sir Albert Thomas, KBE, CMG, DFC

Lambert, Sir Anthony Edward, KCMG

Lambert, Sir Edward Thomas, KBE, CVO

Lambert, Sir John Henry, KCVO, CMG

†Lambert, Sir Peter John Biddulph, Bt. (1711)

Lampl, Sir Frank William, Kt.

Landale, Sir David William Neil, KCVO

Landau, Sir Dennis Marcus, Kt.

Lane, Sir David William Stennis Stuart, Kt.

Lang, Lt.-Gen. Sir Derek Boileau, KCB, DSO, MC

Langham, Sir James Michael, Bt. (1660)

Langley, Maj.-Gen. Sir Henry Desmond Allen, KCVO, MBE

Langrishe, Sir Hercules Ralph Hume, Bt. (I. 1777)

Lapsley, Air Marshal Sir John Hugh, KBE, CB, DFC, AFC

Lapun, Hon. Sir Paul, Kt.

Larcom, Sir (Charles) Christopher Royde, Bt. (1868)

Large, Sir Peter, Kt., CBE

Larmour, Sir Edward Noel, KCMG

Lasdun, Sir Denys Louis, Kt., CBE, FRIBA

Latey, Rt. Hon. Sir John Brinsmead, Kt., MBE

Latham, Hon. Sir David Nicholas Ramsey, Kt.

Latham, Sir Michael Anthony, Kt.

Latham, Sir Richard Thomas Paul, Bt. (1919)

Latimer, Sir (Courtenay) Robert, Kt., CBE

Latimer, Sir Graham Stanley, KBE

Laucke, Hon. Sir Condor Louis, KCMG

Lauder, Sir Piers Robert Dick-, Bt. (s. 1690)

Laughton, Sir Anthony Seymour, Kt.

Laurantus, Sir Nicholas, Kt., MBE

Laurence, Sir Peter Harold, KCMG, MC

Laurie, Sir Robert Bayley Emilius, Bt. (1834)

Lauti, Rt. Hon. Sir Toaripi, GCMG

Lavan, Hon. Sir John Martin, Kt.

Law, Adm. Sir Horace Rochfort, GCB, OBE, DSC

Lawes, Sir (John) Michael Bennet, Bt. (1882)

Lawler, Sir Peter James, Kt., OBE

Lawrence, Sir David Roland Walter, Bt. (1906)

Lawrence, Sir Guy Kempton, Kt., DSO, OBE, DFC

Lawrence, Sir Ivan John, Kt., QC, MP

Lawrence, Sir John Patrick Grosvenor, Kt., CBE

Lawrence, Sir John Waldemar, Bt., OBE (1858)

Lawrence, Sir William Fettiplace, Bt. (1867)

Laws, Hon. Sir John Grant McKenzie, Kt.

Lawson, Sir Christopher Donald, Kt.

Lawson, Col. Sir John Charles Arthur Digby, Bt., DSO, MC (1900)

Lawson, Sir John Philip Howard-, Bt. (1841)

Lawson, Hon. Sir Neil, Kt.

Lawson, Gen. Sir Richard George, KCB, DSO, OBE

Lawton, Prof. Sir Frank Ewart, Kt.

Lawton, Rt. Hon. Sir Frederick Horace, Kt.

Layard, Vice-Adm. Sir Michael Henry Gordon, KCB, CBE

Layden, Sir John (Jack), Kt.

Layfield, Sir Frank Henry Burland Willoughby, Kt., QC

Lazarus, Sir Peter Esmond, KCB

Lea, Vice-Adm. Sir John Stuart Crosbie, KBE

Lea, Sir Thomas William, Bt. (1892)

Leach, Admiral of the Fleet Sir Henry Conyers, GCB

Leach, Sir Ronald George, GBE

Leahy, Sir Daniel Joseph, Kt.

Leahy, Sir John Henry Gladstone, KCMG

Learmont, Gen. Sir John Hartley, KCB, CBE

Leask, Lt.-Gen. Sir Henry Lowther Ewart Clark, KCB, DSO, OBE

Leather, Sir Edwin Hartley Cameron, KCMG, KCVO

Leaver, Sir Christopher, GBE

Le Bailly, Vice-Adm. Sir Louis Edward Stewart Holland, KBE, CB

Le Cheminant, Air Chief Marshal Sir Peter de Lacey, GBE, KCB, DFC

Lechmere, Sir Berwick Hungerford, Bt. (1818)

Ledger, Sir Frank, (Joseph Francis), Kt.

Ledwidge, Sir (William) Bernard (John), KCMG

Lee, Sir Arthur James, KBE, MC

Lee, *Air Chief Marshal* Sir David John Pryer, GBE, CB

Lee, Sir (Henry) Desmond (Pritchard), Kt.

Lee, *Brig.* Sir Leonard Henry, Kt., CBE

Lee, Sir Quo-wei, Kt., CBE

Lee, *Col.* Sir William Allison, Kt., OBE, TD

Leeds, Sir Christopher Anthony, Bt. (1812)

Lees, Sir David Bryan, Kt.

Lees, Sir Thomas Edward, Bt. (1897)

Lees, Sir Thomas Harcourt Ivor, Bt. (1804)

Lees, Sir (William) Antony Clare, Bt. (1937)

Leese, Sir John Henry Vernon, Bt. (1908)

Le Fanu, *Maj.* Sir (George) Victor (Sheridan), KCVO

le Fleming, Sir Quintin John, Bt. (1705)

Legard, Sir Charles Thomas, Bt. (1660)

Legg, Sir Thomas Stuart, KCB, QC

Leggatt, *Rt. Hon.* Sir Andrew Peter, Kt.

Leggatt, Sir Hugh Frank John, Kt.

Leggett, Sir Clarence Arthur Campbell, Kt., MBE

Leigh, Sir Geoffrey Norman, Kt.

Leigh, Sir Neville Egerton, KCVO

†Leigh, Sir Richard Henry, Bt. (1918)

Leighton, Sir Michael John Bryan, Bt. (1693)

Leitch, Sir George, KCB, OBE

Leith, Sir Andrew George Forbes-, Bt. (1923)

Le Marchant, Sir Francis Arthur, Bt. (1841)

Le Masurier, Sir Robert Hugh, Kt., DSC

Lemon, Sir (Richard) Dawnay, Kt., CBE

Leng, *Gen.* Sir Peter John Hall, KCB, MBE, MC

Lennard, *Revd* Sir Hugh Dacre Barrett-, Bt. (1801)

Leon, Sir John Ronald, Bt. (1911)

Leonard, *Revd and Rt. Hon.* Graham Douglas, KCVO

Leonard, *Hon.* Sir (Hamilton) John, Kt.

Lepping, Sir George Geria Dennis, GCMG, MBE

Le Quesne, Sir (Charles) Martin, KCMG

Le Quesne, Sir (John) Godfray, Kt., QC

Leslie, Sir Colin Alan Bettridge, Kt.

Leslie, Sir John Norman Ide, Bt. (1876)

†Leslie, Sir (Percy) Theodore, Bt. (s. 1625)

Leslie, Sir Peter Evelyn, Kt.

Lethbridge, Sir Thomas Periam Hector Noel, Bt. (1804)

Leuchars, Sir William Douglas, KBE

Leupena, Sir Tupua, GCMG, MBE

Levene, Sir Peter Keith, KBE

Lever, Sir (Tresham) Christopher Arthur Lindsay, Bt. (1911)

Levey, Sir Michael Vincent, Kt., MVO

Levine, Sir Montague Bernard, Kt.

Levinge, Sir Richard George Robin, Bt. (I. 1704)

Levy, Sir Ewart Maurice, Bt. (1913)

Lewando, Sir Jan Alfred, Kt., CBE

Lewinton, Sir Christopher, Kt.

Lewis, *Adm.* Sir Andrew Mackenzie, KCB

Lewis, Sir Kenneth, Kt.

Lewthwaite, Sir William Anthony, Bt. (1927)

Ley, Sir Francis Douglas, Bt., MBE, TD (1905)

Leyland, Sir Philip Vyvyan Naylor-, Bt. (1895)

Lickiss, Sir Michael Gillam, Kt.

Lickley, Sir Robert Lang, Kt., CBE, FEng.

Lidbury, Sir John Towersey, Kt.

Lidderdale, Sir David William Shuckburgh, KCB

Liggins, *Prof.* Sir Graham Collingwood, Kt., CBE, FRS

Lighthill, Sir (Michael) James, Kt., FRS

†Lighton, Sir Thomas Hamilton, Bt. (I. 1791)

Lim, Sir Han-Hoe, Kt., CBE

Linacre, Sir (John) Gordon (Seymour), Kt., CBE, AFC, DFM

Lincoln, Sir Anthony Handley, KCMG, CVO

Lindley, Sir Arnold Lewis George, Kt., FEng.

Lindop, Sir Norman, Kt.

Lindsay, Sir James Harvey Kincaid Stewart, Kt.

Lindsay, *Hon.* Sir John Edmund Frederic, Kt.

Lindsay, Sir Ronald Alexander, Bt., (1962)

Lintott, Sir Henry John Bevis, KCMG

Lipworth, Sir (Maurice) Sydney, Kt.

Lithgow, Sir William James, Bt. (1925)

Little, *Most Revd* Thomas Francis, KBE

Littler, Sir (James) Geoffrey, KCB

Livesay, *Adm.* Sir Michael Howard, KCB

Llewellyn, Sir Henry Morton, Bt., CBE (1922)

Llewellyn, *Lt.-Col.* Sir Michael Rowland Godfrey, Bt. (1959)

Llewelyn, Sir John Michael Dillwyn-Venables-, Bt. (1890)

Lloyd, *Rt. Hon.* Sir Anthony John Leslie, Kt.

Lloyd, Sir Ian Stewart, Kt.

Lloyd, Sir (John) Peter (Daniel), Kt.

Lloyd, Sir Nicholas Markley, Kt.

Lloyd, Sir Richard Ernest Butler, Bt. (1960)

Loader, Sir Leslie Thomas, Kt., CBE

Loane, *Most Revd* Marcus Lawrence, KBE

Lobo, Sir Rogerio Hyndman, Kt., CBE

Lock, *Cdr.* Sir (John) Duncan, Kt.

Lockhart, Sir Simon John Edward Francis Sinclair-, Bt. (s. 1636)

Loder, Sir Giles Rolls, Bt. (1887)

Lodge, Sir Thomas, Kt.

Logan, Sir Donald Arthur, KCMG

Logan, Sir Raymond Douglas, Kt.

Lokoloko, Sir Tore, GCMG, GCVO, OBE

Lombe, *Hon.* Sir Edward Christopher Evans-, Kt.

Longden, Sir Gilbert James Morley, Kt., MBE

Longland, Sir John Laurence, Kt.

Longley, Sir Norman, Kt., CBE

Loram, *Vice-Adm.* Sir David Anning, KCB, MVO

Lorimer, Sir (Thomas) Desmond, Kt.

Lousada, Sir Anthony Baruh, Kt.

Love, Sir Makere Rangiatea Ralph, Kt.

Lovell, Sir (Alfred Charles) Bernard, Kt., OBE, FRS

Lovelock, Sir Douglas Arthur, KCB

Loveridge, Sir John Henry, Kt., CBE

Loveridge, Sir John Warren, Kt.

Lovill, Sir John Roger, Kt., CBE

Low, Sir Alan Roberts, Kt.

Low, Sir James Richard Morrison-, Bt. (1908)

Lowe, *Air Chief Marshal* Sir Douglas Charles, GCB, DFC, AFC

Lowe, Sir Thomas William Gordon, Bt. (1918)

Lowry, Sir John Patrick, Kt., CBE

Lowson, Sir Ian Patrick, Bt. (1951)

Lowther, *Maj.* Sir Charles Douglas, Bt. (1824)

Loyd, Sir Francis Alfred, KCMG, OBE

Loyd, Sir Julian St John, KCVO

Lu, Sir Tseng Chi, Kt.

Lucas, Sir Cyril Edward, Kt., CMG, FRS

Lucas, Sir Thomas Edward, Bt. (1887)

Luce, *Rt Hon.* Sir Richard Napier, Kt.

Luckhoo, Sir Lionel Alfred, KCMG, CBE, QC

Lucy, Sir Edmund John William Hugh Cameron-Ramsay-Fairfax-, Bt. (1836)

Luddington, Sir Donald Collin Cumyn, KBE, CMG, CVO

Lumsden, Sir David James, Kt.

Lus, *Hon.* Sir Pita, Kt., OBE

Lush, *Hon.* Sir George Hermann, Kt.

Lushington, Sir John Richard Castleman, Bt. (1791)

Luttrell, *Col.* Sir Geoffrey Walter Fownes, KCVO, MC

Luyt, Sir Richard Edmonds, GCMG, KCVO, DCM

Lyell, *Rt. Hon.* Sir Nicholas Walter, Kt., QC, MP

Lygo, *Adm.* Sir Raymond Derek, KCB

Lyle, Sir Gavin Archibald, Bt. (1929)

Lyons, Sir Edward Houghton, Kt.

Lyons, Sir James Reginald, Kt.

Lyons, Sir John, Kt.

McAdam, Sir Ian William James, Kt., OBE

Macadam, Sir Peter, Kt.
McAlpine, Sir William Hepburn, Bt. (1918)
†Macara, Sir Hugh Kenneth, Bt. (1911)
Macartney, Sir John Barrington, Bt. (I. 1799)
McAvoy, Sir (Francis) Joseph, Kt., CBE
McCaffrey, Sir Thomas Daniel, Kt.
McCall, Sir (Charles) Patrick Home, Kt., MBE, TD
McCallum, Sir Donald Murdo, Kt., CBE, FEng.
McCamley, Sir Graham Edward, Kt., MBE
McCarthy, Rt. Hon. Sir Thaddeus Pearcey, KBE
McClellan, Col. Sir Herbert Gerard Thomas, Kt., CBE, TD
McClintock, Sir Eric Paul, Kt.
McColl, Sir Colin Hugh Verel, KCMG
McCollum, Hon. Sir William, Kt.
McConnell, Sir Robert Shean, Bt. (1900)
McCowan, Rt. Hon. Sir Anthony James Denys, Kt.
McCowan, Sir Hew Cargill, Bt. (1934)
McCrea, Prof. Sir William Hunter, Kt., FRS
McCrindle, Sir Robert Arthur, Kt.
McCullough, Hon. Sir (Iain) Charles (Robert), Kt.
McCusker, Sir James Alexander, Kt.
MacDermott, Rt. Hon. Sir John Clarke, Kt.
McDermott, Sir (Lawrence) Emmet, KBE
MacDonald, Gen. Sir Arthur Leslie, KBE, CB
McDonald, Air Chief Marshal Sir Arthur William Baynes, KCB, AFC
McDonald, Sir Duncan, Kt., CBE, FEng.
Macdonald of Sleat, Sir Ian Godfrey Bosville, Bt. (S. 1625)
Macdonald, Sir Kenneth Carmichael, KCB
Macdonald, Vice-Adm. Sir Roderick Douglas, KBE
McDonald, Sir Tom, Kt., OBE
McDonald, Hon. Sir William John Farquhar, Kt.
MacDougall, Sir (George) Donald (Alastair), Kt., CBE, FBA
McDowell, Sir Eric Wallalce, Kt., CBE
McDowell, Sir Henry McLorinan, KBE
Mace, Lt.-Gen. Sir John Airth, KBE, CB
McEwen, Sir John Roderick Hugh, Bt. (1953)
McFarland, Sir John Talbot, Bt. (1914)
Macfarlane, Sir (David) Neil, Kt.
Macfarlane, Sir George Gray, Kt., CB, FEng.
McFarlane, Sir Ian, Kt.
Macfarlane, Sir James Wright, Kt.
McGeoch, Vice-Adm. Sir Ian Lachlan Mackay, KCB, DSO, DSC
McGrath, Sir Brian Henry, KCVO
Macgregor, Sir Edwin Robert, Bt. (1828)

MacGregor of MacGregor, Sir Gregor, Bt. (1795)
McGregor, Sir Ian Alexander, Kt., CBE, FRS
MacGregor, Sir Ian Kinloch, Kt.
McGrigor, Capt. Sir Charles Edward, Bt. (1831)
McIntosh, Vice-Adm. Sir Ian Stewart, KBE, CB, DSO, DSC
McIntosh, Sir Ronald Robert Duncan, KCB
McIntyre, Sir Donald Conroy, Kt., CBE
McIntyre, Sir Meredith Alister, Kt.
McKaig, Adm. Sir (John) Rae, KCB, CBE
Mackay, Sir (George Patrick) Gordon, Kt., CBE
McKay, Sir John Andrew, Kt., CBE
Mackechnie, Sir Alistair John, Kt.
McKee, Maj. Sir (William) Cecil, Kt., ERD
McKellen, Sir Ian Murray, Kt., CBE
McKenzie, Sir Alexander, KBE
Mackenzie, Sir Alexander Alwyne Henry Charles Brinton Muir-, Bt. (1805)
Mackenzie, Vice-Adm. Sir Hugh Stirling, KCB, DSO, DSC
†Mackenzie, Sir (James William) Guy, Bt. (1890)
Mackenzie, Lt.-Gen. Sir Jeremy John George, KCB, OBE
†Mackenzie, Sir Peter Douglas, Bt. (S. 1673)
†Mackenzie, Sir Roderick McQuhae, Bt. (S. 1703)
McKenzie, Sir Roy Allan, KBE
Mackeson, Sir Rupert Henry, Bt. (1954)
Mackie, Sir Maitland, Kt., CBE
MacKinlay, Sir Bruce, Kt., CBE
McKinnon, Sir James, Kt.
McKinnon, Hon. Sir Stuart Neil, Kt.
McKissock, Sir Wylie, Kt., OBE, FRCS
Macklin, Sir Bruce Roy, Kt., CBE
Mackworth, Cdr. Sir David Arthur Geoffrey, Bt. (1776)
McLaren, Sir Robin John Taylor, KCMG
MacLaurin, Sir Ian Charter, Kt.
Maclean, Sir Donald Og Grant, Kt.
Maclean, Sir Fitzroy Hew, Bt., CBE (1957)
McLean, Sir Francis Charles, Kt., CBE
MacLean, Vice-Adm. Sir Hector Charles Donald, KBE, CB, DSC
Maclean, Sir Lachlan Hector Charles, Bt. (NS 1631)
Maclean, Sir Robert Alexander, KBE
McLennan, Sir Ian Munro, KCMG, KBE
McLeod, Sir Charles Henry, Bt. (1925)
McLeod, Sir Ian George, Kt.
†MacLeod, Hon. Sir John Maxwell Norman, Bt. (1924)
McLintock, Sir Michael William, Bt. (1934)

Maclure, Sir John Robert Spencer, Bt. (1898)
McMahon, Sir Brian Patrick, Bt. (1817)
McMahon, Sir Christopher William, Kt.
Macmillan, Sir (Alexander McGregor) Graham, Kt.
MacMillan, Lt.-Gen. Sir John Richard Alexander, KCB, CBE
McMullin, Rt. Hon. Sir Duncan Wallace, Kt.
Macnab, Brig. Sir Geoffrey Alex Colin, KCMG, CB
Macnaghten, Sir Patrick Alexander, Bt. (1836)
McNamara, Air Chief Marshal Sir Neville Patrick, KBE
Macnaughton, Prof. Sir Malcolm Campbell, Kt.
McNee, Sir David Blackstock, Kt., QPM
McNeice, Sir (Thomas) Percy (Fergus), Kt., CMG, OBE
MacPhail, Sir Bruce Dugald, Kt.
MacPherson, Sir Keith Duncan, Kt.
Macpherson, Sir Ronald Thomas Steward (Tommy), CBE, MC, TD
Macpherson of Cluny, Hon. Sir William Alan, Kt., TD
McQuarrie, Sir Albert, Kt.
MacRae, Sir (Alastair) Christopher (Donald Summerhayes), KCMG
Macrae, Col. Sir Robert Andrew Scarth, KCVO, MBE
Macready, Sir Nevil John Wilfrid, Bt. (1923)
McShine, Hon. Sir Arthur Hugh, Kt.
Mactaggart, Sir John Auld, Bt. (1938)
Macwhinnie, Sir Gordon Menzies, Kt., CBE
McWilliams, Sir Francis, GBE, FEng.
Madden, Adm. Sir Charles Edward, Bt., GCB (1919)
Maddocks, Sir Kenneth Phipson, KCMG, KCVO
Madigan, Sir Russel Tullie, Kt., OBE
Magnus, Sir Laurence Henry Philip, Bt. (1917)
Maguire, Air Marshal Sir Harold John, KCB, DSO, OBE
Mahon, Sir (John) Denis, Kt., CBE
Mahon, Sir William Walter, Bt. (1819)
Maiden, Sir Colin James, Kt., D.Phil.
Main, Sir Peter Tester, Kt., ERD
Maini, Sir Amar Nath, Kt., CBE
Maino, Sir Charles, KBE
Mais, Hon. Sir (Robert) Hugh, Kt.
Maitland, Sir Donald James Dundas, GCMG, OBE
Maitland, Sir Richard John, Bt. (1818)
Makins, Sir Paul Vivian, Bt. (1903)
Malcolm, Sir David Peter Michael, Bt. (S. 1665)
Malet, Sir Harry Douglas St Lo, Bt. (1791)
Mallaby, Sir Christopher Leslie George, GCVO, KCMG

Mallinson, Sir William John, Bt. (1935)
Malone, *Hon.* Sir Denis Eustace Gilbert, Kt.
Mamo, Sir Anthony Joseph, Kt., OBE
Manchester, Sir William Maxwell, KBE
Mander, Sir Charles Marcus, Bt. (1911)
Manduell, Sir John, Kt., CBE
Mann, *Rt. Hon.* Sir Michael, Kt.
Mann, *Rt. Revd* Michael Ashley, KCVO
Mann, Sir Rupert Edward, Bt. (1905)
Mansel, *Revd Canon* James Seymour Denis, KCVO
Mansel, Sir Philip, Bt. (1622)
Mansfield, *Vice-Adm.* Sir (Edward) Gerard (Napier), KBE, CVO
Mansfield, *Prof.* Sir Peter, Kt., FRS
Mansfield, Sir Philip (Robert Aked), KCMG
Mantell, *Hon.* Sir Charles Barrie Knight, Kt.
Manzie, Sir (Andrew) Gordon, KCB
Mara, *Rt. Hon. Ratu* Sir Kamisese Kapaiwai Tuimacilai, GCMG, KBE
Margetson, Sir John William Denys, KCMG
Marjoribanks, Sir James Alexander Milne, KCMG
Mark, Sir Robert, GBE
Markham, Sir Charles John, Bt. (1911)
Marking, Sir Henry Ernest, KCVO, CBE, MC
Marling, Sir Charles William Somerset, Bt. (1882)
Marr, Sir Leslie Lynn, Bt. (1919)
Marriner, Sir Neville, Kt., CBE
Marriott, Sir Hugh Cavendish Smith-, Bt. (1774)
Marsden, Sir Nigel John Denton, Bt. (1924)
Marshall, Sir Arthur Gregory George, Kt., OBE
Marshall, Sir Colin Marsh, Kt.
Marshall, Sir Denis Alfred, Kt.
Marshall, *Prof.* Sir (Oshley) Roy, Kt., CBE
Marshall, Sir Peter Harold Reginald, KCMG
Marshall, Sir Robert Braithwaite, KCB, MBE
Marshall, Sir (Robert) Michael, Kt., MP
Martell, *Vice-Adm.* Sir Hugh Colenso, KBE, CB
Martin, *Vice-Adm.* Sir John Edward Ludgate, KCB, DSC
Martin, *Prof.* Sir (John) Leslie, Kt., ph.D.
Martin, *Col.* Sir (Robert) Andrew (St George), KCVO, OBE
Martin, Sir (Robert) Bruce, Kt., QC
Marychurch, Sir Peter Harvey, KCMG
Masefield, Sir Peter Gordon, Kt.
Mason, *Hon.* Sir Anthony Frank, KBE
Mason, Sir (Basil) John, Kt., CB, D.SC., FRS
Mason, *Prof.* Sir David Kean, Kt., CBE
Mason, Sir Frederick Cecil, KCVO, CMG
Mason, Sir Gordon Charles, Kt., OBE

Mason, Sir John Charles Moir, KCMG
Mason, *Prof.* Sir Ronald, KCB, FRS
Matane, Sir Paulias Nguna, Kt., CMG, OBE
Mather, Sir (David) Carol (Macdonell), Kt., MC
Mather, Sir William Loris, Kt., CVO, OBE, MC, TD
Mathers, Sir Robert William, Kt.
Matheson, Sir (James Adam) Louis, KBE, CMG, FEng.
†Matheson of Matheson, Sir Fergus John, Bt. (1882)
Matthews, Sir Peter Alec, Kt.
Matthews, Sir Peter Jack, Kt., CVO, OBE, QPM
Matthews, Sir Stanley, Kt., CBE
Maud, The Hon. Sir Humphrey John Hamilton, KCMG
†Maxwell, Sir Michael Eustace George, Bt. (s. 1681)
Maxwell, Sir Nigel Mellor Heron-, Bt. (s. 1683)
Maxwell, Sir Robert Hugh, KBE
May, *Hon.* Sir Anthony Tristram Kenneth, Kt.
May, *Rt. Hon.* Sir John Douglas, Kt.
May, Sir Kenneth Spencer, Kt., CBE
Mayhew, *Rt. Hon.* Sir Patrick Barnabas Burke, Kt., QC, MP
Maynard, *Hon.* Sir Clement Travelyan, Kt.
Maynard, *Air Chief Marshal* Sir Nigel Martin, KCB, CBE, DFC, AFC
Medlycott, Sir Mervyn Tregonwell, Bt. (1808)
Megarry, *Rt. Hon.* Sir Robert Edgar, Kt., FBA
Megaw, *Rt. Hon.* Sir John, Kt., CBE, TD
Meinertzhagen, Sir Peter, Kt., CMG
Melhuish, Sir Michael Ramsay, KBE, CMG
Mellon, Sir James, KCMG
Melville, Sir Harry Work, KCB, ph.D., D.SC., FRS
Melville, Sir Leslie Galfreid, KBE
Melville, Sir Ronald Henry, KCB
Mensforth, Sir Eric, Kt., CBE, F.eng.
Menter, Sir James Woodham, Kt., ph.D., SC.D., FRS
Menteth, Sir James Wallace Stuart-, Bt. (1838)
Menzies, Sir Peter Thomson, Kt.
Messervy, Sir (Roney) Godfrey (Collumbell), Kt.
Meyer, Sir Anthony John Charles, Bt. (1910)
Meyjes, Sir Richard Anthony, Kt.
Meyrick, Sir David John Charlton, Bt. (1880)
Meyrick, Sir George Christopher Cadafael Tapps-Gervis-, Bt. (1791)
Miakwe, *Hon.* Sir Akepa, KBE
Michael, Sir Peter Colin, Kt., CBE
Middleton, Sir George Humphrey, KCMG
†Middleton, Sir Lawrence Monck, Bt. (1662)

Middleton, Sir Peter Edward, GCB
Miers, Sir (Henry) David Alastair Capel, KBE, CMG
Milbank, Sir Anthony Frederick, Bt. (1882)
Milburn, Sir Anthony Rupert, Bt. (1905)
Miles, Sir Peter Tremayne, KCVO
Miles, Sir William Napier Maurice, Bt. (1859)
Millais, Sir Geoffrey Richard Everett, Bt. (1885)
Millar, Sir Oliver Nicholas, GCVO, FBA
Millar, Sir Ronald Graeme, Kt.
Millard, Sir Guy Elwin, KCMG, CVO
Miller, Sir Donald John, Kt., FRSE, FEng.
Miller, Sir Douglas Sinclair, KCVO, CBE
Miller, Sir Hilary Duppa (Hal), Kt.
Miller, Sir (Ian) Douglas, Kt.
Miller, Sir John Holmes, Bt. (1705)
Miller, *Lt.-Col.* Sir John Mansel, GCVO, DSO, MC
Miller, Sir (Oswald) Bernard, Kt.
Miller, Sir Peter North, Kt.
Miller, Sir Ronald Andrew Baird, Kt., CBE
Miller, Sir Stephen James Hamilton, KCVO, MD, FRCS
Miller of Glenlee, Sir Stephen William Macdonald, Bt. (1788)
Millett, *Hon.* Sir Peter Julian, Kt.
Millichip, Sir Frederick Albert (Bert), Kt.
Milling, *Air Marshal* Sir Denis Crowley-, KCB, CBE, DSO, DFC
Mills, *Vice-Adm.* Sir Charles Piercy, KCB, CBE, DSC
Mills, Sir Frank, KCVO, CMG
Mills, Sir John Lewis Ernest Watts, Kt., CBE
Mills, Sir Peter Frederick Leighton, Bt. (1921)
Milman, *Lt.-Col.* Sir Derek, Bt. (1800)
Milne, Sir John Drummond, Kt.
Milner, Sir (George Edward) Mordaunt, Bt. (1717)
Milnes Coates, Sir Anthony Robert, Bt. (1911)
Miskin, *Hon.* Sir James William, Kt., QC
Mitchell, *Air Cdre* Sir (Arthur) Dennis, KBE, CVO, DFC, AFC
Mitchell, Sir David Bower, Kt., MP
Mitchell, Sir Derek Jack, KCB, CVO
Mitchell, *Prof.* Sir (Edgar) William John, Kt., CBE, FRS
Mitchell, *Hon.* Sir Stephen George, Kt.
Moate, Sir Roger Denis, Kt., MP
Mobbs, Sir (Gerald) Nigel, Kt.
Moberly, Sir John Campbell, KBE, CMG
Moberly, Sir Patrick Hamilton, KCMG
Moffat, *Lt.-Gen.* Sir (William) Cameron, KBE
Mogg, *Gen.* Sir (Herbert) John, GCB, CBE, DSO
Moir, Sir Ernest Ian Royds, Bt. (1916)
Moller, *Hon.* Sir Lester Francis, Kt.

†Molony, Sir Thomas Desmond, Bt. (1925)
Monro, Sir Hector Seymour Peter, Kt., MP
Montgomery, Sir (Basil Henry) David, Bt. (1801)
Montgomery, Sir (William) Fergus, Kt., MP
Mookerjee, Sir Birendra Nath, Kt.
Moollan, Sir Abdool Hamid Adam, Kt.
Moollan, Hon. Sir Cassam (Ismael), Kt.
Moon, Sir Peter Wilfred Giles Graham-, Bt. (1855)
†Moon, Sir Roger, Bt. (1887)
Moore, Sir Francis Thomas, Kt.
Moore, Sir Henry Roderick, Kt., CBE
Moore, Hon. Sir John Cochrane, Kt.
Moore, Maj.-Gen. Sir (John) Jeremy, KCB, OBE, MC
Moore, Sir John Michael, KCVO, CB, DSC
Moore, Prof. Sir Norman Winfrid, Bt. (1919)
Moore, Sir Patrick William Eisdell, Kt., OBE
Moore, Sir William Roger Clotworthy, Bt., TD (1932)
Moores, Sir John, Kt., CBE
Mootham, Sir Orby Howell, Kt.
Morauta, Sir Mekere, Kt.
Mordaunt, Sir Richard Nigel Charles, Bt. (1611)
Moreton, Sir John Oscar, KCMG, KCVO, MC
Morgan, Maj.-Gen. Sir David John Hughes-, Bt., CB, CBE (1925)
Morgan, Sir Ernest Dunstan, KBE
Morgan, Sir John Albert Leigh, KCMG
Morland, Hon. Sir Michael, Kt.
Morland, Sir Robert Kenelm, Kt.
Morpeth, Sir Douglas Spottiswoode, Kt., TD
Morris, Air Marshal Sir Arnold Alec, KBE, CB, FEng.
Morris, Sir (James) Richard (Samuel), Kt., CBE, FEng.
Morris, Sir Robert Byng, Bt. (1806)
Morrison, Hon. Sir Charles Andrew, Kt.
Morrison, Sir Howard Leslie, Kt., OBE
Morrison, Rt. Hon. Sir Peter Hugh, Kt.
Morritt, Hon. Sir (Robert) Andrew, Kt., CVO
Morrow, Sir Ian Thomas, Kt.
Morse, Sir Christopher Jeremy, KCMG
Morton, Adm. Sir Anthony Storrs, GBE, KCB
Morton, Sir (Robert) Alastair (Newton), Kt.
Morton, Sir William David, Kt., CBE
Moseley, Sir George Walker, KCB
Moser, Prof. Sir Claus Adolf, KCB, CBE, FBA
†Moss, Sir David John Edwards-, Bt. (1868)

Mostyn, Gen. Sir (Joseph) David Frederick, KCB, CBE
†Mostyn, Sir William Basil John, Bt. (1670)
Mott, Sir John Harmer, Bt. (1930)
Mott, Sir Nevill Francis, Kt., FRS
Mount, Sir James William Spencer, Kt., CBE, BEM
†Mount, Sir (William Robert) Ferdinand, Bt. (1921)
Mountain, Sir Denis Mortimer, Bt. (1922)
Mowbray, Sir John, Kt.
Mowbray, Sir John Robert, Bt. (1880)
Moynihan, Sir Noel Henry, Kt.
Muir, Sir John Harling, Bt. (1892)
Muir, Sir Laurence Macdonald, Kt.
Muirhead, Sir David Francis, KCMG, CVO
Mulcahy, Sir Geoffrey John, Kt.
Mullens, Lt.-Gen. Sir Anthony Richard Guy, KCB, OBE
Mummery, Hon. Sir John Frank, Kt.
Munn, Sir James, Kt., OBE
Munro, Sir Alan Gordon, KCMG
Munro, Sir Alasdair Thomas Ian, Bt. (1825)
Munro, Sir Ian Talbot, Bt. (S. 1634)
Munro, Hon. Sir Robert Lindsay, Kt., CBE
Munro, Sir Sydney Douglas Gun-, GCMG, MBE
Murley, Sir Reginald Sydney, KBE, TD, FRCS
Murphy, Sir Leslie Frederick, Kt.
Murray, Rt. Hon. Sir Donald Bruce, Kt.
Murray, Sir Donald Frederick, KCVO, CMG
Murray, Sir James, KCMG
Murray, Sir John Antony Jerningham, Kt., CBE
Murray, Prof. Sir Kenneth, Kt., FRCPath., FRS, FRSE
Murray, Sir Nigel Andrew Digby, Bt. (S. 1628)
Murray, Sir Patrick Ian Keith, Bt. (S. 1673)
†Murray, Sir Rowland William Patrick, Bt. (S. 1630)
Murrie, Sir William Stuart, GCB, KBE
Mursell, Sir Peter, Kt., MBE
Musgrave, Sir Christopher Patrick Charles, Bt. (1611)
Musgrave, Sir Richard James, Bt. (I. 1782)
Musson, Gen. Sir Geoffrey Randolph Dixon, GCB, CBE, DSO
Myers, Sir Kenneth Ben, Kt., MBE
Myers, Sir Philip Alan, Kt., OBE, QPM
Myers, Prof. Sir Rupert Horace, KBE
Mynors, Sir Richard Baskerville, Bt. (1964)
Nabarro, Sir John David Nunes, Kt., MD, FRCP
Naipaul, Sir Vidiadhar Surajprasad, Kt.
Nairn, Sir Michael, Bt. (1904)

Nairn, Sir Robert Arnold Spencer-, Bt. (1933)
Nairne, Rt. Hon. Sir Patrick Dalmahoy, GCB, MC
Nalder, Hon. Sir Crawford David, Kt.
Nall, Sir Michael Joseph, Bt., RN (1954)
Napier, Sir John Archibald Lennox, Bt. (S. 1627)
Napier, Sir Oliver John, Kt.
Napier, Sir Robin Surtees, Bt. (1867)
Napley, Sir David, Kt.
Neal, Sir Eric James, Kt., CVO
Neal, Sir Leonard Francis, Kt., CBE
Neale, Sir Alan Derrett, KCB, MBE
Neale, Sir Gerrard Anthony, Kt.
Neave, Sir Paul Arundell, Bt. (1795)
Nedd, Hon. Sir Robert Archibald, Kt.
Neill, Rt. Hon. Sir Brian Thomas, Kt.
Neill, Sir Francis Patrick, Kt., QC
Neill, Rt. Hon. Sir Ivan, Kt., PC(NI)
Nelson, Maj.-Gen. Sir (Eustace) John (Blois), KCVO, CB, DSO, OBE, MC
†Nelson, Sir Jamie Charles Vernon Hope, Bt. (1912)
Nelson, Air Marshal Sir (Sidney) Richard (Carlyle), KCB, OBE, MD
Nepean, Lt.-Col. Sir Evan Yorke, Bt. (1802)
Ness, Air Marshal Sir Charles Ernest, KCB, CBE
Neubert, Sir Michael John, Kt., MP
Nevile, Capt. Sir Henry Nicholas, KCVO
Neville, Sir Richard Lionel John Baines, Bt. (1927)
New, Maj.-Gen. Sir Laurence Anthony Wallis, Kt., CB, CBE
Newbold, Sir Charles Demorée, KBE, CMG, QC
Newington, Sir Michael John, KCMG
Newman, Sir Francis Hugh Cecil, Bt. (1912)
Newman, Sir Geoffrey Robert, Bt. (1836)
Newman, Sir Jack, Kt., CBE
Newman, Sir Kenneth Leslie, GBE, QPM
Newman, Vice-Adm. Sir Roy Thomas, KCB
Newman, Col. Sir Stuart Richard, Kt., CBE, TD
Newns, Sir (Alfred) Foley (Francis Polden), KCMG, CVO
Newsam, Sir Peter Anthony, Kt.
Newton, Sir (Charles) Wilfred, Kt., CBE
Newton, Sir (Harry) Michael (Rex), Bt. (1900)
Newton, Sir Kenneth Garnar, Bt., OBE, TD (1924)
Newton, Sir (Leslie) Gordon, Kt.
Ngata, Sir Henare Kohere, KBE
Niall, Sir Horace Lionel Richard, Kt., CBE
Nichol, Sir Duncan Kirkbride, Kt., CBE
Nicholas, Sir David, Kt., CBE

Nicholas, Sir Herbert Richard, Kt.,
OBE
Nicholas, Sir John William, KCVO, CMG
Nicholls, *Rt. Hon.* Sir Donald James,
Kt.
Nicholls, *Air Marshal* Sir John
Moreton, KCB, CBE, DFC, AFC
Nicholson, Sir Bryan Hubert, Kt.
†Nicholson, Sir Charles Christian, Bt.
(1912)
Nicholson, *Hon.* Sir David Eric, Kt.
Nicholson, *Hon.* Sir Michael, Kt.
Nicholson, Sir Paul Douglas, Kt.
Nicholson, Sir Robin Buchanan, Kt.,
Ph.D., FRS
Nickson, Sir David Wigley, KBE
Nicoll, Sir William, KCMG
Nicolson, Sir David Lancaster, Kt,
FEng.
Nield, Sir Basil Edward, Kt., CBE, QC
Nield, Sir William Alan, GCMG, KCB
Nightingale, Sir Charles Manners
Gamaliel, Bt. (1628)
Nightingale, Sir John Cyprian, Kt.,
CBE, BEM, QPM
Nimmo, *Hon.* Sir John Angus, Kt.,
CBE
Nixon, Sir Edwin Ronald, Kt., CBE
Nixon, *Revd* Sir Kenneth Michael
John Basil, Bt. (1906)
Noad, Sir Kenneth Beeson, Kt., MD
Noble, Sir David Brunel, Bt. (1902)
Noble, Sir Iain Andrew, Bt., OBE
(1923)
Noble, Sir (Thomas Alexander)
Fraser, Kt., MBE
Nolan, *Rt. Hon.* Sir Michael Patrick,
Kt.
Nombri, Sir Joseph Karl, Kt., ISO, BEM
Norman, Sir Arthur Gordon, KBE, DFC
Norman, Sir Mark Annesley, Bt.
(1915)
Norman, Sir Robert Henry, Kt., OBE
Norman, Sir Robert Wentworth, Kt.
Normanton, Sir Tom, Kt., TD
Norris, *Air Chief Marshal* Sir
Christopher Neil Foxley-, GCB, DSO,
OBE
Norris, Sir Eric George, KCMG
North, Sir Thomas Lindsay, Kt.
North, Sir (William) Jonathan
(Frederick), Bt. (1920)
Norton, *Vice-Adm. Hon.* Sir Nicholas
John Hill-, KCB
Norwood, Sir Walter Neville, Kt.
Nossal, Sir Gustav Joseph Victor, Kt.,
CBE
Nott, *Rt. Hon.* Sir John William
Frederic, KCB
Nourse, *Rt. Hon.* Sir Martin Charles,
Kt.
Nugent, Sir John Edwin Lavallin, Bt.
(I. 1795)
Nugent, *Maj.* Sir Peter Walter James,
Bt. (1831)
Nugent, Sir Robin George Colborne,
Bt. (1806)
Nursaw, Sir James, KCB, QC

Nuttall, Sir Nicholas Keith Lillington,
Bt. (1922)
Nutting, *Rt. Hon.* Sir (Harold)
Anthony, Bt. (1903)
Oakeley, Sir John Digby Atholl, Bt.
(1790)
Oakes, Sir Christopher, Bt. (1939)
Oakshott, Hon. Sir Anthony Hendrie,
Bt. (1959)
Oates, Sir Thomas, Kt., CMG, OBE
Oatley, Sir Charles William, Kt., OBE,
FRS, FEng.
Obolensky, *Prof.* Sir Dimitri, Kt.
O'Brien, Sir Frederick William
Fitzgerald, Kt.
O'Brien, Sir Richard, Kt., DSO, MC
O'Brien, Sir Timothy John, Bt. (1849)
O'Brien, *Adm.* Sir William Donough,
KCB, DSC
O'Connell, Sir Maurice James Donagh
MacCarthy, Bt. (1869)
O'Connor, *Rt. Hon.* Sir Patrick
McCarthy, Kt.
O'Dea, Sir Patrick Jerad, KCVO
Odell, Sir Stanley John, Kt.
Ogden, Sir (Edward) Michael, Kt., QC
Ogilvie, Sir Alec Drummond, Kt.
Ogilvy, Hon. Sir Angus James Bruce,
KCVO
†Ogilvy, Sir Francis Gilbert Arthur, Bt.
(s. 1626)
Ognall, *Hon.* Sir Harry Henry, Kt.
Ohlson, Sir Brian Eric Christopher,
Bt. (1920)
Okeover, *Capt.* Sir Peter Ralph
Leopold Walker-, Bt. (1886)
Olewale, *Hon.* Sir Niwia Ebia, Kt.
Oliphant, Sir Mark (Marcus Laurence
Elwin), KBE, FRS
Oliver, Sir (Frederick) Ernest, Kt.,
CBE, TD
O'Loghlen, Sir Colman Michael, Bt.
(1838)
Olver, Sir Stephen John Linley, KBE,
CMG
O'Neil, *Hon.* Sir Desmond Henry, Kt.
Ongley, *Hon.* Sir Joseph Augustine,
Kt.
Onslow, *Rt. Hon.* Sir Cranley Gordon
Douglas, KCMG, MP
Onslow, Sir John Roger Wilmot, Bt.
(1797)
Oppenheim, Sir Alexander, Kt., OBE,
D.SC., FRSE
Oppenheim, Sir Duncan Morris, Kt.
Oppenheimer, Sir Michael Bernard
Grenville, Bt. (1921)
Oppenheimer, Sir Philip Jack, Kt.
Opperman, *Hon.* Sir Hubert
Ferdinand, Kt., OBE
Orde, Sir John Alexander Campbell-,
Bt. (1790)
O'Regan, *Hon.* Sir John Barry, Kt.
Orlebar, Sir Michael Keith Orlebar
Simpson-, KCMG
Ormond, Sir John Davies Wilder, Kt.,
BEM
Orr, Sir David Alexander, Kt., MC
Orr, Sir John Henry, Kt., OBE, QPM

Osborn, Sir John Holbrook, Kt.
Osborn, Sir Richard Henry Danvers,
Bt. (1662)
Osborne, Sir Peter George, Bt.
(I. 1629)
Osifelo, Sir Frederick Aubarua, Kt.,
MBE
Osman, Sir (Abdool) Raman
Mahomed, GCMG, CBE
Osmond, Sir Douglas, Kt., CBE
Osmond, Sir (Stanley) Paul, Kt., CB
Oswald, *Admiral of the Fleet* Sir (John)
Julian Robertson, GCB
Otton, Sir Geoffrey John, KCB
Otton, *Hon.* Sir Philip Howard, Kt.
Oulton, Sir Antony Derek Maxwell,
GCB, QC
Outram, Sir Alan James, Bt. (1858)
Overall, Sir John Wallace, Kt., CBE, MC
Owen, Sir Geoffrey, Kt.
Owen, Sir Hugh Bernard Pilkington,
Bt. (1813)
Owen, Sir Hugo Dudley Cunliffe-, Bt.
(1920)
Owen, *Hon.* Sir John Arthur Dalziel,
Kt.
Owo, The Olowo of, Kt.
Oxburgh, *Prof.* Sir Ernest Ronald,
KBE, Ph.D., FRS
Oxford, Sir Kenneth Gordon, Kt.,
CBE, QPM
Packard, *Lt.-Gen.* Sir (Charles)
Douglas, KBE, CB, DSO
Padmore, Sir Thomas, GCB
Page, Sir Alexander Warren, Kt., MBE
Page, Sir (Arthur) John, Kt.
Page, Sir Frederick William, Kt., CBE,
FEng.
Page, Sir John Joseph Joffre, Kt., OBE
Paget, Sir Julian Tolver, Bt., CVO
(1871)
Paget, Sir Richard Herbert, Bt. (1886)
Pain, *Lt.-Gen.* Sir (Horace) Rollo
(Squarey), KCB, MC
Pain, *Hon.* Sir Peter Richard, Kt.
Palin, *Air Chief Marshal* Sir Roger
Hewlett, KCB, OBE
Palliser, *Rt. Hon.* Sir (Arthur)
Michael, GCMG
Palmar, Sir Derek James, Kt.
Palmer, Sir (Charles) Mark, Bt. (1886)
Palmer, *Gen.* Sir (Charles) Patrick
(Ralph), KBE
Palmer, Sir Geoffrey Christopher
John, Bt. (1660)
Palmer, *Rt. Hon.* Sir Geoffrey
Winston Russell, KCMG
Palmer, Sir John Chance, Kt.
Palmer, Sir John Edward Somerset,
Bt. (1791)
Palmer, *Maj.-Gen.* Sir (Joseph)
Michael, KCVO
Palmer, Sir Reginald Oswald, GCMG,
MBE
Pantlin, Sir Dick Hurst, Kt., CBE
Paolozzi, Sir Eduardo Luigi, Kt., CBE,
RA
Pararajasingam, Sir Sangarapillai, Kt.
Parbo, Sir Arvi Hillar, Kt.

Parish, Sir David Elmer Woodbine, Kt., CBE

Park, *Hon.* Sir Hugh Eames, Kt.

Parker, Sir (Arthur) Douglas Dodds-, Kt.

Parker, Sir Eric Wilson, Kt.

Parker, *Hon.* Sir Jonathan Frederic, Kt.

Parker, Sir Peter, KBE, LVO

Parker, Sir Richard (William) Hyde, Bt. (1681)

Parker, *Rt. Hon.* Sir Roger Jocelyn, Kt.

Parker, *Vice-Adm.* Sir (Wilfred) John, KBE, CB, DSC

Parker, Sir William Peter Brian, Bt. (1844)

Parkes, Sir Edward Walter, Kt., FEng.

Parkinson, Sir Nicholas Fancourt, Kt.

Parsons, Sir Anthony Derrick, GCMG, MVO, MC

Parsons, Sir (John) Michael, Kt.

Parsons, Sir Richard Edmund (Clement Fownes), KCMG

Partridge, Sir Michael John Anthony, KCB

Pascoe, *Gen.* Sir Robert Alan, KCB, MBE

Pasley, Sir John Malcolm Sabine, Bt. (1794)

Paterson, Sir Dennis Craig, Kt.

Paterson, Sir George Mutlow, Kt., OBE, QC

Paterson, Sir John Valentine Jardine, Kt.

Paton, Sir (Thomas) Angus (Lyall), Kt., CMG, FRS, FEng.

Paton, *Prof.* Sir William Drummond Macdonald, Kt., CBE, DM, FRS, FRCP

Pattie, *Rt. Hon.* Sir Geoffrey Edwin, Kt., MP

Pattinson, *Hon.* Sir Baden, KBE

Pattinson, Sir (William) Derek, Kt.

Paul, Sir John Warburton, GCMG, OBE, MC

Paul, *Air Marshal* Sir Ronald Ian Stuart-, KBE

Payne, Sir Norman John, Kt., CBE, FEng.

Peach, Sir Leonard Harry, Kt.

Peacock, *Prof.* Sir Alan Turner, Kt., DSC

Pearce, Sir Austin William, Kt., CBE, ph.D., FEng.

Pearce, Sir (Daniel Norton) Idris, Kt., CBE, TD

Pearce, Sir Eric Herbert, Kt., OBE

Peard, *Rear-Adm.* Sir Kenyon Harry Terrell, KBE

Pearman, *Hon.* Sir James Eugene, Kt., CBE

Pearson, Sir Francis Nicholas Fraser, Bt. (1964)

Pearson, *Gen.* Sir Thomas Cecil Hook, KCB, CBE, DSO

Peart, *Prof.* Sir William Stanley, Kt., MD, FRS

Pease, Sir (Alfred) Vincent, Bt. (1882)

Pease, Sir Richard Thorn, Bt. (1920)

Peat, Sir Gerrard Charles, KCVO

Peat, Sir Henry, KCVO, DFC

Peck, Sir Edward Heywood, GCMG

Peck, Sir John Howard, KCMG

Pedder, *Vice-Adm.* Sir Arthur Reid, KBE, CB

Pedder, *Air Marshal* Sir Ian Maurice, KCB, OBE, DFC

Peek, Sir Francis Henry Grenville, Bt. (1874)

Peek, *Vice-Adm.* Sir Richard Innes, KBE, CB, DSC

Peel, Sir John Harold, KCVO

Peel, Sir (William) John, Kt.

Peierls, Sir Rudolf Ernst, Kt., CBE, D.SC., D.Phil., FRS

Peirse, Sir Henry Grant de la Poer Beresford-, Bt. (1814)

Peirse, *Air Vice-Marshal* Sir Richard Charles Fairfax, KCVO, CB

Pelgen, Sir Harry Friedrich, Kt., MBE

†Pelly, Sir Richard John, Bt. (1840)

Pemberton, Sir Francis Wingate William, Kt., CBE

Percival, Sir Anthony Edward, Kt., CB

Percival, *Rt. Hon.* Sir (Walter) Ian, Kt., QC

Pereira, Sir (Herbert) Charles, Kt., D.SC., FRS

Perkins, *Surgeon Vice-Adm.* Sir Derek Duncombe Steele-, KCB, KCVO

Perring, Sir Ralph Edgar, Bt. (1963)

Perris, Sir David (Arthur), Kt., MBE

Perry, Sir David Howard, KCB

Perry, Sir (David) Norman, Kt., MBE

Pestell, Sir John Richard, KCVO

Peterkin, Sir Neville, Kt.

Peters, *Prof.* Sir David Keith, Kt., FRCP

Petersen, Sir Jeffrey Charles, KCMG

Petersen, Sir Johannes Bjelke-, KCMG

Petit, Sir Dinshaw Manockjee, Bt. (1890)

Peto, Sir Henry George Morton, Bt. (1855)

Peto, Sir Michael Henry Basil, Bt. (1927)

Petrie, Sir Peter Charles, Bt., CMG (1918)

Pettigrew, Sir Russell Hilton, Kt.

Pettit, Sir Daniel Eric Arthur, Kt.

Philips, *Prof.* Sir Cyril Henry, Kt.

Phillips, *Prof.* Sir David Chilton, KBE, ph.D., FRS

Phillips, Sir Fred Albert, Kt., CVO

Phillips, Sir Henry Ellis Isidore, Kt., CMG, MBE

Phillips, Sir Horace, KCMG

Phillips, *Hon.* Sir Nicholas Addison, Kt.

Phillips, Sir Peter John, Kt., OBE

Phillips, Sir Robin Francis, Bt. (1912)

Pickering, Sir Edward Davies, Kt.

Pickthorn, Sir Charles William Richards, Bt. (1959)

Pidgeon, Sir John Allan Stewart, Kt.

Piers, Sir Charles Robert Fitzmaurice, Bt. (I. 1661)

Pigot, Sir George Hugh, Bt. (1764)

Pigott, Sir Berkeley Henry Sebastian, Bt. (1808)

Pike, Sir Michael Edmund, KCVO, CMG

Pike, Sir Philip Ernest Housden, Kt., QC

Pilcher, Sir (Charlie) Dennis, Kt., CBE

Pilditch, Sir Richard Edward, Bt. (1929)

Pile, Sir Frederick Devereux, Bt., MC (1900)

Pile, Sir William Dennis, GCB, MBE

Pilkington, Sir Antony Richard, Kt.

Pilkington, Sir Lionel Alexander Bethune, (Sir Alastair), Kt., FRS

Pilkington, Sir Thomas Henry Milborne-Swinnerton-, Bt. (s. 1635)

Pill, *Hon.* Sir Malcolm Thomas, Kt.

Pillar, *Adm.* Sir William Thomas, GBE, KCB

Pindling, *Rt. Hon.* Sir Lynden Oscar, KCMG

Pinker, Sir George Douglas, KCVO

Pinsent, Sir Christopher Roy, Bt. (1938)

Pippard, *Prof.* Sir (Alfred) Brian, Kt., FRS

Pirie, *Gp Capt* Sir Gordon Hamish, Kt., CVO, CBE

Pitblado, Sir David Bruce, KCB, CVO

Pitcher, Sir Desmond Henry, Kt.

Pitoi, Sir Sere, Kt., CBE

Pitt, Sir Harry Raymond, Kt., ph.D., FRS

Pitts, Sir Cyril Alfred, Kt.

Pixley, Sir Neville Drake, Kt., MBE, VRD

Plastow, Sir David Arnold Stuart, Kt.

†Platt, Sir (Frank) Lindsey, Bt. (1958)

Platt, *Prof.* Hon. Sir Peter, Bt. (1959)

Playfair, Sir Edward Wilder, KCB

Pliatzky, Sir Leo, KCB

Plowman, *Hon.* Sir John Robin, Kt., CBE

Plumb, *Prof.* Sir John Harold, Kt.

Pohai, Sir Timothy, Kt., MBE

†Pole, Sir (John) Richard (Walter Reginald) Carew, Bt. (1628)

Pole, Sir Peter Van Notten, Bt. (1791)

Pollen, Sir John Michael Hungerford, Bt. (1795)

Pollock, Sir George Frederick, Bt. (1866)

Pollock, Sir Giles Hampden Montagu-, Bt. (1872)

Pollock, *Admiral of the Fleet* Sir Michael Patrick, GCB, MVO, DSC

Pollock, Sir William Horace Montagu-, KCB

Ponsonby, Sir Ashley Charles Gibbs, Bt., KCVO, MC (1956)

Pontin, Sir Frederick William, Kt.

Poore, Sir Herbert Edward, Bt. (1795)

Pope, *Vice-Adm.* Sir (John) Ernle, KCB

Pope, Sir Joseph Albert, Kt., D.SC., ph.D.

Popper, *Prof.* Sir Karl Raimund, Kt., CH, ph.D., FRS

Popplewell, *Hon.* Sir Oliver Bury, Kt.

Portal, Sir Jonathan Francis, Bt. (1901)

Porter, Sir John Simon Horsbrugh-, Bt. (1902)
Porter, Sir Leslie, Kt.
Porter, *Air Marshal* Sir (Melvin) Kenneth (Drowley), KCB, CBE
Porter, *Hon.* Sir Murray Victor, Kt.
Porter, *Rt. Hon.* Sir Robert Wilson, Kt., PC(NI), QC
Posnett, Sir Richard Neil, KBE, CMG
Potter, Sir (Joseph) Raymond (Lynden), Kt.
Potter, *Hon.* Sir Mark Howard, Kt.
Potter, *Maj.-Gen.* Sir (Wilfrid) John, KBE, CB
Potter, Sir (William) Ian, Kt.
Potts, *Hon.* Sir Francis Humphrey, Kt.
Pound, Sir John David, Bt. (1905)
Pountain, Sir Eric John, Kt.
Powell, Sir (Arnold Joseph) Philip, Kt., CH, OBE, RA, FRIBA
Powell, Sir Charles David, KCMG
Powell, Sir Nicholas Folliott Douglas, Bt. (1897)
Powell, Sir Richard Royle, GCB, KBE, CMG
Power, Sir Alastair John Cecil, Bt. (1924)
Powles, Sir Guy Richardson, KBE, CMG, ED
Poynton, Sir (Arthur) Hilton, GCMG
Prendergast, Sir John Vincent, KBE, CMG, GM
Prendergast, Sir (Walter) Kieran, KCVO, CMG
Prentice, *Hon.* Sir William Thomas, Kt., MBE
Prescott, Sir Mark, Bt. (1938)
Preston, Sir Kenneth Huson, Kt.
Preston, Sir Peter Sansome, KCB
Preston, Sir Ronald Douglas Hildebrand, Bt. (1815)
Prevost, Sir Christopher Gerald, Bt. (1805)
Price, Sir Charles Keith Napier Rugge-, Bt. (1804)
Price, Sir David Ernest Campbell, Kt.
Price, Sir Francis Caradoc Rose, Bt. (1815)
Price, Sir Frank Leslie, Kt.
Price, Sir (James) Robert, KBE
Price, Sir Leslie Victor, Kt., OBE
Price, Sir Norman Charles, KCB
Price, Sir Robert John Green-, Bt. (1874)
Prickett, *Air Chief Marshal* Sir Thomas Other, KCB, DSO, DFC
Prideaux, Sir Humphrey Povah Treverbian, Kt., OBE
†Primrose, Sir John Ure, Bt. (1903)
Pringle, *Air Marshal* Sir Charles Norman Seton, KBE, FEng.
Pringle, *Hon.* Sir John, Kt.
Pringle, *Lt.-Gen.* Sir Steuart (Robert), Bt., KCB, RM (S. 1683)
Pritchard, Sir Neil, KCMG
Pritchett, Sir Victor Sawdon, Kt., CH, CBE
Proby, Sir Peter, Bt. (1952)

Proud, Sir John Seymour, Kt.
Prout, Sir Christopher James, Kt., TD, QC, MEP
Pryke, Sir David Dudley, Bt. (1926)
Pugh, Sir Idwal Vaughan, KCB
Pugsley, *Prof.* Sir Alfred Grenvile, Kt., OBE, D.SC., FRS, FEng.
Pullen, Sir William Reginald James, KCVO
Pullinger, Sir (Francis) Alan, Kt., CBE
Pumphrey, Sir (John) Laurence, KCMG
Purchas, *Rt. Hon.* Sir Francis Brooks, Kt.
Purves, Sir William, Kt., CBE, DSO
Purvis, *Vice-Adm.* Sir Neville, KCB
Quennell, Sir Peter, Kt., CBE
Quicke, Sir John Godolphin, Kt., CBE
Quigley, Sir (William) George (Henry), Kt., CB, ph.D.
Quilliam, *Hon.* Sir (James) Peter, Kt.
Quilter, Sir Anthony Raymond Leopold Cuthbert, Bt. (1897)
Quinlan, Sir Michael Edward, GCB
Quinton, Sir James Grand, Kt.
Quirk, *Prof.* Sir (Charles)Randolph, Kt., CBE, FBA
Rabukawaqa, Sir Josua Rasilau, KBE, MVO
Radcliffe, Sir Sebastian Everard, Bt. (1813)
Radford, Sir Ronald Walter, KCB, MBE
Radzinowicz, *Prof.* Sir Leon, Kt., LL D
Rae, *Hon.* Sir Wallace Alexander Ramsay, Kt.
Raeburn, Sir Michael Edward Norman, Bt. (1923)
Raeburn, *Maj.-Gen.* Sir (William) Digby (Manifold), KCVO, CB, DSO, MBE
Raffray, Sir Piat Joseph Raymond Andre, Kt.
Raikes, *Vice-Adm.* Sir Iwan Geoffrey, KCB, CBE, DSC
Raison, *Rt. Hon.* Sir Timothy Hugh Francis, Kt.
Ralli, Sir Godfrey Victor, Bt., TD (1912)
Ramdanee, Sir Mookteswar Baboolall Kailash, Kt.
Ramphal, Sir Shridath Surendranath, GCMG
Ramphul, Sir Baalkhristna, Kt.
Ramphul, Sir Indurduth, Kt.
Rampton, Sir Jack Leslie, KCB
Ramsay, Sir Alexander William Burnett, Bt. (1806)
Ramsay, Sir Allan John (Hepple), KBE, CMG
Ramsay, Sir Thomas Meek, Kt., CMG
Ramsbotham, *Gen.* Sir David John, GCB, CBE
Ramsbotham, *Hon.* Sir Peter Edward, GCMG, GCVO
Ramsden, Sir John Charles Josslyn, Bt. (1689)
Ramsey, Sir Alfred Ernest, Kt.
Randle, *Prof.* Sir Philip John, Kt.
Ranger, Sir Douglas, Kt., FRCS
Rank, Sir Benjamin Keith, Kt., CMG

Rankin, Sir Alick Michael, Kt., CBE
Rankin, Sir Ian Niall, Bt. (1898)
Rasch, *Maj.* Sir Richard Guy Carne, Bt. (1903)
Rashleigh, Sir Richard Harry, Bt. (1831)
Rattee, *Hon.* Sir Donald Keith, Kt.
Rault, Sir Louis Joseph Maurice, Kt.
Rawlins, *Surgeon Vice-Adm.* Sir John Stuart Pepys, KBE
Rawlinson, Sir Anthony Henry John, Bt. (1891)
Read, *Air Marshal* Sir Charles Frederick, KBE, CB, DFC, AFC
Read, *Gen.* Sir (John) Antony (Jervis), GCB, CBE, DSO, MC
Read, Sir John Emms, Kt.
Reade, Sir Clyde Nixon, Bt. (1661)
Reay, *Lt.-Gen.* Sir (Hubert) Alan John, KBE
Redgrave, *Maj.-Gen.* Sir Roy Michael Frederick, KBE, MC
Redmayne, Sir Nicholas, Bt. (1964)
Redmond, Sir James, Kt., FEng.
Redwood, Sir Peter Boverton, Bt. (1911)
Reece, Sir Charles Hugh, Kt.
Reece, Sir James Gordon, Kt.
Reed, *Hon.* Sir Nigel Vernon, Kt., CBE
Rees, Sir (Charles William) Stanley, Kt., TD
Rees, Sir David Allan, Kt., ph.D., D.SC.
Rees, *Prof.* Sir Martin John, Kt., FRS
Reeve, Sir Anthony, KCMG
Reeve, Sir (Charles) Trevor, Kt.
Reeves, *Most Revd* Paul Alfred, GCMG, GCVO
Reffell, *Adm.* Sir Derek Roy, KCB
Refshauge, *Maj-Gen.* Sir William Dudley, Kt., CBE
Reid, Sir Alexander James, Bt. (1897)
Reid, *Hon.* Sir George Oswald, Kt., QC
Reid, Sir (Harold) Martin (Smith), KBE, CMG
Reid, Sir Hugh, Bt. (1922)
Reid, Sir John James Andrew, KCMG, CB, TD
Reid, Sir Norman Robert, Kt.
Reid, Sir Robert Basil, Kt., CBE
Reid, Sir Robert Paul, Kt.
Reiher, Sir Frederick Bernard Carl, KBE, CMG
Reilly, Sir (D'Arcy) Patrick, GCMG, OBE
Reilly, *Lt.-Gen.* Sir Jeremy Calcott, KCB, DSO
Renals, Sir Stanley, Bt. (1895)
Rendell, Sir William, Kt.
Rennie, Sir John Shaw, GCMG, OBE
Renouf, Sir Clement William Bailey, Kt.
Renouf, Sir Francis Henry, Kt.
Renshaw, Sir (Charles) Maurice Bine, Bt. (1903)
Renwick, Sir Richard Eustace, Bt. (1921)
Renwick, Sir Robin William, KCMG
Reporter, Sir Shapoor Ardeshirji, KBE

Reynolds, Sir David James, Bt. (1923)
Reynolds, Sir Peter William John, Kt., CBE
Rhodes, Sir Basil Edward, Kt., CBE, TD
Rhodes, Sir John Christopher Douglas, Bt. (1919)
Rhodes, Sir Peregrine Alexander, KCMG
Rice, *Maj.-Gen.* Sir Desmond Hind Garrett, KCVO, CBE
Richards, Sir (Francis) Brooks, KCMG, DSC
Richards, *Lt.-Gen.* Sir John Charles Chisholm, KCB, KCVO, RM
Richards, Sir Rex Edward, Kt., D.SC., FRS
Richardson, Sir Anthony Lewis, Bt. (1924)
Richardson, *Gen.* Sir Charles Leslie, GCB, CBE, DSO
Richardson, *Rt. Hon.* Sir Ivor Lloyd Morgan, Kt.
Richardson, Sir (John) Eric, Kt., CBE
Richardson, Sir Michael John de Rougemont, Kt.
Richardson, *Lt.-Gen.* Sir Robert Francis, KCB, CVO, CBE
Richardson, Sir Simon Alaisdair Stewart-, Bt. (s. 1630)
Riches, Sir Derek Martin Hurry, KCMG
Riches, *Gen.* Sir Ian Hurry, KCB, DSO
Richmond, Sir Alan James, Kt.
Richmond, *Rt. Hon.* Sir Clifford Parris, KBE
Richmond, Sir John Frederick, Bt. (1929)
Richmond, *Prof.* Sir Mark Henry, Kt., FRS
Rickett, Sir Denis Hubert Fletcher, KCMG, CB
Rickett, Sir Raymond Mildmay Wilson, Kt., CBE, Ph.D.
Ricketts, Sir Robert Cornwallis Gerald St Leger, Bt. (1828)
Riddell, Sir John Charles Buchanan, Bt., CVO (s. 1628)
Ridley, Sir Adam (Nicholas), Kt.
Ridley, Sir Sidney, Kt.
Ridsdale, Sir Julian Errington, Kt., CBE
Rigby, *Lt.-Col.* Sir (Hugh) John (Macbeth), Bt. (1929)
Riley, Sir Ralph, Kt., FRS
Ring, Sir Lindsay Roberts, GBE
Ringadoo, *Hon.* Sir Veerasamy, GCMG
Ripley, Sir Hugh, Bt. (1880)
Risk, Sir Thomas Neilson, Kt.
Risson, *Maj.-Gen.* Sir Robert Joseph Henry, Kt., CB, CBE, DSO, ED
Rix, *Hon.* Sir Bernard Anthony, Kt.
Rix, Sir John, Kt., MBE, FEng.
Roberts, Sir Bryan Clieve, KCMG, QC
Roberts, *Hon.* Sir Denys Tudor Emil, KBE, QC
Roberts, Sir (Edward Fergus) Sidney, Kt., CBE
Roberts, Sir Frank Kenyon, GCMG, GCVO

Roberts, Sir Geoffrey Newland, Kt., CBE, AFC
Roberts, *Brig.* Sir Geoffrey Paul Hardy-, KCVO, CB, CBE
Roberts, Sir Gilbert Howland Rookehurst, Bt. (1809)
Roberts, Sir Gordon James, Kt., CBE
Roberts, *Rt. Hon.* Sir (Ieuan) Wyn Pritchard, Kt., MP
Roberts, Sir Samuel, Bt. (1919)
Roberts, Sir Stephen James Leake, Kt.
Roberts, Sir William James Denby, Bt. (1909)
Robertson, Sir Lewis, Kt., CBE, FRSE
Robertson, *Prof.* Sir Rutherford Ness, Kt., CMG
Robins, Sir Ralph Harry, Kt., FEng.
Robinson, Sir Albert Edward Phineas, Kt.
†Robinson, Sir Christopher Philipse, Bt. (1854)
Robinson, Sir John James Michael Laud, Bt. (1660)
Robinson, *Rt. Hon.* Sir Kenneth, Kt.
Robinson, Sir Niall Bryan Lynch-, Bt., DSC (1920)
Robinson, Sir Wilfred Henry Frederick, Bt. (1908)
Robotham, *Hon.* Sir Lascelles Lister, Kt.
Robson, *Prof.* Sir James Gordon, Kt., CBE
Robson, Sir John Adam, KCMG
Roch, *Rt. Hon.* Sir John Ormond, Kt.
Roche, Sir David O'Grady, Bt. (1838)
Rodgers, Sir (John Fairlie) Tobias, Bt. (1964)
Rodrigues, Sir Alberto Maria, Kt., CBE, ED
Roe, *Air Chief Marshal* Sir Rex David, GCB, AFC
Rogers, Sir Frank Jarvis, Kt.
Rogers, *Air Chief Marshal* Sir John Robson, KCB, CBE
Rogers, Sir Philip James, Kt., CBE
Rogers, Sir Richard George, Kt., RA
Roll, *Revd* Sir James William Cecil, Bt. (1921)
Rooke, Sir Denis Eric, Kt., CBE, FRS, FEng.
Roper, *Hon.* Sir Clinton Marcus, Kt.
Ropner, Sir John Bruce Woollacott, Bt. (1952)
Ropner, Sir Robert Douglas, Bt. (1904)
Roscoe, Sir Robert Bell, KBE
Rose, *Rt. Hon.* Sir Christopher Dudley Roger, Kt.
Rose, Sir Clive Martin, GCMG
Rose, Sir David Lancaster, Bt. (1874)
Rose, Sir Julian Day, Bt. (1872 and 1909)
Rosier, *Air Chief Marshal* Sir Frederick Ernest, GCB, CBE, DSO
Ross, Sir Alexander, Kt.
Ross, Sir Archibald David Manisty, KCMG
Ross, Sir (James) Keith, Bt., RD, FRCS (1960)

Rosser, Sir Melvyn Wynne, Kt.
Rossi, Sir Hugh Alexis Louis, Kt.
Roth, *Prof.* Sir Martin, Kt., MD, FRCP
Rothnie, Sir Alan Keir, KCVO, CMG
Rothschild, Sir Evelyn Robert Adrian de, Kt.
Rougier, *Hon.* Sir Richard George, Kt.
Rous, Sir Anthony Gerald Roderick, KCMG, OBE
Rous, *Lt.-Gen.* the Hon. Sir William Edward, KCB, OBE
Row, *Hon.* Sir John Alfred, Kt.
Rowe, Sir Jeremy, Kt., CBE
Rowell, Sir John Joseph, Kt., CBE
Rowland, *Air Marshal* Sir James Anthony, KBE, DFC, AFC
Rowlands, *Air Marshal* Sir John Samuel, GC, KBE
Rowley, Sir Charles Robert, Bt. (1836)
Rowley, Sir Joshua Francis, Bt. (1786)
Rowling, *Rt. Hon.* Sir Wallace Edward, KCMG
Roxburgh, *Vice-Adm.* Sir John Charles Young, KCB, CBE, DSO, DSC
Royden, Sir Christopher John, Bt. (1905)
Rumbold, Sir Henry John Sebastian, Bt. (1779)
Rumbold, Sir (Horace) Algernon (Fraser), KCMG, CIE
Rumbold, Sir Jack Seddon, Kt.
Runchorelal, Sir (Udayan) Chinubhai Madhowlal, Bt. (1913)
Runciman, *Hon.* Sir James Cochran Stevenson (Sir Steven Runciman), Kt., CH
Rusby, *Vice-Adm.* Sir Cameron, KCB, MVO
Russell, Sir Archibald Edward, Kt., CBE, FRS, FEng.
Russell, Sir Charles Ian, Bt. (1916)
Russell, *Hon.* Sir David Sturrock West-, Kt.
Russell, Sir George, Kt., CBE
Russell, Sir George Michael, Bt. (1812)
Russell, Sir (Robert) Mark, KCMG
Russell, Sir Spencer Thomas, Kt.
Russell, *Rt. Hon.* Sir (Thomas) Patrick, Kt.
Rutter, Sir Frank William Eden, KBE
Rutter, *Prof.* Sir Michael Llewellyn, Kt., CBE, MD, FRS
Ryan, Sir Derek Gerald, Bt. (1919)
Rycroft, Sir Richard Newton, Bt. (1784)
Ryrie, Sir William Sinclair, KCB
Sachs, *Hon.* Sir Michael Alexander Geddes, Kt.
Sainsbury, Sir Robert James, Kt.
St Aubyn, Sir (John) Arscott Molesworth-, Bt. (1689)
St George, Sir George Bligh, Bt. (I. 1766)
St Johnston, Sir Kerry, Kt.
Sainty, Sir John Christopher, KCB
Sakzewski, Sir Albert, Kt.
Salt, Sir Patrick MacDonnell, Bt. (1869)

Salt, Sir (Thomas) Michael John, Bt. (1899)

Sampson, Sir Colin, Kt., CBE, QPM

Samuel, Sir Jon Michael Glen, Bt. (1898)

Samuelson, Sir (Bernard) Michael (Francis), Bt. (1884)

Sandberg, Sir Michael Graham Ruddock, Kt., CBE

Sanders, Sir John Reynolds Mayhew-, Kt.

Sanders, Sir Robert Tait, KBE, CMG

Sanderson, Sir Frank Linton, Bt. (1920)

Sandilands, Sir Francis Edwin Prescott, Kt., CBE

Sarei, Sir Alexis Holyweek, Kt., CBE

Sarell, Sir Roderick Francis Gisbert, KCMG, KCVO

Sargant, Sir (Henry) Edmund, Kt.

Saunders, *Hon.* Sir John Anthony Holt, Kt., CBE, DSO, MC

Saunders, Sir Owen Alfred, Kt., D.SC., FRS, FEng.

Saunders, Sir Peter, Kt.

Sauzier, Sir (André) Guy, Kt., CBE, ED

Savage, Sir Ernest Walter, Kt.

Savile, Sir James Wilson Vincent, Kt., OBE

Saville, *Rt. Hon.* Sir Mark Oliver, Kt.

Say, *Rt. Revd* Richard David, KCVO

Schiemann, *Hon.* Sir Konrad Hermann Theodor, Kt.

Schneider, *Rt. Hon.* Sir Lancelot Raymond Adams-, KCMG

Scholey, Sir David Gerald, Kt., CBE

Scholey, Sir Robert, Kt., CBE, FEng.

Scholtens, Sir James Henry, KCVO

Schubert, Sir Sydney, Kt.

Schuster, Sir (Felix) James Moncrieff, Bt., OBE (1906)

Scipio, Sir Hudson Rupert, Kt.

Scoon, Sir Paul, GCMG, GCVO, OBE

Scopes, Sir Leonard Arthur, KCVO, CMG, OBE

Scott, Sir Anthony Percy, Bt. (1913)

Scott, Sir (Charles) Peter, KBE, CMG

Scott, Sir David Aubrey, GCMG

†Scott, Sir Dominic James Maxwell, Bt. (1642)

Scott, Sir Ian Dixon, KCMG, KCVO, CIE

Scott, Sir James Walter, Bt. (1962)

Scott, Sir Kenneth Bertram Adam, KCVO, CMG

Scott, Sir Michael, KCVO, CMG

Scott, Sir Oliver Christopher Anderson, Bt. (1909)

Scott, *Prof.* Sir Philip John, KBE

Scott, *Rt. Hon.* Sir Richard Rashleigh Folliott, Kt.

Scott, Sir Walter John, Bt. (1907)

Scott, *Rear-Adm.* Sir (William) David (Stewart), KBE, CB

Scowen, Sir Eric Frank, Kt., MD, D.SC., LL D., FRCP, FRCS

Scrivenor, Sir Thomas Vaisey, Kt., CMG

Seale, Sir John Henry, Bt. (1838)

Seaman, Sir Keith Douglas, KCVO, OBE

†Sebright, Sir Peter Giles Vivian, Bt. (1626)

Seccombe, Sir (William) Vernon Stephen, Kt.

Secombe, Sir Harry Donald, Kt., CBE

Seconde, Sir Reginald Louis, KCMG, CVO

Sedley, *Hon.* Sir Stephen John, Kt.

Seely, Sir Nigel Edward, Bt. (1896)

Seeto, Sir Ling James, Kt., MBE

Seeyave, Sir Rene Sow Choung, Kt., CBE

Seligman, Sir Peter Wendel, Kt., CBE

Sells, Sir David Perronet, Kt.

Senior, Sir Edward Walters, Kt., CMG

Sergeant, Sir Patrick, Kt.

Series, Sir (Joseph Michel) Emile, Kt., CBE

Serpell, Sir David Radford, KCB, CMG, OBE

Seton, Sir Iain Bruce, Bt. (s. 1663)

Seton, Sir Robert James, Bt. (s. 1683)

Severne, *Air Vice-Marshal* Sir John de Milt, KCVO, OBE, AFC

Sewell, Sir (John) Allan, Kt., ISO

Seymour, *Cdr.* Sir Michael Culme-, Bt., RN (1809)

Shakerley, Sir Geoffrey Adam, Bt. (1838)

Shakespeare, Sir William Geoffrey, Bt. (1942)

Shapland, Sir William Arthur, Kt.

Sharp, Sir Adrian, Bt. (1922)

Sharp, Sir George, Kt., OBE

Sharp, Sir Kenneth Johnston, Kt., TD

Sharp, Sir Milton Reginald, Bt. (1920)

Sharp, Sir Richard Lyall, KCVO, CB

Sharp, Sir (William Harold) Angus, KBE, QPM

Sharpe, *Hon.* Sir John Henry, Kt., CBE

Sharpe, Sir Reginald Taaffe, Kt., QC

Shattock, Sir Gordon, Kt.

Shaw, Sir Brian Piers, Kt.

Shaw, Sir (Charles) Barry, Kt., CB, QC

Shaw, Sir (George) Neville Bowan-, Kt.

Shaw, Sir (John) Giles (Dunkerley), Kt., MP

Shaw, Sir John Michael Robert Best-, Bt. (1665)

Shaw, Sir Michael Norman, Kt.

Shaw, Sir Robert, Bt. (1821)

Shaw, Sir Roy, Kt.

Shaw, Sir Run Run, Kt., CBE

Sheehy, Sir Patrick, Kt.

Sheen, *Hon.* Sir Barry Cross, Kt.

Sheffield, Sir Reginald Adrian Berkeley, Bt. (1755)

Shehadie, Sir Nicholas Michael, Kt., OBE

Sheil, *Hon.* Sir John, Kt.

Sheldon, *Hon.* Sir (John) Gervase (Kensington), Kt.

Shelley, Sir John Richard, Bt. (1611)

Shelton, Sir William Jeremy Masefield, Kt.

Shepheard, Sir Peter Faulkner, Kt., CBE

Shepherd, Sir Peter Malcolm, Kt., CBE

Sheppard, Sir Allen John George, Kt.

Shepperd, Sir Alfred Joseph, Kt.

Sherlock, Sir Philip Manderson, KBE

Sherman, Sir Alfred, Kt.

Sherman, Sir Louis, Kt., OBE

Shields, Sir Neil Stanley, Kt., MC

Shields, *Prof.* Sir Robert, Kt., MD

Shiffner, Sir Henry David, Bt. (1818)

Shillington, Sir (Robert Edward) Graham, Kt., CBE

Shock, Sir Maurice, Kt.

Short, *Brig.* Sir Noel Edward Vivian, Kt., MBE, MC

Shuckburgh, Sir (Charles Arthur) Evelyn, GCMG, CB

Shuckburgh, Sir Rupert Charles Gerald, Bt. (1660)

Siaguru, Sir Anthony Michael, KBE

Sich, Sir Rupert Leigh, Kt., CB

Siddall, Sir Norman, Kt., CBE, FEng.

Sidey, *Air Marshal* Sir Ernest Shaw, KBE, CB, MD

Sie, Sir Banja Tejan-, GCMG

Simeon, Sir John Edmund Barrington, Bt. (1815)

Simmons, *Air Marshal* Sir Michael George, KCB, AFC

Simmons, Sir Stanley Clifford, Kt., FRCS, FRCOG

Simonet, Sir Louis Marcel Pierre, Kt., CBE

Simpson, *Hon.* Sir Alfred Henry, Kt.

Simpson, Sir Joseph Trevor, KBE

Simpson, Sir William James, Kt.

Sinclair, Sir Clive Marles, Kt.

Sinclair, Sir George Evelyn, Kt., CMG, OBE

Sinclair, Sir Ian McTaggart, KCMG, QC

Sinclair, *Air Vice-Marshal* Sir Laurence Frank, GC, KCB, CBE, DSO

Sinclair, Sir Patrick Robert Richard, Bt. (s. 1704)

Sinclair, Sir Ronald Ormiston, KBE

Singer, *Hon.* Sir Jan Peter, Kt.

Singh, *Hon.* Sir Vijay Raghubir, Kt.

Singhania, Sir Padampat, Kt.

Sinnamon, Sir Hercules, Kt., OBE

Sitwell, Sir (Sacheverell) Reresby, Bt. (1808)

Skeet, Sir Trevor Herbert Harry, Kt., MP

Skeggs, Sir Clifford George, Kt.

Skingsley, *Air Chief Marshal* Sir Anthony Gerald, GBE, KCB

Skinner, Sir (Thomas) Keith (Hewitt), Bt. (1912)

Skipwith, Sir Patrick Alexander d'Estoteville, Bt. (1622)

Skyrme, Sir (William) Thomas (Charles), KCVO, CB, CBE, TD

Slack, Sir William Willatt, KCVO, FRCS

Slade, Sir Benjamin Julian Alfred, Bt. (1831)

Slade, *Rt. Hon.* Sir Christopher John, Kt.

Slaney, *Prof.* Sir Geoffrey, KBE

Slater, *Adm.* Sir John (Jock) Cunningham Kirkwood, GCB, LVO

Sleight, Sir Richard, Bt. (1920)

Slimmings, Sir William Kenneth MacLeod, Kt., CBE
Sloan, Sir Andrew Kirkpatrick, Kt., QPM
Sloman, Sir Albert Edward, Kt., CBE
Smallwood, *Air Chief Marshal* Sir Denis Graham, GBE, KCB, DSO, DFC
Smart, *Prof.* Sir George Algernon, Kt., MD, FRCP
Smart, Sir Jack, Kt., CBE
Smedley, Sir Harold, KCMG, MBE
Smiley, *Lt.-Col.* Sir John Philip, Bt. (1903)
Smith, Sir Alan, Kt., CBE, DFC
Smith, Sir Alexander Mair, Kt., ph.D.
Smith, Sir Andrew Colin Hugh-, Kt.
Smith, Sir Charles Bracewell-, Bt. (1947)
Smith, Sir Christopher Sydney Winwood, Bt. (1809)
Smith, *Prof.* Sir Colin Stansfield, Kt., CBE
Smith, Sir Cyril, Kt., MBE
Smith, *Prof.* Sir David Cecil, Kt., FRS
Smith, *Air Chief Marshal* Sir David Harcourt-, GBE, KCB, DFC
Smith, Sir David Iser, KCVO
Smith, Sir Douglas Boucher, KCB
Smith, Sir Dudley (Gordon), Kt., MP
Smith, *Maj.-Gen.* Sir (Francis) Brian Wyldbore-, Kt., CB, DSO, OBE
Smith, *Prof.* Sir Francis Graham-, Kt., FRS
Smith, Sir (Frank) Ewart, Kt., FEng.
Smith, Sir Geoffrey Johnson, Kt., MP
Smith, Sir Howard Frank Trayton, GCMG
Smith, *Prof.* Sir John Cyril, Kt., CBE, QC, FBA
Smith, Sir John Hamilton-Spencer-, Bt. (1804)
Smith, Sir John Jonah Walker-, Bt. (1960)
Smith, Sir John Kenneth Newson-, Bt. (1944)
Smith, Sir John Lindsay Eric., Kt., CBE
Smith, Sir John Wilson, Kt., CBE
Smith, Sir Joseph William Grenville, Kt., MD, FRCP
Smith, Sir Leslie Edward George, Kt.
Smith, *Rt. Hon.* Sir Murray Stuart-, Kt.
Smith, Sir Raymond Horace, KBE
Smith, Sir Reginald Beaumont, Kt.
Smith, Sir Richard Rathbone Vassar-, Bt., TD (1917)
Smith, Sir (Richard) Robert Law-, Kt., CBE, AFC
Smith, Sir Robert Courtney, Kt., CBE
Smith, Sir Robert Hill, Bt. (1945)
Smith, *Prof.* Sir Roland, Kt.
Smith, *Air Marshal* Sir Roy David Austen-, KBE, CB, DFC
Smith, Sir (Thomas) Gilbert, Bt. (1897)
Smith, *Adm.* Sir Victor Alfred Trumper, KBE, CB, DSC
Smith, Sir William Reardon Reardon-, Bt. (1920)

Smith, Sir (William) Richard Prince-, Bt. (1911)
Smithers, *Prof.* Sir David Waldron, Kt., MD
Smithers, Sir Peter Henry Berry Otway, Kt., VRD, D.Phil.
Smithers, *Hon.* Sir Reginald Allfree, Kt.
Smyth, Sir Thomas Weyland Bowyer-, Bt. (1661)
Smyth, Sir Timothy John, Bt. (1955)
Snelling, Sir Arthur Wendell, KCMG, KCVO
Soame, Sir Charles John Buckworth-Herne-, Bt. (1697)
Sobers, Sir Garfield St Auburn, Kt.
Solomon, Sir David Arnold, Kt., MBE
Solomon, Sir Harry, Kt.
Solomons, *Hon.* Sir (Louis) Adrian, Kt.
Solti, Sir Georg, KBE
Somare, *Rt. Hon.* Sir Michael Thomas, GCMG, CH
Somers, *Rt. Hon.* Sir Edward Jonathan, Kt.
Somerset, Sir Henry Beaufort, Kt., CBE
Somerville, *Brig.* Sir John Nicholas, Kt., CBE
Somerville, Sir Quentin Charles Somerville Agnew-, Bt. (1957)
Sopwith, Sir Charles Ronald, Kt.
Soutar, *Air Marshal* Sir Charles John Williamson, KBE
South, Sir Arthur, Kt.
Southby, Sir John Richard Bilbe, Bt. (1937)
Southern, Sir Richard William, Kt., FBA
Southern, Sir Robert, Kt., CBE
Southey, Sir Robert John, Kt., CMG
Southgate, Sir Colin Grieve, Kt.
Southward, Sir Leonard Bingley, Kt., OBE
Southward, Sir Ralph, KCVO, FRCP
Southwood, *Prof.* Sir (Thomas) Richard (Edmund), Kt., FRS
Southworth, Sir Frederick, Kt., QC
Souyave, *Hon.* Sir (Louis) Georges, Kt.
Sowrey, *Air Marshal* Sir Frederick Beresford, KCB, CBE, AFC
Soysa, Sir Warusahennedige Abraham Bastian, Kt., CBE
Sparkes, Sir Robert Lyndley, Kt.
Sparrow, Sir John, Kt.
Spearman, Sir Alexander Young Richard Mainwaring, Bt. (1840)
Speed, Sir (Herbert) Keith, Kt., RD, MP
Speed, Sir Robert William Arney, Kt., CB, QC
Speelman, Sir Cornelis Jacob, Bt. (1686)
Speight, *Hon.* Sir Graham Davies, Kt.
Speir, Sir Rupert Malise, Kt.
Spencer, Sir Derek Harold, Kt., QC, MP

Spender, *Prof.* Sir Stephen Harold, Kt., CBE
Spicer, Sir James Wilton, Kt., MP
Spicer, Sir Peter James, Bt. (1906)
Spiers, Sir Donald Maurice, Kt., CB, TD
Spooner, Sir James Douglas, Kt.
Spotswood, *Marshal of the Royal Air Force* Sir Denis Frank, GCB, CBE, DSO, DFC
Spratt, *Col.* Sir Greville Douglas, GBE, TD
Spreckley, Sir (John) Nicholas (Teague), KCVO, CMG
Springer, Sir Hugh Worrell, GCMG, GCVO, CBE
Spry, *Brig.* Sir Charles Chambers Fowell, Kt., CBE, DSO
Spry, *Hon.* Sir John Farley, Kt.
Stabb, *Hon.* Sir William Walter, Kt., QC
Stack, *Air Chief Marshal* Sir (Thomas) Neville, KCB, CVO, CBE, AFC
Stainton, Sir (John) Ross, Kt., CBE
Stakis, Sir Reo Argiros, Kt.
Stallard, Sir Peter Hyla Gawne, KCMG, CVO, MBE
Stallworthy, Sir John Arthur, Kt., FRCS
Stamer, Sir (Lovelace) Anthony, Bt. (1809)
Stanbridge, *Air Vice-Marshal* Sir Brian Gerald Tivy, KCVO, CBE, AFC
Stanier, *Brig.* Sir Alexander Beville Gibbons, Bt., DSO, MC (1917)
Stanier, *Field Marshal* Sir John Wilfred, GCB, MBE
Stanley, *Rt. Hon.* Sir John Paul, Kt., MP
†Staples, Sir Thomas, Bt. (I. 1628)
Stapleton, Sir (Henry) Alfred, Bt. (1679)
Stark, Sir Andrew Alexander Steel, KCMG, CVO
Starke, *Hon.* Sir John Erskine, Kt.
Starkey, Sir John Philip, Bt. (1935)
Starrit, Sir James, KCVO
Statham, Sir Norman, KCMG, CVO
Staughton, *Rt. Hon.* Sir Christopher Stephen Thomas Jonathan Thayer, Kt.
Staveley, Sir John Malfroy, KBE, MC
Staveley, *Admiral of the Fleet* Sir William Doveton Minet, GCB
Stear, *Air Chief Marshal* Sir Michael James Douglas, KCB, CBE
Steel, Sir David Edward Charles, Kt., DSO, MC, TD
Steel, *Rt. Hon.* Sir David Martin Scott, KBE, MP
†Steel, *Maj.* Sir (Fiennes) Michael Strang, Bt. (1938)
Steel, Sir James, Kt., CBE
Steele, Sir (Philip John) Rupert, Kt.
Steere, Sir Ernest Henry Lee-, KBE
Stenhouse, Sir Nicol, Kt.
Stening, *Col.* Sir George Grafton Lees, Kt., ED
Stephen, *Rt. Hon.* Sir Ninian Martin, GCMG, GCVO, KBE

Stephenson, Sir Henry Upton, Bt.
(1936)
Stephenson, *Rt. Hon.* Sir John
Frederick Eustace, Kt.
Sternberg, Sir Sigmund, Kt.
Stevens, Sir Laurence Houghton, Kt.,
CBE
Stevenson, *Vice-Adm.* Sir (Hugh)
David, KBE
Stevenson, Sir Simpson, Kt.
Stewart, Sir Alan, KBE
Stewart, Sir Alan d'Arcy, Bt. (I. 1623)
Stewart, Sir David James Henderson-,
Bt. (1957)
Stewart, Sir Edward Jackson, Kt.
Stewart, *Prof.* Sir Frederick Henry,
Kt., Ph.D., FRS, FRSE
Stewart, Sir Houston Mark Shaw-, Bt.,
MC, TD (S. 1667)
Stewart, Sir Hugh Charlie Godfray,
Bt. (1803)
Stewart, Sir James Douglas, Kt.
Stewart, Sir (John) Simon (Watson),
Bt. (1920)
Stewart, Sir Michael Norman Francis,
KCMG, OBE
Stewart, Sir Robertson Huntly, Kt.,
CBE
Stewart, Sir Robin Alastair, Bt. (1960)
Stewart, Sir Ronald Compton, Bt.
(1937)
Steyn, *Rt. Hon.* Sir Johan Van Zyl, Kt.
Stibbon, *Gen.* Sir John James, KCB, OBE
Stirling, Sir Alexander John Dickson,
KBE, CMG
Stockdale, Sir Arthur Noel, Kt.
Stockdale, Sir Thomas Minshull, Bt.
(1960)
Stocker, *Rt. Hon.* Sir John Dexter, Kt.,
MC, TD
Stoddart, *Wg Cdr.* Sir Kenneth
Maxwell, KCVO, AE
Stoker, *Prof.* Sir Michael George
Parke, Kt., CBE, FRCP, FRS, FRSE
Stokes, Sir John Heydon Romaine, Kt.
Stones, Sir William Frederick, Kt.,
OBE
Stonhouse, Sir Philip Allan, Bt. (1628)
Stonor, *Air Marshal* Sir Thomas
Henry, KCB
Storey, *Hon.* Sir Richard, Bt. (1960)
Stormonth Darling, Sir James Carlisle,
Kt., CBE, MC, TD
Stott, Sir Adrian George Ellingham,
Bt. (1920)
Stow, Sir Christopher Philipson-, Bt.,
DFC (1907)
Stow, Sir John Montague, GCMG, KCVO
Stowe, Sir Kenneth Ronald, GCB, CVO
Stracey, Sir John Simon, Bt. (1818)
Strachey, Sir Charles, Bt. (1801)
Straker, Sir Michael Ian Bowstead,
Kt., CBE
Strawson, *Prof.* Sir Peter Frederick,
Kt., FBA
Street, *Hon.* Sir Laurence Whistler,
KCMG
Streeton, Sir Terence George, KBE,
CMG

Stringer, Sir Donald Edgar, Kt., CBE
Strong, Sir Roy Colin, Kt., Ph.D., FSA
Stronge, Sir James Anselan Maxwell,
Bt. (1803)
Stroud, *Prof.* Sir (Charles) Eric, Kt.,
FRCP
Strutt, Sir Nigel Edward, Kt., TD
Stuart, Sir James Keith, Kt.
Stuart, Sir Kenneth Lamonte, Kt.
†Stuart, Sir Phillip Luttrell, Bt. (1660)
Stubblefield, Sir (Cyril) James, Kt.,
D.SC., FRS
Stubbs, Sir James Wilfrid, KCVO, TD
Stucley, *Lt.* Sir Hugh George
Coplestone Bampfylde, Bt. (1859)
Studd, Sir Edward Fairfax, Bt. (1929)
Studd, Sir Peter Malden, GBE, KCVO
Studholme, Sir Henry William, Bt.
(1956)
Style, *Lt.-Cdr.* Sir Godfrey William,
Kt., CBE, DSC, RN
†Style, Sir William Frederick, Bt.
(1627)
Suffield, Sir (Henry John) Lester, Kt.
Sugden, Sir Arthur, Kt.
Sullivan, Sir Desmond John, Kt.
Sullivan, Sir Richard Arthur, Bt.
(1804)
Summerfield, *Hon.* Sir John
Crampton, Kt., CBE
Summers, Sir Felix Roland Brattan,
Bt. (1952)
Sunderland, *Prof.* Sir Sydney, Kt., CMG
Sutherland, *Prof.* Sir James
Runcieman, Kt., FBA
Sutherland, Sir John Brewer, Bt.
(1921)
Sutherland, Sir Maurice, Kt.
Sutherland, Sir William George
MacKenzie, Kt.
Suttie, Sir (George) Philip Grant-, Bt.
(S. 1702)
Sutton, Sir Frederick Walter, Kt., OBE
Sutton, *Air Marshal* Sir John Matthias
Dobson, KCB
Sutton, Sir Richard Lexington, Bt.
(1772)
Swaffield, Sir James Chesebrough, Kt.,
CBE, RD
Swallow, Sir William, Kt.
Swan, Sir John William David, KBE
Swann, Sir Michael Christopher, Bt.,
TD (1906)
Swanwick, Sir Graham Russell, Kt.,
MBE
Swartz, *Hon.* Sir Reginald William
Colin, KBE, ED
Sweetnam, Sir (David) Rodney, KCVO,
CBE, FRCS
Swinburn, *Lt.-Gen.* Sir Richard Hull,
KCB
Swinson, Sir John Henry Alan, Kt.,
OBE
Swinton, *Maj.-Gen.* Sir John, KCVO,
OBE
Swire, Sir Adrian Christopher, Kt.
Swire, Sir John Anthony, Kt., CBE
Swiss, Sir Rodney Geoffrey, Kt., OBE

Swynnerton, Sir Roger John Massy,
Kt., CMG, OBE, MC
Sykes, Sir Francis John Badcock, Bt.
(1781)
Sykes, Sir John Charles Anthony le
Gallais, Bt. (1921)
Sykes, *Prof.* Sir (Malcolm) Keith, Kt.
Sykes, Sir Tatton Christopher Mark,
Bt. (1783)
Symington, *Prof.* Sir Thomas, Kt., MD,
FRSE
Symons, *Vice-Adm.* Sir Patrick
Jeremy, KBE
Synge, Sir Robert Carson, Bt. (1801)
Tait, *Adm.* Sir (Allan) Gordon, KCB,
DSC
Tait, Sir James Sharp, Kt., D.SC., LL D.,
Ph.D.
Tait, Sir Peter, KBE
Talbot, *Vice-Adm.* Sir (Arthur Allison)
FitzRoy, KBE, CB, DSO
Talbot, *Hon.* Sir Hilary Gwynne, Kt.
Talboys, *Rt. Hon.* Sir Brian Edward,
CH, KCB
Tancred, Sir Henry Lawson-, Bt.
(1662)
Tangaroa, *Hon.* Sir Tangoroa, Kt.,
MBE
Tange, Sir Arthur Harold, Kt., CBE
Tapsell, Sir Peter Hannay Bailey, Kt.,
MP
Tate, *Lt.-Col.* Sir Henry, Bt. (1898)
Taukala, Sir David Dawea, Kt., MBE
Tavaiqia, *Ratu* Sir Josaia, KBE
Tavare, Sir John, Kt., CBE
Taylor, *Lt.-Gen.* Sir Allan Macnab,
KBE, MC
Taylor, Sir (Arthur) Godfrey, Kt.
Taylor, Sir Cyril Julian Hebden, Kt.
Taylor, Sir Edward Macmillan
(Teddy), Kt., MP
Taylor, Sir George, Kt., D.SC., FRS,
FRSE
Taylor, Sir Henry Milton, Kt.
Taylor, Sir James, Kt., MBE, D.SC
Taylor, Sir John Lang, KCMG
Taylor, Sir Nicholas Richard Stuart,
Bt. (1917)
Taylor, *Prof.* Sir William, Kt., CBE
Tebbit, Sir Donald Claude, GCMG
Te Heuheu, Sir Hepi Hoani, KBE
Telford, Sir Robert, Kt., CBE, FEng.
Temple, Sir Ernest Sanderson, Kt.,
MBE, QC
Temple, Sir John Meredith, Kt.
Temple, Sir Rawden John Afamado,
Kt., CBE, QC
Temple, *Maj.* Sir Richard Anthony
Purbeck, Bt., MC (1876)
Templeton, Sir John Marks, Kt.
Tennant, *Capt.* Sir Iain Mark, KT
Tennant, Sir Anthony John, Kt.
Tennant, Sir Peter Frank Dalrymple,
Kt., CMG, OBE
Teo, Sir Fiatau Penitala, GCMG, GCVO,
ISO, MBE
Terry, Sir George Walter Roberts,
Kt., CBE, QPM
Terry, Sir John Elliott, Kt.

Terry, Sir Michael Edward Stanley Imbert-, Bt. (1917)

Terry, *Air Chief Marshal* Sir Peter David George, GCB, AFC

Tetley, Sir Herbert, KBE, CB

Tett, Sir Hugh Charles, Kt.

Thatcher, Sir Denis, Bt., MBE, TD (1990)

Thiess, Sir Leslie Charles, Kt., CBE

Thomas, Sir Derek Morison David, KCMG

Thomas, Sir Frederick William, Kt.

Thomas, Sir (Godfrey) Michael (David), Bt. (1694)

Thomas, Sir Jeremy Cashel, KCMG

Thomas, Sir (John) Alan, Kt.

Thomas, Sir John Maldwyn, Kt.

Thomas, *Prof.* Sir John Meurig, Kt., FRS

Thomas, Sir Keith Vivian, Kt.

Thomas, Sir Robert Evan, Kt.

Thomas, *Hon.* Sir Swinton Barclay, Kt.

Thomas, Sir William James Cooper, Bt., TD (1919)

Thomas, Sir (William) Michael (Marsh), Bt. (1918)

Thomas, *Adm.* Sir (William) Richard Scott, KCB, OBE

Thompson, Sir Christopher Peile, Bt. (1890)

Thompson, Sir Donald, Kt., MP

Thompson, Sir Edward Hugh Dudley, Kt., MBE, TD

Thompson, Sir Gilbert Williamson, Kt., OBE

Thompson, *Surgeon Vice-Adm.* Sir Godfrey James Milton-, KBE

Thompson, *Vice-Adm.* Sir Hugh Leslie Owen, KBE, FEng.

Thompson, Sir (Humphrey) Simon Meysey-, Bt. (1874)

Thompson, *Hon.* Sir John, Kt.

Thompson, *Prof.* Sir Michael Warwick, Kt., D.Sc

Thompson, Sir Paul Anthony, Bt. (1963)

Thompson, Sir Peter Anthony, Kt.

Thompson, Sir Richard Hilton Marler, Bt. (1963)

Thompson, Sir (Thomas) Lionel Tennyson, Bt. (1806)

Thomson, Sir Adam, Kt., CBE

Thomson, *Air Chief Marshal* Sir (Charles) John, KCB, CBE, AFC

Thomson, Sir Evan Rees Whitaker, Kt.

Thomson, Sir (Frederick Douglas) David, Bt. (1929)

Thomson, Sir John, KBE, TD

Thomson, Sir John Adam, GCMG

Thomson, Sir John (Ian) Sutherland, KBE, CMG

Thomson, Sir Mark Wilfrid Home, Bt. (1925)

Thomson, Sir Thomas James, Kt., CBE, FRCP

Thorn, Sir John Samuel, Kt., OBE

Thorne, *Maj.-Gen.* Sir David Calthrop, KBE

Thorne, Sir Neil Gordon, Kt., OBE, TD

Thorne, Sir Peter Francis, KCVO, CBE

Thornton, Sir (George) Malcolm, Kt., MP

Thornton, *Lt.-Gen.* Sir Leonard Whitmore, KCB, CBE

Thornton, Sir Peter Eustace, KCB

Thorold, Sir Anthony Henry, Bt., OBE, DSC (1642)

Thorpe, *Hon.* Sir Mathew Alexander, Kt.

Thouron, Sir John Rupert Hunt, KBE

†Throckmorton, Sir Anthony John Benedict, Bt. (1642)

Thwaites, Sir Bryan, Kt., PH.D.

Thwin, Sir U, Kt.

Tibbits, *Capt.* Sir David Stanley, Kt., DSC

Tickell, Sir Crispin Charles Cervantes, GCMG, KCVO

Tidbury, Sir Charles Henderson, Kt.

Tikaram, Sir Moti, KBE

Tilney, Sir John Dudley Robert Tarleton, Kt., TD

Tims, Sir Michael David, KCVO

Tippet, *Vice-Adm.* Sir Anthony Sanders, KCB

Tippett, Sir Michael Kemp, Kt., OM, CH, CBE

Tirvengadum, Sir Harry Krishnan, Kt.

Titman, Sir John Edward Powis, KCVO

Tizard, Sir John Peter Mills, Kt.

Tod, *Air Marshal* Sir John Hunter Hunter-, KBE, CB

Todd, Sir Ian Pelham, KBE, FRCS

Todd, *Hon.* Sir (Reginald Stephen) Garfield, Kt.

Tollemache, Sir Lyonel Humphry John, Bt. (1793)

Tololo, Sir Alkan, KBE

Tomkins, Sir Alfred George, Kt., CBE

Tomkins, Sir Edward Emile, GCMG, CVO

Tomkys, Sir (William) Roger, KCMG

Tomlinson, *Prof.* Sir Bernard Evans, Kt., CBE

Tomlinson, Sir (Frank) Stanley, KCMG

Tooley, Sir John, Kt.

Tooth, Sir (Hugh) John Lucas-, Bt. (1920)

ToRobert, Sir Henry Thomas, KBE

Tory, Sir Geofroy William, KCMG

Touche, Sir Anthony George, Bt. (1920)

Touche, Sir Rodney Gordon, Bt. (1962)

Tovey, Sir Brian John Maynard, KCMG

ToVue, Sir Ronald, Kt., OBE

Townsend, *Rear-Adm.* Sir Leslie William, KCVO, CBE

Townsing, Sir Kenneth Joseph, Kt., CMG

Traherne, Sir Cennydd George, KG, TD

Traill, Sir Alan Towers, GBE

Trant, *Gen.* Sir Richard Brooking, KCB

Travers, Sir Thomas à'Beckett, Kt.

Treacher, *Adm.* Sir John Devereux, KCB

Trehane, Sir (Walter) Richard, Kt.

Trelawny, Sir John Barry Salusbury-, Bt. (1628)

Trench, Sir Nigel Clive Cosby, KCMG

Trench, Sir Peter Edward, Kt., CBE, TD

Trescowthick, Sir Donald Henry, KBE

Trethowan, *Prof.* Sir William Henry, Kt., CBE, FRCP

Trevelyan, Sir George Lowthian, Bt. (1874)

Trevelyan, Sir Norman Irving, Bt. (1662)

Trewby, *Vice-Adm.* Sir (George Francis) Allan, KCB, FEng.

Trippier, Sir David Austin, Kt., RD

Tritton, Sir Anthony John Ernest, Bt. (1905)

†Trollope, Sir Anthony Simon, Bt. (1642)

Trotter, Sir Ronald Ramsay, Kt.

Troubridge, Sir Thomas Richard, Bt. (1799)

Troup, *Vice-Adm.* Sir (John) Anthony (Rose), KCB, DSC

Trowbridge, *Rear-Adm.* Sir Richard John, KCVO

Truscott, Sir George James Irving, Bt. (1909)

Tuck, Sir Bruce Adolph Reginald, Bt. (1910)

Tucker, *Hon.* Sir Richard Howard, Kt.

Tuckey, *Hon.* Sir Simon Lane, Kt.

Tudor, *Hon.* Sir James Cameron, KCMG

Tugendhat, Sir Christopher Samuel, Kt.

Tuita, Sir Mariano Kelesimalefo, Kt., OBE

Tuite, Sir Christopher Hugh, Bt., PH.D. (1622)

Tuivaga, Sir Timoci Uluiburotu, Kt.

Tuke, Sir Anthony Favill, Kt.

Tupper, Sir Charles Hibbert, Kt. (1888)

Turbott, Sir Ian Graham, Kt., CMG, CVO

Turing, Sir John Dermot, Bt. (s. 1638)

Turnbull, Sir Richard Gordon, GCMG

Turner, Sir Colin William Carstairs, Kt., CBE, DFC

Turner, *Hon.* Sir Michael John, Kt.

Tuti, *Revd* Dudley, KBE

Tuzo, *Gen.* Sir Harry Craufurd, GCB, OBE, MC

Twiss, *Adm.* Sir Frank Roddam, KCB, KCVO, DSC

Tyree, Sir (Alfred) William, Kt., OBE

Tyrrell, Sir Murray Louis, KCVO, CBE

Tyrwhitt, Sir Reginald Thomas Newman, Bt. (1919)

Udoma, *Hon.* Sir (Egbert) Udo, Kt.

Unsworth, *Hon.* Sir Edgar Ignatius Godfrey, Kt., CMG

Unwin, Sir (James) Brian, KCB

Ure, Sir John Burns, KCMG, LVO

Urquhart, Sir Brian Edward, KCMG, MBE
Urwick, Sir Alan Bedford, KCVO, CMG
Usher, Sir Leonard Gray, KBE
Usher, Sir Robert Edward, Bt. (1899)
Ustinov, Sir Peter Alexander, Kt., CBE
Utting, Sir William Benjamin, Kt., CB
Vallat, Sir Francis Aimé, GBE, KCMG, QC
Vallings, *Vice-Adm.* Sir George Montague Francis, KCB
Vanderfelt, Sir Robin Victor, KBE
van der Post, Sir Laurens Jan, Kt., CBE
Vane, Sir John Robert, Kt., D.Phil., D.SC., FRS
Vanneck, *Air Cdre* Hon. Sir Peter Beckford Rutgers, GBE, CB, AFC
van Straubenzee, Sir William Radcliffe, Kt., MBE
Vasquez, Sir Alfred Joseph, Kt., CBE, QC
Vaughan, Sir (George) Edgar, KBE
Vaughan, Sir Gerard Folliott, Kt., MP, FRCP
Vavasour, *Cdr.* Sir Geoffrey William, Bt., DSC, RN (1828)
Veale, Sir Alan John Ralph, Kt., FEng.
Verco, Sir Walter John George, KCVO
†Verney, Sir John Sebastian, Bt. (1946)
Verney, *Hon.* Sir Lawrence John, Kt., TD
Verney, Sir Ralph Bruce, Bt., KBE (1818)
Vernon, Sir James, Kt., CBE
Vernon, Sir Nigel John Douglas, Bt. (1914)
Vesey, Sir (Nathaniel) Henry (Peniston), Kt., CBE
Vestey, Sir (John) Derek, Bt. (1921)
Vial, Sir Kenneth Harold, Kt., CBE
Vick, Sir (Francis) Arthur, Kt., OBE, Ph.D.
Vickers, *Lt.-Gen.* Sir Richard Maurice Hilton, KCB, MVO, OBE
Victoria, Sir (Joseph Aloysius) Donatus, Kt., CBE
Vincent, *Field Marshal* Sir Richard Frederick, GBE, KCB, DSO
Vincent, Sir William Percy Maxwell, Bt. (1936)
Vinelott, *Hon.* Sir John Evelyn, Kt.
Vines, Sir William Joshua, Kt., CMG
Vyvyan, Sir John Stanley, Bt. (1645)
Waddell, Sir Alexander Nicol Anton, KCMG, DSC
Waddell, Sir James Henderson, Kt., CB
Wade, *Prof.* Sir Henry William Rawson, Kt., QC, FBA
Wade, *Air Chief Marshal* Sir Ruthven Lowry, KCB, DFC
Wagner, Sir Anthony Richard, KCB, KCVO
Waite, *Rt. Hon.* Sir John Douglas, Kt.
Wake, Sir Hereward, Bt., MC (1621)
Wakefield, Sir (Edward) Humphry (Tyrell), Bt. (1962)
Wakefield, Sir Norman Edward, Kt.

Wakefield, Sir Peter George Arthur, KBE, CMG
Wakeford, *Air Marshal* Sir Richard Gordon, KCB, OBE, MVO, AFC
Wakeley, Sir John Cecil Nicholson, Bt., FRCS (1952)
†Wakeman, Sir Edward Offley Bertram, Bt. (1828)
Walker, *Revd* Alan Edgar, Kt., OBE
Walker, Sir Allan Grierson, Kt., QC
Walker, *Gen.* Sir Antony Kenneth Frederick, KCB
Walker, Sir Baldwin Patrick, Bt. (1856)
Walker, Sir (Charles) Michael, GCMG
Walker, Sir Colin John Shedlock, Kt., OBE
Walker, Sir David Alan, Kt.
Walker, Sir Gervas George, Kt.
Walker, *Rt. Hon.* Sir Harold, Kt., MP
Walker, Sir Harold Berners, KCMG
Walker, *Maj.* Sir Hugh Ronald, Bt. (1906)
Walker, Sir James Graham, Kt., MBE
Walker, Sir James Heron, Bt. (1868)
Walker, *Air Marshal* Sir John Robert, KCB, CBE, AFC
Walker, Sir Michael Leolin Forestier-, Bt. (1835)
Walker, Sir Patrick Jeremy, KCB
Walker, *Gen.* Sir Walter Colyear, KCB, CBE, DSO
Wall, *Dr Hon.* Sir Gerard Aloysius, Kt.
Wall, *Hon.* Sir Nicholas Peter Rathbone, Kt.
Wall, Sir Patrick Henry Bligh, Kt., MC, VRD
Wall, Sir Robert William, Kt., OBE
Wallace, Sir Ian James, Kt., CBE
Waller, *Hon.* Sir (George) Mark, Kt.
Waller, *Rt. Hon.* Sir George Stanley, Kt., OBE
Waller, Sir (John) Keith, Kt., CBE
Waller, Sir John Stainer, Bt. (1815)
Waller, Sir Robert William, Bt. (I. 1780)
Walley, Sir John, KBE, CB
Wallis, Sir Peter Gordon, KCVO
Walsh, Sir Alan, Kt., D.SC., FRS
Walsh, *Prof.* Sir John Patrick, KBE
†Walsham, Sir Timothy John, Bt. (1831)
Walter, Sir Harold Edward, Kt.
Walters, *Prof.* Sir Alan Arthur, Kt.
Walters, Sir Dennis Murray, Kt., MBE
Walters, Sir Frederick Donald, Kt.
Walters, Sir Peter Ingram, Kt.
Walters, Sir Roger Talbot, KBE, FRIBA
Walton, Sir John Robert, Kt.
Wan, Sir Wamp, Kt., MBE
Wanstall, *Hon.* Sir Charles Gray, Kt.
Ward, *Hon.* Sir Alan Hylton, Kt.
Ward, Sir Arthur Hugh, KBE
Ward, Sir Joseph James Laffey, Bt. (1911)
Ward, *Maj.-Gen.* Sir Philip John Newling, KCVO, CBE
Wardale, Sir Geoffrey Charles, KCB

Wardlaw, Sir Henry (John), Bt. (S. 1631)
Wardle, Sir Thomas Edward Jewell, Kt.
Waring, Sir (Alfred) Holburt, Bt. (1935)
Warmington, *Lt.-Cdr.* Sir Marshall George Clitheroe, Bt., RN (1908)
Warner, Sir (Edward Courtenay) Henry, Bt. (1910)
Warner, Sir Edward Redston, KCMG, OBE
Warner, Sir Frederick Archibald, GCVO, KCMG
Warner, *Prof.* Sir Frederick Edward, Kt., FRS, FEng.
Warner, *Hon.* Sir Jean-Pierre Frank Eugene, Kt.
Warnock, Sir Geoffrey James, Kt.
Warren, Sir Brian Charles Pennefather, Bt. (1784)
Warren, Sir Frederick Miles, KBE
Warren, Sir (Harold) Brian (Seymour), Kt.
Wass, Sir Douglas William Gretton, GCB
Waterhouse, *Hon.* Sir Ronald Gough, Kt.
Waterlow, Sir Christopher Rupert, Bt. (1873)
Waterlow, Sir (James) Gerard, Bt. (1930)
Waters, *Gen.* Sir (Charles) John, KCB, CBE
Wates, Sir Christopher Stephen, Kt.
Watkins, *Rt. Hon.* Sir Tasker, VC, GBE
Watson, Sir Bruce Dunstan, Kt.
Watson, Sir Duncan Amos, Kt., CBE
Watson, Sir (James) Andrew, Bt. (1866)
Watson, Sir John Forbes Inglefield-, Bt. (1895)
Watson, Sir Michael Milne-, Bt. (1937)
Watson, Sir (Noel) Duncan, KCMG
Watson, *Vice-Adm.* Sir Philip Alexander, KBE, MVO
Watt, *Surgeon Vice-Adm.* Sir James, KBE, FRCS
Watt, Sir James Harvie-, Bt. (1945)
Watts, Sir Arthur Desmond, KCMG
Watts, *Lt.-Gen.* Sir John Peter Barry Condliffe, KBE, CB, MC
Wauchope, Sir Roger (Hamilton) Don-, Bt. (1667)
Way, Sir Richard George Kitchener, KCB, CBE
Weatherall, *Prof.* Sir David John, Kt., FRS
Weatherall, *Vice-Adm.* Sir James Lamb, KBE
Weatherstone, Sir Dennis, KBE
Weaver, Sir Tobias Rushton, Kt., CB
Webb, *Lt.-Gen.* Sir Richard James Holden, KBE, CB
Webb, Sir Thomas Langley, Kt.
Webber, Sir Andrew Lloyd, Kt.
Webster, *Very Revd* Alan Brunskill, KCVO

Webster, *Vice-Adm.* Sir John Morrison, KCB

Webster, *Hon.* Sir Peter Edlin, Kt.

Wedderburn, Sir Andrew John Alexander Ogilvy-, Bt. (1803)

Wedgwood, Sir (Hugo) Martin, Bt. (1942)

Weinberg, Sir Mark Aubrey, Kt.

Weir, Sir Michael Scott, KCMG

Weir, Sir Roderick Bignell, Kt.

Welby, Sir (Richard) Bruno Gregory, Bt. (1801)

Welch, Sir John Reader, Bt. (1957)

Weldon, Sir Anthony William, Bt. (I. 1723)

Wellings, Sir Jack Alfred, Kt., CBE

Wells, Sir Charles Maltby, Bt., TD (1944)

Wells, Sir John Julius, Kt.

Westbrook, Sir Neil Gowanloch, Kt., CBE

Westerman, Sir (Wilfred) Alan, Kt., CBE

Weston, Sir Michael Charles Swift, KCMG, CVO

Weston, Sir (Philip) John, KCMG

Wheeler, Sir Frederick Henry, Kt., CBE

Wheeler, Sir Harry Anthony, Kt., OBE

Wheeler, *Air Chief Marshal* Sir (Henry) Neil (George), GCB, CBE, DSO, DFC, AFC

Wheeler, *Rt. Hon.* Sir John Daniel, Kt., MP

Wheeler, Sir John Hieron, Bt. (1920)

Wheeler, *Hon.* Sir Kenneth Henry, Kt.

Wheeler, *Lt.-Gen.* Sir Roger Neil, KCB, CBE

Wheler, Sir Edward Woodford, Bt. (1660)

Whishaw, Sir Charles Percival Law, Kt.

Whitaker, *Maj.* Sir James Herbert Ingham, Bt. (1936)

White, Sir Christopher Robert Meadows, Bt. (1937)

White, *Hon.* Sir Christopher Stuart Stuart-, Kt.

White, Sir David Harry, Kt.

White, Sir Frederick William George, KBE, Ph.D., FRS

White, Sir George Stanley James, Bt. (1904)

White, Sir Harold Leslie, Kt., CBE

White, *Wg Cdr.* Sir Henry Arthur Dalrymple-, Bt., DFC (1926)

White, *Adm.* Sir Hugo Moresby, KCB, CBE

White, *Hon.* Sir John Charles, Kt., MBE

White, Sir John Woolmer, Bt. (1922)

White, Sir Lynton Stuart, Kt., MBE, TD

White, *Adm.* Sir Peter, GBE

White, Sir Thomas Astley Woollaston, Bt. (1802)

Whitehead, Sir John Stainton, GCMG, CVO

Whitehead, Sir Rowland John Rathbone, Bt. (1889)

Whiteley, Sir Hugo Baldwin Huntington-, Bt. (1918)

Whiteley, *Gen.* Sir Peter John Frederick, GCB, OBE, RM

Whitfield, Sir William, Kt., CBE

Whitford, *Hon.* Sir John Norman Keates, Kt.

Whitley, *Air Marshal* Sir John René, KBE, CB, DSO, AFC

Whitmore, Sir Clive Anthony, GCB, CVO

Whitmore, Sir John Henry Douglas, Bt. (1954)

Whitteridge, Sir Gordon Coligny, KCMG, OBE

Whittle, *Air Cdre* Sir Frank, OM, KBE, CB, FRS, FEng.

Whittome, Sir Leslie Alan, Kt.

Wickerson, Sir John Michael, Kt.

Wicks, Sir James Albert, Kt.

Wicks, Sir Nigel Leonard, KCB, CVO, CBE

Wigan, Sir Alan Lewis, Bt. (1898)

Wiggin, Sir Alfred William (Jerry), Kt., TD, MP

†Wiggin, Sir Charles Rupert John, Bt. (1892)

Wigglesworth, Sir Vincent Brian, Kt., CBE, MD, FRS

Wigram, *Revd Canon* Sir Clifford Woolmore, Bt. (1805)

Wilbraham, Sir Richard Baker, Bt. (1776)

Wilford, Sir (Kenneth) Michael, GCMG

Wilkes, *Gen.* Sir Michael John, KCB, CBE

Wilkins, Sir Graham John, Kt.

Wilkins, *Lt.-Gen.* Sir Michael Compton Lockwood, KCB, OBE

Wilkinson, Sir (David) Graham (Brook) Bt. (1941)

Wilkinson, *Prof.* Sir Denys Haigh, Kt., FRS

Wilkinson, *Prof.* Sir Geoffrey, Kt., FRS

Wilkinson, Sir Peter Allix, KCMG, DSO, OBE

Wilkinson, Sir Philip William, Kt.

Wilkinson, Sir William Henry Nairn, Kt.

Willatt, Sir (Robert) Hugh, Kt.

Willcocks, Sir David Valentine, Kt., CBE, MC

Williams, Sir Alastair Edgcumbe James Dudley-, Bt. (1964)

Williams, Sir Alwyn, Kt., Ph.D., FRS

Williams, Sir Arthur Dennis Pitt, Kt.

Williams, Sir (Arthur) Gareth Ludovic Emrys Rhys, Bt. (1918)

Williams, *Prof.* Sir Bruce Rodda, KBE

Williams, *Adm.* Sir David, GCB

Williams, *Prof.* Sir David Glyndwr Tudor, Kt.

Williams, Sir David Innes, Kt.

Williams, *Hon.* Sir Denys Ambrose, KCMG

Williams, Sir Donald Mark, Bt. (1866)

Williams, Sir Edgar Trevor, Kt., CB, CBE, DSO

Williams, *Prof.* Sir (Edward) Dillwyn, Kt., FRCP

Williams, *Hon.* Sir Edward Stratten, KCMG, KBE

Williams, Sir Francis John Watkin, Bt., QC (1798)

Williams, Sir Henry Sydney, Kt., OBE

Williams, Sir (John) Leslie, Kt., CBE

Williams, Sir John Robert, KCMG

Williams, Sir Leonard, KBE, CB

Williams, Sir Osmond, Bt., MC (1909)

Williams, Sir Peter Watkin, Kt.

Williams, *Prof.* Sir Robert Evan Owen, Kt., MD, FRCP

Williams, Sir (Robert) Philip Nathaniel, Bt. (1915)

Williams, Sir Robin Philip, Bt. (1953)

Williams, Sir (William) Maxwell (Harries), Kt.

Williamson, *Marshal of the Royal Air Force* Sir Keith Alec, GCB, AFC

Williamson, Sir (Nicholas Frederick) Hedworth, Bt. (1642)

Willink, Sir Charles William, Bt. (1957)

Willis, *Hon.* Sir Eric Archibald, KBE, CMG

Willis, *Vice-Adm.* Sir (Guido) James, KBE

Willis, *Air Marshal* Sir John Frederick, KCB, CBE

Willison, *Lt.-Gen.* Sir David John, KCB, OBE, MC

Willison, Sir John Alexander, Kt., OBE

Wills, Sir David Seton, Bt. (1904)

Wills, Sir (Hugh) David Hamilton, Kt., CBE, TD

Wills, Sir John Vernon, Bt., TD (1923)

Wilmot, Sir Henry Robert, Bt. (1759)

Wilmot, *Cdr.* Sir John Assheton Eardley-, Bt., MVO, DSC, RN (1821)

Wilsey, *Gen.* Sir John Finlay Willasey, KCB, CBE

Wilson, Sir Alan Herries, Kt., FRS

Wilson, *Lt.-Gen.* Sir (Alexander) James, KBE, MC

Wilson, Sir Anthony, Kt.

Wilson, *Vice-Adm.* Sir Barry Nigel, KCB

Wilson, Sir Charles Haynes, Kt.

Wilson, Sir David, Bt. (1920)

Wilson, Sir David Mackenzie, Kt.

Wilson, Sir Geoffrey Masterman, KCB, CMG

Wilson, Sir James William Douglas, Bt. (1906)

Wilson, Sir John Foster, Kt., CBE

Wilson, Sir John Gardiner, Kt., CBE

Wilson, *Brig.* Sir Mathew John Anthony, Bt., OBE, MC (1874)

Wilson, *Hon.* Sir Nicholas Allan Roy, Kt.

Wilson, Sir Patrick Michael Ernest David McNair-, Kt., MP

Wilson, Sir Reginald Holmes, Kt.

Wilson, Sir Robert, Kt., CBE

Wilson, Sir Robert Donald, Kt.

Wilson, *Rt. Revd* Roger Plumpton, KCVO, DD

Wilson, Sir Roland, KBE

Wilson, *Air Chief Marshal* Sir (Ronald) Andrew (Fellowes), KCB, AFC

Wilson, *Hon.* Sir Ronald Darling, KBE, CMG

Wilton, Sir (Arthur) John, KCMG, KCVO, MC

Wiltshire, Sir Frederick Munro, Kt., CBE

Windeyer, Sir Brian Wellingham, Kt.

Wingate, *Capt.* Sir Miles Buckley, KCVO

Winnington, Sir Francis Salwey William, Bt. (1755)

Winskill, *Air Cdre* Sir Archibald Little, KCVO, CBE, DFC

Winterbottom, Sir Walter, Kt., CBE

Wiseman, Sir John William, Bt. (1628)

Wolfson, Sir Brian Gordon, Kt.

Wolseley, Sir Charles Garnet Richard Mark, Bt. (1628)

†Wolseley, Sir James Douglas, Bt. (I. 1745)

Wolstenholme, Sir Gordon Ethelbert Ward, Kt., OBE

Wombwell, Sir George Philip Frederick, Bt. (1778)

Womersley, Sir Peter John Walter, Bt. (1945)

Woo, Sir Leo Joseph, Kt.

Wood, Sir Alan Marshall Muir, Kt., FRS, FEng.

Wood, Sir Anthony John Page, Bt. (1837)

Wood, Sir David Basil Hill-, Bt. (1921)

Wood, Sir Frederick Ambrose Stuart, Kt.

Wood, Sir Henry Peart, Kt., CBE

Wood, *Prof.* Sir John Crossley, Kt., CBE

Wood, *Hon.* Sir John Kember, Kt., MC

Wood, Sir Martin Francis, Kt., OBE

Wood, Sir Russell Dillon, KCVO, VRD

Wood, Sir William Alan, KCVO, CB

Woodcock, Sir John, Kt., CBE, QPM

Woodfield, Sir Philip John, KCB, CBE

Woodhead, *Vice-Adm.* Sir (Anthony) Peter, KCB

Woodhouse, *Rt. Hon.* Sir (Arthur) Owen, KBE, DSC

Wooding, Sir Norman Samuel, Kt., CBE

Woodroffe, *Most Revd* George Cuthbert Manning, KBE

Woodroofe, Sir Ernest George, Kt., ph.D.

Woodruff, *Prof.* Sir Michael Francis Addison, Kt., D.SC., FRS, FRCS

Woods, Sir Colin Philip Joseph, KCVO, CBE

Woods, *Rt. Revd* Robert Wilmer, KCMG, KCVO

Woodward, *Hon.* Sir (Albert) Edward, Kt., OBE

Woodward, *Adm.* Sir John Forster, GBE, KCB

Woolf, Sir John, Kt.

Woollaston, Sir (Mountford) Tosswill, Kt.

Wordie, Sir John Stewart, Kt., CBE, VRD

Worsley, *Gen.* Sir Richard Edward, GCB, OBE

Worsley, Sir (William) Marcus (John), Bt. (1838)

Worsthorne, Sir Peregrine Gerard, Kt.

Wraight, Sir John Richard, KBE, CMG

Wratten, *Air Marshal* Sir William John, KBE, CB, AFC

Wraxall, Sir Charles Frederick Lascelles, Bt. (1813)

Wrey, Sir George Richard Bourchier, Bt. (1628)

Wrigglesworth, Sir Ian William, Kt.

Wright, Sir Allan Frederick, KBE

Wright, Sir Denis Arthur Hepworth, GCMG

Wright, Sir Edward Maitland, Kt., D.Phil., LL D., D.SC., FRSE

Wright, *Hon.* Sir (John) Michael, Kt.

Wright, Sir (John) Oliver, GCMG, GCVO, DSC

Wright, Sir Patrick Richard Henry, GCMG

Wright, Sir Paul Hervé Giraud, KCMG, OBE

Wright, Sir Peter Robert, Kt., CBE

Wright, Sir Richard Michael Cory-, Bt. (1903)

Wrightson, Sir Charles Mark Garmondsway, Bt. (1900)

Wykeham, *Air Marshal* Sir Peter Guy, KCB, DSO, OBE, DFC, AFC

Wylie, Sir Campbell, Kt., ED, QC

Wynn, Sir David Watkin Williams-, Bt. (1688)

Yacoub, *Prof.* Sir Magdi Habib, Kt., FRCS

Yang, *Hon.* Ti Liang, Kt.

Yapp, Sir Stanley Graham, Kt.

Yarranton, Sir Peter George, Kt.

Yarrow, Sir Eric Grant, Bt., MBE (1916)

Yeend, Sir Geoffrey John, Kt., CBE

Yellowlees, Sir Henry, KCB

Yocklunn, Sir John (Soong Chung), KCVO

Yoo Foo, Sir (François) Henri, Kt.

Youens, Sir Peter William, Kt., CMG, OBE

Young, Sir Brian Walter Mark, Kt.

Young, *Lt.-Gen.* Sir David Tod, KBE, CB, DFC

Young, *Rt. Hon.* Sir George Samuel Knatchbull, Bt., MP (1813)

Young, *Hon.* Sir Harold William, KCMG

Young, Sir John Kenyon Roe, Bt. (1821)

Young, *Hon.* Sir John McIntosh, KCMG

Young, Sir Leslie Clarence, Kt., CBE

Young, Sir Norman Smith, Kt.

Young, Sir Richard Dilworth, Kt.

Young, Sir Robert Christopher Mackworth-, GCVO

Young, Sir Roger William, Kt.

Young, Sir Stephen Stewart Templeton, Bt. (1945)

Young, Sir William Neil, Bt. (1769)

Younger, *Maj.-Gen.* Sir John William, Bt., CBE (1911)

Zeeman, *Prof.* Sir (Erik) Christopher, Kt., FRS

Zeidler, Sir David Ronald, Kt., CBE

Zoleveke, Sir Gideon Pitabose, KBE

Zunz, Sir Gerhard Jacob (Jack), Kt., FEng.

Zurenuo, *Rt. Revd* Zurewe Kamong, Kt., OBE

The Military Knights of Windsor

The Military Knights of Windsor take part in all ceremonies of the Noble Order of the Garter and attend Sunday morning service in St George's Chapel, Windsor Castle, as representatives of the Knights of the Garter. The Knights receive a small stipend in addition to their army pensions and quarters in Windsor Castle.

The Knights of Windsor were originally founded in 1348 after the wars in France to assist English knights, who, having been prisoners in the hands of the French, had become impoverished by the payments of heavy ransoms. When Edward III founded the Order of the Garter later the same year, he incorporated the Knights of Windsor and the College of St George into its foundation and raised the number of Knights to 26 to correspond with the number of the Knights of the Garter. Known later as the Alms Knights or Poor Knights of Windsor, their establishment was reduced under the will of King Henry VIII to 13 and Statutes were drawn up by Queen Elizabeth I.

In 1833 King William IV changed their designation to The Military Knights and granted them their present uniform which consists of a scarlet tail-coat with white cross sword-belt, crimson sash and cocked hat with plume. The badges are the Shield of St George and the Star of the Order of the Garter.

Governor, Maj.-Gen. Peter Downward, CB, DSO, DFC
Military Knights, Brig. A. L. Atkinson, OBE; Brig. J. F. Lindner, OBE, MC; Maj. W. L. Thompson, MVO, MBE, DCM; Maj. L. W. Dickerson; Maj. J. C. Cowley, DCM; Lt.-Col. N. L. West; Maj. G. R. Mitchell; MBE, BEM; Lt.-Col. R. L. C. Tamplin; Maj. P. H. Bolton, MBE; Lt.-Col. H. R. Rogers, MBE; Brig. T. W. Hackworth, OBE; Maj. R. J. Moore
Supernumerary, Brig. A. C. Tyler, CBE, MC

The Order of St John

THE MOST VENERABLE ORDER OF THE HOSPITAL OF ST JOHN OF JERUSALEM (1888)

GCStJ, Bailiff/Dame Grand Cross
KStJ, Knight of Justice/Grace
DStJ, Dame of Justice/Grace
ChStJ, Chaplain
CStJ, Commander
OStJ, Officer
SBStJ, Serving Brother
SSStJ, Serving Sister
EsqStJ, Esquire

Mottoes, Pro Fide *and* Pro Utilitate Hominum

The Order of St John, founded in the early 12th century in Jerusalem, was a religious order with a particular duty to care for the sick. In Britain the Order was dissolved by Henry VIII in 1540 but the British branch was revived in the early 19th century. The branch was not accepted by the Grand Magistracy of the Order in Rome but its search for a role in the tradition of the Hospitallers led to the founding of the St

John Ambulance Association in 1877 and later the St John Ambulance Brigade; in 1887 the St John Ophthalmic Hospital was founded in Jerusalem. A royal charter was granted in 1888 establishing the British Order of St John as a British Order of Chivalry with the Sovereign as its head.

Admission to the Order is conferred in recognition of service, usually in St John Ambulance. Membership does not confer any rank, style, title or precedence on a recipient.

SOVEREIGN HEAD OF THE ORDER
HM The Queen

GRAND PRIOR
HRH The Duke of Gloucester, GCVO
Lord Prior, The Lord Vestey
Prelate, The Rt. Revd M. A. Mann, KCVO
Chancellor, Prof. A. R. Mellows, TD
Bailiff of Egle, The Lord Remnant
Headquarters, St John's Gate, Clerkenwell, London ECIM 4DA

Dames Grand Cross and Dames Commanders

Style, 'Dame' before forename and surname, followed by appropriate post-nominal initials. Where such an award is made to a lady already in enjoyment of a higher title, the appropriate initials follow her name
Husband, Untitled
For forms of address, *see* page 220

Dame Grand Cross and Dames Commander are the higher classes for women of the Order of the Bath, the Order of St Michael and St George, the Royal Victorian Order, and the Order of the British Empire. Dames Grand Cross rank after the wives of Baronets and before the wives of Knights Grand Cross. Dames Commanders rank after the wives of Knights Grand Cross and before the wives of Knights Commanders

Honorary Dame Commanders may be conferred on women who are citizens of countries of which The Queen is not head of state

---

LIST OF DAMES *Revised to 31 August 1993*

Women peers in their own right and life peers are not included in this list
If a dame has a double barrelled or hyphenated surname, she is listed under the final element of the name

HM Queen Elizabeth the Queen Mother, KG, KT, CI, GMVO
HRH The Princess Royal, GCVO
HRH The Princess Margaret, Countess of Snowdon, CI, GCVO
HRH The Duchess of Gloucester, GCVO
HRH Princess Alice, Duchess of Gloucester, GCB, CI, GCVO, GBE
HRH The Duchess of Kent, GCVO
HRH Princess Alexandra of Kent, GCVO
Abaijah, Dame Josephine, DBE
Abel Smith, Lady, DCVO
Abergavenny, The Marchioness of, DCVO
Albemarle, The Countess of, DBE
Anderson, *Brig.* Hon. Dame Mary Mackenzie (Mrs Pihl), DBE
Anglesey, The Marchioness of, DBE
Arden, *Hon.* Dame Mary Howarth (Mrs Mance), DBE
Baker, Dame Janet Abbott (Mrs Shelley), DBE
Ballin, Dame Reubina Ann, DBE
Baring, Lady Rose Gwendolen Louisa, DCVO
Barnes, Dame (Alice) Josephine (Mary Taylor), DBE, FRCP, FRCS
Barrow, Dame Jocelyn Anita (Mrs Downer), DBE
Barrow, Dame (Ruth) Nita, GCMG
Basset, Lady Elizabeth, DCVO
Beaurepaire, Dame Beryl Edith, DBE
Berry, Dame Alice Miriam, DBE
Blaize, Dame Venetia Ursula, DBE
Blaxland, Dame Helen Frances, DBE
Booth, *Hon.* Dame Margaret Myfanwy Wood, DBE
Bottomley, Dame Bessie Ellen, DBE
Bowman, Dame (Mary) Elaine Kellett-, DBE, MP
Boyd, Dame Vivienne Myra, DBE
Bracewell, *Hon.* Dame Joyanne Winifred (Mrs Copeland), DBE

Brazill, Dame Josephine (Sister Mary Philippa), DBE
Breen, Dame Marie Freda, DBE
Bridges, Dame Mary Patricia, DBE
Brown, Dame Beryl Paston, DBE
Brown, Dame Gillian Gerda, DCVO, CMG
Browne, Lady Moyra Blanche Madeleine, DBE
Bryans, Dame Anne Margaret, DBE
Bryce, Dame Isabel Graham, DBE
Burnside, Dame Edith, DBE
Buttfield, Dame Nancy Eileen, DBE
Bynoe, Dame Hilda Louisa, DBE
Cartland, Dame Barbara Hamilton, DBE
Cartwright, Dame Mary Lucy, DBE, SC.D., D.Phil., FRS
Cartwright, Dame Silvia Rose, DBE
Casey, Dame Stella Katherine, DBE
Cayford, Dame Florence Evelyn, DBE
Charles, Dame (Mary) Eugenia, DBE
Chesterton, Dame Elizabeth Ursula, DBE
Clay, Dame Marie Mildred, DBE
Clayton, Dame Barbara Evelyn (Mrs Klyne), DBE
Cleland, Dame Rachel, DBE
Clode, Dame (Emma) Frances (Heather), DBE
Coles, Dame Mabel Irene, DBE
Cookson, Dame Catherine Ann, DBE
Cooper, Dame Whina, DBE
Corsar, The Hon. Dame Mary Drummond, DBE
Coulshed, Dame (Mary) Frances, DBE, TD
Cozens, *Brig.* Dame (Florence) Barbara, DBE, RRC
Crowe, Dame Sylvia, DBE
Daws, Dame Joyce Margaretta, DBE
Dell, Dame Miriam Patricia, DBE
Dench, Dame Judith Olivia (Mrs Williams), DBE
de Valois, Dame Ninette, OM, CH, DBE
Digby, Lady, DBE
Donaldson, Dame (Dorothy) Mary (Lady Donaldson of Lymington), GBE
Doyle, *Air Comdt.* Dame Jean Lena Annette Conan (Lady Bromet), DBE

Drake, *Brig.* Dame Jean Elizabeth Rivett-, DBE
Dugdale, Kathryn Edith Helen (Mrs John Dugdale), DCVO
Durack, Dame Mary (Mrs H. C. Miller), DBE
Ebsworth, *Hon.* Dame Ann Marian, DBE
Emerton, Dame Audrey Caroline, DBE
Evison, Dame Helen June Patricia, DBE
Fenner, Dame Peggy Edith, DBE, MP
Fitton, Dame Doris Alice (Mrs Mason), DBE
Fookes, Dame Janet Evelyn, DBE, MP
Fraser, Dame Dorothy Rita, DBE
Friend, Dame Phyllis Muriel, DBE
Frost, Dame Phyllis Irene, DBE
Fry, Dame Margaret Louise, DBE
Gallagher, Dame Monica Josephine, DBE
Gardiner, Dame Helen Louisa, DBE, MVO
Gibbs, Dame Molly Peel, DBE
Giles, *Air Comdt.* Dame Pauline (Mrs Parsons), DBE, RRC
Golding, Dame (Cecilie) Monica, DBE
Goodman, Dame Barbara, DBE
Gordon, Dame Minita Elmira, GCMG, GCVO
Gow, Dame Jane Elizabeth, DBE
Grafton, The Duchess of, GCVO
Green, Dame Mary Georgina, DBE
Grey, Dame Beryl Elizabeth (Mrs Svenson), DBE
Guilfoyle, Dame Margaret Georgina Constance, DBE
Guthardt, *Revd Dr* Dame Phyllis Myra, DBE
Haig, Dame Mary Alison Glen-, DBE
Hall, Dame Catherine Mary, DBE
Hambleden, Patricia, Viscountess, GCVO
Hammond, Dame Joan Hood, DBE
Harris, Dame (Muriel) Diana Reader-, DBE
Heilbron, *Hon.* Dame Rose, DBE
Henderson, Dame Louise Etiennette Sidonie, DBE
Henrison, Dame Anne Elizabeth Rosina, DBE

Herbison, Dame Jean Marjory, DBE, CMG

Hercus, *Hon.* Dame (Margaret) Ann, DCMG

Hetet, Dame Rangimarie, DBE

Hill, Dame Elizabeth Mary, DBE

Hill, *Air Cdre* Dame Felicity Barbara, DBE

Hiller, Dame Wendy (Mrs Gow), DBE

Hird, Dame Thora (Mrs Scott), DBE

Horsman, Dame Dorothea Jean, DBE

Howard, Dame Rosemary Christian, DBE

Hunter, Dame Pamela, DBE

Hurley, *Prof.* Dame Rosalinde (Mrs Gortvai), DBE

Hussey, Lady Susan Katharine, DCVO

Isaacs, Dame Albertha Madeline, DBE

James, Dame Naomi Christine (Mrs Haythorne), DBE

Jenkins, Dame (Mary) Jennifer (Lady Jenkins of Hillhead), DBE

Jessel, Dame Penelope, DBE

Jones, Dame Gwyneth (Mrs Haberfeld-Jones), DBE

Kekedo, Dame Mary, DBE, BEM

Kelleher, Dame Joan, DBE

Kettlewell, *Comdt.* Dame Marion Mildred, DBE

Kilroy, Dame Alix Hester Marie (Lady Meynell), DBE

Kirk, Dame (Lucy) Ruth, DBE

Knight, Dame (Joan Christabel) Jill, DBE, MP

Kramer, *Prof.* Dame Leonie Judith, DBE

Lamb, Dame Dawn Ruth, DBE

Lancaster, Dame Jean, DBE

Lewis, Dame Edna Leofrida (Lady Lewis), DBE

Lister, Dame Unity Viola, DBE

Litchfield, Dame Ruby Beatrice, DBE

Lloyd, *Prof.* Dame June Kathleen, DBE, FRCP

Lowrey, *Air Comdt.* Dame Alice, DBE, RRC

Lympany, Dame Moura, DBE

Lynn, Dame Vera (Mrs Lewis), DBE

Mackinnon, Dame (Una) Patricia, DBE

Macknight, Dame Ella Annie Noble, DBE, MD

McLaren, Dame Anne Laura, DBE, FRCOG, FRS

Macmillan of Ovenden, Katharine, Viscountess, DBE

Maconchy, Dame Elizabeth Violet (Mrs Le Fanu), DBE

Major, Dame Malvina Lorraine (Mrs Fleming), DBE

Mann, Dame Ida Caroline, DBE, D.SC., FRCS

Markova, Dame Alicia, DBE

Martin, Rosamund Mary Holland-, Lady, DBE

Menzies, Dame Pattie Maie, GBE

Metge, *Dr* Dame (Alice) Joan, DBE

Miles, Dame Margaret, DBE

Miller, Dame Mabel Flora Hobart, DBE

Miller, Dame Mary Elizabeth Hedley-, DCVO, CB

Mitchell, Dame Mona, DCVO

Mitchell, *Hon.* Dame Roma Flinders, DBE

Mitchell, Dame Wendy, DBE

Morrison, *Hon.* Dame Mary Anne, DCVO

Mueller, Dame Anne Elisabeth, DCB

Muldoon, Thea Dale, Lady, DBE, QSO

Munro, Dame Alison, DBE

Murdoch, *Hon.* Dame Elisabeth Joy, DBE

Murdoch, Dame (Jean) Iris (Mrs Bayley), DBE

Murray, Dame (Alice) Rosemary, DBE, D.Phil.

Niccol, Dame Kathleen Agnes, DBE

Ollerenshaw, Dame Kathleen Mary, DBE, D.Phil.

Oxenbury, Dame Shirley Anne, DBE

Park, Dame Merle Florence (Mrs Bloch), DBE

Paterson, Dame Betty Fraser Ross, DBE

Penhaligon, Dame Annette, DBE

Plowden, The Lady, DBE

Poole, Dame Avril Anne Barker, DBE

Porter, Dame Shirley (Lady Porter), DBE

Prendergast, Dame Simone Ruth, DBE

Prentice, Dame Winifred Eva, DBE

Preston, Dame Frances Olivia Campbell-, DCVO

Price, Dame Margaret Berenice, DBE

Purves, Dame Daphne Helen, DBE

Pyke, Lady, DBE

Quinn, Dame Sheila Margaret Imelda, DBE

Railton, Dame Ruth (Mrs King), DBE

Rankin, Lady Jean Margaret Florence, DCVO

Raven, Dame Kathleen Annie (Mrs Ingram), DBE

Restieaux, *Dr* Dame Norma Jean, DBE

Riddelsdell, Dame Mildred, DCB, CBE

Ridley, Dame (Mildred) Betty, DBE

Ridsdale, Dame Victoire Evelyn Patricia (Lady Ridsdale), DBE

Rie, Dame Lucie, DBE

Robertson, *Comdt.* Dame Nancy Margaret, DBE

Roe, Dame Raigh Edith, DBE

Rue, Dame (Elsie) Rosemary, DBE

Rumbold, *Rt. Hon.* Dame Angela Claire Rosemary, DBE, MP

Salas, Dame Margaret Laurence, DBE

Saunders, Dame Cicely Mary Strode, OM, DBE, FRCP

Schwarzkopf, Dame Elisabeth Friederike Marie Olga Legge-, DBE

Scott, Dame Catherine Campbell, DBE

Scott, Dame Jean Mary Monica Maxwell-, DCVO

Scott, Dame Margaret, (Dame Catherine Margaret Mary Denton), DBE

Shenfield, Dame Barbara Estelle, DBE

Sherlock, *Prof.* Dame Sheila Patricia Violet, DBE, MD, FRCP

Sloss, *Rt. Hon.* Dame (Ann) Elizabeth (Oldfield) Butler-, DBE

Smieton, Dame Mary Guillan, DBE

Smith, *Hon.* Dame Janet Hilary (Mrs Mathieson), DBE

Smith, Dame Margaret Natalie (Maggie) (Mrs Cross), DBE

Smith, Dame Margot, DBE

Snagge, Dame Nancy Marion, DBE

Soames, Mary, Lady, DBE

Spark, Dame Muriel Sarah, DBE

Steel, *Hon.* Dame (Anne) Heather (Mrs Beattie), DBE

Stephens, *Air Comdt.* Dame Anne, DBE

Stewart, Dame Muriel Acadia, DBE

Sutherland, Dame Joan (Mrs Bonynge), OM, DBE

Szaszy, Dame Miraka Petricevich, DBE

Taylor, Dame Jean Elizabeth, DCVO

Te Atairangikaahu, Te Arikinui, Dame, DBE

Te Kanawa, Dame Kiri Janette (Mrs Park), DBE

Tilney, Dame Guinevere (Lady Tilney), DBE

Tinson, Dame Sue, DBE

Tizard, Dame Catherine Anne, GCMG, DBE

Tokiel, Dame Rosa, DBE

Turner, *Brig.* Dame Margot, DBE, RRC

Tyrwhitt, *Brig.* Dame Mary Joan Caroline, DBE, TD

Uatioa, Dame Mere, DBE

Uvarov, Dame Olga, DBE

Varley, Dame Joan Fleetwood, DBE

Wakehurst, Margaret, Lady, DBE

Wall, (Alice) Anne, (Mrs Michael Wall), DCVO

Wallace, Dame (Georgina Catriona Pamela) Augusta, DBE

Warburton, Dame Anne Marion, DCVO, CMG

Warwick, Dame Margaret Elizabeth Harvey Turner-, DBE, FRCP, FRCPEd.

Waterhouse, Dame Rachel Elizabeth, DBE, ph.D.

Wedega, Dame Alice, DBE

Wedgwood, Dame (Cicely) Veronica, OM, DBE

Weston, Dame Margaret Kate, DBE

Williamson, Dame (Elsie) Marjorie, DBE, ph.D.

Winstone, Dame Dorothy Gertrude, DBE, CMG

Yonge, Dame (Ida) Felicity (Ann), DBE

Chiefs of Clans and Names in Scotland

Only chiefs of whole Names or Clans are included, except certain special instances (marked *) who, though not chiefs of a whole name, were or are for some reason (e.g. the Macdonald forfeiture) independent. Under decision (*Campbell-Gray*, 1950) that a bearer of a 'double or triple-barrelled' surname cannot be held chief of a part of such, several others cannot be included in the list at present.

THE ROYAL HOUSE: HM The Queen

AGNEW: Sir Crispin Agnew of Lochnaw, Bt., 6 Palmerston Road, Edinburgh

ANSTRUTHER: Sir Ralph Anstruther of that Ilk, Bt., KCVO, MC, Balcaskie, Pittenweem, Fife

ARBUTHNOTT: The Viscount of Arbuthnott, CBE, DSC, Arbuthnott House, Laurencekirk, Kincardineshire

BARCLAY: Peter C. Barclay of that Ilk, 28A Gordon Place, London 4JE

BORTHWICK: The Lord Borthwick, TD, Crookston, Heriot, Midlothian

BOYD: The Lord Kilmarnock, 194 Regent's Park Road, London NW1 8XP

BOYLE: The Earl of Glasgow, Kelburn, Fairlie, Ayrshire

BRODIE: Ninian Brodie of Brodie, Brodie Castle, Forres, Morayshire

BRUCE: The Earl of Elgin and Kincardine, KT, Broomhall, Dunfermline, Fife

BUCHAN: David S. Buchan of Auchmacoy, Auchmacoy, Ellon, Aberdeenshire

BURNETT: J. C. A. Burnett of Leys, Crathes Castle, Banchory, Kincardineshire

CAMERON: Sir Donald Cameron of Lochiel, KT, CVO, TD, Achnacarry, Spean Bridge, Inverness-shire

CAMPBELL: The Duke of Argyll, Inveraray, Argyll

CARMICHAEL: Richard J. Carmichael of Carmichael, Carmichael, Thankerton, Biggar, Lanarkshire

CARNEGIE: The Duke of Fife, Elsick House, Stonehaven, Kincardineshire

CATHCART: Maj.-Gen. The Earl Cathcart, CB, DSO, MC, 2 Pembroke Gardens, London W8

CHARTERIS: The Earl of Wemyss and March, KT, Gosford House, Longniddry, East Lothian

CLAN CHATTAN: M. K. Mackintosh of Clan Chattan, Maxwell Park, Gwelo, Zimbabwe

CHISHOLM: Alastair Chisholm of Chisholm (*The Chisholm*), Silver Willows, Beck Row, Bury St Edmunds

COCHRANE: The Earl of Dundonald, Lochnell Castle, Ledaig, Argyllshire

COLQUHOUN: Sir Ivar Colquhoun of Luss, Bt., Camstraddan, Luss, Dunbartonshire

CRANSTOUN: David A. S. Cranstoun of that Ilk, Corehouse, Lanark

CRICHTON: vacant

DARROCH: Capt. Duncan Darroch of Gourock, The Red House, Branksome Park Road, Camberley, Surrey

DEWAR: Kenneth M. J. Dewar of that Ilk and Vogrie, The Dower House, Grayshott, Nr. Hindhead, Surrey

DRUMMOND: The Earl of Perth, PC, Stobhall, Perth

DUNBAR: Sir Jean Dunbar of Mochrum, Bt., 45–55 39th Street, Long Island City, New York, USA

DUNDAS: David D. Dundas of Dundas, 8 Derna Road, Kenwyn 7700, South Africa

DURIE: Raymond V. D. Durie of Durie, Court House, Pewsey, Wilts.

ELIOTT: Mrs Margaret Eliott of Redheugh, Redheugh, Newcastleton, Roxburghshire

ERSKINE: The Earl of Mar and Kellie, Claremont House, Alloa

FARQUHARSON: Capt. A. A. C. Farquharson of Invercauld, MC, Invercauld, Braemar, Aberdeenshire

FERGUSSON: Sir Charles Fergusson of Kilkerran, Bt., Kilkerran, Maybole, Ayrshire

FORBES: The Lord Forbes, KBE, Balforbes, Alford, Aberdeenshire

FORSYTH: Alistair Forsyth of that Ilk, Ethie Castle, by Arbroath, Angus

FRASER: The Lady Saltoun, Cairnbulg Castle, Fraserburgh, Aberdeenshire

*FRASER (OF LOVAT): The Lord Lovat, DSO, MC, TD, Balblair House, Beauly, Inverness-shire

GAYRE: Lt.-Col. Robert Gayre of Gayre and Nigg, 1–3 Gloucester Lane, Edinburgh

GORDON: The Marquess of Huntly, Aboyne Castle, Aberdeenshire

GRAHAM: The Duke of Montrose, Buchanan Auld House, Drymen, Stirlingshire

GRANT: The Lord Strathspey, The House of Lords, London SWIA OPW

GRIERSON: Sir Michael Grierson of Lag, Bt., 40C Palace Road, London

HAIG: The Earl Haig, OBE, Bemersyde, Melrose, Roxburghshire

HALDANE: Alexander N. C. Haldane of Gleneagles, Auchterarder, Perthshire

HANNAY: Ramsey W. R. Hannay of Kirkdale and of that Ilk, Cardoness House, Gatehouse-of-Fleet, Kirkcudbrightshire

HAY: The Earl of Erroll, Wolverton Farm, Wolverton, Basingstoke, Hants.

HENDERSON: John W. P. Henderson of Fordell, 7 Owen Street, Toowoomba, Queensland, Australia

HUNTER: Neil A. Hunter of Hunterston, Tour D'Escas, Carretera d'Escas, La Massana, Andorra

IRVINE OF DRUM: David C. Irvine of Drum, 29 Forest Road, Hoylake, Wirral, Merseyside

JARDINE: Sir Alexander Jardine of Applegirth, Bt., Ash House, Thwaites, Millom, Cumbria

JOHNSTONE: The Earl of Annandale and Hartfell, Raehills, Lockerbie, Dumfriesshire

KEITH: The Earl of Kintore, The Stables, Keith Hall, Inverurie, Aberdeenshire

KENNEDY: The Marquess of Ailsa, OBE, Blanefield, Kirkoswald, Ayrshire

KERR: The Marquess of Lothian, KCVO, Monteviot, Ancrum, Roxburghshire

KINCAID: Mrs Heather V. Kincaid of Kincaid, 4 Watling Street, Leintwardine, Craven Arms, Shropshire

LAMONT: Peter N. Lamont of that Ilk, St Patrick's College, Manly, NSW 2095, Australia

LEASK: Madam Leask of Leask, 1 Vincent Road, Sheringham, Norfolk

LENNOX: Edward J. H. Lennox of that Ilk, Pools Farm, Downton on the Rock, Ludlow, Shropshire

LESLIE: The Earl of Rothes, Tanglewood, West Tytherley, Salisbury, Wilts.

LINDSAY: The Earl of Crawford and Balcarres, PC, Balcarres, Colinsburgh, Fife

LOCKHART: Angus H. Lockhart of the Lee, Newholme, Dunsyre, Lanark

LUMSDEN: Gillem Lumsden of that Ilk and Blanerne, Kinderslegh, Bois Avenue, Chesham Bois, Amersham, Bucks

MacAlester: William St J. S. McAlester of Loup and Kennox, 2 Avon Road East, Christchurch, Dorset

McBain: J. H. McBain of McBain, 7025, North Finger Rock Place, Tucson, Arizona, USA

Malcolm (MacCallum): Robin N. L. Malcolm of Poltalloch, Duntrune Castle, Lochgilphead, Argyll

Macdonald: The Lord Macdonald (*The Macdonald of Macdonald*), Kinloch Lodge, Sleat, Isle of Skye

*Macdonald of Clanranald: Ranald A. Macdonald of Clanranald, Wester Lix Cottage, Killin, Perthshire

*Macdonald of Sleat (Clan Husteain): Sir Ian Bosville Macdonald of Sleat, Bt., Thorpe Hall, Rudston, Driffield, N. Humberside

*MacDonell of Glengarry: Air Cdre Aeneas R. MacDonell of Glengarry, CB, DFC, Elonbank, Castle Street, Fortrose, Ross-shire

MacDougall: vacant

Macdowall: Fergus D. H. Macdowall of Garthland, 16 Tower Road, Nepean, Ontario, Canada

MacGregor: Sir Gregor MacGregor of MacGregor, Bt., Bannatyne, Newtyle, Angus

MacIntyre: James W. MacIntyre of Glenoe, 15301 Pine Orchard Drive, Apartment 3H, Silver Spring, Maryland, USA

Mackay: The Lord Reay, House of Lords, London SW1

Mackenzie: The Earl of Cromartie, Castle Leod, Strathpeffer, Ross-shire

Mackinnon: Madam Anne Mackinnon of Mackinnon, 16 Purleigh Road, Bridgwater, Somerset

Mackintosh: The Mackintosh of Mackintosh, OBE, Moy Hall, Inverness

MacLachlan: Madam Marjorie MacLachlan of MacLachlan, Castle Lachlan, Argyll

MacLaren: Donald MacLaren of MacLaren and Achleskine, Achleskine, Kirkton, Balquidder, Lochearnhead

Maclean: The Hon. Sir Lachlan Maclean of Duart, Bt., Duart Castle, Mull

MacLennan: vacant

MacLeod: J. MacLeod of MacLeod, Dunvegan Castle, Isle of Skye

MacMillan: George MacMillan of MacMillan, Finlaystone, Langbank, Renfrewshire

Macnab: J. C. Macnab of Macnab (*The Macnab*), West Kilmany House, Cupar, Fife

Macnaghten: Sir Patrick Macnaghten of Macnaghten and Dundarave, Bt., Dundarave, Bushmills, Co. Antrim

Macneacail: Iain Macneacail of Macneacail and Scorrybreac, 12 Fox Street, Ballina, NSW, Australia

MacNeil of Barra: Ian R. Macneil of Barra (*The Macneil of Barra*), Kisimul Castle, Barra

Macpherson: The Hon. Sir William Macpherson of Cluny, TD, Newtown Castle, Blairgowrie, Perthshire

MacThomas: Andrew P. C. MacThomas of Finegand, c/o The Clan MacThomas Society, 19 Warriston Avenue, Edinburgh

Maitland: The Earl of Lauderdale, 12 St Vincent Street, Edinburgh

Makgill: The Viscount of Oxfuird, Hill House, St Mary Bourne, Andover, Hants.

Mar: The Countess of Mar, St Michael's Farm, Great Witley, Worcs.

Marjoribanks: Andrew Marjoribanks of that Ilk

Matheson: Maj. Sir Fergus Matheson of Matheson, Bt., Hedenham, Old Rectory, Bungay, Suffolk NR35 2LD

Menzies: David R. Menzies of Menzies, 20 Nardina Crescent, Dalkeith, Western Australia

Moffat: Madam Moffat of that Ilk, St Jasual, Bullocks Farm Lane, Wheeler End Common, High Wycombe, Bucks.

Moncreiffe: vacant

Montgomerie: The Earl of Eglinton and Winton, The Dutch House, West Green, Hartley Wintney, Hants.

Morrison: Dr Iain M. Morrison of Ruchdi, Magnolia Cottage, The Street, Walberton, Sussex

Munro: Patrick G. Munro of Foulis, TD, Foulis Castle, Ross

Murray: The Duke of Atholl, Blair Castle, Blair Atholl, Perthshire

Nicolson: The Lord Carnock, 90 Whitehall Court, London SW1

Ogilvy: The Earl of Airlie, KT, GCVO, PC, Cortachy Castle, Kirriemuir, Angus

Ramsay: The Earl of Dalhousie, KT, GCVO, GBE, MC, Brechin Castle, Angus

Rattray: James S. Rattray of Rattray, Craighall, Rattray, Perthshire

Robertson: Alexander G. H. Robertson of Struan (*Struan-Robertson*), The Breach Farm, Goudhurst Road, Cranbrook, Kent

Rollo: The Lord Rollo, Pitcairns, Dunning, Perthshire

Rose: Miss Elizabeth Rose of Kilravock, Kilravock Castle, Croy, Inverness

Ross: David C. Ross of that Ilk, The Old Schoolhouse, Fettercairn, Kincardineshire

Ruthven: The Earl of Gowrie, PC, Castlemartin, Kilcullen, Co. Kildare, Republic of Ireland

Scott: The Duke of Buccleuch and Queensberry, KT, VRD, Bowhill, Selkirk

Scrymgeour: The Earl of Dundee, Birkhill, Cupar, Fife

Sempill: The Lady Sempill, Druminnor Castle, Rhynie, Aberdeenshire

Shaw: John Shaw of Tordarroch, Newhall, Balblair, By Conon Bridge, Ross-shire

Sinclair: The Earl of Caithness, Churchill, Chipping Norton, Oxford OX7 5UX

Stirling: Fraser J. Stirling of Cader, 17 Park Row, Farnham, Surrey

Sutherland: The Countess of Sutherland, House of Tongue, Brora, Sutherland

Swinton: John Swinton of that Ilk, 123 Superior Avenue SW, Calgary, Alberta, Canada

Urquhart: Kenneth T. Urquhart of that Ilk, 7907 Birch Street, New Orleans, Louisiana 790118, USA

Wallace: Ian F. Wallace of that Ilk, 5 Lennox Street, Edinburgh EH4 1QB

Wedderburn of that Ilk: The Master of Dundee, Birkhill, Cupar, Fife

Wemyss: David Wemyss of that Ilk, Invermay, Forteviot, Perthshire

Decorations and Medals

PRINCIPAL DECORATIONS AND MEDALS
In order of precedence

VICTORIA CROSS (VC), 1856
GEORGE CROSS (GC), 1940

British Orders of Knighthood, etc. (for order in which worn, see pages 174–6)
BARONET'S BADGE
KNIGHT BACHELOR'S BADGE

Decorations
ROYAL RED CROSS CLASS I (RRC), 1883. For ladies
DISTINGUISHED SERVICE CROSS (DSC), 1914. For officers of RN below the rank of Captain, and Warrant Officers
MILITARY CROSS (MC), December 1914. Awarded to Captains, Lieutenants, and Warrant Officers (I and II) in the Army and Indian and Colonial forces
DISTINGUISHED FLYING CROSS (DFC), 1918. For officers and Warrant Officers in the RAF (and Fleet Air Arm from 1941) for acts of gallantry when flying in active operations against the enemy
AIR FORCE CROSS (AFC), 1918. Instituted as preceding, but for acts of courage or devotion to duty when flying, although not in active operations against the enemy (extended to Fleet Air Arm 1941)
ROYAL RED CROSS CLASS II (ARRC)
ORDER OF BRITISH INDIA
KAISAR-I-HIND MEDAL
ORDER OF ST JOHN

Medals for Gallantry and Distinguished Conduct
UNION OF SOUTH AFRICA QUEEN'S MEDAL FOR BRAVERY, in Gold
DISTINGUISHED CONDUCT MEDAL (DCM), 1854 Awarded to warrant officers, non-commissioned officers and men of the Army and RAF
CONSPICUOUS GALLANTRY MEDAL (CGM), 1874. Bestowed upon warrant officers and men of the RN and since 1942 of Mercantile Marine and RAF
THE GEORGE MEDAL (GM), 1940
QUEEN'S POLICE MEDAL FOR GALLANTRY
QUEEN'S FIRE SERVICE MEDAL FOR GALLANTRY
ROYAL WEST AFRICAN FRONTIER FORCE DISTINGUISHED CONDUCT MEDAL
KING'S AFRICAN RIFLES DISTINGUISHED CONDUCT MEDAL
INDIAN DISTINGUISHED SERVICE MEDAL
UNION OF SOUTH AFRICA QUEEN'S MEDAL FOR BRAVERY, in Silver
DISTINGUISHED SERVICE MEDAL (DSM), 1914. For chief petty officers, petty officers and men, of all branches of the Royal Navy, and since 1942 of Mercantile Marine; non-commissioned officers and men of the Royal Marines; all other persons holding corresponding positions in Her Majesty's service afloat
MILITARY MEDAL (MM), 1916. For warrant and non-commissioned officers and men and serving women
DISTINGUISHED FLYING MEDAL (DFM), 1918, and the AIR FORCE MEDAL (AFM). For warrant and non-commissioned officers and men for equivalent services as for DFC and AFC (extended to Fleet Air Arm 1941)
CONSTABULARY MEDAL (IRELAND)

MEDAL FOR SAVING LIFE AT SEA
INDIAN ORDER OF MERIT (Civil)
INDIAN POLICE MEDAL FOR GALLANTRY
CEYLON POLICE MEDAL FOR GALLANTRY
SIERRA LEONE POLICE MEDAL FOR GALLANTRY
SIERRA LEONE FIRE BRIGADES MEDAL FOR GALLANTRY
COLONIAL POLICE MEDAL FOR GALLANTRY (CPM)
QUEEN'S GALLANTRY MEDAL, 1974
ROYAL VICTORIAN MEDAL (RVM), Gold, Silver and Bronze
BRITISH EMPIRE MEDAL (BEM), (formerly the Medal of the Order of the British Empire, for Meritorious Service; also includes the Medal of the Order awarded before 29 December 1922)
QUEEN'S POLICE (QPM) AND QUEEN'S FIRE SERVICES MEDALS (QFSM) FOR DISTINGUISHED SERVICE
QUEEN'S MEDAL FOR CHIEFS

War Medals and Stars (in order of date)

Polar Medals (in order of date)

IMPERIAL SERVICE MEDAL

Police Medals for Valuable Service

BADGE OF HONOUR

Jubilee, Coronation and Durbar Medals

KING GEORGE V, KING GEORGE VI AND QUEEN ELIZABETH II LONG AND FAITHFUL SERVICE MEDALS

Efficiency and Long Service Decorations and Medals
MEDAL FOR MERITORIOUS SERVICE
LONG SERVICE AND GOOD CONDUCT MEDAL (Military)
NAVAL LONG SERVICE AND GOOD CONDUCT MEDAL
ROYAL MARINE MERITORIOUS SERVICE MEDAL
ROYAL AIR FORCE MERITORIOUS SERVICE MEDAL
ROYAL AIR FORCE LONG SERVICE AND GOOD CONDUCT MEDAL
MEDAL FOR LONG SERVICE AND GOOD CONDUCT (ULSTER DEFENCE REGIMENT)
POLICE LONG SERVICE AND GOOD CONDUCT MEDAL
FIRE BRIGADE LONG SERVICE AND GOOD CONDUCT MEDAL
COLONIAL POLICE AND FIRE BRIGADES LONG SERVICE MEDAL
COLONIAL PRISON SERVICE MEDAL
ARMY EMERGENCY RESERVE DECORATION (ERD), 1952
VOLUNTEER OFFICER'S DECORATION (VD)
VOLUNTEER LONG SERVICE MEDAL
VOLUNTEER OFFICER'S DECORATION for India and the Colonies
VOLUNTEER LONG SERVICE MEDAL for India and the Colonies
COLONIAL AUXILIARY FORCES OFFICER'S DECORATION
COLONIAL AUXILIARY FORCES LONG SERVICE MEDAL
MEDAL FOR GOOD SHOOTING (Naval)
MILITIA LONG SERVICE MEDAL
IMPERIAL YEOMANRY LONG SERVICE MEDAL
TERRITORIAL DECORATION (TD), 1908
EFFICIENCY DECORATION (ED)
TERRITORIAL EFFICIENCY MEDAL
EFFICIENCY MEDAL

SPECIAL RESERVE LONG SERVICE AND GOOD
CONDUCT MEDAL
DECORATION FOR OFFICERS, ROYAL NAVY RESERVE
(RD), 1910
DECORATION FOR OFFICERS, RNVR (VRD)
ROYAL NAVAL RESERVE LONG SERVICE AND GOOD
CONDUCT MEDAL
RNVR LONG SERVICE AND GOOD CONDUCT MEDAL
ROYAL NAVAL AUXILIARY SICK BERTH RESERVE LONG
SERVICE AND GOOD CONDUCT MEDAL
ROYAL FLEET RESERVE LONG SERVICE AND GOOD
CONDUCT MEDAL
ROYAL NAVAL WIRELESS AUXILIARY RESERVE LONG
SERVICE AND GOOD CONDUCT MEDAL
AIR EFFICIENCY AWARD (AE), 1942
ULSTER DEFENCE REGIMENT MEDAL
The QUEEN'S MEDAL For champion shots in the RN, RM,
RNZN, Army, RAF
CADET FORCES MEDAL, 1950
COAST LIFE SAVING CORPS LONG SERVICE MEDAL,
1911
SPECIAL CONSTABULARY LONG SERVICE MEDAL
ROYAL OBSERVER CORPS MEDAL
CIVIL DEFENCE LONG SERVICE MEDAL
ROYAL ULSTER CONSTABULARY SERVICE MEDAL
SERVICE MEDAL OF THE ORDER OF ST JOHN
BADGE OF THE ORDER OF THE LEAGUE OF MERCY
VOLUNTARY MEDICAL SERVICE MEDAL, 1932
WOMEN'S ROYAL VOLUNTARY SERVICE MEDAL
COLONIAL SPECIAL CONSTABULARY MEDAL

Foreign Orders, Decorations and Medals (in order of date)

THE VICTORIA CROSS (1856)
FOR CONSPICUOUS BRAVERY

VC

Ribbon, Crimson, for all Services (until 1918 it was blue for
Royal Navy)

Instituted on 29 January 1856, the Victoria Cross was
awarded retrospectively to 1854, the first being held by Lt.
C. D. Lucas, RN, for bravery in the Baltic Sea on 21 June
1854 (gazetted 24 February 1857). The first 62 Crosses were
presented by Queen Victoria in Hyde Park, London, on 26
June 1857.

The Victoria Cross is worn before all other decorations,
on the left breast, and consists of a cross-pattée of bronze,
one and a half inches in diameter, with the Royal Crown
surmounted by a lion in the centre, and beneath there is the
inscription *For Valour.* Holders of the VC receive a tax-free
annuity of £100, irrespective of need or other conditions. In
1911, the right to receive the Cross was extended to Indian
soldiers, and in 1920 to Matrons, Sisters and Nurses, and
the staff of the Nursing Services and other services
pertaining to hospitals and nursing, and to civilians of either
sex regularly or temporarily under the orders, direction or
supervision of the Naval, Military, or Air Forces of the
Crown.

SURVIVING RECIPIENTS OF THE VICTORIA CROSS
as at 31 August 1993

Agansing Rai, *Havildar,* MM (Gurkha Rifles)
  1944 *World War*
Ali Haidar, *Jemadar* (Frontier Force Rifles)
  1945 *World War*
Annand, *Capt.* R. W. (Durham Light Infantry)
  1940 *World War*
Bhan Bhagta Gurung, *Capt.* (2nd Gurkha Rifles)
  1945 *World War*
Bhandari Ram, *Capt.* (Baluch R.)
  1944 *World War*
Chapman, *Sgt.* E. T., BEM (Monmouthshire R.)
  1945 *World War*
Cruickshank, *Flt. Lt.* J. A. (RAFVR)
  1944 *World War*
Cutler, Sir Roden, AK, KCMG, KCVO, CBE (Australia)
  1941 *World War*
Ervine-Andrews, *Lt.-Col.* H. M. (E. Lancs. R.)
  1940 *World War*
Foote, *Maj.-Gen.* H. R. B., CB, DSO (R. Tank R.)
  1942 *World War*
Fraser, *Lt.-Cdr.* I. E., DSC (RNR)
  1945 *World War*
Gaje Ghale, *Subedar* (Gurkha Rifles)
  1943 *World War*
Ganju Lama, *Jemadar,* MM (Gurkha Rifles)
  1944 *World War*
Gardner, *Capt.* P. J., MC (RTR)
  1941 *World War*
Gian Singh, *Jemadar* (Punjab R.)
  1945 *World War*
Gould, *Lt.* T. W. (RN)
  1942 *World War*
Hinton, *Sgt.* J. D. (NZMF)
  1941 *World War*
Jackson, *WO* N. C. (RAFVR)
  1944 *World War*
Jamieson, *Maj.* D. A., CVO (R. Norfolk R.)
  1944 *World War*
Kenna, *Pte.* E. (Australian M. F.)
  1945 *World War*
Kenneally, *C-Q-M-S* J. P. (Irish Guards)
  1943 *World War*
Lachiman Gurung, *Rifleman* (Gurkha Rifles)
  1945 *World War*
Learoyd, *Wg Cdr.* R. A. B. (RAF)
  1940 *World War*
Merritt, *Lt.-Col.* C. C. I., CD (S. Saskatchewan R.)
  1942 *World War*
Norton, *Capt.* G. R., MM (SAMF)
  1944 *World War*
Payne, *WO* K. (Australian Army)
  1969 *Vietnam*
Place, *Rear-Adm.* B. C. G., CB, CVO, DSC (RN)
  1943 *World War*
Porteous, *Col.* P. A. (RA)
  1942 *World War*
Rambahadur Limbu, *Lt.,* MVO (Gurkha Rifles)
  1965 *Sarawak*
Reid, *Flt. Lt.* W. (RAFVR)
  1943 *World War*
Smith, *Sgt.* E. A., CD (Seaforth Highlanders of Canada)
  1944 *World War*
Smythe, *Capt.* Q. G. M. (SAMF)
  1942 *World War*
Speakman-Pitt, *Sgt.* W. (Black Watch)
  1951 *Korea*

Tulbahadur Pun, *WOI* (Gurkha Rifles)
  1944 *World War*
Umrao Singh, *Sub-Major* (IA)
  1944 *World War*
Upham, *Capt.* C. H. (and Bar, 1942), (NZMF)
  1941 *World War*
Watkins, *Maj. Rt. Hon.* Sir Tasker, GBE (Welch R.)
  1944 *World War*
Wilson, *Lt.-Col.* E. C. T. (E. Surrey R.)
  1940 *World War*

THE GEORGE CROSS (1940)
FOR GALLANTRY

GC

Ribbon, Dark blue, threaded through a bar adorned with laurel leaves

Instituted 24 September 1940 (with amendments, 3 November 1942).
The George Cross is worn before all other decorations (except the VC) on the left breast (when worn by a woman it may be worn on the left shoulder from a ribbon of the same width and colour fashioned into a bow). It consists of a plain silver cross with four equal limbs, the cross having in the centre a circular medallion bearing a design showing St George and the Dragon. The inscription *For Gallantry* appears round the medallion and in the angle of each limb of the cross is the Royal cypher 'G VI' forming a circle concentric with the medallion. The reverse is plain and bears the name of the recipient and the date of the award. The cross is suspended by a ring from a bar adorned with laurel leaves on dark blue ribbon one and a half inches wide.
  The cross is intended primarily for civilians; awards to the fighting services are confined to actions for which purely military honours are not normally granted. It is awarded only for acts of the greatest heroism or of the most conspicuous courage in circumstances of extreme danger. From 1 April 1965, holders of the Cross have received a tax-free annuity of £100.
  The royal warrant which ordained that the grant of the Empire Gallantry Medal should cease authorized holders of that medal to return it to the Central Chancery of the Orders of Knighthood and to receive in exchange the George Cross. A similar provision applied to posthumous awards of the Empire Gallantry Medal made after the outbreak of war in 1939. In October 1971 all surviving holders of the Albert Medal and the Edward Medal exchanged those decorations for the George Cross.

SURVIVING RECIPIENTS OF THE GEORGE CROSS
as at 31 August 1993
If the recipient originally received the Empire Gallantry Medal (EGM), the Albert Medal (AM) or the Edward Medal (EM), this is indicated by the initials in parenthesis.

Archer, *Col.* B. S. T., GC, OBE, ERD, 1941
Atkinson, T., GC (EGM), 1939
Baker, J. T., GC (EM), 1929
Baldwin, W. C. G., GC, Ph.D. (EM), 1943
Bamford, J., GC, 1952
Baxter, W. F., GC (EM), 1942

Beaton, J., GC, CVO, 1974
Biggs, *Maj.* K. A., GC, 1946
Bridge, *Cdr.* J., GC, GM, 1944
Butson, *Col.* A. R. C., GC, CD, MD (AM), 1948
Bywater, R. A. S., GC, GM, 1944
Durrani, *Lt.-Col.* M. K., GC, 1946
Easton, J. M. C., GC, 1941
Errington, H., GC, 1941
Fairfax, F. W., GC, 1953
Farrow, K., GC (AM), 1948
Flintoff, H. H., GC (EM), 1944
Gledhill, A. J., GC, 1967
Goad, W., GC (AM), 1943
Goldsworthy, *Lt.-Cdr.* L. V., GC, DSC, GM, 1944
Gregson, J. S., GC (AM), 1943
Hallowes, Mrs O. M. C., GC, MBE, Légion d'Honneur, 1946
Hawkins, E., GC (AM), 1943
Hodge, *Capt.* A. M., GC, VRD (EGM), 1940
Johnson, *WOI* (*SSM*) B., GC, 1990
Kinne, D. G., GC, 1954
Lowe, A. R., GC (AM), 1949
Lynch, J., GC, BEM (AM), 1948
McAloney, *Gp. Capt.* W. S., GC, OBE (AM), 1938
McClymont, J. M., GC (EGM), 1940
Malta, GC, 1942
Manwaring, T. G., GC (EM), 1949
May, P. R. S., GC (AM), 1947
Miller, *Lt.-Cdr.* J. B. P., GC, 1941
Moore, R. V., GC, 1940
Moss, B., GC, 1940
Naughton, F., GC (EGM), 1937
Nix, F. E., GC (EM), 1944
Patton, The Hon. John, GC, CBE, 1940
Pearson, Miss J. D. M., GC (EGM), 1940
Pratt, M. K., GC, 1978
Purves, Mrs M., GC (AM), 1949
Raweng, Awang anak, GC, 1951
Riley, G., GC (AM), 1944
Rimmer, R., GC (EGM), 1931
Rogerson, S., GC, 1946
Rowlands, *Air Marshal* Sir John, GC, KBE, 1943
Sinclair, *Air Vice-Marshal* Sir Laurence, GC, KCB, CBE, DSO, 1941
Stevens, H. W., GC, 1958
Stronach, *Capt.* G. P., GC, 1943
Styles, *Lt.-Col.* S. G., GC, 1972
Sylvester, W. G., GC (EGM), 1940
Taylor, *Lt.-Cdr.* W. H., GC, MBE, 1941
Walker, C., GC, 1972
Walker, C. H., GC (AM), 1942
Walton, E. W. K., GC (AM), 1948
Western, D., GC (AM), 1948
Wilcox, C., GC (EM), 1949
Wiltshire, S. N., GC (EGM), 1930
Yates, P. W., GC (EM), 1932

Precedence

ENGLAND AND WALES

The Sovereign
The Prince Philip, Duke of Edinburgh
The Prince of Wales
The Sovereign's younger sons
The Sovereign's grandsons
The Sovereign's cousins
Archbishop of Canterbury
Lord High Chancellor
Archbishop of York
The Prime Minister
Lord President of the Council
Speaker of the House of Commons
Lord Privy Seal
Ambassadors and High
  Commissioners
Lord Great Chamberlain
Earl Marshal
Lord Steward of the Household
Lord Chamberlain of the Household
Master of the Horse
Dukes, according to their patent of
  creation:
  (1) of England
  (2) of Scotland
  (3) of Great Britain
  (4) of Ireland
  (5) those created since the Union
Ministers and Envoys
Eldest sons of Dukes of Blood Royal
Marquesses, according to their patent
  of creation:
  (1) of England
  (2) of Scotland
  (3) of Great Britain
  (4) of Ireland
  (5) those created since the Union
Dukes' eldest sons
Earls, according to their patent of
  creation:
  (1) of England
  (2) of Scotland
  (3) of Great Britain
  (4) of Ireland
  (5) those created since the Union
Younger sons of Dukes of Blood
  Royal
Marquesses' eldest sons
Dukes' younger sons
Viscounts, according to their patent of
  creation:
  (1) of England
  (2) of Scotland
  (3) of Great Britain
  (4) of Ireland
  (5) those created since the Union
Earls' eldest sons
Marquesses' younger sons
Bishops of London, Durham and
  Winchester
Other English Diocesan Bishops,
  according to seniority of
  consecration

Suffragan Bishops, according to
  seniority of consecration
Secretaries of State, if of the degree of
  a Baron
Barons, according to their patent of
  creation:
  (1) of England
  (2) of Scotland
  (3) of Great Britain
  (4) of Ireland
  (5) those created since the Union
Treasurer of the Household
Comptroller of the Household
Vice-Chamberlain of the Household
Secretaries of State under the degree
  of Baron
Viscounts' eldest sons
Earls' younger sons
Barons' eldest sons
Knights of the Garter
Privy Counsellors
Chancellor of the Exchequer
Chancellor of the Duchy of Lancaster
Lord Chief Justice of England
Master of the Rolls
President of the Family Division
Vice-Chancellor
Lords Justices of Appeal
Judges of the High Court
Viscounts' younger sons
Barons' younger sons
Sons of Life Peers
Baronets, according to date of patent
Knights of the Thistle
Knights Grand Cross of the Bath
Members of the Order of Merit
Knights Grand Commanders of the
  Star of India
Knights Grand Cross of St Michael
  and St George
Knights Grand Commanders of the
  Indian Empire
Knights Grand Cross of the Royal
  Victorian Order
Knights Grand Cross of the British
  Empire
Companions of Honour
Knights Commanders of the Bath
Knights Commanders of the Star of
  India
Knights Commanders of St Michael
  and St George
Knights Commanders of the Indian
  Empire
Knights Commanders of the Royal
  Victorian Order
Knights Commanders of the British
  Empire
Knights Bachelor
Vice-Chancellor of the County
  Palatine of Lancaster
Official Referees of the Supreme
  Court
Circuit judges and judges of the
  Mayor's and City of London Court
Companions of the Bath

Companions of the Star of India
Companions of St Michael and St
  George
Companions of the Indian Empire
Commanders of the Royal Victorian
  Order
Commanders of the British Empire
Companions of the Distinguished
  Service Order
Lieutenants of the Royal Victorian
  Order
Officers of the British Empire
Companions of the Imperial Service
  Order
Eldest sons of younger sons of Peers
Baronets' eldest sons
Eldest sons of Knights, in the same
  order as their fathers
Members of the Royal Victorian
  Order
Members of the British Empire
Younger sons of the younger sons of
  Peers
Baronets' younger sons
Younger sons of Knights, in the same
  order as their fathers
Naval, Military, Air, and other
  Esquires by office

SCOTLAND

The Sovereign
The Prince Philip, Duke of Edinburgh
The Lord High Commissioner to the
  General Assembly (while that
  Assembly is sitting)
The Duke of Rothesay (eldest son of
  the Sovereign)
The Sovereign's younger sons
The Sovereign's cousins
Lords Lieutenant of Counties
Lord Provosts of Counties of Cities
Sheriffs Principal, successively, within
  their own localities and during
  holding of office
Lord Chancellor of Great Britain
Moderator of the General Assembly of
  the Church of Scotland
The Prime Minister
Keepers of the Great Seal and of the
  Privy Seal, successively if Peers
Hereditary Lord High Constable of
  Scotland
Hereditary Master of the Household
Dukes, in same order as in England
Eldest sons of Dukes of the Blood
  Royal
Marquesses, as in England
Dukes' eldest sons
Earls, as in England
Younger sons of Dukes of Blood
  Royal
Marquesses' eldest sons
Dukes' younger sons

Keepers of the Great Seal and of the
  Privy Seal, successively if not Peers
Lord Justice General
Lord Clerk Register
Lord Advocate
Lord Justice Clerk
Viscounts, as in England
Earls' eldest sons
Marquesses' younger sons
Lord-Barons, as in England
Viscounts' eldest sons
Earls' younger sons
Lord-Barons' eldest sons
Knights of the Garter
Privy Counsellors
Senators of College of Justice (Lords of
  Session)
Viscounts' younger sons
Lord-Barons' younger sons
Sons of Life Peers
Baronets
Knights of the Thistle
Knights Grand Cross, Grand
  Commander, and Knight
  Commanders, as in England
Solicitor-General for Scotland
Lord Lyon King of Arms
Sheriffs Principal, except as shown
  above
Knights Bachelor
Sheriffs
Companions of Orders, as in England
Commanders of the Royal Victorian
  Order
Commanders of the British Empire
Eldest sons of younger sons of Peers
Companions of the Distinguished
  Service Order
Lieutenants of the Royal Victorian
  Order
Officers of the British Empire
Baronets' eldest sons
Knights' eldest sons, as in England
Members of the Royal Victorian
  Order
Members of the British Empire
Baronets' younger sons
Knights' younger sons
Queen's Counsel
Barons-feudal
Esquires
Gentlemen

WOMEN

Women take the same rank as their husbands or as their brothers; but the daughter of a peer marrying a commoner retains her title as Lady or Honourable. Daughters of peers rank next immediately after the wives of their elder brothers, and before their younger brothers' wives. Daughters of peers marrying peers of lower degree take the same order of precedence as that of their husbands; thus the daughter of a Duke marrying a Baron becomes of the rank of Baroness only, while her sisters married to commoners retain their rank and take precedence of the Baroness. Merely official rank on the husband's part does not give any similar precedence to the wife.

Peeresses in their own right take the same precedence as peers of the same rank, i.e. from their date of creation.

LOCAL PRECEDENCE

England and Wales – No written code of county or city order of precedence has been promulgated, but in counties the Lord Lieutenant stands first, and secondly (normally) the Sheriff, and therefore in cities and boroughs the Lord Lieutenant has social precedence over the Mayor; but at city or borough functions the Lord Mayor or Mayor will preside. At Oxford and Cambridge the High Sheriff takes precedence of the Vice-Chancellor.

Scotland – The Lord Provosts of the city districts of Aberdeen, Dundee, Edinburgh and Glasgow are Lord Lieutenants for those districts ex officio and take precedence as such.

Forms of address

It is only possible to cover here the forms of address for peers, baronets and knights, their wife and children, and Privy Counsellors. Greater detail should be sought in one of the publications devoted to the subject.

Both formal and social forms of address are given where usage differs; increasingly, the social form is preferred to the formal, though this is used for official documents and on very formal occasions.

F__ represents forename.

S__ represents surname.

BARON - *Envelope (formal)*, The Right Hon. Lord __ ; *(social)*, The Lord __ . *Letter (formal)*, My Lord; *(social)*, Dear Lord __ . *Spoken*, Lord __ .

BARON'S WIFE - *Envelope (formal)*, The Right Hon. Lady __ ; *(social)*, The Lady __ . *Letter (formal)*, My Lady; *(social)*, Dear Lady __ . *Spoken*, Lady __ .

BARON'S CHILDREN - *Envelope*, The Hon. F__S__. *Letter*, Dear Mr/Miss/Mrs S__. *Spoken*, Mr/Miss/Mrs [F__] S__.

BARONESS IN OWN RIGHT - *Envelope*, may be addressed in same way as a Baron's wife or, if she prefers *(formal)*, The Right Hon. the Baroness __ ; *(social)*, The Baroness __ . Otherwise as for a Baron's wife.

BARONET - *Envelope*, Sir F__S__, Bt. *Letter (formal)*, Dear Sir; *(social)*, Dear Sir F__. *Spoken*, Sir F__.

BARONET'S WIFE - *Envelope*, Lady S__. *Letter (formal)*, Dear Madam; *(social)*, Dear Lady S__. *Spoken*, Lady S__.

COUNTESS IN OWN RIGHT - As for an Earl's wife.

COURTESY TITLES - The heir apparent to a Duke, Marquess or Earl uses the highest of his father's other titles as a courtesy title. (For list, *see* pages 169–70.) The holder of a courtesy title is not styled The Most Hon. or The Right Hon., and in correspondence 'The' is omitted before the title. The heir apparent to a Scottish title may use the title 'Master' (*see* below).

DAME - *Envelope*, Dame F__S__, followed by appropriate post-nominal letters. *Letter (formal)*, Dear Madam; *(social)*, Dear Dame F__. *Spoken*, Dame F__.

DUKE - *Envelope (formal)*, His Grace the Duke of __ ; *(social)*, The Duke of __ . *Letter (formal)*, My Lord Duke; *(social)*, Dear Duke. *Spoken (formal)*, Your Grace; *(social)*, Duke.

DUKE'S WIFE - *Envelope (formal)*, Her Grace the Duchess of __ ; *(social)*, The Duchess of __ . *Letter (formal)*, Dear Madam; *(social)*, Dear Duchess. *Spoken*, Duchess.

DUKE'S ELDEST SON – *see* Courtesy titles.

DUKE'S YOUNGER SONS - *Envelope*, Lord F__S__. *Letter (formal)*, My Lord; *(social)*, Dear Lord F__. *Spoken (formal)*, My Lord; *(social)*, Lord F__.

DUKE'S DAUGHTER - *Envelope*, Lady F__S__. *Letter (formal)*, Dear Madam; *(social)*, Dear Lady F__. *Spoken*, Lady F__.

EARL - *Envelope (formal)*, The Right Hon. the Earl (of) __; *(social)*, The Earl (of) __ . *Letter (formal)*, My Lord; *(social)*, Dear Lord __ . *Spoken (formal)*, My Lord; *(social)*, Lord __ .

EARL'S WIFE - *Envelope (formal)*, The Right Hon. the Countess (of) __ ; *(social)*, The Countess (of) __ . *Letter (formal)*, Madam; *(social)*, Lady __ . *Spoken (formal)*, Madam; *(social)*, Lady __ .

EARL'S CHILDREN - *Eldest son*, *see* Courtesy titles. *Younger sons*, The Hon. F__S__ (for forms of address, *see* Baron's children). *Daughters*, Lady F__S__ (for forms of address, *see* Duke's daughter).

KNIGHT (BACHELOR) - *Envelope*, Sir F__S__. *Letter (formal)*, Dear Sir; *(social)*, Dear Sir F__. *Spoken*, Sir F__.

KNIGHT (ORDERS OF CHIVALRY) – *Envelope*, Sir F__S__, followed by appropriate post-nominal letters. Otherwise as for Knight Bachelor.

KNIGHT'S WIFE – As for Baronet's wife.

MARQUESS – *Envelope (formal)*, The Most Hon. the Marquess of __ ; *(social)*, The Marquess of __ . *Letter (formal)*, My Lord; *(social)*, Dear Lord __ . *Spoken (formal)*, My Lord; *(social)*, Lord __ .

MARQUESS'S WIFE – *Envelope (formal)*, The Most Hon. the Marchioness of __ ; *(social)*, The Marchioness of __ . *Letter (formal)*, Madam; *(social)*, Dear Lady __ . *Spoken*, Lady __ .

MARQUESS'S CHILDREN – *Eldest son*, *see* Courtesy titles. *Younger sons*, Lord F__S__ (for forms of address, *see* Duke's younger sons). *Daughters*, Lady F__S__ (for forms of address, *see* Duke's daughter).

MASTER – The title is used by the heir apparent to a Scottish peerage, though usually the heir apparent to a Duke, Marquess or Earl uses his courtesy title rather than 'Master'. *Envelope*, The Master of __ . *Letter (formal)*, Dear Sir; *(social)*, Dear Master of __ . *Spoken (formal)*, Master, or Sir; *(social)*, Master, or Mr S__.

MASTER'S WIFE – Addressed as for the wife of the appropriate peerage style, otherwise as Mrs S__.

PRIVY COUNSELLOR – *Envelope*, The Right (or Rt.) Hon. F__S__. *Letter*, Dear Mr/Miss/Mrs S__. *Spoken*, Mr/Miss/Mrs S__. It is incorrect to use the letters PC after the name, unless the Privy Counsellor is a peer below the rank of Marquess and so is styled The Right Hon. because of his rank. In this case the post-nominal letters may be used in conjunction with the prefix The Right Hon.

VISCOUNT – *Envelope (formal)*, The Right Hon. the Viscount __ ; *(social)*, The Viscount __ . *Letter (formal)*, My Lord; *(social)*, Dear Lord __ . *Spoken*, Lord __ .

VISCOUNT'S WIFE – *Envelope (formal)*, The Right Hon. the Viscountess __ ; *(social)*, The Viscountess __ . *Letter (formal)*, Madam; *(social)*, Dear Lady __ . *Spoken*, Lady __ .

VISCOUNT'S CHILDREN – As for Baron's children.

The Privy Council

The Sovereign in Council, or Privy Council, was the chief source of executive power until the system of Cabinet government developed in the 18th century. Now the Privy Council's main functions are to advise the Sovereign and to exercise its own statutory responsibilities independent of the Sovereign in Council (*see also* page 224).

Membership of the Privy Council is automatic upon appointment to certain government and judicial positions in the United Kingdom, e.g. Cabinet ministers must be Privy Counsellors and are sworn in on first assuming office. Membership is also accorded by The Queen to eminent people in the United Kingdom and independent countries of the Commonwealth of which Her Majesty is Queen, on the recommendation of the British Prime Minister. Membership of the Council is retained for life, except for very occasional removals.

The administrative functions of the Privy Council are carried out by the Privy Council Office (*see* page 344) under the direction of the Lord President of the Council, who is always a member of the Cabinet.

Lord President of the Council, The Rt. Hon. Antony Newton, OBE, MP
Clerk of the Council, N. H. Nicholls, CBE

MEMBERS *as at 31 August 1993*

As at 31 August 1993, the appointment of the following to the Privy Council had been announced but the new members had not been sworn: Sir Denis Henry; Sir John Higgins; Sir John Hobhouse; Sir Mark Saville

HRH The Duke of Edinburgh, 1951
HRH The Prince of Wales, 1977

Aberdare, Lord, 1974
Ackner, Lord, 1980
Adams-Schneider, Sir Lancelot, 1980
Airlie, Earl of, 1984
Aldington, Lord, 1954
Alebua, Ezekiel, 1988
Alison, Michael, 1981
Alport, Lord, 1960
Amery of Lustleigh, Lord, 1960
Anthony, Douglas, 1971
Archer of Sandwell, Lord, 1977
Armstrong, Ernest, 1979

Arnold, Sir John, 1979
Ashdown, Paddy, 1989
Ashley of Stoke, Lord, 1979
Avonside, Lord, 1962
Aylestone, Lord, 1962
Azikiwe, Nnamdi, 1960
Baker, Kenneth, 1984
Balcombe, Sir John, 1985
Barber, Lord, 1963
Barnett, Lord, 1975
Barwick, Sir Garfield, 1964
Beckett, Margaret, 1993
Beith, Alan, 1992
Beldam, Sir Roy, 1989
Belstead, Lord, 1983
Benn, Anthony, 1964
Bennett, Sir Frederic, 1985
Bevins, John, 1959
Biffen, John, 1979
Bingham, Sir Thomas, 1986
Birch, William, 1992
Bird, Vere, 1982
Bisson, Sir Gordon, 1987
Blaker, Sir Peter, 1983
Blanch, Lord, 1975
Blatch, Baroness, 1993
Bolger, James, 1991
Booth, Albert, 1976
Boothroyd, Betty, 1992
Boscawen, Hon. Robert, 1992
Bottomley, Lord, 1952
Bottomley, Virginia, 1992
Boyd-Carpenter, Lord, 1954
Boys, Michael, 1989
Boyson, Sir Rhodes, 1987
Braine, Lord, 1985
Braithwaite, Nicholas, 1991
Brandon of Oakbrook, Lord, 1978
Bridge of Harwich, Lord, 1975
Brightman, Lord, 1979
Brittan, Sir Leon, 1981
Brooke, Peter, 1988
Brown, Sir Simon, 1992
Brown, Sir Stephen, 1983
Browne, Sir Patrick, 1974
Browne-Wilkinson, Lord, 1983
Buckley, Sir Denys, 1970
Butler, Sir Adam, 1984
Butler-Sloss, Dame Elizabeth, 1988
Caithness, Earl of, 1990
Callaghan of Cardiff, Lord, 1964
Cameron of Lochbroom, Lord, 1984
Campbell of Croy, Lord, 1970
Canterbury, The Archbishop of, 1991
Carlisle of Bucklow, Lord, 1979
Carr of Hadley, Lord, 1963
Carrington, Lord, 1959
Casey, Sir Maurice, 1986
Castle of Blackburn, Baroness, 1964
Cato, Robert, 1981
Chalfont, Lord, 1964
Chalker of Wallasey, Baroness, 1987
Chan, Sir Julius, 1981

Channon, Paul, 1980
Charteris of Amisfield, Lord, 1972
Chataway, Christopher, 1970
Clark, Alan, 1991
Clark, Helen, 1990
Clark of Kempston, Lord, 1990
Clarke, Kenneth, 1984
Cledwyn of Penrhos, Lord, 1966
Cockfield, Lord, 1982
Cocks of Hartcliffe, Lord, 1976
Coggan, Lord, 1961
Colman, Fraser, 1986
Colnbrook, Lord, 1973
Colyton, Lord, 1952
Compton, John, 1983
Concannon, John, 1978
Cooke, Sir Robin, 1977
Cooper, Sir Frank, 1983
Cope, Sir John, 1988
Corfield, Sir Frederick, 1970
Cowen, Sir Zelman, 1981
Cradock, Sir Percy, 1993
Crawford and Balcarres, Earl of, 1972
Crickhowell, Lord, 1979
Croom-Johnson, Sir David, 1984
Cumming-Bruce, Sir Roualeyn, 1977
Cunningham, Jack, 1993
Davies, Denzil, 1978
Davison, Sir Ronald, 1978
Dean, Sir Paul, 1991
Deedes, Lord, 1962
Dell, Edmund, 1970
Denham, Lord, 1981
Denning, Lord, 1948
Devonshire, Duke of, 1964
Diamond, Lord, 1965
Dillon, Sir Brian, 1982
Donaldson of Lymington, Lord, 1979
Douglas, Sir William, 1977
du Cann, Sir Edward, 1964
Duff, Sir Antony, 1980
Dunn, Sir Robin, 1980
Eccles, Viscount, 1951
Eden of Winton, Lord, 1972
Eichelbaum, Sir Thomas, 1989
Emery, Sir Peter, 1993
Emslie, Lord, 1972
Ennals, Lord, 1970
Erroll of Hale, Lord, 1960
Esquivel, Manuel, 1986
Evans, Sir Anthony, 1992
Eveleigh, Sir Edward, 1977
Farquharson, Sir Donald, 1989
Fellowes, Sir Robert, 1990
Ferguson, Alan, 1992
Ferrers, Earl, 1982
Floissac, Sir Vincent, 1992
Foot, Michael, 1974
Foster, Derek, 1993
Fowler, Sir Norman, 1979
Fox, Sir Michael, 1981
Fraser, Malcolm, 1976
Fraser of Carmyllie, Lord, 1989

Freeman, John, 1966
Freeman, Roger, 1993
Freeson, Reginald, 1976
Gairy, Sir Eric, 1977
Garel-Jones, Tristan, 1992
Gault, Thomas, 1992
Georges, Telford, 1986
Gibbs, Sir Harry, 1972
Gibson, Sir Peter, 1993
Gibson, Sir Ralph, 1985
Gibson-Watt, Lord, 1974
Gilbert, John, 1978
Gilmour of Craigmillar, Lord, 1973
Glenamara, Lord, 1964
Glendevon, Lord, 1959
Glidewell, Sir Iain, 1985
Goff of Chieveley, Lord, 1982
Goodlad, Alastair, 1992
Gorton, Sir John, 1968
Gowrie, Earl of, 1984
Gray of Contin, Lord, 1982
Griffiths, Lord, 1980
Grimond, Lord, 1961
Gummer, John, 1985
Hailsham of St Marylebone, Lord, 1956
Hamilton, Archie, 1991
Harrison, Walter, 1977
Harvington, Lord, 1971
Hattersley, Roy, 1975
Hayhoe, Lord, 1985
Healey, Lord, 1964
Heath, Sir Edward, 1955
Herbison, Margaret, 1964
Heseltine, Michael, 1979
Heseltine, Sir William, 1986
Hesketh, Lord, 1991
Higgins, Sir Terence, 1979
Hirst, Sir David, 1992
Hoffmann, Sir Leonard, 1992
Hogg, Hon. Douglas, 1992
Holderness, Lord, 1959
Home of the Hirsel, Lord, 1951
Hope, Lord, 1989
Hordern, Sir Peter, 1993
Houghton of Sowerby, Lord, 1964
Howard, Michael, 1990
Howe of Aberavon, Lord, 1972
Howell, David, 1979
Howell, Lord, 1976
Hughes, Lord, 1970
Hunt, David, 1990
Hunt, Jonathan, 1989
Hurd, Douglas, 1982
Hutton, Sir Brian, 1988
Ingraham, Hubert, 1993
Jauncey of Tullichettle, Lord, 1988
Jay, Lord, 1952
Jellicoe, Earl, 1963
Jenkin of Roding, Lord, 1973
Jenkins of Hillhead, Lord, 1964
Jones, Aubrey, 1955
Jopling, Michael, 1979
Joseph, Lord, 1962
Jugnauth, Sir Anerood, 1987
Kaufman, Gerald, 1978
Keith of Kinkel, Lord, 1976
Kelly, Sir Basil, 1984
Kenilorea, Sir Peter, 1979

Kennedy, Sir Paul, 1992
Kerr, Sir Michael, 1981
King, Thomas, 1979
Kingsdown, Lord, 1987
Kinnock, Neil, 1983
Kitto, Sir Frank, 1963
Lamont, Norman, 1986
Lane, Lord, 1975
Lang, Ian, 1990
Lange, David, 1984
Lansdowne, Marquess of, 1964
Latey, Sir John, 1986
Lauti, Sir Toaripi, 1979
Lawson of Blaby, Lord, 1981
Lawton, Sir Frederick, 1972
Leggatt, Sir Andrew, 1990
Leonard, Rt. Revd Graham, 1981
Lever of Manchester, Lord, 1969
Lilley, Peter, 1990
Listowel, Earl of, 1946
Llewelyn-Davies of Hastoe, Baroness, 1975
Lloyd, Sir Anthony, 1984
London, The Bishop of, 1991
Longford, Earl of, 1948
Louisy, Allan, 1981
Lowry, Lord, 1974
Luce, Sir Richard, 1986
Lyell, Sir Nicholas, 1990
Mabon, Dickson, 1977
McCarthy, Sir Thaddeus, 1968
McCowan, Sir Anthony, 1989
MacDermott, Sir John, 1987
MacGregor, John, 1985
MacIntyre, Duncan, 1980
Mackay of Clashfern, Lord, 1979
McKay, Ian, 1992
McKinnon, Donald, 1992
McMullin, Sir Duncan, 1980
Major, John, 1987
Manley, Michael, 1989
Mann, Sir Michael, 1988
Mara, Sir Kamisese, 1973
Marsh, Lord, 1966
Mason of Barnsley, Lord, 1968
Maude of Stratford-upon-Avon, Lord, 1979
Maude, Hon. Francis, 1992
May, Sir John, 1982
Mayhew, Sir Patrick, 1986
Megarry, Sir Robert, 1978
Megaw, Sir John, 1969
Mellish, Lord, 1967
Mellor, David, 1990
Merlyn-Rees, Lord, 1974
Millan, Bruce, 1975
Mitchell, James, 1985
Molyneaux, James, 1983
Moore of Lower Marsh, Lord, 1986
Moore, Michael, 1990
Moore of Wolvercote, Lord, 1977
Morris, Alfred, 1979
Morris, Charles, 1978
Morris, John, 1970
Morrison, Sir Peter, 1988
Moyle, Roland, 1978
Mulley, Lord, 1964
Murray, Hon. Lord, 1974
Murray, Sir Donald, 1989

Murray of Epping Forest, Lord, 1976
Murton of Lindisfarne, Lord, 1976
Mustill, Lord, 1985
Nairne, Sir Patrick, 1982
Namaliu, Robbie, 1989
Neill, Sir Brian, 1985
Newton, Antony, 1988
Nicholls, Sir Donald, 1986
Nolan, Sir Michael, 1991
Nott, Sir John, 1979
Nourse, Sir Martin, 1985
Nugent of Guildford, Lord, 1962
Nutting, Sir Anthony, 1954
Oakes, Gordon, 1979
O'Brien of Lothbury, Lord, 1970
O'Connor, Sir Patrick, 1980
O'Donnell, Turlough, 1979
O'Flynn, Francis, 1987
Oliver of Aylmerton, Lord, 1980
Onslow, Sir Cranley, 1988
Oppenheim-Barnes, Baroness, 1979
Orme, Stanley, 1974
Owen, Lord, 1976
Paeniu, Bikenibeu, 1992
Palliser, Sir Michael, 1983
Palmer, Sir Geoffrey, 1986
Parker, Sir Roger, 1983
Parkinson, Lord, 1981
Patten, Christopher, 1989
Patten, John, 1990
Patterson, Percival, 1992
Pattie, Sir Geoffrey, 1987
Percival, Sir Ian, 1983
Perth, Earl of, 1957
Peyton of Yeovil, Lord, 1970
Pindling, Sir Lynden, 1976
Portillo, Michael, 1992
Powell, Enoch, 1960
Prentice, Lord, 1966
Price, George, 1982
Prior, Lord, 1970
Puapua, Tomasi, 1982
Purchas, Sir Francis, 1982
Pym, Lord, 1970
Raison, Sir Timothy, 1982
Ramsden, James, 1963
Rawlinson of Ewell, Lord, 1964
Redwood, John, 1993
Rees, Lord, 1983
Reigate, Lord, 1961
Renton, Lord, 1962
Renton, Timothy, 1989
Richard, Lord, 1993
Richardson, Sir Ivor, 1978
Richardson of Duntisbourne, Lord, 1976
Richmond, Sir Clifford, 1973
Rifkind, Malcolm, 1986
Rippon of Hexham, Lord, 1962
Robens of Woldingham, Lord, 1951
Roberts, Sir Wyn, 1991
Robinson, Sir Kenneth, 1964
Roch, Sir John, 1993
Rodger of Earlsferry, Lord, 1992
Rodgers of Quarry Bank, Lord, 1975
Rose, Sir Christopher, 1992
Roskill, Lord, 1971
Ross, Hon. Lord, 1985
Rowling, Sir Wallace, 1974

Rumbold, Dame Angela, 1991
Runcie, Lord, 1980
Russell, Sir Patrick, 1987
Ryder, Richard, 1990
Sainsbury, Hon. Timothy, 1992
St John of Fawsley, Lord, 1979
Sandiford, Erskine, 1989
Scarman, Lord, 1973
Scott, Nicholas, 1989
Scott, Sir Richard, 1992
Seaga, Edward, 1981
Seear, Baroness, 1985
Selkirk, Earl of, 1955
Shackleton, Lord, 1966
Shawcross, Lord, 1946
Shearer, Hugh, 1969
Sheldon, Robert, 1977
Shephard, Gillian, 1992
Shepherd, Lord, 1965
Shore, Peter, 1967
Simmonds, Kennedy, 1984
Simon of Glaisdale, Lord, 1961
Sinclair, Ian, 1977
Slade, Sir Christopher, 1982
Slynn of Hadley, Lord, 1992
Smith, John, 1978
Somare, Sir Michael, 1977
Somers, Sir Edward, 1981

Stanley, Sir John, 1984
Staughton, Sir Christopher, 1988
Steel, Sir David, 1977
Stephen, Sir Ninian, 1979
Stephenson, Sir John, 1971
Stewartby, Lord, 1989
Steyn, Sir Johan, 1992
Stocker, Sir John, 1986
Stodart of Leaston, Lord, 1974
Stott, Lord, 1964
Stuart-Smith, Sir Murray, 1988
Talboys, Sir Brian, 1977
Taylor of Gosforth, Lord, 1988
Tebbit, Lord, 1981
Templeman, Lord, 1978
Thatcher, Baroness, 1970
Thomas of Gwydir, Lord, 1964
Thomson, David, 1981
Thomson of Monifieth, Lord, 1966
Thorneycroft, Lord, 1951
Thorpe, Jeremy, 1967
Tizard, Robert, 1986
Tonypandy, Viscount, 1968
Tranmire, Lord, 1955
Trefgarne, Lord, 1989
Trumpington, Baroness, 1992
Varley, Lord, 1974
Waddington, Lord, 1987

Waite, Sir John, 1993
Wakeham, Lord, 1983
Waldegrave, William, 1990
Walker, Sir Harold, 1979
Walker of Worcester, Lord, 1970
Waller, Sir George, 1976
Watkins, Sir Tasker, 1980
Watkinson, Viscount, 1955
Weatherill, Lord, 1980
Wheeler, Sir John, 1993
Whitelaw, Viscount, 1967
Wilberforce, Lord, 1964
Williams, Alan, 1977
Williams of Crosby, Baroness, 1974
Wilson of Langside, Lord, 1967
Wilson of Rievaulx, Lord, 1947
Windlesham, Lord, 1973
Wingti, Paias, 1987
Withers, Reginald, 1977
Woodhouse, Sir Owen, 1974
Woolf, Lord, 1986
Wylie, *Hon.* Lord, 1970
York, The Archbishop of, 1983
Young, Baroness, 1981
Young, Sir George, 1993
Young of Graffham, Lord, 1984
Younger of Prestwick, Lord, 1979
Zacca, Edward, 1992

The Privy Council of Northern Ireland

The Privy Council of Northern Ireland had responsibilities in Northern Ireland similar to those of the Privy Council in Great Britain until the Northern Ireland Act 1974 instituted direct rule and a United Kingdom Cabinet minister became responsible for the functions previously exercised by the Northern Ireland government.

Membership of the Privy Council of Northern Ireland is retained for life. The postnominal initials PC(NI) are used to differentiate its members from those of the Privy Council.

MEMBERS *as at 31 August 1993*

Bailie, Robin, 1971
Bleakley, David, 1971
Bradford, Roy, 1969
Craig, William, 1963
Dobson, John, 1969
Glentoran, The Lord, 1953
Kelly, Sir Basil, 1969
Kirk, Herbert, 1962
Long, William, 1966
Lowry, The Lord, 1971
McConnell, Robert, 1964

McIvor, Basil, 1971
Morgan, William, 1961
Moyola, The Lord, 1966
Neill, Sir Ivan, 1950
Porter, Sir Robert, 1969
Rathcavan, The Lord, 1969
Simpson, Robert, 1969
Taylor, John, MP, 1970
West, Henry, 1960

Parliament

The United Kingdom constitution is not contained in any single document but has evolved in the course of time, formed partly by statute, partly by common law and partly by convention. A constitutional monarchy, the United Kingdom is governed by Ministers of the Crown in the name of the Sovereign, who is head both of the state and of the government.

The organs of government are the legislature (Parliament), the executive and the judiciary. The executive consists of HM Government (Cabinet and other Ministers) (see pages 280–1), government departments (see pages 282–369), local authorities (see Local Government), and public corporations operating nationalized industries or social or cultural services (see pages 282–369). The judiciary (see Law Courts and Offices) pronounces on the law, both written and unwritten, interprets statutes and is responsible for the enforcement of the law; the judiciary is independent of both the legislature and the executive.

THE MONARCHY

The Sovereign personifies the state and is, in law, an integral part of the legislature, head of the executive, head of the judiciary, the commander-in-chief of all armed forces of the Crown and the 'Supreme Governor' of the Church of England. The seat of the monarchy is in the United Kingdom. In the Channel Islands and the Isle of Man, which are Crown dependencies, the Sovereign is represented by a Lieutenant-Governor. In the member states of the Commonwealth of which the Sovereign is head of state, her representative is a Governor-General; in United Kingdom dependencies the Sovereign is usually represented by a Governor, who is responsible to the British Government.

Although the powers of the monarchy are now very limited, restricted mainly to the advisory and ceremonial, there are important acts of government which require the participation of the Sovereign. These include summoning, proroguing and dissolving Parliament, giving royal assent to Bills passed by Parliament, appointing important office-holders, e.g. government ministers, judges, bishops, and governors, conferring peerages, knighthoods and other honours, and granting pardon to a person wrongly convicted of a crime. An important function is appointing a Prime Minister, by convention the leader of the political party which enjoys, or can secure, a majority of votes in the House of Commons. In international affairs the Sovereign as head of state has the power to declare war and make peace, to recognize foreign states and governments, to conclude treaties and to annex or cede territory. However, as the Sovereign entrusts executive power to Ministers of the Crown and acts on the advice of her Ministers, which she cannot ignore, in practice royal prerogative powers are exercised by Ministers, who are responsible to Parliament.

Ministerial responsibility does not diminish the Sovereign's importance to the smooth working of government. She holds meetings of the Privy Council, gives audiences to her Ministers and other officials at home and overseas, receives accounts of Cabinet decisions, reads dispatches and signs state papers; she must be informed and consulted on every aspect of national life; and she must show complete impartiality.

COUNSELLORS OF STATE

In the event of the Sovereign's absence abroad, it is necessary to appoint Counsellors of State under letters patent to carry out the chief functions of the Monarch, including the holding of Privy Councils and giving royal assent to Acts passed by Parliament. The normal procedure is to appoint as Counsellors three or four members of the royal family among those remaining in the United Kingdom.

In the event of the Sovereign on accession being under the age of eighteen years, or at any time unavailable or incapacitated by infirmity of mind or body for the performance of the royal functions, provision is made for a regency.

THE PRIVY COUNCIL

The Sovereign in Council, or Privy Council, was the chief source of executive power until the system of Cabinet government developed. Now its main function is to advise the Sovereign to approve Orders in Council and to advise on the issue of royal proclamations. The Council's own statutory responsibilities (independent of the powers of the Sovereign in Council) include powers of supervision over the registering bodies for the medical and allied professions. A full Council is summoned only on the death of the Sovereign or when the Sovereign announces his or her intention to marry. (For full list of Counsellors, see pages 221–3)

There are a number of advisory Privy Council committees, whose meetings the Sovereign does not attend. Some are prerogative committees, such as those dealing with legislative matters submitted by the legislatures of the Channel Islands and the Isle of Man or with applications for charters of incorporation; and some are provided for by statute, e.g. those for the universities of Oxford and Cambridge and the Scottish universities.

The Judicial Committee of the Privy Council is the final court of appeal from courts of the United Kingdom dependencies, courts of independent Commonwealth countries which have retained the right of appeal, courts of the Channel Islands and the Isle of Man, some professional and disciplinary committees, and church sources. The Committee is composed of all Privy Counsellors who hold, or have held, high judicial office, although usually only three or five hear each case.

Administrative work is carried out by the Privy Council Office under the direction of the Lord President of the Council, a Cabinet Minister.

PARLIAMENT

Parliament is the supreme law-making authority and can legislate for the United Kingdom as a whole or for any parts of it separately (the Channel Islands and the Isle of Man are Crown dependencies and not part of the United Kingdom). The main functions of Parliament are to pass laws, to provide (by voting taxation) the means of carrying on the work of government and to scrutinize government policy and administration, particularly proposals for expenditure. International treaties and agreements are by custom presented to Parliament before ratification.

Parliament emerged during the late thirteenth and early fourteenth centuries. The officers of the King's household and the King's judges were the nucleus of early Parliaments, joined by such ecclesiastical and lay magnates as the King might summon to form a prototype 'House of Lords', and occasionally by the knights of the shires, burgesses and proctors of the lower clergy. By the end of Edward III's reign a 'House of Commons' was beginning to appear; the first known Speaker was elected in 1377.

Parliamentary procedure is based on custom and precedent, partly formulated in the Standing Orders of both Houses (see Standing Orders, page 230), and each House has the right to control its own internal proceedings and to commit for contempt. The system of debate in the two Houses is similar; when a motion has been moved, the Speaker proposes the question as the subject of a debate. Members speak from wherever they have been sitting. Questions are decided by a vote on a simple majority. Draft legislation is introduced, in either House, as a Bill. Bills can be introduced by a Government Minister or a private Member, but in practice the majority of Bills which become law are introduced by the Government. To become law, a Bill must be passed by each House (for parliamentary stages, see Bill, page 228) and then sent to the Sovereign for the royal assent, after which it becomes an Act of Parliament.

Proceedings of both Houses are public, except on extremely rare occasions. The minutes (called Votes and Proceedings in the Commons, and Minutes of Proceedings in the Lords) and the speeches (The Official Report of Parliamentary Debates, Hansard) are published daily. Proceedings are also recorded for transmission on radio and television and stored in the Parliamentary Recording Unit before transfer to the National Sound Archive. Television cameras have been allowed into the House of Lords since January 1985, and into the House of Commons since November 1989; committee meetings may also be televised.

By the Parliament Act of 1911, the maximum duration of a Parliament is five years (if not previously dissolved), the term being reckoned from the date given on the writs for the new Parliament. The maximum life has been prolonged by legislation in such rare circumstances as the two world wars (31 January 1911 to 25 November 1918; 26 November 1935 to 15 June 1945). Dissolution and writs for a general election are ordered by The Queen on the advice of the Prime Minister. The life of a Parliament is divided into sessions, usually of one year in length, beginning and ending most often in October or November.

THE HOUSE OF LORDS
London SW1A 0PW
Tel 071-219 3000

The House of Lords consists of the Lords Spiritual and Temporal. The Lords Spiritual are the Archbishops of Canterbury and York, the Bishops of London, Durham and Winchester, and the 21 senior diocesan bishops of the Church of England. The Lords Temporal consist of all hereditary peers of England, Scotland, Great Britain and the United Kingdom who have not disclaimed their peerages, life peers created under the Life Peerages Act 1958, and those Lords of Appeal in Ordinary created life peers under the Appellate Jurisdiction Act 1876, as amended (law lords). Disclaimants of an hereditary peerage lose their right to sit in the House of Lords but gain the right to vote at Parliamentary elections and to offer themselves for election to the House of Commons (see also page 141). Those peers disqualified from sitting in the House include:

– aliens, i.e. any peer who is not a British citizen, a Commonwealth citizen (under the British Nationality Act 1981) or a citizen of the Republic of Ireland
– peers under the age of 21
– undischarged bankrupts or, in Scotland, those whose estate is sequestered
– peers convicted of treason

Peers who do not wish to attend sittings of the House of Lords may apply for leave of absence for the duration of a Parliament.

Until the beginning of this century the House of Lords had considerable power, being able to veto any Bill submitted to it by the House of Commons, but those powers were greatly reduced by the Parliament Act of 1911 and subsequently by the Parliament Act of 1949 (see Parliament Acts 1911 and 1949, page 229).

Combined with its legislative role, the House of Lords has judicial powers as the ultimate Court of Appeal for courts in Great Britain and Northern Ireland, except for criminal cases in Scotland. These powers are exercised by the Lord Chancellor and the law lords.

Members of the House of Lords are unpaid. However, they are entitled to reimbursement of travelling expenses on parliamentary business within the UK and certain other expenses incurred for the purpose of attendance at sittings of the House, within a maximum for each day of £69.00 for overnight subsistence, £31.00 for day subsistence and incidental travel, and £30.00 for secretarial costs, postage and certain additional expenses.

COMPOSITION as at 13 July 1993
Archbishops and Bishops, 26
Peers by succession, 760 (17 women)
Hereditary Peers of first creation (including the Prince of Wales), 15
Life Peers under the Appellate Jurisdiction Act 1876, 19
Life Peers under the Life Peerages Act 1958, 382 (59 women)
Total 1,202
Of whom:
Peers without Writs of Summons, 84 (2 minors)
Peers on leave of absence from the House, 85

STATE OF PARTIES as at 13 July 1993
About half of the members of the House of Lords take the whip of one of the political parties. The other members sit on the cross-benches or as independents.

Conservative, 470
Labour, 113
Liberal Democrats, 57
Cross-bench, 271
Other (including Bishops), 291

OFFICERS
The House is presided over by the Lord Chancellor, who is ex officio Speaker of the House. A panel of deputy Speakers is appointed by Royal Commission. The first deputy Speaker is the Chairman of Committees, appointed at the beginning of each session, a salaried officer of the House who takes the chair in committee of the whole House and in some select committees. He is assisted by a panel of deputy chairmen, headed by the salaried Principal Deputy Chairman of Committees, who is also chairman of the European Communities Committee of the House.

The permanent officers include the Clerk of the Parliaments, who is in charge of the administrative staff collectively known as the Parliament Office; the Gentleman Usher of the Black Rod, who is also Serjeant-at-Arms in attendance upon the Lord Chancellor and is responsible for security and for accommodation and services in the House of Lords; and the Yeoman Usher who is Deputy Serjeant-at-Arms and assists Black Rod in his duties.

Speaker (£15,532), The Rt. Hon. the Lord Mackay of Clashfern
Private Secretary, M. Ormerod
Chairman of Committees (£46,167), The Lord Ampthill, CBE
Principal Deputy Chairman of Committees (£42,188), The Lord Boston of Faversham, QC
Clerk of the Parliaments (£87,620), M. A. J. Wheeler-Booth
Clerk Assistant and Clerk of the Journals (£62,504–£73,216), J. M. Davies
Reading Clerk (£53,272–£61,280), P. D. G. Hayter, LVO
Counsel to Chairman of Committees (£62,504–£73,216), D. Rippengal, CB, QC
Second Counsel (£53,272–£61,280), Mrs E. Denza, CMG
Third Counsel (£53,272–£61,280), Sir James Nursaw, KCB, QC
Assistant Counsel (£42,689–£57,586), N. J. Adamson, CB, QC
Principal Clerks (£47,871–£61,280), J. A. Vallance White (*Judicial Office and Fourth Clerk at the Table*); M. G. Pownall (*Committees*); B. P. Keith (*Private Bills*); D. R. Beamish (*Clerk of the Journals*)
Chief Clerks (£39,339–£51,540), C. A. J. Mitchell; R. H. Walters, D.Phil.; Dr F. P. Tudor
Senior Clerks (£27,080–£37,769), E. C. Ollard (*seconded as Secretary to the Leader of the House and Chief Whip*); Mrs M. E. Ollard; A. Makower; E. J. J. Wells; T. V. Mohan; S. P. Burton
Clerks (£14,390–£25,013), Mrs M. B. Bloor; D. J. Batt
Clerk of the Records (£39,339–£51,540), D. J. Johnson, FSA
Deputy Clerk of the Records (£30,654–£46,140), S. K. Ellison
Accountant (£27,080–£46,140), C. Preece
Assistant Accountant (£19,832–£27,304), Miss J. M. Lansdown
Judicial Taxing Clerk (£19,832–£27,304), C. G. Osborne
Librarian (£39,339–£51,540), D. L. Jones
Deputy Librarian (£30,654–£46,140), P. G. Davis, PH.D.
Senior Library Clerk (£27,080–£37,769), Miss I. L. Victory, PH.D.
Examiners of Petitions for Private Bills, B. P. Keith; R. J. Willoughby
Gentleman Usher of the Black Rod and Serjeant-at-Arms (£53,272–£61,280), Adm. Sir Richard Thomas, KCB, OBE
Yeoman Usher of the Black Rod and Deputy Serjeant-at-Arms (£27,080–£37,769), Air Cdre A. C. Curry, OBE
Staff Superintendent, Maj. F. P. Horsfall, MBE
Shorthand Writer (fees), Mrs P. J. Woolger
Editor, Official Report (Hansard), (£37,084–£48,553), Mrs M. E. Villiers
Deputy Editor, Official Report (£27,764–£41,701), G. R. Goodbarne

THE HOUSE OF COMMONS
London SW1A 0AA
Tel 071-219 3000

The members of the House of Commons are elected by universal adult suffrage. For electoral purposes, the United Kingdom is divided into constituencies, each of which returns one member to the House of Commons, the member being the candidate who obtains the largest number of votes cast in the constituency. To ensure equitable representation the four Boundary Commissions keep constituency boundaries under review and recommend any redistribution of seats which may seem necessary because of population movements, etc.

The number of seats was raised to 640 in 1945, then reduced to 625 in 1948, and subsequently rose to 630 in 1955, 635 in 1970, 650 in 1983 and 651 in 1992. Of the present 651 seats, there are 524 for England, 38 for Wales, 72 for Scotland and 17 for Northern Ireland.

ELECTIONS

Elections are by secret ballot, each elector casting one vote; voting is not compulsory. When a seat becomes vacant between general elections, a by-election is held.

British subjects and citizens of the Irish Republic can stand for election as Members of Parliament (MPs) provided they are 21 or over and not subject to disqualification. Those disqualified from sitting in the House include:

– undischarged bankrupts
– people sentenced to more than one year's imprisonment
– clergy of the Church of England, Church of Scotland, Church of Ireland and Roman Catholic Church
– members of the House of Lords
– holders of certain offices listed in the House of Commons Disqualification Act 1975, e.g. members of the judiciary, Civil Service, regular armed forces, police forces, some local government officers and some members of public corporations and government commissions

For entitlement to vote in parliamentary elections, *see* Legal Notes section.

A candidate does not require any party backing but his or her nomination for election must be supported by the signatures of ten people registered in the constituency. A candidate must also deposit with the returning officer £500, which is forfeit if the candidate does not receive more than 5 per cent of the votes cast. All election expenses at a general election, except the candidate's personal expenses, are subject to a statutory limit of £4,330, plus 3.7 pence for each elector in a borough constituency or 4.9 pence for each elector in a county constituency.

See pages 234–41 for an alphabetical list of MPs, pages 243–73 for the results of the last General Election, and page 242 for the results of recent by-elections.

STATE OF PARTIES *as at 31 July 1993*
Conservative, 334 (19 women)
Labour, 270 (36 women)
Liberal Democrats, 22 (3 women)
Plaid Cymru, 4
Scottish Nationalist, 3 (1 woman)
Democratic Unionist, 3
Social Democratic and Labour, 4
Ulster Popular Unionist, 1
Ulster Unionist, 9
The Speaker, 1
Total, 651 (60 women)

BUSINESS

The week's business of the House is outlined each Thursday by the Leader of the House, after consultation between the Chief Government Whip and the Chief Opposition Whip. A quarter to a third of the time will be taken up by the Government's legislative programme, and the rest by other business, e.g. question time. As a rule, Bills likely to raise political controversy are introduced in the Commons before going on to the Lords, and the Commons claims exclusive control in respect of national taxation and expenditure. Bills such as the Finance Bill, which imposes taxation, and the Consolidated Fund Bills, which authorize expenditure, must begin in the Commons. A Bill of which the financial provisions are subsidiary may begin in the Lords; and the

Commons may waive its rights in regard to Lords' amendments affecting finance.

The Commons has a public register of MPs' financial and certain other interests. Members must also disclose any relevant financial interest or benefit in a matter before the House when taking part in a debate, in certain other proceedings of the House, or in consultations with other MPs, with Ministers or civil servants.

MEMBERS' PAY AND ALLOWANCES

Since 1911 members of the House of Commons have received salary payments; facilities for free travel were introduced in 1924. Members are entitled to claim income tax relief on expenses incurred in the course of their Parliamentary duties. Salary rates since 1911 are as follows:

1911	£400 p.a.	1979 June	£9,450 p.a.
1931	360	1980 June	11,750
1934	380	1981 June	13,950
1935	400	1982 June	14,510
1937	600	1983 June	15,308
1946	1,000	1984 Jan	16,106
1954	1,250	1985 Jan	16,904
1957	1,750	1986 Jan	17,702
1964	3,250	1987 Jan	18,500
1972 Jan	4,500	1988 Jan	22,548
1975 June	5,750	1989 Jan	24,107
1976 June	6,062	1990 Jan	26,701
1977 July	6,270	1991 Jan	28,970
1978 June	6,897	1992 Jan	30,854

In October 1969 MPs were granted an allowance for secretarial and research expenses. In 1987 this became known as the Office Costs Allowance. From April 1993 the allowance is £40,380.

Since January 1972 MPs can claim reimbursement for the additional cost of staying overnight away from their main residence while on Parliamentary business. This was set at £10,958 for the 1993-4 financial year. Since 1984 this has been non-taxable.

From April 1980 provision was made enabling each MP in receipt of Office Costs Allowance to contribute sums to an approved pension scheme for the provision of a pension, or other benefits, for or in respect of persons whose salary is met by him/her from the Office Costs Allowance.

The cost of travel allowances for 1992-3 was stated in June 1993 to be £7,041,663.

MEMBERS' PENSIONS

Pension arrangements for MPs were first introduced in 1964. The arrangements currently provide a pension of one-fiftieth of salary for each year of pensionable service with a maximum of two-thirds of salary at age 65. Pension is payable normally at age 65, for men and women, or on later retirement. Pensions may be paid earlier, e.g. on ill-health retirement. The widow/widower of a former MP receives a pension of five-eighths of the late MP's pension. Pensions are index-linked. Members currently contribute 6 per cent of salary to the pension fund; there is an Exchequer contribution, currently slightly more than the amount contributed by MPs.

The House of Commons Members' Fund provides for annual or lump sum grants to ex-MPs, their widows or widowers, and children whose incomes are below certain limits. Alternatively, payments of £2,033 per annum to ex-MPs with at least ten years' service and who left the House of Commons before October 1964, and £1,271 per annum to their widows or widowers are made as of right. Members contribute £24 per annum and the Exchequer £215,000 per annum to the fund. The net assets of the fund as at 30 September 1992 amounted to £2,061,301.

OFFICERS AND OFFICIALS

The House of Commons is presided over by the Speaker, who has considerable powers to maintain order in the House. A deputy, the Chairman of Ways and Means, and two Deputy Chairmen may preside over sittings of the House of Commons; they are elected by the House, and, like the Speaker, neither speak nor vote other than in their official capacity.

The staff of the House are employed by a Commission chaired by the Speaker. The heads of House of Commons departments are permanent officers of the House, not MPs. The Clerk of the House is the principal adviser to the Speaker on the privileges and procedures of the House, the conduct of the business of the House, and Committees. The Serjeant-at-Arms is responsible for security, ceremonial, and for accommodation in the Commons part of the Palace of Westminster.

Speaker (£63,047), The Rt. Hon. Betty Boothroyd, MP for West Bromwich West
Chairman of Ways and Means (£51,402), Michael Morris, MP for Northampton South
First Deputy Chairman of Ways and Means (£47,989), Geoffrey Lofthouse, MP for Pontefract and Castleford
Second Deputy Chairman of Ways and Means (£47,989), Dame Janet Fookes, DBE, MP for Plymouth Drake

OFFICES OF THE SPEAKER AND CHAIRMAN OF WAYS AND MEANS

Speaker's Secretary (£39,339-£44,474), N. Bevan, CB
Speaker's Counsel (£54,751-£62,990), H. Knorpel, CB, QC; T. J. G. Pratt, CB
Assistant to Speaker's Counsel (£29,410-£34,735), P. Harvey, CB
Chaplain to the Speaker, The Revd Canon D. Gray, TD
Secretary to the Chairman of Ways and Means, Ms P. A. Helme

DEPARTMENT OF THE CLERK OF THE HOUSE

Clerk of the House of Commons (£90,148), Sir Clifford Boulton, KCB
Clerk Assistant (£64,307-£75,238), D. W. Limon, CB
Clerk of Committees (£64,307-£75,238), J. F. Sweetman, CB, TD
Principal Clerks (£54,751-£62,990)
  Public Bills, W. R. McKay
  Table Office, C. B. Winnifrith
  Select Committees, R. B. Sands
  Overseas Office, G. Cubie
  Journals, A. J. Hastings
  Private Bills, R. J. Willoughby
  Second Clerk of Select Committees, D. G. Millar
  Standing Committees, M. R. Jack, PH.D.
  Domestic Committees, R. W. G. Wilson
  Financial Committees, W. A. Proctor
Deputy Principal Clerks (£39,339-£44,474), S. A. L. Panton; Mrs J. Sharpe; Ms A. Milner-Barry; F. A. Cranmer; R. J. Rogers; C. R. M. Ward, PH.D.; Ms H. E. Irwin; D. W. N. Doig; D. L. Natzler; E. P. Silk; A. R. Kennon; L. C. Laurence Smyth; S. J. Patrick; D. J. Gerhold; C. J. Poyser; D. F. Harrison; S. J. Priestley; A. H. Doherty; P. A. Evans; R. I. S. Phillips; R. G. James
Senior Clerks (£27,080-£31,957), Ms P. A. Helme; D. R Lloyd; R. A. Lambert; B. M. Hutton; J. S. Benger, D.PHIL.; Ms E. C. Samson; N. P. Walker; M. D. Hamlyn; P. C. Seaward, D.PHIL.; C. G. Lee; C. D. Stanton;

A. Y. A. Azad; H. R. Neilson (*acting*); D. Steel (*acting*);
D. J. Clarke (*acting*); P. Bolton (*acting*)
Clerks of Domestic Committees (£27,080–£31,957),
K. J. Brown; P. G. Moon
Examiners of Petitions for Private Bills, R. J. Willoughby;
B. P. Keith
Registrar of Members' Interests, R. B. Sands
Taxing Officer, R. J. Willoughby

Vote Office
Deliverer of the Vote (£39,339–£44,474), H. C. Foster
Deputy Deliverer of the Vote (£27,080–£31,957),
J. F. Collins

DEPARTMENT OF THE SERJEANT-AT-ARMS
Serjeant-at-Arms (£54,751–£62,990) Sir Alan Urwick, KCVO, CMG
Deputy Serjeant-at-Arms (£39,339–£44,474),
P. N. W. Jennings
Assistant Serjeant-at-Arms (£30,654–£39,339),
M. J. A. Cummins
Deputy Assistant Serjeants-at-Arms (£27,080–£31,957),
P. A. J. Wright; J. M. Robertson

PARLIAMENTARY WORKS DIRECTORATE
Director of Works (£49,671), H. P. Webber
Deputy Director of Works (£39,339), B. C. Sewell
Principal Works Officers (£27,080–£31,957), A.
Makepeace; B. R. Hall; R. Bentley; C. Hillier;
M. Moone; G. Goode; J. F. Moore; M. Trott
Senior Professional and Technical Officers (£21,994–
£27,586), J. Stone; S. Howard; B. O'Boyle; C. Brown;
C. Cowell; J. Eaton; T. Fox; T. Jardine

DEPARTMENT OF THE LIBRARY
Librarian (£54,751–£62,990), Miss J. B. Tanfield
Deputy Librarian (£47,871–£49,671), Miss P. J. Baines
Assistant Librarians (£39,339–£44,474), S. Z. Young;
K. G. Cunninghame
Deputy Assistant Librarians (£30,654–£39,339),
Mrs J. M. Wainwright; C. C. Pond, ph.D.;
Mrs C. B. Andrews; R. C. Clements; Mrs J. M. Lourie;
R. J. Ware, D.Phil.; C. R. Barclay; Mrs J. M. Fiddick; Mrs
C. M. Gillie; R. J. Twigger; Mrs G. L. Allen
Senior Library Clerks (£27,080–£31,957), Ms F. Poole;
T. N. Edmonds; R. J. Cracknell; Miss O. M. Gay;
Miss E. M. McInnes; B. K. Winetrobe; Miss M. Baber;
Ms A. Walker; Mrs H. V. Holden; Miss J. Seaton;
Mrs P. L. Carling; A. J. L. Crompton; Miss P. J.
Strickland; Miss V. A. Miller; Ms H. M. Jeffs; S. A. Wise

DEPARTMENT OF FINANCE AND ADMINISTRATION
Director of Finance and Administration (£54,751–£62,990),
J. Rodda
Accountant (£47,871–£49,671), A. J. Lewis
Deputy Accountant (£39,339–£44,474), A. R. Marskell
Assistant Accountants (£27,080–£31,957), M. Fletcher;
Mrs G. Crowther
Head of Establishments Office (£39,339–£44,474),
B. A. Wilson
Head of Finance Office (£30,654–£39,339), M. J. Barram
Financial Accountant (£27,080–£31,957), vacant
Management Accountant (£27,080–£31,957),
R. H. A. Russell
Deputy Head of Establishments Office (£30,654–£39,339),
J. A. Robb
Computer Officer (£39,339–£44,474), R. S. Morgan

Internal Auditor (£27,080–£31,957), A. A. Cameron
Staff Inspector (£30,654–£39,339), R. C. Collins

DEPARTMENT OF THE OFFICIAL REPORT
Editor (£47,871–£49,671), I. D. Church
Deputy Editor (£39,339–£44,474), P. Walker
Principal Assistant Editors (£30,654–£39,339), J. Gourley;
W. G. Garland; Miss H. Hales; R. V. Hadlow
Assistant Editors (£28,220–£34,735), Miss V. Grainger;
Miss V. A. A. Clarke; Miss G. L. Sutherland;
S. Hutchinson; Miss C. Fogarty

REFRESHMENT DEPARTMENT
Director of Catering Services (£39,339–£44,474),
Mrs S. J. Harrison
Catering Accountant (£27,080–£31,957), D. R. W. Wood
Operations Manager (£27,080–£31,957), N. M. Hutson

PARLIAMENTARY INFORMATION

The following is a short glossary of aspects of the work of
Parliament. Unless otherwise stated, references are to House
of Commons procedures.

ADJOURNMENT DEBATE – Usually a half-hour debate
introduced by a back-bencher at the end of business for the
day. The subjects raised are often local or personal issues.

BILL – Proposed legislation is termed a Bill. The stages of
a Public Bill (for Private Bills, *see* page 229) in the House of
Commons are as follows:
First Reading: There is no debate at this stage, which
nowadays merely constitutes an order to have the Bill printed
Second Reading: The debate on the principles of the Bill
Committee Stage: The detailed examination of a Bill, clause
by clause. In most cases this takes place in a Standing
Committee, or the whole House may act as a Committee. A
Special Standing Committee may take evidence before
embarking on detailed scrutiny of the Bill. Very rarely, a Bill
may be examined by a Select Committee (*see* page 230)
Report Stage: Detailed review of a Bill as amended in
Committee
Third Reading: Final debate on a Bill
Public Bills go through the same stages in the House of
Lords, except that in almost all cases the Committee stage is
taken in Committee of the Whole House.
A Bill may start in either House, and has to pass through
both Houses to become law. Both Houses have to agree the
same text of a Bill, so that the amendments made by the
second House are then considered in the originating House,
and if not agreed, sent back or themselves amended, until
agreement is reached.

CHILTERN HUNDREDS – A legal fiction, a nominal office
of profit under the Crown, the acceptance of which requires
an MP to vacate his seat. The Manor of Northstead is similar.
These are the only means by which an MP may resign.

CLOSURE AND GUILLOTINE – To prevent deliberate
waste of time of either House, a motion may be made that
the question be now put. In the House of Commons, if the
Speaker decides that the rights of a minority are not being
prejudiced and 100 members support the closure motion in
a division, if carried, the original motion is put to the House
without further debate.
The guillotine represents a more rigorous and systematic
application of the closure. Under this system, a Bill proceeds
in accordance with a rigid timetable and discussion is limited

to the time allotted to each group of clauses. The closure is hardly ever used in the Lords, and there is no procedure for a guillotine. The completion of business in the Lords is ensured by agreement from all sides of the House.

CONSOLIDATED FUND BILL – A Bill to authorize issue of money to maintain Government services. The Bill is dealt with without debate, but afterwards members may raise topics of public or local importance.

DELEGATED LEGISLATION – Many statutes empower Ministers to make delegated legislation, with little or no reference back to Parliament, usually by means of Statutory Instruments. These fall into four broad categories:
Affirmative Instruments, which are subject to approval by resolutions of both Houses before they can come into or remain in force
Negative Instruments, which are subject to annulment by resolution of either House
General Instruments, which include those not required to be laid before Parliament and those which are required to be so laid but are not subject to approval or annulment
Special Procedure Orders, against which parties outside Parliament may lodge petitions

DISSOLUTION – Parliament comes to an end either by dissolution by the Sovereign, on the advice of the Prime Minister, or on the expiration of the term of five years for which the House of Commons was elected. Dissolution is normally effected by a royal proclamation.

EARLY DAY MOTION – A motion put on the Notice Paper by an MP without in general the real prospect of its being debated. Such motions are expressions of back-bench opinion.

EMERGENCY DEBATE – In the Commons a method of obtaining prompt discussion of a matter of urgency is by moving the adjournment under Standing Order No. 20 for the purpose of discussing a specific and important matter that should have urgent consideration. A member may ask leave to make this motion by giving written notice to the Speaker, usually before 12 noon, and if the Speaker considers the matter of sufficient importance and the House agrees, it is discussed usually at 7 p.m. on the following day.

FATHER OF THE HOUSE – The Member whose continuous service in the House of Commons is the longest. The present Father of the House is the Rt. Hon. Sir Edward Heath, KG, MBE, MP, elected first in 1950.

GENERAL SYNOD MEASURE – A measure passed by the national assembly of the Church of England under the Church of England Assembly (Powers) Act 1919. These measures are considered by the Joint Ecclesiastical Committee, who make a report. They are then considered by both Houses and, if approved, sent for the royal assent.

HANSARD – The official report of debates in both Houses (and in Standing Committees) published by HMSO, normally on the day after the sitting concerned.

HOURS OF MEETING – The House of Commons meets Monday to Thursday at 2.30 p.m., and on Friday at 9.30 a.m. Changes to these hours are under consideration. The House of Lords normally meets at 2.30 p.m. Monday to Wednesday and at 3 p.m. on Thursday. In the latter part of the session, the House of Lords sometimes sits on Fridays at 11 a.m.

HYBRIDITY – Public Bill which is considered to affect specific private or local interests, as distinct from all such interests of a single category, is called a Hybrid Bill and is subject to a special form of scrutiny to enable people affected

to object. In the House of Lords, affirmative instruments (*see* Delegated Legislation above) may also be treated as hybrid.

LEADER OF THE OPPOSITION – In 1937 the office of Leader of the Opposition was recognized and a salary of £2,000 per annum was assigned to the post. Since January 1992 the salary has been £59,736 (including Parliamentary salary of £23,227). The present Leader of the Opposition is the Rt. Hon. John Smith, QC, MP.

THE LORD CHANCELLOR – The Lord High Chancellor of Great Britain is (*ex officio*) the Speaker of the House of Lords. Unlike the Speaker of the House of Commons, he is a member of the Government, takes part in debates and votes in divisions. He has none of the powers to maintain order that the Speaker in the Commons has, these powers being exercised in the Lords by the House as a whole. The Lord Chancellor sits in the Lords on one of the Woolsacks, couches covered with red cloth and stuffed with wool. If he wishes to address the House in any way except formally as Speaker, he leaves the Woolsack.

NAMING – When a member has been named by the Speaker for a breach of order, i.e. contrary to the practice of the House, called by surname and not addressed as the 'Hon. Member for . . . (her/his constituency)', the Leader of the House moves that the offender 'be suspended from the service of the House' for (in the case of a first offence) a period of five sitting days. Should the member offend again, the period of suspension is increased.

OPPOSITION DAY – A day on which the topic for debate is chosen by the Opposition. There are twenty such days in a normal session. On seventeen days, subjects are chosen by the Leader of the Opposition; on the remaining three days by the leader of the next largest opposition party.

PARLIAMENT ACTS 1911 AND 1949 – Under these Acts, Bills may become law without the consent of the Lords.
Since at least the eighteenth century the Commons have had the privilege of having Bills concerned with supply (i.e. taxation and money matters) passed without amendment by the Lords, though until 1911 the Lords retained the right to reject such Bills outright.
By the Parliament Act 1911, a Bill which has been endorsed by the Speaker of the House of Commons as a Money Bill, and has been passed by the Commons and sent up to the Lords at least one month before the end of a session, can become law without the consent of the Lords if it is not passed by them without amendment within a month.
Under the Parliament Acts 1911 and 1949, if the Lords reject any other Public Bill (except one to prolong the life of a Parliament) which has been passed by the Commons in two successive sessions, then that Bill shall (unless the Commons direct to the contrary) become law without the consent of the Lords. The Lords have power, therefore, to delay a Public Bill for thirteen months from its first Second Reading in the House of Commons.

PRIME MINISTER'S QUESTIONS – The Prime Minister answers questions from 3.15 to 3.30 p.m. on Tuesdays and Thursdays. Nowadays the 'open question' predominates. Members tend to ask the Prime Minister what are his or her official engagements for the day; a supplementary question on virtually any topic can then be put.

PRIVATE BILL – A Bill promoted by a body or an individual to give powers additional to, or in conflict with, the general law, and to which a special procedure applies to enable people affected to object.

PRIVATE MEMBERS' BILL – A Public Bill promoted by a Member who is not a member of the Government.

PRIVATE NOTICE QUESTION – A question adjudged of urgent importance on submission to the Speaker (in the Lords, the Leader of the House), answered at the end of oral questions, usually at 3.30 p.m.

PRIVILEGE – The following are covered by the privilege of Parliament:
(i) freedom from interference in going to, attending at, and going from, Parliament
(ii) freedom of speech in Parliamentary proceedings
(iii) the printing and publishing of anything relating to the proceedings of the two Houses is subject to privilege
(iv) each House is the guardian of its dignity and may punish any insult to the House as a whole

PROROGATION – The bringing to an end, by the Sovereign on the advice of the Government, of a session of Parliament. Public Bills which have not completed all their stages lapse on prorogation.

QUEEN'S SPEECH – The speech delivered by The Queen at the State Opening of Parliament, in which the Government's programme for the session is set forth. The speech is drafted by civil servants and approved by the Cabinet.

QUESTION TIME – Oral questions are answered by Ministers in the Commons from 2.30 to 3.30 p.m. every day except Friday. They are also taken at the start of the Lords sittings, with a daily limit of four oral questions.

ROYAL ASSENT – The royal assent is signified by letters patent to such Bills and Measures as have passed both Houses of Parliament (or Bills which have been passed under the Parliament Acts 1911 and 1949). The Sovereign has not given royal assent in person since 1854. On occasion, for instance in the prorogation of Parliament, royal assent may be pronounced to the two Houses by Lords Commissioners. More usually royal assent is notified to each House sitting separately in accordance with the Royal Assent Act 1967. The old French formulae for royal assent are then endorsed on the Acts by the Clerk of the Parliaments.

The power to withhold assent resides with the Sovereign but has not been exercised in the United Kingdom since 1707, in the reign of Queen Anne.

SELECT COMMITTEES – Consisting usually of 10–15 members of all parties, select committees are a means used by both Houses in order to investigate certain matters.

Most select committees in the House of Commons are now tied to departments; each committee investigates subjects within a government department's remit. There are other House of Commons select committees dealing with public accounts (i.e. the spending by the Government of money voted by Parliament) and European legislation, and also domestic committees dealing, for example, with privilege and procedure. Major select committees usually take evidence in public; their evidence and reports are published by HMSO.

The principal select committee in the House of Lords is that on the European Communities, which has, at present, six sub-committees dealing with all areas of Community policy. The House of Lords also has a select committee on science and technology, which appoints sub-committees to deal with specific subjects. In addition, *ad hoc* select committees have been set up from time to time to investigate specific subjects, e.g. overseas trade, murder and life imprisonment. There are also some joint committees of the two Houses, e.g. the Joint Committee on Statutory Instruments.

DEPARTMENTAL COMMITTEES
Agriculture – Chair, Sir Jerry Wiggin, MP; *Clerk*, Mr Walker
Defence – Chair, Sir Nicholas Bonsor, MP; *Clerks*, Mr Natzler; Mr Hennessy

Education – Chair, Sir Malcolm Thornton, MP; *Clerk*, Mr Harrison
Employment – Chair, Hon. Greville Janner, MP; *Clerk*, Mr Phillips
Environment – Chair, Robert Jones, MP; *Clerk*, Mr Priestley
Foreign Affairs – Chair, Rt. Hon. David Howell, MP; *Clerks*, Ms Irwin, Mr Hamlyn
Health – Chair, Marion Roe, MP; *Clerks*, Mr Evans, Mr Reid
Home Affairs – Chair, Sir Ivan Lawrence, MP; *Clerks*, Mr Silk; Mr Devine
National Heritage – Chair, Rt. Hon. Gerald Kaufman, MP; *Clerk*, Mrs Sharpe
Science and Technology – Chair, Sir Giles Shaw, MP; *Clerk*, Mrs Samson
Scottish Affairs – Chair, William McKelvey, MP; *Clerk*, Mr Doherty
Social Security – Chair, Frank Field, MP; *Clerk*, Mr Lloyd
Trade and Industry – Chair, Richard Caborn, MP; *Clerks*, Mr Gerhold, Ms Gardner
Transport – Chair, Rt. Hon. Paul Channon, MP; *Clerks*, Mr Doig, Mr Stanton
Treasury and Civil Service – Chair, John Watts, MP; *Clerks*, Mr Proctor, Mr Lee
Welsh Affairs – Chair, Gareth Wardell, MP; *Clerk*, Mr Hutton

NON-DEPARTMENTAL COMMITTEES
European Legislation – Chair, James Hood, MP; *Clerk*, Mr Rogers
Members' Interests – Chair, Sir Geoffrey Johnson Smith, MP; *Clerk*, Mr Sands
Parliamentary Commissioner – Chair, James Pawsey, MP; *Clerk*, Mr Azad
Procedure – Chair, Rt. Hon. Sir Peter Emery, MP; *Clerk*, Mr Kennon
Public Accounts – Chair, Rt. Hon. Robert Sheldon, MP; *Clerk*, Dr Benger

The Privileges committee had still to be reconstituted at the time of going to press.

THE SPEAKER – The Speaker of the House of Commons is the spokesman and president of the Chamber. He or she is elected by the House at the beginning of each Parliament or when the previous Speaker retires or dies. The Speaker neither speaks in debates nor votes in divisions except when the voting is equal.

STANDING ORDERS – Rules which have from time to time been agreed by each House of Parliament to regulate the conduct of its business. These orders may be amended or repealed, and are from time to time suspended or dispensed with.

STATE OPENING – This marks the start of each new session of Parliament. Parliament is normally opened, in the presence of both Houses, by The Queen in person, who makes the speech from the throne which outlines the Government's policies for the coming session (*see* Queen's Speech). In the absence of The Queen, Parliament is opened by Royal Commission, and The Queen's Speech is read by one of the Lords Commissioners specially appointed by letters patent for the occasion.

STRANGERS – Anyone who is not a Member or Officer of the House is a stranger. Visitors are generally admitted to debates of both Houses but may be excluded if the House so decides. In practice this happens only in time of war.

TEN MINUTE RULE – A colloquial term for Standing Order No. 19, under which back-benchers have an opportunity on Tuesdays and Wednesdays to state for about ten minutes why a Bill on a certain subject should be introduced. Time is also available for a short opposing speech.

VACANT SEATS – When a vacancy occurs in the House of Commons during a session of Parliament, the writ for the by-election is moved by a Whip of the party to which the member whose seat has been vacated belonged. If the House is in recess, the Speaker can issue a warrant for a writ, should two members certify to him that a seat is vacant.

WHIPS – In order to secure the attendance of Members of a particular party in Parliament on all occasions, and particularly on the occasion of an important vote, Whips (originally known as 'Whippers-in') are appointed. The written appeal or circular letter issued by them is also known as a 'whip', its urgency being denoted by the number of times it is underlined. Failure to respond to a three-line whip, headed 'Most important', is tantamount in the Commons to secession (at any rate temporarily) from the party. Whips are officially recognized by Parliament and are provided with office accommodation in both Houses. In both Houses, Government and some Opposition Whips receive salaries from public funds.

PUBLIC INFORMATION SERVICES

HOUSE OF COMMONS – Public Information Office, House of Commons, London SW1A 0AA. Tel: 071-219 4272

HOUSE OF LORDS – The Journal and Information Office, House of Lords, London SW1A 0PW. Tel: 071-219 3107

GOVERNMENT OFFICE

The Government is the body of Ministers responsible for the administration of national affairs, determining policy and introducing into Parliament any legislation necessary to give effect to government policy. The majority of Ministers are members of the House of Commons but members of the House of Lords or of neither House may also hold ministerial responsibility. The Lord Chancellor is always a member of the House of Lords. The Prime Minister is, by current convention, always a member of the House of Commons.

THE PRIME MINISTER

The office of Prime Minister, which had been in existence for nearly 200 years, was officially recognized in 1905 and its holder was granted a place in the table of precedence. The Prime Minister, by tradition also First Lord of the Treasury and Minister for the Civil Service, is appointed by the Sovereign and is usually the leader of the party which enjoys, or can secure, a majority in the House of Commons. Other Ministers are appointed by the Sovereign on the recommendation of the Prime Minister, who also allocates functions amongst Ministers and has the power to obtain their resignation or dismissal individually.

The Prime Minister informs the Sovereign of state and political matters, advises on the dissolution of Parliament, and makes recommendations for important Crown appointments, the award of honours, etc.

As the chairman of Cabinet meetings and leader of a political party, the Prime Minister is responsible for translating party policy into government activity. As leader of the Government, the Prime Minister is responsible to Parliament and to the electorate for the policies and their implementation.

The Prime Minister also represents the nation in international affairs, e.g. summit conferences.

THE CABINET

The Cabinet developed during the eighteenth century as an inner committee of the Privy Council, which was the chief source of executive power until that time. The Cabinet is composed of about twenty Ministers chosen by the Prime Minister, usually the heads of government departments (generally known as Secretaries of State unless they have a special title, e.g. Chancellor of the Exchequer), the leaders of the two Houses of Parliament, and the holders of various traditional offices.

The Cabinet's functions are the final determination of policy, control of government and co-ordination of government departments. The exercise of its functions is dependent upon enjoying majority support in the House of Commons. Cabinet meetings are held in private, taking place once or twice a week during parliamentary sittings and less often during a recess. Proceedings are confidential, the members being bound by their oath as Privy Counsellors not to disclose information about the proceedings.

The convention of collective responsibility means that the Cabinet acts unanimously even when Cabinet Ministers do not all agree on a subject. The policies of departmental Ministers must be consistent with the policies of the Government as a whole, and once the Government's policy has been decided, each Minister is expected to support it or resign.

The convention of ministerial responsibility holds a Minister, as the political head of his or her department, accountable to Parliament for the department's work. Departmental Ministers usually decide all matters within their responsibility, although on matters of political importance they normally consult their colleagues collectively. A decision by a departmental Minister is binding on the Government as a whole.

POLITICAL PARTIES

Before the reign of William and Mary the principal officers of state were chosen by and were responsible to the Sovereign alone and not to Parliament or the nation at large. Such officers acted sometimes in concert with one another but more often independently, and the fall of one did not, of necessity, involve that of others, although all were liable to be dismissed at any moment.

In 1693 the Earl of Sunderland recommended to William III the advisability of selecting a ministry from the political party which enjoyed a majority in the House of Commons and the first united ministry was drawn in 1696 from the Whigs, to which party the King owed his throne. This group became known as the Junto and was regarded with suspicion as a novelty in the political life of the nation, being a small section meeting in secret apart from the main body of Ministers. It may be regarded as the forerunner of the Cabinet and in course of time it led to the establishment of the principle of joint responsibility of Ministers, so that internal disagreement caused a change of personnel or resignation of the whole body of Ministers.

The accession of George I, who was unfamiliar with the English language, led to a disinclination on the part of the Sovereign to preside at meetings of his Ministers and caused the appearance of a Prime Minister, a position first acquired by Robert Walpole in 1721 and retained without interruption for 20 years and 326 days.

DEVELOPMENT OF PARTIES

In 1828 the old party of the Whigs became known as Liberals, a name originally given to it by its opponents to imply laxity of principles, but gradually accepted by the party to indicate its claim to be pioneers and champions of political reform and progressive legislation. In 1861 a Liberal Registration Association was founded and Liberal Associations became widespread. In 1877 a National Liberal Federation was formed, with headquarters in London. The Liberal Party was in power for long periods during the second half of the nineteenth century and for several years during the first quarter of the twentieth century, but after a split in the party the numbers elected were small from 1931. In March 1988, the Liberals and the Social Democratic Party merged under the title Social and Liberal Democrats. Since October 1989 they have been known as the Liberal Democrats.

Soon after the change from Whig to Liberal the Tory Party became known as Conservative, a name traditionally believed to have been invented by John Wilson Croker in 1830 and to have been generally adopted about the time of the passing of the Reform Act of 1832 to indicate that the preservation of national institutions was the leading principle of the party. After the Home Rule crisis of 1886 the dissentient Liberals entered into a compact with the Conservatives, under which the latter undertook not to contest their seats, but a separate Liberal Unionist organization was maintained until 1912, when it was united with the Conservatives.

Labour candidates for Parliament made their first appearance at the general election of 1892, when there were 27 standing as Labour or Liberal-Labour. In 1900 the Labour Representation Committee was set up in order to establish a distinct Labour group in Parliament, with its own whips, its own policy, and a readiness to co-operate with any party which might be engaged in promoting legislation in the direct interest of labour. In 1906 the LRC became known as The Labour Party.

The Council for Social Democracy was announced by four former Labour Cabinet Ministers on 25 January 1981. Subsequently a number of sitting Labour Members of Parliament, together with one Conservative, joined the new group, and on 26 March 1981 the Social Democratic Party was launched. Later that year the SDP and the Liberal Party formed an electoral alliance. In 1988 a majority of the SDP agreed on a merger with the Liberal Party (see above) but a minority continued as a separate party under the SDP title. In June 1990 it was decided to wind up the party organization and its three sitting MPs were known as independent social democrats. None were returned at the 1992 general election.

GOVERNMENT AND OPPOSITION

The government of the day is formed by the party which wins the largest number of seats in the House of Commons at a general election, or which has the support of a majority of members in the House of Commons. By tradition, the leader of the majority party is asked by the Sovereign to form a government, while the largest minority party becomes the official Opposition with its own leader and 'Shadow Cabinet'. Leaders of the Government and Opposition sit on the front benches of the Commons with their supporters (the backbenchers) sitting behind them.

When a party is in opposition and its leadership becomes vacant, it makes its free choice among the various personalities available; but if the party is in office, the Sovereign's choice may anticipate, and in a certain sense forestall, the decision of the party.

PARTIES

The parties included here are those with MPs sitting in the House of Commons in the present Parliament. Addresses of other political parties may be found in the Societies and Institutions section.

CONSERVATIVE AND UNIONIST PARTY
Central Office, 32 Smith Square, London SW1P 3HH
Tel 071-222 9000
Chairman, The Rt. Hon. Sir Norman Fowler, MP
Deputy Chairman, The Rt. Hon. Dame Angela Rumbold, DBE, MP; Gerald Malone, MP
Hon. Treasurers, C. Hambro; T. J. Smith, MP

SCOTTISH CONSERVATIVE AND UNIONIST CENTRAL OFFICE
Suite 1/1, 14 Links Place, Leith, Edinburgh EH6 7EX
Tel 031-555 2900
Chairman, Sir Michael Hirst
Vice-Chairmen, Miss A. Goldie; J. Carlow; R. Robertson, MP
Hon. Treasurers, P. Runciman, CBE; M. Tennant
Director of the Party in Scotland, R. Pratt

LABOUR PARTY
150 Walworth Road, London SE17 1JT
Tel 071-701 1234
Parliamentary Party Leader, The Rt. Hon. John Smith, QC, MP
Deputy Party Leader, The Rt. Hon. Margaret Beckett, MP
Leader in the Lords, The Lord Richard, PC, QC
Chair, A. Clarke
Vice-Chair, David Blunkett, MP
Treasurer, T. Burlison
General Secretary, L. Whitty

SHADOW CABINET *at July 1993*
Leader of the Opposition, The Rt. Hon. John Smith, QC, MP
Leader of the House, The Rt. Hon. Margaret Beckett, MP
Treasury and Economic Affairs, Gordon Brown, MP
Home Affairs, Tony Blair, MP
Trade and Industry, Robin Cook, MP
Employment, Frank Dobson, MP
Transport, John Prescott, MP
National Heritage, Ann Clwyd, MP
Chief Secretary to the Treasury, Harriet Harman, MP
Citizen's Charter and Women, Marjorie Mowlam, MP
Environmental Protection, Chris Smith, MP
Wales, Ron Davies, MP
Education, Ann Taylor, MP
Foreign and Commonwealth Affairs, The Rt. Hon. Jack Cunningham, MP
Development and Co-operation, Michael Meacher, MP
Social Security, Donald Dewar, MP
Health, David Blunkett, MP
Environment (Local Government), Jack Straw, MP
Scotland, Tom Clarke, MP
Defence, Disarmament and Arms Control, David Clark, MP
Food, Agriculture and Rural Affairs, Gavin Strang, MP
Northern Ireland, Kevin McNamara, MP
Chief Whip, The Rt. Hon. Derek Foster, MP
Chair of the Parliamentary Labour Party, Douglas Hoyle, MP

LABOUR WHIPS
House of Lords, The Lord Graham of Edmonton
House of Commons, The Rt. Hon. Derek Foster, MP

LIBERAL DEMOCRATS
4 Cowley Street, London SW1P 3NB
Tel 071-222 7999
President, Charles Kennedy, MP
Hon. Treasurer, T. Razzall

General Secretary, G. Elson
Parliamentary Party Leader, The Rt. Hon. Paddy Ashdown, MP
Leader in the Lords, The Rt. Hon. the Lord Jenkins of Hillhead

LIBERAL DEMOCRAT SPOKESMEN
Deputy Leader, Treasury and Civil Service, Alan Beith, MP
Trade and Industry, Malcolm Bruce, MP
Agriculture and Rural Affairs, Paul Tyler, MP
Environment and Natural Resources, Simon Hughes, MP
Transport, Nicholas Harvey, MP
Home Affairs and National Heritage, Robert Maclennan, MP
England, Local Government and Housing, Nigel Jones, MP
Citizen's Charter and Youth Issues, Matthew Taylor, MP
Women's Issues, Ray Michie, MP
Sport, Menzies Campbell, MP
Scotland, Jim Wallace, MP (also fisheries policy); Ray Michie, MP
Northern Ireland, Lord Holme of Cheltenham
Wales and Employment, Alex Carlile, MP
Social Security, Older People and Disabled People, Archy Kirkwood, MP
Health and Community Care, Liz Lynne, MP
Education and Training, Don Foster, MP
Foreign Affairs, Overseas Development, The Rt. Hon. Sir David Steel, MP
Defence and Disarmament, Menzies Campbell, MP
Europe and East-West Relations, Sir Russell Johnston, MP; Charles Kennedy, MP
Overseas Development, The Lord Bonham Carter

LIBERAL DEMOCRAT WHIPS
House of Lords, The Lord Tordoff
House of Commons, Archy Kirkwood, MP (*Chief Whip*); Simon Hughes, MP (*Deputy Whip*)

WELSH LIBERAL DEMOCRATS
57 St Mary Street, Cardiff CF1 1FE
Tel 0222-382210
Party President, Revd R. Roberts
Party Leader, Alex Carlile, QC, MP
Chairman, G. Williams
Treasurer, B. Lopez
Secretary, Ms K. Lloyd

SCOTTISH LIBERAL DEMOCRATS
4 Clifton Terrace, Edinburgh EH12 5DR
Tel 031-337 2314
Party President, Sir Russell Johnston, MP
Party Leader, Jim Wallace, MP
Chair, Ms S. Grieve
Vice-Chairs, M. Ford; D. Miller
Hon. Treasurer, N. Stephen
Secretary, Ms R. Grant

PLAID CYMRU
51 Cathedral Road, Cardiff CF1 9HD
Tel 0222-231944
Party President, Dafydd Wigley, MP
Chairman, J. Dixon
Hon. Treasurer, C. Bryant
Secretary, D. Williams

SCOTTISH NATIONAL PARTY
6 North Charlotte Street, Edinburgh EH2 4JH
Tel 031-226 3661
Parliamentary Party Leader, Margaret Ewing, MP
Chief Whip, Andrew Welsh, MP
National Convener, Alex Salmond, MP
Senior Vice-Convener, Dr A. Macartney

National Treasurer, T. Chalmers
National Secretary, J. Swinney

NORTHERN IRELAND

SOCIAL DEMOCRATIC AND LABOUR PARTY
Cranmore House, 611 Lisburn Road, Belfast BT9 7GT
Tel 0232-668100
Parliamentary Party Leader, John Hume, MP, MEP
Deputy Leader, Seamus Mallon, MP
Chief Whip, Eddie McGrady, MP
Chairman, M. Durkan
Vice-Chairs, J. Stephenson; Ms G. Leonard
Hon. Treasurer, Ms D. Field
Party Administrator, Mrs G. Cosgrove

ULSTER DEMOCRATIC UNIONIST PARTY
296 Albertbridge Road, Belfast BT5 4GX
Tel 0232-458597
Parliamentary Party Leader, I. Paisley, MP, MEP
Deputy Leader, Peter Robinson, MP
Chairman, W. J. McClure
Deputy Chairman, S. Gibson
Hon. Treasurer, D. F. Herron
General Secretary, N. Dodds

ULSTER UNIONIST COUNCIL
3 Glengall Street, Belfast BT12 5AE
Tel 0232-324601
President, J. Cunningham
Party Leader, The Rt. Hon. James Molyneaux, MP
Chief Whip, William Ross, MP
Chairman, J. Nicholson, MEP
Vice-Chairman, A. J. Wilson
Treasurer, J. Allen
Party Secretary, J. Wilson

MEMBERS OF PARLIAMENT AS AT 31 JULY 1993

For abbreviations, *see* page 243
* Denotes membership of the last Parliament

*Abbott, Ms Diane J. (*b.* 1953) *Lab., Hackney North and Stoke Newington,* maj. 10,727
*Adams, Mrs Irene (*b.* 1948) *Lab., Paisley North,* maj. 9,329
Ainger, Nicholas R. (*b.* 1949) *Lab., Pembroke,* maj. 755
Ainsworth, Peter M. (*b.* 1956) *C., Surrey East,* maj. 17,656
Ainsworth, Robert W. (*b.* 1952) *Lab., Coventry North East,* maj. 11,676
*Aitken, Jonathan W. P. (*b.* 1942) *C., Thanet South,* maj. 11,513
*Alexander, Richard T. (*b.* 1934) *C., Newark,* maj. 8,229
*Alison, Rt. Hon. Michael J. H. (*b.* 1926) *C., Selby,* maj. 9,508
*Allason, Rupert W. S. (*b.* 1951) *C., Torbay,* maj. 5,787
*Allen, Graham W. (*b.* 1953) *Lab., Nottingham North,* maj. 10,743
*Alton, David P. (*b.* 1951) *LD, Liverpool, Mossley Hill,* maj. 2,606
*Amess, David A. A. (*b.* 1952) *C., Basildon,* maj. 1,480
Ancram, Michael A. F. J. K. (Earl of Ancram) (*b.* 1945) *C., Devizes,* maj. 19,712
*Anderson, Donald (*b.* 1939) *Lab., Swansea East,* maj. 23,482
Anderson, Mrs Janet (*b.* 1949) *Lab., Rossendale and Darwen,* maj. 120
*Arbuthnot, James N. (*b.* 1952) *C., Wanstead and Woodford,* maj. 16,885
*Armstrong, Miss Hilary J. (*b.* 1945) *Lab., Durham North West,* maj. 13,987
*Arnold, Jacques A. (*b.* 1947) *C., Gravesham,* maj. 5,493
*Arnold, Sir Thomas (*b.* 1947) *C., Hazel Grove,* maj. 929
*Ashby, David G. (*b.* 1940) *C., Leicestershire North West,* maj. 979
*Ashdown, Rt. Hon. J. J. D. (Paddy) (*b.* 1941) *LD, Yeovil,* maj. 8,833
*Ashton, Joseph W. (*b.* 1933) *Lab., Bassetlaw,* maj. 9,997
*Aspinwall, Jack H. (*b.* 1933) *C., Wansdyke,* maj. 13,341
*Atkins, Robert J. (*b.* 1946) *C., South Ribble,* maj. 5,973
*Atkinson, David A. (*b.* 1940) *C., Bournemouth East,* maj. 14,823
Atkinson, Peter (*b.* 1943) *C., Hexham,* maj. 13,438
Austin-Walker, John E. (*b.* 1944) *Lab., Woolwich,* maj. 2,225
*Baker, Rt. Hon. Kenneth W., CH (*b.* 1934) *C., Mole Valley,* maj. 15,950
*Baker, Nicholas B. (*b.* 1938) *C., Dorset North,* maj. 10,080
*Baldry, Antony B. (*b.* 1950) *C., Banbury,* maj. 16,720
Banks, Matthew (*b.* 1961) *C., Southport,* maj. 3,063
*Banks, Robert G., MBE (*b.* 1937) *C., Harrogate,* maj. 12,589
*Banks, Tony L. (*b.* 1943) *Lab., Newham North West,* maj. 9,171
*Barnes, Harold (*b.* 1936) *Lab., Derbyshire North East,* maj. 6,270
*Barron, Kevin J. (*b.* 1946) *Lab., Rother Valley,* maj. 17,222
Bates, Michael W. (*b.* 1961) *C., Langbaurgh,* maj. 1,564
*Batiste, Spencer L. (*b.* 1945) *C., Elmet,* maj. 3,261
*Battle, John D. (*b.* 1951) *Lab., Leeds West,* maj. 13,828
Bayley, Hugh (*b.* 1952) *Lab., York,* maj. 6,342
*Beckett, Rt. Hon. Margaret M. (*b.* 1953) *Lab., Derby South,* maj. 6,936
*Beggs, Roy (*b.* 1936) *UUP, Antrim East,* maj. 7,422
*Beith, Rt. Hon. Alan J. (*b.* 1943) *LD, Berwick-upon-Tweed,* maj. 5,043
*Bell, Stuart (*b.* 1938) *Lab., Middlesbrough,* maj. 15,784

*Bellingham, Henry C. (*b.* 1955) *C., Norfolk North West,* maj. 11,564
*Bendall, Vivian W. H. (*b.* 1938) *C., Ilford North,* maj. 9,071
*Benn, Rt. Hon. Anthony N. W. (*b.* 1925) *Lab., Chesterfield,* maj. 6,414
*Bennett, Andrew F. (*b.* 1939) *Lab., Denton and Reddish,* maj. 12,084
*Benton, Joseph E. (*b.* 1933) *Lab., Bootle,* maj. 29,442
Beresford, Sir Paul (*b.* 1946) *C., Croydon Central,* maj. 9,650
*Bermingham, Gerald E. (*b.* 1940) *Lab., St Helens South,* maj. 18,209
Berry, Roger L., D.Phil (*b.* 1948) *Lab., Kingswood,* maj. 2,370
Betts, Clive J. C. (*b.* 1950) *Lab., Sheffield, Attercliffe,* maj. 15,480
*Biffen, Rt. Hon. John W. (*b.* 1930) *C., Shropshire North,* maj. 16,211
*Blackburn, John G., PH.D. (*b.* 1933) *C., Dudley West,* maj. 5,789
*Blair, Anthony C. L. (*b.* 1953) *Lab., Sedgefield,* maj. 14,859
*Blunkett, David (*b.* 1947) *Lab., Sheffield, Brightside,* maj. 22,681
*Boateng, Paul Y. (*b.* 1951) *Lab., Brent South,* maj. 9,705
*Body, Sir Richard (*b.* 1927) *C., Holland with Boston,* maj. 13,831
*Bonsor, Sir Nicholas, Bt. (*b.* 1942) *C., Upminster,* maj. 13,821
Booth, Hartley, PH.D. (*b.* 1946) *C., Finchley,* maj. 6,388
*Boothroyd, Rt. Hon. Betty (*b.* 1929) *The Speaker, West Bromwich West,* maj. 7,830
*Boswell, Timothy E. (*b.* 1942) *C., Daventry,* maj. 20,274
*Bottomley, Peter J. (*b.* 1944) *C., Eltham,* maj. 1,666
*Bottomley, Rt. Hon. Virginia H. B. M. (*b.* 1948) *C., Surrey South West,* maj. 14,975
*Bowden, Andrew, MBE (*b.* 1930) *C., Brighton, Kemptown,* maj. 3,056
*Bowis, John C., OBE (*b.* 1945) *C., Battersea,* maj. 4,840
Boyce, James (*b.* 1947) *Lab., Rotherham,* maj. 17,561
*Boyes, Roland (*b.* 1937) *Lab., Houghton and Washington,* maj. 20,808
*Boyson, Rt. Hon. Sir Rhodes (*b.* 1925) *C., Brent North,* maj. 10,131
*Bradley, Keith J. C. (*b.* 1950) *Lab., Manchester, Withington,* maj. 9,735
Brandreth, Gyles D. (*b.* 1948) *C., City of Chester,* maj. 1,101
*Bray, Jeremy W., PH.D. (*b.* 1930) *Lab., Motherwell South,* maj. 14,013
*Brazier, Julian W. H. (*b.* 1953) *C., Canterbury,* maj. 10,805
*Bright, Graham F. J. (*b.* 1942) *C., Luton South,* maj. 799
*Brooke, Rt. Hon. Peter L., CH (*b.* 1934) *C., City of London and Westminster South,* maj. 13,369
*Brown, J. Gordon, PH.D. (*b.* 1951) *Lab., Dunfermline East,* maj. 17,444
*Brown, Michael R. (*b.* 1951) *C., Brigg and Cleethorpes,* maj. 9,269
*Brown, Nicholas H. (*b.* 1950) *Lab., Newcastle upon Tyne East,* maj. 13,877
Browning, Mrs Angela F. (*b.* 1946) *C., Tiverton,* maj. 11,089
*Bruce, Ian C. (*b.* 1947) *C., Dorset South,* maj. 13,508
*Bruce, Malcolm G. (*b.* 1944) *LD, Gordon,* maj. 274
*Budgen, Nicholas W. (*b.* 1937) *C., Wolverhampton South West,* maj. 4,966

Burden, Richard (*b.* 1954) *Lab., Birmingham, Northfield*, maj. 630

*Burns, Simon H. M. (*b.* 1952) *C., Chelmsford*, maj. 18,260

*Burt, Alistair J. H. (*b.* 1955) *C., Bury North*, maj. 4,764

*Butcher, John P. (*b.* 1946) *C., Coventry South West*, maj. 1,436

Butler, Peter (*b.* 1951) *C., Milton Keynes North East*, maj. 14,176

*Butterfill, John V. (*b.* 1941) *C., Bournemouth West*, maj. 12,703

Byers, Stephen J. (*b.* 1953) *Lab., Wallsend*, maj. 19,470

*Caborn, Richard G. (*b.* 1943) *Lab., Sheffield Central*, maj. 17,294

*Callaghan, James (*b.* 1927) *Lab., Heywood and Middleton*, maj. 8,074

Campbell, Mrs Anne (*b.* 1940) *Lab., Cambridge*, maj. 580

*Campbell, Ronald (*b.* 1943) *Lab., Blyth Valley*, maj. 8,044

*Campbell, W. Menzies, CBE, QC (*b.* 1941) *LD, Fife North East*, maj. 3,308

*Campbell-Savours, Dale N. (*b.* 1943) *Lab., Workington*, maj. 10,449

*Canavan, Dennis A. (*b.* 1942) *Lab., Falkirk West*, maj. 9,812

Cann, James (*b.* 1946) *Lab., Ipswich*, maj. 265

*Carlile, Alexander C., QC (*b.* 1948) *LD, Montgomery*, maj. 5,209

*Carlisle, John R. (*b.* 1942) *C., Luton North*, maj. 13,094

*Carlisle, Kenneth M. (*b.* 1941) *C., Lincoln*, maj. 2,049

*Carrington, Matthew H. M. (*b.* 1947) *C., Fulham*, maj. 6,579

*Carttiss, Michael R. H. (*b.* 1938) *C., Great Yarmouth*, maj. 5,309

*Cash, William N. P. (*b.* 1940) *C., Stafford*, maj. 10,900

*Channon, Rt. Hon. H. Paul G. (*b.* 1935) *C., Southend West*, maj. 11,902

*Chapman, Sydney B. (*b.* 1935) *C., Chipping Barnet*, maj. 13,951

Chisholm, Malcolm (*b.* 1949) *Lab., Edinburgh, Leith*, maj. 4,985

*Churchill, Winston S. (*b.* 1940) *C., Davyhulme*, maj. 4,426

Clapham, Michael (*b.* 1943) *Lab., Barnsley West and Penistone*, maj. 14,504

Clappison, W. James (*b.* 1956) *C., Hertsmere*, maj. 18,735

*Clark, David G., PH.D. (*b.* 1939) *Lab., South Shields*, maj. 13,477

*Clark, Dr Michael (*b.* 1935) *C., Rochford*, maj. 26,036

Clarke, Eric L. (*b.* 1933) *Lab., Midlothian*, maj. 10,334

*Clarke, Rt. Hon. Kenneth H., QC (*b.* 1940) *C., Rushcliffe*, maj. 19,766

*Clarke, Thomas, CBE (*b.* 1941) *Lab., Monklands West*, maj. 17,065

*Clelland, David G. (*b.* 1943) *Lab., Tyne Bridge*, maj. 15,210

Clifton-Brown, Geoffrey R. (*b.* 1953) *C., Cirencester and Tewkesbury*, maj. 16,058

*Clwyd, Ms Ann (*b.* 1937) *Lab., Cynon Valley*, maj. 21,364

Coe, Sebastian N., OBE (*b.* 1956) *C., Falmouth and Camborne*, maj. 3,267

Coffey, Ms M. Ann (*b.* 1946) *Lab., Stockport*, maj. 1,422

*Cohen, Harry (*b.* 1949) *Lab., Leyton*, maj. 11,484

*Colvin, Michael K. B. (*b.* 1932) *C., Romsey and Waterside*, maj. 15,304

Congdon, David L. (*b.* 1949) *C., Croydon North East*, maj. 7,473

Connarty, Michael (*b.* 1949) *Lab., Falkirk East*, maj. 7,969

*Conway, Derek L. (*b.* 1953) *C., Shrewsbury and Atcham*, maj. 10,965

*Cook, Francis (*b.* 1935) *Lab., Stockton North*, maj. 10,474

*Cook, R. F. (Robin) (*b.* 1946) *Lab., Livingston*, maj. 8,105

*Coombs, Anthony M. V. (*b.* 1952) *C., Wyre Forest*, maj. 10,341

*Coombs, Simon C. (*b.* 1947) *C., Swindon*, maj. 2,826

*Cope, Rt. Hon. Sir John (*b.* 1937) *C., Northavon*, maj. 11,861

*Corbett, Robin (*b.* 1933) *Lab., Birmingham, Erdington*, maj. 4,735

*Corbyn, Jeremy B. (*b.* 1949) *Lab., Islington North*, maj. 12,784

*Cormack, Patrick T. (*b.* 1939) *C., Staffordshire South*, maj. 22,633

Corston, Ms Jean (*b.* 1942) *Lab., Bristol East*, maj. 2,692

*Couchman, James R. (*b.* 1942) *C., Gillingham*, maj. 16,638

*Cousins, James M. (*b.* 1944) *Lab., Newcastle upon Tyne Central*, maj. 5,288

*Cox, Thomas M. (*b.* 1930) *Lab., Tooting*, maj. 4,107

*Cran, James D. (*b.* 1944) *C., Beverley*, maj. 16,517

*Critchley, Julian M. G. (*b.* 1930) *C., Aldershot*, maj. 19,188

*Cryer, G. Robert (*b.* 1934) *Lab., Bradford South*, maj. 4,902

*Cummings, John S. (*b.* 1943) *Lab., Easington*, maj. 26,390

*Cunliffe, Lawrence F. (*b.* 1929) *Lab., Leigh*, maj. 18,827

Cunningham, James (*b.* 1941) *Lab., Coventry South East*, maj. 1,311

*Cunningham, Rt. Hon. Dr John A. (Jack) (*b.* 1939) *Lab., Copeland*, maj. 2,439

*Currie, Mrs Edwina (*b.* 1946) *C., Derbyshire South*, maj. 4,658

*Curry, David M. (*b.* 1944) *C., Skipton and Ripon*, maj. 19,330

Dafis, Cynog G. (*b.* 1938) *PC, Ceredigion and Pembroke North*, maj. 3,193

*Dalyell, Tam (Sir Thomas Dalyell of the Binns, Bt.) (*b.* 1932) *Lab., Linlithgow*, maj. 7,026

*Darling, Alistair M. (*b.* 1953) *Lab., Edinburgh Central*, maj. 2,126

Davidson, Ian (*b.* 1950) *Lab., Glasgow, Govan*, maj. 4,125

Davies, Bryan (*b.* 1939) *Lab., Oldham Central and Royton*, maj. 8,606

*Davies, Rt. Hon. D. J. Denzil (*b.* 1938) *Lab., Llanelli*, maj. 19,270

*Davies, J. Quentin (*b.* 1944) *C., Stamford and Spalding*, maj. 22,869

*Davies, Ronald (*b.* 1946) *Lab., Caerphilly*, maj. 22,672

*Davis, David M. (*b.* 1948) *C., Boothferry*, maj. 17,535

*Davis, Terence A. G. (*b.* 1938) *Lab., Birmingham, Hodge Hill*, maj. 7,068

*Day, Stephen R. (*b.* 1948) *C., Cheadle*, maj. 15,778

Denham, John V. (*b.* 1953) *Lab., Southampton, Itchen*, maj. 551

Deva, Niranjan J. A. (*b.* 1948) *C., Brentford and Isleworth*, maj. 2,086

*Devlin, Timothy R. (*b.* 1959) *C., Stockton South*, maj. 3,369

*Dewar, Donald C. (*b.* 1937) *Lab., Glasgow, Garscadden*, maj. 13,340

*Dickens, Geoffrey K. (*b.* 1931) *C., Littleborough and Saddleworth*, maj. 4,494

*Dicks, Terence P. (*b.* 1937) *C., Hayes and Harlington*, maj. 53

*Dixon, Donald (*b.* 1929) *Lab., Jarrow*, maj. 17,907

*Dobson, Frank G. (*b.* 1940) *Lab., Holborn and St Pancras*, maj. 10,824

Donohoe, Brian H. (*b.* 1948) *Lab., Cunninghame South*, maj. 10,680

*Dorrell, Stephen J. (*b.* 1952) *C., Loughborough*, maj. 10,883

*Douglas-Hamilton, Lord James (*b.* 1942) *C., Edinburgh West*, maj. 879

*Dover, Densmore (*b.* 1938) *C., Chorley*, maj. 4,246

Dowd, James P. (*b.* 1951) *Lab., Lewisham West*, maj. 1,809

Duncan, Alan J. C. (*b.* 1957) *C., Rutland and Melton*, maj. 25,535

Duncan-Smith, G. Iain (*b.* 1954) *C., Chingford*, maj. 14,938

*Dunn, Robert J. (*b.* 1946) *C., Dartford*, maj. 10,314

*Dunnachie, James F. (b. 1930) Lab., Glasgow, Pollok, maj. 7,883

*Dunwoody, Hon. Mrs Gwyneth P. (b. 1930) Lab., Crewe and Nantwich, maj. 2,695

*Durant, Sir Anthony (b. 1928) C., Reading West, maj. 13,298

*Dykes, Hugh J. (b. 1939) C., Harrow East, maj. 11,098

Eagle, Ms Angela (b. 1961) Lab., Wallasey, maj. 3,809

*Eastham, Kenneth (b. 1927) Lab., Manchester, Blackley, maj. 12,389

*Eggar, Timothy J. C. (b. 1951) C., Enfield North, maj. 9,430

Elletson, Harold D. H. (b. 1960) C., Blackpool North, maj. 3,040

*Emery, Rt. Hon. Sir Peter (b. 1926) C., Honiton, maj. 16,511

*Enright, Derek A. (b. 1935) Lab., Hemsworth, maj. 22,075

Etherington, William (b. 1941) Lab., Sunderland North, maj. 17,004

*Evans, David J. (b. 1935) C., Welwyn Hatfield, maj. 8,465

*Evans, John (b. 1930) Lab., St Helens North, maj. 16,244

Evans, Jonathan P. (b. 1950) C., Brecon and Radnor, maj. 130

Evans, Nigel M. (b. 1957) C., Ribble Valley, maj. 6,542

Evans, Roger (b. 1947) C., Monmouth, maj. 3,204

*Evennett, David A. (b. 1939) C., Erith and Crayford, maj. 2,339

*Ewing, Mrs Margaret A. (b. 1945) SNP, Moray, maj. 2,844

Faber, David J. C. (b. 1961) C., Westbury, maj. 12,606

Fabricant, Michael L. D. (b. 1950) C., Staffordshire Mid, maj. 6,236

*Fairbairn, Sir Nicholas, QC (b. 1933) C., Perth and Kinross, maj. 2,094

*Fatchett, Derek J. (b. 1945) Lab., Leeds Central, maj. 15,020

*Faulds, Andrew M. W. (b. 1923) Lab., Warley East, maj. 7,794

*Fenner, Dame Peggy, DBE (b. 1922) C., Medway, maj. 8,786

*Field, Barry J. A., TD (b. 1946) C., Isle of Wight, maj. 1,827

*Field, Frank (b. 1942) Lab., Birkenhead, maj. 17,613

*Fishburn, J. Dudley (b. 1946) C., Kensington, maj. 3,548

*Fisher, Mark (b. 1944) Lab., Stoke-on-Trent Central, maj. 13,420

*Flynn, Paul P. (b. 1935) Lab., Newport West, maj. 7,779

*Fookes, Dame Janet, DBE (b. 1936) C., Plymouth, Drake, maj. 2,013

*Forman, F. Nigel (b. 1943) C., Carshalton and Wallington, maj. 9,943

*Forsyth, Michael B. (b. 1954) C., Stirling, maj. 703

*Forsythe, Clifford (b. 1929) UUP, Antrim South, maj. 24,559

*Forth, Eric (b. 1944) C., Worcestershire Mid, maj. 9,870

*Foster, Rt. Hon. Derek (b. 1937) Lab., Bishop Auckland, maj. 10,087

Foster, Donald M. E. (b. 1937) LD, Bath, maj. 3,768

*Foulkes, George (b. 1942) Lab., Carrick, Cumnock and Doon Valley, maj. 16,626

*Fowler, Rt. Hon. Sir Norman (b. 1938) C., Sutton Coldfield, maj. 26,036

Fox, Dr Liam (b. 1961) C., Woodspring, maj. 17,509

*Fox, Sir Marcus, MBE (b. 1927) C., Shipley, maj. 12,382

*Fraser, John D. (b. 1934) Lab., Norwood, maj. 7,216

*Freeman, Rt. Hon. Roger N. (b. 1942) C., Kettering, maj. 11,154

*French, Douglas C. (b. 1944) C., Gloucester, maj. 6,058

*Fry, Peter D. (b. 1931) C., Wellingborough, maj. 11,816

*Fyfe, Mrs Maria (b. 1938) Lab., Glasgow, Maryhill, maj. 13,419

*Galbraith, Samuel L. (b. 1945) Lab., Strathkelvin and Bearsden, maj. 3,162

*Gale, Roger J. (b. 1943) C., Thanet North, maj. 18,210

Gallie, Philip (b. 1939) C., Ayr, maj. 85

*Galloway, George (b. 1954) Lab., Glasgow, Hillhead, maj. 4,826

Gapes, Michael J. (b. 1952) Lab., Ilford South, maj. 402

*Gardiner, Sir George (b. 1935) C., Reigate, maj. 17,664

*Garel-Jones, Rt. Hon. (W. A. T.) Tristan (b. 1941) C., Watford, maj. 9,590

Garnier, Edward (b. 1952) C., Harborough, maj. 13,543

*Garrett, John L. (b. 1931) Lab., Norwich South, maj. 6,181

*George, Bruce T. (b. 1942) Lab., Walsall South, maj. 3,178

Gerrard, Neil F. (b. 1942) Lab., Walthamstow, maj. 3,022

*Gilbert, Rt. Hon. Dr John W. (b. 1927) Lab., Dudley East, maj. 9,200

*Gill, Christopher J. F., RD (b. 1936) C., Ludlow, maj. 14,152

Gillan, Ms Cheryl E. K. (b. 1952) C., Chesham and Amersham, maj. 22,220

*Godman, Norman A., PH.D. (b. 1938) Lab., Greenock and Port Glasgow, maj. 14,979

Godsiff, Roger D. (b. 1946) Lab., Birmingham, Small Heath, maj. 13,989

*Golding, Mrs Llinos (b. 1933) Lab., Newcastle under Lyme, maj. 9,839

*Goodlad, Rt. Hon. Alistair R. (b. 1943) C., Eddisbury, maj. 12,697

*Goodson-Wickes, Dr Charles (b. 1945) C., Wimbledon, maj. 14,761

*Gordon, Mrs Mildred (b. 1923) Lab., Bow and Poplar, maj. 8,404

*Gorman, Mrs Teresa E. (b. 1931) C., Billericay, maj. 22,494

*Gorst, John M. (b. 1928) C., Hendon North, maj. 7,122

*Gould, Bryan C. (b. 1939) Lab., Dagenham, maj. 6,733

*Graham, Thomas (b. 1944) Lab., Renfrew West and Inverclyde, maj. 1,744

*Grant, Sir Anthony (b. 1925) C., Cambridgeshire South West, maj. 19,637

*Grant, Bernard A. M. (b. 1944) Lab., Tottenham, maj. 11,968

*Greenway, Harry (b. 1934) C., Ealing North, maj. 5,966

*Greenway, John R. (b. 1946) C., Ryedale, maj. 18,439

*Griffiths, Nigel (b. 1955) Lab., Edinburgh South, maj. 4,176

*Griffiths, Peter H. S. (b. 1928) C., Portsmouth North, maj. 13,881

*Griffiths, Winston J. (b. 1943) Lab., Bridgend, maj. 7,326

*Grocott, Bruce J. (b. 1940) Lab., The Wrekin, maj. 6,648

*Grylls, Sir Michael (b. 1934) C., Surrey North West, maj. 28,394

*Gummer, Rt. Hon. John S. (b. 1939) C., Suffolk Coastal, maj. 19,285

Gunnell, W. John (b. 1933) Lab., Leeds South and Morley, maj. 7,372

*Hague, William J. (b. 1961) C., Richmond (Yorks) maj. 23,504

*Hain, Peter G. (b. 1950) Lab., Neath, maj. 23,975

Hall, Michael T. (b. 1952) Lab., Warrington South, maj. 191

*Hamilton, Rt. Hon. Archibald G. (b. 1941) C., Epsom and Ewell, maj. 20,021

*Hamilton, M. Neil (b. 1949) C., Tatton, maj. 15,860

*Hampson, Dr Keith (b. 1943) C., Leeds North West, maj. 7,671

*Hanley, Jeremy J. (b. 1945) C., Richmond and Barnes, maj. 3,869

*Hannam, Sir John (b. 1929) C., Exeter, maj. 4,045

Hanson, David G. (b. 1957) Lab., Delyn, maj. 2,039

*Hardy, Peter (b. 1931) Lab., Wentworth, maj. 22,449

*Hargreaves, Andrew R. (b. 1955) C., Birmingham, Hall Green, maj. 3,665

*Harman, Ms Harriet (b. 1950) Lab., Peckham, maj. 12,005

*Harris, David A. (b. 1937) C., St Ives, maj. 1,645

Harvey, Nicholas B. (b. 1961) LD, Devon North, maj. 794

*Haselhurst, Alan G. B. (b. 1937) C., Saffron Walden, maj. 17,424

*Hattersley, Rt. Hon. Roy S. G. (*b.* 1932) *Lab., Birmingham, Sparkbrook,* maj. 13,572

Hawkins, Nicholas J. (*b.* 1957) *C., Blackpool South,* maj. 1,667

Hawksley, P. Warren (*b.* 1943) *C., Halesowen and Stourbridge,* maj. 9,582

*Hayes, Jeremy J. J. (*b.* 1953) *C., Harlow,* maj. 2,940

Heald, Oliver (*b.* 1954) *C., Hertfordshire North,* maj. 16,531

*Heath, Rt. Hon. Sir Edward, KG, MBE (*b.* 1916) *C., Old Bexley and Sidcup,* maj. 15,699

*Heathcoat-Amory, David P. (*b.* 1949) *C., Wells,* maj. 6,649

*Henderson, Douglas J. (*b.* 1949) *Lab., Newcastle upon Tyne North,* maj. 8,946

Hendron, Dr Joseph G. (*b.* 1932) *SDLP, Belfast West,* maj. 589

Hendry, Charles (*b.* 1959) *C., High Peak,* maj. 4,819

Heppell, John B. (*b.* 1948) *Lab., Nottingham East,* maj. 7,680

*Heseltine, Rt. Hon. Michael R. D. (*b.* 1933) *C., Henley,* maj. 18,392

*Hicks, Robert (*b.* 1938) *C., Cornwall South East,* maj. 7,704

*Higgins, Rt. Hon. Sir Terence, KBE (*b.* 1928) *C., Worthing,* maj. 16,533

*Hill, S. James A. (*b.* 1926) *C., Southampton, Test,* maj. 585

Hill, T. Keith (*b.* 1943) *Lab., Streatham,* maj. 2,317

*Hinchliffe, David M. (*b.* 1948) *Lab., Wakefield,* maj. 6,590

*Hoey, Ms Catharine (Kate) L. (*b.* 1946) *Lab., Vauxhall,* maj. 10,488

*Hogg, Rt. Hon. Douglas M., QC (*b.* 1945) *C., Grantham,* maj. 19,588

*Hogg, Norman (*b.* 1938) *Lab., Cumbernauld and Kilsyth,* maj. 9,215

*Home Robertson, John D. (*b.* 1948) *Lab., East Lothian,* maj. 10,036

*Hood, James (*b.* 1948) *Lab., Clydesdale,* maj. 10,187

Hoon, Geoffrey W. (*b.* 1953) *Lab., Ashfield,* maj. 12,987

Horam, John R. (*b.* 1939) *C., Orpington,* maj. 12,935

*Hordern, Rt. Hon. Sir Peter (*b.* 1929) *C., Horsham,* maj. 25,072

*Howard, Rt. Hon. Michael, QC (*b.* 1941) *C., Folkestone and Hythe,* maj. 8,910

*Howarth, Alan T., CBE (*b.* 1944) *C., Stratford-upon-Avon,* maj. 22,892

*Howarth, George E. (*b.* 1949) *Lab., Knowsley North,* maj. 22,403

*Howell, Rt. Hon. David A. R. (*b.* 1936) *C., Guildford,* maj. 13,404

*Howell, Sir Ralph (*b.* 1923) *C., Norfolk North,* maj. 12,545

*Howells, Kim S., PH.D. (*b.* 1946) *Lab., Pontypridd,* maj. 19,797

*Hoyle, E. Douglas H. (*b.* 1930) *Lab., Warrington North,* maj. 12,622

Hughes, Kevin M. (*b.* 1952) *Lab., Doncaster North,* maj. 19,813

*Hughes, Robert (*b.* 1932) *Lab., Aberdeen North,* maj. 9,237

*Hughes, Robert G. (*b.* 1951) *C., Harrow West,* maj. 17,897

*Hughes, Royston J. (*b.* 1925) *Lab., Newport East,* maj. 9,899

*Hughes, Simon H. W. (*b.* 1951) *LD, Southwark and Bermondsey,* maj. 9,845

*Hume, John (*b.* 1937) *SDLP, Foyle,* maj. 13,005

*Hunt, Rt. Hon. David J. F., MBE (*b.* 1942) *C., Wirral West,* maj. 11,064

*Hunt, Sir John (*b.* 1929) *C., Ravensbourne,* maj. 19,714

*Hunter, Andrew R. F. (*b.* 1943) *C., Basingstoke,* maj. 21,198

*Hurd, Rt. Hon. Douglas R., CBE (*b.* 1930) *C., Witney,* maj. 22,568

Hutton, John M. P. (*b.* 1955) *Lab., Barrow and Furness,* maj. 3,578

*Illsley, Eric E. (*b.* 1955) *Lab., Barnsley Central,* maj. 19,361

*Ingram, Adam P. (*b.* 1947) *Lab., East Kilbride,* maj. 11,992

*Jack, J. Michael (*b.* 1946) *C., Fylde,* maj. 20,991

Jackson, Ms Glenda, CBE (*b.* 1936) *Lab., Hampstead and Highgate,* maj. 1,440

Jackson, Mrs Helen (*b.* 1939) *Lab., Sheffield, Hillsborough,* maj. 7,068

*Jackson, Robert V. (*b.* 1946) *C., Wantage,* maj. 16,473

Jamieson, David C. (*b.* 1947) *Lab., Plymouth, Devonport,* maj. 7,412

*Janner, Hon. Greville E., QC (*b.* 1928) *Lab., Leicester West,* maj. 3,978

Jenkin, Hon. Bernard (*b.* 1959) *C., Colchester North,* maj. 16,492

*Jessel, Toby F. H. (*b.* 1934) *C., Twickenham,* maj. 5,711

*Johnson Smith, Sir Geoffrey (*b.* 1924) *C., Wealden,* maj. 20,931

*Johnston, Sir Russell (*b.* 1932) *LD, Inverness, Nairn and Lochaber,* maj. 458

*Jones, Gwilym H. (*b.* 1947) *C., Cardiff North,* maj. 2,969

*Jones, Ieuan W. (*b.* 1949) *PC, Ynys Môn,* maj. 1,106

Jones, Jon O. (*b.* 1954) *Lab., Cardiff Central,* maj. 3,465

Jones, Ms Lynne M., PH.D. (*b.* 1951) *Lab., Birmingham, Selly Oak,* maj. 2,060

*Jones, Martyn D. (*b.* 1947) *Lab., Clwyd South West,* maj. 4,941

Jones, Nigel D. (*b.* 1948) *LD, Cheltenham,* maj. 1,668

*Jones, Robert B. (*b.* 1950) *C., Hertfordshire West,* maj. 13,940

*Jones, S. Barry (*b.* 1938) *Lab., Alyn and Deeside,* maj. 7,851

*Jopling, Rt. Hon. T. Michael (*b.* 1930) *C., Westmorland and Lonsdale,* maj. 16,436

Jowell, Ms Tessa (*b.* 1947) *Lab., Dulwich,* maj. 2,056

*Kaufman, Rt. Hon. Gerald B. (*b.* 1930) *Lab., Manchester, Gorton,* maj. 16,279

Keen, Alan (*b.* 1937) *Lab., Feltham and Heston,* maj. 1,995

*Kellett-Bowman, Dame Elaine, DBE (*b.* 1924) *C., Lancaster,* maj. 2,953

*Kennedy, Charles P. (*b.* 1959) *LD, Ross, Cromarty and Skye,* maj. 7,630

Kennedy, Mrs Jane (*b.* 1958) *Lab., Liverpool, Broadgreen,* maj. 7,027

*Key, S. Robert (*b.* 1945) *C., Salisbury,* maj. 8,973

Khabra, Piara C. (*b.* 1924) *Lab., Ealing, Southall,* maj. 6,866

*Kilfedder, Sir James (*b.* 1928) *UPUP, Down North,* maj. 4,934

*Kilfoyle, Peter (*b.* 1946) *Lab., Liverpool, Walton,* maj. 28,299

*King, Rt. Hon. Thomas J., CH (*b.* 1933) *C., Bridgwater,* maj. 9,716

*Kinnock, Rt. Hon. Neil G. (*b.* 1942) *Lab., Islwyn,* maj. 24,728

*Kirkhope, Timothy J. R. (*b.* 1945) *C., Leeds North East,* maj. 4,244

*Kirkwood, Archibald J. (*b.* 1946) *LD, Roxburgh and Berwickshire,* maj. 4,257

*Knapman, Roger M. (*b.* 1944) *C., Stroud,* maj. 13,405

Knight, Mrs Angela A. (*b.* 1950) *C., Erewash,* maj. 5,703

*Knight, Gregory (*b.* 1949) *C., Derby North,* maj. 4,453

*Knight, Dame Jill, DBE (*b.* 1923) *C., Birmingham, Edgbaston,* maj. 4,307

*Knox, Sir David (*b.* 1933) *C., Staffordshire Moorlands,* maj. 7,410

Kynoch, George A. B. (*b.* 1946) *C., Kincardine and Deeside,* maj. 4,495

Lait, Ms Jacqui (*b.* 1947) *C., Hastings and Rye,* maj. 6,634

*Lamont, Rt. Hon. Norman S. H. (*b.* 1942) *C., Kingston upon Thames,* maj. 10,153

*Lang, Rt. Hon. Ian B. (*b.* 1940) *C., Galloway and Upper Nithsdale,* maj. 2,468

*Lawrence, Sir Ivan, QC (b. 1936) C., Burton, maj. 5,996
Legg, Barry (b. 1949) C., Milton Keynes South West, maj. 4,687
*Leigh, Edward J. E. (b. 1950) C., Gainsborough and Horncastle, maj. 16,245
*Leighton, Ronald (b. 1930) Lab., Newham North East, maj. 9,986
*Lennox-Boyd, Hon. Mark A. (b. 1943) C., Morecambe and Lunesdale, maj. 11,509
*Lester, James T. (b. 1932) C., Broxtowe, maj. 9,891
*Lestor, Miss Joan (b. 1931) Lab., Eccles, maj. 13,226
*Lewis, Terence (b. 1935) Lab., Worsley, maj. 10,012
Lidington, David R., PH.D. (b. 1956) C., Aylesbury, maj. 18,860
*Lightbown, David L. (b. 1932) C., Staffordshire South East, maj. 7,192
*Lilley, Rt. Hon. Peter B. (b. 1943) C., St Albans, maj. 16,404
*Litherland, Robert K. (b. 1930) Lab., Manchester Central, maj. 18,037
*Livingstone, Ken (b. 1945) Lab., Brent East, maj. 5,971
*Lloyd, Anthony J. (b. 1950) Lab., Stretford, maj. 11,137
*Lloyd, Peter R. C. (b. 1937) C., Fareham, maj. 24,141
Llwyd, Elfyn (b. 1951) PC, Meirionnydd Nant Conwy, maj. 4,613
*Lofthouse, Geoffrey (b. 1925) Lab., Pontefract and Castleford, maj. 23,495
*Lord, Michael N. (b. 1938) C., Suffolk Central, maj. 16,031
*Loyden, Edward (b. 1923) Lab., Liverpool, Garston, maj. 12,279
Luff, Peter J. (b. 1955) C., Worcester, maj. 6,152
*Lyell, Rt. Hon. Sir Nicholas, QC (b. 1938) C., Bedfordshire Mid, maj. 25,138
Lynne, Ms Elizabeth (b. 1948) LD, Rochdale, maj. 1,839
*McAllion, John (b. 1948) Lab., Dundee East, maj. 4,564
*McAvoy, Thomas M. (b. 1943) Lab., Glasgow, Rutherglen, maj. 15,270
*McCartney, Ian (b. 1951) Lab., Makerfield, maj. 18,118
*McCrea, Revd Dr R. T. William (b. 1948) DUP, Ulster Mid, maj. 6,187
*MacDonald, Calum A. (b. 1956) Lab., Western Isles, maj. 1,703
*McFall, John (b. 1944) Lab., Dumbarton, maj. 6,129
*McGrady, Edward K. (b. 1935) SDLP, Down South, maj. 6,342
*MacGregor, Rt. Hon. John R. R., OBE (b. 1937) C., Norfolk South, maj. 17,565
*Mackay, Andrew J. (b. 1949) C., Berkshire East, maj. 28,680
*McKelvey, William (b. 1934) Lab., Kilmarnock and Loudoun, maj. 6,979
MacKinlay, Andrew S. (b. 1949) Lab., Thurrock, maj. 1,172
*Maclean, David J. (b. 1953) C., Penrith and the Border, maj. 18,449
*McLeish, Henry B. (b. 1948) Lab., Fife Central, maj. 10,578
*Maclennan, Robert A. R. (b. 1936) LD, Caithness and Sutherland, maj. 5,365
*McLoughlin, Patrick A. (b. 1957) C., Derbyshire West, maj. 18,769
*McMaster, Gordon J. (b. 1960) Lab., Paisley South, maj. 9,549
*McNair-Wilson, Sir Patrick (b. 1929) C., New Forest, maj. 20,405
*McNamara, J. Kevin (b. 1934) Lab., Hull North, maj. 15,384
*McWilliam, John D. (b. 1941) Lab., Blaydon, maj. 13,343
*Madden, Maxwell F. (b. 1941) Lab., Bradford West, maj. 9,502
Maddock, Mrs Diana (b. 1945) LD, Christchurch, maj. 16,427
*Madel, W. David (b. 1938) C., Bedfordshire South West, maj. 21,273

*Maginnis, Kenneth (b. 1938) UUP, Fermanagh and South Tyrone, maj. 14,113
*Mahon, Ms Alice (b. 1937) Lab., Halifax, maj. 478
Maitland, Lady Olga (b. 1944) C., Sutton and Cheam, maj. 10,756
*Major, Rt. Hon. John (b. 1943) C., Huntingdon, maj. 36,230
*Mallon, Seamus (b. 1936) SDLP, Newry and Armagh, maj. 7,091
Malone, P. Gerald (b. 1950) C., Winchester, maj. 8,121
Mandelson, Peter B. (b. 1953) Lab., Hartlepool, maj. 8,782
*Mans, Keith D. R. (b. 1946) C., Wyre, maj. 11,664
*Marek, John, PH.D. (b. 1940) Lab., Wrexham, maj. 6,716
*Marland, Paul (b. 1940) C., Gloucestershire West, maj. 4,958
*Marlow, Antony R. (b. 1940) C., Northampton North, maj. 3,908
*Marshall, David (b. 1941) Lab., Glasgow, Shettleston, maj. 14,834
*Marshall, James (b. 1941) Lab., Leicester South, maj. 9,440
*Marshall, John L. (b. 1940) C., Hendon South, maj. 12,047
*Marshall, Sir Michael (b. 1930) C., Arundel, maj. 19,863
*Martin, David J. P. (b. 1945) C., Portsmouth South, maj. 242
*Martin, Michael J. (b. 1945) Lab., Glasgow, Springburn, maj. 14,506
*Martlew, Eric A. (b. 1949) Lab., Carlisle, maj. 3,108
*Mates, Michael J. (b. 1934) C., Hampshire East, maj. 29,165
*Mawhinney, Brian S., PH.D. (b. 1940) C., Peterborough, maj. 5,376
*Maxton, John A. (b. 1936) Lab., Glasgow, Cathcart, maj. 8,001
*Mayhew, Rt. Hon. Sir Patrick, QC (b. 1929) C., Tunbridge Wells, maj. 17,132
*Meacher, Michael H. (b. 1939) Lab., Oldham West, maj. 8,333
*Meale, J. Alan (b. 1949) Lab., Mansfield, maj. 11,724
*Mellor, Rt. Hon. David J., QC (b. 1949) C., Putney, maj. 7,526
Merchant, Piers R. G. (b. 1951) C., Beckenham, maj. 15,285
*Michael, Alun E. (b. 1943) Lab., Cardiff South and Penarth, maj. 10,425
*Michie, Mrs J. Ray (b. 1934) LD, Argyll and Bute, maj. 2,622
*Michie, William (b. 1935) Lab., Sheffield, Heeley, maj. 14,954
Milburn, Alan (b. 1958) Lab., Darlington, maj. 2,798
Miller, Andrew (b. 1949) Lab., Ellesmere Port and Neston, maj. 1,989
Milligan, Stephen (b. 1948) C., Eastleigh, maj. 17,702
*Mills, Iain C. (b. 1940) C., Meriden, maj. 14,699
*Mitchell, Andrew J. B. (b. 1956) C., Gedling, maj. 10,637
*Mitchell, Austin V. (b. 1934) Lab., Great Grimsby, maj. 7,504
*Mitchell, Sir David (b. 1928) C., Hampshire North West, maj. 17,848
*Moate, Sir Roger (b. 1938) C., Faversham, maj. 16,351
*Molyneaux, Rt. Hon. James H. (b. 1920) UUP, Lagan Valley, maj. 23,565
*Monro, Sir Hector, AE (b. 1922) C., Dumfries, maj. 6,415
*Montgomery, Sir Fergus (b. 1927) C., Altrincham and Sale, maj. 16,791
*Moonie, Dr Lewis G. (b. 1947) Lab., Kirkcaldy, maj. 9,126
*Morgan, H. Rhodri (b. 1939) Lab., Cardiff West, maj. 9,291
*Morley, Elliot A. (b. 1952) Lab., Glanford and Scunthorpe, maj. 8,412
*Morris, Rt. Hon. Alfred, AO (b. 1928) Lab., Manchester, Wythenshawe, maj. 11,996
Morris, Ms Estelle (b. 1952) Lab., Birmingham, Yardley, maj. 162
*Morris, Rt. Hon. John, QC (b. 1931) Lab., Aberavon, maj. 21,310

*Morris, Michael W. L. (*b.* 1936) *C., Northampton South,* maj. 16,973

*Moss, Malcolm D. (*b.* 1943) *C., Cambridgeshire North East,* maj. 15,093

*Mowlam, Dr Marjorie (*b.* 1949) *Lab., Redcar,* maj. 11,577

Mudie, George (*b.* 1945) *Lab., Leeds East,* maj. 12,697

*Mullin, Christopher J. (*b.* 1947) *Lab., Sunderland South,* maj. 14,501

*Murphy, Paul P. (*b.* 1948) *Lab., Torfaen,* maj. 20,754

*Needham, Richard F. (The Earl of Kilmorey) (*b.* 1942) *C., Wiltshire North,* maj. 16,388

*Nelson, R. Anthony (*b.* 1948) *C., Chichester,* maj. 20,887

*Neubert, Sir Michael (*b.* 1933) *C., Romford,* maj. 11,420

*Newton, Rt. Hon. Antony H., OBE (*b.* 1937) *C., Braintree,* maj. 17,494

*Nicholls, Patrick C. M. (*b.* 1948) *C., Teignbridge,* maj. 8,856

*Nicholson, David J. (*b.* 1944) *C., Taunton,* maj. 3,336

*Nicholson, Miss Emma H. (*b.* 1941) *C., Devon West and Torridge,* maj. 3,614

*Norris, Steven J. (*b.* 1945) *C., Epping Forest,* maj. 20,188

*Oakes, Rt. Hon. Gordon J. (*b.* 1931) *Lab., Halton,* maj. 18,204

O'Brien, Michael (*b.* 1954) *Lab., Warwickshire North,* maj. 1,454

*O'Brien, William (*b.* 1929) *Lab., Normanton,* maj. 8,950

*O'Hara, Edward (*b.* 1937) *Lab., Knowsley South,* maj. 22,011

Olner, William J. (*b.* 1942) *Lab., Nuneaton,* maj. 1,631

*O'Neill, Martin J. (*b.* 1945) *Lab., Clackmannan,* maj. 8,503

*Onslow, Rt. Hon. Sir Cranley, KCMG (*b.* 1926) *C., Woking,* maj. 19,842

*Oppenheim, Hon. Phillip A. C. L. (*b.* 1956) *C., Amber Valley,* maj. 712

*Orme, Rt. Hon. Stanley (*b.* 1923) *Lab., Salford East,* maj. 11,235

Ottaway, Richard G. J. (*b.* 1945) *C., Croydon South,* maj. 20,425

*Page, Richard L. (*b.* 1941) *C., Hertfordshire South West,* maj. 20,107

*Paice, James E. T. (*b.* 1949) *C., Cambridgeshire South East,* maj. 23,810

*Paisley, Revd Ian R. K. (*b.* 1926) *DUP, Antrim North,* maj. 14,936

*Parry, Robert (*b.* 1933) *Lab., Liverpool, Riverside,* maj. 17,437

*Patchett, Terry (*b.* 1940) *Lab., Barnsley East,* maj. 24,777

*Patnick, C. Irvine, OBE (*b.* 1929) *C., Sheffield, Hallam,* maj. 6,741

*Patten, Rt. Hon. John H. C. (*b.* 1945) *C., Oxford West and Abingdon,* maj. 3,539

*Pattie, Rt. Hon. Sir Geoffrey (*b.* 1936) *C., Chertsey and Walton,* maj. 22,819

*Pawsey, James F. (*b.* 1933) *C., Rugby and Kenilworth,* maj. 13,247

*Peacock, Mrs Elizabeth J. (*b.* 1937) *C., Batley and Spen,* maj. 1,408

*Pendry, Thomas (*b.* 1934) *Lab., Stalybridge and Hyde,* maj. 8,831

Pickles, Eric J. (*b.* 1952) *C., Brentwood and Ongar,* maj. 15,145

Pickthall, Colin (*b.* 1944) *Lab., Lancashire West,* maj. 2,077

*Pike, Peter L. (*b.* 1937) *Lab., Burnley,* maj. 11,491

Pope, Gregory J. (*b.* 1960) *Lab., Hyndburn,* maj. 1,960

*Porter, David J. (*b.* 1948) *C., Waveney,* maj. 6,702

*Porter, G. B. (Barry) (*b.* 1939) *C., Wirral South,* maj. 8,183

*Portillo, Rt. Hon. Michael D. X. (*b.* 1953) *C., Enfield, Southgate,* maj. 15,563

*Powell, Raymond (*b.* 1928) *Lab., Ogmore,* maj. 23,827

*Powell, William R. (*b.* 1948) *C., Corby,* maj. 342

Prentice, Mrs Bridget (*b.* 1952) *Lab., Lewisham East,* maj. 1,095

Prentice, Gordon (*b.* 1951) *Lab., Pendle,* maj. 2,113

*Prescott, John L. (*b.* 1938) *Lab., Hull East,* maj. 18,719

*Primarolo, Ms Dawn (*b.* 1954) *Lab., Bristol South,* maj. 8,919

Purchase, Kenneth (*b.* 1939) *Lab., Wolverhampton North East,* maj. 3,939

*Quin, Miss Joyce G. (*b.* 1944) *Lab., Gateshead East,* maj. 18,530

*Radice, Giles H. (*b.* 1936) *Lab., Durham North,* maj. 19,637

*Randall, Stuart J. (*b.* 1938) *Lab., Hull West,* maj. 10,585

*Rathbone, J. R. (Tim) (*b.* 1933) *C., Lewes,* maj. 12,175

Raynsford, W. R. N. (Nick) (*b.* 1945) *Lab., Greenwich,* maj. 1,357

*Redmond, Martin (*b.* 1937) *Lab., Don Valley,* maj. 13,534

*Redwood, Rt. Hon. John A. (*b.* 1951) *C., Wokingham,* maj. 25,709

*Reid, Dr John (*b.* 1947) *Lab., Motherwell North,* maj. 18,910

Rendel, David D. (*b.* 1949) *LD, Newbury,* maj. 22,055

*Renton, Rt. Hon. R. Timothy (*b.* 1932) *C., Sussex Mid,* maj. 20,528

Richards, Roderick (*b.* 1947) *C., Clwyd North West,* maj. 6,050

*Richardson, Ms Josephine (*b.* 1923) *Lab., Barking,* maj. 6,268

*Riddick, Graham E. G. (*b.* 1955) *C., Colne Valley,* maj. 7,225

*Rifkind, Rt. Hon. Malcolm L., QC (*b.* 1946) *C., Edinburgh, Pentlands,* maj. 4,290

Robathan, Andrew R. G. (*b.* 1951) *C., Blaby,* maj. 25,347

*Roberts, Rt. Hon. Sir Wyn (*b.* 1930) *C., Conwy,* maj. 995

*Robertson, George I. M. (*b.* 1946) *Lab., Hamilton,* maj. 16,603

Robertson, Raymond S. (*b.* 1959) *C., Aberdeen South,* maj. 1,517

*Robinson, Geoffrey (*b.* 1938) *Lab., Coventry North West,* maj. 6,432

Robinson, Mark N. F. (*b.* 1946) *C., Somerton and Frome,* maj. 4,341

*Robinson, Peter D. (*b.* 1948) *DUP, Belfast East,* maj. 7,787

Roche, Mrs Barbara M. R. (*b.* 1954) *Lab., Hornsey and Wood Green,* maj. 5,177

*Roe, Mrs Marion A. (*b.* 1936) *C., Broxbourne,* maj. 23,970

*Rogers, Allan R. (*b.* 1932) *Lab., Rhondda,* maj. 28,816

*Rooker, Jeffrey W. (*b.* 1941) *Lab., Birmingham, Perry Barr,* maj. 8,590

*Rooney, Terence H. (*b.* 1950) *Lab., Bradford North,* maj. 7,664

*Ross, Ernest (*b.* 1942) *Lab., Dundee West,* maj. 10,604

*Ross, William (*b.* 1936) *UUP, Londonderry East,* maj. 18,527

*Rowe, Andrew (*b.* 1935) *C., Kent Mid,* maj. 19,649

*Rowlands, Edward (*b.* 1940) *Lab., Merthyr Tydfil and Rhymney,* maj. 26,713

*Ruddock, Mrs Joan M. (*b.* 1943) *Lab., Lewisham, Deptford,* maj. 12,238

*Rumbold, Rt. Hon. Dame Angela, DBE (*b.* 1932) *C., Mitcham and Morden,* maj. 1,734

*Ryder, Rt. Hon. Richard A., OBE (*b.* 1949) *C., Norfolk Mid,* maj. 18,948

*Sackville, Hon. Thomas G. (*b.* 1950) *C., Bolton West,* maj. 1,079

*Sainsbury, Rt. Hon. Timothy A. D. (*b.* 1932) *C., Hove,* maj. 12,268

*Salmond, Alexander E. A. (*b.* 1954) *SNP, Banff and Buchan,* maj. 4,108

*Scott, Rt. Hon. Nicholas P., MBE (*b.* 1933) *C., Chelsea,* maj. 12,789

*Sedgemore, Brian C. J. (*b.* 1937) *Lab., Hackney South and Shoreditch,* maj. 9,016

*Shaw, David L. (*b.* 1950) *C., Dover,* maj. 833

*Shaw, Sir Giles (*b.* 1931) *C., Pudsey,* maj. 8,972

*Sheerman, Barry J. (*b.* 1940) *Lab., Huddersfield,* maj. 7,258

*Sheldon, Rt. Hon. Robert E. (*b.* 1923) *Lab., Ashton-under-Lyne,* maj. 10,935

*Shephard, Rt. Hon. Gillian P. (*b.* 1940) *C., Norfolk South West,* maj. 16,931

*Shepherd, Colin (*b.* 1938) *C., Hereford,* maj. 3,413

*Shepherd, Richard C. S. (*b.* 1942) *C., Aldridge-Brownhills,* maj. 11,024

*Shersby, J. Michael (*b.* 1933) *C., Uxbridge,* maj. 13,179

*Shore, Rt. Hon. Peter D. (*b.* 1924) *Lab., Bethnal Green and Stepney,* maj. 12,230

*Short, Ms Clare (*b.* 1946) *Lab., Birmingham, Ladywood,* maj. 15,283

Simpson, Alan (*b.* 1948) *Lab., Nottingham South,* maj. 3,181

*Sims, Roger E. (*b.* 1930) *C., Chislehurst,* maj. 15,276

*Skeet, Sir Trevor (*b.* 1918) *C., Bedfordshire North,* maj. 11,618

*Skinner, Dennis E. (*b.* 1932) *Lab., Bolsover,* maj. 20,660

*Smith, Andrew D. (*b.* 1951) *Lab., Oxford East,* maj. 7,538

*Smith, Christopher R., ph.d. (*b.* 1951) *Lab., Islington South and Finsbury,* maj. 10,652

*Smith, Sir Dudley (*b.* 1926) *C., Warwick and Leamington,* maj. 8,935

*Smith, Rt. Hon. John, qc (*b.* 1938) *Lab., Monklands East,* maj. 15,712

Smith, Llewellyn T. (*b.* 1944) *Lab., Blaenau Gwent,* maj. 30,067

*Smith, Timothy J. (*b.* 1947) *C., Beaconsfield,* maj. 23,597

*Smyth, Revd W. Martin (*b.* 1931) *UUP, Belfast South,* maj. 10,070

*Snape, Peter C. (*b.* 1942) *Lab., West Bromwich East,* maj. 2,813

*Soames, Hon. A. Nicholas W. (*b.* 1948) *C., Crawley,* maj. 7,765

*Soley, Clive S. (*b.* 1939) *Lab., Hammersmith,* maj. 4,754

*Spearing, Nigel J. (*b.* 1930) *Lab., Newham South,* maj. 2,502

*Speed, Sir Keith, RD (*b.* 1934) *C., Ashford,* maj. 17,359

Spellar, John F. (*b.* 1947) *Lab., Warley West,* maj. 5,472

Spencer, Sir Derek, qc (*b.* 1936) *C., Brighton, Pavilion,* maj. 3,675

*Spicer, Sir James (*b.* 1925) *C., Dorset West,* maj. 8,010

*Spicer, W. Michael H. (*b.* 1943) *C., Worcestershire South,* maj. 16,151

Spink, Dr Robert M. (*b.* 1948) *C., Castle Point,* maj. 16,830

Spring, Richard J. G. (*b.* 1946) *C., Bury St Edmunds,* maj. 18,787

Sproat, Iain M. (*b.* 1938) *C., Harwich,* maj. 17,159

Squire, Ms Rachel (*b.* 1954) *Lab., Dunfermline West,* maj. 7,484

*Squire, Robin C. (*b.* 1944) *C., Hornchurch,* maj. 9,165

*Stanley, Rt. Hon. Sir John (*b.* 1942) *C., Tonbridge and Malling,* maj. 21,558

*Steel, Rt. Hon. Sir David, KBE (*b.* 1938) *LD, Tweeddale, Ettrick and Lauderdale,* maj. 2,520

*Steen, Anthony D. (*b.* 1939) *C., South Hams,* maj. 13,711

*Steinberg, Gerald N. (*b.* 1945) *Lab., City of Durham,* maj. 15,058

Stephen, B. Michael L. (*b.* 1942) *C., Shoreham,* maj. 14,286

*Stern, Michael C. (*b.* 1942) *C., Bristol North West,* maj. 45

Stevenson, George W. (*b.* 1938) *Lab., Stoke-on-Trent South,* maj. 6,909

*Stewart, J. Allan (*b.* 1942) *C., Eastwood,* maj. 11,688

*Stott, Roger, CBE (*b.* 1943) *Lab., Wigan,* maj. 21,842

*Strang, Gavin S., ph.d. (*b.* 1943) *Lab., Edinburgh East,* maj. 7,211

*Straw, J. W. (Jack) (*b.* 1946) *Lab., Blackburn,* maj. 6,027

Streeter, Gary (*b.* 1955) *C., Plymouth, Sutton,* maj. 11,950

*Sumberg, David A. G. (*b.* 1941) *C., Bury South,* maj. 788

Sweeney, Walter E. (*b.* 1949) *C., Vale of Glamorgan,* maj. 19

Sykes, John D. (*b.* 1956) *C., Scarborough,* maj. 11,734

*Tapsell, Sir Peter (*b.* 1930) *C., Lindsey East,* maj. 11,846

*Taylor, Sir Edward (Teddy) (*b.* 1937) *C., Southend East,* maj. 13,111

*Taylor, Ian C., MBE (*b.* 1945) *C., Esher,* maj. 20,371

*Taylor, Rt. Hon. John D. (*b.* 1937) *UUP, Strangford,* maj. 8,911

*Taylor, John M. (*b.* 1941) *C., Solihull,* maj. 25,146

*Taylor, Matthew O. J. (*b.* 1963) *LD, Truro,* maj. 7,570

*Taylor, Mrs W. Ann (*b.* 1947) *Lab., Dewsbury,* maj. 634

*Temple-Morris, Peter (*b.* 1938) *C., Leominster,* maj. 16,680

Thomason, K. Roy, OBE (*b.* 1944) *C., Bromsgrove,* maj. 13,702

*Thompson, Sir Donald (*b.* 1931) *C., Calder Valley,* maj. 4,878

*Thompson, H. Patrick (*b.* 1935) *C., Norwich North,* maj. 266

*Thompson, John (*b.* 1928) *Lab., Wansbeck,* maj. 18,174

*Thornton, Sir Malcolm (*b.* 1939) *C., Crosby,* maj. 14,806

*Thurnham, Peter G. (*b.* 1938) *C., Bolton North East,* maj. 185

Tipping, S. Paddy (*b.* 1949) *Lab., Sherwood,* maj. 2,910

*Townend, John E. (*b.* 1934) *C., Bridlington,* maj. 16,358

*Townsend, Cyril D. (*b.* 1937) *C., Bexleyheath,* maj. 14,086

*Tracey, Richard P. (*b.* 1943) *C., Surbiton,* maj. 9,639

*Tredinnick, David A. S. (*b.* 1950) *C., Bosworth,* maj. 19,094

Trend, Hon. Michael St J. (*b.* 1952) *C., Windsor and Maidenhead,* maj. 12,928

*Trimble, W. David (*b.* 1944) *UUP, Upper Bann,* maj. 16,163

*Trotter, Neville G. (*b.* 1932) *C., Tynemouth,* maj. 597

*Turner, Dennis (*b.* 1942) *Lab., Wolverhampton South East,* maj. 10,240

*Twinn, Dr Ian D. (*b.* 1950) *C., Edmonton,* maj. 593

Tyler, Paul A., CBE (*b.* 1941) *LD, Cornwall North,* maj. 1,921

*Vaughan, Sir Gerard (*b.* 1923) *C., Reading East,* maj. 14,555

*Vaz, N. Keith A. S. (*b.* 1956) *Lab., Leicester East,* maj. 11,316

*Viggers, Peter J. (*b.* 1938) *C., Gosport,* maj. 16,318

*Waldegrave, Rt. Hon. William A. (*b.* 1946) *C., Bristol West,* maj. 6,071

*Walden, George G. H., CMG (*b.* 1939) *C., Buckingham,* maj. 19,791

*Walker, A. Cecil (*b.* 1924) *UUP, Belfast North,* maj. 9,625

*Walker, Rt. Hon. Sir Harold (*b.* 1927) *Lab., Doncaster Central,* maj. 10,682

*Walker, William C. (*b.* 1929) *C., Tayside North,* maj. 3,995

*Wallace, James R. (*b.* 1954) *LD, Orkney and Shetland,* maj. 5,033

*Waller, Gary P. A. (*b.* 1945) *C., Keighley,* maj. 3,596

*Walley, Ms Joan L. (*b.* 1949) *Lab., Stoke-on-Trent North,* maj. 14,777

*Ward, John D., CBE (*b.* 1925) *C., Poole,* maj. 12,831

*Wardell, Gareth L. (*b.* 1944) *Lab., Gower,* maj. 7,018

*Wardle, Charles F. (*b.* 1939) *C., Bexhill and Battle,* maj. 16,307

*Wareing, Robert N. (*b.* 1930) *Lab., Liverpool, West Derby,* maj. 20,425

Waterson, Nigel C. (*b.* 1950) *C., Eastbourne,* maj. 5,481

*Watson, Michael G. (*b.* 1949) *Lab., Glasgow Central,* maj. 11,019

*Watts, John A. (*b.* 1947) *C., Slough,* maj. 514

*Wells, Bowen (*b.* 1935) *C., Hertford and Stortford,* maj. 20,210

*Welsh, Andrew P. (*b.* 1944) *SNP, Angus East,* maj. 954

*Wheeler, Rt. Hon. Sir John (*b.* 1940) *C., Westminster North,* maj. 3,733

*Whitney, Raymond W., OBE (b. 1930) C., Wycombe, maj. 17,076

Whittingdale, John F. L., OBE (b. 1959) C., Colchester South and Maldon, maj. 21,821

Wicks, Malcolm H. (b. 1947) Lab., Croydon North West, maj. 1,526

*Widdecombe, Miss Ann N. (b. 1947) C., Maidstone, maj. 16,286

*Wiggin, Sir Jerry, TD (b. 1937) C., Weston-super-Mare, maj. 5,342

*Wigley, Dafydd (b. 1943) PC, Caernarfon, maj. 14,476

*Wilkinson, John A. D. (b. 1940) C., Ruislip-Northwood, maj. 19,791

Willetts, David L. (b. 1956) C., Havant, maj. 17,584

*Williams, Rt. Hon. Alan J. (b. 1930) Lab., Swansea West, maj. 9,478

*Williams, Dr Alan W. (b. 1945) Lab., Carmarthen, maj. 2,922

*Wilshire, David (b. 1943) C., Spelthorne, maj. 19,843

*Wilson, Brian D. H. (b. 1948) Lab., Cunninghame North, maj. 2,939

*Winnick, David J. (b. 1933) Lab., Walsall North, maj. 3,824

*Winterton, Mrs J. Ann (b. 1941) C., Congleton, maj. 11,120

*Winterton, Nicholas R. (b. 1938) C., Macclesfield, maj. 22,767

*Wise, Mrs Audrey (b. 1935) Lab., Preston, maj. 12,175

*Wolfson, G. Mark (b. 1934) C., Sevenoaks, maj. 19,154

*Wood, Timothy J. R. (b. 1940) C., Stevenage, maj. 4,888

*Worthington, Anthony (b. 1941) Lab., Clydebank and Milngavie, maj. 12,430

*Wray, James (b. 1938) Lab., Glasgow, Provan, maj. 10,703

Wright, Anthony W., D.Phil. (b. 1948) Lab., Cannock and Burntwood, maj. 1,506

*Yeo, Timothy S. K. (b. 1945) C., Suffolk South, maj. 17,289

*Young, David W. (b. 1930) Lab., Bolton South East, maj. 12,691

*Young, Rt. Hon. Sir George, Bt. (b. 1941) C., Ealing, Acton, maj. 7,007

MEMBERS WITH SMALL MAJORITIES

The following MPs were returned in April 1992 with majorities of fewer than 1,000 votes

*Denotes membership of last Parliament

	Maj.
Walter Sweeney, C., Vale of Glamorgan	19
*Michael Stern, C., Bristol North West	45
*Terry Dicks, C., Hayes and Harlington	53
Phil Gallie, C., Ayr	85
Janet Anderson, Lab., Rossendale and Darwen	120
Jonathan Evans, C., Brecon and Radnor	130
Estelle Morris, Lab., Birmingham Yardley	162
*Peter Thurnham, C., Bolton North East	185
Mike Hall, Lab., Warrington South	191
*David Martin, C., Portsmouth South	242
Jamie Cann, Lab., Ipswich	265
*Patrick Thompson, C., Norwich North	266
*Malcolm Bruce, LD, Gordon	274
*William Powell, C., Corby	342
Mike Gapes, Lab., Ilford South	402
*Sir Russell Johnston, LD, Inverness, Nairn and Lochaber	458
*Alice Mahon, Lab., Halifax	478
*John Watts, C., Slough	514
John Denham, Lab., Southampton Itchen	551

	Maj.
Anne Campbell, Lab., Cambridge	580
*James Hill, C., Southampton Test	585
Dr Joe Hendron, SDLP, Belfast West	589
*Dr Ian Twinn, C., Edmonton	593
Neville Trotter, C., Tynemouth	597
Richard Burden, Lab., Birmingham Northfield	630
*Ann Taylor, Lab., Dewsbury	634
*Michael Forsyth, C., Stirling	703
*Phillip Oppenheim, C., Amber Valley	712
Nick Ainger, Lab., Pembroke	755
*David Sumberg, C., Bury South	788
Nick Harvey, LD, Devon North	794
*Graham Bright, C., Luton South	799
*David Shaw, C., Dover	833
*Lord James Douglas-Hamilton, C., Edinburgh West	879
*Sir Tom Arnold, C., Hazel Grove	929
*Andrew Welsh, SNP, Angus East	954
*David Ashby, C., Leicestershire North West	979
*Sir Wyn Roberts, C., Conwy	995

NEWBURY
(6 May 1993)
E.81,081   *T*.71.25%

D. Rendel, *LD*	37,590
J. Davidson, *C*	15,535
S. Billcliffe, *Lab*	1,151
A. Sked, *Anti-Maastricht Anti Fed.*	601
A. Bannon, *Conservative Candidate*	561
S. Martin, *Commoners Party Movement*	435
Lord Sutch, *Loony*	432
J. Wallis, *Green*	341
R. Marlar, *Referendum*	338
J. Browne, *Conservative Rebel*	267
Ms L. St Clair, *Corrective*	170
W. Board, *Maastricht Referendum for Britain*	84
M. Grenville, *NLP*	60
J. Day. *People and Pensioners*	49
C. Palmer, *21st Century*	40
M. Grbin, *Defence of Children's Humanity Bosnia*	33
A. Page, *SDP*	33
Ms A. Murphy, *Comm. GB*	32
M. Stone, *Give Royal Billions to Schools*	21
LD majority	22,055

CHRISTCHURCH
(29 July 1993)
E.71,868   *T*.74.2%

Mrs D. Maddock, *LD*	33,164
R. Hayward, *C*	16,737
N. Lickley, *Lab*	1,453
A. Sked, *Anti-Maastricht Anti Fed.*	878
Lord Sutch, *Monster Raving Loony Rock-Roll*	404
A. Bannon, *Conservative Candidate*	357
P. Newman, *Sack Graham Taylor*	80
Ms T. B. Jackson, *Buy Daily Sport*	67
P. Hollyman, *Save NHS*	60
J. Crockard, *Highlander IV Wednesday Promotion Night*	48
M. Griffiths, *NLP*	45
M. Belcher, *Ian for King*	23
K. Fitzhugh, *Alfred Chicken*	18
J. Walley, *Rainbow Alliance Coalition*	16
LD majority	16,427

Speakers of the Commons since 1708

The date of appointment given is the day on which the Speaker was first elected by the House of Commons. The appointment requires Royal approbation before it is confirmed and this is usually given within a few days. The present Speaker is the 155th.

PARLIAMENT OF GREAT BRITAIN

Sir Richard Onslow (*Lord Onslow*), 16 November 1708
William Bromley, 25 November 1710
Sir Thomas Hanmer, 16 February 1714
Spencer Compton (*Earl of Wilmington*), 17 March 1715
Arthur Onslow, 23 January 1728
Sir John Cust, 3 November 1761
Sir Fletcher Norton (*Lord Grantley*), 22 January 1770
Charles Cornwall, 31 October 1780
Hon. William Grenville (*Lord Grenville*), 5 January 1789
Henry Addington (*Viscount Sidmouth*), 8 June 1789

PARLIAMENT OF UNITED KINGDOM

Sir John Mitford (*Lord Redesdale*), 11 February 1801

Charles Abbot (*Lord Colchester*), 10 February 1802
Charles Manners-Sutton (*Viscount Canterbury*), 2 June 1817
James Abercromby (*Lord Dunfermline*), 19 February 1835
Charles Shaw-Lefevre (*Viscount Eversley*), 27 May 1839
J. Evelyn Denison (*Viscount Ossington*), 30 April 1857
Sir Henry Brand (*Viscount Hampden*), 9 February 1872
Arthur Wellesley Peel (*Viscount Peel*), 26 February 1884
William Gully (*Viscount Selby*), 10 April 1895
James Lowther (*Viscount Ullswater*), 8 June 1905
John Whitley, 27 April 1921
Hon. Edward Fitzroy, 20 June 1928
Douglas Clifton-Brown (*Viscount Ruffside*), 9 March 1943
William Morrison (*Viscount Dunrossil*), 31 October 1951
Sir Harry Hylton-Foster, 20 October 1959
Horace King (*Lord Maybray-King*), 26 October 1965
Selwyn Lloyd (*Lord Selwyn-Lloyd*), 12 January 1971
George Thomas (*Viscount Tonypandy*), 2 February 1976
Bernard Weatherill (*Lord Weatherill*), 15 June 1983
Betty Boothroyd, 27 April 1992

PARLIAMENTARY CONSTITUENCIES AS AT 9 APRIL 1992

The results of voting in each parliamentary division at the General Election of 9 April 1992 are given below. The majority in the 1987 General Election, and any subsequent by-elections, is given below the 1992 result.

Symbols
E.   Total number of electors in the constituency at the 1992 General Election
T.   Turnout of electors at the 1992 General Election
*   Member of the last Parliament

Abbreviations
All.   Alliance Party (NI)
C.   Conservative
DUP   Democratic Unionist Party
Green   Green Party
Ind.   Independent
Lab.   Labour
L./All.   Liberal Alliance
LD   Liberal Democrat
Lib.   Liberal
PC   Plaid Cymru
SD   Social Democrat
SDLP   Social Democratic and Labour Party
SDP   Social Democrat Party
SF   Sinn Fein
SNP   Scottish National Party
UPUP   Ulster Popular Unionist Party
UUP   Ulster Unionist Party

ADS   After Dinner Speaker
AFE   Anti-Federal Europe
Alt.   Alternative
Anti Fed.   Anti Federalist League
Anti H.   Anti-Heseltine Independent
APAKBI   Anti-Paddy Ashdown Keep Britain Independent

AS   Anglo Saxon
Bastion   Bastion Party
BNP   British National Party
Brewer   Jolly Small Brewers Party
Brit. Ind.   British Independence Party
CD   Christian Democrat
Century   21st Century Party
Choice   People's Choice
CL   Communist League
Comm. GB   Communist Party of Great Britain
CRA   Chauvinist Raving Alliance
CSP   Common Sense Party
C. Thatch.   Conservative Thatcherite
DLC   Democrat Liberal Conservative
DOS   Doctor of Stockwell
EFRA   Epping Forest Residents Association
ERIP   Equal Representation in Parliament
EUVJJ   End Unemployment Vote Justice for the Jobless
FDP   Fancy Dress Party
Fellowship   Fellowship Party
FP   Feudal Party
FTA   Fair Trials Abroad
FTM   Forward to Mars Party
Fun   Funstermentalist
Gremloids   Gremloids
Hardcore   The Altern-8-ive (Hardcore) Party
Homeland   Independent British Homeland Defence
Hove C.   Official Conservative Hove Party
IFM   Irish Freedom Movement
ILP   Independent Labour Party
Ind. U.   Independent Unionist
Int. Comm.   International Communist Party
Islamic   Islamic Party
ISS   Illegal Sunday Shopping
JBR   Justice from British Rail

Loony   Official Monster Raving Loony Party
Loony G.   Loony Green
LP   Lodestar Party
LTU   Labour and Trade Union
MBI   Morecambe Bay Independent
NA   Noise Abatement
Nat.   Nationalist
NF   National Front
NLP   Natural Law Party
Pensioners   Pensioners' Party
PP   People's Party
PPP   Peoples' Peace Party
PR   Proportional Representation
Prog. Soc.   Independent Progressive Socialist
Prot. Ref.   Protestant Reformation
QFL   Quality for Life Party
RAVA   Rainbow Ark Voters Association
RCC   Revolutionary Christian Communist
Real Bean   Real Bean
Rev. Comm.   Revolutionary Communist
Rizz   Rizz Party - Rainbow
Scallywagg   Scallywagg
SML   Scottish Militant Labour
SOADDA   Struck Off and Die Doctor's Alliance
Soc.   Socialist
Soc. Lab.   Socialist Labour
True Lab.   True Labour
UTCHAP   Up The Creek Have A Party
WAR   Workers Against Racism
Wessex   Save Wessex
Whiplash   Whiplash Corrective
WP   Workers' Party
WRP   Workers' Revolutionary Party
WUWC   Wake Up Wokingham Campaign
YSOR   Young Socialist – Occupy Ravenscraig

ENGLAND

ALDERSHOT (Hants)
E.81,754 T.78.71%
*J. Critchley, C.   36,974
A. Collett, LD   17,786
J. Anthony Smith, Lab.   8,552
D. Robinson, Lib.   1,038
C. majority   19,188
(June 1987, C. maj. 17,784)

ALDRIDGE-BROWNHILLS
(W. Midlands)
E.63,404 T.82.55%
*R. Shepherd, C.   28,431
N. Fawcett, Lab.   17,407
S. Reynolds, LD   6,503
C. majority   11,024
(June 1987, C. maj. 12,396)

ALTRINCHAM AND SALE (Greater Manchester)
E.65,897 T.80.66%
*Sir F. Montgomery, C.   29,066
Ms M. Atherton, Lab.   12,275
J. Mulholland, LD   11,601

J. Renwick, NLP   212
C. majority   16,791
(June 1987, C. maj. 14,228)

AMBER VALLEY (Derbys)
E.70,155 T.84.69%
*Hon. P. Oppenheim, C.   27,418
J. Cooper, Lab.   26,706
G. Brocklebank, LD   5,294
C. majority   712
(June 1987, C. maj. 9,500)

ARUNDEL (W. Sussex)
E.79,241 T.77.06%
*Sir M. Marshall, C.   35,405
Dr J. Walsh, LD   15,542
R. Nash, Lab.   8,321
Mrs D. Renson, Lib.   1,103
R. Corbin, Green   693
C. majority   19,863
(June 1987, C. maj. 18,880)

ASHFIELD (Notts)
E.75,075 T.77.70%
G. Hoon, Lab.   32,018
L. Robertson, C.   19,031
J. Turton, LD   7,291
Lab. majority   12,987
(June 1987, Lab. maj. 4,400)

ASHFORD (Kent)
E.71,767 T.79.20%
*K. Speed, C.   31,031
Ms C. Headley, LD   13,672
Ms D. Cameron, Lab.   11,365
Dr A. Porter, Green   773
C. majority   17,359
(June 1987, C. maj. 15,488)

ASHTON-UNDER-LYNE (Greater Manchester)
E.58,701 T.73.87%
*Rt. Hon. R. Sheldon, Lab.   24,550
J. Pinniger, C.   13,615
C. Turner, LD   4,005
C. Hall, Lib.   907

J. Brannigan, *NLP* — 289
Lab. majority — 10,935
(June 1987, Lab. maj. 9,286)

AYLESBURY (Bucks)
E.79,208   T.80.29%
D. Lidington, *C.* — 36,500
Ms S. Bowles, *LD* — 17,640
R. Priest, *Lab.* — 8,517
N. Foster, *Green* — 702
B. D'Arcy, *NLP* — 239
C. majority — 18,860
(June 1987, C. maj. 16,558)

BANBURY (Oxon)
E.71,840   T.81.51%
*A. Baldry, *C.* — 32,215
Ms A. Billingham, *Lab.* — 15,495
G. Fisher, *LD* — 10,602
Dr R. Ticiiati, *NLP* — 250
C. majority — 16,720
(June 1987, C. maj. 17,330)

BARKING (Greater London)
E.50,454   T.69.99%
*Ms J. Richardson, *Lab.* — 18,224
J. Kennedy, *C.* — 11,956
S. Churchman, *LD* — 5,133
Lab. majority — 6,268
(June 1987, Lab. maj. 3,409)

BARNSLEY CENTRAL (S. Yorks)
E.55,373   T.70.53%
*E. Illsley, *Lab.* — 27,048
D. Senior, *C.* — 7,687
S. Cowton, *LD* — 4,321
Lab. majority — 19,361
(June 1987, Lab. maj. 19,051)

BARNSLEY EAST (S. Yorks)
E.54,051   T.72.73%
*T. Patchett, *Lab.* — 30,346
J. Procter, *C.* — 5,569
Ms S. Anginotti, *LD* — 3,399
Lab. majority — 24,777
(June 1987, Lab. maj. 23,511)

BARNSLEY WEST AND
PENISTONE (S. Yorks)
E.63,374   T.75.75%
M. Clapham, *Lab.* — 27,965
G. Sawyer, *C.* — 13,461
I. Nicolson, *LD* — 5,610
D. Jones, *Green* — 970
Lab. majority — 14,504
(June 1987, Lab. maj. 14,191)

BARROW AND FURNESS
(Cumbria)
E.67,764   T.82.11%
J. Hutton, *Lab.* — 26,568
*C. Franks, *C.* — 22,990
C. Crane, *LD* — 6,089
Lab. majority — 3,578
(June 1987, C. maj. 3,928)

BASILDON (Essex)
E.67,585   T.79.61%
*D. Amess, *C.* — 24,159
J. Potter, *Lab.* — 22,679
G. Williams, *LD* — 6,967
C. majority — 1,480
(June 1987, C. maj. 2,649)

BASINGSTOKE (Hants)
E.82,952   T.82.79%
*A. Hunter, *C.* — 37,521
D. Bull, *Lab.* — 16,323
C. Curtis, *LD* — 14,119
Ms V. Oldaker, *Green* — 714
C. majority — 21,198
(June 1987, C. maj. 17,893)

BASSETLAW (Notts)
E.58,583   T.92.97%
*J. Ashton, *Lab.* — 29,061
Mrs C. Spelman, *C.* — 19,064
M. Reynolds, *LD* — 6,340
Lab. majority — 9,997
(June 1987, Lab. maj. 5,613)

BATH (Avon)
E.63,689   T.82.54%
D. Foster, *LD* — 25,718
*Rt. Hon. C. Patten, *C.* — 21,950
Ms P. Richards, *Lab.* — 4,102
D. McCanlis, *Green* — 433
Ms M. Barker, *Lib.* — 172
Dr A. Sked, *Anti Fed.* — 117
J. Rumming, *Ind.* — 79
LD majority — 3,768
(June 1987, C. maj. 1,412)

BATLEY AND SPEN (W. Yorks)
E.76,417   T.79.63%
*Mrs E. Peacock, *C.* — 27,629
Mrs E. Durkin, *Lab.* — 26,221
G. Beever, *LD* — 6,380
C. Lord, *Green* — 628
C. majority — 1,408
(June 1987, C. maj. 1,362)

BATTERSEA (Greater London)
E.68,218   T.76.63%
*J. Bowis, *C.* — 26,390
A. Dubs, *Lab.* — 21,550
R. O'Brien, *LD* — 3,659
I. Wingrove, *Green* — 584
W. Stevens, *NLP* — 98
C. majority — 4,840
(June 1987, C. maj. 857)

BEACONSFIELD (Bucks)
E.64,268   T.82.27%
*T. Smith, *C.* — 33,817
Ms A. Purse, *LD* — 10,220
G. Smith, *Lab.* — 7,163
W. Foulds, *Ind. C.* — 1,317
A. Foss, *NLP* — 196
Ms J. Martin, *ERIP* — 166
C. majority — 23,597
(June 1987, C. maj. 21,339)

BECKENHAM (Greater London)
E.59,440   T.77.86%
P. Merchant, *C.* — 26,323
K. Ritchie, *Lab.* — 11,038
Ms M. Williams, *LD* — 8,038
G. Williams, *Lib.* — 643
P. Shaw, *NLP* — 243
C. majority — 15,285
(June 1987, C. maj. 13,464)

BEDFORDSHIRE MID
E.81,864   T.84.45%
*Rt. Hon. Sir N. Lyell, *C.* — 40,230
R. Clayton, *Lab.* — 15,092

N. Hills, *LD* — 11,957
P. Cottier, *Lib.* — 1,582
M. Lorys, *NLP* — 279
C. majority — 25,138
(June 1987, C. maj. 22,851)

BEDFORDSHIRE NORTH
E.73,789   T.80.03%
*Sir T. Skeet, *C.* — 29,920
P. Hall, *Lab.* — 18,302
M. Smithson, *LD* — 10,014
Ms L. Smith, *Green* — 643
B. Bench, *NLP* — 178
C. majority — 11,618
(June 1987, C. maj. 16,505)

BEDFORDSHIRE SOUTH WEST
E.79,662   T.82.39%
*W. D. Madel, *C.* — 37,498
B. Elliott, *Lab.* — 16,225
M. Freeman, *LD* — 10,988
P. Rollings, *Green* — 689
D. Gilmour, *NLP* — 239
C. majority — 21,273
(June 1987, C. maj. 22,305)

BERKSHIRE EAST
E.90,365   T.81.41%
*A. Mackay, *C.* — 43,898
Ms L. Murray, *LD* — 15,218
K. Dibble, *Lab.* — 14,458
C. majority — 28,680
(June 1987, C. maj. 22,626)

BERWICK-UPON-TWEED
(Northumberland)
E.54,919   T.79.12%
*A. Beith, *LD* — 19,283
Dr A. Henfrey, *C.* — 14,240
Dr G. Adam, *Lab.* — 9,933
LD majority — 5,043
(June 1987, L./All. maj. 13,945)

BETHNAL GREEN AND STEPNEY
(Greater London)
E.55,675   T.65.45%
*Rt. Hon. P. Shore, *Lab.* — 20,350
J. Shaw, *LD* — 8,120
Miss J. Emmerson, *C.* — 6,507
R. Edmonds, *BNP* — 1,310
S. Kelsey, *Comm. GB* — 156
Lab. majority — 12,230
(June 1987, Lab. maj. 5,284)

BEVERLEY (Humberside)
E.81,198   T.79.69%
*J. Cran, *C.* — 34,503
A. Collinge, *LD* — 17,986
C. Challen, *Lab.* — 12,026
D. Hetherington, *NLP* — 199
C. majority — 16,517
(June 1987, C. maj. 12,595)

BEXHILL AND BATTLE (E. Sussex)
E.65,850   T.78.99%
*C. Wardle, *C.* — 31,330
Ms S. Prochak, *LD* — 15,023
F. Taylor, *Lab.* — 4,883
J. Prus, *Green* — 594
Mrs M. Smith, *CSP* — 190
C. majority — 16,307
(June 1987, C. maj. 20,519)

BEXLEYHEATH (Greater London)
E.57,684   T.82.17%
*C. Townsend, C.	25,606
J. Browning, Lab.	11,520
Ms W. Chaplin, LD	10,107
R. Cundy, Ind.	170
C. majority	14,086

(June 1987, C. maj. 11,687)

BILLERICAY (Essex)
E.80,388   T.82.34%
*Mrs T. Gorman, C.	37,406
F. Bellard, LD	14,912
Ms A. Miller, Lab.	13,880
C. majority	22,494

(June 1987, C. maj. 18,016)

BIRKENHEAD (Merseyside)
E.62,682   T.72.96%
*F. Field, Lab.	29,098
R. Hughes, C.	11,485
P. Williams, LD	4,417
Ms T. Fox, Green	543
Ms B. Griffiths, NLP	190
Lab. majority	17,613

(June 1987, Lab. maj. 15,372)

BIRMINGHAM EDGBASTON
(W. Midlands)
E.53,041   T.71.29%
*Dame J. Knight, C.	18,529
J. Wilton, Lab.	14,222
I. Robertson-Steel, LD	4,419
P. Simpson, Green	643
C. majority	4,307

(June 1987, C. maj. 8,581)

BIRMINGHAM ERDINGTON
(W. Midlands)
E.52,398   T.70.15%
*R. Corbett, Lab.	18,549
S. Hope, C.	13,814
Dr J. Campbell, LD	4,398
Lab. majority	4,735

(June 1987, Lab. maj. 2,467)

BIRMINGHAM HALL GREEN
(W. Midlands)
E.60,091   T.78.17%
*A. Hargreaves, C.	21,649
Ms J. Slowey, Lab.	17,984
D. McGrath, LD	7,342
C. majority	3,665

(June 1987, C. maj. 7,621)

BIRMINGHAM HODGE HILL
(W. Midlands)
E.57,651   T.70.82%
*T. Davis, Lab.	21,895
Miss E. Gibson, C.	14,827
S. Hagan, LD	3,740
E. Whicker, NF	370
Lab. majority	7,068

(June 1987, Lab. maj. 4,789)

BIRMINGHAM LADYWOOD
(W. Midlands)
E.56,970   T.65.92%
*Ms C. Short, Lab.	24,887
Mrs B. Ashford, C.	9,604
B. Worth, LD	3,068
Lab. majority	15,283

(June 1987, Lab. maj. 10,028)

BIRMINGHAM NORTHFIELD
(W. Midlands)
E.70,533   T.76.08%
R. Burden, Lab.	24,433
*R. King, C.	23,803
D. Cropp, LD	5,431
Lab. majority	630

(June 1987, C. maj. 3,135)

BIRMINGHAM PERRY BARR
(W. Midlands)
E.72,161   T.71.62%
*J. Rooker, Lab.	27,507
G. Green, C.	18,917
T. Philpott, LD	5,261
Lab. majority	8,590

(June 1987, Lab. maj. 6,933)

BIRMINGHAM SELLY OAK
(W. Midlands)
E.72,150   T.76.61%
Ms L. Jones, Lab.	25,430
*A. Beaumont-Dark, C.	23,370
D. Osborne, LD	5,679
P. Slatter, Green	535
C. Barwood, NLP	178
K. Malik, Rev Comm	84
Lab. majority	2,060

(June 1987, C. maj. 2,584)

BIRMINGHAM SMALL HEATH
(W. Midlands)
E.55,213   T.62.95%
R. Godsiff, Lab.	22,675
A. Qayyum Chaudhary, C.	8,686
H. Thomas, LD	2,575
Ms H. Clawley, Green	824
Lab. majority	13,989

(June 1987, Lab. maj. 15,521)

BIRMINGHAM SPARKBROOK
(W. Midlands)
E.51,677   T.66.80%
*Rt. Hon. R. Hattersley, Lab.	22,116
M. Khamisa, C.	8,544
D. Parry, LD	3,028
C. Alldrick, Green	833
Lab. majority	13,572

(June 1987, Lab. maj. 11,859)

BIRMINGHAM YARDLEY
(W. Midlands)
E.54,749   T.77.98%
Ms E. Morris, Lab.	14,884
*A. D. G. Bevan, C.	14,722
J. Hemming, LD	12,899
Miss P. Read, NF	192
Lab. majority	162

(June 1987, C. maj. 2,522)

BISHOP AUCKLAND (Durham)
E.72,572   T.76.52%
*D. Foster, Lab.	27,763
D. Williamson, C.	17,676
W. Wade, LD	10,099
Lab. majority	10,087

(June 1987, Lab. maj. 7,035)

BLABY (Leics)
E.81,790   T.83.39%
A. Robathan, C.	39,498
Ms E. Ranson, Lab.	14,151

Ms M. Lewin, LD	13,780
J. Peacock, BNP	521
Ms S. Lincoln, NLP	260
C. majority	25,347

(June 1987, C. maj. 22,176)

BLACKBURN (Lancs)
E.73,251   T.75.05%
*J. Straw, Lab.	26,633
R. Coates, C.	20,606
D. Mann, LD	6,332
R. Field, Green	878
Mrs M. Carmichael-Grimshaw, LP	334
W. Ayliffe, NLP	195
Lab. majority	6,027

(June 1987, Lab. maj. 5,497)

BLACKPOOL NORTH (Lancs)
E.58,087   T.77.55%
H. Elletson, C.	21,501
E. Kirton, Lab.	18,461
A. Lahiff, LD	4,786
Sir G. Francis, Loony	178
H. Walker, NLP	125
C. majority	3,040

(June 1987, C. maj. 7,321)

BLACKPOOL SOUTH (Lancs)
E.56,801   T.77.35%
N. Hawkins, C.	19,880
G. Marsden, Lab.	18,213
R. Wynne, LD	5,675
D. Henning, NLP	173
C. majority	1,667

(June 1987, C. maj. 6,744)

BLAYDON (Tyne & Wear)
E.66,044   T.77.69%
*J. McWilliam, Lab.	27,028
P. Pescod, C.	13,685
P. Nunn, LD	10,602
Lab. majority	13,343

(June 1987, Lab. maj. 12,488)

BLYTH VALLEY (Northumberland)
E.60,913   T.80.77%
*R. Campbell, Lab.	24,542
P. Tracey, LD	16,498
M. Revell, C.	7,691
S. Tyley, Green	470
Lab. majority	8,044

(June 1987, Lab. maj. 853)

BOLSOVER (Derbys)
E.66,693   T.78.94%
*D. Skinner, Lab.	33,973
T. James, C.	13,313
Ms S. Barber, LD	5,363
Lab. majority	20,660

(June 1987, Lab. maj. 14,120)

BOLTON NORTH EAST (Greater
Manchester)
E.58,659   T.82.26%
*P. Thurnham, C.	21,644
D. Crausby, Lab.	21,459
B. Dunning, LD	4,971
P. Tong, NLP	181
C. majority	185

(June 1987, C. maj. 813)

BOLTON SOUTH EAST (Greater
Manchester)
E.65,600　T.75.53%
*D. Young, *Lab.*	26,906
N. Wood-Dow, *C.*	14,215
D. Lee, *LD*	5,243
W. Hardman, *Ind. Lab.*	2,894
L. Walch, *NLP*	290
Lab. majority	12,691

(June 1987, Lab. maj. 11,381)

BOLTON WEST (Greater
Manchester)
E.71,344　T.83.53%
*Hon. T. Sackville, *C.*	26,452
C. Morris, *Lab.*	25,373
Ms B. Ronson, *LD*	7,529
Ms J. Phillips, *NLP*	240
C. majority	1,079

(June 1987, C. maj. 4,593)

BOOTHFERRY (Humberside)
E.80,747　T.79.73%
*D. Davis, *C.*	35,266
Ms L. Coubrough, *Lab.*	17,731
J. Goss, *LD*	11,388
C. majority	17,535

(June 1987, C. maj. 18,970)

BOOTLE (Merseyside)
E.69,308　T.72.46%
*J. Benton, *Lab.*	37,464
C. Varley, *C.*	8,022
J. Cunningham, *LD*	3,301
Ms M. Hall, *Lib.*	1,174
T. Haynes, *NLP*	264
Lab. majority	29,442

(June 1987, Lab. maj. 24,477)
(May 1990, Lab. maj. 23,517)
(November 1990, Lab. maj. 19,465)

BOSWORTH (Leics)
E.80,234　T.84.13%
*D. Tredinnick, *C.*	36,618
D. Everitt, *Lab.*	17,524
G. Drozdz, *LD*	12,643
B. Fewster, *Green*	716
C. majority	19,094

(June 1987, C. maj. 17,016)

BOURNEMOUTH EAST (Dorset)
E.75,089　T.72.82%
*D. Atkinson, *C.*	30,820
N. Russell, *LD*	15,997
P. Brushett, *Lab.*	7,541
Ms S. Holmes, *NLP*	329
C. majority	14,823

(June 1987, C. maj. 14,683)

BOURNEMOUTH WEST (Dorset)
E.74,738　T.75.72%
*J. Butterfill, *C.*	29,820
Ms J. Dover, *LD*	17,178
B. Grower, *Lab.*	9,423
A. Springham, *NLP*	232
C. majority	12,642

(June 1987, C. maj. 12,651)

BOW AND POPLAR (Greater
London)
E.56,685　T.65.84%
*Mrs M. Gordon, *Lab.*	18,487
P. Hughes, *LD*	10,083

S. Pearce, *C.*	6,876
J. Tyndall, *BNP*	1,107
S. Petter, *Green*	612
W. Hite, *NLP*	158
Lab. majority	8,404

(June 1987, Lab. maj. 4,631)

BRADFORD NORTH (W. Yorks)
E.66,719　T.73.38%
*T. Rooney, *Lab.*	23,420
M. Riaz, *C.*	15,756
D. Ward, *LD*	9,133
W. Beckett, *Loony*	350
M. Nasr, *Islamic*	304
Lab. majority	7,664

(June 1987, Lab. maj. 1,663)
(November 1990, Lab. maj. 9,514)

BRADFORD SOUTH (W. Yorks)
E.69,914　T.75.61%
*G. R. Cryer, *Lab.*	25,185
A. Popat, *C.*	20,283
B. Boulton, *LD*	7,243
M. Naseem, *Islamic*	156
Lab. majority	4,902

(June 1987, Lab. maj. 309)

BRADFORD WEST (W. Yorks)
E.70,016　T.69.90%
*M. Madden, *Lab.*	26,046
Dr A. Ashworth, *C.*	16,544
Dr. A. Griffiths, *LD*	5,150
P. Braham, *Green*	735
D. Pidcock, *Islamic*	471
Lab. majority	9,502

(June 1987, Lab. maj. 7,551)

BRAINTREE (Essex)
E.78,880　T.83.41%
*Rt. Hon. A. Newton, *C.*	34,415
I. Willmore, *Lab.*	16,921
Ms D. Wallis, *LD*	13,603
J. Abbott, *Green*	855
C. majority	17,494

(June 1987, C. maj. 16,857)

BRENT EAST (Greater London)
E.53,319　T.68.82%
*K. Livingstone, *Lab.*	19,387
D. Green, *C.*	13,416
M. Cummins, *LD*	3,249
Ms T. Dean, *Green*	548
Ms A. Murphy, *Comm. GB*	96
Lab. majority	5,971

(June 1987, Lab. maj. 1,653)

BRENT NORTH (Greater London)
E.58,917　T.70.57%
*Rt. Hon. Sir R. Boyson, *C.*	23,445
J. Moher, *Lab.*	13,314
P. Lorber, *LD*	4,149
T. Vipul, *Ind.*	356
T. Davids, *NLP*	318
C. majority	10,131

(June 1987, C. maj. 15,720)

BRENT SOUTH (Greater London)
E.56,034　T.64.10%
*P. Boateng, *Lab.*	20,662
R. Blackman, *C.*	10,957
M. Harskin, *LD*	3,658
D. Johnson, *Green*	479

C. Jani, *NLP*	166
Lab. majority	9,705

(June 1987, Lab. maj. 7,931)

BRENTFORD AND ISLEWORTH
(Greater London)
E.70,880　T.76.22%
N. Deva, *C.*	24,752
Ms A. Keen, *Lab.*	22,666
Ms J. Salmon, *LD*	5,683
J. Bradley, *Green*	927
C. majority	2,086

(June 1987, C. maj. 7,953)

BRENTWOOD AND ONGAR
(Greater London)
E.65,830　T.84.70%
E. Pickles, *C.*	32,145
Ms E. Bottomley, *LD*	17,000
F. Keohane, *Lab.*	6,080
Ms C. Bartley, *Green*	535
C. majority	15,145

(June 1987, C. maj. 18,921)

BRIDGWATER (Somerset)
E.71,567　T.79.51%
*Rt. Hon. T. King, *C.*	26,610
W. Revans, *LD*	16,894
P. James, *Lab.*	12,365
G. Dummett, *Green*	746
A. Body, *Ind.*	183
Ms G. Sanson, *NLP*	112
C. majority	9,716

(June 1987, C. maj. 11,195)

BRIDLINGTON (Humberside)
E.84,829　T.77.93%
*J. Townend, *C.*	33,604
J. Leeman, *LD*	17,246
S. Hatfield, *Lab.*	15,263
C. majority	16,358

(June 1987, C. maj. 17,321)

BRIGG AND CLEETHORPES
(Humberside)
E.82,377　T.77.98%
*M. Brown, *C.*	31,673
I. Cawsey, *Lab.*	22,404
Ms M. Cockbill, *LD*	9,374
N. Jacques, *Green*	790
C. majority	9,269

(June 1987, C. maj. 12,250)

BRIGHTON KEMPTOWN
(E. Sussex)
E.57,646　T.76.14%
*A. Bowden, *C.*	21,129
Ms G. Haynes, *Lab.*	18,073
P. Scott, *LD*	4,461
Ms E. Overall, *NLP*	230
C. majority	3,056

(June 1987, C. maj. 9,260)

BRIGHTON PAVILION (E. Sussex)
E.57,616　T.76.81%
D. Spencer, *C.*	20,630
D. Lepper, *Lab.*	16,955
T. Pearce, *LD*	5,606
I. Brodie, *Green*	963
Ms E. Turner, *NLP*	103
C. majority	3,675

(June 1987, C. maj. 9,142)

BRISTOL EAST (Avon)
E.62,577   T.80.40%

Ms J. Corston, *Lab.*	22,418
*J. Sayeed, *C.*	19,726
J. Kiely, *LD*	7,903
I. Anderson, *NF*	270
Lab. majority	2,692

(June 1987, C. maj. 4,123)

BRISTOL NORTH WEST (Avon)
E.72,726   T.82.35%

*M. Stern, *C.*	25,354
D. Naysmith, *Lab.*	25,309
J. Taylor, *LD*	8,498
H. Long, *SD*	729
C. majority	45

(June 1987, C. maj. 6,952)

BRISTOL SOUTH (Avon)
E.64,309   T.78.04%

*Ms D. Primarolo, *Lab.*	25,164
J. Bercow, *C.*	16,245
P. Crossley, *LD*	7,892
J. Boxall, *Green*	756
N. Phillips, *NLP*	136
Lab. majority	8,919

(June 1987, Lab. maj. 1,404)

BRISTOL WEST (Avon)
E.70,579   T.74.37%

*Rt. Hon. W. Waldegrave, *C.*	22,169
C. Boney, *LD*	16,098
H. Bashforth, *Lab.*	12,992
A. Sawday, *Green*	906
D. Cross, *NLP*	104
B. Brent, *Rev. Comm.*	92
P. Hammond, *SOADDA*	87
T. Hedges, *Anti Fed.*	42
C. majority	6,071

(June 1987, C. maj. 7,703)

BROMSGROVE (H & W)
E.71,111   T.82.49%

K. R. Thomason, *C.*	31,709
Ms C. Mole, *Lab.*	18,007
Ms A. Cassin, *LD*	8,090
J. Churchman, *Green*	856
C. majority	13,702

(June 1987, C. maj. 16,685)

BROXBOURNE (Herts)
E.72,116   T.79.95%

*Mrs M. Roe, *C.*	36,094
M. Hudson, *Lab.*	12,124
Mrs J. Davies, *LD*	9,244
G. Woolhouse, *NLP*	198
C. majority	23,970

(June 1987, C. maj. 22,995)

BROXTOWE (Notts)
E.73,123   T.83.40%

*J. Lester, *C.*	31,096
J. Walker, *Lab.*	21,205
J. Ross, *LD*	8,395
D. Lukehurst, *NLP*	293
C. majority	9,891

(June 1987, C. maj. 16,651)

BUCKINGHAM
E.56,063   T.84.21%

*G. Walden, *C.*	29,496
T. Jones, *LD*	9,705

K. White, *Lab.*	7,662
L. Sheaff, *NLP*	353
C. majority	19,791

(June 1987, C. maj. 18,526)

BURNLEY (Lancs)
E.68,952   T.74.38%

*P. Pike, *Lab.*	27,184
Mrs B. Binge, *C.*	15,693
G. Birtwistle, *LD*	8,414
Lab. majority	11,491

(June 1987, Lab. maj. 7,557)

BURTON (Staffs)
E.75,292   T.82.43%

*I. Lawrence, *C.*	30,845
Ms P. Muddyman, *Lab.*	24,849
R. Renold, *LD*	6,375
C. majority	5,996

(June 1987, C. maj. 9,830)

BURY NORTH (Greater
Manchester)
E.69,529   T.84.77%

*A. Burt, *C.*	29,266
J. Dobbin, *Lab.*	24,502
C. McGrath, *LD*	5,010
M. Sullivan, *NLP*	163
C. majority	4,764

(June 1987, C. maj. 6,929)

BURY SOUTH (Greater Manchester)
E.65,793   T.82.10%

*D. Sumberg, *C.*	24,873
Ms H. Blears, *Lab.*	24,085
A. Cruden, *LD*	4,832
Mrs N. Sullivan, *NLP*	228
C. majority	788

(June 1987, C. maj. 2,679)

BURY ST EDMUNDS (Suffolk)
E.79,967   T.78.38%

R. Spring, *C.*	33,554
T. Sheppard, *Lab.*	14,767
J. Williams, *LD*	13,814
Ms J. Lillis, *NLP*	550
C. majority	18,787

(June 1987, C. maj. 21,458)

CALDER VALLEY (W. Yorks)
E.74,417   T.82.09%

*Sir D. Thompson, *C.*	27,753
D. Chaytor, *Lab.*	22,875
S. Pearson, *LD*	9,842
Ms V. Smith, *Green*	622
C. majority	4,878

(June 1987, C. maj. 6,045)

CAMBRIDGE
E.69,022   T.73.18%

Mrs A. Campbell, *Lab.*	20,039
M. Bishop, *C.*	19,459
D. Howarth, *LD*	10,037
T. Cooper, *Green*	720
D. Brettell-Winnington, *Loony*	175
R. Chalmers, *NLP*	83
Lab. majority	580

(June 1987, C. maj. 5,060)

CAMBRIDGESHIRE NORTH
EAST
E.79,935   T.79.38%

*M. Moss, *C.*	34,288
M. Leeke, *LD*	19,195
R. Harris, *Lab.*	8,746
C. Ash, *Lib.*	998
Mrs M. Chalmers, *NLP*	227
C. majority	15,093

(June 1987, C. maj. 1,428)

CAMBRIDGESHIRE SOUTH EAST
E.78,600   T.80.57%

*J. Paice, *C.*	36,693
R. Wotherspoon, *LD*	12,883
M. Jones, *Lab.*	12,688
J. Marsh, *Green*	836
Ms B. Langridge, *NLP*	231
C. majority	23,810

(June 1987, C. maj. 17,502)

CAMBRIDGESHIRE SOUTH
WEST
E.84,418   T.81.10%

*Sir A. Grant, *C.*	38,902
Ms S. Sutton, *LD*	19,265
K. Price, *Lab.*	9,378
Ms L. Whitebread, *Green*	699
F. Chalmers, *NLP*	225
C. majority	19,637

(June 1987, C. maj. 18,251)

CANNOCK AND BURNTWOOD
(Staffs)
E.72,600   T.84.21%

A. Wright, *Lab.*	28,139
*G. Howarth, *C.*	26,633
P. Treasaden, *LD*	5,899
M. Hartshorne, *Loony*	469
Lab. majority	1,506

(June 1987, C. maj. 2,689)

CANTERBURY (Kent)
E.75,181   T.78.12%

*J. Brazier, *C.*	29,827
M. Vye, *LD*	19,022
M. Whitemore, *Lab.*	8,936
Ms W. Arnall, *Green*	747
Ms S. Curphey, *NLP*	203
C. majority	10,805

(June 1987, C. maj. 14,891)

CARLISLE (Cumbria)
E.55,140   T.79.39%

*E. Martlew, *Lab.*	20,479
C. Condie, *C.*	17,371
R. Aldersey, *LD*	5,740
Ms N. Robinson, *NLP*	190
Lab. majority	3,108

(June 1987, Lab. maj. 916)

CARSHALTON AND
WALLINGTON (Surrey)
E.65,179   T.80.94%

*F. N. Forman, *C.*	26,243
T. Brake, *LD*	16,300
Ms M. Moran, *Lab.*	9,333
R. Steel, *Green*	614
D. Bamford, *Loony G.*	266
C. majority	9,943

(June 1987, C. maj. 14,409)

CASTLE POINT (Essex)
E.66,229   T.80.50%
Dr R. Spink, *C.*   29,629
D. Flack, *Lab.*   12,799
A. Petchey, *LD*   10,208
Ms I. Willis, *Green*   683
C. majority   16,830
(June 1987, C. maj. 19,248)

CHEADLE (Greater Manchester)
E.66,131   T.84.43%
*S. Day, *C.*   32,504
Ms P. Calton, *LD*   16,726
Ms S. Broadhurst, *Lab.*   6,442
Ms P. Whittle, *NLP*   168
C. majority   15,778
(June 1987, C. maj. 10,631)

CHELMSFORD (Essex)
E.83,441   T.84.61%
*S. Burns, *C.*   39,043
H. Nicholson, *LD*   20,783
Dr R. Chad, *Lab.*   10,010
Ms E. Burgess, *Green*   769
C. majority   18,260
(June 1987, C. maj. 7,761)

CHELSEA (Greater London)
E.42,371   T.63.31%
*Rt. Hon. N. Scott, *C.*   17,471
Ms R. Horton, *Lab.*   4,682
Ms S. Broidy, *LD*   4,101
Ms N. Kortvelyessy, *Green*   485
D. Armstrong, *Anti Fed.*   88
C. majority   12,789
(June 1987, C. maj. 13,319)

CHELTENHAM (Glos)
E.79,808   T.80.32%
N. Jones, *LD*   30,351
J. Taylor, *C.*   28,683
Ms P. Tatlow, *Lab.*   4,077
M. Rendall, *AFE*   665
H. Brighouse, *NLP*   169
M. Bruce-Smith, *Ind.*   162
LD majority   1,668
(June 1987, C. maj. 4,896)

CHERTSEY AND WALTON
(Surrey)
E.70,465   T.80.52%
*Rt. Hon. Sir G. Pattie, *C.*   34,163
A. Kremer, *LD*   11,344
Ms I. Hamilton, *Lab.*   10,791
Ms S. Bennell, *NLP*   444
C. majority   22,819
(June 1987, C. maj. 17,469)

CHESHAM AND AMERSHAM
(Bucks)
E.69,895   T.81.93%
Ms C. Gillan, *C.*   36,273
A. Ketteringham, *LD*   14,053
Ms C. Atherton, *Lab.*   5,931
Ms C. Strickland, *Green*   753
T. Griffith-Jones, *NLP*   255
C. majority   22,220
(June 1987, C. maj. 19,440)

CHESTER, CITY OF
E.63,370   T.83.84%
G. Brandreth, *C.*   23,411
D. Robinson, *Lab.*   22,310

G. Smith, *LD*   6,867
T. Barker, *Green*   448
S. Cross, *NLP*   98
C. majority   1,101
(June 1987, C. maj. 4,855)

CHESTERFIELD (Derbys)
E.71,783   T.77.98%
*A. Benn, *Lab.*   26,461
A. Rogers, *LD*   20,047
P. Lewis, *C.*   9,473
Lab. majority   6,414
(June 1987, Lab. maj. 8,577)

CHICHESTER (W. Sussex)
E.82,124   T.77.77%
*R. A. Nelson, *C.*   37,906
P. Gardiner, *LD*   17,019
Ms D. Andrewes, *Lab.*   7,192
E. Paine, *Green*   876
Ms J. Weights, *Lib.*   643
Ms J. Jackson, *NLP*   238
C. majority   20,887
(June 1987, C. maj. 20,177)

CHINGFORD (Greater London)
E.55,401   T.78.41%
G. I. Duncan-Smith, *C.*   25,730
P. Dawe, *Lab.*   10,792
S. Banks, *LD*   5,705
D. Green, *Lib.*   602
J. Baguley, *Green*   575
Revd C. John, *Ind.*   41
C. majority   14,938
(June 1987, C. maj. 17,955)

CHIPPING BARNET (Greater
London)
E.57,153   T.78.57%
*S. Chapman, *C.*   25,589
A. Williams, *Lab.*   11,638
D. Smith, *LD*   7,247
Ms D. Derksen, *NLP*   222
C. Johnson, *Fun.*   213
C. majority   13,951
(June 1987, C. maj. 14,871)

CHISLEHURST (Greater London)
E.53,782   T.78.89%
*R. Sims, *C.*   24,761
I. Wingfield, *Lab.*   9,485
W. Hawthorne, *LD*   6,683
I. Richmond, *Lib.*   849
Dr F. Speed, *Green*   652
C. majority   15,276
(June 1987, C. maj. 14,507)

CHORLEY (Lancs)
E.78,531   T.82.81%
*D. Dover, *C.*   30,715
R. McManus, *Lab.*   26,469
Ms J. Ross-Mills, *LD*   7,452
P. Leadbetter, *NLP*   402
C. majority   4,246
(June 1987, C. maj. 8,057)

CHRISTCHURCH (Dorset)
E.71,438   T.80.70%
*R. Adley, *C.*   36,627
Revd D. Bussey, *LD*   13,612
A. Lloyd, *Lab.*   6,997
J. Barratt, *NLP*   243

A. Wareham, *CRA*   175
C. majority   23,015
(June 1987, C. maj. 22,374)
See also page 242

CIRENCESTER AND
TEWKESBURY (Glos)
E.88,299   T.82.05%
G. Clifton-Brown, *C.*   40,258
E. Weston, *LD*   24,200
T. Page, *Lab.*   7,262
R. Clayton, *NLP*   449
P. Trice-Rolph, *Ind.*   287
C. majority   16,058
(June 1987, C. maj. 12,662)

CITY OF LONDON AND
WESTMINSTER SOUTH
E.55,021   T.63.08%
*Rt. Hon. P. Brooke, *C.*   20,938
C. Smith, *Lab.*   7,569
Ms J. Smithard, *LD*   5,392
G. Herbert, *Green*   458
P. Stockton, *Loony*   147
A. Farrell, *IFM*   107
R. Johnson, *NLP*   101
C. majority   13,369
(June 1987, C. maj. 12,034)

COLCHESTER NORTH (Essex)
E.86,479   T.79.11%
Hon. B. Jenkin, *C.*   35,213
Dr J. Raven, *LD*   18,721
D. Lee, *Lab.*   13,870
M. Tariq Shabbeer, *Green*   372
M. Mears, *NLP*   238
C. majority   16,492
(June 1987, C. maj. 13,623)

COLCHESTER SOUTH AND
MALDON (Essex)
E.86,410   T.79.22%
J. Whittingdale, *C.*   37,548
I. Thorn, *LD*   15,727
C. Pearson, *Lab.*   14,158
M. Patterson, *Green*   1,028
C. majority   21,821
(June 1987, C. maj. 15,483)

COLNE VALLEY (W. Yorks)
E.72,043   T.81.97%
*G. Riddick, *C.*   24,804
J. Harman, *Lab.*   17,579
N. Priestley, *LD*   15,953
R. Stewart, *Green*   443
Mrs M. Staniforth, *Loony*   160
J. Hasty, *Ind.*   73
J. Tattersall, *NLP*   44
C. majority   7,225
(June 1987, C. maj. 1,677)

CONGLETON (Cheshire)
E.70,477   T.84.47%
*Mrs J. A. Winterton, *C.*   29,163
I. Brodie-Browne, *LD*   18,043
M. Finnegan, *Lab.*   11,927
P. Brown, *NLP*   399
C. majority   11,120
(June 1987, C. maj. 7,969)

COPELAND (Cumbria)
E.54,911   *T*.83.54%
*Dr J. Cunningham, *Lab.*	22,328
P. Davies, *C.*	19,889
R. Putnam, *LD*	3,508
J. Sinton, *NLP*	148
Lab. majority	2,439
(June 1987, Lab. maj. 1,894)

CORBY (Northants)
E.68,333   *T*.82.88%
*W. Powell, *C.*	25,203
A. Feather, *Lab.*	24,861
M. Roffe, *LD*	5,792
Ms J. Wood, *Lib.*	784
C. majority	342
(June 1987, C. maj. 1,805)

CORNWALL NORTH
E.76,844   *T*.81.51%
P. Tyler, *LD*	29,696
*Sir G. Neale, *C.*	27,775
F. Jordan, *Lab.*	4,103
P. Andrews, *Lib.*	678
G. Rowe, *Ind.*	276
Mrs H. Treadwell, *NLP*	112
LD majority	1,921
(June 1987, C. maj. 5,682)

CORNWALL SOUTH EAST
E.73,027   *T*.82.14%
*R. Hicks, *C.*	30,565
R. Teverson, *LD*	22,861
Mrs L. Gilroy, *Lab.*	5,536
Miss M. Cook, *Lib.*	644
A. Quick, *Anti Fed.*	227
Miss R. Allen, *NLP*	155
C. majority	7,704
(June 1987, C. maj. 6,607)

COVENTRY NORTH EAST
(W. Midlands)
E.64,787   *T*.73.20%
R. Ainsworth, *Lab.*	24,896
K. Perrin, *C.*	13,220
V. McKee, *LD*	5,306
*J. Hughes, *Ind. Lab.*	4,008
Lab. majority	11,676
(June 1987, Lab. maj. 11,867)

COVENTRY NORTH WEST
(W. Midlands)
E.50,670   *T*.77.63%
*G. Robinson, *Lab.*	20,349
Mrs A. Hill, *C.*	13,917
Ms A. Simpson, *LD*	5,070
Lab. majority	6,432
(June 1987, Lab. maj. 5,663)

COVENTRY SOUTH EAST
(W. Midlands)
E.48,796   *T*.74.87%
J. Cunningham, *Lab.*	11,902
Mrs M. Hyams, *C.*	10,591
*D. Nellist, *Ind. Lab.*	10,551
A. Armstrong, *LD*	3,318
N. Tompkinson, *NF*	173
Lab. majority	1,311
(June 1987, Lab. maj. 6,653)

COVENTRY SOUTH WEST
(W. Midlands)
E.63,474   *T*.80.14%
*J. Butcher, *C.*	23,225
R. Slater, *Lab.*	21,789
G. Sewards, *LD*	4,666
R. Wheway, *Lib.*	989
D. Morris, *NLP*	204
C. majority	1,436
(June 1987, C. maj. 3,210)

CRAWLEY (W. Sussex)
E.78,277   *T*.79.16%
*Hon. A. N. Soames, *C.*	30,204
Ms L. Moffatt, *Lab.*	22,439
G. Seekings, *LD*	8,558
M. Wilson, *Green*	766
C. majority	7,765
(June 1987, C. maj. 12,138)

CREWE AND NANTWICH
(Cheshire)
E.74,993   *T*.81.87%
*Hon. Mrs G. Dunwoody, *Lab.*	28,065
B. Silvester, *C.*	25,370
G. Griffiths, *LD*	7,315
Ms N. Wilkinson, *Green*	651
Lab. majority	2,695
(June 1987, Lab. maj. 1,092)

CROSBY (Merseyside)
E.82,537   *T*.82.45%
*M. Thornton, *C.*	32,267
Ms M. Eagle, *Lab.*	17,461
Ms F. Clucas, *LD*	16,562
J. Marks, *Lib.*	1,052
S. Brady, *Green*	559
N. Paterson, *NLP*	152
C. majority	14,806
(June 1987, C. maj. 6,853)

CROYDON CENTRAL (Greater London)
E.55,798   *T*.71.73%
Sir P. Beresford, *C.*	22,168
G. Davies, *Lab.*	12,518
Ms D. Richardson, *LD*	5,342
C. majority	9,650
(June 1987, C. maj. 12,617)

CROYDON NORTH EAST (Greater London)
E.64,405   *T*.72.01%
D. Congdon, *C.*	23,835
Ms M. Walker, *Lab.*	16,362
J. Fraser, *LD*	6,186
C. majority	7,473
(June 1987, C. maj. 12,519)

CROYDON NORTH WEST (Greater London)
E.57,241   *T*.70.76%
M. Wicks, *Lab.*	19,152
*H. Malins, *C.*	17,626
Ms L. Hawkins, *LD*	3,728
Lab. majority	1,526
(June 1987, C. maj. 3,988)

CROYDON SOUTH (Greater London)
E.64,768   *T*.77.57%
R. Ottaway, *C.*	31,993
P. Billenness, *LD*	11,568

Miss H. Salmon, *Lab.*	6,444
M. Samuel, *Choice*	239
C. majority	20,425
(June 1987, C. maj. 19,063)

DAGENHAM (Greater London)
E.59,645   *T*.70.65%
*B. Gould, *Lab.*	22,027
D. Rossiter, *C.*	15,294
C. Marquand, *LD*	4,824
Lab. majority	6,733
(June 1987, Lab. maj. 2,469)

DARLINGTON (Durham)
E.66,094   *T*.83.60%
A. Milburn, *Lab.*	26,556
*M. Fallon, *C.*	23,758
P. Bergg, *LD*	4,586
Dr D. Clarke, *BNP*	355
Lab. majority	2,798
(June 1987, C. maj. 2,661)

DARTFORD (Kent)
E.72,366   *T*.83.14%
*B. Dunn, *C.*	31,194
Dr H. Stoate, *Lab.*	20,880
Dr P. Bryden, *LD*	7,584
A. Munro, *FDP*	262
Ms A. Holland, *NLP*	247
C. majority	10,314
(June 1987, C. maj. 14,929)

DAVENTRY (Northants)
E.71,824   *T*.82.75%
*T. Boswell, *C.*	34,734
Ms L. Koumi, *Lab.*	14,460
A. Rounthwaite, *LD*	9,820
R. France, *NLP*	422
C. majority	20,274
(June 1987, C. maj. 19,690)

DAVYHULME (Greater Manchester)
E.61,679   *T*.81.82%
*W. Churchill, *C.*	24,216
B. Brotherton, *Lab.*	19,790
Ms J. Pearcey, *LD*	5,797
T. Brotheridge, *NLP*	665
C. majority	4,426
(June 1987, C. maj. 8,199)

DENTON AND REDDISH (Greater Manchester)
E.68,463   *T*.76.77%
*A. Bennett, *Lab.*	29,021
J. Horswell, *C.*	16,937
Dr F. Ridley, *LD*	4,953
M. Powell, *Lib.*	1,296
J. Fuller, *NLP*	354
Lab. majority	12,084
(June 1987, Lab. maj. 8,250)

DERBY NORTH
E.73,176   *T*.80.65%
*G. Knight, *C.*	28,574
R. Laxton, *Lab.*	24,121
R. Charlesworth, *LD*	5,638
E. Wall, *Green*	383
P. Hart, *NF*	245
N. Onley, *NLP*	58
C. majority	4,453
(June 1987, C. maj. 6,280)

DERBY SOUTH
*E.*66,328 *T.*75.52%

*Mrs M. Beckett, *Lab.*	25,917
N. Brown, *C.*	18,981
S. Hartropp, *LD*	5,198
Lab. majority	6,936
(June 1987, Lab. maj. 1,516)	

DERBYSHIRE NORTH EAST
*E.*70,707 *T.*83.61%

*H. Barnes, *Lab.*	28,860
J. Hayes, *C.*	22,590
D. Stone, *LD*	7,675
Lab. majority	6,270
(June 1987, Lab. maj. 3,720)	

DERBYSHIRE SOUTH
*E.*82,342 *T.*85.49%

*Mrs E. Currie, *C.*	34,266
M. Todd, *Lab.*	29,608
Ms D. Brass, *LD*	6,236
T. Mercer, *NLP*	291
C. majority	4,658
(June 1987, C. maj. 10,311)	

DERBYSHIRE WEST
*E.*71,201 *T.*84.99%

*P. McLoughlin, *C.*	32,879
R. Fearn, *LD*	14,110
S. Clamp, *Lab.*	13,528
C. majority	18,769
(June 1987, C. maj. 10,527)	

DEVIZES (Wilts)
*E.*89,745 *T.*81.67%

M. Ancram, *C.*	39,090
Ms J. Mactaggart, *LD*	19,378
Ms R. Berry, *Lab.*	13,060
S. Coles, *Lib.*	962
D. Ripley, *Green*	808
C. majority	19,712
(June 1987, C. maj. 17,830)	

DEVON NORTH
*E.*68,998 *T.*84.36%

N. Harvey, *LD*	27,414
*A. Speller, *C.*	26,620
P. Donner, *Lab.*	3,410
Ms C. Simmons, *Green*	658
G. Treadwell, *NLP*	107
LD majority	794
(June 1987, C. maj. 4,469)	

DEVON WEST AND TORRIDGE
*E.*76,933 *T.*81.46%

*Miss E. Nicholson, *C.*	29,627
D. McBride, *LD*	26,013
D. Brenton, *Lab.*	5,997
Dr F. Williamson, *Green*	898
D. Collins, *NLP*	141
C. majority	3,614
(June 1987, C. maj. 6,468)	

DEWSBURY (W. Yorks)
*E.*72,839 *T.*80.18%

*Mrs W. A. Taylor, *Lab.*	25,596
J. Whitfield, *C.*	24,962
R. Meadowcroft, *LD*	6,570
Lady J. Birdwood, *BNP*	660
N. Denby, *Green*	471
Mrs J. Marsden, *NLP*	146
Lab. majority	634
(June 1987, Lab. maj. 445)	

DONCASTER CENTRAL (S. Yorks)
*E.*68,890 *T.*74.24%

*Rt. Hon. H. Walker, *Lab.*	27,795
W. Glossop, *C.*	17,113
C. Hampson, *LD*	6,057
M. Driver, *WRP*	184
Lab. majority	10,682
(June 1987, Lab. maj. 8,196)	

DONCASTER NORTH (S. Yorks)
*E.*74,732 *T.*73.92%

K. Hughes, *Lab.*	34,135
R. Light, *C.*	14,322
S. Whiting, *LD*	6,787
Lab. majority	19,813
(June 1987, Lab. maj. 19,938)	

DON VALLEY (S. Yorks)
*E.*76,327 *T.*76.25%

*M. Redmond, *Lab.*	32,008
N. Paget-Brown, *C.*	18,474
M. Jevons, *LD*	6,920
S. Platt, *Green*	803
Lab. majority	13,534
(June 1987, Lab. maj. 11,467)	

DORSET NORTH
*E.*76,718 *T.*81.79%

*N. Baker, *C.*	34,234
Ms L. Siegle, *LD*	24,154
J. Fitzmaurice, *Lab.*	4,360
C. majority	10,080
(June 1987, C. maj. 11,907)	

DORSET SOUTH
*E.*75,788 *T.*76.91%

*I. Bruce, *C.*	29,319
B. Ellis, *LD*	15,811
Dr A. Chedzoy, *Lab.*	12,298
Mrs J. Nager, *Ind.*	673
M. Griffiths, *NLP*	191
C. majority	13,508
(June 1987, C. maj. 15,067)	

DORSET WEST
*E.*67,256 *T.*81.18%

*Sir J. Spicer, *C.*	27,766
R. Legg, *LD*	19,756
J. Mann, *Lab.*	7,082
C. majority	8,010
(June 1987, C. maj. 12,364)	

DOVER (Kent)
*E.*68,962 *T.*83.50%

*D. Shaw, *C.*	25,395
G. Prosser, *Lab.*	24,562
M. Sole, *LD*	6,212
A. Sullivan, *Green*	637
P. Sherred, *Ind.*	407
B. Philp, *Ind. C.*	250
C. Percy, *NLP*	127
C. majority	833
(June 1987, C. maj. 6,541)	

DUDLEY EAST (W. Midlands)
*E.*75,355 *T.*74.96%

*Dr J. Gilbert, *Lab.*	29,806
J. Holland, *C.*	20,606
I. Jenkins, *LD*	5,400
G. Cartwright, *NF*	675
Lab. majority	9,200
(June 1987, Lab. maj. 3,473)	

DUDLEY WEST (W. Midlands)
*E.*86,632 *T.*82.08%

*J. Blackburn, *C.*	34,729
K. Lomax, *Lab.*	28,940
G. Lewis, *LD*	7,446
C. majority	5,789
(June 1987, C. maj. 10,244)	

DULWICH (Greater London)
*E.*55,141 *T.*67.91%

Ms T. Jowell, *Lab.*	17,714
*G. Bowden, *C.*	15,658
Dr A. Goldie, *LD*	4,078
Lab. majority	2,056
(June 1987, C. maj. 180)	

DURHAM, CITY OF
*E.*68,165 *T.*74.61%

*G. Steinberg, *Lab.*	27,095
M. Woodroofe, *C.*	12,037
N. Martin, *LD*	10,915
Ms S. J. Banks, *Green*	812
Lab. majority	15,058
(June 1987, Lab. maj. 6,125)	

DURHAM NORTH
*E.*73,694 *T.*76.08%

*G. Radice, *Lab.*	33,567
Ms E. Sibley, *C.*	13,930
P. Appleby, *LD*	8,572
Lab. majority	19,637
(June 1987, Lab. maj. 18,433)	

DURHAM NORTH WEST
*E.*61,139 *T.*75.58%

*Miss H. Armstrong, *Lab.*	26,734
Mrs T. May, *C.*	12,747
T. Farron, *LD*	6,728
Lab. majority	13,987
(June 1987, Lab. maj. 10,162)	

EALING ACTON (Greater London)
*E.*58,687 *T.*76.03%

*Sir G. Young, *C.*	22,579
Ms Y. Johnson, *Lab.*	15,572
L. Rowe, *LD*	5,487
Ms A. Seibe, *Green*	554
T. Pitt-Aikens, *Ind. C.*	432
C. majority	7,007
(June 1987, C. maj. 12,233)	

EALING NORTH (Greater London)
*E.*63,528 *T.*78.84%

*H. Greenway, *C.*	24,898
M. Stears, *Lab.*	18,932
P. Hankinson, *LD*	5,247
D. Earl, *Green*	554
C. Hill, *NF*	277
R. Davis, *CD*	180
C. majority	5,966
(June 1987, C. maj. 15,153)	

EALING SOUTHALL (Greater London)
*E.*65,574 *T.*75.49%

P. Khabra, *Lab.*	23,476
P. Treleaven, *C.*	16,610
*S. Bidwell, *True Lab.*	4,665
Ms P. Nandhra, *LD*	3,790
N. Goodwin, *Green*	964
Lab. majority	6,866
(June 1987, Lab. maj. 7,977)	

EASINGTON (Durham)
E.65,061   T.72.46%

*J. Cummings, *Lab.*	34,269
W. Perry, *C.*	7,879
P. Freitag, *LD*	5,001
Lab. majority	26,390
(June 1987, Lab. maj. 24,639)	

EASTBOURNE (E. Sussex)
E.76,103   T.80.97%

N. Waterson, *C.*	31,792
*D. Bellotti, *LD*	26,311
I. Gibbons, *Lab.*	2,834
D. Aherne, *Green*	391
Ms T. Williamson, *Lib.*	296
C. majority	5,481
(June 1987, C. maj 16,923)	
(October 1990, LD maj. 4,550)	

EASTLEIGH (Hants)
E.91,736   T.82.91%

S. Milligan, *C.*	38,998
D. Chidgey, *LD*	21,296
Ms J. Sugrue, *Lab.*	15,768
C. majority	17,702
(June 1987, C. maj. 13,355)	

ECCLES (Greater Manchester)
E.64,910   T.74.12%

*Miss J. Lestor, *Lab.*	27,357
G. Ling, *C.*	14,131
G. Reid, *LD*	5,835
R. Duriez, *Green*	521
Miss J. Garner, *NLP*	270
Lab. majority	13,226
(June 1987, Lab. maj. 9,699)	

EDDISBURY (Cheshire)
E.75,089   T.82.55%

*A. Goodlad, *C.*	31,625
Ms N. Edwards, *Lab.*	18,928
D. Lyon, *LD*	10,543
A. Basden, *Green*	783
N. Pollard, *NLP*	107
C. majority	12,697
(June 1987, C. maj. 15,835)	

EDMONTON (Greater London)
E.63,052   T.75.66%

*Dr I. Twinn, *C.*	22,076
A. Love, *Lab.*	21,483
E. Jones, *LD*	3,940
Ms E. Solley, *NLP*	207
C. majority	593
(June 1987, C. maj. 7,286)	

ELLESMERE PORT AND NESTON (Cheshire)
E.71,570   T.84.12%

A. Miller, *Lab.*	27,782
A. Pearce, *C.*	25,793
Ms E. Jewkes, *LD*	5,944
Dr M. Money, *Green*	589
Dr A. Rae, *NLP*	105
Lab. majority	1,989
(June 1987, C. maj. 1,853)	

ELMET (W. Yorks)
E.70,558   T.82.53%

*S. Batiste, *C.*	27,677
C. Burgon, *Lab.*	24,416
Mrs A. Beck, *LD*	6,144

C. majority	3,261
(June 1987, C. maj. 5,356)	

ELTHAM (Greater London)
E.51,989   T.78.72%

*P. Bottomley, *C.*	18,813
C. Efford, *Lab.*	17,147
C. McGinty, *LD*	4,804
A. Graham, *Ind. C.*	165
C. majority	1,666
(June 1987, C. maj. 6,460)	

ENFIELD NORTH (Greater London)
E.67,421   T.77.91%

*T. Eggar, *C.*	27,789
M. Upham, *Lab.*	18,359
Ms S. Tustin, *LD*	5,817
J. Markham, *NLP*	565
C. majority	9,430
(June 1987, C. maj. 14,015)	

ENFIELD SOUTHGATE (Greater London)
E.64,311   T.76.28%

*M. Portillo, *C.*	28,422
Ms K. Livney, *Lab.*	12,859
K. Keane, *LD*	7,080
Ms M. Hollands, *Green*	696
C. majority	15,563
(June 1987, C. maj. 18,345)	

EPPING FOREST (Essex)
E.67,585   T.80.55%

*S. Norris, *C.*	32,407
S. Murray, *Lab.*	12,219
Mrs B. Austen, *LD*	9,265
A. O'Brien, *EFRA*	552
C. majority	20,188
(June 1987, C. maj. 21,513)	
(December 1988, C. maj. 4,504)	

EPSOM AND EWELL (Surrey)
E.68,138   T.80.14%

*Rt. Hon. A. Hamilton, *C.*	32,861
M. Emerson, *LD*	12,840
R. Warren, *Lab.*	8,577
G. Hatchard, *NLP*	334
C. majority	20,021
(June 1987, C. maj. 20,761)	

EREWASH (Derbys)
E.75,627   T.83.78%

Mrs A. Knight, *C.*	29,907
S. Stafford, *Lab.*	24,204
P. Tuck, *LD*	8,606
L. Johnson, *BNP*	645
C. majority	5,703
(June 1987, C. maj. 9,754)	

ERITH AND CRAYFORD (Kent)
E.59,213   T.79.66%

*D. Evennett, *C.*	21,926
N. Beard, *Lab.*	19,587
Ms F. Jamieson, *LD*	5,657
C. majority	2,339
(June 1987, C. maj. 6,994)	

ESHER (Surrey)
E.58,840   T.80.80%

*I. Taylor, *C.*	31,115
J. Richling, *LD*	10,744
Ms J. Reay, *Lab.*	5,685

C. majority	20,371
(June 1987, C. maj. 19,068)	

EXETER (Devon)
E.76,723   T.82.21%

*Sir J. Hannam, *C.*	26,543
J. Lloyd, *Lab.*	22,498
G. Oakes, *LD*	12,059
Ms A. Micklem, *Lib.*	1,119
T. Brenan, *Green*	764
M. Turnbull, *NLP*	98
C. majority	4,045
(June 1987, C. maj. 7,656)	

FALMOUTH AND CAMBORNE (Cornwall)
E.70,702   T.81.10%

S. Coe, *C.*	21,150
Ms T. Jones, *LD*	17,883
J. Cosgrove, *Lab.*	16,732
P. Holmes, *Lib.*	730
K. Saunders, *Green*	466
F. Zapp, *Loony*	327
A. Pringle, *NLP*	56
C. majority	3,267
(June 1987, C. maj. 5,039)	

FAREHAM (Hants)
E.81,124   T.81.85%

*P. Lloyd, *C.*	40,482
J. Thompson, *LD*	16,341
Ms E. Weston, *Lab.*	8,766
M. Brimecome, *Green*	818
C. majority	24,141
(June 1987, C. maj. 18,795)	

FAVERSHAM (Kent)
E.81,977   T.79.71%

*R. Moate, *C.*	32,755
Ms H. Brinton, *Lab.*	16,404
R. Truelove, *LD*	15,896
R. Bradshaw, *NLP*	294
C. majority	16,351
(June 1987, C. maj. 13,978)	

FELTHAM AND HESTON (Greater London)
E.81,221   T.73.90%

A. Keen, *Lab.*	27,660
*P. Ground, *C.*	25,665
M. Hoban, *LD*	6,700
Lab. majority	1,995
(June 1987, C. maj. 5,430)	

FINCHLEY (Greater London)
E.52,907   T.77.64%

H. Booth, *C.*	21,039
Ms A. Marjoram, *Lab.*	14,651
Ms H. Leighter, *LD*	4,568
A. Gunstock, *Green*	564
Ms S. Johnson, *Loony*	130
J. Macrae, *NLP*	129
C. majority	6,388
(June 1987, C. maj. 8,913)	

FOLKESTONE AND HYTHE (Kent)
E.65,856   T.79.61%

*Rt. Hon. M. Howard, *C.*	27,437
Mrs L. Cufley, *LD*	18,527
P. Doherty, *Lab.*	6,347
A. Hobbs, *NLP*	123
C. majority	8,910
(June 1987, C. maj. 9,126)	

FULHAM (Greater London)
E.52,740   T.76.16%
*M. Carrington, C.	21,438
N. Moore, Lab.	14,859
P. Crystal, LD	3,339
Ms E. Streeter, Green	443
J. Darby, NLP	91
C. majority	6,579
(June 1987, C. maj. 6,322)

FYLDE (Lancs)
E.63,573   T.78.50%
*M. Jack, C.	30,639
N. Cryer, LD	9,648
Ms C. Hughes, Lab.	9,382
P. Leadbetter, NLP	239
C. majority	20,991
(June 1987, C. maj. 17,772)

GAINSBOROUGH AND
HORNCASTLE (Lincs)
E.72,038   T.80.87%
*E. Leigh, C.	31,444
N. Taylor, LD	15,199
Ms F. Jones, Lab.	11,619
C. majority	16,245
(June 1987, C. maj. 9,723)

GATESHEAD EAST (Tyne & Wear)
E.64,355   T.73.63%
*Miss J. Quin, Lab.	30,100
M. Callanan, C.	11,570
R. Beadle, LD	5,720
Lab. majority	18,530
(June 1987, Lab. maj. 17,228)

GEDLING (Notts)
E.68,953   T.82.34%
*A. J. B. Mitchell, C.	30,191
V. Coaker, Lab.	19,554
D. George, LD	6,863
Ms A. Miszeweka, NLP	168
C. majority	10,637
(June 1987, C. maj. 16,539)

GILLINGHAM (Kent)
E.71,851   T.80.32%
*J. Couchman, C.	30,201
P. Clark, Lab.	13,563
M. Wallbank, LD	13,509
C. MacKinlay, Ind.	248
D. Jolicoeur, NLP	190
C. majority	16,638
(June 1987, C. maj. 12,549)

GLANFORD AND SCUNTHORPE
(Humberside)
E.73,479   T.78.91%
*E. Morley, Lab.	30,623
Dr A. Saywood, C.	22,211
W. Paxton, LD	4,172
C. Nottingham, SD	982
Lab. majority	8,412
(June 1987, Lab. maj. 512)

GLOUCESTER
E.80,578   T.80.24%
*D. French, C.	29,870
K. Stephens, Lab.	23,812
J. Sewell, LD	10,978
C. majority	6,058
(June 1987, C. maj. 12,035)

GLOUCESTERSHIRE WEST
E.80,007   T.83.89%
*P. Marland, C.	29,232
Ms D. Organ, Lab.	24,274
L. Boait, LD	13,366
A. Reeve, Brit. Ind.	172
C. Palmer, Century	75
C. majority	4,958
(June 1987, C. maj. 11,679)

GOSPORT (Hants)
E.69,638   T.76.79%
*P. Viggers, C.	31,094
M. Russell, LD	14,776
Ms M. Angus, Lab.	7,275
P. Ettie, Pensioners	332
C. majority	16,318
(June 1987, C. maj. 13,723)

GRANTHAM (Lincs)
E.83,463   T.79.29%
*Hon. D. Hogg, C.	37,194
S. Taggart, Lab.	17,606
J. Heppell, LD	9,882
J. Hiley, Lib.	1,500
C. majority	19,588
(June 1987, C. maj. 21,303)

GRAVESHAM (Kent)
E.70,740   T.83.48%
*J. Arnold, C.	29,322
G. Green, Lab.	23,829
D. Deedman, LD	5,269
A. Bunstone, Ind.	273
R. Khilkoff-Boulding, ILP	187
B. Buxton, Soc.	174
C. majority	5,493
(June 1987, C. maj. 8,792)

GREAT GRIMSBY (Humberside)
E.67,427   T.75.28%
*A. V. Mitchell, Lab.	25,895
P. Jackson, C.	18,391
Ms P. Frankish, LD	6,475
Lab. majority	7,504
(June 1987, Lab. maj. 8,784)

GREAT YARMOUTH (Norfolk)
E.68,263   T.77.94%
*M. Carttiss, C.	25,505
Ms B. Baughan, Lab.	20,196
M. Scott, LD	7,225
Ms P. Larkin, NLP	284
C. majority	5,309
(June 1987, C. maj. 10,083)

GREENWICH (Greater London)
E.47,789   T.74.63%
W. R. N. Raynsford, Lab.	14,630
*Mrs R. Barnes, SD	13,273
Mrs A. McNair, C.	6,960
R. McCracken, Green	483
R. Mallone, Fellowship	147
M. Hardee, UTCHAP	103
J. Small, NLP	70
Lab. majority	1,357
(June 1987, SDP/All. maj. 2,141)

GUILDFORD (Surrey)
E.77,265   T.78.48%
*Rt. Hon. D. Howell, C.	33,516
Mrs M. Sharp, LD	20,112
H. Mann, Lab.	6,781
A. Law, NLP	234
C. majority	13,404
(June 1987, C. maj. 12,607)

HACKNEY NORTH AND STOKE
NEWINGTON (Greater London)
E.54,655   T.63.53%
*Ms D. Abbott, Lab.	20,083
C. Manson, C.	9,356
K. Fitchett, LD	3,996
Ms H. Hunt, Green	1,111
J. Windsor, NLP	178
Lab. majority	10,727
(June 1987, Lab. maj. 7,678)

HACKNEY SOUTH AND
SHOREDITCH (Greater London)
E.57,935   T.63.82%
*B. Sedgemore, Lab.	19,730
A. Turner, C.	10,714
G. Wintle, LD	5,533
L. Lucas, Green	772
Ms G. Norman, NLP	226
Lab. majority	9,016
(June 1987, Lab. maj. 7,522)

HALESOWEN AND
STOURBRIDGE (W. Midlands)
E.77,644   T.82.28%
P. W. Hawksley, C.	32,312
A. Hankon, Lab.	22,730
V. Sharma, LD	7,941
T. Weller, Green	908
C. majority	9,582
(June 1987, C. maj. 13,808)

HALIFAX (W. Yorks)
E.73,401   T.78.69%
*Ms A. Mahon, Lab.	25,115
T. Martin, C.	24,637
I. Howell, LD	7,364
R. Pearson, Nat.	649
Lab. majority	478
(June 1987, Lab. maj. 1,212)

HALTON (Cheshire)
E.74,906   T.78.34%
*Rt. Hon. G. Oakes, Lab.	35,025
G. Mercer, C.	16,821
D. Reaper, LD	6,104
S. Herley, Loony	398
N. Collins, NLP	338
Lab. majority	18,204
(June 1987, Lab. maj. 14,578)

HAMMERSMITH (Greater London)
E.47,229   T.71.90%
*C. Soley, Lab.	17,329
A. Hennessy, C.	12,575
J. Bates, LD	3,380
R. Crosskey, Green	546
K. Turner, NLP	89
Ms H. Szamuely, Anti Fed.	41
Lab. majority	4,754
(June 1987, Lab. maj. 2,415)

HAMPSHIRE EAST
E.92,139   T.80.35%
*M. Mates, C.	47,541
Ms S. Baring, LD	18,376

J. Phillips, *Lab.* 6,840
I. Foster, *Green* 1,113
S. Hale, *RCC* 165
C. majority 29,165
(June 1987, C. maj. 23,786)

HAMPSHIRE NORTH WEST
E.73,101 T.80.75%
*Sir D. Mitchell, *C.* 34,310
M. Simpson, *LD* 16,462
M. Stockwell, *Lab.* 7,433
Ms D. Ashley, *Green* 825
C. majority 17,848
(June 1987, C. maj. 13,437)

HAMPSTEAD AND HIGHGATE
(Greater London)
E.58,203 T.73.04%
Ms G. Jackson, *Lab.* 19,193
O. Letwin, *C.* 17,753
D. Wrede, *LD* 4,765
S. Games, *Green* 594
Dr R. Prosser, *NLP* 86
Ms A. Hall, *RAVA* 44
C. Scallywag Wilson, *Scallywag* 44
Captain Rizz, *Rizz* 33
Lab. majority 1,440
(June 1987, C. maj. 2,221)

HARBOROUGH (Leics)
E.76,514 T.82.11%
E. Garnier, *C.* 34,280
M. Cox, *LD* 20,737
Ms C. Mackay, *Lab.* 7,483
A. Irwin, *NLP* 328
C. majority 13,543
(June 1987, C. maj. 18,810)

HARLOW (Essex)
E.68,615 T.82.56%
*J. Hayes, *C.* 26,608
W. Rammell, *Lab.* 23,668
Ms L. Spenceley, *LD* 6,375
C. majority 2,940
(June 1987, C. maj. 5,877)

HARROGATE (N. Yorks)
E.76,250 T.77.98%
*R. Banks, *C.* 32,023
T. Hurren, *LD* 19,434
A. Wright, *Lab.* 7,230
A. Warneken, *Green* 780
C. majority 12,589
(June 1987, C. maj. 11,902)

HARROW EAST (Greater London)
E.74,733 T.77.83%
*H. Dykes, *C.* 30,752
A. McNulty, *Lab.* 19,654
Ms V. Chamberlain, *LD* 6,360
P. Burrows, *Lib.* 1,142
Mrs S. Hamza, *NLP* 212
J. Lester, *Anti Fed.* 49
C. majority 11,098
(June 1987, C. maj. 18,273)

HARROW WEST (Greater London)
E.69,616 T.78.69%
*R. G. Hughes, *C.* 30,240
C. Moraes, *Lab.* 12,343
C. Noyce, *LD* 11,050
G. Aitman, *Lib.* 845

Mrs J. Argyle, *NLP* 306
C. majority 17,897
(June 1987, C. maj. 15,444)

HARTLEPOOL (Cleveland)
E.67,968 T.76.07%
P. Mandelson, *Lab.* 26,816
G. Robb, *C.* 18,034
I. Cameron, *LD* 6,860
Lab. majority 8,782
(June 1987, Lab. maj. 7,289)

HARWICH (Essex)
E.80,260 T.77.70%
I. Sproat, *C.* 32,369
Mrs P. Bevan, *LD* 15,210
R. Knight, *Lab.* 14,511
Mrs E. McGrath, *NLP* 279
C. majority 17,159
(June 1987, C. maj. 12,082)

HASTINGS AND RYE (E. Sussex)
E.71,838 T.74.86%
Ms J. Lait, *C.* 25,573
M. Palmer, *LD* 18,939
R. Stevens, *Lab.* 8,458
Ms S. Phillips, *Green* 640
T. Howell, *Loony* 168
C. majority 6,634
(June 1987, C. maj. 7,347)

HAVANT (Hants)
E.74,217 T.79.01%
D. Willetts, *C.* 32,233
S. van Hagen, *LD* 14,649
G. Morris, *Lab.* 10,968
T. Mitchell, *Green* 793
C. majority 17,584
(June 1987, C. maj. 16,510)

HAYES AND HARLINGTON
(Greater London)
E.54,449 T.79.70%
*T. Dicks, *C.* 19,489
J. McDonnell, *Lab.* 19,436
T. Little, *LD* 4,472
C. majority 53
(June 1987, C. maj. 5,965)

HAZEL GROVE (Greater
Manchester)
E.64,302 T.84.94%
*Sir T. Arnold, *C.* 24,479
A. Stunell, *LD* 23,550
C. McAllister, *Lab.* 6,390
M. Penn, *NLP* 204
C. majority 929
(June 1987, C. maj. 1,840)

HEMSWORTH (W. Yorks)
E.55,679 T.75.91%
*D. Enright, *Lab.* 29,942
G. Harrison, *C.* 7,867
Ms V. Megson, *LD* 4,459
Lab. majority 22,075
(June 1987, Lab. maj. 20,700)
(November 1991, Lab. maj. 11,087)

HENDON NORTH (Greater
London)
E.51,513 T.75.08%
*J. Gorst, *C.* 20,569
D. Hill, *Lab.* 13,447
P. Kemp, *LD* 4,136
Ms P. Duncan, *Green* 430
Ms P. Orr, *NLP* 95
C. majority 7,122
(June 1987, C. maj. 10,932)

HENDON SOUTH (Greater London)
E.48,401 T.72.38%
*J. Marshall, *C.* 20,593
Ms L. Lloyd, *Lab.* 8,546
J. Cohen, *LD* 5,609
J. Leslie, *NLP* 289
C. majority 12,047
(June 1987, C. maj. 11,124)

HENLEY (Oxon)
E.64,702 T.79.84%
*Rt. Hon. M. Heseltine, *C.* 30,835
D. Turner, *LD* 12,443
I. Russell-Swinnerton, *Lab.* 7,676
A. Plane, *Anti H.* 431
Ms S. Banerji, *NLP* 274
C. majority 18,392
(June 1987, C. maj. 17,082)

HEREFORD
E.69,676 T.81.29%
*C. Shepherd, *C.* 26,727
G. Jones, *LD* 23,314
Ms J. Kelly, *Lab.* 6,005
C. Mattingly, *Green* 596
C. majority 3,413
(June 1987, C. maj. 1,413)

HERTFORD AND STORTFORD
E.76,654 T.81.05%
*B. Wells, *C.* 35,716
C. White, *LD* 15,506
A. Bovaird, *Lab.* 10,125
J. Goth, *Green* 780
C. majority 20,210
(June 1987, C. maj. 17,140)

HERTFORDSHIRE NORTH
E.80,066 T.84.44%
O. Heald, *C.* 33,679
R. Liddle, *LD* 17,148
Ms S. Bissett Johnson, *Lab.* 16,449
B. Irving, *NLP* 339
C. majority 16,531
(June 1987, C. maj. 11,442)

HERTFORDSHIRE SOUTH WEST
E.70,836 T.83.76%
*R. Page, *C.* 33,825
Ms A. Shaw, *LD* 13,718
A. Gale, *Lab.* 11,512
C. Adamson, *NLP* 281
C. majority 20,107
(June 1987, C. maj. 15,784)

HERTFORDSHIRE WEST
E.78,573 T.82.36%
*R. Jones, *C.* 33,340
Mrs E. McNally, *Lab.* 19,400
M. Trevett, *LD* 10,464
J. Hannaway, *Green* 674

J. McAuley, *NF* — 665
G. Harvey, *NLP* — 175
C. majority — 13,940
(June 1987, C. maj. 14,924)

HERTSMERE (Herts)
*E.*69,951   *T.*80.89%
W. J. Clappison, *C.* — 32,133
Dr D. Souter, *Lab.* — 13,398
Mrs Z. Gifford, *LD* — 10,681
Ms D. Harding, *NLP* — 373
C. majority — 18,735
(June 1987, C. maj. 18,106)

HEXHAM (Northumberland)
*E.*57,812   *T.*82.37%
P. Atkinson, *C.* — 24,967
I. Swithenbank, *Lab.* — 11,529
J. Wallace, *LD* — 10,344
J. Hartshorne, *Green* — 781
C. majority — 13,438
(June 1987, C. maj. 8,066)

HEYWOOD AND MIDDLETON
(Greater Manchester)
*E.*57,176   *T.*74.92%
*J. Callaghan, *Lab.* — 22,380
E. Ollerenshaw, *C.* — 14,306
Dr M. Taylor, *LD* — 5,262
P. Burke, *Lib.* — 757
Ms A. Scott, *NLP* — 134
Lab. majority — 8,074
(June 1987, Lab. maj. 6,848)

HIGH PEAK (Derbys)
*E.*70,793   *T.*84.62%
C. Hendry, *C.* — 27,538
T. Levitt, *Lab.* — 22,719
S. Molloy, *LD* — 8,861
R. Floyd, *Green* — 794
C. majority — 4,819
(June 1987, C. maj. 9,516)

HOLBORN AND ST PANCRAS
(Greater London)
*E.*64,480   *T.*62.99%
*F. Dobson, *Lab.* — 22,243
A. McHallam, *C.* — 11,419
Ms J. Horne-Roberts, *LD* — 5,476
P. Wolf-Light, *Green* — 959
M. Hersey, *NLP* — 212
R. Headicar, *Soc.* — 175
N. Lewis, *WAR* — 133
Lab. majority — 10,824
(June 1987, Lab. maj. 8,853)

HOLLAND WITH BOSTON (Lincs)
*E.*67,900   *T.*77.93%
*Sir R. Body, *C.* — 29,159
J. Hough, *Lab.* — 15,328
N. Ley, *LD* — 8,434
C. majority — 13,831
(June 1987, C. maj. 17,595)

HONITON (Devon)
*E.*79,223   *T.*80.74%
*Sir P. Emery, *C.* — 33,533
Ms J. Sharratt, *LD* — 17,022
R. Davison, *Lab.* — 8,142
D. Owen, *Ind. C.* — 2,175
S. Hughes, *Loony G.* — 1,442
G. Halliwell, *Lib.* — 1,005

A. Tootill, *Green* — 650
C. majority — 16,511
(June 1987, C. maj. 16,562)

HORNCHURCH (Greater London)
*E.*60,522   *T.*79.78%
*R. Squire, *C.* — 25,817
Ms L. Cooper, *Lab.* — 16,652
B. Oddy, *LD* — 5,366
T. Matthews, *SD* — 453
C. majority — 9,165
(June 1987, C. maj. 10,694)

HORNSEY AND WOOD GREEN
(Greater London)
*E.*73,491   *T.*75.85%
Mrs B. Roche, *Lab.* — 27,020
A. Boff, *C.* — 21,843
P. Dunphy, *LD* — 5,547
Ms L. Crosbie, *Green* — 1,051
P. Davies, *NLP* — 197
W. Massey, *Rev. Comm.* — 89
Lab. majority — 5,177
(June 1987, C. maj. 1,779)

HORSHAM (W. Sussex)
*E.*84,158   *T.*81.27%
*Sir P. Hordern, *C.* — 42,210
Ms J. Stainton, *LD* — 17,138
S. Uwins, *Lab.* — 6,745
Ms J. Elliott, *Lib.* — 1,281
T. King, *Green* — 692
J. Duggan, *PPP* — 332
C. majority — 25,072
(June 1987, C. maj. 23,907)

HOUGHTON AND WASHINGTON
(Tyne & Wear)
*E.*79,325   *T.*70.60%
*R. Boyes, *Lab.* — 34,733
A. Tyrie, *C.* — 13,925
O. Dumpleton, *LD* — 7,346
Lab. majority — 20,808
(June 1987, Lab. maj. 20,193)

HOVE (E. Sussex)
*E.*67,450   *T.*74.26%
*Hon. T. Sainsbury, *C.* — 24,525
D. Turner, *Lab.* — 12,257
A. Jones, *LD* — 9,709
N. Furness, *Hove C.* — 2,658
G. Sinclair, *Green* — 814
J. Morilly, *NLP* — 126
C. majority — 12,268
(June 1987, C. maj. 18,218)

HUDDERSFIELD (W. Yorks)
*E.*67,604   *T.*72.32%
*B. Sheerman, *Lab.* — 23,832
Ms J. Kenyon, *C.* — 16,574
Ms A. Denham, *LD* — 7,777
N. Harvey, *Green* — 576
M. Cran, *NLP* — 135
Lab. majority — 7,258
(June 1987, Lab. maj. 7,278)

HULL EAST
*E.*69,036   *T.*69.29%
*J. Prescott, *Lab.* — 30,092
J. Fareham, *C.* — 11,373
J. Wastling, *LD* — 6,050
C. Kinzell, *NLP* — 323

Lab. majority — 18,719
(June 1987, Lab. maj. 14,689)

HULL NORTH
*E.*71,363   *T.*66.71%
*J. K. McNamara, *Lab.* — 26,619
B. Coleman, *C.* — 11,235
A. Meadowcroft, *LD* — 9,504
G. Richardson, *NLP* — 253
Lab. majority — 15,384
(June 1987, Lab. maj. 12,169)

HULL WEST
*E.*56,111   *T.*65.70%
*S. Randall, *Lab.* — 21,139
D. Stewart, *C.* — 10,554
R. Tress, *LD* — 4,867
B. Franklin, *NLP* — 308
Lab. majority — 10,585
(June 1987, Lab. maj. 8,130)

HUNTINGDON (Cambs)
*E.*92,913   *T.*79.16%
*Rt. Hon. J. Major, *C.* — 48,662
H. Seckleman, *Lab.* — 12,432
A. Duff, *LD* — 9,386
P. Wiggin, *Lib.* — 1,045
Miss D. Birkhead, *Green* — 846
Lord D. Sutch, *Loony* — 728
M. Flanagan, *C. Thatch.* — 231
Lord Buckethead, *Gremloids* — 107
C. Cockell, *FTM* — 91
D. Shepheard, *NLP* — 26
C. majority — 36,230
(June 1987, C. maj. 27,044)

HYNDBURN (Lancs)
*E.*58,539   *T.*83.97%
G. Pope, *Lab.* — 23,042
*K. Hargreaves, *C.* — 21,082
Ms Y. Stars, *LD* — 4,886
S. Whittle, *NLP* — 150
Lab. majority — 1,960
(June 1987, C. maj. 2,220)

ILFORD NORTH (Greater London)
*E.*58,670   *T.*77.98%
*V. Bendall, *C.* — 24,698
Ms L. Hilton, *Lab.* — 15,627
R. Scott, *LD* — 5,430
C. majority — 9,071
(June 1987, C. maj. 12,090)

ILFORD SOUTH (Greater London)
*E.*55,741   *T.*76.83%
M. Gapes, *Lab.* — 19,418
*N. Thorne, *C.* — 19,016
G. Hogarth, *LD* — 4,126
N. Bramachari, *NLP* — 269
Lab. majority — 402
(June 1987, C. maj. 4,572)

IPSWICH (Suffolk)
*E.*67,261   *T.*80.32%
J. Cann, *Lab.* — 23,680
*M. Irvine, *C.* — 23,415
J. White, *LD* — 6,159
Ms J. Scott, *Green* — 591
E. Kaplan, *NLP* — 181
Lab. majority — 265
(June 1987, C. maj. 874)

ISLE OF WIGHT
E.99,838   T.79.76%
*B. Field, C.	38,163
Dr P. Brand, LD	36,336
K. Pearson, Lab.	4,784
C. Daly, NLP	350
C. majority	1,827

(June 1987, C. maj. 6,442)

ISLINGTON NORTH (Greater London)
E.56,270   T.67.26%
*J. Corbyn, Lab.	21,742
Mrs L. Champagnie, C.	8,958
Ms S. Ludford, LD	5,732
C. Ashby, Green	1,420
Lab. majority	12,784

(June 1987, Lab. maj. 9,657)

ISLINGTON SOUTH AND
FINSBURY (Greater London)
E.55,541   T.72.52%
*C. Smith, Lab.	20,586
M. Jones, C.	9,934
C. Pryce, LD	9,387
Ms R. Hersey, JBR	149
Ms M. Avino, Loony	142
M. Spinks, NLP	83
Lab. majority	10,652

(June 1987, Lab. maj. 805)

JARROW (Tyne & Wear)
E.62,611   T.74.44%
*D. Dixon, Lab.	28,956
T. Ward, C.	11,049
K. Orrell, LD	6,608
Lab. majority	17,907

(June 1987, Lab. maj. 18,795)

KEIGHLEY (W. Yorks)
E.66,358   T.82.58%
*G. Waller, C.	25,983
T. Flanagan, Lab.	22,387
I. Simpson, LD	5,793
M. Crowson, Green	642
C. majority	3,596

(June 1987, C. maj. 5,606)

KENSINGTON (Greater London)
E.42,129   T.73.29%
*J. D. Fishburn, C.	15,540
Ms A. Holmes, Lab.	11,992
C. Shirley, LD	2,770
Ms A. Burlingham-Johnson, Green	415
A. Hardy, NLP	90
Ms A. Bulloch, Anti Fed.	71
C. majority	3,548

(June 1987, C. maj. 4,447)
(July 1988, C. maj. 815)

KENT MID
E.74,459   T.79.66%
*A. Rowe, C.	33,633
T. Robson, Lab.	13,984
G. Colley, LD	11,476
G. Valente, NLP	224
C. majority	19,649

(June 1987, C. maj. 14,768)

KETTERING (Northants)
E.67,853   T.82.58%
*R. Freeman, C.	29,115
P. Hope, Lab.	17,961
R. Denton-White, LD	8,962
C. majority	11,154

(June 1987, C. maj. 11,327)

KINGSTON UPON THAMES
(Greater London)
E.51,077   T.78.41%
*Rt. Hon. N. Lamont, C.	20,675
D. Osbourne, LD	10,522
R. Markless, Lab.	7,748
A. Amer, Lib.	771
D. Beaupre, Loony	212
G. Woollcoombe, NLP	81
A. Scholefield, Anti Fed.	42
C. majority	10,153

(June 1987, C. maj. 11,186)

KINGSWOOD (Avon)
E.71,727   T.83.85%
R. Berry, Lab.	26,774
*R. Hayward, C.	24,404
Ms J. Pinkerton, LD	8,960
Lab. majority	2,370

(June 1987, C. maj. 4,393)

KNOWSLEY NORTH (Merseyside)
E.48,761   T.72.81%
*G. Howarth, Lab.	27,517
S. Mabey, C.	5,114
J. Murray, LD	1,515
Mrs K. Lappin, Lib.	1,180
V. Ruben, NLP	179
Lab. majority	22,403

(June 1987, Lab. maj. 21,098)

KNOWSLEY SOUTH (Merseyside)
E.62,260   T.74.77%
*E. O'Hara, Lab.	31,933
L. Byrom, C.	9,922
I. Smith, LD	4,480
M. Raiano, NLP	217
Lab. majority	22,011

(June 1987, Lab. maj. 20,846)
(September 1990, Lab. maj. 11,367)

LANCASHIRE WEST
E.77,462   T.82.55%
C. Pickthall, Lab.	30,128
*K. Hind, C.	28,051
P. Reilly, LD	4,884
P. Pawley, Green	546
B. Morris, NLP	336
Lab. majority	2,077

(June 1987, C. maj. 1,353)

LANCASTER (Lancs)
E.58,714   T.78.78%
*Dame E. Kellett-Bowman, C.	21,084
Ms R. Henig, Lab.	18,131
J. Humberstone, LD	6,524
Ms G. Dowding, Green	433
R. Barcis, NLP	83
C. majority	2,953

(June 1987, C. maj. 6,453)

LANGBAURGH (Cleveland)
E.79,566   T.83.05%
M. Bates, C.	30,018
*A. Kumar, Lab.	28,454

P. Allen, LD	7,615
C. majority	1,564

(June 1987, C. maj. 2,088)
(November 1991, C. maj. 1,975)

LEEDS CENTRAL (W. Yorks)
E.62,058   T.61.29%
*D. Fatchett, Lab.	23,673
Mrs T. Holdroyd, C.	8,653
D. Pratt, LD	5,713
Lab. majority	15,020

(June 1987, Lab. maj. 11,505)

LEEDS EAST (W. Yorks)
E.61,699   T.70.02%
G. Mudie, Lab.	24,929
N. Carmichael, C.	12,232
P. Wrigley, LD	6,040
Lab. majority	12,697

(June 1987, Lab. maj. 9,526)

LEEDS NORTH EAST (W. Yorks)
E.64,372   T.76.89%
*T. Kirkhope, C.	22,462
F. Hamilton, Lab.	18,218
C. Walmsley, LD	8,274
J. Noble, Green	546
C. majority	4,244

(June 1987, C. maj. 8,419)

LEEDS NORTH WEST (W. Yorks)
E.69,406   T.72.84%
*Dr K. Hampson, C.	21,750
Ms B. Pearce, LD	14,079
Ms S. Egan, Lab.	13,782
D. Webb, Green	519
N. Nowosielski, Lib.	427
C. majority	7,671

(June 1987, C. maj. 5,201)

LEEDS SOUTH AND MORLEY
(W. Yorks)
E.63,107   T.72.58%
W. J. Gunnell, Lab.	23,896
R. Booth, C.	16,524
Ms J. Walmsley, LD	5,062
R. Thurston, NLP	327
Lab. majority	7,372

(June 1987, Lab. maj. 6,711)

LEEDS WEST (W. Yorks)
E.67,084   T.71.14%
*J. Battle, Lab.	26,310
P. Bartlett, C.	12,482
G. Howard, LD	4,252
M. Meadowcroft, Lib.	3,980
Ms A. Mander, Green	569
R. Tenny, NF	132
Lab. majority	13,828

(June 1987, Lab. maj. 4,692)

LEICESTER EAST
E.63,434   T.78.40%
*N. K. A. S. Vaz, Lab.	28,123
J. Stevens, C.	16,807
Ms S. Mitchell, LD	4,043
M. Frankland, Green	453
D. Taylor, Homeland	308
Lab. majority	11,316

(June 1987, Lab. maj. 1,924)

LEICESTER SOUTH
E.71,120   T.75.09%

*J. Marshall, *Lab.*	27,934
Dr M. Dutt, *C.*	18,494
Ms A. Crumbie, *LD*	6,271
J. McWhirter, *Green*	554
Ms P. Saunders, *NLP*	154
Lab. majority	9,440
(June 1987, Lab. maj. 1,877)	

LEICESTER WEST
E.65,510   T.73.66%

*Hon. G. Janner, *Lab.*	22,574
J. Guthrie, *C.*	18,596
G. Walker, *LD*	6,402
Ms C. Wintram, *Green*	517
Ms J. Rosta, *NLP*	171
Lab. majority	3,978
(June 1987, Lab. maj. 1,201)	

LEICESTERSHIRE NORTH WEST
E.72,414   T.86.11%

*D. Ashby, *C.*	28,379
D. Taylor, *Lab.*	27,400
J. Beckett, *LD*	6,353
J. Fawcett, *NLP*	229
C. majority	979
(June 1987, C. maj. 7,828)	

LEIGH (Greater Manchester)
E.70,064   T.75.02%

*L. Cunliffe, *Lab.*	32,225
J. Egerton, *C.*	13,398
R. Bleakley, *LD*	6,621
A. Tayler, *NLP*	320
Lab. majority	18,827
(June 1987, Lab. maj. 16,606)	

LEOMINSTER (H & W)
E.70,873   T.81.69%

*P. Temple-Morris, *C.*	32,783
D. Short, *LD*	16,103
C. Chappell, *Lab.*	6,874
Ms F. Norman, *Green*	1,503
Capt. E. Carlisle, *Anti Fed.*	640
C. majority	16,680
(June 1987, C. maj. 14,075)	

LEWES (E. Sussex)
E.73,918   T.81.81%

*J. R. Rathbone, *C.*	33,042
N. Baker, *LD*	20,867
Ms A. Chapman, *Lab.*	5,758
A. Beaumont, *Green*	719
N. Clinch, *NLP*	87
C. majority	12,175
(June 1987, C. maj. 13,620)	

LEWISHAM DEPTFORD (Greater London)
E.57,014   T.65.05%

*Mrs J. Ruddock, *Lab.*	22,574
Miss T. O'Neill, *C.*	10,336
Ms J. Brightwell, *LD*	4,181
Lab. majority	12,238
(June 1987, Lab. maj. 6,771)	

LEWISHAM EAST (Greater London)
E.57,674   T.74.78%

Mrs B. Prentice, *Lab.*	19,576
*Hon. C. Moynihan, *C.*	18,481
J. Hawkins, *LD*	4,877
Ms G. Mansour, *NLP*	196
Lab. majority	1,095
(June 1987, C. maj. 4,814)	

LEWISHAM WEST (Greater London)
E.59,317   T.73.11%

J. Dowd, *Lab.*	20,378
*J. Maples, *C.*	18,569
Ms E. Neale, *LD*	4,295
P. Coulam, *Anti Fed.*	125
Lab. majority	1,809
(June 1987, C. maj. 3,772)	

LEYTON (Greater London)
E.57,271   T.67.38%

*H. Cohen, *Lab.*	20,334
Miss C. Smith, *C.*	8,850
J. Fryer, *LD*	8,180
L. de Pinna, *Lib.*	561
K. Pervez, *Green*	412
R. Archer, *NLP*	256
Lab. majority	11,484
(June 1987, Lab. maj. 4,641)	

LINCOLN
E.78,905   T.79.15%

*K. Carlisle, *C.*	28,792
N. Butler, *Lab.*	26,743
D. Harding-Price, *LD*	6,316
Ms S. Wiggin, *Lib.*	603
C. majority	2,049
(June 1987, C. maj. 7,483)	

LINDSEY EAST (Lincs)
E.80,026   T.78.07%

*Sir P. Tapsell, *C.*	31,916
J. Dodsworth, *LD*	20,070
D. Shepherd, *Lab.*	9,477
Ms R. Robinson, *Green*	1,018
C. majority	11,846
(June 1987, C. maj. 8,616)	

LITTLEBOROUGH AND SADDLEWORTH (Greater Manchester)
E.65,576   T.81.61%

*G. Dickens, *C.*	23,682
C. Davies, *LD*	19,188
A. Brett, *Lab.*	10,649
C. majority	4,494
(June 1987, C. maj. 6,202)	

LIVERPOOL BROADGREEN
E.60,080   T.69.59%

Mrs J. Kennedy, *Lab.*	18,062
Ms R. Cooper, *LD*	11,035
*T. Fields, *Soc. Lab.*	5,952
Mrs H. Roche, *C.*	5,405
S. Radford, *Lib.*	1,211
Mrs A. Brennan, *NLP*	149
Lab. majority	7,027
(June 1987, Lab. maj. 6,047)	

LIVERPOOL GARSTON
E.57,538   T.70.60%

*E. Loyden, *Lab.*	23,212
J. Backhouse, *C.*	10,933
W. Roberts, *LD*	5,398
A. Conrad, *Lib.*	894
P. Chandler, *NLP*	187
Lab. majority	12,279
(June 1987, Lab. maj. 13,777)	

LIVERPOOL MOSSLEY HILL
E.60,409   T.68.52%

*D. Alton, *LD*	19,809
N. Bann, *Lab.*	17,203
S. Syder, *C.*	4,269
B. Rigby, *NLP*	114
LD majority	2,606
(June 1987, L./All. maj. 2,226)	

LIVERPOOL RIVERSIDE
E.49,595   T.54.57%

*R. Parry, *Lab.*	20,550
Dr A. Zsigmond, *C.*	3,113
M. Akbar Ali, *LD*	2,498
L. Brown, *Green*	738
J. Collins, *NLP*	169
Lab. majority	17,437
(June 1987, Lab. maj. 20,689)	

LIVERPOOL WALTON
E.70,102   T.67.40%

*P. Kilfoyle, *Lab.*	34,214
B. Greenwood, *C.*	5,915
J. Lang, *LD*	5,672
T. Newall, *Lib.*	963
D. Carson, *Prot. Ref.*	393
Ms D. Raiano, *NLP*	98
Lab. majority	28,299
(June 1987, Lab. maj. 23,253)	
(July 1991, Lab. maj. 6,860)	

LIVERPOOL WEST DERBY
E.56,718   T.69.84%

*R. Wareing, *Lab.*	27,014
S. Fitzsimmons, *C.*	6,589
Ms G. Bundred, *LD*	4,838
D. Curtis, *Lib.*	1,021
C. Higgins, *NLP*	154
Lab. majority	20,425
(June 1987, Lab. maj. 20,496)	

LOUGHBOROUGH (Leics)
E.75,450   T.78.52%

*S. Dorrell, *C.*	30,064
A. Reed, *Lab.*	19,181
A. Stott, *LD*	8,953
I. Sinclair, *Green*	817
P. Reynolds, *NLP*	233
C. majority	10,883
(June 1987, C. maj. 17,648)	

LUDLOW (Salop)
E.68,935   T.80.87%

*C. Gill, *C.*	28,719
D. Phillips, *LD*	14,567
Ms B. Mason, *Lab.*	11,709
N. Appleton-Fox, *Green*	758
C. majority	14,152
(June 1987, C. maj. 11,699)	

LUTON NORTH (Beds)
E.76,857   T.81.91%

*J. Carlisle, *C.*	33,777
A. McWalter, *Lab.*	20,683
Ms J. Jackson, *LD*	7,570
R. Jones, *Green*	633
K. Buscombe, *NLP*	292
C. majority	13,094
(June 1987, C. maj. 15,573)	

LUTON SOUTH (Beds)
E.73,016   T.79.10%
*G. Bright, C.	25,900
W. McKenzie, Lab.	25,101
D. Rogers, LD	6,020
Ms L. Bliss, Green	550
D. Cooke, NLP	191
C. majority	799

(June 1987, C. maj. 5,115)

MACCLESFIELD (Cheshire)
E.76,548   T.82.29%
*N. Winterton, C.	36,447
Mrs M. Longworth, Lab.	13,680
Dr P. Beatty, LD	12,600
Mrs C. Penn, NLP	268
C. majority	22,767

(June 1987, C. maj. 19,092)

MAIDSTONE (Kent)
E.72,834   T.80.08%
*Miss A. Widdecombe, C.	31,611
Ms P. Yates, LD	15,325
Ms A. Logan, Lab.	10,517
Ms P. Kemp, Green	707
F. Ingram, NLP	172
C. majority	16,286

(June 1987, C. maj. 10,364)

MAKERFIELD (Greater Manchester)
E.71,425   T.76.09%
*I. McCartney, Lab.	32,832
Mrs D. Dickson, C.	14,714
S. Jeffers, LD	5,097
Ms S. Cairns, Lib.	1,309
C. Davies, NLP	397
Lab. majority	18,118

(June 1987, Lab. maj. 15,558)

MANCHESTER BLACKLEY
E.55,234   T.69.31%
*K. Eastham, Lab.	23,031
W. Hobhouse, C.	10,642
S. Wheale, LD	4,324
M. Kennedy, NLP	288
Lab. majority	12,389

(June 1987, Lab. maj. 10,122)

MANCHESTER CENTRAL
E.56,446   T.56.90%
*R. Litherland, Lab.	23,336
P. Davies, C.	5,299
M. Clayton, LD	3,151
A. Buchanan, CL	167
Ms V. Mitchell, NLP	167
Lab. majority	18,037

(June 1987, Lab. maj. 19,867)

MANCHESTER GORTON
E.62,410   T.60.84%
*Rt. Hon. G. Kaufman, Lab.	23,671
J. Bullock, C.	7,392
P. Harris, LD	5,327
T. Henderson, Lib.	767
M. Daw, Green	595
Ms P. Lawrence, Rev. Comm.	108
P. Mitchell, NLP	84
Ms C. Smith, Int. Comm.	30
Lab. majority	16,279

(June 1987, Lab. maj. 14,065)

MANCHESTER WITHINGTON
E.63,838   T.71.27%
*K. Bradley, Lab.	23,962
E. Farthing, C.	14,227
G. Hennell, LD	6,457
B. Candeland, Green	725
C. Menhinick, NLP	128
Lab. majority	9,735

(June 1987, Lab. maj. 3,391)

MANCHESTER WYTHENSHAWE
E.53,548   T.69.68%
*Rt. Hon. A. Morris, Lab.	22,591
K. McKenna, C.	10,595
S. Fenn, LD	3,633
G. Otten, Green	362
Ms E. Martin, NLP	133
Lab. majority	11,996

(June 1987, Lab. maj. 11,855)

MANSFIELD (Notts)
E.66,964   T.82.23%
*J. A. Meale, Lab.	29,932
G. Mond, C.	18,208
S. Thompstone, LD	6,925
Lab. majority	11,724

(June 1987, Lab. maj. 56)

MEDWAY (Kent)
E.61,736   T.80.22%
*Dame P. Fenner, C.	25,924
R. Marshall-Andrews, Lab.	17,138
C. Trice, LD	4,751
M. Austin, Lib.	1,480
P. Kember, NLP	234
C. majority	8,786

(June 1987, C. maj. 9,929)

MERIDEN (W. Midlands)
E.76,994   T.78.85%
*I. Mills, C.	33,462
N. Stephens, Lab.	18,763
Ms J. Morris, LD	8,489
C. majority	14,699

(June 1987, C. maj. 16,820)

MIDDLESBROUGH (Cleveland)
E.58,844   T.69.85%
*S. Bell, Lab.	26,343
P. Rayner, C.	10,559
Ms R. Jordan, LD	4,201
Lab. majority	15,784

(June 1987, Lab. maj. 14,958)

MILTON KEYNES NORTH EAST (Bucks)
E.62,748   T.80.95%
P. Butler, C.	26,212
Ms M. Cosin, Lab.	12,036
P. Gaskell, LD	11,693
A. Francis, Green	529
Mrs M. Kavanagh-Dowsett, Ind. C.	249
M. Simson, NLP	79
C. majority	14,176

(New constituency)

MILTON KEYNES SOUTH WEST (Bucks)
E.66,422   T.77%
B. Legg, C.	23,840
K. Wilson, Lab.	19,153

C. Pym, LD	7,429
Dr C. Field, Green	525
H. Kelly, NLP	202
C. majority	4,687

(New constituency)

MITCHAM AND MORDEN (Greater London)
E.63,723   T.80.32%
*Rt. Hon. A. Rumbold, C.	23,789
Ms S. McDonagh, Lab.	22,055
J. Field, LD	4,687
T. Walsh, Green	655
C. majority	1,734

(June 1987, C. maj. 6,183)

MOLE VALLEY (Surrey)
E.66,949   T.81.97%
*Rt. Hon. K. Baker, C.	32,549
M. Watson, LD	16,599
Dr T. Walsh, Lab.	5,291
Ms J. Thomas, NLP	442
C. majority	15,950

(June 1987, C. maj. 16,076)

MORECAMBE AND LUNESDALE (Lancs)
E.56,426   T.78.35%
*Hon. M. Lennox-Boyd, C.	22,507
Ms J. Yates, Lab.	10,998
A. Saville, LD	9,584
M. Turner, MBI	916
R. Marriott, NLP	205
C. majority	11,509

(June 1987, C. maj. 11,785)

NEWARK (Notts)
E.68,801   T.82.17%
*R. Alexander, C.	28,494
D. Barton, Lab.	20,265
P. Harris, LD	7,342
Ms P. Wood, Green	435
C. majority	8,229

(June 1987, C. maj. 13,543)

NEWBURY (Berks)
E.80,252   T.82.75%
Mrs J. Chaplin, C.	37,135
D. Rendel, LD	24,778
R. Hall, Lab.	3,962
J. Wallis, Green	539
C. majority	12,357

(June 1987, C. maj. 16,658)
See also page 242

NEWCASTLE UNDER LYME (Staffs)
E.66,595   T.80.34%
*Mrs L. Golding, Lab.	25,652
A. Brierley, C.	15,813
A. Thomas, LD	11,727
R. Lines, NLP	314
Lab. majority	9,839

(June 1987, Lab. maj. 5,132)

NEWCASTLE UPON TYNE CENTRAL
E.59,973   T.71.32%
*J. Cousins, Lab.	21,123
M. Summersby, C.	15,835
L. Opik, LD	5,816
Lab. majority	5,288

(June 1987, Lab. maj. 2,483)

NEWCASTLE UPON TYNE EAST
E.57,165   T.70.73%
*N. Brown, *Lab.*   24,342
J. Lucas, *C.*   10,465
A. Thompson, *LD*   4,883
G. Edwards, *Green*   744
Lab. majority   13,877
(June 1987, Lab. maj. 12,500)

NEWCASTLE UPON TYNE
NORTH
E.66,187   T.76.80%
*D. Henderson, *Lab.*   25,121
I. Gordon, *C.*   16,175
P. Maughan, *LD*   9,542
Lab. majority   8,946
(June 1987, Lab. maj. 5,243)

NEW FOREST (Hants)
E.75,413   T.80.76%
*Sir P. McNair-Wilson, *C.*   37,986
Ms J. Vernon-Jackson, *LD*   17,581
M. Shutler, *Lab.*   4,989
Ms F. Carter, *NLP*   350
C. majority   20,405
(June 1987, C. maj. 21,732)

NEWHAM NORTH EAST (Greater
London)
E.59,555   T.60.34%
*R. Leighton, *Lab.*   20,952
J. Galbraith, *C.*   10,966
J. Aves, *LD*   4,020
Lab. majority   9,986
(June 1987, Lab. maj. 8,236)

NEWHAM NORTH WEST (Greater
London)
E.46,471   T.56.02%
*T. Banks, *Lab.*   15,911
M. Prisk, *C.*   6,740
A. Sawdon, *LD*   2,445
Ms A. Standford, *Green*   587
T. Jug, *Loony G.*   252
D. O'Sullivan, *Int. Comm.*   100
Lab. majority   9,171
(June 1987, Lab. maj. 8,496)

NEWHAM SOUTH (Greater
London)
E.51,143   T.60.19%
*N. Spearing, *Lab.*   14,358
Ms J. Foster, *C.*   11,856
A. Kellaway, *LD*   4,572
Lab. majority   2,502
(June 1987, Lab. maj. 2,766)

NORFOLK MID
E.80,336   T.81.64%
*Rt. Hon. R. Ryder, *C.*   35,620
M. Castle, *Lab.*   16,672
J. Gleed, *LD*   13,072
Ms C. Waite, *NLP*   226
C. majority   18,948
(June 1987, C. maj. 18,008)

NORFOLK NORTH
E.73,780   T.80.84%
*R. Howell, *C.*   28,810
N. Lamb, *LD*   16,265
M. Cullingham, *Lab.*   13,850
Ms A. Zelter, *Green*   559

Ms S. Jackson, *NLP*   167
C. majority   12,545
(June 1987, C. maj. 15,310)

NORFOLK NORTH WEST
E.77,438   T.80.67%
*H. Bellingham, *C.*   32,554
Dr G. Turner, *Lab.*   20,990
A. Waterman, *LD*   8,599
S. Pink, *NLP*   330
C. majority   11,564
(June 1987, C. maj. 10,825)

NORFOLK SOUTH
E.81,647   T.83.99%
*Rt. Hon. J. MacGregor, *C.*   36,081
C. Brocklebank-Fowler, *LD*   18,516
C. Needle, *Lab.*   12,422
Ms S. Ross-Wagenknecht, *Green*   702
N. Clark, *NLP*   320
R. Peacock, *Ind.*   304
R. Watkins, *Ind. C.*   232
C. majority   17,565
(June 1987, C. maj. 12,418)

NORFOLK SOUTH WEST
E.77,652   T.79.30%
*Mrs G. Shephard, *C.*   33,637
Ms M. Page, *Lab.*   16,706
J. Marsh, *LD*   11,237
C. majority   16,931
(June 1987, C. maj. 20,436)

NORMANTON (W. Yorks)
E.65,562   T.76.35%
*W. O'Brien, *Lab.*   25,936
R. Sturdy, *C.*   16,986
M. Galdas, *LD*   7,137
Lab. majority   8,950
(June 1987, Lab. maj. 7,287)

NORTHAMPTON NORTH
E.69,139   T.78.52%
*A. Marlow, *C.*   24,865
Ms J. Thomas, *Lab.*   20,957
R. Church, *LD*   8,236
B. Spivack, *NLP*   232
C. majority   3,908
(June 1987, C. maj. 9,256)

NORTHAMPTON SOUTH
E.83,477   T.79.90%
*M. Morris, *C.*   36,882
J. Dickie, *Lab.*   19,909
G. Mabbutt, *LD*   9,912
C. majority   16,973
(June 1987, C. maj. 17,803)

NORTHAVON (Avon)
E.83,496   T.84.16%
*Rt. Hon. Sir J. Cope, *C.*   35,338
Ms H. Larkins, *LD*   23,477
Ms J. Norris, *Lab.*   10,290
Ms J. Greene, *Green*   789
P. Marx, *Lib.*   380
C. majority   11,861
(June 1987, C. maj. 14,270)

NORWICH NORTH (Norfolk)
E.63,308   T.81.82%
*H. P. Thompson, *C.*   22,419
I. Gibson, *Lab.*   22,153
D. Harrison, *LD*   6,706

L. Betts, *Green*   433
R. Arnold, *NLP*   93
C. majority   266
(June 1987, C. maj. 7,776)

NORWICH SOUTH (Norfolk)
E.63,603   T.80.60%
*J. Garrett, *Lab.*   24,965
D. Baxter, *C.*   18,784
C. Thomas, *LD*   6,609
A. Holmes, *Green*   803
B. Parsons, *NLP*   104
Lab. majority   6,181
(June 1987, Lab. maj. 336)

NORWOOD (Greater London)
E.52,496   T.65.87%
*J. Fraser, *Lab.*   18,391
J. Samways, *C.*   11,175
Ms S. Lawman, *LD*   4,087
S. Collins, *Green*   790
M. Leighton, *NLP*   138
Lab. majority   7,216
(June 1987, Lab. maj. 4,723)

NOTTINGHAM EAST
E.67,939   T.70.08%
J. Heppell, *Lab.*   25,026
*M. Knowles, *C.*   17,346
T. Ball, *LD*   3,695
A. Jones, *Green*   667
C. Roylance, *Lib.*   598
J. Ashforth, *NLP*   283
Lab. majority   7,680
(June 1987, C. maj. 456)

NOTTINGHAM NORTH
E.69,494   T.74.98%
*G. Allen, *Lab.*   29,052
I. Bridge, *C.*   18,309
A. Skelton, *LD*   4,477
A. Cadman, *NLP*   274
Lab. majority   10,743
(June 1987, Lab. maj. 1,665)

NOTTINGHAM SOUTH
E.72,796   T.74.22%
A. Simpson, *Lab.*   25,771
*M. Brandon-Bravo, *C.*   22,590
G. D. Long, *LD*   5,408
Ms J. Christou, *NLP*   263
Lab. majority   3,181
(June 1987, C. maj. 2,234)

NUNEATON (Warwicks)
E.70,906   T.83.70%
W. Olner, *Lab.*   27,157
*L. Stevens, *C.*   25,526
Ms R. Merritt, *LD*   6,671
Lab. majority   1,631
(June 1987, C. maj. 5,655)

OLD BEXLEY AND SIDCUP
(Greater London)
E.49,449   T.81.94%
*Rt. Hon. E. Heath, *C.*   24,450
Ms D. Brierly, *Lab.*   8,751
D. Nicolle, *LD*   6,438
B. Rose, *Alt. C.*   733
R. Stephens, *NLP*   148
C. majority   15,699
(June 1987, C. maj. 16,274)

OLDHAM CENTRAL AND
ROYTON (Greater Manchester)
*E.*61,333   *T.*74.20%

B. Davies, *Lab.*	23,246
Mrs T. Morris, *C.*	14,640
Ms A. Dunn, *LD*	7,224
I. Dalling, *NLP*	403
Lab. majority	8,606

(June 1987, Lab. maj. 6,279)

OLDHAM WEST (Greater
Manchester)
*E.*54,063   *T.*75.65%

*M. Meacher, *Lab.*	21,580
J. Gillen, *C.*	13,247
J. Smith, *LD*	5,525
Ms S. Dalling, *NLP*	551
Lab. majority	8,333

(June 1987, Lab. maj. 5,967)

ORPINGTON (Greater London)
*E.*57,318   *T.*83.67%

J. Horam, *C.*	27,421
C. Maines, *LD*	14,486
S. Cowan, *Lab.*	5,512
R. Almond, *Lib.*	539
C. majority	12,935

(June 1987, C. maj. 12,732)

OXFORD EAST
*E.*63,075   *T.*74.59%

*A. Smith, *Lab.*	23,702
Dr M. Mayall, *C.*	16,164
M. Horwood, *LD*	6,105
Mrs C. Lucas, *Green*	933
Miss A. Wilson, *NLP*	101
K. Thompson, *Rev. Comm.*	48
Lab. majority	7,538

(June 1987, Lab. maj. 1,288)

OXFORD WEST AND ABINGDON
*E.*72,328   *T.*76.68%

*Rt. Hon. J. Patten, *C.*	25,163
Sir W. Goodhart, *LD*	21,624
B. Kent, *Lab.*	7,652
M. Woodin, *Green*	660
R. Jenking, *Lib.*	194
Miss S. Nelson, *Anti Fed.*	98
G. Wells, *NLP*	75
C. majority	3,539

(June 1987, C. maj. 4,878)

PECKHAM (Greater London)
*E.*58,269   *T.*53.87%

*Ms H. Harman, *Lab.*	19,391
C. Frazer, *C.*	7,386
Mrs R. Colley, *LD*	4,331
G. Dacres, *WRP*	146
V. Emmanuel, *Whiplash*	140
Lab. majority	12,005

(June 1987, Lab. maj. 9,489)

PENDLE (Lancs)
*E.*64,063   *T.*82.91%

G. Prentice, *Lab.*	23,497
*J. Lee, *C.*	21,384
A. Davies, *LD*	7,976
Mrs V. Thome, *Anti Fed.*	263
Lab. majority	2,113

(June 1987, Lab. maj. 2,639)

PENRITH AND THE BORDER
(Cumbria)
*E.*73,769   *T.*79.67%

*D. Maclean, *C.*	33,808
G. Walker, *LD*	15,359
J. Metcalfe, *Lab.*	8,871
R. Gibson, *Green*	610
I. Docker, *NLP*	129
C. majority	18,449

(June 1987, C. maj. 17,366)

PETERBOROUGH (Cambs)
*E.*87,638   *T.*75.12%

*B. Mawhinney, *C.*	31,827
Ms J. Owens, *Lab.*	26,451
Ms A. Taylor, *LD*	5,208
E. Murat, *Lib.*	1,557
R. Heaton, *BNP*	311
P. Beasley, *PP*	271
C. Brettell, *NLP*	215
C. majority	5,376

(June 1987, C. maj. 9,784)

PLYMOUTH DEVONPORT (Devon)
*E.*65,799   *T.*77.83%

D. Jamieson, *Lab.*	24,953
K. Simpson, *C.*	17,541
M. Mactaggart, *LD*	6,315
H. Luscombe, *SD*	2,152
F. Lyons, *NLP*	255
Lab. majority	7,412

(June 1987, SDP/All. maj. 6,470)

PLYMOUTH DRAKE (Devon)
*E.*51,667   *T.*75.56%

*Dame J. Fookes, *C.*	17,075
P. Telford, *Lab.*	15,062
Ms V. Cox, *LD*	5,893
D. Stanbury, *SD*	476
Ms A. Harrison, *Green*	441
T. Pringle, *NLP*	95
C. majority	2,013

(June 1987, C. maj. 3,125)

PLYMOUTH SUTTON (Devon)
*E.*67,430   *T.*81.17%

G. Streeter, *C.*	27,070
A. Pawley, *Lab.*	15,120
J. Brett-Freeman, *LD*	12,291
J. Bowler, *NLP*	256
C. majority	11,950

(June 1987, C. maj. 4,013)

PONTEFRACT AND
CASTLEFORD (W. Yorks)
*E.*64,648   *T.*74.25%

*G. Lofthouse, *Lab.*	33,546
A. Rockall, *C.*	10,051
D. Ryan, *LD*	4,410
Lab. majority	23,495

(June 1987, Lab. maj. 21,626)

POOLE (Dorset)
*E.*79,221   *T.*79.39%

*J. Ward, *C.*	33,445
B. Clements, *LD*	20,614
H. White, *Lab.*	6,912
M. Steen, *Ind. C.*	1,620
A. Bailey, *NLP*	303
C. majority	12,831

(June 1987, C. maj. 14,808)

PORTSMOUTH NORTH (Hants)
*E.*79,592   *T.*77.05%

*P. Griffiths, *C.*	32,240
A. Burnett, *Lab.*	18,359
A. Bentley, *LD*	10,101
Ms H. Palmer, *Green*	628
C. majority	13,881

(June 1987, C. maj. 18,401)

PORTSMOUTH SOUTH (Hants)
*E.*77,645   *T.*69.09%

*D. Martin, *C.*	22,798
M. Hancock, *LD*	22,556
S. Rapson, *Lab.*	7,857
A. Zivkovic, *Green*	349
W. Trend, *NLP*	91
C. majority	242

(June 1987, C. maj. 205)

PRESTON (Lancs)
*E.*64,158   *T.*71.74%

*Mrs A. Wise, *Lab.*	24,983
S. O'Toole, *C.*	12,808
W. Chadwick, *LD*	7,897
Ms J. Ayliffe, *NLP*	341
Lab. majority	12,175

(June 1987, Lab. maj. 10,645)

PUDSEY (W. Yorks)
*E.*70,847   *T.*80.14%

*Sir G. Shaw, *C.*	25,067
A. Giles, *Lab.*	16,095
D. Shutt, *LD*	15,153
Ms J. Wynne, *Green*	466
C. majority	8,972

(June 1987, C. maj. 6,436)

PUTNEY (Greater London)
*E.*61,914   *T.*77.91%

*Rt. Hon. D. Mellor, *C.*	25,188
Ms J. Chegwidden, *Lab.*	17,662
J. Martyn, *LD*	4,636
K. Hagenbach, *Green*	618
P. Levy, *NLP*	139
C. majority	7,526

(June 1987, C. maj. 6,907)

RAVENSBOURNE (Greater London)
*E.*57,259   *T.*81.24%

*Sir J. Hunt, *C.*	29,506
P. Booth, *LD*	9,792
E. Dyer, *Lab.*	6,182
I. Mouland, *Green*	617
P. White, *Lib.*	318
J. Shepheard, *NLP*	105
C. majority	19,714

(June 1987, C. maj. 16,919)

READING EAST (Berks)
*E.*72,151   *T.*75.02%

*Sir G. Vaughan, *C.*	29,148
Ms G. Parker, *Lab.*	14,593
D. Thair, *LD*	9,528
Ms A. McCubbin, *Green*	861
C. majority	14,555

(June 1987, C. maj. 16,217)

READING WEST (Berks)
*E.*67,937   *T.*77.98%

*Sir A. Durant, *C.*	28,048
P. Ruhemann, *Lab.*	14,750
K. Lock, *LD*	9,572

P. Unsworth, *Green* 613
C. majority 13,298
(June 1987, C. maj. 16,753)

REDCAR (Cleveland)
E.62,494   T.77.73%
*Dr M. Mowlam, *Lab.* 27,184
R. Goodwill, *C.* 15,607
C. Abbott, *LD* 5,789
Lab. majority 11,577
(June 1987, Lab. maj. 7,735)

REIGATE (Surrey)
E.71,853   T.78.54%
*Sir G. Gardiner, *C.* 32,220
B. Newsome, *LD* 14,556
Ms H. Young, *Lab.* 9,150
M. Dilcliff, *SD* 513
C. majority 17,664
(June 1987, C. maj. 18,173)

RIBBLE VALLEY (Lancs)
E.64,996   T.85.73%
N. Evans, *C.* 29,178
*M. Carr, *LD* 22,636
R. Pickup, *Lab.* 3,649
D. Beesley, *Loony G.* 152
Ms N. Holmes, *NLP* 112
C. majority 6,542
(June 1987, C. maj. 19,528)
(March 1991, LD maj. 4,641)

RICHMOND AND BARNES
(Greater London)
E.53,081   T.85.01%
*J. Hanley, *C.* 22,894
Dr J. Tonge, *LD* 19,025
D. Touhig, *Lab.* 2,632
Ms J. Maciejowska, *Green* 376
C. Cunningham, *NLP* 89
R. Meacock, *QFL* 62
Ms A. Ellis-Jones, *Anti Fed.* 47
C. majority 3,869
(June 1987, C. maj. 1,766)

RICHMOND (N. Yorks)
E.82,879   T.78.41%
*W. Hague, *C.* 40,202
G. Irwin, *LD* 16,698
R. Cranston, *Lab.* 7,523
M. Barr, *Ind.* 570
C. majority 23,504
(June 1987, C. maj. 19,576)
(Feb 1989, C. maj. 2,634)

ROCHDALE (Greater Manchester)
E.69,522   T.76.47%
Ms E. Lynne, *LD* 22,776
D. Williams, *Lab.* 20,937
D. Goldie-Scott, *C.* 8,626
K. Henderson, *BNP* 620
V. Lucker, *NLP* 211
LD majority 1,839
(June 1987, L./All. maj. 2,779)

ROCHFORD (Essex)
E.76,869   T.82.99%
*Dr M. Clark, *C.* 38,967
N. Harris, *LD* 12,931
D. Quinn, *Lab.* 10,537
Ms L. Farmer, *Lib.* 1,362
C. majority 26,036
(June 1987, C. maj. 19,694)

ROMFORD (Greater London)
E.54,001   T.78%
*Sir M. Neubert, *C.* 23,834
Ms E. Gordon, *Lab.* 12,414
Ms P. Atherton, *LD* 5,329
F. Gibson, *Green* 546
C. majority 11,420
(June 1987, C. maj. 13,471)

ROMSEY AND WATERSIDE
(Hants)
E.82,628   T.83.15%
*M. Colvin, *C.* 37,375
G. Dawson, *LD* 22,071
Mrs A. Mawle, *Lab.* 8,688
J. Spottiswood, *Green* 577
C. majority 15,304
(June 1987, C. maj. 15,272)

ROSSENDALE AND DARWEN
(Lancs)
E.76,909   T.83.06%
Mrs J. Anderson, *Lab.* 28,028
*D. Trippier, *C.* 27,908
K. Connor, *LD* 7,226
J. Gaffney, *Green* 596
P. Gorrod, *NLP* 125
Lab. majority 120
(June 1987, C. maj. 4,982)

ROTHERHAM (S. Yorks)
E.60,937   T.71.68%
J. Boyce, *Lab.* 27,933
S. Yorke, *C.* 10,372
D. Wildgoose, *LD* 5,375
Lab. majority 17,561
(June 1987, Lab. maj. 16,012)

ROTHER VALLEY (S. Yorks)
E.68,303   T.74.98%
*K. Barron, *Lab.* 30,977
T. Horton, *C.* 13,755
K. Smith, *LD* 6,483
Lab. majority 17,222
(June 1987, Lab. maj. 15,790)

RUGBY AND KENILWORTH
(Warwicks)
E.77,766   T.83.72%
*J. Pawsey, *C.* 34,110
J. Airey, *Lab.* 20,863
J. Roodhouse, *LD* 9,934
S. Withers, *NLP* 202
C. majority 13,247
(June 1987, C. maj. 16,264)

RUISLIP-NORTHWOOD (Greater
London)
E.54,151   T.81.91%
*J. Wilkinson, *C.* 28,097
Ms R. Brooks, *Lab.* 8,306
H. Davies, *LD* 7,739
M. Sheehan, *NLP* 214
C. majority 19,791
(June 1987, C. maj. 16,971)

RUSHCLIFFE (Notts)
E.76,253   T.83.04%
*Rt. Hon. K. Clarke, *C.* 34,448
A. Chewings, *Lab.* 14,682
Dr A. Wood, *LD* 12,660
S. Anthony, *Green* 775

M. Maelor-Jones, *Ind. C.* 611
D. Richards, *NLP* 150
C. majority 19,766
(June 1987, C. maj. 20,839)

RUTLAND AND MELTON (Leics)
E.80,976   T.80.82%
A. Duncan, *C.* 38,603
Ms J. Taylor, *Lab.* 13,068
R. Lustig, *LD* 12,682
J. Berreen, *Green* 861
R. Grey, *NLP* 237
C. majority 25,535
(June 1987, C. maj. 23,022)

RYEDALE (N. Yorks)
E.87,048   T.81.73%
*J. Greenway, *C.* 39,888
Mrs E. Shields, *LD* 21,449
J. Healey, *Lab.* 9,812
C. majority 18,439
(June 1987, C. maj. 9,740)

SAFFRON WALDEN (Essex)
E.74,878   T.83.21%
*A. Haselhurst, *C.* 35,272
M. Hayes, *LD* 17,848
J. Kotz, *Lab.* 8,933
M. Miller, *NLP* 260
C. majority 17,424
(June 1987, C. maj. 16,602)

ST ALBANS (Herts)
E.74,188   T.83.47%
*Rt. Hon. P. Lilley, *C.* 32,709
Ms M. Howes, *LD* 16,305
K. Pollard, *Lab.* 12,016
C. Simmons, *Green* 734
D. Lucas, *NLP* 161
C. majority 16,404
(June 1987, C. maj. 10,881)

ST HELENS NORTH (Merseyside)
E.71,261   T.77.35%
*J. Evans, *Lab.* 31,930
B. Anderson, *C.* 15,686
J. Beirne, *LD* 7,224
Ms A. Lynch, *NLP* 287
Lab. majority 16,244
(June 1987, Lab. maj. 14,260)

ST HELENS SOUTH (Merseyside)
E.67,507   T.73.77%
*G. Bermingham, *Lab.* 30,391
Mrs P. Buzzard, *C.* 12,182
B. Spencer, *LD* 6,933
Dr H. Jump, *NLP* 295
Lab. majority 18,209
(June 1987, Lab. maj. 13,801)

ST IVES (Cornwall)
E.71,152   T.80.29%
*D. Harris, *C.* 24,528
A. George, *LD* 22,883
S. Warran, *Lab.* 9,144
Dr G. Stephens, *Lib.* 577
C. majority 1,645
(June 1987, C. maj. 7,555)

SALFORD EAST (Greater
Manchester)
E.52,616   T.64.36%
*Rt. Hon. S. Orme, *Lab.*	20,327
D. Berens, *C.*	9,092
N. Owen, *LD*	3,836
M. Stanley, *Green*	463
C. Craig, *NLP*	150
Lab. majority	11,235

(June 1987, Lab. maj. 12,056)

SALISBURY (Wilts)
E.75,916   T.79.89%
*S. R. Key, *C.*	31,546
P. Sample, *LD*	22,573
S. Fear, *Lab.*	5,483
Dr S. Elcock, *Green*	609
S. Fletcher, *Ind.*	233
T. Abbott, *Wessex*	117
Ms A. Martell, *NLP*	93
C. majority	8,973

(June 1987, C. maj. 11,443)

SCARBOROUGH (N. Yorks)
E.76,364   T.77.18%
J. Sykes, *C.*	29,334
D. Billing, *Lab.*	17,600
B. Davenport, *LD*	11,133
Dr D. Richardson, *Green*	876
C. majority	11,734

(June 1987, C. maj. 13,626)

SEDGEFIELD (Durham)
E.61,024   T.77.06%
*A. Blair, *Lab.*	28,453
N. Jopling, *C.*	13,594
G. Huntington, *LD*	4,982
Lab. majority	14,859

(June 1987, Lab. maj. 13,058)

SELBY (N. Yorks)
E.77,178   T.80.16%
*Rt. Hon. M. Alison, *C.*	31,067
J. Grogan, *Lab.*	21,559
E. Batty, *LD*	9,244
C. majority	9,508

(June 1987, C. maj. 13,779)

SEVENOAKS (Kent)
E.71,050   T.81.35%
*G. M. Wolfson, *C.*	33,245
R. Walshe, *LD*	14,091
Ms J. Evans, *Lab.*	9,470
Ms M. Lawrence, *Green*	786
P. Wakeling, *NLP*	210
C. majority	19,154

(June 1987, C. maj. 17,345)

SHEFFIELD ATTERCLIFFE
(S. Yorks)
E.69,177   T.71.81%
C. Betts, *Lab.*	28,563
G. Millward, *C.*	13,083
Ms H. Woolley, *LD*	7,283
G. Ferguson, *Green*	751
Lab. majority	15,480

(June 1987, Lab. maj. 17,191)

SHEFFIELD BRIGHTSIDE
(S. Yorks)
E.63,810   T.66.26%
*D. Blunkett, *Lab.*	29,771
T. Loughton, *C.*	7,090

R. Franklin, *LD*	5,273
D. Hyland, *Int. Comm.*	150
Lab. majority	22,681

(June 1987, Lab. maj. 24,191)

SHEFFIELD CENTRAL (S. Yorks)
E.59,059   T.56.12%
*R. Caborn, *Lab.*	22,764
V. Davies, *C.*	5,470
A. Sangar, *LD*	3,856
G. Wroe, *Green*	750
M. Clarke, *EUVJJ*	212
Ms J. O'Brien, *CL*	92
Lab. majority	17,294

(June 1987, Lab. maj. 19,342)

SHEFFIELD HALLAM (S. Yorks)
E.76,584   T.70.83%
*C. I. Patnick, *C.*	24,693
Dr P. Gold, *LD*	17,952
Ms V. Hardstaff, *Lab.*	10,930
M. Baker, *Green*	473
R. Hurford, *NLP*	101
Ms T. Clifford, *Rev. Comm.*	99
C. majority	6,741

(June 1987, C. maj. 7,637)

SHEFFIELD HEELEY (S. Yorks)
E.70,953   T.70.89%
*W. Michie, *Lab.*	28,005
D. Beck, *C.*	13,051
P. Moore, *LD*	9,247
Lab. majority	14,954

(June 1987, Lab. maj. 14,440)

SHEFFIELD HILLSBOROUGH
(S. Yorks)
E.77,343   T.77.19%
Mrs H. Jackson, *Lab.*	27,568
D. Chadwick, *LD*	20,500
S. Cordle, *C.*	11,640
Lab. majority	7,068

(June 1987, Lab. maj. 3,286)

SHERWOOD (Notts)
E.73,354   T.85.48%
S. P. Tipping, *Lab.*	29,788
*A. Stewart, *C.*	26,878
J. Howard, *LD*	6,039
Lab. majority	2,910

(June 1987, C. maj. 4,495)

SHIPLEY (W. Yorks)
E.68,816   T.82.12%
*Sir M. Fox, *C.*	28,463
Ms A. Lockwood, *Lab.*	16,081
J. Cole, *LD*	11,288
C. Harris, *Green*	680
C. majority	12,382

(June 1987, C. maj. 12,630)

SHOREHAM (W. Sussex)
E.71,252   T.81.17%
B. M. L. Stephen, *C.*	32,670
M. King, *LD*	18,384
P. Godwin, *Lab.*	6,123
W. Weights, *Lib.*	459
J. Dreben, *NLP*	200
C. majority	14,286

(June 1987, C. maj. 17,070)

SHREWSBURY AND ATCHAM
(Salop)
E.70,620   T.82.45%
*D. Conway, *C.*	26,681
K. Hemsley, *LD*	15,716
Ms E. Owen, *Lab.*	15,157
G. Hardy, *Green*	677
C. majority	10,965

(June 1987, C. maj. 9,064)

SHROPSHIRE NORTH
E.82,675   T.77.68%
*Rt. Hon. J. Biffen, *C.*	32,443
J. Stevens, *LD*	16,232
R. Hawkins, *Lab.*	15,550
C. majority	16,211

(June 1987, C. maj. 14,415)

SKIPTON AND RIPON (N. Yorks)
E.75,628   T.81.34%
*D. Curry, *C.*	35,937
R. Hall, *LD*	16,607
Ms K. Allott, *Lab.*	8,978
C. majority	19,330

(June 1987, C. maj. 17,174)

SLOUGH (Berks)
E.73,889   T.78.24%
*J. Watts, *C.*	25,793
E. Lopez, *Lab.*	25,279
P. Mapp, *LD*	4,041
J. Clark, *Lib.*	1,426
D. Alford, *Ind. Lab.*	699
A. Carmichael, *NF*	290
M. Creese, *NLP*	153
Ms E. Smith, *ERIP*	134
C. majority	514

(June 1987, C. maj. 4,090)

SOLIHULL (W. Midlands)
E.77,303   T.81.61%
*J. Taylor, *C.*	38,385
M. Southcombe, *LD*	13,239
Ms N. Kutapan, *Lab.*	10,544
C. Hards, *Green*	925
C. majority	25,146

(June 1987, C. maj. 21,786)

SOMERTON AND FROME
(Somerset)
E.71,354   T.82.75%
M. Robinson, *C.*	28,052
D. Heath, *LD*	23,711
R. Ashford, *Lab.*	6,154
Ms L. Graham, *Green*	742
Ms J. Pollock, *Lib.*	388
C. majority	4,341

(June 1987, C. maj. 9,538)

SOUTHAMPTON ITCHEN (Hants)
E.72,104   T.76.93%
J. Denham, *Lab.*	24,402
*C. Chope, *C.*	23,851
J. Hodgson, *LD*	7,221
Lab. majority	551

(June 1987, C. maj. 6,716)

SOUTHAMPTON TEST (Hants)
E.72,932   T.77.40%
*S. J. A. Hill, *C.*	24,504
A. Whitehead, *Lab.*	23,919
Ms D. Maddock, *LD*	7,391

J. Michaelis, *Green* — 535
D. Plummer, *NLP* — 101
C. majority — 585
(June 1987, C. maj. 6,954)

SOUTHEND EAST (Essex)
*E.*56,708   *T.*73.80%
*Sir E. Taylor, *C.* — 24,591
G. Bramley, *Lab.* — 11,480
Ms J. Horne, *LD* — 5,107
B. Lynch, *Lib.* — 673
C. majority — 13,111
(June 1987, C. maj. 13,847)

SOUTHEND WEST (Essex)
*E.*64,198   *T.*77.80%
*Rt. Hon. P. Channon, *C.* — 27,319
Ms N. Stimson, *LD* — 15,417
G. Viney, *Lab.* — 6,139
A. Farmer, *Lib.* — 495
C. Keene, *Green* — 451
P. Warburton, *NLP* — 127
C. majority — 11,902
(June 1987, C. maj. 8,400)

SOUTH HAMS (Devon)
*E.*83,061   *T.*81.09%
*A. Steen, *C.* — 35,951
V. Evans, *LD* — 22,240
Ms E. Cohen, *Lab.* — 8,091
C. Titmuss, *Green* — 846
Mrs L. Summerville, *NLP* — 227
C. majority — 13,711
(June 1987, C. maj. 13,146)

SOUTHPORT (Merseyside)
*E.*71,443   *T.*77.60%
M. Banks, *C.* — 26,081
*R. Fearn, *LD* — 23,018
J. King, *Lab.* — 5,637
J. Walker, *Green* — 545
G. Clements, *NLP* — 159
C. majority — 3,063
(June 1987, L./All. maj. 1,849)

SOUTH RIBBLE (Lancs)
*E.*78,173   *T.*82.99%
*R. Atkins, *C.* — 30,828
Dr G. Smith, *Lab.* — 24,855
S. Jones, *LD* — 8,928
Dr R. Decter, *NLP* — 269
C. majority — 5,973
(June 1987, C. maj. 8,430)

SOUTH SHIELDS (Tyne & Wear)
*E.*59,392   *T.*70.07%
*D. Clark, *Lab.* — 24,876
J. Howard, *C.* — 11,399
A. Preece, *LD* — 5,344
Lab. majority — 13,477
(June 1987, Lab. maj. 13,851)

SOUTHWARK AND BERMONDSEY
(Greater London)
*E.*60,251   *T.*62.62%
*S. Hughes, *LD* — 21,459
R. Balfe, *Lab.* — 11,614
A. Raca, *C.* — 3,794
S. Tyler, *BNP* — 530
T. Blackburn, *NF* — 168
Dr G. Barnett, *NLP* — 113
J. Grogan, *CL* — 56

LD majority — 9,845
June 1987, L./All. maj. 2,779

SPELTHORNE (Surrey)
*E.*69,343   *T.*80.36%
*D. Wilshire, *C.* — 32,627
Ms A. Leedham, *Lab.* — 12,784
R. Roberts, *LD* — 9,202
Ms J. Wassell, *Green* — 580
D. Rea, *Loony* — 338
D. Ellis, *NLP* — 195
C. majority — 19,843
(June 1987, C. maj. 20,050)

STAFFORD
*E.*74,663   *T.*82.91%
*W. Cash, *C.* — 30,876
D. Kidney, *Lab.* — 19,976
Mrs J. Calder, *LD* — 10,702
C. Peat, *Hardcore* — 178
P. Lines, *NLP* — 176
C. majority — 10,900
(June 1987, C. maj. 13,707)

STAFFORDSHIRE MID
*E.*73,414   *T.*85.66%
M. Fabricant, *C.* — 31,227
*Mrs S. Heal, *Lab.* — 24,991
B. Stamp, *LD* — 6,432
Ms D. Grice, *NLP* — 239
C. majority — 6,236
(June 1987, C. maj. 14,654)
(March 1990, Lab. maj. 9,449)

STAFFORDSHIRE MOORLANDS
*E.*75,036   *T.*83.66%
*D. Knox, *C.* — 29,240
J. Siddelley, *Lab.* — 21,830
Ms C. Jebb, *LD* — 9,326
M. Howson, *Anti Fed.* — 2,121
P. Davies, *NLP* — 261
C. majority — 7,410
(June 1987, C. maj. 14,427)

STAFFORDSHIRE SOUTH
*E.*82,758   *T.*81.54%
*P. Cormack, *C.* — 40,266
B. Wylie, *Lab.* — 17,633
I. Sadler, *LD* — 9,584
C. majority — 22,633
(June 1987, C. maj. 25,268)

STAFFORDSHIRE SOUTH EAST
*E.*70,199   *T.*82.05%
*D. Lightbown, *C.* — 29,180
B. Jenkins, *Lab.* — 21,988
Dr G. Penlington, *LD* — 5,540
Miss J. Taylor, *SD* — 895
C. majority — 7,192
(June 1987, C. maj. 10,885)

STALYBRIDGE AND HYDE
(Greater Manchester)
*E.*68,189   *T.*73.46%
*T. Pendry, *Lab.* — 26,207
S. Mort, *C.* — 17,376
I. Kirk, *LD* — 4,740
R. Powell, *Lib.* — 1,199
D. Poyzer, *Loony* — 337
E. Blomfield, *NLP* — 238
Lab. majority — 8,831
(June 1987, Lab. maj. 5,663)

STAMFORD AND SPALDING
(Lincs)
*E.*75,153   *T.*81.16%
*J. Q. Davies, *C.* — 35,965
C. Burke, *Lab.* — 13,096
B. Lee, *LD* — 11,939
C. majority — 22,869
(June 1987, C. maj. 14,007)

STEVENAGE (Herts)
*E.*70,233   *T.*83.03%
*T. Wood, *C.* — 26,652
Ms J. Church, *Lab.* — 21,764
A. Reilly, *LD* — 9,668
A. Calcraft, *NLP* — 233
C. majority — 4,888
(June 1987, C. maj. 5,340)

STOCKPORT (Greater Manchester)
*E.*58,095   *T.*82.27%
Ms M. A. Coffey, *Lab.* — 21,096
*A. Favell, *C.* — 19,674
Ms A. Corris, *LD* — 6,539
Ms J. Filmore, *Green* — 436
D. Saunders, *NLP* — 50
Lab. majority — 1,422
(June 1987, C. maj. 2,853)

STOCKTON NORTH (Cleveland)
*E.*69,451   *T.*76.83%
*F. Cook, *Lab.* — 27,918
S. Brocklebank-Fowler, *C.* — 17,444
Ms S. Fletcher, *LD* — 7,454
K. McGarvey, *Ind. Lab.* — 550
Lab. majority — 10,474
(June 1987, Lab. maj. 8,801)

STOCKTON SOUTH (Cleveland)
*E.*75,959   *T.*82.77%
*T. Devlin, *C.* — 28,418
J. Scott, *Lab.* — 25,049
Ms K. Kirkham, *LD* — 9,410
C. majority — 3,369
(June 1987, C. maj. 774)

STOKE-ON-TRENT CENTRAL
(Staffs)
*E.*65,527   *T.*68.12%
*M. Fisher, *Lab.* — 25,897
N. Gibb, *C.* — 12,477
M. Dent, *LD* — 6,073
N. Pullen, *NLP* — 196
Lab. majority — 13,420
(June 1987, Lab. maj. 9,770)

STOKE-ON-TRENT NORTH
(Staffs)
*E.*73,141   *T.*73.42%
*Ms J. Walley, *Lab.* — 30,464
L. Harris, *C.* — 15,687
J. Redfern, *LD* — 7,167
A. Morrison, *NLP* — 387
Lab. majority — 14,777
(June 1987, Lab. maj. 8,513)

STOKE-ON-TRENT SOUTH (Staffs)
*E.*71,316   *T.*74.33%
G. Stevenson, *Lab.* — 26,380
R. Ibbs, *C.* — 19,471
F. Jones, *LD* — 6,870
Mrs E. Lines, *NLP* — 291
Lab. majority — 6,909
(June 1987, Lab. maj. 5,053)

STRATFORD-UPON-AVON
(Warwicks)
*E.*82,824   *T.*82.07%

*A. Howarth, *C.*	40,251
N. Fogg, *LD*	17,359
Ms S. Brookes, *Lab.*	8,932
R. Roughan, *Green*	729
A. Saunders, *Ind. C.*	573
M. Twite, *NLP*	130
C. majority	22,892

(June 1987, C. maj. 21,165)

STREATHAM (Greater London)
*E.*56,825   *T.*69.03%

K. Hill, *Lab.*	18,925
*Sir W. Shelton, *C.*	16,608
J. Pindar, *LD*	2,858
R. Baker, *Green*	443
A. Hankin, *Islamic*	154
Mrs C. Payne, *ADS*	145
J. Parsons, *NLP*	97
Lab. majority	2,317

(June 1987, C. maj. 2,407)

STRETFORD (Greater Manchester)
*E.*54,467   *T.*68.76%

*A. Lloyd, *Lab.*	22,300
C. Rae, *C.*	11,163
F. Beswick, *LD*	3,722
A. Boyton, *NLP*	268
Lab. majority	11,137

(June 1987, Lab. maj. 9,402)

STROUD (Glos)
*E.*82,553   *T.*84.49%

*R. Knapman, *C.*	32,201
D. Drew, *Lab.*	18,796
M. Robinson, *LD*	16,751
Ms S. Atkinson, *Green*	2,005
C. majority	13,405

(June 1987, C. maj. 12,375)

SUFFOLK CENTRAL
*E.*82,735   *T.*80.26%

*M. Lord, *C.*	32,917
Ms L. Henniker-Major, *LD*	16,886
J. Harris, *Lab.*	15,615
J. Matthissen, *Green*	800
Ms J. Wilmot, *NLP*	190
C. majority	16,031

(June 1987, C. maj. 16,290)

SUFFOLK COASTAL
*E.*79,333   *T.*81.62%

*Rt. Hon. J. Gummer, *C.*	34,680
P. Monk, *LD*	15,395
T. Hodgson, *Lab.*	13,508
A. Slade, *Green*	943
Ms F. Kaplan, *NLP*	232
C. majority	19,285

(June 1987, C. maj. 15,280)

SUFFOLK SOUTH
*E.*84,833   *T.*81.73%

*T. Yeo, *C.*	34,793
Ms K. Pollard, *LD*	17,504
S. Hesford, *Lab.*	16,623
T. Aisbitt, *NLP*	420
C. majority	17,289

(June 1987, C. maj. 16,243)

SUNDERLAND NORTH (Tyne &
Wear)
*E.*72,874   *T.*68.86%

W. Etherington, *Lab.*	30,481
Miss J. Barnes, *C.*	13,477
V. Halom, *LD*	5,389
Ms W. Lundgren, *Lib.*	841
Lab. majority	17,004

(June 1987, Lab. maj. 14,672)

SUNDERLAND SOUTH (Tyne &
Wear)
*E.*72,607   *T.*69.87%

*C. Mullin, *Lab.*	29,399
G. Howe, *C.*	14,898
J. Lennox, *LD*	5,844
T. Scouler, *Green*	596
Lab. majority	14,501

(June 1987, Lab. maj. 12,613)

SURBITON (Greater London)
*E.*42,421   *T.*82.44%

*R. Tracey, *C.*	19,033
Ms B. Janke, *LD*	9,394
R. Hutchinson, *Lab.*	6,384
W. Parker, *NLP*	161
C. majority	9,639

(June 1987, C. maj. 9,741)

SURREY EAST
*E.*57,878   *T.*82.53%

P. Ainsworth, *C.*	29,767
R. Tomlin, *LD*	12,111
Mrs G. Roles, *Lab.*	5,075
I. Kilpatrick, *Green*	819
C. majority	17,656

(June 1987, C. maj. 18,126)

SURREY NORTH WEST
*E.*83,648   *T.*78.27%

*Sir M. Grylls, *C.*	41,772
Mrs C. Clark, *LD*	13,378
M. Hayhurst, *Lab.*	8,886
Ms Y. Hockey, *Green*	1,441
C. majority	28,394

(June 1987, C. maj. 23,575)

SURREY SOUTH WEST
*E.*72,288   *T.*82.77%

*Mrs V. Bottomley, *C.*	35,008
N. Sherlock, *LD*	20,033
P. Kelly, *Lab.*	3,840
N. Bedrock, *Green*	710
K. Campbell, *NLP*	147
D. Newman, *AS*	98
C. majority	14,975

(June 1987, C. maj. 14,343)

SUSSEX MID
*E.*80,827   *T.*82.85%

*Rt. Hon. T. Renton, *C.*	39,524
Ms M. Collins, *LD*	18,996
Ms L. Gregory, *Lab.*	6,951
H. Stevens, *Green*	772
P. Berry, *Loony*	392
P. Hodkin, *PR*	246
Dr A. Hankey, *NLP*	89
C. majority	20,528

(June 1987, C. maj. 18,292)

SUTTON AND CHEAM (Greater
London)
*E.*60,949   *T.*82.39%

Lady O. Maitland, *C.*	27,710
P. Burstow, *LD*	16,954
G. Martin, *Lab.*	4,980
J. Duffy, *Green*	444
Ms A. Hatchard, *NLP*	133
C. majority	10,756

(June 1987, C. maj. 15,718)

SUTTON COLDFIELD
(W. Midlands)
*E.*71,410   *T.*79.51%

*Rt. Hon. Sir N. Fowler, *C.*	37,001
J. Whorwood, *LD*	10,965
Ms J. Bott-Obi, *Lab.*	8,490
H. Meads, *NLP*	324
C. majority	26,036

(June 1987, C. maj. 21,183)

SWINDON (Wilts)
*E.*90,067   *T.*81.46%

*S. Coombs, *C.*	31,749
J. D'Avila, *Lab.*	28,923
S. Cordon, *LD*	11,737
W. Hughes, *Green*	647
R. Gillard, *Loony G.*	236
V. Farrar, *Ind.*	78
C. majority	2,826

(June 1987, C. maj. 4,857)

TATTON (Cheshire)
*E.*71,085   *T.*80.83%

*M. N. Hamilton, *C.*	31,658
J. Kelly, *Lab.*	15,798
Ms C. Hancox, *LD*	9,597
M. Gibson, *FP*	410
C. majority	15,860

(June 1987, C. maj. 17,094)

TAUNTON (Somerset)
*E.*78,036   *T.*82.32%

*D. Nicholson, *C.*	29,576
Ms J. Ballard, *LD*	26,240
Ms J. Hole, *Lab.*	8,151
P. Leavey, *NLP*	279
C. majority	3,336

(June 1987, C. maj. 10,380)

TEIGNBRIDGE (Devon)
*E.*74,892   *T.*83.43%

*P. Nicholls, *C.*	31,272
R. Younger-Ross, *LD*	22,416
R. Kennedy, *Lab.*	8,128
A. Hope, *Loony*	437
N. Hayes, *NLP*	234
C. majority	8,856

(June 1987, C. maj. 10,425)

THANET NORTH (Kent)
*E.*70,978   *T.*76.02%

*R. Gale, *C.*	30,867
A. Bretman, *Lab.*	12,657
Ms J. Phillips, *LD*	9,563
Ms H. Dawe, *Green*	873
C. majority	18,210

(June 1987, C. maj. 17,480)

THANET SOUTH (Kent)
*E.*62,441   *T.*78.17%

*J. Aitken, *C.*	25,253
M. James, *Lab.*	13,740

W. Pitt, *LD*	8,948
Ms S. Peckham, *Green*	871
C. majority	11,513
(June 1987, C. maj. 13,683)	

THURROCK (Essex)
E.69,171　T.78.15%

A. MacKinlay, *Lab.*	24,791
*T. Janman, *C.*	23,619
A. Banton, *LD*	5,145
C. Rogers, *Pensioners*	391
P. Compobassi, *Anti Fed.*	117
Lab. majority	1,172
(June 1987, C. maj. 690)	

TIVERTON (Devon)
E.71,024　T.82.98%

Mrs A. Browning, *C.*	30,376
D. Cox, *LD*	19,287
Ms S. Gibb, *Lab.*	5,950
D. Morrish, *Lib.*	2,225
P. Foggitt, *Green*	1,007
B. Rhodes, *NLP*	96
C. majority	11,089
(June 1987, C. maj. 9,212)	

TONBRIDGE AND MALLING
(Kent)
E.77,292　T.82.66%

*Rt. Hon. Sir J. Stanley, *C.*	36,542
P. Roberts, *LD*	14,984
Ms M. O'Neill, *Lab.*	11,533
J. Tidy, *Green*	612
Mrs J. Hovarth, *NLP*	221
C. majority	21,558
(June 1987, C. maj. 16,429)	

TOOTING (Greater London)
E.68,306　T.74.79%

*T. Cox, *Lab.*	24,601
M. Winters, *C.*	20,494
B. Bunce, *LD*	3,776
Ms C. Martin, *Lib.*	1,340
P. Owens, *Green*	694
F. Anklesalria, *NLP*	119
M. Whitelaw, *CD*	64
Lab. majority	4,107
(June 1987, Lab. maj. 1,441)	

TORBAY (Devon)
E.71,171　T.80.63%

*R. Allason, *C.*	28,624
A. Sanders, *LD*	22,837
P. Truscott, *Lab.*	5,503
R. Jones, *NF*	268
Ms A. Thomas, *NLP*	157
C. majority	5,787
(June 1987, C. maj. 8,820)	

TOTTENHAM (Greater London)
E.68,319　T.65.60%

*B. Grant, *Lab.*	25,309
A. Charalambous, *C.*	13,341
A. L'Estrange, *LD*	5,120
P. Budge, *Green*	903
Ms M. Obomanu, *NLP*	150
Lab. majority	11,968
(June 1987, Lab. maj. 4,141)	

TRURO (Cornwall)
E.75,101　T.82.35%

*M. Taylor, *LD*	31,230
N. St Aubyn, *C.*	23,660

J. Geach, *Lab.*	6,078
L. Keating, *Green*	569
C. Tankard, *Lib.*	208
Ms M. Hartley, *NLP*	108
LD majority	7,570
(June 1987, L./All. maj. 4,753)	

TUNBRIDGE WELLS (Kent)
E.76,808　T.78.11%

*Rt. Hon. Sir P. Mayhew, *C.*	34,162
A. Clayton, *LD*	17,030
E. Goodman, *Lab.*	8,300
E. Fenna, *NLP*	267
R. Edey, *ISS*	236
C. majority	17,132
(June 1987, C. maj. 16,122)	

TWICKENHAM (Greater London)
E.63,072　T.84.27%

*T. Jessel, *C.*	26,804
Dr V. Cable, *LD*	21,093
M. Gold, *Lab.*	4,919
G. Gill, *NLP*	152
D. Griffith, *DLC*	103
A. Miners, *Lib.*	85
C. majority	5,711
(June 1987, C. maj. 7,127)	

TYNE BRIDGE (Tyne & Wear)
E.53,079　T.62.64%

*D. Clelland, *Lab.*	22,328
C. Liddell-Grainger, *C.*	7,118
J. Burt, *LD*	3,804
Lab. majority	15,210
(June 1987, Lab. maj. 15,573)	

TYNEMOUTH (Tyne & Wear)
E.74,955　T.80.39%

*N. Trotter, *C.*	27,731
P. Cosgrove, *Lab.*	27,134
P. Selby, *LD*	4,855
A. Buchanan-Smith, *Green*	543
C. majority	597
(June 1987, C. maj. 2,583)	

UPMINSTER (Greater London)
E.64,138　T.80.46%

*Sir N. Bonsor, *C.*	28,791
T. Ward, *Lab.*	14,970
T. Hurlstone, *LD*	7,848
C. majority	13,821
(June 1987, C. maj. 16,857)	

UXBRIDGE (Greater London)
E.61,744　T.78.87%

*J. M. Shersby, *C.*	27,487
R. Evans, *Lab.*	14,308
S. Carey, *LD*	5,900
I. Flindall, *Green*	538
M. O'Rourke, *BNP*	350
A. Deans, *NLP*	120
C. majority	13,179
(June 1987, C. maj. 15,970)	

VAUXHALL (Greater London)
E.62,473　T.62.35%

*Ms C. Hoey, *Lab.*	21,328
B. Gentry, *C.*	10,840
M. Tuffrey, *LD*	5,678
Ms P. Shepherd, *Green*	803
A. Khan, *DOS*	156
Ms S. Hill, *Rev. Comm.*	152

Lab. majority	10,488
(June 1987, Lab. maj. 9,019)	
(June 1989, Lab. maj. 9,766)	

WAKEFIELD (W. Yorks)
E.69,794　T.76.27%

*D. Hinchliffe, *Lab.*	26,964
D. Fanthorpe, *C.*	20,374
T. Wright, *LD*	5,900
Lab. majority	6,590
(June 1987, Lab. maj. 2,789)	

WALLASEY (Merseyside)
E.65,676　T.82.50%

Ms A. Eagle, *Lab.*	26,531
*Rt. Hon. L. Chalker, *C.*	22,722
N. Thomas, *LD*	4,177
Ms S. Davis, *Green*	650
G. Gay, *NLP*	105
Lab. majority	3,809
(June 1987, C. maj. 279)	

WALLSEND (Tyne & Wear)
E.77,941　T.74.12%

S. Byers, *Lab.*	33,439
Miss M. Gibbon, *C.*	13,969
M. Huscroft, *LD*	10,369
Lab. majority	19,470
(June 1987, Lab. maj. 19,384)	

WALSALL NORTH (W. Midlands)
E.69,604　T.74.98%

*D. Winnick, *Lab.*	24,387
R. Syms, *C.*	20,563
A. Powis, *LD*	6,629
K. Reynolds, *NF*	614
Lab. majority	3,824
(June 1987, Lab. maj. 1,790)	

WALSALL SOUTH (W. Midlands)
E.65,642　T.76.26%

*B. George, *Lab.*	24,133
L. Jones, *C.*	20,955
G. Williams, *LD*	4,132
R. Clarke, *Green*	673
J. Oldbury, *NLP*	167
Lab. majority	3,178
(June 1987, Lab. maj. 1,116)	

WALTHAMSTOW (Greater London)
E.49,140　T.72.35%

N. Gerrard, *Lab.*	16,251
*H. Summerson, *C.*	13,229
P. Leighton, *LD*	5,142
Ms J. Lambert, *Green*	594
V. Wilkinson, *Lib.*	241
A. Planton, *NLP*	94
Lab. majority	3,022
(June 1987, C. maj. 1,512)	

WANSBECK (Northumberland)
E.63,457　T.79.29%

*J. Thompson, *Lab.*	30,046
G. Sanderson, *C.*	11,872
B. Priestley, *LD*	7,691
N. Best, *Green*	710
Lab. majority	18,174
(June 1987, Lab. maj. 16,789)	

WANSDYKE (Avon)
E.77,156　T.84.33%

*J. Aspinwall, *C.*	31,389
D. Norris, *Lab.*	18,048

Ms D. Darby, *LD* 14,834
F. Hayden, *Green* 800
C. majority 13,341
(June 1987, C. maj. 16,144)

WANSTEAD AND WOODFORD
(Greater London)
E.55,821 T.78.28%
*J. Arbuthnot, *C.* 26,204
Ms L. Brown, *Lab.* 9,319
G. Staight, *LD* 7,362
F. Roads, *Green* 637
A. Brickell, *NLP* 178
C. majority 16,885
(June 1987, C. maj. 16,412)

WANTAGE (Oxon)
E.68,328 T.82.68%
*R. Jackson, *C.* 30,575
R. Morgan, *LD* 14,102
V. Woodell, *Lab.* 10,955
R. Ely, *Green* 867
C. majority 16,473
(June 1987, C. maj. 12,156)

WARLEY EAST (W. Midlands)
E.51,717 T.71.72%
*A. Faulds, *Lab.* 19,891
G. Marshall, *C.* 12,097
A. Harrod, *LD* 4,547
A. Groucott, *NLP* 561
Lab. majority 7,794
(June 1987, Lab. maj. 5,585)

WARLEY WEST (W. Midlands)
E.57,164 T.73.90%
J. Spellar, *Lab.* 21,386
Mrs S. Whitehouse, *C.* 15,914
Ms E. Todd, *LD* 4,945
Lab. majority 5,472
(June 1987, Lab. maj. 5,393)

WARRINGTON NORTH (Cheshire)
E.78,548 T.77.38%
*E. D. H. Hoyle, *Lab.* 33,019
C. Daniels, *C.* 20,397
I. Greenhalgh, *LD* 6,965
B. Davies, *NLP* 400
Lab. majority 12,622
(June 1987, Lab. maj. 8,013)

WARRINGTON SOUTH (Cheshire)
E.77,694 T.82.04%
M. Hall, *Lab.* 27,819
*C. Butler, *C.* 27,628
P. Walker, *LD* 7,978
S. Benson, *NLP* 321
Lab. majority 191
(June 1987, C. maj. 3,609)

WARWICK AND LEAMINGTON
E.71,259 T.81.54%
*Sir D. Smith, *C.* 28,093
M. Taylor, *Lab.* 19,158
Ms S. Boad, *LD* 9,645
Ms J. Alty, *Green* 803
R. Newby, *Ind.* 251
J. Brewster, *NLP* 156
C. majority 8,935
(June 1987, C. maj. 13,982)

WARWICKSHIRE NORTH
E.71,473 T.83.82%
M. O'Brien, *Lab.* 27,599
*Hon. F. Maude, *C.* 26,145
N. Mitchell, *LD* 6,167
Lab. majority 1,454
(June 1987, C. maj. 2,829)

WATFORD (Herts)
E.72,291 T.82.34%
*W. A. T. T. Garel-Jones, *C.* 29,072
M. Jackson, *Lab.* 19,482
M. Oaten, *LD* 10,231
J. Hywel-Davies, *Green* 566
L. Davis, *NLP* 176
C. majority 9,590
(June 1987, C. maj. 11,736)

WAVENEY (Suffolk)
E.84,181 T.81.81%
*D. Porter, *C.* 33,174
E. Leverett, *Lab.* 26,472
A. Rogers, *LD* 8,925
D. Hook, *NLP* 302
C. majority 6,702
(June 1987, C. maj. 11,783)

WEALDEN (E. Sussex)
E.74,665 T.80.83%
*Sir G. Johnson Smith, *C.* 37,263
M. Skinner, *LD* 16,332
S. Billcliffe, *Lab.* 5,579
I. Guy-Moore, *Green* 1,002
Dr R. Graham, *NLP* 182
C. majority 20,931
(June 1987, C. maj. 20,110)

WELLINGBOROUGH (Northants)
E.73,875 T.81.89%
*P. Fry, *C.* 32,302
P. Sawford, *Lab.* 20,486
Ms J. Trevor, *LD* 7,714
C. majority 11,816
(June 1987, C. maj. 14,070)

WELLS (Somerset)
E.69,833 T.82.71%
*D. Heathcoat-Amory, *C.* 28,620
H. Temperley, *Lab.* 21,971
J. Pilgrim, *Lab.* 6,126
M. Fenner, *Green* 1,042
C. majority 6,649
(June 1987, C. maj. 8,541)

WELWYN HATFIELD (Herts)
E.72,146 T.84.39%
*D. Evans, *C.* 29,447
R. Little, *Lab.* 20,982
R. Parker, *LD* 10,196
Ms E. Lucas, *NLP* 264
C. majority 8,465
(June 1987, C. maj. 10,903)

WENTWORTH (S. Yorks)
E.64,914 T.74.03%
*P. Hardy, *Lab.* 32,939
M. Brennan, *C.* 10,490
Ms C. Roderick, *LD* 4,629
Lab. majority 22,449
(June 1987, Lab. maj. 20,092)

WEST BROMWICH EAST
(W. Midlands)
E.56,940 T.75.25%
*P. Snape, *Lab.* 19,913
C. Blunt, *C.* 17,100
M. Smith, *LD* 5,360
J. Lord, *NF* 477
Lab. majority 2,813
(June 1987, Lab. maj. 983)

WEST BROMWICH WEST
(W. Midlands)
E.57,655 T.70.41%
*Miss B. Boothroyd, *Lab.* 22,251
D. Swayne, *C.* 14,421
Miss S. Broadbent, *LD* 3,925
Lab. majority 7,830
(June 1987, Lab. maj. 5,253)

WESTBURY (Wilts)
E.87,356 T.82.99%
D. Faber, *C.* 36,568
Ms V. Rayner, *LD* 23,962
W. Stallard, *Lab.* 9,642
P. Macdonald, *Lib.* 1,440
P. French, *Green* 888
C. majority 12,606
(June 1987, C. maj. 10,097)

WESTMINSTER NORTH (Greater
London)
E.58,847 T.75.75%
*Sir J. Wheeler, *C.* 21,828
Ms J. Edwards, *Lab.* 18,095
J. Wigoder, *LD* 3,341
Ms A. Burke, *Green* 1,017
J. Hinde, *NLP* 159
M. Kelly, *Anti Fed.* 137
C. majority 3,733
(June 1987, C. maj. 3,310)

WESTMORLAND AND
LONSDALE (Cumbria)
E.71,865 T.77.76%
*Rt. Hon. M. Jopling, *C.* 31,798
S. Collins, *LD* 15,362
D. Abbott, *Lab.* 8,436
R. Johnstone, *NLP* 287
C. majority 16,436
(June 1987, C. maj. 14,920)

WESTON-SUPER-MARE (Avon)
E.78,839 T.79.75%
*A. W. Wiggin, *C.* 30,022
B. Cotter, *LD* 24,680
D. Murray, *Lab.* 6,913
Dr R. Lawson, *Green* 1,262
C. majority 5,342
(June 1987, C. maj. 7,998)

WIGAN (Greater Manchester)
E.72,739 T.76.16%
*R. Stott, *Lab.* 34,910
E. Hess, *C.* 13,068
G. Davies, *LD* 6,111
K. White, *Lib.* 1,116
Ms A. Taylor, *NLP* 197
Lab. majority 21,842
(June 1987, Lab. maj. 20,462)

WILTSHIRE NORTH
E.85,851   T.81.71%

*R. Needham, *C.*	39,028
Ms C. Napier, *LD*	22,640
Ms C. Reid, *Lab.*	6,945
Ms L. Howitt, *Green*	850
G. Hawkins, *Lib.*	622
S. Martienssen, *Bastion*	66
C. majority	16,388
(June 1987, C. maj. 10,939)	

WIMBLEDON (Greater London)
E.61,917   T.80.23%

*Dr C. Goodson-Wickes, *C.*	26,331
K. Abrams, *Lab.*	11,570
Ms A. Willott, *LD*	10,569
V. Flood, *Green*	860
H. Godfrey, *NLP*	181
G. Hadley, *Ind.*	170
C. majority	14,761
(June 1987, C. maj. 11,301)	

WINCHESTER (Hants)
E.79,218   T.83.46%

P. G. Malone, *C.*	33,113
A. Barron, *LD*	24,992
P. Jenks, *Lab.*	4,917
*J. Browne, *Ind. C.*	3,095
C. majority	8,121
(June 1987, C. maj. 7,479)	

WINDSOR AND MAIDENHEAD
(Berks)
E.77,327   T.81.68%

Hon. M. Trend, *C.*	35,075
J. Hyde, *LD*	22,147
Ms C. Attlee, *Lab.*	4,975
R. Williams, *Green*	510
D. Askwith, *Loony*	236
Miss E. Bigg, *Ind.*	110
M. Grenville, *NLP*	108
C. majority	12,928
(June 1987, C. maj. 17,836)	

WIRRAL SOUTH (Merseyside)
E.61,116   T.82.37%

*G. B. Porter, *C.*	25,590
Ms H. Southworth, *Lab.*	17,407
E. Cunniffe, *LD*	6,581
N. Birchenough, *Green*	584
G. Griffiths, *NLP*	182
C. majority	8,183
(June 1987, C. maj. 10,963)	

WIRRAL WEST (Merseyside)
E.62,453   T.81.57%

*Rt. Hon. D. Hunt, *C.*	26,852
Ms H. Stephenson, *Lab.*	15,788
J. Thornton, *LD*	7,420
Ms G. Bowler, *Green*	700
N. Broome, *NLP*	188
C. majority	11,064
(June 1987, C. maj. 12,723)	

WITNEY (Oxon)
E.78,521   T.81.89%

*Rt. Hon. D. Hurd, *C.*	36,256
J. Plaskitt, *Lab.*	13,688
I. Blair, *LD*	13,393
Ms C. Beckford, *Green*	716
Ms S. Catling, *NLP*	134
Miss M. Brown, *FTA*	119

C. majority	22,568
(June 1987, C. maj. 18,464)	

WOKING (Surrey)
E.80,842   T.79.20%

*Rt. Hon. C. Onslow, *C.*	37,744
Mrs D. Buckrell, *LD*	17,902
J. Dalgleish, *Lab.*	8,080
Mrs T. Macintyre, *NLP*	302
C. majority	19,842
(June 1987, C. maj. 16,544)	

WOKINGHAM (Berks)
E.85,914   T.82.41%

*J. Redwood, *C.*	43,497
P. Simon, *LD*	17,788
N. Bland, *Lab.*	8,846
P. Owen, *Loony*	531
P. Harriss, *WUWC*	148
C. majority	25,709
(June 1987, C. maj. 20,387)	

WOLVERHAMPTON NORTH
EAST (W. Midlands)
E.62,695   T.78%

K. Purchase, *Lab.*	24,106
*Mrs M. Hicks, *C.*	20,167
M. Gwinnett, *LD*	3,546
K. Bullman, *Lib.*	1,087
Lab. majority	3,939
(June 1987, C. maj. 204)	

WOLVERHAMPTON SOUTH EAST
(W. Midlands)
E.56,158   T.72.86%

*D. Turner, *Lab.*	23,215
P. Bradbourn, *C.*	12,975
R. Whitehouse, *LD*	3,881
Ms C. Twelvetrees, *Lib.*	850
Lab. majority	10,240
(June 1987, Lab. maj. 6,398)	

WOLVERHAMPTON SOUTH
WEST (W. Midlands)
E.67,288   T.78.28%

*N. Budgen, *C.*	25,969
S. Murphy, *Lab.*	21,003
M. Wiggin, *LD*	4,470
C. Hallmark, *Lib.*	1,237
C. majority	4,966
(June 1987, C. maj. 10,318)	

WOODSPRING (Avon)
E.77,534   T.83.21%

Dr L. Fox, *C.*	35,175
Ms N. Kirsen, *LD*	17,666
R. Stone, *Lab.*	9,942
N. Brown, *Lib.*	836
Ms R. Knifton, *Green*	801
B. Lee, *NLP*	100
C. majority	17,509
(June 1987, C. maj. 17,852)	

WOOLWICH (Greater London)
E.55,977   T.70.91%

J. Austin-Walker, *Lab.*	17,551
*J. Cartwright, *SD*	15,326
K. Walmsley, *C.*	6,598
Ms S. Hayward, *NLP*	220
Lab. majority	2,225
(June 1987, SDP/All. maj. 1,937)	

WORCESTER
E.74,211   T.80.99%

P. Luff, *C.*	27,883
R. Berry, *Lab.*	21,731
J. Caiger, *LD*	9,561
M. Foster, *Green*	592
M. Soden, *Brewer*	343
C. majority	6,152
(June 1987, C. maj. 10,453)	

WORCESTERSHIRE MID
E.84,269   T.81.07%

*E. Forth, *C.*	33,964
Ms J. Smith, *Lab.*	24,094
D. Barwick, *LD*	9,745
P. Davis, *NLP*	520
C. majority	9,870
(June 1987, C. maj. 14,911)	

WORCESTERSHIRE SOUTH
E.80,423   T.79.99%

*W. M. H. Spicer, *C.*	34,792
P. Chandler, *LD*	18,641
N. Knowles, *Lab.*	9,727
G. Woodford, *Green*	1,178
C. majority	16,151
(June 1987, C. maj. 13,645)	

WORKINGTON (Cumbria)
E.57,597   T.81.52%

*D. Campbell-Savours, *Lab.*	26,719
S. Sexton, *C.*	16,270
Ms C. Neale, *LD*	3,028
D. Langstaff, *Loony*	755
Ms N. Escott, *NLP*	183
Lab. majority	10,449
(June 1987, Lab. maj. 7,019)	

WORSLEY (Greater Manchester)
E.72,244   T.77.74%

*T. Lewis, *Lab.*	29,418
N. Cameron, *C.*	19,406
R. Boyd, *LD*	6,490
P. Connolly, *Green*	677
G. Phillips, *NLP*	176
Lab. majority	10,012
(June 1987, Lab. maj. 7,337)	

WORTHING (W. Sussex)
E.77,540   T.77.41%

*Rt. Hon. T. Higgins, *C.*	34,198
Mrs S. Bucknall, *LD*	17,665
J. Deen, *Lab.*	6,679
Mrs P. Beever, *Green*	806
N. Goble, *Lib.*	679
C. majority	16,533
(June 1987, C. maj. 18,501)	

THE WREKIN (Salop)
E.90,892   T.77.14%

*B. Grocott, *Lab.*	33,865
Mrs E. Holt, *C.*	27,217
A. West, *LD*	8,032
R. Saunders, *Green*	1,008
Lab. majority	6,648
(June 1987, Lab. maj. 1,456)	

WYCOMBE (Bucks)
E.72,564   T.78.01%

*R. Whitney, *C.*	30,081
T. Andrews, *LD*	13,005
J. Huddart, *Lab.*	12,222

J. Laker, *Green*   686
A. Page, *SD*   449
T. Anton, *NLP*   168
C. majority   17,076
(June 1987, C. maj. 13,819)

WYRE (Lancs)
*E.*67,778   *T.*79.54%
*K. Mans, *C.*   29,449
D. Borrow, *Lab.*   17,785
J. Ault, *LD*   6,420
R. Perry, *NLP*   260
C. majority   11,664
(June 1987, C. maj. 14,661)

WYRE FOREST (H & W)
*E.*73,550   *T.*82.36%
*A. Coombs, *C.*   28,983
R. Maden, *Lab.*   18,642
M. Jones, *LD*   12,958
C. majority   10,341
(June 1987, C. maj. 7,224)

YEOVIL (Somerset)
*E.*73,057   *T.*81.98%
*Rt. Hon. J. J. D. Ashdown, *LD* 30,958
J. Davidson, *C.*   22,125
Ms V. Nelson, *Lab.*   5,765
J. Risbridger, *Green*   639

D. Sutch, *Loony*   338
R. Simmerson, *APAKBI*   70
LD majority   8,833
(June 1987, L./All. maj. 5,700)

YORK (N. Yorks)
*E.*79,242   *T.*80.97%
H. Bayley, *Lab.*   31,525
*C. Gregory, *C.*   25,183
Ms K. Anderson, *LD*   6,811
S. Kenwright, *Green*   594
Ms P. Orr, *NLP*   54
Lab. majority   6,342
(June 1987, C. maj. 147)

WALES

ABERAVON (W. Glamorgan)
*E.*51,650   *T.*77.57%
*Rt. Hon. J. Morris, *Lab.* 26,877
H. Williams, *C.*   5,567
Mrs M. Harris, *LD*   4,999
D. Saunders, *PC*   1,919
Capt. Beany, *Real Bean*   707
Lab. majority   21,310
(June 1987, Lab. maj. 20,609)

ALYN AND DEESIDE (Clwyd)
*E.*60,477   *T.*80.08%
*S. B. Jones, *Lab.*   25,206
J. Riley, *C.*   17,355
R. Britton, *LD*   4,687
J. Rogers, *PC*   551
V. Button, *Green*   433
J. Cooksey, *Ind.*   200
Lab. majority   7,851
(June 1987, Lab. maj. 6,383)

BLAENAU GWENT
*E.*55,638   *T.*78.13%
L. Smith, *Lab.*   34,333
D. Melding, *C.*   4,266
A. Burns, *LD*   2,774
A. Davies, *PC*   2,099
Lab. majority   30,067
(June 1987, Lab. maj. 27,861)

BRECON AND RADNOR (Powys)
*E.*51,509   *T.*85.94%
J. P. Evans, *C.*   15,977
*R. Livsey, *LD*   15,847
C. Mann, *Lab.*   11,634
Ms S. Meredudd, *PC*   418
H. Richards, *Green*   393
C. majority   130
(June 1987, L./All. maj. 56)

BRIDGEND (Mid Glamorgan)
*E.*58,531   *T.*80.44%
*W. Griffiths, *Lab.*   24,143
D. Unwin, *C.*   16,817
D. Mills, *LD*   4,827
A. Lloyd Jones, *PC*   1,301
Lab. majority   7,326
(June 1987, Lab. maj. 4,380)

CAERNARFON (Gwynedd)
*E.*46,468   *T.*78.15%
*D. Wigley, *PC*   21,439
P. Fowler, *C.*   6,963
Ms S. Mainwaring, *Lab.*   5,641

R. Arwel Williams, *LD*   2,101
G. Evans, *NLP*   173
PC majority   14,476
(June 1987, *PC maj. 12,812*)

CAERPHILLY (Mid Glamorgan)
*E.*64,529   *T.*77.20%
*R. Davies, *Lab.*   31,713
H. Philpott, *C.*   9,041
L. Whittle, *PC*   4,821
S. Wilson, *LD*   4,247
Lab. majority   22,672
(June 1987, Lab. maj. 19,167)

CARDIFF CENTRAL
(S. Glamorgan)
*E.*57,716   *T.*74.35%
J. O. Jones, *Lab.*   18,014
*I. Grist, *C.*   14,549
Ms J. Randerson, *LD*   9,170
H. Marshall, *PC*   748
C. von Ruhland, *Green*   330
B. Francis, *NLP*   105
Lab. majority   3,465
(June 1987, C. maj. 1,986)

CARDIFF NORTH (S. Glamorgan)
*E.*56,721   *T.*84.15%
*G. H. Jones, *C.*   21,547
Ms J. Morgan, *Lab.*   18,578
Ms E. Warlow, *LD*   6,487
Ms E. Bush, *PC*   916
J. Morse, *BNP*   121
D. Palmer, *NLP*   86
C. majority   2,969
(June 1987, C. maj. 8,234)

CARDIFF SOUTH AND PENARTH
(S. Glamorgan)
*E.*61,484   *T.*77.25%
*A. Michael, *Lab.*   26,383
T. Hunter Jarvie, *C.*   15,958
P. Verma, *LD*   3,707
Ms B. Anglezarke, *PC*   776
L. Davey, *Green*   676
Lab. majority   10,425
(June 1987, Lab. maj. 4,574)

CARDIFF WEST (S. Glamorgan)
*E.*58,898   *T.*77.56%
*H. R. Morgan, *Lab.*   24,306
M. Prior, *C.*   15,015
Ms J. Gasson, *LD*   5,002
Ms P. Bestic, *PC*   1,177

A. Harding, *NLP*   184
Lab. majority   9,291
(June 1987, Lab. maj. 4,045)

CARMARTHEN (Dyfed)
*E.*68,887   *T.* 82.70%
*Dr A. W. Williams, *Lab.*   20,879
R. Thomas, *PC*   17,957
S. Cavenagh, *C.*   12,782
Mrs J. Hughes, *LD*   5,353
Lab. majority   2,922
(June 1987, Lab. maj. 4,317)

**CEREDIGION AND PEMBROKE
NORTH** (Dyfed)
*E.*66,180   *T.*77.36%
C. Dafis, *PC*   16,020
*G. Howells, *LD*   12,827
J. Williams, *C.*   12,718
J. Davies, *Lab.*   9,637
PC majority   3,193
(June 1987, L./All. maj. 4,700)

CLWYD NORTH WEST
*E.*67,351   *T.*78.64%
R. Richards, *C.*   24,488
C. Ruane, *Lab.*   18,438
R. Ingham, *LD*   7,999
T. Neil, *PC*   1,888
Ms M. Swift, *NLP*   158
C. majority   6,050
(June 1987, C. maj. 11,781)

CLWYD SOUTH WEST
*E.*60,607   *T.*81.52%
*M. Jones, *Lab.*   21,490
G. Owen, *C.*   16,549
G. Williams, *LD*   6,027
E. Lloyd Jones, *PC*   4,835
N. Worth, *Green*   351
Mrs J. Leadbetter, *NLP*   155
Lab. majority   4,941
(June 1987, Lab. maj. 1,028)

CONWY (Gwynedd)
*E.*53,576   *T.*78.85%
*Rt. Hon. Sir W. Roberts, *C.* 14,250
Revd R. Roberts, *LD*   13,255
Ms E. Williams, *Lab.*   10,883
R. Davies, *PC*   3,108
O. Wainwright, *Ind. C.*   637
Ms D. Hughes, *NLP*   114
C. majority   995
(June 1987, C. maj. 3,024)

CYNON VALLEY (Mid Glamorgan)
E.49,695   T.76.46%

*Ms A. Clwyd, *Lab.*	26,254
A. Smith, *C.*	4,890
T. Benney, *PC*	4,186
M. Verma, *LD*	2,667
Lab. majority	21,364
(June 1987, Lab. maj. 21,571)	

DELYN (Clwyd)
E.66,591   T.83.40%

D. Hanson, *Lab.*	24,979
M. Whitby, *C.*	22,940
R. Dodd, *LD*	6,208
A. Drake, *PC*	1,414
Lab. majority	2,039
(June 1987, C. maj. 1,224)	

GOWER (W. Glamorgan)
E.57,231   T.81.84%

*G. Wardell, *Lab.*	23,455
A. Donnelly, *C.*	16,437
C. Davies, *LD*	4,655
A. Price, *PC*	1,658
B. Kingzett, *Green*	448
G. Egan, *Loony G.*	114
M. Beresford, *NLP*	74
Lab. majority	7,018
(June 1987, Lab. maj. 5,764)	

ISLWYN (Gwent)
E.51,079   T.81.48%

*Rt. Hon. N. Kinnock, *Lab.*	30,908
P. Bone, *C.*	6,180
M. Symonds, *LD*	2,352
Ms H. Jones, *PC*	1,636
Lord Sutch, *Loony*	547
Lab. majority	24,728
(June 1987, Lab. maj. 22,947)	

LLANELLI (Dyfed)
E.65,058   T.77.80%

*Rt. Hon. D. Davies, *Lab.*	27,802
G. Down, *C.*	8,532
M. Phillips, *PC*	7,878
K. Evans, *LD*	6,404
Lab. majority	19,270
(June 1987, Lab. maj. 20,935)	

MEIRIONNYDD NANT CONWY
(Gwynedd)
E.32,413   T.81.47%

E. Llwyd, *PC*	11,608
G. Lewis, *C.*	6,995
R. Williams, *Lab.*	4,978
Mrs R. Parry, *LD*	2,358
W. Pritchard, *Green*	471
PC majority	4,613
(June 1987, PC maj. 3,026)	

MERTHYR TYDFIL AND
RHYMNEY (Mid Glamorgan)
E.58,430   T.75.84%

*E. Rowlands, *Lab.*	31,710
R. Rowland, *LD*	4,997
M. Hughes, *C.*	4,904
A. Cox, *PC*	2,704
Lab. majority	26,713
(June 1987, Lab. maj. 28,207)	

MONMOUTH (Gwent)
E.59,147   T.86.06%

R. Evans, *C.*	24,059
*H. Edwards, *Lab.*	20,855
Mrs F. David, *LD*	5,562
M. Witherden, *Green/PC*	431
C. majority	3,204
(June 1987, C. maj. 9,350)	
(May 1991, Lab. maj. 2,406)	

MONTGOMERY (Powys)
E.41,386   T.79.87%

*A. Carlile, *LD*	16,031
Mrs J. France-Hayhurst, *C.*	10,822
S. Wood, *Lab.*	4,115
H. Parsons, *PC*	1,581
P. Adams, *Green*	508
LD majority	5,209
(June 1987, L./All. maj. 2,558)	

NEATH (W. Glamorgan)
E.56,392   T.80.58%

*P. Hain, *Lab.*	30,903
D. Adams, *C.*	6,928
Dr D. Evans, *PC*	5,145
M. Phillips, *LD*	2,467
Lab. majority	23,975
(June 1987, Lab. maj. 20,578)	
(April 1991, Lab. maj. 9,830)	

NEWPORT EAST (Gwent)
E.51,603   T.81.21%

*R. J. Hughes, *Lab.*	23,050
Mrs A. Emmett, *C.*	13,151
W. Oliver, *LD*	4,991
S. Ainley, *Green/PC*	716
Lab. majority	9,899
(June 1987, Lab. maj. 7,064)	

NEWPORT WEST (Gwent)
E.54,871   T.82.82%

*P. Flynn, *Lab.*	24,139
A. Taylor, *C.*	16,360
A. Toye, *LD*	4,296
P. Keelan, *PC*	653
Lab. majority	7,779
(June 1987, Lab. maj. 2,708)	

OGMORE (Mid Glamorgan)
E.52,195   T.80.62%

*R. Powell, *Lab.*	30,186
D. Edwards, *C.*	6,359
J. Warman, *LD*	2,868
Ms L. McAllister, *PC*	2,667
Lab. majority	23,827
(June 1987, Lab. maj. 22,292)	

PEMBROKE (Dyfed)
E.73,187   T.82.86%

N. Ainger, *Lab.*	26,253
*N. Bennett, *C.*	25,498
P. Berry, *LD*	6,625
C. Bryant, *PC*	1,627
R. Coghill, *Green*	484
M. Stoddart, *Anti Fed.*	158
Lab. majority	755
(June 1987, C. maj. 5,700)	

PONTYPRIDD (Mid Glamorgan)
E.61,685   T.79.25%

*K. Howells, *Lab.*	29,722
Dr P. Donnelly, *C.*	9,925

Dr D. Bowen, *PC*	4,448
S. Belzak, *LD*	4,180
Ms E. Jackson, *Green*	615
Lab. majority	19,797
(June 1987, Lab. maj. 17,277)	
(Feb. 1989, Lab. maj. 10,794)	

RHONDDA (Mid Glamorgan)
E.59,955   T.76.61%

*A. Rogers, *Lab.*	34,243
G. Davies, *PC*	5,427
J. Richards, *C.*	3,588
P. Nicholls-Jones, *LD*	2,431
M. Fisher, *Comm. GB*	245
Lab. majority	28,816
(June 1987, Lab. maj. 30,596)	

SWANSEA EAST (W. Glamorgan)
E.59,196   T.75.56%

*D. Anderson, *Lab.*	31,179
H. Davies, *C.*	7,697
R. Barton, *LD*	4,248
Ms E. Bonner-Evans, *PC*	1,607
Lab. majority	23,482
(June 1987, Lab. maj. 19,338)	

SWANSEA WEST (W. Glamorgan)
E.59,785   T.73.34%

*Rt. Hon. A. Williams, *Lab.*	23,238
R. Perry, *C.*	13,760
M. Shrewsbury, *LD*	4,620
Dr D. Lloyd, *PC*	1,668
B. Oubridge, *Green*	564
Lab. majority	9,478
(June 1987, Lab. maj. 7,062)	

TORFAEN (Gwent)
E.61,104   T.77.47%

*P. Murphy, *Lab.*	30,352
M. Watkins, *C.*	9,598
M. Hewson, *LD*	6,178
Dr J. Cox, *Green/PC*	1,210
Lab. majority	20,754
(June 1987, Lab. maj. 17,550)	

VALE OF GLAMORGAN
(S. Glamorgan)
E.66,672   T.81.93%

W. Sweeney, *C.*	24,220
*J. Smith, *Lab.*	24,201
K. Davies, *LD*	5,045
D. Haswell, *PC*	1,160
C. majority	19
(June 1987, C. maj 6,251)	
(May 1989, Lab. maj. 6,028)	

WREXHAM (Clwyd)
E.63,720   T.80.71%

*J. Marek, *Lab.*	24,830
O. Paterson, *C.*	18,114
A. Thomas, *LD*	7,074
G. Wheatley, *PC*	1,415
Lab. majority	6,716
(June 1987, Lab. maj. 4,152)	

YNYS MÔN (Gwynedd)
E.53,412   T.80.62%

*I. W. Jones, *PC*	15,984
G. Price Rowlands, *C.*	14,878
Dr R. Jones, *Lab.*	10,126
Ms P. Badger, *LD*	1,891
Mrs S. Parry, *NLP*	182
PC majority	1,106
(June 1987, PC maj. 4,298)	

SCOTLAND

ABERDEEN NORTH (Grampian)
E.60,217   T.66.52%

*R. Hughes, *Lab.*	18,845
J. McGugan, *SNP*	9,608
P. Cook, *C.*	6,836
Dr M. Ford, *LD*	4,772
Lab. majority	9,237

(June 1987, Lab. maj. 16,278)

ABERDEEN SOUTH (Grampian)
E.58,881   T.69.78%

R. Robertson, *C.*	15,808
*F. Doran, *Lab.*	14,291
J. Davidson, *SNP*	6,223
Ms I. Keith, *LD*	4,767
C. majority	1,517

(June 1987, Lab. maj. 1,198)

ANGUS EAST (Tayside)
E.63,170   T.75.03%

*A. Welsh, *SNP*	19,006
Dr R. Harris, *C.*	18,052
G. Taylor, *Lab.*	5,994
C. McLeod, *LD*	3,897
D. McCabe, *Green*	449
SNP majority	954

(June 1987, SNP maj. 1,544)

ARGYLL AND BUTE (Strathclyde)
E.47,894   T.76.19%

*Mrs J. R. Michie, *LD*	12,739
J. Corrie, *C.*	10,117
Prof. N. MacCormick, *SNP*	8,689
D. Browne, *Lab.*	4,946
LD majority	2,622

(June 1987, L./All. maj. 1,394)

AYR (Strathclyde)
E.65,481   T.83.08%

P. Gallie, *C.*	22,172
A. Osborne, *Lab.*	22,087
Mrs B. Mullin, *SNP*	5,949
J. Boss, *LD*	4,067
R. Scott, *NLP*	132
C. majority	85

(June 1987, C. maj. 182)

BANFF AND BUCHAN (Grampian)
E.64,873   T.71.20%

*A. Salmond, *SNP*	21,954
S. Manson, *C.*	17,846
B. Balcombe, *Lab.*	3,803
Mrs R. Kemp, *LD*	2,588
SNP majority	4,108

(June 1987, SNP maj. 2,441)

CAITHNESS AND SUTHERLAND
(Highland)
E.30,905   T.71.93%

*R. Maclennan, *LD*	10,032
G. Bruce, *C.*	4,667
K. MacGregor, *SNP*	4,049
M. Coyne, *Lab.*	3,483
LD majority	5,365

(June 1987, SDP/All. maj. 8,494)

**CARRICK, CUMNOCK AND
DOON VALLEY** (Strathclyde)
E.55,330   T.76.94%

*G. Foulkes, *Lab.*	25,142
J. Boswell, *C.*	8,516

C. Douglas, *SNP*	6,910
Ms M. Paris, *LD*	2,005
Lab. majority	16,626

(June 1987, Lab. maj. 16,802)

CLACKMANNAN (Central)
E.48,963   T.78.34%

*M. O'Neill, *Lab.*	18,829
A. Brophy, *SNP*	10,326
J. Mackie, *C.*	6,638
Ms A. Watters, *LD*	2,567
Lab. majority	8,503

(June 1987, Lab. maj. 12,401)

CLYDEBANK AND MILNGAVIE
(Strathclyde)
E.47,337   T.77.79%

*A. Worthington, *Lab.*	19,637
G. Hughes, *SNP*	7,207
W. Harvey, *C.*	6,654
A. Tough, *LD*	3,216
Ms J. Barrie, *NLP*	112
Lab. majority	12,430

(June 1987, Lab. maj. 16,304)

CLYDESDALE (Strathclyde)
E.61,878   T.77.62%

*J. Hood, *Lab.*	21,418
Ms C. Goodwin, *C.*	11,231
I. Gray, *SNP*	11,084
Ms E. Buchanan, *LD*	3,957
S. Cartwright, *BNP*	342
Lab. majority	10,187

(June 1987, Lab. maj. 10,502)

CUMBERNAULD AND KILSYTH
(Strathclyde)
E.46,489   T.79.06%

*N. Hogg, *Lab.*	19,855
T. Johnston, *SNP*	10,640
I. Mitchell, *C.*	4,143
Ms J. Haddow, *LD*	2,118
Lab. majority	9,215

(June 1987, Lab. maj. 14,403)

CUNNINGHAME NORTH
(Strathclyde)
E.54,803   T.78.21%

*B. Wilson, *Lab.*	17,564
Ms E. Clarkson, *C.*	14,625
D. Crossan, *SNP*	7,813
D. Herbison, *LD*	2,864
Lab. majority	2,939

(June 1987, Lab. maj. 4,422)

CUNNINGHAME SOUTH
(Strathclyde)
E.49,010   T.75.88%

B. Donohoe, *Lab.*	19,687
R. Bell, *SNP*	9,007
S. Leslie, *C.*	6,070
B. Ashley, *LD*	2,299
W. Jackson, *NLP*	128
Lab. majority	10,680

(June 1987, Lab. maj. 16,633)

DUMBARTON (Strathclyde)
E.57,222   T.77.11%

*J. McFall, *Lab.*	19,255
T. Begg, *C.*	13,126

W. McKechnie, *SNP*	8,127
J. Morrison, *LD*	3,425
Ms D. Krass, *NLP*	192
Lab. majority	6,129

(June 1987, Lab. maj. 5,222)

DUMFRIES (D & G)
E.61,145   T.79.97%

*Sir H. Monro, *C.*	21,089
P. Rennie, *Lab.*	14,674
A. Morgan, *SNP*	6,971
N. Wallace, *LD*	5,749
G. McLeod, *Ind. Green*	312
T. Barlow, *NLP*	107
C. majority	6,415

(June 1987, C. maj. 7,493)

DUNDEE EAST (Tayside)
E.58,959   T.72.10%

*J. McAllion, *Lab.*	18,761
D. Coutts, *SNP*	14,197
S. Blackwood, *C.*	7,549
I. Yuill, *LD*	1,725
Ms S. Baird, *Green*	205
R. Baxter, *NLP*	77
Lab. majority	4,564

(June 1987, Lab. maj. 1,015)

DUNDEE WEST (Tayside)
E.59,953   T.69.82%

*E. Ross, *Lab.*	20,498
K. Brown, *SNP*	9,894
A. Spearman, *C.*	7,746
Ms E. Dick, *LD*	3,132
Ms E. Hood, *Green*	432
D. Arnold, *NLP*	159
Lab. majority	10,604

(June 1987, Lab. maj. 16,526)

DUNFERMLINE EAST (Fife)
E.50,179   T.75.62%

*J. G. Brown, *Lab.*	23,692
M. Tennant, *C.*	6,248
J. Lloyd, *SNP*	5,746
Ms T. Little, *LD*	2,262
Lab. majority	17,444

(June 1987, Lab. maj. 19,589)

DUNFERMLINE WEST (Fife)
E.50,948   T.76.44%

Ms R. Squire, *Lab.*	16,374
M. Scott-Hayward, *C.*	8,890
J. Smith, *SNP*	7,563
Ms E. Harris, *LD*	6,122
Lab. majority	7,484

(June 1987, Lab. maj. 9,402)

EAST KILBRIDE (Strathclyde)
E.64,080   T.80.01%

*A. Ingram, *Lab.*	24,055
Ms K. McAlorum, *SNP*	12,063
G. Lind, *C.*	9,781
Ms S. Grieve, *LD*	5,377
Lab. majority	11,992

(June 1987, Lab. maj. 12,624)

EAST LOTHIAN
E.66,699   T.82.37%

*J. Home Robertson, *Lab.*	25,537
J. Hepburne Scott, *C.*	15,501

G. Thomson, *SNP*   7,776
T. McKay, *LD*   6,126
Lab. majority   10,036
(June 1987, Lab. maj. 10,105)

EASTWOOD (Strathclyde)
*E.*63,685   *T.*80.97%
*J. A. Stewart, *C.*   24,124
P. Grant-Hutchison, *Lab.*   12,436
Miss M. Craig, *LD*   8,493
P. Scott, *SNP*   6,372
Dr L. Fergusson, *NLP*   146
C. majority   11,688
(June 1987, C. maj. 6,014)

EDINBURGH CENTRAL (Lothian)
*E.*56,527   *T.*69.26%
*A. Darling, *Lab.*   15,189
P. Martin, *C.*   13,063
Ms L. Devine, *SNP*   5,539
A. Myles, *LD*   4,500
R. Harper, *Green*   630
D. Wilson, *Lib.*   235
Lab. majority   2,126
(June 1987, Lab. maj. 2,262)

EDINBURGH EAST (Lothian)
*E.*45,687   *T.*73.89%
*G. Strang, *Lab.*   15,446
K. Ward, *C.*   8,235
D. McKinney, *SNP*   6,225
D. Scobie, *LD*   3,432
G. Farmer, *Green*   424
Lab. majority   7,211
(June 1987, Lab. maj. 9,295)

EDINBURGH LEITH (Lothian)
*E.*56,520   *T.*71.30%
M. Chisholm, *Lab.*   13,790
Ms F. Hyslop, *SNP*   8,805
M. Bin Ashiq Rizvi, *C.*   8,496
Mrs H. Campbell, *LD*   4,975
*R. Brown, *Ind. Lab.*   4,142
A. Swan, *NLP*   96
Lab. majority   4,985
(June 1987, Lab. maj. 11,327)

EDINBURGH PENTLANDS
(Lothian)
*E.*55,567   *T.*80.18%
*Rt. Hon. M. Rifkind, *C.*   18,128
M. Lazarowicz, *Lab.*   13,838
Ms K. Caskie, *SNP*   6,882
K. Smith, *LD*   5,597
D. Rae, *NLP*   111
C. majority   4,290
(June 1987, C. maj. 3,745)

EDINBURGH SOUTH (Lothian)
*E.*61,355   *T.*72.67%
*N. Griffiths, *Lab.*   18,485
S. Stevenson, *C.*   14,309
B. McCreadie, *LD*   5,961
R. Knox, *SNP*   5,727
G. Manclark, *NLP*   108
Lab. majority   4,176
(June 1987, Lab. maj. 1,859)

EDINBURGH WEST (Lothian)
*E.*58,998   *T.*82.67%
*Lord J. Douglas-Hamilton, *C.*   18,071
D. Gorrie, *LD*   17,192

Ms I. Kitson, *Lab.*   8,759
G. Sutherland, *SNP*   4,117
A. Fleming, *Lib.*   272
Ms L. Hendry, *Green*   234
D. Bruce, *BNP*   133
C. majority   879
(June 1987, C. maj. 1,234)

FALKIRK EAST (Central)
*E.*51,918   *T.*76.91%
M. Connarty, *Lab.*   18,423
R. Halliday, *SNP*   10,454
K. Harding, *C.*   8,279
Miss D. Storr, *LD*   2,775
Lab. majority   7,969
(June 1987, Lab. maj. 14,023)

FALKIRK WEST (Central)
*E.*50,126   *T.*76.77%
*D. Canavan, *Lab.*   19,162
W. Houston, *SNP*   9,350
M. Macdonald, *C.*   7,558
M. Reilly, *LD*   2,414
Lab. majority   9,812
(June 1987, Lab. maj. 13,552)

FIFE CENTRAL
*E.*56,152   *T.*74.33%
*H. McLeish, *Lab.*   21,036
Mrs T. Marwick, *SNP*   10,458
Ms C. Cender, *C.*   7,353
C. Harrow, *LD*   2,892
Lab. majority   10,578
(June 1987, Lab. maj. 15,709)

FIFE NORTH EAST
*E.*53,747   *T.*77.84%
*W. M. Campbell, *LD*   19,430
Mrs M. Scanlon, *C.*   16,122
D. Roche, *SNP*   3,589
Miss L. Clark, *Lab.*   2,319
T. Flynn, *Green*   294
D. Senior, *Lib.*   85
LD majority   3,308
(June 1987, L./All. maj. 1,447)

GALLOWAY AND UPPER
NITHSDALE (D & G)
*E.*54,474   *T.*81.66%
*Rt. Hon. I. Lang, *C.*   18,681
M. Brown, *SNP*   16,213
J. Dowson, *Lab.*   5,766
J. McKerchar, *LD*   3,826
C. majority   2,468
(June 1987, C. maj. 3,673)

GLASGOW CATHCART
(Strathclyde)
*E.*44,689   *T.*75.38%
*J. Maxton, *Lab.*   16,265
J. Young, *C.*   8,264
W. Steven, *SNP*   6,107
G. Dick, *LD*   2,614
Ms K. Allan, *Green*   441
Lab. majority   8,001
(June 1987, Lab. maj. 11,203)

GLASGOW CENTRAL (Strathclyde)
*E.*48,107   *T.*63.05%
*M. Watson, *Lab.*   17,341
B. O'Hara, *SNP*   6,322
E. Stewart, *C.*   4,208

Dr A. Rennie, *LD*   1,921
Ms I. Brandt, *Green*   435
T. Burn, *Comm. GB*   106
Lab. majority   11,019
(June 1987, Lab. maj. 17,253)
(June 1989, Lab. maj. 6,462)

GLASGOW GARSCADDEN
(Strathclyde)
*E.*41,289   *T.*71.13%
*D. Dewar, *Lab.*   18,920
R. Douglas, *SNP*   5,580
J. Scott, *C.*   3,385
C. Brodie, *LD*   1,425
W. Orr, *NLP*   61
Lab. majority   13,340
(June 1987, Lab. maj. 18,977)

GLASGOW GOVAN (Strathclyde)
*E.*45,822   *T.*76.03%
I. Davidson, *Lab.*   17,051
*J. Sillars, *SNP*   12,926
J. Donnelly, *C.*   3,458
R. Stewart, *LD*   1,227
D. Spaven, *Green*   181
Lab. majority   4,125
(June 1987, Lab. maj. 19,509)
(Nov. 1988, SNP maj. 3,554)

GLASGOW HILLHEAD
(Strathclyde)
*E.*57,223   *T.*68.80%
*G. Galloway, *Lab.*   15,148
C. Mason, *LD*   10,322
Ms A. Bates, *C.*   6,728
Miss S. White, *SNP*   6,484
Ms L. Collie, *Green*   558
Ms H. Gold, *Rev. Comm.*   73
D. Patterson, *NLP*   60
Lab. majority   4,826
(June 1987, Lab. maj. 3,251)

GLASGOW MARYHILL
(Strathclyde)
*E.*48,426   *T.*65.16%
*Mrs M. Fyfe, *Lab.*   19,452
C. Williamson, *SNP*   6,033
J. Godfrey, *C.*   3,248
J. Alexander, *LD*   2,215
P. O'Brien, *Green*   530
M. Henderson, *NLP*   78
Lab. majority   13,419
(June 1987, Lab. maj. 19,364)

GLASGOW POLLOK (Strathclyde)
*E.*46,139   *T.*70.74%
*J. Dunnachie, *Lab.*   14,170
T. Sheridan, *SML*   6,287
R. Gray, *C.*   5,147
G. Leslie, *SNP*   5,107
D. Jago, *LD*   1,932
Lab. majority   7,883
(June 1987, Lab. maj. 17,983)

GLASGOW PROVAN (Strathclyde)
*E.*36,560   *T.*65.31%
*J. Wray, *Lab.*   15,885
Ms A. MacRae, *SNP*   5,182
A. Rosindell, *C.*   1,865
C. Bell, *LD*   948
Lab. majority   10,703
(June 1987, Lab. maj. 18,372)

GLASGOW RUTHERGLEN
(Strathclyde)
E.52,709 *T*.75.23%

*T. McAvoy, *Lab.*	21,962
B. Cooklin, *C.*	6,692
J. Higgins, *SNP*	6,470
D. Baillie, *LD*	4,470
Ms B. Slaughter, *Int. Comm.*	62
Lab. majority	15,270

(June 1987, Lab. maj. 13,995)

GLASGOW SHETTLESTON
(Strathclyde)
E.51,910 *T*.68.91%

*D. Marshall, *Lab.*	21,665
Ms N. Sturgeon, *SNP*	6,831
N. Mortimer, *C.*	5,396
Ms J. Orskov, *LD*	1,881
Lab. majority	14,834

(June 1987, Lab. maj. 18,981)

GLASGOW SPRINGBURN
(Strathclyde)
E.45,842 *T*.65.65%

*M. Martin, *Lab.*	20,369
S. Miller, *SNP*	5,863
A. Barnett, *C.*	2,625
R. Ackland, *LD*	1,242
Lab. majority	14,506

(June 1987, Lab. maj. 22,063)

GORDON (Grampian)
E.80,103 *T*.73.86%

*M. Bruce, *LD*	22,158
J. Porter, *C.*	21,884
B. Adam, *SNP*	8,445
P. Morrell, *Lab.*	6,682
LD majority	274

(June 1987, L./All. maj. 9,519)

GREENOCK AND PORT
GLASGOW (Strathclyde)
E.52,053 *T*.73.72%

*N. Godman, *Lab.*	22,258
I. Black, *SNP*	7,279
Dr J. McCullough, *C.*	4,479
C. Lambert, *LD*	4,359
Lab. majority	14,979

(June 1987, Lab. maj. 20,055)

HAMILTON (Strathclyde)
E.61,531 *T*.76.15%

*G. Robertson, *Lab.*	25,849
W. Morrison, *SNP*	9,246
Ms M. Mitchell, *C.*	8,250
J. Oswald, *LD*	3,515
Lab. majority	16,603

(June 1987, Lab. maj. 21,662)

INVERNESS NAIRN AND
LOCHABER (Highland)
E.69,468 *T*.73.27%

*Sir R. Johnston, *LD*	13,258
D. Stewart, *Lab.*	12,800
F. Ewing, *SNP*	12,562
J. Scott, *C.*	11,517
J. Martin, *Green*	766
LD majority	458

(June 1987, L./All maj. 5,431)

KILMARNOCK AND LOUDOUN
(Strathclyde)
E.62,002 *T*.79.99%

*W. McKelvey, *Lab.*	22,210
A. Neil, *SNP*	15,231
R. Wilkinson, *C.*	9,438
Mrs K. Philbrick, *LD*	2,722
Lab. majority	6,979

(June 1987, Lab. maj. 14,127)

KINCARDINE AND DEESIDE
(Grampian)
E.66,617 *T*.78.74%

G. Kynoch, *C.*	22,924
*N. Stephen, *LD*	18,429
Dr A. Macartney, *SNP*	5,927
M. Savidge, *Lab.*	4,795
S. Campbell, *Green*	381
C. majority	4,495

(June 1987, C. maj. 2,063)
(Nov. 1991, LD maj. 7,824)

KIRKCALDY (Fife)
E.51,762 *T*.75.06%

*Dr L. Moonie, *Lab.*	17,887
S. Hosie, *SNP*	8,761
S. Wosley, *C.*	8,476
Ms S. Leslie, *LD*	3,729
Lab. majority	9,126

(June 1987, Lab. maj. 11,570)

LINLITHGOW (Lothian)
E.61,082 *T*.78.66%

*T. Dalyell, *Lab.*	21,603
K. MacAskill, *SNP*	14,577
Ms E. Forbes, *C.*	8,424
M. Falchikov, *LD*	3,446
Lab. majority	7,026

(June 1987, Lab. maj. 10,373)

LIVINGSTON (Lothian)
E.61,092 *T*.74.62%

*R. Cook, *Lab.*	20,245
P. Johnston, *SNP*	12,140
H. Gordon, *C.*	8,824
F. Mackintosh, *LD*	3,911
A. Ross-Smith, *Green*	469
Lab. majority	8,105

(June 1987, Lab. maj. 11,105)

MIDLOTHIAN
E.60,255 *T*.77.87%

E. Clarke, *Lab.*	20,588
A. Lumsden, *SNP*	10,254
J. Stoddart, *C.*	9,443
P. Sewell, *LD*	6,164
I. Morrice, *Green*	476
Lab. majority	10,334

(June 1987, Lab. maj. 12,253)

MONKLANDS EAST (Strathclyde)
E.48,391 *T*.75.07%

*Rt. Hon. J. Smith, *Lab.*	22,266
J. Wright, *SNP*	6,554
S. Walters, *C.*	5,830
P. Ross, *LD*	1,679
Lab. majority	15,712

(June 1987, Lab. maj. 16,389)

MONKLANDS WEST (Strathclyde)
E.49,269 *T*.77.45%

*T. Clarke, *Lab.*	23,384
K. Bovey, *SNP*	6,319

A. Lownie, *C.*	6,074
Ms S. Hamilton, *LD*	2,382
Lab. majority	17,065

(June 1987, Lab. maj. 18,333)

MORAY (Grampian)
E.63,255 *T*.72.46%

*Mrs M. Ewing, *SNP*	20,299
Ms R. Hossack, *C.*	17,455
C. Smith, *Lab.*	5,448
B. Sheridan, *LD*	2,634
SNP majority	2,844

(June 1987, SNP maj. 3,685)

MOTHERWELL NORTH
(Strathclyde)
E.57,290 *T*.76.71%

*Dr J. Reid, *Lab.*	27,852
D. Clark, *SNP*	8,942
R. Hargrave, *C.*	5,011
Miss H. Smith, *LD*	2,145
Lab. majority	18,910

(June 1987, Lab. maj. 23,595)

MOTHERWELL SOUTH
(Strathclyde)
E.50,042 *T*.76.17%

*J. Bray, *Lab.*	21,771
Mrs K. Ullrich, *SNP*	7,758
G. McIntosh, *C.*	6,097
A. Mackie, *LD*	2,349
D. Lettice, *YSOR*	146
Lab. majority	14,013

(June 1987, Lab. maj. 16,930)

ORKNEY AND SHETLAND
E.31,472 *T*.65.53%

*J. Wallace, *LD*	9,575
Dr P. McCormick, *C.*	4,542
J. Aberdein, *Lab.*	4,093
Mrs F. McKie, *SNP*	2,301
Ms C. Wharton, *NLP*	115
LD majority	5,033

(June 1987, L./All. maj. 3,922)

PAISLEY NORTH (Strathclyde)
E.46,403 *T*.73.39%

*Mrs I. Adams, *Lab.*	17,269
R. Mullin, *SNP*	7,940
D. Sharpe, *C.*	5,576
Miss E. McCartin, *LD*	2,779
D. Mellor, *Green*	412
N. Brennan, *NLP*	81
Lab. majority	9,329

(June 1987, Lab. maj. 14,442)
(Nov. 1990, Lab. maj. 3,770)

PAISLEY SOUTH (Strathclyde)
E.47,889 *T*.75.01%

*G. McMaster, *Lab.*	18,202
I. Lawson, *SNP*	8,653
Ms S. Laidlaw, *C.*	5,703
A. Reid, *LD*	3,271
S. Porter, *NLP*	93
Lab. majority	9,549

(June 1987, Lab. maj. 15,785)
(Nov. 1990, Lab. maj. 5,030)

PERTH AND KINROSS (Tayside)
E.65,410 *T*.76.86%

*Sir N. Fairbairn, *C.*	20,195
Ms R. Cunningham, *SNP*	18,101

M. Rolfe, *Lab.* — 6,267
M. Black, *LD* — 5,714
C. majority — 2,094
(June 1987, C. maj. 5,676)

RENFREW WEST AND
INVERCLYDE (Strathclyde)
*E.*58,122   *T.*80.32%
*T. Graham, *Lab.* — 17,085
Ms A. Goldie, *C.* — 15,341
C. Campbell, *SNP* — 9,444
S. Nimmo, *LD* — 4,668
D. Maltman, *NLP* — 149
Lab. majority — 1,744
(June 1987, Lab. maj. 4,063)

ROSS, CROMARTY AND SKYE
(Highland)
*E.*55,524   *T.*73.90%
*C. Kennedy, *LD* — 17,066
J. Gray, *C.* — 9,436
R. Gibson, *SNP* — 7,618
J. MacDonald, *Lab.* — 6,275
D. Jardine, *Green* — 642
LD majority — 7,630
(June 1987, SDP/All. maj. 11,319)

ROXBURGH AND
BERWICKSHIRE (Borders)
*E.*43,485   *T.*77.71%
*A. Kirkwood, *LD* — 15,852
S. Finlay-Maxwell, *C.* — 11,595
M. Douglas, *SNP* — 3,437
S. Lambert, *Lab.* — 2,909
LD majority — 4,257
(June 1987, L./All maj. 4,008)

STIRLING (Central)
*E.*58,266   *T.*82.29%
*M. Forsyth, *C.* — 19,174
Ms K. Phillips, *Lab.* — 18,471
G. Fisher, *SNP* — 6,558
W. Robertson, *LD* — 3,337
W. Thomson, *Green* — 342
R. Sharp, *Loony* — 68
C. majority — 703
(June 1987, C. maj. 548)

STRATHKELVIN AND BEARSDEN
(Strathclyde)
*E.*61,116   *T.*82.33%
*S. Galbraith, *Lab.* — 21,267
M. Hirst, *C.* — 18,105
T. Chalmers, *SNP* — 6,275
Ms B. Waterfield, *LD* — 4,585
D. Whitley, *NLP* — 90
Lab. majority — 3,162
(June 1987, Lab. maj. 2,452)

TAYSIDE NORTH
*E.*55,969   *T.*77.64%
*W. Walker, *C.* — 20,283
J. Swinney, *SNP* — 16,288
S. Horner, *LD* — 3,791
S. Maclennan, *Lab.* — 3,094
C. majority — 3,995
(June 1987, C. maj. 5,016)

TWEEDDALE, ETTRICK AND
LAUDERDALE (Borders)
*E.*39,493   *T.*78.04%
*Rt. Hon. Sir D. Steel, *LD* — 12,296
L. Beat, *C.* — 9,776
Mrs C. Creech, *SNP* — 5,244
A. Dunton, *Lab.* — 3,328
J. Hein, *Lib.* — 177
LD majority — 2,520
(June 1987, L./All. maj. 5,942)

WESTERN ISLES
*E.*22,784   *T.*70.35%
*C. MacDonald, *Lab.* — 7,664
Ms F. MacFarlane, *SNP* — 5,961
R. Heany, *C.* — 1,362
N. Mitchison, *LD* — 552
A. Price, *Ind.* — 491
Lab. majority — 1,703
(June 1987, Lab. maj. 2,340)

NORTHERN IRELAND

ANTRIM EAST
*E.*62,839   *T.*62.46%
*R. Beggs, *UUP* — 16,966
N. Dodds, *DUP* — 9,544
S. Neeson, *All.* — 9,132
Miss M. Boal, *C.* — 3,359
Ms A. Palmer, *NLP* — 250
UUP majority — 7,422
(June 1987, UUP maj. 15,360)

ANTRIM NORTH
*E.*69,124   *T.*65.82%
*Revd I. Paisley, *DUP* — 23,152
J. Gaston, *UUP* — 8,216
S. Farren, *SDLP* — 6,512
G. Williams, *All.* — 3,442
R. Sowler, *C.* — 2,263
J. McGarry, *SF* — 1,916
DUP majority — 14,936
(June 1987, DUP maj. 23,234)

ANTRIM SOUTH
*E.*68,013   *T.*62.10%
*C. Forsythe, *UUP* — 29,956
D. McClelland, *SDLP* — 5,397
J. Blair, *All.* — 5,224
H. Cushinan, *SF* — 1,220
D. Martin, *Loony G.* — 442
UUP majority — 24,559
(June 1987, UUP maj. 19,587)

BELFAST EAST
*E.*52,833   *T.*67.74%
*P. Robinson, *DUP* — 18,437
Dr J. Alderdice, *All.* — 10,650
D. Greene, *C.* — 3,314

Ms D. Dunlop, *Ind. U.* — 2,256
J. O'Donnell, *SF* — 679
J. Bell, *WP* — 327
G. Redden, *NLP* — 128
DUP majority — 7,787
(June 1987, DUP maj. 9,798)

BELFAST NORTH
*E.*55,062   *T.*65.22%
*A. C. Walker, *UUP* — 17,240
A. Maginness, *SDLP* — 7,615
P. McManus, *SF* — 4,693
T. Campbell, *All.* — 2,246
Ms M. Redpath, *C.* — 2,107
S. Lynch, *NA* — 1,386
Ms M. Smith, *WP* — 419
D. O'Leary, *NLP* — 208
UUP majority — 9,625
(June 1987, UUP maj. 8,560)

BELFAST SOUTH
*E.*52,032   *T.*64.54%
*Revd W. M. Smyth, *UUP* — 16,336
Dr A. McDonnell, *SDLP* — 6,266
J. Montgomery, *All.* — 5,054
L. Fee, *C.* — 3,356
S. Hayes, *SF* — 1,123
P. Hadden, *LTU* — 875
P. Lynn, *WP* — 362
Ms T. Mullan, *NLP* — 212
UUP majority — 10,070
(June 1987, UUP maj. 11,954)

BELFAST WEST
*E.*54,609   *T.*73.19%
Dr J. Hendron, *SDLP* — 17,415
*G. Adams, *SF* — 16,826
F. Cobain, *UUP* — 4,766
J. Lowry, *WP* — 750
M. Kennedy, *NLP* — 213
SDLP majority — 589
(June 1987, SF maj. 2,221)

DOWN NORTH
*E.*68,662   *T.*65.47%
*J. Kilfedder, *UPUP* — 19,305
Dr L. Kennedy, *C.* — 14,371
Ms A. Morrow, *All.* — 6,611
D. Vitty, *DUP* — 4,414
A. Wilmot, *NLP* — 255
UPUP majority — 4,934
(June 1987, UPUP maj. 3,953)

DOWN SOUTH
*E.*76,093   *T.*80.92%
*E. McGrady, *SDLP* — 31,523
D. Nelson, *UUP* — 25,181
S. Fitzpatrick, *SF* — 1,843
M. Healey, *All.* — 1,542
Mrs S. McKenzie-Hill, *C.* — 1,488
SDLP majority — 6,342
(June 1987, SDLP maj. 731)

FERMANAGH AND SOUTH
TYRONE
*E.*70,192   *T.*78.53%
*K. Maginnis, *UUP* — 26,923
T. Gallagher, *SDLP* — 12,810
F. Molloy, *SF* — 12,604

D. Kettyles, *Prog. Soc.*	1,094
E. Bullick, *All.*	950
G. Cullen, *NA*	747
UUP majority	14,113
(June 1987, UUP maj. 12,823)	

FOYLE
*E.*74,585   *T.*69.57%

*J. Hume, *SDLP*	26,710
G. Campbell, *DUP*	13,705
M. McGuinness, *SF*	9,149
Ms L. McIlroy, *All.*	1,390
G. McKenzie, *WP*	514
J. Burns, *NLP*	422
SDLP majority	13,005
(June 1987, SDLP maj. 9,860)	

LAGAN VALLEY
*E.*72,645   *T.*67.39%

*Rt. Hon. J. H. Molyneaux, *UUP*	29,772
S. Close, *All.*	6,207
H. Lewsley, *SDLP*	4,626
T. Coleridge, *C.*	4,423
P. Rice, *SF*	3,346
Ms A.-M. Lowry, *WP*	582
UUP majority	23,565
(June 1987, UUP maj. 23,373)	

LONDONDERRY EAST
*E.*75,559   *T.*69.79%

*W. Ross, *UUP*	30,370
A. Doherty, *SDLP*	11,843
Ms P. Davey-Kennedy, *SF*	5,320
P. McGowan, *All.*	3,613
A. Elder, *C.*	1,589
UUP majority	18,527
(June 1987, UUP maj. 20,157)	

NEWRY AND ARMAGH
*E.*67,508   *T.*77.87%

*S. Mallon, *SDLP*	26,073
J. Speers, *UUP*	18,982
B. Curran, *SF*	6,547
Mrs E. Bell, *All.*	972
SDLP majority	7,091
(June 1987, SDLP maj. 5,325)	

STRANGFORD
*E.*68,870   *T.*65.02%

*Rt. Hon. J. Taylor, *UUP*	19,517
S. Wilson, *DUP*	10,606
K. McCarthy, *All.*	7,585
S. Eyre, *C.*	6,782
D. Shaw, *NLP*	295
UUP majority	8,911
(June 1987, UUP maj. 20,646)	

ULSTER MID
*E.*69,071   *T.*79.28%

*Revd Dr R. T. W. McCrea, *DUP*	23,181
D. Haughey, *SDLP*	16,994
B. McElduff, *SF*	10,248
J. McLoughlin, *Ind.*	1,996
Ms A. Gormley, *All.*	1,506
H. Hutchinson, *LTU*	389
T. Owens, *WP*	285
J. Anderson, *NLP*	164
DUP majority	6,187
(June 1987, DUP maj. 9,360)	

UPPER BANN
*E.*67,446   *T.*67.43%

*W. D. Trimble, *UUP*	26,824
Mrs B. Rodgers, *SDLP*	10,661
B. Curran, *SF*	2,777
Dr W. Ramsey, *All.*	2,541
Mrs C. Jones, *C.*	1,556
T. French, *WP*	1,120
UUP majority	16,163
(June 1987, OUP maj. 17,361)	
(May 1990, OUP maj. 13,849)	

COMMONWEALTH PARLIAMENTARY ASSOCIATION (1911)

The Commonwealth Parliamentary Association consists of 122 branches in the national, state, provincial or territorial parliaments in the countries of the Commonwealth. Conferences and general assemblies are held every year in different countries of the Commonwealth.

President (1992–3), His Excellency Alexis Galanos, MP, President of the House of Representatives (*Cyprus*)

Vice-President (1992–3), Hon. John Fraser, PC, QC, MP, Speaker of the House of Commons (*Canada*)

Chairman of the Executive Committee (1990–3), Hon. Clive Griffiths, MLC, President of the Legislative Council (*Western Australia*)

Secretary-General, A. R. Donahoe, QC, 7 Old Palace Yard, London SW1P 3JY

UNITED KINGDOM BRANCH

Hon. Presidents, The Lord Chancellor; Madam Speaker
Chairman of Branch, The Rt. Hon. John Major, MP

Chairman of Executive Committee, C. Shepherd, MP
Secretary, P. Cobb, OBE, Westminster Hall, Palace of Westminster, London, SW1

THE INTER-PARLIAMENTARY UNION (1889)

To facilitate personal contact between members of all Parliaments in the promotion of representative institutions, peace and international co-operation.

Secretary-General, P. Cornillon, Place du Petit-Saconnex, BP 99, 1211 Geneva 19, Switzerland

BRITISH GROUP
Palace of Westminster, London SW1A 0AA

Hon. Presidents, The Lord Chancellor; Madam Speaker
President, The Rt. Hon. John Major, MP
Chairman, Dr M. Clark, MP
Secretary, D. Ramsay

European Parliament

UK MEMBERS AS AT END JULY 1993

* Denotes membership of the last Parliament

*Adam, Gordon J. (b. 1934), Lab., Northumbria, maj. 60,040
*Balfe, Richard A. (b. 1944), Lab. Co-op, London South Inner, maj. 45,018
Barton, Roger (b. 1945), Lab., Sheffield, maj. 69,276
*Beazley, Christopher J. P. (b. 1952), C., Cornwall and Plymouth, maj. 19,817
*Beazley, Peter G., CBE (b. 1922), C., Bedfordshire South, maj. 2,977
*Bethell, The Lord (b. 1938), C., London North West, maj. 7,400
*Bird, John A. W. (b. 1926), Lab. Co-op, Midlands West, maj. 42,364
Bowe, David (b. 1955), Lab., Cleveland and Yorkshire North, maj. 24,092
*Buchan, Mrs Janey O. (b. 1926), Lab., Glasgow, maj. 59,232
*Cassidy, Bryan M. D. (b. 1934), C., Dorset East and Hampshire West, maj. 61,774
*Catherwood, Sir Frederick (b. 1925), C., Cambridge and Bedfordshire North, maj. 32,321
Coates, Kenneth (b. 1939), Lab., Nottingham, maj. 14,513
*Collins, Kenneth D. (b. 1939), Lab., Strathclyde East, maj. 60,317
Crampton, Peter D. (b. 1932), Lab., Humberside, maj. 16,328
*Crawley, Mrs Christine M. (b. 1950), Lab., Birmingham East, maj. 46,948
*Daly, Mrs Margaret E. (b. 1938), C., Somerset and Dorset West, maj. 52,220
David, Wayne (b. 1957), Lab., Wales South, maj. 62,557
Donnelly, Alan J. (b. 1957), Lab., Tyne and Wear, maj. 95,780
*Elles, James E. M. (b. 1949), C., Oxford and Buckinghamshire, maj. 47,518
*Elliott, Michael N. (b. 1932), Lab., London West, maj. 14,808
*Ewing, Mrs Winifred M. (b. 1929), SNP, Highlands and Islands, maj. 44,695
*Falconer, Alec (b. 1940), Lab., Scotland Mid and Fife, maj. 52,157
Fletcher-Vane, see Inglewood
*Ford, J. Glyn (b. 1950), Lab., Greater Manchester East, maj. 34,501
Green, Ms Pauline (b. 1948), Lab. Co-op, London North, maj. 5,837
Harrison, Lyndon (b. 1947), Lab., Cheshire West, maj. 23,201
*Hindley, Michael J. (b. 1947), Lab., Lancashire East, maj. 39,148
*Hoon, Geoffrey W. (b. 1953), Lab., Derbyshire, maj. 33,388
*Howell, Paul F. (b. 1951), C., Norfolk, maj. 20,907
*Hughes, Stephen S. (b. 1952), Lab., Durham, maj. 86,848
*Hume, John, MP (b. 1937), SDLP, Northern Ireland, polled 136,335 votes
Inglewood, The Lord (Richard Fletcher-Vane) (b. 1951), C., Cumbria and Lancashire North, maj. 2,391
*Jackson, Mrs Caroline F. (b. 1946), C., Wiltshire, maj. 46,313
*Jackson, Christopher M. (b. 1935), C., Kent East, maj. 28,961

*Kellett-Bowman, Edward T. (b. 1931), C., Hampshire Central, maj. 27,674
*Lomas, Alfred (b. 1928), Lab., London North East, maj. 47,767
*McGowan, Michael (b. 1940), Lab., Leeds, maj. 42,518
McCubbin, Henry (b. 1942), Lab., Scotland North East, maj. 2,613
McIntosh, Miss Anne C. B. (b. 1954), C., Essex North East, maj. 39,398
*McMahon, Hugh R. (b. 1938), Lab., Strathclyde West, maj. 39,591
*McMillan-Scott, Edward H. C. (b. 1949), C., York, maj. 15,102
*Martin, David W. (b. 1954), Lab., Lothians, maj. 38,826
*Megahy, Thomas (b. 1929), Lab., Yorkshire South West, maj. 65,901
*Moorhouse, C. James O. (b. 1924), C., London South and Surrey East, maj. 30,816
*Morris, Revd David R. (b. 1930), Lab., Wales Mid and West, maj. 51,912
*Newens, A. Stanley (b. 1930), Lab. Co-op, London Central, maj. 11,542
*Newman, Edward (b. 1953), Lab., Greater Manchester Central, maj. 38,867
*Newton Dunn, William F. (b. 1941), C., Lincolnshire, maj. 20,650
Nicholson, James F. (b. 1945), UUP, Northern Ireland, polled 118,785 votes
Oddy, Ms Christine M. (b. 1955), Lab., Midlands Central, maj. 5,093
*O'Hagan, The Lord (b. 1945), C., Devon, maj. 57,298
*Paisley, Revd Ian R. K., MP (b. 1926), DUP, Northern Ireland, polled 160,110 votes
*Patterson, G. Benjamin (Ben) (b. 1939), C., Kent West, maj. 24,050
*Plumb, The Lord (b. 1925), C., The Cotswolds, maj. 45,678
Pollack, Ms Anita J. (b. 1946), Lab., London South West, maj. 518
*Prag, Derek (b. 1923), C., Hertfordshire, maj. 43,342
*Price, Peter N. (b. 1942), C., London South East, maj. 7,590
*Prout, Sir Christopher, TD, QC (b. 1942), C., Shropshire and Stafford, maj. 2,544
Rawlings, Miss Patricia (b. 1939), C., Essex South West, maj. 9,403
Read, Ms Mel (b. 1939), Lab., Leicester, maj. 15,322
*Scott-Hopkins, Sir James (b. 1921), C., Hereford and Worcester, maj. 25,665
*Seal, Barry H. (b. 1937), Lab., Yorkshire West, maj. 37,927
*Seligman, R. Madron (b. 1918), C., Sussex West, maj. 46,233
*Simmonds, Richard J. (b. 1944), C., Wight and Hampshire East, maj. 39,430
*Simpson, Anthony M. H., TD (b. 1935), C., Northamptonshire, maj. 20,447
Simpson, Brian (b. 1953), Lab., Cheshire East, maj. 1,864
Smith, Alexander (b. 1943), Lab., Scotland South, maj. 15,693
*Smith, Llewellyn T. (b. 1944), Lab., Wales South East, maj. 108,488

Spencer, Thomas N. B. (*b.* 1948), *C., Surrey West*, maj. 49,342

Stevens, John C. C. (*b.* 1955), *C., Thames Valley*, maj. 26,491

*Stevenson, George W. (*b.* 1938), *Lab., Staffordshire East*, maj. 31,769

*Stewart, Kenneth A. (*b.* 1925), *Lab., Merseyside West*, maj. 49,817

*Stewart-Clark, Sir John, Bt. (*b.* 1929), *C., Sussex East*, maj. 53,294

Titley, Gary (*b.* 1950), *Lab., Greater Manchester West*, maj. 50,135

*Tomlinson, John E. (*b.* 1939), *Lab., Birmingham West*, maj. 30,860

*Tongue, Miss Carole (*b.* 1955), *Lab., London East*, maj. 27,385

*Turner, Amédée E., QC (*b.* 1929), *C., Suffolk*, maj. 25,693

*Welsh, Michael J. (*b.* 1942), *C., Lancashire Central*, maj. 5,688

*West, Norman (*b.* 1935), *Lab., Yorkshire South*, maj. 91,784

White, Ian (*b.* 1947), *Lab., Bristol*, maj. 9,982

Wilson, Joseph (*b.* 1937), *Lab., Wales North*, maj. 4,460

Wynn, Terence (*b.* 1946), *Lab., Merseyside East*, maj. 76,867

UK CONSTITUENCIES AS AT 15 JUNE 1989

Corr.	Corrective Party
Grn.	Green
Hum.	Humanist Party
ICP	International Communist Party
Lab. RG	Labour for Regional Government
MK	Mebyon Kernow
W. Reg.	Wessex Regionalists

For other abbreviations, *see* page 243

BEDFORDSHIRE SOUTH
E. 569,506

*P. G. Beazley, *C.*	73,406
T. McWalter, *Lab.*	70,429
D. Everett, *Grn*	34,508
W. M. Johnston, *SLD*	8,748
R. Muller, *SDP*	3,067
C. majority	2,977

(June 1984, C. maj. 14,982)

BIRMINGHAM EAST
E. 531,081

*Mrs C. M. Crawley, *Lab.*	96,588
M. J. C. Harbour, *C.*	49,640
P. M. Simpson, *Grn.*	22,589
J. C. Binns, *SDP*	5,424
J. M. E. C. Roodhouse, *SLD*	4,010
M. Wingfield, *NF*	1,471
Lab. majority	46,948

(June 1984, Lab. maj. 21,383)

BIRMINGHAM WEST
E. 515,817

*J. E. Tomlinson, *Lab.*	86,545
C. F. Robinson, *C.*	55,685
J. D. Bentley, *Grn.*	21,384
S. Reynolds, *SLD*	7,673
Lab. majority	30,860

(June 1984, Lab. maj. 6,244)

BRISTOL
E. 562,277

I. White, *Lab.*	87,753
*R. J. Cottrell, *C.*	77,771
D. N. Wall, *Grn.*	39,436
C. Boney, *SLD*	16,309
G. McEwen *W. Reg.*	1,017
Lab. majority	9,982

(June 1984, C. maj. 17,644)

CAMBRIDGE AND
BEDFORDSHIRE NORTH
E. 562,539

*Sir F. Catherwood, *C.*	84,044
M. Strube, *Lab.*	51,723

Ms M. E. Wright, *Grn.*	37,956
A. N. Duff, *SLD*	15,052
C. majority	32,321

(June 1984, C. maj. 47,216)

CHESHIRE EAST
E. 518,311

B. Simpson, *Lab.*	74,721
*Sir T. Normanton, *C.*	72,857
C. C. White, *Grn.*	21,456
Mrs B. Fraenkel, *SLD*	12,344
Lab. majority	1,864

(June 1984, C. maj. 18,376)

CHESHIRE WEST
E. 543,256

L. Harrison, *Lab.*	102,962
*A. Pearce, *C.*	79,761
G. L. Nicholls, *Grn.*	25,933
J. Rankin, *SLD*	9,333
Lab. majority	23,201

(June 1984, C. maj. 9,692)

CLEVELAND AND YORKSHIRE
NORTH
E. 571,254

D. Bowe, *Lab.*	94,953
*Sir P. Vanneck, *C.*	70,861
O. Dumpleton, *Grn.*	17,225
T. M. Mawston, *SLD*	8,470
R. I. Andrew *SDP*	7,970
Lab. majority	24,092

(June 1984, C. maj. 2,625)

CORNWALL AND PLYMOUTH
E. 542,527

*C. J. P. Beazley, *C.*	88,376
P. A. Tyler, *SLD*	68,559
Ms D. Kirk, *Lab.*	41,466
H. Hoptrough, *Grn.*	24,581
C. Lawry, *MK*	4,224
C. majority	19,817

(June 1984, C. maj. 17,751)

THE COTSWOLDS
E. 558,115

*The Lord Plumb, *C.*	94,852
Mrs S. Limb, *Grn.*	49,174
T. Levitt, *Lab.*	48,180
L. A. Rowe, *SLD*	18,196
C. majority	45,678

(June 1984, C. maj. 48,942)

CUMBRIA AND LANCASHIRE
NORTH

E. 561,263

W. R. Fletcher-Vane, *C.*	84,035
J. M. P. Hutton, *Lab.*	81,644
Mrs C. E. Smith, *Grn.*	21,262
E. E. Hill, *SLD*	12,590
J. Bates, *SDP*	4,206
C. majority	2,391

(June 1984, C. maj. 23,795)

DERBYSHIRE
E. 564,429

*G. W. Hoon, *Lab.*	105,018
P. Jenkinson, *C.*	72,630
E. Wall, *Grn.*	20,781
S. Molloy, *SLD*	4,613
Mrs A. M. Ayres, *SDP*	3,858
Lab. majority	33,388

(June 1984, Lab maj. 6,853)

DEVON
E. 596,671

*The Lord O'Hagan, *C.*	110,518
P. S. Christie, *Grn.*	53,220
W. J. Cairns, *Lab.*	40,675
M. Edmunds, *SLD*	23,306
R. Edwards, *SDP*	7,806
S. B. F. Hughes, *LM*	2,241
Lady Rous, *W. Reg.*	385
C. majority	57,298

(June 1984, C. maj. 56,610)

DORSET EAST AND HAMPSHIRE
WEST
E. 608,895

*B. M. D. Cassidy, *C.*	111,469
Ms K. I. Bradbury, *Grn.*	49,695
H. R. White, *Lab.*	38,011
H. R. Legg, *SLD*	21,809
C. majority	61,774

(June 1984, C. maj. 59,891)

DURHAM
E. 530,137

*S. S. Hughes, *Lab.*	124,448
R. Hull, *C.*	37,600
Ms H. I. Lennox, *Grn.*	18,770
P. Freitag, *SLD*	8,369
Lab. majority	86,848

(June 1984, Lab. maj. 61,227)

ESSEX NORTH EAST
E. 598,542

Miss A. C. B. McIntosh, *C.*	92,758
Ms H. J. Bryan, *Lab.*	53,360

C. R. Keene, *Grn.* 45,163
Miss D. P. Wallis, *SLD* 16,939
C. majority 39,398
(June 1984, C. maj. 54,302)

ESSEX SOUTH WEST
E. 569,011
Miss P. E. Rawlings, *C.* 77,408
J. W. Orpe, *Lab.* 68,005
Mrs M. E. Willis, *Grn.* 32,242
T. P. Allen, *SLD* 10,618
C. majority 9,403
(June 1984, C. maj. 16,021)

GLASGOW
E. 487,199
*Mrs J. O. Buchan, *Lab.* 107,818
A. Brophy, *SNP* 48,586
Mrs A. K. Bates, *C.* 20,761
D. L. Spaven, *Grn.* 12,229
J. Morrison, *SLD* 3,887
D. Chalmers, *Comm.* 1,164
J. Simons, *ICP* 193
Lab. majority 59,232
(June 1984, Lab. maj. 65,733)

GREATER MANCHESTER
CENTRAL
E. 481,023
*E. Newman, *Lab.* 86,914
Miss C. E. Gillan, *C.* 48,047
B. Candeland, *Grn.* 19,742
J. H. Mulholland, *SLD* 9,437
S. M. Millson, *SDP* 2,769
S. Knight, *Hum.* 1,045
Lab. majority 38,867
(June 1984, Lab. maj. 28,077)

GREATER MANCHESTER EAST
E. 506,930
*J. G. Ford, *Lab.* 93,294
R. N. Greenwood, *C.* 58,793
M. J. Shipley, *Grn.* 19,090
A. B. Leah, *SLD* 16,645
Lab. majority 34,501
(June 1984, Lab. maj. 8,651)

GREATER MANCHESTER WEST
E. 522,476
G. Titley, *Lab.* 109,228
P. H. Twyman, *C.* 59,093
D. W. Milne, *Grn.* 22,778
A. H. Cruden, *SLD* 6,940
Mrs B. Archer, *SDP* 4,526
Lab. majority 50,135
(June 1984, Lab. maj. 37,698)

HAMPSHIRE CENTRAL
E. 546,630
*E. T. Kellett-Bowman, *C.* 78,651
Ms A. Mawle, *Lab.* 50,977
Mrs S. J. Penton, *Grn.* 33,186
D. W. G. Chidgey, *SLD* 18,418
C. majority 27,674
(June 1984, C. maj. 44,821)
(Dec. 1988, C. maj. 21,442)

HEREFORD AND WORCESTER
E. 595,504
*Sir James Scott-Hopkins, *C.* 87,898
C. A. Short, *Lab.* 62,233
Ms F. M. Norman, *Grn.* 49,296

Mrs J. D. Davies, *SLD* 13,569
C. majority 25,665
(June 1984, C. maj. 39,934)

HERTFORDSHIRE
E. 517,137
*D. N. Prag, *C.* 86,898
V. S. Anand, *Lab.* 43,556
M. F. Ames, *Grn.* 37,277
M. D. Phelan, *SLD* 13,456
Mrs C. Treves Brown, *SDP* 5,048
C. majority 43,342
(June 1984, C. maj. 45,932)

HIGHLANDS AND ISLANDS
E. 313,877
*Mrs W. M. Ewing, *SNP* 66,297
Sir A. McQuarrie, *C.* 21,602
N. MacAskill, *Lab.* 17,848
M. Gregson, *Grn.* 12,199
N. Michison, *SLD* 10,644
SNP majority 44,695
(June 1984, SNP maj. 16,277)

HUMBERSIDE
E. 504,219
P. D. Crampton, *Lab.* 74,163
*R. C. Battersby, *C.* 57,835
Mrs J. C. Clark, *Grn.* 23,835
F. L. Parker, *SLD* 3,989
S. W. Unwin, *SDP* 3,419
Lab. majority 16,328
(June 1984, C. maj. 8,015)

KENT EAST
E. 575,789
*C. M. Jackson, *C.* 85,667
G. N. J. Perry, *Lab.* 56,706
Ms P. A. Kemp, *Grn.* 36,931
A. F. C. Morris, *SLD* 15,470
C. majority 28,961
(June 1984, C. maj. 48,867)

KENT WEST
E. 569,725
*G. B. Patterson, *C.* 82,519
P. L. Sloman, *Lab.* 58,469
J. Tidy, *Grn.* 33,202
J. B. Doherty, *SLD* 16,087
C. majority 24,050
(June 1984, C. maj. 34,630)

LANCASHIRE CENTRAL
E. 537,610
*M. J. Welsh, *C.* 81,125
G. W. T. Smith, *Lab.* 75,437
Mrs H. Ingham, *Grn.* 28,777
Ms J. Ross-Mills, *SLD* 7,378
C. majority 5,688
(June 1984, C. maj. 26,195)

LANCASHIRE EAST
E. 529,740
*M. J. Hindley, *Lab.* 96,926
R. W. Sturdy, *C.* 57,778
S. Barker, *Grn.* 20,728
M. Hambley, *SLD* 12,661
Lab. majority 39,148
(June 1984, Lab. maj. 7,905)

LEEDS
E. 519,631
*M. McGowan, *Lab.* 97,385

J. W. Tweddle, *C.* 54,867
C. R. Lord, *Grn.* 22,558
Mrs J. Ewens, *SLD* 11,720
Lab. majority 42,518
(June 1984, Lab. maj. 10,357)

LEICESTER
E. 579,050
Ms I. M. Read, *Lab.* 90,798
*F. A. Tuckman, *C.* 75,476
C. J. Davis, *Grn.* 33,081
A. G. Barrett, *Ind. C.* 6,996
G. W. Childs, *SLD* 6,791
Lab. majority 15,322
(June 1984, C. maj. 2,892)

LINCOLNSHIRE
E. 586,156
*W. F. Newton Dunn, *C.* 92,043
S. Taggart, *Lab.* 71,393
Ms J. Steranka, *Grn.* 24,908
J. P. Heppell, *SLD* 14,341
C. majority 20,650
(June 1984, C. maj. 45,445)

LONDON CENTRAL
E. 486,558
*A. S. Newens, *Lab. Co-op.* 78,561
Ms H. S. Crawley, *C.* 67,019
Ms N. Kortvelyessy, *Grn.* 28,087
Miss S. A. Ludford, *SLD* 7,864
W. D. E. Mallinson, *SDP* 2,957
'Lord' D. E. Sutch, *LM* 841
Ms L. St-Claire, *Corr.* 707
S. Swinden, *Hum.* 304
Lab. Co-op majority 11,542
(June 1984, Lab. maj. 13,297)

LONDON EAST
E. 530,548
*Miss C. Tongue, *Lab.* 92,803
A. R. Tyrrell, *C.* 65,418
Ms E. L. Crosbie, *Grn.* 21,388
J. K. Gibb, *SLD* 7,341
D. A. O'Sullivan, *ICP* 717
Lab. majority 27,385
(June 1984, Lab. maj. 12,159)

LONDON NORTH
E. 573,043
Ms P. Green, *Lab. Co-op.* 85,536
R. M. Lacey, *C.* 79,699
S. Clark, *Grn.* 30,807
Ms H. F. Leighter, *SLD* 8,917
P. Burns, *Ind.* 2,016
Ms L. Reith, *Comm.* 850
Lab. Co-op. majority 5,837
(June 1984, C. maj. 4,853)

LONDON NORTH EAST
E. 510,138
*A. Lomas, *Lab.* 76,085
M. Trend, *C.* 28,318
Mrs J. D. Lambert, *Grn.* 25,949
S. Banks, *SLD* 9,575
Ms N. C. Temple, *Comm.* 1,129
Lab. majority 47,767
(June 1984, Lab. maj. 52,665)

LONDON NORTH WEST
E. 506,707
*The Lord Bethell, *C.* 74,900

A. K. Toms, *Lab.* 67,500
I. E. Flindall, *Grn.* 28,275
C. D. Noyce, *SLD* 10,553
C. majority 7,400
(June 1984, C. maj. 7,422)

LONDON SOUTH AND SURREY EAST
E. 495,942
*C. J. O. Moorhouse, *C.* 78,256
R. J. E. Evans, *Lab.* 47,440
G. F. Brand, *Grn.* 31,854
P. H. Billenness, *SLD* 14,967
C. majority 30,816
(June 1984, C. maj. 44,657)

LONDON, SOUTH EAST
E. 558,815
*P. N. Price, *C.* 80,619
D. J. Earnshaw, *Lab.* 73,029
Dr E. C. McPhee, *Grn.* 37,576
A. A. Kinch, *SDP* 10,196
Mrs M. C. Williams, *SLD* 9,052
W. E. Turner, *Ind.* 456
C. majority 7,590
(June 1984, C. maj. 20,015)

LONDON, SOUTH INNER
E. 528,188
*R. A. Balfe, *Lab Co-op* 90,378
R. J. Wheatley, *C.* 45,360
Ms P. A. Shepherd, *Grn.* 26,230
M. J. Pindar, *SLD* 10,277
P. N. Power, *Comm.* 1,277
Ms D. Weppler, *Comm. League* 323
Lab. Co-op majority 45,018
(June 1984, Lab. maj. 31,481)

LONDON SOUTH WEST
E. 486,412
Ms A. J. Pollack, *Lab.* 74,298
*Dame S. M. Roberts, *C.* 73,780
Ms M. A. Elson, *Grn.* 35,476
J. C. Field, *SLD* 10,400
Lab. majority 518
(June 1984, C. maj. 6,867)

LONDON WEST
E. 515,581
*M. N. Elliott, *Lab.* 92,959
B. Donnelly, *C.* 78,151
J. R. Hywell-Davies, *Grn.* 32,686
J. G. Parry, *SLD* 9,309
J. Rogers-Davies, *SDP* 2,877
Lab. majority 14,808
June 1984, Lab. maj. 5,229)

LOTHIANS
E. 523,506
*D. W. Martin, *Lab.* 90,840
Mrs C. M. Blight, *C.* 52,014
J. Smith, *SNP* 44,935
R. C. M. Harper, *Grn.* 22,983
K. Leadbetter, *SLD* 9,222
Lab. majority 38,826
(June 1984, Lab. maj. 25,924)

MERSEYSIDE EAST
E. 519,514
T. Wynn, *Lab.* 107,288
E. N. Farthing, *C.* 30,421
R. L. Georgeson, *Grn.* 20,018

R. M. Clayton, *SLD* 5,658
Lab. majority 76,867
(June 1984, Lab. maj. 49,039)

MERSEYSIDE WEST
E. 508,722
*K. A. Stewart, *Lab.* 93,717
M. D. Byrne, *C.* 43,900
L. Brown, *Grn.* 23,052
Mrs H. F. Clucas, *SLD* 16,327
D. J. E. Carson, *PRP* 1,747
Lab. majority 49,817
(June 1984, Lab. maj. 13,197)

MIDLANDS CENTRAL
E. 539,211
Ms C. M. Oddy, *Lab.* 76,736
*J. de Courcy Ling, *C.* 71,643
Ms J. A. Alty, *Grn.* 42,622
I. Cundy, *SLD* 8,450
Lab. majority 5,093
(June 1984, C. maj. 12,729)

MIDLANDS WEST
E. 529,505
*J. A. W. Bird, *Lab. Co-op.* 105,529
M. J. Whitby, *C.* 63,165
J. Raven, *Grn.* 21,787
Mrs F. M. Oborski, *SLD* 6,974
Lab. Co-op majority 42,364
(June 1984, Lab. maj. 19,685)
(March 1987, Lab. maj. 4,025)

NORFOLK
E. 577,576
*P. F. Howell, *C.* 92,385
Ms M. Page, *Lab.* 71,478
M. Macartney-Filgate, *Grn.* 40,575
R. A. Lawes, *SLD* 8,902
S. D. Maxwell, *SDP* 4,934
C. majority 20,907
(June 1984, C. maj. 36,857)

NORTHAMPTONSHIRE
E. 587,733
*A. M. H. Simpson, *C.* 86,695
M. Coyne, *Lab.* 66,248
Ms A. T. Bryant, *Grn.* 43,071
R. Church, *SLD* 11,619
C. majority 20,447
(June 1984, C. maj. 39,859)

NORTHUMBRIA
E. 514,083
*G. J. Adam, *Lab.* 110,688
P. Yeoman, *C.* 50,648
Ms A. Lipman, *Grn.* 24,882
Viscount Morpeth, *SLD* 10,983
Lab. majority 60,040
(June 1984, Lab. maj. 15,700)

NOTTINGHAM
E. 565,354
K. Coates, *Lab.* 92,261
*M. L. Kilby, *C.* 77,748
Mrs S. E. Blount, *Grn.* 34,097
A. Swift, *SLD* 6,693
Lab. majority 14,513
(June 1984, Lab. maj. 16,126)

OXFORD AND
BUCKINGHAMSHIRE
E. 560,730

*J. E. M. Elles, *C.* 92,483
R. Gifford, *Lab.* 44,965
T. H. Andrewes, *Grn.* 42,058
R. Johnston, *SLD* 14,405
R. C. Turner, *Ind.* 3,696
C. majority 47,518
June 1984, C. maj. 49,081)

SCOTLAND MID AND FIFE
E. 534,638
*A. Falconer, *Lab.* 102,246
K. W. MacAskill, *SNP* 50,089
A. Christie, *C.* 46,505
G. Moreton, *Grn.* 14,165
M. Black, *SLD* 8,857
Lab. majority 52,157
(June 1984, Lab. maj. 27,166)

SCOTLAND NORTH EAST
E. 554,408
H. McCubbin, *Lab.* 65,348
Dr A. Macartney, *SNP* 62,735
*J. L. C. Provan, *C.* 56,835
M. Hill, *Grn.* 15,584
S. Horner, *SLD* 12,704
Lab. majority 2,613
(June 1984, C. maj. 9,171)

SCOTLAND SOUTH
E. 491,865
A. Smith, *Lab.* 81,366
*A. H. Hutton, *C.* 65,673
M. Brown, *SNP* 35,155
J. Button, *Grn.* 11,658
J. E. McKercher, *SLD* 10,368
Lab. majority 15,693
(June 1984, C. maj. 3,137)

SHEFFIELD
E. 564,409
R. Barton, *Lab.* 109,677
T. S. R. Mort, *C.* 40,401
P. L. Scott, *Grn.* 26,844
A. H. Rogers, *SLD* 10,910
D. E. Hyland, *ICP* 657
Lab. majority 69,276
(June 1984, Lab. maj. 46,283)

SHROPSHIRE AND STAFFORD
E. 597,554
*C. J. Prout, *C.* 85,896
D. J. A. Hallam, *Lab.* 83,352
R. T. C. Saunders, *Grn.* 29,637
C. Hards, *SLD* 10,568
C. majority 2,544
(June 1984, C. maj. 24,932)

SOMERSET AND DORSET WEST
E. 582,098
*Mrs M. E. Daly, *C.* 106,716
Dr R. H. Lawson, *Grn.* 54,496
Ms D. M. Organ, *Lab.* 46,210
M. Mactaggart, *SLD* 28,662
A. P. B. Mockler *W. Reg.* 930
C. majority 52,220
(June 1984, C. maj. 40,251)

STAFFORDSHIRE EAST
E. 581,127
*G. W. Stevenson, *Lab.* 94,873
M. F. Spungin, *C.* 63,104
S. Parker, *Grn.* 23,415

R. C. Dodson, *SLD*	7,046	A. J. Donnelly, *Lab.*	126,682	R. Bell, *Grn.*	27,525
Lab. majority	31,769	N. C. Gibbon, *C.*	30,902	A. Collinge, *SLD*	12,542
(June 1984, Lab. maj. 7,867)		R. Stather, *Grn.*	18,107	*C. majority*	15,102

STRATHCLYDE EAST
E. 494,274
*K. D. Collins, *Lab.*   109,170
G. A. Leslie, *SNP*   48,853
M. Dutt, *C.*   22,233
A. Whitelaw, *Grn.*   9,749
G. Lait, *SLD*   4,276
Lab. majority   60,317
(June 1984, Lab. maj. 63,462)

STRATHCLYDE WEST
E. 493,067
*H. R. McMahon, *Lab.*   89,627
C. M. Campbell, *SNP*   50,036
S. J. Robin, *C.*   45,872
G. Campbell, *Grn.*   16,461
D. J. Herbison, *SLD*   8,098
Lab. majority   39,591
(June 1984, Lab. maj. 23,038)

SUFFOLK
E. 550,131
*A. E. Turner, *C.*   82,481
M. D. Cornish, *Lab.*   56,788
A. C. Slade, *Grn.*   37,305
P. R. Odell, *SLD*   12,660
C. majority   25,693
(June 1984, C. maj. 47,098)

SURREY WEST
E. 515,881
T. N. B. Spencer, *C.*   89,674
E. Haywood, *Grn.*   40,332
H. G. Trace, *Lab.*   28,313
A. Davies, *SLD*   18,042
B. M. Collignon, *SDP*   3,676
C. majority   49,342
(June 1984, C. maj. 52,588)

SUSSEX EAST
E. 553,536
*Sir John Stewart-Clark, Bt., *C.*   96,388
Ms G. Roles, *Lab.*   43,094
Ms R. Addison, *Grn*   42,316
Mrs D. Venables, *SLD*   16,810
D. Howells, *LM*   1,181
C. majority   53,294
(June 1984, C. maj. 65,621)

SUSSEX WEST
E. 554,664
*R. M. Seligman, *C.*   95,821
I. F. N. Bagnall, *Grn.*   49,588
M. Shrimpton, *Lab.*   32,006
Dr J. M. M. Walsh, *SLD*   24,855
C. majority   46,233
(June 1984, C. maj. 57,502)

THAMES VALLEY
E. 542,855
J. C. C. Stevens, *C.*   73,070
Ms H. B. de Lyon, *Lab.*   46,579
P. Gordon, *Grn.*   36,865
D. B. Griffiths, *SLD*   14,603
C. majority   26,491
(June 1984, C. maj. 38,805)

TYNE AND WEAR
E. 530,953

P. J. Arnold, *SLD*   6,101
T. P. Kilgallon, *SPGB*   919
Lab. majority   95,780
(June 1984, Lab. maj. 49,414)

WALES MID AND WEST
E. 547,740
*Revd D. R. Morris, *Lab.*   105,670
O. J. Williams, *C.*   53,758
Ms B. I. McPake, *Grn.*   29,852
Dr P. J. S. Williams, *PC*   26,063
G. A. Sinclair, *SLD*   10,031
Lab. majority   51,912
(June 1984, Lab. maj. 36,452)

WALES NORTH
E. 540,230
J. Wilson, *Lab.*   83,638
*Miss B. A. Brookes, *C.*   79,178
Dr D. E. Thomas, *PC*   64,120
P. H. W. Adams, *Grn.*   15,832
R. K. Marshall, *SLD*   10,056
Lab. majority   4,460
(June 1984, C. maj. 12,278)

WALES SOUTH
E. 520,911
W. David, *Lab.*   108,550
A. R. Taylor, *C.*   45,993
G. P. Jones, *Grn.*   25,993
P. J. Keelan, *PC*   10,727
P. K. Verma, *SLD*   4,037
D. A. T. Thomas, *SDP*   3,513
Lab. majority   62,557
(June 1984, Lab. maj. 44,258)

WALES SOUTH EAST
E. 561,068
*L. T. Smith, *Lab.*   138,872
R. J. Young, *C.*   30,384
M. J. Witherden, *Grn.*   27,869
Ms J. Evans, *PC*   14,152
P. Nicholls-Jones, *SLD*   4,661
Lab. majority   108,488
(June 1984, Lab. maj. 95,557)

WIGHT AND HAMPSHIRE EAST
E. 574,332
*R. J. Simmonds, *C.*   90,658
Dr A. D. Burnett, *Lab.*   51,228
S. L. Rackett, *Grn.*   40,664
Ms V. A. Rayner, *SLD*   19,569
C. majority   39,430
(June 1984, C. maj. 42,928)

WILTSHIRE
E. 568,875
*Mrs C. F. Jackson, *C.*   93,200
G. A. Harris, *Lab.*   46,887
J. V. Hughes, *Grn.*   46,735
P. N. Crossley, *SLD*   18,302
J. A. Cade, *Ind.*   4,809
C. majority   46,313
(June 1984, C. maj. 26,469)

YORK
E. 542,998
*E. H. C. McMillan-Scott, *C.*   81,453
J. T. Grogan, *Lab.*   66,351

(June 1984, C. maj. 36,402)

YORKSHIRE SOUTH
E. 518,995
*N. West, *Lab.*   121,060
W. J. Clappison, *C.*   29,276
A. Grace, *Grn.*   19,063
B. Boulton, *SLD*   5,039
Lab. majority   91,784
(June 1984, Lab. maj. 67,749)

YORKSHIRE SOUTH WEST
E. 523,322
*T. Megahy, *Lab.*   108,444
G. T. Horton, *C.*   42,543
Mrs S. Leyland, *Grn.*   25,677
J. A. D. Ridgway, *SLD*   10,352
Lab. majority   65,901
(June 1984, Lab. maj. 44,173)

YORKSHIRE WEST
E. 564,001
*B. H. Seal, *Lab.*   108,644
G. T. Hall, *C.*   70,717
N. Parrott, *Grn.*   28,308
P. Wrigley, *SLD*   9,765
Lab. majority   37,927
(June 1984, Lab. maj. 20,854)

NORTHERN IRELAND
E. 1,105,551
*Revd I. R. K. Paisley, MP,
  DUP   160,110
*J. Hume, MP, *SDLP*   136,335
J. F. Nicholson, UUP   118,785
D. Morrison SF   48,914
J. T. Alderdice, *All.*   27,905
A. Kennedy, *C.*   25,789
M. H. Samuel, *Ecol.*   6,569
S. Lynch, *WP*   5,590
M. Langhammer, *Lab. RG*   3,540
B. Caul, *Lab. 87*   1,274

Revd I. R. K. Paisley, J. Hume and
J. F. Nicholson were elected by the
single transferable voting system.

Parliamentary statistics

PRINCIPAL PARTIES IN PARLIAMENT SINCE 1970

	1970	1974 Feb.	1974 Oct.	1979	1983	1987	1992
Conservative	330*	296	276	339	397	375	336
Labour	287	301	319	268	209	229	270
Liberal/LD	6	14	13	11	17	17	20
Social Democrat	—	1	—	—	6	5	—
Independent	5†	1	1	2	—	—	—
Plaid Cymru	—	2	3	2	2	3	4
Scottish Nationalist	1	7	11	2	2	3	3
Democratic Unionist	—	—	—	3	3	3	3
SDLP	—	1	1	1	1	3	4
Sinn Fein	—	—	—	—	1	1	—
Ulster Popular Unionist	—	—	—	—	1	1	1
Ulster Unionist‡	*	11	10	6	10	9	9
The Speaker	1	1	1	1	1	1	1
Total	630	635	635	635	650	650	651

* Including 8 Ulster Unionists
† Comprising: Independent Labour 1, Independent Unity 1, Protestant Unity 1, Republican Labour 1, Unity 1
‡ Comprises:
1974 (February) United Ulster Unionist Council 11
1974 (October) United Ulster Unionist 10
1979 Ulster Unionist 5, United Ulster Unionist 1
1983 Official Unionist 10

PARLIAMENTS SINCE 1970

Assembled	Dissolved	Duration yr	m.	d.
29 June 1970	8 February 1974	3	7	10
6 March 1974	20 September 1974	0	6	14
22 October 1974	7 April 1979	4	5	16
9 May 1979	13 May 1983	4	0	4
15 June 1983	18 May 1987	3	11	3
17 June 1987	16 March 1992	4	8	28
27 April 1992				

MAJORITIES IN THE HOUSE OF COMMONS SINCE 1970

Year	Party	Maj.
1970	Conservative	31
1974 Feb.	No majority	
1974 Oct.	Labour	5
1979	Conservative	43
1983	Conservative	144
1987	Conservative	102
1992	Conservative	21

VOTES CAST AT 1987 AND 1992 GENERAL ELECTIONS*

GENERAL ELECTION 1987

Conservative	13,760,525
Labour	10,029,944
Liberal/SDP Alliance	7,341,152
Scottish Nationalist	416,873
Plaid Cymru	123,589
†Green	89,753
Others	37,576

GENERAL ELECTION 1992

Conservative	14,048,283
Labour	11,559,735
Liberal Democrats	5,999,384
Scottish Nationalist	629,552
Plaid Cymru	154,439
Others	436,207

*Excluding Northern Ireland seats
†Excluding Ecology candidate in Northern Ireland

The Government

THE CABINET AS AT 31 JULY 1993

Prime Minister, First Lord of the Treasury and Minister for the Civil Service
The Rt. Hon. John Major, MP, since November 1990
Lord High Chancellor
The Lord Mackay of Clashfern, PC, since October 1987
Secretary of State for Foreign and Commonwealth Affairs
The Rt. Hon. Douglas Hurd, CBE, MP, since October 1989
Chancellor of the Exchequer
The Rt. Hon. Kenneth Clarke, QC, MP, since May 1993
Secretary of State for the Home Department
The Rt. Hon. Michael Howard, QC, MP, since May 1993
President of the Board of Trade and Secretary of State for Trade and Industry
The Rt. Hon. Michael Heseltine, MP, since April 1992
Secretary of State for Transport
The Rt. Hon. John MacGregor, OBE, MP, since April 1992
Secretary of State for Defence
The Rt. Hon. Malcolm Rifkind, QC, MP, since April 1992
Lord Privy Seal and Leader of the House of Lords
The Lord Wakeham, PC, since April 1992
Lord President of the Council and Leader of the House of Commons
The Rt. Hon. Antony Newton, OBE, MP, since April 1992
Secretary of State for National Heritage
The Rt. Hon. Peter Brooke, MP, since September 1992
Secretary of State for the Environment
The Rt. Hon. John Gummer, MP, since May 1993
Secretary of State for Employment
The Rt. Hon. David Hunt, MBE, MP, since May 1993
Secretary of State for Social Security
The Rt. Hon. Peter Lilley, MP, since April 1992
Chancellor of the Duchy of Lancaster and Minister of Public Service and Science
The Rt. Hon. William Waldegrave, MP, since April 1992
Secretary of State for Scotland
The Rt. Hon. Ian Lang, MP, since November 1990
Secretary of State for Northern Ireland
The Rt. Hon. Sir Patrick Mayhew, QC, MP, since April 1992
Secretary of State for Education
The Rt. Hon. John Patten, MP, since April 1992
Secretary of State for Health
The Rt. Hon. Virginia Bottomley, MP, since April 1992
Minister of Agriculture, Fisheries and Food
The Rt. Hon. Gillian Shephard, MP, since May 1993
Chief Secretary to the Treasury
The Rt. Hon. Michael Portillo, MP, since April 1992
Secretary of State for Wales
The Rt. Hon. John Redwood, MP, since May 1993

LAW OFFICERS

Attorney-General
The Rt. Hon. Sir Nicholas Lyell, QC, MP, since April 1992
Lord Advocate
The Lord Rodger of Earlsferry, PC, QC, since April 1992
Solicitor-General
Sir Derek Spencer, QC, MP, since April 1992

Solicitor-General for Scotland
Thomas Dawson, QC, since April 1992

MINISTERS OF STATE

Agriculture, Fisheries and Food
Michael Jack, MP
Defence
Jonathan Aitken, MP (*Defence Procurement*)
Jeremy Hanley, MP (*Armed Forces*)
Education
The Baroness Blatch, CBE, PC
Employment
Michael Forsyth, MP
Environment
The Rt. Hon. Sir George Young, MP (*Minister for Housing, Inner Cities and Construction*)
David Curry, MP (*Minister for Local Government and Planning*)
Timothy Yeo, MP (*Minister for Environment and Countryside*)
Foreign and Commonwealth Affairs
The Baroness Chalker of Wallasey, PC (*Minister for Overseas Development*)
The Rt. Hon. Douglas Hogg, QC, MP; The Rt. Hon. Alastair Goodlad, MP; David Heathcoat-Amory, MP
Health
Brian Mawhinney, MP (*Minister for Health*)
Home Office
The Earl Ferrers, PC; Peter Lloyd, MP; David Maclean, MP
Northern Ireland Office
Robert Atkins, MP; The Rt. Hon. Sir John Wheeler, MP
Scottish Office
The Lord Fraser of Carmyllie, PC, QC
Social Security
The Rt. Hon. Nicholas Scott, MBE, MP (*Minister for Social Security and Disabled People*)
Trade and Industry
The Rt. Hon. Timothy Sainsbury, MP (*Minister for Industry*)
Richard Needham, MP (*Minister for Trade*)
Timothy Eggar, MP (*Minister for Energy*)
Transport
The Earl of Caithness, PC (*Minister for Aviation and Shipping*)
The Rt. Hon. Roger Freeman, MP (*Minister for Public Transport*)
Treasury
Stephen Dorrell, MP (*Financial Secretary*)
The Rt. Hon. Sir John Cope, MP (*Paymaster-General*)
Anthony Nelson, MP (*Economic Secretary*)
Welsh Office
The Rt. Hon. Sir Wyn Roberts, MP

UNDER-SECRETARIES OF STATE

Agriculture, Fisheries and Food
The Earl Howe; the Hon. Nicholas Soames, MP

Office of the Minister for the Civil Service
David Davis, MP
Defence
Viscount Cranborne
Education
Eric Forth, MP; Timothy Boswell, MP; Robin Squire, MP
Employment
The Viscount Ullswater; Ann Widdecombe, MP
Environment
The Lord Strathclyde; Anthony Baldry, MP
Foreign and Commonwealth Affairs
The Hon. Mark Lennox-Boyd, MP
Health
The Baroness Cumberlege, CBE; The Hon. Thomas
Sackville, MP; John Bowis, OBE, MP
Home Office
Charles Wardle, MP
Lord Chancellor's Department
John Taylor, MP
National Heritage
Iain Sproat, MP
Northern Ireland
The Earl of Arran; Michael Ancram, MP
Scottish Office
Lord James Douglas-Hamilton, MP; Allan Stewart, MP;
Sir Hector Monro, MP
Social Security
The Lord Henley; Alistair Burt, MP; William Hague, MP
Trade and Industry
Neil Hamilton, MP (*Corporate Affairs*)
The Baroness Denton of Wakefield, CBE (*Consumer
Affairs and Small Firms*)
Patrick McLoughlin, MP (*Trade and Technology*)
Transport
Steven Norris, MP (*Minister for Transport in London*)
Robert Key, MP (*Minister for Roads and Traffic*)
Treasury
The Lords Commissioners, *see* Government Whips
Welsh Office
Gwilym Jones, MP

Lord Commissioners
Irvine Patnick, MP; Nicholas Baker, MP; Timothy Wood,
MP; Timothy Kirkhope, MP; Andrew MacKay, MP
Assistant Whips
Robert Hughes, MP; James Arbuthnot, MP; Andrew
Mitchell, MP; Michael Brown, MP; Derek Conway, MP

GOVERNMENT WHIPS

HOUSE OF LORDS

*Captain of the Honourable Corps of Gentlemen-at-Arms
(Chief Whip)*
The Lord Hesketh, PC
*Captain of The Queen's Bodyguard of the Yeomen of the
Guard (Deputy Chief Whip)*
The Earl of Strathmore and Kinghorne
Lords-in-Waiting
The Viscount Long, CBE; The Viscount Astor; The
Viscount St Davids; The Viscount Goschen
Baroness-in-Waiting
The Baroness Trumpington, PC

HOUSE OF COMMONS

Parliamentary Secretary to the Treasury (Chief Whip)
The Rt. Hon. Richard Ryder, OBE, MP
Treasurer of HM Household (Deputy Chief Whip)
Gregory Knight, MP
Comptroller of HM Household
David Lightbown, MP
Vice-Chamberlain of HM Household
Sydney Chapman, MP

Government Departments and Public Offices

MINISTERIAL SALARIES
as at 1 January 1993

Prime Minister	£53,007
Secretary of State	£39,820
Minister of State (Lords)	£44,945
Minister of State (Commons)	£28,175
Parliamentary Under-Secretary (Lords)	£37,689
Parliamentary Under-Secretary (Commons)	£21,384

Ministers who are Members of the House of Commons receive a reduced Parliamentary salary (£23,227 in 1993) in addition to this ministerial salary.

CIVIL SERVICE (BASIC) SALARIES *as at 1 April 1993*

*Secretary of the Cabinet and Head of the Home Civil Service	£112,083
*Permanent Secretary to the Treasury	£104,860
*Head of the Diplomatic Service	£104,860
*Grade 1	£90,148
*Grade 1A	£82,925
*Grade 2	£64,307–£75,328
*Grade 3	£51,360–£59,599
†Grade 4	£44,390–£49,790
†Grade 5	£36,019–£47,921
†Grade 6	£27,660–£42,724
†Grade 7	£24,239–£34,469
Senior Executive Officer	£17,535–£21,932
Higher Executive Officer (D)	£16,028–£20,163
Higher Executive Officer	£14,019–£17,895
Executive Officer	£8,260–£14,307
Administration Trainee	£12,760–£14,848
Administrative Officer	£5,167–£10,513
Administrative Assistant	£4,669–£8,878

London Rates

*Grade 3	£52,751–£60,990
†Grade 4	£46,121–£51,732
†Grade 5	£37,589–£49,790
†Grade 6	£28,904–£44,390
†Grade 7	£25,330–£36,019
Senior Executive Officer	£18,263–£22,844
Higher Executive Officer	£14,601–£18,639
Executive Officer	£8,602–£14,901
Administrative Officer	£5,529–£11,249
Administrative Assistant	£4,995–£9,499

*These grades do not attract London weighting. London weighting, since 1 April 1993, is:

Inner zone	£1,776 a year
Intermediate zone	£1,015 a year
Outer zone	£736 a year
†1992–3 salaries	

The Home Civil Service's unified pay and grading structure for senior personnel represents the following:

Grade	Title
1	Permanent Secretary
1A	Second Permanent Secretary
2	Deputy Secretary
3	Under-Secretary
4	Chief Scientific Officer B, Professional and Technology Directing A
5	Assistant Secretary, Deputy Chief Scientific Officer, Professional and Technology Directing B
6	Senior Principal, Senior Principal Scientific Officer, Professional and Technology Superintending Grade
7	Principal

ADVISORY, CONCILIATION AND ARBITRATION SERVICE
27 Wilton Street, London SW1X 7AZ
Tel 071-210 3000

The Advisory, Conciliation and Arbitration Service (ACAS) is an independent organization set up under the Employment Protection Act 1975 (the provisions now being found in the Trade Union and Labour Relations (Consolidation) Act 1992). ACAS is directed by a Council consisting of a chairman and employer, trade union and independent members, all appointed by the Secretary of State for Employment. The functions of the Service are to provide facilities for conciliation, mediation and arbitration as means of avoiding and resolving industrial disputes, and to provide advisory services to industry on industrial relations and matters affecting the quality of working life.

ACAS also has main offices in Accrington, Birmingham, Bristol, Cardiff, Fleet, Glasgow, Leeds, Liverpool, Manchester, Newcastle upon Tyne and Nottingham, and 25 smaller offices in other parts of Great Britain.

Chairman, J. Hougham
Chief Conciliation Officer (G4), D. Evans
Director of Resources and General Policy Branch (G5), E. Norcross
Director of Conciliation and Arbitration Branch (G5), F. Noonan
Director of Advisory Services Branch (G5), P. Syson

MINISTRY OF AGRICULTURE, FISHERIES AND FOOD
*Whitehall Place, London SW1A 2HH
Tel 071-270 3000

The Ministry of Agriculture, Fisheries and Food is responsible for administering government policies on agriculture, horticulture and fisheries in England and policies relating to the safety and quality of food in the United Kingdom as a whole. In association with the Agriculture Departments of the Scottish, Welsh and Northern Ireland Offices and with the Intervention Board (*see* page 324), the Ministry is responsible for the negotiation and administration of the EC common agricultural and fisheries policies, for matters relating to the single European market, and for international agricultural and food trade policy. It commissions research to assist in the formulation and assessment of policy.

*Unless otherwise stated, this is the main address of divisions of the Ministry

The Ministry administers policies on the control and eradication of animal, plant and fish diseases, and on assistance to capital investment in farm and horticultural businesses; it also has responsibilities relating to the protection and enhancement of the countryside and the marine environment as well as to flood defence and other rural issues.

The Ministry is responsible for ensuring public health standards in the manufacture, preparation and distribution of basic foods, and for planning to safeguard essential food supplies in times of emergency. It is responsible for government relations with the UK food and drink manufacturing industries and the food and drink importing, distributive and catering trades.

The Food Safety Directorate is responsible for many aspects of food safety and quality. These include pesticide safety approval, biotechnology, meat hygiene, animal health and welfare, and related public health issues.

Minister, The Rt. Hon. Gillian Shephard, MP
  Principal Private Secretary (G7), Miss E. J. Wordley
  Private Secretary, D. C. Barnes
  Special Advisers, Dr E. Cottrell; K. Leggatt
  Parliamentary Private Secretary, S. Burns, MP
Minister of State, Michael Jack, MP *(Farming and Fisheries)*
  Private Secretary, S. G. Cane
  Parliamentary Private Secretary, Miss E. Nicholson, MP
Parliamentary Secretary (Lords), The Earl Howe
  (Countryside)
  Private Secretary, J. E. T. Hughes
Parliamentary Secretary, The Hon. Nicholas Soames, MP
  (Food)
  Private Secretary, S. C. Tanner
Parliamentary Clerk, Miss A. Evans
Permanent Secretary (G1), R. J. Packer
  Private Secretary, P. Campbell

ESTABLISHMENT DEPARTMENT
Director of Establishments (G3), D. H. Griffiths

ESTABLISHMENTS (GENERAL) DIVISION
Victory House, 30–34 Kingsway, London WC2B 6TU
Tel 071-405 4310

Head of Division (G6), G. P. Hobrough

WELFARE BRANCH
Victory House, 30–34 Kingsway, London WC2B 6TU
Tel 071-405 4310

Chief Welfare Officer (SEO), D. J. Jones

PERSONNEL DIVISION
Victory House, 30–34 Kingsway, London WC2B 6TU
Tel 071-405 4310

Head of Division (G5), G. P. McLachlan

DEPARTMENTAL HEALTH AND SAFETY UNIT
Head of Unit (G7), Dr D. J. Knowles

†OFFICE SERVICES DIVISION
Head of Division (G5), P. A. Cocking

†STAFF TRAINING BRANCH
Principal (G7), Miss E. M. Berthoud

BUILDING AND ESTATE MANAGEMENT
Eastbury House, 30–34 Albert Embankment,
London SE1 7TL
Tel 071-238 3000

Head of Division (G5), J. S. Buchanan

†At Nobel/Ergon House, 17 Smith Square, London SW1P 3JR. Tel: 071-238 3000

INFORMATION DIVISION
Chief Information Officer (G5), S. Dugdale
Chief Press Officer (G7), M. Smith
Principal Librarian (G7), P. McShane

FINANCE DEPARTMENT
19–29 Woburn Place, London WC1H 0LU
Tel 071-917 1000

Principal Finance Officer (G3), A. R. Cruickshank

FINANCIAL PLANNING DIVISION
Head of Division (G5), P. P. Nash

FINANCIAL MANAGEMENT DIVISION
Head of Division (G5), A. G. Kuyk
Deputy Head of Financial Management (G6), J. M. Lowi

AUDIT CONSULTANCY AND MANAGEMENT SERVICES DIVISION
Director of Audit (G5), D. V. Fisher
Deputy Director of Audit (G6), D. J. Littler

MARKET TESTING AND PROCUREMENT ADVICE
Victory House, 30–34 Kingsway, London WC2B 6TU
Tel 071-405 4310

Director (G5), D. B. Rabey

LEGAL DEPARTMENT
55 Whitehall, London SW1A 2EY
Tel 071-270 3000

Legal Adviser and Solicitor (G2), G. J. Jenkins, CB, QC
Principal Assistant Solicitors (G3), B. T. Atwood; D. J. Pearson

LEGAL DIVISION A1
Assistant Solicitor (G5), Miss D. Wood

LEGAL DIVISION A2
Assistant Solicitor (G5), Mrs C. Davis

LEGAL DIVISION A3
Assistant Solicitor (G5), Miss C. A. Crisham

LEGAL DIVISION A4
Assistant Solicitor (G5), Miss E. A. Stephens

LEGAL DIVISION A5
Assistant Solicitor (G5), L. Gunatilleke

LEGAL DIVISION A6
Assistant Solicitor (G5), P. D. Davis

LEGAL DIVISION B1
Assistant Solicitor (G5), P. Hall

LEGAL DIVISION B2
Assistant Solicitor (G4), Ms S. B. Spence

LEGAL DIVISION B3
Assistant Solicitor (G5), A. I. Corbett

LEGAL DIVISION B4
Assistant Solicitor (G5), Dr M. R. Parke

INVESTIGATION UNIT
Chief Investigation Officer, L. R. Blake

AGRICULTURAL COMMODITIES, TRADE AND FOOD PRODUCTION
Deputy Secretary (G2), D. A. Hadley

EUROPEAN COMMUNITY
Under-Secretary (G3), P. W. Murphy

EUROPEAN COMMUNITY DIVISION I
Head of Division (G5), C. I. Llewelyn

EUROPEAN COMMUNITY DIVISION II
Head of Division (G6), L. G. Mitchell

ARABLE CROPS
Under-Secretary (G3), C. J. Barnes

CEREALS AND SET-ASIDE DIVISION
Head of Division (G5), Ms J. Allfrey

SUGAR, TOBACCO, OILSEEDS AND PROTEINS DIVISION
Head of Division (G5), Mrs A. M. Blackburn

†HORTICULTURE AND POTATOES DIVISION
Head of Division (G5), R. A. Saunderson

MEAT GROUP
Under-Secretary (G3), G. A. Hollis

BEEF DIVISION
Head of Division (G5), T. D. Rossington

SHEEP AND LIVESTOCK SUBSIDIES DIVISION
Head of Division (G5), J. R. Cowan

PIGS, EGGS AND POULTRY DIVISION
Head of Division (G5), G. W. Noble

MILK AND MILK PRODUCTS
Head of Division (G5), B. J. Harding

FOOD, MILK AND MARKETING POLICY
Under-Secretary (G3), J. W. Hepburn

MILK MARKETING AND LEGISLATION DIVISION
Head of Division (G5), P. Elliott

FOOD INDUSTRY, MARKETING AND COMPETITION
POLICY DIVISION
Head of Division (G5), R. E. Melville

EXTERNAL RELATIONS AND TRADE PROMOTION
DIVISION
Head of Division (G5), D. V. Orchard

TRADE POLICY AND TROPICAL FOODS
Head of Division (G5), D. P. Hunter

†MARKET TASK FORCE
Head of Division (G5), H. B. Brown

†ALCOHOLIC DRINKS DIVISION
Head of Division (G5), P. M. Boyling

FOOD SAFETY
Deputy Secretary (G2), C. W. Capstick, CB, CMG

†FOOD SAFETY GROUP
Under-Secretary (G3), B. H. B. Dickinson
Chief Scientist (Fisheries and Food) (G3),
  Dr W. H. B. Denner

CHEMICAL SAFETY OF FOOD DIVISION
Head of Division (G5), R. C. McKinley

CONSUMER PROTECTION DIVISION
Head of Division (G5), C. A. Cockbill

MICROBIOLOGICAL SAFETY OF FOOD DIVISION
Head of Division (G5), Mrs A. M. Pickering

FOOD SCIENCE DIVISION I
Head of Division (G5), Dr J. C. Sherlock

FOOD SCIENCE DIVISION II
Head of Division (G5), Dr J. R. Bell

FOOD SCIENCE LABORATORY
Norwich Research Park, Colney Lane, Norwich NR4 7UQ
Tel 0603-259350
Head of Laboratory (G5), Dr J. Gilbert

TORRY RESEARCH STATION
PO Box 31, 135 Abbey Road, Aberdeen AB9 8DG
Tel 0224-877071
Director (G5), K. Whittle, PH.D.

†CHIEF SCIENTIST'S GROUP (FOOD)
Head of Division (G6), Dr D. G. Lindsay

AGRICULTURAL INPUTS, PLANT
PROTECTION AND EMERGENCIES
Under-Secretary (G3), Mrs E. A. J. Attridge

EMERGENCIES AND FOOD PROTECTION
Head of Division (G5), Dr J. R. Park

PLANT HEALTH DIVISION
Head of Division (G4), G. M. Trevelyan

PLANT VARIETY, RIGHTS OFFICE AND SEEDS DIVISION
White House Lane, Huntingdon Road, Cambridge CB3 0LF
Tel 0223-277151
Head of Division (G5), J. Harvey

†AGRICULTURAL RESOURCES POLICY DIVISION
Head of Division (G5), R. C. Lowson

ANIMAL HEALTH AND VETERINARY GROUP
Government Buildings, Hook Rise South, Tolworth,
Surbiton, Surrey KT6 7NF
Tel 081-330 4411
Under-Secretary (G3), M. T. Haddon
Chief Veterinary Officer (G3), K. C. Meldrum

ANIMAL HEALTH (ZOONOSES) DIVISION
Head of Division (G5), R. J. G. Cawthorne

ANIMAL HEALTH (DISEASE CONTROL) DIVISION
Head of Division (G5), T. E. D. Eddy

ANIMAL HEALTH (INTERNATIONAL TRADE) DIVISION
Head of Division (G5), R. A. Bell

MEAT HYGIENE DIVISION
Head of Division (G5), Mrs K. J. A. Brown

RESOURCE MANAGEMENT DIVISION
Head of Division (G6), R. A. Gregg

ANIMAL WELFARE DIVISION
Tolworth Tower, Surbiton, Surrey KT6 7DX
Tel 081-330 4411
Head of Division (G5), A. J. Perrins

STATE VETERINARY SERVICE
Government Buildings, Hook Rise South, Tolworth,
Surbiton, Surrey KT15 3NB
Tel 081-330 4411
Director of Veterinary Field Services (G3), I. Crawford

LASSWADE VETERINARY LABORATORY
East of Scotland College of Agriculture, The Bush Estate,
Penicuik, Midlothian EH26 0SA
Tel 031-445 5371

COUNTRYSIDE, MARINE ENVIRONMENT AND FISHERIES
Deputy Secretary (G2), C. R. Cann

LAND USE, CONSERVATION AND COUNTRYSIDE
†*Under-Secretary (G3)*, G. R. Waters

†COUNTRYSIDE DIVISION
Head of Division (G5), R. C. McIvor

†LAND USE AND TENURE DIVISION
Head of Division (G5), T. J. Osmond

†CONSERVATION POLICY DIVISION
Head of Division (G5), C. R. Bodrell

†ENVIRONMENT TASK FORCE
Head of Division (G5), J. Robbs

†LAND USE PLANNING UNIT
Head of Division (G5), J. R. Mathias

†FISHERIES DEPARTMENT
Fisheries Secretary (G3), S. Wentworth

FISHERIES DIVISION I
Head of Division (G5), I. C. Redfern

FISHERIES DIVISION II
Head of Division (G5), C. J. Ryder

FISHERIES DIVISION III
Head of Division (G5), R. S. Thomas

FISHERIES DIVISION IV
Head of Division (G6), B. S. Edwards

SEA FISHERIES INSPECTORATE
Chief Inspector (G6), M. G. Jennings

FISHERIES RESEARCH
Pakefield Road, Lowestoft, Suffolk NR33 OHT
Tel 0502-562244
Director of Fisheries Research and Development for Great Britain (G4), D. J. Garrod, PH.D.
Deputy Directors of Fisheries Research (G5),
  Dr J. G. Shepherd; P. W. Greig-Smith

FISHERIES LABORATORY
Pakefield Road, Lowestoft, Suffolk NR33 OHT
Tel 0502-562244

FISHERIES LABORATORY
Remembrance Avenue, Burnham-on-Crouch, Essex
CMO 8HA
Tel 0621-782658

FISHERIES EXPERIMENT STATION
Benarth Road, Conwy, Gwynedd LL32 8UB
Tel 0492-593883

FISH DISEASES LABORATORY
33–33A Albany Road, Granby Industrial Estate,
Weymouth, Dorset DT4 9TU
Tel 0305-772137
Officer-in-Charge (Principal Scientific Officer) (G6),
  B. J. Hill, PH.D.

ENVIRONMENT POLICY
Under-Secretary (G3), M. Madden

†At Nobel/Ergon House, 17 Smith Square, London SW1P 3JR. Tel: 071-238 3000

†ENVIRONMENTAL PROTECTION DIVISION
Head of Division (G5), D. L. Dawson

†MARINE ENVIRONMENTAL PROTECTION DIVISION
Head of Division (G5), G. F. Meekings

†SALMON WHALING AND INLAND FISHERIES
Head of Division (G5), A. R. Burne

FLOOD DEFENCE DIVISION
Eastbury House, 30–34 Albert Embankment, London
SE1 7TL
Tel 071-238 3000
Head of Division (G5), R. A. Hathaway

ECONOMICS AND STATISTICS
Under-Secretary (G3), R. E. Mordue

ECONOMICS (FARM BUSINESS) DIVISION
Senior Economic Adviser (G5), J. P. Muriel

ECONOMICS (INTERNATIONAL) DIVISION
Senior Economic Adviser (G5), Dr J. M. Slater

ECONOMICS (RESOURCE USE) DIVISION
Senior Economic Adviser (G5), R. W. Irving

ECONOMICS AND STATISTICS (FOOD)
Senior Economic Adviser (G5), Dr P. J. Lund

†STATISTICS (AGRICULTURAL COMMODITIES) DIVISION
Chief Statistician (G5), D. Wallage

STATISTICS (CENSUS AND PRICES) DIVISION
Government Buildings, Epsom Road, Guildford,
Surrey GU1 2LD
Tel 0483-68121
Chief Statistician (G5), D. E. Bradbury

†CHIEF SCIENTIFIC ADVISER
Chief Scientific Adviser (G2), P. J. Bunyan, DSC, PH.D.
Chief Scientist (Agriculture and Horticulture) (G3),
  D. W. F. Shannon, PH.D.
Assistant Chief Scientist (Agriculture and Horticulture) (G5),
  Dr M. Parker
Scientific Liaison Officer (Fisheries) (G6), Dr D. G. Smith

RESEARCH POLICY CO-ORDINATION DIVISION
Head of Division (G5), J. Suich

REGIONAL ORGANIZATION
†*Director of Regional Administration (G3)*, D. J. Coates

REGIONAL SERVICES AND AGENCIES SUPPORT
DIVISION
†*Head of Division (G5)*, G. Belchamber

RESOURCE MANAGEMENT STRATEGY UNIT
Government Buildings, Epsom Road, Guildford, Surrey
GU1 2LD
Tel 0483 68121
Head of Division (G5), J. D. Garnett

REGIONAL SERVICE CENTRES
ANGLIA REGION, Block B, Government Buildings,
  Brooklands Avenue, Cambridge CB2 2DR. Tel: 0223-
  462727. *Regional Director (G5)*, D. A. Boreham
EAST MIDLANDS REGION, Government Buildings, Block
  7, Chalfont Drive, Nottingham NG8 3SN. Tel: 0602-
  291191. *Regional Director (G5)*, M. J. Finnigan
NORTH-EAST REGION, Government Buildings, Crosby
  Road, Northallerton, N. Yorks. DL6 1AD. Tel: 0609-
  773751. *Regional Director (G6)*, P. Watson

NORTHERN REGION, Eden Bridge House, Lowther Street, Carlisle, Cumbria CA3 8DX. Tel: 0228-23400. *Regional Director (G5)*, D. E. Jones

NORTH MERCIA REGION, Berkeley Towers, Nantwich Road, Crewe, Cheshire CW2 6PT. Tel: 0270-692II. *Regional Director (G6)*, R. Bettley-Smith

SOUTH-EAST REGION, Block A, Government Buildings, Coley Park, Reading, Berks. RGI 6DT. Tel: 0734-581222. *Regional Director (G5)*, R. Anderson

SOUTH MERCIA REGION, Block C, Government Buildings, Whittington Road, Worcester WR5 2LQ. Tel: 0905-763355. *Regional Director (G6)*, P. G. Gething

SOUTH-WEST REGION, Government Buildings, Alphington Road, Exeter EX2 8NQ. Tel: 0392-77951. *Regional Director (G6)*, M. R. W. Highman

WESSEX REGION, Block 3, Government Buildings, Burghill Road, Westbury-on-Trym, Bristol BSIO 6NJ. Tel: 0272-591000. *Regional Director (G6)*, Mrs A. J. L. Ould

INFORMATION TECHNOLOGY DIRECTORATE
Government Buildings, Epsom Road, Guildford, Surrey
GUI 2LD
Tel 0483-68121

Director (G4), D. Selwood
Assistant Directors (G5), A. G. Matthews; D. J. Dunthorne; *(G6)*, D. D. Brown; R. F. Syrett

EXECUTIVE AGENCIES

CENTRAL VETERINARY LABORATORY
Woodham Lane, New Haw, Addlestone, Surrey KTI5 3NB
Tel 0932-341III

The Central Veterinary Laboratory provides scientific and technical expertise in animal and public health.

Director and Chief Executive (G3), Dr T. W. A. Little
Director of Research (G4), Dr B. J. Shreeve
Director of Operations (G5), R. W. Saunders
Director of Business (G5), Dr J. A. Morris

VETERINARY MEDICINES DIRECTORATE
Woodham Lane, New Haw, Addlestone, Surrey KTI5 3NB
Tel 0932-336911

The Veterinary Medicines Directorate is responsible for all aspects of licensing and control of animal medicines, including the protection of the consumer from hazardous or unacceptable residues.

Chief Executive and Director of Veterinary Medicines (G4), Dr J. M. Rutter
Director (Policy and Finance) (G5), C. J. Lawson
Director (Licensing) (G5), Dr K. N. Woodward
Licensing Manager, Pharmaceuticals and Feed Additives (G6), J. P. O'Brien
Licensing Manager, Immunologicals and Suspected Adverse Reactions (SARS) (G6), Dr A. M. T. Lee

CENTRAL SCIENCE LABORATORY
London Road, Slough, Berks. SL3 7HJ
Tel 0753-534626

Chief Executive (G3), Dr P. I. Stanley
Research Director (G5), Dr A. R. Hardy

AGRICULTURAL DEVELOPMENT AND ADVISORY SERVICE (ADAS)
ADAS Headquarters, Oxford Spires Business Park, The Boulevard, Kidlington, Oxon. OX5 INZ
Tel 0865-842742

The Agricultural Development and Advisory Service (ADAS) provides a comprehensive range of consultancy services to the land-based industries. It also carries out research, performs certain statutory functions and provides advice on policy for MAFF and the Welsh Office.

Chief Executive (G2), Dr J. Walsh
Director of Operations (G3), P. Needham
Research Director (G4), Dr A. D. Hughes
Marketing Director (G5), D. N. Hall
Finance Director (G5), Dr C. Herring
Personnel Director (G5), Ms S. Nason
Director for Wales (G5), W. I. C. Davies
Non-Executive Directors, C. Bystram (*Chairman*); P. Christensen, CBE

PESTICIDES SAFETY DIRECTORATE
Ergon House, 17 Smith Square, London SWIP 3JR
Tel 071-238 6299
Rothamstead, Harpenden, Herts. AL5 2SS
Tel 0582-462100

The Pesticides Safety Directorate is responsible for the evaluation and approval of pesticides and the development of policies relating to them, in order to protect consumers, users and the environment.

Chief Executive (G4), G. K. Bruce
Director (Policy) (G5), J. A. Bainton
Director (Approvals) (G5), Dr A. D. Martin (*based at Harpenden*)

AGRICULTURAL AND FOOD RESEARCH COUNCIL
Polaris House, North Star Avenue, Swindon SN2 IUH
Tel 0793-413200

The Agricultural and Food Research Council (AFRC) is an independent body established by royal charter. It is funded by the Office of Science and Technology, receives commissions from the Ministry of Agriculture, Fisheries and Food, and does research for industry and other bodies.

The Council is responsible for research done in its institutes and in UK university departments funded through its research grants scheme. It advises the Scottish Office Agriculture and Fisheries Department (SOAFD) on research in the Scottish Agricultural Research Institutes. The institutes funded through AFRC and SOAFD, and the university groups supported, form the Agricultural and Food Research Service.

From April 1994, the Council will become the Biotechnology and Biological Sciences Research Council.

Chairman, Sir Alistair Grant
Deputy Chairman and Director-General, Prof. T. L. Blundell, FRS
Members, Dr P. J. Bunyan; C. R. Cann;
  Prof. E. C. D. Cocking, FRS; Prof. J. R. Coggins, FRSE; Sir Sam Edwards, FRS; D. F. R. George, OBE; A. B. N. Gill;
  Prof. R. M. Hicks, OBE; Prof. G. Horn, FRS;
  Prof. W. P. T. James, CBE; R. M. Knapman, MP;
  Prof. J. R. Krebs, FRS; Prof. C. J. Leaver, FRS;
  Dr T. Little; K. J. MacKenzie; Prof. T. Mansfield, FRS;
  J. L. C. Provan; G. T. Pryce; Dr D. W. F. Shannon;
  Prof. W. V. Shaw
Assessors, K. Meldrum; Dr C. McMurray; Prof. H. Smith, FRS; O. Rees, CB; Dr G. W. Robinson; D. Wilkinson;
  Dr E. Buttle; Prof. H. J. Newby; Dr D. A. Rees, FRS;
  Sir Mark Richmond, FRS

Director of Administration, Central Office (G3),
   B. G. Jamieson, PH.D.
Heads of Divisions (G5), S. H. Visscher *(Finance)*; R. J. Price
   (Human Resources); Dr J. N. Wingfield *(Science)*;
   Dr A. V. Harrison *(Policy)*
Commercial Policy Section (G6), S. M. Lawrie
Principal Information Officer (G7), Dr M. A. Winstanley

AFRC COMPUTING DIVISION
West Common, Harpenden, Herts. AL5 2JE
Tel 0582-762271
Head of Division, A. Windram

For institutes and units of the Agricultural and Food Research
Service, *see* page 709

COLLEGE OF ARMS OR HERALDS
COLLEGE
Queen Victoria Street, London EC4V 4BT
Tel 071-248 2762

The College is the official repository of the arms and
pedigrees of English, Northern Irish and Commonwealth
families and their descendants, and its records include official
copies of the records of Ulster King of Arms, the originals of
which remain in Dublin. The 13 officers of the College
specialize in genealogical and heraldic work for their
respective clients.
   Arms have been and still are granted by letters patent
from the Kings of Arms under authority delegated to them
by the Sovereign, such authority having been expressly
conferred on them since at least the fifteenth century. A right
to arms can only be established by the registration in the
official records of the College of Arms of a pedigree showing
direct male line descent from an ancestor already appearing
therein as being entitled to arms, or by making application
through the College of Arms for a grant of arms.
   The College of Arms is open Mon.–Fri. 10–4, when an
Officer of Arms is in attendance to deal with enquiries by the
public, though such enquiries may also be directed to any of
the Officers of Arms, either personally or by letter.
Earl Marshal, His Grace the Duke of Norfolk, KG, GCVO, CB,
   CBE, MC

KINGS OF ARMS
Garter, C. M. J. F. Swan, CVO, PH.D., FSA
Clarenceux, Sir Anthony Wagner, KCB, KCVO, FSA
Norroy and Ulster, J. P. B. Brooke-Little, CVO, FSA

HERALDS
Chester (and Registrar), D. H. B. Chesshyre, LVO, FSA
Windsor, T. D. Mathew
Lancaster, P. L. Gwynn-Jones
Somerset, T. Woodcock, FSA
Richmond, P. L. Dickinson
York, H. E. Paston-Bedingfeld

Earl Marshal's Secretary, Sir Walter Verco, KCVO, Surrey
   Herald Extraordinary

PURSUIVANTS
Rouge Dragon, T. H. S. Duke
Bluemantle, R. J. B. Noel
Portcullis, W. G. Hunt, TD
Rouge Croix, vacant

COURT OF THE LORD LYON
HM New Register House, Edinburgh EH1 3YT
Tel 031-556 7255

The Court of the Lord Lyon is the Scottish Court of Chivalry
(including the genealogical jurisdiction of the *Ri-Sennachie*
of Scotland's Celtic Kings). It adjudicates rights to arms and
administers the Scottish Public Register of All Arms and
Bearings and the Public Register of All Genealogies. The
Lord Lyon presides and judicially establishes rights to
existing arms or succession to chiefship, or for cadets with
scientific 'differences' showing position in clan or family.
Pedigrees are also established by decrees of Lyon Court and
by letters patent. As Royal Commissioner in Armory, he
grants patents of arms (which constitute the grantee and
heirs noble in the Noblesse of Scotland) to 'virtuous and well-
deserving' Scotsmen and to petitioners (personal or corporate) in Her Majesty's overseas realms of Scottish connection,
and issues birthbrieves.
Lord Lyon King of Arms, Sir Malcolm Innes of Edingight,
   KCVO, WS, FSA Scot

HERALDS
Albany, J. A. Spens, RD, WS
Rothesay, Sir Crispin Agnew of Lochnaw, Bt.
Ross, C. J. Burnett, FSA Scot

PURSUIVANTS
Kintyre, J. C. G. George, FSA Scot
Unicorn, Alastair Campbell of Airds, FSA Scot
Carrick, Mrs C. G. W. Roads, MVO, FSA Scot

Lyon Clerk and Keeper of Records, Mrs C. G. W. Roads,
   MVO, FSA Scot
Procurator-Fiscal, I. R. Guild, CBE, FRSE, WS
Herald Painter, Mrs J. Phillips
Macer, A. M. Clark

ARTS COUNCIL OF GREAT BRITAIN
14 Great Peter Street, London SW1P 3NQ
Tel 071-333 0100

The Arts Council, an independent body established in 1946,
is the principal channel for the Government's support of the
arts. It funds the major arts organizations in England, the
Regional Arts Boards and the Scottish and Welsh Arts
Councils. From April 1994 the Scottish and Welsh Arts
Councils will become autonomous and will be funded directly
by the Scottish Office and Welsh Office respectively. The
Arts Council of Great Britain will then become the English
Arts Council (title to be confirmed).
   The Arts Council also provides a service of advice,
information and help to artists, arts organizations and the
general public. Its objectives are to develop and improve the
understanding and practice of the arts and to increase their
accessibility to the public.
   The Council distributes an annual grant from the
Department of National Heritage, and for the year 1993–4
the amount is £225.63 million.
Chairman, Lord Palumbo
Secretary-General, A. Everitt

REGIONAL ARTS BOARDS
EASTERN ARTS BOARD, Cherry Hinton Hall, Cherry
   Hinton Road, Cambridge CB1 4DW. Tel: 0223-215355.
   Chair, Prof. D. Hargreaves

EAST MIDLANDS ARTS BOARD, Mountfields House, Forest Road, Loughborough, Leics. LE11 3HU. Tel: 0509-218292. *Chair*, M. Hutchinson

LONDON ARTS BOARD, Elme House, 133 Long Acre, London WC2E 9AF. Tel: 071-240 1313. *Chair*, C. Priestley

NORTHERN ARTS BOARD, 9–10 Osborne Terrace, Newcastle upon Tyne NE2 1NZ. Tel: 091-281 6334. *Chair*, Mrs S. Robinson

NORTH-WEST ARTS BOARD, 12 Harter Street, Manchester M1 6HY. Tel: 061-228 3062. *Chair* (acting), A. Richardson

SOUTH-EAST ARTS BOARD, 10 Mount Ephraim, Tunbridge Wells, Kent TN4 8AS. Tel: 0892-515210. *Chair*, B. Nicholson

SOUTHERN ARTS BOARD, 13 St Clement Street, Winchester SO23 9DQ. Tel: 0962-855099. *Chair*, D. Reid

SOUTH-WEST ARTS BOARD, Bradninch Place, Gandy Street, Exeter EX4 3LS. Tel: 0392-218188. *Chair*, Ms M. Guillebaud

WEST MIDLANDS ARTS BOARD, 82 Granville Street, Birmingham B1 2LH. Tel: 021-631 3121. *Chair*, R. Southgate

YORKSHIRE AND HUMBERSIDE ARTS BOARD, 21 Bond Street, Dewsbury, W. Yorks. WF13 1AX. Tel: 0924-455555. *Chair*, E. Hall

SCOTTISH ARTS COUNCIL
12 Manor Place, Edinburgh EH3 7DD
Tel 031-226 6051

Chairman, W. Brown

WELSH ARTS COUNCIL
Holst House, 9 Museum Place, Cardiff CF1 3NX
Tel 0222-394 711

Chairman, M. Prichard, CBE

ARTS COUNCIL OF NORTHERN IRELAND
185 Stranmillis Road, Belfast BT9 5DU
Tel 0232-381591

The Arts Council of Northern Ireland is funded by the Department of Education for Northern Ireland. Its function is to develop and improve the accessibility of the arts to the public and to disburse government funds in support of the arts in Northern Ireland.
Chairman, D. Deeny, QC (*from Jan. 1994*)

ART GALLERIES, ETC

ROYAL FINE ART COMMISSION
7 St James's Square, London SW1Y 4JU
Tel 071-839 6537

Established in 1924, the Commission is an autonomous authority on the aesthetic implications of any project or development, primarily but not exclusively architectural, which affects the visual environment.
Chairman, The Lord St John of Fawsley, PC
Commissioners, R. D. Carter, CBE; Dame Elizabeth Chesterton, DBE; Sir Philip Dowson, CBE, RA; M. Girouard, PH.D.; The Duke of Grafton, KG, FSA; D. Hamilton Fraser, RA; M. J. Hopkins, CBE, RA; S. A. Lipton; R. MacCormac; H. T. Moggridge, OBE; Mrs J. Nutting; Sir Philip Powell, CH, OBE, RA;

Prof. J. R. Steer, FSA; J. Sutherland; Miss W. Taylor, CBE; Sir William Whitfield, CBE; J. Winter, MBE
Secretary (G6), S. Cantacuzino, CBE

ROYAL FINE ART COMMISSION FOR SCOTLAND
9 Atholl Crescent, Edinburgh EH3 8HA
Tel 031-229 1109

The Commission was established in 1927 and advises ministers and local authorities on the visual impact and quality of design of construction projects. It is an independent body and gives its opinions impartially.
Chairman, The Hon. Lord Prosser
Commissioners, Prof. G. Benson; Miss K. Borland; W. A. Cadell; Mrs K. Dalyell; Dr Deborah Howard, PH.D., FSA, FSA SCOT.; A. S. Matheson, FRIBA; G. Ogilvie-Laing; Prof. T. Ridley; R. R. Steedman, RSA; Prof. R. Webster; R. Wedgwood
Secretary, C. Prosser

NATIONAL GALLERY
Trafalgar Square, London WC2N 5DN
Tel 071-839 3321

Open weekdays 10–6, Sun. 2–6. Closed on Good Friday, 24–26 December, New Year's Day and May Day Bank Holiday. Admission free.

The National Gallery was founded in 1824, following a parliamentary grant of £60,000 for the purchase and exhibition of the Angerstein collection of pictures. The present site was first occupied in 1838 and enlarged and improved at various times throughout the years. A substantial extension to the north of the building with a public entrance in Orange Street was opened in 1975, and the Sainsbury wing was opened in 1991. Government grant-in-aid for 1993–4 is £17.9 million.

BOARD OF TRUSTEES
Chairman, N. H. Baring
Trustees, Sir Rex Richards, D.PHIL., FRS FRSC; The Lord Alexander of Weedon, QC; F. St J. Gore, CBE; B. Gascoigne, FRSL; P. Troughton; The Countess of Airlie, CVO; Sir Derek Oulton, KCB, QC; E. Uglow; Sir Keith Thomas, FBA; The Hon. Simon Sainsbury; Lady Bingham

OFFICERS
Director (G3), R. N. MacGregor
Chief Curator (G5), Dr C. P. H. Brown
Senior Curators (G6), Dr N. Penny; (*G7*), Dr S. Foister; Dr D. Gordon; J. Leighton
Chief Restorer (G5), M. H. Wyld
Head of Exhibitions (G6), M. J. Wilson
Scientific Adviser (G6), Dr A. Roy
Director of Administration (G5), M. A. Cowdy
Head of Finance and Personnel (G5), T. Tarkowski
Head of Building, Mrs J. Evans
Head of Press and Public Relations, Miss J. Liddiard

NATIONAL PORTRAIT GALLERY
St Martin's Place, London WC2H 0HE
Tel 071-306 0055

Open Mon.–Fri. 10–5, Sat. 10–6, Sun. 2–6. Closed on Good Friday, May Day Bank Holiday, 24–26 December and New Year's Day. Admission free.

A grant was made in 1856 to form a gallery of the portraits of the most eminent persons in British history. The present building was opened in 1896, an extension being opened in 1933. There are four outstations displaying portraits in appropriate settings: Montacute House, Gawthorpe Hall, Beningbrough Hall and Bodelwyddan Castle.

Chairman, The Revd Prof. W. O. Chadwick, OM, KBE, FBA

Trustees, The Lord President of the Council (ex officio); The President of the Royal Academy of Arts (ex officio); Sir Oliver Millar, GCVO, FBA, FSA; J. Roberts, D.Phil.; The Lord Morris of Castle Morris, D.Phil.; H. Keswick; Prof. N. Lynton; The Lord Weidenfeld; Sir Eduardo Paolozzi; J. Tusa; Sir Antony Acland, GCMG, GCVO; Mrs J. E. Benson, LVO, OBE; Mrs W. Tumim; Sir David Scholey, CBE; Mrs C. Tomalin

Director (G3), J. T. Hayes, CBE, Ph.D., FSA *(until Jan. 1994)*

Keeper and Deputy Director (G5), M. Rogers, D.Phil.

TATE GALLERY
Millbank, London SW1P 4RG
Tel 071-821 1313

Open weekdays 10–5.50, Sun. 2–5.50. Closed New Year's Day, Good Friday, May Day Bank Holiday and 24–26 December. Admission free.

The Tate Gallery comprises the national collections of British painting and 20th-century painting and sculpture. The Gallery was opened in 1897, the cost of erection (£80,000) being defrayed by Sir Henry Tate, who also contributed the nucleus of the present collection. The Turner wing was opened in 1910, galleries to contain the collection of modern foreign painting in 1926, and a new sculpture hall in 1937. In 1979 a further extension was built; the latest extension to the Tate Gallery, the Clore Gallery for the Turner Collection, was opened in 1987. The Tate Gallery Liverpool, sited in the Albert Dock, opened in May 1988. The Tate Gallery St Ives opened in June 1993. Total government funding for 1993–4 is £17,075,000.

BOARD OF TRUSTEES
Chairman, D. Stevenson
Trustees, The Countess of Airlie, CVO; The Hon. Mrs J. de Botton; R. Deacon; D. Gordon; C. Le Brun; M. Craig-Martin; Sir Richard Carew Pole; Sir Rex Richards; Mrs P. Ridley; D. Verey

OFFICERS
Director (G3), N. Serota
Deputy Director (G5), F. Carnwath
Keeper of the British Collection (G5), A. Wilton
Keeper of the Modern Collection (G5), R. Morphet
Deputy Keepers (G6), L. A. Parris; J. Lewison

TATE GALLERY LIVERPOOL
Albert Dock, Liverpool L3 4BB
Tel 051-709 3223

Open Tues.–Sun., 10–6. Closed Mondays except Bank Holidays. Admission free.
Curator (G6), L. Biggs

TATE GALLERY ST IVES
Porthmeor Beach, St Ives, Cornwall TR26 1TG
Tel 0736-796226

Opening times vary. Closed Mondays Sept.–May except Bank Holidays, 24–26 December and 1 January. Admission £2.50 (inc. admission to Barbara Hepworth Museum and Sculpture Garden).
Curator (G6), M. Tooby

WALLACE COLLECTION
Hertford House, Manchester Square, London W1M 6BN
Tel 071-935 0687

Open weekdays 10–5, Sun. 2–5. Closed on Good Friday, 24–26 December, 1 January and May Day. Admission free.

The Wallace Collection was bequeathed to the nation by the widow of Sir Richard Wallace, Bt. on her death in 1897, and Hertford House was subsequently acquired by the Government. The collection includes pictures, drawings and miniatures, French furniture, sculpture, bronzes, porcelain, armour and miscellaneous *objets d'art.* The total net expenses for 1993–4 were estimated at £2,224,000.

Director, Miss R. J. Savill
Assistant to Director, P. Hughes
Head of Administration, A. W. Houldershaw

NATIONAL GALLERIES OF SCOTLAND
The Mound, Edinburgh EH2 2EL
Tel 031-556 8921

TRUSTEES
Chairman of the Trustees, A. M. Grossart, CBE
Trustees, J. Packer, OBE; A. R. Cole-Hamilton; Mrs L. W. Gibbs; Lord Macfarlane of Bearsden; Dr T. Johnston; Prof. A. A. Tait; E. Hagman; Prof. E. Fernie; M. Shea

OFFICERS
Director (G4), T. Clifford
Keeper of Conservation (G6), J. P. Dick
Keeper of Information (G7), Miss L. S. Callander
Keeper of Education (G7), M. Cassin
Registrar (G7), Miss A. Buddle
Secretary (G6), Ms S. Edwards
Buildings (G7), C. P. Fotheringham

NATIONAL GALLERY OF SCOTLAND
The Mound, Edinburgh
Tel 031-556 8921

Open Mon.–Sat. 10–5, Sun. 2–5. Closed 25, 26, 27, 31 December, 1–3 January. Admission free.
Keeper (G6), M. Clarke
Assistant Keepers (G7), Ms J. Lloyd Williams; R. M. M. Campbell; Miss H. Smailes

SCOTTISH NATIONAL PORTRAIT GALLERY
1 Queen Street, Edinburgh
Tel 031-556 8921

Hours as for National Gallery of Scotland
Keeper (G6), D. Thomson, Ph.D.
Assistant Keepers (G7), Miss R. K. Marshall, Ph.D.; J. E. Holloway
Curator of Photography, Miss S. F. Stevenson

SCOTTISH NATIONAL GALLERY OF MODERN ART
Belford Road, Edinburgh EH4 3DR
Tel 031-556 8921

Hours as for National Gallery of Scotland
Keeper (G6), R. Calvocoressi
Assistant Keepers (G7), K. S. Hartley; P. Elliott, Ph.D.

For other British Art Galleries, *see* Index

UNITED KINGDOM ATOMIC ENERGY AUTHORITY (AEA TECHNOLOGY)
Harwell, Oxfordshire OX11 0RA
Tel 0235-821111

The UKAEA was established by the Atomic Energy Authority Act 1954. Since April 1986 the UKAEA has been required by the Government to operate on a commercial footing and in 1990 it adopted the trading name AEA Technology. It provides scientific and technical services, products and consultancy in nuclear and non-nuclear fields to governments, utilities and industries world-wide. The UKAEA has six research and engineering centres. Many of the technical staff and activities of the Warren Spring Laboratory will be merged with the environmental capabilities of AEA Technology by mid-1994 to create a National Environmental Technology Centre based within AEA Technology.

Chairman (part-time), Sir Anthony Cleaver
Deputy Chairman and Chief Executive, Dr B. L. Eyre, CBE
Members (part-time), Prof. Sir Peter Hirsch, FRS; J. Bullock; R. Sanderson, OBE; Prof. Sir Roger Elliott, FRS; J. A. Gardiner; Mrs S. Shirley
Secretary, J. R. Bretherton
Executive Director, Finance, P. G. Daffern
Managing Director, Sites and Personnel, A. W. Hills
Managing Director, Industrial Business Group, Dr R. S. Nelson
Managing Director, Nuclear Business Group, Dr D. Pooley

AUDIT COMMISSION FOR LOCAL AUTHORITIES AND THE NATIONAL HEALTH SERVICE IN ENGLAND AND WALES
1 Vincent Square, London SW1P 2PN
Tel 071-828 1212

The Audit Commission was set up in 1983 with responsibility for the external audit of local authorities. This remit was extended from October 1990 to include the audit of the National Health Service bodies in England and Wales. The Commission appoints the auditors, who may be from the District Audit Service or from a private firm of accountants. The Commission is also responsible for promoting value for money in the services provided by local authorities and health bodies.

The Commission has 15–17 members appointed by the Secretary of State for the Environment in consultation with the Secretaries of State for Wales and for Health. Though appointed by the Secretary of State, the Commissioners are responsible to Parliament.

Chairman, Sir David Cooksey
Deputy Chairman, C. M. Stuart
Controller of Audit, A. Foster
Associate Controllers, P. Wilkinson; B. Willmor

COMMISSION FOR LOCAL AUTHORITY ACCOUNTS IN SCOTLAND
18 George Street, Edinburgh EH2 2QU
Tel 031-226 7346

The Commission was set up in 1975. It is responsible for securing the audit of the accounts of Scottish local authorities and certain joint boards and joint committees. Amongst its duties the Commission is required to deal with reports made by the Controller of Audit on items of account contrary to law; on incorrect accounting; and on losses due to misconduct, negligence and failure to carry out statutory duties. Since 1988 the Commission has had responsibility for value-for-money audits of authorities.

Members are appointed by the Secretary of State for Scotland.

Chairman, Prof. J. P. Percy
Controller of Audit, J. Broadfoot
Secretary, J. Ritchie

THE BANK OF ENGLAND
Threadneedle Street, London EC2R 8AH
Tel 071-601 4444

The Bank of England was incorporated in 1694 under royal charter. It is the banker of the Government, on whose behalf it executes monetary policy and manages the note issue and the national debt. It is also responsible for promoting the efficiency and competitiveness of financial services. As the central reserve bank of the country, the Bank keeps the accounts of British banks, who maintain with it a proportion of their cash resources, and of most overseas central banks. (*See also* page 614).

Governor, E. A. J. George
Deputy Governor, R. L. Pennant-Rea
Directors, Sir Adrian Cadbury; A. L. Coleby; Sir Colin Corness; A. D. Crockett; Mrs F. A. Heaton; Sir Christopher Hogg; Sir Martin Jacomb; Sir John Keswick; M. A. King; G. H. Laird, CBE; Sir David Lees; Sir Christopher Morse; B. Quinn; Sir David Scholey, CBE; Prof. Sir Roland Smith; Sir Colin Southgate
Associate Directors, P. H. Kent; H. C. E. Harris; I. Plenderleith
Advisers to the Governor, J. P. Charkham; Sir Peter Petrie; P. C. Peddie; I. G. Watt
Chief of Banking Department (Chief Cashier), G. E. A. Kentfield
Chief Registrar, D. A. Bridger
General Manager, Printing Works, A. W. Jarvis
Secretary, G. A. Croughton
Head of Information Division, J. R. E. Footman
The Auditor, M. J. W. Phillips

BOUNDARY COMMISSIONS

The Commissions are constituted under the Parliamentary Constituencies Act 1986. The Speaker of the House of Commons is ex-officio chairman of all four commissions in the United Kingdom. Each of the four commissions is required by law to keep the parliamentary constituencies in their part of the United Kingdom under review. Each of the three commissions in Great Britain is required by law to keep the European Parliamentary constituencies in their part of Great Britain under review.

ENGLAND
St Catherine's House, 10 Kingsway, London WC2B 6JP
Tel 071-242 0262
Deputy Chairman, The Hon. Mr Justice Knox
Joint Secretaries, R. McLeod; Mrs J. S. Morris

WALES
St Catherine's House, 10 Kingsway, London WC2B 6JP
Tel 071-242 0262
Deputy Chairman, The Hon. Mr Justice Pill
Joint Secretaries, R. McLeod; Mrs J. S. Morris

SCOTLAND
St Andrew's House, Edinburgh EH1 3DG
Tel 031-244 2196/3582
Deputy Chairman, The Hon. Lord Davidson
Secretary, D. K. C. Jeffrey

NORTHERN IRELAND
c/o Northern Ireland Office, Whitehall, London SW1A 2AZ
Tel 071-210 6569

Deputy Chairman, The Hon. Mr Justice Higgins
Secretary, J. R. Fisher

The Secretary, M. Stevenson
Legal Adviser, G. Roscoe

BRITISH BROADCASTING CORPORATION
Broadcasting House, London WIA IAA
Tel 071-580 4468
Television Centre, Wood Lane, London W12 7RJ
Tel 081-743 8000

The BBC was incorporated under royal charter as successor to the British Broadcasting Company Ltd, whose licence expired on 31 December 1926. Its present charter came into force on 1 August 1981, for 15 years (*see also* page 679). The Chairman, Vice-Chairman and other Governors are appointed by The Queen-in-Council. The BBC is financed by revenue from receiving licences for the home services and by grant-in-aid from Parliament for the external services. The total number of receiving licences in the UK at 31 March 1993 was 20,067,114, of which 1,036,320 were for monochrome receivers and 19,030,794 for colour receivers. Annual television licence fees are: monochrome £27.50; colour £83. For services, *see* Broadcasting section.

BOARD OF GOVERNORS *as at 1 July 1993*
Chairman (£57,360), M. Hussey
Vice-Chairman (£14,715), The Lord Cocks of Hartcliffe
National Governors (*each* £14,715), Sir Kenneth Bloomfield,
  KCB (*N. Ireland*); Dr G. Jones (*Wales*); Sir Graham Hills,
  FRSE (*Scotland*)
Governors (*each* £7,360), W. B. Jordan, CBE; Miss J. Glover,
  D.Phil.; Mrs S. Sadeque; Lord Nicholas Gordon Lennox,
  KCMG, KCVO; Mrs M. Spurr

BOARD OF MANAGEMENT
Director-General, J. Birt
*Deputy Director-General and Managing Director, World
  Service*, R. Phillis
Adviser to the Director-General, D. Hatch
Managing Directors, W. Wyatt (*Network Television*); Ms E.
  Forgan (*Network Radio*); R. Neil (*Regional Broadcasting*);
  T. Hall (*News and Current Affairs*); R. Lynch (*Resources
  and Engineering Services*)
Directors, Ms P. Taylor (*Corporate Affairs*); Ms M. Salmon
  (*Personnel*); Ms P. Hodgson (*Policy and Planning*); R.
  Baker-Bates (*Finance and Information Technology*)
Chief Executive, Enterprises, vacant

OTHER SENIOR STAFF
Controller, BBC1, A. Yentob
Controller, BBC2, M. Jackson
Assistant Managing Director, Network Television,
  Ms J. Drabble
Controller, Radio 1, M. Bannister
Controller, Radio 2, Ms F. Line
Controller, Radio 3, N. Kenyon
Controller, Radio 4, M. Green
Controller, Radio 5, Ms P. Ewing
Controller, Scotland, J. McCormick
Controller, Wales, G. Talfan Davies
Controller, N. Ireland, R. Walsh
Controller, European Services, A. Taussig
Controller, Overseas Services, S. Younger
Controller, English Services, Ms E. Smith
Chief Political Adviser, vacant
Controller, Editorial Policy, R. Ayre
Chief Executive Officer, BBC World Service TV, C. Irwin

BRITISH COAL CORPORATION
Hobart House, Grosvenor Place, London SW1X 7AE
Tel 071-235 2020

The British Coal Corporation (formerly the National Coal Board) was constituted in 1946 and took over the mines on 1 January 1947.
Chairman, J. N. Clarke
Deputy Chairman, A. Wheeler, CBE
Executive Members, R. Proctor (*Finance Director*); K. Hunt
  (*Employee Relations*); A. D. J. Horsler (*Marketing
  Director*)
Non-Executive Members, Dr D. V. Atterton, CBE; Dr
  T. J. Parker; D. B. Walker; J. P. Erbé; A. P. Hichens; Sir
  Robert Davidson, FEng.; Sir David Alliance, CBE
Secretary, M. S. Shelton

THE BRITISH COUNCIL
10 Spring Gardens, London SW1A 2BN
Tel 071-930 8466
Medlock Street, Manchester M15
Tel 061-957 7000

The British Council was established in 1934 and incorporated by royal charter in 1940. It is an independent, non-political organization which promotes Britain abroad. It provides access to British ideas, talents and experience in education and training, books and periodicals, the English language, the arts, the sciences and technology.
  The Council is represented in 98 countries and runs 187 offices, 116 libraries and 72 English language schools around the world.
  The Council's annual turnover in 1993–4 is estimated at £416 million, including grants from the Foreign and Commonwealth Office and the Overseas Development Administration. The Council's own revenue now exceeds £120 million.
Chairman, Sir Martin Jacomb
Deputy Chairman, The Lord Chorley
Director-General, J. Hanson, CBE

BRITISH FILM COMMISSION
70 Baker Street, London W1M 1DJ
Tel 071-224 5000

The British Film Commission was established in 1992 to promote the use of British locations, production services, technicians and facilities. It is funded by the Department of National Heritage. It offers a free service to international producers and directs enquiries to local film commissions throughout the UK. It also encourages the development of local commissions where they do not already exist.
Commissioner and Chairman of the Board, S. W. Samuelson,
  CBE
Chief Executive, A. Patrick

BRITISH FILM INSTITUTE
21 Stephen Street, London WIP IPL
Tel 071-255 1444

The British Film Institute was established in 1933 under royal charter. Its aims are to encourage the development of the art of film and its use as a record of contemporary life in Great Britain, and to foster the study, appreciation and use of films for television. It includes the National Film Archive, the National Film Theatre and the Museum of the Moving Image, and it supports a network of 40 regional film theatres. The BFI Library contains the world's largest collection of material relating to film and television. Total government funding for 1993–4 is £15 million.
Chairman, J. Thomas
Director, W. Stevenson

BRITISH PHARMACOPOEIA COMMISSION
Market Towers, 1 Nine Elms Lane, London SW8 5NQ
Tel 071-273 0561

The British Pharmacopoeia Commission sets standards for medicinal products used in human and veterinary medicine. It is responsible for the British Pharmacopoeia (a publicly-available statement of the standard that a product must meet throughout its shelf-life), the British Pharmacopoeia (Veterinary) and the selection of British Approved Names. It also participates in the work of the European Pharmacopoeia on behalf of the United Kingdom. It has 18 members who are appointed by the Secretary of State for Health and the Minister for Agriculture, Fisheries and Food.
Chairman, Prof. D. Ganderton
Vice-Chairman, Prof. P. Turner, CBE
Secretary (G6), Dr R. C. Hutton

BRITISH RAILWAYS BOARD
Euston House, 24 Eversholt Street, PO Box 100, London NWI IDZ
Tel 071-928 5151

The British Railways Board came into being in 1963 under the terms of the Transport Act 1962. The Board is responsible for the provision of railway services in Great Britain and for catering and other related services. For details of operations, *see* Transport section.
Chairman (£232,000), Sir Robert Reid
Members, P. Allen, CBE*; Miss K. T. Kantor*;
J. B. Cameron, CBE*; D. E. Rayner, CBE;
K. H. M. Dixon*; Sir Fred Holliday, CBE*; J. J. Jerram;
E. Sanderson*; Dr P. Watson, OBE; R. Horton*;
A. Norman*; Miss J. Page*
* part-time members

BRITISH STANDARDS INSTITUTION (BSI)
2 Park Street, London WIA 2BS
Enquiry section: BSI, Linford Wood, Milton Keynes
MKI4 6LE
Tel 0908-221166

The British Standards Institution is the recognized authority in the UK for the preparation and publication of national standards for industrial and consumer products. In consulta-tion with the interests concerned, BSI prepares standards relating to nearly every sector of the nation's industry and trade. It also represents the UK at European and international standards meetings. About 80 per cent of its standards work is now internationally linked.

British Standards are issued for voluntary adoption, though in a number of cases compliance with a British Standard is required by legislation. BSI operates certification schemes under which industrial and consumer products are certified as complying with the relevant British Standard and may carry the Institution's certification trade marks, known as the 'Kitemark' and the 'Safety Mark'. It assesses and registers companies which meet the requirements of the quality management standard, BS5750. BSI runs one of the largest testing laboratories in Europe and has an advisory service for exporters, Technical Help to Exporters.

BSI is financed by voluntary subscriptions, an annual government grant, the sale of its publications, and fees for testing and certification. There are more than 27,000 subscribing members of BSI.
Chief Executive, vacant

BRITISH TOURIST AUTHORITY
Thames Tower, Black's Road, London W6 9EL
Tel 081-846 9000

Established under the Development of Tourism Act 1969, the British Tourist Authority has specific responsibility for promoting tourism to Great Britain from overseas. It also has a general responsibility for the promotion and develop-ment of tourism and tourist facilities within Great Britain as a whole, and for advising the Government on tourism matters.
Chairman (*part-time*), Ms A. Biss
Chief Executive (*acting*), A. Jefferson

BRITISH WATERWAYS
Willow Grange, Church Road, Watford, Herts. WDI 3QA
Tel 0923-226422

British Waterways is the navigational authority for over 2,000 miles of canals and river navigations in England, Scotland and Wales. Some 380 miles are maintained and are being developed as commercial waterways for use by freight-carrying vessels. Another 1,200 miles, the cruising waterways, are being developed for boating, fishing and other leisure activities. The remaining 500 miles, the remainder water-ways, are maintained with due regard to safety, public health and the preservation of amenities. Of this remaining mileage, nearly two-thirds is navigable or has been restored to navigation over the past twenty years.
Chairman (*part-time*), D. C. Ingman, CBE
Vice-Chairman (*part-time*), Sir Peter Hutchison, Bt.
Members (*all part-time*), J. Gordon; D. H. R. Yorke;
M. Cairns; D. Porter; Viscountess Cobham
Chief Executive, B. C. Dice
Secretary and Solicitor, R. J. Duffy

BROADCASTING STANDARDS COUNCIL
5–8 The Sanctuary, London SWIP 3JS
Tel 071-233 0544

The Council was set up in 1988 but received its statutory powers under the Broadcasting Act 1990. It monitors the portrayal of violence, sex and matters of taste and decency in any television or radio programme or broadcast advertisement. The Council publishes a code of practice, considers complaints and undertakes relevant research. Members of the Council are appointed by the Secretary of State for National Heritage. The appointments are part-time.

Chair (£38,400), The Lady Howe of Aberavon
Deputy Chairman (£29,000), Dame Jocelyn Barrow, DBE
Members (each £11,550), R. Baker, OBE, RD; Ms R. Bevan; Dr Jean Curtis-Raleigh; Revd C. Robertson; M. Parris
Director, C. Shaw, CBE
Deputy Director, T. Cobley

THE BROADS AUTHORITY
Thomas Harvey House, 18 Colegate, Norwich NR3 1BQ
Tel 0603-610734

The Broads Authority is a special statutory authority set up under the Norfolk and Suffolk Broads Act 1988, with powers and responsibilities similar to those of National Park Authorities. The functions of the Authority are to conserve and enhance the natural beauty of the Broads; to promote the enjoyment of the Broads by the public; and to protect the interests of navigation.

The Authority comprises 35 members, appointed by Norfolk County Council (4); Suffolk County Council (2); Broadland District Council (2); Great Yarmouth Borough Council (2); North Norfolk District Council (2); Norwich City Council (2); South Norfolk District Council (2); Waveney District Council (2); the Countryside Commission (2); English Nature (1); the Great Yarmouth Port Authority (2); the National Rivers Authority (Anglian Region) (1); the Secretary of State for the Environment (9); and two from amongst members of the Authority's statutory Navigation Committee who are not already members of the Authority.

Chairman, J. S. Peel, MC
Chief Executive, M. A. Clark

THE CABINET OFFICE

The Cabinet Office comprises the Secretariat, who support Ministers collectively in the conduct of Cabinet business; and the Office of Public Service and Science (OPSS) which is responsible for the Citizen's Charter initiative, the Next Steps programme, policy on open government, senior Civil Service and public appointments, and the management and organization of the Civil Service and recruitment into it. The OPSS is also responsible for the Civil Service College, the Recruitment and Assessment Services Agency, the Occupational Health Service, HMSO, CCTA (the Government Centre for Information Systems), the Central Office of Information and the Chessington Computer Centre. The Office of Science and Technology also forms part of the OPSS.

The OPSS supports the Prime Minister in his capacity as Minister for the Civil Service, with responsibility for day-to-day supervision delegated to the Chancellor of the Duchy of Lancaster.

PRIME MINISTER'S OFFICE
Prime Minister and Minister for the Civil Service,
    The Rt. Hon. John Major, MP
Principal Private Secretary to the Prime Minister (G3),
    A. Allan

Private Secretaries to the Prime Minister, R. Lyne, CMG
    (*Overseas Affairs*); Mrs M. Francis (*Economic Affairs*);
    W. Chapman (*Parliamentary Affairs*); M. Adams (*Home Affairs*)
Diary Secretary to the Prime Minister, Miss S. Phillips
Secretary for Appointments (G5), J. Holroyd, CB
Foreign Affairs Adviser, Sir Rodric Braithwaite, KCMG
Efficiency and Competition Adviser, Sir Peter Levene, KBE
Political Secretary, J. Hill
Policy Unit, The Hon. Mrs S. Hogg; N. True, CBE;
    A. Rosling; The Lord Poole; Mrs K. Ramsey; Miss
    L. Neville-Rolfe; Ms J. Rutter; D. Green; D. Morris
Chief Press Secretary, A. T. O'Donnell
Deputy Chief Press Secretary, J. Haslam
Assistant Private Secretaries to the Prime Minister, Miss
    A. Hordern; Miss J. L. Wilkinson
Parliamentary Private Secretary, G. Bright, MP
Secretary of the Cabinet and Head of Home Civil Service,
    Sir Robin Butler, GCB, CVO
Private Secretary, Miss M. J. Leech

SECRETARIAT
70 Whitehall, London SW1A 2AS
Tel 071-270 3000

Deputy Secretaries (G2), Miss L. Neville-Jones, CMG;
    P. F. Owen, CB; D. E. Fitchew, CMG
Under-Secretaries (G3), R. Bird; D. J. Gould; R. L. Niven;
    R. J. D. Carden
Grade 5, A. Sandall; J. Sibson; Brig. J. A. J. Budd;
    S. G. Eldon
Grade 6, R. Hope

ESTABLISHMENT OFFICER'S GROUP
Government Offices, Great George Street, London
SW1P 3AL
Tel 071-270 3000

Principal Establishment and Finance Officer (G3),
    R. W. D. Venning
Deputy Establishment Officer (G5), G. S. Royston
Senior Finance Officer (G6), Miss J. M. E. Buchan

HISTORICAL AND RECORDS SECTION
Hepburn House, Marsham Street, London SW1P 4HW
Tel 071-217 6032

Grade 5, Miss P. M. Andrews

CEREMONIAL OFFICER
53 Parliament Street, London SW1A 2NG
Tel 071-210 5056

Grade 6, J. H. Thompson, CB

OFFICE OF PUBLIC SERVICE AND SCIENCE (OPSS)
Horse Guards Road, London SW1P 3AL
70 Whitehall, London SW1A 2AS
Tel 071-270 5811

Chancellor of the Duchy of Lancaster and Minister of Public Service and Science, The Rt. Hon. William Waldegrave,
MP
Principal Private Secretary, A. T. Cahn
Private Secretary, I. Dougal
Special Advisers, Dr J. Nicholson; Sir Peter Levene, KBE;
    I. Wilton
Parliamentary Private Secretary, I. Taylor, MBE, MP
Parliamentary Under-Secretary of State, David Davis, MP
Private Secretary, W. E. Jones
Second Permanent Secretary (G1A), R. C. Mottram
Private Secretary, G. R. Davies

Parliamentary Clerk, Miss T. N. Terry
Press Secretary (G5), P. Rose

CITIZEN'S CHARTER UNIT
Government Offices, Great George Street, London
SWIP 3AL
Tel 071-270 6343

Director (G2), B. Hilton, CB
Deputy Directors (G6), Mrs D. A. Goldsworthy; Mrs
    E. Hunter-Johnson

EFFICIENCY UNIT
70 Whitehall, London SWIA 2AS
Tel 071-260 0273

Prime Minister's Adviser on Efficiency and Effectiveness,
    Sir Peter Levene, KBE
Head of Unit (G3), J. Oughton
Deputy Head of Unit (G5), Ms D. Kahn

ADVISORY UNIT ON MINISTERS' AGENCIES
Adviser, C. M. Brendish
Grade 6, D. R. Wood

MANAGEMENT DEVELOPMENT GROUP
Under-Secretary (G3), vacant
Grade 5, R. D. J. Wright (*Security*); Mrs S. Britton (*Equal
    Opportunities*); Miss S. C. Phippard (*Next Steps Project
    Team*); C. J. Parry (*Development*)

TOP MANAGEMENT PROGRAMME
Director of Programme (G3), Miss M. T. Neville-Rolfe
Course Directors (G5), Mrs P. Clarkson; Mrs M. Chapman

SENIOR AND PUBLIC APPOINTMENTS GROUP AND
EUROPEAN STAFFING
Under-Secretary (G3), A. J. Merifield
Grade 5, D. Laughrin
Grade 6, J. K. Barron

MACHINERY OF GOVERNMENT
Grade 5, A. D. Whetnall

OFFICE OF THE CIVIL SERVICE COMMISSIONERS
(OCSC)
Alencon Link, Basingstoke, Hants. RG21 1JB
Tel 0256-29222

First Commissioner (G2), Mrs A. E. Bowtell, CB (*London*)
Commissioner (G3), M. D. Geddes (*Chief Executive, RAS*)
Commissioners (part-time), Ms U. Prashar; Mrs J. Rubin;
    A. Maddrell; K. E. C. Sorensen
Secretary to the Commissioners and Head of the Office (G5),
    Miss E. M. Goodison

INFORMATION OFFICER MANAGEMENT UNIT
Information Officer (G5), T. J. Perks

CCTA (THE GOVERNMENT CENTRE FOR
INFORMATION SYSTEMS)
Riverwalk House, 157–161 Millbank, London SWIP 4RT
Tel 071-217 3000
Gildengate House, Upper Green Lane, Norwich NR3 1DW
Tel 0603-694620

Director (G3), vacant
Deputy Director (G4), W. Houldsworth

OFFICE OF SCIENCE AND TECHNOLOGY
70 Whitehall, London SWIA 2AS
Tel 071-270 3000
Grove House, 16 Orange Street, London WC2H 7ED
Tel 071-270 6944
Sanctuary Buildings, Great Smith Street, London SWIP 3BT
Tel 071-925 5000

Chief Scientific Adviser and Head of Office, Prof.
    W. D. P. Stewart, FRS, FRSE

Private Secretary (G7), Dr L. Drummond
Director-General of Research Councils (from Jan. 1994),
    vacant

BRANCH A
Grade 3, R. Foster
Grade 5, Dr D. P. Walker (*Domestic science and technology
    issues*); D. A. Warren (*International science and technology
    issues*); Dr J. McGuinness (*ACOST Secretariat*)

BRANCH B
Grade 3, D. A. Wilkinson; Dr D. G. Libby
Grade 5, Dr J. Partington (*General Science Policy*);
    R. P. Ritzema (*International Science*)
Grade 6, Dr K. Root (*Science Budget*); Dr R. Dowdell

EXECUTIVE AGENCIES

OCCUPATIONAL HEALTH SERVICE
18–20 Hill Street, Edinburgh EH2 3NB
Tel 031-220 4177

The Occupational Health Service provides services and
advice to all government departments and executive agencies,
and to other public bodies, on matters relating to the health
of their employees in their working environment.
Medical Adviser and Director, Dr E. C. McCloy
Deputy Medical Adviser, Dr P. Brown

CIVIL SERVICE COLLEGE
Sunningdale Park, Ascot, Berks. SL5 0QE
Tel 0344-634000
11 Belgrave Road, London SWIV 1RB
Tel 071-834 6644

The College provides training in management and profes-
sional skills for civil servants and for those working in the
private sector.
Chief Executive (G3), Miss M. T. Neville-Rolfe
Director of Studies (G5), D. R. Smith
Director of Services and Resources (G5), I. Cameron
Business Group Directors (G5/G6), Ms C. M. Bentley; Ms
    E. Chennells; J. G. Fuller; G. W. Llewellyn;
    P. J. C. O'Connell; P. G. Tebby; Miss J. A. Topham
College Secretary (G6), Miss M. A. Wood

RECRUITMENT AND ASSESSMENT SERVICES (RAS)
Alencon Link, Basingstoke, Hants. RG21 1JB
Tel 0256-29222
24 Whitehall, London SWIA 2ED
Tel 071-210 3000

RAS provides professional recruitment and staff development
services to the Civil Service and other public sector bodies.
Chief Executive, M. D. Geddes
Grade 5, A. A. Carter (*London*)
Grade 6, F. D. Bedford (*London*); K. N. Bastin

CHESSINGTON COMPUTER CENTRE
Government Buildings, Leatherhead Road, Chessington,
Surrey KT9 2LT
Tel 081-391 3800

Director (G5), R. N. Edwards

CENTRAL ADJUDICATION SERVICES
Quarry House, Leeds LS2 7UB
Tel 0532-324000

The Chief Adjudication Officer and Chief Child Support
Officer are independent statutory authorities under the Social
Security Act 1975 (as amended) and the Child Support Act

1991. They are appointed by the Secretary of State for Social Security to give advice to adjudication officers and child support officers, to keep under review the operation of the systems of adjudication, and to report annually to the Secretary of State on adjudication standards.

Adjudication officers make decisions of first instance on all claims for social security cash benefits, and child support officers make decisions of first instance on applications for child maintenance made to the Child Support Agency. Officers of the Chief Adjudication Officer also enter written observations on all appeals made to the Social Security Commissioners, and officers of the Chief Child Support Officer make written observations on appeals to the Child Support Commissioners.

Chief Adjudication Officer and Chief Child Support Officer,
   K. Bellamy, CBE

CENTRAL STATISTICAL OFFICE
Great George Street, London SW1P 3AQ
Tel 071-270 6363/6364

The work of the Central Statistical Office encompasses data collection from businesses; the preparation and publication of macro-economic statistics and social statistics abstracts; statistics relating to institutional sectors and financial statistics; the retail prices index and the family expenditure survey; liaison with international statistical bodies; and central management of the Government Statistical Service (GSS). The Central Statistical Office became an executive agency of the Treasury in November 1991.

Director and Head of the Government Statistical Service
   (G1A), W. McLennan
Private Secretary, Miss H. Shanks
Deputy Director and Director of National Accounts (G3),
   D. C. L. Wroe
Head of GSS and General Division (G3), R. G. Ward
Head of Business Statistics Division (G3), R. Norton
Head of Sector Accounts Division (G3), J. E. Kidgell
Head of Central Services Division (G4), Dr L. Mayhew
Head of Information (G5), I. Scott

GSS AND GENERAL DIVISION
Heads of Branches (G5), D. C. K. Stirling *(GSS policy and management);* Miss J. Church *(Social, regional and household expenditure);* Ms M. Haworth *(Retail Prices Index);* R. J. Scott *(Registers and materials inquiries)*

DEPUTY DIRECTOR'S OFFICE
Heads of Branches (G5), Miss S. P. Carter *(National accounts and economic assessment);* P. B. Kenny *(Statistical methods and quality)*

BUSINESS STATISTICS DIVISION
Heads of Branches (G5), K. Francombe *(Index of production);* C. J. Spiller *(Production censuses and capital expenditure inquiries);* G. D. Walker *(Distribution and services);* R. G. Lynch *(Product prices and sales);* K. Mansell *(Output and expenditure)*

SECTOR ACCOUNTS DIVISION
Heads of Branches (G5), G. Jenkinson *(Current account);* B. J. Buckingham *(Balance of payments);* Mrs P. Walker *(Company and personal sector accounts);* P. Turnbull *(Public sector and financial accounts);* S. Clark *(Financial institutions)*

CENTRAL SERVICES DIVISION
Heads of Branches (G5), Dr J. Ludley *(Information systems);* I. Scott *(Press and publications);* D. R. Lewis *(Personnel and finance)*

CERTIFICATION OFFICE FOR TRADE UNIONS AND EMPLOYERS' ASSOCIATIONS
27 Wilton Street, London SW1X 7AZ
Tel 071-210 3734/5

The Certification Office is an independent statutory authority. The Certification Officer is appointed by the Secretary of State for Employment and is responsible for receiving and scrutinizing annual returns from trade unions and employers' associations; for reimbursing certain costs of trade unions' postal ballots; for dealing with complaints concerning trade union elections; for ensuring observance of statutory requirements governing political funds and trade union mergers; and for certifying the independence of trade unions.

Certification Officer, E. G. Whybrew
Assistant Certification Officer, G. S. Osborne

SCOTLAND
58 Frederick Street, Edinburgh EH2 1LN
Tel 031-226 3224
Assistant Certification Officer for Scotland, J. L. J. Craig

CHARITY COMMISSION
St Alban's House, 57–60 Haymarket, London SW1Y 4QX
Tel 071-210 4477
Graeme House, Derby Square, Liverpool L2 7SB
Tel 051-227 3191
Woodfield House, Tangier, Taunton, Somerset TA1 4BL
Tel 0823-345000

The Charity Commission was established under the Charities Act 1960 with the general function of promoting the effective use of charitable resources in England and Wales. The Commissioners give information and advice to charity trustees to make the administration of their charity more effective, investigate misconduct and the abuse of charitable assets and take or recommend remedial action, and maintain a public register of charities. The Commission does not have at its disposal any funds with which to make grants to organizations or individuals.

At the end of 1992 the total number of registered charities was 170,357.

Chief Commissioner (G3), R. Fries
Commissioners (G3), J. Farquharson; R. M. C. Venables
Commissioners (part-time) (G4), M. Webber; Mrs D. H. Yeo
Deputy Commissioners (G5), J. A. Dutton; J. F. Claricoat;
   G. S. Goodchild; K. M. Dibble; S. Slack
Secretary and Executive Director (G4), Mrs E. A. Shaw
Director of Operations (G5), V. F. Mitchell
Grade 6, Mrs H. M. Phillips; Miss D. F. Taylor; S. K. Sen;
   P. P. White; N. M. Mackenzie; M. J. Harbottle;
   J. Tipping; R. E. Edwards; Miss V. A. Nuttall
Senior Legal Assistants, A. H. Bilbrough; I. M. Davies
Grade 7, R. E. Hatton; A. O. Polak; M. C. T. Seymour;
   K. M. Dickin; M. J. McManus; G. B. Ward;
   J. S. Holdsworth; M. Pearson; P. W. Somerfield;
   R. G. Dawes; Miss G. Fletcher; A. J. George; J. Thorne;
   I. Spencer; Mrs P. D. W. Holt; J. Kilby; R. Jones; Miss
   B. Lythgoe; R. A. V. Corden; J. M. Reid; Ms L. Matlock
Official Custodian for Charities (G6), Mrs S. E. Gillingham
Deputy Official Custodian (G7), M. Fry
Establishment Officer (G5), Mrs J. Cotton

The departments responsible for charities in Scotland and Northern Ireland are:

SCOTLAND – Scottish Home and Health Department, Charities Division, New St Andrews House, Edinburgh EH1 3DE. Tel: 031-244 2206

NORTHERN IRELAND – Department of Finance and Personnel, Charities Branch, Rosepark House, Upper Newtownards Road, Belfast BT4 3NR. Tel: 0232-484567

CHIEF ADJUDICATION OFFICER AND CHIEF CHILD SUPPORT OFFICER
— *see* Central Adjudication Services

CHURCH COMMISSIONERS
1 Millbank, London SW1P 3JZ
Tel 071-222 7010

The Church Commissioners were established in 1948 by the amalgamation of Queen Anne's Bounty (established 1704) and the Ecclesiastical Commissioners (established 1836).

The Commissioners are responsible for the management of most of the Church of England's assets, the income from which is predominantly used to pay, house and pension the clergy. The Commissioners own over 150,000 acres of agricultural land, a number of residential estates in central London, and commercial property in Great Britain and the USA. They also carry out administrative duties in connection with pastoral reorganization and redundant churches, and have been designated by the General Synod as the central stipends authority of the Church of England.

CONSTITUTION
The Commissioners are: the Archbishops of Canterbury and of York; the 41 diocesan bishops; five deans or provosts, ten other clergy and ten lay persons appointed by the General Synod; four lay persons nominated by The Queen; four persons nominated by the Archbishop of Canterbury; the Lord Chancellor; the Lord President of the Council; the First Lord of the Treasury; the Chancellor of the Exchequer; the Secretary of State for the Home Department; the Speaker of the House of Commons; the Lord Chief Justice; the Master of the Rolls; the Attorney-General; the Solicitor-General; the Lord Mayor and two Aldermen of the City of London; the Lord Mayor of York; and one representative from each of the Universities of Oxford and Cambridge.

INCOME AND EXPENDITURE
for year ended 31 December 1992

INCOME	£ million
Stock exchange investments	76.6
Property	63.2
Interest from loans, etc.	28.2
Diocesan/parish contributions for stipends	88.7
Total	£256.7

EXPENDITURE	
Clergy stipends	150.0
Clergy and widows' pensions	63.9
Clergy houses	10.2
Episcopal administration and payments to Chapters	10.8
Church buildings	2.6
Administrative expenses of the Commissioners and related bodies	11.2
Carried forward	8.0
Total	£256.7

Between 1988 and 1992, the value of the Church's assets fell by £800 million.

CHURCH ESTATES COMMISSIONERS
First, Sir Michael Colman, Bt.
Second, The Rt. Hon. Michael Alison, MP
Third, Mrs M. H. Laird

OFFICERS
Secretary, P. Locke
Assistant Secretaries:
The Accountant, G. C. Baines
Management Accountant, B. J. Hardy
Commercial Property, M. G. S. Farrell
Computer Manager, J. W. Ferguson
Secretariat, W. R. Herbert
Estates, P. H. P. Shaw, LVO
Houses, D. J. B. Long
Investments Manager, A. S. Hardy
Pastoral, and Redundant Churches, M. D. Elengorn
Stipends and Allocations, R. S. Hopgood
Senior Architect, J. A. Taylor
Principals, A. W. Atkins; Miss A. M. Mackie; G. Wills;
    J. A. W. Elloy; C. R. Bullen; D. W. H. Lewis;
    N. J. Neil-Smith; J. W. Wallace; R. A. Scott

LEGAL DEPARTMENT
Official Solicitor, J. P. Guy
Deputy Solicitor, Miss S. M. S. Jones
Solicitors, Miss J. M. Bland; J. D. Carter; Miss J. A. Egar;
    R. D. C. Murray; Ms A. R. Usher

CIVIL AVIATION AUTHORITY
CAA House, 45–59 Kingsway, London WC2B 6TE
Tel 071-379 7311

The CAA is responsible for the economic regulation of UK airlines by licensing air routes and air travel organizers and by approving fares; for the safety regulation of UK civil aviation by the certification of airlines and aircraft, and by licensing aerodromes, flight crew and aircraft engineers; and, through the National Air Traffic Services, for the provision of air traffic control and telecommunications services.
Chairman (part-time) (£60,606), The Rt. Hon. C. Chataway
Managing Director, T. Murphy, CBE
Secretary, Miss G. M. E. White

COMMONWEALTH DEVELOPMENT CORPORATION
1 Bessborough Gardens, London SW1V 2JQ
Tel 071-828 4488

The Commonwealth Development Corporation is charged with the task of assisting overseas countries in the development of their economies. Its main activity is providing long-term finance, as loans and risk capital, for projects. The Corporation's area of operations includes British dependent territories and, with ministerial approval, Commonwealth or other developing countries. At present, the Corporation is authorized to operate in more than 60 countries and territories. The Corporation is authorized to borrow up to £850 million.
Chairman (part-time), Sir Peter Leslie
Deputy Chairman (part-time), Sir Michael Caine
Members (part-time), Mrs A. Wright; Prof. M. Faber;
    E. B. Waide, OBE; M. D. McWilliam; Prof. I. Carruthers;
    J. Zochonis
Chief Executive, J. D. Eccles, CBE (*until May 1994*); Dr
    R. Reynolds (*from May 1994*)

COMMONWEALTH SECRETARIAT
— see Index

COMMONWEALTH WAR GRAVES
COMMISSION
2 Marlow Road, Maidenhead, Berks. SL6 7DX
Tel 0628-34221

The Commonwealth War Graves Commission (formerly Imperial War Graves Commission) was founded by royal charter in 1917. It is responsible for the commemoration of 1,694,930 members of the forces of the Commonwealth who fell in the two world wars. More than one million graves are maintained in 23,071 burial grounds throughout the world. Over three-quarters of a million men and women who have no known grave or who were cremated are commemorated by name on memorials built by the Commission.
The funds of the Commission are derived from the six governments participating in its work, i.e. the UK, Australia, Canada, India, New Zealand and South Africa.
President, HRH The Duke of Kent, KG, GCMG, GCVO, ADC
Chairman, The Secretary of State for Defence in the UK
Vice-Chairman, Air Chief Marshal Sir Joseph Gilbert, KCB, CBE
Members, The Secretary of State for the Environment in the UK; The High Commissioners in London for Australia, Canada, India and New Zealand; the Ambassador in London for the Republic of South Africa; Dame Janet Fookes, DBE, MP; Sir Nigel Mobbs; Adm. Sir Nicholas Hunt, GCB, LVO; The Viscount Ridley, KG, TD; Prof. R. J. O'Neill, AO; Mrs L. Golding, MP; Sir Harold Walker, KCMG; Gen. Sir John Akenhurst, KCB, CBE
Director-General and Secretary to the Commission, D. Kennedy
Deputy Directors-General, T. F. Penfold (*Administration*); R. J. Dalley (*Operations*)
Directors, T. V. Reeves (*Finance*); A. Coombe (*Works*); D. C. Parker (*Horticulture*); H. Mackay (*Management Services*); D. R. Parker (*Personnel*); J. P. D. Gee (*Information and Secretariat*)
Legal Adviser and Solicitor, G. C. Reddie
Hon. Artistic Adviser, Prof. Sir Peter Shepheard, CBE
Hon. Botanical Adviser, Prof. G. T. Prance, D.Phil., FLS

IMPERIAL WAR GRAVES ENDOWMENT FUND
Trustees, H. U. A. Lambert (*Chairman*); Air Chief Marshal Sir Joseph Gilbert, KCB, CBE; The Lord Remnant, CVO
Secretary to the Trustees, T. V. Reeves

COUNTRYSIDE COMMISSION
John Dower House, Crescent Place, Cheltenham, Glos.
GL50 3RA
Tel 0242-521381

The Countryside Commission was set up in 1968 and is an independent agency which promotes the conservation and enhancement of landscape beauty in England. It encourages the provision and improvement of facilities in the countryside, and works to secure access for open air recreation. Since 1982 the Commission has been funded by an annual grant from the Department of the Environment. Members of the Commission are appointed by the Secretary of State for the Environment.
Chairman, Sir John Johnson, KCMG

Director-General (G3), M. Dower
Directors (G5), R. Clarke (*Policy*); M. J. Kirby (*Operations*); M. Taylor (*Resources*)
National Heritage Adviser, P. Walshe
Head of Corporate Planning (G7), vacant
Head of Land Use Branch (G7), R. Roberts
Head of Recreation and Access Branch (G7), J. W. B. Worth
Head of Public Affairs (G7), Ms P. Palmer
Head of Finance and Establishments (G7), V. Ellis
Head of National Parks and Planning Branch (G7), R. Lloyd
Head of Environmental Protection Branch (G7), I. Mitchell
Regional Officers (G7), K. Buchanan, (*Newcastle*); Dr M. Carroll (*Cambridge*); Dr S. A. Bucknall (*Leeds*); E. Holdaway (*Bristol*); vacant (*Manchester*); D. E. Coleman (*London*); F. S. Walmsley (*Birmingham*)
Special Initiatives, Dr M. Rawson (*Community Forests*); S. Bell (*National Forest*); T. Allen (*Countryside Stewardship*)

COUNTRYSIDE COUNCIL FOR WALES/
CYNGOR CEFN GWLAD CYMRU
Plas Penrhos, Fford Penrhos, Bangor, Gwynedd LL57 2LQ
Tel 0248-370444

The Countryside Council for Wales took over the functions of the Nature Conservancy Council in Wales and the Countryside Commission in Wales in April 1991. It is the Government's statutory adviser on wildlife, countryside and maritime conservation matters in Wales, and it is the executive authority for the conservation of habitats and wildlife. It promotes the protection of the Welsh landscape and encourages opportunities for public access and enjoyment of the countryside. It provides grant aid to local authorities, voluntary organizations and individuals to pursue countryside management. It is funded by the Welsh Office and accountable to the Secretary of State for Wales, who appoints its members.
Chairman, E. M. W. Griffith, CBE
Chief Executive, Prof. I. Mercer
Director of Science and Policy Development, Prof. G. W. Jones
Director of Resources, R. J. Davies
Director of Operations, I. R. Bonner
Chief Ecologist, Dr M. E. Smith
Head of Interpretation and Education, Dr L. D. Gruffydd

COVENT GARDEN MARKET AUTHORITY
Covent House, New Covent Garden Market, London
SW8 5NX
Tel 071-720 2211

The Covent Garden Market Authority is constituted under the Covent Garden Market Acts 1961 to 1977, the members being appointed by the Minister of Agriculture, Fisheries and Food. The Authority owns and operates the 56-acre New Covent Garden Markets (fruit, vegetables, flowers) which have been trading since 1974.
Chairman (*part-time*), W. P. Bowman, OBE
Members (*part-time*), P. J. Hunt; J. A. Harvey, CBE; R. Smith, OBE; Sir Peter Reynolds, CBE; Mrs A. M. Vinton
General Manager, Dr P. M. Liggins
Secretary, C. Farey

CRIMINAL INJURIES COMPENSATION BOARD
Blythswood House, 200 West Regent Street, Glasgow
G2 4SW
Tel 041-221 0945
Whittington House, 19 Alfred Place, London WC1E 7LG
Tel 071-355 6802

The Board was constituted in 1964 to administer the government scheme for *ex gratia* payments of compensation to victims of crimes of violence.
Chairman (part-time) (£27,385), The Lord Carlisle of Bucklow, PC, QC
Members, J. F. A. Archer, QC; D. Barker, QC, Sir Derek Bradbeer, OBE; D. Brennan, QC; Sir David Calcutt, QC; H. Carlisle, QC; B. W. Chedlow, QC; J. Cherry, QC; M. Churchouse; Miss B. Cooper, QC; Miss D. Cotton, QC; J. D. Crowley, QC; His Hon. Judge da Cunha; T. A. K. Drummond, QC; C. Fawcett, QC; W. Gage, QC; Sir Richard Gaskell; E. Gee; G. M. Hamilton, QC; Sir Arthur Hoole; His Hon. Judge Kingham; J. Law, QC; M. E. Lewer, QC; M. Lewis, QC; C. Lindsay, QC; Lord Macaulay of Bragar, QC; J. M. McGhie, QC, D. Mackay, QC; N. Miscampbell, QC; I. M. S. Park, QC; T. Preston, QC; Miss S. Ritchie, QC; D. B. Robertson, QC; C. Seagroatt, QC; E. Stone, QC; D. M. Thomas, OBE, QC; D. O. Thomas, QC; P. Weitzman, QC; His Hon. Sir David West-Russell; C. H. Whitby, QC; J. Leighton Williams, QC
Director, P. G. Spurgeon

CROFTERS COMMISSION
4-6 Castle Wynd, Inverness IV2 3EQ
Tel 0463-237231

The Crofters Commission is a statutory body established in 1955 which is responsible for reorganizing, developing and regulating crofting in the seven crofting (and former county) areas of Argyll, Caithness, Inverness, Orkney, Ross and Cromarty, Shetland and Sutherland. The Commission keeps under review all matters relating to crofting, advises the Secretary of State for Scotland on crofting matters and liaises with other relevant bodies. The Commission also administers the Crofting Counties Agricultural Grants (Scotland) Scheme 1988.
Chairman, H. A. M. Maclean
Members (part-time), B. T. Hunter; Fr. J. A. Macdonald; Mrs A. Rennie; P. Morrison; A. Cameron; W. Ritchie
Secretary (G6), M. Grantham

CROWN AGENTS FOR OVERSEA GOVERNMENTS AND ADMINISTRATIONS
St Nicholas House, St Nicholas Road, Sutton, Surrey SM1 1EL
Tel 081-643 3311

Incorporated by Act of Parliament, the Crown Agents are commercial, financial and professional agents for over 100 governments and over 300 public authorities, international bodies and other organizations, primarily in the public sector.
Chairman, D. H. Probert
Managing Director, P. F. Berry

CROWN ESTATE
16 Carlton House Terrace, London SW1Y 5AH
Tel 071-210 4377

The land revenues of the Crown in England and Wales have been collected on the public account since 1760, when George III surrendered them and received a fixed annual payment or Civil List. At the time of the surrender the gross revenues amounted to about £89,000 and the net return to about £11,000.

In the year ended 31 March 1993, the gross income from the Crown Estate totalled £119,924,000. The sum of £70,500,000 was paid to the Exchequer in 1992–3 as surplus revenue.

The land revenues in Ireland have been carried to the Consolidated Fund since 1820; from 1 April 1923, as regards the Republic of Ireland, they have been collected and administered by the Irish Government.

The land revenues in Scotland were transferred to the Crown Estate Commissioners in 1833.
First Commissioner and Chairman (part-time), The Earl of Mansfield and Mansfield
Second Commissioner and Chief Executive, C. K. Howes, CB
Commissioners (part-time), R. B. Caws, CBE; P. Sober; G. D. Inge-Innes-Lillingston, CVO, CBE; J. N. C. James, CBE; A. S. Macdonald, CBE; J. H. M. Norris, CBE
Deputy Chief Executives, D. E. Murray (*Property*); D. E. G. Griffiths (*Finance and Administration*)
Crown Estate Surveyor, C. F. Hynes
Asset Managers (Urban Estates), M. W. Dillon; J. S. Ellingford; B. T. O'Connoll; M. Tree
Housing Manager, R. Wyatt
Business Manager, Agricultural Estates, R. J. Mulholland
Asset Managers, Agricultural Estates, J. Stumbke; I. Gorwyn
Business Manager, Marine Estates, F. G. Parrish
Asset Managers, Marine Estates, P. Davies; A. Murray
Information Systems Manager, D. Kingston-Smith
Property Services and Technical Manager, P. Shearmur
Head of Valuation and Investment Analysis, R. Spence
Head of Building Services, R. Turner
Internal Audit Manager, J. E. Ford
Finance Manager, J. G. Lelliott
Corporate Services Manager, M. E. Beckwith
Legal Adviser, M. L. Davies
Deputy Legal Adviser, H. Turnsek
Solicitors, J. B. Postgate; R. T. Hayward; M. Drayton; P. Horner; D. R. Apthorpe
Senior Legal Assistant, M. A. J. Cordingley
Personnel Manager, R. J. Blake
Public Relations and Press Officer, Mrs G. Coates

SCOTLAND
10 Charlotte Square, Edinburgh EH2 4BR
Tel 031-226 2741
Crown Estate Receiver for Scotland, M. J. Gravestock
Asset Managers (Scottish Estates), N. Ruck Keene; I. Pritchard; Ms S. Harvey
Glenlivet Estate Ranger, A. Wells

WINDSOR ESTATE
The Great Park, Windsor, Berks. SL4 2HT
Tel 0753-860222
Surveyor and Deputy Ranger, A. R. Wiseman, MVO
Keeper of Gardens, J. Bond

CROWN PROSECUTION SERVICE
— see pages 378–9

BOARD OF CUSTOMS AND EXCISE
New King's Beam House, 22 Upper Ground, London
SE1 9PJ
Tel 071-620 1313

Commissioners of Customs were first appointed in 1671 and housed by the King in London. The Excise Department was formerly under the Inland Revenue Department and was amalgamated with the Customs Department in 1909.

HM Customs and Excise is responsible for collecting and administering customs and excise duties and value added tax, and advises the Chancellor of the Exchequer on any matters connected with them. The Department is also responsible for preventing and detecting the evasion of revenue laws and for enforcing a range of prohibitions and restrictions on the importation of certain classes of goods. In addition, the Department undertakes certain agency work on behalf of other departments, including the compilation of UK overseas trade statistics from customs import and export documents.

THE BOARD
Chairman (G1), Mrs V. P. M. Strachan, CB
Private Secretaries, J. Wild; Miss J. C. Huneburg
Deputy Chairmen (G2), P. Jefferson Smith, CB;
A. W. Russell
Commissioners (G3), P. R. H. Allen; D. F. O. Battle;
A. C. Sawyer; L. J. Harris; Mrs E. Woods; M. J. Eland;
M. R. Brown

HEADQUARTERS OFFICE
Head of Information Technology (G4), A. G. H. Paynter
Assistant Secretaries (G5), P. Kent; D. A. Walton; I. Walton;
A. Killikelly; M. Peach; K. M. Romanski;
B. E. G. Banks; D. C. Hewett; C. J. Holloway; P. Trevett;
B. G. Dawbarn; Mrs M. Smith; J. Campbell;
V. C. Whittington; C. Arnott; D. P. Child; R. Kellaway;
M. F. Knox, CBE; F. A. D. Rush; W. L. Parker;
L. I. Stark; A. P. Allen; J. Meyler; T. Byrne;
A. Aitchison; D. Layton; S. Kingaby; M. Joyce;
D. Chilver; A. Howard; B. Orr; M. Neuburger;
J. Maclean; C. R. S. Talbot; R. McAfee; M. Norgrove
Head of Information (G7), Ms L. J. Sinclair

VAT CENTRAL UNIT
Controller (G5), D. E. J. Nissen

SOLICITOR'S OFFICE
Solicitor (G2), vacant
Principal Assistant Solicitors (G3), G. Fotherby;
R. D. S. Wylie
Assistant Solicitors (G5), M. Michael; M. A. Cooper;
M. C. K. Gasper; Miss A. E. Bolt; Miss S. G. Linton;
J. A. Quinn; I. D. Napper; D. J. C. McIntyre;
D. M. North; C. Allen; Mrs J. Clarke; J. Tester

ACCOUNTANT AND COMPTROLLER-GENERAL'S OFFICE
Accountant and Comptroller-General (G5), D. C. Hewitt
Deputy Accountants-General (G6), G. B. Fox; B. Wood;
D. J. Coyne

STATISTICAL OFFICE
Controller (G5), A. H. Cowley

INVESTIGATION DIVISION
Chief Investigation Officer (G5), F. D. Tweddle

COLLECTORS OF CUSTOMS AND EXCISE *(G5)*
England and Wales:
Birmingham, R. A. Flavill
Dover, R. Crossley

East Anglia, R. C. Shepherd
East Midlands, M. D. Patten
Leeds, H. Peden
Liverpool, C. Roberts
London Airports, J. Bugge
London Central, Mrs F. Boardman
London North and West, J. Galloway, OBE
London Port, R. L. H. Lawrence
London South, T. S. Archer
Manchester, J. C. Bernard
Northampton, A. R. Ball
Northern England, J. A. Rigby
Southampton, C. J. Packman
South Wales and the Borders, W. I. Stuttle
South-west England, P. B. Grange
Thames Valley, A. Bowen

Scotland:
Edinburgh, W. F. Coghill
Glasgow and Clyde, T. F. Jessop

Northern Ireland:
Belfast, T. W. Logan

OFFICE OF THE DATA PROTECTION REGISTRAR
Wycliffe House, Water Lane, Wilmslow, Cheshire SK9 5AX
Tel 0625-535711 (*administration*); 0625-535777 (*enquiries*)

The Office of the Data Protection Registrar was created by the Data Protection Act 1984. It is the Registrar's duty to compile and maintain the Register of Data Users and Computer Bureaux and to provide facilities for members of the public to examine the Register; to promote observance of data protection principles; to consider complaints made by data subjects; to disseminate information about the Act; to encourage the production of codes of practice by trade associations and other bodies; to guide data users in complying with data protection principles; to co-operate with other parties to the Council of Europe Convention and act as UK authority for the purposes of Article 13 of the Convention; and to report annually to Parliament on the performance of his functions.
Registrar, E. J. Howe, CBE

MINISTRY OF DEFENCE
— *see pages 392–5*

DESIGN COUNCIL
28 Haymarket, London SW1Y 4SU
Tel 071-839 8000

The Design Council's aim is to improve the design of British products and hence their competitiveness by advising companies on up-to-date practice in engineering and industrial design; presenting the annual British Design Awards; publishing information to help manufacturers, designers, and others professionally involved in design; and promoting improvements in design education and training at all levels. The headquarters and main exhibition area are in London and there are offices in Belfast, Birmingham, Glasgow, Leeds, Newcastle upon Tyne and Treforest in Wales. The Design Council is funded partly by a government grant-in-aid and partly by earned revenues.

Chairman (acting), C. Welch
Director-General, I. Owen, CBE

For research centres of the Economic and Social Science Research Council, *see* page 710.

THE DUCHY OF CORNWALL
10 Buckingham Gate, London SW1E 6LA
Tel 071-834 7346

The Duchy of Cornwall was instituted by Edward III in 1337 for the support of his eldest son, Edward, the Black Prince, and since 1503 the eldest surviving son of the Sovereign has, as heir apparent, succeeded to the dukedom by inheritance. It is the oldest of the English duchies. Before elevation to a dukedom, it was an earldom from 1227, when Richard, King of the Romans and younger brother of Henry III, was created Earl of Cornwall.

THE PRINCE'S COUNCIL
HRH The Prince of Wales, KG, KT, GCB; The Lord Ashburton, KCVO (*Lord Warden of the Stannaries*); The Earl Cairns, CBE (*Receiver-General*); R. J. A. Carnwath, QC (*Attorney-General to the Prince of Wales*); J. N. C. James, CBE (*Secretary and Keeper of the Records*); Earl of Shelburne; Cdr. R. J. Aylard, RN; J. E. Pugsley; A. M. J. Galsworthy; C. Howes; W. N. Hood, CBE; The Earl Peel

OTHER OFFICERS
Auditors, Sir Jeffery Bowman; I. Brindle; H. Hughes
Sheriff (1993–4), R. Gilbert

THE DUCHY OF LANCASTER
Lancaster Place, Strand, London WC2E 7ED
Tel 071-836 8277

The estates and jurisdiction known as the Duchy and County Palatine of Lancaster have been attached to the Crown since 1399, when John of Gaunt's son came to the throne as Henry IV. As the Lancaster inheritance it goes back to 1265. Edward III erected Lancashire into a County Palatine in 1351.
Chancellor of the Duchy of Lancaster, The Rt. Hon. William Waldegrave, MP
Attorney-General and Attorney and Serjeant within the County Palatine of Lancaster, T. A. W. Lloyd, QC
Receiver-General, Maj. Sir Shane Blewitt, KCVO
Vice-Chancellor, The Hon. Mr Justice Morritt, CVO
Clerk of the Council, M. K. Ridley, CVO
Solicitor, I. J. Dicker
Chief Clerk, Col. F. N. J. Davies

ECONOMIC AND SOCIAL RESEARCH COUNCIL
Polaris House, North Star Avenue, Swindon SN2 1UJ
Tel 0793-413000

The ESRC is an independent, government-funded body established by royal charter in 1965. It promotes and supports high-quality basic, strategic and applied social science research and related post-graduate training with the aim of increasing understanding of social and economic change and thereby enhancing the UK's industrial competitiveness and quality of life.
Chairman, Prof. H. Newby
Secretary, W. Solesbury

DEPARTMENT FOR EDUCATION
Sanctuary Buildings, Great Smith Street, London SW1P 3BT
Tel 071-925 5000

The Government Department of Education was, until the establishment of a separate office, a committee of the Privy Council appointed in 1839 to supervise the distribution of certain grants which had been made by Parliament since 1834. The Act of 1899 established the Board of Education, with a President and Parliamentary Secretary, and created a Consultative Committee. The Education Act of 1944 established the Ministry of Education. In April 1964 the office of the Minister of Science was combined with the Ministry to form the Department of Education and Science. In July 1992, responsibility for science was transferred to the Office of Public Service and Science and the department was re-named the Department for Education. It has overall responsibility for education in England, and for the Government's relations with universities in England, Wales and Scotland.

A review of the department's role and organization, and of its management, personnel and policies, was due to be completed in October 1993.
Secretary of State for Education, The Rt. Hon. John Patten, MP
  Private Secretary, Miss C. Bienkowska
  Special Adviser, C. Grantham
  Parliamentary Private Secretary, M. Carrington, MP
Minister of State, The Baroness Blatch, CBE, PC
  Private Secretary, T. Linden
  Parliamentary Private Secretary, D. Evennett, MP
Parliamentary Under-Secretaries of State, Erich Forth, MP; Tim Boswell, MP; Robin Squire, MP
Permanent Secretary (G1), Sir Geoffrey Holland, KCB
  Private Secretary, K. Hedger
Deputy Secretaries (G2), R. J. Dawe, CB, OBE; J. M. M. Vereker, CB; J. C. Hedger
Under-Secretaries (G3), P. A. Shaw (*Director of Establishments*); C. A. Clark; D. M. Forrester; R. D. Horne (*Accountant-General*); S. R. C. Jones; E. R. Morgan; B. M. Norbury; M. J. Richardson; R. N. Ricks (*Legal Adviser*); N. J. Sanders; C. H. Saville; N. Summers
Chief Architect (G4), P. Benwell

ESTABLISHMENTS AND ORGANIZATION BRANCH
Assistant Secretaries (G5), Mrs H. Douglas; M. F. Hipkins; A. K. C. Gibson
Senior Principals (G6), H. H. Barrick; G. H. N. Evans; S. Green
Principals (G7), R. Ward; K. R. Fitzgerald; Mrs M. J. Lawrence; S. J. Bishop; Mrs J. M. Craggs; M. L. Lyons; Miss B. M. Smart; A. W. Wilshaw

SCHOOLS BRANCH I
Assistant Secretaries (G5), A. Clarke; A. J. Shaw; A. J. Sargent; J. W. Whitaker
Principals (G7), M. E. Malt; A. G. Short; T. C. Tarrant; Miss L. M. Clarke; N. R. Flint; Mrs A. C. Jeffery; Mrs S. G. Evans; Mrs R. M. King; Ms M. Pedersen; Mrs C. K. Saville; Ms A. Barlow; P. W. Fulford-Jones; Ms M. Moon; K. L. R. English; I. N. Walford

SCHOOLS BRANCH 2
Assistant Secretaries (G5), T. B. Jeffery; Ms
J. F. Cramphorn; Mrs P. A. Masters; P. S. Lewis
Principals (G7), C. Dowe; D. Noble; G. A. Holley;
M. Spearing; Miss S. A. Clarke; S. Dance; J. Ratcliff;
A. B. Thompson; Mrs M. Farthing; S. Jetha; R. Mace;
M. Williams

SCHOOLS BRANCH 3
Assistant Secretaries (G5), M. B. Baker; Mrs
C. M. Chattaway; M. F. Neale; S. R. Williams
Principals (G7), Mrs J. Baker; Ms G. Beauchamp; Ms
N. Bartman; J. Lawrence; Ms E. Casbon; I. C. Loveless;
B. D. Glickman; R. J. Wood

SCHOOLS BRANCH 4
Assistant Secretaries (G5), M. C. Stark; R. L. Smith;
A. D. Adamson; P. J. Thorpe; D. G. Halladay
Senior Principal (G6), Mrs J. M. Craggs
Principals (G7), Mrs P. Bailey; J. Browning; Mrs
L. J. Chapman; C. Dee; A. Eagleton; J. Ford;
R. A. V. Jacobs; J. Moore; Ms A. Rushton; A. Sevier; Ms
E. Slater; A. P. Smith; Mrs S. Todd; Mrs C. E. Treen;
Miss C. Trudgett

ARCHITECTS AND BUILDING BRANCH
Chief Architect (G4), A. J. Branton
Chief Quantity Surveyor (G5), B. G. Whitehouse
Superintending Architects (G5), G. J. Parker; J. J. Wilson
Principal Research Officer (G7), Dr G. B. Kenny
Principal Architects (G7), E. C. Bissell; Mrs D. Holt; Miss
E. J. Lloyd-Jones, OBE; P. Lenssen; D. S. Nightingale;
Miss B. M. T. Sanders; A. J. Benson-Wilson;
J. R. C. Brooke; A. C. Thompson; Miss S. A. Legg
Principal Quantity Surveyors (G7), A. A. Jones;
G. E. Wonnacott
Principal Engineer (G7), M. J. Patel
Principal Furniture Designer (G7), N. J. Carter
SPTO Architects, Miss L. Watson; T. J. Williamson;
W. Beadling; R. H. Bishop; A. V. Brock; R. A. Butler;
Miss F. A. Cowburn; T. Dicken; J. A. Ibikunle; P. Kemp;
Mrs H. C. Nicholls
SPTO Quantity Surveyors, D. F. Ashby; C. H. C. Marshall
SPTO Engineer, R. L. Daniels
SPTO Designer, Miss A. Wadsworth

FURTHER AND HIGHER EDUCATION BRANCH 1
Assistant Secretaries (G5), A. Woollard; R. D. Hull
Principals (G7), A. Sevier; A. Smyth; M. P. Markus;
P. Cohen; A. Callaghan

FURTHER AND HIGHER EDUCATION BRANCH 2
Head of FE Support Unit (G4), B. D. Short
Assistant Secretaries (G5), S. T. Crowne; Mrs I. Wilde
Senior Principals (G6), E. F. H. Brittain; B. J. Smeaton
Principals (G7), Ms S. P. Gane; G. Carters; S. E. Kershaw;
Mrs C. West; R. K. Read

FURTHER AND HIGHER EDUCATION BRANCH 3
Assistant Secretaries (G5), Miss P. Laidlaw; M. D. Phipps;
J. S. Street
Principals (G7), D. D. Cook; J. K. Bushnell; E. D. Foster;
Mrs P. Tansley; Miss J. Spatcher

INFORMATION BRANCH
Grade 4, J. W. Coe
Senior Principal Information Officers (G6), K. B. Kerslake;
M. Paterson
Chief Information Officer (G7), T. Cook
Marketing Manager (G7), J. M. Brown

INTERNATIONAL RELATIONS, YOUTH AND GENERAL
BRANCH
Assistant Secretaries (G5), R. W. Chattaway; Miss
C. E. Hodkinson; Miss M. d'Armenia
Principals (G7), Miss L. Hanmer; J. C. Sheridan; Ms
V. Berkeley; D. Barwick; R. Troedson; D. A. Robins;
N. Cornwell

TEACHERS BRANCH
Assistant Secretaries (G5), Ms S. L. Scales; A. J. Wye;
J. Wilde
Principals (G7), Mrs G. W. Dishart; S. A. Mellor;
M. Barker; P. B. Long; D. F. Miller; N. Cornwell;
T. Dracup; S. M. Hillier

INFORMATION SYSTEMS BRANCH
Assistant Secretary (G5), A. K. C. Gibson
Senior Principals (G6), P. D. Gott; E. Herbert; N. Rudd
Principals (G7), B. Lillburn; Mrs N. A. T. Malt;
M. Midwood; A. P. Thompson; D. Craggs; J. Winkle;
M. Young; J. Fitch; G. Trevena; K. Doherty

ANALYTICAL SERVICES BRANCH
Head of Branch (G4), D. Allnutt
Chief Statisticians (G5), J. W. Gardner; H. M. Dale;
S. J. Walton
Head of Economics (G5), D. J. Thompson
Head of Operations Research Unit (G5), R. B. Ladley
Statisticians (G7), A. J. Barnett; R. K. Jain; S. N. Kew;
J. Pascoe; T. C. Knight; M. J. Davidson; N. Rudoe; Mrs
H. E. Evans; S. K. Cook; Miss A. C. Kennedy; Mrs
J. Airs
Economics Advisers (G7), J. Tarsh; M. Thompson

LEGAL BRANCH
Legal Adviser (G3), R. Ricks
Assistant Legal Advisers (G5), D. J. Aries; A. D. Preston;
M. Harris
Assistant Solicitors (G6), Ms J. L. C. Brooks; A. K. Fraser
Senior Legal Assistant (G6), N. P. Beach

INFORMATION BUREAU AND LIBRARY
Chief Librarian, Miss M. Wilson

FINANCE BRANCH
Assistant Secretaries (G5), Mrs H. M. Williams; P. F. Slade;
R. J. Green; N. J. Thirtle
Senior Principal (G6), P. J. Edwards (*Assistant Accountant-
General*)
Principals (G7), P. L. Jones; D. R. Pollard; R. J. Gardner;
S. N. Jardine; K. Fleay; P. G. Dalgleish; P. V. D. Swift;
J. J. Watson; W. Irvine; S. D. James; S. M. Philpotts

TEACHERS PENSION AGENCY
Staindrop Road, Darlington, Co. Durham DL2 9EE
Tel 0325-392929
An executive agency of the Department for Education.
Chief Executive, Mrs D. Metcalfe
Directors, K. M. Miles; P. M. Bleasdale; A. Allison;
D. G. Sanders

OFFICE FOR STANDARDS IN EDUCATION
(OFSTED)
Elizabeth House, York Road, London SE1 7PH
Tel 071–925 6800

A non-ministerial government department established in
September 1992 to keep the Secretary of State informed
about the standards and management of schools in England,
and to establish and monitor a new independent inspection
system for maintained schools in England.
HM Chief Inspector (G2), Prof. S. Sutherland

Director of Administration (G3), T. Flescher
Director of Inspection (G3), Miss A. C. Millett

INFORMATION BRANCH
Senior Principal (G6), J. Lawson

FINANCE BRANCH
Assistant Secretary (G5), B. G. Townsend
Principals (G7), H. Candappa; I. Tough; P. J. Hodgman

PERSONNEL BRANCH
Assistant Secretary (G5), Miss J. M. Phillips
Principal (G7), Miss A. F. Brown

MANAGEMENT BRANCH
Assistant Secretary (G5), C. J. Payne
Principal (G7), P. Arkell

INSPECTION AND ANALYTICAL SERVICES BRANCH
Assistant Secretary (G5), J. Grewe
Chief Statistician (G6), C. Bryant
Principal (G7), Mrs A. Jolly

INFORMATION SYSTEMS BRANCH
Senior Principal (G6), M. L. Childs

COMPETITION AND COMPLIANCE BRANCH
Principal (G7), C. J. Bramley

WORK PROGRAMME BRANCH
Principal (G7), D. Bradley

HM INSPECTORATE
Deputy Directors of Inspection (G4), A. J. Rose;
M. J. Tomlinson
Assistant Directors of Inspection (G5), Mrs C. A. Agambar;
R. J. Brake; Miss D. H. Chorley; M. J. Convey; Miss
K. Cross; A. Dobson; Mrs G. Everson; R. C. Frost;
G. Goldstein; C. D. Gould; V. Green; J. A. Hertrich; Miss
B. J. Lewis; C. P. Marshall; B. E. Merton; Miss
E. L. Passmore; C. M. Richards; P. Singh; P. R. Smith;
D. E. Soulsby; D. W. Taylor; J. V. Townshend;
D. Trainor; D. E. Walker; D. L. West; T. Wylie
There are 218 Grade 6 Inspectors

OFFICE OF ELECTRICITY REGULATION
Hagley House, Hagley Road, Birmingham B16 8QG
Tel 021-456 2100
48 Vincent Street, Glasgow G2 5TS
Tel 041-248 5917

The Office of Electricity Regulation (OFFER) is the
regulatory body for the electricity supply industry in England,
Scotland and Wales. Headed by the Director-General of
Electricity Supply, OFFER was set up under the Electricity
Act 1989 but is independent of ministerial control.
Director-General of Electricity Supply, Prof. S. C. Littlechild
Deputy Director-General, Miss P. A. Boys
Deputy Director-General for Scotland, C. P. Carter

OFFICE OF ELECTRICITY REGULATION
NORTHERN IRELAND
Brookmount Buildings, 42 Fountain Street, Belfast BT1 5EE
Tel 0232-311575

OFFER NI is the regulatory body for the electricity supply
industry in Northern Ireland.
Director-General of Electricity Supply for Northern Ireland,
G. R. Horton
Deputy Director-General, C. H. Coulthard

EMPLOYMENT DEPARTMENT GROUP
Caxton House, Tothill Street, London SW1H 9NF
Tel 071-273 3000

The Employment Department Group is responsible for
government policies aimed at producing a competitive,
efficient and flexible labour market. Its main objectives are
to help people acquire and improve their skills, tb help
unemployed and other disadvantaged people into work, to
encourage industries to train their workforce, to protect
people at work and the public from industrial risks, and to
promote women's opportunities. The Secretary of State for
Employment is responsible for setting the strategic policy
framework in consultation with the Secretaries of State for
Scotland and Wales. From April 1994, responsibility for
training policy in Scotland and Wales within these strategic
aims will be transferred to the Scottish and Welsh Offices
respectively.

The Employment Department Group's policy interests
are carried out by three bodies, all reporting to the Secretary
of State for Employment. These are the Health and Safety
Commission (*see* page 312) and ACAS (*see* page 282) and,
within the Department, the Employment Service. The
training, enterprise and education functions of the Department are carried out by the Training, Enterprise and
Education Directorate, and the responsibility for planning
and delivering many government-funded training and
enterprise programmes rests with the network of 82
independent Training and Enterprise Councils in England
and Wales and with 22 Local Enterprise Companies in
Scotland (for addresses, see local telephone directories).
Secretary of State for Employment, The Rt. Hon. David
Hunt, MBE
Principal Private Secretary (G5), D. Russell
Special Adviser, M. McManus
Parliamentary Private Secretary, N. Evans, MP
Minister of State, Michael Forsyth, MP
Parliamentary Private Secretary, Mrs A. Browning, MP
Parliamentary Under-Secretaries of State, Ann Widdecombe,
MP; The Viscount Ullswater
Private Secretaries, S. Wood; M. Daly; Ms C. Pride
Parliamentary Clerk, Ms M. East
Permanent Secretary (G1), N. Monck
Private Secretary, A. Virgo
Deputy Secretaries (G2), N. W. Stuart, CB; G. Reid, CB;
I. Johnston
Legal Adviser (G3), H. R. L. Purse
Special Advisers, I. Wilton; Ms C. Stratton

THE EMPLOYMENT SERVICE
An executive agency within the Department of Employment.
The Employment Service is responsible for providing services
and administering programmes to help unemployed people
get back to work as quickly as possible and to make payments
to those entitled to benefit.
Chief Executive (G3+), M. E. G. Fogden
Deputy Chief Executive (G3), J. Turner
Director of Finance and Resources (G4), A. G. Johnson
Director of Field Operations (G4), R. Phillips
Director of Business Development (G4), J. Robertson
Director of Human Resources (G4), D. B. Price

TRAINING, ENTERPRISE AND EDUCATION
DIRECTORATE
Moorfoot, Sheffield S1 4PQ
Tel 0742-753275
Director-General (G2), I. Johnston
Director of Operations (G3), S. Loveman

Head of Financial Control Unit (G5), N. Gregory
Regional Directors (G5), Ms C. Johnson (*Eastern*);
  P. Lauener (*East Midlands*); Ms B. Thomas (*Greater
  Manchester*); W. Harris (*London*); K. Heslop (*Northern*);
  Ms F. Everiss (*North-west*); D. Main (*South-east*); Ms
  J. Henderson (*South-west*); P. Thomas (*West Midlands*);
  J. Walker (*Yorkshire and Humberside*)

Youth and Education
Director (G3), Mrs V. Bayliss
Heads of Branches (G5); R. Wye (*Schools and Partnerships
  Policy*); A. Davies (*Careers Service*); G. Dyche (*Young
  People and Work*); K. Franklin (*Further and Higher
  Education*)

Training Strategy and Infrastructure
Director (G3), D. Grover
Heads of Branches (G5), B. Shaw (*Training Strategy and
  Secretariat*); P. Keen (*Employer Investment*); T. Down
  (*Learning Methods*); C. Capella (*European Training Policy,
  Programmes and Funding*); J. Fuller (*Qualifications and
  Industry Training Organizations*)

Planning
Director (G4), K. White
Heads of Branches (G5), M. Nicholas (*Operational Policy*);
  B. Heatley (*Resource Planning*); L. Ammon (*Operational
  Monitoring*); M. Christie (*The Field Systems*)

Adult Learning
Director (G3), J. Lambert
Head of Branches (G5/G6), D. Tansley (*Adult Training*);
  G. Macnair (*Special Needs and Equal Opportunities*);
  J. Smith (*Individual Commitment*)

Quality Assurance
Director (G3), N. Schofield
Heads of Branches (G5), C. Williams (*Financial Analysis and
  Review*); J. Blizard (*Quality Assurance*); T. Fellows
  (*Quality Policy and Networking*)

*National Advisory Council for Education and Training
Targets (NACETT)*
Director (Special Adviser), Ms C. Stratton

INDUSTRIAL RELATIONS AND INTERNATIONAL
DIRECTORATE
Director (G2), G. Reid
International Division (G3), L. Lewis
Industrial Relations Division I (G3), C. Tucker
Industrial Relations Division II (G3), R. Hillier
Statistical Services Division (G3), P. Stibbard

RESOURCES AND STRATEGY DIRECTORATE
Director (G2), N. W. Stuart, CB
Finance and Resource Management Division (G3),
  M. Addison
Economics, Research and Evaluation Division (G3), Ms
  P. Meadows
Strategy and Employment Policy Division (G3), P. Makeham
Personnel and Development Division (G3), D. Normington
Business Services Division (G4), K. Jordan
Information Branch (G5), B. Sutlieff

ENGLISH HERITAGE
— *see* Historic Buildings and Monuments Commission for
England

ENGLISH NATURE
Northminster House, Peterborough PE1 1UA
Tel 0733-340345

English Nature (the Nature Conservancy Council for
England) was established by Act of Parliament in 1991 as a
result of the dissolution of the Nature Conservancy Council
and the creation of three new independent bodies responsible
for promoting nature conservation in the three component
countries of Great Britain. English Nature is responsible for
advising the Government on nature conservation in England.
It promotes, directly and through others, the conservation of
England's wildlife and natural features. It selects, establishes
and manages National Nature Reserves and identifies and
notifies Sites of Special Scientific Interest. It provides advice
and information about nature conservation, and supports
and conducts research relevant to these functions. Through
the Joint Nature Conservation Committee (*see* page 339), it
works with its sister organizations in Scotland and Wales on
UK and international nature conservation issues.
Chairman, The Earl of Cranbrook
Chief Executive, Dr D. R. Langslow
Chief Scientist, Dr K. L. Duff
Director, Operations, E. T. Idle
Director, Corporate Services, Miss C. E. M. Wood
Director, Policy and Development, Mrs S. Collins
Director, Communications and Corporate Affairs, I. Dair
Environmental Audit Manager, M. R. Felton
Head of Lands, W. J. Hopkin

DEPARTMENT OF THE ENVIRONMENT
2 Marsham Street, London SW1P 3EB
Tel 071-276 3000

The Department of the Environment is responsible for
planning and land use; local government; housing and
construction; inner city areas; new towns; environmental
protection; conservation areas and countryside affairs; energy
efficiency; and property holdings.
Secretary of State for the Environment, The Rt. Hon. John
  Gummer, MP
  Private Secretary, A. G. Riddell
  Special Advisers, T. Burke; Prof. P. Hall; K. Adams
  Parliamentary Private Secretary, J. Paice, MP
Minister for Housing, Inner Cities and Construction, The Rt.
  Hon. Sir George Young, Bt., MP
  Private Secretary, R. Anderson
  Parliamentary Private Secretary, Dr C. Goodson-Wickes,
  MP
Minister for Local Government and Planning, David Curry,
  MP
  Private Secretary, Ms K. Jennings
  Parliamentary Private Secretary, D. French, MP
Minister for Environment and Countryside, Timothy Yeo, MP
  Private Secretary, Ms D. Lamb
  Parliamentary Private Secretary, M. Trend, MP
  Special Adviser to Ministers of State, J. Gray
Parliamentary Under-Secretaries of State, Tony Baldry, MP;
  The Lord Strathclyde
  Private Secretaries, Miss M. Cameron; Miss D. Butler
Lord-in-Waiting, The Viscount Goschen
  Private Secretary, Miss A. Moore
Parliamentary Clerk, D. S. Demorais
Permanent Secretary (G1), R. Wilson, CB
  Private Secretary, Mrs B. Houlden

ORGANIZATION AND ESTABLISHMENTS
Lambeth Bridge House, London SE1 7SB
Tel 071-238 3000

Principal Establishments and Finance Officer (G2), D. J. Burr

PERSONNEL
Director (G3), J. A. Owen
Grade 5, J. Adams; K. G. Arnold; L. B. Hicks
Grade 6, M. A. L. Ross; R. E. Vidler; Miss J. A. Clark;
   J. Kingdom
Chief Welfare Officer (G7), R. J. Lintern

FINANCE CENTRAL
Under-Secretary (G3), W. F. S. Rickett
Heads of Divisions (G5), B. L. Glicksman; I. H. Nicol;
   C. P. Evans; D. L. H. Roberts

ADMINISTRATION RESOURCES
Director (G3), D. A. R. Peel
Grade 4, B. G. Rosser
Grade 5, A. C. Allberry; I. S. Elrick
Grade 6, D. Tridgell; R. Bendall; M. J. Burt; G. Knowles,
   ISO; M. R. Haselip

INFORMATION
Director (G4), M. Granatt
Grade 5, J. Gee

PLANNING, RURAL AFFAIRS AND WATER
Deputy Secretary (G2), P. C. McQuail

PLANNING DIRECTORATE
Director (G3), J. F. Ballard
Grade 5, D. N. Donaldson; R. Jones; R. G. Wakeford;
   C. L. L. Braun; M. R. Ash; J. Zetter; R. C. Mabey;
   A. M. Oliver

DIRECTORATE OF RURAL AFFAIRS
Under-Secretary (G3), R. J. A. Sharp, CB
Grade 5, R. Bunce; R. M. Pritchard; Ms S. Carter

WATER DIRECTORATE
Director (G3), N. W. Summerton
Heads of Divisions (G5), N. Dorling; A. J. C. Simcock;
   J. Vaughan; M. Nelson

Drinking Water Inspectorate
Grade 5, M. G. Healey

PLANNING INSPECTORATE
Tollgate House, Houlton Street, Bristol BS2 9DJ
Tel 0272-218950

An executive agency within the Department of the
Environment.
Chief Executive and Chief Inspector of Planning (G3), S. Crow
Deputy Chief Inspector of Planning (G4), J. I. T. Dunlop
Director of Planning Appeals (G4), A. J. M. Morgan
Assistant Chief Planning Inspectors (G5), M. I. Montague-
   Smith; J. Acton; D. F. Harris; R. E. Wilson;
   M. C. Hurley; J. Greenfield; C. Jenkins; J. Waldron; Mrs
   S. Bruton
Head of Administration (G5), D. A. C. Marshall
Head of Finance and Management Services (G5), M. Brasher

MERSEYSIDE TASK FORCE
Director (G3), J. Stoker
Controllers (G5), S. P. Sage; I. Urquhart; J. Warnock

REGIONAL OFFICES

EASTERN, Bedford – *Regional Director (G3)*, P. F. Emms;
   Regional Controllers (G5), I. C. J. Dunabin; R. A. Bird

EAST MIDLANDS, Nottingham – *Regional Director (G4)*,
   D. J. Morrison; *Regional Controller (G6)*, G. Meynell,
   MBE; R. J. Smith
NORTHERN, Newcastle upon Tyne – *Regional Director
   (G3)*, P. A. Shaw; *Regional Controllers (G5)*, Ms
   D. Caudle; R. G. Bell
NORTH-WEST, Manchester – *Regional Director (G3)*,
   J. P. Plowman; *Regional Controllers (G5)*,
   B. C. Isherwood; P. Styche; (G6), P. Walton; *Chairman,
   Mersey Basin Campaign*, B. Alexander
SOUTH-EAST, London W14 – *Regional Director (G3)*,
   J. W. Fellows; *Regional Controllers (G5)*, J. B. Wilson;
   T. E. Radice; (G6), E. G. Everett
SOUTH-WEST, Bristol – *Regional Director (G3)*, Ms
   E. A. Hopkins; *Regional Controllers (G5)*, S. McQuillin;
   D. N. Donaldson
WEST MIDLANDS, Birmingham – *Regional Director (G3)*,
   D. R. Ritchie; *Regional Controllers (G5)*, J. E. Northover;
   J. Darlington; Mrs P. M. Holland
YORKSHIRE AND HUMBERSIDE, Leeds – *Regional Director
   (G3)*, J. P. Henry; *Regional Controllers (G5)*,
   I. H. Crowther; Mrs E. A. Kerry

LONDON REGIONAL OFFICE
Under-Secretary (G3), Mrs L. A. Heath
Grade 5, A. Buchanan; B. Strong; A. M. Wells; I. J. Scotter

HOUSING AND URBAN GROUP
Deputy Secretary (G2), Miss E. C. Turton
Secretariat (G7), P. G. Tobia

INNER CITIES
Director (G3), M. B. Gahagan
Heads of Divisions (G5), G. L. Laufer; P. F. Unwin; Mrs
   R. Le Guen; R. A. Beattie
Grade 6, D. Stroud

HOUSING POLICY AND PRIVATE SECTOR
Director (G4), N. A. J. Kinghan
Heads of Divisions (G5), P. D. Walton; J. E. Roberts; Mrs
   H. Ghosh
Grade 6, J. S. Gill

HOUSING MONITORING AND ANALYSIS
Under-Secretary (G3), N. J. Glass
Grade 5, J. E. Turner; A. E. Holmans, CBE; Mrs
   J. Littlewood; M. Hughes; D. A. C. Heigham, CBE

HOUSING RESOURCES AND MANAGEMENT
Under-Secretary (G3), Mrs M. McDonald
Heads of Divisions (G5), B. H. Leonard; R. S. Horsman;
   C. H. Bowder; Ms P. E. Alexander
Grade 6, R. Ryder

RELOCATION DIRECTORATE
Director (G3), D. A. McDonald
Grade 5, J. Whaley; J. P. Channing; J. Jacobs; A. M. Wells;
   J. A. McCarthy

PROPERTY HOLDINGS, CONSTRUCTION AND
CENTRAL SUPPORT SERVICES
Deputy Secretary (G2), Miss D. A. Nichols
Under-Secretary (G3), Mrs D. S. Phillips
Director, Property Holdings (G3), N. E. Borrett

DIRECTORATE OF ESTATE PLANNING
Grade 4, D. O. McCreadie
Grade 5, R. J. Dinwiddy
Grade 6, N. Lee; J. H. Bilsby; R. M. D. Smith; M. S. Jennett

DIRECTORATE OF ESTATE OPERATIONS
Head of Operations Division (G5), R. W. P. Brice
Head of Central London Division (G5), A. R. Edwards
Deputy Head of Central London Division (G6), J. Glen

Heads of Outstations (G6), Thames North, A. J. Partridge;
   Thames South, C. G. H. Young
Heads of Outstations (G6), Midlands, M. J. Hathaway;
   North-East, J. C. Lewis; *North-West,* A. R. Jones; *South-West/Wales,* R. M. Barry; *Scotland,* P. R. Stewart

FINANCE
Grade 5, B. Redfern

ADMINISTRATION DIVISION
Head of Division (G6), D. M. Gillen

CENTRAL POLICY DIVISION
Grade 5, M. H. Bowles

CONSTRUCTION POLICY DIRECTORATE
Under-Secretary (G3), P. D. Ward
Heads of Divisions (G5), J. N. Lithgow; P. F. Everall; Dr
   J. F. A. Moore; J. G. Grevatt; M. Leigh-Pollitt
Grade 6, W. J. Marsh; R. F. Window

LOCAL GOVERNMENT
Deputy Secretary (G2), C. J. S. Brearley

LOCAL GOVERNMENT FINANCE POLICY
Director, Local Government Finance Policy (G3),
   P. J. J. Britton
Heads of Divisions (G5), P. Rowsell; Mrs C. Wells;
   M. H. Coulshed; Mrs H. J. Chipping; R. J. Gibson;
   M. J. C. Faulkner

LOCAL GOVERNMENT
Under-Secretary (G3), R. U. Young
Heads of Divisions (G5), H. C. T. Fawcett; Miss L. F. Bell;
   L. G. Packer
Grade 6, T. B. J. Crossley; J. R. Footit

LEGAL
Solicitor and Legal Adviser (G2), Mrs M. A. Morgan
Deputy Solicitors (G3), J. A. Catlin; Ms D. Unerman
Assistant Solicitors (G3), P. J. Szell; (G5), J. L. Comber;
   P. J. Szell; I. D. Day; Mrs S. Headley; Miss R. A. Lester;
   Mrs P. J. Conlon; Mrs G. Hedley-Dent; D. W. Jordan;
   Miss D. C. S. Phillips; N. S. Lefton

ENVIRONMENT PROTECTION
Deputy Secretary (G2), F. A. Osborn, CB

HM INSPECTORATE OF POLLUTION
Director and Chief Inspector (G3), Dr D. H. Slater
Deputy Chief Inspector (G4), Dr A. Duncan
Heads of Division (G5), M. F. Tunnicliffe; Dr K. Speakman;
   L. N. Stuffins; Dr D. J. Bryce; I. C. McBrayne

DIRECTORATE OF AIR, CLIMATE AND TOXIC
SUBSTANCES
Under-Secretary (G3), Dr D. J. Fisk
Heads of Division (G5), A. Davis; Dr N. J. King; R. Mills
Grade 6, Dr A. J. Apling; D. L. Pounder; Dr P. J. Corcoran;
   Dr L. M. Smith; Dr M. Williams

CHIEF SCIENTIST
Chief Scientist (G3), Dr D. J. Fisk
Head of Division (G5), C. L. Robson

DIRECTORATE OF POLLUTION CONTROL AND WASTES
Under-Secretary (G3), R. S. Dudding
Heads of Division (G5), Mrs L. A. C. Simcock; N. Sanders;
   Dr P. Hinchcliffe; J. Cleary; Dr N. Williams

ENVIRONMENTAL POLICY AND ANALYSIS
Director (G3), A. G. Watson
Heads of Division (G5), Mrs H. Hillier; J. S. Stevens;
   A. Ramsey; J. W. M. Rogers

ENERGY EFFICIENCY UNIT
Director-General (G3), J. Hobson
Grade 5, Dr C. J. Myerscough; Dr J. Miles; A. D. Fagin
Grade 6, Mrs A. J. Wandsworth

OTHER EXECUTIVE AGENCIES

QUEEN ELIZABETH II CONFERENCE CENTRE
Broad Sanctuary, London SW1P 3EE
Tel 071-798 4010

Chief Executive (G5), M. C. Buck

BUILDING RESEARCH ESTABLISHMENT
Garston, Watford WD2 7JR
Tel 0923-894040

Chief Executive (G3), R. G. Courtney
Deputy Chief Executives (G4), N. O. Milbank; Dr
   W. D. Woolley
Directors of Groups and Stations (G5), B. O. Hall; Dr
   N. J. Cook, Dr V. H. C. Crisp; C. R. Durham

THE BUYING AGENCY
Royal Liver Building, Pier Head, Liverpool L3 1PE
Tel 051-227 4262

Chief Executive (G5), R. M. Powell

TRANSPORT AND SECURITY SERVICES
St Christopher House, Southwark Street, London SE1 0TE
Tel 071-921 3995

Chief Executive (G5), J. C. King

ROYAL COMMISSION ON ENVIRONMENTAL
POLLUTION
Church House, Great Smith Street, London SW1P 3BZ
Tel 071-276 2080

The Commission was set up in 1970 to advise on matters,
both national and international, concerning the pollution of
the environment; on the adequacy of research in this field;
and the future possibilities of danger to the environment.
Chairman, Sir John Houghton, CBE, FRS
Members, Sir Geoffrey Allen, FRS; Prof. H. Charnock, CBE,
   FRS; Prof. Dame Barbara Clayton, DBE; H. R. Fell;
   P. R. A. Jacques, CBE; Prof. J. H. Lawton, FRS;
   Prof. R. Macrory, FRSA; Prof. J. G. Morris;
   D. A. D. Reeve, CBE; Prof. E. M. Rothschild;
   Prof. Z. A. Silberston, OBE
Secretary, D. R. Lewis

EQUAL OPPORTUNITIES COMMISSION
Overseas House, Quay Street, Manchester M3 3HN
Tel 061-833 9244

Press Office, Swan House, 53 Poland Street, London
WIV 3DF. Tel: 071-287 3953
Regional Offices, St Andrew House, 141 West Nile Street,
Glasgow G1 2RN. Tel: 041-332 8018; Caerwys House,
Windsor Place, Cardiff. Tel: 0222-343552

The Commission was set up by Parliament in 1975 as a result
of the passing of the Sex Discrimination Act. It works towards
the elimination of discrimination on the grounds of sex or
marital status and to promote equality of opportunity
between men and women generally.
Chair (£31,451), Ms K. Bahl
Deputy Chair (£28,119), Mrs J. Bridgeman

Members, Mrs M. Prosser; Lady Brittan; Mrs A. Hasan; Ms B. Hillon; Ms A. Watts; Ms N. Bray; Ms A. Gibson; Mrs B. Kelly; Ms C. Wells; C. Mather
Chief Executive, Ms V. Amos

EQUAL OPPORTUNITIES COMMISSION FOR NORTHERN IRELAND
Chamber of Commerce House, 22 Great Victoria Street, Belfast BT2 7BA
Tel 0232-242752

Chair and Chief Executive, Mrs J. Smyth

EXCHEQUER AND AUDIT DEPARTMENT
— *see* National Audit Office

ECGD (EXPORT CREDITS GUARANTEE DEPARTMENT)
PO Box 2200, 2 Exchange Tower, Harbour Exchange Square, London E14 9GS
Tel 071-512 7000

ECGD (Export Credits Guarantee Department), the official export credit insurer, is a separate government department responsible to the President of the Board of Trade and functions under the Export and Investment Guarantees Act 1991. This enables ECGD to facilitate UK exports by making available export credit insurance to British firms engaged in selling overseas and to guarantee repayment to banks in Britain providing finance for export credit for goods sold on credit terms of two years or more. The Act also empowers ECGD to insure British private investment overseas against political risks such as war, expropriation and restrictions on remittances.
Chief Executive, W. B. Willott
Group Directors (G3), M. T. Hawtin; J. R. Weiss; T. M. Jaffray
Grade 5, R. P. Burnett; P. J. Callaghan; D. C. Cooper; J. C. W. Croall; A. P. Fowell; R. Gotts; R. F. Lethbridge; K. G. Lockwood; V. P. Lunn Rockliffe; R. W. MacGregor; M. E. Maddox; M. D. Pentecost; R. A. Ranson; J. W. Roberts; B. M. Sidwell, TD; J. S. Snowdon
Grade 6, G. Cassell; F. O. H. Coulson; R. O. L. Drummond; I. M. N. Ejiegbu; M. Foster; N. Harington; G. G. Jones; L. S. W. Montgomery; Ms S. Rice; D. I. Robbins; E. Walsby
Grade 7, Ms C. L. Anderson; J. S. Astruc; D. I. Calvert; Mrs A. C. Cowie; D. M. Cox; G. P. Cox; A. B. Coyne; M. J. Crane; M. Cranwell; R. P. D. Crick; S. R. Dodgson; D. L. Dyke; A. C. Faulkner; R. X. Fear; G. C. Fisher; P. C. Gaudoin; N. F. George; R. Hardy; P. F. Henson; P. S. Hillman; M. R. Hodson; P. Jackson; S. J. Johnson; K. Jones; R. Jones; C. King; N. A. Lambert; C. J. Leeds; M. M. Leonard; D. J. M. Lucas; I. Mackay; R. A. J. D. Mayer; S. Merchack; A. J. E. Muckersie; P. L. Neal; G. A. Newhouse; J. K. Peacock; S. C. Pond; P. J. Radford; A. B. Redmayne; D. M. Riley; V. G. M. Robertson; S. Rosenthal; P. J. Rossington; K. R. Smith; R. S. Summers; J. Sweeney; J. A. Sweet; Miss V. M. Taylor; Ms A. V. Thomas; C. M. Thorogood; T. West; J. M. Willis; I. Wilson; D. L. Wyatt; J. A. Youd; G. A. Young

EXPORT GUARANTEES ADVISORY COUNCIL
Chairman, R. T. Fox, CBE
Deputy Chairman, A. G. Gormly, CBE

Other Members, Sir Robert Davidson; G. W. Lynch; J. Melbourn; C. Smallwood; Sir Derek Thomas, KCMG; The Viscount Weir

OFFICE OF FAIR TRADING
Field House, Bream's Buildings, London EC4A 1PR
Tel 071-242 2858

The Office of Fair Trading is a non-ministerial government department, headed by the Director-General of Fair Trading. It keeps commercial activities in the UK under review and seeks to protect consumers against unfair trading practices. The Director-General's consumer protection duties under the Fair Trading Act 1973, together with his responsibilities under the Consumer Credit Act 1974, the Estate Agents Act 1979, and Control of Misleading Advertisements Regulations 1988, are administered by the Office's Consumer Affairs Division. The Competition Policy Division is concerned with monopolies and mergers (under the Fair Trading Act 1973), and the Director-General's other responsibilities for competition matters, including those under the Restrictive Trade Practices Act 1976, the Resale Prices Act 1976, the Competition Act 1980, the Financial Services Act 1986 and the Broadcasting Act 1990. The Office is the UK competent authority on the application of the European Commission's competition rules, and also liaises with the Commission on consumer protection initiatives.
Director-General, Sir Bryan Carsberg
Deputy Director-General (G2), J. W. Preston, CB

CONSUMER AFFAIRS DIVISION
Director (G3), J. F. Mills
Assistant Directors (G5), P. Casey; D. W. Lightfoot; J. Chapman

COMPETITION POLICY DIVISION
Director (G3), Dr M. Howe
Assistant Directors (G5), A. J. White; D. Roots-Parsons; H. L. Emden; C. J. C. Wright

LEGAL DIVISION
Director (G3), A. M. Inglese
Assistant Directors (G5), M. A. Khan; P. T. Rostron

Senior Economic Adviser (G5), D. Elliott
Establishment and Finance Officer (G5), Miss C. Banks
Chief Information Officer (G6), D. Hill

FOREIGN AND COMMONWEALTH OFFICE
Downing Street, London SW1A 2AL
Tel 071-270 3000

The Foreign and Commonwealth Office provides, mainly through diplomatic missions, the means of communication between the British Government and other governments and international governmental organizations for the discussion and negotiation of all matters falling within the field of international relations. It is responsible for alerting the British Government to the implications of developments overseas; for protecting British interests overseas; for protecting British citizens abroad; for explaining British policies to, and cultivating friendly relations with, governments overseas; and for the discharge of British responsibilities to the dependent territories.

DIPLOMATIC SERVICE SALARIES *since 1 April 1993*
Permanent Under-Secretary and Head of the
   Diplomatic Service   £104,860
Senior Grade Salary Point 1 (SP1)   £90,148
Deputy Permanent Under-Secretary   £82,925
Senior Grade Salary Point 2 (SP2)   £75,328
Senior Grade Salary Point 3 (SP3)   £64,307
Senior Grade Salary Point 4 (SP4)   £58,347
Senior Grade Salary Point 5 (SP5)   £52,751
Diplomatic Service Grade 4 (DS4)   £37,589–£55,836

Secretary of State, The Rt. Hon. Douglas Hurd, CBE, MP
   Private Secretary, R. J. Sawers
   Social Secretary, Ms M. Hillsin
   Special Advisers, M. Maclay; M. Fraser
   Parliamentary Private Secretary, D. Martin, MP
Minister of State for Foreign and Commonwealth Affairs
   (Minister for Overseas Development), The Baroness
   Chalker of Wallasey, PC
   Private Secretary, M. Lowcock
   Parliamentary Private Secretary, M. Robinson, MP
Ministers of State for Foreign and Commonwealth Affairs, The
   Rt. Hon. Douglas Hogg, QC, MP; The Rt. Hon. Alastair
   Goodlad, MP; David Heathcoat-Amory, MP
   Private Secretaries, N. S. Archer; P. H. Tibber;
   T. M. Hitchens
   Parliamentary Private Secretaries:
   To Mr Hogg, H. Booth, MP
   To Mr Goodlad, G. Kynoch, MP
   To Mr Heathcoat-Amory, R. Richards, MP
Parliamentary Under-Secretary of State, The Hon. Mark
   Lennox-Boyd, MP
   Private Secretary, P. A. Speller
   Parliamentary Private Secretary, M. Robinson, MP
Parliamentary Relations Unit, R. Thomson (*Head*);
   J. P. Rodgers (*Deputy Head and Parliamentary Clerk*)
*Permanent Under-Secretary of State and Head of the
   Diplomatic Service*, Sir David Gillmore, KCMG
   Private Secretary, S. G. McDonald
Deputy Permanent Under-Secretary and Political Director,
   L. V. Appleyard, CMG
Deputy Under-Secretaries (SP2):
Chief Clerk; A. M. Wood, CMG
Economic Director, B. L. Crowe, CMG
M. Elliott, CMG; Sir John Coles, KCMG; Sir Timothy Daunt,
   KCMG
Assistant Under-Secretaries (SP5):
*Deputy Chief Clerk and Principal Establishment and Security
   Officer*, Mrs V. E. Sutherland, CMG
*Deputy Political Director and UK Perm. Rep. on the Council
   of WEU*, J. Greenstock, CMG
Director of Information Systems, J. Ling, CMG
Principal Finance Officer and Chief Inspector, R. J. S. Muir;
   R. J. Alston, CMG; A. J. Beamish, CMG; Sir Michael
   Burton, KCVO, CMG; M. H. Jay, CMG; R. B. Bone;
   A. M. Goodenough, CMG; D. C. B. Logan, CMG;
   C. O. Hum; J. T. Masefield, CMG; P. Lever, CMG
HM Vice-Marshal of the Diplomatic Corps,
   A. St J. H. Figgis, CMG
Legal Adviser (SP2), F. D. Berman, CMG, QC
Second Legal Adviser, D. H. Anderson, CMG
Deputy Legal Advisers, M. R. Eaton, CMG;
   K. J. Chamberlain, CMG
Legal Counsellors, A. Aust; Mrs A. Glover; Miss S. Brooks;
   Ms E. Wilmshurst; C. Whomersley

HEADS OF DEPARTMENTS (DS4)
*Aid Policy Department, S. Chakrabarti
Arms Control and Disarmament Department,
   P. W. M. Vereker
Aviation and Maritime Department, A. S. Collins
Central European Department, N. J. Thorpe

Commonwealth Co-ordination Department, D. Broad
Commonwealth Foreign and Security Policy Unit,
   A. D. R. Smith
Conference on Security and Co-operation in Europe Unit,
   C. A. Munro
Consular Department, S. F. Howarth
Cultural Relations Department, J. N. Elam
Eastern Adriatic Unit, A. Charlton
Eastern Department, D. G. Manning
*Economic Advisers Department, S. H. Broadbent
*Economic Relations Department, K. Tebbit
Environment Science and Energy Department, G. H. Boyce
Equatorial Africa Department, T. G. Harris
European Community Department (External),
   J. M. Macgregor
European Community Department (Internal), A. J. Cary
Far Eastern Department, G. Fry
Home Estate Department, D. Brown
Hong Kong Department, P. Ricketts
Honours Unit, D. E. Tarling
Human Rights Policy Unit, G. S. Hand
Information Department A. D. Harris, LVO
Information Systems Division (Operations), S. I. Soutar
Information Systems Division (Projects), K. Willis
Information Systems Division (Resources), M. Hodge, MBE
Internal Audit, R. Elias
Joint Assistance Unit (Central Europe), D. Coates
Joint Assistance Unit (Eastern Europe), M. McCulloch
†*Joint Directorate*, M. G. Dougal
Latin America Department, L. G. Faulkner
Library and Records Department, R. Bone
*Management Review Staff, E. C. Glover, MVO;
Medical and Welfare Unit, Miss D. M. Symes, OBE
Middle East Department, P. M. Nixon, CMG, OBE
Migration and Visa Department, D. I. Lewty
Narcotics Control and Aids Department, P. Thomson, CVO
Nationality, Treaty and Claims Department, M. F. Sullivan,
   MBE
Near East and North Africa Department, W. G. Ehrman
News Department, R. N. Culshaw
Non-Proliferation and Defence Department, J. B. Donnelly
North America Department, M. E. Pellew, LVO
Overseas Estate Department, M. H. R. Bertram
Overseas Inspectorate, R. J. S. Muir (*Chief Inspector and
   Principal Finance Officer*)
Overseas Police Adviser, L. Grundy (*Senior Police Adviser*)
Permanent Under-Secretary's Department, I. R. Callan, CMG
Personnel Management Department, P. J. Torry
Personnel Policy Department, J. Poston
Personnel Services Department, R. G. Short, MVO
Policy Planning Staff, R. D. Wilkinson
PROSPER, C. J. Edgerton, OBE
Protocol Department, D. C. B. Beaumont (*First Assistant
   Marshal of the Diplomatic Corps*)
Republic of Ireland Department, G. R. Archer
Research and Analysis Department, Director, B. S. Eastwood
Resource and Finance Department, J. W. Thorp
Royal Matters Unit, J. E. Brook
Security Department, J. W. Hodge
Security Co-ordination Department, J. P. G. Freeman
Security Policy Department, S. J. Gomersall
South Asian Department, L. B. Smith
South Atlantic and Antarctic Department, P. M. Newton
South-East Asian Department, G. Hewitt

---

*Joint Foreign and Commonwealth Office/Overseas Development
Administration department
†Joint Foreign and Commonwealth Office/Department of Trade and
Industry directorate

Southern Africa Department, D. R. C. Christopher
Southern European Department, D. C. A. Madden
South Pacific Department, M. R. J. Guest
Support Services Department, A. E. Gay
Technical Security Department, M. Buckland-Smith
Training Department, I. W. Mackley
United Nations Department, Miss M. G. D. Evans, CMG
Western European Department, M. L. H. Hope
West Indian and Atlantic Department, G. M. Baker

THE SECRET INTELLIGENCE SERVICE (MI6)
Director-General, Sir Colin McColl

GOVERNMENT COMMUNICATIONS HEADQUARTERS (GCHQ)
Priors Road, Cheltenham, Glos. GL52 5AJ
Tel 0242-221491

GCHQ is an autonomous government department under the Secretary of State for Foreign and Commonwealth Affairs.

CORPS OF QUEEN'S MESSENGERS
Foreign and Commonwealth Office, London SW1A 2AH
Tel 071-270 2779

Superintendent of the Corps of Queen's Messengers,
  Maj. I. G. M. Bamber
Queen's Messengers, Maj. J. E. A. Andre;
  Cdr. D. H. Barraclough; Maj. A. N. D. Bols;
  Lt.-Cdr. K. E. Brown; Lt.-Col. W. P. A. Bush;
  Lt.-Col. M. B. de S. Clayton; Capt. G. Courtauld;
  Maj. P. C. H. Dening-Smitherman; Maj. P. T. Dunn;
  Sqn. Ldr. J. S. Frizzell; Capt. N. C. E. Gardner;
  Cdr. P. G. Gregson; Maj. D. A. Griffiths;
  Wg Cdr. J. O. Jewiss; Lt.-Col. P. S. Kerr-Smiley;
  Lt.-Col. J. M. C. Kimmins;
  Lt.-Col. R. C. Letchworth; G. F. Miller;
  Lt.-Col. A. R. Murray; Maj. D. R. Nevile;
  Maj. K. J. Rowbottom; Maj. M. R. Senior;
  Cdr. K. M. C. Simmons, AFC; Maj. P. M. O. Springfield;
  Maj. J. S. Steele; Col. D. W. F. Taylor

FOREIGN COMPENSATION COMMISSION
Old Admiralty Building, London SW1A 2AF
Tel 071-210 6158

The Commission was set up by the Foreign Compensation Act 1950 primarily to distribute, under Orders in Council, funds received from other governments in accordance with agreements to pay compensation for expropriated British property and other losses sustained by British nationals.

The Commission also has the duty of registering claims for British-owned property in contemplation of agreements with other countries, and it has done so in seven instances since 1950.
Chairman, A. W. E. Wheeler, CBE
Commissioner, J. A. S. Hall, DFC, QC
Secretary and Chief Examiner, D. H. Wright

FORESTRY COMMISSION
231 Corstorphine Road, Edinburgh EH12 7AT
Tel 031-334 0303

The Forestry Commission is the government department responsible for forestry policy in Great Britain. It reports directly to forestry ministers (i.e. the Minister of Agriculture, Fisheries and Food, the Secretary of State for Scotland, and the Secretary of State for Wales), to whom it is responsible for advice on forestry policy and for the implementation of that policy in Great Britain. There is a statutorily-appointed Chairman and Board of Commissioners (four full-time and seven part-time) with prescribed duties and powers. The full-time Commissioners form the Executive Board.

In 1992 the Commission implemented a reorganization to distinguish between its departmental, regulatory and management functions. A Policy and Resources Group is responsible for the parliamentary and policy aspects of the Commission's duties as a government department. As the Forestry Authority, the Commission provides advice and sets the standards for the forestry industry, administers the grant-aid schemes for private woodlands, carries out regulatory functions for plant health and felling control and undertakes forest research. As the Forest Enterprise, the Commission manages its forestry estate on a multi-use basis. In discharging their functions, the Forestry Commissioners have a statutory duty to endeavour to achieve a reasonable balance between the needs of forestry and the environment.

In April 1993, the Government set up a task force to review options for the ownership and management of the Commission's forestry estate.
Chairman (part-time) (£31,830), Sir Raymond Johnstone, CBE
Director-General and Deputy Chairman (G2), T. R. Cutler
Commissioner, Policy and Resources (G3), D. S. Grundy
Head of the Forestry Authority (G3), R. T. Bradley
Chief Executive, Forest Enterprise (G3), D. L. Foot
Secretary to the Commissioners (G4). P. J. Clarke, CBE

REGISTRY OF FRIENDLY SOCIETIES
15 Great Marlborough Street, London W1V 2AX
Tel 071-437 9992

The Registry of Friendly Societies is a government department serving three statutory bodies, the Building Societies Commission, the Friendly Societies Commission, and the Central Office of the Registry of Friendly Societies (together with the Assistant Registrar of Friendly Societies for Scotland).

The Building Societies Commission was established by the Building Societies Act 1986. The Commission is responsible for the supervision of building societies and administers the system of regulation. It also advises the Treasury and other government departments on matters relating to building societies.

The Friendly Societies Commission was established by the Friendly Societies Act 1992. Its responsibilities for the supervision of friendly societies parallel those of the Building Societies Commission for building societies.

The Central Office of the Registry of Friendly Societies provides a public registry for mutual organizations registered under the Building Societies Act 1986, Friendly Societies Acts 1974 and 1992, and the Industrial and Provident Societies Act 1965. It is responsible for the supervision of friendly societies and credit unions, and advises the Government on issues affecting those societies. The Chief Registrar has certain powers to arbitrate in disputes between members and registered societies, and acts as the Industrial Assurance Commissioner.

BUILDING SOCIETIES COMMISSION
Chairman, Mrs R. E. J. Gilmore
Deputy Chairman, H. G. Walsh

Commissioners, T. F. Mathews; H. R. C. Walden, CBE;
F. E. Worsley; F. G. Sunderland; N. Fox Bassett

FRIENDLY SOCIETIES COMMISSION
Chairman, D. W. Lee
Commissioners, F. da Rocha; A. Wilson; J. A. Geddes;
P. E. Couse; Dr J. Dine

CENTRAL OFFICE
Chief Registrar, Mrs R. E. J. Gilmore
Assistant Registrars (G4), D. W. Lee; A. J. Perrett

THE REGISTRY
First Commissioner and Chief Registrar (G2), Mrs
R. E. J. Gilmore

BUILDING SOCIETIES COMMISSION STAFF
Grade 3, H. G. Walsh
Grade 4, T. F. Mathews
Grade 5, D. A. W. Stevens; J. M. Palmer; W. Champion;
R. K. Gabbertas
Grade 6, N. F. Digance

FRIENDLY SOCIETIES COMMISSION STAFF
Grade 4, D. W. Lee
Grade 6, F. da Rocha

CENTRAL SERVICES STAFF
Legal Adviser (G4), A. J. Perrett
Establishment and Finance Officer (G5), K. Blackburn
Legal Staff (G6), P. G. Ashcroft; Miss E. Long; R. Caune;
C. Stallard

REGISTRY OF FRIENDLY SOCIETIES, SCOTLAND
58 Frederick Street, Edinburgh, EH2 1NB
Tel 031-226 3224
Assistant Registrar (G5), J. L. J. Craig, WS

GAMING BOARD FOR GREAT BRITAIN
Berkshire House, 168–173 High Holborn, London
WC1V 7AA
Tel 071-240 0821

The Board was established in 1968 and its functions are to ensure that those involved in organizing gaming and lotteries are fit to do so and to keep criminals out of gaming; to ensure that gaming is run fairly and in accordance with the law; and to advise the Home Secretary on developments in gaming so that the law can respond to change.
Chairman (part-time) (£30,575), Lady Littler
Members (part-time) (each £12,260), Sir Richard Barratt, CBE, VRD; Lady Trethowan; W. B. Kirkpatrick;
M. H. Hogan
Secretary, T. Kavanagh

OFFICE OF GAS SUPPLY
Stockley House, 130 Wilton Road, London SW1V 1LQ
Tel 071-828 0898

The Office of Gas Supply (Ofgas) is a regulatory body set up under the Gas Act 1986. It is headed by the Director-General of Gas Supply, who is independent of ministerial control.
The principal function of Ofgas is to monitor British Gas's activities as a public gas supplier and, where necessary, to enforce the conditions of that company's authorization to act as a public gas supplier. Other functions are to investigate complaints on matters where enforcement powers may be exercisable; to fix and publish maximum charges for reselling

gas; to publish information and advice for the benefit of tariff customers; to keep under review developments concerning the gas supply industry, including competition; and to settle the terms on which other suppliers have access to British Gas pipelines in the event of disagreement.
Director-General, vacant
Deputy Director-General, J. Dorken
Legal Adviser, D. R. M. Long
Director, Competition and Tariffs, G. McGregor
Director, Public Affairs, I. Cooke
Director, Consumer Affairs, W. Macleod

GOVERNMENT ACTUARY'S DEPARTMENT
22 Kingsway, London WC2B 6LE
Tel 071-242 6828

The Government Actuary provides a consulting service to government departments, the public sector, and overseas governments. The actuaries advise on social security schemes and superannuation arrangements in the public sector at home and abroad, on population and other statistical studies, and on government supervision of insurance companies and friendly societies.
Government Actuary, C. D. Daykin, CB
Directing Actuaries, D. G. Ballantine; D. H. Loades;
M. A. Pickford
Chief Actuaries, E. I. Battersby; J. L. Field; T. W. Hewitson;
P. H. Hinton; A. I. Johnston; J. C. A. Rathbone;
A. G. Young
Actuaries, W. D. B. Anderson; Ms W. M. Beaver;
A. B. Chughtai; W. H. P. Davies; A. P. Gallop;
Mrs B. J. Hall; C. A. Harris; V. P. Knowles; Mrs
I. W. Lane; D. Lewis; A. J. Macnair; P. Merricks;
P. Noonan; S. M. O'Ceallaigh; A. P. Pavelin; J. W. Peers;
H. J. Prescott; D. E. Purchase; A. H. Silverman;
J. G. Spain; D. I. Tomlinson; D. M. Webber

GOVERNMENT HOSPITALITY FUND
8 Cleveland Row, London SW1A 1DH
Tel 071-210 3000

The Government Hospitality Fund was instituted in 1908 for the purpose of organizing official hospitality on a regular basis, with a view to the promotion of international goodwill.
Minister in Charge, The Rt. Hon. Alastair Goodlad, MP
Secretary, Col. T. Earl

DEPARTMENT OF HEALTH
Richmond House, 79 Whitehall, London SW1A 2NS
Tel 071-210 3000

The Department of Health is responsible for the administration of the National Health Service in England and for the personal social services run by local authorities in England for children, the elderly, the infirm, the handicapped and other persons in need. It has functions relating to public and environmental health, food safety and nutrition. The Department is also responsible for the ambulance and emergency first aid services, under the Civil Defence Act 1948. The Department represents the UK at the World Health Organization.
Secretary of State for Health, The Rt. Hon. Virginia
Bottomley, MP

Principal Private Secretary, R. M. Creighton
Private Secretary, Ms G. Wakeman
Special Adviser, R. Marsh
Parliamentary Private Secretary, K. Mans, MP
Minister of State, Dr Brian Mawhinney, MP
  Private Secretary, Ms T. Ing
  Parlimentary Private Secretary, P. Thompson, MP
Parliamentary Under-Secretaries of State, The Baroness
  Cumberlege, CBE; The Hon. Thomas Sackville, MP; John
  Bowis, OBE
Permanent Secretary (G1), G. A. Hart, CB
  Private Secretary, L. Wilkinson
Chief Medical Officer (G1A), Dr K. Calman
Director of Research and Development, Prof. M. Peckham

NATIONAL HEALTH SERVICE POLICY BOARD
Chairman, The Secretary of State
Deputy Chairman, Sir Roy Griffiths
Members, Dr K. Calman (*Chief Medical Officer*); Sir James
  Ackers; Dr B. Mawhinney, MP (*Minister of State*);
  Prof. C. Chantler; The Baroness Cumberlege, CBE; The
  Hon. T. Sackville, MP; J. Bowis, OBE, MP (*Parliamentary
  Under-Secretaries*); Sir Kenneth Durham; G. A. Hart, CB
  (*Permanent Secretary*); Sir Duncan Nichol, CBE; Sir Robert
  Scholey, CBE; P. Gummer; Mrs Y. Moores; Miss
  K. Jenkins; Ms S. Masters; Sir Timothy Chessels

NATIONAL HEALTH SERVICE MANAGEMENT
EXECUTIVE
Chief Executive, Sir Duncan Nichol, CBE (*until March 1994*)
*Deputy Chief Executive and Director of Performance
  Management*, A. Langlands
Director of Corporate Affairs, J. F. Shaw
Director of Personnel (acting), R. W. D. Venning
Director of Finance and Corporate Information,
  G. Greenshields
Medical Director, Dr G. Winyard
Chief Nursing Officer, Mrs Y. Moores
Director of Research and Development, Prof. M. Peckham

HEALTH AND PERSONAL SOCIAL SERVICES
GROUP
Deputy Secretary (G2), T. S. Heppell, CB

HEALTH ASPECTS OF THE ENVIRONMENT AND FOOD
Under-Secretary (G3), B. Bridges
Assistant Secretaries (G5), C. P. Kendall; R. Cunningham;
  Ms L. Lockyer
Senior Principal (G6), Mrs M. Fry

HEALTH CARE (ADMINISTRATIVE) DIVISION
Under-Secretary (G3), Miss R. D. B. Pease
Assistant Secretaries (G5), A. W. McCulloch; K. Jacobsen;
  I. Jewesbury; N. Boyd

COMMUNITY SERVICES DIVISION
Under-Secretary (G3), T. Luce
Assistant Secretaries (G5), Mrs A. De Peyer; J. A. Parker;
  R. P. S. Hughes, CBE; A. McKeon

HEALTH PROMOTION (ADMINISTRATIVE) DIVISION
Under-Secretary (G3), N. M. Hale, CB
Assistant Secretaries (G5), J. E. Knight; C. A. Muir;
  J. F. Sharpe; J. C. Middleton; R. Tyrrell

HEALTH CARE DIRECTORATE (PRIMARY
CARE)
Deputy Chief Medical Officer (G2), Dr G. Winyard

PERFORMANCE MANAGEMENT DIRECTORATE
(PRIMARY CARE)
Under-Secretary (G3), J. H. Barnes
Principal Medical Officer (G4), Dr P. Leech
Assistant Secretaries (G5), Miss H. Gwynn; D. Hewlett

P DIVISION
Under-Secretary (G3), M. Jeremiah
Assistant Secretaries (G5), S. J. Furniss; J. Thompson;
  M. Siswick; S. Alcock

NHS SUPPLIES AUTHORITY
Chairman, Sir Robin Buchanan
National Director of Supplies, T. Hunt
Directors, E. Sutherland (*Purchasing*); R. Chantler (*Finance
  and Information*); C. Uden (*Human Resources*); Mrs
  R. Sutton (*Communications*)

MEDICAL DEVICES DIRECTORATE
Director (G4), A. B. Barton

EUROPEAN AND STANDARDS BUSINESS
Head of Business (G5), Dr D. C. Potter

DEVICE TECHNOLOGY AND SAFETY
Head of Business (G5), Miss M. N. Duncan

DTS1 COMMUNITY HEALTH, NON-ACUTE AND
DIAGNOSTIC, IMAGING SERVICES
Group Manager (G6), A. D. C. Shipley

DTS2 ACUTE CARE SERVICES
Group Manager (G6), C. S. Bray

DEVICE EVALUATION AND PUBLICATIONS
Head of Business (G6), Dr N. A. Slark

MANUFACTURERS' REGISTRATION SCHEME
Head of Business (G6), R. W. B. Allen

CORPORATE MANAGEMENT
Head of Business (G6), T. F. Crawley

MEDICAL AND NURSING ADVICE
Senior Medical Officers (G5), Dr S. M. Ludgate; Dr
  S. P. Vahl
Nursing Officer (G6), Mrs P. A. Collinson

NHS MANAGEMENT EXECUTIVE
PERSONNEL GROUP
Director of Personnel (G2) (acting), R. W. D. Venning

DIVISION HAP
Under-Secretary (G3), R. M. Drury
Senior Principal (G6), A. W. Edwards
Assistant Secretaries (G5), M. G. Sturges; Miss S. Norman;
  M. Staniforth; J. Ashe; B. A. J. Bennett

INFORMATION SYSTEMS DIRECTORATE
Director of Information Systems (G4), Dr A. A. Holt
Deputy Director (G5), Mrs L. Masterman
Grade 6, Miss S. Blackburn; J. Wormald; P. Cobb;
  J. Watkins

RESEARCH AND DEVELOPMENT DIVISION
Director of Research and Development, Prof. M. Peckham
Director of Research Management (G4), Dr W. J. Burroughs
Deputy Director of Research Management (G4), Dr H. Pickles
Assistant Secretaries (G5), Miss M. Edwards; Mrs J. Griffin;
  Mrs B. Soper; Ms M. Woolley; Dr P. Greenaway
Senior Medical Officers (G5), Dr R. Singh; Dr G. Lewis;
  Dr J. Toy; Dr D. Sharp

Senior Principal Research Officers (G6), Ms A. Kauder;
Dr C. Davies; Ms J. Ennis; Dr C. Henshall
Nursing Officers (G6), Dr E. Meerabeau; Miss E. Scott

SOCIAL SERVICES INSPECTORATE
Chief Inspector (G2), H. Laming, CBE
Deputy Chief Inspectors (G4), D. C. Brand; Miss C. M. Hey
Assistant Chief Inspectors (HQ), Miss J. Baraclough;
J. Kennedy; S. Mitchell; J. G. Smith; Mrs W. Rose
Assistant Chief Inspectors (Regions), S. Allard;
J. K. Corcoran; J. Cypher; D. Gilroy; B. D. Harrison;
A. Jones; D. G. Lambert; Miss A. Taylor; Mrs P. K. Hall;
C. P. Brearley

MEDICAL DIVISIONS (HEALTH AND PERSONAL SOCIAL SERVICES)

Chief Medical Officer (G1A), Dr K. Calman
Deputy Chief Medical Officers (G2), Dr J. S. Metters; Dr
G. Winyard

MEDICAL DIVISIONS UNDER DR METTERS

DIVISIONS HP(M)1-3, CHMU, MEDICAL EDITORIAL
UNIT
Senior Principal Medical Officer (G3), Dr E. Rubery
Principal Medical Officers (G4), Dr G. Lewis; Dr D.
McInnes; Dr J. D. F. Bellamy
Senior Medical Officers (G5), Dr S. Turnbull; Dr
D. Salisbury; Dr J. Hilton; Dr J. Leese; Dr E. Tebbs; Dr
H. Williams; Dr M. Powlson; Dr H. Markowe; Dr
F. Harvey; Dr K. Binysh; Dr V. Press; Dr M. Thorley;
Dr C. M. Wein; Dr D. Ernaelsteen; Dr W. J. Modle; Dr
I. A. Lister-Cheese; Dr S. Shepherd; Dr D. Milner; Dr
R. Stanwell-Smith

DIVISION HEF(M)
Senior Principal Medical Officer (G3), Dr G. Jones
Principal Medical Officers (G4), Dr E. Smales; Dr
G. E. Diggle; Dr R. Skinner; Dr M. Wiseman
Senior Medical Officers (G5), Dr M. Waring; Dr N. Lazarus;
Dr R. L. Maynard; Dr T. Marrs; Dr A. Bulman; Dr
P. Clarke; Dr A. Dawson; Dr L. Robinson; Dr
C. Swinson; Dr A. Wight; Dr C. Van den Bosch; Dr
F. Kennedy; Dr S. Lader

DIVISION E
Principal Medical Officer (G4), Dr J. D. F. Bellamy

HEALTH CARE (MEDICAL) DIVISION
Senior Principal Medical Officer (G3), Dr J. L. Reed, CB
Principal Medical Officers (G4), Dr J. R. W. Hangartner; Dr
R. Jenkins
Senior Medical Officers (G5), Dr J. Ashwell; Dr
D. Rothman; Dr N. Halliday; Dr N. Melia; Dr E. Hills;
Dr P. Furnell; Dr A. Rejman; Dr E. Clissold; Dr
A. Rawson; Dr S. Munday; Dr D. Brooksbank; Dr
D. Kingdon; Dr E. Wilson; Dr P. Mason; Dr G. Parry;
Dr Y. Morris; Dr K. Lloyd; Prof. S. Hollins

MEDICAL DIVISIONS UNDER DR WINYARD

DIVISION HCD-PH
Principal Medical Officer (G4), Dr A. Lakhani
Senior Medical Officers (G5), Dr G. Pollock; Dr J. Rees; Dr
M. Campbell-Stern; Dr G. Thomas; Dr J. Dodge; Dr
B. Rana

DIVISION MME
Senior Principal Medical Officer (G3), Dr P. J. Bourdillon
Senior Medical Officers (G5), Dr R. Cairncross; Dr
R. Wilson; Dr P. I. M. Allen

Assistant Secretary (G5), S. D. Catling
Principals (G7), H. Tolland; T. G. Bennett; R. Haugh

DENTAL DIVISION
Chief Dental Officer, R. B. Mouatt
Senior Dental Officers, C. Howard; C. Audrey; K. A. Eaton

NURSING DIVISION
Chief Nursing Officer/Director of Nursing, Mrs Y. Moores
Deputy Director of Nursing, Mrs S. Williams, RGN, RSCN, RNT
Deputy Chief Nursing Officer, J. Tait, OBE
Principal Nursing Officer/Business Manager, M. Hill
Principal Nursing Officer, Miss S. Norman

PHARMACEUTICAL DIVISION
Chief Pharmaceutical Officer (G4), B. H. Hartley
Deputy Chief Pharmaceutical Officer (G5), J. R. V. Merrills
Senior Principal Pharmaceutical Officer (G6), P. E. Green

INFORMATION DIVISION
Director of Information (G4), Miss R. Christopherson
Deputy Directors (G6), C. P. Wilson (news); Mrs A. Rea
(publicity)

NATIONAL HEALTH SERVICE

REGIONAL HEALTH AUTHORITIES
The chairmen and members of Regional Health Authorities
are appointed by the Secretary of State for Health.

EAST ANGLIA, Union Lane, Chesterton, Cambridge CB4
1RF. Chairman, Sir Colin Walker, OBE; Regional General
Manager, A. Liddell
MERSEY, Hamilton House, 24 Pall Mall, Liverpool L3 6AL.
Chairman, Sir Donald Wilson; Regional General Manager,
G. Scaife
NORTH-EAST THAMES, 40 Eastbourne Terrace, London
W2 3QR. Chairman, Sir William Staveley, GCB; Regional
General Manager, B. Harrison
NORTHERN, Benfield Road, Walker Gate, Newcastle upon
Tyne NE6 4PY. Chairman, P. Carr, CBE; Regional General
Manager, Prof. L. Donaldson
NORTH-WESTERN, Gateway House, Piccadilly South,
Manchester M60 7LP. Chairman, Sir Bruce Martin, QC;
Regional General Manager, D. Allison, CB
NORTH-WEST THAMES, 40 Eastbourne Terrace, London
W2 3QR. Chairman, Sir William Doughty; Regional
General Manager, R. Kerr
OXFORD, Old Road, Headington, Oxford OX3 7LF.
Chairman, Dr S. Burgess, CBE; Regional General Manager,
Ms B. Stocking
SOUTH-EAST THAMES, Thrift House, Collington Avenue,
Bexhill-on-Sea, E. Sussex TN39 3NQ. Chairman,
P. Barker; Regional General Manager, G. Green
SOUTH-WESTERN, King Square House, 26-27 King
Square, Bristol BS2 8EF. Chairman, Ms R. Fritchie;
Regional General Manager, Ms P. Charlwood
SOUTH-WEST THAMES, 40 Eastbourne Terrace, London
W2 3QR. Chairman, Prof. M. Hicks, OBE; Regional General
Manager, C. Spry
TRENT, Fulwood House, Old Fulwood Road, Sheffield S10
3TH. Chairman, Sir Michael Carlisle; Regional General
Manager, Dr K. Woods
WESSEX, Highcroft, Romsey Road, Winchester, Hants.
SO22 5DH. Chairman, Sir Robin Buchanan; Regional
General Manager, K. Jarrold
WEST MIDLANDS, Arthur Thompson House, 146-150
Hagley Road, Birmingham B16 9PA. Chairman,
B. W. Baker; Regional General Manager, B. Edwards, CBE
YORKSHIRE, Park Parade, Harrogate HG1 5AH. Chairman,
Sir Bryan Askew; Regional General Manager, K. McLean

SPECIAL HEALTH AUTHORITIES

HEALTH EDUCATION AUTHORITY, Hamilton House, Mabledon Place, London WC1H 9TX. *Chairman,* Sir Donald Maitland, GCMG, OBE; *Chief Executive,* Dr Spencer Hagard

NHS SUPPLIES AUTHORITY, Apex Plaza, Forbury Road, Reading, Berks. RG1 1AX. *Chairman,* Sir Robin Buchanan

SPECIAL HOSPITALS SERVICE AUTHORITY, Charles House, Kensington High Street, London W14. The Special Hospitals Service is provided by four hospitals: Rampton, Broadmoor, Moss Side and Park Lane. *Chairman,* Dr D. E. Edmond; *Chief Executive,* C. Kaye

NATIONAL HEALTH SERVICE, SCOTLAND
—*see* Scottish Office entry

DEPARTMENTAL RESOURCES AND SERVICES GROUP
Deputy Secretary (G2), J. Pilling

FINANCE AND CORPORATE INFORMATION DIRECTORATE

FINANCIAL MANAGEMENT DIRECTORATE
Director of Finance NHSHE (G2), G. Greenshields

FINANCE BRANCH
Under-Secretary (Health) (G3), Ms M. E. Stuart
Assistant Secretaries (G5), J. M. Brownlee; K. J. Guinness; Miss A. Mithani; Ms G. Fletcher-Cook
Senior Principals (G6), R. J. Tredgett; R. Churchill; A. C. Symes; K. G. Gardner

FINANCE AND CORPORATE INFORMATION DIVISION A
Deputy Director (G3), Mrs J. Firth
Heads of Branch (G5), A. Simkins; C. Dobson; M. A. Harris; A. Angilley

FINANCE AND CORPORATE INFORMATION DIVISION B
Deputy Director (G3), B. Marsden
Heads of Branch (G5), J. Rushfirth; B. J. Derry; J. Tomlinson; M. Ruane; M. Gayton; (G6), R. M. Jordan; P. Macaulay; G. Smith; (G7), J. Dixon

FINANCE DIVISION D
Under-Secretary (Social Security) (G3), J. Tross
Assistant Secretaries (G5), S. Lord; Dr L. Mayhew; G. Foster

STATISTICS AND MANAGEMENT INFORMATION DIVISION (S7)
Director of Statistics and Management Information (G3), Mrs R. J. Butler
Chief Statisticians (G5), Miss P. W. Annesley; R. K. Willmer; G. J. O. Phillpotts

ECONOMICS AND OPERATIONAL RESEARCH DIVISION (HEALTH)
Chief Economic Adviser (G3), C. H. Smee
Senior Economic Advisers (G5), R. J. Churnside; J. W. Hurst

DEPARTMENTAL MANAGEMENT
Principal Establishment Officer (G3), M. G. Lillywhite
Assistant Secretaries (G5), Miss A. Stephenson; Ms P. Allen; Mrs S. Hughes; Ms P. A. Stewart

SOLICITOR'S OFFICE
Solicitor (G2), P. K. J. Thompson
Principal Assistant Solicitor (G3), A. D. Roberts
Proceedings Operational Director (G4), P. C. Nilsson

NHS TRUSTS UNIT
Head of Unit (G3), P. Garland
Operational Manager (G7), Dr V. Billingham

COMMITTEE ON THE SAFETY OF MEDICINES
Market Towers, 1 Nine Elms Lane, London SW8 5NQ
Tel 071-273 0451
Chairman, Prof. M. D. Rawlins

COMMITTEE ON DENTAL AND SURGICAL MATERIALS
Market Towers, 1 Nine Elms Lane, London SW8 5NQ
Tel 071-273 0502
Chairman, Prof. D. E. Poswillo, CBE

ADVISORY COMMITTEE ON THE MICROBIOLOGICAL SAFETY OF FOOD
Room 601A, Skipton House, 80 London Road, London SE1 6LW
Tel 071-972 5049
Chairman, Prof. H. M. Dick

CLINICAL STANDARDS ADVISORY GROUP
Room LG22, Wellington House, 133–155 Waterloo Road, London SE1 8UG
Tel 071-972 4926
Chairman, Sir Gordon Higginson

EXECUTIVE AGENCIES

NHS ESTATES
Euston Tower, 286 Euston Road, London NW1 3DN
Tel 071-388 1188

Chief Executive (G3), J. C. Locke
Estate Policy Director (G5), G. G. Mayers
Director of Business Development (G5), A. R. Tanner
Director of Resources (G5), L. J. Wardle
Head of Consultancy Services (G5), C. Davies
Chief Engineer (G5), L. W. M. Arrowsmith
Manager, Surveying Services (G6), A. Garbutt
Principal Nursing Adviser (G6), Mrs D. Vass

MEDICINES CONTROL AGENCY
Market Towers, 1 Nine Elms Lane, London SW8 5NQ
Tel 071-273 3000

Chief Executive, Dr K. H. Jones
Business Managers, D. O. Hagger; R. K. Alder; B. H. Hartley; Dr D. B. Jefferys; Dr S. M. Wood

NHS PENSIONS
Hesketh House, 200–220 Broadway, Fleetwood, Lancs. F47 8LG
Tel 0253-774506

Chief Executive (G5), A. Cowan

HEALTH AND SAFETY COMMISSION
Baynards House, 1 Chepstow Place, Westbourne Grove, London W2 4TF
Tel 071-243 6000

The Health and Safety Commission was created under the Health and Safety at Work etc. Act 1974, with duties to reform health and safety law, to propose new regulations, and generally to promote the protection of people at work and of the public from hazards arising from industrial and commercial activity, including major industrial accidents and the transportation of hazardous materials.

The Commission members are appointed by the Secretary of State for Employment, although the Commission assists a number of Secretaries of State concerned with aspects of its functions. It is made up of representatives of employers, trades unions and local authorities, and has a full-time chairman.

The Commission can appoint agents, and it works in conjunction with local authorities who enforce the Act in such premises as offices and warehouses.

Chairman, vacant
Members, P. Jacques, CBE; A. Tuffin; R. Symons;
  P. Gallagher; E. Carrick, Dame Rachel Waterhouse, DBE,
  PH.D.; N. J. Pitcher; C. Chope; Dr G. Schofield
Secretary, T. Gates

HEALTH AND SAFETY EXECUTIVE
Baynards House, 1 Chepstow Place, Westbourne Grove,
London W2 4TF
Tel 071-243 6000

The Health and Safety Executive is the Health and Safety Commission's major instrument. Through its inspectorates it enforces health and safety law in the majority of industrial premises, to protect people at work and the public. The Executive advises the Commission in its major task of laying down safety standards through regulations and practical guidance for many industrial processes, liaising as necessary with government departments and other institutions. The Executive is also the licensing authority for nuclear installations. In carrying out its functions the Executive acts independently of the Government, guided only by the Commission as to general health and safety policy.
Director-General (G2), J. D. Rimington, CB (*at G1A*)
Deputy Directors-General (G2), D. C. T. Eves, CB;
  Miss J. H. Bacon

HM FACTORY INSPECTORATE
HM Chief Inspector of Factories (G3), Dr J. T. Carter

HM AGRICULTURAL INSPECTORATE
HM Chief Agricultural Inspector (G3), F. D. Lindsay

HM MINES INSPECTORATE
HM Chief Inspector of Mines (G3), K. Twist

NUCLEAR SAFETY DIVISION
HM Chief Inspector of Nuclear Installations (G3),
  Dr S. A. Harbison

HM RAILWAY INSPECTORATE
HM Chief Inspector of Railways (G3), S. S. J. Robertson

STRATEGY AND GENERAL DIVISION
Director (G3), Dr J. M. McQuaid

TECHNOLOGY AND HEALTH SCIENCES DIVISION
Includes HM Explosives Inspectorate
Director (G3), Dr A. Ellis

SAFETY POLICY DIVISION
Director (G3), R. S. Allison

RESEARCH AND LABORATORY SERVICES DIVISION
Director (G4), Dr A. Roberts

HEALTH POLICY DIVISION
Director of Medical Services (G3), A. W. Brown, CB

SOLICITOR'S OFFICE
Solicitor (G4), B. J. Ecclestone

RESOURCES AND PLANNING DIVISION
Including the Accident Prevention Advisory Unit
Director (G3), D. J. Hodgkins, CB

OFFSHORE SAFETY DIVISION
Chief Executive (G3), A. C. Barrell

HIGHLANDS AND ISLANDS ENTERPRISE
Bridge House, 20 Bridge Street, Inverness IV1 1QR
Tel 0463-234171

Highlands and Islands Enterprise (HIE) was set up in 1991 under the Enterprise and New Towns (Scotland) Act 1991. Its role is to design, direct and deliver enterprise development, training, environmental and social projects and services. In carrying out its role HIE operates through and in conjunction with ten Local Enterprise Companies (LECs) to which many of its individual functions are delegated, in particular those relating to the provision of Enterprise Assistance, Youth Training and the new Training for Work scheme. The LECs also design and develop initiatives at local level covering the wider range of economic and social development, training and environmental improvements.
Chairman, F. Morrison
Chief Executive, I. A. Robertson

HISTORIC BUILDINGS AND MONUMENTS COMMISSION FOR ENGLAND (ENGLISH HERITAGE)
Fortress House, 23 Savile Row, London W1X 1AB
Tel 071-973 3000

Under the National Heritage Act 1983, the duties of the Commission are to secure the preservation of ancient monuments and historic buildings; to promote the preservation and enhancement of conservation areas; and to promote the public's enjoyment of, and advance their knowledge of, ancient monuments and historic buildings and their preservation. The Commission has advisory committees on historic buildings and areas, ancient monuments, cathedrals and churches, and London.
Chairman, J. Stevens, CVO
Commissioners, HRH The Duke of Gloucester;
  Miss J. A. Page (*Chief Executive*); Dr R. W. Brunskill;
  The Lord Cavendish of Furness; Ms B. Cherry; Dr
  N. Cossons; Sir Hugh Cubitt; T. Farrell; Sir David
  Wilson; Mrs C. Lycett-Green; J. Seymour; R. Suddards;
  G. Wilson

HISTORIC BUILDINGS COUNCIL FOR WALES
Brunel House, 2 Fitzalan Road, Cardiff CF2 1UY
Tel 0222-465511

The Council's function is to advise the Secretary of State for Wales through Cadw: Welsh Historic Monuments (*see* page 368), which is an executive agency within the Welsh Office.
Chairman, T. Lloyd, FSA
Members, W. Lindsay Evans; Prof. J. Eynon, OBE, FRIBA, FSA;
  The Earl Lloyd George of Dwyfor; R. Haslam;
  Dr P. Morgan
Secretary, R. W. Hughes

HISTORIC BUILDINGS COUNCIL FOR SCOTLAND
20 Brandon Street, Edinburgh EH3 5RA
Tel 031-244 2966

The Historic Buildings Council for Scotland is the advisory body to the Secretary of State for Scotland on matters related

to buildings of special architectural or historic interest and in particular to proposals for awards by him of grants for the repair of buildings of outstanding architectural or historic interest or lying within outstanding conservation areas.
Chairman, Sir Nicholas Fairbairn, QC, MP
Members, Sir Ilay Campbell, Bt.; Mrs P. Chalmers; Prof. J. D. Dunbar-Nasmith, CBE, FRSA, FRSE; M. Ellington; J. Hunter Blair; I. Hutchison, OBE; K. Martin; J. A. M. Mitchell, CB, CVO, MC; Miss G. Nayler; Revd C. Robertson; Prof. A. J. Rowan; Mrs F. Walker
Secretary, I. G. Dewar

ROYAL COMMISSION ON THE HISTORICAL MONUMENTS OF ENGLAND
Fortress House, 23 Savile Row, London WIX 2JQ
Tel 071-973 3500

The Royal Commission on the Historical Monuments of England was established in 1908. It is the national body charged with the recording and analysing of ancient and historical monuments and buildings. It compiles, preserves and makes publicly available the national archive of such material, which is housed in the National Monuments Record. The Commission is due to move to Swindon in the spring of 1994.
Chairman, The Baroness Park of Monmouth, CMG, OBE
Commissioners, Prof. R. Bradley, FSA; D. J. Keene, PH.D.; Prof. G. H. Martin, CBE, D.Phil., FSA; Prof. G. I. Meirion-Jones, PH.D., FSA; Prof. A. C. Thomas, CBE, D.Litt., FSA; Prof. M. Biddle, FBA, FSA; Mrs B. K. Cherry, FSA; R. D. H. Gem, PH.D., FSA; T. R. M. Longman; R. A. Yorke; Miss A. Riches, FSA; Dr M. Airs, FSA; Prof. M. Fulford, PH.D., FSA; Dr M. Palmer, FSA
Secretary, T. G. Hassall, FSA

ROYAL COMMISSION ON ANCIENT AND HISTORICAL MONUMENTS IN WALES
Crown Building, Plas Crug, Aberystwyth, Dyfed SY23 INJ
Tel 0970-624381

The Commission was established in 1908 to make an inventory of the ancient and historical monuments of Wales and Monmouthshire. It is currently empowered by a royal warrant of 1992 to survey, record, publish and maintain a database of ancient and historical sites, structures and landscapes in Wales. The Commission is also responsible for the National Monuments Record of Wales, which is open daily for public reference.
Chairman, Prof. J. B. Smith
Commissioners, R. W. Brunskill, OBE, PH.D., FSA; Prof. D. Ellis Evans, D.Phil., FBA; Prof. R. A. Griffiths, PH.D.; D. Gruffyd Jones; R. M. Haslam, FSA; Prof. G. B. D. Jones, D.Phil., FSA; Mrs A. Nicol; S. B. Smith; G. J. Wainwright, MBE, PH.D., FSA; E. Wiliam, PH.D., FSA
Secretary, P. R. White, FSA

ROYAL COMMISSION ON THE ANCIENT AND HISTORICAL MONUMENTS OF SCOTLAND
John Sinclair House, 16 Bernard Terrace, Edinburgh EH8 9NX
Tel 031-662 1446

The Commission was established in 1908 and is appointed to provide for the survey and recording of ancient and historical monuments connected with the culture, civilization and conditions of life of the people in Scotland from the earliest times. It compiles and maintains the National Monuments Record of Scotland as the national record of the archaeological and historical environment. The National Monuments Record is open for reference Mon.–Thurs. 9.30–4.30, Fri. 9.30–4.
Chairman, The Earl of Crawford and Balcarres, PC
Commissioners, Prof. J. M. Coles, PH.D., FBA; Prof. J. D. Dunbar-Nasmith, CBE, FRIBA; Prof. Rosemary Cramp, CBE, FSA; Mrs P. E. Durham; Prof. T. C. Smout, PH.D.; The Hon. Lord Cullen; Dr D. J. Howard, FSA; The Hon. P. D. E. M. Moncreiffe; R. A. Paxton
Secretary, R. J. Mercer, FSA

ANCIENT MONUMENTS BOARD FOR WALES
Brunel House, 2 Fitzalan Road, Cardiff CF2 IUY
Tel 0222-465511

The Ancient Monuments Board for Wales advises the Secretary of State for Wales on his statutory functions in respect of ancient monuments.
Chairman, Prof. G. Williams, CBE, FBA, FSA
Members, Prof. R. B. Heaton, OBE, FRIBA; Prof. R. R. Davies, FBA, D.phil.; Dr S. H. R. Aldhouse-Green, FSA; R. G. Keen; Miss F. Lynch, FSA; Prof. W. H. Manning, PH.D., FSA; D. Moore, RD, FSA; Dr P. Smith, FSA; Prof. J. B. Smith
Secretary, S. Morris

ANCIENT MONUMENTS BOARD FOR SCOTLAND
20 Brandon Street, Edinburgh EH3 5RA
Tel 031-244 3108

The Ancient Monuments Board for Scotland advises the Secretary of State for Scotland on the exercise of his functions, under the Ancient Monuments and Archaeological Areas Act 1979, of providing protection for monuments of national importance. Protection may be provided by including a monument in a statutory list of protected monuments, by acquisition, or by guardianship in which the Secretary of State assumes responsibility for maintenance.
Chairman, Prof. E. C. Fernie, FSA, FSA SCOT.
Members, Prof. A. Fenton, CBE, FRSE, FSA SCOT.; J. Simpson, FSA SCOT.; Sir Jamie Stormonth Darling, CBE, MC, TD, WS; Mrs E. V. W. Proudfoot, FSA, FSA SCOT.; Mrs K. Dalyell; J. H. A. Gerrard, FRSA; T. R. H. Godden, CB; L. J. Masters, FSA; Dr A. Richie; R. D. Kernohan, OBE; Dr J. Morgan, FSA SCOT.; Prof. C. D. Morris, FSA, FSA SCOT.; R. J. Mercer, FSA; W. D. H. Sellar, FSA SCOT.; Lady Jane Grosvenor
Secretary, R. A. J. Dalziel
Assessor, D. J. Breeze, PH.D., FSA

HOME-GROWN CEREALS AUTHORITY
Hamlyn House, Highgate Hill, London NI9 5PR
Tel 071-263 3391

Set up under the Cereals Marketing Act 1965, the Authority consists of nine members representing UK cereal growers, nine representing dealers in, or processors of, grain and three independent members. The Authority's functions are

to improve the production and marketing of UK-grown cereals through a research and development programme, to provide a market information service, and to promote UK cereals in export markets. The Authority also undertakes agency work for the Intervention Board in connection with the application in the UK of the Common Agricultural Policy for cereals.
Chairman, G. B. Nelson
General Manager, C. J. Ames

BRITISH CEREAL EXPORTS
Chairman, R. J. Cherrington
Manager, J. B. Rose

HOME OFFICE
50 Queen Anne's Gate, London SW1H 9AT
Tel 071-273 3000

The Home Office deals with those internal affairs in England and Wales which have not been assigned to other government departments. The Home Secretary is particularly concerned with the administration of justice; criminal law; the treatment of offenders, including probation and the prison service; the police; immigration and nationality; passport policy matters; community relations; certain public safety matters; and fire and civil emergencies services. The Home Secretary personally is the link between The Queen and the public, and exercises certain powers on her behalf, including that of the Royal Pardon.

Other subjects dealt with include electoral arrangements; addresses and petitions to The Queen; ceremonial and formal business connected with honours; requests for extradition of criminals; scrutiny of local authority byelaws; granting of licences for scientific procedures involving animals; cremations, burials and exhumations; firearms; dangerous drugs and poisons; general policy on laws relating to shops, liquor licensing, gaming and lotteries, charitable collections and marriage; theatre and cinema licensing; co-ordination of government action in relation to the voluntary social services; and race relations policy.

The Home Secretary is also the link between the UK government and the governments of the Channel Islands and the Isle of Man.
Secretary of State for the Home Department, The Rt. Hon. Michael Howard, QC, MP
  Principal Private Secretary (G5), Miss J. MacNaughton
  Private Secretaries, Mrs S. J. McCarthy; Ms J. D. Walker
  Special Adviser, P. Rock
  Parliamentary Private Secretary, Dr L. Fox, MP
Ministers of State, The Earl Ferrers, PC; Peter Lloyd, MP; David Maclean, MP
  Special Adviser, D. Cameron
  Parliamentary Private Secretaries:
  To Mr Lloyd, D. Wilshire, MP
  To Mr Maclean, J. Arnold, MP
Parliamentary Under-Secretary of State, Charles Wardle, MP
Parliamentary Clerk, Miss R. McCool
Permanent Under-Secretary of State (G1), Sir Clive Whitmore, GCB, CVO
  Private Secretary, C. Dolphin
Chief Medical Officer (at Department of Health), Dr K. Calman

LEGAL ADVISER'S BRANCH
Legal Adviser (G2), M. L. Saunders, CB
Principal Assistant Legal Advisers (G3), D. J. Bentley, CB; Miss P. A. Edwards

Assistant Legal Advisers, R. J. Clayton; Mrs S. A. Evans; J. R. O'Meara; C. M. L. Osborne; D. Seymour
Senior Principal Legal Assistants, H. M. Carter; Ms M. Carter; Miss R. P. Davies; Mrs J. M. Jones; Mrs C. Price

CRIMINAL, RESEARCH AND STATISTICS DEPARTMENTS
Deputy Under-Secretary (G2), J. F. Halliday

CRIMINAL POLICY DEPARTMENT
Assistant Under-Secretary of State (G3), A. P. Wilson
Heads of Divisions (G5), Miss C. Macready; J. M. Potts; Miss C. J. Stewart; R. C. Stoate
Chief Inspector, Drugs Branch (G6), A. McFarlane
Senior Principals (G6), A. Norbury; T. C. Morris; M. Rumble
Principals (G7), R. Allen; Miss D. Collings; P. Dawson; R. G. W. Dyce; D. H. Evans; B. Gange; L. T. Hughes; Ms J. L. Hutcheon; N. Jordon; Mrs P. Lutterloch; Miss H. L. McKinnon; Mrs R. M. Mitev; M. J. Narey; R. D. Parsons; D. Rigby; Ms L. Rogerson; Miss A. M. Rutherford; G. H. H. Sonnenberg; Ms F. Taylor; J. R. Thew; P. Topping; P. F. Vallance

RESEARCH AND STATISTICS DEPARTMENT
Assistant Under-Secretary of State (G3), C. P. Nuttall

RESEARCH AND PLANNING UNIT
Head of Unit (G5), R. Tarling
Grade 6, J. M. Hough; P. J. Jordan; Mrs P. Mayhew; G. R. Walmsley
Principals (G7), A. C. Barton; D. C. Brown; J. A. Ditchfield; Dr P. J. Ekblom; Dr S. Field; Ms M. Fitzgerald; J. H. Graham; Dr P. Grove; Mrs K. E. Howard; T. Marshall; Ms P. M. Morgan; Miss J. W. Mott; Dr G. I. U. Mair; J. F. Mcleod; A. D. Moxon; F. P. E. Southgate; Dr I. P. Williamson

STATISTICS DEPARTMENT
Chief Statisticians (G5), K. Childs; C. G. Lewis; J. L. Walker
Grade 6, Mrs C. L. Lehmann; R. Pape; D. A. Povey; P. Sheriff; P. White
Grade 7, Ms A. Barber; G. G. Barclay; W. Burns; P. F. Collier; L. Davidoff; Mrs P. Dowdeswell; N. Frater; Z. Frosztega; I. Gaskell; Miss G. Goddard; Mrs A. James; K. M. Jackson; Mrs S. Keith; M. Lock; Miss A. Maxwell; Mrs P. A. Penneck; D. A. Povey; P. E. Ramell; P. Sheriff; R. M. Taylor; D. Turner; M. Uglow; P. White; Miss M. Wilkinson

CRIMINAL JUSTICE AND CONSTITUTIONAL DEPARTMENT
Assistant Under-Secretary of State (G3), R. M. Morris
Heads of Divisions (G5), E. A. Grant; P. J. Honour; Miss S. Marshall; P. R. C. Storr
Grade 6, M. P. Cook; R. G. Evans; Miss A. Fletcher; G. H. Marriage
Principals (G7), Mrs P. Baskerville; Mrs M. K. Branwell; Ms J. Cooke; S. L. Cox; Miss R. M. Fletton; J. Glaze; Ms M. Gorman; L. D. Hay; Mrs G. Hetherington; H. D. Hillier; Mrs S. J. McDougall; Mrs S. Mann; Miss S. E. Rae; K. E. R. Rogers; D. Ross; J. Wake; S. M. K. Willmington; R. W. Wootton
Chief Inspector of Probation (G4), G. W. Smith, CBE
Deputy Chief Inspector of Probation (G5), J. C. Haines

ANIMALS (SCIENTIFIC PROCEDURE) INSPECTORATE
Chief Inspector, Dr R. M. Watt

POLICE DEPARTMENT
Deputy Under-Secretary (G2), I. M. Burns, CB

POLICE DEPARTMENT
Assistant Under-Secretaries of State (G3), Miss
M. A. Clayton; Miss C. Sinclair; J. Warne;
G. J. Wasserman
Heads of Divisions (G5), Mrs P. G. W. Catto; Mrs
C. Crawford; J. B. Duke-Evans; Mrs B. Fair;
R. A. Harrington; K. H. Heal; D. A. Hill; A. Holt; Miss
D. Loudon; N. C. Sanderson; E. Soden; R. R. Tilt
Senior Principals (G6), D. R. Birleson; D. Crick;
R. A. Ginman; Dr G. K. Laycock; D. Rowe; Dr
G. Turnbull
Principals (G7), Mrs J. Anderson; R. C. Barron; Dr
B. J. Blain; Mrs J. Bonelle; J. W. Bradley; K. Brennan;
R. Brett; D. Brown; G. Brown; Ms C. Checksfield; Mrs
P. Cocks; G. T. Coulthard; N. Custanco; M. de Pulford;
M. Dexter; Miss J. D. Erwteman; D. Faulks; A. Ford;
N. Hancock; M. J. I. Hill; K. Hopley; G. R. Houghton;
Mrs R. Johnson; A. N. Kent; Dr D. K. Laing;
A. Maclean; E. Maclean; P. Martin; D. Massey;
N. F. Montgomery-Pott; Mrs G. I. Moody; Mrs
B. Moore; D. C. Moulton; M. Phillips; Mrs I. Posen;
C. A. Pounds; P. W. Pugh; Mrs M. Rolfe; Miss
J. B. Rumble; D. G. Skene; P. T. Smith; Mrs
A. R. Stiling; R. Sutcliffe; D. Theobald; G. H. Thomas;
P. Tomlinson; Mrs A. Underhill; R. H. Watt; B. Webb;
P. D. White; G. A. Widdecombe; D. Wright; Dr
J. Youell

POLICE SCIENTIFIC DEVELOPMENT BRANCH
Sandridge Laboratories, Woodcock Hill, Sandridge,
St Albans, Herts. AL4 9HQ
Tel 0727-865051

Head of Laboratory (G6)

Langhurst House, Langhurstwood Road, Nr. Horsham,
Sussex RH12 4WX
Tel 0403-55451

FORENSIC SCIENCE SERVICE HEADQUARTERS
Priory House, Gooch Street North, Birmingham B5 6QQ
Tel 021-666 6606

An executive agency within the Home Office.
Director-General (G3), Dr J. Thompson
Grade 5, vacant
Head of Personnel and Administration (G6), J. P. Emery
Grade 7, Mrs E. Sadler *(policy)*; Mrs D. Grice

POLICE NATIONAL COMPUTER (HENDON DATA
CENTRE)
Aerodrome Road, Colindale, London NW9 5LN
Tel 081-200 2424

Head of Division (G6), J. Ladley
Principals (G7), J. A. Henderson; D. McGarry;
L. D. Watson

DTELS (DIRECTORATE OF TELECOMMUNICATIONS)
DTELS House, Mereway, Ruddington, Nottingham
NG11 6JU
Tel 0602-406161

Head of Directorate (G5), N. F. K. Finlayson
Assistant Director (G6), J. F. Nicholson
Head of Operations (G6), vacant
Head of Marketing (G6), I. Aitken

Head of Engineering Consultancy (G6), vacant
Principals (G7), S. R. Cole; W. Hogg; A. Hulme;
A. N. Kent; T. J. Logan; R. J. Sanders; K. Staves;
R. Tuckley; L. T. Whiteside

HM INSPECTORATE OF CONSTABULARY
HM Chief Inspector of Constabulary (£83,944), T. A. Morris,
CBE, QPM
HM Inspectors (£68,671–£75,899), G. J. Dear, QPM;
D. Elliott, CBE, QPM; B. Hayes, CBE, QPM; Sir Philip
Myers, OBE, QPM; D. J. O'Dowd, QPM; C. Smith, CVO, QPM

POLICE STAFF COLLEGE
Bramshill House, Basingstoke, Hants. RG27 0JW
Tel 025 126-2931

Commandant, Sir Robert Bunyard, KBE, QPM
Deputy Commandant and Director of Courses, J. A. Dickinson
National Director of Police Training, P. Ryan, QPM

THE SECURITY SERVICE (MI5)
PO Box 3255, London SW1P 1AE

The Security Service took over responsibility for mainland
intelligence about Irish terrorism in October 1992. Counter-
terrorism activities account for 70 per cent of its work;
25 per cent involves counter-espionage and counter-
proliferation activities, and the remaining 5 per cent involves
the monitoring of subversive organizations. The Service is
split into two sections, Operations and Administration.
Director-General, Mrs S. Rimington

EQUAL OPPORTUNITIES, IMMIGRATION
AND NATIONALITY DEPARTMENTS
Deputy Under-Secretary (G2), A. J. Langdon

EQUAL OPPORTUNITIES AND GENERAL DEPARTMENT
Assistant Under-Secretary of State (G3), M. E. Head, CVO
Heads of Divisions (G5), N. M. Johnson, CBE; R. Kornicki;
A. Harding
Principals (G7), W. Brandon; Ms C. Dale;
P. R. Edmundson; Mrs J. M. Flascher; Mrs
D. D. Gonsalves; Mrs J. S. Morris; G. Sutton;
R. A. Wright

Voluntary Services Unit
Assistant Secretary (G5), D. J. Hardwick
Principals (G7), R. G. W. Cook; Miss V. R. Hatcher;
F. Smith; Ms N. Williams

IMMIGRATION AND NATIONALITY DEPARTMENT
Lunar House, 40 Wellesley Road, Croydon, Surrey, CR9 2BY
Tel 081-686 0688
Assistant Under-Secretaries of State (G3), W. A. Jeffrey;
A. R. Rawsthorne
Heads of Divisions (G5), E. B. Nicholls; Mrs E. C. L. Pallett;
K. D. Sutton; R. M. Whalley; P. N. Wrench; R. G. Yates
Senior Principals (G6), T. Farrage; C. J. Saunders;
A. Walmsley
Principals (G7), C. A. Allison; G. Brindle; W. F. Bryant;
D. Burgess; J. Casey; J. Couch; A. Cunningham;
W. M. Dawnie; J. Gilbert; D. J. Hunt; Mrs C. Kellas;
C. J. Kelly; B. D. C. Mennell; T. L. Neale; C. Passey; Ms
C. Pelham; T. R. Peters; Miss G. M. Romney; Ms
C. Stewart; J. Sweet; D. Truscott; Mrs F. Webster;
R. B. Woodland

Immigration Service
Director (Ports) (G5), Miss K. J. Collins
Director (Immigration Service Enforcement) (G5),
C. B. Manchip
Deputy Directors (G6), G. Boiling; J. M. de Llanos;
D. J. McDonough

Assistant Directors (G7), B. R. Barrett; Miss G. M. Griffith;
V. Hogg; D. I. Ingham; G. Maguire; D. Mould;
P. Quibell; C. Passey; K. Richardson

EUROPEAN COMMUNITIES UNIT
Head of Division (G5), M. J. Gillespie
Grade 7, Dr S. Hadjipavlou

HM PRISON SERVICE
Cleland House, Page Street, London SW1P 4LN
Tel 071-217 3000

An executive agency within the Home Office.

NON-CIVIL SERVICE GRADE SALARIES

HM Chief Inspector of Prisons	£78,378
Prison Service Governor 1	£45,157
Prison Service Governor 2	£40,776
Prison Service Governor 3	£35,215
Prison Service Governor 4	£27,902–£30,285

THE PRISONS BOARD
Chairman, and Chief Executive of the Prison Service (G2),
D. C. Lewis
Director of Personnel and Finance (G3), A. J. Butler
Director of Inmate Administration (G3), I. Dunbar, CB
Director of Inmate Programmes (G3), A. J. Pearson
Director of Custody (G3), Miss P. C. Drew
Director of Services and Parole (G3), Ms J. Reisz
Director of Prison Health Care (G3), Dr R. Wool
Non-Executive Members, Mrs U. Banerjee; F. W. Bentley

PRISON SERVICE
Heads of Divisions (G5), I. Boon; J. I. Chisholm; Miss
L. F. Gill; Mrs E. J. Grimsey; G. E. Guy; Mrs
V. V. R. Harris; S. B. Hickson; R. C. Masefield;
H. H. Taylor; R. J. Weatherill; P. Wheatley; T. Wilson
Assistant Director of Prison Medical Services (G4), Dr
J. Sinclair
Principal Medical Officers (G4), Dr R. Gooch; Dr
R. Harkness; Dr M. Longfield; Dr P. B. Pattison; Dr
G. Penton; Dr R. Ralli; Dr D. Speed; Dr A. Todd
Senior Principals (G6), D. M. Ackland; Mrs P. Almond; Mrs
H. M. Bayne; P. Cook; R. E. Corrigan; C. F. Drewitt;
B. Johnson; R. W. Lockett; B. S. Luetchford; Dr
C. McDougall; P. Sleightholme; C. L. Spencer
Governors (1), J. W. Dring; G. Gregory-Smith; I. Ward;
C. J. Williams
Principals (G7), C. Allars; J. H. Attridge; A. J. Beasley;
A. D. Burgess; N. Burton; H. M. C. Crudge; P. Done;
J. A. Greenland; Mrs M. Haughey, MBE; N. F. M. Home;
G. P. Hopkins; C. Hudson; M. W. Jarvis; Mrs
V. Keating; R. S. H. Kettle; M. P. Loughlin; Ms
P. Lowe; K. MacKenzie; N. Maclean; K. Marshall;
C. R. Miller; Mrs E. Moody; D. S. Neal; Mrs A. Nelson;
N. Newcomen; J. S. Nottingham; J. Page; S. J. Rimmer;
J. S. Sarjantson; D. Shene; R. E. Smith; D. J. Tallock;
M. Todd; J. M. G. Toon; G. Utteridge; T. A. Ward; Miss
S. Weinel; S. C. Wells; W. F. Whiteing; Ms
A. Wickington; Mrs V. M. Wilsdon; A. Woolfenden;
R. J. Wood; P. Wright
Governors (2), Miss M. Carden; C. Lambert; Miss
S. F. McCormick; M. Morrison; C. Scott; D. Shaw;
A. G. Smith; D. Wilson
Chaplain-General and Archdeacon of the Prison Service,
Ven. D. Fleming
Chief Education Officer (G6), I. G. Benson
Chief Physical Education Officer (G6), M. W. Denton
Governors (3), M. Ainsworth; H. Bagshaw; T. Davies;
J. R. Dovell; W. S. Duff; Mrs M. Eagan; S. Eley; Mrs
S. Fielder; J. Forster; G. Gibson; D. Godfrey;

P. L. Hanaway; Ms U. McCollom; A. Mills; D. Myers;
P. Quinn; Miss P. Scriven; J. Talbot; P. Tebrey;
I. Truffet; R. W. Walker

DIRECTORATE OF WORKS
Abell House, John Islip Street, London SW1P 4LH
Tel 071-217 3000

Director of Works (G4), W. L. Sparks, CBE
Group Managers:
Superintending Architect (G6), S. Mahraj
Chief Civil Structural Engineer (G6), R. W. T. Haines
Chief Mechanical and Electrical Engineer (G6), R. Putland
Grade 6, B. Stickley
Principals (G7), O. Astaniotis; P. J. Attwater; B. J. Bleet;
C. F. Brown; J. K. Chamberlain; R. Chick; M. J. Davies;
J. B. Dawson; R. D'Cruz; J. A. Doohan; P. Enticknap;
J. V. Gleed; M. C. Hayes; G. E. Hickey; J. J. Hurley;
C. J. Lawton; L. P. Lumley; D. Newton; S. Richards;
M. Ryland; M. Sweeny; R. J. Tricker; A. Weeks

DSP3 (PRISON SERVICE INDUSTRIES AND FARMS)
Block A, Whitgift Centre, Wellesley Road, Croydon, Surrey
CR9 3LY
Tel 081-686 8710

Director (G5), P. R. A. Fulton
Group Managers (G6), R. K. Fisher; A. Sweeney; J. Weller
Governor (1), K. M. Brewer
Principals (G7), J. Cairns; R. Daw; J. W. Fallows;
B. D. Feist; P. J. Goulder; J. A. Gillcrist; C. Handley;
G. A. Merrett; D. E. Neville; T. Senior; A. S. Wilson;
R. M. Young

SUPPLY AND TRANSPORT BRANCH
Crown House, 52 Elizabeth Street, Corby, Northants
Tel 0536-202101

Director (G5), D. J. C. Kent
Grade 6, B. J. David
Principals (G7), R. C. Brett; D. J. Brown; M. Fitzgerald;
D. J. Miller

AREA MANAGERS (GOVERNORS I)

Directorate of Custody (DOC)
East Anglia, T. G. Murtagh, OBE
Kent, J. Hunter
London North, Miss A. M. Edwards
London South, P. J. Kitteridge
South Coast, A. Rayfield

Directorate of Inmate Administration (DIA)
Central, J. Blakey
Mercia, D. Curtis
Chilterns, A. de Frisching
Wales and the West, J. Wilkinson
Wessex, R. J. May

Directorate of Inmate Programmes (DIP)
East Midland, J. C. Mullens
North-East, A. H. Papps
North-West, D. I. Lockwood
Trans-Pennine, T. Bone
Yorkshire, M. Codd

PRISONS

ACKLINGTON (DIP), Morpeth, Northumberland
NE65 9XF. *Governor,* F. P. Masserick
ALBANY (DOC), Newport, Isle of Wight PO30 5RS.
Governor, R. Mitchell
ALDINGTON (DOC), Ashford, Kent TN25 7BQ. *Governor,*
D. A. Bratton

ASHWELL (DIA), Oakham, Leics. LE15 7LS. *Governor,* H. Reid

*ASKHAM GRANGE (DIP), Askham Richard, York YO2 3PT. *Governor,* H. E. Crew

BEDFORD (DOC), St Loyes Street, Bedford MK40 1HG. *Governor,* S. P. Moore

BELMARSH (DOC), Western Way, Thamesmead, London SE28 OEB. *Governor,* H. D. Jones

BIRMINGHAM (DIA), Winson Green Road, Birmingham B18 4AS. *Governor,* C. B. Scott

BLAKENHURST (private prison), Hewell Lane, Redditch, Worcs. B97 6QS. *Controller,* P. J. Hanglin

BLANTYRE HOUSE (DOC), Goudhurst, Cranbrook, Kent TN17 2NH. *Governor,* J. Semple

BLUNDESTON (DOC), Lowestoft, Suffolk NR32 5BG. *Governor,* S. Robinson

BRISTOL (DIA), Cambridge Road, Bristol BS7 8PS. *Governor,* R. D. Dixon

BRIXTON (DOC), PO Box 369, Jebb Avenue, London SW2 5XF. *Governor,* Dr A. Coyle

BROCKHILL (DIA), Redditch, Worcs. B97 6RD. *Governor,* B. Stanhope

BULLINGDON (DIA), Padrick Haugh Road, Arncott, Bicester, Oxon. OX6 OPZ. *Governor,* J. Thomas-Ferrand

*BULLWOOD HALL (DOC), High Road, Hockley, Essex SS5 4TE. *Governor,* vacant

CAMP HILL (DOC), Newport, Isle of Wight PO30 5PB. *Governor,* W. A. Wood

CANTERBURY (DOC), Longport, Canterbury, Kent CT1 1PJ. *Governor,* J. L. Harrison

CARDIFF (DIA), Knox Road, Cardiff CF2 1UG. *Governor,* N. D. Clifford

CASTINGTON (DIP), Morpeth, Northumberland NE65 9XF. *Governor,* C. Harder

CHANNINGS WOOD (DIA), Denbury, Newton Abbott, Devon TQ12 6DW. *Governor,* R. S. Brandon

CHELMSFORD (DOC), Springfield Road, Chelmsford, Essex CM2 6LQ. *Governor,* D. B. Sinclair

COLDINGLEY (DIA), Bisley, Woking, Surrey GU24 9EX. *Governor,* J. Capel

*COOKHAM WOOD (DOC), Cookham Wood, Rochester, Kent ME1 3LU. *Governor,* Mrs C. Ellis

DARTMOOR (DIA), Princetown, Yelverton, Devon PL20 6RR. *Governor,* J. Powls

DORCHESTER (DIA), North Square, Dorchester, Dorset DT1 1JD. *Governor,* R. Walker

DOWNVIEW (DOC), Sutton Lane, Sutton, Surrey SM2 5PD. *Governor,* D. Aram

*DRAKE HALL (DIA), Eccleshall, Staffs. ST21 6LQ. *Governor,* R. J. Crouch

*DURHAM (DIP), Old Elvet, Durham DH1 3HU. *Governor,* M. Mogg

*EAST SUTTON PARK (DOC), Sutton Valence, Maidstone, Kent ME17 3DF. *Governor,* W. S. Duff

*ELMLEY (DOC), Church Road, Eastchurch, Sheerness, Kent ME12 4DZ. *Governor,* W. J. Cooper

ERLESTOKE HOUSE (DIA), Devizes, Wilts. SN10 5TU. *Governor,* Ms A. J. Gomme

EVERTHORPE (DIP), Brough, North Humberside HU15 1RB. *Governor,* R. Smith

EXETER (DIA), New North Road, Exeter, Devon EX4 4EX. *Governor,* D. Alderson

FEATHERSTONE (DIA), New Road, Featherstone, Wolverhampton WV10 7PU. *Governor,* L. M. Wiltshire

FORD (DOC), Arundel, W. Sussex BN18 OBX. *Governor,* Maj. B. Smith

FRANKLAND (DIP), Frankland, Brasside, Durham, DH1 5YD. *Governor,* P. Buxton

FULL SUTTON (DIP), Full Sutton, York YO4 1PS. *Governor,* J. W. Staples

GARTH (DIP), Ulnes Walton Lane, Leyland, Preston, Lancs. PR5 3NE. *Governor,* W. Rose-Quirie

GARTREE (DIA), Leicester Road, Market Harborough, Leics. LE16 7RP. *Governor,* R. J. Perry

GLOUCESTER (DIA), Barrack Square, Gloucester GL1 2JN. *Governor,* P. W. Winkley

GRENDON (DOC), Grendon Underwood, Aylesbury, Bucks. HP18 OTL. *Governor,* T. C. Newell

HASLAR (DOC), Dolphin Way, Gosport, Hants. PO12 2AW. *Governor,* J. R. Dovell

HAVERIGG (DIP), Haverigg Camp, Millom, Cumbria LA18 4NA. *Governor,* B. Wilson

HEWELL GRANGE (DIA), Redditch, Worcs. B97 6QQ. *Governor,* D. W. Bamber

HIGH DOWN (DOC), Sutton Lane, Sutton, Surrey SM2 5PJ. *Governor,* S. Pryor

HIGHPOINT (DOC), Stradishall, Newmarket, Suffolk CB8 9YG. *Governor,* C. D. Sherwood

HINDLEY (DIP), Gibson Street, Bickershaw, Hindley, Wigan, Lancs. WN2 5TH. *Governor,* D. Roberts

HOLLESLEY BAY COLONY (DOC), Hollesley, Woodbridge, Suffolk IP12 3JS. *Governor,* M. F. Clarke

*HOLLOWAY (DOC), Parkhurst Road, London N7 ONU. *Governor,* T. M. O'Sullivan

HOLME HOUSE (DIP), Holme House Road, Stockton-on-Tees, Cleveland TS18 2QU. *Governor,* A. K. Rawson

HULL (DIP), Hedon Road, Hull, N. Humberside HU9 5LS. *Governor,* R. Daly

KINGSTON (DOC), Milton Road, Portsmouth PO3 6AS. *Governor,* R. Merricks

KIRKHAM (DIP), Preston, Lancs. PR4 2RA. *Governor,* A. F. Jennings

KIRKLEVINGTON GRANGE (DIP), Yarm, Cleveland TS15 9PA. *Governor,* M. K. Lees

LANCASTER (DIP), The Castle, Lancaster LA1 1YL. *Governor,* D. G. McNaughton

LATCHMERE HOUSE (DOC), Church Road, Ham Common, Richmond, Surrey TW10 5HH. *Governor,* S. O'Neill

LEEDS (DIP), Armley, Leeds LS12 2TJ. *Governor,* A. J. Fitzpatrick

LEICESTER (DIA), Welford Road, Leicester LE2 7AJ. *Governor,* G. Ross

LEWES (DOC), Brighton Road, Lewes, E. Sussex BN7 1EA. *Governor,* J. F. Dixon

LEYHILL (DIA), Wotton-under-Edge, Glos. GL12 8HL. *Governor,* D. T. Williams

LINCOLN (DIP), Greetwell Road, Lincoln LN2 4BD. *Governor,* D. Shaw

LINDHOLME (DIP), Bawtry Road, Hatfield, Woodhouse, Doncaster DN7 6EE. *Governor,* P. Leonard

LITTLEHEY (DOC), Perry, Huntingdon, Cambs. PE18 OSR. *Governor,* M. L. Knight

LIVERPOOL (DIP), 68 Hornby Road, Liverpool L9 3DF. *Governor,* R. H. Jacques

LONG LARTIN (DIA), South Littleton, Evesham, Worcs. WR11 5TZ. *Governor,* P. Atherton

MAIDSTONE (DOC), County Road, Maidstone ME14 1UZ. *Governor,* P. J. Meakings

MANCHESTER (DIP), Southall Street, Manchester M60 9AH. *Governor,* R. P. Halward

MOORLAND (DIP), Hatfield Woodhouse, Doncaster DN7 6BW. *Governor*, C. R. Griffiths

MORTON HALL (DIP), Swinderby, Lincoln LN6 9PS. *Governor*, C. P. A. Bushell

THE MOUNT (DIA), Molyneaux Avenue, Bovingdon, Hemel Hempstead HP3 0NZ. *Governor*, Mrs M. Donnelly

*NEW HALL (DIP), Dial Wood, Flockton, Wakefield, W. Yorks. WF4 4AX. *Governor*, D. England

NORTH SEA CAMP (DIP), Freiston, Boston, Lincs. PE22 0QX. *Governor*, R. Reveley

NORWICH (DIP), Mousehold, Norwich NR1 4LU. *Governor*, Miss J. M. Fowler

NOTTINGHAM (DIP), Perry Road, Sherwood, Nottingham NG5 3AG. *Governor*, L. Lavender

OXFORD (DIA), New Road, Oxford OX1 1LZ. *Governor*, R. J. Talbot

PARKHURST (DOC), Newport, Isle of Wight PO30 5NX. *Governor*, J. R. Marriott

PENTONVILLE (DOC), Caledonian Road, London N7 8TT. *Governor*, W. J. Abbott

PRESTON (DIP), 2 Ribbleton Lane, Preston, Lancs. OR1 5AB. *Governor*, R. Doughty

RANBY (DIP), Ranby, Retford, Notts. DN22 8EU. *Governor*, F. Abbott

*RISLEY (DIP), Warrington Road, Risley, Warrington WA3 6BP. *Governor*, F. B. O'Friel.

ROCHESTER (DOC), Rochester, Kent ME1 3QS. *Governor*, D. Wilson

RUDGATE (DIP), Wetherby, W. Yorks. LS23 7AZ. *Governor*, H. Jones

SEND (DOC), Ripley Road, Send, Woking, Surrey GU23 7LJ. *Governor*, A. French

SHEPTON MALLET (DIA), Cornhill, Shepton Mallet, Somerset BA4 5LU. *Governor*, P. O'Sullivan

SHREWSBURY (DIA), The Dana, Shrewsbury, Salop SY1 2HR. *Governor*, D. J. Bradley

STAFFORD (DIA), 54 Gaol Road, Stafford ST16 3AW. *Governor*, vacant

STANDFORD HILL (DOC), Church Road, Eastchurch, Sheerness, Kent ME12 4AA. *Governor*, D. M. Twiner

STOCKEN (DIP), Stocken Hall Road, Stretton, Nr Oakham, Leics. LE15 7RD. *Governor*, D. Hall

STOCKE HEATH (DIA), Market Drayton, Shropshire TF9 2JL. *Governor*, J. Alldridge

*STYAL (DIP), Wilmslow, Cheshire SK9 4HR. *Governor*, G. Walker

SUDBURY (DIA), Sudbury, Derbys. DE6 5HW. *Governor*, P. E. Salter

SWALESIDE (DOC), Eastchurch, Isle of Sheppey, Kent ME12 4AX. *Governor*, R. Tasker

SWANSEA (DIA), Oystermouth Road, Swansea SA1 2SR. *Governor*, J. Heyes

THORP ARCH (DIP), Wetherby, W. Yorks. LS23 7AY. *Governor*, G. Barnard

USK (DIA), 29 Maryport Street, Usk, Gwent NP5 1XP. *Governor*, N. J. Evans

THE VERNE (DIA), Portland, Dorset DT5 1EQ. *Governor*, T. M. Turner

WAKEFIELD (DIP), Love Lane, Wakefield WF2 9AG. *Governor*, R. S. Duncan

WANDSWORTH (DOC), PO Box 757, Heathfield Road, London SW18 3HS. *Governor*, C. G. Clarke

WAYLAND (DOC), Wayland, Griston, Thetford, Norfolk IP25 6RL. *Governor*, T. C. H. Newth

WELLINGBOROUGH (DOC), Millers Park, Doddington Road, Wellingborough, Northants. NN8 2NH. *Governor*, J. Whetton

WHATTON (DIP), Whatton, Notts. NG13 9FQ. *Governor*, M. A. Lewis

WHITEMOOR (DOC), Longhill Road, March, Cambs. PE15 0PR. *Governor*, A. J. Barclay

WINCHESTER (DOC), Romsey Road, Winchester, Hants. SO22 5DF. *Governor*, M. K. Pascoe

WOODHILL (DOC), Tattenhoe Street, Milton Keynes MK4 4DA. *Governor*, R. B. Clark

WORMWOOD SCRUBBS (DOC), PO Box 757, Du Cane Road, London W12 0AE. *Governor*, J. F. Perris

WYMOTT (DIP), Moss Lane, Ulnes Walton, Leyland, Preston, Lancs. PR5 3LW. *Governor*, J. W. Mullen

YOUNG OFFENDER INSTITUTIONS

AYLESBURY (DIA), Bierton Road, Aylesbury, Bucks. HP20 1EH. *Governor*, C. Welsh

BRINSFORD (DIA), New Road, Featherstone, Wolverhampton WV10 7PY. *Governor*, P. J. Earnshaw

*BULLWOOD HALL (DOC), High Road, Hockley, Essex SS5 4TE. *Governor*, Miss S. Ryan

CASTINGTON (DIP), Morpeth, Northumberland NE65 9XF. *Governor*, C. Harder

DEERBOLT (DIP), Bowes Road Barnard Castle, Co. Durham DL12 9RG. *Governor*, W. J. Ginn

DOVER (DOC), The Citadel, Western Heights, Dover, Kent CT17 9DR. *Governor*, B. W. Sutton

*DRAKE HALL (DIA), Eccleshall, Staffs. ST21 6LQ. *Governor*, R. J. Crouch

*EAST SUTTON PARK (DOC), Sutton Valence, Maidstone, Kent ME17 3DF. *Governor*, W. S. Duff

EASTWOOD PARK (DIA), Falfield, Wotton-under-Edge, Glos. GL12 8DB. *Governor*, P. C. Mortimore

FELTHAM (DOC), Bedfont Road, Feltham, Middx. TW13 4ND. *Governor*, J. Whitty

GLEN PARVA (DIA), Tigers Road, Wigston, Leics. LE8 2TN. *Governor*, C. Williams

GUYS MARSH (DIA), Shaftesbury, Dorset SP7 0AH. *Governor*, P. B. Tucker

HATFIELD (DIP), Hatfield, Doncaster DN7 6EL. *Governor*, W. J. Clark

HOLLESLEY BAY COLONY (DOC), Hollesley, Woodbridge, Suffolk IP12 3JS. *Governor*, M. F. Clarke

HUNTERCOMBE (DIA), Huntercombe Place, Nuffield, Henley-on-Thames RG9 5SB. *Governor*, Miss A. W. Hair

LANCASTER FARMS (DIP), Stone Row Head, off Quernmore Road, Lancaster LA1 3QZ. *Governor*, D. J. Waplington

*NEW HALL (DIP), Dial Wood, Flockton, Wakefield WF4 4AX. *Governor*, D. England

NORTHALLERTON (DIP), East Road, Northallerton, N. Yorks. DL6 1NW. *Governor*, D. P. G. Appleton

ONLEY (DIA), Willoughby, Rugby, Warks. CV23 8AP. *Governor*, J. O'Neill

PORTLAND (DIA), Easton, Portland, Dorset DT5 1DL. *Governor*, D. Brisco

PRESCOED (DIA), 29 Maryport Street, Usk, Gwent NP4 0TD. *Governor*, N. J. Evans

STOKE HEATH (DIA), Market Drayton, Salop TF9 2JL. *Governor*, J. Alldridge

*STYAL (DIP), Wilmslow, Cheshire, SK9 4HR. *Governor*, G. Walker

SWINFEN HALL (DIA), Lichfield, Staffs. WS14 9QS. *Governor*, A. J. Davis

THORN CROSS (DIP), Arley Road, Appleton Thorn, Warrington WA4 4RL. *Governor*, I. Windebank

WERRINGTON (DIA), Stoke-on-Trent ST9 0DX. *Governor*, K. Naisbitt

WETHERBY (DIP), York Road, Wetherby, W. Yorks. LS22 5ED. *Governor*, P. J. Atkinson

---

*Women's establishments/establishments with units for women

REMAND CENTRES

BRINSFORD (DIA), New Road, Featherstone,
Wolverhampton WV10 7PY. *Governor,* P. J. Earnshaw
CARDIFF (DIA), Knox Road, Cardiff CF2 1UG. *Governor,*
N. D. Clifford
EXETER (DIA), New North Road, Exeter, Devon EX4 4EX.
Governor, D. Alderson
FELTHAM (DOC), Bedfont Road, Feltham, Middx.
TW13 4ND. *Governor,* J. Whitty
GLEN PARVA (DIA), Tigers Road, Wigston, Leics.
LE8 2TN. *Governor,* C. Williams
LOW NEWTON (DIP), Brasside, Durham DHI 5SD.
Governor, A. Holman
NORWICH (DOC), Mousehold, Norwich, Norfolk NRI 4LU.
Governor, Miss J. M. Fowler
PUCKLECHURCH (DIA), Bristol BSI7 3QJ. *Governor,*
P. Mortimore
READING (DIA), Forbury Road, Reading, Berks. RGI 3HY.
Governor, P. Dixon
STOKE HEATH (DIA), Market Drayton, Salop TF9 2JL.
Governor, J. Alldridge
THE WOLDS (private remand prison), Everthorpe, Brough,
N. Humberside HUI5 2JZ. *Controller,* Mrs P. Midgley

INSPECTORATE OF PRISONS
HM Chief Inspector of Prisons, His Hon. Judge Tumim
HM Deputy Chief Inspector of Prisons (G5), B. V. Smith
HM Inspectors, C. Allen; J. Gallagher; E. Hornblow;
D. Longley; D. A. Strong; B. J. Wells
Principal (G7), S. E. Bass

ESTABLISHMENT, FINANCE, FIRE AND EMERGENCY PLANNING DEPARTMENTS

Deputy Under-Secretary (G2), T. C. Platt

ESTABLISHMENT DEPARTMENT
Assistant Under-Secretary of State (G3), C. L. Scoble
  (Personnel, Organization and Management Services)
Heads of Divisions (G5), J. F. Acton; M. D. Boyle;
B. W. Buck; B. M. Caffarey; Mrs E. I. France
Senior Principals (G6), R. C. Case; J. G. Daly;
A. W. Gillman; D. J. Grant; D. C. Houghton;
S. E. Wharton
Principals (G7), Miss M. A. Allibone; K. Aylen;
F. Bannister; W. Black; P. Buley; M. Carr; A. Fishwick;
J. Fleming; Mrs S. Fleming; Mrs G. C. Hackett;
R. A. Hemmings; W. Heppolette; M. C. Jennings;
D. G. Jones; A. J. Lewis; R. T. Lewis; Ms
P. B. McFarlane; Miss F. Miller; Mrs J. Morgan; Mrs
B. Moxon; J. T. Neil; H. O'Connor; Miss A. Reece;
R. Ritchie; G. R. Sampher; T. Sargent; N. Shackleford;
A. Silver; P. A. Stanton; M. Walsh; T. Ward;
A. T. Williams; N. L. Willson; Mrs L. Wishart

ASSESSMENT CONSULTANCY UNIT
Director (G5), Miss S. E. Paul
Deputy Director (G6), G. J. Jones
Principal Psychologist (G7), D. J. Murray

PUBLIC RELATIONS BRANCH
Director of Information Services (G4), A. E. Moorey
Deputy Director of Information Services (G6), J. G. Blakeway
Head Publicity Officer (G6), C. Skinner

FINANCE DEPARTMENT
Assistant Under-Secretary of State (Principal Finance Officer)
  (G3), S. G. Norris
Heads of Divisions (G5), B. O. Bubbear; J. L. Haugh;
J. A. Ingman; G. C. Robertson
Senior Principals (G6), K. Cole; P. G. Davies;
T. A. S. Devon; R. Eagle; A. K. Holman; J. Nicholson

Principals (G7), B. D. Bishop; D. Burge; Mrs C. Burrows;
G. Cassell; K. I. Cole; Mrs M. Cooper; R. Daniels;
T. A. S. Daniels; C. I. Dickinson; G. J. Edwards;
F. H. Eggleston; B. Elliott; Mrs D. Grainger; C. Harnett;
C. Harwood; S. Hobbs; P. W. Jones; D. J. Kent;
G. Laing; M. Lee; S. Limpkin; Miss D. Loudon; Ms
C. Pelham; Mrs P. Poyton; R. P. Ritchie; C. Roden;
I. F. Rutherford; P. Sheehan; I. F. Smith; P. T. Smith,
Mrs F. Spencer; Mrs M. Thomas

FIRE AND EMERGENCY PLANNING DEPARTMENT
Assistant Under-Secretary of State (G3), W. J. A. Innes
Civil Emergencies Adviser, D. C. G. Brook, CB, CBE
Heads of Divisions (G5), P.E. Bolton; R. J. Miles; Dr
D. M. S. Peace
Grade 6, D. R. Dewick; D. Meakin
Principals (G7), Dr S. S. Athwal; D. Boyle; Dr G. A. Carr-
Hill; N. M. Clowes; E. Cook; Mrs P. E. Culley;
C. I. Dickinson; R. C. Eaton; J. A. Foster; Dr
J. A. Harwood; A. E. Mantle; M. A. Parker; D. A. Peters;
A. N. Pickersgill; Dr G. E. Scott; R. C. Stephen; Dr
M. D. Thomas; K. Wallace

HM FIRE SERVICE INSPECTORATE
HM Chief Inspector, Sir Reginald Doyle, CBE
HM Inspectors, S. D. Christian; B. T. A. Collins, OBE;
A. F. Kilford; N. Musselwhite, QFSM; E. G. Pearn, QFSM;
K. T. Phillips; D. Ritchie; A. V. Rule, QFSM; D. Spencer;
G. K. Tinley; A. C. Wells, QFSM; D. Wright
Senior Engineering Inspector, R. M. Simpson, OBE
Principal (G7), K. O'Sullivan

FIRE SERVICE COLLEGE
Moreton-in-Marsh, Glos. GL56 0RH
Tel 0608-50831

An executive agency within the Home Office
Chief Executive, B. Fuller, CBE
Deputy Chief Executive, A. Salisbury
Director of Studies, Dr R. Willis-Lee
Secretary (G7), J. A. Gundersen

EMERGENCY PLANNING COLLEGE
The Hawkhills, Easingwold, Yorks. YO6 3EG
Tel 0347-21406

Head of College (G5), J. B. Bettridge, CBE
Vice-Principal, Col. H. H. Evans

PASSPORT AGENCY
Clive House, Petty France, London SW1H 9HD
Tel 071-271 3000

An executive agency within the Home Office
Chief Executive (G5), J. E. Hayzelden
Deputy Chief Executive and Director of Operations (G6), Miss
A. Smith
Director of Planning and Resources (G6), N. S. Benger
Director of Systems (G6), T. Lonsdale
Principals (G7), J. Burgess; M. Copley; E. Downham;
R. G. Le Marechal; R. I. Henderson; J. McColl

HORSERACE TOTALISATOR BOARD
74 Upper Richmond Road, London SW15 2SU
Tel 081-874 6411

The Horserace Totalisator Board was established by the
Betting, Gaming and Lotteries Act 1963, as successor to the
Racecourse Betting Control Board. Its function is to operate
totalisators on approved racecourses in Great Britain, and it

also provides on- and off-course cash and credit offices. Under the Horserace Totalisator and Betting Levy Board Act 1972, it is further empowered to offer bets at starting price (or other bets at fixed odds) on any sporting event. The chairman and members of the Board are appointed by the Home Secretary.

Chairman (£92,000), The Lord Wyatt of Weeford
Members, B. McDonnell (*Chief Executive*); The Hon.
J. Deedes; T. J. Phillips (*Finance*); J. F. Sanderson;
The Hon. D. Sieff; The Lord Swaythling

HOUSING CORPORATION
149 Tottenham Court Road, London WIP OBN
Tel 071-387 9466

Established by Parliament in 1964, the Housing Corporation registers, promotes, funds and supervises housing associations. The Corporation's duties were extended under the provisions of the Housing Act 1988 to cover the payment of capital and revenue grants to housing associations, advice for tenants interested in Tenants' Choice, and the approval and revocation of potential new landlords under this policy.

There are over 2,300 registered associations in England providing more than 600,000 homes for people in need of housing. Housing associations are non-profit making bodies run by voluntary committees. In 1992–3, 62,137 homes were made available for rent or low-cost sale.

Chairman, Sir Christopher Benson
Chief Executive, A. Mayer

HUMAN FERTILIZATION AND EMBRYOLOGY AUTHORITY
Paxton House, 30 Artillery Lane, London EI 7LS
Tel 071-377 5077

The Authority was established under the Human Fertilization and Embryology Act 1990. Its function is to license persons carrying out any of the following activities: the creation or use of embryos outside the body in the provision of infertility treatment services; the use of donated gametes in infertility treatment; the storage of gametes or embryos; and research on human embryos. The Authority also keeps under review information about embryos and, when requested to do so, gives advice to the Secretary of State for Health.

Chairman, Prof. C. Campbell
Deputy Chairman, Lady Brittan
Members, Prof. R. J. Berry; Prof. I. Cooke; Prof. A. Cox; Ms
J. Denton; Ms E. Forgan; Ms J. Harbison; Dr S. Hillier;
PH.D.; Prof. B. Hoggett, QC; The Most Revd
R. Holloway; Ms P. Keith; Ms A. Mays; Dr A. McLaren;
Dr J. Naish; Rabbi Julia Neuberger; Prof. R. W. Shaw;
D. Shilson; Prof. R. Snowden; Ms C. Walby;
Prof. D. Whittingham
Chief Executive, Mrs F. Goldhill

INDEPENDENT REVIEW SERVICE FOR THE SOCIAL FUND
Millbank Tower, 21–24 Millbank, London, SWIP 4QU
Tel 071-217 4799
4th Floor, Centre City Podium, 5 Hill Street,
Birmingham B5 4UB
Tel 021-631 4000

The Social Fund Commissioner is appointed by the Secretary of State for Social Security. The Commissioner

appoints Social Fund Inspectors, who provide an independent review of decisions made by Social Fund Officers in the Benefits Agency of the Department of Social Security.

Social Fund Commissioner, Mrs R. Mackworth

INDEPENDENT TELEVISION COMMISSION
33 Foley Street, London WIP 7LB
Tel 071-255 3000

The Independent Television Commission replaced the Independent Broadcasting Authority at the beginning of 1991 under the terms of the Broadcasting Act 1990. The Commission is responsible for licensing and regulating all commercially funded UK television services.

Chairman (£56,809), Sir George Russell, CBE
Deputy Chairman, J. Stevens
Members, Earl of Dalkeith; Prof. J. F. Fulton; Ms
P. Mathias; Lady Popplewell; Prof. J. Ring; P. Sheth;
R. Goddard; Mrs E. Wynne Jones
Chief Executive, D. Glencross
Secretary, M. Redley

INDUSTRIAL INJURIES ADVISORY COUNCIL
6th Floor, The Adelphi, 1–11 John Adam Street, London
WC2N 6HT
Tel 071-962 8066

The Industrial Injuries Advisory Council is a statutory body under the Social Security Act 1975 which considers and advises the Secretary of State for Social Security on regulations and other questions relating to industrial injuries benefits or their administration.

Chairman, Prof. J. M. Harrington, CBE
Members, P. Arscott; Dr J. Asherson; Miss J. C. Brown; Mrs
J. Carter; Prof. M. J. Cinnamond; Dr D. Coggon;
Prof. A. Dayan; Dr C. P. Juniper; T. Mawer;
Prof. A. J. Newman Taylor; R. Pickering; Dr E. Roman;
Dr C. Taylor; O. Tudor; Ms M. Twomey
Secretary, R. Heigh

CENTRAL OFFICE OF INFORMATION
Hercules Road, London SEI 7DU
Tel 071-928 2345

The Central Office of Information (COI) is the government executive agency which provides publicity and information services to government departments, other executive agencies and public sector bodies. It provides consultancy, design, production, procurement and project management services for a wide range of publicity services in all media. Though the majority of COI's work is for government departments in the UK, it also produces a range of publicity materials for overseas consumption.

Administrative responsibility for the COI rests with the Minister of Public Service and Science, while the ministers whose departments it serves are responsible for the policy expressed in its work.

*Chief Executive and Head of the Government Information
Service* (*G3*), G. M. Devereau
Private Secretary and Parliamentary Clerk, vacant
Senior Personal Secretary, Mrs J. Rodrigues

MANAGEMENT BOARD
Members, G. M. Devereau; J. Bolitho; K. Williamson;
  R. Windsor; D. A. Low
Secretary, Miss K. Gliding

MARKETING AND CLIENT SERVICES GROUP
Group Director (G5), J. Bolitho
*Head, Business Development and Communications Services
  (G7)*, W. Roberts

CAMPAIGNS GROUP
Group Director (G5), R. Windsor
Director, Advertising (G6), M. Brodie
Director, Research (G6), vacant
Director, Direct Marketing (G7), C. Noble

PUBLICATIONS, PRESS AND EXHIBITIONS
Group Director (G5), D. A. Low
Director, Press and PR (G6), vacant
Director, Publications (G6), J. Murray
Director, Reference and Translations (G6), D. Beynon
Director, Exhibitions and Pictures (G6), D. Beynon
Director, Films Television and Radio Division (G6),
  M. Nisbet
Principal Finance Officer (G5), K. Williamson
Principal Establishment Officer (G6), M. Langhorne

NETWORK AND EMERGENCY PLANNING SERVICES
GROUP
Group Director (G5), J. Bolitho

NETWORK OFFICES
EASTERN, Three Crowns House, 72–80 Hills Road,
  Cambridge CB2 1LL. *Network Director (G7)*, Mrs
  V. Burdon
LONDON AND SOUTH-EAST, Lincoln House, Westminster
  Bridge Road, London SE1 7DU. *Network Director (G6)*,
  D. Smith
MIDLANDS, Five Ways Tower, Frederick Road,
  Edgbaston, Birmingham B15 1SH. *Network Director (G6)*,
  O. J. B. Prince-White
NORTH-EAST, Wellbar House, Gallowgate, Newcastle
  upon Tyne NE1 4TB. *Network Director (G7)*, H. Cozens
NORTH-WEST, Sunley Tower, Piccadilly Plaza,
  Manchester M1 4BD. *Network Director (G7)*, Mrs E. Jones
SOUTH-WEST, The Pithay, Bristol BS1 2NF. *Network
  Director (G7)*, B. Garner
YORKSHIRE AND HUMBERSIDE, City House, New Station
  Street, Leeds LS1 4JG. *Network Director (G6)*,
  R. P. Haslam

BOARD OF INLAND REVENUE
Somerset House, London WC2R 1LB
Tel 071-438 6622

The Board of Inland Revenue was constituted under the
Inland Revenue Board Act 1849, by the consolidation of the
Board of Excise and the Board of Stamps and Taxes. In 1909
the administration of excise duties was transferred to the
Board of Customs. The Board of Inland Revenue administers
and collects direct taxes – mainly income tax, stamp duty,
development land tax and petroleum revenue tax – and
advises the Chancellor of the Exchequer on policy questions
involving them.
  The Department is organized into a series of accountable
management units under the Next Steps programme. The
day-to-day operations in assessing and collecting tax and in
providing internal support services are carried out by 34

Executive Offices. The Department's Valuation Office is an
executive agency responsible for valuing property for tax
purposes, for compensation, for compulsory purchase, and
(in England and Wales) for local rating purposes. In 1991–2
the Inland Revenue collected over £79,675 million in tax.

THE BOARD
Chairman (G1), Sir Anthony Battishill, KCB
  Private Secretary, G. Lloyd
  Assistant Private Secretary, Miss F. Huskisson
Deputy Chairmen (G2), S. C. T. Matheson, CB;
  L. J. H. Beighton, CB
Director-General (G2), C. W. Corlett

SUBJECT DIVISIONS
Directors (G3), E. McGivern; M. F. Cayley; B. Mace;
  M. Templeman; P. Lewis; I. R. Spence; E. J. Gribbon
Senior Principal Inspectors of Taxes (G4), R. H. Allen;
  R. E. Creed; R. N. Page, CBE; M. A. Keith; R. M. Elliss;
  R. E. Haigh; D. L. Shaw; P. R. P. Stokes; A. J. O'Brien;
  B. Sadler
Grade 5, R. B. Willis; L. E. Jaundoo; I. Stewart; C. Stewart;
  Miss R. A. Dyall; M. T. Evans; M. D. R. Haigh;
  R. Warden; C. D. Sullivan; J. P. B. Bryce; P. W. Fawcett;
  J. B. Shepherd; M. J. G. Elliott; C. S. McNicol; Miss
  S. P. B. Walker; P. A. Michael; Mrs C. B. Hubbard
Principal Inspectors of Taxes (G5), B. Jones; J. H. Keelty;
  A. P. Beauchamp; Mrs M. E. Williams; R. S. Hurcombe;
  J. E. Morris; M. D. Phelps; M. Waters; A. H. Williams;
  P. H. Linford; J. F. McCormick; Mrs D. Hay; K. Hamer;
  J. F. Gilhooly; S. P. Norris; Dr C. Howard; R. J. Gill;
  R. Thomas

STATISTICS AND ECONOMICS OFFICE
Director (G3), J. R. Calder
Grade 5, Dr G. A. Keenay; Dr G. J. Parker; R. J. Eason;
  E. Ko
Information Technology (G6), Dr R. James
Senior Economics Adviser (G5), W. M. McNie

INFORMATION TECHNOLOGY OFFICE
Director (G3), J. E. Yard
Director, Strategic Partnership Project (G3), G. H. Bush
Divisional Directors (G5), R. A. Assirati; P. W. Booth;
  D. B. Topple; R. H. Wearing

PERSONNEL DIRECTORATE
Director of Personnel (G3), J. Gant
Deputy Directors (G4), R. Neilson; N. C. Munro
Assistant Directors (G5), A. Pardoe; J. Eastman; S. Mitha;
  (G6), M. Jarrett; R. Cartwright; A. J. Walker

MANPOWER AND SUPPORT SERVICES
Director (G4), R. R. Martin
Assistant Directors (G5), J. Gray; R. P. R. Tilley;
  D. E. Adam; T. A. Lawson; S. T. Ayling; *(G6)*,
  M. K. Robins

TRAINING OFFICE
Royal Exchange House, Boar Lane, Leeds LS1 5PG
Controller (G5), D. J. Timmons

CENTRAL DIVISION
Director (G3), M. A. Johns
Grade 5, R. Golding; B. Glassberg

CHANGE MANAGEMENT GROUP
Head (G4), D. A. Smith

CORPORATE COMMUNICATIONS OFFICE
Controller (G5), B. Hooper
Press Secretary (G7), Mrs S. J. Bradley

FINANCE DIVISION
Principal Finance Officer (G3), J. M. Crawley, CB
Grade 5, J. H. Reed; J. R. Cavell; Miss M. A. Hill;
R. F. Moore

INTERNAL AUDIT OFFICE
22 Kingsway, London WC2B 6NR
Chief Internal Auditor (G5), N. R. Buckley

FINANCIAL SERVICES OFFICE
Barrington Road, Worthing, W. Sussex BN12 4XH
Controller (G6), J. D. Easey

FINANCIAL AND MANAGEMENT ACCOUNTING SYSTEMS
OFFICE
Barrington Road, Worthing, W. Sussex BN12 4XH
Controller (G6), C. R. F. Jury

SOLICITOR FOR INLAND REVENUE
Solicitor (G2), B. E. Cleave
Principal Assistant Solicitors (G3), J. D. H. Johnston;
J. G. H. Bates; G. F. Butt
Assistant Solicitors (G5), Miss M. P. E. Boland; A. J. Gunz;
A. K. S. Shaw; A. P. Douglas; W. J. Durrans; S. Bousher;
R. S. Waterson; R. F. Walters; Miss A. Hawkins;
K. Brown; R. W. Thornhill; Miss A. E. Wyman;
R. J. Alderman; Mrs M. A. Gilbert
Board's Advisory Accountant (G5), T. C. Carne

SOLICITOR OF INLAND REVENUE (SCOTLAND)
80 Lauriston Place, Edinburgh EH3 9SL
Solicitor, T. H. Scott

DIRECTORATE, OPERATIONS 1
Director (G3), K. V. Deacon
Deputy Directors (G4), D. W. Muir; R. Massingale
Assistant Directors (G5), T. R. Evans; J. M. Thomas;
J. W. Calder; E. C. Jones; A. McClure; S. J. McManus;
J. P. Gilbody; Dr E. A. Harrison; M. G. Oakley;
D. W. Swift; S. Hartlib

REGIONAL OFFICES
INLAND REVENUE EAST, Midgate House, Peterborough
PE1 1TD
INLAND REVENUE EAST LONDON, New Court, Carey
Street, London WC2A 2JE
INLAND REVENUE GREATER MANCHESTER, Apsley
House, Wellington Road North, Stockport SK4 1EY
INLAND REVENUE MIDLANDS, Chadwick House,
Blenheim Court, Solihull, W. Midlands B91 2AA
INLAND REVENUE NORTH, Corporation House, 73 Albert
Road, Middlesbrough, Cleveland TS1 2RD
INLAND REVENUE NORTH AND WEST LONDON, New
Court, Carey Street, London WC2A 2JE
INLAND REVENUE NORTH-WEST, The Triad, Stanley
Road, Bootle, Merseyside L20 3PD
INLAND REVENUE SOUTH-EAST, Albion House, Chertsey
Road, Woking GU21 1BT
INLAND REVENUE SOUTH LONDON, New Court, Carey
Street, London WC2A 2JE
INLAND REVENUE SOUTH-WEST, Finance House,
Barnfield Road, Exeter EX1 1QX
INLAND REVENUE SOUTH YORKSHIRE, Sovereign
House, 110 Queen Street, Sheffield S1 2DU
INLAND REVENUE WALES, Ty Rodfa, Ty Glas Avenue,
Llanishen, Cardiff CF4 5TS
INLAND REVENUE SCOTLAND, 80 Lauriston Place,
Edinburgh EH3 9SL
INLAND REVENUE NORTHERN IRELAND, Dorchester
House, 52–58 Great Victoria Street, Belfast BT2 7QE

DIRECTORATE, OPERATIONS 2
Director (G3), J. H. Roberts
Deputy Director (G4), P. C. Fielder

SPECIAL COMPLIANCE OFFICE
Angel Court, 199 Borough High Street, London SE1 1HZ
Controller (G4), F. J. Brannigan
Grade 5, J. T. Cawdron; J. Mawson, D. F. Parrett;
G. W. Lunn
Board's Investigating Officer (G6), F. B. Dunbar

CLAIMS BRANCH
St John's House, Merton Road, Bootle L69 9BB
Controller (G5), D. A. Hartnett

CLAIMS BRANCH (SCOTLAND)
Trinity Park House, South Trinity Road, Edinburgh
EH5 3SD
Officer in Charge (G7), J. Duguid

PENSION SCHEMES OFFICE
Lynwood Road, Thames Ditton, Surrey KT7 0DP
Controller (G5), R. G. Lusk, CBE

THE STAMP OFFICE
South-West Wing, Bush House, Strand, London WC2B 4QN
Controller (G6), K. S. Hodgson

THE STAMP OFFICE (SCOTLAND)
Mulberry House, 16 Picardy Place, Edinburgh EH1 3NF
Controller, D. G. Hunter

CAPITAL TAXES OFFICE
Minford House, Rockley Road, London W14 0DF
Controller (G4), B. D. Kent
Deputy Controllers (G5), H. V. Capon; A. G. Nield;
R. J. Draper
Assistant Controllers (G6), D. J. Ferley; B. K. Lakhanpaul;
T. J. Plumb; P. R. Twiddy; C. A. Oldridge; F. A. Cook;
R. J. Shanks; N. S. Tant; M. J. Francis; A. D. Tytherleigh

CAPITAL TAXES OFFICE (SCOTLAND)
Mulberry House, 16 Picardy Place, Edinburgh, EH1 3NB
Registrar (G5), I. Fraser
Deputy Registrar (G6), W. Young
Chief Examiners (G7), Mrs J. A. Templeton; Miss
K. M. Patrick; D. McL. Paterson; T. E. Naysmith;
J. Telford; C. G. Hogg; Miss A. Forbes

OFFICE OF THE INSPECTOR OF FOREIGN DIVIDENDS
Lynwood Road, Thames Ditton, Surrey KT7 0DP
Inspector of Foreign Dividends (G6), T. R. Diggins

OIL TAXATION OFFICE
Melbourne House, Aldwych, London WC2B 4LL
Controller (G4), R. C. Mountain
Grade 5, K. Cartwright; I. M. Griffin; D. Newlyn;
D. J. Slattery; M. Wright

THE VALUATION OFFICE EXECUTIVE AGENCY
New Court, 48 Carey Street, London WC2A 2JE
Tel 071-324 1183/1057
Meldrum House, 15 Drumsheugh Gardens, Edinburgh
EH3 7UN
Tel 031-225 8511

Chief Executive (G2), R. R. B. Shutler, CB
Deputy Chief Executives (G3), A. J. Langford (*Management*);
R. J. Pawley (*Technical*)
Chief Valuer, Scotland (G5), A. MacLaren

INQUIRY INTO EXPORTS OF DEFENCE EQUIPMENT AND DUAL-USE GOODS TO IRAQ
Room 2.2.5, 1 Palace Street, London SW1E 5HE
Tel 071-238 3799; *Media:* 071-238 3809

Lord Justice Scott was asked by the President of the Board of Trade, after the collapse of the Matrix Churchill case in November 1992, to examine the facts in relation to the export from the United Kingdom of defence equipment and dual-use goods to Iraq between December 1984 and 1990 and the decisions reached on the export licence applications for such goods and the basis for them; to report on whether the relevant departments, agencies and responsible ministers operated in accordance with the policies of the Government; to examine and report on decisions taken by the prosecuting authority and by those signing public interest immunity certificates in R. v. Henderson and any other similar cases that Lord Justice Scott considers relevant to the issues of the inquiry; and to make recommendations.
Inquiry headed by The Rt. Hon. Lord Justice Scott
Secretary to the Inquiry (G5), C. P. J. Muttukumaru
Counsel to the Inquiry, Ms P. Baxendale, QC
Assistant Secretary (G7), P. Regan
Media Relations Officer (G6), D. Price

INTERCEPTION COMMISSIONER
c/o The Home Office, 50 Queen Anne's Gate, London SW1H 9AT

The Commissioner is appointed by the Prime Minister. He keeps under review the issue by the Home Secretary of warrants under the Interception of Communications Act 1985 and safeguards made in respect of intercepted material obtained through the use of such warrants. He is also required to give all such assistance as the Interception of Communications Tribunal may require to enable it to carry out its functions, and to submit an annual report to the Prime Minister with respect to the carrying out of his functions.
Commissioner, The Rt. Hon. Sir Thomas Bingham

INTERCEPTION OF COMMUNICATIONS TRIBUNAL
PO Box 44, London SE1 0TX

The Tribunal comprises senior members of the legal profession, who are appointed by The Queen. Under the Interception of Communications Act 1985, the Tribunal is required to investigate applications from any person who believes that communications sent to or by them have been intercepted in the course of their transmission by post or by means of a public telecommunications system.
President, The Hon. Mr Justice Macpherson of Cluny
Vice-President, Sir Cecil Clothier, KCB, QC
Members, Sir David Calcutt, QC; I. Guild, CBE; P. Scott, QC

INTERVENTION BOARD
Fountain House, Queen's Walk, Reading RG1 7QW
Tel 0734-583626

The Intervention Board was established as a government department in 1972 and became operational in 1973. It became an executive agency in April 1990. The Board is responsible for the implementation of European Community regulations covering the market support arrangements of the Common Agricultural Policy. Members of the Board are appointed by and are responsible to the Minister of Agriculture, Fisheries and Food and the Secretaries of State for Scotland, Wales and Northern Ireland.
Chairman, A. J. Ellis, CBE
Chief Executive (G3), G. Stapleton

HEADS OF DIVISIONS
Finance Division (G5), J. N. Diserens
External Trade Division (G5), G. N. Dixon
Crops Division (G5), H. MacKinnon
Livestock Products Division (G5), M. J. Griffiths
Corporate Services Division (G5), J. W. M. Peffers
Legal Division (G5), T. Middleton
Chief Accountant (G6), R. Bryant
External Operations (G6), J. P. Bradbury
Procurement and Supply (G6), P. J. Offer
Information Technology (G6), T. T. Simpson

LAND AUTHORITY FOR WALES
The Custom House, Customhouse Street, Cardiff CF1 5AP
Tel 0222-223444

The Authority is responsible for acquiring and disposing of land for private development in Wales.

Chairman (part-time) (£31,625), Sir Geoffrey Inkin, OBE
Chief Executive, B. Ryan, FRICS

LAND REGISTRIES

HM LAND REGISTRY
Lincoln's Inn Fields, London WC2A 3PH
Tel 071-917 8888

The registration of title to land was first introduced in England and Wales by the Land Registry Act 1862; HM Land Registry operates today under the Land Registration Acts 1925 to 1988. The object of registering title to land is to create and maintain a register of land owners whose title is guaranteed by the state and so to simplify the transfer, mortgage and other dealings with real property. Compulsory registration on sale was introduced in stages affecting only certain areas but it is now compulsory throughout England and Wales. The register, which used to be private and could only be inspected with the consent of the registered proprietor, became open to inspection by the public on 3 December 1990.

HM Land Registry is an executive agency administered under the Lord Chancellor by the Chief Land Registrar. The work is decentralized to a number of regional offices. The Chief Land Registrar is also responsible for the Land Charges Department and the Agricultural Credits Department.

HEADQUARTERS OFFICE
Chief Land Registrar and Chief Executive (G2), J. J. Manthorpe
Solicitor to Land Registry (G3), C. J. West
Senior Land Registrar (G5), Mrs J. G. Totty
Principal Establishment Officer (G4), E. G. Beardsall
Director of Operations (G5), G. N. French
Director of Information Technology (G5), R. J. Fenn
Director of Management Services (G6), P. J. Smith
Land Registrar (G5), M. L. Wood

Deputy Establishment Officer (G6), J. Hodder
Controller of Operations Development (G6), P. R. Laker

BIRKENHEAD DISTRICT LAND REGISTRY
Old Market House, Hamilton Street, Birkenhead L41 5FL
Tel 051-473 1110
District Land Registrar (G5), M. G. Garwood
Area Manager (G6), J. Eccles

COVENTRY DISTRICT LAND REGISTRY
Greyfriars Business Centre, 2 Eaton Road, Coventry CV1 2SD
Tel 0203-632442
District Land Registrar (G5), S. P. Kelway
Area Manager (G6), J. C. Lillistone

CROYDON DISTRICT LAND REGISTRY
Sunley House, Bedford Park, Croydon CR9 3LE
Tel 081-781 9100
District Land Registrar (G5), D. M. J. Moss
Area Manager (G6), V. J. C. Shorney

DURHAM DISTRICT LAND REGISTRY
Southfield House, Southfield Way, Durham DH1 5TR
Tel 091-301 3500
District Land Registrar (G5), C. W. Martin
Area Manager (G6), B. Warriner

GLOUCESTER DISTRICT LAND REGISTRY
Twyver House, Bruton Way, Gloucester GL1 1DQ
Tel 0452-511111
District Land Registrar (G5), W. W. Budden
Area Manager (G6), R. B. Johnson

HARROW DISTRICT LAND REGISTRY
Lyon House, Lyon Road, Harrow, Middx. HA1 2EU
Tel 081-427 8811
District Land Registrar (G5), J. V. Timothy
Area Manager (G6), M. J. Wyatt

KINGSTON UPON HULL DISTRICT LAND REGISTRY
Earle House, Portland Street, Hull HU2 8JN
Tel 0482-223244
District Land Registrar (G5), S. R. Coveney
Area Manager (G6), E. Howard

LAND CHARGES AND AGRICULTURAL CREDITS
DEPARTMENT
Burrington Way, Plymouth PL5 3LP
Tel 0752-779831
Superintendent of Land Charges (G7), H. Myers

LEICESTER DISTRICT LAND REGISTRY
Thames Tower, 99 Burleys Way, Leicester LE1 3UB
Tel 0533-654000
District Land Registrar (G6), Mrs J. A. Goodfellow
Area Manager (G7), G. M. Johns

LYTHAM DISTRICT LAND REGISTRY
Birkenhead House, Lytham St Annes, Lancs. FY8 5AB
Tel 0253-736999
District Land Registrar (G5), J. G. Cooper
Area Manager (G6), B. Elliott

NOTTINGHAM DISTRICT LAND REGISTRY
Chalfont Drive, Nottingham NG8 3RN
Tel 0602-291166
District Land Registrar (G5), P. J. Timothy
Area Manager (G6), W. Whitaker

PETERBOROUGH DISTRICT LAND REGISTRY
Touthill Close, City Road, Peterborough PE1 1XN
Tel 0733-288288
District Land Registrar (G5), L. M. Pope
Area Manager (G6), B. J. Andrews

PLYMOUTH DISTRICT LAND REGISTRY
Plumer House, Tailyour Road, Crownhill, Plymouth PL6 5HY
Tel 0752-701234
District Land Registrar (G5), A. J. Pain
Area Manager(G6), K. Robinson

PORTSMOUTH DISTRICT LAND REGISTRY
St Andrews Court, St Michael's Road, Portsmouth PO1 2JH
Tel 0705-865022
District Land Registrar (G6), S. R. Sehrawat
Area Manager (G7), A. W. Howarth

STEVENAGE DISTRICT LAND REGISTRY
Brickdale House, Swingate, Stevenage, Herts. SG1 1XG
Tel 0438-313003
District Land Registrar (G5), C. Tate
Area Manager (G6), A. D. Gould

SWANSEA DISTRICT LAND REGISTRY
Tybryn Glas, High Street, Swansea SA1 1PW
Tel 0792-458877
District Land Registrar (G5), G. A. Hughes
Area Manager (G6), R. T. Davis

TELFORD DISTRICT LAND REGISTRY
Parkside Court, Hall Park Way, Telford TF3 4LR
Tel 0952-290355
District Land Registrar (G5), M. A. Roche
Area Manager (G6), R. D. Moseley

TUNBRIDGE WELLS DISTRICT LAND REGISTRY
Curtis House, Hawkenbury, Tunbridge Wells, Kent TN2 5AQ
Tel 0892-510015
District Land Registrar (G5), G. R. Tooke
Area Manager (G6), B. S. Crozier

WEYMOUTH DISTRICT LAND REGISTRY
1 Cumberland Drive, Weymouth, Dorset DT4 9TT
Tel 0305-776161
District Land Registrar (G5), Mrs P. M. Reeson
Area Manager (G6), J. Dodd

YORK DISTRICT LAND REGISTRY
James House, James Street, York YO1 3YZ
Tel 0904-450000
District Land Registrar (G6), Mrs R. F. Lovel
Area Manager (G7), P. Wright

COMPUTER SERVICES DIVISION
Burrington Way, Plymouth PL5 3LP
Tel 0752-779831
Head of Services Division (G6), P. A. Maycock
Head of Development Division (G6), R. J. Smith

REGISTERS OF SCOTLAND (EXECUTIVE
AGENCY)
Meadowbank House, 153 London Road, Edinburgh EH8 7AU
Tel 031-659 6111

The Registers of Scotland consist of: General Register of
Sasines and Land Register of Scotland; Register of Deeds in
the Books of Council and Session; Register of Protests;
Register of Judgments; Register of Service of Heirs; Register
of the Great Seal; Register of the Quarter Seal; Register of
the Prince's Seal; Register of Crown Grants; Register of
Sheriffs' Commissions; Register of the Cachet Seal; Register
of Inhibitions and Adjudications; Register of Entails; Register
of Hornings.

The General Register of Sasines and the Land Register of
Scotland form the chief security in Scotland of the rights of
land and other heritable (or real) property.
Keeper of the Registers of Scotland (G4), J. W. Barron
Senior Directors (G5), A. W. Ramage; A. G. Rennie

Senior Assistant Directors (G6), B. J. Corr; A. M. Falconer
Strategy Director (G6), D. Leslie
Assistant Directors (G7), D. G. Cant *(computers)*; R. Glen
(personnel); J. Knox *(Land Register)*; D. McCallum *(Land Register)*; L. J. Mitchell *(management services)*;
A. G. T. New *(Land Register)*; I. M. Nicol *(finance)*; Mrs
P. M. Stewart *(training)*
Assistant Keeper (G7), I. A. Davis
Grade 7, J. Anderson; J. F. Campbell; R. C. Clark; J. Cogle;
A. B. Farmer; J. S. McKinlay; D. Manson; J. B. Marshall;
Mrs A. Moore; W. F. Rankin; J. Rynn; M. J. Wilczynski

LAW COMMISSION
Conquest House, 37–38 John Street, Theobalds Road,
London WC1N 2BQ
Tel 071-411 1220

The Law Commission was set up in 1965, under the Law
Commissions Act 1965, to make proposals to the Government
for the examination of the law in England and Wales and for
its revision where it is unsuited for modern requirements,
obscure, or otherwise unsatisfactory. It recommends to the
Lord Chancellor programmes for the examination of different
branches of the law and suggests whether the examination
should be carried out by the Commission itself or by some
other body. The Commission is also responsible for the
preparation of Consolidation and Statute Law (Repeals) Bills.
Chairman, The Hon. Mr Justice Brooke
Members, J. Beatson; R. Buxton, QC; C. Harpum *(from Jan.
1994)*
Secretary, M. H. Collon

SCOTTISH LAW COMMISSION
140 Causewayside, Edinburgh EH9 1PR
Tel 031-668 2131

The Commission keeps the law in Scotland under review and
makes proposals for its development and reform.
Chairman, The Hon. Lord Davidson
Commissioners (full-time), Dr E. M. Clive; Sheriff
I. D. MacPhail, QC; *(part-time)* Prof. P. N. Love, CBE;
W. Nimmo Smith, QC
Secretary, K. F. Barclay

LAW OFFICERS' DEPARTMENTS
Attorney-General's Chambers, 9 Buckingham Gate,
London SW1E 6JP
Tel 071-828 7155
Attorney-General's Chambers, Royal Courts of Justice,
Belfast BT1 3JY
Tel 0232-235111

The Law Officers of the Crown for England and Wales are
the Attorney-General and the Solicitor-General. The Attorney-General, assisted by the Solicitor-General, is the chief
legal adviser to the Government and is also ultimately
responsible for all Crown litigation. He has overall responsibility for the work of the Law Officers' Departments (the
Treasury Solicitor's Department, the Crown Prosecution
Service, the Serious Fraud Office and the Legal Secretariat
to the Law Officers). He has a specific statutory duty to
superintend the discharge of their duties by the Director of

Public Prosecutions (who is head of the Crown Prosecution
Service) and the Director of the Serious Fraud Office. The
Director of Public Prosecutions for Northern Ireland is
responsible to the Attorney-General for the performance of
his functions. The Attorney-General has additional respon-
sibilities in relation to aspects of the civil and criminal law.
Attorney-General (*£42,314), The Rt. Hon. Sir Nicholas
Lyell, QC, MP
  Parliamentary Private Secretary, T. Devlin, MP
Solicitor-General (*£34,695), Sir Derek Spencer, QC, MP
  Parliamentary Private Secretary, G. Streeter, MP
Legal Secretary (G2), Miss J. L. Wheldon
Deputy Legal Secretary (G4), S. J. Wooler

LEGAL AID BOARD
5th and 6th Floors, 29–37 Red Lion Street, London WC1R 4PP
Tel 071-831 4209

The Legal Aid Board has the general function of ensuring
that advice, assistance and representation are available in
accordance with the Legal Aid Act 1988. In 1989 it took over
from the Law Society responsibility for administering legal
aid. The Board is a non-departmental government body
whose members are appointed by the Lord Chancellor.
Chairman, J. Pitts
Members, S. Orchard *(Chief Executive)*; M. Acland; Ms
D. Beale; P. Jones; D. Sinker; J. Smith; Ms V. Boakes;
F. Collins; Ms K. Markus; G. Pulman, QC; A. Thomas

SCOTTISH LEGAL AID BOARD
44 Drumsheugh Gardens, Edinburgh EH3 7SW
Tel 031-226 7061

The Scottish Legal Aid Board was set up under the Legal
Aid (Scotland) Act 1986. It is responsible for ensuring that
advice, assistance and representation are available in
accordance with the Act. The Board is a non-departmental
government body whose members are appointed by the
Secretary of State for Scotland.
Chairman, Mrs C. A. M. Davis
Members, G. Barrie; Mrs P. A. M. Bolton; Miss L. Clark,
QC; A. Gilchrist; Prof. P. H. Grinyer; G. D. Holmes, CB;
D. A. Leitch; R. J. Livingstone; Mrs I. G. McColl;
C. N. McEachran, QC; Sheriff R. G. McEwan, QC; Mrs
G. M. Peebles; Mrs M. Tait
Chief Executive, A. E. M. Douglas

OFFICE OF THE LEGAL SERVICES
OMBUDSMAN
22 Oxford Court, Oxford Street, Manchester M2 3WQ
Tel 061-236 9532

The Legal Services Ombudsman is appointed by the Lord
Chancellor under the Courts and Legal Services Act 1990 to
oversee the handling of complaints against solicitors,
barristers and licensed conveyancers by their professional
bodies. A complainant must first complain to the relevant
professional body before raising the matter with the
Ombudsman. The Ombudsman is independent of the legal
profession and his services are free of charge.

---

*Excluding reduced Parliamentary salary of £23,227

Legal Services Ombudsman, M. Barnes
Secretary (acting), S. Murray

LIBRARIES

THE BRITISH LIBRARY
2 Sheraton Street, London WIV 4BH
Tel 071-636 1544

The British Library is the UK's national library and occupies the central position in the library and information network. The Library aims to serve scholarship, research, industry, commerce and all other major users of information. Its services are based on collections which include over 18 million volumes, 1 million discs, and 55,000 hours of tape recordings, at 18 buildings in London and one complex in West Yorkshire. The British Library is in the process of moving to purpose-built accommodation at St Pancras, London NWI (open to the public in 1996).

The British Library was established in 1973 and brought together the library departments of the British Museum, the National Central Library, the National Lending Library for Science and Technology, the British National Bibliography Ltd and, in 1974, the Office for Scientific and Technical Information. Subsequently the Library took responsibility for the India Office Library and Records, the HMSO Binderies, and the National Sound Archive.

Access to the Humanities and Social Sciences reading rooms in Great Russell Street is limited to holders of a British Library Reader's Pass, and information about eligibility is available from the Reader Admissions Office. The Aldwych and Holborn reading rooms of the Science Reference and Information Service are open to the general public without charge or formality. The Library's exhibition galleries are housed in the British Museum building in Great Russell Street.

BRITISH LIBRARY BOARD
96 Euston Road, London NWI 2DB
Tel 071-323 7262

Chairman, Sir Anthony Kenny, D.Phil., D.Litt., FBA
Chief Executive and Deputy Chairman (G2), B. Lang
Directors-General (G4), J. M. Smethurst; D. Russon
Part-time Members, The Lord Adrian, MD, FRS; The Lord Windlesham, CVO, PC; Prof. A. S. Forty, Ph.D., D.SC.; Sir Robin Mackworth-Young, KCVO, FSA; R. E. Utiger, CBE; T. J. Rix; Dame Anne Warburton, DCVO, CMG; H. Heaney; D. Peake; The Rt. Revd M. A. Mann, KCVO; E. M. W. Griffith, CBE

BRITISH LIBRARY, BOSTON SPA
Boston Spa, Wetherby, W. Yorks. LS23 7BQ
Tel 0937-546000

Director-General (G4), D. Russon

DOCUMENT SUPPLY CENTRE
Tel 0937-546000
Director (G5), D. Bradbury

NATIONAL BIBLIOGRAPHIC SERVICE
Tel 0937-546585
Director (G6), S. J. Ede
London Unit, 2 Sheraton Street, London WIV 4BH. Tel: 071-323 7077

ACQUISITIONS PROCESSING AND CATALOGUING
Tel 0937-546000
Director (G5), Mrs J. E. Butcher

*COMPUTING AND TELECOMMUNICATIONS
2 Sheraton Street, London WIV 4BH
Tel 071-323 7210
Director (G5), J. R. Mahoney

BRITISH LIBRARY, LONDON
Great Russell Street, London WCIB 3DG
Tel 071-636 1544

Director-General (G4), J. M. Smethurst
St Pancras Project Director (G4), D. Lyman
Director of Project Services St Pancras Planning (G6), Dr R. Coman

ADMINISTRATION
2 Sheraton Street, London WIV 4BH
Tel 071-323 7132
Director (G5), R. Ball

PRESS AND PUBLIC RELATIONS
96 Euston Road, London NWI 2DB
Tel 071-323 7111
Head (G7), M. Jackson

PUBLIC SERVICES
Tel 071-323 7626
Director (G5), Dr D. Clements

EXHIBITIONS AND EDUCATION SERVICE. Tel: 071-323 7595

READER ADMISSIONS. Tel: 071-323 7677

HUMANITIES AND SOCIAL SCIENCES
Tel 071-323 7676
Director (G5), A. Phillips

WEST EUROPEAN COLLECTIONS, SLAVONIC AND EAST EUROPEAN COLLECTIONS, ENGLISH LANGUAGE COLLECTIONS. Tel: 071-323 7676
INFORMATION BRANCH, OFFICIAL PUBLICATIONS AND SOCIAL SCIENCE SERVICE. Tel: 071-323 7676
INFORMATION SCIENCES SERVICE (BLISS), Ridgmount Street, London WCIE 7AE. Tel: 071-323 7688
NEWSPAPER LIBRARY, Colindale Avenue, London NW9 5HE. Tel: 071-323 7353
NATIONAL SOUND ARCHIVE, 29 Exhibition Road, London SW7 2AS. Tel: 071-589 6603

COLLECTIONS AND PRESERVATION
Tel 071-323 7676
Director (G5), Dr M. Foot

PRESERVATION SERVICE (NATIONAL PRESERVATION OFFICE). Tel: 071-323 7612

SPECIAL COLLECTIONS
Tel 071-323 7513
Director (G5), Dr A. Prochaska

ORIENTAL AND INDIA OFFICE COLLECTIONS, 197 Blackfriars Road, London SEI 8NG. Tel: 071-412 7873
WESTERN MANUSCRIPTS. Tel: 071-323 7513
MAP LIBRARY. Tel: 071-323 7700

---

*Scheduled to relocate to Yorkshire by the mid-1990s

MUSIC LIBRARY. Tel: 071-323 7528
PHILATELIC COLLECTIONS. Tel: 071-323 7729

SCIENCE REFERENCE AND INFORMATION SERVICE
25 Southampton Buildings, London WC2A 1AW
Tel 071-323 7494
9 Kean Street, London WC2B 4AT
Tel 071-323 7288
Director (G5), A. Gomersall

RESEARCH AND DEVELOPMENT DEPARTMENT
2 Sheraton Street, London W1V 4BH
Tel 071-323 7060
Director (G6), B. J. Perry

NATIONAL LIBRARY OF SCOTLAND
George IV Bridge, Edinburgh EH1 1EW
Tel 031-226 4531

Opening hours: Reading Room, weekdays, 9.30–8.30 (Wed.,
10–8.30); Sat. 9.30–1. Map Library, weekdays, 9.30–5
(Wed., 10–5); Sat. 9.30–1. Exhibition, weekdays, 10–5; Sat.
10–5; Sun. 2–5. Scottish Science Library, weekdays, 9.30–5
(Wed., 9.30–8).

The Library, which was founded as the Advocates' Library
in 1682, became the National Library of Scotland by Act of
Parliament in 1925. It contains about 6,000,000 books and
pamphlets, 20,000 current periodicals, 230 newspaper titles
and 100,000 manuscripts. It has an unrivalled Scottish
collection.

The Reading Room is for reference and research which
cannot conveniently be pursued elsewhere. Admission is by
ticket issued to an approved applicant.

SALARIES

Librarian	£44,390–£49,790
Keeper	£27,760–£42,724
Curator Grade C	£24,239–£34,469

Chairman of the Trustees, The Earl of Crawford and
    Balcarres, PC
Librarian and Secretary to the Trustees, I. D. McGowan
Secretary of the Library, M. C. Graham
Curators Grade C, A. Cameron; W. Jackson; J. E. McIntyre
Keepers of Printed Books, A. M. Marchbank, PH.D.; Ms
    A. Matheson, PH.D.
Curators Grade C, T. A. Cherry; Ms A. E. Harvey Wood;
    B. P. Hillyard, D.Phil.; S. Holland; W. A. Kelly;
    J. M. Morris
Keeper of Manuscripts, I. C. Cunningham
Curators Grade C, I. G. Brown, PH.D., FSA; R. Duce;
    I. F. Maciver; S. M. Simpson; Ms J. M. Wilkes; Ms
    E. D. Yeo
Director of Computer Services and Research (Keeper),
    B. Gallivan
Curator Grade C, R. F. Guy
Director of Scottish Science Library (Keeper), Ms A. J. Bunch

NATIONAL LIBRARY OF WALES/LLYFRGELL
GENEDLAETHOL CYMRU
Aberystwyth, Dyfed SY23 3BU
Tel 0970-623816

Readers' room open weekdays, 9.30–6 (Sat. 9.30–5); closed
first week of October. Admission by Reader's Ticket.

The National Library of Wales was founded by Royal
Charter in 1907, and is maintained by annual grant from the
Treasury. It contains about 4,000,000 printed books, 40,000
manuscripts, 4,000,000 deeds and documents, numerous
maps, prints and drawings, and an audio-visual collection. It
specializes in manuscripts and books relating to Wales and

the Celtic peoples. It is the repository for pre-1858 Welsh
probate records. It is approved by the Master of the Rolls as
a repository for manorial records and tithe documents, and
by the Lord Chancellor for certain legal records. It is the
Bureau of the Regional Libraries Scheme for Wales.
Librarian, B. F. Roberts, CBE, PH.D., FSA
Heads of Departments, M. W. Mainwaring (*Administration
    and Technical Services*); G. Jenkins (*Manuscripts and
    Records*); J. L. Madden (*Printed Books*); D. H. Owen
    (*Pictures and Maps*)

LIGHTHOUSE AUTHORITIES

CORPORATION OF TRINITY HOUSE
Trinity House, Tower Hill, London EC3N 4DH
Tel 071-480 6601

Trinity House, the first general lighthouse and pilotage
authority in the kingdom, was a body of importance when
Henry VIII granted the institution its first charter in 1514.
The Corporation is the general lighthouse authority for
England, Wales and the Channel Islands, with certain
statutory jurisdiction over aids to navigation maintained by
local harbour authorities. It is also responsible for dealing
with wrecks dangerous to navigation, except those occurring
within port limits or wrecks of HM ships.

The Trinity House Lighthouse Service is maintained out
of the General Lighthouse Fund which is provided from light
dues levied on ships calling at ports of the UK and the
Republic of Ireland. The Corporation is also a deep-sea
pilotage authority and a charitable organization.

The affairs of the Corporation are controlled by a board of
Elder Brethren, who are master mariners with long
experience of command in the Royal Navy or merchant
navy, together with figures from the world of commerce, and
the Secretary. A separate board, which comprises Elder
Brethren, senior staff and outside representatives, currently
controls the Lighthouse Service. The Board is assisted by
administrative and technical staff. The Elder Brethren also
act as nautical assessors in marine cases in the Admiralty
Division of the High Court of Justice.

ELDER BRETHREN
Master, HRH The Duke of Edinburgh, KG, KT
Deputy Master, Capt. P. M. Edge
Elder Brethren, Capt. I. R. C. Saunders; Capt. P. F. Mason,
    CBE; HRH The Prince of Wales, KG, KT; Capt. Sir George
    Barnard, FRSA; Capt. R. N. Mayo, CBE; Capt. Sir David
    Tibbits, DSC, RN; Capt. D. A. G. Dickens; Capt.
    J. E. Bury; Capt. J. A. N. Bezant, DSC, RD, RNR; Capt.
    D. J. Cloke; The Lord Wilson of Rievaulx, KG, OBE, PC,
    FRS; Capt. Sir Miles Wingate, KCVO; The Rt. Hon. Sir
    Edward Heath, KG, MBE, MP; Capt. T. Woodfield, OBE; Sir
    Eric Drake, CBE; The Lord Simon of Glaisdale, PC;
    Admiral of the Fleet the Lord Lewin, KG, GCB, LVO, DSC;
    Capt. D. T. Smith, RN; Cdr. Sir Robin Gillett, GBE, RD,
    RNR; The Lord Shackleton, KG, OBE, PC, FRS; Sir John
    Cuckney; Capt. D. J. Orr; The Lord Carrington, KG,
    GCMG, CH, MC, PC; Sir Brian Shaw; The Lord Mackay of
    Clashfern, PC; Sir Adrian Swire; Capt. N. M. Turner, RD;
    HRH The Duke of York, CVO, ADC; Capt. P. H. King;
    Capt. The Lord Sterling of Plaistow, CBE, RNR; Cdr.
    M. J. Rivett-Carnac, RN; Rear-Adm. P. B. Lowe, CBE, LVO

OFFICERS
Secretary and Director of Administration, M. J. Faulkner
Director of Finance, K. W. Clark

Director of Engineering, D. A. S. Vennings
Personnel and General Services Manager, Mrs B. C. Heesom
Navigation Manager, N. J. Cutmore
Legal and Information Manager, D. I. Brewer
General Manager Operations, Capt. J. M. Barnes
Operations Administration Manager, S. J. W. Dunning
Deputy Director of Engineering, F. E. J. Holden
Senior Inspector of Shipping, J. R. Dunnett
Manager, Corporate Department, R. Dobb
Information Officer, H. L. Cooper

COMMISSIONERS OF NORTHERN LIGHTHOUSES
84 George Street, Edinburgh EH2 3DA
Tel 031-226 7051

The Commissioners of Northern Lighthouses are the general lighthouse authority for Scotland and the Isle of Man. The present board owes its origin to an Act of Parliament passed in 1786. At present the Commissioners operate under the Merchant Shipping Act 1894 and are 19 in number.

The Commissioners control 15 major manned lighthouses, 69 major automatic lighthouses, 108 minor lights and many lighted and unlighted buoys. They have a fleet of two motor vessels.

COMMISSIONERS
The Lord Advocate; the Solicitor-General for Scotland; the Lord Provosts of Edinburgh, Glasgow and Aberdeen; the Provost of Inverness; the Chairman of Argyll and Bute District Council; the Sheriffs-Principal of North Strathclyde, Tayside, Central, Fife, Grampian, Highlands and Islands, South Strathclyde, Dumfries and Galloway, Lothians and Borders, and Glasgow and Strathkelvin; T. Macgill; Capt. A. F. Dickson, OBE; A. J. Struthers; W. F. Hay, CBE; J. Hann, CBE; Capt. D. M. Cowell

OFFICERS
Chief Executive, Capt. J. B. Taylor, RN
Secretary, I. A. Dickson
Engineer-in-Chief, W. Paterson

LOCAL COMMISSIONERS

COMMISSION FOR LOCAL ADMINISTRATION IN ENGLAND
21 Queen Anne's Gate, London SW1H 9BU
Tel 071-222 5622

Local Commissioners (local government ombudsmen) are responsible for investigating complaints from members of the public against local authorities (but not town and parish councils); police authorities; the Commission for New Towns and new town development corporations (housing functions); urban development corporations (town and country planning functions) and certain other authorities. The Commissioners are appointed by the Crown on the recommendation of the Secretary of State for the Environment.

Certain types of action are excluded from investigation, including personnel matters and commercial transactions unless they relate to the purchase or sale of land. Complaints can be sent direct to the Local Government Ombudsman or through a councillor, although the Local Government Ombudsman will not consider a complaint unless the council has had an opportunity to investigate and reply to a complainant.

A free booklet Complaint about the Council? How to Complain to the Local Government Ombudsman is available from the Commission's office.

Chairman of the Commission and Local Commissioner (£90,148), D. C. M. Yardley, LL D, D.Phil., FRSA
Vice-Chairman and Local Commissioner (£65,307), Mrs P. A. Thomas
Local Commissioner (£64,307), E. B. C. Osmotherly, CB
Member (ex officio), The Parliamentary Commissioner for Administration
Secretary (£45,447), G. D. Adams

COMMISSION FOR LOCAL ADMINISTRATION IN WALES
Derwen House, Court Road, Bridgend CF31 1BN
Tel 0656-661325

The Local Commissioner for Wales has similar powers to the Local Commissioners in England. The Commissioner is appointed by the Crown on the recommendation of the Secretary of State for Wales. A free booklet Your Local Ombudsman in Wales is available from the Commission's office.
Local Commissioner, E. R. Moseley
Secretary, D. Bowen
Member (ex officio), The Parliamentary Commissioner for Administration

COMMISSIONER FOR LOCAL ADMINISTRATION IN SCOTLAND
23 Walker Street, Edinburgh EH3 7HX
Tel 031-225 5300

The Local Commissioner for Scotland has similar powers to the Local Commissioners in England, and is appointed by the Crown on the recommendation of the Secretary of State for Scotland.
Local Commissioner, R. G. E. Peggie, CBE
Deputy and Secretary, Ms J. H. Renton

LONDON REGIONAL TRANSPORT
55 Broadway, London SW1H 0BD
Tel 071-222 5600

Subject to the financial objectives and principles approved by the Secretary of State for Transport, London Regional Transport has a general duty to provide or secure the provision of public transport services for Greater London.
Chairman (£111,030), Sir Wilfrid Newton
Deputy Chairman and Chief Executive (£100,000), Dr A. K. Watkins
Member (£79,390), A. J. Sheppeck

LORD ADVOCATE'S DEPARTMENT
2 Carlton Gardens, London SW1Y 5AA
Tel 071-210 3000

The Law Officers for Scotland are the Lord Advocate and the Solicitor-General for Scotland. The Lord Advocate's Department is responsible for drafting Scottish legislation, for providing legal advice to other departments on Scottish questions and for assistance to the Law Officers for Scotland in certain of their legal duties.
Lord Advocate (£50,638), The Lord Rodger of Earlsferry, PC, QC
Solicitor-General for Scotland (£44,342), Thomas C. Dawson, QC
Legal Secretary and First Scottish Parliamentary Counsel (G2), J. C. McCluskie, QC

Assistant Legal Secretaries and Scottish Parliamentary
  Counsel (G3), G. M. Clark; G. Kowalski; P. J. Layden, TD
Assistant Legal Secretaries and Depute Scottish Parliamentary
  Counsel (G5), J. D. Harkness; C. A. M. Wilson
Assistant Legal Secretary and Assistant Scottish Parliamentary
  Counsel (G6/7), Miss M. Mackenzie

LORD CHANCELLOR'S DEPARTMENT
House of Lords, London SW1A OPW
Tel 071-219 3000

The Lord Chancellor is responsible for promoting general reforms in the civil law, for the procedure of the civil courts and for the administration of the Supreme Court (Court of Appeal, High Court and Crown Court) and county courts in England and Wales, and for legal aid schemes. He also has ministerial responsibility for magistrates' courts, which are administered locally. He is advised and assisted in raising performance standards in the Service by the new Magistrates' Courts' Service Inspectorate.

The Lord Chancellor is responsible for advising the Crown on the appointment of judges and certain other officers and is himself responsible for the appointment of Masters and Registrars of the High Court, Judges of the Principal Registry of the Family Division, district judges and magistrates. He is responsible for ensuring that letters patent and other formal documents are passed in the proper form under the Great Seal of the Realm, of which he is the custodian. The work in connection with this is carried out under his direction in the Office of the Clerk of the Crown in Chancery.
Lord Chancellor (£114,083; draws only £110,940), The Lord
  Mackay of Clashfern, PC
  Private Secretary, M. Ormerod
Parliamentary Under-Secretary, John Taylor, MP
  Private Secretary, Ms S. Jones
Permanent Secretary (G1), Sir Thomas Legg, KCB, QC
  Private Secretary, Ms J. Hull

CROWN OFFICE
Clerk of the Crown in Chancery (G1), Sir Thomas Legg, KCB,
  QC
Deputy Clerk of the Crown in Chancery (G2), M. Huebner
Clerk of the Chamber, Miss J. L. Waine

JUDICIAL APPOINTMENTS GROUP
House of Lords, London SW1A OPW
Tel 071-219 4311

Head of Group (G3), R. E. E. Holmes
Grade 5, D. E. Staff; R. A. Vincent; R. V. Grobler;
  G. Norman; P. G. Taylor

LAW AND POLICY GROUPS
Trevelyan House, Great Peter Street, London SW1P 2BY
Tel 071-210 8734

Head of Group (G2), M. Malone-Lee
Grade 5, P. L. Jacob

LEGAL GROUP
Southside, 105 Victoria Street, London SW1E 6QJ
Tel 071-210 3508
Grade 3, R. H. H. White
Grade 5, R. Venne; J. Watherston; M. Kron; J. Gibson

POLICY AND LEGAL SERVICES GROUP
Trevelyan House, Great Peter Street, London SW1P 2BY
Tel 071-210 8769
Grade 3, C. Everett
Grade 5, D. M. Nooney; S. Smith; M. Sayers

COURT SERVICE
Trevelyan House, Great Peter Street, London SW1P 2BY
Tel 071-210 8719

Head (G2), M. Huebner

COURT SERVICE MANAGEMENT GROUP
Grade 3, J. F. Brindley
Grade 5, P. Handcock; R. Sams; Miss J. Killick; Mrs
  M. Pigott; P. White

ESTABLISHMENT AND FINANCE GROUP
Trevelyan House, Great Peter Street, London SW1P 2BY
Tel 071-210 8803

Head of Group (G3), Mrs N. A. Oppenheimer
Grade 5, Ms H. Tuffs; A. Cogbill; P. Matthews
Grade 6, Mrs J. Waters; J. Isaacs; K. Cregeen

MAGISTRATES' COURTS' SERVICE
INSPECTORATE
Southside, 105 Victoria Street, London SW1E 6QJ
Tel 071-210 2169

Chief Inspector (G5), Mrs R. L. Melling

LORD CHANCELLOR'S ADVISORY COMMITTEE ON STATUTE LAW
6 Spring Gardens, London SW1A 2BP
Tel 071-389 3244

The Advisory Committee advises the Lord Chancellor on all matters relating to the revision, modernization and publication of the statute book.
Chairman, The Lord Chancellor
Members, Sir Thomas Legg, KCB, QC; M. A. J. Wheeler-
  Booth; Sir Clifford Boulton, KCB; The Hon. Mr Justice
  Brooke; The Hon. Lord Davidson; Sir Peter Graham,
  KCB, QC; J. C. McCluskie, QC; T. R. Erskine, CB;
  G. Hosker; R. Brodie, CB; R. H. H White; J. Gibson; Dr
  P. Freeman
Secretary, C. E. J. Carey

THE LORD CHANCELLOR'S ECCLESIASTICAL OFFICE
10 Downing Street, London SW1A 2AA
Tel 071-930 4433
Secretary for Ecclesiastical Patronage, J. W. Holroyd
Assistant Secretary for Ecclesiastical Patronage,
  N. C. Wheeler

See also Law Courts and Offices section

LORD GREAT CHAMBERLAIN'S OFFICE
House of Lords, London SW1A OAA
Tel 071-219 3100

The Lord Great Chamberlain is a Great Officer of State, the office being hereditary since the grant of Henry I to the family of De Vere, Earls of Oxford. The Lord Great Chamberlain is responsible for the Royal Apartments of the Palace of Westminster, i.e. The Queen's Robing Room, the Royal Gallery and, in conjunction with the Lord Chancellor and Madam Speaker, Westminster Hall. The Lord Great Chamberlain has particular responsibility for the internal administrative arrangements within the House of Lords for State Openings of Parliament.
Lord Great Chamberlain, The Marquess of Cholmondeley

Secretary to the Lord Great Chamberlain, Admiral Sir
Richard Thomas, KCB, OBE
Clerk to the Lord Great Chamberlain, Mrs S. E. Douglas

LORD PRIVY SEAL'S OFFICE
Privy Council Office, 68 Whitehall, London SW1A 2AT
Tel 071-270 3000

As leader of the House of Lords, the Lord Privy Seal is
responsible to the Prime Minister for the arrangement of
government business in the House. He also has a responsibility to the House itself to advise it on procedural matters
and other difficulties which arise. The Lord Privy Seal has
no departmental portfolio, but chairs a number of domestic
and economic Cabinet committees.
Lord Privy Seal, and Leader of the House of Lords, The Lord
Wakeham, PC
Private Secretary, Mrs J. M. Bailey
Private Secretary (House of Lords), E. C. Ollard

OFFICE OF MANPOWER ECONOMICS
22 Kingsway, London WC2B 6JY
Tel 071-405 5944

The Office of Manpower Economics was set up in 1971. It is
an independent non-statutory organization which is responsible for servicing independent review bodies which advise on
the pay of various public service groups (*see* Review Bodies,
page 348), the Pharmacists Review Panel and the Police
Negotiating Board. The Office is also responsible for servicing
ad hoc bodies of inquiry and for undertaking research into
pay and associated matters as requested by the Government.
Director, M. J. Horsman
Assistant Secretaries (G5), H. E. Miller; P. J. H. Edwards;
G. S. Charles; Mrs S. Webber

MEDICAL RESEARCH COUNCIL
20 Park Crescent, London W1N 4AL
Tel 071-636 5422

The Medical Research Council is the main government
agency for the promotion of medical and related biological
research. The council employs its own research staff and also
provides grants for other institutions and for individuals who
are not members of its own staff, thus complementing the
research resources of the universities and hospitals.
Chairman, Sir David Plastow
Deputy Chairman and Secretary, Sir David Rees, Ph.D., D.Sc.,
FRS
Members, Prof. I. V. Allen, D.Sc., MD, FRCPath.; Prof.
D. T. Baird, D.Sc., FRCP, FRCOG, FRSE; R. P. Bauman;
Prof. C. L. Berry, Ph.D., FRCPath.; Prof.
A. M. Breckenridge, MD, FRCP, FRCPE, FRSE;
K. C. Calman, MD, Ph.D., FRCS(Glas.), FRCP, FRSE; Sir
Michael Carlisle; J. T. Carter, FRCP; P. Doyle, CBE, Ph.D.;
Prof. C. R. W. Edwards, MD, FRCP, FRCPE; Prof.
J. Grimley Evans, MD, DM, FRCP, FFCM; R. E. Kendell,
CBE, MD, FRCP, FRCPsych., FRCPE; Prof. Sir Aaron Klug,
Sc.D., FRS; Prof. M. J. Peckham, FRCP, FRCP(Glas.), FRCR;
Miss E. Nicholson, MP; Prof. J. R. Pattison, DM; Prof.
M. J. Peckham, FRCP, FRCP(Glas.), FRCR; Prof. Sir Michael

Rutter, CBE, MD, FRCP, FRCPsych., FRS; Prof. Sir David
Weatherall, MD, FRCP, FRCPath., FRS
Administrative Secretary, Ms N. F. Morris

NEUROSCIENCES AND MENTAL HEALTH BOARD
Chairman, Prof. Sir Michael Rutter, CBE, MD, FRCP,
FRCPsych., FRS

MOLECULAR AND CELLULAR MEDICINE BOARD
Chairman, Prof. M. Bobrow, D.Sc., FRCP, FRCPath.

PHYSIOLOGICAL MEDICINE AND INFECTIONS BOARD
Chairman, Prof. J. R. Pattison, DM

HEALTH SERVICES AND PUBLIC HEALTH RESEARCH
BOARD
Chairman, Prof. J. Grimley Evans, DM, MD, FRCP, FFCM

HEADQUARTERS OFFICE
Second Secretary, D. Evered, MD, FRCP
Director of Finance, B. C. Dodd
Headquarters Office Services, J. E. A. Hay
Director of Human Resources, D. Smith, Ph.D.
Director of Corporate Affairs, N. H. Winterton
Director of Research Management, D. Dunstan, Ph.D.
Director of Research Planning, M. B. Davies, Ph.D.
Director of Industrial Collaboration and Licensing,
D. A. A. Olsen, Ph.D.
Research Policy Development Manager, M. B. Kemp, Ph.D.
Research Business Manager, J. M. Lee
Executive Board Secretaries, P. Dukes, Ph.D.; A. B. Stone,
D.Phil.; D. J. McLaren, D.Sc.; R. D. Lang, D.Phil.;
A. C. Peatfield, Ph.D.

For units of Medical Research Council, *see* pages 710–11

MENTAL HEALTH ACT COMMISSION
Maid Marian House, 56 Hounds Gate, Nottingham
NG1 6BG
Tel 0602-504040

The Mental Health Act Commission was established in 1983.
Its functions are to keep under review the operation of the
Mental Health Act 1983; to visit and interview patients
detained under the Act; to investigate complaints falling
within the Commission's remit; to operate the consent to
treatment safeguards in the Mental Health Act; to publish a
biennial report on its activities; to monitor the implementa-
tion of the Code of Practice; and to advise ministers.
Commissioners are appointed by the Secretary of State for
Health in the following categories: lay; legal; medical;
nursing; psychology; social worker; and specialist.
Chairman, Sir Louis Blom-Cooper, QC
Vice-Chairman, Prof. E. Murphy
Chief Executive (G6), W. Bingley

MONOPOLIES AND MERGERS COMMISSION
New Court, 48 Carey Street, London WC2A 2JT
Tel 071-324 1467

The Commission was established in 1948 as the Monopolies
and Restrictive Practices Commission and became the
Monopolies and Mergers Commission in 1973. The Commission has the duty of investigating and reporting on
questions referred to it with respect to the existence or
possible existence of monopolies not registrable under the
Restrictive Trade Practices Act 1976 and relating to the

supply of goods or services in the UK, or part of the UK, or to the supply of goods for export; to the transfer of a newspaper or newspaper's assets; and to the creation or possible creation of a merger qualifying for investigation within the meaning of the Fair Trading Act 1973. References may be made to the Commission on the general effect on the public interest of specified monopoly or other uncompetitive practices and of restrictive labour practices.

The Competition Act 1980 provides for the reference to the Commission of particular anti-competitive practices and of questions of efficiency, costs, service provided and possible abuse of monopolies in the public sector. In respect of recently-privatized industries, references to the Commission may be made in certain circumstances by the Director-General of Telecommunications, the Civil Aviation Authority, the Director-General of Gas Supply, the Director-General of Water Services and the Director-General of Electricity Supply, with regard to their respective industries.

Under the Broadcasting Act 1990 the Commission can investigate and report on the competition aspects of networking arrangements between holders of regional Channel 3 licences.

Chairman (£90,150), G. D. W. Odgers
Deputy Chairmen (£31,625), H. H. Liesner, CB; P. H. Dean, CBE; D. G. Goyder
Members (£12,735/*£8,490 each), A. G. Armstrong; C. C. Baillieu; I. Barter; Prof. M. E. Beesley, CBE; Mrs C. Blight; F. E. Bonner, CBE; *P. Brenan; J. S. Bridgeman; Prof. M. Bromwich; R. Davies; Prof. S. Eilon; J. Evans; A. Ferry, MBE; Sir Archibald Forster; Sir Ronald Halstead, CBE; Ms P. A. Hodgson; M. R. Hoffman; D. J. Jenkins, MBE; W. Johnson; *A. L. Kingshott; Miss P. K. R. Mann; G. C. S. Mather; *N. F. Matthews; Prof. J. S. Metcalfe, CBE; Mrs D. Miller, MBE; Prof. P. Minford; J. D. Montgomery; Dr D. J. Morris; B. C. Owens; *Prof. J. Pickering; *L. Priestley; Dr A. Robinson; J. K. Roe; D. P. Thomson; C. A. Unwin, MBE; Prof. G. Whittington
Secretary, S. N. Burbridge, CB

MUSEUMS

MUSEUMS AND GALLERIES COMMISSION
16 Queen Anne's Gate, London SW1H 9AA
Tel 071-233 4200

Established in 1931 as the Standing Commission on Museums and Galleries, the Commission was re-named and took up new functions in September 1981. Its sponsor department is the Department of National Heritage. The Commission advises the Government, including the Department for Education for Northern Ireland, the Scottish Education Department and the Welsh Office, on museum affairs. There are 15 Commissioners, appointed by the Prime Minister.

The Commission's executive functions include providing the services of the National Museums Security Adviser; the allocation of grants to the seven Area Museum Councils in England; funding and monitoring the work of the Museum Documentation Association; and directly administering a capital grant scheme for non-national museums, and various other grant schemes. The Commission administers the arrangements for government indemnities and the acceptance of works of art in lieu of inheritance tax, and it has responsibility for the two purchase grant funds for local museums managed on its behalf by the Victoria and Albert Museum and the Science Museum. The Commission's Conservation Unit advises on conservation and operates

grants schemes for conservators and an Environmental Adviser is drawing up guidelines on environmental standards in museums. A registration scheme for museums in the UK is being implemented by the Commission.
Chairman, G. Greene, CBE
Members, The Marchioness of Anglesey, DBE; F. Atkinson, OBE; J. Baer; The Baroness Brigstocke; The Viscountess Cobham; F. Dunning, OBE; R. Foster; J. Last, CBE; Prof. D. Michie; The Lord O'Neill, TD; The Lord Rees, PC, QC; R. H. Smith; Dame Margaret Weston, DBE; Adm. Sir David Williams, GCB
Director and Secretary, P. Longman

THE BRITISH MUSEUM
Great Russell Street, London WC1B 3DG
Tel 071-636 1555

The British Museum houses antiquities collections, coins and paper money, medals, and prints and drawings. Open daily 10–5; Sun. 2.30–6. Closed on Good Friday, 24–26 December, New Year's Day and the first Monday in May. Admission free. The ethnographical collections are displayed in the Museum of Mankind, 6 Burlington Gardens, London W1. Opening times as above.

The British Museum may be said to date from 1753, when Parliament approved the holding of a public lottery to raise funds for the purchase of the collections of Sir Hans Sloane and the Harleian manuscripts, and for their proper housing and maintenance. The building (Montagu House) was opened in 1759. The present buildings were erected between 1823 and the present day, and the original collection has increased to its present dimensions by gifts and purchases. Government grants for running costs and works and building projects were estimated at £34,102,000 in 1993–4.

BOARD OF TRUSTEES
Appointed by the Sovereign, HRH The Duke of Gloucester, GCVO
Appointed by the Prime Minister, The Lord Windlesham, CVO, PC (*Chairman*); Prof. Gillian Beer, FBA; Sir Matthew Farrer, KCVO; G. C. Greene, CBE; Prof. E. T. Hall, D.Phil., FSA, FBA; C. E. A. Hambro; Sir Peter Harrop, KCB; S. Keswick; Hon. Mrs Marten, OBE; Sir John Morgan, KCMG; The Rt. Hon. Sir Timothy Raison; S. Towneley, D.Phil.; Prof. G. H. Treitel, DCL, FBA, QC; The Lord Weinstock; Prof. Sir William Whitfield, CBE
Nominated by the Learned Societies, The Lord Adrian, MD, FRS (*Royal Society*); A. Jones, RA (*Royal Academy*); Sir Claus Moser, KCB, CBE, FBA (*British Academy*); The Lord Renfrew of Kaimsthorn, FBA, FSA (*Society of Antiquaries*)
Appointed by the Trustees of the British Museum, Sir David Attenborough, CVO, CBE, FRS; Prof. Rosemary Cramp, CBE, FSA; The Lord Egremont; Prof. Sir John Hale, FSA, FBA, FRHistS, FRSA; Prof. P. Lasko, CBE, FSA, FBA

OFFICERS
Director (*G2*), Dr R. G. W. Anderson
Deputy Director (*G4*), Miss J. M. Rankine
Secretary (*G6*), G. B. Morris
Assistant to the Director (*G7*), Ms M. L. Caygill, OBE
Head of Public Services (*G6*), G. A. L. House
Head of Design (*G6*), Miss M. Hall, OBE
Head of Education (*G7*), J. F. Reeve
Head of Press and Public Relations (*SIO*), A. E. Hamilton
Head of Administration (*G5*), C. E. I. Jones
Head of Building and Security Services (*G6*), K. T. Stannard
Head of Architectural and Building Services (*G7*), C. J. Walker
Head of Finance (*G7*), D. E. Williams

Head of Personnel and Office Services (G7),
 Miss B. A. Hughes
Keeper of Prints and Drawings (G5), A. V. Griffiths
Keeper of Coins and Medals (G5), Dr A. M. Burnett
Keeper of Egyptian Antiquities (G5), W. V. Davies
Keeper of Western Asiatic Antiquities (G5), Dr J. E. Curtis
Keeper of Greek and Roman Antiquities (G5), Dr
 D. J. R. Williams
Keeper of Medieval and Later Antiquities (G5),
 N. M. Stratford
Keeper of Prehistoric and Romano-British Antiquities (G5),
 Dr I. H. Longworth
Keeper of Japanese Antiquities (G5), L. R. H. Smith
Keeper of Oriental Antiquities (G5), Dr J. M. Rawson
Keeper of Ethnography (G5), B. J. Mack
Keeper of Scientific Research (G5), Dr S. G. E. Bowman
Keeper of Conservation (G5), W. A. Oddy

NATURAL HISTORY MUSEUM
Cromwell Road and Exhibition Road, London SW7 5BD
Tel 071-938 9123

Open Mon.–Sat. 10–6 (closed New Year's Day and 24–26 December), Sun. 11–6. Admission, £4.50.
 The Natural History Museum originates from the natural history departments of the British Museum. During the 19th century the natural history collections grew extensively and in 1881 they were moved to South Kensington. In 1963 the Natural History Museum became completely independent with its own body of trustees. The Zoological Museum, Tring, bequeathed by the second Lord Rothschild, has formed part of the Museum since 1938. The Geological Museum merged with the Natural History Museum in 1985 (opening times are as given above). Research workers are admitted to the libraries and study collections by Student's Ticket, applications for which should be made in writing to the Director.
 The grant-in-aid for 1992–3 was £28.9 million.

BOARD OF TRUSTEES
Appointed by the Prime Minister: Sir Walter Bodmer, FRS
 (*Chairman*); Sir Owen Green; The Baroness Blackstone,
 PH.D; E. N. K. Clarkson, FRS; Mrs J. M. d'Abo; Sir Denys
 Henderson; Prof. R. May, FRS; Sir Crispin Tickell, GCMG,
 KCVO
Nominated by the Royal Society, Prof. J. L. Harper, FRS
Appointed by the Trustees of the Natural History Museum,
 R. J. Carter; Prof. B. K. Follett, FRS; Sir Anthony
 Laughton, FRS

OFFICERS
Director (G3), N. R. Chalmers, PH.D.
Associate Directors (Scientific Development) (G5),
 Dr S. Blackmore; Dr P. Henderson
Secretary (G5), C. J. E. Legg
Assistant to the Director (G7), Miss R. P. Baillon
Head of Development and Marketing Department (G6),
 Mrs R. Laughton-Scott
Marketing Manager (G6), Ms J. Batchelor
Science Marketing (G6), Mrs A. Wendelaar
Public Relations Manager (G6), Miss J. Bevan
Keeper of Zoology (G5), C. R. Curds, D.SC
 Bird Section, Park Street, Tring, Herts. Tel: 044 282-
 4181. *Grade 6,* I. R. Bishop, OBE
Keeper of Entomology (G5), Dr R. P. Lane
Keeper of Botany (G5), S. Blackmore, PH.D.
Keeper of Palaeontology (G5), L. R. M. Cocks, D.SC
Keeper of Mineralogy (G5), P. Henderson, D.Phil
Head of Finance (G6), J. Card
Personnel Officer (G7), Mrs P. H. I. Orchard

Head of Library Services (G6), R. E. R. Banks
Head of Public Services (G5), R. S. Miles, D.SC
Head of Exhibition and Design (G7), R. M. Bloomfield, PH.D.

THE SCIENCE MUSEUM
South Kensington, London SW7 2DD
Tel 071-938 8000

Open Mon.–Sat. 10–6, Sun. 11–6. Closed 24–26 December. Admission charge. Library open Mon.–Fri. 9.30–7, Sat. 9.30–5.30. Closed on Sundays and Bank Holiday weekends.
 The Science Museum, part of the National Museum of Science and Industry, houses the national collections of science, technology, industry and medicine. The Museum began as the science collection of the South Kensington Museum and first opened in 1857. In 1883 it acquired the collections of the Patent Museum and in 1909 the science collections were transferred to the new Science Museum, leaving the art collections with the Victoria and Albert Museum.
 Some of the Museum's commercial aircraft, agricultural machinery, and road and rail transport collections are at Wroughton, near Swindon, Wilts., and are open for public viewing on selected weekends during the summer. The Museum is also responsible for the Concorde Exhibition at the Fleet Air Arm Museum, Yeovilton.
 The total running expenses, including building costs, of the Museum, the Science Museum Library, the National Railway Museum and the National Museum of Photography, Film and Television are estimated at £26 million for 1993–4.

BOARD OF TRUSTEES
Chairman, Sir Austin Pearce, CBE
Members, HRH The Duke of Kent, KG, GCMG, GCVO, ADC;
 Dr Mary Archer; Prof. Sir Eric Ash, CBE, FRS, FEng.; The
 Lord Brabourne, CBE; The Viscount Downe;
 Miss M. S. Goldring, OBE; Mrs A. Higham; Mrs
 J. Kennedy; Dr Bridget Ogilvie; Sir Michael Quinlan,
 GCB; Sir Denis Rooke, CBE, FRS, FEng.; L. de Rothschild,
 CBE; Prof. Sir John Thomas, FRS; Sir Christopher Wates

OFFICERS
Director, Dr N. Cossons, OBE
Assistant Director and Head of Resource Management
 Division (G5), J. J. Defries
Head of Personnel and Training (G6), C. Gosling
Head of Finance (G6), Ms A. Caine
Assistant Director and Head of Collections Division (G5),
 Dr T. Wright
Head of Physical Sciences Group (G5), Dr D. A. Robinson
Head of Life and Environmental Sciences Group (G5),
 Dr R. F. Bud
Head of Technology Group (G5), Dr E. J. S. Becklake
Head of Collections Management Group (G6), Ms S. Keene
Assistant Director and Head of Public Affairs Division (G5),
 C. M. Pemberton
Assistant Director and Head of Science Communication
 Division (G5), Prof. J. R. Durant
Head of Library and Information Services (G6), Dr L. D. Will
Head of Interpretation and Education (G6), Dr G. Farmelo
Assistant Director and Head of Project Development Division
 (G5), Mrs G. M. Thomas
Head of Design (G6), T. Molloy

NATIONAL RAILWAY MUSEUM
Leeman Road, York YO2 4XJ
Tel 0904-621261

Open Mon.–Sat. 10–6, Sun. 11–6. Admission charge. The Museum, opened in 1975, houses the national rail transport

334 Government Departments and Public Offices

collection. Locomotives, rolling stock and carriages are displayed to illustrate the technical, social and economic story of the development of railways in Britain.
Head of Museum (G5), A. R. G. Dow

NATIONAL MUSEUM OF PHOTOGRAPHY, FILM AND TELEVISION
Pictureville, Bradford BD1 1NQ
Tel 0274-727488

Open Tues.–Sun. 10.30–6, with special exhibition galleries open to 7.30. Admission free. The Museum, opened in 1983, collects, conserves and displays photography, film and television materials and equipment. It has the only IMAX cinema in the UK and the only public Cinerama theatre in the world.
Head of Museum (G5), vacant

VICTORIA AND ALBERT MUSEUM
South Kensington, London SW7 2RL
Tel 071-938 8500

Open Mon. 12–5.50, Tues.–Sun. 10–5.50. Closed 24–26 December, New Year's Day, Good Friday and May Day Bank Holiday. The National Art Library is open Tues.–Sat. 10–5 and the Print Room Tues.–Fri. 10–4.30, Sat. 10–1, 2–4.30. (The National Art Slide Library is now housed at De Montfort University, Leicester.) Admission free, but donations are invited.

A museum of all branches of fine and applied art and design, the Victoria and Albert Museum descends directly from the Museum of Manufactures, which opened in Marlborough House in 1852 after the Great Exhibition of 1851. The Museum was moved in 1857 to become part of the collective South Kensington Museum. It was renamed the Victoria and Albert Museum in 1899. The branch museum at Bethnal Green was opened in 1872 and the building is the most important surviving example of the type of glass and iron construction used by Paxton for the Great Exhibition. The Victoria and Albert Museum also administers the Wellington Museum (Apsley House), and the Theatre Museum.

BOARD OF TRUSTEES
Chairman, The Lord Armstrong of Ilminster, GCB, CVO
Deputy Chairman, Sir Michael Butler, GCMG
Members, The Lord Barnett, PC; Miss N. Campbell; Sir Clifford Chetwood; I. H. Davison; E. Dawe; R. Fitch, CBE; Prof. C. Frayling, PH.D.; Pamela, Lady Harlech; R. Gorlin; Sir Nevil Macready, Bt., CBE; Miss J. Muir, CBE; Miss A. Plowden; Prof. M. Podro, PH.D.; M. Saatchi; Prof. J. Steer, FSA
Secretary to the Board of Trustees (G7), P. A. Wilson

OFFICERS
Director (G3), Mrs E. A. L. Esteve-Coll
Assistant Directors (G5), vacant (*Collections*); J. W. Close (*Administration*)
Head of Buildings and Estate (G5), J. G. Charlesworth
Surveyor of Collections (G5), Mrs G. F. Miles
Head of Conservation Department (G5), Dr J. Ashley-Smith
Head of Finance and Central Services (G5), Miss R. M. Sykes
Development Director, Miss S. Mason
Curator, Ceramics Collection (G6), Dr O. Watson
Curator, Far Eastern Collection (G6), Miss R. Kerr
Curator, Furniture and Woodwork Collection (G6), C. Wilk
Curator, Indian and South-East Asian Collection (G6), Dr D. Swallow
Curator, Metalwork Collection (G6), Mrs P. Glanville
Head of Personnel (G6), Mrs G. Henchley

Curator, Prints, Drawings and Paintings Collection (G6), Miss S. B. Lambert
Head of Public Affairs (G5), R. Cole-Hamilton
Head of Marketing and Public Relations (G7), Miss R. Griffith-Jones
Head of Research (G5), Dr C. R. Saumarez Smith
Curator, Sculpture Collection (G6), P. E. D. Williamson
Curator, Textiles and Dress Collection (G6), Mrs V. D. Mendes
Managing Director, V. & A. Enterprises Ltd, M. Cass

NATIONAL ART LIBRARY
Curator and Chief Librarian (G5), J. F. van den Wateren

BETHNAL GREEN MUSEUM OF CHILDHOOD
Cambridge Heath Road, Bethnal Green, London E2 9PA
Tel 081-980 3204
Open Mon.–Thurs. and Sat. 10–6, Sun. 2.30–6. Closed every Friday, May Day Bank Holiday, 24–26 December and New Year's Day. Admission free but donations are invited.
Head of the Museum (G6), A. P. Burton

THEATRE MUSEUM
1E Tavistock Street, London WC2E 7PA
Tel 071-836 7891
Open Tues.–Sun. 11–7. Closed Mondays, 24–26 December, New Year's Day, Good Friday and May Day Bank Holiday. Admission charge.
Head of the Museum (G6), Ms M. Benton

WELLINGTON MUSEUM (APSLEY HOUSE)
149 Piccadilly, Hyde Park Corner, London W1V 9RA
Tel 071-499 5676
Open Tues.–Sun. 11–5. Closed Mondays. Apsley House is closed for essential works until the end of 1994.
Curator (E), J. R. S. Voak

MUSEUM OF LONDON
London Wall, London EC2Y 5HN
Tel 071-600 3699

Open Tues.–Sat. 10–6, Sun. 12–6. Closed Mondays and 24–25 December. Admission, £3 (three months), £6 (one year); concessions, £1.50.
The Museum of London opened in 1976. It is based on the amalgamation of the former Guildhall Museum and London Museum. The Museum is controlled by a Board of Governors, appointed (nine each) by the Government and the Corporation of London. The exhibition illustrates the history of London from prehistoric times to the present day.
Chairman of Board of Governors, P. Revell-Smith, CBE
Director, M. G. Hebditch, FSA

COMMONWEALTH INSTITUTE
Kensington High Street, London W8 6NQ
Tel 071-603 4535

Open Mon.–Sat. 10–5, Sun. 2–5. Closed Good Friday, May Day Bank Holiday, 24–26 December and New Year's Day. Admission £1.00; con. 50p.
The Commonwealth Institute is an independent statutory body funded by the British government with contributions from other Commonwealth governments. Its purpose is to increase knowledge and understanding of the Commonwealth in Britain. The Institute is controlled by a Board of Governors which includes the High Commissioners of all Commonwealth countries represented in London. It comprises the centre in London, a Northern Regional Centre in Bradford, and the autonomous Scottish Institute in Edinburgh. The Institute has permanent exhibitions on all Commonwealth nations, plus educational resource, information and conference centres.

Director-General, S. Cox
Director of Education, G. Brandt
Chief Administrative Officer, P. Kennedy
Head of Exhibitions, S. Brownlow

IMPERIAL WAR MUSEUM
Lambeth Road, London SE1 6HZ
Tel 071-416 5000

Open daily 10–6. Closed 24–26 December and New Year's Day. Admission £3.70; concessions £2.65/£1.85. Free admission after 4 p.m. daily. The Reference departments are open Mon.–Fri. 10–5, Sat. by appointment only.

The Museum, founded in 1917, illustrates and records all aspects of the two world wars and other military operations involving Britain and the Commonwealth since 1914. It was opened in its present home, formerly Bethlem Hospital or Bedlam, in 1936. The Museum also administers HMS *Belfast* in the Pool of London, Duxford Airfield near Cambridge and the Cabinet War Rooms in Westminster.

Expenses for 1993–4 are estimated at £21,058,000.
Director-General (G4), A. C. N. Borg, CBE, Ph.D., FSA
Deputy Director-General (G5), R. W. K. Crawford
Secretary (G6), J. J. Chadwick
Personnel Officer (G7), P. L. Cracknell
Finance Officer (G7), Mrs P. A. Whitfield
Museum Superintendent (G7), D. A. Needham
Information Systems Officer (G7), J. C. Barrett
Director of Duxford Airfield (G5), E. O. Inman
Director of HMS Belfast (G6), E. J. Wenzel

KEEPERS
Department of Museum Services (G6), C. Dowling, D.Phil
Department of Documents (G6), R. W. A. Suddaby
Department of Exhibits and Firearms (G6), D. J. Penn
Department of Printed Books (G6), G. M. Bayliss, Ph.D.
Department of Art (G6), Miss A. H. Weight
Department of Film (G6), R. B. N. Smither
Department of Photographs (G6), Miss K. J. Carmichael
Department of Sound Records (G6), Mrs M. A. Brooks
Department of Marketing and Training (G6),
   Miss A. Godwin
Curator of the Cabinet War Rooms (G7), P. Reed

NATIONAL MARITIME MUSEUM
Greenwich, London SE10 9NF
Tel 081-858 4422

Open Mon.–Sat., 10–6 (10–5 in winter); Sun. 12–6 (2–5 in winter). Closed 24–26 December. Admission charge. Reference Library open Mon.–Fri., 10–5; Sats. by appointment only; readers' tickets available on written application to the Librarian.

Established by Act of Parliament in 1934, the National Maritime Museum illustrates the maritime history of Great Britain in the widest sense, underlining the importance of the sea and its influence on the nation's power, wealth, culture, technology and institutions. The Museum is in three groups of buildings in Greenwich Park – the main building, the Queen's House (built by Inigo Jones, 1616–35) and the Old Royal Observatory (including Wren's Flamsteed House) – and also includes the *Cutty Sark* and a Special Exhibitions Centre. The collections include paintings, actual craft and ship models, ships' lines, prints and drawings, atlases and charts, navigational and astronomical instruments, clocks, uniforms and relics, books and MSS.
Director, R. L. Ormond

NATIONAL ARMY MUSEUM
Royal Hospital Road, London SW3 4HT
Tel 071-730 0717

Open daily, 10–5.30. Closed 24–26 December, New Year's Day, Good Friday and May Day Bank Holiday. Admission free.

The National Army Museum was established by royal charter in 1960. It covers the history of five centuries of the British Army, including the story of the Indian Army up to independence in 1947. The Indian Army room at the Royal Military Academy Sandhurst, Camberley, Surrey may be viewed by appointment.
Director, I. G. Robertson
Assistant Directors, D. K. Smurthwaite; A. J. Guy;
   Maj. P. R. Bateman

ROYAL AIR FORCE MUSEUM
Grahame Park Way, London NW9 5LL
Tel 081-205 2266

Open daily, 10–6. Closed 24–26 December and New Year's Day. Admission charge.

Situated on the former airfield at Hendon, the Museum illustrates the development of aviation from before the Wright brothers to the present-day RAF. More than 65 historic aircraft are on display. The complex includes the Bomber Command Hall and the 'Battle of Britain Experience'.
Director, Dr M. A. Fopp
Deputy Director, J. D. Freeborn
Keepers, D. C. R. Elliott; P. Elliott; D. F. Lawrence

NATIONAL MUSEUMS AND GALLERIES ON MERSEYSIDE
William Brown Street, Liverpool L3 8EN
Tel 051-207 0001

All museums and galleries are open all year except 24–26 December, New Year's Day and Good Friday. Opening times (except for the Maritime Museum and Museum of Liverpool Life) are Mon.–Sat. 10–5, Sun. 12–5. Admission free. Opening times for the Maritime Museum and Museum of Liverpool Life are 10.30–5.30 (last ticket sold 4.30). These two ventures have a joint admission charge.

The Board of Trustees of the National Museums and Galleries on Merseyside was established in 1986 to take over responsibility for the museums and galleries previously administered by Merseyside County Council. Various stores ancillary to the collections are also the responsibility of the body. It is grant-aided by the Department of National Heritage, and received about £14 million for 1993-4.
Chairman of the Board of Trustees, Sir Leslie Young, CBE
Director, R. Foster
Head of Central Services, P. Sudbury, Ph.D.
Keeper of Art Galleries, J. Treuherz
Keeper of Conservation, J. France

LIVERPOOL MUSEUM, William Brown Street, Liverpool L3 8EN. Keeper, E. Greenwood

MERSEYSIDE MARITIME MUSEUM, Albert Dock, Liverpool L3 4AA; and MUSEUM OF LIVERPOOL LIFE, Mann Island, Liverpool L3 1DG. Keeper, M. Stammers

WALKER ART GALLERY, William Brown Street, Liverpool L3 8EL

LADY LEVER ART GALLERY, Port Sunlight Village, Bebington, Wirral L62 5EQ

SUDLEY (ART GALLERY), Mossley Hill Road, Liverpool
LI8 5BX

NATIONAL MUSEUM OF WALES/
AMGUEDDFA GENEDLAETHOL CYMRU
Main Building, Cathays Park, Cardiff CFI 3NP
Tel 0222-397951

Open Tues.-Sat., 10-5. Sun. 2.30-5. Closed on Mondays
(except Bank Holidays), 24-25 December and New Year's
Day. Admission charge.
President, C. R. T. Edwards
Vice-President, M. C. T. Pritchard, CBE
Director, C. Ford, CBE
Head of Administration, T. Arnold
Keepers, M. G. Bassett, PH.D. (*Geology*); B. A. Thomas, PH.D.
(*Botany*); P. M. Morgan (*Zoology*); H. S. Aldhouse-Green,
PH.D. (*Archaeology*); T. J. Stevens, PH.D. (*Art*)

WELSH FOLK MUSEUM/AMGUEDDFA WERIN CYMRU
St Fagans, Nr. Cardiff
Open April–October, daily 10–5; November–March, Mon.-
Sat. 10–5. Closed 24–25 December and New Year's Day.
Admission charge.
Curator, Dr E. Williams
Keepers, E. Scourfield, PH.D.; J. W. Davies.

ROMAN LEGIONARY MUSEUM, CAERLEON
Caerleon, Gwent
Contains material found on the site of the Roman fortress of
Isca and its suburbs. Open Mon.-Sat. 10–6, Sun. 2–6 (closes
4.30 p.m. mid-October to mid-March). Closed 24–25 De-
cember and New Year's Day. Admission charge.
Officer in Charge, D. Zienkiewicz

TURNER HOUSE ART GALLERY
Plymouth Road, Penarth, Nr. Cardiff
Open Tues.-Fri. 11–12.45 and 2–5, Sun. 2–5. Closed
Mondays except Bank Holidays, Saturdays, 24–25 December
and New Year's Day. Admission free.
Keeper in Charge, T. Stevens, PH.D.

MUSEUM OF THE NORTH
Llanberis, Gwynedd
A multi-media presentation of the history of Wales and the
electricity supply industry. Open June to mid-September
9.30–6; mid-September–October and May, 10–5; November–April, pre-booked parties only. Closed 24–25 December
and New Year's Day. Admission charge.
Keeper, D. Roberts, PH.D.

WELSH SLATE MUSEUM
Llanberis, Gwynedd
Open Easter–30 September daily 9.30–5.30. Admission
charge.
Keeper in Charge, D. Roberts, PH.D.

SEGONTIUM ROMAN FORT MUSEUM
Beddgelert Road, Caernarfon, Gwynedd
Open weekdays at 9.30, Sundays at 2. Closes at 6 from May
to September, at 5.30 in March, April and October (5 on
Suns.), and at 4 from November to February. Closed 24–25
December and New Year's Day.
Officer in Charge, R. J. Brewer

MUSEUM OF THE WELSH WOOLLEN INDUSTRY
Dre-fach Felindre, nr. Llandysul, Dyfed
The museum occupies part of a working mill. Open April–
September, Mon.-Sat. 10–5; October–March, Mon.-Fri. 10-
5. Closed 24–25 December and New Year's Day. Admission
charge.
Keeper in Charge, E. Scourfield, PH.D.

WELSH INDUSTRIAL AND MARITIME MUSEUM
Bute Street, Cardiff
Open Tues.-Sat. 10–5; Sun. 2.30–5. Closed Mondays, 24–
25 December and New Year's Day. Admission charge.
Keeper, S. Owen-Jones, PH.D.

THE GRAHAM SUTHERLAND GALLERY AND PICTON
CASTLE GROUNDS
The Rhos, Haverfordwest
Open Easter–end October, Tues.-Sun. 10.30–12.30, 1.30–
5.00. Closed Mondays except Bank Holidays. Admission
charge.
Officer in Charge, S. Moss

NATIONAL MUSEUMS OF SCOTLAND
Chambers Street, Edinburgh EHI IJF
Tel 031-225 7534

BOARD OF TRUSTEES
Members, Prof. L. Bown, OBE; R. D. Cramond, CBE;
Countess of Dalkeith; Sir Nicholas Fairbairn, QC, MP; Sir
Alistair Grant; Dr H. A. P. Ingram; Prof. P. H. Jones;
D. H. Pringle, CBE; R. Smith; Prof. T. C. Smout

OFFICERS
Director, M. Jones
Museums Administrator, I. Hooper
Keeper, Department of History and Applied Art (G5),
Miss D. Idiens
Keeper, Department of Archaeology, D. V. Clarke, D.phil
Keeper, Department of Geology (G5), W. D. I. Rolfe, PH.D.
Keeper, Department of Natural History (G5), M. Shaw, D.phil
*Keeper, Department of Science, Technology and Working Life
(G5)*, D. J. Bryden
Head, Department of Public Affairs (G6), S. Brock, PH.D.
Head, Department of Museum Services (G6), S. R. Elson

ROYAL MUSEUM OF SCOTLAND
Chambers Street, Edinburgh
Open Mon.-Sat. 10–5, Sun. 12–5. Closed 25–26 December
and 1–2 January. Admission free.

MUSEUM OF ANTIQUITIES
Queen Street, Edinburgh
Open Mon.-Sat. 10–5, Sun. 2–5. Closed 25–26 December
and 1–2 January. Admission free.

SCOTTISH UNITED SERVICES MUSEUM
Edinburgh Castle
Open 1 April–30 September, Mon.-Sat. 9.30–5.50, Sun. 11-
5.50; 1 October–31 March, Mon.-Sat. 9.30–5.05, Sun. 12.30-
4.20. Closed 25–26 December and 1–2 January. Admission
free.
Keeper, S. C. Wood

SCOTTISH AGRICULTURAL MUSEUM
Ingliston, Edinburgh
Open May and September Mon.-Fri. 10–4.30; June–August
Mon.-Sat. 10–4.30. Admission free.
Curator, G. Sprott

MUSEUM OF FLIGHT
East Fortune Airfield, East Lothian
Open Easter–end September daily 10.30–4.30. Admission
charge.
Curator, Sqn. Ldr. R. Major

BIGGAR GASWORKS MUSEUM
Biggar, Lanarkshire
Open June–September daily 2–5. Admission free.
Curator, J. Wood

SHAMBELLIE HOUSE MUSEUM OF COSTUME
New Abbey, nr Dumfries
Open Easter–October daily 11–5. Admission charge.
Keeper, Miss D. Idiens

NATIONAL ADVISORY COUNCIL FOR EDUCATION AND TRAINING TARGETS
Caxton House, Tothill Street, London SW1H 9NF
Tel 071-273 5695

The National Advisory Council for Education and Training Targets was established by the Government in March 1993. It will monitor progress towards the National Targets for Education and Training and advise the Secretaries of State for Employment, Education and Wales on performance and policies which influence progress towards them. It will also promote employer investment in the workforce and communicate the importance of continuous learning for all.
Chairman, P. Davis
Vice-Chairman, M. Heron
Members, Sir Christopher Harding; D. Cadbury; Ms
   C. Galley; A. Cann; M. Walker, OBE; W. Jordan; The
   Baroness Perry; M. Rowarth, OBE; R. Perks, OBE
Ex-officio, E. Roberts; Sir Brian Wolfson

NATIONAL AUDIT OFFICE
157–197 Buckingham Palace Road, London SW1W 9SP
Tel 071-798 7000

The National Audit Office came into existence under the National Audit Act 1983 to replace and continue the work of the former Exchequer and Audit Department. The Act reinforced the Office's total financial and operational independence from the Government and brought its head, the Comptroller and Auditor-General, into a closer relationship with Parliament as an officer of the House of Commons. The National Audit Office provides independent information, advice and assurance to Parliament and the public about all aspects of the financial operations of government departments and many other bodies receiving public funds. This it does by examining and certifying the accounts of these organizations and by regularly publishing reports to Parliament on the results of its value for money investigations of the economy, efficiency and effectiveness with which public resources have been used. The National Audit Office is also the auditor by agreement of the accounts of certain international and other organizations. In addition, the Office authorizes the issue of public funds to government departments.
Comptroller and Auditor-General, Sir John Bourn, KCB
   Private Secretary, J. Rickleton
Deputy Comptroller and Auditor-General, R. N. Le Marechal
Assistant Auditors-General, D. A. Dewar; J. A. Higgins;
   L. H. Hughes; J. Marshall; M. C. Pfleger
Directors, A. G. Brown; C. L. Press; B. D. Baker;
   C. K. Beauchamp; R. M. Bennett; B. Hogg; G. G. Jones;
   A. R. Murray; J. Parsons; J. M. Pearce; A. G. Roberts;
   R. A. Skeen; R. E. Spurgeon; A. Fiander; Ms M. Bibby;
   M. Daynes; Miss C. Mawhood; R. J. Eales; J. Colman;
   B. Payne; G. R. L. Osborne
Associate Directors, C. J. Day; J. J. Jones; D. J. Woodward;
   A. Burchell; J. B. Cavanagh; J. Darling; P. R. Duncombe;
   D. A. Ferguson; N. Gale; T. Griffiths; K. Hawkswell;
   Miss J. Lawler; J. S. McEwen; R. Parker; M. J. Reeves;

N. Sloan; P. G. Woodward; R. Goacher; M. Whitehouse;
P. Cannon; R. Swan; M. Sinclair; R. P. Douglas

NATIONAL CONSUMER COUNCIL
20 Grosvenor Gardens, London SW1W 0DH
Tel 071-730 3469

The National Consumer Council was set up by the Government in 1975 to give an independent voice to consumers in the UK. Its job is to advocate the consumer interest to decision-makers in business, industry, the public utilities, the professions, and central and local government. It does this through a combination of research and campaigning. It is funded by a grant-in-aid from the Department of Trade and Industry.
Chairman, Lady Wilcox
Vice-Chairman, Mrs A. Scully
Members, D. Arculus; Miss B. Brookes; A. Burton, OBE; Ms
   A. Daltrop; Prof. P. Fairest; Miss J. Francis; D. Gilchrist;
   J. Hughes; L. N. Hunter; Mrs D. Hutton; Prof. G. Jones;
   J. Mitchell; Ms M. McAnally; Lady McCollum;
   Mrs J. Varnam; Sir Geoffrey Allen
Director, R. Evans

NATIONAL DEBT OFFICE
— *see* National Investment and Loans Office

DEPARTMENT OF NATIONAL HERITAGE
2–4 Cockspur Street, London SW1Y 5DH
Tel 071-270 3000

The Department of National Heritage was established in 1992 and is responsible for aspects of government policy previously covered by six other government departments. It is responsible for government policy relating to the arts, broadcasting, the press, museums and galleries, libraries, sport and recreation, heritage and tourism. It funds the Arts Council of Great Britain and other arts bodies, including the National Heritage Memorial Fund. It also funds the Museums and Galleries Commission, the national museums and galleries in England, the British Library, the Sports Council, the British Tourist Authority and the English Tourist Board, and the British Film Institute. It is responsible for the issue of export licences on works of art, antiques and collector's items; the Government Art Collection; the built heritage, including the Royal Parks and Historic Royal Palaces Executive Agencies; and statistical services including the International Passenger Survey and broadcasting statistics. The Department is also responsible for policy and implementation of the National Lottery and the Millenium Fund.
Secretary of State for National Heritage, The Rt. Hon. Peter
   Brooke, MP
   Private Secretary, A. Davey
   Special Adviser, D. Loehnis
   Parliamentary Private Secretary, A. Steen, MP
Parliamentary Under-Secretary of State, Iain Sproat, MP
   Private Secretary, N. Mackenzie
Lord-in-Waiting, The Viscount Astor
Parliamentary Clerk, Ms S. Forsyth
Permanent Secretary (G1), G. H. Phillips, CB
   Private Secretary, Miss H. Wilkinson

ARTS GROUP
Head of Group (G3), Ms M. O'Mara
Head of Arts Division (G5), N. Kroll

Head of Libraries and Information Services Division (G5),
    P. Bolt
Director, British Library St Pancras Project (G5), J. Pardey
Head of Museums and Galleries Division (G5), P. Gregory
Director, Government Art Collection (G6), Dr Wendy Baron,
    OBE
Head of Cultural Property Unit (G7), Miss C. Morrison
Head of National Lottery Division (G5), Ms S. A. Booth

BROADCASTING, FILM AND SPORT GROUP
Head of Group (G3), P. Wright
Head of Broadcasting Policy Division (G5), Miss J. Goose,
    CBE
Head of Media Division (G5), P. Edwards
Head of Sport and Recreation Division (G5), Miss A. Stewart

HERITAGE AND TOURISM GROUP
Head of Group (G3), D. Chesterton
Head of Heritage Division (G5), A. Corner
Head of Royal Estate Division (G5), P. Douglas
Head of Tourism Division (G5), C. Leamy

RESOURCES AND SERVICES GROUP
Director (G4), N. Pittman
Director of Finance and Corporate Planning (G5), vacant
Director of Implementation and Review (G5), Dr K. Gray
Director of Personnel (G5), G. Jones

INFORMATION
Head of Information (G5), Miss A. MacLean

HISTORIC ROYAL PALACES AGENCY
The Birdwood Annexe, Hampton Court Palace, East
Molesey, Surrey KT8 9AU
Tel 081-977 7222

An executive agency within the Department of National
Heritage, the Historic Royal Palaces Agency manages the
Tower of London, Hampton Court Palace, Kensington
Palace, Kew Palace with Queen Charlotte's Cottage, and the
Banqueting House, Whitehall.
Chief Executive (G3), D. C. Beeton.
Director of Finance and Resources (G5), Ms B. Darbyshire
Surveyor of the Fabric (G5), S. Bond.
Director of Marketing (G6), P. D. Hammond
Curator, Historic Royal Palaces (G6), Dr S. J. Thurley
Administrator, Hampton Court Palace (G6),
    D. J. C. MacDonald
Resident Governor, HM Tower of London (G5), Maj.-Gen.
    C. Tyler, CB (retd)
Administrator, Kensington Palace (G7), N. J. Arch

ROYAL PARKS EXECUTIVE AGENCY
The Royal Parks Headquarters, Hyde Park, London
W2 2UH
Tel 071-298 2000

An executive agency within the Department of National
Heritage
Chief Executive (G5), D. Welch

NATIONAL HERITAGE MEMORIAL FUND
10 St James's Street, London SW1A 1EF
Tel 071-930 0963

The National Heritage Memorial Fund is an independent
body established in 1980 as a memorial to those who have
died for the UK. The Fund is empowered by the National
Heritage Act 1980 to give financial assistance towards the
cost of acquiring, maintaining or preserving land, buildings,

works of art and other objects of outstanding interest which
are also of importance to the national heritage. The Fund is
administered by up to eleven trustees who are appointed by
the Prime Minister. Its major source of funding is the
Department of National Heritage, which gives an annual
grant.

TRUSTEES
Chairman, The Lord Rothschild
Members, Sir Richard Carew Pole, Bt.; The Lord Crathorne;
    W. L. Evans; Sir Nicholas Goodison; Sir Martin Jacomb;
    The Lord Macfarlane of Bearsden; Prof. P. J. Newbould;
    Mrs J. Nutting; Mrs C. Porteous; Cdr.
    L. M. M. Saunders Watson
Director, Miss G. Nayler

NATIONAL INSURANCE JOINT AUTHORITY
The Adelphi, 1–11 John Adam Street, London WC2N 6HT
Tel 071-962 8000

The Authority's function is to co-ordinate the operation of
social security legislation in Great Britain and Northern
Ireland, including the necessary financial adjustments
between the two National Insurance Funds.
Members, The Secretary of State for Social Security; the
    Head of the Department of Health and Social Services for
    Northern Ireland.
Secretary, Ms G. E. Taylor

NATIONAL INVESTMENT AND LOANS OFFICE
1 King Charles Street, London SW1A 2AP
Tel 071-270 3863

The National Investment and Loans Office was set up in
1980 by the merger of the National Debt Office and the
Public Works Loan Board. The Office provides staff and
services for the National Debt Commissioners and the Public
Works Loan Commissioners.
Director, I. H. Peattie
Establishment Officer, A. G. Ladd

NATIONAL DEBT OFFICE
Comptroller-General, I. H. Peattie

PUBLIC WORKS LOAN BOARD
Chairman, Sir Robin Dent, KCVO
Deputy Chairman, Miss F. M. Cook, CBE
Other Commissioners, Miss V. J. Di Palma, OBE; G. Ross
    Russell; P. Brackfield; D. H. Adams; R. A. Chapman;
    A. Morton; G. G. Williams; R. G. Tettenborn;
    J. E. Scotford, CBE; A. Gillespie
Secretary, I. H. Peattie
Assistant Secretary, Miss L. M. Ashcroft

NATIONAL RADIOLOGICAL PROTECTION BOARD
Chilton, Didcot, Oxon. OX11 ORQ
Tel 0235-831600

The National Radiological Protection Board is an independent statutory body created by the Radiological Protection
Act 1970. It is the national point of authoritative reference

on radiological protection for both ionizing and non-ionizing radiations.
Chairman, Sir Richard Southwood, FRS
Director, Prof. R. H. Clarke

NATIONAL RIVERS AUTHORITY
Rivers House, Waterside Drive, Aztec West, Almondsbury, Bristol BS12 4UD
Tel 0454-624400

The National Rivers Authority (NRA) is an independent body set up under the Water Act 1989. Its responsibilities include monitoring the quality of water, controlling pollution, and the management of water resources, flood defence and fisheries. The NRA has a board of 14 members, two of whom are appointed by the Minister of Agriculture, Fisheries and Food, one by the Secretary of State for Wales, and the rest by the Secretary of State for the Environment.
Chairman, The Lord Crickhowell, PC.
Chief Executive, E. Gallagher
Chief Scientist, Dr J. Pentreath
Director, Water Management, Dr C. Swinnerton
Finance Director, N. Reader
Personnel Director, P. Humphreys
Director of Public Affairs, M. Wilson

DEPARTMENT FOR NATIONAL SAVINGS
Charles House, 375 Kensington High Street, London W14 8SD
Tel 071-605 9300

The Department for National Savings was established as a government department in 1969. The Department is responsible for the administration of a wide range of schemes for personal savers.
For details of schemes, *see* National Savings section.
Director of Savings (G2), C. D. Butler
Deputy Director (G3), D. Howard
Establishment Officer (G5), D. S. Speedie
Finance Officer (G5), M. A. Nicholls
Controllers (G5), Miss A. Nash (*Marketing and Information*); A. S. McGill; D. H. Monaghan; E. B. Senior; P. N. S. Hickman Robertson
Senior Principals (G6), D. W. Kellaway; W. J. Herd; I. Forsyth; M. A. Nicholls; D. Newton; T. Threlfall; P. Anderson; A. Muir; T. J. F. McMahon; J. W. Davison
Principals (G7), D. K. Paterson; A. J. V. Cummings; Dr A. Fort; W. J. Ferrier; H. Johnson; A. B. Wood; P. Finnie; C. E. Funk; I. Jordinson; A. Brown; B. Paley; H. Webster; J. Wheatley; C. McVey; R. A. Nichol; J. B. Dunphy; J. C. Foreman; D. Wilson; P. B. Robinson; G. V. Wise; A. S. Lamond; D. Jeffrey; J. Bolam; R. W. Day; C. Dodsworth; R. R. Hesketh; R. J. McLelland; M. J. Tan; M. McDade; I. Rich; Miss J. S. Clark; M. C. Richards; M. Taylor; J. M. Anderson; W. Brough; C. K. D. Conlan; S. F. Owen; W. Ward

NATURAL ENVIRONMENT RESEARCH COUNCIL
Polaris House, North Star Avenue, Swindon SN2 1EU
Tel 0793-411500

The Natural Environment Research Council was established in 1965 to encourage, plan and conduct research in the physical and biological sciences which relate to the natural environment and its resources. The Council carries out research and training through its own institutes and by grants, fellowships and post-graduate awards to universities and other institutions of higher education.
Chairman, Prof. J. Knill, PH.D., D.SC
Secretary, Dr Eileen Buttle
Director of Earth Sciences, Prof. J. C. Briden, PH.D.
Director of Terrestrial and Fresh Water Sciences, Prof. C. Arme
Director of Marine and Atmospheric Sciences, J. D. Woods, CBE, PH.D.

CENTRAL SERVICES
NERC SCIENTIFIC SERVICES, Polaris House, North Star Avenue, Swindon, Wilts. SN2 1EU. Tel: 0793-411500.
Director, B. J. Hinde, OBE

RESEARCH VESSEL SERVICES, No. 1 Dock, Barry, S. Glamorgan. Tel: 0446-737451. *Head*, Dr C. Fay

NERC COMPUTER SERVICE, Holbrook House, Station Road, Swindon, Wilts. SN1 1DE. Tel: 0793-411500. *Director*, H. J. Down

For research institutes and units of the Natural Environment Research Council, *see* page 711–12

JOINT NATURE CONSERVATION COMMITTEE
Monkstone House, City Road, Peterborough PE1 1JY
Tel 0733-62626

The Committee was established under the Environmental Protection Act 1990 and began work on 1 April 1991. It advises the Government and others on UK and international nature conservation issues and disseminates knowledge on these subjects. It establishes common standards for the monitoring of nature conservation and research, and analyses the resulting information. It commissions research relevant to these roles, and provides guidance to English Nature, Scottish Natural Heritage, the Countryside Council for Wales and the Department of the Environment for Northern Ireland.
Chairman, The Earl of Selborne, KBE, FRS
Chief Officer, C. R. Walker, CB
Director, Life Sciences and Resources, Dr M. W. Pienkowski
Director, Earth and Aquatic Sciences, C. Stevens

NORTHERN IRELAND OFFICE
Whitehall, London SW1A 2AZ
Tel 071-210 3000

The Northern Ireland Office is the office of the Secretary of State for Northern Ireland. It was established in 1972, when the Northern Ireland (Temporary Provisions) Act transferred the legislative and executive powers of the Northern Ireland Government and Parliament to the UK Parliament and a Secretary of State. The Northern Ireland Constitution Act 1973 provided for devolution in Northern Ireland through an assembly and executive, but agreement has not been reached on arrangements for involving locally-elected representatives in the government of Northern Ireland, and so responsibility still rests with the UK Parliament.
In 1985 the Governments of the United Kingdom and the Republic of Ireland signed the Anglo-Irish Agreement,

establishing an intergovernmental conference in which the Irish Government may put forward views and proposals on certain aspects of Northern Ireland affairs.

Secretary of State for Northern Ireland, The Rt. Hon. Sir Patrick Mayhew, QC, MP

Special Adviser, J. Caine

Parliamentary Private Secretary, M. Moss, MP

Ministers of State, Robert Atkins, MP; The Rt. Hon. Sir John Wheeler, MP

Parliamentary Private Secretaries:

To Mr Atkins, J. Hayes, MP

To Sir John Wheeler, J. Evans, MP

Parliamentary Under-Secretaries of State, The Earl of Arran; Michael Ancram, MP

Permanent Under-Secretary of State(G1), J. A. Chilcot, CB

Second Permanent Under-Secretary of State, Head of the NICS, (G1A), D. Fell, CB

NORTHERN IRELAND CIVIL SERVICE (NICS), Stormont Castle, Belfast BT4 3TT. Tel: 0232-520700

DEPARTMENT OF AGRICULTURE FOR NORTHERN IRELAND, Dundonald House, Upper Newtownards Road, Belfast BT4 3SB. Tel: 0232-520100

DEPARTMENT OF ECONOMIC DEVELOPMENT NORTHERN IRELAND, Netherleigh, Massey Avenue, Belfast BT4 2JP. Tel: 0232-529900

DEPARTMENT OF EDUCATION FOR NORTHERN IRELAND, Rathgael House, Balloo Road, Bangor, Co. Down BT19 2PR. Tel: 0247-270077

DEPARTMENT OF THE ENVIRONMENT FOR NORTHERN IRELAND, Parliament Buildings, Stormont, Belfast BT4 3SS. Tel: 0232-520600

DEPARTMENT OF FINANCE AND PERSONNEL, Parliament Buildings, Stormont, Belfast BT4 3SW. Tel: 0232-520400

DEPARTMENT OF HEALTH AND SOCIAL SERVICES NORTHERN IRELAND, Dundonald House, Upper Newtownards Road, Belfast BT4 3SF. Tel: 0232-520500

OCCUPATIONAL PENSIONS BOARD
PO Box 2EE, Newcastle upon Tyne NE99 2EE
Tel 091-225 6414

The Occupational Pensions Board (OPB) is an independent statutory body set up under the Social Security Act 1973 to administer the contracting-out of occupational pensions from the State Earnings Related Pension Scheme (SERPS), and to advise the Secretary of State. Its functions have been extended by subsequent legislation and it is now also responsible for administering equal access, preservation and modification requirements and appropriate personal pension schemes. Following the Social Security Act 1990, the OPB was appointed as Registrar of Occupational and Personal Pension Schemes and granted powers to make grants to approved bodies in the field. The OPB now funds the operation of the Occupational Pensions Advisory Service (OPAS).

Chairman, Miss C. H. Dawes

Deputy Chairman, A. Pickering

Members, R. J. Amy; Mrs R. Brown; R. Ellison; A. U. Lyburn; W. M. R. Ramsey, D.Phil.; K. R. Thomas; A. S. Herbert; M. R. Slack

Secretary to the Board and General Manager of Executive Office (G6), A. Scaife

OMBUDSMAN
— see Local Commissioners *and* Parliamentary Commissioner. For non-statutory Ombudsmen, *see* Index

ORDNANCE SURVEY
Romsey Road, Maybush, Southampton SO9 4DH
Tel 0703-792000

The Ordnance Survey is the national mapping agency for Britain. It became an executive agency in May 1990 and reports to the Secretary of State for the Environment.

The Ordnance Survey has military origins. It produces over 220,000 large scale maps of the country at three basic scales. These are 1:1,250 (50 inches to 1 mile) for urban areas; 1:2,500 (25 inches to 1 mile) for rural areas; and 1:10,000 (6 inches to 1 mile) for mountain and moorland. In addition, Ordnance Survey produces a range of small scale maps and other products for general use.

Director-General, Prof. D. Rhind

Directors:

Surveys and Production, A. S. Macdonald

Marketing, Planning and Development, J. Leonard

Establishments and Finance, I. Lock

Heads of Functions:

Production, D. Davies

Topographic Surveys, D. Toft

Marketing, P. Wesley

Research and Development, I. T. Logan

Finance, D. James

Establishments, D. R. Evans

Information and Computer Service, B. W. Nanson

OS International, E. Gilbert

OVERSEAS DEVELOPMENT ADMINISTRATION
94 Victoria Street, London SW1E 5JL
Tel 071-917 7000
Abercrombie House, Eaglesham Road, East Kilbride, Glasgow G75 8EA
Tel 0355-844000

The Overseas Development Administration deals with British development assistance to overseas countries. This includes both capital aid on concessional terms and technical assistance (mainly in the form of specialist staff abroad and training facilities in the United Kingdom), whether provided directly to developing countries or through the various multilateral aid organizations, including the United Nations and its specialized agencies.

Minister for Overseas Development, The Baroness Chalker of Wallasey, PC

Private Secretary (G7), M. A. B. Lowcock

Permanent Secretary (G1A), T. P. Lankester

Private Secretary, Ms G. J. Lyons

Deputy Secretary (G2), R. M. Ainscow, CB

Under-Secretaries (G3), N. B. Hudson; B. R. Ireton; J. V. Kerby; R. G. Manning; A. J. Bennett; J. B. Wilmshurst; J. L. Faint; P. D. M. Freeman

ECONOMIC AND SOCIAL DIVISION

Head of the Economic Service (G3), J. B. Wilmshurst

Senior Economic Advisers (G5), J. C. H. Morris; B. P. Thomson; J. Roberts; M. Foster; P. Sandersley; P. J. Ackroyd

Economic Advisers (G6), P. L. Owen; (G7), P. D. Balacs; Dr F. C. Clift; J. G. Clarke; D. B. Crapper; P. J. Dearden; D. Donaldson; P. D. Grant; N. F. Gregory; Dr G. Haley; A. B. D. Hall; E. Hawthorn; N. Highton

Economists (G7), J. L. Hoy; W. Kingsmill; M. Lewis;
A. Moon; R. Teuten; Ms R. Turner; Mrs J. White;
A. Whitworth; Ms C. Laing; E. Cassidy;
Ms R. Phillipson; J. Burton; M. Surr; R. Moberly;
Ms J. Alston; P. G. Hill
Senior Small Enterprise Development Adviser (G6),
D. L. Wright
Small Enterprise Development Adviser (G7), J. R. Boulter
Small Business Adviser (G7), D. M. Spence
Chief Statistician (G5), R. M. Allen
Statisticians (G6), A. B. Williams; *(G7)*, J. R. B. King;
P. J. Crook; Ms J. J. Church; M. Dyble
*Principal Finance Management and Administration Adviser
(G5)*, K. L. Sparkhall
*Senior Finance Management and Administration Advisers
(G6)*, Dr R. Thomas; Dr G. Glentworth
Finance Management and Administration Adviser (G7),
Dr M. Greaves
Senior Finance and Management Advisers (G6),
D. W. Heffer; D. J. Wood; D. W. Baker; S. Sharples;
J. G. Clarke
Overseas Policy Adviser (G6), L. Grundy
Chief Social Development Adviser (G5), Dr R. J. Eyben
Senior Social Development Adviser (G6), Dr S. Conlin
Social Development Advisers (G7), Ms P. Holden;
M. Schultz; R. H. Kinnear; Dr Anne Coles
Chief Health and Population Adviser (G5), Dr D. Nabarro
Senior Health and Population Adviser (G6), R. N. Grose
Forestry Adviser (G7), D. Chaffey
Purchasing Adviser (G7), R. H. Marriott

INFORMATION DEPARTMENT
Head of Information (G5), A. Bearpark
Principal Information Officer (G7), R. W. Fosker

ADMINISTRATIVE STAFF
Grade 5, Miss A. M. Archbold; M. Bawden; S. Chakrabarti;
J. H. S. Chard; Ms M. Cund; A. D. Davis; M. J. Dinham;
J. R. Drummond; R. Elias; D. S. Fish; R. M. Graham-
Harrison; B. W. Hammond; Mrs P. J. Hilton; J. Hodges;
Mrs S. Jay; Mrs B. M. Kelly; M. C. McCulloch;
J. C. Machin; V. J. McClean; C. Myhill; M. A. Power;
C. P. Raleigh; S. Ray; D. Sands-Smith; D. L. Stanton;
G. M. Stegmann; D. P. Turner; Ms S. E. Unsworth; Miss
M. Vowles; M. Wickstead; Mrs P. M. Wilkinson;
R. J. Wilson
Grade 6, J. A. Anning; D. R. Curran; K. D. Grimshaw;
D. Richards; D. Trotter; G. A. Williams
Grade 7, G. F. H. Aicken; J. D. Aitken; G. Alexander;
R. Allen; G. A. Armstrong; C. B. Austin; N. Bailey;
D. G. Bell; F. Black; H. Britton; W. A. Brownlie;
P. J. Burton; R. T. Calvert; P. H. Charters; D. J. Church;
Dr J. Cocking; T. F. G. Connor; R. G. Cousins;
G. Crabtree; A. O. Davies; M. J. Ellis; B. Foy;
J. R. Gilbert; M. A. Hammond; Ms V. M. Harris;
B. Hefferon; Ms A. C. Higginbottom; M. I. Holland;
N. Hoult; G. I. James; W. Jardine; Mrs J. Laurence;
D. Lawless; G. G. Leader; J. Lingham; I. M. McKendry;
M. Mallalieu; G. H. Malley; P. S. Mason; J. Maund;
C. A. Metcalf; J. C. H. Millett; D. J. Moran;
M. L. S. Mosselmans; J. D. Moye; G. A. Mustard;
J. Patel; P. T. Perris; V. R. Pheasant; R. J. Plumb;
G. M. Porter; Mrs J. Radice; C. N. Raynor;
S. R. J. Robbins; P. T. Rose; C. R. Roth;
Dr P. W. K. Rundell; Ms P. Schofield; D. A. Scott;
Mrs P. A. Scutt; S. J. Sharpe; R. J. Smith;
Miss R. B. Stevenson; M. J. Sexton; I. D. Stuart;
D. J. C. Taylor; E. C. N. Taylor; N. Thomas;
B. A. Thorpe; R. G. Toulmin; N. A. Tranter; R. Vernon;
Ms S. T. Wardell; C. W. Warren; R. S. White;

J. M. Winter; A. K. C. Wood; M. C. Wood;
Mrs G. B. Wright; M. S. S. Wyatt; P. L. Zoller

ADVISORY AND SPECIALIST STAFF
Chief Education Adviser (G5), Dr R. O. Iredale
Senior Education Advisers (G6), M. D. Francis;
Ms M. Harrison; Dr D. Pennycuick; M. E. Seath;
Dr D. G. Swift
Chief Engineering Adviser (G5), T. D. Pike
Senior Engineering Advisers (G6), A. G. Colley; C. I. Ellis;
D. Gillett; B. Dolton; H. B. Jackson;
P. W. D. H. Roberts; M. F. Sergeant
Engineering Advisers (G7), R. J. Cadwallader; A. Barker;
A. Smallwood; M. McCarthy; D. Robson; C. Hunt
Senior Renewable Energy and Research Adviser (G6), vacant
Senior Electrical and Mechanical Engineering Adviser (G6),
R. P. Jones
Senior Architectural and Physical Planning Advisers (G6),
M. W. Parkes; W. M. Housego-Woolgar
Chief Health and Population Advisers (G6), Dr P. Key, OBE;
Miss J. Isard; Dr M. Kapila; Ms S. Simmonds;
J. Lambert
Chief Natural Resources Adviser (G3), A. J. Bennett
*Deputy Chief Natural Resources and Principal Agricultural
Adviser (G5)*, J. M. Scott
Deputy Chief Natural Resources Adviser (G5),
Dr J. C. Davies, OBE *(Research)*
Senior Natural Resources Advisers (G6), Ms L. C. Brown;
B. E. Grimwood; Dr I. Haines; J. R. F. Hansell;
J. A. Harvey; D. J. Salmon; A. J. Tainsh; D. Trotman;
M. J. Wilson; *(G7)*, G. A. Gilman; Dr H. Potter;
Dr P. Dobie; T. Barrett
Animal Health Advisers (G6), G. G. Freeland;
Dr A. D. Irvin; Ms L. Bell
Senior Fisheries Advisers (G6), Dr J. Tarbit; R. W. Beales
Senior Forestry Advisers (G6), W. J. Howard; R. Jenkin;
P. Wood
Senior Procurement Adviser (G6), R. Davidson
Senior Technical Education Advisers (G6), C. Lewis;
Dr G. R. H. Jones
Industrial Training Advisers (G7), W. Wray; D. G. Marr
Population Adviser (G7), C. Allison
Agricultural Education and Training Adviser (G7), A. Hall

NATURAL RESOURCES INSTITUTE
Central Avenue, Chatham Maritime, Chatham, Kent
ME4 4TB
Tel 0634-880088

An executive agency within the ODA, the NRI provides
scientific and technical expertise in renewable natural
resources for the overseas aid programme.
Director and Chief Executive (G3), G. A. Beattie

OFFICE OF THE PARLIAMENTARY
COMMISSIONER AND HEALTH SERVICE
COMMISSIONER
Church House, Great Smith Street, London SW1P 3BW
Tel 071-276 3000

The Parliamentary Commissioner for Administration (the
Ombudsman) is responsible for investigating complaints
referred to him by Members of the House of Commons from
members of the public who claim to have sustained injustice
in consequence of maladministration by or on behalf of
government departments and certain non-departmental
public bodies. Certain types of action by government
departments or bodies are excluded from investigation.

Actions taken by other public bodies (such as local authorities, the police, the Post Office and nationalized industries) are outside the Commissioner's scope.

The Health Service Commissioners for England, for Scotland and for Wales are responsible for investigating complaints against National Health Service authorities that are not dealt with by those authorities to the satisfaction of the complainant. Complaints can be referred direct by the member of the public who claims to have sustained injustice or hardship in consequence of the failure in a service provided by a relevant body, failure of that body to provide a service or in consequence of any other action by that body. Certain types of action are excluded, in particular, action taken solely in consequence of the exercise of clinical judgment. The three offices are presently held by the Parliamentary Commissioner.

Parliamentary Commissioner and Health Service Commissioner (G1), W. K. Reid, CB
Deputy Parliamentary Commissioner (G3), J. E. Avery
Deputy Health Service Commissioner (G3), R. A. Oswald
Directors (G5), Mrs S. Maunsell; M. D. Randall;
J. C. Bateman; Mrs H. Bates; Mrs P. Newman;
Miss D. Fordham
Principals (G7), G. M. Keil; Mrs C. Bentley; T. J. Corkett;
T. J. Hull (*Establishment Officer*); S. J. Drummond;
B. P. Jones; K. O'Brien; D. Howard; Miss C. Corrigan;
D. S. Coleman; E. J. Drake; S. Lillington;
Miss S. Pearson; Mrs S. Skingley; Mrs L. Boulton;
G. Miller; Miss C. Rees-Jenkins, OBE

NORTHERN IRELAND PARLIAMENTARY COMMISSIONER FOR ADMINISTRATION AND NORTHERN IRELAND COMMISSIONER FOR COMPLAINTS
Progressive House, 33 Wellington Place, Belfast BTI 6HN
Tel 0232-233821

The Commissioner is appointed under legislation with powers to investigate complaints by people claiming to have sustained injustice in consequence of maladministration arising from action taken by a Northern Ireland government department, or any other public body within the Commissioner's remit. Senior executive staff are presently seconded from the Northern Ireland Civil Service.
Commissioner, Mrs J. McIvor, QSM
Senior Director, K. McWilliams
Director, G. R. Dawson
Deputy Directors, S. P. Hughes; D. Rodgers

PARLIAMENTARY COUNSEL
36 Whitehall, London SWIA 2AY
Tel 071-210 6633

Parliamentary Counsel draft all government Bills (i.e. primary legislation) except those relating exclusively to Scotland, the latter being drafted by the Lord Advocate's Department. They also advise on all aspects of parliamentary procedure in connection with such Bills and draft government amendments to them as well as any motions (including financial resolutions) necessary to secure their introduction into, and passage through, Parliament.
First Counsel (£82,780), Sir Peter Graham, KCB, QC
Second Counsel (£73,900), J. C. Jenkins, CB

Counsel (£59,020), J. S. Mason, CB; D. W. Saunders, CB;
E. G. Caldwell, CB; E. G. Bowman, CB; G. B. Sellers, CB;
E. R. Sutherland, CB; P. F. A. Knowles; S. C. Laws;
R. S. Parker

PAROLE BOARD FOR ENGLAND AND WALES
Abell House, John Islip Street, London SWIP 4LH
Tel 071-217 5314

The Board was constituted under the Criminal Justice Act 1967 and continued under the Criminal Justice Act 1991. Its duty is to advise the Secretary of State for the Home Department with respect to matters referred to it by him which are connected with the early release or recall of prisoners. Its functions include giving directions concerning the release on licence of prisoners serving discretionary life sentences and of certain prisoners serving long-term determinate sentences; and making recommendations to the Secretary of State concerning the early release on licence of other prisoners, the conditions of parole and licences and the variation and cancellation of such conditions, and the recall of long-term and life prisoners while on licence.
Chairman, The Lord Belstead, PC
Vice-Chairman, The Hon. Mr Justice Ian Kennedy
Secretary, T. E. Russell

PAROLE BOARD FOR SCOTLAND
Calton House, 5 Redheughs Rigg, Edinburgh EH12 9HW
Tel 031-244 8530

The Board advises the Secretary of State for Scotland on the release of prisoners on licence, and related matters.
Chairman, J. M. Scott
Vice-Chairman, I. McNee
Secretary, Miss W. M. Doonan

PATENT OFFICE
Cardiff Road, Newport, Gwent NP9 IRH
Tel 0633-814000

The Patent Office is an executive agency of the Department of Trade and Industry. The duties of the Patent Office consist in the administration of the Patent Acts, the Registered Designs Act and the Trade Marks Act, and in dealing with questions relating to the Copyright, Designs and Patents Act 1988. The Search and Advisory Service carries out commercial searches through patent information. In 1992 the Office granted 9,421 patents and registered 8,175 designs and 35,137 trade and service marks.
Comptroller-General (G3), P. R. S. Hartnack
Assistant Comptroller, Industrial Property and Copyright Department (G4), A. Sugden
Assistant Comptroller, Patents and Designs (G4),
R. J. Marchant
Assistant Registrar, Trade Marks (G4), Miss A. Brimelow
Head of Marketing and Information (Supt. Examiner),
E. F. Blake
Head of Administration and Resources (G5), T. Cassidy
Head of ADP Unit (G6), G. Bennett

OFFICE OF HM PAYMASTER-GENERAL

HM Treasury, Parliament Street, London SW1P 3AG
Tel 071-270 4349
Sutherland House, Russell Way, Crawley, W. Sussex
RH10 1UH
Tel 0293-560999

The Office of HM Paymaster-General was formed by the consolidation in 1835 of various separate pay departments then existing, some of which dated back at least to 1660. Its function is that of paying agent for government departments other than the revenue departments. Most of its payments are made through banks, to whose accounts the necessary transfers are made at the Bank of England. The payment of over 1.5 million public service pensions is an important feature of its work. The Office became an executive agency on 1 April 1993.

Paymaster-General, The Rt. Hon. Sir John Cope, MP
Assistant Paymaster-General/Chief Executive (G5),
   K. Sullens
Grade 6, G. Harbottle; G. Thomas; M. D. West
Grade 7, D. R. Alexander; Mrs D. F. Ambrose; M. L. Card;
   A. Edwards; T. R. George; R. G. Hollands; M. C. Kirk;
   D. Nunn; Mrs J. Parsons; C. A. Ulph

OFFICE OF THE PENSIONS OMBUDSMAN

11 Belgrave Road, London SW1V 1RB
Tel 071-834 9144

The Pensions Ombudsman is appointed by the Secretary of State for Social Security under the Social Security Act 1990 to deal with complaints against, and disputes with, occupational and personal pension schemes. He is completely independent.

Pensions Ombudsman, M. Platt

POLICE COMPLAINTS AUTHORITY

10 Great George Street, London SW1P 3AE
Tel 071-273 6450

The Police Complaints Authority was established under the Police and Criminal Evidence Act 1984 to introduce a further independent element into the procedure for dealing with complaints by members of the public against police officers in England and Wales. (In Scotland, complaints are investigated by independent public prosecutors.) The Authority has powers to supervise the investigation of certain categories of serious complaints and certain statutory functions in relation to the disciplinary aspects of complaints. It does not as a rule deal with complaints about police operations; these are usually dealt with by the Chief Constable of the relevant force.

Chairman, Sir Leonard Peach
Deputy Chairman (Investigations), J. Cartwright
Deputy Chairman (Discipline), P. W. Moorhouse
Members, Mrs L. Cawsey; M. Chapman; Miss L. Haye;
   G. V. Marsh; W. McCall; L. Spencer; Brig. A. Vivian;
   Miss B. Wallis; E. Wignall; A. Williams

POLITICAL HONOURS SCRUTINY COMMITTEE

Cabinet Office, 53 Parliament Street, London SW1A 2NG
Tel 071-210 5058

The function of the Political Honours Scrutiny Committee is set out in an Order of Council dated 31 May 1979. The Prime Minister submits certain particulars to the Committee about persons proposed to be recommended for honour for their political services. The Committee, after such enquiry as they think fit, report to the Prime Minister whether, so far as they believe, the persons whose names are submitted to them are fit and proper persons to be recommended.

Chairman, The Lord Pym, MC, PC
Members, The Lord Cledwyn of Penrhos, CH, PC; The Lord
   Thomson of Monifieth, KT, PC
Secretary, J. H. Thompson, CB

OFFICE OF POPULATION CENSUSES AND SURVEYS

St Catherine's House, 10 Kingsway, London WC2B 6JP
Tel 071-242 0262

The Office of Population Censuses and Surveys was created by the merger in 1970 of the General Register Office and the Government Social Survey Department. The Registrar-General controls the local registration service in England and Wales in the exercise of its registration and marriage duties. Copies of the original registrations of births, still births, marriages and deaths and a register of adopted children are kept at Southport. Central indexes are compiled annually and certified copies of entries may be obtained, on payment of certain fees, either by personal application from St Catherine's House or by post from Smedley Hydro, Southport PR8 2HH.

Since 1841 the Registrar-General has been responsible for taking the census of population. He also prepares and publishes a wide range of statistics and appropriate commentary relating to population, fertility, births, still births, marriages, deaths and cause of death and infectious diseases. The Registrar-General is also responsible for conducting surveys on a range of subjects for other government departments. He maintains, at Southport, the National Health Service Central Register.

Hours of access to Public Search Room, St Catherine's House, Mon.–Fri., 8.30–4.30.

Director and Registrar-General for England and Wales (G2),
   P. J. Wormald, CB
Deputy Director and Director of Statistics (G3),
   E. J. Thompson
Deputy Director and Chief Medical Statistician (G3),
   A. J. Fox, PH.D.
Deputy Registrar-General (G5), J. V. Ribbins
Principal Finance Officer (G5), B. S. Smith
Principal Establishment Officer (G6), N. E. Auckland
Principal Information Officer (G7), Miss S. Wallace
Heads of Division (G5), I. K. G. Arnold (*Information
   Technology*); M. F. G. Murphy (*Senior Medical
   Statistician*); R. Barnes (*Social Survey Division*); J. Craig
   (*Population Statistics*); Ms K. Dunnell (*Health Statistics*);
   B. H. Mahon (*Census*)
Heads of Division (G6), E. Barton (*NHS Central Register*);
   B. W. Meakings (*Data Services*)

Grade 6, B. S. T. Alcock; Mrs M. Bone; A. M. Clark;
J. Denton, OBE; W. Jenkins; I. B. Knight; D. L. Pearce;
R. McLeod; Mrs J. Martin; Ms J. Matheson
Grade 7, R. I. Armitage; F. L. Ashwood; R. A. P. Bailey;
N. Bateson; R. J. Beacham; D. E. Birch;
Mrs B. J. Botting; A. F. Bradbury; J. A. Brown;
L. Bulusu; D. Capron; R. J. Carpenter; J. R. H. Charlton;
J. Cloyne; B. C. Collett; C. J. Denham; T. L. F. Devis;
J. M. Dixie; Mrs J. C. Dobbs; Ms P. A. Dodd; D. Elliot;
Miss C. M. Ellis; Ms E. M. Goddard; Mrs J. R. Gregory;
P. C. Gregory; J. Haskey; A. J. H. Hayes (*Chief Inspector
of Registration*); P. J. Heady; G. Hughes; Mrs J. Humby;
J. Jackson; S. P. King; I. B. Knight; B. G. Little;
Miss C. S. J. Lloyd; D. Lockyer; W. F. Loomes;
Miss E. M. McCrossan; Mrs I. MacDonald-Davies;
Mrs M. Machin; A. J. Manners; V. A. Mason;
H. I. Meltzer; I. D. Mills; Miss D. Pace; A. Parr;
M. Quinn; A. P. Read; S. Robinson-Grindey;
C. I. Rooney; J. A. Salvetti; C. Savage; Ms J. M. Sharp;
Mrs S. M. Smyth; D. Stewart; P. Stickland;
Mrs L. M. Street; A. D. Teague; A. W. Tester;
Mrs M. J. Wagget; I. S. G. White; A. J. White;
E. W. Williams

PORT OF LONDON AUTHORITY
Devon House, 58–60 St Katharine's Way, London E1 9LB
Tel 071-265 2656

The Port of London Authority is a public trust constituted under the Port of London Act 1908 and subsequent legislation. The Board comprises a chairman and up to seven but not less than four non-executive members appointed by the Secretary of State for Transport, and up to four but not less than one executive members appointed by the Board.

The Port of London Authority is the governing body for the Port of London, covering the tidal portion of the River Thames from Teddington to the seaward limit.
Chairman, Sir Brian Shaw
Vice-Chairman, J. H. Kelly, CBE
Chief Executive, D. Jeffery
Secretary, G. E. Ennals

THE POST OFFICE
148 Old Street, London EC1V 9HQ
Tel 071-490 2888

Crown services for the carriage of government despatches were set up in about 1516. The conveyance of public correspondence began in 1635 and the mail service was made a parliamentary responsibility with the setting up of a Post Office in 1657. Telegraphs came under the Post Office control in 1870 and the Post Office Telephone Service began in 1880. The National Girobank service of the Post Office began in 1968. The Post Office ceased to be a government department in 1969 and responsibility for the running of the postal, telecommunications, giro and remittance services was transferred to a public authority called the Post Office. The 1981 British Telecommunications Act separated the functions of the Post Office, making it solely responsible for postal services and Girobank, which was privatized in 1990.

The chairman, chief executive and members of the Post Office Board are appointed by the Secretary of State for Trade and Industry but responsibility for the running of the Post Office as a whole rests with the Board in its corporate capacity.

FINANCIAL RESULTS	1991–2 £m	1992–3 £m
Post Office Group		
Turnover	5,149	5,345
Trading profit before tax	247	283
Royal Mail		
Turnover	3,911	4,048
Trading profit before tax and interest on long-term loans	205	216
Parcelforce		
Turnover	508	501
Trading loss before tax and interest on long-term loans	15	12
Post Office Counters		
Turnover	1,028	1,061
Trading profit before tax and interest on long-term loans	26	43

POST OFFICE BOARD
Chairman, M. Heron
Chief Executive, W. Cockburn, CBE, TD
Members, P. Howarth (*Managing Director, Royal Mail*);
M. Kitchener (*Managing Director, Parcelforce*); R. Dykes
(*Managing Director, Post Office Counters Ltd*); R. Close
(*Managing Director, Finance*)
Secretary, Miss M. MacDonald, CBE

PRIVY COUNCIL OFFICE
Whitehall, London SW1A 2AT
Tel 071-270 3000

The Office is responsible for the arrangements leading to the making of all royal proclamations and Orders in Council; for certain formalities connected with ministerial changes; for considering applications for the granting (or amendment) of royal charters; for the scrutiny and approval of by-laws and statutes of chartered bodies; and for the appointment of High Sheriffs and many Crown and Privy Council appointments to governing bodies.
*Lord President of the Council (and Leader of the House of
Commons*), The Rt. Hon. Antony Newton, OBE, MP
Private Secretary, G. D. S. Sandeman
Special Adviser, I. Stewart
Parliamentary Private Secretary, J. Marshall, MP
Clerk of the Council (G3), N. H. Nicholls, CBE
Deputy Clerk of the Council (G5), R. P. Bulling
Senior Clerk, J. Laverick

PROCURATOR FISCAL SERVICE
— see pages 381–2

PUBLIC HEALTH LABORATORY SERVICE
61 Colindale Avenue, London NW9 5DF
Tel 081-200 1295

The Public Health Laboratory Service comprises 53 regional or area laboratories in England and Wales, the Central Public Health Laboratory, the Communicable Disease Surveillance Centre, and the Centre for Applied Microbiology and Research. The PHLS provides diagnostic microbiological services to hospitals, and has reference facilities that are available nationally. It collates information on the incidence of infection, and when necessary it institutes special inquiries into outbreaks and the epidemiology of infectious disease. It also undertakes bacteriological surveillance of the quality of food and water for local authorities and others. The PHLS is often called upon to advise central and local government and the hospital service on many aspects of infectious disease. It maintains close contact with veterinary organizations in areas of mutual interest, and collaborates with the World Health Organization and with national laboratory and epidemiological services overseas.

THE BOARD
Chairman, Dr M. P. W. Godfrey, CBE, FRCP
Members, Prof. J. P. Arbuthnott, PH.D.; Dr W. Bogie;
D. F. R. Crofton; Prof. G. Crompton; A. E. Eames;
Prof. C. S. F. Easmon; Dr J. M. Forsythe; J. Godfrey;
A. Graham-Dixon, QC; Dr H. H. John; Prof. M. D. Lilly;
D. Noble, CBE; Dr M. J. Painter; Prof. J. R. Pattison;
Prof. I. Phillips; J. J. Skehel, PH.D., FRS; Prof. P. G. Smith,
D.SC.; Prof. L. Southgate

HEAD OFFICE
Director, Dr Diana Walford, FRCP, FRCpath.
Deputy Directors, Dr E. M. Cooke; Dr C. Roberts
Deputy Director (Administration) and Board Secretary,
K. M. Saunders
Deputy Board Secretary, J. M. Harker

CENTRAL PUBLIC HEALTH LABORATORY
Colindale Avenue, London NW9 5HT
Director, Dr M. C. Timbury

COMMUNICABLE DISEASES SURVEILLANCE CENTRE
Colindale Avenue, NW9 5EQ
Director, Dr C. L. R. Bartlett

CENTRE FOR APPLIED MICROBIOLOGY AND RESEARCH
Porton Down, Salisbury, Wilts. SP4 0JG
Director (acting), Prof. J. Melling, PH.D.

OTHER SPECIAL LABORATORIES AND UNITS
ANAEROBE REFERENCE UNIT, Public Health Laboratory,
Cardiff. *Director,* Prof. B. I. Duerden
CRYPTOSPROIDIUM REFERENCE UNIT, Public Health
Laboratory, Rhyl. *Director,* D. P. Casemore, PH.D.
GONOCOCCUS REFERENCE UNIT, Public Health
Laboratory, Bristol. *Director,* A. E. Jephcott, MD
LEPTOSPIRA REFERENCE LABORATORY, Public Health
Laboratory, Hereford. *Director,* I. R. Fergusson, TD
MALARIA REFERENCE LABORATORY, London School of
Hygiene and Tropical Medicine, London WC1. *Directors,*
Prof. D. J. Bradley, DM; D. C. Warhurst, PH.D., FRCpath.
MENINGOCOCCAL REFERENCE LABORATORY, Public
Health Laboratory, Manchester. *Director,*
D. M. Jones, OBE, MD
MYCOBACTERIUM REFERENCE UNIT, Public Health
Laboratory, Cardiff. *Director,* P. A. Jenkins, PH.D.
TOXOPLASMA REFERENCE LABORATORIES, Public
Health Laboratory, Leeds. *Director,* R. N. Peel; Public
Health Laboratory, Swansea. *Director,* D. H. M. Joynson;
Public Health Laboratory, Tooting, London. *Director,*
R. E. Holliman
WATER AND ENVIRONMENTAL LABORATORY, Public
Health Laboratory, Nottingham. *Director,*
J. V. Lee, PH.D.

REGIONAL LABORATORIES AND DIRECTORS
Birmingham, I. D. Farrell, PH.D.; *Bristol,* A. E. Jephcott;
Cambridge, U. Desselberger, MD, FRCP(G); *Cardiff,*
Prof. B. I. Duerden; *Leeds,* R. N. Peel; *Liverpool,*
J. H. Pennington, MD; *Manchester,* D. M. Jones, MD;
Newcastle, N. F. Lightfoot; *Oxford,* J. B. Selkon, TD;
Portsmouth, O. A. Okubadejo, MD; *Sheffield,* P. Norman

AREA LABORATORIES
Ashford, C. Dulake, TD; *Bangor,* T. Howard; *Bath,*
D. G. White; *Brighton,* B. T. Thom; *Carlisle,*
M. A. Knowles; *Carmarthen,* M. D. Simmons; *Chelmsford,*
R. E. Tettmar, D.Path.; *Chester,* P. Hunter, MD; *Coventry,*
P. R. Mortimer, MD; *Dorchester,* A. Rampling, PH.D.; *Epsom,*
S. A. Chambers; *Exeter,* J. G. Cruickshank, MD; *Gloucester,*
K. A. V. Cartwright; *Guildford,* Prof. R. Y. Cartwright;
Hereford, I. R. Ferguson, TD; *Hull,* S. L. Mawer; *Ipswich,*
P. H. Jones; *Leicester,* C. J. Mitchell; *Lincoln,* E. R. Youngs;
LONDON: *Central Middlesex Hospital,* M. S. Shafi (*acting*);
Dulwich, A. H. C. Uttley, PH.D.; *Tooting,*
Prof. A. R. M. Coates; *Whipps Cross,*
B. Chattopadhyay, MD; *Luton,* Dr S. A. Rousseau (*acting*);
Middlesbrough, E. McKay-Ferguson, MD; *Norwich,*
P. M. B. White; *Nottingham,* M. J. Lewis, MD;
Peterborough, R. S. Jobanputra, MD; *Plymouth,*
P. J. Wilkinson; *Poole,* W. L. Hooper; *Preston,*
D. N. Hutchinson, MD; *Reading,* J. V. Dadswell; *Rhyl,*
D. N. Looker; *Salisbury,* S. Patrick; *Shrewsbury,*
C. A. Morris, MD; *Southampton,* J. A. Lowes; *Stoke-on-Trent,*
J. Gray; *Swansea,* D. H. M. Joynson; *Taunton,*
J. V. S. Pether; *Truro,* W. A. Telfer Brunton; *Watford,*
M. T. Moulsdale; *Wolverhampton,* R. G. Thompson

REGISTRAR OF PUBLIC LENDING
RIGHT
Bayheath House, Prince Regent Street,
Stockton-on-Tees, TS18 1DF
Tel 0642-604699

Under the Public Lending Right system, in operation since 1983, payment is made from public funds to authors whose books are lent out from public libraries. Payment is made once a year (in February) and the amount each author receives is proportionate to the number of times (established from a sample) that each registered book has been lent out during the previous year.

The Registrar of PLR, who is appointed by the Secretary of State for National Heritage, compiles the register of authors and books. Only living authors resident in the UK or Germany are eligible to apply. (The term 'author' covers writers, illustrators, translators, and some editors/compilers.)

A payment of 1.86 pence was made in 1992–3 for each estimated loan of a registered book, up to a top limit of £6,000 for the books of any one registered author; the money for loans above this level is used to augment the remaining PLR payments.

In February 1993, the sum of £3,945,000 was made available for distribution to 17,831 registered authors and assignees as the annual payment of PLR.

The PLR Advisory Committee advises the Secretary of State for National Heritage and the Registrar of Public Lending Right. Its members are appointed by the Secretary of State.
Chairman of Advisory Committee, D. H. Whitaker, OBE
Registrar, Dr J. Parker

PUBLIC RECORD OFFICE
— see pages 346–7

PUBLIC TRUST OFFICE
Stewart House, 24 Kingsway, London WC2B 6JX
Tel 071-269 7000

The Public Trustee is a trust corporation created to undertake the business of executorship and trusteeship; he can act as executor or administrator of the estate of a deceased person, or as trustee of a will or settlement. The Public Trustee is also responsible for the performance of all the administrative, but not the judicial, tasks required of the Court of Protection under Part VII of the Mental Health Act 1983, relating to the management and administration of the property and affairs of persons suffering from mental disorder. The Public Trustee also acts as Receiver when so directed by the Court, usually where there is no other person willing or able so to act.

The Accountant-General of the Supreme Court, through the Court Funds Office, is responsible for the investment and accounting of funds in court for persons under a disability, monies in court subject to litigation and statutory deposits.

The Court Funds Office is at 22 Kingsway, London WC2B 6LE. Tel: 071-936 6000
Public Trustee and Accountant-General, P. J. Farmer
Assistant Public Trustee, H. N. Mather
Investment Manager, H. Stevenson
Chief Property Adviser, A. Nightingale

CLIENT SERVICES SECTOR
Head, E. J. Dober
Receivership Division, Mrs H. Bratton
Protection Division, I. S. Price

INTERNAL SERVICES SECTOR
Head, I. J. MacBean
Court Funds Office, F. J. Eddy

PUBLIC WORKS LOAN BOARD
— *see* National Investment and Loans Office

COMMISSION FOR RACIAL EQUALITY
Elliot House, 10–12 Allington Street, London SW1E 5EH
Tel 071-828 7022

The Commission was established in 1977, under the Race Relations Act 1976, to work towards the elimination of discrimination and promote equality of opportunity and good relations between different racial groups.
Chairman, H. Ouseley
Deputy Chairs, A. Ward; R. Sondhi
Members, R. Kent; Revd E. A. Brown; Dr
M. C. K. Chan, MBE; T. A. Khan; A. Rose, OBE;
R. Purkiss; Dr D. Neil; Ms M. Cunningham; Dr
R. Chandran; Dr Z. Khan; M. Hastings
Chief Executive (acting), D. Sharma

THE RADIO AUTHORITY
Holbrook House, 14 Great Queen Street, London WC2B 5DG
Tel 071-430 2724

The Radio Authority was established in January 1991 under the Broadcasting Act 1990 as one of the two successor bodies to the Independent Broadcasting Authority. Its function is to plan frequencies, to grant licences for the provision of independent radio services, and to regulate the output of the services in accordance with published codes dealing with standards for programming, advertising and sponsorship.

Members of the Authority are appointed by the Secretary of State for National Heritage. Senior executive staff are appointed by the Authority.
Chairman, The Lord Chalfont OBE, MC, PC
Deputy Chairman, Mrs J. McIvor, QSM

Members, Mrs M. Corrigan; J. Grant; R. Hooper; R. Sondhi; M. Moriarty, CB
Chief Executive, P. Baldwin
Deputy Chief Executive and Head of Regulation, P. Brown
Head of Development, D. Vick
Head of Finance, N. Romain
Head of Engineering, M. Thomas
Secretary to the Authority, J. Norrington

RECORD OFFICES

ADVISORY COUNCIL ON PUBLIC RECORDS
Trevelyan House, Great Peter Street, London SW1P 2BY
Tel 071-210 8500

Council members are appointed by the Lord Chancellor, under the Public Records Act 1958, to advise him on matters concerning public records in general and, in particular, on those aspects of the work of the Public Record Office which affect members of the public who make use of it. The Council meets quarterly and produces an annual report which is published alongside the Report of the Keeper of Public Records as a House of Commons sessional paper.
Chairman, The Master of the Rolls
Members, Prof. B. W. E. Alford; Sir John Blelloch; Dr
A. Borg; Mrs L. Brindley; A. C. Carlile, QC, MP; Prof.
R. Chapman; T. A. G. Davis, MP; Prof. R. B. Dobson;
Miss A. Duncan; V. Gray; Mrs L. Lithgow; Prof. Shula
Marks; Prof. R. Skidelsky; D. Sumberg, MP; D. G. Vaisey
Assessor, Mrs S. Tyacke
Secretary, P. Kennedy

THE PUBLIC RECORD OFFICE
Ruskin Avenue, Kew, Richmond, Surrey TW9 4DU
Tel 081-876 3444
Chancery Lane, London WC2A 1LR
Tel 081-876 3444

The Office, originally established in 1838 under the Master of the Rolls, was placed by the Public Records Act 1958 under the direction of the Lord Chancellor. He appoints a Keeper of Public Records, whose duties are to co-ordinate and supervise the selection of records of government departments and the English law courts for permanent preservation, to safeguard the records and to make them available to the public.

The Office holds records of central government dating from the *Domesday Book* (1086) to the present. Under the Public Records Act 1967 they are normally open to inspection when 30 years old, and are then available, without charge, in the reading rooms, Mon.–Fri., 9.30–5. The museum at Chancery Lane is open Mon.–Fri., 10–5 and the Census rooms are open Mon.–Sat., 9.30–5.

The Public Records Office became an executive agency in 1992.
Keeper of Public Records (G3), Mrs S. Tyacke
Central Management Department (G6), Dr D. L. Thomas

PUBLIC SERVICES DIVISION
Director (G5), C. D. Chalmers
Reader Services Department (G6), Mrs A. Nicol
Editorial Services Department (G6), vacant
Publishing and Public Relations Department (G6), Dr
E. Hallam Smith
Preservation Department (G7), Dr H. Forde

ARCHIVAL SERVICES DIVISION
Director (G5), Dr N. G. Cox
Government Services Department (G6), J. L. Walford
Team Leaders (G7), A. H. W. Medlicott; E. J. Higgs;
K. J. Smith; Ms J. Rose

CORPORATE SERVICES DIVISION
Director (G5), Mrs S. E. Tyerman
IT Department (G7), Miss J. K. Lawlor
Finance Department (G7), Ms P. Ewens
Personnel Department (G7), N. J. Smedley
New PRO Sponsor (G7), Dr A. J. McDonald
Office Services Department (G7), J. S. Harley

HOUSE OF LORDS RECORD OFFICE
House of Lords, London SWIA OPW
Tel 071-219 3074

Since 1497, the records of Parliament have been kept within the Palace of Westminster. They are in the custody of the Clerk of the Parliaments. In 1946 a record department was established to supervise their preservation and their availability to the public. The search room of the office is open to the public Mon.–Fri., 9.30–5 (Tues. to 8, by appointment).

Some three million documents are preserved, including Acts of Parliament from 1497, journals of the House of Lords from 1510, minutes and committee proceedings from 1610, and papers laid before Parliament from 1531. Amongst the records are the Petition of Right, the Death Warrant of Charles I, the Declaration of Breda, and the Bill of Rights. The House of Lords Record Office also has charge of the journals of the House of Commons (from 1547), and other surviving records of the Commons (from 1572), which include plans and annexed documents relating to Private Bill legislation from 1818. Among other documents are the records of the Lord Great Chamberlain, the political papers of certain members of the two Houses, and documents relating to Parliament acquired on behalf of the nation. All the manuscripts and other records are preserved in the Victoria Tower of the Houses of Parliament. A permanent exhibition was established in the Royal Gallery in 1979.
Clerk of the Records (£37,589–£49,790), D. J. Johnson, FSA
Deputy Clerk of the Records (£28,904–£44,390),
S. K. Ellison
Assistant Clerk of the Records (£14,071–£21,798),
D. L. Prior

ROYAL COMMISSION ON HISTORICAL MANUSCRIPTS
Quality House, Quality Court, Chancery Lane, London
WC2A IHP
Tel 071-242 1198

The Commission was set up by royal warrant in 1869 to enquire and report on collections of papers of value for the study of history which were in private hands. In 1959 a new warrant enlarged these terms of reference to include all historical records, wherever situated, outside the Public Records and gave it added responsibilities as a central co-ordinating body to promote, assist and advise on their proper preservation and storage. The Commission has published over 200 volumes of reports.

It also maintains the National Register of Archives, which contains almost 36,000 unpublished lists and catalogues of manuscript collections describing the holdings of local record offices, national and university libraries, specialist repositories and others in the UK and overseas. The NRA can be searched using three computerised indices which are available in the Commission's search room.

The Commission also administers the Manorial and Tithe Documents Rules on behalf of the Master of the Rolls.
Chairman, G. E. Aylmer, FBA
Commissioners, The Lord Blake, FBA;
J. P. W. Ehrman, FBA, FSA; Prof. S. F. C. Milsom, FBA;
P. T. Cormack, FSA, MP; D. G. Vaisey, FSA; The Viscount of Arbuthnott, CBE, DSC; The Lord Camoys; The Lord Egremont and Leconfield; Mrs J. Thirsk, FBA;
Sir Matthew Farrer, KCVO; Miss B. Harvey, FBA, FSA;
Sir John Sainty, KCB, FSA; Prof. R. H. Campbell, PH.D.;
Very Revd H. E. C. Stapleton, FSA; Sir Keith Thomas
Secretary, C. J. Kitching, PH.D., FSA

SCOTTISH RECORD OFFICE
HM General Register House, Edinburgh EHI 3YY
Tel 031-556 6585

The history of the national archives of Scotland can be traced back to the 13th century. The present headquarters of the Scottish Record Office, the General Register House, was founded in 1774. Here are preserved the administrative records of pre-Union Scotland, the registers of central and local courts of law, the public registers of property rights and legal documents, and many collections of local and church records and private archives. Certain groups of records, mainly the modern records of government departments in Scotland, the Scottish railway records, the plans collection, and private archives of an industrial or commercial nature are preserved in the branch repository at the West Register House in Charlotte Square. The search rooms in both buildings open Mon.–Fri., 9–4.45. A permanent exhibition at the West Register House and changing exhibitions at the General Register House are open to the public on weekdays, 10–4. The National Register of Archives (Scotland), which is a branch of the Scottish Record Office, is based in the West Register House.

The Scottish Record Office became an executive agency of the Scottish Office in April 1993.
Keeper of the Records of Scotland, P. M. Cadell

CORPORATION OF LONDON RECORDS OFFICE
Guildhall, London EC2P 2EJ
Tel 071-332 1251

The Corporation of London Records Office contains the municipal archives of the City of London which are regarded as the most complete collection of ancient municipal records in existence. The collection includes charters of William the Conqueror, Henry II, and later kings and queens to 1957; ancient custumals: Liber Horn, Dunthorne, Custumarum, Ordinacionum, Memorandorum and Albus, Liber de Antiquis Legibus, and collections of Statutes; continuous series of judicial rolls and books from 1252 and Council minutes from 1275; records of the Old Bailey and Guildhall Sessions from 1603; financial records from the 16th century; the records of London Bridge from the 12th century; and numerous subsidiary series and miscellanea of historical interest. Readers' Room open Mon.–Fri., 9.30–4.45.
Keeper of the City Records, The Town Clerk
City Archivist, J. R. Sewell
Deputy City Archivist, Mrs J. M. Bankes

RED DEER COMMISSION
Knowsley, 82 Fairfield Road, Inverness IV3 5LH
Tel 0463-231751

The Red Deer Commission has the general functions of furthering the conservation and control of red and sika deer

348   Government Departments and Public Offices

in Scotland and of keeping under review all matters relating to roe deer. It has the statutory duty, with powers, to prevent damage to agriculture and forestry by red and sika deer. The Commission also has the power to advise in the interest of conservation any owner of land on questions relating to the carrying of stocks of red deer, sika deer and roe deer on that land, and to carry out research into matters of scientific importance relating to deer.
Chairman (part-time), P. Gordon-Duff-Pennington, OBE
Secretary, A. Rinning
Senior Field Officer, R. W. Youngson

REVENUE ADJUDICATOR'S OFFICE
3rd Floor, Haymarket House, 28 Haymarket, London SW1Y 4SP
Tel 071-930 2292

The Revenue Adjudicator is appointed by the Board of Inland Revenue to consider complaints about how the Inland Revenue or the Valuation Office Agency have handled someone's affairs. The Adjudicator's Office opened on 1 July 1993.
Revenue Adjudicator, Ms E. Filkin
Head of Office, D. I. Richardson

REVIEW BODIES

The secretariat for these bodies is provided by the Office of Manpower Economics (*see* page 331)

ARMED FORCES PAY

The Review Body on Armed Forces Pay was appointed in 1971 to advise the Prime Minister on the pay and allowances of members of naval, military and air forces of the Crown and of any women's service administered by the Defence Council.
Chairman, G. M. Hourston
Members, P. Ball, OBE; C. M. Bolton; J. C. L. Cox; J. Crosby; Ms B. Dean; Sir Richard Trant, KCB; Mrs D. Venables

DOCTORS' AND DENTISTS' REMUNERATION

The Review Body on Doctors' and Dentists' Remuneration was set up in 1971 to advise the Prime Minister on the remuneration of doctors and dentists taking any part in the National Health Service.
Chairman, C. B. Gough
Members, D. G. Boyd; Ms T. Boyden; D. Fredjohn, MBE; Dr E. Nelson; Prof. G. F. Thomason, CBE; A. J. P. Vineall

NURSING STAFF, MIDWIVES, HEALTH VISITORS AND PROFESSIONS ALLIED TO MEDICINE

The Review Body for nursing staff, midwives, health visitors and professions allied to medicine was set up in 1983 to advise the Prime Minister on the remuneration of nursing staff, midwives and health visitors employed in the National Health Service; and also of physiotherapists, radiographers, remedial gymnasts, occupational therapists, orthoptists, chiropodists, dietitians and related grades employed in the National Health Service.
Chairman, M. Bett, CBE
Members, J. Hildreth; Miss A. Mackie, OBE; Dame Anne Mueller, DCB; Mrs R. Pickavance; Prof. G. F. Thomason, CBE; Miss D. Whittingham

SCHOOL TEACHERS

The School Teachers' Review Body (STRB) was established in 1991. It replaced an Interim Advisory Committee which made recommendations on school teachers' pay and conditions from 1988 to 1992. Unlike the other review bodies, the STRB is a statutory body, set up under the School Teachers' Pay and Conditions Act 1991. It is required to examine and report on such matters relating to the statutory conditions of employment of school teachers in England and Wales as may be referred to it by the Secretary of State for Education. The STRB's reports are submitted to the Prime Minister and the Secretary of State and the latter is required to publish them.
Chairman, Sir Graham Day
Members, Mrs B. Amey; Miss F. Cairncross; R. Carter, CBE; A. G. Cox, CBE; P. Halsey, CB, LVO; Mrs G. Rostron; Mrs A. Vinton

SENIOR SALARIES

A Top Salaries Review Body was set up in 1971 to advise the Prime Minister on the remuneration of the higher judiciary and other judicial appointments, senior civil servants, and senior officers of the armed forces. The Review Body was also asked on a number of occasions to advise on the remuneration of Members of Parliament and of Ministers and on the level of parliamentary allowances. In July 1993 its name was changed to the Senior Salaries Review Body, and its remit was officially extended to cover the pay, pensions and allowances of MPs, ministers and others whose pay is determined by a Ministerial and Other Salaries Order, and the allowances of peers. It will also be required to reward performance where appropriate, and to take into account equal opportunities policy.
Chairman, Sir David Nickson, KBE
Members, Prof. G. Bain; Ms L. Botting; Ms A. Burdus; Sir Peter Cazalet; Sir Cecil Clothier, KCB, QC; G. M. Hourston; H. S. Pigott; Sir Anthony Wilson

ROYAL BOTANIC GARDEN EDINBURGH
Inverleith Row, Edinburgh EH3 5LR
Tel 031-552 7171

The Royal Botanic Garden (RBG) Edinburgh originated as the Physic Garden, established in 1670 beside the Palace of Holyroodhouse. Since 1986, RBG Edinburgh has been administered by a Board of Trustees established under the National Heritage (Scotland) Act 1985.

RBG Edinburgh is an international centre for scientific research on plant diversity, maintaining collections of living plants and reference resources, including a herbarium of some two million specimens of preserved plants. Other statutory functions of RBG Edinburgh include the provision of education and information on botany and horticulture, and the provision of public access to the living plant collections.

The Garden moved to its present site at Inverleith, Edinburgh in 1821. There are also three specialist gardens: Younger Botanic Garden Benmore, near Dunoon, Argyllshire; Logan Botanic Garden, near Stranraer, Wigtownshire; and Dawyck Botanic Garden, near Stobo, Peeblesshire. Public opening hours: RBG Edinburgh, daily (except Christmas Day and New Year's Day) November–February 10–4; March–April and September–October 10–6; May–August 10–8; specialist gardens, March–October 10–6.
Chairman of the Board of Trustees, Sir Peter Hutchison, Bt., CBE

Regius Keeper, Prof. D. S. Ingram
Deputy Keeper, Dr D. J. Mann

ROYAL BOTANIC GARDENS KEW
Richmond, Surrey TW9 3AB
Tel 081-940 1171
Wakehurst Place, Ardingly, nr. Haywards Heath,
W. Sussex RH17 6TN
Tel 0444-892701

The Royal Botanic Gardens (RBG) Kew were founded in 1759 by HRH Princess Augusta. In 1965 the garden at Wakehurst Place was acquired; it is owned by the National Trust and managed by RBG Kew. Under the National Heritage Act 1983 a Board of Trustees was set up to administer the Gardens which in 1984 became an independent body supported by a grant-in-aid.

The functions of RBG Kew are to carry out research into plant sciences, to disseminate knowledge about plants and to provide the public with the opportunity to gain knowledge and enjoyment from the Gardens' collections. There are extensive national reference collections of living and preserved plants and a comprehensive library and archive. The main emphasis is on plant conservation and bio-diversity.

Open daily (except Christmas Day and New Year's Day) from 9.30 a.m. The closing hour varies from 4 p.m. in mid-winter to 6 p.m. on weekdays, and 7.30 p.m. on Sundays and Bank Holidays, in mid-summer. Admission (1993), £3.50. Concessionary schemes available. Museums open 9.30 a.m.; Glasshouses, 9.30–4.30 (weekdays); 9.30–5.30 (Sundays and Bank Holidays). No dogs except guide-dogs for the blind.

BOARD OF TRUSTEES
Chairman, R. A. E. Herbert
Members, R. P. Bauman; The Viscount Blakenham;
Prof. W. G. Chaloner, FRS; Prof. E. C. D. Cocking, FRS;
Sir Philip M. Dowson, CBE, RA; Sir Leslie Fowden, FRS;
Mrs A. Lennox-Boyd; Prof. R. May, FRS; J. Pettifer; Jane Renfrew, PH.D.; Mrs V. R. Wakefield
Director, Dr G. T. Prance, FRS

ROYAL COMMISSION FOR THE EXHIBITION OF 1851
Sherfield Building, Imperial College of Science and Technology, London SW7 2AZ
Tel 071-225 6110

The Royal Commission was incorporated by supplemental charter as a permanent Commission after winding up the affairs of the Great Exhibition of 1851. Its object is to promote scientific and artistic education by means of funds derived from its Kensington estate, purchased with the surplus left over from the Great Exhibition.
President, HRH The Duke of Edinburgh, KG, KT, PC
Chairman, Board of Management, Sir Denis Rooke, CBE, FRS
Secretary to Commissioners, M. C. Neale, CB

ROYAL COMMISSION ON CRIMINAL JUSTICE

The setting up of a Royal Commission on Criminal Justice was announced in March 1991 and its members were

announced in May 1991. Members were appointed by The Queen upon advice from the Home Secretary. The Commission undertook a review of the criminal justice system in England and Wales and completed its work in June 1993. For a summary of its recommendations, *see* Index.
Chairman, The Viscount Runciman of Doxford, CB, FBA
Members, Sir Robert Bunyard, CBE, QPM; Prof. Sir John Cadogan, CBE, FRS; Prof. J. Gunn; The Rt. Hon. Sir John May; Mrs Y. Newbold; Ms U. Prashar;
Miss A. Rafferty, QC; Sir John Wickerson; Sir Philip Woodfield, KCB, CBE; Prof. M. Zander

---

THE ROYAL MINT
Llantrisant, nr Pontyclun, Mid Glamorgan CF7 8YT
Tel 0443-222111

The prime responsibility of the Royal Mint is the provision of United Kingdom coinage, but it actively competes in world markets for a share of the available circulating coin business and, on average, two-thirds of the 15,000 tonnes of coins produced annually is exported to more than 100 countries. The Mint also manufactures special proof and uncirculated quality coins in gold, silver and other metals; military and civil decorations and medals; commemorative and prize medals; and royal and official seals.

The Royal Mint became an executive agency responsible to the Chancellor of the Exchequer in April 1990.
Master of the Mint, The Chancellor of the Exchequer (ex officio)
Deputy Master and Comptroller, R. de L. Holmes

ROYAL NATIONAL THEATRE BOARD
South Bank, London, SE1 9PX
Tel 071-928 2033

Chairman, The Lady Soames, DBE
Members, The Hon. P. Benson; The Hon. Lady Cazalet;
M. Codron, CBE; Dame Judi Dench, DBE; Sir John Hannam, MP; S. Lipton; Sir Derek Mitchell, KCB, CVO; D. Nandy; The Rt. Hon. Sir Michael Palliser, GCMG; L. Sieff, OBE; T. Stoppard, CBE; J. Whitney; S. Yassukovich, CBE
Company Secretary and Head of Finance, A. Blackstock
Board and Committee Secretary, M. McGregor

RURAL DEVELOPMENT COMMISSION
141 Castle Street, Salisbury, Wilts. SP1 3TP
Tel 0722-336255

The Rural Development Commission was formed in 1988 by the merger of the Development Commission for Rural England and the Council for Small Industries in Rural Areas. It is a statutory body funded by government grant-in-aid. It advises the Government on economic and social matters affecting rural areas, and its prime aim is to stimulate job creation and the provision of essential services in the countryside.
Chairman, The Lord Shuttleworth
Deputy Chairman, R. Thompson
Chief Executive, R. Butt
Deputy Chief Executive, J. Taylor

SCIENCE AND ENGINEERING RESEARCH COUNCIL
Polaris House, North Star Avenue, Swindon, Wilts. SN2 1ET
Tel 0793-411000

The Science and Engineering Research Council (SERC) is one of five research councils funded through the Office of Science and Technology. Its purposes are to develop the natural and social sciences, including engineering; to maintain a fundamental capacity of research and scholarship; and to support relevant postgraduate education. SERC's role is to encourage and support research and advanced training in UK higher education institutions in all the basic areas of science and engineering.

From 1 April 1994, the SERC will be split into the Engineering and Physical Sciences Research Council and the Particle Physics and Astronomy Research Council.
Chairman, Sir Mark Richmond, FRS
Members, Prof. P. G. Burke; D. A. Davis; Prof.
   A. Donnachie; G. H. Fairtlough; Dr K. W. Gray;
   Prof. R. E. Hester; Sir Gordon Higginson, FEng.;
   Prof. C. J. Humphreys; Dr S. D. Iversen; Dr A. Ledwith;
   Prof. J. S. Mason; D. P. Nash; Prof. Sir Ronald Oxburgh,
   FRS; Dr G. W. Robinson; Prof. R. E. Smallman, FRS;
   Prof. J. T. Stuart, FRS; Prof. J. O. Thomas, FRS;
   Prof. D. J. Wallace, FRS; Prof. A. W. Wolfendale
For research establishments, *see* page 712

SCOTT INQUIRY
— *see* page 324

SCOTTISH COURTS ADMINISTRATION
— *see* page 380

SCOTTISH ENTERPRISE
120 Bothwell Street, Glasgow G2 7JP
Tel 041-248 2700

On 1 April 1991 Scottish Enterprise took over the economic development and environmental improvement functions of the Scottish Development Agency and the training functions of the Training Agency in lowland Scotland. Its remit is to further the development of Scotland's economy, to enhance the skills of the Scottish workforce, to promote Scotland's international competitiveness and to improve the environment. Many of its functions are contracted out to a network of local enterprise companies. Through Locate in Scotland, Scottish Enterprise is also concerned with attracting firms to Scotland.
Chairman, Prof. D. MacKay
Chief Executive, C. Beveridge
Senior Management Team, C. Aitken; R. Crawford;
   R. Griggs; J. Langlands; J. Lord; R. Macfarlane;
   A. Proctor; C. Woods

SCOTTISH HOMES
Thistle House, 91 Haymarket Terrace, Edinburgh EH12 5HE
Tel 031-313 0044

Scottish Homes, the national housing agency for Scotland, aims to improve the quality and choice of housing in Scotland by working in partnership with the public and private sectors.

The agency is a major funder of new and improved housing, as well as one of the biggest landlords in Scotland, with nearly 60,000 houses. Scottish Homes is involved in housing research and in piloting innovative housing solutions. Board Members are appointed by the Secretary of State for Scotland.
Chairman, Sir James Mellon
Deputy Chairman, J. Richards, CBE
Chief Executive, P. McKinlay

SCOTTISH NATURAL HERITAGE
12 Hope Terrace, Edinburgh EH9 2AS
Tel 031-447 4784

Scottish Natural Heritage came into existence on 1 April 1992 under the Natural Heritage (Scotland) Act 1991. It was created by the merger of the Countryside Commission for Scotland and the Nature Conservancy Council for Scotland and combines the functions of those bodies. It provides advice on nature conservation to all those whose activities affect wildlife, landforms and features of geological interest in Scotland, and seeks to develop and improve facilities for the enjoyment of the Scottish countryside.
Chairman, M. Magnusson, KBE
Chief Executive, R. Crofts
Chief Scientific Adviser, M. B. Usher

SCOTTISH OFFICE

The Secretary of State for Scotland is responsible in Scotland for a wide range of statutory functions which in England and Wales are the responsibility of a number of departmental ministers. He also works closely with ministers in charge of Great Britain departments on topics of special significance to Scotland within their fields of responsibility. His statutory functions are administered by five main departments: the Scottish Office Agriculture and Fisheries Department, the Scottish Office Education Department, the Scottish Office Environment Department, the Scottish Office Home and Health Department, and the Scottish Office Industry Department. These departments plus Central Services are collectively known as the Scottish Office.

In addition there are a number of other Scottish departments for which the Secretary of State has some degree of responsibility; these include the Scottish Courts Administration, the Department of the Registrar-General for Scotland (the General Register Office), the Scottish Record Office and the Department of the Registers of Scotland. The Secretary of State also bears ministerial responsibility for the activities in Scotland of several statutory bodies whose functions extend throughout Great Britain, such as the Training Commission and the Forestry Commission.

Dover House, Whitehall, London, SW1A 2AU
Tel 071-270 3000

Secretary of State for Scotland, The Rt. Hon. Ian Lang, MP
   Private Secretary (G5), A. W. Fraser
   Special Advisers, A. Young; G. Mackay
   Parliamentary Private Secretary, S. Coombs, MP
Minister of State, The Lord Fraser of Carmyllie, PC, QC
   *(Education, Health and Home Affairs, and General
   European Issues)*
   Private Secretary, Ms S. J. Morrell
Parliamentary Under-Secretaries of State, Lord James
   Douglas-Hamilton, MP; J. Allan Stewart, MP; Sir Hector
   Monro, MP

SCI - SCO   **351**

Private Secretaries, Ms H. A. Jones (*Lord James Douglas-Hamilton*); M. I. Pringle (*J. Allan Stewart*); A. E. Sim (*Sir Hector Monro*)
Parliamentary Clerk, I. Campbell
Permanent Under-Secretary of State (G1), Sir Russell Hillhouse, KCB
Private Secretary, J. Taylor
Liaison Staff:
Assistant Secretary (G5), E. W. Ferguson

St Andrew's House, Edinburgh EH1 3DG
Tel 031-556 8400

MANAGEMENT GROUP SUPPORT STAFF
Principal (G7), Ms M. M. A. McGinn

CENTRAL SERVICES

Grade 2, G. R. Wilson, CB

PERSONNEL GROUP
16 Waterloo Place Edinburgh, EH1 3DN
Tel 031-556 8400

Principal Establishment Officer (G3), C. C. MacDonald
Assistant Secretaries (G5), G. D. Calder; J. A. Rennie;
 W. R. J. McQueen
Senior Principals (G6), C. D. Henderson; I. C. Henderson;
 W. E. Bennet

ADMINISTRATIVE SERVICES
James Craig Walk, Edinburgh EH1 3BA
Tel 031-556 8400

Director of Administrative Services (G4), R. S. B. Gordon
Assistant Secretary (G5), D. Stevenson
Director of Information Technology (G5), A. M. Brown
Deputy Director (G6), I. W. Goodwin
Director of Telecommunications (G6), K. Henderson
Director of Office Management (G6), B. V. Surridge, ISO
Chief Estates Officer (G6), R. I. K. White, FRICS

FINANCE DIVISION
New St Andrew's House, Edinburgh EH1 3TG
Tel 031-556 8400

Principal Finance Officer (G3), Miss E. A MacKay
Assistant Secretaries (G5), J. S. Aldridge; P. A. Brady;
 S. F. Hampson; D. G. N. Reid; W. T. Tait
Director of Financial Systems Unit (G6), R. Smith

SOLICITOR'S OFFICE
For the Scottish departments and certain UK services, including HM Treasury, in Scotland
Solicitor (G2), R. Brodie, CB
Deputy Solicitor (G3), N. W. Boe
Divisional Solicitors (G5), J. B. Allan; K. F. Barclay
 (*seconded to Scottish Law Commission*); R. Bland;
 G. C. Duke; I. H. Harvie; R. M. Henderson;
 J. L. Jamieson; H. F. Macdiarmid; Mrs L. A. Wallace

SCOTTISH OFFICE INFORMATION DIRECTORATE
For the Scottish departments and certain UK services
Director (G5), Ms E. S. B. Drummond
Deputy Director (G6), W. A. McNeill

SCOTTISH OFFICE AGRICULTURE AND FISHERIES DEPARTMENT
Pentland House, 47 Robb's Loan, Edinburgh EH14 ITY
Tel 031-556 8400

Secretary (G2), K. J. MacKenzie
Under-Secretary (G3), T. A. Cameron
Fisheries Secretary (G3), G. Robson

Assistant Secretaries (G5), P. S. Collings; E. C. Davison;
 D. R. Dickson; J. Duffy; I. W. Gordon; R. A. Grant;
 A. K. MacLeod; K. W. Moore; A. J. Rushworth;
 I. M. Whitelaw
Chief Agricultural Officer (G4), J. F. Hutcheson
Deputy Chief Agricultural Officer (G5), W. A. Macgregor
Assistant Chief Agricultural Officers (G6), D. R. J. Craven;
 J. A. Hardie; J. G. Muir; A. Robb; J. I. Woodrow
Chief Agricultural Economist (G6), J. R. Wildgoose, D.Phil.
Chief Meat and Livestock Inspector (G7), J. Miller
Chief Food and Dairy Officer (G7), D. J. MacDonald
Chief Surveyor (G6), N. Taylor, FRICS
Scientific Adviser (G5), T. W. Hegarty, Ph.D.
Senior Principal Scientific Officers (G6), R. J. Dowdell, Ph.D.;
 D. Thornton

AGRICULTURAL SCIENCE AGENCY
East Craigs, Edinburgh EH12 8NJ
Tel 031-556 8400
An executive agency within the Scottish Office
Director (G5), Dr R. K. M. Hay
Deputy Director (G6), R. S. Cooper
Senior Principal Scientific Officer (G6), M. J. Richardson

FISHERIES RESEARCH SERVICES
Marine Laboratory, PO Box 101,
Victoria Road, Torry, Aberdeen AB9 8DB
Tel 0224-876544
Director of Fisheries Research for Scotland (G4),
 Prof. A. D. Hawkins, Ph.D., FRSE
Deputy Director (G5), D. N. MacLennan
Senior Principal Scientific Officers (G6), R. M. Cook, Ph.D.;
 J. M. Davies, Ph.D.; A. L. S. Munro, Ph.D.;
 P. A. M. Stewart, Ph.D.; C. S. Wardle, Ph.D

Freshwater Fisheries Laboratory
Faskally, Pitlochry, Perthshire PH16 5LB
Tel 0796-472060
Senior Principal Scientific Officers (G6), R. G. J. Shelton,
 Ph.D.; J. E. Thorpe, Ph.D.
Inspector of Salmon and Freshwater Fisheries for Scotland
 (*G7*), R. B. Williamson

Scottish Fisheries Protection Agency
Pentland House, 47 Robb's Loan, Edinburgh EH14 ITW
Tel 031-556 8400
An executive agency within the Scottish Office
Chief Executive (G5), A. K. MacLeod
Director of Policy and Resources (G6), J. B. Roddin
Chief Inspector of Sea Fisheries (G6), J. F. Fenton
Marine Superintendent, Capt. R. M. Mill-Irving

SCOTTISH OFFICE ENVIRONMENT DEPARTMENT
New St Andrew's House, Edinburgh EH1 3TG
Tel 031-556 8400

Secretary (G2), H. H. Mills
Under-Secretaries (G3), J. S. Graham; J. F. Laing;
 A. M. Russell
Assistant Secretaries (G5), M. T. Affolter; M. Batho;
 C. M. Baxter; J. T. Birley; D. J. Chalmers;
 W. J. Fearnley; Dr J. M. Francis; I. C. Freeman;
 J. W. L. Lonie; K. W. McKay; D. F. Middleton;
 J. N. Randall; E. C. Reavley; A. M. Russell

PROFESSIONAL STAFF
Chief Engineer (G3), A. C. Paton
Deputy Chief Engineer (G5), T. D. Macdonald
Assistant Chief Engineers (G6), T. Bolton; D. MacFarlane;
 P. Wright

Director of Building and Chief Architect (G3), J. E. Gibbons,
ph.d., fsascot.
Deputy Director of Building and Deputy Chief Architect (G5),
vacant
Assistant Directors (G6), G. Gray; A. Higgins; A. J. Wyllie
Chief Planner (G4), A. Mackenzie
Deputy Chief Planner (G5), D. R. Dare
Assistant Chief Planners (G6), A. W. Denham; I. R. Duncan;
S. G. Fulton; T. Williamson
HM Chief Industrial Pollution Inspector (G5),
I. W. W. Wright

HISTORIC SCOTLAND
20 Brandon Street, Edinburgh EH3 5RA
Tel 031-244 3144
An executive agency within the Scottish Office
Chief Executive (G3), G. N. Munro
Directors (G5), F. J. Lawrie; D. Macniven, TD; I. Maxwell;
S. Rosie
Chief Inspector of Ancient Monuments, Dr D. J. Breeze
Chief Inspector, Building Division, D. M. Walker, OBE

LOCAL GOVERNMENT FINANCE GROUP
New St Andrew's House, Edinburgh EH1 3TB
Tel 031-556 8400
Assistant Secretaries (G5), C. M. Baxter; K. W. McKay

INQUIRY REPORTERS
16 Waterloo Place, Edinburgh EH1 3DN
Tel 031-556 8400
Chief Reporter (G3), Miss G. Pain
Deputy Chief Reporter (G5), R. M. Hickman

SCOTTISH OFFICE INDUSTRY
DEPARTMENT
New St Andrew's House, Edinburgh EH1 3TG
Tel 031-556 8400
Secretary (G2), P. MacKay, CB
Under-Secretaries (G3), A. D. F. Findlay; E. J. Weeple
Assistant Secretaries (G5), D. A. Brew; D. A. Campbell;
M. J. P. Cunliffe; J. W. Elvidge; I. F. Gray;
P. Heatherington; R. N. Irvine; R. MacEwan; R. Tait
Senior Economic Advisers (G5), A. Goudie; C. L. Wood

PROFESSIONAL STAFF
Director of Roads (G3), J. A. L. Dawson
Deputy Chief Engineers (Roads) (G5), J. A. Howison;
R. D. Udall
Deputy Chief Engineer (Bridges) (G5), J. Innes
Assistant Chief Engineers (G6), N. B. MacKenzie;
I. McIntosh

INDUSTRIAL EXPANSION
Alhambra House, 45 Waterloo Street, Glasgow G2 6AT
Tel 041-248 2855
Under-Secretary (G3), vacant
Industrial Adviser, Dr C. K. Benington
Scientific Adviser, I. McGhee
Assistant Secretaries (G5), J. McGhee; J. Meldrum;
J. Thornton

LOCATE IN SCOTLAND
120 Bothwell Street, Glasgow G2 7JP
Tel 041-248 2700
Director (G4), R. Crawford
Senior Principal (G6), W. Malone
Principal (G7), A. McCabe; J. Wilson
Director (North America), R. Crawford

SCOTTISH OFFICE EDUCATION
DEPARTMENT
New St Andrew's House, Edinburgh EH1 3TG
Tel 031-556 8400

Secretary (G2), G. R. Wilson, CB
Under-Secretaries (G3), W. A. P. Weatherston, CB;
J. S. B. Martin
Assistant Secretaries (G5), D. S. Henderson; R. D. Jackson;
T. J. Kelly; G. McHugh; Miss M. MacLean; K. Macrae;
*Mrs R. Menlowe; *Mrs V. MacNiven; *Mrs
N. S. Munro
Chief Statistician (G5), vacant

* part-time

HM INSPECTORS OF SCHOOLS
Senior Chief Inspector (G3), T. N. Gallacher
Deputy Senior Chief Inspectors (G4), W. T. Beveridge;
D. A. Osler
Chief Inspectors (G5), G. H. C. Donaldson; Miss
K. M. Fairweather; G. P. D. Gordon; R. H. Manser;
J. J. McDonald; A. S. McGlynn; M. Roebuck;
H. M. Stalker; R. M. S. Tuck
There are 96 Grade 6 Inspectors.

SCOTTISH OFFICE HOME AND HEALTH
DEPARTMENT
St Andrew's House, Edinburgh EH1 3DG
Tel 031-556 8400

Secretary (G2), J. Hamill
Under-Secretaries (G3), D. Belfall; N. G. Campbell;
D. J. Essery; Mrs G. M. Stewart
Assistant Secretaries (G5), Mrs M. H. Brannan; J. T. Brown;
Mrs M. B. Gunn; C. M. A. Lugton; C. K. McIntosh;
P. M. Russell; R. H. Scott
Senior Principal (G6), N. MacLeod

NATIONAL HEALTH SERVICE IN SCOTLAND
MANAGEMENT EXECUTIVE
Chief Executive, vacant
Private Secretary, vacant
Director of Strategic Management, G. A. Anderson
Director of Finance, M. Collier
Director of Administration, Dr D. Steel
Director of Information Services, C. B. Knox
Director of Manpower, A. J. Matheson
Assistant Secretaries (G5), W. J. Farquhar; Ms I. M. Low;
W. Moyes; Mrs A. Robson; G. M. D. Thomson;
G. W. Tucker
Assistant Director (G6), H. R. McCallum
Senior Principal (G6), Miss J. McGregor

MEDICAL SERVICES
Chief Medical Officer (G2), Prof. R. E. Kendell, CBE, MD
Deputy Chief Medical Officer (G3), Dr A. B. Young, FRCPE
Principal Medical Officers, Dr J. V. Basson;
Dr C. F. Fleming; Dr Margaret Hennigan; Dr Rosalind
Skinner; Dr Elizabeth Sowler
Senior Medical Officers, Dr R. E. G. Aitken, TD; I. R. Bashford;
P. W. Brooks; S. Capewell; W. Dodd; Dr D. J. Ewing;
Dr A. Findlay; Ms E. Keel; Dr Sheila Lawson; Dr
Patricia Madden; Dr A. MacLeod; B. T. Potter; Dr
R. Simmons; Dr O. A. Thores; Dr M. I. Ullah
Chief Scientist, Prof. I. A. D. Bouchier, CBE, FRCP
Chief Dental Officer, J. R. Wild
Deputy Chief Dental Officer, vacant
Regional Dental Officers, K. J. McKenzie; M. G. Platt; Miss
A. J. Power; G. A. Reid
Chief Nursing Officer, Miss A. Jarvie
Chief Pharmacist (G5), W. Scott

Chief Research Officer, Dr C. P. A. Levein
Senior Principal Research Officers (G6), Mrs B. Doig; Dr
Jacqueline Tombs

SOCIAL WORK SERVICES GROUP
43 Jeffrey Street, Edinburgh EH1 1DN
Tel 031-556 8400
The Social Work Services Group administers the provisions
of the Social Work (Scotland) Act 1968.
Assistant Secretaries (G5), Ms L. J. Clare; J. W. Sinclair;
D. Wishart
Chief Inspector of Social Work Services, A. Skinner
Assistant Chief Inspectors, Mrs H. Dempster;
Ms M. L. Hunt; F. A. O'Leary; D. Pia; I. C. Robertson

MISCELLANEOUS APPOINTMENTS
HM Chief Inspector of Constabulary, Sir Colin
Sampson, KBE, QPM
HM Chief Inspector of Prisons, A. H. Bishop, CB
Commandant, Scottish Police College, H. I. Watson, QPM
HM Chief Inspector of Fire Services, N. Morrison
Commandant, Scottish Fire Service Training School,
C. F. McManus, QFSM
Secretary, Scottish Health Service Advisory Council,
W. J. Farquhar

SCOTTISH PRISON SERVICE
Calton House, 5 Redheughs Rigg, Edinburgh EH12 9HW
Tel 031-556 8400
An executive agency within the Scottish Office
Chief Executive of Scottish Prison Service (G3),
E. W. Frizzell
Deputy Chief Executive and Director of Prisons (G5),
A. R. Walker
Director, Human Resources (G5), J. D. Gallagher
Director, Strategy and Planning (G5), D. A. Stewart
Deputy Director, Regime Services and Supplies (G6),
N. Harvey
Deputy Director, Estates and Buildings (G6),
D. D. Sutherland
Area Director, South and West (G5), J. Milne
Area Director, North and East (G5), J. Pearce
Governor, Scottish Prison Service College, R. L. Houchin

Prisons

Aberdeen, Craiginches, Aberdeen AB9 2HN. *Governor*,
W. A. R. Rattray
Barlinnie, Barlinnie, Glasgow G33 2QX. *Governor*,
P. Withers
Barlinnie Special Unit, Barlinnie, Glasgow G33 2QX.
Governor, I. A. Bannatyne
Castle Huntly Young Offenders Institution, Castle Huntly,
Longforgan, nr Dundee DD2 5HL. *Governor*, Mrs
M. Wood
Cornton Vale, Cornton Road, Stirling FK9 5NY. *Governor*,
P. L. Abernethy
Dumfries Young Offenders Institution, Terregles Street,
Dumfries DG2 9AX. *Governor*, G. Taylor
Dungavel, Dungavel House, Strathaven, Lanarkshire
ML10 6RF. *Governor*, J. Bywalec
Edinburgh, Saughton, Edinburgh EH1 3LN. *Governor*,
J. Durno
Friarton, Friarton, Perth PH2 8DW. *Governor*, R. A. Findlay
Glenochil Prison and Young Offenders Institution, King
O'Muir Road, Tullibody, Clackmannanshire FK10 3AD.
Governor, L. McBain
Greenock, Gateside, Greenock PA16 9AH. *Governor*,
D. E. Gunn
Inverness, Porterfield, Inverness IV2 3HH. *Governor*,
W. Blyth

Longriggend Remand Institution, Longriggend, nr Airdrie,
Lanarkshire ML6 7TL. *Governor*, A. F. King
Low Moss, Low Moss, Bishopbriggs, Glasgow G64 2QB.
Governor, J. Collins
Noranside, Noranside, Fern, By Forfar, Angus DD8 3QY.
Governor, E. Brownsmith
Penninghame, Penninghame, Newton Stewart DG8 6RG.
Governor, H. Ross
Perth, 3 Edinburgh Road, Perth PH2 8AT. *Governor*, R. Kite
Peterhead, Salthouse Head, Peterhead, Aberdeenshire AB4
6YY. *Governor*, A. P. Spencer
Polmont Young Offenders Institution, Brightons, Falkirk,
Stirlingshire FK2 0AB. *Governor*, G. Shearer
Shotts, Shotts ML7 4LF. *Governor*, E. J. Campbell
Shotts Alternative Unit, Shotts ML7 4LF. *Governor*,
A. MacDonald

MENTAL WELFARE COMMISSION FOR SCOTLAND
25 Drumsheugh Gardens, Edinburgh EH3 7NS
Tel 031-225 7034
Chairman, Sheriff H. J. Aronson
Commissioners, Mrs A. Baxter; P. H. Brodie; R. G. Davis;
Mrs A. M. Glen; Ms A. M. Green; Mrs H. L. Grieve;
Mrs J. I. D. Isbister; Mrs M. Jeffcoat; Dr J. McCurley;
J. Murray; Miss L. M. Noble; M. O'Reilly;
J. G. Sutherland
Medical Commissioners, J. A. T. Dyer; A. A. McKechnie
Social Work Commissioner, J. H. L. Richards
Secretary, Mrs M. A. MacLeod

COUNSEL TO THE SECRETARY OF STATE FOR SCOTLAND
UNDER THE PRIVATE LEGISLATION PROCEDURE
(SCOTLAND) ACT 1936
50 Frederick Street, Edinburgh EH2 1EX
Tel 031-226 6499
Senior Counsel, G. S. Douglas, QC
Junior Counsel, N. M. P. Morrison

NATIONAL HEALTH SERVICE, SCOTLAND

HEALTH BOARDS
ARGYLL AND CLYDE, Gilmour House, Paisley. *Chairman*,
R. R. Reid; *General Manager*, I. C. Smith
AYRSHIRE AND ARRAN, PO Box 13, Hunters Avenue,
Ayr. *Chairman*, J. W. G. Donaldson, CBE; *General
Manager*, J. M. Eckford, OBE
BORDERS, Huntlyburn, Melrose, Roxburghshire.
Chairman, D. A. C. Kilshaw; *General Manager*,
D. A. Peters
DUMFRIES AND GALLOWAY, Nithbank, Dumfries.
Chairman, J. A. M. McIntyre, OBE; *General Manager*,
D. Banks
FIFE, Glenrothes House, North Street, Glenrothes.
Chairman, R. Baker, OBE; *General Manager*, vacant
FORTH VALLEY, 33 Spittal Street, Stirling. *Chairman*,
Mrs J. D. Isbister; *General Manager*, Miss L. Barrie
GRAMPIAN, 1–7 Albyn Place, Aberdeen. *Chairman*, Dr
C. MacLeod, CBE; *General Manager*, F. E. L. Hartnett,
OBE
GREATER GLASGOW, 112 Ingram Street, Glasgow.
Chairman, W. S. Fyfe, CBE; *General Manager*,
L. Peterken, CBE
HIGHLAND, Reay House, 17 Old Edinburgh Road,
Inverness. *Chairman*, J. D. M. Robertson, CBE; *General
Manager*, R. R. W. Stewart
LANARKSHIRE, 14 Beckford Street, Hamilton,
Lanarkshire. *Chairman*, I. Livingstone, OBE; *General
Manager*, F. Clark, CBE
LOTHIAN, 148 The Pleasance, Edinburgh. *Chairman*,
Dr J. W. Baynham; *General Manager*, J. Lusby

ORKNEY, Balfour Hospital, New Scapa Road, Kirkwall, Orkney. *Chairman*, J. Leslie; *General Manager*, Dr J. I. Cromarty

SHETLAND, 28 Burgh Road, Lerwick. *Chairman*, Mrs F. Grains; *General Manager*, B. J. Atherton

TAYSIDE, PO Box 75, Vernonholme, Riverside Drive, Dundee. *Chairman*, J. C. MacFarlane, OBE; *General Manager*, Dr R. C. Graham, CBE

WESTERN ISLES, 37 South Beach Street, Stornoway, Isle of Lewis. *Chairman*, A. Matheson; *General Manager*, J. J. Glover

HEALTH EDUCATION BOARD FOR SCOTLAND
Woodburn House, Canaan Lane, Edinburgh EH10 4SG
Chairman, E. Walker
General Manager, Dr A. Tannahill

STATE HOSPITAL
Carstairs Junction, Lanark ML11 8RP
Chairman, P. Hamilton-Grierson
General Manager, R. Manson

COMMON SERVICES AGENCY
Trinity Park House, South Trinity Road, Edinburgh EH5 3SE
Chairman, vacant
General Manager, J. T. Donald

SCOTTISH OFFICE PENSIONS AGENCY
151 London Road, Edinburgh EH8 7TG
Tel 031-556 8400
An executive agency within the Scottish Office
Chief Executive, N. MacLeod

GENERAL REGISTER OFFICE
New Register House, Edinburgh EH1 3YT
Tel 031-334 0380

The General Register Office for Scotland is the office of the Registrar-General for Scotland, who has responsibility for civil registration and the taking of censuses in Scotland and has in his custody the following records: the statutory registers of births, deaths, still births, adoptions, marriages and divorces; the old parish registers (recording births, marriages, deaths, etc., before civil registration began in 1855); and records of censuses of the population in Scotland. Hours of public access: Mon.–Thurs. 9–4.30; Fri. 9–4.
Registrar-General (G4), Dr C. M. Glennie
Deputy Registrar-General (G5), B. V. Philp
Senior Principal (G6), D. A. Orr
Principals (G7), D. B. L. Brownlee; R. C. Lawson; F. D. Garvie
Statisticians (G7), J. Arrundale; G. W. L. Jackson; F. G. Thomas

SEA FISH INDUSTRY AUTHORITY
18 Logie Mill, Logie Green Road, Edinburgh EH7 4HG
Tel 031-558 3331

Chairman, The Lord Mackay of Ardbrecknish
Chief Executive, P. D. Chaplin
Assistant Secretary, D. Robertson
Technical Director, J. E. Tumilty
Marketing Director, R. M. Kennedy
Training Director, K. Waind

THE SECURITY SERVICE COMMISSIONER
c/o The Home Office, 50 Queen Anne's Gate, London SW1H 9AT

The Commissioner is appointed by the Prime Minister. He keeps under review the issue of warrants by the Home Secretary under the Security Service Act 1989, and is required to give the Security Service Tribunal help by investigating complaints which allege interference with property and by offering all such assistance in discharging its functions as it may require. He is also required to submit an annual report on the discharge of his functions to the Prime Minister.
Commissioner, The Rt. Hon. Lord Justice Stuart-Smith

SECURITY SERVICE TRIBUNAL
PO Box 18, London SE1 0TZ

The Security Service Act 1989 established a tribunal of three to five senior members of the legal profession, independent of the Government and appointed by The Queen, to investigate complaints from any person about anything which they believe the Security Service has done to them or to their property.
President, The Rt. Hon. Lord Justice Simon Brown
Vice-President, Sheriff J. McInnes, QC
Member, Sir Richard Gaskell

SERIOUS FRAUD OFFICE
Elm House, 10–16 Elm Street, London, WC1X 0BJ
Tel 071-239 7272

The Serious Fraud Office is an autonomous department under the superintendence of the Attorney-General. Its remit is to investigate and prosecute serious and complex fraud. The scope of its powers covers England, Wales and Northern Ireland. The staff includes lawyers, accountants and other support staff; investigating teams work closely with the police.
Director, G. Staple
Deputy Director, J. Knox

DEPARTMENT OF SOCIAL SECURITY
Richmond House, 79 Whitehall, London, SW1A 2NS
Tel 071-210 3000

The Department of Social Security is responsible for the payment of benefits and the collection of contributions under the National Insurance and Industrial Injuries schemes, and for the payment of child benefit, one-parent benefit, Income Support and Family Credit. It administers the Social Fund, and is responsible for assessing the means of applicants for legal aid. It is also responsible for the payment of war pensions.
Secretary of State for Social Security, The Rt. Hon. Peter Lilley, MP
  Private Secretary, Ms J. Rintoul
  Special Adviser, P. Barnes
  Parliamentary Private Secretary, P. Merchant, MP
Minister of State, Rt. Hon. Nicholas Scott, MBE, MP (*Social Security and Disabled People*)

Private Secretary, I. Spur
Parliamentary Private Secretary, M. Bates, MP
Parliamentary Under-Secretary of State (Lords), The Lord
Henley
Private Secretary, Ms C. Poulson
Parliamentary Under-Secretaries of State (Commons), Alistair
Burt, MP; William Hague, MP
Private Secretaries, Ms J. Simpson; Ms H. Nicholas
*Parliamentary Private Secretary to all the Parliamentary
Under-Secretaries*, I. Bruce, MP
Permanent Secretary (G1), Sir Michael Partridge, KCB
Private Secretary, Ms H. Todd

RESOURCE MANAGEMENT AND PLANNING GROUP
Deputy Secretary (G2), B. Gilmore

CORPORATE, STRATEGIC AND PLANNING DIVISION
Grade 3, S. Hewitt

*ANALYTICAL SERVICES DIVISION
Director (G3), D. Stanton

FINANCE DIVISION
Grade 3, J. Tross

SOCIAL SECURITY POLICY GROUP
Deputy Secretary (G2), R. A. Birch

*SOCIAL SECURITY DIVISION A
Under-Secretary (G3), B. Walmsley
Assistant Secretaries (G5), N. Ward; K. Limm;
J. Groombridge; R. H. Layton; Mrs A. Lingwood

*SOCIAL SECURITY DIVISION B
Under-Secretary (G3), Miss M. Pierson
Assistant Secretaries (G5), J. Moor; Miss L. Richards;
C. Evans

*SOCIAL SECURITY DIVISION C
Under Secretary (G3), D. J. Clark
Assistant Secretaries (G5), Mrs C. Souter; Miss J. Liebling;
D. Hill; Ms J. Clayton

*SOCIAL SECURITY DIVISION D
Under-Secretary (G3), R. Brown
Assistant Secretaries (G5), P. Tansley; Miss N. Bastin;
D. Jackson; M. Lloyd

*SOCIAL SECURITY DIVISION E
Under-Secretary (G3), D. Brereton
Assistant Secretaries (G5), S. Wilcox; A. Woods;
B. Calderwood; Miss S. Fraenkel

MAXWELL PENSIONS UNIT
7 St James's Square, London SW1Y 4JU
Tel 071-839 3599
Director (G3), R. P. Cleasby

INFORMATION DIVISION
Head of Information (G5), S. Reardon
Deputy Head of Information (G6), T. Grace
Principal Information Officer (G7), J. Bretherton
Chief Publicity Officer (G7), Ms H. Midlane

SOLICITOR'S OFFICE
Solicitor (G2), P. K. J. Thompson

*At The Adelphi, 1–11 John Adam Street, London WC2N 6HT. Tel:
071-962 8000

SOLICITOR'S DIVISION A
New Court, 48 Carey Street, London WC2A 2LS
Tel 071-412 1342
Principal Assistant Solicitor (G3), Mrs G. S. Kerrigan

SOLICITOR'S DIVISION B
New Court, 48 Carey Street, London WC2A 2LS
Tel 071-412 1370
Proceedings Operational Director (G4), P. C. Nilsson

EXECUTIVE AGENCIES

BENEFITS AGENCY
Quarry House, Quarry Hill, Leeds LS2 7UA
Tel 0532-324000
Chief Executive (G2), M. Bichard
Private Secretary, S. G. Appleton
Directors (G3), D. Riggs *(finance)*; G. Bardwell *(personnel)*

Benefits Agency Territories
SCOTLAND/NORTHERN ENGLAND, Sandyford House,
Archbold Terrace, Newcastle upon Tyne NE2 1AA.
Director (G3), A. J. Laurance
SOUTHERN ENGLAND, Olympic House, Olympic Way,
Wembley, Middx. HA9 ODL. *Director (G3)*, A. Cleveland
WALES/CENTRAL ENGLAND, Five Ways Tower,
Frederick Road, Edgbaston, Birmingham B15 1ST.
Director (G3), I. Stewart

Benefits Agency Medical Services
Director (G3), Dr P. Castaldi
Principal Medical Officers, Dr M. Aylward; Dr P. Dewis; Dr
C. Hudson; Dr P. Doughty

INFORMATION TECHNOLOGY SERVICES AGENCY
15th Floor, Euston Tower, 286 Euston Road, London
NW1 3DN
Tel 071-306 5051
Chief Executive, I. Magee
Deputy Chief Executive, P. T. F. Dunn
Directors, Ms A. Cleveland; K. Caldwell; G. McCorkell;
S. Williams; J. Thomas; U. Brennan; N. Haighton
Non-Executive Director, J. M. Bankier, CBE

CONTRIBUTIONS AGENCY
Room C1837, DSS Longbenton, Benton Park Road,
Newcastle upon Tyne NE98 1YX
Tel 091-225 7665
Chief Executive (G4), Miss A. Chant
Deputy Chief Executive (G5), G. Bertram
Directors, K. Wilson; S. Heminsley; R. Roberts; D. Gatenby;
A. Cass; I. Hutton
Non-Executive Director, R. Brimblecombe

RESETTLEMENT AGENCY
Euston Tower, 286 Euston Road, London, NW1 3DN
Tel 071-388 1188
Chief Executive (G6), A. J. Ward

CHILD SUPPORT AGENCY
Millbank Tower, 21–24 Millbank, London SW1P 4QU
Tel 071-210 3000
The Agency was set up in April 1993. It is responsible for
setting maintenance payment levels and collecting and
enforcing the payments where necessary.
Chief Executive (G4), Mrs R. Hepplewhite

WAR PENSIONS
An executive agency to be established in April 1994
Chief Executitive-designate, P. Mathison

Central Advisory Committee on War Pensions
Room 1138, The Adelphi, 1–11 John Adam Street, London
WC2N 6HT
Tel 071-962 8028
Secretary, S. Adams

SOCIAL SECURITY ADVISORY COMMITTEE
New Court, Carey Street, London, WC2A 2LS
Tel 071-412 1507

The Social Security Advisory Committee (SSAC) was established by the Social Security Act 1980 to advise the Secretary of State for Social Security and the Department of Health and Social Services for Northern Ireland on all social security matters except those relating to benefits for industrial injuries and diseases and occupational pensions. The Social Security Housing Benefit Act 1982 added housing benefit to the Committee's responsibilities.
Chairman, Sir Peter Barclay, CBE
Members, Mrs J. Anelay, OBE; A. Dilnot; Revd G. H. Good, OBE; D. Guereca; M. Hastings; P. F. Naish; Hon. Mrs R. H. P. Price; Lady Scott, CBE; Dr A. V. Stokes, OBE; Prof. Olive Stevenson; O. Tudor; R. G. Wendt
Secretary, L. C. Smith

SPORTS COUNCIL
16 Upper Woburn Place, London WC1H 0QP
Tel 071-388 1277

The Sports Council, created under royal charter, promotes the development of sport and fosters the provision of facilities for sport and recreation in Great Britain.
Chairman, Sir Peter Yarranton

HMSO (HER MAJESTY'S STATIONERY OFFICE)
St Crispins, Duke Street, Norwich NR3 1PD
Tel 0603-622211

HMSO (Her Majesty's Stationery Office) was established in 1786 and is the government executive agency that provides printing, binding and business supplies to government departments and publicly funded organizations. HMSO is also the Government's publisher, and has bookshops for the sale of government publications in six major cities as well as appointed agents in other cities. HMSO obtains most of its supplies and printing from commercial sources by competitive tender, apart from about 20 per cent of its printing requirement, such as Hansard and Bills and Acts of Parliament, which are produced in its own printing works. HMSO is a self-financing government trading fund and competes for its business with other commercial suppliers.
Controller and Chief Executive, P. I. Freeman, CB
  Executive Assistant, Mrs J. B. Ward
Deputy Chief Executive, M. D. Lynn
Director-General of Corporate Services, P. J. Macdonald

HEADS OF DIVISIONS
Publications, C. N. Southgate
Business Supplies, A. J. Davies
Print Procurement, B. Ekers

Finance and Planning, C. J. Penn
Information Technology, D. C. Kerry
Technological Innovation, J. R. Eveson
Engineering and Estates, W. E. Scott
Human Resources, J. McDonald
Organization Development, V. C. Bell
Quality and Consultancy, A. M. Cole

BIRMINGHAM – *Bookshop*, 258 Broad Street, Birmingham B1 2HE
BRISTOL, Ashton Vale Road, Bristol BS3 2HN – *Bookshop*, 33 Wine Street, Bristol BS1 2BQ
LONDON – *Publications Centre*, 51 Nine Elms Lane, London SW8 5DR. *Bookshop*, 49 High Holborn, London WC1V 6HB
MANCHESTER, Broadway, Chadderton, Oldham, Lancs. OL9 9QH – *Bookshop*, 9–21 Princess Street, Manchester M60 8AS
SCOTLAND, South Gyle Crescent, Edinburgh EH12 9EB. *Director, Edinburgh*, G. W. Bedford – *Bookshop*, 71 Lothian Road, Edinburgh EH3 9AZ
NORTHERN IRELAND, IDB House, Chichester Street, Belfast BT1 4PS. *Director, Belfast*, M. McNeill – *Bookshop*, 16 Arthur Street, Belfast BT1 4GD

STUDENT LOANS COMPANY LTD
100 Bothwell Street, Glasgow G2 7JD
Tel 041-306 2000

The Company was established in 1989 to administer the student loans scheme on behalf of the Government. In 1992–3 more than 340,000 students took out loans with a total value of more than £224 million.
Chief Executive, R. J. Harrison

OFFICE OF TELECOMMUNICATIONS
50 Ludgate Hill, London EC4M 7JJ
Tel 071-634 8700

The Office of Telecommunications (Oftel) is a non-ministerial government department which is responsible for supervising telecommunications activities in the UK. Its principal functions are to ensure that holders of telecommunications licences comply with their licence conditions; to maintain and promote effective competition in telecommunications; and to promote the interests of purchasers and other users of telecommunication services and apparatus in respect of prices, quality and variety.
The Director-General has powers to deal with anti-competitive practices and monopoly situations. He also has a duty to consider all reasonable complaints and representations about telecommunication apparatus and services.
Director-General, D. G. Cruickshank
Director of Competition, Mrs A. Walker
Director of PTO Licensing, Mrs P. Sellers
Director of Consumer and International Affairs, D. G. Hyde
Head of Information, D. C. Redding

TOURIST BOARDS
(For British Tourist Authority, *see* page 292)

The English Tourist Board, the Scottish Tourist Board, the Wales Tourist Board and the Northern Ireland Tourist Board are responsible for developing and marketing the tourist industry in their respective countries. The Boards' main objectives are to promote holidays and to encourage the provision and improvement of tourist amenities.

ENGLISH TOURIST BOARD, Thames Tower, Black's Road, London W6 9EL. Tel: 081-846 9000. *Chief Executive,* J. East

SCOTTISH TOURIST BOARD, 23 Ravelston Terrace, Edinburgh EH4 3EU. Tel: 031-332 2433. *Chief Executive,* T. M. Band

WALES TOURIST BOARD, Brunel House, 2 Fitzalan Road, Cardiff CF2 1UY. Tel: 0222-499909. *Chief Executive,* P. Loveluck, CBE

NORTHERN IRELAND TOURIST BOARD, St Anne's Court, 59 North Street, Belfast BT1 1NB. Tel: 0232-231221. *Chief Executive,* I. Henderson

---

DEPARTMENT OF TRADE AND INDUSTRY

*Ashdown House, 123 Victoria Street, London SW1E 6RB
†Tel 071-215 5000

Enterprise Initiative: Tel 0800-500200
Business in Europe: Tel 0272-444888
Innovation Enquiry Line: Tel 0800-442001

The Department is responsible for:
(a) international trade policy, including the promotion of UK trade interests in the European Community, GATT, OECD, UNCTAD and other international organizations
(b) the promotion of UK exports and assistance to exporters
(c) policy in relation to industry and commerce, including policy towards small firms, regional policy and regional industrial assistance (some of this applying only to England), and policy in relation to British Shipbuilders and the Post Office
(d) competition policy and consumer protection, including relations with the Office of Fair Trading, the Office of Telecommunications and the Monopolies and Mergers Commission; co-ordination of policy on deregulation
(e) the development of national policies in relation to all forms of energy and the development of new sources of energy; international aspects of energy policy. Links with British Coal, the Atomic Energy Authority, the electricity supply industry, the nuclear power construction industry, and the oil and gas industries
(f) policy on science and technology research and development; space; standards, quality and design; the following executive agencies: the Laboratory of the Government Chemist, the National Engineering Laboratory, the National Physical Laboratory, the National Weights and Measures Laboratory, and Warren Spring Laboratory
(g) company legislation and the Companies House executive agency; the Insolvency Service executive agency; the regulation of insurance industries; the Radiocommunications Agency (executive agency); and the Patent Office and Accounts Services executive agencies

President of the Board of Trade and Secretary of State for Trade and Industry, The Rt. Hon. Michael Heseltine, MP
Principal Private Secretary, P. Smith
Private Secretaries, Ms E. Jones; N. Welch

Special Advisers, Lady Strathnever; Dr A. Kemp; Dr W. Eltis
Personal Advisers, The Lord Sainsbury of Preston Candover; Sir Peter Levene, KBE
Parliamentary Private Secretary, R. Ottaway, MP
Minister for Industry, The Rt. Hon. Timothy Sainsbury, MP
Private Secretary, M. Scott
Parliamentary Private Secretary, Mrs A. Knight, MP
Minister for Energy, Timothy Eggar, MP
Private Secretary, M. Baldwin
Parliamentary Private Secretary, P. Luff, MP
Minister for Trade, Richard Needham, MP
Private Secretary, J. Warren
Parliamentary Private Secretary, A. Rowe, MP
Parliamentary Under-Secretary of State for Trade and Technology, Patrick McLoughlin, MP
Principal Private Secretary, J. Walker
Parliamentary Under-Secretary of State for Corporate Affairs, Neil Hamilton, MP
Private Secretary, Ms K. Spall
Parliamentary Under-Secretary of State for Consumer Affairs and Small Firms, The Baroness Denton of Wakefield, CBE
Private Secretary, I. Gibbons
Parliamentary Clerk, T. Williams
British Overseas Trade Board Chairman, Sir Derek Hornby
Permanent Secretary (G1), Sir Peter Gregson, KCB
Private Secretary, C. Parker
Deputy Secretaries (G2), Dr G. Robinson (*Chief Adviser on Science and Technology*); C. W. Roberts, CB; R. Williams, CB; A. Lane; A. Hammond, CB (*The Solicitor*); C. Henderson, CB; R. J. Priddle; A. C. Hutton; A. Macdonald, CB

DIVISIONAL ORGANIZATION

‡AEROSPACE DIVISION
Under-Secretary (G3), A. Nieduszynski
Heads of Branch (G5), Ms R. J. Anderson; M. Ralph; Dr G. Coleman

ATOMIC ENERGY
1 Palace Street, London SW1E 5HE

Under-Secretary (G3), Dr T. E. Walker
Heads of Branch (G5), Dr D. Hauser; P. H. Aggrell; Mrs H. Haddon; Dr D. Lumley; S. D. Spivey; Miss S. Haird

CHEMICALS AND BIOTECHNOLOGY DIVISION
Under-Secretary (G3), Dr E. Finer
Heads of Branch (G5), Ms G. Allister; Dr E. A. M. Baker; Dr J. M. Bird

COAL DIVISION
1 Palace Street, London SW1E 5HE

Under-Secretary (G3), W. I. MacIntyre, CB
Heads of Branch (G5), J. A. V. Collett; N. Hirst; A. Berry

COAL PRIVATIZATION UNIT
1 Palace Street, London SW1E 5HE

Under-Secretary (G3), P. Loughead
Grade 5, Ms F. S. Price

COMPANIES DIVISION
10–18 Victoria Street, London SW1H 0NN

Under-Secretary (G3), A. C. Russell, CB
Heads of Branch (G5), M. J. C. Butcher; N. D. Peace; J. Healey; F. C. Jenkins

---

*Unless otherwise stated, this is the main address of divisions of the Department
†Unless otherwise stated, this is the telephone number of divisions of the Department

‡At 151 Buckingham Palace Road, London SW1W 9SS

COMPETITION POLICY DIVISION
Under-Secretary (G3), Dr C. E. D. Bell
Heads of Branch (G5), J. Alty; A. Cooper; C. C. Bridge

CONSUMER AFFAIRS DIVISION
10–18 Victoria Street, London SWIH ONN

Under-Secretary (G3), C. Kerse
Heads of Branch (G5), D. Jones; P. D. Atkinson;
    M. Oldham; D. W. Hellings

DEREGULATION UNIT
Director (G3), H. V. B. Brown
Heads of Branch (G5), R. M. Watson; Miss M. N. Carter

ECONOMICS AND STATISTICS DIVISION
Chief Economic Adviser (G3), D. R. Coates
Head of Industrial and Regional Economics (G4), Dr
    J. A. S. Robertson
Heads of Energy Economics (G4), N. Hartley
Heads of Branch (G5), Dr D. S. Higham; C. B. Moir;
    M. S. Bradbury; B. M. Nonhebel; J. M. Barber; Dr
    R. Van Slooten; G. C. White; D. J. Hodgson; S. A. Price

ELECTRICITY DIVISION
1 Palace Street, London SWIE 5HE

Under-Secretary (G3), C. C. Wilcock
Heads of Branch (G5), S. F. D. Powell; J. H. T. Green; Dr
    D. Fairmaner; G. G. Bevan; A. Steele; Dr P. Fenwick

‡ELECTRONICS AND ELECTRICAL ENGINEERING
DIVISION
Under-Secretary (G3), R. M. Rumbelow
Heads of Branch (G5), T. J. Soane; (G6) I. J. Lawrenson

ENTERPRISE INITIATIVE DIVISION
Kingsgate House, 66–74 Victoria Street, London SWIE 6SW

Under-Secretary (G3), Mrs S. Brown
Heads of Branch (G5), M. Garrod; Mrs E. Ryle

‡ENVIRONMENT DIVISION
Under-Secretary (G3), Dr D. Evans
Heads of Branch (G5), C. Brewer; M. Cohen; Dr
    A. Eggington; G. Riggs

EUROPEAN COMMUNITY AND TRADE RELATIONS
DIVISION
Under-Secretary (G3), vacant
Heads of Branch (G5), J. Rhodes; D. I. Richardson;
    M. D. C. Johnson

EXPORT SERVICES DIVISION
Kingsgate House, 66–74 Victoria Street, London SWIE 6SW

Director-General of Export Promotion (G3), F. R. Mingay,
    CMG
Heads of Branch (G5), K. R. Timmins; (G6) L. B. Rabstaff;
    A. E. Reynolds

EXPORTS TO ASIA, AFRICA AND AUSTRALASIA DIVISION
Kingsgate House, 66–74 Victoria Street, London SWIE 6SW

Under-Secretary (G3), M. M. Baker
Heads of Branch (G5), M. G. Petter; D. E. Love; G. Hopson

EXPORTS TO EUROPE AND THE AMERICAS DIVISION
Under-Secretary (G3), N. Thornton
Heads of Branch (G4), K. W. N. George; (G5),
    K. D. Levinson; B. Hampton; J. V. Hagestadt

FINANCE AND RESOURCE MANAGEMENT DIVISION
Under-Secretary (G3), M. K. O'Shea
Heads of Branch (G5), W. Stow; D. T. Smith; Mrs M. Bloom

INDUSTRIAL COMPETITIVENESS DIVISION
Under-Secretary (G3), Dr R. Dobbie
Heads of Branch (G5), M. Gibson; G. Dart

INFORMATION DIVISION
Head of Information (G4), Ms J. M. Caines
Head of News (G6), A. Marre

Publicity
Bridge Place, 88–89 Eccleston Square, London SWIV IPT

Grade 5, S. Lyle-Smythe

‡INNOVATION POLICY DIVISION
Under-Secretary, (G3), Dr C. Hicks
Heads of Branch (G5), R. King; I. C. Downing; Dr
    R. Hinder; P. L. Bunn; J. Hobday; Mrs K. Elliott; (G6),
    P. Hills

Innovation Unit
Grade 5, Dr A. Keddie

INSURANCE DIVISION
10–18 Victoria Street, London SWIH ONN

Under-Secretary (G3), J. Spencer
Heads of Branch (G5), R. Allen; R. Hobbs; Ms S. Seymour;
    Miss A. Lambert; Miss V. Evans

INTERNAL AUDIT
1 Palace Street, London SWIE 5HE

Head of Internal Audit (G5), A. C. Elkington

INTERNATIONAL ENERGY UNIT
1 Palace Street, London SWIE 5HE

Grade 4, S. W. Freemantle

INTERNATIONAL TRADE POLICY DIVISION
Under-Secretary (G3), J. Cooke
Heads of Branch (G5), J. Hunt; J. Startup; S. J. Bowen

INVESTIGATIONS DIVISION
Under-Secretary (G3), M. G. Roberts
Grade 4, Mrs T. J. Dunstan
Inspector of Companies (G4), G. Harp
Heads of Branch (G5), S. L. Parkinson; A. Mier; R. Burton;
    H. Bradshaw; Mrs B. Chase; A. Robertshaw

JOINT DIRECTORATE (FCO/DTI)
Kingsgate House, 66–74 Victoria Street, London SWIE 6SW

Under-Secretary (G3), F. R. Mingay, CMG
Directors (G5), D. Saunders; (DS4) M. Dougal

‡MECHANICAL ENGINEERING DIVISION
Under-Secretary (G3), R. M. Rumbelow
Grade 5, Dr H. M. Sutton

OFFSHORE SUPPLIES OFFICE
Alhambra House, 45 Waterloo Street, Glasgow G2 6AS
Tel 041-221 8777
1 Palace Street, London SWIE 5HE
Tel 071-215 5000

Director-General (G3), J. E. d'Ancona
Heads of Branch (G5), A. E. Maule; Mrs R. E. Ebbers;
    H. M. Whiteside; (G6), J. Roddie

OIL AND GAS DIVISION
1 Palace Street, London SWIE 5HE

Under-Secretary (G3), M. J. Michell
Heads of Branch (G5), M. H. Atkinson; J. R. Wakely;
    W. C. F. Butler; (RES2), J. R. V. Brooks; B. Coleman;
    (PS2), G. N. Marriott
Director of Petroleum Engineering (RES1), I. W. G. Hughes
Director of Oil and Gas Royalties Office (G5), J. F. Craven

Gas and Oil Measurement Branch
3 Tigers Road, Wigston, Leicester LE18 4UX
Tel 0533-785354
Director (G5), J. Plant

OVERSEAS TRADE DIVISION 2
Kingsgate House, 66–74 Victoria Street, London SW1E 6SW
Under-Secretary (G3), R. J. Meadway
Grade 5, M. V. Coolican

PERSONNEL DIVISION
1 Palace Street, London SW1E 5HE
Under-Secretary (G3), A. Titchener, CB
Heads of Branch (G5), J. Thompson; R. Rogers; H. Evans;
   A. Mantle

PROJECTS AND EXPORT POLICY DIVISION
Under-Secretary (G3), D. J. Hall
Heads of Branch (G5), C. Robbins; A. G. Atkinson;
   N. Worman

REGIONAL DEVELOPMENT AND INWARD INVESTMENT
DIVISION
Kingsgate House, 66–74 Victoria Street, London SW1E 6SW
Director (G3), B. Bender
Director, IDU (G3), P. Rew
Heads of Branch (G5), R. H. S. Wells; J. C. S. Priston;
   K. Holt; Mrs A. Taylor; Dr H. N. M. Stewart;
   M. A. Wilks; *(G6),* M. P. Briggs

SERVICES MANAGEMENT DIVISION
Kingsgate House, 66–74 Victoria Street, London SW1E 6SW
Under-Secretary (G3), Dr R. Heathcote
Grade 4, R. J. Wheeler
Heads of Branch (G5), Miss D. Gane; K. M. Long

SMALL FIRMS DIVISION
c/o Employment Department, St Mary's House, Level 2,
Moorfoot, Sheffield S1 4PQ
Tel 0742-701356
Kingsgate House, 66–74 Victoria Street, London SW1E 6SW
Tel 071-215 5000
Under-Secretary (G3), Mrs S. Brown
Heads of Branch (G5), Miss S. C. Newton; J. M. Reid

SOLICITOR'S OFFICE
10–18 Victoria Street, London SW1H 0NN
The Solicitor (G2), A. Hammond, CB
Grade 3, P. H. Bovey; R. Woolman; Miss K. Morton;
   J. M. Stanley
Assistant Solicitors (G5), H. D. M. Bailey; M. Bucknill; Mrs
   J. Darvell; R. D. Fayers; Miss P. A. E. Granados;
   R. D. B. Green; A. S. W. Hyett; D. H. M. Ingham;
   D. S. Mangat; I. K. Mathers; S. G. Milligan; R. Nicklen;
   Miss E. N. O'Flynn; S. A. Parker; R. C. Perkins; Miss
   G. Richmond; J. W. Roberts; A. M. Susman; B. Welch

‡STEEL, METALS AND MINERALS DIVISION
Under-Secretary (G3), M. Stanley
Head of Branch (G5), B. F. Harding; H. P. Brown

‡TECHNOLOGY PROGRAMMES AND SERVICES DIVISION
Director (G3), Dr K. C. Shotton
Heads of Branch (G5), C. W. Johnston; Dr I. G. Eddison; Dr
   D. K. Potter; B. N. Steele; J. C. Octon; R. L. Hird; Dr
   M. S. Draper; Dr K. F. Poulter

‡TELECOMMUNICATIONS AND POSTS DIVISION
Under-Secretary (G3), P. Salvidge
Grade 4, S. R. Temple

Heads of Branch (G5), D. D. Sibbick; Mrs L. Brown;
   P. Waller; N. McMillan; J. S. Neilson; D. A. Hendon

‡TEXTILES AND RETAILING DIVISION
Under-Secretary (G3), T. Muir
Heads of Branch (G5), C. M. Cruickshank; T. L. Roberts

‡VEHICLES DIVISION
Under-Secretary (G3), M. Stanley
Heads of Branch (G5), T. M. H. Shearer; H. J. Charman

BRITISH OVERSEAS TRADE BOARD
Kingsgate House, 66–74 Victoria Street, London SW1E 6SW
Tel 071-215 5000

President, The President of the Board of Trade
Chairman, Sir Derek Hornby
Vice-Chairman, HRH The Duke of Kent, KG, GCMG, GCVO
Members, Sir Hugh Bidwell, CBE; G. J. Bull; R. Burman, CBE;
   Sir Colin Chandler; Sir Alan Cockshaw; Mrs
   H. M. Cropper; B. L. Crowe, CMG; I. L. Dale, OBE;
   H. Davies; Mrs J. Hall; Dr A. Hayes, CBE; D. Lanigan;
   R. Mingay, CMG; H. B. G. Montgomery; The Rt. Hon.
   Sir Michael Palliser, GCMG; C. W. Roberts, CB;
   B. D. Taylor, CBE; B. W. Willott
Secretary (G5), D. Saunders

REGIONAL OFFICES

DTI EAST, Westbrook Centre, Milton Road, Cambridge
   CB4 1YG. Tel: 0223-461939. *Regional Director (G5),*
   W. J. Hall
DTI EAST MIDLANDS, Severns House, 20 Middle
   Pavement, Nottingham NG1 7DW. Tel: 0602 506181.
   Regional Director (G5), E. Beston
DTI NORTH-EAST, Stanegate House, 2 Groat Market,
   Newcastle upon Tyne NE1 1YN. Tel: 091-232 4722.
   Regional Director (G3), P. A. Denham; *Regional
   Industrial Adviser (G3),* J. W. Armstrong
DTI NORTH-WEST, Sunley Tower, Piccadilly Plaza,
   Manchester M1 4BA. Tel: 061-236 2171. *Regional Director
   (G3),* J. H. Pownall
DTI SOUTH-EAST, Bridge Place, 88–89 Eccleston Square,
   London SW1V 1PT. Tel: 071-215 5000. *Regional Director
   (G5),* I. Jones
DTI SOUTH-WEST, The Pithay, Bristol BS1 2PB. Tel:
   0272-272666. *Regional Director (G5),* J. M. Bowder
DTI WEST MIDLANDS, 77 Paradise Circus, Queensway,
   Birmingham B1 2DT. Tel: 021-212 5000. *Regional
   Director (G3),* S. G. Linstead
DTI YORKSHIRE AND HUMBERSIDE, 25 Queen Street,
   Leeds LS1 2TW. Tel: 0532 443171. *Regional Director (G3),*
   H. M. Lanyon

EXECUTIVE AGENCIES

ACCOUNTS SERVICES AGENCY
PO Box 100, Caerleon House, Cleppa Park, Newport,
Gwent NP1 9YG
Tel 0633-652271
Director and Chief Executive (G5), D. M. Hoddinott

BRITISH NATIONAL SPACE CENTRE
Dean Bradley House, Horseferry Road, London SW1P 2AG
Tel 071-276 2688

Director-General (G3), D. R. Davis
Deputy Director-General (G4), J. S. Shrimplin

‡At 151 Buckingham Palace Road, London SW1W 9SS

Heads of Branch (G5), Prof. J. E. Harries; Dr R. Jude; K. Inglis; *(G6)*, Dr G. W. D. Findlay; Dr D. Williams; J. Thomas

COMPANIES HOUSE
Companies House, Crown Way, Cardiff CF4 3UZ
Tel 0222-388588
Registrar of Companies for England and Wales (G4), D. Durham
London Search Room, 55–71 City Road, London ECIY IBB
Tel 071-253 9393
102 George Street, Edinburgh EH2 3DJ
Tel 031-225 5774
Registrar for Scotland, J. Henderson

THE INSOLVENCY SERVICE
Bridge Place, 88–89 Eccleston Square, London SWIV IPT
Tel 071-215 5000
Inspector-General of the Insolvency Service and Chief Executive, P. R. Joyce
Deputy Inspectors-General, D. J. Flynn; Mrs J. K. Scoones; Mrs K. D. St John-Brooks

LABORATORY OF THE GOVERNMENT CHEMIST
Queens Road, Teddington, Middx. TWII OLY
Tel 081-943 7000
Government Chemist (G3), Dr R. Worswick

NATIONAL ENGINEERING LABORATORY
East Kilbride, Glasgow G75 OQU
Tel 03552-20222
Chief Executive (G3), W. Edgar

NATIONAL PHYSICAL LABORATORY
Teddington, Middx. TWII OLW
Tel 081-977 3222
Chief Executive and Director (G3), Dr P. B. Clapham

NATIONAL WEIGHTS AND MEASURES LABORATORY
Stanton Avenue, Teddington, Middx. TWII OJZ
Tel 081-943 7272
Chief Executive (G5), Dr S. Bennett

PATENT OFFICE
— *see* page 342

RADIOCOMMUNICATIONS AGENCY
Waterloo Bridge House, Waterloo Road, London SEI 8UA
Tel 071-215 2150
Chief Executive (G3), J. Norton
Heads of Branch (G5), M. Goddard; R. Louth; R. A. Bedford; D. Reed; R. M. Skiffins; *(G6)*, B. A. Maxwell

WARREN SPRING LABORATORY
Gunnels Wood Road, Stevenage, Herts. SGI 2BX
Tel 0438-741122
(To form part of a new National Environmental Technology Centre by mid-1994)
Director and Chief Executive (G3), Dr D. Cormack

DEPARTMENT OF TRANSPORT
2 Marsham Street, London SWIP 3EB
Tel 071-276 3000

The Department of Transport is responsible for land, sea and air transport, including sponsorship of the rail and bus industries; airports; domestic and international civil aviation; shipping and the ports industry; navigational lights, pilotage, HM Coastguard and marine pollution; motorways and other trunk roads; oversight of road transport including vehicle standards, registration and licensing, driver testing and licensing, bus and road freight licensing, regulation of taxis and private hire cars and road safety; and oversight of local authorities transport planning, including payment of Transport Supplementary Grant.

Secretary of State for Transport, The Rt. Hon. John MacGregor, OBE, MP
Private Secretary, P. J. Coby
Special Advisers, Mrs E. Laing; Sir Idris Pearce; R. Salmon; J. Swift; Sir Christopher Foster
Parliamentary Private Secretary, G. Riddick, MP
Minister of State for Public Transport, The Rt. Hon. Roger Freeman, MP
Private Secretary, Ms S. M. Watkins
Parliamentary Private Secretary, B. Wells, MP
Minister of State for Aviation and Shipping, The Earl of Caithness, PC
Private Secretary, A. Ferguson
Parliamentary Private Secretary, B. Wells, MP
Parliamentary Under-Secretaries, Robert Key, MP *(Roads and Traffic)*; Steven Norris, MP *(Transport in London)*
Private Secretaries, J. Nicholls; Miss S. Gray
Parliamentary Private Secretary to Parliamentary Under-Secretaries, B. Wells, MP
Parliamentary Clerk, N. Duncan
Permanent Under-Secretary of State (G1), A. P. Brown
Private Secretary, Ms J. Osborne

INFORMATION
Head of Information (G5), M. J. Helm

CENTRAL SERVICES
Principal Establishment and Finance Officer (G2), E. B. C. Osmotherley, CB

PERSONNEL
Lambeth Bridge House, London SEI 7SB
Tel 071-238 3000
Director of Personnel (G3), R. A. Allan
Grade 5, Mrs M. Clare; R. T. Bishop
Chief Welfare Officer (G7), Miss E. T. Haines
Grade 6, K. A. Wyatt; K. Wight; B. Meakins; B. Donaldson

FINANCE
Under-Secretary (G3), C. R. Grimsey
Heads of Division (G5), R. D. Bayly; M. N. Lambirth; S. K. Reeves
Accounting Adviser (G4), A. R. Allum

EXECUTIVE AGENCIES DIRECTORATE
Under-Secretary (G3), J. Phillips
Grade 5, M. J. Fuhr; J. L. Gansler

INTERNAL AUDIT
Ashdown House, Sedlescombe Road North, Hastings, E. Sussex TN37 7GA
Tel 0424-458306
Head of Branch (G5), M. J. Reece

CENTRAL SERVICES UNIT
Ashdown House, Sedlescombe Road North, Hastings, E. Sussex TN37 7GA
Tel 0424-458306
Grade 4, M. R. Newey
Heads of Division (G5), D. E. Bridge; G. L. Jones
Grade 6, I. Harris

ECONOMICS
Chief Economic Adviser (G3), M. J. Spackman
Grade 5, T. E. Worsley; M. C. Mann

STATISTICS
Romney House, 43 Marsham Street, London SWIP 3PY
Tel 071-276 8513

Under-Secretary (G3), D. W. Flaxen
Grade 5, Miss B. J. Wood; H. Collings; P. J. Capell;
    R. P. Donachie

CHIEF SCIENTIST
Chief Scientist (G4), Dr D. H. Metz

PUBLIC TRANSPORT
Deputy Secretary (G2), N. L. J. Montagu, CB

RAILWAYS I
Under-Secretary (G3), D. J. Rowlands, CB
Heads of Division (G5), A. Burchell; N. K. McDonald;
    M. R. Fawcett; S. P. Connolly

RAILWAYS 2
Under-Secretary (G3), P. Wood
Heads of Division (G5), A. T. Baker; P. H. McCarthy;
    B. Wadsworth; R. S. Peal; R. C. Bennett

PUBLIC TRANSPORT LONDON
Under-Secretary (G3), H. M. G. Stevens
Heads of Division (G5), A. B. Murray; G. J. Skinner

URBAN AND GENERAL
Under-Secretary (G3), J. R. Coates, CB
Heads of Division (G5), P. E. Pickering; D. R. Instone;
    M. R. Pitwood; C. C. Thame

HIGHWAYS, SAFETY AND TRAFFIC
Director-General, Highways (G2), J. W. S. Dempster

ROAD PROGRAMME
Friars House, Manor House Drive, Coventry CVI 2TV
Tel 0203-535117

Director (G3), A. Whitfield
Grade 5, N. E. Firkins

MOTORWAY WIDENING UNIT
Friars House, Manor House Drive, Coventry CVI 2TV
Tel 0203-535101

Director (G4), D. York
Grade 5, D. E. Oddy

CONSTRUCTION PROGRAMME DIVISION
EASTERN, Bedford – *Director (G4)*, J. A. Kerman; *Grade 5*,
    J. P. Boud
NORTH-WEST, Manchester – *Director (G4)*, A. J. Homer;
    Grade 5, E. A. Sherwin
SOUTH-EAST, Dorking – *Director (G4)*, B. A. Sperring;
    Grade 5, M. G. Quinn
SOUTH-WEST, Bristol – *Director (G4)*, P. E. Nutt; *Grade 5*,
    G. D. Rowe
WEST MIDLANDS, Birmingham – *Director (G4)*,
    P. E. Nutt; *Grade 5*, J. M. Bradley
YORKSHIRE AND HUMBERSIDE, Leeds – *Director (G4)*,
    A. J. Homer; *Grade 5*, R. R. Bineham

NETWORK MANAGEMENT AND CONSTRUCTION
EAST MIDLANDS, Nottingham – *Director (G5)*, S. Rose
NORTHERN, Newcastle upon Tyne – *Director (G5)*,
    D. W. Ward

NETWORK MANAGEMENT AND MAINTENANCE
2 Monck Street, London SWIP 2BQ
Tel 071-276 2716

Under-Secretary (G3), B. J. Billington
Heads of Division (G5), A. S. D. Whybrow; R. S. Wilson;
    Dr R. M. Kimber; M. R. Fawcett

HIGHWAYS POLICY AND RESOURCES
Grade 3, H. C. S. Derwent
Grade 5, D. J. Kershaw; J. B. W. Robins; R. W. Linnard;
    P. G. Collis; Mrs E. A. Baker; M. A. Walsh; Miss
    P. M. Williams

ENGINEERING POLICY
St Christopher House, Southwark Street, London SEI OTE
Tel 071-928 3666

Director and Chief Highway Engineer (G3), T. A. Rochester
Grade 5, P. H. Dawe; R. Eastman; N. S. Organ

ROAD AND VEHICLE SAFETY
Under-Secretary (G3), Miss S. J. Lambert
Heads of Division (G5), I. R. Jordan; Dr P. H. Martin;
    P. E. Butler
Grade 6, J. Winder
Departmental Medical Adviser (G4), Dr J. F. Taylor
Head of Medical Advisory Board (G5), Dr R. J. M. Irvine

TRAFFIC AREA OFFICES
Licensing Authorities and Traffic Commissioners
EASTERN (Nottingham and Cambridge), Brig. C. M. Boyd
NORTH-EASTERN (Newcastle upon Tyne and Leeds),
    K. R. Waterworth
NORTH-WESTERN (Manchester), M. S. Albu
SCOTTISH (Edinburgh), Brig. M. W. Betts
SOUTH-EASTERN AND METROPOLITAN (Eastbourne),
    Brig. M. H. Turner
SOUTH WALES (Cardiff), J. M. C. Pugh
WESTERN (Bristol), Air Vice-Marshal R. G. Ashford, CBE
WEST MIDLANDS (Birmingham), J. M. C. Pugh

CHIEF MECHANICAL ENGINEER'S OFFICE
Director and Chief Mechanical Engineer (G5), M. Fendick

LONDON REGION
Under-Secretary (G3), I. Yass, CB
Grade 4, D. A. Holland
Heads of Division (G5), R. J. Mance; Dr S. Chatterjee; Dr
    J. C. Miles; D. M. Smith; S. C. Whiteley; G. R. Emes

REGIONAL OFFICES
EASTERN, Bedford – *Regional Director (G3)*,
    P. F. Emms; *Director, Network Management (G5)*,
    R. T. Thorndike
EAST MIDLANDS, Nottingham – *Regional Director (G4)*,
    D. J. Morrison; *Director Network Management and
    Construction (G5)*, S. Rose
NORTHERN, Newcastle upon Tyne – *Regional Director
    (G3)*, B. H. Leonard; *Director, Network Management and
    Construction (G5)*, D. W. Ward
NORTH-WEST, Manchester – *Regional Director (G3)*,
    J. P. Plowman; *Director, Network Management (G5)*,
    M. M. Niven
SOUTH-EAST, London – *Regional Director (G3)*,
    J. W. Fellows; *Director, Network Management (G5)*,
    A. D. Rowland
SOUTH-WEST, Bristol – *Regional Director (G3)*,
    Ms E. A. Hopkins; *Director, Network Management (G5)*,
    A. P. Moss
WEST MIDLANDS, Birmingham – *Regional Director (G3)*,
    D. R. Ritchie; *Director, Network Management (G5)*,
    W. S. C. Wadrup

YORKSHIRE AND HUMBERSIDE, Leeds – *Regional Director (G3)*, J. P. Henry; *Director, Network Management (G5)*, J. R. Wilkins

AVIATION, SHIPPING AND INTERNATIONAL
Deputy Secretary (G2), G. R. Sunderland, CB

CIVIL AVIATION POLICY DIRECTORATE
Under-Secretary (G3), H. B. Wenban-Smith
Grade 5, E. C. Neve; A. G. Thorning; Ms A. Munro

INTERNATIONAL AVIATION DIRECTORATE
Under-Secretary (G3), A. J. Goldman
Heads of Division (G5), D. B. Cooke; M. L. Fielder; R. S. Balme

AIR ACCIDENTS INVESTIGATION BRANCH
Royal Aerospace Establishment, Farnborough, Hants. GU14 6TD
Tel 0252-510300
Chief Inspector of Air Accidents (G4), K. P. R. Smart
Grade 5, R. C. McKinlay

INTERNATIONAL AND FREIGHT DIRECTORATE
Under-Secretary (G3), J. D. Henes
Grade 5, P. D. Burgess; J. R. Fells
Grade 6, D. J. Blackman

CHANNEL TUNNEL SAFETY UNIT
Church House, Great Smith Street, London SW1P 3BL
Tel 071-276 2014
Grade 3, E. Ryder, CB
Deputy Chief Inspector of Mines and Quarries, A. Hall

SHIPPING POLICY, EMERGENCIES AND SECURITY DIRECTORATE
Under-Secretary (G3), R. E. Clarke
Heads of Division (G5), A. Fortnam; H. Ditmas; J. Jack, MBE; L. S. Moyle; J. F. Wall
Grade 7, A. Crosswell

MARINE DIRECTORATE
Spring Place, 105 Commercial Road, Southampton SO1 0ZD
Tel 0703-329100
Under-Secretary (G3), M. W. Jackson
Grade 5, P. R. Smith

MARINE EMERGENCY OPERATIONS AND MARINE POLLUTION CONTROL UNIT
Spring Place, 105 Commercial Road, Southampton SO1 0ZD
Tel 0703-329100
Director, and Chief Executive-designate of the Marine Emergency Operations Executive Agency (G4), C. J. Harris
Chief Coastguard (G5), Cdr. D. T. Ascona, RN (retd)
Surveyor-General, and Chief Executive-designate of the Surveyor-General's Organization Executive Agency (G4), R. M. Bradley
Grade 5, P. J. Hambling; W. A. Graham; Capt. D. Bell

MARINE ACCIDENTS INVESTIGATION BRANCH
5–7 Brunswick Place, Southampton SO1 2AN
Tel 0703-232424
Chief Inspector of Marine Accidents (G5), Capt. P. B. Marriott

EXECUTIVE AGENCIES

VEHICLE INSPECTORATE
Berkeley House, Croydon Street, Bristol BS5 0DA
Tel 0272-543274
Chief Executive (G4), R. J. Oliver

Deputy Chief Executive (G5), J. A. T. David
Director of Administration (G6), K. Walton

DRIVING STANDARDS AGENCY
Stanley House, Talbot Street, Nottingham NG1 5GU
Tel 0602-474222
Chief Executive (G5), Dr C. M. Woodman

TRANSPORT RESEARCH LABORATORY
Crowthorne, Berks. RG11 6AU
Tel 0344-773131
Chief Executive (G3), H. J. Wootton
Operations Director (G4), Dr R. S. Hinsley
Grade 5, Dr P. H. Bly; G. Maycock; J. Porter; D. H. Goody; D. A. Lynam; G. M. Clarke; P. B. Hunt

DRIVER AND VEHICLE LICENSING AGENCY
Longview Road, Morriston, Swansea SA6 7JL
Tel 0792-782318
Chief Executive (G3), S. R. Curtis
Heads of Division (G5), R. J. Verge; T. J. Horton; Dr R. J. M. Irvine; I. R. Heawood
Grade 6, P. G. Desborough

DRIVERS, VEHICLES AND OPERATORS INFORMATION TECHNOLOGY AGENCY
Oldway Centre, 36 Orchard Street, Swansea SA99 5AX
Tel 0792-304578
The agency is expected to be privatized by the end of 1993.
Chief Executive (G4), D. Evans
Grade 5, J. K. Griffiths

VEHICLE AND CERTIFICATION AGENCY
1 Eastgate Office Centre, Eastgate Road, Bristol BS5 6XX
Tel 0272-515151
Chief Executive (G5), D. W. Harvey

THE TREASURY
Parliament Street, London SW1P 3AG
Tel 071-270 3000

The Office of the Lord High Treasurer has been continuously in commission for well over 200 years. The Lord High Commissioners of HM Treasury consist of the First Lord of the Treasury (who is also the Prime Minister), the Chancellor of the Exchequer and five junior Lords. This Board of Commissioners is assisted at present by the Chief Secretary, a Parliamentary Secretary who is also the government Chief Whip, a Financial Secretary, an Economic Secretary, the Paymaster-General, and the Permanent Secretary.

The Prime Minister and First Lord is not primarily concerned in the day-to-day aspects of Treasury business. The junior lords are government whips in the House of Commons. The management of the Treasury devolves upon the Chancellor of the Exchequer and, under him, the Chief Secretary, the Financial Secretary, the Economic Secretary and the Paymaster-General.

The Chief Secretary is responsible for the control of public expenditure; pay in the public sector, including nationalized industries but excluding the Civil Service; parliamentary pay; export credit; and efficiency in the public sector.

The Financial Secretary discharges the traditional responsibility of the Treasury for the largely formal procedure for the voting of funds by Parliament. He also has responsibility for other parliamentary financial business; the legislative programme; Inland Revenue duties and taxes; privatization policy; competition and deregulation policy; and Civil Service pay, management and industrial relations.

The Paymaster-General is responsible for Customs and Excise duties and taxes; procurement policy; environment; women's issues; charities; the environment (including energy efficiency); the EC budget; general accounting issues; the Office of HM Paymaster-General; and ministerial correspondence.

The Economic Secretary has responsibility for monetary policy; the Royal Mint; the financial system (including banks, building societies and other financial institutions); the Central Office of Information; the Government Actuary's Department; Forward (the Civil Service catering organization); the Central Statistical Office; international financial business; Economic and Monetary Union; stamp duties; the Valuation Office; the Department for National Savings; the Registry of Friendly Societies; the National Investment and Loans Office; public expenditure casework; and the Treasury Bulletin and Economic Briefing.

The Office of HM Paymaster-General (*see* page 343) acts as a clearing bank and provides financial information for all government departments; it has particular responsibility for public sector pensions. All Treasury Ministers are concerned in tax matters.

Prime Minister and First Lord of the Treasury,
  The Rt. Hon. John Major, MP
Chancellor of the Exchequer (*£39,820),
  The Rt. Hon. Kenneth Clarke, QC, MP
  Principal Private Secretary, J. Heywood
  Private Secretary, O. M. Barder
  Special Adviser, Mrs T. Keswick
  Parliamentary Private Secretary, P. Oppenheim, MP
Chief Secretary to the Treasury (*£39,820), The
  Rt. Hon. Michael Portillo, MP
  Private Secretary, P. T. Wanless
  Special Adviser, D. Ruffley
  Parliamentary Private Secretary, D. Amess, MP
Financial Secretary to the Treasury (*£28,175), Stephen
  Dorrell, MP
  Private Secretary, W. Nye
  Parliamentary Private Secretary, G. Brandreth, MP
Paymaster-General (*£28,175), The Rt. Hon. Sir John Cope,
  MP
  Private Secretary, D. Hubbard
  Parliamentary Private Secretary, Dr I. Twinn, MP
Economic Secretary (*£21,384), Anthony Nelson, MP
  Private Secretary, S. G. W. Jones
*Parliamentary Secretary to the Treasury and Government
  Chief Whip* (*£33,142), The Rt. Hon. Richard Ryder,
  OBE, MP
  Private Secretary, M. Maclean
Treasurer of HM Household and Deputy Chief Whip
  (*£28,175), Gregory Knight, MP
Lord Commissioners of the Treasury (*£28,175), I. Patnick,
  OBE, MP; N. Baker, MP; T. Wood, MP; T. J. R. Kirkhope,
  MP; A. J. MacKay, MP
Assistant Whips (*£18,130), R. Hughes, MP;
  J. Arbuthnot, MP; A. Mitchell, MP; M. Brown, MP;
  D. Conway, MP
Parliamentary Clerk, D. S. Martin
Panel of Independent Economic Advisers to the Treasury,
  W. Godley; G. Davies; T. Congdon; A. Britton;
  A. Sentance; D. Currie; P. Minford

*In addition to a reduced parliamentary salary of £23,227

Permanent Secretary to the Treasury (*G1*), Sir Terence Burns
  Private Secretary, P. W. Owen
Second Permanent Secretaries (*G1A*), Sir Nigel Wicks, KCB,
  CVO, CBE (*Overseas Finance*); A. Turnbull, CB, CVO (*Public
  Expenditure*)

*Head of Government Economics Service and Chief Economic
  Adviser to the Treasury,* Prof. A. Budd
*Head of Government Accountancy Service and Chief
  Accountancy Adviser to the Treasury,* Sir Alan Hardcastle
Deputy Secretaries (*G2*), R. P. Culpin (*Public Finance*);
  H. P. Evans, CB (*Overseas Finance*); A. J. C. Edwards
  (*Public Services, and General Expenditure*); S. A. Robson
  (*Industry*); R. Mountfield, CB (*Civil Service Management
  and Pay*); Mrs J. R. Lomax (*Financial Services*)

CENTRAL DIVISIONS

ESTABLISHMENT AND ORGANIZATION DIVISION
Under-Secretary (*G3*), B. M. Fox
Assistant Secretaries (*G5*), E. I. Cooper; A. J. T. MacAuslan;
  Dr R. Kosmin; Ms C. Slocock
Senior Principals (*G6*), J. W. Stevens; B. J. Porteus, OBE;
  D. J. Baker; D. N. Walters; P. Tickner

INFORMATION DIVISION
Assistant Secretary (*G5*), A. Hudson
Deputy Head of Division (*G6*), D. Deaton

INDUSTRY

INDUSTRY, AGRICULTURE AND EMPLOYMENT GROUP
Under-Secretary (*G3*), M. L. Williams
Assistant Secretaries (*G5*), M. C. Mercer; D. Revolta;
  C. R. Pickering; T. J. Sutton

PUBLIC ENTERPRISES GROUP
Under-Secretary (*G3*), I. P. Wilson
Assistant Secretaries (*G5*), S. Sargent; T. R. Fellgett

HOME AND EDUCATION GROUP
Under-Secretary (*G3*), M. Whippman
Assistant Secretaries (*G5*), J. Graham; D. J. Batt

PUBLIC SERVICES

SOCIAL SERVICES AND TERRITORIAL GROUP
Under-Secretary (*G3*), Miss G. M. Noble
Assistant Secretaries (*G5*), J. Halligan; J. W. Grice; S. Kelly

LOCAL GOVERNMENT GROUP
Under-Secretary (*G3*), J. Beastall
Assistant Secretaries (*G5*), N. J. Ilett; R. Bent

CENTRAL UNIT ON PURCHASING
Director, P. Forshaw, CBE
Deputy Director, M. J. Hoare

TREASURY OFFICER OF ACCOUNTS GROUP
Under-Secretary (*G3*), T. J. Burr
Assistant Secretary (*G5*), I. S. Thomson

GENERAL EXPENDITURE

GENERAL EXPENDITURE POLICY GROUP
Under-Secretary (*G3*), C. W. Kelly
Assistant Secretaries (*G5*), J. Hibberd; F. K. Jones;
  I. W. V. Taylor

DEFENCE POLICY, MANPOWER AND MATERIEL GROUP
Under-Secretary (*G3*), Ms A. Perkins
Assistant Secretaries (*G5*), R. J. Devereux; M. E. Donnelly

OVERSEAS FINANCE

INTERNATIONAL FINANCE GROUP
Under-Secretary (*G3*), P. N. Sedgwick
Assistant Secretaries (*G5*), D. Owen; Ms E. Young;
  J. S. Cunliffe

AID AND EXPORT FINANCE GROUP
Under-Secretary (G3), J. E. Mortimer
Assistant Secretaries (G5), S. N. Wood; M. G. Richardson

EUROPEAN COMMUNITY GROUP
Under-Secretary (G3), D. J. Bostock
Assistant Secretaries (G5), M. E. Corcoran; P. M. Rayner

GOVERNMENT ACCOUNTANCY SERVICE
MANAGEMENT UNIT AND ACCOUNTANCY ADVICE
GROUP
Grade 4, D. Cooke
Assistant Secretaries (G5), D. Jamieson; K. E. Bradley
Senior Principals (G6), C. Butler; P. M. Rowley

TREASURY REPRESENTATIVES IN USA
Economic Minister and UK Representative IMF/IBRD,
   D. L. C. Peretz

CHIEF ECONOMIC ADVISER'S SECTOR
FORECASTS AND ANALYSIS GROUP
Under-Secretary (G3), C. J. Mowl
Senior Economic Advisers (G5), C. M. Kelly; S. Brooks

MEDIUM TERM AND POLICY ANALYSIS GROUP
Under-Secretary (G3), C. Riley
Assistant Secretaries (G5), D. Savage; S. W. Matthews

PUBLIC SERVICES ECONOMICS DIVISION
Under-Secretary (G3), Dr J. H. Rickard
Assistant Secretaries (G5), R. Weeden; M. A. Parsonage

ECONOMIC BRIEFING DIVISION
Assistant Secretary (G5), P. L. Patterson

PUBLIC FINANCE
FISCAL POLICY GROUP
Under-Secretary (G3), Mrs A. F. Case
Assistant Secretaries (G5), A. Sharples; R. P. Short

MONETARY GROUP
Under-Secretary (G3), P. R. C. Gray
Assistant Secretaries (G5), S. J. Davies; J. P. McIntyre

FINANCIAL INSTITUTIONS AND MARKETS GROUP
BANKING GROUP
Under-Secretary (G3), E. J. W. Gieve
Assistant Secretaries (G5), C. Farthing; J. M. G. Taylor

SECURITIES AND INVESTMENT GROUP
Under-Secretary (G3), A. Whiting
Grade 5, Dr J. P. Compton; Miss R. Thompson; Mrs
   P. C. Diggle

PUBLIC SECTOR FINANCE
Assistant Secretary (G5), A. W. Ritchie
Statistician (G7), S. C. Knight

CIVIL SERVICE MANAGEMENT AND PAY
CIVIL SERVICE PAY
Under-Secretary (G3), S. W. Boys-Smith
Assistant Secretaries (G5), Mrs S. D. Brown; R. J. Evans

PERSONNEL POLICY GROUP
Under-Secretary (G3), B. A. E. Taylor
Assistant Secretaries (G5), D. G. Pain; D. W. Rayson;
   J. Dixon; J. Strachan

MANAGEMENT POLICY
Under-Secretary (G3), R. I. G. Allen
Assistant Secretary (G5), M. Perfect

SPECIALIST SUPPORT GROUP
Grade 4, C. J. A. Chivers
Grade 5, J. B. Jones
Grade 6, J. A. Barker

FORWARD (CIVIL SERVICE CATERING)
Executive Director (G4) (acting), B. Bloxham

THE TREASURY SOLICITOR
DEPARTMENT OF HM PROCURATOR-GENERAL AND
TREASURY SOLICITOR
Queen Anne's Chambers, 28 Broadway, London SW1H 9JS
Tel 071-210 3000

The Treasury Solicitor's Department provides legal services
for many government departments. Those that do not have
their own lawyers are given legal advice, and both they and
other departments are provided with litigation and conveyancing services. The Department also deals with Bona
Vacantia. The Treasury Solicitor is also the Queen's Proctor.
HM Procurator-General and Treasury Solicitor (G1),
   G. A. Hosker, CB, QC
Deputy Treasury Solicitor (G2), D. Hogg

CENTRAL ADVISORY DIVISION
Principal Assistant Solicitor (G3), M. A. Blythe
Assistant Solicitors (G5), Mrs P. A. Dayer; M. J. Hemming;
   Mrs V. Collett; Mrs I. G. Letwin
Grade 6, C. J. Gregory; Miss P. F. Henderson;
   C. A. R. Bird; A. K. Fraser; Ms S. Grundy; Ms
   S. Cochrane

LITIGATION DIVISIONS
Principal Assistant Solicitor (G3), P. Ridd
Grade 4, F. L. Croft; D. Brummell
Assistant Solicitors (G5), A. D. Lawton; A. Leithead;
   A. J. Sandal; P. F. O. Whitehurst; R. J. Phillips;
   M. Sturdy; P. R. Messer; J. B. C. Oliver; D. F. Pascho
Grade 6, A. P. M. Aylett; P. Carroll; Miss R. M. Caudwell;
   M. R. M. Davis; J. N. Desai; P. D. F. Grant;
   J. D. Howes; D. Palmer; Miss A. J. Rees;
   H. O. J. R. Shepheard; D. A. Stalker; A. Turek;
   R. J. Walter
Principals (G7), T. C. Adcock; C. Ashford; M. Benney;
   L. Blake; R. Brown; A. P. Chapman; J. M. Crane;
   H. Fassnidge; J. Gladysz; M. P. Gold; A. Goodfellow;
   L. John-Charles; Mrs K. Lester; Miss C. R. Manuel;
   J. B. Matthews; P. J. Moran; Miss J. A. Murnane;
   Miss C. R. Musaala-Mukasa; S. Nasser; L. Nicoll;
   A. C. Nwanodi; F. G. O'Connell; L. O'Dea;
   R. C. J. Opie; R. M. Pierce; M. E. Robinson;
   D. Trinchero; G. Tuttle; J. C. Youdell; J. Ziegel

QUEEN'S PROCTOR DIVISION
Queen's Proctor, G. A. Hosker, CB, QC
Assistant Queen's Proctor, Mrs D. Babar

ESTABLISHMENTS, FINANCE AND DEPARTMENTAL
SERVICES DIVISION
*Principal Establishment and Finance and Security Officer
   (G5)*, A. J. E. Hollis
*Departmental Services Manager and Deputy Establishment
   and Security Officer (G7)*, P. Pegler
Departmental Personnel Manager (G7), Ms H. Donnelly
Chief Accountant (G7), R. B. Smith

Head of Information Systems Development (G7),
  G. N. Younger
Business Support Manager (G7), P. Hoadly

BONA VACANTIA DIVISION
Assistant Solicitor (G5), Miss S. L. Sargant
Senior Legal Assistant, M. R. M. Davies
Grade 7, Mrs P. L. Woods; Mrs A. Evans; I. Adams;
  D. Reid; N. Gajjar

EUROPEAN DIVISION
Principal Assistant Solicitor (G3), J. E. G. Vaux
Grade 5, J. E. Collins; D. Macrae
Grade 6, S. T. Harker; Miss R. Caudwell
Grade 7, Miss S. L. Hudson; J. D. Colahan

NATIONAL HERITAGE DIVISION
Grade 5, P. C. Jenkins
Grade 6, F. D. W. Clarke; C. A. R. Bird

OFFICE OF PUBLIC SERVICE AND SCIENCE DIVISION
Grade 5, M. C. Carpenter
Grade 6, P. Kilgarriff

MINISTRY OF DEFENCE BRANCH
Neville House, Page Street, London SW1P 4LS
Tel 071-218 4691
Principal Assistant Solicitor (G3), D. F. W. Pickup
Grade 5, J. R. J. Braggins; R. Batstone
Grade 6, Mrs A. Morris; P. Visagie; Miss V. F. Dewhurst
Grade 7, Miss E. Polledri; M. Truran; G. Brzezina;
  M. Pulver; J. Cooper; J. Ziegel

DEPARTMENT FOR EDUCATION BRANCH
Sanctuary Buildings, Great Smith Street, London SW1P 3BT
Tel 071-925 5000
Principal Assistant Solicitor (G3), R. N. Ricks
Assistant Solicitors (G5), D. J. Aries; M. Harris;
  A. D. Preston
Grade 6, Miss J. L. C. Brooks; A. K. Fraser; N. P. Beach
Grade 7, C. J. Reay; C. J. Hales

DEPARTMENT OF EMPLOYMENT BRANCH
Caxton House, Tothill Street, London SW1H 9NF
Tel 071-273 3000
Principal Assistant Solicitor (G3), H. R. L. Purse
Assistant Solicitors (G5), R. J. Baker; C. House;
  Mrs A. Leale; N. A. D. Lambert
Grade 6, R. H. Britten; P. H. Kilgarriff; J. K. Winayak;
  M. W. Smith; A. W. Stewart
Grade 7, Mrs K. Booth; S. J. Gibbon; Miss C. Smith;
  R. Creasy

DEPARTMENT OF TRANSPORT BRANCH
2 Marsham Street, London SW1P 3EB
Tel 071-276 3000
Principal Assistant Solicitor (G3), M. C. P. Thomas
Assistant Solicitors (G5), R. G. Bellis; P. D. Coopman;
  C. W. M. Ingram; A. G. Jones; R. Lines
Grade 6, G. W. M. Galliford; A. Lancaster;
  A. M. H. Prosser; S. W. Rock; N. C. Thomas;
  V. Edwards; J. Hall; G. Claydon; J. Jones; J. Jordan
Senior Legal Assistants, B. J. Hammersley; A. K. Johnston
Grade 7, R. C. Drabble; B. Golds; Mrs A. Heilpern;
  R. J. R. Jones; N. Magyar; M. S. Esdale

GOVERNMENT PROPERTY LAWYERS
Riverside Chambers, Castle Street, Taunton, Somerset TA1 4AP
Tel 0823-345200
An executive agency within the Treasury Solicitor's Department

Chief Executive (G3), A. D. Osborne
Group Directors (G5), M. Benmayor; Miss G. Gilder;
  P. L. Noble; P. F. Nockles; M. F. Rawlins; A. M. Scarfe
Director of Lands Advisory (G6), R. C. Paddock
Deputy Director of Lands Advisory (G7), T. P. Baker
Assistant Group Directors (G6), D. G. Ager; M. V. Cooper;
  R. L. Coward; R. F. Good; R. D. Harris; P. K. Hicks;
  J. B. Howe; R. S. Lugg; P. Page; I. Parker; A. W. Prior;
  P. A. Redgrove; R. J. B. Stenhouse; T. Sylvester Jones;
  B. D. Thurley
Senior Legal Assistants, T. Forrester; A. R. Lilleystone
Grade 7, S. R. Bould; Miss G. Bowles; A. M. Cross;
  Ms J. K. Dabbs; H. S. Davis; Miss M. F. Davitt;
  Mrs A. M. Foxhuntley; M. J. Hair; Q. J. Hawkes;
  T. J. Howe; C. R. Irving; P. S. Jaskolski; J. H. Leggatt;
  J. L. Leonard; Miss S. Lomas; P. J. Lowe; D. Roberts;
  M. D. Savage; Miss J. C. Shotter; R. C. Stewart;
  J. P. Trent
Finance and Personnel Director (G7), M. J. Robbins

COUNCIL ON TRIBUNALS
7th Floor, 22 Kingsway, London WC2B 6LE
Tel 071-936 7045

The Council on Tribunals is an independent statutory body. It keeps under review the constitution and working of the various tribunals which have been placed under its general supervision, and considers and reports on administrative procedures relating to statutory inquiries. It is consulted by government departments on proposals for legislation affecting tribunals and inquiries, and on proposals where the need for an appeals procedure may arise. It also offers advice on draft primary legislation.

Some 60 tribunals are currently under the Council's supervision. The matters with which they deal range from agriculture to immigration, pensions, road traffic, taxation, and the allocation of school places.

The Scottish Committee of the Council generally considers Scottish tribunals and matters relating only to Scotland.

Members of the Council are appointed by the Lord Chancellor and the Lord Advocate. The Scottish Committee is composed partly of members of the Council designated by the Lord Advocate and partly of others appointed by him. The Parliamentary Commissioner for Administration is ex officio a member of both the Council and the Scottish Committee.

Chairman, The Lord Archer of Sandwell, PC, QC
Members, The Parliamentary Commissioner for
  Administration; Mrs A. Anderson; G. A. Anderson;
  T. N. Biggart, CBE, WS (*Chairman of the Scottish
  Committee*); M. B. Dempsey; Prof. D. L. Foulkes;
  Mrs S. Friend; T. R. H. Godden, CB; C. Heaps; B. Hill,
  CBE; Prof. M. J. Hill; W. N. Hyde; R. H. Jones, CVO; Dr
  C. A. Kaplan; L. F. Read, QC
Secretary, J. D. Saunders

SCOTTISH COMMITTEE
20 Walker Street, Edinburgh EH3 7HR
Tel 031-220 1236
Chairman, T. N. Biggart, CBE, WS
Members, The Parliamentary Commissioner for
  Administration; G. A. Anderson; W. J. Campbell;
  Mrs C. A. M. Davis; T. R. H. Godden, CB; J. Langan; Ms
  M. Burns
Secretary, Ms L. Wilkie

TRIBUNALS
— *see* pages 384–7

UNRELATED LIVE TRANSPLANT
REGULATORY AUTHORITY
Department of Health, Room 520, Eileen House,
80–94 Newington Causeway, London SE1 6EF
Tel 071-972 2739

The Unrelated Live Transplant Regulatory Authority
(ULTRA) is a statutory body established on 1 January 1990.
In every case where the transplant of an organ within the
definition of the Human Organ Transplants Act 1989 is
proposed between a living donor and a recipient who are not
genetically related, the proposal must be referred to ULTRA.
Applications must be made by registered medical practi-
tioners.
    The Authority comprises a chairman and ten members
appointed by the Secretary of State for Health. The secretariat
is provided by Department of Health Officials.
Chairman, Prof. M. Bobrow
Members, Revd Prof. G. R. Dunstan; Dr P. A. Dyer;
    Mrs D. Eccles; Prof. M. G. McGeown; S. G. Macpherson;
    Dr N. P. Mallick; Prof. J. R. Salaman; Miss F. Smithers;
    Miss S. M. Taber; J. Wellbeloved
Administrative Secretary, P. Pudlo
Medical Secretary, Dr E. Hills

URBAN REGENERATION AGENCY
c/o Department of the Environment, 2 Marsham Street,
London SW1P 3EB
Tel 071-276 4704

The agency is likely to begin work during the second half of
1993, its primary aim being to bring 150,000 acres of vacant
and derelict land in towns and cities back into use and ease
the pressure for development in the countryside.
Chairman, The Lord Walker of Worcester, MBE, PC
Chief Executive, D. Taylor

WALES YOUTH AGENCY
Leslie Court, Lon-y-Llyn, Caerphilly, Mid Glamorgan
CF8 1BQ
Tel 0222-880088

The Wales Youth Agency is a non-departmental public body
funded by the Welsh Office. Its functions include the
encouragement and development of the partnership between
statutory and voluntary agencies relating to young people;
the promotion of staff development and training; and
the extension of marketing and information services in the
relevant fields. The board of directors is appointed by the
Secretary of State for Wales; directors do not receive a salary.
Chairman of the Board of Directors, G. Davies
Vice-Chairman of the Board of Directors, Dr H. Williamson
Executive Director, B. Williams

OFFICE OF WATER SERVICES
Centre City Tower, 7 Hill Street, Birmingham B5 4UA
Tel 021-625 1300

The Office of Water Services (Ofwat) was set up under the
Water Act 1989. Its role is to support the Director-General

of Water Services, who regulates the economic framework of
the water industry in England and Wales. His main duties
are to ensure that water companies (*see* page 508) comply
with the terms of their appointments (or licences) and to
protect the interests of water consumers. The Director-
General has established ten regional customer service
committees which investigate complaints and identify customer concerns. The Ofwat National Customer Council is a
non-statutory body set up by the Director-General in March
1993 to represent the views of water customers nationally.
    The Director-General is independent of ministerial control
and directly accountable to Parliament.
Director-General of Water Services, I. C. R. Byatt

WELSH DEVELOPMENT AGENCY
Pearl House, Greyfriars Road, Cardiff CF1 3XX
Tel 0222-222666

The Welsh Development Agency was established under the
Welsh Development Agency Act 1975 and came into
existence on 1 January 1976. Its remit is to help further the
regeneration of the economy and improve the environment
in Wales, a task that is carried out by business divisions
working from the Agency's head office in Cardiff and through
a network of six regional offices. The Agency's main activities
include helping to boost the growth, profitability and
competitiveness of indigenous Welsh companies; building
speculative and bespoke factories and encouraging investment by the private sector in site development; grant-aiding
land reclamation; and stimulating quality urban and rural
regeneration and development. Through Welsh Development International it also promotes inward investment into
Wales.
Chairman, D. Rowe-Beddoe
Deputy Chairman, Dr R. Bichan
Chief Executive, P. Head

WELSH OFFICE

The Welsh Office has responsibility in Wales for ministerial
functions relating to health and personal social services;
education, except for terms and conditions of service and
student awards; training, including training policy from April
1994; the Welsh language, arts and culture; the implementation of the Citizen's Charter in Wales; local government;
housing; water and sewerage; environmental protection;
sport; agriculture and fisheries; forestry; land use, including
town and country planning and countryside and nature
conservation; new towns; non-departmental public bodies
and appointments in Wales; ancient monuments and historic
buildings, and, from April 1994, the Welsh Arts Council;
roads; tourism; financial assistance to industry; the Strategic
Development Scheme in Wales and the Programme for the
Valleys; the operation of the European Regional Development Fund in Wales and other European Community
matters; civil emergencies; and all financial aspects of these
matters, including Welsh rate support grant. It has oversight
responsibilities for economic affairs and regional planning in
Wales.

Gwydyr House, Whitehall, London SW1A 2ER
Tel 071-270 3000

Secretary of State for Wales, The Rt. Hon. John Redwood,
    MP
    Private Secretary, Miss J. C. Simpson
    Parliamentary Private Secretary, D. Evans, MP

Minister of State, The Rt. Hon. Sir Wyn Roberts, MP
  Private Secretary, H. O. Jones
  Parliamentary Private Secretary, D. Tredinnick, MP
Parliamentary Under-Secretary, Gwilym Jones, MP
  Private Secretary, Ms J. Allen
Parliamentary Clerk, V. R. Watkin
Permanent Secretary (G1), M. C. Scholar, CB
  Private Secretary, R. Shearer

Cathays Park, Cardiff CF1 3NQ
Tel 0222-825111

LEGAL DIVISION
Legal Adviser (G3), D. G. Lambert
Assistant Solicitors (G5), P. J. Murrin; J. H. Turnbull
Lawyers (G6), H. D. Evans; J. D. H. Evans;
  Miss A. L. Ferguson; C. P. Jones; C. G. Longville;
  A. J. Park; Mrs A. T. Parkes; A. J. Watkins;
  A. Widdrington
Senior Legal Assistant, D. H. J. Williams
Lawyers (G7), Mrs K. R. Davies; T. R. E. Heywood;
  Ms T. L. Jones; Miss K. Nicholas; M. Partridge;
  Mrs P. Turnbull; Miss E. Stallard; Mrs R. J. Wiles

INFORMATION DIVISION
Director of Information (G5), H. G. Roberts
Chief Press Officer (G7), R. Lehnert
Principal Publicity Officer (G7), W. J. Edwards

ESTABLISHMENT GROUP
Principal Establishment Officer (G3), G. C. G. Craig
Heads of Divisions (G5), R. M. Abel; G. A. Thomas;
  Ms H. Angus
Senior Economic Adviser (G5), M. G. Phelps
Chief Statistician (G5), Dr M. P. G. Pepper
Head of Health Intelligence Unit (G6), M. R. Brand
Head of Training and Education Intelligence Unit (G6),
  J. D. Kinder
Principals (G7), R. J. Callen; J. F. Bowley; Mrs J. Leitch;
  P. Lunn; Mrs B. Hollick; M. Stevenson; P. H. Skellon;
  C. Tudor; D. D. Baird; Mrs J. Blamire
Economic Adviser (G7), V. W. F. McPherson
Principal Research Officers (G7), E. Darwin;
  Mrs M. A. J. Gronow
Statisticians (G7), P. J. Fullerton; E. Swires Hennessy;
  J. D. James; H. M. Jones; R. Jones; Mrs K. M. Phillips;
  Dr G. W. Thomas; Miss D. R. Carter; P. J. Demery;
  Miss C. M. Roberts; Mrs S. Leake; R. T. Kilpatrick
Medical Director of Cancer Registry, Dr M. Cotter
NHS (G9) Secondee, A. M. Jackson

FINANCE GROUP
Principal Finance Officer (G3), R. A. Wallace
Heads of Divisions (G5), D. W. Jones; L. A. Pavelin;
  Mrs E. A. Taylor
Grade 6, M. G. Horlock
Principals (G7), B. R. Davies; M. H. Harper; Mrs H. Usher;
  D. A. Powell; H. F. Rawlings; P. J. Higgins; W. F. Atwill
Head of Internal Audit (G7), D. Howarth

NATIONAL HEALTH SERVICE DIRECTORATE
Director of the NHS in Wales, J. W. Owen
Heads of Divisions (G5), D. H. Jones; D. A. Pritchard;
  N. E. Thomas; B. Wilcox; R. C. Williams
Senior Principal (G6), R. O'Sullivan
Principals (G7), Mrs J. D. Annand; M. A. C. Brooke;
  M. D. Chown; P. Davenport; J. Duggan; R. J. Dodd;
  J. Morgan; R. A. Williams; D. W. Evans; Mrs C. Lines;
  D. Boyland; I. Heppenstall; M. F. Webb; J. Toman;
  W. Evans; J. H. Grainger; E. J. McDonald; R. A. Jones;
  Ms J. Plastow; Mrs J. E. Wood; K. Orchard; K. S. Sleight

HEALTH AUTHORITIES
CLWYD, Preswylfa, Hendy Road, Mold, Clwyd CH7 1PZ.
  Chief Executive Director, B. F. Jones
EAST DYFED, Starling Park House, Johnstown,
  Carmarthen, Dyfed SA31 3HL. Managing Director,
  M. Ponton
GWENT, Brecon House, Mamhilad Park Estate, Pontypool,
  Gwent. Joint Chief Executive, J. Hallett
GWYNEDD, Coed Mawr, Bangor, Gwynedd LL57 4IP.
  District General Manager, C. H. Thomas
MID GLAMORGAN, District Headquarters, Albert Road,
  Pontypridd CF37 1LA. District General Manager,
  E. J. Thomas
PEMBROKESHIRE NHS TRUST, Meyler House, St
  Thomas Green, Haverfordwest, Dyfed SA61 1QP. Chief
  Executive, B. J. Davies
POWYS, Mansion House, Bronllys, Brecon, Powys LD3 OLS.
  District General Manager, Dr D. Bevan
SOUTH GLAMORGAN, Temple of Peace and Health,
  Cathays Park, Cardiff CF1 3NW. District General Manager,
  G. L. Harrhy
WEST GLAMORGAN, The Oldway Centre, 36 Orchard
  Street, Swansea SA1 5AQ. Chief Executive Director,
  A. Beddow

AGRICULTURE, INDUSTRY AND ECONOMIC
DEVELOPMENT AND TRAINING
Deputy Secretary (G2), J. F. Craig

AGRICULTURE DEPARTMENT
Head of Department (G3), O. Rees, CB
Heads of Divisions (G5), G. Podmore; D. R. Thomas;
  L. K. Walford
Principals (G7), Mrs B. Harding; A. G. Huws; Ms
  A. Jackson; R. F. Patterson; C. E. Taylor; B. E. Price;
  P. N. S. Wolfenden; A. Agett
Divisional Executive Officers (G7), W. K. Griffiths
  (Carmarthen); E. Hughes (Caernarfon); J. C. Alexander
  (Llandrindod Wells)

ECONOMIC DEVELOPMENT AND TRAINING GROUP
Head of Group (G3), M. J. Cochlin
Head of Training, Education and Enterprise Department (G4),
  C. L. Jones
Heads of Divisions (G5), M. E. Bevan; M. J. Clancy;
  Miss E. N. M. Davies; M. L. Evans; H. Evans
Senior Principals (G6), H. D. Brodie; M. Betenson;
  J. D. Kinder
Principals (G7), D. Beames; M. H. Bendon; C. J. Burdett;
  Dr M. C. Dunn; Ms J. M. Gordon; A. D. Lansdown;
  Miss J. E. Paulett; J. N. Roberts; M. A. J. Roberts;
  A. J. Davies; Dr J. Milligan; P. F. Brown; R. O. Evans;
  Mrs C. Fullerton; Dr I. I. Thomas; R. Keveren

INDUSTRY DEPARTMENT
Director (G3), C. D. Stevens
Industrial Director (G4), J. Cameron
Heads of Divisions (G5), D. T. Richards; G. T. Evans
Business Services Division Director (G6), Dr R. J. Loveland
Principals (G7), N. Barry; C. F. Francis; J. A. Grimes;
  G. Jones; J. A. Atkins; K. Smith; R. Waller;
  J. W. Wallington; G. Madden; I. Shuttleworth

EDUCATION, HOUSING, HEALTH AND SOCIAL
SERVICES, TRANSPORT, PLANNING AND
ENVIRONMENT
Deputy Secretary (G2), J. W. Lloyd, CB

EDUCATION DEPARTMENT
Head of Department (G3), S. H. Martin
Heads of Divisions (G5)°, W. G. Davies; H. Evans;
    B. J. Mitchell; R. C. Simpson
Principals (G7)°, Mrs J. Booker; P. F. Brown; D. A. Bullen;
    Mrs L. L. Changkee; B. Dare; R. O. Evans;
    Mrs J. Hopkins; G. R. Jones; Mrs C. Peat;
    M. G. Richards; D. M. Rolph

OFFICE OF HM CHIEF INSPECTOR FOR SCHOOLS IN
WALES
Chief Inspector (G4)°, R. L. James
Staff Inspectors (G5)°, S. J. Adams; J. R. N. Evans;
    T. E. Parry; G. Thomas; P. Thomas; Mrs I. Thomas;
    M. J. F. Wynn
There are 46 Grade 6 Inspectors.
Head of Administration (G7), Ms C. M. Owen

HOUSING, HEALTH AND SOCIAL SERVICES POLICY
GROUP
Head of Group (G3), R. W. Jarman
Heads of Divisions (G5), D. Adams; R. J. Davies;
    Mrs B. J. M. Wilson; A. G. Thornton
Chief Inspector, Social Services Inspectorate (Wales) (G5),
    D. G. Evans
Deputy Chief Inspectors, J. F. Mooney; R. C. Woodward
Grade 6, A. C. Elmer; M. J. Shanahan
Principals (G7), Mrs K. Cassidy; L. Conway; C. Coombs;
    P. Godden-Kent; D. B. Hilbourne; D. Hobbs;
    Miss E. M. Jones; J. Kilner; R. Norris; I. Price Jones
Social Services Inspectors (G7), D, Barker; D. A. Brushett;
    G. H. Davies; Miss R. E. Evans; I. Forster;
    Mrs J. Jenkins; C. D. Vyvyan; Mrs P. White
Principal Professional and Technology Officers (G7),
    G. N. Harding; W. Ross

HEALTH PROFESSIONAL GROUP
Chief Medical Officer (G3), Dr D. J. Hine

Public Health Sub Group (HPG M1)
Deputy Chief Medical Officer (G4), Dr A. M. George
Senior Medical Officers (G5), Dr J. Ludlow; Dr B. Fuge; Dr
    J. G. Avery

Hospital Services Sub Group (HPG M2)
Principal Medical Officer (acting) (G4), Dr D. W. Owen
Senior Medical Officers (G5), Dr B. Davies; Dr D. Salter;
    (part-time) Dr J. N. P. Hughes

Community and Primary Care Services Sub Group (HPG M3)
Principal Medical Officer (G4), Dr J. K. Richmond
Senior Medical Officers (G5), Dr A. K. Thomas;
    D. E. Davies; Dr R. Owen; Dr H. N. Williams
Divisional Medical Officer (G5), Dr D. E. Davies
Medical Officers (G6), Dr J. W. Crossley; Dr J. D. Andrews;
    Dr H. Williams; Dr T. Lyons; Dr T. I. Evans;
    Dr N. E. Thomas
Chief Dental Officer (G5), D. M. Heap
Senior Dental Officer (G5), vacant
Dental Officer (G6), J. D. O. Parkholm
Chief Scientific Adviser (G5), Dr J. A. V. Pritchard
Deputy Scientific Adviser (G6), Dr E. O. Crawley
Chief Pharmaceutical Adviser (G5), Dr G. B. A. Veitch
Deputy Pharmaceutical Adviser (G6), Mrs D. Kay Roberts
Chief Environmental Health Adviser (G5), R. Alexander
Deputy Environmental Health Adviser (G6), vacant

NURSING DIVISION
Chief Nursing Officer, Miss M. Bull
Deputy Chief Nursing Officer, Mrs B. Melvin
Nursing Officers, Mrs R. Cohen; Mrs S. M. Drayton;
    P. Johnson; Mrs J. Sait; M. F. Tonkin

TRANSPORT, PLANNING AND ENVIRONMENT GROUP
Head of Group (G3), P. R. Gregory
Director of Highways (G4), K. J. Thomas°
Deputy Director of Highways (G5), J. G. Evans★
Heads of Divisions (G5), A. H. H. Jones; D. I. Westlake°;
    H. R. Bollington°
Superintending Engineers (G6), J. R. Rees; B. H. Hawker,
    OBE★
Chief Estates Adviser (G6), G. K. Hoad
Senior Principal (G6), P. R. Marsden
Scientific Adviser (G6), Dr H. Prosser
Chief Planning Adviser (G6), W. P. Roderick
Principals (G7), P. M. Bishop; M. D. Evans; T. W. Hunter;
    H. R. Payne; Mrs C. R. Jones; G. R. Jones; D. Hadfield°;
    R. D. Macey; G. Quarrell; D. C. Quinlan
Principal Planning Officers (G7), D. B. Courtier; L. Owen;
    J. V. Spear
Principal Research Officers (G7), A. S. Dredge;
    Ms L. J. Roberts
Principal Estates Officer (G7), R. W. Wilson
*Principal Professional and Technology Officers, Highways
    Directorate (G7)*, M. J. Gilbert; I. A. Grindulais;
    A. P. Howcroft; A. L. Perry; R. H. Powell; S. C. Shouler;
    J. Collins; K. J. Alexander; R. H. Hooper; R. K. Cone;
    J. Dawkins; T. Dorken; R. Shaw; M. J. A. Parker;
    V. S. Pownall

LOCAL GOVERNMENT REORGANIZATION GROUP
Head of Group (G3), J. D. Shortridge
Principals (G7), I. R. Miller; A. C. Wood; Dr
    H. F. Rawlings

HM INSPECTORATE OF POLLUTION FOR WALES
11th Floor, Brunel House, 2 Fitzalan Road, Cardiff CF2 ITI
Tel 0222-49558

Inspector, Hazardous Wastes (G7), G. Taylor
Inspector, Radiation and Chemicals (G7) (acting),
    Dr C. Hardman
Inspector, Water (G7), A. A. Houlden

EXECUTIVE AGENCIES

CADW: WELSH HISTORIC MONUMENTS
Brunel House, Fitzalan Road, Cardiff CF2 IUY
Tel 0222-465511

Chief Executive, E. A. J. Carr
Director of Properties in Care, J. H. Pavitt
Director of Policy and Administration, R. W. Hughes
Conservation Architect (G6), J. D. Hogg
*Principal Inspector of Ancient Monuments and Historic
    Buildings*, J. R. Avent
Inspectors of Ancient Monuments and Historic Buildings,
    J. K. Knight; A. D. McLees; Dr S. E. Rees;
    R. C. Turner; M. J. Yates

PLANNING INSPECTORATE
Cathays Park, Cardiff CFI 3NQ
Tel 0222-823892

Chief Executive and Chief Planning Officer (G3), H. S. Crow
Assistant Chief Planning Inspector (G5), D. F. Harris

Based at:
°Ty Glan Road, Llanishen, Cardiff CF4 5WE. Tel: 0222-761456
★Government Buildings, Dinerth Road, Rhos on Sea, Colwyn Bay
LL28 4UL. Tel: 0492-44261

WOMEN'S NATIONAL COMMISSION
Level 4, Caxton House, Tothill Street, London SW1H 9NF
Tel 071-273 5486

The Women's National Commission is an advisory committee to the Government whose remit is to ensure by all possible means that the informed opinions of women are given their due weight in the deliberations of the Government. The Commission's fifty members are all women who are elected or appointed by national organizations with a large and active membership of women. The organizations include the women's sections of the major political parties, trades unions, religious groups, professional women's organizations and other bodies broadly representative of women.
Government Co-Chairman, The Baroness Denton of
  Wakefield, CBE (*nominated by the Prime Minister* 1992)
Elected Co-Chairman, Ms M. Rooney (*elected* 1993)
Joint Secretaries, Ms J. Bailey; Ms W. Brown

WOMEN'S ROYAL VOLUNTARY SERVICE
234–244 Stockwell Road, London SW9 9SP
Tel 071-416 0146

The Women's Royal Voluntary Service (WRVS) assists government departments, local authorities and voluntary bodies in organizing and carrying out welfare and emergency work for the community on a nationwide network operated through divisional, county, metropolitan, district and London borough organizers. Activities include work for the elderly and handicapped, for young families, and for offenders and their families; non-medical work in hospitals; welfare work for HM Forces and for Service families; and trained teams to assist in international, national and local emergencies.
National Chairman, Mrs E. Toulson

Law Courts and Offices

THE JUDICIAL COMMITTEE OF THE PRIVY COUNCIL

The Judicial Committee of the Privy Council is the final court of appeal from courts of the United Kingdom dependencies and courts of independent Commonwealth countries which have retained the right of appeal (Antigua and Barbuda, the Bahamas, Barbados, Belize, Brunei, Dominica, The Gambia, Jamaica, Kiribati, Mauritius, New Zealand, Singapore, St Christopher and Nevis, St Lucia, St Vincent and the Grenadines, Trinidad and Tobago, and Tuvalu). The Committee also hears appeals from courts of the Channel Islands and the Isle of Man, the disciplinary and health committees of the medical and allied professions, and some ecclesiastical appeals under the Pastoral Measure 1983.

The Judicial Committee includes the Lord Chancellor, the Lords of Appeal in Ordinary (*see* below) and other members of the Privy Council who hold or have held high judicial office, and certain judges from the Commonwealth. Commonwealth appeals are usually heard by a board of five judges.

PRIVY COUNCIL OFFICE (JUDICIAL COMMITTEE), Downing Street, London SW1A 2AJ. Tel: 071-270 0483
Registrar of the Privy Council, D. H. O. Owen
Chief Clerk, K. N. Stringer

The Judicature of England and Wales

The legal system of England and Wales is separate from those of Scotland and Northern Ireland and differs from them in law, judicial procedure and court structure, although there is a common distinction between civil law (disputes between individuals) and criminal law (acts harmful to the community).

The supreme judicial authority for England and Wales is the House of Lords, which is the ultimate Court of Appeal from all courts in Great Britain and Northern Ireland (except criminal courts in Scotland). As a Court of Appeal it consists of the Lord Chancellor and the Lords of Appeal in Ordinary (Law Lords).

The Supreme Court of Judicature comprises the Court of Appeal, the Crown Court and the High Court of Justice. The High Court of Justice is the superior civil court and is divided into three divisions. The Chancery Division is concerned mainly with equity, bankruptcy and contentious probate business; the Queen's Bench Division deals with commercial and maritime law, with civil cases not assigned to other courts, and hears appeals from lower courts; and the Family Division deals with matters relating to family law. Sittings are held at the Royal Courts of Justice in London or at 26 Crown Court centres outside the capital. High Court judges sit alone to hear cases at first instance. Appeals from lower courts are heard by two or three judges, or by single judges of the appropriate division. The Restrictive Practices Court, set up under the Restrictive Trade Practices Act 1956, and the Official Referees' Courts, which deal almost exclusively

with cases concerning the construction industry, are also part of the High Court.

Questions concerning the interpretation and application of European Community law, including preliminary rulings requested by British courts and tribunals, are decided by the European Court of Justice (*see* pages 761–2).

The decision to prosecute in the majority of cases rests with the Crown Prosecution Service, an independent prosecuting body established in 1986 to serve all of England and Wales (*see* pages 378–9). At the head of the service is the Director of Public Prosecutions, who discharges her duties under the superintendence of the Attorney-General. Certain categories of offence continue to require the Attorney-General's consent for prosecution.

Minor criminal offences (summary offences) are dealt with in magistrates' courts, which usually consist of three unpaid lay magistrates (Justices of the Peace) sitting without a jury, who are advised on points of law and procedure by a legally-qualified clerk to the justices. There were 29,686 Justices of the Peace at 1 January 1993. In busier courts a full-time, salaried and legally-qualified stipendiary magistrate presides alone. Cases involving people under 16 are heard in youth courts, specially constituted magistrates' courts which sit apart from other courts. Preliminary proceedings in a serious case to decide whether there is evidence to justify committal for trial in the Crown Court are also held in the magistrates' courts. Appeals from magistrates' courts against sentence or conviction are made to the Crown Court. Appeals upon a point of law are made to the High Court, and may go on to the House of Lords.

The Crown Court sits in about 90 centres, divided into six circuits, and is presided over by High Court judges, full-time circuit judges, and part-time recorders, sitting with a jury in all trials which are contested. It deals with trials of the more serious criminal offences, the sentencing of offenders committed for sentence by magistrates' courts (when the magistrates consider their own power of sentence inadequate), and appeals from lower courts. Magistrates usually sit with a circuit judge or recorder to deal with appeals and committals for sentence. Appeals from the Crown Court, either against sentence or conviction, are made to the Court of Appeal (Criminal Division), presided over by the Lord Chief Justice. A further appeal from the Court of Appeal to the House of Lords can be brought if a point of law of general public importance is considered to be involved.

Most minor civil cases are dealt with by the county courts, of which there are about 300 (details may be found in the local telephone directory). For cases involving small claims there are special arbitration facilities and simplified procedures. Where there are financial limits on county court jurisdiction, claims which exceed those limits may be tried in the county courts with the consent of the parties, or in certain circumstances on transfer from the High Court. Outside London, bankruptcy proceedings can be heard in designated county courts. Magistrates' courts can deal with certain classes of civil case and committees of magistrates license public houses, clubs and betting shops. For the implementation of the Children Act 1989, a new structure of hearing centres was set up in October 1991 for family proceedings cases, involving magistrates' courts (family proceedings courts), divorce county courts, family hearing centres and care centres.

Appeals in family matters heard in the family proceedings courts go to the Family Division of the High Court; affiliation appeals and appeals from decisions of the licensing committees of magistrates go to the Crown Court. Appeals from the High Court and county courts are heard in the Court of Appeal (Civil Division), presided over by the Master of the Rolls, and may go on to the House of Lords.

Coroners' courts investigate violent and unnatural deaths or sudden deaths where the cause is unknown. Cases may be brought before a local coroner (a senior lawyer or doctor) by doctors, the police, various public authorities or members of the public. Where a death is sudden and the cause is unknown, the coroner may order a post-mortem examination to determine the cause of death rather than hold an inquest in court.

THE HOUSE OF LORDS
AS FINAL COURT OF APPEAL

The Lord High Chancellor
The Rt. Hon. the Lord Mackay of Clashfern, *born* 1927, *apptd* 1987

Lords of Appeal in Ordinary (each £103,790)

Rt. Hon. Lord Keith of Kinkel, *born* 1922, *apptd* 1977
Rt. Hon. Lord Templeman, MBE, *born* 1920, *apptd* 1982
Rt. Hon. Lord Goff of Chieveley, *born* 1926, *apptd* 1986
Rt. Hon. Lord Jauncey of Tullichettle, *born* 1925, *apptd* 1988
Rt. Hon. Lord Lowry, *born* 1919, *apptd* 1988 (until Jan. 1994)
Rt. Hon. Lord Browne-Wilkinson, *born* 1930, *apptd* 1991
Rt. Hon. Lord Mustill, *born* 1931, *apptd* 1992
Rt. Hon. Lord Slynn of Hadley, *born* 1930, *apptd* 1992
Rt. Hon. Lord Woolf, *born* 1933, *apptd* 1992
Rt. Hon. Lord Lloyd, *born* 1929, *apptd* 1993
Rt. Hon. Lord Nolan, *born* 1928, *apptd* 1994 (from Jan. 1994)
Registrar, The Clerk of the Parliaments (*see* page 228)

SUPREME COURT OF JUDICATURE

COURT OF APPEAL

The Master of the Rolls (£103,790), The Rt. Hon. Sir Thomas Bingham, *born* 1933, *apptd* 1992
Secretary, Miss V. Seymour
Clerk, D. G. Grimmett

Lords Justices of Appeal (each £99,510)

Rt. Hon. Sir Brian Dillon, *born* 1923, *apptd* 1982
Rt. Hon. Sir Brian Neill, *born* 1923, *apptd* 1985
Rt. Hon. Sir Martin Nourse, *born* 1932, *apptd* 1985
Rt. Hon. Sir Iain Glidewell, *born* 1924, *apptd* 1985
Rt. Hon. Sir John Balcombe, *born* 1925, *apptd* 1985
Rt. Hon. Sir Ralph Gibson, *born* 1922, *apptd* 1985
Rt. Hon. Sir Patrick Russell, *born* 1926, *apptd* 1987
Rt. Hon. Dame Elizabeth Butler-Sloss, DBE, *born* 1933, *apptd* 1988
Rt. Hon. Sir Murray Stuart-Smith, *born* 1927, *apptd* 1988
Rt. Hon. Sir Christopher Staughton, *born* 1933, *apptd* 1988
Rt. Hon. Sir Michael Mann, *born* 1930, *apptd* 1988
Rt. Hon. Sir Donald Farquharson, *born* 1928, *apptd* 1989
Rt. Hon. Sir Anthony McCowan, *born* 1928, *apptd* 1989

Rt. Hon. Sir Roy Beldam, *born* 1925, *apptd* 1989
Rt. Hon. Sir Andrew Leggatt, *born* 1930, *apptd* 1990
Rt. Hon. Sir Richard Scott, *born* 1934, *apptd* 1991
Rt. Hon. Sir Johan Steyn, *born* 1932, *apptd* 1992
Rt. Hon. Sir Paul Kennedy, *born* 1935, *apptd* 1992
Rt. Hon. Sir David Hirst, *born* 1925, *apptd* 1992
Rt. Hon. Sir Simon Brown, *born* 1937, *apptd* 1992
Rt. Hon. Sir Anthony Evans, *born* 1934, *apptd* 1992
Rt. Hon. Sir Christopher Rose, *born* 1937, *apptd* 1992
Rt. Hon. Sir Leonard Hoffman, *born* 1934, *apptd* 1992
Rt. Hon. Sir John Waite, *born* 1932, *apptd* 1993
Rt. Hon. Sir John Roch, *born* 1934, *apptd* 1993
Rt. Hon. Sir Peter Gibson, *born* 1934, *apptd* 1993
Rt. Hon. Sir John Hobhouse, *born* 1932, *apptd* 1993
Rt. Hon. Sir Denis Henry, *born* 1931, *apptd* 1993
Rt. Hon. Sir Mark Saville, *born* 1936, *apptd* 1994 (from Jan. 1994)
Ex officio Judges, The Lord High Chancellor; the Lord Chief Justice of England; the Master of the Rolls; the President of the Family Division; and the Vice-Chancellor

COURT OF APPEAL (CRIMINAL DIVISION)
Judges, The Lord Chief Justice of England; the Master of the Rolls; Lords Justices of Appeal; and Judges of the High Court of Justice

COURTS-MARTIAL APPEAL COURT
Judges, The Lord Chief Justice of England; the Master of the Rolls; Lords Justices of Appeal; and Judges of the High Court of Justice

HIGH COURT OF JUSTICE

CHANCERY DIVISION

President, The Lord High Chancellor
The Vice-Chancellor (£99,510), The Rt. Hon. Sir Donald Nicholls, *born* 1933, *apptd* 1991
Clerk, W. Northfield, BEM

Judges (each £90,148)

Hon. Sir John Vinelott, *born* 1923, *apptd* 1978
Hon. Sir Jean-Pierre Warner, *born* 1924, *apptd* 1981
Hon. Sir Jeremiah Harman, *born* 1930, *apptd* 1982
Hon. Sir John Knox, *born* 1925, *apptd* 1985
Hon. Sir Peter Millett, *born* 1932, *apptd* 1986
Hon. Sir Andrew Morritt, CVO, *born* 1938, *apptd* 1988
Hon. Sir William Aldous, *born* 1936, *apptd* 1988
Hon. Sir John Mummery, *born* 1938, *apptd* 1989
Hon. Sir Donald Rattee, *born* 1937, *apptd* 1989
Hon. Sir Francis Ferris, TD, *born* 1932, *apptd* 1990
Hon. Sir John Chadwick, ED, *born* 1941, *apptd* 1991
Hon. Sir Jonathan Parker, *born* 1937, *apptd* 1991
Hon. Sir John Lindsay, *born* 1935, *apptd* 1992
Hon. Dame Mary Arden, DBE, *born* 1947, *apptd* 1993
Hon. Sir Edward Evans-Lombe, *born* 1937, *apptd* 1993

HIGH COURT OF JUSTICE IN BANKRUPTCY
Judges, The Vice-Chancellor and judges of the Chancery Division of the High Court

COMPANIES COURT
Judges, The Vice Chancellor and judges of the Chancery Division of the High Court

PATENT COURT (APPELLATE SECTION)
Judges, The Hon. Mr Justice Aldous; The Hon. Mr Justice Mummery; The Hon. Mr Justice Morritt

QUEEN'S BENCH DIVISION

The Lord Chief Justice of England (£112,083) The Rt. Hon.
  the Lord Taylor of Gosforth, *born* 1930, *apptd* 1992
Private Secretary, E. Adams
Clerk, J. Bond

Judges (each £90,148)

Hon. Sir Haydn Tudor Evans, *born* 1920, *apptd* 1974
Hon. Sir Ronald Waterhouse, *born* 1926, *apptd* 1978
Hon. Sir Maurice Drake, DFC, *born* 1923, *apptd* 1978
Hon. Sir Christopher French, *born* 1925, *apptd* 1979
Hon. Sir Charles McCullough, *born* 1931, *apptd* 1981
Hon. Sir John Leonard, *born* 1926, *apptd* 1981
Hon. Sir Oliver Popplewell, *born* 1927, *apptd* 1983
Hon. Sir William Macpherson, TD, *born* 1926, *apptd* 1983
Hon. Sir Philip Otton, *born* 1933, *apptd* 1983
Hon. Sir Michael Hutchison, *born* 1933, *apptd* 1983
Hon. Sir Swinton Thomas, *born* 1931, *apptd* 1985
Hon. Sir Richard Tucker, *born* 1931, *apptd* 1985
Hon. Sir Robert Gatehouse, *born* 1924, *apptd* 1985
Hon. Sir Patrick Garland, *born* 1929, *apptd* 1985
Hon. Sir Michael Turner, *born* 1931, *apptd* 1985
Hon. Sir John Alliott, *born* 1932, *apptd* 1986
Hon. Sir Harry Ognall, *born* 1934, *apptd* 1986
Hon. Sir Konrad Schiemann, *born* 1937, *apptd* 1986
Hon. Sir John Owen, *born* 1925, *apptd* 1986
Hon. Sir Humphrey Potts, *born* 1931, *apptd* 1986
Hon. Sir Richard Rougier, *born* 1932, *apptd* 1986
Hon. Sir Ian Kennedy, *born* 1930, *apptd* 1986
Hon. Sir Nicholas Phillips, *born* 1938, *apptd* 1987
Hon. Sir Robin Auld, *born* 1937, *apptd* 1988
Hon. Sir Malcolm Pill, *born* 1938, *apptd* 1988
Hon. Sir Stuart McKinnon, *born* 1938, *apptd* 1988
Hon. Sir Mark Potter, *born* 1937, *apptd* 1988
Hon. Sir Henry Brooke, *born* 1936, *apptd* 1988
Hon. Sir Igor Judge, *born* 1941, *apptd* 1988
Hon. Sir Edwin Jowitt, *born* 1929, *apptd* 1988
Hon. Sir Scott Baker, *born* 1937, *apptd* 1988
Hon. Sir Michael Morland, *born* 1929, *apptd* 1989
Hon. Sir Mark Waller, *born* 1940, *apptd* 1989
Hon. Sir Roger Buckley, *born* 1939, *apptd* 1989
Hon. Sir Anthony Hidden, *born* 1936, *apptd* 1989
Hon. Sir Michael Wright, *born* 1932, *apptd* 1990
Hon. Sir Charles Mantell, *born* 1937, *apptd* 1990
Hon. Sir John Blofeld, *born* 1932, *apptd* 1990
Hon. Sir Peter Cresswell, *born* 1944, *apptd* 1991
Hon. Sir Anthony May, *born* 1940, *apptd* 1991
Hon. Sir John Laws, *born* 1945, *apptd* 1992
Hon. Dame Ann Ebsworth, DBE, *born* 1937, *apptd* 1992
Hon. Sir Simon Tuckey, *born* 1941, *apptd* 1992
Hon. Sir David Latham, *born* 1942, *apptd* 1992
Hon. Sir John Kay, *born* 1943, *apptd* 1992
Hon. Sir Christopher Holland, *born* 1937, *apptd* 1992
Hon. Sir Richard Curtis, *born* 1933, *apptd* 1992
Hon. Sir Stephen Sedley, *born* 1939, *apptd* 1992
Hon. Dame Janet Smith, DBE, *born* 1940, *apptd* 1992
Hon. Sir Anthony Colman, *born* 1938, *apptd* 1992
Hon. Sir Anthony Clarke, *born* 1943, *apptd* 1993
Hon. Sir John Dyson, *born* 1943, *apptd* 1993
Hon. Sir Thayne Forbes, *born* 1938, *apptd* 1993
Hon. Sir Michael Sachs, *born* 1932, *apptd* 1993
Hon. Sir Stephen Mitchell, *born* 1941, *apptd* 1993
Hon. Sir Rodger Bell, *born* 1939, *apptd* 1993
Hon. Sir Michael Harrison, *born* 1939, *apptd* 1993
Hon. Sir Bernard Rix, *born* 1944, *apptd* 1993
Hon. Dame Anne Steel, DBE, *born* 1940, *apptd* 1993
Hon. Sir Richard Buxton, *born* 1938, *apptd* 1993

FAMILY DIVISION

President (£99,510) Rt. Hon. Sir Stephen Brown, *born* 1929,
  apptd 1988
Secretary, Mrs S. Leung
Clerk, Mrs S. Bell

Judges (each £90,148)

Hon. Sir John Wood, MC, *born* 1922, *apptd* 1977
Hon. Dame Margaret Booth, DBE, *born* 1933, *apptd* 1979
Hon. Sir Anthony Ewbank, *born* 1925, *apptd* 1980
Hon. Sir Anthony Hollis, *born* 1927, *apptd* 1982
Hon. Sir Mathew Thorpe, *born* 1938, *apptd* 1988
Hon. Sir Edward Cazalet, *born* 1936, *apptd* 1988
Hon. Sir Alan Ward, *born* 1938, *apptd* 1988
Hon. Sir Robert Johnson, *born* 1933, *apptd* 1989
Hon. Sir Douglas Brown, *born* 1931, *apptd* 1989
Hon. Dame Joyanne Bracewell, DBE, *born* 1934, *apptd* 1990
Hon. Sir Michael Connell, *born* 1939, *apptd* 1991
Hon. Sir Peter Singer, *born* 1944, *apptd* 1993
Hon. Sir Nicholas Wall, *born* 1945, *apptd* 1993
Hon. Sir Andrew Kirkwood, *born* 1944, *apptd* 1993
Hon. Sir Nicholas Wilson, *born* 1945, *apptd* 1993
Hon. Sir Christopher Stuart-White, *born* 1933, *apptd* 1993

RESTRICTIVE PRACTICES COURT

Judge, The Hon. Mr Justice Warner
Lay Members, B. M. Currie; Sir Lewis Robertson, CBE;
  R. Garrick, CBE; S. J. Ahearne; J. A. Graham;
  Mrs D. H. Hatfield; S. McDowall; J. A. Scott

OFFICIAL REFEREES' COURTS
St Dunstan's House, 133–137 Fetter Lane, London
EC4A 1HD
Tel 071-936 7429

Judges (each £78,378)

His Hon. Judge Newey, QC (*Senior Official Referee*)
His Hon. Judge Lewis, QC
His Hon. Judge Fox-Andrews, QC
His Hon. Judge Bowsher, QC
His Hon. Judge Loyd, QC
His Hon. Judge Hicks, QC
His Hon. Judge Havery, QC

Chief Clerk, Miss B. Joy

LORD CHANCELLOR'S DEPARTMENT
— *see* Government Departments and Public Offices

SUPREME COURT DEPARTMENTS AND OFFICES
Royal Courts of Justice, London WC2A 2LL
Tel 071-936 6000

ADMINISTRATOR'S OFFICE
Administrator (*G5*), G. A. Calvett
Deputy Administrator (*G6*), I. Hyams
Secretary to the Family Division (*G6*), R. P. Knight

ADMIRALTY AND COMMERCIAL REGISTRY AND MARSHAL'S OFFICE
Registrar (£54,035), P. Miller
Marshal and Chief Clerk (*G7*), A. Ferrigno

BANKRUPTCY DEPARTMENT

Chief Registrar (£65,912), G. L. Pimm
Bankruptcy Registrars (£54,035), W. S. James;
  J. A. Simmonds; D. G. Scott
Chief Clerk (SEO), M. Brown

CENTRAL OFFICE OF THE SUPREME COURT

*Senior Master of the Supreme Court (QBD), and Queen's
  Remembrancer (£65,912)*, W. K. Topley
Masters of the Supreme Court (QBD) (£54,035),
  P. B. Creightmore; D. L. Prebble; G. H. Hodgson;
  R. L. Turner; J. Trench; M. Tennant; P. Miller;
  N. O. G. Murray; I. H. Foster; G. H. Rose; P. G. Eyre
Chief Clerk (Central Office) (G7), C. F. Jones

CHANCERY DIVISION

Chief Clerk (G7), P. Emery

CHANCERY CHAMBERS

Chief Master of the Supreme Court (£65,912),
  J. M. Dyson
Masters of the Supreme Court (£54,035), J. S. Gowers;
  G. A. Barratt; J. I. Winegarten; J. A. Moncaster
Chief Clerk (SEO), G. Robinson
Conveyancing Counsel of the Supreme Court, J. Monckton;
  S. G. Maurice; M. J. Roth

COMPANIES COURT

Registrar (£54,035), M. Buckley
Chief Clerk (SEO), A. Roberts

COURT OF APPEAL CIVIL DIVISION

Registrar (£65,912), J. D. R. Adams
Chief Clerk (SEO), Miss H. M. Goddard

COURT OF APPEAL CRIMINAL DIVISION

Registrar (£65,912), M. McKenzie, QC
Deputy Registrar (G5), M. N. Farmer
Chief Clerk (G7), K. M. Dickerson

COURTS-MARTIAL APPEALS OFFICE

Registrar (£65,912), M. McKenzie, QC
Chief Clerk (G7), K. M. Dickerson

CROWN OFFICE OF THE SUPREME COURT

*Master of the Crown Office, and Queen's Coroner and
  Attorney (£65,912)*, M. McKenzie, QC
Head of Crown Office (G5), Mrs L. Knapman
Chief Clerk (G7), K. M. Dickerson

EXAMINERS OF THE COURT

Empowered to take examination of witnesses in all
Divisions of the High Court

M. F. Meredith-Hardy; B. Rathbone; N. W. Briggs;
R. Jacob

RESTRICTIVE PRACTICES COURT

Clerk of the Court, M. Buckley
Chief Clerk (SEO), A. Roberts

SUPREME COURT TAXING OFFICE

Chief Master (£65,912), P. T. Hurst
Masters of the Supreme Court (£54,035), C. R. N. Martyn;
  C. A. Prince; M. Ellis; T. H. Seager Berry (*Taxing
  Master*); C. C. Wright; P. A. Rogers
Chief Clerk (Administration) (G7), R. Cuthbert
Chief Taxing Officer (G7), T. J. Ryan

COURT OF PROTECTION

Stewart House, 24 Kingsway, London WC2B 6HD
Tel 071-269 7000

Master (£65,912), Mrs A. B. Macfarlane

ELECTION PETITIONS OFFICE

Room E218, Royal Courts of Justice, Strand, London
WC2A 2LL
Tel 071-936 6131

The office accepts petitions and deals with all matters relating
to the questioning of Parliamentary, European Parliament
and local government elections, and with applications for
relief under the Representation of the People legislation.

Prescribed Officer, W. K. Topley
Chief Clerk, C. I. P. Denyer

OFFICE OF THE LORD CHANCELLOR'S VISITORS

Trevelyan House, 30 Great Peter Street, London SW1P 2BY
Tel 071-210 8563

Legal Visitor, A. R. Tyrrell
Medical Visitors, A. G. Fullerton; F. E. Kenyon; K. Khan;
  P. A. Morris; D. Parr; J. Roberts

OFFICIAL RECEIVERS' DEPARTMENT

21 Bloomsbury Street, London WC1B 3SS
Tel 071-323 3090

Senior Official Receiver, J. R. Donnison
Official Receivers, M. J. Pugh; L. T. Cramp;
  M. W. A. Sanderson; G. J. A. Harp

OFFICIAL SOLICITOR'S DEPARTMENT

81 Chancery Lane, London WC2B 6HD
Tel 071-911 7105

Official Solicitor to the Supreme Court, P. M. Harris
Deputy Official Solicitor, H. J. Baker
Chief Clerk (G7), R. Lancaster

PRINCIPAL REGISTRY (FAMILY DIVISION)

Somerset House, London WC2R 1LP
Tel 071-936 6000

Senior District Judge (£65,912), G. B. N. A. Angel
District Judges (£54,035), T. G. Guest; J. E. Artro-Morris;
  R. B. Rowe; B. P. F. Kenworthy-Browne;
  Mrs K. T. Moorhouse; D. T. A. Davies; Mrs N. Pearce;
  M. J. Segal; R. Conn; Miss I. M. Plumstead; G. J. Maple;
  Miss H. C. Bradley; K. J. White; A. R. S. Bassett-Cross
Secretary (G6), R. P. Knight

District Probate Registrars

Birmingham and Stoke-on-Trent, C. Marsh
Brighton and Maidstone, M. N. Emery
Bristol, Exeter and Bodmin, P. L. Speyer
Ipswich, Norwich and Peterborough, E. R. Alexander
Leeds, Lincoln and Sheffield, A. P. Dawson
Liverpool, Lancaster and Chester, B. J. Thomas
Llandaff, Bangor, Carmarthen and Gloucester, R. F. Yeldam
Manchester and Nottingham, M. A. Moran
Newcastle, Carlisle, York and Middlesbrough, P. Sanderson
Oxford, R. R. Da Costa
Winchester, A. K. Biggs

OFFICE OF THE JUDGE ADVOCATE OF THE
FLEET

The Law Courts, Barker Road, Maidstone ME16 8EQ
Tel 0622-754966

Judge Advocate of the Fleet, His Hon. Judge Waley, VRD, QC

OFFICE OF THE JUDGE ADVOCATE-GENERAL OF THE FORCES
(*Joint Service for the Army and the Royal Air Force*)
22 Kingsway, London WC2B 6LE
Tel 071-305 6649

Judge Advocate-General (£78,378), His Hon. Judge
J. W. Rant, QC
Vice-Judge Advocate-General (£65,912), G. L. Chapman
Assistant Judge Advocates-General (£42,850–£49,450),
E. G. Moelwyn-Hughes; A. P. Pitts; D. M. Berkson;
M. A. Hunter; T. R. King; T. G. Pontius; J. P. Camp
Deputy Judge Advocates (£30,000–£42,050), Miss S. E.
Woollam; R. C. C. Seymour

HIGH COURT AND CROWN COURT CENTRES

First-tier centres deal with both civil and criminal cases and are served by High Court and circuit judges. Second-tier centres deal with criminal cases only and are served by High Court and circuit judges. Third-tier centres deal with criminal cases only and are served only by circuit judges.

MIDLAND AND OXFORD CIRCUIT
First-tier – Birmingham, Lincoln, Nottingham, Oxford, Stafford, Warwick
Second-tier – Leicester, Northampton, Shrewsbury, Worcester
Third-tier – Coventry, Derby, Grimsby, Hereford, Peterborough, Stoke-on-Trent, Wolverhampton
Circuit Administrator, L. Oates, 2 Newton Street, Birmingham B4 7LU. Tel: 021–627 1700
Courts Administrators: Birmingham Group, V. C. Grove; *Nottingham Group*, Mrs E. A. Folman; *Stafford Group*, A. F. Parker

NORTH-EASTERN CIRCUIT
First-tier – Leeds, Newcastle upon Tyne, Sheffield, Teesside
Second-tier – York
Third-tier – Doncaster, Durham
Circuit Administrator, S. W. L. James, 17th Floor, West Riding House, Albion Street, Leeds LS1 5AA. Tel: 0532–441841
Courts Administrators: Leeds Group, P. Delany; *Newcastle upon Tyne Group*, K. Budgen; *Sheffield Group*, G. Bingham

NORTHERN CIRCUIT
First-tier – Carlisle, Liverpool, Manchester, Preston
Third-tier – Barrow-in-Furness, Bolton, Burnley, Lancaster
Circuit Administrator, R. A. Vincent, 15 Quay Street, Manchester M60 9FD. Tel: 061–833 1005
Courts Administrators: Manchester Group, P. G. Walsh; *Liverpool Group*, D. A. Beaumont; *Preston Group*, Mrs A. Prior

SOUTH-EASTERN CIRCUIT
First-tier – Chelmsford, Lewes, Norwich
Second-tier – Ipswich, London (Central Criminal Court), Luton, Maidstone, Reading, St Albans
Third-tier – Aylesbury, Bury St Edmunds, Cambridge, Canterbury, Chichester, Guildford, King's Lynn, London (Croydon, Harrow, Inner London Session House, Isleworth, Kingston upon Thames, Knightsbridge, Middlesex Guildhall, Snaresbrook, Southwark and Wood Green, Woolwich), Southend
The High Court in Greater London sits at the Royal Courts of Justice.
Circuit Administrator, B. Cooke, New Cavendish House, 18 Maltravers Street, London WC2R 3EU. Tel: 071–936 7235
Deputy Circuit Administrator, P. Stockton
Courts Administrators: Chelmsford Group, M. Littlewood; *Maidstone Group*, Mrs H. Hartwell; *Kingston Group*, J. L. Powell; *London (Civil)*, P. Risk; *London (Crime)*, G. F. Addicott

WALES AND CHESTER CIRCUIT
First-tier – Caernarfon, Cardiff, Chester, Mold, Swansea
Second-tier – Carmarthen, Merthyr Tydfil, Newport, Welshpool
Third-tier – Dolgellau, Haverfordwest, Knutsford, Warrington
Circuit Administrator, D. Howe, Churchill House, Churchill Way, Cardiff CF1 4HH. Tel: 0222–396925
Courts Administrators: Cardiff Group, G. Jones; *Chester Group*, T. D. Beckett

WESTERN CIRCUIT
First-tier – Bristol, Exeter, Truro, Winchester
Second-tier – Dorchester, Gloucester, Plymouth
Third-tier – Barnstaple, Bournemouth, Devizes, Newport (IOW), Portsmouth, Salisbury, Southampton, Swindon, Taunton
Circuit Administrator, R. J. Clark, CBE, Bridge House, Sion Place, Clifton, Bristol BS8 4BN. Tel: 0272–743763
Courts Administrators: Bristol Group, A. C. Butler; *Exeter Group*, J. Ardern; *Winchester Group*, D. Ryan

CIRCUIT JUDGES

*Senior Circuit Judges, each £78,378
Circuit Judges, each £65,912

MIDLAND AND OXFORD CIRCUIT
Senior Presiding Judge, Hon. Mr Justice Rougier
W. A. L. Allardice; F. A. Allen; Miss C. Alton;
B. J. Appleby, QC; M. J. Astill; R. S. A. Benson;
I. J. Black, QC; R. W. A. Bray; D. W. Brunning;
F. A. Chapman; F. L. Clark, QC; R. R. B. Cole; P. F. Crane;
*P. J. Crawford, QC (*Recorder of Birmingham*)*;
I. T. R. Davidson, QC; P. N. de Mille; T. M. Dillon, QC;
C. H. Durman; J. F. Evans, QC; B. A. Farrer, QC;
Miss E. N. Fisher; J. E. Fletcher; R. J. H. Gibbs, QC;
H. G. A. Gosling; J. Hall; S. T. Hammond;
G. C. W. Harris, QC; M. K. Harrison-Hall; T. R. Heald;
J. R. Hopkin; R. H. Hutchinson; J. E. M. Irvine;
R. P. V. Jenkins; J. G. Jones; A. W. P. King; J. T. C. Lee;
M. H. Mander; K. Matthewman, QC; W. D. Matthews;
R. G. May; H. R. Mayor, QC; N. Micklem; P. R. Morrell;
A. J. H. Morrison; M. D. Mott; A. J. D. Nicholl;
R. T. N. Orme; J. F. F. Orrell; D. S. Perrett, QC;
C. J. Pitchers; R. F. D. Pollard; F. M. Potter; D. P. Pugsley;
J. R. Pyke; D. E. Roberts; J. A. O. Shand; J. R. S. Smyth;
P. J. Stretton; G. C. Styler; H. C. Tayler, QC; A. B. Taylor;
K. J. Taylor; M. B. Ward; R. L. Ward, QC; D. J. R. Wilcox;
H. Wilson; J. W. Wilson; K. S. W. Wilson Mellor, QC;
B. Woods; C. G. Young

NORTH-EASTERN CIRCUIT
Senior Presiding Judge, Hon. Mr Justice Waller
J. Altman; T. G. F. Atkinson; G. Baker, QC;
P. M. Baker, QC; T. W. Barber; J. M. A. Barker;

G. N. Barr Young; D. R. Bentley, QC; A. N. J. Briggs;
D. M. A. Bryant; J. W. M. Bullimore; B. Bush; M. C. Carr;
M. L. Cartlidge; P. J. Charlesworth; P. J. Cockroft;
G. J. K. Coles, QC; J. Crabtree; M. T. Cracknell;
W. H. R. Crawford, QC; Mrs J. Davies; E. J. Faulks;
P. J. Fox, QC; A. N. Fricker, QC; M. S. Garner;
S. P. Grenfell; W. Hannah; G. F. R. Harkins;
J. A. Henham; D. Herrod, QC; P. M. L. Hoffman; R. Hunt;
A. E. Hutchinson, QC; N. H. Jones, QC; G. H. Kamil;
T. D. Kent-Jones, TD; C. F. Kolbert; G. M. Lightfoot;
A. G. McCallum; A. C. Macdonald;
Miss M. B. M. MacMurray, QC; M. K. Mettyear;
A. L. Myerson, QC; D. A. Orde; Miss H. E. Paling;
*D. M. Savill, QC; R. M. Scott; A. Simpson; J. Stephenson;
*R. A. R. Stroyan, QC; Mrs L. Sutcliffe; R. C. Taylor;
G. M. Vos; M. Walker; P. H. C. Walker

NORTHERN CIRCUIT

Senior Presiding Judge, Hon. Mr Justice Morland
H. H. Andrew, QC; J. F. Appleton; A. W. Bell;
R. C. W. Bennett; Miss I. Bernstein; M. S. Blackburn;
R. Brown; I. B. Campbell; F. B. Carter, QC; B. I. Caulfield;
D. Clark; D. M. Clifton; G. P. Crowe, QC; *R. E. Davies, QC
(*Recorder of Manchester*); M. Dean, QC; Miss A. E. Downey;
B. R. Duckworth; S. B. Duncan; D. M. Evans, QC;
S. J. D. Fawcus; D. S. Gee; J. A. D. Gilliland, QC;
R. G. Hamilton; J. A. Hammond; R. J. Hardy;
F. D. Hart, QC; M. Hedley; T. D. T. Hodson;
F. R. B. Holloway; Miss M. Holt; N. J. G. Howarth;
G. W. Humphries; P. M. Kershaw, QC (*Commercial Circuit
Judge*); H. L. Lachs; C. N. Lees; J. M. Lever, QC;
R. J. D. Livesey, QC; R. Lockett; J. H. Lord; D. Lynch;
D. I. Mackay; D. G. Maddison; B. C. Maddocks;
C. J. Mahon; J. A. Morgan; M. O'Donoghue;
F. D. Owen, TD; R. E. I. Pickering; D. A. Pirie;
A. J. Proctor; J. H. Roberts; Miss G. D. Ruaux;
H. S. Singer; Miss E. M. Steel; I. R. Taylor, QC;
C. B. Tetlow; J. P. Townend; L. C. Trigger;
P. W. Urquhart; I. S. Webster; W. R. Wickham (*Recorder of
Liverpool*); B. Woodward

SOUTH-EASTERN CIRCUIT

Senior Presiding Judge, Hon. Mr Justice Garland (Hon. Mr
Justice Blofeld from Jan. 1994)
J. R. S. Adams; F. J. Aglionby; J. A. Baker; J. B. Baker, QC;
M. J. D. Baker; P. V. Baker, QC; A. F. Balston;
G. S. Barham; C. J. A. Barnett, QC; K. Bassingthwaighte;
G. A. Bathurst Norman; P. J. L. Beaumont, QC;
N. E. Beddard; G. J. Binns; J. E. Bishop; B. M. B. Black;
P. C. Bowsher, QC; A. V. Bradbury; P. N. Brandt;
L. J. Bromley, QC; A. E. Brooks; R. G. Brown;
J. M. Bull, QC; G. N. Butler, QC; *N. M. Butter, QC;
H. J. Byrt, QC; C. V. Callman; B. E. Capstick, QC;
B. L. Charles, QC; A. W. Clark; D. J. Clarkson, QC;
P. C. Clegg; M. Cohen, QC; S. H. Colgan; P. H. Collins;
C. C. Colston, QC; S. S. Coltart; Viscount Colville of
Culross, QC; J. S. Colyer, QC; C. D. Compston;
T. A. C. Coningsby, QC; R. D. Connor; M. J. Cook;
R. A. Cooke; G. H. Coombe; M. R. Coombe; A. Cooray;
Dr E. Cotran; R. C. Cox; D. L. Croft, QC; G. L. Davies;
I. H. Davies, TD; W. L. M. Davies, QC; W. N. Denison, QC;
J. E. Devaux; K. M. Devlin; M. N. Devonshire, TD;
A. E. J. Diamond, QC; A. H. Durrant; C. M. Edwards;
Q. T. Edwards, QC; F. P. L. Evans; J. K. Q. Evans;
S. J. Evans; J. D. Farnworth; P. Fingret; J. J. Finney;
P. Ford; J. J. Fordham; G. C. F. Forrester; J. Fox-
Andrews, QC; Ms D. A. Freedman; R. Gee; L. Gerber;
Miss A. F. Goddard, QC; S. A. Goldstein; P. W. Goldstone;

M. B. Goodman; C. G. M. Gordon; J. B. Gosschalk;
J. H. Gower, QC; M. Graham, QC; B. S. Green, QC;
P. B. Greenwood; D. J. Griffiths; G. D. Grigson;
R. B. Groves, TD, VRD; N. T. Hague, QC;
A. B. R. Hallgarten, QC; Miss G. Hallon; P. J. Halnan;
J. Hamilton; R. E. Hammerton; C. R. H. Hardy;
B. Hargrove, OBE, QC; J. P. Harris, DSC, QC; M. F. Harris;
R. O. Havery, QC; R. G. Hawkins, QC; R. J. Haworth;
A. H. Head; J. C. Hicks, QC; A. N. Hitching; D. Holden;
A. C. W. Hordern, QC; R. W. Howe;
Sir David Hughes-Morgan, Bt., CB, CBE; J. G. Hull, QC;
J. Hunter; M. J. Hyam; D. A. Inman; Dr P. J. E. Jackson;
C. P. James; M. Kennedy, QC; A. M. Kenny; L. G. Krikler;
L. H. C. Lait; P. St J. H. Langan, QC;
Capt. J. B. R. L. Langdon, RN; G. F. B. Laughland, QC;
R. Laurie; T. Lawrence; D. M. Levy, QC; E. Lewis, QC;
D. T. Lloyd; F. R. Lockhart; D. B. D. Lowe; R. H. Lownie;
Mrs N. M. Lowry; R. J. Lowry, QC; J. A. T. Loyd, QC;
R. D. Lymbery, QC (*Common Serjeant*); Capt. S. Lyons;
K. M. McHale; K. A. Machin, QC; M. B. McMullan;
K. C. Macrae; J. R. Main, QC; B. A. Marder, QC;
F. J. M. Marr-Johnson; L. A. Marshall; N. A. Medawar, QC;
D. J. Mellor; G. D. Mercer; A. L. Mildon, QC; D. Q. Miller;
D. Morton Jack; J. I. Murchie; Mrs N. F. Negus;
M. H. D. Neligan; J. H. R. Newey, QC;
C. W. F. Newman, QC; Mrs M. F. Norrie;
Ms S. F. Norwood; P. W. O'Brien; C. R. Oddie;
M. A. Oppenheimer; D. A. Paiba; R. H. S. Palmer;
M. C. Parker, QC; Miss V. A. Pearlman; J. R. Peppitt, QC;
F. H. L. Petre; A. J. Phelan; N. A. J. Philpot; D. C. Pitman;
J. R. Platt; P. B. Pollock; H. C. Pownall, QC;
R. J. C. V. Prendergast; J. E. Previté, QC; B. H. Pryor, QC;
J. E. Pullinger; J. W. Rant, QC; E. V. P. Reece; G. K. Rice;
M. S. Rich, QC; K. A. Richardson, QC; G. Rivlin, QC;
J. H. P. Roberts; D. A. H. Rodwell, QC; J. W. Rogers, QC;
G. H. Rooke, TD, QC; P. C. R. Rountree; J. H. Rucker;
T. R. G. Ryland; R. B. Sanders;
Maj.-Gen. D. H. D. Selwood; J. L. Sessions; J. D. Sheerin;
D. R. A. Sich; A. G. Simmons; K. T. Simpson;
P. R. Simpson; M. Singh, QC; J. K. E. Slack, TD;
S. P. Sleeman; P. M. J. Slot; F. B. Smedley, QC;
C. M. Smith, QC; S. A. R. Smith; R. J. Southan;
S. B. Spence; *R. O. C. Stable, QC; E. Stockdale;
C. J. Sumner; W. F. C. Thomas; A. G. Y. Thorpe;
A. H. Tibber; C. H. Tilling; A. M. Troup; S. Tumim;
J. T. Turner; C. J. M. Tyrer; Mrs A. P. Uziell-Hamilton;
J. E. van der Werff; Sir Lawrence Verney, TD (*Recorder of
London*); A. O. R. Vick, QC; T. L. Viljoen;
Miss M. S. Viner, QC; A. F. Waley, VRD, QC; R. Walker;
D. B. Watling, QC; V. B. Watts; F. J. White;
S. R. Wilkinson; S. M. Willis; C. G. F. Woodford;
G. N. Worthington; E. G. Wrintmore; K. H. Zucker, QC

WALES AND CHESTER CIRCUIT

Senior Presiding Judge, Hon. Mr Justice Pill (Hon. Mr
Justice Curtis from Jan. 1994)
M. R. Burr; T. R. Crowther, QC; G. H. M. Daniel;
R. D. G. David, QC; J. B. S. Diehl, QC; D. E. H. Edwards;
G. O. Edwards, QC; Lord Elystan-Morgan; D. R. Evans, QC;
T. M. Evans, QC; *M. Gibbon, QC; D. M. Hughes;
G. J. Jones; H. D. H. Jones; G. E. Kilfoil;
T. E. I. Lewis-Bowen; D. G. Morgan; D. C. Morton;
T. H. Moseley; D. A. Phillips; P. J. Price, QC;
E. J. Prosser; H. W. J. ap Robert; H. E. P. Roberts, QC;
S. M. Stephens, QC; D. B. Williams, TD, QC;
H. V. Williams, QC; R. G. Woolley

WESTERN CIRCUIT

Senior Presiding Judge, Hon. Mr Justice Auld

M. F. Addison; S. T. Bates, QC; P. T. S. Batterbury;
J. F. Beashel; C. L. Boothman; M. J. L. Brodrick;
J. M. J. Burford, QC; R. D. H. Bursell, QC; J. R. Chalkley;
M. G. Cotterill; Ms H. Counsell; J. A. Cox;
S. C. Darwall Smith; Mrs S. P. Darwall Smith;
Mrs L. H. Davies; M. Dyer; *P. Fallon, QC; P. D. Fanner;
D. L. Griffiths; Mrs C. M. A. Hagen; I. S. Hill, QC;
G. B. Hutton; R. E. Jack, QC; A. G. H. Jones;
D. McCarraher, VRD; Miss S. M. D. McKinney;
I. S. McKintosh; I. G. McLean; J. G. McNaught;
T. J. Milligan; E. G. Neville; S. K. O'Malley;
S. K. Overend; R. C. Pryor, QC; J. N. P. Rudd;
R. M. Shawcross; D. A. Smith, QC; W. E. M. Taylor;
P. M. Thomas; A. A. R. Thompson, QC;
H. J. M. Tucker, QC; D. M. Webster, QC; J. H. Weeks, QC;
J. R. Whitley; J. A. J. Wigmore; K. M. Willcock, QC;
J. C. Willis; J. H. Wroath

RECORDERS (each £315 per day)

J. D. R. Adams; R. J. P. Aikens, QC; J. F. Akast;
I. D. G. Alexander, QC; C. D. Allen; M. P. Allweis;
W. P. Andreae-Jones, QC; P. J. Andrews, QC;
R. A. Anelay, QC; A. R. L. Ansell; J. T. Anthony;
Ms L. E. Appleby, QC; J. F. A. Archer, QC;
Lord Archer of Sandwell, PC, QC; A. J. Arlidge, QC;
E. K. Armitage; R. Ashton; P. Ashworth, QC;
J. M. Aspinall; E. G. Aspley; B. Atchley; N. J. Atkinson, QC;
M. G. Austin-Smith, QC; W. S. Aylen, QC;
J. F. Badenoch, QC; A. B. Baillie; M. F. Baker, QC;
N. R. J. Baker, QC; C. G. Ball, QC; A. Barker, QC;
B. J. Barker, QC; D. Barker, QC; G. E. Barling, QC;
R. O. Barlow; D. N. Barnard; D. M. W. Barnes, QC;
H. J. Barnes; T. P. Barnes; W. E. Barnett, QC;
R. A. Barratt, QC; J. E. Barry; R. Bartfield;
G. R. Bartlett, QC; J. C. T. Barton; D. C. Bate;
S. D. Batten, QC; J. J. Baughan, QC; R. A. Bayliss;
C. H. Beaumont; C. O. M. Bedingfield, TD, QC;
C. O. J. Behrens; R. W. Belben; The Hon. M. J. Beloff, QC;
D. P. Bennett; H. P. D. Bennett, QC; J. M. Bennett;
P. Bennett, QC; K. C. Bentall; H. L. Bentham;
D. M. Berkson; M. Bethel, QC; J. P. V. Bevan;
J. C. Beveridge, QC; M. G. Binning; P. V. Birkett, QC;
W. J. Birtles; P. W. Birts, QC; H. O. Blacksell;
J. A. Blair-Gould; A. N. H. Blake; C. Bloom, QC;
D. J. Blunt, QC; J. G. Boal, QC; D. R. L. Bodey, QC;
G. T. K. Boney, QC; Miss J. A. M. Bonvin; D. J. Boulton;
S. N. Bourne-Arton; P. H. Bowers; J. J. Boyle;
W. T. S. Braithwaite, QC; A. G. B. Breen; D. J. Brennan, QC;
M. L. Brent, QC; G. J. B. G. Brice, QC; J. N. W. Bridges-
Adams; A. J. Brigden; P. J. Briggs; R. P. Brittain;
J. Bromley-Davenport; S. C. Brown, QC; J. N. Browne;
A. J. N. Brunner; A. Bueno, QC; D. L. Bulmer;
J. P. Burgess; J. K. Burke, QC; J. P. Burke, QC;
H. W. Burnett, QC; M. J. Burton, QC; K. Bush;
A. J. Butcher, QC; A. N. L. Butterfield, QC; C. W. Byers;
M. D. Byrne; Mrs B. A. Calvert, QC; D. Calvert-Smith;
R. Camden Pratt, QC; Miss S. M. C. Cameron, QC;
A. N. B. Campbell; J. Q. Campbell; G. M. C. Carey, QC;
A. C. Carlile, QC, MP; The Lord Carlisle of Bucklow, PC, QC;
H. B. H. Carlisle, QC; J. J. Carter-Manning, QC;
R. Carus, QC; B. E. F. Catlin; J. J. Cavell; J. A. Chadwin, QC;
N. M. Chambers, QC; D. C. Champion; B. W. Chedlow, QC;
J. M. Cherry, QC; J. R. Cherryman, QC; C. F. Chruszcz, QC;
C. H. Clark, QC; C. S. C. S. Clarke, QC; D. C. Clarke, QC;
P. W. Clarke; S. P. Clarke; A. S. L. Cleary;
R. N. B. Clegg, QC; W. Clegg, QC; M. F. Coates;
W. P. Coates; D. J. Cocks, QC; J. J. Coffey; T. A. Coghlan;
W. J. Coker; J. R. Cole; N. J. Coleman; N. B. C. Coles, QC;

A. R. Collender, QC; P. N. Collier, QC; A. D. Collins, QC;
J. M. Collins; Ms M. Colton; Mrs J. R. Comyns;
G. D. Conlin; J. G. Connor; C. S. Cook; A. E. M. Cooper;
Miss B. P. Cooper, QC; P. J. Cooper, QC; P. E. Copley;
S. M. Corkhill; T. G. E. Corrie; P. J. Cosgrove;
G. W. A. Cottle; Miss D. R. Cotton, QC; J. S. Coward, QC;
P. R. Cowell; B. R. E. Cox, QC; P. J. Cox, DSC, QC;
D. I. Crigman, QC; M. L. S. Cripps; C. A. Critchlow;
J. F. Crocker; D. R. Crome; I. W. Crompton;
J. D. Crowley, QC; E. J. R. Crowther, OBE;
W. R. H. Crowther, QC; H. M. Crush; D. M. Cryan;
T. S. Culver; Miss E. A. M. Curnow, QC; J. T. Curran;
P. D. Curran; J. W. O. Curtis; M. J. Curwen; K. C. Cutler;
Ms J. M. P. Daley; A. J. G. Dalziel; G. W. Davey;
C. P. M. Davidson; A. R. M. Davies; D. T. A. Davies;
J. T. L. Davies; A. W. Dawson; D. H. Day, QC; J. J. Deave;
J. B. Deby, QC; P. G. Dedman; Mrs P. A. Deeley;
C. F. Dehn, QC; P. A. de la Piquerie; M. A. de Navarro, QC;
W. E. Denny, CBE, QC; R. L. Denyer, QC; S. C. Desch, QC;
H. A. D. de Silva; C. E. Dines; A. D. Dinkin, QC;
I. J. Dobkin; R. A. M. Doggett; Ms B. Dohmann, QC;
A. M. Donne; A. K. Dooley; S. M. Duffield;
P. R. Dunkels, QC; W. H. Dunn, QC; R. T. Dutton;
D. Eady, QC; Ms D. B. Eaglestone; T. K. Earnshaw;
H. W. P. Eccles, QC; Miss S. M. Edwards, QC;
D. F. Elfer, QC; G. Elias, QC; B. J. Elliott; E. A. Elliott;
D. R. Ellis; C. Elwen; R. M. Englehart, QC; G. A. Ensor;
D. A. Evans, QC; D. H. Evans, QC; G. W. R. Evans;
Sir Graham Eyre, QC; W. D. Fairclough; R. B. Farley, QC;
D. J. Farrer, QC; K. J. Farrow; R. Fernyhough, QC;
P. S. Fish; D. P. Fisher; G. D. Flather, CBE, QC;
P. E. J. Focke, QC; J. D. Foley; R. A. Fordham, QC;
A. J. Forrest; J. R. Foster, QC; R. M. Foster;
R. H. K. Frisby, QC; J. H. Fryer-Spedding, OBE;
M. T. Fugard, CB; W. M. Gage, QC; M. Gale, QC;
C. J. E. Gardner; J. W. Gaskell; R. C. Gaskell;
S. A. G. L. Gault; J. R. B. Geake; A. C. Geddes;
A. H. Gee, QC; D. S. Geey; W. George; J. S. Gibbons;
C. A. H. Gibson; N. B. D. Gilmour, QC; L. Giovene;
A. T. Glass, QC; H. B. Globe; H. K. Goddard, QC;
H. A. Godfrey, QC; Ms L. S. Godfrey, QC;
J. J. Goldberg, QC; J. B. Goldring, QC; A. R. Goldsack, QC;
P. H. Goldsmith, QC; L. C. Goldstone, QC;
I. F. Goldsworthy; A. J. J. Gompertz, QC; A. A. Gordon;
J. P. Gorman, QC; T. J. C. Goudie, QC; C. O. G. Gould;
A. A. Goymer; G. Gozem; A. S. Grabiner, QC; R. A. Grant;
C. A. St J. Gray, QC; G. Gray, QC; J. M. Gray;
R. M. K. Gray, QC; H. Green, QC; J. C. Greenwood;
J. G. Grenfell; R. D. Grey, QC; J. C. Griffiths, CMG, QC;
J. P. G. Griffiths; L. Griffiths; J. D. Griggs; M. G. Grills;
M. S. E. Grime, QC; Mrs H. M. Grindrod, QC; P. Grobel;
M. A. W. Grundy; S. J. Gullick; A. S. Hacking, QC;
M. F. Haigh; J. W. Haines; D. R. Halbert; D. J. Hale;
V. E. Hall; J. P. N. Hallam; D. T. Hallchurch;
Ms H. C. Hallett, QC; A. W. Hamilton, QC;
D. R. D. Hamilton; G. M. Hamilton, TD, QC; J. Hampton;
J. L. Hand, QC; Miss R. S. A. Hare, QC; R. D. Harman, QC;
P. J. Harrington; D. M. Harris, QC; R. M. Harrison, QC;
H. M. Harrod; C. P. Hart-Leverton, QC; B. Harvey;
C. S. Harvey, MBE, TD; M. L. T. Harvey, QC;
T. S. A. Hawkesworth, QC; R. W. P. Hay;
Prof. D. J. Hayton; R. Hayward-Smith, QC; A. J. Healey;
M. J. Heath; T. B. Hegarty; G. E. Heggs;
R. A. Henderson, QC; R. H. Q. Henriques, QC;
P. J. M. Heppel; R. C. Herman; M. S. Heslop;
R. B. Hickman; B. J. Higgs, QC; E. M. Hill, QC;
J. W. Hillyer; A. J. H. Hilton, QC; Ms E. J. Hindley;
W. T. J. Hirst; J. D. Hitchen; S. A. Hockman, QC;
C. R. Hodson; The Hon. Mary Hogg, QC;

A. J. C. Hoggett, QC; Ms B. M. Hoggett, QC;
D. A. Hollis, VRD, QC; E. J. Holman, QC; R. C. Holman;
C. J. Holmes; J. F. Holt; R. M. Hone; A. T. Hoolahan, QC;
A. Hooper, QC; The Lord Hooson, QC; P. J. C. R. Hooton;
K. A. D. Hornby; M. Horowitz, QC; C. P. Hotten;
B. F. Houlder; R. Houlker, QC;
The Rt. Hon. M. Howard, QC, MP; M. N. Howard, QC;
C. I. Howells; M. J. Hubbard, QC; M. Hucker;
A. P. G. Hughes, QC; P. T. Hughes, QC; R. P. Hughes;
T. M. Hughes; J. Hugill, QC; L. D. Hull; D. P. Hunt;
D. R. N. Hunt, QC; P. J. Hunt, QC; I. G. A. Hunter, QC;
M. Hussain, QC; B. A. Hytner, QC; A. B. Issard-Davies;
D. G. A. Jackson; M. R. Jackson; R. M. Jackson, QC;
I. E. Jacob; P. J. Jacobs; C. E. F. James;
N. F. B. Jarman, QC; J. M. Jarvis, QC; A. H. Jeffreys;
D. A. Jeffreys, QC; J. Jeffs, QC; J. D. Jenkins, QC;
D. B. Johnson, QC; M. H. Johnson; G. R. Jones;
R. A. Jones, QC; S. E. Jones; T. G. Jones; T. J. C. Joseph;
W. H. Joss; H. M. Joy; P. S. L. Joyce, QC;
M. D. L. Kalisher, QC; M. L. Kallipetis, QC; S. S. Katkhuda;
M. R. Kay, QC; M. L. Keane; D. N. Keating, QC;
K. R. Keen, QC; D. W. Keene, QC; B. R. Keith, QC;
C. L. Kelly; C. J. B. Kemp; D. A. M. Kemp, QC;
D. Kennett Brown; L. D. Kershen, QC; G. M. Khayat, QC;
R. I. Kidwell, QC; T. R. King; T. R. A. King, QC;
W. M. Kingston, QC; R. C. Klevan, QC; B. J. Knight, QC;
M. S. Knott; Miss P. E. Knowles; S. E. Kramer;
Miss L. J. Kushner, QC; P. E. Kyte; L. P. Laity;
P. M. Lakin; C. A. Lamb; D. G. Lane, QC;
G. J. H. Langley, QC; R. B. Latham, QC; S. W. Lawler, QC;
I. J. Lawrence, QC, MP; M. H. Lawson, QC; G. S. Lawson
Rogers; L. D. Lawton, QC; D. Lederman, QC;
M. K. Lee, QC; B. W. T. Leech; I. Leeming, QC;
C. H. de V. Leigh, QC; Sir Godfrey Le Quesne, QC;
A. P. Lester, QC; H. B. G. Lett; B. H. Leveson, QC;
S. Levine; A. E. Levy, QC; M. E. Lewer, QC;
A. K. Lewis, QC; B. W. Lewis; M. ap G. Lewis, QC;
R. S. Lewis; C. C. D. Lindsay, QC; S. J. Linehan, QC;
J. S. Lipton; B. J. E. Livesey, QC; C. G. Llewellyn-Jones, QC;
H. J. Lloyd, QC; S. H. Lloyd; J. Lloyd-Eley, QC;
A. J. C. Lodge, QC; A. C. Longmore, QC; D. C. Lovell-
Pank, QC; R. P. Lowden; G. W. Lowe; N. H. Lowe;
G. W. Lowther; F. D. L. Loy; G. Lumley;
Rt. Hon. Sir Nicholas Lyell, QC, MP; E. Lyons, QC;
D. L. McCarthy; A. W. McCreath; A. G. MacDuff, QC;
D. D. McEvoy, QC; R. D. Machell, QC; B. M. McIntyre;
C. C. Mackay, QC; T. N. MacKean; D. L. Mackie;
I. McLeod; N. R. B. Macleod, QC; N. J. C. McLusky;
J. B. MacMillan; T. Maher; A. R. Malcolm;
The Baroness Mallalieu, QC; J. H. Mance, QC;
M. E. Mann, QC; The Hon. G. R. J. Mansfield;
A. C. B. Markham-David; A. S. Marron, QC;
R. G. Marshall-Andrews, QC; D. N. N. Martineau;
H. R. A. Martineau; C. G. Masterman; D. Matheson, QC;
P. R. Matthews; P. B. Mauleverer, QC; R. B. Mawrey, QC;
R. Maxwell, QC; M. Meggeson; D. B. Meier;
N. F. Merriman, QC; J. T. Milford, QC; R. A. Miller;
S. M. Miller, QC; J. B. M. Milmo, QC;
N. A. Miscampbell, QC, MP; C. R. Mitchell; D. C. Mitchell;
F. I. Mitchell; N. J. Mitchell; J. E. Mitting, QC;
E. G. Moelwyn-Hughes; C. R. D. Moger, QC;
H. J. Montlake; R. J. Moore; M. J. Moore-Bick, QC;
M. G. C. Moorhouse; H. M. Morgan; G. E. Moriarty, QC;
T. R. A. Morison; A. P. Morris; D. G. Morris; The
Rt. Hon. J. Morris, QC, MP; J. I. Morris; W. P. Morris;
C. Morris-Coole; T. J. Mort; A. G. Moses; C. J. Moss;
R. T. Moss; P. C. Mott, QC; R. W. Moxon-Browne, QC;
J. H. Muir; J. Mulcahy, QC; F. J. Muller, QC;
I. P. Murphy, QC; M. J. A. Murphy; N. J. Mylne, QC;

H. G. Narayan; T. M. E. Nash; R. F. Nelson, QC;
D. E. Neuberger, QC; R. E. Newbold;
A. R. H. Newman, QC; G. M. Newman, QC; G. Nice, QC;
C. A. A. Nicholls, QC; C. V. Nicholls; M. C. Nicholson;
A. S. T. E. Nicol; B. Nolan, QC; Col. A. P. Norris, OBE;
P. H. Norris; J. G. Nutting; D. P. O'Brien, QC;
E. M. Ogden, QC; B. R. Oliver; S. Oliver-Jones;
C. P. L. Openshaw, QC; R. C. C. O'Rorke; G. V. Owen, QC;
R. M. Owen, QC; S. R. Page; D. C. J. Paget;
A. O. Palmer, QC; A. W. Palmer, QC; A. D. W. Pardoe, QC;
S. A. B. Parish; A. E. W. Park, QC; G. C. Parkins, QC;
G. E. Parkinson; M. P. Parroy, QC; D. J. Parry;
D. J. T. Parry; E. O. Parry; M. A. Parry Evans;
N. S. K. Pascoe, QC; A. Patience, QC; J. G. Paulusz;
Mrs N. Pearce; Prof. D. S. Pearl; R. J. Pearse Wheatley;
B. P. Pearson; D. H. Penry-Davey, QC; Sir Ian Percival, QC;
J. Perry, QC; M. Pert, QC; B. J. Phelvin; J. A. Phillips;
W. B. Phillips; J. C. Phipps; M. A. Pickering, QC;
C. J. Pitchford, QC; The Hon. B. M. D. Pitt; A. P. Pitts;
Miss E. F. Platt, QC; J. R. Playford; A. G. S. Pollock, QC;
T. G. Pontius; D. A. Poole, QC; A. R. Porten, QC;
L. R. Portnoy; W. D. C. Poulton; M. J. Pratt, QC; S. Pratt;
T. W. Preston, QC; G. A. L. Price, QC; J. A. Price, QC;
N. P. L. Price, QC; R. N. M. Price; A. C. Pugh, QC;
G. V. Pugh, QC; C. P. B. Purchas, QC; R. M. Purchas, QC;
N. R. Purnell, QC; P. O. Purnell, QC; Q. C. W. Querelle;
D. A. Radcliffe; D. W. Radford; Ms A. J. Rafferty, QC;
A. Rankin, QC; A. D. Rawley, QC; P. R. Raynor;
L. F. Read, QC; A. R. F. Redgrave; J. Reeder, QC; P. Rees;
J. R. Reid, QC; P. C. Reid; M. P. Reynolds; P. C. Rhodes;
R. E. Rhodes; D. G. Rice; D. W. Richards;
H. A. Richardson; N. P. Riddell; S. V. Riordan, QC;
Miss J. H. Ritchie, QC; Miss S. A. Ritchie, QC;
S. D. Robbins; J. A. Roberts, QC; J. D. Roberts;
J. M. G. Roberts, QC; P. B. Roberts; P. E. Robertshaw;
V. Robinson, QC; D. E. H. Robson, QC; G. W. Roddick, QC;
Miss D. J. Rodgers; J. M. T. Rogers, QC; K. S. Rokison, QC;
J. G. Ross Martyn; P. C. Rouch; J. J. Rowe, QC;
R. J. Royce, QC; R. J. Rubery; A. A. Rumbelow, QC;
A. P. Russell; R. R. Russell; A. Rutherford; G. C. Ryan, QC;
J. R. T. Rylance; J. E. A. Samuels, QC; A. T. Sander;
G. R. Sankey, QC; H. B. Saunders, QC; M. P. Sayers, QC;
R. J. Scholes, QC; A. R. G. Scott-Gall; R. J. Seabrook, QC;
C. Seagroatt, QC; H. M. Self, QC; M. R. Selfe; O. M. Sells;
J. S. Sennitt; D. Serota, QC; A. J. Seys-Llewellyn;
A. R. F. Sharp; P. P. Shears; S. J. Sher, QC;
J. M. Shorrock, QC; S. R. Silber, QC; P. F. Singer;
J. C. N. Slater, QC; E. Slinger; A. T. Smith, QC;
R. D. H. Smith, QC; R. S. Smith, QC; W. P. Smith;
Ms Z. P. Smith; S. M. Solley, QC; R. F. Solman; E. Somerset
Jones, QC; R. C. E. Southwell; Miss J. M. Southworth;
M. H. Spence, QC; Sir Derek Spencer, QC, MP;
J. Spencer, QC; M. G. Spencer, QC; R. V. Spencer Bernard;
S. M. Spencer, QC; L. Spittle; J. A. C. Spokes, QC;
R. W. Spon-Smith; D. P. Stanley; D. W. Steel, QC;
D. Steer, QC; M. T. Steiger; D. H. Stembridge, QC;
Mrs L. J. Stern, QC; A. W. Stevenson, TD;
J. S. H. Stewart, QC; R. M. Stewart, QC; G. J. C. Still;
D. A. Stockdale; D. M. A. Stokes, QC; M. G. T. Stokes;
E. D. R. Stone, QC; P. L. Storr; T. M. F. Stow, QC;
D. M. A. Strachan, QC; M. Stuart-Moore, QC; F. R. C. Such;
A. B. Suckling, QC; J. M. Sullivan, QC; Ms L. E. Sullivan;
D. M. Sumner; P. C. Sumption, QC; P. J. Susman;
D. R. Swift; L. Swift, QC; M. R. Swift, QC; C. J. M. Symons;
J. A. Tackaberry, QC; R. K. K. Talbot; G. F. Tattersall, QC;
E. Taylor; N. Taylor, QC; J. J. Teare; A. D. Temple, QC;
V. B. A. Temple, QC; M. I. Tennant;
D. M. Thomas, OBE; D. O. Thomas, QC;
R. J. L. Thomas, QC; R. L. Thomas; R. U. Thomas, QC;

P. J. Thompson; A. C. L. Thornton, QC; J. Tiley;
M. B. Tillett; J. W. Tinnion; R. N. Titheridge, QC;
J. K. Toulmin, QC; R. G. Toulson, QC; J. B. S. Townend, QC;
C. M. Treacy, QC; H. B. Trethowan; A. D. H. Trollope, QC;
H. W. Turcan; D. A. Turner, QC; P. A. Twigg, QC;
A. R. Tyrrell, QC; J. G. G. Ungley; N. P. Valios, QC;
A. R. Vandermeer, QC; M. J. D. Vere-Hodge;
C. D. Voelcker; J. P. Wadsworth, QC; D. St J. Wagstaff;
S. P. Waine; J. J. Wait; R. Wakefield; R. M. Wakerley, QC;
W. H. Waldron, QC; J. D. G. Walford; R. A. Walker, QC;
R. J. Walker, QC; T. E. Walker, QC; J. J. Walker-Smith;
S. P. Waller; B. Walsh, QC; C. T. Walton; J. C. Warner;
J. Warren; D. E. B. Waters; Sir James Watson, Bt.;
C. D. G. Waud; B. J. Waylen; A. R. Webb; R. S. Webb, QC;
P. A. Webster; M. Weisman; P. Weitzman, QC;
C. P. C. Whelon; G. Whitburn, QC; C. H. Whitby, QC;
W. J. M. White; D. R. B. Whitehouse, QC;
P. G. Whiteman, QC; P. J. M. Whiteman, TD;
A. Whitfield, QC; D. G. Widdicombe, QC; R. Wigglesworth;
J. S. Wiggs; A. D. F. Wilcken; K. H. P. Wilkinson;
N. V. M. Wilkinson; D. B. Williams;
G. H. G. Williams, QC; Lord Williams of Mostyn, QC;
J. G. Williams, QC; J. L. Williams, QC; The
Hon. J. M. Williams, QC; M. J. Williams;
W. L. Williams, QC; S. W. Williamson, QC;
A. M. Wilson, QC; C. Wilson-Smith, QC; G. W. Wingate-
Saul, QC; M. E. Wolff; J. S. Wolstenholme; H. Wolton, QC;
D. A. Wood, QC; D. R. Wood; N. A. Wood; W. R. Wood;
L. G. Woodley, QC; Miss S. Woodley; J. T. Woods;
W. C. Woodward, QC; D. R. Woolley, QC; N. G. Wootton;
A. M. Worrall, QC; N. J. Worsley, QC; P. F. Worsley, QC;
D. E. M. Young, QC

STIPENDIARY MAGISTRATES

PROVINCIAL (each £54,035)

Cheshire, P. K. Dodd, OBE, *apptd* 1991
East and West Sussex, P. C. Tain, *apptd* 1992
Greater Manchester, W. D. Fairclough, *apptd* 1982;
   C. T. Latham, OBE, *apptd* 1976; Miss J. E. Hayward,
   apptd 1991
Hampshire, T. G. Cowling, *apptd* 1989
Humberside, N. H. White, *apptd* 1985
Lancashire/Merseyside, J. Finestein, *apptd* 1992
Merseyside, N. G. Wootton, *apptd* 1976; D. R. G. Tapp,
   apptd 1992
Middlesex, N. A. McKittrick, *apptd* 1989; S. Somjee, *apptd*
   1991; S. N. Day, *apptd* 1991
Mid Glamorgan, B. R. Oliver, *apptd* 1983; J. T. Curran,
   apptd 1990
North-East London, G. E. Cawdron, *apptd* 1993
Nottinghamshire, P. F. Nuttall, *apptd* 1991; M. L. R. Harris,
   apptd 1991
South Glamorgan, vacant
South Yorkshire, I. W. Crompton, *apptd* 1983; J. A. Browne,
   apptd 1992; J. E. Barry, *apptd* 1985; W. D. Thomas,
   apptd 1989
Staffordshire, P. G. G. Richards, *apptd* 1991
West Midlands, W. M. Probert, *apptd* 1983; B. Morgan,
   apptd 1989; I. Gillespie, *apptd* 1991; M. F. James, *apptd*
   1991
West Yorkshire, F. D. L. Loy, *apptd* 1972; Mrs P. A. Hewitt,
   apptd 1990

METROPOLITAN
*Chief Metropolitan Stipendiary Magistrate and Chairman of
   Committee of Magistrates for Inner London Area* (£69,924),
   P. G. N. Badge, *apptd* 1992 (*Bow Street*)

Magistrates (each £54,035)
Bow Street, The Chief Magistrate; R. D. Bartle, *apptd* 1972;
   J. G. Connor, *apptd* 1979; C. S. F. Black, *apptd* 1993
Camberwell Green, C. P. M. Davidson, *apptd* 1984;
   Mrs H. Mitcham, *apptd* 1986; T. H. Workman, *apptd*
   1986; H. Gott, *apptd* 1992; P. S. Wallis, *apptd* 1993
Clerkenwell, M. L. R. Romer, *apptd* 1972; C. J. Bourke,
   apptd 1972; B. Loosley, *apptd* 1989
Greenwich and Woolwich, Mrs K. R. Keating, *apptd* 1987;
   W. A. Kennedy, *apptd* 1991; D. A. Cooper, *apptd* 1991
Highbury Corner, D. Barr, *apptd* 1976; Miss D. Quick, *apptd*
   1986; G. Wicks, *apptd* 1987; D. B. Meier, *apptd* 1985
Horseferry Road, A. R. Davies, *apptd* 1985; R. T. Moss,
   apptd 1984; T. Maher, *apptd* 1983; G. Breen, *apptd* 1986
Marlborough Street, J. Q. Campbell, *apptd* 1981; Sir Bryan
   Roberts, KCMG, QC, *apptd* 1982
Marylebone, G. L. J. Noel, *apptd* 1975; A. C. Baldwin, *apptd*
   1990; T. English, *apptd* 1986; K. Maitland-Davies, *apptd*
   1984
Old Street, Miss G. B. Babington-Browne, *apptd* 1991;
   M. A. Johnstone, *apptd* 1980
South-Western, S. G. Clixby, *apptd* 1981; C. D. Voelcker,
   apptd 1982; A. Ormerod, *apptd* 1988
Thames, D. M. Fingleton, *apptd* 1980; Miss D. Wickham,
   apptd 1989; G. E. Parkinson, *apptd* 1982; N. Crichton,
   apptd 1987
Tower Bridge, Mrs J. R. Comyns, *apptd* 1982; R. D. Philips,
   apptd 1989; M. Kelly, *apptd* 1992
Wells Street, Miss A. M. Jennings, *apptd* 1972; I. M. Baker,
   apptd 1990; C. L. Pratt, *apptd* 1990
West London, H. J. Cook, *apptd* 1975; D. Kennett Brown,
   apptd 1982
Unattached Magistrates, D. L. Thomas, *apptd* 1990; I. Bing,
   apptd 1989; A. Evans, *apptd* 1990; D. Simpson, *apptd*
   1993; M. J. Read, *apptd* 1993

COMMITTEE OF MAGISTRATES FOR INNER
LONDON AREA
65 Romney Street, London SW1P 3RD
Tel 071-799 3332
Principal Chief Clerk and Clerk to the Committee (£53,023),
   I. Fowler, OBE
Chief Clerk (*Training*) (£47,848), P. Unwin

CROWN PROSECUTION SERVICE
50 Ludgate Hill, London EC4M 7EX
Tel 071-273 8000

The Crown Prosecution Service (CPS) is responsible for the
independent review and conduct of criminal proceedings
instituted by police forces in England and Wales (with the
exception of cases conducted by the Serious Fraud Office and
certain minor cases).
   The Director of Public Prosecutions is the head of the CPS
and discharges her statutory functions under the superintendence of the Attorney-General.
   The CPS comprises a headquarters office and 13 areas
covering England and Wales. Each of the CPS areas is
supervised by a Chief Crown Prosecutor.

For salaries, *see* page 282

Director of Public Prosecutions (G1), Mrs B. Mills, QC

Principal Establishment and Finance Officer (G3),
D. J. Wiblin, CB
Director (Casework) (G3), C. Newell
Director (Operations) (G3), G. Duff
Director (Policy) (G3), K. Ashken

CPS AREAS

CPS ANGLIA, Queens House, 58 Victoria Street, St Albans
ALI 3HZ. Tel: 0727-844753. *Chief Crown Prosecutor (G4)*,
R. J. Chronnell
CPS EAST MIDLANDS, 2 King Edward Court, King
Edward Street, Nottingham NGI IEL. Tel: 0602-480480.
Chief Crown Prosecutor (G4), B. T. McArdle
CPS HUMBER, Belgrave House, 47 Bank Street, Sheffield
SI 2EH. Tel: 0742-761601. *Chief Crown Prosecutor (G4)*,
D. Adams
CPS LONDON, 24th Floor, Portland House, Stag Place,
London SWIE 5BH. Tel: 071-828 9050. *Chief Crown
Prosecutor (G3)*, G. D. Etherington
CPS MERSEY/LANCASHIRE, 7th Floor (South), Royal
Liver Building, Pier Head, Liverpool L3 IHN. Tel: 051–
236 7575. *Chief Crown Prosecutor (G4)*, E. C. Woodcock

CPS MIDLANDS, 6th Floor, Dale House, 31 Dale End,
Birmingham B4 7LN. Tel: 021-233 3133. *Chief Crown
Prosecutor (G4)*, T. M. McGowran
CPS NORTH, Benton House, 136 Sandyford Road,
Newcastle upon Tyne NE2 IQE. Tel: 091-230 0800. *Chief
Crown Prosecutor (G4)*, D. V. Dickenson
CPS NORTH-WEST, PO Box 377, 8th Floor, Sunlight
House, Quay Street, Manchester M60 3LU. Tel: 061-837
7402. *Chief Crown Prosecutor (G4)*, A. R. Taylor
CPS SEVERN/THAMES, Orchard House, Victoria Square,
Droitwich, Worcester WR9 8QT. Tel: 0905-779502. *Chief
Crown Prosecutor (G4)*, A. S. R. Clarke
CPS SOUTH-EAST, Stoke Mill, Woking Road, Guildford,
Surrey GUI IAQ. Tel: 0483-573255. *Chief Crown
Prosecutor (G4)*, D. E. J. Dracup
CPS SOUTH-WEST, Hawkins House, Pynes Hill, Rydon
Lane, Exeter EX2 5SS. Tel: 0392-422555. *Chief Crown
Prosecutor (G4)*, P. Boeuf
CPS WALES, 21st Floor, Pearl Assurance House,
Greyfriars Road, Cardiff CFI 3PL. Tel: 0222-382777.
Chief Crown Prosecutor (G4), R. A. Prickett
CPS YORKSHIRE, 6th Floor, Ryedale Building, 60
Piccadilly, York YOI INS. Tel: 0904-610726. *Chief Crown
Prosecutor (G4)*, D. M. Sharp

The Scottish Judicature

Scotland has a legal system separate from and differing
greatly from the English legal system in enacted law, judicial
procedure and the structure of courts.

There is in Scotland a system of public prosecution headed
by the Lord Advocate which is independent of the police,
who have no say in the decision to prosecute. The Lord
Advocate, discharging his functions through the Crown
Office in Edinburgh, is responsible for prosecutions in the
High Court, sheriff courts and district courts. Prosecutions
in the High Court are prepared by the Crown Office and
conducted in court by one of the law officers, by an advocate-
depute, or by a solicitor advocate. In the inferior courts the
decision to prosecute is made and prosecution is preferred
by procurators fiscal, who are lawyers and full-time civil
servants, subject to the directions of the Crown Office. A
permanent legally-qualified civil servant known as the Crown
Agent is responsible for the running of the Crown Office and
the organization of the Procurator Fiscal Service, of which he
is the head.

Scotland is divided into six Sheriffdoms, each with a full-
time Sheriff Principal. The Sheriffdoms are further divided
into sheriff court districts, each of which has a legally-
qualified, resident sheriff or sheriffs, who are the judges of
the court.

In criminal cases sheriffs principal and sheriffs have the
same powers; sitting with a jury of 15 members, they may try
more serious cases on indictment, or, sitting alone, may try
lesser cases under summary procedure. Minor summary
offences are dealt with in district courts which are administered by the district and the islands local government
authorities and presided over by lay justices of the peace (of
whom there are about 4,400) and, in Glasgow only, by
stipendiary magistrates. Juvenile offenders (children under
16) may be brought before an informal children's hearing
comprising three local lay people. The superior criminal
court is the High Court of Justiciary which is both a trial and
an appeal court. Cases on indictment are tried by a High

Court judge, sitting with a jury of 15, in Edinburgh and on
circuit in other towns. Appeals from the lower courts against
conviction or sentence are heard also by the High Court,
which sits as an appeal court only in Edinburgh. There is no
further appeal to the House of Lords in criminal cases.

In civil cases the jurisdiction of the sheriff court extends to
most kinds of action. Appeal against decisions of the sheriff
may be made to the Sheriff Principal and thence to the Court
of Session, or direct to the Court of Session, which sits only
in Edinburgh. The Court of Session is divided into the Inner
and the Outer House. The Outer House is a court of first
instance in which cases are heard by judges sitting singly,
sometimes with a jury of 12. The Inner House, itself
subdivided into two divisions of equal status, is mainly an
appeal court. Appeals may be made to the Inner House from
the Outer House as well as from the sheriff court. An appeal
may be made from the Inner House to the House of Lords.

The judges of the Court of Session are the same as those
of the High Court of Justiciary, the Lord President of the
Court of Session also holding the office of Lord Justice
General in the High Court. Senators of the College of Justice
are Lords Commissioners of Justiciary as well as judges of
the Court of Session.

The office of coroner does not exist in Scotland. The local
procurator fiscal inquires privately into sudden and suspicious
deaths and may report findings to the Crown Agent. In some
cases a fatal accident inquiry may be held before the sheriff.

COURT OF SESSION AND HIGH COURT OF JUSTICIARY

The Lord President and Lord Justice General (£103,790)
The Rt. Hon. Lord Hope (David Hope), *born* 1938, *apptd*
1989

INNER HOUSE

Lords of Session (each £99,510)

FIRST DIVISION

The Lord President
Hon. Lord Allanbridge (William Stewart), *born* 1925, *apptd* 1977
Hon. Lord Cowie (William Cowie), *born* 1926, *apptd* 1977
Hon. Lord Mayfield (Ian MacDonald, MC), *born* 1921, *apptd* 1981

SECOND DIVISION

Lord Justice Clerk (£100,510), The Rt. Hon. Lord Ross (Donald Ross), *born* 1927, *apptd* 1985
Rt. Hon. Lord Murray (Ronald Murray), *born* 1922, *apptd* 1979
Hon. The Lord McCluskey, *born* 1929, *apptd* 1984
Hon. Lord Morison (Alastair Morison), *born* 1931, *apptd* 1985

OUTER HOUSE

Lords of Session (each £90,148)

Hon. Lord Davidson (Charles Davidson) *(seconded to Scottish Law Commission)*, *born* 1929, *apptd* 1983
Hon. Lord Sutherland (Ranald Sutherland), *born* 1932, *apptd* 1985
Hon. Lord Weir (David Weir), *born* 1931, *apptd* 1985
Hon. Lord Clyde (James Clyde), *born* 1932, *apptd* 1985
Hon. Lord Cullen (Douglas Cullen), *born* 1935, *apptd* 1986
Hon. Lord Prosser (William Prosser), *born* 1934, *apptd* 1986
Hon. Lord Kirkwood (Ian Kirkwood), *born* 1932, *apptd* 1987
Hon. Lord Coulsfield (John Cameron), *born* 1934, *apptd* 1987
Hon. Lord Milligan (James Milligan), *born* 1934, *apptd* 1988
Hon. The Lord Morton of Shuna, *born* 1930, *apptd* 1988
Hon. Lord Caplan (Philip Caplan), *born* 1929, *apptd* 1989
Rt. Hon. The Lord Cameron of Lochbroom, *born* 1931, *apptd* 1989
Hon. Lord Marnoch (Michael Bruce), *born* 1938, *apptd* 1990
Hon. Lord MacLean (Ranald MacLean), *born* 1938, *apptd* 1990
Hon. Lord Penrose (George Penrose), *born* 1938, *apptd* 1990
Hon. Lord Osborne (Kenneth Osborne), *born* 1937, *apptd* 1990
Hon. Lord Abernethy (John Cameron), *born* 1938, *apptd* 1992

COURT OF SESSION AND HIGH COURT OF JUSTICIARY

Parliament House, Parliament Square, Edinburgh EH1 1RQ
Tel 031-225 2595

Principal Clerk of Session and Justiciary (£36,019–£47,921), H. S. Foley
Deputy Principal Clerk of Justiciary and Administration (£27,660–£42,724), E. Cumming
Deputy Principal Clerk of Session and Principal Extractor (£27,660–£42,724), M. Weir
Deputy Principal Clerk (Keeper of the Rolls) (£27,660–£42,724), M. G. Bonar
Depute Clerks of Session and Justiciary (£17,535–£24,780), T. D. McIntosh; A. Hogg; N. J. Dowie; J. M. Clark; I. Smith; J. A. R. Cowie; T. Higgins; T. B. Cruickshank; Q. Oliver; F. Shannly; R. D. Sinclair; Mrs A. Leighton; T. M. Thomson; D. D. Mackay; A. S. Moffat;

J. Atkinson; D. J. Shand; G. Ellis; Mrs G. McKeand; D. G. Lynn; R. Cockburn; W. Dunn; A. Finlayson

SCOTTISH COURTS ADMINISTRATION

26–27 Royal Terrace, Edinburgh EH7 5AH
Tel 031-556 0755

Director, G. Murray

SHERIFF COURT OF CHANCERY

16 North Bank Street, Edinburgh EH1 2NH
Tel 031-226 7181

The Court settles disputes related to unclaimed estates of deceased persons, and other related matters.
Sheriff of Chancery, C. G. B. Nicholson, QC

HM COMMISSARY OFFICE

16 North Bank Street, Edinburgh EH1 2NJ
Tel 031-226 7181

The Office is responsible for issuing confirmation, a legal document entitling a person to execute a deceased person's will, and other related matters.
Commissary Clerk, I. E. Scott

SCOTTISH LAND COURT

1 Grosvenor Crescent, Edinburgh EH12 5ER
Tel 031-225 3595

The court deals with disputes relating to agricultural and crofting land in Scotland.
Chairman (£78,378), The Hon. Lord Philip (Alexander Philip), QC
Members, D. D. McDiarmid; D. M. MacDonald; J. Kinloch *(part-time)*
Principal Clerk, K. H. R. Graham

SHERIFFDOMS

SALARIES

Sheriff Principal	£78,378
Sheriff	£65,912
Regional Sheriff Clerk	£27,660–£42,724
Sheriff Clerk	£14,019–£47,921

*Floating Sheriff

GRAMPIAN, HIGHLANDS AND ISLANDS

Sheriff Principal, D. J. Risk
Regional Sheriff Clerk, J. Robertson

SHERIFFS AND SHERIFF CLERKS

Aberdeen and Stonehaven, D. W. Bogie; G. C. Warner; D. Kelbie; L. A. S. Jessop; *Sheriff Clerks*, J. Rodden; W. A. Mouser
Peterhead and Banff, K. A. McLernan; *Sheriff Clerk*, H. Hempseed; *Sheriff Clerk Depute*, W. H. Connon
Elgin, N. McPartlin; *Sheriff Clerk*, A. Lynch
Inverness, Lochmaddy, Portree, Stornoway, Dingwall, Tain, Wick and Dornoch, W. J. Fulton; D. Booker-Milburn; J. O. A. Fraser; E. Stewart; *Sheriff Clerk*, J. Robertson
Kirkwall and Lerwick, G. S. MacKenzie; *Sheriff Clerks Depute*, Miss H. M. Phillips; A. C. Norris
Fort William, D. Noble (also *Oban and Campbeltown*); *Sheriff Clerk Depute*, C. Morrison

TAYSIDE, CENTRAL AND FIFE

Sheriff Principal, J. J. Maguire, QC
Regional Sheriff Clerk, J. S. Doig

SHERIFFS AND SHERIFF CLERKS

Arbroath and Forfar, K. A. Veal; G. N. R. Stein; *Sheriff Clerks*, M. Herbertson; P. Dougan
Dundee, G. L. Cox; A. L. Stewart; *Sheriff Clerk*, J. S. Doig
Perth, J. F. Wheatley; J. C. McInnes, QC; *Sheriff Clerk*, W. Jones
Falkirk, A. V. Sheehan; A. J. Murphy; *Sheriff Clerk*, D. Nicoll
Stirling, A. Pollock; R. E. G. Younger; *Sheriff Clerk*, P. Crow
Alloa, R. E. G. Younger; *Sheriff Clerk*, J. M. Murphy
Cupar, C. Smith (also *Dundee*); *Sheriff Clerk*, B. Sullivan
Dunfermline, J. S. Forbes; W. M. Reid; *Sheriff Clerk*, J. Ross
Kirkcaldy, W. J. Christie; Mrs L. G. Patrick; *Sheriff Clerk*, I. Hay

LOTHIAN AND BORDERS

Sheriff Principal, C. G. B. Nicholson, QC
Regional Sheriff Clerk, I. E. Scott

SHERIFFS AND SHERIFF CLERKS

Edinburgh, N. E. D. Thomson; J. L. M. Mitchell; P. G. B. McNeill, PH.D., QC; Miss H. J. Aronson, QC; R. G. Craik, QC; G. I. W. Shiach; Miss I. A. Poole; R. J. D. Scott; A. M. Bell; J. M. S. Horsburgh, QC; G. W. S. Presslie; *J. A. Farrell; A. Lothian; *Sheriff Clerk*, I. E. Scott
Peebles, N. E. D. Thomson, CBE (also *Edinburgh*); *Sheriff Clerk*, I. E. Scott
Linlithgow, M. Stone; G. R. Fleming; *Sheriff Clerk*, R. Sinclair
Haddington, G. W. S. Presslie (also *Edinburgh*); *Sheriff Clerk*, B. W. S. Manthorpe
Jedburgh and Duns, J. V. Paterson; *Sheriff Clerk*, J. W. Williamson
Selkirk, J. V. Paterson; *Sheriff Clerk*, L. McFarlane

NORTH STRATHCLYDE

Sheriff Principal, R. C. Hay, CBE
Regional Sheriff Clerk, A. A. Brown

SHERIFFS AND SHERIFF CLERKS

Oban and Campbeltown, D. Noble (also *Fort William*); *Sheriff Clerk Deputes*, W. M. Cochrane; K. L. Graham
Dumbarton, J. T. Fitzsimons; T. Scott; S. W. H. Fraser; *Sheriff Clerk*, N. R. Weir
Paisley, R. G. Smith; C. N. Stoddart; J. Spy; C. K. Higgins; C. W. Palmer; *C. G. McKay; *Sheriff Clerk*, A. A. Brown
Greenock, J. Herald (also *Rothesay*); Sir Stephen Young; *Sheriff Clerk*, P. G. Corcoran
Kilmarnock, T. M. Croan; D. B. Smith; T. F. Russell; *Sheriff Clerk*, J. Shaw
Dunoon, A. Noble (also *Dumbarton*); *Sheriff Clerk Depute*, Mrs C. Carson

GLASGOW AND STRATHKELVIN

Sheriff Principal, N. D. MacLeod, QC
Regional Sheriff Clerk, C. McLay

SHERIFFS AND SHERIFF CLERKS

Glasgow, A. C. Horsfall, QC (*seconded to Scottish Lands Tribunal*); A. A. Bell, QC; B. Kearney; G. H. Gordon, QC;

A. C. McKay; J. C. M. Jardine; Mrs D. J. B. Robertson; B. A. Lockhart; I. G. Pirie; Mrs A. L. A. Duncan; W. G. Stevenson, QC; G. J. Evans; E. H. Galt; F. J. Keane; A. C. Henry; J. K. Mitchell; A. G. Johnston; J. P. Murphy; M. Sischy; S. A. O. Raeburn; A. B. Wilkinson; *Sheriff Clerk*, C. McLay

SOUTH STRATHCLYDE, DUMFRIES AND GALLOWAY

Sheriff Principal, J. S. Mowat, QC
Regional Sheriff Clerk, H. Findlay

SHERIFFS AND SHERIFF CLERKS

Hamilton, L. S. Lovat; A. C. MacPherson; W. F. Lunny; D. G. Russell; V. J. Canavan (also *Airdrie*); W. E. Gibson; H. Stirling; *C. B. Miller; *Sheriff Clerk*, J. Cumming
Lanark, J. D. Allan; *Sheriff Clerk*, D. M. Cameron
Ayr, N. Gow, QC; R. G. McEwan, QC; *Sheriff Clerk*, G. W. Waddell
Stranraer and Kirkcudbright, J. R. Smith; *Sheriff Clerk*, N. L. Hodgson; *Sheriff Clerk Depute*, B. Lindsay
Dumfries, K. G. Barr; L. Cameron; *Sheriff Clerk*, P. McGonigle
Airdrie, J. H. Stewart; V. J. Canavan (also *Hamilton*); R. H. Dickson; I. C. Simpson; *Sheriff Clerk*, H. Findlay

---

STIPENDIARY MAGISTRATES

GLASGOW

R. Hamilton, *apptd* 1984; J. B. C. Nisbet, *apptd* 1984; R. B. Christie, *apptd* 1985; Mrs J. A. M. MacLean, *apptd* 1990

PROCURATOR FISCAL SERVICE

CROWN OFFICE
Regent Road, Edinburgh EH7 5BL
Tel 031-557 3800

Crown Agent (£67,600), J. D. Lowe
Deputy Crown Agent (†£46,122), A. D. Vannet

PROCURATORS FISCAL

†SALARIES

Regional Procurator Fiscal–grade 3	£48,000
Regional Procurator Fiscal–grade 4	£46,122
Procurator Fiscal–upper level	£34,667–£39,402
Procurator Fiscal–lower level	£24,928–£33,921

†as at August 1992

GRAMPIAN, HIGHLANDS AND ISLANDS REGION

Regional Procurator Fiscal, S. W. Lockhart, CBE (*Aberdeen*)
Procurators Fiscal, E. K. Barbour (*Stonehaven*); A. J. M. Colley (*Banff*); I. S. McNaughtan (*Peterhead*); G. K. Buchanan (*Elgin*); A. N. MacDonald (*Wick*); C. B. McClory (*Portree and Lochmaddy*); Mrs D. Wilson (*Stornoway*); H. T. Westwater (*Dornoch and Tain*); W. W. Orr (*Inverness*); D. K. Adam (*Kirkwall and Lerwick*); Mrs A. Neizer (*Fort William*); D. R. Hingston (*Dingwall*)

TAYSIDE, CENTRAL AND FIFE REGION
Regional Procurator Fiscal, B. K. Heywood (*Dundee*)
Procurators Fiscal, Mrs B. Bott (*Arbroath*); A. L. Ingram
(*Forfar*); I. A. McLeod (*Perth*); G. E. Scott (*Falkirk*);
K. Valentine (*Stirling*); I. D. Douglas (*Alloa*);
E. B. Russell (*Cupar*); R. T. Hamilton (*Dunfermline*);
F. R. Crowe (*Kirkcaldy*)

LOTHIAN AND BORDERS REGION
Regional Procurator Fiscal, R. F. Lees (*Edinburgh*)
Procurators Fiscal, R. F. Lees (*Peebles*); H. R. Annan
(*Linlithgow*); A. J. P. Reith (*Haddington*); A. R. G. Fraser
(*Duns* and *Jedburgh*); D. McNeill (*Selkirk*)

NORTH STRATHCLYDE REGION
Regional Procurator Fiscal, J. D. Friel (*Paisley*)
Procurators Fiscal, I. Henderson (*Campbeltown*); J. Cardle
(*Dumbarton*); C. C. Donnelly (*Greenock* and *Rothesay*);
D. L. Webster (*Dunoon*); J. G. MacGlennan
(*Kilmarnock*); B. R. Maguire (*Oban*)

GLASGOW AND STRATHKELVIN REGION
Regional Procurator Fiscal, A. C. Normand (*Glasgow*)

SOUTH STRATHCLYDE, DUMFRIES AND
GALLOWAY REGION
Regional Procurator Fiscal, W. G. Carmichael (*Hamilton*)
Procurators Fiscal, S. R. Houston (*Lanark*); N. G. O'Brien
(*Ayr*); F. Walkingshaw (*Stranraer*); D. J. Howdle
(*Dumfries* and *Kirkcudbright*); A. T. Wilson (*Airdrie*)

Northern Ireland Judicature

In Northern Ireland the legal system and the structure of courts closely resemble those of England and Wales; there are, however, often differences in enacted law.

The Supreme Court of Judicature of Northern Ireland comprises the Court of Appeal, the High Court of Justice and the Crown Court. The practice and procedure of these courts is similar to that in England. The superior civil court is the High Court of Justice, from which an appeal lies to the Northern Ireland Court of Appeal; the House of Lords is the final civil appeal court.

The Crown Court, served by High Court and county court judges, deals with criminal trials on indictment. Cases are heard before a judge and, except those involving offences specified under emergency legislation, a jury. Appeals from the Crown Court against conviction or sentence are heard by the Northern Ireland Court of Appeal; the House of Lords is the final court of appeal.

The decision to prosecute in cases tried on indictment and in summary cases of a serious nature rests in Northern Ireland with the Director of Public Prosecutions, who is responsible to the Attorney-General. Minor summary offences are prosecuted by the police.

Minor criminal offences are dealt with in magistrates' courts by a full-time, legally qualified resident magistrate and, where an offender is under 17, by juvenile courts each consisting of a resident magistrate and two lay members specially qualified to deal with juveniles (at least one of whom must be a woman). There are 974 Justices of the Peace in Northern Ireland. Appeals from magistrates' courts are heard by the county court, or by the Court of Appeal on a point of law or an issue as to jurisdiction.

Magistrates' courts in Northern Ireland can deal with certain classes of civil case but most minor civil cases are dealt with in county courts. Judgments of all civil courts are enforceable through a centralized procedure administered by the Enforcement of Judgments Office.

SUPREME COURT OF JUDICATURE
The Royal Courts of Justice, Belfast BT1 3JF
Tel 0232-235111

Lord Chief Justice of Northern Ireland (£103,790),
The Rt. Hon. Sir Brian Hutton, *born* 1931, *apptd* 1988

Lords Justices of Appeal (each £99,510)
Rt. Hon. Sir Basil Kelly, *born* 1920, *apptd* 1984
Rt. Hon. Sir John MacDermott, *born* 1927, *apptd* 1987
Rt. Hon. Sir John Higgins, *born* 1927, *apptd* 1993

Puisne Judges (each £90,147)
Hon. Sir Robert Carswell, *born* 1934, *apptd* 1984
Hon. Sir Michael Nicholson, *born* 1933, *apptd* 1986
Hon. Sir William McCollum, *born* 1933, *apptd* 1987
Hon. Sir Anthony Campbell, *born* 1936, *apptd* 1988
Hon. Sir John Sheil, *born* 1938, *apptd* 1989
Hon. Sir Brian Kerr, *born* 1948, *apptd* 1993
Hon. Sir John Pringle, *born* 1929, *apptd* 1993

LORD CHIEF JUSTICE'S OFFICE
Principal Secretary to the Lord Chief Justice and Clerk of the Crown for Northern Ireland, J. A. L. McLean, QC
Legal Secretary to the Lord Chief Justice,
Mrs. D. M. Kennedy

MASTERS OF SUPREME COURT (each £54,035)
Master, Queen's Bench and Appeals, J. W. Wilson, QC
Master, High Court, vacant
Master, Office of Care and Protection, F. B. Hall
Master, Chancery Office, vacant
Master, Bankruptcy and Companies Office, J. B. C. Glass
Master, Probate and Matrimonial Office, R. T. Millar
Master, Taxing Office, J. C. Napier

COUNTY COURTS

RECORDERS (each £78,377)
Belfast, vacant
Londonderry, Judge Higgins, QC

JUDGES (each £78,377)
Rt. Hon. Judge Sir Robert Porter, QC; Judge Russell, QC;
Judge Curran, QC; Judge McKee, QC; Judge Gibson, QC;
Judge Hart, QC; Judge Petrie, QC; Judge Smyth, QC;
Judge Martin, QC; Judge Burgess

MAGISTRATES COURTS

RESIDENT MAGISTRATES (each £54,035)
There are 17 resident magistrates in Northern Ireland.

CROWN SOLICITOR'S OFFICE
PO Box 410, Royal Courts of Justice, Belfast BT1 3JY
Tel 0232–235111

Crown Solicitor, N. P. Roberts

DEPARTMENT OF THE DIRECTOR OF PUBLIC PROSECUTIONS
Royal Courts of Justice, Belfast BT1 3NX
Tel 0232–235111

Director of Public Prosecutions, A. Fraser, CB, QC
Deputy Director of Public Prosecutions, D. Magill

Ecclesiastical Courts

Original jurisdiction is exercised by the consistory court of each diocese in England, presided over by the Chancellor of that diocese. Appellate jurisdiction is exercised by the provincial courts detailed below, by the Court for Ecclesiastical Causes Reserved, and by commissions of review (the membership of these being newly constituted for each case).

COURT OF ARCHES (PROVINCE OF CANTERBURY)
Registry, 16 Beaumont Street, Oxford OX1 2LZ
Tel 0865–241974

Dean of the Arches, The Rt. Worshipful Sir John Owen

COURT OF THE VICAR-GENERAL OF THE PROVINCE OF CANTERBURY

Registry, 16 Beaumont Street, Oxford OX1 2LZ
Tel 0865–241974

Vicar-General, The Rt. Worshipful Miss S. Cameron, QC

CHANCERY COURT OF YORK
Registry, 1 Peckitt Street, York YO1 1SG
Tel 0904–623487

Auditor, The Rt. Worshipful Sir John Owen

THE VICAR-GENERAL OF THE PROVINCE OF YORK
Registry, 1 Peckitt Street, York YO1 1SG
Tel 0904–623487

Vicar-General, His Honour the Worshipful Judge T. A. C. Coningsby, QC

COURT OF FACULTIES
Registry, 1 The Sanctuary, London SW1P 3JT
Tel 071–222 5381

Office for the use of special and common marriage licences, appointment of notaries public, etc. Office hours, Monday–Friday, 10–4.

Master of the Faculties, The Rt. Worshipful Sir John Owen

Tribunals

AGRICULTURAL LAND TRIBUNALS

c/o Land Use and Tenure Division, Ministry of Agriculture,
Fisheries and Food, Nobel House, 17 Smith Square,
London SW1P 3JR
Tel 071-238 3000

Agricultural Land Tribunals were set up under the Agriculture Act 1947 and settle disputes and other issues between agricultural landlords and tenants. They also settle drainage disputes between neighbours.

There are seven tribunals covering England and one covering the whole of Wales. For each tribunal the Lord Chancellor appoints a chairman and one or more deputies, who must be barristers or solicitors of at least seven years standing. The Lord Chancellor also appoints lay members to three statutory panels of members: the 'landowners' panel, the 'farmers' panel and the 'drainage' panel.

Each of the eight tribunals is an independent statutory body with jurisdiction only within its own area. A separate tribunal is constituted for each case, and consists of a chairman (who may be the chairman or one of the deputy chairmen) and two lay members nominated by the chairman. The chairmen and deputy chairmen are entitled to claim a fee of £221 per day.

Chairmen (England), W. D. Greenwood; K. J. Fisher; The
Hon. Mr Justice Evans-Lombe; C. H. Beaumont;
N. J. Worsley; G. L. Newsom; His Hon. Judge Robert
Taylor
Chairman (Wales), W. J. Owen

COMMONS COMMISSIONERS

Golden Cross House, Duncannon Street, London WC2N 4JF
Tel 071-210 4584

The Commons Commissioners are responsible for deciding disputes arising under the Commons Registration Act 1965 and the Common Land (Rectification of Registers) Act 1989. They also enquire into the ownership of unclaimed common land. Commissioners are appointed by the Lord Chancellor.
Chief Commons Commissioner (£78,377), M. Roth
Commissioners, I. L. R. Romer; D. M. Burton;
P. G. Langdon-Davies
Clerk, Miss F. A. A. Buchan

COPYRIGHT TRIBUNAL

Room 4/6, Hazlitt House, 45 Southampton Buildings,
London WC2A 1AR
Tel 071-438 4776

The Copyright Tribunal is the successor to the Performing Right Tribunal which was established by the Copyright Act 1956 to resolve various classes of copyright dispute, principally in the field of collective licensing. Its jurisdiction was extended by the Copyright, Designs and Patents Act 1988 and the Broadcasting Act 1990.

The chairman and two deputy chairmen are appointed by the Lord Chancellor. Up to eight ordinary members are appointed by the Secretary of State for Trade and Industry.

Chairman, J. M. Bowers
Secretary, Mrs K. M. Adams

DATA PROTECTION TRIBUNAL

c/o The Home Office, Queen Anne's Gate, London
SW1H 9AT
Tel 071-273 3755

The Data Protection Tribunal was established under the Data Protection Act 1984 to determine appeals against decisions of the Data Protection Registrar. The chairman and two deputy chairmen are appointed by the Lord Chancellor and must be legally qualified. Lay members are appointed by the Home Secretary to represent the interests of data users or data subjects.

A tribunal consists of a legally-qualified chairman sitting with equal numbers of the lay members appointed to represent the interests of data users and data subjects. The chairman and members receive an *ad hoc* daily fee when the tribunal is sitting.
Chairman, J. A. C. Spokes, QC
Secretary, S. Bucher-Jones

EMPLOYMENT APPEAL TRIBUNAL

Central Office, Audit House, 58 Victoria Embankment,
London EC4Y ODS
Tel 071-273 1041
Divisional Office, 11 Melville Crescent, Edinburgh
EH3 7LU
Tel 031-225 3963

The Employment Appeal Tribunal was established as a superior court of record under the provisions of the Employment Protection Act 1975, hearing appeals on a question of law arising from any decision of an industrial tribunal.

A tribunal consists of a legally-qualified chairman and two lay members, one from each side of industry. They are appointed by The Queen on the recommendation of the Lord Chancellor and the Secretary of State for Employment.
President, The Hon. Mr Justice Wood
Scottish Chairman, The Hon. Lord Coulsfield
Registrar, Miss V. J. Selio

IMMIGRATION APPELLATE AUTHORITIES

Thanet House, 231 Strand, London WC2R 1DA
Tel 071-353 8060

The Immigration Appeal Adjudicators hear appeals from immigration decisions concerning the need for, and refusal of, leave to enter or remain in the UK, decisions to make deportation orders and directions to remove persons subject to immigration control from the UK. The Immigration Appeal Tribunal hears appeals direct from decisions to make deportation orders in matters concerning conduct contrary to the public good. Its principal jurisdiction is, however, the hearing of appeals from adjudicators by the party (Home

Office or individual) who is aggrieved by the decision. Appeals are subject to leave being granted by the tribunal.

An adjudicator sits alone. The tribunal sits in divisions of three – normally a legally qualified member and two lay members. Members of the tribunal and adjudicators are appointed by the Lord Chancellor.

IMMIGRATION APPEAL TRIBUNAL
President (£64,064), G. W. Farmer
Vice-Presidents, Prof. D. C. Jackson; Mrs J. Chatwani

IMMIGRATION APPEAL ADJUDICATORS
Chief Adjudicator (£63,103) M. Patey, MBE
Deputy Chief Adjudicator, R. G. Care

INDEPENDENT TRIBUNAL SERVICE
City Gate House, Finsbury Square, London EC2A IUU
Tel 071-814 6500

The service is the administrative authority which exercises judicial and administrative control over the independent social security and child support appeal tribunals, medical appeal tribunals, vaccine damage tribunals and disability appeal tribunals.
President (£69,500), His Hon. Judge Thorpe
Chief Executive, Mrs V. Willcocks

INDUSTRIAL TRIBUNALS

CENTRAL OFFICE (ENGLAND AND WALES)
93 Ebury Bridge Road, London SW1W 8RE
Tel 071-730 9161

Industrial Tribunals for England and Wales sit in 11 regions. The tribunals deal with matters of employment law, redundancy, dismissal, sexual and racial discrimination and related areas of dispute which may arise in the workplace. The tribunals are funded by the Department of Employment.

Chairmen, who may be full-time or part-time, are legally qualified. They are appointed by the Lord Chancellor. Tribunal members are nominated by the CBI and TUC, and appointed by the Secretary of State for Employment.
President (£78,377), His Hon. Judge T. Lawrence

CENTRAL OFFICE (SCOTLAND)
St Andrew House, 141 West Nile Street, Glasgow GI 2RU
Tel 041-331 1601

Tribunals in Scotland have the same remit as those in England and Wales. Chairmen are appointed by the Lord President of the Court of Session and lay members by the Secretary of State for Employment.
President (£65,250), Mrs D. Littlejohn

INDUSTRIAL TRIBUNALS AND THE FAIR EMPLOYMENT TRIBUNAL (NORTHERN IRELAND)
Long Bridge House, 20–24 Waring Street, Belfast BTI 2EB
Tel 0232-327666

The industrial tribunal system in Northern Ireland was set up in 1965 and is similar to the system operating in the rest of the UK. The main legislation in Northern Ireland giving jurisdiction to industrial tribunals to hear complaints relating to employment matters corresponds to legislation enacted in

Great Britain, except that there is no equivalent legislation to the Race Relations Act.

Since 1 January 1990 there has been a separate Fair Employment Tribunal in Northern Ireland. The Fair Employment Tribunal hears and determines individual cases of alleged religious or political discrimination in employment. Employers can also appeal to the Fair Employment Tribunal if they consider the directions of the Fair Employment Commission to be unreasonable, inappropriate or unnecessary, and the Fair Employment Commission can make application to the Tribunal for the enforcement of undertakings or directions with which an employer has not complied.

The president, vice-president and part-time chairmen of the Fair Employment Tribunal are appointed by the Lord Chancellor. The full-time chairman and the part-time chairmen of the industrial tribunals and the panel members to both the industrial tribunals and the Fair Employment Tribunal are appointed by the Department of Economic Development Northern Ireland.
President of the Industrial Tribunals and the Fair Employment Tribunal (£78,377), J. Maguire
Vice-President of the Industrial Tribunals and the Fair Employment Tribunal (£65,912), Mrs M. Perceval-Price
Secretary, J. Murphy

LANDS TRIBUNAL
48–49 Chancery Lane, London WC2A IJR
Tel 071-936 7200

The Lands Tribunal is an independent judicial body constituted by the Lands Tribunal Act 1949 for the purpose of determining a wide range of questions relating to the valuation of land, rating appeals from local valuation courts and the discharge or modification of restrictive covenants. The Act also empowers the tribunal to accept the function of arbitration under references by consent. The tribunal consists of a president and a number of other members, who are appointed by the Lord Chancellor.
President (£69,412), His Hon. Judge Marder, QC
Members (£65,912), Dr T. Hoyes, FRICS; M. S. J. Hopper, FRICS
Members (part-time) (£300 per day), J. C. Hill, TD; His Hon. Judge O'Donoghue; His Hon. Judge Rich, QC; A. P. Musto, FRICS; P. H. Clarke, FRICS
Registrar, C. A. McMullan

LANDS TRIBUNAL FOR SCOTLAND
1 Grosvenor Crescent, Edinburgh EH12 5ER
Tel 031-225 7996

The Lands Tribunal for Scotland was constituted by the Lands Tribunal Act 1949. Its remit is the same as the tribunal for England and Wales but also covers questions relating to tenants rights. The president is appointed by the Lord President of the Court of Session.
President (£78,377), The Hon. Lord Philip, QC
Members (£65,912), Sheriff A. C. Horsfall, QC; A. R. MacLeary; J. Devine (*full-time*); R. A. Edwards, CBE, WS (*part-time*)
Clerk, D. Pentland

MENTAL HEALTH REVIEW TRIBUNALS

The Mental Health Review Tribunals are independent judicial bodies established under the Mental Health Act 1959 and which now operate under the Mental Health Act 1983. They are responsible for reviewing the cases of patients compulsorily detained under the Act's provisions. They have the power to discharge the patient and, in the case of unrestricted patients, to re-classify the patient, to recommend leave of absence, delayed discharge, transfer to another hospital, or that a guardianship order be made. There are 14 Tribunals in England, each headed by a regional chairman who is appointed by the Lord Chancellor's Department on a part-time basis. In practice there are ten chairmen covering the 14 regions, some with more than one region. Each tribunal is made up of at least three members, and must include a lawyer, who acts as president (£221 per day), a medical member (£217.40 per day) and a lay member (£91 per day).

The Medical Health Review Tribunals' secretariat is based in five regional offices:

LONDON (NORTH) , Spur 5, Block I, Government Buildings, Honeypot Lane, Stanmore, Middx. HA7 IAY. Tel: 071-972 2373. *Clerk*, P. Barnett

LONDON (SOUTH) , Spur B, Block 3, Crown Offices, Kingston Bypass Road, Surbiton, Surrey KT6 5QN. Tel: 081-398 4166. *Clerk*, Mrs J. Innes

LIVERPOOL, 3rd Floor, Cressington House, 249 St Mary's Road, Garston, Liverpool L19 0NF. Tel: 051-494 0095. *Clerk*, Mrs B. Foot

NOTTINGHAM , Spur A, Block 5, Government Buildings, Chalfont Drive, Western Boulevard, Nottingham NG8 3RZ. Tel: 0602-294222. *Clerk*, M. Chapman

WALES , 1st Floor, New Crown Buildings, Cathays Park, Cardiff CF1 3NQ. Tel: 0222-825328. *Clerk*, Mrs C. Thomas

NATIONAL HEALTH SERVICE TRIBUNAL

The NHS Tribunal inquires into representations that the continued inclusion of a family practitioner (doctor, dentist, pharmacist or optician) on a Family Practitioner Committee's list would be prejudicial to the efficiency of the services concerned. The tribunal sits when required, about eight times a year, and usually in London.
Chairman, R. Bell, QC
Clerk, I. D. Keith, East Hookers, Twineham, nr Haywards Heath, W. Sussex RH17 5NN. Tel: 0444-881345

NATIONAL HEALTH SERVICE TRIBUNAL (SCOTLAND)
33 Queen Street, Edinburgh EH2 ILE
Tel 031-226 6541

The tribunal was set up under the National Health Service (Scotland) Act 1978, and exists to consider representations that the continued inclusion of a registered medical practitioner, dental practitioner, optometrist or pharmacist on a health board's list would be prejudicial to the continuing efficiency of the service in question.

The tribunal meets when required and is composed of a chairman, one lay member, and one practitioner member drawn from a representative professional panel. The chairman is appointed by the Lord President of the Court of Session, and the lay member and the members of the professional panel are appointed by the Secretary of State for Scotland. The chairman and members receive an *ad hoc* daily fee when the tribunal is sitting.

Chairman, W. C. Galbraith, QC
Lay member, J. D. M. Robertson
Clerk to the Tribunal, D. G. Brash, WS

PENSIONS APPEAL TRIBUNALS

CENTRAL OFFICE (ENGLAND AND WALES)
48-49 Chancery Lane, London WC2A 1JR
Tel 071-936 7034

The Pensions Appeal Tribunals are responsible for hearing appeals from ex-servicemen or women and widows who have had their claims for a war pension rejected by the Secretary of State for Social Security. The Entitlement Appeal Tribunals hear appeals in cases where the Secretary of State has refused to grant a war pension. The Assessment Appeal Tribunals hear appeals against the Secretary of State's assessment of the degree of disablement caused by an accepted condition.

The tribunal members are appointed by the Lord Chancellor.
President (£55,777), J. R. T. Holt
Secretary, Miss A. Gibson

PENSIONS APPEAL TRIBUNALS FOR SCOTLAND
20 Walker Street, Edinburgh EH3 7HS
Tel 031-220 1404
President, A. C. Hamilton, QC

OFFICE OF THE SOCIAL SECURITY AND CHILD SUPPORT COMMISSIONERS
Harp House, 83-86 Farringdon Street, London EC4A 4DH
Tel 071-353 5145

23 Melville Street, Edinburgh EH3 7PW
Tel 031-225 2201

The Social Security Commissioners are the final statutory authority to decide appeals relating to entitlement to social security benefits. The Child Support Commissioners are the final statutory authority to decide appeals relating to child support. Appeals may be made in relation to both matters only on a point of law. The Commissioners' jurisdiction covers England, Wales and Scotland. The commissioners are all qualified lawyers.
Chief Social Security Commissioner and Chief Child Support Commissioner (£78,000), His Hon. Judge Machin, QC
Secretary, Mrs M. White (*London*); R. Lindsay (*Edinburgh*)

OFFICE OF THE SOCIAL SECURITY AND CHILD SUPPORT COMMISSIONERS FOR NORTHERN IRELAND
Lancashire House, 5 Linenhall Street, Belfast BT2 8AA
Tel 0232-332344

The role of Northern Ireland Social Security and Child Support Commissioners is similar to that of the Commissioners in Great Britain.
Chief Commissioner (£78,377), His Hon. Judge Chambers, QC
Registrar of Appeals, W. D. Pollock

THE SOLICITORS' DISCIPLINARY TRIBUNAL
16 Bell Yard, London WC2A IPL
Tel 071–242 0219

The Solicitors' Disciplinary Tribunal was constituted under the provisions of the Solicitors Act 1974. It is an independent statutory body whose members are appointed by the Master of the Rolls. The tribunal considers applications made to it alleging either professional misconduct and/or a breach of the statutory rules by which solicitors are bound against an individually named solicitor, former solicitor, or registered foreign lawyer. The tribunal's jurisdiction extends to solicitor's clerks, in respect of whom they may make an order restricting that clerk's employment by solicitors.
President, G. B. Marsh
Clerk, Mrs S. C. Elson

SPECIAL COMMISSIONERS OF INCOME TAX
15–19 Bedford Avenue, London WCIB 3AS
Tel 071–631 4242

The Special Commissioners are an independent body appointed by the Lord Chancellor to hear appeals concerning income taxes, etc.
Presiding Special Commissioner (£78,378), His Hon. Stephen Oliver, QC
Special Commissioners (£54,035), T. H. K. Everett; D. A. Shirley
Deputy Special Commissioners, D. C. Potter, QC; R. H. Widdows, CB
Clerk (£22,618), R. P. Lester

TRAFFIC COMMISSIONERS
c/o Western Traffic Area, The Gaunt's House, Denmark Street, Bristol BSI 5DR
Tel 0272-755065

The Traffic Commissioners are responsible for the licensing of operators of heavy goods and public service vehicles, and they also have responsibility for appeals relating to the licensing of operators and for disciplinary cases involving the conduct of drivers of these vehicles. There are seven Commissioners in the eight traffic areas covering Great Britain. For Traffic Area Offices and Commissioners, *see* page 361. Each Traffic Commissioner constitutes a tribunal for the purposes of the Tribunals and Inquiries Act 1971.
Senior Traffic Commissioner, Air Vice-Marshal R. G. Ashford, CBE

TRANSPORT TRIBUNAL
48–49 Chancery Lane, London, WC2A IJR
Tel 071–936 7494

The Transport Tribunal was set up in 1947 and hears appeals against decisions made by Traffic Commissioners at public inquiries. The tribunal consists of a legally-qualified president, two legal members who may sit as chairmen, and four lay members. The president and legal members are appointed by the Lord Chancellor and the lay members are appointed by the Secretary of State for Transport.

President (part-time), His Hon. Judge H. Wilson
Legal members (£221 per day), His Hon. Judge Brodrick *(part-time)*; R. Owen, QC
Lay members (£177 per day), T. W. Hall; J. W. Whitworth; G. Simms; Miss E. B. Haran
Secretary, P. Harris

VALUATION TRIBUNALS
c/o Warwickshire Valuation Tribunal, 2nd Floor, Walton House, 11 Parade, Leamington Spa, Warks. CV32 4DG
Tel 0926-421875

The Valuation Tribunals hear appeals concerning the council tax, non-domestic rating and land drainage rates in England and Wales. They also have residual jurisdiction to hear appeals concerning the community charge, the pre-1990 rating list, disabled rating and mixed hereditaments. There are 56 Valuation Tribunals in England, and eight in Wales. Each tribunal is a separate independent body; those in England are funded by the Department of the Environment and those in Wales by the Welsh Office. A separate tribunal is constituted for each hearing, and normally consists of a chairman and two other members. Members are appointed by the local authority/authorities, and serve on a voluntary basis. A National Committee of Valuation Tribunals considers all matters affecting Valuations Tribunals in England, and the Council of Wales, Valuation Tribunal Presidents, performs the same function in Wales.
President, National Committee of Valuation Tribunals, A. W. H. Kennard
Secretary, National Committee of Valuation Tribunals, B. P. Massen
President, Council of Wales, Valuation Tribunal Presidents, T. W. Jones

VAT TRIBUNALS
15–19 Bedford Avenue, London WCIB 3AS
Tel 071–631 4242

VAT Tribunals are administered by the Lord Chancellor's Department in England and Wales, and by the Secretary of State in Scotland. They are independent and decide disputes between taxpayers and the Commissioners of Customs and Excise, who manage VAT. In England and Wales, the president and chairmen are appointed by the Lord Chancellor, and members are appointed by the Treasury. Chairmen in Scotland are appointed by the Lord President of the Court of Session.
President (£78,378), His Hon. Stephen Oliver, QC
Vice-President, Scotland (£54,035), R. A. Bennett, CBE, QC
Registrar, R. P. Lester

TRIBUNAL CENTRES
LONDON (including Belfast), 15–19 Bedford Avenue, London WCIB 3AS. Tel: 071–631 4242
EDINBURGH, 44 Palmerston Place, Edinburgh EHI2 5BJ. Tel: 031–226 3551
MANCHESTER, Warwickgate House, Warwick Road, Old Trafford, Manchester MI6 OGP. Tel: 061–872 6471

The Police Service

There are 52 police forces in the United Kingdom, each responsible for law enforcement in its area. Most forces' area is conterminous with an English or Welsh county or Scottish region, though there are several combined forces. Law enforcement in London is carried out by the Metropolitan Police and the City of London Police; in Northern Ireland by the Royal Ulster Constabulary; and by the Isle of Man, States of Jersey, and Guernsey forces in their respective islands and bailiwicks. The National Criminal Intelligence Service (*see* below) was set up in April 1992.

Each police force is maintained by a police authority. The authorities of English and Welsh forces comprise committees of local councillors and magistrates; in Scotland, the regional and islands councils are the authorities. The authority for the Metropolitan Police is the Home Secretary. In Northern Ireland the Secretary of State appoints the police authority.

Police authorities are financed by central and local government. Subject to the approval of the Home Secretary and to regulations, they appoint the chief constable, decide the maximum size of the force and provide buildings and equipment.

The Home Secretary and the Secretaries of State for Scotland and Northern Ireland are responsible for the organization, administration and operation of the police service. They make regulations covering matters such as police ranks, discipline, hours of duty, and pay and allowances.

All police forces (including the Metropolitan Police at the request of the Commissioner) are subject to inspection by HM Inspectors of Constabulary, who report to the respective Secretary of State.

The investigation of a serious complaint against a police officer is supervised by the Police Complaints Authority (*see* page 343) in England and Wales. An officer may appeal against the finding of an investigation, or against the resulting punishment, to the Home Secretary; appeals are heard by private Police Appeal tribunals consisting of a chairman (a barrister or solicitor) and two retired police officers appointed on an *ad hoc* basis. In Scotland, complaints are investigated by independent public prosecutors, and in Northern Ireland by the Independent Commission for Police Complaints.

For details of the government White Paper on the police and the Sheehy report on police pay and conditions, *see* Index.

BASIC RATES OF POLICE PAY
as at 1 September 1993

Chief Constable	£56,313–£71,580
Deputy Chief Constable	£49,605–£57,264
Assistant Chief Constable	£47,241
Chief Superintendent	£40,071–£42,549
Superintendent	£36,042–£39,135
Chief Inspector	£26,496–£29,472
Inspector	£23,337–£26,496
Sergeant	£20,343–£23,337
Constable	£12,744–£21,267

Metropolitan Police
(excluding London weighting and London allowance)

Metropolitan Commissioner	£90,148
Deputy Commissioner	£76,266
Assistant Commissioner	£67,281
Deputy Assistant Commissioner	£53,826

Commander	£47,241
Chief Superintendent	£40,071–£42,549
Superintendent	£36,960–£39,135
Chief Inspector	£27,768–£30,732
Inspector	£24,591–£27,768
Sergeant	£20,343–£23,337
Constable	£12,744–£21,267

THE SPECIAL CONSTABULARY

The Special Constabulary is the part-time volunteer branch of the police force. Special Constables have full police powers within their force area and undertake regular officers' routine policing duties when required, thus freeing regulars at times of emergency for those tasks which only they can perform. There were 19,243 Special Constables in England and Wales at the end of 1992.

NATIONAL CRIMINAL INTELLIGENCE SERVICE

Headquarters: PO Box 8000, Spring Gardens, Tinworth Street, London SE11 5EN
Tel 071-238 8000

The function of the National Criminal Intelligence Service (NCIS) is to gather, collate and disseminate information and intelligence on serious crime of a regional, national and international nature. It is independent of any other police organization.
Director-General, A. H. Pacey, QPM
Director (Intelligence), S. R. W. Crawshaw, QPM
Director, Drugs Division, S. Wesley
Director of Resources, R. Creedon

POLICE AUTHORITIES

Strength: actual strength of force as at mid June 1993
Chair: Chairman/Convener of the Police Authority/Police Committee

ENGLAND

AVON AND SOMERSET CONSTABULARY, *HQ*, PO Box 37, Valley Road, Portishead, Bristol BS20 8QJ. Tel: 0272-818181. *Strength*, 3,056; *Chief Constable*, D. J. Shattock, QPM; *Chair*, D. Heath

BEDFORDSHIRE POLICE, *HQ*, Woburn Road, Kempston, Bedford MK43 9AX. Tel: 0234-841212. *Strength*, 1,173; *Chief Constable*, A. Dyer, QPM; *Chair*, elected at each meeting

CAMBRIDGESHIRE CONSTABULARY, *HQ*, Hinchingbrooke Park, Huntingdon, Cambs. PE18 8NP. Tel: 0480-456111. *Strength*, 1,224; *Chief Constable*, I. H. Kane, QPM; *Chair*, J. Fitch

CHESHIRE CONSTABULARY, *HQ*, Castle Esplanade, Chester, CH1 2PP. Tel: 0244-350000. *Strength*, 1,892; *Chief Constable*, J. M. Jones, QPM; *Chair*, J. H. Collins, OBE

CLEVELAND CONSTABULARY, *HQ*, PO Box 70, Ladgate Lane, Middlesbrough, Cleveland TS8 9EH. Tel: 0642-326326. *Strength*, 1,466; *Chief Constable*, B. D. D. Shaw; *Chair*, I. Jeffrey

CUMBRIA CONSTABULARY, *HQ*, Carleton Hall, Penrith, Cumbria CA10 2AU. Tel: 0768-64411. *Strength*, 1,196; *Chief Constable*, A. G. Elliott; *Chair*, R. Watson

DERBYSHIRE CONSTABULARY, *HQ*, Butterley Hall, Ripley, Derbyshire DE5 3RS. Tel: 0773-570100. *Strength*, 1,811; *Chief Constable*, J. F. Newing, QPM; *Chair*, E. H. Swain

DEVON AND CORNWALL CONSTABULARY, *HQ*, Middlemoor, Exeter EX2 7HQ. Tel: 0392-52101. *Strength*, 2,960; *Chief Constable*, J. S. Evans, QPM; *Chair*, O. A. May

DORSET POLICE FORCE, *HQ*, Winfrith, Dorchester, Dorset DT2 8DZ. Tel: 0929-462727. *Strength*, 1,302; *Chief Constable*, B. H. Weight, QPM; *Chair*, Sir Stephen Hammick, Bt.

DURHAM CONSTABULARY, *HQ*, Aykley Heads, Durham DH1 5TT. Tel: 091-386 4929. *Strength*, 1,376; *Chief Constable*, F. W. Taylor, QPM; *Chair*, J. Richardson

ESSEX POLICE, *HQ*, PO Box 2, Springfield, Chelmsford CM2 6DA. Tel: 0245-491491. *Strength*, 2,955; *Chief Constable*, J. H. Burrow, CBE; *Chair*, G. W. Rice

GLOUCESTERSHIRE CONSTABULARY, *HQ*, Holland House, Lansdown Road, Cheltenham, Glos. GL51 6QH. Tel: 0242-521321. *Strength*, 1,137; *Chief Constable*, A. J. P. Butler, PH.D.; *Chair*, C. Hay

GREATER MANCHESTER POLICE, *HQ*, PO Box 22 (S. West PDO), Chester House, Boyer Street, Manchester M16 0RE. Tel: 061-872 5050. *Strength*, 7,039; *Chief Constable*, D. Wilmot, QPM; *Chair*, S. Murphy

HAMPSHIRE CONSTABULARY, *HQ*, West Hill, Winchester, Hants. SO22 5DB. Tel: 0962-868133. *Strength*, 3,267; *Chief Constable*, J. C. Hoddinott, QPM; *Chair*, vacant

HERTFORDSHIRE CONSTABULARY, *HQ*, Stanborough Road, Welwyn Garden City, Herts. AL8 6XF. Tel: 0707-331177. *Strength*, 1,684; *Chief Constable*, B. H. Skitt, BEM, QPM; *Chair*, F. Peacock

HUMBERSIDE POLICE, *HQ*, Queens Gardens, Kingston upon Hull, N. Humberside HU1 3DJ. Tel: 0482-26111. *Strength*, 2,027; *Chief Constable*, D. A. Leonard, QPM; *Chair*, I. A. Cawsey

KENT CONSTABULARY, *HQ*, Sutton Road, Maidstone, Kent ME15 9BZ. Tel: 0622-690690. *Strength*, 3,140; *Chief Constable*, J. D. Phillips; *Chair*, Sir John Grugeon

LANCASHIRE CONSTABULARY, *HQ*, PO Box 77, Hutton, Preston PR4 5SB. Tel: 0772-614444. *Strength*, 3,188; *Chief Constable*, R. B. Johnson, CBE, QPM; *Chair*, Mrs R. B. Henig

LEICESTERSHIRE CONSTABULARY, *HQ*, PO Box 999, Leicester LE99 1AZ. Tel: 0533-530066. *Strength*, 1,833; *Chief Constable*, K. Povey, QPM; *Chair*, B. Singh

LINCOLNSHIRE POLICE, *HQ*, PO Box 999, Lincoln LN5 7PH. Tel: 0522-532222. *Strength*, 1,196; *Chief Constable*, vacant; *Chair*, B. Fippard

MERSEYSIDE POLICE, *HQ*, PO Box 59, Canning Place, Liverpool L69 1JD. Tel: 051-709 6010. *Strength*, 4,766; *Chief Constable*, J. Sharples, QPM; *Chair*, G. Bundred, CBE

NORFOLK CONSTABULARY, *HQ*, Martineau Lane, Norwich NR1 2DJ. Tel: 0603-768769. *Strength*, 1,428; *Chief Constable*, K. R. Williams, QPM; *Chair*, vacant

NORTHAMPTONSHIRE POLICE, *HQ*, Wootton Hall, Northampton NN4 0JQ. Tel: 0604-700700. *Strength*, 1,190; *Chief Constable*, E. Crew, QPM; *Chair*, Dr M. Dickie

NORTHUMBRIA POLICE, *HQ*, Ponteland, Newcastle upon Tyne NE20 0BL. Tel: 0661-872555. *Strength*, 3,620; *Chief Constable*, J. A. Stevens, QPM; *Chair*, G. Gill

NORTH YORKSHIRE POLICE, *HQ*, Newby Wiske Hall, Newby Wiske, Northallerton, N. Yorks. DL7 9HA. Tel: 0609-783131. *Strength*, 1,386; *Chief Constable*, D. M. Burke, QPM; *Chair*, elected at each meeting

NOTTINGHAMSHIRE CONSTABULARY, *HQ*, Sherwood Lodge, Arnold, Nottingham NG5 8PP. Tel: 0602-670999. *Strength*, 2,357; *Chief Constable*, D. Crompton, QPM; *Chair*, C. P. Winterton

SOUTH YORKSHIRE POLICE, *HQ*, Snig Hill, Sheffield S3 8LY. Tel: 0742-768522. *Strength*, 3,400; *Chief Constable*, R. Wells, QPM; *Chair*, Sir John Layden

STAFFORDSHIRE POLICE, *HQ*, Cannock Road, Stafford ST17 0QG. Tel: 0785-57717. *Strength*, 2,165; *Chief Constable*, C. H. Kelly, CBE, QPM; *Chair*, T. J. Meir

SUFFOLK CONSTABULARY, *HQ*, Martlesham Heath, Ipswich IP5 7QS. Tel: 0473-613500. *Strength*, 1,234; *Chief Constable*, A. T. Coe, QPM; *Chair*, C. C. Jones

SURREY POLICE, *HQ*, Mount Browne, Sandy Lane, Guildford, Surrey GU3 1HG. Tel: 0483-571212. *Strength*, 1,763; *Chief Constable*, D. J. Williams, QPM; *Chair*, A. C. Tisdall

SUSSEX POLICE, *HQ*, Malling House, Church Lane, Lewes, E. Sussex BN7 2DZ. Tel: 0273-475432. *Strength*, 2,994; *Chief Constable*, P. Whitehouse, QPM; *Chair*, J. P. Sheridan

THAMES VALLEY POLICE, *HQ*, Oxford Road, Kidlington, Oxon. OX5 2NX. Tel: 0865-846000. *Strength*, 3,944; *Chief Constable*, C. Pollard, QPM; *Chair*, C. F. Robinson, OBE

WARWICKSHIRE CONSTABULARY, *HQ*, PO Box 4, Leek Wootton, Warwick CV35 7QB. Tel: 0926-415000. *Strength*, 1,037; *Chief Constable*, P. D. Joslin, QPM; *Chair*, M. Singh

WEST MERCIA CONSTABULARY, *HQ*, PO Box 55, Hindlip Hall, Hindlip, Worcester WR3 8SP. Tel: 0905-723000. *Strength*, 2,048; *Chief Constable*, D. C. Blakey, QPM; *Chair*, P. H. Fallows, TD

WEST MIDLANDS POLICE, *HQ*, PO Box 52, Lloyd House, Colmore Circus, Queensway, Birmingham B4 6NQ. Tel: 021-626 5000. *Strength*, 7,092; *Chief Constable*, R. Hadfield, QPM; *Chair*, L. V. Jones

WEST YORKSHIRE POLICE, *HQ*, PO Box 9, Laburnum Road, Wakefield, W. Yorks. WF1 3QP. Tel: 0924-375222. *Strength*, 5,024; *Chief Constable*, K. Hellawell, QPM; *Chair*, T. Brennan

WILTSHIRE CONSTABULARY, *HQ*, London Road, Devizes, Wilts. SN10 2DN. Tel: 0380-722341. *Strength*, 1,163; *Chief Constable*, W. R. Girven, QPM; *Chair*, Mrs J. M. Wood

WALES

DYFED–POWYS POLICE, *HQ*, PO Box 99, Llangunnor, Carmarthen, Dyfed SA31 2PF. Tel: 0267-236444. *Strength*, 969; *Chief Constable*, R. White, QPM; *Chair*, D. R. Irving

GWENT CONSTABULARY, *HQ*, Croesyceiliog, Cwmbran, Gwent NP44 2XJ. Tel: 0633-838111. *Strength*, 995; *Chief Constable*, J. E. Over, QPM; *Chair*, B. Sutton

NORTH WALES POLICE, *HQ*, Glan-y-Don, Colwyn Bay, Clwyd LL29 8AW. Tel: 0492-517171. *Strength*, 1,369; *Chief Constable*, D. Owen, CBE, QPM; *Chair*, W. E. Conway

SOUTH WALES CONSTABULARY, *HQ*, Cowbridge Road, Bridgend, Mid Glamorgan CF31 3SU. Tel: 0656-655555. *Strength*, 3,172; *Chief Constable*, W. R. Lawrence, QPM; *Chair*, R. Jones

SCOTLAND

CENTRAL SCOTLAND POLICE, *HQ*, Randolphfield, Stirling FK8 2HD. Tel: 0786-456000. *Strength*, 651; *Chief Constable*, W. J. M. Wilson, QPM; *Convener*, H. Brown

DUMFRIES AND GALLOWAY CONSTABULARY, *HQ*, Cornwall Mount, Dumfries DG1 1PZ. Tel: 0387-52112.

Strength, 384; *Chief Constable*, G. A. Esson, QPM; *Chair*, R. Brown

FIFE CONSTABULARY, *HQ*, Wemyss Road, Dysart, Kirkcaldy, Fife KY1 2YA. Tel: 0592-652611. *Strength*, 772; *Chief Constable*, W. M. Moodie, CBE, QPM; *Chair*, C. J. Groom

GRAMPIAN POLICE, *HQ*, Queen Street, Aberdeen AB9 1BA. Tel: 0224-639111. *Strength*, 1,174; *Chief Constable*, I. T. Oliver, QPM, Ph.D.; *Chair*, Dr J. K. A. Thomaneck

LOTHIAN AND BORDERS POLICE, *HQ*, Fettes Avenue, Edinburgh EH4 1RB. Tel: 031-311 3131. *Strength*, 2,500; *Chief Constable*, Sir William Sutherland, QPM; *Chair*, R. B. Martin

NORTHERN CONSTABULARY, *HQ*, Perth Road, Inverness IV2 3SY. Tel: 0463-239191. *Strength*, 654; *Chief Constable*, H. C. MacMillan, QPM; *Chair*, Mrs I. C. Rhind

STRATHCLYDE POLICE, *HQ*, 173 Pitt Street, Glasgow G2 4JS. Tel: 041-204 2626. *Strength*, 6,805; *Chief Constable*, L. Sharp, QPM; *Chair*, J. Jennings

TAYSIDE POLICE, *HQ*, PO Box 59, West Bell Street, Dundee DD1 9JU. Tel: 0382-23200. *Strength*, 1,093; *Chief Constable*, J. W. Bowman, CBE, QPM; *Chair*, W. Smith

NORTHERN IRELAND

ROYAL ULSTER CONSTABULARY, *HQ*, Brooklyn, Knock Road, Belfast BT5 6LE. Tel: 0232-650222. *Strength*, 8,468; *Chief Constable*, Sir Hugh Annesley, QPM; *Chair*, T. Rainey

ISLANDS

ISLAND POLICE FORCE, *HQ*, St Peter Port, Guernsey, Channel Islands. Tel: 0481-725111. *Strength*, 149; *Chief Officer*, M. Le Moignan, QPM; *President, States Committee for Home Affairs*, M. Torode

STATES OF JERSEY POLICE, *HQ*, Rouge Bouillon, PO Box 789, St Helier, Jersey, Channel Islands JE2 3ZA. Tel: 0534-69996. *Strength*, 232; *Chief Officer*, R. H. Le Breton; *Chair*, M. Wavell

ISLE OF MAN CONSTABULARY, *HQ*, Glencrutchery Road, Douglas, Isle of Man. Tel: 0624-631212. *Strength*, 212; *Chief Constable*, R. E. N. Oake; *Minister for Home Affairs*, The Hon. A. A. Callin

---

METROPOLITAN POLICE SERVICE
New Scotland Yard, Broadway, London SW1H 0BG
Tel 071-230 1212

Establishment, 28,472
Commissioner, P. Condon, QPM
Deputy Commissioner, J. A. Smith, QPM
Receiver, G. L. Angel

TERRITORIAL OPERATIONS DEPARTMENT
Assistant Commissioner, R. A. Hunt, OBE, QPM
Deputy Assistant Commissioner, T. J. Siggs, OBE
Commanders, J. J. Allinson; D. N. Stevens, QPM

AREA HEADQUARTERS
Deputy Assistant Commissioners, M. B. Taylor, QPM; D. J. Osland, QPM; A. G. Fry, QPM; L. T. Roach, QPM; A. J. Speed, QPM; D. Flanders; M. J. Sullivan, QPM; W. J. R. Johnston, QPM
Commanders, T. O. Jones, MBE; J. A. Coo, QPM; L. J. Poole; D. M. T. Kendrick, QPM; J. F. Purnell, CGM; B. J. Luckhurst; T. D. Laidlaw; A. V. Comben;

B. S. Plaxton; J. Townshend; H. N. L. Blenkin; R. C. Adams; C. R. Pearman; A. L. Rowe

SPECIALIST OPERATIONS DEPARTMENT
Assistant Commissioner, W. Taylor, QPM
Deputy Assistant Commissioners, D. M. Meynell, OBE; J. A. Hawley, QPM; D. C. Veness
Commanders, K. G. Churchill-Coleman, QPM; P. R. Nove; R. A. Penrose, QPM; D. C. Stockley; D. Buchanan; R. C. Marsh, QPM; D. M. Tucker; B. G. Moss; J. G. D. Grieve

Metropolitan Police Laboratory
Director, Dr B. Sheard
Deputy Directors, G. J. O. Lee; M. R. Loveland; P. D. Martin; Dr W. D. C. Wilson

PERSONNEL DEPARTMENT
Director of Personnel, E. Mitchell, QPM
Director of Civil Staff Personnel Management, R. M. Gregory
Director of Police Personnel Management, C. A. Couch
Director of Manpower Planning and Personnel Policy, J. S. Steele
Director of Catering, A. Thompson
Director of Occupational Health, Dr A. Johnson

MEDICAL AND DENTAL BRANCH
Chief Medical Officer, Dr E. C. A. Bott, CBE

INSPECTION AND REVIEW
Assistant Commissioner, P. J. J. Winship, QPM
Deputy Assistant Commissioner, J. E. Metcalfe
Commander, J. D. Gibson

COMPLAINTS INVESTIGATION BUREAU
Commander, E. Humphrey, QPM

CENTRAL STAFF
Commander, M. Briggs

DIRECTORATE OF PUBLIC AFFAIRS
Director of Public Affairs, Ms S. Cullum

DIRECTORATE OF PERFORMANCE REVIEW AND MANAGEMENT SERVICES
Director, Mrs S. M. Merchant

SOLICITOR'S DEPARTMENT
Solicitor, C. S. Porteous, CBE

FINANCE DEPARTMENT
Director of Finance, J. A. Crutchlow

PROPERTY SERVICES DEPARTMENT
Director of Property Services, T. G. Lawrence

DEPARTMENT OF TECHNOLOGY
Director of Technology, N. Boothman

CITY OF LONDON POLICE
26 Old Jewry, London EC2R 8DJ
Tel 071-601 2222

Strength (June 1993), 862
Commissioner (£74,745), O. Kelly, QPM
Assistant Commissioner (£56,841), C. Coxall, QPM
Commander (£47,709), H. J. Moore, QPM
Chief Superintendents (£39,480–£42,540):
  'B' *Division*, G. Marshall
  'C' *Division*, P. Eskriett
  CID, T. Dickinson

Company Fraud, R. Knevett
Management Support, R. Friend
Operational Support, T. Hillier

BRITISH TRANSPORT POLICE
15 Tavistock Place, London WC1H 9SJ
Tel 071-388 7541

Strength (August 1993), 2,123
The Force provides a policing service to the British Railways
Board and London Underground Ltd. Police stations are
located throughout England, Wales and Scotland. The Chief
Constable reports to the British Transport Police Committee,
a statutory body set up under the Transport Act 1962. The
members of the Committee are appointed by the British
Railways Board and London Underground Ltd.
Chief Constable, D. O'Brien, OBE, QPM
Deputy Chief Constable, A. Parker
Assistant Chief Constables:
  Support Services, G. K. Miller
  Operations, W. I. McGregor, QPM
  Scottish Area, S. Mannion
  Communications and Technology, A. Horn

MINISTRY OF DEFENCE POLICE
Ministry of Defence, Empress State Building,
Lillie Road, London SW6 1TR
Tel 071-385 1244

Strength (May 1993), 5,035
The Ministry of Defence Police is a statutory police force
directly responsible to the Secretary of State for Defence for
the policing of all military land, stations and establishments
in the United Kingdom. It is due to become a defence agency
in 1994.
Chief Constable, J. Reddington, QPM
Deputy Chief Constable, W. E. E. Boreham, OBE
Head of Secretariat, J. A. Smallwood
Assistant Chief Constables:
  Corporate Development, S. G. Edwards, QPM
  Operations, R. E. Murray
  Personnel and Training, B. J. Smith
  Scotland, J. Reade
  Support, P. A. Bedwell

ROYAL PARKS CONSTABULARY
The Old Police House, Hyde Park, London W2 2UH
Tel 071-298 2054

Strength (August 1993), 190
The Royal Parks Constabulary is maintained by the
Department of National Heritage and is responsible for the
policing of 21 Royal Parks in and around London. These
comprise an area in excess of 6,300 acres. Officers of the
Force are appointed under the Parks Regulations Act 1872,
as amended by the Parks Regulations (Amendment) Act
1974.
Chief Officer, W. Ross
Deputy Chief Officer, M. J. Loader

UNITED KINGDOM ATOMIC ENERGY
AUTHORITY CONSTABULARY
Building E6, Culham Laboratory, Abingdon,
Oxon. OX14 3DB
Tel 0235-463760

Strength (June 1993), 509
The Constabulary is responsible for policing United Kingdom
Atomic Energy Authority and British Nuclear Fuels PLC
establishments and for escorting nuclear material between
establishments.
The Chief Constable is responsible, through the Atomic
Energy Authority Police Committee, to the President of the
Board of Trade.
Chief Constable, H. J. McMorris, QPM
Deputy Chief Constable, E. H. Miller

STAFF ASSOCIATIONS

ASSOCIATION OF CHIEF POLICE OFFICERS OF
ENGLAND, WALES AND NORTHERN IRELAND, Room
311, Wellington House, 67–73 Buckingham Gate,
London SW1E 6BE. Tel: 071-230 7148. Represents the
Chief Constables, Deputy Chief Constables and Assistant
Chief Constables of England, Wales and Northern
Ireland, and officers of the rank of Commander and
above in the Metropolitan and City of London Police.
General Secretary, Miss M. C. E. Barton
THE POLICE SUPERINTENDENTS' ASSOCIATION OF
ENGLAND AND WALES, 67A Reading Road,
Pangbourne, Reading RG8 7JD. Tel: 0734-844005.
Represents officers of the rank of Superintendent and
Chief Superintendent. *Secretary*, Chief Supt. P. G. Wall
THE POLICE FEDERATION OF ENGLAND AND WALES,
15–17 Langley Road, Surbiton, Surrey KT6 6LP. Tel: 081-
399 2224. Represents officers up to and including the
rank of Chief Inspector. *General Secretary*, L. Williams;
Chairman, R. Coyles
ASSOCIATION OF CHIEF POLICE OFFICERS IN
SCOTLAND, Police Headquarters, Fettes Avenue,
Edinburgh EH4 1RB. Tel: 031-311 3051. Represents the
Chief Constables, Deputy Chief Constables and Assistant
Chief Constables of the Scottish police forces. *Hon.
Secretary*, Sir William Sutherland, QPM
THE ASSOCIATION OF SCOTTISH POLICE
SUPERINTENDENTS, Secretariat, 173 Pitt Street,
Glasgow G2 4JS. Tel: 041-221 5796. Represents officers of
the rank of Superintendent and Chief Superintendent.
Hon. Secretary, Chief Supt. J. Urquhart
THE SCOTTISH POLICE FEDERATION, 5 Woodside Place,
Glasgow G3 7QF. Tel: 041-332 5234. Represents officers
up to and including the rank of Chief Inspector. *General
Secretary*, D. J. Keil
THE SUPERINTENDENT ASSOCIATION OF NORTHERN
IRELAND, Ormiston House, Hawthornden Road, Belfast
BT4 3JW. Tel: 0232-700129. Represents Superintendents
and Chief Superintendents in the RUC. *Hon. Secretary*,
Chief Supt. A. Donald
THE POLICE FEDERATION FOR NORTHERN IRELAND,
Royal Ulster Constabulary, Garnerville, Garnerville
Road, Belfast BT4 2NX. Tel: 0232-760831. Represents
officers up to and including the rank of Chief Inspector.
Secretary, D. A. McClurg

Defence

MINISTRY OF DEFENCE
Main Building, Whitehall, London SW1A 2HB
Tel 071-218 9000

The Ministry of Defence is concerned with the control, administration, equipment and support of the Armed Forces of the Crown. The research, development, production and purchase of weapons systems and equipment is the concern of the Procurement Executive.

SALARIES 1993–4

Secretary of State	£39,820*
Minister of State	£28,175*
Parliamentary Under-Secretary	£37,689*
Grade 1	£90,148
Grade 1A	£82,925
Grade 2	£64,307–£75,328
Grade 3	£51,360–£59,599†
Grade 4	£44,390–£49,790†‡
Grade 5	£36,178–£47,921†‡

*In addition to a reduced parliamentary salary of £23,227
†Plus London weighting (see page 282); Grade 3s in London also receive a £2,000 London allowance
‡1992–3 figures
For Services salaries, see pages 402–4

Secretary of State for Defence, The Rt. Hon. Malcolm Rifkind, QC, MP
  Private Secretary (G5), J. Pitt-Brooke
  Special Advisers, C. Blunt; C. Littmoden
  Parliamentary Private Secretary, H. Bellingham, MP
Minister of State for the Armed Forces, Jeremy Hanley, MP
  Private Secretary (G7), Miss O. Muirhead
  Parliamentary Private Secretary, R. Gale, MP
Minister of State for Defence Procurement, The Rt. Hon. Jonathan Aitken, MP
  Private Secretary (G7), J. Wright
  Parliamentary Private Secretary, S. Milligan, MP
Parliamentary Under-Secretary of State, Viscount Cranborne
  Private Secretary (SEO), Miss H. Davies
Permanent Under-Secretary of State (G1), Sir Christopher France, KCB
  Private Secretary (G7), B. R. Mann
Chief of the Defence Staff, Marshal of the RAF Sir Peter Harding, GCB, ADC

THE DEFENCE COUNCIL
The Defence Council is responsible for running the Armed Forces. It is chaired by the Secretary of State for Defence and consists of: the Ministers of State; the Permanent Under-Secretary of State; the Chief of the Defence Staff and the Vice-Chief of the Defence Staff; the Parliamentary Under-Secretary of State; the Chief Scientific Adviser; the Chief of Defence Procurement; the Second Permanent Under-Secretary of State; the Chief of the Naval Staff; the Chief of the General Staff; and the Chief of the Air Staff.

DEFENCE STAFF

Vice-Chief of the Defence Staff, Adm. Sir Jock Slater, GCB, LVO
Deputy Under-Secretary (Policy) (G2), D. B. Omand
Defence Services Secretary, Maj.-Gen. B. T. Pennicott
Deputy CDS (Commitments), Vice-Adm. the Hon. Sir Nicholas Hill-Norton, KCB

Asst Under-Secretary (Commitments) (G3), W. D. Reeves, CB
Asst CDS (Overseas), Air Vice-Marshal N. B. Baldwin
Asst CDS (Logistics), Rear-Adm. F. B. Goodson
Deputy CDS (Systems), Air Marshal Sir Roger Austin, KCB, AFC
Head of Manpower Structure Study Team, Air Vice-Marshal A. L. Roberts, CBE, AFC
Asst CDS, Operational Requirements (Sea), Rear-Adm. R. F. Cobbold
Asst CDS, Operational Requirements (Land), Maj.-Gen. S. Cowan, CBE
Asst CDS, Operational Requirements (Air), Air Vice-Marshal I. D. Macfadyen, CB, OBE
Asst CDS (CIS), Maj.-Gen. W. J. P. Robins, OBE
Asst CDS (Policy and Nuclear), Rear-Adm. J. J. R. Tod, CBE
Asst Under-Secretary (Policy) (G3), I. D. Dawson
Deputy CDS (Programmes and Personnel), Lt.-Gen. the Hon. Sir Thomas Boyd-Carpenter, KBE
Asst CDS (Programmes), Air Vice-Marshal T. Garden
Surgeon-General and Director-General, Army Medical Services, Lt.-Gen. Sir Peter Beale, KBE, QHP
Deputy Surgeon-General (Health Services) and Director-General, Medical Services (RAF), Air Vice-Marshal J. M. Brook, QHS
Deputy Surgeon-General (Ops. and Plans) and Medical Director-General (Naval), Surgeon Rear-Adm. A. L. Revell
Director, Defence Nursing Services and Director, Nursing Services (Royal Navy), Commandant Nursing Officer Miss J. Titley
Director, Army Nursing Services, Brig. H. S. Dixon-Nuttal, QHNS
Director, Defence Dental Services, Air Vice-Marshal J. Mackey, QHDS
Head of Medical Services (Finance and Secretariat Division) (G5), P. G. Schulte
Director, Army Medicine and Consultant Physician, Brig. G. O. Cowan, OBE, QHP
Director, Army Surgery and Consultant Surgeon, Brig. I. R. Haywood
Director, Army Psychiatry and Consultant Psychiatrist, Col. R. M. L. Anderson

DEFENCE INTELLIGENCE STAFF
Director, Defence Intelligence (Secretariat) (G5), P. Bailey

NAVAL DEPARTMENT
Chief of the Naval Staff and First Sea Lord, Adm. Sir Benjamin Bathurst, KCB
Asst Chief of Naval Staff, Rear-Adm. J. R. Brigstocke
Commandant-General Royal Marines, Lt.-Gen. R. J. Ross, CB, OBE
Chief of Naval Personnel and Second Sea Lord, Vice-Adm. Sir Michael Layard, KCB, CBE
Naval Secretary, Rear-Adm. M. G. Rutherford, CBE
Director-General, Naval Manpower and Training, Rear-Adm. N. J. Wilkinson
Asst Under-Secretary (Naval Personnel) (G3), J. M. Moss
Chief of Fleet Support, Vice-Adm. Sir Neville Purvis, KCB
Asst Under-Secretary (Fleet Support) (G3), A. J. D. Pawson
Director-General, Ship Refitting (G3), B. V. Babbington
Director-General, Supplies and Transport (N) (G3), D. G. Jones

Principal Director, Supplies and Transport (Ops.) (G4), W. N. Cooke
Principal Director, Supplies and Transport (Stores and Victualling) (G4), G. E. Miller
Principal Director, Supplies and Transport (Armaments) (G4), M. A. Holder
Director-General, Fleet Support (Operations and Plans), Rear-Adm. J. H. Dunt
Director, Naval Shore Telecommunications (G5), M. Frowde
Director-General, Aircraft (Navy), Rear-Adm. R. C. Moylan-Jones
Chaplain of The Fleet, Ven. M. W. Bucks, QHC

HYDROGRAPHIC OFFICE
Taunton, Somerset TAI 2DN
Tel 0823-337900

The Hydrographic Office was established as a defence support agency in April 1990 and provides charts and publications for the Royal Navy and other customers in the UK and overseas.

Hydrographer of the Royal Navy and Chief Executive, Hydrographic Office, Rear-Adm. J. A. L. Myres, CB (*until Feb. 1994*); Rear-Adm. N. R. Essenhigh (*from Feb. 1994*)

ARMY DEPARTMENT
Chief of the General Staff, Gen. Sir Peter Inge, KCB, ADC (*Gen.*)
Asst Chief of the General Staff, Maj.-Gen. M. J. D. Walker
Director-General, TA, Maj.-Gen. A. I. J. Kennedy, CBE
Director-General, Army Training, Maj.-Gen. R. W. M. McAfee
Inspector-General, Doctrine and Training, Lt.-Gen. P. R. Duffell, CBE, MC
Director, Royal Armoured Corps, Maj.-Gen. R. J. Hayman-Joyce, CBE (*until Jan. 1994*)
Director, Royal Artillery, Maj.-Gen. M. T. Tennant
Director, Infantry, Maj.-Gen. B. H. Dutton, CBE
Director, Army Air Corps, Maj.-Gen. S. W. St J. Lytle
Engineer in Chief (Army), Maj.-Gen. G. W. Field
Director-General, Communications and Information Systems (Army) and Signals Officer in Chief (Army), Maj.-Gen. A. H. Boyle
Military Secretary, Maj.-Gen. R. J. Hayman-Joyce, CBE (*from Jan. 1994*)
Adjutant-General, Gen. Sir Michael Wilkes, KCB, CBE
Asst Under-Secretary (Command Secretary, HQ UK Land Forces) (G3), D. Dreher
Director-General, Army Manning and Recruiting, Maj.-Gen. J. F. Deverell
Director, Staff and Personal Services (Army), Brig. C. Geal, OBE
Director-General, Personal Services (Army), Maj.-Gen. M. D. Jackson, MBE
Provost Marshal (Army), Brig. I. Cameron
Director, Army Legal Services, Maj.-Gen. M. H. F. Clarke
Director, Educational and Training Services (Army), Brig. J. M. Macfarlane
Quartermaster-General, Lt.-Gen. the Hon. Sir William Rous, KCB, OBE (*from Jan. 1994*)
Asst Under-Secretary (Quartermaster) (G3), N. J. Beaumont
Director-General, Logistics Policy (Army), Maj.-Gen. P. J. Sheppard, CBE
Director, Royal Army Veterinary Corps, Brig. A. H. Parker-Bowles, OBE
Director-General, Management and Support of Intelligence, Maj.-Gen. A. L. Meier, OBE
Director-General, Equipment Support (Army), Maj.-Gen. M. S. Heath

Director, Women, Brig. J. M. Roulstone
Chaplain General, Revd J. Harkness, OBE, QHC

MILITARY SURVEY
Elmwood Avenue, Feltham, Middx. TW13 7AH
Tel 081-890 3622

Military Survey was established as a defence support agency in April 1991. Its role is to give the armed forces the geographic support required to enable them to plan, train and fight effectively.

Director-General, Maj.-Gen. R. Wood

AIR FORCE DEPARTMENT
Chief of the Air Staff, Air Chief Marshal Sir Michael Graydon, GCB, CBE
Asst Chief of Air Staff, Air Vice-Marshal A. J. C. Bagnall
Chief Executive, National Air Traffic Services (G3), D. J. McLauchlan
Director-General, Policy and Planning, Air Vice-Marshal M. J. Gibson, OBE
Air Member for Personnel, Air Chief Marshal Sir Andrew Wilson, KCB, AFC, ADC
Air Secretary, Air Vice-Marshal R. J. Honey, CB, CBE
Director-General, Training and Personnel (RAF), Air Vice-Marshal P. G. Beer, CBE, LVO
Director, Legal Services (RAF) Air Vice-Marshal G. W. Carleton
Asst Under-Secretary (Personnel (Air)) (G3), M. D. Tidy
Air Member for Supply and Organization, Air Chief Marshal Sir Michael Alcock, KCB
Director-General, Support Services (RAF), Air Vice-Marshal R. H. Kyle, MBE
Director-General, Support Management (RAF), Air Vice-Marshal C. G. Terry, OBE
Asst Under-Secretary (Supply and Organization (Air)) (G3), H. Griffiths
Chaplain-in-Chief (RAF), Ven. B. H. Lucas, CB, QHC

RAF SUPPORT COMMAND MAINTENANCE GROUP
RAF Brampton, Huntingdon, Cambs. PE18 8QL
Tel 0480-52151

The Group became a defence support agency in April 1991. It supplies engineering, warehousing, transportation and communications services to the RAF and some other UK and NATO services.

Chief Executive, Air Vice-Marshal D. R. French, CB

DEFENCE SCIENTIFIC STAFF
Chief Scientific Adviser (G1A), Prof. D. Davies, CBE
Deputy Chief Scientific Adviser (G2), Dr G. G. Pope, CB
Asst Chief Scientific Advisers (G3), Dr G. D. Coley (*Projects*); G. H. B. Jordan (*Capabilities*); P. M. Sutcliffe (*Research*); (*G4*) A. L. C. Quigley (*Nuclear*)
Chief Executive, Defence Operational Analysis Centre (G3), Dr D. Leadbeater
Director, Science Ballistic Missile Defence Directorate (G5), P. Varnish

OFFICE OF MANAGEMENT AND BUDGET
Second Permanent Under-Secretary of State (G1A), J. M. Stewart, CB
Deputy Under-Secretaries (G2), J. F. Howe, OBE (*Civilian Management*); R. L. L. Facer, CB (*Personnel and Logistics*); R. T. Jackling, CBE (*Resources and Programmes*); vacant (*Security and Common Services*)
Asst Under-Secretaries (G3), T. J. Brack (*General Finance*); I. D. Fauset (*Civilian Management (Personnel*)); Dr M. J. Harte (*Resources*); A. J. Cragg (*Director-General of Management Audit*); A. Walker (*Service Personnel*);

vacant (*Programmes*); D. Fisher (*Systems*); B. F. Rule (*Director-General, Information Technology Services*); B. W. Stanley (*Director, Works Services*); T. F. W. B. Knapp (*Infrastructure and Logistics*)
Chief Statistical Adviser and Chief Executive of Defence Analytical Services Agency, P. Altobell
Chief of Ministry of Defence Police, J. Reddington, QPM

DIRECTORATE-GENERAL OF DEFENCE ACCOUNTS
Warminster Road, Bath BA1 5AA
Tel 0225-828106

This defence support agency was established in April 1991 and is responsible for providing accounting services to the MOD.
Chief Executive (G4), M. J. Dymond

PUBLIC RELATIONS
Chief of Public Relations (G4), Ms G. Samuel
Deputy Chief of Public Relations (G5), A. Armstrong
Director, Public Relations (Navy), Capt. C. Esplin-Jones
Director, Public Relations (Army), Brig. P. Trousdell
Director, Public Relations (RAF), Air Cdre G. McRobbie

PROCUREMENT EXECUTIVE

Chief of Defence Procurement (G1), Dr M. K. McIntosh
    Private Secretary (G7), S. H. Lowe

PROCUREMENT EXECUTIVE POLICY AND ADMINISTRATION
Deputy Under-Secretary (Defence Procurement) (G2), M. J. V. Bell
Asst Under-Secretary (Business Strategy) (G3), J. A. Gulvin
Asst Under-Secretary (Finance) (G3), Ms D. J. Seammen
President of the Ordnance Board, Maj.-Gen. C. R. S. Notley, CBE
Director-General, Test and Evaluation (G3), B. Miller
Director-General, Defence Contracts (G3), G. E. Roe
Principal Director, Pricing and Quality Services (G4), J. V. A. Crawford
Director, Intellectual Property Rights (G4), D. J. Isaaks
Director, Test and Evaluation (Air Systems), Air Cdre J. E. Houghton, AFC

DEFENCE RESEARCH AGENCY
Farnborough, Hants. GU14 6TD
Tel 0252-392000

The Defence Research Agency (DRA) was set up on 1 April 1991. It incorporated the Royal Aerospace Establishment, the Admiralty Research Establishment, the Royal Armament Research and Development Establishment, and the Royal Signals and Radar Establishment.
Chief Executive (G2), J. A. R. Chisholm
Directors (G3), Dr A. L. Mears (*technical and quality*); Dr D. C. Tyte (*rationalization*); M. Goodfellow (*commercial*); Dr D. J. L. Smith (*group services*); G. Love (*finance*); (*G5*), R. Hack (*personnel*)
Managing Director, Maritime Division (G3), P. D. Ewins
Managing Director, Military and Aeronautics Division (G3), Dr R. H. Warren
Managing Director, Electronics Division (G3), Dr V. G. Roper
Managing Director (Operations) (G3), P. D. Ewins
Head of Marketing Intelligence, Dr B. Milsom
Company Secretary (G5), Mrs E. Peace

CHEMICAL AND BIOLOGICAL DEFENCE ESTABLISHMENT
Porton Down, Salisbury, Wilts. SP4 0JQ
Tel 0980-613000

This defence support agency was established in April 1991 and is the United Kingdom's scientific and technical authority on chemical and biological defence matters. It carries out research, provides advice and support to the MOD and other government departments, and assists the development and production in industry of appropriate equipment for the armed forces.
Chief Executive (G3), Dr G. S. Pearson, CB

NUCLEAR PROGRAMMES
Deputy Controller (Nuclear) (G3), G. N. Beaven
Chief Executive, Atomic Weapons Establishment (G2), B. H. Richards

SEA SYSTEMS CONTROLLERATE
Controller of the Navy, Adm. Sir Kenneth Eaton, KCB
Head of Material Co-ordination (Naval) (G5), vacant
Principal Director, Navy and Nuclear Contracts (G4), A. T. Phipps
Director-General, Submarines and Deputy Controller, Rear-Adm. R. Walmsley
Director-General, Surface Ships (G3), C. V. Betts
Director-General, Surface Weapons (G4), Cdre F. P. Scourse, MBE
Naval Ships Acceptance, Cdre S. Taylor
Director (Finance and Secretariat), Underwater Systems (G3), J. A. Kenny
Director-General, Underwater Weapons (G4), D. McArthur
Director, Naval Architect (G5), P. Davies
Chief, Strategic Systems Executive, Rear-Adm. R. D. Irwin
Deputy Chief, Strategic Systems Executive, Cdre N. R. Hodgson
Director-General, Strategic Weapons Systems, Dr J. P. Catchpole
Director (Finance and Secretariat), Strategic Systems (G5), D. M. T. Lewis
Director, Naval Support Command Implementation (G5), J. Read
Director (Finance and Secretariat), Abovewater Systems (G5), J. C. Cox
Director, Future Projects (G5), P. C. Bryan

LAND SYSTEMS CONTROLLERATE
Master-General of the Ordnance, Lt.-Gen. Sir Jeremy Blacker, KCB, CBE
Director-General, Policy and Special Projects, J. G. H. Walker
Principal Director, Contracts (Ordnance) (G4), R. C. Harford
Director-General, Guided Weapons and Electronic Systems (G3), J. D. Maines
Director-General, Land Fighting Systems, Maj.-Gen. A. C. P. Stone

AIR SYSTEMS CONTROLLERATE
Controller, Aircraft, Sir Donald Spiers, CB, TD
Principal Director, Contracts (Air) (G4), S. L. Porter
Director-General, Aircraft 1, (G3), J. A. Gordon
Director-General, Aircraft 2, Air Vice-Marshal P. C. Norriss, AFC
Director-General, Avionics Weapons and Information Systems (G3), J. C. Mabberley

DEFENCE EXPORT SERVICES ORGANIZATION
Head of Defence Export Services (G2), Sir Alan Thomas
Military Deputy to Head of DES, Rear-Adm. J. F. T. G. Salt

Director-General, Saudi Armed Forces Project, Air Marshal
Sir William Wratten, KBE, CB, AFC
Director-General, Marketing (G3), N. Paren
Asst Under-Secretary (Export Policy and Finance) (G3),
C. T. Sandars
Malaysian Project Office (G5), J. B. Taylor

METEOROLOGICAL OFFICE
London Road, Bracknell, Berks. RG12 2SZ
Tel 0344-420242

The Meteorological Office is the national meteorological
service. It became an executive support agency within the
Ministry of Defence in April 1990. It provides meteorological
services for the Services departments and civilian aviation,
shipping, public services, the press, industry and the general
public. It collects, distributes and publishes meteorological
information from all parts of the world and undertakes
research related to meteorology and climate.
Chief Executive (G2), Prof. J. Hunt, FRS
Director of Operations (G3), Dr P. Ryder
Director of Research (G4), Dr P. Mason

The Royal Navy

LORD HIGH ADMIRAL OF THE UNITED KINGDOM, HM
The Queen

ADMIRALS OF THE FLEET

HRH The Prince Philip, Duke of Edinburgh, KG, KT, OM,
GBE, AC, QSO, PC, *apptd* 1953
Sir Varyl Begg, GCB, DSO, DSC, *apptd* 1968
The Lord Hill-Norton, GCB, *apptd* 1971
Sir Michael Pollock, GCB, LVO, DSC, *apptd* 1974
Sir Edward Ashmore, GCB, DSC, *apptd* 1977
The Lord Lewin, KG, GCB, LVO, DSC, *apptd* 1979
Sir Henry Leach, GCB, *apptd* 1982
Sir William Staveley, GCB, *apptd* 1989
Sir Julian Oswald, GCB, *apptd* 1993

ADMIRALS

Bathurst, Sir Benjamin, GCB, ADC *(Chief of the Naval Staff
and First Sea Lord)*
Slater, Sir Jock, GCB, LVO, *(Vice-Chief of the Defence Staff)*
Kerr, Sir John, GCB, ADC *(C.-in-C. Naval Home Command)*
White, Sir Hugo, KCB, CBE *(C.-in-C. Fleet)*
Eaton, Sir Kenneth, KCB *(Controller of the Navy)*

VICE-ADMIRALS

Coward, Sir John, KCB, DSO *(Commandant, Royal College of
Defence Studies)*
Hill-Norton, The Hon. Sir Nicholas, KCB *(Deputy CDS
(Commitments))*
Purvis, Sir Neville, KCB *(Chief of Fleet Support)*
Dobson, Sir David, KBE *(Chief of Staff to Commander, Allied
Naval Forces Southern Europe)*
Newman, Sir Roy, KCB *(Flag Officer Plymouth and Naval
Base Comd. Devonport)*
Woodhead, Sir Peter, KCB
Layard, Sir Michael, KCB, CBE *(Chief of Naval Personnel and
Second Sea Lord)*
Biggs, Sir Geoffrey, KCB *(Deputy Comd. Fleet)*
Morgan, C. C. *(Flag Officer Scotland and N. Ireland)*
Frere, R. T. *(Flag Officer Submarines and Comd. Sub. Area
East Atlantic, until Dec. 1993)*
Abbott, P. C. *(Deputy Supreme Allied Commander Atlantic)*

REAR-ADMIRALS

Tod, J. J. R., CBE *(Asst CDS (Policy and Nuclear))*
Walmsley, R. *(Director-General, Submarines)*
Myres, J. A. L., CB *(Hydrographer of the Navy and Chief
Executive, Hydrographic Office Defence Support Agency,
until Feb. 1994)*
Hoddinott, A. P., OBE *(Commander, British Naval Staff
Washington, Naval Attaché Washington and UK National
Liaison Representative to SACLANT)*
Woodard, R. N. *(Flag Officer Royal Yachts)*
Moore, M. A. C., LVO *(Maritime Adviser to the Supreme
Allied Commander Europe)*
Wilkinson, N. J. *(Director-General, Naval Manpower and
Training)*
Brigstocke, J. R. *(Asst Chief of Naval Staff)*
Cobbold, R. F. *(Asst CDS Operational Requirements (Sea
Systems))*
Boyce, M. C., OBE *(Flag Officer Surface Flotilla)*
Shiffner, J. R. *(Director-General, Fleet Support (Equipment
and Systems))*
Lang, J. S. *(Director-General, Intelligence (Assessments))*
Sanders, J. T., OBE *(Flag Officer Gibraltar)*
Moylan-Jones, R. C. *(Director-General, Aircraft (Navy))*
Rankin, N. E., CBE *(Flag Officer Portsmouth)*
England, T. J. *(Chief Staff Officer (Support)/Fleet)*
Tolhurst, J. G. *(Flag Officer Sea Training)*
Garnett, I. D. G. *(Flag Officer Naval Aviation)*
Rutherford, M. G., CBE *(Naval Secretary)*
Irwin, R. O. *(Chief, Strategic Systems Executive)*
Goodson, F. B., OBE *(Asst CDS (Logistics))*
Blackham, J. J. *(Chief of Staff to C.-in-C. NAVHOME)*
Gretton, M. P. *(Commander, UK Task Group)*
Dunt, J. H. *(Director-General, Fleet Support (Operations and
Plans))*
Lane-Nott, R. C. *(Flag Officer Submarines, from Dec. 1993)*
Essenhigh, N. R. *(Hydrographer of the Navy and Chief
Executive, Hydrographic Office Defence Support Agency,
from Feb. 1994)*

HM FLEET AS AT 1 APRIL 1993

SUBMARINES

TRIDENT
Operational: Vanguard

POLARIS
Operational: Renown, Repulse, Resolution

FLEET
Operational: Sceptre, Spartan, Splendid, Superb, Talent,
Tireless, Torbay, Trenchant, Triumph, Turbulent,
Valiant
Refitting/standby: Sovereign, Trafalgar

TYPE 2400
Operational: Unicorn*, Upholder†
Refitting/standby: Unseen, Ursula

OBERON CLASS
Operational: Opossum, Opportune
Refitting/standby: Oracle

ANTI-SUBMARINE WARFARE (ASW)
CARRIERS

Operational: Ark Royal, Invincible
Refitting/standby: Illustrious

ASSAULT SHIPS

Operational: Fearless
Refitting/standby: Intrepid

DESTROYERS

TYPE 42
Operational: Birmingham, Cardiff, Edinburgh, Exeter,
Glasgow, Liverpool, Manchester, Newcastle,
Nottingham, Southampton, York
Refitting/standby: Gloucester

FRIGATES

TYPE 23
Operational: Argyll, Iron Duke†, Lancaster†, Marlborough,
Monmouth†, Montrose*, Norfolk, Westminster*

TYPE 22
Operational: Battleaxe, Beaver, Boxer, Brazen, Brilliant,
Broadsword, Campbelltown, Chatham, Cornwall,
Coventry, Cumberland, London, Sheffield
Refitting/standby: Brave

TYPE 21
Operational: Active, Alacrity, Amazon, Ambuscade, Arrow,
Avenger

LEANDER CLASS
Operational: Andromeda, Scylla

OFFSHORE PATROL

CASTLE CLASS
Operational: Dumbarton Castle, Leeds Castle

ISLAND CLASS
Operational: Alderney, Anglesey, Guernsey, Jersey,
Lindisfarne, Orkney, Shetland

MINESWEEPERS

RIVER CLASS[1]
Operational: Arun, Blackwater, Carron, Dovey, Helford,
Humber, Itchen, Orwell, Spey, Waveney
Refitting/standby: Helmsdale, Ribble

MINEHUNTERS TON CLASS
Operational: Brinton, Nurton, Sheraton, Wilton (Dartmouth
Navigation Training Ship)
Refitting/standby: Iveston, Kellington

HUNT CLASS
Operational: Atherstone, Berkeley, Bicester, Brocklesby,
Cattistock, Chiddingfold, Cottesmore, Dulverton,
Hurworth, Ledbury, Middleton, Quorn
Refitting/standby: Brecon

SINGLE ROLE MINEHUNTER
Operational: Bridport*, Cromer†, Inverness†, Sandown,
Walney†

PATROL CRAFT

BIRD CLASS
Operational: Cygnet, Kingfisher, Redpole

COASTAL TRAINING CRAFT[2]
Operational: Biter, Blazer, Charger, Dasher, Puncher,
Pursuer
Refitting/standby: Archer, Smiter

PEACOCK CLASS
Operational: Peacock, Plover, Starling

GIBRALTAR SEARCH AND RESCUE CRAFT
Operational: Ranger, Trumpeter

ROYAL YACHT/HOSPITAL SHIP

Operational: Britannia

TRAINING SHIPS

FLEET TENDERS
Operational: Messina

ICE PATROL SHIP

Operational: Endurance

SURVEY SHIPS

Operational: Bulldog, Gleaner, Hecla, Herald, Roebuck
Refitting/standby: Beagle

SOLD/DECOMMISSIONED 1992–3

Argonaut, Ariadne, Blue Rover, Hermione, Juno, Jupiter,
Minerva, Osiris, Regent, Revenge, Sentinel, Sirius

*   Under construction at 1 April 1993 and planned to enter
service 1993–4
†   Engaged in trials or training at 1 April 1993
1   River Class vessels, apart from HMS *Blackwater*, are
operated by the RNR
2   Coastal training craft are operated by the RNR and
University Royal Naval Units

ROYAL FLEET AUXILIARY (RFA)

The Royal Fleet Auxiliary supplies ships of the fleet with
fuel, food, water, spares and ammunition while at sea. Its
ships are manned by merchant seamen.

FLEET AIR ARM

The Fleet Air Arm was established in 1937 and operates
aircraft and helicopters for the Royal Navy.

ROYAL NAVAL RESERVE (RNR)

The Royal Naval Reserve is a totally integrated part of the
Royal Navy. It comprises about 6,000 men and women
nationwide who volunteer to train in their spare time for a
variety of sea and shore tasks which they would carry out in
time of tension or war.
Chief Staff Officer, Capt. C. W. Pile

ROYAL NAVAL AUXILIARY SERVICE (RNXS)

The RNXS is a uniformed, unarmed and, in peacetime,
volunteer civilian service of some 2,700 men and women,
under the direction of the Commander-in-Chief Naval Home
Command. Members train in their spare time in units around
the coasts of the United Kingdom for duties in times of
tension and war. Their role includes manning port headquarters in support of the Naval Control of Shipping Organization,
and providing crews for vessels engaged in the defence of
ports and anchorages.
Patron and Hon. Auxiliary Commodore, HRH Prince
Michael of Kent
Captain, Capt. J. M. Neville-Rolfe, RN

ROYAL MARINES

The Army

The Corps of Royal Marines was formed in 1664 and is part of the Naval Service. The Royal Marines provide Britain's sea soldiers and in particular 3 Commando Brigade Royal Marines, which is trained and equipped for arctic warfare. Royal Marines also serve in HM Ships, provide landing craft crews, special boat sections and other detachments for naval and amphibious operations. They also provide the Naval Band Service. The Corps is about 7,000 strong.

Commandant-General, Royal Marines, Lt.-Gen. R. J. Ross, CB, OBE

Major-Generals, A. M. Keeling (*MGRM*); J. S. Chester, OBE (*Royal College Defence Studies*)

ROYAL MARINES RESERVE (RMR)

The Royal Marines Reserve is a force of commando-trained volunteers who train to combat-readiness in order to support the regular Royal Marines should the need arise. About 50 per cent are trained and equipped for arctic warfare and most regular Royal Marine specializations are open to the reservist. There are RMR centres in London, Glasgow, Bristol, Liverpool and Newcastle, each with a number of outlying detachments. The present strength of the RMR is about 1,200.

Director, Brig. R. S. Tailyour

QUEEN ALEXANDRA'S ROYAL NAVAL NURSING SERVICE

The first nursing sisters were appointed to naval hospitals in 1884 and the Queen Alexandra's Royal Naval Nursing Service (QARNNS) gained its current title under the patronage of Queen Alexandra in 1902. Nursing ratings were introduced in 1960 and men were integrated into the Service in 1982; both men and women serve as officers and ratings. Female medical assistants were introduced in 1987. Qualified staff and learners are mainly based at the UK Royal Naval Hospitals, and continue their responsibility for the health and fitness of naval personnel. The strength is about 600.

Patron, HRH Princess Alexandra, the Hon. Lady Ogilvy
Matron-in-Chief, Commandant Nursing Officer Miss J. Titley

WOMEN'S ROYAL NAVAL SERVICE

Originally founded in 1917, the Women's Royal Naval Service (WRNS) was temporarily disbanded between the First and Second World Wars. The contribution of the Service is now established as a professional and integral part of the Royal Navy with personnel serving in the United Kingdom and abroad in a wide range of specialist roles. From 6 February 1990, the role of the WRNS was expanded to include sea service, and from 1 January 1991 to include aircrew. WRNS officers adopted Royal Navy rank titles from 1 December 1990. The strength of the WRNS is about 4,500. Commandant Spencer is not being replaced when she retires in October 1993, and it is thought that the WRNS will then be abolished as a separate Service.

Chief Commandant, HRH The Princess Royal
Director, Commandant A. C. Spencer, ADC (*retires Oct. 1993*)

THE QUEEN

FIELD MARSHALS

HRH The Prince Philip, Duke of Edinburgh, KG, KT, OM, GBE, AC, QSO, PC, *apptd* 1953
Sir James Cassels, GCB, KBE, DSO, *apptd* 1968
The Lord Carver, GCB, CBE, DSO, MC, *apptd* 1973
Sir Roland Gibbs, GCB, CBE, DSO, MC, *apptd* 1979
The Lord Bramall, KG, GCB, OBE, MC, *apptd* 1982
Sir John Stanier, GCB, MBE, *apptd* 1985
Sir Nigel Bagnall, GCB, CVO, MC, *apptd* 1988
Sir Richard Vincent, GBE, KCB, DSO (*Chairman of NATO's Military Committee*), *apptd* 1991
Sir John Chapple, GCB, CBE (*Governor and C.-in-C. Gibraltar*), *apptd* 1992
HRH The Duke of Kent, KG, GCMG, GCVO, ADC, *apptd* 1993

GENERALS

Inge, Sir Peter, GCB, ADC (*Gen.*), Col. Green Howards, Col. Cmdt. APTC (*Chief of the General Staff*)
Waters, Sir John, KCB, CBE, ADC (*D. SACEUR*)
Guthrie, Sir Charles, KCB, LVO, OBE, ADC (*Gen.*), Col. Cmdt. Int. Corps (*C.-in-C. BAOR and Comdt. Northern Army Group*)
Jones, Sir Edward, KCB, CBE, Col. Cmdt. 2 RGJ (*UK Military Rep. to NATO*)
Learmont, Sir John, KCB, CBE, Col. Cmdt. AAC, Col. Cmdt. RA (*Quartermaster-General, until Jan. 1994*)
Johnson, Sir Garry, KCB, OBE, MC, Col. 10 GR, Col. Cmdt. The Light Division (*C.-in-C. AFNORTH*)
Wilkes, Sir Michael, KCB, CBE, Col. Cmdt. Hon. Artillery Company (TA) (*Adjutant-General*)
Wilsey, Sir John, KCB, CBE, Col. Cmdt POW Division, Col. Cmdt. Royal Logistic Corps (*C.-in-C. UK Land Forces*)

LIEUTENANT-GENERALS

Swinburn, Sir Richard, KCB (*GOC S District*)
Blacker, Sir Jeremy, KCB, CBE, Col. Cmdt. RTR, Col. Cmdt. RAC (*Master-General of the Ordnance*)
Rous, The Hon. Sir William, KCB, OBE (*Quartermaster-General, from Jan. 1994*)
Mackenzie, Sir Jeremy, KCB, OBE, Col. Cmdt. AG Corps (*Cmdt. NATO Rapid Reaction Corps*)
Duffell, Sir Peter, KCB, CBE, MC (*Inspector-General, Doctrine and Training*)
Beale, Sir Peter, KBE, QHP (*Surgeon-General*)
Boyd-Carpenter, the Hon. Sir Thomas, KBE (*Deputy CDS (Programmes and Personnel)*)
Wheeler, Sir Roger, KCB, CBE (*GOC Northern Ireland*)
Rose, H. M., CBE, QGM (*Comd. UK Land Forces*)

MAJOR-GENERALS

Corbett, R. J. S., CB (*GOC London District*)
Hayman-Joyce, R. J., CBE (*Military Secretary, from Jan. 1994*)
Cowan, S., CBE, Col. QGS (*Asst Chief of the Defence Staff OR (Land)*)
Pennicott, B. T. (*Defence Services Secretary*)
Barr, J. A. J. P., CB, CBE, Col. Cmdt. Corps of Royal Engineers
Crawford, I. P., GM, QHP, FFCM
Grist, R. D., OBE, Col. Gloucesters (*Director-General, AG Corps*)

Thomson, D. P., CB, CBE, MC, Col. The Argyll and Sutherland Highlanders (Princess Louise's) (*Senior Army Member, Royal College of Defence Studies*)

Denison-Smith, A. A., MBE (*GOC 4 Armd Division*)

Field, G. W., CB, CBE, Col. Cmdt. Royal Logistic Corps (*Engineer-in-Chief (Army)*)

Stone, A. C. P., CB, Col. Cmdt. Royal Regiment of Artillery (*Director-General, Land Fighting Systems*)

Wallace, C. B. Q., OBE, Col. Cmdt. RMP (*Comdt. Staff College*)

Harley, A. G. H., CB, OBE (*Comd. British Forces Cyprus*)

Baskervyle-Glegg, J., MBE (*SBLSO RAO*)

Smith, R. A., DSO, OBE, QGM, Col. Cmdt. Parachute Regiment, Col. Cmdt. REME Equipment Support Organization (*Asst CDS (Operations/Security)*)

Wood, R., FRICS (*Director-General, Military Survey*)

Courage, W. J., MBE (*Chief of Joint Services Liaison Organization Bonn*)

Mayes, F. B., QHS, FRCS (*Director-General, Army Medical Services*)

Toyne Sewell, T. P. (*Cmdt. RMAS*)

Tennant, M. T. (*Director, Royal Artillery*)

Heath, M. S., CBE (*Director-General, Equipment Support (Army)*)

Burton, E. F. G., OBE (*Cmdt. RMCS*)

Grove, D. A., OBE (*Team Leader, AG Study Group*)

Meier, A. L., OBE (*Director-General, Management and Support of Intelligence, MOD*)

Pett, R. A., MBE (*Deputy Chief of Staff (Support) AFNORTH*)

Grant, S. C. (*Team Leader, Command Structure Review*)

Gordon, J., CBE (*Chief of Staff HQ UK Land Forces*)

Sheppard, P. J., CBE (*Director-General, Logistics Policy (Army)*)

Walker, M. J. D., CBE, Col. Cmdt. The Queen's Division (*Asst Chief of General Staff*)

Regan, M. D., OBE (*GOC Wales and W District*)

Freer, I. L., CBE, Col. Staffords (*CLF and DD Ops. N. Ireland*)

Foley, J. P., CB, OBE, MC (*Comd. BFHK and Maj.-Gen. Brigade of Gurkhas*)

Hollands, G. S. (*Cmdt. Artillery 1 (Br) Corps*)

Lytle, S. W. St J. (*Director, Army Air Corps*)

Notley, C. R. S., CBE (*President, Ordnance Board*)

Dutton, B. H., CBE (*Director, Infantry*)

Pike, H. W. R., DSO, MBE, Col. SASC (*GOC UK Division*)

Carr-Smith, S. R. (*Chief C3 NACISA*)

Clarke, M. F. H. (*Director, Army Legal Services*)

Jackson, M. D., CBE (*Director-General, Personal Services (Army)*)

Kennedy, A. I. G., CBE (*Director-General, TA*)

Burden, D. L., CBE (*Director-General, Logistic Support (Army)*)

Craig, R. P., MD, FRCS, QHS (*Cmdt. MED. UK Land Forces*)

Boyle, A. H. (*Director-General, CCCIS (Army) and Signal Officer-in-Chief (Army)*)

Cordingley, P. A. J., DSO (*GOC E District*)

Robins, W. J. P., OBE (*Asst CDS (CCCIS)*)

Willcocks, M. A. (*Director-General, Land Warfare*)

McAfee, R. W. M. (*Director-General, Army Training*)

Scott, M. I. E., CBE, DSO, Col. Cmdt. The Scottish Division (*GOC Scotland*)

Deverell, J. F., OBE (*Director-General, Army Manning and Recruiting*)

Mackay-Dick, I. C., MBE (*Comd. British Forces Falkland Islands*)

Pigott, A. D., CBE (*Chief of Staff HQ ACE Rapid Reaction Corps*)

White, M. S., CBE (*Director of Support LANDCENT*)

Cowan, G. O. (*Cmdt. Royal Army Medical College*)

Cordy-Simpson, R. A. (*Chief of Staff HQ BAOR*)

CONSTITUTION OF THE BRITISH ARMY

The regular forces include the following arms, branches and corps. Soldiers' record offices are shown at the end of each group; records of officers are maintained at the Ministry of Defence.

THE ARMS

HOUSEHOLD CAVALRY – The Household Cavalry Regiment (The Blues and Royals and The Life Guards). *Records*, Horse Guards, London SW1.

ROYAL ARMOURED CORPS – Cavalry Regiments: 1st The Queen's Dragoon Guards; The Royal Scots Dragoon Guards (Carabiniers and Greys); The Royal Dragoon Guards; The Queen's Royal Hussars (The Queen's Own and Royal Irish); 9th/12th Royal Lancers (Prince of Wales's); The King's Royal Hussars; The Light Dragoons; The Queen's Royal Lancers; Royal Tank Regiment comprising two regular regiments. *Records*, Queen's Park, Chester.

ARTILLERY – Royal Regiment of Artillery. *Records*, Imphal Barracks, Fulford Road, York.

ENGINEERS – Corps of Royal Engineers. *Records*, Kentigern House, Brown Street, Glasgow.

SIGNALS – Royal Corps of Signals. *Records*, Kentigern House, Brown Street, Glasgow.

THE INFANTRY

The Foot Guards and Regiments of Infantry of the Line are grouped in Divisions as follows:

GUARDS DIVISION – Grenadier, Coldstream, Scots, Irish and Welsh Guards. *Divisional HQ*, HQ Household Division, Horse Guards, London SW1. *Depot*, Pirbright Camp, Brookwood, Surrey. *Records*, Imphal Barracks, Fulford Road, York.

SCOTTISH DIVISION – The Royal Scots (The Royal Regiment); The Royal Highland Fusiliers (Princess Margaret's Own Glasgow and Ayrshire Regiment); The King's Own Scottish Borderers; The Black Watch (Royal Highland Regiment); Queen's Own Highlanders (Seaforth and Camerons); The Gordon Highlanders; The Argyll and Sutherland Highlanders (Princess Louise's). *Divisional HQ*, The Castle, Edinburgh. *Depots*, Scottish Divisional Depots, Glencorse, Milton Bridge, Midlothian; Albemarle Barracks, Ouston, Newcastle. *Records*, Imphal Barracks, Fulford Road, York.

QUEEN'S DIVISION – The Princess of Wales's Royal Regiment (Queen's and Royal Hampshire's); The Royal Regiment of Fusiliers; The Royal Anglian Regiment. *Divisional HQ* and *Depot*, Bassingbourn Barracks, Royston, Herts. *Records*, Higher Barracks, Exeter, Devon.

KING'S DIVISION – The King's Own Royal Border Regiment; The King's Regiment; The Prince of Wales's Own Regiment of Yorkshire; The Green Howards (Alexandra, Princess of Wales's Own Yorkshire Regiment); The Queen's Lancashire Regiment; The Duke of Wellington's Regiment (West Riding). *Divisional HQ*, Imphal Barracks, York. *Depots*, The King's Division Depot (Yorkshire), Queen Elizabeth Barracks, Strensall, Yorks.; Albemarle Barracks, Ouston, Newcastle. *Records*, Imphal Barracks, Fulford Road, York.

PRINCE OF WALES'S DIVISION – The Devonshire and Dorset Regiment; The Cheshire Regiment; The Royal

Welch Fusiliers; The Royal Regiment of Wales (24th/41st Foot); The Gloucestershire Regiment; The Worcestershire and Sherwood Foresters Regiment (29th/45th Foot); The Staffordshire Regiment (The Prince of Wales's); The Duke of Edinburgh's Royal Regiment (Berkshire and Wiltshire). *Divisional HQ* and *Depot*, Whittington Barracks, Lichfield, Staffs. *Records*, Imphal Barracks, Fulford, York.

LIGHT DIVISION – The Light Infantry; The Royal Green Jackets. *Divisional HQ* and *Depot*, Sir John Moore Barracks, Winchester, Hants. *Records*, Higher Barracks, Exeter.

BRIGADE OF GURKHAS – 2nd King Edward VII's Own Gurkha Rifles (The Sirmoor Rifles); 6th Queen Elizabeth's Own Gurkha Rifles; 7th Duke of Edinburgh's Own Gurkha Rifles; 10th Princess Mary's Own Gurkha Rifles; The Queen's Gurkha Engineers; Queen's Gurkha Signals; Gurkha Transport Regiment. *Brigade HQ*, HMS *Tamar*, Hong Kong, BFPO 1. *Depot*, Training Depot, Brigade of Gurkhas, Malaya Lines, Sek Kong, BFPO 1. *Records*, Record Office, Brigade of Gurkhas, Hong Kong, BFPO 1.

THE ROYAL IRISH REGIMENT (two general service and seven home service battalions) – 27th (Inniskilling), 83rd, 87th and the Ulster Defence Regiment. *Depot*, St Patrick's Barracks, Ballymena, N. Ireland. *Records*, Imphal Barracks, Fulford Road, York.

THE PARACHUTE REGIMENT (three regular battalions) – *Depot*, Browning Barracks, Aldershot, Hants. *Records*, Higher Barracks, Exeter.

SPECIAL AIR SERVICE REGIMENT – *Regimental HQ*, Duke of York's Headquarters, Sloane Square, London SW3. *Depot*, Stirling Lines, Hereford. *Records*, Higher Barracks, Exeter, Devon.

ARMY AIR CORPS – Regimental HQ and *Depot*, Middle Wallop, Hants. *Records*, Higher Barracks, Exeter.

THE SERVICES

Royal Army Chaplain's Department – *Regimental HQ* and *Depot*, Bagshot Park, Surrey.

Royal Logistic Corps – formed in April 1993 to subsume the functions of the Royal Corps of Transport, the Royal Army Ordnance Corps, the Royal Pioneer Corps, the Army Catering Corps, and the Postal and Courier Service of the Royal Engineers.

Royal Army Medical Corps, Royal Army Dental Corps and Queen Alexandra's Royal Army Nursing Corps. – *Records*, Queen's Park, Chester.

Adjutant-General's Corps – *Depot*, Worthy Down, Winchester, Hants. *Records*, Queen's Park, Chester.

Corps of Royal Electrical and Mechanical Engineers Equipment Support Organization – *Records*, Glen Parva Barracks, Saffron Road, Wigston, Leicester.

Small Arms School Corps – *Records*, Higher Barracks, Exeter.

General Service Corps – *Records*, Imphal Barracks, Fulford Road, York.

Corps of Royal Military Police, Royal Army Pay Corps, Royal Army Veterinary Corps, Intelligence Corps, Army Physical Training Corps, Sandhurst, Officers Training Corps – *Records*, Higher Barracks, Exeter, Devon.

THE TERRITORIAL ARMY (TA)

The Territorial Army is designed to provide a highly-trained and well-equipped force which will complete the Regular Army order of battle in a time of national emergency. Its establishment is approximately 91,000, reducing to 65,000, due to TA restructuring, by 1995.

QUEEN ALEXANDRA'S ROYAL ARMY NURSING CORPS

The Queen Alexandra's Royal Army Nursing Corps (QARANC) was founded in 1902 as Queen Alexandra's Imperial Military Nursing Service (QAIMNS) and gained its present title in 1949. The QARANC has trained nurses for the register and roll since 1950 and has eight other employment categories. A non-nursing officer element was introduced in 1959 for personnel work. Since 1 April 1992 men have been eligible to join the QARANC. The Corps provides service in military hospitals in the United Kingdom (including Northern Ireland), BAOR, Hong Kong, Cyprus, Falkland Islands and Belize.

Colonel-in-Chief, HRH The Princess Margaret, Countess of Snowdon, GCVO, CI

Matron-in-Chief (Army) and Director, Army Nursing Services, Brig. H. Dixon-Nuttal

WOMEN'S ROYAL ARMY CORPS

Formed 1 February 1949; disbanded April 1992.

The Royal Air Force

THE QUEEN

MARSHALS OF THE ROYAL AIR FORCE

HRH The Prince Philip, Duke of Edinburgh, KG, KT, OM, GBE, AC, QSO, PC, *apptd* 1953
Sir John Grandy, GCB, GCVO, KBE, DSO, *apptd* 1971
Sir Denis Spotswood, GCB, CBE, DSO, DFC, *apptd* 1974
Sir Michael Beetham, GCB, CBE, DFC, AFC, *apptd* 1982
Sir Keith Williamson, GCB, AFC, *apptd* 1985
Lord Craig of Radley, GCB, OBE, *apptd* 1988
Sir Peter Harding, GCB, ADC (*Chief of the Defence Staff*), *apptd* 1993

AIR CHIEF MARSHALS

Graydon, Sir Michael, GCB, CBE (*Chief of the Air Staff*)
Stear, Sir Michael, KCB, CBE (*Deputy C.-in-C. Allied Forces Central Europe*)
Thomson, Sir John, KCB, CBE, AFC (*AOC.-in-C. Strike Command and C.-in-C. UK Air Forces*)
Wilson, Sir Andrew, KCB, AFC, ADC (*Air Member for Personnel*)
Alcock, Sir Michael, KCB (*Air Member for Supply and Organization*)

AIR MARSHALS

Walker, Sir John, KCB, CBE, AFC (*Chief of Defence Intelligence*)
Austin, Sir Roger, KCB, AFC (*Deputy CDS (Systems)*)
Harris, Sir John, KCB, CBE (*AOC No. 18 Group*)
Wratten, Sir William, KBE, CB, AFC (*Director-General, Saudi Armed Forces Project*)
Willis, Sir John, KCB, CBE (*AOC.-in-C. RAF Support Command*)
Johns, R. E., CB, CBE, LVO (*Chief of Staff and Deputy C.-in-C. Strike Command*)

AIR VICE-MARSHALS

Roberts, A. L., CB, CBE, AFC (*Head of Manpower Structure Study Team*)

Honey, R. J., CB, CBE (*Air Secretary and AOC RAF Personnel Management Centre*)

Blackley, A. B., CBE, AFC (*Air Officer Scotland and N. Ireland*)

Harding, P. J., CB, CBE, AFC (*Deputy Chief of Staff (Operations) Allied Air Forces Central Europe*)

Cousins, D., CB, AFC (*Cmdt. RAF College, Cranwell*)

Allison, J. S., CBE (*AOC No. 11 Group*)

Dodworth, P., OBE, AFC (*Defence Attaché and Head of British Defence Staff, Washington*)

Garden, T., CB (*Asst CDS (Programmes)*)

Baird, J. A., QHP (*Principal Medical Officer Strike Command*)

Beer, P. G., CBE, LVO (*Director-General, Training and Personnel (RAF)*)

Clark, P. D., CB (*Air Officer Engineering Strike Command*)

Ferguson, G. M., CB, CBE (*Air Officer Admin. Strike Command*)

French, D. R., CB, MBE (*Chief Executive, RAF Support Command Maintenance Group*)

Gibson, M. J., OBE (*Director-General, Policy and Planning*)

Macfadyen, I. D., CB, OBE (*Asst CDS Operational Requirements (Air)*)

Saunders, D. J., CBE (*Asst CDS (Logistics)*)

Squire, P. T., DFC, AFC (*AOC No. 1 Group*)

Robertson, G. A., CBE (*AOC No. 2 Group*)

Lucas, Ven. B. H., QHC (*Chaplain-in Chief (RAF)*)

Davison, D. J., QHS (*Dean of Air Force Medicine*)

Brook, J. M., QHS (*Director-General, Medical Services (RAF)*)

Chapple, R., QHP (*Principal Medical Officer, RAF Support Command*)

Cheshire, J. A., CBE (*Asst COS (Policy), SHAPE*)

Kyle, R. H., MBE (*Director-General, Support Services (RAF)*)

Mackey, J., QHDS (*Director, Defence Dental Services*)

Norriss, P. C., AFC (*Director-General, Aircraft 2*)

Rae, W. M., CB (*Senior Director of Staff, Royal College of Defence Studies*)

Sherrington, T. B., OBE (*Air Officer Admin., RAF Support Command*)

Carleton, G. W. (*Director, Legal Services (RAF)*)

Coville, C. C. C. (*Air Officer Training RAF Support Command*)

O'Brien, R. P., OBE (*Cmdt. Joint Service Defence College*)

May, J. A. G., CBE

Bagnall, A. J. C., OBE (*Asst Chief of Air Staff*)

Baldwin, N. B., CBE (*Asst CDS (Overseas)*)

Donaldson, M. P., MBE (*Cmdt. RAF Staff College, Bracknell*)

Terry, C. G., OBE (*Director-General, Support Management (RAF)*)

CONSTITUTION OF THE ROYAL AIR FORCE

The RAF currently consists of two Commands: Strike Command and Support Command. On 1 April 1993 RAF Germany became No. 2 Group of Strike Command. From April 1994, the RAF will consist of Strike Command, Logistics Command, and Personnel and Training Command. The two new Commands will take over the functions of Support Command, the Air Member for Personnel, and the Air Member for Supply and Organization. Strike Command is the RAF's operational command for the UK and designated locations abroad (including Germany); its roles include

strike/attack, air defence, control and reporting, maritime surveillance, air reconnaissance, air-to-air refuelling, offensive support, air transport, aero-medical facilities, and search and rescue. Logistics Command will be responsible for all logistics, engineering support, and maintenance. Personnel and Training Command will be responsible for air and ground training, hospitals, and personnel administration.

To carry out its tasks, the Royal Air Force is equipped (as at 1 April 1993) with:

Aircraft – 8 Victor, 274 Tornado, 24 Buccaneer, 6 Hunter, 7 Sentry, 56 Harrier, 53 Jaguar, 19 Canberra, 29 Nimrod, 19 VC10, 9 Tristar, 55 Hercules, 118 Hawk, 30 Jet Provost, 104 Tucano, 63 Chipmunk, 118 Bulldog

Helicopters – 37 Puma, 37 Wessex, 17 Sea King, 26 Chinook, 28 Gazelle

Miscellaneous communications aircraft, etc.

Rapier missiles

ROYAL AUXILIARY AIR FORCE (RAUXAF)

Formed in 1924, the Auxiliary Air Force served with great distinction in the Second World War and in recognition of its war record King George VI conferred the prefix 'Royal' in 1947. Following a major reduction of units in the late 1950s, the benefits to be gained by using auxiliary forces in certain roles has resulted in a subsequent expansion. Today, the Royal Auxiliary Air Force supports the RAF in maritime air operations, air and ground defence of major airfields, air movements and aero-medical evacuation.

Air Commodore-in-Chief, HM The Queen

Director of Personnel Management (Airmen) and Director of Reserve Forces (RAF), Air Cdre D. T. Davies

ROYAL AIR FORCE VOLUNTEER RESERVE (RAFVR)

The Royal Air Force Volunteer Reserve was created in 1936 with the object of providing training for the increased number of aircrew who were seen as necessary for the forthcoming conflict. The RAFVR was reconstituted in 1947 following war service and today is a small but important part of the Air Force Reserve. The RAFVR provides specialist personnel who fill specific wartime intelligence support, photo interpretation and public relations appointments. A small number of RAFVR aircrew are employed to augment regular crews on Nimrod (Maritime Reconnaissance) aircraft in wartime.

Director of Personnel Management (Airmen) and Director of Reserve Forces (RAF), Air Cdre D. T. Davies

PRINCESS MARY'S ROYAL AIR FORCE NURSING SERVICE

The Princess Mary's Royal Air Force Nursing Service (PMRAFNS) is open to both male and female candidates. Commissions are offered to those who are Registered General Nurses (RGN) with a minimum of two years experience after obtaining RGN and normally with a second qualification. RGNs with no additional experience or qualification are also recruited as non-commissioned officers in the grade of Staff Nurse.

Air Chief Commandant, HRH Princess Alexandra, the Hon. Lady Ogilvy, GCVO

Matron-in-Chief, Group Captain V. M. Hand (*from Jan. 1994*)

WOMEN'S ROYAL AIR FORCE

Formed on 1 April 1918, the Women's Royal Air Force (WRAF) was disbanded on 1 April 1920 and re-formed on 1 February 1949 from the Women's Auxiliary Air Force, the Second World War service which had been formed on 28 June 1939, and from the RAF companies of the Auxiliary Territorial Service.

WRAF officers and airwomen serve in most of the RAF branches and trades including as aircrew and as pilots of combat jets. WRAF personnel are employed at RAF stations and higher formations at home and abroad, and they compete on equal terms with their RAF counterparts for appointments, promotion and places on training courses.

Commandant-in-Chief, HM Queen Elizabeth The Queen Mother

Air Chief Commandant, HRH Princess Alice, Duchess of Gloucester

Director, Air Commodore R. M. B. Montague, ADC

ROYAL OBSERVER CORPS
Established in 1925; stood down 31 March 1992

ARMED FORCES STRENGTHS

AS AT 1 JULY 1993

All Services	270,912
Men	252,148
Women	18,764
Royal Naval Services	58,513
Men	54,092
Women	4,421
Army	133,058
Men	125,507
Women	7,551
Royal Air Force	79,341
Men	72,549
Women	6,792

DEFENCE CUTS

Cuts and restructuring are intended to achieve the following strengths by the mid 1990s:

Royal Navy	52,500
Army	119,000
Royal Air Force	70,000

SERVICE SALARIES AND PENSIONS

The following rates of pay have been introduced as part of the 1993 pay award for service personnel.

The increasing integration of women in the armed services is reflected in equal pay for equal work and the X factor addition is now the same for men and women (11.5 per cent).

Annual salaries are derived from daily rates in whole pence and rounded to the nearest £.

The pay rates shown are for Army personnel. The rates apply also to personnel of equivalent rank and pay band in the other services.

OFFICERS' SALARIES

MAIN SCALE

Rank	Daily	Annual
Second Lieutenant	£34.55	£12,611
Lieutenant		
On appointment	45.69	16,677
After 1 year in the rank	46.88	17,111
After 2 years in the rank	48.08	17,549
After 3 years in the rank	49.28	17,987
After 4 years in the rank	50.48	18,425
Captain		
On appointment	58.14	21,221
After 1 year in the rank	59.71	21,794
After 2 years in the rank	61.29	22,371
After 3 years in the rank	62.86	22,944
After 4 years in the rank	64.43	23,517
After 5 years in the rank	66.01	24,094
After 6 years in the rank	67.58	24,667
Major		
On appointment	73.27	26,744
After 1 year in the rank	75.09	27,408
After 2 years in the rank	76.91	28,072
After 3 years in the rank	78.72	28,733
After 4 years in the rank	80.54	29,397
After 5 years in the rank	82.36	30,061
After 6 years in the rank	84.17	30,722
After 7 years in the rank	85.99	31,386
After 8 years in the rank	87.81	32,051

Rank	Daily	Annual
Special List Lieutenant-Colonel	£101.03	£36,876
Lieutenant-Colonel		
On appointment with less than 19 years service	102.79	37,518
After 2 years in the rank or with 19 years service	105.50	38,508
After 4 years in the rank or with 21 years service	108.21	39,497
After 6 years in the rank or with 23 years service	110.92	40,486
After 8 years in the rank or with 25 years service	113.63	41,475
Colonel		
On appointment	119.72	43,698
After 2 years in the rank	122.87	44,848
After 4 years in the rank	126.01	45,994
After 6 years in the rank	129.16	47,143
After 8 years in the rank	132.31	48,293
Brigadier	146.85	53,600
Major-General	155.37	56,710
Lieutenant-General	177.65	64,842
General	246.98	90,148
Field Marshal	307.08	112,084

SALARIES OF OFFICERS COMMISSIONED FROM THE RANKS (LIEUTENANTS AND CAPTAINS ONLY)

YEARS OF COMMISSIONED SERVICE	YEARS OF NON-COMMISSIONED SERVICE FROM AGE 18					
	Less than 12 years		12 years but less than 15 years		15 years or more	
	Daily	Annual	Daily	Annual	Daily	Annual
On appointment	£63.89	£23,320	£67.14	£24,506	£70.39	£25,692
After 1 year service	65.52	23,915	68.77	25,101	71.45	26,079
After 2 years service	67.14	24,506	70.39	25,692	72.50	26,462
After 3 years service	68.77	25,101	71.45	26,079	73.56	26,849
After 4 years service	70.39	25,692	72.50	26,462	74.61	27,233
After 5 years service	71.45	26,079	73.56	26,849	75.67	27,620
After 6 years service	72.50	26,462	74.61	27,233	76.72	28,003
After 8 years service	73.56	26,849	75.67	27,620	77.78	28,390
After 10 years service	74.61	27,233	76.72	28,003	77.78	28,390
After 12 years service	75.67	27,620	77.78	28,390	77.78	28,390
After 14 years service	76.72	28,003	77.78	28,390	77.78	28,390
After 16 years service	77.78	28,390	77.78	28,390	77.78	28,390

The pay structure below officer level is divided into pay bands. Jobs at each rank are allocated to bands according to their score in the job evaluation system.

Scale A: committed to serve/have completed less than 6 years

Scale B: committed to serve/have completed 6 years but less than 9 years

Scale C: committed to serve/have completed more than 9 years

Daily rates of pay effective from 1 April 1993 are:

SALARIES OF WARRANT OFFICERS AND SENIOR NCOs

RANK	SCALE A				SCALE B				SCALE C			
	Band 4	Band 5	Band 6	Band 7	Band 4	Band 5	Band 6	Band 7	Band 4	Band 5	Band 6	Band 7
Sergeant	£42.47	£46.69	£51.31	£ —	£42.77	£46.99	£51.61	£ —	£43.23	£47.45	£52.07	£ —
Staff Sergeant	44.90	49.13	53.75	59.34	45.21	49.43	54.06	59.64	45.66	49.89	54.52	60.10
Warrant Officer												
Class 2	48.02	52.24	57.95	63.64	48.32	52.55	58.25	63.95	48.78	53.00	58.71	64.40
Class 1	51.21	55.43	61.19	66.89	51.51	55.73	61.50	67.19	51.97	56.19	61.96	67.65

SALARIES OF ADULT PERSONNEL OF THE RANK OF CORPORAL AND BELOW

RANK	SCALE A			SCALE B			SCALE C		
	Band 1	Band 2	Band 3	Band 1	Band 2	Band 3	Band 1	Band 2	Band 3
Private									
Class 4	£21.62	£ —	£ —	£21.92	£ —	£ —	£22.38	£ —	£ —
Class 3	24.22	28.13	32.46	24.52	28.43	32.76	24.98	28.89	33.22
Class 2	27.09	31.01	35.34	27.39	31.31	35.65	27.85	31.77	36.10
Class 1	29.39	33.30	37.64	29.70	33.61	37.94	30.16	34.06	38.40
Lance-Corporal									
Class 3	29.39	33.30	37.64	29.70	33.61	37.94	30.16	34.06	38.40
Class 2	31.40	35.32	40.00	31.71	35.63	40.31	32.17	36.08	40.76
Class 1	33.79	37.71	42.39	34.09	38.01	42.69	34.55	38.47	43.15
Corporal									
Class 2	36.29	40.19	44.88	36.59	40.50	45.19	37.05	40.96	45.64
Class 1	38.95	42.86	47.55	39.25	43.17	47.86	39.71	43.62	48.31

Relative Rank – Armed Forces

	Royal Navy		*Army*		*Royal Air Force*
1	Admiral of the Fleet	1	Field Marshal	1	Marshal of the RAF
2	Admiral (Adm.)	2	General (Gen.)	2	Air Chief Marshal
3	Vice-Admiral (Vice-Adm.)	3	Lieutenant-General (Lt.-Gen.)	3	Air Marshal
4	Rear-Admiral (Rear-Adm.)	4	Major-General (Maj.-Gen.)	4	Air Vice-Marshal
5	Commodore (1st & 2nd Class) (Cdre)	5	Brigadier (Brig.)	5	Air Commodore (Air Cdre)
6	Captain (Capt.)	6	Colonel (Col.)	6	Group Captain (Gp Capt)
7	Commander (Cdr.)	7	Lieutenant-Colonel (Lt.-Col.)	7	Wing Commander (Wg Cdr.)
8	Lieutenant-Commander (Lt.-Cdr.)	8	Major (Maj.)	8	Squadron Leader (Sqn. Ldr.)
9	Lieutenant (Lt.)	9	Captain (Capt.)	9	Flight Lieutenant (Flt. Lt.)
10	Sub-Lieutenant (Sub-Lt.)	10	Lieutenant (Lt.)	10	Flying Officer (FO)
11	Acting Sub-Lieutenant (Acting Sub-Lt.)	11	Second Lieutenant (2nd Lt.)	11	Pilot Officer (PO)

SERVICE RETIRED PAY ON COMPULSORY RETIREMENT

Those who leave the services having served at least five years, but not long enough to qualify for the appropriate immediate pension, now qualify for a preserved pension and terminal grant, both of which are payable at age 60. The tax-free resettlement grants shown below are payable on release to those who qualify for a preserved pension and who have completed nine years service from age 21 (officers) or 12 years from age 18 (other ranks).

The annual rates for army personnel are given. The rates apply also to personnel of equivalent rank in the other services, including the nursing services.

OFFICERS (applicable to officers who give full pay service on the active list on or after 31 March 1993)

No. of years reckonable service over age 21	Capt. and below*	Major*	Lt.-Col.	Col.	Brigadier	Major-General	Lieutenant-General	General
16	£ 7,030	£ 8,378	£10,975	£ —	£ —	£ —	£ —	£ —
17	7,354	8,776	11,483	—	—	—	—	—
18	7,678	9,174	11,991	13,964	—	—	—	—
19	8,003	9,573	12,498	14,555	—	—	—	—
20	8,327	9,971	13,006	15,146	—	—	—	—
21	8,651	10,369	13,514	15,738	—	—	—	—
22	8,975	10,767	14,022	16,329	18,849	—	—	—
23	9,300	11,165	14,529	16,920	19,445	—	—	—
24	9,624	11,563	15,037	17,511	20,040	21,203	—	—
25	9,948	11,962	15,545	18,102	20,636	21,833	—	—
26	10,272	12,360	16,053	18,693	21,232	22,463	—	—
27	10,596	12,758	16,561	19,284	21,827	23,093	26,405	—
28	10,921	13,156	17,068	19,875	22,423	23,723	27,125	—
29	11,245	13,554	17,576	20,466	23,018	24,354	27,846	—
30	11,569	13,952	18,084	21,058	23,614	24,984	28,566	39,716
31	11,893	14,351	18,592	21,649	24,209	25,614	29,287	40,718
32	12,218	14,749	19,099	22,240	24,805	26,244	30,007	41,719
33	12,542	15,147	19,607	22,831	25,400	26,874	30,728	42,721
34	12,866	15,545	20,115	23,422	25,996	27,504	31,448	43,722

Field Marshal – active list retired pay at the rate of £54,361 a year

*Including Quartermaster

WARRANT OFFICERS, NCOS AND PRIVATES (applicable to soldiers who give full pay service on or after 21 March 1993)

Number of years reckonable service	Below Corporal	Corporal	Sergeant	Staff Sergeant	Warrant Officer Class II	Warrant Officer Class I
22	£4,082	£5,216	£5,732	£6,524	£ 6,744	£ 7,452
23	4,224	5,398	5,932	6,752	6,983	7,720
24	4,367	5,580	6,132	6,979	7,222	7,988
25	4,509	5,762	6,332	7,207	7,461	8,256
26	4,652	5,944	6,532	7,435	7,700	8,524
27	4,794	6,126	6,732	7,663	7,939	8,792
28	4,937	6,308	6,932	7,890	8,178	9,060
29	5,079	6,490	7,132	8,118	8,417	9,328
30	5,222	6,673	7,333	8,346	8,656	9,595
31	5,364	6,855	7,533	8,574	8,895	9,863
32	5,507	7,037	7,733	8,801	9,134	10,131
33	5,649	7,219	7,933	9,029	9,375	10,399
34	5,792	7,401	8,133	9,257	9,612	10,667
35	5,934	7,583	8,333	9,485	9,851	10,935
36	6,077	7,765	8,533	9,712	10,090	11,203
37	6,219	7,947	8,733	9,940	10,329	11,471

TERMINAL GRANTS AND GRATUITIES

Terminal grants are in each case three times the rate of retired pay or pension. There are special rates of retired pay for chaplains and certain other ranks not shown above. Lower rates are payable in cases of voluntary retirement.

A gratuity of £2,355 is payable for officers with short service commissions for each year completed. Resettlement grants are: officers £8,101; non-commissioned ranks £5,357.

The Christian Churches

The Church of England

The Church of England is the established (i.e. state) church in England and the mother church of the Anglican Communion. It originated in the conflicts between church and state throughout the Middle Ages, culminating in the Act of Supremacy issued by Henry VIII in 1534. This repudiated papal supremacy and declared the King to be the supreme head of the Church in England. Since 1559 the English monarch has been termed the Supreme Governor of the Church of England. The Thirty-Nine Articles, a set of doctrinal statements defining the position of the Church of England, were adopted in their final form in 1571 and include the emphasis on personal faith and the authority of the scriptures common to the Protestant Reformation throughout Europe.

The Church of England is divided into the two provinces of Canterbury and York, each under an archbishop. The two provinces are subdivided into 44 dioceses. Decisions on matters concerning the Church of England are made by the General Synod, established in 1970. It also discusses and expresses opinion on any other matter of religious or public interest. The General Synod has 574 members in total, divided between three houses: the House of Bishops, the House of Clergy and the House of Laity. It is presided over jointly by the Archbishops of Canterbury and York and normally meets twice a year. The Synod has the power, delegated by Parliament, to frame statute law (known as a Measure) on any matter concerning the Church of England. A Measure must be laid before both Houses of Parliament, who may accept or reject it but cannot amend it. Once accepted the Measure is submitted for Royal Assent and then has the full force of law. The Synod appoints a number of committees, boards and councils which deal with, or advise on, a wide range of matters. In addition to the General Synod, there are synods of clergy and laity at diocesan level.

In 1990 the Church of England had an electoral roll membership of 1.4 million, of whom about 1.1 million regularly attended Sunday services. There are (1992 figures) two archbishops, 104 diocesan, suffragan and (stipendiary) assistant bishops, 10,141 male and 707 female full-time stipendiary clergy, and over 16,000 churches and places of worship. (The Diocese in Europe is not included in these figures.)

THE ORDINATION OF WOMEN

On 11 November 1992, the General Synod of the Church of England voted to permit the ordination of women as priests. In the House of Bishops there were 39 votes (75 per cent) in favour of the legislation and 13 (25 per cent) against; in the House of Clergy, 176 (70.4 per cent) in favour and 74 (29.6 per cent) against; and in the House of Laity, 169 (67.3 per cent) in favour and 82 (32.7 per cent) against. The legislation therefore received the required two-thirds majority in all three houses.

The most important stages leading to the legislation being passed were:

1975   A motion that 'there are no fundamental objections to the ordination of women to the priesthood' was passed in the General Synod

1984   The General Synod agreed to 'bring forward legislation to permit the ordination of women to the priesthood'

1985   A motion permitting the ordination of women as deacons was carried

1987   A motion asking the standing committee to prepare draft legislation was carried
      The first women deacons were ordained

1988   Draft legislation to enable the ordination of women to the priesthood was approved and sent to a revision committee

1989   The revised legislation was amended and carried

1990   A majority of the 44 diocesan synods approved the legislation in the Diocesan House of Clergy and the Diocesan House of Laity

1992

June   The House of Bishops of the General Synod debated the final draft of the legislation and passed it on unaltered

July   The legislation was 'claimed' for debate and approved on a simple majority in the separate Houses of the Convocations of Canterbury and York (which together form the House of Bishops and the House of Clergy of the General Synod) and in the House of Laity of the General Synod

Nov   Final Approval debate and vote in the General Synod (*see above*)

The case for the ordination of women as priests was supported by the Archbishop of Canterbury (Dr George Carey), who said in the General Synod debate that this would not be a break with tradition, and that 'we must draw on all available talent if we are to be a credible church engaged in a mission to an increasingly confused and lost world'. Supporters of the legislation appealed to scripture to show that both men and women are made in the image of God, and said that the legislation should be passed for theological, practical and financial reasons. Opposition to the measure was led by the Bishop of London (Dr David Hope), who said that he was committed to women's full-time ministry, but was not convinced that this should be in the context of the ministerial priesthood and episcopate. Other opponents said that the legislation was confused and divisive, that 2,000 years of tradition should not be broken, and that the maleness of Christian priesthood was supported by scripture.

The legislation was presented to the Ecclesiastical Committee of Parliament in early 1993. The Committee found the legislation expedient, and it will be debated in both Houses of Parliament in the autumn of 1993. If either House votes the legislation down, the General Synod has the right to present it for a second time. If the legislation receives royal assent, the petition to promulgate the canon will be submitted to the Crown. When the canon has been promulgated (proclaimed) in the General Synod, which is likely to be in February 1994, the first women may be ordained as priests.

A clause of the Priests (Ordination of Women) Measure allows the bishop of a diocese to declare that women may not be ordained within his diocese, and that a woman ordained outside the diocese may not officiate or act as a priest within it. After the measure was passed, organizations opposed to women priests proposed that a system of 'alternative episcopal oversight' be set up, under which priests in dioceses where the bishop ordained women would be able to petition the nearest diocesan bishop opposed to women priests to oversee their ministry. This was rejected by the House of Bishops, who in January 1993 unanimously agreed a plan to appoint up to three 'provincial visitors' to work with those who are unable to accept the ministry of bishops ordaining women priests. The provincial visitors, who would be suffragan bishops, would be allowed to carry out confirmations and ordinations in parishes opposed to women priests, as long as they had the permission of the diocesan bishop. Diocesan bishops would also be able to depute a suffragan to ordain women; authorize a suffragan to minister to clergy and parishes whose views differ from his own; or make similar arrangements with bishops in neighbouring dioceses. The plan was welcomed by all the Anglo-Catholic diocesan bishops, and by the Archbishop of Canterbury, who said: 'We want to reject the idea of a church within a church, and to retain the geographical unity of each diocese'.

In June 1993 the House of Bishops drew up a draft Act of Synod setting out the practical arrangements to provide pastoral care for all, irrespective of their views on the ordination of women to the priesthood. The draft Act will go before the General Synod in November 1993 but will not be enshrined in a supplementary Measure which would be put before Parliament. Clergy who still feel compelled to leave the ministry will be entitled to generous financial assistance.

GENERAL SYNOD OF THE CHURCH OF ENGLAND, Church House, Dean's Yard, London SW1P 3NZ. Tel: 071-222 9011. *Secretary-General*, P. Mawer

HOUSE OF BISHOPS: *Chairman*, The Archbishop of Canterbury; *Vice-Chairman*, The Archbishop of York

HOUSE OF CLERGY: *Joint Chairmen*, The Archdeacon of Leicester; Canon J. Stanley

HOUSE OF LAITY: *Chairman*, Prof. J. D. McClean; *Vice-Chairman*, Dr Christina Baxter

STIPENDS 1993–4

Archbishop of Canterbury	£43,550
Archbishop of York	£38,150
Bishop of London	£35,560
Bishop of Durham	£31,380
Bishop of Winchester	£26,160
Other Diocesan Bishops	£23,610
Suffragan Bishops	£19,410
Deans and Provosts	£19,410
Residentiary Canons	£15,870

Province of Canterbury

CANTERBURY

103RD ARCHBISHOP AND PRIMATE OF ALL ENGLAND
Most Revd and Rt. Hon. George L. Carey, PH.D., *cons.* 1987, *trans.* 1991, *apptd* 1991; Lambeth Palace, London SE1 7JU. *Signs* George Cantuar:

BISHOPS SUFFRAGAN
Dover, Rt. Revd John R. A. Llewellin, *cons.* 1985, *apptd* 1992; Upway, St Martin's Hill, Canterbury, CT1 1PR
Maidstone, Rt. Revd Gavin H. Reid, *cons.* 1992, *apptd* 1992; Bishop's House, Pett Lane, Charing, Ashford TN27 0DL

ASSISTANT BISHOPS
Rt. Revd Ross Hook, MC, *cons.* 1965, *apptd* 1986; Rt. Revd William Franklin, OBE, *cons.* 1972, *apptd* 1987; Rt. Revd Richard Say, KCVO, *cons.* 1961, *apptd* 1988

DEAN
Very Revd John Arthur Simpson, *apptd* 1986

CANONS RESIDENTIARY
J. H. R. De Sausmarez, *apptd* 1981; P. Brett, *apptd* 1983; Ven. M. Till, *apptd* 1986
Organist, D. Flood, FRCO, *apptd* 1988

ARCHDEACONS
Canterbury, Ven. M. Till, *apptd* 1986
Maidstone, Ven. P. Evans, *apptd* 1989

Stipendiary Male Clergy, 189
Stipendiary Women Deacons, 11

Vicar-General of Province and Diocese, Chancellor S. Cameron, QC
Commissary-General, His Honour Judge Newey, QC, *apptd* 1971
Joint Registrars of the Province, F. E. Robson, OBE, 16 Beaumont Street, Oxford; B. J. T. Hanson, Church House, Dean's Yard, London SW1P 3NZ
Registrar of the Diocese of Canterbury, A. O. E. Davies, 9 The Precincts, Canterbury CT1 2EE

LONDON

131ST BISHOP
Rt. Revd and Rt. Hon. David M. Hope, D.Phil., *cons.* 1985, *trans.* 1991, *apptd* 1991; 8 Barton Street, London SW1P 3NE. *Signs* David Londin:

AREA BISHOPS
Edmonton, Rt. Revd Brian J. Masters, *cons.* 1982, *apptd* 1984; 1 Regent's Park Terrace, London NW1 7EE
Kensington, Rt. Revd John Hughes, PH.D., *cons.* 1987, *apptd* 1987; 19 Campden Hill Square, London W8 7JY
Stepney, Rt. Revd Richard C. Chartres; 63 Coborn Road, London E3 2DB
Willesden, Rt. Revd Graham G. Dow; 173 Willesden Lane, London NW6 7YN

BISHOP SUFFRAGAN
Fulham, Rt. Revd C. John Klyberg, *cons.* 1985, *apptd* 1985; 4 Cambridge Place, London W8 5PB

ASSISTANT BISHOPS
Rt. Revd Maurice Wood, DSC, *cons.* 1971, *apptd* 1985; Rt. Revd Michael Marshall, *cons.* 1975, *apptd* 1984

DEAN OF ST PAUL'S
Very Revd T. Eric Evans, *apptd* 1988

CANONS RESIDENTIARY
Ven. G. Cassidy, *apptd* 1987; C. J. Hill, *apptd* 1989; R. J. Halliburton, *apptd* 1990; M. J. Saward, *apptd* 1991
Registrar and Receiver of St Paul's, Brig. R. W. Acworth, CBE
Organist, J. Scott, FRCO, *apptd* 1990

ARCHDEACONS
Charing Cross, Rt. Revd C. J. Klyberg, *apptd* 1989
Hackney, Ven. C. Young, *apptd* 1992
Hampstead, Ven. R. A. W. Coogan, *apptd* 1985
London, Ven. G. Cassidy, *apptd* 1987
Middlesex, Ven. T. J. Raphael, *apptd* 1983
Northolt, Ven. M. Colclough, *apptd* 1992

Stipendiary Male Clergy, 568
Stipendiary Women Deacons, 49

Chancellor and Commissary of the Dean and Chapter, Miss S. Cameron, QC, *apptd* 1992
Registrar, D. W. Faull, OBE, 35 Great Peter Street, London SW1P 3LR

WESTMINSTER
The Collegiate Church of St Peter (A Royal Peculiar)

DEAN
Michael Clement Otway Mayne, *apptd* 1986

SUB DEAN AND ARCHDEACON
A. E. Harvey, *apptd* 1987

CANONS OF WESTMINSTER
A. E. Harvey, *apptd* 1982; D. C. Gray, *apptd* 1987;
C. D. Semper, *apptd* 1987; P. S. Bates, *apptd* 1990

Chapter Clerk and Receiver-General, Rear-Adm. K. A. Snow,
   CB, *apptd* 1987
Organist, M. Neary, FRCO, *apptd* 1988
Legal Secretary, C. L. Hodgetts, *apptd* 1973
Registrar, S. J. Holmes, MVO, *apptd* 1984, 20 Dean's Yard,
   London SW1P 3PA

WINCHESTER

95TH BISHOP
Rt. Revd Colin C. W. James, *cons.* 1973, *trans.* 1977 and
1985, *apptd* 1985; Wolvesey, Winchester SO23 9ND. *Signs*
Colin Winton:

BISHOPS SUFFRAGAN
Basingstoke, vacant; Bishop's Lodge, Skippetts Lane West,
   Basingstoke RG21 3HP
Southampton, Rt. Revd John F. Perry, *cons.* 1989, *apptd*
   1989; Ham House, The Crescent, Romsey SO51 7NG

ASSISTANT BISHOPS
Rt. Revd Hassan Dehqani-Tafti, *cons.* 1961, *apptd* 1982; Rt.
Revd Leslie Rees, *cons.* 1980, *apptd* 1986

DEAN
Very Revd Trevor R. Beeson, *apptd* 1987

Dean of Jersey (A Peculiar), Very Revd John Seaford, *apptd*
   1993
Dean of Guernsey (A Peculiar), Very Revd Jeffery Fenwick,
   apptd 1989

CANONS RESIDENTIARY
E. G. Job, *apptd* 1979; P. A. Britton, *apptd* 1980;
A. K. Walker, *apptd* 1987; Ven. A. F. Knight, *apptd* 1991
Organist, D. Hill, FRCO, *apptd* 1988

ARCHDEACONS
Basingstoke, Ven. A. F. Knight, *apptd* 1990
Winchester, Ven. A. G. Clarkson, *apptd* 1984

Stipendiary Male Clergy, 252
Stipendiary Women Deacons, 9

Chancellor, C. Clark, *apptd* 1993
Registrar and Legal Secretary, P. M. White, 19 St Peter
   Street, Winchester SO23 8BU

BATH AND WELLS

76TH BISHOP
Rt. Revd James L. Thompson, *cons.* 1978, *apptd* 1991; The
Palace, Wells BA5 2PD. *Signs* James Bath & Wells

BISHOP SUFFRAGAN
Taunton, Rt. Revd J. H. Richard Lewis, *cons.* 1992, *apptd*
1992; Sherford Farm House, Sherford, Taunton TA1 3RF

DEAN
Very Revd Richard Lewis, *apptd* 1990

CANONS RESIDENTIARY
C. E. Thomas, *apptd* 1983; P. de N. Lucas, *apptd* 1988;
G. O. Farran, *apptd* 1985
Organist, A. Nethsingha, FRCO, *apptd* 1993

ARCHDEACONS
Bath, Ven. J. E. Burgess, *apptd* 1975
Taunton, Ven. R. M. C. Frith, *apptd* 1992
Wells, Ven. R. Ackworth, *apptd* 1993

Stipendiary Male Clergy, 253
Stipendiary Women Deacons, 13

Chancellor, T. Briden, *apptd* 1993
Registrar, Secretary and Chapter Clerk, T. Berry, Diocesan
   Registry, Market Place, Wells BA5 2RE

BIRMINGHAM

7TH BISHOP
Rt. Revd Mark Santer, *cons.* 1981, *apptd* 1987; Bishop's
Croft, Harborne, Birmingham B17 0BG. *Signs* Mark
Birmingham

BISHOP SUFFRAGAN
Aston, Rt. Revd John Austin, *cons.* 1992, *apptd* 1992;
Strensham House, 8 Strensham Hill, Moseley,
Birmingham B13 8AG

STIPENDIARY ASSISTANT BISHOP
Rt. Revd Michael Whinney, *cons.* 1982, *apptd* 1989

ASSISTANT BISHOP
Rt. Revd Anthony Dumper, *cons.* 1977, *apptd* 1993

PROVOST
Very Revd Peter A. Berry, *apptd* 1986

CANONS RESIDENTIARY
Ven. C. J. G. Barton, *apptd* 1990; A. H. F. Luff, *apptd* 1992
Organist, M. Huxley, FRCO, *apptd* 1986

ARCHDEACONS
Aston, Ven. C. J. G. Barton, *apptd* 1990
Birmingham, Ven. J. F. Duncan, *apptd* 1985
Coleshill, Ven. J. L. Cooper, *apptd* 1990

Stipendiary Male Clergy, 210
Stipendiary Women Deacons, 15

Chancellor, His Honour Judge Aglionby, *apptd* 1970
Registrar and Legal Secretary, H. Carslake, St Philip's
   House, St Philip's Place, Birmingham B3 2PP

BRISTOL

54TH BISHOP
Rt. Revd Barry Rogerson, *cons.* 1979, *apptd* 1985; Bishop's
House, Clifton Hill, Bristol BS8 1BW. *Signs* Barry Bristol

BISHOP SUFFRAGAN
Malmesbury, Rt. Revd Peter J. Firth, *cons.* 1983, *apptd* 1983;
7 Ivywell Road, Bristol BS9 1NX

DEAN
Very Revd Dr A. Wesley Carr, *apptd* 1987

CANONS RESIDENTIARY
J. Rogan, *apptd* 1983; A. L. J. Redfern, *apptd* 1987;
J. L. Simpson, *apptd* 1989; P. F. Johnson, *apptd* 1990

Organist, C. Brayne, *apptd* 1990

ARCHDEACONS
Bristol, Ven. D. J. Banfield, *apptd* 1990
Swindon, Ven. M. Middleton, *apptd* 1992

Stipendiary Male Clergy, 162
Stipendiary Women Deacons, 19

Chancellor, Sir David Calcutt, QC, *apptd* 1971
Registrar and Secretary, T. R. Urquhart, 30 Queen Charlotte
Street, Bristol BS13 8HE

CHELMSFORD

7TH BISHOP
Rt. Revd John Waine, *cons.* 1975, *apptd* 1986; Bishopscourt,
Margaretting, Ingatestone CM4 0HD. *Signs* John
Chelmsford

BISHOPS SUFFRAGAN
Barking, Rt. Revd Roger F. Sainsbury, *cons.* 1991, *apptd*
1991; 110 Capel Road, Forest Gate, London E7 0JS
Bradwell, Rt. Revd Laurence Green, *cons.* 1993, *apptd* 1993;
The Vicarage, Orsett Road, Horndon-on-the-Hill,
Stanford-le-Hope, Essex SS17 8NS
Colchester, Rt. Revd Michael E. Vickers, *cons.* 1988, *apptd*
1988; 1 Fitzwalter Road, Lexden, Colchester CO3 3SS

PROVOST
Very Revd John H. Moses, PH.D., *apptd* 1982

CANONS RESIDENTIARY
P. G. Brett, *apptd* 1985; P. G. Southwell-Sander, *apptd* 1985;
T. Thompson, *apptd* 1988; B. P. Thompson, *apptd* 1988

Organist, Dr G. Elliott, PH.D., FRCO, *apptd* 1981

ARCHDEACONS
Colchester, Ven. E. C. F. Stroud, *apptd* 1983
Harlow, Ven. M. J. Fox, *apptd* 1993
Southend, Ven. D. Jennings, *apptd* 1992
West Ham, Ven. T. J. Stevens, *apptd* 1991

Stipendiary Male Clergy, 496
Stipendiary Women Deacons, 27

Chancellor, Miss S. M. Cameron, QC, *apptd* 1970
Diocesan Registrar, B. Hood, 53 New Street, Chelmsford
CM1 1NG

CHICHESTER

102ND BISHOP
Rt. Revd Eric W. Kemp, DD, *cons.* 1974, *apptd* 1974; The
Palace, Chichester PO19 1PY. *Signs* Eric Cicestr:

BISHOPS SUFFRAGAN
Horsham, Rt. Revd John W. Hind, *cons.* 1991, *apptd* 1991;
Bishop's Lodge, Worth, nr. Crawley RH10 4RT
Lewes, Rt. Revd Ian P. M. Cundy, *cons.* 1992, *apptd* 1992;
Beacon House, Berwick, Polegate BN26 6ST

ASSISTANT BISHOPS
Rt. Revd William Hunt, *cons.* 1955, *apptd* 1980; Rt. Revd
Mark Green, *cons.* 1972, *apptd* 1982; Rt. Revd Simon

Phipps, *cons.* 1968, *apptd* 1987; Rt. Revd Edward Knapp-
Fisher, *cons.* 1960, *apptd* 1987; Rt. Revd Morris Maddocks,
cons. 1972, *apptd* 1987; Rt Revd Christopher Luxmoore,
cons. 1984, *apptd* 1991; Rt. Revd Michael Marshall, *cons.*
1975, *apptd* 1992

DEAN
Very Revd John D. Treadgold, LVO, *apptd* 1989

CANONS RESIDENTIARY
R. T. Greenacre, *apptd* 1975; J. F. Hester, *apptd* 1985

Organist, A. J. Thurlow, FRCO, *apptd* 1980

ARCHDEACONS
Chichester, Ven. M. Brotherton, *apptd* 1991
Horsham, Ven. W. C. L. Filby, *apptd* 1983
Lewes and Hastings, Ven. H. Glaisyer, *apptd* 1991

Stipendiary Male Clergy, 362
Stipendiary Women Deacons, 5

Chancellor, His Honour Judge Q. T. Edwards, QC, *apptd*
1978
Legal Secretary to the Bishop, and Diocesan Registrar,
C. L. Hodgetts, 5 East Pallant, Chichester PO19 1TS

COVENTRY

7TH BISHOP
Rt. Revd Simon Barrington-Ward, *cons.* 1985, *apptd* 1985;
The Bishop's House, 23 Davenport Road, Coventry
CV5 6PW. *Signs* Simon Coventry

BISHOP SUFFRAGAN
Warwick, Rt. Revd George C. Handford, *cons.* 1990, *apptd*
1990; 139 Kenilworth Road, Coventry CV4 7AF

ASSISTANT BISHOPS
Rt. Revd John Daly, *cons.* 1935, *apptd* 1968; Rt. Revd
Vernon Nicholls, *cons.* 1974, *apptd* 1984

PROVOST
Very Revd John F. Petty, *apptd* 1987

CANONS RESIDENTIARY
P. Oestreicher, *apptd* 1986; M. Sadgrove, *apptd* 1987;
G. T. Hughes, *apptd* 1989

Organist, A. P. Leddington Wright (from March 1994)

ARCHDEACONS
Coventry, Ven. H. I. L. Russell, *apptd* 1989
Warwick, Ven. M. J. J. Paget-Wilkes, *apptd* 1990

Stipendiary Male Clergy, 186
Stipendiary Women Deacons, 12

Chancellor, W. M. Gage, *apptd* 1980
Registrar, D. J. Dumbleton, 8 The Quadrant, Coventry
CV1 2EL

DERBY

5TH BISHOP
Rt. Revd Peter S. Dawes, *cons.* 1988, *apptd* 1988; The
Bishop's House, 6 King Street, Duffield, Derby
DE56 4EU. *Signs* Peter Derby

BISHOP SUFFRAGAN
Repton, Rt. Revd F. Henry A. Richmond, *cons.* 1986, *apptd*
1986; Repton House, Lea, Matlock DE4 1JP

PROVOST
Very Revd Benjamin H. Lewers, *apptd* 1981

CANONS RESIDENTIARY
G. A. Chesterman, *apptd* 1989; Ven. I. Gatford, *apptd* 1992;
G. O. Marshall, *apptd* 1992; R. M. Parsons, *apptd* 1993
Organist, P. Gould, *apptd* 1982

ARCHDEACONS
Chesterfield, Ven. G. R. Phizackerley, *apptd* 1978
Derby, Ven. I. Gatford, *apptd* 1992

Stipendiary Male Clergy, 201
Stipendiary Women Deacons, 12

Chancellor, J. W. M. Bullimore, *apptd* 1981
Registrar, J. S. Battie, Derby Church House, Full Street,
    Derby DEI 3DR

ELY

67TH BISHOP
Rt. Revd Stephen W. Sykes, *cons.* 1990, *apptd* 1990; The
    Bishop's House, Ely CB7 4DW. *Signs* Stephen Ely

BISHOP SUFFRAGAN
Huntingdon, Rt. Revd William G. Roe, D.Phil., *cons.* 1980,
    apptd 1980; 14 Lynn Road, Ely, Cambs. CB6 IDA

DEAN
Very Revd Michael Higgins, *apptd* 1991

CANONS RESIDENTIARY
D. J. Green, *apptd* 1980; J. Rone, *apptd* 1989
Organist, P. Trepte, FRCO, *apptd* 1991

ARCHDEACONS
Ely, Ven. J. Watson, *apptd* 1993
Huntingdon, Ven. R. K. Sledge, *apptd* 1978
Wisbech, Ven. D. Fleming, *apptd* 1984

Stipendiary Male Clergy, 170
Stipendiary Women Deacons, 7

Chancellor, W. Gage, QC
Registrar, W. H. Godfrey, 18 The Broadway, St Ives,
    Huntingdon PE17 4BS
Joint Registrar (Legal Secretary), P. F. B. Beesley, 1 The
    Sanctuary, London SWIP 3JT

EXETER

69TH BISHOP
Rt. Revd G. Hewlett Thompson, *cons.* 1974, *apptd* 1985;
    The Palace, Exeter EXI IHY. *Signs* Hewlett Exon:

BISHOPS SUFFRAGAN
Crediton, Rt. Revd Peter E. Coleman, *cons.* 1984, *apptd*
    1984; 10 The Close, Exeter EXI IEZ
Plymouth, Rt. Revd Richard S. Hawkins, *cons.* 1988, *apptd*
    1988; 31 Riverside Walk, Tamerton Foliot, Plymouth PL5
    4AQ

ASSISTANT BISHOPS
Rt. Revd Ronald Goodchild, *cons.* 1964, *apptd* 1983; Rt.
    Revd Philip Pasterfield, *cons.* 1974, *apptd* 1984; Rt. Revd
    Richard Cartwright, *cons.* 1972, *apptd* 1988; Rt. Revd Colin
    Docker, *cons.* 1975, *apptd* 1991

DEAN
Very Revd Richard Montague Stephens Eyre, *apptd* 1981

CANONS RESIDENTIARY
A. C. Mawson, *apptd* 1979; Ven. J. Richards, *apptd* 1981;
K. C. Parry, *apptd* 1991
Organist, L. A. Nethsingha, FRCO, *apptd* 1973

ARCHDEACONS
Barnstaple, Ven. T. Lloyd, *apptd* 1989
Exeter, Ven. J. Richards, *apptd* 1981
Plymouth, Ven. R. G. Ellis, *apptd* 1982
Totnes, Ven. A. F. Tremlett, *apptd* 1988

Stipendiary Male Clergy, 280
Stipendiary Women Deacons, 10

Chancellor, Sir David Calcutt, QC, *apptd* 1971
Registrar, R. K. Wheeler, 18 Cathedral Yard, Exeter
    EXI IHE

GIBRALTAR IN EUROPE

BISHOP
Vacant; 5A Gregory Place, London W8 4NG. *Signs* –
    Gibraltar

BISHOP SUFFRAGAN
In Europe, Rt. Revd Edward Holland, *apptd* 1986

AUXILIARY BISHOPS
Rt. Revd E. M. H. Capper, OBE, *cons.* 1967, *apptd* 1973; Rt.
    Revd D. de Pina Cabral, *cons.* 1967, *apptd* 1976; Rt. Revd
    A. W. M. Weeks, CB, *cons.* 1977, *apptd* 1988; Rt. Revd E.
    Devenport, *apptd* 1992

Vicar-General, Revd W. G. Reid
Bishop's Commissaries, Canon L. Tyzack; Canon
    J. D. Beckwith; Canon D. H. Palmer; A. M. Apostol
Dean, Cathedral Church of the Holy Trinity, Gibraltar, Very
    Revd B. W. Horlock, OBE
Chancellor, Pro-Cathedral of St Paul, Valletta, Malta, Canon
    P. Cousins
*Chancellor, Pro-Cathedral of the Holy Trinity, Brussels,
    Belgium*, vacant

ARCHDEACONS
Aegean, Ven. G. B. Evans
North-West Europe, Ven. G. G. Allen
North France, Ven. M. B. Lea
Gibraltar, Rt. Revd D. de Pina Cabral
Italy, Rt. Revd E. Devenport
Riviera, Ven. J. Livingstone
Scandinavia, Ven. G. A. C. Brown
Switzerland, Ven. P. J. Hawker

Chancellor, Sir David Calcutt, QC
Diocesan Registrar and Legal Secretary, J. G. Underwood,
    37A Walbrook, London EC4 8BS

GLOUCESTER

39TH BISHOP
Rt. Revd David Bentley, *cons.* 1986, *apptd* 1993;
    Bishopscourt, Gloucester GLI 2BQ. *Signs* David Gloucester

BISHOP SUFFRAGAN
Tewkesbury, Rt. Revd G. D. Jeremy Walsh, *cons.* 1986,
    apptd 1986; Green Acre, Hempsted, Gloucester GL2 6LG

DEAN
Very Revd Kenneth N. Jennings, *apptd* 1982

CANONS RESIDENTIARY
R. D. M. Grey, *apptd* 1982; R. P. Greenwood, *apptd* 1986;
N. Chatfield, *apptd* 1992

Organist, Dr J. D. Sanders, FRCO, *apptd* 1967

ARCHDEACONS
Cheltenham, Ven. J. A. Lewis, *apptd* 1988
Gloucester, Ven. C. J. H. Wagstaff, *apptd* 1982

Stipendiary Male Clergy, 185
Stipendiary Women Deacons, 12

Chancellor and Vicar-General, Ms D. J. Rogers, *apptd* 1990
Registrar, C. G. Peak, 34 Brunswick Road, Gloucester
  GL1 1JJ

GUILDFORD

7TH BISHOP
Rt. Revd Michael E. Adie, *cons.* 1983, *apptd* 1983; Willow
  Grange, Woking Road, Guildford GU4 7QS. *Signs* Michael
  Guildford

BISHOP SUFFRAGAN
Dorking, Rt. Revd David P. Wilcox, *cons.* 1986, *apptd* 1986;
  13 Pilgrims Way, Guildford GU4 8AD

DEAN
Very Revd Alexander G. Wedderspoon, *apptd* 1987

CANONS RESIDENTIARY
F. S. Telfer, *apptd* 1973; P. G. Croft, *apptd* 1983;
R. D. Fenwick, *apptd* 1990

Organist, A. Millington, FRCO, *apptd* 1982

ARCHDEACONS
Dorking, Ven. C.W. Herbert, *apptd* 1990
Surrey, Ven. J. S. Went, *apptd* 1989

Stipendiary Male Clergy, 194
Stipendiary Women Deacons, 15

Chancellor, His Hon. Judge Goodman
Legal Secretary and Registrar, P. F. B. Beesley, 1 The
  Sanctuary, London SW1P 3JT

HEREFORD

103RD BISHOP
Rt. Revd John Oliver (until Dec. 1993), *cons.* 1990, *apptd*
  1990; The Palace, Hereford HR4 9BN. *Signs* John
  Hereford

BISHOP SUFFRAGAN
Ludlow, Rt. Revd Ian M. Griggs, *cons.* 1987, *apptd* 1987;
  Bishop's House, Halford, Craven Arms, Shropshire SY7
  9BT

DEAN
Very Revd Robert A. Willis, *apptd* 1992

CANONS RESIDENTIARY
P. Iles, *apptd* 1983; J. Tiller, *apptd* 1984

Organist, Dr R. Massey, FRCO, *apptd* 1974

ARCHDEACONS
Hereford, Ven. L. G. Moss, *apptd* 1992
Ludlow, Ven. J. C. Saxbee, *apptd* 1992

Stipendiary Male Clergy, 129
Stipendiary Women Deacons, 9

Chancellor, J. M. Henty
Joint Registrars, V. T. Jordan, 44 Bridge Street, Hereford;
  P. Beesley, 1 The Sanctuary, London SW1P 3JT

LEICESTER

5TH BISHOP
Rt. Revd Thomas F. Butler, PH.D., *cons.* 1985, *apptd* 1991;
  Bishop's Lodge, 10 Springfield Road, Leicester LE2 3BD.
  Signs Thomas Leicester

STIPENDIARY ASSISTANT BISHOP
Rt. Revd Godfrey Ashby, *cons.* 1980, *apptd* 1988

ASSISTANT BISHOP
Rt. Revd John Mort, CBE, *cons.* 1952, *apptd* 1972

PROVOST
Very Revd Derek Hole, *apptd* 1992

CANONS RESIDENTIARY
M. T. H. Banks, *apptd* 1988; M. Wilson, *apptd* 1988

Organist, P. G. White, FRCO, *apptd* 1968

ARCHDEACONS
Leicester, Ven. R. D. Silk, *apptd* 1980
Loughborough, Ven. I. Stanes, *apptd* 1992

Stipendiary Male Clergy, 180
Stipendiary Women Deacons, 12

Chancellor, N. Seed, *apptd* 1989
Registrars, P. C. E. Morris, 35 Great Peter Street, London
  SW1P 3LR; R. H. Bloor, 23 Friar Lane, Leicester LE1 5QQ

LICHFIELD

97TH BISHOP
Rt. Revd Keith N. Sutton, *cons.* 1978, *apptd* 1984; Bishop's
  House, The Close, Lichfield WS13 7LG. *Signs* Keith
  Lichfield

BISHOPS SUFFRAGAN
Shrewsbury, Rt. Revd John D. Davies, *cons.* 1987, *apptd*
  1987; Athlone House, 68 London Road, Shrewsbury SY2
  6PG
Stafford, Rt. Revd Michael C. Scott-Joynt, *cons.* 1987, *apptd*
  1987; Ash Garth, Broughton Crescent, Barlaston ST12
  9DD
Wolverhampton, Rt. Revd Michael G. Bourke, *cons.* 1993,
  apptd 1993; 61 Richmond Road, Wolverhampton WV3
  9JH

ASSISTANT BISHOPS
Rt. Revd Ronald O. Bowlby, *cons.* 1973, *apptd* 1991; Rt.
  Revd Kenneth C. Oram, *cons.* 1974, *apptd* 1987

DEAN
Very Revd Tom Wright, *apptd* 1993 (from Dec. 1993)

CANONS RESIDENTIARY
Ven. R. B. Ninis, *apptd* 1974; A. N. Barnard, *apptd* 1977;
W. J. Turner, *apptd* 1983; J. Howe, *apptd* 1988

Organist, A. Lumsden, *apptd* 1992

ARCHDEACONS
Lichfield, Ven. R. B. Ninis, *apptd* 1974
Salop, Ven. G. Frost, *apptd* 1987

Stoke-on-Trent, Ven. D. Ede, *apptd* 1989

Stipendiary Male Clergy, 406
Stipendiary Women Deacons, 41

Chancellor, His Honour Judge Shand
Diocesan Registrar, J. P. Thorneycroft, St Mary's House,
The Close, Lichfield WS13 7LD

LINCOLN

70TH BISHOP
Rt. Revd Robert M. Hardy, *cons.* 1980, *apptd* 1987;
Bishop's House, Eastgate, Lincoln LN2 1QQ. *Signs* Robert
Lincoln

BISHOPS SUFFRAGAN
Grantham, Rt. Revd William Ind, *cons.* 1987, *apptd* 1987;
Fairacre, Barrowby High Road, Grantham NG31 8NP
Grimsby, Rt. Revd David Tustin, *cons.* 1979, *apptd* 1979;
Bishop's House, Church Lane, Irby-upon-Humber,
Grimsby DN37 7JR

ASSISTANT BISHOPS
Rt. Revd Gerald Colin, *cons.* 1966, *apptd* 1979; Rt. Revd
Harold Darby, *cons.* 1975, *apptd* 1989

DEAN
Very Revd Brandon D. Jackson, *apptd* 1989

CANONS RESIDENTIARY
B. R. Davis, *apptd* 1977; A. J. Stokes, *apptd* 1992

Organist, C. S. Walsh, FRCO, *apptd* 1988

ARCHDEACONS
Lincoln, Ven. M. P. Brackenbury, *apptd* 1988
Lindsey, Ven. J. H. C. Laurence, *apptd* 1985
Stow, Ven. R. J. Wells, *apptd* 1989

Stipendiary Male Clergy, 244
Stipendiary Women Deacons, 21

Chancellor, His Honour Judge Goodman, *apptd* 1971
Registrar and Legal Secretary, D. M. Wellman, 28 West
Parade, Lincoln LN1 1JT

NORWICH

70TH BISHOP
Rt. Revd Peter J. Nott, *cons.* 1977, *apptd* 1985; Bishop's
House, Norwich, NR3 1SB. *Signs* Peter Norvic:

BISHOPS SUFFRAGAN
Lynn, vacant; The Old Vic, Castle Acre, King's Lynn
PE32 2AA
Thetford, Rt. Revd Hugo F. de Waal, *cons.* 1992, *apptd*
1992; Rectory Meadow, Bramerton, Norwich NR14 7DW

DEAN
Very Revd John P. Burbridge, *apptd* 1983

CANONS RESIDENTIARY
M. S. McLean, *apptd* 1986; M. F. Perham, *apptd* 1992

Organist, M. B. Nicholas, FRCO, *apptd* 1971

ARCHDEACONS
Lynn, Ven. A. C. Foottit, *apptd* 1987
Norfolk, Ven. A. M. Handley, *apptd* 1993
Norwich, vacant

Stipendiary Male Clergy, 237
Stipendiary Women Deacons, 10

Chancellor, His Honour J. H. Ellison, VRD, *apptd* 1955
Registrar and Secretary, J. W. F. Herring, Francis House,
3–7 Redwell Street, Norwich NR2 4TJ

OXFORD

41ST BISHOP
Rt. Revd Richard D. Harries, *cons.* 1987, *apptd* 1987;
Diocesan Church House, North Hinksey, Oxford
OX2 0NB. *Signs* Richard Oxon:

AREA BISHOPS
Buckingham, Rt. Revd Simon H. Burrows, *cons.* 1974, *apptd*
1974; Sheridan, Grimms Hill, Great Missenden HP16 9BD
Dorchester, Rt. Revd Anthony J. Russell, *cons.* 1988, *apptd*
1988; Holmby House, Sibford Ferris, Banbury, Oxon.
OX15 5RG
Reading, Rt. Revd John F. E. Bone, *cons.* 1989, *apptd* 1989;
Greenbanks, Old Bath Road, Sonning, Reading RG4 0SY

ASSISTANT BISHOPS
Rt. Revd Kenneth Cragg, DD, *cons.* 1970, *apptd* 1982; Rt.
Revd Leonard Ashton, CB, *cons.* 1974, *apptd* 1984; Rt. Revd
Richard Watson, *cons.* 1970, *apptd* 1988; Rt. Revd Peter
Walker, *cons.* 1972, *apptd* 1990; Rt. Revd Maurice Wood,
cons. 1971, *apptd* 1991; Rt. Revd Stephen Verney, *cons.*
1977, *apptd* 1991

DEAN OF CHRIST CHURCH
Very Revd John H. Drury, *apptd* 1991

CANONS RESIDENTIARY
Ven. F. V. Weston, *apptd* 1982; O. M. T. O'Donovan,
D.Phil., *apptd* 1982; J. M. Pierce, *apptd* 1987; J. S. K. Ward,
apptd 1991; Rt. Revd A. R. M. Gordon, *apptd* 1991

Organist, S. Darlington, FRCO, *apptd* 1985

ARCHDEACONS
Berkshire, Ven. M. A. Hill, *apptd* 1992
Buckingham, Ven. J. A. Morrison, *apptd* 1989
Oxford, Ven. F. V. Weston, *apptd* 1982

Stipendiary Male Clergy, 449
Stipendiary Women Deacons, 36

Chancellor, P. T. S. Boydell, QC, *apptd* 1958
Registrar and Legal Secretary, Dr F. E. Robson, OBE,
16 Beaumont Street, Oxford OX1 2LZ

WINDSOR
*The Queen's Free Chapel of St George within Her Castle of
Windsor (A Royal Peculiar)*

DEAN
Very Revd Patrick R. Mitchell, FSA, *apptd* 1989

CANONS RESIDENTIARY
J. A. White, *apptd* 1982; D. M. Stanesby, PH.D., *apptd* 1985;
A. A. Coldwells, *apptd* 1987; M. A. Moxon, *apptd* 1990

Chapter Clerk, Lt.-Col. N. J. Newman, *apptd* 1990
Organist, J. Rees-Williams, FRCO, *apptd* 1991

PETERBOROUGH

36TH BISHOP
Rt. Revd William J. Westwood, *cons.* 1975, *apptd* 1984; The Palace, Peterborough PE1 1YA. *Signs* William Petriburg:

BISHOP SUFFRAGAN
Brixworth, Rt. Revd Paul E. Barber, *cons.* 1989, *apptd* 1989; 4 The Avenue, Dallington, Northampton NN1 4RZ

DEAN
Very Revd Michael Bunker, *apptd* 1992

CANONS RESIDENTIARY
T. R. Christie, *apptd* 1980; J. Higham, *apptd* 1983; T. Willmott, *apptd* 1989

Organist, C. S. Gower, FRCO, *apptd* 1977

ARCHDEACONS
Northampton, Ven. M. R. Chapman, *apptd* 1991
Oakham, Ven. B. Fernyhough, *apptd* 1977

Stipendiary Male Clergy, 186
Stipendiary Women Deacons, 9

Chancellor, T. A. C. Coningsby, QC, *apptd* 1989
Registrar and Legal Secretary, R. Hemingray, 4 Holywell Way, Longthorpe, Peterborough PE3 6SS

PORTSMOUTH

7TH BISHOP
Rt. Revd Timothy J. Bavin, *cons.* 1974, *apptd* 1985; Bishopswood, Fareham, Hants. PO14 1NT. *Signs* Timothy Portsmouth

PROVOST
Vacant

CANONS RESIDENTIARY
M. D. Doe, *apptd* 1989; C. J. Bradley, *apptd* 1990; D. T. Isaac, *apptd* 1990; Jane Hedges, *apptd* 1993

Organist, A. Lucas, FRCO, *apptd* 1990

ARCHDEACONS
Isle of Wight, Ven. A. H. M. Turner, *apptd* 1986
Portsmouth, Ven. G. P. Knowles, *apptd* 1993

Stipendiary Male Clergy, 138
Stipendiary Women Deacons, 9

Chancellor, His Honour Judge Aglionby, *apptd* 1978
Registrar, Miss H. A. G. Tyler, 132 High Street, Portsmouth PO1 2HR

ROCHESTER

105TH BISHOP
Rt. Revd Michael A. Turnbull, *cons.* 1988, *apptd* 1988; Bishopscourt, Rochester ME1 1TS. *Signs* Michael Roffen:

BISHOP SUFFRAGAN
Tonbridge, Rt. Revd Brian A. Smith, *cons.* 1993, *apptd* 1993; Bishop's Lodge, St Botolph's Road, Sevenoaks TN13 3AG

ASSISTANT BISHOP
Rt. Revd Colin Buchanan, *cons.* 1985, *apptd* 1989

DEAN
Very Revd Edward F. Shotter, *apptd* 1990

CANONS RESIDENTIARY
E. R. Turner, *apptd* 1981; R. J. R. Lea, *apptd* 1988; J. Armson, *apptd* 1989; N. Warren, *apptd* 1989

Organist, B. Ferguson, FRCO, *apptd* 1977

ARCHDEACONS
Bromley, Ven. E. R. Francis, *apptd* 1979
Rochester, Ven. N. L. Warren, *apptd* 1989
Tonbridge, Ven. R. J. Mason, *apptd* 1977

Stipendiary Male Clergy, 226
Stipendiary Women Deacons, 20

Chancellor, His Honour Judge M. B. Goodman, *apptd* 1971
Registrar, O. R. Woodfield, The Precinct, Rochester ME1 1SZ

ST ALBANS

8TH BISHOP
Rt. Revd John B. Taylor, *cons.* 1980, *apptd* 1980; Abbey Gate House, St Albans AL3 4HD. *Signs* John St Albans

BISHOPS SUFFRAGAN
Bedford, vacant; 168 Kimbolton Road, Bedford MK41 8DN
Hertford, Rt. Revd Robin J. N. Smith, *cons.* 1990, *apptd* 1990; Hertford House, Abbey Mill Lane, St Albans AL3 4HE

ASSISTANT BISHOPS
Rt. Revd The Lord Runcie, *cons.* 1970, *apptd* 1991; Rt. Revd David J. Farmbrough, *cons.* 1981, *apptd* 1994 (from 1994)

DEAN
Very Revd Christopher Lewis, *apptd* 1993

CANONS RESIDENTIARY
C. B. Slee, *apptd* 1982; C. Garner, *apptd* 1984; G. R. S. Ritson, *apptd* 1987; M. Sansom, *apptd* 1988

Organist, Dr B. Rose, *apptd* 1988

ARCHDEACONS
Bedford, vacant
St Albans, Ven. P. B. Davies, *apptd* 1987

Stipendiary Male Clergy, 323
Stipendiary Women Deacons, 26

Chancellor, His Honour Judge Bursell, QC, *apptd* 1992
Registrar and Legal Secretary, D. N. Cheetham, Holywell Lodge, 41 Holywell Hill, St Albans AL1 1HE

ST EDMUNDSBURY AND IPSWICH

8TH BISHOP
Rt. Revd John Dennis, *cons.* 1979, *apptd* 1986; Bishop's House, 4 Park Road, Ipswich IP1 3ST. *Signs* John St Edmundsbury and Ipswich

BISHOP SUFFRAGAN
Dunwich, Rt. Revd Jonathan S. Bailey, *cons.* 1992, *apptd* 1992; The Old Vicarage, Stowupland, Stowmarket IP14 4BQ

PROVOST
Very Revd Raymond Furnell, *apptd* 1981

CANONS RESIDENTIARY
A. M. Shaw, *apptd* 1989; M. E. Mingins, *apptd* 1993

ARCHDEACONS
Ipswich, Ven. T. A. Gibson, *apptd* 1987
Sudbury, Ven. R. Garrard, *apptd* 1992
Suffolk, Ven. N. Robinson, *apptd* 1987

Stipendiary Male Clergy, 192
Stipendiary Women Deacons, 11

Chancellor, His Honour Sir John Blofeld, QC, *apptd* 1974
Registrar, J. D. Mitson, 22–28 Museum Street, Ipswich
IP1 1JA

SALISBURY

77TH BISHOP
Rt. Revd David S. Stancliffe, *cons.* 1993, *apptd* 1993 (to be
enthroned early 1994); South Canonry, The Close,
Salisbury SP1 2ER. *Signs* David Sarum

BISHOPS SUFFRAGAN
Ramsbury, Rt. Revd Peter St G. Vaughan, *cons.* 1989, *apptd*
1989; Bishop's House, Urchfont, Devizes, Wilts. SN10 4QH
Sherborne, Rt. Revd John D. G. Kirkham, *cons.* 1976, *apptd*
1976; Little Bailie, Sturminster Marshall, Wimborne BH21
4AD

ASSISTANT BISHOP
Rt. Revd John Cavell, *cons.* 1972, *apptd* 1988

DEAN
Very Revd the Hon. Hugh G. Dickinson, *apptd* 1986

CANONS RESIDENTIARY
D. J. C. Davies, *apptd* 1985; J. R. Stewart, *apptd* 1990;
D. M. K. Durston, *apptd* 1992

Organist, R. G. Seal, FRCO, *apptd* 1968

ARCHDEACONS
Dorset, Ven. G. E. Walton, *apptd* 1982
Sarum, Ven. B. J. Hopkinson, *apptd* 1986
Sherborne, Ven. P. C. Wheatley, *apptd* 1991
Wilts, Ven. B. J. Smith, *apptd* 1980

Stipendiary Male Clergy, 260
Stipendiary Women Deacons, 11

Chancellor of the Diocese, His Honour J. H. Ellison, VRD,
apptd 1955
Registrar and Legal Secretary, F. M. Broadbent, 42 Castle
Street, Salisbury SP1 3TX

SOUTHWARK

8TH BISHOP
Rt. Revd Robert K. Williamson, *cons.* 1984, *trans.* 1991,
apptd 1991; Bishop's House, 38 Tooting Bec Gardens,
London SW16 1QZ. *Signs* Robert Southwark

BISHOPS SUFFRAGAN
Croydon, Rt. Revd Wilfred D. Wood, DD, *cons.* 1985, *apptd*
1985; St Matthew's House, George Street, Croydon CRO
1PE
Kingston upon Thames, Rt Revd Martin Wharton, *cons.*
1992, *apptd* 1992; *Office*, Whitelands College, West Hill,
London SW15 3SN

Woolwich, Rt. Revd Albert P. Hall, *cons.* 1984, *apptd* 1984;
8B Hilly Fields Crescent, London SE4 1QA

ASSISTANT BISHOPS
Rt. Revd Edmund Capper, OBE, *cons.* 1967, *apptd* 1981; Rt.
Revd John Hughes, *cons.* 1956, *apptd* 1986; Rt. Revd Hugh
Montefiore, *cons.* 1970, *apptd* 1987; Rt. Revd Simon Phipps,
cons. 1976, *apptd* 1987; Rt. Revd Michael Nazir-Ali, *cons.*
1984, *apptd* 1990

PROVOST
Very Revd David L. Edwards, *apptd* 1983

CANON RESIDENTIARY
D. Painter, *apptd* 1991

Organist, P. Wright, FRCO, *apptd* 1989

ARCHDEACONS
Croydon, vacant
Lambeth, Ven. C. R. B. Bird, *apptd* 1988
Lewisham, Ven. G. Kuhrt, *apptd* 1989
Reigate, Ven. P. B. Coombs, *apptd* 1988
Southwark, Ven. D. L. Bartles-Smith, *apptd* 1985
Wandsworth, Ven. D. Gerrard, *apptd* 1989

Stipendiary Male Clergy, 404
Stipendiary Women Deacons, 34

Chancellor, R. M. K. Gray, QC, *apptd* 1990
Joint Registrars, D. W. Faull, OBE, and P. Morris, 35 Great
Peter Street, London SW1P 3LR

TRURO

13TH BISHOP
Rt. Revd Michael T. Ball, *cons.* 1980, *apptd* 1990; Lis
Escop, Truro TR3 6QQ. *Signs* Michael Truro

BISHOP SUFFRAGAN
St Germans, Rt. Revd Graham R. James, *cons.* 1993, *apptd*
1993; 32 Falmouth Road, Truro TR1 2HX

ASSISTANT BISHOP
Rt. Revd Conrad Meyer, *cons.* 1979, *apptd* 1991

DEAN
Very Revd David J. Shearlock, *apptd* 1982

CANONS RESIDENTIARY
Ven. R. L. Ravenscroft, *apptd* 1988; R. O. Osborne, *apptd*
1988

Organist, D. J. Briggs, FRCO, *apptd* 1989

ARCHDEACONS
Cornwall, Ven. R. L. Ravenscroft, *apptd* 1988
Bodmin, Ven. R. D. C. Whiteman, *apptd* 1989

Stipendiary Male Clergy, 149
Stipendiary Women Deacons, 2

Chancellor, P. T. S. Boydell, QC, *apptd* 1957
Registrar and Secretary, M. J. Follett, Messrs Follett
Stock, Riverside Business Centre, Malpas Road,
Truro TR1 1QH

WORCESTER

111TH BISHOP
Rt. Revd Philip H. E. Goodrich, *cons.* 1973, *apptd* 1982;
The Bishop's House, Hartlebury Castle, Kidderminster
DY11 7XX. *Signs* Philip Worcester

BISHOP SUFFRAGAN
Dudley, Rt. Revd Dr Rupert Hoare, *cons.* 1993, *apptd* 1993;
The Bishop's House, Brooklands, Halesowen Road,
Cradley Heath B64 7JF

ASSISTANT BISHOPS
Rt. Revd John Maund, CBE, MC, *cons.* 1950, *apptd* 1984; Rt.
Revd Kenneth Woollcombe, *cons.* 1971, *apptd* 1989; Rt.
Revd George Briggs, *cons.* 1973, *apptd* 1990; Rt. Revd
Derek Bond, *cons.* 1976, *apptd* 1992

DEAN
Very Revd Robert M. C. Jeffery, *apptd* 1987

CANONS RESIDENTIARY
Ven. F. Bentley, *apptd* 1984; D. G. Thomas, *apptd* 1987;
I. M. MacKenzie, *apptd* 1989
Organist, Dr D. Hunt, FRCO, *apptd* 1975

ARCHDEACONS
Dudley, Ven. J. Gathercole, *apptd* 1987
Worcester, Ven. F. Bentley, *apptd* 1984

Stipendiary Male Clergy, 150
Stipendiary Women Deacons, 14

Chancellor, P. T. S. Boydell, QC, *apptd* 1959
Registrar, M. Huskinson, Diocesan Registry, 8 Sansome
Walk, Worcester WR1 1LW

Province of York

YORK

95TH ARCHBISHOP AND PRIMATE OF ENGLAND
Most Revd and Rt. Hon. John S. Habgood, PH.D., *cons.*
1973, *trans.* 1983, *apptd* 1983; Bishopthorpe, York
YO2 1QE. *Signs* John Ebor:

BISHOPS SUFFRAGAN
Hull, Rt. Revd Donald G. Snelgrove, TD, *cons.* 1981, *apptd*
1981; Hullen House, Woodfield Lane, Hessle, Hull HU13
OES
Selby, Rt. Revd Humphrey V. Taylor, *cons.* 1991, *apptd*
1991; 10 Precentor's Court, York YO1 2ES
Whitby, Rt. Revd Gordon Bates, *cons.* 1983, *apptd* 1983;
60 West Green, Stokesley, Middlesbrough TS9 5BD

ASSISTANT BISHOPS
Rt. Revd George Cockin, *cons.* 1959, *apptd* 1969; Rt. Revd
Richard Wimbush, *cons.* 1963, *apptd* 1977; Rt. Revd
Richard Wood, *cons.* 1973, *apptd* 1985; Rt. Revd Graham
Foley, *cons.* 1982, *apptd* 1989; Rt. Revd David Galliford,
cons. 1975, *apptd* 1991; Rt. Revd Clifford Barker, *cons.* 1976,
apptd 1991

DEAN
Very Revd John E. Southgate, *apptd* 1984

CANONS RESIDENTIARY
R. A. Hockley, *apptd* 1976; R. Mayland, *apptd* 1982; J. Toy,
PH.D., *apptd* 1983; R. Metcalfe, *apptd* 1988
Organist, P. Moore, FRCO, *apptd* 1983

ARCHDEACONS
Cleveland, Ven. C. J. Hawthorn, *apptd* 1991
East Riding, Ven. H. F. Buckingham, *apptd* 1988
York, Ven. G. B. Austin, *apptd* 1988

Stipendiary Male Clergy, 329

Stipendiary Women Deacons, 23

Official Principal and Auditor of the Chancery Court,
J. A. D. Owen, QC
Chancellor of the Diocese, His Honour Judge Coningsby, QC,
apptd 1977
*Vicar-General of the Province and Official Principal of the
Consistory Court*, His Honour Judge Coningsby, QC
Registrar and Legal Secretary, L. P. M. Lennox, 1 Peckitt
Street, York YO1 1SG

DURHAM

92ND BISHOP
Rt. Revd David E. Jenkins (until June 1994), *cons.* 1984,
apptd 1984; Auckland Castle, Bishop Auckland DL14 7NR.
Signs David Dunelm

BISHOP SUFFRAGAN
Jarrow, Rt. Revd Alan Smithson, *cons.* 1990, *apptd* 1990;
The Old Vicarage, Hallgarth, Pittington, Durham
DH6 1AB

DEAN
Very Revd John R. Arnold, *apptd* 1989

CANONS RESIDENTIARY
M. C. Perry, *apptd* 1970; R. L. Coppin, *apptd* 1974; Ven. J.
D. Hodgson, *apptd* 1983; D. W. Brown, *apptd* 1990;
G. S. Pedley, *apptd* 1993
Organist, J. B. Lancelot, FRCO, *apptd* 1985

ARCHDEACONS
Auckland, Ven. G. G. Gibson, *apptd* 1993
Durham, Ven. J. D. Hodgson, *apptd* 1993

Stipendiary Male Clergy, 266
Stipendiary Women Deacons, 22

Chancellor, His Honour Judge Bursell, QC, *apptd* 1989
Registrar and Legal Secretary, D. M. Robertson, Diocesan
Registry, Auckland Castle, Bishop Auckland DL14 7QJ

BLACKBURN

7TH BISHOP
Rt. Revd Alan D. Chesters, *cons.* 1989, *apptd* 1989; Bishop's
House, Ribchester Road, Blackburn BB1 9EF. *Signs* Alan
Blackburn

BISHOPS SUFFRAGAN
Burnley, vacant; Dean House, 449 Padiham Road, Burnley
BB12 6TE
Lancaster, Rt. Revd John Nicholls, *cons.* 1990, *apptd* 1990;
Wheatfields, 7 Dallas Road, Lancaster LA1 1TN

PROVOST
Very Revd David Frayne, *apptd* 1992

CANONS RESIDENTIARY
J. M. Taylor, *apptd* 1976; G. I. Hirst, *apptd* 1987;
M. A. Kitchener, *apptd* 1990
Organist, D. A. Cooper, FRCO, *apptd* 1983

ARCHDEACONS
Blackburn, Ven. W. D. Robinson, *apptd* 1986
Lancaster, Ven. K. H. Gibbons, *apptd* 1981

Stipendiary Male Clergy, 262

Stipendiary Women Deacons, 8

Chancellor, J. W. M. Bullimore, *apptd* 1990
Registrar, T. A. Hoyle, Diocesan Registry, Cathedral Close,
    Blackburn BBI 5AB

BRADFORD

8TH BISHOP
Rt. Revd David J. Smith, *cons.* 1987, *apptd* 1992;
    Bishopscroft, Ashwell Road, Heaton, Bradford BD9 4AU.
    Signs David Bradford

PROVOST
Very Revd John S. Richardson, *apptd* 1990

CANONS RESIDENTIARY
K. H. Cook, *apptd* 1977; C. G. Lewis, *apptd* 1993
Organist, A. Horsey, FRCO, *apptd* 1986

ARCHDEACONS
Bradford, Ven. D. H. Shreeve, *apptd* 1984
Craven, vacant

Stipendiary Male Clergy, 134
Stipendiary Women Deacons, 11

Chancellor, D. M. Savill, QC, *apptd* 1976
Registrar and Secretary, J. G. H. Mackrell, 6–14 Devonshire
    Street, Keighley BD21 2AY

CARLISLE

65TH BISHOP
Rt. Revd Ian Harland, *cons.* 1985, *apptd* 1989; Rose Castle,
    Dalston, Carlisle CA5 7BZ. *Signs* Ian Carliol:

BISHOP SUFFRAGAN
Penrith, Rt. Revd George L. Hacker, *cons.* 1979, *apptd*
    1979; The Rectory, Great Salkeld, Penrith CAII 9NA

DEAN
Very Revd Henry E. C. Stapleton, *apptd* 1988

CANONS RESIDENTIARY
R. A. Chapman, *apptd* 1978; R. C. Johns, *apptd* 1989;
D. T. I. Jenkins, *apptd* 1991; Ven. D. C. Turnbull, *apptd*
    1993
Organist, J. Suter, FRCO, *apptd* 1991

ARCHDEACONS
Carlisle, Ven. D. C. Turnbull, *apptd* 1993
West Cumberland, Ven. J. R. Packer, *apptd* 1991
Westmorland and Furness, Ven. L. J. Peat, *apptd* 1989

Stipendiary Male Clergy, 169
Stipendiary Women Deacons, 8

Chancellor, His Honour Judge Aglionby, *apptd* 1991
Registrar and Secretary, Mrs S. Holmes, Woodside, Great
    Corby, Carlisle CA4 8LL

CHESTER

39TH BISHOP
Rt. Revd Michael A. Baughen, *cons.* 1982, *apptd* 1982;
    Bishop's House, Chester CHI 2JD. *Signs* Michael Cestr:

BISHOPS SUFFRAGAN
Birkenhead, Rt. Revd Michael L. Langrish, *cons.* 1993,
    apptd 1993; 67 Bidston Road, Oxton, Birkenhead L43
    6TR
Stockport, Rt. Revd Frank P. Sargeant, *cons.* 1984, *apptd*
    1984; Bishop's Lodge, Back Lane, Dunham Town,
    Altrincham, Cheshire WAI4 4SG

DEAN
Very Revd Stephen S. Smalley, *apptd* 1986

CANONS RESIDENTIARY
R. M. Rees, *apptd* 1990; C. J. Bennetts, *apptd* 1990;
O. A. Conway, *apptd* 1991
Organist, R. Fisher, FRCO, *apptd* 1968

ARCHDEACONS
Chester, Ven. G. M. Turner, *apptd* 1993
Macclesfield, Ven. J. S. Gaisford, *apptd* 1986

Stipendiary Male Clergy, 300
Stipendiary Women Deacons, 13

Chancellor, H. H. Lomas, *apptd* 1977
Registrar and Legal Secretary, A. K. McAllester, Friars,
    20 White Friars, Chester CHI IXS

LIVERPOOL

6TH BISHOP
Rt. Revd David S. Sheppard, *cons.* 1969, *apptd* 1975;
    Bishop's Lodge, Woolton Park, Liverpool L25 6DT. *Signs*
    David Liverpool

BISHOP SUFFRAGAN
Warrington, Rt. Revd Michael Henshall, *cons.* 1976, *apptd*
    1976; Martinsfield, Elm Avenue, Great Crosby, Liverpool
    L23 2SX

ASSISTANT BISHOPS
Rt. Revd Graham Chadwick, *cons.* 1976, *apptd* 1990; Rt.
    Revd James Roxburgh, *cons.* 1983, *apptd* 1991

DEAN
Very Revd Rhys D. C. Walters, *apptd* 1983

CANONS RESIDENTIARY
M. M. Wolfe, *apptd* 1982; D. J. Hutton, *apptd* 1983;
K. J. Riley, *apptd* 1983; H. Thomas, *apptd* 1988
Organist, Prof. I. Tracey, *apptd* 1980

ARCHDEACONS
Liverpool, Ven. S. Durant, *apptd* 1991
Warrington, Ven. C. D. S. Woodhouse, *apptd* 1981

Stipendiary Male Clergy, 274
Stipendiary Women Deacons, 23

Chancellor, R. G. Hamilton
Registrar and Cathedral Chapter Clerk, R. H. Arden,
    I Hanover Street, Liverpool LI 3DW

MANCHESTER

10TH BISHOP
Rt. Revd Christopher J. Mayfield, *cons.* 1985, *apptd* 1993;
    Bishopscourt, Bury New Road, Manchester M7 OLE. *Signs*
    Christopher Manchester

BISHOPS SUFFRAGAN
Bolton, Rt. Revd David Bonser, *cons.* 1991, *apptd* 1991;
    4 Sandfield Drive, Lostock, Bolton BL6 4DU
Hulme, Rt. Revd Colin J. F. Scott, *cons.* 1984, *apptd* 1984;
    1 Raynham Avenue, Didsbury, Manchester M20 0BW
Middleton, vacant; The Hollies, Manchester Road,
    Rochdale OL11 3QY

ASSISTANT BISHOP
Rt. Revd Edward Wickham, *cons.* 1959, *apptd* 1982

DEAN
Vacant

CANONS RESIDENTIARY
Ven. R. B. Harris, *apptd* 1980; J. R. Atherton, PH.D., *apptd*
1984; B. Duncan, *apptd* 1986; A. E. Radcliffe, *apptd* 1991

Organist, C. Stokes, *apptd* 1992

ARCHDEACONS
Bolton, Ven. L. M. Davies, *apptd* 1992
Manchester, Ven. R. B. Harris, *apptd* 1980
Rochdale, Ven. J. M. M. Dalby, *apptd* 1991

Stipendiary Male Clergy, 377
Stipendiary Women Deacons, 16

Chancellor, G. C. H. Spafford, *apptd* 1976
Registrar and Bishop's Secretary, M. Darlington,
    90 Deansgate, Manchester M3 2GH

NEWCASTLE

10TH BISHOP
Rt. Revd Andrew A. K. Graham, *cons.* 1977, *apptd* 1981;
    Bishop's House, 29 Moor Road South, Gosforth,
    Newcastle upon Tyne NE3 1PA. *Signs* A. Newcastle

ASSISTANT BISHOP
Rt. Revd Kenneth Gill, *cons.* 1972, *apptd* 1980

PROVOST
Very Revd Nicholas G. Coulton, *apptd* 1990

CANONS RESIDENTIARY
R. Langley, *apptd* 1985; P. R. Strange, *apptd* 1986;
I. F. Bennett, *apptd* 1988; Ven. P. Elliott, *apptd* 1993

Organist, T. G. Hone, FRCO, *apptd* 1987

ARCHDEACONS
Lindisfarne, Ven. M. E. Bowering, *apptd* 1987
Northumberland, Ven. P. Elliott, *apptd* 1993

Stipendiary Male Clergy, 175
Stipendiary Women Deacons, 10

Chancellor, His Honour A. J. Blackett-Ord, CVO, *apptd* 1971
Registrar and Secretary, R. R. V. Nicholson, 46 Grainger
    Street, Newcastle upon Tyne NE1 5LB

RIPON

11TH BISHOP
Rt. Revd David N. de L. Young, *cons.* 1977, *apptd* 1977;
    Bishop Mount, Ripon HG4 5DP. *Signs* David Ripon

BISHOP SUFFRAGAN
Knaresborough, Rt. Revd Malcolm J. Menin, *cons.* 1986,
    apptd 1986; 16 Shaftesbury Avenue, Roundhay, Leeds
    LS8 1DT

ASSISTANT BISHOPS
Rt. Revd Ralph Emmerson, *cons.* 1972, *apptd* 1986; Rt.
Revd Derek A. Rawcliffe, *cons.* 1974, *apptd* 1991

DEAN
Very Revd Christopher R. Campling, *apptd* 1984

CANONS RESIDENTIARY
D. G. Ford, *apptd* 1980; P. J. Marshall, *apptd* 1985;
M. R. Glanville-Smith, *apptd* 1990

Organist, R. Perrin, FRCO, *apptd* 1966

ARCHDEACONS
Leeds, Ven. J. M. Oliver, *apptd* 1992
Richmond, Ven. K. Good, *apptd* 1993

Stipendiary Male Clergy, 174
Stipendiary Women Deacons, 17

Chancellor, His Honour Judge Grenfell, *apptd* 1992
Registrar and Legal Secretary, J. R. Balmforth, York House,
    York Place, Knaresborough HG5 0AD
Diocesan Secretary, G. M. Royal, Diocesan Office, St Mary's
    Street, Leeds LS9 7DP

SHEFFIELD

5TH BISHOP
Rt. Revd David R. Lunn, *cons.* 1980, *apptd* 1980;
    Bishopscroft, Snaithing Lane, Sheffield S10 3LG. *Signs*
    David Sheffield

BISHOP SUFFRAGAN
Doncaster, Rt. Revd. Michael F. Gear, *cons.* 1993, *apptd*
    1993; Bishops Lodge, Hooton Roberts, Rotherham S65
    4PF

ASSISTANT BISHOPS
Rt. Revd Kenneth Skelton, CBE, *cons.* 1962, *apptd* 1984; Rt.
Revd Kenneth Pillar, *cons.* 1982, *apptd* 1989

PROVOST
Very Revd John W. Gladwin, *apptd* 1988

CANONS RESIDENTIARY
T. M. Page, *apptd* 1982; Ven. S. R. Lowe, *apptd* 1988;
C. M. Smith, *apptd* 1991; Jane E. M. Sinclair, *apptd* 1993

Organist, P. Brough, FRCO, *apptd* 1991

ARCHDEACONS
Doncaster, Ven. D. Carnelley, *apptd* 1985
Sheffield, Ven. S. R. Lowe, *apptd* 1988

Stipendiary Male Clergy, 216
Stipendiary Women Deacons, 16

Chancellor, Prof. J. D. McClean, *apptd* 1992
Registrar and Legal Secretary, C. P. Rothwell, 30 Bank
    Street, Sheffield S1 2DS

SODOR AND MAN

79TH BISHOP
Rt. Revd Noel D. Jones, CB, *cons.* 1989, *apptd* 1989; The
    Bishop's House, Quarterbridge Road, Douglas, IOM.
    Signs Noel Sodor and Man

CANONS
B. H. Kelly, *apptd* 1980; B. H. Partington, *apptd* 1985;
J. Sheen, *apptd* 1991; F. H. Bird, *apptd* 1993

ARCHDEACON
Isle of Man, Ven. D. A. Willoughby, *apptd* 1982

Stipendiary Male Clergy, 21

Vicar-General and Registrar, P. W. S. Farrant, 24 Athol
Street, Douglas, IOM

SOUTHWELL

9TH BISHOP
Rt. Revd Patrick B. Harris, *cons.* 1973, *apptd* 1988; Bishop's
Manor, Southwell NG25 0JR. *Signs* Patrick Southwell

BISHOP SUFFRAGAN
Sherwood, Rt. Revd Alan W. Morgan, *cons.* 1989, *apptd*
1989; Sherwood House, High Oakham Road, Mansfield
NG18 5AJ

PROVOST
Very Revd David Leaning, *apptd* 1991

CANONS RESIDENTIARY
D. P. Keene, *apptd* 1981; I. G. Collins, *apptd* 1985;
M. Austin, *apptd* 1992

Organist, P. Hale, *apptd* 1981

ARCHDEACONS
Newark, Ven. D. C. Hawtin, *apptd* 1992
Nottingham, Ven. T. O. Walker, *apptd* 1991

Stipendiary Male Clergy, 212
Stipendiary Women Deacons, 9

Chancellor, J. Shand, *apptd* 1981
Registrar, C. C. Hodson, Diocesan Office, Westgate,
Southwell NG25 0JL

WAKEFIELD

11TH BISHOP
Rt. Revd Nigel S. McCulloch, *cons.* 1986, *apptd* 1992;
Bishop's Lodge, Woodthorpe Lane, Wakefield WF2 6JL.
Signs Nigel Wakefield

BISHOP SUFFRAGAN
Pontefract, Rt. Revd John T. Finney, *cons.* 1993, *apptd* 1993;
Pontefract House, Manygates Lane, Wakefield WF2 6AX

PROVOST
Very Revd John E. Allen, *apptd* 1982

CANONS RESIDENTIARY
R. D. Baxter, *apptd* 1986; I. C. Knox, *apptd* 1989;
D. O'Connor, *apptd* 1992; G. Nairn-Briggs, *apptd* 1992

Organist, J. Bielby, FRCO, *apptd* 1972

ARCHDEACONS
Halifax, Ven. D. Hallatt, *apptd* 1989
Pontefract, Ven. J. Flack, *apptd* 1992

Stipendiary Male Clergy, 196
Stipendiary Women Deacons, 14

Chancellor, P. Collier, QC, *apptd* 1992
Registrar and Secretary, E. Chapman, Burton Street,
Wakefield WF1 2DA

The Anglican Communion

The Anglican Communion consists of 30 independent
provincial or national Christian Churches throughout the
world, many of which are in Commonwealth countries and
originated from missionary activity by the Church of England.
There is no single world authority linking the Communion,
but all recognize the leadership of the Archbishop of
Canterbury and have strong ecclesiastical and historical links
with the Church of England. Every ten years all the bishops
in the Communion meet at the Lambeth Conference,
convened by the Archbishop of Canterbury. The Conference
has no policy-making authority but is an important forum for
the discussion of issues of common concern. The Anglican
Consultative Council was set up in 1968 to function between
conferences and the meeting of the Primates every two years.

There are about 70 million Anglicans and 700 archbishops
and bishops world-wide.

THE CHURCH IN WALES

The Anglican Church was the established church in Wales
from the 16th century until 1920, when the estrangement of
the majority of Welsh people from Anglicanism, in particular
in favour of Presbyterianism, resulted in disestablishment.
Since then the Church in Wales has been an autonomous
province consisting of six sees, with one of the diocesan
bishops being elected Archbishop of Wales by an electoral
college comprising elected lay and clerical members.

The legislative body of the Church in Wales is the
Governing Body, which has 347 members in total, divided
between the three orders of bishops, clergy and laity. It is
presided over by the Archbishop of Wales and meets twice
annually. Its decisions are binding upon all members of the
Church. There are 105,661 members of the Church in Wales,
with six bishops, about 700 clergy and 1,142 parishes.

THE GOVERNING BODY OF THE CHURCH IN WALES,
39 Cathedral Road, Cardiff CF1 9XF. Tel: 0222–231638.
Secretary-General, J. W. D. McIntyre

10TH ARCHBISHOP OF WALES, Most Revd Alwyn
R. Jones (Bishop of St Asaph), *elected* 1991

THE RT. REVD BISHOPS
Bangor (79th), Rt. Revd Barry C. Morgan, *b.* 1947, *cons.*
1993, *apptd* 1992; Tŷ'r Esgob, Bangor LL57 2SS. *Signs*
Barry Bangor. *Stipendiary clergy*, 69
Llandaff (101st), Rt. Revd Roy T. Davies, *b.* 1934, *cons.*
1985, *apptd* 1985; Llys Esgob, The Cathedral Green,
Llandaff, Cardiff CF5 2YE. *Signs* Roy Landav. *Stipendiary
clergy*, 168
Monmouth (8th), Rt. Revd Rowan D. Williams, *b* 1950, *cons.*
1992, *apptd* 1992; Bishopstow, Stow Hill, Newport NP9
4EA. *Signs* Rowan Monmouth. *Stipendiary clergy*, 110
St Asaph (74th), Most Revd Alwyn R. Jones, *b.* 1934, *cons.*
1982, *apptd* 1982; Esgobty, St Asaph, Clwyd LL17 0TW.
Signs Alwyn Cambrensis. *Stipendiary clergy*, 112
St David's (125th), Rt. Revd J. Ivor Rees, *b.* 1926, *cons.*
1988, *apptd* 1991; Llys Esgob, Abergwili, Dyfed SA31 2JG.
Signs Ivor St Davids. *Stipendiary clergy*, 132
Swansea and Brecon (7th), Rt. Revd Dewi M. Bridges, *b.*
1933, *cons.* 1988, *apptd* 1988; Ely Tower, Brecon, Powys
LD3 9DE. *Signs* Dewi Swansea & Brecon. *Stipendiary
clergy*, 100

The stipend of a diocesan bishop of the Church in Wales is
£23,610 a year from 1994.

THE EPISCOPAL CHURCH IN SCOTLAND

The Episcopal Church in Scotland was founded after the Act of Settlement (1690) established the presbyterian nature of the Church of Scotland. The Episcopal Church is in full communion with the Church of England but is autonomous. The governing authority is the General Synod, an elected body of 160 members which meets once a year. The diocesan bishop who convenes and presides at meetings of the General Synod is called the Primus and is elected by his fellow bishops.

There are 56,742 members of the Episcopal Church in Scotland, of whom 34,909 are communicants. There are seven bishops, 207 clergy, and 341 churches and places of worship.

THE GENERAL SYNOD OF THE EPISCOPAL CHURCH IN SCOTLAND, 21 Grosvenor Crescent, Edinburgh EH12 5EE. Tel: 031-225 6357. *Secretary-General,* J. Simpson

PRIMUS OF THE EPISCOPAL CHURCH IN SCOTLAND, Most Revd Richard F. Holloway (Bishop of Edinburgh), *elected* 1992

THE RT. REVD BISHOPS
Aberdeen and Orkney, A. Bruce Cameron, *b.* 1941, *cons.* 1992, *apptd* 1992. *Clergy* 14
Argyll and the Isles, Douglas M. Cameron, *b.* 1935, *cons.* 1992, *apptd* 1992. *Clergy* 10
Brechin, Robert T. Halliday, *b.* 1932, *cons.* 1990, *apptd* 1990. *Clergy* 15
Edinburgh, Richard F. Holloway, *b.* 1933, *cons.* 1986, *apptd* 1986. *Clergy* 65
Glasgow and Galloway, John M. Taylor, *b.* 1932, *cons.* 1991, *apptd* 1991. *Clergy* 45
Moray, Ross and Caithness, vacant. *Clergy* 16
St Andrews, Dunkeld and Dunblane, Michael G. Hare-Duke, *b.* 1925, *cons.* 1969, *apptd* 1969. *Clergy* 30

The stipend of a diocesan bishop of the Episcopal Church in Scotland was £16,840 in 1993

THE CHURCH OF IRELAND

The Anglican Church was the established church in Ireland from the 16th century but never secured the allegiance of a majority of the Irish and was disestablished in 1871. The Church in Ireland is divided into the provinces of Armagh and Dublin, each under an archbishop. The provinces are subdivided into 12 dioceses.

The legislative body is the General Synod, which has 660 members in total, divided between the House of Bishops and the House of Representatives. The Archbishop of Armagh is elected by the House of Bishops; other episcopal elections are made by an electoral college.

There are about 375,000 members of the Church of Ireland, with two archbishops, ten bishops, about 600 clergy and about 1,000 churches and places of worship.

CENTRAL OFFICE, Church of Ireland House, Church Avenue, Rathmines, Dublin 6. Tel: 0001-978422. *Assistant Secretary of the General Synod,* J. F. Buttimore

PROVINCE OF ARMAGH

ARCHBISHOP OF ARMAGH AND PRIMATE OF ALL IRELAND, Most Revd Robert H. A. Eames, PH.D., *b.* 1937, *cons.* 1975, *trans.* 1986. *Clergy* 57

THE RT. REVD BISHOPS
Clogher, Brian D. A. Hannon, *b.* 1936, *cons.* 1986, *apptd* 1986. *Clergy* 33
Connor, Samuel G. Poyntz, PH.D., *b.* 1926, *cons.* 1978, *trans.* 1987. *Clergy* 116
Derry and Raphoe, James Mehaffey, PH.D., *b.* 1931, *cons.* 1980, *apptd* 1980. *Clergy* 54
Down and Dromore, Gordon McMullan, PH.D., *b.* 1934, *cons.* 1980, *trans.* 1986. *Clergy* 111
Kilmore, Elphin and Ardagh, Michael H. G. Mayes, *b.* 1941, *cons.* 1993, *apptd* 1993. *Clergy* 30
Tuam, Killala and Achonry, John R. W. Neill, *b.* 1945, *cons.* 1986, *apptd* 1986. *Clergy* 9

PROVINCE OF DUBLIN

ARCHBISHOP OF DUBLIN, BISHOP OF GLENDALOUGH, AND PRIMATE OF IRELAND, Most Revd Donald A. Caird, DD, *b.* 1925, *cons.* 1970, *trans.* 1976, 1985. *Clergy* 92

THE RT. REVD BISHOPS
Cashel and Ossory, Noel V. Willoughby, *b.* 1926, *cons.* 1980, *apptd* 1980. *Clergy* 38
Cork, Cloyne and Ross, Robert A. Warke, *b.* 1930, *cons.* 1988, *apptd* 1988. *Clergy* 24
Limerick and Killaloe, Edward F. Darling, *b.* 1933, *cons.* 1985, *apptd* 1985. *Clergy* 22
Meath and Kildare, Most Revd Walton N. F. Empey, *b.* 1934, *cons.* 1981, *trans.* 1985. *Clergy* 21

Anglican Communion Overseas

ANGLICAN CHURCH OF AOTEAROA, NEW ZEALAND AND POLYNESIA

PRIMATE AND ARCHBISHOP OF NEW ZEALAND, The Most Revd Brian N. Davis (Bishop of Wellington), *cons.* 1980, *apptd* 1986

THE RT. REVD BISHOPS
Aotearoa, Whakahuhui Vercoe, *cons.* 1981, *apptd* 1981
Auckland, Bruce Gilberd, *cons.* 1985, *apptd* 1985
Christchurch, David Coles, *cons.* 1990, *apptd* 1990
Dunedin, Penelope Jamieson, *cons.* 1990, *apptd* 1990
Nelson, Derek Eaton, *cons.* 1990, *apptd* 1990
Polynesia, Jabez Bryce, *cons.* 1975, *apptd* 1975
Waiapu, Murray Mills, *cons.* 1991, *apptd* 1991
Waikato, David Moxon, *cons.* 1993, *apptd* 1993
Wellington, see above

ANGLICAN CHURCH OF AUSTRALIA

PRIMATE OF AUSTRALIA, The Most Revd Keith Rayner (Archbishop of Melbourne), *cons.* 1969, *apptd* 1991

PROVINCE OF NEW SOUTH WALES

METROPOLITAN
Archbishop of Sydney, The Most Revd R. Harry Goodhew, *cons.* 1982, *apptd* 1993

THE RT. REVD BISHOPS
Armidale, Peter Chiswell, *cons.* 1976, *apptd* 1976
Bathurst, Bruce W. Wilson, *cons.* 1984, *apptd* 1989

Canberra and Goulburn, George V. Browning, *apptd* 1993
Grafton, Bruce A. Schultz, *cons.* 1985, *apptd* 1985
Newcastle, Roger A. Herft, *apptd* 1993
Riverina, Bruce Q. Clark, *apptd* 1993

PROVINCE OF QUEENSLAND

METROPOLITAN
Archbishop of Brisbane, The Most Revd Peter Hollingworth,
 cons. 1985, *apptd* 1990

THE RT. REVD BISHOPS
Carpentaria, Anthony F. B. Hall-Matthews, *cons.* 1984
North Queensland, John Lewis, *cons.* 1971
Northern Territory, Richard F. Appleby, *cons.* 1992
Rockhampton, George A. Hearn, *cons.* 1981

PROVINCE OF SOUTH AUSTRALIA

METROPOLITAN
Archbishop of Adelaide, The Most Revd Ian G. C. George,
 cons. 1989, *apptd* 1991

THE RT. REVD BISHOPS
The Murray, Graham H. Walden, *cons.* 1981, *apptd* 1989
Willochra, W. David H. McCall, *cons.* 1987, *apptd* 1987

PROVINCE OF VICTORIA

METROPOLITAN
Archbishop of Melbourne, The Most Revd Keith Rayner,
 cons. 1969, *apptd* 1990 *(see above)*

THE RT. REVD BISHOPS
Ballarat, vacant
Bendigo, vacant
Gippsland, Colin D. Sheumack, *cons.* 1987, *apptd* 1987
Wangaratta, Robert G. Beal, *cons.* 1985, *apptd* 1985

PROVINCE OF WESTERN AUSTRALIA

METROPOLITAN
Archbishop of Perth, The Most Revd Peter F. Carnley,
 PH.D., *cons.* 1981, *apptd* 1981

THE RT. REVD BISHOPS
Bunbury, Hamish J. U. Jamieson, *cons.* 1974, *apptd* 1984
North-West Australia, Anthony Nicholls, *cons.* 1992, *apptd*
 1992

EXTRA-PROVINCIAL DIOCESE

Bishop of Tasmania, Rt. Revd Phillip K. Newell, AO, *cons.*
 1982, *apptd* 1982

EPISCOPAL ANGLICAN CHURCH OF BRAZIL
Igreja Episcopal Anglicana Do Brasil

PRIMATE *(acting),* The Most Revd Claudio V. S. Gastal
 (Bishop of Southern Brazil), *cons.* 1984, *acting since* 1993

THE RT. REVD BISHOPS
Brasilia, Almir dos Santos, *cons.* 1989, *apptd* 1989
Central Brazil, Sydney A. Ruiz, *cons.* 1985, *apptd* 1985
Northern Brazil, Clovis E. Rodrigues, *cons.* 1985, *apptd* 1986
Pelotas, Luiz O. P. Prado, *cons.* 1987, *apptd* 1989
South Central Brazil, Glauco Soares de Lima, *cons.* 1989,
 apptd 1989
Southern Brazil, see above, *apptd* 1984

South-Western Brazil, Jubal P. Neves, *cons.* 1993, *apptd*
 1993

CHURCH OF THE PROVINCE OF BURUNDI

ARCHBISHOP OF PROVINCE, The Most Revd Samuel
 Sindamuka (Bishop of Matana), *cons.* 1975, *apptd* 1989

THE RT. REVD BISHOPS
Bujumbura, Pie Ntukamazina, *cons.* 1990, *apptd* 1990
Buye, Samuel Ndayisenga, *apptd* 1979
Gitega, Jean Nduwayo, *apptd* 1985
Matana, see above

ANGLICAN CHURCH OF CANADA

ARCHBISHOP AND PRIMATE, The Most Revd Michael
 G. Peers, *cons.* 1977, *trans.* 1986

PROVINCE OF BRITISH COLUMBIA

METROPOLITAN
vacant

THE RT. REVD BISHOPS
British Columbia, Barry Jenks, *cons.* 1992, *elected* 1992
Caledonia, John Hannen, *cons.* 1981, *elected* 1981
Cariboo, James Cruickshank, *cons.* 1992, *elected* 1992
Kootenay, David Crawley, *cons.* 1990, *elected* 1990
New Westminster, vacant
Yukon, Ronald Ferris, *cons.* 1981, *elected* 1981

PROVINCE OF CANADA

METROPOLITAN
Archbishop of Western Newfoundland, Most Revd Stewart
 S. Payne, *cons.* 1978, *elected* 1990

THE RT. REVD BISHOPS
Central Newfoundland, Edward Marsh, *cons.* 1990, *elected*
 1990
Eastern Newfoundland and Labrador, Donald Harvey, *cons.*
 1993, *elected* 1992
Fredericton, George Lemon, *cons.* 1989, *elected* 1989
Montreal, Andrew Hutchison, *cons.* 1990, *elected* 1990
Nova Scotia, Arthur Peters, *cons.* 1982, *elected* 1982
Quebec, Bruce Stavert, *cons.* 1991, *elected* 1991
Western Newfoundland, see above

PROVINCE OF ONTARIO

METROPOLITAN
Archbishop of Huron, The Most Revd Percival O'Driscoll,
 cons. 1987, *elected* 1993

THE RT. REVD BISHOPS
Algoma, Leslie Peterson, *cons.* 1983, *elected* 1983
Huron, see above
Moosonee, Caleb Lawrence, *cons.* 1980, *elected* 1980
Niagara, Walter Asbil, *cons.* 1990, *elected* 1990
Ontario, Peter Mason, *cons.* 1992, *elected* 1992
Ottawa, John Baycroft, *cons.* 1985, *elected* 1993
Toronto, Terence Finlay, *cons.* 1986, *elected* 1990

PROVINCE OF RUPERT'S LAND

METROPOLITAN
Archbishop of Rupert's Land, The Most Revd Walter H. Jones, *cons.* 1970, *elected* 1988

THE RT. REVD BISHOPS
Arctic, J. C. R. Williams, *cons.* 1987, *elected* 1991
Athabasca, John Clarke, *cons.* 1992, *elected* 1992
Brandon, Malcolm Harding, *cons.* 1992, *elected* 1992
Calgary, Barry Curtis, *cons.* 1983, *elected* 1983
Edmonton, Kenneth Genge, *cons.* 1988, *elected* 1988
Keewatin, Thomas Collings, *cons.* 1991, *elected* 1991
Qu' Appelle, Eric Bays, *cons.* 1986, *elected* 1986
Rupert's Land, *see* above
Saskatchewan, vacant
Saskatoon, Thomas Morgan, *cons.* 1985, *elected* 1993

CHURCH OF THE PROVINCE OF CENTRAL AFRICA

ARCHBISHOP OF PROVINCE, The Most Revd Walter P. K. Makhulu (Bishop of Botswana), *cons.* 1979, *apptd* 1980

THE RT. REVD BISHOPS
Botswana, *see* above
Central Zambia, Clement Shaba, *cons.* 1984, *apptd* 1984
Harare, Ralph Hatendi, *cons.* 1979, *apptd* 1981
Lake Malawi, Peter Nyanja, *cons.* 1978, *apptd* 1978
The Lundi, Jonathan Siyachitema, *cons.* 1981, *apptd* 1981
Lusaka, Stephen Mumba, *cons.* 1981, *apptd* 1981
Manicaland, Elijah Masuko, *cons.* 1981, *apptd* 1981
Matabeleland, Theophilus Naledi, *cons.* 1987, *apptd* 1987
Northern Zambia, Bernard Malango, *cons.* 1988, *apptd* 1988
Southern Malawi, Nathaniel Aipa, *cons.* 1987, *apptd* 1987

CHURCH OF THE PROVINCE OF THE INDIAN OCEAN

ARCHBISHOP OF PROVINCE, The Most Revd French Chang-Him (Bishop of Seychelles), *cons.* 1979, *apptd* 1984

THE RT. REVD BISHOPS
Antananarivo, Remi Rabenirina, *cons.* 1984, *apptd* 1984
Antsiranana, Keith Benzies, OBE, *cons.* 1982, *apptd* 1982
Mauritius, Rex Donat, *cons.* 1984, *apptd* 1984
Seychelles, *see* above
Toamasina, Donald Smith, *cons.* 1990, *apptd* 1990

THE HOLY CATHOLIC CHURCH IN JAPAN
Nippon Sei Ko Kai

PRIMATE, The Most Revd Christopher I. Kikawada (Bishop of Osaka), *cons.* 1975, *apptd* 1986

THE RT. REVD BISHOPS
Chubu, Samuel W. Hoyo, *cons.* 1987, *apptd* 1987
Hokkaido, Augustine H. Amagi, *cons.* 1987, *apptd* 1987
Kita Kanto, James T. Yashiro, *cons.* 1985, *apptd* 1985
Kobe, John J. Furumoto, *cons.* 1992, *apptd* 1992
Kyoto, John T. Okano, *cons.* 1991, *apptd* 1991
Kyushu, Joseph N. Iida, *cons.* 1982, *apptd* 1982

Okinawa, Paul S. Nakamura, *cons.* 1972, *apptd* 1972
Osaka, *see* above
Tohoku, William T. Murakami, *cons.* 1993, *apptd* 1993
Tokyo, John M. Takeda, *cons.* 1988, *apptd* 1988
Yokohama, Raphael S. Kajiwara, *cons.* 1984, *apptd* 1984

THE EPISCOPAL CHURCH IN JERUSALEM AND THE MIDDLE EAST

PRESIDENT-BISHOP, Rt. Revd Samir Kafity, *apptd* 1986

THE RT. REVD BISHOPS
Jerusalem, Samir Kafity, *cons.* 1984
Iran, Iraj Mottahedeh, *cons.* 1990
Egypt, Ghais A. Malik, *cons.* 1984
Cyprus and the Gulf, John Brown, *cons.* 1986

CHURCH OF THE PROVINCE OF KENYA

ARCHBISHOP OF PROVINCE, The Most Revd Manasses Kuria (Bishop of Nairobi), *cons.* 1970, *apptd* 1980

THE RT. REVD BISHOPS
Eldoret, Stephen Kewasis, *apptd* 1992
Embu, Moses Njue
Katakwa, Eliud Okiring
Kirinyaga, David Gitari, *cons.* 1975, *apptd* 1975
Machakos, Benjamin Nzimbi, *cons.* 1985, *apptd* 1985
Maseno North, James Mundia, *cons.* 1970, *apptd* 1970
Maseno South, Henry Okullu, *cons.* 1974, *apptd* 1974
Maseno West, Joseph Wesonga, *apptd* 1991
Mombasa, Crispus Nzano, *cons.* 1975, *apptd* 1981
Mount Kenya Central, John Mahiaini, *cons.* 1984, *apptd* 1984
Mount Kenya South, George Njuguna, *cons.* 1984, *apptd* 1985
Nairobi, *see* above
Nakuru, Stephen M. Nijihia, *apptd* 1992
Nambale, Isaac Namango, *cons.* 1984, *apptd* 1987

CHURCH OF THE PROVINCE OF KOREA

ARCHBISHOP OF PROVINCE, The Most Revd Bundo Kim (Bishop of Pusan), *apptd* 1993

THE RT. REVD BISHOPS
Pusan, *see* above, *apptd* 1988
Seoul, Simon Kim
Taejon, Paul Hwan Yoon, *apptd* 1988

CHURCH OF THE PROVINCE OF MELANESIA

ARCHBISHOP OF PROVINCE, The Most Revd Amos S. Waiaru (Bishop of Central Melanesia), *cons.* 1981, *apptd* 1988

THE RT. REVD BISHOPS
Central Melanesia, *see* above
Hanuato'o, James Mason, *cons.* 1991, *apptd* 1991
Malaita, Raymond Aumae, *cons.* 1990, *apptd* 1990
Temotu, Lazarus Munamua, *cons.* 1987, *apptd* 1987
Vanuatu, Michael Tavoa, *cons.* 1990, *apptd* 1990
Ysabel, Ellison Pogo, *cons.* 1981, *apptd* 1981

CHURCH OF THE PROVINCE OF MYANMAR

ARCHBISHOP OF PROVINCE, The Most Revd Andrew
Mya Han (Bishop of Yangon), *cons.* 1988, *apptd* 1988

THE RT. REVD BISHOPS
Hpa'an, Daniel Hoi Kyin, *cons.* 1992, *apptd* 1992
Mandalay, Andrew Hla Aung, *cons.* 1988, *apptd* 1988
Myitkyina, Timothy Mya Wah, *cons.* 1984, *apptd* 1984
Sittwe, Barnabas Theaung Hawi, *cons.* 1978, *apptd* 1980
Taungoo, George Kyaw Mya, *cons.* 1979, *apptd* 1979
Yangon (Rangoon), *see above*

CHURCH OF THE PROVINCE OF NIGERIA

ARCHBISHOP OF THE PROVINCE, The Most Revd Joseph
Adetiloye (Bishop of Lagos), *apptd* 1991

THE RT. REVD BISHOPS
Aba, A. O. Iwuagwu, *apptd* 1985
Abuja, Peter Akinole, *apptd* 1989
Akoko, J. O. K. Olowokure, *apptd* 1986
Akure, Emmanuel Gbonigi, *apptd* 1983
Asaba, Roland Nwosu, *apptd* 1977
Awka, Maxwell Anikwenwa, *apptd* 1987
Bauchi, Emmanuel O. Chukwuma, *apptd* 1990
Benin, John George, *apptd* 1985
Calabar, W. G. Ekprikpo
Egbado, Timothy Bolaji
Egba-Egbado, T. I. Akintayo, *apptd* 1977
Ekiti, C. A. Akinbola, *apptd* 1986
Enugu, Gideon Otubelu, *apptd* 1969
Ibadan, Gideon Olajide, *apptd* 1988
Ife, Gabriel Oloniyo
Ijebu, Abraham Olowoyo, *apptd* 1990
Ijebu Remo, E. O. I. Ogundana, *apptd* 1984
Ilesha, E. A. Ademowo, *apptd* 1989
Jos, B. A. Kwashi
Kaduna, Titus Ogbonyomi, *apptd* 1975
Kafanchan, William Diya, *apptd* 1990
Kano, B. O. Omoseibi, *apptd* 1990
Katsina, J. S. Kwasu, *apptd* 1990
Kwara, Herbert Haruna, *apptd* 1974
Lagos, *see above*, *apptd* 1985
Maiduguri, E. K. Mani, *apptd* 1990
Makurdi, Nathan Nyom
Minna, Nathaniel Yisa, *apptd* 1990
The Niger, Jonathan Onyemelukwe, *apptd* 1975
Niger Delta, Samuel Elenwo, *apptd* 1981
Okigwe/Orlu, Samuel Ebo, *apptd* 1984
Ondo, Samuel Aderin, *apptd* 1981
Osun, Seth Fagbemi, *apptd* 1987
Owerri, Benjamin Nwankiti, *apptd* 1968
Owo, Abraham Awosan, *apptd* 1983
Sokoto, J. A. Idowu-Fearon, *apptd* 1990
Uyo, Ebenezar Nglass
Warri, Nathaniel Enuku
Yola, Chris O. Efobi, *apptd* 1990

ANGLICAN CHURCH OF PAPUA NEW GUINEA

ARCHBISHOP OF PROVINCE, The Most Revd Bevan
Meredith (Bishop of New Guinea Islands), *cons.* 1967,
elected 1990

THE RT. REVD BISHOPS
Aipo Rongo, Paul Richardson, *cons.* 1987, *elected* 1987
Dogura, Tevita Talanoa, *cons.* 1992, *elected* 1992
New Guinea Islands, *see above*, *elected* 1977
Popondota, Walter Siba, *cons.* 1990, *elected* 1990
Port Moresby, Isaac Gadebo, *cons.* 1983, *elected* 1983

PHILIPPINE EPISCOPAL CHURCH

PRIME BISHOP, The Most Revd Narciso V. Ticobay, *cons.*
1986, *apptd* 1993

THE RT. REVD BISHOPS
Central Philippines, Manuel C. Lumpias, *cons.* 1977, *apptd*
1978
North Central Philippines, Joel A. Pachao, *cons.* 1993, *apptd*
1993
Northern Luzon, Ignacio C. Soliba, *cons.* 1990, *apptd* 1990
Northern Philippines, Robert L. Longid, *cons.* 1983, *apptd*
1986
Southern Philippines, James B. Manguramas, *cons.* 1993,
apptd 1993

CHURCH OF THE PROVINCE OF RWANDA

ARCHBISHOP OF THE PROVINCE, The Most Revd
Augustin Nshamihigo (Bishop of Shyira), *apptd* 1992

THE RT. REVD BISHOPS
Butare, Justin Ndandali, *apptd* 1992
Byunba, Onesphore Rwaje
Cyangugu, Daniel Nduhura
Kigali, Adonia Sebununguri, *cons.* 1965
Kigeme, Norman Kayumba
Shyira, *see above*, *apptd* 1984
Shyogwe, Samuel Musubyinare

CHURCH OF THE PROVINCE OF SOUTHERN
AFRICA

METROPOLITAN
Archbishop of Cape Town, The Most Revd Desmond
M. B. Tutu, *cons.* 1976, *trans.* 1986

THE RT. REVD BISHOPS
Bloemfontein, Thomas Stanage, *cons.* 1978, *apptd* 1982
Christ the King, Peter Lee, *cons.* 1990, *apptd* 1990
George, Derek Damant, *cons.* 1985, *apptd* 1985
Grahamstown, David Russell, *cons.* 1986, *apptd* 1987
Johannesburg, Duncan Buchanan, *cons.* 1986, *apptd* 1986
Kimberley and Kuruman, W. N. Ndungane, *cons.* 1991,
apptd 1991
Klerksdorp, David Nkwe, *cons.* 1990, *apptd* 1990
Lebombo, Dinis Sengulane, *cons.* 1976, *apptd* 1976
Lesotho, Philip Mokuku, *cons.* 1978, *apptd* 1978
Namibia, James Kauluma, *cons.* 1978, *apptd* 1981
Natal, Michael Nuttall, *cons.* 1975, *apptd* 1982
Niassa, Paulino Manhique, *cons.* 1986, *apptd* 1986
Port Elizabeth, Eric Pike, *cons.* 1989, *apptd* 1993
Pretoria, Richard Kraft, *cons.* 1982, *apptd* 1982
St Helena, John Ruston, *cons.* 1985, *apptd* 1991
St John's, Jacob Dlamini, *cons.* 1980, *apptd* 1985
St Mark the Evangelist, Rollo Le Feuvre, *cons.* 1987, *apptd*
1987

422   The Christian Churches

South-Eastern Transvaal, David Beetge, *cons.* 1990, *apptd* 1990
Swaziland, Lawrence Zulu, *cons.* 1975, *apptd* 1993
Umzimvubu, Geoffrey Davies, *cons.* 1987, *apptd* 1991
Zululand, Peter Harker, *cons.* 1993, *apptd* 1993

Order of Ethiopia, Sigqibo Dwane, *cons.* 1983, *apptd* 1983

ANGLICAN CHURCH OF THE SOUTHERN CONE OF AMERICA

PRESIDING BISHOP, Rt. Revd Colin Bazley (Bishop of Chile), *cons.* 1969

THE RT. REVD BISHOPS
Argentina, David Leake, *cons.* 1969, *apptd* 1990
Chile, see above, *apptd* 1977
Northern Argentina, Maurice Sinclair, *cons.* 1990, *apptd* 1990
Paraguay, John Ellison, *cons.* 1988, *apptd* 1988
Peru, Alan Winstanley, *cons.* 1988, *apptd* 1988
Uruguay, Harold Godfrey, *cons.* 1986, *apptd* 1986

PROVINCE OF THE EPISCOPAL CHURCH OF THE SUDAN

ARCHBISHOP OF PROVINCE, The Most Revd Benjamin W. Yugusuk (Bishop of Juba)

THE RT. REVD BISHOPS
Bor, Nathaniel Garang
Juba, see above
Kadugli, Mubarek Khamis
Kajokeji, Manaseh Dawidi
Khartoum, Bulus Idris
Malakal, Kedekia Mabior
Maridi, Joseph Marona
Mundri, Eluzai Munda
Red Sea, Butrus Kowa Kori
Rumbek, Gabriel Jur
Wau, Henry Riak
Yambio, Daniel Zindo, *cons.* 1984, *apptd* 1984
Yei, Seme Solomona

CHURCH OF THE PROVINCE OF TANZANIA

ARCHBISHOP OF PROVINCE, The Most Revd John A. Ramadhani (Bishop of Zanzibar and Tanga), *cons.* 1980, *apptd* 1984

THE RT. REVD BISHOPS
Central Tanganyika, Godfrey Mhogolo, *cons.* 1989, *apptd* 1989
Dar es Salaam, Basil Sambano, *cons.* 1992, *apptd* 1992
Kagera, Edwin Nyang'ubi, *cons.* 1993, *apptd* 1993
Mara, Gershom Nyaronga, *cons.* 1985, *apptd* 1985
Masasi, Christopher Sadiki, *cons.* 1992, *apptd* 1992
Morogoro, Dudley Mageni, *cons.* 1987, *apptd* 1987
Mount Kilimanjaro, Simon Makundi, *cons.* 1991, *apptd* 1991
Mpwapwa, Simon Chiwanga, *cons.* 1991, *apptd* 1991
Rift Valley, Alpha Mohamed, *cons.* 1982, *apptd* 1991
Ruaha, Donald Mtetemela, *cons.* 1982, *apptd* 1990
Ruvuma, Stanford Shauri, *cons.* 1989, *apptd* 1989
South-West Tanganyika, Charles Mwaigoga, *cons.* 1983, *apptd* 1983

Tabora, Francis Ntiruka, *cons.* 1989, *apptd* 1989
Victoria Nyanza, John Changae, *cons.* 1993, *apptd* 1993
Western Tanganyika, George Mpango, *cons.* 1983, *apptd* 1983
Zanzibar and Tanga, see above

CHURCH OF THE PROVINCE OF UGANDA

ARCHBISHOP OF THE PROVINCE, The Most Revd Dr Yona Okoth (Bishop of Kampala), *cons.* 1972, *apptd* 1984

THE RT. REVD BISHOPS
Bukedi, Nicodemus Okille, *apptd* 1984
Bunyoro-Kitara, Wilson Turumanya, *apptd* 1981
Busoga, Cyprian Bamwoze, *apptd* 1972
East Ankole, Elisha Kyamugambi, *cons.* 1992, *apptd* 1992
Kampala, see above
Karamoja, Peter Lomongin, *apptd* 1987
Kigezi, William Rukirande
Lango, Melchizedek Otim, *apptd* 1976
Luwero, M. Bugimbi, *cons.* 1990, *apptd* 1990
Madi and West Nile, Caleb Nguma, *apptd* 1991
Mbale, Israel Koboyi, *cons.* 1992, *apptd* 1992
Mityana, Wilson Mutebi, *apptd* 1977
Muhabura, Ernest M. Shalita, *cons.* 1990, *apptd* 1990
Mukono, Livingstone Mpalanyi-Nkoyoyo, *apptd* 1985
Namirembe, Misaeri Kauma, *apptd* 1985
Nebbi, Henry L. Orombi, *cons.* 1993, *apptd* 1993
North Mbale, Peter Mudonyi, *cons.* 1992, *apptd* 1992
North Kigezi, Yustasi Ruhindi, *apptd* 1981
Northern Uganda, Allan Oboma
Ruwenzori, Eustace Kamanyire, *apptd* 1981
Soroti, Geresom Ilukor, *apptd* 1976
South Ruwenzori, Zebidee Masereka
West Ankole, Yorumu Bamunoba, *apptd* 1977
West Buganda, Christopher Senyonjo, *apptd* 1974

EPISCOPAL CHURCH IN THE USA

PRESIDING BISHOP AND PRIMATE, Most Revd Edmond Lee Browning, DD, *cons.* 1968, *apptd* 1986

RT. REVD BISHOPS
(*missionary diocese)

Province I
Connecticut, Clarence Coleridge, *cons.* 1981, *apptd* 1994
Maine, Edward C. Chalfant, *cons.* 1984, *apptd* 1986
Massachusetts, David E. Johnson, *cons.* 1985, *apptd* 1986
New Hampshire, Douglas E. Theuner, *cons.* 1986, *apptd* 1986
Rhode Island, George N. Hunt, *cons.* 1980, *apptd* 1980
Vermont, Mary A. Mcleod, *cons.* 1993, *apptd* 1993
Western Massachusetts, Robert S. Denig, *cons.* 1993, *apptd* 1993

Province II
Albany, David S. Ball, *cons.* 1984, *apptd* 1984
Central New York, David B. Joslin, *cons.* 1991, *apptd* 1992
Europe, Convocation of American Churches in, Matthew P. Bigliardi, *cons.* 1974, *apptd* 1988
Haiti, Zaché Duracin, *cons.* 1993, *apptd* 1994
Long Island, Orris Walker, *cons.* 1988, *apptd* 1991
New Jersey, G. P. Mellick Belshaw, *cons.* 1975, *apptd* 1983
New York, Richard Grein, *cons.* 1981, *apptd* 1989

Newark, John S. Spong, *cons.* 1976, *apptd* 1979
Rochester, William G. Burrill, *cons.* 1984, *apptd* 1984
*Virgin Islands, Don. E. Taylor, *cons.* 1987, *apptd* 1987
Western New York, David C. Bowman, *cons.* 1986, *apptd* 1987

Province III

Bethlehem, J. Mark Dyer, *cons.* 1982, *apptd* 1983
Central Pennsylvania, Charlie F. McNutt, *cons.* 1980, *apptd* 1982
Delaware, C. Cabell Tennis, *cons.* 1986, *apptd* 1986
Easton, Martin G. Townsend, *cons.* 1992, *apptd* 1993
Maryland, A. Theodore Eastman, *cons.* 1982, *apptd* 1986
North-Western Pennsylvania, Robert D. Rowley jun., *cons.* 1989, *apptd* 1991
Pennsylvania, Allen L. Bartlett, *cons.* 1986, *apptd* 1987
Pittsburgh, Alden M. Hathaway, *cons.* 1981, *apptd* 1983
Southern Virginia, Frank Vest, *cons.* 1985, *apptd* 1991
South-Western Virginia, Arthur H. Light, *cons.* 1979, *apptd* 1979
Virginia, Peter J. Lee, *cons.* 1984, *apptd* 1985
Washington, Ronald Haines, *cons.* 1986, *apptd* 1990
West Virginia, John H. Smith, *cons.* 1989, *apptd* 1989

Province IV

Alabama, Robert O. Miller, *cons.* 1988, *apptd* 1988
Atlanta, Frank K. Allen, *cons.* 1988, *apptd* 1989
Central Florida, John Howe, *cons.* 1989, *apptd* 1990
Central Gulf Coast, Charles F. Duvall, *cons.* 1981, *apptd* 1981
East Carolina, B. Sidney Sanders, *cons.* 1979, *apptd* 1983
East Tennessee, Robert G. Tharp, *cons.* 1991, *apptd* 1992
Florida, Frank S. Cerveny, *cons.* 1974, *apptd* 1975
Georgia, Harry W. Shipps, *cons.* 1984, *apptd* 1985
Kentucky, David B. Reed, *cons.* 1964, *apptd* 1974
Lexington, Don A. Wimberley, *cons.* 1984, *apptd* 1985
Louisiana, James B. Brown, *cons.* 1976, *apptd* 1976
Mississippi, Alfred C. Marble jun., *cons.* 1991, *apptd* 1993
North Carolina, Robert W. Estill, *cons.* 1980, *apptd* 1983
South Carolina, Edward Salmon jun., *cons.* 1990, *apptd* 1990
South-East Florida, Calvin O. Schofield jun., *cons.* 1979, *apptd* 1980
South-West Florida, Roger Harris, *cons.* 1989, *apptd* 1989
Tennessee, Bertram N. Herlong, *cons.* 1993, *apptd* 1993
Upper South Carolina, William A. Beckham, *cons.* 1979, *apptd* 1979
West Tennessee, Alex D. Dickson jun., *cons.* 1983, *apptd* 1983
Western Louisiana, Robert Hargrove jun., *cons.* 1989, *apptd* 1990
Western North Carolina, Robert Johnson, *cons* 1989, *apptd* 1990

Province V

Chicago, Frank T. Griswold III, *cons.* 1985, *apptd* 1987
Eau Claire, William C. Wantland, *cons.* 1980, *apptd* 1980
Fond Du Lac, William L. Stevens, *cons.* 1980, *apptd* 1980
Indianapolis, Edward W. Jones, *cons.* 1977, *apptd* 1977
Michigan, R. Stewart Wood, *cons.* 1990, *apptd* 1990
Milwaukee, Roger J. White, *cons.* 1984, *apptd* 1985
Missouri, Hayes Rockwell, *cons.* 1991, *apptd* 1993
Northern Indiana, Francis C. Gray, *cons.* 1986, *apptd* 1987
Northern Michigan, Thomas K. Ray, *cons.* 1982, *apptd* 1982
Ohio, James R. Moodey, *cons.* 1983, *apptd* 1984
Quincy, Edward Macburney, *cons.* 1988, *apptd* 1988
Southern Ohio, Herbert Thompson jun., *cons.* 1988, *apptd* 1992
Springfield, Donald M. Hultstrand, *cons.* 1982, *apptd* 1982
Western Michigan, Edward L. Lee jun., *cons.* 1989, *apptd* 1989

Province VI

Colorado, William Winterrowd, *cons.* 1991, *apptd* 1991
Iowa, C. Christopher Epting, *cons.* 1988, *apptd* 1988
Minnesota, James Jelinek, *cons.* 1993, *apptd* 1993
Montana, Charles I. Jones, *cons.* 1986, *apptd* 1986
Nebraska, James E. Krotz, *cons.* 1989, *apptd* 1989
*North Dakota, Andrew H. Fairfield, *cons.* 1990, *apptd* 1990
South Dakota, vacant
Wyoming, Bob G. Jones, *cons.* 1977, *apptd* 1977

Province VII

Arkansas, vacant
Dallas, James Stanton, *cons.* 1993, *apptd* 1993
Fort Worth, Clarence C. Pope jun., *cons.* 1985, *apptd* 1986
Kansas, William E. Smalley, *cons.* 1989, *apptd* 1989
North-West Texas, Sam B. Hulsey, *cons.* 1980, *apptd* 1980
Oklahoma, Robert M. Moodey, *cons.* 1988, *apptd* 1989
Rio Grande, Terence Kelshaw, *cons.* 1989, *apptd* 1989
Texas, Maurice M. Benitez, *cons.* 1980, *apptd* 1980
West Missouri, John C. Buchanan, *cons.* 1989, *apptd* 1989
West Texas, John H. MacNaughton, *cons.* 1986, *apptd* 1987
Western Kansas, John F. Ashby, *cons.* 1981, *apptd* 1981

Province VIII

Alaska, Stephen Charleston, *cons.* 1991, *apptd* 1991
Arizona, Robert R. Shahan, *cons.* 1992, *apptd* 1993
California, William E. Swing, *cons.* 1979, *apptd* 1980
El Camino Real, Richard L. Skimpfky, *cons.* 1990, *apptd* 1990
Eastern Oregon, Rustin R. Kimsey, *cons.* 1980, *apptd* 1980
Hawaii, Donald P. Hart, *cons.* 1986, *apptd* 1986
Idaho, John Thornton, *cons.* 1990, *apptd* 1990
Los Angeles, Frederick L. Borsch, *cons.* 1988, *apptd* 1988
*Navajoland Area Mission, Steven T. Plummer, *cons.* 1989, *apptd* 1989
Nevada, Stewart C. Zabriskie, *cons.* 1986, *apptd* 1986
Northern California, Jerry A. Lamb, *cons.* 1991, *apptd* 1992
Olympia, Vincent W. Warner, *cons.* 1989, *apptd* 1990
Oregon, Robert L. Ladehoff, *cons.* 1985, *apptd* 1986
San Diego, Gethin B. Hughes, *cons.* 1992, *apptd* 1992
San Joaquin, John-David Schofield, *cons.* 1988, *apptd* 1989
Spokane, Frank Terry, *cons.* 1990, *apptd* 1991
*Taiwan, John C. T. Chien, *cons.* 1988, *apptd* 1988
Utah, George E. Bates, *cons.* 1986, *apptd* 1986

Province IX

*Central Ecuador, Neptali L. Moreno, *cons.* 1990, *apptd* 1990
*Colombia, Bernardo Merino-Botero, *cons.* 1979, *apptd* 1979
Cuernavaca, Jose G. Saucedo, *cons.* 1958, *apptd* 1989
*Dominican Republic, Julio C. Holguin, *apptd* 1991
*Guatemala, Armando Guerra-Soria, *cons.* 1982, *apptd* 1982
*Honduras, Leopold Frade, *cons.* 1984, *apptd* 1984
*Mexico, Sergio Cananga-Gomez, *cons.* 1989, *apptd* 1989
*Nicaragua, Sturdie W. Downs, *cons.* 1985, *apptd* 1985
*Northern Mexico, German Martinez, *cons.* 1987, *apptd* 1987
*Panama, James H. Ottley, *cons.* 1984, *apptd* 1984
*El Salvador, Martin Barahona, *cons.* 1992, *apptd* 1992
*South-East Mexico, Claro H. Rames, *cons.* 1980, *apptd* 1989
*Western Mexico, Samuel Espinoza-Venegas, *cons.* 1981, *apptd* 1983

Extra-Provincial

Costa Rica, Cornelius J. Wilson, *cons.* 1978, *apptd* 1978
Puerto Rico, David Alvarez, *cons.* 1987, *apptd* 1987
Venezuela, Onell A. Soto, *cons.* 1987, *apptd* 1987

CHURCH OF THE PROVINCE OF WEST AFRICA

ARCHBISHOP OF PROVINCE, vacant

THE RT. REVD BISHOPS
Accra, Francis Thompson, *cons.* 1983, *apptd* 1983
Bo, Michael Keili, OBE, *cons.* 1981, *apptd* 1981
Cape Coast, Kobina Quashie, *apptd* 1992
Freetown, Prince Thompson, *cons.* 1981, *apptd* 1981
Gambia, Solomon Johnson, *cons.* 1990, *apptd* 1990
Guinea, vacant
Koforidua, Robert Okine, *cons.* 1981, *apptd* 1981
Kumasi, Edmund Yeboah, *cons.* 1985, *apptd* 1985
Liberia, vacant
Sekondi, Theophilus Annobil, *cons.* 1981, *apptd* 1981
Sunyani/Tamale, Joseph Dadson, *cons.* 1981, *apptd* 1981

The Anglican Church of Cameroon is a missionary area of the Province

CHURCH IN THE PROVINCE OF THE WEST INDIES

ARCHBISHOP OF PROVINCE, The Most Revd Orland Lindsay (Bishop of North-Eastern Caribbean and Aruba), *cons.* 1970, *apptd* 1986

THE RT. REVD BISHOPS
Barbados, Drexel Gomez, *cons.* 1972, *apptd* 1972
Belize, Desmond Smith, *cons.* 1989, *apptd* 1989
Guyana, Randolph George, *cons.* 1976, *apptd* 1980
Jamaica, Neville de Souza, *cons.* 1973, *apptd* 1979
Nassau and the Bahamas, Michael Eldon, CMG, *cons.* 1971, *apptd* 1972
North-Eastern Caribbean and Aruba, *see* above
Trinidad and Tobago, Clive Abdulah, *cons.* 1970, *apptd* 1970
Windward Islands, Philip Elder, *cons.* 1966

CHURCH OF THE PROVINCE OF ZAIRE

ARCHBISHOP OF THE PROVINCE, The Most Revd Byanka Njojo (Bishop of Boga-Zaire), *apptd* 1992

THE RT. REVD BISHOPS
Boga-Zaire, *see* above, *apptd* 1980
Bukavu, Balufuga Dirokpa, *apptd* 1982
Kisangani, Sylvestre Mugera, *apptd* 1980
Nord Kivu, Methusela Musubaho
Shaba, Emmanuel Mbona

OTHER CHURCHES AND EXTRA-PROVINCIAL DIOCESES

ANGLICAN CHURCH OF BERMUDA, Rt. Revd William Down, *apptd* 1990
EPISCOPAL CHURCH OF CUBA, Rt. Revd Emilio H. Albalate
HONG KONG AND MACAO, Rt. Revd Peter Kwong
KUCHING, Rt. Revd Datuk John Leong Chee Yun
SABAH, Rt. Revd Yong Ping Chung, *apptd* 1991
SINGAPORE, Rt. Revd Moses Leng Kong Tay, *apptd* 1982

WEST MALAYSIA, Rt. Revd Tan Sri John Savarimuthu, *apptd* 1973
LUSITANIAN CHURCH (*Portuguese Episcopal Church*), Rt. Revd Fernando Soares, *apptd* 1971
SPANISH REFORMED CHURCH, Rt. Revd Arturo Sánchez Galan, *apptd* 1982

The Church of Scotland

The Church of Scotland is the established (i.e. state) church of Scotland. The Church is Reformed and evangelical in doctrine, and presbyterian in constitution. In 1560 the jurisdiction of the Roman Catholic Church in Scotland was abolished and the first assembly of the Church of Scotland ratified the Confession of Faith, drawn up by a committee including John Knox. In 1592 Parliament passed an Act guaranteeing the liberties of the Church and its presbyterian government. James VI (James I of England) and later Stuart monarchs attempted to restore episcopacy, but a presbyterian church was finally restored in 1690 and secured by the Act of Settlement (1690) and the Act of Union (1707). The Free Church of Scotland was formed in 1843 in a dispute over patronage and state interference; in 1900 most of its ministers joined with the United Presbyterian Church (formed in 1847) to form the United Free Church of Scotland. In 1929 most of this body rejoined the Church of Scotland to form the united Church of Scotland.

The Church of Scotland is presbyterian in its organization, i.e. based on a hierarchy of councils of ministers and elders and, since 1990, of members of a diaconate. At local level the kirk session consists of the parish minister and ruling elders. At district level the presbyteries, of which there are 47, consist of all the ministers in the district, one ruling elder from each congregation, and those members of the diaconate who qualify for membership. The General Assembly is the supreme authority, and is presided over by a Moderator chosen annually by the Assembly. The Sovereign, if not present in person, is represented by a Lord High Commissioner who is appointed each year by the Crown.

The Church of Scotland has about 753,000 members, 1,260 ministers and 1,700 churches. There are about 100 ministers and other personnel working overseas.

Lord High Commissioner (1993), The Lord Macfarlane of Bearsden
Moderator of the General Assembly (1993), Rt. Revd J. L. Weatherhead
Principal Clerk, Revd A. G. McGillivray
Deputy Clerk, Revd F. A. J. MacDonald
Procurator, A. Dunlop, QC
Law Agent and Solicitor of the Church, R. A. Paterson
Parliamentary Agent, I. McCulloch (*London*)
General Treasurer, W. G. P. Colledge
CHURCH OFFICE, 121 George Street, Edinburgh EH2 4YN. Tel: 031-225 5722

PRESBYTERIES
Clerks

Edinburgh, Revd W. P. Graham
West Lothian, Revd D. Shaw
Lothian, Revd J. Ritchie

Melrose and Peebles, Revd C. A. Duncan
Duns, Revd I. G. Wotherspoon
Jedburgh, Revd N. R. Combe

Annandale and Eskdale, Revd C. B. Haston

Dumfries and Kirkcudbright, Revd G. M. A. Savage
Wigtown and Stranraer, Revd D. Dutton

Ayr, Revd J. Crichton
Irvine and Kilmarnock, Revd C. G. F. Brockie
Ardrossan, Revd D. Broster

Lanark, Revd I. D. Cunningham
Paisley, Revd J. P. Cubie
Greenock, Revd D. Mill
Glasgow, Revd A. Cunningham
Hamilton, Revd J. H. Wilson
Dumbarton, Revd D. P. Munro

South Argyll, Revd R. H. McNidder
Dunoon, Revd R. Samuel
Lorn and Mull, Revd W. M. Ritchie

Falkirk, Revd D. E. McClements
Stirling, Revd G. A. McCutcheon

Dunfermline, Revd W. E. Farquhar
Kirkcaldy, Revd B. L. Tomlinson
St Andrews, Revd J. W. Patterson

Dunkeld and Meigle, Revd A. F. Chisholm
Perth, Revd G. G. Stewart
Dundee, Revd J. A. Roy
Angus, Revd A. F. M. Downie

Aberdeen, Revd A. M. Douglas
Kincardine and Deeside, Revd J. W. S. Brown
Gordon, Revd I. U. Thomson
Buchan, Revd R. Neilson
Moray, Revd J. T. Stuart

Abernethy, Revd J. A. I. MacEwan
Inverness, Revd R. J. V. Logan
Lochaber, Revd A. Ramsay

Ross, Revd R. M. MacKinnon
Sutherland, Revd J. L. Goskirk
Caithness, Revd M. G. Mappin
Lochcarron/Skye, Revd A. I. Macarthur
Uist, Revd A. P. J. Varwell
Lewis, Revd T. S. Sinclair

Orkney (Finstown), Revd D. A. Williams
Shetland (Lerwick), Revd M. Cheyne
England (London), Revd W. A. Cairns
Europe (Portugal), Revd R. Hill

The Roman Catholic Church

The Roman Catholic Church is one world-wide Christian Church acknowledging as its head the Bishop of Rome, known as the Pope (Father). The Pope is held to be the successor of St Peter and thus invested with the power which was entrusted to St Peter by Jesus Christ. A direct line of succession is therefore claimed from the earliest Christian communities. Papal authority over the doctrine and jurisdiction of the Church in western Europe developed early and was unrivalled after the split with the Eastern Orthodox Church until the Protestant Reformation in the 16th century. With the fall of the Roman Empire the Pope also became an important political leader. His temporal power is now limited to the 107 acres of the Vatican City State.

The Pope exercises spiritual authority over the Church with the advice and assistance of the Sacred College of Cardinals, the supreme council of the Church. He is also advised about the concerns of the Church locally by his ambassadors, who liaise with the Bishops' Conference in each country.

In addition to advising the Pope, those members of the Sacred College of Cardinals who are under the age of 80 also elect a successor following the death of a Pope. The assembly of the Cardinals at the Vatican for the election of a new Pope is known as the Conclave in which, in complete seclusion, the Cardinals elect by a secret ballot; a two-thirds majority is necessary before the vote can be accepted as final. When a Cardinal receives the necessary votes, the Dean of the Sacred College formally asks him if he will accept election and the name by which he wishes to be known. On his acceptance of the office the Conclave is dissolved and the First Cardinal Deacon announces the election to the assembled crowd in St Peter's Square. On the first Sunday or Holyday following the election, the new Pope assumes the pontificate at High Mass in St Peter's Square. A new pontificate is dated from the assumption of the pontificate.

The number of cardinals was fixed at 70 by Pope Sixtus V in 1586, but has been steadily increased since the pontificate of John XXIII and now stands at 153 (as at end May 1993).

The Roman Catholic Church universally and the Vatican City State are run by the Curia, which is made up of the Secretariat of State, the Sacred Council for the Public Affairs of the Church, and various congregations, secretariats and tribunals assisted by commissions and offices. The congregations are permanent commissions for conducting the affairs of the Church and are made up of cardinals, one of whom occupies the office of prefect. Below the Secretariat of State and the congregations are the secretariats and tribunals, all of which are headed by cardinals. (The Curial cardinals are analagous to ministers in charge of government departments.)

The Vatican State has its own diplomatic service, with representatives known as nuncios. Papal nuncios with full diplomatic recognition are given precedence over all other ambassadors to the country to which they are appointed; where precedence is not recognized, as in Britain, the Papal representative is known as a pro-nuncio. Where the representation is only to the local churches and not to the government of a country, the Papal representative is known as an apostolic delegate. The Roman Catholic Church has an estimated 890,907,000 adherents world-wide.

SOVEREIGN PONTIFF

His Holiness Pope John Paul II (Karol Wojtyla), *born* Wadowice, Poland, 18 May 1920; *ordained priest* 1946; *appointed Archbishop* of Krakow 1964; *created Cardinal* 1967; *assumed pontificate* 16 October 1978

SECRETARIAT OF STATE
Secretary of State, HE Cardinal Angelo Sodano
First Section (General Affairs), Mgr G. Re, Archbishop of Vescovio
Second Section (Relations with other states), Mgr J. L. Tauran, Archbishop of Telepte

BISHOPS' CONFERENCE
The Roman Catholic Church in England and Wales is governed by the Bishops' Conference, membership of which includes the Diocesan Bishops, the Apostolic Exarch of the Ukrainians, the Bishop of the Forces and the Auxiliary Bishops. The Conference is headed by the President (Cardinal Basil Hume, Archbishop of Westminster) and Vice-President (the Archbishop of Liverpool). There are five departments, each with an episcopal chairman: the Department for Christian Life and Worship (the Archbishop of Southwark), the Department for Mission and Unity (the Bishop of East Anglia), the Department for Catholic Education and Formation (the Bishop of Leeds), the Department for Christian Responsibility and Citizenship

(the Bishop of Middlesbrough), and the Department for International Affairs (the Bishop of Salford).

The Bishops' Standing Committee, made up of all the Archbishops and the chairman of each of the above departments, has general responsibility for continuity and policy between the plenary sessions of the Conference. It prepares the Conference agenda and implements its decisions. It is serviced by a General Secretariat. There are also agencies and consultative bodies affiliated to the Conference.

The Bishops' Conference of Scotland has as its president Archbishop Winning of Glasgow and is the permanently constituted assembly of the Bishops of Scotland. To promote its work, the Conference establishes various agencies which have an advisory function in relation to the Conference. The more important of these agencies are called Commissions and each one has a Bishop President who, with the other members of the Commissions, are appointed by the Conference.

The Irish Episcopal Conference has as its acting president Archbishop Connell of Dublin. Its membership comprises all the Archbishops and Bishops of Ireland and it appoints various Commissions to assist it in its work. There are three types of Commissions: (a) those made up of lay and clerical members chosen for their skills and experience, and staffed by full-time expert secretariats; (b) Commissions whose members are selected from existing institutions and whose services are supplied on a part-time basis; and (c) Commissions of Bishops only.

The Roman Catholic Church in Britain and Ireland has an estimated 8,992,092 members, 11 archbishops, 67 bishops, 12,698 priests, and 8,588 churches and chapels open to the public.

Bishops' Conferences secretariats:

ENGLAND AND WALES, 39 Eccleston Square, London SWIV IPD. Tel: 071-630 8220. *General Secretary*, Revd Philip Carroll

SCOTLAND, Candida Casa, 8 Corsehill Road, Ayr, Scotland KA7 2ST. Tel: 0292-256750. *General Secretary*, Rt. Revd Maurice Taylor, Bishop of Galloway

IRELAND, Iona, 67 Newry Road, Dundalk, Co. Louth. *Executive Secretary*, Revd Gerard Clifford

---

GREAT BRITAIN

APOSTOLIC PRO-NUNCIO TO THE UNITED KINGDOM OF GREAT BRITAIN AND NORTHERN IRELAND
The Most Revd Luigi Barbarito

ENGLAND AND WALES

THE MOST REVD ARCHBISHOPS
Westminster, HE Cardinal Basil Hume, *cons.* 1976
   Auxiliary, Victor Guazzelli, *cons.* 1970
   Auxiliary, Vincent Nichols, *cons.* 1992
   Auxiliary, James J. O'Brien, *cons.* 1977
   Auxiliary, Patrick O'Donoghue, *cons.* 1983
   Clergy, 839
Birmingham, Maurice Couve de Murville, *cons.* 1982, *apptd* 1982
   Auxiliary, Terence Brain, *cons.* 1991
   Auxiliary, Philip Pargeter, *cons.* 1989
   Clergy, 426
Cardiff, John A. Ward, *cons.* 1981, *apptd* 1983
   Clergy, 163
Liverpool, Derek Worlock, *cons.* 1965, *apptd* 1976
   Auxiliary, John Rawsthorne, *cons.* 1981

   Auxiliary, Vincent Malone, *cons.* 1989
   Clergy, 515
Southwark, Michael Bowen, *cons.* 1970, *apptd* 1977
   Auxiliary, Charles Henderson, *cons.* 1972
   Auxiliary, Howard Tripp, *cons.* 1980
   Auxiliary, John Jukes, *cons.* 1980
   Clergy, 518

THE RT. REVD BISHOPS
Arundel and Brighton, Cormac Murphy-O'Connor, *cons.* 1977. *Clergy*, 255
Brentwood, Thomas McMahon, *cons.* 1980, *apptd* 1980. *Clergy*, 188
Clifton, Mervyn Alexander, *cons.* 1972, *apptd* 1975. *Clergy*, 242
East Anglia, Alan Clark, *cons.* 1969, *apptd* 1976. *Clergy*, 112
Hallam, Gerald Moverley, *cons.* 1968, *apptd* 1980. *Clergy*, 100
Hexham and Newcastle, Michael Ambrose Griffiths, *cons.* 1992. *Clergy*, 309
   Auxiliary, Owen Swindelhurst, *cons.* 1977
Lancaster, John Brewer, *cons.* 1971, *apptd* 1985. *Clergy*, 228
Leeds, David Konstant, *cons.* 1977, *apptd* 1985. *Clergy*, 225
Menevia (Wales), Daniel Mullins, *cons.* 1970, *apptd* 1987. *Clergy*, 59
Middlesbrough, John Crowley, *cons.* 1986, *apptd* 1992. *Clergy*, 201
   Auxiliary, Thomas O'Brien, *cons.* 1981
Northampton, Patrick Leo McCartie, *cons.* 1977. *Clergy*, 123
Nottingham, James McGuinness, *cons.* 1972, *apptd* 1975. *Clergy*, 224
Plymouth, Christopher Budd, *cons.* 1986. *Clergy*, 168
Portsmouth, F. Crispian Hollis, *cons.* 1987, *apptd* 1989. *Clergy*, 282
Salford, Patrick Kelly, *cons.* 1984. *Clergy*, 455
Shrewsbury, Joseph Gray, *cons.* 1969, *apptd* 1980. *Clergy*, 226
Wrexham (Wales), James Hannigan, *cons.* 1983, *apptd* 1987. *Clergy*, 94

SCOTLAND

THE MOST REVD ARCHBISHOPS
St Andrews and Edinburgh, Keith Patrick O'Brian, *cons.* 1985
   Auxiliary, Kevin Rafferty, *cons.* 1990
   Clergy, 213
Glasgow, Thomas Winning, *cons.* 1971, *apptd* 1974
   Clergy, 338

THE RT. REVD BISHOPS
Aberdeen, Mario Conti, *cons.* 1977. *Clergy*, 59
Argyll and the Isles, Roderick Wright, *cons.* 1990. *Clergy*, 35
Dunkeld, Vincent Logan, *cons.* 1981. *Clergy*, 67
Galloway, Maurice Taylor, *cons.* 1981. *Clergy*, 75
Motherwell, Joseph Devine, *cons.* 1977, *apptd* 1983. *Clergy*, 190
Paisley, John A. Mone, *cons.* 1984, *apptd* 1988. *Clergy*, 98

IRELAND

There is one hierarchy for the whole of Ireland. Several of the dioceses have territory partly in the Republic of Ireland and partly in Northern Ireland.

NUNCIO TO IRELAND
   Most Revd Emanuele Gerada (titular Archbishop of Nomenta)

THE MOST REVD ARCHBISHOPS
Armagh, HE Cardinal Cahal B. Daly, *cons.* 1990
  Auxiliary, Gerard Clifford, *cons.* 1991
  Clergy, 271
Cashel, Dermot Clifford, *cons.* 1986
  Clergy, 122
Dublin, Desmond Connell, *cons.* 1988, *apptd* 1988
  Auxiliary, Donal Murray, *cons.* 1982
  Auxiliary, Dermot O'Mahony, *cons.* 1975
  Auxiliary, James Moriarty, *cons.* 1992
  Auxiliary, Eamonn Walsh, *cons.* 1990
  Auxiliary, Desmond Williams, *cons.* 1985
  Clergy, 994
Tuam, Joseph Cassidy, *cons.* 1979, *apptd* 1987
  Auxiliary, Michael Neary, *cons.* 1992
  Clergy, 165

THE MOST REVD BISHOPS
Achonry, Thomas Flynn, *cons.* 1975. *Clergy*, 55
Ardagh and Clonmacnois, Colm O'Reilly, *cons.* 1983.
  Clergy, 108
Clogher, Joseph Duffy, *cons.* 1979. *Clergy*, 124
Clonfert, Joseph Kirby, *cons.* 1988. *Clergy*, 76
Cloyne, John Magee, *cons.* 1987. *Clergy*, 155
Cork and Ross, Michael Murphy, *cons.* 1976. *Clergy*, 360
  Auxiliary, John Buckley, *cons.* 1984
Derry, Edward Daly, *cons.* 1974. *Clergy*, 149
  Auxiliary, Francis Lagan, *cons.* 1988
Down and Connor, Patrick J. Walsh, *cons.* 1991. *Clergy*, 324
  Auxiliary, Anthony Farquhar, *cons.* 1983
  Auxiliary, William Philbin, *cons.* 1991
Dromore, Francis Brooks, *cons.* 1976. *Clergy*, 71
Elphin, Dominic Conway, *cons.* 1970. *Clergy*, 104
Ferns, Brendon Comiskey, *cons.* 1980. *Clergy*, 148
Galway and Kilmacduagh, James McLoughlin, *cons.* 1993
Kerry, Dermot O'Sullivan, *cons.* 1985. *Clergy*, 143
Kildare and Leighlin, Laurence Ryan, *cons.* 1984.
  Clergy, 225
Killala, Thomas Finnegan, *cons.* 1970. *Clergy*, 51
Killaloe, Michael Harty, *cons.* 1967. *Clergy*, 186
Kilmore, Francis McKiernan, *cons.* 1972. *Clergy*, 103
Limerick, Jeremiah Newman, *cons.* 1974. *Clergy*, 234
Meath, Michael Smith, *cons.* 1984, *apptd* 1990. *Clergy*, 270
Ossory, Laurence Forristal, *cons.* 1980. *Clergy*, 125
Raphoe, Seamus Hegarty, *cons.* 1984. *Clergy*, 102
Waterford and Lismore, Michael Russell, *cons.* 1965.
  Clergy, 206

RESIDENTIAL ARCHBISHOPRICS
THROUGHOUT THE WORLD

This list is set out with the name of the relevant country first;
then the name of the diocese; and finally the Archbishop's
name. It does not include England and Wales, Scotland or
Ireland which are above.

ALBANIA
Durrës-Tirana, Brok K. Mirdita
Shkodër, Frano Illia

ALGERIA
Algiers, Henri Teissier

ANGOLA
Huambo, Francisco Viti
Luanda, HE Cardinal Alexandre do Nascimento
Lubango, Manuel Franklin da Costa

ARGENTINA
Bahia Blanca, Romulo Garcia
Buenos Aires, HE Cardinal Antonio Quarracino
Córdoba, HE Cardinal Raúl Francisco Primatesta
Corrientes, Fortunato A. Rossi
La Plata, Carlos Galán
Mendoza, Candido Genaro Rubiolo
  Coadjutor, Jose M. Grancibia
Paraná, Estanislao Esteban Karlic
Resistencia, vacant
Rosario, Jorge Manuel López
Salta, Moises J. Blanchoud
San Juan de Cuyo, Italo Severino Di Stefano
Santa Fe, Edgardo Gabriel Storni
Tucumán, Horatio A. Bozzoli

AUSTRALIA
Adelaide, Leonard Anthony Faulkner
Brisbane, John A. Bathersby
Canberra, Francis P. Carroll
Hobart, Joseph E. D'Arcy
Melbourne, Thomas Francis Little
Perth, Barry J. Hickey
Sydney, HE Cardinal Edward B. Clancy

AUSTRIA
Salzburg, Georg Eder
Vienna, HE Cardinal Hans Hermann Groer

BANGLADESH
Dhaka, Michael Rozario

BELARUS
Minsk-Mohilev Archdiocese, Kazimierz Swiatek

BELGIUM
Malines-Bruxelles, HE Cardinal Godfried Danneels

BENIN
Cotonou, Isidore de Souzá

BOLIVIA
Cochabamba, Rene Fernandez Apaza
La Paz, Luis Sainz Hinojosa
Santa Cruz de la Sierra, Julio T. Sandoval
Sucre, Jesus G. Pérez Rodriguez

BOSNIA HERCEGOVINA
Vrhbosna, Sarajevo, Vinko Pubjić

BRAZIL
Aparecida, Geraldo Maria de Morais Penido
Aracaju, Luciano José Cabral Duarte
Bélem do Pará, Vicente Joaquim Zico
Belo Horizonte, Serafim Fernandes de Araújo
Botucatu, Antonio M. Mucciolo
Brasilia, HE Cardinal Jose Freire Falcao
Campinas, Gilberto Pereira Lopes
Campo Grande, Vitorio Pavanello
Cascavel, Armando Cirio
Cuiaba, Bonifacio Piccinini
Curitiba, Pedro Antonio Fedalto
Diamantina, Geraldo Majelo Reis
Florianópolis, Eusebio Oscar Scheid
Fortaleza, HE Cardinal Aloisio Lorscheider
Goiania, Antonio Ribeiro de Oliveira
Juiz de Fora, Clovis Frainer
Londrina, Albano Bortoletto Cavallin
Maceió, Edvaldo G. Amaral
Manaus, Luiz S. Vieira
Mariana, Luciano Mendes de Almeida
Maringá, Jaime Luis Coelho
Natal, Alair V. Fernandes de Melo

Niteroi, Carlos A. Navarro
Olinda and Recife, José Cardoso Sobrinho
Paraiba, José M. Pires
Porto Alegre, Altamiro Rossato
Porto Velho, José Martins da Silva
Pouso Alegre, João Bergese
Ribeirão Preto, Arnaldo Ribeiro
São Luis do Maranhão, Paulo Eduardo de Andrade Ponte
São Paulo, HE Cardinal Paulo Evaristo Arns
São Salvador da Bahia, HE Cardinal Lucas Moreira Neves
São Sebastião do Rio de Janeiro, HE Cardinal Eugenio de
    Araújo Sales
Sorocaba, José Lambert
Teresina, Miguel F. Camara Filho
Uberaba, Benedito de Ulhôa Vieira
Vitória, Silvestre L. Scandian

BURKINA
Ouagadougou, HE Cardinal Paul Zoungrana

BURUNDI
Gitega, Joachim Ruhuna

CAMEROON
Bamenda, Paul Verdzekov
Douala, HE Cardinal Christian W. Tumi
Garoua, Antoine Ntalou
Yaoundé, Jean Zoa

CANADA
Edmonton, Joseph N. MacNeil
Gatineau-Hull, Roger Ebacher
Grouard-McLennon, Henri Légaré
Halifax, Austin-Emile Burke
Keewatin-Le Pas, Peter Alfred Sutton
Kingston, Francis John Spence
Moncton, Donat Chiasson
Montreal, Jean-Claude Turcotte
Ottawa, Marcel A. Gervais
Quebec, Maurice Couture
Regina, Charles Halpin
Rimouski, Bertrand Blanchet
St Boniface, Antoine Hacault
St Johns, Newfoundland, James H. MacDonald
Sherbrooke, Jean Marie Fortier
Toronto, Aloysius Matthew Ambrosic
Vancouver, Adam J. Exner
Winnipeg, Leonard J. Wall; (Ukrainian Rite), Michael Bzdel

CENTRAL AFRICAN REPUBLIC
Bangui, Joachim N'Dayen

CHAD
Ndjamena, Charles Vandame

CHILE
Antofagasta, Patricio Infante Alfonso
Concepción, Antonio M. Casamitjana
La Serena, Francisco J. Cox Huneeus
Puerto Montt, Savino B. Cazzaro Bertollo
Santiago de Chile, Carlos Oviedo Cavada

CHINA
Anking, Huai-Ning, vacant
Canton, Dominic Tang Yee-Ming
Changsha, vacant
Chungking, vacant
Foochow, Min-Hou, vacant
Hangchow, vacant
Hankow, vacant
Kaifeng, vacant
Kunming, vacant
Kweyang, vacant

Lanchow, vacant
Mukden, vacant
Nanchang, vacant
Nanking, vacant
Nanning, vacant
Peking (Beijing), vacant
Sian, vacant
Suiyüan, Francis Wang Hsueh-Ming
Taiyuan, vacant
Tsinan, vacant

COLOMBIA
Barranquilla, Felix Maria Torres Parra
Bogotá, HE Cardinal Mario Revollo Bravo
Bucaramanga, Dario Castrillon Hoyos
Cali, Pedro Rubiano Sáenz
Cartagena, Carlos José Ruiseco Vieira
Ibague, Juan S. Jaramillo
Manizales, José de Jesús Pimiento Rodriguez
Medellin, Hector Rueda Hernández
Nueva Pamplona, Rafael Sarmiento Peralta
Popayán, Alberto G. Jaramillo
Santa Fe de Antioquia, Ignacio Gomez Afistizabal
Tunja, Augusto Trujillo Arango

CONGO
Brazzaville, Barthélémy Batantu

COSTA RICA
San José, Román Arrieta Villalobos

CÔTE D'IVOIRE
Abidjan, HE Cardinal Bernard Yago

CROATIA
Rijeka-Senj, Anton Tamarut
Split-Makarska, Ante Juric
Zadar, Marijan Oblak
Zagreb, HE Cardinal Franjo Kuharić

CUBA
San Cristóbal de la Habana, Jaime Lucas Ortega y Alamino
Santiago de Cuba, Pedro Meurice Estiu

CYPRUS
Cyprus (Maronite Seat at Nicosia), Boutros Gemayel

CZECH REPUBLIC
Olomouc, Jan Graubner
Praha, Miloslav Vlk

DOMINICAN REPUBLIC
Santo Domingo, HE Cardinal Nicolás de Jesús López
    Rodriguez

ECUADOR
Cuenca, Alberto Luna Tobar
Guayaquil, Ignacio Larrea Holguin
Quito, Antonio J. González Zumárraga

EQUATORIAL GUINEA
Malabo, Idlefonso Obama Obono

ETHIOPIA
Addis Ababa, HE Cardinal Paul Tzadua

FRANCE
Aix, Bernard Panafieu
Albi, Roger Meindre
Auch, Gabriel Vanel
Avignon, Raymond Bouchex
Besançon, Lucien Daloz
Bordeaux, Pierre Eyt
Bourges, Pierre Plateau
Cambrai, Jacques Delaporte

Chambéry, Claude Feidt
Lyon, HE Cardinal Albert Decourtray
Marseilles, HE Cardinal Robert Coffy
Paris, HE Cardinal J. M. Lustiger
Reims, Jean Balland
Rennes, Jacques Jullien
Rouen, Joseph Duval
Sens, Gérard Defois
Strasbourg, Charles Amarin Brand
Toulouse, André Collini
Tours, Jean Honoré

FRENCH POLYNESIA
Papeete, Michel Coppenrath

GABON
Libreville, André Fernand Anguilé

GERMANY
Bamberg, Elmar Maria Kredel
Cologne, HE Cardinal Joachim Meisner
Freiburg im Breisgau, Oskar Saier
Munich and Freising, HE Cardinal Friedrich Wetter
Paderborn, Johannes Joachim Degenhardt

GHANA
Accra, Dominic K. Andoh
Cape Coast, Peter Kodwo A. Turkson
Tamale, Peter Poreiku Dery

GREECE
Athens, Nicholaos Foscolos
Corfu, Antonio Varthalitis
Naxos, Nicolaos Printesis
Rhodes, vacant (Apostolic Administrator, Nicholaos Foscolos)

GUATEMALA
Guatemala, Prospero Penados del Barrio

GUINEA
Conakry, Robert Sarah

HAITI
Cap-Haitien, François Gayot
Port au Prince, François-Wolff Ligondé

HONDURAS
Tegucigalpa, Oscar A. Maradiaga

HONG KONG
Hong Kong, HE Cardinal J. B. Wu Cheng Chung

HUNGARY
Eger, Istvan Seregely
Esztergom, HE Cardinal Laslo Paskai
Kalocsa, Laszlo Danko

INDIA
Agra, Cecil de Sa
Bangalore, Alphonsus Mathias
Bhopal, Eugene D' Souza
Bombay, HE Cardinal I. Pimenta
Calcutta, Henry Sebastian D'Souza
Changanacherry, Joseph Powathil
Cuttack-Bhubaneswar, Raphael Cheenath
Delhi, Alan de Lastic
Ernakulam, HE Cardinal Anthony Padiyara
Goa and Daman, Raul Nicolau Gonsalves
Hyderabad, Saminini Arulappa
Madras and Mylapore, Casimir Gnanadickam
Madurai, Marianus Arokiasamy
Nagpur, Leobard D'Souza
Pondicherry and Cuddalore, Michael Augustine
Ranchi, Telesphore P. Toppo

Shillong-Gauhati, Hubert D'Rosario
Trivandrum (Syrian Melekite Rite), Benedict Varghese Gregorios Thangalathil
Verapoly, Cornelius Elanjikal

INDONESIA
Ende, Donatus Djagom
Jakarta, Leo Soekoto
Kupang, Gregorius Manteiro
Medan, Alfred Gonti Pius Datubara
Merauke, Jacobus Duivenvoorde
Pontianak, Hieronymus Herculanus Bumbun
Semarang, Julius R. Darmaatmadja
Ujung Pandang, R. P. Francis van Roessel

IRAN
Ahváz, Hanna Zora
Tehran, Youhannan Semaan Issayi
Urmyâ, Thomas Meram

IRAQ
Arbil, Stephane Babaca
Baghdad (Latin Rite), Paul Dahdah; (Syrian Rite), Athanase M. S. Matoka; (Armenian Rite), Paul Coussa
Basra, Yousif Thomas
Kirkuk, André Sana
Mosul, Georges Garmo

ISRAEL
Akka (Greek Melekite Catholic Rite), Maximos Salloum

ITALY
Acerenza, Michele Scandiffio
Amalfi, Beniamino De Palma
Ancona, Franco Festorazzi
Bari, Mariano Magrassi
Benevento, Serafino Sprovieri
Bologna, HE Cardinal Giacomo Biffi
Brindisi, Settimio Todisco
Cagliari, Otterino Pietro Alberti
Camerino, vacant
Campobasso-Boiano, Ettore Di Filippo
Capua, Luigi Diligenza
Catania, Luigi Bommarito
Catanzaro, Antonio Cantisani
Chieti, Antonio Valentini
Conza, Mario Milano
Cosenza, Dino Trabalzini
Crotone-Santa Severina, Giuseppe Agostino
Fermo, Cleto Bellucci
Ferrara, Luigi Maverna
Florence, HE Cardinal Silvano Piovanelli
Foggia, Giuseppe Casale
Gaeta, Vincenzo Farano
Genoa, HE Cardinal Giovanni Canestri
Gorizia and Gradisca, Antonio Vitale Bommarco
Lanciano, Enzio d'Antonio
L'Aquila, Mario Peressin
Lecce, Cosmo F. Ruppi
Lucca, Bruno Tommasi
Manfredonia, Vincenzo D'Addario
Matera, Antonio Ciliberti
Messina, Ignazio Cannavó
Milan, HE Cardinal Carlo Maria Martini
Modena, Santo B. Quadri
Monreale, Salvatore Cassisa
Naples, HE Cardinal Michele Giordano
Oristano, Pier Luigi Tiddia
Otranto, Francesco Cacucci
Palermo, HE Cardinal Salvatore Pappalardo
Perugia, Ennio Antonelli

Pescara-Penne, Francesco Cuccarese
Pisa, Alessandro Plotti
Potenza, Ennio Appignanesi
Ravenna, Luigi Amaducci
Reggio Calabria, Vittorio L. Mondello
Rossano-Cariati, Andrea Cassone
Salerno, Gerardo Pierro
Sassari, Salvatore Isgrò
Siena, Gaetano Bonicelli
Siracusa, Giuseppe Costanzo
Sorrento, Felice Cece
Spoleto, Antonio Ambrosanio
Taranto, Luigi Papa
Turin, HE Cardinal Giovanni Saldarini
Trani and Barletta, Carmelo Cassati
Trento, Giovanni Sartori
Udine, Alfredo Battisti
Urbino, Donato U. Bianchi
Vercelli, Tarcisio Bertone

JAMAICA
Kingston, Samuel Emmanuel Carter

JAPAN
Nagasaki, Francis Xavier Shimamoto
Osaka, Paul Hisao Yasuda
Tokyo, Peter Seiichi Shirayanagi

JORDAN
Petra and Filadelfia (Greek Melekite Catholic Rite), George
  El-Murr

KAZAKHSTAN
Karaganda Apostolic Administration (Latin Rite), Apostolic
  Administrator, Mgr Jan Lenga (titular Bishop of Arba)

KENYA
Kisumu, Zaccharus Okoth
Mombasa, John Njenga
Nairobi, HE Cardinal Maurice Otunga
Nyeri, Nicodemus Kirima

KOREA
Kwangju, Victorinus Kong-Hi Youn
Seoul, HE Cardinal Stephen Sou Hwan Kim
Taegu, Paul Moun-Hi Ri

LATVIA
Riga, Jānis Pujats

LEBANON
Antelias (Maronite Rite), Joseph Mohsen Bechara
Baalbek, Eliopoli (Greek Melekite Catholic Rite), Salim
  Bustros
Baniyas (Greek Melekite Catholic Rite), Antoine Hayek
Beirut (Greek Melekite Catholic Rite), Habib Bacha;
  (Maronite Rite), Khalil Abinader
Saïda (Greek Melekite Catholic Rite), Georges Kwaiter
Tripoli (Maronite Rite), Antoine Joubeir; (Greek Melekite
  Catholic Rite), Elias Nijmé
Tyre (Greek Melekite Catholic Rite), Jean A. Haddad;
  (Maronite Rite), Maroun Sader
Zahle and Furzol (Greek Melekite Catholic Rite), Andre
  Haddad

LESOTHO
Maseru, Bernard Mohlalisi

LIBERIA
Monrovia, Michael Kpakala Francis

LITHUANIA
Kaunas, HE Cardinal Vincentas Sladkevicius
Vilnius, Audris J. Bačkis

LUXEMBOURG
Luxembourg, Fernand Franck

MADAGASCAR
Antananarive, HE Cardinal Victor Razafimahatratra
Antsiranana, Albert Joseph Tsiahoana
Fianarantsoa, Philibert Randriambololona

MALAYSIA
Kuala Lumpur, Anthony S. Fernandez
Kuching, Peter Chung Hoan Ting

MALI
Bamako, Luc Auguste Sangaré

MALTA
Malta, Joseph Mercieca

MARTINIQUE
Fort de France, Maurice Marie-Sainte

MAURITIUS
Port Louis, HE Cardinal Jean Margeot

MEXICO
Acapulco, Rafael Bello Ruiz
Antequera, Bartolomé Carrasco Briseno
Chihuahua, José Fernández Arteaga
Durango, José M. Perez
Guadalajara, vacant
Hermosillo, Carlos Quintero Arce
Jalapa, Sergio Obeso Rivera
Mexico City, HE Cardinal Ernesto Corripio Ahumada
Monterrey, Adolfo Suarez Rivera
Morelia, Estanislao Alcarez Figueroa
Puebla de los Angeles, Rosendo Huesca Pacheco
San Luis Potosi, Arturo A. Szymanski Ramirez
Tlalnepantla, Manuel P. Gil Gonzalez
Yucatán, Manuel Castro Ruiz

MONACO
Monaco, Joseph-Marie Sardou

MOROCCO
Rabat, Hubert Michon
Tangier, Antonio J. Peteiro Freire

MOZAMBIQUE
Beira, Jaime P. Goncalves
Maputo, HE Cardinal Alexandre José Maria dos Santos
Nampula, Manuel Vieira Pinto

MYANMAR (BURMA)
Mandalay, Alphonse U. Than Aung
Yangon (Rangoon), Gabriel Thohey Mahn Gaby

NETHERLANDS
Utrecht, HE Cardinal Adrianus J. Simonis

NEW ZEALAND
Wellington, HE Cardinal Thomas Stafford Williams

NICARAGUA
Managua, HE Cardinal Miguel Obando Bravo

NIGERIA
Kaduna, Peter Yariyok Jatau
Lagos, Anthony Okogie
Onitsha, Stephen Nweke Ezeanya

OCEANIA
Agaña, Anthony Sablan Apuron
Honiara, Adrian Thomas Smith
Nouméa, Michel-Marie-Bernard Calvet
Samoa, Apia and Tokelau, HE Cardinal Pio Taofino'u
Suva, Petero Mataca

PAKISTAN
Karachi, HE Cardinal Joseph Cordeiro
  Coadjutor, Simeon Pereira

PANAMA
Panama, Marcos Gregorio McGrath

PAPUA NEW GUINEA
Madang, Benedict To Varpin
Mount Hagen, Michael Meier
Port Moresby, Peter Kurongku
Rabaul, Karl Hesse

PARAGUAY
Asuncion, Felipe Santiago B. Avalos

PERU
Arequipa, Fernando Vargas Ruiz de Somocurcio
Ayacucho o Huamanga, vacant
Cuzco, Alcides Mendoza Castro
Huancayo, vacant
Lima, Augusto Vargas Alzamora
Piura, Oscar Rolando Cantuarias Pastor
Trujillo, Manuel Prado Pérez-Rosas

PHILIPPINES
Caceres, Leonardo Legazpi
Cagayan de Oro, Jesus B. Tuquib
Capiz, Onesimo C. Gordoncillo
Cebu, HE Cardinal Ricardo Vidal
Cotabato, Philip Frances Smith
Davao, Antonio Mabutas
Jaro, Alberto J. Piamonte
Lingayen-Dagupan, Oscar V. Cruz
Lipa, Gaudencio B. Rosales
Manila, HE Cardinal Jaime L. Sin
Nueva Segovia, Orlando Quevedo
Ozamiz, Jesus Dosado
Palo, Pedro R. Dean
San Fernando, Paciano Aniceto
Tuguegarao, Diosdado A. Talamayan
Zamboanga, Francisco Raval Cruces

POLAND
Bialystok, Stanislaw Szymecki
Czestochowa, Stanislaw Nowak
Gdańsk, Tadeusz Goclowski
Gniezno, Henryk Muszyński
Katowice, Damian Zimoń
Kraków, HE Cardinal Franciszek Macharski
Lodz, Wladyslaw Ziolek
Lublin, Boleslaw Pylak
Poznań, Jerzy Stroba
Przemyśl of the Latins, Jozef Michalik
Szczecin-Kamień, Marian Przykucki
Warmia, Edmund Piszcz
Warsaw, HE Cardinal Józef Glemp
Wrocław, HE Cardinal Henryk Roman Gulbinowicz

PORTUGAL
Braga, Eurico Dias Nogueira
Evora, Maurilio Jorge Quintal de Gouveia

PUERTO RICO
San Juan, HE Cardinal Luis Aponte Martinez

ROMANIA
Alba Julia (Latin Rite), Lajos Balint
Bucareşti, Ioan Robu
Fagaras and Alba Julia (Romanian Byzantine Rite), HE
  Cardinal Alexandru Todea

RUSSIA
Moscow Apostolic Administration (covering European
  Russia), Apostolic Administrator, Archbishop Tadeusz
  Kondrusiewicz
Novosibirsk Apostolic Administration (covering Siberia),
  Apostolic Administrator, Mgr Joseph Werth, SJ (titular
  Bishop of Bulna)

RWANDA
Kigali, Vincent Nsengiyumva

EL SALVADOR
San Salvador, Arturo Rivera Damas

SENEGAL
Dakar, HE Cardinal Hyacinthe Thiandoum

SIERRA LEONE
Freetown and Bo, Joseph Ganda

SINGAPORE
Singapore, Gregory Yong Sooi Ngean

SLOVAK REPUBLIC
Trnava, Jan Sokol

SLOVENIA
Ljubljana, Alojzij Suštar

SOUTH AFRICA
Bloemfontein, Peter John Butelezi
Cape Town, Lawrence Patrick Henry
Durban, Wilfrid Fox Napier
Pretoria, George Francis Daniel

SPAIN
Barcelona, Ricardo Maria Carles Gordó
Burgos, Santiago Martinez Acebes
Granada, José Méndez Asensio
Madrid, HE Cardinal Angel Suquia Goicoechea
Oviedo, Gabino Diaz Merchán
Pamplona, Fernando S. Aquilar
Santiago de Compostela, Antonio Rouco Varela
Sevilla, Carlos Amigo Vallejo
Tarragona, Ramon Torrella Cascante
Toledo, HE Cardinal Marcelo González Martin
Valencia, Agustin Garcia-Gasco Vicente
Valladolid, José Delicado Baeza
Zaragoza, Elíaz Yanez Alvarez

SRI LANKA
Colombo, Nicholas Marcus Fernando

SUDAN
Khartoum, Gabriel Zubeir Wako

SYRIA
Alep, Beroea, Halab (Greek Melekite Catholic Rite),
  Néophytes Edelby; (Syrian Rite), Raboula A. Beylouni;
  (Maronite Rite), Pierre Callaos; (Armenian Rite),
  Boutros Marayati
Baniyas (Greek Melekite Catholic Rite), Antoine Hayek
Bosra, Bostra, Boulos Nassif Borkhoche
Damascus (Greek Melekite Catholic Rite), vacant; (Syrian
  Rite), Eustache J. Mounayer; (Maronite Rite), Hamid A.
  Mourany
Hassaké-Nisibi, Georges Habib Hafouri
Homs, Emesa (Greek Melekite Catholic Rite), Abraham
  Nehmé; (Syrian Catholic Rite), Jean Dahi
Laodicea (Greek Melekite Catholic Rite), Michel Yatim

TAIWAN
Taipei, Joseph Ti-Kang

TANZANIA
Dar es Salaam, Polycarp Pengo
Mwanza, Antony Mayala

Songea, Norbert W. Mtega
Tabora, Mario E. A. Mgulunde

THAILAND
Bangkok, HE Cardinal Michael Michai Kitbunchu
Tharé and Nonseng, Lawrence Khai Saen-Phon-On

TOGO
Lomé, Philippe F. K. Kpodzro

TRINIDAD
Port of Spain, Gordon Anthony Pantin

TURKEY
Diarbekir, Paul Karatas
Istanbul (Constantinople), Jean Tcholakian
Izmir, Giuseppe G. Bernardini

UGANDA
Kampala, Emmanuel Wamala

UKRAINE
Lvov (Latin Rite), Marian Jaworski (Archbishop of Lvov of the Latins); (Ukrainian Rite), HE Cardinal Myroslav I. Lubachivsky (Major Archbishop of Lvov of the Ukrainians)

URUGUAY
Montevideo, José Gottardi Cristelli

USA
Anchorage, Francis Thomas Hurley
Atlanta, vacant
Baltimore, William Henry Keeler
Boston, HE Cardinal Bernard F. Law
Chicago, HE Cardinal Joseph L. Bernardin
Cincinnati, Daniel E. Pilarczyk
Denver, James Francis Stafford
Detroit, Adam J. Maida
Dubuque, Daniel W. Kucera
Hartford, Daniel A. Cronin
Indianapolis, Daniel Mark Buechlein
Kansas City, Ignatius J. Strecker
Los Angeles, HE Cardinal Roger M. Mahony
Louisville, Thomas C. Kelly
Miami, Edward A. McCarthy
Milwaukee, Rembert G. Weakland
Mobile, Oscar H. Lipscomb
Newark, Theodore E. McCarrick
New Orleans, Francis B. Schulte
New York, HE Cardinal John J. O'Connor
Oklahoma City, Eusebius Joseph Beltran
Omaha, Elden Curtiss
Philadelphia, HE Cardinal Anthony J. Bevilacqua; (Ukrainian Rite), Stephen Sulyk
Pittsburgh (Byzantine Rite), Thomas V. Dolinay
Portland (Oregon), William J. Levada
St Louis (Missouri), vacant
St Paul and Minneapolis, John Robert Roach
San Antonio, Patrick F. Flores
San Francisco, John R. Quinn
Santa Fe, Administrator, Michael Sheehan
Seattle, Thomas J. Murphy
Washington, HE Cardinal James A. Hickey

VENEZUELA
Barquisimeto, Julio Manuel Chirivella Varela
Caracas, HE Cardinal José Ali Lebrún Moratinos; (Greek Melekite Catholic Rite), Pierre Rai
Ciudad Bolivar, Medardo Luzardo Romero
Cumana, Alfredo J. R. Figueroa
Maracaibo, Ramon O. Perez Morales
Mérida, Baltazar P. Cardozo
Valencia, Jorge Liberato Urosa Savino

VIETNAM
Hanoi, vacant
Hue, vacant
Thanh-Phô Hôchiminh, Paul Nguyên Van Binh

WEST INDIES
Castries, Kelvin Edward Felix, OBE

YUGOSLAV FEDERAL REPUBLIC
Bar, Petar Perkolić
Belgrade, Franc Perko

ZAIRE
Bukavu, Mulindwa Mutabesha Mweru
Kananga, Bakole wa Ilunga
Kinshasa, HE Cardinal Frederick Etsou-Nzabi-Bamungwabi
Kisangani, Laurent Monsengwo Pasinya
Lubumbashi, Kabanga Songasonga
Mbandaka-Bikoro, Joseph Kumuondala Mbimba

ZAMBIA
Kasama, James Spaita
Lusaka, Adrian Mungandu

ZIMBABWE
Harare, Patrick Chakaipa

PATRIARCHS IN COMMUNION WITH THE ROMAN CATHOLIC CHURCH

Alexandria, HB Stephanos II Ghattas (Patriarch for Catholic Copts)
Antioch, HB Ignace Antoine II Hayek (Patriarch for Syrian Rite Catholics); HB Maximos V. Hakim (Patriarch for Greek Melekite Rite Catholics); HB Nasrallah Pierre Sfeir (Patriarch for Maronite Rite Catholics)
Jerusalem, HB Michel Sabbah (Patriarch for Latin Rite Catholics)
Babilonia of the Chaldeans, HB Raphael I Bidawid
Cilicia of the Armenians, HB Jean Pierre XVIII Kasparian (Patriarch for Armenian Rite Catholics)
Oriental India, Archbishop Raul Nicolau Gonsalves
Lisbon, HE Cardinal Antonio Ribeiro
Venice, HE Cardinal Marco Ce

Other Churches in the UK

AFRICAN AND AFRO-CARIBBEAN CHURCHES

There are more than 160 Christian churches or groups of African or Afro-Caribbean origin in the United Kingdom. These include the Apostolic Faith Church, the Cherubim and Seraphim Church, the New Testament Church Assembly, the New Testament Church of God and the Wesleyan Holiness Church.

The Council of African and Allied Churches was initiated by the Most Revd Father Olu Abiola in 1979 to give one voice to the various Christian churches of African origin in the UK. Membership increased in the early 1980s and some churches of Caribbean origin also joined, resulting in 1986 in the change of name to the Council of African and Afro-Caribbean Churches UK. The Council is the medium through which the member churches can work jointly to provide services they cannot easily provide individually.

There are about 68,500 adherents of African and Afro-Caribbean churches in the United Kingdom, and about 950 churches. The Council has 30 member churches, with 70 congregations, 12,000 members and 200 ministers.
Council Chairman, His Grace The Most Revd Father Olu A. Abiola, 31 Norton House, Sidney Road, London SW9 OUJ. Tel: 071-274 5589

ASSOCIATED PRESBYTERIAN CHURCHES OF SCOTLAND

The Associated Presbyterian Churches came into being in 1989 as a result of a division within the Free Presbyterian Church of Scotland. Following two controversial disciplinary cases, the culmination of deepening differences within the Church, a Deed of Separation was drawn up by several members of the Church's synod. This held that the Church, in contravention of its constitution, had denied its members freedom of judgement in matters relating to the application of the Christian faith to daily living. A presbytery was formed calling itself the Associated Presbyterian Churches (APC). The APC claims that it represents the Free Presbyterian Church of Scotland as constituted in 1893. The Associated Presbyterian Churches has about 20 churches, 1,000 members and 13 ministers.
Clerk of the Scottish Presbytery, D. K. Laing, 1 Golden Square, Aberdeen AB9 IHA. Tel: 0862-87541

THE BAPTIST CHURCH

Baptists trace their origins to John Smyth, who in 1609 in Amsterdam reinstituted the baptism of conscious believers as the basis of the fellowship of a gathered church. Members of Smyth's church established the first Baptist church in England in 1612. They came to be known as 'General' Baptists and their theology was Arminian, whereas a later group of Calvinists who adopted the baptism of believers came to be known as 'Particular' Baptists. The two sections of the Baptists were united into one body, the Baptist Union of Great Britain and Ireland, in 1891. In 1988 the title was changed to the Baptist Union of Great Britain.
Baptists emphasize the complete independence of the local church, although individual churches are linked in various kinds of associations. There are international bodies (such as the Baptist World Alliance) and national bodies, but many Baptist churches belong to neither. However, in Great Britain the majority of churches and associations belong to the Baptist Union of Great Britain. There are also Baptist Unions in Wales, Scotland and Ireland which are much smaller than the Baptist Union of Great Britain, and there is some overlap of membership.
There are over 38 million Baptist church members world-wide; in the Baptist Union of Great Britain there are 160,000 members, 1,779 pastors and 2,118 churches. In the Baptist Union of Scotland there are 16,212 members, 130 pastors and 166 churches. In the Baptist Union of Wales there are 27,700 members, 117 pastors and 560 churches. In the Baptist Union of Ireland there are 8,505 members, 72 pastors and 103 churches.
President of the Baptist Union of Great Britain (1993-4), Revd Dr B. Haymes
General Secretary, Revd D. R. Coffey, Baptist House, PO Box 44, 129 Broadway, Didcot, Oxon. OX11 8RT. Tel: 0235-512077

THE CHURCH OF CHRIST, SCIENTIST

The Church of Christ, Scientist, was founded by Mary Baker Eddy in the United States of America in 1879 to 'reinstate primitive Christianity and its lost element of healing'. Christian Science is concerned with spiritual regeneration and salvation from sin, but is best known for its reliance on prayer alone in the healing of sickness. Adherents believe that such healing is in direct line with that practised by Jesus Christ (revered, not as God, but as the Son of God) and by the early Christian Church.
The denomination consists of the First Church of Christ, Scientist, in Boston, Massachusetts, USA (the Mother Church) and its branch churches in over 60 countries world-wide. Branch churches are democratically governed by their members. There is also a five-member Board of Directors which oversees Church matters. There are no clergy. Those engaged in full-time healing ministry are called practitioners, of whom there are 3,500 world-wide.
No membership figures are available, since Mary Baker Eddy felt that numbers are no measure of spiritual vitality and ruled that such statistics should not be published. There are over 2,500 branch churches world-wide, including 210 in the United Kingdom.
CHRISTIAN SCIENCE COMMITTEE ON PUBLICATION, 108 Palace Gardens Terrace, London W8 4RT. Tel: 071-221 5650. *District Manager for Great Britain and Ireland,* G. Phaup

THE CONGREGATIONAL FEDERATION

The Congregational Federation was founded by members of Congregational churches in England and Wales who did not join the United Reformed Church (q.v.) in 1972. There are also churches in Scotland and Australia. The Federation exists to encourage congregations of believers to worship in free assembly, but has no authority over them and emphasizes their right to independence and self-government.
The Federation has 9,455 members, 117 ministers, 36 pastors, about 330 lay preachers and 287 churches.
President of the Federation (1993-4), Revd Dr R. W. Cleaves
General Secretary, G. M. Adams, The Congregational Centre, 4 Castle Gate, Nottingham NG1 7AS. Tel: 0602-413801

THE FREE CHURCH OF ENGLAND

The Free Church of England, also known as the Reformed Episcopal Church, traces its beginnings to a dispute over the influence of the Oxford Movement in the established church between the Bishop of Exeter and one of his clergy, James Shore, in 1843. The Church defined its beliefs in 1863, accepting the Church of England's Thirty-Nine Articles and recognizing the legitimacy of the principle of episcopacy. Although its government was at first presbyterian, the Church later became affiliated to the Reformed Episcopal Church in the USA (a connection which has not been maintained) and adopted episcopal organization.
The Free Church of England has 1,700 members, 35 ministers and 30 churches in England. It also has three churches and three ministers in New Zealand, and one church and one minister in St Petersburg, Russia.

General Secretary, Revd W. J. Lawler, 45 Broughton Road, Wallasey, Merseyside L45 1JP. Tel: 051-638 2564

THE FREE CHURCH OF SCOTLAND

The Free Church of Scotland was formed in 1843 when over 400 ministers withdrew from the Church of Scotland as a result of interference in the internal affairs of the church by the civil authorities. In 1900, all but 26 ministers joined with others to form the United Free Church (most of which rejoined the Church of Scotland in 1929). In 1904 the remaining 26 ministers were recognized by the House of Lords as continuing the Free Church of Scotland.

The Church maintains strict adherence to the Westminster Confession of Faith (1648) and accepts the Bible as the sole rule of faith and conduct. Its General Assembly meets annually. It also has links with Reformed Churches overseas. The Free Church of Scotland has about 20,000 members, 110 ministers and 140 churches.

General Treasurer, I. D. Gill, The Mound, Edinburgh EH1 2LS. Tel: 031-226 5286

THE FREE PRESBYTERIAN CHURCH OF SCOTLAND

The Free Presbyterian Church of Scotland was formed in 1893 by two ministers of the Free Church of Scotland who refused to accept a Declaratory Act passed by the Free Church General Assembly in 1892. The Free Presbyterian Church of Scotland is Calvinistic in doctrine and emphasizes observance of the Sabbath. It adheres strictly to the Westminster Confession of Faith of 1648.

The Church has about 4,000 members in Scotland and about 11,000 in overseas congregations. It has 22 ministers and 34 churches.

Moderator, Revd D. MacLean, 104 Barronald Drive, Glasgow G12 0HE. Tel: 041-357 2315.

Clerk of Synod, Revd D. B. MacLeod, 8 Colinton Road, Edinburgh EH10 5DS. Tel: 031-447 1920

THE INDEPENDENT METHODIST CHURCHES

The Independent Methodist Churches seceded from the Wesleyan Methodist Church in 1805 and remained independent when the Methodist Church in Great Britain was formed in 1932. They are mainly concentrated in the industrial areas of the north of England.

The churches are Methodist in doctrine but their organization is congregational. All the churches are members of the Independent Methodist Connexion of Churches. The controlling body of the Connexion is the Annual Meeting, to which churches send delegates. The Connexional President is elected annually. Between annual meetings the affairs of the Connexion are handled by departmental committees. Ministers are appointed by the churches and trained through the Connexion. The ministry is open to both men and women and is unpaid.

There are 3,600 members, 126 ministers and 103 churches in Great Britain.

Connexional President (1993–4), H. Porter
General Secretary, Revd J. M. Day, The Old Police House, Croxton, Stafford ST21 6PE. Tel: 063-082 671

THE LUTHERAN CHURCH

Lutheranism is based on the teachings of Martin Luther, the German leader of the Protestant Reformation. The authority of the scriptures is held to be supreme over Church tradition and creeds, and the key doctrine is that of justification by faith alone.

Lutheranism is one of the largest Protestant denominations and it is particularly strong in northern Europe and the USA. Some Lutheran churches are episcopal, while others have a synodal form of organization; unity is based on doctrine rather than structure. Most Lutheran churches are members of the Lutheran World Federation, based in Geneva.

Lutheran services in Great Britain are held in many languages to serve members of different nationalities. English-language congregations are members either of the Lutheran Church in Great Britain–United Synod, or of the Evangelical Lutheran Church of England. The United Synod and most of the various national congregations are members of the Lutheran Council of Great Britain.

There are over 70 million Lutherans world-wide; in Great Britain there are 27,000 members, 45 ministers and 100 churches.

Chairman of the Lutheran Council of Great Britain, Very Revd R. J. Patkai, 8 Collingham Gardens, London SW5 0HW. Tel: 071-373 1141

THE METHODIST CHURCH

The Methodist movement started in England in 1729 when the Revd John Wesley, an Anglican priest, and his brother Charles met with others in Oxford and resolved to conduct their lives and study by 'rule and method'. In 1739 the Wesleys began evangelistic preaching and the first Methodist chapel was founded in Bristol in the same year. In 1744 the first annual conference was held, at which the Articles of Religion were drawn up. Doctrinal emphases included repentance, faith, the assurance of salvation, social concern and the priesthood of all believers. After John Wesley's death in 1791 the Methodists withdrew from the established Church to form the Methodist Church. Methodists gradually drifted into many groups, but in 1932 the Wesleyan Methodist Church, the United Methodist Church and the Primitive Methodist Church united to form the Methodist Church in Great Britain as it now exists.

The governing body and supreme authority of the Methodist Church is the Conference, but there are also 33 district synods, consisting of all the ministers and selected lay people in each district, and circuit meetings of the ministers and lay people of each circuit.

There are over 54 million Methodists world-wide; in Great Britain (1992 figures) there are 408,107 members, 3,601 ministers, 10,414 lay preachers and 6,950 churches.

President of the Conference in Great Britain (1993–4), Revd B. E. Beck

Vice-President of the Conference (1993–4), Mrs S. M. Howdle
Secretary of the Conference, Revd B. E. Beck, Methodist Church, Conference Office, 1 Central Buildings, Storeys Gate, London SW1H 9NH. Tel: 071-222 8010

THE METHODIST CHURCH IN IRELAND

The Methodist Church in Ireland is closely linked to British Methodism but is autonomous. It has 19,217 members, 196 ministers, 296 lay preachers and 234 churches.

President of the Conference in Ireland (1993–4), Revd R. H. Taylor
Secretary of the Conference in Ireland, Revd E. T. I. Mawhinney, 1 Fountainville Avenue, Belfast BT9 6AN. Tel: 0232-324554

THE ORTHODOX CHURCH

The Orthodox Church (or Eastern Orthodox Church) is a communion of self-governing Christian churches recognizing the honorary primacy of the Oecumenical Patriarch of Constantinople.

In the first millennium of the Christian era the faith was slowly formulated. Between AD 325 and 787 there were seven Oecumenical Councils at which bishops from the entire Christian world assembled to resolve various doctrinal disputes which had arisen. The estrangement between East and West began after Constantine moved the centre of the Roman Empire from Rome to Constantinople, and it gained momentum after the temporal administration was divided. Linguistic and cultural differences between Greek East and Latin West served to encourage separate ecclesiastical developments which became pronounced in the tenth and early eleventh centuries.

The administration of the church was divided between five ancient patriarchates: Rome and all the West, Constantinople (the imperial city – the 'New Rome'), Jerusalem and all Palestine, Antioch and all the East, and Alexandria and all Africa. Of these, only Rome was in the Latin West and after the Great Schism in 1054, Rome developed a structure of authority centralized on one source, the Papacy, while the Orthodox East maintained the style of localized administration.

To the older patriarchates were later added the Patriarchates of Russia, Georgia, Serbia, Bulgaria and Romania. The Orthodox Church also includes autocephalous (self-governing) national churches in Greece, Cyprus, Poland, Albania, Czechoslovakia and Sinai, and autonomous national churches in Finland and Japan. The Estonian and Latvian Orthodox Churches are in practice part of the Moscow Patriarchate. The Belorussians and Ukrainians have recently been given greater autonomy by Moscow, but some Ukrainians have broken away to establish an independent Ukrainian Patriarchate. In Macedonia the local hierarchy has declared itself independent of the Serbian Patriarchate. The Russian dioceses in the diaspora fall into four groups: those under the direct control of the Moscow Patriarchate; the Russian Orthodox Church Outside Russia, sometimes known as the Synod in Exile; the Russian Archdiocese centred at the cathedral in rue Daru, Paris, which is part of the Patriarchate in Constantinople; and the Orthodox Church in America, which was granted autocephalous status in 1970.

The position of Orthodox Christians is that the faith was fully defined during the period of the Oecumenical Councils. In doctrine it is strongly trinitarian, and stresses the mystery and importance of the sacraments. It is episcopal in government. The structure of the Orthodox Christian year differs from that of Western Churches (*see* page 82).

Orthodox Christians throughout the world are estimated to number about 150 million.

PATRIARCHS
Archbishop of Constantinople, New Rome and Oecumenical Patriarch, Bartholomew, *elected* 1991
Pope and Patriarch of Alexandria and All Africa, Parthenios III, *elected* 1987

Patriarch of Antioch and All the East, Ignatios IV, *elected* 1979
Patriarch of Jerusalem and All Palestine, Diodoros, *elected* 1981
Patriarch of Moscow and All Russia, Alexei II, *elected* 1990
Archbishop of Tbilisi and Mtskheta, Catholicos-Patriarch of All Georgia, Ilia II, *elected* 1977
Archbishop of Pec, Metropolitan of Belgrade and Karlovci, Patriarch of Serbia, Paul, *elected* 1990
Archbishop of Bucharest and Patriarch of Romania, Teoctist, *elected* 1986
Metropolitan of Sofia and Patriarch of Bulgaria, Maxim, *elected* 1971
Patriarch of Kiev and All Ukraine, Mstyslav, *elected* 1990 (not officially recognized by other national Orthodox churches)

ORTHODOX CHURCHES IN THE UK

THE GREEK ORTHODOX CHURCH (PATRIARCHATE OF CONSTANTINOPLE)
The presence of Greek Orthodox Christians in Britain dates back to 1677 when Archbishop Joseph Geogirenes of Samos fled from Turkish persecution and came to London, where a church was built for him in Soho. The present Greek cathedral in Moscow Road, Bayswater, was opened for public worship in 1879 and the Diocese of Thyateira and Great Britain was established in 1922. There are now 87 parishes in Great Britain, served by eight bishops and 87 churches.

In Great Britain the Patriarchate of Constantinople is represented by Archbishop Gregorios of Thyateira and Great Britain, 5 Craven Hill, London W2 3EN. Tel: 071-723 4787.

THE RUSSIAN ORTHODOX CHURCH (PATRIARCHATE OF MOSCOW) AND THE RUSSIAN ORTHODOX CHURCH OUTSIDE RUSSIA
The earliest records of Russian Orthodox Church activities in Britain date from the visit to England of Tsar Peter I at the beginning of the 18th century. Clergy were sent from Russia to serve the chapel established to minister to the staff of the Imperial Russian Embassy in London.

After 1917 the Church of Russia was persecuted. The Patriarch of Moscow, St Tikhon the New Martyr, anathematized both the atheistic persecutors of the Church and all who collaborated with them. Because of the civil war normal administrative contact with Russian Orthodox Christians outside the country was impossible, and he therefore authorized the establishment of a higher church administration, i.e. a synod in exile, by Russian bishops who were then outside Russia. This is the origin of the Russian Orthodox Church Outside Russia. The attitude of the Church of Russia to the former Soviet regime was always a source of contention between the two hierarchies; tensions are now lessening but remain unresolved.

In Britain the Patriarchate of Moscow is represented by Metropolitan Anthony of Sourozh, 67 Ennismore Gardens, London SW7 1NH. Tel: 071-584 0096. He is assisted by one archbishop, one bishop and about 13 priests. There are 15 parishes.

The Russian Orthodox Church Outside Russia is represented by Archbishop Mark of Richmond and Great Britain (who is also Archbishop of Berlin and Germany), 14 St Dunstan's Road, London W6 8RB. Tel: 081-748 4232. There are eight parishes and two monasteries, served by six priests.

THE SERBIAN ORTHODOX CHURCH (PATRIARCHATE OF SERBIA)
There was a small congregation of Orthodox Christian Serbs in London before the Second World War, but most Serbian

parishes in Britain have been established since 1945. There is no resident bishop as the parishes are part of the Serbian Orthodox Diocese of Western Europe, which has its centre in Germany. There are five main parishes in Britain and several smaller communities served by seven priests.

In Britain the Patriarchate of Serbia is represented by the Episcopal Vicar, the Very Revd Milun Kostic, 89 Lancaster Road, London W11 1QQ. Tel: 071-727 8367.

OTHER NATIONALITIES
Latvian, Polish and some Belorussian Orthodox parishes in Britain are under the care of the Patriarchate of Constantinople. The Patriarchates of Antioch, Bulgaria and Romania are represented by one priest each. Both the Ukrainian Autocephalous Orthodox Church and the Belorussian Autocephalic Orthodox Church have a few parishes in Britain.
ORTHODOX CHURCH PUBLIC RELATIONS OFFICE, St George Orthodox Information Service, 64 Prebend Gardens, London W6 0XU. Tel: 081-741 9624. *Secretary*, A. Bond

---

PENTECOSTAL CHURCHES

Pentecostalism is inspired by the descent of the Holy Spirit upon the apostles at Pentecost. The movement began in Los Angeles, USA, in 1906 and is characterized by baptism with the Holy Spirit, divine healing, speaking in tongues (glossolalia), and a literal interpretation of the scriptures. The Pentecostal movement in Britain dates from 1907. Initially, groups of Pentecostalists were led by laymen and did not organize formally. However, in 1915 the Elim Foursquare Gospel Alliance (more usually called the Elim Pentecostal Church) was founded in Ireland by George Jeffreys and in 1924 about 70 independent assemblies formed a fellowship, the Assemblies of God in Great Britain and Ireland. The Apostolic Church grew out of the 1904–5 revivals in South Wales and was established in 1916, and the New Testament Church of God was established in England in 1953. In recent years many aspects of Pentecostalism have been adopted by the growing charismatic movement within the Roman Catholic Church and Protestant and Eastern Orthodox churches.

There are about 22 million Pentecostalists world-wide, with about 115,000 adult adherents in Great Britain and Ireland.
THE APOSTOLIC CHURCH, International Administration Offices, PO Box 389, 24–27 St Helens Road, Swansea, West Glamorgan SA1 1ZH. Tel: 0792-473992. *President*, Pastor P. Cawthorne; *Administrator*, Pastor M. Davies. The Apostolic Church has about 130 churches, 5,500 adherents and 83 ministers
THE ASSEMBLIES OF GOD IN GREAT BRITAIN AND IRELAND, General Offices, 106–114 Talbot Street, Nottingham NG1 5GH. Tel: 0602-474525. *General Superintendent*, W. Shenton; *General Administrator*, B. D. Varnam. The Assemblies of God has 614 churches, about 70,000 adherents (including children) and 627 accredited ministers
THE ELIM PENTECOSTAL CHURCH, PO Box 38, Cheltenham, Glos. GL50 3HN. Tel: 0242-519904. *General Superintendent*, Pastor I. W. Lewis; *Administrator*, Pastor B. Hunter. The Elim Pentecostal Church has about 470 churches, 50,000 adherents and 475 accredited ministers
THE NEW TESTAMENT CHURCH OF GOD, Main House, Overstone Park, Overstone, Northampton NN6 0AD. Tel: 0604-645944. *National Overseer*, Revd Dr S. E. Arnold. The New Testament Church of God has

106 organized congregations, 7,042 baptized members, about 20,000 adherents and 216 accredited ministers

---

THE PRESBYTERIAN CHURCH IN IRELAND

The Presbyterian Church in Ireland is Calvinistic in doctrine and presbyterian in constitution. Presbyterianism was established in Ireland as a result of the Ulster plantation in the early 17th century, when English and Scottish Protestants settled in the north of Ireland.

There are 21 presbyteries and five regional synods under the chief court known as the General Assembly. The General Assembly meets annually and is presided over by a Moderator who is elected for one year. The ongoing work of the Church is undertaken by 18 boards under which there are a number of specialist committees.

There are about 330,000 Presbyterians in Ireland, mainly in the north, in 562 congregations and with 400 ministers.
Moderator (1993–4), Rt. Revd Dr A. Rodgers
Clerk of Assembly and General Secretary, Revd S. Hutchinson, Church House, Belfast BT1 6DW. Tel: 0232-322284

THE PRESBYTERIAN CHURCH OF WALES

The Presbyterian Church of Wales or Calvinistic Methodist Church of Wales is Calvinistic in doctrine and presbyterian in constitution. It was formed in 1811 when Welsh Calvinists severed the relationship with the established church by ordaining their own ministers. It secured its own confession of faith in 1823 and a Constitutional Deed in 1826, and since 1864 the General Assembly has met annually, presided over by a Moderator elected for a year. The doctrine and constitutional structure of the Presbyterian Church of Wales was confirmed by Act of Parliament in 1931–2.

The Church has 57,876 members, 118 ministers and 971 churches.
Moderator (1993–4), A. C. Davies
General Secretary, Revd D. H. Owen, 53 Richmond Road, Cardiff CF2 3UP. Tel: 0222-494913

THE RELIGIOUS SOCIETY OF FRIENDS (QUAKERS)

Quakerism is a movement, not a church, which was founded in the 17th century by George Fox and others in an attempt to revive what they saw as 'primitive Christianity'. The movement was based originally in the Midlands, Yorkshire and north-west England, but there are now Quakers in 36 countries around the world. The colony of Pennsylvania, founded by William Penn, was originally Quaker.

Emphasis is placed on the experience of God in daily life rather than on sacraments or religious occasions. There is no church calendar. Worship is largely silent and there are no appointed ministers; the responsibility for conducting a meeting is shared equally among those present. Social reform and religious tolerance have always been important to Quakers, together with a commitment to non-violence in resolving disputes.

There are 213,800 Quakers world-wide, with over 19,000 in Great Britain and Ireland. There are 464 meeting houses in Great Britain.

CENTRAL OFFICES: (GREAT BRITAIN) Friends House, Euston Road, London NW1 2BJ. Tel: 071-387 3601; (IRELAND) Swanbrook House, Morehampton Road, Dublin 4. Tel: 0001-683684

THE SALVATION ARMY

The Salvation Army was founded by a Methodist minister, William Booth, in the east end of London in 1865, and has since become established in 95 countries world-wide. It was first known as the Christian Mission, and took its present name in 1878 when it adopted a quasi-military command structure intended to inspire and regulate its endeavours and to reflect its view that the Church was engaged in spiritual warfare. Salvationists emphasize evangelism, social work and the relief of poverty.

The world leader, known as the General, is elected by a High Council composed of the Chief of the Staff and senior ranking officers known as commissioners.

There are about 1.5 million soldiers, 16,455 active officers (full-time ordained ministers) and 14,068 corps (churches) world-wide. In Great Britain and Ireland there are 55,000 soldiers, 1,807 active officers and 992 worship centres.

International Leader, B. Tillsley

UK Territorial Commander, Commissioner D. Pender

INTERNATIONAL AND TERRITORIAL HEADQUARTERS, PO Box 249, 101 Queen Victoria Street, London EC4P 4EP. Tel: 071-236 5222

THE SEVENTH-DAY ADVENTIST CHURCH

The Seventh-day Adventist Church was founded in 1863 in the USA. Its members look forward to the second coming of Christ and observe the Sabbath as a day of rest, worship and ministry. The Church bases its faith and practice wholly on the Bible and has developed 27 fundamental beliefs.

The World Church is divided into 12 divisions, each made up of unions of churches. The Seventh-day Adventist Church in the British Isles is known as the British Union of Seventh-day Adventists and is a member of the Trans-European Division. In the British Isles the administrative organization of the church is arranged in three tiers: the local churches; the regional conferences for south England, north England, Wales, Scotland and Ireland, which are held every three years; and the national 'union' conference which is held every five years.

There are over 7 million Adventists and 34,363 churches in 201 countries world-wide. In the United Kingdom and Ireland there are 18,200 members, 155 ministers and 242 churches.

President of the British Union Conference (1991–6), Pastor C. Perry

BRITISH ISLES HEADQUARTERS, Stanborough Park, Watford WD2 6JP. Tel: 0923-672251

UNDEB YR ANNIBYNWYR CYMRAEG
The Union of Welsh Independents

The Union of Welsh Independents was formed in 1872 and is a voluntary association of Welsh Congregational Churches

and personal members. It is entirely Welsh-speaking. Congregationalism in Wales dates back to 1639 when the first Welsh Congregational Church was opened in Gwent. Member Churches are Calvinistic in doctrine and congregationalist in organization. Each church has complete independence in the government and administration of its affairs.

The Union has 48,000 members, 120 ministers and 610 chapels.

President of the Union (1993–4), Revd J. G. Jones

General Secretary, Revd D. Morris Jones, Tŷ John Penry, 11 Heol Sant Helen, Swansea SA1 4AL. Tel: 0792-467040

UNITARIAN AND FREE CHRISTIAN CHURCHES

Unitarianism has its historical roots in the Judaeo-Christian tradition but denies the exclusive divinity of Christ and the doctrine of the trinity. It allows the individual to embrace insights from all the world's faiths and philosophies, as there is no formal creed. It is accepted that beliefs may evolve in the light of personal experience.

Unitarian communities first became established in Poland and Transylvania in the 16th century. The first avowedly Unitarian place of worship in the British Isles opened in London in 1774. The General Assembly of Unitarian and Free Christian Churches came into existence in 1928 as the result of the amalgamation of two earlier organizations.

There are about 10,000 Unitarians in Great Britain and Ireland, and 150 Unitarian ministers. About 250 self-governing congregations and fellowship groups, including a small number overseas, are members of the General Assembly.

GENERAL ASSEMBLY OF UNITARIAN AND FREE CHRISTIAN CHURCHES, Essex Hall, 1–6 Essex Street, Strand, London WC2R 3HY. Tel: 071-240 2384. *General Secretary*, Dr R. W. Smith

THE UNITED REFORMED CHURCH

The United Reformed Church was formed by the union of most of the Congregational churches in England and Wales with the Presbyterian Church of England in 1972.

Congregationalism dates from the mid 16th century. It is Calvinistic in doctrine, and its followers form independent self-governing congregations bound under God by covenant, a principle laid down in the writings of Robert Browne (1550–1633). From the late 16th century the movement was driven underground by persecution, but the cause was defended at the Westminster Assembly in 1643 and the Savoy Declaration of 1658 laid down its principles. Congregational churches formed county associations for mutual support and in 1832 these associations merged to form the Congregational Union of England and Wales.

The Presbyterian Church in England also dates from the mid 16th century, and was Calvinistic and evangelical in its doctrine. It was governed by a hierarchy of courts.

In the 1960s there was close co-operation locally and nationally between Congregational and Presbyterian Churches. This led to union negotiations and a Scheme of Union, supported by Act of Parliament in 1972. In 1981 a further unification took place, with the Reformed Association of Churches of Christ becoming part of the URC. In its basis the United Reformed Church reflects local church initiative and responsibility with a conciliar pattern of oversight. The

General Assembly is the central body, and is made up of equal numbers of ministers and lay members.

The United Reformed Church is divided into 12 Provinces, each with a Provincial Moderator who chairs the Synod, and 70 Districts. There are 115,000 members, 730 full-time ministers and 1,800 local churches.

General Secretary, Revd A. G. Burnham, 86 Tavistock Place, London WC1H 9RT. Tel: 071-916 2020

THE WESLEYAN REFORM UNION

The Wesleyan Reform Union was founded by Methodists who left or were expelled from Wesleyan Methodism in 1849 following a period of internal conflict. Its doctrine is Methodist but its organization is congregational, each church having complete independence in the government and administration of its affairs. The main concentration of churches is in Yorkshire.

The Union has 2,698 members, 20 ministers, 143 lay preachers and 122 churches.

President (1993-4), B. S. Pratt

General Secretary, Revd E. W. Downing, Wesleyan Reform Church House, 123 Queen Street, Sheffield S1 2DU. Tel: 0742-721928

Popes since 1800

The family name is in italics

Pius VII, *Chiaramonti*, elected 1800
Leo XII, *della Genga*, elected 1823
Pius VIII, *Castiglioni*, elected 1829
Gregory XVI, *Cappellari*, elected 1831
Pius IX, *Mastai-Ferretti*, elected 1846
Leo XIII, *Pecci*, elected 1878
Pius X, *Sarto*, elected 1903
Benedict XV, *della Chiesa*, elected 1914
Pius XI, *Ratti*, elected 1922

Pius XII, *Pacelli*, elected 1939
John XXIII, *Roncalli*, elected 1958
Paul VI, *Montini*, elected 1963
John Paul I, *Luciani*, elected 1978
John Paul II, *Wojtyla*, elected 1978

Adrian IV is the only Englishman to be elected pope. He was born Nicholas Breakspear at Langley, near St Albans, and was elected Pope in 1154 on the death of Anastasius IV. He died in 1159.

Archbishops of Canterbury since 1414

Henry Chichele (1362–1443), translated 1414
John Stafford (?–1452), translated 1443
John Kemp (c.1380–1454), translated 1452
Thomas Bourchier (c.1410–86), translated 1454
John Morton (c.1420–1500), translated 1486
Henry Deane (?–1503), translated 1501
William Warham (1450–1532), translated 1503
Thomas Cranmer (1489–1556), translated 1533
Reginald Pole (1500–58), translated 1556
Matthew Parker (1504–75), translated 1559
Edmund Grindal (c. 1519–83), translated 1576
John Whitgift (c.1530–1604), translated 1583
Richard Bancroft (1544–1610), translated 1604
George Abbot (1562–1633), translated 1611
William Laud (1573–1645), translated 1633
William Juxon (1582–1663), translated 1660
Gilbert Sheldon (1598–1677), translated 1663
William Sancroft (1617–93), translated 1678
John Tillotson (1630–94), translated 1691
Thomas Tenison (1636–1715), translated 1695
William Wake (1657–1737), translated 1716

John Potter (c. 1674–1747), translated 1737
Thomas Herring (1693–1757), translated 1747
Matthew Hutton (1693–1758), translated 1757
Thomas Secker (1693–1768), translated 1758
Hon. Frederick Cornwallis (1713–83), translated 1768
John Moore (1730–1805), translated 1783
Charles Manners-Sutton (1755–1828), translated 1805
William Howley (1766–1848), translated 1828
John Bird Sumner (1780–1862), translated 1848
Charles Longley (1794–1868), translated 1862
Archibald Campbell Tait (1811–82), translated 1868
Edward White Benson (1829–96), translated 1883
Frederick Temple (1821–1902), translated 1896
Randall Thomas Davidson (1848–1930), translated 1903
Cosmo Gordon Lang (1864–1945), translated 1928
William Temple (1881–1944), translated 1942
Geoffrey Fisher (1887–1972), translated 1945
Arthur Ramsey (1904–88), translated 1961
Donald Coggan (1909–), translated 1974
Robert Runcie (1921–), translated 1980
George Carey (1935–), translated 1991

Archbishops of York since 1606

Tobias Matthew (1546–1628), translated 1606
George Montaigne (1569–1628), translated 1628
Samuel Harsnett (1561–1631), translated 1629
Richard Neile (1562–1640), translated 1632
John Williams (1582–1650), translated 1641
Accepted Frewen (1588–1664), translated 1660
Richard Sterne (1596–1683), translated 1664
John Dolben (1625–86), translated 1683
Thomas Lamplugh (1615–91), translated 1688
John Sharp (1645–1714), translated 1691
William Dawes (1671–1724), translated 1714
Launcelot Blackburn (1658–1743), translated 1724
Thomas Herring (1693–1757), translated 1743
Matthew Hutton (1693–1758), translated 1747
John Gilbert (1693–1761), translated 1757
Robert Hay Drummond (1711–76), translated 1761

William Markham (1719–1807), translated 1777
Edward Venables Vernon Harcourt (1757–1847), translated 1808
Thomas Musgrave (1788–1860), translated 1847
Charles Longley (1794–1868), translated 1860
William Thomson (1819–90), translated 1862
William Connor Magee (1821–91), translated 1891
William Dalrymple Maclagan (1826–1910), translated 1891
Cosmo Gordon Lang (1864–1945), translated 1909
William Temple (1881–1944), translated 1929
Cyril Garbett (1875–1955), translated 1942
Arthur Ramsey (1904–88), translated 1956
Donald Coggan (1909–), translated 1961
Stuart Blanch (1918–), translated 1975
John Habgood (1927–), translated 1983

Non-Christian Faiths

BUDDHISM

Buddhism originated in northern India, in the teachings of Siddharta Gautama, who was born near Kapilavastu about 560 BC. After a long spiritual quest he experienced enlightenment beneath a tree at the place now known as Bodhgaya, and began missionary work.

Fundamental to Buddhism is the concept that there is no such thing as a permanent soul or self; when someone dies, consciousness is the only one of the elements of which they were composed which is lost. All the other elements regroup in a new body and carry with them the consequences of the conduct of the earlier life (known as the law of *karma*). This cycle of death and rebirth is broken only when the state of *nirvana* has been reached. Buddhism steers a middle path between belief in personal immortality and belief in death as the final end.

The Four Noble Truths of Buddhism (*dukkha*, suffering; *tanha*, a thirst or desire for continued existence which causes dukkha; *nirvana*, the final liberation from desire and ignorance; and *ariya*, the path to nirvana) are all held to be universal and to sum up the *dhamma* or true nature of life. Necessary qualities to promote spiritual development are *sila* (morality), *samadhi* (meditation) and *panna* (wisdom).

There are two main schools of Buddhism: *Theravada* Buddhism, the earliest extant school, which is more traditional, and *Mahayana* Buddhism, which began to develop about 100 years after the Buddha's death and is more liberal; it teaches that all people may attain Buddahood. Important schools which have developed within Mahayana Buddhism are *Zen* Buddhism, *Nichiren* Buddhism and Pure Land Buddhism or *Amidism*. There are also distinctive Tibetan forms of Buddhism. Buddhism began to establish itself in the West at the beginning of the 20th century.

The scripture of Theravada Buddhism is the *Pali Canon*, which dates from the first century BC. Mahayana Buddhism uses a Sanskrit version of the Pali Canon but also has many other works of scripture.

There is no set time for Buddhist worship, which may take place in a temple or in the home. Worship centres around *paritta* (chanting), acts of devotion centring on the image of the Buddha, and, where possible, offerings to a relic of the Buddha. Buddhist festivals vary according to local traditions and within Theravada and Mahayana Buddhism. For religious purposes Buddhists use solar and lunar calendars, the New Year being celebrated in April. Other festivals mark events in the life of the Buddha.

There is no supreme governing authority in Buddhism. In the United Kingdom communities representing all schools of Buddhism have developed and operate independently. The Buddhist Society was established in 1924; it runs courses and lectures, and publishes books about Buddhism. It represents no one school of Buddhism.

There are estimated to be at least 300 million Buddhists world-wide, with about 200 groups, an estimated 25,000 adherents and 15 temples or monasteries in the United Kingdom.

THE BUDDHIST SOCIETY, 58 Eccleston Square, London SW1V 1PH. Tel: 071-834 5858. *General Secretary,* R. C. Maddox

HINDUISM

Hinduism has no historical founder but is known to have been highly developed in India by about 1200 BC. Its adherents originally called themselves Aryans; Muslim invaders first called the Aryans 'Hindus' (derived from the word 'Sindhu', the name of the river Indus) in the eighth century.

Hinduism's evolution has been complex and it embraces many different religious beliefs, mythologies and practices. Most Hindus hold that *satya* (truthfulness), *ahimsa* (non-violence), honesty, physical labour and tolerance of other faiths are essential for good living. They believe in one supreme spirit (*Brahman*), and in the transmigration of *atman* (the soul). Most Hindus accept the doctrine of *karma* (consequences of actions), the concept of *samsara* (successive lives) and the possibility of all atmans achieving *moksha* (liberation from samsara) through *jnana* (knowledge), *yoga* (meditation), *karma* (work or action) and *bhakti* (devotion).

Most Hindus offer worship to *murtis* (images or statues) representing different aspects of Brahman, and follow their *dharma* (religious and social duty) according to the traditions of their *varna* (social class), *ashrama* (stage in life), *jati* (caste) and *kula* (family).

Hinduism's sacred texts are divided into *shruti* ('heard' or divinely inspired), including the *Vedas*; or *smriti* ('remembered' tradition), including the *Ramayana*, the *Mahabharata*, the *Puranas* (ancient myths), and the sacred law books. Most Hindus recognize the authority of the *Vedas*, the oldest holy books, and accept the philosophical teachings of the *Upanishads*, the *Vedanta Sutras* and the *Bhagavad-Gita*.

Brahman is formless, limitless and all-pervading, and is represented in worship by murtis which may be male or female and in the form of a human, animal or bird. Brahma, Vishnu and Shiva are the most important gods worshipped by Hindus; their respective consorts are Saraswati, Lakshmi and Durga or Parvati, also known as Shakti. There are held to have been ten *avatars* (incarnations) of Vishnu, of whom the most important are Rama and Krishna. Other popular gods are Ganesha, Hanuman and Subrahmanyam. All gods are seen as aspects of the supreme God, not as competing deities.

Orthodox Hindus revere all gods and goddesses equally, but there are many sects, including the Hare-Krishna movement (ISKCon), the Arya Samaj, the Swami Narayan Hindu mission and the Satya Sai-Baba movement. Worship in the sects is concentrated on one deity to the exclusion of others. In some sects a human *guru* (spiritual teacher), usually the head of the organization, is revered more than the deity, while in other sects the guru is seen as the source of spiritual guidance.

Hinduism does not have a centrally-trained and ordained priesthood. The pronouncements of the *shankaracharyas* (heads of monasteries) of Shringeri, Puri, Dwarka and Badrinath are heeded by the orthodox but may be ignored by the various sects.

The commonest form of worship is a *puja*, in which offerings of red and yellow powders, rice grains, water, flowers, food, fruit, incense and light are made to the image of a deity. Puja may be done either in a home shrine or a *mandir* (temple). For details of the Hindu calendar, main festivals etc, *see* pages 84–5.

The largest communities of Hindus in Britain are in Leicester, London, Birmingham and Bradford, and developed as a result of immigration from India, east Africa and Sri Lanka. Many Hindus now are British by birth, with English as their first language; the main ethnic languages are Gujarati, Hindi, Punjabi, Tamil, Bengali and Marathi.

There are an estimated 650 million Hindus world-wide; there are about 350,000 adherents and over 150 temples in the UK.

ARYA PRATINIDHI SABHA (UK), 69A Argyle Road, London W13 0LY

BHARATIYA VIDYA BHAVAN, Old Church Building, 4A Castletown Road, London W14 9HQ. Tel: 071-381 3086

INTERNATIONAL SOCIETY FOR KRISHNA CONSCIOUSNESS (ISKCon), Bhakti Vedanta Manor, Radlett, Herts. Tel: 0923-857244

NATIONAL COUNCIL OF HINDU TEMPLES, 559 St Alban's Road, Watford, Herts. WD2 6JH

SWAMI NARAYAN HINDU MISSION, 54 Meadow Garth, London NW10 8HD. Tel: 081-965 2651

VISHVA HINDU PARISHAD (UK), 5 Rosemary Drive, Redbridge, Ilford, Essex IG4 5JD

ISLAM

Islam (which means 'peace arising from submission to the wisdom of Allah' in Arabic) is a monotheistic religion which originated in Arabia through the prophet Muhammad, who was born in Mecca in AD 570. Islam spread to Egypt, North Africa, Spain and the borders of China in the century following the prophet's death, and is now the predominant religion in Indonesia, the Near and Middle East, North and parts of West Africa, Pakistan, Bangladesh, Malaysia and some of the republics of the former Soviet Union. There are also large Muslim communities in many other countries.

For Muslims (adherents of Islam), God (*Allah*) is one and holds absolute power. His commands were revealed to mankind through the prophets, who include Abraham, Moses and Jesus, but his message was gradually corrupted until revealed finally and in perfect form to Muhammad by the angel *Jibril* (Gabriel) over a period of 23 years. This last, incorruptible message has been recorded in the *Qur'an* (Koran), which contains 114 divisions called *surahs*, each made up of *ayahs*, and is held to be the essence of all previous scriptures. The *Hadith* is the record of the prophet Muhammad's deeds and sayings (the *Sunnah*) as recounted by his immediate followers. A culture and a system of law and theology based on the Hadith and the Qur'an gradually developed to form a distinctive Islamic civilization. Islam makes no distinction between sacred and worldly affairs and provides rules for every aspect of human life.

The 'five pillars of Islam' are *shahada* (a declaration of faith in the oneness and supremacy of Allah); *salat* (formal prayer, to be performed five times a day facing the holy city of Mecca); *zakat* (alms-giving); *saum* (fasting during the month of Ramadan); and *hajj* (pilgrimage to Mecca); some Muslims would add *jihad* (striving for the cause of good and resistance to evil). Together with other prescriptions, the five pillars make up the *Shari'a* (sacred law) of Islam.

Two main groups, with distinct legal and theological characteristics, developed among Muslims. *Sunni* Muslims accept the legitimacy of Muhammad's first four *caliphs* (successors as head of the Muslim community) and the authority of the Muslim community as a whole. About 90 per cent of Muslims are *Sunni* Muslims. *Shi'ites* recognize

only Muhammad's son-in-law Ali as his rightful successor and the *Imams* (descendants of Ali, not to be confused with *imams* (prayer leaders or religious teachers)) as the principal legitimate religious authority. The largest group within *Shi'ism* is *Twelver Shi'ism*, which has been the official religion of Iran since the 16th century, and other subsects include the *Ismailis* and the *Druze* (the latter being an offshoot of the Ismailis and differing considerably from the main body of Muslims).

There is no organized priesthood, but holy men such as *ulama, imams* and *ayatollahs* are accorded great respect. The *Sufis* are the mystics of Islam. Mosques are centres for worship and teaching and also for social and welfare activities. For details of the Muslim calendar and festivals, *see* page 86.

Islam was first known in western Europe in the eighth century AD when 800 years of Muslim rule began in Spain. Later, Islam spread to eastern Europe. More recently, Muslims came to Europe from Africa, the Middle East and Asia in the late 19th century. Both the Sunni and Shi'ah traditions are represented in Britain, but the majority of Muslims in Britain adhere to Sunni Islam.

The largest communities are in London, Liverpool, Manchester, Birmingham, Bradford, Cardiff, Edinburgh and Glasgow. There is no central organization, but the Islamic Cultural Centre, which is the London Central Mosque, and the Imams and Mosques Council are influential bodies; there are many other Muslim organizations in Britain.

There are at least 700 million Muslims world-wide. The estimated number of adherents in Britain is between one and two million, with over 350 mosques.

ISLAMIC CULTURAL CENTRE, 146 Park Road, London NW8 7RG. Tel: 071-724 3363. *Director,* Dr M. A. al-Ghamdi

IMAMS AND MOSQUES COUNCIL, 20–22 Creffield Road, London W5 3RP. Tel: 081-992 6636. *Director of the Council and Principal of the Muslim College,* Dr M. A. Z. Badawi

JUDAISM

Judaism is the oldest monotheistic faith. The primary authority of Judaism is the Hebrew Bible or *Tanakh*, which records how the descendants of Abraham were led by Moses out of their slavery in Egypt to Mount Sinai where God's law (*Torah*) was revealed to them as the chosen people. The *Talmud*, which consists of commentaries on the *Mishnah* (the first text of rabbinical Judaism), is also held to be authoritative, and may be divided into two main categories: the *halakah* (dealing with legal and ritual matters) and the *Aggadah* (dealing with theological and ethical matters not directly concerned with the regulation of conduct). The *Midrash* comprises rabbinic writings containing biblical interpretations in the spirit of the *Aggadah*. The *halakah* has become a source of division; Orthodox Jews regard Jewish law as derived from God and therefore unalterable; Reform and Liberal Jews seek to interpret it in the light of contemporary considerations; and Conservative Jews aim to maintain most of the traditional rituals but to allow changes in accordance with that tradition. Reconstructionist Judaism, a 20th-century movement, regards Judaism as a culture rather than a theological system and therefore accepts all forms of Jewish practice.

The family is the basic unit of Jewish ritual, with the synagogue playing an important role as the centre for public worship and religious study. A synagogue is led by a group of laymen who are elected to office; there are no priestly roles. The Rabbi is primarily a teacher and spiritual guide. The Sabbath is the central religious observance. For details of the Jewish calendar, fasts and festivals, *see* page 85. Most British Jews are descendants of either the *Ashkenazim* of central and eastern Europe or the *Sephardim* of Spain and Portugal.

The Chief Rabbi of the United Hebrew Congregations of the Commonwealth is appointed by a Chief Rabbinate Conference, and is the rabbinical authority of the Orthodox sector of the Ashkenazi Jewish community. His authority is not recognized by the Reform Synagogues of Great Britain (the largest progressive group), the Union of Liberal and Progressive Synagogues, the Union of Orthodox Hebrew Congregations, the Federation of Synagogues, the Sephardi community, or the Assembly of Masorti Synagogues. He is, however, generally recognized both outside the Jewish community and within it as the public religious representative of the totality of British Jewry.

The *Beth Din* (Court of Judgment) is the rabbinic court. The *Dayanim* (Assessors) adjudicate in disputes or on matters of Jewish law and tradition; they also oversee dietary law administration. The Chief Rabbi is President of the *Beth Din* of the United Synagogue.

The Board of Deputies of British Jews was established in 1760 and is the representative body of British Jewry. The basis of representation is mainly synagogal, but communal organizations are also represented. It watches over the interests of British Jewry and seeks to counter anti-Jewish discrimination.

There are over 12.5 million Jews world-wide; in Great Britain and Ireland there are an estimated 300,000 adherents and about 350 synagogues. Of these, 185 congregations and about 150 rabbis and ministers are under the jurisdiction of the Chief Rabbi. A further 99 orthodox congregations have a more independent status, and 72 congregations do not recognize the authority of the Chief Rabbi.

Chief Rabbi, Dr Jonathan Sacks
CHIEF RABBINATE, Adler House, Tavistock Square, London WC1H 9HN. Tel: 071-387 1066. *Executive Director*, J. Kestenbaum
BETH DIN (COURT OF THE CHIEF RABBI), Adler House, Tavistock Square, London WC1H 0EP. Tel: 071-387 5772. *Registrar*, J. Phillips; *Dayanim*, Rabbi C. Ehrentreu; Rabbi I. Binstock; Rabbi C. D. Kaplin; Rabbi I. D. Berger
UNITED SYNAGOGUE HEAD OFFICE, Woburn House, Tavistock Square, London WC1H 0EZ. Tel: 071-387 4300. *Chief Executive*, J. M. Lew
REFORM SYNAGOGUES OF GREAT BRITAIN, The Sternberg Centre, Manor House, 80 East End Road, London N3 2SY. Tel: 081-349 4731. *Executive Director*, R. M. Goldman
UNION OF LIBERAL AND PROGRESSIVE SYNAGOGUES (JEWISH RELIGIOUS UNION), 109 Whitfield Street, London W1P 5RP. Tel: 071-580 1663. *Director*, Mrs R. Rosenberg
UNION OF ORTHODOX HEBREW CONGREGATIONS, 40 Queen Elizabeth's Walk, London N16 0HH. Tel: 081-802 6226. *Executive Director*, B. Steinhart
FEDERATION OF SYNAGOGUES, 65 Watford Way, London NW4 3AQ. Tel: 081-202 2263. *Administrator*, G. Kushner
SPANISH AND PORTUGUESE JEWS' CONGREGATION, 2 Ashworth Road, London W9 1JY. Tel: 071-289 2573. *Chief Executive*, Mrs J. Velleman
ASSEMBLY OF MASORTI SYNAGOGUES, 766 Finchley Road, London NW11 7TH. Tel: 081-201 8772. *Administrator*, Mrs G. Miller

BOARD OF DEPUTIES OF BRITISH JEWS, Woburn House, Tavistock Square, London WC1H 0EZ. Tel: 071-387 3952. *President*, His Hon. I. Finestein, QC; *Chief Executive*, N. A. Nagler

SIKHISM

The Sikh religion dates from the birth of Guru Nanak in the Punjab in 1469. The word 'guru' means teacher, but in Sikh tradition it has come to represent the divine presence of God giving inner spiritual guidance. Nanak's role as the human vessel of the divine guru was passed on to nine successors, the last of whom (Guru Gobind Singh) died in 1708. The immortal guru is now held to reside in the sacred scripture, *Guru Granth Sahib*, and so to be present in all Sikh gatherings.

Guru Nanak taught that there is one God and that different religions are like different roads leading to the same destination. He condemned religious conflict, ritualism and caste prejudices. The fifth Guru, Guru Arjan, compiled the Sikh Holy Book, a collection of hymns (*gurbani*) known as the *Adi Granth*. It contains the writings of the first five Gurus and selected writings of Hindu and Muslim saints whose views are in accord with the Guru's teachings. Guru Arjan also built the Golden Temple at Amritsar, the centre of Sikhism. The tenth Guru, Guru Gobind Singh, passed on the guruship to the sacred scripture, Guru Granth Sahib. He also founded the *Khalsa*, an order intended to fight against tyranny and injustice. Male initiates to the order added 'Singh' to their given names and women added 'Kaur'. Guru Gobind Singh also made five symbols obligatory: *kaccha* (a special undergarment), *kara* (a steel bangle), *kirpan* (a small sword), *kesh* (long unshorn hair, and consequently the wearing of a turban), and *kangha* (a comb). These practices are still compulsory for those Sikhs who are initiated into the *Khalsa* (the *Amritdharis*). Those who do not seek initiation are known as *Sahajdharis*.

There are no professional priests in Sikhism; anyone with a reasonable proficiency in the Punjabi language can conduct a service. Worship can be offered individually or communally, and in a private house or a *gurdwara* (temple). Sikhs are forbidden to eat meat prepared by ritual slaughter; they are also asked to abstain from smoking, alcohol and other intoxicants. For details of the Sikh calendar and main celebrations, *see* page 86.

Sikhs first came to Britain in the 1950s, mainly for economic and political reasons. The largest Sikh communities are in London, Bradford, Leeds, Huddersfield, Birmingham, Nottingham, Coventry and Wolverhampton. Every gurdwara manages its own affairs and there is no central body in the UK. The Sikh Missionary Society UK works for the advancement of Sikhism and provides an information service.

There are about 12.5 million Sikhs world-wide and an estimated 400,000 adherents and 170 gurdwaras in Great Britain.

SIKH MISSIONARY SOCIETY UK, 10 Featherstone Road, Southall, Middx. UB2 5AA. Tel: 081-574 1902. *Hon. General Secretary*, H. S. Kular

Education

For addresses of national education departments, *see* Government Departments and Public Offices. For other addresses, *see* Education Directory

Responsibility for education in the United Kingdom is largely decentralized. Overall responsibility for all aspects of education in England lies with the Secretary of State for Education; in Wales with the Secretary of State for Wales; in Scotland with the Secretary of State for Scotland acting through the Scottish Office Education Department; and in Northern Ireland with the Secretary of State for Northern Ireland.

The main concerns of the education departments (the Department for Education (DFE), the Welsh Office, the Scottish Office Education Department (SOED), and the Department of Education for Northern Ireland (DENI)) are the formulation of national policies for education, and the maintenance of consistency in educational standards. They are responsible for the broad allocation of resources for education, for the rate and distribution of educational building and for the supply, training and superannuation of teachers. Hitherto, none of the education departments have run any schools or colleges directly, nor employed any teachers. However, under the provisions of the Education Reform Act 1988 and the Self-Governing Schools etc. (Scotland) Act 1989, the Department for Education in England until March 1994, the Welsh office and the Scottish Office Education Department fund individual schools which have opted out of local education authority control and applied for direct funding from the Secretaries of State. In addition, the Department for Education, in association with sponsors from industry, funds the new City Technology Colleges (CTCs) and the City Colleges for the Technology of the Arts. Technology Academies are proposed on a similar basis in Scotland.

Schools in Northern Ireland providing integrated education are able to apply for grant-maintained status from the Department of Education for Northern Ireland.

EXPENDITURE

The Department for Education, the Welsh Office, the Scottish Office and the Northern Ireland Office act within a framework of estimates approved by Parliament.

In real terms expenditure on education by central government departments was as follows (£ million):

	1992–3 estimated outturn	1993–4 planned
DFE	7,200	9,523
Welsh Office	151.5	403.6
SOED	678	1,182
DENI	1,199	1,234

The discontinuity between the expenditure profiles of the DFE, Welsh Office and SOED for the years 1992–3 and 1993–4 is due to the transfer of resources to the Higher Education Funding Councils and the Further Education Funding Councils.

In the United Kingdom in 1990–1, central government provisional expenditure on education was apportioned as follows (£million):

Schools	15,579
Further and higher education	6,833
Other education and related expenditure	2,458

Most of this expenditure is incurred by local authorities, which make their own expenditure decisions according to their local situations and needs and which, until April 1993, were also responsible for funding most further education courses. The bulk of direct expenditure by the DFE, the Welsh Office and SOED is directed towards supporting higher education in universities and colleges through the three Higher Education Funding Councils and further education and sixth form colleges through the Further Education Funding Councils in England and Wales and directly from central government in Scotland. In addition, the DFE funds grant-maintained schools (from April 1994 through the Funding Agency for Schools (FAS)) and CTCs in the schools sector.

The Welsh Office also funds grants for higher and further education, grant-maintained schools, educational services and research and supports bilingual education and the Welsh language.

In Scotland, as in England and Wales, the bulk of expenditure on education is at a local level by the regional and islands councils. In addition to those outlined above, the main elements of central government expenditure are grant-aided special schools, self-governing schools, student awards, curriculum development, special educational needs and community education.

The Department of Education for Northern Ireland finances higher education, teacher education, teacher salaries and superannuation, student awards, grant-maintained integrated schools, and voluntary grammar schools. Remaining expenditure is by education and library boards at local level.

Current net expenditure on education by local education authorities in England and Wales, regional and islands councils in Scotland, and education and library boards in Northern Ireland is as follows (£million):

	1992–3 estimated outturn	1993–4 planned
England	22,576	16,854
Wales	1,336.5	1,234.4
Scotland	2,583	2,425
Northern Ireland	856	880

LOCAL EDUCATION ADMINISTRATION

The education service at present is a national service in which the provision of most school education is locally administered; its administration is still largely decentralized.

ENGLAND AND WALES – In England and Wales the education service is administered by local education authorities (LEAs), which carry the day-to-day responsibility for providing most state primary and secondary education in their areas, although the planning and supply of school places is to be shared with the newly established Funding Agency for Schools (FAS) as the number of pupils in grant-maintained schools grows. They also share with the FEFCs the duty to provide adult education to meet the needs of their areas.

Each local education authority was formerly required by statute to appoint an education committee, or committees, authorized to exercise on its behalf any of the authority's functions with respect to education, except the power to borrow money, but the passing of the Education Act 1993 removed this requirement and LEAs are now free to organize themselves as they think fit.

The LEAs own and maintain schools and colleges, build new ones and provide equipment. Most of the public money spent on education is disbursed by the local authorities. LEAs are financed largely from the council tax and Aggregate External Finance (AEF) from the Department of the Environment in England and the Welsh Office in Wales.

The powers of local education authorities as regards the control of schools have been modified in recent years. The Education (No. 2) Act 1986 legislated for equal numbers of parents and local authority representatives as governors in most maintained schools. The process was continued by the Education Reform Act 1988, which delegated control of their budgets directly to all schools by April 1994. It also provided for schools to opt out of local authority control and to be funded by central government, from April 1994 through the Funding Agency for Schools in England. The Schools Funding Council for Wales will take over from the Welsh Office when the number of grant-maintained schools warrants the change. The Education Act 1993 has facilitated this process and also enabled primary schools to apply for grant-maintained status as a group as well as individually. It also provided for an Education Association to be set up to take over the management of failing schools where both the LEA and the governing body have not brought about the improvements identified as necessary.

SCOTLAND – The duty of providing education locally in Scotland rests with the nine regional and three islands councils. They are responsible for the construction of buildings, the employment of teachers and other staff, and the provision of equipment and materials, but management is to be devolved to the schools themselves by April 1996. Their responsibility for the curricula taught in schools is shared with headteachers under the guidance of the Secretary of State for Scotland and the Scottish Consultative Council on the Curriculum.

The powers of local authorities over educational institutions under their control have been reduced also in Scotland. Under the School Boards (Scotland) Act 1988, education authorities are required to establish school boards consisting of parents and teachers as well as co-opted members, responsible among other things for the appointment of staff. The Self-Governing Schools etc. (Scotland) Act 1989 provides for schools to withdraw from local authority control and become self-governing; for the institution of Technology Academies directly funded by central government; and for the composition of further education college councils on which at least half the members are employers, and for the delegation of substantial functions to these new councils.

NORTHERN IRELAND – Education is administered locally in Northern Ireland by five education and library boards, although a review of educational administration is taking place. All grant-aided schools include elected parents and teachers on their boards of governors. Provision has been made for schools wishing to provide integrated education to have grant-maintained integrated status from the outset. All secondary schools and colleges of further education, and most primary schools, have full responsibility for their own budgets, including staffing costs. Full delegation was phased in for the remaining primary schools from April 1993.

The Council for Catholic Maintained Schools forms an upper tier of management for Catholic schools and provides advice on matters relating to management and administration.

THE INSPECTORATE

Under the Education (Schools) Act 1992, the Office for Standards in Education (OFSTED), headed by HM Chief Inspector of Schools in England (HMCI) was created separately from the DFE. Its counterpart in Wales is the Office of HM Chief Inspector of Schools in Wales (OHMCISW). OFSTED's remit is to inspect, report on and improve standards of achievement and quality of education through regular independent inspection, public reporting and informed advice. OFSTED's major and most urgent task is to set up the new system of inspection by independent registered inspectors. The new system provides a full inspection for all state schools every four years, beginning in September 1993 for secondary schools and one year later for primary and special schools. OFSTED will select the teams of independent inspectors following bids for the contracts. A summary of the inspection report must be sent to parents of each pupil, followed by a copy of the governors' action plan thereon. HM Inspectorate in Scotland carries out the inspection of schools in that country, and in addition requires schools to produce a document setting out their educational targets for the two years ahead and a report on progress over the previous two years. The inspection of further and higher education is the responsibility of inspectors appointed to the Further and Higher Education Funding Councils. Inspection is carried out in Northern Ireland by the Education and Training Inspectorate of the Department of Education which also performs an advisory function to the Secretary of State for Northern Ireland.

There were, in 1992–3, 300 HMIs in England, 58 in Wales, 108 in Scotland and 61 members of the Inspectorate in Northern Ireland.

Schools and Pupils

Schooling is compulsory in the United Kingdom for all children between five and 16 years. Some provision is made for children under five and many pupils remain at school after the minimum leaving age. No fees are charged in any publicly maintained school in England, Wales and Scotland. In Northern Ireland, fees are paid by pupils in preparatory departments of grammar schools, but pupils admitted to the secondary departments of grammar schools do not pay fees.

In the United Kingdom, parents have a right to express a preference for a particular school and have a right to appeal if dissatisfied. Parental choice has been increased by the introduction of a policy known as more open enrolment whereby schools are required to admit children up to the limit of their capacity if there is a demand for places, and to publish their criteria for selection if they are over-subscribed, in which case parents have a right of appeal.

Schools are now required to make available information about themselves, their public examination and key stage 2 national curriculum test results, truancy rates, and destination of leavers. Corporal punishment is no longer legal in publicly maintained schools in the United Kingdom.

FALL AND RISE IN NUMBERS

In primary education, and increasingly in secondary education, pupil numbers in the United Kingdom have declined. In nursery and primary schools pupil numbers reached their lowest figure of 4.5 million in 1990. Numbers are expected to increase gradually year by year until by 2000 they reach about 5.5 million. In secondary schools pupil numbers rose to 4.6 million in 1981. They stood at 3.5 million in 1991 and are projected to rise to 4 million in 2000.

ENGLAND AND WALES

There are two main categories of school in England and Wales: those maintained by local education authorities, which charge no fees; and independent schools, which charge fees (see page 447). To these categories may be added two more as a result of the Education Reform Act 1988, consisting of grant-maintained schools funded directly by the Secretary of State in England until March 1994, thereafter through the Funding Agency for Schools (FAS), and by the Welsh office in Wales. These comprise primary and secondary schools which, although still providing free education, have applied to opt out of local education authority control in favour of grant-maintained status; and City Technology Colleges (*see* below). There are 32,119 schools in the maintained sector and 2,508 independent schools.

Maintained schools are of two types: (i) county schools (16,958 in 1992) which are owned by LEAs and wholly funded by them. They are non-denominational and provide primary and secondary education; (ii) voluntary schools (7,538 in 1992) which also provide primary and secondary education. Although the buildings are in many cases provided by the voluntary bodies (mainly religious denominations) they are financially maintained by an LEA.

Voluntary schools are of three kinds: controlled (3,132), aided (4,406) and special agreement (67). In controlled schools the LEA bears all costs. In aided schools the building is usually provided by the voluntary body. The managers or governors are responsible for repairs to the outside of the school building and for improvements and alterations to it, though the Department for Education may reimburse part of approved capital expenditure, while the LEA pays for internal maintenance and other running costs. Special agreement schools are those where the LEA may, by special agreement, pay between one-half and three-quarters of the cost of building a new, or extending an existing, voluntary school, almost always a secondary school. There are no special agreement schools in Wales. In voluntary schools the majority of the managers or governors are appointed by the voluntary body and at least one by the LEA. The managers or governors control the appointment of teachers. Expenditure is normally apportioned between the authority and the voluntary body.

All publicly maintained schools have a governing body usually made up of a number of parent representatives, governors appointed by the LEA if the school is LEA maintained, the headteacher (unless he or she chooses otherwise), and serving teachers. The passing of the Education Act 1993 allows schools to appoint up to four sponsor governors from business who will be expected to provide financial and managerial assistance. Parental involvement in the running of schools has increased considerably in recent years, and parents have also been given the power to decide by ballot whether their child's school should opt out of local authority control and become self-governing (grant-maintained). Governors are responsible for the overall policies of schools and their academic aims and objectives; they also now control matters of school discipline and the appointment and dismissal of staff. Under the Education (Schools) Act 1992, governing bodies select inspectors for their schools, are responsible for action as a result of inspection reports and are required to make these reports and their action plans thereon available to parents. The Education Reform Act 1988 delegated control of the administration of the major part of school budgets, including staffing costs, from LEAs directly to schools under an initiative known as Local Management of Schools (LMS).

Technology schools and Technology Colleges – The technology schools initiative, launched in December 1991, provides capital and project funding for a network of schools committed to offering innovative technology teaching of a vocational nature. In 1993–4 £23 million of capital funding has been made available to 122 schools which submitted successful bids. A similar initiative was launched for Wales in May 1993 for which funding of £2.24 million has been earmarked for the financial years 1993–4 and 1994–5. In autumn 1993 the Government will publish a detailed prospectus for schools wishing to become Technology Colleges which will specialize in the teaching of technology, mathematics and science.

Grant-maintained (GM) schools (self-governing state schools) – All secondary and primary schools are eligible to apply for grant-maintained status, subject to a ballot of parents. GM schools are maintained directly by the Secretary of State and the Welsh office, not the LEA, and are wholly run by their own governing body. The Funding Agency for Schools (FAS) is being set up from April 1944 to take over the payment of grants to grant-maintained schools in England. The Schools Funding Council for Wales will be instituted when the number of GM schools justifies the change in funding arrangements. By April 1994 there are projected to be at least 1,000 GM schools. Of the 493 schools operating in June 1993, 388 were secondary schools, and 105 were primary schools.

City Technology Colleges (CTCs) and *City Colleges for the Technology of the Arts (CCTAs)* are state-aided but independent of LEAs. Their aim is to widen the choice of secondary education in disadvantaged urban areas and to teach a broad curriculum with an emphasis on science, technology, business understanding and arts technologies. Capital costs are shared by government and sponsors from industry and commerce, and running costs are covered by a per capita grant from the DFE in line with comparable costs in an LEA maintained school.

The first city technology college opened in September 1988 in Solihull. By September 1993 there were fifteen. The first CCTA, known as Britschool, opened in Croydon in September 1991.

SCOTLAND

Schools in Scotland fall into three main categories: education authority schools (3,796) (known as public schools), which are managed by the regional and islands councils and financed jointly by the councils and central government; grant-aided schools (8), conducted by voluntary managers who receive grants direct from the Scottish Office Education Department; and independent schools (123), which receive no direct grant and charge fees, but are subject to inspection and registration. An additional category is created under the provisions of the Self-Governing Schools etc. (Scotland) Act 1989, of schools opting to be managed entirely by a board of management consisting of the headmaster, parent and staff representatives and co-opted members. The change of status will require a ballot of parents and the publication of proposals by the board, and the achievement of self-government is subject to a final decision by the Secretary of State. These schools will remain in the public sector and will be funded by direct government grant set to match the resources the school would have received under education authority management. None has yet been established.

Under the School Boards (Scotland) Act 1988, education authorities are required to establish school boards to participate in the administration and management of schools. These boards consist of elected parents and staff members as well as co-opted members.

Technology Academies (TAs) – The Self-Governing Schools etc. (Scotland) Act 1989 provides for setting up technology academies in areas of urban deprivation. These secondary schools are intended to be so placed as to draw on a wide catchment, and will offer a broad curriculum with an emphasis on science and technology. They are to be founded and managed in partnership with industrial sponsors, with central government meeting the running costs by grant-aid thereafter. None has yet been set up.

NORTHERN IRELAND

There are three main categories of grant-aided school in Northern Ireland: controlled schools (706), which are controlled by the education and library boards with all costs paid from public funds; voluntary maintained schools (584), mainly under Roman Catholic management, which receive grants towards capital costs and running costs in whole or in part; and voluntary grammar schools (52), which may be under Roman Catholic or non-denominational management and receive grants from the Department of Education for Northern Ireland. All grant-aided schools include elected parents and teachers on their boards of governors, whose responsibilities also include financial management under the Local Management of Schools (LMS) initiative. Legislation is being brought forward under which voluntary maintained and voluntary grammar schools will be able to apply for designation as a new category of voluntary school, which will be eligible for 100 per cent grant. Such schools will be managed by a board of governors on which no single interest group will have a majority of nominees. There are also 17 independent schools in Northern Ireland.

The majority of children in Northern Ireland are educated in schools which in practice are segregated on religious lines. The Education Reform (Northern Ireland) Order 1989, however, makes provision for parents to opt for integrated education more easily. These provisions include arrangements to fund new integrated schools from the outset and procedures for balloting parents in existing segregated schools to determine whether they want instead to have integrated schools. By September 1993, 21 integrated schools had been established, four of them secondary.

THE STATE SYSTEM

NURSERY EDUCATION – Nursery education is for children from two to five years and is not compulsory. In the United Kingdom it takes place in nursery schools or nursery classes in primary schools. In 1990–1, 799,100 pupils under five years of age were receiving education in maintained nursery and primary schools, an increase of 30,000 on the previous year. Of the total, 84,400 were in nursery schools, 660,500 in primary schools, and 47,800 in non-maintained nursery schools. Expressed as a percentage of the population aged three and four years, the 799,100 represented 53 per cent, compared to 51 per cent in the previous year.

Many children also attend pre-school playgroups organized by parents and voluntary bodies such as the Pre-School Playgroups Association.

PRIMARY EDUCATION – Primary education begins at five years and is almost always co-educational. In England, Wales and Northern Ireland the transfer to secondary school is generally made at 11 years. In Scotland, the primary school course lasts for seven years and pupils transfer to secondary courses at about the age of 12.

Primary schools consist mainly of infants' schools for children aged five to seven, junior schools for those aged seven to 11, and combined junior and infant schools for both age groups. First schools in some parts of England cater for ages five to ten as the first stage of a three-tier system: first, middle and secondary. Many primary schools provide nursery classes for children under five (see above).

The number of primary schools in the United Kingdom in 1990–1 was 24,135, which was 133 fewer than in 1989–90, with 4,989,000 full- and part-time pupils, of which 660,500 were under five. Between 1990 and 2000 primary school pupil numbers are projected to rise by about 10 per cent.

Pupil-teacher ratios in maintained primary schools in the United Kingdom are:

	1989–90	1990–1
England	21.8	22.0
Wales	22.3	22.3
Scotland	19.7	19.5
Northern Ireland	23.2	22.9
UK	21.7	21.8

The average size of classes 'as taught' fell to 23.8 in 1991 but rose to 25.5 in 1992.

MIDDLE SCHOOLS – Middle schools (which take children from first schools), mostly in England, cover varying age ranges between eight and 14 and usually lead on to comprehensive upper schools.

SECONDARY EDUCATION – Secondary schools are for children aged 11 to 16 and for those who choose to stay on to 18. At 16, many students prefer to move on to tertiary or sixth form colleges (see page 451). Most secondary schools in England, Wales and Scotland are co-educational. The largest secondary schools have over 2,000 pupils but only 2.8 per cent of the schools take over 1,000 pupils.

In England and Wales the main types of secondary schools are: comprehensive schools (85.7 per cent of pupils in England, 99.2 in Wales), whose admission arrangements are without reference to ability or aptitude; middle deemed secondary schools for children aged variously between eight and 14 years who then move on to senior comprehensive schools at 12, 13 or 14 (6.4 per cent of pupils in England only); secondary modern schools (3.3 per cent of pupils in England only) providing a general education with a practical bias; secondary grammar schools (3.6 per cent of pupils in England only) with selective intake providing an academic course from 11 to 16–18 years; and technical schools (0.1 per cent in England only), providing an integrated academic and technical education.

In January 1991 there were in England and Wales 3,154,000 pupils in maintained secondary schools, including 12.2 per cent in England and 12.1 per cent in Wales who were 16 or over. After falling by 16 per cent between 1987 and 1991, numbers are projected to rise 10.3 per cent by 2000.

Pupil-teacher ratios improved steadily from 15.7 in 1987 to 15.3 in 1990 in England and Wales, then rose to 15.7 again in 1992. The average class size in England was 21.2 in 1992. In Wales the average class size in 1992 was 21.5.

In Scotland all pupils in education authority secondary schools attend schools with a comprehensive intake. Most of these schools provide a full range of courses appropriate to all levels of ability from first to sixth year. In 1991–2 there were 296,446 pupils in education authority schools, of whom 21.9 per cent were 16 or over. Numbers are projected to increase to 326,000 in 2000. Pupil-teacher ratios worsened from 12.4 in 1991 to 12.6 in 1992. The average class size in 1992 was 18.9.

In most areas of Northern Ireland there is a selective system of secondary education with pupils transferring either to grammar schools or secondary schools at 11–12 years of age. Parents can choose the school they would like their children to attend and all those who apply must be admitted if they meet the criteria. If a school is over-subscribed beyond its statutory admissions number, selection is on the basis of published criteria, which, for most grammar schools, place emphasis on performance in the transfer procedure tests which are centrally administered by the Department for Education. When parents consider that a school has not applied its criteria fairly they have access to independent appeals tribunals. Grammar schools provide an academic type of secondary education with A-levels at the end of the seventh year, while secondary non-grammar schools follow a curriculum suited to a wider range of aptitudes and abilities.

In 1992 there were 143,300 pupils in public sector secondary schools, of whom 87,525 (61.1 per cent) attended non-grammar secondary and 55,770 (38.9 per cent) attended grammar schools. Of all pupils 35.4 per cent were 16 or over. Pupil-teacher ratios in Northern Ireland were 15.3 in 1992.

SPECIAL EDUCATION – Special education is provided for children with special educational needs, usually because they have a disability which either prevents or hinders them from making use of educational facilities of a kind generally provided for children of their age in schools within the area of the local authority concerned. However, wherever possible, such children are now educated in ordinary schools, taking the parents' wishes into account and schools are required to publish their policy for pupils with special educational needs. Maintained special schools are run by education authorities which pay all the costs of maintenance, and by April 1994 Local Management of Schools (LMS) will be extended to those that are able and wish to manage their own budgets. Non-maintained special schools are run by voluntary bodies; they may receive some grant from central government for capital expenditure and for equipment, but their current expenditure is met primarily from the fees charged to the education authorities for pupils placed in the schools. Some independent schools provide education wholly or mainly for children with special educational needs and are required to meet similar standards to those for maintained and non-maintained special schools. The national curriculum also applies to children with a statement of special needs, but there is provision for them to be exempt from it, or for it to be modified to suit their capabilities. The Education Act 1993 gives parents greater choice of schools and extends their right of appeal by establishing the Special Educational Needs (SEN) Tribunal.

In January 1991 in the United Kingdom there was a total of 111,700 full-time pupils in special schools (of whom 900 were in hospital schools in England, Wales and Northern Ireland). Of the total, 94,500 were in England, 3,600 in Wales, 8,700 in Scotland and 4,000 in Northern Ireland. Numbers have decreased since 1975–6 as education authorities in England, Wales and Northern Ireland must now ensure that children with special needs are educated as far as possible in ordinary schools with support teaching.

In Scotland, school placing is a matter of agreement between education authorities and parents. Parents have the right to say which school they want their child to attend, and a right of appeal where their wishes are not being met. Whenever possible, children with special needs are integrated into ordinary schools. However, for those who require a different environment or specialized facilities, there are special schools, both grant-aided by central government and independent, and special classes within ordinary schools. The Self-Governing Schools etc. (Scotland) Act 1989 obliges education authorities to respond to reasonable requests for independent special schools, and provides for them to send children with special needs to schools outside Scotland if appropriate provision is not available within the country. A new centre has been opened which practices conductive education methods for children with motor impairments.

ALTERNATIVE PROVISION

There is no legal obligation on parents in the United Kingdom to educate their children at school provided that the local education authority is satisfied that the child is receiving full-time education suited to its age, abilities and aptitudes. The education authority need not be informed that a child is being educated at home unless the child is already registered at a state school. In this case the parents must arrange for the child's name to be removed from the school's register (by writing to the headteacher) before education at home can begin. Failure to de-register a child leaves the parents liable to prosecution for condoning non-attendance.

In most cases an initial visit is made by an education adviser or education welfare officer, and sometimes subsequent inspections are made, but practice varies according to the individual education authority. There is no requirement for parents educating their children at home to be in possession of a teaching qualification.

Further advice on educating children other than at school can be obtained from Education Otherwise (*see* page 460).

INDEPENDENT SCHOOLS

Independent schools receive no grants from public funds. They charge fees, and are owned and managed under special trusts, with profits being used for the benefit of the schools concerned. There is a wide variety of provision, from kindergartens to large day and boarding schools, and from experimental schools to traditional institutions. A number of independent schools have been instituted by religious and ethnic minorities.

All independent schools in the United Kingdom are open to inspection by approved inspectors (*see* page 444) and must register with the appropriate government education department. The education departments lay down certain minimum standards and can make schools remedy any unacceptable features of their building or instruction and exclude any unsuitable teacher or proprietor. Most independent schools offer a similar range of courses to state schools and enter pupils for the same public examinations. Introduction of the national curriculum and the associated education targets and assessment procedures is not obligatory in the independent sector.

The term public schools is often applied to those independent schools in membership of the Headmasters' Conference, the Governing Bodies Association or the Governing Bodies of Girls' Schools Association. Most public schools are single-sex (about half of them for girls) but there are some mixed schools and an increasing number of schools have mixed sixth forms.

Preparatory schools are so-called because they prepare children for the Common Entrance Examination to senior independent schools. Most cater for boys from about seven to 13 years, some are for girls, and an increasing number are co-educational. The Common Entrance Examination is set by the Common Entrance Examination Board, but marked by the independent school to which the pupil intends to go. It is taken at 13 by boys, and from 11 to 13 by girls.

In 1992 there were in England 2,256 independent schools with 566,700 full-time pupils and a pupil-teacher ratio of 10.6.

In Wales in 1991–2 there were 68 independent schools, with 11,913 pupils and a pupil-teacher ratio of 9.7.

In Scotland in 1991–2 there were 123 registered independent schools with 33,500 pupils and a pupil-teacher ratio of 11.4. Most independent schools in Scotland follow the English examination system, i.e. GCSE followed by A-levels, although some take the Scottish Education Certificate at Ordinary/Standard grade followed by Highers.

There are 17 independent schools in Northern Ireland with 1,023 pupils and a pupil-teacher ratio of 11.9.

ASSISTED PLACES SCHEME
The Assisted Places Scheme enables children to attend independent secondary schools which their parents could not otherwise afford. The scheme provides help with tuition fees and other expenses, except boarding costs, on a sliding scale depending on the family's income. The take-up rate for places available at age 11 to 13 at the 303 participating schools in England and Wales is around 99 per cent, and the proportion of pupils receiving full fee remission is about 36 per cent. Over 35,000 places were offered in England and Wales in the academic year 1992–3. The 58 participating schools in Scotland admitted about 3,000 pupils on the scheme in 1992–3, which, unlike that in England and Wales, is cash-limited. The proportion of pupils receiving full fee remission is expected to be about 50 per cent.

The scheme is administered and funded in England by the Department for Education, in Wales by the Welsh Office, and in Scotland by the Scottish Office Education Department. The scheme does not operate in Northern Ireland as the independent sector admits non-fee-paying pupils. There is, however, a similar scheme known as the Talented Children's Scheme to help pupils gifted in music and dance.

Further information can be obtained from the Independent Schools Information Service (*see* page 460).

THE CURRICULUM

ENGLAND AND WALES
The Education Reform Act 1988 legislated for the progressive introduction of a national curriculum in primary and secondary schools from autumn 1989. During the period of compulsory schooling for children aged five to 16 the curriculum includes mathematics, English and science as core subjects and history, geography, technology, music, art, physical education and (for pupils in secondary schools) a modern foreign language as foundation subjects. For the core and foundation subjects attainment targets have been identified and standard assessment tests are being instituted at the end of each key stage, at the ages of 7, 11, 14 and 16. It was planned to use the SATS results in compiling publicly available comparative tables of schools, but this has met with resistance from schools and is being reconsidered. The first assessment tests took place in 1991 for seven year-olds. Pilot tests were carried out in 1992 for 14 year-olds and are planned in 1994 for 11 year-olds. Teachers have, however, expressed dissatisfaction with the tests since their inception. In response to their concerns the Government's interim review of the manageability of the national curriculum and the testing system has announced that there will be fewer and shorter tests and that the compulsory curriculum will be reduced. A final report is due in December 1993. The 1993 tests were boycotted by many schools, some of which substituted their own examinations, while others carried out the tests but did not report the results. At 16 the GCSE will be the main form of assessment. It is intended that pupils with special educational needs should have access to as much of the national curriculum as possible. Religious education is required to be available in schools, with the curriculum devised locally, but parents have the right to remove their children if they wish.

In Wales in 1991–2 the Welsh language was in use as the main or secondary medium of instruction in 33.3 per cent of primary and 31.4 per cent of secondary schools. Following the introduction of the national curriculum it will constitute a core subject in Welsh-speaking schools and a foundation subject in the others, although there is provision for exemptions to be made.

In England the School Curriculum and Assessment Authority (SCAA), funded by the Department for Education, is responsible for the promotion and support of curriculum development, in addition to advising the Secretary of State on the national curriculum. The Authority replaced the National Curriculum Council and the School Examinations and Assessment Council in October 1993. In Wales its functions are performed by the Curriculum Council for Wales, funded by the Welsh Office, which will undertake additional functions and be renamed the Curriculum and Assessment Authority for Wales from April 1994.

SCOTLAND
The content and management of the curriculum in Scotland is the responsibility of education authorities and individual headteachers. Advice and guidance is provided by the Scottish Office Education Department and the Scottish Consultative Council on the Curriculum. Scotland effectively has a national curriculum for 14–16 year-olds, who are required to study English, mathematics and a science subject plus five other subjects. These form the core area, supplemented by other activities forming the elective area. There is a recommended percentage of class time to be devoted to each area over the two years. Provision is made for teaching in Gaelic in Gaelic-speaking areas.

The Scottish Consultative Council on the Curriculum, which is responsible for development and advisory work on the curriculum in Scotland, has undertaken a major review of the balance of the primary curriculum, and produced new guidelines for each of the subject areas for the age group five to 14. There are new guidelines on assessment across the whole curriculum, and standardized tests are being phased in for English language and mathematics at five stages for this age group which are taken when teachers think the pupils are ready. For 16–18 year-olds, there is available a modular system of vocational courses in addition to academic courses.

NORTHERN IRELAND
Major programmes of curriculum review and development are in progress in primary and secondary schools. A curriculum common to all schools is being introduced over a four-year period to 1994–5, with six broad areas of study within which ten subjects will be compulsory; religious education will also be a compulsory part of the curriculum. The Irish language will be a compulsory subject in Irish-medium primary schools and can be chosen as the compulsory foreign language in secondary schools. Arrangements for the assessment of pupils, broadly in line with those in England and Wales, are proposed at the ages of eight, 11, 14 and 16. Voluntary pilot assessments were carried out by June 1993 for 11 and 14 year-olds and in May 1994 for 8 year-olds. In Northern Ireland, as in England and Wales, teachers are dissatisfied with the assessment arrangements.

The Northern Ireland Curriculum Council (NICC) advises the Government on all matters concerning the curriculum for grant-aided schools in Northern Ireland. From April 1994 it will amalgamate with the Northern Ireland Schools Examination and Assessment Council (NISEAC) to form the Northern Ireland Council for the Curriculum, Assessment and Examinations (NICCAE).

RECORDS OF ACHIEVEMENT
The National Records of Achievement sets down the range of a school-leaver's achievements and activities both inside and outside the classroom, including those not tested by examination. It is issued to all those leaving school in England

and Wales and will be introduced in Scotland. Under the Education (Schools) Act 1992, parents in England and Wales must receive a written yearly progress report on all aspects of their children's achievements. There is a similar commitment for Northern Ireland. In Scotland the school report card has been reformed to give parents more information on their children's progress; the new format was introduced in schools in September 1993.

TECHNICAL AND VOCATIONAL EDUCATION INITIATIVE

The Technical and Vocational Education Initiative (TVEI), administered and funded by the Department of Employment in England, the Welsh Office in Wales and the Scottish Office Industry Department in Scotland, operates across the curriculum within a framework of general education. It aims to make the secondary curriculum more relevant to adult life and work. Following pilot projects, it is now a national scheme with newly established criteria which complement and are compatible with the requirements of the new national curriculum in England and Wales. Participation is voluntary, and is open to all maintained schools and colleges providing for young people of all abilities aged 14–18. TVEI is not an examination or a qualification.

THE PUBLIC EXAMINATION SYSTEM

ENGLAND, WALES AND NORTHERN IRELAND

Until the end of 1987, secondary school pupils at the end of compulsory schooling around the age of 16, and others, took the General Certificate of Education (GCE) Ordinary-level or the Certificate of Secondary Education (CSE). From 1988 these were replaced by a single system of examinations, the General Certificate of Secondary Education (GCSE), which is usually taken after five years of secondary education. The first examinations took place in summer 1988. From summer 1994, the GCSE will be used to assess the performance of pupils in all national curriculum subjects required to be assessed at the end of compulsory schooling and the structure of the exam is being adapted in accordance with national curriculum requirements.

The GCSE differs from its predecessors in that there are syllabuses based on national criteria covering course objectives, content and assessment methods; differentiated assessment (i.e. different papers or questions for different ranges of ability); and grade-related criteria (i.e. grades awarded on absolute rather than relative performance).

The GCSE certificates are at present awarded on a seven-point scale, A to G, although a ten-level scale is under discussion. Grades A to C are the equivalent of the corresponding O-level grades A to C, or CSE grade 1. Grades D, E, F and G record achievement at least as high as that represented by CSE grades 2 to 5. There is no restriction on entry to any examination. All GCSE syllabuses, assessments and grading procedures are monitored by the School Curriculum and Assessment Authority (*see* pages 448, 450) to ensure that they conform to the national criteria.

Of school leavers in the United Kingdom who left school without A-levels or SCE H-grades in 1990–1, 48.9 per cent had achieved one or more graded GCSE or SCE O or Standard grade results.

From September 1991, many maintained schools have offered BTEC Firsts (*see* page 452) and it is hoped that more schools will offer BTEC Nationals than do so at present. National Vocational Qualifications in the form of General NVQs have been available to students in schools from September 1992 (*see* page 453).

Advanced levels – Advanced (A-level) examinations are taken by those who choose to continue their education after GCSE. A-level courses last two years and have traditionally provided the foundation for entry to higher education. A-levels are marked on a seven-point scale, from A to E (narrow failure) and U (unclassified), which latter grade will not be certificated.

Advanced Supplementary levels – As an alternative to, and to complement, A-level examinations, Advanced Supplementary level (AS-level) examinations were introduced in September 1987, with the first examinations taking place in summer 1989. AS-levels are for full-time students but are also open to other students. An AS-level syllabus covers not less than half the amount of ground covered by the corresponding A-level syllabus and, where possible, is related to it. An AS-level course lasts two years and requires not less than half the teaching time of the corresponding A-level course, and two AS-levels are equivalent to one A-level. AS-level courses are intended to supplement and broaden A-level studies, and examinations are held at the same time as A-levels. AS-level passes are graded A to E, with grade standards related to the A-level grades.

A mixture of A-level courses in the subjects to be specialized in and AS-levels will form the standard for admission to higher education.

In the United Kingdom in 1990–1, 28 per cent of all 17 year-olds (26 per cent of boys, 30 per cent of girls) achieved one or more A-level or SCE H-grade result. This figure includes those continuing their education in maintained further education establishments including tertiary colleges, as well as school leavers.

Of school leavers alone (661,000), 23.2 per cent achieved at least one A-level or SCE H-grade (21.7 per cent of boys, 24.7 per cent of girls). Of those in Great Britain obtaining two or more A-levels, or three or more SCE H-grades, 13 per cent studied sciences (18 per cent of boys, 8 per cent of girls), 45 per cent studied arts/social studies (35 per cent of boys, 54 per cent of girls), and 43 per cent (47 per cent of boys, 38 per cent of girls) studied a combination of science and arts/social studies.

S-levels – Most examining boards allow the option of an additional paper of greater difficulty to be taken by A-level candidates to obtain what is known as a Special-level or Scholarship-level qualification. S-level papers are available in most of the traditional academic subjects and are marked on a three-point scale, grade A or 1, grade B or 2, and unclassified.

The Diploma of Vocational Education – The City and Guilds Diploma of Vocational Education superseded Foundation programmes and the Certificate of Pre-Vocational Education (CPVE) in schools and colleges in England, Wales and Northern Ireland from September 1992. It is intended for a wide ability range, including pupils who might not go on to A-levels but would like to continue their education on completion of compulsory secondary schooling. The qualification is offered by the City and Guilds of London Institute.

The City and Guilds Diploma of Vocational Education provides recognition of achievement at three levels: foundation, intermediate and national; the two latter broadly corresponding to the one- and two-year CPVE programmes, and linked with the GNVQ (*see* page 453) at levels 2 and 3. Within guidelines schools and colleges design their own courses, which stress activity-based learning, core skills of application of numbers, communication and information technology, and work experience. The City and Guilds Diploma of Vocational Education is mainly for those who want to find out what aptitudes they may have and to prepare themselves for work, but who are not yet committed to a particular occupation. It can be taken alongside other courses such as GCSEs, A- or AS-levels. The City and Guilds Diploma of Vocational Education will be phased out at intermediate and national levels as GNVQs are introduced. The Diploma at foundation level will continue.

CO-ORDINATION AND ADVISORY BODIES

The School Curriculum and Assessment Authority (SCAA) advises the Government on all school curriculum examination and assessment matters in England. It was formed by the amalgamation of the Schools Examination and Assessment Council with the National Curriculum Council in October 1993 and is funded wholly by the Department for Education.

The Curriculum Council for Wales advises on the curriculum in Wales. From April 1994 it will take on additional functions from SCAA and be renamed the Curriculum and Assessment Authority for Wales.

The Northern Ireland Schools Examinations and Assessment Council (NISEAC) performs the same function in Northern Ireland. In April 1994 it will amalgamate with the Northern Ireland Curriculum Council (NICC) to form a single new body the Northern Ireland Council for the Curriculum, Assessment and Examinations (NICCEA). Both NISEAC and its successor are funded by the Department of Education for Northern Ireland.

SCOTLAND

The system of public examinations in Scotland is different from that elsewhere in the United Kingdom. At the end of the fourth year of secondary education (equivalent to the fifth year in the rest of the United Kingdom), at about the age of 16, pupils take either the Ordinary grade of the Scottish Certificate of Education Examination (corresponding to the old GCE Ordinary level) or the Standard grade. By 1994–5, the Ordinary grade will have been replaced by Standard grade courses and examinations, which have been designed to suit every level of ability, with assessment against nationally determined standards of performance.

For most courses there are three separate examination papers at the end of the two-year Standard grade course. They are set at Credit (leading to awards at grade 1 or 2), General (leading to awards at grade 3 or 4) and Foundation (leading to awards at grade 5 or 6) levels. Grade 7 is available to those who, although they have completed the course, have shown no significant level of attainment. Normally pupils will take examinations covering two pairs of grades, either grades 1–4 or grades 3–6.

Pupils may attempt as many of a wide range of subjects as they are capable of, on either the Ordinary/Standard grades, or on the Higher grade which is normally taken one year after Ordinary/Standard grades, at the age of 17 or thereabouts. The shorter course means that Higher grades are normally studied to a lesser depth than A-levels; on the other hand it is common for pupils to be presented for four or more Higher grades at a single diet of the examination.

The Certificate of Sixth Year Studies (CSYS) is designed to give direction and purpose to sixth-year work by encouraging pupils who have completed their main subjects at Higher grade to study a maximum of three of these subjects in depth. Pupils may also use the sixth year to gain improved or additional Higher grades or Ordinary/Standard grades. The Scottish Office Education Department is proposing a number of changes in the system of Highers and CSYS as a result of recommendations made in the report of the Howie Committee in 1992.

The examining body for the Scottish Certificate of Education and the Certificate of Sixth Year Studies is the Scottish Examination Board.

National Certificates – National Certificates were introduced in 1984–5 as an alternative to, and to complement, Highers and CSYS. They are awarded to pupils normally over the age of 16 who have successfully completed a programme of vocational courses based on modular study units, and the assessment system is based on national criteria. National Certificates are validated by the Scottish Vocational Education Council (*see also* page 452).

THE INTERNATIONAL BACCALAUREATE

The International Baccalaureate is an internationally recognized two-year pre-university course and examination designed to facilitate the mobility of students and to promote international understanding. Candidates must offer one subject from each of six subject groups, at least three at higher level and the remainder at subsidiary level. Single subjects can be offered, for which a certificate is received. There are 27 schools and colleges in the United Kingdom which offer the International Baccalaureate diploma.

TEACHERS

ENGLAND AND WALES

Teachers are appointed by local education authorities, school governing bodies, or school managers. Those in publicly maintained schools must be approved as qualified by the Department for Education. To become a qualified teacher it is necessary to have successfully completed a course of initial teacher training, usually either a Bachelor of Education (B.Ed.) degree or the Postgraduate Certificate of Education (PGCE), but a one-year course is being considered which will qualify certain non-graduates to teach at nursery and infant level. Teacher training has hitherto been largely integrated with the rest of higher education, with training places concentrated in universities and institutes or colleges of education, but it is now to become largely school-based, with student teachers on secondary PGCE courses spending two-thirds of their training in the classroom by September 1994. From September 1993 secondary schools or consortia of schools and CTCs will be invited to bid for funds from the DFE to carry out their own teacher training, including recruitment of students, subject to approval of their proposed training programme. Funds will be given to schools to meet the costs of designing and delivering the courses, and students will receive flat-rate bursaries equivalent in value to the PGCE student grant plus loan. Changes are also to be introduced by September 1994 in primary phase teacher training with a view to making it more school-based and giving schools a role in course design and delivery. Under the articled teacher scheme, graduates are paid a bursary in addition to a salary to complete a school-based PGCE course over two years involving a progressively increasing teaching load. From September 1993, this scheme was restricted to primary phase teacher training only.

With certain exceptions the profession at present has an all-graduate entry. Teachers in further education are not required to have qualified teacher status, though roughly half have a teaching qualification and most have industrial, commercial or professional experience.

The licensed teacher scheme is designed to attract into the teaching profession entrants over 24 years of age without formal teaching qualifications but with relevant training and experience. All licensees are required to have the equivalent of two years' higher education in the United Kingdom and the equivalent of grade C in GCSE maths and English. Local education authorities will be involved in devising a suitable two-year training programme for any licensed teachers they may appoint to their schools; for grant-maintained schools and City Technology Colleges this will be a matter for the schools themselves. LEAs have discretion to recommend qualified teacher status after one year for a licensee with at least two years' experience as an instructor prior to becoming a licensed teacher.

SCOTLAND

All teachers in maintained schools must be registered with the General Teaching Council for Scotland. They are registered provisionally for a two-year probationary period which can be extended if necessary. Only graduates are accepted as entrants to the teaching profession in Scotland. As a result of a review of initial teacher training instituted in 1992 a greater proportion of training is to be classroom-based. The colleges of education provide both in-service and pre-service training for teachers and are funded by the Scottish Higher Education Funding Council.

NORTHERN IRELAND

Teacher training in Northern Ireland is provided by the two universities and two colleges of education. The colleges are concerned with teacher education mainly for the primary school sector. They also provide B.Ed. courses for intending secondary school teachers of religious education, commercial studies, and craft, design and technology. With these exceptions, the training of teachers for secondary schools is provided in the education departments of the universities. A review of primary and secondary teacher training is taking place.

ACCREDITATION OF TRAINING INSTITUTIONS

The Council for the Accreditation of Teacher Education (CATE) advises central government on the accreditation, content and quality of initial teacher training courses in England, Wales and Northern Ireland, monitoring and disseminating good practice.

In Scotland all training courses in colleges of education must be approved by the Scottish Office Education Department and a validating body.

NEWLY-TRAINED TEACHERS

Of teachers who in 1990 had successfully completed initial training courses in the United Kingdom, 10,800 had completed a postgraduate course and 7,000 a course for non-graduates.

Because of a shortage of teachers in a number of secondary subjects, a tax-free bursary scheme for trainee teachers on one- or two-year courses has been introduced. The subjects are: physics, chemistry, biology, or any combination of these three; mathematics; modern languages (including Welsh in Wales); technology; craft, design and technology (CDT). The bursary is £1,000 a year.

SERVING TEACHERS

In 1990-1 there were 560,000 teachers (full-time and full-time equivalent) in public sector schools and establishments of further education in the United Kingdom. Of these, 463,000 were in maintained schools and 91,000 in further education. There were 210,000 full-time teachers in public sector primary schools, 234,000 in public sector secondary schools and 19,000 in special schools.

SALARIES

Qualified teachers in England and Wales, other than heads and deputy heads, are paid on an 18-point scale ranging from £11,224 to £18,837 (September 1993 figures). Entry points and placement depend on qualifications, experience, responsibilities, excellence and recruitment and retention factors as calculated by the relevant body, i.e. in grant-maintained

schools and LEA schools with delegated budgets, the governing body; otherwise the LEA. Headteachers' salaries range from £23,505 to £50,682 and deputy headteachers' salaries range from £22,404 to £36,855. Qualified teachers in Northern Ireland are paid on a ten-point scale as of April 1993 ranging from £11,244 to £18,942. Salaries for principals range from £23,505 to £46,398 and vice-principals from £22,404 to £33,789. There is a statutory superannuation scheme in maintained schools.

Teachers in Scotland are paid (April 1993 figures) on a ten-point scale from £11,562 to £19,218. The entry point depends on type of qualification, and additional allowances are payable under certain circumstances. Headteachers are paid on a scale from £24,375 to £45,150 and deputy headteachers from £24,375 to £33,783, depending on whether the school is primary or secondary and the size of school roll.

Further Education

The Education Reform Act 1988 defines further education as all provision outside schools to people aged over 16 of education up to and including A-level and its equivalent. The Further Education Funding Councils for England and Wales, the Scottish Office Education Department and the Education and Library Boards in Northern Ireland have a duty to secure provision of adequate facilities for further education in their territories.

ENGLAND AND WALES

The Further and Higher Education Act 1992 removed all further education and sixth form colleges from local authority control as of April 1993, and provided for them to be funded directly by central government through the Further Education Funding Council for England (FEFC) and the Further Education Funding Council for Wales (FEFCW). These councils are also responsible for the assessment of quality. The colleges are controlled by autonomous further education corporations with substantial representation from business, which own their own assets and employ their own staff. Their funding is determined in part by the number of students recruited.

In England and Wales further education courses are taught at a variety of institutions. These range from universities which were formerly polytechnics and colleges of higher education and colleges of further education (most of which also offer higher education courses) to tertiary colleges and sixth form colleges, which concentrate on the provision of normal sixth form school courses as well as a range of vocational courses. A number of institutions specific to a particular form of training, e.g. the Royal College of Music, are also involved. Until April 1993, all such courses were funded by local education authorities, including further education courses in universities and colleges of higher education. Funding is now provided by the Further Education Funding Councils.

Every institution providing full-time further education under a further education scheme is required to appoint a board of governors which has the power to appoint staff and manage budgets under the local management of further and higher education colleges initiative, duties devolved from local education authorities in 1989. From April 1993, governing boards and principals have had total responsibility and accountability for their institutions. At least half the governors must represent employment interests or be independent of local authority or college interests.

Teaching staff in further education establishments are not necessarily required to have teaching qualifications although many do so, but they are subject to regular appraisal of teaching performance.

Much of the post-school provision outside the higher education sector is broadly vocational in purpose. It ranges from lower-level technical and commercial courses through courses for those aiming at higher-level posts in industry, commerce and administration, to professional courses. Facilities for GCSE courses, Diploma of Vocational Education, AS-levels and A-level courses are also provided (see page 449). These courses can form the foundation for progress to higher education qualifications (see below).

The main courses and examinations in the vocational field, all of which link in with the NVQ framework, are offered by the following bodies, but there are also many others:

The Business and Technology Education Council (BTEC) provides programmes of study across a wide range of subject areas. The main qualifications are: the BTEC First Certificate; the BTEC First Diploma; the BTEC National Certificate and the BTEC National Diploma; BTEC intermediate and advanced GNVQs (which are being introduced progressively in 14 vocational sectors over the next few years); and BTEC foundation, intermediate and advanced GNVQs in some vocational areas.

City and Guilds of London Institute (C&G) offers a wide range of technical and vocational qualifications all of which link in with the GNVQ framework, and has sole responsibility for administering the Diploma of Vocational Education (see page 449). Most courses are part-time for students already in employment, but some full-time courses are available.

RSA (Royal Society of Arts) Examinations Board schemes cover a wide range of vocational qualifications, including business administration, management, language schemes, information technology and teaching qualifications. Many schemes are offered at levels matching those established by the NCVQ (see below), and a policy operates of credit accumulation, so that candidates can take a single unit or complete qualifications.

There are 413 further education establishments in England and Wales and 2,656 adult education centres. In 1991–2 there were 495,000 full-time and sandwich students and 808,000 part-time students on further education courses.

SCOTLAND

Further education comprises non-advanced courses up to SCE Highers grade, GCE A-level and SCOTVEC vocational courses. Under the Further and Higher Education (Scotland) Act 1992 funding of further education colleges was transferred to central government from the education authorities in April 1993; a further education funding council is proposed at a later stage. Courses are taught mainly at colleges of further education, including technical colleges, and in some schools.

The Self-Governing Schools etc. (Scotland) Act 1989 legislated for Further Education College Councils to be set up with extensive powers to run their colleges; from April 1993 when the colleges became self-governing the Councils became boards of management. These run the colleges and employ staff. They include the Principal and staff and student representatives among their 10–16 members, and at least half the members must have experience of commerce, industry or the practice of a profession.

The Scottish Vocational Education Council (SCOTVEC) provides qualifications for most occupations (paralleling the work of the Business and Technology Education Council, City and Guilds of London Institute, the Royal Society of Arts and other bodies in England, Wales and Northern Ireland). It provides at non-advanced level the National Certificate which is completely comprehensive and covers

the whole range of non-advanced further education provision in Scotland. Students may study for the National Certificate on a full-time, part-time, open learning or work-based learning basis. The system is based on modules and National Certificate modules and modular programmes can be taken in further education colleges, secondary schools and other centres, normally from the age of 16 onwards. SCOTVEC also offers modular advanced level HNC/HND qualifications and a few post-graduate or post-experience qualifications which are available in further education colleges and higher education institutions. Scottish Vocational Qualifications (SVQs) combine programmes of SCOTVEC's National Certificate modules or Higher National Units. They correspond to the system of NVQs which operates in the rest of the UK and were introduced in schools, further education colleges and other centres from August 1992.

The Record of Education and Training (RET) has been introduced to provide a single certificate recording SCOTVEC achievements; an updated version is provided as and when necessary.

In 1990–1 there were 37,923 full-time and sandwich students and 93,981 part-time students on non-advanced vocational courses of further education in the 49 further education colleges, 15 central institutions and five colleges of education then in existence.

NORTHERN IRELAND

The Education and Library Boards are obliged to prepare and submit for approval to the Department of Education for Northern Ireland, schemes setting out the principles to be applied by the boards in planning the further education provision to be made by colleges under their management.

The colleges of further education are at present maintained by the Education and Library Boards, but financial powers and responsibilities are delegated to the boards of governors of the colleges. The boards of governors must include at least 50 per cent membership from the professions, local business or industry, or other fields of employment relevant to the activities of the college. The review of further education provision which took place during 1992–3 recommended that from 1995 further education should be planned and funded centrally and that college and course provision should be rationalized by the amalgamation of some colleges from March 1994.

On reaching school-leaving age, pupils may attend colleges of further education to pursue the same type of vocational courses as are provided in colleges in England and Wales, administered by the same examining bodies.

Northern Ireland has 24 institutions of further education with 309 out-centres. In 1990–1 there were 20,468 full-time students and 55,440 part-time students on non-advanced vocational courses of further education.

COURSE INFORMATION

Applications for further education courses are generally made directly to the colleges concerned. Information on further education courses in the United Kingdom and addresses of colleges can be found in the Directory of Further Education published annually by the Careers Research and Advisory Centre.

NATIONAL COUNCIL FOR VOCATIONAL QUALIFICATIONS

The National Council for Vocational Qualifications (NCVQ) was set up by the Government in October 1986 to achieve a coherent national framework for vocational qualifications in England, Wales and Northern Ireland. The Council does not award qualifications but works with and through the established examining and awarding bodies to reform the existing vocational qualifications system and introduce simplified arrangements. SCOTVEC (*see* above) performs similar functions in Scotland, but its role includes the awarding of qualifications.

The name and style National Vocational Qualification is accorded to qualifications accredited by NCVQ. The NVQ framework is currently based on five levels incorporating qualifications up to and including the Higher National standard. From September 1992 General National Vocational Qualifications were introduced into colleges and schools. They cover broad categories in the NVQ framework and are aimed at those wishing to familiarize themselves with a range of opportunities. Advanced GNVQ or the vocational A-level (formerly level 3) is designed to be equivalent to two A-levels; intermediate (formerly level 2) is equivalent to four or five good GCSEs. Foundation GNVQs (formerly level 1) are being piloted.

The National Record of Achievement (NRA) replaced the National Record of Vocational Achievement (NRVA) in autumn 1993. The NRA is intended to be a record of achievement, both formal and informal, in education, training and employment, in a single format.

Higher Education

The term higher education is used to describe education above A-level, Higher grade and their equivalent, which is provided mainly in universities and colleges of higher education.

The Further and Higher Education Act 1992 and parallel legislation in Scotland marked the end of the so-called 'binary' system in higher education in Great Britain; a unitary system has always existed in Northern Ireland, where the funding of higher education is undertaken by DENI. The Acts removed the distinction between higher education provided by the universities, which were funded by the Universities Funding Council (UFC), and that provided in England and Wales by the polytechnics and colleges of higher education, funded by the Polytechnics and Colleges Funding Council (PCFC), and in Scotland by the central institutions and other institutions funded by central government. All are now brought under a single funding structure, the Higher Education Funding Councils for England, Wales and Scotland. The HEFCs took over from the UFC, PCFC and Scottish Office in April 1993. The Acts also provided for other changes to bring the non-university sector in line with the universities, including the right for all polytechnics, and other higher education institutions which satisfy the necessary criteria, to award their own taught course and research degrees and to adopt the title of university, subject to Privy Council approval of the proposed new name. The change of name does not affect the legal constitution of the institutions.

In 1990–1, there were 748,600 full-time and sandwich students in higher education in the United Kingdom, of whom 80,200 were from overseas. The number of part-time students in the United Kingdom, including the Open University, was 428,000. The proportion of 16- to 20-year-olds entering full-time higher education in Great Britain rose from 16.1 per cent in 1985–6 to 19.9 per cent in 1990–1. The number of mature entrants (those aged 21 and over when starting an undergraduate course and 25 and over when starting a postgraduate course) to higher education in Great Britain in 1990 (excluding those at the Open University) was 237,000, up by 77 per cent on 1980. The number of full-time students on science courses in 1990–1 was 124,700, of whom 43,700 were female.

The universities are self-governing institutions established by royal charter or Act of Parliament. They have academic freedom and are responsible for their own academic appointments, curricula and student admissions and award their own degrees.

Responsibility for universities in England rests with the Secretary of State for Education, and in their territories with the Secretaries of State for Scotland, Wales and Northern Ireland. Advice to the Government on matters relating to the universities is provided by the Higher Education Funding Councils for England, Wales and Scotland, and by the Northern Ireland Higher Education Council. The HEFCs receive a block grant from central government which they allocate to the universities and colleges. The grant is allocated directly by central government in Northern Ireland.

There are now 86 universities in the United Kingdom, where only 48 existed prior to the Further and Higher Education Acts 1992. Of these 86, 70 are in England (including one federal university), two (one a federal institution) in Wales, 12 in Scotland and two in Northern Ireland.

The universities which pre-date the 1992 Acts each have their own system of internal government, but broad similarities exist. Most are run by two main bodies: the senate, which deals primarily with academic issues and consists of members elected from within the university; and the council, which is the supreme body and is responsible for all appointments and promotions, and bidding for and allocation of financial resources. At least half the members of the council are drawn from outside the university. Joint committees of senate and council are becoming increasingly common.

In 1991–2, at the 48 universities which then existed in the United Kingdom (two in Northern Ireland, eight in Scotland, a single federal university in Wales), there were 401,657 full-time students (19,369 from EC countries; 44,044 from other overseas countries) and 66,438 part-time students. Women formed 44.3 per cent of the full-time total and 44.7 per cent of the part-time total.

Those universities which were formerly polytechnics and the colleges of higher education are run by Higher Education Corporations (HECs), which are controlled by boards of governors whose members were initially appointed by the Secretaries of State but which will subsequently make their own appointments. At least half the members of each board must be drawn from industry, business, commerce and the professions.

In England and Wales, there were 336,637 students in the 33 polytechnics in 1990–1. Of these, 324,301 were on higher education courses, of whom 225,794 were full-time or sandwich course students. In the 50 colleges of higher education in England and Wales in 1990–1, there were 619,313 students, 131,296 of these on higher education courses and of whom 83,201 were full-time or sandwich course students.

In 1990–1 there were 413 major establishments in higher education (maintained, assisted by LEAs, in receipt of direct grant from the DFE, or voluntary) outside the PCFC sector. In England and Wales in 1990–1 they catered for 114,575 students on higher education courses funded by the PCFC, including 23,548 on full-time or sandwich courses. The higher education courses in these establishments are now, as a result of the 1992 Act, funded by the HEFCs for England and Wales, while their further education courses are funded through the FEFCs.

The non-residential Open University provides courses nationally leading to degrees. Teaching is through a combination of television and radio programmes, correspondence, tutorials, short residential courses and local audio-visual centres. No qualifications are needed for entry. The Open University offers a modular programme of undergraduate courses by credit accumulation and post-experience and postgraduate courses, including a programme of higher degrees which comprise B.Phil., M.Phil. and Ph.D. through research, and MA, MBA and M.Sc. through taught courses. The Open University throughout the UK is funded by the Higher Education Funding Council for England. In 1993, about 86,000 undergraduates were registered at the Open University, of whom about 41,000 were women and 43,000 were men. Estimated cost (year 1993) of a six-credit degree was around £2,750.

The independent University of Buckingham provides a two-year course leading to a bachelor's degree and its tuition fees were £8,456 for 1993. It receives no capital or recurrent income from the Government but its students are eligible for mandatory awards from local education authorities. Its academic year consists of four terms of ten weeks each.

ACADEMIC STAFF

Each university and college appoints its own academic staff on its own conditions. There is, however, a common salary structure and, except for Oxford and Cambridge, a common career structure in universities; and a common salary structure for the former PCFC sector. The Education Reform Act 1988 appointed the University Commissioners to secure changes to university statutes abolishing the granting of tenure, thus enabling staff to be dismissed for good cause and for redundancy.

The Education Reform Act 1988 took polytechnics and higher education colleges in England and Wales out of local education authority control, turning them into employers on their own account. The Polytechnics and Colleges Employers' Forum was set up to look after terms and conditions of employment and has negotiated the introduction of an academic contract similar to that obtaining in the universities which pre-dated the Higher and Further Education Act 1992.

Teaching staff in higher education require no formal teaching qualification, but teacher trainers are required to spend a certain amount of time in schools to ensure that they have sufficient recent practical experience.

In 1991–2, when the binary system still operated, there were 57,600 full-time and part-time academic staff in universities in the United Kingdom and 125,927 in public sector further and higher education.

Salary scales for staff in the pre-existing universities differ from those in the former polytechnics and colleges; it is hoped to amalgamate them over the next three years. The 1993–4 salary scales for non-clinical academic staff in universities are:
lecturer grade A, £13,601–£18,855
lecturer grade B, £19,642–£25,107
senior lecturer, £26,359–£29,788
professor, £30,358 (minimum)
The salaries of clinical academic staff are kept broadly comparable to those of doctors and dentists in the National Health Service.

Salary scales for lecturers in the former polytechnics, now universities, and colleges of further and higher education are (September 1992):
lecturer, £11,163–£20,235
senior lecturer, £19,536–£24,423
principal, from £25,986
The same scales apply in Northern Ireland. The salary scales for staff in Scotland are (April 1993):

lecturer, £13,875–£24,903
senior lecturer, £22,842–£29,526
head of department/professorial, from £30,453

FINANCE

Although universities and colleges are expected to look to a much wider range of funding sources than before, and to generate additional revenue in collaboration with industry, they are still largely financed, directly or indirectly, from government resources.

In the academic year 1991–2 the total recurrent income of the 48 universities then existing in the United Kingdom was £4,870 million (£4,422 million in 1990–1). The exchequer grant was £1,564 million (£1,590 million in 1990–1), forming 32.1 per cent of total income (36.6 per cent in 1990–1), compared to 1976–7 when it formed 75 per cent. Income from research grants and contracts in 1991–2 was £941 million, an increase of 7.3 per cent on the previous year.

In the academic year 1991–2 the PCFC recurrent grant to institutions and LEAs for higher education courses was £842 million (£988.8 million in 1990–1).

COURSES

In the United Kingdom all universities, including the Open University, and some colleges award their own degrees and other qualifications and can act as awarding and validating bodies for neighbouring colleges which are not yet accredited. These functions, and the accreditation of institutions to award their own degrees, were formerly effected by the Council for National Academic Awards until it ceased to operate in October 1992. The Higher Education Quality Council (HEQC), to be funded by institutional contributions, has now been set up to advise the Secretaries of State on applications for degree-awarding powers.

Higher education courses last full-time for at least four weeks or, if part-time, involve more than 60 hours of instruction. Facilities exist for full-time and part-time study, day release, sandwich or block release. Credit Accumulation and Transfer (CATS) is a system of study which is now becoming widely available. It allows a student to achieve a final qualification by accumulating credits for courses of study successfully achieved, or even professional experience, over a period. Credit transfer information and values are carried on an electronic database called ECCTIS 2000, which is available in most careers offices and many schools and colleges.

Higher education courses include: first degree and postgraduate (including research); Diploma in Higher Education (Dip.HE); Higher National Diploma (HND) and Higher National Certificate (HNC); preparation for professional examinations; and the in-service training of teachers.

The Diploma of Higher Education (Dip.HE) is a two-year diploma usually intended to serve as a stepping-stone to a degree course or other further study. The Dip.HE is awarded by the institution itself if it is accredited; by an accredited institution of its choice if not. The BTEC Higher National Certificate (HNC) is awarded after two years part-time study. The BTEC Higher National Diploma (HND) is awarded after two years full-time, or three years sandwich or part-time study.

With the exception of certain Scottish universities where master is sometimes used for a first degree in arts subjects, undergraduate courses lead to the title of Bachelor – Bachelor of Arts (BA) and Bachelor of Science (B.Sc.) being the most common – and for a higher degree, Master of Arts (MA), Master of Science (M.Sc.) (usually taught courses) and the research degrees of Master of Philosophy (M.Phil.) and Doctor of Philosophy (Ph.D. or, at a few universities, D.Phil.).

Most undergraduate programmes at British universities and colleges of higher education run for three years, except in Scotland and at the University of Keele where they may take four years. Professional courses in subjects such as medicine, dentistry and veterinary science take longer. Details of courses on offer and of predicted entry requirements for the following year's intake are provided in *University and College Entrance* published annually by Universities and Colleges Admissions Service (UCAS), which includes degree, Dip.HE and HND courses at all universities (excluding the Open University) and most colleges of HE (for address, see page 462).

Postgraduate programmes vary in length. Taught courses which lead to certificates, diplomas or master's degrees usually take one year full-time or two years part-time. Research degrees take from two to three years full-time and much longer if completed on a part-time basis. Details of taught courses and research degree opportunities can be found in *Graduate Studies* published annually for the Careers Research and Advisory Centre (CRAC) by Hobsons Publishing PLC (for address, see page 462).

Post-experience short courses are forming an increasing part of higher education provision, reflecting the need to update professional and technical training. Most of these courses fund themselves.

ADMISSIONS

Apart from quotas for medical, dental and veterinary students, there are no limits set for student intakes and the individual university or college decides which students to accept. The formal entry requirements to most degree courses are two A-levels at grade E or above (or equivalent), and to HND courses one A-level (or equivalent). In practice, most offers of places require qualifications in excess of this, higher requirements usually reflecting the popularity of a course. These requirements do not, however, exclude applications from students with a variety of non-GCSE qualifications or unquantified experience and skills.

For admission to a degree, Dip.HE or HND, potential students apply through a central clearing house. All universities and most colleges providing higher education courses in the United Kingdom are members of the Universities and Colleges Admission Service (UCAS), which operates for the first time for 1994 entry and replaces the former Universities Central Council on Admissions (UCCA) and Polytechnics Central Admissions System (PCAS). (The only exception among universities is the Open University, which conducts its own admissions.) Applicants are supplied with an application form and a *UCAS Handbook*, available from schools, colleges and careers offices or direct from UCAS, and may apply to a maximum of eight institutions on the UCAS form.

There are a number of studio-based art and design courses for which applications should be made through the Art and Design Admissions Registry. Initial teacher training courses in Scotland are at present applied to through the Teacher Education Admissions Clearing House (TEACH), which will, however, be wound up after handling the intake for session 1994-5. Applications for undergraduate teacher training courses will thereafter be made through UCAS; procedures for admission to postgraduate teacher training courses have yet to be decided.

For admission as a postgraduate student, universities and colleges normally require a good first degree in a subject related to the proposed course of study or research, but other experience and qualifications will be considered on merit. Most applications are made to individual institutions but there are two clearing houses of relevance. Postgraduate teacher training courses in England, Wales and Northern Ireland utilise the Graduate Teacher Training Registry (see page 462) and for social work the Social Work Admissions System operates (see page 462).

SCOTLAND

As a result of changes brought about by the Further and Higher Education (Scotland) Act 1992, the Scottish Higher Education Funding Council (SHEFC) now funds 23 institutions of higher education, including 12 universities. The universities are broadly managed as described above and each institution of higher education is managed by an independent governing body which includes representatives of industrial, commercial, professional and educational interests. Most of the courses outside the universities have a vocational orientation and a substantial number are sandwich courses.

In 1990-1, there were 77,475 students enrolled on courses of higher education outside the universities. Of these, 36,924 attended the 15 central institutions, 6,999 the five colleges of education, and 33,164 the 49 education authority colleges. Of the total number, 55 per cent were on full-time or sandwich courses.

Applications to institutions of higher education in Scotland are made through UCAS, except for applications for teacher training which are made through TEACH (see page 462) up to and including student intake for the session 1994-5. Details of initial teacher training courses can be obtained from colleges of education and those universities offering such courses, and from the Committee of Scottish Higher Education Principals (COSHEP).

NORTHERN IRELAND

In Northern Ireland advanced courses are provided by 24 institutions of further education and by the two universities. As well as offering first and postgraduate degrees, the University of Ulster offers courses leading to the BTEC Higher National Diploma and professional qualifications. Applications to undertake courses of higher education other than degree courses are made to the institutions direct. Applications for degree courses are made through UCAS.

In 1990-1, 4,095 students were enrolled on advanced courses of higher education in the institutions of further education, 43.5 per cent of whom were women. There were 951 students on full-time or sandwich courses.

FEES

The tuition fees for students with mandatory awards (*see* page 456) are paid by the grant-awarding body. Students from member states of the European Community pay fees at home student rates. Since 1980-1 students from outside the EC have paid fees that are meant to cover the cost of their education, but financial help is available under a number of schemes. Information about these schemes is available from British Council offices world-wide.

Although universities are free to set their own charges, the Committee of Vice-Chancellors and Principals recommend minimum fees for students from non-EC countries which, however, do not apply to those institutions formerly in the PCFC sector. Fees for 1993-4 are £5,550 for arts students, £7,360 for science students, and £13,550 for students following clinical courses in medicine, dentistry and veterinary science. These compare with undergraduate fees for home and EC students of £1,300 for arts courses, £2,770 for laboratory or workshop based courses, mainly science, and £4,985 for clinical courses in the academic year 1993-4.

All institutions of higher education charge the same fees for home students and EC nationals.

For postgraduate students, the maximum tuition fee that will be reimbursed through the awards system is £2,260 in 1993–4.

GRANTS FOR STUDENTS

Students in the United Kingdom who plan to take a full-time or sandwich course of further study after leaving school may be eligible for a grant. A parental contribution is deductible on a sliding scale dependent on income. For married students this may be deducted from their spouse's income instead. However, parental contribution is not deducted from the grant to students over 25 years of age who have been self-supporting for at least three years. The main rates of mandatory grant have been frozen from 1991–2, as it is envisaged that students will increasingly support themselves by loans (*see* below). Tuition fees are paid in full for all students in receipt of a grant, regardless of parental income, and they are usually paid direct to the university or college by the education authority.

Grants are paid by local education authorities in England, Wales and Northern Ireland, which are reimbursed for 100 per cent of the cost by central government, and by the Scottish Office Education Department in Scotland. Applications are made to the authority in the area in which the student normally lives. Applications should not, however, be made earlier than the January preceding the start of the course.

TYPES OF GRANT

Grants are of two kinds: mandatory and discretionary. Mandatory grants are those which awarding authorities must pay to students who are attending designated courses (*see* below) and who can satisfy certain other conditions. Such a grant is awarded normally to enable the student to attend only one designated course and there is no general entitlement to an award for any particular number of years. Discretionary grants are those for which each awarding authority has discretion to decide its own policy.

Designated courses are those full-time or sandwich courses leading to: a degree; the Diploma of Higher Education; the BTEC Higher National Diploma; initial teacher-training courses, including those for the postgraduate certificate of education and the art teachers' certificate or diploma; a university certificate or diploma course lasting at least three years; other qualifications which are specifically designated as being comparable to first degree courses; and the SCOTVEC Higher National Diploma.

To be eligible for a mandatory grant, students admitted to a designated course must usually have been ordinarily resident in the United Kingdom for the three years immediately preceding the academic year in which the course begins; have not previously attended a course of advanced further education of more than two years' duration; and apply for the grant before the end of the first term of the course. The local education authority should be consulted for advice about eligibility.

Students taking designated courses who do not satisfy the residency condition may be eligible for a mandatory grant if they come from other member states of the EC and can establish migrant worker status, or their parents are migrant workers; or if they, or their spouse and children, are asylees or refugees.

A means-tested maintenance grant, usually paid once a term, covers periods of attendance during term as well as the Christmas and Easter vacations, but not the summer vacation. It is subject to deduction on account of the student's own income and her/his parents' or spouse's income. The basic grant rates are: £2,845 if living in a hall of residence or lodgings and studying within the London area; £2,265 as above but outside the London area; £1,795 if living at the parental home. Additional allowances are available if, for example, the course requires a period of study abroad.

Education authority and Scottish Office Education Department expenditure on student fees and maintenance in 1991–2 was £2,368 million; 649,360 mandatory awards were made.

STUDENT LOANS

The Education (Student Loans) Act 1990 legislated for interest-free but indexed top-up loans of up to £940 in 1993–4 to be made available to eligible students in the United Kingdom. The government expects that at least £276.8 million will be taken up in loans in 1993–4.

Students apply direct to the Student Loans Company Ltd (see page 356), which will require a certificate of eligibility from their place of study. Loans are available to students on designated courses within the scope of mandatory awards and the same residency conditions apply. Repayment is normally over five to seven years, although it can be deferred if income is low.

ACCESS FUNDS

Access Funds are allocated by education departments to the appropriate Funding Councils in England, Wales and Scotland and administered by further and higher education institutions. In Northern Ireland they are allocated by central government to the institutions direct. They are available to students whose access to higher education might otherwise be inhibited by financial considerations or where real financial difficulties are faced. For the academic year 1993–4, provision in the United Kingdom will be £29.7 million. The purpose and operation of access funds was under review in late 1993.

POSTGRADUATE AWARDS

Unlike funding for undergraduates, which is mandatory for most degree and equivalent level courses, grants for postgraduate study are usually discretionary. Grants are also often dependent on the class of first degree, especially for research degrees.

A number of schemes of postgraduate bursaries or studentships for residents in England and Wales are funded by the Department for Education, the five government research councils, the Ministry of Agriculture, Fisheries and Food, and the British Academy, which awards grants for study in the humanities.

In Scotland postgraduate funding is provided by the Scottish Office Education Department, the Scottish Office Agriculture and Fisheries Department, and the research councils as in England and Wales.

Awards in Northern Ireland are made by the Department of Education for Northern Ireland, the Department of Agriculture for Northern Ireland, and the Medical Research Council.

In 1990–1 in the United Kingdom 26,200 awards were made. The national rates for twelve-month studentships in 1993–4 were: £5,340 in college or lodgings in London; £4,245 in college or lodgings outside London; £3,130 for those living with parents or spouse's parents. The rates for 30-week bursaries for 1993–4 were: £3,170 in college or lodgings in London; £2,500 in college or lodgings outside London; £1,890 if living with parents or spouse's parents.

Adult and Continuing Education

The term adult education covers a broad spectrum of educational activities ranging from non-vocational courses of general interest, through the acquiring of special vocational skills needed in industry or commerce, to study for a degree at the Open University.

Until the passing of the Further and Higher Education Act 1992, local education authorities were the main providers of adult and continuing education in England and Wales and had a statutory duty to do so. The Further Education Funding Councils are now responsible for, and fund, those courses which take place in their sector and lead to academic and vocational qualifications, prepare students to undertake further or higher education courses, or confer basic skills. Advanced courses of continuing education are funded by the Higher Education Funding Councils. Courses which do not fall within the remit of the funding councils continue to be the responsibility of the LEAs. Arrangements for funding in Scotland and Northern Ireland are unchanged, through the regional and islands education authorities in Scotland and the education and library boards in Northern Ireland.

PROVIDERS

Courses specifically for adults are provided by many bodies. They include, in the statutory sector: local education authorities in England and Wales; the regional and islands education authorities in Scotland and the Scottish Office Education Department; education and library boards in Northern Ireland; further education colleges; higher education colleges; universities, especially the Open University and Birkbeck College of the University of London; residential colleges; the BBC, independent television and local radio stations. There are also a number of voluntary bodies.

The local education authorities in England and Wales operate through 'area' adult education centres (2,656 in 1991), institutes or colleges, and the adult studies departments of colleges of further education. The regional and islands education authorities in Scotland fund adult education, including that provided by the universities and the Workers' Educational Association, at vocational further education colleges (46 in 1991). In addition, the Scottish Office Education Department provides grants to a number of voluntary organizations. Provision in the statutory sector in Northern Ireland is the responsibility of the universities and the education and library boards, which operate 24 further education colleges and a number of community schools.

The involvement of universities in adult education and continuing education has diversified considerably and is supported by a variety of administrative structures ranging from dedicated departments to a devolved approach. Birkbeck College in the University of London caters solely for part-time students. Those institutions and colleges formerly in the PCFC sector in England and Wales, because of their range of courses and flexible patterns of student attendance, provide opportunities in the field of adult and continuing education. The New Universities and Polytechnics Association for Continuing Education promotes collaboration between institutions of higher education active in this area. The Open University, in partnership with the BBC, provides distance teaching leading to first degrees, and also offers post-experience and higher degree courses (*see* page 470).

Of the voluntary bodies, the biggest is the Workers' Educational Association (WEA) which operates throughout the United Kingdom, reaching about 180,000 adult students annually. The Further Education Funding Councils for England and Wales, Scottish Office Education Department, Department of Education for Northern Ireland and local education authorities make grants towards provision.

The National Institute of Adult Continuing Education (England and Wales) (NIACE) provides information and advice to organizations and individuals on all aspects of adult continuing education. NIACE conducts research, project and development work, and is funded by the DFE, the Welsh Office, the LEAs and other funding bodies. The Welsh committee, NIACE Cymru, receives financial support from the Welsh Office, support in kind from the Welsh Joint Education Committee, and advises government, voluntary bodies and education providers on adult continuing education and training matters in Wales. In Scotland advice on adult and community education, and promotion thereof, is provided by the Scottish Community Education Council. The Northern Ireland Council for Adult Education has an advisory role. Its membership includes representatives of the education and library boards and of most organizations involved in the field, together with an assessor appointed by DENI.

Membership of the Universities Association for Continuing Education is open to any university or university college in the United Kingdom. It promotes university continuing education, facilitates the interchange of information, and supports research and development work in continuing education.

COURSES

Although lengths vary, most courses are part-time. Long-term residential colleges grant-aided by the DFE, the Welsh Office or the Scottish Office provide full-time courses lasting one or two years. Some colleges and centres offer short-term residential courses, lasting from a few days to a few weeks, in a wide range of subjects. Local education authorities directly sponsor many of the colleges, while others are sponsored by universities or voluntary organizations. A list, *Residential Short Courses*, is published by NIACE.

GRANTS

Although full-time courses at degree level attract mandatory awards, for courses below that level all students over the age of 19 must pay a fee. However, discretionary grants may be available. Adult education bursaries for students at the long-term residential colleges of adult education are the responsibility of the colleges themselves. The awards are administered for the colleges by the Awards Officer of the Residential Colleges Committee for students resident in England and are funded by the Further Education Funding Council for England in English colleges; for colleges in Wales they are funded and administered by the Further Education Funding Council for Wales; for colleges in Scotland by the Scottish Office Education Department; and for colleges in Northern Ireland by the Department of Education for Northern Ireland. A booklet *Adult Education Bursaries* can be obtained from the Awards Officer, Adult Education Bursaries, c/o Ruskin College (*see* page 473).

NUMBERS

There are no comprehensive statistics covering all aspects of adult education. However, enrolments on evening courses in the United Kingdom numbered 1,791,000 in 1990–1 (66.7 per cent women). This number included 1,026,000 students at adult education centres. In 1991–2, liberal adult education and professional updating short courses organized by university departments were attended by 870,491 students, an increase of 8.8 per cent on the previous year.

Education Directory

LOCAL EDUCATION AUTHORITIES

ENGLAND

COUNTY COUNCILS

AVON, PO Box 57, Avon House North, St James Barton, Bristol BS99 7EB. Tel: 0272-290777. *Director*, G. Badman
BEDFORDSHIRE, County Hall, Cauldwell Street, Bedford MK42 9AP. Tel: 0234-363222. *Director*, D. G. Wadsworth
BERKSHIRE, Shire Hall, Shinfield Park, Reading RG2 9XE. Tel: 0734-233401. *Chief Education Officer*, S. R. Goodchild
BUCKINGHAMSHIRE, County Hall, Aylesbury HP20 1UZ. Tel: 0296-395000. *Chief Education Officer*, S. Sharp
CAMBRIDGESHIRE, Castle Court, Shire Hall, Cambridge CB3 0AP. Tel: 0223-317667. *Director*, J. Ferguson
CHESHIRE, County Hall, Chester CHI ISF. Tel: 0244-602424. *Director*, D. Cracknell
CLEVELAND, Woodlands Road, Middlesbrough TS1 3BN. Tel: 0642-248155. *County Education Officer*, B. Worthy
CORNWALL, County Hall, Truro TR1 3AY. Tel: 0872-74282. *Secretary of Education*, D. W. Fryer
CUMBRIA, 5 Portland Square, Carlisle CA1 1PU. Tel: 0228-23456. *Director*, Ms P. Black
DERBYSHIRE, County Offices, Matlock DE4 3AG. Tel: 0629-580000. *Chief Education Officer (acting)*, R. Taylor
DEVON, County Hall, Exeter EX2 4QG. Tel: 0392-382059. *Chief Education Officer*, S. W. Jenkin
DORSET, County Hall, Dorchester DT1 1XJ. Tel: 0305-251000. *Director*, R. H. Ely
DURHAM, County Hall, Durham DH1 5UJ. Tel: 091-386 4411. *Director*, K. Mitchell
EAST SUSSEX, PO Box 4, County Hall, St Anne's Crescent, Lewes BN7 1SG. Tel: 0273-481000. *County Education Officer*, D. Mallen
ESSEX, Threadneedle House, Market Road, Chelmsford CM1 1LD. Tel: 0245-492211. *County Education Officer*, R. M. Sharp
GLOUCESTERSHIRE, Shire Hall, Gloucester GL1 2TP. Tel: 0452-425301. *Director*, K. D. Anderson
HAMPSHIRE, The Castle, Winchester SO23 8UJ. Tel: 0962-841841. *County Education Officer*, P. J. Coles
HEREFORD AND WORCESTER, Castle Street, Worcester WR1 3AG. Tel: 0905-763763. *County Education Officer*, vacant
HERTFORDSHIRE, County Hall, Hertford SG13 8DF. Tel: 0992-555827. *County Education Officer*, Mrs H. du Quesnay
HUMBERSIDE, County Hall, Cross Street, Beverley HU17 9BA. Tel: 0482-867131. *Director*, Dr M. W. Garnett
ISLE OF WIGHT, County Hall, Newport PO30 1UD. Tel: 0983-823400. *Director*, Dr J. A. Williams
KENT, Springfield, Maidstone ME14 2LJ. Tel: 0622-671411. *Director*, R. Pryke
LANCASHIRE, PO Box 61, County Hall, Preston PR1 8RJ. Tel: 0772-254868. *Chief Education Officer*, A. J. Collier
LEICESTERSHIRE, County Hall, Glenfield, Leicester LE3 8RF. Tel: 0533-323232. *Director*, K. H. Wood-Allum
LINCOLNSHIRE, County Offices, Newland, Lincoln LN1 1YL. Tel: 0522-552222. *Director*, A. M. Ridings
NORFOLK, County Hall, Martineau Lane, Norwich NR1 2DL. Tel: 0603-222300. *Director*, M. H. Edwards

NORTHAMPTONSHIRE, Northampton House, Northampton NN1 2HX. Tel: 0604-236236. *Director*, R. Atkinson
NORTHUMBERLAND, County Hall, Morpeth NE61 2EF. Tel: 0670-533000. *Director*, C. C. Tipple
NORTH YORKSHIRE, County Hall, Racecourse Lane, Northallerton DL7 8AE. Tel: 0609-780780. *Director*, F. F. Evans
NOTTINGHAMSHIRE, County Hall, West Bridgford, Nottingham NG2 7QP. Tel: 0602-823823. *Director*, P. J. Housden
OXFORDSHIRE, Macclesfield House, New Road, Oxford OX1 1NA. Tel: 0865-815449. *Chief Education Officer*, Mrs J. Stephens
SHROPSHIRE, The Shirehall, Abbey Foregate, Shrewsbury SY2 6ND. Tel: 0743-254302. *County Education Officer*, P. B. Cates
SOMERSET, County Hall, Taunton TA1 4DY. Tel: 0823-333451. *Chief Education Officer*, Mrs J. Wisker
STAFFORDSHIRE, Tipping Street, Stafford ST16 2DH. Tel: 0785-223121. *Chief Education Officer*, Dr P. J. Hunter
SUFFOLK, St Andrew House, County Hall, St Helen Street, Ipswich IP4 2JS. Tel: 0473-230000. *County Education Officer*, D. J. Peachey
SURREY, County Hall, Penrhyn Road, Kingston upon Thames KT1 2DJ. Tel: 081-541 9501. *County Education Officer*, Ms J. H. Burrow
WARWICKSHIRE, PO Box 24, 22 Northgate Street, Warwick CV34 4SR. Tel: 0926-410410. *Director*, Ms M. Maden
WEST SUSSEX, County Hall, Chichester PO19 1RF. Tel: 0243-777100. *Director*, R. D. C. Bunker
WILTSHIRE, County Hall, Trowbridge BA14 8JB. Tel: 0225-753641. *Director*, Dr K. Robinson

METROPOLITAN DISTRICT COUNCILS

BARNSLEY, Berneslai Close, Barnsley. Tel: 0226-770770. *Director (acting)*, M. Warrington
BIRMINGHAM, Council House, Margaret Street, B3 3BU. Tel: 021-235 2590/2872. *Chief Education Officer*, T. Brighouse
BOLTON, Paderborn House, Civic Centre, BL1 1JW. Tel: 0204-22311. *Education Officer*, B. Hughes
BRADFORD, Flockton House, Flockton Road, BD4 7RY. Tel: 0274-751700. *Education Officer*, Mrs S. Conway
BURY, Athenaeum House, Market Street, BL9 0BN. Tel: 061-705 5000. *Chief Education Officer*, J. Beech
CALDERDALE, Northgate House, Halifax HX1 1UN. Tel: 0422-357257. *Director*, Miss J. Tonge
COVENTRY, The Council House, Earl Street, CV1 5RR. Tel: 0203-831500. *Chief Education Officer*, C. Farmer
DONCASTER, PO Box 266, The Council House, DN1 3AD. Tel: 0302-737222. *Director*, A. M. Taylor
DUDLEY, Westox House, 1 Trinity Road, DY1 1JB. Tel: 0384-452200. *Chief Education Officer*, R. K. Westerby
GATESHEAD, Civic Centre, Regent Street, NE8 1HH. Tel: 091-477 1011. *Director*, D. Arbon
KIRKLEES, Oldgate House, 2 Oldgate, Huddersfield HD1 6QW. Tel: 0484-422133. *Chief Education Officer*, Ms J. Devlin
KNOWSLEY, Huyton Hey Road, Huyton, Merseyside L36 5YH. Tel: 051-443 3220. *Education Officer*, A. Culley
LEEDS, Merrion House, 110 Merrion Centre, LS2 8DT. Tel: 0532-348080. *Chief Education Officer*, Mrs J. A. M. Strong

LIVERPOOL, 14 Sir Thomas Street, LI 6BJ. Tel: 051-227 3911. *Director*, M. F. Cogley

MANCHESTER, Cumberland House, Crown Square, M60 3BB. Tel: 061-234 7121. *Education Officer*, R. Jobson

NEWCASTLE UPON TYNE, Civic Centre, NE99 2BN. Tel: 091-232 8520. *Education Officer*, N. Purser

NORTH TYNESIDE, Stephenson House, Stephenson Street, North Shields NE30 1QA. Tel: 091-257 5544. *Education Officer*, C. Benneworth

OLDHAM, Old Town Hall, Middleton Road, Chadderton, OL9 6PP. Tel: 061-678 4200. *Education Officer*, W. R. Kneen, PH.D.

ROCHDALE, PO Box 70, Municipal Offices, Smith Street, OL16 1YD. Tel: 0706-47474. *Director*, Mrs D. Cavanagh

ROTHERHAM, Norfolk House, Walker Place, Rotherham, S60 1QT. Tel: 0709-382121. *Education Officer*, B. H. Yemm

ST HELENS, Rivington Centre, Rivington Road WAIO 4ND. Tel: 0744-24061. *Director*, B. M. Mainwaring

SALFORD, Chapel Street, M3 5LT. Tel: 061-832 9751. *Chief Education Officer*, D. Johnston

SANDWELL, PO Box 41, Shaftesbury House, 402 High Street, West Bromwich B70 9LT. Tel: 021-525 7366. *Director*, S. Gallacher

SEFTON, Town Hall, Oriel Road, Bootle, Merseyside L20 7AE. Tel: 051-933 6003. *Education Officer*, J. A. Marsden

SHEFFIELD, PO Box 67, Leopold Street, SI 1RJ. Tel: 0742-734420/1. *Director*, Ms A. Muller

SOLIHULL, PO Box 20, Council House, B91 3QU. Tel: 021-704 6674. *Director*, C. J. Trinick

SOUTH TYNESIDE, Town Hall and Civic Offices, Westoe Road, South Shields NE33 2RL. Tel: 091-427 1717. *Education Officer*, I. L. Reid

STOCKPORT, Stopford House, Piccadilly, SKI 3XE. Tel: 061-474 3808. *Director*, M. K. J. Hunt

SUNDERLAND, PO Box 101, Civic Centre, SR2 7DN. Tel: 091-567 6161. *Education Officer*, D. A. Bowers

TAMESIDE, Council Offices, Wellington Road, Ashton-under-Lyne OL6 6DL. Tel: 061-342 8355. *Director*, A. M. Webster

TRAFFORD, Town Hall, Tatton Road, Sale M33 1YR. Tel: 061-872 2101. *Director*, A. Lee

WAKEFIELD, County Hall, WFI 2QW. Tel: 0924-290900. *Education Officer*, A. Lenney

WALSALL, Civic Centre, Darwall Street, WSI 1DQ. Tel: 0922-650000. *Education Officer*, M. J. Quinn

WIGAN, Gateway House, Standishgate, WNI 1AE. Tel: 0942-44991. *Education Officer*, J. K. Hampson

WIRRAL, Hamilton Building, Conway Street, Birkenhead L41 4FD. Tel: 051-666 2121. *Director*, D. Rigby

WOLVERHAMPTON, Civic Centre, St Peter's Square, WVI 1RR. Tel: 0902-27811. *Director*, Ms C. Adams

LONDON

*Inner London borough

BARKING AND DAGENHAM, Town Hall, Barking, Essex IGII 7LU. Tel: 081-592 4500. *Education Officer*, A. Larbalastier

BARNET, Town Hall, Friern Barnet Lane, Friern Barnet, NII 3DL. Tel: 081-368 1255. *Education Officer*, vacant

BEXLEY, Hill View, Hill View Drive, Welling, Kent DAI6 5RY. Tel: 081-303 7777. *Director*, P. McGee

BRENT, Chesterfield House, 9 Park Lane, Wembley, Middx. HA9 7RW. Tel: 081-900 5443. *Director*, G. Banham

BROMLEY, Town Hall, Widmore Road, Bromley, Kent BRI 1SB. Tel: 081-464 3333. *Director*, A. Baxter

*CAMDEN, Crowndale Centre, 218–220 Eversholt Street, NWI 1BD. Tel: 071-911 1525. *Education Officer*, P. Mitchell

*CITY OF LONDON, Education Department, Corporation of London, PO Box 270, Guildhall, EC2P 2EJ. Tel: 071-332 1750. *City Education Officer*, D. Smith

*CITY OF WESTMINSTER, City Hall, Victoria Street, SWIE 6QP. Tel: 071-828 8070. *Education Officer*, Mrs D. Tuck

CROYDON, Taberner House, Park Lane, CR9 1TP. Tel: 081-686 4433. *Director*, P. Benians

EALING, Perceval House, 14–18 Uxbridge Road, W5 2HL. Tel: 081-579 2424. *Director*, M. Herrman

ENFIELD, PO Box 56, Civic Centre, Silver Street, ENI 3XQ. Tel: 081-967 9257. *Director*, G. Hutchinson

*GREENWICH, Riverside House, Woolwich High Street, Woolwich, SE18 6DN. Tel: 081-854 8888. *Director*, J. Kramer

*HACKNEY, Edith Cavell Building, Enfield Road, NI 5AZ. Tel: 071-214 8400. *Director*, G. John

*HAMMERSMITH AND FULHAM, Cambridge House, Cambridge Grove, W6 4LE. Tel: 081-748 3020. *Director*, Ms C. Whatford

HARINGEY, 48 Station Road, N22 4TY. Tel: 081-975 9700. *Director*, R. L. Jones

HARROW, PO Box 22, Civic Centre, Harrow HAI 2UW. Tel: 081-863 5611. *Director*, Mrs C. Gilbert

HAVERING, Mercury House, Mercury Gardens, Romford RMI 3DR. Tel: 0708-766999. *Director*, C. Hardy

HILLINGDON, Civic Centre, Uxbridge, Middx. UB8 1UW. Tel: 0895-250528. *Education Officer*, Ms K. Higgins

HOUNSLOW, Civic Centre, Lampton Road, TW3 4DN. Tel: 081-862 5301. *Director*, J. D. Trickett

*ISLINGTON, Laycock Street, NI 1TH. Tel: 071-457 5753. *Education Officer*, C. Webb

*KENSINGTON AND CHELSEA, Town Hall, Hornton Street, W8 7NX. Tel: 071-937 5464. *Education Officer*, M. Stoten

KINGSTON UPON THAMES, Guildhall, KTI 1EU. Tel: 081-547 5280. *Director*, W. Dickinson

*LAMBETH, Blue Star House, 234–244 Stockwell Road, SW9 9SP. Tel: 071-926 2248. *Chief Education Officer*, Mrs B. Burchell

*LEWISHAM, Laurence House, 1 Catford Road, SE6 4RY. Tel: 081-695 6000. *Director*, L. Fullick

MERTON, Civic Centre, London Road, Morden, Surrey SM4 5DX. Tel: 081-545 3251. *Director*, Ms L. Kant

NEWHAM, Broadway House, 322 High Street, E15 1AJ. Tel: 081-555 5552. *Director*, I. Harrison

REDBRIDGE, Lynton House, 255–259 High Road, Ilford, IGI 1NN. Tel: 081-478 3020. *Director*, K. G. M. Ratcliffe

RICHMOND UPON THAMES, Regal House, London Road, Twickenham, TWI 3QB. Tel: 081-891 1411. *Director*, G. Alexander

*SOUTHWARK, 1 Bradenham Close, SE17 2QA. Tel: 071-525 5000. *Education Officer*, G. Mott

SUTTON, The Grove, Carshalton, Surrey SM5 3AL. Tel: 081-770 5000. *Director*, C. Blurton

*TOWER HAMLETS, Mulberry Place, 5 Clove Crescent, E14 2BG. Tel: 071-512 4200. *Education Officer*, Mrs A. Sofer

WALTHAM FOREST, Municipal Offices, High Road, Leyton E10 5QJ. Tel: 081-527 5544. *Director*, A. Lockhart

*WANDSWORTH, Town Hall, Wandsworth High Street, SWI8 2PU. Tel: 081-871 7890. *Director*, D. Naismith

WALES

COUNTY COUNCILS

CLWYD, Shire Hall, Mold CH7 6ND. Tel: 0352-702500. *Director*, K. McDonogh

DYFED, Pibwrlwyd, Carmarthen SA31 2NH. Tel: 0267-233333. *Director,* J. G. Ellis
GWENT, County Hall, Cwmbran NP44 2XD. Tel: 0633-838838. *Director,* J. D. Griffiths
GWYNEDD, County Offices, Caernarfon LL55 1SH. Tel: 0286-672255. *Director,* G. E. Humphreys
MID GLAMORGAN, County Hall, Cathays Park, Cardiff CF1 3NE. Tel: 0222-820820. *Director,* E. Roberts
POWYS, County Hall, Llandrindod Wells LD1 5LG. Tel: 0597-826000. *Director,* M. R. J. Barker
SOUTH GLAMORGAN, County Hall, Atlantic Wharf, Cardiff CF1 5UW. Tel: 0222-872000. *Director,* T. Parry Davies
WEST GLAMORGAN, County Hall, Swansea SA1 3SN. Tel: 0792-471111. *Director,* H. G. Roberts

SCOTLAND

REGIONAL AND ISLANDS COUNCILS

BORDERS, Regional Headquarters, Newtown St Boswells, Melrose TD6 0SA. Tel: 0835-23301. *Director,* I. Dutton
CENTRAL, Regional Council Offices, Viewforth, Stirling FK8 2ET. Tel: 0786-442000. *Director,* I. Collie
DUMFRIES AND GALLOWAY, 30 Edinburgh Road, Dumfries DG1 1JQ. Tel: 0387-61234. *Director,* W. C. Fordyce
FIFE, Fife House, North Street, Glenrothes KY7 5LT. Tel: 0592-754411. *Director,* B. Welsh
GRAMPIAN, Summerhill Education Centre, Stronsay Drive, Aberdeen AB2 6JA. Tel: 0224-664600. *Director,* J. Graham
HIGHLAND, Regional Buildings, Glenurquhart Road, Inverness IV3 5NX. Tel: 0463-702081. *Director,* Dr C. E. Stewart
LOTHIAN, 40 Torphichen Street, Edinburgh EH8 8JB. Tel: 031-229 9166. *Director,* Ms E. Reid
ORKNEY, Council Offices, Kirkwall KW15 1NY. Tel: 0856-873535. *Director,* J. Anderson
SHETLAND, 1 Harbour Street, Lerwick ZE1 0LS. Tel: 0595-3535. *Director,* J. Halcrow
STRATHCLYDE, 20 India Street, Glasgow G2 4PF. Tel: 041-249 4150. *Director,* F. Pignatelli
TAYSIDE, Tayside House, 28 Crichton Street, Dundee DD1 3RJ. Tel: 0382-23281. *Director,* A. B. Watson
WESTERN ISLES, Council Offices, Sandwick Road, Stornoway, Isle of Lewis PA87 2BW. Tel: 0851-703773. *Director,* N. R. Galbraith

NORTHERN IRELAND

EDUCATION AND LIBRARY BOARDS

BELFAST, Board Headquarters, 40 Academy Street, Belfast BT1 2NQ. Tel: 0232-329211. *Chief Executive,* T. G. J. Moag
NORTH EASTERN, County Hall, 182 Galgorm Road, Ballymena, Co. Antrim BT42 1HN. Tel: 0266-653333. *Chief Executive,* G. Topping
SOUTH EASTERN, 18 Windsor Avenue, Belfast BT9 6EF. Tel: 0232-381188. *Chief Executive,* T. Nolan, OBE
SOUTHERN, 3 Charlemont Place, The Mall, Armagh BT61 9AX. Tel: 0861-523811. *Chief Executive,* J. G. Kelly
WESTERN, 1 Hospital Road, Omagh, Co. Tyrone BT79 0AW. Tel: 0662-240240. *Chief Executive,* M. H. F. Murphy, OBE

ISLANDS

GUERNSEY, PO Box 32, Grange Road, St Peter Port. Tel: 0481-710821. *Director,* J. D. Stephenson

JERSEY, PO Box 142, St Saviour JE4 8QJ. Tel: 0534-509500. *Director,* B. Grady
ISLE OF MAN, Department of Education, Murray House, Mount Havelock, Douglas. Tel: 0624-685685. *Director,* G. Baker
ISLES OF SCILLY, Town Hall, St Mary's TR21 0LW. Tel: 0720-22537. *Secretary for Education,* P. S. Hygate

ADVISORY BODIES

SCHOOLS

EDUCATION OTHERWISE, PO Box 120, Leamington Spa, Warks. CV32 7ER. *Helpline,* tel: 0926-886828
INTERNATIONAL BACCALAUREATE, Examinations Office, Pascal Close, St Mellons, Cardiff CF3 0YP. Tel: 0222-770770. *Director of Examinations,* C. Carthew

INDEPENDENT SCHOOLS

ASSISTED PLACES COMMITTEE, 26 Queen Anne's Gate, London SW1H 9AN. Tel: 071-222 9595. *Secretary,* Mrs M. L. Shaw
COMMON ENTRANCE BOARD, Jordan House, Christchurch Road, New Milton, Hants. BH25 6QJ. Tel: 0425-621111. *Secretary,* Mrs J. Williams
GOVERNING BODIES ASSOCIATION, Windleshaw Lodge, Withyham, Nr. Hartfield, E. Sussex TN7 4DB. Tel: 0892-770879. *Secretary,* D. G. Banwell
GOVERNING BODIES OF GIRLS' SCHOOLS ASSOCIATION, Windleshaw Lodge, Withyham, Nr. Hartfield, E. Sussex TN7 4DB. Tel: 0892-770879. *Secretary,* D. G. Banwell
INDEPENDENT SCHOOLS INFORMATION SERVICE, 56 Buckingham Gate, London SW1E 6AG. Tel: 071-630 8793. *National Director,* D. J. Woodhead

FURTHER EDUCATION

FURTHER EDUCATION UNIT, Unit 3, Citadel Place, Tinworth Street, London SE11 5BR. Tel: 071-962 1280. *Chief Officer,* G. Stanton
NATIONAL COUNCIL FOR VOCATIONAL QUALIFICATIONS, 222 Euston Road, London NW1 2BZ. Tel: 071-387 9898. *Chief Executive,* J. Hillier

Regional Advisory Councils

ASSOCIATION OF COLLEGES IN THE EASTERN REGION, Merlin Place, Milton Road, Cambridge CB4 4DP. Tel: 0223-424022. *Chief Officer,* A. Young
CENTRA (NORTH WESTERN REGIONAL ADVISORY COUNCIL FOR FURTHER EDUCATION), Walkden Road, Worsley, Manchester M28 4QE. Tel: 061-702 8700. *Manager,* R. S. Welsh
EMFEC (EAST MIDLAND FURTHER EDUCATION COUNCIL), Robins Wood House, Robins Wood Road, Aspley, Nottingham NG8 3NH. Tel: 0602-293291. *Chief Executive,* R. Ainscough
LASER ADVISORY COUNCIL (LONDON AND SOUTH EAST), Chenies House, 21 Bedford Square, London WC1B 3HH. Tel: 071-637 3073. *Director,* L. South
NORTHERN COUNCIL FOR FURTHER EDUCATION, 5 Grosvenor Villas, Grosvenor Road, Newcastle upon Tyne NE2 2RU. Tel: 091-281 3242. *Director,* J. F. Pearce
SOUTHERN REGIONAL COUNCIL FOR EDUCATION AND TRAINING, The Mezzanine Suite, Civic Centre, Reading RG1 7TD. Tel: 0734-390592. *Chief Officer,* B. J. Knowles
SOUTH WEST ASSOCIATION FOR FURTHER EDUCATION AND TRAINING, Bishops Hull House, Bishops Hull,

Taunton, Somerset TA1 5RA. Tel: 0823-335491. *Secretary,* F. S. Fisher

WELSH JOINT EDUCATION COMMITTEE, 245 Western Avenue, Cardiff CF5 2YX. Tel: 0222-561231. *Secretary,* C. Heycock

YORKSHIRE AND HUMBERSIDE ASSOCIATION FOR FURTHER AND HIGHER EDUCATION, 13 Wellington Road East, Dewsbury, W. Yorks. WF13 1XG. Tel: 0924-450900. *Chief Executive,* Ms P. Cole

HIGHER EDUCATION

ASSOCIATION OF COMMONWEALTH UNIVERSITIES, John Foster House, 36 Gordon Square, London WC1H 0PE. Tel: 071-387 8572. *Secretary-General,* Dr A. Christodoulou, CBE

COMMITTEE OF VICE-CHANCELLORS AND PRINCIPALS OF THE UNIVERSITIES OF THE UNITED KINGDOM, 29 Tavistock Square, London WC1H 9EZ. Tel: 071-387 9231. *Chairman,* Dr K. Edwards

HIGHER EDUCATION QUALITY COUNCIL, 344-354 Gray's Inn Road, London WC1X 8BP. Tel: 071-837 2223. *Company Secretary,* G. L. Middleton

NORTHERN IRELAND HIGHER EDUCATION COUNCIL, c/o Department of Education for Northern Ireland, Rathgael House, Balloo Road, Bangor BT19 7PR. Tel: 0247-270077. *Chairman,* Sir Kenneth Bloomfield

CURRICULUM COUNCILS, ETC.

CURRICULUM COUNCIL FOR WALES/CURRICULUM AND ASSESSMENT AUTHORITY FOR WALES, Castle Buildings, Womanby Street, Cardiff CF1 9SX. Tel: 0222-344946. *Chief Executive,* B. Jones

NORTHERN IRELAND CURRICULUM COUNCIL, Stranmillis College, Stranmillis Road, Belfast BT9 5DY. Tel: 0232-381414. *Chief Executive,* Mrs C. Coxhead

SCHOOL CURRICULUM AND ASSESSMENT AUTHORITY, Newcombe House, 45 Notting Hill Gate, London W11 3JB. Tel: 071-243 9238. *Chairman,* Sir Ron Dearing. *Chief Executive,* C. Woodhead

SCOTTISH CONSULTATIVE COUNCIL ON THE CURRICULUM, Gardyne Road, Broughty Ferry, Dundee DD5 1NY. Tel: 0382-455053. *Chief Executive,* C. E. Harrison

TVEI UNIT, Training Agency, Employment Department, Room E435, Moorfoot, Sheffield S1 4PQ. Tel: 0742-593857

EXAMINING BODIES

GCSE

NORTHERN EXAMINATIONS AND ASSESSMENT BOARD, Devas Street, Manchester M15 6EX. Tel: 061-953 1180. *Chief Executive,* Ms K. Tattersall

NORTHERN IRELAND SCHOOLS EXAMINATIONS AND ASSESSMENT COUNCIL, Beechill House, 42 Beechill Road, Belfast BT8 4RS. Tel: 0232-704666. *Chief Executive,* W. J. Caves

SOUTHERN EXAMINING GROUP, Stag Hill House, Guildford, Surrey GU2 5XJ. Tel: 0483-506506/0865-510085. *Joint Secretaries,* J. A. Day; J. Pailing

UNIVERSITY OF LONDON EXAMINATIONS AND ASSESSMENT COUNCIL, The Lindens, 139 Lexden Road, Colchester CO3 3RL. Tel: 0206-549595; Stewart House, 32 Russell Square, London WC1B 5DN. Tel: 071-331 4000. *Chief Executive,* A. Smith

WELSH JOINT EDUCATION COMMITTEE, 245 Western Avenue, Cardiff CF5 2YX. Tel: 0222-561231. *Secretary,* C. Heycock

WEST MIDLANDS EXAMINATIONS BOARD, Mill Wharf, Mill Street, Birmingham B6 4BU. Tel: 021-628 2000. *Secretary,* B. Swift

A-LEVEL

ASSOCIATED EXAMINING BOARD, Stag Hill House, Guildford, Surrey GU2 5XJ. Tel: 0483-506506. *Secretary-General,* J. A. Day

NORTHERN EXAMINATIONS AND ASSESSMENT BOARD, Devas Street, Manchester M15 6EX. Tel: 061-953 1180. *Chief Executive,* Ms K. Tattersall

NORTHERN IRELAND SCHOOLS EXAMINATIONS AND ASSESSMENT COUNCIL, Beechill House, 42 Beechill Road, Belfast BT8 4RS. Tel: 0232-704666. *Chief Executive,* W. J. Caves

OXFORD AND CAMBRIDGE SCHOOLS EXAMINATION BOARD, Purbeck House, Purbeck Road, Cambridge CB2 2PU. Tel: 0223-411211. *Secretary-General,* H. F. King

OXFORD AND CAMBRIDGE SCHOOLS EXAMINATION BOARD, Elsfield Way, Oxford OX2 8EP. Tel: 0865-54421. *Secretary (acting),* J. G. Lloyd

UNIVERSITY OF CAMBRIDGE LOCAL EXAMINATIONS SYNDICATE, Syndicate Buildings, 1 Hills Road, Cambridge CB1 2EU. Tel: 0223-61111. *Secretary,* M. P. Halstead

UNIVERSITY OF LONDON EXAMINATIONS AND ASSESSMENT COUNCIL, Stewart House, 32 Russell Square, London WC1B 5DN. Tel: 071-331 4000. *Chief Executive,* A. Smith

UNIVERSITY OF OXFORD DELEGACY OF LOCAL EXAMINATIONS, Ewert House, Ewert Place, Summertown, Oxford OX2 7BZ. Tel: 0865-54291. *Secretary,* J. Pailing

WELSH JOINT EDUCATION COMMITTEE, 245 Western Avenue, Cardiff CF5 2YX. Tel: 0222-561231. *Secretary,* C. Heycock

SCOTLAND

SCOTTISH EXAMINATION BOARD, Ironmills Road, Dalkeith, Midlothian EH22 1LE. Tel: 031-663 6601. *Chief Executive,* H. A. Long, PH.D.

SCOTTISH VOCATIONAL EDUCATION COUNCIL, Hanover House, 24 Douglas Street, Glasgow G2 7NQ. Tel: 041-248 7900. *Chief Executive,* T. J. McCool

FURTHER EDUCATION

BUSINESS AND TECHNOLOGY EDUCATION COUNCIL, Central House, Upper Woburn Place, London WC1H 0HH. Tel: 071-413 8400. *Chief Executive,* J. E. Sellars

CITY AND GUILDS OF LONDON INSTITUTE, 76 Portland Place, London W1N 4AA. Tel: 071-278 2468. *Director-General,* Dr N. Carey

RSA EXAMINATIONS BOARD, Westwood Way, Coventry CV4 8HS. Tel: 0203-470033. *Chief Executive,* M. F. Cross

VOCATIONAL EDUCATION UNIT, 46 Britannia Street, London WC1X 9RG. Tel: 071-278 2468. *Chairman,* P. Wates; *Division Manager,* Ms H. Aylett

---

FUNDING COUNCILS

SCHOOLS

FUNDING AGENCY FOR SCHOOLS, Albion Wharf, 25 Skeldergate, York YO1 2XL. Comes into operation in April 1994

FURTHER EDUCATION

FURTHER EDUCATION FUNDING COUNCIL FOR
ENGLAND, Sheriffs Orchard, Greyfriars Road, Coventry
CUI 3PJ. Tel: 0203-530300. *Chief Executive,*
W. H. Stubbs
SCOTTISH FURTHER EDUCATION FUNDING UNIT,
Scottish Office Education Department, 43 Jeffrey Street,
Edinburgh EHI IDN. *Director,* J. G. Henderson
WELSH FUNDING COUNCIL, FURTHER EDUCATION
DIVISION, Lambourne House, Cardiff Business Park,
Llanishen, Cardiff CF4 5GL. Tel: 0222-761861. *Chief
Executive,* Prof. J. A. Andrews

HIGHER EDUCATION

HIGHER EDUCATION FUNDING COUNCIL FOR
ENGLAND, Northavon House, Coldharbour Lane,
Bristol BS16 1QD. Tel: 0272-317317. *Chief Executive,* Prof.
G. Davies, FEng.
SCOTTISH HIGHER EDUCATION FUNDING COUNCIL,
Donaldson House, 97 Haymarket Terrace, Edinburgh
EH12 5HD. Tel: 031-244 5345. *Chief Executive,*
Prof. J. Sizer
WELSH FUNDING COUNCIL, HIGHER EDUCATION
DIVISION, Lambourne House, Cardiff Business Park,
Llanishen, Cardiff CF4 5GL. Tel: 0222-761861. *Chief
Executive,* Prof. J. A. Andrews

ADMISSIONS AND COURSE INFORMATION

ART AND DESIGN ADMISSIONS REGISTRY, Penn House,
9 Broad Street, Hereford HR4 9AP. Tel: 0432-266653.
Registrar, T. W. M. Gourdie
CAREERS RESEARCH AND ADVISORY CENTRE
(CRAC), Sheraton House, Castle Park, Cambridge
CB3 OAX. Tel: 0223-460277. *Director,* D. Blandford.
Publishers, Hobsons Publishing PLC, Bateman Street,
Cambridge CB2 ILZ
COMMITTEE OF SCOTTISH HIGHER EDUCATION
PRINCIPALS (COSHEP), St Andrews House, 141 West
Nile Street, Glasgow G2 2RN. Tel: 041-353 1880.
Secretary, Dr R. L. Crawford
GRADUATE TEACHER TRAINING REGISTRY, Fulton
House, Jessop Avenue, Cheltenham GL50 3SH
SOCIAL WORK ADMISSIONS SYSTEM, Fulton House,
Jessop Avenue, Cheltenham GL50 3SH. Tel: 0242-
225977. *Admissions Officer,* Ms M. Griffiths
TEACHER EDUCATION ADMISSIONS CLEARING HOUSE
(TEACH) (Scotland only), PO Box 165, Holyrood Road,
Edinburgh EH8 8AT. *Registrar,* Miss R. C. Williamson
UNIVERSITIES AND COLLEGES ADMISSIONS SERVICE,
Fulton House, Jessop Avenue, Cheltenham GL50 3SH.
Tel: 0242-222444. *Chief Executives,* M. A. Higgins
(*Corporate Affairs*); P. A. Oakley (*Applications*).
Application materials from PO Box 67, Cheltenham
GL50 3SF

UNIVERSITIES

THE UNIVERSITY OF ABERDEEN (1495)
Regent Walk, Aberdeen AB9 IFX
Tel 0224-272000
Full-time Students (1992–3), 8,600

Chancellor, Sir Kenneth Alexander, FRSE (1987)
Principal, Prof. J. Maxwell Irvine, PH.D.
Secretary, N. R. D. Begg
Rector, vacant

ANGLIA POLYTECHNIC UNIVERSITY (1992)
Victoria Road South, Chelmsford, Essex CMI ILL
Tel 0245-493131
Full-time Students (1992–3), 7,863
Chancellor, The Lord Prior, PC
Vice-Chancellor, M. J. Salmon
Head of Student Administration, D. Davis

ASTON UNIVERSITY (1966)
Aston Triangle, Birmingham B4 7ET
Tel 021-359 3611
Full-time Students (1992–3), 4,240
Chancellor, Sir Adrian Cadbury (1979)
Vice-Chancellor, Prof. Sir Frederick Crawford, PH.D., D.Eng.,
D.SC., FEng.
Registrar and Secretary, R. D. A. Packham

THE UNIVERSITY OF BATH (1966)
Claverton Down, Bath BA2 7AY
Tel 0225-826826
Full-time Students (1992–3), 5,000
Chancellor, Sir Denys Henderson (1993)
Vice-Chancellor, Prof. V. D. VanderLinde
Secretary and Registrar, R. M. Mawditt, OBE, FRSA

THE UNIVERSITY OF BIRMINGHAM (1900)
Edgbaston, Birmingham B15 2TT
Tel 021-414 3344
Full-time Students (1992–3), 13,000
Chancellor, Sir Alexander Jarratt, CB (1983)
Vice-Chancellor, Prof. Sir Michael Thompson, D.SC.
Registrar and Secretary, D. R. Holmes

BOURNEMOUTH UNIVERSITY (1992)
(formerly Bournemouth Polytechnic)
Poole House, Talbot Campus, Fern Barrow,
Dorset BHI2 5BB
Tel 0202-524111
Full-time Students (1992-3), 8,000
Chancellor, The Baroness Cox (1992)
Vice-Chancellor, Dr B. R. MacManus
Secretary and Registrar, Miss B. Chamberlain

THE UNIVERSITY OF BRADFORD (1966)
Bradford BD7 IDP
Tel 0274-733466
Full-time Students (1992–3), 5,765
Chancellor, Sir Trevor Holdsworth (1992)
Vice-Chancellor, Prof. D. J. Johns, PH.D., D.SC. (1989)
Registrar and Secretary, D. W. Granger, MBE

THE UNIVERSITY OF BRIGHTON (1992)
(formerly Brighton Polytechnic)
Mithras House, Lewes Road, Brighton BN2 4AT
Tel 0273-600900
Full-time Students (1992–3), 8,806
Chairman of the Board, M. J. Aldrich
Director, Prof. D. J. Watson
Deputy Director, D. E. House

THE UNIVERSITY OF BRISTOL (1909)
Senate House, Tyndall Avenue, Bristol BS8 ITH
Tel 0272-303030
Full-time Students (1992–3), 10,000

Chancellor, Sir Jeremy Morse, KCMG (1989)
Vice-Chancellor, Sir John Kingman, FRS
Registrar, vacant
Secretary, J. H. M. Parry

BRUNEL UNIVERSITY (1966)
Uxbridge, Middx. UB8 3PH
Tel 0895-274000
Full-time Students (1992–3), 5,690
Chancellor, The Earl of Halsbury, FRS (1966)
Vice-Chancellor, Prof. M. J. H. Sterling
Secretary-General and Registrar, D. Neave

THE UNIVERSITY OF BUCKINGHAM (1983)
Founded 1976 as University College at Buckingham
Buckingham MK18 1EG
Tel 0280-814080
Full-time Students (1992–3), 908
Chancellor, The Baroness Thatcher, OM, PC, FRS (1992)
Vice-Chancellor, The Rt. Hon. Sir Richard Luce (1992)
Registrar and Secretary, M. Lavis, PH.D.

THE UNIVERSITY OF CAMBRIDGE
University Offices, The Old Schools, Cambridge CB2 1TN
Tel 0223-337733
Number of undergraduates in residence 1993–4: *Men*,
6,108; *Women*, 4,348

UNIVERSITY OFFICERS, ETC.
Chancellor, HRH The Duke of Edinburgh, KG, KT, OM, GBE,
PC (1977)
Vice-Chancellor, Prof. Sir David Williams (*Wolfson*) (1989)
High Steward, The Lord Runcie, PC, DD (1991)
Deputy High Steward, The Lord Richardson of
Duntisbourne, PC, MBE, TD (1983)
Commissary, The Lord Oliver of Aylmerton, PC (*Trinity
Hall*) (1989)
Proctors, P. Echlin (*Clare Hall*); F. J. J. Leeper, PH.D.
(*Emmanuel*) (1993)
Orator, A. J. Bowen (*Jesus*) (1993)
Registrary, S. G. Fleet, PH.D. (*Downing*) (1983)
Deputy Registrary, N. J. B. A. Branson, PH.D. (*Darwin*)
(1993)
Librarian, F. W. Ratcliffe, PH.D. (*Corpus Christi*) (1980)
Treasurer, Ms J. Womack (*Trinity*) (1993)
Secretary-General of the Faculties, D. A. Livesey,
PH.D. (*Emmanuel*) (1992)
Director of the Fitzwilliam Museum, S. S. Jervis (*Corpus
Christi*) (1990)

COLLEGES AND HALLS, ETC.
with dates of foundation

CHRIST'S (1505), *Master*, Prof. Sir Hans Kornberg, PH.D.,
D.SC., SC.D., FRS (1983)
CHURCHILL (1960), *Master*, Prof. A. N. Broers, PH.D., FRS
(1990)
CLARE (1326), *Master*, Prof. B. A. Hepple (1993)
CLARE HALL (1966), *President*, Prof. D. A. Low, PH.D.
(1987)
CORPUS CHRISTI (1352), *Master*, M. W. McCrum (1980)
DARWIN (1964), *Master*, Prof. G. E. R. Lloyd, PH.D., FBA
(1989)
DOWNING (1800), *Master*, P. Mathias, CBE, Litt.D., FBA
(1987)
EMMANUEL (1584), *Master*, The Lord St John of Fawsley,
PC, PH.D. (1991)
FITZWILLIAM (1966), *Master*, Prof. A. W. Cuthbert, PH.D.,
FRS (1991)

GIRTON (1869), *Mistress*, Mrs J. J. d'A. Campbell, CMG
(1992)
GONVILLE AND CAIUS (1348), *Master*, Prof. P. Gray, SC.D.,
FRS (1988)
HOMERTON (1824) (for B.Ed. students), *Principal*,
Mrs K. B. Pretty, PH.D. (1991)
HUGHES HALL (1885), (for post-graduate students),
President, J. T. Dingle, D.SC. (1993)
JESUS (1496), *Master*, Prof. the Lord Renfrew of
Kaimsthorn, SC.D. (1986)
KING'S (1441), *Provost*, Prof. P. P. G. Bateson, SC.D., FRS
(1987)
*LUCY CAVENDISH COLLEGE (1965) (for women research
students and mature and affiliated undergraduates),
President, Dame Anne Warburton, DCVO, CMG (1985)
MAGDALENE (1542), *Master*, Sir David Calcutt, QC (1985)
*NEW HALL (1954), *President*, Mrs V. L. Pearl, PH.D. (1981)
*NEWNHAM (1871), *Principal*, Ms O. S. O'Neill (1992)
PEMBROKE (1347), *Master*, Sir Roger Tomkys, KCMG (1992)
PETERHOUSE (1284), *Master*, Prof. Sir John Meurig
Thomas, FRS (1993)
QUEENS' (1448), *President*, Revd J. C. Polkinghorne, SC.D.,
FRS (1989)
ROBINSON (1977), *Warden*, Prof. the Lord Lewis of
Newnham, SC.D., FRS (1977)
ST CATHARINE'S (1473), *Master*, Prof. Sir Terence English
(1993)
ST EDMUND'S (1896), *Master*, R. M. Laws, CBE, PH.D.
(1986)
ST JOHN'S (1511), *Master*, Prof. R. A. Hinde, SC.D., FRS
(1989)
SELWYN (1882), *Master*, D. Harrison, CBE, SC.D., F.Eng.
(1993)
SIDNEY SUSSEX (1596), *Master*, Prof. G. Horn, SC.D., FRS
(1992)
TRINITY (1546), *Master*, Sir Michael Atiyah, PH.D., FRS,
FRSE (1990)
TRINITY HALL (1350), *Master*, Sir John Lyons, PH.D.
(1984)
WOLFSON (1965), *President*, J. Tusa (1993)
*Colleges for women only

THE UNIVERSITY OF CENTRAL ENGLAND
IN BIRMINGHAM (1992)
(formerly Birmingham Polytechnic)
Perry Barr, Birmingham B42 5SU
Tel 021-331 5000
Full-time Students (1992–3), 11,900
Vice-Chancellor, Dr P. C. Knight
Secretary and Registrar, Ms M. Penlington

THE UNIVERSITY OF CENTRAL LANCASHIRE
(1992)
(formerly Lancashire Polytechnic)
Preston PRI 2TQ
Tel 0772-201201
Full-time Students (1992–3), 11,102
Rector and Chief Executive, B. Booth
Secretary, Ms P. M. Ackroyd

THE CITY UNIVERSITY (1966)
Northampton Square, London ECIV OHB
Tel 071-477 8000
Full-time Students (1992–3), 5,833
Chancellor, The Rt. Hon. the Lord Mayor of London
Vice-Chancellor and Principal, Prof. R. N. Franklin, D.Phil.,
D.SC.
Registrar, A. H. Seville, PH.D.
Secretary, M. M. O'Hara

COVENTRY UNIVERSITY (1992)
(formerly Coventry Polytechnic)
Priory Street, Coventry CVI 5FB
Tel 0203-631313
Full-time Students (1992–3), 14,000
Vice-Chancellor, M. Goldstein, PH.D., D.SC.
Registrar, J. Gledhill, PH.D.
Secretary, Ms L. Arlidge

DE MONTFORT UNIVERSITY (1992)
(formerly Leicester Polytechnic)
The Gateway, Leicester LEI 9BH
Tel 0533-551551
Full-time Students (1991–2), 14,500
Chancellor, Dame Anne Mueller
Vice-Chancellor and Chief Executive, Prof. K. Barker
Registrar, J. Wools
Secretary, A. Denny

THE UNIVERSITY OF DERBY (1993)
(formerly Derbyshire College of Higher Education)
Kedleston Road, Derby DE22 1GB
Tel 0332-622222
Full-time Students (1992–3), c. 5,700
Vice-Chancellor, Prof. R. Waterhouse
Academic Registrar, Mrs J. Fry

THE UNIVERSITY OF DUNDEE (1967)
Dundee DDI 4HN
Tel 0382-23181
Full-time Students (1992–3), 6,340
Chancellor, Sir James Black, FRCP, FRS (1992)
Vice-Chancellor, Prof. M. J. Hamlin, FRSE, FEng.
Secretary, R. Seaton
Rector, S. Fry (1992–5)

THE UNIVERSITY OF DURHAM
Founded 1832; re-organized 1908, 1937 and 1963
Old Shire Hall, Durham DHI 3HP
Tel 091-374 2000
Full-time Students (1992–3), 6,742
Chancellor, Sir Peter Ustinov, CBE, FRSL
Vice-Chancellor and Warden, Prof. E. A. V. Ebsworth, PH.D.,
  D.SC., FRSE
Registrar and Secretary, J. C. F. Hayward

COLLEGES
COLLINGWOOD, *Principal*, G. H. Blake, PH.D.
GRADUATE SOCIETY, *Principal*, M. Richardson, PH.D.
GREY, *Master*, V. E. Watts
HATFIELD, *Master*, J. P. Barber, PH.D.
ST AIDAN'S, *Principal*, R. J. Williams
ST CHAD'S, *Principal*, E. Halladay
ST CUTHBERT'S SOCIETY, *Principal*, S. G. C. Stoker
ST HILD AND ST BEDE, *Principal*, J. V. Armitage, PH.D.
ST JOHN'S, *Principal*, D. V. Day
ST MARY'S, *Principal*, Miss J. M. Kenworthy
TREVELYAN, *Principal*, Miss D. Lavin
UNIVERSITY, *Master*, E. C. Salthouse, PH.D.
USHAW, *President*, Rt. Revd Mgr R. Atherton, OBE
VAN MILDERT, *Principal*, Dr J. Turner

THE UNIVERSITY OF EAST ANGLIA (1963)
Norwich NR4 7TJ
Tel 0603-56161
Full-time Students (1992–3), 5,751

Chancellor, Revd Prof. W. O. Chadwick, OM, KBE, DD, FBA
  (1985)
Vice-Chancellor, Prof. D. C. Burke, PH.D.
Registrar and Secretary, M. G. E. Paulson-Ellis, OBE

THE UNIVERSITY OF EAST LONDON (1992)
(formerly Polytechnic of East London)
Romford Road, London E15 4LZ
Tel 081-590 7722
Full-time Students (1992–3), 8,200
Vice-Chancellor, Prof. F. Gould
Registrar, Ms S. Millard

THE UNIVERSITY OF EDINBURGH (1583)
Old College, South Bridge, Edinburgh EH8 9YL
Tel 031-667 1011
Full-time Students (1992–3), 13,700
Chancellor, HRH The Prince Philip, Duke of Edinburgh,
  KG, KT, OM, GBE, PC, FRS (1952)
Vice-Chancellor and Principal, Sir David Smith, D.Phil., FRS,
  FRSE
Registrar and Secretary, M. J. B. Lowe, PH.D.
Rector, D. Munro (1991–4)

THE UNIVERSITY OF ESSEX (1964)
Wivenhoe Park, Colchester CO4 3SQ
Tel 0206-873333
Full-time Students (1992–3), 4,580
Chancellor, The Rt. Hon. Sir Patrick Nairne, GCB, MC (1983)
Vice-Chancellor, Prof. R. J. Johnston, PH.D.
Registrar and Secretary, A. F. Woodburn

THE UNIVERSITY OF EXETER (1955)
Northcote House, The Queen's Drive, Exeter EX4 4QJ
Tel 0392-263263
Full-time Students (1992–3), 7,409
Chancellor, Sir Rex Richards, D.SC., FRS (1981)
Vice-Chancellor, D. Harrison, CBE, PH.D., SC.D., FEng.
Academic Registrar and Secretary, I. H. C. Powell

GLAMORGAN UNIVERSITY (1992)
(formerly Polytechnic of Wales)
Pontypridd, Mid Glamorgan CF37 1DL
Tel 0443-480480
Full-time Students (1992–3), 7,664
Vice-Chancellor, Prof. A. L. Webb
Academic Registrar, J. O'Shea
Secretary, J. L. Bracegirdle

THE UNIVERSITY OF GLASGOW (1451)
Glasgow G12 8QQ
Tel 041-339 8855
Full-time Students (1991–2), 13,054
Chancellor, Sir Alexander Cairncross, KCMG, FBA (1972)
Vice-Chancellor, Sir William Fraser, GCB, LL D, FRSE
Registrar, J. M. Black
Secretary, R. Ewen, OBE, TD
Rector, J. Ball (1993–6)

GLASGOW CALEDONIAN UNIVERSITY
Cowcaddens Road, Glasgow G4 OBA
Tel 041-331 3000
Full-time Students (1992–3), 8,800
Chancellor, Sir David Nickson, KBE
Vice-Chancellor, Prof. J. S. Mason
Secretary, B. M. Fraser, PH.D.

THE UNIVERSITY OF GREENWICH (1992)
(formerly Thames Polytechnic)
Wellington Street, Woolwich, London SE18 6PF
Tel 081-316 8000
Full-time Students (1991–2), 9,700
Chancellor, The Baroness Young
Vice-Chancellor, Dr D. Fussey
Academic Registrar, A. I. Mayfield
Secretary, J. Charles

HERIOT-WATT UNIVERSITY (1966)
Riccarton, Edinburgh EH14 4AS
Tel 031-449 5111
Full-time Students (1992–3), c.8,550
Chancellor, The Lord Mackay of Clashfern, PC, QC, FRSE
(1979)
Principal and Vice-Chancellor, Prof. A. G. J. MacFarlane,
CBE, ph.d., FRS, FRSE, FEng. (1989)
Registrar, D. Sturgeon
Secretary, P. L. Wilson

THE UNIVERSITY OF HERTFORDSHIRE
(1992)
(formerly Hatfield Polytechnic)
College Lane, Hatfield, Herts. AL10 9AB
Tel 0707-279000
Full-time Students (1992–3), 10,128
Chancellor, Sir Brian Corby
Vice-Chancellor, Prof. N. K. Buxton
Registrar and Secretary, P. G. Jeffreys

THE UNIVERSITY OF HUDDERSFIELD (1992)
(formerly Polytechnic of Huddersfield)
Queensgate, Huddersfield HD1 3DH
Tel 0484-422288
Full-time Students (1992–3), 8,520
Chancellor, R. C. Cross, OBE
Vice-Chancellor and Rector, Prof. K. J. Durrands, CBE
Academic Registrar, M. E. Bond
Secretary, D. J. Lock

THE UNIVERSITY OF HULL (1954)
Cottingham Road, Hull HU6 7RX
Tel 0482-46311
Full-time Students (1992–3), 8,289
Chancellor, The Lord Wilberforce, CMG, OBE, PC (1978)
Vice-Chancellor, Prof. D. Dilks, FRSL
Registrar and Secretary, P. A. Bolton

THE UNIVERSITY OF HUMBERSIDE (1992)
(formerly Humberside Polytechnic)
Cottingham Road, Hull HU6 7RT
Tel 0482-440552
Full-time Students (1992–3), 10,085
Pro-Chancellor, Dr Harry Hooper
Vice-Chancellor, Prof. R. King
Registrar, Mrs P. Jackson
Secretary, Miss M. Harries-Jenkins

THE UNIVERSITY OF KEELE (1962)
Keele, Newcastle under Lyme, Staffs. ST5 5BG
Tel 0782-621111
Full-time Students (1992–3), 4,925
Chancellor, Sir Claus Moser, KCB, CBE, FBA (1986)
Vice-Chancellor, Prof. B. E. Fender, CMG, ph.d.
Registrar, D. Cohen, ph.d.

THE UNIVERSITY OF KENT AT CANTERBURY
(1965)
Tanglewood, Giles Lane, Canterbury CT2 7LX
Tel 0227-764000
Full-time Students (1992–3), 5,982
Chancellor, R. Horton (1990)
Vice-Chancellor, D. J. E. Ingram, CBE, D.Phil., D.SC.
Registrar, T. Mead, ph.d.

KINGSTON UNIVERSITY (1992)
(formerly Kingston Polytechnic)
Penrhyn Road, Kingston upon Thames,
Surrey KT1 2EE
Tel 081-547 2000
Full-time Students (1992-3), 8,804
Vice-Chancellor, R. C. Smith, CBE, ph.d.
Academic Registrar, Miss A. Hynes
Secretary, E. Lang

THE UNIVERSITY OF LANCASTER (1964)
Lancaster LA1 4YW
Tel 0524-65201
Full-time Students (1992–3), 6,133
Chancellor, HRH Princess Alexandra, the Hon. Lady
Ogilvy, GCVO (1964)
Vice-Chancellor, Prof. H. J. Hanham, ph.d.
Secretary, G. M. Cockburn

THE UNIVERSITY OF LEEDS (1904)
Leeds LS2 9JT
Tel 0532-431751
Full-time Students (1992–3), 15,210
Chancellor, HRH The Duchess of Kent, GCVO (1966)
Vice-Chancellor, Prof. A. G. Wilson
Registrar, E. Newcomb

LEEDS METROPOLITAN UNIVERSITY
(formerly Leeds Polytechnic)
Calverley Street, Leeds LS1 3HE
Tel 0532-832600
Full-time Students (1992–3), 13,777
Principal and Chief Executive, C. Price
Secretary, M. Wilkinson

THE UNIVERSITY OF LEICESTER (1957)
Leicester LE1 7RH
Tel 0533-522522
Full-time Students (1992–3), 7,551
Chancellor, The Lord Porter of Luddenham, OM, ph.d.,
SC.D., FRS (1985)
Vice-Chancellor, K. J. R. Edwards, ph.d.
Registrar, K. J. Julian

THE UNIVERSITY OF LIVERPOOL (1903)
PO Box 147, Liverpool L69 3BX
Tel 051-794 2000
Full-time Students (1992–3), 11,560
Chancellor, The Viscount Leverhulme, KG, TD (1980)
Vice-Chancellor, Prof. P. N. Love, CBE
Registrar and Secretary, M. D. Carr

LIVERPOOL JOHN MOORES UNIVERSITY
(1992)
(formerly Liverpool Polytechnic)
Rodney House, 70 Mount Pleasant, Liverpool L3 5UX
Tel 051-231 2121
Full-time Students (1992–3), 19,000
Chancellor, vacant
Vice-Chancellor, Prof. P. Toyne
Registrar, Ms A. Richardson
Secretary, P. Blackburn

THE UNIVERSITY OF LONDON (1836)
Senate House, London WC1E 7HU
Tel 071-636 8000
Internal Students (1992–3), 64,744, External Students, 16,807
Visitor, HM The Queen in Council
Chancellor, HRH The Princess Royal, GCVO, FRS (1981)
Vice-Chancellor, Prof. S. R. Sutherland
Chairman of the Court, The Lord Rippon of Hexham, PC, QC
Chairman of Convocation, Prof. C. D. Cowan, CBE, Ph.D.
Principal, P. Holwell

SCHOOLS OF THE UNIVERSITY

BIRKBECK COLLEGE, Malet Street, London
   WC1E 7HX. *Master*, The Baroness Blackstone, Ph.D.
GOLDSMITHS' COLLEGE, Lewisham Way, New Cross,
   London SE14 6NW. *Warden*, Prof. K. J. Gregory, Ph.D.
IMPERIAL COLLEGE OF SCIENCE, TECHNOLOGY AND
   MEDICINE (includes St Mary's Hospital Medical School),
   Prince Consort Road, London SW7 2AZ. *Rector*, Prof. Sir
   Ronald Oxburgh, KBE, FRS
INSTITUTE OF EDUCATION, 20 Bedford Way, London
   WC1H 0AL. *Director*, Sir Peter Newsam
KING'S COLLEGE LONDON (includes King's College
   School of Medicine and Dentistry), Strand, London
   WC2R 2LS. *Principal*, Prof. A. Lucas, Ph.D.
LONDON SCHOOL OF ECONOMICS AND POLITICAL
   SCIENCE, Houghton Street, London WC2A 2AE. *Director*,
   J. M. Ashworth, Ph.D., D.SC.
QUEEN MARY AND WESTFIELD COLLEGE, Mile End
   Road, London E1 4NS. *Principal*, Prof. G. Zellick, Ph.D.
ROYAL HOLLOWAY, Egham Hill, Egham, Surrey TW20
   0EX. *Principal*, Prof. N. Gowar
ROYAL VETERINARY COLLEGE, Royal College Street,
   London NW1 0TU. *Principal and Dean*,
   Prof. L. E. Lanyon, Ph.D.
SCHOOL OF ORIENTAL AND AFRICAN STUDIES,
   Thornhaugh Street, London WC1H 0XG. *Director*,
   M. D. McWilliam
SCHOOL OF PHARMACY, 29–39 Brunswick Square,
   London WC1N 1AX. *Dean*, Prof. A. T. Florence, Ph.D.,
   FRSE
UNIVERSITY COLLEGE LONDON (including UCL Medical
   School), Gower Street, London WC1E 6BT. *Provost*,
   Dr D. H. Roberts, CBE, FRS
WYE COLLEGE, Wye, Ashford, Kent TN25 5AH. *Principal*,
   Prof. J. H. D. Prescott, Ph.D.
*HEYTHROP COLLEGE, Kensington Square, London
   W8 5HQ. *Principal*, Revd B. A. Callaghan, SJ

*Not in receipt of HEFCE grants

MEDICAL SCHOOLS

CHARING CROSS AND WESTMINSTER MEDICAL
   SCHOOL, The Reynolds Building, St Dunstan's Road,
   London W6 8RP. *Dean*, J. E. H. Pendower, FRCS
THE LONDON HOSPITAL MEDICAL COLLEGE, Turner
   Street, London E1 2AD. *Dean*, Prof. R. Duckworth, CBE,
   MD, FRCS, FRCPath
ROYAL FREE HOSPITAL SCHOOL OF MEDICINE,
   Rowland Hill Street, London NW3 2PF. *Dean*,
   Prof. A. J. Zuckerman, MD, FRCP
ST BARTHOLOMEW'S HOSPITAL MEDICAL COLLEGE,
   West Smithfield, London EC1A 7BE. *Dean*, L. H. Rees,
   MD, FRCP
ST GEORGE'S HOSPITAL MEDICAL SCHOOL, Cranmer
   Terrace, London SW17 0RE. *Dean*, Prof. A. W. Asscher,
   MD, FRCP, FRCPath.

UNITED MEDICAL AND DENTAL SCHOOLS OF GUY'S
   AND ST THOMAS' HOSPITALS, Guy's, London Bridge,
   London SE1 9RT; St Thomas', Lambeth Palace Road,
   London SE1 7EH. *Principal*, Prof. C. Chantler

POSTGRADUATE MEDICAL INSTITUTIONS

LONDON SCHOOL OF HYGIENE AND TROPICAL
   MEDICINE, Keppel Street, London WC1E 7HT. *Dean*,
   Prof. R. G. Feachem, Ph.D, D.SC.(Med)
ROYAL POSTGRADUATE MEDICAL SCHOOL, Du Cane
   Road, London W12 0SH. *Dean*, Prof. Sir Colin
   Dollery, FRCP
BRITISH POSTGRADUATE MEDICAL FEDERATION
   (University of London), 33 Millman Street, London
   WC1N 3EJ. *Director*, Dr M. Green, DM, FRCP
Comprises:
HUNTERIAN INSTITUTE, Royal College of Surgeons of
   England, Lincoln's Inn Fields, London
   WC2A 3PN. *Master*, Prof. Sir Stanley Peart, FRS, FRCP;
   Academic Dean, Dr N. Wedderburn
INSTITUTE OF CANCER RESEARCH, Royal Cancer
   Hospital, 17A Onslow Gardens, London
   SW7 3AL. *Director*, Prof. P. B. Garland, Ph.D., FRSE
INSTITUTE OF CHILD HEALTH, 30 Guilford Street,
   London WC1N 1EH. *Dean*, Prof. R. J. Levinsky, MD, FRCP
INSTITUTE OF DENTAL SURGERY, Eastman Dental
   Hospital, Gray's Inn Road, London WC1X 8LD. *Dean*,
   Prof. G. B. Winter, D.ch.
INSTITUTE OF NEUROLOGY, National Hospital, Queen
   Square, London WC1N 3BG. *Dean*, Prof. D. N. Landon
INSTITUTE OF OPHTHALMOLOGY, 11–43 Bath Street,
   London EC1V 9EL. *Dean*, N. S. C. Rice, MD, FRCS
INSTITUTE OF PSYCHIATRY, De Crespigny Park,
   Denmark Hill, London SE5 8AF. *Dean*, S. A. Checkley,
   FRCPsych.
NATIONAL HEART AND LUNG INSTITUTE, Dovehouse
   Street, London SW3 6LI. *Dean*, Prof. T. Clark, MD, FRCP

SENATE INSTITUTES

BRITISH INSTITUTE IN PARIS, 9–11 Rue de Constantine,
   75007, Paris. *Director*, Prof. C. L. Campos, L-ès-L., Ph.D.
   London office: Senate House, Malet Street, London
   WC1E 7HU
CENTRE FOR DEFENCE STUDIES, King's College London,
   Strand, London WC2R 2LS. *Director*, Prof. L. Freedman
COURTAULD INSTITUTE OF ART, North Block, Somerset
   House, Strand, London WC2R 2LS. *Director*,
   Prof. C. M. Kauffmann, Ph.D, FSA
INSTITUTE OF ADVANCED LEGAL STUDIES, Charles
   Clore House, 17 Russell Square, London
   WC1B 5DR. *Director*, Prof. T. C. Daintith
INSTITUTE OF CLASSICAL STUDIES, 31–34 Gordon
   Square, London WC1H 0PY. *Director*,
   Prof. R. R. K. Sorabji, FBA
INSTITUTE OF COMMONWEALTH STUDIES, 27–28
   Russell Square, London WC1B 5DS. *Director*, Prof. Shula
   E. Marks, Ph.D.
INSTITUTE OF GERMANIC STUDIES, 29 Russell Square,
   London WC1B 5DP. *Hon. Director*, Prof. M. W. Swales,
   Ph.D.
INSTITUTE OF HISTORICAL RESEARCH, Senate House,
   Malet Street, London WC1E 7HU. *Director*,
   Prof. P. K. O'Brien, D.phil.
INSTITUTE OF LATIN AMERICAN STUDIES, 31 Tavistock
   Square, London WC1H 9HA. *Director*, Prof. V. G. Bulmer-
   Thomas, D.phil.

INSTITUTE OF ROMANCE STUDIES, Senate House, Malet Street, London WC1E 7HU. *Hon. Director*, Prof. A. Lavers, L-ès-L, Ph.D.
INSTITUTE OF UNITED STATES STUDIES, Senate House, Malet Street, London WC1E 7HU. *Director*, G. L. McDowell, Ph.D.
INSTITUTE OF ZOOLOGY, Royal Zoological Society, Regent's Park, London NW1 4RY. *Director*, Prof. A. P. F. Flint, Ph.D., D.Sc.
SCHOOL OF SLAVONIC AND EAST EUROPEAN STUDIES, Senate House, Malet Street, London WC1E 7HU. *Director*, Prof. M. A. Branch, Ph.D.
WARBURG INSTITUTE, Woburn Square, London WC1H OAB. *Director*, Prof. C. N. J. Mann, Ph.D.

INSTITUTIONS HAVING RECOGNIZED TEACHERS
JEWS' COLLEGE, 44A Albert Road, London NW4 2SJ. *Principal*, Rabbi Dr I. Jacobs
LONDON BUSINESS SCHOOL, Sussex Place, London NW1 4SA. *Principal*, Prof. G. Bain, D.Phil.
ROYAL ACADEMY OF MUSIC, Marylebone Road, London NW1 5HT. *Principal*, L. Harrell
ROYAL COLLEGE OF MUSIC, Prince Consort Road, London SW7 2BS. *Director*, M. G. Matthews, FRSA, FRCM
TRINITY COLLEGE OF MUSIC, Mandeville Place, London W1M 6AQ. *Principal*, P. Jones, CBE, FRCM

LONDON GUILDHALL UNIVERSITY
31 Jewry Street, London EC3N 2EY
Tel 071-320 1000
Full-time Students (1992–3), 8,235
Provost, Prof. R. Floud, D.Phil.
Registrar, B. High

LOUGHBOROUGH UNIVERSITY OF TECHNOLOGY (1966)
Loughborough LE11 3TU
Tel 0509-263171
Full-time Students (1992–3), 7,688
Chancellor, Sir Denis Rooke, CBE, FRS, FEng (1989)
Vice-Chancellor, Prof. D.Wallace, Ph.D., FRS, FRSE
Registrar, D. E. Fletcher, Ph.D.
Academic Secretary, N. A. McHard

UNIVERSITY OF LUTON (1993)
(formerly Luton College of Higher Education)
Park Square, Luton LU1 3JU
Tel 0582-34111
Full-time Students (1992–3), 10,825
Chancellor, Sir David Plastow
Vice-Chancellor, Dr A. Wood
Admissions Tutor, P. Vachon

THE UNIVERSITY OF MANCHESTER
(Founded 1851; re-organized 1880 and 1903)
Oxford Road, Manchester M13 9PL
Full-time Students (1992–3), c.14,000
Chancellor, B. Redhead
Vice-Chancellor, Prof. M. B. Harris, CBE, Ph.D.
Registrar and Secretary, K. E. Kitchen

UNIVERSITY OF MANCHESTER INSTITUTE OF SCIENCE AND TECHNOLOGY (1824)
PO Box 88, Manchester M60 1QD
Tel 061-236 3311
Full-time Students (1992–3), 5,635
President, Sir John Mason, CB, D.Sc., FRS (1986)
Principal, Prof. H. C. A. Hankins, Ph.D.
Secretary and Registrar, P. C. C. Stephenson

MANCHESTER METROPOLITAN UNIVERSITY
(formerly Manchester Polytechnic)
All Saints, Manchester M15 6BH
Tel 061-247 2000
Full-time Students (1992–3), 21,354
Chancellor, The Duke of Westminster
Director, Sir Kenneth Green
Registrar, J. Karczewski-Slowikowski
Secretary, R. O. Yeo

MIDDLESEX UNIVERSITY (1992)
(formerly Middlesex Polytechnic)
White Hart Lane, London N17 8HR
Tel 081-362 5000
Full-time Students (1992–3), 13,500
Chancellor, The Baroness Platt of Writtle
Vice-Chancellor, Prof. D. Melville, Ph.D.
Registrar, G. Jones

NAPIER UNIVERSITY (1992)
(formerly Napier Polytechnic)
219 Colinton Road, Edinburgh EH14 1DJ
Tel 031-444 2266
Full-time Students (1992–3), 7,500
Chancellor, The Lord Younger of Prestwick, KCVO, TD, PC, FRSE
Vice-Chancellor, Prof. W. Turmeau, CBE, FRSE
Secretary and Registrar, I. J. Miller

THE UNIVERSITY OF NEWCASTLE UPON TYNE
(Founded 1852; re-organized 1908, 1937 and 1963)
6 Kensington Terrace, Newcastle upon Tyne NE1 7RU
Tel 091-222 6000
Full-time Students (1992–3), 10,943
Chancellor, The Viscount Ridley, KG, TD (1989)
Vice-Chancellor, J. R. G. Wright
Registrar, D. E. T. Nicholson

THE UNIVERSITY OF NORTH LONDON (1992)
(formerly Polytechnic of North London)
166–220 Holloway Road, London N7 8DB
Tel 071-607 2789
Full-time Students (1992–3), 9,770
Vice-Chancellor, L. Wagner
Academic Registrar, Dr M. Storey
Secretary, C. Wragg

THE UNIVERSITY OF NORTHUMBRIA AT NEWCASTLE
(formerly Newcastle upon Tyne Polytechnic)
Newcastle upon Tyne NE1 8ST
Tel 091-232 6002
Full-time Students (1992–3), 12,000
Chancellor, The Lord Glenamara, CH, PC
Vice-Chancellor, Prof. L. Barden, CBE, Ph.D., D.Sc.
Registrar and Secretary, R. A. Bott

THE UNIVERSITY OF NOTTINGHAM (1948)
University Park, Nottingham NG7 2RD
Tel 0602-484848
Full-time Students (1992–3), 10,500
Chancellor, Sir Ron Dearing, CB (1993)
Vice-Chancellor, Prof. C. M. Campbell
Registrar, G. E. Chandler

NOTTINGHAM TRENT UNIVERSITY
Burton Street, Nottingham NG1 4BU
Tel 0602-418418

Full-time Students (1991–2), 12,260
Vice-Chancellor, Prof. R. Cowell, PH.D.
Academic Registrar, A. E. Foster

THE UNIVERSITY OF OXFORD
University Offices, Wellington Square, Oxford OX1 2JD
Tel 0865-270001
Number of students in residence 1992–3:
Men, 8,871; *Women*, 5,723

UNIVERSITY OFFICERS, ETC.

Chancellor, The Lord Jenkins of Hillhead, PC
(*Balliol*), *elected* 1987
High Steward, The Lord Goff of Chieveley, PC (*Lincoln and New College*), *elected* 1990
Vice-Chancellor, Dr P. M. North, CBE, FBA (*Jesus*), *elected* 1993
Proctors, P. A. Allen (*St Cross*); Ms E. A. Fallaize (*St John's*), *elected* 1993
Assessor, J. S. Rowett, D.phil. (*Brasenose*), *elected* 1993
Public Orator, J. Griffin (*Balliol*), *elected* 1992
Bodley's Librarian, D. G. Vaisey (*Exeter*), *elected* 1986
Keeper of Archives, J. Hackney (*Wadham*), *elected* 1988
Director of the Ashmolean Museum, C. J. White (*Worcester*), *elected* 1985
Registrar of the University, A. J. Dorey, D.phil. (*Linacre*), *elected* 1979
Surveyor to the University, P. M. R. Hill, *elected* 1993
Secretary of Faculties, A. P. Weale (*Worcester*), *elected* 1984
Secretary of the Chest, I. G. Thompson (*Merton*), *elected* 1986
Deputy Registrar (Administration), P. W. Jones (*Green*), *elected* 1991

OXFORD COLLEGES AND HALLS
with dates of foundation

ALL SOULS (1438), *Warden*, Sir Patrick Neill, QC (1977)
BALLIOL (1263), *Master*, B. S. Blumberg (1989)
BRASENOSE (1509), *Principal*, The Lord Windlesham, CVO, PC (1989)
CHRIST CHURCH (1546), *Dean*, Very Revd J. H. Drury (1991)
CORPUS CHRISTI (1517), *President*, Prof. Sir Keith Thomas, FBA (1986)
EXETER (1314), *Rector*, vacant
GREEN (1979), *Warden*, Sir Crispin Tickell, GCMG, KCVO (1990)
HERTFORD (1874), *Principal*, Prof. Sir Erik Zeeman, KBE, FRS (1988)
JESUS (1571), *Principal*, Dr P. M. North, CBE, FBA (1984)
KEBLE (1868), *Warden*, G. B. Richardson, CBE (1989)
LADY MARGARET HALL (1878), *Principal*, D. M. Stewart (1979)
LINACRE (1962), *Principal*, Sir Bryan Cartledge, KCMG (1988)
LINCOLN (1427), *Rector*, Sir Maurice Shock (1987)
MAGDALEN (1458), *President*, A. D. Smith, CBE (1988)
MERTON (1264), *Warden*, J. M. Roberts, D.phil. (1985)
NEW COLLEGE (1379), *Warden*, H. McGregor, QC, DCL (1985)
NUFFIELD (1937), *Warden*, Sir David Cox, FRS (1988)
ORIEL (1326), *Provost*, E. W. Nicholson, DD, FBA (1990)
PEMBROKE (1624), *Master*, Prof. R. Stevens, DCL (1993)
QUEEN'S (1340), *Provost*, G. Marshall (1993)
REWLEY HOUSE (1990), *President*, G. P. Thomas, ph.D. (1990)
ST ANNE'S (1952) (Originally Society of Oxford Home-Students (1879)), *Principal*, Mrs R. L. Deech (1991)
ST ANTONY'S (1950), *Warden*, The Lord Dahrendorf, KBE, ph.D., FBA (1987)

ST CATHERINE'S (1962), *Master*, G. C. K. Peach (*acting*)
ST CROSS (1965), *Master*, R. C. Repp, D.phil. (1987)
ST EDMUND HALL (*c.* 1278), *Principal*, J. C. B. Gosling (1983)
*ST HILDA'S (1893), *Principal*, Miss E. Llewellyn-Smith, CB (1990)
ST HUGH'S (1886), *Principal*, D. Wood, QC (1991)
ST JOHN'S (1555), *President*, W. Hayes, D.phil. (1987)
ST PETER'S (1929), *Master*, J. P. Barron, D.phil. (1991)
SOMERVILLE (1879), *Principal*, Mrs C. E. Hughes, CMG (1989)
TRINITY (1554), *President*, Sir John Burgh, KCMG, CB (1987)
UNIVERSITY (1249), *Master*, W. J. Albery, D.phil., FRS (1989)
WADHAM (1612), *Warden*, J. S. Flemming (1993)
WOLFSON (1966), *President*, Sir David Smith, D.phil. (1994)
WORCESTER (1714), *Provost*, R. G. Smethurst (1991)
CAMPION HALL (1896), *Master*, Revd J. A. Munitiz (1989)
GREYFRIARS (1910), *Warden*, Revd M. W. Sheehan, D.phil. (1990)
MANCHESTER (1786), *Principal*, Revd R. Waller, ph.D. (1990)
MANSFIELD (1886), *Principal*, D. J. Trevelyan, CB (1989)
REGENT'S PARK (1810), *Principal*, Revd P. S. Fiddes, D.phil. (1989)
ST BENET'S HALL (1897), *Master*, Revd H. Wansbrough, OSB (1991)

* College for women only

OXFORD BROOKES UNIVERSITY
Headington, Oxford OX3 0BP
Tel 0865-741111
Full-time Students (1992–3), 8,500
Chancellor, vacant
Vice-Chancellor, Dr C. Booth
Registrar, R. M. Tulloch
Secretary, B. Summers

THE UNIVERSITY OF PAISLEY (1992)
(formerly Paisley College of Technology)
High Street, Paisley PA1 2BE
Tel 041-848 3000
Full-time Students (1992–3), 5,107
Chancellor, Sir Robert Easton, CBE
Vice-Chancellor, Prof. R. W. Shaw
Registrar, D. Rigg
Secretary, J. Fraser

UNIVERSITY OF PLYMOUTH (1992)
(formerly Polytechnic SouthWest)
Drake Circus, Plymouth PL4 8AA
Tel 0752-600600
Full-time Students (1992–3), 15,000
Vice-Chancellor, Prof. J. Bull
Registrar, Dr C. J. Sparrow
Deputy Vice-Chancellor (Secretariat), Dr R. M. Thorpe

PORTSMOUTH UNIVERSITY (1992)
(formerly Portsmouth Polytechnic)
University House, Winston Churchill Avenue, Portsmouth PO1 2UP
Tel 0705-827681
Full-time Students (1992–3), 10,298
Chancellor, The Lord Palumbo
Vice-Chancellor, N. Merritt
Academic Registrar, R. Moore
Secretary, D. Hunt

THE QUEEN'S UNIVERSITY OF BELFAST
(1908)
Belfast BT7 1NN
Tel 0232-245133
Full-time Students (1992–3), 9,875
Chancellor, Sir David Orr
President and Vice-Chancellor, G. Beveridge, ph.d., FRSE
Academic Secretary, Dr G. Baird

THE UNIVERSITY OF READING (1926)
Whiteknights, PO Box 217, Reading RG6 2AH
Tel 0734-875123
Full-time Students (1992–3), 8,816
Chancellor, The Lord Carrington, KG, GCMG, CH, MC, PC
 (1992)
Vice-Chancellor, Prof. E. Williams
Registrar, D. C. R. Frampton

THE ROBERT GORDON UNIVERSITY (1992)
(formerly Robert Gordon Institute of Technology)
Schoolhill, Aberdeen AB9 1FR
Tel 0224-262000
Full-time Students (1992–3), 5,239
Chancellor, Sir Bob Reid
Vice-Chancellor and Principal, Dr D. A. Kennedy
Academic Registrar, Mrs H. Douglas
Secretary, D. Caldwell

THE UNIVERSITY OF ST ANDREWS (1411)
College Gate, St Andrews KY16 9AJ
Tel 0334-76161
Full-time Students (1992–3), 4,461
Chancellor, Sir Kenneth Dover, D.Litt., FRSE, FBA (1981)
Vice-Chancellor, Prof. S. Arnott, ph.d., FRS, FRSE
Registrar, R. Douglas
Secretary of Court, D. J. Corner
Rector, N. Campbell (1991–4)

THE UNIVERSITY OF SALFORD (1967)
Salford M5 4WT
Tel 061-745 5000
Full-time Students (1992–3), 5,538
Chancellor, HRH The Duchess of York (1990)
Vice-Chancellor, Prof. T. M. Husband, ph.d, FEng.
Registrar (acting), M. D. Winton, ph.d.

THE UNIVERSITY OF SHEFFIELD (1905)
Western Bank, Sheffield S10 2TN
Tel 0742-768555
Full-time Students (1991–2), 10,723
Chancellor, The Lord Dainton, ph.d., SC.D., FRS (1979)
Vice-Chancellor, Prof. G. G. Roberts
Registrar and Secretary, Dr J. S. Padley

SHEFFIELD HALLAM UNIVERSITY
(formerly Sheffield Polytechnic)
Pond Street, Sheffield S1 1WB
Tel 0742-720911
Full-time Students (1992–3), 15,417
Chancellor, Sir Bryan Nicholson
Vice-Chancellor, J. Stoddart
Registrar, Ms J. Tory
Secretary, Ms S. Neocosmos

THE UNIVERSITY OF SOUTHAMPTON (1952)
Highfield, Southampton S09 5NH
Tel 0703-595000
Full-time Students (1992–3), 9,160

Chancellor, The Earl Jellicoe, KBE, DSO, MC, PC, FRS (1984)
Vice-Chancellor, Sir Gordon Higginson, ph.d, FEng.
Secretary and Registrar, J. F. D. Lauwerys
Academic Registrar, Miss A. E. Clarke

SOUTH BANK UNIVERSITY (1992)
(formerly South Bank Polytechnic)
103 Borough Road, London SE1 0AA
Tel 071-928 8989
Full-time Students (1991–2), 10,627
Chairman of the Board of Governors, C. McLaren
Vice-Chancellor, Prof. G. Bernbaum
Registrar, N. Andrew
Secretary, Ms L. Gander

STAFFORDSHIRE UNIVERSITY (1992)
(formerly Staffordshire Polytechnic)
College Road, Stoke-on-Trent ST4 2DE
Tel 0782-744531
Full-time Students (1992–3), 9,169
Chancellor, The Lord Ashley of Stoke, CH, PC
Vice-Chancellor, K. B. Thompson
Academic Registrar, Miss F. Francis
Secretary, K. Sproston

THE UNIVERSITY OF STIRLING (1967)
Stirling FK9 4LA
Tel 0786-73171
Full-time Students (1992–3), 4,510
Chancellor, The Lord Balfour of Burleigh, FRSE (1988)
Principal and Vice-Chancellor, Prof. A. J. Forty, CBE, ph.d.,
 D.SC., FRSE
Registrar, D. J. Farrington, D.phil.
Secretary, R. G. Bomont

THE UNIVERSITY OF STRATHCLYDE (1964)
16 Richmond Street, Glasgow G1 1XQ
Tel 041-552 4400
Full-time Students (1992–3), 12,246
Chancellor, The Lord Tombs, LL D, D.SC., FEng. (1990)
Principal and Vice-Chancellor, Prof. J. P. Arbuthnott
Secretary, P. W. A. West

THE UNIVERSITY OF SUNDERLAND (1992)
(formerly Sunderland Polytechnic)
Langham Tower, Ryhope Road, Sunderland SR2 7EE
Tel 091-515 2000
Full-time Students (1992–3), 10,060
Vice-Chancellor, A. Wright, ph.d.
Registrar, S. Porteous
Secretary, J. D. Pacey

THE UNIVERSITY OF SURREY (1966)
Guildford, Surrey GU2 5XH
Tel 0483-300800
Full-time Students (1992–3), 5,255
Chancellor, HRH The Duke of Kent, KG, GCMG, GCVO
 (1977)
Vice-Chancellor, Prof. A. Kelly, CBE, SC.D., FRS, FEng.
Secretary, H. W. B. Davies

THE UNIVERSITY OF SUSSEX (1961)
Falmer, Brighton BN1 9RH
Tel 0273-678416
Full-time Students (1992–3), 7,346
Chancellor, The Duke of Richmond and Gordon (1985)
Vice-Chancellor, Prof. G. Conway
Registrar and Secretary, G. Lockwood, D.phil.

THE UNIVERSITY OF TEESSIDE (1992)
(formerly Teesside Polytechnic)
Middlesbrough, Cleveland TS1 3BA
Tel 0642-218121
Full-time Students (1992–3), 6,995
Chancellor, Sir Leon Britten
Vice-Chancellor, Prof. D. Fraser
University Secretary, J. M. McClintock

THAMES VALLEY UNIVERSITY (1992)
(formerly Polytechnic of West London)
St Mary's Road, Ealing, London W5 5RF
Tel 081-579 5000
Full-time Students (1992–3), 10,393
Chancellor, P. Hamlyn
Vice-Chancellor, Dr M. Fitzgerald
Secretary, Ms M. Joyce

THE UNIVERSITY OF ULSTER (1984)
(Amalgamation of New University of Ulster and Ulster
Polytechnic)
Cromore Road, Coleraine BT52 1SA
Tel 0265-44141
Full-time Students (1992–3), 13,234
Chancellor, vacant
Vice-Chancellor, Prof. T. A. Smith
Academic Registrar, K. Millar, PH.D.
Secretary, J. A. Hunter

THE UNIVERSITY OF WALES (1893)
King Edward VII Avenue, Cathays Park, Cardiff CF1 3NS
Tel 0222-382656
Chancellor, HRH The Prince of Wales, KG, KT, GCB, PC
(1976)
Vice-Chancellor, Prof. K. O. Morgan, D.PHIL., FBA
Acting Registrar, J. D. Pritchard

COLLEGES

ST DAVID'S UNIVERSITY COLLEGE, Lampeter, Dyfed
SA48 7ED. Tel: 0570-422351. *Principal*, Prof. K. Robbins,
D.LITT., D.PHIL., FRSE (1992)
UNIVERSITY COLLEGE OF NORTH WALES, Bangor,
Gwynedd LL57 2DG. Tel: 0248-351151. *Principal*, Prof.
E. Sunderland, PH.D. (1984)
UNIVERSITY COLLEGE OF SWANSEA, Singleton Park,
Swansea SA2 8PP. Tel: 0792-205678. *Principal*, Prof.
B. L. Clarkson, PH.D. (1982)
UNIVERSITY COLLEGE OF WALES, Old College, King
Street, Aberystwyth, Dyfed SY23 2AX. Tel: 0970-623111.
Principal, Prof. K. O. Morgan, D.PHIL., FBA (1979)
UNIVERSITY OF WALES COLLEGE OF CARDIFF, PO Box
920, Cardiff CF1 3XP. Tel: 0222-874000. *Principal*,
E. B. Smith, PH.D., D.SC. (1993)
UNIVERSITY OF WALES COLLEGE OF MEDICINE, Heath
Park, Cardiff CF4 4XN. Tel: 0222-747747. *Provost*, Prof.
Sir Herbert Duthie, MD, CH.M., FRCS (1979)

THE UNIVERSITY OF WARWICK (1965)
Coventry CV4 7AL
Tel 0203-523523
Full-time Students (1992–3), 9,666
Chancellor, Sir Shridath Surendranath Ramphal, GCMG, QC
(1989)
Vice-Chancellor, Sir Brian Follett, FRS, D.SC.
Registrar, M. L. Shattock, OBE

THE UNIVERSITY OF WESTMINSTER (1992)
(formerly Polytechnic of Central London)
309 Regent Street, London W1R 8AL
Tel 071-911 5000
Full-time Students (1992–3), 6,000
Rector, Prof. T. E. Burlin
Deputy-Rector, Dr G. M. Copland
Registrar, Ms J. Hopkinson

THE UNIVERSITY OF THE WEST OF
ENGLAND, BRISTOL (BRISTOL UWE) (1992)
(formerly Bristol Polytechnic)
Coldharbour Lane, Frenchay, Bristol BS16 1QY
Tel 0272-656261
Full-time Students (1992–3), 10,625
Vice-Chancellor, A. C. Morris
Academic Registrar, Ms M. J. Carter
Secretary, W. Evans

THE UNIVERSITY OF WOLVERHAMPTON
(1992)
(formerly Wolverhampton Polytechnic)
Molineux Street, Wolverhampton WV1 1SB
Tel 0902-321000
Full-time Students (1992–3), 15,128
Chancellor, The Earl of Shrewsbury and Waterford
Vice-Chancellor/Director, Prof. M. J. Harrison

THE UNIVERSITY OF YORK (1963)
Heslington, York YO1 5DD
Tel 0904-430000
Full-time Students (1992–3), 5,026
Chancellor, Dame Janet Baker, DBE
Vice-Chancellor, Prof. R. U. Cooke
Registrar, D. J. Foster

CRANFIELD UNIVERSITY (1969)
Cranfield, Bedford MK43 0AL
Tel 0908-672974
Cranfield University (formerly the Cranfield Institute of
Technology) grants degrees in applied science, engineering,
technology and management.
Full-time Students (1992–3), 2,120
Chancellor, The Lord Kings Norton, PH.D., FEng. (1969)
Vice-Chancellor, Prof. F. R. Hartley, D.SC.
Secretary and Registrar, J. K. Pettifer

THE OPEN UNIVERSITY (1969)
Walton Hall, Milton Keynes MK7 6AA
Tel 0908-274066
Students and clients (1993), 200,000
Tuition by correspondence linked with special radio and
television programmes, video and audio cassettes, residential
schools and a locally-based tutorial and counselling service.
The University awards degrees of BA, B.PHIL., MA, MBA, M.SC.,
M.PHIL., PH.D., D.SC. and D.LITT. There are eight faculties: arts;
education; health, welfare and community education; man-
agement; mathematics and computing; science; social sci-
ences; technology; and a wide range of qualification courses
and study packs.
Chancellor, The Lord Briggs, FBA (1978)
Vice-Chancellor, Dr J. S. Daniel
Secretary, D. J. Clinch

THE ROYAL COLLEGE OF ART (1837)
Kensington Gore, London SW7 2EU
Tel 071-584 5020
Under royal charter (1967) the Royal College of Art grants
the degrees of Doctor, Doctor of Philosophy, Master of Arts,

Master of Design and Master of Design (Engineering) (RCA).
Students (1991–2), 700 (all postgraduate)
Provost, The Earl of Gowrie, PC (1986)
Registrar, A. Selby

SCOTTISH CENTRALLY-FUNDED COLLEGES

DUNCAN OF JORDANSTONE COLLEGE OF ART, Perth Road, Dundee DD1 4HT. Tel: 0382-23261. *Principal*, Dr C. Carter
DUNDEE INSTITUTE OF TECHNOLOGY, Bell Street, Dundee DD1 1HG. Tel: 0382-308012. *Principal*, Prof. B. King
EDINBURGH COLLEGE OF ART, Lauriston Place, Edinburgh EH3 9DF. Tel: 031-229 9311. *Principal*, Prof. A. J. Rowan, PH.D.
GLASGOW SCHOOL OF ART, 167 Renfrew Street, Glasgow G3 6RQ. Tel: 041-332 9797. *Director*, Prof. D. Cameron
QUEEN MARGARET COLLEGE, Clerwood Terrace, Edinburgh EH12 8TS. Tel: 031-317 3000. *Principal*, Prof. D. F. Leach
ROYAL SCOTTISH ACADEMY OF MUSIC AND DRAMA, 100 Renfrew Street, Glasgow G2 3DB. Tel: 041-332 4101. *Principal*, Dr P. Ledger, CBE, FRSE
SAC: THE NATIONAL COLLEGE FOR FOOD, LAND AND ENVIRONMENTAL STUDIES, Central Office, West Mains Road, Edinburgh EH9 3JG. Tel: 031-662 1303. Campuses at Aberdeen, Auchincruive, and Edinburgh. *Principal and Chief Executive*, Prof. P. C. Thomas
SCOTTISH COLLEGE OF TEXTILES, Netherdale, Galashiels, Selkirkshire TD1 3HF. Tel: 0896-3351. *Principal*, Prof. C. E. R. Maddox, PH.D.

COLLEGES

It is not possible to name here all the colleges offering courses of higher or further education. The list of English colleges that follows is confined to those in the Higher Education Funding Council for England sector; there are many more colleges in England providing higher education courses, some with HEFCFE funding.
The list of colleges in Wales, Scotland and Northern Ireland includes institutions providing at least one full-time course leading to a first degree granted by an accredited validating body. It does not include colleges forming part of a polytechnic or a university, nor does it include Scottish centrally-funded colleges.

ENGLAND

BATH COLLEGE OF HIGHER EDUCATION, Newton Park, Newton St Loe, Bath BA2 9BN. Tel: 0225-873701. *Director and Chief Executive*, B. L. Gomes da Costa
BISHOP GROSSETESTE COLLEGE, Lincoln LN1 3DY. Tel: 0522-527347. *Principal*, Prof. L. Marsh, OBE, D.Phil.
BOLTON INSTITUTE OF HIGHER EDUCATION, Deane Road, Bolton BL3 5AB. Tel: 0204-28851. *Principal*, R. Oxtoby, PH.D.
BRETTON HALL, West Bretton, Wakefield, W. Yorks. WF4 4LG. Tel: 0924-830261. *Principal*, Prof. G.H. Bell

BUCKINGHAMSHIRE COLLEGE, Queen Alexandra Road, High Wycombe, Bucks. HP11 2JZ. Tel: 0494-522141. *Director*, P. B. Mogford
CANTERBURY CHRIST CHURCH COLLEGE, North Holmes Road, Canterbury, Kent CT1 1QU. Tel: 0227-767700. *Principal*, M. H. A. Berry, TD
THE CENTRAL SCHOOL OF SPEECH AND DRAMA, Embassy Theatre, Eton Avenue, London NW3 3HY. Tel: 071-722 8183. *Principal*, R. S. Fowler
CHELTENHAM AND GLOUCESTER COLLEGE OF HIGHER EDUCATION, PO Box 220, The Park, Cheltenham, Glos. GL50 2QF. Tel: 0242-532700. *Director*, Miss J. O. Trotter, OBE
CHESTER COLLEGE, Cheyney Road, Chester CH1 4BJ. Tel: 0244-375444. *Principal*, Revd E. V. Binks
COLLEGE OF ST MARK AND ST JOHN, Derriford Road, Plymouth PL6 8BH. Tel: 0752-761110. *Principal*, J. E. Anderson
DARTINGTON COLLEGE OF ARTS, Totnes, Devon TQ9 6EJ. Tel: 0803-862224. *Principal*, Prof. K. Thompson
EDGE HILL COLLEGE OF HIGHER EDUCATION, St Helens Road, Ormskirk, Lancs. L39 4QP. Tel: 0695-575171. *Director*, Prof. R. Gee
FALMOUTH SCHOOL OF ART AND DESIGN, Woodlane, Falmouth, Cornwall TR11 4RA. Tel: 0326-211077. *Principal*, Prof. A. G. Livingston
HARPER ADAMS AGRICULTURAL COLLEGE, Newport, Shropshire TF10 8NB. Tel: 0952-820280. *Principal*, A. G. Harris, OBE
HOMERTON COLLEGE, Cambridge CB2 2PH. Tel: 0223-411141. *Principal*, Mrs K. Pretty, PH.D.
INSTITUTE OF ADVANCED NURSING, Royal College of Nursing, 20 Cavendish Square, London W1M 0AB. Tel: 071-355 1396. *Principal*, J. C. A. Wells
KENT INSTITUTE OF ART AND DESIGN, Oakwood Park, Oakwood Road, Maidstone ME16 8AG (*also* New Dover Road, Canterbury CT1 3AN; and Fort Pitt, Rochester ME1 1DZ). Tel: 0622-757286. *Director*, P. I. Williams
KING ALFRED'S COLLEGE, Winchester SO22 4NR. Tel: 0962-841515. *Principal*, Prof. J. P. Dickinson
LIVERPOOL INSTITUTE OF HIGHER EDUCATION, PO Box 6, Stand Park Road, Liverpool L16 9JD. Tel: 051-737 3000. *Rector*, J. Burke, OBE, PH.D.
THE LONDON INSTITUTE, 65 Davies Street, London W1Y 2AA. *Rector*, Prof. J. C. McKenzie
Comprising:
Camberwell College of Arts, Peckham Road, London SE5 8UF
Central St Martins College of Art and Design, Southampton Row, London WC1B 4AP
Chelsea College of Art and Design, Manresa Road, London SW3 6LS
London College of Fashion, 20 John Prince's Street, London W1M 9HE
London College of Printing and Distributive Trades, Elephant and Castle, London SE1 6SB
LOUGHBOROUGH COLLEGE OF ART AND DESIGN, Radmoor, Loughborough, Leics. LE11 3BT. Tel: 0509-261515. *Principal*, I. Pugh
LSU COLLEGE OF HIGHER EDUCATION, The Avenue, Southampton SO9 5HB. Tel: 0703-228761. *Principal*, Dr A. C. Chitnis
NENE COLLEGE, Park Campus, Boughton Green Road, Northampton NN2 7AL. Tel: 0604-735500. *Director*, S. M. Gaskell, PH.D.
NEWMAN COLLEGE, Genners Lane, Bartley Green, Birmingham B32 3NT. Tel: 021-476 1181. *Principal*, Joan S. Cuming, PH.D.

RAVENSBOURNE COLLEGE OF DESIGN AND
COMMUNICATION, Walden Road, Chislehurst, Kent
BR7 5SN. Tel: 081-468 7071. *Director,* N. J. Frewing
ROEHAMPTON INSTITUTE, Senate House, Roehampton
Lane, London SW15 5PU. Comprises Digby Stuart
College, Froebel Institute College, Southlands College
and Whitelands College. Tel: 081-392 3000. *Rector,*
S. C. Holt, PH.D
ROSE BRUFORD COLLEGE OF SPEECH AND DRAMA,
Lamorbey Park, Burnt Oak Lane, Sidcup, Kent
DA15 9DF. Tel: 081-300 3024. *Principal,* R. Ely
ROYAL ACADEMY OF MUSIC, Marylebone Road, London
NW1 5HT. Tel: 071-935 5461. *Principal,* L. Harrell
ROYAL COLLEGE OF MUSIC, Prince Consort Road,
London SW7 2BS. Tel: 071-589 3643. *Director,*
J. Ritterman, PH.D.
ROYAL NORTHERN COLLEGE OF MUSIC, 124 Oxford
Road, Manchester M13 9RD. Tel: 061-273 6283.
Principal, Sir John Manduell, CBE
S. MARTIN'S COLLEGE, Lancaster LA1 3JD. Tel: 0524-
63446. *Principal,* D. Edynbry, PH.D.
ST MARY'S COLLEGE, Strawberry Hill, Twickenham
TW1 4SX. Tel: 081-892 0051. *Principal,* Dr A. Naylor
SALFORD COLLEGE OF TECHNOLOGY, Frederick Road,
Salford M6 6PU. Tel: 061-736 6541. *Principal,* J. Squires
SOUTHAMPTON INSTITUTE OF HIGHER EDUCATION,
East Park Terrace, Southampton SO9 4WW. Tel: 0703-
229381. *Director,* D. G. Leyland
TRINITY AND ALL SAINTS' COLLEGE, Brownberrie Lane,
Horsforth, Leeds LS18 5HD. Tel: 0532-584341. *Principal,*
Dr G. L. Turnbull
TRINITY COLLEGE OF MUSIC, 11–13 Mandeville Place,
London WIM 6AQ. Tel: 071-935 5773. *Principal,* P. Jones,
CBE
UNIVERSITY COLLEGE OF RIPON AND YORK ST JOHN,
Lord Mayor's Walk, York YO3 7EX. Tel: 0904-656771.
Principal, Prof. G. P. McGregor
UNIVERSITY COLLEGE SCARBOROUGH, THE NORTH
RIDING COLLEGE, Filey Road, Scarborough,
N. Yorks. YO11 3AZ. Tel: 0723-362392. *Principal,*
R. A. Withers, PH.D.
WESTHILL COLLEGE, Hamilton Building, Weoley Park
Road, Selly Oak, Birmingham B29 6LL. Tel: 021-472
7245. *Principal,* Dr J. G. Priestley
WEST LONDON INSTITUTE OF HIGHER EDUCATION,
Lancaster House, Borough Road, Isleworth,
Middx. TW7 5DU. Tel: 081-568 8741/891 0121. *Principal,*
Prof. J. E. Kane, OBE, PH.D.
WESTMINSTER COLLEGE, Oxford OX2 9AT. Tel: 0865-
247644. *Principal,* Revd Dr K. B. Wilson, OBE
WEST SURREY COLLEGE OF ART AND DESIGN, Falkner
Road, The Hart, Farnham, Surrey GU9 7DS. Tel: 0252-
722441. *Director,* N. J. Taylor
WEST SUSSEX INSTITUTE OF HIGHER EDUCATION,
College Lane, Chichester, West Sussex PO19 4PE. Tel:
0243-787911. *Director,* Dr J. F. Wyatt
WINCHESTER SCHOOL OF ART, Park Avenue,
Winchester, Hants. SO23 8DL. Tel: 0962-842500.
Principal, M. Sadler-Forster
WORCESTER COLLEGE OF HIGHER EDUCATION,
Henwick Grove, Worcester WR2 6AJ. Tel: 0905-748080.
Principal, Ms D. Urwin

WALES

BANGOR NORMAL COLLEGE OF HIGHER EDUCATION,
Bangor, Gwynedd LL57 2PX. Tel: 0248-370171. *Principal,*
R. Williams

CARDIFF INSTITUTE OF HIGHER EDUCATION, Western
Avenue, Llandaff, Cardiff CF5 2YB. Tel: 0222-551111.
Director, J. D. Winslow
GWENT COLLEGE OF HIGHER EDUCATION, College
Crescent, Caerleon, Newport, Gwent NP6 1XJ. Tel: 0633-
430088. *Principal,* Dr K. J. Overshott
INSTITUTE OF HEALTH CARE STUDIES, University
Hospital of Wales, Heath Park, Cardiff CF4 4XW. TEL:
0222-747747. *Manager,* J. Connelly
THE NORTH EAST WALES INSTITUTE (NEWI Plas
Coch), Mold Road, Wrexham, Clwyd LL11 2AW. Tel:
0978-290666. Also NEWI Cartrefle at Cefn Road,
Wrexham LL13 9NL, NEWI College of Art and Design
Technology at Regent Street, Wrexham LL11 and NEWI
Deeside at Kelsterton Road, Connah's Quay, Deeside
CH5 4BR. *Principal,* Prof. J. O. Williams, PH.D, D.SC.
SWANSEA INSTITUTE OF HIGHER EDUCATION, Townhill
Road, Swansea SA2 OUT. Tel: 0792-203482. *Principal,*
Prof. G. Stockdale
TRINITY COLLEGE, Carmarthen, Dyfed, SA31 3EP. Tel:
0267-237971. *Principal,* D. C. Jones-Davies, OBE
WELSH AGRICULTURAL COLLEGE, Llanbadarn Fawr,
Aberystwyth, Dyfed SY23 3AL. Tel: 0970-624471.
Principal, Dr J. H. Harries
WELSH COLLEGE OF MUSIC AND DRAMA, Castle
Grounds, Cathays Park, Cardiff CF1 3ER. Tel: 0222-
342854. *Principal,* E. Fivet

SCOTLAND

BELL COLLEGE OF TECHNOLOGY, Almada Street,
Hamilton, Lanarkshire ML3 OJB. Tel: 0698-283100.
Principal, J. Reid
MORAY HOUSE COLLEGE OF EDUCATION, Holyrood
Campus, Holyrood Road, Edinburgh EH8 8AQ. Tel: 031-
556 8455. *Principal,* Prof. G. Kirk
NORTHERN COLLEGE OF EDUCATION, Hilton Place,
Aberdeen AB9 1FA. Tel: 0224-283500; Gardyne Road,
Dundee DD5 1NY. Tel: 0382-464000. *Principal,*
D. A. Adams
ST ANDREW'S COLLEGE OF EDUCATION, Duntocher
Road, Bearsden, Glasgow G61 4QA. Tel: 041-943 1424.
Principal, B. J. McGettrick

NORTHERN IRELAND

ST MARY'S COLLEGE, 191 Falls Road, Belfast BT12 6FE.
Tel: 0232-327678. *Principal,* Revd M. O'Callaghan
STRANMILLIS COLLEGE, Stranmillis Road, Belfast
BT9 5DY. Tel: 0232-381271. *Principal,* Dr R. McMinn

ADULT AND CONTINUING EDUCATION

NATIONAL INSTITUTE OF ADULT CONTINUING
EDUCATION, 19B De Montfort Street, Leicester LE1 7GE.
Tel: 0533-551451. *Director,* A. Tuckett
NIACE CYMRU, 245 Western Avenue, Cardiff CF5 2YX.
Tel: 0222-571201. *National Officer for Wales,* Ms
A. Poole
NORTHERN IRELAND COUNCIL FOR ADULT
EDUCATION, c/o Western Education and Library Board,
1 Hospital Road, Omagh, Co. Tyrone BT79 OAW. Tel:
0662-240240. *Chairman,* M. H. F. Murphy, OBE
THE NEW UNIVERSITIES AND POLYTECHNICS
ASSOCIATION FOR CONTINUING EDUCATION,
Educational Development Officer, Polytechnic of Wales,
Pontypridd, Mid Glam. CF37 1DL. Tel: 0443-480480.
Secretary, P. Race

THE RESIDENTIAL COLLEGES COMMITTEE, c/o Ruskin College, Oxford OX1 2HE. Tel: 0865-56360. *Awards Officer*, Mrs F. A. Bagchi
SCOTTISH COMMUNITY EDUCATION COUNCIL, Rosebery House, 9 Haymarket Terrace, Edinburgh EH12 5EZ. Tel: 031-313 2488. *Executive Director*, C. McConnell
THE UNIVERSITIES ASSOCIATION FOR CONTINUING EDUCATION, Department of Continuing Education, Westwood Site, The University of Warwick, Coventry CV4 7AL. Tel: 0203-523835/27. *Hon. Secretary*, Prof. C. Duke, PH.D.
THE WORKER'S EDUCATIONAL ASSOCIATION, Temple House, 17 Victoria Park Square, London E2 9PB. Tel: 081-983 1515. *General Secretary*, R. Lochrie

LONG-TERM RESIDENTIAL COLLEGES FOR ADULT EDUCATION
COLEG HARLECH, Harlech, Gwynedd LL46 2PU. Tel: 0766-780363. *Warden*, J. W. England
CO-OPERATIVE COLLEGE, Stanford Hall, Loughborough, Leics. LE12 5QR. Tel: 0509-852333. *Principal*, Dr R. Houlton
FIRCROFT COLLEGE, 1018 Bristol Road, Selly Oak, Birmingham B29 6LH. Tel: 021-472 0116. *Principal*, K. Jackson
HILLCROFT COLLEGE, South Bank, Surbiton, Surrey KT6 6DF. Tel: 081-399 2688. For women only. *Principal*, Ms E. Aird
NEWBATTLE ABBEY COLLEGE, Dalkeith, Midlothian EH22 3LL. Tel: 031-663 1921. *Principal*, W. M. Conboy
NORTHERN COLLEGE, Wentworth Castle, Stainborough, Barnsley, S. Yorks. S75 3ET. Tel: 0226-285426. *Principal*, R. H. Fryer
PLATER COLLEGE, Pullens Lane, Oxford OX3 ODT. Tel: 0865-741676. *Principal*, M. Blades
RUSKIN COLLEGE, Walton Street, Oxford OX1 2HE. Tel: 0865-54331. *Principal*, S. Yeo, D.Phil.

Professional Education

Excluding postgraduate study

The organizations listed below are those which, by providing specialist training or conducting examinations, control entry into a profession, or organizations responsible for maintaining a register of those with professional qualifications in their sector.

Many professions now have a largely graduate entry, and possession of a first degree can exempt entrants from certain of the professional examinations. Enquiries about obtaining professional qualifications should be made to the relevant professional organization(s). Details of higher education providers of first degrees may be found in *University and College Entrance*.

ACCOUNTANCY

The main bodies granting membership on examination after a period of practical work are:
INSTITUTE OF CHARTERED ACCOUNTANTS IN ENGLAND AND WALES, Chartered Accountants' Hall, PO Box 433, Moorgate Place, London EC2P 2BJ. Tel: 071-920 8100. *Secretary and Chief Executive*, A. J. Colquhoun
INSTITUTE OF CHARTERED ACCOUNTANTS OF SCOTLAND, 27 Queen Street, Edinburgh EH2 1LA. Tel: 031-479 4809. *Chief Executive*, P. W. Johnston

CHARTERED ASSOCIATION OF CERTIFIED ACCOUNTANTS, 29 Lincoln's Inn Fields, London WC2A 3EE. Tel: 071-242 6855. *Secretary*, Mrs A. L. Rose
CHARTERED INSTITUTE OF MANAGEMENT ACCOUNTANTS, 63 Portland Place, London W1N 4AB. Tel: 071-637 2311. *Secretary*, Sir George Vallings, KCB
CHARTERED INSTITUTE OF PUBLIC FINANCE AND ACCOUNTANCY, 3 Robert Street, London WC2N 6BH. Tel: 071-895 8823. *Secretary*, N. P. Hepworth, OBE

ACTUARIAL SCIENCE

Two professional organizations grant qualifications after examination:
INSTITUTE OF ACTUARIES, Staple Inn Hall, High Holborn, London WC1V 7QJ. Tel: 071-242 0106. *Secretary-General*, A. G. Tait. Enquiries to Actuarial Education Service, Napier House, 4 Worcester Street, Oxford OX1 2AW. Tel: 0865-794144
FACULTY OF ACTUARIES IN SCOTLAND, 23 St Andrew Square, Edinburgh EH2 1AQ. Tel: 031-557 1575. *Secretary*, W. W. Mair

ARCHITECTURE

The Education and Professional Development Committee of the Royal Institute of British Architects sets standards and guides the whole system of architectural education throughout the United Kingdom. Courses at Schools recognized by the RIBA exempt students from the RIBA's own examinations.
THE ROYAL INSTITUTE OF BRITISH ARCHITECTS, 66 Portland Place, London W1N 4AD. Tel: 071-580 5533. *President*, Dr F. Duffy; *Director-General*, The Lord Rodgers of Quarry Bank, PC
Schools of architecture outside the universities include:
THE ARCHITECTURAL ASSOCIATION, 34–36 Bedford Square, London WC1B 3ES. *Secretary*, E. A. Le Maistre

BANKING

Professional organizations granting qualifications after examination are:
CHARTERED INSTITUTE OF BANKERS, 10 Lombard Street, London EC3V 9AS. Tel: 071-623 3531. *Secretary-General*, E. Glover
CHARTERED INSTITUTE OF BANKERS IN SCOTLAND, 19 Rutland Square, Edinburgh EH1 2DE. Tel: 031-229 9869. *Chief Executive*, Dr C. W. Munn

BIOLOGY, CHEMISTRY, PHYSICS

Professional qualifications are awarded by:
INSTITUTE OF BIOLOGY, 20–22 Queensberry Place, London SW7 2DZ. Tel: 071-581 8333. *President*, Prof. C. R. W. Spedding, CBE; *General Secretary*, Dr R. H. Priestley
ROYAL SOCIETY OF CHEMISTRY, Burlington House, Piccadilly, London W1V OBN. Tel: 071-437 8656. *President*, Prof. C. W. Rees, FRS; *Secretary-General*, Dr T. Inch

INSTITUTE OF PHYSICS, 47 Belgrave Square, London SW1X 8QX. Tel: 071-235 6111. *Chief Executive,* Dr A. Jones

BUILDING

Examinations are conducted by:
CHARTERED INSTITUTE OF BUILDING, Englemere, King's Ride, Ascot, Berks. SL5 8BJ. Tel: 0344-23355. *Chief Executive,* K. Banbury
INSTITUTE OF BUILDING CONTROL, 21 High Street, Ewell, Epsom, Surrey KT17 1SB. Tel: 081-393 6860. *Director,* Ms R. Raywood
INSTITUTE OF CLERKS OF WORKS OF GREAT BRITAIN, 41 The Mall, London W5 3TJ. Tel: 081-579 2917/8. *Secretary,* A. P. Macnamara

BUSINESS, MANAGEMENT AND ADMINISTRATION

Professional bodies conducting training and/or examinations in business, administration, management or commerce include:
AMETS (ASSOCIATION FOR MANAGEMENT EDUCATION AND TRAINING IN SCOTLAND), c/o University of Stirling, Stirling FK9 4LA. Tel: 0786-450906. *Vice-Chairman,* M. Makower
CAM FOUNDATION (COMMUNICATIONS, ADVERTISING AND MARKETING EDUCATION FOUNDATION), Abford House, 15 Wilton Road, London SW1V 1NJ. Tel: 071-828 7506. *Registrar,* Ms K. Hutchinson
CHARTERED INSTITUTE OF MARKETING, Moor Hall, Cookham, Maidenhead, Berks. SL6 9QH. Tel: 0628-524922. *Director-General,* J. McAinsh
CHARTERED INSTITUTE OF PURCHASING AND SUPPLY, Easton House, Easton on the Hill, Stamford, Lincs. PE9 3NZ. Tel: 0780-56777. *Director-General,* P. Thomson
CHARTERED INSTITUTE OF TRANSPORT, 80 Portland Place, London W1N 4DP. *Director-General,* R. P. Botwood
FACULTY OF SECRETARIES AND ADMINISTRATORS, PO Box 7, Godalming, Surrey GU7 1PR. Tel: 0483-425144. *Secretary,* Mrs D. M. Rummery
INSTITUTE OF ADMINISTRATIVE MANAGEMENT, 40 Chatsworth Parade, Petts Wood, Orpington, Kent BR5 1RW. Tel: 0689-875555. *Chief Executive,* Ms C. Hayhurst
INSTITUTE OF CHARTERED SECRETARIES AND ADMINISTRATORS, 16 Park Crescent, London W1N 4AH. Tel: 071-580 4741. *Secretary,* M. J. Ainsworth
INSTITUTE OF CHARTERED SHIPBROKERS, 3 Gracechurch Street, London EC3V 0AT. Tel: 071-626 3058. *Secretary,* J. H. Parker
INSTITUTE OF EXPORT, Export House, 64 Clifton Street, London EC2A 4HB. Tel: 071-247 9812. *Director-General,* I. J. Campbell
INSTITUTE OF HEALTH SERVICES MANAGEMENT, 75 Portland Place, London W1N 4AN. Tel: 071-580 5041. *Director,* R. Rowden
INSTITUTE OF HOUSING, Octavia House, Westwood Business Park, Westwood Way, Coventry CV4 8JP. Tel: 0203-694433. *Chief Executive,* P. McGurk
INSTITUTION OF MANAGEMENT, Management House, Cottingham Road, Corby, Northants. NN17 1TT. Tel: 0536-204222. *Chief Executive,* R. Young

INSTITUTE OF PERSONNEL MANAGEMENT, IPM House, Camp Road, London SW19 4UX. Tel: 081-946 9100. *Director-General,* G. Armstrong
INSTITUTE OF PRACTITIONERS IN ADVERTISING, 44 Belgrave Square, London SW1X 8QS. Tel: 071-235 7020. *Secretary,* J. Raad
HENLEY MANAGEMENT COLLEGE, Greenlands, Henley-on-Thames, Oxon. RG9 3AU. Tel: 0491-571454. *Principal,* Prof. R. Wild
LONDON BUSINESS SCHOOL, Sussex Place, Regent's Park, London NW1 4SA. Tel: 071-262 5050. *Principal,* Prof. G. Bain, PH.D.
MANCHESTER BUSINESS SCHOOL, Booth Street West, Manchester M15 6PB. Tel: 061-275 6333. *Director,* Prof. A. Cockerill
LONDON CHAMBER OF COMMERCE AND INDUSTRY EXAMINATIONS BOARD, Marlowe House, Station Road, Sidcup, Kent DA15 7BJ. Tel: 081-302 0261. *Chief Executive,* L. Swords

DANCE

ROYAL ACADEMY OF DANCING, 36 Battersea Square, London SW11 3RA. Tel: 071-223 0091. *Chief Executive,* D. Watchman; *Artistic Director,* J. Byrne
ROYAL BALLET SCHOOL, 155 Talgarth Road, London W14 9DE. Tel: 081-748 6335. Also at White Lodge, Richmond Park, Surrey TW10 5HR. Tel: 081-876 5547. *Director,* Dame Merle Park, DBE
IMPERIAL SOCIETY OF TEACHERS OF DANCING, Euston Hall, Birkenhead Street, London WC1H 8BE. Tel: 071-837 9967. *General Secretary,* M. J. Browne

DEFENCE

ROYAL NAVAL COLLEGES
ROYAL NAVAL COLLEGE, Greenwich, London SE10 9NN. Tel: 081-858 2154. *Admiral President,* Vice-Adm. Sir Michael Layard, KCB, CBE; *Dean of the College,* Prof. D. C. C. Gibbs
BRITANNIA ROYAL NAVAL COLLEGE, Dartmouth, Devon TQ6 0HJ. Tel: 0803-832141. Provides general and academic officer training. *Captain,* Capt. S. Moore
ROYAL NAVAL ENGINEERING COLLEGE, Manadon, Plymouth PL5 3AQ. Provides BA, B.Eng., M.Sc. and specialist training in naval engineering. Students are selected uniformed officers of the Royal Navy, Commonwealth and foreign navies, and civilians. *Captain,* Capt. D. G. Littlejohns, CBE; *Dean,* Capt. B. M. Leavey; *Executive Officer,* Cdr. S. P. C. Westwood

MILITARY COLLEGES
STAFF COLLEGE, Camberley, Surrey GU15 4NP. Tel: 0276-412691. *Commandant,* Maj.-Gen. C. B. Q. Wallace, OBE
ROYAL MILITARY ACADEMY SANDHURST, Camberley, Surrey GU15 4PQ. Tel: 0276-63344. *Commandant,* Maj.-Gen. T. P. Toyne Sewell
ROYAL MILITARY COLLEGE OF SCIENCE, Shrivenham, Swindon, Wilts. SN6 8LA. Tel: 0793-785434. Students from UK and overseas study from degree to postgraduate levels in management, science and technology. There is an increasing range of research and consultancy activity as the College is now a Faculty of Cranfield University.

Commandant, Maj.-Gen. E. F. B. Burton, OBE; *Principal*, Prof. A. C. Baynham, PH.D.
DIRECTORATE OF EDUCATIONAL AND TRAINING SERVICES, Director-General Adjutant General's Corp, Worthydown, Winchester, Hants SO21 2RG. Tel: 0962-887672/3. *Director*, Brig. J. M. Macfarlane

ROYAL AIR FORCE COLLEGES
ROYAL AIR FORCE STAFF COLLEGE, Bracknell, Berks. RG12 3DD. Prepares selected senior officers for high-grade command and staff appointments. Two-thirds of the students are RAF officers; the others are officers from the other UK Services and overseas air forces. *Air Officer Commanding and Commandant*, Air Vice-Marshal M. P. Donaldson
ROYAL AIR FORCE COLLEGE, Cranwell, Sleaford, Lincs. NG34 8HB. Provides initial officer training for officers of the RAF, WRAF and PMRAFNS. The initial specialist training for officers of the Engineer and Supply Branches, advanced specialist training for officers of the General Duties, Engineer and Supply Branches and basic flying training for pilots of the General Duties Branch are also conducted at Cranwell. *Air Officer Commanding and Commandant*, Air Vice-Marshal D. Cousins, CB, AFC
ROYAL AIR FORCE SCHOOL OF EDUCATION AND TRAINING SUPPORT, RAF Newton, Nottingham NG13 8HL. Tel: 0949-20771. *Commanding Officer*, Gp Capt J. Rennie

DENTISTRY

To be entitled to be registered in the Dentists Register, a person must hold the degree or diploma in dental surgery of a university in the United Kingdom or the diploma of any of the licensing authorities (The Royal College of Surgeons of England and of Edinburgh, and the Royal College of Physicians and Surgeons of Glasgow). Nationals of an EC member state holding an appropriate European diploma, and holders of certain overseas diplomas, may also be registered. The Dentists Register is maintained by:
THE GENERAL DENTAL COUNCIL, 37 Wimpole Street, London WIM 8DQ. Tel: 071-486 2171. *Registrar*, N. T. Davies, MBE

DIETETICS
See also FOOD AND NUTRITION SCIENCE

The professional association is The British Dietetic Association. Full membership is open to dietitians holding a recognized qualification, who may also become State Registered Dietitians through the Council for Professions Supplementary to Medicine (*see* Medicine)
THE BRITISH DIETETIC ASSOCIATION, 7th Floor, Elizabeth House, 22 Suffolk Street, Queensway, Birmingham BI ILS. Tel: 021-643 5483

DRAMA

The national validating body for courses providing training in drama for the professional theatre is the National Council for Drama Training. It currently has accredited courses at the following: Academy of Live and Recorded Arts; Arts Educational Schools; Birmingham School of Speech Training & Dramatic Art; Bristol Old Vic Theatre School; Central School of Speech and Drama; Drama Centre, London; Drama Studio; Guildford School of Acting; Guildhall School of Music and Drama; London Academy of Music and Dramatic Art; Manchester Polytechnic School of Theatre; Mountview Theatre School; Rose Bruford College of Speech and Drama; Royal Academy of Dramatic Art; Royal Scottish Academy of Music and Drama; Webber Douglas Academy of Dramatic Art; Welsh College of Music and Drama.
The accreditation of a course in a school does not necessarily imply that other courses of different type or duration in the same school are also accredited
THE NATIONAL COUNCIL FOR DRAMA TRAINING, 5 Tavistock Place, London WCIH 9SS. *Secretary*, Miss E. M. McKay

ENGINEERING

The Engineering Council supervises the engineering profession through the 42 nominated engineering institutions who are represented on its Board for Engineers' Registration. Working with and through the institutions, the Council sets the standards for the registration of individuals, and also the accreditation for academic courses in universities and colleges and the practical training in industry.
THE ENGINEERING COUNCIL, 10 Maltravers Street, London WC2R 3ER. Tel: 071-240 7891. *Secretary*, L. Chelton
The principal qualifying bodies are:
BRITISH COMPUTER SOCIETY, PO Box 1454, Station Road, Swindon SNI ITG. Tel: 0793 480269. *Chief Executive*, G. Kirkpatrick
CHARTERED INSTITUTION OF BUILDING SERVICES ENGINEERS, Delta House, 222 Balham High Road, London SW12 9BS. Tel: 081-675 5211. *Secretary*, A. V. Ramsay
INSTITUTION OF CHEMICAL ENGINEERS, The Davis Building, 165–171 Railway Terrace, Rugby, Warks. CV21 3HQ. Tel: 0788-578214. *General Secretary*, Dr T. J. Evans
INSTITUTION OF CIVIL ENGINEERS, Great George Street, London SWIP 3AA. Tel: 071-222 7722. *Secretary*, R. Dobson
INSTITUTION OF ELECTRICAL ENGINEERS, Savoy Place, London WC2R OBL. Tel: 071-240 1871. *Secretary*, Dr J. C. Williams, FEng.
INSTITUTE OF ENERGY, 18 Devonshire Street, London WIN 2AU. Tel: 071-580 7124. *Secretary*, J. E. H. Leach
INSTITUTE OF GAS ENGINEERS, 17 Grosvenor Crescent, London SWIX 7ES. Tel: 071-245 9811. *Secretary*, D. J. Chapman
INSTITUTE OF MARINE ENGINEERS, The Memorial Building, 76 Mark Lane, London EC3R 7JN. Tel: 071-481 8493. *Secretary*, J. E. Sloggett
INSTITUTE OF MATERIALS, 1 Carlton House Terrace, London SWIY 5DB. Tel: 071-839 4071. *Secretary*, Dr J. A. Catterall
INSTITUTE OF MEASUREMENT AND CONTROL, 87 Gower Street, London WCIE 6AA. Tel: 071-387 4949. *Secretary*, M. J. Yates
INSTITUTION OF MECHANICAL ENGINEERS, 1 Birdcage Walk, London SWIH 9JJ. Tel: 071-222 7899. *Director-General*, Dr R. Pike
INSTITUTION OF MINING ENGINEERS, Danum House, 6A South Parade, Doncaster DNI 2DY. Tel: 0302-320486. *Secretary*, W. J. W. Bourne, OBE

INSTITUTION OF MINING AND METALLURGY, 44 Portland Place, London WIN 4BR. Tel: 071-580 3802. *Secretary*, M. J. Jones

INSTITUTION OF STRUCTURAL ENGINEERS, 11 Upper Belgrave Street, London SWIX 8BH. Tel: 071-235 4535. *Secretary*, D. J. Clark

ROYAL AERONAUTICAL SOCIETY, 4 Hamilton Place, London WIV 0BQ. Tel: 071-499 3515. *Director*, R. J. Kennett

ROYAL INSTITUTION OF NAVAL ARCHITECTS, 10 Upper Belgrave Street, London SWIX 8BQ. Tel: 071-235 4622. *Secretary*, J. Rosewarn

FOOD AND NUTRITION SCIENCE

See also DIETETICS

Scientific and professional bodies include:

INSTITUTE OF FOOD SCIENCE & TECHNOLOGY, 5 Cambridge Court, 210 Shepherd's Bush Road, London W6 7NL. Tel: 071-603 6316. *Executive Secretary*, Ms H. G. Wild

NUTRITION SOCIETY, 10 Cambridge Court, 210 Shepherds Bush Road, London W6 7NJ. Tel: 071-602 0228. *Hon. Secretary*, Dr R. F. Grimble

FORESTRY AND TIMBER STUDIES

Professional organizations include:

ROYAL FORESTRY SOCIETY OF ENGLAND, WALES AND NORTHERN IRELAND, 102 High Street, Tring, Herts., HP23 4AF. Tel: 0442-822028. *Director*, J. E. Jackson, ph.D.

ROYAL SCOTTISH FORESTRY SOCIETY, Camsie House, Charlestown, Dunfermline, Fife KY11 3EE. Tel: 0383-873014. *Director*, M. Osborne

INSTITUTE OF CHARTERED FORESTERS, 7A St Colme Street, Edinburgh EH3 6AA. Tel: 031-225 2705. *Secretary*, Mrs M. W. Dick

COMMONWEALTH FORESTRY ASSOCIATION, c/o Oxford Forestry Institute, South Parks Road, Oxford OX1 3RB. Tel: 0865-275072. *Chairman*, P. J. Wood

FUEL AND ENERGY SCIENCE

The principal professional bodies are:

INSTITUTE OF ENERGY, 18 Devonshire Street, London WIN 2AU. Tel: 071-580 7124. *Secretary*, J. Leach

INSTITUTION OF GAS ENGINEERS, 17 Grosvenor Crescent, London SWIX 7ES. Tel: 071-245 9811. *Secretary*, D. J. Chapman

INSTITUTE OF PETROLEUM, 61 New Cavendish Street, London WIM 8AR. Tel: 071-636 1004. *Director-General*, I. Ward

HOTELKEEPING, CATERING AND INSTITUTIONAL MANAGEMENT

See also DIETETICS, and FOOD and NUTRITION SCIENCE

The qualifying professional body in the subjects is:

HOTEL CATERING AND INSTITUTIONAL MANAGEMENT ASSOCIATION, 191 Trinity Road, London SW17 7HN. Tel: 081-672 4251. *Chief Executive*, J. Logie

INDUSTRIAL AND VOCATIONAL TRAINING

There are 120 Industry Training Organizations, employer-led independent organizations whose role includes setting the standards of National and Scottish Vocational Qualifications.

NATIONAL COUNCIL OF INDUSTRY TRAINING ORGANIZATIONS, 5 George Lane, Royston, Herts. SG8 9AR. Tel: 0763-247285. *Chairman*, P. Morley; *Administrator*, Mrs C. Armstrong

INSURANCE

Organizations conducting examinations and awarding diplomas are:

ASSOCIATION OF AVERAGE ADJUSTERS, HQS *Wellington*, Temple Stairs, Victoria Embankment, London WC2R 2PN. Tel: 071-240 5516. *Secretary*, Mrs P. J. Albano

CHARTERED INSURANCE INSTITUTE, 20 Aldermanbury, London EC2V 7HY. Tel: 071-606 3835. *Director-General*, Dr D. E. Bland

CHARTERED INSTITUTE OF LOSS ADJUSTERS, Manfield House, 376 The Strand, London WC2R 0LR. Tel: 071-240 1496. *Director*, A. F. Clack

JOURNALISM

Courses for trainee newspaper journalists are available at 20 centres. One-year full-time courses are available for selected students. Particulars of all these courses are available from the National Council for the Training of Journalists. Short courses for experienced journalists are also arranged by the National Council.

For periodical journalists, there are six centres running courses approved by the Periodicals Training Council.

THE NATIONAL COUNCIL FOR TRAINING OF JOURNALISTS, Latton Bush Centre, Southern Way, Harlow, Essex CM18 7BL. Tel: 0279-430009. *Chief Executive*, K. Hall

THE PERIODICALS TRAINING COUNCIL, Imperial House, 15–19 Kingsway, London WC2B 6UN. Tel: 071-836 8798. *Executive Director*, D. Longbottom, MBE

LAW

THE BAR

Admission to the Bar of England and Wales is controlled by the Inns of Court and admission to the Bar of Northern Ireland by the Honorable Society of the Inn of Court of Northern Ireland, which are the governing bodies of barristers in England and Wales and Northern Ireland respectively. Admission as an Advocate of the Scottish Bar is controlled by the Faculty of Advocates.

THE GENERAL COUNCIL OF THE BAR, 3 Bedford Row, London WCIR 4DB. Tel: 071-242 0082. The governing body of the barristers' branch of the legal profession in England and Wales. *Chairman*, J. Rowe, QC; *Chief Executive*, J. Mottram, CB, LVO, OBE

The Inns of Court

THE INNER TEMPLE, London EC4Y 7HL. Tel: 071-797 8175/7. *Treasurer,* The Rt. Hon. Sir John May; *Sub-Treasurer,* Capt. P. T. Sheehan, CBE, RN.

THE MIDDLE TEMPLE, London EC4Y 9AT. *Treasurer,* Rear-Adm. J. R. Hill; *Deputy Treasurer,* M. J. P. Spain

GRAY'S INN, 8 South Square, London WC1R 5EU. *Treasurer,* C. Sparrow, QC, FSA; *Under-Treasurer,* D. Machin

LINCOLN'S INN, London WC2A 3TL. Tel: 071-405 1393. *Treasurer,* The Lord Oliver of Aylmerton, PC; *Under-Treasurer,* Capt. P. M. Carver, RN

The education and examination of students for the Bar of England and Wales is superintended by the COUNCIL OF LEGAL EDUCATION, Inns of Court School of Law, 39 Eagle Street, London WC1R 4AJ. Tel: 071-404 5787. *Chairman,* The Hon. Mr Justice Phillips; *Dean, Inns of Court School of Law,* Mrs M. A. Phillips

FACULTY OF ADVOCATES, Advocates Library, Parliament House, Edinburgh EH1 1RF. Tel: 031-226 5071. *Dean,* A. C. M. Johnston, QC; *Clerk,* J. A. Doherty

THE HONORABLE SOCIETY OF THE INN OF COURT OF NORTHERN IRELAND, Royal Courts of Justice, Belfast BT1 3JF. Tel: 0232-235111. *Treasurer* (1993), The Hon. Mr Justice Campbell; *Under-Treasurer,* J. A. L. McLean, QC

SOLICITORS

Qualifications for solicitor are obtainable only from one of the Law Societies, which control the education and examination of articled clerks, and the admission of solicitors.

LAW SOCIETY OF ENGLAND AND WALES, 113 Chancery Lane, London WC2A 1PL. Tel: 071-242 1222. *President* (1993-4), R. J. Pannone; *Vice-President* (1993-4), R. C. Elly; *Secretary-General,* J. W. Hayes

THE COLLEGE OF LAW provides courses for the Law Society examinations at Braboeuf Manor, St Catherine's, Guildford, Surrey GU3 1HA; 14 Store Street, London WC1E 7DE; Christleton Hall, Chester CH3 7AB; Bishopthorpe Road, York YO2 1QA

THE SOLICITORS COMPLAINTS BUREAU, Victoria Court, 8 Dormer Place, Leamington Spa, Warks CV31 1HE. Tel: 0926-820082. The Bureau is an independent arm of the Law Society set up to handle complaints about solicitors.

LAW SOCIETY OF SCOTLAND, Law Society's Hall, 26 Drumsheugh Gardens, Edinburgh EH3 7YR. Tel: 031-226 7411. *President* (1993-4), I. D. Dunbar; *Secretary,* K. W. Pritchard, OBE

LAW SOCIETY OF NORTHERN IRELAND, Law Society House, 90–106 Victoria Street, Belfast BT1 3JZ. Tel: 0232-231614. *Secretary,* M. C. Davey

---

LIBRARIANSHIP AND INFORMATION SCIENCE/MANAGEMENT

The Library Association accredits degree and/or postgraduate courses in library and information science which are offered by 16 universities in the UK. A full list of accredited degree and postgraduate courses is available from the Education Department. The Association also maintains a professional register of Chartered Members open to graduate ordinary members of the Association.

THE LIBRARY ASSOCIATION, 7 Ridgmount Street, London WC1E 7AE. Tel: 071-636 7543. *Chief Executive,* R. Shimmon

---

MATERIALS STUDIES

The qualifying body is:

INSTITUTE OF MATERIALS, 1 Carlton House Terrace, London SW1Y 5DB. Tel: 071-839 4071. *Secretary,* Dr J. A. Catterall

---

MEDICINE

LICENSING CORPORATIONS GRANTING DIPLOMAS

SOCIETY OF APOTHECARIES OF LONDON, Black Friars Lane, London EC4V 6EJ. Tel: 071-236 1189. *Clerk,* Maj. J. C. O'Leary; *Registrar,* A. M. Wallington-Smith

SCOTTISH TRIPLE QUALIFICATION BOARD, Nicolson Street, Edinburgh EH8 9DW, tel: 031-556 6206; and 242 St Vincent Street, Glasgow, tel: 041-221 6072

COLLEGES HOLDING POSTGRADUATE MEMBERSHIP AND DIPLOMA EXAMINATIONS

ROYAL COLLEGE OF ANAESTHETISTS, 48–49 Russell Square, London WC1B 4JY. Tel: 071-813 1900. *President,* Prof. A. Spence, CBE. *Chief Executive,* Sir Geoffrey de Deney, KCVO

ROYAL COLLEGE OF GENERAL PRACTITIONERS, 14 Princes Gate, London SW7 1PU. Tel: 071-581 3232. *President,* Dr A. Donald; *Secretary,* Dr M. McBride

ROYAL COLLEGE OF OBSTETRICIANS AND GYNAECOLOGISTS, 27 Sussex Place, London NW1 4RG. Tel: 071-262 5425. *President,* Prof. G. V. P. Chamberlain, RD, FRCOG; *Secretary,* Prof. W. Dunlop, FRCOG

ROYAL COLLEGE OF PATHOLOGISTS, 2 Carlton House Terrace, London SW1Y 5AF. Tel: 071-930 5863. *President,* Prof. A. J. Bellingham, FRCP, FRCPath.; *Secretary,* K. Lockyer

ROYAL COLLEGE OF PHYSICIANS, 11 St Andrews Place, London NW1 4LE. Tel: 071-935 1174. *President,* Prof. L. A. Turnberg; *Secretary,* D. B. Lloyd

ROYAL COLLEGE OF PHYSICIANS OF EDINBURGH, 9 Queen Street, Edinburgh EH2 1JQ. Tel: 031-225 7324. *President,* Dr A. D. Toft; *Secretary,* Dr J. StJ. Thomas

ROYAL COLLEGE OF PHYSICIANS AND SURGEONS OF GLASGOW, 234–242 St Vincent Street, Glasgow G2 5RJ. Tel: 041-221 6072. *President,* Prof. D. Campbell, CBE; *Hon. Secretary,* Dr B. Williams

ROYAL COLLEGE OF PSYCHIATRISTS, 17 Belgrave Square, London SW1X 8PG. Tel: 071-235 2351. *President,* Dr F. Caldicott; *Secretary,* Mrs V. Cameron

ROYAL COLLEGE OF RADIOLOGISTS, 38 Portland Place, London W1N 3DG. Tel: 071-636 4432. *President,* Dr C. H. Paine; *Secretary,* A. J. Cowles

ROYAL COLLEGE OF SURGEONS OF ENGLAND, 35–43 Lincoln's Inn Fields, London WC2A 3PN. Tel: 071-405 3474. *President,* Prof. N. L. Browse, PRCS; *Secretary,* R. H. E. Duffett

ROYAL COLLEGE OF SURGEONS OF EDINBURGH, Nicolson Street, Edinburgh EH8 9DW. Tel: 031-556 6206. *President,* Prof. P. S. Boulter; *Secretary,* I. B. Macleod, FRCSEd.

PROFESSIONS SUPPLEMENTARY TO MEDICINE

The standard of professional education in chiropody, dietetics, medical laboratory sciences, occupational therapy, orthoptics, physiotherapy and radiography is the responsibility of seven professional boards, which also publish an annual register of qualified practitioners. The work of the Boards is co-ordinated by the Council for Professions Supplementary to Medicine.

THE COUNCIL FOR PROFESSIONS SUPPLEMENTARY TO MEDICINE, Park House, 184 Kennington Park Road, London SEII 4BU. Tel: 071-582 0866. *Registrar*, R. Pickis

CHIROPODY

Professional recognition is granted by the Society of Chiropodists and Podiatrists to students who are awarded B.Sc. degrees in Podiatry or Podiatric medicine after attending a course of full-time training for three or four years at one of the 14 recognized schools in the UK (11 in England and Wales, two in Scotland and one in Northern Ireland). Qualifications granted and degrees recognized by the Society are approved by the Chiropodists Board for the purpose of State Registration, which is a condition of employment within the National Health Service.

THE SOCIETY OF CHIROPODISTS AND PODIATRISTS, 53 Welbeck Street, London WIM 7HE. Tel: 071-486 3381. *General Secretary*, J. G. C. Trouncer

See also DIETETICS

MEDICAL LABORATORY SCIENCES

Qualifications from higher or further education establishments and training in medical laboratories are required for progress to the professional examinations and qualifications of the INSTITUTE OF MEDICAL LABORATORY SCIENCES, 12 Queen Anne Street, London WIM 0AU. Tel: 071-636 8192. *Chief Executive*, A. Potter

OCCUPATIONAL THERAPY

Professional qualifications are awarded by the College of Occupational Therapists upon completion of one of the 27 training courses approved by the College

THE COLLEGE OF OCCUPATIONAL THERAPISTS, 6–8 Marshalsea Road, London SEI IHL. Tel: 071-357 6480. *Secretary*, M. D. Hall, OBE, GM

See also OPHTHALMIC OPTICS

ORTHOPTICS

Orthoptists undertake the diagnosis and treatment of all types of squint and other anomalies of binocular vision, working in close collaboration with ophthalmologists. The training and maintenance of professional standards are the responsibility of the Orthoptists Board of the Council for the Professions Supplementary to Medicine. The professional body is the British Orthoptic Society. Training is at degree level.

THE BRITISH ORTHOPTIC SOCIETY, Tavistock House North, Tavistock Square, London WCIH 9HX. *Secretary*, Mrs A. Charnock

PHYSIOTHERAPY

Full-time three- or four-year degree courses are available at 31 recognized schools in the UK. Information about courses leading to eligibility for Membership of the Chartered Society of Physiotherapy and to State Registration is available from THE CHARTERED SOCIETY OF PHYSIOTHERAPY, 14 Bedford Row, London WCIR 4ED. Tel: 071-242 1941. *Secretary*, T. Simon

RADIOGRAPHY AND RADIOTHERAPY

In order to practise both diagnostic and therapeutic radiography in the United Kingdom, it is necessary to have successfully completed a course of education and training recognized by the Privy Council. Such courses are offered by universities and colleges throughout the United Kingdom and lead to the award of either a degree in radiography or the Diploma of the College of Radiographers. Further information is available from THE COLLEGE OF RADIOGRAPHERS, 14 Upper Wimpole Street, London WIM 8BN. Tel: 071-935 5726. *Chief Executive*, B. Macey

MERCHANT NAVY TRAINING SCHOOLS

OFFICERS

MARITIME OPERATIONS CENTRE, Southampton Institute of Higher Education, Newtown Road, Warsash, Southampton SO3 9ZL. Tel: 0489-576161. *Head of Centre*, Capt. G. B. Angas

SEAFARERS

INDEFATIGABLE SCHOOL, Plas Llanfair, Llanfairpwll, Anglesey LL61 6NT. Tel: 0248-714338. *Headmaster*, Capt. P. White

NATIONAL SEA TRAINING COLLEGE, Denton, Gravesend, Kent DA12 2HR. Tel: 0474-363656. *Principal*, M. Bolton

MUSIC

ASSOCIATED BOARD OF THE ROYAL SCHOOLS OF MUSIC, 14 Bedford Square, London WCIB 3JG. Conducts music examinations in centres throughout the world for the Royal Academy of Music and the Royal College of Music in London, the Royal Northern College of Music, Manchester and the Royal Scottish Academy of Music and Drama, Glasgow. *Chief Executive*, R. Morris

ROYAL ACADEMY OF MUSIC, Marylebone Road, London NWI 5HT. Tel: 071-935 5461. *Principal*, L. Harrell

ROYAL COLLEGE OF MUSIC, Prince Consort Road, London SW7 2BS. Tel: 071-589 3643. *Director*, Dr J. Ritterman

ROYAL NORTHERN COLLEGE OF MUSIC, 124 Oxford Road, Manchester M13 9RD. Tel: 061-273 6283. *Principal*, Sir John Manduell, CBE

ROYAL SCOTTISH ACADEMY OF MUSIC AND DRAMA, 100 Renfrew Street, Glasgow G2 3DB. Tel: 041-332 4101. *Principal*, Dr P. Ledger, CBE

ROYAL COLLEGE OF ORGANISTS, 7 St Andrew Street, London EC4A 3LQ. Tel: 071-936 3606. *Clerk*, V. Waterhouse

GUILDHALL SCHOOL OF MUSIC AND DRAMA, Silk Street, London EC2Y 8DT. Tel: 071-628 2571. *Principal*, I. Horsbrugh

LONDON COLLEGE OF MUSIC, Thames Valley University, St Mary's Road, London W5 5RF. Tel: 081-231 2364. *General Manager*, R. D. Roberts

TRINITY COLLEGE OF MUSIC, 11–13 Mandeville Place, London WIM 6AQ. Tel: 071-935 5773. *Principal*, P. Jones, CBE

NURSING

Courses leading to registration as a nurse are at least three years in length. There are also some programmes which are combined with degrees. Students study in colleges of nursing or in institutions of higher education. Courses offer a combination of theoretical and practical experience in a wide variety of settings. Depending on the type of course, students will register in adult, child, mental health or mental handicap (learning disabilities) nursing. A wide variety of specialist programmes are available after registration, for example in district nursing or occupational health nursing.

UK CENTRAL COUNCIL FOR NURSING, MIDWIFERY AND HEALTH VISITING, 23 Portland Place, London WIN 3AF. Tel: 071-637 7181. *Registrar and Chief Executive*, C. Ralph

ENGLISH NATIONAL BOARD FOR NURSING, MIDWIFERY AND HEALTH VISITING, Victory House, 170 Tottenham Court Road, London WIP OHA. Tel: 071-388 3131. *Chief Executive Officer*, A. P. Smith

WELSH NATIONAL BOARD FOR NURSING, MIDWIFERY AND HEALTH VISITING, Floor 13, Pearl Assurance House, Greyfriars Road, Cardiff CFI 3AG. Tel: 0222-395535. *Chief Executive Officer*, D. A. Ravey

NATIONAL BOARD FOR NURSING, MIDWIFERY AND HEALTH VISITING FOR SCOTLAND, 22 Queen Street, Edinburgh EH2 IJX. Tel: 031-226 7371. *Chief Executive Officer*, Mrs L. Mitchell

NATIONAL BOARD FOR NURSING, MIDWIFERY AND HEALTH VISITING FOR NORTHERN IRELAND, RAC House, 79 Chichester Street, Belfast BTI 4JE. Tel: 0232-238152. *Chief Executive Officer*, Dr O. D'A. Slevin.

OPHTHALMIC OPTICS

Professional bodies are:

THE BRITISH COLLEGE OF OPTOMETRISTS, IO Knaresborough Place, London SW5 OTG. Tel: 071-373 7765. Grants qualifications as an optometrist. *General Secretary*, P. D. Leigh

THE ASSOCIATION OF BRITISH DISPENSING OPTICIANS, 6 Hurlingham Business Park, Sulivan Road, London SW6 3DU. Tel: 071-736 0088. Grants qualifications as a dispensing optician. *Registrar*, D. G. Baker

PHARMACY

Information may be obtained from the Secretary and Registrar, ROYAL PHARMACEUTICAL SOCIETY OF GREAT BRITAIN, I Lambeth High Street, London SEI 7JN. *Secretary and Registrar*, J. Ferguson

PHOTOGRAPHY

The professional body is:

BRITISH INSTITUTE OF PROFESSIONAL PHOTOGRAPHY, Fox Talbot House, 2 Amwell End, Ware, Herts. SG12 9HN. Tel: 0920-464011. *Chief Executive*, A. Mair

PRINTING

Details of courses in general and technical design can be obtained from the Institute of Printing and the British Printing Industries Federation. In addition to these examining and organizing bodies, examinations are held by various independent regional examining boards in further education.

BRITISH PRINTING INDUSTRIES FEDERATION, II Bedford Row, London WCIR 4DX. Tel: 071-242 6904. *Director-General*, C. Stanley

INSTITUTE OF PRINTING, 8 Lonsdale Gardens, Tunbridge Wells, Kent TNI INU. Tel: 0892-538118. *Secretary-General*, C. F. Partridge

SOCIAL WORK

The Central Council for Education and Training in Social Work promotes education and training for social work and social care throughout the UK. It approves education and training programmes, including those leading to its qualifying award, the Diploma in Social Work.

THE CENTRAL COUNCIL FOR EDUCATION AND TRAINING IN SOCIAL WORK, Derbyshire House, St Chad's Street, London WCIH 8AD. Tel: 071-278 2455. *Chairman*, J. Greenwood; *Director*, T. Hall

SPEECH THERAPY

The College of Speech and Language Therapists provides details of courses leading to qualification as a speech and language therapist. The College also sponsors advanced clinical courses. Other professionals may become Associates of the College. A directory of registered members is published annually.

THE COLLEGE OF SPEECH AND LANGUAGE THERAPISTS, 7 Bath Place, London EC2A 3DR. Tel: 071-613 3855. *Director*, Mrs S. Davis

SURVEYING

The qualifying professional bodies include:

ROYAL INSTITUTION OF CHARTERED SURVEYORS (incorporating The Institute of Quantity Surveyors), Surveyor Court, Westwood Way, Coventry CV4 8JE. Tel: 0203-694757. *Chief Executive*, M. Pattison

ARCHITECTS AND SURVEYORS INSTITUTE, 15 St Mary Street, Chippenham, Wilts. SNI5 3JN. Tel: 0249-444505. *Chief Executive.*, B. A. Hunt

ASSOCIATION OF BUILDING ENGINEERS, Jubilee House, Billing Brook Road, Weston Favell, Northampton NN3 4NW. Tel: 0604-404121. *Chief Executive*, B. D. Hughes

INSTITUTE OF REVENUES, RATING AND VALUATION, 41 Doughty Street, London WCIN 2LF. Tel: 071-831 3505. *Director*, C. Farrington

INCORPORATED SOCIETY OF VALUERS AND AUCTIONEERS (1968), 3 Cadogan Gate, London SWIX OAS. Tel: 071-235 2282. *Chief Executive*, H. Whitty

TEACHING

To become a qualified teacher it is necessary to have successfully completed a course of initial teacher training. Non-graduates usually qualify by way of a three- or four-year course leading to a Bachelor of Education (B.Ed.) honours degree, but some universities offer first degree courses (BA, B.Sc.) taken concurrently with a certificate of education.

Graduates take a one-year postgraduate certificate of education (PGCE). Increasingly, it is possible to train in schools whilst working as a teacher.

Details of courses in England and Wales are contained in the *Handbook of Degree and Advanced Courses* published annually by the National Association of Teachers in Further and Higher Education.

Applications for B.Ed. courses in England and Wales at institutions other than universities are made through UCAS. For all PGCE courses in England and Wales, applications are handled by the Graduate Teacher Training Registry. (For addresses, *see* page 462).

Details of courses in Scotland can be obtained from the colleges of education and from TEACH through which applications are made (*see* page 462). Details of courses in Northern Ireland can be obtained from the Department of Education for Northern Ireland. Applications for teacher training courses in Northern Ireland are made to the institutions direct.

TEXTILES

THE TEXTILE INSTITUTE, 10 Blackfriars Street, Manchester M3 5DR. Tel: 061-834 8457. *Chief Executive*, R. G. Denyer

THEOLOGICAL COLLEGES

The number of students training for the ministry for the academic year 1992–3 is shown in parenthesis.

ANGLICAN

CHICHESTER THEOLOGICAL COLLEGE, Chichester, W. Sussex PO19 1SG. (25). *Principal*, Revd Canon P. Atkinson

CRANMER HALL, St John's College, Durham DH1 3RJ. (77). *Warden*, Revd J. Pritchard

LINCOLN THEOLOGICAL COLLEGE, Drury Lane, Lincoln LN1 3BP. (65). *Warden*, Revd Canon W. M. Jacob, PH.D.

OAK HILL COLLEGE, Chase Side, London N14 4PS. (87). *Principal*, Revd Canon G. Bridger

COLLEGE OF THE RESURRECTION, Mirfield, W. Yorks. WF14 0BW. (37). *Principal*, Revd Dr D. J. Lane

RIDLEY HALL, Cambridge CB3 9HG. (60). *Principal*, Revd G. A. Cray

RIPON COLLEGE, Cuddesdon, Oxford OX9 9EX. (65). *Principal*, Revd Canon J. H. Garton

ST JOHN'S COLLEGE, Chilwell Lane, Bramcote, Nottingham NG9 3DS. (120). *Principal*, Revd Dr J. Goldingay

ST MICHAEL'S THEOLOGICAL COLLEGE, Llandaff, Cardiff CF5 2YJ. (38). *Warden*, Revd Canon J. H. L. Rowlands

ST STEPHEN'S HOUSE, 16 Marston Street, Oxford OX4 1JX. (55). *Principal*, Revd E. R. Barnes

SALISBURY AND WELLS THEOLOGICAL COLLEGE, 19 The Close, Salisbury SP1 2EE. (60). *Principal*, Revd Canon P. A. Crowe

THEOLOGICAL INSTITUTE OF THE SCOTTISH EPISCOPAL CHURCH, Coates Hall, Rosebery Crescent, Edinburgh EH12 5JT. (45). *Principal*, Revd Canon K. Mason

TRINITY COLLEGE, Stoke Hill, Bristol BS9 1JP. (130). *Principal (acting)*, Revd M. Roberts

WESTCOTT HOUSE, Jesus Lane, Cambridge CB5 8BP. (50). *Principal*, Revd Dr R. W. N. Hoare

WYCLIFFE HALL, 54 Banbury Road, Oxford OX2 6PW. (70). *Principal*, Revd Dr R. T. France

BAPTIST

BRISTOL BAPTIST COLLEGE, Woodland Road, Bristol BS8 1UN. (24). *Principal*, vacant

NORTHERN BAPTIST COLLEGE, Northern Federation for Training in Ministry, Luther King House, Brighton Grove, Rusholme, Manchester M14 5JP. (40). *Principal*, Revd Dr B. Haymes

NORTH WALES BAPTIST COLLEGE, Ffordd Ffriddoedd, Bangor, Gwynedd LL57 2EH. (3). *Principal*, Revd J. R. Rowlands

REGENT'S PARK COLLEGE, Oxford OX1 2LB. (25). *Principal*, Revd Dr P. S. Fiddes

THE SCOTTISH BAPTIST COLLEGE, 12 Aytoun Road, Glasgow G41 5RT. (14). *Principal*, Revd Dr I. J. W. Oakley

SOUTH WALES BAPTIST COLLEGE, 54 Richmond Road, Cardiff CF2 3UR. (23). *Principal*, Revd D. H. Matthews

SPURGEON'S COLLEGE, South Norwood Hill, London SE25 6DJ. (140). *Principal*, Revd M. Quicke

CHURCH OF SCOTLAND

CHRIST'S COLLEGE, Aberdeen AB1 1YD. (28). *Master*, Revd Prof. A. Main, TD, PH.D.

NEW COLLEGE, Mound Place, Edinburgh EH1 2LU. (54). *Principal*, Revd Prof. D. B. Forrester

TRINITY COLLEGE, 4 The Square, University of Glasgow, Glasgow G12 8QQ. (65). *Principal*, Revd Prof. G. M. Newlands

CONGREGATIONAL

COLLEGE OF THE WELSH INDEPENDENTS, 38 Pier Street, Aberystwyth, Dyfed. *Principal*, Revd Dr E. S. John

SCOTTISH CONGREGATIONAL COLLEGE, Rosebery Crescent, Edinburgh EH12 5YN. (12). *Principal*, Revd Dr J. W. S. Clark

ECUMENICAL

QUEEN'S COLLEGE, Somerset Road, Edgbaston, Birmingham B15 2QH. (75). *Principal*, Revd Dr J. B. Walker

METHODIST

EDGEHILL THEOLOGICAL COLLEGE, 9 Lennoxvale, Belfast BT9 5BY. (13). *Principal*, Revd D. Cooke, PH.D.

HARTLEY VICTORIA COLLEGE, Northern Federation for Training in Ministry, Luther King House, Brighton Grove, Manchester M14 5JP. (24). *Principal*, Revd G. Slater

LINCOLN THEOLOGICAL COLLEGE, Drury Lane, Lincoln LN1 3BP. (65). *Warden*, Revd Canon W. M. Jacob, PH.D.

WESLEY COLLEGE, College Park Drive, Henbury Road, Bristol BS10 7QD. (62). *Principal*, Dr H. McKeating

WESLEY HOUSE, Cambridge CB5 8BJ. (34). *Principal*, Revd Dr I. H. Jones

WESLEY STUDY CENTRE, 55 The Avenue, Durham DH1 4EB. (18). *Director*, Revd P. Luscombe, PH.D.

NON-DENOMINATIONAL

ST MARY'S COLLEGE, The University, St Andrews, Fife KY16 9JU. (180). *Principal*, Dr R. A. Piper

PRESBYTERIAN

UNION THEOLOGICAL COLLEGE, Belfast BT7 1JT. (76). *Principal*, Revd Prof. T. S. Reid

PRESBYTERIAN CHURCH OF WALES

UNITED THEOLOGICAL COLLEGE, Aberystwyth SY23 2LT.
(58). *Principal*, Revd Prof. E. ap Nefydd Roberts

ROMAN CATHOLIC

ALLEN HALL COLLEGE, 28 Beaufort Street, London
SW3 5AA. (63). *Principal*, Revd K. Barltrop, STL
CAMPION HOUSE COLLEGE, 112 Thornbury Road,
Isleworth, Middx. TW7 4NN. (35). *Principal*,
Revd M. Barrow, SJ
OSCOTT COLLEGE, Chester Road, Sutton Coldfield,
W. Midlands B73 5AA. (67). *Rector*, Rt. Revd
Mgr P. McKinney, STL
SCOTUS COLLEGE, 2 Chesters Road, Bearsden, Glasgow
G61 4AG. (50). *Rector*, Rt Revd Mgr M. J. Conway
ST JOHN'S SEMINARY, Wonersh, Guildford, Surrey
GU5 0QX. (35). *Rector*, Rt. Revd Mgr P. Smith
USHAW COLLEGE, Durham DH7 9RH. (92). *Principal*,
Rt. Revd Mgr R. Atherton, OBE

UNITARIAN

UNITARIAN COLLEGE, Northern Federation for Training
in Ministry, Luther King House, Brighton Grove,
Rusholme, Manchester M14 5JP. (5). *Principal*, Revd
L. Smith, PH.D.

UNITED REFORMED

BALA-BANGOR INDEPENDENT COLLEGE, Bangor
LL57 2EH. (15). *Principal*, R. T. Jones, D.Phil., DD
MANSFIELD COLLEGE, Mansfield Road, Oxford OX1 3TF.
(27). *Principal*, D. J. Trevelyan, CB
NORTHERN COLLEGE, Northern Federation for Training
in Ministry, Luther King House, Brighton Grove,
Rusholme, Manchester M14 5JP. (34). *Principal*, Revd Dr
D. R. Peel
WESTMINSTER COLLEGE, Madingley Road, Cambridge
CB3 0AA. (35). *Principal*, Revd M. H. Cressey

JEWISH

JEWS' COLLEGE, Albert Road, London NW4 2SJ. (20).
Principal, Rabbi Dr I. Jacobs
LEO BAECK COLLEGE, Sternberg Centre for Judaism, 80
East End Road, London N3 2SY. (22). *Principal*, Rabbi
Dr J. Magonet

TOWN AND COUNTRY PLANNING

Degree and diploma courses in town planning are accredited
by the Royal Town Planning Institute.
THE ROYAL TOWN PLANNING INSTITUTE, 26 Portland
Place, London W1N 4BE. Tel: 071-636 9107. *Secretary-
General*, D. Fryer

TRANSPORT

Qualifying examinations in transport management and
logistics leading to chartered professional status are con-
ducted by the Chartered Institute of Transport.
THE CHARTERED INSTITUTE OF TRANSPORT, 80
Portland Place, London W1N 4DP. Tel: 071-636 9952.
Director, A. M. J. Pomeroy

Independent Schools

The following pages list those independent schools whose
Head is a member of the Headmasters' Conference, the
Society of Headmasters and Headmistresses of
Independent Schools or the Girls' Schools Association

THE HEADMASTERS' CONFERENCE

Chairman (1994), R. J. Wilson (Trinity School, Surrey)
Secretary, V. S. Anthony, 130 Regent Road, Leicester
LEI 7PG. Tel: 0533-854810
Membership Secretary, R. N. P. Griffiths, 1 Russell House,
Bepton Road, Midhurst, W. Sussex GU29 9NB. Tel: 0730-
815635. The annual meeting is, as a rule, held at the end
of September

* Woodard Corporation School, 1 The Sanctuary, London
SWIP 3JT. Tel: 071-222 5381
† Girls in VI form
‡ Co-educational
° 1992 figures

Name of School	Founded	No. of pupils	Annual fees £ Boarding	Day	Head (with date of appointment)
ENGLAND AND WALES					
Abbotsholme School, Staffs.	1889	240‡	10,251	6,906	D. J. Farrant (1984)
Abingdon School, Oxon.	1256	750	9,036	4,794	M. St J. Parker (1975)
Ackworth School, W. Yorks.	1779	430‡	8,673	5,022	D. S. Harris (1989)
Aldenham School, Herts.	1597	350†	10,600	7,200	M. Higginbottom (1983)
Alleyn's School, London SE22	1619	903‡	—	5,340	Dr C. H. R. Niven (1992)
Allhallows School, Dorset	1515	240‡	10,686	5,343	P. S. Larkman, LVO (1983)
Ampleforth College (*RC*), Yorks.	1802	632	10,860	5,700	Revd G. F. L. Chamberlain, OSB (1993)
*Ardingly College, W. Sussex	1858	447‡	10,710	8,505	J. W. Flecker (1980)
Arnold School, Blackpool	1896	815‡	6,837	3,385	W. T. Gillen (1993)
Ashville College, Harrogate	1877	368‡	8,172	4,386	M. H. Crosby (1987)
Bablake School, Coventry	1560	804†	—	3,312	Dr S. Nuttall (1991)
Bancroft's School, Essex	1727	716‡	—	5,094	Dr P. C. D. Southern (1985)
Barnard Castle School, Co. Durham	1883	500†	7,614	4,506	F. S. McNamara (1980)
Batley Grammar School, W. Yorks.	1612	595	—	3,228	C. S. Parker (1986)
Bedales School, Hants.	1893	374‡	11,901	8,529	R. E. I. Newton (1992)
Bedford School	1552	713	10,080	6,300	Dr I. P. Evans (1990)
Bedford Modern School	1566	980	7,632	3,987	P. J. Squire (1977)
Berkhamsted School, Herts.	1541	651	10,083	6,198	Revd K. H. Wilkinson (1989)
Birkenhead School, Merseyside	1860	750	—	3,234	S. J. Haggett (1988)
Bishop's Stortford College, Herts.	1868	°360†	°9,520	°6,880	S. G. G. Benson (1984)
*Bloxham School, Oxon.	1860	340†	10,665	7,995	D. K. Exham (1991)
Blundell's School, Devon	1604	380†	10,500	6,250	J. Leigh (1992)
Bolton School	1524	870	—	4,191	A. W. Wright (1983)
Bootham School, York	1823	340‡	9,500	6,300	I. M. Small (1988)
Bradfield College, Berks.	1850	580†	11,475	8,606	P. B. Smith (1985)
Bradford Grammar School	1662	1,000†	—	3,666	D. A. G. Smith (1974)
Brentwood School, Essex	1557	1,038†	9,156	5,232	J. A. B. Kelsall (1993)
Brighton College, E. Sussex	1845	480‡	10,800	7,101	J. D. Leach (1987)
Bristol Cathedral School	1542	483†	—	3,789	K. J. Riley (1994)
Bristol Grammar School	1532	1,220‡	—	3,591	C. E. Martin (1986)
Bromsgrove School, Worcs.	1553	610‡	9,285	5,805	T. M. Taylor (1986)
Bryanston School, Dorset	1928	650‡	12,255	8,169	T. D. Wheare (1983)
Bury Grammar School, Lancs.	1634	690	—	3,432	K. Richards (1990)
Canford School, Dorset	1923	494†	11,440	8,580	J. D. Lever (1992)
Caterham School, Surrey	1811	450†	9,513	5,181	S. R. Smith (1974)
Charterhouse, Surrey	1611	700†	11,910	9,825	P. Hobson (1993)
Cheadle Hulme School, Cheshire	1855	910‡	—	3,780	D. J. Wilkinson (1990)
Cheltenham College, Glos.	1841	559†	11,370	8,595	P. D. V. Wilkes (1990)
Chetham's School of Music, Manchester	1653	274‡	14,844	11,496	Revd P. F. Hullah (1992)
Chigwell School, Essex	1629	400†	8,844	5,817	A. R. M. Little (1989)
Christ College, Brecon	1541	366†	8,697	6,591	S. W. Hockey (1982)
Christ's Hospital, W. Sussex	1553	835‡	varies	—	R. C. Poulton (1987)

Name of School	Founded	No. of pupils	Annual fees £ Boarding	Day	Head (with date of appointment)
Churcher's College, Hants.	1722	561‡	8,700	4,650	G. W. Buttlc (1988)
City of London, London EC4	1442	850	—	5,391	B. G. Bass (1990)
City of London Freemen's School, Surrey	1854	365‡	8,370	5,373	D. C. Haywood (1987)
Clifton College, Bristol	1862	660‡	11,355	7,962	H. Monro (1990)
Colfe's School, London SE12	1652	710†	—	4,455	Dr D. Richardson (1990)
Colston's Collegiate School, Bristol	1710	350†	8,130	4,905	S. B. Howarth (1988)
Cranleigh School, Surrey	1863	545†	11,625	8,715	A. Hart (1984)
Culford School, Suffolk	1881	357‡	9,156	5,952	J. Richardson (1992)
Dame Allan's School, Newcastle upon Tyne	1705	460†	—	3,276	T. A. Willcocks (*Principal*) (1988)
Dauntsey's School, Wiltshire	1543	615‡	9,717	5,985	C. R. Evans (1985)
Dean Close School, Cheltenham	1884	439‡	11,070	7,740	C. J. Bacon (1979)
*Denstone College, Staffs.	1873	290‡	9,972	7,110	H. C. K. Carson (1990)
Douai School (*RC*), Berks.	1903	238‡	9,735	6,270	Revd E. Power (1993)
Dover College, Kent	1871	300‡	10,500	5,970	M. P. G. Wright (1991)
Downside School (*RC*), Somerset	1607	378	10,320	7,118	Dom. A. Bellenger (1991)
Dulwich College, London SE21	1619	1,250	11,670	5,835	A. C. F. Verity (*Master*) (1986)
Durham School	1414	362†	10,815	7,209	M. A. Lang (1982)
Eastbourne College, E. Sussex	1867	512†	10,908	8,067	C. M. P. Bush (1993)
*Ellesmere College, Shropshire	1884	350†	9,600	6,600	D. R. du Croz (1988)
Eltham College, London SE9	1842	580†	10,558	4,998	D. M. Green (1990)
Emanuel School, London SW11	1594	760	—	4,215	P. F. Thomson (1984)
Epsom College, Surrey	1855	664†	10,620	7,890	A. H. Beadles (1993)
Eton College, Berks.	1440	1,270	11,934	—	Dr W. E. K. Anderson (1980)
Exeter School	1633	735†	7,116	3,756	N. W. Gamble (1992)
Felsted School, Essex	1564	350†	11,418	9,018	S. C. Roberts (1993)
Forest School, London E17	1834	810‡	7,923	5,046	A. Boggis (*Warden*) (1992)
Framlingham College, Suffolk	1864	440‡	9,000	5,775	J. F. X. Miller (1989)
Frensham Heights, Surrey	1925	295‡	10,920	6,990	P. de Voile (1993)
Giggleswick School, N. Yorks.	1512	304‡	10,776	7,086	A. P. Millard (1993)
Gresham's School, Norfolk	1555	456‡	10,800	7,550	J. H. Arkell (1991)
Haberdashers' Aske's School, Herts.	1690	1,118	—	5,028	K. Dawson (1987)
Haileybury, Herts.	1862	626†	11,775	8,535	D. J. Jewell (1987)
Hampton School, Middx.	1557	909	—	4,254	G. G. Able (1988)
Harrow School, Middx.	1571	780	12,360	—	N. R. Bomford (1991)
Hereford Cathedral School	1384	586‡	7,365	4,185	Dr H. C. Tomlinson (1988)
Highgate School, London N6	1565	575	10,416	6,525	R. P. Kennedy (1989)
Hulme Grammar School, Oldham	1611	740	—	3,315	G. F. Dunkin (1987)
*Hurstpierpoint College, W. Sussex	1849	350	10,605	8,475	S. A. Watson (1986)
Hymers College, Hull	1889	940	—	3,180	J. C. Morris (1990)
Ipswich School, Suffolk	1390	620†	7,839	4,581	I. G. Galbraith (1993)
John Lyon School, Middx.	1876	520	—	4,950	Revd T. J. Wright (1986)
Kelly College, Devon	1877	305‡	10,485	6,750	C. H. Hirst (1985)
Kent College, Canterbury	1885	540‡	9,183	5,145	R. J. Wicks (1980)
Kimbolton School, Cambs.	1600	550‡	8,175	4,740	R. V. Peel (1987)
King Edward VI School, Southampton	1553	956†	—	4,305	T. R. Cookson (1990)
King Edward VII School, Lytham	1908	530	—	3,345	P. J. Wilde (1993)
King Edward's School, Bath	1552	680†	—	3,744	P. J. Winter (1993)
King Edward's School, Birmingham	1552	870	—	4,074	H. R. Wright (*Chief Master*) (1991)
King Edward's School, Witley, Surrey	1553	515‡	8,295	5,085	R. J. Fox (1988)
King Henry VIII School, Coventry	1545	830‡	—	3,312	G. R. James (1991)
*King's College, Taunton	1880	465‡	10,500	7,290	R. S. Funnell (1988)
King's College School, London SW19	1829	680	—	5,760	R. M. Reeve (1980)
King's School, Bruton, Somerset	1519	308†	10,245	7,260	R. I. Smyth (1993)
King's School, Canterbury	600	700‡	11,820	8,160	Revd Canon A. C. J. Phillips (1986)
King's School, Chester	1541	500	—	4,048	A. R. D. Wickson (1981)
King's School, Ely, Cambs.	970	379‡	10,413	6,975	R. H. Youdale (1992)
King's School, Macclesfield	1502	1,000†	—	3,875	A. G. Silcock (1987)
King's School, Rochester, Kent	604	311†	10,167	5,955	Dr I. R. Walker (1986)
King's School, Tynemouth	1860	900‡	—	3,309	Dr D. Younger (1993)
King's School, Worcester	1541	770‡	8,439	4,917	Dr J. M. Moore (1983)
Kingston Grammar School, Surrey	1561	590‡	—	4,890	C. D. Baxter (1991)

484   Education

Name of School	Founded	No. of pupils	Annual fees £ Boarding	Day	Head (with date of appointment)
Kingswood School, Bath	1748	446‡	10,164	6,609	G. M. Best (1987)
*Lancing College, W. Sussex	1848	532†	11,175	8,400	C. J. Saunders (1993)
Latymer Upper School, London w6	1642	970	—	5,055	C. Diggory (1991)
Leeds Grammar School	1552	1,130	—	3,909	B. W. Collins (1986)
Leighton Park School, Reading	1890	350†	10,350	7,767	J. A. Chapman (1986)
The Leys School, Cambridge	1875	400†	11,070	8,190	Revd J. C. A. Barrett (1990)
Liverpool College	1840	650‡	—	3,702	B. R. Martin (1992)
Llandovery College, Dyfed	1848	245‡	8,463	5,523	Dr C. E. Evans (Warden) (1988)
Lord Wandsworth College, Hants.	1912	435†	8,712	6,804	G. de W. Waller (1993)
Loughborough Grammar School	1495	920	7,587	4,068	D. N. Ireland (1984)
Magdalen College School, Oxford	1480	500	—	4,380	P. M. Tinniswood (Master) (1991)
Malvern College, Worcs.	1865	669‡	11,400	8,295	R. de C. Chapman (1983)
Manchester Grammar School	1515	1,450	—	3,792	J. G. Parker (High Master) (1985)
Marlborough College, Wilts.	1843	816‡	11,658	8,219	E. J. H. Gould (1993)
Merchant Taylors' School, Liverpool	1620	728	—	3,456	S. J. R. Dawkins (1986)
Merchant Taylors' School, Middx.	1561	725	10,050	6,130	J. R. Gabitass (1991)
Mill Hill School, London NW7	1807	570†	10,584	7,014	E. A. M. MacAlpine (1992)
Monkton Combe School, Bath	1868	325‡	10,860	7,695	M. J. Cuthbertson (1990)
Monmouth School, Gwent	1614	546	7,596	4,560	R. D. Lane (1982)
Mount St Mary's College (RC), Sheffield	1842	320‡	8,343	5,637	P. Fisher (1991)
Newcastle under Lyme School	1874	1,185‡	—	3,276	Dr R. M. Reynolds (Principal) (1990)
Norwich School	1250	593	7,680	4,080	C. D. Brown (1984)
Nottingham High School	1513	840	—	4,119	D. T. Witcombe, ph.D. (1970)
Oakham School, Rutland	1584	800‡	10,530	5,820	G. Smallbone (1985)
The Oratory School (RC), Berks.	1859	365	10,926	7,635	S. W. Barrow (1992)
Oundle School, Northants	1556	820‡	12,021	—	D. B. McMurray (1984)
Pangbourne College, Berks.	1917	360†	10,440	7,320	A. B. E. Hudson (1988)
Perse School, Cambridge	1615	486†	—	4,044	Dr G. M. Stephen (1986)
Plymouth College	1877	621	7,935	4,140	A. J. Morsley (1992)
Pocklington School, York	1514	600‡	7,995	4,368	J. N. D. Gray (1992)
Portsmouth Grammar School	1732	775‡	—	4,035	A. C. V. Evans (1983)
Prior Park College (RC), Bath	1830	449‡	9,423	5,211	J. W. R. Goulding (1989)
Queen Elizabeth GS, Wakefield	1591	744†	—	3,792	R. P. Mardling (1985)
Queen Elizabeth's GS, Blackburn	1567	1,100†	—	3,788	P. F. Johnston (1978)
Queen Elizabeth's Hospital, Bristol	1590	520	6,360	3,624	Dr R. Gliddon (1985)
Queen's College, Taunton	1843	650‡	8,475	5,535	C. T. Bradnock (1991)
Radley College, Oxon.	1847	607	11,430	—	R. M. Morgan (Warden) (1991)
Ratcliffe College (RC), Leicester	1844	462‡	8,409	5,607	Revd K. A. Tomlinson (1993)
Reading Blue Coat School	1646	560†	8,535	4,680	Revd A. Sanders (1974)
Reed's School, Surrey	1813	350†	9,468	7,155	D. E. Prince (1983)
Reigate Grammar School, Surrey	1675	815†	—	4,425	J. G. Hamlin (1982)
Rendcomb College, Glos.	1920	230‡	9,639	7,632	J. Tolputt (1987)
Repton School, Derby	1557	600‡	10,770	8,070	G. E. Jones (1987)
RNIB New College, Worcester	1987	126‡	20,400	13,600	Revd B. R. Manthorp (1980)
Rossall School, Lancs.	1844	460‡	10,500	5,250	R. D. W. Rhodes (1987)
Royal Grammar School, Guildford	1552	820	—	5,274	T. M. S. Young (1992)
Royal Grammar School, Newcastle upon Tyne	1545	973	—	3,312	A. S. Cox (1972)
Royal Grammar School, Worcester	1291	780	—	4,104	W. A. Jones (1993)
Rugby School, Warwicks.	1567	655‡	11,865	8,898	M. B. Mavor, cvo (1990)
Rydal School, Clwyd	1885	333‡	9,039	6,819	N. W. Thorne (1991)
Ryde School, Isle of Wight	1921	424‡	7,716	3,864	M. D. Featherstone (1990)
St Albans School, Herts.	1570	640†	—	4,920	A. R. Grant (1993)
St Ambrose College, Cheshire	1946	680	—	2,928	G. E. Hester (1991)
St Anselm's College (RC), Birkenhead	1933	630	—	2,967	C. Cleugh (1993)
St Bede's College (RC), Manchester	1876	944‡	—	3,543	J. Byrne (1983)
St Bees School, Cumbria	1583	285‡	9,609	6,612	P. A. Chamberlain (1988)
St Benedict's School (RC), London w5	1902	592†	—	4,425	Dr A. J. Dachs (1987)
St Dunstan's College, London se6	1888	570	—	4,836	J. D. Moore (1993)
St Edmund's College (RC), Herts.	1568	475‡	8,586	5,493	D. J. J. McEwen (1984)

Name of School	Foun-ded	No. of pupils	Annual fees £ Boarding	Day	Head (with date of appointment)
St Edmund's School, Canterbury	1749	315‡	11,820	7,230	J. V. Tyson (1978)
St Edward's College (RC), Liverpool	1853	660‡	—	°3,150	J. E. Waszek (1992)
St Edward's School, Oxford	1863	571†	11,430	8,595	D. Christie (Warden) (1988)
St George's College (RC), Surrey	1869	475†	—	6,075	P. A. Johnson, D.Phil. (1992)
St John's School, Surrey	1851	400†	9,300	6,600	C. H. Tongue (1993)
St Lawrence College, Kent	1879	360‡	10,200	6,870	J. H. Binfield (1983)
St Mary's College (RC), Merseyside	1919	564‡	—	3,402	W. Hammond (1991)
St Paul's School, London SW13	1509	750	11,685	7,485	R. S. Baldock (High Master) (1992)
St Peter's School, York	627	470‡	9,576	5,700	R. N. Pittman (1985)
Sedbergh School, Cumbria	1525	460	10,770	7,537	Dr R. G. Baxter (1982)
Sevenoaks School, Kent	1418	940‡	10,701	6,507	R. P. Barker (1981)
Sherborne School, Dorset	1550	650	11,700	8,940	P. H. Lapping (1988)
Shrewsbury School	1552	680	11,388	8,034	F. E. Maidment (1988)
Silcoates School, W. Yorks.	1820	492‡	8,772	5,022	A. P. Spillane (1991)
Solihull School, Warwicks	1560	820†	—	3,931	A. Lee (1983)
Stamford School, Lincs.	1532	572	7,446	3,723	G. J. Timm (1978)
Stockport Grammar School	1487	1,005‡	—	3,636	D. R. J. Bird (1985)
Stonyhurst College (RC), Lancs.	1593	397†	10,608	6,342	Dr R. G. G. Mercer (1985)
Stowe School, Bucks.	1923	570†	12,000	8,400	J. G. L. Nichols (1989)
Sutton Valence School, Kent	1576	340‡	10,341	6,621	M. R. Haywood (1980)
Taunton School	1847	515‡	10,650	6,810	B. B. Sutton (1987)
Tettenhall College, Staffs.	1863	300‡	8,670	5,340	W. J. Dale (1968)
Tonbridge School, Kent	1553	640	11,820	8,340	J. M. Hammond (1990)
Trent College, Derbys.	1868	756‡	9,630	5,871	J. S. Lee (1988)
Trinity School, Surrey	1596	840	—	4,722	R. J. Wilson (1972)
Truro School	1879	890‡	7,950	4,269	G. A. G. Dodd (1993)
University College School, London NW3	1830	520	—	6,270	G. D. Slaughter (1983)
Uppingham School, Leics.	1584	620†	11,850	7,110	S. C. Winkley (1991)
Warwick School	914	800	8,985	4,185	P. J. Cheshire (1988)
Wellingborough School, Northants.	1595	413‡	8,130	4,890	F. R. Ullmann (1993)
Wellington College, Berks.	1856	807†	11,505	8,400	C. J. Driver (1989)
Wells Cathedral School, Somerset	1180	620‡	8,196	4,815	J. S. Baxter (1986)
West Buckland School, Devon	1858	459‡	8,142	4,416	M. Downward (1979)
Westminster School, London SW1	1560	664†	11,850	8,850	D. M. Summersale (1986)
Whitgift School, Surrey	1596	960	—	5,034	C. A. Barnett, D.Phil. (1991)
William Hulme's GS, Manchester	1887	790‡	—	3,816	P. A. Briggs (1987)
Winchester College, Hants.	1382	664	12,270	9,204	J. P. Sabben-Clare (1985)
Wisbech Grammar School, Cambs.	1379	630‡	—	4,125	R. S. Repper (1988)
Wolverhampton Grammar School	1512	655‡	—	4,269	B. St J. Trafford (1990)
Woodbridge School, Suffolk	1662	520‡	8,208	4,998	S. H. Cole (1994)
Woodhouse Grove School, Bradford	1812	560‡	7,995	4,785	D. W. Welsh (1991)
*Worksop College, Notts.	1895	350‡	9,876	6,816	R. D. V. Knight (1990)
Worth School (RC), W. Sussex	1959	311	10,800	8,100	Fr C. Jamison (1994)
Wrekin College, Shropshire	1880	320‡	10,470	7,185	P. Johnson (1991)
Wycliffe College, Glos.	1882	301‡	11,085	7,740	D. C. M. Prichard (1994)

SCOTLAND

Daniel Stewart's and Melville College, Edinburgh	1832	785	7,500	3,843	P. J. F. Tobin (Principal) (1989)
Dollar Academy, Clackmannanshire	1818	750‡	7,869	3,549	L. Harrison (Rector) (1984)
Dundee High School	1239	1,100‡	—	3,549	R. Nimmo, OBE (Rector) (1977)
The Edinburgh Academy	1824	851†	10,194	4,821	A. J. D. Rees (Rector) (1992)
Fettes College, Edinburgh	1870	343‡	11,385	7,650	M. T. Thyne (1988)
George Heriot's School, Edinburgh	1659	978‡	—	3,489	K. P. Pearson (1983)
George Watson's College, Edinburgh	1741	1,256‡	7,578	3,798	F. E. Gerstenberg (Principal) (1985)
Glasgow Academy	1845	605‡	—	3,900	C. W. Turner (Rector) (1983)
Glenalmond College, Perthshire	1841	274†	11,100	7,395	I. G. Templeton (Warden) (1992)
Gordonstoun School, Moray	1934	465‡	11,160	7,200	M. C. S.-R. Pyper (1990)
Hutchesons' Grammar School, Glasgow	1641	1,117‡	—	3,303	D. R. Ward (Rector) (1987)
Kelvinside Academy, Glasgow	1878	630	—	4,050	J. H. Duff (Rector) (1980)

Name of School	Foun-ded	No. of pupils	Annual fees £		Head (with date of appointment)
			Boarding	Day	
Loretto School, E. Lothian	1827	312†	10,575	7,050	Revd N. W. Drummond (1984)
Merchiston Castle School, Edinburgh	1833	380	10,590	6,870	D. M. Spawforth (1981)
Morrison's Academy, Crieff	1860	690‡	9,192	3,321	H. A. Ashmall (Rector) (1979)
Robert Gordon's College, Aberdeen	1729	928‡	7,700	3,500	G. A. Allan (1978)
Strathallan School, Perthshire	1913	400‡	9,990	6,660	A. McPhail (1993)
NORTHERN IRELAND					
Bangor Grammar School, Co. Down	1856	900	—	354	T. W. Patton (1979)
Belfast Royal Academy	1785	1,320‡	—	185	W. M. Sillery (1980)
Campbell College, Belfast	1894	650	4,900	900	Dr R. J. I. Pollock (1987)
Coleraine Academical Institution	1856	850	5,120	2,285	R. S. Forsythe (1984)
Methodist College, Belfast	1868	1,727‡	5,016	2,316	T. W. Mulryne (1988)
Portora Royal School, Enniskillen	1618	420	2,901	nil	R. L. Bennett (1983)
Royal Belfast Academical Institution	1810	990	—	300	R. M. Ridley (1990)
CHANNEL ISLANDS AND ISLE OF MAN					
Elizabeth College, Guernsey	1563	570†	5,760	2,280	J. H. F. Doulton (1988)
King William's College, Isle of Man	1668	298‡	9,825	7,020	S. A. Westley (1989)
EUROPE					
Aiglon College, Switzerland	1949	273‡	Fr.40,485	Fr.27,825	P. Parsons (1976)
British School in the Netherlands	1935	540‡	—	Gld.18,350	M. J. Cooper (Principal) (1990)
British School of Brussels	1970	1,020‡	—	Fr.561,000	Ms J. M. Bray (1993)
British School of Paris, France	1954	°280‡	—	Fr.68,825	A. Slesser (1992)
The English School, Nicosia, Cyprus	1900	830‡	—	C£1,500	A. M. Hudspeth (1988)
The International School of Geneva	1924	2,750‡	Fr.40,000	Fr.17,000	G. Walker, OBE (Director-General) (1991)
The International School of Paris	1964	210‡	—	Fr.75,000	N. M. Prentki (1988)
St Columba's College, Dublin	1843	291‡	IR£5,310	IR£2,970	T. E. Macey (Warden) (1988)
St George's English School, Rome	1958	450‡	—	L17.3m	Dr R. B. Guthrie (acting)
Sir James Henderson School, Milan	1969	°170†	—	°L12.4m	C. T. G. Leech (1986)

OTHER OVERSEAS MEMBERS

AFRICA

FALCON COLLEGE, PO Esigodini, Zimbabwe. Head, P. N. Todd

HILTON COLLEGE, Natal 3245, SA. Head, P. Marsh

MICHAELHOUSE, Balgowan, Natal 3275, SA. Head, J. H. Pluke

PETERHOUSE, Marondera, Zimbabwe. Head, Revd Dr A. J. Megahey

ST GEORGE'S COLLEGE, Harare, Zimbabwe. Head, M. F. Hackett

DIOCESAN COLLEGE, Rondebosch, SA. Head, J. B. Gardener

ST JOHN'S COLLEGE, Johannesburg, SA. Head, W. Macfarlane

ST STITHIAN'S COLLEGE, Randburg, SA. Head, D. B. Wylde

AUSTRALIA

ANGLICAN CHURCH GRAMMAR SCHOOL, Brisbane. Head, C. V. Ellis

BRIGHTON GRAMMAR SCHOOL, Brighton, Victoria. Head, R. L. Rofe

CAMBERWELL GRAMMAR SCHOOL, Balwyn, Victoria 3101. Head, C. F. Black

CANBERRA GS, Red Hill, ACT 2603. Head, T. C. Murray

CAULFIELD GRAMMAR SCHOOL, East St Kilda, Victoria. Head, Revd A. S. Holmes

CHRIST CHURCH GRAMMAR SCHOOL, Claremont 6010, W. Australia. Head, J. J. S. Madin

CHURCH OF ENGLAND GRAMMAR SCHOOL, Melbourne. Head, A. J. de V. Hill

CHURCH OF ENGLAND GRAMMAR SCHOOL, Sydney, NSW. Head, R. A. I. Grant

CRANBROOK SCHOOL, Sydney, NSW. Head, Dr B. N. Carter

GEELONG CHURCH OF ENGLAND GRAMMAR SCHOOL, Corio. Head, J. E. Lewis

THE GEELONG COLLEGE, Geelong, Victoria. Head, A. P. Sheahan

GUILDFORD GRAMMAR SCHOOL, W. Australia. Head, J. M. Moody

HAILEYBURY COLLEGE, Keysborough, Victoria 3175. Head, A. H. M. Aikman

HALE SCHOOL, Wembley Downs, W. Australia. Head, K. G. Tregonning

KING'S SCHOOL, Parramatta, NSW. Head, J. A. Wickham

KINROSS WOLAROI SCHOOL, NSW. Head, A. E. S. Anderson

KNOX GS, Wahroonga 2076, NSW. Head, Dr I. Paterson

NEWINGTON COLLEGE, Stanmore, NSW. Head, A. J. Rae

THE PENINSULA SCHOOL, Mt Eliza, Victoria. Head, H. A. Macdonald

ST PETER'S COLLEGE, St Peter's, S. Australia. *Head*,
Dr A. J. Shinkfield
SCOTCH COLLEGE, Adelaide, S. Australia. *Head*,
W. M. Miles
SCOTCH COLLEGE, Hawthorn, Melbourne, Victoria. *Head*,
Dr F. G. Donaldson
SCOTCH COLLEGE, Swanbourne, W. Australia. *Head*,
W. R. Dickinson
SCOTS COLLEGE, Sydney, NSW. *Head*, G. A. W. Renney
THE SOUTHPORT SCHOOL, Southport, Queensland. *Head*,
B. A. Cook
SYDNEY GRAMMAR SCHOOL, NSW. *Head*,
Dr R. D. Townsend
WESLEY COLLEGE, Melbourne. *Head*, D. H. Prest

CANADA

BRENTWOOD COLLEGE SCHOOL, Vancouver, BC. *Head*,
W. T. Ross
GLENLYON-NORFOLK SCHOOL, Victoria, BC. *Head*,
D. Brooks
HILLFIELD-STRATHALLAN COLLEGE, Hamilton, Ontario.
Head, M. B. Wansbrough
PICKERING COLLEGE, Newmarket, Ontario. *Head*,
S. H. Clark
ST ANDREW'S COLLEGE, Aurora, Ontario. *Head*,
R. P. Bedard
TORONTO FRENCH SCHOOL. *Head*, A. S. Troubetzkoy
TRINITY COLLEGE SCHOOL, Port Hope, Ontario. *Head*,
R. C. N.Wright
UPPER CANADA COLLEGE, Toronto. *Head*, J. D. Blakey

HONG KONG

ISLAND SCHOOL, Borrett Road. *Head*, D. J. James
KING GEORGE V SCHOOL, Kowloon. *Head*,
M. J. Behennah

INDIA

BIRLA PUBLIC SCHOOL, Pilani 333 031, Rajasthan. *Head*,
B. K. Sood
LAWRENCE SCHOOL, Lovedale, Nilgiris. *Head*,
B. S. Bhatnagar
LAWRENCE SCHOOL, Sanawar. *Head*, Sumer Singh
THE SCINDIA SCHOOL, GWALIOR. *Head*, Dr S. D. Singh

NEW ZEALAND

CHRIST'S COLLEGE, Christchurch, Canterbury. *Head*,
Dr M. J. Rosser
KING'S COLLEGE, Auckland. *Head*, J. S. Taylor
ST ANDREW'S COLLEGE, Christchurch, Canterbury. *Head*,
Dr A. J. Rentoul
RATHKEALE COLLEGE, Masterton. *Head*, B. R. Levick
THE COLLEGIATE SCHOOL, Wanganui. *Head*,
T. S. McKinlay
WAITAKI BOYS' HIGH SCHOOL, Oamaru. *Head*,
B. R. Gollop

SOUTH AMERICA

ACADEMIA BRITANICA CUSCATLECA, El Salvador. *Head*,
A. J. McGuiggan
MARKHAM COLLEGE, Lima, Peru. *Head*, W. J. Baker
ST ANDREW'S SCOTS SCHOOL, Argentina. *Head*, K. Prior
ST GEORGE'S COLLEGE, Quilmes, Argentina. *Head*,
N. P. O. Green
ST PAULS' SCHOOL, São Paulo, Brazil. *Head*,
M. T. M. C. McCann
THE BRITISH SCHOOLS, Montevideo, Uruguay. *Head*,
J. H. Sidwell

ADDITIONAL MEMBERS

The headteachers of some maintained schools are by
invitation Additional Members of the HMC. They include
the following:

DURHAM JOHNSTONE SCHOOL, Durham. *Head*,
J. Dunford
EGG BUCKLAND COMMUNITY COLLEGE, Plymouth.
Head, H. Green
HABERDASHERS' ASKE'S HATCHAM BOYS' SCHOOL,
Pepys Road, London SE14 5SF. *Head*, G. J. Walker
HAYWARDS HEATH SIXTH FORM COLLEGE, W. Sussex.
Head, B. W. Derbyshire
THE JUDD SCHOOL, Tonbridge, Kent. *Head*,
K. A. Starling
KING EDWARD VI CAMP HILL SCHOOL FOR BOYS,
Birmingham. *Head*, R. Dancey
LISKEARD SCHOOL, Cornwall. *Head*, A. D. Wood
THE LONDON ORATORY SCHOOL, London SW6. *Head*,
J. C. McIntosh
PRESCOT SCHOOL, Merseyside. *Head*, P. A. Barlow
PRINCE HENRY'S GRAMMAR SCHOOL, Otley, W Yorks.
Head, M. Franklin
PRINCE WILLIAM SCHOOL, Oundle, Cambs. *Head*,
C. J. Lowe
THE ROYAL GRAMMAR SCHOOL, Lancaster. *Head*,
P. J. Mawby
ST BARTHOLOMEW'S SCHOOL, Newbury, Bucks. *Head*,
R. P. H. Mermagen
ST JOHN'S SCHOOL, Marlborough, Wilts. *Head*, J. Price
STOWMARKET HIGH SCHOOL, Suffolk. *Head*,
Dr R. J. Montgomery
WESTMINSTER CITY SCHOOL, London SW1. *Head*,
M. Billingham

SOCIETY OF HEADMASTERS AND HEADMISTRESSES OF INDEPENDENT SCHOOLS

The Society was founded in 1961 and, in general, represents smaller boarding schools.

Hon. Secretary, A. E. R. Dodds, Mantons, Park Road, Winchester, Hants. SO23 7BE. Tel: 0962-862579

Headmasters of the following schools are members of both HMC and SHMIS; details of these schools appear in the HMC list: Abbotsholme School, Ackworth School, Bedales School, Churcher's College, City of London Freemen's School, Colston's Collegiate School, King's School, Tyne-mouth, Lord Wandsworth College, Pangbourne College, Reading Blue Coat School, Reed's School, Rendcomb College, Ryde School, St George's College, Silcoates School, Tettenhall College, West Buckland School, Wisbech Grammar School, Woodbridge School

* Woodard Corporation School

† Girls in VI form

‡ Co-educational

Name of School	Foun-ded	No. of pupils	Annual fees £		Head (with date of appointment)
			Boarding	Day	
Austin Friars School (*RC*), Carlisle	1951	302‡	6,915	4,132	Revd T. Lyons, OSA (1981)
Bearwood College, Berks.	1827	265	9,300	5,175	Dr R. J. Belcher (1993)
Bedstone College, Shropshire	1948	165‡	9,000	5,610	M. S. Symonds (1990)
Belmont Abbey (*RC*), Hereford	1926	180	8,115	4,680	Revd D. C. Jenkins, OSB (1988)
Bembridge School, Isle of Wight	1919	180‡	8,490	4,230	J. High (1986)
Bentham School, N. Yorks	1726	260‡	7,794	3,891	N. K. D. Ward (1992)
Bethany School, Kent	1866	275‡	8,814	5,640	W. M. Harvey (1988)
Box Hill School, Surrey	1959	297‡	9,390	5,820	Dr R. A. S. Atwood (1987)
Carmel College (*Jewish*), Oxon.	1948	224‡	12,450	7,200	P. D. Skelker (1984)
Claremont Fan Court School, Surrey	1932	377‡	8,340	5,250	J. H. Scott (1987)
Clayesmore School, Dorset	1896	301‡	10,440	7,305	D. J. Beeby (1986)
Cokethorpe School, Oxon.	1957	200‡	10,950	7,200	D. G. Crawford (1989)
Duke of York's Royal Military School, Dover	1803	473	—	—	Col. G. H. Wilson (1992)
Embley Park School, Romsey, Hants.	1946	225†	8,885	5,490	D. F. Chapman (1987)
Ewell Castle School, Surrey	1926	320†	—	3,900	R. A. Fewtrell (1983)
Friends' School, Essex	1702	270‡	9,126	5,664	Miss S. H. Evans (1989)
Fulneck Boys' School, W. Yorks.	1753	317†	8,310	4,365	I. D. Cleland (1980)
*Grenville College, Devon	1954	250	9,030	4,428	M. C. V. Cane, PH.D. (1992)
Halliford School, Middx.	1956	320†	—	4,020	J. R. Crook (1984)
Hipperholme Grammar School, Halifax	1648	362‡	—	3,024	C. C. Robinson (1988)
Keil School, Dumbarton	1915	225‡	8,082	4,527	J. A. Cummings (1993)
Kingham Hill School, Oxon.	1886	195‡	8,181	4,908	M. Payne (*Warden*) (1990)
King's School, Gloucester	1541	350‡	8,100	4,800	P. Lacey (1993)
Kirkham Grammar School, Lancs.	1549	510‡	6,147	3,276	B. Stacey (1991)
Licensed Victuallers' School, Ascot, Berks.	1803	670‡	8,910	5,010	Mrs P. M. Cowley (1992)
Lord Mayor Treloar College, Hants.	1908	228‡	33,384	25,038	H. Heard (1990)
Milton Abbey School, Dorset	1954	250	10,620	7,080	R. H. Hardy (1987)
Oswestry School, Shropshire	1407	283‡	8,340	4,920	J. V. Light (1992)
Pierrepont School, Surrey	1947	170‡	9,465	5,699	N. Taylor (1993)
The Purcell School (music), Middx.	1962	150‡	13,446	7,950	K. J. Bain (1984)
Rannoch School, Perthshire	1959	270‡	9,585	5,430	M. Barratt (1982)
Rishworth School, W. Yorks.	1724	475‡	8,610	4,455	M. J. Elford (1992)
Rougemont School, Gwent	1919	236‡	—	4,227	G. R. Sims (1991)
Royal Hospital School, Ipswich	1712	602‡	7,200	—	M. A. B. Kirk (1983)
Royal Russell School, Surrey	1853	450‡	9,150	4,830	R. D. Balaam (1981)
Royal School, Dungannon, N. Ireland	1614	650‡	5,505	85	P. D. Hewitt (1984)
Royal Wolverhampton School	1850	320‡	8,310	4,755	P. Gorring (1985)
Ruthin School, Clwyd	1574	170‡	8,985	5,685	J. S. Rowlands (1993)
St Bede's School, E. Sussex	—	360‡	10,455	6,450	R. A. Perrin (1978)
St David's College, Gwynedd	1965	235	8,640	5,625	W. Seymour (1991)
Scarborough College, N. Yorks.	1898	418‡	8,775	4,758	D. S. Hempsall, PH.D. (1985)
Seaford College, W. Sussex	1884	300†	9,030	5,550	R. C. Hannaford (1990)
Shebbear College, Devon	1841	260‡	8,460	4,620	R. J. Buley (1983)
Shiplake College, Oxon.	1959	325	10,500	7,350	N. V. Bevan (1988)
Sidcot School, Avon	1808	300‡	8,925	5,355	C. J. Greenfield (1986)
Stafford Grammar School, Staffs.	1982	290‡	—	3,636	M. James (1992)
Stanbridge Earls School, Hants.	1952	180‡	10,785	8,100	H. Moxon (1984)
Warminster School, Wilts.	1707	323‡	8,310	4,905	T. D. Holgate (1990)
Yarm School, Cleveland	1978	430†	—	4,350	R. Neville Tate (1978)

GIRLS' SCHOOLS ASSOCIATION

THE GIRLS' SCHOOLS ASSOCIATION, 130 Regent Road, Leicester LEI 7PG. Tel: 0533-541619
President (1993-4), Miss J. Jefferson
Secretary, Miss A. C. Parkin

CSC Church Schools Company, 1A Doughty Street, London WCIN 2PH. Tel: 071-404 3134
§ Girls Public Day School Trust, 26 Queen Anne's Gate, London SW1H 9AN. Tel: 071-222 9595
* Woodard Corporation School
† Boys in VI form
‡ Co-educational
° 1992 figures

Name of School	Founded	No. of pupils	Annual fees £ Boarding	Day	Head (with date of appointment)
ENGLAND AND WALES					
Abbey School, Reading	1887	760	—	3,780	Miss B. C. L. Sheldon (1991)
Abbot's Hill, Herts.	1912	170	9,435	5,565	Mrs J. Kingsley (1979)
Adcote School, Shropshire	1907	70	8,385	4,725	Mrs S. B. Cecchet (1979)
Alice Ottley School, Worcester	1883	600	—	4,260	Miss C. Sibbit (1986)
Amberfield School, Ipswich	1952	179	—	3,630	Mrs L. A. Lewis (1992)
Ashford School, Kent	1910	428	8,178	4,716	Mrs P. Metham (1992)
Atherley School, Southampton (CSC)	1926	320	—	3,915	Mrs M. Williams (1988)
Badminton School, Bristol	1858	355	10,350	5,700	C. J. T. Gould (1981)
§Bath High School	1875	407	—	3,600	Miss M. A. Winfield (1985)
Battle Abbey School, E. Sussex	1912	120‡	8,565	5,295	D. J. A. Teall (1982)
Bedford High School	1882	800	8,101	4,282	Mrs D. M. Willis (1987)
Bedgebury School, Kent	1860	373	9,879	6,114	Mrs M. E. A. Kaye (1987)
Beechwood School (RC), Kent	1915	152	9,810	5,775	J. A. Fallon, Ph.D. (1979)
§Belvedere School, Liverpool	1880	439	—	3,600	Mrs C. H. Evans (1992)
Benenden School, Kent	1923	418	11,730	—	Mrs G. D. duCharme (1985)
Berkhamsted School, Herts.	1888	454	8,472	4,986	Miss V. E. M. Shepherd (1980)
§Birkenhead High School	1901	732	—	3,600	Mrs K. R. Irving (1986)
§Blackheath High School, London SE3	1880	341	—	4,200	Miss R. K. Musgrave (1989)
Bolton School, Lancs.	1877	936	—	4,190	Mrs M. A. Spurr (1979)
Bradford Girls' Grammar School	1875	646	—	3,744	Mrs L. J. Warrington (1986)
§Brighton and Hove High School	1876	500	—	3,600	Miss R. A. Woodbridge (1989)
Brigidine School, Windsor	1948	260	—	3,993	Mrs M. B. Cairns (1987)
§Bromley High School, Kent	1883	552	—	4,200	Mrs E. J. Hancock (1989)
Bruton School, Somerset	1900	510	6,201	3,357	Mrs J. M. Wade (1987)
Burgess Hill School, W. Sussex	1906	365	8,280	4,980	Mrs R. F. Lewis (1992)
Bury Grammar School, Lancs.	1884	820	—	3,432	Miss J. M. Lawley (1987)
Casterton School, Cumbria	1823	335	8,388	5,256	A. F. Thomas (1990)
§Central Newcastle High School	1895	582	—	3,600	Mrs A. M. Chapman (1985)
Channing School, London N6	1885	310	—	5,235	Mrs I. R. Raphael (1984)
§Charters-Ancaster School, E. Sussex	1906	220	8,220	4,080	Mrs K. Lewis (1990)
Cheltenham Ladies' College, Glos.	1853	830	10,725	6,810	Miss E. Castle (Principal) (1987)
City of London School for Girls, London EC2	1894	538	—	4,626	Lady France (1986)
Clifton High School, Bristol	1877	463	7,710	4,035	Mrs J. D. Walters (1985)
Cobham Hall, Kent	1962	175	11,520	7,731	Mrs R. J. McCarthy (1989)
Colston's Girls' School, Bristol	1891	600	—	3,273	Mrs J. P. Franklin (1989)
Combe Bank School, Kent	1868	415	—	5,010	Miss N. Spurr (1993)
Commonweal Lodge School, Surrey	1916	150	—	4,125	Miss J. M. Brown (1982)
Cranford House School, Oxon.	1931	195	—	4,260	Mrs A. B. Gray (1992)
Croft House School, Dorset	1941	130	8,910	6,288	M. P. Hawkins (1993)
Croham Hurst School, Surrey	1899	330	—	3,900	Miss J. M. Shelmerdine (1986)
§Croydon High School, Surrey	1874	706	—	4,200	Mrs P. E. Davies (1990)
Dame Alice Harpur School, Bedford	1882	780	—	3,765	Mrs R. Randle (1990)
Dame Allan's Girls' School, Newcastle upon Tyne	1705	453†	—	3,267	T. A. Willcocks (Principal) (1988)

Name of School	Foun-ded	No. of pupils	Annual fees £ Boarding	Day	Head (with date of appointment)
Derby High School	1892	316	—	3,990	Dr G. H. Goddard (1983)
Downe House, Berks.	1907	520	11,385	8,250	Miss S. Cameron (1989)
Dunottar School, Surrey	1926	295	—	4,020	Miss J. Burnell (1985)
Durham High School	1884	271	—	3,630	M. L. Walters (1992)
Edgbaston Church of England College	1886	215	—	4,020	Mrs A. Varley-Tipton (1992)
Edgbaston High School	1876	521	—	3,960	Mrs S. J. Horsman (1987)
Edgehill College, Devon	1884	368	8,505	4,635	Mrs E. M. Burton (1987)
Elmslie Girls' School, Lancs.	1918	300	—	3,516	Miss E. M. Smithies (1978)
Eothen School, Surrey (CSC)	1892	160	—	4,407	Mrs A. Coutts (1992)
Farlington School, W. Sussex	1896	234	8,400	5,190	Mrs P. Mawer (1992)
Farnborough Hill, Hants.	1889	500	—	3,873	Sr E. McCormack (1988)
Farringtons, Kent	1911	280	8,379	4,587	Mrs B. J. Stock (1987)
Felixstowe College, Suffolk	1929	200	10,155	6,330	Mrs B. Patterson (1993)
Fernhill Manor School, Hants.	1890	144	7,500	4,770	Revd A. J. Folks (1985)
Francis Holland School, London NW1	1878	365	—	4,710	Mrs P. H. Parsonson (1988)
Francis Holland School, London SW1	1881	170	—	5,205	Mrs J. A. Anderson (1982)
Gateways School, Leeds	1941	200	—	3,240	Miss L. M. Brown (1984)
Godolphin School, Wilts.	1726	360	9,900	5,880	Mrs H. Fender (1990)
Godolphin and Latymer School, London W6	1905	703	—	5,190	Miss M. Rudland (1986)
Greenacre School, Surrey	1933	°376	—	°4,272	Mrs P. M. Wood (1990)
The Grove School, Hindhead, Surrey	1877	206	8,862	5,544	C. Brooks (1984)
Guildford High School (CSC)	1888	450	—	4,611	Mrs S. H. Singer (1991)
Haberdashers' Aske's School for Girls, Herts.	1873	847	—	3,015	Mrs P. Penney (1991)
Haberdashers' Monmouth School, Gwent	1891	543	7,380	4,065	Mrs D. L. Newman (1992)
Harrogate Ladies' College	1893	395	8,325	5,595	Mrs J. A. Smith (1993)
Headington School, Oxford	1915	545	8,181	4,335	Miss E. M. Tucker (1982)
Heathfield School, Ascot, Berks.	1900	210	11,415	—	Mrs J. Benammar (1992)
§Heathfield School, Pinner, Middx.	1900	344	—	4,200	Mrs J. Merritt (1988)
Hethersett Old Hall School, Norwich	1928	207	7,560	3,945	Mrs V. M. Redington (1983)
Highclare School, W. Midlands	1932	261†	—	3,380	Mrs C. A. Hanson (1973)
Hollygirt School, Nottingham	1877	185	—	3,330	Mrs M. R. Banks (1985)
Holy Child School, Birmingham	1933	200	—	4,065	Mrs J. Hill (acting)
Holy Trinity College, Bromley	1886	280	—	3,846	Sr B. Wetz (1986)
Holy Trinity School, Kidderminster	1903	180	—	4,050	Mrs S. M. Bell (1990)
Howell's School, Denbigh, Clwyd	1859	220	9,330	6,039	Mrs M. Steel (1991)
§Howell's School, Llandaff, Cardiff	1860	571	—	3,600	Mrs C. J. Fitz (1991)
Hull High School (CSC)	1890	163	5,795	3,648	Miss C. M. B. Radcliffe (1976)
Hulme Grammar School, Oldham	1895	520	—	3,315	Miss M. S. Smolenski (1992)
§Ipswich High School	1878	419	—	3,600	Miss V. MacCuish (1993)
James Allen's Girls' School, London SE22	1741	745	6,732	4,190	Mrs B. Davies (1984)
Kent College	1885	234‡	10,020	5,940	Miss B. Crompton (1990)
King Edward VI High School for Girls, Birmingham	1883	548	—	3,780	Miss E. W. Evans (1977)
King's HS for Girls, Warwick	1879	556	—	3,582	Mrs J. M. Anderson (1987)
Kingsley School, Warwicks.	1884	431	—	3,855	Mrs M. A. Webster (1988)
Lady Eleanor Holles School, Middx.	1711	630	—	4,530	Miss E. M. Candy (1981)
La Retraite School, Wilts.	1953	200	—	°3,840	Mrs M. Paisey (1986)
La Sagesse Convent High School, Newcastle upon Tyne	1906	350	—	3,381	Mrs D. C. Parker (1988)
La Sagesse Convent School, Hants.	1896	°125	—	°2,600	Sr Thomas Cox (1977)
Lavant House School, W. Sussex	1952	126	9,150	5,595	Mrs Y. Graham (1990)
Lawnside, Worcs.	1818	100	9,585	5,685	Miss J. Harvey (1991)
Leeds Girls' High School	1876	615	—	3,954	Miss P. A. Randall (1977)
Leicester High School	1906	304	—	3,750	Mrs P. A. Watson (1992)
Loughborough High School	1850	525	5,793	3,663	Miss J. E. L. Harvatt (1978)
Luckley-Oakfield School, Berks.	1895	304	7,470	4,647	R. C. Blake (1984)
Malvern Girls' College, Worcs.	1893	485	10,602	7,068	Dr V. B. Payne (1986)
Manchester High School	1874	725	—	3,600	Miss M. M. Moon (1983)
Manor House School, Little Bookham, Surrey	1927	260	—	4,974	Mrs L. Mendes (1989)
Maynard School, Exeter	1877	553	—	3,684	Miss F. Murdin (1980)
Merchant Taylors' School, Liverpool	1888	640	—	3,456	Miss E. J. Panton (1988)
Micklefield School, E. Sussex	1910	120	9,270	5,325	E. Reynolds (1987)
Moira House School, E. Sussex	1875	300	9,630	6,216	A. R. Underwood (1975)

Name of School	Founded	No. of pupils	Annual fees £ Boarding	Day	Head (with date of appointment)
More House School, London sw1	1953	240	—	5,040	Miss M. Connell (1991)
Moreton Hall, Shropshire	1913	275	10,125	7,020	J. Forster (1992)
Mount School, York	1831	252	9,060	6,030	Miss B. J. Windle (1986)
Newcastle upon Tyne Church HS	1885	399	—	3,330	Mrs P. E. Davies (1974)
New Hall School, Essex	1642	450	9,864	6,318	Sr Margaret Mary Horton (1986)
Northampton High School	1878	535	—	3,825	Mrs L. A. Mayne (1988)
North Foreland Lodge, Hants.	1909	180	9,900	—	Miss D. L. Matthews (1983)
North London Collegiate School	1850	725	—	4,401	Mrs J. L. Clanchy (1987)
Northwood College, Middx.	1878	525	—	4,428	Mrs J. A. Mayou (1991)
§Norwich High School	1875	641	—	3,600	Mrs V. C. Bidwell (1985)
§Nottingham High School	1875	807	—	3,600	Mrs C. Bowering (1984)
§Notting Hill and Ealing High School	1873	560	—	4,200	Mrs S. M. Whitfield (1991)
Ockbrook School, Derby	1799	220	5,802	3,156	Ms M. Rennie, ph.d. (1987)
Old Palace School, Surrey	1887	600	—	3,570	Miss K. L. Hilton (1974)
§Oxford High School	1875	559	—	3,600	Mrs J. Townsend (1981)
Palmers Green High School, London n21	1905	320	—	3,675	Mrs S. Grant (1989)
Park School, Somerset	1851	°93	°7,620	°4,380	Mrs M. J. Hannon (1987)
Parsons Mead, Surrey	1897	250	8,610	4,485	Miss E. B. Plant (1990)
Penrhos College, Clwyd	1880	236	8,670	5,940	C. M. J. Allen (1993)
Perse School for Girls, Cambridge	1881	530	—	4,020	Miss H. S. Smith (1989)
*Peterborough High School	1939	200	7,560	3,765	Mrs A. Storey (1977)
Pipers Corner School, Bucks.	1930	370	8,535	5,100	Dr M. M. Wilson (1986)
Polam Hall, Co. Durham	1848	350	8,223	4,023	Mrs H. C. Hamilton (1987)
§Portsmouth High School	1882	542	—	3,600	Mrs J. M. Dawtrey (1984)
Princess Helena College, Herts.	1820	150	9,240	6,450	Miss H. Davidson-Wall (1990)
Prior's Field, Surrey	1902	230	8,685	5,685	Mrs J. M. McCallum (1987)
§Putney High School, London sw15	1893	571	—	4,200	Mrs E. Merchant (1991)
Queen Anne's School, Berks.	1698	373	10,200	6,450	Mrs D. Forbes (1993)
Queen Ethelburga's College, York	1912	250	9,085	5,685	Mrs G. L. Richardson (1993)
Queen Margaret's School, York	1901	355	9,375	5,940	Dr G. A. H. Chapman (1993)
Queen Mary School, Lytham, Lancs.	1930	550	—	3,345	Miss M. C. Ritchie (1981)
Queen's College, London w1	1848	390	6,570	5,370	Lady Goodhart (1991)
Queen's Gate School, London sw7	1891	210	—	4,710	Mrs A. M. Holyoak (Principal) (1987)
Queen's School, Chester	1878	416	—	3,879	Miss D. M. Skilbeck (1989)
Queenswood, Herts.	1894	406	10,680	6,318	Mrs A. M. B. Butler (1981)
Redland High School, Bristol	1882	480	—	3,633	Mrs C. Lear (1989)
Red Maids' School, Bristol	1634	500	6,990	3,525	Miss S. Hampton (1987)
Rickmansworth Masonic School, Herts.	1788	520	7,677	4,401	Mrs I. M. Andrews (1992)
Roedean School, Brighton	1885	440	11,985	—	Mrs A. R. Longley (1984)
Rosemead, W. Sussex	1919	130	8,970	5,160	Mrs H. Kingham (Principal) (1991)
Royal Naval School, Surrey	1840	250	8,820	5,598	Dr J. L. Clough (1987)
Royal School, Bath	1864	305	10,371	6,615	Mrs E. McKendrick (1994)
Runton and Sutherland School, Norfolk	1875	120	9,705	5,670	Mrs D. J. Buckenham (1993)
Rye St Antony School (RC), Oxford	1930	400	7,725	4,650	Miss A. M. Jones (1990)
St Albans High School, Herts.	1889	520	—	4,299	Miss E. M. Diggory (1983)
St Andrew's School, Bedford	1897	170	—	3,012	Mrs J. E. Stephen (1991)
St Anne's School, Cumbria	1863	265	8,685	5,760	C. M. G. Jenkins (1993)
St Antony's-Leweston School (RC), Dorset	1891	285	9,363	6,105	Miss C. Denley Lloyd (1993)
St Catherine's School, Surrey	1885	450	8,580	5,235	J. R. Palmer (1982)
*School of St Clare, Penzance	1889	100	7,665	4,050	I. Halford (1986)
St David's School, Middx.	1716	246†	8,295	4,785	Mrs J. G. Osborne (1985)
St Dunstan's Abbey, Devon	1850	210	7,399	5,089	R. A. Bye (1991)
St Elphin's School, Derbys.	1844	180	9,111	5,307	A. P. C. Pollard (1979)
St Felix School, Suffolk	1897	265	9,627	6,189	Mrs S. R. Campion (1991)
St Francis' College (RC), Herts.	1933	205	8,850	4,575	Miss M. Hegarty (1993)
S. Gabriel's School, Berks.	1929	170	—	4,497	D. Cobb (1990)
St George's School, Ascot, Berks.	1923	295	10,950	6,150	Mrs A. M. Griggs (1989)
School of S. Helen and S. Katharine, Oxon.	1903	520	7,200	3,750	Mrs C. L. Hall (1993)
St Helen's School, Middx.	1899	571	8,187	4,341	Mrs Y.A. Burne, ph.d. (1987)
*S. Hilary's School, Cheshire	1880	188	—	3,735	Mrs J. Tracey (1985)

Name of School	Founded	No. of pupils	Annual fees £		Head (with date of appointment)
			Boarding	Day	
St James's and the Abbey, Worcs.	1896	200	9,600	6,399	Miss E. M. Mullenger (1986)
St Joseph's Convent School (RC), Berks.	1909	420	—	3,540	Mrs V. Brookes (1990)
St Joseph's School, Lincoln	1905	210	7,245	3,645	Mrs A. Scott (1983)
St Leonards-Mayfield School, E. Sussex	1850	525	9,360	6,240	Sr J. Sinclair (1980)
St Margaret's School, Bushey, Herts.	1749	380	8,040	5,085	Miss M. de Villiers (1993)
*St Margaret's School, Exeter	1904	370	5,805	3,540	Mrs M. D'Albertanson (1993)
St Martin's School, Solihull, W. Midlands	1941	245	—	4,230	Mrs S. J. Williams (1989)
*School of St Mary and St Anne, Abbots Bromley, Staffs.	1874	240	9,900	6,597	A. Grigg (1989)
St Mary's Convent School, Worcester	1934	350	—	3,075	Mrs M. Kilbride (1986)
St Mary's Hall, Brighton	1836	227	8,487	5,439	Mrs P. J. James (1992)
St Mary's School (RC), Ascot, Berks.	1885	338	10,995	6,597	Sr M. M. Orchard (1982)
St Mary's School, Calne, Wilts.	1872	321	10,530	6,240	Miss D. H. Burns (1985)
St Mary's School, Cambridge	1898	590	6,180	3,450	Miss M. Conway (1989)
St Mary's School, Colchester	1908	260	—	3,336	Mrs G. M. G. Mouser (1981)
St Mary's School, Gerrards Cross	1872	325	—	4,575	Mrs J. P. G. Smith (1984)
St Mary's School (RC), Shaftesbury	1945	290	8,970	5,730	Sr M. Campion Livesey (1985)
St Mary's School, Wantage, Oxon.	1873	270	9,900	—	Revd Mrs P. H. Johns (1980)
St Maur's Convent School, Weybridge	1898	750	—	4,500	Mrs M. E. Dodds (1991)
*S. Michaels Burton Park, W. Sussex	1844	130	8,970	5,970	Mrs L. J. Griffin (1991)
St Michael's, Limpsfield, Surrey	1850	131	9,521	5,528	Ms M. J. Hustler, PH.D. (1989)
St Paul's Girls' School, London w6	1904	620	—	5,538	Miss J. Gough (High Mistress) (1992)
St Swithun's School, Winchester	1884	448	10,275	6,210	Miss J. E. Jefferson (1986)
St Teresa's School, Dorking	1928	360	9,330	4,590	L. Allan (1987)
Selwyn School, Glos.	—	230	8,025	4,575	A. Beatson (1990)
§Sheffield High School	1878	540	—	3,600	Mrs M. A. Houston (1989)
Sherborne School for Girls, Dorset	1899	457	10,350	6,900	Miss J. M. Taylor (1985)
§Shrewsbury High School	1885	406	—	3,600	Miss S. Gardner (1990)
Sir William Perkins's School, Surrey	1725	504	—	°3,315	Mrs A. F. Darlow (1982)
§South Hampstead High School, London NW3	1876	593	—	4,200	Mrs J. G. Scott (1993)
Stamford High School, Lincs.	1876	730	7,488	3,744	Miss G. K. Bland (1978)
Stonar School, Wilts.	1921	450	8,910	4,935	Mrs S. Hopkinson (1986)
Stover School, Devon	1932	260	°7,290	°3,825	Mrs W. E. Lunel (1984)
Stratford House School, Kent	1912	230	—	4,260	Mrs A. A. Williamson (1974)
§Streatham Hill and Clapham High School, London sw2	1887	391	—	4,200	Miss G. M. Ellis (1979)
Sunderland High School (CSC)	1884	230‡	—	3,600	Miss C. Rendle-Short (1993)
Surbiton High School (CSC), Surrey	1884	510	—	4,428	Miss G. Perry (1993)
§Sutton High School, Surrey	1884	557	—	4,200	Miss A. E. Cavendish (1980)
§Sydenham High School, London se26	1887	488	—	4,200	Mrs G. Baker (1988)
Talbot Heath, Dorset	1886	439	7,911	4,509	Mrs C. Dipple (1991)
Teesside High School, Cleveland	1970	375	—	3,393	Mrs H. Coles (1982)
Tormead School, Surrey	1905	450	—	4,635	Mrs H. E. M. Alleyne (1992)
Truro High School	1880	350	7,341	4,023	J. Graham-Brown (1992)
Tudor Hall School, Oxon.	1850	262	9,510	5,925	Miss N. Godfrey (1984)
Upper Chine, Isle of Wight	1799	138	8,415	4,485	Dr H. Harvey (1990)
Ursuline Convent School, Kent	1904	300	7,881	4,596	Sr M. Murphy (1977)
Ursuline High School, Ilford	1903	408	—	4,020	Miss J. Reddington (1990)
Wadhurst College, E. Sussex	1930	165	9,855	6,270	Miss A. M. Phillips (1991)
Wakefield Girls' High School	1878	900	—	3,792	Mrs P. A. Langham (1987)
Walthamstow Hall, Kent	1838	375	9,810	5,280	Mrs J. S. Lang (1984)
Wentworth Milton Mount, Dorset	1962	280	8,064	5,040	Miss S. Coe (1991)
Westfield School, Newcastle upon Tyne	1962	205	—	3,771	Mrs M. Farndale (1990)
West Heath, Kent	1867	129	10,500	7,380	Mrs R. A. Ditchburn (1993)
Westholme School, Lancs.	1923	650	—	3,195	Mrs L. Croston (Principal) (1988)
Westonbirt, Glos.	1928	250	9,975	6,420	Mrs G. Hylson-Smith (1986)
§Wimbledon High School, London sw19	1880	539	—	4,200	Mrs E. M. Baker (1992)
Wispers School, Surrey	1946	165	8,442	5,442	L. H. Beltran (1979)
Withington Girls' School, Manchester	1890	480	—	3,465	Mrs M. Kenyon (1986)

Name of School	Founded	No. of pupils	Annual fees £		Head (with date of appointment)
			Boarding	Day	
Woldingham School, Surrey	1842	453	10,404	6,300	Ms P. Dineen, ph.d. (1985)
Wroxall Abbey School, Warwick	1872	100	9,075	5,325	Mrs J. M. Gowen (1993)
Wychwood School, Oxford	1897	160	6,420	4,020	Mrs M. L. Duffill (1981)
Wycombe Abbey School, Bucks.	1896	485	11,538	—	Mrs J. M. Goodland (1989)
Wykeham House School, Fareham, Hants.	1913	250	—	3,546	Mrs E. M. Moore (1983)
York College for Girls (CSC)	1908	147	—	4,041	Mrs J. L. Clare (1982)
SCOTLAND					
Kilgraston School, Perthshire	1930	236	8,700	4,725	Mrs J. L. Austin (1993)
Laurel Bank School, Glasgow	1903	385	—	3,870	Miss L. G. Egginton (1984)
Mary Erskine School, Edinburgh	1694	630	7,750	3,843	P. F. J. Tobin (Principal) (1989)
Park School, Glasgow	1880	365	—	3,627	Mrs M. E. Myatt (1986)
St Denis and Cranley School, Edinburgh	1858	150	8,400	4,170	Mrs J. M. Munro (1984)
St George's School, Edinburgh	1888	540	7,926	4,101	Dr J. McClure (1994)
St Leonards School, St Andrews	1877	270	11,100	5,850	Mrs L. E. James (1988)
St Margaret's School, Aberdeen	1846	218	—	3,360	Miss L. M. Ogilvie (1989)
St Margaret's School, Edinburgh	1890	400	7,759	3,782	Mrs M. J. Cameron (1984)
Wellington School for Girls, Ayr	1849	°300	°8,160	°4,095	Mrs D. A. Gardner (1988)
CHANNEL ISLANDS					
The Ladies' College, Guernsey	1872	346	—	1,890	Miss M. Macdonald (1992)

Social Welfare

National Health Service

and Local Authority Personal Social Services

The National Health Service came into being on 5 July 1948, as a result of the National Health Service Act 1946. The Act placed a duty on the Secretary of State for Social Services to promote the establishment in England and Wales of a comprehensive health service designed to secure improvement in the mental and physical health of the people and the prevention, diagnosis and treatment of illness. The Secretary of State for Wales administers the National Health Service in Wales. There are separate Acts for Scotland and Northern Ireland, where the health services are run on very similar lines and the respective Secretaries of State are responsible to Parliament.

The National Health Service covers a comprehensive range of hospital, specialist, family practitioner (medical, dental, ophthalmic and pharmaceutical), artificial limb and appliance, ambulance, and community health services. Everyone normally resident in this country is entitled to use any of these services, there are no contribution conditions and the charges made (except those for amenity beds) are reduced or waived in cases of hardship.

In addition, the Secretary of State for Social Services is responsible under the Local Authority Social Services Act 1970 for the provision by local authorities of social services for the elderly, the disabled, those with mental disorders and for families and children.

The NHS is financed mainly from taxation and the cost met from moneys voted by Parliament. The present level of expenditure is £30.5 billion per annum.

STRUCTURE

The National Health Service and Community Care Act 1990 introduced wide-ranging reforms in management and patient care. The Act provides for more streamlined Regional and District Health Authorities and Family Health Services Authorities, and for the establishment of NHS Trusts, which operate as self-governing health care providers. One result of the Act is that health care is provided through NHS contracts, where one body (the purchaser) is responsible for obtaining the appropriate health care for its population from another body (the provider). From 1 April 1993, the Community Care Reforms introduced major changes in the way care is administered for the elderly, the mentally ill, the physically handicapped and people with learning disabilities.

The 14 Regional Health Authorities (RHAs) in England are responsible for regional planning, the allocation of resources to District Health Authorities, Family Health Services Authorities and general practitioner fundholders, and the promotion of national policies and priorities. They are directly accountable to the Secretary of State for Health and provide the link between the DHAs and FHSAs, and the NHS Management Executive.

The 145 District Health Authorities (DHAs) are responsible for purchasing health care for the people who live within their areas, and for the operational management of health services and planning within regional and national strategic guidelines. DHAs' resources are allocated by RHAs, to which they are also accountable for their performance. As a result of the reforms, some DHAs have merged to form larger bodies, allowing them to increase their purchasing power and make better use of resources.

THE HEALTH SERVICES

FAMILY DOCTOR SERVICE

In England and Wales the Family Doctor Service (or General Medical Services) is managed by 90 Family Health Services Authorities (FHSAs) which also organize the general dental, pharmaceutical and ophthalmic services for their areas. There is a Family Health Services Authority for one or more District Health Authorities. In England the chairman is appointed by the Secretary of State and the non-executive members by the Regional Health Authority. In Wales the chairman and non-executive members are appointed by the Secretary of State. There are nine non-executive members: a general medical practitioner, a general dental practitioner, a community pharmacist, a nurse, and five lay members.

Any doctor may take part in the Family Doctor Service (provided the area in which he/she wishes to practise has not already an adequate number of doctors) and about 28,000 general practitioners in England and Wales do so. They may at the same time have private fee-paying patients. Family doctors are paid for their Health Service work in accordance with a scheme of remuneration which includes *inter alia* a basic practice allowance, capitation fees, reimbursement of certain practice expenses and payments for out-of-hours work.

The National Health Service and Community Care Act 1990 enables general practitioner practices with at least 7,000 patients to apply for fundholding status (a number of smaller practices form units in order to achieve fundholding status). This makes the practice responsible for its own NHS budget for a specified range of goods and services. There are currently 1,120 fundholding units, comprising 1,235 practices. Fundholding practices are monitored by the FHSAs on behalf of the Regional Health Authorities.

Everyone aged 16 or over can choose their doctor (parents or guardians choose for children under 16) and the doctor is also free to accept a person or not as he or she chooses. A person may change their doctor if they wish, by going to the surgery of a general practioner of their choice who is willing to accept them, and either handing in their medical card to register or filling in a form. When people are away from home they can still use the Family Doctor Service if they ask to be treated as temporary residents, and in an emergency, if a person's own doctor is not available, any doctor in the service will give treatment and advice.

Patients are treated either in the doctor's surgery or, when necessary, at home. Doctors may prescribe for their patients all drugs and medicines which are medically necessary for their treatment and also a certain number of surgical appliances (the more elaborate being provided through hospitals).

DENTAL SERVICE

Dentists, like doctors, may take part in the National Health Service and also have private patients. About 16,000 of the dentists available for general practice in England provide

NHS general dental services. They are responsible to the Family Health Services Authorities in whose areas they provide services.

Patients are free to go to any dentist who is taking part in the Service and willing to accept them. Dentists are paid a capitation fee for patients registered with them who are under 18 years of age. They receive payment for items of treatment for individual adult patients and, in addition, a continuing care payment for those registered with them.

Patients are asked to pay 80 per cent of the cost of NHS dental treatment. The maximum charge for a course of treatment is £250. There is no charge for arrest of bleeding, repairs to dentures, home visits by the dentist or re-opening a surgery in an emergency (in these two cases, payment will be for treatment given in the normal way). The following are exempt from dental charges:

(i) young people under 18
(ii) full time students under 19
(iii) expectant mothers who were pregnant when accepted for treatment
(iv) women who have had a child in the previous 12 months

People receiving Income Support or Family Credit, and members of the same family as someone receiving Income Support or Family Credit, are automatically entitled to full remission of charges.

Leaflet AB11 available from post offices and leaflet D11 available from local social security offices explain how other people on a low income can, depending on their financial circumstances, get free treatment or help with charges.

PHARMACEUTICAL SERVICE

Patients may obtain medicines, appliances and oral contraceptives prescribed under the NHS from any pharmacy whose owner has entered into arrangements with the Family Health Services Authority to provide this service. Almost all pharmacy owners have done so and display notices that they dispense under the NHS; the number of these pharmacies in England and Wales at the end of 1990 was about 10,400. There are also some appliance suppliers who only provide special appliances. In country areas where access to a pharmacy may be difficult, patients may be able to obtain medicines, etc., from their doctor.

Except for contraceptives (for which there is no charge), a charge of £4.25 is payable for each item supplied unless the patient is exempt and the declaration on the back of the prescription form is completed. Exemptions cover:

(i) children under 16
(ii) full-time students under 19
(iii) men aged 65 and over
(iv) women aged 60 and over
(v) pregnant women
(vi) mothers who have had a baby within the last 12 months
(vii) people suffering from certain medical conditions
(viii) people who receive Income Support or Family Credit and their dependants
(ix) people who hold an AG2 certificate issued by the Health Benefits Unit, and their dependants
(x) war pensioners (for their accepted disablements)

Prepayment certificates (£22 valid for four months, £60.60 valid for a year) may be purchased by those patients not entitled to exemption who require frequent prescriptions. Further information about the exemption and prepayment arrangements is given in leaflet P11.

GENERAL OPHTHALMIC SERVICES

General Ophthalmic Services, which are administered by Family Practitioner Committees, form part of the ophthalmic services available under the National Health Service. The NHS sight test is available free to:

(i) children under 16
(ii) full-time students under the age of 19
(iii) people in receipt of Income Support and Family Credit, and their partners
(iv) people prescribed complex lenses
(v) the registered blind and partially sighted
(vi) diagnosed diabetic and glaucoma patients
(vii) close relatives aged 40 or over of diagnosed glaucoma patients

Those on a low income may qualify for help with the cost.

Certain groups are automatically entitled to help with the purchase of glasses under an NHS voucher scheme:

(i) children under 16
(ii) full-time students under 19
(iii) people in receipt of Income Support or Family Credit, and their partners
(iv) people wearing certain complex lenses
(v) people whose spectacles are lost or damaged as a result of their disability, injury or illness

The value of the voucher depends on the lenses required. Vouchers may be used to help pay for the glasses or contact lenses of the patient's choice. People with a low income may claim help on form AG1. Glasses or contact lenses should not be purchased until the result of a claim is known as no refunds can be given. Booklet G11 gives further details.

Diagnosis and specialist treatment of eye conditions is available through the Hospital Eye Service as well as the provision of glasses of a special type. Testing of sight may be carried out by any ophthalmic medical practitioner or ophthalmic optician and can cost up to £18. The optician must hand the prescription, and a voucher if eligible, to the patient who can take this to any supplier of glasses of his/her choice to have dispensed. However, only registered opticians can supply glasses to children and to people registered as blind or partially sighted.

PRIMARY HEALTH CARE SERVICES

Primary health care services include the general medical, dental, ophthalmic and pharmaceutical services and the family doctor service. They also include community services run by district health authorities, health centres and clinics, family planning outside the hospital service, and preventive activities in the community including vaccination, immunization and fluoridation.

The district nursing and health visiting services include community psychiatric nursing for mentally ill people living outside hospital, and school nursing for the health surveillance of schoolchildren of all ages. Ante- and post-natal care and chiropody are also an integral part of the primary health care service.

COMMUNITY CHILD HEALTH SERVICES

Pre-school services, usually at child health clinics, provide regular surveillance of children's physical, mental and emotional health and development, and advice to parents on their children's health and welfare.

The School Health Service provides for the medical and dental examination of schoolchildren, and advises the local education authority, the school, the parents and the pupil of any health factors which may require special consideration during the pupil's school life. GPs are increasingly undertaking child health surveillance to improve the preventive health care of children.

HOSPITALS AND OTHER SERVICES

The Secretary of State for Health has a duty to provide, to such extent as he/she considers necessary to meet all reasonable requirements, hospital and other accommodation; medical, dental, nursing and ambulance services; other facilities for the care of expectant and nursing mothers and young children; facilities for the prevention of illness and the care and after-care of persons suffering from illness; and such other services as are required for the diagnosis and treatment of illness. Rehabilitation services (occupational therapy, physiotherapy and speech therapy) may also be provided for those who need it and surgical and medical appliances are supplied in appropriate cases.

Specialists and consultants who take part in the Health Service can engage in private practice, including the treatment of their private patients in NHS hospitals.

Trusts

The National Health Service and Community Care Act 1990 enables hospitals and other providers of health care, to become independent of health authority control as self-governing NHS Trusts run by boards of directors. The Trusts derive their income principally from contracts to provide health services to health authorities and fund-holding general practitioners. In April 1993 there were 292 NHS Trusts, and applications from hospitals wishing to become Trusts in April 1994 are currently under consideration.

Charges

In a number of hospitals, accommodation is available for the treatment of private in-patients who undertake to pay the full costs of hospital accommodation and services and (usually) separate medical fees to a specialist as well. The amount of the medical fees is a matter for agreement between doctor and patient. Hospital charges for private resident patients are determined by District Health Authorities or Trusts, either on a local basis or in line with a central 'model' list.

Certain hospitals have accommodation in single rooms or small wards which, if not required for patients who need privacy for medical reasons, may be made available to patients who desire it as an amenity. These patients are still NHS patients and are treated as such.

There is no charge for drugs supplied to National Health hospital in-patients but out-patients pay £4.25 per item unless they are exempt.

With certain exceptions, hospital out-patients have to pay fixed charges for dentures, contact lenses and certain appliances. Glasses may be obtained either from the hospital or an optician and the charge will be related to the type of lens prescribed and the choice of frame.

LOCAL AUTHORITY PERSONAL SOCIAL SERVICES

Local authorities are responsible for the organization, management and administration of the personal social services and each authority has a Director of Social Services and a Social Services Committee responsible for the social services functions placed upon them by the Local Authority Social Services Act 1970.

National Insurance and Related Cash Benefits

The State insurance and assistance schemes, comprising schemes of national insurance and industrial injuries insurance, national assistance, and non-contributory old age pensions came into force from 5 July 1948. The Ministry of Social Security Act 1966 replaced national assistance and non-contributory old age pensions with a scheme of non-contributory benefits, termed supplementary allowances and pensions. These, and subsequent measures relating to social security provision in Great Britain, were consolidated by the Social Security Act 1975; the Social Security (Consequential Provisions) Act 1975; and the Industrial Injuries and Diseases (Old Cases) Act 1975. Corresponding measures were passed for Northern Ireland. The Social Security Pensions Act 1975 introduced a new State pensions scheme, which came into force on 6 April 1978, and the graduated pension scheme 1961 to 1975 has been wound up, existing rights being preserved. The Pensioners' Payments and Social Security Act 1979 provided for a £10 bonus for pensioners in 1979 and for the payment of a bonus in succeeding years at levels then to be determined. The Child Benefit Act 1975 replaced family allowances (introduced 1946) with child benefit and one parent benefit.

Some of the above legislation has been superseded by the provisions of the Social Security Acts 1968 to 1992.

NATIONAL INSURANCE SCHEME

The National Insurance scheme operates under the Social Security Contributions and Benefits Act 1992 and the Social Security Administration Act 1992, and orders and regulations made thereunder. The scheme is financed by contributions payable by earners, employers and others (such as non-employed persons, paying voluntary contributions). It provides the funds required for paying benefits payable under the Social Security Acts out of the National Insurance Fund and not out of other public money and for the making of payments towards the cost of the National Health Service. In 1991 the Redundancy Fund was absorbed into the National Insurance Fund. The yearly Treasury supplement to the National Insurance Fund was abolished in April 1989.

CONTRIBUTIONS

Contributions are of four classes:

Class 1 contributions

These are earnings-related, based on a percentage of the employee's earnings.
(a) primary Class 1 contributions are payable by employed earners and office-holders over age 16 with gross earnings at or above the lower earnings limit of £56.00 per week. For those with gross earnings at or above this level, contributions are payable on all earnings up to an upper limit of £420.00 per week. 'Gross earnings' include overtime pay, commission, bonus, etc., without deduction of any superannuation contributions.
(b) secondary Class 1 contributions are payable by employers of employed earners, and by the appropriate authorities in the case of office-holders. On 6 October 1985 the upper earnings limit for employers' contributions was abolished and secondary contributions are payable on all

the employee's earnings if they reach or exceed £56.00 per week.

Women who marry for the first time no longer have a right to elect not to pay the full contribution rate. Married women and widows who before 12 May 1977 elected not to pay contributions at the full rate retain the right to pay a reduced rate over the same earnings range, which includes a contribution to the National Health Service. They lose this right if, after 5 April 1978, there are two consecutive tax years in which they receive no earnings on which primary Class 1 contributions are payable and in which they have not been at any time self-employed earners. No primary contributions are due on earnings paid for a period on or after the employee's pension age, even when retirement is deferred.

Primary contributions are deducted from earnings by the employer and are paid, together with the employer's contributions, to the Inland Revenue along with income tax collected under the PAYE system. On 6 October 1985 several lower percentage rates of contribution for lower paid employees and their employers were introduced.

Class 2 contributions

These are flat-rate, paid weekly by self-employed earners over age 16. Those with earnings below £3,140 a year for the tax year 1993-4 can apply for exemption from liability to pay Class 2 contributions. People who while self-employed are exempted from liability to pay contributions on the grounds of small earnings may pay either Class 2 or Class 3 contributions voluntarily. Self-employed earners (whether or not they pay Class 2 contributions) may also be liable to pay Class 4 contributions based on profits or gains within certain limits. There are special rules for those who are concurrently employed and self-employed.

Married women and widows can no longer choose not to pay Class 2 contributions. Those who elected not to pay Class 2 contributions before 12 May 1977 retain the right until there is a period of two consecutive tax years after 5 April 1978 in which they were not at any time either self-employed earners or had earnings on which primary Class 1 contributions were payable.

Class 2 contributions may be paid by direct debit through a bank or National Giro account or by stamping a contribution card.

Class 3 contributions

These are voluntary flat-rate contributions payable by persons over school-leaving age who would otherwise be unable to qualify for retirement pension and certain other benefits because they have an insufficient record of Class 1 or Class 2 contributions. Married women and widows who on or before 11 May 1977 elected not to pay Class 1 (full rate) or Class 2 contributions cannot pay Class 3 contributions while they retain this right.

Payment may be made by stamping a contribution card or by direct debit through a bank or National Giro account.

Class 4 contributions

These are payable by self-employed earners, whether or not they pay Class 2 contributions, on annual profits or gains from a trade, profession or vocation chargeable to income tax under Schedule D, where these fall between £6,340 and £21,840 a year. The maximum Class 4 contribution, payable on profits or gains of £21,840 or more, is £976.50.

Class 4 contributions are generally assessed and collected by the Inland Revenue along with Schedule D income tax. Self-employed persons under 16, or who at the beginning of a tax year are over pension age even where retirement is deferred, are not liable to pay Class 4 contributions. There

are special rules for people who have more than one job, or who pay Class 1 contributions on earnings which are chargeable to income tax under Schedule D.

Regulations state the cases in which earners may be exempted from liability to pay contributions, and the conditions upon which contributions are credited to persons who are exempted. Leaflet NI 208 is obtainable from local social security offices.

The Secretary of State for Social Services is empowered by the Social Security Acts to alter certain rates of contributions by order approved by both Houses of Parliament, and is required by the same enactments to make annual reviews of the general level of earnings in order to determine whether such an order should be made.

For the period 6 April 1993 to 5 April 1994 the earnings brackets determining Class 1 contributions are:

	Weekly earnings
1	£56.00– 94.99
2	95.00–139.99
3	140.00–194.99
4	195.00–420.00
5	over 420.00

Contribution rates for the period 6 April 1993 to 5 April 1994 are:

CLASS 1 CONTRIBUTIONS – NOT CONTRACTED OUT

Employee's rates

Earnings bracket	Percentage of reckonable income			
	On first £56.00		On earnings from £56.00–£420.00	
	standard	reduced	standard	reduced
1	2	3.85	9	3.85
2	2	3.85	9	3.85
3	2	3.85	9	3.85
4	2	3.85	9	3.85
5	*2	*3.85	*9	*3.85

*to a maximum of £420.00 per week

The employee's rate is scheduled to go up to 10 per cent from 7 April 1994

CLASS 1 CONTRIBUTIONS – CONTRACTED OUT

(*see also* page 499)

Employee's rates

Earnings bracket	On first £56.00		On earnings from £56.00–£420.00	
	standard	reduced	standard	reduced
1	2	3.85	7.2	3.85
2	2	3.85	7.2	3.85
3, 4, 5	2	3.85	7.2	3.85

Employer's rates

Earnings bracket	On first £56.00	On earnings from £56.00–£420.00	On any earnings over £420.00
1	4.6	1.6	0
2	6.6	3.6	0
3	8.6	5.6	0
4	10.4	7.4	0
5	10.4	7.4	10.4

	Weekly flat rate
CLASS 2 CONTRIBUTIONS	£5.55

CLASS 3 CONTRIBUTIONS   £5.45

CLASS 4 CONTRIBUTIONS   6.3% of profits or gains
                               (7.4% from 7 April 1994)

From 5 October 1989 there was a change in the assessment of National Insurance contributions for employees. Where earnings were paid or were due to be paid on or after 5 October 1989, employees' contributions were paid at 2 per cent of earnings at the lower earnings limit (£56.00 a week or equivalent) plus 9 per cent (not contracted out) or 7.2 per cent (contracted out) of earnings between the lower earnings limit up to and including the employees' upper earnings limit (£420.00 a week or equivalent). Employees contributing at the reduced rate continue to pay contributions at 3.85 per cent on all earnings up to and including the employees' upper earnings limit.

The Social Security (Contributions) Act 1991 added a new class of contributions: IA, payable in respect of car fuel by persons liable to pay secondary Class 1 contributions. It has effect with regard to the 1991–2 tax year and thereafter.

Employees earning less than the lower earnings limit continue not to pay any contributions.

There was no change in the assessment of employers' contributions.

THE STATE EARNINGS RELATED PENSION SCHEME (SERPS)

The Social Security Pensions Act 1975, which came into force in April 1978, aims to reduce reliance upon means-tested benefit in old age, in widowhood and in chronic ill-health by providing better pensions; to ensure that occupational pension schemes which are contracted out of part of the State scheme fulfil the conditions of a good scheme; that pensions are adequately protected against inflation; and that in both the State and occupational schemes men and women are treated equally. Retirement, widow's and invalidity pensions under the new scheme started to be paid in April 1979. Since 6 April 1979 flat-rate retirement and other State pensions have been augmented for employed earners by additional pensions related to earnings, but it will be twenty years before these additional pensions become payable at the full rate.

Under the scheme, retirement, invalidity and widow's pensions for employees are related to the earnings on which national insurance contributions have been paid. For employees of either sex with a complete insurance record, the scheme provides a category A retirement pension in two parts, a basic and an additional pension. The basic pension corresponds to the old personal flat-rate national insurance pension. The additional pension is 1.25 per cent of average earnings between the lower weekly earnings limit for Class 1 contribution liability and the upper earnings limit for each year of such earnings under the scheme, and will thus build up to 25 per cent in twenty years.

The additional pension will be calculated in a different way for individuals who reach pension age after 6 April 1999. The changes are to be phased in over ten years. From 2010 a lifetime's earnings will be included in the calculation and for years from 1988–9 onwards the accrual rate on these surplus earnings will be 20 per cent. The accrual rate on surplus earnings for the years from 1978–9 to 1987–8 will remain at 25 per cent.

Actual earnings are to be revalued in terms of the earnings level current in the last complete tax year before pension age (or death or incapacity). Both components of pensions in payment will be uprated annually in line with the movement of prices. Graduated retirement pensions in payment, and rights to such pensions earned by people who are still working, will be brought into the annual review of benefits.

Self-employed persons pay contributions towards the basic pension. The non-employed and employees with earnings below the lower limit may contribute voluntarily for basic pension. Although no primary Class 1 contributions or Class 2 or Class 4 contributions are payable by persons who work beyond pension age (65 for men, 60 for women), the employer's liability for secondary Class 1 contributions continues if earnings are at or above the lower earnings limit. Class 4 contributions are still payable up to the end of the tax year during which pension age is reached.

Widows will get the whole of any additional pensions earned by their husbands with their widowed mother's allowances or widow's pensions; and can add to the retirement pensions earned by their own contributions any additional pensions earned by their husbands up to the maximum payable on one person's contributions. Men whose wives die when they are both over pension age can add together their own and their wives' pension rights in the same way as widows.

Among the steps taken to give women equal treatment in benefit provision, the State scheme permits sharing of home responsibilities to reduce the number of qualifying years (since 1978) needed for retirement pension, widowed mother's allowance and widow's pension; and the 'half-test', by which a married woman who married before age 55 could not qualify for a Category A retirement pension unless she had contributed on earnings at the basic level in at least half the years between marriage and pension age, has been abolished with effect from 22 December 1984. The range of short-term social security benefits and industrial injury benefits under the Social Security Act 1975 continues with only minor changes.

CONTRACTED-OUT AND PERSONAL PENSION SCHEMES

Members of occupational pension schemes which meet the standards laid down in the Social Security Pensions Act 1975 can be contracted-out of the earnings related part of the state scheme relating to retirement and widows' benefits. Regulations made under the Act require employers to consult employees and their organizations and inform them of their intention to contract out. (Leaflets relating to pensions and guidance for employers about contracting-out are available from local social security offices.) The Act also contains provisions ensuring equal access to membership of schemes for men and women.

Until 6 April 1988 occupational pension schemes could only contract out if they promised a pension that was related to earnings. These are known as contracted-out salary related schemes. They must provide a pension that is not less than the guaranteed minimum pension (GMP), which is broadly equivalent to the state earnings related pension. However, new options were introduced by the Social Security Act 1986. Since 6 April 1988 occupational pension schemes which promise a minimum level of contributions have also been able to contract out. These are known as contracted-out money purchase schemes. They provide a pension based on the fund built up in the scheme over the years plus the results of the way they have been invested.

In addition, since July 1988 employees whose employers do not provide a pension scheme have been able to start their own personal pension instead of staying in the state earnings related pension scheme. Since 6 April 1988, this choice has been open to all employees even if their employer does have a pension scheme. A personal pension, like a contracted-out money purchase scheme, provides a pension based on the fund built up in the scheme over the years plus the results of the way they have been invested.

The decision on whether or not an occupational pension scheme may become contracted-out lies with the Occupational Pension Board, an independent statutory body which has a general responsibility for supervising contracting-out. They also consider and approve personal pension schemes which can be used instead of state additional pension.

The State earnings related pension payable to a member of a contracted-out salary related scheme, or his widow, will be reduced by the amount of GMP payable (which in the case of a widow must be at least half of the late husband's GMP entitlement). Members of contracted-out money purchase schemes and personal pension schemes, or their widows, have no GMP entitlement as such. But the state earnings related pension payable will be reduced by an amount equivalent to a GMP (or widow's GMP).

Since 6 April 1988 contracted-out salary related schemes must also provide a widower's GMP which must be at least half of the late wife's GMP entitlement built up from 6 April 1988. (A scheme need not provide entitlement to a GMP for widowers of earners dying before April 1989.) Contracted-out money purchase schemes and personal pension schemes must provide half-rate widower's benefit.

In contracted-out schemes, both the employee and the employer pay the full ordinary rate of contribution on the first £56.00 (1993–4 figure) of earnings but earnings above that amount attract a lower rate of contribution from the employee, and from the employer where the employee's earnings are under £420.00; where the employee's earnings exceed this amount, the full ordinary rate of contribution is payable only by the employer and the employee has no liability for contributions on these earnings (*see also* page 497).

An employee who chooses a personal pension in place of SERPS or their employer's pension scheme must pay National Insurance contributions at the full ordinary rate (the employer's share must be paid at the same rate). The DSS pays the difference between the lower contracted-out rate and the full ordinary rate directly into the personal pension scheme.

NATIONAL INSURANCE FUND

The National Insurance Fund receives all social security contributions (less only the National Health Service and Redundancy Fund and Maternity Pay Fund allocations and the National Insurance surcharge for taxation purposes) and it bears the cost of all contributory benefits provided by the Social Security Acts and the cost of administration.

Approximate receipts and payments of the National Insurance Fund for the year ended 31 March 1992, were as follows:

Receipts	£'000
Balance, 1 April 1991	11,791,856
Contributions under the Social Security Acts (net of SSP/SMP)	32,474,390
Compensation from Consolidated Fund for SSP/SMP recoveries	1,055,000
Income from investments	1,109,426
Other receipts	37,284
	46,467,956

Payments	£'000	£'000
Unemployment benefit	1,603,815	
Sickness benefit	273,512	
Invalidity benefit	5,485,418	
Maternity allowance	30,951	
Widow's benefit	1,010,599	
Guardian's allowance and child's special allowance	1,471	
Retirement pension	25,543,024	
Pensioners' lump sum payments	114,324	34,063,114
Personal pensions		2,451,867
Transfers to Northern Ireland		125,000
Administration		1,201,541
Other payments		9,682
Redundancy payments		283,452
Balance, 31 March 1992		8,333,300
		46,467,956

NB: There have been changes to the National Insurance Fund. Payments will no longer be paid into surcharges or the Maternity Pay Fund. However, residual payments are still being paid in respect of late paid contributions for premium years.

BENEFITS

The benefits payable under the Social Security Acts are as follows:

CONTRIBUTORY BENEFITS

Unemployment benefit
Sickness benefit
Invalidity pension and allowance
Maternity allowance
Widow's benefit, comprising widow's payment, widowed mother's allowance and widow's pension
Retirement pensions, categories A and B

NON-CONTRIBUTORY BENEFITS

Child benefit
One parent benefit
Guardian's allowance
Invalid care allowance
Mobility allowance
Severe disablement allowance
Attendance allowance
Disability Living Allowance
Disability Working Allowance
Retirement pensions, categories C and D
Income Support
Family Credit
Social Fund

BENEFITS FOR INDUSTRIAL INJURIES, DISABLEMENT AND DEATH

OTHER

Statutory sick pay
Statutory maternity pay

Leaflets relating to the various benefits and payments are obtainable from local social security offices.

The Social Security Acts empower the Secretary of State to increase certain rates of benefit by order approved by both Houses of Parliament, and require him to increase certain rates by such an order if an annual review shows that they have not retained their value in relation to the general level of prices obtaining in Great Britain as measured by the Retail Price Index.

The latest order providing for increases in benefit rates took effect from the week commencing 6 April 1993. It did not apply to all benefits.

CONTRIBUTORY BENEFITS

Entitlement to contributory benefits depends on contribution conditions being satisfied either by the client or by some other person (depending on the kind of benefit). The class or classes of contribution which for this purpose are relevant to each benefit are as follows:

Short-term benefits

Unemployment benefit	Class 1
Sickness benefit	Class 1 or 2
Maternity allowance	Class 1 or 2

Long-term benefits

Widow's benefits	
Category A retirement pension	Class 1, 2 or 3
Category B retirement pension	
Invalidity benefit	Class 1 or 2

The system of contribution conditions relates to yearly levels of earnings on which contributions have been paid. The contribution conditions for different benefits are set out in summary form in leaflets available at local social security offices.

UNEMPLOYMENT BENEFIT

Benefit is payable in a period of interruption of employment for up to 312 days (a year, excluding Sundays). Spells of unemployment and sickness not separated by more than eight weeks count as one period of interruption of employment. A person who has exhausted benefit requalifies when he/she has again worked as an employed earner for at least 16 hours a week for 13 weeks. These weeks need not be consecutive but must generally fall within 26 weeks prior to the date of the claim.

There are disqualifications from receiving benefit, e.g. for a period not exceeding 26 weeks if a person has lost their employment through misconduct, or has voluntarily left employment without just cause, or has, without good cause, refused an offer of employment or training.

SICKNESS BENEFIT

Sickness benefit is payable for up to 28 weeks of sickness in a period of interruption of employment and is then replaced by invalidity benefit (*see* below).

There are disqualifications from receiving sickness or invalidity benefit for a period not exceeding six weeks if a person has become incapable of work through his/her own misconduct or fails without good cause to attend for or submit himself/herself to prescribed medical or other examination or treatment, or observe prescribed rules of behaviour.

Statutory sick pay (SSP) was introduced from 6 April 1983 and was payable for up to eight weeks. Since 6 April 1986 employers are responsible for paying SSP to their employees for up to 28 weeks of sickness in any period of incapacity for work. SSP replaces the employee's entitlement to State Sickness Benefit, which is not payable as long as any SSP liability remains. SSP is subject to PAYE and to NI deductions. From 6 April 1991 employers can recover 80 per cent (previously 100 per cent) of the SSP they have paid out. Employees who cannot get SSP can claim State Sickness Benefit instead.

INVALIDITY BENEFIT

Normally, after 28 weeks of sickness, sickness benefit (or SSP where the underlying conditions for sickness benefit are satisfied) is replaced by an invalidity pension. In addition, an invalidity allowance is payable if incapacity for work begins more than five years before pension age. The allowance varies according to the age at which invalidity began, and if still in payment at pension age will continue as an addition to retirement pension. From 16 September 1985 invalidity allowance has been offset by entitlement to an additional earnings-related pension and/or a guaranteed minimum pension.

MATERNITY BENEFIT

Statutory maternity pay (SMP) is administered by employers. The state maternity allowance scheme covers women who are self-employed or otherwise do not qualify for SMP.

In general, employers pay SMP to pregnant women who have been employed by them for at least 26 weeks and earned at least the lower earnings limit for the payment of NI contributions. For those who have been employed for at least two years, payment of SMP for the first six weeks is related to earnings, followed by up to twelve weeks at a standard rate of £47.95. Those who have been employed for at least 26 weeks but less than two years receive payment at standard rate only for the 18 weeks. Part-time working women also qualify for the earnings-related element if employed for at least five years. Women have some choice in deciding when to begin maternity leave but SMP is not payable for any week in which work is done.

A woman may qualify for maternity allowance (MA) if she has been working and paying contributions at the full rate for at least 26 weeks in the 52-week period which ends 15 weeks before the baby is due. She also has an element of choice in deciding when to stop work and receive MA, which is not payable for any period she works.

WIDOW'S BENEFITS

Only the late husband's contributions of any class count for widow's benefit in any of its three forms.

Widow's Payment – may be received by a woman who at her husband's death is under 60, or whose husband was not entitled to a Category A retirement pension when he died.

Widowed Mother's Allowance – payable to a widow if she is entitled or treated as entitled to child benefit, or if she is expecting her husband's baby.

Widow's Pension – a widow may receive this pension if aged 45 or over at the time of her husband's death or when her widowed mother's allowance ends. If aged 55 or over she will receive the full widow's pension rate.

Widow's benefit of any form ceases upon re-marriage or during a period in which she lives with a man as his wife.

RETIREMENT PENSION – CATEGORIES A AND B

A Category A pension is payable for life to men or women on their own contributions if they are over pension age (65 for a man and 60 for a woman).

Where a person defers making a claim at 65 (60 for a woman) or later opts to be treated as if he/she had not made a claim, and does not draw a Category A pension, the weekly rate of pension is increased, when he or she finally makes a claim or reaches the age of 70 (65 for a woman), in respect of weeks when pension is forgone during the five years after reaching minimum pension age. Details of the increase in the rate of pension due to deferred retirement are given in leaflet NP46, available at social security offices. If a married man defers his own Category A pension, his wife has to defer receiving her Category B pension based on his contribution record. During this time she earns increments to the

Category B pension, provided she does not claim retirement pension or Graduated Retirement Benefit in her own right, which is payable to her (and not her husband) when they both claim their pensions.

A Category B pension is normally payable for life to a woman on her husband's contributions when he has claimed, or is over 70, and has qualified for his own Category A pension, and she has reached 60. It is also payable on widowhood after 60 whether or not the late husband had retired and qualified for his own pension. The weekly pension is payable at the rate of the increase for a wife while the husband is alive, and at the single person's rate on widowhood after 60. Where a woman is widowed before she reaches 60, a Category B pension is paid to her on reaching 60 at the same weekly rate as her widow's pension if she claims. If a woman qualifies for a pension of each category she receives whichever pension is the larger. Details of the increase in the rate of pension due to deferred retirement are given in leaflet NP46, available at social security offices.

The earnings rule which stated that a man aged 65 to 70, or a woman aged 60 to 65, who has qualified for pension would have it reduced if he or she earned more than a certain amount was abolished on 1 October 1989. Where an adult dependant is living with the client, an Adult Dependants Allowance will only be payable if the dependant's earnings do not exceed the standard rate of unemployment benefit for a single person under pensionable age (*see* below). For the purpose of the dependency rule only, earnings will include payments by way of occupational or personal pension. The earnings of a separated spouse affect the increase of retirement pension if they exceed £31.25 a week.

Unemployment, sickness or invalidity benefit is payable to men between 65 and 70, and women between 60 and 65 who have not claimed their retirement pension and who would have been entitled to a retirement pension if they had claimed at pension age. This applies in the case of sickness and invalidity benefit if incapacity for work is the result of an industrial accident or prescribed disease. These rates of benefit for people over pension age are shown in leaflet NI 196. A retirement pension will be increased by the amount of any invalidity allowance the pensioner was getting within the period of eight weeks and one day before reaching minimum pension age but this will be offset against any Additional Pension or Guaranteed Minimum Pension. An age addition of 25p per week is payable if a retirement pensioner is aged 80 or over.

GRADUATED RETIREMENT BENEFIT

Graduated National Insurance contributions were first payable from April 1961 and were calculated as a percentage of earnings between certain bands. They were discontinued in April 1975. Any graduated pension which an employed person over 18 and under 70 (65 for a woman) had earned by paying graduated contributions will be paid when the contributor claims retirement pension or at 70 (65 for a woman), in addition to any retirement pension for which he or she qualifies.

Graduated retirement benefit is at the rate of 7.35p a week (April 1993) for each 'unit' of graduated contributions paid by the employee (half a unit or more counts as a whole unit). A unit of contributions is £7.50 for men and £9.00 for women of graduated contributions paid.

A wife can get a graduated pension in return for her own graduated contributions, but not for her husband's. A widow, or a widower whose wife died after 5 April 1979 when they were both over pensionable age, gets a graduated addition to his/her retirement pension equal to half of any graduated additions earned by his/her late spouse, plus any additions earned by his/her own graduated contributions. If a person

defers making a claim beyond 65 (60 for a woman), entitlement may be increased by one seventh of a penny per £1 of its weekly rate for each complete week of deferred retirement, as long as the retirement is deferred for a minimum of seven weeks.

RATES OF BENEFITS
from week commencing 6 April 1993

	Weekly rate
Unemployment Benefit: standard rate	
Person under pension age	£44.65
Increase for wife/other adult dependant	27.55
*Person over pension age	56.10
Increase for wife/other adult dependant	33.70
Sickness Benefit: standard rate	
Person under pension age	42.70
Increase for wife/other adult dependant	26.40
*Person over pension age	53.80
Increase for wife/other adult dependant	32.30
Invalidity Pension	
Person (under or over pension age)	56.10
Increase for wife or adult dependant	33.70
Invalidity Allowance: maximum amount payable	
Higher rate	11.95
Middle rate	7.50
Lower rate	3.75
Maternity Allowance	43.75
Widow's Benefits	
Widow's Payment (lump sum)	1,000.00
*Widowed Mother's Allowance	56.10
*Widow's Pension	56.10
Retirement pension: categories A and B	
Single person	56.10
Increase for wife or adult dependant	33.70

*These benefits attract an increase for each dependent child (in addition to child benefit) of £9.80 for the first or only child and £10.95 for each subsequent child

NON-CONTRIBUTORY BENEFITS

CHILD BENEFIT

Child benefit is payable for virtually all children aged under 16, and for those aged 16 to 18 who are studying full-time up to and including A-level or equivalent standard. It is also payable for a short period if the child has left school recently and is registered for work or youth training at a careers office.

ONE PARENT BENEFIT

This benefit may be paid to a person in receipt of Child Benefit who is responsible for bringing up one or more children on his/her own. It is a flat rate non-means tested, non-contributory benefit payable for the eldest child.

GUARDIAN'S ALLOWANCE

Where the parents of a child are dead, the person who has the child in his/her family may claim a guardian's allowance in addition to child benefit. The allowance, in exceptional circumstances, is payable on the death of only one parent.

INVALID CARE ALLOWANCE

Invalid care allowance is payable to persons of working age, who are not gainfully employed because they are regularly and substantially engaged in caring for a severely disabled person who is receiving attendance allowance, the middle or highest rate of disability living allowance or constant attendance allowance with either a war or services pension, industrial disablement workman's compensation, or an allowance under the Pneumoconiosis, Byssinosis and Miscellaneous Diseases Benefit Scheme.

SEVERE DISABLEMENT ALLOWANCE

Persons under pensionable age who have been continuously incapable of work for a period of at least 28 weeks but who do not qualify for a contributory invalidity pension may be entitled to severe disablement allowance. People who first become incapable of work after their twentieth birthday must be at least 80 per cent disabled.

ATTENDANCE ALLOWANCE

This is payable to disabled people over 65 who need a lot of care or supervision because of physical or mental disability for a period of at least six months. People not expected to live for six months because of an illness do not have to wait six months. The allowance has two rates: the lower rate is for day or night care, and the higher rate is for day and night care.

DISABILITY LIVING ALLOWANCE

This is payable to disabled people under 65 who have personal care and mobility needs because of an illness or disability for a period of at least three months. People not expected to live for six months because of an illness do not have to wait three months. The allowance has two components: the care component, which has three rates of help, and the mobility component, which has two rates. The amount payable depends on the care and mobility needs of the claimant. The mobility component is payable only to those aged five or over.

DISABILITY WORKING ALLOWANCE

This is a tax-free, income-related benefit for people who are working 16 hours a week or more but have an illness or disability which puts them at a disadvantage in getting a job. To qualify a person must be aged 16 or over and must, at the date of the claim, have one of the 'qualifying benefits', such as Disability Living Allowance. The amount payable depends on the size of the family and weekly income. DWA is not payable if any savings exceed £16,000.

NON-CONTRIBUTORY RETIREMENT PENSION – CATEGORIES C AND D

A Category C pension is provided, subject to a residence test, for persons who were over pensionable age on 5 July 1948, and for women whose husbands are so entitled if they are over pension age, with increases for adult and child dependants. A Category D pension is provided for others when they reach 80 if they are not already getting a retirement pension of any category or if they are getting that pension at less than these rates. An age addition of 25p per week is payable if persons entitled to retirement pension are aged 80 or over.

RATES OF BENEFITS

from week commencing 6 April, 1993

	Weekly rate
Child Benefit (first child)	£10.00
Each subsequent child	8.10
One Parent Benefit	
First or only child of certain lone parents	6.05
Guardian's Allowance (eldest child)	9.80
Each subsequent child	10.95

	Weekly rate
*Severe Disablement Allowance	
†Basic rate	£33.70
Under 40	11.95
40–49	7.50
50–59	3.75
Increase for wife/other adult dependant	20.15
*Invalid Care Allowance	33.70
Increase for wife/other adult dependant	20.15
Attendance Allowance	
Higher rate	44.90
Lower rate	30.00
Disability Living Allowance	
Care component	
Higher rate	44.90
Middle rate	30.00
Lower rate	11.95
Mobility component	
Higher rate	31.40
Lower rate	11.95
Disability Working Allowance	
Single person	43.95
Couple or single parent	60.95
Child aged under 11	10.75
aged 11–15	17.85
aged 16–17	22.20
aged 18	31.00
‡*Applicable amount* (income threshold)	
Single person	41.40
Couple or single parent	69.00
*Retirement Pension: Categories *C and D*	
Single person	33.70
Increase for wife/other adult dependant	20.15
(not payable with Category D pension)	

* These benefits attract an increase for each dependent child (in addition to child benefit) of £9.80 for the first or only child and £10.95 for each subsequent child
† The age addition applies to the age when incapacity began
‡ 70 pence is deducted from the maximum DWA payable (this is obtained by adding up the appropriate allowance for each person in the family) for every pound coming in each week over the appropriate applicable amount. Where weekly income is below the applicable amount, maximum DWA is payable

INCOME SUPPORT

Income Support is a benefit for those aged 18 and over (although certain vulnerable 16- and 17-year-olds may be eligible) whose income is inadequate and who are unemployed. Others who may be eligible include people who are: over 60; bringing up children alone; unable to work through sickness; caring for a disabled person; or working part-time. Except in special cases Income Support is not available to those who work for more than 16 hours per week or who have a partner who works for more than 16 hours per week.

Income Support is not payable if the claimant, or claimant and partner, have capital or savings in excess of £8,000. The rate of benefits is affected by possession of capital or savings in excess of £3,000 and may be affected by a claimant's earnings.

Sums payable depend on fixed allowances laid down by law for people in different circumstances. Special rates may apply to some people living in residential care or nursing homes. Details are available from local social security offices.

Applications for Income Support are made on form IS1, available from post offices; Income Support claim forms, available from social security offices; or on form B1 (for the unemployed), available from unemployment benefit offices. If both partners are entitled to Income Support, either may claim it for the couple. People receiving Income Support will be able to receive Housing Benefit, help with mortgage or home loan interest and help with health care. They may also be eligible for help with exceptional expenses, from the Social Fund. Leaflet IS20 gives a detailed explanation of Income Support.

INCOME SUPPORT PREMIUMS

Income Support Premiums are additional weekly payments for those with special needs. They are payable as part of the Income Support scheme. People qualifying for more than one premium will normally only receive the highest single premium for which they qualify. However Family Premium, Disabled Child's Premium, Severe Disability Premium and Carer Premium are payable in addition to other premiums.

People with children qualify for a Family Premium if they have at least one child; a Disabled Child's Premium if they have a child who receives Attendance Allowance or certain components of Disability Living Allowance or is registered blind; or a Lone Parent Premium if they are bringing up one or more children alone. If someone receives Invalid Care Allowance, they qualify for the Carer Premium.

Long-term sick or disabled people qualify for a Disability Premium if they or their partner are receiving certain benefits because they are disabled or cannot work; are registered blind; or if the claimant, but not their partner, has been sending in doctor's statements for at least 28 weeks stating inability to work through sickness. If someone is living alone and they are in receipt of Attendance Allowance or Disability Living Allowance, without anyone receiving Invalid Care Allowance for looking after them, they may qualify for a Severe Disability Premium in addition to a Disability Premium.

People qualify for a Pensioner Premium if they or their partner are aged between 60 and 79, and for a Higher Pensioner Premium if they or their partner are aged 80 or over. A Higher Pensioner Premium is also payable to people aged between 60 and 79 who receive Attendance Allowance, Mobility Allowance, Invalidity Benefit or Severe Disablement Allowance, or who are registered blind. A Higher Pensioner Premium may be paid as well as a Severe Disability Premium. Enhanced Pensioner Premium is payable to pensioners aged between 75 and 79 in addition to Pensioner Premium.

RATES OF BENEFIT
from week commencing 6 April 1993

	Weekly rate
Income Support	
Single people	
aged 16–17	£26.45
aged 16–17 (certain circumstances)	34.80
aged 18–24	34.80
aged 25 and over	44.00
aged 18 and over and a single parent	44.00
Couples*	
both under 18	52.40
both aged 18 or over	69.00
For each child in a family	
under 11	15.05
aged 11–15	22.15
†aged 16–17	26.45
†aged 18 and over	34.80

	Weekly rate
Premiums	
Family Premium	9.65
Disabled Child's Premium	18.45
Lone Parent Premium	4.90
Disability Premium	
Single	18.45
Couple	26.45
Severe Disability Premium	
Single	33.70
Couple (one person qualified)	33.70
Couple (both qualified)	67.40
Pensioner Premium	
Single	17.30
Couple	26.25
Higher Pensioner Premium	
Single	23.55
Couple	33.70
Enhanced Pensioner Premium	
Single	19.30
Couple	29.00

*Where one or both partners are aged under 18, their personal allowance will depend on their situation
†If in full-time education up to A-level or equivalent standard

FAMILY CREDIT

Family Credit is a tax-free benefit for working families with children. It is not a loan and does not have to be paid back. To qualify, a family must include at least one child under 16 (under 19 if in full-time education up to A-level or equivalent standard), and the claimant, or partner (if there is one), must be working for at least 16 hours per week. It does not matter which partner is working and they may be employed or self-employed. The right to Family Credit does not depend on NI contributions and the same rates of benefit are paid to one- and two-parent families. Family Credit is not payable if the claimant, or claimant and partner, have capital or savings in excess of £8,000. The rate of benefit is affected if capital or savings in excess of £3,000 are held. The rate of benefit payable depends upon the claimant's (and partner's) net income (excluding Child Benefit), number of children, and children's ages. Family Credit, One Parent Benefit, and the first £15.00 of any maintenance in payment are paid for 26 weeks and the amount payable will usually remain the same throughout this period, regardless of change of circumstances. Payment is made weekly via post offices or every four weeks directly into a bank or building society account. Family Credit is claimed by post. A claim pack FC1 which includes a claim form can be obtained at a post office or social security office or call the Family Credit Helpline on 0253-500050. In two-parent families the woman should claim.

RATES OF BENEFIT
from week commencing 6 April 1993

	Weekly rate

The maximum amount will be payable where net income is no more than £69.00 per week. Where net income exceeds that amount, the maximum credit is reduced by 70 per cent of the excess and the result is the Family Credit payable. The maximum rate consists of:

Adult credit (for one or two parents)	£42.50
plus for each child	
aged under 11	10.75
aged 11–15	17.85
aged 16–17	22.20
aged 18	31.00

CLAIMS AND QUESTIONS

With a few exceptions, claims and questions relating to Social Security benefits are decided by statutory authorities who act independently of the Department of Social Security and Department of Employment.

The first of the statutory authorities, the Adjudication Officer, determines entitlement to benefit. A client who is dissatisfied with that decision has the right of appeal to a Social Security Appeal Tribunal. There is a further right of appeal to a Social Security Commissioner against the Tribunal's decision but leave to appeal must first be obtained. Appeals to the Commissioner must be on a point of law. Provision is also made for the determination of certain questions by the Secretary of State for Social Services.

Disablement questions are decided by adjudicating medical authorities or Medical Appeal Tribunals. Appeal to the Commissioner against a tribunal's decision is with leave and on a point of law only.

Leaflet NI246, which is available from social security offices, explains how to appeal, and leaflet NI260 is a guide to reviews and appeals.

THE SOCIAL FUND

The Social Fund helps people with expenses which are difficult to meet from regular income. Regulated Maternity, Funeral and Cold Weather payments are decided by Adjudication Officers and are not cash-limited. Discretionary Community Care Grants, and Budgeting and Crisis Loans are decided by Social Fund Officers and come out of a yearly budget which is allocated to each district (1993–4, grants £95 million; loans £250 million).

REGULATED PAYMENTS

Maternity Payments

A payment of up to £100 for each baby expected, born or adopted. It is payable to people on Income Support and Family Credit and is non-repayable.

Funeral Payments

Payable for reasonable funeral expenses incurred by people receiving Income Support, Family Credit or Housing Benefit. It is recoverable from the estate of the deceased.

Cold Weather Payments

£6 for any consecutive seven days when the average temperature is 0°C or below. Paid to people on Income Support who are pensioners, disabled or parents with a child under the age of five. It is non-repayable.

DISCRETIONARY PAYMENTS

Community Care Grants

They are intended to help people on Income Support to move into the community or avoid institutional care; ease exceptional pressures on families; and/or meet certain essential travelling expenses. They are usually non-repayable.

Budgeting Loans

These are interest-free loans to people who have been receiving Income Support for at least six months, for intermittent expenses that may be difficult to budget for.

Crisis Loans

These are interest-free loans to anyone, whether receiving benefit or not, who is without resources in an emergency, where there is no other means of preventing serious risk or damage to health or safety.

Loans are normally repaid over a period of up to 78 weeks at 15, 10 or 5 per cent of Income Support (less housing costs), depending on other commitments.

SAVINGS

Savings over £500 (£1,000 for people aged 60 or over) are taken into account for Maternity and Funeral Payments, Community Care Grants and Budgeting Loans. All savings are taken into account for crisis loans.

APPEALS AND REVIEWS

For regulated payment there is a right of appeal to an independent Social Security Appeal and thereafter to a Social Security Commissioner. For discretionary payments there is a review system where persons can ask for a review at the local office with a further right of review to an independent Social Fund Inspector.

INDUSTRIAL INJURIES, DISABLEMENT AND DEATH BENEFITS

The Industrial Injuries scheme, administered under the Social Security Contributions and Benefits Act 1992, provides a range of benefits designed to compensate for disablement resulting from an industrial accident (i.e. an accident arising out of and in the course of an employed earner's employment) or from a prescribed disease due to the nature of a person's employment. Rates of benefit are increased periodically.

BENEFITS

Disablement Benefit is normally payable 15 weeks (90 days) after the date of accident or onset of disease if the employed earner suffers from loss of physical or mental faculty such that the resulting disablement is assessed at not less than 14 per cent. The amount of disablement benefit payable varies according to the degree of disablement (in the form of a percentage) assessed by an adjudicating medical authority or medical appeal tribunal.

Disablement assessed at less than 14 per cent does not normally attract basic benefit except for certain chest diseases. A weekly pension is payable where the assessment of disablement is between 14 and 100 per cent (assessments of 14 to 19 per cent are payable at the 20 per cent rate). Payment can be made for a limited period or for life.

The basic rates are applicable to adults and to juveniles entitled to an increase for a child or adult dependant; other juveniles receive lower rates.

Basic rates of pension are not related to the pensioner's loss of earning power, and are payable whether he/she is in work or not. There is provision for increases of pension if the pensioner requires constant attendance or if his/her disablement is exceptionally severe. A pensioner may draw SSP, sickness or invalidity benefit as appropriate, in addition to disablement pension, during spells of incapacity for work.

Regulations impose certain obligations on clients and beneficiaries and on employers, including, in the case of clients for disablement benefit, that of submitting themselves for medical examination.

SUPPLEMENTARY ALLOWANCES

Special schemes under the Industrial Injuries and Diseases (Old Cases) Act 1975 provide supplementary allowances to those entitled to receive weekly payments of workmen's compensation for loss of earnings due to injury at work, or disease contracted during employment before 5 July 1948 when the Industrial Injuries scheme was introduced. Other schemes under the Act provide allowances to those who contracted slowly-developing diseases during employment before July 1948 where neither workmen's compensation nor Industrial Injuries Benefits are payable. A lump sum death benefit of up to £300 may also be payable to a dependant of such a person. Leaflet NI196 provides details relating to these allowances.

RATES OF BENEFITS

from April 1993

	Weekly rate
*Disablement Benefit/Pension	
Degree of disablement	
100 per cent	£91.60
90	82.44
80	73.28
70	64.12
60	54.96
50	45.80
40	36.64
30	27.48
20	18.32
†Unemployability supplement	56.10
Addition for adult dependant (subject to earnings rule)	33.70
Reduced earnings allowance (maximum)	35.36
Constant Attendance allowance (normal maximum rate)	36.70
Exceptionally severe disablement allowance	36.70

*There is a weekly benefit for those under 18 with no dependants which is set at a lower rate
†This benefit attracts an increase for each dependent child (in addition to child benefit) of £9.80 for the first child and £10.95 for each subsequent child

CLAIMS AND QUESTIONS

Provision is made for the determination of certain questions by the Secretary of State for Social Security, and of 'disablement questions' by a medical board (or a single doctor) or, on appeal, by a medical appeal tribunal. An appeal on a point of law against a medical appeal tribunal decision is determined by the Social Security Commissioner.

Claims for benefit and certain questions arising in connection with a claim for or award of benefit (e.g. whether the accident arose out of and in the course of the employment) are determined by an adjudication officer appointed by the Secretary of State, or a Social Security Appeal Tribunal, or in certain circumstances, on further appeal, by the Commissioners.

War Pensions

War pensions are awarded under The Naval, Military and Air Forces, Etc. (Disablement and Death) Service Pensions Order 1983, which was a consolidation of the previous Royal Warrants, Orders in Council and Orders by Her Majesty.

The Department of Social Security (DSS) awards war pensions to members of the armed forces in respect of the periods 4 August 1914 to 30 September 1921 and subsequent to 3 September 1939 (including present members of the armed forces). There is also a scheme for civilians and civil defence workers in respect of the 1939–45 war, and other schemes for groups such as merchant seamen, and Polish armed forces who served under British command.

War pensions for the period 1 October 1921 to 2 September 1939 are dealt with by the Ministry of Defence, which is also responsible for the Armed Forces Pension Scheme.

PENSIONS

War disablement pension is awarded for the disabling effects of any injury, wound or disease which is attributable to, or has been aggravated by, conditions of service in the armed forces. It cannot be paid until the serviceman or woman has left the armed forces.

Disablement is assessed by comparison of the disabled person's health with that of a normal, healthy person of the same age and sex, without taking into account the disabled person's earning capacity or occupation, and is expressed on a percentage scale up to 100 per cent. Disablement of 20 per cent and above, for which a pension is awarded, is assessed in steps of 10 per cent. Maximum assessment does not necessarily imply total incapacity. For assessment of less than 20 per cent a lump sum is payable. No award is made where disablement in respect of noise-induced sensorineural hearing loss is assessed at less than 20 per cent.

The Dependency Allowance, formerly payable in respect of a wife or child, was abolished in April 1992 and an equivalent amount incorporated into the basic War Disablement Pension.

War widow's pension is awarded where death occurs as a result of service or where a war disablement pensioner was receiving constant attendance allowance at the time of his death, or would have been receiving it if he were not in hospital, in which case his widow has automatic entitlement to a war widow's pension, regardless of the cause of death.

Additional allowances are payable for dependent children, in addition to child benefit.

A reduced weekly rate is payable to war widows of men below the rank of Lieutenant-Colonel who are under the age of 40, without children and capable of maintaining themselves. This is increased to the standard rate at age 40.

Rank additions and gratuities to disablement and widow's pensions may be paid where the rank held was above that of private (or equivalent).

CLAIMS

Where a claim is made no later than seven years after the termination of service, the client does not have to prove that the disablement or death on which the claim is based is related to service and receives the benefit of any reasonable doubt. Where a claim is made more than seven years after the termination of service the claimant has to show that disablement or death is related to service. However, the claim succeeds if reliable evidence is produced which raises a reasonable doubt whether or not disablement or death is related to service. There is no time limit for making a claim for war pension.

SUPPLEMENTARY ALLOWANCES

A number of supplementary allowances may be awarded to a war pensioner which are intended to meet the various needs such as mobility, unemployability, constant nursing care, which may result from disablement or death and take account of its particular effect on the pensioner or spouse.

The principal supplementary allowances are:

Unemployability supplement – with additional allowances for dependants, this may be paid to a war pensioner whose pensioned disablement is so serious as to make him unemployable. In addition, an invalidity allowance may be payable if the incapacity for work began more than five years before normal retirement age.

Allowance for lowered standard of occupation – this may be awarded to a partially disabled pensioner whose pensioned disablement permanently prevents him from following his pre-service occupation and from doing another job of equivalent financial standard. The allowance, together with the basic war disablement pension, must not exceed pension at the 100 per cent rate.

Constant attendance allowance– this may be awarded if the pensioner is receiving a pension at the 80 per cent rate or more and needs a great deal of care because of the disability.

Widow's age allowance – this is paid at three different rates according to age, 65–69, 70–79 and over 80.

Widow's child's allowance – this may be paid in addition to child benefit.

Other supplementary allowances include exceptionally severe disablement allowance, severe disablement occupational allowance, mobility supplement, comforts allowance, clothing allowance, age allowance and education allowance. There is a supplementary rent allowance available on a war widow's pension.

Decisions on supplementary allowances are made on a discretionary basis on behalf of the Secretary of State and there is no provision for a statutory right of appeal against them. However, war pensioners may discuss any aspect of their pension position with their local War Pensions Committee, which may be able to arrange help or make representations to the DSS.

WAR PENSIONERS ABROAD

The DSS is responsible for the payment of war pensions, and, where necessary, meeting the cost of treatment for accepted disablement, to pensioners who reside overseas. They receive the same pension rates as war pensioners in this country and benefit from the same annual upratings.

SOCIAL SECURITY BENEFITS

When a war disablement pensioner is sick, unemployed or retired, the appropriate social security benefits are paid in addition to the basic war disablement pension.

Any sickness, invalidity, unemployment benefit or retirement pension for which a war widow qualifies on her own contributions, and any graduated retirement benefit, or additional earnings related pension inherited from her husband, can be paid in addition to her war widow's pension.

A war pensioner or war widow who claims Income Support, Family Credit or Disability Working Allowance has the first £10 of pension disregarded. A similar provision operates for housing benefit and council tax benefit; but the local authority may, at its discretion, disregard any or all of the balance.

PENSIONS APPEAL TRIBUNALS

There are independent Pensions Appeal Tribunals, set up by the Lord Chancellor's office, which hear appeals against the decisions of the DSS on entitlement, and assessment of disablement, in respect of the 1939–45 war and subsequent service cases. There are no time limits within which an entitlement appeal must be made but there are time limits within which an assessment appeal should be made. However, there are now no rights of appeal in the 1914–21 war disablement cases, the great majority of which were given final assessment in the 1920s with a 12 months' right of appeal at the time. An appeal by a 1914 war widow must be made within twelve months of the date on which the rejection of the claim is notified.

WAR PENSIONERS WELFARE SERVICE

The DSS operates a war pensioners welfare service to advise and assist war pensioners and their widows on any matters affecting their welfare. Welfare officers are attached to War Pensioners' Welfare Offices located in the major towns, and work closely with central and local government agencies as well as the various ex-service organizations. The service is available on call to any war pensioner or war widow who needs it.

RATES OF PENSIONS AND ALLOWANCES

from week commencing 6 April 1993

	Weekly rates
War Disablement pension	
(for Private or equivalent rank)	
Degree of disablement:	
100 per cent	£97.20
90 per cent	87.48
80 per cent	77.76
70 per cent	68.04
60 per cent	58.32
50 per cent	48.60
40 per cent	38.88
30 per cent	29.16
20 per cent	19.44
Unemployability supplement	
Personal allowance	59.55
Increase for wife/other adult dependant	33.70
Increase for first child	9.80
Increase for other children	10.95
Allowance for lowered standard of occupation	
(maximum)	36.64
Widow's pension	
(widow of Private or equivalent rank)	
Standard rate	72.90
Increase for first child	13.85
Increase for other children	15.00
Childless widow under 40	16.83
Widow's age allowance	
aged 65–69	8.35
aged 70–79	16.10
aged 80 and over	23.95

The current rates of all war pensions and allowances are listed in leaflet MPL154 *Rates of War Pensions and Allowances*, obtainable from War Pensioners Welfare Offices or the Leaflets Unit, PO Box 21, Stanmore, Middx. HA7 1AY, or phone the War Pension Helpline on 0253-858858.

New Towns in Great Britain

COMMISSION FOR THE NEW TOWNS
Glen House, Stag Place, London SW1E 5AJ
Tel 071-828 7722

The Commission was established under the New Towns Act
1959. Its remit is to:
(a) take over and, with a view to its eventual disposal, to
hold, manage and turn to account the property of
development corporations transferred to the Commission
(b) dispose of property so transferred and any other property
held by it, as soon as it considers it expedient to do so
In carrying out its remit the Commission must have due
regard to the convenience and welfare of persons residing,
working or carrying on business there and, until disposal, the
maintenance and enhancement of the value of the land held
and return obtained from it.
The Commission has such responsibilities in Basildon,
Bracknell, Central Lancashire, Corby, Crawley, Harlow,
Hatfield, Hemel Hempstead, Milton Keynes, Northampton,
Peterborough, Redditch, Skelmersdale, Stevenage, Telford,
Warrington and Runcorn, Washington, and Welwyn Garden
City. These properties are administered through four
regional offices.
The Commission has minimal responsibilities (principally
financial and litigation) in Aycliffe and Peterlee, and
Cwmbran following the wind-up of their development
corporations in 1988.

Chairman, Sir Neil Shields, MC
Deputy Chairman, The Lord Finsberg, MBE
Members, R. B. Caws, CBE; W. J. Mackenzie, OBE;
Sir Gordon Roberts, CBE; The Lord Bellwin; Sir Brian
Jenkins, GBE; M. H. Mallinson; R. W. P. Luff;
F. C. Graves, OBE; J. Trustram Eve; Ms W. Luscombe;
Lady Marsh
Chief Executive, N. J. Walker

REGIONAL OFFICES

NORTH (Central Lancashire, Skelmersdale, Warrington
and Runcorn, Washington, Aycliffe and Peterlee) –
Office, New Town House, Buttermarket Street,
Warrington WA1 2LF. Tel: 0925-51144. *Director,* J. Leigh
MILTON KEYNES – *Office,* Saxon Court, 502 Avebury
Boulevard, Central Milton Keynes MK9 3HS. Tel: 0908-
692692. *Director,* J. Napleton
WEST MIDLANDS (Redditch, Telford) – *Office,* Jordan
House West, Hall Court, Hall Park Way, Telford
TF3 4NN. Tel: 0952-293131. *Director,* C. Mackrell

SOUTH (Basildon, Bracknell, Corby, Crawley, Harlow,
Hatfield, Hemel Hempstead, Northampton,
Peterborough, Stevenage, Welwyn Garden City) – *Office,*
Glen House, Stag Place, London SW1E 5AJ. Tel: 071-828
7722. *Director,* G. D. Johnston

DEVELOPMENT CORPORATIONS

WALES
DEVELOPMENT BOARD FOR RURAL WALES – Formed
1977. *Chairman,* G. Davies. *Offices,* Ladywell House,
Newtown, Powys SY16 1JB. Tel: 0686-626965

SCOTLAND
CUMBERNAULD, Strathclyde – Formed 1956. *Chairman,*
D. W. Mitchell, CBE. *Chief Executive,* D. Millan.
Headquarters, Cumbernauld House, Cumbernauld
G67 3JH. Area, 7,788 acres. Population, 50,600.
Estimated eventual population, 60,000
EAST KILBRIDE, Strathclyde – Formed 1947. *Chairman,*
J. A. Denholm, CBE. *Managing Director,* J. C. Shaw.
Offices, Atholl House, East Kilbride, Glasgow G74 1LU.
Area, 10,250 acres. Population, 70,300. Estimated
eventual population, 71,600
GLENROTHES, Fife – Formed 1948. *Chairman,*
Prof. C. Blake, CBE. *General Manager,*
J. A. F. McCombie. *Offices,* Balgonie Road, Markinch,
Glenrothes KY7 6AH. Area, 5,760 acres. Population,
38,950. Estimated eventual population, 48,000
IRVINE, Ayrshire – Formed, 1966. *Chairman,* M. Crichton.
Managing Director, Brig. R. A. Rickets. *Offices,* Perceton
House, Irvine, Ayrshire KA11 2AL. Area, 16,000 acres.
Population, 56,000. Estimated eventual population,
70,000
LIVINGSTON, West Lothian – Formed 1962. *Chairman,*
R. S. Watt, CBE. *Chief Executive,* J. A. Pollock. *Offices,*
Sidlaw House, Almondvale, Livingston, West Lothian
EH54 6QA. Area, 6,868 acres. Population, 44,800.
Estimated eventual population, 70,000

The Water Industry

ENGLAND AND WALES

In England and Wales the Secretaries of State for the Environment and for Wales and the Director-General of Water Services are responsible for the general oversight of the industry and for ensuring that the private water companies fulfil their statutory obligation to provide water supply and sewerage services.

The Minister of Agriculture, Fisheries and Food and the Secretary of State for Wales are responsible for policy relating to land drainage, flood protection, sea defences and the protection and development of fisheries.

The National Rivers Authority is responsible for water quality and the control of pollution, the management of water resources and nature conservation. The Drinking Water Inspectorate and local authorities are responsible for the quality of drinking water.

THE WATER COMPANIES

Until the end of 1989, nine regional water authorities in England and the Welsh Water Authority in Wales were responsible for water supply and the development of water resources, sewerage and sewage disposal, pollution control, freshwater fisheries, flood protection, water recreation, and environmental conservation. The Water Act 1989 provided for the creation of a privatized water industry under public regulation.

Of the 99 per cent of the population of England and Wales who are connected to a public water supply, 75 per cent are supplied by the water companies (through their principal operating subsidiaries, the water service companies), which have replaced the regional water authorities. The remaining 25 per cent are supplied by statutory water companies which were already in the private sector. Most of these have now converted to public limited company (PLC) status. The ten water service companies are also responsible for sewerage and sewage disposal throughout England and Wales.

Water Service Companies

ANGLIAN WATER SERVICES LTD, Compass House, Chivers Way, Histon, Cambs. CB4 4ZY
DWR CYMRU (WELSH WATER), Cambrian Way, Brecon, Powys LD3 7HP
NORTHUMBRIAN WATER LTD, Abbey Road, Pity Me, Durham DH1 5FS
NORTH WEST WATER LTD, Dawson House, Liverpool Road, Great Sankey, Warrington WA5 3LW
SEVERN TRENT WATER LTD, 2297 Coventry Road, Sheldon, Birmingham B26 3PU
SOUTHERN WATER SERVICES LTD, Southern House, Yeoman Road, Worthing, W. Sussex BN13 3NX
SOUTH WEST WATER SERVICES LTD, Peninsula House, Rydon Lane, Exeter EX2 7HR
THAMES WATER UTILITIES LTD, Nugent House, Vastern Road, Reading RG1 8DB
WESSEX WATER SERVICES LTD, Wessex House, Passage Street, Bristol BS2 0JQ
YORKSHIRE WATER SERVICES LTD, West Riding House, 67 Albion Street, Leeds LS1 5AA

REGULATORY BODIES

The Director-General of Water Services is appointed by the Secretaries of State for the Environment and for Wales. Independent of ministers and directly accountable to Parliament, his main duties are to ensure that the water companies comply with the terms of their appointments (or licences) and to protect the interests of the consumer. All the water companies are subject to a system of price control which sets a limit on the average increase in their prices each year. The Office of Water Services (*see* page 366) was set up to support the director-general's activities.

An independent national body, the National Rivers Authority (*see* page 339) was established under the Water Act 1989 to take over the regulatory and river management functions of the regional water authorities. It has statutory duties and powers in relation to water resources, pollution control, flood defence, fisheries, recreation, conservation and navigation in England and Wales.

The Drinking Water Inspectorate (*see* page 304) was established under the Water Act 1989, and is responsible for assessing the quality of the drinking water supplied by all the water companies in England and Wales and for inspecting the companies themselves. The inspectors look at records, check operational manuals, visit laboratories and water treatment works, and question company officials. They also investigate any accidents affecting drinking water quality. The Chief Inspector presents an annual report to the Secretaries of State for the Environment and for Wales.

METHODS OF CHARGING

In England and Wales, most householders have up to now paid for domestic water supply and sewerage services through charges based on the assessed value of their property under the old domestic rating system. Industrial and most commercial users are charged according to consumption, which is recorded by meter.

The abolition of domestic rates necessitated new methods of charging the private consumer for water and sewerage services. The Water Industry Act 1991 gives the water companies until the end of the century to decide on and introduce a suitable method of charging. Three options under consideration are a flat-rate licence fee, property banding, and metering. Trials of domestic metering are currently taking place.

SCOTLAND

Overall responsibility for national water policy in Scotland rests with the Secretary of State for Scotland. Most aspects of water policy are administered through the Scottish Office Environment Department, but fisheries and certain aspects of land drainage are the responsibility of the Scottish Office Agriculture and Fisheries Department. The supply of water and sewerage services and the development of water resources are administered by separate authorities from those responsible for the control of water pollution.

Water supply and sewerage services are at present local authority responsibilities and are provided by the nine Regional Councils and the three Islands Councils.

In November 1992 the Government published a consultation paper which set out eight options for the future structure of water and sewerage services in Scotland, ranging from privatization to retention of the services in local authority control. Following the consultation, the Secretary of State announced in July 1993 that three public water authorities would be established to own and operate current water and sewerage assets and to arrange new investment to maximize private sector involvement. The authorities will be in place by April 1996, with a new independent representative body being set up to protect consumers' interests.

Seven river purification boards and the Islands Councils of Orkney, Shetland and the Western Isles have the specific duty of promoting the cleanliness of Scotland's rivers, lochs and coastal waters and conserving water resources. They are responsible for the prevention and control of pollution within their own areas.

The Central Scotland Water Development Board was established in 1967 with the main statutory function of developing new sources of water supply for the purpose of providing water in bulk to water authorities whose limits of supply are within the board's area, i.e. Central, Fife, Lothian, Strathclyde and Tayside Regional Councils.

Along with the council tax, which was introduced in April 1993, a council water charge is set by each Regional and Islands Council.

CENTRAL SCOTLAND WATER DEVELOPMENT BOARD, Balmore, Torrance, Glasgow G64 4AJ. *Director,* W. G. Mitchell

NORTHERN IRELAND

In Northern Ireland ministerial responsibility for water services lies with the Secretary of State for Northern Ireland. The Department of the Environment for Northern Ireland, operating through the Water Executive, is responsible for policy and co-ordination with regard to supply and distribution of water, and provision and maintenance of sewerage services.

The Water Executive is divided into four regions, the Eastern, Northern, Western and Southern Divisions. These are based in Belfast, Ballymena, Londonderry and Craigavon respectively.

On major issues the Department of the Environment for Northern Ireland seeks the views of the Northern Ireland Water Council, a body appointed to advise the Department on the exercise of its water and sewerage functions. The Council includes representatives from agriculture, angling, industry, commerce, tourism, trade unions and local government.

Usually householders do not pay directly for water and sewerage services; the costs of these services are allowed for in the Northern Ireland regional rate. Water consumed by industry, commerce and agriculture in excess of 100 cubic metres (22,000 gallons) per half year is charged through meters. Traders operating from industrially derated premises are required to pay for the treatment and disposal of the trade effluent which they discharge into the public sewerage system.

HM Coastguard

Founded in 1822, originally to guard the coasts against smuggling, HM Coastguard's role today is the very different one of guarding and saving life at sea. The Service is responsible for co-ordinating all civil marine search and rescue operations around the 2,500 mile coastline of Great Britain and Northern Ireland and 1,200 miles into the Atlantic. In addition, it co-operates with search and rescue organizations of neighbouring countries in western Europe and around the Atlantic seaboard. The Service maintains a 24-hour radar watch on the Dover Strait, providing a Channel navigation information service for all shipping in one of the busiest sea lanes in the world. The Service is administered by the Department of Transport.

Since 1978 HM Coastguard has been organized into six regions, each with a Regional Controller, operating from a Maritime Rescue Co-ordination Centre. Each region is subdivided into districts under District Controllers, operating from Maritime Rescue Sub-Centres. In all there are 21 of these centres. They are on 24-hour watch and are fitted with a comprehensive range of communications and rescue equipment. They are supported by some 350 smaller stations manned by Auxiliary Coastguards under the direction of Regulars, each of which keeps its parent centre fully informed of day-to-day casualty risk, particularly on the more remote danger spots around the coast.

Between 1 January and 31 December 1992, the 500 Regular and 4,000 Auxiliary Coastguards co-ordinated 8,532 incidents requiring search and rescue facilities, resulting in assistance being given to 14,528 persons. All distress telephone and radio calls are centralized on the 21 centres, which are on the alert for people or vessels in distress, shipping hazards and oil slicks. Using modern telecommunications equipment, including satellite, they can alert and co-ordinate the most appropriate rescue facilities; RNLI lifeboats, Royal Navy, RAF or Coastguard helicopters, fixed-wing aircraft, naval vessels, ships in the vicinity, or Coastguard shore and cliff rescue teams.

For those who regularly sail in local waters or make longer passages, the Coastguard Yacht and Boat Safety Scheme provides a valuable free service. Its aim is to give the Coastguard a record of the details of craft, their normal operating areas and their passage plans. Yacht and Boat Safety Scheme cards are available from all Coastguard stations, harbourmasters' offices, and most yacht clubs and marinas.

Members of the public who see an accident or a potentially dangerous incident on or around the coast should dial 999 and ask for the Coastguard.

Energy

COAL: SUPPLY AND DEMAND   *million tonnes*

	1986	1987	1988	1989	1990	1991
Supply						
Production of deep-mined coal	90.4	86.0	83.8	79.6	72.9	73.4
Production of opencast coal	14.3	15.8	17.9	18.7	18.1	18.6
Recovered slurry, fines, etc.	3.5	2.8	2.4	2.8	3.4	4.2
Imports	10.6	9.8	11.7	12.1	14.8	19.5
Change in colliery stocks	+0.3	−1.1	+0.7	+1.3	−0.9	+2.8
Change in stocks at opencast sites	−0.8	−1.5	+0.5	+1.5	−0.1	−0.8
Total supply	119.2	116.9	114.6	110.6	108.1	117.6
Home consumption						
Electricity supply industry	82.7	86.2	82.5	80.6	82.6	82.0
Coke ovens	11.1	10.9	10.9	10.8	10.9	10.0
Low temperature carbonization plants	1.0	1.0	0.8	0.8	0.8	0.8
Manufactured fuel plants	1.0	1.0	1.2	0.9	0.8	0.7
Railways	—	—	—	—	—	—
Collieries	0.3	0.2	0.2	0.1	0.1	0.1
Industry (disposals to users)	8.2	8.0	8.1	7.5	7.4	7.0
Domestic (disposals to users)	8.4	7.2	6.6	5.7	4.5	5.7
Public services	1.3	1.2	1.0	0.9	0.9	0.8
Miscellaneous	0.2	0.2	0.2	0.2	0.3	0.3
Total home consumption	114.2	115.9	111.5	107.6	108.3	107.5
Overseas shipments and bunkers	2.7	2.4	1.8	2.0	2.5	1.7
Total consumption and shipments	116.9	118.2	113.3	109.6	110.8	109.2
*Change in distributed stocks	+4.0	−2.8	+1.7	+0.4	−0.4	+3.6
†Balance	−1.8	+1.3	−0.4	+0.6	−2.3	+4.8

*Stock change excludes industrial and domestic stocks
†This is the balance between supply and consumption, shipments and changes in known distributed stocks

Source: HMSO - *Annual Abstract of Statistics 1993*

FUEL INPUT AND GAS OUTPUT: GAS SALES   *million therms*

	1986	1987	1988	1989	1990	1991
Fuel input to gas industry						
Petroleum (*million tonnes*)	0.1	0.1	—	—	—	—
*Petroleum gases	36	6	1	3	1	1
Natural gas	—	—	—	—	—	—
Coke oven gas	—	—	—	—	—	—
Total to gas works	55	20	6	3	1	1
Natural gas for direct supply	19,747	20,198	19,083	18,826	19,231	21,087
Total fuel input	19,802	20,218	19,089	18,829	19,232	21,083
Gas output and sales						
Gas output:						
Town gas	18	13	4	1	1	1
Natural gas supplied direct	19,775	20,205	19,083	18,826	19,231	21,087
Gross total available	19,793	20,218	19,087	18,827	19,232	21,088
Own use	−152	−137	−120	−101	−81	−103
†Statistical difference	−613	−708	−328	−377	−223	−691
Total sales	18,496	19,373	18,639	18,349	18,928	20,294
Analysis of gas sales						
Power stations	75	357	381	395	396	467
Final users:						
Iron and steel industry	419	465	446	467	461	404
Other industries	4,804	4,997	4,515	4,606	4,779‡	4,519
Domestic	10,242	10,500	10,255	9,914	10,250	11,395
Public administration	1,286	1,326	1,242	1,188	1,204	1,365
Agriculture	24	29	30	32	34	35
Miscellaneous	1,597	1,636	1,725	1,699	1,760	2,050

*Butane, propane, ethane and refinery tail gases
†Supply greater than recorded demand (−). Includes losses in distribution

‡Includes 27 million therms by independent gas suppliers
Source: HMSO - *Annual Abstract of Statistics 1993*

THE ELECTRICITY SUPPLY INDUSTRY

Under the Electricity Act 1989 twelve new public electricity supply companies were formed from the twelve Area Electricity Boards in England and Wales. These companies were floated on the stock market in 1990. Four new companies were formed from the Central Electricity Generating Board: three new generating companies (National Power PLC, Nuclear Electric PLC and PowerGen PLC) and the National Grid Company PLC. National Power PLC and PowerGen PLC were floated on the stock market in 1991, Government retaining a 40 per cent holding in both companies.

In Scotland, there are three new companies: Scottish Power PLC, Scottish Hydro-Electric PLC and Scottish Nuclear Ltd. Flotation of Scottish Power PLC and Scottish Hydro-Electric PLC on the stock market took place in 1991.

A new trade and representational organization, the Electricity Association, was created by the newly formed British electricity companies; its principal subsidiaries were Electricity Association Services Ltd (for representational and professional services) and Electricity Association Technology Ltd (for distribution and utilization research, development and technology transfer). Electricity Association Technology Ltd (now renamed EA Technology Ltd) left the Electricity Association group of companies in April 1993.

ELECTRICITY ASSOCIATION SERVICES LTD, 30 Millbank, London SW1P 4RD. Tel: 071-344 5700. *Chief Executive*, R. Farrance
EA TECHNOLOGY LTD, Capenhurst, Chester CHI 6ES. Tel: 051-339 4181. *Managing Director*, Dr S. F. Exell

CEGB SUCCESSOR COMPANIES

THE NATIONAL GRID COMPANY PLC, National Grid House, Kirby Corner Road, Coventry CV4 8JY. Tel: 0203-537777. *Chief Executive*, B. Kerss
NATIONAL POWER PLC, Senator House, 85 Queen Victoria Street, London EC4V 4DP. Tel: 071-454 9494. *Chief Executive*, J. Baker
NUCLEAR ELECTRIC PLC, Barnett Way, Barnwood, Glos GL4 7RS. Tel: 0452-652222. *Chairman*, J. Collier
POWERGEN PLC, 53 New Broad Street, London EC2M IJJ. Tel: 071-638 5742. *Chief Executive*, E. Walliss

REGIONAL ELECTRICITY COMPANIES

EASTERN ELECTRICITY PLC, PO Box 40, Wherstead, Ipswich IP2 9AQ
EAST MIDLANDS ELECTRICITY PLC, PO Box 4 North PDO, 398 Coppice Road, Arnold, Nottingham NG5 7HX
LONDON ELECTRICITY PLC, Templar House, 81–87 High Holborn, London WCIV 6NU
MANWEB PLC, Sealand Road, Chester CHI 4LR
MIDLANDS ELECTRICITY PLC, Mucklow Hill, Halesowen, W. Midlands B62 8BP
NORTHERN ELECTRIC PLC, Carliol House, Newcastle upon Tyne NE99 ISE
NORWEB PLC, Talbot Road, Manchester MI6 0MQ
SEEBOARD PLC, Grand Avenue, Hove, E. Sussex BN3 2LS
SOUTHERN ELECTRIC PLC, Littlewick Green, Maidenhead, Berks SL6 3QB
SOUTH WALES ELECTRICITY PLC, St Mellons, Cardiff CF3 9XW
SOUTH WESTERN ELECTRICITY PLC, 800 Park Avenue, Aztec West, Almondsbury, Avon BSI2 4SE
YORKSHIRE ELECTRICITY GROUP PLC, Scarcroft, Leeds LSI4 3HS

SCOTTISH COMPANIES

SCOTTISH HYDRO-ELECTRIC PLC, 16 Rothesay Terrace, Edinburgh EH3 7SE. Tel: 031-225 1361. *Chief Executive*, R. Young
SCOTTISH NUCLEAR LTD, Minto Building, 6 Inverlair Avenue, Glasgow G44 4AD. Tel: 041-633 1166. *Chief Executive*, Dr R. C. Jeffrey
SCOTTISH POWER PLC, Cathcart House, Spean Street, Glasgow G44 4BE. Tel: 041-637 7177. *Chief Executive*, Dr I. Preston

GENERATION, SUPPLY AND CONSUMPTION
gigawatt-hours

	1990	1991
Electricity generated		
All generating companies: total	318,979	322,132
Conventional steam stations	245,732	245,227
Nuclear stations	65,747	70,543
Gas turbines and oil engines	432	355
Hydro-electric stations:		
Natural flow	5,080	4,482
Pumped storage	1,982	1,523
Other (mainly wind)	4	3
Electricity used on works: total	19,583	20,083
Major generating companies	17,891	18,420
Other generators	1,691	1,663
Electricity supplied (gross)		
All generating companies: total	299,396	302,050
Conventional steam stations	233,366	233,042
Nuclear stations	58,664	62,761
Gas turbines and oil engines	403	310
Hydro-electric stations:		
Natural flow	5,067	4,469
Pumped storage	1,892	1,465
Other (mainly wind)	3	3
Electricity used in pumping		
Major generating companies	2,626	2,109
Electricity supplied (net): total	296,770	299,942
Major generating companies	277,978	280,649
Other generators	18,792	19,293
Net imports	11,943	16,407
Electricity available	308,713	316,349
Losses in transmission, etc	24,293	25,508
Electricity consumption: total	284,420	290,841
Fuel industries	9,986	9,794
Final users: total	274,434	281,048
Industrial sector	100,643	99,570
Domestic sector	93,793	98,098
Other sectors	79,997	83,380

Source: HMSO - *Annual Abstract of Statistics 1993*

THE GAS INDUSTRY

The gas industry in the United Kingdom was nationalized in 1949 under the Gas Act 1948, and operated as the Gas Council. The Gas Act 1972 replaced the Gas Council with the British Gas Corporation and led to greater centralization of the industry. The British Gas Corporation was privatized in 1986 as British Gas PLC and remains the main supplier of gas in Great Britain.

The principal business of British Gas is the purchase, transmission and sale of natural gas to domestic, industrial and commercial customers in Great Britain. British Gas has hydrocarbon exploration and production operations offshore and onshore, both in Great Britain and overseas, and it has an interest in gas-related activities world-wide.

BRITISH GAS PLC, Rivermill House, 152 Grosvenor Road, London SW1V 3JL. Tel: 071-821 1444. *Chairman*, R. Evans, CBE; *Chief Executive*, C. H. Brown

REGIONS

The Regions are largely concerned with the management of the gas business locally, including distribution and sale of gas, installation and servicing of appliances, meter reading, and the maintenance of emergency services.

EASTERN, Star House, Potters Bar, Herts. EN6 2PD
EAST MIDLANDS, PO Box 145, De Montfort Street, Leicester LEI 9DB
NORTH-EASTERN, New York Road, Leeds LS2 7PE
NORTHERN, PO Box 1GB, Killingworth, Newcastle upon Tyne NE99 1GB
NORTH THAMES, North Thames House, London Road, Staines, Middx. TW18 4AE
NORTH-WESTERN, Welman House, Altrincham, Cheshire WA15 8AE
SCOTLAND, Granton House, 4 Marine Drive, Edinburgh EH5 1YB
SOUTH-EASTERN, Katherine Street, Croydon CR9 1JU
SOUTHERN, 80 St Mary's Road, Southampton SO9 7GL
SOUTH-WESTERN, Riverside, Temple Street, Keynsham, Bristol BS19 1EQ
WALES, Helmont House, Churchill Way, Cardiff CF1 4NB
WEST MIDLANDS, Wharf Lane, Solihull, W. Midlands B91 2JP

SUPPLY AND TRANSMISSION

British Gas obtains natural gas from fields on mainland Britain, in coastal waters and in the North Sea. It also imports gas from other countries. In 1992 total production from UK continental shelf fields of gas contracted to British Gas was 55,666 million cubic metres, of which 55,397 million cubic metres was offshore production and 289 million cubic metres was onshore production.

The mainland national transmission system is operated by British Gas, with other gas suppliers entering contracts with British Gas to use the system. British Gas operates six reception terminals. The length of mains in use in 1992 was 255,200 km: 242,900 km of distribution mains and 17,900 km of transmission mains.

SALES 1992

Total gas sold and used:	GWh
Domestic	330,100
Commercial	92,625
Industrial	132,081
Released	2,651
Used for own purposes	3,547
Total	561,004

Charges for domestic use from 1 Oct. 1992:	pence
Standing charge per day	10.10
Unit charges	pence per kilowatt hour
Annual consumption	
First 146,536 KWh	1.477
146,537–293,071 KWh	1.409
293,072–439,607 KWh	1.375
439,608–732,678 KWh	1.341

BRITISH GAS FINANCE

	£ million	
	1991	1992
Turnover		
UK gas supply	8,423	8,129
Overseas gas supply	879	883
Exploration and production	980	995
UK marketing activities	774	786
Other activities	105	184
Less: intra-group sales	(676)	(723)
Total	10,485	10,254
Operating costs include:		
UK gas supply (includes levy)	3,834	3,033
Overseas gas supply	581	567
Payroll costs	1,647	1,672
Current cost depreciation less replacement expenditure	786	772
Current cost working capital adjustments	88	50
Total	8,812	8,825
Current cost operating profit	1,673	1,429
Gearing adjustment	39	41
Net interest payable	(243)	(311)
Current cost profit before tax	1,469	846
Current cost profit after tax	913	475
Minority shareholders' interest	8	(2)
Current cost profit attributable to British Gas shareholders	921	473
Dividends	(571)	(613)
Current cost profit retained	350	(140)

Transport

GOODS TRANSPORT IN GREAT BRITAIN

	1986	1987	1988	1989	1990	1991
TOTAL TONNE KILOMETRES (*thousand millions*)	187.2	195.2	218.8	222.8	218.8	212.2
Road	105.4	113.3	130.2	137.8	136.3	130.0
Rail (British Rail only)	16.6	17.3	18.2	17.3	15.8	15.2
Water: coastwise oil products*	33.9	31.6	34.2	34.1	32.1	31.3†
Water: other*	20.9	22.5	25.1	23.8	23.6	24.6†
Pipelines (except gases)	10.4	10.5	11.1	9.8	11.0	11.1
TOTAL (*million tonnes*)	1,836	1,909	2,163	2,206	2,163	1,984
Road	1,473	1,542	1,758	1,812	1,749	1,600
Rail (British Rail only)	140	141	150	146	141	135
Water: coastwise oil products*	46	43	47	46	44	44†
Water: other*	98	100	109	109	108	100†
Pipelines (except gases)	79	83	99	93	121	105

*'Coastwise' includes all sea traffic within the UK, Isle of Man and Channel Islands. 'Other' means other coastwise plus inland waterway traffic and one-port traffic
†provisional
Source: HMSO – *Annual Abstract of Statistics 1993*

SEAPORT TRAFFIC OF GREAT BRITAIN   *Million gross tonnes*

	1986	1987	1988	1989	1990	1991
FOREIGN TRAFFIC: *Imports*						
Bulk fuel traffic	61.7	57.3	62.9	64.2	75.1	78.0
Other bulk traffic	37.3	42.0	45.0	47.0	45.1	43.1
Container and roll-on traffic	31.1	34.0	38.0	40.9	40.5	40.2
Semi-bulk traffic	15.8	16.9	18.9	18.1	17.3	15.5
Conventional traffic	1.5	1.6	1.6	1.2	1.8	1.3
All imports	147.4	151.8	166.4	171.4	179.8	178.1
FOREIGN TRAFFIC: *Exports*						
Bulk fuel traffic	101.9	100.2	91.1	72.9	80.3	84.7
Other bulk traffic	21.1	20.4	18.5	19.5	19.0	19.6
Container and roll-on traffic	22.1	23.9	26.5	29.4	30.8	32.4
Semi-bulk traffic	4.0	5.0	4.6	4.6	4.3	5.1
Conventional traffic	1.2	1.2	1.0	0.7	1.1	0.9
All exports	150.4	150.6	141.7	127.1	135.7	142.7
DOMESTIC TRAFFIC						
Bulk fuel traffic	112.3	108.3	115.5	108.5	101.7	102.1
Other bulk traffic	32.7	34.8	41.1	45.5	44.0	41.1
Container and roll-on traffic	6.2	7.3	7.6	8.1	8.0	8.2
Semi-bulk traffic	0.2	0.2	0.3	0.3	0.3	0.4
Conventional traffic	0.3	0.3	0.3	0.4	0.3	0.4
Non-oil traffic with UK offshore installations	3.3	3.5	3.9	4.2	5.5	4.8
All domestic traffic	154.9	154.4	168.8	166.9	159.8	157.0
TOTAL FOREIGN AND DOMESTIC TRAFFIC	452.7	456.8	476.9	465.4	475.3	477.8

Source: HMSO – *Annual Abstract of Statistics 1993*

PASSENGER TRANSPORT IN GREAT BRITAIN   *Thousand million passenger kilometres (estimated)*

	1986	1987	1988	1989	1990	1991†
TOTAL	568	604	640	684	694	689
Air	4	4	5	5	5	5
Rail*	37	39	41	40	41	38
Road: Public service vehicles	47	47	46	47	46	45
Cars, vans and taxis	467	501	536	581	591	590
Motorcycles	8	7	7	6	6	6
Pedal cycles	5	6	5	5	5	5

*Including London Regional Transport and Passenger Transport Executive railway systems
†provisional
Source: HMSO – *Annual Abstract of Statistics 1993*

AIR PASSENGERS BY TYPE OF OPERATOR 1992

	Total terminal & transit	*Scheduled		*Charter	
		Terminal	Transit	Terminal	Transit
ALL UK AIRPORTS: TOTAL	107,803,780	78,820,169	1,229,081	27,303,183	451,347
LONDON AREA AIRPORTS: TOTAL	69,744,368	57,921,836	309,313	11,364,742	148,477
Battersea Heliport	3,959	—	—	3,959	—
Gatwick	19,968,401	10,934,103	32,466	8,070,378	94,964
Heathrow	45,242,604	44,742,141	272,649	225,841	1,973
London City	186,175	183,334	22	2,819	—
Luton	1,976,179	443,185	1,402	1,499,875	31,717
Southend	16,460	419	—	16,011	30
Stansted	2,354,549	1,618,654	2,774	713,328	19,793
OTHER UK AIRPORTS: TOTAL	38,055,453	20,898,333	919,768	15,934,482	302,870
Aberdeen	2,182,117	1,250,502	27,924	902,980	711
Barrow-in-Furness	627	243	—	384	—
Belfast	2,257,361	1,793,853	715	447,422	15,371
Belfast City	612,110	611,076	—	1,034	—
Bembridge	77	—	—	59	18
Benbecula	34,499	31,735	1,733	1,031	—
Birmingham	3,827,659	2,003,288	153,163	1,648,320	22,888
Blackpool	109,815	68,887	1,009	39,767	152
Bournemouth	109,104	24,723	723	80,211	3,447
Bristol	1,068,604	343,231	28,600	682,679	14,094
Cambridge	23,329	19,266	—	4,063	—
Cardiff	698,623	127,704	19,480	525,232	26,207
Carlisle	955	—	—	934	21
Coventry	9,299	7,436	241	1,622	—
Dundee	21,362	11,188	8,307	1,859	8
East Midlands	1,264,782	450,898	3,837	799,644	10,403
Edinburgh	2,678,937	2,324,642	137,321	213,914	3,060
Exeter	174,372	73,868	875	93,347	6,282
Glasgow	4,785,181	3,114,876	75,699	1,554,169	40,437
Gloucester/Cheltenham	9,646	4,297	1,263	4,075	11
Hawarden	1,185	—	—	1,166	19
Humberside	174,131	82,877	22,233	67,713	1,308
Inverness	229,318	210,543	16,079	2,606	90
Islay	18,989	17,590	624	775	—
Isle of Man	475,365	455,243	15,205	4,375	542
Isles of Scilly–St Mary's	102,318	102,318	—	—	—
–Tresco	21,675	20,445	1,230	—	—
Kirkwall	115,486	98,593	9,822	6,399	672
Leeds/Bradford	708,868	481,255	1,299	217,949	8,365
Lerwick (Tingwall)	5,062	2,305	126	2,604	27
Liverpool	455,869	408,254	9,848	36,778	989
Londonderry	27,567	26,568	—	999	—
Lydd	4,592	2,546	—	2,046	—
Manchester	12,051,220	4,779,651	292,323	6,898,285	80,961
Manston	7,385	633	79	5,826	847
Newcastle	1,996,998	799,289	31,946	1,142,268	23,495
Norwich	189,215	131,843	4,932	51,314	1,126
Penzance Heliport	89,719	89,041	176	502	—
Plymouth	84,362	65,564	16,634	2,164	—
Prestwick	17,134	4,791	950	6,340	5,053
Scatsta	14,112	—	—	14,097	15
Shoreham	2,087	277	—	1,810	—
Southampton	404,954	383,682	997	20,098	177
Stornoway	85,898	85,627	36	235	—
Sumburgh	440,937	93,822	61	312,452	34,602
Teesside	336,628	255,440	25,486	54,274	1,428
Tiree	6,026	5,078	843	105	—
Unst	80,194	2,131	15	78,048	—
Wick	39,700	31,214	7,934	508	44
CHANNEL IS. AIRPORTS: TOTAL	2,484,976	2,275,469	54,446	153,297	1,764
Alderney	78,550	78,280	1	266	3
Guernsey	787,354	744,383	32,723	10,034	214
Jersey	1,619,072	1,452,806	21,722	142,997	1,547

*UK and overseas   Source: Civil Aviation Authority

AERODROMES/AIRPORTS

The following aerodromes in the UK, the Isle of Man and the Channel Islands are either state owned or licensed for use by civil aircraft. A number of unlicensed aerodromes not included in this list are also available for private use by special permission. Aerodromes designated as Customs airports are printed in small capitals. Customs facilities are available at certain other aerodromes by special arrangement.

BAA   Owned by BAA PLC
H   Licensed for helicopters
HIAL   Operated by Highland and
         Islands Airports Ltd
J   Military aerodromes – civil
         availability by prior
         permission
M   Owned by municipal authority
P   Private ownership
S   Government owned and
         operated

ENGLAND AND WALES

Aberporth, Dyfed   J
Andrewsfield, Essex
Barrow (Walney Island), Cumbria
Bedford/Thurleigh   J
Bembridge, IOW
Benson, Oxon   J
Beverley/Linley Hill, N. Humberside
BIGGIN HILL, Kent   P
BIRMINGHAM, W. Midlands   P
Blackbushe, Hants
BLACKPOOL, Lancs   P
Bodmin, Cornwall
Boscombe Down, Wilts   S
Bourn, Cambridge
BOURNEMOUTH, Dorset   P
BRISTOL, Avon   P
Brize Norton, Oxford   J
Brough, N. Humberside
Caernarfon, Gwynedd
CAMBRIDGE   P
CARDIFF, S. Glamorgan   P
Carlisle, Cumbria   M
Chichester (Goodwood), Sussex
Chivenor, Devon   J
Church Fenton, N. Yorks   J
Clacton, Essex
Compton Abbas, Dorset
Cosford, Wolverhampton   J
COVENTRY, W. Midlands   M
Cranfield, Beds
Cranwell, Lincs   J
Crowfield, Suffolk
Culdrose, Cornwall   J
Deenethorpe, Northants
Denham, Bucks
Dishforth, N. Yorks   J
Dunkeswell, Devon
Dunsfold, Surrey   M
Duxford, Cambs   M
Eaglescott, Devon
Earls Colne, Halstead
EAST MIDLANDS, Derbys   P

Elstree, Herts
EXETER, Devon
Fairoaks, Surrey
Farnborough, Hants   S
Fenland, Lincs
Filton, Bristol
Finningley, S. Yorks   J
Fowlmere, Cambs
Gloucestershire (Staverton)   P
Great Yarmouth (North Denes),
   Norfolk   H
Halfpenny Green, Staffs
Halton, Bucks   J
Hatfield, Herts
Haverfordwest, Dyfed   M
Hawarden, Clwyd
Hucknall, Notts
HUMBERSIDE   P
Ipswich, Suffolk
Isle of Wight/Sandown
Land's End (St Just), Cornwall
Lashenden, Headcorn, Kent
Leavesden, Herts
LEEDS/BRADFORD, Yorks   P
Lee-on-Solent, Hants   J
Leicester, Leics
Linton-on-Ouse, Yorks   J
Little Gransden, Beds
LIVERPOOL, Merseyside   P
Llanbedr, Gwynedd   J
LONDON/CITY
LONDON/GATWICK   BAA
LONDON/HEATHROW   BAA
LONDON/STANSTED   BAA
London/Westland Heliport   H
LUTON, Beds   P
LYDD, Kent
Lyneham, Wilts   J
MANCHESTER   P
Manchester (Barton)
MANSTON, Kent   J
Marston Moor, York
Mona, Gwynedd   J
Netherthorpe, S. Yorks
NEWCASTLE, Tyne and Wear   P
Newton, Notts   J
Northampton (Sywell), Northants
Northolt, Middx   J
NORWICH, Norfolk   M
Nottingham, Notts
Old Sarum, Wilts
Oxford (Kidlington), Oxfordshire
Penzance, Cornwall   H
Perranporth, Cornwall
Peterborough (Conington)
Peterborough (Sibson), Cambs
PLYMOUTH (ROBOROUGH), Devon
Portland Naval, Dorset   JH
Redhill, Surrey
Retford/Gamston, Notts
Rochester, Kent
St Mawgan, Cornwall   J
Sandtoft, Humberside
Scilly Isles (St Mary's)   M
Seething, Norfolk
Shawbury, Shropshire   J
Sherburn-in-Elmet, N. Yorks
Shipdham, Norfolk
Shobdon, Herefordshire
SHOREHAM, W. Sussex   P

Silverstone, Northants
Sleap, Shropshire
SOUTHAMPTON/Eastleigh, Hants   P
SOUTHEND, Essex   P
Stapleford, Essex
Sturgate, Lincs
Swansea, W. Glam   M
TEESSIDE, Cleveland   P
Thruxton, Hants
Tresco, Isles of Scilly   H
Turweston, Northants
Valley, Gwynedd   J
Warton, Lancs
Wattisham, Suffolk   J
Wellesbourne Mountford, Warwick
Welshpool, Powys
Weston, Avon   H
White Waltham, Berks
Wickenby, Lincs
Woodford, Gtr Manchester
Woodvale, Merseyside   J
Wycombe Air Park (Booker), Bucks
Yeovil, Somerset
Yeovilton, Somerset   J

SCOTLAND

ABERDEEN (DYCE)   BAA
Barra, Hebrides
Benbecula, Hebrides   HIAL
Cumbernauld, Strathclyde
Dounreay (Thurso)   S
Dundee, Angus   M
Eday   M
EDINBURGH   BAA
Fair Isle
Fife/Glenrothes   M
Flotta, Orkneys
GLASGOW   BAA
Inverness (Dalcross)   HIAL
Islay (Port Ellen)   HIAL
Kirkwall   HIAL
Lerwick (Tingwall)   M
Leuchars, Fife   J
Machrihanish, Kintyre   J
North Ronaldsay, Orkneys   M
Papa Westray, Orkneys   M
Perth (Scone)
PRESTWICK,   BAA
Sanday, Orkneys   M
Scatsta
Stornoway, Hebrides   HIAL
Stronsay, Orkneys   M
SUMBURGH, Shetlands   HIAL
Tiree   HIAL
Unst, Shetlands   M
West Freugh, Dumfries   S
Westray, Orkneys   M
Whalsay, Shetlands
Wick   HIAL

NORTHERN IRELAND

BELFAST (ALDERGROVE)   S
Belfast (City)
Enniskillen (St Angelo)   P
Londonderry (Eglinton)   M
Newtownards

ISLANDS

ALDERNEY, CI   S
GUERNSEY, CI   S
JERSEY, CI   S
RONALDSWAY, IOM   S

RAILWAYS

The British Railways Board was set up by the Transport Act 1962, and assumed its responsibilities on 1 January 1963. (For members, see Government Departments and Public Offices section.)

Management of the railways is organized into the business sectors of InterCity, Network SouthEast, Regional Railways, Trainload Freight and Railfreight Distribution. A new organization, European Passenger Services Ltd, has been set up to manage international rail services through the Channel Tunnel. Under the Government's plans for the privatization of British Rail, ownership of track and land would be vested in a new body, Railtrack. Operation of passenger and freight rail services would be divided into a number of train-operating units, which would gradually be transferred to the private sector by franchising or sale.

FINANCIAL RESULTS

The profit and loss account for 1992–3 showed a deficit of £163.9 million after interest and extraordinary items, compared with a deficit of £144.7 million in 1991–2. The railway operating surplus was £13.4 million compared with a deficit of £101.4 million for the previous year.

	£ million
Railways	1992–3
Gross receipts	
Passenger (including grants)	2,862.6
Freight (incl. parcels and mails)	751.4
Other	109.3
Total	3,723.3
Working expenses	
Train services	1,669.8
Terminals	464.5
Miscellaneous traffic expenses	186.3
Track and signalling	625.8
General expenses	360.4
Depreciation	246.3
Other expenses	156.8
Total expenditure	3,709.9
Railway operating surplus	13.4
Interest and exceptional items	(177.3)
Group deficit	(163.9)

STAFF

On 31 March 1993 British Rail employed 124,791 staff (133,060 at 31 March 1992). Including subsidiaries, the group total at 31 March 1993 was 129,990 (138,001 at 31 March 1992).

OPERATING STATISTICS

At 31 March 1993, British Rail had 23,446 miles of standard gauge lines and sidings in use, representing 10,270 miles of route of which 3,051 miles were electrified. Standard rail on main line has a weight of 110 lb per yard. British Rail had 1,991 locomotives (2 diesel, 1,754 diesel-electric and 235 electric); 1,925 diesel multiple-unit vehicles, 6,629 electric multiple-unit vehicles and 2,630 locomotive-hauled vehicles.

Loaded train miles run in passenger service totalled 228.3 million. Passenger journeys made during the year totalled 744.8 million, including 361.3 million made by holders of season tickets. The average distance of each passenger journey on ordinary fare was 36.1 miles; and on season ticket, 16.2 miles. Passenger stations in use in 1993 numbered 2,482 and freight terminals 61.

FREIGHT

There were 15,912 freight vehicles and 1,241 other vehicles in the non-passenger-carrying stock. Train miles run in freight service totalled 31 million.

ACCIDENTS ON RAILWAYS

	1990*	1991–2
Train accidents: total	1,283	960
Persons killed: total	4	11
Passengers	0	2
Railway staff	1	2
Others	3	7
Persons injured: total	243	391
Passengers	157	307
Railway staff	73	65
Others	13	19
Other accidents through movement of railway vehicles		
Persons killed	75	73
Persons injured	2,658	2,360
Other accidents on railway premises		
Persons killed	4	10
Persons injured	6,815	6,900
Trespassers and suicides		
Persons killed	285	242
Persons injured	123	92

* Calendar year

ROADS

HIGHWAY AUTHORITIES

The powers and responsibilities of highway authorities in England and Wales are set out in the Highways Acts 1980; for Scotland there is separate legislation.

Responsibility for trunk road motorways and other trunk roads in Great Britain rests in England with the Secretary of State for Transport, in Scotland with the Secretary of State for Scotland, and in Wales with the Secretary of State for Wales. The costs of construction, improvement and maintenance are paid for by central government. The highway authority for non-trunk roads in England and Wales is, in general, the county council, metropolitan district council or London borough council in whose area the roads lie, and in Scotland the regional or islands council. In Northern Ireland the Northern Ireland Department of the Environment is responsible for public roads and their maintenance and construction.

EXPENDITURE

Transport Supplementary Grant (TSG) is a block grant and was introduced in England and Wales in 1975 to replace a variety of specific grants paid towards local transport expenditure.

In England grant was paid towards capital and current spending on transport by county councils and the GLC from 1975–6 to 1984–5. Since 1985 TSG has only been paid towards capital spending on highways and the regulation of traffic, current expenditure having been subsumed by rate support grant. Since the abolition of the GLC and the metropolitan county councils in 1986, grant has been paid to London boroughs, the Common Council of the City of London and metropolitan district councils. Since 1991 TSG has also been paid towards capital spending on bridge assessment and strengthening; since 1992 towards structural maintenance on the Primary Route Network; and since 1 April 1993 towards all principal 'A' roads. In Wales grant was also paid to the Welsh county councils towards current and capital expenditure on transport. In 1982 TSG became payable on capital expenditure only, current expenditure having been subsumed by rate support grant. In 1990 the grant for Wales was renamed Transport Grant.

Grant rates are determined by the respective Secretaries of State; at present, grant is paid at 50 per cent of expenditure accepted for grant in England and Wales.

For the financial year 1993–4 local authorities in England will receive £431 million in TSG. Total estimated expenditure on building and maintaining motorways and trunk roads in 1991–2 was £1.85 billion in England; estimated outturn for 1992–3 is £1.98 billion.

In the financial year 1993–4, local authorities in Wales will receive £36.5 million in TG. Total expenditure on roads in Wales in 1991–2 was £268 million.

Total capital expenditure on local roads in 1991–2 was £156 million in Scotland, and total expenditure on building and maintaining trunk roads was £208 million.

ROAD LENGTHS (in miles) as at April 1992

	Total roads	Trunk roads (including motorways)	Motorways*
England	171,924	6,571	1,684
Wales	20,836	1,063	74
Scotland	32,343	1,987	167
N. Ireland	15,039	1,373†	69
UK	240,142	10,994	1,994

*There were in addition 42 miles of local authority motorway in England and 15 miles in Scotland
†'A' roads; there are no designated trunk roads in N. Ireland

MOTORWAYS
The network in England and Wales is based on five main routes:

M1	London to Yorkshire
M4	London to South Wales
M5	Birmingham, Bristol, Exeter
M6	Birmingham to Carlisle
M62	Lancashire to North Humberside

Other important motorways include:

M2	Medway towns
M3	London to Winchester
M11	London to Cambridge
M18	Rotherham to Goole
M20	London to Folkestone
M25	London orbital route
M40	London to Birmingham
M56	North Cheshire
M180	South Humberside

Motorways in Scotland include:

M8	Edinburgh, Glasgow, Greenock
M9	Edinburgh to Stirling
M73	Maryville to Mollisburn
M74	Nether Abington to Maryville
M80	Stirling to Haggs/Glasgow (M8) to Stepps
M85	Perth to Friarton Bridge
M90	Perth to Inverkeithing
M876	Dennyloanhead to Kincardine Bridge

DRIVING TESTS
The number of driving tests conducted in Great Britain in 1992 was 1,650,436, of which 50.38 per cent resulted in a pass. In addition a total of 67,034 LGV/PCV (Large goods vehicle/Passenger carrying vehicle) tests were undertaken, of which 53 per cent were successful.

MOTOR VEHICLES
The number of vehicles in Great Britain with current licences in 1992 was:

Private and light goods	22,344,000
Motor cycles, scooters, mopeds	688,000
Public transport vehicles	108,000
Heavy goods vehicles	437,000
Agricultural tractors	324,000
Others	59,000
Total	24,851,000

This total includes 891,000 Crown vehicles and vehicles exempt from licensing.

BUSES AND COACHES 1991–2 (Great Britain)

Number of vehicles (31 March 1992)	71,200
Vehicle kilometres (millions)	3,873
Local bus passenger journeys (millions)	4,669
Passenger receipts (£ million)	2,966

ROAD ACCIDENTS 1992

Road accidents	233,025
Vehicles involved:	
Pedal cycles	25,285
Motor vehicles	391,311
Total casualties	310,673
Pedestrians	51,587
Vehicle users	259,086
Killed*	4,229
Pedestrians	1,347
Pedal cycles	204
All two-wheeled motor vehicles	469
Cars and taxis	1,978
Others	231

*Died within 30 days of accident

	Killed	Injured
1965	7,952	389,985
1970	7,499	355,869
1975	6,366	318,584
1980	6,010	323,000
1985	5,165	312,359
1990	5,217	335,924
1991	4,568	306,701
1992	4,229	306,444

LICENCES

VEHICLE LICENSES
Since 1974 registration and first licensing of vehicles has been through local offices (known as Vehicle Registration Offices) of the Department of Transport's Driver and Vehicle Licensing Centre in Swansea. The records of existing vehicles are held at Swansea. Local facilities for relicensing are available as follows:

(i) with a licence reminder (form V11) in person at any post office which deals with vehicle licensing, or post it to the post office shown on the form
(ii) with a vehicle licence renewal (form V10). You may normally apply in person at any licensing post office. You will need to take your vehicle registration document with you; if this is not available you must complete form V62 which is held at post offices. Postal applications can be made to the post offices shown on form V100, available at any post office. This form also provides guidance on registering and licensing vehicles.

Details of the present duties chargeable on motor vehicles are available at post offices and Vehicle Registration Offices. The Vehicles (Excise) Act 1971 provides *inter alia* that any vehicle kept on a public road but not used on roads is chargeable to excise duty as if it were in use.

Rates of duty for motor car and motor cycle licences are shown below.

	12 months £	6 months £
Motor Cars		
Those first constructed before 1 January		
1947	70.00	38.50
Others	125.00	68.75
Motor Cycles		
With or without sidecar, not exceeding		
150 cc	15.00	—
With or without sidecar, 150–250 cc	35.00	—
Others	55.00	30.25
Three Wheelers		
Not over 150 cc	15.00	—
Others	55.00	30.25
Hackney Carriages		
Seating less than 9 persons	125.00	68.75
Seating 9–16 persons	150.00	82.50
Seating 17–35 persons	200.00	110.00
Seating 36–60 persons	300.00	165.00
Seating over 60 persons	450.00	247.50

DRIVING LICENCE FEES
On or after 1 February 1993

Full Licence
First full licence — £21.00
Changing a provisional to a full licence after passing a driving test — free
Renewal of licence issued after 30 September 1982 — £6.00
Medical renewal — free
Medical renewal (over 70) — £6.00
Removing endorsements — £6.00
New licence after a period of disqualification — £12.00

Provisional Licence
First provisional licence — £21.00
Renewal of provisional licence issued before 1 October 1982 — £21.00

Duplicate Licence — £6.00

Exchange Licence — £6.00

The minimum age for driving motor cars, light goods vehicles and motor cycles is 17 (moped, 16).

DRIVING TEST FEES (weekday rate/Saturday rate)

For cars — £26/£36
*For motor cycles — £34/£45
For lorries, buses — £60/£77.50
For invalid carriages — free

*The first part of the motor cycle test, now known as Compulsory Basic Training, is no longer conducted by the Department of Transport but by appointed motor cycle training organizations, who conduct the majority of Basic Training tests within the framework of their own training courses and are free to set their own fee. The fee for a certificate of completion of a Compulsory Basic Training course is £5

An extended driving test was introduced in 1992 for those convicted of dangerous driving. The fee is £48.50/£77.50 (car) or £57/£92 (motorcycle)

MoT TESTING
Cars, motor cycles, motor caravans, light goods and dual-purpose vehicles more than three years old must be covered by a current MoT test certificate. Copies of the legislation governing MoT testing can be obtained from any bookshop which stocks HMSO publications. The legislation comprises the Road Traffic Act 1988 (Sections 45 and 46), the Motor Vehicles (Test) Regulations 1981, and subsequent amendments.

PRINCIPAL MERCHANT FLEETS OF THE WORLD

Flag	1982		1987		1991		1992	
	No.	Gross tonnage	No.	Gross tonnage	No.	Gross tonnage	No.	Gross tonnage
Liberia	2,189	70,718,439	1,574	51,412,029	1,605	52,426,516	1,672	55,166,948
Panama	5,032	32,600,278	5,136	43,254,716	4,953	44,949,330	5,217	49,629,986
Japan	10,652	41,593,612	9,822	35,932,177	10,063	26,406,930	10,091	25,403,270
Greece	3,501	40,035,204	1,948	23,559,852	1,863	22,752,919	1,872	24,542,087
Norway	2,409	21,861,635	1,979	6,359,349	2,577	23,585,661	2,499	22,583,133
Cyprus	557	2,149,869	1,341	15,650,207	1,359	20,297,661	1,416	20,385,718
Bahamas	96	432,502	469	9,105,182	973	17,541,196	1,061	20,054,161
China, People's Republic of	1,108	8,056,849	1,773	12,341,477	2,382	14,298,912	2,390	13,946,326
China, Republic of (Taiwan)	511	2,225,377	594	4,512,749	644	5,888,100	649	6,103,581
*United States of America	6,133	1,911,092	6,427	20,178,236	6,222	20,290,520	5,737	18,228,470
Russia	—	—	—	—	—	—	4,543	15,632,698
Malta	93	425,563	271	1,725,984	702	6,916,325	889	10,126,848
Singapore	849	7,183,326	700	7,098,116	854	8,488,172	946	9,247,352
Philippines	882	2,773,855	1,394	8,681,227	1,465	8,625,561	1,499	8,448,711
(USSR)	—	—	—	—	—	—	2,272	8,109,752
Italy	1,663	10,374,966	1,571	7,817,353	1,652	8,121,595	1,636	7,730,054
Korea (South)	1,652	5,529,398	1,899	7,214,070	2,136	7,820,532	2,138	7,518,485
Hong Kong	255	3,498,512	409	8,034,668	355	5,875,825	387	6,925,724
India	644	6,213,489	803	6,725,776	890	6,516,780	888	6,457,275
United Kingdom	2,826	22,505,265	2,165	8,504,605	1,949	6,610,633	1,747	6,016,868
Denmark	1,152	5,214,063	1,256	4,873,465	1,290	5,870,589	1,276	5,780,551
Brazil	666	5,678,111	718	6,324,059	669	5,882,528	635	5,573,175
Germany	1,782	7,706,661	1,414	4,317,616	1,522	5,971,254†	1,375	5,552,094†
Iran	235	1,312,734	370	3,976,873	401	4,583,179	403	4,558,219
Saint Vincent	34	25,966	145	699,947	698	2,709,794	881	4,380,956
Netherlands	1,228	5,393,104	1,307	3,908,231	1,249	3,872,301	1,230	4,250,456
France	1,171	10,770,880	954	5,371,273	910	3,988,072	890	4,205,310
Turkey	631	2,127,921	852	3,336,093	880	4,107,075	880	4,186,083
Romania	345	2,203,317	430	3,263,823	469	3,828,034	439	3,266,168
Spain	2,635	8,130,693	2,350	4,949,387	2,305	3,617,151	2,190	3,224,604
Poland	816	3,650,615	719	3,469,670	673	3,348,443	644	3,162,140
Bermuda	68	474,402	105	1,925,297	100	3,036,987	94	3,139,164
Sweden	697	3,787,567	642	2,269,541	684	3,174,274	664	3,081,166
Australia	558	1,875,316	690	2,404,559	714	2,571,867	695	2,676,087
Canada	1,299	3,212,562	1,238	2,971,155	1,204	2,684,614	1,185	2,642,795
Indonesia	1,319	1,846,824	1,734	2,120,531	1,991	2,336,880	2,014	2,338,604
Vanuatu	9	3,035	88	540,088	287	2,172,621	280	2,154,913
Marshall Islands	—	—	—	—	28	1,698,051	35	2,098,671
Malaysia	329	1,195,411	498	1,688,523	508	1,755,279	552	2,015,562
Kuwait	217	2,014,379	236	2,087,856	197	1,372,976	209	1,910,180
Luxembourg	—	—	—	—	51	1,703,482	54	1,580,695
Bulgaria	193	1,248,210	205	1,551,176	226	1,366,792	222	1,346,085
Latvia	—	—	—	—	—	—	261	1,235,573
Egypt	341	635,801	428	1,074,192	444	1,256,641	444	1,200,054
Finland	354	2,376,995	257	1,122,249	266	1,052,980	263	1,186,691
Mexico	545	1,251,630	651	1,532,485	649	1,195,517	635	1,109,683
Saudi Arabia	347	4,301,789	349	2,692,044	309	1,321,464	301	1,016,127

*Including ships of the United States Reserve Fleet
†Including the former German Democratic Republic

Classification with Lloyd's Register of Shipping: As at 30 June 1992, 8,620 ships with an aggregate gross tonnage of 96 million were classed or were to be classed with Lloyd's Register

Source: Lloyd's Register of Shipping

MERCHANT SHIPS COMPLETED DURING 1992

Country of Build	No.	Gross tonnage	For Registration in	No.	Gross tonnage
Japan	568	7,581,728	Liberia	117	4,947,193
Korea (South)	105	4,766,704	Panama	160	3,958,543
*China, People's Republic of	38	360,735	Japan	378	1,366,909
China, Republic of (Taiwan)	13	698,932	Norway	54	1,236,128
Germany	94	903,555	Singapore	60	731,805
Denmark	40	599,878	Bahamas	32	713,010
Spain	70	478,971	China, People's Republic of	28	146,175
Italy	43	391,735	China, Republic of (Taiwan)	10	425,408
Croatia	12	384,186	Germany	70	479,438
Poland	44	340,728	Kuwait	4	449,513
Brazil	11	285,668	Cyprus	24	447,387
Romania	18	200,634	Italy	54	442,040
Finland	9	196,385	Denmark	40	375,852
Netherlands	55	173,860	Netherlands	43	244,110
Norway	54	168,967	France	19	204,316
United Kingdom	28	152,307	Finland	7	192,252
*Ukraine	7	129,333	Hong Kong	12	189,397
France	17	116,161	Korea (South)	19	147,671
Belgium	9	108,114	United Kingdom	25	142,078
Portugal	10	93,057	Malaysia	19	139,481
Singapore	42	66,866	Poland	10	136,495
Bulgaria	6	60,004	Bermuda	2	125,878
India	10	57,060	Russia	20	125,758
Turkey	15	56,657	Saint Vincent	2	122,634
United States of America	27	54,033	Greece	5	121,410
Indonesia	8	23,902	Belgium	11	118,314
Malaysia	29	23,017	India	14	116,341
Sweden	6	22,791	Brazil	9	115,808
*Russia	3	20,863	Sweden	7	113,310
Other countries	115	116,056	Other countries	251	558,233
World Total	1,506	18,632,887	**World Total**	1,506	18,632,887

*Information incomplete

Source: Lloyd's Register of Shipping

Of the ships completed in the world during the year
2,909,865 gross tonnage (15.6 per cent) was to be classed
with Lloyd's Register

Communications

Postal Services

On 1 October 1969 the Post Office ceased to be a government department. The responsibility for running postal services was transferred to a public authority called the Post Office, which also administered telecommunications in the United Kingdom. The British Telecommunications Act 1981 separated the postal and telecommunications functions and gave the Secretary of State for Trade and Industry powers to suspend the monopoly of the Post Office in certain areas and to issue licences to other bodies to provide an alternative service. Non-Post Office bodies are now permitted to transfer mail between document exchanges and to deliver letters, provided that a minimum fee of £1 per letter is charged. Charitable organizations are allowed to carry and deliver Christmas and New Year cards.

INLAND POSTAL SERVICES AND REGULATIONS

Inland Letter Post Rates*

Not over	1st class	2nd class
60 g	24p	18p
100 g	36p	28p
150 g	45p	34p
200 g	54p	41p
250 g	64p	49p
300 g	74p	58p
350 g	85p	66p
400 g	96p	75p
450 g	£1.08	84p
500 g	£1.20	93p
600 g	£1.50	£1.15
700 g	£1.80	£1.35
750 g	£1.95	£1.40 (not
800 g	£2.05	admissible
900 g	£2.25	over 750 g)
1,000 g	£2.40	
Each extra 250 g or part thereof	60p	

Postcards travel at the same rates

UK Parcel Rates

Not over		Not over	
1 kg	£2.60	8 kg	£5.50
2 kg	£3.25	10 kg	£6.50
4 kg	£4.25	30 kg	£8.10
6 kg	£4.80		

Stamps

There is a two-tier postal delivery system in the UK with first class letters normally being delivered the following day and second class post within three days.

Postage stamps are sold in values of 1p, 2p, 3p, 4p, 5p, 6p, 10p, 18p, 20p, 24p, 28p, 30p, 33p, 34p, 35p, 39p, 50p, 75p, £1, £1.50, £2.00, £5.00, and £10.00.

* The Post Office has proposed an increase in 1st and 2nd class inland letter post (to 25p and 18p respectively) and in rates for other services from 1 November 1993. At the time of going to press no decision had been made

Books of stamps costing 50p or £1, or single first or second class stamps, are available from electronic vending machines at some main post offices. At post office counters books are sold containing ten first class stamps (£2.40) and ten second class stamps (£1.80). Rolls of 24p and 18p stamps are also sold. Mixed value rolls are only available on special order from post offices. The sale of postage stamps has been extended to outlets other than post offices, including stationers and newsagents.

PREPAID STATIONERY

Aerogrammes to all destinations, 34p.
Forces Aerogrammes, free to certain destinations. Other mail charged at a concessionary rate.
Registered Prepaid Letter Envelopes in three sizes:
  G, 156 × 95mm, £2.30
  H, 203 × 120mm, £2.35
  K, 292 × 152mm, £2.45
Printed postage stamps cut from envelopes, postcards, newspaper wrappers, etc., may be used as stamps in payment of postage, provided that they are not imperfect or defaced.

POSTAL ORDERS

Postal Orders (British pattern) are issued and paid at nearly all post offices in the UK. They are also paid in the Irish Republic, and issued and/or paid in many other countries overseas.

Postal orders are printed with a counterfoil for denominations of 50p and £1, followed by £1 steps to £10, £15 and £20. Postage stamps may be affixed in the space provided to increase the value of the postal order by up to 49p.

Charges (in addition to the value of the postal order): Up to £1, 25p; £2–£4, 42p; £5–£7, 55p; £8–£10, 60p; £15, 75p; £20, 80p.

The name of the payee must be inserted on the postal order. If not presented within six months of the last day of the month of issue, orders must be sent to the local customer services manager of Post Office Counters Ltd (the address and telephone number can be found in the telephone directory), to ascertain whether the order may still be paid, although if the counterfoil has been retained postal orders not more than four years out of date may be paid when presented with the counterfoil at a post office.

OTHER SERVICES

Cash on Delivery Service

(Inland, excluding Irish Republic and HM ships). A trade charge (amount to be collected) up to £500 can, under certain conditions, be collected from addresses and remitted to the sender of a parcel containing an invoice. Invoice values of over £100 are only collectable at Post Office premises.

Charge per parcel (exclusive of postage and registration): Customers under contract, £1.70; other customers, £2.00; COD enquiry, £1.70.

Certificate of Posting

Issued free on request at time of posting.

Compensation

(Royal Mail inland only): compensation up to a maximum of £24 may be paid where it can be shown that a letter was

522   Communications

damaged or lost in the post due to the fault of the Post Office, its employees or agents. The onus of making up properly any parcel sent by post lies with the sender. The Post Office does not accept any responsibility for loss arising from faulty packing.

Parcelforce: compensation up to £20 per parcel will be paid for loss or damage if a certificate of posting has been obtained. A Compensation Fee Certificate of Posting can also be obtained; 65p, up to £150 compensation, £1.15, up to £500 compensation.

Newspaper Post

Copies of newspapers registered at the Post Office may be posted by the publisher or their agents in wrappers open at both ends, in unsealed envelopes approved by the Post Office, or without covers and tied by string which can be removed without cutting. Wrappers and envelopes must be prominently marked 'newspaper post' in the top left-hand corner. No writing or additional printing is permitted, other than the words 'with compliments', name and address of sender, request for return if undeliverable and a reference to a page. Items receive first class letter service.

Newspapers posted by the public, or supplements to registered newspapers dispatched apart from their ordinary publications, are transmitted under the conditions governing the first or second class letter services.

Prohibited Articles

Prohibitions include offensive or dangerous articles, packets likely to impede Post Office sorters, and certain kinds of advertisement.

Recorded Delivery

The recorded delivery service provides a record of posting and delivery of inland letters and ensures a signature on delivery. No compensation is available for money or jewellery sent by this service. Charge, 55p. To confirm delivery, call LocalCall 0645-272100 and quote the number on the bar-coded receipt. (Also for Registered and Special Delivery.)

Redirection

(i) By agent of addressee – mail other than parcels, business reply and freepost items may be reposted free not later than the day after delivery (not counting Sundays and public holidays) if unopened and if original addressee's name is unobscured. Parcels may be redirected free of charge within the same time limits only if the original and substituted address are in the same local parcel delivery area (or within the London postal area). Registered packets, which must be taken to a post office, are re-registered free only up to the day after delivery.
(ii) By the Post Office – requests for redirection of mail should be made on printed forms obtainable from the Post Office and must be signed by the person to whom the letters are to be addressed. A fee is payable for each different surname on the application form.

Charges: Up to 1 calendar month, £3.50; up to 3 calendar months, £7.75; up to 12 calendar months, £18.75; up to 12 calendar months where redirection has already been in operation for 12 months or more, £65.00.

Registration

(Inland first class letters only). All packets intended for registration must be handed to the post office and a certificate of posting obtained. The registration fee is £3.00, which includes a 30p compensation premium (for up to a £500 claim). Registered Plus service is available for items worth between £500 and £2,200.

Consequential Loss Insurance provides cover up to £10,000 for items worth more than their material value:

Compensation up to	Standard fee in addition to registered fee and postage
£1,000	£0.45
£2,500	£0.60
£5,000	£0.85
£7,500	£1.10
£10,000	£1.35

Compensation in respect of currency or other forms of monetary worth is given only if money is sent by registered letter post in one of the special envelopes sold officially (see Prepaid Stationery). Compensation cannot be paid in the case of any packet containing anything not legally transmissible by post. Compensation is paid for fragile articles only if they have been adequately packed. No compensation is paid for deterioration due to delay of perishable articles or for damage to exceptionally fragile articles.

Special Delivery

Offers the same next-day delivery service as Registered Post but with no compensation service. Charge, £2.70.

Undelivered Mail

Undelivered mail is returned to the sender provided the return address is indicated either on the outside of the envelope or inside. If the sender's address is not available, items not containing property are destroyed. If the packet contains something of value it is retained for up to three months. Exceptionally, items in the minimum weight step on which a rebate of postage has been allowed are destroyed unopened unless there is a return address shown on the outside of the cover. In addition, undeliverable second class mail which contains newspapers, magazines or commercial advertising is destroyed.

Unpaid Mail

All unpaid or underpaid letters are treated as second class mail. The recipient is charged the amount of underpayment plus 14p per item. The same rates apply to parcels.

SPECIAL DELIVERY SERVICES

Datapost

A guaranteed service for the delivery of documents and packages: (i) Datapost Sameday offers same-day collection and delivery in many areas; (ii) Datapost 10 and Datapost 12 offer next day delivery nationwide. Datapost 10 for delivery before 10 a.m. and Datapost 12 for delivery before noon are available to certain destinations only. Items may be collected or handed in at post offices. There are also Datapost links with a number of overseas countries. Parcelforce 24 and 48 offer a similar guaranteed service to Datapost, 24 being delivered the following day and 48 the day after.

Royal Mail Special Delivery

This service offers special messenger treatment, where necessary, to ensure next day delivery of first class letters and packets. The fee of £2.70 is refunded if next working day delivery is not achieved, provided that items are posted before latest recommended posting times.

Swiftair

Express delivery of airmail letters and packets up to 2 kg anywhere in the world. Items normally arrive at least one day in advance of normal air mail. Charge (in addition to postage), £2.70.

OVERSEAS POSTAL SERVICES AND REGULATIONS

OVERSEAS SURFACE MAIL RATES

Letters and Postcards

Not over		Not over	
20 g	28p	450 g	£2.44
60 g	48p	500 g	£2.70
100 g	69p	750 g	£4.00
150 g	92p	1,000 g	£5.30
200 g	£1.18	1,250 g	£6.60
250 g	£1.42	1,500 g	£7.90
300 g	£1.66	1,750 g	£9.20
350 g	£1.92	2,000 g	£10.50
400 g	£2.18		

AIRMAIL LETTER RATES

Europe: Letters and Postcards

Not over		Not over	
20 g	24p	260 g	£1.60
20 g non EC	28p	280 g	£1.71
40 g	39p	300 g	£1.82
60 g	50p	320 g	£1.93
80 g	61p	340 g	£2.04
100 g	72p	360 g	£2.15
120 g	83p	380 g	£2.26
140 g	94p	400 g	£2.37
160 g	£1.05	420 g	£2.48
180 g	£1.16	440 g	£2.59
200 g	£1.27	460 g	£2.70
220 g	£1.38	480 g	£2.81
240 g	£1.49	*500 g	£2.92
* Max. 2 kg			

Outside Europe: Letters

	Not over 10 g	Not over 20 g	Each extra 20 g
Zone 1	39p	57p	32p
Zone 2	39p	57p	42p

For airmail letter zones outside Europe, *see* pages 527–8

OTHER SERVICES

Cash on Delivery

Applicable to parcels only, but not to all countries, nor to British naval, military and RAF forces serving overseas.

A charge starting at £5.00 per parcel must be prepaid in addition to the postage for outward parcels. The trade charge (amount to be collected) may not exceed £1,500 but to most non-European countries the limit is lower. The addressee has also to pay on delivery, besides Customs charges if any, a further charge which is not prepayable. If the trade charge cannot be collected special rules apply for undeliverable COD parcels.

Compensation

If a certificate of posting is produced, compensation may be given for loss or damage in the UK to uninsured parcels to or from most overseas countries. No compensation will be paid for any loss or damage due to the action of the Queen's Enemies.

Export Restrictions

Under Department of Trade and Industry regulations the exportation of some goods by post is prohibited except under Department of Trade licence. Enquiries should be addressed to the Export Data Branch, Overseas Trade Divisions, Department of Trade and Industry, 1 Victoria Street, London SW1H 0ET. Tel: 071-215 5000.

Insurance

Packets containing valuable papers, documents or articles such as jewellery can be insured as letters, or as parcels if the country of destination does not accept dutiable goods in the letter post. For HM ships abroad and also members of the Army and RAF overseas using BFPO numbers, parcels only are insurable up to £140 at a fee of £1.20.

Charges: Cover up to £150, £1.90; up to £300, £2.15; up to £450, £2.40; up to £600, £2.65; to a limit of £3.90 for £1,500 coverage.

International Reply Coupons

Coupons are used to prepay replies to letters. They are exchangeable abroad for stamps representing the minimum surface mail letter rate from the country concerned to the UK. Charge, 60p each.

Poste Restante

Solely for the convenience of travellers and for three months only in any one town. A packet may be addressed to any post office, except town sub-offices, and should have the words 'Poste Restante' or 'to be called for' in the address. Redirection from a Poste Restante is undertaken for up to three months. Letters at a seaport for an expected ship are kept for two months; otherwise letters are kept for two weeks, or for one month if originating from abroad. At the end of this period mail is treated as undeliverable, unless bearing a request for return.

Registration

(Except for parcels and printed paper items posted in bulk). Registration is available to all countries except the British Indian Ocean Territory and the Republic of the Maldives. No compensation is payable for loss or damage to valuable articles sent in an unregistered letter. Charge in addition to postage, £3.00.

Small Packets Post

This service permits the transmission of goods up to 2 kg to all countries, in the same mails as printed papers (NB: To Australia, Cuba, Myanmar (Burma) and Papua New Guinea there is a limit of 500 g, and to Italy 1 kg). Packets can be sealed and can contain personal correspondence if it relates to the contents of the packet. Registration is allowed as insurance as long as the item is packed in a way which complies with appropriate insurance regulations. A customs declaration is required and the packet must be endorsed 'small packet' and marked with a return address.

Instructions for the disposal of undelivered packets must be given at the time of posting. A packet which cannot be delivered will be returned to the sender at his/her expense.

SMALL PACKETS POST RATES

Surface Mail: World-wide

Not over		Not over	
100 g	45p	450 g	£1.50
150 g	60p	500 g	£1.65
200 g	75p	750 g	£2.30
250 g	90p	1,000 g	£2.95
300 g	£1.05	1,500 g	£4.15
350 g	£1.20	2,000 g	£5.35
400 g	£1.35		

Public Telecommunications Services

Under the British Telecommunications Act 1981 the functions of the Post Office were divided between two separate organizations. The Post Office retained control of postal services and British Telecom (now BT) was created to provide a telecommunications service. The Act also provided for a limited relaxation of the telecommunications monopoly. This was further advanced by the Telecommunications Act 1984, which removed BT's monopoly on running the public telecommunications system. British Telecom was privatized as a public limited company in 1984.

The Telecommunications Act 1984 also established the Office of Telecommunications (Oftel) as the independent regulatory body for the telecommunications industry. (*See also* Government Departments and Public Offices.)

PUBLIC TELECOMMUNICATIONS OPERATORS

Until recently there were three licensed fixed-link public telecommunications operators (PTOs) in the UK: BT, Mercury Communications Ltd, and Kingston Communications (Hull) PLC. In 1988 the Government announced its intention to license up to six other operators to provide one-way satellite communications systems; during 1989 three of these operators were granted temporary licences and the Government announced that such operators could offer services throughout Europe, rather than in the UK only, as previously indicated. In March 1991 the Government announced that it was opening up the existing duopoly of the two major fixed-link operators and would be encouraging applications for telecommunications licences. Since then there have been four recipients of major licences (Ionica, COLT, Energis, and Scottish Hydro-Electric) included in the 23 licences issued by the Department of Trade and Industry. There are 35 applications under consideration.

BT's obligations under its operating licence include the provision of a universal telecommunications service; a service in rural areas; and essential services, such as public call boxes and emergency services.

Mercury Communications is licensed to provide national and international public telecommunications services for residential and business customers. These services utilize the digital network created by Mercury. Mercury can also provide the following services: (i) public and private telephone services; (ii) national and international telex; (iii) international switched data services; (iv) electronic messaging (electronic mail and access to telex via a personal computer); (v) data network services; (vi) customer equipment; (vii) mobile communications services; and (viii) Mercury paging.

PRIVATE TELEPHONE SERVICES

There are over 260 private telephone companies which offer information on a variety of subjects such as the weather, stock market analysis, horoscopes, etc., on the BT network. Other services are available on Mercury's network.

The lines and equipment are provided by BT under condition that services adhere to the codes of practice of the Independent Committee for the Supervision of Standards of Telephone Information Practice. All services are charged at 48p per minute (peak and standard rate) or 36p per minute (cheap rate).

MOBILE TELEPHONE SYSTEMS

Cellular telephone network systems, in existence since 1985, allow calls to be made to and from mobile telephones. The two companies licensed by the Department of Trade and Industry to provide competing cellular telephone systems

are Cellnet, jointly owned by BT and Securicor, and Racal Vodafone Ltd, owned by the Racal Electronics Group. Cellular phones can be identified by the number prefixes 0831, 0836, 0850, 0860, or 0881 and calls to them are charged at the 'm' rate.

INLAND TELEPHONES

Since December 1986 an individual customer can install an extension telephone socket or apparatus in their own home without the need to buy the items from any of the licensed public telecommunications operators. However, it is necessary to possess a special style of master-socket which must be supplied by the public network operator. Although an individual need not buy or rent an apparatus from a PTO, a telephone bought from a retail outlet must be of an approved standard compatible with the public network (indicated by a green disc on the label).

BT CHARGES

EXCHANGE LINE RENTALS (*excluding VAT*)

	Per quarter
Residential, exclusive	£19.54
Supportline, exclusive	£9.77
Business, exclusive	£31.65
Telephone apparatus rental	
Residential	from £3.80
Business	from £4.70
Private payphone	from £36.50

EXCHANGE LINE CONNECTION AND TAKE-OVER CHARGES (*including VAT*)

	Residential	Business
New customer	£116.32	£116.32
Removing customer	£116.32	£116.32
Take-over of existing lines	£0.00	£0.00
Non-simultaneous take-over of lines	£36.78	£36.78

Local and dialled national calls are charged in 4.2p units when made from ordinary lines and in 10p units when made from payphones. All charges are subject to VAT except those from payphones which are VAT inclusive. VAT charges on ordinary lines are calculated as a percentage of the total quarterly bill.

The length of time per unit depends on the distance of the call and the time of day:

Local rate

'a' rate – up to 35 miles (56 km)
'b1' rate – frequently used routes over 35 miles (56 km)
'b' rate – over 35 miles (56 km) (incl. Channel Islands and Isle of Man)
'm' rate – dialled calls to mobile phones
'p1' rate – calls to Callstream service

*Greater London has an exceptionally large 'local' call area

Peak rate: Monday to Friday, 9 a.m.–1 p.m.
Standard rate: Monday to Friday, 8 a.m.–9 a.m. and 1 p.m.– 6 p.m.

Telecommunications 525

Cheap rate: Monday to Friday, 6 p.m.–8 a.m. All day Saturday and Sunday and also Christmas Day, Boxing Day and New Year's Day

DIALLED CALL UNIT TIME (*excluding VAT*)

Seconds per unit at 4.2p

Local rate
Peak	57.5
Standard	80
Cheap	220

'a' rate
Peak	27
Standard	36.15
Cheap	80.8

'b1' rate
Peak	23.9
Standard	32
Cheap	50.35

'b' rate
Peak	19.2
Standard	25.6
Cheap	37.9

'm' rate
Peak	7.61
Standard	7.61
Cheap	11.4

'p1' rate
Peak	6.2
Standard	6.2
Cheap	8.25

PREFIXED CALL CHARGES

0800 – free
0345 – charged at the local rate
0831, 0860 and Callstream 0077 services – charged at 'm' rate (and some 0836 calls also)
0839, 0898 and 08364 – charged at 'p1' rate

OPERATOR-CONNECTED CALLS

Operator-connected calls from ordinary lines are generally subject to a three-minute minimum charge (and thereafter by the minute) which varies with distance and time of day. Operator-connected calls from payphones are charged in three-minute periods at the payphone tariff. For calls that have to be placed through the operator because a dialled call has failed, the charge is equivalent to the dialled rate, subject normally to the three-minute minimum.

Higher charges apply to other operator-connected calls, including special services calls and those to mobile phones, the Irish Republic and the Channel Islands.

PHONECARDS

Phonecards to the value of £2, £4, £10 and £20 are available from post offices and other outlets for use in specially designated public telephone boxes. Each phonecard unit is equivalent to a 10p coin in a payphone.

Special public payphones at major railway stations and airports also accept commercial credit cards.

INTERNATIONAL TELEPHONES

All UK customers have access to International Direct Dialling (IDD) and can dial direct to numbers on most exchanges in over 200 countries world-wide. Details about how to make calls are given in dialling code information and in the International Telephone Guide.

For countries without IDD, calls have to be made through the International Operator. All operator-connected calls are subject to a three-minute minimum charge. Thereafter the call is charged by the minute.

Countries which can be called on IDD fall into one of 13 international charge bands depending on location. Charges in each band also vary according to the time of day; cheap rate dialled calls are available to all countries at certain times, but there is no reduced rate for operator-connected calls. Details of current international telephone charges can be obtained from the International Operator.

For International Dialling Codes, *see* pages 527–8

OTHER TELECOMMUNICATIONS SERVICES

Telex Service
There are now 208 countries that can be reached by the BT telex service from the UK, over 200 of them by direct dialling.

For most customers, direct dialled calls to international destinations are charged in six-second units. Units cost between 4.5p and 13.5p depending upon the country called. Calls via the BT operator are charged in one-minute steps with a three-minute minimum, plus a surcharge of £1.30 a call. Operator-connected calls are charged at between 39p and £1.60 a minute depending upon the country called.

Calls made via BT's Telex Plus store and forward facility attract normal telex charges and a handling charge of 13p for inland delivered messages and 30p for international delivered messages.

Telemessage
Telemessages can be sent by telephone or telex within the UK for 'hard copy' delivery the next working day, including Saturdays. To achieve this, a telemessage must be telephoned/telexed before 10 p.m. Monday to Saturday (7 p.m. Sundays and Bank Holidays). Dial 100 (190 in London, Birmingham and Glasgow) and ask for the Telemessage Service or see the telex directory for codes.

A telemessage costs £5 for the first 50 words and £2.75 for each subsequent group of 50 words – the name and address are free. A sender's copy costs 85p. A selection of cards is available for special occasions at 80p per card. All prices are subject to VAT.

International Telemessage
Telemessage is also available to the USA. For next working day delivery a telemessage must be filed by 10 p.m. UK time Monday to Saturday (7 p.m. Sundays and Bank Holidays). US addresses must include the ZIP code. Charges are £7.25 for the first 50 words and £3.60 for each subsequent group of 50 words. The name and address are free but all charges are subject to VAT.

BT SERVICES

OPERATOR SERVICES – 100
For difficulties
For the following call services: alarm calls (booking charge £2.15); advice of duration and charge (charge 75p); charge card calls (charge 25p); freefone calls; international personal calls (charge £2.15–£4.30); transferred charge calls (charge 40p); subscriber controlled transfer (All charges exclude VAT).

INTERNATIONAL OPERATOR – 155
DIRECTORY ENQUIRIES
  For numbers in the London postal area, 142
  For numbers outside the London postal area, including
  the Irish Republic, 192
INTERNATIONAL DIRECTORY ENQUIRIES – 153
EMERGENCY SERVICES – 999
  Services include fire service; police service; ambulance
  service; coastguard; lifeboat; cave rescue; mountain
  rescue
FAULTS – 151
TELEMESSAGE – 100 (190 in London, Birmingham and
  Glasgow)

INTERNATIONAL TELEMESSAGE – 100 (190 in London,
  Birmingham and Glasgow). The service is only available
  to the USA
INTERNATIONAL TELEGRAMS – 100 (190 in London,
  Birmingham and Glasgow). The service is available
  world-wide
MARITIME SERVICES – 100
  Includes Ship's Telegram Service and Ship's Telephone
  Service
BT INMARSAT SATELLITE SERVICE – 155
ALL OTHER CALL ENQUIRIES – 191

Forecast Services

WEATHERCALL SERVICE

To obtain local weather forecasts, dial the prefix code
0891 500 followed by the appropriate regional code

Greater London	401
Kent, Surrey and Sussex	402
Dorset, Hampshire and IOW	403
Devon and Cornwall	404
Wiltshire, Glos., Avon and Somerset	405
Berks., Bucks. and Oxfordshire	406
Beds., Herts. and Essex	407
Norfolk, Suffolk and Cambridgeshire	408
West, Mid and South Glamorgan and Gwent	409
Salop, Hereford and Worcester	410
Central Midlands	411
East Midlands	412
Lincolnshire and Humberside	413
Dyfed and Powys	414
Gwynedd and Clwyd	415
North-west England	416
West and South Yorkshire	417
North-east England	418
Cumbria and the Lake District	419
South-west Scotland	420
West Central Scotland	421
Edinburgh, South Fife, Lothian and Borders	422
East Central Scotland	423
Grampian and East Highlands	424
North-west Scotland	425
Caithness, Orkney and Shetland	426
Northern Ireland	427
Yorkshire Dales	748

Calls are charged at 36p per minute cheap rate, 48p at all
other times, as at June 1993

MARINECALL SERVICE

To obtain information about weather conditions up to twelve
miles off the coast, dial the prefix code 0891 500, followed
by the appropriate area code

Scotland North	451
Scotland East	452
North-east	453
East	454
Anglia	455
Channel East	456
Mid-Channel	457
South-west	458
Bristol Channel	459
Wales	460
North-west	461
Clyde	462
Caledonia	463
Minch	464
Ulster	465
Southern North Sea	991
English Channel	992

Calls are charged at 36p per minute cheap rate, 48p at all
other times, as at June 1993

Airmail and IDD Codes

AIRMAIL ZONES (AZ)
The table includes airmail letter zones for countries outside Europe, and destinations to which European and European Community airmail letter rates apply (*see also* page 523). (*Source: Post Office*)

1   airmail zone 1
2   airmail zone 2
e   Europe
cc European Community

INTERNATIONAL DIRECT DIALLING (IDD)
International dialling codes are composed of four elements which are dialled in sequence:

(i)   the international code
(ii) the country code (*see* below)
(iii) the area code
(iv) the customer's telephone number

Calls to some countries must be made via the international operator. (*Source: BT*)

†   Calls must be made via the international operator
p   A pause in dialling is necessary whilst waiting for a second tone
p*   Only in Bruges, Ostende and Veurne
°   Second tone may not always be audible
*   Varies in some areas

Country	AZ	IDD from UK	IDD to UK
Afghanistan	1	010 93	†
Albania	e	010 355	†
Algeria	1	010 213	00p44
Andorra	ec	010 33 628	0p44
Angola	1	010 244	†
Anguilla	1	010 1 809	001 44
Antigua and Barbuda	1	010 1 809	011 44
Argentina	1	010 54	00 44
Armenia	e	010 7	810 44
Aruba	1	010 297	†
Ascension Island	1	010 247	
Australia	2	010 61	00 11 44
Austria	e	010 43	00 44
Azerbaijan	e	010 7	810 44
Azores	ec	010 351	00 44
Bahamas	1	010 1 809	011 44
Bahrain	1	010 973	0 44
Bangladesh	1	010 880	00 44
Barbados	1	010 1 809	011 44
Belarus	e	010 7	810 44
Belgium	ec	010 32	00p44*
Belize	1	010 501	†
Benin	1	010 229	00p44
Bermuda	1	010 1 809	1 44
Bhutan	1	010 975	00 44
Bolivia	1	010 591	00 44
Bosnia-Hercegovina	e	010 38	99 44
Botswana	1	010 267	00 44
Brazil	1	010 55	00 44
British Virgin Islands	1	010 1 809 49	011 44
Brunei	1	010 673	00 44
Bulgaria	e	010 359	00 44
Burkina Faso	1	010 226	
Burundi	1	010 257	90 44
Cambodia	1	†	†
Cameroon	1	010 237	00 44
Canada	1	010 1	011 44
Canary Islands	ec	010 34	07p44
Cape Verde	e	010 238	†
Cayman Islands	1	010 1 809	0 44
Central African Republic	1	010 236	†
Chad	1	010 235	†
Chile	1	010 56	00 44
China	2	010 86	00 44
Colombia	1	010 57	90 44
Comoros	1	010 269	†
Congo	1	010 242	00 44
Cook Islands	2	010 682	00 44
Costa Rica	1	010 506	00 44
Côte d'Ivoire	1	010 225	00 44
Croatia	e	010 38	99 44
Cuba	1	010 53	
Cyprus	e	010 357	00 44
Czech Republic	e	010 42	00 44
Denmark	ec	010 45	009 44
Djibouti	1	010 253	00 44
Dominica	1	010 1 809	011 44
Dominican Republic	1	010 1 809	†
Ecuador	1	010 593	00 44
Egypt	1	010 20	00 44
Equatorial Guinea	1	010 240	†
Estonia	e	010 7	810 44
Ethiopia	1	010 251	
Falkland Islands	1	010 500	01 44
Faroe Islands	e	010 298	009 44
Fiji	2	010 679	05 44
Finland	e	010 358	990 44
France	ec	010 33	19p44°
French Guiana	1	010 594	†
French Polynesia	2	010 689	00 44
Gabon	1	010 241	00 44
The Gambia	1	010 220	00 44
Georgia	e	010 7	810 44
Germany	ec	010 49	00 44
Ghana	1	010 233	
Gibraltar	ec	010 350	00 44
Greece	ec	010 30	00 44
Greenland	e	010 299	009 44
Grenada	1	010 1 809	011 44
Guadeloupe	1	010 590	†
Guam	2	010 671	00 44
Guatemala	1	010 502	00 44
Guinea	1	010 224	†
Guinea-Bissau	1	010 245	†
Guyana	1	010 592	011 44
Haiti	1	010 509	†
Honduras	1	010 504	00 44
Hong Kong	1	010 852	001 44
Hungary	e	010 36	00 44
Iceland	e	010 354	90 44
India	1	010 91	00 44
Indonesia	1	010 62	00 44
Iran	1	010 98	00 44
Iraq	1	010 964	00 44
Irish Republic	ec	010 353	00 44
Dublin		0001	
Israel	1	010 972	00 44
Italy	ec	010 39	00 44
Jamaica	1	010 1 809	†
Japan	2	010 81	001 44
Jordan	1	010 962	00 44*
Kazakhstan	e	010 7	810 44

Country	AZ	IDD from UK	IDD to UK
Kenya	1	010 254	000 44
Kiribati	2	010 686	09 44
Korea, North	2	010 850	†
Korea, South	2	010 82	001 44
Kuwait	1	010 965	00 44
Kyrgystan	e	010 7	810 44
Laos	1	†	†
Latvia	e	010 7	810 44
Lebanon	1	010 961	00 44
Lesotho	1	010 266	00 44
Liberia	1	010 231	00 44
Libya	1	010 218	00 44
Liechtenstein	e	010 41 75	00 44
Lithuania	e	010 7	810 44
Luxembourg	ec	010 352	00 44
Macao	1	010 853	00 44
Madagascar	1	010 261	†
Madeira	ec	010 351 91	00 44*
Malawi	1	010 265	101 44
Malaysia	1	010 60	00 44
Maldives	1	010 960	
Mali	1	010 223	00 44
Malta	e	010 356	00 44
Mariana Islands, Northern	2	010 670	
Marshall Islands	2	010 692	
Martinique	1	010 596	†
Mauritania	1	010 222	†
Mauritius	1	010 230	
Mayotte	1	010 269	
Mexico	1	010 52	98 44
Micronesia, Federated States of	2	010 691	
Moldova	e	010 7	810 44
Monaco	ec	010 33 93	19p44
Mongolia	2	†	†
Montserrat	1	010 1 809	†
Morocco	1	010 212	00p44
Mozambique	1	010 258	†
Myanmar	1	010 95	†
Namibia	1	010 264	091 44
Nauru	2	010 674	00 44
Nepal	1	010 977	00 44
Netherlands	ec	010 31	09p44
Netherlands Antilles	1	010 599	00 44
New Caledonia	2	010 687	00 44
New Zealand	2	010 64	00 44
Nicaragua	1	010 505	00 44
Niger	1	010 227	00 44
Nigeria	1	010 234	009 44
Niue	2	010 683	
Norfolk Island	2	010 672	
Norway	e	010 47	095 44
Oman	1	010 968	00 44
Pakistan	1	010 92	00 44
Palau	2	010 6809	
Panama	1	010 507	00 44
Papua New Guinea	2	010 675	31 44
Paraguay	1	010 595	002 44 / 003 44
Peru	1	010 51	00 44
Philippines	2	010 63	00 44
Poland	e	010 48	0p044
Portugal	ec	010 351	00 44
Puerto Rico	1	010 1 809	135 44
Qatar	1	010 974	044
Réunion	1	010 262	19p44
Romania	e	010 40	

Country	AZ	IDD from UK	IDD to UK
Russia	e	010 7	810 44
Rwanda	1	010 250	†
St Helena	1	010 290	†
St Kitts and Nevis	1	010 1 809	†
St Lucia	1	010 1 809	0 44
St Pierre and Miquelon	1	010 508	†
St Vincent and the Grenadines	1	010 1 809	0 44
El Salvador	1	010 503	00 44
Samoa, American	2	010 684	144
San Marino	ec	010 39 549	00 44
São Tomé and Príncipe	1	010 23 912	†
Saudi Arabia	1	010 966	00 44
Senegal	1	010 221	00p44
Seychelles	1	010 248	0 44
Sierra Leone	1	010 232	†
Singapore	1	010 65	005 44
Slovak Republic	e	010 42	00 44
Slovenia	e	010 38	99 44
Solomon Islands	2	010 677	00 44
Somalia	1	010 252	†
South Africa	1	010 27	09 44
Spain	ec	010 34	07p44
Sri Lanka	1	010 94	00 44
Sudan	1	010 249	†
Suriname	1	010 597	001 44
Swaziland	1	010 268	00 44
Sweden	e	010 46	009 44p
Switzerland	e	010 41	00 44
Syria	1	010 963	00 44
Taiwan	2	010 886	002 44
Tajikistan	e	010 7	810 44
Tanzania	1	010 255	†
Thailand	1	010 66	001 44
Tibet	1	010 86	00 44
Togo	1	010 228	
Tonga	2	010 676	0 44
Trinidad and Tobago	1	010 1 809	01 44
Tristan da Cunha	1	†	
Tunisia	1	010 216	00 44
Turkey	1	010 90	9p944
Turkmenistan	e	010 7	810 44
Turks and Caicos Islands	1	010 1 809	†
Tuvalu	2	010 688	†
Uganda	1	010 256	†
Ukraine	e	010 7	810 44
United Arab Emirates	1	010 971	00 44
Uruguay	1	010 598	00 44
USA	1	010 1	011 44
Alaska		010 1 907	
Hawaii		010 1 808	
Uzbekistan	e	010 7	810 44
Vanuatu	2	010 678	†
Vatican City State	ec	010 39 66982	
Venezuela	1	010 58	00 44
Vietnam	1	010 84	†
Virgin Islands (US)	1	010 1 809	011 44
Western Samoa	2	010 685	†
Yemen			
north	1	010 967	00 44
south	1	010 969	00 44
Yugoslav Fed. Rep.	e	010 38	99 44
Zaire	1	010 243	00 44
Zambia	1	010 260	00 44
Zimbabwe	1	010 263	110 44

Local Government

The Local Government Acts of 1972 and 1985, the Local Government (Scotland) Act 1973 and the London Government Act 1963 are the main Acts which have brought about the present structure of local government in Great Britain. This structure has been in effect in England and Wales since 1974, with alterations in 1986 with the abolition of the metropolitan counties and the Greater London Council; and in Scotland since 1975.

The structure is based on two tiers of local authorities (county or regional councils and district councils) in the non-metropolitan areas; and a single tier of metropolitan and London borough councils in the six metropolitan areas of England and in London respectively.

The two-tier structure of local government in England is currently being reviewed by the Local Government Commission. The Government has published proposals for the establishment of a single tier of unitary authorities in Wales and Scotland.

Local authorities are empowered or required by various Acts of Parliament to carry out functions in their areas. The legislation concerned comprises public general Acts and 'local' Acts which local authorities have promoted as private bills.

ELECTIONS

Local elections are normally held on the first Thursday in May. Generally, all British subjects or citizens of the Republic of Ireland of 18 years or over who are resident on the qualifying date in the area for which the election is being held, are entitled to vote at local government elections. A register of electors is prepared and published annually by local electoral registration officers.

A returning officer has the overall responsibility for an election. Voting takes place at polling stations, arranged by the local authority and under the supervision of a presiding officer specially appointed for the purpose. Candidates, who are subject to various statutory qualifications and disqualifications designed to ensure that they are suitable persons to hold office, must be nominated by electors for the electoral area concerned.

In England, the Local Government Boundary Commission keeps the areas and electoral arrangements under review, and makes proposals to the Secretary of State for changes found necessary. In Wales and Scotland there are separate Local Government Boundary Commissions which carry out this task.

INTERNAL ORGANIZATION

The council as a whole is the final decision-making body within any authority. Councils are free to a great extent to make their own internal organizational arrangements.

Normally, questions of major policy are settled by the full council, while the administration of the various services is the responsibility of committees of councillors. Day-to-day decisions are delegated to the council's officers, who act within the policies laid down by the councillors.

FINANCE

Local government in England, Wales and Scotland is financed from three sources: the council tax, non-domestic rates and government grants. (For arrangements in Northern Ireland, *see* page 533.)

COUNCIL TAX

Under the Local Government Finance Act 1992, from 1 April 1993 the council tax replaced the community charge (which had been introduced in April 1989 in Scotland and April 1990 in England and Wales in place of domestic rates).

The council tax is a local tax levied by each local council. Liability for the council tax bill usually falls on the owner-occupier or tenant of a dwelling which is their sole or main residence. Council tax bills may be reduced because of the personal circumstances of people resident in a property, and there are discounts in the case of dwellings occupied by fewer than two adults.

In England and Wales, each county council and each district council sets its own council tax rate. The district councils collect the combined council tax and the county councils claim their share from the district councils' collection funds. In Scotland the regional and islands councils levy the council tax and the district councils claim a share.

The tax relates to the value of the dwelling. Each dwelling is placed in one of eight valuation bands, ranging from A to H, based on the property's estimated market value as at 1 April 1991.

The valuation bands and ranges of values in England, Wales and Scotland are:

England

A	Up to £40,000	E	£88,001–£120,000
B	£40,001–£52,000	F	£120,001–£160,000
C	£52,001–£68,000	G	£160,001–£320,000
D	£68,001–£88,000	H	Over £320,000

Wales

A	Up to £30,000	E	£66,001–£90,000
B	£30,001–£39,000	F	£90,001–£120,000
C	£39,001–£51,000	G	£120,001–£240,000
D	£51,001–£66,000	H	Over £240,000

Scotland

A	Up to £27,000	E	£58,001–£80,000
B	£27,001–£35,000	F	£80,001–£106,000
C	£35,001–£45,000	G	£106,001–£212,000
D	£45,001–£58,000	H	Over £212,000

The council tax within a local area varies between the different bands according to proportions laid down by law. The charge attributable to each band as a proportion of the Band D charge set by the council is:

A	67%	E	122%
B	78%	F	144%
C	89%	G	167%
D	100%	H	200%

The band D rate is given in the tables on pages 551–7 (England), 563 (London), 566 (Wales), and 570–1 (Scotland). There may be variations from the given figure within each district council area because of different parish precepts being levied.

NON-DOMESTIC RATES

Non-domestic (business) rates have been collected since 1 April 1990 by billing authorities, i.e. district councils in England and Wales, and regional and islands councils in Scotland. The Local Government Finance Act 1988 provides for liability for rates to be assessed on the basis of a poundage (multiplier) tax on the rateable value of property (hereditaments). The multiplier is set by central government and rates are collected by the billing authority for the area where a property is located. Rate income collected by billing authorities is paid into a national non-domestic rating (NNDR) pool and redistributed to individual authorities on the basis of the adult population figure as prescribed by the Secretary of State. For the years 1990–1 to 1994–5 actual payment of rates in certain cases are subject to transitional arrangements, to phase in the larger increases and reductions in rates resulting from the combined effects of the 1990 revaluation and the introduction of a uniform national business rate (UBR). The transitional arrangements were altered in 1992–3 and 1993–4 to freeze the increases for those going towards higher bills and ensure those going towards lower bills reached their true bill sooner.

Rateable values for the rating lists came into force on 1 April 1990. They are derived from the rental value of property as at 1 April 1988 and determined on certain statutory assumptions by valuation officers of the Valuation Office Agency. New property which is added to the list, and significant changes to existing property, necessitate amendments to the rateable value on the same basis. Rating lists remain in force until the next general revaluation, which is scheduled for 1 April 1995.

Certain types of property are exempt from rates, e.g. agricultural land and buildings, and places of public religious worship. Charities and other non-profit-making organizations may receive full or partial relief. Specified classes of empty property are liable to pay rates at 50 per cent.

GOVERNMENT GRANTS

In addition to specific grants in support of revenue expenditure on particular services, central government pays revenue support grant to local authorities. This grant is paid to each county/regional and district council so that if each authority spends at a level sufficient to provide a standard level of service, it can set the same council tax.

COMPLAINTS

Commissioners for Local Administration in England, Wales and Scotland (see page 329) are responsible for investigating complaints from members of the public who claim to have suffered injustice as a consequence of maladministration in local government.

The Northern Ireland Commissioner for Complaints fulfils a similar function in Northern Ireland, investigating complaints about local authorities and certain public bodies.

QUEEN'S REPRESENTATIVES

The Lord Lieutenant of a county is the permanent local representative of the Crown and as such takes precedence in the county. The Lord Lieutenant is appointed by the Sovereign on the recommendation of the Prime Minister. The title was created in 1557, when the Lord Lieutenant was given a range of responsibilities including the maintenance of an efficient militia. Some of the rights and duties of the post were abolished in 1871, but the Lord Lieutenant's duties still include attending on royalty during official visits to the county, acting as head of the county's commission of the peace (which recommends the appointment of magistrates for the county bench), raising the militia in times of need, and appointing deputy lieutenants. Lord Lieutenants must retire at the age of 75 if they do not choose to do so before reaching that age.

The office of Sheriff (from the Old English shire-reeve) of a county was created in the tenth century. The Sheriff was the special nominee of the Sovereign, and the office reached the peak of its influence under the Norman kings. The Provisions of Oxford (1258) laid down a yearly tenure of office. Since the mid-16th century the office has been purely civil, with military duties taken over by the Lord Lieutenant of the county. The Sheriff (commonly known as 'High Sheriff') attends on royalty during official visits to the county, acts as the returning officer during parliamentary elections in county constituencies, attends the opening ceremony when a High Court judge goes on circuit, executes High Court writs, and appoints under-sheriffs to act as deputies. The appointments and duties of the High Sheriffs in England and Wales are laid down by the Sheriffs Act 1887.

The serving High Sheriff submits a list of names of possible future sheriffs to a tribunal which chooses three names to put to the Sovereign. The tribunal nominates the High Sheriff annually on 12 November and the Sovereign pricks the name of the Sheriff to succeed in the following year. The term of office runs from 25 March to the following 24 March (the civil and legal year before 1752). No person may be chosen twice in three years if there is any other suitable person in the county.

CIVIC DIGNITIES

District councils may petition for a royal charter granting borough or 'City' status to the district.

In England and Wales the chairman of a borough council may be called a mayor, and the chairman of a city council a Lord Mayor. Parish councils in England and Wales may call themselves 'town councils', in which case their chairman is the town mayor.

In Scotland the chairman of a district council may be known as a convenor; a provost is the equivalent of a mayor. The chairmen of the councils for the cities of Aberdeen, Dundee, Edinburgh and Glasgow are Lord Provosts.

ENGLAND
(For London, see below)

England outside Greater London is divided into counties. Each county is divided into districts. There are 39 non-metropolitan counties; each of these is divided into non-metropolitan districts, of which there are 296. These districts have populations broadly in the range of 60,000 to 100,000; some however, have larger populations, because of the need to avoid dividing large towns, and some in mainly rural areas have smaller populations.

Six metropolitan counties cover the main conurbations outside Greater London; Tyne and Wear, West Midlands, Merseyside, Greater Manchester, West Yorkshire and South Yorkshire. They are divided into 36 metropolitan districts, most of which have a population of over 200,000.

There are also about 10,000 parishes, in 219 of the non-metropolitan and 18 of the metropolitan districts.

ELECTIONS

For districts, non-metropolitan counties, and for about 8,000 parishes, there are elected councils, consisting of directly elected councillors. The councillors elect annually one of their number as chairman.

Generally, councillors serve four years and there are no elections of district and parish councillors in county election years. In metropolitan districts, one-third of the councillors for each ward are elected each year except in the year of county elections. Non-metropolitan districts can choose whether to have elections by thirds or whole council elections. In the former case, one-third of the council, as nearly as may be, is elected in each year of metropolitan district elections.

If whole council elections are chosen, these are held in the year midway between county elections.

FUNCTIONS

In non-metropolitan areas, functions are divided between the districts and counties, those requiring the larger area or population for their efficient performance going to the county. The metropolitan district councils, with the larger population in their areas, already had wider functions than non-metropolitan councils, and following abolition of the metropolitan county councils were given most of their functions also. A few functions continue to be exercised over the larger area by joint bodies, made up of councillors from each district.

The allocation of functions is as follows:

County councils: education; strategic planning; traffic, transport and highways; police; fire service; consumer protection; refuse disposal; smallholdings; social services; libraries

Non-metropolitan district councils: local planning; housing; highways (maintenance of certain urban roads and off-street car parks); building regulations; environmental health; refuse collection; cemeteries and crematoria

Metropolitan district councils: their functions are all those listed above, except that fire, civil defence, police and passenger transport (and in some cases, refuse disposal) are exercised by joint bodies

Concurrently by county and district councils: recreation (parks, playing fields, swimming pools); museums; encouragement of the arts, tourism and industry

PARISH COUNCILS

Parishes with 200 or more electors must generally have parish councils, which means that over three-quarters of the parishes have councils. A parish council comprises at least five members, the number being fixed by the district council. Elections are held every four years, in the year in which the local district council is elected. All parishes have parish meetings, comprising the electors of the parish. Where there is no council, the meeting must be held at least twice a year.

Parish council functions include: allotments; encouragement of arts and crafts; community halls, recreational facilities (e.g. open spaces, swimming pools); cemeteries and crematoria; and many minor functions. They must also be given an opportunity to comment on planning applications. They may, like county and district councils, spend limited sums for the general benefit of the parish. They levy a precept on the district councils for their funds.

FINANCE

Aggregate external finance for 1993–4 was originally determined at £33,180 million. Of this, specific grants were estimated at £3,981 million and special grants at £588 million (mainly the community charge special grant). £17,051 million was in respect of revenue support grant and £11,559 million was support from the national non-domestic rate pool. Total standard spending by local authorities considered for grant purposes was £41,168 million.

The average council taxes, expressed in terms of Band C, two-adult properties for 1993–4, were: inner London boroughs £502; outer London boroughs £492; London £496; metropolitan districts £566; non-metropolitan districts £488. The average for England was £505.

National non-domestic rate (or uniform business rate) for 1993–4 is 41.6p. The amount estimated to be raised is £11.8 billion. Total rateable value held on local authority lists at 31 December 1992 was £31.1 billion.

EXPENDITURE

Local authority budgeted net revenue expenditure for 1992–3 was (1992–3 cash prices):

Service	£m
Education	18,531
School catering	410
Libraries, museums and art galleries	721
Personal social services	5,698
Police	5,513
Fire	1,197
Other Home Office services	768
Local transport	2,378
Local environmental services	5,098
Agricultural services	34
Consumer protection and trading standards	135
Employment	183
Non-housing revenue account housing	380
Housing benefits	3,418
Parish precepts	108
New net current expenditure	44,574
Capital charges	2,788
Capital charged to revenue	588
Other non-current expenditure	2,830
Interest receipts	−732
Gross revenue expenditure	50,048
Specific grants outside AEF	−7,399
Other income	−61
Revenue expenditure	42,588
Specific grants inside AEF	−4,563
Net revenue expenditure	38,025

AEF = aggregate external finance

LONDON

Since the abolition of the Greater London Council in 1986, the Greater London area has not had a single local government body. The area is divided into 32 borough councils, which have a status similar to the metropolitan district councils in the rest of England, and the Corporation of the City of London.

LONDON BOROUGH COUNCILS

The London boroughs have whole council elections every four years, in the year immediately following the county council election year. The next elections will be held on 6 May 1994.

The borough councils have responsibility for the following functions: building regulations; cemeteries and crematoria; consumer protection; education; youth employment; environmental health; electoral registration; food; drugs; housing; leisure services; libraries; local planning; local roads; museums; parking; recreation (parks, playing fields, swimming pools); refuse collection and street cleansing; social services; town planning; and traffic management.

THE CORPORATION OF THE CITY OF LONDON
(*see also* pages 558–60)

The Corporation of the City of London is the local authority for the City of London. Its legal definition is 'The Mayor and Commonalty and Citizens of the City of London'. It is governed by the Court of Common Council, which consists of the Lord Mayor, 24 other aldermen, and 132 common councilmen. The Lord Mayor and two sheriffs are nominated annually by the City guilds (the livery companies) and elected by the Court of Aldermen. Aldermen and councilmen are elected by businesses in the 25 wards into which the City is divided; councilmen must stand for re-election annually. The Council is a legislative assembly, and there are no political parties.

The Corporation has the same functions as the London borough councils. In addition, it runs the City of London Police; is the health authority for the Port of London; has health control of animal imports throughout Greater London, including at Heathrow airport; owns and manages public open spaces throughout Greater London; runs the Central Criminal Court; and runs Billingsgate, Smithfield and Spitalfields markets.

THE CITY GUILDS (LIVERY COMPANIES)
The livery companies of the City of London grew out of early medieval religious fraternities and began to emerge as trade and craft guilds, retaining their religious aspect, in the 12th century. From the early 14th century, only members of the trade and craft guilds could call themselves citizens of the City of London. The guilds began to be called livery companies, because of the distinctive livery worn by the most prosperous guild members on ceremonial occasions, in the late 15th century.

By the early 19th century the power of the companies within their trades had begun to wane, but those wearing the livery of a company continued to play an important role in the government of the City of London. Liverymen still have the right to nominate the Lord Mayor and sheriffs, and most members of the Court of Common Council are liverymen (*see also* page 560).

GREATER LONDON SERVICES
After the abolition of the Greater London Council (GLC) in 1986, the London boroughs took over most of its functions. Successor bodies have also been set up for certain functions.

The London Residuary Body (LRB) was set up in 1986 to deal with residual matters of the GLC which could not easily be transferred elsewhere. The LRB completed its work in relation to the GLC in 1990, when it became responsible for residual matters relating to the Inner London Education Authority, which was abolished on 1 April 1990. The LRB has now transferred most residual greater London-wide matters to the London Borough of Bromley and inner London-wide matters to the Royal Borough of Kensington and Chelsea. Its sole remaining responsibility is the disposal of County Hall.

LONDON RESIDUARY BODY, c/o Town Hall, Royal Borough of Kensington and Chelsea, Hornton Street, London W8 7NX. Tel: 071-938 4028.

WALES

Since 1974 Wales, including the former Monmouthshire, has been divided into eight counties. Each county is divided into districts, of which there are 37.

The arrangements for Welsh counties and districts are generally similar to those for English non-metropolitan counties and districts. There are some differences in functions; Welsh district councils have refuse disposal as well as refuse collection functions, and they may provide on-street as well as off-street car parks with the consent of the county council. A few districts have also been designated as library authorities.

COMMUNITY COUNCILS
In Wales parishes have been replaced by communities. Unlike England, where many areas are not in any parish, communities have been established for the whole of Wales, approximately 865 communities in all. Community meetings may be convened as and when desired.

Community councils exist in 734 communities and further councils may be established at the request of a community meeting. Community councils have broadly the same range of powers as English parish councils. Community councillors are elected en bloc at the same time as a district council election and for a term of four years.

FINANCE
Aggregate external finance for 1993–4 is £2,344.2 million. This comprises revenue support grant of £1,669.3 million, specific grants of £204.7 million, and support from the national non-domestic rate pool of £470.2 million. Total standard spending by local authorities considered for grant purposes is £2,599.8 million.

The average council tax levied in Wales for 1993–4 is £328, comprising county councils £267 and district councils £61.

National non-domestic rates (or uniform business rate) in Wales for 1993–4 is 44p. The amount estimated to be raised is £470.2 million. Total rateable value held on local authority lists at 31 December 1992 was £1,087 million.

SCOTLAND

Since 1975, mainland Scotland has been divided for local government purposes into nine regions within which there are 53 districts. In the three islands areas, Orkney, Shetland and the Western Isles, there are single-tier islands councils responsible for most local authority functions.

ELECTIONS
For the regional, islands and district councils, there are councils consisting of directly elected councillors. The councillors serve for four years, elections to district councils taking place midway between regional council elections. The next elections for regional councils are in 1994. In 1995 there will be elections for the shadow unitary authorities in advance of local government reform.

In 1993 the register showed 3,930,286 electors in Scotland.

FUNCTIONS
Regional councils: education; social work; strategic planning; the provision of infrastructure such as roads, water and sewerage; consumer protection; flood prevention; coast protection; valuation and rating; the police and fire services; civil defence; electoral registration; public transport; registration of births, deaths and marriages

District councils: housing; leisure and recreation, including tourism, parks, libraries, museums and galleries; development control and building control; environmental health, including cleansing, refuse collection and disposal, food hygiene, inspection of shops, offices and factories, clean air, markets and slaughterhouses, burial and cremation; licensing, including liquor, cinemas and theatres, taxis, street traders, betting and gaming, and charitable collections; allotments; public conveniences; the administration of district courts

COMMUNITY COUNCILS
Unlike the parish councils of England or community councils of Wales, Scottish community councils are not local

authorities. Their purpose as defined in statute is to ascertain and express the views of the communities which they represent, and to take in the interests of their communities such action as appears to be expedient or practicable. Over 1,000 community councils have been established under schemes drawn up by district and islands councils in Scotland.

FINANCE

In 1991–2 a total of £1,332.9 million was received from non-domestic rates by local authorities. The average non-domestic rate levied was 58.1p. Total non-domestic water rate income was £17,611,000 and the average non-domestic water rate levied was 4.9p. Income from the non-domestic sewerage rate was £93,115,000 and the average non-domestic sewerage rate levied was 4.5p. Total metered water income was £77,961,000 and the average metered water rate levied was 36.7p.

The 1991–2 community charge income received by local authorities totalled £790,801,000 and the average personal community charge levied was £247.36 (after the £140 reduction). The community water charge receipts were £88,828,000 and the average community water charge levied was £28.64.

Provisional figures for 1992–3 show total receipts from non-domestic rates of £1,137.07 million and £982.33 million from the community charge. The average non-domestic rate per £ levied for 1992–3 was 55p and the average personal community charge payable in Scotland was £297.46.

rateable value). Rates are collected by the Department of the Environment for Northern Ireland and consist of a regional rate made by the Department of Finance and Personnel and a district rate made by individual district councils.

In 1991–2 a total of £321 million was raised in domestic rates in Northern Ireland and the total rateable value was £203.6 million. The average domestic poundage levied was 145.44p and the average non-domestic rate poundage was 239.44p.

NORTHERN IRELAND

For the purpose of local government Northern Ireland has a system of 26 single-tier district councils.

ELECTIONS

There are 566 members of the councils, elected for periods of four years at a time on the principle of proportional representation.

FUNCTIONS

The district councils have three main roles. These are:
Executive: responsibility for a wide range of local services including building regulations; community services; consumer protection; cultural facilities; environmental health; miscellaneous licensing and registration provisions, including dog control; litter prevention; recreational and social facilities; refuse collection and disposal; street cleansing; and tourist development
Representative: nominating representatives to sit as members of the various statutory bodies responsible for the administration of regional services such as drainage, education, electricity, fire, health and personal social services, and libraries
Consultative: acting as the medium through which the views of local people are expressed on the operation in their area of other regional services, notably conservation (including water supply and sewerage services), planning, and roads, provided by those departments of central government which have an obligation, statutory or otherwise, to consult the district councils about proposals affecting their areas

FINANCE

Local government in Northern Ireland is funded by a system of rates (a local property tax calculated by using the rateable value of a property multiplied by an amount per pound of

Political Composition of Local Councils

AS AT END MAY 1993

Abbreviations:
C.	Conservative
Com.	Communist
Dem.	Democrat
Green	Green
Ind.	Independent
Lab.	Labour
Lib.	Liberal
LD	Liberal Democrat
MK	Mebyon Kernow
NP	Non-political/Non-party
PC	Plaid Cymru
RA	Ratepayers'/Residents' Associations
SD	Social Democrat
SNP	Scottish National Party

ENGLAND

COUNTY COUNCILS

Avon	*Lab.* 33, *C.* 25, *LD* 18
Bedfordshire	*Lab.* 31, *C.* 28, *LD* 13, *Ind.* 1
Berkshire	*LD* 33, *Lab.* 24, *C.* 16, *Ind.* 2, *Lib.* 1
Buckinghamshire	*C.* 39, *LD* 16, *Lab.* 13, *Ind.* 2, *RA* 1
Cambridgeshire	*C.* 33, *Lab.* 21, *LD* 21, *Ind.* 1, *Lib.* 1
Cheshire	*Lab.* 35, *C.* 22, *LD* 14
Cleveland	*Lab.* 51, *C.* 14, *LD* 12
Cornwall	*LD* 42, *Ind.* 21, *Lab.* 8, *C.* 6, *Lib.* 1, *MK* 1
Cumbria	*Lab.* 39, *C.* 28, *LD* 14, *Ind.* 2
Derbyshire	*Lab.* 55, *C.* 21, *LD* 7, *Ind.* 1
Devon	*LD* 40, *Lab.* 21, *C.* 19, *Ind.* 4, *Lib.* 1
Dorset	*LD* 38, *C.* 29, *Lab.* 6, *Ind.* 4
Durham	*Lab.* 56, *C.* 6, *LD* 6, *Ind.* 4
East Sussex	*LD* 30, *C.* 22, *Lab.* 18
Essex	*Lab.* 33, *C.* 32, *LD* 32, *Ind.* 1
Gloucestershire	*LD* 30, *Lab.* 18, *C.* 10, *Ind. C.* 2, *Others* 3
Hampshire	*LD* 48, *C.* 29, *Lab.* 24, *Ind.* 1
Hereford and Worcester	*C.* 25, *Lab.* 24, *LD* 23, *Ind.* 4
Hertfordshire	*Lab.* 30, *C.* 27, *LD* 19, *Ind. RA* 1
Humberside	*Lab.* 43, *C.* 22, *LD* 10
Isle of Wight	*LD* 28, *C.* 9, *Ind.* 4, *Others* 2
Kent	*C.* 41, *Lab.* 30, *LD* 28
Lancashire	*Lab.* 52, *C.* 35, *LD* 10, *vacant* 2
Leicestershire	*Lab.* 37, *C.* 31, *LD* 17
Lincolnshire	*C.* 32, *Lab.* 25, *LD* 15, *Ind.* 4
Norfolk	*C.* 33, *Lab.* 32, *LD* 16, *Ind.* 2
Northamptonshire	*Lab.* 36, *C.* 27, *LD* 5
Northumberland	*Lab.* 40, *C.* 14, *LD* 11, *Ind.* 1
North Yorkshire	*LD.* 35, *C.* 29, *Lab.* 23, *Ind.* 8, *Ind. Lab.* 1
Nottinghamshire	*Lab.* 58, *C.* 24, *LD* 6
Oxfordshire	*C.* 25, *Lab.* 24, *LD* 20, *Green* 1
Shropshire	*C.* 26, *Lab.* 23, *LD* 14, *Ind.* 2, *Ind. Lab.* 1
Somerset	*LD* 41, *C.* 13, *Lab.* 2, *Ind.* 1
Staffordshire	*Lab.* 53, *C.* 22, *LD* 4, *Ind.* 1, *RA* 1, *Ratepayer* 1
Suffolk	*Lab.* 31, *C.* 26, *LD* 19, *Ind.* 4
Surrey	*C.* 34, *LD* 29, *Lab.* 8, *RA* 3, *Ind.* 2
Warwickshire	*Lab.* 30, *C.* 19, *LD* 10, *Ind.* 3
West Sussex	*LD* 34, *C.* 26, *Lab.* 10, *Ind.* 1
Wiltshire	*LD* 33, *C.* 18, *Lab.* 17

METROPOLITAN DISTRICT COUNCILS

GREATER MANCHESTER

Bolton	*Lab.* 39, *C.* 16, *Lib.* 4, *LD* 1
Bury	*Lab.* 24, *C.* 22, *LD* 2
Manchester	*Lab.* 78, *LD* 14, *C.* 5, *Ind. Lab.* 2
Oldham	*Lab.* 32, *LD* 19, *C.* 7, *Ind. Lab.* 1, *Ind. LD* 1
Rochdale	*Lab.* 23, *LD* 20, *C.* 16, *Ind.* 1
Salford	*Lab.* 53, *C.* 6, *vacant* 1
Stockport	*LD* 26, *C.* 17, *Lab.* 17, *Ind.* 3
Tameside	*Lab.* 46, *C.* 8, *Others* 2, *vacant* 1
Trafford	*C.* 37, *Lab.* 22, *LD* 4
Wigan	*Lab.* 63, *LD* 6, *C.* 2, *Ind. Lab.* 1

MERSEYSIDE

Knowsley	*Lab.* 59, *C.* 3, *Ind.* 2, *Ind. Lab.* 1, *vacant* 1
Liverpool	*Lab.* 40, *LD* 37, *C.* 2, *Lib.* 1, *SD* 1, *Others* 18
St Helens	*Lab.* 29, *LD* 14, *C.* 6, *Others* 5
Sefton	*Lab.* 27, *C.* 25, *LD* 17
Wirral	*Lab.* 31, *C.* 29, *LD* 6

SOUTH YORKSHIRE

Barnsley	*Lab.* 61, *C.* 2, *Ind.* 1, *vacant* 2
Doncaster	*Lab.* 54, *C.* 9
Rotherham	*Lab.* 63, *C.* 3
Sheffield	*Lab.* 65, *C.* 11, *LD* 11

TYNE AND WEAR

Gateshead	*Lab.* 55, *LD* 8, *C.* 1, *Ind.* 1, *Lib.* 1
Newcastle upon Tyne	*Lab.* 61, *LD* 11, *C.* 6
North Tyneside	*Lab.* 36, *C.* 16, *LD* 8
South Tyneside	*Lab.* 56, *LD* 3, *Ind.* 1
Sunderland	*Lab.* 64, *C.* 8, *LD* 3

WEST MIDLANDS

Birmingham	*Lab.* 61, *C.* 43, *LD* 13
Coventry	*Lab.* 40, *C.* 13, *vacant* 1
Dudley	*Lab.* 37, *C.* 35
Sandwell	*Lab.* 42, *C.* 24, *LD* 6
Solihull	*C.* 24, *Lab.* 15, *LD* 6, *RA* 6
Walsall	*C.* 23, *Lab.* 23, *LD* 9, *Ind.* 4, *vacant* 1
Wolverhampton	*Lab.* 29, *C.* 28, *LD* 3

WEST YORKSHIRE

Bradford	*Lab.* 50, *C.* 38, *LD* 2
Calderdale	*C.* 24, *Lab.* 22, *LD* 7, *Ind. C.* 1
Kirklees	*Lab.* 41, *C.* 18, *LD* 10, *RA* 2, *Others* 1
Leeds	*Lab.* 67, *C.* 23, *LD* 8, *Ind.* 1
Wakefield	*Lab.* 55, *C.* 6, *Ind.* 2

NON-METROPOLITAN DISTRICT COUNCILS

* denotes councils where one-third of councillors retire each year except the year of county council elections

*Adur	LD 22, C. 14, RA 2, Lab. 1
Allerdale	Lab. 30, C. 11, Ind. 11, LD 3
Alnwick	LD 15, C. 7, Ind. 5, Lab. 2
*Amber Valley	Lab. 21, C. 16, Ind. 3, Others 2, vacant 1
Arun	C. 36, LD 12, Lab. 7, Ind. 1
Ashfield	Lab. 32, C. 1
Ashford	C. 29, LD 12, Lab. 4, Ind. 1, Others 3
Aylesbury Vale	C. 27, LD 24, Ind. 6, Lab. 1
Babergh	C. 16, Ind. 9, Lab. 6, LD 5, Others 6
*Barrow-in-Furness	C. 18, Lab. 18, Ind. 2
*Basildon	C. 25, Lab. 13, LD 3, vacant 1
*Basingstoke and Deane	C. 35, Lab. 11, LD 7, Ind. 2, Others 2
*Bassetlaw	Lab. 30, C. 17, Ind. 2, LD 1
*Bath	C. 24, LD 17, Lab.7
Berwick-upon-Tweed	LD 11, Ind. 7, C. 5, Lab. 1, Others 4
Beverley	C. 31, Lib. 19, Lab. 2, Ind. 1
Blaby	C. 30, LD 4, Ind. 3, Lab. 1
*Blackburn	Lab. 36, C. 19, LD 4, Ind. 1
Blackpool	Lab. 27, C. 11, LD 5, vacant 1
Blyth Valley	Lab. 30, LD 17
Bolsover	Lab. 35, RA 2
Boothferry	C. 18, Lab. 12, Ind. 5
Boston	C. 12, Lab. 8, LD 8, Ind. 6
Bournemouth	LD 25, C. 21, Lab. 6, Ind. 5
Bracknell Forest	C. 32, Lab. 7, LD 1
Braintree	C. 24, Lab. 21, Ind. 9, LD 6
Breckland	C. 33, Ind. 12, Lab. 8
*Brentwood	LD 24, C. 13, Ind. 1, Lab. 1
Bridgnorth	C. 12, Ind. 8, LD 3, Ind. Lab. 2, NP 2, Lab. 1, Others 5
*Brighton	Lab. 25, C. 22, Ind. Lab. 1
*Bristol	Lab. 38, C. 22, LD 6, Others 2
*Broadland	C. 27, Ind. 8, LD 8, Lab. 6
Bromsgrove	C. 26, Lab. 14, LD 1
*Broxbourne	C. 36, Lab. 4, LD 2
Broxtowe	C. 27, Lab. 15, LD 6, Ind. 1
*Burnley	Lab. 33, C. 8, LD 7
*Cambridge	Lab. 20, LD 12, C. 9, vacant 1
*Cannock Chase	Lab. 30, C. 8, Dem. 2, Ind. 1, Ind. Lib. 1
Canterbury	LD 22, Lab. 19, Lab. 8
Caradon	Ind. 21, LD 8, C. 7, RA 4, Lab. 1
*Carlisle	Lab. 30, C. 18, LD 2, Ind. 1
Carrick	LD 20, C. 9, Ind. 8, Lab. 4, Ind. C. 1, Others 2, vacant 1
Castle Morpeth	Ind. 9, Lab. 9, LD 9, C. 7
Castle Point	C. 37, Lab. 2
Charnwood	C. 35, Lab. 15, Ind. 1, LD 1
Chelmsford	C. 29, LD 21, Ind. 4, Lab. 2
*Cheltenham	LD 23, C. 12, Ind. 3, Lab. 3
*Cherwell	C. 33, Lab. 15, LD 3, Ind. 1
*Chester	C. 23, Lab. 19, LD 16, Ind. 2
Chesterfield	Lab. 31, LD 12, C. 3, vacant 1
Chester-le-Street	Lab. 27, Ind. 5, C. 1
Chichester	C. 33, LD 14, Ind. 3
Chiltern	C. 39, LD 9, RA 2
*Chorley	Lab. 22, C. 20, LD 3, Ind. C. 2, Ind. 1
Christchurch	C. 13, Ind. 12

Cleethorpes	Lab. 16, C. 13, LD 10, Ind. 1, vacant 1
*Colchester	LD 30, C. 21, Lab. 7, RA 2
*Congleton	LD 19, C. 16, Lab. 9, vacant 1
Copeland	Lab. 28, C. 19, Ind. 3, vacant 1
Corby	Lab. 23, C. 2, Ind. 1, LD 1
Cotswold	Ind. 15, C. 10, LD 6, Lab. 1, Others 13
*Craven	C. 13, LD 10, Ind. 5, Lab. 3, Ind. C. 1, Lib. 1, vacant 1
*Crawley	Lab. 22, C. 8, Ind. 1, LD 1
*Crewe and Nantwich	Lab. 31, C. 24, LD 2
Dacorum	C. 37, Lab. 16, LD 4, Ind. C. 1
Darlington	Lab. 30, C. 18, Ind. 2, SD 2
Dartford	C. 25, Lab. 20, RA 2
*Daventry	C. 19, Lab. 11, LD 3, Ind. 2
*Derby	C. 22, Lab. 22
Derbyshire Dales	C. 26, LD 9, Lab. 4
Derwentside	Lab. 37, Ind. 14, C. 2, vacant 2
Dover	C. 28, Lab. 20, LD 6, Ind. 1, vacant 1
Durham	Lab. 29, LD 14, Ind. 6
Easington	Lab. 40, Ind. 4, Lib. 4, Ind. Lab. 3
*Eastbourne	LD 17, C. 12, vacant 1
East Cambridgeshire	Ind. 24, C. 5, LD 5, Ind. C. 1, Lab. 1, vacant 1
East Devon	C. 41, LD 11, Green 2, Ind. 2, Ind. C. 1, Lib. 1, Others 2
East Dorset	C. 18, LD 14, RA 2, Others 2
East Hampshire	LD 21, C. 15, Ind. 6
East Hertfordshire	C. 33, LD 11, Ind. 3, Lab. 2, RA 1
*Eastleigh	C. 20, LD 19, Lab. 5
East Lindsey	Ind. 44, C. 6, LD 5, Lab. 4, Green 1
East Northamptonshire	C. 24, Lab. 9, LD 3
East Staffordshire	Lab. 23, C. 18, LD 4, vacant 1
East Yorkshire	C. 16, Ind. 13, LD 6, Lab. 5, SD 3
Eden	Ind. 32, LD 4, vacant 1
*Ellesmere Port and Neston	Lab. 30, C. 11
*Elmbridge	C. 22, RA 19, LD 10, Lab. 8, Ind. 1
*Epping Forest	C. 31, Lab. 13, RA 10, LD 3, SD 2
Epsom and Ewell	RA 30, Lib. 6, Lab. 3
Erewash	Lab. 27, C. 22, Ind. 2, LD 1
*Exeter	Lab. 16, C. 14, LD 5, Lib. 1
*Fareham	C. 30, LD 8, Lab. 4
Fenland	C. 25, Lab. 6, Ind. 4, LD 3, vacant 2
Forest Heath	C. 12, Ind. 9, LD 3, Lab. 1
Forest of Dean	Lab. 25, Ind. 16, LD 7, Others 1
Fylde	C. 23, Ind. 11, RA 9, LD 4, Green 1, Lab. 1
Gedling	C. 38, Lab. 15, LD 3, Ind. 1
*Gillingham	C. 16, LD 15, Lab. 9, Ind. LD 2
Glanford	C. 22, Ind. 9, Lab. 7, Green 3
*Gloucester	Lab. 16, C. 13, LD 5, Ind. 1
*Gosport	LD 16, C. 8, Ind. 3, Lab. 3
Gravesham	C. 22, Lab. 22
*Great Grimsby	Lab. 28, C. 13, LD 2, Ind. 1, vacant 1
*Great Yarmouth	Lab. 29, C. 18, LD 1
Guildford	C. 20, LD 18, Lab. 6, Ind. 1
*Halton	Lab. 44, LD 7, C. 2

Hambleton — *C.* 24, *Ind.* 13, *LD* 5, *SD* 3, *Lab.* 2

Harborough — *C.* 18, *LD* 12, *Ind.* 4, *Lab.* 3

*Harlow — *Lab.* 31, *C.* 8, *LD* 3

*Harrogate — *LD* 31, *C.* 22, *Lab.* 4, *Ind.* 2, *Green* 1

*Hart — *C.* 16, *LD* 12, *Ind.* 7

*Hartlepool — *Lab.* 28, *C.* 12, *LD* 6, *Ind.* 1

*Hastings — *C.* 14, *Lab.* 9, *LD* 9

*Havant — *C.* 19, *Lab.* 12, *LD* 6, *Ind.* 5

*Hereford — *LD* 22, *Lab.* 4, *C.* 1

*Hertsmere — *C.* 23, *Lab.* 12, *LD* 3, *Ind.* 1

High Peak — *Lab.* 17, *C.* 14, *LD* 10, *Ind.* 3

Hinckley and Bosworth — *C.* 22, *LD* 8, *Lab.* 3, *Ind.* 1

Holderness — *Ind.* 24, *LD* 6, *vacant* 1

Horsham — *C.* 27, *LD* 14, *Ind.* 2

Hove — *C.* 21, *Lab.* 6, *LD* 3

*Huntingdonshire — *C.* 41, *LD* 7, *Lab.* 4, *Ind.* 1

*Hyndburn — *Lab.* 31, *C.* 12, *LD* 3, *vacant* 1

*Ipswich — *Lab.* 33, *C.* 15

Kennet — *C.* 17, *Ind.* 13, *LD* 8, *Lab.* 1, *vacant* 1

Kerrier — *LD* 15, *Lab.* 12, *Ind.* 10, *C.* 5, *Lib.* 2

Kettering — *Lab.* 18, *C.* 11, *LD* 8, *Ind.* 6, *Others* 2

King's Lynn and West Norfolk — *C.* 38, *Lab.* 15, *LD* 5, *Ind.* 1, *vacant* 1

*Kingston upon Hull — *Lab.* 56, *LD* 3, *C.* 1

Kingswood — *Lab.* 25, *C.* 18, *LD* 5, *Ind.* 1, *Ind. Lab.* 1

Lancaster — *Lab.* 24, *C.* 15, *Ind. Lab.* 11, *LD* 6, *Ind.* 2, *Ind. C.* 1

Langbaurgh on Tees — *Lab.* 29, *C.* 22, *LD* 7, *Ind. Lab.* 1

Leicester — *Lab.* 37, *C.* 12, *LD* 7

*Leominster — *Ind.* 24, *LD* 9, *Lab.* 2, *Green* 1

Lewes — *LD* 27, *C.* 18, *Ind.* 3

Lichfield — *C.* 37, *Lab.* 15, *Ind. Lab.* 3, *Ind.* 1

*Lincoln — *Lab.* 30, *C.* 3

Luton — *Lab.* 29, *C.* 9, *LD* 9, *Ind. C.* 1

*Macclesfield — *C.* 34, *LD* 13, *Lab.* 10, *RA* 3

*Maidstone — *C.* 26, *LD* 15, *Lab.* 8, *Ind.* 6

Maldon — *C.* 14, *Ind.* 11, *LD* 4, *vacant* 1

Malvern Hills — *Ind.* 17, *LD* 16, *C.* 15, *Lab.* 1, *Others* 1

Mansfield — *Lab.* 39, *C.* 5, *LD* 2

Medina — *C.* 18, *LD* 13, *Ind.* 2, *Lab.* 2, *vacant* 1

Melton — *C.* 18, *LD* 8

Mendip — *LD* 19, *C.* 13, *Ind.* 7, *Lab.* 3, *vacant* 1

Mid Bedfordshire — *C.* 43, *LD* 4, *Ind.* 3, *Lab.* 3

Mid Devon — *Ind.* 28, *LD* 8, *Lib.* 2, *Lab.* 1, *Ind. SD* 1

Middlesbrough — *Lab.* 37, *C.* 9, *LD* 5, *Ind.* 1, *vacant* 1

Mid Suffolk — *C.* 17, *LD* 10, *Lab.* 9, *Ind. C.* 4

*Mid Sussex — *C.* 34, *LD* 13, *Ind.* 5, *Lab.* 2

*Milton Keynes — *Lab.* 21, *C.* 15, *LD* 9, *Ind.* 1

*Mole Valley — *LD* 18, *C.* 13, *Ind.* 9, *Lab.* 1

Newark and Sherwood — *Lab.* 28, *C.* 18, *LD* 5, *Ind.* 3

Newbury — *LD* 24, *C.* 20, *vacant* 1

*Newcastle under Lyme — *Lab.* 36, *C.* 10, *LD* 10

New Forest — *LD* 30, *C.* 22, *Ind.* 6

Northampton — *Lab.* 21, *C.* 18, *LD* 4

Northavon — *LD* 25, *C.* 20, *Lab.* 11, *Ind.* 1

*North Bedfordshire — *C.* 25, *Lab.* 15, *LD* 10, *Ind.* 3

North Cornwall — *Ind.* 29, *LD* 6, *Lab.* 2, *C.* 1

North Devon — *LD* 29, *Ind.* 12, *C.* 3

North Dorset — *Ind.* 21, *LD* 12

North East Derbyshire — *Lab.* 34, *C.* 12, *Ind.* 4, *LD* 3

*North Hertfordshire — *C.* 27, *Lab.* 16, *LD* 3, *RA* 3, *Ind.* 1

North Kesteven — *NP* 26, *Lab.* 6, *LD* 5, *Ind.* 2

North Norfolk — *C.* 16, *LD* 7, *Ind.* 6, *Lab.* 6, *Others* 11

North Shropshire — *Ind.* 31, *C.* 5, *Lab.* 4

North Warwickshire — *Lab.* 20, *C.* 12, *Ind.* 2

North West Leicestershire — *Lab.* 26, *C.* 11, *Ind.* 3

North Wiltshire — *LD* 30, *C.* 15, *Ind.* 3, *Lab.* 3, *Others* 1

*Norwich — *Lab.* 35, *LD* 10, *C.* 3

Nottingham — *Lab.* 37, *C.* 17, *Green* 1

*Nuneaton and Bedworth — *Lab.* 36, *C.* 9

*Oadby and Wigston — *LD* 19, *C.* 7

Oswestry — *Ind.* 10, *C.* 9, *Lab.* 6, *LD* 4

*Oxford — *Lab.* 35, *C.* 10, *LD* 5, *Ind.* *LD* 1

*Pendle — *Lab.* 27, *Lib.* 17, *C.* 7

*Penwith — *C.* 12, *Lab.* 9, *Ind.* 8, *LD* 3, *Ind. Lab.* 1, *MK* 1

*Peterborough — *C.* 21, *Lab.* 18, *LD.* 6, *Ind.* 3

Plymouth — *Lab.* 41, *C.* 18, *LD* 1

Poole — *LD* 20, *C.* 16

*Portsmouth — *C.* 17, *Lab.* 14, *LD* 7, *vacant* 1

*Preston — *Lab.* 32, *C.* 20, *LD* 5

*Purbeck — *C.* 12, *Ind.* 5, *LD* 5

*Reading — *Lab.* 29, *C.* 11, *LD* 4, *Others* 1

*Redditch — *Lab.* 20, *C.* 9

*Reigate and Banstead — *C.* 24, *Lab.* 11, *LD* 10, *RA* 3, *Ind.* 1

Restormel — *LD* 29, *Ind.* 12, *C.* 2, *Lab.* 1

Ribble Valley — *C.* 23, *LD* 15, *Lab.* 1

Richmondshire — *Ind.* 26, *C.* 4, *LD* 4

Rochester upon Medway — *C.* 22, *Lab.* 21, *LD* 7

*Rochford — *LD* 18, *C.* 12, *Ind. Lab.* 7, *RA* 2, *Ind.* 1

*Rossendale — *Lab.* 21, *C.* 15

Rother — *C.* 18, *LD* 16, *Ind.* 8, *Lab.* 3

*Rugby — *C.* 19, *Lab.* 16, *Ind.* 8, *LD* 3, *Ind. C.* 1, *vacant* 1

*Runnymede — *C.* 28, *Lab.* 7, *Ind.* 6, *Green* 1

Rushcliffe — *C.* 43, *LD* 6, *Lab.* 5

*Rushmoor — *C.* 30, *LD* 9, *Lab.* 6

Rutland — *Ind.* 9, *C.* 7, *LD* 4

Ryedale — *LD* 20, *Ind.* 14, *C.* 6, *Lab.* 2

*St Albans — *LD* 24, *C.* 22, *Lab.* 8, *Ind.* 1, *vacant* 2

St Edmundsbury — *C.* 26, *Lab.* 11, *LD* 5, *Ind.* 2

Salisbury — *C.* 33, *Ind.* 11, *LD* 8, *Lab.* 6

Scarborough — *C.* 16, *Lab.* 16, *Ind.* 9, *LD* 8

*Scunthorpe — *Lab.* 33, *C.* 6, *SD* 1

Sedgefield — *Lab.* 31, *LD* 8, *Ind.* 4, *C.* 2, *Others* 2, *vacant* 2

Sedgemoor — *C.* 26, *Lab.* 12, *LD* 7, *Ind.* 4

Selby — *C.* 22, *Lab.* 13, *Ind.* 10, *LD* 3, *Ind. Lab.* 2

Sevenoaks — *C.* 31, *LD* 11, *Ind.* 9, *Others* 2

Shepway — *LD* 32, *C.* 19, *Lab.* 3, *Ind.* 2

*Shrewsbury and Atcham — *C.* 20, *Lab.* 17, *Ind.* 6, *LD* 5

*Slough — *Lab.* 28, *C.* 5, *Lib.* 5, *vacant* 1

*Southampton — *Lab.* 30, *C.* 8, *LD* 6, *vacant* 1

*South Bedfordshire — *C.* 37, *Lab.* 9, *LD* 6, *Ind.* 1

South Bucks — *C.* 30, *Ind.* 10, *LD* 1

*South Cambridgeshire — *C.* 26, *Ind.* 21, *Lab.* 5, *LD* 3

South Derbyshire	*Lab.* 20, *C.* 11, *Ind.* 2, *Others* 1
*Southend-on-Sea	*C.* 25, *LD* 8, *Lab.* 6
South Hams	*C.* 24, *Ind.* 8, *NP* 6, *LD* 4,
	Ind. C. 1, *Lab.* 1
*South Herefordshire	*Ind.* 29, *C.* 5, *LD* 4, *RA* 1
South Holland	*Lab.* 10, *C.* 7, *Ind.* 2, *Others* 19
South Kesteven	*C.* 24, *Lab.* 13, *Ind.* 10, *LD* 9,
	Lib. 1
*South Lakeland	*C.* 17, *LD* 15, *Ind.* 14, *Lab.* 6
South Norfolk	*C.* 22, *LD.* 22, *Ind.* 3
South Northamptonshire	*C.* 29, *Ind.* 9, *Lab.* 2
South Oxfordshire	*C.* 28, *LD* 8, *Ind.* 5, *Lab.* 5, *RA* 3,
	vacant 1
South Ribble	*C.* 33, *Lab.* 15, *LD* 6
South Shropshire	*NP* 25, *C.* 5, *Ind.* 5, *LD* 3,
	Ind. C. 1, *Lab.* 1
South Somerset	*LD* 41, *C.* 14, *Ind.* 5
South Staffordshire	*C.* 37, *Lab.* 9, *LD* 3, *Ind.* 1
South Wight	*LD* 10, *C.* 7, *Ind.* 7
Spelthorne	*C.* 33, *Lab.* 4, *LD* 2, *Ind.* 1
Stafford	*C.* 29, *Lab.* 18, *LD* 11, *Ind.* 2
Staffordshire	*RA* 24, *C.* 13, *Lab.* 8, *Ind.* 5, *Lib.* 4,
Moorlands	*Others* 1, *vacant* 1
*Stevenage	*Lab.* 32, *C.* 4, *LD* 3
Stockton-on-Tees	*Lab.* 26, *C.* 17, *LD* 11, *Ind.*
	Lab. 1
*Stoke-on-Trent	*Lab.* 49, *C.* 11
*Stratford-upon-Avon	*C.* 27, *LD* 19, *Ind.* 6, *Ind. C.* 1,
	Lab. 1, *vacant* 1
*Stroud	*C.* 22, *Lab.* 14, *LD* 10, *Green* 5,
	Ind. 3, *vacant* 1
Suffolk Coastal	*C.* 37, *Ind.* 7, *Lab.* 6, *LD* 5
Surrey Heath	*C.* 31, *LD* 4, *Lab.* 1
*Swale	*C.* 20, *Lab.* 14, *LD* 14, *Ind.* 1
*Tamworth	*Lab.* 21, *C.* 8, *Ind.* 1
*Tandridge	*C.* 20, *LD* 18, *Lab.* 4
Taunton Deane	*LD* 29, *C.* 13, *Lab.* 7, *Ind.* 4
Teesdale	*Ind.* 21, *Lab.* 8, *C.* 2
Teignbridge	*Ind.* 22, *C.* 18, *Lib.* 14, *Lab.* 4
Tendring	*LD* 21, *C.* 19, *Lab.* 12, *Ind.* 8
Test Valley	*C.* 26, *LD* 16, *Ind.* 1, *NP* 1
Tewkesbury	*Ind.* 20, *C.* 7, *LD* 6, *Lab.* 3
*Thamesdown	*Lab.* 34, *C.* 13, *LD* 6, *Ind.* 1
Thanet	*C.* 30, *Lab.* 14, *Ind.* 8, *LD* 2
*Three Rivers	*C.* 21, *LD* 18, *Lab.* 9
*Thurrock	*Lab.* 29, *C.* 7, *Ind. C.* 2, *Others* 1
*Tonbridge and Malling	*C.* 32, *LD* 17, *Lab.* 6
*Torbay	*LD* 20, *C.* 13, *Lab.* 2, *Others* 1
Torridge	*Ind.* 16, *C.* 5, *LD* 5, *Lab.* 4,
	Ind. C. 3, *Green* 1, *Others* 2
*Tunbridge Wells	*C.* 29, *LD* 15, *Lab.* 3, *Ind.* 1
Tynedale	*C.* 18, *Lab.* 14, *LD* 9, *Ind.* 6
Uttlesford	*C.* 23, *LD* 12, *Ind.* 6, *Lab.* 1
Vale of White Horse	*C.* 30, *LD* 17, *Ind.* 2, *Lab.* 2
Vale Royal	*Lab.* 31, *C.* 24, *LD* 3, *Ind.* 1,
	vacant 1
Wansbeck	*Lab.* 44, *Lib.* 2
Wansdyke	*C.* 22, *Lab.* 20, *Ind.* 3, *LD* 2
Warrington	*Lab.* 42, *LD* 9, *C.* 8, *Ind. Lab.* 1
Warwick	*C.* 24, *Lab.* 10, *LD* 8, *RA* 3
*Watford	*Lab.* 22, *C.* 10, *LD* 4
*Waveney	*Lab.* 26, *C.* 17, *LD* 5
Waverley	*C.* 28, *LD* 27, *Lab.* 2
Wealden	*C.* 44, *LD* 9, *Ind.* 5
Wear Valley	*LD* 28, *Lab.* 8, *Ind.* 4
Wellingborough	*C.* 19, *Lab.* 12, *Ind.* 3
*Welwyn Hatfield	*C.* 24, *Lab.* 23
West Devon	*Ind.* 16, *LD* 7, *C.* 5, *Green* 1,
	Lab. 1

West Dorset	*C.* 17, *LD* 12, *Ind.* 7, *Lab.* 3, *SD*
	1, *Others* 15
*West Lancashire	*C.* 27, *Lab.* 27, *LD* 1
*West Lindsey	*Ind.* 11, *C.* 10, *LD* 9, *Ind. Lab.* 7
*West Oxfordshire	*Ind.* 20, *C.* 14, *LD* 8, *Lab.* 6,
	vacant 1
West Somerset	*Ind.* 23, *C.* 5, *Lab.* 3, *LD* 1
West Wiltshire	*LD* 23, *C.* 9, *Lib.* 5, *Ind.* 2, *Lab.*
	2, *Others* 1, *vacant* 1
*Weymouth and	
Portland	*C.* 10, *Lab.* 10, *LD* 10, *Ind.* 5
*Winchester	*C.* 24, *LD* 22, *Lab.* 6, *Ind.* 3
Windsor and	
Maidenhead	*C.* 26, *LD* 25, *RA* 7
*Woking	*C.* 19, *LD* 11, *Lab.* 5
*Wokingham	*C.* 33, *LD* 19, *Lab.* 1, *vacant* 1
Woodspring	*C.* 36, *LD* 15, *Ind.* 4, *Lab.* 3,
	Green 1
*Worcester	*C.* 22, *Lab.* 12, *Ind.* 1, *LD* 1
*Worthing	*C.* 22, *LD* 14
Wrekin	*Lab.* 33, *C.* 10, *LD* 2, *Ind.* 1
Wychavon	*C.* 32, *LD* 10, *Lab.* 6, *Ind.* 1
Wycombe	*C.* 37, *LD* 11, *Lab.* 9, *Ind.* 2,
	RA 1
Wyre	*C.* 32, *Lab.* 17, *LD* 5, *Ind.* 1,
	RA 1
*Wyre Forest	*Lab.* 21, *LD* 11, *C.* 9, *Ind.* 1
*York	*Lab.* 34, *C.* 7, *LD* 4

GREATER LONDON BOROUGHS

Barking and Dagenham	*Lab.* 44, *RA* 3, *LD* 1
Barnet	*C.* 39, *Lab.* 18, *LD* 3
Bexley	*C.* 34, *Lab.* 18, *LD* 9, *Ind.* 1
Brent	*C.* 33, *Lab.* 22, *LD* 7, *Ind.* 2,
	Green 1, *vacant* 1
Bromley	*C.* 42, *Lab.* 11, *LD* 7
Camden	*Lab.* 42, *C.* 15, *LD* 2
City of Westminster	*C.* 45, *Lab.* 15
Croydon	*C.* 40, *Lab.* 30
Ealing	*C.* 39, *Lab.* 31
Enfield	*C.* 35, *Lab.* 31
Greenwich	*Lab.* 42, *C.* 12, *SD* 4, *Ind.* 2,
	LD 2
Hackney	*Lab.* 41, *C.* 8, *LD* 7, *Ind. Lab.* 2,
	Others 1, *vacant* 1
Hammersmith and	
Fulham	*Lab.* 27, *C.* 22, *vacant* 1
Haringey	*Lab.* 43, *C.* 16
Harrow	*C.* 35, *Lab.* 13, *LD* 12, *Ind.* 3
Havering	*Lab.* 26, *C.* 19, *RA* 13, *LD* 5
Hillingdon	*C.* 35, *Lab.* 34
Hounslow	*Lab.* 44, *C.* 15, *LD* 1
Islington	*Lab.* 47, *LD* 4, *C.* 1
Kensington and Chelsea	*C.* 39, *Lab.* 15
Kingston upon Thames	*C.* 25, *LD* 18, *Lab.* 7
Lambeth	*Lab.* 26, *C.* 18, *LD* 9, *Others* 10,
	vacant 1
Lewisham	*Lab.* 58, *C.* 6, *LD* 3
Merton	*Lab.* 29, *C.* 22, *RA* 2, *Ind. Lab.*
	1, *Others* 3
Newham	*Lab.* 54, *C.* 4, *LD* 2
Redbridge	*C.* 43, *Lab.* 17, *LD* 3
Richmond upon Thames	*LD* 49, *C.* 3
Southwark	*Lab.* 35, *LD* 22, *C.* 6, *Ind.* 1
Sutton	*LD* 32, *C.* 18, *Lab.* 6
Tower Hamlets	*LD* 29, *Lab.* 21
Waltham Forest	*Lab.* 30, *C.* 15, *LD* 11, *Ind.* 1
Wandsworth	*C.* 48, *Lab.* 13

WALES

COUNTY COUNCILS

Clwyd	Lab. 32, Ind. 15, C. 8, Others 8, vacant 1
Dyfed	Ind. 31, Lab. 22, LD 8, PC 7, C. 1, RA 1
Gwent	Lab. 55, C. 6, LD 1, PC 1
Gwynedd	Ind. 27, PC 18, Lab. 9, LD 7, C. 1
Mid Glamorgan	Lab. 60, PC 10, Ind. 3, C. 1
Powys	Ind. 35, Lab. 6, LD 4, Others 1
South Glamorgan	Lab. 40, C. 12, LD 8, Ind. Lab. 1, PC 1
West Glamorgan	Lab. 47, Ind. 5, C. 3, LD 3, PC 1, RA 1, SD 1

DISTRICT COUNCILS

Aberconwy	Lab. 11, LD 10, C. 9, Ind. 6, PC 1, Others 4
Alyn and Deeside	Lab. 27, C. 8, Ind. 5, LD 2, Ind. Lab. 1
Arfon	Ind. 14, PC 14, Lab. 8, LD 2, Others 1
Blaenau Gwent	Lab. 32, RA 5, Ind. 3, PC 2, C. 1, Lib. 1
Brecknock	Ind. 29, Lab. 13, LD 2
Cardiff	Lab. 39, C. 16, LD 9, Ind. 1
Carmarthen	Ind. 27, Lab. 6, PC 2, LD 1, RA 1
Ceredigion	Ind. 30, LD 9, PC 4, Lab. 1
Colwyn	LD 12, Ind. 11, C. 7, Lab. 3, vacant 1
Cynon Valley	Lab. 25, PC 10, Ind. Lab. 2, Others 1
Delyn	Ind. 22, Lab. 12, Others 8
Dinefwr	Lab. 15, PC 5, Ind. Lab. 2, NP 1
Dwyfor	PC 7, Others 22
Glyndŵr	Ind. 26, Lab. 6, LD 2, PC 1
Islwyn	Lab. 30, PC 5
Llanelli	Lab. 19, LD 4, Green 2, PC 2, Ind. 1, Others 7
Lliw Valley	Lab. 22, Green 5, PC 4, C. 1, Others 1
Meirionnydd	PC 13, Lab. 5, Ind. 1, Others 22
Merthyr Tydfil	Lab. 20, RA 8, Ind. 2, PC 1, Others 2
Monmouth	C. 22, Lab. 14, Ind. 3, LD 1
Montgomeryshire	Ind. 38, LD 4, Lab. 2, C. 1, PC 1
Neath	Lab. 25, PC 5, LD 2, Ind. 1, Others 1
Newport	Lab. 40, C. 7
Ogwr	Lab. 38, C. 9, Ind. Lab. 1, LD 1
Port Talbot	Lab. 21, RA 6, SD 2, Ind. 1, LD 1
Preseli Pembrokeshire	Ind. 36, Lab. 2, C. 1, LD 1
Radnorshire	NP 26, Lab. 4, LD 2, Green 1
Rhondda	Lab. 26, PC 4, RA 3
Rhuddlan	Ind. 21, Lab. 11
Rhymney Valley	Lab. 27, PC 13, Ind. 3, NP 3
South Pembrokeshire	NP 26, Lab. 2, PC 2
Swansea	Lab. 30, C. 10, Ind. 6, LD 6
Taff-Ely	Lab. 19, PC 14, Ind. 4, C. 2, LD 2, RA 1, SD 1
Torfaen	Lab. 36, Ind. 3, LD 3, C. 1, Others 1
Vale of Glamorgan	Lab. 20, C. 18, PC 3, Others 4, vacant 1
Wrexham Maelor	Lab. 29, Ind. 6, LD & Lib. 6, C. 4, PC 1
Ynys Môn	Ind. 25, PC 8, Lab. 5, C. 1

SCOTLAND

REGIONAL AND ISLANDS COUNCILS

Borders	Ind. 14, LD 5, C. 2, SNP 2
Central	Lab. 22, SNP 6, C. 5, Ind. 1
Dumfries and Galloway	Lab. 11, Ind. 9, NP 6, SNP 4, Lib. 2, C. 1, Ind. Lab. 1, Others 1
Fife	Lab. 29, LD 11, C. 2, SNP 2, Com. 1, Ind. 1
Grampian	Lab. 17, SNP 14, C. 13, LD 9, Ind. 3, Ind. Lab. 1
Highland	Ind. 34, Lab. 10, LD 3, SNP 2, C. 1, Green 1, Ind. LD 1
Lothian	Lab. 34, C. 12, LD 2, SNP 1
Orkney	Ind. 23, SNP 1
Shetland	Ind. 17, Lab. 2, Others 6
Strathclyde	Lab. 87, C. 5, LD 4, Ind. 3, Ind. Lab. 2, SNP 2
Tayside	Lab. 18, C. 13, SNP 10, LD 3, Ind. 1, Ind. Lab. 1
Western Isles	NP 30

DISTRICT COUNCILS

Aberdeen	Lab. 27, LD 13, C. 10, SNP 2
Angus	SNP 11, C. 7, Ind. 2, Others 1
Annandale and Eskdale	LD 10, NP 5, Lab. 1
Argyll and Bute	Ind. 10, NP 6, C. 4, LD 3, SNP 2, Lab. 1
Badenoch and Strathspey	Ind. C. 11
Banff and Buchan	Ind. 11, SNP 7
Bearsden and Milngavie	C. 5, LD 4, Lab. 1
Berwickshire	C. 7, Ind. 3, LD 1, vacant 1
Caithness	Ind. 14, Ind. Lib. 1, Lab. 1
Clackmannan	Lab. 8, SNP 3, C. 1
Clydebank	Lab. 8, SNP 2, C. 1, Ind. 1
Clydesdale	Lab. 7, SNP 4, C. 3, Ind. 2
Cumbernauld and Kilsyth	Lab. 7, SNP 5
Cumnock and Doon Valley	Lab. 10
Cunninghame	Lab. 20, C. 6, SNP 3, Ind. 1
Dumbarton	Lab. 8, C. 5, SNP 2, NP 1
Dundee	Lab. 26, C. 12, SNP 6
Dunfermline	Lab. 22, LD 5, SNP 4, C. 2, Others 1
East Kilbride	Lab. 12, C. 2, SNP 2
East Lothian	Lab. 9, C. 7, SNP 1
Eastwood	C. 8, RA 2, Lab. 1, LD 1
Edinburgh	Lab. 30, C. 23, LD 7, SNP 2
Ettrick and Lauderdale	Ind. 15, SNP 1
Falkirk	Lab. 16, SNP 12, Ind. 5, C. 3
Glasgow	Lab. 54, C. 5, Ind. 4, SNP 2, LD 1
Gordon	Ind. 9, LD 5, C. 2
Hamilton	Lab. 15, C. 2, LD 2, Ind. Lab. 1
Inverclyde	Lab. 11, LD 8, C. 1
Inverness	Ind. 13, Lab. 8, LD 5, Lib. 1, SNP 1
Kilmarnock and Loudoun	Lab. 8, SNP 7, C. 3

Kincardine and Deeside	*C.* 5, *Ind.* 5, *LD* 1, *SNP* 1
Kirkcaldy	*Lab.* 24, *SNP* 7, *Ind.* 3, *C.* 2, *LD* 2, *Others* 2
Kyle and Carrick	*C.* 16, *Lab.* 9
Lochaber	*Ind.* 8, *Lab.* 3, *SNP* 3, *Ind. Lab.* 1
Midlothian	*Lab.* 12, *C.* 2, *SNP* 1
Monklands	*Lab.* 17, *SNP* 3
Moray	*Ind.* 9, *SNP* 7, *C.* 1, *Lab.* 1
Motherwell	*Lab.* 22, *SNP* 4, *C.* 2, *Ind.* 1, *NP* 1
Nairn	*Ind.* 8, *C.* 1, *SNP* 1
Nithsdale	*Lab.* 9, *Ind.* 8, *C.* 5, *SNP* 5, *LD* 1
North East Fife	*LD* 13, *C.* 4, *Ind.* 1
Perth and Kinross	*C.* 16, *SNP* 5, *Ind.* 3, *Lab.* 3, *Lib.* 2
Renfrew	*Lab.* 22, *SNP* 12, *C.* 8, *LD* 2, *Ind.* 1
Ross and Cromarty	*Ind.* 15, *SNP* 4, *Lab.* 2, *C.* 1
Roxburgh	*Ind.* 8, *LD* 5, *C.* 2, *SNP* 1
Skye and Lochalsh	*Ind.* 10, *SNP* 1
Stewartry	*Ind.* 11, *C.* 1
Stirling	*C.* 10, *Lab.* 10
Strathkelvin	*Lab.* 8, *C.* 6, *vacant* 1
Sutherland	*Ind.* 14
Tweeddale	*Ind.* 6, *LD* 2, *Lab.* 1, *SNP* 1
West Lothian	*Lab.* 11, *SNP* 10, *C.* 2, *Ind.* 1
Wigtown	*Ind.* 10, *SNP* 2, *C.* 1, *Lab.* 1

540

England

POSITION AND EXTENT

The Kingdom of England lies between 55° 46' and 49° 57' 30" N. latitude (from a few miles north of the mouth of the Tweed to the Lizard), and between 1° 46' E. and 5° 43' W. (from Lowestoft to Land's End). England is bounded on the north by the Cheviot Hills; on the south by the English Channel; on the east by the Straits of Dover (Pas de Calais) and the North Sea; and on the west by the Atlantic Ocean, Wales and the Irish Sea. It has a total area of 50,377 sq. miles (130,478 sq. km): land 50,085 sq. miles (129,720 sq. km); inland water 293 sq. miles (758 sq. km).

POPULATION

The population at the 1991 Census was 46,382,050 (males 22,469,707; females 23,912,343). The average density of the population in 1991 was 3.6 persons per hectare.

FLAG

The cross of St George, the patron saint of England (cross gules in a field argent), has been used since the 13th century.

RELIEF

There is a marked division between the upland and lowland areas of England. In the extreme north the Cheviot Hills (highest point, The Cheviot, 2,674 ft) form a natural boundary with Scotland. Running south from the Cheviots, though divided from them by the Tyne Gap, is the Pennine range (highest point, Cross Fell, 2,930 ft), the main orological feature of the country. The Pennines culminate in the Peak District of Derbyshire (Kinder Scout, 2,088 ft). West of the Pennines are the Cumbrian mountains, which include Scafell Pike (3,210 ft), the highest peak in England, and to the east are the Yorkshire Moors, their highest point being Urra Moor (1,490 ft).

In the west, the foothills of the Welsh mountains extend into the bordering English counties of Shropshire (the Wrekin, 1,334 ft; Long Mynd, 1,694 ft) and Hereford and Worcester (the Malvern Hills – Worcestershire Beacon, 1,394 ft). Extensive areas of high land and moorland are also to be found in the south-western peninsula formed by Somerset, Devon and Cornwall: principally Exmoor (Dunkery Beacon, 1,704 ft), Dartmoor (High Willhays, 2,038 ft) and Bodmin Moor (Brown Willy, 1,377 ft). Ranges of low, undulating hills run across the south of the country, including the Cotswolds in the Midlands and south-west, the Chilterns to the north of London, and the North (Kent) and South (Sussex) Downs of the south-east coastal areas.

The lowlands of England lie in the Vale of York, East Anglia and the area around the Wash. The lowest-lying are the Cambridgeshire Fens in the valleys of the Great Ouse and the River Nene, which are below sea-level in places. Since the 17th century extensive drainage has brought much of the Fens under cultivation. The North Sea coast between the Thames and the Humber, low-lying and formed of sand and shingle for the most part, is subject to erosion and defences against further incursion have been built along many stretches.

HYDROGRAPHY

The Severn is the longest river in Great Britain, rising in the north-eastern slopes of Plynlimon (Wales) and entering England in Shropshire with a total length of 220 miles (354 km) from its source to its outflow into the Bristol Channel, where it receives on the east the Bristol Avon, and on the west the Wye, its other tributaries being the Vyrnwy, Tern, Stour, Teme and Upper (or Warwickshire) Avon. The Severn is tidal below Gloucester, and a high bore or tidal wave sometimes reverses the flow as high as Tewkesbury (13½ miles above Gloucester). The scenery of the greater part of the river is very picturesque and beautiful, and the Severn is a noted salmon river, some of its tributaries being famous for trout. Navigation is assisted by the Gloucester and Berkeley Ship Canal (16¾ miles), which admits vessels of 350 tons to Gloucester. The Severn Tunnel was begun in 1873 and completed in 1886 at a cost of £2,000,000 and after many difficulties from flooding. It is 4 miles 628 yards in length (of which 2¼ miles are under the river). The Severn road bridge between Haysgate, Gwent, and Almondsbury, Glos., with a centre span of 3,240 ft, was opened in 1966.

The longest river wholly in England is the Thames, with a total length of 215 miles (346 km) from its source in the Cotswold hills to the Nore, and is navigable by ocean-going ships to London Bridge. The Thames is tidal to Teddington (69 miles from its mouth) and forms county boundaries almost throughout its course; on its banks are situated London, Windsor Castle, the oldest royal residence still in regular use, Eton College, the first of the public schools, and Oxford, the oldest university in the kingdom.

Of the remaining English rivers those flowing into the North Sea are the Tyne, Wear, Tees, Ouse and Trent from the Pennine Range, the Great Ouse (160 miles), which rises in Northamptonshire, and the Orwell and Stour from the hills of East Anglia. Flowing into the English Channel are the Sussex Ouse from the Weald, the Itchen from the Hampshire Hills, and the Axe, Teign, Dart, Tamar and Exe from the Devonian hills. Flowing into the Irish Sea are the Mersey, Ribble and Eden from the western slopes of the Pennines and the Derwent from the Cumbrian mountains.

The English Lakes, noteworthy for their picturesque scenery and poetic associations, lie in Cumbria, the largest being Windermere (10 miles long), Ullswater and Derwentwater.

ISLANDS

The Isle of Wight is separated from Hampshire by the Solent. The capital, Newport, stands at the head of the estuary of the Medina, Cowes (at the mouth) being the chief port. Other centres are Ryde, Sandown, Shanklin, Ventnor, Freshwater, Yarmouth, Totland Bay, Seaview and Bembridge.

Lundy (the name means Puffin Island), 11 miles northwest of Hartland Point, Devon, is about two miles long and about half a mile broad (average), with a total area of about 1,116 acres, and a population of about 20. It became the property of the National Trust in 1969 and is now principally a bird sanctuary.

The Isles of Scilly consist of about 140 islands and skerries (total area, 6 sq. miles/10 sq. km) situated 28 miles southwest of Land's End. Only five are inhabited: St Mary's, St Agnes, Bryher, Tresco and St Martin's. The population is 1,978. The entire group has been designated a Conservation Area, a Heritage Coast, and an Area of Outstanding Natural Beauty, and has been given National Nature Reserve status by the Nature Conservancy Council because of its unique flora and fauna. Tourism and the winter/spring flower trade for the home market form the basis of the economy of the Isles. The island group is a recognized rural development area.

EARLY HISTORY

Prehistoric Inhabitants

Archaeological evidence suggests that England has been inhabited since at least the Palaeolithic period, though the extent of the various Palaeolithic cultures was dependent upon the degree of glaciation. The succeeding Neolithic and Bronze Age cultures have left abundant remains throughout the country, the best-known of these being the henges and stone circles of Stonehenge (ten miles north of Salisbury, Wilts.) and Avebury (Wilts.), both of which are believed to have been of religious significance. In the latter part of the Bronze Age the Goidels, a people of Celtic race, and in the Iron Age other Celtic races of Brythons and Belgae, invaded the country and brought with them Celtic civilization and dialects, place names in England bearing witness to the spread of the invasion over the whole kingdom.

The Roman Conquest

The Roman conquest of Gaul (57–50 BC) brought Britain into close contact with Roman civilization, but although Julius Caesar raided the south of Britain in 55 BC and 54 BC, conquest was not undertaken until nearly 100 years later. In AD 43 the Emperor Claudius dispatched Aulus Plautius, with a well-equipped force of 40,000, and himself followed with reinforcements in the same year. Success was delayed by the resistance of Caratacus (Caractacus), the British leader from AD 48–51, who was finally captured and sent to Rome, and by a great revolt in AD 61 led by Boudicca (Boadicea), Queen of the Iceni; but the south of Britain was secured by AD 70, and Wales and the area north to the Tyne by about AD 80.

In AD 122, the Emperor Hadrian visited Britain and built a continuous rampart, since known as Hadrian's Wall, from Wallsend to Bowness (Tyne to Solway). The work was entrusted by the Emperor Hadrian to Aulus Platorius Nepos, legate of Britain from AD 122 to 126, and it was intended to form the northern frontier of the Roman Empire.

The Romans administered Britain as a province under a Governor, with a well-defined system of local government, each Roman municipality ruling itself and surrounding territory, while London was the centre of the road system and the seat of the financial officials of the Province of Britain. Colchester, Lincoln, York, Gloucester and St Albans stand on the sites of five Roman municipalities, and Wroxeter, Caerleon, Chester, Lincoln and York were at various times the sites of legionary fortresses. Well-preserved Roman towns have been uncovered at (or near) Silchester (*Calleva Atrebatum*), ten miles south of Reading, Wroxeter (*Viroconium Cornoviorum*), near Shrewsbury, and St Albans (*Verulamium*) in Hertfordshire.

Four main groups of roads radiated from London, and a fifth (the Fosse) ran obliquely from Lincoln through Leicester, Cirencester and Bath to Exeter. Of the four groups radiating from London, one ran south-east to Canterbury and the coast of Kent, a second to Silchester and thence to parts of western Britain and south Wales, a third (later known as Watling Street) ran through Verulamium to Chester, with various branches, and the fourth reached Colchester, Lincoln, York and the eastern counties.

In the fourth century Britain was subject to raids along the east coast by Saxon pirates, which led to the establishment of a system of coast defence from the Wash to Southampton Water, with forts at Brancaster, Burgh Castle (Yarmouth), Walton (Felixstowe), Bradwell, Reculver, Richborough, Dover, Lympne, Pevensey and Porchester (Portsmouth). The Irish (Scoti) and Picts in the north were also becoming more aggressive; from about AD 350 incursions became more

frequent and more formidable. As the Roman Empire came under attack increasingly towards the end of the fourth century, many troops were removed from Britain for service in other parts of the empire. The island was eventually cut off from Rome by the Teutonic conquest of Gaul, and with the withdrawal of the last Roman garrison early in the fifth century, the Romano-British were left to themselves.

Saxon Settlement

According to legend, the British King Vortigern called in the Saxons to defend him against the Picts, the Saxon chieftains being Hengist and Horsa, who landed at Ebbsfleet, Kent, and established themselves in the Isle of Thanet; but the events during the one and a half centuries between the final break with Rome and the re-establishment of Christianity are unclear. However, it would appear that in the course of this period the raids turned into large-scale settlement by invaders traditionally known as Angles (England north of the Wash and East Anglia), Saxons (Essex and southern England) and Jutes (Kent and the Weald), which pushed the Romano-British into the mountainous areas of the north and west, Celtic culture outside Wales and Cornwall surviving only in topographical names. Various kingdoms were established at this time which attempted to claim overlordship of the whole country, hegemony finally being achieved by Wessex (capital, Winchester) in the ninth century. This century also saw the beginning of raids by the Vikings (Danes), which were resisted by Alfred the Great (871–899), who fixed a limit to the advance of Danish settlement by the Treaty of Wedmore (878), giving them the area north and east of Watling Street, on condition that they adopt Christianity.

In the tenth century the kings of Wessex recovered the whole of England from the Danes, but subsequent rulers were unable to resist a second wave of invaders. England paid tribute (*Danegeld*) for many years, and was invaded in 1013 by the Danes and ruled by Danish kings from 1016 until 1042, when Edward the Confessor was recalled from exile in Normandy. On Edward's death in 1066 Harold Godwinson (brother-in-law of Edward and son of Earl Godwin of Wessex) was chosen King of England. After defeating (at Stamford Bridge, Yorkshire, 25 September) an invading army under Harald Hadraada, King of Norway (aided by the outlawed Earl Tostig of Northumbria, Harold's brother), Harold was himself defeated at the Battle of Hastings on 14 October 1066, and the Norman conquest secured the throne of England for Duke William of Normandy, a cousin of Edward the Confessor.

Christianity

Christianity reached the Roman province of Britain from Gaul in the third century (or possibly earlier); Alban, traditionally Britain's first martyr, was put to death as a Christian during the persecution of Diocletian (22 June 303), at his native town Verulamium; and the Bishops of Londinium, Eboracum (York), and Lindum (Lincoln) attended the Council of Arles in 314. However, the Anglo-Saxon invasions submerged the Christian religion in England until the sixth century when conversion was undertaken in the north from 563 by Celtic missionaries from Ireland led by St Columba, and in the south by a mission sent from Rome in 597 which was led by St Augustine, who became the first archbishop of Canterbury. England appears to have been converted again by the end of the seventh century and followed, after the Council of Whitby in 663, the practices of the Roman Church, which brought the kingdom into the mainstream of European thought and culture.

PRINCIPAL CITIES

BIRMINGHAM

Birmingham (West Midlands) is Britain's second city. It is a focal point in national communications networks with a rapidly expanding International Airport. The generally accepted derivation of 'Birmingham' is the *ham* (dwelling-place) of the *ing* (family) of *Beorma*, presumed to have been a Saxon. During the Industrial Revolution the town grew into a major manufacturing centre. In 1889 Birmingham was granted City status.

Despite the decline in manufacturing, Birmingham is still a major hardware trade and motor component industry centre. As well as the National Exhibition Centre and the Aston Science Park, recent developments include the International Convention Centre and the National Indoor Arena. An Urban Development Agency was set up in 1986.

The principal buildings are the Town Hall (1832–4); the Council House (1879); Victoria Law Courts (1891); the University (1909); the 13th century Church of St Martin-in-the-Bullring (rebuilt 1873); the Cathedral (formerly St Philip's Church) (1711) and the Roman Catholic Cathedral of St Chad (1839–41).

BRADFORD

Bradford (West Yorkshire) lies on the southern edge of the Yorkshire Dales National Park, including within its boundaries the village of Haworth, home of the Brontë sisters, and Ilkley Moor.

Originally a Saxon township, Bradford received a market charter in 1251 but developed only slowly until the industrialization of the textile industry brought rapid growth during the 19th century. The prosperity of that period is reflected in much of the city's architecture, particularly the public buildings: City Hall (1873), Wool Exchange (1867), St George's Hall (Concert Hall, 1853), Cartwright Hall (Art Gallery, 1904) and the Technical College (1882). Other chief buildings are the Cathedral (15th century) and Bolling Hall (14th century).

Textiles still play an important part in the city's economy but industry is now more broadly based, including engineering and micro-electronics. The city has a strong financial services sector, and a growing tourism industry.

BRISTOL

Bristol (Avon) was a Royal Borough before the Norman Conquest. The earliest form of the name is *Bricgstow*. In 1373 it received from Edward III a charter granting it county status.

The chief buildings include the 12th century Cathedral (with later additions), with Norman chapter house and gateway, the 14th century Church of St Mary Redcliffe, Wesley's Chapel, Broadmead, the Merchant Venturers' Almshouses, the Council House (1956), Guildhall, Exchange (erected from the designs of John Wood in 1743), Cabot Tower, the University and Clifton College. The Roman Catholic Cathedral at Clifton was opened in 1973.

The Clifton Suspension Bridge, with a span of 702 feet over the Avon, was projected by Brunel in 1836 but was not completed until 1864. Brunel's SS *Great Britain*, the first ocean-going propeller-driven ship, is now being restored in the City Docks from where she was launched in 1843. The docks themselves have been extensively restored and redeveloped.

CAMBRIDGE

Cambridge, a settlement far older than its ancient University, lies on the River Cam or Granta. The city is a county town and regional headquarters. Its industries include electronics, flour milling, cement making, the manufacture of scientific instruments and the growing area of biotechnology. Among its open spaces are Jesus Green, Sheep's Green, Coe Fen, Parker's Piece, Christ's Pieces, the University Botanic Garden, and the Backs, or lawns and gardens through which the Cam winds behind the principal line of college buildings. East of the Cam, King's Parade, upon which stand Great St Mary's Church, Gibbs' Senate House and King's College Chapel with Wilkins' screen, joins Trumpington Street to form one of the most beautiful throughfares in Europe.

University and college buildings provide the outstanding features of Cambridge architecture but several churches (especially St Benet's, the oldest building in the City, and St Sepulchre's, the Round Church) also are notable. The modern Guildhall (1939) stands on a site of which at least part has held municipal buildings since 1224.

CANTERBURY

Canterbury, the Metropolitan City of the Anglican Communion, has a history going back to prehistoric times. It was the Roman *Durovernum Cantiacorum* and the Saxon *Cant-wara-byrig* (stronghold of the men of Kent). Here in 597 St Augustine began the conversion of the English to Christianity, when Ethelbert, King of Kent, was baptized.

Of the Benedictine St Augustine's Abbey, burial place of the Jutish Kings of Kent (whose capital Canterbury was), only extensive ruins remain. St Martin's Church, on the eastern outskirts of the city, is stated by Bede to have been the place of worship of Queen Bertha, the Christian wife of King Ethelbert, before the advent of St Augustine.

In 1170 the rivalry of Church and State culminated in the murder in Canterbury Cathedral, by Henry II's knights, of Archbishop Thomas Becket, whose shrine became a great centre of pilgrimage, as described by Chaucer in his *Canterbury Tales*. After the Reformation pilgrimages ceased, but the prosperity of the city was strengthened by an influx of Huguenot refugees, who introduced weaving. The Elizabethan poet and playwright Christopher Marlowe was born and reared in Canterbury, and there are literary associations also with Defoe, Dickens, Joseph Conrad and Somerset Maugham.

The Cathedral, with architecture ranging from the 11th to 15th centuries, is world famous. Modern pilgrims are attracted particularly to the Martyrdom, the Black Prince's Tomb, the Warriors' Chapel and the many examples of medieval stained glass.

The medieval city walls are built on Roman foundations and the 14th century West Gate is one of the finest buildings of its kind in the country.

The 1,000 seat Marlowe Theatre is the base for the Canterbury International Festival of the Arts each autumn.

CARLISLE

Carlisle is situated at the confluence of the River Eden and River Caldew, 309 miles north-west of London and about ten miles from the Scottish border. It was granted a charter in 1158.

The city stands at the western end of Hadrian's Wall and dates from the original Roman settlement of *Luguvalium*. Granted to Scotland in the tenth century, Carlisle is not included in the Domesday Book. William Rufus reclaimed the area in 1092 and the castle and city walls were built to guard Carlisle and the western border; the citadel is a Tudor addition to protect the south of the city. Until the Union of the Crowns in 1603, Carlisle changed hands several times and was frequently besieged. During the Civil War the city remained Royalist; in 1745 it supported the Young Pretender.

The Cathedral, originally a 12th century Augustinian priory, was enlarged in the 13th and 14th centuries after the diocese was created in 1133. To the south is a restored Tithe Barn and nearby the 18th century church of St Cuthbert, the third to stand on a site dating from the seventh century.

Carlisle is the major shopping, commercial and agricultural centre for the area, and industries include the manufacture of metal goods, biscuits and textiles. However, the largest employer is the services sector, notably in retailing and transport. The city has an important communications position at the centre of a network of major roads, as an important stage on the main west coast rail services, and with its own airport at Crosby.

CHESTER

Chester is situated on the River Dee, and was granted Borough and City status in 1974. Its recorded history dates from the first century when the Romans founded the fortress of *Deva*. The city's name is derived from the Latin *castra* (a camp or encampment). During the Middle Ages, Chester was the principal port of north-west England but declined with the silting of the Dee estuary and competition from Liverpool. The city was also an important military centre, notably during Edward I's Welsh campaigns and the Elizabethan Irish campaigns. During the Civil War, Chester supported the King and was besieged from 1643 to 1646. Chester's first charter was granted *c.*1175 and the city was incorporated in 1506. The office of Sheriff is the earliest created in the country (*c.*1120s), and in 1992 the Mayor was granted the title of Lord Mayor. He/she also enjoys the title 'Admiral of the Dee'.

The city's architectural features include the city walls (an almost complete two-mile circuit), the unique Rows (covered galleries above the street-level shops), the Victorian Gothic Town Hall (1869), the Castle (rebuilt 1788 and 1822) and numerous half-timbered buildings. The Cathedral was a Benedictine abbey until the Dissolution. Remaining monastic buildings include the chapter house, refectory and cloisters and there is a modern free-standing bell tower. The Norman church of St John the Baptist was a cathedral church in the early Middle Ages.

Chester is primarily a regional service centre and has considerable tourist appeal. In 1984 the city was awarded Development Area status, which has attracted a range of nationally-known companies to expand or locate in Chester.

COVENTRY

Coventry (West Midlands) is an important industrial centre, producing vehicles, machine tools, agricultural machinery, man-made fibres, aerospace components and telecommunications equipment. New investment has come from the financial services, power transmission, professional services and educational sectors.

The city owes its beginning to Leofric, Earl of Mercia, and his wife Godiva who, in 1043, founded a Benedictine monastery. The guildhall of St Mary dates from the 14th century, three of the city's churches date from the 14th and 15th centuries, and 16th century almshouses may still be seen. Coventry's first cathedral was destroyed at the Reformation, its second in the 1940 blitz (the walls and spire remain) and the new cathedral designed by Sir Basil Spence, consecrated in 1962, now draws innumerable visitors.

Coventry is the home of the University of Warwick and its Science Park, Coventry University, the rapidly-expanding Westwood Business Park and the Museum of British Road Transport.

DERBY

Derby stands on the banks of the River Derwent, and its name dates back to 880 when the Danes settled in the locality and changed the original Saxon name of *Northworthy* to *Deoraby*.

Derby has a wide range of industries: its products include aero engines, pipework, specialized mechanical engineering equipment, textiles, chemicals, plastics and the Royal Crown Derby porcelain. The city is an established railway centre, the site of British Rail's Technical Centre with its research laboratories.

Buildings of interest include St Peter's Church and the Old Abbey Building (14th century), the Cathedral (1525), St Mary's Roman Catholic Church (1839) and the Industrial Museum, formerly the Old Silk Mill (1721). The traditional city centre is complemented by the new Eagle Centre and 'out-of-centre' retail developments. In addition to the Derby Playhouse, the Assembly Rooms are a multi-purpose venue.

The first charter granting a Mayor and Aldermen was that of Charles I in 1637. Previous charters date back to 1154. It was granted City status in 1977.

DURHAM

The city of Durham is a district in the county of Durham and a major tourist attraction because of its prominent Norman Cathedral and Castle set high on a wooded peninsula overlooking the River Wear. The Cathedral was founded as a shrine for the body of St Cuthbert in 995. The present building dates from 1093 and among its many treasures is the tomb of the Venerable Bede (673-735). Durham's Prince Bishops had unique powers up to 1836, being lay rulers as well as religious leaders. As a palatinate Durham could have its own army, nobility, coinage and courts. The Castle was the main seat of the Prince Bishops for nearly 800 years; it is now used as a college by the University. The University, founded on the initiative of Bishop William Van Mildert, is England's third oldest. Its students live in 14 colleges spread across the city.

Among other buildings of interest is the Guildhall in the Market Place which dates originally from the 14th century. Much work has been carried out to conserve this area, forming part of the city's major contribution to the Council of Europe's Urban Renaissance Campaign. Annual events include Durham's Regatta in June (claimed to be the oldest rowing event in Britain) and the Annual Gala (formerly Durham Miners' Gala) in July.

In the past 20 years the economy of Durham has undergone a significant change with the replacement of mining as the dominant industry by 'white collar' employment. Although still a predominantly rural area, the industrial and commercial sector is growing and a wide range of manufacturing and service industries are based on industrial estates in and around the city.

EXETER

Exeter lies on the River Exe ten miles from the sea. It was granted a Royal Charter by Henry II. The Romans founded *Isca Dumnoniorum* in the first century AD, and in the third century a stone wall (most of which remains) was built, providing protection against Saxon, and then Danish invasions. After the Conquest, the city led resistance to William in the west, until reduced by siege. The Normans built the ringwork castle of Rougemont, the gatehouse and one tower of which remain, although the rest was pulled down in 1784. The first bridge across the Exe was built in the 13th century. The city's role as a port declined due to the silting of the river, but was somewhat restored by the construction in the 1560s of the first true canal in England. Exeter was the Royalist headquarters in the west during the Civil War.

The diocese of Exeter was established by Edward the Confessor in 1050, although a minster existed near the Cathedral site from the late seventh century. A new cathedral was built in the 12th century but the present building was begun c.1275, although incorporating the Norman towers, and completed about a century later. The Guildhall dates from the 12th century and there are many other medieval buildings in the city, as well as architecture in the Georgian and Regency styles, and the Custom House (1680). Damage suffered by bombing in 1942 led to the redevelopment of the city centre.

Exeter's prosperity from medieval times was based on trade in wool and woollen cloth (commemorated by Tuckers Hall), which remained at its height until the late 18th century when export trade was hit by the French wars. Subsequently Exeter has developed as an administrative and commercial centre, notably in the distributive trades, light manufacturing industries and tourism.

KINGSTON UPON HULL

Hull (officially Kingston upon Hull) lies in the mostly rural county of Humberside, at the junction of the River Hull with the Humber, 22 miles from the North Sea. It is one of the great seaports of the United Kingdom. It has docks covering a water area of 172 acres, equipped to handle cargoes by unit-load techniques, and is a departure point for car ferry services to continental Europe. There is a great variety of industry and service industries, as well as increasing tourism and conference business.

The city, restored after very heavy air raid damage during the Second World War, has good office and administrative buildings, its municipal centre being the Guildhall, its educational centre the University of Hull and its religious centre the Parish Church of the Holy Trinity. The old town area is being renovated and includes a new marina and shopping complex. Just west of the city is the Humber Bridge, the world's longest single span suspension bridge.

Kingston upon Hull was so named by Edward I. City status was accorded in 1897 and the office of Mayor raised to the dignity of Lord Mayor in 1914.

LEEDS

Leeds (West Yorkshire), situated in the lower Aire Valley, is a junction for road, rail, canal and air services and an important commercial centre. Seventy-three per cent of employment is in services, notably the distributive trades, public administration, medical services and business services. The main manufacturing industries are mechanical engineering, printing and publishing, metal goods and furniture.

The principal buildings are the Civic Hall (1933), the Town Hall (1858), the Municipal Buildings and Art Gallery (1884) with the Henry Moore Gallery (1982), the Corn Exchange (1863) and the University. The Parish Church (St Peter's) was rebuilt in 1841; the 17th century St John's Church has a fine interior with a famous English Renaissance screen; the last remaining 18th century church in the city is Holy Trinity in Boar Lane (1727). Kirkstall Abbey (about three miles from the centre of the city), founded by Henry de Lacy in 1152, is one of the most complete examples of Cistercian houses now remaining. Temple Newsam, birthplace of Lord Darnley, was acquired by the Council in 1922. The present house was largely rebuilt by Sir Arthur Ingram in about

1620. Adel Church, about five miles from the centre of the city, is a fine Norman structure.

Leeds was first incorporated by Charles I in 1626. The earliest forms of the name are Loidis or Ledes, the origins of which are obscure.

LEICESTER

Leicester is situated geographically in the centre of England. It dates back to pre-Roman times and was one of the five Danish Burghs. In 1589 Queen Elizabeth I granted a Charter to the City and the ancient title was confirmed by Letters Patent in 1919. Under local government reorganization Leicester retained its designation as a City.

The principal industries of the city are hosiery, knitwear, footwear manufacturing and engineering. The growth of Leicester as a hosiery centre increased rapidly from the introduction there of the first stocking frame in 1670 and today it has some of the largest hosiery factories in the world.

The principal buildings in the city are the Town Hall, the New Walk Centre, the University of Leicester, De Montfort University, De Montfort Hall, one of the finest concert halls in the provinces seating over 2,750 people, and the Granby Halls, an indoor sports facility. The ancient Churches of St Martin (now Leicester Cathedral), St Nicholas, St Margaret, All Saints, St Mary de Castro, and buildings such as the Guildhall, the 14th century Newarke Gate, the Castle and the Jewry Wall Roman site still exist. The Haymarket Theatre was opened in 1973 and The Shires, a new shopping centre, was opened in 1992.

LINCOLN

Situated 40 miles inland on the River Witham, Lincoln derives its name from a contraction of Lindum Colonia, the settlement founded in AD 48 by the Romans to command the crossing of Ermine Street and Fosse Way. Sections of the third century Roman city wall can be seen, including an extant gateway (Newport Arch), and excavations have discovered traces of a sewerage system unique in Britain. The Romans also drained the surrounding fenland and created a canal system, laying the foundations of Lincoln's agricultural prosperity, and also of the city's importance in the medieval wool trade as a port and Staple town.

As one of the Five Boroughs of the Danelaw, Lincoln was an important trading centre in the ninth and tenth centuries and medieval prosperity from the wool trade lasted until the 14th century, enabling local merchants to build parish churches (of which three survive), and attracting in the 12th century a Jewish community (Jew's House and Court, Aaron's House). However, the removal of the Staple to Boston in 1369 heralded a decline from which the city only recovered fully in the 19th century when improved fen drainage made Lincoln agriculturally important, and improved canal and rail links led to industrial development, mainly in the manufacture of machinery, components and engineering products.

The castle was built shortly after the Conquest and is unusual in having two mounds; on one motte stands a Keep (Lucy's Tower) added in the 12th century. The Cathedral was begun c.1073 when the first Norman bishop moved the see of Lindsey to Lincoln, but was mostly destroyed by fire and earthquake in the 12th century. Rebuilding was begun by St Hugh and completed over a century later. The Wren library contains manuscripts including one of the four surviving originals of the Magna Carta. Other notable architectural features of the city are the 12th century High Bridge, the oldest in Britain still to carry buildings, and the Guildhall situated above the 15th–16th century Stonebow gateway.

LIVERPOOL

Liverpool (Merseyside) on the right bank of the River Mersey, three miles from the Irish Sea, is the United Kingdom's foremost port for the Atlantic trade. Tunnels link Liverpool with Birkenhead and Wallasey.

There are 2,100 acres of dockland on both sides of the river and the Gladstone and Royal Seaforth Docks can accommodate the largest vessels afloat. Annual tonnage of cargo handled is approximately 27.8 million tonnes. The main imports are crude oil, grain, ores, edible oils, timber, containers and break-bulk cargo. Liverpool Free Port, Britain's largest, was opened in 1984.

Liverpool was created a free borough in 1207 and a city in 1880. From the early 18th century it expanded rapidly with the growth of industrialization and the Atlantic trade. Surviving buildings from this date include the Bluecoat Chambers (1717, formerly the Bluecoat School), the Town Hall (1754, rebuilt to the original design 1795), and buildings in Rodney Street, Canning Street and the suburbs. Notable from the 19th and 20th centuries are the Anglican Cathedral, built from the designs of Sir Giles Gilbert Scott (the foundation stone was laid in 1904, and the building was completed only in 1980), the Catholic Metropolitan Cathedral (designed by Sir Frederick Gibberd, consecrated 1967) and St George's Hall (1838–54), regarded as one of the finest modern examples of classical architecture. The recently refurbished Albert Dock (designed by Jesse Hartley) contains the Merseyside Maritime Museum and Tate Gallery, Liverpool.

In 1852 an Act was obtained for establishing a public library, museum and art gallery: as a result Liverpool had one of the first public libraries in the country. The Brown, Picton and Hornby libraries now form one of the country's major libraries. The Victoria Building of Liverpool University, the Royal Liver, Cunard and Mersey Docks & Harbour Company buildings at the Pier Head, the Municipal Buildings and the Philharmonic Hall are other examples of the City's fine buildings. Britain's first International Garden Festival was held in Liverpool in 1984.

MANCHESTER

Manchester (the *Mamucium* of the Romans, who occupied it in AD 79) is a commercial and industrial centre with a population engaged in the engineering, chemical, clothing, food processing and textile industries and in education. Banking, insurance and a growing leisure industry are among the prime commercial activities. The city is connected with the sea by the Manchester Ship Canal, opened in 1894, 35½ miles long, and accommodating ships up to 15,000 tons. Manchester Airport handles more than 11 million passengers yearly.

The principal buildings are the Town Hall, erected in 1877 from the designs of Alfred Waterhouse, together with a large extension of 1938; the Royal Exchange (1869, enlarged 1921); the Central Library (1934); Heaton Hall; the 17th century Chetham Library; the Rylands Library (1900), which includes the Althorp collection; the University precinct; the 15th century Cathedral (formerly the parish church); G-MEX and the Free Trade Hall. Manchester is the home of the Hallé Orchestra, the Royal Northern College of Music, the Royal Exchange Theatre and seven public art galleries. Metrolink, the new light rail system, opened in 1992.

The town received its first charter of incorporation in 1838 and was created a city in 1853. The title of City was retained under local government reorganization.

NEWCASTLE UPON TYNE

Newcastle upon Tyne (Tyne and Wear), on the north bank of the River Tyne, is eight miles from the North Sea. A Cathedral and University city, it is the administrative, commercial and cultural centre for north-east England and the principal port. It is an important manufacturing centre with a wide variety of industries.

The principal buildings include the Castle Keep (12th century), Black Gate (13th century), Blackfriars (13th century), West Walls (13th century), St Nicholas's Cathedral (15th century, fine lantern tower), St Andrew's Church (12th–14th century), St John's (14th–15th century), All Saints (1786 by Stephenson), St Mary's Roman Catholic Cathedral (1844), Trinity House (17th century), Sandhill (16th century houses), Guildhall (Georgian), Grey Street (1834–9), Central Station (1846–50), Laing Art Gallery (1904), University of Newcastle Physics Building (1962) and Medical Building (1985), Civic Centre (1963), Central Library (1969) and Eldon Square Shopping Development (1976). Open spaces include the Town Moor (927 acres) and Jesmond Dene. Eight bridges span the Tyne at Newcastle.

The City derives its name from the 'new castle' (1080) erected as a defence against the Scots. In 1400 it was made a County, and in 1882 a City.

NORWICH

Norwich (Norfolk) grew from an early Anglo-Saxon settlement near the confluence of the Rivers Yare and Wensum, and now serves as provincial capital for the predominantly agricultural region of East Anglia. The name is thought to relate to the most northerly of a group of Anglo-Saxon villages or *wics*. The city's first known Charter was granted in 1158 by Henry II.

Norwich serves its surrounding area as a market town and commercial centre, banking and insurance being prominent among the city's businesses. From the 14th century until the Industrial Revolution, Norwich was the regional centre of the woollen industry, but now the biggest single industry is financial services and principal trades are engineering, printing, shoemaking, double glazing, and the production of chemicals, clothing, confectionery and other foodstuffs. Norwich is accessible to seagoing vessels by means of the River Yare, entered at Great Yarmouth, 20 miles to the east.

Among many historic buildings are the Cathedral (completed in the 12th century and surmounted by a 15th century spire 315 feet in height), the keep of the Norman castle (now a museum and art gallery), the 15th century flint-walled Guildhall (now a tourist information centre), some thirty medieval parish churches, St Andrew's and Blackfriars' Halls, the Tudor houses preserved in Elm Hill and the Georgian Assembly House. The University of East Anglia is located on a site at Earlham on the city's western boundary.

NOTTINGHAM

Nottingham stands on the River Trent in one of the most valuable coalfields of the country and connected by canal with the Atlantic Ocean and the North Sea. *Snotingaham* or *Notingeham*, literally the homestead of the people of Snot, is the Anglo-Saxon name for the Celtic settlement of *Tigguoco-bauc*, or the house of caves. In 878, Nottingham became one of the Five Boroughs of the Danelaw following a treaty signed by Alfred the Great and the Danish King Guthrum. William the Conqueror ordered the construction of Nottingham Castle, while the town itself developed rapidly under Norman rule. Its laws and rights were later formally recognized by Henry II's Charter in 1155. The Castle became a favoured residence of King John. In 1642 King Charles I raised his personal standard at Nottingham Castle at the start of the Civil War.

Nottingham is a major sporting centre, home to Nottingham Forest FC, Notts County FC (the world's oldest Football league side), Nottingham Racecourse and the National Watersports Centre. The principal industries include textiles, pharmaceuticals, food manufacturing, engineering and telecommunications. There are two universities within the city boundaries.

Architecturally, Nottingham has a wealth of notable buildings, particularly those designed in the Victorian era by T. C. Hine and Watson Fothergill. The City Council owns the Castle, of Norman origin but restored in 1878, Wollaton Hall (1580–8), Newstead Abbey (home of Lord Byron), the Guildhall (1888) and Council House (1929). St Mary's, St Peter's and St Nicholas's Churches are of interest, as is the Roman Catholic Cathedral (Pugin, 1842–4).

Nottingham was granted City status in 1897.

OXFORD

Oxford is a University city, an important industrial centre, and a market town. Industry played a minor part in Oxford until the motor industry was established in 1912.

It is for its architecture that Oxford is of most interest to the visitor, its oldest specimens being the reputedly Saxon tower of St Michael's church, the remains of the Norman castle and city walls, and the Norman church at Iffley. It is chiefly famous, however, for its Gothic buildings, such as the Divinity Schools, the Old Library at Merton College, William of Wykeham's New College, Magdalen College and Christ Church and many other college buildings. Later centuries are represented by the Laudian quadrangle at St John's College, the Renaissance Sheldonian Theatre by Wren, Trinity College Chapel, and All Saints Church; Hawksmoor's mock-Gothic at All Souls College, and the 18th century Queen's College. In addition to individual buildings, High Street and Radcliffe Square, just off it, both form architectural compositions of great beauty. Most of the Colleges have gardens, those of Magdalen, New College, St John's (designed by 'Capability' Brown) and Worcester being the largest.

PLYMOUTH

Plymouth is situated on the borders of Devon and Cornwall at the confluence of the Rivers Tamar and Plym. The city has a long maritime history; it was the home port of Sir Francis Drake and the starting point for his circumnavigation of the world, as well as the last port of call for the *Mayflower* when the Pilgrim Fathers sailed for the New World in 1620. Today Plymouth is host to many international yacht races. The Barbican harbour area has many Elizabethan buildings and on Plymouth Hoe stands Smeaton's lighthouse, the third to be built on the Eddystone Rocks 13 miles offshore.

Following extensive war damage, the city centre, comprising a large shopping centre, municipal offices, law courts and public buildings, has been rebuilt. The main employment is provided at the naval base, though many new industrial firms and service industries have become established in the postwar period and the city is a growing tourism centre. In 1982 the Theatre Royal was opened. In conjunction with the Cornwall County Council, the Tamar Bridge was constructed linking the city by road with Cornwall.

PORTSMOUTH

Portsmouth occupies Portsea Island, Hampshire, with boundaries extending to the mainland. It is a centre of industry and commerce, including many high technology and manufacturing industries. It is the British headquarters of several major international companies. The Royal Navy base still has a substantial work force, although this has decreased in recent years. The commercial port and continental ferry port is owned and run by the City Council, and carries passengers and vehicles to France and northern Spain.

A major port since the 16th century, Portsmouth is also a thriving seaside resort catering for thousands of visitors annually. Among many historic attractions are Lord Nelson's flagship, HMS *Victory*, the Tudor warship *Mary Rose*, Britain's first 'ironclad', HMS *Warrior*, the D-Day Museum, Charles Dickens' birthplace at 393 Old Commercial Road, the Royal Naval and Royal Marine museums, Southsea Castle (built by Henry VIII), the Round Tower and Point Battery, which for hundreds of years have guarded the entrance to Portsmouth Harbour, Fort Nelson on Portsdown Hill and the Sealife Centre.

ST ALBANS

The origins of St Albans, situated on the River Ver, stem from the Roman town of *Verulamium*. Named after the first Christian martyr in Britain, who was executed here, St Albans has developed around the Norman Abbey and Cathedral Church (consecrated 1115), built partly of materials from the old Roman city. The museums house Iron Age and Roman artefacts and the Roman Theatre, unique in Britain, has a stage as opposed to an amphitheatre. Archaeological excavations in the city centre continue also to reveal evidence of pre-Roman, Saxon and medieval occupation.

The town's significance grew to the extent that it was a signatory and venue for the drafting of the Magna Carta. It was also the scene of riots during the Peasants' Revolt, the French King John was imprisoned there after the Battle of Poitiers, and heavy fighting took place there during the Wars of the Roses.

Previously controlled by the Abbot, the town achieved a Royal Charter in 1553 and City status in 1877. The street market, first established in 1553, is still an important feature of the city, as are many hotels and inns which survive from the days when St Albans was an important coach stop. Tourist attractions include historic churches and houses, and a 15th century clock tower.

The city now contains a wide range of firms, with special emphasis on micro-technology and electronics, particularly in the medical field. In addition, it is the home of the Royal National Rose Society, and of Rothamsted Park, agricultural research centre.

SHEFFIELD

Sheffield (South Yorkshire), the centre of the special steel and cutlery trades, is situated at the junction of the Sheaf, Porter, Rivelin and Loxley valleys with the River Don. Though its cutlery, silverware and plate have long been famous, Sheffield has other and now more important industries: special and alloy steels, engineering, tool-making and financial services. Research in glass, metallurgy and other fields is carried out.

The parish church of St Peter and St Paul, founded in the 12th century, became the Cathedral Church of the Diocese of Sheffield in 1914. The Roman Catholic Cathedral Church of St Marie (founded 1847) was created Cathedral for the new diocese of Hallam in 1980. Parts of the present building date from *c*.1435. The principal buildings are the Town Hall (1897, 1923 and 1977), the Cutlers' Hall (1832), the University (1905 and recent extensions, including 19-storey Arts Tower), City Hall (1932), Graves Art Gallery (1934), Mappin Art Gallery and the Crucible Theatre. The restored 19th century Lyceum theatre opened in 1990.

Sheffield was created a city in 1893 and in 1974 retained its city status.

Master Cutler (1993-4) of the Company of Cutlers in Hallamshire, Derrick Willingham

SOUTHAMPTON

Southampton is the leading British deep-sea port on the Channel and is situated on one of the finest natural harbours in the world. The first Charter was granted by Henry II and Southampton was created a county of itself in 1447. In 1964 it was granted city status by Royal Charter.

There were Roman and Saxon settlements on the site of the city, which has been an important port since the time of the Conquest due to its natural deep-water harbour. The oldest church is St Michael's (1070) which has a black tournai marble font and an unusually tall spire built in the 18th century as a landmark for navigators of Southampton Water. Other buildings and monuments within the city walls are the Tudor House, God's House Tower, Bargate Museum, the Tudor Merchants Hall, the Weigh-house, West Gate, King John's House, Long House, Wool House, the ruins of Holy Rood Church, St Julien's Church and the Mayflower Memorial. The medieval town walls, built for artillery, are among the most complete in Europe. Public open spaces total over 1,000 acres in extent and comprise 9 per cent of the city's area. The Common covers an area of 328 acres in the central district of the city and is mostly natural parkland.

STOKE-ON-TRENT

Stoke-on-Trent (Staffordshire), standing on the River Trent and familiarly known as The Potteries, is the main centre of employment for the population of North Staffordshire. The city is the largest clayware producer in the world (china, earthenware, sanitary goods, refractories, bricks and tiles) and has a considerable coal mining output drawn from one of the richest coalfields in western Europe. The city has steelworks, foundries, chemical works, engineering plants, rubber works, paper mills, and a very wide range of manufactures. Extensive reconstruction has been carried on in recent years.

The city was formed by the federation in 1910 of the separate municipal authorities of Tunstall, Burslem, Hanley, Stoke, Fenton, and Longton, all of which are now combined in the present City of Stoke-on-Trent.

WINCHESTER

Winchester, the ancient capital of England, is situated on the River Itchen. The city is rich in architecture of all types but the Cathedral takes pride of place. The longest Gothic cathedral in the world, it was built in 1079-93 and exhibits examples of Norman, Early English and Perpendicular styles. Winchester College, founded in 1382, is one of the most famous public schools, the original building (of 1393) remaining largely unaltered. St Cross Hospital, another great medieval foundation, lies one mile south of the city. The almshouses were founded in 1136 by Bishop Henry de Blois, and Cardinal Henry Beaufort added a new almshouse of 'Noble Poverty' in 1446. The chapel and dwellings are of great architectural interest, and visitors may still receive the 'Wayfarer's Dole' of bread and ale.

Recent excavations have done much to clarify the origins and development of Winchester. Part of the forum and several of the streets of the Roman town have been discovered; and excavations in the Cathedral Close have uncovered the entire site of the Anglo-Saxon cathedral (known as the Old Minster) and parts of the New Minster, built by Alfred's son Edward the Elder and the burial place of the Alfredian dynasty. The original burial place of St Swithun, before his remains were translated to a site in the present cathedral, was also uncovered.

Excavations in other parts of the city have thrown much light on Norman Winchester, notably on the site of the Royal Castle, adjacent to which the new Law Courts have been built, and in the grounds of Wolvesey Castle, where the great house built by Bishops Giffard and Henry de Blois in the 12th century has been uncovered. The Great Hall, built by Henry III between 1222 and 1236 survives. It houses the Arthurian Round Table.

YORK

The city of York (North Yorkshire) is an archiepiscopal seat. Its recorded history dates from AD 71, when the Roman Ninth Legion established a base under Petilius Cerealis which later became the fortress of *Eburacum.* In Anglo-Saxon times the city was the royal and ecclesiastical centre of Northumbria, and after capture by a Viking army in AD 866 it became the capital of the Viking kingdom of Jorvik. By the 14th century the city had become a great mercantile centre, mainly owing to its control of the wool trade, and was used as the chief base against the Scots. Under the Tudors its fortunes declined, though Henry VIII made it the headquarters of the Council of the North. Recent excavations on many sites, including Coppergate, have greatly expanded knowledge of Roman, Viking and medieval urban life.

With its development as a railway centre in the 19th century the commercial life of York expanded. The principal industries are the manufacture of chocolate, railway coaches, scientific instruments, and sugar. It is the location of several government departments.

The city is rich in examples of architecture of all periods. The earliest church was built in AD 627 and, in the 12th to 15th centuries, the present Minster was built in a succession of styles. Other examples within the city are the medieval city walls and gateways, churches and guildhalls. Domestic architecture includes the Georgian mansions of The Mount, Micklegate and Bootham. Its museums include York Castle Museum, the National Railway Museum and the Jorvik Viking Centre.

English Counties and Shires

LORD LIEUTENANTS AND HIGH SHERIFFS

County/Shire	Lord Lieutenant	High Sheriff, 1993–4
Avon	Sir John Wills, Bt., TD	H. H. Bayntun-Coward
Bedfordshire	S. C. Whitbread	E. Fountain, OBE
Berkshire	J. R. Henderson, CVO, OBE	Maj. T. C. Gore
Buckinghamshire	Cdr. the Hon. J. T. Fremantle	D. V. Palmer
Cambridgeshire	J. G. P. Crowden	The Hon. Lady Hastings
Cheshire	W. Bromley-Davenport	The Hon. R. H. Cornwall-Legh
Cleveland	The Lord Gisborough	D. Manners
Cornwall	The Viscount Falmouth	R. J. Gilbert
Cumbria	Maj. Sir Charles Graham, Bt.	Mrs M. H. Washington
Derbyshire	Col. Sir Peter Hilton, KCVO, MC	R. H. Turner
Devon	Lt.-Col. the Earl of Morley	Sir John Boles, MBE
Dorset	The Lord Digby	R. G. G. de Pelet
Durham	D. J. Grant, CBE	Mrs E. A. Jennings
East Sussex	Adm. Sir Lindsay Bryson, KCB	A. K. Stewart-Roberts
Essex	The Lord Braybrooke	C. S. Gosling
Gloucestershire	H. W. G. Elwes	C. G. M. Lloyd-Baker
Greater London	Field Marshal the Lord Bramall, GCB, OBE, MC	A. C. Everett, OBE
Greater Manchester	Col. J. B. Timmins, OBE, TD	L. D. Lawton
Hampshire	Lt.-Col. Sir James Scott, Bt.	C. N. Wilson
Hereford and Worcester	Capt. T. R. Dunne	S. Webb
Hertfordshire	S. A. Bowes Lyon	F. E. Harvey
Humberside	R. A. Bethell	P. W. Barker, CBE
Isle of Wight	*The Lord Mottistone, CBE	D. B. B. Cheverton, OBE
Kent	The Lord Kingsdown, PC	Hon. R. Dennison-Pender
Lancashire	S. Towneley	Col. R. R. Craik, OBE, TD
Leicestershire	T. G. M. Brooks	R. H. Murray-Philipson
Lincolnshire	Capt. Sir Henry N. Nevile, KCVO	A. G. Jarvis
Merseyside	vacant	Cdre R. H. Walker
Norfolk	T. J. Colman	R. E. Buscall
Northamptonshire	J. L. Lowther, CBE	J. G. Church
Northumberland	The Viscount Ridley, KG, TD	R. Errington
North Yorkshire	Sir Marcus Worsley, Bt.	M. D. Abrahams, MBE
Nottinghamshire	Sir Andrew Buchanan, Bt.	Mrs J. L. Mortensen
Oxfordshire	Sir Ashley Ponsonby, Bt., KCVO, MC	Sir David Black, Bt.
Shropshire	J. R. S. Dugdale	Capt. R. M. Gabb
Somerset	Col. Sir Walter Luttrell, KCVO, MC	The Hon. J. H. Jolliffe
South Yorkshire	J. H. Neill, CBE, TD	C. S. Barker
Staffordshire	J. A. Hawley, TD	C. H. Mitchell
Suffolk	Sir Joshua Rowley, Bt.	C. J. H. Gurney
Surrey	R. E. Thornton, OBE	Rear-Adm. Sir Peter Anson, Bt., CB
Tyne and Wear	Sir Ralph Carr-Ellison, TD	Sir David Chapman, Bt.
Warwickshire	Capt. the Viscount Daventry	D. C. Wasdell
West Midlands	The Earl of Aylesford	J. I. Westwood
West Sussex	The Duke of Richmond and Gordon	R. H. Goring
West Yorkshire	J. Lyles	G. F. Armitage
Wiltshire	Field Marshal Sir Roland Gibbs, GCB, CBE, DSO, MC	Lt.-Gen. Sir Maurice Johnston, KCB, OBE

* Lord Lieutenant and Governor

COUNTY COUNCILS: Area, Population, Finance

Council	Administrative headquarters	Area (hectares)	Population 1991	Total demand upon collection fund 1993
Avon	Avon House North, St James Barton, Bristol	134,628	962,000	£158,000,000
Bedfordshire	County Hall, Bedford	123,468	534,200	349,276,000
Berkshire	Shire Hall, Reading	125,901	752,500	124,853,000
Buckinghamshire	County Hall, Aylesbury	188,279	640,200	104,300,000
Cambridgeshire	Shire Hall, Cambridge	340,181	669,900	94,507,000
Cheshire	County Hall, Chester	233,325	966,400	165,860,256
Cleveland	Municipal Buildings, Middlesbrough	59,079	557,500	78,948,287
Cornwall	County Hall, Truro	356,442*	475,200	74,807,000
Cumbria	The Courts, Carlisle	682,451	489,700	80,638,000
Derbyshire	County Offices, Matlock	263,098	939,700	150,448,263
Devon	County Hall, Exeter	671,096	1,040,000	594,058,743
Dorset	County Hall, Dorchester	265,433	662,900	107,242,800
Durham	County Hall, Durham	243,369	604,300	76,801,000
East Sussex	Pelham House, St Andrews Lane, Lewes	179,530	716,500	113,826,000
Essex	County Hall, Chelmsford	367,167	1,548,800	229,324,000
Gloucestershire	Shire Hall, Gloucester	264,270	538,700	84,226,000
Hampshire	The Castle, Winchester	378,022	1,578,700	916,000,000
Hereford and Worcester	County Hall, Worcester	392,650	686,000	101,442,107
Hertfordshire	County Hall, Hertford	163,601	989,500	162,612,000
Humberside	County Hall, Beverley, N. Humberside	351,256	874,500	266,000,000
Isle of Wight	County Hall, Newport, IOW	38,063	126,600	21,072,626
Kent	County Hall, Maidstone	373,063	1,538,800	233,000,000
Lancashire	County Hall, Preston	306,957	1,408,300	219,567,974
Leicestershire	County Hall, Leicester	255,297	890,800	114,978,900
Lincolnshire	County Offices, Lincoln	591,791	592,600	82,355,560
Norfolk	County Hall, Norwich	537,482	759,400	110,225,196
Northamptonshire	County Hall, Northampton	236,721	587,100	77,822,400
Northumberland	County Hall, Morpeth	503,165	307,100	47,000,000
North Yorkshire	County Hall, Northallerton	831,236	720,800	108,500,000
Nottinghamshire	County Hall, Nottingham	216,090	1,015,400	151,611,000
Oxfordshire	County Hall, Oxford	260,798	579,600	93,800,000
Shropshire	The Shirehall, Shrewsbury	349,013	412,600	59,346,000
Somerset	County Hall, Taunton	345,233	469,400	75,449,200
Staffordshire	County Buildings, Stafford	271,616	1,047,400	135,344,200
Suffolk	County Hall, Ipswich	379,664	661,900	484,000,000
Surrey	County Hall, Kingston upon Thames	167,924	1,035,500	181,000,000
Warwickshire	Shire Hall, Warwick	198,052	489,900	82,832,315
West Sussex	County Hall, Chichester	198,935	713,600	385,700,000
Wiltshire	County Hall, Trowbridge	347,883	575,100	90,135,000

* Including Isles of Scilly

THE ISLES OF SCILLY

The islands of the Scillies group are administered by the Council of the Isles of Scilly, a 21-member non-political body, which combines the powers and duties of a county council and a district council under the Local Government Act 1972 and the Isles of Scilly Orders 1978. Legislation is specifically applied to the Isles of Scilly by Special Order. The Council is responsible for education, fire services, highways, planning, social services, water, and the airport. The police service is administered by the Devon and Cornwall Police Authority, of which the Council is a member. The Isles are part of the St Ives electoral division.

Administrative Headquarters, Town Hall, St Mary's, Isles of Scilly TR21 0LW

Chairman of the Council, J. P. Greenlaw

Clerk and Chief Executive, P. S. Hygate

Chief Technical Officer, B. M. Lowen

COUNTY COUNCILS: Officers and Chairman

Council	Chief Executive	County Treasurer	Chairman of County Council
Avon	B. D. Smith	D. G. Morgan	T. Walker
Bedfordshire	D. Cleggett	‡B. Phelps	A. Brewer
Berkshire	A. J. Allen	vacant	R. J. Day
Buckinghamshire	C. M. Garrett	J. Beckerlegg	C. F. Robinson
Cambridgeshire	A. G. Lister	‡D. Earle	C. Bradford
Cheshire	M. E. Pitt	J. E. H. Whiteoak	P. Walker
Cleveland	B. Stevenson	†P. Riley	E. Wood
Cornwall	G. K. Burgess	S. F. Nicol	P. B. Locks, CBE
Cumbria	J. E. Burnet	R. F. Mather	R. Strike
Derbyshire	*J. S. Raine	P. Swaby	J. McKay
Devon	R. D. Clark	J. Glasby	D. W. Lentell
Dorset	P. K. Harvey	A. P. Peel	Mrs P. A. Hymers
Durham	°K. W. Smith	J. Kirkby	J. Mackintosh
East Sussex	R. M. Beechey	J. Davies	D. Bellotti
Essex	R. W. Adcock, CBE	K. D. Neale	Mrs B. A. Barton
Gloucestershire	M. Honey	J. R. Cockroft	F. R. Thompson
Hampshire	A. R. Hodgson	J. E. Scotford	J. Maynard
Hereford and Worcester	J. W. Turnbull	P. Middleborough	J. W. Wardle, MBE
Hertfordshire	B. Briscoe	‡W. D. Ogley	M. D. Colne
Humberside	J. A. Parkes	‡G. T. Southern	D. Rose
Isle of Wight	J. S. Horsnell	J. B. W. Proctor	Mrs V. A. Anderson
Kent	P. R. Sabin	‡P. Martin	B. Clark
Lancashire	G. A. Johnson	B. G. Aldred	H. Caunce
Leicestershire	D. Prince	R. Hale	D. Lucas
Lincolnshire	R. J. D. Procter	M. Spink	R. Rainsforth
Norfolk	B. J. Capon, CBE	R. D. Summers	J. F. B. Donaldson
Northamptonshire	A. J. Greenwell, CBE	‡R. Paver	Mrs E. M. Dicks
Northumberland	K. Morris	‡K. Morris	W. E. Ashbridge
North Yorkshire	R. A. Leyland	D. Martin	F. Robson
Nottinghamshire	M. T. Lyons	R. Latham	Mrs N. Smedley
Oxfordshire	J. Harwood	C. Gray	J. E. Jones
Shropshire	A. Barnish	N. Pursey	G. Raxster
Somerset	B. M. Tanner	C. N. Bilsland	C. Clarke
Staffordshire	B. A. Price	R. G. Tettenborn	J. O'Leary
Suffolk	P. F. Bye	P. B. Atkinson	Maj. L. A. Henniker
Surrey	D. J. Thomas	R. Wolstenholme	Mrs C. Gerard
Warwickshire	I. G. Caulfield	S. R. Freer	J. Haynes
West Sussex	B. Fieldhouse	D. P. Rigg	C. Robinson
Wiltshire	I. A. Browning	‡D. Chalker	Mrs P. Rugg

* County Director
° Principal Executive Officer
‡ Director of Finance
† County Finance Officer

Metropolitan Councils

SMALL CAPITALS denote CITY status

Council	Population 1991	Band D charge 1993	Chief Executive	Mayor (a) Lord Mayor 1993-4
Greater Manchester	2,561,600			
Bolton	262,900	£594.12	B. Collinge	C. Benjamin
Bury	179,100	607.81	D. J. Burton	G. Sharkey
MANCHESTER	432,700	738.00	A. Sandford	(a) W. Risby
Oldham	219,700	621.00	C. Smith	B. J. Mather
Rochdale	205,200	664.90	J. F. D. Pierce	A. Bagnall
SALFORD	227,400	706.87	J. C. Willis	R. Heron
Stockport	288,100	646.11	A. L. Wilson	B. P. Harrison
Tameside	220,000	698.40	M. Greenwood	A. E. Hatton
Trafford	216,000	513.00	W. A. Lewis	R. E. Crosbie
Wigan	310,500	650.00	S. M. Jones	J. Clarke
Merseyside	1,441,000			
Knowsley	154,500	654.99	D. G. Henshaw	G. Bundred, CBE
LIVERPOOL	474,600	725.20	P. Bounds	(a) M. Black
St Helens	180,800	612.32	Mrs C. A. Hudson	J. Molyneux
Sefton	295,100	618.78	G. J. Haywood	G. H. Mann
Wirral	336,100	690.15	A. White	P. Corcoran
South Yorkshire	1,292,700			
Barnsley	224,200	595.94	J. A. Edwards, OBE	G. Hadfield
Doncaster	293,600	577.46	J. P. Hale	J. Quinn
Rotherham	254,700	686.34	J. Bell	C. A. Kelly
SHEFFIELD	520,300	639.90	Mrs P. Gordon	(a) Q. Hussain
Tyne and Wear	1,125,500			
Gateshead	203,100	693.00	L. N. Elton	S. Henderson
NEWCASTLE UPON TYNE	273,300	791.81	G. N. Cook	(a) J. M. Lamb
North Tyneside	195,400	706.90	*B. Drew	K. Conroy
			*J. Foster	
			*V. Gallant	
			*C. Roberts	
			*D. Wright	
South Tyneside	157,200	654.66	S. Clark	T. A. Bamford
SUNDERLAND	296,300	600.01	C. Sinclair	(a) B. Charlton
West Midlands	2,619,000			
BIRMINGHAM	994,500	657.00	R. M. W. Taylor	(a) P. Tilsley
COVENTRY	306,300	685.80	I. Roxburgh	(a) A. Boyd
Dudley	309,200	582.99	A. V. Astling	Miss M. Whitehouse
Sandwell	295,100	611.43	F. N. Summers	G. I. Wyton
Solihull	201,400	510.00	J. Scampion	P. Llewellyn
Walsall	263,400	591.48	D. C. Winchurch	E. Moorman
Wolverhampton	249,200	554.40	N. H. Perry, PH.D.	R. F. Whitehouse
West Yorkshire	2,066,200			
BRADFORD	468,700	517.65	R. Penn	(a) R. Sowman
Calderdale	194,100	613.02	M. Ellison	A. D. J. Mazey
Kirklees	381,200	627.00	R. V. Hughes	J. Mernagh
LEEDS	706,300	599.65	J. P. Smith	(a) K. Loudon
WAKEFIELD	315,900	635.84	R. Mather	H. Clark

* Lead Officer

Non-Metropolitan Councils

SMALL CAPITALS denote CITY status
§ denotes Borough status

Council	Population 1991	Band D charge 1993	Chief Executive	Chairman 1993–4 (a) Mayor (b) Lord Mayor
Adur, West Sussex	58,900	£575.74	F. M. G. Staden	Mrs S. Bucknall
Allerdale, Cumbria	96,700	573.66	*C. J. Hart	(a) J. E. Fryer
Alnwick, Northumberland	30,600	621.01	L. St Ruth	Mrs S. E. Bolam
§Amber Valley, Derbyshire	112,800	585.72	P. M. Carney	(a) C. Cutting
Arun, West Sussex	131,500	505.87	I. Sumnall	G. E. Bird
Ashfield, Nottinghamshire	109,700	586.54	S. Beedham	D. Shooter
§Ashford, Kent	93,800	487.15	E. H. W. Mexter	(a) G. H. Turner
Aylesbury Vale, Bucks.	148,300	480.20	B. J. Quoroll	W. G. Lapham
Babergh, Suffolk	80,600	450.75	D. C. Bishop	C. M. Spence
§Barrow-in-Furness, Cumbria	73,700	696.48	T. O. Campbell (acting)	(a) D. H. Edwards
Basildon, Essex	162,400	656.73	°J. C. Rosser	T. G. Leask
§Basingstoke and Deane, Hants.	146,300	434.49	D. W. Pilkington, RD	(a) K. J. Brant
Bassetlaw, Notts.	105,200	597.82	M. S. Havenham	B. Yeoman
BATH, Avon	84,600	510.31	N. C. Abbott	(a) Mrs E. H. Bradley
§Berwick-upon-Tweed, Northumberland	26,900	579.72	E. D. Cawthorn	(a) P. Herdman
§Beverley, Humberside	113,600	601.42	M. Rice	(a) T. B. Pearson
Blaby, Leics.	83,500	479.96	†E. Hemsley	A. C. M. Pullen
§Blackburn, Lancs.	137,800	620.65	G. L. Davies	(a) P. N. Browne
§Blackpool, Lancs.	150,100	649.53	D. Wardman	(a) J. L. Preston
§Blyth Valley, Northumberland	80,300	676.14	D. Crawford	(a) R. B. Anderson
Bolsover, Derbys.	71,300	611.64	J. R. Fotherby	R. Brooks
§Boothferry, Humberside	64,800	558.79	J. W. Barber	(a) M. Deneley
§Boston, Lincs.	53,700	524.27	I. Ward	(a) K. Dobson
§Bournemouth, Dorset	159,100	504.00	D. Newell	(a) R. Whittaker
§Bracknell Forest, Berks.	98,500	519.16	A. J. Targett	(a) Mrs I. Mattick
Braintree, Essex	119,800	513.57	C. R. Daybell	M. F. Hall
Breckland, Norfolk	108,600	485.27	R. Garnett	D. R. M. Sanyer
Brentwood, Essex	70,900	500.58	C. P. Sivell	(a) L. Bottomley
Bridgnorth, Salop	50,800	524.98	A. L. Bain	M. G. Pate
§Brighton, East Sussex	153,900	535.91	G. Jones	(a) D. Lepper
BRISTOL, Avon	392,600	699.11	M. Robinson	(b) J. Channon
Broadland, Norfolk	107,400	505.89	J. H. Bryant	H. Bowyer
Bromsgrove, Hereford and Worcs.	92,300	503.54	R. P. Bradshaw	M. J. Scanlan
§Broxbourne, Herts.	82,400	527.86	M. J. Walker	(a) K. G. Holliday, DFC
§Broxtowe, Notts.	108,800	557.55	M. Brown	(a) Mrs L. Ball
§Burnley, Lancs.	92,100	627.59	R. Ellis	(a) J. Greenwood
CAMBRIDGE	105,700	575.05	R. Hammond	(a) A. Maceachern
Cannock Chase, Staffs.	90,000	567.65	M. G. Kemp	C. H. Harris
CANTERBURY, Kent	130,700	542.86	C. Gay	(b) R. Ruston
Caradon, Cornwall	77,500	556.54	J. Neal	B. E. de St Paër-Gotch
CARLISLE, Cumbria	102,000	618.16	R. S. Brackley	(a) Miss J. Prewitt
Carrick, Cornwall	84,000	558.47	P. M. Talbot	D. C. Hancock
§Castle Morpeth, Northumberland	50,300	641.35	P. Wilson	(a) G. M. Green
§Castle Point, Essex	87,200	624.66	B. Rollinson	Mrs E. V. M. Wood
§Charnwood, Leics.	147,900	552.86	S. M. Peatfield	R. J. Shepherd
§Chelmsford, Essex	154,400	527.22	R. M. C. Hartley	(a) C. J. C. Kingsley
§Cheltenham, Glos.	107,700	588.01	C. Nye	(a) R. Wilson
Cherwell, Oxon.	125,700	500.67	G. J. Handley	N. A. Matthews
CHESTER, Cheshire	118,300	606.26	P. F. Durham	(b) M. Byatt
§Chesterfield, Derbyshire	100,300	624.94	D. R. Shaw	(a) G. A. Wright
Chester-le-Street, Co. Durham	53,200	574.33	J. A. Greensmith	M. G. Briscoe
Chichester, West Sussex	103,100	447.89	C. E. Evans	Capt. S. A. Stuart, CBE
Chiltern, Bucks.	89,900	532.33	D. G. Sainsbury	A. Dibbo
§Chorley, Lancs.	97,100	613.00	J. W. Davies	(a) D. E. Simkin

* General Manager
° Town Manager
† Finance and General Manager

Council	Population 1991	Band D charge 1993	Chief Executive	Chairman 1993-4 (a) Mayor (b) Lord Mayor
§Christchurch, Dorset	41,300	£491.20	C. H. Dewsnap	(a) Mrs J. J. Payne
§Cleethorpes, Humberside	69,800	666.12	P. Daniel	(a) K. M. Bradley
§Colchester, Essex	146,600	531.76	J. Cobley	(a) I. Truster
§Congleton, Cheshire	85,300	575.28	Miss C. L. Pointer	(a) G. Baxendale
§Copeland, Cumbria	72,000	600.00	R. G. Smith	(a) C. Blair
Corby, Northants.	53,600	522.21	T. Simmons	(a) R. Telfer
Cotswold, Glos.	75,200	586.48	D. A. Sketchley	Mrs M. F. Brown
Craven, North Yorks.	50,800	498.67	††H. H. Crabtree	Mrs V. M. Cutter
§Crawley, West Sussex	88,700	544.36	M. D. Sander	(a) A. G. Nickson
§Crewe and Nantwich, Cheshire	105,300	601.20	A. Wenham	(a) R. Ellwood
§Dacorum, Herts.	133,900	510.02	K. Hunt	(a) Mrs Appleby
§Darlington, Co. Durham	100,000	588.35	H. R. C. Owen	(a) E. A. Richmond
§Dartford, Kent	81,000	525.17	C. R. Shepherd	(a) Mrs A. Allen
Daventry, Northants.	63,200	479.58	R. J. Symons, RD	C. J. Over
DERBY	222,500	582.50	R. H. Cowlishaw	(a) R. Wood
Derbyshire Dales	67,900	602.21	D. Wheatcroft	Mrs P. V. Edwards, MBE
Derwentside, Co. Durham	87,000	702.54	N. F. Johnson	E. Coulson
Dover, Kent	105,700	532.72	J. P. Moir, TD	R. R. Chesterfield
DURHAM	86,000	552.12	C. G. Firmin	(a) M. Cranthorne
Easington, Co. Durham	99,000	633.21	*P. Innes	J. Goodwin
§Eastbourne, East Sussex	85,200	591.40	Dr M. Blanch	A. E. Leggett
East Cambridgeshire	61,300	456.33	T. T. G. Hardy	L. W. Neal
East Devon	118,700	497.34	F. J. Vallender	F. A. C. Pinney, OBE
East Dorset	79,300	514.84	A. Breakwell	Mrs P. H. Batstone
East Hampshire	104,700	469.15	B. P. Roynon	S. M. E. Halstead
East Hertfordshire	118,000	514.97	R. J. Bailey	R. J. F. Tucker
§Eastleigh, Hants.	107,100	478.48	C. Tapp	(a) M. Kyrle
East Lindsey, Lincs.	118,800	469.51	‡P. Haigh	R. F. Dickinson
East Northamptonshire	69,000	468.40	R. K. Heath	H. E. Gregory
East Staffordshire	98,500	434.22	F. W. Saunders	G. Callister
§East Yorkshire, Humberside	85,400	558.00	J. H. Gibson	(a) J. Ireland
Eden, Cumbria	46,000	589.45	I. W. Bruce	E. S. C. Woolf
§Ellesmere Port and Neston, Cheshire	81,500	616.14	S. Ewbank	(a) J. A. Sherlock
§Elmbridge, Surrey	114,700	600.15	D. W. L. Jenkins	(a) D. A. S. Brooke
Epping Forest, Essex	117,100	517.69	J. Burgess	W. A. G. Easton, OBE
§Epsom and Ewell, Surrey	68,000	524.85	D. J. Smith	(a) H. H. Upton
§Erewash, Derbyshire	107,400	726.00	R. M. Fletcher	(a) Mrs M. E. Henshaw
EXETER, Devon	104,700	543.44	B. Frowd	(a) M. J. Rich
§Fareham, Hants.	100,600	443.97	A. A. Davies	(a) Mrs D. Burton-Jenkins
Fenland, Cambs.	75,600	511.86	N. R. Topliss	A. R. German
Forest Heath, Suffolk	65,300	460.19	S. W. Catchpole	W. J. Bishop
Forest of Dean, Glos.	76,200	619.00	‡R. A. Willis	B. W. Hobman
§Fylde, Lancs.	72,600	594.94	J. P. Johnson	(a) Miss J. Wilding
§Gedling, Notts.	111,100	590.13	W. Brown	(a) Mrs E. M. Hindle
§Gillingham, Kent	96,600	504.86	J. A. McBride	(a) K. Webber
§Glanford, Humberside	72,400	603.98	D. D. H. Cameron	(a) K. Vickers
GLOUCESTER	103,600	526.69	G. Garbett	(a) Mrs E. Hedge
§Gosport, Hants.	77,200	492.36	M. S. Friend	(a) M. G. Russell
§Gravesham, Kent	93,800	475.78	E. V. J. Seager	(a) F. J. Eve
§Great Grimsby, Humberside	91,800	685.00	R. S. G. Bennett	(a) S. J. Norton
§Great Yarmouth, Norfolk	89,000	519.20	vacant	(a) C. Burrows
§Guildford, Surrey	126,900	543.38	D. T. Watts	(a) R. Marks
§Halton, Cheshire	124,700	645.00	M. Cuff	(a) J. Pimblett
Hambleton, North Yorks.	80,200	435.00	C. Spencer	R. G. Horner
Harborough, Leics.	68,200	569.87	B. B. Bowen (acting)	J. Shaw
Harlow, Essex	75,500	724.56	*D. Byrne	H. Talbot
§Harrogate, North Yorks.	146,300	579.00	P. M. Walsh	(a) R. M. Whitfield
Hart, Hants.	81,700	438.10	G. R. Jelbart	P. Carr
§Hartlepool, Cleveland	91,400	655.05	B. J. Dinsdale	(a) B. Smith
§Hastings, East Sussex	83,700	536.37	R. A. Carrier	(a) R. Stevens

* General Manager
‡ Director of Central Services
†† Head of Paid Service

Council	Population 1991	Band D charge 1993	Chief Executive	Chairman 1993–4 (a) Mayor (b) Lord Mayor
§Havant, Hants.	120,600	£512.28	D. E. Ridley	(a) Mrs J. Carruthers
HEREFORD	51,300	497.50	C. E. S. Willis	(a) R. E. G. Alford
§Hertsmere, Hertfordshire	88,900	537.22	†P. Copland	(a) A. R. Gattward
§High Peak, Derbyshire	86,000	602.19	R. P. H. Brady	(a) J. Francis
§Hinckley and Bosworth, Leics.	97,200	427.44	vacant	(a) Mrs A. Wainwright
§Holderness, Humberside	51,400	590.13	A. Johnson	(a) F. J. Gledhill
Horsham, West Sussex	110,400	460.63	M. J. Pearson	G. Godwin
§Hove, East Sussex	90,000	525.20	J. P. Teasdale	(a) P. B. Martin
Huntingdonshire, Cambs.	149,600	422.29	T. J. Gee	Mrs J. Day
§Hyndburn, Lancs.	79,000	633.96	M. J. Wedgeworth	(a) Mrs S. M. Bramley-Haworth
§Ipswich, Suffolk	118,800	632.43	J. D. Hehir	(a) Mrs M. D. Alderton
Kennet, Wilts.	70,400	490.67	P. L. Owens	D. J. Godwin
Kerrier, Cornwall	89,400	572.24	G. G. Cox	G. J. J. Stephens
§Kettering, Northants.	77,000	515.70	P. S. Williams	(a) C. J. Groome
§King's Lynn and West Norfolk	132,300	495.47	A. E. Pask	(a) C. A. Matkin
KINGSTON UPON HULL, Humberside	262,900	633.81	D. Stephenson	(b) L. Harvey
§Kingswood, Avon	90,600	582.43	A. Smith	(a) C. A. Rickards
LANCASTER, Lancs.	130,300	615.45	W. Pearson	(a) Mrs J. Taylor
§Langbaurgh-on-Tees, Cleveland	146,400	528.31	K. Abigail	(a) V. Teesdale
LEICESTER	280,500	650.89	I. Farookhi	(b) H. Dundhy
Leominster, Hereford and Worcs.	40,000	505.67	G. R. Chilton	Mrs G. Wright
Lewes, East Sussex	88,700	540.57	J. N. Crawford	Mrs A. D. G. Stiles
Lichfield, Staffs.	93,500	507.80	J. T. Thompson	M. B. Hession
LINCOLN	83,600	525.22	C. J. Thomas	(a) W. Crumblehulme
§Luton, Beds.	174,600	511.77	J. C. Southwell	(a) Mrs J. Fensome
§Macclesfield, Cheshire	151,500	584.51	B. W. Longden	(a) C. H. T. Cleaver
§Maidstone, Kent	137,700	541.09	J. D. Makepeace	(a) P. Oldham
Maldon, Essex	53,000	508.74	E. A. P. Plumridge	F. Delderfield
Malvern Hills, Hereford and Worcs.	89,200	540.63	M. J. Jones	D. J. Young
Mansfield, Notts.	101,600	677.59	R. P. Goad	Mrs F. Spate
§Medina, Isle of Wight	72,100	536.38	*J. Sprake	(a) Mrs R. Hames
§Melton, Leics.	45,600	480.14	°P. J. G. Herrick	(a) M. C. R. Graham
Mendip, Somerset	97,900	541.61	G. Jeffs	W. Mackay
Mid Bedfordshire	113,300	511.43	C. A. Tucker	Mrs C. M. Barnes
Mid Devon	65,300	533.81	M. I. R. Bull	Mrs M. E. Turner
§Middlesbrough, Cleveland	144,500	637.22	J. R. Foster	(a) Mrs I. Berryman
Mid Suffolk	79,600	482.73	H. McFarlane	Air Cdre. J. B. Wellingham
Mid Sussex	122,700	496.24	B. J. Grimshaw	W. E. Knighton
§Milton Keynes, Bucks.	178,800	580.03	M. J. Murray	(a) L. B. Hostler
Mole Valley, Surrey	79,800	517.35	A. A. Huggins	H. M. Sewill
Newark and Sherwood, Notts.	103,700	630.63	†R. G. Dix	T. P. Crewe
Newbury, Berks.	139,900	520.00	P. E. McMahon	K. H. Lock
§Newcastle under Lyme, Staffs.	122,100	543.62	D. F. Hill	(a) Mrs E. Ashley, OBE
New Forest, Hants.	162,200	464.45	P. A. D. Hyde	Mrs J. K. Vernon-Jackson, MBE
§Northampton	184,400	541.80	R. J. B. Morris	(a) A. Howes
Northavon, Avon	132,900	585.41	F. Maude	R. M. McGurk
§North Bedfordshire	137,400	505.42	L. W. Gould	(a) D. A. Jones
North Cornwall	74,400	521.40	D. H. Westwell	K. F. White
North Devon	85,700	450.32	R. D. Hall	M. J. Edmunds
North Dorset	54,100	443.95	A. J. Bridgeman	B. R. Clarke
North East Derbyshire	98,700	632.20	Mrs C. A. Gilbey	Mrs T. M. Lide
North Hertfordshire	113,200	517.84	S. Philp	R. S. Flatman
North Kesteven, Lincs.	81,400	500.00	S. Lamb	T. E. Ball, MBE
North Norfolk	92,600	495.11	T. V. Nolan	P. D. Blaxell
North Shropshire	54,000	545.57	K. Flood	Mrs S. Lewis
§North Warwickshire	61,300	643.72	D. Monks	(a) P. F. Morson
North West Leicestershire	81,400	487.06	J. E. White	D. T. Williamson
North Wiltshire	114,600	498.47	H. Miles	A. S. R. Jackson

* General Manager
† Managing Director
° Clerk

Council	Population 1991	Band D charge 1993	Chief Executive	Chairman 1993-4 (a) Mayor (b) Lord Mayor
NORWICH, Norfolk	125,200	£595.61	J. R. Packer	(b) R. Durrant
NOTTINGHAM	276,000	630.56	E. F. Cantle	(b) M. Ibrahim
§Nuneaton and Bedworth, Warwicks.	118,100	658.37	‡‡J. Walton	(a) M. Kedwards
§Oadby and Wigston, Leics.	53,100	534.78	Mrs R. E. Hyde	(a) M. Griffiths
§Oswestry, Shropshire	34,600	529.55	D. A. Towers	(a) W. S. Keable
OXFORD	127,600	587.79	R. S. Block	(b) J. G. Power
§Pendle, Lancs.	85,700	652.55	S. Barnes	(a) R. Clarkson
Penwith, Cornwall	60,000	551.99	‡M. J. Furneaux	T. A. Harvey
PETERBOROUGH, Cambs.	155,200	531.73	W. E. Samuel	(a) Mrs K. Coppen
PLYMOUTH, Devon	254,500	565.02	Mrs A. Stone	(b) J. Richards
§Poole, Dorset	135,400	481.50	J. W. Brooks	(a) B. R. V. Grant-Braham
PORTSMOUTH, Hants.	185,200	454.95	N. Gurney	(b) A. M. Bentley
§Preston, Lancs.	129,900	651.82	G. Driver	(a) K. J. Hudson
Purbeck, Dorset	43,400	468.51	P. B. Croft	D. B. Humphry
§Reading, Berks.	134,600	607.76	Ms S. Pierce	(a) R. Sohpal
§Redditch, Hereford and Worcs.	78,900	558.75	Ms S. Manzie	(a) K. L. Somner
§Reigate and Banstead, Surrey	119,000	554.11	M. Bacon	(a) N. Spiers
§Restormel, Cornwall	88,000	541.79	D. Brown	(a) G. H. Netherton
§Ribble Valley, Lancs.	52,100	597.22	O. Hopkins	(a) T. Jackson
Richmondshire, North Yorks.	46,200	492.49	H. Tabiner	K. Jones
ROCHESTER UPON MEDWAY, Kent	147,100	498.00	R. I. Gregory	(a) R. D. Cox
Rochford, Essex	75,900	497.34	P. W. Hughes	T. Fawell
§Rossendale, Lancs.	66,100	668.61	J. S. Hartley	(a) G. Atkinson
Rother, East Sussex	83,200	541.44	D. F. Powell	G. A. Swift
§Rugby, Warwicks.	86,000	590.35	J. S. R. Lawton	(a) Mrs C. A. Lane
§Runnymede, Surrey	74,900	470.00	T. N. Williams	(a) Mrs E. W. Meany
§Rushcliffe, Notts.	99,300	569.95	J. Saxton	(a) E. J. Bonham
§Rushmoor, Hants.	86,000	455.05	R. Upton	(a) T. R. Davies
Rutland, Leics.	33,400	517.27	K. R. Emslie	P. R. Holloway
Ryedale, North Yorks.	92,000	480.38	M. Walker	K. J. R. Binks
ST ALBANS, Herts.	126,900	644.51	E. A. Hackford	(a) Mrs S. Burton
§St Edmundsbury, Suffolk	93,100	499.47	G. R. N. Toft	(a) E. G. Spooner
Salisbury, Wilts.	107,900	474.38	D. R. J. Rawlinson	W. R. Moss
§Scarborough, North Yorks.	109,600	495.00	J. M. Trebble	(a) E. W. Dixon
§Scunthorpe, Humberside	62,500	653.23	I. M. Hutchinson	(a) Mrs C. Pearson
Sedgefield, Co. Durham	91,500	561.49	A. J. Roberts	G. Ferguson
Sedgemoor, Somerset	99,400	532.99	A. G. Lovell	P. H. Daniel
Selby, North Yorks.	92,500	490.00	J. C. Edwards	J. W. Bramall
Sevenoaks, Kent	109,600	527.00	B. C. Cova, MBE	M. H. L. Whitehouse
Shepway, Kent	93,800	560.86	R. J. Thompson	P. Rossiter
§Shrewsbury and Atcham	92,800	520.66	D. Bradbury	(a) L. N. Morris
§Slough, Berks.	102,400	468.00	°A. Bhattacharya	(a) Mrs S. Thorpe
SOUTHAMPTON, Hants.	204,500	500.00	E. A. Urquhart	(a) J. Martin
South Bedfordshire	109,900	543.88	T. D. Rix	Mrs E. A. Luckhurst-Matthews
South Bucks.	62,600	502.63	C. Furness	Prof. C. A. Hogarth
South Cambridgeshire	122,500	442.93	J. S. Ballantyne	E. W. Bullman
South Derbyshire	72,900	587.40	T. Day	G. S. Knight
§Southend-on-Sea, Essex	162,900	516.72	°D. Moulson	(a) J. Tobin
South Hams, Devon	78,700	493.10	F. G. Palmer	D. J. Andrews
South Herefordshire	52,400	484.34	A. Hughes	E. R. Vines
South Holland, Lincs.	67,900	504.31	C. J. Simpkins	Mrs A. M. Newton
South Kesteven, Lincs.	110,200	499.50	K. R. Cann	R. Briggs
South Lakeland, Cumbria	99,300	608.29	°A. F. Winstanley	Mrs E. M. Braithwaite
South Norfolk	104,100	484.82	A. G. T. Kellett	Mrs K. Rogers
South Northamptonshire	71,600	537.32	K. Whitehead	F. Pinny
South Oxfordshire	120,800	539.98	R. Watson	Mrs E. A. Ducker
§South Ribble, Lancs.	102,900	602.46	J. B. R. Leadbetter	(a) J. C. Hughes
South Shropshire	38,700	511.59	G. C. Biggs	J. McCormick

° Clerk
‡‡ Borough Manager
‡Director of Central Services

Council	Population 1991	Band D charge 1993	Chief Executive	Chairman 1993–4 (a) Mayor (b) Lord Mayor
South Somerset	144,000	£539.90	M. Usher	R. Madelin
South Staffordshire	106,400	434.22	L. Barnfild	B. R. Edwards
§South Wight, IOW	54,500	547.10	D. W. Jaggar	(a) Mrs A. E. Cardew
§Spelthorne, Surrey	91,400	528.43	M. B. Taylor	(a) G. Paterson-Borland
§Stafford	120,300	508.26	°J. K. M. Krawiec	(a) A. B. Compton
Staffordshire Moorlands	96,000	553.25	A. W. Law	A. R. Williamson
§Stevenage, Herts.	76,000	605.83	H. L. Miller	(a) R. A. Clark
§Stockton-on-Tees, Cleveland	175,300	628.54	°F. F. Theobalds	(a) J. Vaughan
STOKE-ON-TRENT, Staffs.	249,700	562.05	B. Smith	(b) Mrs M. Beckett
Stratford-upon-Avon, Warwicks.	106,200	562.66	I. B. Prosser	J. W. Sharp
Stroud, Glos.	104,700	615.22	R. M. Ollin	Mrs S. M. Bruce
Suffolk Coastal	116,000	479.16	T. K. Griffin	K. R. Burnett
§Surrey Heath	80,200	527.91	N. M. Pughe	(a) D. A. V. Martell
§Swale, Kent	116,900	487.57	W. Croydon, CBE	(a) B. Austen
§Tamworth, Staffs.	70,900	507.24	G. Morrell	(a) B. D. Jenkins
Tandridge, Surrey	77,600	540.88	P. J. D. Thomas	M. J. Kelly
§Taunton Deane, Somerset	95,900	489.33	*Mrs S. Douglas	(a) T. G. Smith
Teesdale, Co. Durham	24,500	464.84	C. E. Fell	E. T. Scott
Teignbridge, Devon	110,200	542.13	P. B. Young	K. A. Beer
Tendring, Essex	127,200	530.63	D. Mitchell-Gears	J. Hewitt
§Test Valley, Hants.	103,400	444.56	G. Blythe	(a) G. E. King
§Tewkesbury, Glos.	71,500	458.53	R. A. Wheeler	(a) D. M. M. Davies
§Thamesdown, Wilts.	173,000	561.10	D. M. Kent	(a) G. D. Dart
Thanet, Kent	127,300	526.16	I. G. Gill	Mrs M. Mortlock
Three Rivers, Herts.	79,600	562.14	A. Robertson	T. Palmer
§Thurrock, Essex	129,600	549.51	K. Barnes	(a) P. Rice
§Tonbridge and Malling, Kent	102,700	528.30	T. Thompson	(a) Mrs M. Cole
§Torbay, Devon	122,800	567.00	D. P. Hudson	(a) B. Spencer
Torridge, Devon	53,200	515.71	R. K. Brasington	Mrs P. D. Biggs
§Tunbridge Wells, Kent	102,200	536.02	R. J. Stone	(a) Mrs A. Sturley
Tynedale, Northumberland	57,500	610.12	A. Baty	A. Rubery
Uttlesford, Essex	66,200	507.46	K. Ivory	J. A. Wright
Vale of White Horse, Oxon.	113,200	510.34	D. J. Heavens	K. H. Davies
§Vale Royal, Cheshire	114,700	611.26	W. R. T. Woods	(a) J. S. Chesworth
Wansbeck, Northumberland	61,500	691.99	A. G. White	J. Smith
Wansdyke, Avon	80,800	616.81	*P. May	D. Hamblin
§Warrington, Cheshire	185,100	575.88	M. I. M. Sanders	(a) J. Taylor
Warwick	118,200	575.00	J. V. Picking	A. W. Boxley
§Watford, Herts.	75,800	570.65	D. Plank	M. Jackson
Waveney, Suffolk	108,500	493.02	M. Berridge	J. Reynolds
§Waverley, Surrey	116,100	536.00	G. W. Nuttall	(a) Mrs C. Savage
Wealden, East Sussex	132,000	548.50	D. R. Holness	P. Clifford
Wear Valley, Co. Durham	63,400	628.10	†Mrs E. M. Ashness	H. Russell
§Wellingborough, Northants.	68,500	244.71	W. B. Veal	(a) A. W. Robertson
Welwyn Hatfield, Herts.	94,900	587.70	D. Riddle	F. Matthews
§West Devon	46,200	521.14	J. S. Ligo	(a) R. B. Tait
West Dorset	87,500	503.63	R. C. Rennison	Mrs J. D. Cockerill
West Lancashire	109,100	609.75	B. A. Knight	B. Gannaway-James
West Lindsey, Lincs.	77,000	522.12	R. W. Nelsey	Mrs J. E. Tilney-Bassett
West Oxfordshire	92,400	491.47	N. J. B. Robson	C. R. M. Fox
West Somerset	32,200	495.10	C. Rockall	N. Edwards
West Wiltshire	109,200	517.80	D. G. Latham	J. B. Wesley
§Weymouth and Portland, Dorset	62,800	535.46	M. N. Ashby	(a) A. Martindale
WINCHESTER, Hants.	99,300	432.37	D. H. Cowan	(a) Mrs S. Glasspool
§Windsor and Maidenhead, Berks.	135,100	499.50	G. B. Blacker	(a) M. Scott
§Woking, Surrey	87,200	532.11	P. Russell	(a) Mrs R. Sharpley
Wokingham, Berks.	141,800	550.39	N. B. J. Gurney	G. Parkinson
Woodspring, Avon	180,500	599.60	C. A. Stephens	Mrs J. W. B. Young
WORCESTER	83,900	550.51	††D. Wareing	(a) Mrs H. S. License
§Worthing, West Sussex	98,200	523.23	M. J. Ball	(a) P. Bennett
Wrekin, Shropshire	141,700	629.54	D. G. Hutchinson	Mrs J. Noel

* General Manager
† Director of Administration
° Clerk
††Head of Paid Service

Council	Population 1991	Band D charge 1993	Chief Executive	Chairman 1993–4 (a) Mayor (b) Lord Mayor
Wychavon, Hereford and Worcs.	102,400	£498.94	T. Du Sautoy	P. Coley
Wycombe, Bucks.	160,500	510.11	R. J. Cummins	(a) D. Morris
§Wyre, Lancs.	103,300	601.41	M. Brown	(a) Mrs S. Preston
Wyre Forest, Hereford and Worcs.	95,700	547.49	A. S. Dick	J. L. Gordon
YORK, North Yorks.	103,300	516.29	J. Cairns	(b) Mrs A. Reid

The Cinque Ports

As their name implies, the Cinque Ports were originally five in number: Hastings, New Romney, Hythe, Dover and Sandwich. They were formed during the eleventh century to defend the Channel coast and, after the Norman Conquest, were recognized as a Confederation by a charter of 1278. The "antient towns" of Winchelsea and Rye were added at some time after the Conquest. The other members of the Confederation, known as Limbs, are Lydd, Faversham, Folkestone, Deal, Tenterden, Margate and Ramsgate.

Until 1855 the duty of the Cinque Ports was to provide ships and men for the defence of the state in return for considerable privileges, such as tax exemptions and the framing of by-laws. Of these privileges only jurisdiction in Admiralty remains.

The Barons of the Cinque Ports have the ancient privilege of attending the Coronation ceremony and are allotted special places in Westminster Abbey.

Lord Warden of the Cinque Ports, HM Queen Elizabeth the Queen Mother

Judge, Court of Admiralty, G. Darling, RD, QC

Registrar, I. G. Gill, LVO, PO Box 9, Margate, Kent CT9 1XZ. Tel: 0843-225511

LORD WARDENS OF THE CINQUE PORTS *since* 1904

The Marquess Curzon	1904
The Prince of Wales	1905
The Earl Brassey	1908
The Earl Beauchamp	1913
The Marquess of Reading	1934
The Marquess of Willingdon	1936
Winston Churchill	1941
Sir Robert Menzies	1965
HM Queen Elizabeth the Queen Mother	1978

Roman Names of English Towns and Cities

Bath	*Aquae Sulis*	Leicester	*Ratae Corieltauvorum*
Canterbury	*Durovernum Cantiacorum*	Lincoln	*Lindum*
Carlisle	*Luguvalium*	London	*Londinium*
Chelmsford	*Caesaromagus*	Manchester	*Mamucium*
Chester	*Deva*	Newcastle upon Tyne	*Pons Aelius*
Chichester	*Noviomagus Regnensium*	Pevensey	*Anderetium*
Cirencester	*Corinium Dobunnorum*	Rochester	*Durobrivae*
Colchester	*Camulodunum*	St Albans	*Verulamium*
Doncaster	*Danum*	Salisbury (Old Sarum)	*Sorviodunum*
Dorchester	*Durnovaria*	Silchester	*Calleva Atrebatum*
Dover	*Dubris*	Winchester	*Venta Belgarum*
Exeter	*Isca Dumnoniorum*	Wroxeter	*Viroconium Cornoviorum*
Gloucester	*Glevum*	York	*Eburacum*

London

THE CORPORATION OF LONDON
(see also page 531)

The City of London is the historic centre at the heart of London known as 'the square mile' around which the vast metropolis has grown over the centuries. The City's residential population is 4,100 (1991 Census). The civic government is carried on by the Corporation of the City of London through the Court of Common Council.

The City is the financial and business centre of London and includes the head offices of the principal banks, insurance companies and mercantile houses, in addition to buildings ranging from the historic interest of the Roman Wall and the 15th century Guildhall, to the massive splendour of St Paul's Cathedral and the architectural beauty of Wren's spires.

The City of London was described by Tacitus in AD 62 as 'a busy emporium for trade and traders'. Under the Romans it became an important administration centre and hub of the road system. Little is known of London in Saxon times, when it formed part of the kingdom of the East Saxons. In 886 Alfred recovered London from the Danes and reconstituted it a burgh under his son-in-law. In 1066 the citizens submitted to William the Conqueror who in 1067 granted them a charter, which is still preserved, establishing them in the rights and privileges they had hitherto enjoyed.

THE MAYORALTY

The Mayoralty was probably established about 1189, the first Mayor being Henry Fitz Ailwyn who filled the office for 23 years and was succeeded by Fitz Alan (1212–14). A new charter was granted by King John in 1215, directing the Mayor to be chosen annually, which has ever since been done, though in early times the same individual often held the office more than once. A familiar instance is that of 'Whittington, thrice Lord Mayor of London' (in reality four times, 1397, 1398, 1406, 1419); and many modern cases have occurred. The earliest instance of the phrase 'Lord Mayor' in English is in 1414. It was used more generally in the latter part of the 15th century and became invariable from 1535 onwards. At Michaelmas the liverymen in Common Hall choose two Aldermen who have served the office of Sheriff for presentation to the Court of Aldermen, and one is chosen to be Lord Mayor for the following mayoral year.

LORD MAYOR'S DAY

The Lord Mayor of London was previously elected on the feast of St Simon and St Jude (28 October), and from the time of Edward I, at least, was presented to the King or to the Barons of the Exchequer on the following day, unless that day was a Sunday. The day of election was altered to 16 October in 1346, and after some further changes was fixed for Michaelmas Day in 1546, but the ceremonies of admittance and swearing-in of the Lord Mayor continued to take place on 28 and 29 October respectively until 1751. In 1752, at the reform of the calendar, the Lord Mayor was continued in office until 8 November, the 'New Style' equivalent of 28 October. The Lord Mayor is now presented to the Lord Chief Justice at the Royal Courts of Justice on the second Saturday in November to make the final declaration of office, having been sworn in at Guildhall on the preceding day. The procession to the Royal Courts of Justice is popularly known as the Lord Mayor's Show.

REPRESENTATIVES

Aldermen are mentioned in the 11th century and their office is of Saxon origin. They were elected annually between 1377 and 1394, when an Act of Parliament of Richard II directed them to be chosen for life.

The Common Council, elected annually on the first Friday in December, was, at an early date, substituted for a popular assembly called the Folkmote. At first only two representatives were sent from each ward, but the number has since been greatly increased.

OFFICERS

Sheriffs were Saxon officers; their predecessors were the wic-reeves and portreeves of London and Middlesex. At first they were officers of the Crown, and were named by the Barons of the Exchequer; but Henry I (in 1132) gave the citizens permission to choose their own Sheriffs, and the annual election of Sheriffs became fully operative under King John's charter of 1199. The citizens lost this privilege, as far as the election of the Sheriff of Middlesex was concerned, by the Local Government Act 1888; but the liverymen continue to choose two Sheriffs of the City of London, who are appointed on Midsummer Day and take office at Michaelmas.

The office of Chamberlain is an ancient one, the first contemporary record of which is 1237. The Town Clerk (or Common Clerk) is mentioned in 1274.

ACTIVITIES

The work of the Corporation is assigned to a number of committees which present reports to the Court of Common Council. These Committees are: City Lands and Bridge House Estates, Policy and Resources, Finance, Planning and Communications, Central Markets, Billingsgate and Leadenhall Markets, Spitalfields Market, Police, Port and City of London Health and Social Services, Libraries, Art Galleries and Records, Boards of Governors of Schools, Music and Drama (Guildhall School of Music and Drama), Establishment, Housing, Gresham (City side), Hampstead Heath Management, Epping Forest and Open Spaces, West Ham Park, Privileges, Barbican Residential and Barbican Centre (Barbican Arts and Conference Centre).

The City's estate, in the possession of which the Corporation of London differs from other municipalities, is managed by the City Lands and Bridge House Estates Committee, the chairmanship of which carries with it the title of Chief Commoner. Chairman (1993), C. D. Woodward, OBE.

The Honourable the Irish Society (The Irish Chamber, Guildhall, London EC2P 2EJ. Clerk, S. J. Murrells), which manages the Corporation's estates in Ulster, consists of a Governor and five other Aldermen, the Recorder, and 19 Common Councilmen, of whom one is elected Deputy Governor.

THE LORD MAYOR 1992–3*

The Rt. Hon. the Lord Mayor (1992-3), Sir Francis McWilliams, GBE

Secretary, Air Vice-Marshal M. Dicken, CB

THE SHERIFFS 1993–4

L. J. Chalstrey (Alderman, Vintry) and J. M. B. Gotch; elected, 8 July 1993; assumed office, 28 September 1993

OFFICERS

Town Clerk, S. Jones, apptd 1991
Chamberlain, B. P. Harty, apptd 1983

* The Lord Mayor for 1993-4 was elected on Michaelmas Day. See Stop-press

THE ALDERMEN

Name and Ward	CC	Ald.	Shff.	Lord Mayor
Cdr. Sir Robin Gillett, Bt., GBE, RD, *Bassishaw*	1965	1969	1973	1976
Sir Peter Gadsden, GBE, *Farringdon Wt.*	1969	1971	1970	1979
Sir Christopher Leaver, GBE, *Dowgate*	1973	1974	1979	1981
Sir Alan Traill, GBE, *Langbourn*	1970	1975	1982	1984
Sir David Rowe-Ham, GBE, *Bridge*	—	1976	1984	1986
Sir Greville Spratt, GBE, TD, *Castle Baynard*	—	1978	1984	1987
Sir Christopher Collett, GBE, *Broad Street*	1973	1979	1985	1988
Sir Hugh Bidwell, GBE, *Billingsgate*	—	1979	1986	1989
Sir Alexander Graham, GBE, *Queenhithe*	1978	1979	1986	1990
Sir Brian Jenkins, GBE, *Cordwainer*	—	1980	1987	1991
Sir Francis McWilliams, GBE, *Aldersgate*	1978	1980	1988	1992

All the above have passed the Civic Chair

Paul Newall, TD, *Walbrook*	1980	1981	1989
Christopher Walford, *Farringdon Wn.*	—	1982	1990
Neil Young, *Bread Street*	1980	1982	1991
Roger Cork, *Tower*	1978	1983	1992
Bryan Toye, *Lime Street*	—	1983	
Richard Nichols, *Candlewick*	1983	1984	
Peter Bull, *Cheap*	1968	1984	
Sir Peter Levene, KBE, *Portsoken*	1983	1984	
Leonard Chalstrey, *Vintry*	1981	1984	1993
Clive Martin, OBE, TD, *Aldgate*	—	1985	
David Howard, *Cornhill*	1972	1986	
James Oliver, *Bishopsgate*	1980	1987	
Gavyn Arthur, *Cripplegate*	1988	1991	
Robert Finch, *Coleman Street*	—	1992	

THE COMMON COUNCIL OF LONDON

Deputy: Each Common Councilman so described serves as deputy to the Alderman of her/his ward

Angell, E. H. (1991)	*Cripplegate Wt.*
Anstee, N. J. (1987)	*Aldersgate*
Archibald, *Deputy* W. W. (1986)	*Cornhill*
Ballard, K. A., MC (1969)	*Castle Baynard*
Balls, *Deputy* H. D. (1970)	*Cripplegate Wt.*
Barker, J. A. (1981)	*Cripplegate Wt.*
Barnes-Yallowley, H. M. F. (1986)	*Coleman Street*
Beale, M. J. (1979)	*Lime Street*
Bird, J. L. (1977)	*Bridge*
Biroum-Smith, P. L. (1988)	*Dowgate*
Block, S. A. A. (1983)	*Cheap*
Bradshaw, D. J. (1991)	*Cripplegate Wn.*
Bramwell, F. M. (1983)	*Langbourn*
Brewer, D. W. (1992)	*Bassishaw*
Brighton, R. L. (1984)	*Portsoken*
Brooks, W. I. B. (1988)	*Billingsgate*
Brown, *Deputy* D. T. (1971)	*Walbrook*
Cassidy, *Deputy* M. J. (1989)	*Coleman Street*
Catt, B. F. (1982)	*Farringdon Wn.*
Challis, G. H., CBE (1978)	*Langbourn*
Clements, *Deputy* G. E. I. (1960)	*Farringdon Wt.*
Cohen, Mrs C. M. (1986)	*Lime Street*
Cole, Lt.-Col. Sir Colin, KCB, KCVO, TD (1964)	*Castle Baynard*

Collinson, Miss A. H. (1991)	*Farringdon Wt.*
Cope, Dr J. (1963)	*Farringdon Wt.*
Cotgrove, C. B. (1991)	*Lime Street*
Coven, *Deputy* Mrs E. O., CBE (1972)	*Dowgate*
Currie, Miss S. E. M. (1985)	*Cripplegate Wt.*
Daily-Hunt, R. B. (1989)	*Cripplegate*
David, C. P. (1984)	*Aldgate*
Davis, C. B. (1991)	*Bread Street*
de Silva, D., QC (1980)	*Farringdon Wt.*
Dowson, G. R. (1992)	*Cripplegate Wn.*
Dunitz, A. A. (1984)	*Portsoken*
Edwards, R. D. K. (1978)	*Bassishaw*
Eskenzi, A. N. (1970)	*Farringdon Wn.*
Evans, Mrs J. (1975)	*Farringdon Wt.*
Eve, R. A. (1980)	*Cheap*
Everett, K. M. (1984)	*Candlewick*
Falk, F. A., TD (1984)	*Farringdon Wt.*
Farthing, R. B. C. (1981)	*Aldgate*
Fell, J. A. (1982)	*Queenhithe*
FitzGerald, R. C. A. (1981)	*Bread Street*
Floyd-Ewin, *Deputy* Sir David, LVO, OBE (1963)	*Castle Baynard*
Forbes, G. B. (1993)	*Bishopsgate*
Frankenberg, P. B. (1989)	*Cordwainer*
Frappell, *Deputy* C. E. (1973)	*Bread Street*
Fraser, W. B. (1981)	*Vintry*
Frazer, C. M. (1986)	*Farringdon Wt.*
Galloway, A. D. (1981)	*Broad Street*
Ginsburg, S. (1990)	*Bishopsgate*
Gold, R. (1965)	*Castle Baynard*
Gowman, Miss A. (1991)	*Dowgate*
Graves, A. C. (1985)	*Bishopsgate*
Halliday, Mrs P. (1992)	*Walbrook*
Harding, N. H. (1970)	*Farringdon Wn.*
Hardwick, Dr P. B. (1987)	*Aldgate*
Hart, *Deputy* M. G. (1970)	*Bridge*
Haynes, J. E. H. (1986)	*Cornhill*
Henderson, *Deputy* J. S., OBE (1975)	*Langbourn*
Henderson-Begg, M. (1977)	*Coleman Street*
Hill-Smith, A. G. L. (1992)	*Farringdon Wt.*
Holland, *Deputy* J. (1972)	*Aldgate*
Horlock, *Deputy* H. W. S. (1969)	*Farringdon Wn.*
Hughesdon, J. S. (1991)	*Bread Street*
Ide, W. R. (1972)	*Castle Baynard*
Jackson, L. St J. T. (1978)	*Bassishaw*
Jennings, I. G. (1988)	*Cripplegate Wn.*
Keep, Mrs B. (1987)	*Cripplegate Wn.*
Kellett, Mrs M. W. F. (1986)	*Tower*
Kemp, D. L. (1984)	*Coleman Street*
Knowles, S. K. (1984)	*Candlewick*
Langmead, A. D. G., TD (1982)	*Tower*
Langton Way, J. H. (1992)	*Cripplegate Wt.*
Lawrence, D. W. O., TD (1979)	*Bridge*
Lawson, G. C. H. (1971)	*Portsoken*
MacLellan, A. P. W. (1989)	*Walbrook*
McNeil, I. D. (1977)	*Lime Street*
Malins, J. H., QC (1981)	*Farringdon Wt.*
Martin, R. C. (1986)	*Queenhithe*
Mayhew, Miss J. (1986)	*Queenhithe*
Mitchell, C. R. (1971)	*Castle Baynard*
Mizen, *Deputy* D. H. (1979)	*Broad Street*
Mobsby, D. J. L. (1985)	*Billingsgate*
Morgan, *Deputy* B. L., CBE (1963)	*Bishopsgate*
Moss, A. D. (1989)	*Tower*
Nash, *Deputy* Mrs J. C. (1983)	*Aldersgate*
Neary, J. E. (1982)	*Aldgate*
Newman, Mrs P. B. (1989)	*Aldersgate*
Northall-Laurie, P. D. (1975)	*Walbrook*
Owen, Mrs J. (1975)	*Langbourn*
Owen-Ward, J. R. (1983)	*Bridge*

Packard, Brig. J. J. (1972)   *Cripplegate Wn.*
Parmley, A. C. (1992)   *Vintry*
Pembroke, *Deputy* Mrs A. M. F. (1978)   *Cheap*
Ponsonby of Shulbrede, The Lady
   (1981)   *Farringdon Wt.*
Pulman, G. A. G. (1983)   *Tower*
Reed, *Deputy* J. L., MBE (1967)   *Farringdon Wn.*
Revell-Smith, *Deputy* P. A., CBE (1959)   *Vintry*
Rigby, P. P., CBE (1972)   *Farringdon Wn.*
Robinson, Mrs D. C. (1989)   *Bishopsgate*
Rodgers, Miss E. H. L. (1987)   *Vintry*
Roney, *Deputy* E. P. T., CBE (1974)   *Bishopsgate*
Samuel, *Deputy* Mrs I. (1971)   *Portsoken*
Sargant, K. A. (1991)   *Cornhill*
Saunders, *Deputy* R. (1975)   *Candlewick*
Savory, M. B. (1980)   *Broad Street*
Scriven, R. G. (1984)   *Candlewick*
Sellon, S. A., TD, OBE (1990)   *Cordwainer*
Shalit, D. M. (1972)   *Farringdon Wn.*
Sharp, *Deputy* Mrs I. M. (1974)   *Queenhithe*
Sherlock, M. R. C. (1992)   *Dowgate*
Shindler, *Deputy* A. B. (1966)   *Billingsgate*
Simpson, A. S. J. (1987)   *Aldersgate*
Simpson, Mrs S. G. (1992)   *Aldersgate*
Smithers, H. J. (1986)   *Billingsgate*
Snyder, M. J. (1986)   *Cordwainer*
Spanner, J. H., TD (1984)   *Broad Street*
Stitcher, *Deputy* G. M., CBE (1966)   *Farringdon Wt.*
Swan, N. E. B. (1985)   *Coleman Street*
Taylor, J. A. F., TD (1991)   *Bread Street*
Walsh, S. (1989)   *Farringdon Wt.*
White, J. W. (1986)   *Cornhill*
Williams, G. M. E. (1985)   *Aldersgate*
Willoughby, P. J. (1985)   *Bishopsgate*
Wilmot, *Deputy* R. T. D. (1973)   *Cordwainer*
Wilson, A. B., CBE (1984)   *Cheap*
Wixley, G. R. A., TD (1964)   *Bassishaw*
Woodward, *Deputy* C. D., OBE (1971)   *Cripplegate Wn.*
Wooldridge, F. D. (1988)   *Farringdon Wn.*

The City Guilds (Livery Companies)

The constitution of the livery companies has been unchanged for centuries. There are three ranks of membership; freemen, liverymen and assistants. A person can become a freeman by patrimony (through a parent having been a freeman); by servitude (through having served an apprenticeship to a freeman); or by redemption (by purchase).

Election to the livery is the prerogative of the company, who can elect any of its freemen as liverymen. Assistants are usually elected from the livery and form a Court of Assistants which is the governing body of the company. The Master (in some companies called the Prime Warden) is elected annually from the assistants.

As at June 1993, 22,995 liverymen of the guilds were entitled to vote at elections at Common Hall.

The order of precedence, omitting extinct companies, is given in parenthesis after the name of each company in the list below.

THE TWELVE GREAT COMPANIES
In order of civic precedence

MERCERS (*1*). *Hall*, Ironmonger Lane, London EC2V 8HE. *Livery*, 250. *Clerk*, G. M. M. Wakeford. *Master*, F. R. Baden-Powell
GROCERS (*2*). *Hall*, Princes Street, London EC2R 8AD. *Livery*, 305. *Clerk*, C. G. Mattingley, CBE. *Master*, Viscount Glenapp
DRAPERS (*3*). *Hall*, Throgmorton Street, London EC2N 2DQ. *Livery*, 238. *Clerk*, A. L. Lang, MBE. *Master*, R. P. St G. Cazalet
FISHMONGERS (*4*). *Hall*, London Bridge, London EC4R 9EL. *Livery*, 363. *Clerk*, M. R. T. O'Brien. *Prime Warden*, D. T. Young
GOLDSMITHS (*5*). *Hall*, Foster Lane, London EC2V 6BN. *Livery*, 276. *Clerk*, R. D. Buchanan-Dunlop, CBE. *Prime Warden*, Dr A. M. Stirling.
MERCHANT TAYLORS (*6/7*). *Hall*, 30 Threadneedle Street, London EC2R 8AY. *Livery* 317. *Clerk*, Capt. D. A. Wallis, RN. *Master*, Sir Edward Studd, Bt.
SKINNERS (*6/7*). *Hall*, 8 Dowgate Hill, London EC4R 2SP. *Livery*, 370. *Clerk*, Capt. D. H. Dyke, CBE, LVO, RN. *Master*, Sir John Leahy, KCMG
HABERDASHERS (*8*). *Hall*, Staining Lane, London EC2V 7DD. *Livery*, 300. *Clerk*, Capt. M. E. Barrow, DSO, RN. *Master*, B. E. Sturgess
SALTERS (*9*). *Hall*, 4 Fore Street, London EC2Y 5DE. *Livery*, 153. *Clerk*, Col. M. P. Barneby. *Master*, The Lord Porter of Luddenham, OM, FRS
IRONMONGERS (*10*). *Hall*, Shaftesbury Place, Barbican, London EC2Y 8AA. *Livery*, 217. *Clerk*, J. A. Oliver. *Master*, R. B. Brayne, MBE
VINTNERS (*11*). *Hall*, Upper Thames Street, London EC4V 3BJ. *Livery*, 324. *Clerk*, Brig. G. Read, CBE. *Master*, C. de C. P. Paynter
CLOTHWORKERS (*12*). *Hall*, Dunster Court, Mincing Lane, London EC3R 7AH. *Livery*, 185. *Clerk*, M. G. T. Harris. *Master*, G. P. Purefoy

OTHER CITY GUILDS
In alphabetical order

ACTUARIES *(91)*. *Livery*, 175. *Clerk*, P. D. Esslemont, 16A Cadogan Square, London SW1X 0JU. *Master*, A. V. Hall
AIR PILOTS AND AIR NAVIGATORS, GUILD OF *(81)*. *Livery*, 390. *Grand Master*, HRH The Prince Philip, Duke of Edinburgh, KG, KT. *Clerk*, Gp Capt J. W. Tritton, AFC, Cobham House, 291 Gray's Inn Road, London WC1X 8QF. *Master*, Capt. C. E. Elton
APOTHECARIES, SOCIETY OF *(58)*. *Hall*, Black Friars Lane, London EC4V 6EJ. *Livery*, 1,250. *Clerk*, Lt.-Col. R. J. Stringer. *Master*, M. P. Ward, CBE, MD, FRCS
ARBITRATORS *(93)*. *Livery*, 190. *Clerk*, Lt.-Col. I. R. P. Green, 2 Bolts Hill, Castle Camps, Cambs. CB1 6GL. *Master*, A. P. G. Borley
ARMOURERS AND BRASIERS *(22)*. *Hall*, 81 Coleman Street, London EC2R 5BJ. *Livery*, 120. *Clerk*, Lt.-Col. R. R. F. Cowe. *Master*, Brig. G. L. D. Duckworth
BAKERS *(19)*. *Hall*, Harp Lane, London EC3R 6DP. *Livery*, 415. *Clerk (acting)*, J. W. Tompkins. *Master*, H. Gould
BARBERS *(17)*. *Hall*, Monkwell Square, London EC2Y 5BL. *Livery*, 224. *Clerk*, Col. A. B. Harfield, CBE. *Master*, R. J. Pincham, CBE
BASKETMAKERS *(52)*. *Livery*, 430. *Clerk*, A. Gillett, 7 Kinghorn Street, London EC1A 7HT. *Prime Warden*, A. K. Brown, MBE, MB, FRCS
BLACKSMITHS *(40)*. *Livery*, 275. *Clerk*, R. C. Jorden, 27 Cheyne Walk, Grange Park, London N21 1DB. *Prime Warden*, Lt.-Col. D. D. Dennis, OBE
BOWYERS *(38)*. *Livery*, 107. *Clerk*, A. Black, CBE, 2 Serjeant's Inn, Fleet Street, London EC4Y 1LL. *Master*, C. Ballenden
BREWERS *(14)*. *Hall*, Aldermanbury Square, London EC2V 7HR. *Livery*, 130. *Clerk*, C. W. Dallmeyer. *Master*, J. H. Morgan
BRODERERS *(48)*. *Livery*, 156. *Clerk*, P. J. C. Crouch, 11 Bridge Road, East Molesey, Surrey KT8 9EU. *Master*, D. N. Smedley
BUILDERS MERCHANTS *(88)*. *Livery*, 215. *Clerk*, Miss S. Robinson, TD, 14 Charterhouse Square, London EC1M 6AX. *Master*, M. Pares
BUTCHERS *(24)*. *Hall*, 87 Bartholomew Close, London EC1A 7EB. *Livery*, 800. *Clerk*, A. H. Emus. *Master*, F. J. Mallion
CARMEN *(77)*. *Livery*, 447. *Clerk*, Lt.-Col. G. T. Pearce, MBE, 35–37 Ludgate Hill, London EC4M 7JN. *Master*, E. R. Britt
CARPENTERS *(26)*. *Hall*, 1 Throgmorton Avenue, London EC2N 2JJ. *Livery*, 150. *Clerk*, Maj.-Gen. P. T. Stevenson, OBE. *Master*, V. F. Browne
CHARTERED ACCOUNTANTS *(86)*. *Livery*, 345. *Clerk*, G. H. Kingsmill, The Grove, Hinton Parva, Swindon SN4 0DH. *Master*, Mrs B. M. Culverhouse
CHARTERED ARCHITECTS *(98)*. *Livery*, 118. *Clerk*, L. W. Groome, OBE, 5 Claylands Place, London SW8 1NZ. *Master*, B. A. Barker, OBE
CHARTERED SECRETARIES AND ADMINISTRATORS *(87)*. *Livery*, 235. *Hon. Clerk*, G. H. Challis, CBE, St Dunstan's House, Carey Lane, London EC2V 8AA. *Master*, F. J. Bergin
CHARTERED SURVEYORS *(85)*. *Livery*, 340. *Clerk*, Mrs A. L. Jackson, 16 St Mary-at-Hill, London EC3R 8EE. *Master*, A. Gordon-James
CLOCKMAKERS *(61)*. *Livery*, 285. *Hall*, St Dunstan's House, Carey Lane, London EC2V 8AA. *Clerk*, P. H. Gibson, MBE. *Master*, J. N. W. Smith

COACHMAKERS AND COACH-HARNESS MAKERS *(72)*. *Livery*, 400. *Clerk*, Maj. W. H. Wharfe, 149 Banstead Road, Ewell, Epsom, Surrey KT17 3HL. *Master*, P. C. K. O'Ferrall, OBE
CONSTRUCTORS *(99)*. *Livery*, 105. *Clerk*, A. W. J. Appleton, Graves End House, Woodbury, Salterton, Exeter EX5 1PG. *Master*, R. H. Rooley
COOKS *(35)*. *Livery*, 75. *Clerk*, M. C. Thatcher, 35 Great Peter Street, London SW1P 3LR. *Master*, S. J. Herbage
COOPERS *(36)*. *Hall*, 13 Devonshire Square, London EC2M 4TH. *Livery*, 260. *Clerk*, J. A. Newton. *Master*, C. S. Griffin
CORDWAINERS *(27)*. *Livery* 150. *Clerk*, Cdr. C. Shears, CVO, OBE, Eldon Chambers, 30 Fleet Street, London EC4Y 1AA. *Master*, T. M. A. Upfill-Brown
CURRIERS *(29)*. *Livery*, 93. *Clerk*, Gp Capt F. J. Hamilton, Kestrel Cottage, East Knoyle, Salisbury SP3 6AD. *Master*, M. Simmonds
CUTLERS *(18)*. *Hall*, Warwick Lane, London EC4M 7GR. *Livery*, 100. *Clerk*, K. S. G. Hinde, TD. *Master*, P. R. W. Roberts
DISTILLERS *(69)*. *Livery*, 250. *Clerk*, C. V. Hughes, 71 Lincoln's Inn Fields, London WC2A 3JF. *Master*, N. C. Strofton
DYERS *(13)*. *Hall*, Dowgate Hill, London EC4R 2ST. *Livery*, 125. *Clerk*, J. R. Chambers. *Prime Warden*, D. G. Mathieson
ENGINEERS *(94)*. *Livery*, 286. *Clerk*, Cdr. B. D. Gibson, 1 Carlton House Terrace, London SW1Y 5DB. *Master*, G. Clerehugh, OBE
ENVIRONMENTAL CLEANERS *(97)*. *Livery*, 185. *Clerk*, S. J. Holt, Whitethorns, Rannoch Road, Crowborough, E. Sussex TN6 1RA. *Master*, J. A. Howard
FAN MAKERS *(76)*. *Livery*, 216. *Clerk*, Lt.-Col. I. R. P. Green, 2 Bolts Hill, Castle Camps, Cambs. CB1 6GL. *Master*, J. R. P. Hammond
FARMERS *(80)*. *Hall*, 3 Cloth Street, London EC1A 7LD. *Livery*, 278. *Clerk*, vacant. *Master*, A. Tritton
FARRIERS *(55)*. *Livery*, 375. *Clerk*, H. W. H. Ellis, 37 The Uplands, Loughton, Essex IG10 1NQ. *Master*, R. J. D. Thompson
FELTMAKERS *(63)*. *Livery*, 170. *Clerk*, Lt.-Col. C. J. Holroyd, Providence Cottage, Chute Cadley, Andover, Hants. SP11 9EB. *Master*, B. D. S. Burgess
FLETCHERS *(39)*. *Hall*, 3 Cloth Street, London EC1A 7LD. *Livery*, 102. *Clerk*, J. R. Garnett. *Master*, P. L. Whiting
FOUNDERS *(33)*. *Hall*, 1 Cloth Fair, London EC1A 7HT. *Livery*, 170. *Clerk*, A. J. Gillett. *Master*, B. D. Farmer
FRAMEWORK KNITTERS *(64)*. *Livery*, 212. *Clerk*, D. A. Tate, Apothecaries' Hall, Black Friars Lane, London EC4V 6EL. *Master*, R. A. Wessel
FRUITERERS *(45)*. *Livery*, 275. *Clerk*, Cdr. M. T. H. Styles, Denmead Cottage, Chawton, Alton, Hants. GU34 1SB. *Master*, M. C. Wallis
FUELLERS *(95)*. *Livery*, 85. *Clerk*, Wg Cdr. H. F. C. Squire, OBE, 4 Maycross Avenue, Morden, Surrey SM4 4DA. *Master*, Dr P. W. Glover
FURNITURE MAKERS *(83)*. *Livery*, 268. *Clerk*, Wg Cdr. G. Acklam, MBE, 30 Harcourt Street, London W1H 2AA. *Master*, B. Perringe
GARDENERS *(66)*. *Livery*, 243. *Clerk*, Col. N. G. S. Gray, 25 Luke Street, London EC2A 4AR. *Master*, E. M. Upward
GIRDLERS *(23)*. *Hall*, Basinghall Avenue, London EC2V 5DD. *Livery*, 80. *Clerk*, N. Wyldbore-Smith. *Master*, I. W. Fairclough
GLASS-SELLERS *(71)*. *Livery*, 167. *Hon. Clerk*, B. J. Rawles, 43 Aragon Avenue, Thames Ditton, Surrey KT7 0PY. *Master*, P. C. Northam

GLAZIERS AND PAINTERS OF GLASS (53). *Hall*, 9 Montague Close, London SE1 9DD. *Livery*, 281. *Clerk*, P. R. Batchelor. *Master*, N. Burston

GLOVERS (62). *Livery*, 287. *Clerk*, Mrs M. Hood, 71 Ifield Road, London SW10 9AU. *Master*, C. J. Wood

GOLD AND SILVER WYRE DRAWERS (74). *Livery*, 330. *Clerk*, J. R. Williams, 50 Cheyne Avenue, London E18 2DR. *Master*, N. E. B. Swan

GUNMAKERS (73). *Livery*, 269. *Clerk*, F. B. Brandt, The Proof House, 48–50 Commercial Road, London E1 1LP. *Master*, Dr C. Swan, CVO, FSA

HORNERS (54). *Livery*, 290. *Clerk*, S. J. Holt, Whitethorns, Rannoch Road, Crowborough, E. Sussex TN6 1RA. *Master* J. D. Spofforth

INFORMATION TECHNOLOGISTS (100). *Livery*, 225. *Clerk*, R. A. Laidlaw, Epworth House, 25 City Road, London EC1Y 1AA. *Master*, P. R. E. Monson

INNHOLDERS (32). *Hall*, College Street, London EC4R 2SY. *Livery*, 135. *Clerk*, J. R. Edwardes Jones. *Master*, Sir Malcolm Chaplin, CBE

INSURERS (92). *Hall*, 20 Aldermanbury, London EC2V 7HY. *Livery*, 360. *Clerk*, V. D. Webb. *Master*, J. S. Greig

JOINERS AND CEILERS (41). *Livery*, 139. *Clerk*, D. A. Tate, Parkville House, Bridge Street, Pinner, Middx. HA5 3JD. *Master*, W. E. Gale

LAUNDERERS (89). *Hall*, 9 Montague Close, London SE1 9DD. *Livery*, 193. *Clerk*, P. E. Coombe. *Master*, J. G. Crisp

LEATHERSELLERS (15). *Hall*, 15 St Helen's Place, London EC3A 6DQ. *Livery*, 150. *Clerk*, Rear-Adm. P. B. Rowe, CBE, LVO. *Master*, J. G. Curtis

LIGHTMONGERS (96). *Livery*, 122. *Clerk*, S. H. Birch, 53 Leithcote Gardens, London SW16 2UX. *Master*, R. J. Seabrook

LORINERS (57). *Livery*, 380. *Clerk*, J. R. Williams, 50 Cheyne Avenue, London E18 2DR. *Master*, R. C. A. Fitzgerald

MAKERS OF PLAYING CARDS (75). *Livery*, 145. *Clerk*, M. J. Smyth, 6 The Priory, Godstone, Surrey RH9 8NL. *Master*, C. J. F. Latham

MARKETORS (90). *Livery*, 240. *Clerk*, B. F. Catt, 42 Tottenham Lane, London N8 7EA. *Master*, J. A. E. Hathrell, OBE

MASONS (30). *Livery*, 125. *Clerk*, T. F. Ackland, 261 Green Lanes, London N13 4XS. *Master*, R. A. Waters

MASTER MARINERS, HONOURABLE COMPANY OF (78). HQS *Wellington*, Temple Stairs, London WC2R 2PN. *Livery*, 253. *Clerk*, J. A. V. Maddock. *Admiral*, HRH The Duke of Edinburgh, KG, KT. *Master*, Capt. A. D. Braithwaite, RD

MUSICIANS (50). *Livery*, 307. *Clerk*, M. J. G. Fletcher, 1 The Sanctuary, Westminster, London SW1P 3JT. *Master*, J. C. Iles

NEEDLEMAKERS (65). *Livery*, 250. *Clerk*, M. G. Cook, 17 Southampton Place, London WC1A 2EH. *Master*, D. S. Anslow-Wilson

PAINTER-STAINERS (28). *Hall*, 9 Little Trinity Lane, London EC4V 2AD. *Livery*, 380. *Clerk*, Wg Cdr. B. C. Pratt. *Master*, M. L. Giles

PATTENMAKERS (70). *Livery*, 200. *Clerk*, P. Merritt, 25 Wellesley Road, London W4 4BU. *Master*, G. R. A. Andrews

PAVIORS (56). *Livery*, 267. *Clerk*, R. F. Coe, 154 Dukes Avenue, New Malden, Surrey KT3 4HR. *Master*, V. J. Willey

PEWTERERS (16). *Hall*, Oat Lane, London EC2V 7DE. *Livery*, 107. *Clerk*, Maj.-Gen. J. St J. Grey, CB. *Master*, Sir Frank Layfield, QC

PLAISTERERS (46). *Hall*, 1 London Wall, London EC2Y 5JU. *Livery*, 209. *Clerk*, H. Mott. *Master*, G. C. Grover

PLUMBERS (31). *Livery*, 360. *Clerk*, Cdr. A. J. Roberts, OBE, 49 Queen Victoria Street, London EC4N 4SE. *Master*, G. E. Banks

POULTERS (34). *Livery*, 178. *Clerk*, A. W. Scott, 23 Orchard Drive, Chorleywood, Herts. WD3 5QN. *Master*, D. C. Butcher

SADDLERS (25). *Hall*, 40 Gutter Lane, London EC2V 6BR. *Livery*, 70. *Clerk*, K. M. Oliver. *Master*, A. D. G. Welch

SCIENTIFIC INSTRUMENT MAKERS (84). *Hall*, 9 Montague Close, London SE1 9DD. *Livery*, 208. *Clerk*, F. G. Everard. *Master*, D. R. Coleman

SCRIVENERS (44). *Livery*, 146. *Clerk*, H. J. W. Harman, Westminster Bank Chambers, 11 Bridge Road, East Molesey, Surrey KT8 9EU. *Master*, B. J. Ducker

SHIPWRIGHTS (59). *Livery*, 450. *Clerk*, Capt. R. F. Channon, RN, Ironmongers' Hall, Barbican, London EC2Y 8AA. *Permanent Master*, HRH The Duke of Edinburgh, KG, KT. *Prime Warden*, Sir Brian Shaw

SOLICITORS (79). *Livery*, 287. *Clerk*, Miss S. M. Robinson, TD, 14 Charterhouse Square, London EC1M 6AX. *Master*, C. R. Walford

SPECTACLE MAKERS (60). *Livery*, 360. *Clerk*, C. J. Eldridge, Apothecaries' Hall, Black Friars Lane, London EC4V 6EL. *Master*, M. Jalie

STATIONERS AND NEWSPAPER MAKERS (47). *Hall*, Ave Maria Lane, London EC4M 7DD. *Livery*, 450. *Clerk*, Capt. P. Hames, RN. *Master*, P. T. Rippon

TALLOW CHANDLERS (21). *Hall*, 4 Dowgate Hill, London EC4R 2SH. *Livery*, 180. *Clerk*, Brig. W. K. L. Prosser, CBE, MC. *Master*, D. G. Milne, CBE

TIN PLATE WORKERS alias Wire Workers (67). *Livery*, 150. *Clerk*, S. J. Holt, Whitethorns, Rannoch Road, Crowborough, E. Sussex TN6 1RA. *Master*, R. G. Vincent

TOBACCO PIPE MAKERS AND TOBACCO BLENDERS (82). *Livery*, 180. *Clerk*, I. J. Kimmins, Bouverie House, 154 Fleet Street, London EC4A 2HX. *Master*, A. G. Alton

TURNERS (51). *Livery*, 152. *Clerk*, R. G. Woodwark, DSC, 33A Hill Avenue, Amersham, Bucks. HP6 5BX. *Master*, P. F. W. Venn

TYLERS AND BRICKLAYERS (37). *Livery*, 130. *Clerk*, F. A. G. Rider, 6 Martin Lane, Cannon Street, London EC4R 0DP. *Master*, N. H. Carter

UPHOLDERS (49). *Livery*, 200. *Clerk*, W. R. Wallis, Charrington House, The Causeway, Bishop's Stortford CH23 2EW. *Master*, Judge R. Cole

WAX CHANDLERS (20). *Hall*, Gresham Street, London EC2V 7AD. *Livery*, 80. *Clerk*, T. Wood. *Master*, H. R. C. Riches, FRCP

WEAVERS (42). *Livery*, 125. *Clerk*, J. G. Ouvry, 1 The Sanctuary, Westminster, London SW1P 3JT. *Upper Bailiff*, G. E. L. Yeandle

WHEELWRIGHTS (68). *Livery*, 246. *Clerk*, M. R. Francis, Greenup, Milton Avenue, Gerrards Cross, Bucks. SL9 8QW. *Master*, K. A. Wells

WOOLMEN (43). *Livery*, 125. *Clerk*, F. Allen, Hollands, Hedsor Road, Bourne End, Bucks. SL8 5EE. *Master*, R. J. R. Cousins

PARISH CLERKS (No livery). *Members*, 104. *Clerk*, B. J. N. Coombes, 1 Dean Trench Street, London SW1P 3HB. *Master*, L. R. R. Miller

WATERMEN AND LIGHTERMEN (No livery). *Craft Owning Freemen*, 350. *Hall*, 16 St Mary-at-Hill, London EC3R 8EE. *Clerk*, Lt.-Col. C. P. Cameron, MC. *Master*, P. D. T. Roberts

In certain companies the election of Master or Prime Warden for the year does not take place till the autumn. In such cases the Master or Prime Warden for 1992–3 is given.

LONDON BOROUGH COUNCILS

Council	Municipal offices	Population 1991	Band D charge 1993	Chief Executive (*Managing Director)	Mayor (a) Lord Mayor 1993-4
Barking and Dagenham	°Dagenham, RMIO 7BN	145,200	£504.00	W. C. Smith	J. White
Barnet	†The Burroughs, Hendon, NW4 4BG	298,200	549.52	M. M. Caller	V. Lyon
Bexley	‡Bexleyheath, Kent DA6 7LB	218,100	515.00	T. Musgrave	A. W. Charlton
Brent	†Forty Lane, Wembley, HA9 9EZ	247,200	597.60	C. Wood	A. Steel
Bromley	°Bromley, BRI 3UH	293,000	510.00	N. T. Palk	R. Egington
§Camden	†Euston Road, NWI 2RU	177,900	717.54	J. Smith	R. Bhattacharyya
§CITY OF WESTMINSTER	City Hall, Victoria Street, SWIE 6QP	182,400	295.00	*M. C. Montacute	(a) Mrs J. Bianco
Croydon	Taberner House, Park Lane, Croydon CR9 3JS	317,200	515.00	D. Wechsler	P. Hecks
Ealing	°Uxbridge Road, W5 2HL	280,100	570.00	Ms J. Hunt	M. Mallam
Enfield	°Enfield, ENI 3XA	261,500	587.50	Ms M. Arnold	Ms N. Conway
§Greenwich	†Wellington Street, SEI8 6PW	212,000	696.00	C. Roberts	Ms A. Barratt
§Hackney	†Mare Street, E8 IEA	183,500	698.54	J. White	J. Lamb
§Hammersmith and Fulham	†King Street, W6 9JU	152,000	548.74	N. Newton (acting)	Ms J. Caruana
Haringey	°Wood Green, N22 4LE	206,800	726.55	G. Singh	R. Rice
Harrow	°Harrow, HAI 2UH	203,000	553.00	A. G. Redmond	E. W. H. Feakins
Havering	†Romford, RMI 3BD	231,200	535.00	D. R. Bradley	Mrs M. Edwards
Hillingdon	°Uxbridge, UB8 IUW	235,300	525.00	C. Rippingale	G. Booth
Hounslow	°Lampton Road, Hounslow, TW3 4DN	207,700	612.99	R. Kerslake	L. Bawn
§Islington	†Upper Street, NI 2UD	169,600	697.08	E. W. Dear	Ms A. Gilman
§Kensington and Chelsea (RB)	†Hornton Street, W8 7NX	141,300	489.00	R. A. Taylor	D. Harney, OBE
Kingston upon Thames (RB)	Guildhall, Kingston upon Thames KTI IEU	136,800	522.66	T. Hornsby	Ms J. Smith
§Lambeth	†Brixton Hill, SW2 IRW	249,900	629.84	H. Gilby	Ms M. Schumann
§Lewisham	†Catford, SE6 4RU	235,700	515.99	T. Hanafin	S. Mani
Merton	°London Road, Morden, SM4 5DX	170,800	496.81	Ms H. Rabbats	M. de Villiers
Newham	†East Ham, E6 2RP	217,000	599.00	D. Stevenson	Ms J. Reeves
Redbridge	†Ilford, IGI IDD	229,800	525.00	M. J. Frater	R. J. Watts
Richmond upon Thames	°York Street, Twickenham, TWI 3AA	163,400	540.79	R. L. Harbord	Ms G. Mackinney
§Southwark	†Peckham Road, SE5 8UB	222,200	756.00	Ms A. Whyatt	C. Lothian
Sutton	‡St Nicholas Way, Sutton, SMI IEA	170,300	520.74	Ms P. Hughes	F. Sharp
§Tower Hamlets	107 Commercial Street, EI 6BG	165,100	631.55	A. Golding	J. Snooks
Waltham Forest	†Forest Road, Walthamstow, EI7 4JF	216,200	589.50	A. Tobias	N. S. Matharoo
§Wandsworth	†Wandsworth, SWI8 2PU	258,700	145.89	G. K. Jones	M. Johnson

§   Inner London Borough
RB Royal Borough
°   Civic Centre
†   Town Hall
‡   Civic Offices

Wales

POSITION AND EXTENT

The Principality of Wales (Cymru) occupies the extreme west of the central southern portion of the island of Great Britain, with a total area of 8,018 sq. miles (20,766 sq. km): land 7,968 sq. miles (20,636 sq. km); inland water 50 sq. miles (130 sq. km). It is bounded on the north by the Irish Sea, on the south by the Bristol Channel, on the east by the English counties of Cheshire, Shropshire, Hereford and Worcester, and Gloucestershire, and on the west by St George's Channel.

Across the Menai Straits is the Welsh island of Ynys Môn (Anglesey) (276 sq. miles), communication with which is facilitated by the Menai Suspension Bridge (1,000 ft. long) built by Telford in 1826, and by the tubular railway bridge (1,100 ft. long) built by Stephenson in 1850. Holyhead harbour, on Holy Isle (north-west of Anglesey), provides accommodation for ferry services to Dublin (70 miles).

POPULATION

The population at the 1991 Census was 2,811,865 (males 1,356,886; females 1,454,979). The average density of population in 1991 was 1.36 persons per hectare.

RELIEF

Wales is a country of extensive tracts of high plateau and shorter stretches of mountain ranges deeply dissected by river valleys. Lower-lying ground is largely confined to the coastal belt and the lower parts of the valleys. The highest mountains are those of Snowdonia in the north-west (Snowdon, 3,559 ft), Berwyn (Aran Fawddwy, 2,971 ft), Cader Idris (Pen y Gadair, 2,928 ft), Dyfed (Plynlimon, 2,467 ft), and the Black Mountain, Brecon Beacons and Black Forest ranges in the south-east (Carmarthen Van, 2,630 ft, Pen y Fan, 2,906 ft, Waun Fâch, 2,660 ft).

HYDROGRAPHY

The principal river rising in Wales is the Severn (see page 540), which flows from the slopes of Plynlimon to the English border. The Wye (130 miles) also rises in the slopes of Plynlimon. The Usk (56 miles) flows into the Bristol Channel, through Gwent. The Dee (70 miles) rises in Bala Lake and flows through the Vale of Llangollen, where an aqueduct (built by Telford in 1805) carries the Pontcysyllte branch of the Shropshire Union Canal across the valley. The estuary of the Dee is the navigable portion, 14 miles in length and about five miles in breadth, and the tide rushes in with dangerous speed over the 'Sands of Dee'. The Towy (68 miles), Teifi (50 miles), Taff (40 miles), Dovey (30 miles), Taf (25 miles) and Conway (24 miles), the last named broad and navigable, are wholly Welsh rivers.

The largest natural lake in Wales is Bala (Llyn Tegid) in Gwynedd, nearly four miles long and about one mile wide. Lake Vyrnwy is an artificial reservoir, about the size of Bala, and forms the water supply of Liverpool; Birmingham is supplied from a chain of reservoirs in the Elan and Claerwen valleys.

WELSH LANGUAGE

According to the 1991 Census results, the percentage of persons of three years and over able to speak Welsh was:

Clwyd	18.2	Powys	20.2
Dyfed	43.7	S. Glamorgan	6.5
Gwent	2.4	W. Glamorgan	15.0
Gwynedd	61.0		
Mid Glamorgan	8.5	Wales	18.7

FLAG

A red dragon on a field divided white over green (per fess Argent and Vert a dragon passant Gules). The flag was augmented in 1953 by a royal badge on a shield encircled with a riband bearing the words *Ddraig Goch Ddyry Cychwyn* and imperially crowned. Only the unaugmented flag is flown on Government offices in Wales and, where appropriate, in London. Both flags continue to be used elsewhere.

EARLY HISTORY

CELTS AND ROMANS

The earliest inhabitants of whom there is any record appear to have been subdued or exterminated by the Goidels (a people of Celtic race) in the Bronze Age. A further invasion of Celtic Brythons and Belgae followed in the ensuing Iron Age. The Roman conquest of southern Britain and Wales was for some time successfully opposed by Caratacus (Caractacus or Caradog), chieftain of the Catuvellauni and son of Cunobelinus (Cymbeline). South-east Wales was subjugated and the legionary fortress at Caerleon-on-Usk established by about AD 75-77; the conquest of Wales was completed by Agricola about AD 78. Communications were opened up by the construction of military roads from Chester to Caerleon-on-Usk and Caerwent, and from Chester to Conwy (and thence to Carmarthen and Neath). Christianity was introduced during the Roman occupation, in the fourth century.

ANGLO-SAXON ATTACKS

The Anglo-Saxon invaders of southern Britain drove the Celts into the mountain stronghold of Wales, and into Strathclyde (Cumberland and south-west Scotland) and Cornwall, giving them the name of *Waelisc* (Welsh), meaning 'foreign'. The West Saxons' victory of Deorham (AD 577) isolated Wales from Cornwall and the battle of Chester (AD 613) cut off communication with Strathclyde and northern Britain. In the eighth century the boundaries of the Welsh were further restricted by the annexations of Offa, King of Mercia, and counter-attacks were largely prevented by the construction of an artificial boundary from the Dee to the Wye (Offa's Dyke).

In the ninth century Rhodri Mawr (844-878) united the country and successfully resisted further incursions of the Saxons by land and raids of Norse and Danish pirates by sea, but at his death his three provinces of Gwynedd (north), Powys (mid) and Deheubarth (south) were divided among his three sons, Anarawd, Mervyn and Cadell. Cadell's son Hywel Dda ruled a large part of Wales and codified its laws but the provinces were not united again until the rule of Llewelyn ap Seisyllt (husband of the heiress of Gwynedd) from 1018 to 1023.

THE NORMAN CONQUEST

After the Norman conquest of England, William I created palatine counties along the Welsh frontier, and the Norman barons began to make encroachments into Welsh territory. The Welsh princes recovered many of their losses during the civil wars of Stephen's reign and in the early 13th century Owen Gruffydd, prince of Gwynedd, was the dominant figure in Wales. Under Llywelyn ap Iorwerth (1194-1240) the Welsh united in powerful resistance to English incursions and Llywelyn's privileges and *de facto* independence were recognized in Magna Carta. His grandson, Llywelyn ap Gruffydd, was the last native prince; he was killed in 1282 during hostilities between the Welsh and English, allowing Edward I of England to establish his authority over the country. On 7 February 1301, Edward of Caernarvon, son of Edward I, was created Prince of Wales, a title which has subsequently been borne by the eldest son of the sovereign.

Strong Welsh national feeling continued, expressed in the early 15th century in the rising led by Owain Glyndŵr, but the situation was altered by the accession to the English throne in 1485 of Henry VII of the Welsh House of Tudor. Wales was politically assimilated to England under the Act of Union of 1535, which extended English laws to the Principality and gave it parliamentary representation for the first time.

EISTEDDFOD

The Welsh are a distinct nation, with a language and literature of their own, and the national bardic festival (Eisteddfod), instituted by Prince Rhys ap Griffith in 1176, is still held annually (for date, see page 12). These *Eisteddfodau* (sessions) form part of the *Gorsedd* (assembly), which is believed to date from the time of Prydian, a ruling prince in an age many centuries before the Christian era.

PRINCIPAL CITIES

CARDIFF

Cardiff (South Glamorgan), at the mouth of the Rivers Taff, Rhymney and Ely, is the capital city of Wales and one of

Britain's major administrative, commercial and business centres. It has many industries, including steel and cigars, and is a flourishing port with a substantial and varied trade.

There are many fine buildings in the civic centre, including the City Hall, the National Museum of Wales, University Buildings, Law Courts, Welsh Office, County Hall, Police Headquarters and the Temple of Peace and Health. Also in the city are Llandaff Cathedral, the Welsh National Folk Museum at St Fagans, Cardiff Castle, the New Theatre, the Sherman Theatre and the Cardiff College of Music and Drama. New buildings include St David's Hall, a concert and conference hall, and the Welsh National Ice Rink.

SWANSEA

Swansea (*Abertawe*) is a city and a seaport of West Glamorgan. The Gower peninsula was brought within the city boundary under local government reform in 1974. The trade of the port includes coal, steel products, containerized goods and the import and export of petroleum products and petrochemicals.

The principal buildings are the Norman Castle (rebuilt c.1330), the Royal Institution of South Wales, founded in 1835 (including Library), the University College at Singleton, and the Guildhall, containing the Brangwyn panels. New buildings include the Industrial and Maritime Museum, the new Maritime Quarter and Marina and the leisure centre.

Swansea was chartered by the Earl of Warwick, c.1158–84, and further charters were granted by King John, Henry III, Edward II, Edward III and James II, Cromwell (two) and the Marcher Lord William de Breos.

Welsh Counties

LORD LIEUTENANTS AND HIGH SHERIFFS

County	Lord Lieutenant	High Sheriff, 1993-4
Clwyd	Sir William Gladstone, Bt.	P. Cauldfield
Dyfed	D. C. Mansel Lewis	Mrs P. Rooney
Gwent	R. Hanbury-Tenison	S. Boyle
Gwynedd	R. E. Meuric Rees, CBE	Sir Richard Williams-Bulkeley, Bt.
Mid Glamorgan	M. A. McLaggan	B. M. Ladbrooke
Powys	M. L. Bourdillon	A. J. Gibson-Watt
South Glamorgan	Capt. N. Lloyd-Edwards	J. Curteis
West Glamorgan	Lt.-Col. Sir Michael Llewellyn, Bt.	A. Aylesbury, OBE

COUNTY COUNCILS: AREA, POPULATION, FINANCE

Council	Administrative headquarters	Area (hectares)	Population 1991	Total demand upon collection fund 1993
Clwyd	Shire Hall, Mold	243,015	413,700	£41,619,000
Dyfed	County Hall, Carmarthen	576,575	350,800	38,400,000
Gwent	County Hall, Cwmbran	137,652	446,900	35,171,900
Gwynedd	County Offices, Caernarfon	386,331	240,000	23,310,000
Mid Glamorgan	County Hall, Cathays Park, Cardiff	101,749	541,500	36,532,782
Powys	County Hall, Llandrindod Wells	507,716	118,600	11,310,000
South Glamorgan	County Hall, Atlantic Wharf, Cardiff	41,622	405,800	31,576,000
West Glamorgan	County Hall, Swansea	81,960	368,700	34,847,000

566   Local Government

COUNTY COUNCILS: OFFICERS AND CHAIRMAN

Council	Chief Executive *County Clerk	County Treasurer	Chairman of County Council
Clwyd	E. R. Davies	A. Bell	H. O. Clarke
Dyfed	W. J. Phillips	H. Morse	H. Jones
Gwent	M. J. Perry	J. P. Walsh	P. Geraghty
Gwynedd	H. V. Thomas	T. D. Heald	T. I. Morris
Mid Glamorgan	*D. H. Thomas, CBE	L. M. James	L. Lewis
Powys	N. M. Pringle	†J. Wrightson	D. M. J. James
South Glamorgan	B. Davies	K. Bray	D. J. Francies
West Glamorgan	A. G. Corless	°S. G. Dunster	V. C. Alexander

† County Finance Officer
° Director of Finance

District Councils

SMALL CAPITALS denote CITY status
§ denotes Borough status

Council	Population 1991	Band D charge 1993	Chief Executive	Chairman 1993-4 (a) Mayor (b) Lord Mayor
§Aberconwy, Gwynedd	53,900	£335.00	A. G. Carr	(a) Miss E. Jones
Alyn and Deeside, Clwyd	74,500	382.72	D. Salisbury	E. Bagnall
§Arfon, Gwynedd	56,100	315.19	D. L. Jones	(a) H. Jones
§Blaenau Gwent, Gwent	76,900	296.90	R. Leadbeter	(a) M. Mochan
§Brecknock, Powys	41,600	304.99	R. O. Doylend	(a) E. T. Morgan
CARDIFF, South Glamorgan	290,000	289.56	R. E. Paine	(b) V. Riley
Carmarthen, Dyfed	56,100	316.38	R. R. Morgan	J. R. Davies
Ceredigion, Dyfed	66,700	354.00	D. Morgan	H. G. Evans
§Colwyn, Clwyd	56,600	359.44	C. D. Barker	(a) T. Stott
§Cynon Valley, Mid Glamorgan	65,800	285.66	T. B. Roberts	(a) P. M. David
§Delyn, Clwyd	68,300	381.82	P. J. McGreevy	(a) Mrs H. E. D. Jones
§Dinefwr, Dyfed	39,100	340.69	E. W. Harries	(a) D. R. Harris
Dwyfor, Gwynedd	27,200	313.67	E. M. Royles	D. B. Evans
Glyndŵr, Clwyd	42,300	350.30	J. H. Parry	E. C. Edwards
§Islwyn, Gwent	66,900	306.00	B. Bird	(a) S. Jenkins
§Llanelli, Dyfed	75,300	406.32	D. B. Parry-Jones	(a) H. W. Jenkins
§Lliw Valley, West Glamorgan	63,700	351.74	G. C. Sambrook	(a) D. Lewis
Meirionnydd, Gwynedd	33,100	344.86	G. W. Hughes	E. Williams
§Merthyr Tydfil, Mid Glamorgan	59,900	281.30	R. V. Morris	(a) Mrs L. Matthews
§Monmouth, Gwent	76,600	317.40	G. Cummings	(a) A. W. Breeze
Montgomeryshire, Powys	53,200	290.15	N. J. Bardsley	D. R. Jones
§Neath, West Glamorgan	66,000	389.15	S. Penny	(a) K. C. Palmer
§Newport, Gwent	135,500	309.86	R. D. Blair	(a) Mrs J. Jepps
§Ogwr, Mid Glamorgan	133,600	285.04	J. G. Cole	(a) K. F. King
§Port Talbot, West Glamorgan	51,300	351.10	I. K. Lewis	(a) T. P. Crowley
Preseli Pembrokeshire, Dyfed	71,300	327.45	I. W. R. David	W. H. Hitchings
Radnorshire, Powys	24,000	289.64	G. C. Read	L. V. Lewis
§Rhondda, Mid Glamorgan	79,300	280.05	G. Evans	(a) D. Morgan
§Rhuddlan, Clwyd	55,300	367.68	E. O. Lake	(a) P. E. Williams
Rhymney Valley, Mid Glamorgan	104,500	278.66	P. A. Bennett	L. R. Rees
South Pembrokeshire, Dyfed	42,400	309.38	G. H. James	M. Williams
SWANSEA, West Glamorgan	187,700	360.79	A. K. B. Boatswain	(b) W. Dyer
§Taff-Ely, Mid Glamorgan	98,400	288.86	D. Gethin	(a) C. Hughes
§Torfaen, Gwent	91,200	300.30	M. B. Mehta	(a) F. H. Bacon
§Vale of Glamorgan, South Glamorgan	115,800	275.02	M. P. A. Smith	(a) Mrs L. S. Hughes
§Wrexham Maelor, Clwyd	116,700	361.88	R. J. Dutton, CBE	(a) Mrs W. Williams
§Ynys Môn (Isle of Anglesey), Gwynedd	69,800	335.00	E. L. Gibson	(a) J. M. Davies

Scotland

POSITION AND EXTENT

The Kingdom of Scotland occupies the northern portion of the main island of Great Britain and includes the Inner and Outer Hebrides, and the Orkney, Shetland, and many other islands. It lies between 60° 51′ 30″ and 54° 38′ N. latitude and between 1° 45′ 32″ and 6° 14′ W. longitude, with England to the south, the Atlantic Ocean on the north and west, and the North Sea on the east.

The greatest length of the mainland (Cape Wrath to the Mull of Galloway) is 274 miles, and the greatest breadth (Buchan Ness to Applecross) is 154 miles. The customary measurement of the island of Great Britain is from the site of John o' Groats house, near Duncansby Head, Caithness, to Land's End, Cornwall, a total distance of 603 miles in a straight line and approximately 900 miles by road.

The total area of Scotland is 30,420 sq. miles (78,789 sq. km); land 29,767 sq. miles (77,097 sq. km), inland water 653 sq. miles (1,692 sq. km).

POPULATION

The population at the 1991 Census was 4,998,567 (males 2,391,961; females 2,606,606). The average density of the population in 1991 was 0.65 persons per hectare.

RELIEF

There are three natural orographic divisions of Scotland. The southern uplands have their highest points in Merrick (2,766 ft), Rhinns of Kells (2,669 ft), and Cairnsmuir of Carsphairn (2,614 ft), in the west; and the Tweedsmuir Hills in the east (Hartfell 2,651 ft, Dollar Law 2,682 ft, Broad Law 2,756 ft).

The central lowlands, formed by the valleys of the Clyde, Forth and Tay, divide the southern uplands from the northern Highlands, which extend most from the extreme north of the mainland to the central lowlands, and are divided into a northern and a southern system by the Great Glen.

The Grampian Mountains, which entirely cover the southern Highland area, include in the west Ben Nevis (4,406 ft), the highest point in the British Isles, and in the east the Cairngorm Mountains (Cairn Gorm 4,084 ft, Braeriach 4,248 ft, Ben Macdui 4,296 ft). The north-western Highland area contains the mountains of Wester and Easter Ross (Carn Eige 3,880 ft, Sgurr na Lapaich 3,775 ft).

Created, like the central lowlands, by a major geological fault, the Great Glen (60 miles long) runs between Inverness and Fort William, and contains Loch Ness, Loch Oich and Loch Lochy. These are linked to each other and to the north-east and south-west coasts of Scotland by the Caledonian Canal, providing a navigable passage between the Moray Firth and the Inner Hebrides.

HYDROGRAPHY

The western coast of Scotland is fragmented by peninsulas and islands, and indented by fjords (sea-lochs), the longest of which is Loch Fyne (42 miles long) in Argyll. Although the east coast tends to be less fractured and lower, there are several great drowned inlets (firths), e.g. Firth of Forth, Firth of Tay, Moray Firth, as well as the Firth of Clyde in the west.

The lochs are the principal hydrographic feature of Scotland. The largest in Scotland and in Great Britain is Loch Lomond (27 sq. miles), in the Grampian valleys; the longest and deepest is Loch Ness (24 miles long and 800 feet deep), in the Great Glen; and Loch Shin (20 miles long) and Loch Maree in the northern Highlands.

The longest river in Scotland is the Tay (117 miles), noted for its salmon. It flows into the North Sea, with Dundee on the estuary, which is spanned by the Tay Bridge (10,289 ft) opened in 1887 and the Tay Road Bridge (7,365 ft) opened in 1966. Other noted salmon rivers are the Dee (90 miles) which flows into the North Sea at Aberdeen, and the Spey (110 miles), the swiftest flowing river in the British Isles, which flows into Moray Firth. The Tweed, which gave its name to the woollen cloth produced along its banks, marks in the lower stretches of its 96-mile course the border between Scotland and England.

The most important river commercially is the Clyde (106 miles), formed by the junction of the Daer and Portrail water, which flows through the city of Glasgow to the Firth of Clyde. During its course it passes over the picturesque Falls of Clyde, Bonnington Linn (30 ft), Corra Linn (84 ft), Dundaff Linn (10 ft) and Stonebyres Linn (80 ft), above and below Lanark. The Forth (66 miles), upon which stands Edinburgh, the capital, is spanned by the Forth (Railway) Bridge (1890), which is 5,330 feet long, and the Forth (Road) Bridge (1964), which has a total length of 6,156 feet (over water) and a single span of 3,000 feet.

The highest waterfall in Scotland, and the British Isles, is Eas a'Chùal Aluinn with a total height of 658 feet (200 m), which falls from Glas Bheinn in Sutherland. The Falls of Glomach, on a head-stream of the Elchaig in Wester Ross, have a drop of 370 feet.

GAELIC LANGUAGE

According to the 1991 Census, 1.4 per cent of the population of Scotland, mainly in the Highlands and western coastal regions, were able to speak the Scottish form of Gaelic.

FLAG

A white diagonal cross (the cross of St Andrew, the patron saint of Scotland) on a blue field (saltire Argent in a field Azure).

THE SCOTTISH ISLANDS

The Hebrides did not become part of the Kingdom of Scotland until 1266, when they were ceded to Alexander III by Magnus of Norway. Orkney and Shetland fell to the Scottish Crown as a pledge for the unpaid dowry of Margaret of Denmark, wife of James III, in 1468, the Danish claims to suzerainty being relinquished in 1590 when James VI married Anne of Denmark.

ORKNEY

The Orkney Islands (total area 375½ sq. miles) lie about six miles north of the mainland, separated from it by the Pentland Firth. Of the 90 islands and islets (holms and skerries) in the group, about one-third are inhabited.

The total population at the 1981 Census was 19,040; the 1981 populations of the islands shown here include those of smaller islands forming part of the same civil parish.

Mainland, 14,299	Shapinsay, 345
Eday, 154	South Ronaldsay, 1,188
Hoy and Graemsay, 80	Stronsay, 462
Papa Westray, 94	Walls and Flotta, 761
Rousay and Egilsay, 264	Westray, 741
Sanday and North Ronaldsay, 652	

The islands are rich in Pictish and Scandinavian remains, the most notable being the Stone Age village of Skara Brae, the burial chamber of Maeshowe, the many brochs (Pictish towers) and St Magnus Cathedral. Scapa Flow, between the Mainland and Hoy, was the war station of the British Grand Fleet from 1914 to 1919 and the scene of the scuttling of the surrendered German High Seas Fleet (21 June 1919).

Most of the islands are low-lying and fertile, and farming (principally beef cattle) is the main industry. Flotta, to the south of Scapa Flow, is now the site of the oil terminal for the Piper, Claymore and Tartan fields in the North Sea. The capital is Kirkwall (population 6,881) on Mainland.

SHETLAND

The Shetland Islands have a total area of 551 sq. miles and a population at the 1981 Census of 27,271. They lie about 50 miles north of the Orkneys, with Fair Isle about half-way between the two groups. Out Stack, off Muckle Flugga, one mile north of Unst, is the most northerly part of the British Isles (60° 51' 30" N. lat.).

There are over 100 islands, of which 16 are inhabited. Populations at the 1981 census were:

Mainland, 22,184	Muckle Roe, 101
Bressay, 335	Out Skerries, 79
East and West Burra	Papa Stour, 29
and Trondra, 930	Unst, 1,206
Fair Isle, 69	Whalsay, 1,026
Fetlar, 102	Yell, 1,168
Foula, 39	

Shetland's many archaeological sites include Jarlshof, Mousa and Clickhimin, and its long connection with Scandinavia has resulted in a strong Norse influence on its place-names and dialect.

Industries include fishing, knitwear and farming. In addition to the fishing fleet there are fish processing factories, while the traditional handknitting of Fair Isle and Unst is supplemented now with machine-knitted garments. Farming is mainly crofting, with sheep being raised on the moorland and hills of the islands. Latterly the islands have become an important centre of the North Sea oil industry, with pipelines from the Brent and Ninian fields running to the terminal at Sullom Voe, the largest of its kind in Europe. Lerwick is the main centre for supply services for offshore oil exploration and development.

The capital is Lerwick (population 7,901) on Mainland.

THE HEBRIDES

Until the closing years of the 13th century the Hebrides included other Scottish islands in the Firth of Clyde, the peninsula of Kintyre (Argyllshire), the Isle of Man, and the (Irish) Isle of Rathlin. The origin of the name is stated to be the Greek *Eboudai*, latinized as *Hebudes* by Pliny, and corrupted to its present form. The Norwegian name *Sudreyjar* (Southern Islands) was latinized as *Sodorenses*, a name that survives in the Anglican bishopric of Sodor and Man.

There are over 500 islands and islets, of which about 100 are inhabited, though mountainous terrain and extensive peat bogs mean that only a fraction of the total area is under cultivation. Stone, Bronze and Iron Age settlement has left many remains, including those at Callanish on Lewis, and Norse colonization has influenced language, customs and place-names. Occupations include farming (mostly crofting and stock-raising), fishing and the manufacture of tweeds and other woollens. Tourism is also an important factor in the economy.

The Inner Hebrides lie off the west coast of Scotland and relatively close to the mainland. The largest and best-known is Skye (area 643 sq. miles; chief town, Portree), which contains the Cuillin Hills (Sgurr Alasdair 3,257 ft), the Red Hills (Beinn na Caillich 2,403 ft), Bla Bheinn (3,046 ft) and The Storr (2,358 ft). Skye is also famous as the refuge of the Young Pretender in 1746. Other islands in the Highland Region include Raasay (pop. 182), Rum, Eigg and Muck.

Islands in the Strathclyde Region include Arran (pop. 4,726) containing Goat Fell (2,868 ft); Coll and Tiree (pop. 933); Colonsay and Oronsay (pop. 137); Islay (area 235 sq.

miles; pop. 3,997); Jura (area 160 sq. miles; pop. 239) with a range of hills culminating in the Paps of Jura (Beinn-an-Oir, 2,576 ft, and Beinn Chaolais, 2,477 ft); and Mull (area 367 sq. miles; pop. 2,605; chief town Tobermory) containing Ben More (3,171 ft).

The Outer Hebrides, separated from the mainland by the Minch, now form the Western Isles Islands Council area (area 1,119 sq. miles; population at the 1981 Census 31,842). The main islands are Lewis with Harris (area 770 sq. miles, pop. 23,390), whose chief town, Stornoway (pop. 13,409), is the administrative headquarters; North Uist (pop. 1,454); South Uist (pop. 2,223); Benbecula (pop. 1,988) and Barra (pop. 1,232). Other inhabited islands include Bernera (292), Berneray (134), Eriskay (219), Grimsay (206), Scalpay (461) and Vatersay (108).

EARLY HISTORY

PREHISTORIC INHABITANTS

The Picts, believed to be of non-Aryan origin, seem to have inhabited the whole of northern Britain and to have spread over the north of Ireland. Remains are most frequent in Caithness and Sutherland and the Orkney Islands.

Celts arrived from Belgic Gaul during the latter part of the Bronze Age and in the early Iron Age, and except in the extreme north of the mainland and in the islands, the civilization and speech of the people were definitely Celtic at the time of the Roman invasion of Britain.

THE ROMAN INVASION

In AD 79–80 Julius Agricola extended the Roman conquests in Britain by advancing into Caledonia and building a line of fortifications across the isthmus between the Forth and Clyde, but after a victory at Mons Graupius he was recalled. Hadrian's Wall, mostly complete by AD 130, marked the frontier until about AD 143 when the frontier moved north to the Forth–Clyde isthmus and was secured by the Antonine Wall. From about AD 155 the Antonine Wall was damaged by frequent attacks and by the end of the second century the northern limit of Roman Britain had receded to Hadrian's Wall.

THE SCOTS

After the withdrawal or absorption of the Roman garrison of Britain there were many years of tribal warfare between the Picts and Scots (the Gaelic tribe then dominant in Ireland), the Brythonic Waelisc (Welsh) of Strathclyde (south-west Scotland and Cumberland), and the Anglo-Saxons of Lothian. The Waelisc were isolated from their kinsmen in Wales by the victory of the West Saxons at Chester (613), and towards the close of the ninth century the Scots under Kenneth Mac Alpin became the dominant power in Caledonia. In the reign of Malcolm I (943–954) Strathclyde was brought into subjection, the English lowland kingdom (Lothian) being conquered by Malcolm II (1005–1034).

From the late 11th century until the mid 16th century there were constant wars between Scotland and England, the outstanding figures in the struggle being William Wallace, who defeated the English at Stirling Bridge (1297) and Robert Bruce, who won the victory of Bannockburn (1314). James IV and many of his nobles fell at the disastrous battle of Flodden (1513).

THE JACOBITE REVOLTS

In 1603 James VI of Scotland succeeded Elizabeth I on the throne of England (his mother, Mary Queen of Scots, was the great-granddaughter of Henry VII), his successors reigning as sovereigns of Great Britain, although political union of the two countries did not occur until 1707. After the abdication (by flight) in 1688 of James VII and II, the crown devolved upon William III (grandson of Charles I) and Mary (elder daughter of James VII and II). In 1689 Graham of Claverhouse roused the Highlands on behalf of James VII and II, but died after a military success at Killiecrankie.

After the death of Anne (younger daughter of James VII and II), the throne devolved upon George I (great-grandson of James VI and I). In 1715, armed risings on behalf of James Stuart (the Old Pretender) led to the indecisive battle of Sheriffmuir, and the Jacobite movement died down until 1745, when Charles Stuart (the Young Pretender) defeated the Royalist troops at Prestonpans and advanced to Derby (1746). From Derby, the adherents of 'James VIII and III' (the title claimed for his father by Charles Stuart) fell back on the defensive, and the movement was finally crushed at Culloden (16 April 1746).

PRINCIPAL CITIES

ABERDEEN

Aberdeen, 130 miles north-east of Edinburgh, received its charter as a Royal Burgh from William the Lion in 1179. Scotland's third largest city, Aberdeen is the second largest Scottish fishing port and the main centre for offshore oil exploration. It is also an ancient university town and distinguished research centre. Other industries include engineering, shipbuilding, food processing, textiles, paper manufacturing and chemicals.

Places of interest include King's College, St Machar's Cathedral, Brig o' Balgownie, Duthie Park and Winter Gardens, Hazlehead Park, the Kirk of St Nicholas, Mercat Cross, Marischal College and Marischal Museum, Provost Skene's House, Art Gallery, James Dun's House (children's museum), Satrosphere Hands-On Discovery Centre, and Provost Ross's House (maritime museum).

DUNDEE

Dundee, a Royal Burgh, is situated on the north bank of the Tay estuary. The city's port and dock installations are important to the offshore oil industry and the airport also provides servicing facilities. Principal industries include textiles, computers and other electronic industries, lasers, printing, tyre manufacture, food processing, carpets, engineering and clothing manufacture. Six sites have Enterprise Zone status, including the Technology Park, airport and port.

The unique City Churches – three churches under one roof, together with the 15th century St Mary's Tower – are the most prominent architectural feature. RRS *Discovery*, the ship which took Captain Scott to the Antarctic and which was built in Dundee in 1901, is berthed in Discovery Quay.

EDINBURGH

Edinburgh is the capital of and seat of government in Scotland. The city is built on a group of hills and contains in Princes Street one of the most beautiful thoroughfares in the world.

The principal buildings are the Castle, which includes St Margaret's Chapel, the oldest building in Edinburgh, and near it, the Scottish National War Memorial; the Palace of Holyroodhouse; Parliament House, the present seat of the judicature; three universities (Edinburgh, Heriot-Watt, Napier); St Giles' Cathedral (restored 1879–83); St Mary's (Scottish Episcopal) Cathedral (Sir Gilbert Scott); the General Register House (Robert Adam); the National and the Signet Libraries; the National Gallery; the Royal Scottish Academy; and the National Portrait Gallery.

GLASGOW

Glasgow, a Royal Burgh, is the principal commercial and industrial centre in Scotland. The city occupies the north and south banks of the Clyde, formerly one of the chief commercial estuaries in the world. The principal industries include engineering, electronics, finance, chemicals and printing. The city has also developed recently as a tourism and conference centre.

The chief buildings are the 13th century Gothic Cathedral, the University (Sir Gilbert Scott), the City Chambers, the Royal Concert Hall, St Mungo Museum of Religious Life and Art, Pollok House, the School of Art (Mackintosh), Kelvingrove Art Galleries, the Burrell Collection museum and the Mitchell Library. The city is home to the Scottish National Orchestra, Scottish Opera and Scottish Ballet.

LORD LIEUTENANTS

Region	Title	Name
Borders	Berwickshire	Maj.-Gen. Sir John Swinton, KCVO, OBE
	Roxburgh, Ettrick and Lauderdale	The Duke of Buccleuch and Queensberry, KT, VRD
	Tweeddale	Lt.-Col. A. M. Sprot of Haystoun, MC
Central	Clackmannan	The Earl of Mar and Kellie
	Stirling and Falkirk	Lt.-Col. J. Stirling of Garden, CBE, TD
Dumfries and Galloway	Dumfries	Capt. R. C. Cunningham-Jardine
	The Stewartry of Kirkcudbright	Sir Michael Herries, OBE, MC
	Wigtown	Maj. E. S. Orr Ewing
Fife	Fife	The Earl of Elgin and Kincardine, KT
Grampian	Aberdeenshire	Capt. C. A. Farquharson
	Banffshire	J. A. S. McPherson, CBE
	Kincardineshire	The Viscount of Arbuthnott, CBE, DSC, FRSE
	Morayshire	Capt. Sir Iain Tennant, KT

Region	Title	Name
Highland	Caithness	The Viscount Thurso
	Inverness	Lt.-Cdr. L. R. D. Mackintosh of Mackintosh, OBE
	Nairn	The Earl of Leven and Melville
	Ross and Cromarty	Capt. R. W. K. Stirling of Fairburn, TD
	Sutherland	Maj.-Gen. D. Houston, CBE
Lothian	East Lothian	Sir Hew Hamilton-Dalrymple, Bt., KCVO
	Midlothian	Capt. G. W. Burnett, LVO
	West Lothian	The Earl of Morton
Strathclyde	Argyll and Bute	vacant
	Ayrshire and Arran	Maj. R. Y. Henderson, TD
	Dumbartonshire	Brig. D. D. G. Hardie, TD
	Lanarkshire	H. B. Sneddon, CBE
	Renfrewshire	Maj. J. D. M. Crichton Maitland
Tayside	Angus	The Earl of Airlie, KT, GCVO, PC
	Perth and Kinross	Maj. Sir David Butter, KCVO, MC
Orkney	Orkney	Brig. M. G. Dennison
Shetland	Shetland	M. M. Shearer
Western Isles	Western Isles	The Earl Granville, MC

The Lord Provosts of the four city districts of Aberdeen, Dundee, Edinburgh and Glasgow are Lord Lieutenants for those districts *ex officio*

Scottish Regions and Islands

REGIONAL AND ISLANDS COUNCILS: Area, Population, Finance

Council	Administrative headquarters	Area (hectares)	Population (latest estimate)	Band D charge 1993	Band D water charge per household 1993
Borders	Newtown St Boswells	471,253	103,881	£365.00	£86.00
Central	Stirling	263,455	272,800	416.00	47.00
Dumfries and Galloway	Dumfries	639,561	148,400	378.00	84.00
Fife	Glenrothes	131,201	345,900	445.00	59.00
Grampian	Aberdeen	869,772	514,400	389.00	89.00
Highland	Inverness	2,539,759	204,004	396.00	81.00
Lothian	Edinburgh	171,595	750,500	730.30	70.00
Orkney	Kirkwall	97,581	19,580	400.00	116.00
Shetland	Lerwick	143,268	22,522	397.62	106.05
Strathclyde	Glasgow	1,350,283	2,306,000	371.00	75.00
Tayside	Dundee	749,165	383,848	415.00	64.00
Western Isles	Stornoway, Lewis	289,798	29,600	463.00	183.00

REGIONAL AND ISLAND COUNCILS: Officers and Conveners

Council	Chief Executive	Director of Finance	Convener
Borders	K. J. Clark, CBE	P. Jeary	The Earl of Minto, OBE
Central	D. Sinclair	S. C. Craig	Mrs A. Wallace
Dumfries and Galloway	I. F. Smith	J. C. Stewart	D. R. Robinson
Fife	Dr J. A. Markland	A. E. Taylor	R. Gough, CBE
Grampian	A. G. Campbell	A. McLean	R. Middleton
Highland	R. H. Stevenson	J. W. Bremner	D. J. McPherson, CBE
Lothian	G. M. Bowie, CBE	D. B. Chynoweth	E. Milligan
Orkney	R. H. Gilbert	R. H. Gilbert	J. A. Tait
Shetland	M. E. Green	A. Matthews	E. Thomason, OBE
Strathclyde	N. McIntosh	A. Gillespie	Dr D. Sanderson
Tayside	R. W. Black	I. B. McIver	Dr G. W. Buckman
Western Isles	B. W. Stewart	R. Bennie	D. Macleod

District Councils

Council	Administrative headquarters	Population (latest estimate)	Band D charge 1993	Chief Executive	Chairman (a) Convener (b) Provost (c) Lord Provost
Aberdeen City (5)	Aberdeen	211,080	£155.50	D. Macdonald	(c) J. Wyness
Angus (9)	Forfar	94,480	99.00	P. B. Regan	(b) B. M. C. Milne
Annandale and Eskdale (3)	Annan	36,361	118.00	W. J. Davidson	(a) D. T. R. Wilson
Argyll and Bute (8)	Lochgilphead	65,140	170.00	M. A. J. Gossip, CBE	G. McMillan
Badenoch and Strathspey (6)	Kingussie	11,900	99.00	Mrs J. M. Fraser	A. Gordon
Banff and Buchan (5)	Banff	85,020	94.50	R. M. Blackburn	(a) W. R. Cruickshank, OBE
Bearsden and Milngavie (8)	Bearsden	40,900	126.00	I. C. Laurie	(b) I. J. Miller
Berwickshire (1)	Duns	19,120	64.80	R. A. Christie	Capt. J. Evans
Caithness (6)	Wick	26,790	96.00	A. Beattie	(a) J. M. Young, OBE
Clackmannan (2)	Alloa	47,470	165.03	R. Allan	(a) J. Watson
Clydebank (8)	Clydebank	44,700	193.00	J. T. McNally	(b) A. Macdonald
Clydesdale (8)	Lanark	46,000	198.00	P. W. Daniels	(a) Mrs E. Logan
Cumbernauld and Kilsyth (8)	Cumbernauld	64,100	145.00	J. Hutton	(b) C. Combe
Cumnock and Doon Valley (8)	Cumnock	42,950	118.22	K. W. Inch	(a) E. Ross
Cunninghame (8)	Irvine	138,069	154.00	B. Devine	(a) S. Dewar
Dumbarton (8)	Dumbarton	77,173	199.00	‡M. J. Watters	(b) P. O'Neill
Dundee City (9)	Dundee	172,120	208.00	A. Stephen	(c) T. M. McDonald
Dunfermline (4)	Dunfermline	130,000	117.00	K. Drennan	(b) Ms M. Millar
East Kilbride (8)	East Kilbride	82,777	171.00	D. Liddell	(b) S. Crawford
East Lothian (7)	Haddington	84,114	135.00	M. Duncan	G. M. Wanless
Eastwood (8)	Giffnock	62,380	79.00	M. D. Henry	(b) L. M. Rosin
Edinburgh City (7)	Edinburgh	418,914	219.30	P. Lowenberg	(c) Rt. Hon. N. Irons
Ettrick and Lauderdale (1)	Galashiels	34,000	100.80	C. M. Anderson	(b) W. Hardie
Falkirk (2)	Falkirk	143,200	80.00	W. Weir	(b) J. Constable
Glasgow City (8)	Glasgow	689,210	234.00	T. J. Monaghan	(c) Rt. Hon. R. Innes
Gordon (5)	Inverurie	77,130	86.00	M. C. Barron	(b) R. G. Bisset
Hamilton (8)	Hamilton	105,202	156.00	M. Docherty	(b) S. Casserly
Inverclyde (8)	Greenock	91,600	167.00	R. McPherson	(b) A. Robertson
Inverness (6)	Inverness	62,490	90.00	B. Wilson	(b) W. A. E. Fraser
Kilmarnock and Loudoun (8)	Kilmarnock	81,350	155.14	R. W. Jenner	(b) D. Coffey
Kincardine and Deeside (5)	Stonehaven	53,710	58.50	T. Hyder	(a) Mrs D. Ewing
Kirkcaldy (4)	Kirkcaldy	147,053	150.00	§D. A. Watt	(a) R. King, OBE
Kyle and Carrick (8)	Ayr	112,658	220.42	I. R. D. Smillie	(b) G. T. Macdonald
Lochaber (6)	Fort William	20,000	141.00	D. A. B. Blair	D. Purdon
Midlothian (7)	Dalkeith	79,990	125.00	T. Muir	(a) D. Molloy
Monklands (8)	Coatbridge	102,379	200.00	M. V. P. Hart	(b) R. Gilson
Moray (5)	Elgin	83,616	90.00	L. Morgan	(a) E. Aldridge
Motherwell (8)	Motherwell	144,750	166.00	J. Bonomy	(b) W. Wilson
Nairn (6)	Nairn	10,420	108.00	†A. M. Kerr	(b) J. Cattanach
Nithsdale (3)	Dumfries	57,140	129.00	T. Orr	(b) Mrs J. McMurdo
North-East Fife (4)	Cupar	65,100	158.00	R. G. Brotherton	Mrs I. M. Carter
Perth and Kinross (9)	Perth	128,369	110.00	H. Robertson	(b) Mrs J. McCormack
Renfrew (8)	Paisley	201,030	180.00	*A. I. Cowe	(b) W. Orr
Ross and Cromarty (6)	Dingwall	49,197	136.00	R. Mair	(a) Maj. A. Cameron, MBE
Roxburgh (1)	Hawick	35,340	99.00	K. W. Cramond	Mrs M. S. Turnbull
Skye and Lochalsh (6)	Portree	12,541	109.00	D. H. Noble	J. F. Munro
Stewartry (3)	Kirkcudbright	23,550	67.50	J. C. Howie	(a) J. Nelson, MBE, TD
Stirling (2)	Stirling	81,280	186.00	G. Bonner	(a) Mrs P. Greenhill
Strathkelvin (8)	Kirkintilloch	85,191	199.00	C. Mallon	(b) R. M. Coyle
Sutherland (6)	Golspie	13,050	102.00	†J. Allison	Mrs A. Magee
Tweeddale (1)	Peebles	15,375	95.00	G. H. T. Garvie	D. Suckling
West Lothian (7)	Bathgate	146,430	87.00	A. M. Linkston	(a) J. McGinley
Wigtown (3)	Stranraer	30,254	123.00	A. Geddes	W. Service

‡ District Secretary
§ General Manager
* Managing Director
† Director of Administration

Regions
(1) Borders
(2) Central
(3) Dumfries and Galloway
(4) Fife
(5) Grampian
(6) Highland
(7) Lothian
(8) Strathclyde
(9) Tayside

Northern Ireland

Northern Ireland has a total area of 5,461 sq. miles (14,144 sq. km): land, 5,215 sq. miles (13,506 sq. km); inland water and tideways, 246 sq. miles (638 sq. km).

The population of Northern Ireland at the 1991 Census was 1,577,836 (males, 769,071; females, 808,765). The average density of population in 1991 was 1.11 persons per hectare.

In 1991 the number of persons in the various religious denominations (expressed as percentages of the total population) were: Roman Catholic, 38.4; Presbyterian, 21.4; Church of Ireland, 17.7; Methodist, 3.8; others 7.7; none, 3.7; not stated, 7.3.

PRINCIPAL CITIES

BELFAST

Belfast, the administrative centre of Northern Ireland, is situated at the mouth of the River Lagan at its entrance to Belfast Lough, owing to its easy access by sea to Scottish coal and iron, to be a great industrial centre.

The principal buildings are of a relatively recent date and include the Parliament Buildings at Stormont, the City Hall, the Law Courts, the Public Library and the Museum and Art Gallery.

Belfast received its first charter of incorporation in 1613 and was created a city in 1888; the title of Lord Mayor was conferred in 1892.

LONDONDERRY

Londonderry, situated on the River Foyle, was reputedly founded in AD 546 by St Columba. Londonderry (formerly Derry) has important associations with the City of London. The Irish Society, under its royal charter of 1613, fortified the city and was for long closely associated with its administration.

The city is famous for the great siege of 1688–9, when for 105 days the town held out against the forces of James II until relieved by sea. The city walls are still intact and form a circuit of almost a mile around the old city.

Interesting buildings are the Protestant Cathedral of St Columb's (1633) and the Guildhall, reconstructed in 1912 and containing a number of beautiful stained glass windows, many of which were presented by the livery companies of London.

CONSTITUTION AND GOVERNMENT

As part of the United Kingdom, Northern Ireland is subject to the same fundamental constitutional provisions which apply to the rest of the United Kingdom. However, the Northern Ireland Constitution Act 1973 and the Northern Ireland Act 1982 provide for a measure of devolved government in Northern Ireland. This arrangement was last in force in January 1974, following agreement between the Northern Ireland political parties to form a power-sharing executive. However, this arrangement collapsed in May 1974 and there has been no devolution since.

In the interim, Northern Ireland continues to be governed by direct rule under the provisions of the Northern Ireland

Act 1974. This allows Parliament to approve all laws for Northern Ireland and places the Northern Ireland departments under the direction and control of the Secretary of State for Northern Ireland.

Attempts have been made by successive governments to find a means of restoring a widely acceptable form of devolved government to Northern Ireland. A 78-member Assembly was elected by proportional representation in 1982. However, four years later it was dissolved after it ceased to discharge its responsibilities of making proposals for the resumption of devolved government and of monitoring the work of the Northern Ireland Departments.

In January 1990 further dialogue between the Government and the constitutional political parties in Northern Ireland was established as a means of exploring the extent of the common ground which existed between them at that time. A formula, known as the three-stranded approach, for political talks about the future of Northern Ireland and its relationship with the United Kingdom and the Republic of Ireland was agreed in 1991. Strand 1 of the new talks between the Government and the four main local constitutional political parties began in April 1992. Strand 2, involving the government of the Republic of Ireland, began in July 1992. Though a settlement had not been reached when the talks ended in November 1992, progress had been made and the Government hopes that discussions will restart soon. (*See also* Events of the Year.)

FLAG

The official national flag is the Union Flag. The flag formerly in use (a white, six-pointed star in the centre of a red cross on a white field, enclosing a red hand and surmounted by a crown) has not been used since the imposition of direct rule.

FINANCE

Taxation in Northern Ireland is largely imposed and collected by the United Kingdom government. After deducting the cost of collection and of Northern Ireland's contributions to the European Community the balance, known as the Attributed Share of Taxation, is paid over to the Northern Ireland Consolidated Fund. Northern Ireland's revenue is insufficient to meet its expenditure and is supplemented by a grant-in-aid.

	1992–3*	1993–4**
Public income	£5,300,604,492	£5,982,100,000
Public expenditure	5,319,603,886	5,982,100,000

* Outturn
** Estimate

PRODUCTION

The products of the engineering, shipbuilding and aircraft industries, which employed 33,500 persons in 1990, were valued at £1,695 million. The textile industries, employing about 10,500 persons, produced products valued at approximately £412 million. The food and drink industry, employing about 20,700 persons, produced goods valued at £3,355 million.

In 1991 1,316 persons were employed in mining and quarrying operations in Northern Ireland and the minerals raised (19,073,832 tonnes) were valued at £37,567,234.

COMMUNICATIONS

road passenger services) and Northern Ireland Railways. Road freight services are also provided by a large number of hauliers operating competitively under licence.

SEAPORTS

The total tonnage handled by Northern Ireland ports in 1992 was 17.5 million. Regular ferry, freight and container services operate to ports in Great Britain and Europe from 18 ports including Belfast, Coleraine, Larne, Londonderry and Warrenpoint.

ROAD AND RAIL

The Northern Ireland Transport Holding Company is largely responsible for the supervision of the subsidiary companies, Ulsterbus and Citybus (which operate the public

AIR

Belfast International Airport, which is due to be privatized during 1994, is operated by Northern Ireland Airports Ltd, a subsidiary of the Northern Ireland Transport Holding Company. It has substantial passenger and freight handling facilities and provides scheduled and chartered services on domestic and international routes.

Scheduled services also operate from Belfast City Airport to 19 UK destinations and from Eglinton Airport to two UK destinations.

Northern Ireland Counties

County	Area* (sq. miles)	Lord Lieutenant	High Sheriff, 1993
Antrim	1,093	Sir Richard Dobbs, KCVO	P. D. Cooke
‡Belfast City	25	Col. J. E. Wilson, OBE	J. Walker
Armagh	484	The Earl of Caledon	J. N. Greenlee
Down	945	Col. W. S. Brownlow	S. B. Cunningham
Fermanagh	647	The Earl of Erne	W. R. Dickson
†Londonderry	798	Col. M. W. McCorkell, OBE, TD	K. H. Greeves
‡Londonderry City	3.4	J. T. Eaton, CBE, TD	T. E. W. Huey
Tyrone	1,211	The Duke of Abercorn	G. R. A. Darling, QC

* Excluding inland waters and tideways
‡ Denotes County Borough
† Excluding the City of Londonderry

District Councils

§ Denotes Borough Council

Council	Population (30 June 1991)	Net Annual Value	Council Clerk	Chairman †Mayor 1993
§Antrim, Co. Antrim	45,400	£6,611,649	S. J. Magee	†T. E. Wallace
§Ards, Co. Down	65,000	7,663,758	D. J. Fallows	†W. Magill
Armagh, Co. Armagh	51,800	5,185,016	D. R. D. Mitchall	P. Brannigan
§Ballymena, Co. Antrim	56,600	8,293,838	M. G. Rankin	†Revd R. Coulter
§Ballymoney, Co. Antrim	24,200	2,626,353	J. C. Alderdice	†C. J. Cousley
Banbridge, Co. Down	33,500	3,651,303	R. Gilmore	J. F. Dobson
Belfast, Co. Antrim and Co. Down	287,100	55,270,064	I. Macdonald	R. Empey (Lord Mayor)
§Carrickfergus, Co. Antrim	33,100	4,478,264	R. Boyd	†J. L. Neeson
§Castlereagh, Co. Down	61,500	8,175,226	J. White	†T. Jeffers
§Coleraine, Co. Londonderry	51,200	7,566,221	W. E. Andrews	†D. McClarty
Cookstown, Co. Tyrone	30,900	3,108,381	M. McGuckin	S. A. Glasgow
§Craigavon, Co. Armagh	75,400	10,565,555	E. A. McKinley	†Mrs A. A. J. Savage
Derry, Co. Londonderry	97,100	12,046,002	J. Keanie	†Mrs A. Courtney
Down, Co. Down	58,800	6,019,037	O. O'Connor	Miss M. M. Ritchie
Dungannon, Co. Tyrone	45,300	4,562,524	W. J. Beattie	P. Daly
Fermanagh, Co. Fermanagh	54,400	5,619,283	G. Burns, MBE	B. Kerr
§Larne, Co. Antrim	29,500	3,969,281	G. McKinley	†Mrs R. G. Armstrong
§Limavady, Co. Londonderry	29,700	2,896,569	J. K. Stevenson	†A. Doherty

Council	Population (30 June 1991)	Net Annual Value	Council Clerk	Chairman † Mayor 1993
§Lisburn, Co. Antrim and Co. Down	101,100	13,251,541	M. S. Fielding	†S. A. Close
Magherafelt, Co. Londonderry	36,100	3,585,929	J. A. McLaughlin	P. A. Kilpatrick
Moyle, Co. Antrim	14,700	1,514,384	R. G. Lewis	M. McSparran
Newry and Mourne, Co. Down and Co. Armagh	83,100	8,273,433	K. O'Neill	J. Savage
§Newtownabbey, Co. Antrim	74,500	11,234,637	J. Campbell	†J. A. Kell
§North Down, Co. Down	72,900	9,472,934	A. McDowell	†B. A. S. Wilson
Omagh, Co. Tyrone	46,000	4,494,364	J. P. McKinney	P. J. McGowan, MBE
Strabane, Co. Tyrone	35,500	3,135,065	Dr V. R. Eakin	E. Turner

Patron Saints

ST GEORGE
Patron Saint of England

St George is believed to have been born in Cappadocia, of Christian parents, in the latter part of the third century and to have served with distinction as a soldier under the Emperor Diocletian, including a visit to England on a military mission. When the persecution of Christians was ordered, St George sought a personal interview to remonstrate with the Emperor and after a profession of faith resigned his military commission. Arrest and torture followed and he was martyred at Nicomedia on 23 April 303, a day ordered to be kept in remembrance as a national festival by the Council of Oxford in 1222, although it was not until the reign of Edward III that he was made patron saint of England.

St George's connection with a dragon seems to date from the close of the sixth century and to be due to the transfer of his remains from Nicomedia to Lydda, close to the scene of the legendary exploit of Perseus in rescuing Andromeda and slaying the sea monster, credit for which became attached to the Christian martyr.

ST DAVID
Patron Saint of Wales

St David is believed to have been born towards the beginning and to have died towards the end of the sixth century. St David was an eloquent preacher, who founded the monastery at Menevia, now St David's. He became the patron of Wales,

but there is no record of any papal canonization before 1181. His annual festival is observed on 1 March.

ST ANDREW
Patron Saint of Scotland

St Andrew, one of the Christian Apostles and brother of Simon Peter, was born at Bethsaida on the Sea of Galilee and lived at Capernaum. He preached the Gospel in Asia Minor and in Scythia along the shores of the Black Sea and became the patron saint of Russia. It is believed that he suffered crucifixion at Patras in Achaea, on a *crux decussata* (now known as St Andrew's Cross) and that his relics were removed from Patras to Constantinople and thence to St Andrews, probably in the eighth century, since which time he has been the patron saint of Scotland. The festival of St Andrew is held on 30 November.

ST PATRICK
Patron Saint of Ireland

St Patrick was born, probably in England, about 389 and was carried off to Ireland as a slave about 16 years later, escaping to Gaul at the age of 22. He was ordained deacon at Auxerre and having been consecrated Bishop in 432 was despatched to Wicklow to reorganize the Christian communities in Ireland. He founded the see of Armagh and introduced Latin into Ireland as the language of the Church. He died *c.*461 and his festival is celebrated on 17 March.

The Isle of Man

Ellan Vannin

The Isle of Man is an island situated in the Irish Sea, in latitude 54° 3′–54° 25′ N. and longitude 4° 18′–4° 47′ W., nearly equidistant from England, Scotland and Ireland. Although the early inhabitants were of Celtic origin, the Isle of Man was part of the Norwegian Kingdom of the Hebrides until 1266, when this was ceded to Scotland. Subsequently granted to the Stanleys (Earls of Derby) in the 15th century and later to the Dukes of Atholl, it was brought under the administration of the Crown in 1765. The island forms the bishopric of Sodor and Man.

The total land area is 221 sq. miles (572 sq. km). The report on the 1991 Census showed a resident population of 69,788 (males, 33,693; females, 36,095). The main language in use is English. There are no remaining native speakers of Manx Gaelic but 643 people are able to speak the language.

CAPITAL – ΨDouglas; population (1991), 22,214. ΨCastletown (3,152) is the ancient capital; the other towns are ΨPeel (3,829) and ΨRamsey (6,496)

FLAG – Three conjoined armoured legs in white and gold on a red ground

TYNWALD DAY – 5 July.

GOVERNMENT

The Isle of Man is a self-governing Crown dependency, having its own parliamentary, legal and administrative system. The British Government is responsible for international relations and defence. The island has a limited relationship with the European Community (UK Act of Accession, Protocol 3). The Lieutenant-Governor is The Queen's personal representative in the island.

The legislature, Tynwald, is the oldest parliament in the world in continuous existence. It has two branches: the Legislative Council and the House of Keys. The Council consists of the President of Tynwald, the Bishop of Sodor and Man, the Attorney-General (who does not have a vote) and eight members elected by the House of Keys. The House of Keys has 24 members, elected by universal adult suffrage. The branches sit separately to consider legislation and sit together, as Tynwald Court, for most other parliamentary purposes.

The presiding officer in Tynwald Court is the President of Tynwald, elected by the members, who also presides over sittings of the Legislative Council. The presiding officer of the House of Keys is Mr Speaker, who is elected by members of the House.

The principal members of the Manx Government are the Chief Minister and nine departmental ministers, who· comprise the Council of Ministers.

Lieutenant-Governor, His Excellency Air Marshal Sir
  Laurence Jones, KCB, AFC
  ADC to the Lieutenant-Governor, M. M. Wood
President of Tynwald, The Hon. Sir Charles Kerruish, OBE
Speaker, House of Keys, The Hon. J. C. Cain
The First Deemster and Clerk of the Rolls, His Honour
  J. W. Corrin
Clerk of Legislative Council, T. A. Bawden
*Clerk of Tynwald, Secretary to the House of Keys and Counsel
  to the Speaker*, Prof. T. St J. N. Bates
Attorney-General, T. W. Cain, QC
Chief Minister, The Hon. M. R. Walker
Chief Secretary, J. F. Kissack
Chief Financial Officer, J. A. Cashen

ECONOMY

Most of the income generated in the island is earned in the services sector with financial and business services being considerably larger than the traditional industry of tourism. Manufacturing industry is also a major generator of income whilst the island's other traditional industries of agriculture and fishing now play a smaller role in the economy.

Under the terms of Protocol 3, the island has free access to EC markets for its products.

A 20-acre freeport has been developed adjacent to the main airport at Ronaldsway.

The island's unemployment rate is approximately 4 per cent and price inflation is around 2 per cent per annum.

FINANCE

The island's Budget for 1993–4 provided for net expenditure of £202,046,000. The principal sources of government revenue are taxes on income and expenditure. Income tax is payable at a rate of 15 per cent on the first £17,000 of taxable income of resident individuals and 20 per cent on the balance, after personal allowances. The rate of income tax is 20 per cent on the whole taxable income of non-residents and companies. By agreement with the British Government, the island keeps most of its rates of indirect taxation (Value Added Tax and duties) the same as those in the United Kingdom, but this agreement may be terminated by either party. A reciprocal agreement on national insurance benefits and pensions exists between the Governments of the Isle of Man and the United Kingdom. Taxes are also charged on property (rates), but these are comparatively low.

The major government expenditure items are health, social security and education, which account for 59 per cent of the government budget. The island makes a voluntary annual contribution to the United Kingdom for defence and other external services.

Although the island has a limited relationship with the European Community, it neither contributes money to nor receives funds from the EC Budget.

The Channel Islands

The Channel Islands, situated off the north-west coast of France (at distances of from ten to thirty miles), are the only portions of the Dukedom of Normandy now belonging to the Crown, to which they have been attached ever since the Conquest. The islands consist of Jersey (28,717 acres/11,630 ha), Guernsey (15,654 acres/6,340 ha), and the dependencies of Guernsey: Alderney (1,962 acres/795 ha), Brechou (74/30), Great Sark (1,035/419), Little Sark (239/97), Herm (320/130), Jethou (44/18) and Lihou (38/15) – a total of 48,083 acres/19,474 ha, or 75 sq. miles/121 sq. km. In 1991 the population of Jersey was 84,082; and of Guernsey, 58,867; Alderney, 2,297 and Sark, 575.

GOVERNMENT

The islands are Crown dependencies with their own legislative assemblies (the States in Jersey, Guernsey and Alderney, and the Court of Chief Pleas in Sark), and systems of local administration and of law, and their own courts. Acts passed by the States require the sanction of The Queen-in-Council. The British Government is responsible for defence and international relations.

In both Bailiwicks the Lieutenant-Governor and Commander-in-Chief, who is appointed by the Crown, is the personal representative of The Queen and the channel of communication between the Crown (via the Privy Council) and the island's government.

The Bailiffs of Jersey and Guernsey, also appointed by the Crown, are President of the States and of the Royal Courts of their respective islands.

The government of each Bailiwick is conducted by committees appointed by the States. Justice is administered by the Royal Courts of Jersey and Guernsey, each consisting of the Bailiff and 12 elected Jurats.

Each Bailiwick constitutes a deanery under the jurisdiction of the Bishop of Winchester (see Index).

ECONOMY

A mild climate and good soil have led to the development of intensive systems of agriculture and horticulture, which form a significant part of the economy of the Channel Islands. Equally important are invisible earnings, principally from the tourist trade and from banking and finance, the low rate of income tax (20p in the £ in Jersey and Guernsey; no tax of any kind in Sark) and the absence of super-tax and death duties making the Channel Islands a popular tax-haven.

Principal exports are agricultural produce and flowers; imports are chiefly machinery, manufactured goods, food, fuel and chemicals. Trade with the UK is regarded as internal trade.

British currency is legal tender in the Channel Islands but each Bailiwick issues its own coins, and some notes (see page 613). They also issue their own postage stamps; UK stamps are not valid.

LANGUAGE

The official languages are English and French, but French is gradually being supplanted by English, which is the language in daily use. In country districts of Jersey and Guernsey and throughout Sark a Norman-French patois is also in use, though to a declining extent.

JERSEY

Lieutenant-Governor and Commander-in-Chief of Jersey, His Excellency Air Marshal Sir John Sutton, KCB, *apptd* 1990
Secretary and ADC, Cdr. D. M. L. Braybrooke, LVO
Bailiff of Jersey, Sir Peter Crill, CBE
Deputy Bailiff, vacant
Attorney-General and Receiver-General, P. M. Bailhache, QC
Solicitor-General, T. C. Sowden, QC
Greffier of the States, G. H. C. Coppock
States Treasurer, G. M. Baird

FINANCE

Year to 31 Dec.	1991	1992
Revenue	£354,010,485	£377,235,237
Revenue expenditure	297,812,924	377,331,511
Capital expenditure	62,701,000	51,106,748
Public debt	0	0

CHIEF TOWN – ΨSt Helier, on the south coast of Jersey
FLAG – A white field charged with a red saltire cross, and the coat of arms of Jersey in the upper centre

GUERNSEY AND DEPENDENCIES

Lieutenant-Governor and Commander-in-Chief of the Bailiwick of Guernsey and its Dependencies, His Excellency Lt.-Gen. Sir Michael Wilkins, KCB, OBE, *apptd* 1990
Secretary and ADC, Capt. D. P. L. Hodgetts
Bailiff of Guernsey, Sir Graham Dorey
Deputy Bailiff, de V. G. Carey
HM Procureur and Receiver-General, A. C. K. Day, QC
HM Comptroller, G. R. Rowland, QC
States Supervisor, M. J. Brown

FINANCE

Year to 31 Dec.	1991	1992
Revenue	£149,453,687	£157,145,000
Expenditure	132,621,840	140,661,000

CHIEF TOWNS – ΨSt Peter Port, on the east coast of Guernsey; St Anne on Alderney
FLAG – White, bearing a red cross of St George, with a gold cross overall in the centre

ALDERNEY

President of the States, J. Kay-Mouat
Clerk of the States, D. V. Jenkins
Clerk of the Court, A. Johnson

SARK

Seigneur of Sark, J. M. Beaumont
The Seneschal, L. P. de Carteret
The Greffier, J. P. Hamon

OTHER DEPENDENCIES

Brechou, Lihou and Jethou are leased by the Crown. Herm is leased by the States of Guernsey.

Conservation and Heritage

Countryside Conservation

NATIONAL PARKS

ENGLAND AND WALES

The ten National Parks of England and Wales were established in the 1950s under the provisions of the National Parks and Access to the Countryside Act 1949. The National Parks were set up to conserve and protect scenic landscapes from inappropriate development and to provide access to the land for public enjoyment.

The Countryside Commission is the statutory body which has the power to designate National Parks in England and the Countryside Council for Wales is responsible for National Parks in Wales. The designation of National Parks in England is considered and confirmed by the Secretary of State for the Environment, and the designation of National Parks in Wales by the Secretary of State for Wales. The designation of a National Park does not affect the ownership of the land, nor does it remove the rights of the local community. Although the parks are administered through local government, the majority of the land is owned by private landowners (74 per cent) or by other bodies like the National Trust (7 per cent) and the Forestry Commission (7 per cent). The National Park Authorities own only 2.3 per cent of the land in the National Parks.

Under the Local Government Act 1972, National Park Authorities (NPAs) are the authorities responsible for park administration. They also influence land use and development, and deal with planning applications.

Two-thirds of the members of each authority are appointed by the county and district councils within whose boundaries the parks lie. One-third of the members are appointed by the Secretary of State for the Environment or the Secretary of State for Wales with advice from the Countryside Commission or the Countryside Council for Wales.

In the Peak District and the Lake District the NPAs are special boards: the Peak Park Joint Planning Board and the Lake District Special Planning Board. These are autonomous authorities which are financially independent, unlike the authorities in the other eight parks which are county council committees. The NPAs appoint the National Park Officer for the National Park they administer.

Central government provides 75 per cent of the funding for the parks through the National Park Supplementary Grant. The remaining 25 per cent is supplied by the local authorities concerned. Forecast net expenditure for all National Parks in England and Wales in 1993-4 was £28,241,660.

The Countryside Commission has stated that other areas are regarded as being worthy of National Parks status. Two areas considered as having equivalent status are the Broads and the New Forest (see page 578).

The National Parks in England and Wales (with date designation confirmed) are:

BRECON BEACONS (1957), 1,351 sq. km/522 sq. miles – The park lies in Powys (66 per cent), Dyfed, Gwent and Mid Glamorgan. The park is centred on the Beacons, Pen y Fan, Corn Du and Cribyn, but also includes the valley of the Usk, the Black Mountains to the east and the Black Mountain to the west. There are information centres at Brecon, Craig-y-nos Country Park, Abergavenny and Llandovery, a study centre at Danywenallt and a day visitor centre near Libanus. *Information Office,* 7 Glamorgan Street, Brecon, Powys LD3 7DP. Tel: 0874-624437. *National Park Officer,* M. Fitton

DARTMOOR (1951), 954 sq. km/368 sq. miles – Dartmoor lies wholly in Devon. Dartmoor consists of moorland and rocky granite tors, and is rich in prehistoric remains. There are information centres at Newbridge, Tavistock, Bovey Tracey, Steps Bridge, Princetown and Postbridge. *Information Office,* Parke, Haytor Road, Bovey Tracey, Devon TQ13 9JQ. Tel: 0626-832093. *National Park Officer,* N. Atkinson

EXMOOR (1954), 693 sq. km/268 sq. miles – Exmoor lies in Somerset (71 per cent) and Devon. Exmoor is a moorland plateau inhabited by wild ponies and red deer. There are many ancient remains and burial mounds. There are information centres at Lynmouth, County Gate, Dulverton and Combe Martin. *Information Office,* Exmoor House, Dulverton, Somerset TA22 9HL. Tel: 0398-23665. *National Park Officer,* K. Bungay

LAKE DISTRICT (1951), 2,292 sq. km/885 sq. miles – The Lake District lies wholly in Cumbria. The Lake District includes England's highest mountains (Scafell Pike, Helvellyn and Skiddaw) but it is most famous for its glaciated lakes. There are information centres at Keswick, Waterhead, Hawkshead, Seatoller, Bowness, Grasmere, Coniston, Glenridding and Pooley Bridge, an information van at Gosforth and a park centre at Brockhole, Windermere. *Information Office,* Busher Walk, Kendal, Cumbria LA9 4RH. Tel: 0539-724555. *National Park Officer,* J. Toothill

NORTHUMBERLAND (1956), 1,049 sq. km/405 sq. miles – The Northumberland National Park lies wholly in Northumberland. The park is an area of hill country stretching from Hadrian's Wall to the Scottish Border. There are information centres at Ingram, Once Brewed, Rothbury, Housesteads, Harbottle and Kielder, and an information caravan at Cawfields. *Information Office,* Eastburn, South Park, Hexham, Northumberland NE46 1BS. Tel: 0434-605555. *National Park Officer,* G. Taylor

NORTH YORK MOORS (1952), 1,436 sq. km/554 sq. miles – The North York Moors lie in North Yorkshire (96 per cent) and Cleveland. The park consists of woodland and moorland, and includes the Hambleton Hills and the Cleveland Way. There are information centres at Danby, Pickering, Sutton Bank, Ravenscar, Helmsley and Hutton-le-Hole, and a day study centre at Danby. *Information Office,* The Old Vicarage, Bondgate, Helmsley, York YO6 5BP. Tel: 0439-70657. *National Park Officer,* D. Statham

PEAK DISTRICT (1951), 1,438 sq. km/555 sq. miles – The Peak District lies in Derbyshire (64 per cent), Staffordshire, South Yorkshire, Cheshire, West Yorkshire and Greater Manchester. The Peak District is composed of the gritstone moors of the 'dark peak' and the limestone dales of the 'white peak'. There are information centres at Bakewell, Edale, Fairholmes and Castleton, and information points at Torside (in the Longdendale Valley) and at Hartington (former station). *Information Office*, Aldern House, Baslow Road, Bakewell, Derbyshire DE45 1AE. Tel: 0629-814321. *National Park Officer*, C. Harrison

PEMBROKESHIRE COAST (1952), 584 sq. km/225 sq. miles – The Pembrokeshire Coast National Park lies wholly in Dyfed. The park consists of cliffs, open moorland and Skomer Island. There are information centres at Tenby, St David's, Pembroke, Newport, Kilgetty, Haverfordwest and Broad Haven. *Information Office*, County Offices, Haverfordwest, Dyfed SA61 1QZ. Tel: 0437-764591. *National Park Officer*, N. Wheeler

SNOWDONIA (1951), 2,142 sq. km/817 sq. miles – Snowdonia lies wholly in Gwynedd. It is an area of deep valleys and rugged mountains in northern Wales. There are information centres at Aberdovey, Bala, Betws y Coed, Blaenau Ffestiniog, Conwy, Harlech, Dolgellau and Llanberis. *Information Office*, Penrhyndeudraeth, Gwynedd LL48 6LS. Tel: 0766-770274. *National Park Officer*, A. Jones

YORKSHIRE DALES (1954), 1,769 sq. km/683 sq. miles – The Yorkshire Dales National Park lies in North Yorkshire (88 per cent) and Cumbria. The Yorkshire Dales are composed primarily of limestone overlaid in places by millstone grit. The three peaks of Ingleborough, Whernside and Pen-y-Ghent are within the park. There are information centres at Clapham, Grassington, Hawes, Aysgarth Falls, Malham and Sedbergh. *Information Office*, Yorebridge House, Bainbridge, Leyburn, North Yorkshire DL8 3BP. Tel: 0969-50456. *National Park Officer*, R. Harvey

Two other areas considered to have equivalent status to national parks are the Broads and the New Forest. The Broads Authority, a special statutory authority, was established in 1989 to develop, conserve and manage the Norfolk and Suffolk Broads (*see also* Government Departments and Public Offices). The Government declared in 1992 its intention of giving the New Forest a status equivalent to that of a National Park by declaring it an 'area of national significance'.

THE BROADS (1989), 303 sq. km/117 sq. miles – The Broads are located between Norwich and Great Yarmouth on the flood plains of the five rivers flowing through the area to the sea. The area is one of fens, winding waterways, woodland and marsh. The forty or so broads are man-made, the flooded remains of medieval peat pits, and are connected to the rivers by dykes, providing over 200 km of navigable waterways. There are information centres at Beccles, Hoveton, North-west Tower (Yarmouth), Ranworth and Toad Hole. *Broads Authority*, Thomas Harvey House, 18 Colegate, Norwich NR3 1BQ. Tel: 0603-610734. *Chief Executive*, A. Clark

THE NEW FOREST, 376 sq. km/145 sq. miles – The area has been protected since 1079 when it was declared a royal hunting forest. The landscape consists of forest, ancient woodland and heathland which is grazed by New Forest ponies and cattle. Much of the Forest is managed by the Forestry Commission, which provides several camp-sites. The main villages are Brockenhurst, Burley and Lyndhurst, which has a visitor centre.

The Forestry Commission, Office of the Deputy Surveyor of the New Forest, The Queen's House, Lyndhurst, Hants. SO43 7NH. Tel: 0703-284149

SCOTLAND AND NORTHERN IRELAND

The National Parks and Access to the Countryside Act 1949 dealt only with England and Wales, and made no provision for Scotland or Northern Ireland. Although there are no national parks in these two countries, there is power to designate them in Northern Ireland under the Amenity Lands Act 1965 and the Nature Conservation and Amenity Lands Order (Northern Ireland) 1985; and in 1989 the Scottish Office asked Scottish Natural Heritage to report on whether national parks should be designated in Scotland.

AREAS OF OUTSTANDING NATURAL BEAUTY

ENGLAND AND WALES

Under the National Parks and Access to the Countryside Act 1949, provision was made for the designation of Areas of Outstanding Natural Beauty (AONBs) by the Countryside Commission. The Countryside Act 1968 further defines the role of AONBs, suggesting that they should show due regard for the interests of other land users, such as agriculture and forestry groups. The Countryside Commission continues to be responsible for AONBs in England but since April 1991 the Countryside Council for Wales has been responsible for the Welsh AONBs. Designations in England are confirmed by the Secretary of State for the Environment and those in Wales by the Secretary of State for Wales.

Although less emphasis is placed upon the provision of open-air enjoyment for the public than in the national parks, AONBs are seen as areas which are no less beautiful and require the same degree of protection to conserve and enhance the natural beauty of the countryside. This includes protecting flora and fauna, geological and other landscape features.

In AONBs planning and management responsibilities are split between county and district councils (there are 17 which cross county boundaries). Finance for the AONBs is provided by grant-aid.

Thirty-nine Areas of Outstanding Natural Beauty have been designated since 1956. They are (with date designation confirmed):

ANGLESEY (1967), 221 sq. km/85 sq. miles – The designated area extends along the entire coastline of the island, except for breaks around the urban areas and in the vicinity of Wylfa

ARNSIDE AND SILVERDALE (1972), 75 sq. km/29 sq. miles – The area embraces the upper half of Morecambe Bay, the Kent estuary, and includes extensive tidal flats in the Bay

BLACKDOWN HILLS (1991), 370 sq. km/143 sq. miles – An area of greensand ridges in Devon and Somerset extending from Cullompton in the west to Chard in the east, south of Taunton to north of Honiton

CANNOCK CHASE (1958), 68 sq. km/26 sq. miles – An area of high heathland in Staffordshire. Deer continue to roam over the Chase

CHICHESTER HARBOUR (1964), 74 sq. km/29 sq. miles – The area extends from Hayling Island to Apuldram and includes Thorney Island

CHILTERNS (1965; extended 1990), 833 sq. km/322 sq. miles – Chalk downlands running from South

Oxfordshire north-eastwards to Bedfordshire, including the outlying group of hills beyond Luton

CLWYDIAN RANGE (1985), 157 sq. km/61 sq. miles – A prominent ridge extending southwards from Prestatyn on the north Wales coast. Offa's Dyke runs along the crest of the range

CORNWALL (1959; Camel estuary 1983), 958 sq. km/370 sq. miles – A number of separate areas including Bodmin Moor, most of the Land's End peninsula, the coast between St Michael's Mount and St Austell (with Falmouth omitted), the Fowey estuary; in north Cornwall most of the coast to Bedruthan Steps and between Perranporth and Godrevy Towans, plus the Camel estuary

COTSWOLDS (1966; extended 1990), 2,038 sq. km/787 sq. miles – The area of limestone hills above the Vales of Gloucester and Evesham

CRANBORNE CHASE AND WEST WILTSHIRE DOWNS (1983), 983 sq. km/379 sq. miles – A mainly chalkland and greensand area covering parts of Wiltshire, Dorset, Hampshire and Somerset, including the wooded remnants of the ancient Chase

DEDHAM VALE (1970; extended 1978, 1991), 90 sq. km/35 sq. miles – The area on the Essex/Suffolk border where John Constable painted

EAST DEVON (1963), 268 sq. km/103 sq. miles – The coastline between Exmouth and Lyme Regis, with Sidmouth, Beer and Seaton omitted. Inland, Gittisham Hill, East Hill and Woodbury and Aylebeare Commons are included

NORTH DEVON (1960), 171 sq. km/66 sq. miles – Includes most of the North Devon coastline, from just north of Bude to the boundary of the Exmoor National Park

SOUTH DEVON (1960), 337 sq. km/130 sq. miles – Includes the coast between Bolt Head and Bolt Tail, Salcombe, Slapton Sands and Dartmouth, and the estuaries and valleys of the Yealm, Erme, Avon and Dart

DORSET (1959), (1,129 sq. km/436 sq. miles – The coastline between Lyme Regis and Poole, with the Isle of Portland and Weymouth omitted, stretching inland to include the Purbeck Hills and the downs of Hardy county

FOREST OF BOWLAND (1964), 802 sq. km/310 sq. miles – A moorland area mostly in Lancashire running westward from the River Ribble, with a small outlying area east of the Ribble which includes Pendle Hill

GOWER (1956), 188 sq. km/73 sq. miles – A peninsula in West Glamorgan, South Wales, known for its coastline

EAST HAMPSHIRE (1962), 383 sq. km/148 sq. miles – A chalkland area stretching from the outskirts of Winchester to the Sussex border at a distance of about 10 miles inland

SOUTH HAMPSHIRE COAST (1967), 77 sq. km/30 sq. miles – 14 miles of coastline between Hurst Castle and Calshot Castle, extending inland up the River Beaulieu for about six miles

HIGH WEALD (1983), 1,460 sq. km/564 sq. miles – The area covers parts of East and West Sussex, Kent and Surrey. It is predominantly wooded, and includes larger heathland areas like Ashdown Forest, the remnants of the old Wealden forests

HOWARDIAN HILLS (1987), 204 sq. km/79 sq. miles – Wooded hills which rise above the Vales of York and Pickering

KENT DOWNS (1968), 878 sq. km/339 sq. miles – Running east and south-east from the Surrey border near Westerham to the coast near Dover and Folkestone, with a coastal outlier at South Foreland and a narrow strip of the old sea cliff escarpment west of Hythe overlooking Romney Marsh

LINCOLNSHIRE WOLDS (1973), 558 sq. km/215 sq. miles – The area extends in a south-east direction from Laceby and Caistor in the north to the region of Spilsby, about ten miles west of the coast

LLEYN (1957), 161 sq. km/62 sq. miles – The peninsula forming the westernmost part of the county of Gwynedd

MALVERN HILLS (1959), 105 sq. km/40 sq. miles – The whole range of the Malvern Hills in the county of Hereford and Worcester, just touching Gloucestershire

MENDIP HILLS (1972; extended 1989), 198 sq. km/76 sq. miles – Comprising over half of the Mendip Hills, the area stretches from Bleadon Hill to the A39 road north of Wells and includes Cheddar Gorge and Wookey Hole

NORFOLK COAST (1968), 451 sq. km/174 sq. miles – An almost continuous coastal strip three to five miles in depth from Hunstanton to Bacton, with a further small strip between Sea Palling and Winterton-on-Sea. The area includes part of the Sandringham estate

NORTH PENNINES (1988), 1,998 sq. km/766 sq. miles – The northern limit of the Pennine chain, covering parts of Cumbria, Co. Durham and Northumberland

NORTHUMBERLAND COAST (1958), 135 sq. km/52 sq. miles – Stretches from just south of Berwick to Amble and includes Holy Island and the Farne Islands

QUANTOCK HILLS (1957), 99 sq. km/38 sq. miles – A range of sandstone hills in Somerset

ISLES OF SCILLY (1976), 16 sq. km/6 sq. miles – About 140 islands and skerries in the Scillies group of which only five are inhabited. There are a number of Sites of Special Scientific Interest

SHROPSHIRE HILLS (1959), 804 sq. km/310 sq. miles – Most of south-west Shropshire between the Welsh border and the boundary with Hereford and Worcester, including the region around Clun, the area of the Stiperstones, the Long Mynd and Wenlock Edge, with the tongues of land running north-east to the Wrekin and south towards Ludlow

SOLWAY COAST (1964), 115 sq. km/44 sq. miles – A stretch of coastline in Cumbria from Maryport to the estuaries of the Rivers Eden and Esk (with Silloth omitted) backed by the Solway Plain

SUFFOLK COAST AND HEATHS (1970), 403 sq. km/156 sq. miles – The area includes 38 miles of coastline and parts of the Stour and Orwell estuaries, while the Rivers Deben, Alde and Blyth flow through it

SURREY HILLS (1958), 419 sq. km/162 sq. miles – An area of hills to the east and south of Guildford, including the Hog's Back and the ridge of the North Downs

SUSSEX DOWNS (1966), 983 sq. km/379 sq. miles – The area includes the chalk escarpment of the South Downs from Beachy Head to the Hampshire border, and stretches down to the coast between Eastbourne and Seaford

NORTH WESSEX DOWNS (1972), 1,730 sq. km/668 sq. miles – An upland area in Hampshire, Wiltshire, Oxfordshire and Berkshire, bounded by the Marlborough and Lambourn Downs in the west, the Chiltern Hills in the east and Salisbury Plain in the south

ISLE OF WIGHT (1963), 189 sq. km/73 sq. miles – A number of separate areas comprising stretches of coastline, the Yar Valley, the high downland behind Ventnor and the chalk ridge which runs from Newport to Culver Cliff and Foreland

WYE VALLEY (1971), 326 sq. km/126 sq. miles – The deep, wooded, river valley running through the counties of Gwent, Gloucestershire, and Hereford and Worcester

Proposals for further designations include: the Tamar valley, Devon/Cornwall and Nidderdale, North Yorkshire.

NORTHERN IRELAND

The Department of the Environment for Northern Ireland, with advice from the Council for Nature Conservation and the Countryside, designates Areas of Outstanding Natural Beauty in Northern Ireland. At present there are nine and these cover a total area of approximately 284,948 hectares (704,121 acres).

ANTRIM COAST AND GLENS, Co. Antrim, 70,600 ha/ 174,452 acres
CAUSEWAY COAST, Co. Antrim, 4,200 ha/10,378 acres
LAGAN VALLEY, Co. Down, 2,072 ha/5,119 acres
LECALE COAST, Co. Down, 3,108 ha/7,679 acres
MOURNE, Co. Down, 57,012 ha/140,876 acres
NORTH DERRY, Co. Londonderry, 12,950 ha/31,999 acres
RING OF GULLION, Co. Armagh, 15,353 ha/37,938 acres
SPERRIN, Co. Tyrone/Co. Londonderry, 101,006 ha/ 249,585 acres
STRANGFORD LOUGH, Co. Down, 18,647 ha/46,077 acres

NATIONAL SCENIC AREAS

No Areas of Outstanding Natural Beauty are designated in Scotland. However, National Scenic Areas have a broadly equivalent status.

Scottish Natural Heritage recognizes areas of national scenic significance. At present there are 40, covering a total area of 1,001,800 hectares (2,475,448 acres).

Development within National Scenic Areas is dealt with by the local planning authority, who are required to consult Scottish Natural Heritage for certain categories of development within these areas. Land management uses can also be modified in the interest of scenic conservation. The Secretary of State for Scotland has limited powers of intervention should a planning authority and Scottish Natural Heritage disagree.

	hectares	acres
BORDER		
Eildon and Leaderfoot	3,600	8,896
Upper Tweeddale	10,500	25,945
CENTRAL		
*Loch Lomond	11,200	27,675
*Loch Rannoch and Glen Lyon	1,300	3,212
The Trossachs	4,600	11,367
DUMFRIES AND GALLOWAY		
East Stewartry Coast	4,500	11,119
Fleet Valley	5,300	13,096
Nith Estuary	9,300	22,980
GRAMPIAN		
*The Cairngorm Mountains	29,800	73,636
*Deeside and Lochnagar	32,200	79,566
HIGHLAND		
Assynt-Coigach	90,200	222,884
*Ben Nevis and Glen Coe	79,600	196,692
*The Cairngorm Mountains	37,400	92,415
The Cuillin Hills	21,900	54,115
Dornoch Firth	7,500	18,532
Glen Affric	19,300	47,690
Glen Strathfarrar	3,800	9,390
Kintail	15,500	38,300
Knoydart	39,500	97,604
Kyle of Tongue	18,500	45,713
Loch Shiel	13,400	33,111
Morar, Moidart and Ardna- murchan	13,500	33,358
North-west Sutherland	20,500	50,655
The Small Isles	15,500	38,300
Trotternish	5,000	12,355
Wester Ross	145,300	359,036
ORKNEY ISLANDS		
Hoy and West Mainland	14,800	36,571
SHETLAND ISLANDS		
Shetland	11,600	28,664
STRATHCLYDE		
*Ben Nevis and Glen Coe	17,500	43,242
Jura	21,800	53,868
Knapdale	19,800	48,926
Kyles of Bute	4,400	10,872
*Loch Lomond	16,200	40,030
Loch na Keal, Isle of Mull	12,700	31,382
Lynn of Lorn	4,800	11,861
North Arran	23,800	58,810
Scarba, Lunga and the Garvel- lachs	1,900	4,692
TAYSIDE		
*Ben Nevis and Glen Coe	4,500	11,119
*Deeside and Lochnagar	7,800	19,274
*Loch Rannoch and Glen Lyon	47,100	116,384
Loch Tummel	9,200	22,733
River Earn	3,000	7,413
River Tay	5,600	13,838
WESTERN ISLES		
St Kilda	900	2,224
South Lewis, Harris and North Uist	109,600	270,821
South Uist Machair	6,100	15,073
TOTAL	1,001,800	2,475,448

*National Scenic Areas in more than one region

Nature Conservation Areas

SITES OF SPECIAL SCIENTIFIC INTEREST

Site of Special Scientific Interest (SSSI) is a legal designation applied to land in England, Scotland or Wales which English Nature (EN), Scottish Natural Heritage (SNH), or the Countryside Council for Wales (CCW) identifies as being of special interest because of its flora, fauna, geological or physiographical features. In some cases, SSSI are managed as nature reserves.

EN, SNH and CCW must notify the designation of a SSSI to the local planning authority, every owner/occupier of the land, and the Secretary of State for the Environment (or Secretary of State for Scotland or for Wales where applicable). Forestry and agricultural departments and a number of other bodies are also informed of this designation.

Objections to the designation of a SSSI can be made and ultimately considered at a full meeting of the Council of EN or the Site Safeguard Committee of CCW. In Scotland an objection will be dealt with by the appropriate regional board or the main board of SNH, depending on the nature of the objection. Unresolved objections on scientific grounds must be referred to the Advisory Committee for SSSI.

The protection of these sites depends on the co-operation of individual landowners and occupiers. Owner/occupiers must consult EN, SNH or CCW and gain written consent before they can undertake certain listed activities on the site. Funds are available through management agreements and grants to assist owners and occupiers in conserving sites' interests. As a last resort a site can be purchased.

As at 31 March 1993 there were 5,927 SSSI in Britain, covering 1,861,558 hectares (4,599,909 acres).

	no.	hectares	acres
England	3,707	839,309	2,073,932
Scotland	1,350	816,596	2,017,808
Wales	870	205,653	508,168

NORTHERN IRELAND

In Northern Ireland 41 Areas of Special Scientific Interest (ASSIs) have been established by the Department of the Environment for Northern Ireland. These cover a total area of 47,832 hectares (118,145 acres).

NATIONAL NATURE RESERVES

National Nature Reserves are defined in the National Parks and Access to the Countryside Act 1949 as land designated for the study and preservation of flora and fauna, or of geological or physiographical features.

English Nature (EN), Scottish Natural Heritage (SNH) or the Countryside Council for Wales (CCW) can designate as a National Nature Reserve land which is being managed as a nature reserve under an agreement with one of the statutory nature conservation agencies; land held and managed by EN, SNH or CCW; or land held and managed as a nature reserve by another approved body. EN, SNH or CCW can turn to the appropriate Secretary of State to impose by-laws for the protection of the reserves from undesirable development.

As at 31 March 1993 there were 258 National Nature Reserves in Britain, covering 182,795 hectares (451,686 acres).

	no.	hectares	acres
England	140	57,151	141,220
Scotland	69	112,247	277,362
Wales	49	13,397	33,103

NORTHERN IRELAND

National Nature Reserves are established and managed by the Department of the Environment for Northern Ireland, with advice from the Council for Nature Conservation and the Countryside. There are 45 National Nature Reserves covering 4,574 hectares (11,297 acres).

LOCAL NATURE RESERVES

Local Nature Reserves are defined in the National Parks and Access to the Countryside Act 1949 as land designated for the study and preservation of flora and fauna, or of geological or physiographical features. The Act gives local authorities in England and Wales and district councils in Scotland the power to acquire, declare and manage local nature reserves in consultation with English Nature, Scottish Natural

Heritage and the Countryside Council for Wales. Conservation trusts can also own and manage non-statutory local nature reserves.

As at 31 March 1993 there were 364 designated Local Nature Reserve areas in Britain, covering 20,266 hectares (50,077 acres).

	no.	hectares	acres
England	337	13,977	34,537
Scotland	8	2,866	7,081
Wales	19	3,423	8,458

An additional 17.19 km of linear trails are designated as Local Nature Reserves.

FOREST NATURE RESERVES

Forest Enterprise (part of the Forestry Commission) has created Forest Nature Reserves from conservation sites within its estate. These are like other nature reserves in that their purpose is to protect and conserve special forms of natural habitat, flora and fauna existing in forested areas.

Forest Enterprise has 397 SSSI on its estates and has chosen 46 as Forest Nature Reserves. They extend in size from under 50 hectares (124 acres) to 500 hectares (1,236 acres). The largest include the Black Wood of Rannoch, by Loch Rannoch; Cannop Valley Oakwoods, Forest of Dean; Culbin Forest, near Forres; Glen Affric, near Fort Augustus; Kylerhea, Skye; Pembrey, Carmarthen Bay; Starr Forest, in Galloway Forest Park; and Wyre Forest, near Kidderminster.

NORTHERN IRELAND

There are 36 Forest Nature Reserves in Northern Ireland, covering 1,759 hectares (4,346 acres). They are designated and administered by the Forest Service, a division of the Department of Agriculture for Northern Ireland. There are also 15 National Nature Reserves on Forest Service-owned property.

MARINE NATURE RESERVES

The Wildlife and Countryside Act 1981 gives the Secretary of State for the Environment (and the Secretaries of State for Wales and for Scotland where appropriate) power to designate Marine Nature Reserves, and English Nature, Scottish Natural Heritage and the Countryside Council for Wales powers to select and manage these reserves. Interested parties at a national and at a local level are consulted prior to the confirmation of an area.

Marine Nature Reserves provide protection for marine flora and fauna, and geological and physiographical features on land covered by tidal waters or parts of the sea in or adjacent to Great Britain. Reserves also provide opportunities for study and research.

Statutory Marine Nature Reserves are:

LUNDY (1986), Bristol Channel
SKOMER (1990), Dyfed

Other areas proposed for designation as reserves are: the Isles of Scilly, the Menai Strait, Bardsey Island, and part of the Lleyn peninsula, Gwynedd.

A number of non-statutory marine reserves have been set up by conservation groups.

Wildlife Conservation

PROTECTED SPECIES

The Wildlife and Countryside Act 1981 gives legal protection to a wide range of animals and wild plants. Subject to parliamentary approval, the Secretary of State for the Environment may vary the animals and plants given legal protection. The most recent variation of Schedules 5 and 8 came into effect in October 1992.

ANIMALS, ETC.

Under Schedule 5 of the Act it is illegal without a licence to kill, injure, take, possess or sell any of the animals mentioned below (whether alive or dead) and to disturb its place of shelter and protection or to destroy that place.

†Adder (*Vipera berus*)
§Allis shad (*alosa alosa*)
Anemone, Ivell's Sea (*Edwardsia ivelli*)
Anemone, Startlet Sea (*Nematosella vectensis*)
Apus (*Triops cancriformis*)
Bat, Horseshoe (*Rhinolophidae*, all species)
Bat, Typical (*Vespertilionidae*, all species)
Beetle (*Graphoderus zonatus*)
Beetle (*Hypebaeus flavipes*)
Beetle (*Paracymus aeneus*)
Beetle, Lesser Silver Water (*Hydrochara caraboides*)
§§Beetle, Mire Pill (*Curimopsis nigrita*)
Beetle, Rainbow Leaf (*Chrysolina cerealis*)
Beetle, Violet Click (*Limoniscus violaceus*)
Burbot (*Lota lota*)
*Butterfly, Adonis Blue (*Lysandra bellargus*)
*Butterfly, Black Hairstreak (*Strymonidia pruni*)
*Butterfly, Brown Hairstreak (*Thecla betulae*)
*Butterfly, Chalkhill Blue (*Lysandra coridon*)
*Butterfly, Chequered Skipper (*Carterocephalus palaemon*)
*Butterfly, Duke of Burgundy Fritillary (*Hamearis lucina*)
*Butterfly, Glanville Fritillary (*Melitaea cinxia*)
Butterfly, Heath Fritillary (*Mellicta athalia* (or *Melitaea athalia*))
Butterfly, High Brown Fritillary (*Argynnis adippe*)
Butterfly, Large Blue (*Maculinea arion*)
*Butterfly, Large Copper (*Lycaena dispar*)
*Butterfly, Large Heath (*Coenonympha tullia*)
*Butterfly, Large Tortoiseshell (*Nymphalis polychloros*)
*Butterfly, Lulworth Skipper (*Thymelicus acteon*)
*Butterfly, Marsh Fritillary (*Eurodryas aurinia*)
*Butterfly, Mountain Ringlet (*Erebia epiphron*)
*Butterfly, Northern Brown Argus (*Aricia artaxerxes*)
*Butterfly, Pearl-bordered Fritillary (*Boloria euphrosyne*)
*Butterfly, Purple Emperor (*Apatura iris*)
*Butterfly, Silver Spotted Skipper (*Hesperia comma*)
*Butterfly, Silver-studded Blue (*Plebejus argus*)
*Butterfly, Small Blue (*Cupido minimus*)
Butterfly, Swallowtail (*Papilio machaon*)
*Butterfly, White Letter Hairstreak (*Stymonida w-album*)

*the offence relates to 'sale' only
**the offence relates to 'taking' and 'sale' only
†the offence relates to 'killing and injuring' only
‡the offence relates to 'killing, injuring and sale'
§the offence relates to 'killing, injuring and taking'
§§the offence relates only to damaging, destroying or obstructing access to a shelter or protection, or disturbing during occupation of such

*Butterfly, Wood White (*Leptidea sinapis*)
Cat, Wild (*Felis silvestris*)
Cicada, New Forest (*Cicadetta montana*)
**Crayfish, Atlantic Stream (*Austropotamobius pallipes*)
Cricket, Field (*Gryllus campestris*)
Cricket, Mole (*Gryllotalpa gryllotalpa*)
Dolphin (*Cetacea*)
Dormouse (*Muscardinus avellanarius*)
Dragonfly, Norfolk Aeshna (*Aeshna isosceles*)
*Frog, Common (*Rana temporaria*)
Grasshopper, Wart-biter (*Decticus verrucivorus*)
Hatchet Shell, Northern (*Thyasira gouldi*)
Lagoon Snail (*Paludinella littorina*)
Lagoon Snail, De Folin's (*Caecum armoricum*)
Lagoon Worm, Tentacled (*Alkmaria romijni*)
Leech, Medicinal (*Hirudo medicinalis*)
Lizard, Sand (*Lacerta agilis*)
‡Lizard, Viviparous(*Lacerta vivipara*)
Marten, Pine (*Martes martes*)
Moth, Barberry Carpet (*Pareulype berberata*)
Moth, Black-veined (*Siona lineata* (or *Idaea lineata*))
Moth, Essex Emerald (*Thetidia smaragdaria*)
Moth, New Forest Burnet (*Zygaena viciae*)
Moth, Reddish Buff (*Acosmetia caliginosa*)
Moth, Sussex Emerald (*Thalera fimbrialis*)
Moth, Viper's Bugloss (*Hadena irregularis*)
Mussel, Freshwater Pearl (*Margaritifera margaritifera*)
Newt, Great Crested (or Warty) (*Triturus cristatus*)
*Newt, Palmate (*Triturus helveticus*)
*Newt, Smooth (*Triturus vulgaris*)
Otter, Common (*Lutra lutra*)
Porpoise (*Cetacea*)
Sandworm, Lagoon (*Armandia cirrhosa*)
Sea Fan, Pink (*Eunicella verrucosa*)
Sea-Mat, Trembling (*Victorella pavida*)
Sea Slug, Lagoon (*Tenellia adspersa*)
Shrimp, Fairy (*Chirocephalus diaphanus*)
Shrimp, Lagoon Sand (*Gammarus insensibilis*)
‡Slow-worm (*Anguis fragilis*)
Snail, Glutinous (*Myxas glutinosa*)
Snail, Sandbowl (*Catinella arenaria*)
‡Snake, Grass (*Natrix natrix* (*Natrix helvetica*))
Snake, Smooth (*Coronella austriaca*)
Spider, Fen Raft (*Dolomedes plantarius*)
Spider, Ladybird (*Eresus niger*)
Squirrel, Red (*Sciurus vulgaris*)
Sturgeon (*Acipenser sturio*)
*Toad, Common (*Bufo bufo*)
Toad, Natterjack (*Bufo calamita*)
Turtle, Marine (*Dermochelyidae* and *Cheloniidae*, all species)
Vendace (*Coregonus albula*)
Walrus (*Odobenus rosmarus*)
Whale (*Cetacea*)
Whitefish (*Coregonus lavaretus*)

PLANTS

Under Schedule 8 of the Wildlife and Countryside Act 1981, it is illegal without a licence to pick, uproot, sell or destroy any of the plants mentioned below and, unless authorized, to uproot any wild plant.

Adder's tongue, Least (*Ophioglossum lusitanicum*)
Alison, Small (*Alyssum alyssoides*)
Blackwort (*Southbya nigrella*)
Broomrape, Bedstraw (*Orobanche caryophyllacea*)
Broomrape, Oxtongue (*Orobanche loricata*)

Broomrape, Thistle (*Orobanche reticulata*)
Cabbage, Lundy (*Rhynchosinapis wrightii*)
Calamint, Wood (*Calamintha sylvatica*)
Caloplaca, Snow (*Caloplaca nivalis*)
Catapyrenium, Tree (*Catapyrenium psoromoides*)
Catchfly, Alpine (*Lychnis alpina*)
Catillaria, Laurer's (*Catellaria laureri*)
Centaury, Slender (*Centaurium tenuiflorum*)
Cinquefoil, Rock (*Potentilla rupestris*)
Cladonia, Upright Mountain (*Cladonia stricta*)
Clary, Meadow (*Salvia pratensis*)
Club-rush, Triangular (*Scirpus triquetrus*)
Colt's-foot, Purple (*Homogyne alpina*)
Cotoneaster, Wild (*Cotoneaster integerrimus*)
Cottongrass, Slender (*Eriophorum gracile*)
Cow-wheat, Field (*Melampyrum arvense*)
Crocus, Sand (*Romulea columnae*)
Crystalwort, Lizard (*Riccia bifurca*)
Cudweed, Broad-leaved (*Filago pyramidata*)
Cudweed, Jersey (*Gnaphalium luteoalbum*)
Cudweed, Red-tipped (*Filago lutescens*)
Diapensia (*Diapensia lapponica*)
Dock, Shore (*Rumex rupestris*)
Earwort, Marsh (*Jamesoniella undulifolia*)
Eryngo, Field (*Eryngium campestre*)
Fern, Dickie's bladder (*Cystopteris dickieana*)
Fern, Killarney (*Trichomanes speciosum*)
Flapwort, Norfolk (*Leiocolea rutheana*)
Fleabane, Alpine (*Erigeron borealis*)
Fleabane, Small (*Pulicaria vulgaris*)
Frostwort, Pointed (*Gymnomitrion apiculatum*)
Galingale, Brown (*Cyperus fuscus*)
Gentian, Alpine (*Gentiana nivalis*)
Gentian, Dune (*Gentianella uliginosa*)
Gentian, Early (*Gentianella anglica*)
Gentian, Fringed (*Gentianella ciliata*)
Gentian, Spring (*Gentiana verna*)
Germander, Cut-leaved (*Teucrium botrys*)
Germander, Water (*Teucrium scordium*)
Gladiolus, Wild (*Gladiolus illyricus*)
Goosefoot, Stinking (*Chenopodium vulvaria*)
Grass-poly (*Lythrum hyssopifolia*)
Grimmia, Blunt-leaved (*Grimmia unicolor*)
Gyalecta, Elm (*Gyalecta ulmi*)
Hare's-ear, Sickle-leaved (*Bupleurum falcatum*)
Hare's-ear, Small (*Bupleurum baldense*)
Hawk's-beard, Stinking (*Crepis foetida*)
Hawkweed, Northroe (*Hieracium northroense*)
Hawkweed, Shetland (*Hieracium zetlandicum*)
Hawkweed, Weak-leaved (*Hieracium attenuatifolium*)
Heath, Blue (*Phyllodoce caerulea*)
Helleborine, Red (*Cephalanthera rubra*)
Helleborine, Young's (*Epipactis youngiana*)
Horsetail, Branched (*Equisetum ramosissimum*)
Hound's-tongue, Green (*Cynoglossum germanicum*)
Knawel, Perennial (*Scleranthus perennis*)
Knotgrass, Sea (*Polygonum maritimum*)
Lady's-slipper (*Cypripedium calceolus*)
Lecanactis, Churchyard (*Lecanactis hemisphaerica*)
Lecanora, Tarn (*Lecanora archariana*)
Lecidea, Copper (*Lecidea inops*)
Leek, Round-headed (*Allium sphaerocephalon*)
Lettuce, Least (*Lactuca saligna*)
Lichen, Arctic Kidney (*Nephroma arcticum*)
Lichen, Ciliate Strap (*Heterodermia leucomelos*)
Lichen, Coralloid Rosette (*Heterodermia propagulifera*)
Lichen, Ear-lobed Dog (*Peltigera lepidophora*)
Lichen, Forked Hair (*Bryoria furcellata*)
Lichen, Golden Hair (*Teloschistes flavicans*)

Lichen, Orange Fruited Elm (*Caloplaca luteoalba*)
Lichen, River Jelly (*Collema dichotomum*)
Lichen, Scaly Breck (*Squamarina lentigera*)
Lichen, Stary Breck (*Buellia asterella*)
Lily, Snowdon (*Lloydia serotina*)
Liverwort (*Petallophyllum ralfsi*)
Liverwort, Lindenberg's Leafy (*Adelanthus lindenbergianus*)
Marsh-mallow, Rough (*Althaea hirsuta*)
Marshwort, Creeping (*Apium repens*)
Milk-parsley, Cambridge (*Selinum carvifolia*)
Moss (*Drepanocladius vernicosus*)
Moss, Alpine Copper (*Mielichoferia mielichoferi*)
Moss, Baltic Bog (*Sphagnum balticum*)
Moss, Blue Dew (*Saelania glaucescens*)
Moss, Blunt-leaved Bristle (*Orthotrichum obtusifolium*)
Moss, Bright Green Cave (*Cyclodictyon laetevirens*)
Moss, Cordate Beard (*Barbula cordata*)
Moss, Cornish Path (*Ditrichum cornubicum*)
Moss, Derbyshire Feather (*Thamnobryum angustifolium*)
Moss, Dune Thread (*Bryum mamillatum*)
Moss, Glaucous Beard (*Barbula glauca*)
Moss, Green Shield (*Buxbaumia viridis*)
Moss, Hair Silk (*Plagiothecium piliferum*)
Moss, Knothole (*Zygodon forsteri*)
Moss, Large Yellow Feather (*Scorpidium turgescens*)
Moss, Millimetre (*Micromitrium tenerum*)
Moss, Multifruited River (*Cryphaea lamyana*)
Moss, Nowell's Limestone (*Zygodon gracilis*)
Moss, Rigid Apple (*Bartramia stricta*)
Moss, Round-leaved Feather (*Rhyncostegium rotundifolium*)
Moss, Schleicher's Thread (*Bryum schleicheri*)
Moss, Triangular Pygmy (*Acaulon triquetrum*)
Moss, Vaucher's Feather (*Hypnum vaucheri*)
Mudwort, Welsh (*Limosella australis*)
Naiad, Holly-leaved (*Najas marina*)
Naiad, Slender (*Najas flexilis*)
Orache, Stalked (*Halimione pedunculata*)
Orchid, Early Spider (*Ophrys sphegodes*)
Orchid, Fen (*Liparis loeselii*)
Orchid, Ghost (*Epipogium aphyllum*)
Orchid, Lapland Marsh (*Dactylorhiza lapponica*)
Orchid, Late Spider (*Ophrys fuciflora*)
Orchid, Lizard (*Himantoglossum hircinum*)
Orchid, Military (*Orchis militaris*)
Orchid, Monkey (*Orchis simia*)
Pannaria, Caledonia (*Pannaria ignobilis*)
Parmelia, New Forest (*Parmelia minarum*)
Parmentaria, Oil Stain (*Parmentaria chilensis*)
Pear, Plymouth (*Pyrus cordata*)
Penny-cress, Perfoliate (*Thlaspi perfoliatum*)
Pennyroyal (*Mentha pulegium*)
Pertusaria, Alpine Moss (*Pertusaria bryontha*)
Physcia, Southern Grey (*Physcia tribacioides*)
Pigmyweed (*Crassula aquatica*)
Pine, Ground (*Ajuga chamaepitys*)
Pink, Cheddar (*Dianthus gratianopolitanus*)
Pink, Childling (*Petroraghia nanteuilii*)
Plantain, Floating Water (*Luronium natans*)
Pseudocyphellaria, Ragged (*Pseudocyphellaria lacerata*)
Psora, Rusty Alpine (*Psora rubiformis*)
Ragwort, Fen (*Senecio paludosus*)
Ramping-fumitory, Martin's (*Fumaria martinii*)
Rampion, Spiked (*Phyteuma spicatum*)
Restharrow, Small (*Ononis reclinata*)
Rock-cress, Alpine (*Arabis alpina*)
Rock-cress, Bristol (*Arabis stricta*)
Rustworth, Western (*Marsupella profunda*)
Sandwort, Norwegian (*Arenaria norvegica*)
Sandwort, Teesdale (*Minuartia stricta*)

Saxifrage, Drooping (*Saxifraga cernua*)
Saxifrage, Marsh (*Saxifrage hirulus*)
Saxifrage, Tufted (*Saxifraga cespitosa*)
Solenopsora, Serpentine (*Solenopsora liparina*)
Solomon's-seal, Whorled (*Polygonatum verticillatum*)
Sow-thistle, Alpine (*Cicerbita alpina*)
Spearwort, Adder's-tongue (*Ranunculus ophioglossifolius*)
Speedwell, Fingered (*Veronica triphyllos*)
Speedwell, Spiked (*Veronica spicata*)
Star-of-Bethlehem, Early (*Gagea bohemica*)
Starfruit (*Damasonium alisma*)
Stonewort, Bearded (*Chara canescens*)
Stonewort, Foxtail (*Lamprothamnium papulosum*)
Strapwort (*Corrigiola litoralis*)
Turpswort (*Geocalyx graveolens*)
Violet, Fen (*Viola persicifolia*)
Viper's-grass (*Scorzonera humilis*)
Water-plantain, Ribbon-leaved (*Alisma gramineum*)
Wood-sedge, Starved (*Carex depauperata*)
Woodsia, Alpine (*Woodsia alpina*)
Woodsia, Oblong (*Woodsia ilvensis*)
Wormwood, Field (*Artemisia campestris*)
Woundwort, Downy (*Stachys germanica*)
Woundwort, Limestone (*Stachys alpina*)
Yellow-rattle, Greater (*Rhinanthus serotinus*)

WILD BIRDS

The Wildlife and Countryside Act 1981 lays down a close season for wild birds (other than game birds) from 1 February to 31 August inclusive, each year. Exceptions to these dates are made for:

Capercaillie and (except Scotland) *Woodcock* – 1 February–30 September
Snipe – 1 February–11 August
Wild Duck and *Wild Goose* (below high water mark) – 21 February–31 August

Birds which may be killed or taken outside the close season (except on Sundays and on Christmas Day in Scotland, and on Sundays in prescribed areas of England and Wales) are the above-named, plus coot, certain wild duck (gadwall, goldeneye, mallard, pintail, pochard, shoveler, teal, tufted duck, wigeon), certain wild geese (Canada, greylag, pink-footed, white-fronted (in England and Wales only)), moorhen, golden plover and woodcock.

Certain wild birds may be killed or taken at any time by authorized persons: crow, collared dove, gull (great and lesser black-backed or herring), jackdaw, jay, magpie, pigeon (feral or wood), rook, sparrow (house), and starling.

All other British birds are fully protected by law throughout the year.

CLOSE SEASONS AND TIMES

GAME BIRDS

In each case the dates are inclusive:

Black game – 11 December–19 August (31 August in Somerset, Devon and New Forest)
Grouse – 11 December–11 August
Partridge – 2 February–31 August
Pheasant – 2 February–30 September
Ptarmigan – (Scotland only) 11 December–11 August

* It is also unlawful in England and Wales to kill this game on a Sunday or Christmas Day

HUNTING AND GROUND GAME

There is no statutory close time for fox-hunting or rabbit-shooting, nor for hares. However, by an Act passed in 1892 the sale of hares or leverets in Great Britain is prohibited from 1 March to 31 July inclusive under a penalty of £1. The recognized date for the opening of the fox-hunting season is 1 November, and it continues till the following April.

DEER

The statutory close seasons for deer (all dates inclusive) are:

	England and Wales	Scotland
Fallow deer		
Male	1 May–31 July	1 May–31 July
Female	1 Mar.–31 Oct.	16 Feb.–20 Oct.
Red deer		
Male	1 May–31 July	21 Oct.–30 June
Female	1 Mar.–31 Oct.	16 Feb.–20 Oct.
Roe deer		
Male	1 Nov.–31 Mar.	21 Oct.–31 Mar.
Female	1 Mar.–31 Oct.	1 April–20 Oct.
Sika deer		
Male	1 May–31 July	21 Oct.–30 June
Female	1 Mar.–31 Oct.	16 Feb.–20 Oct.
Red/Sika hybrids		
Male	—	21 Oct.–30 June
Female	—	16 Feb.–20 Oct.

ANGLING

Where local by-laws neither specify nor dispense with an annual close season, the following are statutory close times (dates inclusive):

Coarse fishing – 15 March–15 June
Game fishing – Trout, 1 October–end February; salmon, 1 November–31 January

Close seasons vary in accordance with local by-laws. It is now necessary in all cases to check with the National Rivers Authority regional office covering the area (details can be found in the local telephone directory).

The NRA introduced in 1992 an annual national rod fishing licence which replaced more than 100 regional licences, as well as removing the need for separate licences for game and coarse fish. Purchase of a national rod fishing licence is legally required of anglers wishing to fish with rod and line for salmon, migratory trout (sea trout), trout, char, grayling and other freshwater fish (coarse fish) and eels, in all waters within the area of the NRA. The full licence, valid 1 April to 31 March, costs £13.25 in 1993–4. Seven day licences and concessionary licences (for senior citizens aged 60 and over, registered disabled and juniors aged 12–16) are available at £6.75.

Historic Monuments

ENGLAND

The following is a select list of monuments, most of which are in the care of English Heritage or the National Trust. Charges for admission are those obtaining in 1993–4. Concessionary rates are available for children, etc. Standard hours of opening are:

1 April–30 September   10–6
1 October–31 March   10–4

* Monuments open all year. Other monuments open from 1 April to 30 September only. All monuments are closed on 24–26 December and 1 January. Some smaller sites may close for the lunch-hour, which is normally 1–2 p.m. During the winter season, many English Heritage monuments are closed on Mondays.

*AVEBURY, Wilts. Adm. free. Remains of stone circles constructed 4,000 years ago surrounding the later village of Avebury. Also AVEBURY MUSEUM, adm. £1.30

*BATTLE ABBEY, E. Sussex. £2.70. Remains of the abbey founded by William the Conqueror on the site of the Battle of Hastings

*BEESTON CASTLE, Cheshire. £2.00. Thirteenth-century inner ward with gatehouse and towers, and considerable remains of large outer ward

*BOLSOVER CASTLE, Derbyshire. £2.00. Notable for its interesting 17th-century buildings

*BOSCOBEL HOUSE, Shropshire. £3.00. Timber-framed early 17th-century hunting lodge with later alterations. A descendent of Charles II's 'Royal Oak' is nearby

BRINKBURN PRIORY, Northumberland. £1.20. A house of Augustinian canons; the church (c.1200, repaired 1858) and parts of the cloister buildings survive

*BYLAND ABBEY, North Yorkshire. £1.20. Considerable remains of church and conventual buildings date from the abbey's foundation in 1177 by the Cistercians

*CARISBROOKE CASTLE, Isle of Wight. £3.20. Norman castle, the prison of Charles I from 1647–8

*CARLISLE CASTLE, Cumbria. £2.00. Medieval castle, prison of Mary Queen of Scots. Inner and outer wards enclosing a 12th century keep

*CASTLE ACRE PRIORY, Norfolk. £2.00. Extensive remains include the 12th century church and the prior's lodgings

*CASTLE RISING CASTLE, Norfolk. £1.20. A 12th century keep standing in a massive earthwork with its gatehouse and bridge

*CHESTERS ROMAN FORT, Northumberland. £2.00. Fine example of a Roman cavalry fort

*CHYSAUSTER ANCIENT VILLAGE, Cornwall. £1.30. Romano–Cornish village, 2nd and 3rd century AD, probably on a late Iron Age site

*CLEEVE ABBEY, Somerset. £1.70. Much of the claustral buildings survive including timber-roofed frater, but only foundations of the church

*CLIFFORD'S TOWER, York. £1.20. Thirteenth-century tower built on a mound

*CORBRIDGE ROMAN SITE, Northumberland. £2.00. Excavations have revealed the central area of a Roman town and successive military bases

*CORFE CASTLE, Dorset. £2.80. Feb.–Oct., daily. Nov.–Jan., weekends only, PM. Ruined former royal castle dating back to the 11th century

*DEAL CASTLE, Kent. £2.00. The largest and most complete of the forts erected by Henry VIII for coastal defence

*DOVER CASTLE, Kent. £5.00. One of the strongest British castles, with Roman, Saxon and Norman features

*DUNSTANBURGH CASTLE, Northumberland. £1.20. The 14th century castle standing on a cliff above the sea has a substantial gatehouse-keep

*FARLEIGH HUNGERFORD CASTLE, Somerset. £1.20. Late 14th century castle of two courts. The chapel contains fine tomb of Sir Thomas Hungerford

FARNHAM CASTLE KEEP, Surrey. £1.50. Built by the Bishops of Winchester, the motte of the castle is dominated by a large 12th century shell keep. Foundations of a Norman tower

*FOUNTAINS ABBEY, nr. Ripon, North Yorkshire. £3.50. Closed Fri. Nov.–Jan. Ruined monastery founded by Cistercian monks in 1132. Eighteenth-century landscaped garden at Studley Royal

*FRAMLINGHAM CASTLE, Suffolk. £1.70. Impressive castle (c.1200) with high curtain walls enclosing an almshouse of 1639

*FURNESS ABBEY, Cumbria. £2.00. Founded in 1123 by Stephen, afterwards King of England; extensive remains of church and conventual buildings

*GLASTONBURY ABBEY, Somerset. £2.00. Ruined abbey built in AD 708 by the Saxon Ina, on the site of an earlier monastery

*GOODRICH CASTLE, Hereford and Worcester. £1.70. Extensive remains of 13th and 14th century castle incorporating 12th century keep

*GRIMES GRAVES, Norfolk. £1.20. Extensive group of flint mines dating from the Neolithic period. One shaft can be descended

*HAILES ABBEY, Gloucestershire. £1.80. Ruins of a Cistercian monastery founded in 1246. Museum contains some fine architectural fragments

*HELMSLEY CASTLE, North Yorkshire. £1.70. Twelfth century keep and curtain wall with 16th century domestic buildings. Spectacular earthwork defences

*HOUSESTEADS ROMAN FORT, Northumberland. £2.00. Excavation has exposed this infantry fort on Hadrian's Wall with its extra-mural civilian settlement

*KENILWORTH CASTLE, Warwickshire. £1.70. One of the most extensive castles in Britain, showing many styles of building from 1155 to 1649

LANERCOST PRIORY, Cumbria. 80p. The nave of the Augustinian priory church, c.1166, is still used and there are remains of other claustral buildings

*LINDISFARNE PRIORY, Northumberland. £2.00 (subject to tide). The bishopric of the Northumbrian kingdom destroyed by the Danes; re-established in 11th century as a Benedictine priory, now ruined

*LULLINGSTONE ROMAN VILLA, Kent. £1.70. A large villa occupied through much of the Roman period; fine mosaics

*MIDDLEHAM CASTLE, North Yorkshire. £1.20. Childhood home of Richard III. The 12th century keep stands within later fortifications and domestic buildings

*MOUNT GRACE PRIORY, North Yorkshire. £2.00. Carthusian monastery, founded 1398, with remains of monastic buildings

NETLEY ABBEY, Hampshire. £1.20. Extensive remains of Cistercian abbey, founded 1239, with ruined Tudor house

*OLD SARUM, Wiltshire. £1.30. Large earthworks enclosing the excavated remains of the castle and the first Salisbury cathedral, begun in 1078

*ORFORD CASTLE, Suffolk. £1.70. Circular keep of c.1170 and remains of coastal defence castle built by Henry II

*PENDENNIS CASTLE, Cornwall. £2.00. Well-preserved castle erected by Henry VIII for coastal defence

*PEVENSEY CASTLE, East Sussex. £1.70. Walls of a 4th century Roman fort enclosing remains of an 11th century castle

*PEVERIL CASTLE, Derbyshire. £1.20. In a picturesque and nearly impregnable position, this 12th century castle is defended on two sides by precipitous rocks

*PORTCHESTER CASTLE, Hampshire. £1.70. Walls of a late Roman fort enclosing a Norman keep and an Augustinian priory church

*RICHBOROUGH CASTLE, Kent. £1.70. The landing-site of the Claudian invasion in AD 43, with massive 3rd century stone walls

*RICHMOND CASTLE, North Yorkshire. £1.70. This 12th century keep, with 11th century curtain wall and gatehouse, commands Swaledale

*RIEVAULX ABBEY, North Yorkshire. £2.00. Founded c.1132. Extensive remains include an early Cistercian nave and fine 13th century choir and claustral buildings

*ROCHESTER CASTLE, Kent. £1.70. Eleventh century castle partly founded on the Roman city wall, with a square keep of c.1130

*ST AUGUSTINE'S ABBEY, Kent. £1.20. Remains of Benedictine monastery, with Norman church, on site of abbey founded by St Augustine in AD 598

*ST MAWES CASTLE, Cornwall. £1.30. Coastal defence castle built by Henry VIII consisting of central tower and three bastions

*SCARBOROUGH CASTLE, North Yorkshire. £1.70. Remains of 12th century keep and curtain walls dominating the town

*STONEHENGE, Wiltshire. £2.70. Prehistoric monument consisting of a series of concentric stone circles surrounded by a ditch and bank

*TILBURY FORT, Essex. £1.70. One of Henry VIII's coastal forts, extended by Charles II

*TINTAGEL CASTLE, Cornwall. £2.00. 12th century castle on cliff top. Dark Age settlement site

*TYNEMOUTH PRIORY and CASTLE, Tyne and Wear. £1.20. Remains of a Benedictine priory, founded 1090, on Saxon monastic site. Coastal batteries with reconstructed First World War magazine

*WALMER CASTLE, Kent. £2.70. (Closed when Lord Warden is in residence.) One of Henry VIII's coastal defence castles, now the residence of the Lord Warden of the Cinque Ports

*WALTHAM ABBEY, Essex. Adm. free. Ruined abbey including the nave of the former Abbey church c.1120, 'Harold's Bridge' and late 14th-century gatehouse. Traditionally, burial place of Harold II (1066)

*WARKWORTH CASTLE, Northumberland. £1.70. 15th century keep amidst earlier ruins with a 14th century hermitage upstream

*WHITBY ABBEY, North Yorkshire. £1.20. 13th and 14th century Benedictine church on site of monastery founded in AD 657

*WROXETER ROMAN CITY, Shropshire. £1.70. The 2nd century public baths and part of the forum remain of the Roman town of Viroconium

WALES

The following is a select list of monuments under the control of Cadw: Welsh Historic Monuments. Charges for admission are those obtaining in 1993–4; concessionary rates are available for children, etc.

Standard hours of admission:

	Weekdays	Sundays
29 March–24 October	9.30–6.30	9.30–6.30
25 October–28 March	9.30–4.00	2.00–4.00

All monuments are closed on Christmas Eve, Christmas Day, Boxing Day and New Year's Day.

BEAUMARIS CASTLE, Anglesey, Gwynedd. £1.50. The finest example of the concentrically planned castle in Britain, it is still almost intact

CAERLEON ROMAN AMPHITHEATRE, Gwent. £1.25. Late 1st century oval arena surrounded by bank for spectators

CAERLEON ROMAN FORTRESS BATHS, Gwent. £1.25, joint ticket £2.00 (with National Museum of Wales). Rare example of a legionary bath-house

CAERNARFON CASTLE, Gwynedd. £3.50. The most important of the Edwardian castles, built together with the town wall between 1283 and 1330

CAERPHILLY CASTLE, Mid Glamorgan. £2.00. Concentrically planned castle (c.1270) notable for its great scale and use of water defences

CASTELL COCH, S. Glamorgan. £2.00. Rebuilt 1875–90 on medieval foundations

CHEPSTOW CASTLE, Gwent. £2.90. Fine rectangular keep in the middle of extensive fortifications

CONWY CASTLE, Gwynedd. £2.90. Built by Edward I to guard the Conwy ferry

CRICCIETH CASTLE, Gwynedd. £1.80. A native Welsh castle of the early 13th century, much altered by Edward I

DENBIGH CASTLE, Clwyd. £1.50. The remains of the castle, which dates from 1282–1322, include an unusual triangular gatehouse

HARLECH CASTLE, Gwynedd. £2.90. Well-preserved Edwardian castle with a concentric plan sited on a rocky outcrop above the former shore-line

RAGLAN CASTLE, Gwent. £1.80. Extensive remains of 15th century castle with moated hexagonal keep

ST DAVID'S, BISHOP'S PALACE, Dyfed. £1.50. Extensive remains of principal residence of Bishop of St David's dating from 1280–1350

TINTERN ABBEY, Gwent. £2.00. Extensive remains of 13th century church and conventual buildings of this Cistercian monastery

TRETOWER COURT, Powys. £1.80. Medieval house with remains of castle nearby

SCOTLAND

The following is a select list of monuments under the control of Historic Scotland.

Except where indicated differently, charges are: adults £1.00, concessions (con.) 50p.

Monuments open at any reasonable time are indicated by *. Standard hours of opening (marked †) are:

	Weekdays	Sundays
April–September	9.30–6.30	2.00–6.30
October–March	9.30–4.30	2.00–4.30

*ABERLEMNO SCULPTURED STONES, Tayside. Adm. free. Four Pictish stones

*ANTONINE WALL, Central and Strathclyde regions. Adm. free. Built about AD 142, consists of ditch, turf rampart and road, with forts every two miles

†BLACKHOUSE ARNOL, Western Isles. Closed Sun. £1.50, con. 80p. Traditional Lewis thatched house

†BONAWE IRONWORKS, Strathclyde. Closed in winter. £1.50, con. 80p. Charcoal-fuelled ironworks

*BROCH OF BIRSAY, Orkney. Adm. free. Remains of Norse church

†CAERLAVEROCK CASTLE, Dumfries and Galloway. £1.70, con. 90p. One of the finest examples of early classical Renaissance building in Scotland

†CAIRNPAPPLE HILL, Lothian. Closed in winter. A prehistoric ritual complex and Bronze Age cairn

*CALLANISH, Western Isles. Adm. free. Standing stones in a cross-shaped setting, dating back to 3000 BC

*CATERTHUNS (BROWN AND WHITE), Tayside. Adm. free. Iron Age hill forts

*CLAVA CAIRNS, Highland. Adm. free. Late Neolithic or early Bronze Age cairns

†DRYBURGH ABBEY, Borders. £2.00, con. £1.00. Twelfth-century abbey containing tomb of Sir Walter Scott

EDINBURGH CASTLE, including Scottish National War Memorial, Scottish United Services Museum and historic apartments. Open April–September 9.30–6, October–March 9.30–5. Adm. to War Memorial, free; to all other areas £4.00, con. £2.00

†EDZELL CASTLE, Tayside. Closed Tuesday p.m. and Friday in winter. £1.70, con. 90p. A late medieval tower house incorporated into a 16th-century courtyard mansion. Walled garden

†ELGIN CATHEDRAL, Grampian. Closed Thursday p.m. and Friday in winter. £1.20, con. 60p. Thirteenth-century cathedral with fine chapterhouse

†FORT GEORGE, Highland. £2.30, con. £1.20. A complete view of the defensive system of an 18th-century artillery fort

†GLASGOW CATHEDRAL, Strathclyde. Adm. free. Medieval cathedral with elaborately vaulted crypt

*GLENELG BROCHS, Highland. Adm. free. Two broch towers with well-preserved structural features

†HERMITAGE CASTLE, Borders. Closed weekdays in winter. £1.20, con. 60p. Extensive ruined castle dating back to the 14th century

†HUNTLY CASTLE, Grampian. Closed Thursday p.m. and Friday in winter. £1.70, con. 90p. Ruin of a house built in the 16th and 17th centuries

†JARLSHOF, Shetland. Closed all winter. £1.70, con. 90p. Remains of Bronze Age village

†JEDBURGH ABBEY, Borders. £2.00, con. £1.00. Romanesque and early Gothic style church founded about 1138

†KELSO ABBEY, Borders. Adm. free. Remains of west end of great abbey church founded 1128

†LINLITHGOW PALACE, Lothian. £1.70, con. 90p. Ruin of royal palace set in its own park. Birthplace of Mary, Queen of Scots

*LOANHEAD STONE CIRCLE, Grampian. Adm. free. Recumbent stone circle enclosing a ring cairn

†MAES HOWE, Orkney. £1.70, con. 90p. Prehistoric tomb

†MEIGLE MUSEUM, Tayside. Closed all winter. Pictish stones

†MELROSE ABBEY, Borders. £2.00, con. £1.00p. Ruin of Cistercian abbey founded about 1136

*MOUSA BROCH, Shetland. Adm. free. Finest surviving Iron Age broch tower

*NETHER LARGIE CAIRNS, Argyll and Bute. Adm. free. Bronze Age and Neolithic cairns

†NEW ABBEY CORN MILL, Dumfries and Galloway. Closed Thursday p.m. and Friday in winter. £1.50, con. 80p. Water-powered oatmeal mill in working order

*RING OF BROGAR, Orkney. Adm. free. Late Neolithic circle of upright stones with an enclosing ditch spanned by causeways

*RUTHWELL CROSS, Dumfries and Galloway. Adm. free. Seventh-century Anglian cross

†ST ANDREWS CASTLE AND CATHEDRAL, Fife. Separate adm. fee for Cathedral; £1.50, con. 80p. Ruins of 13th-century castle and remains of the largest cathedral in Scotland

†SKARA BRAE, Orkney. £2.00, con. £1.00. Prehistoric village

†SMAILHOLM TOWER, Borders. Closed in winter. £1.50, con. 80p. Well-preserved rectangular tower

STIRLING CASTLE, Central. Open April–September 9.30–6, October–March 9.30–5. £2.50, con. £1.30/£1.00. Great Hall and gatehouse of James IV, palace of James V, Chapel Royal remodelled by James VI, artillery fortifications

†TANTALLON CASTLE, Lothian. £1.70, con. 90p. Closed Thursday p.m. and Friday in winter. Fortification with earthwork defences and a 14th-century curtain wall with towers

†THREAVE CASTLE, Dumfries and Galloway. Adm. includes ferry trip. Closed in winter. £1.20, con. 60p. Late 14th-century tower with an artillery fortification. On an island; approached by boat, long walk to castle

Historic Houses and Castles

Dates of opening and admission fees shown are those which obtained in 1993, and are subject to modification. Specific opening hours are not given but may be checked by telephone. Most houses have concessionary rates for certain categories of visitor.

Space permits only a selection of some of the more noteworthy houses in the UK which are open to the public.
* Property of the National Trust
Adm. admission
PM open in afternoons only

*A LA RONDE, Exmouth. 1 April–31 Oct. Sun.–Thurs. Adm. £3.00. Tel: 0395-265514. Unique 16-sided house built in 1796

ALNWICK CASTLE, Northumberland. Maundy Thursday–mid Oct. Adm. £3.60. Tel: 0665-510777. The second largest inhabited castle in England, with Italian Renaissance-style interior

ALTHORP, Northants. Opening times and prices subject to change. Contact Lord Spencer. House originally built in early 16th century. Fine art collection

*ANGLESEY ABBEY, Cambs. 27 March–17 Oct. Wed.–Sun. and Bank Holiday Mons. Closed Good Fri. PM. Adm. £4.50. Gardens only Adm. £2.50. Tel: 0223-811200. House built about 1600; bought by Lord Fairhaven in early 20th century. Outstanding grounds with unique statuary

ARUNDEL CASTLE, W. Sussex. 1 April–29 Oct. daily (not Sat.). PM. Adm. charge. Tel: 0903-883136. Castle dating from the Norman Conquest. Seat of the Dukes of Norfolk

BALMORAL CASTLE, Grampian. 1 May–31 July, daily (not Sun.). Adm. £1.75. Tel: 03397-42334. Mid 19th-century Baronial-style castle built for Queen Victoria and Prince Albert. The Queen's private Highland residence

BANQUETING HOUSE, Whitehall, London. Daily (not Sun. or Bank Holidays). Adm. £2.75. Tel: 071-839 3787. Designed by Inigo Jones; ceiling paintings by Rubens. Site of the execution of Charles I

*BASILDON PARK, Berks. April–Oct. (not Mon. except Bank Holidays; not Tues., not Good Friday). Adm. £3.50. Grounds £2.50. Tel: 0734-843040. Palladian house built in 1776; unusual octagonal room

BEAULIEU, Hants. Daily (not Christmas). Adm. charge. Tel: 0590-612345. House and gardens, Beaulieu abbey and exhibition of monastic life, National Motor Museum (see also page 592)

*BELTON HOUSE, Grantham. April–Oct. Wed.–Sun. and Bank Holiday Mons. Closed Good Friday. PM. Adm. £4.00. Tel: 0476-66116. Fine 17th-century country house in landscaped park

BELVOIR CASTLE, nr. Grantham. 1 April–1 Oct. daily (not Mon., Fri. except Bank Holidays). Adm. £3.50. Tel: 0476-870262. Seat of the Dukes of Rutland; early 19th-century Gothic-style castle

BERKELEY CASTLE, Glos. April–Sept. daily (not Mon. except Bank Holidays). PM only except May–Aug., Tues.–Sat. and Bank Holidays 11–5. Oct. Sun. PM only. Adm. £3.70. Tel: 0453-810332. Completed 1153; site of the murder of Edward II in 1327. Elizabethan terraced gardens and tropical butterfly house

BLAIR CASTLE, Tayside. April–last Fri. in Oct. daily (Sun. April, May and Oct PM.). Adm. £4.00. Tel: 0796-481207. Seat of the Duke of Atholl; mid 18th-century mansion with 13th-century tower

BLENHEIM PALACE, Oxon. Mid-March–31 Oct. daily. Adm. charge. Tel: 0993-811325. Seat of the Duke of Marlborough and Winston Churchill's birthplace; designed by Vanbrugh

BOUGHTON HOUSE, Northants. Aug.–1 Sept. daily PM. Staterooms by prior booking. Grounds 1 May–30 Sept. daily (not Fri.) PM. Adm. charge. Tel: 0536-515731. French-style 17th-century house with fine state apartments

BOWHILL, Selkirk. House 1 July–31 July daily PM; Grounds early May to late summer daily (not Fri.) PM. Adm. £3, Grounds only, £1. Tel: 0750-20732. Seat of the Duke of Buccleuch and Queensberry. Fine collection of paintings including portrait miniatures

BROADLANDS, Hants. Easter–end Sept. daily (not Fri. except Aug. and Good Friday). Adm. £5.00 Tel: 0794-516878. Palladian mansion set in Capability Brown parkland. Mountbatten exhibition

BRONTË PARSONAGE, Haworth, W. Yorks. Daily (not Christmas or mid Jan.–mid Feb.). Adm. £3.50. Tel: 0535-642323. Home of the Brontë sisters; museum and memorabilia

BROUGHTON CASTLE, Oxon. 19 May–12 Sept. Wed., Sun. (also Thurs. in July and Aug.) and Bank Holiday Suns and Mons PM. Adm. £3.00. Tel: 0295-262624. Moated medieval mansion; important Civil War role

BUCKFAST ABBEY, Devon. Daily. Adm. free. Tel: 0364-43301. Abbey church erected between 1907 and 1938

BUCKINGHAM PALACE, London SW1. Open daily for eight weeks from early August, annually until further notice. Adm. £8. Tel: 071-930 5526. The Queen's official London residence. Eighteen state rooms on view, including the throne room and dining-room; also the picture gallery, housing the Royal Collection

*BUCKLAND ABBEY, Devon. 1 April–31 Oct. daily except Thurs. Nov.–March Wed., Sat., Sun. (Wed. pre-booked parties only) PM. Adm. £4.00. Tel: 0822-853607. Thirteenth-century Cistercian monastery. Home of Sir Francis Drake

BURGHLEY HOUSE, Stamford. 1 April–3 Oct. (closed 4 Sept) daily. Adm. £4.80. Tel: 0780-52451. Late Elizabethan house; vast state apartments

*CALKE ABBEY, Derbyshire. 3 April–end Oct., Sat.–Wed. Closed Good Friday. PM. Adm. £4.20 by timed ticket only. Tel: 0332-863822. Baroque early 18th-century mansion

CARDIFF CASTLE . Daily (not Christmas, New Year). Adm. charge. Tel: 0222-822086. Castle built on the site of a Roman fort; spectacular towers and rich interior

*CARLYLE'S HOUSE, Chelsea, London. April–end Oct. Wed.–Sun. and Bank Holiday Mons (not Good Friday). Adm. £2.50. Tel: 071-352 7087. Home of Thomas Carlyle, Scottish historian and philosopher

*CASTLE COOLE, Enniskillen. Easter period, daily; June, July, Aug. daily (not Thurs.); Sat., Sun. and Bank Holidays in April, May, Sept. PM. Adm. £2.30, Grounds April–Sept. free. Tel: 0365-322690. Eighteenth-century mansion by James Wyatt

*CASTLE DROGO, Devon. April–Oct. daily except Fri. Adm. £4.60. Grounds only £2.00. Tel: 064743-3306. Granite castle designed by Lutyens

CASTLE HOWARD, N. Yorks. 19 March–31 Oct., daily. Adm. £5.50. Tel: 065384-333. Designed by Vanbrugh 1699–1726; mausoleum designed by Hawksmoor

CAWDOR CASTLE, Inverness. May–3 Oct., daily. Adm. £3.50, Grounds £1.80. Tel: 06677-615. Fourteenth-century tower-house with mainly 17th-century additions

*CHARTWELL, Kent. Open three days each week. Times vary. Adm. £4.20, Grounds only £2.00. Tel: 0732-866368. Home of Sir Winston Churchill

CHATSWORTH, Derbyshire. 21 March-31 Oct. daily. Grounds 21 March-3 Oct., daily. Adm. charge. Tel: 0246-582204. Tudor mansion with later additions, in magnificent parkland

CHICHELEY HALL, nr. Newport Pagnell. 11 April-30 May, Aug. Sun. and Bank Holidays PM. Adm. £3.00. Tel: 023065-252. Early Georgian house with notable brickwork and a Palladian hall

*CLIVEDEN, Maidenhead. House, April-31 Oct., Thurs. and Sun. PM. Gardens March-Dec. daily. Adm. £3.50, £1.00 extra for house. Tel: 0628-605069. Former home of the Astors, now an hotel. About 375 acres of garden and woodland

*COMPTON CASTLE, nr. Paignton. April-31 Oct. Mon., Wed., Thurs. daily. Adm. £2.60. Tel: 0803-872112. Fortified manor house with notable façade

*CROFT CASTLE, Herefordshire. Easter Bank Holiday weekend (not Fri.), May-Sept. Wed.-Sun., Bank Holiday Mons., April and Oct. weekends. PM. Adm. £2.80. Tel: 056885-246. Border castle mentioned in the Domesday Book; Georgian-Gothic interior

DICKENS HOUSE, London, WC1. Daily (not Sun., Christmas and Bank Holidays). Adm. £2.00. Tel: 071-405 2127. House occupied by Dickens 1837-9; manuscripts, furniture and portraits

DR JOHNSON'S HOUSE, London, EC4. Daily (not Sun. and Bank Holidays). Adm. £2.00. Tel: 071-353 3745. Home of Samuel Johnson, built in 1700

DRUMLANRIG CASTLE, Dumfries. May-Aug., daily (not Thurs.). Sun., PM. Adm. charge. Tel: 0848-31682. Castle with baroque decorative features and notable art and furniture collections

GLAMIS CASTLE, Tayside. 4 April-11 Oct., daily. Adm. £4.00, grounds only £2.00. Tel: 03784-242. A royal residence and seat of the Lyon family (later earls of Strathmore and Kinghorne) since 1372

GREENWICH, London SE10. ROYAL OBSERVATORY, daily (Sun., PM). Closed 24-26 Dec. Adm. charge. Former Royal Observatory (founded 1675) where the time ball and zero meridian of longitude can be seen. THE QUEEN'S HOUSE, daily (Sun., PM). Closed 24-26 Dec. Adm. charge. Tel: 081-858 4422. Designed for Anne of Denmark, wife of James I, by Inigo Jones; begun in 1616. PAINTED HALL AND CHAPEL, daily (not Thurs.), PM. Visitors are also admitted to Sunday service in the Chapel at 11 a.m. except during Royal Naval College vacations

HADDON HALL, Derbyshire. 1 April-30 Sept. Tues.-Sun., and Bank Holidays. Closed Sun. in July and Aug. (except Bank Holiday weekends). Adm. £3.40. Tel: 0629-812855. Well-maintained 12th-century manor house

*HAM HOUSE, Richmond, Surrey. House re-opens after restoration on 3 April 1994. April-Oct. Sat.-Wed. Nov.-Dec. weekends only. Adm. £4.00. Garden all year (except Mon). Adm. free. Tel: 081-940 1950. Stuart house with fine interior decoration

HAMPTON COURT PALACE, East Molesey, Surrey. Daily (closed 24-26 Dec.). Adm. £5.90. Tel: 081-781 9500. Sixteenth-century palace built by Cardinal Wolsey, with additions by Sir Christopher Wren. Beautiful gardens with maze; Tudor tennis court (summer only)

*HARDWICK HALL, Derbyshire. 1 April-31 Oct. House Wed., Thurs., Sat., Sun., Bank Holiday Mons. Garden daily to end Oct. (not Good Friday). PM. Adm. £5.00, Garden only, £2.00. Tel: 0246-850430. Built 1591-7 by Bess of Hardwick; notable furniture and tapestries

HAREWOOD HOUSE, Leeds. 3 April-31 Oct. daily. Adm. charge. Tel: 0532-886331. Eighteenth-century house designed by John Carr and Robert Adam; park landscaped by Capability Brown

HATFIELD HOUSE, Herts. 25 March-10 Oct. daily (not Mon. except Bank Holidays, not Good Friday). PM except Bank Holidays. Grounds, times vary. Adm. charge. Tel: 0707-262823. Jacobean house built by Robert Cecil, and the family home of the Cecils. Surviving wing of Royal Palace of Hatfield (1497)

HEVER CASTLE, Kent. 16 March-7 Nov., daily PM. Grounds 11-6. Adm. charge. Tel: 0732-865224. Thirteenth-century double-moated castle, childhood home of Anne Boleyn

HOLKER HALL, Cumbria. 1 April-31 October daily (not Sat.). Adm. charge. Tel: 05395-58328. Former home of the Dukes of Devonshire; award-winning gardens

HOLKHAM HALL, Norfolk. 30 May-30 Sept. Sun.-Thurs. and Easter, Spring and Summer Bank Holidays. PM, except Bank Holidays. Adm. £2.70. Tel: 0328-710227. Fine Palladian mansion

HOPETOUN HOUSE, nr. Edinburgh. 9 April-3 October, daily. Adm. £3.50. Tel: 031-331 2451. House designed by Sir William Bruce, enlarged by William Adam

HOUGHTON HALL, Norfolk. Easter Sun.-27 Sept., Sun., Thurs. and Bank Holidays. Opening times to be announced. Adm. £4.00. Tel: 0485-528569. Home of the Marquess of Cholmondeley; built for Sir Robert Walpole in the 18th century; fine example of Palladian architecture

*HUGHENDEN MANOR, High Wycombe. April-end Oct. (not Good Friday), Wed.-Sun. and Bank Holiday Mons PM. March, weekends only. Adm. £3.30. Tel: 0494-532580. Home of Benjamin Disraeli; small formal garden

INVERARAY CASTLE, Argyll. 1st Sat. in April-2nd Sun. in Oct. daily (not Fri., except July-Aug.), Sun., PM. Adm. £3.00. Woods open all year. Tel: 0499-2203. Seat of the Dukes of Argyll; Gothic-style 18th-century castle

IONA ABBEY, Inner Hebrides. Daily. Adm. £2.00. Tel: 06817-404. Monastery founded by St Columba in AD 563 and restored by the Iona community

JANE AUSTEN'S HOUSE, Chawton, Hants. April-Oct. daily, Jan. and Feb. weekends, Nov., Dec. and March, Wed.-Sun. (not Christmas). Adm. £1.50. Tel: 0420-83262. Jane Austen's home from 1809 until 1817

KEATS HOUSE, Hampstead, London. April-Oct. daily (Sun. and Bank Holidays, PM). Nov.-March, daily (Mon.-Fri. and Sun., PM). (Not Christmas, New Year, Good Friday, Easter Eve, 4 May.) Adm. free. Tel: 071-435 2062. Home of John Keats from 1818 to 1820

KELMSCOTT MANOR, nr. Lechlade, Glos. April-Sept., Wed. only. Thurs., Fri. by written application. Adm. (Wed.) £4.50. Summer home of William Morris, containing many products of Morris and Co. Tel: 0367-252486

KENSINGTON PALACE, London W8. Daily (closed 24-26 Dec., 1 Jan. and Good Friday). Adm. £3.90. Tel: 071-937 9561. Built in 1605 and bought by William and Mary in 1689; enlarged by Wren. Birthplace of Queen Victoria

KENWOOD, Hampstead Heath, London. Daily (closed 24-25 Dec.). Adm. free. Tel: 081-348 1286. Adam villa housing the Iveagh Bequest of paintings and furniture. Open air concerts in summer

KEW PALACE, Surrey. April-Sept. daily. Adm. £1.20. Tel: 081-940 3321. Built in 1631 as the Dutch House; residence of George III. Also QUEEN CHARLOTTE'S COTTAGE. April-Sept., weekends and Bank Holidays only. Adm. 70p. Joint ticket Palace and Cottage £1.50

*KINGSTON LACY HOUSE, Dorset. 3 April–31 Oct., PM.
Sat.–Wed. Adm. £5.00, Grounds only £2.00. Tel: 0202–
883402. Seventeenth-century house with 18th- and 19th-
century alterations; important collection of paintings
KNEBWORTH HOUSE, Herts. 3 April–31 May, Sat., Sun.,
School and Bank Holidays, 1 June–5 Sept. daily (not
Mon.). PM. Weekends only to 3 Oct. (Closed 16–19 July).
Adm. £4.00, Grounds only, £2.50. Tel: 0438–812661.
Tudor manor house concealed by 19th-century Gothic
decoration; Lutyens gardens
*KNOLE, Kent. April–Oct. Wed., Fri.–Sun. and Bank
Holiday Mons. Thurs., PM. Adm. £4.00, Garden 50p.
Tel: 0732–450608. House dating from 15th century set
in magnificent parkland; fine art treasures
LEEDS CASTLE, Kent. 15 March–end Oct. daily. Nov.–
March, weekends only. Adm. charge. Tel: 0622–765400.
Castle dating from 9th century, on two small islands in
the middle of a lake. Former royal palace
LINCOLN CASTLE, Daily (closed 25–26 Dec.). Adm. £1.40.
Tel: 0522–511068. Built by William the Conqueror in
1068
*LITTLE MORETON HALL, Cheshire. April–30 Sept.,
Wed.–Sun. and Bank Holiday Mons (not Good Friday).
Oct. weekends, Wed. PM. Adm. £2.50, weekends and
Bank Holidays. £3.50. Tel: 0260–272018. Timber-
framed moated manor house with a knot garden
LONGLEAT HOUSE, Warminster. House daily (not
Christmas). Safari Park mid-March–Oct. Adm. charge.
Tel: 0985–844551. Elizabethan house (1580) in the
Italian Renaissance style
LUTON HOO, Beds. April–Oct., Fri.–Sun., PM and Bank
Holiday Mondays. Adm. £4.50. Tel: 0582–22955.
Houses the Wernher collection of china, glass, pictures
and other objets d'art
MARBLE HILL HOUSE, Twickenham, Middx. All year,
daily (not 24, 25 Dec.). Adm. free. Tel: 081–892 5115.
English Palladian villa with early Georgian paintings and
furniture
MICHELHAM PRIORY, E. Sussex. 25 March–31 Oct. daily.
Nov. and March, Sun. only. Adm. £3.30. Tel: 0323–
844224. Tudor house built onto an Augustinian priory
*MONTACUTE HOUSE, Yeovil. 1 April–31 Oct. daily (not
Tues.) PM. Closed Good Friday. Grounds open all year
(not Tues.). Adm. £4.60, Grounds only £2.50. Tel:
0935–823289. Elizabethan house built of Ham Hill stone
*MOUNT STEWART, Co. Down. Times vary. Adm. House,
Garden, Temple £3.30, Garden and Temple only £2.70.
Tel: 024774–387. Eighteenth-century house, childhood
home of Lord Castlereagh
OSBORNE HOUSE, IOW. 1 April–31 Oct. daily. Adm.
£5.40. Tel: 0983–200022. Queen Victoria's seaside
residence
*OSTERLEY PARK HOUSE, Isleworth, Middx. April–Oct.
Wed.–Sat. PM. Sun., Bank Holiday Mon. 11–5. (Closed
Good Fri.). Adm. £3.50, Grounds (open all year) free.
Tel: 081–560 3918. Elizabethan mansion set in parkland
PALACE OF HOLYROODHOUSE, Edinburgh. Open daily
(not Sun. in winter, and not when The Queen is in
residence). Adm. charge. Tel: 031–556 7371. The
Queen's official Scottish residence. Main part of the
palace built 1671–9
*PENRHYN CASTLE, Bangor. 1 April–31 Oct. daily (not
Tues.) PM. Adm. £4.20, Garden £2.00. Tel: 0248–
353084. Neo-Norman castle built in the 19th century.
Industrial Railway Museum
PENSHURST PLACE, Kent. 27 March–4 Oct. daily PM.
Adm. £4.50, Grounds only £3.00. Tel: 0892–870307.
Stately home with medieval Baron's Hall and 14th-
century gardens

*PETWORTH HOUSE, W. Sussex. April–Oct. Tues.–Sun.,
Bank Holiday Mons., Good Friday. PM. Adm. £4.00. Tel:
0798–42207. Late 17th-century house set in deer park
*POLESDEN LACY, Surrey. April–Oct. Wed.–Sun., also
Bank Holidays and preceding Suns. March and Nov.,
weekends only. PM. Grounds open daily all year. Adm.
charge. Tel: 0372–458203. Regency villa remodelled in
the Edwardian era. Fine paintings, tapestries and
furniture
PORTMEIRION, Gwynedd. All year daily. Adm. £2.90
(April–Oct.) £1.45 (Nov.–March). Tel: 0766–770228.
Village in Italianate style
POWDERHAM CASTLE, Exeter. Easter–Oct. Sun.–Fri.
Adm. charge. Tel: 0626–890243. Medieval castle with
18th- and 19th-century alterations
*POWIS CASTLE, Powys. 1 April–30 June, 1 Sept.–31 Oct.
Wed.–Sun.; July and Aug. Tues.–Sun. Open Bank
Holiday Mons. PM. Adm. £5.80, Museum, garden £3.60.
Tel: 0938–554336. Medieval castle with interior in
variety of architectural styles. Fine 17th-century gardens
and Clive of India museum
RABY CASTLE, Durham. Easter (Sat.–Wed.), 1 May–30
June, Wed. and Sun., July–Sept. daily (not Sat.). Also
Bank Holiday Sat.–Tues. PM. Adm. £3.00, Grounds
£1.00. Tel: 0833–60202. Fourteenth-century castle with
extensive walled gardens
RAGLEY HALL, Warks. 10 April–26 Sept. daily (not Mon.,
Fri.). PM. Open Bank Holidays. Adm. £4.50, Garden
£3.50. Tel: 0789–762090. Seventeenth-century house
with gardens, park and lake
ROCKINGHAM CASTLE, Northants. Easter Sunday–30
Sept., Sun., Thurs., (also Bank Holiday Mon. and Tues.
and Tues. in Aug.). PM. Adm. £3.50, Gardens only
£2.00. Tel: 0536–770240. Built by William the
Conqueror; former royal castle
ROYAL PAVILION, Brighton. Daily (closed 24–25 Dec.).
Adm. charge. Tel: 0273–603005. Palace of George IV.
Chinoiserie interiors with much of the original furniture
*RUFFORD OLD HALL, Lancashire. 1 April–31 Oct. daily
(not Fri.). PM. Adm. £2.70. Tel: 0704–821254. Fifteenth-
century hall with unique screen
*ST MICHAEL'S MOUNT, Cornwall. April–Oct. Mon.–Fri.
Nov.–March, guided tours or free flow as tide, weather
and circumstances permit (no regular ferry service in
winter). Adm. £2.90. Tel: 0736–710507. Fourteenth-
century castle with later additions and alterations, off the
coast at Marazion
SANDRINGHAM, Norfolk. 11 April–3 Oct. (closed 19 July–7
Aug.) Daily; Sun. PM. Closed when Royal Family in
residence. Adm. £3.00, Grounds only £2.00. Tel: 0553–
772675. The Queen's private residence; a neo-Jacobean
house built in 1870 with attractive gardens
SCONE PALACE, Perth. Good Friday–mid Oct., daily. Sun.,
PM except July and Aug. Adm. £4.00. Tel: 0738–52300.
House built between 1802 and 1813 on the site of a former
medieval palace
SHERBORNE CASTLE, Dorset. Easter Sat.–end Sept.
Thurs., Sat., Sun. and Bank Holiday Mons. PM. Adm.
charge. Tel: 0935–813182. Built by Sir Walter Raleigh
*SHUGBOROUGH, Staffs. 27 March–31 Oct., daily. Adm.
£7.50 (House, Museum, Farm; House only, £3.00). Tel:
0889–881388. Elegant house set in 18th-century park
with monuments, temples and pavilions in the Greek
Revival style
SKIPTON CASTLE, N. Yorks. Open all year (not Christmas
Day). Daily. (Sun., PM). Adm. £2.60. Tel: 0756–792442.
D-shaped castle with six round towers and beautiful inner
courtyard

*SMALLHYTHE PLACE, Kent. April–Oct. Sat.–Wed. PM. Open Good Friday. Adm. £2.50. Tel: 05806-2334. Half-timbered 16th-century house; home of Ellen Terry 1899–1928

STANFORD HALL, Leics. Easter Sat.–end Sept. Sat., Sun., Bank Holidays (Mon. and Tues.). PM. Adm. £2.90. Tel: 0788-860250. Elegant William and Mary house with unique collection of Stuart portraits. Motorcycle museum

STONELEIGH ABBEY, Warks. Open by prior appointment only, Mon.–Fri. Tel: 0926-52116. Italianate mansion built in the early 18th century on the site of a former Cistercian abbey

STONOR PARK, Oxon. Times vary. Adm. £3.30. Tel: 0491-63587. Large medieval house with Georgian façade. Centre of Roman Catholicism after the Reformation

*STOURHEAD, Wilts. 3 April–31 Oct., Sat.–Wed. PM. Gardens all year, daily. Adm. House £4.00; Gardens £4.00. Tel: 0747-840348. English Palladian mansion with famous Italian landscape gardens

STRATFIELD SAYE HOUSE, nr. Reading. 1 May–last Sun. in Sept. daily (not Fri.). Wellington Country Park March–Oct. daily, Nov.–Feb. weekends only. Adm. charge. Tel: 0256-882882. House built between 1630 and 1640; home of the Dukes of Wellington since 1817

SUDELEY CASTLE, Glos. April–Oct. daily, PM. Adm. £4.75. Tel: 0242-602308. Castle built in 1442; a royal palace between 1469 and 1547. Restored in the 19th century

SULGRAVE MANOR, Northants. March–31 Dec., daily (not Wed.), Closed Christmas. Adm. £3.00. Tel: 0295-760205. Sixteenth-century manor house

SYON HOUSE, Brentford, Middx. 1 April–29 Sept., Wed.–Sun. and Bank Holiday Mons. Also Sun. in Oct. PM. Adm. charge. Tel: 081-560 0881. Built on the site of a former monastery; magnificent Adam interior

TOWER OF LONDON. Daily, March–Oct. 9–6, Nov.–Feb. 9.30–5. Closed 1 Jan., Good Friday and 24–26 Dec. (Jewel House closed all Jan.). Adm. charge. Tel: 071-709 0765. Royal palace and fortress begun by William the Conqueror in 1078. Home of the Crown Jewels since the reign of Henry III, and of the national collection of arms and armour

*TRERICE, Cornwall. 1 April–31 Oct. daily (not Tues.). Adm. £3.60. Tel: 0637-875404. Small Elizabethan manor house

WARWICK CASTLE. Daily (not Christmas Day). Adm. £6.75. Tel: 0926-408000. Fine medieval castle in Capability Brown parkland

WILTON HOUSE, Wilts. 5 April–17 Oct. daily 11–6, Sun. PM. Adm. £5.00. Tel: 0722-743115. Grey stone house completed in 1653 on site of former Tudor house and Saxon abbey

WINDSOR CASTLE, Berks. Daily (but State apartments closed when The Queen is in residence). Adm. charge, including the castle precincts. Tel: 0753-868286. Official residence of The Queen and the oldest royal residence still in regular use. State apartments, Queen Mary's Dolls' House, Exhibition of The Queen's Presents and Royal Carriages. Restoration work in progress on fire-damaged state rooms (which may still be viewed). Also ST GEORGE'S CHAPEL. Tel: 0753-865538. Adm. free. Also ROYAL MAUSOLEUM, Frogmore Gardens. Tel: 0753-831118 for recorded information

WOBURN ABBEY, Beds. 29 March–31 Oct. daily. 1 Jan.–28 March, weekends only. Adm. £6.00. Tel: 0525-290666. Built on site of a former Cistercian abbey; home of the Dukes of Bedford since the 17th century. Important art collection; deer park with wildlife

Museums and Galleries

Adm. admission; con. concessionary rate (prices are mostly those obtaining in 1993)

BARNARD CASTLE, Co. Durham – *The Bowes Museum.* European art from the late medieval period to 19th century. Fine porcelain and glass, tapestries and furniture. Music and costume galleries. English period rooms from Elizabeth I to Victoria; French decorative arts of 18th and 19th centuries; local antiquities. Temporary exhibitions. Open weekdays: May–Sept., 10–5.30, March, April, Oct., 10–5, Nov.–Feb., 10–4. Sun., 2–5 (summer); 2–4 (winter). Adm. charge

BATH – *Roman Baths Museum.* Roman baths complex of 1st century AD. Open daily, 9–6. Adm. (including adjoining 18th century Pump Room), £4.00, con. £1.90
Museum of Costume, Assembly Rooms. Fashion from 16th century to date. Adm. £2.50, con. £1.30
American Museum in Britain, Claverton Manor. American decorative arts from late 17th to mid 19th centuries. Open end March to end Oct., daily (not Mon.), 2–5, Bank Hol. Mons. and preceding Suns. 11–5. During winter only on application. Adm. charge
Victoria Art Gallery, Bridge Street. Open Mon.–Fri. 10–5.30, Sat. 10–5. Closed Sun., Bank Hols. Adm. free

BEAMISH – *The North of England Open Air Museum*, Beamish, Co. Durham. Re-creates northern life *c.*1900. Local buildings have been rebuilt and furnished, including the Town with houses, shops, etc., the Colliery Village, the Railway Station and Home Farm complete with agricultural machinery, animals and exhibitions. Open daily: 14 March–31 Oct., 10–6, 1 Nov.–13 March, 10–4 (not Mon. or Fri.). Check for Christmas opening

BEAULIEU – *National Motor Museum.* Displays of vehicles dating from 1895 to present. Open daily (not Christmas Day), 10–6 (winter, 10–5). Adm. charge

BELFAST – *Ulster Museum*, Botanic Gardens. Collections of Irish antiquities, natural and local history, fine and applied arts. Open Mon.–Fri. 10–5, Sat. 1–5, Sun. 2–5
Ulster Folk and Transport Museum, Holywood. Indoor and outdoor exhibits. Open Oct.–March, weekdays 9.30–4, weekends 12.30–4.30 (April–Sept. 9.30–5, Sat. 10.30–6, Sun. 12–6). July, Aug. 10.30–6, Sun. 12–6. Adm. £2.60, con. £1.30

BEVERLEY, N. Humberside. – *Museum of Army Transport.* Exhibits include field workshop, amphibious assault landing, railway section and aircraft. Open 10–5. Closed Christmas period. Adm. £2.50, con. £1.50

BIRMINGHAM – *City Museum and Art Gallery.* European art 14th to 20th centuries (particularly Pre-Raphaelites), sculpture, European gold, silver and jewellery, metalwork, glass, pottery and porcelain, furniture, textiles and costume, archaeology, local and natural history. Open Mon.–Sat. 9.30–5, Sun. 2–5. Closed Christmas Day, Boxing Day and New Year's Day. Adm. free
Museum of Science and Industry, Newhall Street. From the Industrial Revolution to the present; many working machines. Open Mon.–Sat. 9.30–5, Sun. 2–5. Adm. free
Also *Aston Hall, Blakesley Hall, Birmingham Nature Centre, Jewellery Quarter Discovery Centre, Sarehole Mill*, and *Weoley Castle*

BRADFORD – *Cartwright Hall Art Gallery*, Lister Park. British 19th and 20th century fine art
Bolling Hall, off Wakefield Road, a furnished period house, mainly 17th and 18th century

Industrial and Horses at Work Museum, Moorside Road, illustrates the local industries and transport in an old mill, with mill owner's and workers' houses and stables with shire horses
Cliffe Castle, Keighley. Natural history, minerals and folk life material, and period rooms
Manor House, Ilkley. Archaeology, local history and contemporary fine art. Open 10–5 (April–Sept. 10–6, except Industrial Museum). Closed Good Friday, Christmas Day, Boxing Day and Mon. (except Bank Hols.). Adm. free

BRIGHTON – *Museum and Art Gallery*, Church Street. Old master paintings; Willett pottery and porcelain collection, 20th century art and furniture, ethnography, archaeology, local history, musical instruments, costume gallery. Open Mon.–Sat. 10–5, Sun. 2–5. Closed Wed., Good Friday, 25, 26 Dec. and 1 Jan. Adm. free
Preston Manor, Preston Park. Thomas-Stanford/ Macquoid bequests of English period furniture, china and silver. Servants quarters. Open Tues.–Sat. and Bank Hol. Mon. 10–5, Sun. 2–5. Closed Mon., 25, 26 Dec. and Good Friday. Adm. charge
The Booth Museum of Natural History, Dyke Road. Open 10–5, Sun. 2–5. Closed Thurs., Good Friday, 25, 26 Dec. and 1 Jan. Adm. free

BRISTOL – *City Museum and Art Gallery*, Queen's Road. Collections include geology, natural history, archaeology, Egyptology, ethnography, applied art, fine art, and oriental art. Displays include Bristol ceramics and the Bristol school of artists, silver, Japanese and Chinese ceramics
Also *Red Lodge, Blaise Castle House Museum, Georgian House, Bristol Industrial Museum, Maritime Heritage Centre*. Adm. charges. Times vary, tel: 0272-223571

CAMBRIDGE – *Fitzwilliam Museum.* Egyptian, Greek, Near Eastern and Roman antiquities, coins and medals, medieval manuscripts, paintings and drawings, prints, sculpture, Oriental and Occidental fans, pottery and porcelain, textiles, arms and armour, medieval and renaissance objects of art, and a library. Open Tues.–Sat., Lower Galleries 10–2, Upper Galleries 2–5; Sun. 2.15–5. Closed 24 Dec.–1 Jan., Good Friday, Mon. incl. May Day Bank Hol. but not Easter and Bank Hol. Mons. Adm. free

CANTERBURY – *Royal Museum and Art Gallery*, and *Buffs Regimental Museum.* Military artefacts and pictures. Open Mon.–Sat. 10–5. Adm. free
Canterbury Heritage, a museum of the city's history in the medieval Poor Priest's Hospital, Stour Street. Open Mon.–Sat. 10.30–5, Sun. (June–Oct.) 1.30–5. Adm. £1.40, con. £1.00
Roman Museum. Open Mon.–Sat., 10.30–5, Sun. (June–Oct.) 1.30–5. Adm. £1.40, con. £1.00
West Gate Museum. Arms and armour and views of the city from the battlements. Open Mon.–Sat., 11–12.30 and 1.30–3.30. Adm. 60p, con. 40p

CARLISLE – *Tullie House Museum and Art Gallery*, Castle Street. Collections of archaeology, natural and social history, fine and decorative arts in Jacobean house with Victorian and modern extensions. Open Mon.–Sat. 10–5, Sun. 12–5
Guildhall Museum, Greenmarket. Civic and guild history and artefacts. Contact Tullie House Museum for information. Tel: 0228-34781

CHESTER – *Grosvenor Museum*, Grosvenor Street. Roman collections, silver gallery, natural history, art and folk-life. Open weekdays 10.30–5, Sun. 2–5
Chester Heritage Centre, St Michael's Church, Bridge Street Row. Displays Chester's history and architecture. Open weekdays 11–5, Sun. 12–5. Adm. charge
King Charles Tower, City Walls. Civil War displays
Water Tower, City Walls. Camera obscura. Open Mon.–Sat. 11–5, Sun. 12–5. Adm. charge
COLCHESTER – *Colchester Castle*. Local archaeological antiquities, especially from Roman Colchester. Tours of Roman vaults, castle walls, chapel and prisons. Open Mon.–Sat. 10–5, Sun. March–Nov., 2–5. Closed 24–26 Dec. Adm. £2.00, con. £1.00
Hollytrees Museum. 18th and 19th century costume, toys and social history. Open Tues.–Sat. 10–5. Closed Good Friday and Christmas period. Adm. free
Natural History Museum, All Saints Church. Open April–Oct., Tues.–Sat., 10–5. Adm. free
Social History Museum, Holy Trinity Church. Domestic life and crafts. Open as Natural History Museum
Tymperleys Clock Museum. Open as Natural History Museum. Adm. free
COVENTRY – *Herbert Art Gallery and Museum*, Jordan Well. City's history exhibition, natural history gallery, fine and decorative art. Open weekdays 10–5.30, Sun. 2–5. Closed Christmas period
Museum of British Road Transport, St Agnes Lane, Hales Street. Open daily 10–5. Adm. £2.95, con. £1.95
Lunt Roman Fort, Baginton. Open Easter–mid-July, Sat.–Sun., 10–5, mid-July–end Sept., Wed.–Sun., 10–5. Adm. £2.50, con. £1.25
CRICH, nr. Matlock, Derbyshire – *National Tramway Museum*. Open-air working museum with tram-rides. Open April–Oct. weekends and Bank Hols. 10–6.30. May–Sept., open daily (not Fri. in May and Sept.) 10–5.30
DERBY – *Museum and Art Gallery*, The Strand. Archaeology, geology, military, natural history, paintings by Joseph Wright of Derby, Derby porcelain. Open Mon. 11–5, Tues.–Sat. 10–5, Sun. and Bank Hols. 2–5. Adm. free
Industrial Museum, Silk Mill, Full Street. Rolls-Royce collection of aero engines, a railway engineering gallery. Open as above. Adm. 30p, con. 10p
Pickford's House, Friargate. 18th and 19th century period room settings, social history, decorative arts, costume and textiles. Open as above. Adm. 30p, con. 10p
DORCHESTER – *Dorset County Museum*. Geology, archaeology, local and natural history and rural crafts of Dorset. Collection of Thomas Hardy's manuscripts, books, notebooks and drawings. Open Mon.–Sat. 10–5, closed 24, 25 Dec. Adm. £1.95, con. 95p
DURHAM – *Light Infantry Museum and Art Gallery*. Display of County regiment's 200-year history, arts and crafts exhibitions. Open weekdays (except Mon.) 10–5, Sun. and Bank Hol. Mon. 2–5. Closed Christmas Day and Boxing Day. Adm. 75p, con. 35p
Oriental Museum, Elvet Hill. Collections ranging from Ancient Egypt to China and Japan
Cathedral Treasury and Dormitory Museum. Relics of St Cuthbert, church plate, medieval seals, manuscripts and vestments. Open weekdays 10–4.30, Sun. 2–4.30. Adm. 80p, con. 20p
Old Fulling Mill Museum. Archaeological material from local excavations. Open Nov.–March, daily 12.30–3, April–Oct., daily 11–4. Adm. 50p, con. 25p
EDINBURGH – *City Art Centre*, 2 Market Street. Late 19th and 20th century art, mostly Scottish, and temporary

exhibitions. Open weekdays 10–5 (June–Sept. 10–6). Adm. free
People's Story, Canongate Tolbooth, Canongate. Courthouse and prison, now museum of Edinburgh life. Open weekdays 10–5 (June–Sept. 10–6). Adm. free
Huntly House, Canongate. Local history, collections of Edinburgh silver, glass and Scottish pottery. Open weekdays 10–5 (June–Sept. 10–6). Adm. free
Lady Stair's House, Lawnmarket. Mon.–Sat. 10–5 (June–Sept. 10–6)
Lauriston Castle, Cramond Road South. April–Oct. daily (except Fri.), 11–5; Nov.–March, weekends only
Museum of Childhood, High Street. Open weekdays 10–5 (June–Sept. 10–6). Adm. free
For *National Galleries of Scotland* and *National Museums of Scotland*, *see* Government Departments and Public Offices section
EXETER – *Exeter Maritime Museum*, The Haven. Collection of boats. Open daily, April–Sept., 10–5. Adm. charge
Royal Albert Memorial Museum and Art Gallery, Queen Street. Fine art, Exeter silver, ceramics, ethnography, natural and local history. Open Tues.–Sat. 10–5.30. Adm. free
Underground Passages, High Street. Medieval water supply
Connections Discovery Centre, Rougemont House. Hands-on centre for schools and groups
St Nicholas' Priory, The Mint. Norman priory
FORT WILLIAM – *West Highland Museum*, Cameron Square. Historical, natural history and folk exhibits, including those of the 1745 Rising. Daily (except Sun.) 10–5; July and Aug. 9.30–5.30, Sun 2–5. Closed lunchtime in winter
GLASGOW – *Art Gallery and Museum*, Kelvingrove. Old Masters, 19th century French paintings, archaeology and natural history, collection of armour
People's Palace, Glasgow Green. History of city from 1175 to present
The Burrell Collection, Pollok Country Park. Textiles, furniture, ceramics, stained glass, silver and paintings, especially 19th century
Pollok House, Pollok Country Park. Spanish paintings, furniture, silver, ceramics
Haggs Castle Museum, St Andrews Drive. Children's museum with activity workshops
Provand's Lordship, Castle Street. Oldest house in Glasgow, period furniture displays
Rutherglen Museum, King Street. History of former royal burgh of Rutherglen
Museum of Transport, Kelvin Hall
St Mungo Museum of Religious Life and Art, Castle Street
All open Mon.–Sat. 10–5, Sun. 11–5. Adm. free
Also *McLellan Galleries*, Sauchiehall Street. Major exhibition venue for large-scale temporary exhibitions. Adm. charge
HULL – *Ferens Art Gallery*. European art, especially Dutch 17th century, British portraits from 17th to 20th centuries, Humberside marine paintings, live art space and changing exhibitions
Wilberforce House. Jacobean merchant's house, birthplace of Wilberforce; slavery relics, period furniture, costume and ceramics
Streetlife. Museum of Transport; public service vehicles from the stage-coach to the last surviving Hull tram
Hull and East Riding Museum. Closed for two years from 8 Sept. 1993
Town Docks Museum. Whaling, fishing, trawling, ships and shipping

Old Grammar School. Hull's oldest secular building with story of Hull displays
Spurn Lightship, built 1927, restored 1986. Closed Mon. and Tues. in winter
All open Mon.–Sat. 10–5, Sun. 1.30–4.30
HUNTINGDON – *Cromwell Museum.* Remaining portion of the 12th century Hospital of St John; portraits of Cromwell, his family and parliamentary notables, and Cromwelliana. Open April–Oct., Tues.–Fri. 11–5, Sat, Sun. 11–4 (closed 1–2); Nov.–March, Tues.–Fri. 1–4, Sat. 11–1, 2–4, Sun. 2–4. Closed 1–2, Bank Hols. other than Good Friday. Adm. free
IPSWICH – *Ipswich Museum.* Suffolk geology, archaeology, natural history and ethnology. Temporary exhibitions. Open Tues.–Sat. 10–5
Christchurch Mansion. Tudor house containing furniture, Suffolk portraits, English porcelain, pottery and glass. Collections of paintings (local artists, Gainsborough, Constable). Victorian room displays
Wolsey Art Gallery, temporary exhibitions. Open Tues.–Sat. 10–5, Sun. and Bank Hol. Mons 2.30–4.30. Closed Good Friday, 24–26 Dec., 1 Jan. Adm. free
LEEDS – *City Art Gallery.* English watercolours. British and European painting, modern sculpture, Henry Moore gallery, Print Room. Open Tues.–Fri. 10–5.30, Sat. 9.30–4
Temple Newsam House. Tudor/Jacobean house, furnished in style of 17th and 18th centuries; silver, European porcelain and pottery, pictures, etc. Open daily (not Mon. except Bank Hols.) 10.30–6.15, Weds. (May–Sept.) 10.30–8.30. Adm. £1.00, con. 45p
Lotherton Hall, Gascoigne art and silver collection, oriental gallery, costume collection, 19th century furniture, ceramics; park and gardens. Open daily (not Mon. except Bank Hols.) 10.30–6.15, Thurs. (May–Sept.) 10.30–8.30. Adm. £1.00, con. 45p
Abbey House Museum. Folk museum including three full-sized streets. Open Mon.–Sat. 9.30–5. Sun. 2–5
City Museum. Geology, archaeology, ethnography and natural history
Also *Armley Mills Industrial Museum, Thwaite Mills*
LEICESTER – *Leicestershire Museum and Art Gallery,* New Walk. Natural history, geology, Egyptology, 15th–20th century European art, ceramics, silver
Newarke Houses, The Newarke. Social history of Leicestershire from 1485, musical instruments, local clocks, Gimson furniture collection
Jewry Wall Museum, St Nicholas Circle. Archaeology, Roman Jewry Wall and Baths, mosaics
Belgrave Hall, Church Road. Queen Anne house with furniture and garden
Museum of the Royal Leicestershire Regiment, Oxford Street
Museum of Technology, Corporation Road. Horse-drawn and motor vehicles, beam engines, motive power galleries, site narrow gauge railway
Wygston's House Museum of Costume, Applegate. Costume from 1789 to the present
All museums open weekdays 10–5.30, Sun. 2–5.30. Closed Christmas Day, Boxing Day and Good Friday.
Snibston Discovery Park, Ashby Road, Colville. Science and industry museum on site of historic coal mine. Open daily (except 25, 26 Dec.) 10–6. Adm. charge
LEWES – *Museum of Sussex Archaeology,* Barbican House, near Castle. Open weekdays, 10–5.30, Sun. 11–5.30. Adm. (including Castle and Lewes Living History Model) £2.80, con. £1.50
Museum of Local History, Anne of Cleves House, Southover. Local history and folk museum. Open April–

Oct., weekdays 10–5.30, Sun. 2–5.30. Adm. £1.60, con. 80p
LINCOLN – *Usher Gallery.* Watches, miniatures, porcelain, silver, etc., Peter de Wint collection of oils and watercolours, Lincolnshire topographical drawings, personalia associated with Tennyson family. Open weekdays 10–5.30, Sun. 2.30–5
City and County Museum, Broadgate. Geology and archaeology of Lincolnshire. Open Mon.–Fri. 10–5.30, Sun. 2.30–5
Museum of Lincolnshire Life. Covers the last 200 years; large agricultural collection. Open weekdays 10–5.30, Sun. 2–5.30
National Cycle Museum, Brayford Wharf. Vintage cycles. Open daily, except Christmas week, 10–5
Lincoln Castle, 11th century, features Victorian Silent System Prison Chapel, Magna Carta. Open daily
LIVERPOOL – For *National Museums and Galleries on Merseyside, see* Government Departments and Public Offices section
LONDON: GALLERIES – *Courtauld Institute Galleries,* Somerset House, Strand, WC2. The galleries of the University of London containing many collections of major works of art. Open weekdays 10–6, Sun. 2–6. Adm. £3.00, con. £1.50
Dulwich Picture Gallery, College Road, SE21. Built by Sir John Soane to house the Bourgeois collection. Open Tues.–Fri. 10–1, 2–5, Sat. 11–5, Sun. 2–5. Adm. £2.00, con. £1.00
Percival David Foundation of Chinese Art, 53 Gordon Square, WC1. Open Mon.–Fri. 10.30–5. Adm. free
The Queen's Gallery, Buckingham Palace, SW1. Changing selection of works of art from the royal collection. Open Tues.–Sat. and Bank Hols. 10–5, Sun. 2–5. Adm. charge
Ranger's House, Chesterfield Walk (Greenwich Park), SE10. The villa houses the Suffolk collection of English portraits and the Dolmetsch Collection of musical instruments. Open daily 1 Oct.–Maundy Thursday 10–4 (not 24, 25 Dec.), Good Friday–30 Sept. 10–6. Adm. free
Whitechapel Art Gallery, Whitechapel High Street, E1. Temporary exhibitions, mainly of modern art. Open Tues.–Sun. 11–5, Wed. 11–8. Adm. free for most exhibitions
For *National Gallery, National Portrait Gallery, Tate Gallery* and *Wallace Collection, see* Government Departments and Public Offices section
LONDON: MUSEUMS – *Bank of England Museum,* public entrance Bartholomew Lane, EC2. History of the Bank from 1694. Open Mon.–Fri. 10–5, Sun. and Bank Hols. (summer only) 11–5. Adm. free
Design Museum, Butlers Wharf, SE1. Illustrates development of design and mass-production of consumer objects. Open Mon.–Fri. 10.30–5.30, Sat.–Sun. 10.30–6.30. Adm. £3.50, con. £2.50
Geffrye Museum, Kingsland Road, E2. Series of English period rooms dating from 1600 to 1939 with decorative arts exhibits. Open Tues.–Sat. 10–5, Sun. and Bank Hols. 2–5. Adm. free
Horniman Museum and Gardens, London Road, SE23. Museum of ethnography, musical instruments, and natural history. Reference library (not Mon.). Open Mon.–Sat. 10.30–5.30, Sun. 2–5.30 (not Christmas). Adm. free
Jewish Museum. Moves from Woburn House, Tavistock Square, WC1 to 129 Albert Street, NW1 in 1994, reopening June. Illustrates Jewish life, history and religion. Tues.–Thurs. 10–4; Fri., Sun. 10–1. Adm. £1. Closed public and Jewish holidays

London Transport Museum, Covent Garden, WC2. Reopens Dec. 1993, daily 10–6. Adm. charge
MCC Museum, Lord's Ground, St John's Wood Road, NW8. Open match days, Mon.–Sat. 10.30–5, Sun. 1–5. Adm. £1.00, con. 50p. Conducted tours by appointment with Tours Manager
Museum of the Moving Image, South Bank, SE1. The history of the moving image in cinema and television. Open daily 10–6 (not 24–26 Dec.). Adm. £5.50, con. £4/4.70
The Royal Mews, Buckingham Palace, SW1. Open 5 Jan.–23 March Wed. 12–4, 29 March–29 Sep. Tues.–Thurs. 12–4, 5 Oct.–21 Dec. Wed. 12–4. Adm. charge.
Information line: 071-799 2331
Sherlock Holmes Museum, 221B Baker Street, NW1. Open daily 10–6. Adm. £5.00, con. £3.00
Sir John Soane's Museum, 13 Lincoln's Inn Fields, WC2. Containing Sir John Soane's collections of art and antiques. Open Tues.–Sat. 10–5, first Tues. in month 6–9. Adm. free. Tours must be booked in advance
Tower Bridge Walkway and Museum, SE1. Centenary exhibition, panoramic high-level viewing gallery, original Victorian steam machinery. Open daily from 10 (not Christmas Eve). Adm. £3.50, con. £2.50
Wellington Museum, Apsley House, 149 Piccadilly, W1 (Hyde Park Corner). Known as 'No. 1 London', the home of the 1st Duke of Wellington, housing paintings, sculptures, services of porcelain and silver plate and personal relics. Reopening June 1994. Adm. charge
Wimbledon Lawn Tennis Museum, Church Road, SW19. Open Tues.–Sat. 10.30–5, Sun. 2–5. Adm. £2.00, con. £1.00
For the *British Museum, Natural History Museum, Museum of London, Science Museum, Victoria and Albert Museum, Imperial War Museum, National Maritime Museum, National Army Museum* and *RAF Museum*, see Government Departments and Public Offices section
MANCHESTER – *City Art Galleries*, Mosley Street and Princess Street. Old Masters, Turner, Pre-Raphaelites; sculpture, furniture, porcelain, silver. Changing exhibitions. Weekdays 10–5.45, Sun. 2–5.45
Whitworth Art Gallery, University of Manchester, Oxford Road. Watercolours, drawings, prints, textiles and wallpaper collections, 20th century British art. Mon.–Sat. 10–5 (Thurs. 10–9), closed Suns, Good Friday and Christmas week. Adm. free
Museum of Science and Industry, Liverpool Road, Castlefield. Working machinery and displays in world's oldest passenger railway station. Open daily 10–5
Gallery of English Costume, Platt Hall, Platt Fields, Rusholme. Exhibits from 16th century to present. Times vary
Also *Heaton Hall*, Prestwich, *Wythenshawe Hall*, Northenden. Times vary, tel: 061-236 5244
NEWCASTLE UPON TYNE – *Laing Art Gallery*, Higham Place. Fine art from 17th century, pottery, glass, silver and metalwork. Open Tues.–Fri. 10–5.30, Sat. 10–4.30, Sun. 2.30–5.30
Castle Keep, St Nicholas Street. Oct.–March, Tues.–Sun. 9.30–4.30 (April–Sept. 9.30–5.30)
Trinity Maritime Centre and *Trinity House*, Broad Chare. Centre open April–Oct., Mon.–Fri. 11–4, 16–30 Oct. 11–2.30. Trinity House, April–Nov. (chapel and entrance hall only) Tues.–Thurs. 2–4
John George Joicey Museum, City Road. Military and social history. Open Tues.–Sat. 10–5.30 (Sat. 10–4.30)
Museum of Science and Engineering, West Blandford Square. Tues.–Fri. 10–5.30, Sat. 10–4.30

Newburn Hall Motor Museum, Townfield Gardens. Tues.–Sun. 10–6
NEWMARKET – *National Horseracing Museum*. Six galleries of displays relating to horseracing, horses and people connected with the sport. Sporting art galleries. Equine Tours. Open April–Dec., Tues.–Sat. 10–5, Sun. 12–5. Closed Mon. except Bank Hols, July, Aug. Adm. £2.50, con. £1.50/75p
NORWICH – *Castle Museum*. Exhibits of art (including Norwich school), archaeology, natural history, silver and glass, Twining teapot gallery, battlement and dungeon tours. Open Mon.–Sat., 10–5, Sun. 2–5
Strangers' Hall, Charing Cross. Medieval mansion with period room settings from Tudor to Victorian times, toy display and costumes. Open Mon.–Sat. 10–5
Bridewell Museum of Local Industries, Bridewell Alley. Open Mon.–Sat. 10–5
St Peter Hungate Church Museum, Princes Street. 15th century church used for display of church art and antiquities. Open Mon.–Sat. 10–5
Royal Norfolk Regimental Museum, Market Avenue. History of the regiment from 1685 to the present. Open Mon.–Sat., 10–5, Sun. 2–5
NOTTINGHAM – *Castle Museum and Art Gallery*. Paintings and drawings 17th–20th centuries. Selection of decorative arts, interactive 'Story of Nottingham' exhibition, and Sherwood Foresters' regimental collection. Conducted tours of Mortimer's Hole caves
Industrial Museum, Wollaton Park. Lacemaking machinery, steam engines, transport
Canal Museum, Canal Street. History of local canals and river transport
Natural History Museum, Wollaton Hall. Tudor building and park
Museum of Costumes and Textiles, Castlegate
Brewhouse Yard Museum, Castle Boulevard. Everyday life from the 17th century to the present
Green's Mill and Science Centre, Sneinton. Working windmill and interactive science centre
Also the *Lace Hall* and the *Robin Hood Centre*
OAKHAM – *Rutland County Museum*, Catmos Street. Archaeology, local history, craft tools and agricultural implements. Open Mon.–Sat. 10–5, Sun. (April–Oct.) 2–5 (Nov.–March) 2–4
OXFORD – *Ashmolean Museum*, Beaumont Street. The University's collections of European and Oriental fine and applied arts, Classical and Near-Eastern archaeology and numismatics. Open Tues.–Sat. 10–4, Sun. 2–4. Bank Hol. Mon. Adm. free
PLYMOUTH – *City Museum and Art Gallery*, Drake Circus. Fine art including Reynolds' portraits, Plymouth porcelain, archaeology, local and natural history. Tues.–Sat. 10–5.30, Sun. 2–5. Also Bank Holiday Mons. Adm. free
Elizabethan House, 32 New Street
Merchant's House, 33 St Andrew's Street. 16th century
The Dome, the Hoe. Maritime history museum
PORTSMOUTH – *City Museum*, Museum Road
Natural Science Museum and Butterfly House, Eastern Parade
Southsea Castle and Museum, *D-Day Museum*, Clarence Esplanade
All open daily 10.30–5.30, except 24–26 Dec. Adm. charge
Charles Dickens' Birthplace Museum, Old Commercial Road. Open 1 March–31 Oct., daily 10.30–5.30. Adm. charge

Naval Heritage Area. Tells the story of the Royal Navy using Henry VIII's *Mary Rose*, HMS *Victory* and the ironclad HMS *Warrior* (1860)
Royal Naval Museum. Open daily (except Christmas Day). Adm. charge
ST ALBANS – *Museum of St Albans*, Hatfield Road. Story of St Albans since Roman times. Open weekdays 10–5, Sun. 2–5
Verulamium Museum, St Michael's. Iron Age and Roman Verulamium including wall plasters, jewellery, mosaics. Open weekdays 10–5.30, Sun. 2–5.30. Adm. £2.40, con. £1.40
SHEFFIELD – *City Museum*, Weston Park. Includes the Bateman collection of antiquities from Peak District, cutlery and old Sheffield plate, local geology and wildlife
Mappin Art Gallery, Weston Park. Paintings and sculpture of 18th–20th centuries (mainly British school) and contemporary works
Abbeydale Hamlet, Abbeydale Road South. A late 18th to early 19th century scythe and steel works with associated housing
Kelham Island Industrial Museum. Sheffield's industrial past
Shepherd Wheel, Whiteley Wood. Water-powered cutlery grinding establishment
Bishops' House, Meersbrook Park. Museum of local history in Tudor yeoman's house. Opening times vary. Tel: 0742–768588
STOKE-ON-TRENT – *City Museum and Art Gallery*, Bethesda Street, Hanley. Major ceramic collections. Open daily 10–5, Sun. 2–5
Chatterley Whitfield Mining Museum, Tunstall. Guided tours underground. Open March–Oct. 10–5; Nov.–Feb., Tues.–Sat. 11–4, Sun. 10–5
Gladstone Pottery Museum, Longton. A working Victorian pottery
Pottery factory tours are available Mon.–Fri., except during factory holidays, at the following: *Royal Doulton*, Nile Street, Burslem; *Spode*, Church Street, Stoke; *Beswick*, Gold Street, Longton; *Royal Grafton China*, Marlborough Road, Longton; *Coalport*, Park Street, Fenton, *Wedgwood's*, Barlaston; *Aynsley*, Uttoxeter Road, Longton
STRATFORD-UPON-AVON – *Shakespeare's Birthplace.* Period furniture, rare books, MSS and memorabilia; Shakespeare Centre nearby
Anne Hathaway's Cottage, Shottery. Home of Shakespeare's wife
Mary Arden's House, Wilmcote. Tudor farmhouse home of Shakespeare's mother
New Place, where Shakespeare died
Hall's Croft. Shakespeare's daughter's home
Grammar School attended by Shakespeare
Royal Shakespeare Theatre. Burnt down 1926, rebuilt 1932. *Swan Theatre*, opened in 1986
STYAL – *Quarry Bank Mill*, Cheshire. History of the cotton industry, weaving demonstrations at water-powered cotton mill. Restored Apprentice House. Open all year. Closed Mon., Oct.–March. Open Bank Hols. Adm. charge
WINCHESTER – *City Museum.* Weekdays 10–5, Sun. 2–5 (closed Mon. in winter)
Cathedral Library and *Triforium Gallery.* Illuminated manuscripts, sculpture, wood- and metalwork from 12th to 19th centuries. Times vary. Closed Mon. morning and Suns. Adm. charge
WORCESTER – *City Museum and Art Gallery.* Natural history of Worcestershire, changing art exhibitions; also

military museum. Open Mon.–Wed., Fri. 9.30–6, Sat. 9.30–5
The Commandery, Sidbury. Civil War centre. Weekdays 10.30–5, Sun. 1.30–5.30
Tudor House Museum, Friar Street. Local history. Mon.–Wed., Fri., Sat. 10.30–5
Dyson Perrins Museum and Royal Worcester Porcelain Works, Severn Street. Mon.–Fri. 9.30–5, Sat. 10–5
YORK – *Castle Museum.* Everyday life of the last three centuries. Open weekdays 9.30–5.30, Sun. 10–5.30 (closes 6.30 April–Oct., 4.45 Nov.–March). Adm. £3.80, con. £2.70
Jorvik Viking Centre, Coppergate. Reconstruction of Viking York. Open daily. Adm. £3.80, con. £1.90
Yorkshire Museum and Gardens, Museum Street, Roman Life gallery, archaeology, decorative arts, geology, natural history. Open weekdays 10–5, Sun. 1–5. Adm. £2.50, con. £1.25, family ticket £6.00. Gardens, Roman, Anglian and medieval ruins. Open weekdays 7.30–dusk (summer 7.30–8), Sun. 10–dusk
Art Gallery, Exhibition Square. European paintings, 14th to 20th century; watercolours and prints of Yorkshire; modern English stoneware pottery. Open weekdays 10–5, Sun. 2.30–5. Adm. free
Treasurer's House, Chapter House Street. Open 26 March–30 Oct. 10.30–5. Adm. £3.00, con. £1.50

Hallmarks

Hallmarks are the symbols stamped on gold, silver or platinum articles to indicate that they have been tested at an official Assay Office and that they conform to one of the legal standards. With certain exceptions, all gold, silver, or platinum articles are required by law to be hallmarked before they are offered for sale. Hallmarking was instituted in England in 1300 under a statute of Edward I.

MODERN HALLMARKS

Normally a complete modern hallmark consists of four symbols – the sponsor's mark, the assay office mark, the standard mark and the date letter. Additional marks have been authorized from time to time.

SPONSOR'S MARK

Instituted in England in 1363, the sponsor's mark was originally a device such as a bird or fleur-de-lis. Now it consists of the initial letters of the name or names of the manufacturer or firm. Where two or more sponsors have the same initials, there is a variation in the surrounding shield or style of letters.

STANDARD MARK

The standard mark indicates that the content of the precious metal in the alloy from which the article is made, is not less than the legal standard. The legal standard is the minimum content of precious metal by weight in parts per thousand, and the standards are:

Gold	916.6	(22 carat)
	750	(18 carat)
	585	(14 carat)
	375	(9 carat)
Silver	958.4	(Britannia)
	925	(sterling)
Platinum	950	

The metals are marked as follows, if they are manufactured in the United Kingdom:

GOLD – a crown followed by the millesimal figure for the standard, e.g. 916 for 22 carat (see table above)

SILVER – Britannia silver: a full-length figure of Britannia. Sterling silver: a lion passant (England) or a lion rampant (Scotland)

Britannia Silver

Sterling Silver (England)

Sterling Silver (Scotland)

PLATINUM – an orb

ASSAY OFFICE MARK

This mark identifies the particular assay office at which the article was tested and marked. The existing assay offices in Britain are:

LONDON, Goldsmiths' Hall, London EC2V 8AQ.
Tel: 071-606 8975

BIRMINGHAM, Newhall Street, Birmingham B3 1SB.
Tel: 021-236 6951

Gold and platinum

Silver

SHEFFIELD, 137 Portobello Street, Sheffield S1 4DS.
Tel: 0742-755111

EDINBURGH, 9 Granton Road, Edinburgh EH5 3QJ.
Tel: 031-551 2189

Assay offices formerly existed in other towns, e.g. Chester, Exeter, Glasgow, Newcastle, Norwich and York, each having its own distinguishing mark.

DATE LETTER

The date letter shows the year in which an article was assayed and hallmarked. Each alphabetical cycle has a distinctive style of lettering or shape of shield. The date letters were different at the various assay offices and the particular office must be established from the assay office mark before reference is made to tables of date letters.

The table on page 604 shows specimen shields and letters used by the London Assay Office on silver articles in each period from 1498. The same letters are found on gold articles but the surrounding shield may differ. Since 1 January 1975, each office has used the same style of date letter and shield for all articles.

OTHER MARKS

FOREIGN GOODS

Since 1842 foreign goods imported into Britain have been required to be hallmarked before sale. The marks consist of the importer's mark, a special assay office mark, the figure denoting fineness (fineness mark) and the annual date letter.

The following are the assay office marks for gold imported articles. For silver and platinum the symbols remain the same but the shields differ in shape.

London

Birmingham

Sheffield

Edinburgh

CONVENTION HALLMARKS

Special marks at authorized assay offices of the signatory countries of the International Convention (Austria, Denmark, Finland, Ireland, Norway, Portugal, Sweden, Switzerland and the UK) are legally recognized in the United Kingdom as approved hallmarks. These consist of a sponsor's mark, a common control mark, a fineness mark (arabic numerals showing the standard in parts per thousand), and an assay office mark. There is no date letter.

The fineness marks are:

Gold	750	(18 carat)
	585	(14 carat)
	375	(9 carat)
Silver	925	(sterling)
Platinum	950	

The common control marks are:

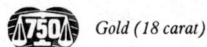 Gold (18 carat)

 Silver

Platinum

DUTY MARKS

In 1784 an additional mark of the reigning sovereign's head was introduced to signify that the excise duty had been paid. The mark became obsolete on the abolition of the duty in 1890.

COMMEMORATIVE MARKS

There are three other marks to commemorate special events, the Silver Jubilee of King George V and Queen Mary in 1935, the Coronation of Queen Elizabeth II in 1953, and her Silver Jubilee in 1977.

LONDON (GOLDSMITHS' HALL) DATE LETTERS FROM 1498

		from	to
	Black letter, small	1498–9	1517–8
	Lombardic	1518–9	1537–8
	Roman and other capitals	1538–9	1557–8
	Black letter, small	1558–9	1577–8
	Roman letter, capitals	1578–9	1597–8
	Lombardic, external cusps	1598–9	1617–8
	Italic letter, small	1618–9	1637–8
	Court hand	1638–9	1657–8

		from	to
	Black letter, capitals	1658–9	1677–8
	Black letter, small	1678–9	1696–7
	Court hand	1697	1715–6
	Roman letter, capitals	1716–7	1735–6
	Roman letter, small	1736–7	1738–9
	Roman letter, small	1739–40	1755–6
	Old English, capitals	1756–7	1775–6
	Roman letter, small	1776–7	1795–6
	Roman letter, capitals	1796–7	1815–6
	Roman letter, small	1816–7	1835–6
	Old English, capitals	1836–7	1855–6
	Old English, small	1856–7	1875–6
	Roman letter, capitals [A to M square shield N to Z as shown]	1876–7	1895–6
	Roman letter, small	1896–7	1915–6
	Black letter, small	1916–7	1935–6
	Roman letter, capitals	1936–7	1955–6
	Italic letter, small	1956–7	1974
	Italic letter, capitals	1975	

Sports Records

All the world records given below have been accepted by the International Amateur Athletic Federation except those marked with an asterisk* which are awaiting homologation. Fully automatic timing to 1/100th second is mandatory up to and including 400 metres. For distances up to and including 10,000 metres, records will be accepted to 1/100th second if timed automatically, and to 1/10th if hand timing is used.

MEN'S EVENTS

TRACK EVENTS	hr.	min.	sec.
100 metres			9.86
Carl Lewis, USA, 1991			
200 metres			19.72
Pietro Mennea, Italy, 1979			
400 metres			43.29
Harry Reynolds, USA, 1988			
800 metres		1	41.73
Sebastian Coe, GB, 1981			
1,000 metres		2	12.18
Sebastian Coe, GB, 1981			
1,500 metres		3	28.86
Noureddine Morceli, Algeria, 1993			
1 mile		3	44.39
Noureddine Morceli, Algeria, 1993			
2,000 metres		4	50.81
Saïd Aouita, Morocco, 1987			
3,000 metres		7	28.96
Moses Kiptanui, Kenya, 1992			
5,000 metres		12	58.39
Saïd Aouita, Morocco, 1987			
10,000 metres		26	58.38
Yobes Ondieki, Kenya, 1993			
20,000 metres		56	55.6
Arturo Barrios, Mexico, 1991			
21,101 metres (13 miles 196 yards 1 foot)	1	00	00.0
Arturo Barrios, Mexico, 1991			
25,000 metres	1	13	55.8
Toshihiko Seko, Japan, 1981			
30,000 metres	1	29	18.8
Toshihiko Seko, Japan, 1981			
110 metres hurdles (3 ft 6 in)			12.91
Colin Jackson, GB, 1993			
400 metres hurdles (3 ft 0 in)			46.78
Kevin Young, USA, 1992			
3,000 metres steeplechase		8	02.08
Moses Kiptanui, Kenya, 1992			

RELAYS		min.	sec.
4 × 100 metres			37.40
USA, 1992, 1993			
4 × 200 metres		1	19.11
Santa Monica TC, 1992			
4 × 400 metres		2	54.29
USA, 1993			
4 × 800 metres		7	03.89
GB, 1982			
4 × 1,500 metres		14	38.8
Federal Republic of Germany, 1977			

FIELD EVENTS	metres	ft	in
High jump	2.45	8	0¼
Javier Sotomayor, Cuba, 1993			
Pole vault	6.13	20	1½
Sergei Bubka, CIS, 1992			
Long jump	8.95	29	4½
Mike Powell, USA, 1991			
Triple jump	17.97	58	11½
Willie Banks, USA, 1985			
Shot	23.12	75	10¼
Randy Barnes, USA, 1990			
Discus	74.08	243	0
Jürgen Schult, GDR, 1986			
Hammer	86.74	284	7
Yuriy Sedykh, USSR, 1986			
Javelin	95.66*	313	10
Jan Zelezny, Czech Rep., 1993			
Decathlon†	8,891 pts		
Dan O'Brien, USA, 1992			

† Ten events comprising 100 m, long jump, shot, high jump, 400 m, 110 m hurdles, discus, pole vault, javelin, 1500 m

WALKING (TRACK)	hr.	min.	sec.
20,000 metres	1	18	35.2
Stefan Johansson, Sweden, 1992			
29,572 metres (18 miles 660 yards)	2	00	00.0
Maurizio Damilano, Italy, 1992			
30,000 metres	2	01	44.1
Maurizio Damilano, Italy, 1992			
50,000 metres	3	41	38.4
Raul Gonzalez, Mexico, 1979			

WOMEN'S EVENTS

TRACK EVENTS		min.	sec.
100 metres			10.49
Florence Griffith-Joyner, USA, 1988			
200 metres			21.34
Florence Griffith-Joyner, USA, 1988			
400 metres			47.60
Marita Koch, GDR, 1985			
800 metres		1	53.28
Jarmila Kratochvilova, Czechoslovakia, 1983			
1,500 metres		3	52.47
Tatyana Kazankina, USSR, 1980			
1 mile		4	15.61
Paula Ivan, Romania, 1989			
3,000 metres		8	22.62
Tatyana Kazankina, USSR, 1984			
5,000 metres		14	37.33
Ingrid Kristiansen, Norway, 1986			
10,000 metres		30	13.74
Ingrid Kristiansen, Norway, 1986			
100 metres hurdles (2 ft 9 in)			12.21
Yordanka Donkova, Bulgaria, 1988			
400 metres hurdles (2 ft 6 in)			52.74
Sally Gunnell, GB, 1993			

RELAYS		min.	sec.
4 × 100 metres			41.37
GDR, 1985			
4 × 200 metres		1	28.15
GDR, 1980			
4 × 400 metres		3	15.17
USSR, 1988			
4 × 800 metres		7	50.17
USSR, 1984			

FIELD EVENTS	metres	ft	in
High jump	2.09	6	10¼
Stefka Kostadinova, Bulgaria, 1987			
Long jump	7.52	24	8¼
Galina Chistiakova, USSR, 1988			
Triple jump	15.09	49	6¼
Ana Biryukova, Russia, 1993			
Shot	22.63	74	3
Natalya Lisovskaya, USSR, 1987			
Discus	76.80	252	0
Gabriele Reinsch, GDR, 1988			
Javelin	80.00	262	5
Petra Felke, GDR, 1988			
Heptathlon†			7,291 pts
Jackie Joyner–Kersee, USA, 1988			

†Seven events comprising 100 m hurdles, shot, high jump, 200 m, long jump, javelin, 800 m

ATHLETICS NATIONAL (UK) RECORDS
AS AT 3 SEPTEMBER 1993

Records set anywhere by athletes eligible to represent Great Britain and Northern Ireland

MEN

TRACK EVENTS	hr.	min.	sec.
100 metres			9.87
Linford Christie, 1993			
200 metres			19.94
John Regis, 1993			
400 metres			44.47
David Grindley, 1992			
800 metres		1	41.73
Sebastian Coe, 1981			
1,000 metres		2	12.18
Sebastian Coe, 1981			
1,500 metres		3	29.67
Sebastian Coe, 1985			
1 mile		3	46.32
Steve Cram, 1985			
2,000 metres		4	51.39
Steve Cram, 1985			
3,000 metres		7	32.79
David Moorcroft, 1982			
5,000 metres		13	00.41
David Moorcroft, 1982			
10,000 metres		27	23.06
Eamonn Martin, 1988			
20,000 metres		57	28.7
Carl Thackery, 1990			
20,855 metres	1		
Carl Thackery, 1990			
25,000 metres	1	15	22.6
Ron Hill, 1965			

30,000 metres	1	31	30.4
Jim Alder, 1970			
3,000 metres steeplechase		8	07.96
Mark Rowland, 1988			
110 metres hurdles			12.91
Colin Jackson, 1993			
400 metres hurdles			47.82
Kriss Akabusi, 1992			

RELAYS		min.	sec.
4 × 100 metres			37.77
GB team, 1993			
4 × 200 metres		1	21.29
GB team, 1989			
4 × 400 metres		2	57.53
GB team, 1991			
4 × 800 metres		7	03.89
GB team, 1982			

FIELD EVENTS	metres	ft	in
High jump	2.37	7	9¼
Steve Smith, 1992, 1993			
Pole vault	5.65	18	6½
Keith Stock, 1981			
Long jump	8.23	27	0
Lynn Davies, 1968			
Triple jump	17.57	57	7¾
Keith Connor, 1982			
Shot	21.68	71	1½
Geoff Capes, 1980			
Discus	64.32	211	0
William Tancred, 1974			
Hammer	77.54	254	5
Martin Girvan, 1984			
Javelin	91.46	300	1
Steve Backley, 1992			
Decathlon			8,847 points
Daley Thompson, 1984			

WALKING (TRACK)	hr.	min.	sec.
20,000 metres	1	23	26.5
Ian McCombie, 1990			
30,000 metres	2	19	18
Christopher Maddocks, 1984			
50,000 metres	4	05	44.6
Paul Blagg, 1990			
2 hours	26,037 metres (16 miles 315 yards)		
Ron Wallwork, 1971			

WOMEN

TRACK EVENTS		min.	sec.
100 metres			11.10
Kathy Cook, 1981			
200 metres			22.10
Kathy Cook, 1984			
400 metres			49.43
Kathy Cook, 1984			
800 metres		1	57.42
Kirsty Wade, 1985			
1,500 metres		3	59.96
Zola Budd, 1985			
1 mile		4	17.57
Zola Budd, 1985			
3,000 metres		8	28.83
Zola Budd, 1985			

5,000 metres	14	48.07
Zola Budd, 1985		
10,000 metres	30	57.07
Liz McColgan, 1991		
100 metres hurdles		12.82
Sally Gunnell, 1988		
400 metres hurdles		52.74
Sally Gunnell, 1993		

RELAYS	min.	sec.
4 × 100 metres		42.43
GB team, 1980		
4 × 200 metres	1	31.57
GB team, 1977		
4 × 400 metres	3	22.01
GB team, 1991		
4 × 800 metres	8	23.8
GB team, 1971		

FIELD EVENTS	metres	ft	in
High jump	1.95	6	4¾
Diana Elliott, 1982			
Long jump	6.90	22	7¾
Beverley Kinch, 1983			
Triple jump	13.75	45	1½
Michelle Griffith, 1993			
Shot	19.36	63	6¼
Judy Oakes, 1988			
Discus	67.48	221	5
Margaret Ritchie, 1981			
Javelin	77.44	254	1
Fatima Whitbread, 1986			
Heptathlon	6,623 points		
Judy Simpson, 1986			

SWIMMING WORLD RECORDS
AS AT 31 AUGUST 1993

MEN	min.	sec.
50 metres freestyle		21.81
Tom Jager, USA		
100 metres freestyle		48.42
Matt Biondi, USA		
200 metres freestyle	1	46.69
Giorgio Lamberti, Italy		
400 metres freestyle	3	45.00
Evgueni Sadovyi, CIS		
800 metres freestyle	7	46.60
Kieren Perkins, Australia		
1,500 metres freestyle	14	43.48
Kieren Perkins, Australia		
100 metres breaststroke	1	00.95
Karoly Guttler, Hungary		
200 metres breaststroke	2	10.16
Mike Barrowman, USA		
100 metres butterfly		52.84
Pablo Morales, USA		
200 metres butterfly	1	55.69
Melvin Stewart, USA		
100 metres backstroke		53.86
Jeff Rouse, USA		
200 metres backstroke	1	57.30
Martin Lopez-Zubero, Spain		
200 metres medley	1	59.36
Tamás Darnyi, Hungary		

400 metres medley	4	12.36
Tamás Darnyi, Hungary		
4 × 100 metres freestyle relay	3	16.53
USA		
4 × 200 metres freestyle relay	7	11.95
CIS		
4 × 100 metres medley relay	3	36.93
USA		

WOMEN	min.	sec.
50 metres freestyle		24.79
Yang Wenyi, China		
100 metres freestyle		54.48
Jenny Thompson, USA		
200 metres freestyle	1	57.55
Heike Friedrich, GDR		
400 metres freestyle	4	03.85
Janet Evans, USA		
800 metres freestyle	8	16.22
Janet Evans, USA		
1,500 metres freestyle	15	52.10
Janet Evans, USA		
100 metres breaststroke	1	07.91
Silke Hörner, GDR		
200 metres breaststroke	2	25.35
Anita Nall, USA		
100 metres butterfly		57.93
Mary Meagher, USA		
200 metres butterfly	2	05.96
Mary Meagher, USA		
100 metres backstroke	1	00.31
Krisztina Egerszegi, Hungary		
200 metres backstroke	2	06.62
Krisztina Egerszegi, Hungary		
200 metres medley	2	11.65
Li Lin, China		
400 metres medley	4	36.10
Petra Schneider, GDR		
4 × 100 metres freestyle relay	3	39.46
USA		
4 × 200 metres freestyle relay	7	55.47
GDR		
4 × 100 metres medley relay	4	02.54
USA		

The Olympic Games

Venues of the modern Olympic Games

I	Athens, Greece	1896
II	Paris, France	1900
III	St Louis, USA	1904
*	Athens	1906
IV	London, Britain	1908
V	Stockholm, Sweden	1912
†VI	Berlin, Germany	1916
VII	Antwerp, Belgium	1920
VIII	Paris, France	1924
IX	Amsterdam, Netherlands	1928
X	Los Angeles, USA	1932
XI	Berlin, Germany	1936
†XII	Tokyo, Japan, then Helsinki, Finland	1940
†XIII	London, Britain	1944
XIV	London, Britain	1948
XV	Helsinki, Finland	1952
§XVI	Melbourne, Australia	1956
XVII	Rome, Italy	1960
XVIII	Tokyo, Japan	1964
XIX	Mexico City, Mexico	1968
XX	Munich, West Germany	1972
XXI	Montreal, Canada	1976
XXII	Moscow, USSR	1980
XXIII	Los Angeles, USA	1984
XXIV	Seoul, South Korea	1988
XXV	Barcelona, Spain	1992
XXVI	Atlanta, USA	1996
XXVII	Sydney, Australia	2000

* The 'Intercalated' Games
† These Games were scheduled but did not take place owing to World Wars
§ Equestrian events were held in Stockholm, Sweden

WINTER OLYMPIC GAMES

I	Chamonix, France	1924
II	St Moritz, Switzerland	1928
III	Lake Placid, USA	1932
IV	Garmisch-Partenkirchen, Germany	1936
V	St Moritz, Switzerland	1948
VI	Oslo, Norway	1952
VII	Cortina d'Ampezzo, Italy	1956
VIII	Squaw Valley, USA	1960
IX	Innsbruck, Austria	1964
X	Grenoble, France	1968
XI	Sapporo, Japan	1972
XII	Innsbruck, Austria	1976
XIII	Lake Placid, USA	1980
XIV	Sarajevo, Yugoslavia	1984
XV	Calgary, Canada	1988
XVI	Albertville, France	1992
XVII	Lillehammer, Norway	1994
XVIII	Nagano, Japan	1998

The Commonwealth Games

The Games were originally called the British Empire Games. From 1954 to 1966 the Games were known as the British Empire and Commonwealth Games, and from 1970 to 1974 as the British Commonwealth Games. Since 1978 the Games have been called the Commonwealth Games.

BRITISH EMPIRE GAMES

I	Hamilton, Canada	1930
II	London, England	1934
III	Sydney, Australia	1938
IV	Auckland, New Zealand	1950

BRITISH EMPIRE AND COMMONWEALTH GAMES

V	Vancouver, Canada	1954
VI	Cardiff, Wales	1958
VII	Perth, Australia	1962
VIII	Kingston, Jamaica	1966

BRITISH COMMONWEALTH GAMES

IX	Edinburgh, Scotland	1970
X	Christchurch, New Zealand	1974

COMMONWEALTH GAMES

XI	Edmonton, Canada	1978
XII	Brisbane, Australia	1982
XIII	Edinburgh, Scotland	1986
XIV	Auckland, New Zealand	1990
XV	Victoria, Canada	1994
XVI	Kuala Lumpur, Malaysia	1998

AVERAGE AND GENERAL VALUES 1991–3 (JUNE)

	Rainfall (mm)				Temperature (°C)				Bright Sunshine (hrs per day)			
	Average 1961–90	1991	1992	1993	Average 1961–90	1991	1992	1993	Average 1961–90	1991	1992	1993
ENGLAND AND WALES												
January	77	92	48	113	3.8	3.9	4.2	6.3	1.6	2.2	1.7	1.3
February	55	63	47	15	3.8	2.0	5.9	5.2	2.3	2.3	2.3	1.8
March	63	75	85	26	5.6	8.1	7.6	6.8	3.5	2.9	2.5	3.8
April	53	68	73	93	7.7	8.3	8.9	9.7	4.9	5.1	4.2	4.1
May	56	14	49	86	10.9	10.9	13.5	11.6	6.2	4.7	8.2	5.7
June	58	92	38	68	13.9	12.4	15.8	15.0	6.4	4.7	7.2	6.4
July	56	68	83	–	15.7	17.0	16.6	–	6.0	6.2	5.3	–
August	68	31	130	–	15.6	17.0	15.9	–	5.7	6.9	5.3	–
September	70	62	92	–	13.6	14.7	13.8	–	4.5	5.9	3.9	–
October	77	77	84	–	10.7	10.2	8.3	–	3.2	2.8	3.1	–
November	81	95	138	–	6.6	6.7	7.9	–	2.2	1.8	1.9	–
December	82	49	83	–	4.7	4.7	4.2	–	1.5	1.5	1.4	–
YEAR	796	786	950	–	9.4	9.7	10.2	–	4.0	3.9	3.9	–
SCOTLAND												
January	117	146	139	291	3.1	3.2	4.7	4.8	1.3	1.7	1.4	0.9
February	78	83	167	67	3.1	2.6	5.5	6.2	2.3	2.3	1.9	1.3
March	94	128	208	120	4.6	6.7	6.2	5.9	3.2	2.7	2.3	3.1
April	60	121	119	113	6.5	7.5	7.4	7.9	4.8	5.2	3.2	3.6
May	67	43	81	114	9.3	10.4	11.7	9.6	5.6	5.1	7.4	4.6
June	67	121	39	75	12.1	11.0	14.3	12.7	5.6	5.2	6.1	3.9
July	74	91	91	–	13.6	15.3	14.0	–	4.9	4.8	4.0	–
August	92	67	221	–	13.5	14.9	13.3	–	4.6	4.8	4.6	–
September	111	131	177	–	11.5	11.9	11.7	–	3.5	5.0	3.2	–
October	120	165	123	–	9.1	8.7	6.9	–	2.6	2.1	2.4	–
November	118	227	212	–	5.3	5.6	6.0	–	1.7	1.5	1.5	–
December	116	141	159	–	3.9	4.7	3.7	–	1.0	0.8	0.9	–
YEAR	1114	1464	1736	–	7.9	8.5	8.8	–	3.4	3.4	3.2	–

WEATHER RECORDS

WORLD RECORDS

Maximum air temperature	57.8°C/136°F
San Louis, Mexico, 11 August 1933	
Minimum air temperature	–89.2°C/–128.56°F
Vostok, Antarctica, 21 July 1983	
Greatest rainfall in one day	1870 mm/73.62 in
Cilaos, Isle de Réunion, 16 March 1952	
Greatest rainfall in one calendar month	9300 mm/366.14 in
Cherrapunji, Assam, July 1861	
Greatest annual rainfall total	22,990 mm/905.12 in
Cherrapunji, 1861	
Highest gust of wind	201 knots/231 mph
Mt Washington Observatory, USA, 12 April 1934	

UNITED KINGDOM RECORDS

Maximum air temperature	37.1°C/98.8°F
Cheltenham, Glos., 3 August 1990	
Minimum air temperature	–27.2°C/–17°F
Braemar, Grampian, 11 February 1895 and 10 January 1982	
Greatest rainfall in one day	280 mm/11 in
Martinstown, Dorset, 18 July 1955	
Greatest annual rainfall total	6528 mm/257 in
Sprinkling Tarn, Cumbria, 1954	
Highest gust of wind	150 knots/173 mph
Cairngorm, Highland, 20 March 1986	
Highest low-level gust*	123 knots/141.7 mph
Fraserburgh, Grampian, 13 February 1989	
Highest mean hourly speed	92 knots/106 mph
Great Dun Fell, Cumbria, December 1974	
Highest low-level mean hourly speed*	72 knots/83 mph
Shoreham-by-Sea, Sussex, 16 October 1987	

* below 200 m/656 ft

WIND FORCE MEASURES

The *Beaufort Scale* of wind force has been accepted internationally and is used in communicating weather conditions. Devised originally by Admiral Sir Francis Beaufort in 1805, it now consists of the numbers 0–17, each representing a certain strength or velocity of wind at 10 m (33 ft) above ground in the open.

Scale no.	Wind Force	mph	knots
0	Calm	1	1
1	Light air	1–3	1–3
2	Slight breeze	4–7	4–6
3	Gentle breeze	8–12	7–10
4	Moderate breeze	13–18	11–16
5	Fresh breeze	19–24	17–21
6	Strong breeze	25–31	22–27
7	High wind	32–38	28–33
8	Gale	39–46	34–40
9	Strong gale	47–54	41–47
10	Whole gale	55–63	48–55
11	Storm	64–72	56–63
12	Hurricane	73–82	64–71
13	–	83–92	72–80
14	–	93–103	81–89
15	–	104–114	90–99
16	–	115–125	100–108
17	–	126–136	109–118

The Queen's Awards

The Queen's Award for Export Achievement and The Queen's Award for Technological Achievement were instituted by Royal Warrant in 1976. The two separate awards took the place of The Queen's Award to Industry, which had been instituted in 1965. In 1992 the scheme was extended with the launch of a third award, The Queen's Award for Environmental Achievement.

The awards are designed to recognize and encourage outstanding achievements in exporting goods or services from the United Kingdom and in advancing process or product technology. The purpose of the new award is to recognize and encourage product and process development which has major benefit for the environment and which is commercially successful.

The awards differ from a personal royal honour in that they are given to a unit as a whole, management and employees working as a team. They may be applied for by any organization within the United Kingdom, the Channel Islands or the Isle of Man producing goods or services which meet the criteria for the awards. Eligibility is not influenced in any way by the particular activities of the unit applying, its location, or size. Units or agencies of central and local government with industrial functions, as well as research associations, educational institutions and bodies of a similar character, are also eligible, provided that they can show they have contributed to industrial efficiency.

Each award is formally conferred by a grant of appointment and is symbolized by a representation of its emblem cast in stainless steel and encapsulated in a transparent acrylic block.

Awards are held for five years and holders are entitled to fly the appropriate award flag and to display the emblem on the packaging of goods produced in this country, on the goods themselves, on the unit's stationery, in advertising and on certain articles used by employees. Units may also display the emblem of any previous current awards during the five years.

Awards are announced on 21 April (the birthday of The Queen) and published formally in a special supplement to the London Gazette.

AWARDS OFFICE

All enquiries about the scheme and requests for application forms (completed forms must be returned by 31 October) should be made to: The Secretary, The Queen's Awards Office, Dean Bradley House, 52 Horseferry Road, London SW1P 2AG. Tel: 071–222 2277.

EXPORT ACHIEVEMENT

The criterion upon which recommendations for an award for export achievement is based is a substantial and sustained increase in export earnings to a level which is outstanding for the products or services concerned and for the size of the applicant unit's operations. Account will be taken of any special market factors described in the application. Applicants for the award will be expected to explain the basis of the achievement (e.g. improved marketing organization or new initiative to cater for export markets) and this will be taken into consideration. Export earnings considered will include receipts by the applicant unit in this country from the export of goods produced in this country, and the provision of services to non-residents. Account will be taken of the overseas expenses incurred other than marketing expenses. Income from profits (after overseas tax) remitted to this country from profits (after overseas tax) remitted to this country from the applicant unit's direct investments in its overseas branches, subsidiaries or associates in the same general line of business will be taken into account, but not receipts from profits on other overseas investments or by interest on overseas loans or credits.

In 1993, The Queen's Award for Export Achievement was conferred on the following concerns:

Rotherham and Bradford Branch of AES Engineering Ltd, Rotherham, South Yorkshire
ASM (Orchestra) Ltd (t/a The Academy of St Martin-in-the-Fields), London E1
Advent Communications Ltd, Chesham, Bucks
Airwair Ltd, Wellingborough, Northants
Appletise PLC, Woking, Surrey
A. E. Arthur Ltd, King's Lynn, Norfolk
Autovalet Systems International Ltd, London NW10
BCB International Ltd, Cardiff
BT & D Technologies Ltd, Ipswich
Edward Baker Ltd, Sudbury, Suffolk
Banque Paribas Export Finance Unit, London W1
Bioscot Ltd, Edinburgh
Booster Electric Vehicles Ltd, Huddersfield, West Yorkshire
Borden Decorative Products Ltd (Transprints Division), Morecambe, Lancs
CADCentre Ltd, Cambridge
Canadian Pizza Crust Co. (UK) Ltd, Salford
Carron Bathrooms Ltd, Carron, Falkirk
Caterham Cars Ltd, Caterham, Surrey
Chadwicks of Bury Ltd, Bury, Lancs
Churchill Tableware Ltd, Stoke-on-Trent
ConvaTec Ltd, Deeside, Clwyd
Cookson Entek Ltd, Newcastle upon Tyne
The Copyrights Company Ltd, Milton, Banbury, Oxon
Croda Kerr Ltd, Liverpool
Derwent MacDee Ltd, Doncaster, South Yorkshire
Desurvey Ltd, Birkenhead, Merseyside
Dunphy Combustion Ltd, Rochdale, Lancs
Dynacast International Ltd, Alcester, Warks
Epitaxial Products International Ltd, Cardiff
Europalite Ltd, Mansfield, Notts
Europressings Ltd, Cardiff
FMC Corporation (UK) Ltd, Wellhead Equipment Division, Dunfermline, Fife
Financial Times Group Ltd, London SE1

Ford Motor Company Ltd, Brentwood, Essex
Foster Refrigerator (UK) Ltd, Kings Lynn, Norfolk
Foster Wheeler Energy Ltd, Reading, Berks
GEC ALSTHOM Transmission & Distribution Projects Ltd (TaDPoLe), Stafford
Gaffney, Cline & Associates Ltd, Alton, Hants
The Good Book Guide Ltd, London WCI
Griffith Laboratories, European Group Bakery Business Unit, Somercotes, Derby
Hanover Displays Ltd, Lewes, East Sussex
Harrison & Sons Ltd, High Wycombe, Bucks
Hilditch & Key Ltd (Wholesale Division), Glenrothes, Fife
A. E. Holt (Leicester) Ltd, Leicester
John Horsfall & Sons (Greetland) Ltd, Halifax, West Yorkshire
Howmet Ltd, Exeter Casting, Exeter
ICL Mid Range Systems, Bracknell, Berks
IXI Ltd, Cambridge
It's At (UK) Ltd, London WI
Johnson Matthey PLC, Catalytic Systems Division, European Autocatalyst Group, Royston, Herts
Jotun-Henry Clark Ltd, London EC3
Junior Hagen Ltd, London NWIO
Justerini & Brooks Ltd, London NWI
KCC Process Equipment Ltd, Sunbury-on-Thames, Middx
Kacy Ltd, London NI7
John Laing International Ltd, Hemel Hempstead, Herts
Lightfoot Surfaces Ltd, Great Doddington, Northants
Linnhoff March Ltd, Knutsford, Cheshire
Lion Cabinets Ltd, Leeds
Lofthouse of Fleetwood Ltd, Fleetwood, Lancs
Lothian Coated Fabrics Ltd, Prestonpans, East Lothian
Lowndes Lambert Group Holdings PLC, London EC3
Macallan-Glenlivet PLC, Craigellachie, Banffshire
Madge Networks Ltd, Chalfont St Giles, Bucks
Marks and Spencer PLC, London WI
Mayflower Glass Ltd, East Boldon, Tyne and Wear
R. Mears & Co. Ltd, London EC3
Morane Ltd, Banbury, Oxon
National Pig Development Company Ltd, Driffield, East Yorkshire
Newey Goodman Ltd, Textile Division, Tipton, West Midlands
Newsround International Airfreight Ltd, High Wycombe, Bucks
Nissan Motor Manufacturing (UK) Ltd, Sunderland
Nylon Hosiery Company Ltd, Hinckley, Leics
Omega Diagnostics Ltd, Alloa, Clackmannanshire
Otodynamics Ltd, Hatfield, Herts
PED (Staden) Ltd, Earls Barton, Northants
PPE Ltd, Harlow, Essex
Pauls Malt Ltd, Newmarket, Suffolk
Pearsalls Sutures, Taunton, Somerset
Peboc Ltd, Llangefni, Gwynedd
Pfizer Ltd, Sandwich, Kent
Pig Improvement Company UK Ltd, Abingdon, Oxon
Pilkington Micronics Ltd, Deeside, Clwyd
Pointing Ltd, Prudhoe, Northumberland
Porton Speywood Ltd, Wrexham, Clwyd
Powell Duffryn International Fuels Ltd, Harpenden, Herts
Psygnosis Ltd, Liverpool
Racal Radar Defence Systems Ltd, Chessington, Surrey
Randox Laboratories Ltd, Crumlin, Co. Antrim
The Really Useful Group Ltd, London WC2
Redwood International Ltd (Uniplex), Hemel Hempstead, Herts
Reyrolle Ltd, Hebburn, Tyne and Wear
Riggarna UK Ltd, Christchurch, Dorset
Felix Rosenstiel's Widow & Son Ltd, London SW3

STC Submarine Systems, London SEIO
St Brendans Irish Cream Liqueur Company Ltd, Londonderry
Schroder Capital Management International, London EC2
Shelbourne Reynolds Engineering Ltd, Bury St Edmunds, Suffolk
Fokker Division of Short Brothers PLC, Belfast
Sigmaform UK Ltd, Wellingborough, Northants
Silent Channel Products Ltd, Huntingdon, Cambs
E. Slinger & Sons Ltd – The Slinger Group, Blackburn
Stewart Hughes Ltd, Eastleigh, Hants
TSS (UK) Ltd, Weston-on-the-Green, Oxon
Tacolin Ltd, Winsford, Cheshire
Charles W. Taylor & Son Ltd, South Shields, Tyne and Wear
Edward Thompson (Printers) Ltd, Sunderland
Thor Ceramics Ltd, Glasgow
Titus International Ltd, Iver, Bucks
Torquemeters Ltd, Ravensthorpe, Northants
Transatlantic Clothing Company Inc. Aero Leathers, Galashiels, Selkirkshire
University of Strathclyde Graduate Business School, Glasgow
Vascutek Ltd, Inchinnan, Renfrewshire
Vauxhall Motors Ltd, Luton
Voltech Instruments Ltd, Abingdon, Oxon
Vosper Thornycroft Holdings PLC, Southampton, Hants
Warwick Fabrics UK Ltd, Cheltenham, Glos
West Merchant Bank Ltd, London EC3

TECHNOLOGICAL ACHIEVEMENT

The criterion upon which recommendations for an award for technological achievement is based is a significant advance, leading to increased efficiency, in the application of technology to a production or development process in British industry or the production for sale of goods which incorporate new and advanced technological qualities.

In 1993 The Queen's Award for Technological Achievement was conferred on the following concerns:

BT Laboratories (BTL) Optical Research Division, Ipswich, Suffolk – *metal organic vapour phase epitaxy for making semiconductor devices for the optoelectronics industry*
Bridon Ropes Ltd, Brifen Department, Doncaster, South Yorkshire – *Brifen wire rope safety fence*
Marine Technology, Castrol Ltd, Pangbourne, Berks – *Castrol Marine Cyltech 80 - diesel cylinder lubricant*
The Darwen Site of Crown Berger Ltd, Darwen, Lancs – *loop process for continuous manufacture of emulsion polymers suitable for the production of paints and adhesives*
Glacier Vandervell Ltd, Kilmarnock, Strathclyde – *crankshaft bearing materials for highly loaded applications*
Holroyd, Rochdale, Lancs – *computer numerically controlled (CNC) tool and cutter grinding machinery*
Huntleigh Healthcare (Cardiff) Ltd, Cardiff – *a range of pocket diagnostic instruments for vascular and obstetric investigations*
ICL Corporate Systems, Gorton, Manchester – *Series 39 SX mainframe computer systems*
Insignia Solutions Ltd, High Wycombe, Bucks – *SoftPC, software emulation system*
Intavent Ltd, Pangbourne, Berks – *laryngeal mask for anaesthetics purposes*
Joint Replacement Instrumentation Ltd, London WI – *hydroxy-apatite ceramic-coated total hip prosthesis*

Kelvin Hughes Ltd, a Smiths Industries company, Ilford, Essex – *RSR 1000 river radar*
Land Rover Power Train, Solihull – *200 TDi diesel engine*
Martin-Baker Aircraft Company Ltd, Uxbridge, Middx – *Navy aircrew common ejection seat (NACES)*
NextBase Ltd, Ashford, Middx – *computerized route planning systems*
Oxford Applied Research Ltd, Oxford – *reactive atom-radical beam source*
P. P. Payne Ltd, Nottingham – *Supastrip pressure-sensitive adhesive tear tape*
Pitman-Moore Ltd, Uxbridge, Middx – *automatic cattle wormer*
pneuPAC Ltd, Luton – *small portable lung ventilators*
Raychem Ltd Corporate Technology Europe, Swindon – *heat-shrinkable fabric-based telecommunications splice cases*
S & S International Ltd, Berkhamsted, Herts – *Dr Solomon's Anti-virus Toolkit, an anti-virus program for computers*
Smiths Industries Aerospace & Defence Systems – Integrated Display Systems, Cheltenham, Glos – *multi-purpose cockpit colour display system for high performance aircraft*
Solid State Logic Ltd, Oxford – *digital audio post-production systems*
Tronic Electronic Services Ltd, Ulverston, Cumbria – *controlled environment underwater mateable electrical connector*
Zeneca Ltd, Zeneca FCMO Grangemouth Works, Grangemouth, Stirlingshire – *manufacture of Hexaconazole and Flutriafol, systemic fungicides*

Kerry Ultrasonics Ltd, Hitchin, Herts – *development of cleaning systems in which ozone-depleting CFCs are replaced by environment-friendly aqueous and semi-aqueous cleaning liquids*
Pilkington Glass Ltd (Basic Glass), St Helens, Merseyside – *Pilkington K Glass – an energy-saving glass*
Ricardo Consulting Engineers Ltd, Shoreham-by-Sea, West Sussex – *tumbling air motion in gasoline engines for cars*
Ricoh UK Products Ltd, Telford, Shropshire – *recycling and CFC elimination in selenium drum production*
Sericol Ltd, Broadstairs, Kent – *water-based screen printing inks*

ENVIRONMENTAL ACHIEVEMENT

The criterion upon which recommendations for an award for environmental achievement is based is a significant advance in the application by British industry of the development of products, technology or processes which offer major benefits in environmental terms compared to existing products, technology or processes. An award is only granted for products, technology or processes which have achieved commercial success.

The Queen's Award for Environmental Achievement was conferred for the first time on 21 April 1993, and was awarded to the following:

Agricultural Genetics Co. Ltd, MicroBio Division, Royston, Herts – *development of insect pathogenic nematode products as alternative products to synthetic pesticides*
BEWT (Water Engineers) Ltd, Alcester, Warks – *Chemelec electrolytic metal recovery systems for the control of industrial pollution*
Edwards High Vacuum International, Crawley, West Sussex – *DP160V chemical dry pump, which reduces polluting emissions in the chemical processing industry*
FKI Babcock Robey Ltd, Oldbury, West Midlands – *development of the EURONOX high efficiency low NOx emission range of steam and hot water boilers*
The Non-Ferrous Metal Treatment Team of the Foundry Division of Foseco (FS) Ltd, Tamworth, Staffs – *rotary degassing of aluminium and its alloys in the foundry industry*
Horticulture Research International, Wellesbourne, Warks – *development of insect parasitic nematode products as alternative products to synthetic pesticides*
Johnson Matthey PLC Catalytic Systems Division, Royston, Herts – *autocatalysts for the control of vehicle exhaust emissions*

Nobel Prizes

For prize winners for the years 1901–89, *see* earlier editions of *Whitaker's Almanack*.

The Nobel Prizes are awarded each year from the income of a trust fund established by the Swedish scientist Alfred Nobel, the inventor of dynamite, who died on 10 December 1896, leaving a fortune of £1,750,000. The prizes are awarded to those who have contributed most to the common good in the domain of:

Physics
  awarded by the Royal Swedish Academy of Sciences;
Chemistry
  awarded by the Royal Swedish Academy of Sciences;
Physiology or Medicine
  awarded by the Karolinska Institute;
Literature
  awarded by the Swedish Academy of Arts;
Peace
  awarded by a five-person committee elected by the Norwegian Storting;
Economic Sciences (instituted 1969)
  awarded by the Royal Swedish Academy of Sciences.

The first awards were made in 1901 on the fifth anniversary of Nobel's death. The prizes are awarded every year on 10 December, the anniversary of Nobel's death.

The Trust is administered by the board of directors of the Nobel Foundation, Stockholm, consisting of five members and three deputy members. The Swedish Government appoints a chairman and a deputy chairman, the remaining members being appointed by the awarding authorities.

The awards have been distributed as follows:
Physics
American 55, British 20, German 19 (1948–90, West German 8), French 11, Soviet 7, Dutch 6, Swedish 4, Austrian 3, Danish 3, Italian 3, Japanese 3, Chinese 2, Swiss 2, Canadian 1, Indian 1, Irish 1, Pakistani 1.
Chemistry
American 37, German 27 (1948–90, West German 10), British 23, French 7, Swiss 5, Swedish 4, Canadian 2, Dutch 2, Argentinian 1, Austrian 1, Belgian 1, Czech 1, Finnish 1, Hungarian 1, Italian 1, Japanese 1, Norwegian 1, Soviet 1.
Physiology or Medicine
American 69, British 22, German 14 (1948–90, West German 4), French 7, Swedish 7, Danish 5, Swiss 5, Austrian 4, Belgian 4, Italian 3, Australian 2, Canadian 2, Dutch 2, Hungarian 2, Russian 2, Argentinian 1, Japanese 1, Portuguese 1, South African 1, Spanish 1.
Literature
French 12, American 9, British 8, Swedish 7, German 6 (1948–90, West German 1), Italian 5, Spanish 5, Danish 3, Norwegian 3, Soviet 3, Chilean 2, Greek 2, Irish 2, Polish 2, Swiss 2, Australian 1, Belgian 1, Colombian 1, Czech 1, Egyptian 1, Finnish 1, Guatemalan 1, Icelandic 1, Indian 1, Israeli 1, Japanese 1, Mexican 1, Nigerian 1, South African 1, Trinidadian 1, Yugoslav 1, Stateless 1.
Peace
American 17, Institutions 16, British 9, French 9, Swedish 5, German 4 (1948–90, West German 1), Belgian 3, Swiss 3, Argentinian 2, Austrian 2, Norwegian 2, South African 2, Soviet 2, Burmese 1, Canadian 1, Costa Rican 1, Danish 1, Dutch 1, Egyptian 1, Guatemalan 1, Irish 1, Israeli 1, Italian 1, Japanese 1, Mexican 1, Polish 1, Tibetan 1, Vietnamese 1, Yugoslav 1.
Economics
American 19, British 6, Norwegian 2, Swedish 2, Dutch 1, French 1, Soviet 1.

Prize	1990	1991	1992
Physics	Prof. J. Friedman (American) Prof. H. Kendall (American) Prof. R. Taylor (Canadian)	Prof. P.-G. de Gennes (French)	Prof. G. Charpak (French)
Chemistry	Prof. E. Corey (American)	Prof. R. Ernst (Swiss)	Prof. R. Marcus (American)
Physiology or Medicine	Dr J. Murray (American) Dr E. D. Thomas (American)	E. Neher (German) B. Sakmann (German)	Dr E. Krebs (American) Dr E. Fischer (American)
Literature	O. Paz (Mexican)	N. Gordimer (South African)	D. Walcott (Trinidadian)
Peace	Pres. M. Gorbachev (Soviet)	Aung San Suu Kyi (Burmese)	Sra R. Menchú (Guatemalan)
Economics	Prof. H. Markowitz (American) Prof. M. Miller (American) Prof. W. Sharpe (American)	Prof. R. Coase (British)	G. S. Becker (American)

The Cost of Living

The first cost-of-living index to be calculated in Great Britain was the one which took July 1914 as 100 and was based on the pattern of expenditure of working class families in 1904. Since 1947 the General Index of Retail Prices has superseded the cost-of-living index, although the older term is still often popularly applied to it. This index is designed to reflect the month-by-month changes in the average level of retail prices of goods ar.d services purchased by the 'majority' of households in the United Kingdom, including practically all wage-earners and most small and medium salary-earners. For spending coming within the scope of the index, a representative list of items is selected and the prices actually charged for these items are collected at regular intervals. In working out the index figure, the price changes are 'weighted' – that is, given different degrees of importance – in accordance with the pattern of consumption of the average family.

A more widely used guide when considering changes in the average level of prices of all consumer goods and services, particularly over a number of years, is the consumer price index, now renamed the consumers' expenditure deflator. This index, which has been calculated back to 1938, covers the expenditure of all consumers as defined for national income purposes, and compares the price of goods and services actually purchased in a given year with the prices of the same goods and services in a base year.

During 1973 the Central Statistical Office constructed an annual index of prices of consumer goods and services over the period 1914 to 1972. This index has been constructed by linking together the pre-war cost-of-living index for the period 1914-38, the consumers' expenditure deflator for the period 1938 and 1946-62 and the General Index of Retail Prices for the period 1962-72.

In August 1979, the tax and price index (TPI) was introduced in order to provide a statistic which incorporates the effects of direct and indirect taxation, as well as prices, on taxpayers. The TPI is not directly concerned with the purchasing power of money, however, but with the purchasing power of pre-tax income. The General Index of Retail Prices thus retains its function of measuring the changes in the prices of goods and services purchased by households (from their post-tax income), and therefore as an indicator of the purchasing power of money.

	Long term index of consumer goods and services (Jan. 1987 = 100)	Comparable purchasing power of £1 in 1992
1914	2.8	49.46
1915	3.5	39.57
1920	7.0	19.79
1925	5.0	27.70
1930	4.5	30.78
1935	4.0	34.63
1938	4.4	31.48

There are no official figures for 1939-45

1946	7.4	18.72
1950	9.0	15.39
1955	11.2	12.37
1960	12.6	10.99
1965	14.8	9.36
1970	18.5	7.49
1975	34.2	4.05
1976	39.8	3.48
1977	46.1	3.00
1978	50.0	2.77
1979	56.6	2.45
1980	66.8	2.07
1981	74.8	1.85
1982	81.2	1.71
1983	84.9	1.63
1984	89.2	1.55
1985	94.6	1.46
1986	97.8	1.42
1987	101.9	1.36
1988	106.9	1.30
1989	115.2	1.20
1990	126.1	1.10
1991	133.5	1.04
1992	138.5	1.00

By employing this table an annual purchasing power of the pound index may be derived by taking the inverse of the price index. So, for example, if the purchasing power of the pound is taken to be 100p in 1975, then its comparable purchasing power in 1992 would be:

$$100 \times \frac{34.2}{138.5} = 24.7p$$

It should be noted that these figures can only be approximate.

Countries of the World

The total population of the world in mid-1990 was estimated at 5,292 million, compared with 3,019 million in 1960 and 2,070 million in 1930.

Continent, etc.	Area sq. miles '000	Area sq. km '000	Estimated population mid-1990
Africa	11,704	30,313	642,000,000
North America[1]	8,311	21,525	276,000,000
Latin America[2]	7,933	20,547	448,000,000
Asia[3]	10,637	27,549	3,113,000,000
Europe[4]	1,915	4,961	498,000,000
Former USSR	8,649	22,402	289,000,000
Oceania[5]	3,286	8,510	26,500,000
TOTAL	52,435	135,807	5,292,000,000

[1] Includes Greenland and Hawaii
[2] Mexico and the remainder of the Americas south of the USA
[3] Includes European Turkey, excludes former USSR
[4] Excludes European Turkey and former USSR
[5] Includes Australia, New Zealand and the islands inhabited by Micronesian, Melanesian and Polynesian peoples
Source: UN Demographic Yearbook 1990 (pub. 1992)

A United Nations report (*The Future Growth of World Population*) in 1958 stated that the population of the world had increased since the beginning of the 20th century at an unprecedented rate: in 1850 it was estimated at 1,094 million and in 1900 at 1,500 million, an increase of 42 per cent in 50 years. By 1925 it had risen to 1,907 million (23 per cent in 25 years) and by 1950 it had reached 2,500 million, an increase of 31 per cent in 25 years. Levels of population and the trend in distribution of the population by continents as forecast for the year 2000 were:

Continents, etc.	Estimated population	per cent
Africa	517,000,000	8.2
North America	312,000,000	5.0
Latin America[1]	592,000,000	9.4
Asia (excluding USSR)	3,870,000,000	61.8
Europe (including USSR)	947,000,000	15.1
Oceania	29,000,000	0.5
TOTAL	6,267,000,000	100

[1] Mexico and the remainder of the Americas south of USA

No complete survey of many countries has yet been achieved and consequently accurate area figures are not always available. Similarly, many countries have not recently, or have never, taken a census. The areas of countries given below are derived from estimated figures published by the United Nations. The conversion factors used are:
(i) to convert square miles to square km, multiply by 2·589988
(ii) to convert square km to square miles, multiply by 0·3861022
Population figures for countries are derived from the most recent estimates available. Accurate and up-to-date data for the populations of capital cities are scarce, and definitions of cities' extent differ. The figures given below are the latest estimates available, and where it is known that the figure applies to an urban agglomeration this is indicated.

  *   latest census figure
  Ψ   seaport
  u.a.   urban agglomeration

AFRICA

COUNTRY	AREA sq. miles	sq. km	POPULATION	CAPITAL	POPULATION OF CAPITAL
Algeria	919,595	2,381,741	25,660,000	Ψ Algiers	3,250,000
Angola	481,354	1,246,700	10,303,000	Ψ Luanda	3,000,000
Benin	43,484	112,622	4,889,000	Ψ Porto Novo	208,258
Botswana	224,607	581,730	1,348,000	Gaborone	137,174
Burkina	105,869	274,200	9,242,000	Ouagadougou	441,514
Burundi	10,747	27,834	5,620,000	Bujumbura	215,243
Cameroon	183,569	475,442	12,239,000	Yaoundé	635,670
Cape Verde Islands	1,557	4,033	382,000	Ψ Praia	57,748*
Central African Republic	240,535	622,984	3,127,000	Bangui	473,817
Chad	495,755	1,284,000	5,819,000	Ndjaména	402,000
Comoros	838	2,171	570,000	Moroni	17,267*
Congo	132,047	342,000	2,346,000	Brazzaville	596,200*
Côte d'Ivoire	124,503	322,463	12,464,000	Ψ Abidjan	3,500,000
Djibouti	8,494	22,000	520,000	Ψ Djibouti	340,700
Egypt	386,662	1,001,449	54,688,000	Cairo	14,000,000
Equatorial Guinea	10,830	28,051	356,000	Ψ Malabo	30,418
Eritrea	36,170	93,679	3,500,000	Asmara	275,000
Ethiopia	471,778	1,221,900	49,883,000	Addis Ababa	1,793,000
Gabon	103,347	267,667	1,212,000	Ψ Libreville	251,000
Gambia	4,361	11,295	884,000	Ψ Banjul (u.a.)	109,986

COUNTRY	AREA sq. miles	sq. km	POPULATION	CAPITAL	POPULATION OF CAPITAL
Ghana	92,100	238,537	15,509,000	Ψ Accra (u.a.)	1,781,100
Guinea	94,926	245,857	5,931,000	Ψ Conakry	763,000
Guinea-Bissau	13,948	36,125	984,000	Ψ Bissau	109,214*
Kenya	224,961	582,646	25,905,000	Nairobi	1,400,000
Lesotho	11,720	30,355	1,826,000	Maseru	288,951*
Liberia	43,000	111,369	2,705,000	Ψ Monrovia	425,000
Libya	679,362	1,759,540	4,712,000	Ψ Tripoli	1,000,000
Madagascar	226,669	587,041	11,493,000	Antananarivo	1,250,000
Malawi	45,747	118,484	8,556,000	Lilongwe	233,973*
Mali	478,791	1,240,000	9,507,000	Bamako	658,275
Mauritania	397,955	1,030,700	2,036,000	Nouakchott	850,000
Mauritius	790	2,045	1,022,456	Ψ Port Louis	142,505
Mayotte (Fr.)	144	372	94,410	Mamoundzou	12,000
Morocco	172,414	446,550	27,575,000	Ψ Rabat	1,494,000
Western Sahara	102,703	266,000	183,000	Laayoune	96,784*
Mozambique	309,495	801,590	16,084,000	Ψ Maputo	1,150,000
Namibia	318,261	824,292	1,837,000	Windhoek	110,000
Niger	489,191	1,267,080	7,984,000	Niamey	410,000
Nigeria	356,669	923,768	112,163,000	Abuja	378,671
Réunion (Fr.)	969	2,510	598,000	St Denis	122,000
Rwanda	10,169	26,338	7,491,000	Kigali	156,000
St Helena (UK)	47	122	5,644	Ψ Jamestown	1,332
Ascension Island	34	88	1,117	Ψ Georgetown	—
Tristan da Cunha	38	98	295	Ψ Edinburgh	—
São Tomé and Príncipe	372	964	124,000	Ψ São Tomé	25,000
Senegal	75,750	196,192	7,533,000	Ψ Dakar	1,000,000
Seychelles	108	280	68,000	Ψ Victoria	24,324
Sierra Leone	27,699	71,740	4,260,000	Ψ Freetown	470,000
Somalia	246,201	637,657	7,691,000	Ψ Mogadishu	1,000,000
South Africa	471,445	1,221,031	36,070,000	{ Pretoria (u.a.) Ψ Cape Town (u.a.)	822,925 1,911,521
Sudan	967,500	2,505,813	25,941,000	Khartoum (u.a.)	3,000,000
Swaziland	6,704	17,363	817,000	Mbabane	38,290
Tanzania	364,900	945,087	28,359,000	Dodoma	88,474
Togo	21,925	56,785	3,643,000	Ψ Lomé	366,476
Tunisia	63,170	163,610	8,362,000	Ψ Tunis	1,394,749
Uganda	91,259	236,036	19,517,000	Kampala (u.a.)	750,000
Zaire	905,567	2,345,409	36,672,000	Kinshasa	2,778,281*
Zambia	290,586	752,614	8,780,000	Lusaka (u.a.)	1,000,000
Zimbabwe	150,804	390,580	10,019,000	Harare	681,000

AMERICA

North America

Canada	3,849,646	9,970,537	27,296,859	Ottawa (u.a.)	313,987*
Greenland (Den.)	840,004	2,175,600	55,385	Ψ Godthab	8,425
Mexico	761,605	1,972,547	87,836,000	Mexico City (u.a.)	14,987,051
St Pierre and Miquelon (Fr.)	93	242	6,300	Ψ St Pierre	—
United States	3,787,318	9,809,108	248,709,873*	Washington DC	606,900

Central America and the West Indies

Anguilla (UK)	35	91	8,800*	The Valley	1,400
Antigua and Barbuda	170	440	65,962	Ψ St John's	30,000
Aruba (Neth.)	75	193	59,000	Ψ Oranjestad	20,000
Bahamas	5,380	13,935	258,000	Ψ Nassau	171,000*
Barbados	166	431	255,000	Ψ Bridgetown	7,466
Belize	8,867	22,965	169,392*	Belmopan	3,558*
Bermuda (UK)	20	53	58,460	Ψ Hamilton	1,617
Cayman Islands (UK)	100	259	29,700	Ψ George Town	15,000
Costa Rica	19,575	50,700	3,000,000	San José (u.a.)	1,068,206
Cuba	42,804	110,861	10,736,000	Ψ Havana	2,096,000

AREA

COUNTRY	sq. miles	sq. km	POPULATION	CAPITAL	POPULATION OF CAPITAL
Dominica	290	751	72,000	Ψ Roseau	15,850
Dominican Republic	18,816	48,734	7,321,000	Ψ Santo Domingo (u.a.)	1,313,172*
Grenada	133	344	84,000	Ψ St George's	10,000
Guadeloupe (Fr.)	687	1,779	386,600	Ψ Basse-Terre	14,000
Guatemala	42,042	108,889	9,745,000	Guatemala City	1,675,589
Haiti	10,714	27,750	6,625,000	Ψ Port au Prince	1,000,000
Honduras	43,277	112,088	4,915,900	Tegucigalpa	670,100
Jamaica	4,244	10,991	2,460,700	Ψ Kingston (u.a.)	696,300
Martinique (Fr.)	425	1,102	359,800	Ψ Fort de France	101,540
Montserrat (UK)	38	98	11,000	Ψ Plymouth	2,500
Netherlands Antilles (Neth.)	371	961	189,000	Ψ Willemstad	50,000
Nicaragua	50,193	130,000	3,999,000	Managua	615,000
Panama	29,762	77,082	2,370,000	Ψ Panama City	1,063,565
Puerto Rico (USA)	3,435	8,897	3,336,000	Ψ San Juan (u.a.)	437,745
St Christopher and Nevis	101	261	44,000	Ψ Basseterre	15,000
St Lucia	238	616	153,000	Ψ Castries	56,000
St Vincent and the Grenadines	150	388	117,000	Ψ Kingstown	33,694
El Salvador	8,124	21,041	5,376,000	San Salvador	497,644
Trinidad and Tobago	1,981	5,130	1,253,000	Ψ Port of Spain	59,649
Turks and Caicos Is. (UK)	166	430	12,400	Ψ Grand Turk	3,700
Virgin Islands:					
British (UK)	59	153	16,108*	Ψ Road Town	3,983*
US (USA)	132	342	101,809	Ψ Charlotte Amalie	11,756
South America					
Argentina	1,068,302	2,766,889	32,370,298*	Ψ Buenos Aires	2,955,002
Bolivia	424,165	1,098,581	6,440,000*	La Paz	1,115,000*
Brazil	3,286,488	8,511,965	150,368,000	Brasilia	1,803,478
Chile	292,258	756,945	13,386,000	Santiago	4,385,481
Colombia	439,737	1,138,914	33,613,000	Bogotá	5,000,000
Ecuador	109,484	283,561	10,851,000	Quito	1,387,887
Falkland Islands (UK)	4,700	12,173	2,121	Ψ Stanley	1,643
French Guiana (Fr.)	35,135	91,000	114,900	Ψ Cayenne	41,000
Guyana	83,000	214,969	800,000	Ψ Georgetown	187,056
Paraguay	157,048	406,752	4,397,000	Asunción (u.a.)	729,307
Peru	496,225	1,285,216	22,465,000	Lima (u.a.)	6,459,000
South Georgia (UK)	1,580	4,092	—	—	—
Suriname	63,037	163,265	429,000	Ψ Paramaribo (u.a.)	182,100
Uruguay	68,037	176,215	3,116,802	Ψ Montevideo	1,383,660
Venezuela	352,144	912,050	20,226,000	Caracas (u.a.)	2,784,000

ASIA

Afghanistan	250,000	647,497	16,430,000	Kabul	2,000,000
Bahrain	240	622	516,000	Ψ Manama	108,684*
Bangladesh	55,598	143,998	108,000,000	Dhaka	6,000,000
Bhutan	18,147	47,000	1,551,000	Thimphu	15,000
Brunei	2,226	5,765	260,863	Bandar Seri Begawan	46,229
Cambodia	69,898	181,035	8,442,000	Ψ Phnom Penh	920,000
China[1]	3,705,408	9,596,961	1,171,000,000	Beijing (Peking) (u.a.)	10,860,000
Hong Kong (UK)	416	1,074	5,900,000	Ψ Victoria	—
India	1,269,346	3,287,590	843,930,861	Delhi	8,375,188
Indonesia	735,358	1,904,569	187,765,000	Ψ Jakarta	7,885,519
Iran	636,296	1,648,000	55,762,000	Tehran	6,042,584
Iraq	167,925	434,924	19,581,000	Baghdad	3,205,665
Israel[2]	8,019	20,770	5,090,000	Tel Aviv	1,781,500
Japan	145,834	377,708	123,921,000	Tokyo (u.a.)	11,935,700
Jordan	37,738	97,740	4,145,000	Amman	1,100,000
Kazakhstan	1,049,155	2,716,626	16,700,000	Alma Ata	1,128,000
Korea, DPR (North)	46,540	120,538	23,193,000	Pyongyang	1,500,000
Korea, Rep. of (South)	38,025	98,484	43,268,000	Seoul	9,991,089
Kuwait	6,880	17,818	1,000,000	Ψ Kuwait (city)	400,000

Country	Area sq. miles	sq. km	Population	Capital	Population of Capital
Kyrgyzstan	76,642	198,501	4,367,000	Biskek	616,000
Laos	91,429	231,800	4,262,000	Vientiane	120,000
Lebanon	4,015	10,400	2,745,000	Ψ Beirut	702,000
Macao (*Port.*)	6	16	479,000	Ψ Macao	—
Malaysia	127,317	329,749	18,333,000	Kuala Lumpur	1,103,200
Maldives	115	298	223,000	Ψ Malé	46,334
Mongolia	604,250	1,565,000	2,156,000	Ulan Bator	600,500
Myanmar (Burma)	261,218	676,552	42,561,000	Ψ Yangon (Rangoon) (*u.a.*)	3,973,872
Nepal	54,342	140,747	19,605,000	Kathmandu	300,000
Oman	82,030	212,457	1,559,000	Ψ Muscat	400,000
Pakistan	307,374	746,045	115,524,000	Islamabad (*u.a.*)	350,000
Philippines	115,831	300,000	62,868,000	Ψ Manila	1,876,195
Qatar	4,247	11,000	381,000	Ψ Doha	220,000
Saudi Arabia	830,000	2,149,640	16,929,294	Riyadh	2,000,000
Singapore	247	639	3,002,800	—	—
Sri Lanka	25,332	65,610	17,243,000	Ψ Colombo	1,963,000
Syria	71,498	185,180	12,993,000	Damascus	1,378,000
Tajikistan	55,251	143,100	4,969,000	Dushanbe	595,000
Taiwan	13,800	35,742	20,536,233	Taipei	2,719,659
Thailand	198,457	514,000	56,923,000	Ψ Bangkok	5,876,000
Turkey[3]	301,382	780,576	60,777,000	Ankara	3,236,626
Turkmenistan	188,456	488,100	3,809,000	Ashkhabad	398,000
United Arab Emirates	32,278	83,600	1,909,000	Abu Dhabi	450,000
Uzbekistan	172,742	447,229	20,300,000	Tashkent	2,073,000
Vietnam	127,242	329,556	71,267,000	Hanoi	2,150,000
Yemen	203,850	527,696	12,302,000	Sana'a	427,150

[1] Including Tibet
[2] Including East Jerusalem, the Golan Heights and Israeli citizens on the West Bank
[3] Including Turkey in Europe

EUROPE

Albania	11,099	28,748	3,331,000	Tirana	239,381
Andorra	180	468	58,000	Andorra La Vella	22,205
Armenia	11,306	29,271	3,645,000	Erevan	1,119,000
Austria	32,374	83,849	7,897,800	Vienna	1,539,848*
Azerbaijan	33,436	86,565	7,136,000	Baku	1,757,000
Belarus	80,300	207,897	10,260,000	Minsk	1,589,000
Belgium	11,781	30,513	9,928,000	Brussels (*u.a.*)	960,324*
Bosnia–Hercegovina	19,735	51,129	4,100,000	Sarajevo	447,000
Bulgaria	42,823	110,912	8,982,000	Sofia	1,107,613
Croatia	21,823	56,538	4,760,344	Zagreb	950,000
Cyprus	3,572	9,251	706,900	Nicosia	177,410
Czech Republic	30,372	78,664	10,302,000	Prague	1,215,076
Denmark	16,629	43,069	5,146,469	Ψ Copenhagen (*u.a.*)	1,337,114
Faroe Islands	540	1,399	47,449	Ψ Thorshavn	10,726
Estonia	17,413	45,082	1,574,955	Talinn	484,400
Finland	137,851	337,032	5,029,000	Ψ Helsinki	492,200
France	211,208	547,026	56,614,000	Paris (*u.a.*)	9,318,800
Georgia	26,911	69,673	5,401,000	Tbilisi	1,211,000
Germany	137,738	365,755	80,372,000	Berlin	3,376,800
Gibraltar (*UK*)	2	6	28,848	Ψ Gibraltar	—
Greece	50,944	131,944	10,256,464	Athens (*u.a.*)	3,096,775
Hungary	35,919	93,030	10,335,000	Budapest	2,004,000
Iceland	39,768	103,000	259,581	Ψ Reykjavik (*u.a.*)	99,653
Ireland, Republic of	27,136	70,283	3,525,719	Ψ Dublin	478,389
Italy	116,304	301,225	57,052,000	Rome (*u.a.*)	2,693,383
Latvia	24,695	63,935	2,606,000	Riga	900,000
Liechtenstein	61	157	29,856	Vaduz	4,874
Lithuania	26,173	67,761	3,761,000	Vilnius	596,000
Luxembourg	998	2,586	389,800	Luxembourg	75,400
Macedonia	9,925	25,713	2,034,000	Skopje	448,229

AREA

COUNTRY	sq. miles	sq. km	POPULATION	CAPITAL	POPULATION OF CAPITAL
Malta	122	316	362,950	Ψ Valletta	9,199
Moldova	13,912	36,018	4,361,000	Kishinev	665,000
Monaco	0.4	1	28,000	Monaco-Ville	1,234
Netherlands	15,770	40,844	15,240,000	Ψ Amsterdam (u.a.)	1,034,562
Norway[1]	125,181	324,219	4,262,000	Ψ Oslo	467,090
Poland	120,725	312,677	38,300,000	Warsaw	1,655,063
Portugal[2]	35,553	92,082	10,582,000	Ψ Lisbon	2,128,000
Romania	91,699	237,500	22,760,449	Bucharest	2,064,474
Russia[3]	6,593,391	17,070,289	148,800,000	Moscow	8,967,000
San Marino	23	61	24,000	San Marino	—
Slovak Republic	18,932	49,035	5,274,335	Bratislava	440,421
Slovenia	7,816	20,251	2,020,000	Ljubljana	268,000
Spain[4]	194,897	504,782	38,872,268	Madrid (u.a.)	4,947,555
Sweden	173,732	449,964	8,635,000	Ψ Stockholm (u.a.)	669,485
Switzerland	15,943	41,293	6,833,750	Berne	135,600
Ukraine	233,090	603,700	52,000,000	Kiev	2,577,000
United Kingdom[5]	94,227	244,046	56,467,000*	Ψ London (u.a.)	6,679,699
England	50,363	130,439	49,890,000	—	—
Wales	8,018	20,768	2,811,865*	Ψ Cardiff	290,000
Scotland	30,414	78,772	4,998,567*	Ψ Edinburgh	418,914
Northern Ireland	5,452	14,121	1,577,836*	Ψ Belfast (u.a.)	287,100
Vatican City State	0.2	0.44	1,000	Vatican City	—
Yugoslavia, Fed. Rep. of	39,506	102,350	10,410,000	Belgrade	1,455,000

[1] Excludes Svalbard and Jan Mayen Islands (approx. 24,101 sq. miles (62,422 sq. km) and 3,000 population)
[2] Includes Madeira (314 sq. miles) and the Azores (922 sq. miles)
[3] Includes Russia in Asia
[4] Includes Balearic Islands, Canary Islands, Ceuta and Melilla
[5] Includes Isle of Man (227 sq. miles (588 sq. km), 69,788* population), and Channel Islands (75 sq. miles (195 sq. km), 142,949* population)

OCEANIA

Australia	2,967,909	7,686,848	17,482,600*	Canberra	284,000*
Norfolk Island	14	36	1,912	Ψ Kingston	—
Fiji	7,055	18,274	776,000	Ψ Suva	69,665
French Polynesia (Fr.)	1,544	4,000	206,000	Ψ Papeete	24,200
Guam (USA)	212	549	132,152	Agaña	—
Kiribati	281	728	68,000	Tarawa	17,921
Marshall Islands	70	181	45,569	Majuro	20,000
Micronesia, Fed. States of	271	701	101,000	Palikir	—
Nauru	8	21	9,000	Ψ Nauru	—
New Caledonia (Fr.)	7,358	19,058	167,000	Ψ Noumea	65,000
New Zealand	103,736	268,676	3,435,000	Ψ Wellington (u.a.)	325,682
Cook Islands	91	236	17,185*	Avarua	—
Niue	100	259	2,239	Alofi	—
Ross Dependency[1]	286,696	750,310	—	—	—
Tokelau	5	12.9	1,578	—	—
Northern Mariana Islands (USA)	184	476	43,555	Saipan	39,090
Palau (USA)	192	497	15,105	Koror	10,493
Papua New Guinea	178,260	461,691	3,772,000	Ψ Port Moresby	173,500
Pitcairn Islands (UK)	1.9	5	65	—	—
Samoa, Eastern (USA)	76	197	46,773	Ψ Pago Pago	3,075
Solomon Islands	10,983	28,446	330,000	Ψ Honiara	30,499*
Tonga	270	699	94,000	Ψ Nuku'alofa	30,000
Tuvalu	10	25	9,000	Ψ Funafuti	2,856
Vanuatu	4,706	12,190	163,000	Ψ Port Vila	19,400
Wallis and Futuna Islands (Fr.)	106	274	13,705	Ψ Mata-Utu	—
Western Samoa	1,097	2,842	162,000	Ψ Apia	36,000

[1] Includes permanent shelf ice

Presidents of the USA

Name (*with Native State*)	Party	Born	Inauguration	Died	Age
George Washington, *Va.*	Federation	22 February 1732	1789	14 December 1799	67
John Adams, *Mass.*	Federation	30 October 1735	1797	4 July 1826	90
Thomas Jefferson, *Va.*	Republican	13 April 1743	1801	4 July 1826	83
James Madison, *Va.*	Republican	16 March 1751	1809	28 June 1836	85
James Monroe, *Va.*	Republican	28 April 1758	1817	4 July 1831	73
John Quincy Adams, *Mass.*	Republican	11 July 1767	1825	23 February 1848	80
Andrew Jackson, *SC*	Democrat	15 March 1767	1829	8 June 1845	78
Martin Van Buren, *NY*	Democrat	5 December 1782	1837	24 July 1862	79
William Henry Harrison†, *Va.*	Whig	9 February 1773	1841	4 April 1841	68
John Tyler (*a*), *Va.*	Whig	29 March 1790	1841	17 January 1862	71
James Knox Polk, *NC*	Democrat	2 November 1795	1845	15 June 1849	53
Zachary Taylor†, *Va.*	Whig	24 November 1784	1849	9 July 1850	65
Millard Fillmore (*a*), *NY*	Whig	7 January 1800	1850	8 March 1874	74
Franklin Pierce, *NH*	Democrat	23 November 1804	1853	8 October 1869	64
James Buchanan, *Pa.*	Democrat	23 April 1791	1857	1 June 1868	77
Abraham Lincoln†§, *Ky.*	Republican	12 February 1809	1861	15 April 1865	56
Andrew Johnson (*a*), *NC*	Republican	29 December 1808	1865	31 July 1875	66
Ulysses Simpson Grant, *Ohio*	Republican	27 April 1822	1869	23 July 1885	63
Rutherford Birchard Hayes, *Ohio*	Republican	4 October 1822	1877	17 January 1893	70
James Abram Garfield†§, *Ohio*	Republican	19 November 1831	1881	19 September 1881	49
Chester Alan Arthur (*a*), *Vt.*	Republican	5 October 1830	1881	18 November 1886	56
Grover Cleveland, *NJ*	Democrat	18 March 1837	1885	24 June 1908	71
Benjamin Harrison, *Ohio*	Republican	20 August 1833	1889	13 March 1901	67
Grover Cleveland, *NJ*	Democrat	18 March 1837	1893	24 June 1908	71
William McKinley†§, *Ohio*	Republican	29 January 1843	1897	14 September 1901	58
Theodore Roosevelt (*a*), *NY*	Republican	27 October 1858	1901	6 January 1919	60
William Howard Taft, *Ohio*	Republican	15 September 1857	1909	8 March 1930	72
Woodrow Wilson, *Va.*	Democrat	28 December 1856	1913	3 February 1924	67
Warren Gamaliel Harding†, *Ohio*	Republican	2 November 1865	1921	2 August 1923	57
Calvin Coolidge (*a*), *Vt.*	Republican	4 July 1872	1923	5 January 1933	60
Herbert Clark Hoover, *Iowa.*	Republican	10 August 1874	1929	20 October 1964	90
Franklin Delano Roosevelt†‡, *NY*	Democrat	30 January 1882	1933	12 April 1945	63
Harry S. Truman (*a*), *Missouri*	Democrat	8 May 1884	1945	26 December 1972	88
Dwight David Eisenhower, *Texas*	Republican	14 October 1890	1953	28 March 1969	78
John Fitzgerald Kennedy, *Mass.*†§	Democrat	29 May 1917	1961	22 November 1963	46
Lyndon Baines Johnson (*a*), *Texas*	Democrat	27 August 1908	1963	22 January 1973	64
Richard Milhous Nixon, *California*	Republican	9 January 1913	1969		
Gerald Rudolph Ford (*b*), *Nebraska*	Republican	14 July 1913	1974		
James Earl Carter, *Georgia*	Democrat	1 October 1924	1977		
Ronald Wilson Reagan, *Illinois*	Republican	6 February 1911	1981		
George Herbert Walker Bush, *Mass.*	Republican	12 June 1924	1989		
William Jefferson Blythe IV Clinton, *Ark.*	Democrat	19 August 1946	1993		

† Died in office
(*a*) Elected as Vice-President
§ Assassinated
‡ Re-elected 5 November 1940, the first case of a third term; re-elected for a fourth term 7 November 1944.
(*b*) Appointed under the provisions of the 25th Amendment

Events of the Year

1 September 1992–31 August 1993

SEPTEMBER 1992

3. The Chancellor of the Exchequer (Norman Lamont) said that the Government would borrow £7,200 million in foreign currencies from a group of international banks in order to buy sterling and maintain its position within the exchange rate mechanism (ERM). The Prime Minister (John Major) rejected a request from the Leader of the Opposition (John Smith) for Parliament to be recalled to debate the crises in Yugoslavia and Iraq and the state of the economy. Kevin Maxwell was declared bankrupt with debts of £406 million, the largest-ever bankruptcy in Britain. **6.** A small IRA bomb exploded in London. **10.** The Prime Minister said that devaluation of sterling would be a betrayal of Britain's future and repeated the Government's commitment to membership of the ERM. **13.** The Liberal Democrat annual conference opened in Harrogate. **16.** As sterling's position in the ERM worsened, bank base rates rose from 10 per cent to 12 per cent and then to 15 per cent. Sterling fell below the permitted lowest level against the Deutsche Mark (DM 2.7780) and was quoted at DM 2.7400 by close of trading in London. The Chancellor of the Exchequer announced at 7.45 p.m. that sterling's membership of the ERM had been suspended and that bank base rates had returned to 12 per cent. Sterling was permitted to float on the currency markets. The Prime Minister agreed to recall Parliament on 24 September to discuss the crisis. **17.** Bank base rates were lowered to 10 per cent and sterling closed at DM 2.6323. Firebombs exploded at the Imperial War Museum, Madame Tussaud's and the London Planetarium. **21.** Sterling fell to a record low of DM 2.5456 by close of trading in London. **22.** Bank base rates were cut to 9 per cent. **24.** Parliament was recalled for an emergency debate on the economic crisis. A government motion in support of its handling of the economy was passed by 322 votes to 296 in the House of Commons. More than 60 Conservative MPs signed an early day motion welcoming Britain's departure from the ERM. David Mellor resigned as Secretary of State for National Heritage after press revelations that a family holiday in September 1990 had been paid for by the daughter of the PLO's head of finance (*see also* Crimes and Legal Affairs below). **25.** An emergency debate on foreign policy was held in the House of Commons, after which Parliament went back into recess. **28.** The Labour Party annual conference

opened in Blackpool. **30.** A letter from the president of the German Bundesbank to the Treasury, denying that the Bundesbank's actions had contributed to the sterling crisis, was leaked to the press by the German Embassy in London. Sterling closed at DM 2.5046.

OCTOBER 1992

2. Sterling fell to DM 2.4450. **6.** The Conservative Party annual conference opened in Brighton. **7.** Two small IRA bombs exploded in London. **8–10.** Small IRA bombs exploded in London on each day. **12.** A man was killed and several people injured when an IRA bomb exploded in a pub in Covent Garden, London. **13.** The President of the Board of Trade (Michael Heseltine) and the chairman of British Coal (Neil Clarke) announced the closure of 31 pits by the end of March 1993, six of them to close on 16 October, and the loss of 30,000 jobs. A storm of protest greeted the announcement. **15.** Downing Street said that the decision to close 31 pits was taken by a small group of ministers and not the full Cabinet. An emergency application by the National Union of Mineworkers and NACODS, the pit deputies' union, for a temporary injunction to stop the closures was made to the High Court in London; on 20 October the hearing was adjourned (*see* 21 December). **16.** In the High Court the UDM won the right to seek a judicial review of the decision to close eight pits. An EC summit meeting was held in Birmingham. Bank base rates were cut to 8 per cent. **19.** After an emergency Cabinet meeting the President of Board of Trade announced that only ten pits would close, after a 90-day consultation period, and that a moratorium until the new year would be introduced for the other 21 pits, after which the closures, if confirmed, would be phased in. The Queen and the Duke of Edinburgh arrived in Germany for a five-day State visit. Two small IRA bombs exploded in London. **20.** The Prime Minister said that there would be a 'full and open review' of pit closures and of the market for coal. In the House of Lords peers voted in favour of an opposition motion calling for an independent inquiry into the future of the coal industry. **21.** After a debate in the House of Commons, during which the President of the Board of Trade said that there would be a complete review of the Government's energy policy, an opposition motion calling for all 31 pits to remain open pending a review of the future of the coal industry was defeated. About 50,000 miners and their supporters marched in London in protest at the pit closures. Three small IRA bombs exploded in London. **22.** The report of the official inquiry headed by Lord Justice Bingham into the collapse of the Bank of Credit and Commerce International (BCCI) was published; it was highly critical of the supervision of the Bank of England. **23.** A report commissioned by the Government recommended the closure of 15 hospitals in London. **25.** About 150,000 people marched through London to protest at the planned pit closures. A small IRA bomb exploded in London. **27.** The London Ambulance Service's new computer-aided dispatch system was shut down after repeated problems on 26–27 October. The report of the inquiry into the conduct of the Orkney child ritual sex abuse allegations in February 1991 was published; it was highly critical of the social workers and police involved. **28.** About 70 lb of Semtex explosive was found by police at a house in Leytonstone, London. **30.** An IRA car bomb exploded in Whitehall, London, after a minicab driver was forced at gunpoint to drive it there.

NOVEMBER 1992

2. The Prince and Princess of Wales arrived in South Korea for a five-day official visit; current speculation continued about the state of their marriage. **3.** The Sultan of Brunei arrived in Britain for a four-day State visit. The Isle of Man parliament voted to abolish capital punishment. **4.** The Government won a vote allowing the bill ratifying the Maastricht Treaty to proceed. **5.** The Prime Minister said that the Maastricht Treaty bill would not have its final reading in the Commons until after the Danish referendum in May 1993. **9.** President Yeltsin of Russia arrived in Britain for a two-day State visit. **11.** The General Synod of the Church of England voted by 384 votes to 169, with the required majority of 66 per cent in each of the three Houses, to permit the ordination of women as priests. **12.** The Chancellor of the Exchequer presented his autumn financial statement (see page 1164). The Ministry of Defence announced that Portland Naval Base in Dorset would close by 1996. **13.** Bank base rates were cut to 7 per cent. **14.** A policeman was shot and wounded after stopping a lorry containing 2,000 lb of IRA explosives in north London. **18.** The Department for Education published 1992 GCSE and A-level results for 4,600 state schools and 260 independent schools; the 'league tables' were attacked for being inaccurate and misleading. **23.** The Secretary of State for National Heritage (Peter Brooke) said that the costs of rebuilding the state apartments at Windsor Castle (see Accidents and Disasters) would be met wholly from government funds; the announcement caused widespread protests. **24.** In a speech at the Guildhall in the City of London, The Queen said that 1992 had been an 'annus horribilis'. **26.** The Prime Minister announced that The Queen had offered to pay tax on private income from April 1993 and to refund Civil List payments for most members of the royal family (see page 130). The Sun published details of an unpaid credit card bill on the account of the Chancellor of the Exchequer; on 30 November two staff of the Threshers off-licence chain were suspended after

they admitted falsely alleging that Mr Lamont had purchased champagne and cigarettes from their branch on 16 November. **28.** The Treasury confirmed that £4,700 of the legal costs incurred by the Chancellor of the Exchequer in evicting a tenant from his London home in 1991 were met from public funds.

DECEMBER 1992

1. The west end of London was evacuated after an IRA warning; police found a van loaded with explosives near Tottenham Court Road. **2.** The Government announced that the Cammell Laird shipyard, Birkenhead, would close in 1993. **3.** Two IRA bombs exploded in central Manchester, injuring 64 people. **8.** The Shree Khrishna Hindu temple in West Bromwich was destroyed by an arson attack in the wake of communal violence in India, Pakistan and Bangladesh. **9.** The Prime Minister announced in the House of Commons that the Prince and Princess of Wales had decided to separate. An IRA bomb exploded in London. The Duchess of York and John Bryan were awarded £90,500 damages and costs by a French court over the publication of intimate photos by *Paris Match* magazine in August 1992. **10.** Ten people were injured when two IRA bombs exploded at Wood Green shopping centre, London. **11–12.** A two-day EC summit meeting on the Maastricht Treaty was held in Edinburgh (see pages 1097–8). **12.** The Princess Royal married Commander Timothy Laurence at Crathie Church, Balmoral. **16.** Two IRA bombs exploded in London. The European Court of Justice ruled that restrictions on Sunday trading are legal under EC law. **21.** The High Court ruled that the Government's pit closure programme was unlawful and that miners and their unions had a right to be fully consulted. The President of the Board of Trade said that coal production would not resume at the ten pits which had already closed. **22.** An IRA bomb exploded in London. **23.** The *Sun* published a transcript of The Queen's Christmas broadcast.

JANUARY 1993

2. Sean Devereux, a British aid worker, was shot dead in Somalia. **3.** Princess Margaret was admitted to hospital suffering from pneumonia. **6.** The Foreign Secretary (Douglas Hurd) arrived in Argentina for a four-day visit, the first by a Cabinet minister since the 1982 conflict. Four IRA incendiary bombs exploded in shops in central London. **11.** British Airways issued an unconditional apology to Virgin airlines and its owner Richard Branson, and agreed to pay £610,000 damages and up to £3 million costs in settlement of a libel action in which Virgin had alleged that BA was conducting a 'dirty tricks' campaign against it. Blizzards caused disruption in Scotland and northern England. **12.** The chairman of the Press Complaints Commission (Lord McGregor of Durris) said that he had evidence that the Princess of Wales had provided information about the state of her marriage to selected tabloid newspapers. An

Australian magazine, *New Idea*, published a transcript of an intimate telephone conversation allegedly between the Prince of Wales and his friend Camilla Parker Bowles in 1989; the transcript was later published by sections of the British press. More than 2,000 people had to be rescued from their vehicles in blizzards in eastern Scotland. **13.** A soldier serving with the Cheshire Regiment in Bosnia, L/Cpl Wayne Edwards, was killed by a sniper while escorting a civilian ambulance. Gale force winds caused disruption and at least two deaths in southern England. **15.** Five people were killed in accidents when gales hit northern England and Scotland. **17.** Flooding and gales caused disruption in Scotland. **22.** An official report criticized corruption and malpractice at Lambeth Council, London. **26.** Bank base rates were cut to 6 per cent. **28.** The Prime Minister issued writs for libel against two magazines, *New Statesman and Society* and *Scallywag*, over articles mentioning rumours that he was having an affair with Clare Latimer, a caterer; Ms Latimer also issued writs. A small IRA bomb exploded outside Harrods, London.

FEBRUARY 1993

1. Sterling fell to DM 2.3757; on 2 February it fell to DM 2.3746 and on 3 February to DM 2.3595. On 4 February sterling recovered after German interest rates were cut by 0.5 per cent. **2.** Solicitors acting for The Queen began legal proceedings against the *Sun* over its publication of the text of her 1992 Christmas broadcast two days before transmission. On 11 February a writ was served on the newspaper, and on 14 February the *Sun* apologized to The Queen and offered to make a donation to charity; this was accepted. **3.** The Defence Secretary announced that the strength of the Army would be reduced to 119,000, rather than the planned 116,000, and that four regiments would not be amalgamated. DAF, the Anglo-Dutch lorry manufacturer with 5,500 employees at its British branch Leyland DAF, went into receivership. In a speech at the Carlton Club, the Prime Minister suggested that the unemployed should be required to work for their benefits, sparking a controversy about the possible introduction of 'workfare' schemes in Britain. Two small IRA bombs exploded in London. Chris Patten, the governor of Hong Kong, underwent heart surgery. **5.** Sir Ranulph Fiennes and Dr Michael Stroud set a world record for the longest unsupported polar journey after they walked 1,257 miles across Antarctica; on 7 February they became the first people to cross the Antarctic land mass on foot. **9.** Sterling fell to DM 2.3490. The Secretary of State for Defence announced that the naval dockyards at Devonport and Rosyth would be kept open. **10.** A small IRA bomb exploded in London. **12.** The Prime Minister and Clare Latimer reached out-of-court settlements in their libel actions against the newsagent John Menzies and the printers and distributors of *New Statesman and Society*. The Prince of Wales left London for a seven-day official visit to the USA and Mexico. **16.** The Government

published a report, *Making London Better*, in response to the Tomlinson report on health services in London; it approved the closure of five hospitals and proposed merging or closing other hospitals over the next six years. **21.** Hundreds of people were evacuated from their homes when high tides and gales caused widespread flooding along the east coast of England. **24.** The Duke of Westminster resigned from the Conservative Party in protest at the Government's proposed leasehold reform legislation. **26.** PC Mark Toker was shot and wounded by an IRA gunman in Warrington, Cheshire. Three bombs subsequently caused a huge explosion at a gasworks in the town and a motorist was kidnapped at gunpoint. Two men were arrested and the motorist was freed; one terrorist escaped but was later arrested. **27.** At least 15 people were injured when an IRA bomb exploded in Camden High Street, north London.

MARCH 1993

2. The Princess of Wales and the Minister for Overseas Development (Baroness Chalker) arrived in Nepal for a five-day official visit. **4.** The Prime Minister announced changes to the honours system, including a new system of public nominations for awards. **8.** The Bishop of Gloucester, the Rt. Revd Peter Ball, resigned after being cautioned by police for committing an act of gross indecency with a novice monk. **9.** The NAS/UWT teaching union voted to boycott statutory testing and assessment procedures in all subjects in summer 1993. EC commissioners ruled that the £44.4 million 'sweetener' paid by the Government to British Aerospace during the BAe takeover of the Rover Group should be repaid with interest; on 26 May BAe agreed to repay £57.6 million less tax relief, a total of 42.2 million. **11.** The chief executive of the Stock Exchange, Peter Rawlins, resigned after work on the Taurus computerized share transfer system was stopped because of its complexity and expense. **16.** The Chancellor of the Exchequer presented the last spring budget (*see* pages 1166–7). The Prince of Wales visited British troops in Bosnia. **20.** Three-year-old Johnathan Ball was killed and 56 people were injured when two IRA bombs exploded in the centre of Warrington. Twelve-year-old Timothy Parry, who was injured in the blast, died on 25 March. **26.** More than 200 fishing boats blockaded Plymouth harbour in protest at the Sea Fish (Conservation) Act, which will limit the number of days trawlers can spend at sea. **28.** A French trawler, *La Calypso*, abducted three members of a Royal Navy boarding party, part of a prolonged dispute over Britain's six-mile fishing limit around the Channel Islands; the men were later returned to their ship. On 2 April the trawler was placed under arrest.

APRIL 1993

2. A 24-hour strike was held by the Rail, Maritime and Transport union, the National Union of Mineworkers and bus crews in London, in protest at compulsory redundancies, pit closures and pay cuts. 7. A memorial service for Johnathan Ball and Timothy Parry was held in Warrington and attended by Prince Philip, the President of Ireland, the Prime Minister and the Leader of the Opposition. A small IRA bomb exploded in London. 14. The governing body of the Anglican Church in Wales voted in favour of a bill permitting the ordination of women as priests; the final vote will be held in 1994. 23. A small IRA bomb exploded at an oil depot in North Shields, Tyne and Wear. 24. A newspaper photographer was killed and 37 people injured when an IRA bomb exploded in the City of London, causing extensive damage. Two minicabs were later hijacked by suspected IRA terrorists in separate incidents in London. The drivers were ordered to take bombs to Downing Street and New Scotland Yard but alerted police before reaching their destinations; both bombs exploded in north London, causing minor damage. Leyland DAF's van plant was bought from the receivers by its management; on 11 June the lorry plant was also bought by its management. 26. Statistics were published showing that GDP rose by 0.2 per cent in the first quarter of 1993, ending 30 months of declining or flat production. 28. George Walker, the former chairman of the Brent Walker leisure group, was declared bankrupt with debts of £180 million. 29. A man died after setting fire to himself in Parliament Square, Westminster, in protest at western policy in former Yugoslavia.

MAY 1993

4. The Queen and the Duke of Edinburgh arrived in Hungary for a four-day State visit. The inquiry headed by Lord Justice Scott into the Government's implementation of sanctions on the export of military equipment to Iraq opened in London. 6. In the Newbury by-election the Liberal Democrats took the seat from the Conservatives with a swing of 28 per cent. In the county council elections in England and Wales, the Conservatives lost control of 15 councils; Labour took control of one council, and the Liberal Democrats took control of two councils. 10. A British sailor, Tom McNally, completed a crossing of the Atlantic in his 5 ft 4½ in boat *Vera Hugh*, the smallest vessel ever to complete the journey. 11. The Education Secretary (John Patten) announced that national curriculum testing would be radically reduced from 1994, but that the 1993 tests would still take place. 12. A small IRA bomb was found in Oxford city centre. 13. Swan Hunter, the Tyneside shipbuilders, went into receivership two days after the Government awarded £170 million order to Vickers. The National Union of Teachers voted not to implement national curriculum testing. 17. Rebecca Stephens became the first British woman to climb Mount Everest. The Prince of Wales arrived in Poland for a four-day official visit. 21. Queen Elizabeth the Queen Mother underwent an operation to remove a piece of food from her throat. 24. In evidence to the Scott inquiry the former Conservative

MP Sir Hal Miller said that the former Attorney-General, Sir Patrick Mayhew, had tried to prevent evidence that officials had known about the export of military equipment to Iraq reaching court. Sir Patrick denied the claim, and repeated his denial in evidence to the inquiry on 27 May. 27. In a Cabinet reshuffle, Norman Lamont resigned as Chancellor of the Exchequer and was replaced by Kenneth Clarke. Michael Howard was appointed Home Secretary. The Queen received the President of Ireland (Mary Robinson) at Buckingham Palace, the first meeting between a British sovereign and an Irish head of state since 1937. 28. The Queen and the Duke of Edinburgh attended events in Liverpool commemorating the 50th anniversary of the Battle of the Atlantic; on 30 May the Prince and Princess of Wales attended a commemoration service at Liverpool Anglican Cathedral.

JUNE 1993

4. The Holbeck Hall Hotel, Scarborough, began to slip over the cliff as half a mile of coastline crumbled into the sea. 9. In a speech in the House of Commons Norman Lamont, the former Chancellor, strongly criticized the Prime Minister, accusing him of giving 'the impression of being in office but not in power'. A small IRA bomb exploded at a British Gas depot in Gateshead, Tyne and Wear; two small IRA bombs later exploded at a disused Esso oil depot in North Shields. 10-11. Torrential rain caused flooding in many parts of Britain, particularly north Wales and Cornwall. 11. The Queen visited Northern Ireland. 15. After a bitter five-month industrial dispute, Timex announced that it would close down its factory in Dundee by the end of 1993. 21. Michael Heseltine, the President of the Board of Trade, suffered a mild heart attack in Venice. 22. Lloyd's of London announced record losses of £2.91 billion for 1990. 24. Michael Mates resigned as minister of state at the Northern Ireland Office over his links with fugitive businessman Asil Nadir. The Government awarded the £5 billion contract for refitting Trident nuclear submarines to the Devonport dockyard. 28. Buckingham Palace announced that the Duke and Duchess of York had agreed the terms of their legal separation. 29. In a speech in the House of Commons, Michael Mates accused the Serious Fraud Office of mishandling the investigation into Asil Nadir's finances and putting improper pressure on the trial judge; he continued with his speech in spite of repeated warnings from the Speaker (Betty Boothroyd) that it could prejudice any future trial.

JULY 1993

5. A British aid worker, Christine Witcutt, was shot dead in Bosnia. 6. Fifteen women scaled the walls of Buckingham Palace in a protest about nuclear testing; they were arrested in the grounds. The *New Statesman and Society* said that the Prime Minister and Clare Latimer had accepted £1,001 damages each over the allegedly libellous articles published in January 1993.

Mr Major and Miss Latimer later dropped their libel actions against *Scallywag*, which said it would not repeat the allegations. The Queen opened the Queen Elizabeth Gate in honour of the Queen Mother at Hyde Park Corner, London. **14.** A suspected IRA member was arrested at a bus stop in north London in possession of the components of a large bomb. It was announced that inflation had fallen to 1.2 per cent in June 1993, the lowest level for 30 years. **15.** A former civil servant told the Scott inquiry that Foreign Office ministers had relaxed the guidelines on exports to Iraq in 1989 and subsequently misled Parliament and the public. **19.** Lord Rees-Mogg secured permission in the High Court for a judicial review of the legitimacy of the ratification process in Britain of the Maastricht Treaty. The Government said that it would not ratify the treaty until the court proceedings were completed; the hearing started on 26 July. **20.** The European Communities (Amendment) Bill received royal assent. In London about 20,000 policemen held a protest rally against the proposals in the Sheehy report on police employment conditions. Nuclear Electric announced the closure of the Magnox plant at Trawsfynydd. **22.** A debate on the social chapter to the Maastricht Treaty was held in the House of Commons. The government's main motion was defeated by 324 votes to 316; the Prime Minister announced that he would table a motion of confidence in the Government's policy on the social chapter the following day. **23.** The Government won the vote of confidence. **25.** The *Observer* newspaper reported a leaked recording of the Prime Minister speaking in derogatory terms about three Cabinet colleagues in an off-camera conversation with a journalist. **29.** In the Christchurch by-election the Liberal Democrats took the seat from the Conservatives with a swing of 35 per cent. **30.** The action brought by Lord Rees-Mogg challenging the legality of the ratification of the Maastricht Treaty failed in the High Court.

AUGUST 1993

2. The United Kingdom ratified the Maastricht Treaty. The Government announced that the national curriculum would be streamlined, that testing would be simplified, and that 'league tables' would not be produced on pupils' performance at the ages of 7 and 14. **6.** Buckingham Palace was opened to the public for the first time, for an eight-week season. **9.** An injured five-year-old Bosnian girl, Irma Hadzimuratovic, was flown from Sarajevo to London and underwent an operation at Great Ormond Street Hospital. 'Operation Irma' was then set up to airlift the seriously injured from Sarajevo, but a row developed between British and UN officials over whether children should be given priority. A further 21 evacuees arrived in Britain on 15 August. A small IRA bomb exploded on Bournemouth pier and six incendiary devices exploded in the town. **18.** An application by the Islamia primary school, London, to become Britain's first voluntary-aided Muslim school was rejected. **26.** The South Birmingham

Health Authority said that an inquiry had revealed errors of diagnosis involving at least 24 cancer patients and that the cases of more than 2,000 patients would be reviewed.

ACCIDENTS AND DISASTERS

SEPTEMBER 1992

2. Tidal waves caused by an undersea earthquake off the coast of Nicaragua killed over 118 and left 13,000 homeless. **10.** Torrential rain caused flooding in northern Pakistan. By 16 September the death toll was over 2,000, and two million were homeless. **11.** Hurricane Iniki hit Hawaii. **22.** Over 70 people were killed when violent storms and heavy rain caused flooding in south-east France. **28.** A Pakistan airbus crashed in Nepal, killing all 167 passengers and crew.

OCTOBER 1992

1. Five people were killed and 15 injured when the US aircraft carrier *Saratoga* fired two missiles by mistake at a Turkish destroyer in the Aegean Sea. **4.** About 70 people were killed when an El Al cargo plane crashed into a block of flats in a suburb of Amsterdam and burst into flames. **12.** An earthquake registering between 5.5 and 5.9 on the Richter scale hit Cairo, leaving over 540 dead.

NOVEMBER 1992

20. The state apartments at Windsor Castle were severely damaged by fire. **24.** All 141 passengers and crew were killed when a Boeing 737 crashed near Guilin, China. **25.** Twenty people were injured when two trains collided outside London Bridge station in the morning rush hour. **26.** Four soldiers were killed when two military helicopters crashed in mid air over Bessbrook Mill military base in Co. Armagh. **27.** The Hofburg palace in Vienna was severely damaged by fire. **30.** Five people were killed when a train was derailed outside Amsterdam.

DECEMBER 1992

2. A coal tip collapsed, covering the grounds of Tredegar Comprehensive School, south Wales, six miles from Aberfan. **12.** An earthquake registering 6.8 on the Richter scale hit eastern Indonesia, killing over 1,500. **21.** Fifty-four people were killed when a Dutch DC10 split in two and burst into flames while landing in a thunderstorm at Faro, Portugal. **22.** All 159 people aboard a Libyan Boeing 727 were killed in a mid-air collision with a military aircraft near Tripoli.

JANUARY 1993

9. All 165 passengers and crew survived when an Indian Airlines plane crashed, turned over, broke into sections and burst into flames at Delhi airport. **14.** Fifty-four people drowned when a Polish ferry capsized off the north German coast. **15.** Nine people, including a British scientist, were killed when the Galeras volcano in Colombia erupted as they were walking along its inner rim. An earthquake registering 7.5 on the Richter scale hit northern Japan, killing two people and injuring 360.

FEBRUARY 1993

3. Ash emissions and lava flows from Mount Mayon, the Philippines, killed at least 48 people. **8.** A plane collided with a military jet after take-off at Tehran airport, Iran, killing all 132 on board.

MARCH 1993

13-14. Tornadoes, blizzards and hurricane-force winds hit the east coast of the USA, killing over 67 people. **22.** Four teenagers from a school in Plymouth drowned when their canoes capsized off the Dorset coast.

APRIL 1993

9-12. At least 21 people were killed in road accidents over the Easter holiday period. **28.** Thirty people, including most of the Zambian national football squad, were killed when their plane crashed after take-off at Libreville, Gabon, en route to a world cup qualifying match in Senegal.

MAY 1993

10. At least 210 people were killed when fire destroyed a toy factory in Bangkok. About 200 people were feared dead in a landslide at Las Brisas de Nambija, Ecuador. **19.** All 132 people on a Boeing 727 died when the plane crashed in central Colombia. **27.** Nine aircrew were killed when an RAF Hercules crashed in the Scottish Highlands.

JUNE 1993

3. Nine people were killed when the BP tanker *British Trent* collided with a cargo ship and caught fire off the coast of Belgium. **25.** Eighteen people were killed and 32 injured when fire broke out at a psychiatric clinic near Rennes, Brittany.

JULY 1993

1-31. At least 1,750 people were killed and 250,000 left homeless when monsoon rains caused floods and landslides in Nepal. The rains also caused flash flooding in six states in India, where at least 700 people were killed, hundreds were missing and two million were left homeless; in Bangladesh more than 300 people were killed and millions left homeless. **4-31.** After a month of flooding, heavy rain caused the Mississippi and Missouri rivers to burst their banks in the mid-west of the USA. At least 50 people were killed and 70,000 left homeless, millions of acres of land were flooded and an estimated $12 billion worth of damage caused. The flooding began to subside on 10 August. **12.** Over 80 people were killed after an earthquake registering 7.8 on the Richter scale hit northern Japan.

AUGUST 1993

5. Two explosions caused by a leak of nitric acid killed over 70 people and injured hundreds in Shenzhen, China. **12.** Three air cadets were killed when an RAF Wessex helicopter crashed into a lake in Snowdonia. **18.** Three miners were killed and three others were rescued in a roof collapse at Bilsthorpe colliery, Notts. The 13th-century Kapellbruecke at Lucerne, Switzerland, was destroyed by fire. **27.** At least 263 people were killed and 180 were missing after water breached the Gouhou reservoir dam in Qinghai province, China.

ARTS, SCIENCE AND MEDIA

SEPTEMBER 1992

7. The new national radio station Classic FM went on the air. **28.** A new institute of architecture set up by the Prince of Wales opened in Regent's Park, London. **29.** The two-day sale of the contents of Pitchford Hall, Shropshire, raised £1.3 million. On 6 October the house was sold to an overseas buyer for over £750,000.

OCTOBER 1992

1. An Arts Council report criticized the management of the Royal Opera House. **12.** Rifat Ozbek was named Designer of the Year at the British Fashion Awards. **26.** The chairman of English Heritage, Jocelyn Stevens, announced a new management strategy, including plans for the privatization of about 200 ancient monuments and buildings.

NOVEMBER 1992

19. The Government announced that Britain would not contribute to research into fast breeder nuclear reactors after March 1993. **24.** The Government published a Green Paper on the future of the BBC (*see* page 679). The Turner Prize for contemporary art was awarded to the sculptor Grenville Davey. **26.** The BBC launched a policy review document, *Extending Choice (see* page 679).

DECEMBER 1992

3. The BBC announced a £58 million overspend since 1991. **11.** The Secretary of State for National Heritage (Peter Brooke) announced that from 1994 responsibility for funding 42 arts organizations, including the Bristol Old Vic and the Manchester Royal Exchange, would pass from the Arts Council to the regional arts boards. **15.** The Tate Gallery announced that it would split its collections, British art remaining at its present site and a new Tate Gallery of Modern Art being created elsewhere in London. **18.** The Independent Television Commission refused to award the fifth national television licence to the sole bidder, a consortium led by Thames Television, on the grounds that it did not have sufficient 'investor commitment'.

JANUARY 1993

1. John Birt took over as director-general of the BBC. **11.** John Birt announced a reorganization of the BBC's management, several new appointments (*see* page 1086) and a programme strategy review. **14.** The Calcutt report on press regulation was published (*see* page 686). A £200,000 donation from the Clore Foundation saved the Dulwich Picture Gallery from closure.

FEBRUARY 1993

22. A painting by Turner was sold by Royal Holloway College to the J. Paul Getty Museum in Los Angeles for £11 million. **28.** The *Independent on Sunday* revealed that John Birt was employed by the BBC on a freelance basis; on 1 March Mr Birt joined the staff of the BBC.

MARCH 1993

5. Two portraits by Gainsborough and Reynolds stolen from Lincoln's Inn, London, in 1990, were recovered when they were taken to Sotheby's for valuation. **24.** The actress Kim Basinger was ordered by a court in Los Angeles to pay Main Line Pictures $8.9 million after pulling out of the lead role in the film *Boxing Helena* a month before filming was due to start. **29.** A consortium of independent television companies headed by Carlton Communications took control of ITN.

APRIL 1993

2. A report by the Medical Research Council said that the drug AZT did not delay the onset of Aids in people infected with the HIV virus. **29.** The editor of the *Observer* newspaper announced that the paper would be sold to the Guardian and Manchester Evening News group for an undisclosed sum. **30.** The first national commercial pop radio station, Virgin 1215, went on the air.

MAY 1993

11. The Prime Minister met Salman Rushdie at the House of Commons. **27.** A car bomb exploded outside the Uffizi Gallery in Florence, damaging the building and many works of art.

JUNE 1993

8. Lord Rix resigned from the Arts Council in protest at its level of funding, its relationship with the Government and its manner of operation. **19.** Inger Dam-Jensen won the Cardiff Singer of the World competition. **23.** The Prince of Wales opened the new Tate Gallery at St Ives, Cornwall.

JULY 1993

2. At least 40 people were killed when Muslim fundamentalists set fire to a hotel in central Turkey where a translator of *The Satanic Verses* was staying. **8.** The Arts Council said that it would fund only two of London's four orchestras from April 1994 and that its drama budget would be cut in favour of the visual

arts, contemporary dance and education. **9.** Scientists said that they were 98.5 per cent certain that bones found in a grave in Yekaterinburg in July 1991 were those of Tsar Nicholas II and four members of his family. **13.** Mark Tully, the BBC's India correspondent, made a speech in which he strongly criticized the corporation's director-general, John Birt, and the changes instituted by him; Mr Birt defended his reforms in a speech the following day. **15.** Scientists in Maryland, USA, said that they had discovered evidence of a genetic component to homosexuality. **21.** The National Heritage Secretary said that the Arts Council would in future be accountable to Parliament for its decisions, that its administrative costs had to be cut by 10 per cent, and that its membership would be cut from 20 to 16. The closure of Elstree Studios was announced. **22.** Thieves broke into the British Museum and stole priceless Roman jewels and coins; many of the items were recovered on 27 July after a man was arrested while attempting another break-in. **27.** Two car bombs in Rome caused damage to the Basilica of St John Lateran and the Church of San Giorgio al Velabro.

AUGUST 1993

8. The Radio 1 disc jockey Dave Lee Travis announced on the air his resignation from the BBC in protest at recent changes.

CRIMES AND LEGAL AFFAIRS

SEPTEMBER 1992

19. Dr Nigel Cox was convicted at Winchester Crown Court of the attempted murder in August 1991 of Mrs Lillian Boyes, to whom, at her request, he administered a fatal injection in order to relieve her suffering. On 21 September he was given a 12-month prison sentence suspended for one year. On 17 November the General Medical Council decided not to take any disciplinary action against him. **22.** The jury were unable to reach a verdict in a libel action brought against Mirror Group Newspapers by Mona Bauwens, the daughter of the Palestine Liberation Organization's head of finance, who had paid for a holiday for the Secretary of State for National Heritage (David Mellor) and his family. **25.** Kiranjit Ahluwalia, who was convicted in 1989 of murdering her violent husband, was convicted of manslaughter on the grounds of diminished responsibility at her retrial at the Central Criminal Court, and sentenced to three years and four months' imprisonment; she had already served this time and was released from prison immediately. **30.** Paintings and antiques worth over £10 million were stolen from Houghton Hall, Norfolk.

OCTOBER 1992

1. The Home Secretary (Kenneth Clarke) announced that he would not recommend a posthumous pardon for Derek Bentley, who was hanged in 1953 for his part in the murder of a policeman. **8.** Seven-year-old Nikki Allen, who had gone missing on 7 October, was found battered to death near her home in Sunderland. On 19 October a man was charged with her murder. **12.** Frank Crichlow was awarded more than £50,000 damages in the High Court after suing the Metropolitan Police Commissioner for false imprisonment, battery and malicious prosecution in relation to his arrest on drugs charges in 1988. After an emergency High Court ruling, surgeons at a London hospital performed a Caesarean operation on a woman against her will in an attempt to save the life of her baby. **14.** Andrei Chikatilo was convicted in Rostov-on-Don, Russia, of murdering 52 people between 1978 and 1990. On 15 October he was sentenced to death. **15.** The libel damages of £150,000 awarded to Teresa Gorman, MP, in July 1991 (*see* Whitaker's Almanack 1992) were reduced in the Court of Appeal to £50,000. **20.** The bodies of Petra Kelly, founder of the German Green Party, and her partner Gert Bastian were found at their home in Bonn. **23.** Jean-Pierre Allain, professor of transfusion medicine at Cambridge University and honorary director of the East Anglian Regional Blood Transfusion Service, was sentenced at a court in Paris to four years' imprisonment, two of them suspended, for allowing blood contaminated with the HIV virus to be given to hundreds of haemophiliacs in France in 1985. **26.** Detective Constable Bob Window's left hand was severed with a samurai sword in an attack in north London; the hand was later sewn back on, and a man was charged with attempted murder.

NOVEMBER 1992

9. At the Central Criminal Court, the trial of three businessmen accused of exporting military equipment to Iraq in breach of the UN embargo collapsed after the former trade minister Alan Clark said in evidence that he had given advice to assist the exports. On 10 November the Prime Minister announced an independent judicial inquiry into the affair. **12.** Associated Newspapers, the publishers of the *Mail on Sunday*, and two journalists were fined a total of £60,000 for contempt of court for publishing details of the deliberations of the jury in the Blue Arrow fraud trial. **19.** The President of the Family Division of the High Court (Sir Stephen Brown) ruled that doctors would be acting lawfully if they discontinued the artificial feeding of Anthony Bland, a victim of the Hillsborough football stadium disaster who had been in 'persistent vegetative state' since 1989. The Official Solicitor, acting for Mr Bland, lodged an appeal against the decision; the appeal was dismissed by three appeal court judges on 9 December and a second appeal was dismissed on 4 February 1993 in the House of Lords. Doctors stopped feeding Mr Bland on 22 February and he died on 3 March.

DECEMBER 1992

7. Nicholas Vernage was sentenced at the Central Criminal Court to five terms of life imprisonment for the murders of Lorna Bogle, Javaid Iqbal and Police Sergeant Alan King in November 1991. **10.** Stephen Miller, Tony Paris and Yusuf Abdullahi, who were sentenced to life imprisonment in November 1990 for the murder of Lynette White in Cardiff, were released by the Court of Appeal, which found the convictions to have been 'unsafe and unsatisfactory'. **14.** The Crown Prosecution Service said that bribery and corruption charges against the Conservative MP Harry Greenway had been dropped. **16.** Lorrain Osman was extradited to Hong Kong to face fraud charges after spending seven years in Brixton prison on remand. **18.** Sixteen-year-old Suzanne Capper, who was found wandering naked and with severe burns in Romiley, Stockport, on 14 December, died in hospital; she had been kidnapped, tortured, covered with petrol and set on fire. Six people were later charged with her murder. **26.** The body of 14-year-old Johanna Young, who had gone missing on 23 December, was found in a water-filled pit near Watton, Norfolk. **27.** A policewoman was stabbed in the heart with a screwdriver when tackling a suspected burglar in Wavertree, Liverpool; a man was later charged with attempted murder.

JANUARY 1993

2. A 14-year-old boy was shot dead in a take-away food shop in Moss Side, Manchester. **8.** George Walker, the former chairman and chief executive of Brent Walker, was charged with stealing £12.5 million from the company. **15.** Criminal proceedings against Ann Griffin and George Hadjioannou over the violent death of their baby daughter Kim in September 1992 were dropped because of insufficient evidence when they invoked their right to silence. **18.** Sixteen-year-old Claire Tiltman was stabbed to death in an alley in Greenhithe, Kent. **29.** A police constable was stabbed seven times after stopping a man for questioning in Deptford, London.

FEBRUARY 1993

3. In a debate in the House of Lords the Lord Chief Justice (Lord Taylor of Gosforth) attacked plans to reduce eligibility for legal aid. **5.** A judge at Newport Crown Court ordered a 15-year-old boy convicted of raping a female classmate to pay his victim £500 for a holiday rather than imposing a custodial sentence on him. On 11 March the Court of Appeal increased the sentence to two years' detention. **10.** James Canning, a member of the IRA, was sentenced at the Central Criminal Court to 30 years' imprisonment for conspiring to cause explosions in Britain. **12.** Two-year-old James Bulger was abducted from a shopping centre in Liverpool; his body was found on a railway embankment two days later. On 20 February two ten-year-old boys were charged with his murder. **13.** Darius Guppy and Benedict Marsh were convicted at Snaresbrook Crown Court of a £1.8 million jewellery insurance fraud. On 25 March they were sentenced to five years' imprisonment each and fined £539,000 and £535,000 respectively. **15.** Thomas Ward, an American lawyer, was cleared at the Central Criminal Court of stealing £5.2 million from Guinness during its takeover of Distillers in 1986. **18.** In the House of Lords, in a case brought by Derbyshire County Council over articles in the *Sunday Times* in 1989, five law lords ruled that democratically-elected bodies have no right to sue for libel.

MARCH 1993

12. Derek Hatton, the former deputy leader of Liverpool City Council, was cleared at Mold Crown Court of conspiring to defraud the council in land deals. The chief executive of National Car Parks, Gordon Layton, was cleared at the Central Criminal Court of conspiracy to defraud in financing an industrial espionage campaign against a rival company. **21.** Police Sergeant William Forth was stabbed to death near Gateshead, Tyne and Wear. On 23 March two people were charged with his murder. **25.** Jean Bradley, a businesswoman, was stabbed to death in a street in Acton, London. **29.** Paul Magee, an IRA terrorist on the run from a life sentence, was convicted at the Central Criminal Court of murdering Special Constable Glen Goodman in June 1992. On 30 March he was sentenced to 30 years' imprisonment. **31.** Benjamin Laing was sentenced at the Central Criminal Court to life imprisonment for the murder of Matthew Manwaring and his daughter Alison in April 1992. The Court of Appeal cut from £250,000 to £110,000 the libel damages awarded in 1991 to Esther Rantzen, the television presenter and chairman of Childline, after claims that she had protected an alleged paedophile.

APRIL 1993

2. Mr Justice Mantell ruled in the High Court that members of the NAS/UWT had no statutory duty to test children under the Education Reform Act 1988 and that they were involved in a legitimate trade dispute; the ruling was confirmed in the Court of Appeal on 23 April. **4.** Nessan Quinlivan, who escaped from Brixton prison in 1991 while awaiting trial on terrorist charges, was arrested in Co. Tipperary. On 9 April Pearse McAuley, who escaped at the same time, was arrested in Dublin. **18.** A man armed with a shotgun was shot dead by police during a siege in Cheshunt, Herts. **22.** Eighteen-year-old Stephen Lawrence was murdered by white youths in a racially-motivated attack in Eltham, London. **28.** Sixteen-month-old Constantine Georgopolous was kidnapped from his home in St John's Wood, London; he was found unharmed in a van in Kilburn on 29 April. **30.** A woman was shot dead in a street in Luton; her baby daughter was kidnapped and later shot dead. A man was charged with the murders.

MAY 1993

4. The bankrupt chairman of the Polly Peck group, Asil Nadir, who was on £3.5 million bail awaiting trial on charges of theft and false accounting involving more than £30 million, jumped bail and flew to northern Cyprus. **13.** The Home Secretary (Kenneth Clarke) announced that fundamental changes would be made to the provisions of the Criminal Justice Act 1991, including the scrapping of the unit fines system in magistrates' courts, and the restoration of the right of courts to take into account all a defendant's previous convictions when sentencing. A gunman took 20 children and a teacher hostage in a nursery school in Paris; he later released 14 of the children. On 15 May a police squad stormed the school, shot the gunman dead and released the remaining children and the teacher. **17.** A hospital nurse, Beverley Allitt, was convicted at Nottingham Crown Court of the murder of four babies in her care at Grantham and Kesteven Hospital in 1991, the attempted murder of three other babies, and causing grievous bodily harm to six others; on 28 May she was given 13 life sentences. **19.** Three former detectives were cleared at the Central Criminal Court of conspiring to pervert the course of justice by fabricating confession evidence against one of the Guildford Four in 1975. **29.** Frederic Blancke was sentenced at a court in Beauvais, France, to 15 years' imprisonment for the murder of Fiona Jones, a British schoolteacher, in August 1989.

JUNE 1993

4. Pte Lee Clegg of the Parachute Regiment was sentenced at a court in Belfast to life imprisonment for the murder of 18-year-old Karen Reilly, who was shot dead in a stolen car in west Belfast in September 1990. Pte Barry Aindow was sentenced to seven years' imprisonment for the attempted murder of the car's driver, 17-year-old Martin Peake, who was also shot dead in the incident. **7.** The film director Woody Allen failed to win custody of his three children after a bitter court case against his former partner Mia Farrow. **10.** At Norwich Crown Court two men were sentenced to five years' imprisonment for kidnapping and threatening a youth they suspected of being involved in local thefts; on 28 June the sentences were cut to six months by the Court of Appeal. **11.** Michelle and Lisa Taylor, who were sentenced to life imprisonment in 1991 for the murder of Alison Shaughnessy, were released by the Court of Appeal after their convictions were found to be 'unsafe and unsatisfactory'. **15.** A man was found strangled at his home in south London; police warned that he was the fifth victim of a murderer targeting homosexual men in London. **21.** The conviction of 15-year-old Ivan Fergus, who served six months of a 15-month youth custody sentence for assault with intent to rob, was quashed by the Court of Appeal and found to be 'wholly false'. **30.** Michael Hunt, the former deputy chairman of Nissan UK, was sentenced to eight years' imprisonment for his part in a £55 million tax fraud between 1983 and 1991.

JULY 1993

6. The report of the Royal Commission on Criminal Justice was published. John Matthews, who was arrested in April 1993 and charged with causing an IRA bomb explosion in London, was released 'without a blemish on his character' after the prosecution could offer no evidence against him; he was later served with an exclusion order and expelled from mainland Britain. **7.** Three High Court judges ruled that the former Home Secretary (Kenneth Clarke) had 'erred in law' when he refused in October 1992 to grant a conditional posthumous pardon to Derek Bentley; on 30 July the Home Secretary (Michael Howard) granted Bentley a pardon limited to sentence. **8.** Michael Sams was given four life sentences at Nottingham Crown Court for the kidnap and murder of 18-year-old Julie Dart in 1991 and the kidnap and unlawful imprisonment of Stephanie Slater in January 1992. A gunman shot dead a German tourist and wounded members of his family near Stranraer. **13.** A teenager was acquitted at the Central Criminal Court on charges of murder and manslaughter after admitting that he stabbed to death a man who had caught him slashing tyres and chased him holding a hammer; the jury accepted his plea of self-defence. **19.** An Englishman, Vincent Wood, was sentenced at the Central Criminal Court to 22 years' imprisonment for possessing IRA explosives with intent to endanger life. Eight-year-old Sean Williams was found murdered in a lift in a block of flats in East Finchley, London. **20.** Karyn Smith and Patricia Cahill, two young British women who had been sentenced to 25 and 18 years imprisonment respectively in Thailand for drug smuggling in 1990, were granted a royal pardon. **22.** Robin Pask, who murdered a lecturer at an Open University summer school in July 1992, was ordered to be detained indefinitely in a secure unit after he was found unfit to stand trial because of a serious depressive illness. **25.** Nine-year-old Akhlaq Razzaq was found strangled in a park in Slough where he had gone to watch a game of cricket. **27.** A 1991 Appeal Court ruling that a former Home Secretary, Kenneth Baker, had been in contempt of court when he had illegally deported a Zairean asylum-seeker during legal proceedings was upheld by five law lords.

AUGUST 1993

1. Joy Gardner, a Jamaican woman who collapsed after a violent struggle with police serving her with a deportation order at her home in north London on 28 July, died in hospital; on 3 August the three detectives involved and Scotland Yard's central aliens and deportation unit were suspended. **17.** A man was charged with the murder of Rachel Nickell on Wimbledon Common in July 1992. **20.** Police in Los Angeles started an investigation into allegations by a 13-year-old boy that he had been sexually abused by the pop star Michael Jackson. Ronald Godfrey was charged in Oxford with battering his wife, daughter and mother-in-law to death with a hammer.

31. Twenty-one-year-old Sharon Pritchard was beaten to death in a playing field after seeing her babysitter home in Croeserw, West Glamorgan. A man was later charged with her murder.

ENVIRONMENT

SEPTEMBER 1992

22. An unconditional ban on dumping nuclear waste at sea was agreed by 12 European countries; Britain and France agreed only a 15-year moratorium.

OCTOBER 1992

4-7. The hole in the ozone layer over Antarctica extended over the coast of South America and the Falkland Islands for the first time.

NOVEMBER 1992

25. The Court of Justice of the EC ruled that Britain was in breach of EC standards on drinking water.

DECEMBER 1992

1. English Nature designated more than 25,000 acres of The Wash a national nature reserve. **3.** The Greek tanker *Aegean Sea* ran on to rocks off the coast of north-west Spain, causing a 60-mile oil slick. **14.** A firebomb attack at the research headquarters of the Forestry Commission in Hampshire destroyed 30 years' research on tree diseases. **16.** EC environment ministers advanced the deadline for phasing out the production of CFCs to 1 January 1995.

JANUARY 1993

5. The Liberian-registered oil tanker *Braer*, carrying 85,000 tonnes of light crude oil, ran aground in storms off Garths Ness, Shetland, causing a six-mile oil slick; oil continued to pour from the vessel for a week, with salvage work hampered by hurricane-force winds. On 12 January the tanker broke up and spilled almost all its remaining oil into the sea, causing a 20-mile slick. By 14 January the oil had largely dispersed.

MARCH 1993

31. The Government announced a review of options for the ownership and management of land owned by the Forestry Commission.

APRIL 1993

6. A tank of radioactive waste exploded at a weapons plant in Tomsk, Siberia, contaminating over 2,500 acres with radiation. **20.** The ruling council of the National Trust rejected a resolution passed by Trust members in 1990 to ban deer-hunting on its land.

MAY 1993

18. Norway announced that it would resume commercial hunting of minke whales.

JULY 1993

7. The Transport Secretary (John MacGregor) announced that plans to build a road through Oxleas Wood in south-east London had been abandoned. 21. The Environment Secretary (John Gummer) published a consultation paper, *UK Strategy for Sustainable Development*. 22. The Transport Secretary announced plans to add twin three-lane link roads to parts of the M25 London orbital motorway. Six protesters were sentenced to 28 days' imprisonment for defying an injunction to stay away from the M3 extension being built across Twyford Down, Hants.

NORTHERN IRELAND

SEPTEMBER 1992

4. An unarmed Roman Catholic youth was shot dead by soldiers after running away from an army checkpoint in Belfast; two soldiers were charged with his murder and remanded in military custody. 5. A man was shot dead by the UVF in east Belfast. 7. A Roman Catholic man and his wife were shot dead by the UVF in Moy, Co. Tyrone. 11. A man was shot dead by the IPLO in Belfast. 21. The three-day Dublin phase of talks on the political future of Northern Ireland opened at Dublin Castle; delegates from the Ulster Unionist Party attended but the talks were boycotted by the Democratic Unionist Party. The DUP rejoined the talks on 30 September at Stormont Castle. 23. A 2,000 lb IRA bomb severely damaged the Northern Ireland forensic science laboratory and surrounding buildings in Belfast. 27. A Roman Catholic man was shot dead by the UFF in north Belfast. 30. A man was shot dead in south Belfast.

OCTOBER 1992

9. A Protestant man was shot dead by the loyalist Red Hand Commandos in east Belfast. 16. A woman member of Sinn Fein was shot dead in a hotel bar in Belfast. 20. A member of the Royal Irish Regiment (RIR) was shot dead in Rasharkin, Co. Antrim.

NOVEMBER 1992

1. A member of the IPLO was shot dead by the IRA in Belfast. 4. A Roman Catholic man was shot dead by the UFF in south Belfast. 10. The talks on the political future of Northern Ireland ended without agreement. The chairman, Sir Ninian Stephen, said that informal consultations would continue. 13. A bomb explosion severely damaged the centre of Coleraine, Co. Londonderry. 14. Two men were shot dead and ten injured when a UFF gunman opened fire in a betting shop in north Belfast. 19. A part-time member of the RIR was shot dead in Portadown, Co. Armagh. A man was killed and three seriously injured when UVF gunmen opened fire in a pub in Kilcoo, Co. Down. 22. A man was found shot dead in

Londonderry; the IRA claimed responsibility and said that he was an informer for British Intelligence. 24. In a BBC documentary, a former police informer said that he had taken part in the murder of an off-duty soldier in Belfast in 1991. 25. A member of the IRA was shot dead by police in west Belfast.

DECEMBER 1992

1. Twenty-five people were injured when an IRA bomb exploded in the centre of Belfast. 8. A man was shot by the IRA in Londonderry; he died on 13 December. 12. A member of Sinn Fein was shot by the UFF in Ballymoney, Co. Antrim; he died on 13 December. 20. A Roman Catholic man was shot dead by the UVF in north Belfast. 30. A member of the RIR was shot dead in north Belfast.

JANUARY 1993

3. A Roman Catholic man and his son were shot dead by the UVF in Lisnagleer, Co. Tyrone. 11. A man was shot dead by the IRA near Dungannon, Co. Tyrone. 14. A Roman Catholic man was shot dead by the UDA in south Belfast. 17. A Roman Catholic woman was shot dead at the home of her Protestant boyfriend in Belfast. 21. A Protestant man was shot dead by the INLA in north Belfast. 23. A member of the RUC was shot dead in Londonderry. 28. A Roman Catholic man was killed by a UVF bomb in Cookstown, Co. Tyrone.

FEBRUARY 1993

2. A Roman Catholic man was shot dead in Ballyronan, Co. Londonderry. 9. In Armagh one soldier was killed and four injured by IRA bombs. 11. A Roman Catholic man was shot dead by the UVF in Derrymagowan, Co. Tyrone. 12. A man was shot dead by the IRA near Castlederg, Co. Tyrone. 15. An off-duty member of the RIR was shot dead in west Belfast. 21. Three Roman Catholic taxi drivers were wounded when two UFF gunmen opened fire on a taxi rank in the Falls Road area of Belfast. 25. An RUC officer died when his car was blown up by a bomb in Loughgall, Co. Armagh; another officer was shot dead by the IRA near Crossmaglen, Co. Armagh.

MARCH 1993

8. A man was killed when three IRA mortar bombs were fired at the joint RUC-Army security base in Keady, Co. Armagh. 10. A Protestant man was shot dead in a shop in north Belfast. 15. A Roman Catholic man was shot dead by the UFF in Belfast. 17. A soldier of the Royal Scots Regiment was shot dead in south Armagh. 25. Four Roman Catholic men were shot dead by the UFF in Castlerock, Co. Londonderry. A Roman Catholic man was shot dead by the UFF in west Belfast.

APRIL 1993

5. A former member of the UDA was shot dead in Portavogie, Co. Down. 6-7. The Prime Minister visited Northern Ireland. 7. Gordon Wilson, whose

daughter was killed in the IRA bombing at Enniskillen in 1987, met IRA representatives as part of a personal peace initiative. **25.** A former member of the UDR was killed by a booby-trap bomb near Pomeroy, Co. Tyrone.

MAY 1993

1. A man was shot dead in Belfast by the UFF, who had intended to attack Alec Maskey, a Sinn Fein councillor. **17.** Six paratroopers were cleared of charges resulting from clashes with civilians in Coalisland, Co. Tyrone, in May 1992. Five of the men were bound over to keep the peace. **20.** A 1,000 lb IRA bomb exploded in Belfast, injuring 21 people and causing extensive damage to the Grand Opera House. **22.** A 1,000 lb IRA bomb exploded in Portadown, Co. Armagh, injuring six people and causing widespread damage. **23.** A 300 lb IRA bomb exploded in Magherafelt, Co. Londonderry, causing extensive damage. **30.** A Roman Catholic man was shot dead at his home in east Belfast. **31.** A part-time member of the RIR was killed by a car bomb near Moneymore, Co. Londonderry.

JUNE 1993

2. A Roman Catholic man was shot dead by the UFF near Comber, Co. Down. **17.** A former RUC officer was shot dead in the York Hotel, Belfast. **24.** A Protestant man was shot dead in Lurgan, Co. Armagh. **26.** A soldier of the Duke of Edinburgh's Royal Regiment was shot dead in Belfast. Twenty-eight people, including 12 police officers, were injured when a grenade exploded during an Orange Order parade in west Belfast. The grenade carrier, a member of the UVF, died from his injuries on 29 June. **28.** The Secretary of State for Northern Ireland apologized for making an insensitive remark a few hours after the grenade explosion on 26 June.

JULY 1993

2. A bomb exploded in Strabane, Co. Tyrone, causing widespread damage. **5.** Fifteen people were injured when a large IRA bomb exploded in Newtownards, Co. Down, causing extensive damage. **17.** A soldier of the Duke of Edinburgh's Royal Regiment was shot dead in Crossmaglen, South Armagh. **20.** A UFF bomb exploded under the car of Dr Joe Hendron, MP for West Belfast; no one was injured.

AUGUST 1993

8. The son of a Sinn Fein councillor was shot dead in Belfast. **11.** A Roman Catholic man was beaten to death in a sectarian attack in Belfast. **12.** Police intercepted a 3,000 lb IRA bomb near Portadown, Co. Armagh. **30.** A Roman Catholic woman was shot dead by the UFF in north Belfast. **31.** Two large IRA bombs exploded in Derriaghy on the outskirts of Belfast, injuring two police officers and causing extensive damage.

SPORT

SEPTEMBER 1992

2. Bobby Fischer and Boris Spassky began a chess match in Montenegro. On 5 November Fischer completed a 10-5 victory over Spassky in the final game of the 'rematch', in Belgrade. **3.** The Paralympic Games opened in Barcelona. **6.** Four players from the Hereford United football team were sent off in a match against Northampton. **7.** David Gower was omitted from the England cricket team selected for the winter tour of India and Sri Lanka. **13.** Nigel Mansell said that he would retire from Formula One motor racing at the end of the season, and on 18 September signed to compete in the American Indy Car World Series 1992-3. **17.** The National Football League announced the suspension of the World League of American Football for the 1992-3 season. **22.** The Lawn Tennis Association announced that attempts to revive the Wightman Cup, last staged in 1989, had been abandoned. **23.** Allan Lamb was fined £5,000 by the Test and County Cricket Board (TCCB) for writing an unauthorized article on 26 August in which he accused Pakistani bowlers of cheating. In November the fine was reduced by £1,000. **24.** Surrey were fined £1,000, suspended for two years, by the TCCB for repeated infringements of the regulation covering ball-tampering. **27.** Nigel Mansell won the Portuguese grand prix in Estoril, his ninth grand prix win of the season and a world record. Imran Khan, the former Pakistan captain, announced his retirement from cricket. **30.** Wimbledon footballer Vinnie Jones was charged by the Football Association with bringing the game into disrepute for his part in a video, *Soccer's Hard Men.* On 17 November he was fined £20,000.

OCTOBER 1992

1. The Al-Maktoum family said that it would reduce its involvement in British horse-racing. **26.** The National and Olympic Sports Congress of South Africa withdrew its support for a tour of England by the South African rugby union team starting on 4 November. **27.** The manager of Liverpool football club, Graeme Souness, was suspended for five European fixtures by UEFA for comments he made to the referee after a match against Spartak Moscow on 22 October. **31.** The jockey Lester Piggott was injured and his horse Mr Brooks was destroyed after a fall in the Breeders' Cup Sprint in Florida, USA. The British Amateur Weightlifting Association said that no action would be taken against Andrew Davies and Andrew Saxton, the British weightlifters sent home from the 1992 Olympic Games for alleged drug abuse.

NOVEMBER 1992

6. Birmingham City football club went into receivership. **14.** The first rugby union match against South Africa in Britain since 1969 was held at Twickenham. **22.** American yachtsman Mike Plant was missing, presumed dead, after his yacht capsized en route to the start of the Vendée Globe Challenge round-the-world race. **23.** Barnet football club was fined £50,000 by the Football League for breaches of League regulations. **26.** British yachtsman Nigel Burgess died after abandoning his yacht during a gale in the Vendée Globe Challenge round-the-world race. **30.** The Football Association ordered Peterborough United to replay their first-round FA Cup tie against Kingstonian, which they won 9-1, because the Kingstonian goalkeeper had been injured after being struck on the head by a missile thrown by a spectator; Peterborough won the replay 1-0.

DECEMBER 1992

3. In Ohio, USA, Harry 'Butch' Reynolds, the 400 metres world record holder, was awarded $27.3 million damages against the International Amateur Athletics Association (IAAF) over his suspension for drug abuse in 1990; the IAAF said that it was not bound by the decisions of US courts and started an appeal against the ruling. **5.** Charlton Athletic football club returned to The Valley after seven years of ground-sharing. **14.** Lennox Lewis became the first British heavyweight boxing champion since 1897 when Riddick Bowe was stripped of the WBC title for refusing to defend it against Lewis. **23.** The sprinter Jason Livingston was suspended for four years by the British Athletic Federation and banned for life by the British Olympic Association after a drugs test proved positive in July 1992.

JANUARY 1993

7. The Arsenal and England footballer Ian Wright was suspended for three matches by the Football Association for throwing a punch at a player during a match in December 1992. The Arsenal manager George Graham was fined £500 for making improper remarks to the referee of the same match. **11.** The Indian Cricket Board cancelled the one-day match between India and England at Ahmadabad on 16 January because of religious violence in the city. **23.** Third division rugby union club St Peter's caused a major upset by beating Cardiff 16-14 in the Welsh Cup. **26.** In a Test match in Adelaide, West Indies beat Australia by one run, the closest victory margin in the history of Test cricket. **27.** After a special general meeting of the MCC in London, a motion of no confidence in the England cricket selectors was defeated by 4,600 to 6,135. **30.** Nigel Short became the first British chess world championship contender for over 100 years when he beat Jan Timman in Spain.

FEBRUARY 1993

19. The FA Premier League agreed a £2 million four-year sponsorship deal with Bass. **20.** Graeme Hick scored 178 runs, his first Test century, against India in Bombay. **25.** Pakistan were 43 all out against West Indies in Cape Town, the lowest total recorded in a one-day international. **26.** Garry Kasparov and Nigel Short rejected the authority of the World Chess Federation (FIDE) and said that they would stage a world championship under the auspices of a new body, the Professional Chess Association (PCA); on 23 March FIDE disqualified both players. Allan Border, the Australian cricket captain, became the highest-scoring batsman in Test history when he took his career total of runs to 10,161 in a match against New Zealand in Christchurch.

MARCH 1993

5. The Canadian sprinter Ben Johnson, who was banned for two years and stripped of his 100 metres title after a positive drugs test at the 1988 Olympic Games, was banned for life by the IAAF after failing a drugs test in Montreal. **15.** Sean Lavelle, a rugby union player, died after allegedly being punched during a match at Hendon, London, on 13 March. **21.** Nigel Mansell, the world Formula One motor racing champion, won his Indycar racing debut in Surfers Paradise, Australia. **27.** Cambridge won the Boat Race for the first time since 1986. **30.** The German Athletics Federation reduced the ban on Katrin Krabbe for alleged drug abuse from four years to one year.

APRIL 1993

3. The Grand National was declared void after all but nine of the riders failed to realize that a second false start had been indicated; seven horses completed both circuits of the course. After a stewards' inquiry it was said that no recall flag had been shown. On 5 April the Jockey Club announced an inquiry into the day's events; the inquiry report was published on 13 June and blamed human error, outdated starting equipment and an inadequate recall system. **5.** Members of the Jockey Club voted to establish a new body, the British Horseracing Board, to take over all its responsibilities except licensing and discipline from May 1993. **6.** The champion jockey Peter Scudamore announced his retirement from racing. **9.** Four members of the Pakistan cricket team, including its captain Wasim Akram, were arrested in Grenada at the beginning of a tour in the West Indies and charged with drugs offences. On 12 April the charges were dropped. The start of the first Test against the West Indies in Trinidad was delayed by one day as a result of the incident. **16.** The WBO featherweight champion, Reuben Palacio, was stripped of his title after testing positive for the HIV virus. **21.** The French yachtsman Bruno Peyron completed a record 79-day circumnavigation of the world in his catamaran *Commodore Explorer.* **26.** Nottingham Forest football club said that Brian Clough would retire as manager at the end of the season. **29.** William Vincent, a crewman competing in the British Steel Challenge round-the-world yacht race, was missing, feared drowned, after diving overboard in the south Atlantic. **30.** The tennis player Monica Seles was stabbed in the back by a man at a tournament in Hamburg.

MAY 1993

2. Britain was relegated from the world group of the Davis Cup after losing 3–2 to Hungary. **13.** Terry Venables was sacked as chief executive of Tottenham Hotspur football club by its chairman, Alan Sugar. Venables was granted an emergency High Court injunction temporarily reinstating him but on 14 June the High Court upheld the club's right to sack him. **20.** Arsenal won the FA Cup final replay against Sheffield Wednesday, becoming the first team to win the League (Coca-Cola) Cup and FA Cup in the same season. **21.** Robin Smith achieved the highest score by an England batsman in international one-day cricket with an innings of 167 against Australia at Edgbaston.

JUNE 1993

4–13. Eleven motorcyclists, including one competitor, were killed during the Isle of Man TT week. **7.** Graham Gooch became the first England cricketer to be given out for handling the ball when he knocked the ball away from the wicket with his free hand in the first Test match against Australia. **14.** FIDE announced that a world championship match would be held to rival the match staged by the PCA (*see* above) in September 1993; Garry Kasparov and Nigel Short were stripped of their FIDE international ratings. **17.** A competitor at the Hexham Horse Trials died when his horse fell at a fence; he was the third rider to be killed at trials in less than three weeks. **22.** A German spectator was banned from the Wimbledon tennis championships after shouting abuse at Steffi Graf.

JULY 1993

6. Graham Thorpe made a century in his first Test match for England, with an innings of 114 not out against Australia. **15.** Rangers football club signed Duncan Ferguson from Dundee United for a record British transfer fee of about £4 million. **18.** Greg Norman won the Open golf championship with a record 13 under par aggregate of 267. **19.** Ian Botham retired from first-class cricket after playing for Durham against Australia. **26.** The England cricket captain Graham Gooch resigned after England's eighth defeat in nine Test matches; on 28 July Mike Atherton was appointed captain.

AUGUST 1993

1. England won the women's cricket World Cup, beating New Zealand at Lord's. **9.** The chairman of the England cricket selectors, Ted Dexter, resigned. **15.** At the world athletics championships in Stuttgart, Linford Christie won the 100 metres with a time of

9.87 seconds. On 16 August Chinese runners took the first three places in the women's 3,000 metres. On 19 August Sally Gunnell won the 400 metres hurdles in a world record time of 52.74 seconds. On 20 August Colin Jackson won the 110 metres hurdles in a world record time of 12.91 seconds. On 22 August the USA set a new 4 × 400 metres world record of 2 minutes 54.29 seconds. **19.** At the cycling world championships in Norway, Graeme Obree won the 4,000 metres pursuit title in a world record time of 4 minutes 20.894 seconds. **21.** Graham Gooch became the highest-scoring Test player for England, reaching a total of 8,293 runs in the match against Australia at the Oval. **23.** The England cricket team won its first Test match since July 1992. **26.** Peter Reid was sacked as manager of Manchester City football club. **31.** Ian Folley, the former Lancashire and Derbyshire spin bowler, died after being hit in the face by a ball while playing for Whitehaven against Workington.

APPOINTMENTS AND RESIGNATIONS

In addition to those mentioned above, the following appointments, resignations, etc., were announced:

1992

12 October: Charles Moore was appointed editor of the *Sunday Telegraph*

22 October: David Montgomery was appointed chief executive of Mirror Group Newspapers

15 November: Richard Stott was dismissed as editor of the *Daily Mirror* and replaced by David Banks; Bridget Rowe was appointed editor of the *People*, with Colin Mylor replacing her as editor of the *Sunday Mirror*

25 November: Gerald Ratner resigned as chief executive of Ratners

1 December: Ian Phillips resigned as finance director of the BBC

10 December: Jonathan Powell resigned as controller of BBC1

1993

11 January: Robert Phillis was appointed deputy director-general of the BBC; Liz Forgan was appointed managing director of BBC network radio

25 January: Martin Dunn, the editor of *Today*, was appointed editor of the *Boston Herald*

31 January: Richard Stott was appointed editor of *Today*

5 February: Lord King retired as chairman of British Airways and was succeeded by Sir Colin Marshall

18 February: Frances Heaton was appointed the first female director of the Bank of England

26 February: Alan Yentob was appointed controller of BBC1

26 March: Louis Gerstner was appointed chairman and chief executive of IBM

30 March: Paul Foot resigned as a columnist on the *Daily Mirror* and Lord Hollick resigned from the board of Mirror Group Newspapers
1 April: Michael Jackson was appointed controller of BBC2
5 April: David Gordon was appointed chief executive of ITN
14 May: Jonathan Fenby was appointed editor of the *Observer*
24 May: Sir Colin Davis was appointed principal conductor of the London Symphony Orchestra from 1995
30 June: The Bishop of Durham announced that he would retire in June 1994
19 August: Martin Taylor was appointed chief executive of Barclays Bank
31 August: Kenneth Branagh was appointed to the board of the British Film Institute

AFRICA

SEPTEMBER 1992

7. Ciskei armed forces fired on 70,000 African National Congress demonstrators who were marching on the capital Bisho, killing over 29 and injuring 200. **26.** President de Klerk of South Africa and the ANC president Nelson Mandela held a meeting in an attempt to restart the constitutional negotiations which had collapsed in June. **27.** The *Inkatha* leader Chief Buthelezi rejected the ANC-government agreement to fence off Zulu migrant hostels and ban the carrying of cultural weapons, and withdrew from constitutional negotiations in protest. **30.** In Angolan parliamentary elections the ruling MPLA government won the largest number of seats; in the presidential elections President Dos Santos won 49.5 per cent of the vote and the UNITA leader Jonas Savimbi 40.5 per cent.

OCTOBER 1992

4. President Chissano of Mozambique and Alfonso Dhlakama, leader of the Renamo rebels, signed a peace settlement in Rome ending the 16-year civil war. **19.** The ANC published an abridged version of a report by its own lawyers which showed that it was guilty of murder, torture and other abuses against detainees in its camps. **20.** Nigerian aircraft and warships bombarded the port of Buchanan, Liberia, held by rebels fighting the West African peace-keeping force. The South African Parliament passed the Constitution Amendment Act, which allows blacks to serve in the cabinet for the first time. **30.** Fighting between Angolan government and UNITA forces broke out in Luanda and in the centre of the country after UNITA disputed the election results.

NOVEMBER 1992

2. A UN-brokered cease-fire came into effect in the Angolan capital Luanda. **3.** The incumbent president,

Flt. Lt. Jerry Rawlings, won the presidential election in Ghana, though electoral fraud was alleged by opposition politicians. **6.** UNITA forces advanced on Luanda and other government-held cities in Angola as civil war broke out again. **18.** The Nigerian President, General Babangida, announced that the planned transfer from military to civilian rule in January 1993 had been postponed for a further seven months. **26.** President de Klerk of South Africa announced that multiracial elections would be held by April 1994. **27.** Angola's first elected parliament, composed mainly of MPLA members, was sworn in at a ceremony in Luanda boycotted by UNITA members. **29.** In South Africa eight whites were killed and 17 injured in two separate attacks by blacks using hand grenades and automatic weapons.

DECEMBER 1992

1. President Mobutu of Zaire dissolved the country's pro-democracy cabinet in an attempt to regain dictatorial powers. **3.** The UN Security Council authorized the use of force by a US-led international coalition of peace-keeping forces to ensure the safe delivery of food and medical supplies in Somalia. **8.** An advance party of US marines went ashore in Somalia. **10.** Two gunmen were shot dead and five wounded by French troops in Mogadishu. **11.** US troops in Somalia brought together the rival warlords Muhammed Farrah Aideed and Ali Mahdi Muhammed, who signed an agreement to end hostilities and end the division of Mogadishu. **15.** UN-mandated troops in Somalia moved to Baidoa to protect relief supplies. **20.** US marines and Belgian paratroopers secured control of Kismayu in southern Somalia. **27.** Rival Somali leaders Muhammed Farrah Aideed and Ali Mahdi Muhammed publicly proclaimed an end to the civil war. **29.** The incumbent president, Daniel arap Moi, won the first multi-party presidential elections in Kenya for 26 years amid allegations of vote-rigging and electoral irregularities.

JANUARY 1993

3. The UN Secretary-General was forced to leave Mogadishu after being besieged in the UN compound by stone-throwing crowds. **6.** Fighting erupted throughout Angola between MPLA and UNITA forces. **7.** US marines fought Somali gunmen in Mogadishu and captured a large cache of heavy weapons. **8.** In Addis Ababa Somali faction leaders signed a tentative agreement calling for a cease-fire and a national conference. **14.** The interim Zairean parliament, the High Council of the Republic, declared President Mobutu guilty of treason for undermining moves towards democracy. **15.** The Somali peace talks closed with an agreement that armed supporters would be sent to designated compounds and heavy weapons placed under the control of the UN-mandated forces. **20.** UNITA forces in Angola captured Soyo and its oil refinery. **29.** Army factions clashed in the Zairean capital Kinshasa.

FEBRUARY 1993

5. The Zairean Prime Minister Etienne Tshisekedi refused to accept his dismissal by President Mobutu or the blame for the army riots. **12.** The South African government and the ANC agreed the basis of a timetable for establishing a Government of national unity and moves to multiracial democracy. **20.** President de Klerk announced the appointment of the first non-whites to the South African cabinet. **23.** UN-mandated troops in Somalia forced gunmen to leave Kismayo and to disarm in a designated area. **24.** Rioting and disturbances occurred in Mogadishu after General Aideed accused US forces of supporting a rival. Zairean troops besieged Kinshasa and held MPs captive in an attempt to force them to recognize as legal tender new notes with which they had been paid by President Mobutu. **25.** Clashes between Somali gunmen and UN-mandated troops left ten gunmen dead and led to the suspension of aid distribution in Mogadishu.

MARCH 1993

4. A state of emergency was declared in Zambia and leading opposition politicians were arrested after the discovery of a plan by UNIP, the former ruling party, to overthrow President Chiluba. **7.** After weeks of heavy fighting, UNITA forces defeated Angolan government troops to take control of Huambo. **20–22.** Five whites were killed in South Africa in an upsurge of violence by the armed wing of the Pan Africanist Congress. **28.** In UN-brokered negotiations in Addis Ababa, rival Somali factions agreed to disarm and form a transitional government.

APRIL 1993

1. Negotiations on the constitutional future of South Africa resumed after an eleven-month break. **2.** Ntsu Mokhehle was sworn in as Prime Minister of Lesotho after the Basotho Congress Party won the general election which ended seven years of military rule. **10.** Chris Hani, leader of the South African Communist Party and an ANC national executive member, was shot dead. **11–19.** Violence in South Africa following Hani's murder left 31 people dead. **25.** Over 99 per cent of Eritreans voted for independence from Ethiopia in a referendum.

MAY 1993

4. The UN officially took command of the multinational peace-keeping force in Somalia. **23.** Eritrea became an independent state. **25.** South African police arrested 73 senior officials of the Pan-Africanist Congress and its armed wing in connection with attacks on white farms over the previous four months.

JUNE 1993

5. Twenty-two UN peace-keepers were killed in ambushes in Mogadishu by supporters of General Aideed. **12.** Elections for a civilian President were held in Nigeria; on 23 June the military government declared the elections invalid. **13.** Pakistani UN

soldiers in Mogadishu opened fire on a demonstration, killing 14 and wounding 23. **14.** In a referendum in Malawi the electorate voted in favour of a multiparty democracy. **15.** The Inkatha Freedom Party and right-wing groups walked out of the South African constitutional negotiations, refusing to agree a date for multiracial elections because of alleged government-ANC collusion. **17.** UN forces captured General Aideed's headquarters in Mogadishu; 19 Somalis and five UN troops died. **25.** Armed right-wing extremists held delegates at South Africa's constitutional negotiations hostage for three hours, demanding a separate Afrikaner homeland.

JULY 1993

2. The Inkatha Freedom Party and the right-wing Conservative Party negotiators walked out of South Africa's constitutional negotiations in protest at an election date of 27 April 1994 being set before an interim constitution had been agreed. **12.** Four journalists were killed by Somalis in Mogadishu after UN forces had attacked a stronghold of General Aideed, killing 13 Somalis. **14.** The governments of Italy, Kuwait, Saudi Arabia and the United Arab Emirates refused to deploy troops on offensive UN operations in Somalia, objecting to the aggressiveness of the US-led UN operation to destroy General Aideed's forces. **25.** Twelve people were killed and 53 wounded in an attack on a church in Cape Town. **26.** A draft of South Africa's first multiracial constitution was tabled for debate at the constitutional negotiations.

AUGUST 1993

10. Fierce fighting between government and UNITA forces for control of Cuito in Angola left over 200 people dead. **25.** Pro-democracy demonstrations demanding an end to military government brought Lagos to a standstill. **26.** President Babangida of Nigeria resigned and transferred power to an interim president and government.

THE AMERICAS

SEPTEMBER 1992

13. Abimael Guzman, the leader of Peru's Shining Path terrorist group, was captured after 12 years on the run. **29.** The Brazilian House of Representatives voted to authorize the Senate to impeach President Collor de Mello for corruption.

OCTOBER 1992

1. Ross Perot announced his re-entry into the US presidential election as an independent candidate. **2.** The Brazilian Vice-President Itamar Franco was sworn in as acting president following President Collor de Mello's suspension. **5.** Dr Cheddi Jagan defeated the incumbent president Desmond Hoyte in the presidential election in Guyana. **26.** In a national referendum Canadians rejected a proposed new constitution, known as the Charlottetown accord.

NOVEMBER 1992

3. Governor Bill Clinton defeated the incumbent president George Bush and the independent candidate Ross Perot in the US presidential election. **8.** President Gaviria of Colombia declared a 90-day state of emergency after left-wing guerrillas killed more than 100 people. **22.** Parties supporting President Fujimori won the majority of seats in elections to a new constituent assembly in Peru. **27.** Venezuelan troops loyal to the government defeated a coup attempt by army rebels.

DECEMBER 1992

2. The Brazilian Senate voted to indict President Collor de Mello for corruption. **24.** President Bush announced pardons for the former defence secretary Caspar Weinberger and five other officials in the Reagan administration who were to stand trial over the Iran-Contra affair. **29.** Collor de Mello resigned as President of Brazil and interim President Itamar Franco was formally sworn in.

JANUARY 1993

17. The Haitian army announced that it had agreed to UN-mediated negotiations on the restoration of democracy with exiled President Jean-Bertrand Aristide. **20.** William Jefferson Clinton was inaugurated as the 42nd President of the USA. **22.** President Clinton's nominee for the office of attorney-general, Zoe Baird, was forced to withdraw after revealing that she had hired illegal immigrants as domestic help.

FEBRUARY 1993

5. President Clinton's second nominee as attorney-general, Kimba Wood, withdrew because she had hired illegal immigrants as domestic help. **15.** President Clinton gave a televised address announcing a serious effort to cut the federal budget deficit through tax increases and spending cuts. **24.** The Canadian Prime Minister Brian Mulroney resigned as leader of the ruling Progressive Conservative Party. **26.** Five people were killed and over 1,000 injured when a bomb exploded in a car park beneath the World Trade Centre in New York, causing fires and extensive structural damage.

MARCH 1993

1. Four agents of the US Treasury department were killed as they attempted to storm the fortified ranch of a religious sect in Waco, Texas. **25.** The US Senate approved by 54 votes to 45 President Clinton's $500 billion (£340 billion) programme of tax increases and spending cuts. **30.** The incumbent People's National Party won the Jamaican general election; 13 people were killed in politically-motivated violence during the campaign.

APRIL 1993

17. Two of the four officers accused of beating the black motorist Rodney King were found guilty of violating his civil rights; the other two were acquitted. **19.** The 51-day siege of the Branch Davidian cult compound at Waco ended; 87 cult members died in fires as FBI agents stormed the compound.

MAY 1993

9. Juan Carlos Wasmosy was elected President of Paraguay. **20.** The Venezuelan Supreme Court voted to charge President Perez with embezzlement from public funds. **25.** President Serrano of Guatemala suspended the country's constitution, dissolved the Congress and announced that he would rule by decree to purge state corruption. **27.** The US House of Representatives approved by 219 votes to 213 President Clinton's programme of tax increases and spending cuts.

JUNE 1993

1. President Serrano was ousted by the Guatemalan military. The Canadian government signed an agreement granting self-government to Canadian Eskimos in their own territory, to be created from part of the Northwest Territories. **4.** The Venezuelan Congress elected Ramon Velasquez as interim President. **6.** Ramon de Leon Carpio was elected President of Guatemala by Congress. **6.** The opposition National Revolutionary Movement won presidential and Congressional elections in Bolivia. **13.** Kim Campbell was elected leader of Canada's ruling Progressive Conservative Party and was sworn in as Prime Minister on 25 June. **23.** The UN Security Council imposed economic sanctions on Haiti after the military government did not meet a deadline to reinstate President Aristide.

JULY 1993

4. The Haiti military government and the exiled President Aristide signed a UN-mediated agreement to restore Aristide to power by 30 October 1993. **23.** Nicaraguan government forces retook the northern town of Esteli from former Sandinista rebels after two days of fighting.

AUGUST 1993

8. President Clinton's deficit-cutting budget was finally passed when the Senate passed a compromise version of the differing Senate and House of Representatives draft bills on the casting vote of Vice-President Gore. **20.** Nicaraguan government forces surrounded a camp where Contra guerrillas were holding military officers and government officials hostage to try to force the government to dismiss the Sandinista army commander Humberto Ortega; on 21 August Sandinistas took hostage 50 politicians, including Vice-President Vaglio, in Managua in protest at the hostage-taking by the Contra guerrillas. All the hostages were released on 26 August.

ASIA

SEPTEMBER 1992

13. Pro-democracy parties emerged victorious in the Thai general election, at the expense of pro-military parties that had supported the May 1992 military crackdown. 27. The Myanmar government lifted most martial law decrees and released detainees imprisoned since the May 1990 military take-over of power.

OCTOBER 1992

7. The Governor of Hong Kong (Chris Patten) presented plans for the extension of democracy in the colony. 12. The 14th Chinese Communist Party congress opened with a speech by party leader Jiang Zemin calling for a 'socialist market economy'. 18. The Chinese Communist Party congress closed with the replacement of elderly conservative leaders, including eight of the 14 Politburo members, by economic reformers.

NOVEMBER 1992

8. Talks in Beijing (Peking) to try to rescue the peace process in Cambodia ended in deadlock after the Khmer Rouge refused to disarm before the planned elections. 11. An angry debate in Hong Kong's Legislative Council ended with a vote in favour of the democratic reforms proposed by the Governor. 15. The Khmer Rouge failed to meet a UN deadline to rejoin the Cambodian peace process and refused to disarm its fighters. 18. The Pakistani government expelled opposition leader Benazir Bhutto from Islamabad after violent clashes between opposition supporters and police. 23. The Chinese government warned the Hong Kong Governor to withdraw proposals for greater democracy in the colony or China would end talks on the colony's future. 30. The UN Security Council voted unanimously to impose economic sanctions on the Khmer Rouge. In direct contravention of the 1984 Anglo-Chinese treaty on Hong Kong, the Chinese government announced that all contracts, leases and agreements signed by the Hong Kong government without Chinese approval would be declared invalid after the 1997 handover of power.

DECEMBER 1992

6. Thousands of Hindu fundamentalists marched on the north Indian town of Ayodhya and destroyed a mosque. 7. Rioting and fighting between Muslims and Hindus spread throughout India, Pakistan and Bangladesh following the destruction of the Ayodhya mosque. 8. As rioting continued, the Indian government arrested leaders of the BJP Hindu fundamentalist party and promised to rebuild the Ayodhya mosque. 9. The Indian parliament was adjourned and MPs returned to their constituencies in an attempt to calm the continuing unrest, in which over

600 people had died. Fighting in the Afghan capital Kabul between rival groups left 100 people dead. 11. Amid the worst economic downturn in the Japanese economy for 20 years, Prime Minister Kiichi Miyazawa replaced all but two of his Cabinet ministers. 15. The Indian government dismissed three state governments led by the BJP and imposed direct rule. 18. Kim Young-sam won the South Korean presidential election.

JANUARY 1993

3. Burhanuddin Rabbani was sworn in as President of Afghanistan. 6–11. Clashes between Hindus and Muslims in Bombay left 167 people dead. 16. The Indian government resigned en masse to enable the Prime Minister to form a new government and restore government authority after the Hindu-Muslim clashes.

FEBRUARY 1993

1. Government forces launched an offensive against Khmer Rouge guerrillas in central and eastern Cambodia. 7. Fighting erupted in Kabul between rival mujahidin groups. 9. Hong Kong's Executive Council approved the constitutional reform proposals of the Governor. 25. In New Delhi, Indian security forces prevented thousands of BJP supporters from staging a rally which had been banned.

MARCH 1993

7. Rival mujahidin groups in Kabul signed a peace accord whereby Burhanuddin Rabbani would remain President for 18 months and the Hezb-i-Islami leader Gulbuddin Hekmatyar would become Prime Minister. 12. The Governor of Hong Kong finally tabled his democratic reform plans for debate in the Legislative Council, after continually delaying the move in an unsuccessful attempt to persuade China to resume negotiations. Thirteen bomb blasts in Bombay caused 300 deaths and over 1,000 injuries, and led to the imposition of a nation-wide state of emergency by the Indian government. 16. A bomb exploded in the centre of Calcutta, killing 45 people. 17. The Chinese government announced that it would disband Hong Kong's legislature in 1997 and form its own government and legislature in the territory. 23. The Chinese government refused to continue six-monthly meetings with the UK government over Hong Kong and called for the dismissal of Governor Patten. 28. The Chinese National People's Congress elected Jiang Zemin as the country's President.

APRIL 1993

8. Four of the UN peace-keeping force in Cambodia were killed in Khmer Rouge attacks. 13. Britain and China announced that talks on the future of Hong Kong would resume after China ended its insistence that democratic reform proposals should be withdrawn. 18. The President of Pakistan dismissed the government and dissolved parliament.

MAY 1993

1. President Premadasa of Sri Lanka was assassinated by a suicide bomber in Colombo. **12.** Fighting between rival mujahidin groups around Kabul left 70 dead. **24.** Chinese security forces fought thousands of Tibetans demonstrating against Chinese rule in Lhasa. **28.** The five-day UN-supervised elections in Cambodia ended with a 90 per cent turn-out and only sporadic attempts by the Khmer Rouge to disrupt the elections.

JUNE 1993

9. Crown Prince Naruhito of Japan married diplomat Masako Owada in Tokyo. **12.** Members of the defeated Cambodian People's Party declared the secession of seven provinces in eastern Cambodia and attacked UN officials and FUNCIPEC supporters in the region; on 15 June the secessionists fled to Vietnam. **16.** Prince Sihanouk formed a coalition government with himself as head of state of Cambodia, and the Royalist Party leader Prince Ranariddh and the Communist Party leader Hun Sen as co-chairmen of the government. **18.** The Japanese parliament was dissolved and a general election called after the government was defeated in a confidence vote.

JULY 1993

5. David Rowbottom and Tania Miller were kidnapped by Kurdish guerrillas while travelling in eastern Turkey; they were released unharmed on 10 August. **18.** In the Japanese general election the Liberal Democratic Party lost its majority in the lower house of parliament for the first time since 1955; on 22 July the Liberal Democrat government resigned. Moeen Qareshi was named as caretaker Prime Minister of Pakistan after President Ghulam Ishaq Khan and Prime Minister Nawaz Sharif both resigned after months of feuding.

AUGUST 1993

6. The leader of the Japan New Party, Morihiro Hosokawa, was elected Prime Minister by the Japanese parliament; the new Cabinet was sworn in on 9 August. **18.** Cambodian government forces launched assaults on Khmer Rouge positions in eastern Cambodia. **22.** Two British tourists were kidnapped by Kurdish guerrillas in eastern Turkey; they were released on 24 August after Turkish soldiers shot dead eight of the guerrillas. **29.** Ong Teng Cheong was elected President of Singapore.

AUSTRALASIA AND THE PACIFIC

SEPTEMBER 1992

13. Papua New Guinean soldiers raided the Solomon Islands in an attempt to cut off supplies to secessionists on Bougainville Island.

OCTOBER 1992

3. The Labour state government in Victoria, Australia, lost the state election to the conservative opposition. **5.** The Australian Prime Minister (Paul Keating) announced that Australia was formally discontinuing the British honours system. **23.** Papua New Guinean troops and riot police attacked and besieged rebel strongholds on Bougainville Island.

NOVEMBER 1992

18. The incumbent president of Nauru, Bernard Dowiyogo, was re-elected by the country's parliament.

DECEMBER 1992

17. The Australian Prime Minister announced that new citizens would no longer swear an oath of allegiance to The Queen.

FEBRUARY 1993

4. In the Tongan general election, seven of the nine elected parliamentary seats were won by candidates supporting a reduction in the power of the monarchy and aristocracy. **14.** Papua New Guinean forces attacked the secessionist-held town of Arawa, Bougainville. **25.** Eight Papua New Guinean soldiers were killed in an ambush by separatist rebels in Bougainville.

MARCH 1993

13. The Labor Party won a fifth successive general election victory in Australia.

APRIL 1993

12. The Solomon Islands formally protested to Papua New Guinea over raids into Solomon Island territory by Papuan forces. **27.** Papua New Guinean and Solomon Islands' patrol boats clashed off Bougainville in a border dispute. **28.** The Australian Prime Minister announced the appointment of a committee of eminent persons to advise on the changes needed to convert Australia to a republic.

EUROPE

SEPTEMBER 1992

4. The former Communist president of Bulgaria, Todor Zhivkov, was convicted of embezzlement and abuse of power, and gaoled for seven years. **10.** The Italian Prime Minister (Giuliano Amato) asked parliament for emergency economic powers to deal with chronic economic chaos and a currency crisis. **17.** The German government, faced with increasing numbers of asylum-seekers, announced that it had agreed with the Romanian government to send back to Romania all those whose asylum requests were rejected.

OCTOBER 1992

1. The Czechoslovak federal parliament voted to maintain a new, looser federation and rejected plans for a division of the country. **5.** The Estonian Riigikogu elected Lennart Meri as the country's first post-Soviet president. **11.** The incumbent president of Romania, Ion Iliescu, was re-elected for a second term. **19.** Mart Laar became Prime Minister of Estonia at the head of a coalition government. **28.** The last former Soviet troops left Poland, though a skeleton transport and communications force remained to assist the withdrawal from east Germany. **29.** The Bulgarian government resigned after losing a parliamentary vote of confidence over arms smuggling allegations.

NOVEMBER 1992

4. Nicolae Vacarion was appointed Prime Minister of Romania. **5.** The Irish government lost a confidence motion in the Dail and was forced to resign and call a general election. **6.** The Norwegian Prime Minister Gro Harlem Brundtland announced her resignation as Labour Party leader for personal reasons, but continued as Prime Minister. **11.** In Berlin the trial began of Erich Honecker and five of his colleagues on charges of manslaughter. **16.** The Democratic Party of Labour (formerly the Communist Party) won the second round of parliamentary elections in Lithuania. **18.** The Swedish parliament voted to ratify the European Economic Area agreement between the EC and EFTA states. **19.** Sweden abandoned the pegging of its currency to the ECU after intense currency speculation. **25.** The Czechoslovak federal parliament passed a bill authorizing the partition of the country into separate Czech and Slovak republics from 1 January 1993. In the Irish general election, the Labour Party emerged holding the balance of power in the Dail. **27.** The German government outlawed the neo-Nazi Nationalist Front in an attempt to reduce attacks on asylum-seekers.

DECEMBER 1992

2. The Greek Prime Minister sacked his entire cabinet after months of feuding over economic and foreign policy. The Lithuanian parliament elected Bronislovas Lubys as Prime Minister. **6.** In a referendum, Switzerland voted by 50.3 per cent to 49.7 per cent to reject the European Economic Area agreement between the EC and EFTA states. **10.** Norway abandoned the pegging of its currency to the ECU following currency speculation. **13.** In a referendum, Liechtenstein voted in favour of ratifying the European Economic Area agreement. **14.** The separatist Lombardy League and anti-Mafia La Rete parties made large gains in the Italian local elections at the expense of the Christian Democrat and Socialist parties.

JANUARY 1993

1. Czechoslovakia separated into two new independent states, the Czech Republic and the Slovak Republic. **12.** The Irish Dail endorsed the Fianna Fail-Labour coalition government. The Icelandic parliament voted to ratify the European Economic Area agreement between the EC and EFTA states. The former East German leader Erich Honecker flew to Chile after his trial on charges of manslaughter collapsed when he was judged too ill to stand trial. **14.** The Danish Prime Minister Poul Schluter resigned after a judicial inquiry accused him of lying about measures taken to prevent Tamil refugees from Sri Lanka entering Denmark. **25.** A new Danish coalition government led by Poul Rasmussen was sworn in. **27.** Nexhnije Hoxha, the widow of former Albanian dictator Enver Hoxha, was found guilty of corruption and sentenced to nine years in gaol.

FEBRUARY 1993

10. The Italian Justice Minister Claudio Martelli resigned after coming under investigation for corruption. **12.** The Italian Socialist Party leader Bettino Craxi resigned after being implicated in a Milan bribery scandal. **14.** Glafcos Clerides defeated the incumbent George Vassilliou in the Cypriot presidential election. The former Communist Party leader Algirdas Brazaukas was elected President of Lithuania. **15.** Michal Kovac was elected by the Slovak parliament as the state's first president. **19.** The Italian finance minister Giovanni Goria and health minister Francesco de Lorenzo resigned after magistrates said that both were under investigation for corruption. **25.** As corruption inquiries in Italy spread, the coalition government survived a parliamentary vote of confidence.

MARCH 1993

3. The Belgian parliament voted to end the King's power to nominate and appoint a prime minister and to dissolve parliament. **4.** The German cabinet agreed an economic consolidation package, including tax increases and cuts in subsidies and social services, to raise DM 150 billion a year to cover unification costs. **10.** Fighting broke out in the Italian Senate between government and opposition members over alleged corruption involving leading politicians. **14.** German federal, state and opposition leaders, employers and trade unions reached agreement on a 'solidarity pact' of spending cuts, tax increases, pay restraint and investment increases to fund unification. **16.** The Italian government survived a vote of confidence in the Chamber of Deputies after fighting had broken out and the Liberal Party leader Renato Altissimo had resigned over alleged involvement in corruption. **21.** The ruling French Socialist Party was defeated in the first round of legislative elections by the right-wing RPR-UDF alliance. **23.** The Belgian coalition government offered its resignation to King Baudouin after failing to agree budget cuts. The King asked the government to continue in office and attempt to reach agreement. The coalition agreed budget cuts and on 30 March the King rejected the resignation and reappointed the ministers. In Dublin a demonstration by 15,000 people demanded an end to IRA violence in the wake of the Warrington bombing. **29.** Edouard Balladur was appointed Prime Minister after the RPR-UDF alliance won the French legislative elections.

APRIL 1993

17. President Turgut Ozal of Turkey died of a heart attack. **19.** In a referendum in Italy an overwhelming majority voted to change the voting system for three-quarters of the Senate seats from proportional representation to a first-past-the-post system. **22.** The Italian government resigned. **28.** A new Italian coalition government headed by Carlo Ciampi was announced. **29.** Five ministers resigned from the Italian government in protest at parliament's vote not to lift the immunity from prosecution on corruption charges of the former Prime Minister Bettino Craxi.

MAY 1993

6. The German Transport Minister Gunther Krause resigned after his involvement in a scandal over the misuse of public funds. **13.** The Italian Senate voted to lift the immunity from prosecution of former Prime Minister Giulio Andreotti, who faced charges of collusion with the Mafia. **19.** Anti-Maastricht protesters fought with police in Copenhagen. **27.** A bomb suspected to have been planted by the Mafia exploded in Florence, killing six people and severely damaging parts of the Uffizi gallery. **28.** The Polish government was defeated in a parliamentary vote of confidence. **29.** German neo-Nazi youths killed five Turks in an arson attack in Solingen. **30.** Thousands of Turks rioted in Solingen to protest at the arson attack.

JUNE 1993

1. Riots by Turks, anarchists and extremists spread throughout Germany. **3.** Turks rioted in Cologne and Nuremberg after the funeral service for the victims of the arson attack on 29 May. **6.** Latvia held legislative elections, which were won by the moderate Latvian Way coalition. The Socialist Party retained power in the Spanish general election but lost its parliamentary majority. **13.** Tansu Ciller was elected leader of the ruling True Path Party in Turkey, becoming Turkey's first woman Prime Minister. **21.** Two ETA car bombs exploded in central Madrid killing seven people.

JULY 1993

27. Five people were killed when three car bombs exploded in Milan and Rome. **31.** King Baudouin of Belgium died.

AUGUST 1993

4. The Italian Chamber of Deputies passed electoral reform legislation to replace proportional representation by a first-past-the-post system for 75 per cent of the seats. **31.** The last Russian troops left Lithuania.

THE FORMER SOVIET UNION

SEPTEMBER 1992

1. Fighting broke out between Georgian government forces and separatist rebels in the Abkhazia region. Opposition supporters seized control of the presidential palace in Dushanbe, capital of Tajikistan, and took several government ministers hostage. **4.** Government troops and rebel forces clashed in Dushanbe, leaving hundreds dead; Russia, Uzbekistan, Kyrgyzstan and Kazakhstan sent troops to seal the former Soviet border with Afghanistan to prevent arms entering Tajikistan. **7.** President Nabiev of Tajikistan was forced to resign by opposition forces. **15.** Seven former Soviet republics took steps towards restoring central co-ordination with the establishment of an inter-parliamentary assembly in St Petersburg. **27.** Rival armed factions in Tajikistan took 30 Russian troops hostage in an attempt to seize their heavy weapons. **28.** Russia reinforced its military presence in Tajikistan to prevent rival factions from obtaining military weaponry. **30.** The Ukrainian Prime Minister Vitold Fokin resigned after increasing pressure from the opposition over the slow pace of economic reforms.

OCTOBER 1992

1. Russia launched its mass privatization scheme, based on distributing vouchers to all the population. **2.** The Ukrainian parliament passed a vote of no confidence in the government, forcing it out of office. **3.** Separatist rebels in the Abkhazia region of Georgia captured the town of Gaga from government forces. **6.** Separatists in Abkhazia, allied to Cossack and Muslim volunteers from Russia, defeated Georgian government troops and gained control of all land north-west of Sukhumi. **7.** The Azerbaijani parliament voted against ratifying the republic's membership of the CIS. **9.** Russia, Belarus, Kazakhstan, Uzbekistan, Armenia and Kyrgyzstan agreed at a CIS summit to create a rouble zone. **11.** Eduard Shevardnadze was elected chairman of Georgia's parliament and State President. **13.** Leonid Kuchma was appointed Prime Minister of the Ukraine. **24.** Armed forces loyal to ousted President Nabiev of Tajikistan overthrew the acting coalition government of Islamic and democratic groups. **26.** Tajik government forces defeated forces loyal to former President Nabiev and forced them out of Dushanbe. **29.** President Yeltsin suspended the withdrawal of Russian troops from the Baltic states because of alleged human rights violations against ethnic Russians in the republics.

NOVEMBER 1992

2. President Yeltsin imposed direct rule in the Russian republics of North Ossetia and Ingush after clashes between the two republics. **5.** A cease-fire came into effect in North Ossetia after fighting between Ingush and Ossetians had left 150 people dead. **19.** The acting President of Tajikistan, Akbarsho Iskandarov, was voted out of office by the parliament and replaced by Imamali Rakmanov. **20.** Fighting erupted in the southern Kurgan-Tyube region of Tajikistan between supporters of the former Communist government and the Islamic-democratic coalition.

DECEMBER 1992

3. Fighting broke out in the Russian Congress of People's Deputies between economic reformers and conservatives over constitutional changes to determine the balance of power between the president and the Congress. **9.** The Congress of People's Deputies rejected President Yeltsin's nomination of Yegor Gaidar as Prime Minister. **10.** Pro-Communist forces loyal to ex-President Nabiev seized control of Dushanbe after heavy fighting with Islamic-democratic coalition forces. **12.** President Yeltsin and the Congress chairman, Ruslan Khasbulatov, tried to end the growing constitutional crisis and suggested a referendum be held on a new constitution in April 1993. **14.** President Yeltsin was forced by the Congress to accept the conservative Viktor Chernomyrdin as Prime Minister. **19.** President Yeltsin returned early from a visit to China to prevent the sacking of economic reformers in the Russian cabinet by the conservative wing of the Congress. **23.** President Yeltsin and Prime Minister Chernomyrdin announced a new Russian cabinet that included most of the economic reformers from the previous government.

JANUARY 1993

4. The heads of state of the five Central Asian republics of the CIS held a summit in Tashkent and announced their intention to form a union of Central Asian people. **22.** At a summit of CIS leaders in Minsk, seven members signed a charter on closer cooperation but three members refused to sign. **26.** The Azerbaijani Prime Minister Ragim Guseinov resigned and was replaced by Ali Masimov.

FEBRUARY 1993

2. President Ter-Petrossian of Armenia dismissed Prime Minister Arutunyan for failing to implement economic reforms, and appointed Grant Bagratyan acting Prime Minister. **18.** Armenian forces captured five villages in the disputed Nagorno-Karabakh enclave in the continuing war with Azerbaijan. **21.** Government forces seized control of the Garm region in Tajikistan from Islamic rebels. **23.** Thousands of Communists and right-wing nationalists marched through central Moscow to protest against President Yeltsin's reformist government.

MARCH 1993

10. An emergency session of the Russian Congress of People's Deputies convened to resolve the power struggle between President Yeltsin and the legislature. **12.** President Yeltsin and his entire cabinet stormed out of the Russian Congress after deputies voted to restrict the government's powers. **16.** President Schevardnadze of Georgia claimed that

Russian troops and aircraft had supported Abkhazian separatists in an attack on Georgian government forces. **19.** Georgian forces shot down a Russian fighter aircraft believed to have been aiding Abkhazian separatists. **20.** President Yeltsin imposed emergency 'special rule' in Russia and called a referendum on the constitution for 25 April to resolve his continuing power struggle with the Congress. **23.** The Russian Constitutional Court declared President Yeltsin's imposition of 'special rule' illegal. **28.** In the Congress of People's Deputies a motion to impeach President Yeltsin failed to gain the necessary two-thirds majority.

APRIL 1993

4. Azerbaijani forces suffered a heavy defeat by Armenian forces and lost control of a large area of Azerbaijan. **13.** The trial of the leaders of the failed August 1991 coup against Soviet President Gorbachev began in Moscow. The UN began to airlift aid to Azeri refugees displaced by Armenian advances. **15.** The Turkish government announced that it had started to ship armaments to Azerbaijan to help it in the war against Armenia. **25.** President Yeltsin won the referendum on constitutional reform, with 58 per cent of voters supporting the President and 54 per cent supporting continued economic reform.

MAY 1993

1. Communists and nationalists fought with police in central Moscow as they were prevented from marching to Red Square. **10.** Kyrgyzstan left the rouble zone and introduced its own currency, the som. **18.** The trial of the leaders of the August 1991 coup was suspended indefinitely by the judges after the dismissal of the prosecuting team. **20.** The Ukrainian Prime Minister Leonid Kuchma resigned when parliament and President Kravchuk refused to extend his extraordinary powers to enable a faster pace of economic reform. **21.** The Ukrainian parliament refused to support an attempt by President Kravchuk to take over control of the government and reinstated Prime Minister Kuchma but without extraordinary powers.

JUNE 1993

5. President Yeltsin opened a constitutional assembly charged with amending and approving a draft constitution prepared by the Russian government. **7.** A rebellion by discontented sections of the army broke out in Azerbaijan, with rebels capturing the city of Gyandzha and calling for the President's and government's dismissal. **15.** The Ukraine's President Kravchuk acceded to demands for a referendum on his leadership and early parliamentary elections. The Azerbaijani parliament elected the former Communist leader Heidar Aliyev as its chairman and effective head of state to appease the military rebels. **16.** President Kravchuk took control of the Ukraine government and set up a special commission headed by the Prime Minister to stabilize the economy after

Almanack
Whitaker's
QUIZ
£2,000 worth of prizes to be won

QUIZ RULES

1 Employees of Whitaker or anyone else involved in the quiz and their families are excluded.

2 Entries are limited to one per person.

3 The closing date for entries is 31st January 1994 and all entries must be received by that date addressed to Whitaker's Almanack 1994 Quiz, 12 Dyott Street, London WC1A 1DF.

4 The first prize will be £1,000. There will be five prizes of £150 each and 10 runner up prizes of a free copy of Whitaker's Almanack 1995 edition, on publication.

5 The prizes will be awarded to the first 16 correct entries that are drawn.

6 Prize winners will be notified by 4th March 1994. The names of winners may be publilished.

7 A list of prize winners and the correct answers to the questions will be available on request from Whitaker, 12 Dyott Street, London WC1A 1DF, after 4th March 1994. A stamped addressed envelope marked 'Prize Winners List' should accompany such requests.

8 In all matters concerning this quiz, the decision of the Editor will be final, and no correspondence will be entered into.

Name ....

(BLOCK LETTERS)

Address ....

(BLOCK LETTERS)

....

.... Postcode ....

Tel No ....

Signed ....

QUIZ QUESTIONS

Answer   Page No

15 Who was translated in 1452?

16 What do these have in common?

   (a) WAR, Fun, Bastion

   (b) The Friend, The Inquirer, Reform

   (c) Carlton, Meridian, Westcountry

17 Which European country's territories include

   (a) the Åland Archipelago?

   (b) the Sheep Islands?

   (c) Peter the First Island?

18 Who was the sculptor of

   (a) Captain Scott?

   (b) 'Bomber' Harris?

   (c) Zeus (at Olympia)?

19 If 1994 is the dog, what is

   (a) 1996?

   (b) 1998?

   (c) 2000?

20 Which confederation is called five, numbers seven and has seven Limbs?

the parliament had rejected strikers' demands for a referendum. **21.** President Kravchuk rescinded a decree which placed him in charge of the Ukrainian government. **22.** Military rebels led by Colonel Suret Guseinov entered the Azerbaijani capital Baku without resistance from government forces. **27.** The Azerbaijani military rebels pledged allegiance to acting President Heidar Aliyev and promised to withdraw from Baku. **30.** The military rebel leader Colonel Suret Guseinov was elected Prime Minister of Azerbaijan by the parliament.

JULY 1993

2. Abkhazian separatists shelled the city of Sukhumi held by Georgian government forces. The new Azerbaijani regime launched a counter-offensive to retake villages in Nagorno-Karabakh recently lost to Armenian forces. **6.** President Shevardnadze of Georgia imposed martial law in Abkhazia. **12.** The Russian constitutional assembly approved the draft constitution. **14.** Tajik rebels based in Afghanistan, supported by Afghan mujahidin, launched a raid into Tajikistan; they were resisted by Tajik government and Russian troops. **16.** Georgian government forces launched an offensive against Abkhazian separatists after they had rejected an ultimatum to retreat from two villages. Ethnic Russians in the Estonian cities of Narva and Sillamäe voted in referendums for autonomy for their local regions. **21.** Tajik rebels in Afghanistan shelled military posts on the Tajik-Afghan border. **28.** Russian and Tajik government forces destroyed a force of Tajik rebels and mujahidin crossing into Tajikistan from Afghanistan.

AUGUST 1993

5. The Moldovan parliament failed to ratify the state's membership of the CIS. **6.** The Georgian government resigned amid economic chaos and the parliament asked President Shevardnadze to form a government. **15.** Georgian government forces and Abkhazian separatists began disengaging their forces around the Abkhazian capital of Sukhumi under the terms of a Russian-sponsored peace plan. **23.** Armenian forces captured the Azerbaijani town of Fizuli.

THE FORMER YUGOSLAVIA

SEPTEMBER 1992

3. The permanent conference on Yugoslavia, agreed upon at the London conference in August, opened in Geneva, co-chaired by Lord Owen for the EC and Cyrus Vance for the UN. **4.** A UN aid convoy reached Goradze, Bosnia. The parliament of the unrecognized Yugoslav federation voted to accept the London peace agreement. **15.** Bosnian Serb forces launched an attack on Sarajevo in an attempt to cut off Muslim forces. **20.** The UN Security Council voted to deny the new Yugoslav federation of Serbia and Montenegro former Yugoslavia's seat at the UN.

OCTOBER 1992

6. The UN Security Council voted unanimously to prepare evidence for the trial of war crimes in the former Yugoslavia. **9.** The UN Security Council voted unanimously to ban all military flights over Bosnia-Hercegovina. **21.** Fighting broke out around the Bosnian town of Vitez between Croats and Muslims, previously allies, over Croatian attempts to form a breakaway state. **27.** The UN and EC peace negotiators Cyrus Vance and Lord Owen proposed a new constitution for Bosnia-Hercegovina with a central government and ten autonomous regions. **28.** The Bosnian town of Jajce was captured by Serb forces.

NOVEMBER 1992

2. The Bosnian Serb delegation withdrew from the Geneva peace talks and rejected proposals for dividing Bosnia-Hercegovina into autonomous provinces. **11.** The main British contingent of the UN protection force arrived in Split, Croatia. **16.** The UN Security Council voted to tighten economic sanctions against the Yugoslav federation. **19.** British troops escorted relief supplies to the besieged Bosnian town of Tuzla. **29.** A UN relief convoy reached the besieged Muslim-held town of Srebrenica in Bosnia, the first aid since May.

DECEMBER 1992

6. In Slovenia, Milan Kucan was re-elected president, and the ruling Liberal Democratic Party was returned to power in the general election. **8.** Bosnian Serb forces took control of the road from Sarajevo to its airport. **11.** The UN Security Council ordered peace-keeping troops to Macedonia to set up checkpoints on the borders with Albania and Kosovo to prevent the spread of fighting. **20.** Slobodan Milosevic was re-elected president of Serbia in a general election that was deemed flawed and unfair by international observers. **29.** The parliament of the Yugoslav federation passed a vote of no confidence in Prime Minister Milan Panic and voted him out of office. **31.** The UN Secretary-General was booed by residents when he visited Sarajevo.

JANUARY 1993

2. The UN-EC conference on the former Yugoslavia reopened in Geneva with the presentation by co-chairmen Cyrus Vance and Lord Owen of plans (the Vance-Owen peace plan) for Bosnia-Hercegovina to become a federal republic of ten autonomous regions. **4.** The Vance-Owen peace plan was accepted by the Bosnian Croats and partially accepted by the Muslims. **13.** A British soldier, L/Cpl Wayne Edwards, was killed in crossfire between Croat and Muslim forces in Gornji Vakuf. **18.** Fighting began between Muslim and Croat forces in Gornji Vakuf after Croat leaders in the area ordered Muslim forces to put themselves under Croat rather than Bosnian government control. **22.** Fighting began again in Croatia after a year's peace as Croatian troops attacked the Serb-held area of Krajina, Croatia, to gain control of a strategic bridge. **23.** Serbs in Krajina raided UN depots to obtain artillery and other weapons to fight the Croatian offensive. **25.** Croat forces in Krajina won control of the strategic bridge of Maslenica and the airport at Zemunik, reopening transport and communications links with the Dalmatian coast. **30.** Talks in Geneva ended without agreement by the Bosnian Muslims and Bosnian Serbs to the Vance-Owen peace plan.

FEBRUARY 1993

9. Cyrus Vance and Lord Owen presented their peace plan to the UN Security Council. **11.** The Bosnian government announced that no more aid would be allowed into Sarajevo until aid also reached starving Muslims in eastern Bosnia. **16.** Bosnian Muslim forces lost control of Kamenica to Bosnian Serb forces. **19.** The UN Security Council approved a resolution putting the entire UN operation in the former Yugoslavia under chapter seven of the UN Charter, which allows the use of force to ensure compliance with UN resolutions. **21.** A UN aid convoy reached the besieged Muslim-held town of Zepa in Bosnia after being held up by Serb forces for seven days. **28.** US transport aircraft dropped food and medicines by parachute to besieged Muslim enclaves in eastern Bosnia.

MARCH 1993

2. Cerska was captured by Bosnian Serb forces. **3.** The Bosnian Muslim government agreed to the military accord to end hostilities, part of the Vance-Owen plan. **5.** Bosnian Serb forces opened two routes from Cerska and Kamenica to Muslim-held Tuzla to allow Muslim refugees to flee. **12.** General Philippe Morillon, the UN commander, was prevented from leaving Srebrenica by women and children who wanted the UN to send aid and armed personnel to the enclave. The first war crimes trial opened in Sarajevo; two Bosnian Serb soldiers stood trial for murder, rape and looting, and on 30 March they were sentenced to death after being found guilty. **19.** A UN aid convoy led by General Morillon reached Srebrenica. **25.** Bosnian Muslim President Izetbegovic signed the Vance-Owen peace plan, which left the Bosnian Serbs the only group not to sign. **29.** A UN convoy which had delivered aid to Srebrenica returned to Tuzla crammed with refugees.

APRIL 1993

2. The Bosnian Serbs rejected the territorial proposals of the Vance-Owen peace plan. **4–6.** Muslim soldiers in Srebrenica prevented UN lorries from evacuating people trapped in the enclave. **6.** Croatian and Serb forces signed a cease-fire which ended fighting in Krajina. **16.** Fighting broke out between Muslim and Croat forces in central Bosnia which closed aid convoy routes. **18.** Muslim defenders and Serb besiegers of Srebrenica agreed to allow the evacuation of civilians, and the sick and wounded, and the establishment of a UN 'safe area'. Fighting between Muslims and Croats spread in central Bosnia as Croat forces ordered Muslim forces in areas designated as Croat under the Vance-Owen plan to submit to Croat control. **27.** Croatian Serb forces attacked the Bosnian Muslim enclave of Bihac.

MAY 1993

1. Thorvald Stoltenberg of Norway replaced Cyrus Vance as the UN peace negotiator. A peace conference on Bosnia-Hercegovina opened in Athens attended by the leaders of Bosnia's Muslims, Croats and Serbs, the presidents of the Yugoslav federation, Serbia, Montenegro and Croatia, and the UN and EC peace negotiators. **2.** The Bosnian Serb leader Radovan Karadzic signed the UN-EC peace plan, conditional on ratification by the Bosnian Serb parliament. **4.** Bosnian Serb forces attacked Zepa. **5.** The Bosnian Serb parliament effectively rejected the UN-EC peace plan by attaching unacceptable conditions. **6.** The UN Security Council declared Sarajevo, Tuzla, Zepa, Goradze, Bihac and Srebrenica to be UN safe areas. **9.** Fighting broke out in Mostar between Muslim and Croat forces. **15.** Bosnian Serbs rejected the UN-EC peace plan in a referendum. **22.** The USA, EC and Russia agreed to defend UN safe areas and enforce tougher sanctions, signalling their awareness that the Vance-Owen plan was defunct. **30.** Bosnian Serb forces attacked Goradze and Sarajevo. **31.** The Yugoslav federation President Dobrica Cosic was ousted by no-confidence votes in both houses of the federal parliament.

JUNE 1993

7. Muslim forces captured Travnik from Bosnian Croats. **11.** British soldiers protecting an aid convoy shot dead two Bosnian Croats who opened fire on the convoy. **16.** Muslim forces took control of Kakanj from Bosnian Croats. **23.** Peace talks on Bosnia-Hercegovina opened in Geneva on a Serb and Croat plan to partition the state according to military gains. **27.** Fighting broke out around Maglaj as Muslim and Croat forces ended their local alliance against Serb forces and fought each other.

JULY 1993

2. An alliance of Bosnian Serb and Croat forces captured Zepce from Muslim forces. **9.** Bosnian President Izetbegovic rejected the Serb-Croat partition plan. **15.** Croatian Serbs launched attacks on the Croatian towns of Osijek, Rijeka and Karlovac after Croatia decided to reopen the Maslenica Bridge. **16.** Bosnian Muslim forces captured Fojnica from Croat forces. **19.** Fighting broke out between Bosnian Serbs and Muslims for control of Mount Igman, overlooking Sarajevo. **26.** Muslim forces captured Bugojno from Bosnian Croat forces. **27.** Peace negotiations on Bosnia-Hercegovina reopened in Geneva between the presidents of Serbia, Montenegro, Croatia and Bosnia-Hercegovina, and the Bosnian Croat and Serb leaders; a preliminary agreement was reached on 30 July.

AUGUST 1993

1. Serb forces in Krajina shelled the Maslenica bridge after Croat forces refused to hand control of the area to UN troops. **2.** Muslim forces captured Gornji Vakuf from Bosnian Croat forces. **4.** Bosnian Serb forces captured most of Mount Igman, near Sarajevo. **10.** Bosnian Serb forces partially withdrew and handed over parts of Mount Igman and Mount Bjelasnica to UN forces, but later retook control of the mountains. **15.** UN troops replaced Bosnian Serb forces as they withdrew from Mount Igman and Mount Bjelasnica. Wounded Bosnian Muslims were flown out of Sarajevo for treatment in Britain and Sweden. **20.** New constitutional arrangements and territorial divisions for Bosnia-Hercegovina were presented by Lord Owen and Thorvald Stoltenberg to the Bosnian Muslim, Serb and Croat leaders in Geneva. **21.** A UN relief convoy arrived at the besieged Muslim-held eastern part of Mostar, the first for three months. **24.** US aircraft dropped relief supplies to eastern Mostar after Bosnian Croat forces refused to allow through any more UN convoys. **25.** A UN aid convoy was allowed into the Muslim part of Mostar after it had distributed aid to Croat areas of the city. **26.** The UN aid convoy was prevented from leaving Mostar by Muslims, to stop further Croat bombardments. **28.** The Bosnian Muslim and Bosnian Croat parliaments accepted the Geneva peace plan, conditional on changes to the territorial divisions and constitutional principles; the Bosnian Serb parliament accepted the plan. **31.** The Bosnian government and Bosnian Serb leaders announced a provisional agreement on ending hostilities and exchanging prisoners. UN personnel trapped in Mostar were allowed to leave.

EUROPEAN COMMUNITY

SEPTEMBER 1992

2. The European Commission conceded that the United Kingdom could retain passport controls after 1 January 1993. **13.** The currencies of the European monetary system (EMS) were realigned, the lira being devalued by 3.5 per cent and all other currencies being revalued by 3.5 per cent. **17.** After intense currency speculation, the British and Italian governments were forced to withdraw the pound and the lira respectively from the exchange rate mechanism (ERM) of the EMS and the Spanish peseta was devalued by 5 per cent. **20.** In a referendum, the French electorate voted by 51 per cent to 49 per cent in favour of ratifying the Maastricht Treaty. **23.** Amid continued currency speculation, France and Germany spent billions of pounds defending the French franc, while Spain reintroduced capital controls.

OCTOBER 1992

1. The Italian government announced that it was asking the EC for an £8 billion loan to enable the lira

to return to the ERM. **16.** An EC heads of government summit meeting was held in Birmingham and agreed on a declaration emphasizing their commitment to 'subsidiarity' (minimum interference in national life). **28.** The Danish government announced the changes to the Maastricht Treaty that they considered necessary before a second referendum on ratification could be held; these included protocols enabling Denmark to opt out of a common currency, a common defence policy and common EC citizenship. **29.** The Italian House of Deputies voted by 403 to 46 to ratify the Maastricht Treaty, confirming the Senate's vote in favour.

NOVEMBER 1992

4. The Belgian Senate voted by 115 to 26 to ratify the Maastricht Treaty, confirming an earlier vote in the Chamber of Deputies. **5.** The EC Agriculture Commissioner, Ray MacSharry, resigned from his position as negotiator in the GATT talks, accusing the European Commission President Jacques Delors of sabotaging a GATT agreement. **9.** France's attempt to retaliate against increased US agricultural tariffs was outvoted in the EC Council of Ministers, and the Council ordered the Commission to accelerate negotiation of a GATT agreement. **10.** Ray Mac-Sharry was reinstated as the chief EC GATT negotiator after President Delors agreed to the reopening of GATT negotiations with the USA. **18.** The European Commission announced that plans to abolish all passport and immigration controls within the EC by 1 January 1993 had been delayed by at least one year. **19.** The Norwegian parliament voted to apply for EC membership. **22.** After currency speculation, the Spanish peseta and Portuguese escudo were devalued by 5 per cent within the ERM. **25.** The French National Assembly voted by 301 to 251 to declare unacceptable the GATT agreement reached with the USA over agriculture; farmers demonstrated and fought street battles with police in Paris. The upper house of the Cortes voted by 222 to 0 to ratify the Maastricht Treaty, completing Spain's ratification.

DECEMBER 1992

1. In Strasbourg 50,000 French farmers protesting at the GATT agreement on agriculture clashed with police. **10.** Portugal's Assembly voted by 200 to 21 to ratify the Maastricht Treaty. **11.** A two-day summit meeting opened in Edinburgh (*see* below). **15.** The Netherlands States-General voted to ratify the Maastricht Treaty. **18.** The German Bundesrat voted to ratify the Maastricht Treaty; in an earlier vote, the Bundestag had ratified the treaty but reserved its right to vote again on a single currency at the time of implementation.

THE EDINBURGH AGREEMENT

– Denmark to be allowed to opt out of the single currency, of a common defence policy, of European

citizenship, and of the new immigration, asylum and policing pillar of the Community
- no deadlines for ratification of the Maastricht Treaty by Denmark or the UK
- the EC budget to rise in phases, from 1.2 per cent of Community GDP in 1992 to 1.27 per cent in 1999. The UK's budget rebate to remain unchanged
- a co-ordinated strategy for economic growth to be adopted
- Strasbourg confirmed as the site of plenary sessions of the European Parliament. From 1994 the Parliament will expand from 518 to 567 members
- decision on siting the new European Central Bank delayed for six months
- enlargement negotiations to begin with Austria, Sweden, Finland and Norway in 1993
- agreement on subsidiarity; decision-making to occur at the appropriate national, regional or local level
- the single market declared to be an irreversible achievement, complete in all essential respects

JANUARY 1993

1. The Single European Market came into being. **30.** The Irish government devalued the punt by 10 per cent against other currencies in the ERM after intense currency speculation.

FEBRUARY 1993

1. The European Community formally opened membership negotiations with Austria, Finland and Norway. **15.** EC finance ministers agreed that, because of the economic recession, the date by which member countries should meet the Maastricht convergence criteria for economic and monetary union should be delayed to the end of 1996.

MARCH 1993

17. Officials from the twelve EC states signed a protocol to enable the European Economic Area Agreement between the EC and six of the seven EFTA states to come into force before the end of 1993. **30.** The European Community came under suspicion of mass agricultural fraud when a senior agriculture official who was under investigation for corruption committed suicide.

APRIL 1993

29. The new French government announced that it would not ratify the agreement to abolish border controls because no effective measures were being introduced against drug trafficking.

MAY 1993

13. The Spanish and Portuguese governments were forced to devalue the peseta and escudo by 8 per cent and 6½ per cent respectively after currency speculation. **18.** In a referendum the Danish electorate voted by 57 per cent to 43 per cent to ratify the Maastricht Treaty, subject to the opt-outs agreed at the Edinburgh summit.

JUNE 1993

8. The French government ended its threat to veto an EC-US agreement on trade in oilseed reached in November 1992. **11.** The German government admitted that, contrary to the Treaty of Rome, it had signed a trade agreement with the USA whereby German telecommunications firms would not face the US sanctions faced by other EC firms. **30.** EC members apart from the UK, Denmark and Ireland agreed to abolish border controls between the nine states from December 1993.

JULY 1993

1. The German constitutional court began hearing a series of appeals claiming that ratifying the Maastricht Treaty would be constitutionally illegal. **30.** Community central banks spent an estimated £31 billion in an attempt to defend the ERM from the worst currency speculation in its history.

AUGUST 1993

1. An emergency meeting of EC finance ministers agreed to allow six of the remaining ERM currencies to fluctuate within margins of 15 per cent above or below the central rate in an attempt to protect the ERM from currency speculation. (The Deutsche Mark and Dutch Guilder remained with 2.25 per cent margins.) **2.** The United Kingdom ratified the Maastricht Treaty.

THE MIDDLE EAST

SEPTEMBER 1992

1. The Russian government announced that it would send two warships to the Gulf as a contribution to the international effort to tighten sanctions against Iraq. **2.** The leader of the UN weapons inspectorate team in Iraq stated that the Iraqi nuclear arms programme had been totally dismantled and destroyed. A Briton, Michael Wainwright, was gaoled for ten years in Iraq for illegally entering the country during a cycling trip. **10.** The Israeli Prime Minister Yitzhak Rabin said that Israel was ready to exchange part of the Golan Heights for a peace agreement with Syria. **24.** Leaders of 17 Iraqi opposition groups met in the Kurdish enclave in northern Iraq to seek agreement on forming a democratic government and overthrowing President Saddam Hussein. **29.** Fighting on the Iraqi border left 27 Turkish soldiers and 174 Kurdish guerrillas dead.

OCTOBER 1992

2. The UN Security Council voted to seize Iraqi assets in foreign banks and to use the money to provide compensation for Gulf War victims, to fund relief operations in Iraq and to finance the destruction of Iraqi weapons of mass destruction. **6.** Candidates from a coalition of opposition groups won a majority

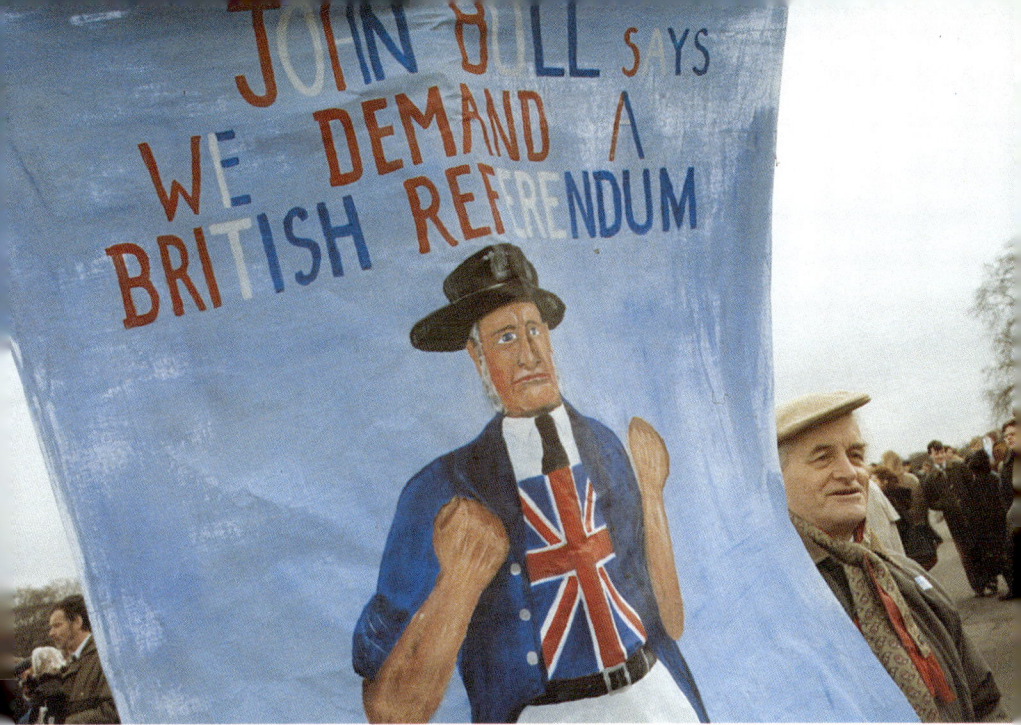

MAASTRICHT TREATY
The Government pushed through ratification of the Maastricht Treaty despite fierce opposition, including from within its own party (*Rex Features*)

THE ECONOMY
The Government came under constant criticism throughout the year over its handling of the economy and the pit closures (*Rex Features*)

CURRENCY CRISIS
Sterling was withdrawn from the ERM in September 1992, weakened by currency speculation. The ERM virtually collapsed after renewed speculation in July 1993 (*Rex Features*)

CHANCELLOR SACKED
Norman Lamont lost his job in May 1993, as the recession dragged on without any sign of his 'green shoots of recovery' (*Rex Features*)

IRA Bombings
IRA bombs caused fatalities in the City of London (above) in April and in Warrington in March 1993 (*Rex Features*)

YUGOSLAVIA
Desperate Bosnians escaped from besieged towns in UN aid lorries as Serbian forces tightened their grip on Bosnian territory (*Rex Features*)

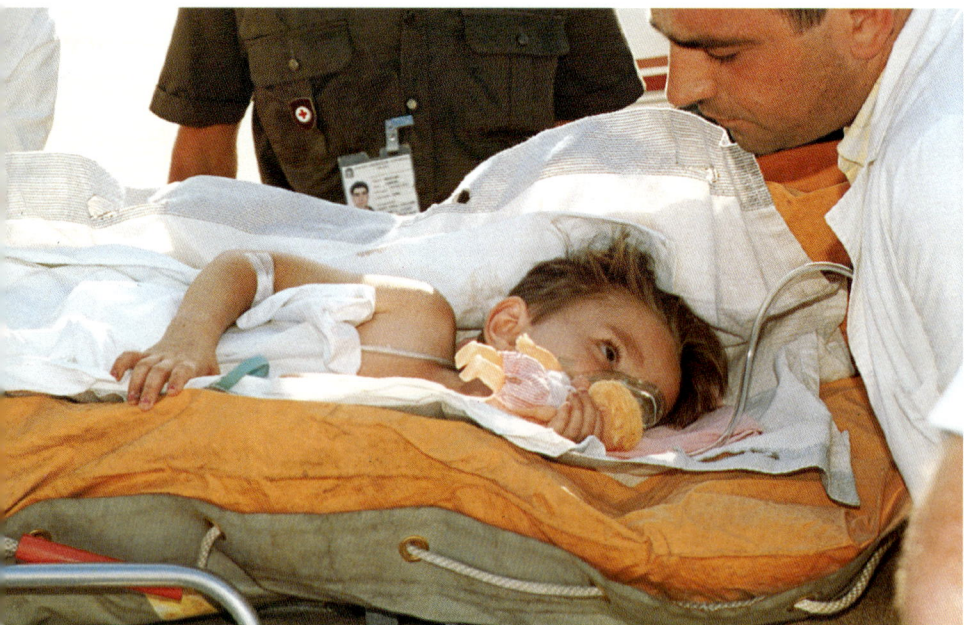

LITTLE IRMA
The plight of Irma Hadzimuratovic led to the evacuation of some of the severely wounded from Sarajevo to the west in August 1993 (*Rex Features*)

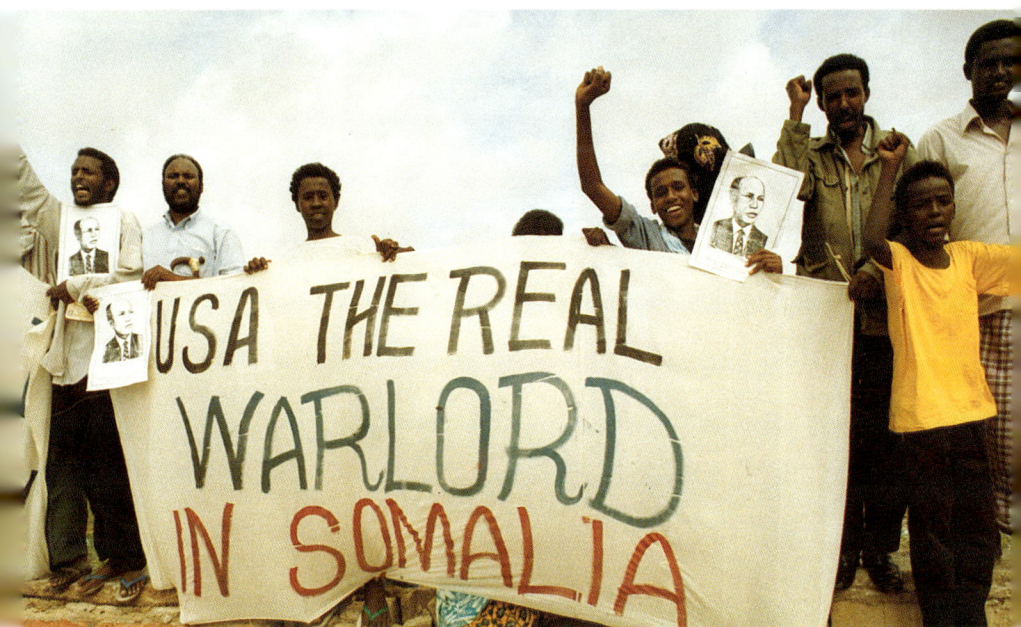

SOMALIA
UN intervention in the Somali civil war was ineffectual and increasingly resented as UN troops were drawn into the conflict (*Rex Features*)

INDIA
Religious tensions ran high in India throughout the year after the destruction of the Ayodhya mosque by Hindu extremists provoked retaliatory attacks (*Rex Features*)

PALESTINIAN DEPORTEES
Deportees from the Occupied Territories spent nine months in no man's land on the Israeli-Lebanon border before Israel agreed to their return home in August 1993 (*Rex Features*)

MIDDLE EAST PEACE ACCORD
In September 1993 Israel and the PLO signed agreements recognizing each other and giving Palestinians a degree of self-government (*Rex Features*)

SOUTH AFRICA
Demonstrations and rioting followed the assassination and funeral of Chris Hani, a Communist and ANC leader, by white extremists in April 1993 (*AP*)

TURMOIL IN ITALY
The bombing of historic buildings in Florence and Rome in summer 1993 was linked to the political turmoil caused by investigations into corrupt politicans (*Rex Features*)

RACISM IN EUROPE
Increasing racism in Europe, especially Germany, led to murder, violent demonstrations, and the desecration of Commonwealth war graves (*Rex Features*)

USA FLOODING
Flood waters in the mid-west American states in spring 1993 covered an area larger than Britain (*Rex Features*)

WINDSOR CASTLE FIRE
The fire in November 1992 contributed to The Queen's 'annus horribilis' and the financing of repairs added to the controversy surrounding the royal family in 1992–3 (*Rex Features*)

OBITUARIES
Deaths during the year included those of Rudolf Nureyev (top left), Willi Brandt (top right), Audrey Hepburn (bottom left) and Les Dawson (*Rex Features*)

NATIONAL DISASTER
The failure of the recall after a false start in the 1993 Grand National led to the race being declared void (*Mercury Press Agency*)

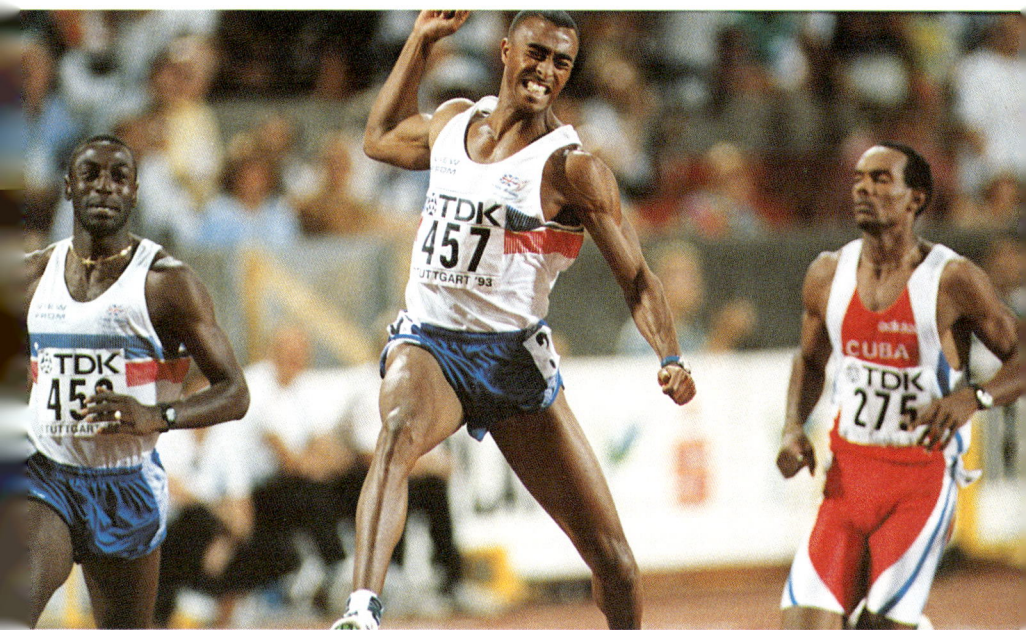

ATHLETICS TRIUMPH
Colin Jackson won his first gold medal and set a new 110 metre hurdles world record at the World Championships in Stuttgart (*Allsport*)

GOLDEN GIRL
Sally Gunnell became world as well as Olympic champion and set a new 400 metre hurdles world record in Stuttgart (*Allsport*)

of the 50 seats in parliamentary elections in Kuwait. **8.** The Israeli government made procedural concessions for future rounds of the Middle East peace talks, lifting its boycott on two multinational sections of the talks and accepting the participation of Palestinians from outside the Occupied Territories. **22.** President Hrawi of Lebanon appointed Rafic Hariri Prime Minister. The UN and Iraq signed an accord enabling Iraq to sell oil, the proceeds from which will be used for a relief programme. **23.** Turkish commandos entered northern Iraq in an attempt to destroy Kurdish guerrilla units.

NOVEMBER 1992

9. The seventh round of the Middle East peace negotiations began in Washington. **10.** Israeli defence forces and Hizbollah guerrillas exchanged rocket and artillery fire in southern Lebanon.

DECEMBER 1992

7. Members of Hamas, a Palestinian Islamic movement, shot dead three Israeli soldiers in the Gaza Strip on the fifth anniversary of the beginning of the *intifada*. **15.** The body of an Israeli police sergeant was found by a roadside near Jerusalem two days after he was kidnapped by Hamas. **17.** Arab delegates boycotted the Middle East peace talks in Washington in response to the deportation from Israel to southern Lebanon of 418 alleged Hamas members. **18.** The Palestinian deportees in southern Lebanon were attacked by the pro-Israeli South Lebanese Army as they tried to return to the Occupied Territories. **27.** US aircraft patrolling the air exclusion zone over southern Iraq shot down an Iraqi MiG fighter.

JANUARY 1993

6. The USA, Britain and France told the Iraqi government to remove the anti-aircraft missile batteries stationed in the air exclusion zone in southern Iraq or they would be destroyed. **8.** Iraq removed its anti-aircraft missile batteries from the air exclusion zone, and then banned UN aircraft from flying in Iraq. **10.** Iraqi soldiers carried out a raid into Kuwait, seizing missiles and other military equipment. **11.** Iraqi soldiers carried out a second raid into Kuwait, dismantling prefabricated warehouses and removing them to Iraq. **13.** US, British and French aircraft attacked and destroyed Iraqi missile sites and radar installations in response to the Iraqi incursions along the border with Kuwait. **15.** US troops began to arrive in Kuwait to boost security along the frontier with Iraq. **17.** After continued Iraqi refusals to guarantee the safety of UN weapons inspectors' flights into Iraq, the US navy destroyed a suspected nuclear weapons plant with cruise missiles. **18.** US, British and French aircraft destroyed Iraqi missile sites and radar installations in southern and northern Iraq. **19.** The USA moved more naval forces and missiles to the Gulf and bombed anti-aircraft missiles in northern Iraq. The Israeli parliament voted to repeal the ban on Israeli citizens meeting PLO

officials. **21.** UN weapons inspection teams arrived in Iraq after the Iraqi government was forced to agree to their return. **23.** Seventeen of the Palestinians deported to southern Lebanon were flown back to Israel by RAF helicopters; they were either seriously ill or had been mistakenly identified as Hamas members.

FEBRUARY 1993

5. The UN Security Council voted to send to the Iraq–Kuwait frontier peace-keeping soldiers permitted to use force to repel incursions. **13.** The UN Security Council accepted the Israeli offer to repatriate 101 of the 415 alleged Hamas members deported to Lebanon, and ended its threat to impose UN trade sanctions on Israel. **26.** Palestinian delegates to Middle East peace talks rejected attempts to restart negotiations until Israel allowed the 415 Palestinian deportees in Lebanon to return home.

MARCH 1993

10. Thirteen Islamic extremists were killed and 15 injured by Egyptian police in gun fights in Cairo and Aswan. The Palestinian delegation to the Middle East peace talks again refused to attend the next round of talks until Israel allowed the 415 Palestinian deportees in Lebanon to return home. **24.** The Knesset elected Ezer Weizman President of Israel.

APRIL 1993

9. US aircraft bombed Iraqi anti-aircraft artillery in the northern air exclusion zone after coming under fire. **16.** The Palestinian deportees in southern Lebanon were shelled by Israeli artillery as they tried to march to the Israeli border. **26.** The Palestinian deportees in southern Lebanon were again shelled by Israeli artillery as they protested at the resumption of peace talks. **27.** The ninth round of peace talks opened in Washington, attended by Arab states and PLO delegates. **30.** The first of 30 Palestinians deported by Israel between 1967 and 1987 were allowed to return to the West Bank.

MAY 1993

10. The Palestinian negotiators withdrew from the Middle East peace talks in Washington in protest at Israel reneging on promises to accept the return of deportees from southern Lebanon and to respect human rights in the Occupied Territories. **13.** The UN announced the withdrawal of its armed guards for aid convoys in Kurdish areas of northern Iraq as it had no funds to maintain them there. **14.** The ninth round of Middle East peace talks ended in Washington without progress. **25.** The Iranian Air Force attacked bases of the Iranian opposition inside Iraq in retaliation for attacks on Revolutionary Guards units in Iran. **27.** An Egyptian military court sentenced six Muslim extremists to death for terrorist bombings.

JUNE 1993

11. President Rafsanjani of Iran was re-elected for a second four-year term. **26.** The USA destroyed the headquarters of the Iraqi intelligence service in Baghdad in retaliation for an Iraqi plot to kill ex-President Bush when he visited Kuwait in April.

JULY 1993

8. Seven Muslim fundamentalists were hanged in Cairo after being found guilty of attacks on tourist buses and Nile cruise ships. **11.** A UN weapons team left Iraq after an unsuccessful attempt to close two missile-testing sites. Two days of fighting in southern Lebanon between Israeli forces and Hezbollah guerrillas left five Israeli soldiers dead. **19.** The Iraqi government accepted UN demands for cameras and monitoring equipment to be installed at two missile-testing ranges. **25.** Israel launched air, sea and land attacks on Hezbollah and Palestinian bases in southern Lebanon after repeated Hezbollah artillery and rocket attacks on northern Israel. **31.** The Israeli defence forces ended a seven-day bombardment of southern Lebanon which killed 130 people.

AUGUST 1993

15. The Palestinian deportees banished in southern Lebanon agreed to Israel's proposal that they return in stages by December. **18.** The Egyptian Interior Minister Hassan al-Alfi was seriously injured in a bomb attack by Muslim fundamentalists. **19.** Nine Israeli soldiers were killed by Hezbollah bomb attacks in southern Lebanon, which led to Israel bombing Hezbollah bases. Iraqi forces fired at US aircraft patrolling the northern air exclusion zone; in retaliation US aircraft destroyed missile sites and radar installations. **30.** The Israeli cabinet voted in favour of an agreement with the PLO which would grant Palestinians self-government in the Gaza Strip and Jericho.

INTERNATIONAL RELATIONS

SEPTEMBER 1992

11. El Salvador and Honduras agreed to abide by an International Court of Justice decision ending a border dispute. **14.** The Russian government announced that the Soviet Union and later Russia had been producing bacteriological weapons until March 1992 in violation of a 1972 Treaty. **15.** China announced that it would boycott multilateral talks on Middle East arms control because of US plans to sell military aircraft to Taiwan.

OCTOBER 1992

2. The NATO Rapid Reaction Corps, based in Bielefeld, Germany, came into operation. **19.** President Yeltsin of Russia signed a decree extending Russia's nuclear arms test moratorium to July 1993.

22. Talks between the EC and the USA about the failed GATT negotiations broke down because of the French refusal to reduce agricultural subsidies to the level requested by the USA. **29.** The head of the UN mission in Somalia, Muhammed Sahnuon, resigned after criticizing the UN's slow response to the war and starvation in the country.

NOVEMBER 1992

4. The US government made an official request to the GATT governing council to place tariffs on $1 billion of EC goods after the collapse of the Uruguay round of GATT talks. **9.** Britain and Russia signed a friendship treaty, the first since 1766, and several other agreements. **20.** US and EC negotiators reached agreement on agricultural subsidies, paving the way for a GATT agreement. Greece joined the Western European Union as a full member, with Turkey, Norway and Iceland becoming associate members and Denmark and the Irish Republic observers.

JANUARY 1993

3. In Moscow President Bush and President Yeltsin signed the START 2 treaty which reduces US and Russian strategic nuclear weapons by 72 per cent. **12.** Representatives of 120 countries gathered in Paris to sign the Chemical Weapons Convention 1993, which bans the storage, production and use of chemical weapons. **19.** The Czech Republic and the Slovak Republic were admitted to membership of the UN as two independent states.

FEBRUARY 1993

16. OPEC oil ministers agreed to cut crude oil production by 1.4 million barrels per day to 23.6 million barrels per day in an attempt to increase prices.

MARCH 1993

1. An internal UN report stated that the organization was rife with corruption, waste, bureaucratic patronage and overmanning. **12.** North Korea renounced its accession to the Nuclear Non-Proliferation Treaty after refusing to allow the International Atomic Energy Authority to inspect sites in the country for possible nuclear weapons production. The US trade representative Mickey Kantor announced the unilateral ending of US–EC trade negotiations because of EC public procurement policies. **22.** Bosnia-Hercegovina brought cases of genocide and war crimes against Serbia and Montenegro in the International Court of Justice at The Hague. **31.** Greece blocked an attempt by the former Yugoslav republic of Macedonia to join the UN, disputing the republic's proposed name and flag.

APRIL 1993

1. The IAEA declared North Korea to be in violation of an agreement on safeguarding nuclear materials and referred the issue to the UN. **2.** Nineteen western states announced a rescheduling of Russia's £52 billion foreign debt. **8.** The International Court of Justice ruled that the rump Yugoslav state should stop committing genocide in Bosnia-Hercegovina. The UN General Assembly voted to accept Macedonia as a UN member under the compromise name of 'The Former Yugoslav Republic of Macedonia'. **15.** The G7 group of industrialized nations announced a $43.4 billion aid package for Russia.

MAY 1993

5. The director-general of the World Health Organization, Dr Hiroshi Nakajima, was re-elected for a second term despite western opposition and claims of financial irregularities. **13.** Japan threatened to leave the International Whaling Commission after its members voted to reject a lifting of the commercial whaling moratorium. **28.** Monaco and Eritrea joined the UN.

JUNE 1993

11. North Korea announced that it would remain a party to the Nuclear Non-Proliferation Treaty. **25.** Jacques Attali, the president of the European Bank for Reconstruction and Development, resigned after criticism of spending on the Bank's headquarters, which was twice the amount that the Bank had lent to Eastern Europe.

JULY 1993

1. The former European Community commissioner Peter Sutherland replaced Arthur Dunkel as director-general of the GATT. **6.** The Japanese government officially requested a permanent seat on the UN Security Council. **9.** The G7 Tokyo summit ended with agreement on market access for certain categories of trade in the GATT negotiations, a $3 billion aid package for Russia, and a US–Japanese trade accord. **19.** North Korea agreed to negotiate with the IAEA on international supervision of suspected nuclear weapons installations. **29.** A former Pakistani army chief, General Aslam Beg, confirmed that Pakistan had acquired the ability to construct nuclear weapons in 1987.

AUGUST 1993

18. The USA notified the Sudanese government that the Sudan was being placed on a list of countries sponsoring international terrorism and banned all US trade with the country. **25.** The USA imposed trade sanctions on China and Pakistan because of Chinese exports of missile parts to Pakistan in contradiction of the Missile Technology Control Regime.

Obituaries

Ademola, Rt. Hon. Sir Adetokunbo, KBE, Chief Justice of Nigeria 1958–72, aged 86 – 29 January 1993

Adley, Robert, MP, Conservative MP for Bristol North East 1970–4 and for Christchurch since 1974, aged 58 – 13 May 1993

Airey of Abingdon, Baroness, aged 73 – 27 November 1992

al-Alami, Saad al-Din, Mufti of Jerusalem since 1953, aged 82 – 6 February 1993

Allison, Rt. Revd Falkner, Bishop of Chelmsford 1951–61, Bishop of Winchester 1961–74, aged 86 – 31 May 1993

Amherst, 5th Earl, MC, soldier, journalist and airline executive, aged 96 – 4 March 1993

Andrews, Dana, American film actor, aged 83 – 17 December 1992

Argyll, Margaret, Duchess of, socialite, aged 80 – 25 July 1993

Ashby, Lord, D.SC., FRS, botanist and academic administrator, aged 88 – 22 October 1992

Ashe, Arthur, American tennis player and 1975 Wimbledon champion, aged 49 – 6 February 1993

Bacon, Baroness (Alice), CBE, PC, Labour MP for Leeds North East 1945–55 and for Leeds South East 1955–70, aged 83 – 24 March 1993

Bangor, 7th Viscount (Edward Ward), journalist, broadcaster and writer, aged 87 – 8 May 1993

Barcelona, Don Juan de Borbon y Battenberg, Count of, aged 79 – 1 April 1993

Barnett, Charles, cricketer, aged 82 – 28 May 1993

Barnett, Air Chief Marshal Sir Denis, GCB, CBE, DFC, air commander in the Suez campaign 1956, aged 86 – 31 December 1992

Baudouin, King of the Belgians since 1951, aged 62 – 31 July 1993

Benson, Ivy, bandleader of the All Girls Band, aged 79 – 6 May 1993

Bérégovoy, Pierre, prime minister of France April 1992 to March 1993, aged 67 – committed suicide 1 May 1993

Berkeley, Baroness (17th in line), aged 87 – 17 October 1992

Bernstein, Lord (Sidney), founder of Granada Television and the Granada Group, aged 94 – 5 February 1993

Box, Donald, Conservative MP for Cardiff North 1959–66, aged 75 – 12 July 1993

Boyle, Marshal of the RAF Sir Dermot, GCB, KCVO, KBE, AFC, aged 88 – 5 May 1993

Braden, Bernard, Canadian-born actor and broadcaster, aged 76 – 2 February 1993

Brandt, Willi, mayor of West Berlin 1957–66, chancellor of West Germany 1969–74, aged 78 – 8 October 1992

Bresslaw, Bernard, comic actor, aged 59 – 11 June 1993

Browne, George, archbishop of the Province of West Africa since 1982, aged 59 – 14 February 1993

Bruntisfield, 1st Baron, MC, aged 93 – 14 January 1993

Bullard, Tony, British UN worker in Afghanistan, aged 35 – killed 1 February 1993

Bunce, Cyril, Labour MP for Dunbartonshire East 1951–70, aged 89 – 7 September 1992

Burnham, 5th Baron, soldier and amateur sailor, aged 72 – 18 June 1993

Burton, Richard, VC, aged 70 – 11 July 1993

Bute, 6th Marquess, KBE, landowner, charity executive, Lord Lieutenant of Argyll and Bute since 1990, aged 60 – 21 July 1993

Cahn, Sammy, songwriter, aged 79 – 15 January 1993

Carey, Joyce, OBE, actress, aged 94 – 28 February 1993

Carrick, 9th Earl, aged 61 – 5 October 1992

Cawdor, 6th Earl, aged 60 – 20 June 1993

Chaplin, Judith, OBE, MP, Conservative MP for Newbury since 1992, aged 53 – 19 February 1993

Charteris, Leslie, writer, creator of *The Saint*, aged 85 – 15 April 1993

Chirwa, Orton, Malawian barrister, politician and political prisoner, in prison, aged 73 – 20 October 1992

Christoff, Boris, Bulgarian-born opera singer, aged 79 – 28 June 1993

Clark Hutchinson, Michael, Conservative MP for Edinburgh South 1957–79, aged 79 – 21 March 1993

Cobham, Cdr Anthony, GC, aged 83 – 14 May 1993

Copperwheat, Lt.-Cdr Dennis, GC, aged 78 – 8 September 1992

Cotton, Henry, Lord Lieutenant of Merseyside since 1989 and Chancellor of Liverpool John Moores University since 1992, aged 64 – 3 August 1993

Cowley, Lt.-Gen. Sir John, GC, KBE, CB, aged 87 – 7 January 1993

Craigton, Lord, CBE, PC, Conservative MP 1950–9 and minister of state, Scottish Office 1959–64, aged 88 – 28 July 1993

Craven, Danie, South African rugby administrator, aged 82 – 4 January 1993

Croker, Ted, secretary of the Football Association 1973–89, aged 68 – 25 December 1992

Dawson, Les, comedian, aged 60 – 10 June 1993

de Ramsey, 3rd Baron, KBE, TD, aged 83 – 31 March 1993

Decies, 6th Baron, aged 77 – November 1992

Devereux, Sean, Irish UNICEF official in Somalia, aged 28 – murdered 2 January 1993

Dickens, Monica, MBE, author, aged 77 – 25 December 1992

Douglas Home, William, playwright and author, aged 80 – 28 September 1992

Dowding, 2nd Baron, aged 73 – 22 November 1992

Dubcek, Alexander, first secretary of the Czechoslovak Communist Party during the 1968 Prague Spring reform movement and subsequent Soviet invasion, aged 70 – 7 November 1992

Dunleath, 4th Baron, TD, aged 59 – 9 January 1993

Eastham, Sir Michael, High Court judge (Family Division) since 1978, aged 72 – 4 March 1993

Eckstine, Billy, American singer and bandleader, aged 78 – 8 March 1993

Edmund-Davies, Lord, PC, Lord of Appeal in Ordinary 1974–81, aged 86 – 27 December 1992

Edwards, L/Cpl Wayne, British soldier killed in Bosnia, aged 26 – 13 January 1993

Eisler, Paul, engineer widely regarded as inventor of the printed circuit, aged 85 – 26 October 1992

Elliott, Denholm, CBE, actor, aged 70 – 6 October 1992

Elworthy, Marshal of the Royal Air Force Lord, KG, GCB, CBE, DSO, LVO, DFC, AFC, Chief of Defence Staff 1967–71, aged 82 – 4 April 1993

Evans, Sir Geraint, CBE, opera singer, aged 70 – 19 September 1992

Ewart-Biggs, Baroness, a Labour whip in the House of Lords, aged 63 – 7 October 1992

Fernyhough, The Rt. Hon. Ernest, Labour MP for Jarrow 1947–79, aged 84 – 16 August 1993

Fortescue, 7th Earl, aged 70 – 7 March 1993

Forteviot, 3rd Baron, MBE, aged 87 – 25 March 1993

Fowler, Gerald, Labour MP for the Wrekin 1966–70 and 1974–9, rector of the Polytechnic of East London 1982–92, aged 58 – 1 May 1993

Franks, Lord, OM, GCMG, KCB, KCVO, CBE, PC, FBA, civil servant, diplomat, banker and academic, aged 87 – 15 October 1992

Freyberg, 2nd Baron, OBE, MC, soldier, aged 69 – 26 May 1993

Frink, Dame Elisabeth, CH, DBE, RA, sculptor, aged 62 – 18 April 1993

Frost, Maj.-Gen. John, CB, DSO and Bar, MC, commander of 2nd Parachute Battalion at Arnhem 1944, aged 80 – 21 May 1993

Garrett, Ted, Labour MP for Wallsend 1964–92, aged 73 – 30 May 1993

Gillespie, Dizzy, jazz trumpeter, aged 75 – 6 January 1993

Gilliat, Lt.-Col. Sir Martin, GCVO, MBE, private secretary to the Queen Mother since 1956, aged 80 – 27 May 1993

Gilliatt, Penelope, writer, aged 61 – 9 May 1993

Gish, Lillian, American actress, aged 99 – 27 February 1993

Golding, Sir William, CBE, novelist and Nobel laureate, aged 81 – 19 June 1993

Gordon, Esmé, RSA, architect, aged 82 – 31 May 1993

Gormley, Lord (Joe), OBE, president of the National Union of Mineworkers 1971–82, aged 75 – 27 May 1993

Granard, 9th Earl, AFC, aviator and businessman, aged 77 – 19 November 1992

Granger, Stewart, actor, aged 80 – 16 August 1993

Grantham, Admiral Sir Guy, GCB, OBE, DSO, aged 92 – 8 September 1992

Gray, HE Cardinal Gordon, Roman Catholic Archbishop of St Andrews and Edinburgh 1951–85, aged 82 – 19 July 1993

Hani, Martin Thembisile (Chris), general secretary of the South African Communist Party and member of the ANC national executive committee, aged 50 – assassinated 10 April 1993

Hasluck, Rt. Hon. Sir Paul, KG, GCMG, GCVO, governor-general of Australia 1969–74, aged 87 – 9 January 1993

Hassett, Lindsay, MBE, Australian cricketer, aged 79 – 16 June 1993

Hatch of Lusby, Lord, Labour peer, aged 74 – 11 October 1992

Hayes, Helen, American stage and film actress, aged 92 – 17 March 1993

Hearst, William Randolph, jnr, American newspaper magnate and journalist, aged 85 – 14 May 1993

Hellyer, Arthur, MBE, FLS, horticulturist and writer, aged 90 – 28 January 1993

Henderson, Admiral Sir Nigel, GBE, KCB, aged 84 – 2 August 1993

Hepburn, Audrey, film actress and UNICEF ambassador, aged 63 – 20 January 1993

Hersey, John, American war correspondent and novelist, aged 78 – 24 March 1993

Hilder, Rowland, OBE, painter, aged 87 – 21 April 1993

Holley, Robert, American biochemist and winner of Nobel prize for medicine (1968) for unravelling the genetic code of RNA, aged 71 – 11 February 1993

Hughes, Charlotte, oldest person in Britain, aged 115 – 17 March 1993

Hughes, Mark, Labour MP for Durham 1970–83 and for the City of Durham 1983–7, aged 60 – 19 March 1993

Hunt, James, world Formula 1 motor racing champion 1976 and television commentator, aged 45 – 15 June 1993

Huxley, Anthony, botanist, horticulturist and author, aged 72 – 26 December 1992

Idris, Shawish Taha, GC, aged 93 – 31 May 1993

Jacob, Lt.-Gen. Sir Ian, GBE, CB, military assistant secretary to the War Cabinet 1939–46, director-general of the BBC 1952–60, aged 93 – 24 April 1993

Jobe, Tom, American dancer and choreographer, aged 39 – 8 December 1992

Johns, Mervyn, actor, aged 93 – 6 September 1992

Johnson, Marv, American soul singer, aged 54 – 16 May 1993

Joicey, 4th Baron, country landowner, aged 68 – 14 June 1993

Jones, Sir Edward, PC, Attorney-General for Northern Ireland 1964–8 and Lord Justice of Appeal in Northern Ireland 1973–84, aged 80 – 18 March 1993

Joseph, Helen, campaigner against apartheid in South Africa, aged 87 – 25 December 1992

Kadoorie, Lord, CBE, Hong Kong businessman, aged 94 – 25 August 1993

Keeler, Ruby, American dancer and actress, aged 83 – 28 February 1993

Kelly, Petra, founding member and former leader of German Green Party, aged 44 – found dead 12 October 1992

Kenyon, 5th Baron, CBE, chairman of the trustees of the National Portrait Gallery 1966–88, aged 75 – 16 May 1993

Kroger, Helen, 1950s Soviet spy, aged 79 – late December 1992

Kusch, Polykarp, American physicist and Nobel laureate, aged 82 – 20 March 1993

Lamborghini, Ferruccio, founder of Lamborghini car company, aged 76 – 20 February 1993

Langford-Holt, Sir John, Conservative MP for Shrewsbury 1945–83, aged 77 – 23 July 1993

Leatherland, Lord, OBE, aged 94 – 18 December 1992

Litchfield, Captain John, OBE, RN, Conservative MP for Chelsea 1959–66, aged 89 – 31 May 1993

Lloyd of Hampstead, Lord, QC, Ll.D., barrister and professor of jurisprudence at London University 1956–82, aged 77 – 31 December 1992

Macclesfield, 8th Earl, aged 78 – 7 December 1992

McClintock, Barbara, American geneticist and Nobel laureate, aged 90 – 2 September 1992

MacMillan, Sir Kenneth, choreographer, aged 62 – 29 October 1992

McNair-Wilson, Sir Michael, Conservative MP for Walthamstow East 1969–74 and for Newbury 1974–92, aged 62 – 28 March 1993

Mankiewicz, Joseph, screenwriter and film director and producer, aged 83 – 5 February 1993

Mann, Sunnie, wife of the former Beirut hostage, Jackie Mann, aged 79 – 30 November 1992

Maskell, Dan, CBE, tennis champion, coach and commentator, aged 84 – 10 December 1992

Massereene (13th) and Ferrard (6th), Viscount, landowner, aged 78 – 27 December 1992

Mikardo, Ian, Labour MP for Reading 1945–50 and 1955–9, Reading South 1950–5, Poplar 1964–74, Bethnal Green and Bow 1974–83, Bow and Poplar 1983–7, and a former party chairman, aged 84 – 6 May 1993

Mills, Nat, variety and radio star, aged 93 – 13 August 1993

Mills, Sir Peter, Conservative MP for Torridge (renamed Devon West, then Torridge and West Devon) 1964–87, aged 71 – 16 August 1993

Mnouchkine, Alexandre, French film producer, aged 85 – 3 April 1993

Moore, Bobby, OBE, footballer, captain of England's 1966 World Cup winning team, aged 51 – 24 February 1993

Mott-Radclyffe, Sir Charles, Conservative MP for Windsor 1942–70, aged 80 – 25 November 1992

Nolan, Sir Sydney, OM, AC, CBE, Australian painter, aged 75 – November 1992

Norman, Leslie, film producer and director, aged 81 – 18 February 1993

Norman, Sir Richard, KBE, FRS, chemist, Rector of Exeter College, Oxford, since 1987, aged 61 – 6 June 1993

Nureyev, Rudolf, ballet dancer, aged 54 – 6 January 1993

Oort, Prof. Jan, Dutch astronomer, aged 92 – November 1992

O'Reilly, Bill, Australian spin bowler, aged 86 – 5 October 1992

Ozal, Turgut, prime minister of Turkey 1983–9 and president since 1989, aged 66 – 17 April 1993

Parkinson, Prof. C. Northcote, author, historian, economist and originator of Parkinson's Law, aged 83 – 9 March 1993

Pennock, Lord, industrialist, aged 72 – 23 February 1993

Perkins, Anthony, American film actor, aged 60 – 12 September 1992

Phomvihane, President Kaysone, prime minister of Laos 1975–91, president since 1991 and leader of the Laotian Communist Party since 1955, aged 71 – 21 November 1992

Pizey, Admiral Sir Mark, GBE, CB, DSO, aged 93 – 17 May 1993

Plaidy, Jean (Eleanor Hibbert), who also wrote as Victoria Holt, Philippa Carr, etc., novelist, aged about 83 – 18 January 1993

Poole, 1st Baron, CBE, TD, PC, a former chairman of the Conservative Party, aged 81 – 28 January 1993

Poulson, John, architect, imprisoned for bribery and corruption in the 1970s, aged 82 – 31 January 1993

Powis, 7th Earl, aged 68 –13 August 1993

Premadasa, Ranasinghe, president of Sri Lanka since 1989, aged 69 – assassinated 1 May 1993

Price, Prof. William, FRS, physicist and spectroscopist, aged 83 – 10 March 1993

Pyke, Magnus, scientist and television presenter, aged 83 – 19 October 1992

Railton, Brig. Dame Mary, DBE, director of Women's Royal Army Corps 1954–7, aged 86 – 12 November 1992

Rice, Peter, structural engineer, aged 57 – 25 October 1992

Ridgway, General Matthew, commander of US 82nd Division 1942–5, UN supreme commander in Korea 1951–2, US Army chief of staff 1953–5, aged 98 – 26 July 1993

Ridley of Liddesdale, Lord (Nicholas), PC, Conservative politician and former minister, aged 64 – 4 March 1993

Rimington, Claude, FRS, biochemist, aged 90 –
8 August 1993
Roach, Hal, American film producer, aged 100 –
2 November 1992
Robinson, Prof. Sir Austin, CMG, OBE, FBA,
economist, aged 95 – June 1993
Robinson, Cardew, actor and comedian, aged 75 –
27 December 1992
Rochdale, 1st Viscount, OBE, TD, textile magnate,
financier and industrialist, aged 86 – 24 May
1993
Rodgers, Sir John, Bt., Conservative MP for
Sevenoaks 1950–79, aged 86 – 29 March 1993
Rodney, 9th Baron, aged 72 –13 October 1992
Ross of Newport, Lord, Liberal MP for the Isle of
Wight 1974–87, aged 66 –10 May 1993
Rothenstein, Michael, artist and printmaker,
aged 85 – 6 July 1993
Rowallan, 3rd Baron, aged 73 – July 1993
Sauvé, Jeanne, governor-general of Canada 1984–
90, aged 70 – 26 January 1993
Shawn, William, editor of the *New Yorker* 1952–87,
aged 85 – 8 December 1992
Sheybal, Vladek, Polish-born actor, writer and
director, aged 69 – 16 October 1992
Slater, Jim, general secretary of the National Union
of Seamen 1974–86, aged 69 – 30 May 1993
Smith, Dr E. Lester, FRS, research scientist who
discovered vitamin B12, aged 88 – December
1992
Smith, T. Dan, former Newcastle council leader
gaoled in 1974 for corruption in Poulson affair,
aged 78 – 27 July 1993
Sobell, Sir Michael, businessman and philanthropist,
aged 100 – 31 August 1993
Soref, Harold, Conservative MP for Ormskirk
1970–4, aged 76 – 14 March 1993
Stark, Dame Freya, DBE, writer and traveller,
aged 100 – 9 May 1993
Strauss, Lord, PC, Labour MP for Lambeth North
1929–31, 1934–50, and for Lambeth Vauxhall
1950–79, and a minister 1945–51, aged 91 –
5 June 1993
Summerson, Sir John, CH, CBE, FBA, FSA,
architectural historian, aged 87 – 10 November
1992
Sutton, Prof. John, FRS, geologist, aged 73 –
6 September 1992
Tambo, Oliver, president of the African National
Congress 1978–91, aged 75 – 24 April 1993
Thompson, E. P., historian and author, aged 69 –
28 August 1993
Tilston, Col. Fred, VC, CD, aged 86 – 22 September
1992
Todd, Ann, film actress and documentary film-
maker, aged 84 – 6 May 1993
Trace, Christopher, *Blue Peter* presenter 1958–67,
aged 59 – 5 September 1992
Treurnicht, Andries, leader of the South African
Conservative Party, aged 72 – 22 April 1993
Twitty, Conway, American rock and country and
western singer, aged 59 – 5 June 1993

Tytler, Rt. Revd Donald, Suffragan Bishop of
Middleton since 1982, aged 67 – November 1992
Underhill, Lord, CBE, deputy leader of the
Opposition in the House of Lords 1982–9,
aged 78 – 12 March 1993
Underwood, Michael (John Michael Evelyn), crime
story-writer and barrister, aged 76 – January 1993
Van Fleet, Gen. James, American Second World
War general, aged 100 – 23 September 1992
Vaughan, Dame Janet, DBE, FRS, principal of
Somerville College, Oxford, 1945–67, aged 93 –
9 January 1993
Wang Zhen, vice-president of the People's Republic
of China, aged 85 – 12 March 1993
Warriss, Ben, comedian and actor, aged 83 –
14 January 1993
Watts, Sir Roy, CBE, chairman of Thames Water
since 1983, aged 67 – found dead 5 May 1993
Westall, Robert, children's writer, aged 63 –
15 April 1993
Whitcomb, Noel, newspaper columnist, aged 73 –
11 June 1993
White, Sir Dick, KCMG, KBE, director-general of MI5
1953–6 and director-general of MI6 1956–68,
aged 86 – 20 February 1993
Williams, R. H., rugby union player, aged 62 –
27 January 1993
Willis, Lord (Ted), playwright, politician and
author, aged 78 – 22 December 1992
Winstanley, Lord, Liberal MP for Cheadle 1966–70
and Hazel Grove February to October 1974, and
chairman of the Countryside Commission 1978–
80, aged 74 – 18 July 1993
Witcutt, Christine, British aid worker killed in
Sarajevo, aged 56 – 5 July 1993
Woddis, Roger, satiric writer and versifier,
aged 76 – 16 July 1993
Woods, The Most Revd Frank, KBE, Archbishop of
Melbourne 1957–77, Primate of Australia 1971–7,
aged 85 – 29 November 1992
Yates, Jess, former television personality and
producer, aged 74 – 9 April 1993
Young, Jack, Middlesex and England slow bowler,
aged 80 – 5 February 1993
Younger, William, GC, aged 83 – 6 February 1993
Zuckerman, Lord, OM, KCB, FRS, chief scientific
adviser to the Secretary of State for Defence
1960–6, chief scientific adviser to the
Government 1964–71, aged 88 – 1 April 1993

Index

Ashton-under-Lyne, MP 243–4
Ash Wednesday 9, 83
Asia:
  area 111
  continent 111
  countries 611–12
  events (1992–3) 632–3
  migration to UK 119
Assessment Appeal Tribunals 387
Assisted Places Scheme 448
Associated Presbyterian Churches of
  Scotland 433
Aston:
  Archdeacon 407
  Bishop Suffragan 407
  University 462
Astronomical constants 75
Astronomical notes 72
Astronomical phenomena (1994) 16, 20, 24,
  etc., 71
Astronomical predictions (1994) 16–63
Astronomical unit 75
Astronomy, Particle Physics and, Research
  Council 350, 1173
Atcham, Shrewsbury and 536, 555
  MP 261
Atomic Energy Authority, UK 289–90
  constabulary 391
Atomic time 74
Attendance allowance 502
Attercliffe (Sheffield), MP 261
Attorney-General 280, 326, 370
  departments 326
Auckland, Archdeacon 414
Audit Commission for England and Wales
  290
Audit Office, National 337
Australasia:
  countries 613
  events (1992–3) 633
  migration to UK 119
Australia 111
  Anglican Church 418–19
  Archbishops (RC) 427
  continent 111
Austria, Archbishops (RC) 427
Autumn:
  defined 15
  equinox 15, 81
Avon 534, 549, 550
  Education Authority 458
Avon and Somerset, Police Authority 388
Aylesbury, MP 244
Aylesbury Vale 535, 552
Ayr, MP 269

Babergh 535, 552
Badenoch and Strathspey 538, 571
Ballymena 573
Ballymoney 573
Banbridge 573
Banbury, MP 244
Banff and Buchan 538, 571
  MP 269
Bangladesh, Archbishop (RC) 427
Bangor:
  Bishop 417
  University College of 470
Bank holidays 87
  (1994) 10
  (1995) 11
Banking, professional organizations 473
Bank of England 290
  Museum 594
Bankruptcy, High Court 371
Banqueting House 588
Banstead, Reigate and 536, 555

Baptist Church 433
Barking:
  Bishop (Suffragan) 408
  MP 244
Barking and Dagenham 537, 563
  Education Authority 459
Barnes, Richmond and, MP 260
Barnet 537, 563
  Education Authority 459
Barnsley 534, 551
  Education Authority 458
  MPs 244
Barnstaple, Archdeacon 409
Bar of England and Wales 476–7
Bar of Northern Ireland 477
Baronesses:
  form of address 161, 220
  in own right 161
  Life 166–7
Baronets 178–209
  form of address 177, 220
  premier 142, 179, 184, 185
Barons:
  courtesy titles 169–70
  form of address 152, 220
  hereditary 152–61
  life 162–6
  premier 142, 154, 155, 157
Barony, premier 154
Barristers' training 476–7
Barrow and Furness, MP 244
Barrow-in-Furness 535, 552
Basildon 507, 535, 552
  MP 244
Basingstoke:
  Archdeacon 407
  Bishop (Suffragan) 407
  MP 244
Basingstoke and Deane 535, 552
Bassetlaw 535, 552
  MP 244
Bath (city) 535, 552
  MP 244
  University 462
Bath, Archdeacon 407
Bath, Order of 174
  Dames 211–12
  Knights 178–209
Bath and Wells, Bishop 168, 407
Batley and Spen, MP 244
Battersea, MP 244
Battle, Bexhill and, MP 244
BBC 291
Beaconsfield, MP 244
Bearsden, Strathkelvin and, MP 270
Bearsden and Milngavie 538, 571
Beaufort scale 603
Beckenham, MP 244
Bedford:
  Archdeacon 412
  Bishop (Suffragan) 412
Bedfordshire 534, 549, 550
  Education Authority 458
  MEPs 275
  Mid 536, 554
  MPs 244
  North 536, 554
  Police Authority 388
  South 536, 555
Bedworth, Nuneaton and 536, 555
Belarus, Archbishop (RC) 427
Belfast 572, 573
  airports 515
  Education and Library Board 460
  MPs 272
  Queen's University 469
Belgium, Archbishop (RC) 427
Benefits:
  Agency 355

Benefits continued
  contributory 500–1
  non-contributory 501–2
Benin, Archbishop (RC) 427
Berkshire 534, 549, 550
  Archdeacon 411
  East, MP 244
  Education Authority 458
Bermondsey, Southwark and, MP 262
Bermuda, Bishop (Anglican) 424
Berwickshire 538, 571
  Roxburgh and, MP 272
Berwick-upon-Tweed 535, 552
  MP 244
Bethnal Green and Stepney, MP 244
Bethnal Green Museum of Childhood 334
Beverley 535, 552
  MP 244
Bexhill and Battle, MP 244
Bexley 537, 563
  Education Authority 459
Bexleyheath, MP 245
Biggar Gasworks Museum 336
Biggin Hill airport 515
Billericay, MP 245
Bills, Parliamentary 225, 226, 228
Biological Sciences, Biotechnology and,
  Research Council 286
Biology, qualifying body 473
Biotechnology and Biological Sciences
  Research Council 286
Birkenhead:
  Bishop (Suffragan) 415
  MP 245
Birmingham 534, 542, 551
  airport 515
  Archbishop (RC) 426
  Archdeacon 407
  Bishop 167, 407
  Education Authority 458
  MEPs 275
  MPs 245
  University 462
  University of Central England 463
Births:
  registration 343
  Scotland 354
  statistics 120
Bishop Auckland, MP 245
Bishops:
  Anglican, overseas 418–24
  Church of England 167–8, 405–17
  Roman Catholic 426
  Suffragan 405–17
Blaby 535, 552
  MP 245
Blackburn 535, 552
  Archdeacon 414
  Bishop 167, 414
  MP 245
Blackley (Manchester), MP 257
Blackpool 535, 552
  airport 515
  MPs 245
Black Rod:
  Gentleman Usher 126, 174, 226
  Yeoman Usher 226
Blaenau Gwent 538, 566
  MP 267
Blaydon, MP 245
Blue Rod 175
Blyth Valley 535, 552
  MP 245
Board of Trade (BOTB) 359
  President 280, 357, 359
Bodmin, Archdeacon 413
Bolivia, Archbishops (RC) 427
Bolsover 535, 552
  MP 245

Stop-press

CHANGES SINCE PAGES WENT TO PRESS

ROYAL HOUSEHOLD
Captain, The Honorable Corps of Gentlemen-at-Arms, The Viscount Ullswater
Gentlemen of the Corps, Col. Sir Brian Barttelot, Bt. replaces Maj. J. R. E. Nelson
The Queen's Bodyguard of the Yeomen of the Guard Lieutenant, Col. G. W. Tufnell
Clerk of the Cheque and Adjutant, Col. R. S. Longsdon
Ensign, Maj. C. R. Marriott
Exon, Maj. M. Wills

PEERAGE
Lord Hawke married
Died: 15th Earl of Westmorland; Lord Alexander of Potterhill; Lord Galpern

BARONETAGE AND KNIGHTAGE, DAMES
Died: Sir Owen Aisher; Sir David Brown; Sir Bayard Dill, CBE; Rt. Hon. Sir John Higgins; Sir John Moores, CBE; Sir William Montagu-Pollock, KCMG; Sir John Prendergast, KBE, CMG, GM; Brig. Dame Margot Turner

DECORATIONS AND MEDALS
Sydney Rogerson, GC, died

THE GOVERNMENT
Captain of the Honorable Corps of Gentlemen-at-Arms (Chief Whip in the House of Lords), The Viscount Ullswater (formerly Parliamentary Under-Secretary, Employment)

GOVERNMENT DEPARTMENTS AND PUBLIC OFFICES
Cabinet Office: OPSS, Special Adviser to William Waldegrave and David Davis, C. Brendish
Department of Environment: Drinking Water Inspectorate, Grade 5, M. Rouse; *Northern Region, Regional Director*, B. H. Leonard
Office of Gas Supply: Director-General, Ms C. Spottiswoode
Monopolies and Mergers Commission: Secretary, A. Nieduszynski (formerly at DTI)
Scottish Office: NHS Management Executive, Chief Executive, G. Scaife (formerly chief executive of Mersey Regional Health Authority)

LAW COURTS AND OFFICES
Justices of the High Court – appointed: R. R. H. Jacob (Chancery Division); W. M. Gage (Queen's Bench Division); W. A. Blackburne (Chancery Division); retired: Mr Justice Wood
Circuit Judges – appointed: M. Lee (Midland and Oxford); retired: D. Roberts; J. Evans; J. Lee (Midland and Oxford); R. D. Lymbery, Common Serjeant; J. Hunter; H. Palmer (South-Eastern); R. Woolley (Wales and Chester)
Recorders – died: Lt.-Col. B. Elliott
Stipendiary Magistrates – appointed: *Provincial*, G. R. Watkins (S. Glamorgan); M. A. Rosenberg (S. Yorks); *Metropolitan*, M. J. Read; P. S. Wallis
Northern Ireland: Lord Justice Higgins (Rt. Hon. Sir John Higgins) died

TRIBUNALS
President, Employment Appeal Tribunal, The Hon. Mr. Justice Mummery

ANGLICAN COMMUNION
Assistant Bishops, Coventry, John Daly died
Bishop of Gibraltar in Europe, Rt. Revd John Hind (formerly Suffragan Bishop of Horsham)
Archdeacon of Norwich, Revd Clifford Offer
Archdeacon of Bedford, Canon Malcolm Lesiter
Suffragan Bishop of Burnley, Revd Martyn Jarrett
Dean of Manchester, Revd Canon Kenneth Riley
Bishop of Ballarat, Victoria, Australia, Ven. David Silk (formerly Archdeacon of Leicester)

LOCAL GOVERNMENT
Lord Mayor of London 1993–4, Alderman Paul Newall
Attorney-General of Jersey, M. C. St J. Birt

TRADE UNIONS
The EETPU section of the Amalgamated Engineering and Electrical Union reaffiliated with the TUC, 9 September

INTERNATIONAL ORGANIZATIONS
CIS: Azerbaijan parliament voted to rejoin 20 September; economic union agreement signed by nine members (not Turkmenistan and Ukraine) 24 September

COUNTRIES OF THE WORLD
Algeria: new government under Redha Malek appointed 21 August
Angola: UN imposed sanctions on UNITA from 25 September
Azerbaijan: parliament voted to rejoin CIS 20 September
Bosnia: Prime Minister Akmadzic sacked 27 August
Brazil: new Cruzeiro (= 1,000 Cruzeiros) introduced August
Cambodia: Prince Sihanouk elected King, new constitution promulgated, UN mandate ended 24 September
Canada: federal general election called for 25 October
Central African Republic: new President, Ange-Felix Patasse, elected 27 September
Georgia: parliament agrees to President Shevardnadze's demands, dissolves itself for three months and declares state of emergency 14 September; civil war restarts 24 September; Abkhazian separatists capture Sukhumi 26 September
Greece: general election called for 10 October
Haiti: new pro-Aristide government under Robert Malval appointed 30 August
Iraq: government reshuffle 5 September, Ahmad Hussein appointed Prime Minister
Israel: Declaration of Principles on an Interim Self-government Arrangement signed in Washington DC by Israel and PLO 13 September. Set of principles for a peace agreement signed by Israel and Jordan 14 September
New Zealand: general election called for 6 November
Norway: general election on 13 September won by Labour Party
Poland: former Communist Party and allies have parliamentary majority after general election on 19 September
South Africa: parliament voted to approve the Transitional Executive Council; UN sanctions lifted 24 September
Ukraine: Prime Minister Kachma resigns and President Kravchuk takes control of government; presidential and parliamentary elections called for June 1994

BRITISH DEPENDENT TERRITORIES
Hong Kong: Hon. Anson Chan appointed Chief Secretary

SPORTS RECORDS
Athletics: Women
1,500 metres, Qu Yunxia (China), 3 min 50.46 sec
3,000 metres, Wang Junxia (China), 8 min 06.11 sec
10,000 metres, Wang Junxia (China), 29 min 31.78 sec
All await ratification

EVENTS
SEPTEMBER 1993
6. More than 700 inmates rioted at Wymott Prison, Lancs.
9. Israel and the PLO exchanged letters of recognition. Over
50 Somalis were killed in Mogadishu by armed UN
helicopters after 300 Somali militiamen attacked a Pakistani
UN unit. **13.** Israel and the PLO signed a 'Declaration of
Principles' peace accord at the White House in Washington
DC. **14.** Israel and Jordan signed a set of principles for a
formal peace treaty. **16.** The British National Party won its
first local council seat in an election on the Isle of Dogs, east
London. **19.** The former Communist Party and its allies won
parliamentary elections in Poland. Nigel Mansell won the
IndyCar world series championship. **20.** Salman Rushdie's
1981 novel *Midnight's Children* won the Booker of Bookers
Prize. **21.** President Yeltsin dissolved the Russian parlia-
ment, calling new parliamentary elections for December.
The parliament stripped Yeltsin of his powers and swore in
Vice-President Rutskoi as President. **22.** At least 44 people
were killed when a train was derailed on a bridge and
plunged into a swamp in Alabama, USA. **23.** The Congress
of People's Deputies voted to impeach President Yeltsin.
The International Olympic Committee awarded the Olympic
Games 2000 to Sydney, Australia. **24.** A siege began at the
Russian parliament as President Yeltsin ordered armed
troops to surround the building. Prince Sihanouk was elected
King of Cambodia. All remaining sanctions against South
Africa began to be lifted, apart from the arms embargo.
28. The Labour Party annual conference in Brighton
approved a one-member-one-vote system of selecting pro-
spective parliamentary candidates. The Labour MP George
Foulkes resigned as a defence spokesman. **30.** An estimated
22,000 people were killed and thousands injured when an
earthquake hit Maharashtra state, western India.

DEATHS
SEPTEMBER 1993
1. Hew Lorimer, CBE, RSA, sculptor, aged 86
2. Rt. Hon. Sir John (Eoin) Higgins, a judge of the High
   Court of Northern Ireland since 1984, aged 66
8. 15th Earl of Westmorland, GCVO, Master of the Horse
   1978–91 and chairman of Sothebys 1980–2, aged 69
9. Lord Alexander of Potterhill, Ph.D., general secretary of
   Association of Education Committees 1945–77, aged 87
12. Raymond Burr, American actor, aged 76
    Harold Innocent, actor, aged 60
20. Leonard Parkin, former ITN newscaster, aged 64
23. Lord Galpern, Labour MP for Glasgow Shettleston
    1959–79, aged 90
    Sydney Rogerson, GC, aged 78
25. Sir John Moores, CBE, founder of the Littlewoods
    Organization and chairman 1924–77 and 1980–2, aged
    97
26. James Boyden, Labour MP for Bishop Auckland 1959–
    79, aged 82
30. Alex Lyon, Labour MP for York 1966–83 and junior
    minister, aged 61